ENGLISH RECUSANT LITERATURE
1558–1640

Selected and Edited by
D. M. ROGERS

Volume 313

THOMAS HESKYNS
The Parliament of Chryste
1566

THOMAS HESKYNS

The Parliament of Chryste

1566

The Scolar Press

1976

ISBN 0 85967 325 1

Published and printed in Great Britain by
The Scolar Press Limited, 59-61 East Parade,
Ilkley, Yorkshire and
39 Great Russell Street,
London WC1

THE
PARLIAMENT
OF CHRYSTE AVOV-
CHING AND DECLARING THE ENAC-

ted and receaued trueth of the presence of his bodie and bloode in the
blessed Sacrament, and of other articles concerning the same, impugned in a wicked sermon by M. Iuell, Collected and seth-
furth by Thomas Heskyns Doctour
of dyuinitie.

Wherin the reader shall fynde all the scripturs comonlie alleaged oute of the newe Testament,
touching the B. Sacrament, and some of the olde Testament, plainlie and truely expownded
by a nombre of holie learned Fathers and Doctours.

Ecclesiast. viii.

Non te pretereat narratio seniorum, ipsi enim didicerunt à patribus suis. Quoniam
ab ipsis disces intellectum, & in tempore necessitatis dare responsum.

Go not from the doctryne of the elders, for they haue learned of their fathers. For of them thowe
shalt learn vnderstanding, so that thowe maist make answer in tyme of nede.

Avgvst. lib. i. *de moribus Eccle.* cap. xxv.

Avdite doctos catholicæ Ecclesiæ viros tanta pace animi, & eo voto, quo ego vos
audiui.
Heare ye the learned men of the catholique Churche with as quiet a mynde, and with socht
desyre as I haue heard yowe.

SCRVTA MINI

Imprinted in Antvverpe,
At the golden Angell, by VVilliam Silvius prynter to the Kynges
Maiestie. M. D. LXVI.
VVith Priuilege.

THE NAMES OF SOCHE AVTHOVRS AS BE

ALLEAGED IN THIS BOOKE OF THE PARLIA-
ment of Chryſte, placed as yt vvere in tvvo houſes, that ys to vvitte, ſoche as vvere
before a thouſand years or verie neer, in the higher houſe, ſoche as vvere ſince, in
the lovver houſe.

Ieſus Chriſtus.

Apoſt. &
Euangeliſt.

Ioannes.
Marcus.
Paulus.

Latines of the hi-
gher houſe.

Clemens.
Alexander.
Sixtus,
Pius.
Soter.
Tertullianus.
Fabianus.
Cyprianus.
Silueſter.
Iuuencus.
Hilarius.
Optatus.
Ambroſius.
Hieronimus.
Auguſtinus.
Primaſius.
Vincentius lirinen.
Sedulius.
Leo primus.
Hilarius PP.
Caſsiodorus
Gregorius
Iſidorus.

Latines of the lo
wer houſe.

Beda
Haymo.
Remigius
Paſchaſius
Lanfrancus
Algerus
Guitmundus
Anſelmus.
Hugo de S. vict.
Rupertus
Bernardus
Petrus Clu.
Innocentius.3
Thomas de Aqui.
Nicolaus lyra
Hugo Cardinalis
Holkot.
Roffenſis
Titelmannus

Apoſt. &
Euangeliſt.

Mattheus.
Lucas.
Andreas.

Grecians of the hi-
gher houſe.

Martialis.
Abdias.
Anacletus.
Ignatius.
Dionyſius Areop.
Teleſphorus,
Iuſtinus.
Irenęus.
Origenes.
Euſebius Cęſarien.
Athanaſius.
Euſebius emiſ.
Baſilius.
Gregorius Niſſ.
Gregorius Nazian.
Efrem.
Iſichius.
Chryſoſtomus.
Theophilus Alexan.
Amphilochius
Didymus.
Proclus
Cyrillus.
Euthymius
Theodoretus

Grecians of the lo-
wer houſe.

Damaſcenus.
Theophilactus.
Oecumenius
Nicolaus Methonen.
Nicolaus Cabiſila.
Germanus
Beſſario

Promifed
Ioan. 6

Inftituted.
Math. 26

Praԁtized
Iac in Miḹ.

Prophecied.
malach. 1.

Referued.
Clem̄ epiſt

Figured
Exod. 16.

Continued.
1. Cor. 11.

Adored.

Priuilegium.

Regiæ Maiestatis diplomate permissum est Thomæ Heskins S. Theologiæ professori, vti per aliquem Typographorū in hisce omnibus ditionis suæ Regionibus admißorum, imprimendum curet librum, inscriptum: The Parliament of Chryste auouching and declaring, &c. Inhibitumque alijs omnibus intra eandem ditionem, ne ante triennium proximum absque ipsius Thomæ licentia imprimant, aut alibi impreßum diuendant: sub pœna in eodem diplomate expreßa.   Datum Bruxellæ 7. Iulij. 1565. Subsign.

Burgeois,
&
Facuwez.

A

DETESTING your heresie, yet louing your person, and therfor wishing your reformaciõ and correctiõ, I haue, M. Iuell cõpilled this booke, wherbie as I trust the vanitie of your bragge ys and shalbe disclosed and perceaued: so do I wish that by the same both yowe and soch as haue erred, maie be reduced from your foule errour, and all the people of my natiue contrie, for whose cause especia lie I haue také these labours, so staied in faith, that by your manifold vntru- eths they be not seduced. Yow haue not onelie enwrapped your self in er- rour, but also to maintein the same cõmitted three heinouse offences. One is the abuse and contépt of the authoritie ãd doctrine of the holie Fathers of the primitiue ãd aunciét Church. Those Fathers youe do not onelie truncate lie alleage, ãd with craftie sleight abuse ãd falsifie: but also although yowe e- uidétlie see thé impugning your doctrine and heresie, yet without all regard

B of their great learning ãd authoritie, of their perpetual cõsent ãd agreement, of their reueréd antiquitie, of their famouse holinesse, yowe runne stil in the race of your deuised inuencion, and phantasie, vtterlie cõténing whatsoeuer hath ben by thé saied or doen contrarie to your blinde affection, and wicked opinion. Now to vse to yowe the woords of the holie Father *Leo* to *Eutyches*: *Quid iniquius, quàm impia sapere, & sapientioribus doctoribusque non credere?* What ys more wicked then to haue vngodlie opinions, and not to beleue thé that be wiser and better learned? *Decet enim sequi patres nostros, nec cõmutare definitioné eorû perpetuã, quorû regulã secundùm sacras scripturas esse didicimus.* Yt becometh vs (saieth *Flauianus*) to folowe our Fathers, and not to chaunge their perpetuall defini- tion, whose rule we haue learned to be according to the scripturs.

But yow staied not here. Yt was not enough for yow to cõténe or abusethe perpetuall definitiõ of the Fathers, but youe proceaded to the second offéce eué to mocke ãd skorn the learned ãd holie Fathers of Chrysts Church not onelie thé of the later daies, but soch as liued a thousand years agon, wherof some were famouse for their learning, some so constant in their faith and per

C fect in life that of the vniuersal Church thei haue bé hitherto, ãd yet be repu ted ãd esteemed blessed Saincts. Soch I saie as God hath exalted to his glo- rie, soch, as in heaué be honourable, soch haue yow in earth dishonoured yea mockt ãd skorned, ãd as moch as in yow laie, made despicable to the worlde. Thus haue yow vsed or raither abused S. Siluester, who liued in the time of Cõstãtine the great, a mã right vertueouse ãd holie, ãd so reported in al good histories, as yourself know, ãd so esteemed ãd reueréced of the whol Church. Thus haue yow vsed S. *Isidore*, a mã of great fame, ãd an holie bishoppe in the time of S. Gregorie. Thus haue you vsed *Innocétius*, the third, *Thomas de Aquino* ãd Roffensis all mé of singular vertue, ãd in learning not inferiour to yowe, I am sure, but a great waie befor yow, wherfor no soch as yow aught to deride and mock. As for the Bishoppe of Rochester, who both learnedlie ãd godlie wrote against both Luther and *Oecolãp*, his works stand yet vntouched, but of your mock, not able to be impugned by any *Lutherã, Oecolãpadiã Caluinist*, or other like, for of which sect yow be, I think yow disclose not. In this yourmoc krie yow are the right imitatour of *Porphirius* the enemie of all chrystianitie.

D For he (as *Euseb.* ãd *Niceph.* wittnesse) derided the *Euãgelists* ãd Apostles the writ ers of the scripturs: yow deride the holie Bishops ãd saincts their successours, writers vpõ the script. He cõténed the holie scripturs, he reprehended them, imagining cõtradictiõs inthé, he reputed thé (saith *Niceph.*) as things of naught:

yowe conténe the learned cómentaries ãd writings of the Sainſts of God v- **E**
pō the ſcripturs,ãd matters incidét ãd apperteining to the ſcripturs,with ſkof
fes yowe trauail to reprehéd their graue authoritie ãd godlie writings.Yowe
plaie and dallie with them before the people like a ioung *Porphirie*,as though
they were things of naught.Thus yow maie ſee,as all that be wiſe and ſtaied
by Gods grace doo ſee,howe fullie herin yowe bear the image,and iuſtlie fo
lowe the ſteppes of him,that fiercelie(as yowe doe)perſecuted with deadlie
hatred the church and religion of Chryſte.

   Your third offence ys yet worſe and more heinouſe,wher yowe haue vttered ſo manie vntrueths and lies euen *aduerſus Dominũ,⁊ aduerſus Chriſtũ eius,*
againſt our Lord,ãd againſt his Chryſte,againſt his holie goſpell,and againſt
his holie woord.Ys yowr matter ſoch(M.Iuell)as yt can not be mainteined
without lies? and(as the holie man Iob ſaied) *Nunquid Deus indiget veſtro menda*
*cio?*Hath God nede of your lies?No,ſo litle nede hath he of lies,that he will
deſtroie al thē that ſpeak lies,as the pſalmiſt ſaieth.But that I ſeē not to charg
yowe without proof,as yowe do other,ys not one of your chalenging articles againſt the preſence of Chryſts bodie and blood in the bleſſed Sacr? ys
not thē doctrine yowe teach and preache in that poinct directlie contrarie **F**
to the doctrine of our Sauiour Chryſt?Whē he ſaieth:*This ys my bodie, This ys*
*my blood:*and yowe auouche and teache that yt ys verie bread and verie wine
ys not this a contrarie doctrine to his ? ys yt not plain againſt his manifeſt
woorde?ys yt not in effect to charge him with vntrueth,though yowe daie
not yet in flat woordes ſaie that he lied?The craftie ſleight yowe vſe in hand
ling the ſcripture,wher the trueth of Chryſts doctrin doeth appeare,ãd your
wieſlie ſuppreſsiō of thoſe woords which cheiſlie declare the ſame trueth, ãd
opē yowr vntrueth,doe wel proue youre wicked meening to be none other.
For taking the woords of S.Paule for the theme of your ſermō, yowe produ
ced thē truncatedlie,and paſſed thē with moch ſleight.Thus yowe vtter thē:
I haue receaued of the Lord that thing,which alſo I deliuered vnto yow:that ys,that the lord
*Ieſus in the night that he was betraied took bread,*ãd ther yowe end.Wher,although
yowe pretēted to teach the firſt inſtituciō of the Sacr.yet either of malice to
ſuppreſſe Chriſts trueth,or for feare to diſcloſe your own vntrueth,you wold
not or durſt not reherſe the verie words of the inſtituciō,which I wiſh al mē
to note, but both in the latin ãd ingliſh,as your faith ſtaeth in bread , and as **G**
yow wold the faith of your audiēce ſhould do the like,your theme ended in
bread,in ſo moch as whē yowe come to your laſt matter,to ſpeak of priuate
Maſſe(as yow tearm yt,though falſelie,for ther ys none ſoch) and ,to proue
yowr Cōmuniō,beginne again to repete the woords of the inſtituciō, Lord,
what ſhift yowe make to ſuppreſſe the words of Chryſt:*This ys my bodie,This ys*
my blood in the which lieth al the effect of his inſtituciō. Theſe woords yowe
flie,as frō a ſerpét,yowe cã not abide the ſownd of thē,ãd therfor with ſham-
ful craft,yowe paſſe thē ſaing thus:*Chryſt in the laſt ſupper ordeined a Cōmuniō,ãd ſhe*
wed no maner token of priuate Maſſe,as maie plainlie appeare both by the woordes that he
ſpake,and alſo by the order of his doings.For he tooke the bread,brake yt,deuided yt,ãd gaue
*yt to his Diſciples,and ſaied:Drinke ye all herof.*Theſe be yowr own woords. Yowe
pretēded to proue your matter by Chryſts woords ãd order,but whē yowe
come to the verie point yowe do not as moch as touch his woords,but ſkip-
pe ouer thē,ſo well maie your prof appeare bi thē,ãd ſo loath are yowe to vt
ter Chriſt words,that his trueth might appear,ãd your falſhead be diſcloſed.
Againſt your firſt offéce(which ys your abuſe of the doctours in mutilating **H**
their ſaings,as yow doo *Anacletus*:in falſifieng their meening,as yow do *Ter-*
*tullian,*and S.Cyprian:in craftie alleaging two or three woordes,that apparantlie maie ſeem to make for yowe , leauing oute the reſt that mightilie

lie maketh againſt yowe , as yowe doe ſainct Auguſtine : in corrupting
A authours by putting woordes to their ſaings, which they haue not, as yowe
doe with *Leo*: wherbie euidentlie appeareth yowr contēpt of their autoritie,
whom by ſo manie means yowe labour to abuſe, to ſhadowe, and hide the
trueth by them ſo clerelie ſettfurth) I come in right vſe, reuerentlie alleaging them, whollie and fullie producing them, truelie reporting them, and
their mening, iuſtlie letting euerie of them plainlie to teſtifie that, whiche
he hath written , and cauſing euerie one to ſpeake his owne woordes without corruption. And that yowe maie perceaue that the catholique Churche ys ſtrong, againſt the whiche the gates of hell, the power of hereſie ſhall
not preuaill , knowe yowe, that yt ys *Terribilis caſtorum acies ordinata, a terrible*
fortreſſe in moſt goodlie order appoincted . Oute of the which fortreſſe in goodlie
order ys comed a great nombre againſt yowe, marching by cooples , eche
coople to ſhewe the vnitie of trueth and faith profeſſed in bothe Churches,
being one of the greke church, and other of the latine churche , and the ſe-
niours for the moſt part placed in the forewarde . Theſe haue I brought
furth not one alone and by piece meale ſo to rume awaie with the matter,
B as yowe doo, but in good nombres, and with their full ſaings, and the ſame
doo I oftentimes conferr together, that the full and perfect cleerneſſe of the
trueth in ther conſonant ſentences maie appear, and ſhine to all that liſt to
looke therat, and be diſpoſed to knowe the trueth.

Againſt yowr ſecond offence, which ys the mocking of holie writers and
Saincts, wherbie yowe ſeke to diſhonour and deface bothe them and the re
ligion they profeſſed, I come with due reuerence and honour of them, whō
I knowe by Chryſts promeſſe to be honourable before theFather in heauen
for their conſtant confeſsion of his holie name whileſt they liued here vpon
earth. Wherfor as being vpon the earth they were not geſts and ſtraungers
but the felowes of Saincts, and of the houſe of God, I tearme them as ſena
tours of the Parliament houſe of Chryſte, as knowing the enacted and recea
ued trueth of the matters of faith perteining to that houſe. For this cauſe I
regard all their writings which the catholique Churche hath allowed, conſi
dering that the ſame Churche that hath taught me that the goſpell , that ys
C the verie woorde of God written by the mocion and inſtruction of his holie
Spirit , hath taught me that theſe mens wiritings vpon the ſame are good
and commendable. And as with S. Auguſtine I ſaie, that I wolde not beleue
the Goſpell but that the authoritie of the Churche moueth me therunto:
no more wolde I beleue the Fathers expownding the ſcripturs, but that ther
vnto I am moued by the Churche . Then yt foloweth well that as I ought
to beleue the Goſpell for the authoritie of the Churche: ſo ought I to beleue the doctours for the autoritie of the Churche . And here to ouerthrowe your contempt of them and your ſelf alſo, I do oftentimes conferre the
expoſitions of the later Fathers with the expoſitions of the elder fathers, and
finding them alltogether grauelie againſt youre euell doctrine to conſent,
and yt to confute as hereticall and deueliſh, I let your light mockes and skor-
nes flie home again to yowe as fleſhflies to their carien.

Againſt your thirde wickedneſſe, I meen your cōtempt abuſe and vntrue
handling of the holie ſcripturs, I come in euerie place, where mencion ys
made of the bleſſ. Sacrament, with the wholl proceſſe ther conteined. In the
vi of S. Iohn, the xxvi. of S. Matth the xxiiii, of S. Luke, the x. and xi. of the
firſt epiſtle to the Corinth, the v. to the Epheſians, and the xiii to the Hebru
D es, ſomoch as the Fathers expownd to appertein to the holie Sacr. I produce
not truncatelie and falſelie, but fullie and trulie euery ſentence, and euery
woord, ſubmitting my ſelf to the authoritie of gods woord, ād not bi ſleight
ſubdewing yt to mine owne autoritie.   ¶ iiii   But

But here the learned perchaunce maie merueill, that I wold ioin with yowe in the scripturs considering the auncient counsell of Tertullian, who **E** wolde not that anie catholique shoulde entre into disputacion with an heretique with the scripturs. *Nihil proficit congreßio scripturarum cum hæreticis, nisi planè vt aut stomachi quis meat euersionem aut cerebri &c.* To ioin (saieth he) *in disputacion with heretiques with scripturs yt doeth nothing auaill, except a man will turne vppe side down either his stomacke or his brain. what shall thowe gain, thowe great learned man in the scripturs, when yf thowe defend anie thing yt shall be denied of the contrarie part: yf thowe denie anie thing, yt shall be defended &c.* And after he concludeth thus: *Ergo non ad scripturas prouocandum est &c. We maie not therfor appeall to the scripturs, neither maie we appoinct our disputacion in them, in the which ther ys either none or vnceten victorie, or not verie certen.* For this cause, and for that S. Hierom saieth that *Scripturæ non in legendo côsistunt, sed in intelligendo* the scripturs côsist not in reading but in vnderstanding: I haue trauailed by diligent searching of the fathers from the Apostles to this our time, to trie oute by ther common consent howe the scripturs are to be vnderstanded, and so haue I (as by a line drawen from hand to hand) descended from age to age, that the true vnderstanding of **F** them receaued and approued in all that diuersitie of ages and places, might be perceaued and knowen.

In this my doing I haue fulfilled the counseill of *Vincentius lyrinen.* who for remidies against errours among other willeth, that if anie errour hath ben committed in the olde time, either by certain men, or by anie one wholl citie, or by anie Prouince, to reforme that, the decrees of auncient generall Councells must be sought, and yf none soche can be founde (*as in these daies though they be fownd, they be not regarded*) then (saieth he) *operam dabit, vt collatas inter se maiorum consulat, interrogetque sententias &c.* He shall geue diligence to seke and learn the iudgemêts of the elders, and côferr the to gether but of those elders onelie, which although they were in diuerse times and places abiding: yet in the Cômunion and faith of one catholique Churche, were allwaies allowed as masters, or men of autoritie. And what soeuer he shall knowe, what not one or two of them, but what alltogether with one consent haue holden, written, and taught openlie, cômonlie, and continuallie, let him vnderstand, that that ys without all doubt to be beleued. Thus he. As this counseill ys on my part fulfilled in that I haue searched and conferred the iudgements of the fathers, and **G** fownd them (though they were in diuerse ages and places) fullie and wholie agreeng in the matters of the presence of Chrysts bodie and blood in the blessed Sacrament, of the oblacion of the same, and of other articles apperteining ther to, whiche (as in this worke yt maie be clerlie perceaued) not one or two, but euery one of them haue, not obscurely but manifestlie, not in one place, or at one time, but cômonlie and continuallie, holden, taught, and written: So wolde wolde I that yowe, M. Iuell, if yowe regarde the Fathers of the primitiue Churche in dede, as yowe bragge in woorde, that yowe (I saie) shoulde receaue and embrace these scripturs as expownded and deliuered to yowe by their hands, and their expositions to accept as a cleer and certen vndoubted trueth, whiche trueth so opened by thê, I bring furth against your vntrueths, and not the bare scripture alone, as *Tertullian* wolde I shoulde not. This, I trust, yowe shall well perceaue, if leauing your corruted affection apart, yowe will with a cleer eie and vpright iudgement read this worke, wherin yowe shall see all the Fathers that commonlie haue, ex- **H** pownding the scripturs, written of these articles of the Sacrament, whiche yowe in your iolitie (I will not saie more arrogantlie than as a chrystian preacher should, mekelie and lowlie, more rashlie, then wiselie or aduisedlie) with so great bragge wttered in your sermon, all soche Fathers, I saie, shall

yowe

yowe fee, afwell grekes as latines, afwell auncient, as of later time, with one

A cômon confent and agreement, fo expownding the fcripturs as though they had ben in one time, and had côfpired vpon one fenfe and vnderftâding: all thofe fhall yowe fee impugning your negatiues, âd by the fcripturs affirming the catholike doctrine, and faith catholiquelie and vniuerfallie profeffed, âd thus fhal the trueth of the fcripturs ouerthrow the vntruethof your herefies.

Nowe I haue in a generall maner fhewed your offences, whiche moued me to write againft yowe: in like generalitie I haue fhewed howe I do proceead againft yowe: the fpecialitie of your offences and of the proceffe aunfwe rable to the fame, yowe fhall finde in this worke, though fimplie without coolour, yet plainlie without craft, declared. Yf my trauaill herein obtein not his entêded effect, namelie your conuerfiô and amêdement, and to doo yowe that good that yow maie be ftaied frô running to pertual damnacion: yet ftaing other that by your peftilent herefies might be brought to that wo full daûger, I fhall not onelie do thê that good I wifh, but alfo helpe to make your dânaciô the eafier, whiche howe greuoufe yt fhall be, he knoweth beft, that knoweth howe manie foules yowe haue brought to damnaciô. Yf yowe

B being obdurated perfift in your impietie, yt cã not be auoided but yowe doe yt of malice, hauing ben aduertifed and admonifhed of your wicked errours and herefies hertofore by doctour Harding and other, and nowe by me. Yowe knowe who faieth: *Hæreticum hominem &c. after one or two admonicions flie the companie of an heretique, knowing that foche one ys fubuerted, for fomoche as he ys euen by his owne iudgement condemned.* In dede being, as I faied, thus admonifhed, and feing with all your wicked doctrine by the whol multitude here alleaged, fo plainlie and cleerly condemned, yt can not be but by your owne indgemêt yowe muft be condêned. For this ys fo euidêtlie true that yowe or any man can not denie yt, that no doctrine, nowe holdê of the catholique Churche for a trueth, and impugned by the Sacramentaries, was euer yet at anie time by the churche, or by any catholique writer, reputed as herefie or errour. Again this ys as true that euerie doctrine holden of the Sacramentaries, and nowe impugned by the catholiques, hath ben before time of the catholique Church and wtiters reputed and adiudged erour and herefie, a fewe late in

C uencions onelie excepted, which alfo are now by catholikes impugned, and by plain teftimonies of the auncient Church proued to be erours and here fies, and fo condemned.

To make good the firft faing, I will reherfe certain catholiq; propofitions: *Chryfts bodie ys verilie in the bleffed Sacrament. Chryfts bodie ys offred in facrifice in the Maffe. The holie Sacrament ys to be referued for the cômunion of the ficke. The bleffed Sacrament maie be receaued vnder one kinde. The bodie of Chryfte in the Sacrament ys to be adored. Sainfts in glorie praie for vs and are to be praied vnto by vs. The dead receaue great benefitte by the facri fice of the Maffe. Praier and almofe dedes doen for the dead doe auaill them*. Thefe and foche like the catholiques doe holde, the heretiques denie. I will not here proclame againft yowe, but I will ioine this iffue with yowe, that if yowe can bring anie catholique Coûcell or catholique doctour impugning thefe or anie of thê, as hereticall or erroneous, I will fubfcribe vnto yowe and faie as yowe faie : yf yowe can not (as I am fure yowe can not) thê will I faie, as I maie well, that your doctrine ys erroneous, hereticall, and deuelifh. Nowe to faue your doctrine frô this fowle reproache, proue by foche teftimonie as I haue faied, that our doctrine ys erroneous, or ells the fhame will be on your fide that teach the contrarie

D To make good my fecond affertion, I will alfo reherfe certain propofitions of your doctrine: *Chryfts bodie ys not reallie in the Sacrament. The Sacrament ys onelie a figure of Chryfte and not his bodie. The fubftance of bread ys not by due confecra-*

tion chaunged, turned, tranfmuted, nor tranfelementated into the fubftance of the bodie of Chryfte. Ther ys no facrifice of Chryftes bodie offred in the Maffe. Praier and almofe dedes nothing auaile the dead, neither the facrifice of the Maffe. Thefe and foche like do yowe and your likes teache and defend, for the whiche I will ioin this iffue with yowe, that if I haue not in this booke fufficientlie proued, or can not hereafter, if I be required, more fullie proue euerie of thefe to be erroneous and hereticall, and long agon for foche to haue ben condemned, I will fub-fcribe to them, and confeffe thē to be good? Yf I haue or can euidentlie pro ue thē fo to be, then confeffe yowe thē to be naught and deuelifh. Yf yowe refufe thus to doo: yet for the defence of your doctrine, yf yt maie be defen ded, doo that to vs, that I haue doen to yowe. I haue doen to yowe in this booke three things. Firft, I haue fhewed yowe the beginning of the doctri-ne of the bleff. Sacramēt, the progreffe and cōtinuance of yt, and the defence of yt. Secōdlie, of the Maffe which ys the folēne facrifice of Chryfts Church, I haue fhewed yowe good prefidents, certē and affured practifes, and thefe right auncient. Thirdlie, for the Sacramētaries doctrine, I haue fhewed whē yt began, by whō yt was inuēted, whē and wher yt was condēned, and fo ce affed, and by whom yt was raifed again in thefe our daies, in the whiche yt ys alfo laufullie again condēned. Nowe doo yowe the like, for your doctrine, and againft ours, Shew the beginning, progreffe, cōtinuance and defence of your Sacramentaries doctrine. Shewe the originalls and aunciēt prefidents of your Cōmunion, which ys the kaie, and note of your religion, and cōfer re thē as we haue done the Maffe, with the aunciēt prefidents of the primiti ue Churche. Shew howe all your innouacions, whiche within thefe fewe years were in no place of the chriftian world vfed, were put down, howe and by whō that was compafed: in what Popes time and Emperours reign they were fuffred to be doen, yf anie fuffred perfecuciō or exile for thē, who ftoo de againft thefe that ouerthrewe them, who wrote againft thē that banifhed your religiō, and wher be the bookes, Yf your doctrine be fo notablie good and ours fo notablie wicked as yowe teache and preache yt to be, fo great an alteraciō and decaie of religion frō fo great a good to fo grete an euell, coul-de not be doē in the world withoute greate note, without large teftimonies of hiftores and cronicles of fo lamentable a chaūge. Bring furth therfor yf yowe can the monimētes and teftimonies of thischaunge: Yf yowe can not, wife mā will thinke and beleue that ther was neuer none foche: Yf ther was none, thē be your procedings but nouelties, inuēted in thefe later daies, and neuer before in vfe, and therfor well tearmed the newe religiō, newe doctri ne, newe faith, newe churche, newe Communion.

Two things, M Iuell, I doubt not, but yowe knowe. Thone, that in the pri mitiue and auncient church ther arofe no notable herefie, but yt was fpede-lie impugned: Thother, that of the originall and progreffe of euerie foch ther were notes made and moniments for memorie left. As concerning the firft, yt ys certē, that euē in the beginning of Chryftes Church *Ebion* and *Ce-rinthus* fowing their herefie were ftreight impugded by S. Iohn, againft whō he was moued to write his gofpell and epiftles. Againft the fame alfo with other, as *Valentinus, Marcion, Cerdon, Symon Samarites Bafilides, Carpocrates,* and foch like, wrote the holie Father *Irenæus* not long after, who, as in his workes yt maie be feen in diuerfe places, vfed for an argument againft thofe hereti-ques, the prefence of Chryfts bodie in the Sacramēt, and yet the fame *Irenæus* was neuer noted of errour for his fo affirming and teaching. *Origen* his works being fownde infperfed with diuerfe errours, was noted for them, but wher he teftifieth the prefence of Chryftes bodie in the bleff. Sacrament, he was

neuer

neuer blamed : Ciprian the holie martir was verie vehemēt againſt *Nouatus*

A the heretique, and his ſect, he diligentlie laboured to cut of ſoche weedes. This holie mā in the matter of the preſence wrote ſo plainlie as no mā more plainlie, he wrote alſo of baptiſme. In the matter of the preſence, the church hath allowed him, in the matter of Baptiſme notwithſtanding his holineſſe they haue refuſed him. To be ſhort *Epiphanius* and S. Auguſtine wrote bookes of the hereſies of them that were before and in their times, and although manie beſides the fore mēcioned had ſpoken ſo plainlie of the bleſſed Sacr. that they cleerly cōfeſſed the preſence of Chryſts bodie in the ſame, as *Martialis, Ignatius, Iuſtinus, Tertullianus, Hilarius,* and manie other: yet be none of all theſe nor none other for that doctrine nōbred ther amōg heretiques, which vndoubtedlie they ſhould haue ben, if the matter had ſo deſerued. But trulie yt was neuer yet red in anie god writer, nor ſomoche as dreamed, that the cōfeſſiō of the preſēce of Chryſte in the bleſſ. Sacramēt ys hereſie or errour.

Nowe as touching hiſtories witneſſing the wicked beginning the miſerable progreſſe, and open end and confuſion of hereſies, yt were ſuperfluouſe for me to write, ſith ther hath ben no notable hereſie or heretique, which

B are not recorded either by *Euſebius, Teodoret, Soʒomenus, Nicephorus, Aeneus Siluius,* and ſoche other whoſe bookes be dailie in mens hands. By whom when your Sacramētaries hereſie begā we knowe, howe lōg yt continued openlie we knowe, who withſtood yt and wrote againſt yt we knowe, in howe manie Councells yt hath be cōdemned we knowe. Furder who haue renewed the ſame in theſe later daies we knowe, when and howe *Luther* reigned we knowe: howe *Oecolampadius* folowed, though an other waie, we knowe, howe *Caluine* hath cōtroled both catholiques and heretiques we knowe, what the doings of theſe and their complices haue ben and be, we knowe, and that they haue ben and be condēned for heretiques we know. To be ſhort, ther hath ben no notable alteracion or moleſtacion in religion by hereſie, but yt ys committed to memorie in hiſtories. Yf thē your doctrine and faith, your religion and profeſsion, your notable Cōmunion, or raither confuſiō, were once good and catholique, yt can not be but of ſo great an alteracion as to make catholique faith damnable hereſie, or holie cōmunion wicked diuiſiō

C ther muſt be ſome notable mencion in hiſtories or ſome auncient monimēt in writing to declare yt. Yf yowe haue anie ſoche bring them furth, and thē yowe ſhall doo ſōwhat to allure wiſe men vnto yowe. For in this poinct I hold him nothing wiſe that will repute either your doctrine, faith, religion or communion to be good and catholique vntill yowe ſhewe good teſtimonies and preſidents of the catholique vſe of them, which I am certen yowe can neuer doo. As for ſoche euidences as your ſelf nowe and your auncetours heretofore haue picked oute of the right and true euidences of the catholique Churche, I meen the holie ſcripturs, Councells, doctours, and approued hiſtories, and with great boldneſſe haue ſhewed thē to the world and auouched them to be yours and to aſſure your cauſe, they are allreadie well knowē ād tried not to be yours in dede, but to make all for the catholique faith and religiō, and mightilie againſt your ſingular phāſies and to ouer throw your wicked hereſies, when they be plainlie opened, and deliuered frō your craftie corruptions, as they haue ben by ſondrie and manie famouſe learned men as well in this age, as before our time. And I, to my power, haue in this booke, for ſoche matters as I hādle, detected your forgerie, and

D corrupting of the euidences therto appertening, by your wreſting, gloſing, cutting, peicing, diminiſhing, adding, and other wiſe falſifieng the right, cleer, wholl, perfect, godlie and true teſtimonies of the ſcripturs, Councells ād auunciēt doctours. And ſoch as be ſo flatte againſt your cauſe, as yowe can

haue

haue no aide of them, but be forced therfor either to depraue their authori
tie with mocking aud skorning, or flatlie to denie their workes, they are de- E
fended, and holdé in their woorthie eftimacions, and their denied works re
ftored to the right authours. The firft therfor, that ys the fcripturs Coūcells
and aunciét doctours yowe can no more abufe for fhame and chaleng to be
on your fide, whé being fifted frō your fleights, and clered frō your falfhead
all mé maie perceaue thé not to be your right euidéce, making, as thei do, fo
plainlie againft yowe, ād mightilie ouerthrowing your caufe. The other, that
ys, the later learned writers and holie fathers, yow maie no lōger contemne
being proued to agree, as they doe, with their elders and approued, as they
be of the church, to be catholique and holie writers, your skoffes and mocks
againft them, will ftand for no reafon before wife men.

Nowe yowe vnderftand, M. Iuell, what I haue here doen, to the whiche
yf either yowe or anie other for yowe fhall by railing Rethorike make
a pretenfed anfwer, I do yowe to witte, that I will not vouchfafe to
putt my penne to the papire for that kinde of anfwer. For I haue begonne with yowe in an other fort, and like a diuine, railing I haue left to ruffins F
and skoldes, and coolours of perfuafions to rethoricians, directlie according
to my profefsion with all plain trueth haue I proceaded. Yf anfwere therfor
fhall be made, let yt be either a direct anfwere or none. Direct anfwer ys foche as I make to yow, where yowe abufe the vnderftāding of the fcripture, or
doctour, to proue the fame vnto yowe: where yowe falfilie, to alleage the pla
ce truely: where yowe corrupt, to fhewe the right faing: when yowe adde
and put to, to declare what yowe adde and put to: whé yowe leaue oute, to
exprefle the woordes fo by yowe left oute. And finallie, by full, plain, and
exprefle teftimonie of fcripturs, Councells, or doctours, as the condiciō of
the matter requireth, to open and declare the trueth, and by like authoritie
to proue and cōfirme the fame. Thus haue I doé to yowe in plétifull maner,
in euery matter here by me handled, fo that the trueth of euerie thing ys fo
fullie opened, and by good authoritie fo confirmed, that I truft, euerie man
that will fee maie fee, and euerie man that will vnderftand, maie vnderftand,
where the weight of the trueth ys.

Read therfor, M. Iuell, and diuorcing your felf frō vainglorie to the which
ye haue hen a lōg time maried, let your vnderftāding be captiuated vnto the G
feruice of Chryfte, Let not your vain eftimaciō in errour and herefie detein
yowe to come to the honorable eftimacion, that ys gotten in the profefsing
of Gods trueth. Lét yt not be faied of yowe, as the holie father and Pope *Leo*
faied of *Eutiches: Noluit intelligere vt bene ageret. Iniquitaté meditatus eft in cubili fuo.*
My good will was that this mi doing fhould haue bé in your hāds a lōg time
er this, for yt was finifhed full three years paft, but ficknefle, pouertie, and lac
ke of oportunitie to printe yt haue thus long ftaied yt. But fith nowe at the
laft yt ys by Gods helpe comed abroad, I hefeche him of his great goodnefle
to graūt that it maie be to his honour, ād to the helpe of his people ād that it
maie be a medicine of health to yow, ād all that by your falfe doctrine ād fleight, haue bé entrapped ād deceaued. Yowe promifed that yow wolde yelde
to him that wolde bringfurth to yowe one fcripture, or one doctour, or one
Coūcell &c. as yow knowe: This being nowe doé by me ād other I wifh that
yow maie yeld your felf prifoner, not in warrelike maner to vs, but in lowlie
maner to Chrifte, ād his dere fpoufe the catholiq; Churche, by acknowleging
their faith, and profefsing their religion to faue your foule, which we fhal be H
moft ioifull to vnderftād, ād for your foch cōuerfiō yelde to God moft hūble
thanks. Yf yow doo not, yet let me wifh yow for fome better ftaie of your felf
hereafter, to haue this olde faing in minde: *Ante victoriam ne canas triumphum.*

B

He Phylyſtynes (gentle Reader) moued ſore and great warre againſt the Iſraelites: The heretikes againſt the catholique Chruche of God . from whome ys comed furth a newe Golyath mightie in hys owne cōceit, with reprochfull woordes to reuyle the hoſte of oure lyuyng God, and to blaſpheme hys holie name, to raill at hys holie myſteryes and to comdemne hys holie ordinãces, who with impudēt mouthe (truſting,in the ſtrēght of ſpere and ſheilde)bluſtereth oute ſoche blaſphemouſe woordes,as the like.to my knowledge(Crã, mer hys auncetour onelie excepted) neuer dyd phyliſtyne before hym.

Hæretiques moue Ware againſt the Churche.

He alone cometh oute, and prouokyng Iſraël to battaill, makéth proclamation thus: *Yf any learned man of all our Aduerſaryes , or yf all the learned men that be a lyue , be hable to bring anye one ſuffycyent ſentence , oute of anye olde catholique Doctour, or father : or oute of anye olde generall Councell : or oute of the holye ſcriptures of God:or anye one example of the primatyue churche, wherbye yt may be elerely,and playnly, proued, that ther was anye pryuate maſſe in the wholl worlde at that tyme, for the ſpace of ſyx hundreth years after Chryſte &c. and a fewe articles recited, he proceadeth thus: orthat the people were then taught to beleue , that Chryſte bodye ys reallie , ſubſtantiallye , corporallye , carnallye or naturallye in the Sacrament : or that hys bodie ys ,or may be in a thouſand places, or mo,at one tyme :* and ſofurth proceadeng to laye oute hys matters.enombreth xv.articles,all whiche(foure onelie excepted)be agaynſt the holie Sacrament of Chriſtes bleſſed bodie and bloode, And for that he wolde not ſeem to faynte in hys doyng, he ſaieth, that he for hys parte wolde not onelie not call in anye thing that he had then ſaied , but alſo wolde laie more matter to the ſame, and ſo addeth he twelue mo artycles to the former, all whiche (one onelie excepted) be alſo againſt the bleſſed Sacramēt,and the mynyſtraciō of the ſame.whiche hys proclamation with the addycion he knytteth vppe thus: *Yf any one of all oure Aduerſaries , be able to auouche anye one of all theſe articles by anye ſoch ſuffycient authorytie of Scriptures , Doctours, or Councells,as I haue required , as I ſaied before , ſo ſaie I nowe agayn : I am content to yeldé vnto hym,and to ſubſcrybe.*

Proclamacion of the newe Goliath

VVhiche ſtoute bragge as ſome of hys likes (I ſuppoſe) myſlyked, and manye good catholique men(I knowe) thought yt arrogant : So I thynking the ſame , like litle Dauid, not in faith,might,aud powre : not in vertue and ſyngular fauour of God : but as the leaſt and yongeſt of my breatheren , in the houſe of my ffather, not bearyng thys vyle reproche ſo arrogantlie, and ſhameleſlie made againſt the hoſte of God , of a good zeale hauyng ſure truſt in my lord God (whoſe cauſe for my powre, I wolde gladlie defende) hanyng ſome ſtones gathered together in my ſheperdes bagge, I come in the name of God againſt thys Goliath,and for thys tyme putting thys ſtone oute of my bagge into my ſlyng,I caſt yt at hym,whiche,I truſt,ſhall ſo hytte hym in the forehead, wher ys the ſeat of ſhamefaſtneſſe, yf anye be in the man,that he ſhall be aſhamed ſo to reuyle the wholl churche of God agayn. I ſaie the wholl Churche, for theiſe, hys lucyferouſe woordes, be not ſpoken onelie againſt ſoche as were or be of the catholique Churche in Englōde : but to the contumelye of all the wholl catholique Churche of Chryſtendome , wherſoeuer ys or hath ben profeſſed , and taught the reall preſence of Chryſtes bleſſed bodie and blood ir the holie Sacrament.

A   And

And for that hys cheif force ys bent agaynſt that Sacrament, whyche ys **H**
our comforte, foode, and nutryment to euerlaſting life: I haue alſo bent my
ſelf therin cheiflie to withſtande hym, not medling moche with anye other
matter.

Wherunto yet when I prepared my ſelf, and conſydered one of the Arti-
clesof hys proclamaciõ,wher in effect he ſaieth,that neuer mã was condemned as an herytyke, for ſaynge that the Sacrament was a fygure, a pledge, a
tokẽ, or a remẽbrance of Chryſtes bodie: I began to be abaſſhed,Firſt at his
craft ãd ſubletie vſed in ſo weightie matter of faith, wher all ſymplycitie and **I**
playn dealing ſhoud be vſed. for if he referre theiſe his woordes to the ſyxe
hondreth yeares next aftcr Chryſt,that in thoſe ther was neuer man cõdemned for ã heretike,that ſaied that the Sacramẽt was a figure,a pledge,a tokẽ a
remẽbrãce.yt ys true.for in all that tyme neuer was ther heretike that ſo ſaied
in that ſenſe that this proclamer ãd his likes doo ſaye yt.wherfor that ys but a
craftie toye to'bleer the eye of the hearer to make him beleue that mẽ in tho
ſe daies were not for ſo ſaing cõdemned,wher in dede none did ſo ſaye, and
where none did ſo ſaie none coulde be condemned for yt. Moche like argu- **K**
mẽt might a felõ make for hym ſelf in theſe daies ſaing that Chryſte, intwhõ
afert his reſurrectiõ, was the fullneſſe of auctoritie and power,as he hym ſelf
wittneſſeth, dyd neuer cõdemne anye of his Apoſtles or dyſciples to deathe
for felonye.wherfore he being a chryſtian man aught not be condemned for
felonye.This argument hath a trueth,for Chryſte cõdemned none of them.
for none of them were felons : but yt lacketh force, for though they not ſo
offending were not condemned: yet thys felon ſo offending maye iuſtly be
condemned.Likewiſe though none with in thoſe ſyxe hondreth years,for as **L**
muche as they ſo ſaied not, were not condemned ꞉ yet this proclamer ſo
ſainge maye wel be condemned And here I willioyn iſſue with hym that
if he can bring one within thoſe ſixe hondereth yeares that ſaied, as he
ſaieth & was not condemned, I will ſubſcrybe. Secundly I abaſshed at hys
impudencye. for if the man be ſo impudent as to ſaie, that neuer man was
yet hitherto indged and condemned for an heretyke, that ſaied the Sacrament was a figure in that ſenſe that he,and hys complyces do take yt,name-
lie tobe a figure withoute the verie preſence of the bodie of Chriſt,the con- **M**
trarye wherof ys knowen to all the worlde, and therfor not vnknowen to
hym:what ſhall yt awaill me to buckle with ſo impudent a man?

Sacramen-
taries con-
demned by
eight Coun-
cels.

For ſoche ſaiers haue ben condẽned by eight Coũcells all readie, as he-
retykes, and theyr hereſie ſo deteſted, hated, and abhorred of all chriſtians,
that the catholique learned men, yf they had but a ſuſpicion, of anye that
dyd in anie one title ſwarue from the verytie of Chryſtes bodie in the Sacramẽt, they furth with addreſſed them ſelues to their pennes,and with the
ſwoorde of Gods trueth,vanquyſhed,and ouerthrewe yt. **N**

Paſchaſi⁹.
Bertramus
wrote obſ-
curelie and
ſuſpiciouſly
of the Sa-
crament.

Thys (as yt ys thought)moued *Paſchaſius* towryte in the matter of the Sa-
crament.for that *Bertramus* had in the tyme of kyng Charles wrytten therof
ſuſpycyouſlie,and yet in ſuche ſorte,as no mã coulde be certẽ what he aſſuredlie ment.Nowe that the treuth of the matter of the Sacramẽt,ſhoulde not
be obſcured with ſoche doubtfull wryting, *Paſchaſius* wrotte a booke of the
preſence of the verie bodie of Chryſt in the Sacrament, in ſoche expreſſe
and playn woordes, as the ſymple man maye preceaue what was the faith of
the Chruche in that tymeof that matter.

And for that, he was ſo playn, *Gaſtius*, one of thys proclamers facion, ha **O**
uyng gotten an olde exemplar of that worke (as yt ys appertynent to the
ſyncerytie

A ſyncerytie of ſoche men) he raced yt, he blotted yt, yea, he cutte oute wholl chapiters of yt. and that doen (that yt might to the woorlde appeare, that *Paſchaſius*, who wrotte ſo long agone, wrotte yet nothing againſt the Sacramentaries) he ſett yt furthe, ſo mutylated, ſo torn and ſo defaced, to be prynted.

But to return to ſpeake of thys proclamer,conſydering,as I ſaied, the Artycle wherin he ſaieth neuer man was condemned for an heretike, that affirmed the Sacraméte to be a figure,ſign &c. I was ſo abaſſhed at hys impude-

B cye,that I was partelye mynded not to haue ioyned with hym.

But remembryng that yt was more impudencye to denye Chryſtes preſence in the Sacrament, whiche ys tanght by Chryſtes owne woordes delyuered by ſainĉte Paule,beleued in the primytiue Churche, ſo receaued of holie men, wrytten by an infynyte nombre of learned wryters, confyrmed by Councells,and embraced and ſtaied vpon,by all chryſtyan nacions; I corrected my ſelf, ſayng that yf I wolde not ſpare to ioyn with hym in thys wicked aſſertyon,moche leſſe ſhoulde I ſpare to ioyn with hym in that other.

C Wherfore reſumynge my former pourpoſe, I wyll in thys alſo ioyn with hym.and ſhewyng from the begynnyng of the fyrſt Aucthour of thys hereſie eué vnto thys Proclamer, that they were all iudged for heretikes, whiche affyrmed and taught that the Sacrament ys a figure, (as thys Aduerſarie and hys complyces do) I ſhall with all open the vanytie of hys bragge, wherin he ſaieth,that the catholique Churche .haith not one ſcrypture,not one doĉtour,&c. for the mayntenance of their faith.

For the playn openyng of whiche mattter,yt ys certen,by teſtymonye of

D manie learned mé,that though ſome dyd ſo cófuſedlie wryte in thys matter, that they might be ſuſpeĉted, or dyd ſecretlie (as men fearyng the goodneſſeof their cauſe) whiſper in corners, whiche were very fewe: yet amonge all that rightlie beleued in Chryſt, as God and man, *Berengarius* was the fyrſt, that dyd openly wryte and teache, denyeng (as thys proclamer doth) the reall preſence of Chryſtes bodie and bloode in the Sacrament.

Whiche *Berengarius* was about the yeare of our lorde a thouſande ãd three ſcore, and So by computacion fyue hondreth yeares agon,& more, a man,

E as ſundrye wryters teſtyfie) neither excellent in learnyng, nor commendable in life : who publyſhing thys doĉtryne by poure ſcholers, to whome he gaue ſtypende for that pourpoſe, he ſpredde yt abroad in corners.

Whiche when yt came to the knowledge of *Leo* then Pope, a man (as *Platina* ſaieth) of ſyngular ſanĉtymonye,and holyneſſe of life:he condemned *Berengarius* in a Councell.

The woordes of *Platina*, for the certen declaracion of the matter, I ſhall not refuſe to reporte.Thus he wryteth: *Ad Leonem redeo virũ ceriè pietate,inno-*

F *centia, benignitate, gratiâ, hoſpitalitate, adeô inſignem, vt eius Domus peregrinis, & pauperibus ſemper patuerit. Nam cum ſemel ante fores ſuas leproſum pauperem inueniſſet, cunq; præ miſericordia collocari in leĉto ſuo mãdaſſet,apertis manè foribus à ianitore,nuſquã pauper inuentus eſt.Chriſtum pauperis nomine,eo loci recubuiſſe creditum.In rebus præterea ad religionem pertinentibus,tanta diligentia.& ſolertia vſus eſt, vt & in Concilio Vercellenſi Berengarium hereſeos autorem damnauerit.*

I come agayn to Leo,a man trulie in godlyneſſe,in innocécye,benygnytie, grace,and hoſpytalytie ſo notable excellent, that to ſtraũgers,and poure peo

G ple hys houſe was allways open. For when vpon a tyme he fownde a poure man,a leapre,lyeng before hys gate,and through mercye had godlie commaunded hym to be layed in hys bedde, in the mornyng when the gates were

A ij   opened

Beréngarius firſt openlie impugned the ſacrament.

Beréngarius neither excellent in learning nor cõmédable in life. Leo nonus Platina

opened of the porter, the poor man was in no place fownde. And ſo yt was **H**
thought that Chryſte in the maner of a poor man was layed ther.

Berēgarius condemned in the Coūcell of Vercells, at Rome, ād two other Coūcells.
Beſydes thys in matters apperteynyng to religyon he vſed ſo moche dyligence and wyſe cyrcumſpection, that in the Councell at *Vercells* he condemned *Berengarius* the Author of an hereſye. Thus farr Platina. This condénacion notwithſtandyng, the wicked man perſyſted in hys impyetie, wherfore an other Councell was holden at Towres, wher by dyuerſe learned Fathers he was conuynced, and ſo abiured hys hereſie.

Berēgarius recanteth and abiureth.
And in à Councell holden at Rome, wher were cxiij. Byſhops (as *Lanfrācus* **I**
who then lyued teſtyfieth) he recanted alſo hys hereſyes.

And yet all thys notwiſtāding, though thys cākre of hereſie ſemed in the outwarde parte to be cured: yet yt fretted inwardlie, and grewe to an newe ſore, that wher before he had taught that the Sacrament was but onelye a figure of the bodie of Chryſt (as thys proclamer alſo tracheth) nowe he begā a newe doctryne, affyrmyng that in the Sacrament was the verye bodie of Chriſt: but that ther was alſo the Subſtāce of bread, with the Subſtāce of the bodie of Chryſt. Wherupon ther was an other councell called vnder **K**

Gregorius. 7.
Gregorye the vij, in the whichę the ſaid *Berengarius* beyng conuinced, dyd acknowledge hys errour, and by expreſſe woordes recanted the ſame.

Not onelie theſe foure Councells condemned the hereſye of *Berengarius* againſt the Sacrament. but alſo the learned men that were in that tyme, peyned them ſelues to wryte wholl bookes to the confutacion of the ſaid *Berengarius*, and hys hereſies.

Lanfrancus. Tritemius.
For againſt hym wrote *Lanfrancus* ſomtyme Archbyſhope of Cantorburye, of whom *Tritemius* ſaied: that he was *vir in diuinis ſcripturis eruditiß. et non mi-* **L**
nus ſanctitate, quam ſcientia clarus. a man in the dyuyne ſcryptures moſt excellentlie learned, and no leſſe in holyneſſe, then in knoweledge notable.

Algerus Guitmundus.
Againſt the ſame alſo wrote *Algerus*, and *Guitmundns.* men not by my commédacion onelie to be accepted, but by the Iudgement of *Eraſmus* alſo, a man not only knowen to the worlde, but alſo ſpecyallie famouſe in thys Realme of Englonde, who openyng to vs what theſe two men were, ſheweth therwtih the benefitt of God that cometh to hys churche by hys ſufferāce of errours, and hereſyes to growe. And enombryng dyuerſe hereſies cōceaued againſt the bleſſed Sacrament he ſaieth thus : *Et tamen horum omnium* **M**

Eraſ. in epiſtola ad Balthaſarum Epiſc. Hildeſūm.
error in hoc profecit, vt in tanti myſterij cognitionem, magis ac magis tū erudita, tum conſir mata ſit eccleſia. Nulli tamē plus debet quàm Berēgario. imo nō Berēgario, ſed Chriſti ſapiē-
tiæ, qui malitiā hominū vertit in bonū ſponſæ ſuæ. Quos & qualiū virorū calamos excitauit
impudens error Berengarij? Nuper exijt opus Guitmundi, ex monacho Benedictino epiſcopi
Auerſenſis . Nunc prodit Algerus ex ſcholaſtico monachus eiuſdem inſtituti . Guitmundus
acrior eſt & ardētior, & plus habet ſpiritus Rethorici: hic ſedatior eſt ac religioſior, vterq;
tum Dialecticas, tum reliquæ philoſophiæ bellè peritus, licet citra oſtētationem: vterq; in ca- **N**
nonicis ſcripturis, ac priſcis illis doctoribus, Cypriano, Hilario, Ambroſio, Hieronimo, Augu-
ſtino, Baſilio , Chriſoſtomo (quorum ſcripta plurimùm adhuc referunt ſpiritus Apoſtolici)
ſtudioſè verſatus : vterq; tantum habet eloquentiæ, quantum requirere à theologo par eſt.
Certè dictionis argutiam , & collectionis acumen, nuſquam in eis deſidere. Agunt

Chriſt turneth the malice of Heretiques to the profett of his Church.
ſolidis rationibus, nec (vt nunc quidam faciunt) bonam voluminis partem rixis, &
contentionibus occupant, aut ſophiſticis ratiunculis rem tractant . And yet the erroure of all theſe (ſaieth *Eraſmus*) dyd profytt in this, that in the hnowledge of ſo great a myſterye, the Churche ſhoulde be both more and more inſtru- **O**
cted, and alſo confyrmed, Yet ys ſhe to none more bownde then to *Berengarius*, yet not to *Berēgarius*, but to the wyſdō of Chryſte, who turneth the malice

of

A of men to the profett of his fpoufe . what writing , iea and of what men hath this impudent errour of *Berengarius* ftirred vppe ? Of late went oute the woorke of *Quitmundus* fomtyme a benedyctyne Monke, and Bifhoppe of Auergne : nowe commeth furth the worke of *Algerus* of a fcholer, made a monke of thefame ordre: *Guitmundus* ys fharpe and vehement, and hath more of the rethoricall fpiritte: the other milde , and religioufe, bothe of them well learned both in logike and philofophie , although withoute oftetation; both of them well ftudied both in the canonicall fcriptures and in the olde

Erafmus calleth the errour of Berengarius impudent.

B doctors Cyprian, Hillarie, Ambrofe, Hierom, Auguftin, Bafill, and Chrifoftome. whofe writinges do yet declare moche of the Apoftolicall fpiritte : Bothe of thē haue as moch eloquence as ys meet to be required of a diuine. As for wittie fpeache, and fharpeneffe of collection, ther ys no lacke in them in anie place. They go to yt with fubftanciall reafons, neither do they as fome whiche occupie a good parte of ther bookes, with braulinges , and contenciōs, and handle the matter with fophifticall difputacions & reafons. Thus moche *Erafmus*.

C I haue the more willinglie tranfcribed thus moche of *Erafmus* bicaufe the Aduerfaries haue had him in good price, and regarded his fainges. Yf this champion do the like, let him diligentlie obferue that *Erafmus* calleth the errour of *Berengarius*, an impudent errour . Whiche fo being, forfomoch as this man ys drowned in the fame , and mainteineth the fame , maie we not iuftlie faie , that he impudentlie mainteineth an impudent errour? Let him alfo note , howe he commendeth thefe men, and what Iudgement he hath of their learning bothe in liberall fciences, in Scriptures, and doctours. whō

Errour of the Proclamer impudent.

D he doth alfo no leffe extoll, but that by their writinges God hath doen a great benefet to his Churche. whiche fo ftanding yt can not be but that the Scriptures, and doctours be plain , and euident for the proof of the veritie of the reall prefence of Chriftes bodie in the Sacrament . whiche fcriptures and doctours adduced by thefe learned men be mo then one, or one fcore, and yet this Proclamer crieth: bring one doc &c.

Yf their writing be a benefett then this chalengers doimge ys a detriment.

After *Berengarius* rofe one *Petrus Waldo* a citizen of Lions, a man vnlearned, yet as vnlearned as he was , when he had newlie fkoured the ruftie condem-

E ned herefie of *Berēgarius*(in foch rude maner as yt was) manie were fo folifh, and fo readie to fall from faith to herefie, from life to death and damnacion, from teaching of the learned to the teaching of the ignorarūt , that thei chofe raither to folowe the phantafie of this one rude man void of knowledge, than to remain in the Subftancial tried doctrine of a nombre of holie , and moft excellent learned men of Chriftes Churche. Thus (more pietie yt was) a mombre folowed hym, and became his difciples, and were called *Waldenfes*. Vnto whom becomminge an Aucthor and blinde guide, according to Chri-

Petrus Waldo fkoureth the eftie herefie of Berēgarius

Waldenfes. Heretiques condēned

F ftes faing, he led them fo , as both fell into the ditche . This fecte and herefie of this *Waldo*, was not fuffred to ftand, but (as Guido faieth) was condemned in a Councell holden at Rome . And yet this Proclamer faieth ther was neuer man indged for an heretike that faied the Sacrament was a figure , a token, &c.

In the tyme of fainate Bernarde Satan wolde moue yet fome more trooble to the Churche. and therfor raifed one *Peter de Bruis* whom he taught to fell theife lies to the people for trueths , that though Chrift in his laft fupper

Petrus Brufian . his herefie.

G did in the Sacramēt, geue hys bodie to his Apoftles: yet no preift doth fo nowe, by the power of his woorde, as yt ys faied that they doe. For neuer ani one (quoth he) but Chrift alone did geue his bodie in the Sacrament.

Although

Althongh thys herefie geuing foche preeminence to Chrift that,bycaufe he H
faied,thys ys my bodye, teacheth that he in dede gaue to hys Apoftles hys
verye bodie,ys woorthy of more fauour thē the herefie whiche thys Procla
mer teacheth(for not withftanding that our Sauiour Chryft faied : Thys ys
my bodie,yet thys Aduerfarie teacheth yt ys not)yet paffed not this herefie
awaie in fcylence,but was wrytten againft by dyuerfe. Among whyche *Pe-*
Petrus
Cluniacen.
trus Gluniacenfis whofe commendation ys fo moche fettfurth in dyuerfe Epiftles of faynē Bernarde,that he nedeth not myne to commend hym) wrote
a booke in the matter of the Sacrament againft the fe&t of the fame Peter de I
Bruys,called Petrobrufians,and other cleauing to them,calledHenrycyans,
Almari-
cus a Sacra
mentarie
condemned
iu the Coũ-
cell of late-
ran.
In the whiche booke, I am certen, ther be mo then one fcripture, one doctour &c. alleaged and brought furth. Yt ys faied that one *Almaricus* amóge
other herefies, dyd alfo fette furth thys herefie againft the Sacrament, who
with thys hys herefie and hys other,as Bernardus de Lutzēburgo faith,were
condemned in the great Lateran Councell.

After all thefe commeth the famoufe heretike Ihon Wycleff oure
contrey man,whom God fuffred with manye peftylent herefies to trouble K
Iohn wi-
cleff oure cõ
trie man
an hereti-
que cõdē-
ned.
Ioānes hus
condēned.
Horoni-
mus de Pra
ga condem-
ned.
Luther
Oecolam-
pad.
the Churche . Amonge whiche herefies he helde two or three againft
the Sacrament . All whofe articles being in nombre fortie and fiue,
Ioannes Hus, befides other of hys owne inuencion dyd holde and mayn-
teyn, auouching them to be good and godlie. And as he embraced the
do&tryn of *VVycleff.*So dyd *Hierom de Praga* both the do&tryne of *Wycleff* and
of the faid *Ioannes Hus*,who being conuented for the fame in the Couuncell
of Conftance,dyd fyrft,as Berengarius dyd,abiure hys herefies.After,to declare what conftancie was in hym,he reuoked hys abiuracion, ād auouched L
the do&trine of *Wicleff* and *Hus*.All whiche three with their herefieswere in
that Councell of Conftance condemned.

Luther and *Oecolampadius*,although repugnaunt one to the other, in this
our time,they haue faied and doen as moche as this champyon can doe,and
thought themfelues as mightie as he.An yet they haue not onely bē impug
ned by writers : but alfo condemned as heretikes in the generall Councell
of Trydent.

Thus haue ye nowe feen the wholl defcent of this herefie againft the blef M
fed Sacrament, euen from Berengarius the firft open teacher of the fame,vn
to *Luther* and *Oecolampadius* the newe furbufhers and fkourers of the fame:Ye
perceaue that from time to time,they were euer condemned by Councells
as heretikes,that taught the bleffed Sacrament to be but a figure or token
of Chriftes bodie,and not the bodie yt felf:ye haue feen that learned mē ha
ue written againft them , and with learning beaten them downe, for that
they reputed,efteemed,and iudged them as heretikes , and the enemies of
gods trueth,as the breakers,fubuerters, and deftroyers of peace, and diffol- N
uers of the vnitie of Chriftes churche.

Maye I not therfore well faie,that this proclamer ys an impudent man ,a
fhamelefle man,which feareth not to fpeake fo openlie,to preache fo boldelie,to write fo fhamelefllie fo manyfeft an vntrueth, as to faie in effe&te , that
neuer man was iudged an heretike,that denied the prefence of Chriftes bodie in the Sacrament,when they were neuer yet otherwife iudged? But to
ende this parte of the matter,this dare I faie(for that I knowe I fhall fpeake
yt trulie)that to this daie ther was neuer man iudged or condemned by any O
generall Councell that euer was , to be an heretike that faied , that Chriftes
bodie ys reallie and fubftanciallie in the Sacrament . Nowe yf this do&tri

ne

A ne neuer, and the other euer, hath ben condemned, yt ys eafie to iudge, what eche of thefe doctrines ys.

To come to this our time, befide the condemnacion of the herefies of Lu ther and *Oecolampadius* in the matter of the Sacrament, as before ys faied, Euē as *Lanfrancus, Algerus, & Guitmundus* did aginft *Berengarius*, auouche the catho like doctrine by their workes and Boorkes fett furth for the fame pourpo- fe: Euen fo a great nombre as well of owre contrie men, as other, haue by fcriptures, Councells, and doctours, againft the faid *Luther* and *Oecolampadius*,
B doen the like.

For to beginne with our contrie men firft, hath not the learned, graue, and reuerend Father Ihon fomtime Byfhoppe of Rochefter, encountred a- gainft them, and with Scriptures, Coūcells, and doctours fo mightilie and in- uiuciblie ouerthrowen them, that neuer till this daie any Philiftin durft ta- ke weapon in hāde againft hym to helpe vppe and recouer ther *Goliaths* and champions? And can not this Goliath fee one fcripture, one Councell, nor one doctour in all thofe his woorkes written to that pourpofe? Tonftall of
C durefme, and Stephen of winchefter, bothe reuerend Fathers, men not one lie in Englonde, but alfo in other nacions right famoufe, haue they not left their woorthie monumentes behinde them, replenifhed with fcriptures, Councels, and doctours, for the affertion of their faithe in this matter of the Sacramēt, to the cōfufiō of the aduerfaries. Alfo Ihon late of winchefter, hathe he not collected into one booke two hundereth wittneffes of fcrip- tures, Councells and doctours, for the veritie of Chriftes bodie in the Blef fed Sacrament?

D Doctour watfon Bifhoppe of Lincolne, as he ys right woorthely learned: So to hys moche prayfe hath he writtē godlie, and learned Sermons of the bleffed Sacramēt, in the whiche be mo plain teftimonies of fcriptures, Coū- cells, and doctours, alleaged for the trueth of this matter of the Sacrament, then the proteftantes can bring apparaunt for their herifie. Doctour Albane Langdale Archdeacon of Chycheftre in the confntacion of the determina- cion made by Redleye, at the difputacion holden at Cambridge for the mat ter of the Sacrament, ys fo plentyfull in fcriptures, Councells, and doctours,
E and fo pythie withall, and fo plainlie laieth them furth for that pourpofe, that this Goliath with all his blafphemoufe, and prowde woordes fhal neuer be able to conuince him.

Yf herefie were not by election, and election of fingularitie, and fingulari- tie fett not more by her owne phantafie, then by moft mens iudgementes, be they neuer fo graue, neuer fo wyfe, neuer fo well learned, the iudgement of thefe men in the fcriptures, Councells, and docturs, whiche they alleadge as fentēces euidēt, and plain, certēlie and clerely prouing the reall prefence
F of Chriftes bodie in the Sacrament mighte fuffice to pull downe the peacoc kes taile of this fingular man. But in the iudgement of them that be wyfe I doubte not, but hys bragge femeth more prowde than true.

Befydes all thefe, to fpeake of other that be ftraungers hath not this man hearde of the fame of *Alfonfus*, who not long fence was here in Englonde, and wrote here parte of his booke, which he hath written and fett furthe a- gainft al herefies, in the whiche he inueyeth againft this newe Goliath and all like Philiftines, their adherents, and complices. yea and againft all their
G Auncetours. Where he maketh reherfall of thii ten fundrie herefies inuen ted by that wicked generacion againft this holie and bleffed Sacrament and conuinceth them all as well with fcriptures, and Councells, as with many

A iiij   holie

Rofenfius neuer yet aunfwered.

Tonftallus Dunelmen Steph. wint

Ioā wyntō.

watfonus Lincoln.

Albanus Lāgdallus.

Herefie ys by election.

Alfonfus.

Thirtē fun drie here- fies againft the Sacra- ment.

holie doctours and famouse writers, and yet this proclamer cryeth: bring **H**
furth one fcripture, one Councell, one doctour, one example, &c.

The time wolde not ferue to nombre all that haue written in this matter,
and tedyoufneffe wolde encombre the Reader, wherfore leauing manie, as
Gropperus. Gropperus, who right learnedlie, and largelie hath hãdled and fetfurthe the
faithe of the Churche in all times of the high pointes of the Sacramẽt, auou-
Vernierus. ching the fame by fcriptures, doctours, and Councells: And Wernierus, who
like vnto the Nycen Councell, hath made Collection of three hondreth
eighten places of fcriptures, doctours, and Councells, for the affertion of the **I**
Tauerne- trueth of the Sacrament: And alfo, Tauernerius, Eckius, Pighius, Hoffmeiſterus, Ga-
rius. retius, with other manie: I will onelie bring two, who be foche as, I fuppofe,
Eckius. this man will better regard, and better like their iudgementes in this mat-
Pighius. ter, then of thefe before mencioned.
Hoffmei-
ſter. The one of them fhall be, Erafmus who in hys epiſtle aboue alleaged wry-
Garetius. teth thus: Ex euangelio habemus, Hoc eſt corpus meum, quod pro vobis traditur. Ex Pau
Erafmus lo habemus: Ego enim accepi à Domino quod & tradidi vobis, &c. Et qui ederit, & bibe-
ad Balthas rit indignè reus erit corporis & fanguinis Domini. Hoc nobis immobile fundamentum. **K**
Epiſcop. Oute of the Gofpell we haue: This ys my bodie, whiche ys delyuered for
yowe. Oute of Paule we haue: I haue receaued of our lorde, which I delyue
Erafmus red alfo vnto yowe, and fo furthe. And he that eateth and drinketh vnwour-
his iudge- thylie fhall be giltie of the bodie and blood of our lorde. This ys vnto vs an
ment of the vnmoueable foundacion. And after a fewe woordes he faieth: Cum igitur tam
Sacramẽt. euidens à Chriſto & Paulo habeamus teſtimonium, quum per hos viros euidentiſsimè decla
ratum fit prifcos, quibus non fine caufa tantum auctoritatis tribuit ecclefia, concorditer fenfiffe in Euchariſtia veram effe fubſtantiam corporis & fanguinis Domini, quum ijs om- **L**
nibus etiã acceſſerit Synodorũ conſtãs autoritas, tantusque populi Chriſtiani cõfenfus, fimus et
nos concordes in tam cæleſti myſterio, & hic fub enigmate edamus de pane et calice Domini,
donec aliter edamus, & bibamus, in regno Dei. Vtinam autem qui Berengarium fecuti funt
errantem, fequantur & pænitentem. Seing then we haue both of Chriſt and of
Paule fo euident teſtimonie, feing alfo by thefe men (meening, Guitmundus
and Algerus) yt ys moſt euidentlie declared, that the olde auncyent Fathers
(vnto whom the Churche not withoute caufe yeldeth fo moche authoritie)
haue agreablie vnderſtand the verie fubſtãce of the bodie and blood of our **M**
Lorde to be in the Sacrament: Seing alfo that to all theife agreeth the conſtant Authoritie of the Councells, and fo great a confent of Chriſtian people, let vs alfo agree in fo heauenly a myſterie, and lẽt vs here in a darke maner, as vnder a couert, eate of the bread, and drinke of the cuppe of ourlorde,
vntill otherwyfe we maye eate and drinke in the kingdom of God. Wolde
to God that all they that hane folowed, Berengarius in errour, wolde folowe
hym alfo in penaunce. Thus farre Erafmus: Note gentle Reader, and I wolde
the Aduerfarie fhoulde note alfo, that here ys moſt euident teſtimonie affir- **N**
med, and auouched out of Chriſt, and Paule, and the common concorde of
all the doctours, the conſtante Authoritie of Councells, the vniuerfall and
wholl confente of Chriſtian people, all agreyng, beleuing, and teaching the
very fubſtance of Chriſtes bodie and blood to be in the Sacrament. Forafmoch then as here ys produced afmoche and more to, then thys chalenger
did require (for he did require but anye one fcripture, one doctour, one coũ
cell) and here be produced fundrie fcriptures, all the olde doctours the Authortie of the Councels, and befydes thefe the common and vniuerfall con- **O**
fent of the Chriſtian orbe, yf ther be anye trueth in thys man, he will perfourme his promiffe and fubfcribe to this trueth, whiche wolde to God were
doen

A doen by him, that (to conclude with Erafmus his fayng) he might folowe, *Berengarius* in penaunce, as he hath folowed hym in erroure. Nowe to the better confirmacion of this matter, and to the more confutacion of this hys impudent boaft, and fhamefull blafphemye, I fhall ioyn his owne fchoole with hym, I meen the learned of the Germanes, whiche write thus: *Decimus Articulus approbatus eft, in quo confitemur nos fentire, quod in cœna Domini verè & fubftantialiter adfint corpus & fanguis Chryfti, & verè exhibeantur cum illis rebus quæ videntur, pane & vino, his qui facramentum accipiunt. Hanc fententiam conftanter defenderunt concionatores noftri. Et comperimus non tantùm Romanam ecclefiam affirmare corporalem præfentiam Chryfti, fed idem & nunc fentire, & olim fenfiffe Græcam ecclefiã, vt teftatur canon Miffæ apud Græcos. Et extant quorundam fcriptorum teftimonia. Nam Cyrillus in Ioannem cap. xv. inquit Chryftũ nobis corporaliter exhiberi in cœna. Sic enim ait: Non tamen negamus rectà nos fide, charitatéque fyncera Chryfto fpiritualiter coniungi. Sed nullam nobis coniunctionis rationem fecundùm carnem cum illo effe, id profectò pernegamus, idque à fcripturis diuinis omnino alienũ dicimus. An fortaffe putãt ignotã nobis myfti-*

B *ce benedictionis virtutẽ effe, quæ cum in nobis fit, nónne corporaliter quoq; facit cõmunicatione carnis Chryfti, Chryftũ in nobis habitare? Et paulo poft: Vnde confiderandũ eft, non habitudine folùm, quæ per charitatẽ intelligitur, Chryftũ in nobis effe, verumetiam participatione naturali, etc. Hæc recitauimus, vt clarius perfpicerent, qui ifta legent, nos defendere receptam in tota ecclefia fententiam, quòd in cœna Domini, verè et fubftantialiter adfint corpus, et fanguis Chryfti.* The tenthe article ys approued, in the whiche we confeffe that we beleue that in the fupper of our Lorde be verilie and fubftantiallie prefent, the bodie and blood of Chryft, and that they be verilie geuen with thofe thinges that be feẽ, that ys, with bread and wine, vnto them that receaue the Sacramẽt Thys fentẽce haue our preachers cõftantlie defended, And we finde not onelie the churche of Rome to affirme the corporall prefence of Chryft in the Sacramẽt, but alfo the greke churche both nowe to beleue, and of olde time to haue beleued the fame, as the Canõ of the Maffe emõg the grekes dothe teftifie. And ther be alfo extant the teftimonie of certain writers. For *Cyrillus* vpon Iohn in the fiuetene chapter faieth, that Chryft ys corporallie deliuered vnto vs in the Supper. Thus he faieth: We do not denie

C that we be fpirituallie ioyned vnto Chryft by faith and fyncere charitie. But that we haue no maner of cõiunctiõ with him after the flefh, that we verilie, denie, and that we faie, ys altogether againft the fcriptures. Doth he thinke the power of the myftical benediction to be vnknowen vnto vs? which whẽ yt ys doen in vs, doth yt not alfo by the communication of Chryftes flefh, make Chryft corporallie to dwell in vs? And a litle after he faieth: Wherfor yt ys to be confydered, that not by inward difpofition onelie, wihiche ys vnderftand by charitie, Chryft dwelieth in vs: but alfo by naturall participaciõ, &c. Thefe thinges haue we recited, that what foeuer they be that fhall read thys, they fhoulde the more clearly perceaue, that we defende the doctrine receaued in all the Churche, whiche ys, that in the fupper of our Lorde are verilie and fubftanciallie prefent the bodie and bloode of Chryft. Thus moche the Germans in their Apologie. I fuppofe this proclamer will nowe take a better minde with him, and fomwhat contracte and drawe in the large fales of his great bragge, fo vehementlie puffed vppe with a mightie vain glorioufe winde, when he feeth the learned of Germanie fo franklie and plainly

D publifhing their faith, whiche, though yt be not in euery point fownde, yet auouche they the contrarie to the doctrine of this proclamer, and encoũter with him in this chalenge.

For firft they cõfeffe the very fubftãciall prefence of the bodie and blood

of Chryft

Apologia Confeff. Auguft.

Cyrillus

The Germanes acknowlege the verie prefence of Chryft in the Sacrament.

The greke and latine Churches, both nowe and in olde time affirme the corporall prefence.

Chryft dwelleth in vs corporallie not onlie fpirituallie

The receaued doctrine in all the Church ys, that Chryft ys verily, and fubftã tiallie prefent in the Sacramẽt.

of Chryſt in the Sacrament. Secondarely they confirme the ſame by the au- E
thoritie of all the Chriſtian churche, as well the latin, as the greke church, for
that in them both, not nowe onely, but of olde time alſo, yt hath ben ſo
taught, receaued, and beleūed. Thirdly they alleadge a clere and moſt plain
place oute of Cyrill, whiche by their iudgement, as yt dothe appeare, doth
manifeſtly and inuinciblie proue the corporall preſence of Chryſt in the Sacrament. And as yt ſo doth by their iudgement: ſo doth yt by the iudgement of all catholike men, not onelie withſtand this prowde Goliath, But
yt plainly ouerthroweth hym. Of the force of whiche ſentence, more ſhall
be ſaied hereafter. Fourthlie earneſtly acknowledging this trueth, and willing yt to be knowen to all the worlde, they declare that the cauſe of their
thus writing ys, that all men might knowe, that they do defende the trueth
receaued of all the Churche, which ys (ſaie they (that the bodie and blood
of Chryſt be verilie and ſubſtanciallie in the Sacrament.

This then being a treuth, that ys and hath ben receaued of all the wholl
Church of Chryſte, as beſides theſe mens confeſsion, all catholique people F
through oute all chriſtendome do acknowlege yt ſo to be, I praie thee (good
Reader) what parte doth this mã take to defende, who with might and main
dothe maintein the cõtrarie: And impugneth that, that the whollChurche re
ceaueth, reuileth that, that the whol Church reuerenceth: blaſphemeth that,
that the wholl Churche honoureth? and that ſo arrogantlie and impudẽtlie?

The Pro-
clamer ys
to be pi-
tied.

Yt ys pittie that ther ys ſo moche impudencie, and ſo moche arrogancie
mixed with vntrueth in him. I ſaie pittie for that he ys Gods creature, and in
Baptiſme once profeſſed Chriſtes name, in this reſpecte charitie moueth me
to pittie him, and the more for that he receauing the plentifull giftes of
God, doth ſo wickedlie to the more encreaſe of his damnacion abuſe them,
and forſaking God and his trueth, becometh enemie to them bothe, which
he well declareth in that with ſoche violence he impugneth, and blaſphemeth them both.

In this parte and reſpecte as I cã not ioin with him: ſo for my maſters cauſe,
and the defence of my Mother the catholique Churche, in whoſe houſe I
deſire to cõtinewe, I cõtende with him, and contẽne him, yea and hate him, G
not the ſubſtance that God hath created in him, but the wicked hereſie that

Hereſie ma
keth mã e-
nemie to
God.
Pſalm. 148

the Deuell hath breathed into him, by which as he ys become enemie to
God: ſo muſt all the people of God become enemies to him, as of the Prophet Dauid we haue good example. Do not I, o lord (ſaeth he) hate them,
that hate thee? And am not I greiued with thoſe that ryſe vppe againſt thee?
Yea, I hate them right ſore, euen as though they were my enemies. And yet
as I moue my penne againſt him: So ſhall I moue my tounge to praye for
him. Poſsible yt ys that he being in the higheſt of his miſchief, maye be ſtry-
ken downe as Paule was in the hygheſt of his rage of perſecucion.

Saincte Auguſtine when he walked in hereſie, and did moſt ſtowtly con-
tempne the catholique profeſsiõ of Chriſtes name: yt pleaſed God, ſodenlie
as yt were, to geue him a newe minde, and cauſed him to reuerence that, that
before he deſpiced.

The like happie chaunce I wiſhe this mã, againſt whom yf I haue ben, or in
this boke ſhall ſeme to be ſharpe, let yt be referred to the euel cauſe wich the
man defendeth, and not the perſon himſelf. The doctrine ys ſo wicked, ſo di- H
rectly againſt Gods holie woord, ſo diſcrepant from the holie Councells, ſo
diſſonant from the auncient Fathers, ſo diſſenting frõ the common conſent
of Chriſtian people, ſo iniurouſe, and contumeliouſe to the wholl Churche
that

A that hath ben from Chrift vntill this daie, that yt ys by nō means tollerable.

Nowe Reader, I truft thowe feift, that as moche as this iolie Chalenger required, ys nowe perfourmed to him, let him therfor perfourme his promeſ ſe, and fubſcribe to the catholique faith, and confeſſe Chriſtes reall preſence in the Sacrament. Yf he will yet maliciouſlie perſift, and faie, ther ys no ſcripture, nor doctour, nor Councell brought furth, that plainly proueth yt, thē we muſt prouoke to iudges. Yf he will not beleue the Germanes being Proteftantes, not *Eraſmus*, who ys accompted of them an vppright man, not the Catholiques of our owne contrie, and of other contries, not the Councells, which be alleaged, not Cyrills plain and manifeſt fentēce, not the cōmon re ceaued faith of the wholl Churche, as well of that of the olde time, as that, that ys nowe, bothe of the latines, and of the grekes, not the plain woordes of Chrift, who plainlie faith: *This ys my bodie*: Whiche woordes Eraſmus faieth be owre ſure and vmmoueable fundacion. I praie thee, Reader, whome will he beleue befides himſelf? Who ſhal bringe furth that one ſcripture, doctour,

B or Councell, that he will accept, as plainlie prouing the matter? None but he himſelf, or his likes, moche like to the Felon that pleadeth not giltie, and ſtoutlie crieth to be tried by God, and the contrie. And when by verdict of the iurie and ſentence of the iudge he ys cōdēned, he defieth thē all calling bothe iudge and q̄ſt falſe harlotts, ad faieth, that true mē wolde neuer haue cōdēned him. But the true mē that he meeneth be ſoche as he ys himſelf. So che true mē they be nowe alſo, that this mā wil creditte in this matter, euē ſo che as he ys himſelf, yf he doe refuſe all theſe kindes of mē aboue produced.

But howeſoeuer he ſhall take this, and the reſt of my booke in outwarde countenance, I truft yt ſhal touche his conſcience. And then (as Chryſoftom faieth) *Leuis erit conſolatio, ybi conſcientiæ ſentiunt ſe eſſe confuſas.* Yt ys but a light or ſmall comfort, when the conſciences of men perceaue them ſelues confownded.

God of his mercie reduce him and all, that be gone aſtraie, home to hys folde again, that they be not in his terrible iudgement confownded before him and all his Angells.

C Nowe, Reader, that the order of this my rude worke maye be knowen vn to thee, vnderſtād that wher the enemie of Gods trueth, hath in his ſaied ſer mō made his boaſt, that he ys ſure, that not one fentēce cā be brought by the catholiq̄s to proue the Articles, ther by him rehersed, amōge the which, befi de the reall and fubſtāciall preſence of Chriſt in the Sacramēt, he addeth ma nie other thinges apperteininge to the ſame, which he ioineth together vnder one predicamēt, that ys, that we haue no proof for them : that he maye be perceaued to be a vain and falſe man; I will proue yt by ſcriptures, doctours, and Councells. And incidentlie diuerſe other of his rehersed matters, to this principal apperteining, Whiche, allthough I ouerpaſſe them not in ſo che maner as he doth, onelie to faie, and nothing to proue or improue thē, as they be of him vttered : yet ye ſhall finde thē anſwered, wher occaſion ys miniſtred to ſpeake of ſoche matter.

And although manie profownde, and excellent learned men, whoſe latchettes of their ſhoes I am not woorthie to looſe, haue woorthlie written in

D this matter: yet for that none of them, to my knowledge, hathe after this ma ner proceaded orderlie to expownde the ſcriptures, that treact of the Sacrament, whiche methinke to the confutacion of this man ys neceſſarie, I will, by the helpe of God, that waie proceade, and not by mine owne phantaſie, but by the verie mindes of the doctours, truely ſeke oute the true vnderſtan

Smalle con forte wher conſcience ys con founded.

Ordre of the Booke.

The contens, and ordre of this work.

ding of them. And for that thefe fcriptures be in three fundrie bookes of the E Bible, that ys, in the olde Teftament, in the Gofpells, and in the epiftles: ther for the matter beinge lõg, I haue diuided this rude worke into three bookes. In the firft booke are opened foche promiffes, figures, and prophecies of the olde Teftament, as appertein to the Sacrament. The feconde booke geueth yow vnderftanding of the fcriptures apperteininge to the fame, conteined in the vj. of fainct Ihon his Gofpell, the xxvj of fainct Matthew, and in the xxiiij. of faincte Luke. The thirde booke expowndeth fo moche of the tenth, and the eleuenth chapiter of the firft epiftle to the Corinthians, as toucheth that matter, and alfo one fentence of the epiftle to the Ephefians, and one other to the Hebrues.

In this expofition, to the more confutacion of the Aduerfaire, and confirmacion of the catholique, I, for the moft part, bringinge fundrie, and diuerfe doctours vpon euerie text, doe ioin a greke doctour and a latine together, that the concord and agreement of bothe churches maye well appeare, and fullie be feen. So haue I alfo ioined the doctours that haue written within F the compaffe of thefe nine hondreth yeares, to them that haue written before, that yt maie be iudged, whether that thefe of the later time doo differ, or diffent from them of the auncient time in the fubftanciall poinctes of our faith, as the aduerfarie faieth they doo.

By which proceffe, gẽtle Reader, thow fhalt, I truft, perceaue, that where the arrogante Philiftine both blafphemouflie, and vntruelie hathe faid of the Catholique Church of the liuing God, that yt hathe not one fcripture, one doctour, nor one Councell: yt hathe vñdoubtedly, as touching the bleffed Sacramẽt, and other articles apperteining to the fame, not onelie al the holie Scriptures that treact of that holie myfterie, but alfo the holie Fathers, and Councells, that fpeake of the fame, both Grekes and latines, and them afwel of the auncient time before a thoufand yeares, as thẽ, that were of the later time, within the cõpaffe of a thoufand yeares. So that the fcriptures being thus explained by the common confent of fo manie doctours, and all the fame alfo confpiring vpon this one trueth (as yt fhall be perceaued, not by a vain bragge, withoute proofe, but by euident and plain teftimonie) we maie as truelie G as boldlie, returning his bragge into his owne lappe, faie, that this philiftine and his cõplices, for the maintenance of their herefie againft the prefence of Chrift in the bleffed Sacramẽt, haue not one fcripture, one doctour, nor one Catholiq Coũcel to make for thẽ. Which thĩge, I dare faie, the indifferẽt Reader, whẽ he fhal haue perufed this booke, wil not feare to auouche with me.

Catholique Church Chriftes Parliamẽt houfe.

And wifhinge that this my laboure might be profitable to the fimple and vnlearned, for whofe helpe I haue moft fpeciallie taken yt, I haue framed my writing, as neare as the matter will fuffre, to their capacities. And wher in ciuill, and politike regiment, Lawes, Actes and ftatutes haue their force by Councells and Parliamentes, therfor wher the veritie of Chriftes reall prefence in the Sacrament, ys a trueth eftabliffed, enacted, and receaued by Chriftes Parliament houfe (I meen the catholique Churche) yt liketh me oftentimes to allude to the name, and therto agreablie to name this booke. I haue not entẽded to fall one heere breadth frõ the faith of the catholiq Churche. Yf anie thing hath flipped from me, I fubmitte yt to the correction of Chriftes catholique Churche, and my felf aifo, Prainge thee, god Reader, to accept my labours in good part, and remembre me in thy prayers. Vale.

Title of the booke.

THE FIRST CHAPITER VPON OCCASION THAT

This adversarie, this Proclamer, and chalen-
ger wolde haue the scriptures red of all men (presupposing the same to be
easie to be vnderstanded) entreth , as by preamble, to treact of the difficultie of the scriptures , and to prooue that they aught not of all men to
be red, without an hable interpretour or teacher.

AVING in pourpose to declare by the testimonie of the noble men of Christes Parliament house , the enacted and receaued treuth, or true meening of all, or most of soche scriptures, as
treact of the blessd Sacrament of the bodie and bloode of our
B   Sauioure Christe, ther cometh to my minde the doctrine of Lu
ther, the great Progenitour of this Aduersarie, who in his booke. *De seruo ar-*   *Luther. de*
bitrio (as other his ympes likewise in their bookes) teacheth, that the scriptu-   *seruo ar-*
res of them selues be easie of all men to be vnderstanded , and nede no in-   *bitr.*
terpretour.

Wherunto also (the more to infatuate the people) he addeth, that we be
all, *Theodidacti*, that ys to saie, taught of God, and of his Spirit, so that yt shall
not nede for one man to teache an other, or for one to learn of an other. Of
whiche mynde this Aduersarie semeth also to be, in that he woolde the scriptures shoulde be commō to all men. Whiche doctrine yf yt were true, then
ys my pourpose here vain and superfluouse , which ys to seke oute the true
meening of the scriptures by the holie fathers and doctours.

Wherfore, as a preamble to this rude worke, I haue thought good to discusse, and by discussion to make plain to the vnlearned Reader, that the scriptures be obscure, darke, and harde to be vnderstāded, and for that cause not
of all men indifferentlie to be red. Wherbie yt shall appeare, that my pour-
C pose shall be to good effecte. And for the better cōpasing therof, I minde to
shewe to the vnlearned the waie to atteign to the true vnderstanding of the
scriptures, and that doen, to proceade to my matter principallie intended.

And wher our cheif pourpose ys, to treact of the blessed Sacrament this   *1.*
maie iustlie be the first argument, that the controuersies therof in theise ou-   *Scriptures*
re daies moued (whiche be to manie) do make yt more then manifest , that   *to be hard*
ther be difficulties in the scriptures .Yf difficulties, then be they not plain.   *prooued by*

The secōde: the disciples whiche heard Christes owne disputacion of this   *seuen argu-*
mentes
mysterie, proceading oute of his owne mouthe , as oute of the liuelie welf-   *2.*
pring, ād who, for that they were disciples, shoulde better haue disgested Cri-
stes woordes, then the people of the Iewes, who grosslie saied: *Quomodo potest*
hic dare nobis carnem suam ad manducandum ? howe can this man geue vs his flesh   *Ioan.6.*
to eate? Yet they (*the disciples I meen*) in the ende of the disputacion saied: *Du-*   *The disci-*
rus est hic sermo, quis potest eum audire? This ys an hard saieng, who can abide to   *ples vnder-*
heare him? So that neither the people of the Iewes, nor yet the verie disci-   *stode not*
ples of Christe, whiche shoulde moch haue exceaded the other, did atteign   *Christes*
D to the trewe vnderstanding of Christes woordes , carnall reason preuailing   *owne woor-*
des.
against humble and lowlie submission to faithe.

Vpon the whiche woordes of the disciples, Chrystome saieth; *Quid ergo est,*   *Chrysost, in*
Durus? difficilis intellectu , & quē capere non posset eorum imbecillitas, plenus formidinis.   *6.Ioan.*

What then ys this woorde, *harde*? A faieng not eafie to be vnderftanded, and **E** whiche being full of dread, their imbecillitie coulde not beare or take. Yf then the woordes whiche Chrifte fpake, being the gofpell (although vnwritten) were (as Chrifoftome faieth) not eafie to be vnderftanded, what more eafineffe maie we thinke to be in thē nowe being the gofpel written?

3.

Luc.24.

Jbid.

And further yf we trulie faie that the fcriptures be eafie, and plain for euerie man to vnderftande, yt fhoulde appeare, that yt was no great benefet, that Chrifte did to his Apoftles, in opening their wittes, that thei might vnderftande the fcriptures. Neither was it anye great matter that he did to the two difciples that went to *Emaus*. vnto whome beginning at Moyfes, and the prophettes he interpreted in all fcriptures whiche were written of him.

Chriftes interpreting of the fcripturs, and opēnig of wittes to vnderftād them argueth the difficultie.
2.Petr.3.
4.
Acto.8.

But certenlie yt was a great benefet, that Chrifte did at theife two fundrie tymes geue, in openyng theyr wittes to vnderftand the fcriptures to the one: and in interpreting the fcriptures to the other. For withoute this benefet neither the one, nor the other coulde haue atteigned to that gifte. **F** Wherfore the depeneffe of the fcriptures weighed, and oure infirmitie confidered, we maie verie well conclude with fainde Peter, that as (he wittneffing) the epiftles of fainde Paule be hard: fo be the reft of the fcriptures harde.

Of this the chamberlain of queen *Candace*, of whome ys made mencion in the actes of the Apoftles, beinge fo well affected to the fcriptures, that paffing from Hierufalem homewarde, and fitting in his chariette he was reading them, and yet vnderftoode them not, had good experience. That he vnderftoode them not yt dothe well appeare by his owne confeffion. For Philippe beinge mcued by the Spirit of God to ioin him felf to his chariette, heard him reade Efaie the Prophete, and afked him faing: vnderftandeft thowe, what thowe readeft? and he aunfwered and faied: howe can I, except I had a guide? wherefore when Philippe was with him in his chariette, and the fcripture was red, the camberlain afked him faieng: I praic thee, of whome fpeaketh the Prophet this? of him felf, or of fome other man? Philippe opened his mouthe, and beganne at the fame fcripture **G** and preached vnto him Iefus.

Philippe fent by the holie Goft to expownd the Scriptures to the Eunuche.

This place teacheth vs, that not onelie by the faing, and doing of the chamberlain, but alfo by the doing of the holie Gofte, the fcriptures be obfcure and harde. For the holie Spirit of God dothe nothing in vain. wherfore when the fame Spirit mercifullie beholding the good affection of this man, and knowing the fcriptures to be foche, as he coulde not vnderftand them withoute an interpretour, did fend Philippe vnto him, to open and declare that vnto him, that was obfcure and dake before, yt dothe inuinciblie proue oure pourpofe. Whiche facte of the holie Gofte had ben vainlie doen, yf the fcriptures were plain and eafie of all men to be vnderftanded. Nowe yf this man coulde not vnderftande them withoute an interpretour, no more can anie other common man doo. And then what dothe yt auaill the fcriptures to be commonlie red withoute an interpretour?

5.
Ioan.16.
The Apoftles vnder ftood not Chriftes liuelie voice,

The Apoftles them felues, when our fauiour Chrifte fpake vnto them of his paffion and refurrection (as yt appeareth in the xvj. of Iohn) coulde **H** not vnderftande him. For when he faied vnto them: After a while ye fhall not fee me, and again after a while ye fhall fee me. For I go to the Father: then faied fome of them emongeft them felues: what ys this that he faieth vnto vs, after a while ye fhall not fee me, and again after a while ye fhall fee me?

A me? and that I go to the father? they saied therfore, what ys this that he saieth after a while? we can not tell what he saieth.

As this maner of speache beinge vttered by the liuelie voice of Chriſte was darke vnto the Apoſtles: ſo the ſame beinge nowe written in deade letters, ys yt not (trowe ye) as darke to manie as yt was to them, till yt be opened and declared? yf yt were not eaſie to them that heard Chriſte him ſelf ſpeake yt: howe ſhoulde yt be eaſie to the vnlearned, that do but read yt?

For as ſaincte Hierom ſaieth: *Habet neſcio quid latentis ænergiæ viua vox, & in aures diſcipuli de Autoris ore transfuſa, fortius ſonat. Vnde & AEſchines, cum Rhodi exularet, & legeretur illa Demoſthenis oratio, quam aduerſus eum habuerat, mirantibus cunctis atque laudantibus, ſuſpirans, ait: Quid ſi ipſam audiſſetis Beſtiam ſua verba reſonantem:* The liuelie voice (ſaieth ſaincte Hierom) hath I wote not what an hidden vertue, or cIereneſſe of demonſtration, and beyng vttered from the mouthe of the Authour into the eares of the diſciple, yt haith a more

B force in ſownde. wherfore Aeſchynes, when he was a banisſhed man at the Rhodes, and the oration, which *Demoſthenes* made againſt him was red, when all men did wonder at yt, and praiſe yt, ſithing he ſaied: what yf ye had heard the beaſt him ſelf vttering his owne woordes? Thus moche ſaincte Hierom.

Hieron ad Paulinum.

The liuelie voice hath a more force in the eare then the dead letter in the eye.

In the whiche ſaieng he declareth, that ther ys more clereneſſe in a ſentence liuelie ſpoken from the mouth of the Authour, and the hearers ſhall more eaſelie preceaue yt, and ſooner vnderſtande yt, then they ſhall onelie reading the ſame in the dead letter. Yt maie therfore be concluded, that the goſpell as yt, ys written ys more hard to be vnderſtanded, then as yt was of the mouthe of Chriſte ſpoken. But as yt was ſpoken yt was hard to be vnderſtanded, wherfore being written yt ys more harde to be vnderſtanded.

Saincte Paule enombring the giftes of the Spirit, ſaieth: To one ys geuen the vtterance of wiſdome: to an other the vtterance of knowledge: to an other ys geuen faith: to an other the giftes of healing: to an other po-

C wer to do miracles: to an other prophecie: to an other iudgment to diſcern ſpirites: to an other diuerſe tounges: to an other interpretació of toûges. All theiſe (ſaieth he) woorketh one and the ſelf ſame Spirit, diuiding to euerie man a ſeuerall gifte euen as he will.

6. 1.Cor. 12.

In the whiche diſtinction of giftes, ye perceaue that the vtterance of wiſdome, the vtterance of knowledge, the gifte of tounges, be ſeuerall giftes. And that they be not geuen to all men indifferentlie, but ſome to one, ſome to other, as yt pleaſeth the holie will of that bleſſed Spirit, that ys the Authour and diſtributour of the ſame giftes. For ſaincte Paule in the ende of the ſame chapiter, wher the former alleaged woordes be writté, ſaieth: Are all Apoſtles? are all prophetes? are all teachers? are all doers of miracles? haue all the giftes of healing? doo all ſpeake with toûges? doo all interprete? &c. whiche his maner of queſtioninge includeth a negatiue, that euerie man hath not all theiſe.

Then foraſmuche as euerie man hath not the gifte of vtterance, of know-

D ledge, nor the gifte of prophecie, nor the gifte of interpretacion &c. Euerie man hath not the vnderſtanding of the ſcriptures, Neither then be the ſcriptures eaſie to be vnderſtanded of euerie man. For vnto him, that hath the gifte of knowledge, prophecie, and interpretacion of ſcriptures, the ſame be eaſie; But euerie man hath not theſe giftes, wherfore the ſcriptures to all mē be not eaſie.

Interpretation of Scripture not geuen to euerie man.

B iiij   This

7.
1.Cor. 12.

This also fainte Paule proueth verie well by the ordre and difpofition   E
of the naturall bodie, from whiche he diduceth and taketh an argument to
proue an order in the mifticall bodie the Churche. Ye are (faieth he) the
bodie of Chrifte, and membres one of an other. And God hath alfo ordeined in the Congregacion: Firft Apoftles, fecondarelie prophetes, thirdlie Teachers, then them that doo miracles, after that the gifte of healinge
&c. In the whiche defcription of the order in Chriftes Churche, ye fee
that the three cheifeft, and higheft ftates be Apoftles, Prophetes, and teachers. Nowe if the Scriptures be eafie for euerie mans vnderftanding then
either thefe ftates be fuperfluoufe, bicaufe euerie man vnderftanding the
Scriptures, ther nedeth no teacher, nor Prophete : Or ells forafmoche as
euery man vnderftandeth the fcriptures, he ys in this ftate to be a teacher,
and a prophete, whiche ys directlie againft fainte Paules doctrine. For he
faieth all be not Prophetes, neither be all teachers.

*All be not
Prophets,
nor teac-
hers.*

Forafmoche then as Chrifte hath appointed, as one of the cheifeft ftates of his Churche, the ftate of teachers, there muft be of neceffitie a great   F
nombre of inferiour membres, that muft be hearers, and learners. And
whie fhoulde they fo be, but that the fcriptures being harde, and obfcure,
by the teachers they muft be opened and declared, that other maie learn. So that as by this fcripture yt maye be perceaued and learned that
euery man hath not the gifte of knowledge, and therfore no eafie vnderftanding of the fcriptures : So by all the other before alleaged yt ys mofte
manifeft that the fcriptures be harde and full of difficulties, whiche fhall
alfo by other means well appeare to the Reader, in the proceffe enfewinge.

THE SECVNDE CHAPITER TO PROVE THAT

THE SCRIPTVRES BE NOT EASIE, RECITETH CER-
tain hard and obfcure places of the olde teftament.

L B E I T that this, that ys all readie faied, ys fufficiét to proue the
fcriptures to be hard, and not playn, ne eafie to be vnderftanded : yet that ye maye fee yt more manyfeftlie before yowe face,   G
certain places fhall be laied before yowe, whiche for their obfcuritie and difficultie, fhall compell and enforce yowe to confeffe that they be not eafie for euerie mans vndeftanding.

And firft fhall be brought fome places of the olde Teftament, oute of the
whiche I might bring, not places, but wholl bookes, and of them not a fewe,
as all the Prophetes, as well the greater, as the leffe, the Booke of Iob, the
booke of pfalmes, the booke of the Preacher, and *Cantica canticorum*, englifhed
the Ballett of ballettes of Salomon. All whiche bookes, certen I am, be

Acto.8.

of foche difficultie, hardneffe, and obfturitie, that, as queen *Candaces* Chã-
amberlain faied, they can not be vnderftanded with oute a guide, or ells
fpeciall infpiracion of god.

*Hieron
prefa. in
Ezech.
Genefis mi
ght not be
red of the
Iewes befo-
re thirtie
yeares of
age.*

As for *Genefis*, although it be counted fo eafie, and fo plain a booke : yet
the Iewes (as fainte Hierome witneffeth) might not read yt before they were thirtie yeares of age, as in whiche were many thinges verie harde to be
vnderftanded, whiche required a ftaied heade, of mature, rype, and graue
Iudgement, foberlie to feke the true fenfe, and vnderftanding of them, whi-   H
che rafh youthe wolde fooen ouerpaffe, and frame an vnderftanding at
their pleafure, foche as they phantafied, as manye do nowe a daies.

Oute of this booke, although fainte Auguftin, and other that haue trauailed

A uailed in the expofition of the fame do mooue manie and fundrie doubtes:
yet I fhall ouerpaffe them, wisfhinge the Reader to confider the 49. chapiter, in the whiche are côteined the bleffinges of Iacob to his twelue Sonnes, and let him trie howe he can waid through the vnderftanding of them,
as for example : In the bleffing of *Iuda*, *Iacob* faied : *Iuda* ys a lions whelpe,   *Gen.49.*
from thefpoill, my fonne, thowe arte comed on high.He laied him dowen,
and couched him felf as a lion, and as a lioneffe, who wil ftire him vppe?
And after a litle : He fhall binde his fole to the vine, and his Affes colte to
the braunch. He wafhed his garment in wine , and his mantle in the
bloode of grapes. His eies are reader then wine, and his teeth whiter then
milke. Soche like be the other . Howe eafie theife be for the vnlearned
to vnderftande I referre yt to thy iudgement, Reader.

    Exodus, and *Leuiticus*, withe the reft of *Pentateuchon*, although they require
an higher fenfe for a Chriftian to vnderftand, then the letter fowndeth
(as Origen declareth) whiche not all the learned atteign vnto, befides the
B applicacion of the figures to the things figured in the newe teftament by
Allegories, as fainct Paule dothe in the Epiftle to the Galatians, and in his
Epiftle to the Hebrues : yet they conteyn diuerfe obfcure fenfes, feming
almoft to haue no reafon in them, as this in *Leuiticus* : Ye fhall kepe my or-
denances . Thowe fhalt not let cattle gendre with a contrarie kinde , nei-   *Leuit.19.*
ther fowe thy felde with mingled feede . Neither fhalt thow put on anie
garment of linnen, and wollen.

    And in *Deutronomio*, God thus commaunded: Yf thowe chaunce vpon a
birdes neft by the waie, in whatfoener tree yt be, or on the grownde, whe-   *Deut.22.*
ther they be younge or egges, and the dame fitting vpon the younge, or
vpon the egges : Thowe fhalt not take the dame with the younge but fhalt
in any wife let the dame go, and take the young to thee, that thowe maift
profper and prolong thy daies . Thowe fhalt not fowe thy vineyeard with   *Ibid.23.*
diuerfe feedes , left the fruicte of thy vineyeard be defiled. Thowe fhalt not
plowe with an oxe and an affe together. And again in an other place: Tho-
C we fhalt not mofell the oxe that treadeth oute the corne in the Bearn.

    Shall we take theife places in their grammaticall fenfe ? dothe the high
prouidence of God occupie yt felf in making ordeinances for birdes neftes?
And by gods ordeinance , fhall a man profper, and prolong his daies that
taketh not the dame with the younge? dothe the wifdom of God ioin foche
rewardes, to foche trifles ? And making the ordeinance for the threffing
oxe, dothe God (as fainct Paule alleaging the fame afketh) take thought for   *1.Cor.9.*
oxen? No. yt hath an other vnderftanding, as ther fainct Paule alleaging this
ordeinance of God, applieth yt vnto.

    Yt were enough to make a iuft volume, yf all the obfcure places fhoulde
be recited, that be in the olde Teftament . But as by theife yt maie be perceaued, that the fcriptures be not fo eafie, as men phanfie them to be: So truly yt ys perilous that they (as the aduerfaries wolde) fhoulde be handeled
commonlie of them, whofe vnderftanding atteigning to none other fenfe,
then the grammaticall fenfe, and oftentymes not to that neither, doo wounderfullie abufe them , to the great difhonour of God , and plain côtempt of
D the fcriptures, his holie woorde. As yf the rude and fimple fhoulde read theife fentences aboue alleaged oute of *Genefis, Leuiticus, and Deutronomium*, wolde
he not faie they were fond and trifeling thinges?

    And wher as wifedom and knowledge be the goodlie gifes of God: yf the   *Eccls.1.*
vnlearned fhoulde reade the booke of the Preacher wher yt ys faied : I com-
moned

moned with my owne heart faieng:lo,I am comed to a great ſtate,and haue **E** gotten more wiſdom then all that haue ben before me in Hieruſalem. yea my hearte hath great experience of wiſdome and knowledge, for therunto I applied my minde, that I might knowe what were wiſdom and vnderſtandinge,what were errour and fooliſhneſſe, and I perceaued that this alſo was but a vexaciõ of minde . For wher moche wiſdome ys,ther ys alſo great trauaill,and diſquitnes &c.Yf the vnlearned(I ſaie)ſhoulde reade this, might he not take occaſion to contẽpne bothe wiſdome and knowledge,and ſo diſhonour God in his giftes ? wherunto appeareth more occaſion to be geuen in the next chapiter folowing,wher yt ys writen thus:

Ibid. 2. Then I tourned me to conſider wiſdome,errour, and fooliſhnes,for who ys he emonge men that might be compared to me the kinge in ſoche workes?and I ſawe that wiſdome excelleth fooliſhnes,as farre as light dothe dark neſſe.For a wiſe man hathe his eies in his head· but the foole goeth in darknes . I perceaued alſo that they bothe had one ende . Then thought I in my minde: Yf yt happen to the foole,as yt doth vnto me, what neadeth me thẽ **F** to labour any more for wiſdome ? So I confeſſed within my heart, that this alſo was but vanitie.

What maie appeare more vehement, to diſſuade a man from wiſdom? Howe moche ys wiſdom the goodlie gifte of God, abaſed to appearance in this ſaing? Howe ys the gift of God magnified to the aduancement of gods honour, when in appearance Salomon accompteth the labour for yt to be but vanitie ? I ſaie to yowe before God,whom I call to wittnes, that I ſpeake trueth.I heard a man of woorſhippe, of grauitie, of wiſdom, of godlie life, and of competent learning, able to vnderſtand, and likewiſe excercyſed in in the ſcriptures, vpon the reading of this booke, and conference had betwixt hym and me for the ſame, earneſtlie ſaye, that yt was a naughtie booke. Yf he dyd thus, what will the rude, the raſhe vnlearned, and the vngodlie reader doe?

Howe litle incitament of vertue appeareth to be in the Ballettes of Salomon? Yea raitheir howe vngodlie and wanton ſeme they to be ? raither in the outwarde face teaching, and prouoking wantonneſſe, then godlyneſſe **G** Cant.1. of life.In the firſt chapiter ye reade thus : O howe faire arte thowe my loue, howe fair arte thowe.Thowe haueſt doues eies, Ohowe fair arte thowe, my beloued,howe well fawoured arte thowe. Owre bed ys deckt with flowres, the ſyllinges of oure houſe are Cedre tree.And again: O ſtand vppe my loue my beautifull and come.For lo ; the wynter ys nowe paſt, the rain ys awaie and gone . The flowres are comed vppe in the feldes, the tyme of the birdes ſyngynge ys comed, and the voice of the Turtle doue ys heard in oure lande.The figge tree bringeth furthe her figges, and the Vines beare bloſſomes,and haue a good ſmell.O ſtande vppe my loue, my beautyfull, and come my doue oute of the caues of the Rockke, oute of the holls of the walls. O let me ſee thy coũtenãce, and heare thy voice.For ſwete ys thie voice,and fair ys thie face,&c. Like vnto this ys all that booke.What can the vnlearned finde,or vnderſtande here?any thinge to edificacion of godlie life? or rather (as ys ſaied) a prouocation to wanton life?

Yet Ieſus Sonne of Syrac ſemeth to haue more vnſemelie woordes then **H** theiſe, yea ſo vnſemelie, as an honeſt mẽ wolde be aſhamed to ſpeake them, as I alſo wolde be aſhamed to wryte thẽ,yf they were not ſcripture. He ſpeaEccleſiaſt. king of an harlotte, writeth thus:Like as one that goeth by the waie, and ys 62. thriſtie,ſo ſhall ſhe open her mouth,and drynke of euerie next water,that ſhe

maie

A maie gette. By euerie hedge fhall fhe fitte her downe, and open her quoiuer
to euerie arrowe.

What trifeling, what ieftyng, what paftime, I haue heard and feen vpon
the reading, and rcherfall of this texte, and what vnfeemlie, and vnchaift
woordes haue fallen oute by occafiõ of the fame, yt ys vnmeete in this place to be reherfed. But this I will reporte, for that as trulie as God liueth, I
knowe yt to be true. This texte was fpoken in the prefence of a good vertueoufe gentlewoman, and one that feared God, and fhe mifliking the
fame, yt was auouched to her to be fcripture. The booke was turned, the
place was red, fhe exclamed, and faied: that yf the fcripture had foche
bawdie woordes, fhe wolde no more beleue the fcripture. for yt was naught.
with mo foche like woordes, which nowe memorie reteyneth not.

Maye not this grieue a chriftian heart, that the fcriptures Gods holie
woorde fhoulde be thus blafphemed? And what ys the caufe of yt? verilie
bicaufe they be made common to their handes, that vnderftande them not.

B That this place was not vnderftanded of them that handeled the fame, as ys
afore faied, yt ys more manifeft then I nede reporte. For the effecte well
proueth yt.

Nowe to put a conclufion to this, that ys here faied : litle dothe yt awaill
them to reade the fcriptures, that vnderftand not what they reade. But
raither (as *Origen* faieth) they maye as well take occafion of euell as of good
by reading the fcriptures, and not in their true fenfe and meeming vnderftand them. whofe fentence for the better declaracion therof, I haue
here noted:

Opera carnis diuinorum voluminũ hiftoria continet, non valde eos iuuans, qui fic eam　Origen.
intelligunt vt fcripta eft. Quis enim non docebitur feruire luxuriæ, & fornicationem ha-　.:o.li.
bere pro nihilo, cum Iudam ad meretricem legerit ingredientem, & Patriarchas mul-　Strom.
tas pariter habuiffe vxores? Quomodo non ad idololatrian prouocabitur, qui fanguinem
taurorum, & cæteras Leuitici victimas, non plus quàm in litera fonat, putauerit indicare?　Gene.38.
Quod autem inimicitias in aperto pofitus fcripturæ fermo, doceat, & ex hoc loco probatur:　Pfal.136.
Filia Babylonis mifera, beatus qui retribuet tibi retributionem, quam retribuifti nobis.　Pfal.100.
C *Beatus qui tenebit, & allidet paruulos fuos ad petram. Et ex illo : In matutino interficie-*
bam omnes peccatores terræ : et ex ijs fimilibus, de contentionibus videlicet, æmulatione,
ira, rixis, diffentionibus. Ad quæ, fi non altius aliquid fentiamus, pronocant nos magis hifto-
riæ exempla quàm prohibent. Hærefes quoque magis de carnali fcripturæ intellectu, quam
de opera carnis noftræ (vt plurimi æftimant) fubftiterunt. Nec non ebrietates, et inuidiam,
per legis literam difcimus. Inebriatur Noë poft Diluuium, et Patriarchæ apud fratrem
Iofeph in Ægypto. The hiftories of Gods books (faieth *Origen*) contein the
workes of the flesfh. whiche hiftorie dothe not moche helpe them, whiche
doofo vnderftande yt, as yt ys written. For who fhall not be taught to ferue voluptuoufe pleafure, and to accompte fornycation for nothinge, when
he fhall reade Iudas to haue taken an harlotte, and the Patriarkes to haue
had manie wifes at once? Howe fhall he not be prouoked to Idolatrie, who
fhall thinke the blood of Bulls, and other Leuiticall facrifices, no more to
fhewe vnto him then the letter fowndeth? That the plain fainge of the
fcripture teacheth enemities, yt ys proued both by this place : Daughter of
Babilon, thowe fhalt come to myferie thy felf : yea happie fhall he be that
D rewardeth thee, as thowe haueft ferued vs. Bleffed fhall he be that taketh
thy children, and throweth them againft the ftones. And alfo by that place:
I fhall foon deftroie all the vngodlie that are in the lande. And by foche
other like vnto theife, as of contencion, enuie wrathe, brawlinges diffen-
tions

*Diuerſe
hiſtories of
Scripture
literallie
taken, doe
more prouo
ke ſinne,
than for-
bidde yt.*

tions vnto the whiche yf ye vnderſtand not ſome higher thing, the exam- E
ples of the hiſtories do more prouoke vs then forbidde vs. Hereſies alſo
haue ben more by the carnall vnderſtanding of the ſcriptures, then by the
worke of our fleſh, as manie do thinke. We learn alſo by the letter of the
lawe dronkennes, and enuie . Noë after the flood was dronken. And the
Patriarkes alſo were droncken, being with their Brother Ioſeph in AEgypte. Thus Origen.

Nowe then as in this chapiter ye haue heard a nombre of bookes and
places of ſcripture recited, whiche well proue the obſcuritie and hardneſſe
of the ſame: So yn the ende ye haue heard Origen declaring his minde,
that to vnderſtand but the carnall ſenſe of yt, ys raither hurtfull to edificacion, then profitable. Peraduenture ſome will graunte that thē olde Teſtament ys darke and hard, but the newe Teſtament (they will ſaie) ys eaſie
and plain: But that this likwiſe, ys not eaſie for euerie man to vnderſtande,
the chapiter folowing ſhall declare?

THE THIRDE CHAPITER TO DECLARE F
*the newe Teſtament not to be eaſie to be vnderſtanded bringeth
diuerſe obſcure places of the ſame.*

T H A T the newe Teſtament ys hard to be vnderſtanded yt ys
ſufficientlie proued in the friſt chapiter . Neuertheleſſe that
the Reader maie haue ſome experiéce of that, that by Authoritie ys ſaied : I ſhall laie before hym certain places, whiche
ſhall enforce hym to confeſſe, that by his owne iudgement to
be true, whiche by the ſcriptures he hath allreadie heard taught and affirmed.

And firſt let him beginne with the Genealogie of Chryſte deſcribed vnto
vs by two Euangeliſtes, Matthew, and Luke. And let them be compared to
gether, and triall made, whether yt be eſaie to concile them or no.

Matthewe beginneth at the elders, as at Abraham, and ſo deſcendeth to
Chryſte: Luke beginneth at Chryſte and aſcendeth vppe to the elders, euen G
vnto Adā, and ſo to God. In the whiche Genealogie Luke ſaieth that Chryſt

*The Euan
geliſtes
Mathew,
and Luke
ſeem to va-
rie in the
genealogie
of Chryſt .*

was the ſuppoſed ſonne of *Ioſeph*, and that *Ioſeph* was the ſonne of *Heli* : Matthewe ſaieth that *Iacob* begatte *Ioſeph* the husband of Mary, of whō was born
Ieſus, whiche ys called Chryſte. So that Luke ſaieth: that *Ioſep* was the ſonne
of Heli, and Matthew ſaieth he was the ſonne of *Iacob*. Which dyſagrement
Iulianus Auguſtus, the Apoſtata, as ſainčte Hierō ſaieth, obiečted vnto vs. Which
obiečtion although it be ſolued by ſainčte Hierō: yet ther remaineth a great
difficultie howe theſe Genealogies ſhoulde be true, and both pertain to
Chryſte: ſeing that from *Ioſeph*, to *Dauid* ther ys none agrement betwixt thē,
as by comparing of the Euāgeliſtes together, ye ſhal eaſilie perceaue. Which
I ſaie not as that ther ys in dede no agrement or conſonant trueth betwixt
thē: But that yt maie the raither appeare and be wel knowen, that the trueth
of the hiſtorie of the Goſpell lieng hid , yt ys not eaſie for euery man to fin
de oute the ſame.

*Chryſoſtō.
ın pri.
Matth.*

Chryſoſtom alſo findeth an other obſcure place, for thus he ſaieth : *Illud
quoque inter occulta numeratur, quomodo Elizabeth de Leuitica exiſtens tribu Mariæ co-* H
gnata dicatur. That alſo ys to be enombred emonge the hid thinges, howe
that Elyſabeth being of the tribe of Leui, maye be called the coſine of Mary
Foraſmuche as the lawe was, that men ſhoulde marrie within their owne
tribes

A tribes yt dothe, appeare that Elifabeth being married to *Zacharie*, fhe was of
the fame tribe. Likewife that *Iofeph* being of the tribe of *Iuda*, and marrieng
the virgen Mary, that fhe was of the fame trybe. Whiche thinge ys declared
by faincte Hierom and Chryfoftom alfo in foluing this double: Why the
Euangeliftes do bring the ordre of the genealogie of Chrift to *Iofeph*, feing
that *Iofeph* was not the father of Chrift in dede, but his putatiue or fuppofed father? To this they anfwere, that *Iofeph* and Mary being of one tribe, the
Genealogie commeth right to Chrifte.

So then Mary being of the tribe of Iuda, and Elifabeth of the trybe of Leui, the doubte ftãdeth howe the virgen Marie fhoulde be coufin to Elifabeth.
And yet the Euangelift faincte Luke recitinge the woordes of the Angell,
faieth: *Et ecce Elizabeth cognata tua, & ipfa concepit filium in fenectute fua.* And be-　　*Luc. 1.*
holde thy coufin Elifabeth fhe alfo hath conceaued a fonne in her olde age.

Alfo yt ys not withoute Doubte that ys faied of our mafter Chryfte (as
the Euangelift faincte Marke reciteth) wher he fpeaking of the coming of　　*Marc. 13.*
B the Sonne of man to the general iugement faieth: *De die autẽ illa, & hora, nemo*
nouit, neq; Angeli in cælo, neq; filius, nifi pater, But of that daie and howre knoweth
no mã, no not the Angells which are in heauẽ, neither the Sonne himfelf, faue
the Father oneli. Whiche doubte ys liuelie opened ãd fett furth by the holie
father Chryfoftom in the xlviij homelie vpon faincte Matthew, wher emong
other godlie woordes as touchinge this matter he faieth thus: *Quis hæc vnquã*　　*Chryfoft.*
dicere potuit? Patrem filius optimè nouit, & eo prorfus pacto, quo pater filium: diem au-　　*hom. 48.*
tem illum ignorat? Præterea, Spiritus dei profunda inueftigat: Filius verò nec tempus
nouit? ed quomodò quidem iudicare oporteat, non fugit eum, & archana fingulorum clam
eo non funt, quod autem multo vilius eft, id ignorat? Adhuc, quomodò is per quem omnia
facta funt, & fine quo factum eft nihil diem illum ignorabit? Qui enim fecula fecit, is pro-
iecto creauit & tempora, & diem produxit, quomodò igitur quæ ipfe produxit, ignorat?
Who coulde at any time (faieth Chryfoftom) faie thefe thinges? The Sonne
knoweth the Father verie well, and euẽ the verie fame waye that the Father
knoweth the Sonne, and dothe he not knowe that daie? Moreouer the
Spirit of God fearcheth the depe Botomes of the fecretes of God, and do-
C the not the Sonne knowe the time? But howe he muft Iudge the worlde, he
ys not ignorante, and the fecretes of all men are not hidden from hym· and
ys he ignorante of that, that ys not fo wourthie a thinge? Howe alfo dothe
he by whom all thinges are made, and withoute whom nothing was made,
not knowe that daie? he that made the worldes, he trulie created the tymes,
and brought furthe the daie, howe thẽ doth he not knowe that, that he produced? Thus moche Chryfoftome, wherby ye maie fee what doubte ther ys
in the text, Whiche yf yt fhoulde be vnderftanded as yt lieth, what errour
and herefie fhoulde fpring oute of yt?

Thus as many a man fwimming aboue vpon the fmoothe of the water
feeth not the depe botome therof: So manie a man readinge the fmoothe
face of the Scripture, feeth not the depe doubtes of the fame.

Algafia and *Hedibia* women bothe vertueufe, and ftudioufe by their ftu-　　*Hieron. ad*
dies perceaued many darke places in the fcriptures, whiche they not taking　　*Alg. qn. 1.*
vpõ them rafhlie to explicate, as perfuading them felues that the fcriptures
were not eafie and plain, fent from the fordeft partes of Fraunce to fain-
D cte Hierom then being at *Bethleem*, the one of them twelue queftions: The
other eleuen queftions, whiche all be of the newe Teftament, as well of the
gofpells, as of the Epiftles.

Algafia moueth this doubte: whie faincte Iohn the Baptift being in pri-
　　　　　　　　　　　　　　　　　　　　C　　　fon

Luc. 7.
Ioan. 1.

son sent hys disciples to Chryste asking him this questiō: Arte thowe he that E shall come, or do we looke for an other? seing before he had appointed him with his fingar, saienge of him. *Ecce agnus Dei, ecce qui tollit peccata mundi* Beholde the lābe of god, beholde him that taketh awaie the sinnes of the worlde.

Yt augmēteth the doubte also, that Ihon had baptised Chryste, at which time he knowing him to be Chryst the verie Messias, did not onelie saie to

Matth. 3.

Chryst, I haue nede to be Baptised of thee, and comest thowe to me? But also sawe the heauens open and the Spirite of God descending like a doue, and lighting vpō him, and heard also the voice from heauen saieng: Thys ys my beloued Sonne, in whō I am wel pleased: howe then dothe he aske this, whether he be the Messias that shoulde come, or that they must looke for an other? Thys (as I suppose) maie well appeare to be a doubte to a simple reader, and not withoute consultacion of learned men to be dissolued.

Ioan. 20.
Matth. 28
Hed. qn. 5.
Hieron. ad

Hedibia moueth this doubte emōg other in the gospell, Howe sainĉte Matthew saieth, Mary Magdalen with the other Mary fell downe at the feete of Christ after his resurreĉtion, and helde his feet : Seinge that sainĉt Iohn E saieth, that Christ forbod her saieng: Touche me not, For I haue not yet ascended to my Father. Yt semeth that one of theise must be vntrue.

An other doubte moche like vnto this ther ys betwixt sainĉte Iohn and

Marc. 16.

sainĉte Marke. Sainĉt Marke saieth : when the Sabboth was past, Mary Magdalen, and Mary Iacobi, and Salome, bought swete odoures, that they might come and anoynt Iesus. And early in the morning the first daie of the Sabboth, they came to the Sepulchre, when the Sunne was risen . Sainĉte

Ioan. 20.

Iohn saieth : The first daie of the Sabboth came Mary Magdalen earlie in the morning when yt was yet darke . Yt ys not verie easie for an vnlearned reader to agree theise two.

Matth. 28
Ioan. 20.
Marc . 16.

In the storie of the resurreĉtion of Christe, ther be a great nombre of apparant contrarieties: as of the time of the resurreĉtiō : of the appearinge of the Angells in the Sepulchre: of their nombre: of their place : and soche other, whiche all generallie to enombre yt were to long.

Hieron. ad
Hed. q. 9.
Ioan. 20.
Act. 1.

The same *Hedibia* moueth also this doubte : whether that Chryste breathinge on his Apostles (as sainĉt Iohn saieth) and saieng: Take ye the holie G Goste, gaue them then the holie Goste : Seing that sainĉte Luke saieth, immediatelie before his ascension, he promised that he wolde send them the holie Goste. Yf he gaue thē the holie Goste before his ascensiō, yt appeareth that he wolde not, or neded not to send him to thē after his ascension.

Tus yt maie be seē that ther be obscure and darke places in the Gospel. To conclude ther be innumerable places hauing moche doubte, whiche sainĉte Austen with great labour and trauaill doth right learnedlie dissolue, making for that pourpose a great volume intiteled , *De consensu Euangelistarum.* of the consent of the Euangelistes, whiche had ben vain and superfluouse, yf the gospells were easie & plain for euery man to vnderstand.

What neaded the commentaries of sainĉte Hierom. and of sainĉte Ambrose vpon the Euangelistes : The homelies of Chrysostom , and sainĉte Austen vpo the same: The expositions also of a great nombre of famouse and learned men, whiche with great studie, labour, and trauaill haue made their workes , yf the scriptures be so plain and easie? H

I haue brought but a fewe places of the Gospells to make a litle shewe, and to aduertise the reader, by these fewe to be circumspeĉte in medling. For the scripturs be a depth of a great profunditie. And nowe will I doo the like oute of the Epistles.

THE

A THE FOVRTH CHAPITER CON-
taineth certain harde places of the Epiſtles.

TO beginne with the Epiſtle of ſainɛte Paule to the Romans, whiche as yt ys firſt in the ordre of the epiſtles, ſo ſhall yt be here firſt ſpoken of,yt ys more eaſie ther to finde obſcure and darke places,loaden with difficulties and doubtes, then yt ys to finde eaſie and plain places.Ther ys diſputed the matter of iuſtification,whiche howe harde a matter yt ys,yf ther were none other argument to proue yt,the controuerſies that be thervpon riſen in this oure time,might ſuffice to declare yt.

In the epiſtle to the Romans be mo obſcure than plain places.

And yet yt ys not eaſie for all men, that reade that ſame epiſtle,well to vnderſtand this place of ſainɛte Paule:Arbitramur iuſtificari hominem per fidem,ſine operibus legis.We holde that a man ys iuſtified by faithe, withoute the workes of the lawe:ſeinge ſainɛt Iames in his epiſtle ſaieth:What auaileth yt my brethrē,though a man ſaie,he hath faithe,yf he haue no works,can faith ſaue him?After he concludeth thus : Euen ſo faith, if yt haue no workes, yt ys dead in yt ſelf.

Rom. 3.

Iaco. 2.

Again ſainɛt Paule ſaieth:We ſaie that faith was recknid to Abraham for righteouſneſſe.And ſainɛte Iames ſaieth:Was not Abraham our Father iuſtified by workes?

Rom 4.

Iaco. 2.

In that epiſtle alſo ys ſett furthe the reieɛtion of the Iewes, and the calling of the gentiles.In the diſcourſe wherof ſainɛt Paule ſaieth thus,alleaging the Prophete Eſaie for the calling of the gētiles:I am fownde of thē that ſought me not,I am manifeſted vnto them,that aſked not after me.But againſt Iſrael he ſaieth:All daie long haue I ſtretched furthe my handes vnto a people, that beleueth not,but ſpeaketh againſt me. And yet afterwarde he asketh thus:hath God caſt awaie his people?He aunſwereth : God forbidde : And yet he ſaieth again in the ſame chapiter,ſpeaking of the Iewes:Yf the caſting awaie of them be the reconciling of the worlde, &c. Wherbie he ſheweth that the Iewes be caſt awaie.

Rom. 10.

In that ſame chapiter alſo he asketh this queſtion: Nunquid ſic offenderunt,vt caderent?Haue they ſo offended or ſtumbled,that they ſhoulde fall?He aunſwereth:God forbidde.And yet within a fewe lynes after he ſaieth : Propter incredulitatem fraɛti ſunt.Bicauſe of vnbeleif they were broken of.

Theiſe matters require a clearer ſeight of vnderſtanding,and heades of deper ſtudie,and iudgemēt to deciſe thē,then haue the cōmō ſorte of readers, which oftentimes are moſt buſie,thinking thē ſelues to ſee,whē in dede they ſee nothing at all.God geue thē grace and open their eies to ſee their owne ignorance , that they maye walke within their compaſſe , and not ſtreign aboue their reache,

In the matter of predeſtinacion,wher vpon ſainɛte Paule entreth depely to diſpute,ther ys no ſentence withoute difficultie. So that , as wher ther be a great nōbre of thinges a man ſtaieth,not knowing whiche to take firſt:Euen ſo I,in this great multitude of difficulties, knowe not wher to beginne, or whiche to take firſt?But at the laſt I take one of the leaſt which ys this : Non eſt volentis,neque currentis,ſed miſerentis Dei.Yt lyeth not in the will of man , nor the runninge of man , but in the mercie of God.

Rom. 9.

This ſentence beſydes manie other,hath this doubte:that ſainɛt Paule in a chapiter before ſaieth:Velle adiacet mihi,perficere autē bonum non inuenio . Will ys preſent with me,but I finde no means to that,whiche ys good.

Supra ca.7

The ſame ſainɛte Paule ſaieth alſo: Deus vult omnes homines ſaluos fieri, & ad
C ij　　agnitionem

1.Thim. 2

agnitionem veritatis venire? God will haue all men to be faued, and to come to E
the knowledge of the trueth. Yf God fo will, and (as the fame fainéte Paule

Rom. 9.

faieth in an other place) *voluntati eius quis refiftet?* Who can withftand his wil?
Why then walke fo manie in the broade waie to perdition ? And whie be
ther fo manie Infidells, that come not to the knowledge of the treuth? And
fo manie heretikes that forfake the trueth? And again : yf God will haue all
men to be faued, how ftandeth the trueth of this fcripture? *Multi vocati , pauci
eleéti:* Manie be called, but fewe chofen. Yf God will haue all faued, then all
muft be chofen. For whome he will haue faued, him he chofeth.

*Hieron. ad
Alg. q. 9.
Algafia
moueth
great doub
tes to fainét
Hierom.
Sup. 8.*

Algafia alfo moueth a doubte to fainéte Hierom in the fame chapiter of
the epiftle of fainéte Paule to the Romans. What (faeth fhe) meeneth fainéte
Paule by this faieng: I haue wifhed my felf to be curfed from Chryfte for my
kinfmen as perteining to the flefh?

To the whiche fainét, Hierom aunfwering, openeth the queftiõ and faieth:
In very dede yt ys a great queftion, how the Apoftle, who before had faied:
who fhall feparate vs from the loue of God? fhall tribulation? or anguyfhe? F
or perfecution? or hungar? either perill? either fwoorde? And again: I am fure
that neither death, neither life, neither Angells, neither Rule, neither power,
neither thinges prefent, neither thinges to come , neither height, neither lowght, neither any other creature fhall be able to departe vs from
the loue of God, whiche we haue in Chryfte Iefus our Lorde. Nowe vnder
an othe he faieth: I faie the treuth in Chryfte, and lie not, my confcience alfo bearing me wittneffe by the holie Goft, that I haue great heauineffe by
continuall forowe in my heart. For I haue wifhed my felf to be curfed from
Chryfte for my brethren my kinfmen after the flefh. Yf he be of fo great loue
to God , that neither for feare of death , neither for the hope of life, neither for perfecution, hungar, nakedneffe , perill, nor fwoorde, he maye be fe
parated from his loue: And if Angells alfo, and powers, and thinges prefent,
and thinges to come, and all the ftrenght of the heauens, and if the heightes
alfo, and the dephts, with the vniuerfall creature fhoulde come againft him
(whiche can not be) yet wolde he not be feperated from the loue of God,
whiche he hath in Iefus Chryft: what ys this great mutacion or chaunge, yea G
rayther a wyfdom neuer heard of before , that for the loue of Chryft he
wolde not haue Chryft? And leaft peraduenture we fhoulde not beïeue
him, he fweareth and confirmeth yt by Chryft, and calleth the holie Goft to
wittnes of hys confcience , that he hath no light , nor fmall, but great and
incredible heauineffe, not forowe that ftingeth or vexeth for an howre, but
that continuallie abideth in his heart. Whether tendeth this heauineffe ?
to what auaileth this inceffant forowe ? He wifheth to be curfed,
from Chryfte and to perifh, that other maie be faued. Thus moche fainéte
Hierom.

In the whiche woordes he openeth a great doubte that fainéte Paule, who
fo feruentlie loued Chryft that nothing either in heauen, or in earthe, coulde feparate him from Chryfte, nowe femeth to wifh for the loue he bare to
the Iewes to be diuided from Chryft. Whiche might be an argument, that
he loued the Iewes aboue Chryft.

As this, after the fentence of fainéte Hierom, ys a great doubte: So ys ther

*Hieron. ad
Alg. qn. 7.*

an other by the fame *Algafia* moued vpon the fame epiftle to the Romans, H
In what fenfe (faieth fhe) ys that to be taken, that fainét Paule writeth to the
Romãs: *Vix enim pro iufto quis moritur. Nã pro bono forfitan quis audet mori.* For fkar
ce will any man die for the righteoufe man . Peraduenture for a good man
durft a man die.   This

A　This sentence semeth so plain, and the natiue sense therof so easie to be perceaued, that saincte Hierom saieth for lacke of the true vnderstanding of yt, two horrible heresies being diuerse, and vnlike in sentence, but like in impietie and wickednesse, tooke here moche occasion.

Marcion by this maketh two Gods: one the iust God, and creatour of the Lawe, ād the Prophetes: The other the good God, which ys the God of the Gospell, and the Apostles, whose Sonne ys Chryste. For the iust God (saieth he) fewe or none haue died. But for the good God (whiche ys Chryst) ther haue been innumberable Martyrs.

Arrius the other heretike (saieth saincte Hierom) contrariwise, calleth Chryst the iust God, and for his so saieng alleageth scripture oute of the Psalmes, wher *Dauid* prophecieng of Chryst saied: Geue the king thy iudgementes (to. God) and thy righteousnes vnto the kinges Sonne. The good God he calleth the Father of heauen, of whom (saieth he) Chryst him self saieth: what callest thow me good? ther ys none good, but one God, the Father.

B　As theise heretikes for the obscuritie of this sentence of saincte Paule (for yt ys a darke maner of speache in dede, to saie: for a iust man scarce a man wil die: But for a good man, a man will peraduenture die, as though ther were a great difference betwen the iust and the good mā) through theyr wicked rashnesse and headinesse, haue vpō yt mainteined two notable, and abhominable heresies, manifestlie repugnant: So likewise haue some in this oure time, through their arrogant willfullnes vpon one sentence fownded two conttarie heresies, as moche repugnant as these. But leauing the further opening of this to a more conuenient place, I will proceade in that ys here appoincted to the doen.

Amandus a preist writeth to sainct Hierom, desiring to be resolued in foure questions. Of the whiche one ys vpon the epistle of saincte Paule to the Corinthians, wher disputing of the resurrection, he cometh to this place: He must reign till he hath put al his enemies vnder his feet. The last enemie that shall be destroied ys deathe. For he hath put all thinges vnder his feet. But when he saieth all thinges are put vnder him, yt ys manifest that he ys excep-C　ted, whiche did put all thinges vnder him. When all thinges are subdued vnder him, then shall the Sonne also himself be subiect vnto him, that put all thinges vnder him, that God maie be all in all.

Besides manie doubtes, whiche maie be moued vpon this scripture, this ys one verie notable for the mainteining of the Arrians heresie, wher he saieth that when all thinges be subdued, then shall the Sonne himself also be subiecte vnto him, as though the Sonne of God in Godhead, were subiecte to God the Father. Whiche maner of saing, for somoche as the holie catholique faith confesseth that he ys equall to the Father, ys to be taken detestable hericicall. This proposition ys learnedlie handeled, and treacted of by saincte Hillarie in his eleuenth booke againstt the Arrians, and this doubte ther dissolued. Yt were to tediouse, and all most vnpossible for me to rehearse all the darke places of the epistles. Therfor one, or two mo, and so an ende.

To the Collosians Saincte Paule writeth thus: Nowe ioye I in my suffrin-D　ges for yowe, and fulfill that, whiche ys behind of the passions of Chryste in my flesh, for hys bodies sake, whiche ys the churche. In the which sentence, he semeth to make the passion of Chryste insufficient, in that he saieth, that he fulfilleth that, that wanteth of the passions of Chryst.

To the Hebrues he hath this sentence: For yt can not be, that they, which

B iij　　　were

Two contrarie heresies grownded vpō one scripture.

Marcion

Arrius.

Psalm.71.

Luc.18.

Amādus.

1.Cor.15.

Hila.li.11. de Trinitā.

Colloss.1.

Hebr.6.

were once lightened,and haue tasted of the heauenlie gifte, and were beco- **E**
me partakers of the holieGoste,and haue tasted of the goodwoorde of God,
and of the promisse of the worlde to cõme,yf they fall awaie, and as concerning themselues crucifie the Sõne of God a fresh, and make a mocke of him
that they shoulde be renewed again by penaunce.And again in the same epi

Ibid. 10. stle he saieth:For if we sinne wilfullie,after that we haue receaued the know
ledge of the truthe,ther remaineth no more sacrifice for sinne, but a fearfull
looking for iudgement, and violét fire whiche shal deuour the Aduersaries.

　　Theise two sentences,yf they had no fauourablier interpretacion,thẽ they
seem to beare in their grammaticall sense,all Chrystendome might wail and
mourne,For the former sentence semeth to teache,that yf a Christian fall in
to mortall sinne,after that he ys christened,and hath receaued the giftes of
God therunto appertaining,that he can not be reconciled by penaũce, and
so were all hope of mercie for the remission of sinnes clean taken awaie.

Nouatus Which thing one *Nouatus* by occasiõ of this scripture vnderstãding yt in the
sense,that yt semeth in the first face to haue,taught verie stoutelie, and so **F**
becam the Authour of a wofull,and wicked heresie.Against whiche *Athana-*

Athanas. *sius* wrote an epistle to *Serapio*,wher he declareth that the same saincte Paule
receaued the incestiouse Corinthian,and also the Galathians,that had erred
in faith,to whom he saied:*O insensati Galatæ,quis vos fascinauit,non obedire verita-*
*ti?*O infensate Galathians,who hath bewitched yowe , that ye shoulde not

Galat. 3.
Ibid.4. obey the treuth?And yet afterwarde he saied:*Filioli mei,quos iterum parturio,do-*
nec formetur in vobis Chryst9. O my litle children, of whom I trauaill again in
byrth vntil Chryste be fashyoned in yowe.

　　The second sentence also semeth vtterlie to denie all means to atteign to
gods mercie, after we haue wilfullie fallen to sinne, whiche sentence yf yt
shoulde be vnderstanded as it sowndeth,desperaciõ shoulde reign,and hope
shoulde be abandoned.

　　What shall I saie for the vnderstanding of the scripturs by the common
people vnlearned,when not onelie manie other learned men through their
euell or wrong vnderstanding of them,haue swarued , and fallẽ into sundrie
and diuerse heresies:But also saincteHierom,and saincte Augustin,two ligh- **G**
tes and pillers of the Christian orbe,haue dissented vpon the vnderstanding

Galat.2. of a sayeng of saincte Paule to the Galathians,wher he saieth : When Peter
was comed tóAntioche, I withstoode him openlie,bicause he was wourthie
to be blamed.In the which their disagrement ther was nothing committed,
that either charitie betwixt thẽ was empaired , or yet anie heresie obstinate
lie defended:but raither the treuth learnedlie enquired and searched.

　　Wherfor,Reader,I saie vnto thee:*Noli altũ sapere,sed time.* Be not high minded but feare For arrogácie is mother of errour.Put on therfore anhũble spi
Rom.11.
Arrogã -
cie mother
of errour. rit, and in reading of the scriptures submitte thy self to the teaching of thy
Mother the churche.For the loulie bowing man maie easelie go withoute
harme,wher the stowte high looker shall breake his browe. Be humble therfore and feare to trust thine owne iudgement in the exposition of the scrip-
Esay.66. tures,and so will the Spirit of God rest vpon thee.For vpon whome (saieth
he) shall my Spirit rest, but vpon him that ys humble, and fearing my
woordes?　　　　　　　　　　　　　　　　　　　　　　　　　　　　　**H**
　　　　　　　　　　　　　　　　　　　　　　　　　　　　　　　　The

A THE FIFT CHAPITRE DECLARING THE MIN-
des and Iudgementes of the Fathers and doctours vpon the difficultie of the Scriptures.

T nedeth not to trauaill anye more in this matter, when (as I
suppose) the Reader ys by this that ys allreadie saied, so perswaded, that he wil with hand and foote (as they saie) go with
me, and ioin with me in one sentence, and minde. Yet that the
arrogancie of the stoute ignorant and vnlearned, and the vntrueth of the learned maie be confownded, and suffer their
wourthie shame : the Reader shall heare the iudgement of the famouse learned Fathers, and doctours, as touching the difficultie, and obscuritie of the
scriptures. Wherbie the impudencie of soche arrogant persons maie clerlie and manifestlie be perceaued, and they, if they haue not (as the Prophet
Hieremie in the voice of God saieth of the people of Israell) gotten an whoo   *Hierem 3.*
B res forehead, and will not be ashamed, maye then in dede be ashamed.

    Origen, a man both auncient, and famouse in learning handeling this pla-   *Galat. 5.*
ce of saincte Paule to the Galathians: *Vos in libertatē vocati estis fratres.* Brethe-   *Orig 19.li.*
ren ye are called vnto libertie, saieth thus : *Difficilis locus est et ita à nobis disse-*   *Storm.*
rendus videtur. An hard place this ys, and thus vnto me yt semeth to be expownded. And after a long discourse in the exposition of the same texte,
he saieth thus : *Quamobrem spiritum scripturæ, fructusq; quæramus, qui non dicuntur*
esse manifesti. Multo quippe labore, et sudore, et digno cultu in scripturis fructus spiritus
inuenitur. Vnde arbitror Paulum, diligenter, et cautè de scripturæ sensibus dixisse carnali-
bus: Manifesta sunt opera carnis. De spiritualibus vero, non vt ibi posuisse; Manifestus est
fructus, Sed ita: Fructus autem spiritus est charitas, gaudium, pax etc. Wherfore let us
seke the Spirit of the scripture, and the fruicts of the same, whiche are not   *Scripture*
saied to be manifest. For trulie the fruicte of the Spirit ys fownde in the   *must be stu*
scriptures with moche labour, and swette, and wourthie trauaill. Wherfo-   *died withe*
re I thinke Paule diligentlie and warelie of the carnall senses of the scriptu-   *moche la-*
res to haue saied; the workes of the flesh are manifest. But of the spirituall   *bour.*
C senses not to haue putte as in the other, The fruicte of the Spirit ys manifest;
but thus : The fruicte of the Spirit ys charitie, ioye, peace, &c. Hitherto *Ori-*
gen.

    In the whiche saing, first by expresse and plain woordes, ye perceaue hym
to saie of that place of saincte Paule ther alleaged, that yt ys an harde place.
And afterwarde he concludeth of the wholl scripture, that the spirituall senses, and vnderstandinges therof are not manifest, but are to be sought with
moche labour, swette, and wourthie trauaill. Whiche he proueth by saincte
Paule.

    Nowe thinges that be easie, and plain are acquired and gotten with mo-
che facilitie without Laboure, or with verie easie labour: hard thinges
be not so gotten but contrarie wise. Wherfor by *Origen* yt maie be concluded that forasmoche as the right senses, whiche he calleth the spirituall sense,
or vnderstanding of the scripture, are to be gotten with moche labour, swette and wourthie trauaill, they be not easie, but raither hard.

D   Sainct Hierom exhorting *Paulinus* to the studie of the scriptures as well
by the exāples of Ethnickes and Philosophers, as *Plato, Pithagoras, Apollonius,*
and soche other, whiche for knowledge trauailed ouer seas and contries : as
also by the examples of christians, as of Saint Paule, Timothie, Tyte and soche other, maketh it not an easie matter, but raither teacheth howe moch dif
              B iiij   ficultie

ficultie ys therin. To the whiche pourpofe he faieth: *Aperiebantur cœli Ezechie-* E
li, qui populo peccatori clauſi erant. Reuela (inquit Dauid) oculos meos, et conſiderabo mira-
bilia de lege tua. Lex enim ſpiritualis eſt, et reuelatione opus eſt ʋt intelligatur, ac reuelata
facie gloriam Dei contemplemur. Liber in Apocalypſi ſeptem ſigillis ſignatus oſtenditur,
quem ſi dederis homini ſcienti literas ʋt legat, reſpondebit tibi; Non poſſum. Signatus eſt
enim. Quanti hodie putant ſe noſce literas, et tenent ſignatum librũ, nec aperire poſſunt, niſi
ille reſerauerit, qui habet clauem Dauid, qui aperit, et nemo claudit: claudit, et nemo aperit?
In Actis Apoſtolorum ſanctus Eunuchus, imò ʋir (ſic enim eum ſcriptura cognominat) cum
legeret Eſaiam, interrogatus à Philippo; Putáſne intelligis quæ legis? Reſpondit; Quomodò
poſſum, niſi aliquis me docuerit? Ego(ʋt de me loquar interim) nec ſanctior ſum hoc Eu-
nucho, nec ſtudioſior, qui de Aethiopia, id eſt, de extremis mundi ſinibus ʋenit ad templũ,
reliquit aulam, et tantus amator legis diuinæq; ſcientiæ fuit, ʋt etiam in ʋehiculo ſacras li-
teras legeret, et tamen cum librum teneret, et ʋerbum Domini cogitatione conciperet, lingua
volueret, labijs perſonaret, ignorabat eum, quem in libro neſciens ʋenerabatur. Venit Phi-
lippus, oſtendit ei Ieſum, qui clauſus latebat in litera. O mira doctoris ʋirtus, eâdem hora
credit Eunuchus, baptiſatur, et ſanctus factus eſt. The heauens were open to Eze- F
chiel, whiche to the ſinfull people were ſhette. Dauid ſaith: Open thowe
mine eies, and I ſhall ſee the wonderfull thinges of thy lawe. The lawe ys
ſpirituall, and yt hathe nede of reuclacion, that yt maye be vnderſtanded,
and that with open face, we maie beholde the glorie of God. The booke in
the Apocalips ys ſhewed ſigned, or faſtened with ſeũ ſcales, whiche if thow
geue to a man hauing knowledge of letters, that he maye read it, he

Manie
nowe a dai-
es holde the
booke of
ſcripture
ſcaled.

will aunſwer; I can not. For it ys ſealed. Howe manie nowe a daies thinke
them ſelues learned? and do holde the booke ſealed, neither yet can open
it, except he onlocke it, which ſhetteth, and noman openeth, openeth, and
no man ſhetteth. In the Actes of the Apoſtles the holie Eunuche, yea raither a man (for ſo the ſcripture doth call him) when he did reade Eſaie the
Prophet, being aſked of Philippe; Thinkeſt thow, thow vnderſtandeſt, what
thow readeſt? he anſwered: howe can I, except ſome bodie ſhall teache me?
As for me (that I maie ſpeake ſomthing of my ſelf) I am neither more holie,
then this Eunuch, nor more ſtudiouſe, whiche came from Aethiope, that
ys from the furtheſt coaſtes of the worlde, vnto the Téple. He left the Cour G
te, and was ſo great a louer of the lawe, and godlie Science, that he wolde
euen in his Chariett read the holie ſcriptures. And yet when he helde the
booke, and conceaued in his minde the woord of God, when he ſpake it
with his tounge, and ſownded it with his lipps, he knew not him whom
vnwitting he woorſhipped in the booke. Philippe came, he ſhewed him Ieſus, who laie hidde in the letter. O great vertue of a teacher. The ſame howre the Eunuch beleued, he was baptiſed, and made faithfull, and holie,
Thus farre ſaincte Hierom.

In whoſe ſentence marke well howe many ſcriptures this holie doctour
hath brought forth to declare, and proue, that the ſcriptures be obſcure,
and therfore of neceſſitie require to haue ſome exerciſed and learned in
them, to open and declare them, as ſainct Hierom declaring the cauſe whie,
alleageth theſe ſcriptures, whiche ye haue heard, and immediately addeth
and ſaieth: *Hæc à me breuiter perſtricta ſunt, ʋt intelligeres te in ſcripturis ſanctis ſine*
præuio, et monſtrante ſemitam non poſſe ingredi. Theiſe thinges are breiſtie tou- H
ched of me to the entent thow ſhouldeſt vnderſtande, that withoute a
leader, and one ſhewing the path, thow canſt not entre in to the ſcriptures.

Not moche vnlike to this, declaring the obſcuritie and hardneſſe of the
olde

A olde Teſtament he writeth in his epiſtle to *Algaſia* : *Quæstiunculæ tuæ de Euan-* *Hieron. ad Algaſia*
gelio tantum, & de Apoſtolo propoſitæ, indicant, te veterem ſcripturam aut non ſatis
legere, aut non ſatis intelligere, quæ tantis obſcuritatibus, & futurorum typis obuoluta eſt,
vt omnis interpretatione egeat. Thy queſtions propownded onelie out of the
goſpell and the Apoſtle, doo declare, that either thowe haueſt not ſufficientlie red the olde ſcripture, or ells doeſt not ſufficientlie vnderſtand yt.
whiche ys enwrapped with ſo manie obſcurities, and figures of thinges to
come, that euery parte of yt had nede of interpretacon. Thus moche ſaincte
Hierom.

Saincte Baſill teacheth that all the ſcriptures are not to be publiſhed,
and made cõmon, for that ſome parte of them ſemeth to require a ſcilence
or cloſeneſſe for their obſcuritie. Wherfor he diuideth the ſcriptures into
two ſortes, or partis ſaieng : *Aliud eſt Dogma, aliud Prædicatio. Dogmata ſilentur:* *Baſil. li. de*
Prædicationes verò publicantur. Silentij autem ſpecies eſt & obſcuritas, qua vtitur ſcri- *Sp.S.ca.27*
ptura, ita dogmatum ſententiam conſtruens, vt ægrè aſſequi poſsis. The pointes of
B learning be one thing, and morall inſtruction ys an other. Pointes of learning, be kept cloſe or ſecret: Morall inſtructions are publiſhed, and openlie
taught. A kinde of ſcilence alſo ys the obſcuritie, whiche the ſcripture vſeth,
ſo framing the meening of the ſecret pointes of learning, that a man maye
hardlie atteign therto.

Saint Ambroſe alſo in a fewe woordes ſaieth moche to this matter, cal- *Lib 7. epiſt 44.*
ling the ſcripture of God the great ſea, hauing in yt a depeneſſe withoute
Botome of depe ſenſes and vnderſtãdinges into the whiche manie flouddes
doo entre.

Chryſoſtom alſo vpon this text: *Væ vobis qui clauditis regnum cælorum,* Wo be *Math 23. Chryſoſt. oinel.44. in Matth.*
to yow whiche ſhett vppe the kingdom of heauen : ſaieth thus : *Regnum eſt
beatitudo cæleſtis. Ianua autem eius eſt ſcriptura, per quam intratur ad eam. Clauicularij
autem ſunt ſacerdotes, quibus creditum eſt verbum docendi, et interpretandi ſcripturas.
Clauis autem eſt verbum ſcientiæ ſcripturarum, per quam aperitur hominibus ianua veritatis. Adapertio autem eſt interpretatio vera. Videte, quia non dixit : Væ vobis qui non
aperitis regnum cælorum, ſed qui clauditis. Ergo non ſunt ſcripturæ clauſæ, ſed obſcuræ qui-*
C *dem, vt cum labore inueniantur, non autem clauſæ vt nullo modo inueniantur. Propterea
dicit Petrus in epiſtola ſua de ſcripturarum obſcuritate, quia non ſicut võluit homo, locutus
eſt ſpiritus: ſed ſicut voluit ſpiritus, ita locutus eſt homo. Ratio autem obſcuritatis multi-
plex eſt : tamen ſatisfactionis cauſa dicimus duas. Obſcurata eſt notitia veritatis, ne non
tam vtilis inueniatur, quàm contemptibilis. Contemptibilis enim eſt, ſi ab illis intelligatur,
à quibus nec amatur, nec cuſtoditur.* The kingdom ys the heauenlie bleſſe. The *Preiſtes are the keie bearers of the ſcri ptures.*
gates of yt ys the ſcripture, by the whiche we entre into yt. The keibearers
are the preiſtes, vnto whom the woorde ys committed, to teache and interprete the ſcriptures. The keie ys the woorde of the knowledge of the
ſcriptures, by the whiche the gate of trueth ys opened vnto men. The opening ys the true interpretacion. Marke ye that he did not ſaie: Wo be vnto
yowe, that do not open the kingdom of heauen: but to yowe whiche do
ſhette yt. Therfore the ſcriptures be not ſhett vppe, but obſcure, that with
labour they maye be fownd, but not ſhette vppe, that by no meanes they
maie be fownd. Therfor Peter ſaieth in his epiſtle of the obſcuritie of the
ſcriptures : Not as man wolde, hathe the Spirit ſpoken, but as the Spirit
D wolde, ſo ſpake man. Ther be manie cauſes of the obſcuritie of yt. But to
ſatisfie I tell twain : The knowledge of the trueth ys obſcured, leaſt yt
ſhoulde not be fownd as profitable, as contemptible, yf yt maie be vnder-
ded of thoſe, of whõ yt ys neither loued, nor kept. Thus moche Chryſoſtõ.

         Who

Who alſo geueth an other cauſe of the obſcuritie ofthe ſcriptures,whiche E
I reſerue to be declared in the next chapiter , minding to heare the ſaieng
of ſainct Gregorie,forſomoche as yt ys moche like,and agreable to the ſainge of Chryſoſtome.

Gregorius
ſuper
Ezech.
hom.9.

Magnæ vtilitatis eſt ipſa obſcuritas eloquiorum Dei, quia exercet ſenſum, vt fatiga-
tione dilatetur, & exercitatus capiat, quod capere non poteſt ocioſus. Habet quoque ad-
huc maius aliud, quia ſi ſcripturæ ſacræ intelligentia in cunctis eſſet aperta, vileſceret, quæ
in quibuſdam locis obſcurioribus tanta maiore dulcedine,inuenta reficit, quanto maiore la-
bore fatigat animum, quæſita. The obſcuritie of the woordes of God (ſaieth
ſaincte Gregorie) ys of great profit. For yt dothe exerciſe the vnderſtandinge, that by wearineſſe yt maie be ſtretched oute, and being exerciſed yt
maie take that,that yt coulde not take being idle. Yt hath yet an other greater thing. For yf the vnderſtanding of the ſcriptures were in all thinges
open and plain, yt ſhoulde waxe vile. The whiche vnderſtanding in certain
obſture places being fownde, dothe with ſo moche the more pleaſure or
ſweteneſſe delight, as with the more labour, being ſought yt wearyeth the F
minde.Thus moche Saincte Gregorie.

I might euen to wearineſſe load the Reader, with ſaienges of the Fathers, teſtifieng the obſcuritie of the ſcriptures. But for that I haue entred
into this matter to vſe yt but as a preparatiue to that, that ys here principa-
pallie entended to be treacted of, I will not tarie vpon yt, but heare the teſtimonie of ſaincte Hierom , as concerning the leſſer epiſtles, called canonicall, I meen the epiſtles of Iames, Peter, Iohn, and Iude, of the whiche he
ſaieth thus: *Iacobus, Petrus , Ioannes , & Iudas Apoſtoli ſeptem epiſtolas ædiderunt,*
tam myſticas quàm ſuccinctas, & breues pariter et longas . Breues in verbis , longas in
ſententijs, vt rarus ſit qui in eorum lectione non cæcutiat. The Apoſtles,Iames, Peter,
Iohn ,and Iude , made ſeuen epiſtles , as miſticall, as ſuccincte, and bothe
ſhort and long. Shorte in woordes, but long in Sentences. So as he ys a rare man, that in the reading of them doth not want ſeight of vnderſtandinge. Thus moche ſaincte Hierom.

Hieron ad
Paulin.
Fewe doe
well vnder
ſtand the
epiſtles of
Peter
James, Io-
hum &c.

Ye haue nowe heard the cenſure and iudgement of diuerſe famouſe Fathers,as touching the difficultie,and obſcurytie of the ſcriptures,the contra- G
rie wherof hath not onelie moſt falſlie, and ſhamfullie ben taught by Luther, as I haue ſaied, But alſo with like fooliſh arrogancie , hath ben pratled
by his pettie diſciples to the entrapping,and ſnaring of manie a ſimple Soule. For thei being perſuaded that the ſcriptures were eaſie to be vnderſtanded, proceaded with raſh boldeneſſe to vnderſtand euery ſcripture, as their
phanſie moued them, vſing the ſcriptures as ſimple children do the bells,
phataſing them to ſownd , euen as their phanſie conceaueth , according to
the common ſaieng : As the childe doth ſing : So dothe the bell ring. By
the whiche arrogant preſumption hereſie hath at this daie onerrunne , yea
almoſt ouerwhelmed a great parte of chriſtendome. Whiche howe lamentable yt ys, the charitable chriſtian heart feleth and perceyueth.

Hereſie
through
arrogancie
hath al-
moſt ouer-
runne Chri
ſtendom.

But nowe conſider with me(gentle Reader) two thinges. Firſte their arrogancie, and after their blindeneſſe. Their arrogancie ys to manifeſt, that
wher the ſcriptures them ſelues (as ye haue heard) doo teſtifie, that they are
obſcure and hard : And ſainte Peter by moſt plain woordes teacheth, that
the epiſtles of ſaincte Paule be hard to be vnderſtanded : the common con- H
ſent and iudgement of the nobleſt learned men of Chryſtes Churche be
agreable to the ſame, the experience alſo not only of this our myſerable
time, but of diuerſe other times, in the whiche hereſies haue vexed the
churche

A churche, whiche haue rifen vpon the ohfcuritie of fcriptures (as Ifidore faieth) doth proue yt, and conuince yt: yet thcfe arrogant heretikes will auouche them to be eafie and plain. Ys yt not more then impudent arrogancye, to ftand againft fo manie true, fubftanciall and inuincible wittneffes? ys yt not wi ked that faincte Peter faing that faincte Paules epiftles be hard, Luther, and his difciples, yea his verie petties, that can but read, and yet not that well, fhall faie that they be efaie and plain? Ys ther anie credite to be geuê to theife wicked men in other matters, that fo arrogantlie againft all treuth teache this? Howe litle will they basfh in foome other matter, wher they maie through the darkneffe and obfcuritie of the fcriptures, fomwhat cloake and fhadow their falfhood, whê in fo manifeft a matter as this ys they basfh neuer one whitte?

As touching their blindneffe, the ignorant, that through ignorance can nothing faie, dothe not more open his blindneffe then thefe men do theirs, in fainge that the fcriptures be efaie and plain. For as learning, witte and

B knowledge, moue queftion, Scruple, and doubte : So ignorante blindneffe doth perceaue nothing but plaineffe, eafineffe, and faiftie.

The learned medleth with the fcriptures, with feare, diligence and painfull ftudie : The ignorant with boldneffe necligence and flackeneffe. wherbie yt cometh to paffe, that ys commonlie faied : who ys bolder then blind biarde?

Ignorance as bolde, as blinde.

As then *Origen*, Hierom, Ambrofe, Auguftin, Chryfoftome, and Gregorie through knowledge and learning holpen with grace did finde perceaue, and fee the fcriptures refperfed with manie difficulties and doubtes : So Luther and his offpring, through blinde arrogancie deftitute and void of grace fee no other but that the fcriptures be eafie and plain for euerie man to read and vnderftande, and findeth neither Scruple, ne doubte.

Wherfore, Reader, I wifh thee to be aduertifed raiher to folowe Origen Hierom, and the other holie Fathers, and with them to perceaue that the fcriptures be hard, and fo with circumfpection, and inftruction of the learned to read, or ells contenting thy felf to heare, to forbear reading, raither

C then to folowe the blinde, and fo withoute miftruft walke in rough places, and ther ftumbling fall into the ditche.

But here perchaunce ye will obiect and faie: why teache ye the fcriptures to the hard, and therby difwade men from the reading of them : feing that Chryfoftom in a nombre of places mofte earneftlie exhorteth men to the reading of the fcripturs, and doth not feare them with the obfcuritie and difficultie therof?

An obiection.

I am not ignorante (gentle Reader) that Chryfoftom doth fo. Neither do I forgett that Erafmus being very earneft that the fcriptures fhould be red of the common people, vfeth for this pourpofe, both the doyng and authoritie of Chryfoftom. Wherfore I fhall firft aunfwer thee for Chryfoftom, and after Erafmus.

An aunfwere.

Although Chryfoftom exhorteth yow to read, yet he maketh yow no warrantife of the eafineffe of the fcriptures, that ye maie vnderftand, interprete, and expownd them, and frame to your felf a doctrine, foch one as

D fhall like your phantafie. But (as all ready ye haue heard) he teacheth that the fcriptures be hard and obfcure. But ther be two caufes why Chryfoftom willed the people to read. One that he expownding the fcriptures to his people, he thought it fhoulde be commodioufe to them for the better vnderftanding of the fcripturs, if they wolde read that fcripture before they

camme

came to hym,whiche he wolde expōde vnto them.An other that they ſhou- E
de read them to folowe thē . To theſe pourpoſes,and with this entent,with
the remembrance alſo , that they be full of difficulties , and therfore cir-
cumſpeĉtlie to be red,it were tollerable they ſhoulde be red. But otherwiſe
to folowe their phantaſies,to be doĉtours and framers of a faith and doĉtrine tothem ſelues,with the contempte of them, whom God hath called and
placed to be teachers , that Chryſoſtom willeth not as in the next chapiter
folowing,ye ſhall heare him ſaie.

Alfonſus

As for aunſwer to Eraſmus ther neadeth no better to be made,thē *Alfon-*
ſus maketh.And yet firſt to ſaie to Eraſmus, yt ys merueilouſe that he, cōfeſ-
ſing the ſcripture to be hard , as he dothe in the argument of the epiſtle of
ſainĉt hierom to *Paulinus* , and in the argument of the epiſtle of ſainĉte Paule to the Romans , wher he dothe with ſoche maner of woordes ſet furth
the difficultie of that epiſtle (and yet truely) that it wolde raither diſcoura-
ge a man from the reading of it , then otherwiſe moue or prouoke him to
read:yt ys merueilouſe(I ſaie,)that he wolde the cōmō,rude and vnlearned F
people ſhoulde read that, that he teacheth to be ſo hard. In the whiche for
lacke of vnderſtanding manie of them , either they ſpend their labour in
vain, or ells vainly abuſe the ſcriptures to errour, and hereſie, according to
the vanitie of their minde. So that to confeſſe the ſcriptures to be hard,and
withall to will them to be common to the rude people yt hath but litle
ſhewe of reaſon . Yf they were eaſie and plain (as *Luther* falſlie teacheth)
yt might ſeme conſonante to reaſon that the people might medle with
them , for that , that for the eaſyneſſe therof they might wade through
them.

Alfonſus aunſwereth thus: that although ſaynĉte Chryſoſtom wolde the
the people ſhoulde read the ſcriptures, as in that tyme, yt ys no good colle-
ĉtion, that it aught to be ſo at this time . For oftentimes yt ys ſeen , that an
order of a lawe taken & reputed to be good for the maners of the people,
and condicion of the tyme, at one tyme , ys lefte and not put in execution
at an other time . As in olde tyme yt was vſed to kepe night watches at the
monumētes of holie Martyrs , the name wherof(whiche we call *Vigills*) yet G
remaneth . Vnto the hwich all maner of ages,men, women, bachelers,mai
dens,and children repaired and came. Whiche thing was ſo eſtemed in the
time of ſainĉte Hierom , that when *Vigilantius* depraued yt, ſainĉte Hierom
wrote verie ſharpelie againſt him for yt. And yet afterward (the maners of
of the people ſo requiring) theſe *Vigills* were lefte . Why then dothe not
Eraſmus as well ſeke to haue theſe *Vigills* reuiued and reſtored, ſeing they
were vſed in the tyme of ſainĉt Hierom , and of Chryſoſtome as well as the
other was?

In the time of ſainĉt Auguſtin, children were communicated. but nowe
yt ys not in vſe.

The Apoſtles made an ordinaunce at Hieruſalem that ſtrangled andblo
ode , ſhoulde be forborne, and not eaten of, but yet yt ys not nowe in vſe,
for that the condicon of the tyme,and of the people ys otherwiſe,

Diſcipline and publike penance were in vſe in the olde daies in the churche,but we be loth now to haue yt again in vſe.

So,true yt ys that the people in the time of Chryſoſtom did read the ſcri- H
ptures , but yt foloweth not therfore that yt ys good and expedient that yt
be ſo nowe.For the condicion of the time,and maners of the people be farꝛ
different.Whiche two oftentimes,as they do alter & chaunge, cauſe altera-

cion

A cion of orders and lawes, as yt femeth to the rulars expedient. Yt ys the offi
ce of the people to heare, and learn, and fo by that mean to knowe the lawe
of their Lord God as the fcriptures do teftifie, and putting yt in practife, to
vfe due obedience toward God, and his officers, as the next chapiter more
at large fhall declare.

THE SYXTE CHAPITER DECLARING HOWE
the people fhall come to the vnderftanding of the fcriptures.

Lmightie God, who in mofte goodlie wife difpofith all thinges,
and ordeineth nothing in vain, hathe thus appointed that the la
we fhoulde be in the mouthe of ther preift, and that the people
fhoulde learne yt of him, as yt ys written : Yf ther ryfe a matter
to harde for thee in iudgemēt betwene bloode and bloode, be-
twē plee, and plee, betwē plague, ād plague, and the matters come to ftrife wi
B thin thy gates: Thē fhalt thow rife, ād get thee vppe vnto the place, which the
Lorde thy God hath chofen, and come vnto the preiftes the leuites, and vnto the iudge that fhall be in thofe daies, and aske, and they fhall fhewe thee
the fentence of iudgement. And thow muft doo according to that whiche
they of that place, which the Lorde had choofen, fhewe thee. And thowe
fhalt obferue to doe according to all that they enforme thee, accordinge to
the fentence of the Lawe, which they teache thee, and according to the iudgement which they tell thee, fhalt thowe doo and bowe not frō that whiche
they fhewe thee, neither to the right hande neither to the lefte. And that
man that will do prefumptuouflie, and will not harken to the preift that ftan
deth ther before the Lorde thy God to miniftre, or vnto the iudge, that man
fhall die, and thowe fhalt put awaie euell from Ifrael. And all the people fhall
heare, and feare, and fhall doo no more prefumptuouflie.

Accordinglie to this alfo allmightie God faieth by his prophet Malachie.
*Labia facerdotis cuftodient fcientiam, et legem requirent ex ore eius , quia Angelus domini
exercituum eft.* The lippes of the preift fhall kepe knowledge, and they fhall re
C quire the lawe at his mouthe. For he ys the meffenger of the Lorde of hoftes.

And forfomoche as yt ys fo, God willed the prophet *Aggæus*, to aske the
the preiftes the law, faieng: *Interroga facerdotes legē*, Aske the preiftes the lawe.
Vpon the which texte faieth fainɗe Hierome: *Confidera facerdotū effe officij , de
lege interroganti refpondere. Si facerdos eft, fciat legem Domini: fi ignorat legem, ipfe fe ar-
guit non effe Domini facerdotem. Sacerdotis eft enim fcire legem, & ad interrogationē refpondere de lege.* Cōfider (faieth fainɗ Hierō) that yt ys the office of a preift,
to aūfweer him, that asketh of the Lawe. Yf he be a preift, let him knowe the
lawe of God : yf he be ignoraunte he argueth himfelf that he ys not the
preift of God. For yt ys appertaining to a preift to knowe the lawe, and to
aunfwer vnto a queftion , oute of the lawe. Thus moche fainɗe
Hierome.

This ordre thus appoinɗed in the olde lawe, fo farre was yt from the min
de of our Sauiour Chryfte to breake yt in the newe lawe, that although the
D preiftes were of corrupte maners, and wicked life: Yet he willed their authoritie to be obeyed, and their office to be regarded. The Scribes and the Pharifeis (faieth he) fitte in Moyfes feate. All therfore what foeuer they bidde
yowe obferue, that obferue and doo: But doo not ye after their workes , for
they faie, and doo not,

Deuteron.
17
*Matters of
doubt muft
be refered
to the prei-
ftes.*

*He that wil
not heare
the preift
fhall die.*

Malac. 2.

Agga. 2.

*Hieron. in
2. Agg.
Office of
preiftes ys
to knowe,
and expo-
wnd the
fcripture.*

*Authori-
tie ys to be
obied wher
corruption
of life reig-
neth.*

D　　　Whiche

Hieron. in
Hggai. c.2

Whiche thing alſo ſainᶜte Hierom by expreſſe woordes teacheth to be con **E**
tinewed in the newe lawe,and that by ſainᶜte Paules ordre to *Timothee* , and
Titus,ſaing.*Et ne forſitan in veteri ſolùm inſtrumento hæc præcepta videatur,loquitur &*
1.Tim . 3.   *Apoſtolus ad Timotheü:Epiſcopũ non ſolum irreprehenſibilê eſſe debere, & vnius vxoris*
virũ,& ſapientê,& pudicũ,et ornatũ,et hoſpitalê: ſed etiã doᶜtorê.Et ne caſu hoc dixiſſe
videatur,ad Titum quoq; ſuper presbyteris (quos et Epiſcopos intelligi vult)ordinandis, ea-
Tit.1.   *dê cautela ſeruatur.Propter hoc reliqui te Cretæ,vt quæ reſidua erant corrigeres,et ordina-*
res per ciuitates presbyteros,ſicut ego præcepi tibi:Si quis eſt irreprehenſibilis, vnius vxoris
vir,filios habens fideles,non in accuſatione luxuriæ,vel inſubieᶜtos . Oportet enim Epiſcopũ
irreprehenſibilê eſſe,ſicut Dei diſpenſatorê,non procacê,non iracundũ,nõ vinolentũ,nõ per-
cuſſorê,non turpis lucri cupidũ,ſed hoſpitalê,benignũ,iuſtum,ſanᶜtũ,cõtinentê,habentê in do
ᶜtrina ſermonê fidelê,vt poſsit cohortari in doᶜtrina ſana, et eos qui contradicunt arguere.
Sunt enim multi non ſubieᶜti,vaniloqui,et ſeduᶜtores,maximè qui de circumciſione ſunt: qui
bus oportet imponere ſilentiũ.Hæc prolixius poſui,vt tam ex veteri,quàm ex nouo Teſtamê
to,ſacerdotum eſſe officiũ nouerimus,ſcire legê Dei,et reſpondere ad quæ fuerint interrogati.

And leſte peraduᶜture(ſaieth ſainᶜte Hierom)theiſe thinges maie ſeme to **F**
be cõmaunded onelie in the olde Teſtament , the Apoſtle alſo ſpeaketh to
Bishops ãd   Timothie that a Biſhoppe ſhoulde not onelie be irreprehenſible,and the huſ
preiſtes de   band of one wife,aȵd wiſe,ſobre,diſcrete,and a keper of hoſpitalitie:But alſo
ſcribed.   a teacher.And leſte peraduenture he ſhoulde ſeme to haue ſpoken this by
happe or chaunce,the ſame cautele ys obſerued vnto Tite,for the ordring of
preiſtes, whome alſo he wil to be vnderſtanded Biſhoppes.For this cauſe ha
ue I lefte thee at Crete,that thowe ſhouldeſt reſourme the thinges , that are
vnperfeᶜte,and ſhouldeſt ordein preiſtes in euerie citie, as I haue commaun-
·ded thee.Yf anie be blameleſſe,the husbande of one wife , hauing faithfull
children,whiche are not ſlaundered of riotte,neither are diſſobedient. For **a**
Biſhoppe muſt be blameleſſe,as the Stewarde of God, not ſtobbourne, not
angrie,not geuen to moche wine,no fighter,not geuen to filthie lucre, but **a**
keper of hoſpitalitie,one that loueth goodneſſe,ſobre,righteouſe,godlie,tem
perate,and ſoche as hathe the true woorde of doᶜtrine, that he maie be able
alſo to exhorte by holſome learning,and to reproue them, that ſaie againſt
yt.For ther are manie vnrulie,and talkers of vanitie,and deceiuours of min- **G**
des,ſpeciallie they that are of the circũciſion,whoſe mouthes muſt be ſtopt.
Theiſe thinges I haue ſette furthe at lenght, that we might knowe as well
oute of the newe teſtament,as oute of the olde,that the office of the preiſtes
ys to knowe the lawe of God,and to aunſwer to ſoche thinges as they be aſ
ked of.Thus moche ſainᶜte Hierome.

1.Cor . 12.   To this alſo maye be added,that ſainᶜte Paule ſaieth to the Corinthians,
Gods ordre   that god hath ſo ordered his Churche,that he hath appointed ſome Apoſt-
in hys   les,ſome prophetes,ſome doᶜtours and teachers.
Church.

All that ys hitherto alleaged,as well of the ſcriptures, as of ſainᶜte Hierome teacheth and includeth thre thinges.The firſt ys the duetie,and office of
a preiſt:The ſeconde that the ſcriptures haue doubtes,and difficulties . The
thirde that the people muſt be taught them,and learn of the preiſtes.

As touchinge the firſt, the duetie of à preiſt ys to be learned in the lawe
Duetie ãd   of god, and godlie life alſo, To bothe whiche ſainᶜte Paule moueth *Titus*
office of   in one ſentence, ioininge them together, euen as they anght to be iointlie
preiſtes.   in him that ys a preiſt. In all thinges(ſaith he)ſhewe thy ſelf an enſample of **H**
good workes, in the doᶜtrine with honeſtic and grauitie, and with the hol-
Tit.2.   ſome woorde, whiche can not be rebuked, that he whiche withſtandeth
maye be aſhamed, hauing no euell thing to ſaic of yowe.

                                        As

A   As for the office of a preiſt, ſainct Paule declareth yt to Timothee: I teſtifie (ſaieth he) before God, and before oure Lorde Ieſu Chryſt, preache
thowe the woorde, be feruent in ſeaſon, and oute of ſcaſon, improue rebuke,
exhorte, with all long ſuffringe and doctrine, doo the worke of an Euangeliſt, fulfill thine office to the wttermoſte.

As here the office and duetie of a preiſt ys breiflie and truelie declared:
So wiſſhe I that they maie as breiflie and trulie be planted, and take good
roote in all that beare that office. For I write this with the greif of my heart
before God that yt greueth me to ſee the great lacke of theſe two partes in
thoſe that take the office vpon them, of the whiche manie lacke bothe good
liuing and good learning. God take mercie vpon his people, and ſend them
faithfull paſtours, whiche maye feede his ſhepe with the holſom foode of
true doctrine, and example of godlie liuing, that God bothe in his paſtours
and people maie be glorified.

As cōcerning the ſecond, that the ſcriptures haue doubtes and difficulties:
B   Yt appeareth by the expreſſe woorde of God, when he ſaieth: Yf ther riſe a
matter to hard for thee in iudgemēt,&c. Thow ſhalt get thee vppe to the prei
ſtes the Leuites. But forſomoch as this matter ys allready ſufficiētlie treacted
of and proued, yt ys enough here nowe to haue touched yt and ſo to paſſe
to the third: Which ys that the people muſt be taught, and learn the lawes of
god of the preiſtes. Which thīg ys ſo manifeſtlie declared ād in ſo plain woor
des opened in the ſcriptures alleaged, that I ſhal not nede to make any further declaraciō therof: foraſmuche as yt ys plainlie ther ſaied, that the doubtes of the people in the lawe of God muſt be diſſolued bi the preiſtes, to who
ſe ſentēce and iudgemēt they muſt in any wiſe ſtande, and not decline frō yt
neither on the right hand, nor on the left, and that on the pain of deathe.

In the which ſaing of God yt ys euidēt, howe moche God wolde that the
determinaciō of his church in the doubtes of his lawe ſhould be eſtemed ād
reuerēced, and his preiſtes in that reſpecte obeid. Which howe moche yt ys
nowe diſdained and contēned, and gods ordre and cōmaūdemēt neclected,
his holie faith and religion infringed and violated, yt ys more with Sithes
C   and teares to be lamented, then beinge ſo manifeſt as yt ys, nedefull to be o-
pened and declared.

Of whoſe mouthe the people ſhould learn the lawe, AlmightieGod by his
prophete Malachie telleth. Likewiſe that of the preiſtes the people ſhould aſke the lawe, God by the Prophete Aggæus cōmaundeth. Who ſhoulde teach
the people, the newe Teſtamēt he alſo preſcribeth, Appointing ſome Apoſt
les, ſome Prophetes, ſome Doctours or teachers, who to theiſe offices are ap
pointed to rule and inſtruct the people, In ijs quæ ad Deū pertimēt, in thoſe thinges that appertein to God. But nowe al this ordre ys inuerted in manie places. The people teache the preiſtes, and not the preiſtes the people. The peo
ple diſſolue the doubts of the lawe, the preiſtes not being asked for. The peo
ple ſpeake, the preiſtes holde their peace. The peoplemake lawes in religion,
the preiſtes are cōpelled to obeie. The people take in hande the thinges that
appertain to God, the preiſtes are put to ſcilence.

A moch like ſtate we finde in the time of Moyſes emōge the children of
Iſrael in the time when Moyſes was in the moūt with God. For they percei-
D   uing him to be lōg abſent, and thinking that he wolde no more come, they
began to take the rule vpō thēſelues. And wheras Aarō before cōmaūded
and taught thē the religiō of the true God, nowe they taking the rule, and in
uerting the ordre, cōmaunded Aaron, and taught him ſoche Religion as ly-
ked them, of a falſe God.   D ij   When

2.Tim.4.

Scriptures
ful of doub
res.

*Doubtes in
the lawe of
God muſt
be diſſolued
by the prei
ſtes.*

*People
muſt learn
of the prei-
ſtes.*

*God his or-
dre inuer-
ted.*

Exod. 32.

When the people sawe (saieth the booke of *Exodus*)that yt was long er E
Moyses came downe oute of the Mountain,they gathered themselfes togea
ther vnto Aaron,and saied vnto him:Vppe make vs Gods to go before vs.
For of this Moifes the felowe,that brought vs oute of the lande of Aegypte,
we wote not what ys become.

Hereby maie yt be perceiued,what religion shall be,when the ordre that
God appointed being broken,they will teache and commaunde , which in
matters to godwarde,shoulde be taught and commaunded.

Plagues for
breaking
Gods ap-
pointed or
dre in reli-
giō and my
nisterie.

But with all yt ys to be remembred,that for this wickednes the wrathe of
God waxed hote againft the people,and notwithftanding that ther was immediatelie a greate slaughter of the people,aboute the nōbre of three thousand,and that Moyses made intercefsion to God for the people:Yet allmigh
tie God in the ende saied:Neuer the latter in the daie when I vifet,I will viset their sinne vpon them,and the Lorde plagued the people bicause of the
calfe whiche Aaron made.

Wherfore seinge that the moche like trangrefsion ys committed emonge F
the Chryftian people,yt ys to be feared, that the wrathe of God will waxe
hote againft vs.But God graūte vs a Moyses,that by earneft intercefsiō,maie
yet mittigate the plague of God that shall come for this wickednesse.

Num .16.

The plague,I feare me,will be fore vpon *Corah*,*Dathan*,and *Abiron*,and vpon
the capitanes of the multitude,whiche be the great and famouse mē in the
congregacion,which haue gathered thē selues together againft Moyses, and
Aaron,and cā not contēt thē selues with soche ordre,as God hath put in his
Church, ānd which by hys pleasure hath so long continued:But yet they co
me to Moyses,and Aaron,and saie,ye make muche to doo,seing all the multitude are holie,euery one of them,and the Lorde ys emonge them . Whie
heaue ye your selues vppe aboue the Congregacion of the Lorde.

I muft ftaie my hand, I shall ells be to tediouse to the reader in this matter,in the whiche I thought not to haue writtē the fourth parte of that that
ys written,and for expedicion leaue vnto him to reade the ftrory in the boo
ke of Nombres,and so further to confider yt.

And wher ther be manie ftories declaring the difpleafures of God to ha- G
ue commed vppon the people bicause they wolde not submitte them selues
to the ordeinaunce of him, and his miniftres , but wolde vsurpe vpon them
both:Yet I will speake but of one,in the firft booke of the kinges, which ys,
that where God appointed *Samuel*,his beloued and holie Prophet to be the

1. Reg . 8.

ruler of the people,they being a ftiffnecked and difobedient people, to gods
ordre so long before)vfed,al the elders gathered themfelues together,and ca
me to *Samuel*,and saied vnto him:Beholde thowe arte olde, and thy Sonnes
walke not in thy waies,Nowe therfore make vs a king to iudge vs,as al other
nacions haue.

See their phantafticall prouidence,and therwith their difobediéce.They
take in hande to prouide for their common wealth, as though God coulde
not prouide them as good a ruler after *Samuel* , as he did in prouiding of *Samuel*.And therfore (the ruler whiche God appointed reiected) make vs, saie
they,a kinge.But what saied Almightie God to *Samuel* ? Heare the voice of
the people,for they haue not caft thee awaye , but me , that I shoulde not

1.Reg. 12.

reign ouer them. H

And after that they had a kinge,*Samuel*,to caufe them to vnderftand, that
their offence was great,faied: I will call vnto the Lorde , and he shall send
thunder,and rain,that ye maie perceaue and see howe that yower wicked-

nesse

A neſſe ys great,which ye haue doen in thee ſeight of the Lorde, in asking yowe a king.And they ſaied, Praye for vs thy ſeruauntes vnto the Lorde thy
God that we die not,for we haue ſinned in asking vs a king.

As theiſe people offended for that they abidde not in the ordre that God
appointed thē:So oure people nowe a daies folowing the inuentiōs of their
heades,and caſtinge awaie their rulers,which God hathe appointed,and takinge ſoche as God hath not appointed,reieĉtinge alſo the holie religiō and
faith of God vniuerſallie receaued, and framinge thēſelues a faith and Religiō newlie inuēted,and but priuately vſed,haue not onelie offended, but(as
ſainĉt Auguſtine ſaieth)they haue ſhewed their great madneſſe. *Si quid diuinæ*
ſcripturæ præſcribit autoritas,non eſt dubitandū,quin ita facere debeamus,vt legimus.Simi
liter etiam ſi quid per orbem frequentat Eccleſia.Nam hoc quin ita faciendum ſit diſputare,
*inſolentiſsimæ inſaniæ eſt.*Yf the authoritie of the ſcripture of God dothe preſcri
be anie thing, yt ys not to be doubted but that we aught to do as we read.
Likewiſe what ſo euer the Churche through the worlde dothe obſerue for
B to diſpute but that this aught ſo to be done , yt ys moſt arrogant or fooliſh
madneſſe.

Aug.ad.
Ianuar.
Epla. 118.

As,I ſaie,oure people haue offended with the childrē of Iſrael in theiſe and
other before mencioned:So God graūte thē to be cōtended with Gods ordre,and to repēt with the childrē of Iſraell and ſaie:*peccauimus*,we haue offen
ded,ād ſo their eies through mekenes opened,theymaie mekelie ſe their igno
raunce,and acknowledging the ſame,maie iudge thēſelues more mete to hea
re then to ſpeake,to learn then to teache,to obie then to rule,as the authori
tie and exāples of the moſt famouſe fathers and men of Chryſtes Churche
maie moue.Of whiche ſome ſhalbe ſhewed in the next chapiter.

THE SEVENTH CHAPITER DECLARING THE
ſame by examples of the Fathers and autorities of the Doĉtours of the Churche.

Oyſes,when his death drewe nere, willing that the great woū
ders that God had wrought ſhoulde not by obliuiō , be wiped
oute of memorie,not onelie to the childrē of Iſrael that thē liued,but to al their poſteritie,as wel their ſpiritual,as carnal chil
C drē,he gaue this rule:*Interroga patrem tuum,& annunciabit tibi, ma*
*iores tuos & dicent tibi.*Aske thy father and he will ſhewe thee,thy Elders and
they will tell thee.

Deut.32.

Although Moyſes had writtē fiue bookes,wherin he had moſt excellētlye
declared the mightie workes,and wounderful miracles of God : Yet he did
not ſende all the people onelie thither to learn,but he willed thē to learn of
their Elders,what were the great workes of God:Euē ſo nowe a daies all mē
maie not be ſent to the ſcriptures to learn , but they muſt learn of their fathers,what be the goodlie workes of God conteined in the Scriptures.

Yf ye aske all the holie auncient Fathers of whome they learned,they wil
aunſwere,of their teachers,Fathers,and Elders.

The Apoſtles learned of our maſter Chryſte,who were not in a ſoddein abſolutelie,and perfectlie learned,but were three yeares and more in learning,
although they learned of ſo noble a Schoolemaſter , whom yt pleaſed ſo to
vſe his Scholers the holie Apoſtles,as therby to inſinuate vnto thē , that the
D knowledge of the ſcriptures ys not raſhlie to be had,either with a daies hearinge,or with a yeares ſtudieng,but yt ys(as Origen ſaieth)with greate ſtudie
and praier to be gotten.*Non ſtudiū ſolū nobis adhibendū eſt,ad diſcendas ſacras literas,*
verùm & ſupplicandū Domino,& diebus ac noĉtibus obſecrandū , vt veniat Agnus ex
*tribu Iuda,& ipſe accipiēs librū ſignatū,dignetur aperire.*Not onelie ſtudie(ſaieth O-

Scripture
muſt be lear
ned of the
Fathers.
The Fa-
thers lear-
ned of their
elders.
The Apo
ſtles lear-
ned of
Chryſt.
Praier re-
qnired to
vnderſtād
the ſcriptu-
res.

D iij　　　　rigen

rigen)ys to be applied to learn the holie fcriptures,but fupplicacion muft be **E**
made vnto our Lorde,and praier vfed daies and nightes,that the Lābe of the
Tribe of Iuda maie come , and that he takinge the fealed booke, maie vouchefaif to open yt . Thus moche *Origen.*

Fathers of the Church learned of their Elders.

After this maner the holie difciples ād fathers did learn of their Seniours as
the hiftories do declare.So did *Marke,Clemens, Linus,* and *Cletus* learn of fainde
Peter.So did *Titus,Timothius, Lucas,* and *Dionyfius* of fainde Paule.*Ignatius, Policarpus,* and *Papias* of fainde Ihon.*Of Papias,Tertulian.* Of *Pantenus Origen.* Of *Origen,Dionyfius Alexandrinus.* Of *Tertulian,Cyprian.* Of *Dydimus* and *Gregorie Nazian-
ʒen,* fainde Hierō.Of *Theophilus,* fainde Cyrill.Of fainde *Ambrofe,* fainde *Auguftin.* Of fainde *Auguftin,Primafius,* and *Orofius.* And fo a great nōbre of other,
which did not onelie with holie life,ād deuoute praier applie their great and
plainfull ftudie:but alfo trauailed manie and diuerfe cōtries to feke famoufe
and holie learned mē,of whome they might be inftruded in the Scriptures.

*Ecclef.hift.
li.11.ca. 9.
Sainde Ba-
fill and Gre-
go.Naziā.
howe they
learned the
fcriptures.*

The Ecclefiaftical hiftorie declareth that two notable learned holie Fathers
Bafil, and *Gregorie Nazianzen* laie thirtene years in a Monafterie, in the ftudie **F**
of the Scriptures,and yet prefumed not of their owne heades, but vfed the
learned helpe and inftrudiō of their elders,whofe learninge and authoritie,
they diligentlie and obediētlie folowed.The woordes of the hiftorie be the
fe:*Gregorius cum fe totum dei feruitio mancipaffet,tantum de collegæ amore præfumpfit,
vt fedentē Bafiliū de dodoris cathedra deponeret,ac fecū ad Monafteriū manu inieda per-
duceret,ibíque per annos(vt aiunt) tredecim, omnibus Græcorū fæculariū libris remotis,folis
diuinæ fcripturæ voluminibus operā dabāt, eorumóue intelligentiā,non ex propria præfum
ptione,fed ex maiorū fcriptis,& autoritate fequebantur,quos & ipfos ex apoftolica fuccef-
fione intelligendi regulā fufcepiffe,conftabat.* Gregorie,when he had geuen and boū
de himfelf whollie to the feruice of God,prefumed fo moche vpon the loue
of his felowe,that he putte Bafille fitting,from the chaire of a dodour or tea
cher,and taking him by the hande led him with him to the Monafterie, and
ther by the fpace of thirtene yeares (as yt ys reported) all prophane or fecu-
lar bookes of the Grecians remoued,they applied their diligéce and laboure
to the onelie bookes of Gods Scripture,and pourfewed the vnderftāding of
the fame,not of their owne prefumption,but by the writinges and autoritie **G**
of their Elders,who alfo themfelues (as yt was wel knowē (receaued the rule of vnderftanding by fuccefsion frō the Apoftles.Thus moche the hiftorie.

*Hier . ad
Domnion,
et Rogatiā
Sainēt Hie-
rom howe
he learned
the fcriptu
res.*

Sainde Hierome of himfelf faieth:*Nobis curæ fuit,cum eruditifsimis Hebræorum
hunc laborē fubire,vt circumiremus Prouinciā,quam vniuerfæ ecclefiæ Chrifti fonāt. Fateor
enim mi Domnion & Rogatiane charifsimi, nunquam me in diuinis voluminibus proprijs
viribus credidiffe,nec habuiffe opinionē meā,fed ea etiā,de quibus fcire me arbitrabar, inter
rogare me folitū.Quantomagis in ijs,de quibus anceps eram?* This care had I,that with
the beft learned of the Hebrues I wolde go rownde aboute the Prouince,
whiche all the churches of Chryfte do fpeake of.For I acknowledge (my dea-
reft beloued Domnion,and Rogatian) that I neuer trufted moche to my
owne iudgement in the ftudie of gods bookes, neither haue I had my owne
opinion,but I haue vfed to afke of other,yea euen thofe thinges,whiche I
thought I did vnderftande,howe moche more thófe thinges of the whiche
I was doubtfull.Thus moche fainde Hierom.

*Rafhe rea
ders, and
arrogant
teachers
maie be
abaffhed.*

By the which faienge, howe maie they bafhe and be afhamed who hauing
fkant anic tafte of learninge,take vpō thē not onelie to reade the fcriptures, **H**
but alfo to determin,to expownde,to aunfwer,to diffolue , yea withoute all
ftoppe to wade through all matters of the fcriptures; wher fainde Hierom a
man of great learninge,and famoufe in knowledge, did not fo farre prefume

in

A in matters,that he did thinke himmself to vnderſtãde,but he wolde cõsult,and learn the iudgement of his Elders beinge learned, and moche more wolde he ſo do in doubtefull matters.

Although in the time of Sainẽte Hierom manie did ſtudie the ſcriptures, whiche if the people coulde nowe reuerentlie and mekelie vſe, taking no more vpon thẽ, then becometh them, and as to their calling apperteineth, might be tollerated,but the arrogant abuſe,then beginning emõge the peo ple,whiche nowe hath inuaded and troubled a great parte of the Churche, that ys, that euerie man wolde be a teacher before he haith learned ſainẽte Hierom coulde not conteine, but complain and exclame vpon yt ſainge: *Ad minores artes veniam,& quæ non tam lingua, quàm manu adminiſtrantur. Agricolæ, cemẽtarij,fabri metallorum, lignorumúe cæſores, lanarij quoque & fullones,& ceteri,qui variam ſupellectilem , & vilia opuſcula fabricant , abſque doctore non poſſunt eſſe quod cupiunt.Quod medicorum eſt,promittunt medici,tractant fabrilia fabri. Sola ſcripturarum ars eſt,quam ſibi paſsim omnes vẽdicant.Scribimus indocti,doctiq́; poëmata paſsim. Hanc*

B *garrula anus,hanc delirus ſenex, hanc ſophiſta verboſus,hanc vniuerſi præſumunt,lacerãt, docent antequam diſcant. Alij a ducto ſupercilio grandia verba trutinantes,inter mulier- culas de ſacris literis philoſophantur .* I wil come to the lower ſciẽces,and ſoche as are excerciſed, not ſo moche with tounge as with hande.Plowmẽ,Maſons, metall Smiths,Carpenters,Wollmen,fullers, and other whiche do make di uerſe thinges of houſholde, and vile workes, without a teacher they can not be that they wolde be .Phiſitions promiſſe what to Phiſitions appertei neth,Craſtes men handle thinges to craſtes men apperteininge. Yt ys onlie the ſcience of the ſcripture, whiche all men euerie wher chalenge , and ta- ke vpon them . Learned and vnlearned, we write Poëtes workes euerie wher. This ſcience of the ſcripture , the chatering olde wief,this ſcience the olde dotinge man , this ſcience the bablinge Sophiſtre, this ſcience all men preſume on , they teare yt , they teache yt before rhey can learn yt. Some with high looke and great pride weighing graue woordes,vtter ther wiſdõ oute of the ſcriptures emongeſt womẽ.Thus moche ſainẽt Hierome.Who- ſe woordes if a man will applie to this our time, he ſhall perceaue them , in

C euerie parte to be trewe And by theiſe woordes the Reader maie well per- ceaue howe moche yt miſliked ſainẽt Hierome , that all maner of people woulde be prattelers,bablers,manglers,and mincers of the ſcriptures,med- ling,reaſoninge,and diſputinge of thinges they cã no ſkill of,and preſuming to teache before they haue learned. Whiche great abuſe.I wolde to God it were yet no more in this our time,then yt was in ſainẽt Hieroms time.

Note further(whiche ys the thinge that ys intended here to be ſpokẽ of) that willinge no man ſhoulde be his owne maſter and teacher in the vnder- ſtanding of the ſcriptures, he bringeth furth for an example mechanicall ar- tes, or handy craſtes, whiche (he ſaieth) be not perfectlie learned withoute a teacher , as though he ſhoulde therbie conclude, that the ſcriptures can moche leſſe be learned , except the reader haue a teacher . He proueth the ſame alſo by the ſciences liberall , for the obteininge of whiche, manie phi- loſophers haue trauailed diuerſe and manie farre contries to heare famou- ſe men teache the ſame.

D Likewiſe in the ſame epiſtle when he had by diuerſe ſcriptures proued the difficultie of the ſame, he aſſigneth the cauſe of his ſo doinge, as ys be- fore ſhewed in the firſt chapiter, by theſe woordes . *Hæc à me breuiter per ſtricta ſunt, vt intelligeres te in ſcripturis ſanctis , ſine præuio & monſtrante ſemitam non poſſe ingredi.* Theiſe thinges (ſaieth he) are of me breiſli touched, that thowe

Many pre ſume to tea che before they learn. Hieron.ad Prulinum.

Preſump- tuouſe tea- chers.

No man maie be his owne tea- cher in the ſcriptures.

Ibidm.

D iiij   ſhouldeſt

shouldest vnderstande, that without a foreleader and a shewer, thowe canst E
not entre the path into the holie scriptures.

Nowe wher this Proclamer wolde, that yt shoulde be proued by some
auncient writers, that the laie people were forbidden to reade the woorde
of God in their owne toung, as though the Churche had nowe forbidden
them, and wolde therbie bring the Churche in hatred with the people:
I let him vnderstande that I neuer knewe anye soche prohibicion geuen to
the laie people vniuersallie. For yf ther had ben any soche, ther shoulde not

Proclamer
chargeth
the Chur-
che with an
vntrueth.

haue ben so manie learned laie men, bothe in this Realme, and in other,
as ther haue ben, and be, whiche haue bothe red, and written of the scriptures in their natiue tounges, and set their doinges abroad to the common
reading of all people, as well before theise daies, as nowe, and were not
reprehended for their so doinge, yf yt were well doen, I meen accordinge
to the catholique faith. Wherfore I saie that he chargeth the Churche in this
point with an vntreuth,

But this I saie that the Churche hath feared the abuse of the scriptures, F
by soche of the laitie as be vnlearned, and therwith rashe, and therfore
hath rebuked yt from time to time, as ye maie perceaue, sainēte Hierom
did in his time. And I wolde learn of the Aduersarie, whether yt be not
better for the laie people to heare and learn, then to read and read with

Mysunder
stāding ma-
keth heresie
Hilarius.

misunderstanding, forasmoche as misunderstanding maketh heresie, and
heresie condemnacon. *De intelligentia enim hæresis, non de scriptura est*, saieth
Hillarye. Heresie riseth vpon the vnderstanding of the scripture, not vpon
the scripture yt self.

Scripture
ys full of
hardnesse
and diuerse
senseis.

Seing then, as yt ys proued, and yet more shall, that the scriptures be full
of obscurities, ful of difficulties, and heardnes; seing also the scriptures haue
manie senses, and in some places require Tropes and figures, in some none,
in some place they beare one sense, in some other place they wil not beare
the same: And the vnframed capacitie of the vnlearned, can not therunto
atteign: shall yt not be better for them, to learn the true vnderstanding
of the scriptures by hearing, then by reading to fall into misunderstanding?

Maruaill not, Reader, at this that I saie. For the learned, yf they be rash G
fall into this daunger. For the *Arrians*, the *Macedonians*, the *Nestorians*, the
Eutichians, the *Pelagians*, the *Lutherans*, the *Oecolampadians* (of the which secte
this proclamer ys) were learned men, and yet folowing their owne arrogaunt phantasie fell in to the misunderstandind of the scriptures, and
by misunderstanding into heresie. Moche sooner the vnlearned maye thus

knowledge
of misteri-
es not com-
mon to all.
Hierō. prę
fa. in Eze-
ch.

fall.

Yt hathe ben vsed emong most people of sundrie sortes, not to make the
knowledge of their high thinges common of all to be handeled.

The Iewes were forbidden to read *Genesis* and the Balletts of Salamon,
before they were thirtie yeares of age. Among the Romans, the Bookes of
the Sibells were red but of certain selected, and speciall choosen men.
Emong the Philosophers, Morall philosophie, and speciallie Metaphisick,
was not to be handeled of all men, but of soche as were thought mete for
that studie. Howe moche more then ys the scripture of God, with reuerence and fear to be handeled of the chrystians: not that I wolde yt should
not be knowen of all, as yt aught to be knowen, but that yt shoulde not be H
red of all, and therbie through misunderstanding God to be dishonoured,
the scripture abused, and not onelie they that read but other also by them
deceaued. And thus Reader I wish thee to perceaue the godlie meening
of

A　of the Churche, to fee the fhaunder of this proclamer againſt yt, and with all to vnderſtand that the ſcriptures be hard. Whiche meenyng ys not to be imagined nowe to be in theiſe latter daies inuented (as this Proclamer ſemeth to charge the Churche) but the weightie conſideracion of this mat ter, that the people ſhoulde raither learn then read them ſelues, was not onelie in the latin churche (as it appeareth by ſainct Hierom) but alſo in the greke churche, as yt appeareth by Chryſoſtom. For he declaring the cauſes of the obſcurities of the ſcriptures, and alleaging this for the firſt, ſaieth:

Primum, quia voluit Deus alios eſſe doctores, alios diſcipulos. Si autem omnes omnia ſcirent, doctor neceſſarius non erat, & ideò eſſet rerum ordo confuſus. Nam ad eos quidē, quos voluit eſſe doctores, ſic Deus dicit per Eſaiam prophetam : Loquimini ſacerdotes in cordibus populi. Ad eos autem, quos voluit diſcendo cognoſcere myſteria veritatis, ſic di-cit in Cantico : Interroga patrem tuum & dicet tibi, presbyteros tuos, & annunciabunt tibi. Et ſicut ſacerdotes, ne ſi omnem veritatem manifeſtauerint in populo, dabunt ratio-

Chryſ.omel 44. in Matth. Eſay.40. Deutr.32.

B　*nem in die Iudicij, ſicut dicit Dominus ad Ezechielem : Ecce ſpeculatorem te poſui domui Iſraël, ſi non dixeris impio vt à vijs ſuis prauis diſcedat, ipſe quidem in peccatis ſuis morie-tur, animam autem eius de manu tua requiram : ſic & populus niſi à ſacerdotibus didicerit, & cognouerit veritatem, dabit rationem in die Iudicij. Sic enim dicit Sapientia ad populum : Et extendebam ſermones meos, & non audiebatis. Ideò & ego in veſtra perditione ridebo. Sicut enim paterfamilias cellarium aut veſtiarium ſuũ non habet cunctis expoſitum, ſed alios habet in domo qui dant, alios autem qui accipiunt: ſic & in domo Dei alij ſunt qui docent, alij qui diſcunt.* Firſt bicauſe God wolde ſome ſhoulde*

why God wolde the ſcriptures to be obſcu re.

be teachers, ſome learners. Yf all men ſhould knowe all thinges, a teacher were not neceſſarie, and therfor ſhoulde the ordre of thinges be confown-ded. For vnto them, whome he wolde ſhoulde be doctours or teachers, God ſaieth thus by Eſaye the Prophete : Speake ye preiſtes in the heartes of the people. But vnto them whom he wolde to haue knowledge of the miſteries of trueth by learning of other, he ſaieth thus in the Canticle : Aske thy father and he ſhall tell thee, thy elders, and they ſhall ſhewe thee. And enen as the preiſtes, except they open all treuth to the people, they

C　ſhall make an accompte in the daie of Iugement, as our Lorde ſaieth to Ezechiell : Beholde I haue ſett thee a watch man to the houſe of Iſrael. Yf thow ſaie not to the wicked, that he maie departe from his naughtie waies, he ſhall die in his ſinnes, but I ſhall require his ſowle at thy hande : So alſo the people except they learn of the preſtes, and ſhall know the trueth, they ſhall make an accompte in the daie of iudgement. So ſaieth Sapience vnto the peole: I did ſette furth my wordes, and ye did not heare. Therfor ſhall I alſo laugh in your perdicion. As the houſholder dothe not make his ſtore-houſe or his wardrobbe common to all men, but he hath in his houſe ſo-me that deliuer, ſome that receaue: So in the howſe of God, ther be ſome that teache, ſome that learn. Thus moche Chryſoſtome.

The ſtore-houſe of God not co mon to all.

Whoſe ſaieng I nede not to expownde yt ys ſo plain of yt ſelf. Ye percea-ue that he teacheth yowe, that God hath ſette this ordre, that the pre-iſtes ſhoulde be teachers, and the people learners, and that for this cauſe God hath willed the ſcriptures ſhoulde be obſcure. Whiche in the ende of his ſaing he cõmendeth vnto vs to be remembred by à goodlie Similitude

D　that the houſholder maketh not his ſtorehouſe, and wardrobbe cõmon to all but certain do deliuer, and other do receaue, no more thē ys deliuered.

Scripture the ſtore-houſe of God.

The Storehouſe ys the ſcripture, wher in for the feading and cloathing of mans ſowle, ys repoſed great plentie of knowledge, whiche yet God haith

hath not made common to all men, to take at their owne pleafures. But he E
hath appointed officiers to be kepers of this ftore, which be his preiftes, to
geue yt furthe to the people in due tyme, and in due maner and forme.

As all men haue not difcrecion to vfe plentie well, but fome will waft yt,
fome will abufe yt, and turne yt to other vfes then yt was made or appointed for & therfore they haue not acceffe vnto yt : So all men hauing not
grace, and difcrecion to vfe the plentie of Gods knowledge in the fcriptures
well, they waft yt, that ys they fett litle by yt, they do but bable and talke
of yt, yt runneth aboute their lippes, as the meate doth aboute the childes
mouthe, bofom, and cloathes, and ys wafted, but yt entreth not into their
ftomackes, I meen into their folues, ther to fede them, and make them lu-
ftie and fatte, that yt maie appeare in their faces, in their outwarde conuerfacion, and godlie liuing. Theife be the verie wafters in dede, not wourthie
to haue acceffe to treafure houfes, ftorehoufes and places of plentie.

Some other likewife lacking grace and difcrecion abufe thinges of plentie. As the father leauing to the Sonne great treafure for the mainteinäce of F
his liuing, and the mercifull releiuing of foche as haue nede, the fonne abufeth and abfumeth the fame, in mainteining of quarrells, Suites, contencions, and moleftations of his bretheren and other, for whiche caufe better
yt had ben that foche treafure had ben deliuered vnto him as he had neded
yt, to helpe his neceffitie, than he hauing the libertie of the wholl, wickedlie fhoulde abufe yt : Euen fo men withoute grace and difcrecion hauinge
libertie to come to the treafure of the fcripturs, wher yt was geuen them to
good vfe, as to maintein the godlie life that they fhoulde lead in Chrift, and
by counfell to relieue thê, that haue nede of yt, they abufe yt to Scifme and
Herefie, wherby cometh contencion, Sectes, and diuifion, to the great
moleftacion of their chriften bretheren. Wherfore were yt not better, that
this treafure were deliuered vnto them, by foche as God hath appointed,
and fo to vfe yt well, then hauing libertie of the wholl to abufe all? Howfoeuer then this Proclamer, to winne the people by flatterie, wolde haue
the fcriptures common to all fortes, yet as to the auncient Fathers yt hath
appeared the beft waie, that yt fhoulde be deliuered : So fhall our mifera- G
ble experience teach vs at the laft, that yt ys the beft waie?

Valdo 　Valdo, a man alltogether vnlearned hauing a defire to côme into this
ftorehoufe of God, caufed certain bookes of the fcripture to be tranflated,
Valdenfes, 　whiche he reading withoute vnderftanding, fell into diuerfe herefies, and
fiue Paupe 　became an Authour of herefie, hauing many foloweing, as his Secte, which
res de Lug 　were called after his name *Valdenfes*. and by an other name *Pauperes de Lug-*
duno. 　*duno*, the poor men or people of Lions.

Begardi 　Oute of the fame fountain of ignorance (faieth *Alfonfus*) fprang an other
Turelupini 　forte of Heretikes called *Begradi Turelupini* men plainlie ignorante, and clere
withoute all learning. All whiche mens errours proceeded of a peruerfe
fenfe, and wrong vnderftanding of the fcriptures, whiche they through
ignorance mixed with malice, framed to them felues according to their
phanfies?

Luther äd 　Nowe Reader, hauing heard the mindes of the great learned and holie
Zuig. their 　Fathers of the Churche, as touchinge the difficultie of the fcriptures, the
ftraunge 　reading alfo, and vnderftanding of the fame, of whom alfo and at whofe H
doctrines 　handes ye muft learne the vnderftanding of them : what trueth ys to be
Luther. in 　thought in *Luther*, and *Zuinglius*, whiche fo plainlie to the contrarie, arro-
Affertiõ. 　gantlie affirme the fcriptures to be eafie and plain for all men to vnderftand
make

A make yt free for all men to read and expowde them, teache that not onelie men, but alfo womé maye openlie preache the woorde of God? And for the mainteinance of the fame moft wickedlie auouche all chryften men and women to be preiftes : and to all theife mifcheiuoufe and wicked herefies adde this moft peftilent herefie, that as well a childe and a woman abfolueth, as the Bifhoppe:

O Lord how manifeftlie repugnante be theife peftiferoufe affertions vnto the fcriptures? howe moche confownding and breaking the orde of the catholique Churche? howe farre diffenting from all the holie Fathers? yea and in fome of theife how moche dothe Luther diffent from him felf. *Luther cõtrarie to himfelf.*

In one booke he teacheth (as ys faied before) that ther ys no difficultie in the fcriptures, and boafting himfelf to be ignorant in no parte of them provoketh all men to bring him anie one place that he can not expownde. This ys one mete to be an Herefiarch in Satans Sinagog, that to gett him *lib.deferuo arbitrio. Luthers prowdbragges and lies*

B credite with his difciples extolleth him felf with Luciferane pride accõpanied with falfhood and lieng, euen vnto the heauens.

But fainёte Auguftine endewed with an other Spirit and depreffing and making himfelf lowe, faieth of himfelf thus : *Fateor me in fcripturis Dei, plura nefcire quam fcire.* I acknowledge mifelf, not to knowe mo thinges in the fcriptures of God, then to knowe. Thus faieth fainёte Auguftin. And yt ys eafie for all men to iudge, that betwixt theife two their ys no comparifon, whether ye haue refpeёte to excellencie of learning, or fanёtimony of lief.

But what trueth ys yn this faieng of Luther, his owne woordes in an other place fhall be iudge, thus he faieth : *Quocirca ingenuè me confiteri oportet, me ignorare, an legitimam habeam pfalmorum intelligentiam.* wherfor I muft francklie confeffe, that I am ygnorant whether I haue the lawfull vnderftanding of the pfalmes or no. And a litle after that he faieth again : *Scio impudentifsimæ temeritatis eum effe, qui audeat profiteri vnum librum fcripturæ, à fe in omnibus partibus intelleёtum.* I knowe him to be (faieth Luther) of moft impudent *Luther, in præfatione fuper pfalmos.*

C rafhneffe or foolifh blodneffe, that dare faie that he vnderftandeth anie one booke of the fcripture in all partes. Conferr theife two faienges with his other fentence before, and then iudge of the Spirit of the man. wolde ye not thinke them the fainges raither of two men, the one fobre, and the other drunke, or the one fobre, and the other ftark madde? When I conferred him in his firft faing with fainёte Auguftin yt femed to me that I hearde Goliath and Dauid, the condicions of the parties, fo well refembled eche other. *Luther fpeaketh diuerfelie, as thongh he were not one, but two diuerfe mẽ.*

Neuertheleffe howe wicked fo euer his Spirit and doёtrine ys. ther haue ben, and yet be to manie, that embrace and folowe the fame. For haue not the people, vpon this perfuafion of the eafineffe of the fcriptures, taken a great boldneffe, to read and difpute of the higheft and hardeft matters of all the fcriptures? Wil they not difpute, and determine in predeftinacon? Ys yt not a common matter almoft at euerie meting, that man hath no free will? Do not the Tauerns fownde of iuftificacion? Are not Barbre Shopps Schooles, teaching God to be caufe of Sinne? doo not Innes and Alehoufes *The peoples arrogante irreuerẽcie to diuiue matters.*

D fwarme with difputers of the Sacramentes, Howe manie ther be, what ys the force of them, what ys the Sacrament of the Altare, what ys the woorthineffe of yt, And what yt conteineth? Do not the mouthes of women, boies, and Girles, breath oute moft filthie ftincking, and abhominable

Blafphemie,

Blafphemie, againft this bleffed Sacrament and the miniftracon of the fame **E** in ftreetes, high waies and feldes? Ah Lord ys this the reuerence that aught to be geuen to the holie fcriptures, and to the high mifteries of God? Be theife matters mete foode for all kinde of people? Yf ther be any ftrong meat in all the fcripturs this ys ftrong meat. And fainɗe Paule faieth : *Perfeɗorum eſt ſolidus cibus, eorum, qui pro ipſa conſuetudine exercitatos habent ſenſus ad diſcretionem boni et mali.* Strong meat belongeth to them that be perfeɗe, euen thofe, whiche by reafon of vfe , haue their wittes exercifed to difcern bothe good and enell.

Hebr .5.

Agreablie to Saint Paule, faieth Gregorie Nazianzen. *Non cuiuſuis Chriſtiani eſt, de Deo diſſerere, non adeò res hec eſt vilis : neque eorum , qui humi ſerpentes terrenis ſtudijs occupantur. Quoniam eorum tantùm eſt, qui habito deleɗu, ad tantum munus videntur idonei, quiɋ; contemplandi acumine cæteros antecellunt, qui iam antè corpus et animam ab affeɗu purgarunt.* Yt ys not apperteining to euery chriſtian to reafon and difpute of God. This ys not fo vile a matter : nether ys yt apperteyning to them, whiche creping vpon the grownde, are occupied in earthlie **F** ftudies. For yt belongeth onelie to them, which beyng chofen, are perceaued to be mete for fo great an office, and whiche alfo in fharpeneffe of perceauing do excell other, whiche haue allready pourged both bodie and foule from affeɗion. Thus moche Gregorie.

Grego. Nazian lib.1. Theolog.

Euerie chriſtian maye not reaſon and diſpute of God.

In whiche fentence ye maie percceaue what difference in Iudgement ther ys betwen theife deſtroiers of religion and order, and this holie aunci-ent Father, for the medling with matters apperteining to God. Yet the wicked confownders haue not onelie wrought this mifcheif, but they haue alfo brought the people to foche contempte, that laie men haue in diuerfe famoufe places, openlie preached, and not onely foche as haue folowed ftudie, but plain Artificers, Bricklaiers Shoomakers, Tanners, Stacionars, Groffers, and foche like men all void of learning, but filled with pride and arrogancie. Yet Luther defirous to haue all order broken, and nothing to be doen in order, he geueth libertie alfo to women to preache. doo ye not fee a wonderfull confufion? And yet ther ys more . For yt ys knowen that diuerfe laie men haue miniftred Sacramentes, afwell Baptifme as **G** other, and haue not abafhed to miniftre them openlie in churches.

Laie men haue vſurped the office both of preaching and miniſtring of Sacramentes.

O Reader dothe yt not lothe thee to read thefe thinges, as yt greiueth me to write them ? Time will not fuffer me to go fo farre in the reherfall of thefe abhominacõns, as greif wolde enforce me. And yet fee how farre greif hath drawen me , and as yt were by force and violence thruft me on, when **I** wolde haue ftaied.

But God open ther eyes to fee in the fcriptures, whiche they be fo deficroufe to read, the plagues that God hath fent vpon them, that haue vfurped the preiftes office, being not called therunto, as theife doo, and that they maie beholde the order that our Sauiour Chrift began in choofing his Apoftles, and difciples, and geuing them autoritie to execute their office : to beholde alfo the imitation of the fame in fainɗe Paule in the inftitution of Bifhopps and preiftes with his owne hande , and the order prefcribed to other to be circumfpeɗ before they did laie on their handes : And then fhall they perceaue, that not euery man for his owne phantafie maye intrude him felf, but onelie foche as be called. **H**

Paral. 26. Luc.6. ibid.10. Aɗ.14. 1.Tim.4. &c.5. None maie exerciſe the office of a preiſt but he that ys called.

A   THE EIGHT CHAPITER EXHORTETH MEN
to heare, or to read the expositions of the scriptures, and not to
presume vpon their owne vnderstanding.

IT omnis homo (saieth sainct Iames) *velox ad audiendum, tardus autem ad loquendum, et tardus ad iram.* Let euery mã be swifte to heare, but slow to speake, and slow to wrathe. This counsel truly ys verie good and profitable. For as in the man of manie woordes ther lacketh not of fence: So the (foole as the wise man saieth) yf he holde his peace, he shalbe reputed wise, and to haue vnderstanding, when he shetteth his lipps. And whie, for he hath the propertie of a wise man. For as Salomon saieth he ys wise and discreet that tempereth his woordes.

Iacob. 1.

Prou. 10.
Ibid. 17.
Ibid. 17.

As by scilence, ys shewed wisdom: So by hearing wisdom ys gotten. For (as Salomon saieth) *Audiens sapiens, sapiētior erit, & intelligēs gubernacula possidebit.* By hearing the wise man shall come by more wisdom, and hauing vnder-

B standing shall atteign to gouernment. Vpon the whiche place sainct Hierom hath a goodlie saieng: *Quód autē ait, sapientem cum audierit verbum, sapientiorē effici : ostendit neminem in hac vita ita sapientem fieri posse, cuius sapientia nequeat augeri, semperq; moris esse sapientum, vt dictis maiorum, aliquando etiam minorum auscultent, & quicquid in illis vtilitatis audierint, ad se replicent, suóque in corde recondant. Denique audiuit sapiens minor maiorem, regina Saba Salomonem, & sapiētior redijt. Audiuit Moises socerum, multo inferiorem sublimior, et sapientior redditus est. Audierunt discipuli Christum, & spiritum sapientiæ percipere meruerunt. Audiuit Nicodemus, audiuit Gamaliel, audiuit discipulus eius, tunc Saulus, nunc Apostolus Paulus, sapientes vtique verbum Euangelij, & sapientiores sunt facti. Qui etiam Paulus cum ad tertium cælum raptus audiuisset ea, quæ non licet hominibus verba loqui, nihilominus ad terram reuersus aiebat: Quia ex parte cognoscimus, & ex parte prophetamus.*

Hieron. in ca. primi Prou.

Wheras he saieth the wise man to be made wiser, when he heareth the woord, he sheweth that no man in this life can be made so wise, whose wisdom maie not be encreaced, And further he sheweth yt to be alwaie the maner of wisemen, to take hede to the sainges of their betters, and somtime also

C of their inferiours, that what profitt so euer they finde in them, they maie replie yt to themselues, and laie yt vppe in their heart. To be brief, the lesser wise heard the greater, the queen of Saba Salomon, and she retourned wyser, Moyses hearde his father in lawe, the higher the farre lower, and he was made the wiser. The disciples heard Chryst, and they reccaued the Spirit of wisdom. Nichodemus heard, Gamaliel heard, Saulus being then his disciple, nowe the Apostle Paul heard, all these being wise men heard the woord of the gospell, and they were made wiser. The which Paul also when he was rapt into the third heauen, and had heard those woordes, which yt ys not laufull for a man to speake, yet being retourned to the earth he saied: Oure knowledge ys vnperfect, and oure prophecieng ys vnperfecte. Thus moche sainte Hierom.

The wise man by hearing maie be wiser.

In the whiche sentence two thinges maie emong other be noted: the one ys, that be ye neuer so wise, yet ye maie be wiser. Wherfore disdain not to learn either by hearing, or by reading. The other that all these, which S. Hierom bringeth in for example, contented them selues to heare, and by hearin

D ge came to more wisdõ. Let not then the prowde cr arrogant, be singular in his owne conceat, for the superiour maie heare and learn of the inferiour, as here ye haue perceaued Moyses to doo of Ietro, his wifes Father.

Yf thē we should hear ãd learn of al mē, moche more should we heare and

E   learn

learn of them,whome God hath appointed in his Churche,to be paſtours ãd E
teachers,whom of deutie we aught to heare,as being cõmended vnto vs by
God and his Church,and preaching vnto vs nowe by their bookes , as ſoim-
time they did by their mouthes,whoſe holineſ and learning was ſoche , that
they maie verie wel be takē for the elders that Ieſus Sirach ſpeaketh of ſaing:
Ne deſpicias narrationē presbyterorũ ſapientiũ,& in prouerbijs eorũ conuerſare . Ab ipſis
enim diſces ſapientiã & doctrinãintellectus, &c. Deſpiſe not the ſermons of ſoche
elders,as haue vnderſtãdinge,but acqueint thy ſelf with the wiſe ſentēces of
thē.For of them ſhalt thow learn wiſdom,and the doctrine of vnderſtãding.

Eccleſ.8.

But for aſmuche as men maie appoincte to thē ſelues ſoche elders,as they
phantaſie,as ſaincte Paule propheci"eng both of ſoche maſters and diſciples
ſaith:The time ſhall come,when they ſhall not ſuffer holſome doctrine, but
after their owne luſtes ſhall they,whoſe eares doo ytche,gett them an heape
of teachers,and ſhall withdrawe their eares frõ the trueth,and ſhal be turned
to fables:yt ys expediēt that we learn of the wiſe what elders we ſhal folowe.

2.Tim.4.

Ieſus Syrach teacheth vs to learn of ſoche elders, as had learned of their F
Fathers.*Ne te prætereat narratio ſeniorum,ipſi enim didicerũt à patribus ſuis , quoniã ab*
ipſis diſces intellectum,& in tēpore neceſſitatis dare reſponſum. Go not from the doctri
ne of the elders,for they haue learned yt of their fathers.For of them thowe
ſhalt learn vnderſtãding,ſo that thow maiſt make aũſwer in the time of nede

Ibid.8.

In this godlie counſel ye perceaue the cauſe geuen,why ye ſhoulde learn of
your elders,bicauſe(ſaieth he)they haue learned of their Fathers . As who
might ſaie,the learning that ys learned of the Fathers,ys no new inuēted do
ctrine,yt ys no ſtraunge doctrine vnknowē to the cõgregacion,of the which
S.Paule geueth yow admonitiõ,ſaieng.*Doctrinis varijs,et peregrinis nolite abduci.*
*Optimũ eſt enim gratia ſtabilire cor.*Be not caried awaie with diuerſe and ſtraũge
doctrines,for yt ys a good thing that the heart be eſtabliſhed with grace:But
yt ys a doctrine tried and continued frõ ſucceſsiõ to ſuceſsiõ,a doctrine that
ys permanent,through all ages.

Eldersthat
are to be
folowed.

Straũge do
ctrines are
not to be
folowed.

Therfor go not frõ that doctrine,neither choſe yow anie other elders to
learn of,but ſoche as haue learned of their fathers.Therfor choſe not ſoche
elders,as be inuētours of their owne doctrine, as the Lutherãs choſe Luther, G
who teaching that womē maie preache,teacheth an inuēted doctrine againſt
the ſcripture.For S.Paule ſaieth.*Mulieres in eccleſiis taceant, non enin permittitur eis*
*loqui,etc.*Let your women kepe ſcilence in the congregacion,for yt ys not per
mitted vnto them to ſpeake,but to be vnder obedience,as ſaieth the law.Yf
they will learn anie thing let thē aske their husbandes at home . For yt ys a
ſhame for women to ſpeake in the eongregacion.

Eldersthat
are not to
be folowed

1.Cor.14.

Luther taught that cõtritiõ maketh a man a more ſinner.And that the righ
teouſe man doth in euerie good worke,that he dothe,mortallie offende.Lu
ther alſo taught that euery chriſtian man ys a preiſt for the cõmon miniſtrie.
Theſe be ſtraunge doctrines,bothe to the ſcriptures, and to oure elders, and
therfore we maie not learn of him,for he hath not learned of the Fathers.

In aſſert.
art . 6.
Ibid.ar.31
Luthers
ſtraunge
doctrine.
In libell.de
Baptiſmo.

Zuinglius taught that original offēce ys no ſinne.Yet Dauid in the pſalme hũ
blie confeſſeth.*Ecce in iniquitatibus conceptus ſum,et in peccatis concepit me mater mea.*
Behold(ſaieth he)I was conceaued in iniquitie,and in ſinne hath my mother
conceaued me.And ſaincte Paule ſaieth:*Natura ſumus filij iræ.*of nature we be
the children of wrathe or damnacion.Zuinglius taught alſo,that the children H
of chriſten men nede not to be Baptiſed,but yf they die withoute Baptiſme,
they ſhall be ſaued : yet Chryſt ſaieth : *Niſi quis renatus fuerit ex aqua et ſpiritu*
ſancto , non poteſt introire in regnum Dei . Except a man be born again

Pſalm.50.
Zuinglius
ſtraunge
doctrine
In articulis
in fine.
Ioan. 3.

of the

A of the water, and the holie goste, he can not entre into the kingdõ of God.

Of this man therfore maie ye not learn, neither doo ye heare him, for whie he hath not learned of the fathers. Whiche thinge moſt arrooantlie, euen Luther(like as yt becometh a Lucyferan) folowing his maſter Lucifer prowdelie proteſteth not a fewe times, and ſaieth, that he will not be taught of men but of God.

Luthers luciferouſt priſde.

O deueliſh and wicked ſaing. This ys a ſecond Paule. The firſt Paule ſaieth ſpeaking of the goſpell. *Neque ab homine accepi illud, neque didici, ſed per reuelationem Ieſu Chriſti.* Nether haue I receaued yt of man, nether learned yt, but by the reuelation of Ieſus Chryſt. The ſecond Paule ſaieth that he will not learn of man, but of God. But as ther ys a firſt Adam, and a ſeconde, the one earthlie, the other heauenlie: And as in the firſt Adam all doo die, and in the ſecõde all be reuiued. So our firſt Paule ys heauenlie: this ſecond earthlie that firſt leadeth to ſaluation; This ſeconde to damnacion.

In lib. cõt. Canon.

1.Cor.15.

B Zuinglius wrote *de claritate verbi Dei*, of the clereneſſe of the woorde of God, an whol booke, to the entent to make you ſuppoſe hard thinges to be eaſie, and ſo to paſſe through thẽ not as the trueth woulde lead yowe, which ys hard to finde, but as yowre phantaſie ſhould moue you, which ys at hãde, and that he might with like facilitie bringe yowe to errour, ſciſme, and hereſie, and ſo conſequentlie to damnacion. Wherof he being ſoche a ſecõd Paule, ys the right miniſtre. Howe falſelie that booke ys compiled, this that ys here ſaied dothe manifeſtlie declare, and inuincible proue.

Zuinglius wrote a boo ke of the clereneſſe of ſcripture

What ſhoulde I troble thee, Reader, with reherſall of the falſe doctrine of *Oecolãpadius* of *Bullingerus*, of *Caluinus*, of *Bucer.* ãd of ſoche like? Who although they diſſent emong themſelues in manie thinges: yet in manie they agree, ãd ſpecialle in this, that they be all mortall enemies to the catholique Churche.

Heretiques diſſẽt emõg themſelues but conſpire al againſt the Church

Of theiſe fathers hath this our Aduerſarie learned his doctrine, of the which he ys a ſtowte mainteiner as ye haue partlie heard. But maye we hope to drinke ſwete water, oute of a ſtinking puddle? Maie we gather (as our Sauiour Chryſt ſaieth) grapes of thornes, or figges of thiſtles? Maie we hope to learn the wholſom trueth of him, who hath ſucked the lothſom poyſon of C Hereſie, of Luther and Zuinglius, of whoſe deteſtable doctrines ye haue heard, of many their wicked aſſertions, a fewe reherſed, that by thẽ ye maie iudge of the reſt.

Heretiques what Fathers they folowe. Math.7.

He that foloweth ſoche doctors and buildeth vpõ ſoche ſandes, forſaketh the ſtrong rocke: he alſo leaueth the fountain of the water of life, and pudd-leth in the fowle puddles which they haue digged, whiche can not holde water. Wherfor as they be not to be folowed, no more ys this Aduerſarie, being certen, that none of thẽ all haue taught the doctrine that they learned of holie catholike Fathers, but of ſoche fathers as be of the nõbre of the elders, ãd teachers that faincte Peter ſpake of, whiche ſhoulde come emong vs. *Fuerunt in populo Pſeudoprophetæ ſicut & in vobis erunt magiſtri mendaces, qui introducent ſectas perditionis, etc.* Ther were falſe Prophetes in the people, as emõg yow ther ſhal be falſe teachers or lieng maſters, which ſhall bring in damnable ſectes euen denieng the Lorde, that hath bought thẽ, ãd ſhal bring vpõ thẽ ſelfs ſwifte dã nation. Wherfor coũt thẽ not as elders mete to learn of, leeſt ye be of the nõ bre of thẽ, that faincte Peter immediatlie ſpeaketh of: And manie (ſaieth he) D ſhal folow their dãnable waies, bi whõ the waie of truth ſhal be blaſphemed

Heretiques whie they are not to be folow.

2.Pet.2.

Of theiſe folowers ther be ſome, that folowing the arrogancie of their ma ſters, wil aſſeble cõpanies in corners, ãd being rude ãd illiterate, not brought vppe in the ſtudie of ſciẽce, but onelie in trade of worldlie craftes wil take vpon thẽ to teache before they learn as S. Hierõ ſaieth.　　　E ij　　And

Corner teachers.

And this emong other ys lamentable, that mē will sett so litle by the faith E of their Lord God: so litle by the doctrine of Gods Churche: so litle finallie by their owne sowles, that they will hassard all these vpon the credite of soche an ignorāte vppestarte, who neuer learned of his Fathers, neither knewe what the Fathers had taught.

But be not so light (o Brethren) be not so light, haue a more staie in you, be not so easilie caried awaie frō your Lord God, to your destruction. Yf ye haue cōmitted your selfs to soche light masters, open nowe your eyes, ād be holde howe ye haue ben deceaued. And to exhorte you with sainde Paules woordes, frō hencefurth be no more babes, wauering, and caried aboute with euerie winde of doctrine, by the wilinesse of mē, through craftinesse, wherwith they laie in wait for yowe, to deceaue yowe. But folow the trueth in charitie, and in all thinges growe in him which ys the head, euen Chryste.

Ephes.4.

And this shall yowe the better do yf ye wil well regard the counsel of Salomon, who saieth thus to euerie one of yowe: *Audi fili mi disciplinam patris tui, et ne dimittas legem matris tuæ.* My Sonne heare thy fathers doctrine, and forsa- F ke not the lawe of thy Mother. Vpon the which text sainct Hierom saieth thus: *Notandum, quod ita nos disciplinam patris audire præcipit, vt legem quoque matris nullo modo dimittamus, quia non sufficit vt quis se Deum diligere, & eius præceptis obtemperare dicat, si vnitatem Ecclesiæ fraterna charitate nō sequatur.* Yt ys to be noted, that he commaundeth vs so to heare the doctrine of the father, that we also by no means forsake the lawe of the Mother. For yt sufficeth not that anie mā shall saie that he loueth God, and obeyeth his commaundementes, yf with brotherlie charitie he folowe not the vnitie of the Churche.

Teachers meet to be beleued. Prou.1.

Hier.ibid.

Note well, Reader, this note of sainde Hierom, and by this learne to knowe bothe when your teacher ys good, and when his learninge ys good, yf your teacher remain in the vnitie of the Churche, and his learning swarue not from the same, nor teache dissention from that, that in yt ys taught, then ys your teacher, and his learninge soche, as ye maie withoute daūger accept. Yf otherwise, flee yt, as from a serpent.

Howe to know good teachers.

And yf ye wolde learn or being learned wolde be resolued in doubtes (as ys before said) seke not onelie soche as be onelie learned, but seke soche G as being best learned, haue learned of their Fathers, and abiding in the same do so embrace the doctrine of their Fathers, that they in no poincte forsake the lawe of their mother the Churche, as by this Aduersary ye are taught to doo. For yf all christēdom maie be called the Churche, thē teacheth he yow to forsake the lawe of your mother the Church. For wher ys this doctrine of his professed through oute the Churche, and not raither the contrarie? Befo re these fewe yeares, where was yt taught in all the Christian worlde, that Chrystes bodie ys not in the Sacrament? that yt ys not to be offred for the quick and the dead? that yt ought not to be reserued for the commoditie of the sick? that yt aught not to be honoured? that soules departed are not to be praied for? that we maie not make requestes to Sainctes to praie for vs? ād manie soche other.

Straunge doctrines

Seing thē he forsaketh the lawe of his mother, though he pretende to haue learned of the Fathers: yet ys he not to be folowed, bicause he hath not bo- the theise two, that ys, bothe the learning of his father, and also the lawe of his mother. For they onelie are to be folowed, that haue both theise. Thus H shall ye finde the holie Fathers to haue doen, as first for exāple sainde Hierō, a mā not of the cōmon sorte of learned mē, but an excellēt, and singular mā, who neither hauinge affiance in his owne iudgement, notwithstanding his

Teachers not meet to be beleued.

great

A great learning neither seking obscure teachers, but most famouse, reporteth this of himself: *Non ab adolescētia aut legere vnquam, aut doctos viros ea, quæ nesciebā, interrogare cessaui, & meipsum tātùm(vt pleriq;)habui magistrū. Deniq; nuper ob hāc vel maximè causam, Alexādriā perrexi, vt viderē Didymū, & ab eo in scripturis omnibus, quæ habebā dubia, sciscitarer.* I haue not frō my youth ceassed at any time, either to read, or ells to aske of learned men, soche thinges as I knewe not. Nether haue I had or vsed my self(as manie do)as master to my self. But of late euē speciallie for this cause I wēt to Alexādria, that I might se *Didymus,* ād that I might aske of him, soche doubtes as I had in all the scriptures. Thus sainct Hierom.

Hieron. in Prohemio Epist. ad Eph. ad Paul. & Eusto. Saincte Hierom howe he learned the scriptures.

　In the which reporte ye do heare(howe cleresoeuer *Luther* and *Zuinglius* make the scriptures)that saincte Hierō fownde doubtes therin, and for dissolution of thē trauailed to Alexandria to *Didymus.* In which facte also yt maie be learned that yf sainct Hierō so notable a mā, sought a famouse mā to learn him, yt maie well beseme other so to doo. Did not *Damasus* being Bishoppe of Rome send to saincte Hierō to be aunswered in certain doubtes, and dis-

B deined not to learn of him? Did not sainct Augustin go to Millen to saincte Ambrose to heare him, and to learn of him? Howe many that were learned worte to sainct Augustin to be taught of him in diuerse matters of scripture? Yt wolde well fill an whollvolume to nōbre vppe those that haue trauailed cōtries, to heare and learn of good holie learned men, and that haue written to other for the like. And therfore to conclude this matter, I will no more but bringe in the saieng of sainct Clement the holie Martyr, and disciple of saincte Peter the Apostle, and then enter into the matter, which principallie I haue in pourpose to treacte of.

Damasus learned of S. Hierom. S. Augustin of S. Amb. Many learned of S. Aug.

　Saincte Clement in his fiste epistle writeth thus: *Relatū est nobis, quòd quidā in vestris partibus cōmorantes, aduersantur sanis doctrinis, & prout eis videtur, & non secū diū traditiones patrū, sed secundū suū sensum docere videntur. Multas enim quidā (vt audiuimus) vestrarū partium, secundum ingeniū hominū, ex ijs quæ legunt verisimilitudines capiunt. Et ideò diligenter obseruandū est, vt lex Dei cum legitur, non secundum propriā intelligentiā legatur, vel doceatur. Sunt enim multa verba in diuinis scripturis, quæ possunt trahi ad eum sensum, quem sibi vnusquisque spontè præsumpsit. Sed fieri non oportet. Non enim*

C *sensū, quē extrinsecus adulteretis, alienū & extraneū debetis quærere, aut quoquo modo ipsū ex scripturarū autoritate confirmare, sed ex ipsis scripturis sensum capere veritatis. Et ideò oportet ab eo intelligentiā discere scripturarum, qui à maioribus secundum veritatem sibi traditam seruauit, vt & ipse possit ea, quæ rectè suscepit, competenter asserere.*

Clemens epist. 5.

　Yt ys reported vnto vs, that some duelling in your partes, are aduersaires to wholsom doctrines, and are perceaued to teache euē as yt liketh thēselues, ād not according to the traditiōs of the Fathers, but according to their own vnderstanding. Some of your countries(as we haue heard)take many likelihoodes of those thinges, that they do read, according to the witte of men. And therfore yt ys diligentlie to be looked vnto, that the lawe of God whē yt ys red, be not red or taught according to mens owne vnderstanding. For ther be manie woordes in the scriptures of God, which maie be drawen to that vnderstāding, that euery mā at his own pleasure hath chosen. But it maie not so be doen. For ye ought not to seke an vnderstanding diuerse and straunge, which ye maie adulterate, or by any maner of means by autoritie of the scrip-

Scripture maie be drawen to diuerse sensés.

D turs in the outwarde face to confirme, but of the scriptures themselues to take the true vnderstanding. And therfore ye must learn the vnderstanding of the scriptures of him, who kepeth yt according to the trueth deliuerid vnto him frō his elders, that he maie also agreablie teache, that he hath well receaued. Thus farre Sainct Clement.

To take and embrace this ordre,I meen,to miftruft oure owne iudgemétes, E
ãd therfore to heare our Fathers,ãd vpõ their iudgemétes,not vpõ our own
phãtafies,to ftaie our felues in the true vnderftãding of the fcriptures,I haue
yf my iudgement faill me not geuen thee(gentle Reader)god occafion.For
firft to remoue and difproue the falfe faing of Luther and Zuinglius,who ha
ue taught that the fcriptures be eafie and plain to be vnderftanded(wherun
to this proclamer willing the fcriptures to be common,femeth to agree,and
confent,I haue proued by diuerfe and fondrie places,yea and by whol bookes of the olde Teftament,that thefame ys verie harde,and full of difficulties
not able to be diffolued,but by a mã wel exercifed in the reading and know
ledge of the fame.And the like haue I doen of the gofpells.

As for the epiftles of fainéte Paule,yt ys proued by the inuincible teftimonie of fainét Peter,that they be harde,ãd be depraued of manie to their own
damnaciõ.And that this might fullie appeare to thee I haue at large opened
and proued thefame,not onelie by the faing and iudgementes of the beft ãd
moft auncient fathers of Chryftes Churche,as cf fanéte Clement , Hierom, F
Chryfoftome and other:but alfo by their maner of atteigning to the vnderftanding of the fcriptures for that they be hard. Whiche their maner I haue
alfo declared by their owne teftimonie.

The difficultie of the fcriptures thus proued,cõtrarie to the fainges of Lu
ther and Zuinlius, I haue proceaded to declare by the fcriptures firft,and after by the famoufe learned Fathers,howe we fhall come to the vnderftãding
therof.Wher yt ys made manifeft that we muft atteign therunto by the teaching of the preiftes,which God hath appointed to be paftours ãd teachers,
and Fathers of the people,to feede thé,to teache thé,and to bring thé vppe
in God.And yet maie we not learn of euery one that taketh vpon him the
name of a paftour,teacher or Father,but of foche as teache the lawe of our
heauélie Father,and ther withall forgetteth not the lawe of our mother the
holie churche.Theife two propreties he muft haue iointlie,for the one withoute the other fufficeth not in a teacher,as by fainét Hierom yt ys declared.
Who alfo(as fainéte Clement teacheth)muft be foche one as teacheth the
vnderftanding of the fcriptures according to the trueth that he hath recea- G
ued and learned of his elders.

According to which counfell I minding to fearche the vnderftanding of
certain fcriptures which be in controuerfie,I will repair to them that be the
elders of Chriftes Churche , whiche I terme his Parliament houfe , and to
learn of them the true vnderftanding of thofe fcriptures. I wifh therfore the
reader,to fubmitte his iudgement vnto them, as I will doo,and all affeétion
fett aparte,to learn of them,we ought to learn of,who,I doubte not, will fo
well and clerely open to vs the trueth of that matter , that we feke , that except we will not fee,we fhall perceaue yt.

The holie fpirit of God geue vs the gifte of vnderftanding,and an humble
and docible heart to receaue and embrace his trueth.

THE NINGHT CHAPITER DECLARING

that oure redemption was prenunciated by promiffes,figures, and prophecies,
and what the promiffes be,and to whome they were made.

Lmightie God beholding the miferable ruine of man,and mer- H
cifullie entending the repaire of the fame,by his prouident wifdome,*quæ difponit omnia fuauiter*, which difpofeth all things louinglie,according to his foreknowledge,whiche was from euer,
declared vnto man the mean , howe by whom, and when hys
laps

Teachers
meet to be
folowed.

Sap.8.

A　laps or fall fhoulde be reftored, affuring hym of hys redemption, euen
by the woorde of hys owne mouthe, that wher man through hys
fall had experience of the fore burden of Gods iuftice , he might alfo haue
a tafte and hope of his mercie, and beholdinge the goodlie contéperament
of bothe in God, might frame alfo in him felf a right temperature of feare
and loue,fearing for iuftice,and louing for mercie,and therby in good ordre
of fpirituall melodie,yoifullie finge with the Prophete Dauid: *Mifericordiam
et iudiciū cantabo tibi Domine.*Mercie and iudgement will I fing to thee,o Lord. *Pfal. 102.*
For *Mifericors Dominus et iuftus.*Oure Lord ys mercifull and righteoufe.

Thus I faie Man hauing in practife that God ys a God of iuftice, left he *Affurāce*
fhoulde be ouerwhelmed and depreffed with defperacion for lacke of mer- *of mercie*
cie, Before the ful fentence of Gods iuftice was pronōūced, affurāce of mer *promifed*
cie was made,that mā being nowe preffed with the one, fhould be releiued *to man be-*
with the other. *Inimicitias ponam inter te,et inter mulierem, et femē tuū & femē illius: fore full*
ipfa conteret caput tuum. I will put enemitie (faid allmightie God to the Serpēt) *fentence of*
B　betwen thee, and the woman, betwen thie feed and her feed,the fame fhal *iuftice was*
tread downe thine head. By the whiche woordes affuredlie our firft Paren- *pronoun-*
tes conceaued a firme hope of a Meffias, of a Redemer, and of a Sauiour to *ced.*
come of the feed of a woman, that as the Enemie the Deuell had craftelie *Gen.3.*
fupplāted,and therbie ouerthrowē mā:So he by noble victorie wrought on
the croffe,and accepted and approued by the iuftice of God,fhoulde debel
the enemie the deuell and take the fpoill from him, whiche was mankinde.

And as our righteoufe, and neuer the leffe our mercifull Lord God had
fignified this gladde tidinges of Redémption to oure firft Parentes,that they
might vnderftand the mercie of God, and therby conceaue and haue hope
and comforth : Euen fo likewife did he to our Fathers the holie Patriarkes,
and other our elders notifie the fame by diuerfe means, as by promiffes,
figures, and prophecies. Of the whiche three I fhall by Gods helpe feuerallie fpeake. And firft as the order leadeth, I will treacte of promiffes.

To our Father Abraham God declared the gladde tidinges of our Re-
demption by promiffe, faing thus: *In femine tuo benedicentur omnes nationes terræ. Gen.22.*
C　In thy feede fhall all the nacions of the earth be bleffed.Who was this feede,
by whom al nacions fhoulde be bleffed, and howe they fhoulde atteign *Promiffe*
vnto yt,faincte Paule to the Galathians by the teaching of the holie Gofte, *made to*
declareth faiēg: To Abrahā and his feed were the promiffes made.He faieth *Abrahā.*
not, in thie feedes,as to manie : but yn thy feed as of one which ys Chrifte.

As faincte Paule here by the inftruction of the holie Gofte, expowndeth
this promiffe to be made of Chrifte : So doubte ye not but the fame holie *Galat.3.*
Spiritie, had breathed the like breath into the holie Patriarke Abrahā,wher-
bie he vnderftood, that Chrift after the flefh fhoulde defcend from him,and
that this bleffing fhoulde by him happen to all nacions. For all nacions fhall
atteign to this bleffing , that beleue with faithful Abraham (as faincte Paule
declareth in the fame chapiter : The fcripture (faieth he) feing before hand
that God wolde iuftifie the heathen through faithe, fhewed before hande *Ibid.3.*
glad tidinges to Ahraham, faing : In thee fhall all nacions be bleffed. So
then they whiche be of faith are bleffed with faithfull Abraham.

D　In the whiche declaracion we maie learn, that the promeffe was made to
Abraham : the fullfillinge of the faid promiffe fhoulde be doen by Chrifte,
who ys that one feed : the receauers of this promiffe are the faithfull,

To kinge Dauid alfo he opened the fame by promiffe faienge : *De fructu*
ventris tui ponam fuper fedem tuam. Of the fruicte of thy bodie, fhall I feete vppe

vpon thy feat. whiche woordes of the pfalme, are a reherfall of the promiffe E
made to king Dauid in the fecond booke of the kinges, wher yt ys writren
thus : I will fett vppe thy feed, whiche fhall proceade of thy bodie, and will
ftablifh his kingdom, he fhall builde an houfe for my name, and I will ftablifh the feat of his kingdom for euer.

2 Reg.7.

Whiche promiffe although the Ieues wolde haue to be vnderftanded and
perfourmed in Salamon : yet yt can not fo be, for that thefe woordes *I will
ftablifh the feat of his kingdom for euer* can not be veryfied in Salomon, whofe
worldlie kingdom ys finifhed, and vtterly extingnisfhed, and was fo before
the coming of Chrifte, according to the prophecie of the holy Patriarke Iacob, who prophecied thus : *Non auferetur fceptrum de Iuda, & dux de femore eius,
donec veniat qui mittendus eft : & ipfe erit expectatio gentium .* The fcepter fhall
not be taken from Iuda, and the lawegeuer from betwixt his feet, vntill he
comme that fhall be fent, and he yt fhal be, whom the gentiles fhall looke
for.

Gen.49.

By whiche prophecie yt ys manifeft, that at the coming of Chrifte, the F
kingdom of the Iewes fhoulde ceaffe, wherby yt ys confequent, that the
promiffe of God made to Dauid, tendeth not to Salomõ and his Succeffiõ,
whofe kingdom muft haue an ende, as the prophecie of Iacob fignified :
But yt refpecteth Chrifte, who lineallie defcended from Dauid. *Qui factus eft
ei ex femine Dauid fecundum carnem,* whiche was borne to him of the feed of Dauid after the flefh as fainct Paule faieth, whofe kingdom ys euerlafting accordinge to the prophecie: *Super folium Dauid, et fuper regnum eius fedebit , vt
confirmet et corroboret illud in iudicio et iuftitia, amodò et vfque in fempiternũ.* He fhall
fitte vpon the feat of Dauid, and in his kingdome to fett vppe the fame,
and to eftablifh yt with equitie and righteonfueffe from hence furth for
euermore.

*Chrift ys
the feed
Promifed
to Dauid
and not
Salomon.*
Rom.1.

Efay .9.

That this ys to be vnderftanded onely of Chrifte, the reft of the fentence
goinge immediatelie before dothe make yt fo plain, that all men of iudgement muft nedes confeffe, that yt can not admitte any other vnderftanding.
For thus the prophete ordereth the woll fentéce: Vnto vs a childe ys born,
and vnto vs a Sonne ys geuen, vpon his fhoulder dothe the kingdom lie, and G
he ys called by his owne name, wounderfull, the geuer of counfell, the
mightie God, the euerlafting father, the prince of peace, he fhall make none ende to encreafe the kingdom, and peace. And fhall fitte vpon the feat
of Dauid, and in his kingdõ, to fette vppe the fame, and to ftablifh yt with
equitie and righteoufneffe from hencefurth for euer more.

Who ys he that ys a childe born to vs, that ys or maye be called the migh
tie God, and the euerlafting Father, but our Meffias, our Sauiour Chrifte,
God and man? who ys the Sonne geuen to vs, that fhall fitte vpon the feat
of Dauid, for euer more, making no ende to encreafe his kingdom, and
ftablifhe yt with equitie and righteoufneffe for euer more, but IefusChrifte,
oure verie Meffias, the verie naturall Sonne of our heauenlie Father, which
ys geuen to vs to be our Redemption, iuftificacion, and fanctification?
Who geuing his commiffion to the Apoftles, to preache his Gofpell appointed them no termes, limittes or bowndes, neither did he make anie
difference of creatures or people, but *Ite, (faied he) in vniuerfum mundum, et
prædicate Euangelium omni creaturæ* Go ye through oute all the worlde, and H
preache the Gofpell to all creatures. whiche thing they fo doinge, *In omnem
terram exiuit fonus eorum, et in fines orbis terræ verba eorum.* Their found ys gon
into all londes, and their woordes into the endes of the worlde.

1.Cor.1.

Mar. vlt.

Pfal.18.

His

A His kingdom ys wounderfullie encreaced, so that the prophecie of Malachie ys fullfilled: *Ab ortu solis vsque ad occasum magnum est nomen meum in gentibus, et in omni loco sacrificatur, et offertur nomini meo oblatio munda.* From the rising of the Sunne vnto the goinge downe of the same my name ys great emōge the gentiles, yea in euerie place ys ther sacrifice doen, and a clean meat offing offerd vppe vnto my name.

Malac. 1

Yt ys to be noted that the Prophete saieth: To the name of God in euery place shall sacrifice be doen, whiche maner of doing of sacrifice, being mēt of the Sacrifice of Christes Church so to be doē eueriewher, well declareth the great encreace of Christes kingdom. Whiche must nedes so be, For *Dominabitur à mari vsque ad mare, et à flumine vsque ad terminos orbis terrarum.* His dominion shall be from the one sea to the other, and from the flood vnto the woorldes ende. They that dwell in the wildernes shall knele before him, his enemies shall licke the dust. The kinges of Tharses, and of the Iles shall geue presenttes, and the kinges of Arabie and Saba shall bring giftes. All kinges

Psal. 71.

B shall fall downe before him, all nacions shall do him seruice.

Here *Iacobus de valentia* expounding the dominion of Christe, whiche shal be from one sea to an other, saieth that yt ys from the Sea Mediterranian vnto bothe he Ocean Seas, and vnto the Southe, and so yt comprehendeth all Affrike, and vnto the north Sea, and so yt comprehendeth all Europe: And he shall haue dominion from the flood *Nilus* and *Tanays*, vnto the endes of the worlde that be toward the Easte, whiche comprehendeth all Asia, and so his dominion ys ouer all the worlde. For being ouer these three partes, all whiche three receaued Christes faith, and submitted them selues to his holie religion, in to the whiche three partes the wholl worlde ys diuided, yt maie well be saied, that hys dominion, ys ouer all the worlde.

Iacobus de Valentia.

Christe then alone and no pure earthlie kinge ys he, that ys promised to Dauid, to sitt vpon his seat for euer, and to dilate his kingdom, so that ther shall be none ende of the encreace of yt

Chryst, not Salomon promised to Dauid. Act. 13.

That in this promisse made vnto Dauid was ment Christe, sainte Paule,
C also in the Actes of the Apostles declareth. *Inueni Dauid filium Iesse virum secundùm cor meum, qui faciet omnes voluntates meas. Huius ex semine Deus secundùm promissionem eduxit Israëli saluatorem Iesum.* I haue fownde (saith allmightie God) Dauid the Sonne of Iesse, a man after my owne heart, which shall fullfill all my will. Of this mans seed (saieth sainte Paule) hath God, according as he had promised brought furth to Israël a Sauiour Iesus. By which woordes sainte Paule teacheth plainlie that Iesus our Sauioure, was promised to comne of Dauid.

And for that the promisse was made both to Abraham and to Dauid (as yt ys declared) that Messias shoulde descend from them both: Therfore the Euangelist sainte Matthew describing the Genealogie of oure Sauiour Christe after the flesh, beginneth the same at Abraham and Dauid, calling Christ the Sonne of Dauid and Abraham, saing: *Liber generationis Iesu Christi, filij Dauid, filij Abraham.* The booke of the generacion of Iesus Christ the Sōne of Dauid, the Sonne of Abraham.

And to conclude, two prophetes of the newe Testament, namelie the
D most excellent Prophetisse the virgen Marie, the muther of that promised seed Christe, and Zacharias the Father of Iohn the Baptist, do testifie this also. She saieth: *Suscepit Israël puerum suum, etc.* He hath holpen his seruannt Israël in remembrance of his mercie, enen as he promised to owre Farhers,

Luc. 1.

Abraham

Abraham and his feed for euer. The other faieth : *Et erexit cornu falutis nobis,* E
in domo Dauid &c. And he hath raifed vppe an horn of faluacion to vs in the
houfe of his feruannt Dauid, Euen as he promifed by the mouthe of his holie Prophetes, whiche were fence the worlde began.

In the whiche prophecies we maie perceaue, that the holie Gofte did
ftrike an vniforme fownde in thefe two inftrumentes fownding that the
promiffes made to Abraham and Dauid, and fpoken by the Prophetes fence the worlde began, were nowe fullfilled in that, that Chrift the Sauioure
of the worlde was conceaued and incarnate in the wombe of the immaculate virgen Mary, by whom the blefsing promiffed, fhoulde come to all the
nacions of the earth, as nowe we haue feen profourmed.

THE TENTH CHAPITER TOVCHETH THE FI-
gures of Chriftes Incarnation, pafsion, Refurrection, and Afcenfion.

S vnto thefe two noble Fathers before fpoken of, God by ma- F
nifeft promiffe opened the ioyfull coming of our Sauioure
into fhefh: So to other did he defcribe, and painte by figures,
all the mifterie of our Redemption to be wrought, doen, and
perfected, by the fame oure Sauiour. wherby their faith in
Chrifte to come was moche nourifhed, and they by hope of redemption in
Gods mercy moche comforted.

Iudic.13.   Vnto the wife of Manoah, the Angell of God appeared and faied. *Ecce*
Figures of *fterilis es, concipies, & paries filum.* Beholde as yet thow arte barren, or haft
Chryfts in had no childe before. Thowe fhalt conceaue, and bring furth a Sonne. This
carnation. was a figure of the Salutacõ of the Angell to the virgẽ the mother of Chrifte
Ecce(faied the Angell to the virgen) *concipies & paries filum* . Beholde thowe
fhalt conceaue and bring furth a Sonne.

Obferue and note the conformitie, and likeneffe of both meffagcs. Wherin
note by whom the meffages were doen, to whom they were doen, and
what maner of perfons they were doen, vnto by vhom the thing promifed
fhoulde be perfourmed, of what force value and wourthineffe the thinges G
promifed be, And then fhall ye perceaue, howe liuelie the figure (for that
part that yt ys a figure) painteth and fetteth furthe the thing that ys
Figures be figured.
not in eue-   Note alfo that I faie, that a figure for that parte that yt ys a figure, dothe
rie point paint and fett furth the thing figurated, For enery ftorie conteining a figure,
cõparable ys not a figure for the wholl ftorie, neither the perfons of the figure, are in
to the thin al poinctes to be likened, compared , or affembled to the thinge figurated.
ges figura- As for example.
ted.
Gen.38.   Iofeph being folde of his bretheren for money, was a figure of Chrifte
Iofeph and folde by Iudas to the Iewes for moneie. In the whiche figure application
Chryft cõ- maye not fo be made, that the perfon, who ys the figure, fhall expreffe or
pared toge- aunfwere the thing figured in all pointes and euery condicion : or that the
ther. perfon, who ys the figure, fhal counteruaill the wourthineffe of the perfon
figured. For Iofeph the perfon in this figure was a pure man: Chrifte the
perfon figured God and man. Iofeph fubiecte vnto finne : Chrift free from
finne. Iofeph folde not to die, but to be faued from death : Chrifte folde H
not to be faued from death, but to die. wherfore Iofeph in thefe partes and
cõfideracõs, ys not a figure of Chrift, but in this parte, that as Iofeph being
innocent, his bretheren confpired againft him : So Chrift being innocent,
Iudas

A Iudas with the pharifeies confpired againft him. Iofeph was folde of his bretheren : Chrifte of Iudas his elect Apoftle , and brother. Iofeph was called the Sauiour of the worlde : Chrifte was called, and ys the Sauioure of the worlde. *Vocabis nomen eius Iefum : ipfe enim faluum faciet populum fuum à peccatis eorum,* Thowe fhalt call his name Iefus, faieth the Angell. For he fhall faue his people from their finnes. In thefe poinctes Iofeph ys a figure of Chrifte.

Math . 1.

So the Mother of Sampfon, and Sampfon himfelf being the perfons of the figure, maie not aunfwere the perfons figured in all partes. For the mother of Sampfon conceaued by man : The mother of Chrifte withoute man. Sampfon a finfull man : Chrifte void of finne. Therfor let vs confider the figure in that parte that yt ys a figure. and firft by whome the meffage of the conception of thofe childeren was doen.

The conception of Sampfon was declared by an Angell : The conceptiõ of Chrifte likwife by an Angell. The Angell faied to the mother of Sam- B pfom : *Ecce concipies & paries filum.* Beholde thow fhalt conceaue, and bring furthe a Sonne : The Angell to the virgen faied, *Ecce concipies & paries filum.* Behoholde thow fhalt conceaue, and bring furth a Sonne . The Mother of Sampfon was alone when the Angell appeared to her : The mother of Chrifte was alone, when the Angell faluted her.

Sampfons conception and Chryftes compared to gether.

Secondlie, confider what maner of perfons they were, to whome thefe meffages were fent. Yt ys to be fuppofed that the mother of Sampfon was in Gods fauour, to whome he did vouchefaif to fende his Angell with a meffage inoche defiered : Yt ys to be beleued that the mother of Chrifte was certenlie in Gods fauoure, who fanctified her in her mothers wombe, and appoincted her to be the mother of his owne Sonne, and certifiied her ther of by the Angell . The mother of Sampfon had neuer childe before : The mother of Chrifte had neuer childe before.

Mother of Sampfon compared with the mother of Chryft. Bernardus epift. 174.

Nowe thirdlie. Let vs cõfider by whom the thinges promifed, that ys the conception of theife children fhoulde be perfourmed. The mother of Sãpfon being barren, wher the ordre of nature coulde not caufe her to concea- C ue, conceaued by Gods difpofition helping nature : The mother of Chrifte beinge a virgen, and not knowing man, coulde not by the courfe of nature conceaue, but conceaued by the power of God, and operacon of the holie Gofte. *Spiritus fanctus fuperueniet in te, & virtus altifsimi obumbrabit tibi.* The holie Gofte fhall come vpon thee, and the power of the higheft fhall ouerfhadow thee.

Luc .1.

Fourthlie and laft, let vs fearche of what wourthineffe thefe childeren promifed were. Sampfon was an a Nazarite vnto God from his youthe : Chrift moft acceptable to God from his youthe. Sampfon began to deliuer the children of Ifrael oute of the handes of the Philiftines tirannouflie reigning ouer them : Chrift began to deliuer the people oute of the handes of the Deuell tirannouftie reigninge ouer them. Thus beholding and weighing, howe goodlie the ordre of the conception of Chrift aunfwereth the ordre and maner of the conception of Sampfon, we maie well perceaue the one did prefigurate the other.

Sãpfon and Chryft cõpared. together.

D As the conception of our Sauioure Chrifte was thus prefigurated : So was his paffiõ and deathe alfo. Abraham hauing bi t his onelie begottẽ Sonne and beft beloued Ifaac, yet at the commaundement of God, willing to flaye him, and offer him, he was a figure of the mercifull will of God the Father, who hauing but his onelie begotten, and beloued Sonne Iefus Chrifte

Gen.22.

Chrifte, was willing that he fhoulde fuffer death and be offred for vs.

Ifaac a figu
re of Chrift
Philip. 2. Ifaac bearing the woodde to the place of Sacrifice, and obedient to his fathers will, therto be flain and offred, was a figure of Chrifte bearing the woodde of his croffe to the place wher he fhoulde fuffer, and being obedient to his Fathers will did fuffer death, euen the deathe vpon the croffe.

Nū. 21. ca.
Joan. 3. In whiche facte he did not onelie fulfill the Scriptures, but alfo aunfwereth the figures, whiche prefigurated that this his death fhoulde be the faluaciō of them, that fhoulde beleue in him. Whiche figure ys the fetting vppe of the Brafen Serpent mencioned in the booke of Nombres. Of the whiche figure he himfelf maketh mencion in the Gofpell, applieng yt to him felf, faing : *Sicut Moifes exaltauit ferpentem in deferto, ita exaltari oportet filium hominis, vt omnis qui credit in ipfum, non pereat, fed habeat vitam æternam* , As Moyfes lifted vppe the ferpent in the wildernefe : Euen fo muft the Sonne of man be lifted vppe, that who foeuer béleueth in him maie not perifh but haue eternall life.

As God opened the mifterie of our redemption by thefe and foche other F like figures to the Fathers in their owē perfons: So did he the like by fundrie and manifolde figures in ceremonies and facrifices of the lawe of Moifes. What was the wholl preifthood of Aron, with all the facrifices therto apperteining, but a prefiguracion of the facrifice doen by our Sauiour Chrifte vpon the Altar of the croffe? Wherof fainct Paule being not ignorant, doth at large treacte in his epiftle to the Hebrues, not onelie conferring and comparing the thing figurated to the figure : but alfo therby prouing the excellencie, wourthineffe, value and force of Chriftes facrifice, confirmeth and eftablifheth the placing and continuance of the newe Teftament fo fet fur the by the fame newe facrifice to endure for euer . In the ninght chapiter he teacheth that the olde lawe had ordinaunces, and feruinges of God Hebr. 9. and defcribeth the ordre of the tabernacle, and the ordre alfo of thinges therin conteined in a brief maner, of whiche he faieth, he can not fpeake particularlie.

And after that he had in a like compendioufe forte, touched the maner of facrifices doen as well in the firft Tabernacle, as in the fecond, into the G whiche the high preift alone entred once euery yeare, and that not with oute blood whiche thinges were figures of better thinges to come, as ther he faieth, that the holie Gofte by thefe thinges fignified, that the waie of holie thinges was not yet opened, he defcendeth to the thinges fignified and figurated.

But Chrift (faieth he) being an high preift of good things to come, came by a greater, and a more perfect tabernacle, not made with handes, that ys to faie, not of this buildinge, neither by the bloode of goates, and calues, but by his owne blood he entred once into the holie place, and fownde eternall redemption. In the which faieng yt ys woorthie to be noted, howe wounderfullie well he adapted the thinges figurated to the figures, and therwith declareth the excellencie of them, aboue theife.

In whiche applicacion this we maie learn, that the high preift of the lawe figured Chrifte our high preift. The tabernacle by which he entred into Chryfoft. in
9. ad Heb. the holie place, figured the tabernacle of Chriftes bodie, by whiche he entred into the holie place. The blood wherwith the preift entred, figured the H blood of Chrifte. The entring and facrificing of the high preift once in the yeare, figured the facrificing of Chrift, and his entringe into the holy place of heauen once for all. The cleinfing and purifieng of the people by vertue

of

A   of the facrifice of the high preiſt whiche (as ſaincte Paule ſaieth) purified
the vnclean as touching the purifieng of the fleſh, figured the clenſing and
purifieng of the conſciences of the beleuers, from dead workes, and all filthineſſe of finne For *Lauit nos à peccatis noſtris in ſanguine ſuo.* he hath waſhed vs
from our ſinnes in his bloode (ſaieth ſaincte Ihon)   *Apoca.1.*

As the death and blood ſhedding of kiddes and calues, and ſoche other, ād
the ſacrifices doen by thē, did figure the paſſiō, and bloodſhedding of Chriſt
ād the holie ſacrifice offred by him (for he was *ſacerdos & victima,* both preiſt
and ſacrifice) by the whiche the beleuing people in Chryſt to come, were inſtructed, that the Sauiour of the woorlde ſhoulde die for the finnes of the ſa
me: So by figures alſo were they taught, that he ſhould riſe again the third
daie: As by that figure which Chryſt applieth to him ſelf for that pourpoſe
in the Goſpell: *Sicut enim Ionas fuit in ventre ceti tribus diebus,& tribus noctibus: ſic e-*
rit filius hominis in corde terr.e,&c. As Ionas (ſaieth he) was three daies and three   *Matth.12*
nightes in the whalls bellie: So ſhal the Sonne of man be thre daies, ād three
B   nightes in the heart of the earth.

Which figure liuelie declareth not onelie that Chryſt ſhoulde be three
nightes in the earth, as Ionas was in the belly of the whall: But that as Ionas
the third daie cā oute of the whalls bellie aliue : So Chriſt the third daie
ſhoulde riſe oute of the earth aliue. Whiche thing to be verified, and ſo
doen in Chryſt all the Euangeliſtes do teſtifie.

As his buryall, and abode in the graue, and his reſurrection was figured
by Ionas: So was his Aſcenſion by the takinge vppe of Elias in a chariett of
fyre into heauen. Elias went to heauen by the powre of God: Chryſt aſcended into heauen by the power of his Godhead.

Tediouſnes that ſhould moche offende the Reader, moueth me to ſtaie
to bring in anie mo figures of Chryſte, at this preſent to this pourpoſe. Wher
fore I will ceaſſe at this time any farder to procead therin, and treat of the
like matter by prophecies, which ys the third waie, by which God vſed in
ſundrie times and ages, to reueill the miſterie of our redemption.

THE ELEVENTH CHAPITER DECLARETH
C   *by the Prophetes of what line Meſsias ſhoulde come, with his conception,*
birth, paſsion, and deathe.

I N the ſhewing ād opening of the prophecies I wil obſerue this
ordre before vſed. Firſt, to ſet furthe of what line Meſsias ſhall
come. Secondlie, of his conception and birth, Thirdlie, of his paſ
ſiō and death. Fourthlie, of his reſurrectiō, and laſt of his aſcēſiō.

As cōcerning the firſt: As God promiſed that the ſame Meſsias, Sauiour of   *Prophecie*
the worlde ſhould be of the ſeede of Abrahā, ād of the fruict of the bodie of   *of the line*
Dauid: So long after their times, by his prophet Eſaie did he manifeſtlie ſpeak   *and ſtock*
the ſame *Egredietur virga de radice Ieſſe, et flos de radice eius aſcēdet.* Ther ſhal come   *of Chriſt.*
a rodde oute of the kinred of Ieſſe, ād a bloſſom, or flowre ſhal flowriſh oute
of his roote. Who ys the roote, the rodde, and the flower, S. Ambroſe expoū   *Eſay.11.*
deth, ſaing. *Radix, familia Iudæorū: virga, Maria: flos Mariæ Chriſtus eſt, qui fœtorē mun*   *Ambr.de*
danæ colluuionis aboleuit, et odorē vitæ æternæ infudit. The roote ys the familie, of the   *Benedict*
Iewes: The rod ys Marie: The flower of Marie ys Chriſt, who hath takē awaie   *Patriach.*
the ſtinke, and hath powred in, the odoure of euerlaſting life.   *ca.4.*

D   That Chriſt ys that flower, that the Prophete ſpeaketh of, the ſcriptures al
ſo, that do ther immediatelie folowe, do euidentlie proue. Whiche to auoid
prolixitie, and in conſideracion that I writte not to Iewes, but to Chriſtē mē
I leaue to induce, referring the Reader to the place of the Prophet, which he

maie eaſelie peruſe , ſuppoſing yt ſufficiét to ſhew how Gods woords ãd his E
trueth ys conſtante,vnifourme,and permanente in all ages,and howe agreable his woorde ſpoken by his prophete ys to his promiſſemade to Abraham,
and Dauid as before ys mencioned.

*Prophecie
of the cõcep
tiõ of Chriſt
Eſay.7.*
Nowe therfor let vs procead to weigh other prophecies , howe they will
aunſwer the figures. And firſt the prophecie of the conception.What the figure was ye haue heard.The Prophet Eſaie being taught of God thus ſaied:
*Ecce virgo cõcipiet,& pariet filiũ.*Behold a virgé ſhal cõceaue,and beare a Sõne.
As the perſon of the figure,for that,that nature failed, cõceaued ãd brought
furth a childe by Gods power:So a virgen,wher nature hath not her ordre
to conceaue,hath beſides nature,and againſt the ordre of nature,conceaued
by Gods power.

And this prophecie of Eſaie doth wel opé ãd declare the former prophecie.
He ſaied a Rod ſhal come furth of the kinred of Ieſſe, ãd a flower ſhal floriſh
oute of his roote.*Virga virgo eſt.*The rodde ys the virgé,the floriſhing flower
ys the Sõne of the virgé.What maner of Sõne yt ys, the Prophete immedia- F
*Matth.1.*telie declareth: *Et vocabitur nomé eius Emanuel.*And his name ſhall be called E-
manuel.What Emanuel ys the Euãgeliſt declareth: *Quod interpretatur nobiſcum
Deus,*which, yf a mã interprete, ys as moche to ſaie,as God with vs. Whiche
*Baruch.3.*interpretaciõ geueth vs to vnderſtãd,that the Sõne of this wirgé ys the verie
Meſsias God and man,who was God with vs: For *In terris viſus eſt,& cum hominibus cõuerſatus eſt.*He was ſeen in the earth and was cõuerſaunt with mé, or
dwelt with men.So thé wher the prophete ſaid:A rodde ſhall bring furth a
flower,nowe by plain woordes he ſaieth:A virgen ſhall bring furth a Sonne
called Emanuel.

*Math.1.*And that this was fulfilled as yt was prefigured and prophecied, the Euã
geliſt teſtifieth:*Cùm eſſet deſpõſata mater Ieſu Maria Ioſeph,antequam cõuenirét,inuen
ta eſt in vtero habés de ſpiritu ſanĉto.*Whé Marie the mother of Ieſus was maried
to Ioſeph,before they came to dwel together,ſhe was founde with child by
the holie Goſte.

*Ibidem.*That ſhe cõceaued by the holie Goſte,the Angel teſtified to Ioſeph: *Ioſeph
fili Dauid,noli timere accipere Mariã coniugé tuã.Quod enim in ea natũ eſt, de ſpiritu ſan- G
ĉto eſt:*Ioſeph the ſõne of Dauid (ſaieth the Angel) feare not to take vnto thee
Marie thy wief.For that,that ys cõceaued in her,cometh of the holie Goſte.
And to cõclude thus the Euãgeliſt ſaieth.*Hoc auté totũ faĉtũ eſt, vt adimpleretur
quod diĉtũ eſt à Domino per Prophetã dirété: Ecce virgo cõcipiet,& pariet filiũ,& voca
*Eſay.7.*bũt nomé eius Emanuel.*Al this was doé that yt might be fulfilled which was ſpo
ké of oure Lord by the Prophete:ſaieng:Beholde a maide ſhal be with child,
ãd ſhall bring furth a ſonne,And they ſhal cal his name Emanuel.In this pro
ceſſe yt ys eaſie to be perceaued,how the prophecie aũſwereth the figure,ãd
the Euãgeliſt aũſwereth both figure,ãd prophecie,certifieng vs that to be ful
*Chriſts paſ
ſion and all
notable par
tes therof
conferred
to the pro-
phecies.
Ioan.3.
Eſaie.53.
Prophecie
of Chriſtes
paſsion.*filled ãd doé in faĉte,that thei promiſed,the one in figure the other inwoord

We haue heard of Chryſtes cõminge into fleſh by his cõception ãd birth:
Now let vs procead to ſpeake of the third,which ys his paſsiõ ãd death.And
for étrie therũto,firſt let vs ſearch by the prophecies wherfor he cã into fleſh
Chryſte himſelf ſaieth:*Venit filius hominis quærere,et ſaluũ facere quod perierat.*The
Sõne of mã came to ſeke,ãd ſaue that,that had periſhed.But by what meanes
was yt his pleaſure to ſaue that,that had periſhed? The Prophet declareth, H
ſaieng.*Ipſe auté vulneratus eſt propter iniquitates noſtras, attritus eſt propter ſcelera no-
ſtra.Diſciplina pacis noſtræ ſuper eũ,et liuore eius ſanati ſumus.*He was woũded for our
offences,ãd ſmitté for our wickednes.For the chaiſteſemét of our peace was
laied vpon him,and with his ſtripes are we healed.By what means did he co

A me to his paſsion?and howe came he into the hãdes of his enemies? By the
treaſon of one of his Apoſtles, who(as by the figure was prefigurated) ſolde
him to the Iewes, as the Brethren of Ioſeph ſolde him to the Iſmaelites.

But that prolixitie maie be auoided, and yet ſo notable a matter not o-
mitted,as wherbie the faithfull maie take occaſion to reioice in the ſownde-
neſſe of their faith,and therin glorifie God,I will by the helpe of God, paſſe
through the ſtorie of the Paſsiõ,as yt ys written of the Euangeliſtes,compa-
ringe euery notable parte of yt with the prophecies, wherby ſhall appeare,
that the faith of the chryſtians,beleuing Chryſt to haue died for the ſinnes
of the woorlde,and by that death to haue wrought the redemption of the
ſame,ys a ſure,ſubſtancial, and a grownded faith,fownded vpon the vnmoueable trueth of Gods woorde.

As yt was by his foreknowledge,by his holie prophetes liuelie and plain
lie ſpoken,howe,and by what means Meſsias ſhould woorke the ſaluaciõ of
mã:Euẽ ſo plainly and liuelie hath our Meſsias wrought and doen the ſame
B in faĉte,that was before ſpoken in woorde,as by this brief compariſon enſe-
wing yt ſhall appeare.

And to beginne,the howre of the paſsiõ of our Lorde drawing nere,which
he right wel knewe:*Sciens Ieſus quia venit hora eius,vt tranſeat ex hoc mundo ad Pa-*
*trem,*Ieſus knowing that his howre was cõmed, that he ſhould departe oute
of this worlde to the father,he prepared him,and willinglie went to Hieruſa *Ioan.13.*
lẽ.*Appropinquante horâ paſsionis,appropinquare voluit loco paſsionis.* The howre of
his paſsion drawing nere,he wolde alſo drawe nere to the place of his paſ-
ſion.And therfore(as S.Matthew ſaieth)he going vppe to Hieruſalem,tooke *Gregor.*
the xii.diſciples aſide in the waie,and ſaied to them.Beholde we go vppe to
Hieruſalem,and the Sonne of man ſhall be betraied vnto the chief preiſtes,
and vnto the Scribes,and they ſhall condemne him to death and ſhall deliuer him to the gentiles to be mocked,to be ſcourged,and to be crucified,ãd *Matth.20*
the thirde daie he ſhall riſe again.

By the which his ſaieng and doing yt appeareth,that he willinglie went
to ſuffer his paſsion.Which yet at the inſtant of the ſame, when Iudas with
C his companie came to the garden,wher he and his diſciples were, he did mo
re plainlie ſhewe in effeĉte.For(as S.Iohn ſaieth)*Sciens Ieſus omnia quæ ventura*
*erant,proceſsit,et dixit eis.*Ieſus knowing all thinges that ſhoulde come on him, *Ioan.18.*
wente furth and ſaied,whome ſeke ye?They ſaied: Ieſus of Nazareth . Ieſus
ſaieth to them:I am he.As ſoen as he ſaied vnto them:I am he,they wẽt back
ward ãd fel to the grownd.Wherbie yt ys manifeſt both in that,that he came
to mete them,ãd alſo in that,at his meting with thẽ,with his onelie woorde *Ibid.*
he threwe thẽ on the grownd,that he with like power might haue eſchaped *Zach.26.*
their hãdes,yf yt had not ben his will to haue ſuffred. In further argument
wherof alſo,when Peter drewe his ſworde,and cutte of the eare of Malchus,
Ieſus ſaied vnto him:Putte vppe thy ſworde into the ſheath. Shall I not drin
ke of the cuppe which my Father hath geuen me?And(as S. Matthew teſtifieth)ſaied further to Peter:Thinkeſt thowe that I can not now praie to my
Father,and he ſhall geue me by and by more then twelue legiõs of Angels?
But howe then ſhall the ſcriptures be fulfilled?for thus muſt yt be.

By all whiche proceſſe,yt dothe moſt euidentlie appeare , that willinglie
D he ſuffred his paſsion.So did God by his Prophet foreſaie that he ſhoulde
doo.*Oblatus eſt,quia voluit.*He was offred vppe bicauſe he wolde.

Iudas betraied him with a kiſſe: *Iuda,oſculo filium hominis tradis* ? Iudas be *Eſay.53.*
traieſt thowe the Sonne of man with a kiſſe?The prophecie ſaied lõg before
       F ij   that

that yt fhoulde fo be. *Homo pacis mea in quo fperaui, qui edebat panes meos, magnifi-* E
cauit fuper me fupplantationem, My owne familiar frende, whom I trufted, which
did alfo eate of my bread, hath laied great wait for me.

That this prophecie was fpoken of Iudas, Chryfte him felf ys wittneffe,
who fpeakinge of Iudas in the Gofpell alleageth this fame fcripture : *Qui*
manducat mecum panem, leuabit cōtra me calcaneum fuum. He that eateth bread with
me, fhall lifte vppe his hele againft me.

To procead in the ftory of the pafsion, when the Iewes laied handes vpon
him, and apprehended him, *Difcipuli omnes relicto eo fugerunt.* All his difciples
fledde and forfooke him. Whiche thing allmightie God had fpoken by hys
Prophet Zacharie, that fo yt fhoulde come to paffe: *Percutiam paftorem, & difper*
gentur oues gregis. I will fmite the fheaperd, and the fhepe of the flocke fhall be
fcatered. That this prophecie ys thus to be vnderftanded. Chrifte ys witneffe, who in the Gofpell of fainéte Marke, applieth yt to the fame pourpofe.

In the houfe of Caiphas they entreaéted our Sauiour very cuell. For F
emongeft other thinges: *Expuerunt in faciem eius.* They did fpitte in his face. Of
the whiche the Prophete Efaie fpake, as though yt had ben doen to hys own
perfon: *Faciem non auerti ab increpantibus & confpuentibus in me.* I turned not my
face from fhame and fpitting on me.

That in the morninge the cheif preiftes and the elders of the people had
a councell againft Iefus to pntte him to deathe, yt was not ouerpaffed withoute prophecie. For the Prophete Dauid fpeaketh thus of yt in the perfon
of Chryfte: *Circumdederunt me canes multi, concilium malignantium obfedit me.* Manie
dogges compafed me rownde aboute, the councell of the wicked laied fiege
againft me.

When Iudas (as yt foloweth in the ftorie) feing Chryfte condemned,
brought the moncie again, fainge: I haue offended betrayeng an innocent
bloode, and that the cheif preiftes wolde not putte thefe filuer plates into
the treafurie, bicaufe yt was the price of blood, but tooke coūfell, and bought
with them a potters fielde to burie ftraungers : the Euangelift himfelf affirmeth the prophecie therby to be fulfilled, faing. Then was that fulfilled, G
whiche was fpoken of by the Prophet Hieremie fainge: And they tooke thir
tie filuer peices, the price of him that was valued, whom they bought of the
children of Ifraell, and gaue them for the potters feilde.

Theife woordes be not fownde in Hieremie after the tranflation of the
Bibles that nowe be comonly vfed: yet this prophecie maie well be alleaged
oute of Hieremie. For fainéte Hierom faieth, that he hath red a booke of
Hieremie in the Hebrue tounge, in the whiche this fentence ys conteined
woord for woorde.

But emōge the prophetes that we haue in vfe nowe, Zacharie hath yt moft
plainlie, wher we read yt thus: Yf ye thinke yt good bring hether my price:
Yf no, then leaue. So they weighed down thirtie filuer pcices, the value that
I was priced at. And the Lorde faid vnto me: Caftyt vnto the potter, a good
lie price for me to be valued at of them. And I tooke the thirtie filuer peices
and caft them vnto the potter. Thus moche Zacharie.

In whofe woordes ye perceaue the price of him that was folde, whichwas
thirtie filuer plates, for the whiche fumme our fauiour was folde. Ye percea- H
ue further more what was doen with thofe thirtie plates. In the prophecie
they were caft to the potter. And the cheif preiftes caft thē likewife to the pot
ter, for they bought a porters feilde with thē, to burie ftrangers in. Thus maie
　　　　　　　　　　　　　　　　　　　　　　　　　　　　　　　ye fe

Pfal. 40.

Ioan. 13.

Matth. 26

Zach. 14.

Mat.h. 26
Efay. 50.

Mat. 21.

Pfal. 21.

Mat. 27

Zachar. 11

Matt. 27

ye se how agreable thinges doen in the Gospell, be with the prophecie, and how liuelie and well the one aunswereth the other.

Pilate hearing that Iesus was a man of Galilie, which belonged to the iurisdiction of Herode, he sent him to Herode, before whom the high preistes and Scribes accused him straitlie. But Herode with his men of warre, when they had despised him, they sent him again cloathed in a white garment, vnto Pilate, Wherby the prophecie was fulfilled which saied. *Quare fremuerunt gē Psal.2.* *tes, & populi meditati sunt inania? Astiterunt reges terræ, & principes conuenerunt in vnum, aduersus Dominum, et aduersus Christum eius.* Whie do the heathē so furiouslie rage together, and why dothe the people ymagen vain thinges? The kinges of the earthe stand vppe, and the rulers take counsell together against the Lorde, and against hys enointed.

That this prophecie of Dauid was here fullfilled, the holie Goste by the holie multitude testifieth in the actes of the Apostles, which in their praier to God praied thus: *Domine, tu es qui fecisti cælum et terram, etc.* Lorde thow arte *Act. 4.*
B God, which hast made heauē and earthe, the Sea ād all that in thē ys. Which in the holie Gost by the mouth of thy seruaūt Dauid our father haueст saied: why did the heathē rage, and the people ymagen vain thinges? The Kinges of the earth stoode vppe, and the rulers came together against the Lorde, ād against his enointed. And of trueth against thy holie childe Iesus, whom thow haueст enointed, both Herode, and also PoncePilate with the gentiles ād the people of Israell gathered thē selfs together in this Citie, to doo what soeuer thy hādes, and thy counseil determined before to be doen. Thus ye se not onelie the Gospel aunswereth the prophecie, but also by mē full of the holie Goste, yt ys so taken, vnderstāded, and applied.

To procead in the storie. When Chryst was before Herode, who questio ned withe him manie woordes, he aunswered nothing, as S. Luke testifieth: *Luc.23.* So being before Pilate, when he was accused of the cheif preistes and elders, *Matth.27.* as S. Mathew wittnesseth, he aunswered nothinge, And whē Pilate also saied to him, doest thowe not heare how manie wittnesses they laye against thee? And he aunswered him neuer one woorde, insomoche as the deputie mer *Esay.53.*
C uciled greatlie. Wherbie was fulfilled the prophecie which saieth. *Tanquam ouis ad occisionē ducetur, et tanquam agnus corā tondente se obmutescet, et non aperiet os suū.* He shall be led as a shepe to be slain, yet shall he be as still as a lambe, before the sherer, and not open his mouth.

This ys the prophecie which the Chāberlain of queen Candace, did read *Act.8.* sitting in his chariet, retourning frō Hierusalē. To whose chariett the Spirit of God cōmaunded Philippe to ioin himself, who hearing him reading this place, asked him : vnderstandeст thow what thowe readeст? &c. And Philippe went yppe into the chariette, and began at the same scripture, and preached vnto him Iesus. By the which yt ys manifeст that this scripture or prophecie ys to be vnderstanded of our Sauioure Chryст Iesus.

When Pilate (as yt foloweth in the storie) sate in iudgemēt, and asked the people, what he shoulde doo with Iesus, which was called Chryste, They all *Math. 27,* saied: Let him be crucified. Whē Pilate saied: what hath he doēn? They cried the more, let him be crucified. Whē Pilate called for water, and wasshed his
D handes, saieng: I am innocent, of the blood of this iuст person, their feircenes se, and crueltie was so great, that they cried: His bloode be vpon vs, and on owre children. Which their lionlike crueltie and fiercenesse was foreseen by God, and spokē by the Prophete in the psalm: *Aperuerūt super me os suū sicut leo rapiēs et rugiēs.* They haue opened their mouth vpō me, as yt were a rāping, ād roringe Lion. F iij When

Whē Pilate fawe their importunitie, he willing to cōtēt the people, let Bar　E
rabas loofe vnto thē, ād whē he had fcourged Iefus, deliuered him to be cruci

Efay.50.
fied. Accordinlie faieth the Prophete: *Corpus meū dedi percutientibus, et genas meas vellentibus*. I offred my backe to the fmiters, and my chekes to the nippers.

Which prophecie dothe not onelie declare the fcourginges that Chryfte
fhoulde fuftein in his bodie, but alfo the buffettes and blowes, that he fuffred on the face in the houfe of the high preift, and of other miniftres, as the
Euangelift doth declare.

Matth.26.
Mar.15.
Luc.22.
Then Iudas feing that Chryft was condemned, he hanged him felf, fullfil-
ling the prophecie whiche faieth: *Fiant dies eius pauci, et epifcopatum eius accipiat al
ter.* Let his daies be fewe, and let an other take hys office.

That this was prophecied of Iudas fainéte Peter dothe teftifie, faing : Ye

Acto.1.
men and bretheren, this fcripture muft nedes haue ben fullfilled, whiche the
holie Goft through the mouthe of Dauid fpake before of Iudas, whiche was
guide of them that tooke Iefus, &c. And when he was hanged he bruft in
fundre, and his bowels gufhed oute. For yt ys writtē in the booke of pfalms.　F
Fiat Commoratio, &c.

After all theife perfecutions, when Chryft was deliuered to the foldiers to
be crucified, they led him into the common haul, wher they entreaéted him
like a moft vile man, putting on him a purple Robe, and pleétinge a Crowne
of thornes vpon his head, and a rede in his hand, and they on their knees,
faing : Haill king of Iewes.

Efay.53.
Wherin was verified the prophecie of Efaie, fpoken in the perfon of the Ie
wes: We haue recknid him fo vile, that we haue turned our faces frō him: yea
he was defpifed, ād therfor we regarded him not. So that our Sauiour might
verie well faie, at that fame time, with his owne mouthe, that the Prophet

Pfal.21.
Dauid fpake before by the fpirit of prophecie in the perfon of Chryfte: *Ego
fum vermis, et non homo, opprobriū hominū, et abieétio plebis.* I am a woorme and no
man, a verie fcorne of men, and the outcaft of the people.

Thofe cruell handlinges of him doen, yet moft cruellie to his vnfpeakeable pain, percinge hys moft blefled, and fwete handes and feete, they crucified him, in this alfo fulfilling the fcripture prophecieng that yt fhould fo be,　G

Ibid.
and fpeaking yt in the perfon of Chrifte, who fuffred yt: *Foderunt manus meas,
& pedes meos, & dinumerauerunt omnia offa mea.* They perced my handes, and
my feet. I maie tell al my bones. What prophecies coulde more liuelie expref
fe this parte of Chryftes pafsion, then this dothe?

But I fhall hafte me to other fpeaking as plainlie as this. And to folow the
ordre after the narration of fainéte Luke, they crucified with him two euell
doers, one on hys right hand, the other on hys left, fulfilling the prophecie

Efay.53.
Marc.15.
which faieth: *Et cum iniquis reputatus eft.* And he was reputed with the wicked.
Whiche prophecie S. Marke applieth to this pourpofe, fainge yt here to be
fullfilled.

When he was thus crucified, they parted his garment, and caft lottes for

Pfal.21.
Math.27.
yt. The prophecie agreablie faieth: *Diuiferunt fibi veftimenta mea, et fuper veftem
meam miferunt fortem.* They parted my garments amōg them, and vpon my ve
fture they caft lottes. That this prophecie ys fulfilled by this faéte, S. Matthew ys wittneffe, who faieth : They parted hys garmentes, and caft lottes,
that yt might be fulfilled which was fpoken by the Prophet, &c.　　　　　H

When this was doen they paffed by, reuiling him, and wagging their heades. Accordinglie was yt prophecied and fpoken in the perfon of Chryfte.

Pfal.21.
Omnes videntes me deriferunt me, locuti funt labijs, et mouerunt caput. All that
did

A did see me, laught me to skorne, they spake with their lipps, and wagged their heades.

Likewise the high priestes with the Scribes and the elders mocked him, *Math. 27.* and saied : He saued other, himself he can not saue . He trusted in God, let him deliuer him nowe yf he wil haue him. Nowe beholde if the prophecie *Psal. 21.* haue not almoste euen the same woordes : *Sperauit in Domino, eripiat eum, saluū faciat eum, quoniam vult eum.* He trusted in God that he wolde deliuer him. let him deliuer him, if he will haue him.

All these their wicked mockes, and cruell tormentes not with standinge, hanging vpon the crosse he praied for them to his Father, sainge: *Pater dimitte* *Luc. 23.* *illis, non enim sciunt quid faciunt .* Father forgeue them, for they knowe not what they doo. Herin also he fullfilled the prophecie, whiche saied of him , *Pro* *Esay. 53.* *transgressoribus orauit* , He made intercession for misdoers. And when the sixt howre was commed , darknesse arose ouer all the earth vntill the ningth howre (as sainte Marke writeth) Iesus cried with a loude voice saing:

B *Eloy Eloy Lamasabathani,* whiche ys if one interprete. My God my God, why *Mar. 15.* haueft thow forsaken me ? In the whiche crie, Christ spake the verie woordes of the prophecie : *Deus, Deus meus respice in me, quare me dereliquisti ?* My *Psal. 21.* God, my God, looke vpon me, why haueft thow forsaken me? When he *Mar. 15.* had thus cried, one ranne, and filled a sponge with vineagre, and put yt vppō a Reed, and gaue him to drincke. Sainte Matthew saieth, that they gaue *Math. 27* him vineagre mingled with gall, which fullie aunswereth the prophecie which saieth : *Dederunt in escam meam sel, & in siti mea potauerunt me aceto.* They *Psal. 68.* gaue me gall to eate, and when I was thirstie, they gaue me vineagre to drinke. Sainte Iohū concludinge here the wholl storie of the passion saieth *Ioan. 19.* thus. *Postea sciens Iesus quia omnia consummata etc.* After these thinges Iesus knowing, that all thinges were nowe perfourmed, that the scripture might be fullfilled he saied : I thirst. Ther stoode a vessell by full of vineagre. Therfore they filled a sponge with vineagre , and wounde yt aboute with Isope and put yt to his mouth. As sooen as Iesus receaued the vineagre he saied: Yt ys finished : and bowed downe his head, and gaue vppe the Goste:

C In this woord, *Consummatum est,* yt ys finished, Christe, who saied, that all *Ioan. 19.* must nedes be fullfilled, which was written of him in the Lawe of Moises, *Luc. 24.* and in the prophetes, and in the Psalmes, perceauing that all those that spake of his incarnacion, conuersation, and passion (the ende of whiche passion was instante) were fullfilled in him, and by him, signified to vs the ende of the same. whiche ende was that all thinges be doen in dede, as these bookes forespake by woorde in figures and prophecies . Nowe the end of these bookes being commed, and therfore well finished, as one that had doen his worke appoincted at his own pleasure, he gaue himself to rest, and yelded vppe his most blessed Spirit.

THE TVVELVETH CHAPITER BRIEFLIE TOV-
cheth a prophecie or two of Christs Resurrection and Ascension.

D Owe (gentle Reader) thowe haueft heard the goodlie storie of the passion of our Sauiour Iesus Christe, not according to the woorthinesse of soche a matter treacted of, and handled, but for the avoiding of tediousnes breiflie, and as yt were in a transcourse ouerrunne. Wherin yet yf you well note the conference and applicacion of the storie of the Gospell to the prophecies, and

weigh well, howe the one aunſwereth the other, yt will occaſion yowe (as E
I ſuppoſe) to honour God in his prouident wiſedom , and foreknowledge, and to reuerence his holie myſteries in the ſcriptures alſo, teaching vs
the ſame.

Nowe to perfourme my promiſſe, I will bringe furth a prophecie or two
of his Reſurrection, and aſcenſion, and ſo end this matter.

Prophecie
of Chryſtes
reſurrect.
and aſcēſiō

1.Cor . 15.

Pſal.15.

As the ſtorie of the Goſpell hath ſufficientlie wittneſſed that Chriſte our
Sauiour gaue vppe the goſt vppon the croſſe, and ther (to declare himſelf a
mortall man) died: So doth yt teſtifie vnto vs, that he was buried, and that
the third daie he roſe again, and that (as ſainct Paule ſaieth) accordinge to
the Scriptures. And for aſmoche as the Goſpell was not perchaunce then
written, or receaued as of autoritie to proue that article to vnbeleuing men:
yt ys to be ſuppoſed, that ſainete Paule ment the Scriptures of the Prophetes, whiche did prophecie the reſurrection of Chriſte. of the whiche matter we read thus in the pſalme: I haue ſett God allwais before me, for he ys
on my right hand. therfor I ſhall not fall. wherfore my hearte was gladde, F
and my tounge reioced, my fleſh alſo ſhall reſt in hope . for whie ? Thowe
ſhallt not, leaue my ſowle in Hell, nether ſhalt thowe ſuffer thy holie one
to ſee corruption.

a Acto.2.

That this prophecie ſpeaketh of the reſurrection of Chriſte, ſainete Peter
in the firſt ſermon that he made, after he hadde receaued the holie Goſte,
whiche was enen the ſame daie of Pentecoſt, dothe alleage the ſame ſcripture by the teaching of the ſame holie Spirit to proue the reſurrectiō of Chriſte,
wher he ſaieth thus : Ye men of Iſraell heare theſe woordes. Ieſus of Nazareth a man approued of God emong yowe with miracles , wonders, and
ſignes, which God did by him in the middeſt of yowe (as ye your ſelues
knowe) him haue ye taken by the handes of vnrighteouſe perſons, after he
was deliuered by the determinate counſeill, and foreknowledge of God,
and haue crucified and ſlain him , whom God hath rayſed vppe, and looſed the ſorowes of death, bycauſe yt was vnpoſsible that he ſhoulde be holden of yt. For Dauid ſpeaketh of him before hand : I ſawe God allwais before me &c. as ys before alleadged.   G

And proceading in this matter, noteth the ſpeciall poinctes of this Prophecie, that doo proue the reſurrection of Chriſte and ſaieth : Therfor
ſeing he was a Prophete (ſpeking of Dauid) and knewe that God had ſworne with an othe to him , that Chriſte (as concerninge the fleſh) ſhoulde
come of the fruicte of his loines, and ſhoulde ſitte on his ſeat, he knowing
this before ſpake of the reſurrection of Chriſte, that his ſowle ſhowlde not
be lefte in hell, neither his fleſh ſhoulde ſee corruption. This Ieſus hath God
raiſed vppe wherof all we are wittneſſes.

In the whiche wholl ſentence and ſaieng of ſainete Peter two thinges are
to this pourpoſe to be noted. Firſt, that before the allegacion of the prophete Dauid he ſaieth thus, ſpeaking of Chriſte: whom God hath raiſed vppe,
and looſed the ſorowes of death. Yf ye aſke the holie Apoſtle, the cauſe whie
God hath raiſed him from deathe, he aunſwereth : Bicauſe yt was vnpoſsible that he ſhoulde be holden of yt. Yf ye proceaad to aſke him why yt was
vnpoſsible. he aunſwereth : For Dauid ſpeaketh of him. Wherin he noteth
the immutabilitie of God, and the certentie of his woorde . As who ſhould H
ſaie, forſomoch as God hath ſpoken by his Prophete Dauid that he wolde raiſe vppe Chriſte again, yt ys vnpoſsible but he muſt be raiſed, and ther
fore he was raiſed.

The

A The fecond thing to be noted in the Apoftle ys, that he noteth, as yt were with his fingar, the verie fpeciall woordes of the prophecie of Dauid, that forefpake the refurrection of Chrifte, where the Apoftle fpeking of Dauid, faied : He knowing of this before fpake of the refurrection of Chrifte, that his fowle fhoulde not be left in Hell, nether his flefh fhoulde fee corruption.

This fentence ys yt, that plainlie proueth the refurrection. Wherfore the Apoftle, to conferre the fullfilling of the prophecie to the prophecie yt felf, concludeth the fentence thus : This Iefus hath God raifed vppe, wherof we all are wittneffes. Albeit the learned Fathers alleage other places alfo: yet for fo moche as I hafte to the matter principallie entended, I will ftaie my hande in this matter, Mindinge with like expedicion to finifh the reft that remaineth to be doen by my promeffe, that ys onelie to declare the afcenfion of Chrift by prophecie, as I haue doen by figure.

Of the Afcenfion of our Sauiour Chrifte the Prophete Dauid alfo in the
B pfalme dothe Prophecie thus : *Afcendifti in altum, cepifti captiuitatem, accepifti dona in hominibus* . Thow arte gon vppe on high, thowe haueft led captiuitie captiue, and receaued giftes for men. That the Prophete did in this fentence fpeake and prophecie of the afcenfion of Chrifte, fainct Paule ys wittneffe, who alleaging this prophecie proceadeth vppon yt thus *Vnicuique noftru data eft gratia fecundum menfuram donationis Chrifti. Propter quod dicit: Afcendés in altum, captiuam duxit captiuitatem , dedit dona hominibus , &c* . vnto euerie one of vs ys geuen grace, according to the meafure of the gifte of Chrifte. wher fore he faieth : when he went vppe on high, he led captiuitie captiue and gaue giftes vnto men. That he afcended, what meeneth yt, but that he alfo defcended firft into the loweft partes of the earth ? He that defcended ys enen the fame alfo that afcended vppe aboue all heauens, to fullfill all thinges.

By the whiche woordes, that fainct Paule taketh the fainge of Dauid to be a prophecie of Chriftes Afcencion, yt ys more manifeft, then yt neadeth anie further probacion of me or anie other man.

C But this fcruple perchaunce maie moue a diligente reader, that the Pfalme faieth: Thowe arte gon vppe on high, thowe haueft led captiuitie captiue, and receaued giftes for men, or emonge men: *Accepifti dona in hominibus*: And the Apoftle faieth : *Dedit dona hominibus* . He hath geuen giftes to men. betwixte geuinge and receauing ther ys a great difference.

This doubte doth fainct Auguftine diffolue, writting in this wife : *Sed cum Propheta dixerit, Accepifti dona in hominibus: Apoftolus maluit dicere, Dedit dona hominibus, vt ex vtroque fcilicet verbo, vno Phrophetico, Apoftolico altero, (quia in vtroque eft diuini fermonis autoritas) fenfus pleniffimus redderetur. Vtrúque enim verum eft, & quia dedit hominibus, et quia accepit in hominibus. Dedit hominibus, tanquã caput membris fuis : accepit in hominibus, idem ipfe vtique in membris fuis, propter quæ membra fua clamauit de cœlo, Saule, Saule, quid me perfequeris?* But when the Prophete hath faied : Thowe haueft receaued giftes in men, or emong men: the Apoftle hath chofen to faie : Thow haueft geuen giftes to men, that oute of both fainges, the one of the Prophete, the other of the Apoftle (by caufe that in bothe ys the autoritie of Gods woord) a moft full and perfecte fenfe
D might be geuen. For both be true, bothe that he gaue giftes vnto men, and alfo receaued giftes in men . He gaue giftes vnto men, as the head to the membres, the felf fame alfo receaued giftes in his membres, for the whiche his membres he cried from heauen: Saul, Saul, why doeft thowe perfequute

te

Pfal. 67.
Prophecie
of the Afcé
fion.

Ephef.4.

Aug.l.15
de Trinit.

te me ? Thus moche fainct Auguftin.

Albeit the Scriptures be topioufe and plentifull of Prophecies as well of this matter as of other, all teachinge vs one trueth, though they be vtterred by diuerfe organs, or inftrumentes of the holie Gofte, forbicaufe the holie Gofte the Schoolemafter of all trueth ys but one : Yet I will not moleft the Reader with the reherfall of anie mo, well knowing, that the truthe ys as perfecte, as fure, and as fubftacial in one fentece of the holy Gofte, as in tweti : Neuertheleffe he that ys defieroufe to read mo prophecies of this matter I referre him to the xlvj. pfame, to the lxiij. chapiter of Eafie, and to the fecond of Micheas, as the holie learned fathers haue taught me.

Holie Goft
fchoolmaf-
ter of all
trueth.

Thus (praife be to God) I haue through his helpe profourmed that, that I entended : namely, declared that the mifteries of our Redemptio were by diuerfe meanes, that ys to faie, by promiffes, figures, and prophecies reueiled vnto the Fathers by Allmightie God, and that in diuerfe ages, and times, as in the time of the lawe of Nature, in the time of the lawe of Moyfes, All whiche promiffes, figures, and prophecies, promifed, figured and prophecied foche thinges, as by our Sauiour Chrifte, were fullfilled, accoplifhed, and ended. whiche fo beinge they haue their ende, according as Chrift him felf faied : *Etenim quæ de me fcripta funt, finem habent.* For the thinges, whiche are written of me, haue an ende.

F

Luc.22.

THE THIRTENE CHAPITER HOW THAT MELCHI
fedech was a figure of Chrifte bothe in preifthood, and facrifice.

Owe to approche to the matter in this firft booke principallie entended : Wheras Allmightie God, did paint, open, and fhewe the mifterie of our Redemption, by promifes, figures, and prophecies in the olde teftament to the great comforth of thé, that liued in that teftament, whiche Redemption ys alredie wrought, doen and perfected : Euen fo hath he by figures, and prophecies, fhadowed, and fpoken before of thinges that fhal be doen in the new Teftament, as a perpetuall memoriall of the fame redemption, to the great and fpirituall comforth of them that liue vnder the newe teftament. whiche memoriall ys nowe in the Churche of Chriftendom, vfed and continned. For as by his bloodfheding vpon the Croffe, he did the verie thing in dede, that the legall Sacrifices did prefigurate, & fhadowe in the olde teftament : So by the fame blood he (as being the thing yt felf, and the verie light caufing ge figure to ceaffe, and the fhadow to be remoued) abolifhed the olde Tefta ment, and eftablifhed and confirmed a newe Teftament, not to remayn for a feafon, as the other was appointed to do, when Moifes faied : *Hic fanguis Teftamenti, quod mandauit ad vos Deus.* This ys the bloode of the Teftament, whiche God hath made with yowe : But a newe euerlafting Teftament, according as fainéte Paule faieth.

G

Exod.24.
Hebr.9.
Hebr.13.
Æternum
Teftametu

This euerlafting Teftament hath accordinglie an euerlafting preift, and an euerlafting facrifice. The euerlafting preift ys our Sauiour Chrifte, as wittneffeth fainct Paule : *Nec Chriftus femetipfum glorificauit, vt pontifex fieret, fed qui dixit ad eum : Filius meus es tu, ego hodie genui te. Quemadmodum & in alio loco dicit : Tu es facerdos in æternum fecundum ordinem Melchifedech.* Neither did Chrifte glorifie him felf, to be made the high preift, but he that faied vnto him : Thowe arte my Sonne, this daie haue I begotté thee, As he faieth alfo in an other place : Thowe arte a preift for euer after the order of Melchifedech.

Hebr.5.

H

The

A　　The euerlasting sacrifice ys the verie bodie aud bloode of the same our
Sauiour Iesus Christe. whiche as he, according to the ordre of his preisthood, did sacrifice in his last Supper vnder the formes of bread and wine:
So did he geue auctoritie and commandement to the Apostles and ministres
of his Churche to do the same saing : *Hoc facite in meam commemoratione.* This
do ye in the remembrance of me.

Christes bodie and blood an euerlasting sacrifice. Luc.22.

The continuance of the doing of this thing in the remembrance of him,
sainct Paule declareth saing: *Donec veniat.* vntill he come, vnderstande to the
general iudgemet. wherbie yt doth appeare that this sacrifice, ad preisthood,
shall continewe vnto the worldes ende.

1.Cor. 11.

These be the thinges, whiche I saied before, that God had sheued, by
figures, and prophecies. Whiche figures and prophecies, being doen and
past, and ment of these thinges, must as necessarelie be fullfilled, as the
other before mencioned figures, and prophecies were fullfiled of the Authour, and Institutour of them.

B　　The figures and prophecies before mencioned were of thinges, whiche
as touchinge the facte (not the vertue, efficacie, and merite, which haue
none ende) were ended in Christe. As his incarnacion ys doen and ended,
his passion, resurrection, and ascension be doen, and ended in facte, not in
vertue, efficacie, and meritte.

But the newe Testament, wherin the vertue, efficacie, and merites of these
factes be continued, and applied, ys begonne and confirmed in Christes
bloode. The preisthood also of the same, whiche he ordeined in that newe
lawe or Testament. For a newe lawe must nedes haue a newe preisthood,
and a newe preisthood most haue a newe lawe, as saincte Paule maketh
this argument of necessitie, that *Translato sacerdotio, necesse est vt legis translatio
fiat.* The preisthood being taken awaie, the lawe must nedes be taken awaie.
For lawe and preisthood go together. And with a newe preisthood cometh
a newe sacrifice. For the diuersitie of preisthood standeth in the diuersitie
of sacrifice. These three shall endure, and remain, as the figures and prophecies of the same shall manifestlie declare, and proue.

A new lawe a newe preisthood Heb. 7.

A newe preisthood a newe sacrifice.

C　　Of these thinges ther be figures in the lawe of nature, and in the lawe
of Moyses. In the lawe of nature, albeit that Seth, Noe, and other holie men,
did offer sacrifices vnto God : yet were they not figures of this Sacrifice,
vsed nowe in Christes church, but raither of Christes Sacrifice offred vpon
the Crosse after the maner of Aaron. For the whiche cause saincte Iohn
saieth, he ys *Agnus, qui occisus est ab origine mundi.* the Lambe that was slain from
the beginning of the worlde, Both for that he was figured in the sacrifices
doen to God from the beginnig of the worlde, & also that he gaue vertue
to all soche sacrifices.

Apoca. 13.

But the first that figureth bothe the preisthood and sacrifice of the newe
lawe, ys *Melchisedech,* of whome we read thus : And *Melchisedech,* king of
Salem brought furth bread and wine (for he was the preist of the most high
God) and blessed him saieng : Blessed be Abraham vnto the high God,
possessour of heauen and earth. And blessed be the high God whiche hath
deliuered thine enemies into thy handes. And Abraham gaue him tithes
D　of all.

To proue this *Melchisedech* to be the verie figure of Christe, we can haue
no better argument, then the applicacion which S. Paule maketh by the holie Goste, in the epistle to the Hebrues, wher in the ende of the sixte chapiter he saieth thus: Wher the forerenner ys for vs entred, euen Iesus, that ys

Heb.6. &.7. Christ and Melchise-dech compa-red togethe

made

made an high preiſt for euer, after the ordre of *Melchiſedech*. And then yt fo- E
loweth in the beginning of the next chapiter: This *Melchiſedech* king of Salé,
who being preiſt of the moſt high God, mette Abraham, as he returned
again from the ſlaughter of the kinges, and bleſſed him, to whom alſo
Abraham gaue tithes of all thinges, firſt ys called by interpretation king of
righteouſneſſe, after king of Salem, that ys to ſaie, king of peace, without
Father, without mother withoute kinred, And hath neither beginning of
daies, neither ende of life, but ys likened to the Sonne of God, and continueth a preiſt for euer.

In the whiche ſentence ſainĉte Paule firſt reciteth the ſtorie, and after
doth interprete the woordes, and applie the ſame to Chriſte, as the figure
to the thing figured.

Firſt (ſaieth he) ys he called the king of righteouſnes, wher in ſainĉte
Paule dothe interprete the name of *Melchiſedech* For as the learned in the
tounges ſaie, *Melec*, doth ſignifie kinge, and *Sedech* righteouſneſſe, and ſo
ſainĉte Paule by the name of *Melchiſedech* calleth him king of righteouſneſſe. F
After, king of Salem. Salem by interpretatiō ys peace. And therfore ſainĉte
Paule ſaieth king of Salem, that ys to ſaie, of peace.

Yet ther was a Cittie in dede called Salem, of the whiche *Melchiſedech* (as
the Hebrues do ſaie) being the eldeſt Sonne of Noë, whome the ſcripture
Hierom.in
Eſay.41. otherwiſe calleth Sem, was the verie king. In the whiche (as ſainĉte Hierom
dothe teſtifie) ther remain the ruines of his palace, which doth teſtifie what
a goodlie thinge yt was.

Whiche *Melchiſedech* notwithſtanding that he was a king, he was alſo a
preiſt. For (as ſainĉte Hierom doth alſo ſaie) the eldeſt or firſt born ſonnes in
the lawe of nature were preiſtes. And therfore yt dothe appeare that he was
an eldeſt Sonne.

Sainĉt Paule goeth on, and ſaieth, that he was withoute father, and with
oute mother: By the whiche, ſainĉte Paule meeneth not, that he had no
father, nor mother, but that the Scripture maketh no menciō of his father,
nor mother.

Likewiſe ys that to be vnderſtanded whiche foloweth, wher he ſaieth: G
that *Melchiſedech* was withoute kin, hauing neither beginning of daies nor
yet endinge. In dede he had bothe, but the Scripture maketh no mencion
of them. But all theſe thinges doth ſainĉte Paule inferre to declare howe
liuely *Melchiſedech* as a figure of Chriſte, doth expreſſe him.

As Firſt, wher *Melchiſedech* ys called king of righteouſneſſe, he figureth
Chriſte verie well. For Chriſte ys that righteouſe kinge, who according to
Eſay.11. the ſaieng of the Prophete Eſaie : *Non ſecundùm viſionem oculorũ iudicabit, neque
ſecundùm auditum aurium arguet, ſed iudicabit in iuſtitia pauperes &c*. He ſhall not
geue ſentence after the thing, that ſhal be brought before his eies, neither
reproue a matter at the firſt hearinge, but with righteouſnes ſhall he iudge
Id.9. the poor . And again the Prophete ſaieth: He ſhall ſitte vpon the ſcat of
Dauid, and in his kingdom, to ſett vppe the ſame, and to eſtabliſh yt with
equitie and righteouſnes, for the whiche cauſe (as the Prophete ſaieth) *vo-
cabunt eum, Dominus iuſtus noſter* . They ſhall call his name, owre righteouſe Lord.

Ioan.5. And wourthilie ys he ſo called. For dailie dothe he righteouſlie, for that H
that *Pater omne iudicium dedit Filio*. The Father hath geuen all iudgement to
2.Cor.5. the Sonne. Before whome, *Omnes nos manifeſtari oportet , vt referat vnuſquiſque
prout geſsit in corpore, ſiue bonum, ſiue malum*. We muſt all appeare, that enery
　　　　　　　　　　　　　　　　　　　　　　　　　　　　　　　　man

A man maie receaue the workes of his bodie, according to that he hath doen, be yt good or euell. At the whiche time : *Procedent, qui bona fecerunt, in resur-* *rectionem vitæ, qui vero mala egerunt, in resurrectionē iudicij .* They shall come furth that haue don good, vnto the resurrection of life, and they that haue doen euell vnto the resurrection of damnacion.   *Ioan.5.*

Thus maie ye perceaue that *Melchisedech* being called the king of righteous nesse, figureth well Christ our righteouse king.

He ys called also, *Rex Salem*, king of peace, wherin he doth wonde- rons well figure Christe, who of the Prophet ys called: *Princeps pacis, cuius regnum multiplicabitur , & pacis non erit finis* . The prince of peace, whose kingdom shall be multiplied, and there shall be no ende of peace. Wher- fore the Angells at his birth sange : *Et in terra pax hominibus bonæ volun- tatis* . And in earth peace vnto men of a good will. For (as sainĉte Paule saieth) *Annunciauit pacem ijs, qui longè erant , & pacem ijs qui propè.* He preac- hed peace to those that were a farre of, and to them that were nigh. For *Esay.9.* *Luc.2.* *Ephes.2.*

B why? *Ipse est pax nostra,* he ys our peace.

In this then howe well *Melchisedech* figureth Christe, though no admo- nicion were geuen, the thing will shewe yt self, and howe well Christe aun- swereth *Melchisedech.*

In this also that he saieth. *Mechisedech* to be withoute father and withoute mother, he ys also a right figure of Christ. For as *Melchisedech* ys not fownde in the Scriptures to haue anie naturall father in the earthe : Nomore hath Christe in very dede anie naturall father in the earthe. And as *Melchisedech* hath no mother, So Christe proprelie hath no naturall mother, calling a na- turall mother, a woman that conceaueth by naturall course and ordre . For a woman that conceaueth aboue nature, and bringeth furth a child aboue nature, ys also a mother aboue nature. And being a mother aboue nature, properlie ys no mother natural. For that ys natural that ys conteined within thecōpasse of nature. And thus in this respect he had no natural mother. Yet maie she be called a naturall mother, for that she imparted to him her natu- ral fleshe, and her naturall bloode to the worke of his incarnacion . Wherby

C also he in that respecte that he had naturall flesh, and naturall blood of man, was and ys a naturall man.   *Mariechri stes mother by nature and aboue nature.*

Melchisedech also (saieth sainĉt Paule) was without kynred : wherin he ys also likened to Chryst, who although as touching his flesh, he hath a genealo gie, as Matthew and Luke declare. Yet as concerning his Godhead ithe Pro- phete saieth: *Generationem eius quis enarrabit?* Who can declare, or nombre hys generacion? As who shoulde saie, No man can declare, howe God the Fa- ther begatte God the Sonne . Yt ys inexplicable. And after thys maner Chryste trulie answereth his figure *Melchisedech,* for that in the Godhead he hath no kinne.   *Esay.53.*

Melchisedech, hathe neither beginning of daies, nor ende of life : So Chryste, as God, hath neither beginning nor endinge. For he saieth: *Ego sum alpha & omega, primus & nouissimus, princip:um & finis.* I am alpha and omega, the first and the last, the beginning an the endinge. And sainĉte Paule: *Iesus Chri stus he- ri et hodie, ipse et in secula.* Iesus Chryste ys yesterdaie, and to daie, and the same continueth for euer.   *Apoc.22.* *Heb.13*

D When sainĉt Paule had enombred all these thinges to declare therbie that Mechisedech was a figure of Chryste, he saieth : *Assimulatus est filio Dei.* He ys likened to the Sonne of God. Which ys as moche to saie, as he ys the figure of Chryst the Sonne of God.   *Ibidem. 6.*

Augu. de
Gen. ad li-
teram.

Of the which matter ſaincte Auguſtin ſpeaketh vpon the ſame pla- E
ce : *Locus diligenti conſideratione digniſſimus . Cum enim per Melchiſedech , in
quo huius rei futuræ figura præceſſerat,diſcerneret ſacerdotium Chriſti, à ſacerdotio Leui, vi
dete ergo (inquit) qualis hic eſt , cui & decimam partem Abraham dedit de primitijs,
Patriarcha.* A place moſt woorthie diligent conſideracion.For when by Melchiſedech,in whom the figure of the thing to come went before, he wolde
diſcern the preiſthood of Chryſt,from the preiſthoode of Leui,See therfore
(ſaieth he)what maner of man this ys,vnto whom Abraham the Patriarke
gaue the tithes of his firſt fruites.

But forſomoche as here ys no controuerſie, but that *Melchiſedech* ys a figure of Chryſt, and of Chryſts preiſthood, I will not trauaill here,nor hinder the reader with allegacion of manie doctours,vntill we come to the
handling of the Prophecie,whiche ſhall aunſwer the figure according to the
ordre,which I haue vſed in other figures heretofore brought furthe, for the
declaracion and ſetting furthe of other miſteries of Chryſt. But I ſhall go on
to bringe in an other figure of the lawe of nature. F

THE FOVRTENE CHAPITER DECLARETH,
*after the minde of Chryſoſtom, that Iob was a figure of Chryſte, for the
deſire his ſeruantes had to eate his fleſh.*

Iob. 31.
Deſire of
the eating
of the fleſh
of Iob ap-
plied to the
deſire to
eate Chry-
ſtes fleſh.

I N Iob we do read,that the men of his owne houſholde ſhould
ſaie:*Quis det de carnibus eius, vt ſaturemur?* Who ſhall geue vs of his
fleſh , that we maie be fylled or ſatisfied ? or as the common
tranſlation ys, Who ſhall let vs haue our bellies full of hys
fleſh?

As they that were of the houſholde of Iob,for the great loue they bare
vnto him, wolde euen haue eaten of his fleſh : So they that be of the
houholde of Chryſte,for the loue they beare to him , wolde eate of hys
fleſh.

Chryſo.in 6
Ioan.omel.
45.

The deſire of the eating of the fleſh of Chryſte,Chryſoſtome applieth to
the deſire of thoſe that were of the houſholde of Iob,whiche deſired to eate
the fleſh of Iob,as a thinge figuringe or ſignifienge the eatinge of Chriſtes
fleſh,thus ſaieth he:*Vt autem non ſolùm per dilectionem,ſed reipſa in carnem illam con* G
*uertamur,per cibum id efficitur, quem nobis largitus eſt. Cum enim ſuum in nos amorem
indicare vellet,per corpus ſuum ſe nobis commiſcuit, & in vnum nobiſcum redegit, vt corpus cum capite vniretur.Hoc enim amantium maximè eſt. Hoc Iob ſignificabat de ſeruis,
à quibus maximè amabatur,qui ſuum amorem præ ſe ferentes dicebant : Quis daret nobis,
vt eius carnibus impleremur?Quod Chriſtus fecit,vt maiori nos charitate aſtringeret, & vt
ſuum in nos oſtenderet deſiderium,non ſe tantùm videri permittens deſiderantibus , ſed &
tangi,et manducari,et dentes carni ſuæ infigi,et deſiderio ſui omnes impleri. Ab illa igitur
menſa tanquam leones ignem ſpirantes ſurgamus, Diabolo formidoloſi , et caput noſtrum
intelligamus,et quam in nos præ ſe tulit charitatem.Parentes ſæpenumerò liberos ſuos alijs
alendos dederunt:ego autem mea carne alo,me ijs exhibeo,omnibus faueo,omnibus optimam
de futuris ſpem præbeo.Qui in hac vita ita ſe nobis exhibet,multo magis in futura . Veſter
ego frater eſſe volui,et communicaui carnem propter vos, et ſanguinem , et per quæ vobis
coniunctus ſum,ea rurſum vobis exhibui.*

*Chryſt and
we ioined
two maner
of waies.*

That we ſhould be turned into that fleſh (ſpeaking of the fleſh of
Chryſte)not by loue onelie, but in verie dede, *yt ys doen by the meat whiche
he hath graunted vs.*For when he wolde ſhewe his loue to vs , he mixed him- H
ſelf with vs by hys bodie, and made himſelf one with vs, that the head
might be vnited with the bodie. This did Iob ſignifie by his ſeruantes , of
whom he was greatlie beloued , whiche declaring their loue, did ſaie:
Who

A Who will geue vs of his flesh that we maie be filled: The which thing Christ did, that with a more greater charitie and loue he might bind vs to him, and also that he might shewe his desyre that he had to vs, he doth not onelie suffer him self to be seen of these that desire him, but also *to be touched, and eaten, and their teeth to be fastned in his flesh*, and them all to be filled with the desyre of him. Let vs therfore rise from that table as lions breathing oute fyre, being fearfull to the Deuell, and let vs consider our head, and what charitie he hath declared vnto vs. Parentes oftentimes haue deliuered their children vnto other to be fedde. But I do feade with my *owne flesh.* Vnto these I exhibit and geue my self. I loue and fauour all, I geue a good hope to all of thinges to come. He that thus exhibiteth and geueth himself to vs in this life, moche more he will geue himself to vs in the life to come. I wolde be your brother, And I tooke flesh and bloode with yowe, for your sakes. And by what thinges I was ioined to yow, the same again I geue to yowe. Thus moche Chrysostome.

Chrisst geueth himselfe to be toched, and eaten in the Sacramēt.

B In the which sentence, that thinges woorthie of note be not with to moche negligence ouerpassed, yt ys to be obserued, that this learned Father (besyde the declaraeion of the ardente loue of Christe toward vs, for the which he did vouchsaif to geue vs *his verie flesh to eate*, to the entēt we should be turned into yt, as the seruantes of Iob, who for ther great loue vnto him, desired to eate his flesh, that they might be all one with hym, whiche verie well signified the mutuall loue of Chryst and hys seruantes, He for loue geuing his flesh to be eaten, and they desiering through loue to eate the same) in the beginning of the sentence also saieth, that to the entent we shoulde be ioined to Chryste, not onelie by loue, but by the thing yt self in verie dede, that ys hrought to passe by the meat which he hath graunted vs.

we be ioined to Chrisst.two waies.

In the which woordes yt ys verie euident that we are ioined to Chryste two maner of waies, that ys by loue, and by the thing yt self. Which in other termes ys called spirituallie, and reallie. Spirituallie we are ioined to Chryste by charitie and faith, and therby incorporated to hys mystical bodie: Reallie or substanciallie we are ioined to him, when by eating hys verie substanciall flesh in the Sacrament, *the substance of oure flesh ys turned into the substance of his flesh*, and therby so ioined to him, as we are made one flesh with him, of the which we will speake more at large, whē we shal come to the sentence of S. Hilary.

Oure flesh ys turned into the flesh of Christ by receipt of the Sacrament.

Here by the waie note that Chrystes flesh ys not disgested in our bodies after the maner of naturall disgestion of otheir meates, and so passeth through the bodie accordinglie, as the Stercoranites of our tyme haue blasphemed. But as the meate ys celestiall, and yet substanciall, and not nowe proprelie terrestriall, being a glorified bodie and flesh: So yt draweth vs vppewarde to yt, conuerting and turning vs into yt, according to the nature of a celestiall thing, and not terrestriallie depressing vs to the earthward.

Chrisstes flesh ys not digestedin vs as other meates.

But principallie to the cheif entent and pourpose of the thinge that this part of the sentence moueth vs to note, Marke that, where the Sacramentaries of our time wolde haue none other receauing of Ghrystes bodie, but onelie a spirituall receauing: this holie Father teacheth vs, the faithe of Chrystes Churche in his time, whiche was before anye controuersie or heresie was rysen aboute the Sacrament, that we be ioined to Chryste

Stercoranites of our time.

C

D

G ij not

not onelie fpirituallie by loue (which maie be and ys doen withoute the re- E
ceipt of meate) But we are alfo ioined to Chryfte, *reipfa*, that ys, by the
thing yt felf, or in verie deed, by the receipt of a certain meate. And therfor
he faieth: *Id efficitur per cibum, quem nobis largitus eft*, This ioining of vs to Chryft
in verie dede, ys brought to paffe by the meate, whiche he hath graunted vs.

What the meate ys he openeth mediatelie when he faieth: that he might

Chrift ys ioined to vs corporallie by oure re- ceipt of hys bodie in the Sacrament

declare his loue towarde vs. *Per corpus fuum fe nobis commifcuit*. He hath myn-
gled him felf to, or with vs *by his bodie*. So his bodie then ys the meat, wherbie, when we receaue yt, we are in verie deed ioined to Chryfte.

That this was his minde he liuelie declareth, applieng the ftorie of Iob, as a
thing fignifieng this matter, in the whiche the feruantes of Iob defiered in
verie dede, to eate his verie flefh, reallie, and fubftanciallie, and not fpiritual
lie onelie.

Whiche thinge yet more manifeftlie he openeth in the ende of the fen-

Chrift ge- ueth vs the fame flesh by which he was ioi- ned to vs.

tence, fpeaking in the perfon of Chryfte and fainge: I wolde be your brother, F
and for your fakes, I did take flefh and bloode with yowe, And the fame thin
ges (*that ys to faie flesh and bloode*) by the which I was ioined to yowe, I gaue to
yowe again.

Note that Chryfte geueth vs thofe thinges in the facramēt by the which
he was ioined to vs. He was ioined to vs by verie fubftancial flefh and blood,
wherfore he geueth vs verie fubftanciall flefh and bloode. Yf he fhoulde geue
him felf to vs onelie fpirituallie, then he fhould not geue vs thofe thinges, by
the whiche he was ioined to vs. For Chriftes flefh and blood fpirituallie, and
his flefh and blood fubftanciallie or reallie, be as farre different as flefh and
fpirite.

Albeit this Authour hath declared that, that was fpoken by me as concer
ning the eating of the flefh of Chryfte figured by Iob, and therto added o-
ther fentences moft euidentlie declaring the veritie of Chryftes bodie and
blood in the Sacramēt: Yet, that ye maie perceaue in him bothe conftancie,
and confonancie, in vttering the fubftāciall poinctes of our faith, I fhall bring
in one other place of the fame, wher he handeleth the fame place of Iob to G
the pourpofe before mencioned. *Medio draconis ventre rupto atq; difcerpto, ex*

Chryf. in 10 1. Cor. o- mel. 24.

adytis clarifsimus euafit, & radios non ad hoc vfque cœlum, fed ad ipfum fupernum thro-
num dimifit. Illuc namque ipfum extulit, quod nobis etiam exhibuit, & vt teneremus, et mā
ducaremus, quod maximum dilectionis fignum eft. Quos enim amamus, nonnunquàm etiam
morfu petimus. Quare Iob, vt feruorū in fe amorē oftenderet, dicebat illos nimio in fe amore
dixiffe: Quis det de carnibus eius vt faturemur? Ita & Chriftus fuam carnē dedit nobis, vt
ea faturemur . Quo nos in plurimum fui amorem allexit. The beallie of the dragon
being braft, and torne in the middle, frō the darke place he came furth moft
bright and clere, and fent oute his beames, not vnto this heauē, but vnto the
verie high Throne. Thyther hath he caried vppe that, which alfo he hath geuen vnto vs, that we fhoulde holde and eate yt, which ys the greateft token
of loue. For whome we loue, oftentimes we defire to byte. Therfor Iob, that
he might declare the loue of his feruantes towardes him, faied, that they for
the exceading loue, that they bare towards him, haue oftentimes faied: Who
will geue vs of his flefh, that we maie be filled? *Euen fo Chrift hath geuen vs hys*
flesh, that we might be fylled withal, wherbie he hath allured vs vnto his H
great loue.

In the which fentēce (gentle Reader) thow feift and perceaueft fyrft, howe
Chryfoftome reherfeth the ftorie of Iob, and fecondlie, how he applieth yt

vnto

A vnto Chryſt,ſaing:*Euen ſo Chriſt hath geuen vs his fleſh* to holde,and to eate.The which his applicaciō doth verifie my ſaing , that Iob was in this behalfa figure that Chriſtes fleſh ſhoulde be eaten,and that not ſpirituallie onelie, but reallie and ſubſtāciallie,which Chryſoſtome ſignifieth by this woorde (Ita,euen ſo)as who ſhould ſaie:As the very ſubſtanciall fleſh of Iob was de ſired to be eaten:Euen ſo *Chryſt hath geuen vs his verie ſubſtanciall fleſh to be eaten.*

Thus am I not onelie moued to vnderſtand Chryſoſtō for the cauſe now mencioned:But I am therunto compelled by that,that in him immediatelie foloweth:*Ad eum igitur cum feruore accedamus, & dilectione quàm vehementiſsima, ne grauius ſubeamus ſupplicium.Quanto enim maius beneficium accepimus,tanto magis pu-niemur,quando eo indigni apparebimus.*Let vs therfore come vnto him with feruēt

deſire,and moſte vehement loue,leſte we ſuffer more greuouſe puniſhment. For the more great benefet we haue receaued, the more ſhall we be puni-ſhed,yf we be fownde vnwoorthie of yt.And he addeth: *Hoc corpus in præſepi reueriti ſunt Magi,&c.*This bodie did the wiſe men reuerence or honour in

B the maunger.Wherby he declareth what bodie of Chryſt he moueth vs to come vnto,here in this his concluſion.Wherbie alſo we maie vnderſtande, what fleſh of Chryſte he ment in the former ſentence,by the applicacion of the figure to the thing figured.But this maie ſuffice for the figures in the law of nature.

THE FIFTENE CHAPITER DECLARETH BY
ſcripturs,that the eating of the Paſchall lambe was a figure of the eating of Chryſt our Paſchall Lambe.

OWe that I haue ſpoken of ſoche ſcriptures, as declare ſoche thinges to haue ben doen in the law of nature, which by other ſcriptures,and holie Fathers,are applied and taken,as figures of Chryſtes preiſthood and myſterie:I will go forwarde to the fi-gures in the time of the lawe of Moyſes,of the which I will ſpea

ke and treact of foure , whiche be figures of this myſterie. Which be : The

C Paſchall Lambe , Manna , The Shewbread , and the Stone flowing oute water.

Of the fyrſt,that ys of the Paſchall Lābe we read thus:In the tenth daie of this moneth euery mā ſhall take vnto him a lambe,accordinge to their hou-ſes and families,&c.And let the lambe of yours be withoute blemiſh,a male of a yeare olde , whiche ye ſhall take oute from emonge the Shepe,and ye ſhall kepe him vntill the xiiij. daie of the ſame moneth. And euery man of the multitude of the children of Iſraell ſhall kill him at euen. And they ſhall take the bloode,and ſtrike yt on the two ſyde poſtes , and on the vpper doer poſte,euen in the houſes wher they ſhall eate hym. And they ſhall eate the fleſh that ſame night roſted with fyre , and with vnleauened bread,and with ſowre herbes they ſhall eate yt. See that ye eate not therof rawe,nor ſoddē in water, but roſted with fyre,the head,feet and purtenaūce therof.

In this declaracion of the maner, of eating the Paſchall Lambe , ther be

D two principall partes.The one ys of the killinge of yt : The other of the ea-tinge of yt.

The condicion and maner of the lambe , and the killing of the ſame,fi-gureth the condicion of Chryſte , and the crucifyeng of hym . And al-beit that other beaſtes being taken to be ſacrificed , as oxe , cowe, calf,

and kilde,did figure the pafsion of Chryfte:Yet none of thefe doth fo liue- **E**
lie,and expreffedlie figure Chryfte and hys death,as the lambe dothe. For

Chrift and the Paf-chall lambe compared together.

the lambe was but younge:Chryft was but younge. The lambe was withoute blemifh:Chryfte was withoute finne . The lambe was taken from e-
monge the fhepe : Chryfte from emonge hys Apoftles.   By the offringe
of that lambe , the people of Ifraell were deliuered from the feruitute of
Aegypte:By the offringe of Chryft the people are deliuered from the feru-
tude of the deuell and finne. Their daile facrifice was a lambe: Owre daile

Chrift mo-re often cal led a Labe then by na-me of anie other beaft

facrifice ys Chryfte. And for this confideracion Chryft ys more oftentymes called a lambe in the fcripture,then by the name of other beaftes,which
were facrificed,and figured Chryft the euerlafting facrifice.

Joan.1.

Wherfore faincte Ihon the Baptift applieng the figure of the lambe , as
a thing moft fpeciallie and fullie figuring Chryfte , pointed him , with his
fyngar , fainge . *Ecce Agnus Dei , ecce qui tollit peccata mundi* . Beholde the
Lambe of God , beholde him that taketh awaie the finnes of the
woorlde.   **F**

The Prophet alfo calleth him a lambe : *Tanquam ouis ad occifionem duce-*

Efai.53.

tur , & tanquam agnus coram tondente fe obmutefcit . He fhall be led awaie
like a fhepe to be flain , and as a lambe before the fherer fhall he holde hys
peace?

For like confideracion fainct Ihon being inftructed by the reuelacion of the holie Goft,dothe fo call him after he had fulfilled the figure by
fuffring of his pafsion . I beheld (faieth he) and lo, a great multitude,

Apoca. 7.

whiche no man coulde nombre of all nacions,people,and tounges ftood
before the feat,and before the Lambe, cloathed in long white garmentes,
and palmes in their handes. And they cried with a Loude voice , fainge:
Saluacion be afcribed vnto him,that fitteth on the Seate of our lorde God,
and vnto the lambe which Lambe ys Chryfte.

Apocal 5.

Of whome again he faieth by plain woordes : I beheld and lo , in the
middeft of the feate,and of the foure beaftes,and in the middeft of the elders
ftoode a lambe,as though he hadde ben killed. And when he had taken the
booke,the foure beaftes,and the xxiiij.elders fell down before the labe,and **G**
with inftrumentes fang a newe fonge,faing:Thow arte woorthie to take the
booke,and open the fcales therof.For thow was killed and haueft redemed
vs with thy bloode.

But forafmoche as this parte of the figure,namely the pafsion of Chrifte,
ys allreadie treacted of,and of this ther ys no controuerfie : I fhall diuert me
to fpeake of the other parte of the figure,which ys of the eatinge of the lam-
be.Whiche figureth the eatinge of our Pafchall lambe,in the inftitucion of
the newe pafsouer . And of yt alfo , nowe fo frequented and vfed in the
churche of the fame Lambe our Sauiour Chrifte,and that by his commandement,whervpon ftandeth nowe the controuerfie.

In this matter to make a comparifon:As the lambe killed, was a figure of
Chrifte verelie killed:So the fame lambe being verilie eaten , ys a figure of
Chrift verilie eaten.As the Lambe was eaten reallie and fubftanciallie:So ys
Chrifte eaten reallie and fubftanciallie.

That the eating of this lambe was a figure of the eating of Chrift our
lambe in his laft Supper,Chrift himfelf doth wittneffe, who fpeaking of the **H**
verie Pafchall Lambe faied : *Defiderio defideraui hoc Pafcha manducare vobifcum*

Luc.22.

antequam patiar I haue Inwardlie defiderd to eate this Pafouer with yowe
before that I fuffer.

This

A   This was not fpoken of the olde pafouer, whiche he had eaten with them before, but of the newe, whiche was figured by yt, whiche he entred immediatelie to inftitute, to anfwere the figure and to fullfill the Scripturs.

Therfore fainte Paule confidering bothe the principall partes of the figure the lambe, that he muft be bothe offred in facrifice, and alfo eaten, applieth them bothe vnto Chrifte, and ioineth the together, fainge : *Pafcha noftru immolatus eft Chriftus, itaque epulemur.* Chrifte our pafouer ys offered vppe for vs(behold here the facrifice)Therfore lett vs eate(note here the eating of Chrift)For as the lambe that was offred for the paffouer, was alfo eaten : So Chrift (as fainte Paule faieth) was alfo offred vppe for our paffouer,therfor let vs eate. The fame lambe that was offred for the figure was eaten : The fame Chrifte that was offred to anfwer the figure, was and ys eaten.

And for further probacion of his matter, note that in good thinges, the thing figured ys better, then the thing, that ys the figure. And cotrarie wyfe
B   the figure in euell thinges ys better, then the thing figured. Or more proprelie and trulie to faie: In euell thinges the thing figured ys woorfe then the thing, whiche ys the figure. As for example firft of this latter, that we maie with the other procead.

King Pharao tirannouflie reigning ouer the children of Ifraell. ys a figure ofthe Deuell tirannouflie reiginge ouer finfull men, and with holdinge them from the due feruice of God. The feruitude, that the childeren of Ifraell were in, ys a figure of the feruitude of finne that man was in.

The bretheren of *Iofeph* confpiring the fale of him, were a figure of *Iudas,* and the Iewes confpiring the like matter againft Chrifte.

In the whiche, as in other of like forte, ye maie note and preceaue, that Pharo being the figure of the deuell, and the feruitude of Egipte, being the figure of the feruitude of finne, And the bretheren of Iofeph being the figure of Iudas and the Iewes, the thinges figured are woorfe, then the figures. For the Deuell the thing figured, ys woorfe, then Pharao the figure. The feruitude of finne being the thing figured, ys woorfe then the feruitude of
C   Egipte being the figure. Iudas and the Iewes confpiring againft our Sauiour Chrifte being the thinges figured, are woorfe, then the bretheren of Iofeph being the figure. So fhall ye finde in all other figures of the olde lawe of thinges that be not good, that the thing figured ys allwaies woorfe, then the thing that ys the figure.

But as for goodthinges, the thing figured ys better, then the thing that ys the figure. As for example : Abraham ys a figure of God the Father, Ifaac a figure of Chrift Gods fonne : God the Father and Chrift his fonne, the thinges figured,are withoute comparifon better, then the thinges that be the figures.

The rodde of Aaron, and the bloffomme of the fame, are figures of the virgen Marie, and Chrift the bloffome of the fame. The Brafen Serpent vpon the pole ys a figure of Chrifte vpon the croffe. Ionas in the beallie of the whall, a figure of Chrifte in the heart of the earth : In euerie of thefe, the thinges figured be better, then the thing that ys the figure, as by com-
D   parifon ye maie perceaue.

Nowe then to the pourpofe: As the Pafchall Lambe beind offered was a figure of Chrifte offred: So the lambe eaten, ys a figure of Chrift by vs eate. Wherfore as Chrifte offred being the thing figured, ys better then the lambe offred being the figure: So of confequence muft the paffeouer figured

August in Pfal 77: Figures in good thinges not fo god, as the thinges figured : Figures in euell thinges not fo euell.

Paffouer of the Chriftians more excellent then the Paffouer of the Iewes.

being eaten, be better then the paſſouer, the figure whiche was eaten. Yf **E** the paſſeouer, which ys nowe eaten, be but a peice of bread, a bare ſigne, or figure (as the Sacramentaries do affirme) then the Paſchall lambe ys the figure of a peice of bread, which bread in ſpecial thinges hath no ſimilitude, to anſwer the figure, as all thinges figured doo. And ſo alſo ſhall not the thing figured in the newe Teſtament, be better, then the figure, whiche ys in the olde teſtament, whiche maie not be.

But that the Reader, that hath ben ſeduced and drawen from the catholique faith, conceaue no ſiniſtre opinion of me, and thinke that I go aboute to deceaue him with rules of mine owne inuencion, as thinges feigned beſides the Scriptures : Let the ſame vnderſtande, that this rule: that thinges figured be better, then the figures, as ys aboue declared, ys not the dreame of mine own head, but a ſubſtanciall trueth grownded vpon the ſure foundacion of Gods woorde. I meen vpon the cheif argument of Saincte Paules epiſtle to the Hebrues. For what dothe ſaincte Paule in that epiſtle trauaill to proue more, than that Chriſte, and the newe Teſtament, and all thinges **F** therin conteyned, doo farre excell *Melchiſedech*, Moiſes, and the olde Teſtament, and all the ceremonies and ſacrifices of the ſame.

Argumẽt of S. Pauls epiſtle to the Hebr.

As firſt, in the firſt chapter he declareth the excellencie of the newe Teſtament aboue the olde, for that yt was geuen by Chriſte the Sonne of God, by whome God ſpake to vs, who excelleth Angels, Fathers, and Prophetes, by the whiche God ſpake in the olde Teſtament as ther he proueth.

Heb. 1.

Thẽ after he declareth Chriſte to be a preiſt, after the ordre of *Melchiſedech*. But he proueth him to be farre more excellent, then *Melchiſedech*.

Ibid. 7.

This doen he deſcendeth to the preiſt of the olde lawe, and comparinge the officie of Chriſte to the office of the preiſt of the lawe, and teaching yt to be vnperfecte, proueth the office of Chriſte by all meanes to be preferred.

Ibid. 8.
Ibid. 9.

Then he maketh mencion in a brief reherſall of the religion, and high ſeruice of Goſt among the Iewes, teaching, that they hadde a fore Tabernacle, and what thinges ther were within conteined. And alſo a ſeconde Ta- **G** bernacle, whiche was called. *Sanctum ſanctorũ*, and what was therin conteined, with their Ceremonies, ſeruices, and Sacrifices doen in eche of thoſe.

Which doẽ, he cõpareth the high preiſt to the high preiſt, Tabernacle to tabernacle, Sacrifice to Sacrifice, blood to blood, effecte of blood to effect of blood, clenſing ãd purifieng, to clenſing, ãd purifieng holy place, to holie place, and allwaies according to his principall entẽt, and argument, proueth all the figured things of the newe Teſtament, to be farre better then their figu res in the olde Teſtament. And finalie, to conclude and knitte vppe all the wholl diſputacion of the olde Teſtament withe one woorde, he ſaieth: *Vm_ bram habens Lex futurorum bonorum, non ipſam imaginem rerum &c*. The Lawe hathe but a ſhadow of good thinges to cõme, and not the veric faſhion of the thinges them ſelues.

Heb. 10. The olde la we had but the ſhad - dowes : the newe lawe hath the ve rie thinges

In the whiche woordes, as yt were in a brief, he deſcribeth the condicion and ſtate of bothe lawes, whiche ys, that the olde lawe hathe the figures of good thinges, and the newe lawe hath the good thinges them ſelues.

By the whiche proceſſe yt ys not onelie euident, and proued, that the **H** thinges figured be better, then the figure: But alſo by this laſt concluſion of ſaincte Paule yt ys improued, that the thinges of the newe Teſtament ſhoulde be but bare figures. But they are in dede the good thinges (as he

dothe

A doth terme thē) and the verie thinges of the figures and fhadowes, whiche haue gon before in the olde Teftament,

Wherbie alfo I maie conclude. that the Sacrament of Chriftes bodie and blood (being according to Chriftes inftitution confecrated to be offred and receaued in the memoriall of Chriftes paffion and death: being alfo as *Diony-* *fius Areopagita in his ecclefiafticall Hierarchie faieth, Omnium facramentorum confum-* *matifsimum & auguftifsimum*, of all Sacramentes moft perfecte, and nobleft, withoute the whiche no miniftracion almoft fhoulde de doen, but that this diuine Sacrament fhould ende yt) ys not a bare figure, as the Pafchall lābe, being the figure of this, was: but ys the verie good thing in dede, that ys, the verie bodie and bloode of owre immaculate Pafchall Lābe of the newe Teftament figured by that Pafchall Lambe of the olde Teftament. For ells the figure fhoulde not be a figure of a good thing (as faincte Paule faieth) but the figure fhoulde be the figure of a bare figure, whiche ys inconue-nient, and againft faincte Paule, and againft the worthineffe of the newe

B Teftamente, and the excellencie of the fame, whiche in a great parte con-fifteth in the Sacramentes, whiche haue the verie thinges, and trueth of the figures and Shadowes of the olde Teftament.

And albeit, I haue (as yt femeth to me, and fo, I trufte, yt appeareth to anie right chriftian reader) fufficientlie proued by the Scriptures, that the Pafchall Lambe eaten, was a figure of owre Pafchall Lambe Chrifte eatē in the Sacrament: yet left anie man maliciouftie maie cauille, faing that I haue vfed the Scriptures at my owne pleafure, and wrefted them to my owne phantafie, and perchaunce that fome weake man maie be better fatif-fied, I will reforte to the Parliament houfe of Chriftes Churche, and learn of them whiche ys the verie trueth determined and enacted, approued, and receaued ther.

Dionyf. Ec-
cle. Hie-
rarch.
Parte. 3.

THE SIXTENE CHAPITER TEACHETH THIS
matter by Tertullian and Ifychius.

C Nd firft for the applicacion of the figure of the Pafchall Lambe to the thinge figured : I will conferre with Tertullian a man of great learninge. Who alfo ys fo anncient, that he ys of fome accompted the eldeft writer of the latin churche. He was verie neare to the time of the Apoftles, aboute the 166. yeare after Chrift. Whome faincte Cyprian fo highlie efteemed, that no daie paffed, in the whiche Tertullian was not in his hande, and fome parte of him redde.

This man being a noble man of Chriftes Parlament houfe, can certifie vs, what was enacted and receaued as a truthe through oute all the houfe of Chrifte in his tyme. Therfore we will heare what he faieth in this matter. He did write againft one Marcion an heretike, and in that booke he faieth thus: *Profeffus itaque fe concupifcentia concupifcere edere Pafcha vt fuum (indignū enim vt quid alienum concupifceret Deus) acceptum panem, & diftributum difcipulis, corpus fuū illum fecit.* Therfore when he had openlie faied, that with defire he had de-fiered to eate the paffouer as his own paffouer (for yt was vnmete that God

D fhould defire anie ftraung thing) *he made that bread*, that he did take and diftri-bute to his difciples, *his bodie*.

Tertu. li.4
cont. Mar-
cion.

Remembre (gentle Reader) what ys before faied, that the Pafchall Lābe of the olde lawe, as touching that, that he was offred, was a figure of the
oblaciō

oblacion of our Lambe Chrift, whiche ys withoute all controuerfie : But **E**
whether the eating of the lambe reallie, and fubftanciallie did figure, that
Chrifte our Pafchall Lambe fhoulde be eaten reallie, and fubftanciallie in
the Sacrament, ys the verie controuerfie. Wherin what this auncient man
of Chriftes Parliament houfe hath faied, yowe haue heard.

In the whiche his faing yf yowe haue noted, yowe maye preceaue, that
he maketh mencio of two paffouers : One that was not proprelie his, which
he did not fo earneftlie defire to eate : An other that was proprelie his owne,
whiche he did earneftlie defire to eate. Wherbie he toucheth the the figuratiue Paffouer, and the true paffouer. What the true Paffouer ys, he plainlie declareth when he faieth : The bread that he did take, and diftribute to
his difciples, *he made his bodie.*

Heretiqs barck againft the trueth as dogges do againft the Moone.

I can not contein but to breake, oute to declare, that I do not a litle
wonder to fee the obftinate blindneffe of the enemies of Gods trueth, that
hearing and feing fo manifeft, fo plain, and fo cleare a fentence, fpoken and
vttered withoute anie confufe, or obfcure tearmes, breiflie knitte, and com- **F**
pacte, withoute anie long ambages, hearing will not heare, and feing will
not fee, but wilfullie will be blinde, and not vnderftande, and yet maliciouftie barke againft the clear light, whiche they can not extinguifh, As the
dogges doo againft the Moone, whiche they can not vanquifh. But lett the
brak as long as they lift, *Veritas Domini manet in æternum.* The trueth of our

Pfalm 116

Lorde abideth for euer. To the whiche God geue them grace to turne.

But let the true Chriftian heare and marke what enacted and receaued
truth was in the parliament houfe of Chriftes Churche, nowe opened and
teftified by the Auncient elder of the fame, whiche ys that Chrifte made
the bread, which he did take, and diftribute to his difciples, his bodie.

Heretiqs build tehir faith vpon reafon and fenfes.

whiche was, and ys the true Pafcall Lambe, figured by the olde Pafchall
lambe. And by this let him coforte him felf, in the true faith that the hath
receaued, ad cofirme him felf to be mightie againft all the affauts of herefie,
how moche fo euer their fainges fhall delight, or pleafe reafon, or the knowe
ledge of our fenfes, wherpon they do fo builde their faith, that they wolde
haue no poincte ne parte therof directlie repugnant to reafon, or Iudgment **G**
of fenfe, as Cranmer, or the Authour of that booke, which ys fett furth in
his name, with moche boldeneffe affirmeth,

Cranmers fenfuall fentence Li. 2.

Whofe verie woordes for the triall, I will afcribe. Thus fhall ye ther
read : But to conclude in fewe woordes, the Papiftes fhal neuer be able to
fhewe one article of our faith, fo directlie contrarie to our fenfes, that all our
fenfes by daile experience fhall affirme a thinge to be, And yet our faith
fhall teache vs the contrarie therunto. Thus he.

In whiche faing (gentle Reader) yowe maie perceaue that thefe fenfuall
men were fo moche captiue to fenfuall knowledge, that not cotent to haue
faith a knowledge aboue, or at lefte equall with reafon, whiche in dede fur

Faith fur- mounteth reafon, or fenfes.

mounteth, and paffeth all reafon, wolde abafe her to be an hand maiden to
the knowledge of our fenfes, as one that fhoulde teach no article contrarie
to them, which yet teacheth all aboue the knowledge of fenfes, and moche
directlie contrarie. As for example.

Owre fenfes by dailie experiece teach vs that men do die. And that fome

Faith teac- heth many thinges con trarie to the fenfes.

of their bodies being burned, ther ys nothing lefte but Afhes blowe abro- **H**
ad with the winde. And fome confumed of the foules of the aire : Some of
the fifhes of the fea : Some vtterly doo putrifie in the earth, as thinges that
fhoulde neuer be the fame flefh, the fame fubftance, the fame man again.

And

A And yet faith teacheth vs directlie contrarie. that ys, that the thing which the senses Iudge to be dead, whiche ys so diuided and separated from life, that yt shall neuer liue, the same thing in nombre again, that in dede yt ys not dead, but sleapeth, and shall be the same in person again that yt was before.

The senses taught none other but that the woundes whiche Christe had in his bodie after the resurrection, and specially the wounde of his side, into the which he willed Thomas to pute his hande, were verie sore and painfull: and yet faith saieth directlie contrarie. For a glorified bodie yt not passible.

Thus these men building ther faith vpon their senses, when their senses perished, their sensuall faith preished with all, Wherfor cleaue not to soche a faith whiche neadeth to be mainteined with vntruthe, and false sensuall knowledge. But embrace that faith, whiche ys grownded vpon Christ, and lined oute, and tried by the sure and streight piller of truthe the Catholique B Churche.

But perchaunce the Aduersarie will saie, that although the sentence of Tertullian for so moche as I haue brought in, sowndeth plainlie to my pourpose: yet yf I had brought in the wholle sentéce, yt wolde haue ouerthrowé the same. Wherfore I deale not sincerelie, but vse crafte. To this I saie, that this, that ys alleadged oute of Tertulliã, ys his verie saing, ãd neadeth no dependence to make yt perfecte, but ys of yt self a perfecte propofition, and therfore hath yn yt self a trueth, or falshood, and maie then well be alleaged to confirme my pourpose. *Obiection out of Tertull.*

And yet I haue not so omitted yt, as though I wolde not see yt, but I haue reserued yt to be handled, wher we shall seke the exposition of his texte: *Hoc est corpus meum.*

But that we maie perceaue in the meã while, that Tertullian in his place minded no other wise, then these his woordes alleaged pourporte (*I meen that Chrifts bodie ys made present in the Sacrament, aud in the same geuen, and dipensed*) I shall bring himself to wittnesse in an other place, wher he testifieth, that C the flesh, that ys to saie, the naturalman eateth the bodie of Christ: *Caro (inquit) abluitur, vt anima emaculetur. Caro vngitur, vt anima consecretur. Caro signatur, vt anima muniatur. Caro corpore & sanguine vescitur, vt anima de Deo saginetur.* The flesh (saith Tertullian) ys washed, that the Soule maie be pourged. The flesh ys enoynted, that the soule maie be consecrated. The flesh ys signed, that the soule maie be defended. *The flesh eateth the bodie and bloode of Chrifte*, that the soule maie be made fatte, or lustie in God. Thus Tertullian. *Note that the flesh eateth the bodie and blood of Chryst.*

In the whiche woordes he teacheth, that as verilie, as we be washed with verie water, and enointed with verie oile, and signed with the verie signe of the crosse, and not with the figures of these : So be we fedde with the *verie bodie and blood of our Sauiour Chrifte*, and not with the figures of them. *The flesh (saieth he) eateth the bodie, and blood of Chrift*, and not the spirit onlie. Nowe then that yowe haue heard one of the one side of the parliamét house, yowe shall heare one of the other side.

Iyschius an aunciente author, Disciple to the great learned father Gregorie Na- D ziancen. saieth thus: *Non oportet eos, qui Pascha euangelicum celebrant, quod nobis tradidit Ecclesia, legale Pascha peragere, quod bouem, & ouem, legislator dicens, significauit, quia hæc præcepit Moises in die Pascha, quod traditum est Iudæis immolare.* They, that doe celebrate the euangelicall Passouer, whiche the Churche hath deliuered vs, maie not celebrate the legall Passouer, whiche the lawegeuer comma- *Iyschius in Le. lib. 6. cap. 22.*

commaunding, hath declared to be an oxe and a shepe. For Moises hath E
commaunded to offer these thinges in the daie of the passeouer, that ys appointed to the Iewes.

And a litle after foloweth : *Non ergo oportere nos, habentes in manibus, & con-
summantes verum mysterium, sequi figuras, quæ prædicta sunt, demonstrant. Neque enim
est eiusdem temporis, Sed aliud quidem pertinere ad figuram, aliud autem ad veritatem,
qui vtraque sanciuit, præcepit. Propter quod & Christus primùm celebrauit figuratum
Pascha. Post cænam autem intelligibilem tradit, & angustante eam tempore, pro die horâ
immutauit, vel magis etiam diem. Sic enim ad vesperam quartæ decimæ diei cæna Iudaicæ
Paschalis festiuitatis celebratur. Post hoc autè Christus propriam tradidit cænam.* The thin
ges therfore, which are afore saied, doe declare, that we, hauing present,
and doinge the true misterie, maie not folowe figures. Neither ys yt apperteining to the same time. But he that ordeined both, commaunded one time
to appertein to the figure, an other time to the veritie. Wherfore Crist also
did first celebrate the figuratiue passeouer, but after supper *he deliuered the intelligible Supper,* and the time straicting the same, he chaunged an howre for a F
daie, or raither also the daie. For so in the euening of the fourtenth daie,
the Supper of the Iewish Paschall solemnitie ys celebrated. And after this
Christe deliuered his owne Supper. Thus farre Isychius.

In whose woordes yt maie be perceaued : first, what was the Iewish
Paschall offring, whiche was an oxe or à shepe, whiche were a figure of
Christ our Paschall oblation.

Secondlie, he teacheth, that we nowe hauing the true misterie, maie not
folowe figures. In whiche woordes note (gentle Reader) that he saieth that
we nowe haue the true misterie, wherby we are taught, that we haue in our
Paschall solemnitie, the verie or true presence of Christe. For he putteh
here this terme (*true misterie*) to answere the figuratiue presence in the figure. The figure hath but the shadowe of the thing, but that, that ys figured,
hath the thing yt self. The Paschall Lambe of the Iewes eaten in their Passouer, was a figure of Christ our Paschall lambe eaten in our Passouer. Wher
for, as the Iewes had a verie earthlie lambe, the figure, in their supper: So we
haue the verie heauenlie Lambe Christ, the truthe of that figure in our G
Supper.

*Verie
Christ in
oure Passo-
uer.*

Whiche thing this Authour in the woordes folowinge doth plainlie de-
clre. For (saieth he) one time serueth not for the figure, and the thing figured : but ther ys one time for the figure, an other time for the veritie. Note
then again that he calleth the thing figured the veritie. what ys the veritie,
but the verie thing in dede, that the figure did perfigurate? The lambe
the figure did perfigurate Christ : Wherfore *verie Christe ys in our passouer.*

This ys not fallen from this Authour as a thing vnwittinglie spoken, but
proceading aduisedlie in the matter, and applieng the thinge figurated, and
declaring the accomplishing of the thing by Christe, he saieth : Wherfore
Christ also did first celebrate the figuratiue Passouer. But after supper he deliuered the intelligible Supper.

What ys meat by the intelligible Supper, ye shall better perceaue by other
places of this Authour, wher he vseth this woorde, whiche he doth almost
in every leaf. As in his same chapiter, shewing wherof Aegipte ys a figure, he
saieth : *Et enim Ægyptus intelligibilis, præsens mundus, quia Ægyptus cõtenebratio inter* H
pretatur. The intelligible Aegipt ys this present worlde, For Aegipt, by interpretacion, ys called a darkning.

Likewise vpon this text of Leuiticus, wher Allmightie God saied to the
childrẽ

Paschal lã-
be ad christ
compared.

Isych. Ibid.

A children of Ifrael by Moyfes : When ye fhall come into the land, *Iebitic.23.* whiche I will geue vnto yowe, and reape downe the harueft therof, ye fhall bring a fheife of the firft frudts of your harueft vnto the preift, who fhall waue the fheife before the Lorde , to be accepted for yowe. Firft teaching who were figured by the fheiues he faieth : *Illi enim funt & Ific.li.6.* *mefſores,et intelligibiles fegetes,ad quos Dominus dicebat:Meſſis quidem multa , operarij* *ca.23.* *autē pauci,etc.*They be both the reapers,and the intelligible fheiues, to whom *Matth. 9.* our lord faid : The harueft trulie ys great, but the woorkmen , or reapers are fewe.

And likewife opening,who was figured by the preift, that fhoulde make their oblacion accepted of God for them,he faieth:*Manipulum autem primitia-* *rum intelligibilis facerdos Chriſtus,corpus proprium offerebat .* The intelligible preift Chryft did offer his owne bodie a fheif of firft fruidts.

Again in the fame chapiter vpon this text:And ye fhall offer that daie when ye waue the fheife an he lambe withoute blemifh,of a yeare olde, for B a burnt offring vnto the Lorde , he faieth : *Volens nos in die, qua celebramus* *Domini refurrectionem , et manipuli intelligibilem oblationem celebramus , non ob-* *liuifci dominici facrificij , ex quo nobis eſt oblatio manipuli : fed cædere agnum im-* *maculatum , anniculum , in holocauſtum Domino , intelligibilem agnum, Domini tra-* *ditionem immolantes myſticè,et offerentes,ipſius autem , vt facrificium cædentes , memo-* *riamfecit.* Owre Lorde willing vs, in the daie, wherin we do celebrate the refurrection of him , and do celebrate the intelligible oblacion of the fheif,not to forgett our Lordes facrifice,of the which we haue the oblacion of the fheif, but to offer vppe a lambe withoute fpotte of one yeare olde, for a burnt facrifice to our Lorde,myfticallie *facrificing , and offring the intelligi-* *ble lambe,being the tradicion of our Lorde,* in the doing of this facrifice , he hath made his memoriall.

In an other place alfo,wher almightie God faied:A man that hath finned *Ifich.li. 7.* through ignorance,and hath doen againft the lawe, and knoweth himfelf *ca.5.* giltie,fhall offer an vnfpotted Ramme vnto the preift : *Recte intelligibilis aries* *Chriſtus, huius peccatum,in facrificio pro eo oblatus,diluit.*Euen verie wel Chryfte the C intelligible ramme, being offred for him in facrifice, wipeth awaie the finne of this man.

In all thefe places, thefe woordes, the intelligible Egypte , the intelli- gible fheiues, the intelligible preift,the intelligible oblacion, the intelligi- ble lambe,the intelligible Ramme,what doe thefe ells fignifie , but the ve- rie thinges fhadowed,and fignified by the figures ? Wherby we maie con- clude by this authour,that the legall Supper , and the lambe therin eaten, were the figures of Chryftes Supper, and the lambe therin eaten beinge the verie thinges in dede , that ys *Chryſtes owne Supper , and hys owne* *bleſſed bodie ,* whiche ys the intelligible lambe , that was and ys therin eaten.

And that this fhall be fo plain , that the Aduerfarie fhall not againft faie *Leuit. 24.* yt , heare this Authour clerelie opening the matter . Expownding *Ifich in Le* howe Aaron,and hys children,were touched with the bloode of the Ram- *uit .li.2.* me,that was facrificed for them,and applieng yt to that,that yt was a figure *ca.8.* of,he faieth : *Sed tamen primus facerdos fanguine , & poſt eum filij eius fecundùm* D *legem vngebantur : quia ipfe Dominus primus in cæna myſtica intelligibilem accepit* *fanguinem , atque deinde calicem Apoſtolis dedit . Sed ecce legiſlator hic poſt* *vnctionem Aaron & filiorum fubdidit:De fanguine reliquum fudit fuper altari per cir-* *cuitum . Quod et Chriſtum feciſſe inuenimus . Bibens enim ipfe, et Apoſtolis bibere*

H   *dans,*

dans , tunc intelligibilem ſanguinem ſuper altare , videlicet ſuum corpus effudit . E
Corpus autem Chriſti, Eccleſia eſt, et omnis plebs eius . Quod ſpecialiter dicentem Marcum
inuenimus: Et ſumens, gratias agens, dedit eis, et biberunt ex eo omnes, et dixit eis : Hic eſt
ſanguis meus noui teſtamenti , qui pro multis effuſus eſt . But firſt the preiſt , and
after him his Sonnes were according to the lawe anoincted with blood.
For our Lorde him ſelf alſo firſt in the miſticall Supper , did *take the intelligi-*
*ble blood,*and then gaue the cuppe to hys Apoſtles But yet lo, this lawgeuer
after the enoincting of Aaron,and his ſonnes,ſaieth:The reſt of the blood he
powred rownde aboute vpon the Altar.Whiche thing alſo we finde Chryſt

to haue doen . For he drinking and geuing his Apoſtles to drinke , then
*he powred the intelligible bloode vpon the altar,*that ys to ſaie,vpon his bodie. The
bodie of Chryſt ys the Churche,and all his people.Whiche thinge we finde
Marke ſpeciallie ſainge.And he tooke the cuppe,and gaue thankes, and gaue
yt to them,and they all dranke of yt,and he ſaied vnto them : Thys ys my
blood of the newe Teſtament, whiche ys ſhedde for manie . Thus moche
Iſychius.　　　　　　　　　　　　　　　　　　　　　　　　　　　　　　F

I ſhall not nede to note any thing in this place of this Authour , wher

euery parte of his ſaieng ys ſo plain.Yt ys verie manifeſt,that he ſaieth , that
*Chriſt gaue vnto the Apoſtles his bloode,*whiche he calleth, as before ys declared,
*the intelligible bloode.*Which ys as moche to ſaie,as the bloode of Chryſt figured by the bloode of the lambe,and alſo of the Ramme offred for Aaron
ad his Sonnes.Whiche bloode(as Chryſoſtõ alſo together with this Author
wittneſſe)Chryſt himſelf,becauſe his Apoſtles beleuing yt verilie, according
to the woorde of their maſter,to be bloode,ſhoulde not therfore loathe to
drinke of yt,dranke firſt vnto them,and then dranke all they. Yf Chryſt dran
ke his owne blood,he dranke yt either ſpirituallie or corporallie. Spirituallie
he could not,wherfore he dranke yt corporallie.

As touching this wittnes of Chryſoſtome,more ſhall be ſaied in the ſe-

cond booke.And although this place conuinceth the Proclamer, who ſaith,
that we can not bringe anie one olde catholique Doctour or Father: Yet in
the thirde booke (ſhall be brought oute of this father diuerſe and many places,more plainlie teaching Gods truthe,then this doth . Wherfore leauing
him with his ioint felowe, who haue plainly teſtified Chryſtes verie preſen-　G
ce in the Sacrament ,for that the figure muſt be aunſwered by the verie
thing,and truthe,wherof yt ys the figure:I ſhall cal two other mo wittneſſes
to teſtifie the ſame.

THE SEVENTENE CHAPITER PROCEADETH
in the ſame matter by ſainct Cyprian, and Euthymius.

Aincte Cyprian martir,Biſhoppe of Carthage , a man in learninge,
and vertuouſe conuerſacion moſt excellent, and in propinquitie of
time to Chryſt,right aunciente,as *Euſebius* doth teſtifie,whom ſainct
Auguſtine in his workes doth moche reuerence,who liued aboute
256.yeares after Chryſte,whome I make to folowe emong the latines, Tertullian,for that he ſo moche eſteemed and loued him,as ys before ſaied , In　H
this matter he ſpeaketh after this ſorte.

Cœna itaque diſpoſita inter ſacramentales epulas , obuiarunt ſibi inſtituta noua , &
antiqua , & conſumpto agno , quem antiqua traditio proponebat , inconſumptibilem
cibum

A *cibum magifter apponit difcipulis. Nec iam ad elaborata impenfis , et arte conuiuia populi inuitantur , fed immortalitatis alimonia datur , à communibus cibis differens, corporalis fubftantiæ retinens fpeciem, fed virtutis Diuinæ inuifibili efficientia probans adeffe præfentiam.* The Supper therfore beinge ordered, emonge the facramental meates, their mett together the olde ordeinances and the newe. And when the lambe was confumed or eaten, which the olde tradition did fett furth, the mafter did put before hys difciples, *the inconfumptible meate.* Neither nowe be the people bidden to feaftes prepared with conninge, and charges, but here ys geuen *the food of immortalitie* , differing from common meates, reteining the forme of corporall fubftance, but prouinge by the inuifible efficiencie, the prefence of Gods power to be therin.   Thus fainct Cyprian.

In the which woordes of this holy Father, ye perceaue, firft, the comparifon of the two paffouers. Which he calleth the olde ordeinaunce, and the newe, that mette together emong the facramentall meates. Secondarelie, ye

B maie perceaue the difference of thé bothe. For the olde Paffouer was a lãbe, which was cõfumed. Whiche he teacheth when he faieth. *Et confumpto agnó,* and when the lambe was confumed, which the olde tradicion dyd fett furth. The other ys a meate, whiche neuer ys able to be confumed, whiche he plainlie vttereth thus. The mafter (*meening Chryft*) did put before his difciples *inconfumptible meat.*

Nowe note howe different the Sacramentaries be from this holie elder of Chryftes church. They faie ther ys put, or fett before vs but bread, which ys confumptible, as the pafchall lambe was: but this Father faieth : The mafter put before hys difciples inconfumptible meat.

Neither maie they here vfe their feigned glofing, fainge that we do receaue inconfumptible meate in the Supper of the Lorde, for we receaue Chryft fpirituallie, that ys, the merite and grace of his paffion . For neither thefe woordes will beare that glofe, neither the woordes that folowe . For thefe woordes faie, that the mafter *did putte before them inconfumptible meate* . He did not putte the merite of his paffion before them.   For yt ys not a thing of

C that nature, that yt maie be taken by hand , and laied before men in feight, but yt ys taken by the inward man onelie.   But this meate was put before them.

And the woordes that do folowe, do yet more clearlie fhewe the matter, and wype awaie their glofe , for yt foloweth that this meate, whiche Chryfte putte before his difciples, did differ from cõmon meates, and yet yt reteined the forme of naturall fubftance. Yf yt did differ from common meates, then yt can not be taken for the bread vfed in the Sacrament . For that bread (as Cranmer, or the Authour of that booke faieth) differeth not from other meates. For yt ys verie pure materiall breade, hauing no more holineffe, then other creatures haue, for that, that dome creatures are no partakers of holineffe.

And further this meat (as Ciprian faieth) differing frõ other meates, reteineth the forme of corporall fubftance. Yf this meat alfo doth retein the forme of corporall fubftance, then ys yt not that fpirituall meate, whiche they call the merite of Chriftes paffion, or the belief that Chryft hath fuffred for

D vs, for that meat reteineth not the forme of corporall fubftance.

So that this newe ordeinaunce that was inftituted by our Sauiour Chrift, to mete, and to aunfwer the olde ordeinaunce of the Pafchall Lambe , was no bare bread, for that neither differeth from other meates, neither yt

H ij   ys meat

Christ gaue his difciples incon fumptible meat : Sacramentaries giue ther difciples confumptile meat.

Sacramentaries glofe vpon S. Cyprian ouerthrowen.

Meate of Chriftes fupper differeth frõ common meates.

H.3. Bread of the hereticall comunion differeth not frõ common bread. Chriftes meat reteining the forme of corporall fubftãce cã not be the fpirituall meat of the Sacramentaries.

ys meat inconfumptible,neither ys yt the fpirituall meate of the merite of E
Chriftes pafsion.For that reteineth not the forme of corporall fubftance.
Wherfore I maie be bolde to affyrme,that yt ys the verie reall and fubftanciall bodie of our Sauiour Iefus Chrift,which ys the inconfumptible meate
as the Churche in the praife of God,for hys wonderfull worke in this Sacrament,fingeth:*Sumit vnus,fumunt mille,tantum ifti, quantum ille, nec fumptus ab-
fumitur.*One dothe eate,and a thoufande do eate, as moche do thefe eate as
he,and yet receaued,he ys not abfumed.

    This alfo ys that foode of immortalitie that Ciprian fpeaketh of,which cã
not be bare materiall bread, but yt ys the bread of life, euen the flefh of
Chryfte,which ys the medicine of immortalitie,as faieth holie *Ignatius*,difci-
ple of fainct Ihon the Euangelift,who exhorting the Ephefians, whome he
wrote vnto,fpeaketh verie aptlie to the matter here nowe entreated . Be ye
taught (faieth he) of the comforter,obediéce to the Byfhoppe, and the preift
with vnfwaruing,or ftable minde,breakinge the bread,whiche ys the medicine of immortalitie,the perferuatiue of not dieng, but of liuinge by Iefus F
Chryfte.Thus *Ignatius.*

    Note nowe that he calleth the bread that ys broken in the Sacrament,
the medicine of immortalitie, the preferuatiue from death . Whiche effectes can not
be attributed to the facramentall bread of the Sacramentaries,but to the hea
uenlie bread of the Catholiques,which ys the bodie of Chrifte.

    This *inconfumptible meate*,this *foode of immortalitie*,reteineth the forme of cor
porall fubftance. For the bodie of Chryfte in the Sacrament reteineth and
ys couered with the formes of the corporall fubftances of bread and wine.
Whiche meat ys not fo prepared to vs,and for vs (faieth Ciprian) by the con
ning of man, but by the inuifible woorking of God, wherby being made
a meat of foche excellencie,and fingular prerogatiue,yt proueth the prefence of Gods power to be ther,whiche prefence ys not,that his general prefen
ce,wherby he ys euery wher,but yt ys afpeciall maner of prefence, as yt was
with the virgen,when the Angell faied:*Et virtus Altifsimi obumbrabit tibi.* And
the power of the higheft fhall ouerfhadowe thee.

    Wheigh nowe with me(chriftian Reader) what maner of thing this new G
meate ys,which Chryfte hath fett in the place of the olde meate , I meen,of
the Pafchall lambe: *Yt ys an inconfumptible meate.yt ys a foode of immortalitie , yt ys
wrought by the inuifible woorkinge of God , yt hath a fpeciall prefence of gods power.*
All which declare yt a thing moche more honorable,moche more excellent,
then the Pafchall lambe,which excellent tearmes can be verified in no one
thing of this Sacramét,but in him onelie that faied:*Caro mea verè eſt cibus.*My
flefh ys verilie meate.Wherfor this excellent meate ys his verie flefh,whiche
ys our verie Pafchall Lambe of the newe Teftamét,not onelie verilie offred,
but alfo verilie eaten to aunfwer the figure, whiche was both offred, and
eaten.

    And that the Aduerfarie fhall not faie,that I feign and make foche an ex-
pofition of S.Cyprians woordes,as liketh me,or make him to meen as pleafeth me,he fhall perceaue the fame Cyprian himfelf,with one fhorte fentence of the fame fermon,in the which the former fentence ys conteined , to
expownde yt,as I haue doen,which ys this:*Panis ifte,quem Dominus difcipulis por
rigebat, non effigie , fed natura mutatus , omnipotentia Verbi factus eſt caro. Et ficut in
perfona Chrifti humanitas videbatur,et latebat diuinitas: ita facramento vifibili ineffabiliter fe diuina infudit effentia.*This bread,which oure Lorde gaue to his difciples,
chaunged, not in outwarde fhape, but in nature, *by the allmightineffe of the
woorde*

*D.Tho.
Aquin.*

*Ignatius in
epiſtola ad
Ephef.*

*The bread
broken in
the bleffed
Sacrament
ys the medi
cine of im-
mortalitie.*

Luc.1.

*Honorable
ãd worthie
titles of the
Sacrament*

Joan. 6.

*Cyprian.eo
dem.ferm.
de Cana.*

E

F

G

H

A *woorde ys made flesh* And as in the person of Chryste the humanitie was seen, and the Godhead laye hidden: Euen so the diuine nature inspeakeablie powreth, and putteth yt self in the visible Sacrament. Thus moche Saincte Cyprian.

    In the former sentence he speaketh of a meate, geuen to the disciples in the last Supper. Here he speaketh of the same meate, geuen at that same time to the disciples. Ther he saied, that that meate ys an inconsumptible meate, meate of immortalitie, diffring from other meates, but yet reteining the forme of corporall substance: Here he saieth, that being chaunged in nature, but not in outward forme, by the omnipotécie of the woord yt *ys made flesh*. Ther he saied, that the preséce of the diuine powr was proued to be present: Here he saieth, that the diuine nature vnspeakablie putteth yt self in the visible Sacramét, So that, that he called before indeterminatelie incósumptible meat: Here he calleth yt determinatelie *flesh*, into the which the nature of breade ys turned. Before indeterminatelie he saied, that the meat reteineth

B the forme of corporall substance: Here he determinatelie saieth, that the breade *which ys made flesh*, nowe being flesh, reteineth the outwarde forme still. In the other sentence he saied, that the feast ys not prepared with arte and charges of man: In this he saieth determinatelie, by what mean yt ys prepared, *By the omnipontencie of the woord* (saieth he) *yt ys made flesh*.

    Note further what Similitude he vseth for the declaracion of Christes inuisible being in the Sacrament: As in the person of Chryste, the humanitie was seen, and the Godhead was hidden: Euen so the diuine nature (which ys Chryst verie God) vnspeakablie putteth yt self in the visible Sacramét. Wherby he teacheth, that as the Godheade was hidden vnder the humanitie: So Chryste ys hidden vnder the visible Sacrament, that ys, vnder the formes of bread and wine, which are seen.

    And wher the Aduersaries being sore pressed with this manifest, and most plain sentence, haue gon aboute to elude yt with a glose vpon this woorde, *nature*, saieng that nature ys here taken for the propertie of nature, and not for the substance of nature: that glose ys ouerthrowen by these woordes

C ther immediatelie folowing: *Factus est caro*, was made flesh.

    Nowe ye haue heard holie Cyprians faith in this matter, so plainlie vttered, that his testimonie alone were sufficient to make the aduersarie to rubbe his forehead for shame, yf anie shame be in him, ád to cal in his proclamació, for asmoche as he heareth the matter so clerelie, and so manifestlie spoké, ád vttered, as neither he, ne anie of his likes can well fasten any darke, or blinde glose to take awaie the clearnesse of this sentence. But trusting that the thing yt self confowndeth sufficiently the arrogancie of the Aduersaries: I will proccad and bring furth one of the other side of Chrystes Parliamét house, who shall be *Euthymius*, a man so auncient, and so famed emong learned men, that I nede not here to stand moche in his commendacion.

    As touching this matter he saieth thus, speaking of our Sauiour Chrystes doing in his last Supper. *Egit gratias, & nunc ante pané, & postmodú ante poculum, docens quòd gratias agere oportet ante huiusmodi mysterium, quod perfectum est ad præ-*

D *standum naturæ nostræ beneficium. Si enim agni figuratiui immolatio ab interfectione liberationem, & à seruitute libertatem Iudæis præstitit, quanto maiora præstabit Christianis veri agni immolatio? Simul etiam ostendens, quòd vltroneus ad pasionem veniret, & præterea docens nos gratias agere in omnibus quæ patimur. Sicut autem pictores in vna tabula, & lineas supponunt, & picturas adumbrant, et colores superinducunt, ac formant: ita quoque Christus in eadem*

                       H iij   *mensa*

The bread i the blessed Sacrament by the omnipotencie of the word ys made flesh.

S. Cyprian his similitude to declare Chrystes presence in the Sacrament.

Sacramétaries glose vpon S. Cyprian ouerthrowen.

Euthym in Matth.26

menſa et figuratiuum ac vmbratile Paſcha ſubſcripſit, et verum , ac perfectum appoſuit. E
He gaue thankes,bothe nowe before the bread , and afterward before the
cuppe,teachinge that we muſt geue thankes before ſoche a miſtery , as was
doen to geue a benefet to owre nature.For yf the ſacrificinge of the figuratiue lambe gaue vnto the Iewes deliuerance from being ſlain , and libertie
from ſeruitude:Howe moche greater benefettes ſhall the ſacrificing of the
trew lambe geue vnto the Chriſtians?Shewing alſo withall , that he came
willinglie to his paſsion, and beſides that , teaching that we ſhoulde geue
thankes in all thinges , that we ſuffer. As painters in one table firſt drawe
their lines, and ſhadowe their paintinges , and then laie on their colours,
and ſett yt oute in forme or faſhion:Euen ſo alſo Chryſt in that one table
ſette oute the figuratiue and ſhadolike paſſouer,an then putte vnto them *the
true,and perfect paſſeouer.* Hitherto *Euthymius.*

In whoſe ſentence ye maie firſt perceaue, that he teacheth that the
lambe eaten of the Iewes, was the figure and ſhadowe of the true paſchall lambe,that Chryſt gaue to hys Apoſtles. Secondarelie, that yt ys to
be côſidered, that he calleth Chryſtes Paſſouer,in reſpect of the Iewes paſſo
uer,a perfight and true Paſſouer. F

Sacramen-
taries opi-
nions.
Nowe the Aduerſaries teache,that the good Iewes eating their Paſchall
Lambe receaued Chryſte Spirituallie:And they ſaie likewiſe, that the good
Chryſtians,eating the ſacramentall bread(as they terme yt)receaue Chryſt
alſo but Spirituallie,They ſaie alſo that the Iewes receaued Chryſte in a ſigne,or figure:They ſaie that the Chriſtians likewiſe , receaue Chryſte but in
ſigne,or figure.Howe then riſeth thys difference, that their Paſchall feaſt
ys called but a ſhadow , or figure, and owre ys called the true, and perfecte paſchall feaſt ? And yet, according to the Aduerſaries doctrine,ther
ys no more in the one,then in other,but bothe be figures, bothe be ſigns,
and Chryſt but ſpirituallie receaued in bothe.

Wher ys then the trueth,that maketh our paſchall feaſt,a true feaſt ? And
wher ys the perfection , that maketh yt perfecte , as thys authour tear-
menth yt?

Chriſt in
the iudai-
call feaſt
imperfect-
lie in our
feaſt per-
fectie.
Yt can not be,but that in Chriſtes Supper ther muſt be the trneth, and ve G
rie thing of that , that was figured in the iudaicall Supper.And that perfect
thinge,in perfecte maner , whiche in the Iewes Supper was vnperfectlie,
as ye haue hearde,that that lambe,and Supper was a figure of Chryſte oure
lambe,and our Supper.Wherfore then yt muſt nedes folowe,that as Chryſt
was in that Supper but in a figure,and therfore vnperfectlie: So muſt he be
preſent in our Supper,more then in a figure,euen by verie true,and reall pre
ſence,and ſo perfectlie.

And that this Authour(as I haue declared) meant of ſoche a perfecte
reall preſence of Chryſt in the ſacramẽt,not onelie his own woords allreadie
reherſed do wel proue, but this his ſaieng alſo in the ſame chapiter:*Sicut vetus
Teſtamentum hoſtias et ſanguinem habebat:Ita ſanè et nouũ,corpus videlicet,et ſanguinem
Domini.*Euen as the olde Teſtament had ſacrifices and bloode:So trulie hath
the newe alſo , that ys to witte, *the bodie and bloode of our lorde,*Thus *Euthymius.*

A plain
place for
maſter Iuel
Ys not this ſaieng plain ynough?can the Proclamer finde anie tropes, or
darke figures,to ſaie that this ys not a plain ſentence,declaring the verie real
preſence of Chriſtes bleſſed bodie , and bloode in the Sacrament, foraſ- H
moche as he ſaieth not onelie that the newe Teſtament hathe the bodie
and bloode of Chryſte : But yt hathe them as the propre ſacrifice of the
ſame.

Neither

A   Neither maie the Proclamer drawe this faing & pinche yt to meen the
facrifice of the croffe. For this authour proceadeth immediatelie in the proif
of Chriftes reall prefence in the Sacrament, by Chriftes owne woordes:
This ys my bodie, And teacheth, that not onelie fignes of Chriftes bodie and
bloode be ther, But his verie bodie and blood, as in the fecond booke,
where we fhall haue a more apte, and couenient place to fpeake of thefe
woordes, more at large oute of this Authour Yt fhall be declared.

And for this place, fuppofing enoughe to be faied as côcerning the minde
of thefe two Authours, for the applicacion of the figure of the Pafchall Lâbe
to Chrifte our Pafchall Lambe, and howe the one ys but the figure, the
other the veritie, And that therfore the thing in dede, that was figured,
whiche ys Chriftes verie bodie ys otherwife prefent, then in a figure: I will
leaue thefe, and call other two of Chriftes Parliament houfe, to heare ther
teftimonie alfo, what the enacted trueth of this matter ys.

B   THE EIGHTENE CHAPITER TREACTETH OF
the fame matters by fainſte Hierom, and Chryfoſtome.

A monge the elders of the latin churche, whiche remain I will
firſt heare fainſte Hierom, a man in fame fo excellent, in learning fo deape, and profownde, in liuing fo holie, in time fo
auncient, as being born the yeare of our Lorde 331. of diuerfe
holie men fo highlie commended, of all true Chtiftians fo well
accepted, and receaued, that his teftimonie in this matter can not be refu-
fed. Thus faieth he: *Poſtquam typicum Pafcha fuerat impletum, & agni carnes cum*   *Hieron. in*
Apoſtolis comediſſet, aſſumit panẽ, qui confortat cor hominis, & ad verum Pafchæ tranf-   *26.*
greditur facramentum, vt quomodò in præfiguratione illius Melchifedech, fummi Dei fa-   *Matth.*
cerdos, panem & vinum offerens, fecerat, ipſe quoque veritatem fui corporis, & fangui-
nis repræfentaret. After that the figuratiue Paſſouer was fulfilled, and he had
eaten the flefh of the lambe with his Apoſtles, he taketh breade, whiche
côforteth the heart of man, and goeth to the true Sacramẽt of the Paſſouer,
C   that as *Melchifedech* the preiſt of the highe God, in offringe bread and wine,
did in the prefiguracion of the fame, he alfo might reprefent the veritie of
his bodie and bloode. Thus moche fainſte Hierom.

I nede not here to note the applicacion of the olde Pafchall Lambe to the
newe, as of the figure to the thinge figured. For this Authour fpeaketh yt fo
plainlie, that yt nede not be noted to him, that will fee, perceaue, and vnderftande. But forafmoch as the weightieſt parte of the controuerfie confifteth in the thing figured, what yt fhoulde be, whether yt be breade, the
figure of Chriftes bodie, or Chriftes verie bodie and bloode in dede, and
trueth, verilie prefent, and reallie, in the Sacrament: therfore I will weigh
the fainge of this Authour, wher he fpeaketh of yt.

He faieth, that as *Melchifedech* did offer bread and wine, Chrifte alfo wolde reprefent the truthe of his bodie and bloode. The aduerfaries perchaun-   *Obiection*
ce will triumphe, and faie, that Sainſte Hierõ ys here on their fide, for that   *of the Ad*
he faieth not plainlie, that Chrift did geue his verie bodie, but that he did   *uerfaries*
D   reprefẽt his verie bodie. And reprefenting (faie they) ys a fhewing of a thing   *oute of S.*
by figne, or figure, and not by the thing yt felf. Wherfor Chrift by the bre-   *Hierom-*
ad, as by a figure, did reprefent his bodie, but not verilie, and realie geue yt
to the Difciples.

To aunfwer this obieſtion, I wolde learn of them, yf emong learned mẽ
H iiij   this

this verbe be so striected, as oneli to signifie, to shewe a thing by figure or E
sign. And whether this be the propre significatiõ of the woorde or no. And
yf they be ygnorant therof, let them woorthilie take the taunte, that Luther the fownder of Sectes in our time, vnwoorthilie gaue to King Henrie
the eight, that ys, let them go looke the Vocabularies.

But bicause their trauaill shall be eased, I will shewe them, howe they
shall finde yt yn two sundrie editions of Calepine. In the first thus: *Repræsento præsentem* sisto. that ys, I represent, I sett, or make present. In the which
signification Collumella also vseth this verbe *Repræsento*, as by his saing ther
alleaged, yt ys manifest. For thus he saieth: *Itaque villicus curabit vt iusta reddã-
tur. Istaque non ægrè consequetur, si semper se repræsentauerit.* Therfore shall the bai-
lif see, that dueties be paied. And these shall be easilie atteign, yf he allwaies
represent himself. Thus he. Wher yt ys euident, that *Repræsentarit* in the
latine, or represent in the english, signifieth not a figuratiue representing,
but a verie reall and personal representing of the bailiff in his owne verie per-
són. And in moche like signification, the same Calepine in an other place F
hath yt thus: *Repræsento, id est præsens affero.* I presentlie bring. Whiche signification ys often vsed in the lawes, as when they saie : *Repræsentare rei precium,*
and *repræsentare mercedem.*

In the english Dictionarie *Repræsento* ys to represent, to rendre, to bring in
presence, to present a thing, to laie before one, to shewe or declare. By all
these places yt ys manifest, that *Repræsento* signifieth not onelie to shew a thig
by figure sign, or token, but by the verie thing yt self present. And thus by
their Grammar, their argument of representation ys not onelie aunswered,
and they of ignorance reprehended, that wolde frame yt to confirme their
wicked assertion : but also the true meening of the woord, *Repræsento*,
moche opened to the better vnderstanding of this Authour here alleaged.

Wherfor, gentle Reader, vnderstand, that when sainct Hierom had declared, that the figuratiue Paschall Lambe was a figure of the true Paschall
Lambe Christ, who in the same was presented, as in a sign : And likewise
had saied of the bread, whiche Melchisedech offred in the prefigu-
ration of Christ, wherby also Christ was once presented, as in his figure: G
Nowe he saieth, Christ wolde in veritie present himself again, in whiche
veritie ys vnderstanded his verie bodie, and verie blood. As by plain, and
brief woordes he might saie: *Melchisedech* in bread, and wine did figuratiuelie present the bodie and blood of Christ, but Christ hath presented again
verilie, and truelie his bodie, and blood.

To this vnderstanding, the woorde, *veritie* in saincte Hierom enforceth
vs. For if he had meant, that Christ had sette or laied before his Apostles,
but a signe, he might haue saied: *Ipse quoque corpus, & sanguinem suum repræsentaret.* He also might represent his bodie and blood. But when he saieth: *Ipse
quoque veritatem coporis, & sanguinis sui repræsentaret.* He wolde represent the
veritie of his bodie and bloode, this woorde, *veritie*, bannisheth signes and
figures, and geueth vs to vnderstande a verie and reall presence whiche
Christe, according to the significacion of the woorde, wolde shewe or declare to this Apostles.

And for the further declaracion that this ys the meening of saincte Hierom: Note that when he first spake of the lambe, he calleth yt *Typicum Pas-* H
cha the figuratiue passouer. When he speaketh of the figured passeouer, he
calleth yt, *verum Pascha. the true Passouer.* So likewise when he did speake of
bread and wine, which *Melchisedech* offred, he saieth, he did yt *in præfiguratione,*

in

Marginal notes:

Represent what yt si-gnisieth.

Chryst, in in the lawe presented in figure: in the Gospel in veritie.

A in the prefiguration.When he fpeaketh of Chriftes doinge, he faieth, he did geue the veritie. So that Chrift was prefented twice:once in figure ãd again in veritie. Wherfor fainct Hierom faied verie well,that he wolde reprefent, that ys, he wolde prefent himfelf again.

This maie appeare alfo by the Scripture whiche fainct Hierom ther alleageth, fainge : *Affumit panem, qui confortat cor hominis.*He taketh the bread,that comforteth the heart of man. To what pourpofe? To celebrate the Sacrament of the true Paffouer. What ys the true paffouer? The bodie and blooe de of Chrift. Whiche ys the verie right bread, that comforteth the hearte of man in verie dede, with that fpirituall and heauenlie cõforte, that ys permanent,whiche ys the right and true comforte.

Forafmoche as yt ys moft manifeft, that this fentence of the Pfalme ys to be vnderftanded of Chrift, that excellent bread of life,for that the Prophete Dauid in that Pfalme dothe fpeake of the greate prouidence of God, in ordering, and difpofing all thinges in heauen, in earthe, and in the Seas,fig-

B nifieng therby in the fpirite of prophecie, the goodlie difpofition of thinges in the Church of Chrifte, beautified, adorned, and confirmed with Sacramentes, in moft goodlie wife, of the which Chrifte, and his Churhe, ys the wheil prophecie of that booke, as here after more at large fhall be declared, amonge the whiche facramentes , fpeaking of the Sacrament of Chriftes bodie and bloode the prophet faied. *Vt educas panem de terra,⁊ vinum lætificet cor hominis, ⁊ panis cor hominis confirmet.* That thow maift bringe furthe foode oute of the earth, and wine,that maketh gladde the heart of man,and bread to ftrenghthen màns hearte: yt fhall fuffice for this prefent to declare the fame by the woordes alleaged of fainte Hierom. For he, ther declaring the ceaffing of the olde Pafchall lambe, and the beginning of the newe, whiche he calleth the true Paffouer, in the beginning of the fame, faieth thus: *Affumit panem, qui confortat cor hominis,* He taketh bread, whiche comforteh the hearte of man. *Pfalm. 103*

Yt was moft certen(as fainte Ciprian faieth) that *Manducauerunt de eodem pane fecundùm formam vifibilem.* They had eaten of the fame bread after a vifi-

C ble maner. But to that bread fo eaten, fainct Hierome wolde not applie the fainge of the Prophete,but wher he beginneth to fhewe howe Chrifte commeth to the inftitucion of this bleffed Sacrament,in the whiche they fhoulde eate the true Pafchall Lambe, the bodie of Chrifte, the verie bread of life, and comforth , Ther he applieth the propheicie, of the Prophete, to the verie thing that yt prophecied of, and faieth : He taketh the breade,that comforteth the heart of man.

Thus the placing, and applicacon of that Scripture well confidered, and weighed of the reader, fhall caufe him well to perceaue, howe the fame ys to be vnderftanded, as ys by me before faied.

And nowe, altough fainte Hierom hath fufficientlie declared his faith in this matter of the veritie enacted, and receaued throughout all the houfe of Chrifte in his time: Yet for the fatisfieng of them, that thirft for the trueth, I will bring in fainte Hierom in an other place, fpeaking fo plain woordes, as neither the enemie can withftãde fo euident a trueth, nor other men take occafiõ of doubte. *Abfit* (faieth he) *vt de ijs quicquam finiftrũ loquar , qui apoftolico*

D *gradui fuccedentes, Chrifti corpus facro ore conficiunt.* God forbidde, that I fhoulde fpeake anie euell of them , whiche fucceading the Apoftolike degree, with their holie mouth do *confecrate the bodie of Chrifte.* *Hieron.ad Heliodorũ epiftola. 1. Chriftes bodie ys cõ fecrated of the preift.*

In the whiche fainge ye maie perceaue that fainct Hieroms faith was(being

ſo taught of the churhe wherin he liued) that he preiſt doth *conſecrate the bo-* E
die of Chriſte. wherby alſo then yt ys moſt manifeſt, that Chriſtes verie bodie
ys in the Sacrament.

eAmb. de
ſacr. lib.4.
caſ.Euſeb.
Emiſe hō.
paſch.
Chry. de
prod.
Hom.30.

And this alſo ys not to be ouerpaſſed, that the he ſaieth , *the preiſtes doo*
with their holie mouth conſecrate the ſame bodie of Chriſt : For hereby ys reiected that
fooliſh hereſie , void aſwell of reaſon, as of authoritie, which taught that
the faith of the receauer made the preſence of Chriſt in the Sacrament. for
yt ys as S. Ambroſe , Euſebius, and Chryſoſtom ſaie, the holie woord of
Chriſt ſpoken, as ſancte Hierom here ſaieth, by the mouth of the preiſt, that
conſecrateth the bodie of Chriſt. And thus alſo, if by the mouth of the preiſt the bodie of Chriſt be conſecrated, then ys that bodie verilie preſent.

Preiſtes
aught to be
reuereced.
for their
ordre and
office.

And further yt maie be learned of this great learned, and holie father, that
the ordre of preiſthoode ys not to be contemned, but reuerenced, who
with a maner of ſpeache of vehemencie, ſaieth: God forbidde, that I ſhoulde ſpeake anie euell of them &c. By whiche maner of ſpeache he noteth yt
to be a greate crime to ſpeake euell of them. The cauſes why he wolde not F
ſpeake euell of them be : that they ſucceade the Apoſtles in office, whiche
ys an high degree, and that the worke of their miniſtraciō ys great, and that
they do *conſecrate the bodie of Chriſte*.

Chryſoſtom
his woor-
thineſſe of
learning,
holineſſe,
conſtancie,
and aunci-
entie.

And nowe that this noble mā hath ſo plainlie opened the treuthe enacted and receaued of the one ſide of Chriſtes Parliament houſe : we will alſo
heare what one of the other ſide will ſaie. Whiche ſhall be golden mouthed
Chriſoſtome, who ys wourthie ſo to be called for the golden ſentences that
proceade oute of his mouthe. Who alſo ys woorhie to be beleued, not onelie for his holineſſe, and great learning : But alſo for his conſtancie of faith,
and auncientie in time. Who being in the time of the hereſie of the Arriās,
aboute the yeare of Chriſte 350· and therfore aboute 1200 yeares a gone,
gaue no place to yt, neither for Princes, neither for the loſſe of his Biſhop-
perick, neither for baniſhment, neither for anie perſecucion, that did come
to him for his conſtancie in faithe, but ſtood immoueable, inflexible, and
ſtreight vpright by the right piller of trueth Wherfore we maie conceaue a
good opinion of him that he will doo and hath doen the like in teachinge G
vs the matter, that we nowe ſeke. Let vs therfore heare. Thus he ſaieth:

Omel.de
prodi.
Juda.

Sed per hoc etiam aliud maius beneficium monſtrabatur, quòd ille agnus futuri agni fuit
typus, & ille ſanguis dominici ſanguinis monſtrabat aduentum, & cuis illa ſpiritalis ouis
fuit exemplū.Ille agnus vmbra fuit: Hic veritas. Sed poſtquam ſol iuſticiæ radiauit, vmbra
ſoluitur luce. & ideò in ipſa menſa vtrūque Paſcha, & typi, & veritatis celebratū eſt.Nā
ſicut pictores pingendam tabulam veſtigijs quibuſdam adumbrare ſolent, et ſic colorū varie
tate perficere: ita & Chriſtus fecit in menſa, & typū Paſchæ deſcripſit, et Paſcha verita-
tis oſtendit. Vbi vis paremus tibi comedere Paſcha? Iudaicum Paſcha erat, ſed vmbra lu-
mini cedat, aduectata imago veritate ſuperetur. But by that alſo an other great benefitte was ſhewed, that that lambe was a figure of the lambe to come, and
that bloode declared the cominge of our Lordes bloode, and that ſhepe
was an exāple of the ſpirituall ſhepe. That lābe was a ſhaddow: This lābe the

The olde
Paſchal
lambe a
ſhaddowe,
oure lambe
the trueth.

trueth. But after that the Sūne of righteouſnes ſhewed furth his beames, the
ſhadowe ys put awaie with the light. And therfor in that tablebothe the paſ
ſeouers, both of the figure, ād of the trueth, were celebrated. For as the pain
ters are wont to ſhaddowe the table, that ys to be paincted, with certain H
ſignes and lineamentes, and ſo with varietie of colours to make yt perfecte:
Euen ſo Chriſt did in the table . He did both deſcribe the figure of the paſſo
uer, and alſo ſhewed the poſſouer of the truth. Wher willt thowe that we
make

A make readie for thee to eate the paſſouer? That was the Iudaicall Paſſouer. But let the ſhadowe geue place to the light. And the ymage be ouer-
cõmed of the truthe. Thus Chriſoſtom.

What neadeth me here to trauaill to open the Authours mening, where
he himſelf vſeth ſo plain ſpeche, that he neadeth no interpretour? He hath
not onelie made a iuſt compariſon betwen the olde Paſchall lambe and our
Paſchall lambe, but alſo by tearmes applied to them, he hathe declared the
contentes of thẽ, and what they be. That lambe (ſaieth he) was, a ſhaddow:
This lambe the trueth. That lambe a figuratiue paſſouer, this the true
Paſſouer.

I wolde to God all that haue romed aſtraie in the matter of this bleſſed
Sacrament, wolde open their eies and clerelie beholde, howe by theſe
woordes (*true, and trueth*) whiche Chriſoſtom in this ſentence ſo often hath
vſed, the true faith, and the trueth of the faith of the Churche, the piller of
trueth, ys taught, maintened, and aduaunced, and the falſed of the falſe
B prophetes, and preachers weakened, and conuinced. Theſe preachers teache
that the Sacrament ys but a figure, a ſign or token of Chriſtes bodie: Chriſoſtom ſaieth that the olde Paſchall lambe was but a figure, but our Paſchall
lambe eaten in the Sacrament ys the trueth. That the ſhaddowe: This the
light. Yf then the olde Paſchall lambe were the figure and the ſhaddow, and
our newe Paſchall lambe the trueth and the light, thẽ are they moche more
then bare figures and ſignes, for they are the verie thinges.

But to make an euaſion from this argument, they will ſaie that Chriſt ys
our true Paſchall lãbe, and ys truelie eaten in the receipte of the Sacrament.
And therfore we ſaie with Chriſoſtom, we haue the trueth, and the verie
true Paſchall lambe ys receaued of the faithfull, euen the very bodie of
Chriſte. But if yowe procead to demaunde of them, yf the verie bodie of
Chriſte be conſecrated on the Altar, and deliuered by the preiſt to the hande or mouthe of the faithfull, and ſo receaued: here they ſtarte backe, and
can not abide this voice, that yt ſhoulde be on the Altar, but onelie in the
heart of the godlie receauer.

C But Chriſoſtome ſaieth, that his true Paſſeouer (wherbye he meneth the
bodie of Chriſt) was on the table, where the olde paſſeouer was. In that
table (ſaieth he) both the Paſſeouer, of the figure and of the trueth were
celebrated.

And that none occaſion of miſunderſtandig or wreſting of his woordes
ſhoulde be taken, he ſpeaketh the ſame ſentẽce after warde in more plain
woordes ſaing: Chriſt in the table did bothe deſcribe the figure of the Paſſeouer, and ſhewed alſo the true Paſſeouer.

Note then, bothe that Chriſte did ſhewe the true Paſſeouer, And that he
did ſhewe yt in the table. whiche bothe do importe a reall preſence, For to
ſhewe the true thing ys to ſhewe the verie thing yt ſelf: to ſhewe the verie
thing yt ſelf, ys to ſhewe the reall preſence of the thinge. To ſhewe yt in or
vpon the table importeth a ſubſtanciall maner of beinge farre differente frõ
their ſpirituall maner of beinge, whiche ys onelie in the hearte. For yt ys
outwardlie vpon the table, and therfore neadeth a preſence reall.

D And here ſomwat more to preſſe the Proclamer, yt wolde be learned of
him, why S. Hierom, and S. Chriſoſtom call not the iudaicall Paſſouer the
light, the trueth, ãd the veritie, as they do oure Paſchall lambe, ſeing (as he
and his likes do ſaic) they receaued Chriſt as well aſ we, and we in our Sacrament no more them they. for they ſpirituallie, and we ſpirituallie, and
　　　　　　　　　　　　　　　　　　　　　　　　　　　　　　　　　our

*Heretiques
euaſion frõ
Chryſoſtõ.*

*Figuratiue
paſſouer ãd
true Paſſo-
uer both in
one table.*

our Sacrament no better then theirs.

But vnderſtand(Reader) that they ſo ſaing ſpeak lies, and deceaue thee. The holie Fathers calling the olde ſacramẽtes figures and ſhaddowes, and ours the light, the trueth, and the thinges in dede, teache that thoſe ſacramentes had not the verie preſence of Chriſt, and that our Sacrament hath.

And that ye maie the better perceaue that Chriſoſtom meneth, as here ys declared: ye ſhal heare him in an other place vttering his minde and faith, yea the faithe of the Churche in his time, in more plain and expreſſe woordes. Thus he writeth: *Ipſa namque menſa animæ noſtræ vis eſt, nerui mentis, fiduciæ* *Homeli. in 10.1. Corin.* *vinculum, fundamentum, ſpes, ſalus, lux, vita noſtra. Si hinc hocſacrificio muniti migrabimus, maxima cum fiducia ſanctum aſcendemus veſtibulum, tanquam aureis quibusdam veſtibus contecti. Et quid futura commemoro? Nam dum in hac vita ſumus, vt terra nobis cœlum ſit, facit hoc myſteriũ. Aſcende ad cœli portas, & diligenter attende, imò non cœli, ſed cœli cœlorum, & tunc quod dicimus intueberis. Etenim quod ſummo honore dignum eſt, id tibi in terra oſtendam. Nam quemadmodum in regijs, non parietes, non tectum aureum, ſed regium corpus in throno ſedens omniũ eſt præſtantiſsimũ: ita quoque in cœlis regium corpus, quod nunc in terra videndum tibi proponitur. Neque Angelos, neque Archangelos, non cœlos, non cœlos cœlorum, ſed ipſum horum tibi omnium Dominum oſtendo. Animaduertis quónam pacto quod omnium maximũ eſt, atque præcipuum, in terra non conſpicaris tantũ, ſed tangis: neque tangis ſolũ, ſed comedis, & eo accepto domũ redis. Abſterge igitur ab omni ſorde animã tuã, præpara mentẽ tuã ad horũ myſterioriũ ſuſceptionem. Etenim ſi puer regius purpura, & diademate ornatus tibi ferẽdus traderetur, nõnne omnibus humi abiectis eum ſuſciperes? Verùm nunc, cum nõ hominis regiũ pueriũ, ſed vnigenitũ Dei filium accipias, dic quæſo, non horreſcis, & omnium ſecularium reriũ amorẽ abiicis?*

That table ys the ſtrenght of our ſoule, the Sinnewes of the minde, the bande of truſt, the fundacion, hope, health, light, and our life. Yf we beinge defended with this ſacrifice ſhall departe hence, with moſt great truſt we ſhall, as couered with certain golden garmentes, aſcend to the holie place. But what do I reherſe thinges that be to come? For while we be in this life, this miſterie cauſeth that the earth ys an heauen vnto vs. Go vppe therfor vnto the gates of heauen, but not of heauen, bnt of the heauen of heauens, *The thing woorthie of moſt honour ys in the Sacrament* and diligentlie marke, And then thowe ſhalt beholde what we ſaie. For G trulie that, *that ys woorthie of moſt higheſt honour, that ſhall I ſhewe thee in earthe.* For as in Kinges howſes, not the walls, not the golden Rooffe, but the Kinges bodie ſitting in Throne ys moſt cheif and woorthieſt of all: Euen ſo alſo do I ſhewe thee, neither Angells, nor Archangells, not heauens, nor the heauen of heauens, *but the Kinges bodie whiche ys in heauen, whiche* *The verie bodie of Chriſt ys. ſetfurth before vs in earth.* *nowe ys ſetfurth before thee in earth to be ſeen, the lorde of all theiſe doo I ſhewe thee.* Doeſt thowe marke howe thowe doeſt not onelie beholde in earth that, that ys greateſt and cheifeſt of all thinges, But thowe doeſt touche yt, neither doeſt thowe onelie touche yt, but thowe doeſt eate yt, And that receaued thowe goeſt home? Wipe therfore and make clean thy ſoule from all filthineſſe, prepare thy minde to the receipt of theſe miſteries. For yf the Kinges childe, being deckt in purple, and Diadeame, were deliuered to thee to be caried, woldeſt thowe not caſt all down vpon the grownde, and take him? But nowe when thowe takeſt, not the childe of a kinge being a *The onlie begotten Sonne of God receiued in the Sacramẽt.* man, but *the onelie begotten Sonne of God,* Saie (I beſeche thee) arte thowe not afraied? And doeſt thowe not caſt awaie the loue of all worldelie thinges? H Thus moche Chriſoſt.

Among ſo manie goodlie notes, as this ſentence dothe contein, let me (gentle Reader) with thy pacience note two or three, whiche be verilie
woorthie

A woorthie of note and confideracion.

The firft fhall be, that we obferue the notable titles that he geueth to the table: This note hathe two partes . For firft he calleth yt life &c. after in the fentéce next adioined he calleth yt afacrifice. Wherfore we fhall firft fpea ke of the titles in the firft fentence, and then of the title in the next fentence.

In the firft fentence he calleth yt *the ftrenght of our fowle , our fundacion, hope, health, light, and life.* Whiche thinges for that they can not be attributed to the materiall table, yt ys eafie for euery man to perceaue that the Authour meneth them of the thing, that ys, of the meat or foode vpon the table, after the maner of our common fpeache, whiche faieth: Soche a man kepeth a good table, wherbie ys ment the good fare on the table. *Honorable and woor= thie titles of the Sa= crament.*

Nowe then yf the thinge on the table be a thing of foche woorthineffe, that yt maie be called *our ftrenght, health, hope, light, and life:* yt can not be a peice of breade, but he that ys fo in verie dede, Iefus Chryft our Sauiour God and mã. Yt ys he that ys our ftréght, according to the Pfalmift. *Dominus fortitudo* B *plebis fuæ.* Owre Lorde ys the ftrength of his people. He ys our health and faluacion. for *Ipfe faluum faciet populum fuum à peccatis eorum.* He fhall faue his people from ther finnes. He ys our light. For he ys *Lux vera, quæ illuminat omnem hominem venientem in hunc mundum.* The verie light that lightneth euery man comminge into this worlde. He ys our life, For he ys *Via, veritas, & vita* the waie, the trueth, and the life. *Pfalm. 27. Matth. 1. Ioan. 1.*

Ibid. 14.

Wherfore feing that thefe titles appropriated onelie to Chrift, are by this auncient father declared to be applied to the thing vpon the Altar or table, yt muft of necefsitie be concluded, that the thing vpon the Altar or table ys verilie Chryfte. *Chryft ys verilie vpõ the Altar.*

The further proofe wherof appeareth in the fentence immediatelie folo- wing, whiche ys the feconde of the notes before mencioned, wher he faieth thus Yf we fhall departe hence being defended with this facrifice, we fhall with moft great truft go vppe to the holie place. In the whiche fainge, what he before called the table, he calleth yt nowe the facrifice. Wherbie ys de- clared the firft parte of the note that he ment not the materiall table , but C the thing vpon the table . Secondarelie calling yt a facrifice by the whiche with greate truft we go vppe to the holie place, he plainlie teacheth that the thing vpon the table ys Chryfte, who ys our verie and moft woor- thie facrifice, who by his oblacion founde eternall redemption, of the which more hereafter. *Heb. 9.*

The feconde note ys, that he faieth: *Trulie that, that ys wourthie of moft high ho- nour, that will I fhewe thee in earth.* What thinge ys that, that ys woorthie of moft high, honour, but that, that fainct Paule fpeaketh of when he faieth: *Regi fecu lorum immortali, inuifibili, foli Deo honor & gloria,* Vnto God king euerla- ftinge, immortall, inuifible, be onlie honour and praife for euer ? What ys the moft highe honour, but that honour whiche the learned call *Latriam,* the honour due to God alone? whiche honour confifteth in faith , beleuin- ge that he ys the creatour, and conferuatour of all thinges : in hoope , tru- fting by him to be faued: in Charitie, louinge him aboue all thinges crea- ted, yea euen aboue our owne felues , through the whiche loue we are rea- D die louinglie to obey his moft holie commaundementes : in Sacrifice, as wherbie we exhibitte and teftifie outwardlie our feruice to our onely Lorde God, to be geuen, vfed, and frequented, whiche facrifice, whether yt be of praife or thankes geuing , or of the offring vppe of our owne bo- dyes , or anie other thing appoincted of God , ys (as fainct Paule te- *1 Tim. 1. Honour due to God alone cal- led Latria, wherin yt confifteth .*

Rom. 12.

I   ftifieth)

ſtifieth) called our reaſonable ſeruing of God.

The thing woorthie moſt high honoure ys in the Sacrament.
Yf thē that, that ys ſhewed in earth, be woorthie of this moſt high honour, and the ſhewing therof ys in the table, of the whiche Chryſoſtom ſpake in the beginning of the this ſentence, what ells doth he meen, or what ells can yt be, *but Chryſt God and man verilie preſent in the Sacrament, who ys wourthie of this honour.*

But what neadeth me to trauaill to expownde Chryſoſtome, and to decla re what the thing ys, that he woulde ſhewe in earth, ſeing that he himſelf ſo clerelie expowndeth him ſelf in his owne woordes that do folow? For as in kinges howſes (ſaieth he) not the walls, not the golden Rooffe, but the Kin ges bodie ſitting in the Throne ys the cheifeſt and woorthiſt of all : Euen ſo alſo the Kinges bodie which ys in heauen, whiche ys nowe ſett furth befo re thee to be ſeen in earth, not Angells, nor Archangells, not heauens, nor the heauens of heauens, *but the verie Lorde of all theſe doo I ſhewe thee.*

In whiche woordes ye maie clerelie perceaue, that the thing, whiche he ſaieth ys to be ſhewed in earthe, ys the kinges bodie, which ys in heauen, the F verie lorde of Angells, and Archangells, the Lorde of heauens, and of the heauen of heauens. Which ys not preſent in figure, and abſent in dede : but ys verilie preſent in ſo true a maner, *verie Chryſt, verie God, and verie man*, that he ſo being with vs in miſterie here in earth, maketh the ſame earth (ſaieth Chryſoſtom) to be an heauen vnto vs, whiche coulde not ſo be, but by the preſence of him, who ys Lorde of heauens, whoſe graciouſe preſence ma keth heauen wher yt pleaſeth the ſame graciouſlie to be.

Crāmer his gloſe vpon Chryſoſto-me.
Li.4.ca.8.
Yf this place of Chryſoſtome, with the notes of the ſame, be diligentlie weighed, yt ſhall eaſelie appeare to the reader, how vain the gloſe of Can torburie vpon this and all the like ſaings of Chryſoſtom, ys, wherin of hys abſolute authoritie without proofe, he ſaieth, that wher Chryſoſtome ſaieth, that we ſee Chryſt with our eyes, we touche him with oure handes, we re ccaue him with our mouthes, be not to be vnderſtanded of the verie fleſh and blood of Chryſte, but of the bread and wine, whiche be the ſignes of them. But for that this gloſe confowndeth the texte yt ys to be reiected for the woordes of Chryſoſtom can not beare yt. For he ſaieth not that G thowe ſeiſt bread and wine, but the kinges bodie whiche ys in heauē, which ys now ſett furthe before thee in earth to be ſeen.

What ys ſeen in the Sacrament
Yf we ſhouide aske of Chryſoſtome, what we do ſee in the Sacrament here vpon earth, he aunſwereth, *the kinges bodie.* Yf ye aske again which kinges bodie? He anſwereth *the Kinges bodie whiche ys in heauen.* Yf ye proceade asking, where do we ſee yt? he aunſwereth, before thee. So that he maketh no mencion of bread or wine. Wherfore I wolde knowe, what warrant this *Crūmer glo ſeth with-oute war-rant.* man had, to geue ſoche a gloſe to Chryſoſtome. Yf Chryſoſtome ment as this man gloſeth, ſtraunge yt ys, that he wolde ſpeake ſo plain con trary to his mening, as to ſaie, yt ys *the kinges bodie* and ment yt was not.

Obiection.
Anſwer.
Yf the Aduerſarie ſaie, the bodie of Chryſt cānot be ſeē: No more (ſaie I) cā the ſubſtance of mā be ſeen. And yet we ſaie we ſee ſoche a man, when we ſee but the outward accidentes of man, we ſaie we ſee the king, when we ſee no parte of him, but the garment that he hath vpon him, and ſo of other thin *Cap.62.*
A ignorāt obiection of the Ad-uerſaries. kes, when we ſee ther outwarde formes, and conſider ther ſubſtance, we ſaie, H and that truly, we ſee the thing. But I will ſpeake of this, more in the ſecond booke.

But here the Aduerſarie will further obiecte and ſaie : Yf that thing be in the Sacrament,that ys woorthie of moſt high honour (as Chryſoſtom ſaieth,and one parte of that high honour ys to be ſacrificed vnto , Then Chryſte ys not in the Sacrament.For(as your ſelues ſaie) Chryſt ys your ſacrifice.Who being in the Sacrament,ye offer vnto that thing that ys in the Sacrament.And ſo foloweth this abſurditie , that the Sacrifice , and he to whome the Sacrifice ys offred,ys all one.

This obiection conuinceth the obiectour of ignorance of the faith of the church,or ells of malice againſt the receaued faith of the ſame.For yf he had either red what S.Auguſtine writeth in this matter,or yf he haue red yt , he wolde not arrogantly and maliciouſlie contemne the ſame, he wolde either not thus obiecte,or ſooen be by ſainct Auguſtine ſatiſfied. To aunſwer this thus ſaieth he:*Chriſtus vnus manet cum illo,cui offert, & vnum ſe facit cum illis ,pro quibus ipſe ſe offert,& vnus eſt cum illis,qui offerunt,& vnum cum illo,quod offertur.* Chryſte(ſaieth he)abideth one with him to whome he offreth , and he maketh him ſelf one with them,for whom he dothe offer , and he ys one with them which do offer,and one with that,that ys offred.Thus S.Auguſtine. *The anſwere.* / *Li.4. de trini ca.14*

Weighe with me)gentle Reader)eche parte of this ſentece. Firſt he ſaieth, that Chryſte abideth one with him,to whom he offreth . In whiche ſainge note that Chryſte dothe both offer, and ys alſo he to whome he offreth . For *Chryſte,as man,offreth hys owne bodie in ſacrifice to him ſelf as God. Et tamen Deus & homo vnus eſt Chriſtus* (as ſaieth *Athanaſius*) And yet God and man ys one Chryſte. *Chriſt doth both offre and ys offred vnto.*

Wherby ys aunſwered in fewe woordes the obiection of the Aduerſarie. For Chryſte ys bothe he to whome the ſacrifice ys made, And he him ſelf alſo ys the Sacrifice yt ſelf,that ys made,as the latter parte of ſainct Auguſtines ſainge dothe ſhewe.*Et vnum eſt cum illo,quod offertur.*He ys one with yt,that ys offred. In the whiche ſaing yow maie perceaue, *that Chryſt ys the preiſt that offreth , he ys the Sacrifice that ys offred , and he ys he , to whome the ſacrifice ys offred.* *In Simbolo*

Perchance the Aduerſarie, who ſeketh by all meanes to impugne, And therbie to flee from the truth and his ſaluacion, will ſaie : that ſainct Auguſtin ſpeaketh this of the Sacrifice offred vpon the Croſſe,and not of the Sacrifice offred in the Maſſe. *Obiectiõ.*

In caſe yt ſo were,yet the former maliciouſe obiection of him ys not onelie perceaued,but alſo ſoluted.For in dede Chryſt making his ſacrifice vpon the croſſe,was bothe the preiſt,the ſacrifice,and alſo he to whom the ſacrifice was made.And therfor falleth that argument, that ſhoulde proue that Chryſt ys not in the Sacrament,bicauſe he was the ſacrifice that was offred to him ſelf in the Sacrament,who (as Chryſoſtome ſaied) ys moſt woorthie of the higheſt honoure. *Anſwer.*

But that this was ſpoken of the Sacrifice offred in the Maſſe,the ſelfe ſame ſentence of ſainct Auguſtin,ſhall declare and proue. For firſt, yt ys manifeſt that no man did offer Chryſt vpon the Croſſe in conſideracion of a ſacrifice,but he him ſelf.But here ſainct Auguſtine ſpeaketh not onelie of the ſacrifice of Chryſt by him ſelf, but by other alſo , as yt ys euident when he ſaieth. *Et vnus eſt cum illis qui offerunt.* And he ys one withe them that doo offer.

Now ioining the whol ſentece together,and not taking yt truncatelie,or by peice meall,as heretikes doo,to maintein there hereſies, and to deceaue the ſimple,wher ys ther any ſacrifice the which ys offred of manie,with the which, and them that offer,and with the Sacrifice offred,and with him to whom yt

ys offred, Chryſt ys one, but in the Sacrifice of the Maſſe, in the which the **E**
Churche being they that doo offer, which Churche ys the bodie of Chryſt,
and Chryſte beinge the heade of the ſame bodie, be one with yt? And therfore when the Churche dothe offer that ſacrifice, Chryſte as one with yt
offreth alſo. And ſo by this wonderfull connexion of the head and the bodie
yt cometh to paſſe, that bothe *the Churche ys offred by Chryſte*, and *Chryſt by the
Churche*, as ſaincte Auguſtin doth ſaie, *Sacerdos ipſe eſt, ipſe offerens, ipſe oblatio.
Cuius rei ſacramentum, quotidianum voluit eſſe Eccleſiæ ſacrificium, cum ipſius corporis
ipſe ſit caput,& ipſius capitis ipſa ſit corpus,tam ipſa per ipſum, quàm ipſe per ipſam con-
ſuetus offerri.* He ys the preiſt, he ys the offerer, and the oblaciō . The ſacramēt
of the which thinge, he willed the dailie Sacrifice of the Churche to be, foraſmoche as of that bodie he ys the head, and of that head, ſhe ys the bodie,
being vſed or accuſtomed, aſwell ſhe by him, as he by her to be offred.
Thus ſaincte Auguſtine.

*Chriſt is
offered of
his Church
and the
Churche of
Chriſt.*

*De ciuit.
Dei.li. 10.
cap. 20.*

*Chriſts bo
die the
dailie Sa-
crifice of
the Church*

Nowe yowe ſee, not only their inuented obiections ſoluted, but alſo the
trueth taught, and confirmed by auncient Authoritie, that ys, *that Chryſtes bo-* **F**
die, which ys in heauen, ys alſo in earth in the Sacrament, as Chryſoſtō teacheth) which
bodie ys ſo verilie preſent, that ys ys *the dailie Sacrifice of the Churche,* not a ſacri
fice of mans inuention, inuented to the derogacion of Chriſtes bleſſed ſacrifice vpō the Croſſe (as the Aduerſaries blaſpheme) but a Sacrifice that Chriſt
him ſelf wolde haue dailie frequented in the Churche, as ſainct Auguſtin tea
cheth as a ſacrament of that bleſſed Sacrifice paſt and doen.

Although, chriſtian Reader, the plentifullneſſe of this matter, and the delectacion of the ſame, and the earneſt deſire that I haue, that all men wolde
be obedient to Gods trueth, aud bringe their imaginacions into captiuitie,
to the obedience of Chryſte, and ſpecially my bretheren, and contrie
men after the fleſh, for whome I wolde wiſh my ſelf accurſed that they
might be ſaued, doth carie me awaie, making me to forgett my ſelf in long
tarieng vpon this one Author: yet nowe I will ſtaie my ſelf, and breiflie note
the thirde note of Chryſoſtom, and then procead to other.

The thirde note ys the ſimilitude whiche Chryſoſtome vſeth in exhortacion to moue vs to the woorthy receauing of ſo glorioùſe a thinge. Yf the **G**
kinges ſonne (ſaieth he) deckt with purple and diademe, were deliuered to
thee to be born, woldeſt thowe not caſt all thinges down on the grounde ād
receaue him? But nowe when thowe takeſt not the ſonne of a king being **a**
man, but the onelie begotten Sonne of God, ſaie, I praie thee, arte thowe
not afraied.

Note then that ye receaue not in the Sacrament a bare peice of bread,
but ye receaue the onelie begotten ſonne of God, Ieſus Chryſt, God and man . At whoſe
preſence we aught to tremble and feare, leſt anie filthineſſe ſhoulde remain
in our conſciences, wherwith the eyes of his maieſtie ſhoulde be offended.

In the receipt of a peice of bread we nede not to tréble, or quake, neither
in the receipt of the merite of Chryſtes paſsion, which ys the ſpirituall recea
uing of Chryſt. For in receauing of that, we receaue great comforth with al,
and no feare, but raither we ſhoulde feare yf we receaue yt not. For
then are we deſtitute of our ſaluacion whiche commeth to vs by the paſſiō
of Chryſte. **H**

*Trembling
at the re-
ceipt of the
Sacr. proo-
ueth the
preſence of
Chriſt.*

But Chryſoſtome asketh yf we *tremble* not, when we receaue the *onelie begotten Sonne of God,* which muſt nedes be at the preſence of ſo high a maieſtie
for conſideracion aboue ſaied, as Peter did vpon the contemplacion of the
                                                                                    powre

A powre of Chryſte,in wourking the miracle of the taking ef the great nom- *Luc.5.*
bre of fiſhes,who fell down at his feet and ſaied:*Exi à me Domine,quia homo pec*
*cator ſum.*Lorde go from me,for I am a ſinfull man.And Centurio likewiſe: *Matth. 8.*
Domine,non ſum dignus, vt intres ſub teƈtum meum. I am not wourthie o Lorde,
that thow ſhouldeſt enter into my houſe. *Luc.7.*

Mary *Magdalen*,though in the preſence of Chriſte ſhe humbled her ſelf,
hauing(no doubte) both feare and ſorowe for her ſinnes committed. Yet,I
dare ſaie,ſhe trébled neuer a whitte at this ioifull voice:*Remittuntur tibi peccata*
*tua.*Thy ſinnes be forgeuen thee,but ſhe reioiced, and was gladde in God.
So vndoubtedlie a man beinge certified by the Spirit of God , that he ys a
partaker of the merittes of Chryſtes paſsion,and therby through the receauing of the Sacramentes ys made a liuelie membre of Chryſt,can not at the
receipt of ſo high a benefit tremble and quake,but ioye,and be gladde, and
praiſe God with manie other that receaued benefits at Chryſtes hand , of
whom the Goſpell maketh mencion.Wherfor yt ys euident, that yt ys the

B the *verie reall preſence of Chryſtes bodie,that we aught to tremble* at, and feare when
we receaue yt,leſt peraduenture anie ſinne ſhoulde be in vs , which ſhoulde
offende his bleſſed Maieſtie,wherbie we might receaue him to our damna-
cion:And not at the receipt of the Chryſte ſpirituallie.

THE NINGHTENE CHAPITER CONTINVETH
the proofe of the ſame matter by S.Auguſtin,and S.Cyrill.

 N the chapiter before ye hearde two famouſe Fathers,not diſſenting,but conſenting,but conſenting,not infirming but confirming the ſainges of the other anciét elders before brought
furth:Nowe will we likewiſe heare other two,whiche will plainlie declare,what was enaƈted ãd receaued in the houſe of God,
for the verie trueth of this matter.

The firſt ſhall be ſainƈte Auguſtine , a miracle of chryſtendom , paſsing *S. Auguſti*
withoute controuerſie all writers,that haue written,both Grekes, and Lati- *ne cómend*
C nes in profownde learninge, and in nombre of bookes, a man ſo famouſe, *ded by this*
that euery childe almoſt in chriſtendom hath ſainƈtAuguſtin in his mouthe. *Authour.*
A man of ſoƈhe grauitie and authoritie,that all Chryſten men do reuerence
him,and ſtaie vpon the ſaing of him:A man of ſoƈhe zeale to the trueth of
Chryſtes faith,that by his learned trauaill he pourged Affrick of the hereſies
of the *Manicheis,* the *Donatiſtes,*and the *Pelagians.*And with all he ys ſo anciét,
being born aboute the yeare of our lorde 354.that he ys withoute ſuſpicion
of corruption in this matter,of our controuerſie.

To declare what the trueth of this matter ys, he ſaieth thus: *Aliud eſt Paſ-* *Cót. literas*
chal , quod adhuc Iudæi celebrant de oue:Aliud autem, quod nos in corpore & ſanguine *Petiliani*
Domini celebramus Yt ys an other Paſſouer , that the Iewes do yet celebrate
with a ſhepe:an other that we doo celebrate in the bodie and bloode of
Chriſte.

In the which ſainge,ye do firſt perceaue,that he doth firſt declare a difference of the Iudaicall Paſſeouer,and the Chryſtian Paſſeouer , yet compa-
D ring them together,as the figure to the thing figured,and by expreſſe woordes ſheweth what they be.The Iudaicall Paſſeouer was a ſhepe :*our Paſſeouer*
ys the bodie and bloode of Chryſte. *An obie-*
Ƈtion.
What more plain woordes wolde theProclamer wiſh to be ſpoké for the
determinacion of this controuerſie ? And yet yt maie be that the enemie

An obie-
Ction.

will here delude the simple,and holde in the arrogant with one of hys com **E**
mon aunswers,that Chryste spirituallie ys our spirituall Paschall Lambe,
but not Chryst reallie present in the Sacrament . For ther ys no soche , neither dothe saincte Augustine saye anye soche thinge here.

The an-
swer.

But to answere this , although the place yt self dothe sufficientlie
teache the verie reall presence of Chrystes bodie and bloode in the Sacra-
ment:Yet by openinge of the difference of the olde Passeouer , and our
newe Passeouer,and by comparyson,of them eche to other,yt shall be more
plain and easie to perceaue the same.   For as Chryst verilie and corporallie dienge, did aunswere the dienge of the lambe : So he being verilie
and corporallie eaten,as our true Paschall Lambe,dothe aunswer the eating
of the Iewesh Passeouer,whiche was both for the dienge, and eatinge , the
verie figure of Chryst.

Yf we re-
ceiue
Christ but
spirituallie,
as the Iues
did our
Passeouers
be all one.

But to ioin nearer with the Aduersarie, yf Chryste spirituallie receaued
onelie,ys our Paschall Lambe,And the Iewes also (as before ys saied) did
euen so receaue Chryste spirituallie in their Paschall feast , How standeth **F**
that difference which saincte Augustine here maketh betwen our Paschall
Lambe and theirs,yf yt be all one,that ys receaued in bothe?Yf saincte Augu
stine had saied yt ys an other Passeouer that the Iewes do kepe with a shepe,
and an other that we do kepe with a peice of bread, and wine , though we
had bothe receaued Chryst spirituallie:Yet the difference might haue stand
in the outwarde signes.But sainge as he doth,yt must nedes be , that as the
Iewes passeouer was a verie shepe in dede,So ys our passeouer *the very bodie*

Christes
reall bodie
oure Passeo
uer.

of Christe in dede.

And althoughe this might suffice for aunswere to the Aduersarie : Yet yt
shal be by an other setece of the same S.Augustin made so plain,that he shal
not be able to denie,but that S.Augustin taught a real presence in the Sacra

Cot.Faust.
Man. Li.
20.ca.18.

met.Hys sentece ys this.*Hebrei autem in victimis pecorum,quas offerebant Deo mul
tis et varijs modis, sicut re tanta dignum erat, prophetiam celebrabant future victi-
me, quam Christus obtulit. Vnde iam Christiani , peracti eiusdem sacrificij memoriam
celebrant sacrosancta oblatione , et participatione corporis et sanguinis Christi .* The He-

Sacrifice of
the Chri-
stians in
oblacio and
participa-
cion.

brues in the sacrifices of beastes, whiche they did offer vnto God manye **G**
and diuerse waies,as for so great a thing yt was meet, did openlie declare a
prophecie of the sacrifice to come,whiche Chryste did offer.Wherfor nowe
the chrystians do celebrate the memorie of the same Sacrifice past, *by the holie oblacion,and participacion of the bodie and blood of Chryste :* Thus moche sainct
Augustine.

Yf this woorde participacion had ben alone in this sencence,he shoulde
haue had (spirituallie) on the backe of him immediatelie, and so by violence haue ben wrested to sownde to the euell tuned notes of the Aduersaries.   But praised be the holie Spirit of God , the Spirit of consent,
and agreement , who so kaied thys woorde,*participacion,* with the woorde , *oblacion* , that yt can not be wrested to sownde any other sounde,
then the reall presence of Chrystes blessed bodie in the Sacrament.Which
bodie the Chrystians(saieth S.Augustin)do offer in sacrifice in the remembrance of the Sacrifice of Chryst don vpon the Crosse.

By whiche maner of sainge of sainct Augustin, all the obiections of the
aduersaries,whiche are made against the Sacrifice of the Masse, are clean wi- **H**
ped awaie,as more at large in the third booke,by the helpe of Godes grace,
yt shall be declared.

Yt

A   Yt ys well knowen to all men bothe true Chryſtians, and Pſeudochryſtians, that if Chryſtes bodie be offred of vs in ſacrifice or oblaciō (as ſainct
Auguſtine doth here affirme) ther muſt nedes be a reall preſence of the ſame
bodie ſo offred, or ells yt muſt nedes be a mathematicall ſacrifice.

Ye haue nowe heard ſainct Auguſtine reporting ſoche trueth, as was ena
cted and receaued in Chryſtes Parliament houſe. Nowe will we heare an
other of the other ſide of the ſame houſe reporte the ſame trueth, whiche *Cyrillus
ſhall be the holie Father Cyrill, a man profowdlie ſeen in the ſtatutes of the* *cōmēded of
houſe of Chryſte. Who for his excellent wourthineſſe in holineſſe, grauitie,* *the Aut-
and learning, was preſident in the great Councell Epheſine, whiche was* *hour.*
one of the foure principall Councells of the whiche ſain<e Gregorie ſpeaketh ſo móch praiſe, wherin the hereſie of *Neſtorius* was confownded, and
condemned.

Whiche Cyrill alſo through cōſtancie in faithe wrote againſt the Arrians
both learnedlie and godlie, as his woorkes do teſtifie, he liued aboute the
B yeare of our lorde 4 2 0. And therfor for his auncientie woorthie to be beleued, being after this ſupputacion 1136. yeares agon.

This man ſaieth after this ſorte: *Nec putet ex tarditate mentis ſuæ Iudæus, inaudi-* *li. 4. in .6.*
ta nobis excogitata eſſe myſteria. Videbit enim, ſi attentius quærat, hoc ipſum à Moiſis *Ioan.*
temporibus factitatum fuiſſe. Quid enim maiores eorum à morte, & pernitie Aegyptiaca *cap. 14.*
*liberauit, quando mors in primogenita Aegypti deſæuiebat? Nónne omnibus palam eſt, quia
diuina inſtitutione perdocti, agni carnes manducauerunt, ac poſtes, et ſuperliminaria agni
ſanguine perunxerunt, propterea mortem ab eis diuertiſſe? Pernities namque, id eſt, mors
huius carnis, aduerſus humanum genus, propter primi hominis tranſgreſſionem fure-
bat. Terra enim es, & in terram reuerteris, propter peccatum audiuimus. Verùm quoniam per carnem ſuam Chriſtus atrocem hunc euerſurus erat Tyrannum, propterea id myſterio apud priſcos obumbratur, & ouinis carnibus, & ſanguine ſancti
ficati, Deo ita volente, pernitiem effugiebant. Quid igitur, Iudæe, turbaris, præ-
figuratam iam diu veritatem videns? Cur, inquam, turbaris, ſi Chriſtus dicit: Niſi
manducaueritis carnem filij hominis & biberitis eius ſanguinē, non habebitis vitā in vobis,
quum oporteret te Moſaicis legibus inſtitutum, & priſcis vmbris ad credendum perdoctū,
C ad intelligenda hæc myſteria paratiſſimum eſſe? Vmbram, & figuram noſti, diſce ergo
ipſam rei veritatem. Caro (inquit) mea verè eſt cibus, & ſanguis meus verè eſt potus.*
Let not the Iewe, by ſlackneſſe of minde thinke, that we haue inuented
myſteries neuer heard of before. He ſhall ſee (yf he will with better heede
ſeke) euen the ſame often doen from the time of Moiſes. For what did deliuer ther elders from death and deſtruction of Aegipte, when death raiged
very ſore vpon the firſt born of Aegipte? ys yt not knowen to all men that
they being taught by the commaundemet of God, did eate the fleſh of the
lambe, and with the bloode of the lambe did anoincte the poſtes, and the
vpper dore poſtes, and therfor death diuerted from them? Deſtruction, that
ys to ſaie, the deathe of this fleſh, for the tranſgreſſion of the firſt man, raiged ſore againſt mankinde. For ſinne we hearde: Thowe arte earth, and
into earth thowe ſhalt retourn. But for aſmoche as Chryſt woolde ouerthrowe by his fleſh this cruell Tyranne, therfore that was ſhadowed among
the olde Fathers in a miſterie, and they being ſanctified withe the fleſh and
D blood of a ſhepe (God ſo willing) did eſcape the plague ād deſtructiō. Wher
for then, thowe Iewe art thow troubled, ſeing nowe the trueth long before
prefigurated? why, I ſaie, arte thowe troubled, yf Chryſte do ſaie: *Except ye
eate the fleſh of the ſonne of man, and drink his bloode, ye ſhall haue no life in yowe:* ſeing
yt behoueth thee beinge inſtructed in Moiſes lawes, ād taught, by the olde

                 I iiij   ſhaddowes

ſhaddowes to beleue, to be moſt readie to vnderſtãd theſe miſteries.Thowe   E
haeſt knowen the ſhaddowe ãd the figure: *Learn therfor the veritie of the thing.*
My fleſh(ſaieth he) ys verilie meat, and my blood ys verilie drinke. Thus
farre Cyrill.

 Whome ye haue hearde at lenght declaring the figuratiue Paſchall lãbe,
and the benefit that the Iewes had by the ſame.Likewiſe ye haue heard him
declaring the true Paſchall Lambe, and the benefite that commeth to vs
therbie . And when he hath applied the figure to the thing figured, whiche
ys the trueth of the figure as a matter ſufficiẽtlie taught ther, to be beleued
of the Iewes : He falleth into a wonder at the incredulitie of thẽ,and repro-
uinge them all in the perſon of one ,ſaieth : Why arte thowe (o Iewe) troubled, ſeing nowe the verie veritie long before this preſigurated? Yt behoued thee being inſtructed by Moiſes Lawes , and verie well taught
by the olde ſhadowes to beleue, to be moſt readie to vnderſtande theſe
miſteries.

 Yf Cyrill did ſo earneſtlie reproue the Iewes for their incredulitie, being   F
taught but by Moyſes, and the figures , howe wolde he reprouc our men
who well inſtructed,not by Moyſes,but by Chryſte : not by ſhaddowes,and
figures,but by the goſpell of treuth and veritie not moued (as the Iewes
ſemed to be) to beleue a ſtraunge noueltie,but an aunciente ſaithe recea-
Falſe Chri ſtians wort hilie repro- ued for ſa- king their faith. red of antiquitie: Yf the Iewes(I ſaie) be woorthie of reproche who knowe
not the true faithe, whiche they neuer yet had by plain knowledge recea-
ued : how moche more be our falſe Chryſtians to be reproued, which,the
faithe that they were brought vppe in, that they once embraced and receaued that they earneſtlie beleued : nowe haue maliciouſlie not onelie contemned, but alſo Reuiled, deteſted and abiected?

 God that ys the verie light, lighten their heartes, that they maie ſee into
howe depe damnacion they haue deiected and caſt them ſelues, by their
forſaking of the catholique faith, being nowe bare, and void of all excuſe,
forſomoche as they did once knowe the trueth, whiche nowe deueliſhlie
they blaſpheme. *Si non veniſſem, & locutus eis fuiſſem , peccatum non haberent,nũc*
Ioan 15. *autem excuſationem non habent de peccato ſuo.*Yf I had not commed (ſaied Chryſt)   G
and ſpokẽ to them,they ſhoulde not haue had ſinne : but nowe they haue
none excuſe of their ſinne.

 God, I ſaie, therfore haue mercie vpon them, whileſt time of mercie for
them endureth, and geue them grace dailie with the Prophett Dauid to crie
Pſal. 12. and ſaie: *Reſpice, & exaudi me Domine Deus meus. Illumina oculos meos ne vnquam*
obdormiam in morte, ne quando dicat inimicus meus, prævalui aduerſus eum. Conſider
and heare me , o Lorde , my God lighten mine eies that I ſheape not
in death , leſt mine enemis ſaie, I haue preuailed againſt him.

 What a preie and Spoill ys yt to our goſtlie enemie, and howe moche
dothe he reioice, when he deceaueth one that hath ben in the true faith,
and berieueth him of the ſame, and ſo driueth him from God? No doubte
he counteth yt a great Spoill, and reioiceth moch at yt , as the verſe of the
ſame pſalme immediatelie folowing dothe ſaie: *Qui tribulant me exultabunt,ſi*
motus fuero. They that trouble me, will reioice at yt, yf I becaſt down. Return
therfor in time, and cleaue hard to the ſtreight and ſtrong piller of trueth.
For if ye be caſt downe ye ſhall fall verie lowe, and ſinke depe.   H

Math. 10. Chryſte ſending his Apoſtles to preache, taught them thus : Into what
cittie ſoeuer ye ſhall come, enquire who ys worthie in yt, and ther abide
till ye go thence, and whoſoeuer ſhall not receaue yowe, nor will heare
                    yowe

A yowe preachinge, when ye departe oute of that houfe or cittie, fhake of the duft of yowe feete. Verilie I faie vnto yowe, yt fhall be eafier for the lande of Sodom, and Gomorre, in the daie of Iudgement, then for that citte.

Confider therfor and heauie hand of God vpon Sodom, and gomorre, which in foche terrible forte being fonke, and deftroied, with fire and Brimftone from heauen, argueth a more terrible damnacion to enfewe, and folowe, and yet yt fhall be more eafie to them in the daie of Iudgement, then to foche as will not receaue faith: Howe moche more greuoufe then fhall yt be to them which forfake that faith, that not onelie they them felues haue receaued, but the wholl Churche of Chryft throughoute all Chryftendom, whiche faithe, although yt hath diuerfe times ben impugned (as nowe in theife daies yt ys) Yet, God be praifed, yt was neuer ouerthowen, nor neuer fhall be, and will cleaue to an herefie, whiche hath ben not onelie fundrie and diuerfe times ympugned, but ouerthrowen, condemned, curfed,

B and extincted? Surelie as their reproche ys moche in this worlde, for their fo doing. So fhall yt be moche more before the face of God and his electe, in the daie of his terrible iudgement.

But I will retourn from whence I haue digreffed, and touche one note more of Cyrill and fo paffe to other. After he had thus rebuked theIewes, for their hardneffe of beleue, he faied: *Vmbram & figuram nofti, difce ergo ipfam rei veritatem.* Thow haueft knowen the Shaddow and the figure, *learn therfore the verie thinge.*

Note here again, as before in Chryfoftom ys noted, that the olde Pafchall lambe was a figure, and owre Pafchall Lambe the verie thinge. Then yt ys not a peice of bread, a bare fign or figure of Chryft, for then thefe fainges of the learned Fathers were not true, whiche faie plainlie, that yt ys the verie thinge.

And this Father, when he had willed the Iewes to learn the verie thing, he declared furthwith what the verie thing ys: *Caro mea verè eft cibus, & fanguis meus verè eft potus.* My flefh (faieth Chryft) ys verilie meat, and my

C bloode ys verilie drinke. This (faieth Cyrill) ys the verie thing of the figure *the verie flesh and bloode of Chrift* whiche be verilie meat and verilie drinke.

Howe this texte, and other apperteining to the fame matter in the fixte of S.Iohn, haue ben wrefted and wried, and violentliie drawen by the enemies of gods trueth from their natiue and true fenfe, yt fhall be fhewed more at large in the fecond booke.

But nowe that the Aduerfarie ys preffed fo fore, he ys driuen to his common refuge, of the woorde, *Spirituallie,* and will peraduenture. faie that the bread in the Sacrament ys not the verie thinge that aunfwereth the figure of the Pafchall lambe, but the flefh and bloode of Chryft (as Cyrill here alleageth) Spirituallie receaued.

But howe farre this their common glofe diffenteth from the truthe, yt fhall by Gods helpe ftreight waie euidentlie appeare.

Firft, this ys moft certen, that the faithfull people of the olde Teftament, *1.Cor. 10.* whiche through faithe in Chryfte to come, were the children of faithfull

D Abraham, did eate the flefh and drincke the bloode of Chryft fpirituallie, as faincte Paule wittneffeth: *Omnes eandem efcam fpiri uale manducauerunt, & omnes eundem potum fpiritualem biberunt, bibebant autem de fpirituali confequente eos petra. Petra autem erat Chriftus.* All our Fathers did eate of one fpirituall meat, and

and

and did all drinke of one maner of fpirituall drinke. For they drancke of **E** that fpirituall Rocke that folowed them, whiche Rocke was Chryft.

Yf Chryft was then fpirituallie eaten and dronken of the fathers, the fpirituall eatinge and drinknige of Chryfte, or Chryfte fpirituallie eaten and dronken was not figured by the Pafchall läbe, neither can the Pafcall Läbe be applied to Chryfte fpirituallie eatē as the propre figure to the thing figured. And this fhall be proued : For all the Sacramentes and Ceremonies of the olde Lawe were figures of thinges to come, and to be doen, and fullfilled in the newe lawe. Aud if Chryft were receaued fpirituallie of the Fathers in the olde lawe, then was the Pafchall lambe no figure of Chryft to be fpirituallie receaued in the newe lawe.

That the Sacrifices and Ceremonies of the law were figures of thinges to come, S. Paule teftifieth : *Vmbram habens lex futurorum bonorum &c.* The lawe hauing the fhaddowe of good thinges to come, and not the verie fafhion of the thinges them felues &c.

Hebr. 10.

And fainēte Auguftine alfo (as before ys alleaged) faieth that the facrifi- **F** ces of the Hebrues were prophecies of the facrifices to come, whiche Chrift did offer.

Math. 5.

Wherunto Chryft him felf, who came to fullfill the lawe, hauing regarde, faied : *Iota vnum, aut vnus apex non præteribit à lege, donec omnia fiant.* One iotte or one title of the lawe fhall not fcape, till all be fullfilled. Whiche maner of fpeache fhoulde not nede: yf the thinges that were figured, were doen allreadie. Wherfor feing the fpirituall receauing of Chryft was not a thing to comme, but was in vfe euen with the figuts in the time of the lawe : And alfo forfomoche as the Sacramentall bread (as they do terme yt) whiche ys but a fign or a figure of Chryft, ys not the thing that ys figured, For the thinge that ys figured muft nedes be Chryft, and as yt ys nowe proued yt can not be Chryft fpirituallie : therfor of neceffitie yt muft be verie Chryft reallie. And therfore to conclude, when Cirill faied in the ende of his fentence : Thowe haueft knowen the figure, learn therfor the verie thinge: And alleageth this Scripture: *My flesh ys verilie meate, and my blood ys verilie drinke* Bothe he and the Scripture meen the verie thinge, whiche ys the *reall and* **G** *fubftanciall flesh of Chrift and his verie bloode,* and not the fpiritual flefh and blood onely.

Ioan. 6.

THE TWENTETH CHAPITER IOINETH
fainct Gregorie, and Damafcen to confirme the fame matter.

E haue all readie heard certain cooples of the two fides of the higher houfe of Parliament. whiche howe they agree within them felues, and howe Iuftlie and trulie they reporte the enacted veritie of the fame, and therwith howe mightilie they ouerthrowe the peftilent fectes of the wicked, I truft the gentle Reader dothe well perceaue.

Nowe though this great mafter of herefie will not accept the Authours that haue written within the compaffe of theife nime hondreth yeares, whiche therfore I diuide from the other that did write within fixe hondreth years after Chryft. calling them of the lower houfe, and theife of the higher houfe: yet for afmoche as I write as well for the comforth of the true bele- **H** uing Chryftian, as for the confutacon of the falfe Chryftian : I will confult with an other coople, of the whiche the one ys laft of the higher houfe, and the other one of the firfte or cheifeft of the lower houfe. and after with

o ther

A   other of the lower houſe, that the trueth reported of manie, maye the more ioifullie be embraced, and they that refuſe them, and their authoritie,
wourthilie defaced . For yf theſe of the lower houſe, do agree with them of
the higher houſe, and haue all one tune and ſownde with them in the trueth
then both their prowde arrogancie, whiche haue ſo contemptuouſlie reie-
ĉted ſo manie verteuouſe and learned mens authorities, ys condignelie to
be rebuked, and alſo their falſe impoſture, teaching that the Churche hath
ſiuerued from the trueth and lien in erronr ſo manie yeares, to thentente
that they getting eſtimacon as the Inuentours of trueth, might ſell their lies
vnder the colour of truth, maie the better be perceaued.

   This Authour whom I called the laſt of the higher houſe ys ſainĉt Gregorie, who ſomtime was cheif head vnder Chryſt of the howſe, a man both
learned, and vertuouſe, as appeareth not onelie by him that ſetteth oute his
life in ſtorie, but alſo by his own woorkes, ſauouring as well of vertue and
holineſſe, as of learning and faithfull trueth.

Sainĉt Gre
gorie hys
cõmēdaciõ.

B   This holie learned Father in a Paſchall homelie, comparing the olde
Paſchall Lambe to the newe ſaieth thus : *Quæ videlicet cunĉta magnam nobis ædi-
ficationem pariunt, ſi fuerint myſtica interpretatione diſcuſſa. Quid namque ſit ſanguis agni,
non iam audiendo, ſed bibendo didiciſtis. Qui ſanguis ſuper vtrunque poſtem ponitur, quãdo
non ſolùm ore corporis, ſed etiam ore cordis hauritur. Nam qui ſic redemptoris ſui ſanguinē
ſumit, vt imitari paſſionem eius necdum velit, in vno poſte ſanguinem poſuit.* All whiche
thinges do bring furth to vs great edificacion, yf they ſhall be with a miſticall
interpretacion diſcuſſed. What the bloode of the lãbe ys, ye haue not onelie by hearing, but by drinking learned. Whiche blood ys put vpon bothe
the poſtes, when not onelie with the mouthe of the bodie, but alſo with the
mouthe of the heart yt ys receaued. For he that doth ſo receaue the bloode
of his redemer, that he wolde not yet folowe his paſſion, he hath put the
bloode but vpon one poſte. Thus moche ſainĉte Gregorie.

Omil . 22.
Paſcha.

   As in this ſaing he hath made mencion of the bloode of Chryſt, So pro-
ceadinge vpon the ſame matter in the ſame homelie, he ſpeaketh of the
eating of the olde Paſchall Lambe, and of the eating of Chryſtes bodie our
C   true Paſchall lambe. *In noĉte quippe (inquit) agnum comedimus , quia in ſacramento
modò Dominicum corpus accipimus, quando adhuc inuicem noſtras conſcientias non videmus.* In the night (ſaieth he) do we eate the lambe, forſomoche as we do
nowe receaue *our lordes bodie in the Sacrament,* when as yet we doe not ſee one
an others conſcience:

Chryſtes
bodie and
blood recei
ued with
mouth of
bodie and
ſoule both .

   In this his ſainge, ys not onelie perceaued the applicacion of the figuratiue Paſchall Lambe, to the verie true Paſchall Lambe, but to the full agreement with other holie Fathers before alleaged, he doth moſt plainlie teſtifie the reall preſence, bothe by his woordes, *terming yt the bloode of our Redemer
and the bodie of our lorde,* and alſo by the maner of the receauinge of yt. In the
whiche note that he teacheth that the bodie and bloode of Chryſt ys receaued by two diſtinĉted and diuerſe maners of receauinge. One maner ys
with the mouthe of the bodie , whiche argueth the reall preſence : The
other maner ys with the mouthe of the hearte, and that ys the ſpirituall maner of receauing.

   So that the learned men in Chryſtes faithe, doo teache the good Chryſti-
D   an man to receaue Chryſtes bodie both corporallie, and ſpirituallie. But the
maliciouſe learned man againſt Chryſtes faith, teacheth that the good Chry
ſtian man receaueth Chryſte but onelie ſpiritualiie, and ſo robbeth him of
the other, the contrarie of the whiche Doĉtrine ye ſee here auouched by
                                                                        ſainĉt

fainct Gregorie as yt was alfo by other before alleaged, with whom he well **E**
agreeth,

To this fainct Gregorie fhall be yoined Damafcen one of the other fide
of the Parliament houfe of Chryft, that ys, of the greke church, and of the
lowe houfe, but one of the firft and cheif in that place, as ys before faied, a
man fo excellentlie will feen in the ftatutes of Chryftes Parliament houfe,
that ys to faie in the knowledge of the receaued trueth of Chryftes faithe,
that he did write foure bookes of the fame both learnedlie and godlie, and
in the fourthe booke of his workes , emong other explicacions of matters of
faith, he declareth alfo the faithe of the Churche in this matter of the Sacrament at large, wher as touching the fame matter he faieth thus:

Li.4. de or-
thod.fid. c.
14.

Natiuitas nobis per fpiritum donata eft, per fanctum dico baptifmum. Cibus verò ipfe
panis vitæDominus nofter Iefus Chriftus, qui de cœlo defcendit. Nam fufcepturus volunta-
riam pro nobis mortem, in nocte qua feipfum obtulit, teftamentum nouum difpofuit fanctis
Difcipulis & Apoftolis, & per ipfos omnibus alijs in ipfum credentibus . In cœnaculo
fanctæ & gloriofæ Sion antiquum Pafcha cum Difcipulis manducans, et implens inftrumē- **F**
tum antiquum , lauit pedes Difcipulorum, fignum fancti baptifmatis præbens. Deinde fran-
gens panem dedit illis dicens : Accipite , & comedite, Hoc eft corpus meum, quod pro
vobis tradetur in remifsionem peccatorum. Similiter accipiens calicem ex vino & aqua,
tradidit illis dicens : Bibite ex eo omnes, hic eft fanguis meus noui teftamenti, qui pro vobis
effunditur in remifsionem peccatorum . Hoc facite in meam cōmemorationem. Quotiefcun-
que enim manducabitis panem hunc, & calicem bibetis, mortem filij hominis annunciatis,
& refurrectionem eius cōfitemini donec veniat. Si igitur verbum dei viuens eft & efficax,
& omnia quæcunque voluit Deus, fecit: Si dixit, Fiat lux, & facta eft lux : Fiat firma-
mentum, & factum eft : Si verbo Dei cœli firmati funt, & fpiritu oris eius omnis virtus
eorum: Si cœlum, terra, aqua, ignis, & aer, & omnis ornatus eorum verbo Dei perfecta
funt, & homo ipfe vbique diuulgatum animal: Si volens ipfe Deus Verbum, factus eft
homo, &c. Non poteft panem fuum ipfius corpus facere, & vinum cum aqua fanguinem?
Dixit in principio Deus : Producat terra herbam virentem , & vfque nunc pluuia facta
producit germina , diuino coädiuta & vigorata præcepto. Dixit Deus: Hoc eft corpus
meum, & hic eft fanguis meus, & hoc facite in meam commemoratiōe, & omnipotenti
eius præcepto donec veniat, efficitur.

A néwe birth ys geuen to vs , by the Spirit and the water, I faie, by holie **G**
Baptifme, but *the meat ys the verie bread of life our lorde Iefus Chrift,* who defcended from heauen. For willing to take for vs a willing death, in the night , in
the whiche he offred vppe him felf, he difpofed a newe teftamēt to his holie

Chryftes
cuppe cōtei-
ned wine ād
Water.

Difciples and Apoftles, and by them to all other beleuing in him. In the parlour therfore of holie glorioufe Sion, eating the olde Paffeouer with his
difciples, and fulfilling the olde lawe, he wafhed the feet of his difciples, geuing a fign of holie Baptifme . Afterwarde breaking bread he gaue yt to thē
faing : Take eate, This ys my bodie, whiche fhall be deliuered for yowe in
the remiffion of finnes. Likewife taking the cuppe *of wine and water,* he deliuered yt vnto them faing: Drinke ye all of this. This ys my bloode of the newe Teftament, whiche fhall be fhedde for yowe in the remiffion of Sinnes,
This do ye in my remembrāce. For as often times as ye fhall eate this bread,
ād drinke this cuppe, ye fhew furth the death of the Sōne of mā, ād acknowledge his refurrectiō vntill he come. Yf then the woorde of God be liuing, ād
mightie in operaciō, and al thinges , whatfoeuer he hath willed he hath doē, **H**
Yf he faied, The light be made, and the light was made: The firmament be
made, and yt was made: Yf by the woorde of God the heauens were made,
and all the power of them, with the breath of his mouthe: Yf heauen, earth,

water,

A water, fire and the Ayer, and al the furniture of them, by the woorde of God were made perfect, and man himself, being euery where a knowen liuing creature: Yf God the Sonne himself being willing was made man, &c. *Can not he make breade his owne bodie? and wine and water his bloode?* God faied at the beginning: Let the earth bring furth green herbe, And vntill this daie, being holpen and made ftrong with Gods commaundement, the rain comming, yt bringeth furth fruicts. God faied: This ys my bodie, and this ys my blood and this do ye in the remembrance of me: *And by hys allmightie commaunde-ment yt ys fo made and brought to effecte vntill he come* . Thus farre Da-mafcen.

Effect of Chryftes woordes of confecracio

Whofe faing ys long, but as pithie and weightie as yt ys long. In the which he hath not onelie declared hys faith, but the faith of Chryft receaued in his Churche, which ys the wholl matter, and onelie argument of hys worke, as the title of the fame doth purporte.

And to the matter, which we haue in hande, he geueth woorthie teftimo
B nie, declaring the accomplifhment of the olde lawe, in eating the olde Paf-chall Lambe, and the beginning of the newe teftament, with the newe Paf-chall Lambe. Which Pafchall Lambe, how yt was, and what yt was, and how yt ys wrought ãd made, he leaueth yt not vndeclared. He tooke bread (faieth he, *mening Chryft*) and brake yt, and gaue yt to his difciples faing : Take, eate, This ys my bodie.

And that he might leaue no place to the enemies to mifconftrue him, and to wreft him to their pourpofe, he addeth the probacion of yt by the powre of God in other of hys workes, which ys alfo a moft plain declaracion of hys faith, That as God by his woorde made heauen, and earth and all thinges in them conteined: So by his woorde faing: *Thys ys my bodie*, yt ys euen fo made in dede, as yt ys faied. For can not he (faieth Damafcen) make *the bread his bo-die? and the wine and water his bloode?* Which woordes being fo plain nede no in terpretaciõ. For he affirmeth that God by hys woord, and allmightie powre dothe make *the bread his bodie, and the wine and water his bloode.*

Chryft tur ned the bread into his bodie, and the wy ne and wa-ter into his blood.

And wher the Aduerfarie hath againft this, faied: that he doubteth not of
C the power of God, but that he ys able to do yt, yf he will, or yf yt be his plea-fure: but we finde not (faieth he) in the fcripture that his pleafure ys, that the preift pronouncing the woordes, fhoulde by gods power confecrate the bo-die of Chryfte. This ys their ignoraunt fcruple. But if they had, leuing all arrogancie, mekelie confulted with thys Damafcẽ, they fhoulde haue fownd yt in the fcripture, that Gods pleafure ys, *that the bodie of Chryfte fhoulde be confe-crated by the poower of God, and by the preift as his mynifter* . For God) faieth Da-mafcen) faied at the beginning: Let the earth bring furth grene herbe, and vn till this time the earth being holpen with Godes commaundement doth bringe furth fruict. God faied: This ys my bodie, this ys my bloode , this doe ye in remembrance of me, And by his allmightie commaundement, yt ys fo made.

Chryft com maunded his bodie to be cõfecra-ted.

Note then, that when Chryft by his powre had of bread made his bodie, for he faied yt was his bodie, and his faing ys making, Then he gaue com-maundement to his myniftres faing: *Hoc facite*. This doo ye , by the whiche allmightie commaundement (faieth Damafcen) yt ys doen.
D But nowe when the fcripture ys produced and laied before their face, ha-uing no good will to accept the trueth, they procead to queftioning, and af-ke: howe proue ye that Chryft by thefe woordes , commaunded the confe-cracion.

How the queftion of the faithlef fe answered

K   Ytys

Yt ys as mete a queſtion as wher we heard that God ſaied : let the earth E
bring furth grene herbe, to ſaie : Howe proue ye that the earth by Gods
commaundement bringeth furth grene herbe?For God ſaied: this ys my bodie,and this do ye,whiche ys as plain as the other.

But to aunſwer to them I ſaie:Euē as they proue that theſe woordes, *Hoc
facite,This do ye* , be ſcripture:So do I with Damaſcen affirme, that by them
Chryſte commaunded the conſecracion of his bodie.

*The Chur-
che that
teacheth vs
which be
ſcripturs,
teacheth vs
alſo the vn-
derſtāding
of the ſame*

The proof that they cā,ād the cheifeſt that they haue ys,that the Church
hath ſo taught,and deliuered yt to them.And by the ſame proof ſaie I, that
the Churche, that taught them that yt ys ſcripture, hath taught me that
this ys the meening of yt.And as good authoritie,and knowledge hath ſhe
to teache me the mening of the ſcripture, as to teach them that yt ys
ſcripture.

And that they ſhall not thinke,that this ys onely the opiniō of Damaſcē,
and of the Churche when he liued,which they haue ſnſpected according to
the vanitie of their minde,not to be withoute corruption(although by ſom F
mens computacion,Damaſcen liued aboue a thouſand yeares agone) they
ſhall heare Chryſoſtom,who vndoubtedlie liued wellnigh twelue hondreth
yeares agon,agreing with this Authour in this matter. Thus writeth he . *Et*

*Chryſoſt.
hom.30.de
prodition.
Iudæ.*

*nunc ille præſtò eſt Chriſtus,qui illam ornauit menſam,ipſe iſtā quoque conſecrat. Non enim
homo eſt,qui propoſita de conſecratione menſæ Domini,corpus Chriſti facit & ſanguinem,
ſed ille qui pro nobis crucifixus eſt Chriſtus.Sacerdotis ore verba proferuntur,ſed Dei virtu
te conſecrantur,& gratia.Hoc eſt (ait) corpus meū.Hoc verbo propoſita conſecrantur . Et
ſicut illa vox quæ dixit,Creſcite & multiplicamini,ſemel quidem dicta eſt , ſed omni tempore ſentit effectum ad generationem,operante natura: ita vox illa ſemel quidem dicta eſt,
ſed per omnes menſas Eccleſiæ vſque ad hodiernum diem,et vſque ad eius aduentum præſtat
ſacrificio firmitatem.*

*Chryſt,not
man doth
conſecrate
his body
and blood.*

And nowe that ſame Chryſt ys preſent which did furniſh that table, he
alſo dothe conſecrate this.Yt ys not man that maketh the thinges ſettfurth
the bodie and bloode of Chryſt by the *conſecracion* of the table, but he that
was crucified for vs,euen Chryſt.*The woordes are ſpoken by the mouth of the preiſt:
But the thinges are conſecrated by the power and grace of God.Thys ys(ſaieth he) my bo-
die.By this woorde the things ſettfurth are conſecrated.*And as that voice , the which G
ſaieth:Growe ye,and be multiplied,was but once ſpoken,but yet yt feeleth
allwaie effecte,nature woorking with yt vnto generacion: Euē ſo that voice
alſo was but once ſpoken,but throughout all the tables of the Church vntill this preſent daie,and vntill his cōming yt geueth to the ſacrifice ſtréght.
Thus moche Chryſoſtom.

Doe ye not marke here,that no mā,but Chryſt maketh the things ſett furth
vpon the table(which be bread and wine)his bodie and blood?Doth not he
agree with Damaſcē who ſaieth by interrogaciō:Cā he not make the bread
his owne bodie,and the wine and water his blood?By which maner of queſtion he meeneth that Chryſt doth make his bodie and bloode of the

*Chryſt cō-
maunded
his bodie
and blood
to be conſe-
ſecrated.*

bread and wine . Doth not Chryſoſtom declare the execucion of
Gods commaundement to the myniſter as concerning conſecracion, ſo
farre as to his office apperteineth, and that God doth woorke the thing
by his power , when he ſaieth : *The woordes are ſpoken by the mouth of the preiſt*
(note here the execucion of the commaundement *Hoc facite , This do ye*)*ſed Dei virtute* H
conſecrantur & gratia : but they are conſecrated by Godes power and grace . Behold,
the doing and woorking of the thing apperteineth to God. Doth not nowe
Chryſoſtome agree with Damaſcen, and Damaſcen with Chryſoſtom, ſo as
　　　　　　　　　　　　　　　　　　　　　　　　　they

A they ſaie all one thing in effecte, though they vſe diuerſe ſimilitudes to proue that the power of the conſecracion of Chryſtes bodie and bloode ys of force, and ſhall continue vntill Chryſt come?

    Nowe then (gentle Reader) yf thowe by errour haueſt diſſented from the trueth, return again, and come to the houſe of God, wher ys conſent of one trueth. Yf this like thee not, wilt thow beleue Luther the Patriarke, or more trulie, the Hereſiarke of your faith? Hear what he ſaieth: *Conſecrandi officium inſtituit, dum dicit : Hoc facite. Facere enim eſt hoc totum imitari, quod ipſe tunc fecit.* He inſtituted the office of conſecracion when he ſaied. Thys do ye. For to doe, ys by imitacion to doe all that he then did. Thus Luther.

Office of conſecratiõ inſtituted by Chriſt, ſaieth Luther.

    And thus ye perceaue that he alſo was of the minde, that Chryſt did inſtitute the conſecracion by theſe woordes, *Hoc facite.* This do ye.

    Yf ye will yet procead, and vſe this common queſtion (howe) whiche (with lamentacion I ſaie yt) ys to moche vſed nowe a daies in matters of

Howe, the queſtion to moche vſed nowe a daie:

B faith, and aske how the breade ys made the bodie of Chryſt, Damaſcen alſo doth aunſwer you, ſainge· *Quomodò fiet iſtud, dicit ſancta virgo, quoniam virum non cognoſco? Reſpondit Gabriel Archangelus: Spiritus ſanctus ſuperueniet in te, & virtus Altiſsimi obumbrabit tibi. Itaque ſi & nunc interrogas, quomodò panis ſit corpus Chriſti, et vinum, et aqua ſanguis Chriſti : Reſpondeo et ego tibi : Spiritus ſanctus obumbrat, et hæc ſupra ſermonem et intelligentiam operatur.* The holie virgen ſaied. Howe ſhall this be doen, for I knowe not a man? The Archaungell Gabriel aunſwered: The holie Goſt ſhall come vpon thee, and the powre of *the higheſt ſhall ouerſhadow thee.Therfor yf thow aſkeſt* nowe, howe the bread ys made the bodie of Chryſt, and the wine and water hys blood, I alſo aunſwere thee. *The holie Goſt doth ouer ſhaddowe and woorketh theſe thinges aboue that maie be ſpoken or vnderſtanded.* Thus Damaſcen.

Damaſc. ibid.

The holie Goſt. woorketh the conſecratiõ aboue our vnderſtanding.

    O mercifull God howe lowlie was the ſubmiſsion of mens hearts and vnderſtanding in thoſe daies to faith, who were aunſwered, ſatiſſied, and fullie contented with a fewe woordes ? But in this our time, ſo puffed vppe be the heartes of men, ſo high in ſingularitie be their vnder-

C ſtandinges, that manie aunſwers, manie writings, manie bookes, yea manie great volumes will not content, nor ſtaie them . This Authonr hath ſaied ſo moche as maie well aunſwer a man that will be aunſwered. For firſt he declared that our true Paſchall Lambe, ys the verie bodie of Chryſt . Secondarelie, that Chryſt himſelf, as he was in powre able, So by hys powre in the Supper he made the bread hys owne bodie, and the wine and water his bloode. Thirdlie, that by hys ſaied allmightie commaundement, and power, the ſaid conſecracion of hys bodie and blood ys and ſhall be vſed and doen till he come to the generall iudgement. Fourthlie, yf we will knowe howe, and by what means the conſecracion ys doen, he hath taught vs that yt ys doen by the holie Goſt. Whiche vndoubtedlie ys the verie true catholique faith, that euery true chryſtian muſt profeſſe, and acknowledge, yf he will be partaker of the merites of the ſame Chryſte crucified.

                    K ij   THE

D

THE ONE AND TWENTETH CHAPITER CON-
cludeth this matter of the figure of the paschall lambe by Haymo and Cabasila.

He nombre ys great,that might be called oute of this lower house , whiche for that yt wolde make thys rude worke to growe into to great a volume , I will content my self and staie,after I haue brought furth one coople mo , and so leaue this figure.

The first of theise shall be *Haymo* , for that he ys the elder , being aboute the yeare of Chryst 734.and so aboue eight hundreth yeares agon , before the time of *Berengarius*,who was the first open and notable Aduersaire of this Sacrament,that laboured to take awaie the reall presence of Chryste. Ther-for this learned Father maie wel be cōsulted with all,who being before this controuersie was moued,ys to be thought to speake vpprightlie,ād not par-

Haymo in 26. Matt.
ciallie.In his exposition therfore vpon S.Matthew,he saieth thus: *Cœnantibus* F *autem eis,accepit Iesus panem,&c.Expletis solemnijs veteris Paschæ, transit Dominus ad sacramenta noui Paschæ demonstranda.Postquam cœnauit,dedit eis panem et vinum,in my sterio videlicet corporis et sanguinis sui. Quia enim panis cor hominis confirmat, vinum au-get sanguinem in homine,meritò idem panis in carnem Domini mutatur , et idem vinum in*

Bread and wine chaŭ-ged into the bodie and blood of Chryst,not in figure, but in tru-eth.
sanguinem Domini transfertur,non per figuram,neque per vmbram,sed per veritatem.Cre dimus enim quia in veritate caro est Christi,similiter et sanguis. As they were eating at Supper,*Iesus* tooke bread , &c. When the Solemnities of the olde Passouer were fullfilled,our Lorde goeth to shewe furthe the Sacrament of the newe Passouer.After he hadde Supped he gaue them bread and wine, in mysterie of his bodie and bloode . For bicause bread doth strenghten the hearte of man,and wine encreaseth the bloode in man, *the same bread ys woorthilie chaun ged into the flesh of our Lorde,and that same wine transferred into the bloode of our Lorde, not by figure,nor by shaddowe,but by the verie trueth. For we beleue that in trueth yt ys the flesh of Chryst,and likewise his bloode.*Thus farre *Haymo.*

The two principall pointes here enquired, this holie Father hath agrea-blie bothe to the elders of the higher house, and also to them of the lower G house, declared. First , hys comparing of the olde Passeouer to the newe ys easie to be perceaued.　　And then,what the newe Passeouer ys, he doth most plainlie manifest.　Yf he had left the matter of the newe Passeouer, when he had said:He deliuered bread and wine in mysterie of hys bodye and bloode, then the Aduersaries wolde haue vsed their accustomed vio-lence to haue drawen him by force to be a wittnesse of their syde . I saie by force, bicause this Authour not mening as they do,as after yt shall appeare,

Heretiques how they al leage the Fathers.
yet they wolde with great boast haue saied that he had mened as they doo.

Sacramēta ries can not bring one Father tea ching the Sacrament to be only a figure.
Which maner of doinge(Reader)ys their cōmō practise.For wher they in their workes alleage the holie Fathers, they alleadge thē in doubtful places, wher they vse the common termes of Sacrament, mysterie, and soch other, whiche,when controuersie and contencion ys raised by wicked men , maie be drawen to either parte,Albeit the Authours intended and ment, but the onelie one true waie,of Chrystes trueth and faith,as this Authour nowe al-leaged did.　　　　　　　　　　　　　　　　　　　　　　　　　H

But,gentle reader,yf thow perusest their bokes,and findest that they bring anie allowed Authour saing by expresse woordes, and plain sentence , that the Sacrament ys but a figure or a sign , or by plain deniall shall saie that
　　　　　　　　　　　　　　　　　　　　　　　　　　　Christes

A Chryftes bodie ys not in the Sacrament reallie or in verie dede, we fhall yelde and geue them the victorie, for certen I am that they can not.

But on our fyde, that ys on the parte of the catholique faithe of Chryftes Churche, ye fhall heare à nombre that by expreffe woordes fhall affirme the verie prefence of Chryftes bodie, of whiche nôbre ye haue allreadie heard-fome, And by like expreffe woordes fhall denie that yt ys but a figure, as this Authour dothe. The contrarie wher of this Proclamer, and other Sacramentaries are not afhamed to teache, although they be (if ther were anie fhame in them) ouercharged with nôbre of wittneffes, fo that they maie be afhamed of theyr herefie.

Thys Authour(God be prayfed) when he had faied, that Chryft gaue hys Apoftles bread and wyne in myfterie of hys bodie and bloode : leeft thys myfterie fhoulde be made a myfterie of nothing (as the Sacrametaries make yt) he declareth yt to be a myfterie of fomwhat. And faieth that the bread and wyne be chaunged into the bodie and blode of our lorde . And *Bread and*

B yet that none of the common hereticall glofes fhoulde take place, he faieth *wine cha-* further by plain exclufion, that they be chaunged in to Chriftes *unged not* flefh and bloode neither by figure, ner by fhaddowe but by verie *in figure* trueth. *but in*

Wolde to God that they that be yet deteined in this naughtie herefie, *trueth.* wolde well note, weigh, and remembre this fainge, and looke whether they haue anie foche plain, manifeft, and expreffe fentence, of anie Authour Autenticall to maintein their herefie, as this ys for the trueth.

And yet to knitte vppe the matter that this ys no fingular opinion, or whifpered inuention, but a fure and vndoubted faith commonlie, and generallie receaued, he concludeth, not in his owne perfon, but in the perfon of the beleuing Churche, and faieth: *Credimus, &c. We beleue that yt ys in trueth and in verie dede the flesh of Chryft, and likewife his bloode.*

As this Authour hath teftified not onelie his owne faithe but the faith *Heretiq,s* of the Churche: So wolde I that the Aduerfarie fhoulde regarde not hys *haue no* priuate opinion (whiche he calleth a faith, and ys none in dede) But the *faith but*

C faith of the Churche, whiche ys a fure faith in dede, builded vpon a fure *opinions.* rocke.

Nowe to make vppe the coople we pourpofed here to induce, we will heare this Authours iocke felow in faith, *Cabafila,* one of the fame lower hou fe of Parliament, but of the other fide therof, that ys, of the greke churche, a man of fingular learninge . Who expowndinge the Maffe of the Grekes vfed in their churches, declareth why Chryfte willed his memorie to be had, and the Maffe to be doen in remembrance of him . Thus he faieth: *Huius autem conferuundæ memoriæ homines multas rationes excogitarunt, fepulchra, Nicolaus. ftatuas, columnas, dies feftos & celebres, certamina, quorum omnium vnum eft inftitutum, Cabafila: non finere vt viri præclari & præftanti virtute obliuioni mandentur. Tale eft etiam ca.9. quod dicit Seruator: Alij quidem alia obliuionis quærunt remedia, vt recordentur eorum, qui ipfos beneficio affecerunt, vos autem in meam recordationem hoc facite . Et quemadmodum ciuitates, fortium virorum, per quos victoriam affecuti funt, vel qui eis falu tem attulerunt, aut res eorum recte gefferunt, columnis infcribunt : ita etiam in ijs donis*

D *nos mortem Domini afcribimus, in qua vniuerfa fita fuit aduerfus malignum victoria. Et per ftatuas quidem ciuitates folùm habent figuram corporis benefactorum : Nos au tem ab hac oblatione non habemus figuram corporis, fed ipfum corpus eius, qui fe gefsit fortifsimè. Hoc ipfum etiam antiquis conftituit, vt in figura facerent id, quod nunc eft in rerum veritate. Id enim erat Pafcha, & agni occifio, quæ memoriam reuocat*

K iij *cædis*

E

cædis illius ouis & ſanguinis, qui ſeruauit Hebræis in Ægypto primogenita.

To conſerue this memorie, men haue deuiſed manie waies or means, as Tumbes, ymages, pillers, feaſtfull and Solemne daies, exerciſes, of all whiche ther ys one pourpoſe, not to ſuffer, that noble men of excellent vertue ſhoulde be forgotten. Soche maner of thing yt ys, that our Sauioure ſaieth: Some ſeke other remedies againſt obliuion, that they maie remembre them, that haue doen them good: But in the remembrance of me, this doo ye. And as cities do write in pillers the noble actes of mightie men, by whom they ha ue gotten victorie, or that haue ſaued them, or haue doen their affaires or bu ſineſſe wel: Euē ſo alſo do we in theſe giftes imprinte the death of our Lord, in the which was all the victorie againſt the wicked one had or gotten. Now the cities haue by their images but the onelie figure of the bodie of their be nefactours: *but we in this oblacion hane not the figure of the bodie, but the bodie yt ſelf of him, euen that ſame that ys nowe in veritie of thing.* For that was the Paſſeouer, and the killing of the lambe which dothe call again the memorie of that ſhepe and bloode, whiche ſaued the firſt born of the Hebrues. Hither to Cabaſila.

We haue the verie bo die in the Sacramēt, not the figu re.

Of whom as we haue learned the faith of the greke churche, as yt was in the time of the auncient Fathers, *Chryſoſtom, Cyrill, Iſychius, Damaſcen, Euthymius,* and ſoche other, as touching the preſence of Chryſtes bleſſed bodie in the Sacrament: Euen ſo do we learn of him the ſame faith, and none other new-lie inuented, but euen the ſame continued, euer approued vnto his time in all the greke churche.

F

Monumen tes and me mories of ho lie, ād woor thie men de faced.

This authour allthough minding to ſett furth a cauſe why the memoriall of Chryſtes death ſhoulde be reteined and kept emong vs, by the bringing in examples of our elders, whiche by diuerſe means cōtinued the memorie of noble, vertueouſe, or other wourthie men, he doth therin geue good occa ſion to rebuke the inſolencie of manie of this our time, which defacing how ſes, ſpoiling churches, ouerthrowing monumentes, diſparſing the bones ād reliques of holie ſainctes, and ſoche other a great ſorte like, do moſt earneſtlie labour to extinguiſh and clean put oute of all memorie the noble actes, the holie dedes, the godly liues of many vertueouſe, and wourthie men, which to Gods honoure, to their praiſe, and to owre exāple of vertue, ſhoulde and ought to haue remained: Yet minding not to take euery ſoche occaſiō, I will leaue yt, and folowe my matter here principallie entended.

G

As heretofore I haue doen: So alſo wil I nowe both declare that the Paſ chall Lambe was a figure of Chryſt, and alſo that the veritie or verie thing by that lambe figured, ys the bodie of Chryſt reallie and ſubſtanciallie in the Sacrament.

Olde lawe had the fi gure: the newe lawe hath the th ing in trueth.

As for the firſt, this Authour ſaieth, that God appoincted with the olde fathers, that they ſhoulde haue a figure of Chryſt. And that (ſaieth he) was the Paſſeouer, and the killing of the lambe. In which his ſainge he nothing diſſenteth, but moche and whollie agreeth as well with the grekes, as the la tines before alleaged, and declared.

As for the ſeconde parte, that yt ys a figure of Chryſte reallie in the Sacra-ment, this Authour alſo very plainlie teacheth. Marke therfore wel his woor des, thus he ſaieth: *Hoc ipſum & antiquis conſtituit vt in figura facerent id, quod nunc eſt in rerum veritate.* The ſame thing God appoincted the olde Fathers to doo in a figure, which thing ys nowe in trueth or verie dede.

H

Note I praie yow that he appointeth the figure of Chryſt to the Fathers of the lawe of Moyſes, to vs that be nowe in the lawe of Chryſt, he appoin-teth not the figure, but the thing yt ſelf, euen verie Chryſtes bodie.

But

A But the ferpent ys a wilie beaft, and fekinge fome litle holle or crannie to flippe through, and to flide awaie from this fentence, that preffeth him fo fore, will, to delude the Simple, graunt that we, whiche be in the lawe of Chryft, haue verilie Chryft, euen that fame that was born of the virgen Mary, that was curcified, that rofe from death to life, that afcended into heauen.

Thefe be gaie glorioufe woordes. But take heade, reader, ther ys a fnake vnder thefe fair flowres. Looke diligentlie vpon them, and afke him howe we haue him, that was born of the virgen &c. And thowe fhalt fee him by and by betraie him felf, and runne to his olde and common fhift, and faie that he ys ther facramentallie. Which maner of being or prefence (as Iohn Frith our contrie man, and many other mafters of that herefie do teache) ys as moche as ys the prefence of the wine in the Iuie garlande at the tauern doore, or the loue of the hufbande in the ringe, whiche he geueth to his wife : Whiche maner of prefence ys next doore to nothing, for all their glorioufe woordes.

Crāmer his glorioufe woordes, to cloake euell meening. lib. 4. Iohn frith his herefie.

B Yf ye porcead, and vrge him, faing, that after this forte he was in all the figures of the lawe, that were figures of him : But this Authour appointing that maner of prefence to the lawe : faieth, that his prefence with vs ys in verie dede. whiche ys a maner of prefence other, and more then they vnder the lawe had.

Nowe he muft to his cheifeft refuge, and faie that we haue him fpirituallie . Here to mete with him again, ye maie faie, and that trulie as before ys faied, and proued in the xix capiter of this booke, that fo the Iewes in the lawe receaued him and had him fpirituallie in their Pafchall lambe, fo that by this maner of prefence, ther ys no perrogatiue, nor difference, of our Sacrament and the prefence of Chryft ther in aboue theirs, nor from theirs. The contrarie wherof all chatholique Fathers do teache.

heretiques refuges in reafoning.

Nowe ys he commed to his laft refuge, that ys that the Iewes receaued him fpirituallie, as yet to come, but we receaue him fpirituallie as allready comed.

C Yf this be all, what neadeth this difference of fpeache, that this Authour vfeth, faing : God appointed the Fathers of the lawe to do that thing in a figure, that we do nowe in verie dede ? Ys to doe a thinge in figure, and to doe a thing in dede all one maner of doinge ? A verie babe will not graunt that.

Thus I fuppofe, yt ys eafie to be perceaued, that the Aduerfaries faith ys foche, that when he hath fpoken the beft of yt, yt will not, nor can ioin with the faith of the learned men of Chryftes Parliament houfe : But ys as farre diftant from them and their faith, as falfhood from trueth. Wherof ye fhall haue yet better experience, and further prooff by an other parte of this Aut hours fentence, when yt ys noted to yowe, and the aduerfaries doctrine conferred with yt.

That other parte ys this : *Citties* (faieth he) *by the ymages of foche as haue doen them good, haue onelie bnt their figures : we haue by this oblacion, not the figure of Chriftes bodie, but the bodie yt felf, whiche moft ftoutlie handled yt felf.*

D Note well this conference : The citties had but the figures of foche wourthie men, as had noblie doen for them : We haue, not the figure of Chrift but the bodie yt felf whiche wrought vs the great benefitt of our Redemption.

Remembre, I praie yowe, what the latin Authour before alleadged faied,

that this man being of the greke churche, and conferred with him, yt maie **E**
appear what agreement in doctrine and faithe in this matter,ther ys yn both
the churches.

Not the fi-
gure, but
verie bodie
of Chriſt ys
yn the Sa-
crament.

The latin Authour ſaied thus : *The bread ys chaunged into the fleſh of our Lorde,*
and the wine into his bloode not by a figure , or in a ſhaddowe, but in verie dede: This
greke Authour ſaieth, *that we haue not the figure of Chriſt,* but his *verie bodie , euen*
that whiche ſo mightilie ſought for vs.

See ye not a conſonant agreement betwen theſe two ? do thiey not both
teache the verie preſence of Chriſtes bodie in the Sacramēt ? and ther with
by a plain negatiue denie the figure? Maie not our Proclamer , our newe
Goliath well ſee, and trulie ſaie , that here be two plain ſentences againſt
him? Let them be conferred, and yt will planlie appeare.

Doctrine
of the Sa-
cramētari-
es confer-
red with
the Fa-
thers.

Theſe Authours ſaie that the Sacrament conteineth not a figure onelie:
The Aduerſarie ſaieth, that yt hath no more but a figure . Theſe ſaie that the
Sacrament conteineth the very bodie of Chriſte:The Aduerſarie ſaieth that
yt ys Ieweſh ſo to thinke and that they be groſſe Capharnaites, that ſaie that **F**
the bodie of Chriſt ys ſubſtanciallie in the Sacrament.

In this conference ye maie ſee the ſtowte repugnance of the Aduerſarie
againſt catholique writers. In the ſame ye ſee the ſaid writers by expreſſe
woordes denie the doctrine of the Aduerſarie, that wher he ſaieth,yt ys a figure, they ſaie, yt ys not a figure.

Iſſue ioined
with the
Proclamer
tonching
the preſēce.

And here will I yoin an yſſue withe the Proclamer that yf he cā bring any
Scripture, anie catholique Councell , or anie one approued doctour, that
by expreſſe and plain woordes doth denie the reall preſēce of Chryſte in the
Sacrament, as theſe writers doo denie his figure, or figuratiue preſence, then
will I geue ouer, and ſubſcribe to him.

But wher he vntrulie hath ſaied, that he was ſure that we coulde bring
furthe no one approued Authour to teſtifie the reall preſence of Chriſt
in the Sacrament : I will ſaie trulie, that I am ſure that neither he, nor
all the Aduerſaries can bring anie one, teaching by expreſſe woordes the
contrarie.

Obiection.

Yf percaſe anie man will obiecte here to me, that though theſe men denie
the figure, and teache that Chryſtes verie bodie ys preſent in the Sacramēt: **G**
yet they ſaie not ſo moche as your Aduerſarie requireth, that his bodie ys
ſubſtanciallie and reallie preſent.

Anſwer.

The aunſwer to this ys eaſie, whiche the Aduerſarie will graunte, that yf
the bodie of Chryſt be in the Sacrament, not by a figure, but in verie dede,
then yt muſt nedes be ther reallie and ſubſtāciallie. For the Aduerſarie hathe

Sacramen-
taries ma-
ke two ma-
ner of pre-
ſences of
Chryſt.

two maner of beinges of Chryſt, the one ys in the Sacrament,wher he ſaieth
Chryſte ys as in a ſign , token, or figure, but not in veritie. The other maner
of being ys not in the Sacramēt, but in the receauer of yt,in whom he ſaieth
Chryſt ys ſpirituallie.

As for this ſeconde maner of being euerie good Chryſtian will graunte,
that euerie wourthie receauer of the Sacrament, receaueth Chryſte ſpirituallie, but not onelie ſpirituallie,as the Aduerſarie teacheth, but he alſo receaueth Chryſtes verie real ād ſubſtācial bodie.So that in this ſecōd maner,
he diſſenteth in part from the catholike faith : But in the firſt maner of beinge he diſſenteth whollie. for ther he denieth Chryſtes bodie to be verilie **H**
in the Sacrament, which the catholique faith doth affirme and teache.

Nowe (gentle reader) thowe haueſt hearde, this figure of the Paſchall
Lambe, both by great auncient Authours that were aboue a thouſand years agon,

A years agon, or within the compaſſe of ſixe hundreth years after Chryſt,
and alſo by Authours that were within the compaſſe of theſe nine hundreth years, applied to the thing figured. Whiche thing figured, by one
conſent, and by one mouth, as yt were, and by conſonante and vniforme
teſtimonie, they haue teſtified and taught, not onelie to be Chryſtes bodie
vpon the croſſe, for that in that parte yt aunſwereth the death and bloode
ſheding of the lambe : but alſo the bodie of Chryſt being in the Sacrament,
not as in a ſhaddowe, ſigne, or token, but verilie, ſubſtanciallie and reallie,
and ſo not ſpirituallie onelie eaten and receaued, But of all good chriſtians,
both ſpirituallie with the mouth of the ſoule, and alſo reallie with the mouthe of the bodie, taken, eaten, and reccaued, herin alſo aunſweringe the figure, that as the lambe was eaten in the remembrance of the ſauing of the
firſt born, and of their deliuerance from the tirannie of Pharao, and of their
paſsing oute of Aegipte by the mightie hand of God : So the true faithfull
of Chryſt ſhoulde eate the verie Paſchall lambe of the newe Teſtament,
B whiche ys the verie bodie of that immaculate Lambe our Sauiour Ieſus
Chryſt reallie and ſubſtanciallie in the Sacrament, and ſo receaue yt in
the remembrance of our deliueraunce from our cruell Pharao the Deuell,
and from the miſerable ſeruitude of Aegipt, whiche ys ſinne. Whiche benefittes as they haue happened to vs by the death of that bleſſed Lambe, aught by the eating of him in the Sacramēt to be remēbred. And thus moche
for the figure of the Paſchall Lambe.

THE TWO AND TWENTETH CHAPITER BE-
*ginneth the applicacion of the ſhewe bread to the Sacrament, as of the figure
to the veritie by ſainct Hierom, and Damaſcen.*

Nowe ther remaineth three other figures to be treacted of,
which be Manna, the water flowing oute of the Rocke, and the
ſhewe bread. But for ſomoche as ſainct Paule maketh mencion
of two of them, that ys of Manna, and of the water, and I wolde
not gladlie grieue the reader with reading of one matter twice,
C I ſhall differ theiſe two, vntill we come to treacte of the ſainges of ſainct Paule, whiche ſhall be in the third booke.

Wherfore nowe I will paſſe them ouer, and treacte here of the figure
of the ſhewe bread. Of this ſhewe bread we firſt read thus : Thowe
ſhalt ſett vpon the table ſhewe breade before me allwaie. Theſe woordes
Allmightie God ſpake vnto Moyſes, after he had tolde him the maner and *Exod. 25.*
faſhion of the table, howe yt ſhoulde be made and graniſhed, vpon the which
table this ſhewe breades ſhoulde allway be ſett.

But of the making of the breads, and the ordre of them we reade in *Leuit. 24.*
Leuiticus thus : *And thowe ſhalt take fine flowre, and bake twelue waſſells therof, two tenth deals ſhall be in one waſſell . And thowe ſhalt ſett them in
two rowes, that they maie be bread of remembrance, and an offring vnto thy
Lord God enery Sabboth . He ſhall put them in rowes before thy Load God euermore. Of the children of Iſraël ſhall they be offred for an euerlaſting couenante . And
they ſhall be Aarons and his Sonnes, whiche ſhall eate them in the holie place.*
D *For they are moſt holie vnto him, of the offringes of the Lorde by a perpetuall
ſtatute.*

In the whiche ſaing of God, ye firſt perceaue the place of theiſe breades, whiche ys vpon the table in the tabernacle . Ye vnderſtande alſo
the

the continuance of them, whiche ys that they muſt be before the Lorde E allwaie.

Further, this bread was made of fine flowre, and yt was the bread of remembrance, and an offring vnto the Lord . Yt was no common bread, but an holie bread, wherof the preiſtes onelie might eate, and no defiled perſon·

1.Reg.21. Wherfore when Dauid and his men were verie hungrie, and came to Abimelech the preiſt, and deſired him to geue them ſome bread, he aunſwered him, that he hadd no common bread vnder his hand, but hallowed bread, neuertheleſſe he conſidering their neceſſitie, aſked Dauid if the men had kept them ſelues from vnclaen thinges eſpeciallie from womē: And when Dauid had aunſwered that they werie clean from womē aboute three daies, the preiſt gaue them of the bread.

Nowe all the Ceremonialls of the lawe of Moyſes, were figures of Chryſt, and his Churche, as by ſainct Auguſtine before ys declared. And for ſo moche as the Shewe bread was a ſollemne offring in the olde lawe: F Yt muſt nedes be a figure of ſome thing in the newe lawe. For no iotte nor title of the olde lawe ſhall eſcape (ſaieth Chryſt) vntill yt be fullfilled in the newe lawe

Shewbread a figure of the Sacrament. Ther ys therfor ſomething in the newe lawe, that aunſwereth and fulfilleth this figure of the olde lawe. And that ys vndoubtedlie, that moſt bleſſed and heauenlie bread of life, the verie bodie of our Sauiour Chriſt in the Sacrament, vnder the forme of bread . Whiche bleſſed bread aunſwereth the figure the Shewe bread verie aptelie and iuſtilie, as by compariſon in diſcourſe and applicacion of them we ſhall perceaue.

Shew bread applied to the Sacrament. The Shewe bread was placed vpon the table in the tabernacle : This bread ys placed on the Altar in the Churche . That bread neuer failed, but was allwaies reſerued : This bread allwaies remaineth and ys reſerued. That bread was a bread of remembrance : This bread ys a bread of remembrance , bothe of Chryſtes death , and of the great benefett pourchaſed by the ſame death. That bread was an offringe to God: This bread ys a moſt holie oblacion and ſacrifice to God . That bre- G ad might no defiled perſon eate : This bread maie no defiled ſinner eate. For Quicunque manducauerit panem Domini, & biberit calicem indignè, reus erit corporis, & ſanguinis Domini, &c. he that eateth the breade of our Lorde , and

1.Cor.11. drinketh of his cuppe vnwourthilie, ſhalbe giltie of the bodie of our Lorde. Therfor let a man examin himſelf, and ſo let him eate of that bread, and drinke of that cuppe ſaieth ſainct Paule.

Thus ye ſee howe well the thing figured aunſwereth the figure . And albeit that no mã can bring anie other thing in the newe teſtamēt, that ys figured by the Shewe bread, but our heauēlie bread before ſaied: Yet, for that I will not chalēge to me any ſoche credite or Authoritie, that by cauſe I ſaie yt ys ſo, therfor yt ys ſo (as manie of our Pheudochryſtians doe) I ſhall repair to the holie elders of Chryſtes parliament houſe, and teache by them what was the enacted and receaued trueth in his matter.

Hieron.ca. And firſt, I will heare what ſainct Hierom ſaieth : Si autem Laicis impe-

1.adTitū. ratur, vt propter orationem abſtineant ſe ab vxorum coitu, quid de Epiſcopo ſentiendum eſt, qui quotidie pro ſuis populíque peccatis, illibatas oblaturus eſt vi- H ctimas? Relegamus Regum libros, & inueniemus ſacerdotem Abimelech de panibus propoſitionis noluiſſe dare Dauid, & pueris ſuis, niſi interrogaret vtrum mundi

eſſent

A　*eſſent pueri à muliere, non vtique aliena, ſed coniuge. Et niſi audiſſet eos ab heri*
& nudiustertiùs vacaſſe ab opere coniugali, nequaquam panes, quos prius nega-
uerat conceſſiſſet. Tantum intereſt inter propoſitionis panes, & corpus Chriſti, quantum
inter, vmbram & corpora, inter imaginem, & veritatem, inter exemplaria futurorum, &
ea ipſa, quæ per exemplaria præfigurabantur. Quomodò itaque manſuetudo, patientia, ſo-
brietas, moderatio, abſtinentia lucri, hoſpitalitas quoque & benignitas præcipuè eſſe debent
in Epiſcopo, & inter cunctos laicos eminentia: ſic & caſtitas propria, & (vt ita dicam)
pudicitia ſacerdotalis, vt non ſolùm ſe ab immundo opere abſtineat, ſed etiam à iactu oculi,
& cogitationis errore mens Chriſti corpus confectura ſit libera.

　　Yf the laye men (ſaieth ſainct Hierom be cõmanded that for praier they
abſtein frõ the cõpanieng with their wiues, what ys to be thought of the Biſhoppe, whiche dailie for his owne ſinnes, and the peoples, ſhall offer vnto
God vndefiled ſacrifices? Let vs reade the bookes of the kĩges and we ſhall finde that Abimelech the preiſt wolde not geue to Dauid and his ſeruãtes the
ſhewe breade, before he aſked, wether the ſeruãtes were cleã, not frõ a ſtraun-

B　ge womã, but frõ their viues. And except he had heard, that frõ yeſteraie, and
the daie before they had abſteined from the worke of matrimonie, he had
not graunted them the bread, whiche before he had denied. *Ther ys as great*
difference betwene the Shewe bread, and the bodie of Chriſte, as ys betwene the
Shaddow and the bodies, betwene the ymage and the trueth: betwene the exemplars
of the thinges to come, and the thinges themſelues, that were perfigurated by the exem-
plars. Therfor as mekeneſſe, pacience, ſobrietie, moderacion, abſtinence frõ
lucre, hoſpitalitie alſo and benignitie ſhoulde be chieflie in a Biſhoppe, and
emõg all laie men a ſurmoũting eminécie: So alſo a propre or peculiar chai-
ſtitie, and (as I might ſaie) a preiſtlie ſhamefeſtnes, that not onelie he ſhoulde
whith holde himſelf frõ the vnclean worke, but alſo that the minde whiche
ſhall *conſecrate the bodie of Chriſte* maie from the caſting of the eie, and from
wandring of thought be free. Hither to ſaincte Hierom.

　　In whiche woordes cõcerning the thing which ys nowe principallie ſought, wher as he ſaieth, ther ys as great differéce betwene the Shew bread and
the bodie of Chriſt, as betwẽ the ſhaddow ãd the bodies, betwen the ymage

C　and the trueth, What ells dothe he geue vs to vnderſtãde, but that the Shew
bread ys the figure, ãd the bodie of Chryſt in the Sacrament the thing figured. Whiche thing figured (yf yt were alſo but a figure, as of late the people be
taught) howe coulde ther be ſo great differéce betwne a figure, and a figure,
as betwene the ſhaddowe and the bodie? betwene the ymage and the trueth?

　　Wherfore contrariewiſe let euerie man perceaue, that (as this holie learned mã in the ſtatutes of Chryſtes enacted faithe, doth teache) as the Shewe
bread was the ſhaddowe, So ys the bodie of Chryſt in the Sacrament a verie
bodie, and as the Shewe breade was the ymage: So ys the thing repreſented
the verie tueth.

　　But peraduẽture ſome captiouſe falſe Chryſtã will ſaie: I adde more then
my Authour ſpeaketh of, and wreſt him to my pourpoſe. For wher this Authour ſaieth, that ther ys as moche difference betwene the ſhewe bread,
and the bodie of Chryſt, I adde and ſaie: the bodie of Chryſt in the Sacrament Whiche ſainct Hierom ſpeaketh not.

D　　I adde nothing to the Authours mening. For although he ſaieth the
bodie of Chryſt abſolutelie withoute anie addicion of the maner of the
bodie here or ther, in plain viſion or in myſterie (whiche maner what
ſoeuer yt be, the ſubſtance ys all one) yet he meneth of the bodie of
Chryſt in myſterie, or in Sacrament. For by the example of the puritie

Laie men
cõmãuded
for praier
times to ab-
ſtein from
their wie-
ues.

Difference
betwixt
the Shew
bread and
the bodie
of Chryſt.

Chaſtitie
required in
a preiſt.

Obiection

Anſwer.

puritie of life, that was required to the eating of the Shewe breade in the **E**
olde lawe, he moueth the Bishopps of the newe lawe to soche puritie and
cleannesse of life, as to that lawe ys meet to be had.

Preistes
must confe-
crate,offre,
ãd receaue
And forsomoche as the office of a Bishoppe aboute the Sacrament,
standeth in thre pointes, that ys, yn consecracion,oblacion, and reauing,he
frameth an exhortaciõ to this pourpose thus,that seing they in the olde lawe
which shoulde eate of the Shew breade, must haue soche puritie , that they
might not for a time knowe their one, vieues,moche more they that cõsecra
te,offer,and reccaue the bodie of Cryste,whiche as farre excelleth the Shew
bread, as the bodie dothe he shaddowe, must excell them of the olde lawe
in puritie and cleannesse of life. Nowe then,when sainte Hierom speaketh
of the bodie of Chryste that ys cõsecrated by the Bishoppe, and so offred in
sacrifice and receaued, dothe he not meen of the bodie of Chryst in the Sacrament? And when he speaketh of the bodie consecrated, dothe he not
meen the verie bodie of Chryst , reallie in the Sacrament, as the holie
Churche doth teache and beleue?   **F**

Wanton lu
stes of Bi-
shoppes and
preistes re-
proue d.
In this sentence also sainct Hierom doth not onelie impugne the heresie
of the Sacramétaries, in that he teacheth the veritie of Chrystes bodie in the
Sacrament : but he also reproueth the fleshlie wanttõnesse of our Bishoppes
and preistes in these daies, who against all lawe and ordre being preistes take
wieues (as they terme thé) and vnder the countenáce of pretenfed matrimonie continewe their vnchaist, and vicioufe life, who shoulde excell all the
people in puritie and cleannesse of life, to thintent they might cõsecrate the

Cõsecraciõ
and facrifi-
ce put awai
for to kepe
women.
bodie of Chryste, and dailie offer pure facrifice to God for thé selues and for
the people,as sainct Hierõ saieth they should. But bicaufe these high fũctiõs,
and the keping of womé cã not ioin together,raither thé they will put awaie
ther womé, they haue deuifed to putte awaie the cõsecracion of the bodie
of Chryst,and the facrifice also whiche they shoulde offer. Of whiche matter,
for that yt ys impertinente to my pourpofe, I will not speake, but ouerpasse
yt, and not medle withall.

Nowe haue ye here heard one wittnesse of the one fide of the higher house **G**
of Parliament, reporting the trueth of this matter: We will heare one of the
Li.4.c.14.
de ortho-
dox. fid.
other fide and of the lower house to reporte the fame trueth, who shall be
Damafcen . Thus he saieth : *Hunc panem, panes figurabant propofitionis* . This
bread(mening the bodie of Chryst in the Sacrament) did the Shew bread
figure . That he speake of the bodie of Chryst, the learned reader shall
fooen perceaue, if he will perufe this place in Damafcen, wher he shall
finde, that after he mofte plainly had affirmed the verie reall prefence of Chrystes bodie in the Sacramét,by the woordes of our Sauiour Chryst
in the vj. of Iohn, and in the other Euangeliftes : he cometh to exhortacion
for the wourthie receauing of the fame, faing thus : *Proinde cum omni timore,*
& confcientia pura, & indubitabili fide accedamus, & veneremur ipfum omni puritate
Dam. ibi.
animi & corporis . Accedamus ei defiderio ardenti , manus in modum crucis forman-
tes , crucifixi corpus fufcipiamus? Therfor let vs comme to yt with all feare,
and pure confcience, and with a fure faith , and let vs woorfhippe him
whith all puritie of minde and bodie . Let vs go to him whith burning de-
fire, *fafhioning our handes in maner of a croffe* , let vs receaue *the body of him that was* **H**
crucified.

And after a fewe scriptures alleaged, he speaketh the woordes whiche I before recited , that the Shewe bread did figure this bread. Wherby yt ys
euident, that he meneth that he Shewe bread was a figure, not of a figure,
but

A　but of Chryſt him ſelf, who promiſed that the bread, that he wolde geue, ſhoulde be his fleſh, whiche fleſh he wolde geue for the life of the woorlde. *Ioan. 6.*

THE THREE AND TWENTHETH CHAPIT.

ceadeth in the proof of the ſame by S. Auguſtine and Iſychius.

Lthough the Authours alleaged might ſuffice for the declaracion and proof of this matter nowe entreacted of: yet for the ful contentacion of the reader, ſome mo ſhall be brought to make the thing more plain, and the truthe more certen.

The firſt of theſe ſhall be ſainct Auguſtin, who ſaied thus: *Dicit ceſſiſſe pani* *Ad Ca-* *pecus, tanquam neſciens, & tunc in Domini menſa panes Propoſitionis poni ſolere, et nunc* *ſulanum* *ſe de agni immaculati corpore partem accipere. Dicit ceſſiſſe poculo ſanguinē, non cogitans et* *epiſt. 86.* *nunc ſe accipere in poculo ſanguinē. Quanto ergo melius et congruentius vetera tranſiſſe, et* *noua in Chriſto facta eſſe ſic diceret, vt cederet altare altari, gladius gladio, ignis igni, panis*

B　*pani, pecus pecori, ſanguis ſanguini? Videmus in ijs omnibus carnalem vetuſtatem ſpiritali* *cedere nouitati.* He ſaieth that the beaſt hath geuen place to the breade, as though he knewe not that euen then the Shew breades were wounte to be putte vpon the table of our lorde, *and that nowe he dothe take parte of the bodie of* *that vndefiled lambe.* He ſaied that bloode hathe geuen place to the cuppe, *not* *remembring that he alſo nowe doth receaue blood in the cuppe.* Howe moche better therfor, and more agreablie ſhoulde he ſaie, that the olde are goen, and new be made in Chryſt, ſo as the Altar gaue place to the Altar, the ſwoord to the ſwoorde, fire to fire, breade to breade, beaſt to beaſt, bloode to bloode ? We doo ſee in all theſe, the carnall oldeneſſe to geue place, to the ſpirituall neweneſſe. Thus farre S. Auguſtin.

In theſe woordes S. Auguſtin correcting the euell ſaing of one that ſaied, that in the coming of the newe Teſtament, the Sacrifices of the olde lawe, whiche were doen in beaſtes, as ſheepe, lābes, kiddes, heckfers, oxē, and ſoche other did geue place to breade(*meening the Sacrament*)dothe declare, that theſe proprelie did not geue place to yt. As though he ſhould ſaie, that theſe bea

C　ſtes wer not figures of the Sacramēt, but of the blooddie Sacrifice of Chryſt offred vppō the croſſ, after the maner of Aarō. But he ſaieth the ſhew breads gaue place to our bread. And therfore he ſaieth that the Aduerſarie ſaing, that the beaſtes gaue place to bread, he ſpake yt as though he knew not, that the Shewe breades, were wounte to be putte vpon the table of our Lord, mening that the Shew breades were a figure of the Sacrament. And therfore when the truth came, thoſe breades, as the figure, muſt nedes geue place to the true bread, which ys Chryſt in the bleſſed Sacrament.

And therfore S. Auguſtin teaching this man, to make due applicacion of eche figure to the thing figured, ſaieth: that he ſhould better haue ſaied, that the Altar gaue place to the Altar, ſignifieng that the Altar of the Iewes, was a figure of the Altar of the Chryſtians : and that bread gaue place to breade, ſignifieng that the Shew bread was a figure of our bleſſed breade.

But here perchaunce the Aduerſarie will ſaie, that ſainct Augu-　*Obiection* ſtin calleth the Sacrament but breade, mening that the Shew bread　*oute of S.*

D　was a figure of the Sacramentall breade. I wolde to God the Ad-　*Auguſtin.* uerſarie (who being aduerſarie to Gods trueth, ys moſt aduerſarie to hys owne ſowles health) wolde in ſoche ſentences of holie Fathers,　*Anſwer.* as narrowlie looke, and eſpie the trueth whiche they do teache,

L　　as he

as he dothe for fome one woorde to make fome apparant fhew to maintein   E
his herefie, and falfe doctrine.

Trueth yt ys that S. Auguftin doth call yt bread, to fhewe the iuft applicacion of the figure to the thing figured. That bread was the figure of bread, for outwardlie yt appeareth bread, and inwardlie yt ys the true breade , that ys, the bread of life.

But marke fainct Auguftin well, and ye fhall haue nede of no expofitour to knowe his faith, and mening in this faing. For in the beginning : he faieth that the beaft hath geuen place to the bread , as though he knewe not , that the fhewe breades were wount to be fett vpon the table of our Lorde , and that nowe he doth take parte of the bodie of the vndefiled lambe to whiche bodie and not to facramentall bread, the Shewe bread gaue place.

Note well fainct Auguftin therefor here, that fpeaking what thing he dothe receaue, doth faie, not facramentall breade , *but the bodie of the vndefiled lambe,* which ys the lambe that tooke awaie the finnes of the worlde.
So that which he firft called bread, nowe he calleth yt the bodie of the vnde   F
filed lambe, who ys the bread of life.

And that the Aduerfarie fhoulde not haue anie place to put in his glofing woorde (fpirituallie) and to faie that he receaueth the bodie of the vndefiled lambe fpirituallie : S. Auguftin maketh a ftoppe in the woordes that folowe, faing : he dothe faie (mening vibicus) that blood hath geuen place to the cuppe, not remébring that he alfo nowe *doth receaue blood in the cuppe.* Which faing of fainte Auguftin openeth the true faith of the catholique Churche, and wipeth oute the falfe faithe of the malignant Churche.
For they well vnderftande, that to receaue the bloode of Chryfte in the cuppe teacheth a reall prefence of the fame. And as yt ys manifeft by S . Auguftin, that *the bloode ys receaued reallie:* So ys the flefh of the bodie of the immaculate lambe receaued reallie. For as the one ys receaued, fo ys the other.

Thus ye haue hearde fainct Auguftine his wittneffe of the trueth of this matter : Nowe fhall be ioined to him *Ifychius,* who beareth full teftimonie of the fame trueth. Thys man (as the learned knowe) applieng the leuiticall Sacrifices, and Ceremonies, to the thinges, which they figured in the euangelicall lawe, dothe at large expownd this place, and figure of the Shewe breads.   G
Whofe expofition though yt be long, yet forafmoche as yt ys fructfull , my truft ys, that yt fhall not be tedioufe, but euen as I, for the readers commoditie, did with good will tranfcribe yt. So I truft that he wil, with like good wil reade yt.
And that the wholl matter maie be knowen to the Reader, I will alleadge ād bringe the wholl text of the fcripture, as this Authour hath yt, ād then putto his expofitiō, wherby yt fhal be feen how euerie parte of the text ys applied.
Thus alleageth he the text : *Accipies quoque fimilam , & coques ex ea duo-*
Ifychius li. *decim panes , qui finguli habebunt duas Decimas , quorum fenos altrinfecus fuper*
7.64.24. *menfam purifsimam coram Domino ftatues, & pones fuper eos thus lucidifsimum , vt fit panis in monimentum oblationis Domini . Per fingula Sabbata mutabuntur coram Domino, fufcepti à filijs Ifraël fœdere fempiterno. Eruntque Aaron et filiorum eius , vt comedant eos in loco fancto, quia Sanctum Sanctorum eft de facrificio Domini iure perpetuo.*
And thowe fhalt take fine flowre and bake twelue loaues therof , two
tenth deales fhall be in one loaff . And thowe fhallt fett them in   H
two rowes , fixe on a rowe vpon the pure table of thy Lorde. And
putte pure frankencenfe vpon the rowes , that they maye be breades of re
membrance, and an offring to thy Lorde . Euery Sabboth fhall he putte
them

A them in rowes before thy Lorde for euermore. Of the children of Iſraell ſhall they be offred, for an euerlaſting couenaunte. And they be Aarons and his ſonnes, whiche ſhall eate them in the holie place. For they are moſt holie to him of the offringes of thy Lorde, by a perpetuall ſtature.

Vpon this text thus writeth *Iſychius : Vocat ad contemplationem mandati nos ipſe panum numerus, ſed & propoſitio, & quia non & ipſos, quemadmodum ea quæ ſunt de ſartagine, & craticula, & clibano, holocauſtum fieri præcipit, ſed poni quidem in menſa altrinſecus, & ſolis eos licere ſacerdotibus, non & Leuitis edere , vt tamen & ab ipſis in loco ſanéto comedantur. Sed & quia Sanctu ſanctorum appellati ſunt (intellige quæ dicuntur , dabit enim tibi Dominus intellectum) memento myſticæ menſæ , de qua nulli præſumere præceptum eſt , excepto intelligibili Aaron, id eſt, Chriſto (Ipſe enim eam primus initiauit) ſed & filijs eius, qui ab eo facti ſunt Chriſti, & induti ſunt eo, quam tamen comedere in loco ſanéto iuſſi ſunt . Eſt verò et Sanétum ſanctorum , vt ſanctificationem habeant præcipuam et indeſpicabilem . Illi panes ex duabus decimis (Dei enim et hominis ſunt , eiuſdem in vtroque perfecti) ponuntur ſeni altrinſe-*
B *cus. Myſtica menſa ponitur quidem hic, ponitur etiam in futuro ſeculo . Sex autem panes propoſitio vna, quia perfectus numerus, ſicut & myſterium ipſum perfectum eſt , & perfectos facit eos , qui hoc fruuntur. In ſex autem diebus hæc viſibilis facta eſt creatura: ſextaque die homo productus eſt, propter quem Chriſtus myſticam præparauit menſam. Veruntamen & omnes ſimul recté duodecim panes ſunt , quia primi dominicam cœnauerunt Apoſtoli, qui erant duodecim numero.*

The verie nombre of the loaues doth call vs to the contemplacion or deligent beholding of the commaundement. So doth alſo the ſetting furthe of them, and that he doth not commaunde them to be made a burnt ſacrifice, as thoſe thinges whiche be of the frieng panne, of the gridiron, and fornace, but that they ſhall be put vpon the table on the one parte, and to be laufull to the preiſtes alone , and not to the Leuites to eate them , and yet they maie not be eaten of them, but in the holie place. But alſo bicauſe they be called moſt holie, vnderſtande theſe thinges that be ſaied, Owre Lorde ſhall geue thee vnderſtanding. *Remembre the myſticall table of whiche yt ys commaunded no man to eate , except the intelligible Aaron*, that ys to ſaie Chryſt,
C he firſt began this table, except alſo his children, whiche of him were made Chryſtes, and were cloathed with him , whiche table yet they were commaunded to eate in the holie place. Yt ys alſo moſt holie, that they ſhoulde haue a principall and reuerente holineſſe. Thoſe loaues are of two tenth deales, that ys of God and man, perfecte in both. Six loaues are ſett on a rowe. For the myſticall table ys ſett here , and ys ſett alſo in the worlde to come. Sixe loaues ys one rowe, for yt ys a perfect nombre , as the myſterie ys alſo perfect, and maketh them perfecte, that do vſe yt. In ſixe daies the viſible creature was made, the ſixte daie alſo man was created, for whom Chryſte prepared the myſticall table. And yet for all that , all the loaues together are verie well twelue . For the Apoſtoles , that firſt ſupped at the Supper of our Lorde , were in nombre twelue Thus moche *Iſychius.*

Of whome we learne a full applicacion of the figure to the thing : of the Shew bread to Chryſt. For beginning to open the figure , and to ſett furthe the thing figured by the Shew bread, he ſaieth: *Memeto myſticæ menſæ. Remēbre the myſtical table.* Wherbie he meeneth the bleſſed bread of the table of Chriſt
D which after he openeth with verie plain woordes, whē he ſaieth: The Shew breades were made of two tēths deales: Chryſt the verie bread ys made of the Godhead and the manhead, in both perfecte , perfect God and perfecte man.

Shewbread applied to the Sacrament.

Yf this applicacion were not plain enough I wolde tarie longer vpon yt. **E**
But yt ys eafie to perceaue that by the Shewbread ys figured that bread that
ys made of two tenth deales, as that was, by which tenth deales he vnderftã-
In Symbole deth the Godhead and manheade of Chryft. For (as *Athanafius* faieth) *Sicut
anima rationalis & caro vnus eft homo: ita Deus & homo vnus eft Chriftus.* As the reafonable Soule, and the flefh ys one man : Euen fo God and man ys one
Chryfte.

Nowe this loaf made of thefe two tenth deales, of the Godhead, and of
the manhead, wher ys yt, but *in myftica menfa,* in the myfticall table? So that
here ys taught, more plainlie then can be denied, that which the rude heretike with wonder fomtime asketh, faing: What? ys Chryfte God and man
in the Sacrament, vnder the formes of fo litle a peice of bread? Which rude
man if he wolde leaue reafoning and queftioning (which make him dout-
fullie to wonder at the workes of God) and wolde fubdue his vnderftanding to the faithe of Chryft and harken to this Father and foche other of the
Parliament houfe of Chryfte as teache his enacted and receaued faith, he **F**
fhoulde foone by the helpe of Gods grace ceaffe with incredulitie to wonder, and with reuerence to embrace this mifterie.

And that ye maie the fooner fo doo, note yet more, how this auncient Fa
ther expowndeth this figure: The loaues made of two tenth deales were fet
in two fondrie rowes: The bleffed loaf Chryfte, that ys of two tenth deales
of his Godhead and of his manhead ys fett in two fondrie rowes, as thys
Authour applieth yt: *Seni ponuntur altrinfecus: Myftica menfa ponitur quidem hic, po
nitur & in futuro feculo.* The breades are putte fixe in a rowe. The myfticall table ys fett here, and ys fett in the woorld to come.

In which Applicacion note that as the Shew bread was fette in fondrie
rowes: *So Chryft figured by the fame bread, ys fett both here and in heauen.* And that the
Glofe of the Aduerfarie fhall not delude thee by his common glofe, faing: that Chryft by
Sacramen- his godhead ys here in the worlde, but not by Godhead and manhead in
taries for the Sacrament. Remembre the wholl applicacion of the figure, that yt ys
Chryftes for the prefence of Chryft in the Sacrament, as yt dothe well appeare by **G**
prefence. that that foloweth immediatelie.

In fixe daies (faieth he) this vifible creature was made, and in the fixt daie
man was created, for whom Chryft prepared this myfticall table. And yet all
thefe breades together are verie well twelue. For the Apoftles which firft
fupped at our Lordes Supper were twelue. So that this figure ys cõtinuallie
applied to the Sacrament.

The table Wherin to proue the prefence of Chryfte, if ye defire more plain and eui
of Chryft dent teftimonie, note this that he faieth immediatelie : *Hæc munda eft primùm
pourgeth,* *quidem ficut mundans: deinde ficut nihil mendacij, nec infectionis, qualia funt in myfterijs*
&c. *Paganorum, habens.* This table ys clean, Firift, *as clenfing or making clean:* fecondlie
as hauing no lie or vntrueth nor infection, as the myfteries of the Pagans
haue.

In which fainge note well, that he faieth, *that this table ys a table, that pourgeth
clenfeth, or maketh clean.* What doth yt make clean but the foule? What ys yt to
make the foule clean, but to remitte and wipe awaie finnes, which be the vn
cleanneffe, and filthineffe of the fowle? Who remitteth and taketh awaie fin **H**
ne, but God, our Sauiour and Redemer Chryft Iefus? For (as the Iewes
Luc. 5. faied) *Quis poteft peccata remittere nifi folus Deus?* who can remitte finne but God
alone?

Seing then in this table ys that, that clenfeth vs, and taketh awaie our
fin̄es

A　finnes,we maie boldelie point with our fingar to this bleſſed table, wher
Chryſt ys preſent in myſterie,and yet verilie,as Iohn the Baptiſt did point
to him being in viſible forme,and ſaie: *Ecce agnus Dei,ecce qui tollit peccata mun-* Joan.1.
*di.*Beholde the Lambe of God,beholde him,that taketh awaie the ſinnes of
the woorlde.And humbling our ſelues before him ther preſent , with meke
ſupplicacion of the catholique Churche, praie God,and ſaie . *O Lambe of*
*God that takeſt awaie the ſinnes of the worlde,haue mercie vpon vs.*This maie we boldelie doe,for(as yt foloweth in this Authour)in this table ys no lie or vntrueth,as in the myſteries of the Pagans,but here ys in verie dede Chryſte,
God and man , verilie and trulie , as ys before by this Authour teſtified.

　In my iudgement this veritie of the bleſſed Sacramẽt ys by this Authour
allready both pithilie and plainlie teſtified:and the figure well and iuſtilie
applied. But will ye yet ſee in the ende of the applicacion, a more plain ſentence?Thus he ſaieth: *Inſuper eleuans eius gloriam,&* *myſterij dignitatem efferens in*
B　*ſublime,addit:Sanctum ſanctorum eſt de ſacrificio Domini iure perpetuo . Ergo ſancta eſt*
oratio,ſancta ſcripturæ diuinæ lectio , & *interpretationis auditio , ſancta ſunt (vt breuiter*
dicam) omnia quæ in eccleſiis Dei ſecundùm legem eius dicuntur, & *aguntur. Sancta*
autem ſanctorum de ſacrificio Domini , de omnibus videlicet quæ offeruntur , & *agun-*
tur ad eius gloriam,menſa eſt,quam de ſacrificio ſuo Chriſtus proponit . Moreouer exal-　Table of
ting the glorie of yt , and extolling the dignitie of the myſtery vnto the　the Sacrifi
height he addeth:*Yt ys the moſt holie of the Sacrifice of the Lorde , by a* perpetuall　ce moſt ho
ſtatute.Nowe praier ys holie,the reading of Gods ſcripture ys hólie,and the　lie thing in
hearing of the interpretacion of the ſcripture ys holie , and (breifly to ſaie)　the church
All thinges that according to his lawe, are either ſaied , or doen in the
churches of God are holie.But of all thinges,whiche be either offred or doẽ
to his glorie,*the moſt holie of all ys the table,whiche Chryſte hath ſett furth of his ſacrifi-*
*ce.*Hitherto Iſychius.

　Doe ye not here ſee, whiche ys the holieſt thing in all the church of
God , aboue praier,aboue the reading of the ſcriptures, aboue the hearing of the interpretacion of the ſcriptures,yea generallie aboue all thinges
C　that be doen or offred to the glorie of God?The bleſſed Shewe bread , the
bodie of Chryſte,which ys the bread of life ys the holieſt of all.

　Thus,Reader,thowe maiſt ſee,how yt hath pleaſed God by the figure,
to extoll and magnifie the thing figured,that ys the bleſſed bodie of Chryſt
in the Sacrament,with theſe great woordes, caling yt , *the moſt holie of the of-*
*fringes of God.*A greablie wherunto ye ſee this Authour ſo moche eſteme and
repute the woorthines and holineſſe of the Sacrament, that he declareth yt
to Sourmounte and excell all the holie thinges,what ſoeuer they be, that be
doen to the glorie of God in his Churche.

　Iudge then what ells can atteign to ſoche holineſſe in the Sacrament,but
the bodie of Chryſt.For the bread and wine(as the aduerſaries ſaie)being
dumme creatures are not able to take holineſſe. Conclude then with this
Authour,that the Shew bread was a figure of the bleſſed Sacrament, which
for that yt ys holieſt of all other,yt proueth yt well to be the verie bodie of
Chryſt.

D　　This Authour by plain woordes conuinceth the wicked opinion of Oe-　Oecolãpad
colampadius,who in his booke of the Supper of our lorde ſaieth , that the Sa-　conuinced
cramẽt ys no holier,nor otherwiſe ſanctifieth then praiers doo.Theſe be his　by thautori
woordes : *Hæc verò creatura panis ita ſanctiſsimo vſui ſeruiens , vt &* *corpus*　tie of Iſychius.
　　　　　　　　　L　iij　　　　　　　　Chriſti

Chriſti, quod repræſentat, appelletur, vtentesque ſanctificat non ſua quidem natura, ſed vten E
tium ſanctimonia, hoc eſt, fide, & affectu ſancto. Non minùs enim verè hoc quis de Eucha-
riſtia affirmat, quàm de precibus, quæ vſu ſuo hominem ſanctificant. This creature of
bread ys ſo ſanctified, ſeruing to a moſt holie vſe, that yt maie alſo be called
the bodie of Chryſt, whiche yt dothe repreſent. And yt doth ſanctifie them
that vſe yt, not of the owne nature: But by the ſanctimonie of the vſers, that
ys, by faith, and holie affection. Thus he.

In whoſe woordes ys plain contradiction. For firſt he ſaieth *that the bread ys*
Oecolamp. *ſanctified,* And yet he ſaieth again, *yt hath no holineſſe in yt.* Again he ſaieth,
his contra- *yt ſanctifieth the receauers:* And after he ſaieth, *yt doth not,* but their own ſanctimo
diction. nie ſanctifieth them. Thirdlie he ſaieth, yt ſanctifieth as praiers do : and praiers, if theye be deuoute, pourchaſe ſanctificacion but ſanctifie not of them ſel
ues: but the bodie of Chryſt ſanctifieth of yt ſelf.

Nowe yf he meen this of the bread as yt ys handled nowe a daies of men
Comunion of this ſecte, I thinke he ſaieth trueth. For nether ys that holie of yt ſelf, ne-
bread of the ther dothe yt ſanctifie the receauers. For they by their corrupted faith, are ra F
Sacramen- ther defiled. But if he ſpeake of the Sacrament, as yt ys vſed emõg the catho-
taries ſan- lique people, then he fowlie erreth. For that bread ſanctifieth , and maketh
ctifieth not vs clean, as this Authour before hath ſaied. And yt ys of yt ſelf moſt holie,
as this ſame Authour in his laſt ſentence taught. And ſo againſt this wicked
Oecolampadius, yt ys holier then praier , or anie other thing in the churche
of God.

Nowe when we ſee this man, and Cantorburie and ſoch other ſo plainly
repugnante to the olde auncient Fathers, what ſhoulde we ells do but reiect
them, and vtterlie deteſt them as men framing them ſelfes a faith vpon their
hereticall election, and not vpon the faithe of Chryſt declared by the Auncient Fathers of the catholique Churche.

Although *Iſychius* be right plain in this place alleaged: yet ſhall yow heare
him hereafter ſpeake more plainlie.

THE FOVRE AND TWENTETH CHAPITER AP-
plieng the continuall reſeruing of the Shewe bread to the reſeruacion of the Sacra
ment, proueth theſame reſeruacion by the olde Fathers, and by the perpe- G
tuall practiſe of the Church.

T ys oute of all doubte by the teſtimonie of the Fathers before alleaged, that the Shewe bread was a figure of the holie Sacrament:
Plain yt ys that the ſame Shewe bread was ſett furth bicauſe yt
ſhoulde be continuallie reſerued in the temple, and to no vſe more
was yt appointed, then to be reſerued . Wherfore God commaunded that
euerie Sabboth, daie hott bread ſhoulde be ſett furth vpõ the table, and that
Shewe Aaron and his Sonnes the preiſtes ſhoulde eate the ſtale bread.
bread ap-
pointed Now the figure muſt be aunſwered by the thing figured, ſpeciallie in that
for three parte, that ys the cheif and principall parte of the figure. The principall par-
thinges. te of the Shew bread and the cheif cauſe of the appointement of yt was for
three things. The firſt (as the text alleaged declareth) that yt ſhould be alwais
remaining in the temple vpon the table: The ſecond , *vt ſit panis in monimentũ*
oblationis Domini, that yt ſhould be a bread of remẽbrance of the offring of the H
Lord · The third, that yt ſhould be eaten onelie of Aaron, and his Sonnes.

Seing then the Sacrament ys the thing figured yt muſt anſwer the figure in theſe poinctes, whiche be the principall parte of the figure.
So

A So then as the Shewe bread was referued , So likewife maie the Sacra- *Shewe*
ment be referued : As the Shewe bread was a bread of remenbrance of *bread ap-*
the oblaciō or offring of the Lorde: So ys the Sacramēt the breade of remē- *plied to the*
brāce of the offring of Chryft our lorde . As the Shwe bread was to be eatē *Sacramēt.*
onely of Aron and his Sonnes: So ys the Sacrament of none to be receaued but of our fpirituall Aron and his Sonnes, whiche folowe their father
in holie faith, and like conuerfation.

    This goodlie agreement, and iuft anfwering of the thing figured to the
figure therof, doth very well proue the thing fo to be.

    The Aduerfarie can not denie, but that the Shewe breade was a figure of
the Sacrament . For that ys teftified by the holie Fahers. And the referuaciō
of the Shew breade being a figure of fome thing in the newe Teftamēt (*For
all the Leuiticall facrifices , and Ceremonies, were figures of thinges of the newe Teftament*)
wherof can yt be a figure , but of the referuacion of the Sacrament, as the
bread yt felf was a figure of the Sacrament yt felf?

B   Let the aduerfarie bring furth the thinge figured by the referuaciō of the
Shew bread yf he cā, yf he can not (as certē yt ys that he cā not) for fomuche *God ap-*
as God appointed no vain figure, voide of all fignificaciō, and he hath ordei- *pointed no*
ned alfo, that *iota vnū, aut vnus apex non præteribit à lege, donec omnia fiāt.* one iotte *vainfigure.*
or one title fhall not fcape till all be fullfilled: maugre of the Aduerfaries he- *Math.5.*
arte, this parte of the figure ys aunfwered by the referuacion of this bleffed Sacrament , for the memoriall of the offring of Chrift vpon the croffe,
and to be eaten of his good faithfull children.

    Now wher one of the membres of the proclamaciō of this Aduerfarie ys *One mēbre*
againft the referuacion of the bleffed Sacramēt: ye maie fee that was made, *of mafter*
more by felf will then by lawe, for the lawe ys againft him, as by that, that ys *Iuells pro-*
faied, yt dothe well appeare. *clamacion*

    But to this further confufion, I fhall declare and proue that this matter *againft Re-*
hathe ben putte in execucion in fundrie and diuerfe ages, frō the beginning *feruaciō m*
of Chryftes Churche. And for that this Aduerfarie alleadgeth the epiftle of *proued.*
fainct Clement, written to fainčte Iames called the brother of Chryft: ther-
C for fhall I alfo alleadg the fame epiftle, and beginning with yt , defcende to
our daies.

    Sainčt Clemēt the difciple of faincte Peter the Apoftle, and an holie mar- *Phill.4.*
tir of Chryfte, of whome faincte Paule maketh mencion , declaring the or- *Clemens*
dre aboute the bleffed Sacrament vfed in his time , faith thus: *Tribus gradibus* *Epift.1.*
cōmiffa funt facramenta diuinorum fecretorum: prefbytero, Diacono, & miniftro. Qui cum
timore, & tremore reliquias corporis Domini debent cuftodire fragmentorum, ne qua pu-
tredo in facrario inueniatur, ne cùm negligenter agitur, portioni corporis Domini grauis
inferatur iniuria . The Sacramentes of the diuine fecrettes are committed
to three degrees : to the Preift, to the Deacon, and to the miniftre . which
aught with feare and trembling to kepe the leauinges of the peices *of the bodie*
of our Lorde, leeft anie corruption be fownde in the holie place, leeft when
any thinge ys necligentlie doen, great wrong be doen to *the porcion of our Lor-*
des bodie. Thus fainct Clement.

    In whiche faing we haue not onelie to confider, that this ys the bare fa-
D ing of faincte Clement but that yt ys foche learr ing as he had learned of his
maftre, and of the Apoftles, and was both in their times, and after, and ys
yet taught, and practifed in the catholique Churche.

    And fecondarelie, we haue to note, that he calleth the Sacrament that ys
left, the procion of owre Lordes bodie.

Thirdlie, he doth not onelie by fo calling yt, teache vs that yt ys the bodie **E** of Chryft, but alfo by the facte, that ys, by the comaundement of the reue-rent keping of yt, whiche ys that they to whome thefe myfteries are com mitted, fhoulde kepe them *with feare and tremblinge,* which feare and trembling importeth the prefence of an other maner of thing then of a peice of bread.

Fourtlie, ye perceaue, that the Sacrament was appointed to be kept, and that not for an howre or a daie, but for a loger time, or ells they fhoul-de not be aduertifed to be circufpecte, that no corruptio fhoulde be fownde in the holie place, or anie wrong thorough necligece, fhoulde be doe to the porcio of Chriftes bodie. So that by this yt ys manifeftlie taught, that the Sacramet ys not onelie the bodie of Chryft: but alfo that in the time of the Apoftles yt was referued ad kept with great reuerece, diligece, ad circufpectio

Refuruati-on of the Sacrament in the Apo-ftles tyme.

But here perchaunce the aduerfarie will obiecte, and faie that fainete Cle ment immediatelie maketh againft me. For he faieth : *Tata in altario holocaufta offeratur, quata populo fufficere debet. Quòd fi remaferint, in craftinu nō referuetur, fed cu timore & tremore clericorum diligentia confumantur.* Let ther be fo many hoftes **F** offred on the Altar, as maie fuffice the people : And yf anie of them remain let them not be referued till the morowe, but by the diligence of the clerkes, with feare and trembling fpent.

Obiection out of S. Clement.

I graunt that this ys in the epiftle of fainte Clemet, and that within a fewe lines after the former fainge by me alleaged. But the aduerfarie can not re-proue me of falfe allegacion. For certen I am, that yt ys euen in that epiftle, as I haue alleaged.

But to anfwer the Aduerfarie, thinketh he that fainete Clemet was a foole, or fo forgettfull, that within fixe lines he wolde againft faie that he had before faied ? Yt can not be dinied, but that in the beginning of the Epiftle he geueth an ordre for the reuerent keping of the Sacrament. Yt maie not then be thought that he wolde geue a contrarie ordre within fo fewe lines, as ys faied. But geuing firft an ordre for the reuerend keping of that, that ys referued : in the fecond fentece he geueth ordre, that in the dailie Sacrifice referuacio fhoulde not be made. For fo ther fhoulde be more the neaded to be referued, whiche were not meet. As euer in the ca-tholique Churche, wher fufficiet ys appointed for referuacio, the miniftres **G** in ther quotidian miniftracion do not put more to that, that ys referued, but dailie as they cofecrate, dailie receaue. And (as by ordre they be appointed) whe time requireth, they receaue that, that was referued, ad put other in place

Aunfwer

S.Clement his faing o-pened.

The church at this daie hath in vfe that which S Clement comauded.

So that yt appeareth to me that the catholique churche at this daie hath that in vfe, that fainete Clemet in his epiftle comaunded, both for the refer-uacio, and ordre of dailie Sacrifice withoute referuacion.

That fainct Clement did not abfolutelie forbidde referuacion, but rai-ther willed yt to be in vfe, the practife of the primitiue church doth verie wel proue. For wher ther was a varietie of obferuacio of Eafter, and faft, betwixt the latin churche and the greke churche, neither wolde the grekes coforme the felues to the maner receaued in the latin churche : Victor the Pope being the xiij. after Peter, not bearing the cotumacie of the, being fo ofte and log called on, to come to coformitie, and euer refifting, did excommunicate the churches of Afia.

Victor ex-comunica-ted the churches of Afia.

Whiche thinge as yt was mifliked of manie Bifhopps : So was yt for feare **H** of the loffe of fo manie churhes mifliked of *Irenæus,* who therwith moued wroted to Victor an epiftle in that matter. In the whiche (as *Eufebius* wittneffeth) *Irenæus* reporting howe *Anicetus, Pius, Higinus, Telefphorus, and* *Xiftus*

Ecclefiaft. hift.li.5.c. 14.

A *Xiſtus* did beare with them, although they did not receaue that ordre, and did communicate with them, ſaied: *Nunquam tamen ob hoc repulſi ſunt ab Ec-cleſiæ ſocietate, aut venientes ab illis partibus non ſunt ſuſcepti : imò potiùs & omnes presbyteri, qui fuerunt ante te, omnibus ſemper, qui non ita obſeruabant, presbyteris eccle-ſiarum Euchariſtiam ſolemniter tranſmittebant.* Neuer for all that were they for this repulſed from the felowſhippe of the Church, or ells cōming frō thoſe par-ties were not receaued, but raither all Biſhopps, that were before thee, to all Biſhopps of the churches, whiche did not ſo obſerue, they did allwaies ſo-lemnelie ſende the Sacrament.

By this ſentence yt doth appeare (as of the learned yt ys noted) that the Biſhoppes of Rome accuſtometh, that yf anie Biſhoppes came thither, that were catholique, they wolde in tokē of chriſtiā vnitie, ſende the Sacra-ment to them, that they might cōmunicate together, for that they were of one Cōmunion. Wherby yt ys euident, that the Sacrament was allwais reſerued, to be readie for ſoche pourpoſes.

B Tertulliā writing (as ſome thinke) to his owne wife, declareth the maner of good chryſtian people aboute the Sacrament in that time, ſaing thus: *An* ・*Lib.2.* *arbitrare (ò vxor) ita geſturam te, vt clam viro ſint, quæ facis ? Non ſciet ille quid ſecretò ante omnem cibum guſtes? et ſi ſciuerit, non panem illum credit eſſe, qui dicitur.* Doeſt thowe thinke (o wife) ſo to handle thy ſelf that thoſe thinges, ・*Tertulliā with, one ſa-* that thowe doeſt, ſhall be vnknowen to thy houſbande ? Shal not he know, ・*ing ouer-* what before all meates thow doeſt ſecretly receaue ? And yf he ſhall knowe ・*throweth* yt, he beleueth not yt to be that bread, that yt ys ſaied to be. Hitherto Ter- ・*three aſſer-* tul. Whoſe litle ſentence, although yt doth ouerthrowe thre or foure aſſer- ・*tions of the* tions of the Auerſaries in this matter of the Sacrament: Yet we ſhall here ・*Sacramen-* touche but two, that be to the pourpoſe here. ・*taries.*

The firſt ys, that good deuoute godlie people had the Sacrament reſerued in their houſes, ofte to receaue, as their deuotiō to God moued thē, ſecretly by them ſelfs. For at that time the churche was not ſo ſettled, nor had ・*The Sacra-* ſoche peace, that the chryſten people might frelie come together, and ・*ment reſer-* receaue openlie. Wherfor for the excerc.iſing of their faith and deuociō, and ・*ued in pri-* **C** doing of their duetie to God, they had the Sacrament home to their houſes ・*uate houſes* and ther reſerued yt to receaue when they thought good. And this maie ye ・*mitiue* verie well gather of this that Tertullian ſaieh: *ſhall not thy houſband knowe what* ・*church.* *thowe ſecretlie doeſt receaue, before all meat?*

For the better vnderſtāding of whiche ſaing, yowe muſt ſuppoſe and kno we that Tertulian writeth to this woman, as though ſhe had an infidell to her houſbande, and ſhe a Chryſtian. Vnto whom ſhe wolde not haue her doinges knowē in this behalf, Nowe to couer this matter frō ſoche an yn-fidel, good people wolde ſecretlie by thē ſelues receaue that they for ſoche pourpoſe reſerued, and ſo yt appeareth, that for ſoche cauſe reſeruacion of the Sacrament might be and was moche vſed in the primitiue churche.

The ſeconde note ys for the preſence, whiche ys wher he ſaieth : *And* ・*Ioan.* *yf he knoweth yt, yet he beleueth not yt to be the bread, that yt ys ſaid to be.* Wherby ・*De lapſis* we are taught, that yt ys an other maner of bread, then yt appea- ・*ſerm.5.* reth. For yt appeareth to be but earthlie bread. but in dede yt ys heauenly ・*A mira-* bread the bread of life, euen that bread yt ſelf tnat ſaied : *The bread which I will* ・*cle wrought* **D** *geue, ys my fleſh, which I will geue for the life of the worlde.* ・*in the Sa-*

But to return to the matter of reſeruacion, we haue plain teſtimonie ther ・*crament re-* of in ſainct Cyprian, who reporteth thus : *Cùm quædam arcam ſuam, in qua Do-* ・*ſerued.* *mini Sanctum erat, manibus indignis tentaſſet aperire, igne inde ſurgente deterrita eſt,* ・*ne ne auderet contingere*. When a certain woman did attempte with vnwourthie handes to open her coafer, in whiche was *the holie thing of our Lorde*, ther arose thence a fire, and so feared her, that she durst not touche yt. Thus sainct Ciprian.

Do ye not heare that this woman had the Sacrament kept in her coafer? Perceaue ye not the great power of yt, that wher she wolde but ope the coafer with vnclea handes, she was feared awaie with a fire that rose frō thence? Ys ther anie mean for the Aduersarie, to auoid this?

Perchaunce he will cauille and saie, that Ciprian speaketh not of the Sacrament, but of some other thing, whiche he calleth, the holie thing of our Lorde. But yf he wolde so seke to auoide, he shoulde shewe him self to vain. For Ciprian speaketh ther alltogether of the Sacrament, in somoche as he reporteth foure miracles together, which God had wrought aboute the Sacrament.

Oecolamp. and Cranmers doctrine reproued by S. Cipr. Vide sup. cap. 23.

And albeit in this sentence, he dothe not by expresse woordes call yt the bodie of our Lorde, as he dothe in manie other places, yet he so termeth yt, **F** as he reproueth the doctrine of *Oecolampadius*, and Cranmer, and very likly of this Proclamer also, For he calleth yt *the holie thing of our Lorde*: and they saie ther ys no holinesse yn yt. For yt ys a dumme creature. Thus though in woordes they pretende to folowe the olde Fathers: yet in very dede they flatlie against saie them.

Ambr. in oratione fu nebr, de obi tu fratris sui.

Satyr. had part of the Sacrament reserued in the shippe and was sa. ued ther by from drow ning.

But to proceade in the prooff of reseruaciō, yt maketh moche for yt, that sainct Ambrose reporteth of his bother *Satyrus*, who, as he saieth, being a singular mā in godlinesse, and affiance toward God, and being in danger vpō the sea yet not fearing death, but desierouse not to be destitute of that blessed Sacramēt (yf yt should so please God to call him) went to the christians that were ther in the shippe ād desired to haue that Godlie Sacramēt of the faith full, not that he wolde please his curiouse eies in loking vpō soche a mistery, but that by soche a Sacramēt, he might obtein the helpe of his faith. Whiche whē yt was geuē him, he caused yt to bownde in a stole, ād so hāged yt aboute his necke, ād whē shippwracke happened, he sought not for a loose boorde **G** of the shippe to swimme vpon, and so to helpe him self, but for that he had sought the armour of faith alone, he did so committe him self to the sea, and thinking him self safe enough by the helpe of the Sacrament, he desiered no other helpe, and (as sainct Ambrose saieth) his hope did not forsake him nor deceaue him. For he was the first that escaped oute of the sea, ād came to the land. Thus moche in effect reporteth sainct Ambrose.

In whiche his reporte yt ys more thē manifest, that the Sacramēt was reserued, and as yt maie be supposed for a good time. Yf yt maie be reserued three or foure daies, why maie yt not be reserued longer?

As the wholl reporte (for that yt ys made by so holie, and woorthie a man) vs woorthie to be remembred: So be two or three things wourthie of speciall note.

The first ys, that this good man, the Brother of saincte Ambrose wēt to the chrystians in the shippe ād obteined of thē, to haue, ād to carie the Sacramēt with him. Yf to reserue the Sacrament had ben so heinouse a matter, as this Proclamer, and his complices make yt, wolde they (trowe ye) haue **H**

Sacrament reserued in the shippe.

cōmitted soche an offēce as to haue yt reserued in the shippe, ād to deliuer yt to Satirus to be so reserued? And further yf the reseruing of this Sacrament had ben against the ordre of the churche, wolde Saincte Ambrose to the praise of his Brother report yt as a thing well and Godlie doen? No trulie,

yt

A yt ys not to be thought in fo godlie and fo learned a father: but raither yt ys tobe thought that the Brother of fainct Ambrofe doing no other thing but that was by the fame fainct Ambrofe cōmended, did agreable to the maner of the Churche.

Therfor fain&e Ambrofe, to his Bothers praife, and to the example of the pofteritie to doo foche like vertuonfe workes, did write this matter, and made a boke to remain to kepe the thing in memorie. By this then yt maie appeare, that the referuacion of the Sacrament was in vfe in the churche in thofe daies.

S. Ambro-fe cōmēded the doing of his bro-the Satyr.

An other thing woorthie of note in this reporte of fainɛte Ambrofe ys, that he with cōmēdaciō declareth the affiāce that his brother had in the Sacrament. Whiche was foche that feing imminēt perill, and remēbring what he had aboute him, did not feke earthlie or worldly helpe, but repofing his truft in the Sacramēt that he had aboute him, he perfwaded him felf to haue helpe enough, and nothing diftrufting refted onelie vpon that helpe, and in B that hope committed him felf to the fearfull, and terrible vaiues of the fea.

I praie thee(good Reader) weigh this well, ād iudge whether this good mā the brother of fainɛt Ambrofe, did thinke or beleue, the Sacramēt to be but a peice of bread, a figure or fign of Chryft onelie. Wolde he(thinke yowe)in that great daūger & perill, haue cōmitted the fauing of his life(all other helpes fett a parte) te a poour dūme creature, a litle peice of bread? And aboue this, wold that good mā in that agonie, fo endaūgered his foule, as to cōmitte fo horrible ydolatrie, in placing and putting that his great truft in a peice of bread, whiche aught onelie to haue ben repofed in God? No, yt ys not to be thought, but this raither, that he being a faithfull and godlie man folowed the example of faithfull Peter, who, being in a fhippe, and hearing Chryft whom he fawe walking on the fea faing to them that were in the fhippe : be of good truft, yt ys I, be not afraied, faied to him : yf yt be thowe lorde cōmaunde me to come to thee vpon the waters. And he went out of the fhippe and walked vpon the fea toward Chryft: Euen fo this man by faith knowing his mafter Chryft to be at hand with him prefent-C lie in the facrament, he cōmitted him felf with Peter to the fea, and was the firft that was faued.

Matth. 14

Adde vnto this, that whiche ys an other thing to be noted, that fainɛt Ambrofe cōmending this brother for the great faith, truft, and affiance that he had in the Sacrament, well declareth alfo his ownę faithe, that he alfo beleued the verie prefence of Chryft in the Sacrament. Holie men commēde not the misbeleif of mē to the worlde, no not by mouthe, moche leffe by bookes, whiche muft remain.

For that then that fainct Ambrofe hath written this, no dowbte afwell to our Imitaciō, as to the cōmendaciō of his brother : bothe the faith of the Churche beleuing Chryftes prefence in the Sacrament, ys to be approued, and the referuacion of the fame Sacrament, for the comforth of vs, being feke or wholl, ys not to be diffalowed.

And yet ys ther a more euident teftimonie of this matter of referuaciɔn in an epiftle of Chrifoftom to *Innocentius*, wherin he maketh complainte of D the calamitie that happened in his churche of Conftantinople by wicked Soldiers, and emong other thinges reporteth thns : *Ipfo magno Sabbato collecta manus militum, ad vefperam diei in ecclefias ingreßa, clerum omnem, qui nobifcum erat, vi eiecit, & armis gradum vndique muniuit. Mulieres quoq; quæ per illud tēpus fe exuerant vt baptifarentur, metu grauiorum infidiarum nudæ aufugerunt:*

Chryfoft. epiſt.ad ʃn nocent.

neque

neque enim concedebatur vt se velarent, sicut mulieres honestas decet, multæ etiam E
acceptis vulneribus eijciebanttur, & sanguine implebantur natatoria, & sancto
cruore rubescebant fluenta . Neque hic rerum finis erat . Nam & sanctuaria in-
greßi sunt milites, quorum aliquos scimus nullis initiatos mysteris, & viderunt omnia,
quæ intus erant , quin & sanctißimus Christi sanguis, sicut in tali tumultu con-
tingit, in prædictorum militum vestes effusus est . Euen vpon the great Sabboth
daie (meaning Eafter daie) at the euentide, an Armie of Soldiers entred
the churche , and by violence caft oute all foche as were with vs of the cleargie. And kept with ftrêght the entrie. The womê alfo, whiche at that time
had put of their cloathes to be baptifed , for feare of more daûger, fled naked awaie. Nether were they fuffred to couer the felues, as becometh honeft
women , manie of them alfo being wounded were caft oute, and the fontes prepared to baptife them in, were full of bloode, and the waters of

Chryftes blood in the Sacr. shed vpon the foldiers. cloathes. the fontes were made red with bloode . But this was not the ende of the
bufineffe. For the Soldiers alfo went into the holie places, of the whiche, F
we knowe, fome to haue receaued no parte of the chryftian religion, and
they fawe all the thinges that were within . And befides that *the most holie*
bloode of Chryft (as yt doth happen in foche tumulte) *was shedde vpon the garmêts*
of the Soldiers. Thus facre Chriloftom.

In this complaint, firft note when thefe wycked foldiers entred vpon the
churche , they entred in the euening. At whiche time they entring into the
Sanctuarie, Ye perceaue they fownde the Sacrament ther, for he faieth that
yt was fhedde vpô the cloathes of the Soldiars. In the time of Chrifoftô yt
was not in vfe to côfecrate the Sacramêt in the after noone, but onely in the
morning. This then being kept in the Sanctuarie, and fhed vpon the garmêt
of the Soldiers in the euening, yt proueth inuinciblie, and moft plainly that

Prefence of Chryftes blood in the Sacra. and referuation auouched by Chry-foft. the Sacrament was referued.

Yf ye will alfo knowe what the Sacrament was, whether yt was a figure onely or the thing yt felf , Chriftoftom by as plain woordes teacheth vs that *yt was the bloode of Chrift*, And that we fhould perceaue yt
was fo in dede, he côtented not him felf onelie to cal yt the blood of Chryft, G
but *the moft holie blood of Chryft.* By Chrifoftom then, the referuacion of the
Sacrament ys fo plainly wittneffed , that the Proclamer can not denie yt,
& the very prefence of Chriftes bloode in the fame ys fo auouched,
that the Sacramentary ys confounded . Yt ys with moche reuerence
termed and called *the moft holie blood of Chryft*, wherby the vurcuerent and
fpitefull railing and raiging of the blafphemer ys reproued and rebuked.

Referuatiõ in S. Hie-roms time. But let vs yet proceade further, maie we not finde the referuacion of the
Sacrament in S . Hieromes time ? Yes verilie. For he wittneffeth yt
him felf declaring to one *Rufticus*, the godlie life and great libertie of *Exu-*
perius Bifhoppe of Toloife , and fignifieng the great contempt of worldelie thinges the fame had , and his great pleafure in heauenly thinges , writeth thus . *Nihil illo ditius , qui corpus Domini in caniftro vimineo,*
fanguinem portat in vitro . Ther ys no man richer then he, who beareth
the bodie of our Lorde in a wicker basket, and his bloode in a glaffe . As who might
faie: So litle regardeth this good Bifhoppe *Exuperius* the riches of the worl-

Hiero . ad Rufticum. de, that geuing awaie all his fubftance , and bearing aboute him the bodie H
of our Lord but in a litle wicker bafkett, and the blood of our Lord in a glaffe, and fo hauing thefe, he thinketh that no man vs richer then he, as I alfo
thinke ther ys not.

In thefe woordes fainthe Hierõ ys a double helpe to vs, for he dothe not
onelie

A onelie teftifie that this holy Bifhoppe, referued and caried the Sacrament in foche veffell, but alfo teftifieth what yt ys, and that by as plain woordes as can be fpoken, calling yt *the bodie and bloode of our lorde*. Wherby the Proclamer hath a double blowe. bothe for the referuacion, and alfo for the prefence.

The Proclamer wolde haue plain woordes, yf thefe be not plain enough, to call yt *the bodie and the bloode of our lorde*. I can not tell what plaineffe he wolde haue.

But as touching referuacion, and the vfe therof, we reade alfo in the Ecclefiafticall Hiftorie, a practife whiche well proueth them, wher we finde yt written thus of one Serapion, that he lieng in extreamis and wifhing to die faied: *Quoufque me detinetis? Quæfo vos, cito aliquis Presbyterum roget, vt poßim aliquando dimitti, et cùm hæc dixiffet, rurfum fine voce permanfit. Abijt curfu puer ad presbyterum noctis tempore, infirmabatur presbyter, venire non potuit. Parum Euchariftiæ puero, qui ad fe venerat, dedit, quod infufum iußit feni præberi.* Howe long will yow detein me? I befeche yowe let one quickly defire

B the preift, that I maie be let departe. And when he had fpoken thefe woordes, he remained again fpeche leffe. A feruant ranne to the preift in the night time, the preift was ficke and coulde not come. Wherfor he deliuered of the Sacrament to the feruant that came vnto him, whiche infufed he commaunded to be geuen to the olde man. Thus moche the ftorie.

Confider nowe reader, that the Meffenger came to the preift in the night time, confidre alfo that the preift was ficke, and coulde not come, fo that for vnfemelineffe of time, and fpeciallie for fickeneffe he coulde not then celebrate that holie miniftracion, and yet he fent of the Sacrament to the olde ficke man. Ys yt not plain enough by this hiftorie, that the Sacrament was referued, whiche in the night time was fo readie to be fent?

As for the maner of the place wher yt was referued I ftand not in yt, as the Proclamer in his trifling maner, difdainfullie for fo weightie a matter faieth: *that yt can not be proued, that yt shoulde be hanged vppe vnder a canopie*. The maner

C of the place ys diuerfe, as he himfelf knoweth, in the contries wher he hath trauailed. But the fubftance of the matter, whiche ys the referuacion of the Sacrament, in all the catholique Churche ys one. But as yt ys in prouerbe: *Simia femper fimia.* An ape ys allwais an ape. An hereticall contemner of bleffed myfteries will allwaies fo be, and fhewe him felf allwais like himfelf, whẽ he will trifle in the vtterance of foche matters, for the whiche fo lamentable a diuifion ys in the Churche. Yf he faie he trifeleth not, thẽ I faie he femeth either to graunt the referuacion, or ells couertlie to impugne yt, as fearing openly to doo yt, for that he knoweth he coulde not fo ftand in yt, but foen be ouerthrowen.

But let the matter go on, and let vs fee more of the vfe of the referuacion of the Sacrament. As yt maie be gathered, Satan the great enemie of the peace of Chryftes Churche, as a roring lion feking whom he might deuoure, at laft fownde fome, that did not, as ftrong men in faithe, refift him. Who yet he durft not in that time of vertue, when fo moche godlineffe, and fo mo

D che reuerẽce to the Sacramẽt floorifhed, incite and moue to fpeake directly againft the prefence of Chryfte in the Sacramẽt, as the doth in this time, but onelie that the Sacrament was not of force, nor vertue yf yt were referued but vntill the next daie. But note howe good this doctrine was. As foen as the holy father and Bifhope Cyrill heard of yt, he wrote againft yt, and with vehemencie impuged yt, as by his owne woordes ye fhall well

                M   perceiue

Cyrill.ad Ca
losirium.

perceiue. Thus he writeth: *Audio quod dicunt illi mysticam benedictionem , si ex ea remanserint in sequentem diem reliquiæ ad sanctificationem inutilem esse.Sed insaniunt hæc dicentes, non enim alius fit Christus , neque sanctum eius corpus mutabitur, sed benedictionis virtus & viuifica gratia perpetuò manent in illo .* I do heare, that they saie , that the mysticall benediction, yf the leauinges therof remain vntill the next daie folowing, ys vnprofitable to sanctificacion. *But they are madde saing these thinges. For ther ys not made an other Chryst , nether shall his holie bodie be chaunged, but the powre or vertue of the benediction and the liuelie grace doo perpetuallie abide in yt.* Thus Cyrille.

As yt maie be thought,to make awaie reseruacion of the Sacrament frō the Churche,wherby the honour of God, and of our Sauiour Chryste was moche caused to be in the heartes of people , and wherby also sicke people had moche comforte, and manie were wonne from the Deuell , and their soules sent to God,which ells perchaūce had perished,the Deuell,as I saied, not bearing this did inuent this heresie against reseruacion of the Sacramēt, and breathed yt into some vessells of perdicion.

But this doctrine was so reasonable, and so agreable to the woorde of God,that Cyrill saieth they be madde that affirme yt : Yf they were iustlie accompted madde,that taught soche doctrine in those daies, what be they, that teache the like nowe in these daies ?

But holie Cyrill teacheth vs the holsome and sobre doctrine of the Churche,and saieth,yf the Sacrament be reserued vntill the next daie,yt ys of like force,power,& vertue as yt was when yt was consecrated.

Reseruaciō
in vse befo-
re S.Cirills
time.

This sentence of Cyrill doth also presuppose, that reseruacion of the Sacramēt was in vse befooe he wrote,or ells why shoulde these naughtie men, of whom he maketh mencion,speake against yt ? Men vse not to impugne a thing that ys not.Wherfore yt must nedes be,that reseruacion being impugned,was then in vse.Yt doth also teache that reseruacion ys not vnlawfull, and a thing that maie not be doen, but raither, saing the thing continueth of like force,power and vertue,teacheth that reseruacion ys to be vsed.

Ye haue nowe hearde of the practise and vse of the reseruacion of the Sacrament,in the primitiue Churche,euē from the time of the Apostles to the time of Cyrill , for the space of more then foure hundreth yeares, whiche was the purest time of the Churche.Wherby we maie well conclude against the Aduersarie,that reseruacion ys laufull,and aught,by example of this that we haue hearde,to be vsed of all good chrystiā Churches, not withstanding the vain barking of heretikes against yt. To auoid tediousnesse', I do not tarie to note howe notablie he speaketh of the presence of Chryst in the Sacrament. But yet for so moche as yt ys so goodlie a place, and so euidentlie plain,I praie thee,Reader,cōsider yt,and well weigh yt. For I haue somwhat more to saie for reseruacion.

A plain pla
ce for Ma-
ster Iuell.

THE FIVE AND TWENTETH CHAP. PRO-
ueth the same by Councells that haue ben nearer to our time.

The church
arrogantlie
charged
with errou-
re.

Forasmoche as the Proclamer more arrogantlie then semely , chargeth, the Churche withe errour these nine hondreth yeares and aboue, and chalengeth to him and his likes the restauring of the trueth , which during all these yeares hath ben lacking, as though Chryst were false of his promisse, who promised to lead his Church into all treuth,and taketh vpō him to reiecte all Fathers,to contēne all Coūcells,and
breiflie

E breiflie to faie, to fruftrate and adnihilate all that hath ben writen, decreed, determined, or doen in matters of religion thefe ix. hondreth yeares, whiche ys a ftraung enterprife: I will therfore produce certain decrees made as well by fome other of authoritie, as by Councells, to make a triall, howe the practife of the auncient Church will agree with the decrees and practife of the Church that hath folowed and continued, whiche he fo moch reproueth.

Among the whiche I finde alleaged *Iuftinian* the Emperour, who hauing a good zeale to godlie religion made a conftitucion, that monafteries of virgens fhoule haue libertie to choofe a preift, who fhoulde bring vnto them the holie communion.

Iuftinian. conft. 123. *de Nouuel.*

This conftitucion appointeth not the preift, that fhoulde be chofen by thefe virgens, to celebrate the holie myfterie, but that he fhoulde bring them the holie communion, when they were difpofed to communicate. And yf yt were brought, yt argueth for the time a referuacion.

F In the decrees alfo ys alleaged the Councell of worms, which was holden aboute the time of Charles the great, in whiche foche a Canon was made: *Presbyter Euchariftiam femper habeat paratam, vt fi quis infirmatus fuerit, ftatim eum communicet, ne fine communione moriatur.* Let the preift allwaies haue the Sacrament in a readineffe, that yf anie man be ficke he maie furthwith receaue the Sacrament, that he die not withoute the communion.

De conf. dift 2. *cap. Prefbyter.* The preift muft allwaies haue the Sacramêt readie for the ficke

I nede not to make here any note to the reader for his better vnderftanding, for the decree ys plain enough for the confutacion of the Aduerfarie.

But the Aduerfarie that eftemeth not the generall Councells, perchaunce will with moche more contempt reiecte this Councell, faing that yt was but a prouinciall Councell. Yt was but a prouinciall Councell in dede, and although a prouinciall Councell hath not authoritie to binde the wholl Churche by their priuate decrees: yet yt hath authoritie to fett furth a G trueth. And that thys decree was not againft the ordre receaued in the wholl Churche this proueth yt inuinciblie, for that yt was neuer by any generall Councell condemned.

Ther was neuer prouinciall Councell that decreed anie thing contrary to the generall receaued faith, but yt was noted, and by fome generall Councell confuted.

Hereticall Councells allwaies fuppreffed.

The Arrians called manie Councells, befides that whiche they kept in *Nicæa Thraciæ*, but they coulde neuer take place nor authoritie, neither did the Churche fuffer them to be publifhed, but fuppreffed, impugned, confuted, and conuinced them.

The feconde Ephefine Councell, although ther was ther a great affemblie: yet yt was ouerthrowen by the generall Councell of Calcedon.

What fhall I nede to protracte this matter with mo examples? Certen yt ys, that yf this Councell had decreed any thing againft the trueth of the catholique faith, or againft the receaued ordre of the Churche in matters H of Religion, yt fhoulde haue ben impugned manie years, er this Aduerfarie had ben born. But for afmoche as yt hath continned fomany yeares not confuted by anie generall Councell, nor impugned by anie cattholique learned man, and ys agreable afwell to the order receaued in the aunciente Churche (as by that that ys faied in the laft chap. yt dothe well appeare) as to the order of the catoliq Churche that hath bê and ys in this our time (for all

these reasons and consideracions yt can not be but that the Decree of the **A**
Councell before alleaged ys catholique, good and alowable.

And yf all this weigh not in the conceat of the Aduersarie: yet he can not
denie, but that reseruacion was then in vse, whiche well appeareth also by

Concil. Re-
men.
the Councell called *Concilium Remense*, as yt ys alleaged in the same decrees,
and same distinction. Whiche for the reuerence of the Sacrament, straictlie
forbiddeth the preist to deliuer the same to aniclaie man or woman, to carie
yt to any sicke person, but straictlie commaundeth that the preist go him
self, and minister to the sicke.

After these Councells was the generall Councell of Lateran, whiche was
a notable and a great Coūcell, wherin were present besides a great nōbre of

Concil. La-
teran.
Bishoppes, the foure Patriarkes, as some writers testifie, and manie grecians
aswell as latines. This Councell was celebrated vnder *Innocentius* the thirde,
the yeare of our lorde M. CC. XV. and so CCC. XLVI. years agone.   In

Canon 20.
whiche great Councel this I finde ther Decreed: *Statuimus in cunctis eccle-*
siis, vt Chrysma & Eucharistia, sub fideli custodia conseruentur. We doo ordein **B**
that in all Churches, the holie oile, and the Sacrament be kept vnder
faithfull custodie. Here ye see howe the reseruacion being in vse in the
beginning, ys in this Councel appointed to be cōtinued, and that not in some Churches, but in all.

Howe so euer yt shall like the Proclamer to accepte or to reiect this
Councell: yet the sobre chrystian considering howe great a Councell
yt was, and that of the learned men as well of the greke Churche as of
the latin Churche, whiche coulde, and did knowe as well as the Proclamer, and see what ys to be doen as well as he doth: And considering also
that yt was holden more then three hondreth yeares agon, at whiche present time (althoug before and after) their was no publique or open controuersie in that point: and also that yt ys an ordinaunce agreable to the vse
of the primitiue Churche, will regarde yt, and with humble maner obeie
yt, or at the leest wish yt to be obeyed.

Luther his
fonde opi-
nion of the
presence.
After this Councell in the time of Leo the tenth, Martyr Luther, a newe **C**
Heresiarke, or inuentour of heresie, rose vppe, who affirming the presence
of Chryst in the Sacrament but verie fondlie without all authoritie of Scripture, Doctour, or Councell, taught that the presence of Chryst was in the
Sacrament yf yt were receaued: Yf not, ther was no presence. And vpon this
reseruacion of the Sacrament was of him denied.

Carolstad.
Oute of this Luther sprang first Corolstadins, who impugned his masters
doctrine, and taught, as our Proclamer teacheth, that ther ys no presence of

Oecolamp.
Zuinglius.
Chryst in the Sacrament. With whom shortlie ioined *Oecolampadius*, and
Zuinglius. Whiche first among all other wrote and sett oute their bookes
against the Sacrament and denieng the wholl (as of consequence yt must
be) they denied the parte also.

And for that the Lutherans, and the named Sacramentaries did pietifullie disturbe, rent, teare and diuide those contries of Saxonie, and Helue
tia, with other in Getmanie with these rehersed heresies, and an infinite
nombre mo, whiche dailie grewe vppe to the great endammaginge of ma- **D**
nie chrysten Soules: Paule the thirde then Bishoppe of Rome, to re-
presse these heresies, called a Councell at Trident, wher emonge manie other good and godlie determinacions as touching the matter of the

Conci. Tri-
dent.
reseruacion whiche we haue nowe in hande, ys this Canon:

Consuetudo asseruandi in sacrario sanctam Eucharistiam, adeò antiqua est, vt eam
seculum

E *seculum etiam Niceni Concilij agnouerit.Porro deferri ipsam sacram Euchariſtiam ad infir-*
mos, & in hunc vsum diligenter in ecclesijs conseruari, præterquam quòd cum summa
æquitate & ratione conunctum eſt, tum multis in Concilijs præceptum inuenitur, &
vetuſtiſsimo catholicæ Eccleſiæ more obseruatum.Quare hæc sancta Synodus retinendum
omnino salutarem hunc, & necessarium morem ſtatuit. The cuſtome to kepe the
holy Sacrament in the holie place ys of soche antiquitie, that the worlde
in tyme of the Nicen Councell did agnise yt. Moreouer that the Sacrament ſhoulde be caried to them that are sicke, and for this pourpose to be
diligentlie kept in Churches,be side that yt ys agreable to equitie and reason, yt ys also fownde to be commended in manie Councells, and in the
moſt auncient maner of the catholique Churche obserued. Wherfor
this holie Synode hath commaunded this holsom and necessarie maner
to be reteined and kept ſtill. Thus moche the Councell.

*Nycê Coñ-
cell did ag-
niſe Reſer-
uacion.*

I wiſh that the reader taking these woordes as the woordes and saing
of a Councell,and as the agreable saing of a great nombre of learned
F men, wolde marke and learn ther in, firſt, that the vse of the reseruacion
ys of great antiquitie. Secondly, that reseruacion, to the entent the Sacrament ſhoulde be allwais readie for the sicke, ys here teſtified to be
commaunded by manie Councells. Thirdlie,that this Councell iudgeth
meet and consonant to reason that yt ſhoulde be doen. Fourtly, that by
the autoritie of a Councell they haue commaunded this vse of reseruacion
to be reteined and continued. Yf all these be (as they ought to be) well
weighed, why ſhoulde they not conteruaill, yea and so weightilie weigh
down all contrarie sainges, as these ſhoule be as a light feather, in respecte of a thousande weight, when they be in lanceis to be weighed
together.

Yf a Parlament of a Realme geue soche authoritie to the Actes and Statu-
tes ther made,that the priuate talke of rebelliouse, and disobedient persons,
though they be manie, can not diſſolue them: Why ys not the like pre-
G eminence geuen to the Parlament of Chryſtes catholique Churche. Wher
decrees are made not by the people of one Realme, but of manie, yea of all
chriſtian Realmes,that liſt to come, and theie not vulearned but learned. Yf
the one doth binde,why not the other?

*Yf a Parla
ment be of
force to bin
de, why not
a Councell.*

But not minding to enter into the disputacion of so large a matter, and
ther by to make, to long digreſſion from my pourpose, I will ſtaie and yet
wiſh the reader to consider what foloweth in the same Councell decreed
againſt soche as ſhall contemptuouſlie speake againſt this matter of reseruacion. Soche a Canon ther I finde. *Si quis dixerit non licere sacram Eucha-*
riſtiam in sacrario reseruari, sed ſtatim poſt consecrationem aſtantibus necessariò diſtri-
buendam: aut non licere vt illa ad infirmos honorificè deferatur: Anathema sit. Yf
anie man ſhall saie that yt ys not laufull to reserue the holie Sacrament
but that ſtreight waie after the consecracion yt ys of neceſſitie to be diſtributed to them that be present, and that yt ys not laufull reuerently to carie
yt to them that be sicke,accurſed be he.

Canon 7.

*Deniers of
reseruacion
accurſed.*

H Although(I knowe) the Aduersarie contemneth thys heauie sentence,
forsamoche as he vilipédeth and derideth the Councells: Yet(I thanke God
of that his grace)I regard them,I reuerence their sentence,I feare and dread
the same, hauing in minde the sainge of our Sauiour Chryſte : *Qui non*
*audiuerit Eccleſiam, sit tibi sicut Ethnicus, & publicanus.*He that will not heare the
Churche, let him be to thee, as an ethnicke and publicane.And again. *Qui*
vos ſpernit,me ſpernit: et qui me ſpernit,ſpernit eũ qui me miſit. He that deſpiſeth yow

Math. 18.

Luc.10.

M iij　　deſpiſeth

despiseth me:and he that despiseth me,despiseth him that sent me.

This being spoken and ment of the Apostles and their successours, the spirituall rulars of the Churche,the Proclamer and hys likes so doing, what doo they ells,but,as Chryst saieth, contemne him and hys Father? yf they saie they contemne not the rulars of the Churche,but obeie them:let them answere me.Whom did their great fathers *Luther, Carolstadius, Oecolampadius, Zuinglius, Bullinger, &c.* obey in the Churche? yf ye wyll saie they coulde obeye none of all the wholl Churche that was then and before, for yt was no Churche:well let this your false aunswere stande.Yf then your Churche began with *Luther,*he being sole head,why did *Carolstadius,Oecolampadius,* and the rest disobeie him? Yf all they were the Churche,why did *Thomas Monetarius,*and *Sweckfeldius* disobey them,and not heare them:But to be shorte,good Reader, they obey none, neither will they heare anie, but onelie soche as saye as they saie. And this ys propre to euery secte of them,so that the *Oecolampadians* will not heare the *Lutheraus,*the *Anabaptistes,*will not heare the *Oecolampadians,*the *Swenckfeldians* will heare none of all these.

Yet euery of these sectes saie, they be the Churche, and euery of them saie,they haue the very woorde of God,and therupon,they saie,they builde. And yet the woorde of God as yt ys one, so hath yt one trueth, whiche euery one of these forsaking, do miserablie adulterate that holie and blesset woorde of God,and in stede of trueth sell vnto the people their hereticall lies,vnder the pretence of Gods woorde and his trueth.

I am lothe to entre any further in the opening of the rebelliouse diuisions, sectes, and factions that be emonge them. And they be so manie as wolde require a iust volume to sette them furth,soch ys the consent,agreemēt and obedience emong them selues. wiche ys euen the iust plague of God. For as man falling from the obedience of God,fownde by Gods permission, a merueillouse rebellion in his owne bodie and membres: So these men falling from the obedience of God in his Church, fall to continuall disobedience,and implacable rebellion among them selues.

But ther was a Churche before Luther began his malignant Churche. C whiche former Churche being fownded vpon Christe continueth, for that yt ys builded vpon à sure stone.And this ys that Churche that must be hearde and obeied. Against thys Churche *Berengarius,*(as before ys saied) began to be disobedient,but he humbled him self and desired to be restored again. *Wiclef* and *Husse* also rebelled,and moued warre,but they coulde not preuaill. And allthough for our sinnes God suffred the Philystines nowe to make warre against Israell,as he did against the carnall Israell: yet nothing mistrusting his mercie, and hauing sure affiance in his promesse that *Portæ inferi non præualebunt aduersus eã,*the gates of hell shall not preuaill against his Churche, I doubte not but he will at his mercifull pleasure looke vpon yt, and send peace to yt.

And nowe to return to that from which, I haue a litle digressed: I saie, I do regarde the sentence of the Churche.for yt ys terrible to be cutte offrom that mysticall bodie of Chryst, and to be made a dead membre, like vnto a rotten or dead sticke meit for no pourpose but to be cast in the fire and D burnt.

Perchaunce the aduersarie will saie, he feareth not to dissent from the Churche,wher the Church dissenteth from the Scripture,as yt doth in this matter of reseruacion.

Yere will I again ioin yssue with the proclamer, that if he can bring any
plain

Obedience of the newe Churches how yt stādeth.

Euery sect of Protestātes chalenge to thē the woorde of God,and the name of the Churche.

Berēgarius Wicleff. Hus.

Math. 16.

Issue ioined with the proclamer touching re seruacion.

E plain scripture,catholique Doctour, or Councell, that by expresse woordes forbiddeth reseruacion, I will subscribe, and come to him. Yf he can bringe yone soche,what shamelesse rashnesse ys yt for him to calumniate the Churche for that thing,for the whiche he hath no good warrant . Ys he so imperiall ouer the Churche,that he maie and will haue yt to leaue of reseruacion of the Sacrament at his pleasure, which yt hath vsed from the beginning, an can shewe no scripture, no catholique Doctour, no auncient Councel that forbiddeth yt ? Ys this woorde of the disciples of *Pythagoras* (*ipse dixit, he saied yt*) a sufficient warrant for vs ? Shall we so lightlie cast awaie the orders,rites, customes, and maners of so long time receaued, vsed, and through all the Churche frequented for soche mens bare woorde? Yf he finde any thing amisse let him reforme yt by scriptures, Doctours,or Councells,andwe shall heare:otherwise yt shall be more easey for the Churche , to repell his obiections, then yt shall be for him to proue them.

Auncient and godlie customes, are not to be left for the bare saing of à Protestāt.

F And methinke,nay I do not onelie thynk yt,but I saie yt ys a shame for him to enterprise soche prohibition,and to crie out vpon the Churche as though she had committed most high treason against God,aswell in other thinges,as in the vse of reseruacio,whiche ye haue hearde to be cōmaunded by decrees with in these nine hondreth yeares made to be continued as yt was vsed in the primitiue Churche , and by the space of manie yeares after , and to bring no peice of lawe to charge her by, and iustlie to proue that she hathe offended.

THE SIXE AND TWENTETH CHA-
pit. aunswereth the cheif obiection of the aduersaries.

G YF anie thing maie be obiected against reseruacion of the Sacramēt this ys yt,whiche ys *Achilles* with them,and euen ther common argument aswell against reseruacion, as other rites,and orders of the Churche in the ministration of the Sacraments.In the institution of the Sacrament ther ys no mencion made of reseruacion,wher for(saie they)yt aught not to be vsed.

Will ye see the great force of this argument : Ther ys no mencion made of praier in the institution of the Sacrament of Baptisme, when Chryst was baptised,Ergo,ther aught to be no praier made in the ministration of yt nowe. Again ther ys no mencion made of the Baptising of children in the institucio of Baptisme,Ergo,children aught not to be chrystened . Ther were no wittnesses as godfathers , or godmothers to Chryste,Ergo,ther aught none to be in the ministracion of Baptisme to children. Ther is no mencion made of this terme,Sacrament,as calling Babtisme or the Supper of our lorde a Sacrament,Ergo they ought not so to be called. Likwise , ther ys no mencion made of praiers in the institucion of the Supper of our lorde,Ergo, ther aught none to be said at the ministracion ther of. Ther is no mencion made that any women were at Chrystes Supper , Ergo ther aught no women to

Protestāts argumētes of negatiues eluded.

H come to the communion.Ther is no mencion made in the institucion of the Sacrament that yt shoulde be done in the daie time,Ergo,yt ought not so to be doen. And a great nombre of soche might in this wise be inferred,wher by yt dothe well appeare howe fonde the argument ys.

And yet this ys a common and inuincible maner of argument with these people. For in other matters they vse yt thus: Ther is no mencion of purgatorie in the scripture,Ergo,ther ys none.Ther ys no mencion in the scripture

The procla mer vseth the same maner of disputaciō. he denieth all and proueth no-thing.

M iiij   to praie

to praie for the dead, Ergo they are not to be praied for. There ys no men- **A**
cion in scripture of the inuocacion of sainctes, Ergo, rhey are not to be
praied vnto. Ther ys prescribed no daies of fasting in the scripture, Ergo, we
are not bownde to fast. This ys the maner of disputacion of that Schoole.

*Three ma-
ner of doin-
ges as tou-
ching the
Scripture.*
    I.

But to ioine with thē in the soluciō of their argumēt. Ther be thre maner
of doinges as concerning the Scripture: One ys to do so moche as the Scri-
ture biddeth. An other to do against that the Scripture biddeth. The thirde
ys to do something besides that the Scripture biddeth.

As concerning the first, wher Chryst toke bread, and made yt his bodie,
and wine and made yt his bloode, And commaunded them to be eaten, and
dronken in the remembrance of his passion and death. Yf the true chrystian
to whom Authoritie ys geuen, doth take the like matter of bread and wine,
and doth consecrate yt according to Chrystes commaundement, *Hoc facite:
This do ye,* and so eate yt and drinke, yt in the remembrance of Chrystes passion and death: this man hath doen as moche as the scripture biddeth him,
and therfor ys he blamelesse in this respect. **B**

II.   An other maner of doinge ys when a man dothe contrarie to the scripture, as when men will not vse soche matter as Chryst appointed of whiche for
te ther haue ben diuerse.

*August. l.
de hæresib.*
The Manyches hauing wicked opinions, among whiche one was that all
our foode ys vnclean, and therupon taking common bread to be vnclean,
they vsed flower in the Sacrament, mingled with water and other lothsom
matter. And so did contrarie to the scripture, not vsing pure bread, but other
matter then Chryste appointed.

Ibid. ca. 64
Other ther were, that for a singular sobrietie whiche they semed to professe, wolde not vse wine in the ministracion of the Sacrament, but onely water, whiche therfore saincte Augustine calleth *Aquarios,* watrie men. Against
these men did saincte Cyprian write, and Chrysostome also, and diuerse
other.

*Concil. Cõ-
stant. 6. ca.*
The sixte generall Councell holden at Constantinople condemneth the **C**
Armenians, whiche did vse wine alone in the ministracion with oute water.
For confutacion of whiche erroure, they alleaged the Masse of saincte Ia-
mes, of Basill, the Decree of the Councell of Cartage, and Chrysostome.

Bothe these then, not vsing soche matter, as Chryst did vse in the Sacrament, are reproued and condemned, as doing contraie to the institucion of
Chryste. For to celebrate either with wine alone, or with water alone, ys a
*Alexand.
primus.
Not wine
alone, not
water alone
in our lor-
des cuppe.
Master
Iuell calleth
for exãples
of the pri-
mitiue
Church for
Doctours,
and Coun-
cells but he
will beleue,
and folowe
none.*
plain conrrarie doinge to the institutiõ of Chryste. For as *Alexander* the sixte
Bishoppe of Rome after Peter, saieth: *Non debet (vt à patribus accepimus, & ipsa
ratio docet) in calice Domini aut vinũ solum, aut aqua sola offerri, sed vtrumque permixtũ,
quia vtrumque ex latere eius in passione sua profluxisse legitur.* As we haue receaued
of our Fathers, and verie reason also teacheth, ther aught not to be offred
in the cuppe of our lorde either wine alone, or water alone, but both mixed
together. For yt ys redde, that in his passion both ranne oute of his side.
Thus Alexander.

Note here that this Father saieth, that he receaued yt of his Fathers. Then
he being the sixte, and as some accompte the fifte from Peter, who were his **D**
Fathers but the Apostles? By this then yt maie be pereeaued, that euen from
the beginning of Chrystes Churche yt hath ben vsed to mixte water with
wine in the ministracion of the Sacrament.

Nowe this Proclamer calleth for examples of the primitiue Churche, for
Doctours and Councells and all these be against him and his complices for
that

E that they vse but wine alone, and yet obstinately they persist in ther erroure and disobedience. Why do yow call for the examples of the primitiue Churche, for auncient Doctours, and Councells, as though yowe wolde be ruled by them, and yet in so euident a matter ye spurn against them, and do what yowe list, and not what yowe are taught ? yowe contemne the rules and orders of the auncient Churche in your dedes howe so euer glosinglie yow speake of them in woordes. In your owne traditions yow are verie straight.

    I remembe the Somer before I wrote this rude woorke, I was nere vnto this man (whom I terme the Proclamer) within whose iurisdictiō one of his ministres ministring the communion to a woman, gaue her to drinke a cuppe of ale in stead of wine. Whiche when this man vnderstoode, no entreatie, no desire, no letters of mē of woorshippe of the Same contrie might appease his displeasure, nor obtein pardon for the offender, but open penance must he do in diuerse places. And certen I am that he was so inioined, and did parte er I departed the contrie. I mislike not that an offender was punished, but I moche mislike that they so straictlie punishe the breach of their

Ale geuen in stead of wine at a Cōmunion.

F disordre, and they them selues breake the ordre of the catholique Churche. When I heard of this correction, ther came to my minde the straunge conscience of the high preistes of the Iewes, who made no conscience in the compasing of the deathe of Chryst, and yet when Iudas brought the moneie again to them whiche they gaue him to betraie his master, here their consciences were spiced, and they saied, those pence might not be cast in the Threasurie, bycause yt ys the price of bloode. Their consciences suffred them to make awaie Chryste, whiche was incomparablie a more heinouse offence, and yet their consciences grudged that those plates shoulde be put in to the treasurie, whiche was but a small matter.

Math. 25.

    So to impugne the trueth of Chryst, to take awaie his bodie and bloode from vs in the Sacrament, and as yt were, to make Chryst awaie, to transgresse the ordre of the holie institucion of Chryste, contēptuouslie to leaue the order of the catholique Churche, yt ys easie ynough to their cōsciences.

G But when they haue taken the fatte and swete of the Sacrament awaie, and left nothing but lean bread, and bare wine, yf then wine be not ministred howe greate an offence ys committed?

Sacramentaries take awaie the fatt and sweet of the Sacramēt.
Mat. 23.

    Thus ye streign oute a guatte, and swallowe (as Chryste saied) a Cammell. And as the prouerbe ys, ye stomble at a strawe, and leape ouer a blocke. Ye are curiouse in tithing minte, anise, and commin, but ye omitte the weightier matters of the lawe: ye are busie in bread and wine and leaue oute the bodie and bloode of Chryst, the weightier matters of the lawe of the Gospell. Ye cast awaie the kernell, and fight for the shale. And thus ye transgresse the commaundement of God for your traditions. And ye do not onelie transgresse the commaundement and order of Chryst, as ys saied, but also inexcusablie ye transgresse the ordre of our Seniours and elders of the primitiue Churche, in that ye vse wine alone in the ministracion of the Sacrament. And therfor leauing yowe amonge them, that be of this seconde sorte of doers mencioned in our distinction, I shall diuert me to speake of the thirde

They stoble at a strawe and leape ouer a block
Ibid. 15.

H maner of doing, whiche ys to doo some thing beside the Scripture.

    This maner of doing, for the readers better vnderstanding, maie be diuerse waies. One ys when the substauce of the institucion ys doen according to the scriptures, but the maner of the doing ys varied and altered. An other ys when, the institucion being accordinglie doen, some thing ys added for the more deuoute, and semelie doing of the same.

III.

    As

The Sub-
ſtance of a
Sacrament
muſt be ob-
ſerued the
maner of
miniſtring
maie be al-
tered.
Mat. 28.

As touchinge the firſt waie, yt ys certen that the ſubſtance of the inſtitu- **A** cion of a Sacrament being obſerued, ther ys none offence comitted by the Churche to alter the maner of the miniſtracion therof. As for example.

Chryſte in the inſtitucion of Baptiſme was baptiſed in the Riuer Iordain, and geuing commiſſion to his Apoſtles to baptiſe, the matter of Baptiſme nowe preſuppoſed, whiche ys the one parte of the Subſtance of the Sacrament, he taught them the forme, which ys the other parte of the Subſtance of the Sacrament ſaing: *Euntes, Baptiſate eos, Iu nomine Patris, & Filij, et Spiritus ſancti.* Go ye and chryſten them in the name of the Father, and of the Sonne, and of the holie Goſte. The one parte of Baptiſme then ys water, the other ys the woorde: *I baptiſe thee in the name of the Father and of the Sonne etc.* Theſe two things beinge the Subſtance of the Sacrament muſt neades be doen. But the maner of the doing of theſe maie be altered, as the practiſe of the primitiue Churche, as well as of the Churche euer ſynce wery well proueth.

For the maner of the inſtitucion was to baptiſe in a Riuer, and that in the **B** Riuer of Iordan. This maner was altered by the Apoſtles. For Peter being at Hieruſalem vpon the daie of the comming of the holie Goſte in to the Apoles, called the daie of Pentecoſt, at one ſermon the ſame daie couerted three thouſand to Chryſt, and baptiſed them furtwith, and nether went to Iordan, non other Riuer.

The Churche alſo nowe and of long time hath vſed no riuer, but ſemelie veſſels with water, and ſo baptiſe them that are to be baptiſed. Yf we ſhoulde be ſtreict obſeruers of the maner, and ther in folowe our Maſter Chryſt, the Authour of the Sacrament, then for that he was then a perfecte man, and thirtie yeares of age, none ſhoulde be baptiſed vntill they were of the ſame age.

Chryſts ma
ner in mini
ſtring the
bleſſed Sa-
crament
hath no cō-
maūdemēt.

Euen ſo the inſtituciō of the Sacramēt of the bodie and blood of Chryſt, as yt had by him a Subſtance apoincted, as ys before ſaied: So he vſed alſo about yt ſoche maner as pleaſed him for that time to vſe. This maner as yt had no commaundement for the obſeruacion of yt from Chryſt: So **C** hath yt no neceſſite to be obſerued. Wherfor as ys ſaied of the maner of Baptiſme: So the practiſe of the primitiue Churche proueth, that this alſo maie be altered.

Chryſtes maner in the inſtitucion of the Sacrament was, that he did diſtribute yt to twelue. This maner bindeth not, that yt muſt allwais be imparted to twelue, and to none other nombre. Theſe twelue alſo were Apoſtles: this likewiſe bindeth not, that the diſciples and other chryſtians of inferioure ſorte ſhoulde not communicate. So to come to the pourpoſe, Chryſt diſtributed his bodie and bloode to his Apoſtles, and reſerued nothing of that, that was conſecrated: This alſo beinge a parte of the maner, and not of the Subſtance of the Sacrament, bindeth no more then theſe that folowe. Chryſte miniſtred his bodie and bloode at night: yt bindeth not vs to do the like. For the Church vſeth yt in the daie. The Sacrament was miniſtred when they had ſupped with the Paſchall lambe, the Churche euen from the beginninge hath and doth yt faſtinge. **D**

And notwitſtanding that yt was vſed certain yeares after Chryſt to be receaued after meat, as the Epiſtle to the Corynthians doth well proue: yet ſaincte Auguſtine aſcribeth the chaunge of that maner to the holie

Ad Ianua.
epiſt. 118. Goſt. *Placuit enim Spiritui ſancto, vt in honorem tanti Sacramenti in os chriſtiani prius Dominicum corpus intraret quàm exteri cibi.* Yt hath pleaſed the holie Goſte

(ſaieth

A　(faieth he)that into the mouthe of a Chryften man, firft fhoulde enter the bodie of owre lorde,then other outwarde meates.

Seing then all thefe maners of the miniftracion be altered, and the receauing of the Sacrament immediatelie vpon the confecracion, ys not of the fubftance of the Sacrament,but of the maner of yt,why maie yt not withoute perill be altered,as well as the other be?

Sainct Auguftine geuing a caufe of that maner of receauing declareth that the order of receauingwas left to the Apoftles to difpofe.*Saluator quò vehemétius commendaret myfterij altitudinem,vltimum hoc voluit infigere cordibus, & memoriæ Difcipulorum, à quibus ad paffionem digreffurus erat. Et ideò non præcepit quo deinceps ordine fumeretur, vt Apoftolis, per quos erat eclcefias difpofiturus, feruaret hunc locum.*Owre Sauiour,wherbie he might the more vehementlie commédethe great excellencie of the myftery,wolde laft of all fixe this in the heartes and memorie of his difciples,from whom he was aboute to departe to his paffió. *And therfore he did not giue commaundement in,or after what ordre yt fhoulde be afterward receaued,*for that vnto his Apoftles,by whome he wolde fet his Churche B　in ordre he wolde referue that place.Thus faiucte Auguftin.

In whiche fentence we are firft taught,that Chryft did not geue *his bodie and bloode to his Apoftles after Supper,*bycaufe yt fhoulde fo be doen ftill, nether bicaufe yt was ftreigt waie receaued after he confecrated yt, that yt fhoulde be fo ftill:but both thefe were doen than, bycaufe they fhoulde be his laft factes before his paffion,doé to his difciples,that the myfterie might therby better remain in their memories.

Note again that faincte Auguftine faieth : *That he gaue no commaundement, in what maner yt fhoulde afterwarde be receaued,* So that the maner that Chryft vfed then was not as a commaundement to binde vs to euery thing precifelie and annfwerablie as he did yt. But the fubftanciall parte being obferued,the maner was lefte to the difpofition of his Churche.

Wherfore we maie conclude, that, notwithftanding the argument of the Aduerfary,that referuacion ys not mencioned in the Scripture, therfore yt C　aught not to be vfed,we maie celebrate the bleffed myfterie in the morning, though he did yt at night: We maie receaue yt fafting, though he gaue yt to his Apoftles after fupper: So maie we receaue yt long after the confecracion,though yt were miniftred to the Apoftles immediatelie after.For I faie, we are bownde to the fubftance of the Sacrament,and not to the maner.

And here will I ioin again with the Proclamer in this pointe, that yf he can vpon the inftitucion of the Sacrament proue,that we maie not as well referue the fame after yt ys confecrate,as we maie alter the time of miniftracion and receauing therof,I will geue place to him in this controuerfie.

And fo in the mean time I dare conclude this, that to referue the Sacrament ys not a thinge againft the inftitucion of the fame. Wherfore leauinge this as fufficientlie fpoken of for this time,I will fpe ake breiflie of the other parte of this diuifion.

The feconde parte was,that fome thinges be added to the miniftració,not altering,or chaunging the Subftance of yt,but to caufe and prouoke deuoció D　and femely behauiour towarde fo woorthie an inftitucion. As for example: In the Baptifme of Chryft,ther were neither exorcifmes,neither praiers,neither geuing of name,neither anie like Ceremonies.In the Baptifme wher Peter baptifed three thoufáde, we reade of no Ceremonies vfed,neither praiers.

Likewife in the laft fupper,we finde not manny Ceremonies.This we reade that : *Surgit à cœna & ponit veftimenta fua,& cùm accepiffet lintheum præcinxit fe.* He rofe

Aug. ibi.

Chryft left the maner of miniftracion of the Sacrament to be difpofed by his Apoftles.

Chryftes maner in miniftring the bleffed Sacrament hath no cõmaũdemét.

Iffue ioined with the Proclamer touching referuacion. Referuació ys not againft the inftitucion of Chryft.

Act.2.

Ioan.13.

He rofe from fupper, and laied a fide his garmentes, and when he had taken **E**
a towell, he girded him felf, and putting water in to a bafen he beganne
to wafhe the feet of his Difciles. And after he had wafhed them, he puteth
on his garmentes again, and fatte down to the Supper of the inftitucion of
the Sacrament. In the whiche we neither read that any praies were made,
nor that Chryft had any other then his owne garmentes vpon him, when
he miniftred. Nowe the Churche hath in vfe, not onelie that the minifter
hath fome other garmentes vpon him, befide his vfuall garmentes, in the
miniftracion of thefe Sacramentes, but vfeth alfo certain Ceremonies, and
praiers not vfed in the inftitucion of them, whiche all are doen to helpe our
infirmitie, imbecillitie, and weakneffe, and to lifte vs vppe to fome higher cō-
fideracion, and eftimacion of thefe Sacramētes, then we fhulde atteing vnto,
yf they were but barelie miniftred.

Soche ys our groffeneffe, that wher we fee no difference in externe and
outwarde cowntenance, we iudge the thinges internlie, or inwardlie to be
of like condicion, or at the leeft not moche better the one then the other. **F**
Wher then thefe Ceremonies be added to the fubftance of the Sacrament
for caufes before faied, yt ys not therfor to be faied that Chryftes inftitucion ys altered, whiche in fubftance ftill remaineth wholl, neither ys
the Churche to be exclamed vpon therfor with reproche, no more then
yt ys for that yt ordeineth the Sacrament to be receaued fafting, for the
whiche fainĉte Auguftine faieth: *Liquidè apparet, quando primum acceperunt Difci-*
Ad Ian.   *puli corpus & fanguinem Domini, non eos accepiffe ieiunos. Nunquid tamen propterea*
calumniandum eft vniuerfæ Ecclefiæ, quòd à ieiunis femper accipitur? Yt doth plainlie
appeare that whē the Apoftles did firft receaue *the bodie and bloode of Chryft*, they
did not receaue thē fafting. Ys therfor the vniuerfall Churche to be reproued
bycaufe the fame bodie and blod of Chryft ys nowe receaued fafting?

Yf the Churche, by the iudgement of fainĉte Auften, ys not to be reproued, though yt altered the maner of the receauing of the bodie and blood of
Chryfte: howe moche leffe ys yt to be reproued for the adding or putting to
of certain godlie Ceremonies for the better, and more deuoute maner of **G**
receauing?

Seing then the vniuerfall Churche hath, putte to the miniftracion of the
Sacramētes afwell of Baptifme as of the bodie and bloode of Chryft, certain
praiers, and garmētes, for the admoniciō of the people, that heauēlie thinges
be in doinge, and fo to ftirre vppe their deuociō, and not therbie altering the
fubftance of the Sacramentes: they be without all doubte to be accepted,
regarded, and reuerenced, and the Church therfor not to be reproued.

THE SEVEN AND TWENTETH CHAP. AVNSWE-
ring other argumentes, and obieĉtions of the Proclamer.

I Haue, as me femeth, fatisfied the requeft of the Proclamer.
For in this matter I haue produced the examples of the primitiue Churche, the fainges of diuerfe of the auncient Fathers:
the decrees of fondrie Councells: Whiche be not obfcure, or **H**
doubefull fentences, but plain, and manifeft.

And nowe that we haue proued the doinges of the Churche in this behalf
to be laufull, and weldoē: let vs nowe heare what proof he bringeth againft
the Churche.

In his fermon, amonge other thinges conteined in the exclamaciō ther, he
faied

A ſaieth thus: *Yf anie learned man of all our Aduerſaries, or yf all the learned men that be a liue, be hable to bringe anie one ſufficient ſentence, oute of any catholique doctour, or oute of anie olde generall Councell, or oute of the holie ſcriptures of God, or anie one example of the primitiue churche, wherbie yt maie be clerelie and plainlie proued, that the Sacrament was then, or nowe aught to be hanged vppe vnder a Canopie, I promiſed then that I wolde geue ouer, and ſubſcribe vnto him.*

The office and callinge of him that ſpake theſe woordes, the place they were ſpoken in the weight of the matter, that was ſpoken of, will not ſuffer the man (as I ſuppoſe) to fauoure reſeruacion couertlie, and with a gibing mocke onelie to inweigh againſt the maner of reſeruacion. I neuer knewe anie of his opinion, and doctrine, denieng the preſence, but he made clean worke, and denied all the reſt, that apperteineth to the Sacrament. Yt ys then to be thought that this article of the proclamacion impugneth as well reſeruacion yt ſelf, as the maner of yt.

But this Proclamacion including a lawe, that no ſoche reſeruacion ſhoulde be in the Churche, what prof, what grownde hath yt annexed? Yt ys no
B ſmall matter to improue the ordre of the wholl Churche obſerued nine hundret yeares and aboue. Wherfor yt ys like that he hath made ſome great proof againſt yt, and ſpecially his office and place withall conſidered.

I neuer ſawe a man diſpoſſeſſed, that had ben in poſſeſſion time oute of minde, but he ſhould ſhewe good matter that wolde diſpoſſeſſe him, and the other onelie to ſtande to his poſſeſſion, and not be driuen to ſhewe his euidence. What ſheweth this proclamer? trulie nothinge. what no ſcripture? no doctour? no Councell? that the Churche ſhoulde breake this ordre? None at all, but his bare proclamacion, and yet therwith driueth the Churche to ſhewe. An imperiouſe maner. After this maner he maie breake mo good ordres in one daie, thē he will make while he liueth. Well, bycauſe yt ys to ſhamefull to break ancient orders of the Church, without ſome proof: I will applie one of his great proues made in his ſermō to one pourpoſe, to ſerue this alſo.

In his ſaied ſermon to improue priuate Maſſe (as he liſt to tearme yt) he
C alleageth this ſaing of Chryſte, *Hoc facite.* Doo this: wherunto he addeth his expoſition ſaing: *that ys to ſue, practiſe this, that I haue here doen, and that in ſoche forme and ſorte, as ye haue ſeen me doo yt.* Thus moch this Proclamer.

As by this his expoſition, yf yt were aught wourth, he maie ſeem to proue, that foraſmoche as Chryſt did not receane alone, but gaue alſo to the Apoſtles, the miniſtre maie not reccaue alone, but muſt alſo geue to other: So likewiſe yt proueth aſwell, that foraſmoche as Chryſte reſerued no parte of the Sacrament, no more ſhoulde the Churche nowe.

Yt ys a great libertie that this man taketh vnto him ſelf, to make ſoche expoſitions as liketh him ſelf, and vpon his owne expoſition to grownd an argnment to condemne the practiſe of the wholl Church, as though yt were *Locus Topycus*, a ſure grownded argument, when yt ys ſownded but vpon his owne authoritie. I haue not redde this maner of expoſition in anie catholike Authour, auncient, or of the later daies, that theſe woordes of Chryſt (do this) ſhoulde be a charge and commaundement to celebrate the memoriall
D of Chryſtes death in the ſame ſorte and maner, that Chryſt did: but raither that his bodie and blood ſhoulde be receaued in the Sacrament, as the Subſtance wherupon the memoriall ſhould be grownded, withoute anie charge geuen of the maner and forme. So doth Saincte Hierom expownde theſe woordes, referring the commaundement to the doing of the thing, and not to the doinge of the maner for the memoriall of Chryſte.

N　　This

The Proclamer impugned Reſeruaciō without reaſō or authoritie.

Fol. 34.

In 11. cap.
1.Cor.

E

This ys his saing : *Ideò hoc Saluator tradidit Sacramentum, vt per hoc semper com-memoremus,quia pro nobis est mortuus.Nam & ideò cùm accipimus, à sacerdotibus com-monemur quia corpus & sanguis est Christi , vt beneficijs eius non existamus memrati.* Therfor our Sauiour deliuered this Sacrament, that by this we shoulde allwaies remember that he died for vs. For therfore also,when we receaue, we are putte in minde by the preistes that yt ys *the bodie and bloode of Chryste,* that we shoulde not be vnthankfull for the benefittes receaued . Thus sainct Hierom.

In 11.1.Co.

Chrysostom also dissenteth not from this maner of exposition. For thus he saieth: *Deinde de cœna illa referens, præsentia his, quæ tunc fuerant, copulat, vt quemadmodum in illa ipsa vespera, & mensa dispositi, ab ipso Christo hoc acceperunt sacrificium : ita & nunc disponerentur, & inquit: Quotiescunque comederitis panem hunc, & sanguinem hunc biberitis, mortem Domini annunciabitis donec veniat. Quemadmodum Christus & in pane, & in calice,in commemorationem hoc facite, dixit, causam nobis aperiens, quare mysterium daret, cum alijs hanc esse dicens sufficientem nobis ad pietatem . Nam cùm intelliges, quid propter te Dominus passus est, sapientior* E *efficieris. Ita & ipse iterum inquit: Quotiescunque manducaueritis, mortem eius annun-ciabitis. Et hæc illa Cœna est.* Afterward speaking of that supper he coopleth thinges present, to those that then were , that as in the same euentide and table,they being disposed did receaue of Chryste him self this sacrifice: euen so nowe also they shoulde be disposed, and saied. *As often as ye shall drinke this bloode* , ye shall declare the death of our Lorde vntill he come. For as Chryst both at the bread, and at the cuppe saied : Do this in my remembrance, opening a cause why he wolde geue the mysterie among other,saied this to be sufficient to godlinesse . For when thowe shalt vnder-stande what our Lorde hath suffred for thee,thowe shalt be made the wiser: Euen so he also saieth again: As often as ye shall eate, ye shall declare his death, and this ys euen the same Supper.Thus farre Chrysost.

Chrystes
woordes,
This do ye,
&c. Be re-
ferred to
the substã-
ce,not to
the maner.

In whose woordes,as well as in saincte Hieroms, we see this commaun-dement of Chryst (*Hoc facite,* do this) to be referred to the Substance, that ys ,to the bodie and bloode of Chryste to be receaued for his memoriall, G and not to the maner of receauing.

And by the waie (gentle reader) note and beare awaie these woordes of saincte Hierom , that he saieth , that *when we receaue, we are admonished of the preistes that yt ys the bodie and bloode of Chryste,* wherby we are taught both wherunto tendeth the commaundement of Chryste , and also what we re-ceaue in that holie and honorable Sacrament.

What S.
Paule cal-
leth the
cuppe Chry
sost.calleth
yt to bloode

I wishe also that Chrysostome might be noted, howe he vttereth the woordes of saincte Paule. Sainct Paule saieth thus: *As often as ye shall eate this bread , and drinke this cuppe :* Chrysostom thus : *As often as ye shall eate this bread , and drinke this bloode:* not reporting euery wher the verie woordes of saincte Paule, but raither the sense,and vnderstanding . So wher saincte Paule calleth yt the cuppe of ourLorde,this mã expownding S.Paule calleth yt the blood of Chryst, wherby we are taught,what ys in the cuppe of our Lorde,euẽ the bloode of Chryste,and not bare wine,yf yt be so in that parte of the Sacramẽt,thẽ in the other ys the bodie of Chryst,and not bare bread. H

Euth.in 26
Matth.

But to return to our pourpose : *Euthymius* also expowndinge the saied woordes of Chryst,vnderstandeth them not of the maner,but of the Substã-ce These be his woordes: *Ait autem Lucas hoc quoque dixisse Christum : Hoc facite in mei recordationem,hoc, inquit, nouum mysterium, & non illud vetus illud my-sterium in recordationem inductum est salutis Hebræorum primogenitorum in Aegypto,*
ac libertatis

A *ac libertatis Hebræorum: hoc autem in recordatiouem Domini. Per tale enim sacrificium reminiscimur, quòd corpus suum in mortem tradiderit, & sanguinem suum effuderit, ac ita continuitate, memoriam renouamus.* Luke saieth that our Lorde also saied: *Do ye this in my remembrance. This newe mystery* (saieth he) *and not that olde.* For trulie that olde mysterie was instituted in the remembrance of the sauing of the first born of the Hebrues, and of the deliuerance of the Hebrues. But this ys in the remembrance of our Lorde. *By soche a sacrifice we remembre that he deliuered his bodie to death, and shed furth his bloode, and so by continuance we renewe memorie.* Thus moche *Euthymius.* Who as the other Fathers aboue alleaged, vnderstandeth Chrystes commaundement of the substance of the Sacrament no mencion made of the maner.

After these to see some of the later writers, howe they vnderstood these woordes, yt shall not be amisse, that hauing the mindes of men of diuerse ages, what the true vnderstanding ys, yt maie the better appeare.

Sainct Thomas, among learned and holie men, that haue ben with in these foure hundreth yeares, a man right famouse saieth thus: *Hoc facite &c.*

B *Iniungit vsum huius Sacramenti, dicens: Hoc facite, quotiescunque sumetis in meam commemorationem, id est, in memoriam meæ passionis.* Do this &c. He commaundeth the vse of the Sacramēt, saing: This do ye as often as ye shall receaue, in my commemoracion, that ys in the memorie of my passion.   *Tho.Aqui. in 11.1.Co.*

And again he saieth: *Mortem Domini annunciabitis repræsentando eam, per hoc Sacramentum.* Ye shall shewe furth the death of our Lorde, representing yt by this Sacrament.

Hauing no regarde of the contempt of the Aduersarie contemning the learned men of the later age, I will among manie that maie be brought, for the auoiding of tediousnesse, and yet to shewe the conformitie of doctrine in this age, with the auncient age, bring the exposition of one named Hugo, whose saing ys this. *Dixerat quòd sumerent corpus Domini, & sanguinem in commemorationem eius, hic determinat in quam: quia in Dominicæ passionis.* He had saied, that they shoulde receaue the bodie and blood of oure   *Hugo Car. in 11.1.Co.*

C Lorde in the remembrance of him. Here he determineth in what remembrance. In the remembrance (saieth he) of our Lordes passion.

Nowe ye haue heard diuerse expownding these woordes, *Hoc facite* (do this) all agreing that they are to be refered, and vnderstanded to and of the substance and vse of the Sacrament, that ys, that yt shoulde be receaued in the remembrance of Chrystes passion and deathe. But that we are by those woordes commaunded to obserue that maner and forme, that our Sauiour obserued in his ministracion, otherwise then ys saied both in the last chapiter, and in this also, ther ys no one title in these Authours.   *The Proclamer vseth his owne authoritie in expounding the scriptures for he hath none other.*

By this then yt maie well be thought and supposed, that this man vsing his absolute authoritie, for lacke of other helpe, had iuuented and framed soche an exposition vpon this scripture, as was not knowen to the auncient expositours, nor yet to them of the later time, and so verie like neuer seen written, or heard spoken before this time. And yet with a pretense of simplicitie and synceritie, yt ys commended to the people, as

D the trew syncere woorde of God, when yt hath neither Gods woorde, nor aide of holie Fathers to bear yt, but ys a plain inuencion of his owne, void of all trueth.

Thus moche being doen by authoritie, I shall also by good reason proue his exposition false. For he him self graunteth that for fiue or sixe hundreth yeares after Chryste, the Churche vsed the institucion of Chryst purelie   *The Proclamer his exposition impugned by reason.*

N ij   and

and well, withoute the breach of Chryſtes woorde or commaundement. **E**
But for the moſt parte of that time they did not obſerue the practiſe of
Chryſtes inſtitucion in ſoche forme and ſorte as he did him ſelf. Wherfor
to practiſe that,that Chryſte did in his laſt ſupper in ſome other maner or
ſorte then he did,ys not the breach of his woorde. Yf yt be not the breach
of his woorde, then ys this mans expoſition falſe.

Maſſes in the primi-tiue church varied frō the forme and maner of Chryſtes inſtitucion.

    That the primitiue and auncient Church vſed an other forme and maner
in the miniſtracion of the Sacramēt,then Chryſt did in the inſtitucion of the
ſame,the Maſſe of ſaincte Iames, of the whiche this man maketh mencion,
the Maſſe of ſaincte Baſill,the Maſſe of Chryſoſtome,the Maſſe vſed in Millan by ſainct Ambroſe, with the wholl practiſe as well of the Apoſtles, as of
other doth moſte manifeſtlie teſtifie. And theſe Maſſes vſed in the primitiue and auncient Churche did all agree in the Subſtance of the Sacrament:
But in the forme,maner,and ſorte of miniſtracion , ther was great diuerſitie,
one moche varieng from an other,and euerie one of them varieng from the
maner that Chryſte vſed,and yet euery one godlie and good. We maie then **F**
conclude that either the primitiue and auncient Churche,varieng from the
forme and ſorte of Chryſtes miniſtracion,did offende, which ys not to be
thought, or ells that this Proclamer ſo wreſting the ſcripture to main-
tien his falſe Doctine , hath offended, which I dare auouche,maie well
be ſaied.

Proclamer his reaſon impugned by his owne practiſe.

    We maie alſo impugne this expoſition,by this mans owne practiſe, who
being ſoche a preciſe reformer of the abuſes of the Church (as he termeth
yt) will not in his doinges committe anie notoriouſe abuſe,howe ſo euer he
doth in his woordes.Yt ys notoriouſe that he miniſtreth in other ſorte and
forme then Chryſt did. Wherfor yf ther be no abuſe in his doing,ther ys
abuſe in his ſainge. For his ſaing, and doing in this matter be plainly contrarie. He ſaieth we muſt practiſe in ſoche ſort and forme as Chryſte did,but his
doinges be not in ſoche ſort and forme as Chryſt did. That his forme
ys not ſoche as Chryſt vſed, yt ys more manifeſt then I neade to make
reherſall.   **G**

I am not certen but I iudge the beſt.

    For Chryſt miniſtred when the Apoſtles had eaten : this man when the
people be faſting.Chryſte in the euening : this man in the morning.Chryſte
with vſuall vuleauened bread: this man withe wafer cakes. Chryſte withoute any other ſtraung garment then his owne vſuallie worn : this man
in other garmentes appoincted to that pourpoſe. Chryſt did ſitte with
the twelue : this man ſtandeth with an vncertain nombre, with manie
other like.

    And here yf this expoſitour will haue his expoſition ſtreictly laied
to all the forme & ſorte of Chryſtes doing in his ſupper:I wolde learn of
him , whether I knowing a man to be farre vnworthie to receaue the bleſſed Sacrament,ſhall admitte him to the table, and miniſtre vnto him notwithſtanding his vnwoorthineſſe, bycauſe that Chryſt did knowe Iudas to
be vnwoorthie and yet miniſtred to him.

Chryſtes maner in miniſtraciō of the Sa-cramēt ne-uer ſince vſed.

    But to return, ye maie perceaue that the forme and ſorte,which this
man vſeth in his communion, ys moche in many thinges diſcrepant from **H**
the doinges of Chryſt in his ſupper . And yet I ſuppoſe, that he thinketh
well of him ſelf in his ſo doing. Yf then his doing be good: then ys his
expoſition naught.

    And to cōclude,ſeing the Apoſtles,the Fathers of the primitiue Churche,
the auncièt doctours that were within three,foure,and fiue hundreth yeares
of Chryſt

A of Chryſt, obſerued not the forme and ſort that Chryſte vſed in the miniſtracion of his Supper, nor any other age ſince that time , neither this
man himſelf hath or dothe practiſe the ſame, we maie boldelie ſaie , that
yt ys no charge geuen of Chryſte to do all thinges in the miniſtracion
in ſoche ſorte and forme as he did , but the ſubſtance doen, the other thinges be of no neceſſitie , but be at the libertie of the Churche to diſpoſe
and ordre, as yt hath doen . Then as manie thinges haue ben doen aboute
the miniſtracion , whiche Chryſt did not : So maie reſeruacion be doen,
though Chryſte did yt not.

This argument then being, as I truſt, fullie ſolued, I finde nothing in his
ſermon, that he obiecteth againſt this matter of reſeruacion directlie . But I
finde a prettie ſleight that he vſeth , as therby to make his audience beleue,
that to reſerue the Sacramēt ys an abuſe, whiche ſleight when I haue opened
to the reader, he ſhall I truſt perceaue, that vnder the pretence and cowntenance of ſynceritie, and ſimplicitie, he iugleth with craft and ſubtletie.

For the better perceiuing of this ſleight, yf ye do not remember what ys
B alleaged oute of Tertullian, and ſaincte Ciprian in the xxiiij. chapter of this
booke, haue recourſe thither, and reade them. This Proclamer being preſſed with thoſe places (for they make mightilie and directlie againſt him in
this matter) cnombring diuerſe and ſondrie abuſes of the Sacramentes of
Baptiſme, & of the bodie and bloode of Chryſt, yt liked him to putte that,
that Tertullian and Ciprian ſpake of the Sacrament reſerued and receaued
of good women, among his abuſes, wherin in dede he moche abuſeth him
ſelf. His woordes be theſe:

In the time of Tertullian and ſaincte Cyprian , whiche was a thouſande and foure
hundreth yeares agon , women commonly tooke the Sacrament home with them in their
napkins , and laied yt in their cheſtes, and receaued a porcion of yt in the morning
before other meates.

A ſleight of the Procla-mer to abu-ſe Tertul. and S. Cy-prian.

See ye not howe by this ſleight, he wolde daſell the eyes and iudgement
of the reader, that when he ſhoulde happe to read theſe places , he ſhoulde
C repute and eſteem thē, not as good examples, but as abuſes, and ſo ſhaddowe
the matter of reſeruacion whiche they proue. But dothe he finde this ſpoken
of Tertullian as an abuſe? Dothe Tertullian ſo terme yt? Naie I am ſure
he doth not. Yf Tertulliā doo not ſo accōpt yt, whie dothe this newe maker
of abuſes ſo terme yt? Tertulian ſpeaketh of yt as a thing well doen , what
commiſſion then aboue Tertullian had this man to ſaie yt ys euell doen.

As for ſaincte Ciprian the Aduerſarie perhappe wolde gloſe yt a litle, and
proue yt an abuſe, bycauſe the woman, whē ſhe opened her coaſer, wher the
holie Sacrament laie, ther ſprang oute a fire that feared her, that ſhe durſt not
touch yt. But let the Proclamer veiue that place of ſaincte Cyprian well,
and he ſhall finde none other abuſe mencioned ther of him , but that
the woman wolde haue preſumed to touche *the holie thinge of our Lorde* (as
he termeth yt) with vnwoorthie hādes. This ys the abuſe that S. Cyprian reherſeth ther. But that ſhe reſerued yt, he accompteth yt no abuſe. For ther ys
no ſoche woorde in ſaincte Cyprian. Wherfore Reader, be ware of ſoche
D ſleightes, and by this perceaue, that all ys not trewth, that this man ſo
glorious lie ſetteth furth.

And yf he accompt yt an abuſe, bycauſe they carie d yt home, what will he
ſaie to the vſe of the Churche in the time of *Iuſtinus* Martyr? was not then
the Sacrament caried home to ſoche as were abſent? This holie man
ſo teſtifieth ſaing thus : *Cùm autem is qui præeſt gratias egerit, & totus populus*

Iuſt. in Apologia.

　　　　　　N iij　　*approbauerit,*

approbauerit, hi,qui vocantur apud nos Diaconi, diſtribuunt vnicuique præſentium , vt E
participent de pane, in quo gratiæ actæ ſunt,et de vino et aqua,et ijs qui non ſunt præſentes

The Sacra
mēt caried
home to thē
that were
abſent.

deſerūt domū. Whē he that ys cheif hath geuē thankes,and all the people hath
cōſented to yt,theſe,that with vs be called Deacons,do diſtribute of the cōſecrated bread,and of the wine and water,to euery one that ys preſent to receaue,and to thoſe that be abſent they carie yt home. Thus *Iuſtinus.*

Sainct Baſill alſo wittneſſeth that holie men liuing in wilderneſſe did reſerue the Sacrament in their Cells, and as deuocion moued them,receaued

Epiſt.ad
Cæſariam
Patriciam.

yt. Thus he ſaieth: *Omnes in eremis ſolitariam vitam agentes,vbi non eſt ſacerdos Cōmu-
nionem domi ſeruantes,à ſeipſis communicant,* All that lead ſolitarie liues in the wilderneſſe,wher ther ys no preiſt,keping the Sacrament in their houſes,recea-
ue yt by them ſelues. Thus ſainct Baſill.

Sainct Hierom alſo in his Apologie againſt Iouinian , teſtifieth that the
people of Rome in his time vſed to kepe the Sacrament in their houſes, and

The Sacr.
reſerued in
Rome.in S.
Hieroms ti
me.

receaued yt by them ſelues.

Nowe yf the Sacrament were caried to the houſes of ſoche as were abſent F
(as appareth by Iuſtinus) and of diuerſe kept to be receaued as deuocion ſer-
ued(as ys wittneſſed by ſainct Baſill,and ſainct Hierom) And ſo to doo was
thē the vſe of the Churche,yt doth well appeare that for ſoche godlie pourpoſes, to carie yt home and to reſerue yt, ys no abuſe . Wherfor in this that
the Proclamer accompted yt an abuſe bycauſe yt was caried from the Churche,and receaued at home(as before ys ſaied) in making that accompte he
moche abuſeth him ſelf.

And here,Reader,beſide that good vſe to carie the Sacrament to ſoche
as neaded yt, ys ther not in Iuſtine a good argument for reſeruacion ? was
not the Sacrament,when all the Communion was doen in the Churche,re-
ſerued to be caried to them that were abſent? Nowe yf yt maie be reſerued
but ſo long time,why maie yt not be kept a longer time? Yf not a longer time,let the Proclamer bring furthe the iuſt preſcript time oute of the Scriptu
res,the Doctours,or Councells,and we ſhall regarde the preſcription , yf he
can not (as I am ſure that he can not) let him ceaſſe with theſe his vain in- G
uēted trifles to vexe,diſturbe,diuide,moleſt and ſlaunder the catholikeChur-
che,and let him acknowledge that theChurche in theſe our daies,cariēg the
Sacrament to ſoche as be ſicke, and to ſoche as cā not come to the Church,
offendeth not,neither abuſeth the Sacrament in ſo doing,but foloweth the
godlie example of the auncient catholique Churche,as nowe ye haue heard
to the full teſtified.

The church
nowe reſer-
uing the Sa
cr.and ſen-
ding yt to
the ſick of-
fendeth not

And wher the Churche kepeth and reſerued the Sacrament on the altar,
or ells wher,let him knowe by ſainct Baſill,and ſainct Hierom , that ſo yt
was in their time,and from the beginning likewiſe reſerued and kept, ſo that
the Churche neither in ſending the Sacrament to ſicke folkes , or other
abſent in their neceſſitie, neither in keping yt in the churche , dothe other
wiſe then was doen in the primitiue Churche.

Wherfor I wiſhe thee(gentle Reader)to ſtaie thy ſelf,and not to ſuffer thy
ſelf to be caried awaie with ſoche vain,diuerſe, and ſtraunge Doctrines, but
conſider well the practiſe of the Churche declared vnto thee in this matter. H
Conſider the vſe of reſeruacion through oute all the Churche vntill this
time of Sciſme and hereſie , to be doen not onelie in Englonde , but in all
Realms Chryſtened , whiche being ſo vniuerſallie receaued,maie not be
thought to be euell doen , or anie abuſe to be therin committed : but yt
aught with all humbleneſſe to be obeied,receaued,and folowed.

For

A　For two thinges by the doctrine of fainte Auguftine muft we obferue: the one ys what fo euer ys taught vs of the Scripture: the other, what we finde obferued throughoute all the Churche. Soche rule gaue he to *Ianua-rius* : *Si quid diuinæ fcripturæ præfcribit autoritas, non eft dubitandum, quin ita facere debeamus vt legimus. Similiter etiam fi quid per orbem frequentat Ecclefia. Nam hoc quin ita faciendum fit, difputare, infolentiſſimæ infaniæ eſt* . What foeuer the au-thoritie of the diuine fcripture prefcribeth vnto vs, ther ys no doubte but we aught euen fo to doo as we read,likewife what foeuer the Churche vfith throughoute the worlde. For to difpute whether this fhoulde be fo doen or no,yt ys a moft prefumptuoufe madneffe. Thus fainct Auguftin,

Ad Ianua. Epift.118. *What foeuer the Churche vfeth throu ghout the worlde yt ys to be ob-ferued.*

Seing then referuacion ys and hath ben vfed through oute all the Chur-che: And yet nowe this Proclamer withoute anie authoritie maketh his pro-clamacion againft yt,ys not he conuinced by the fentence of fainte Augu-ftine, to be a prefumtuoufe madde man, or prefumptuouflie madde? For although the fcripture geueth no commaundement for referuacion,as yt doth not alfo for receauing in the morning , and before meate,yet the vfe and cu-

B　ftome of the people of God,and the commaundement of the elders are to be holden for a lawe, as fainte Auguftine faieth in an other place: *In his rebus, de quibus nihil certi ſtatuit fcriptura diuina , mos populi Dei, vel inſtituta maiorum pro lege tenenda funt . Et ficut prævaricatores Diuinarum legum : ita contemptores ecclefia-ſticarum confuetudinum coercendi funt . Si quis autem videtur contentiofus effe, nos talem confuetudinem non habemus , neque Ecclefia Dei.* In thefe thinges of the whiche the fcripture of God hath determined nothing certen, the cuftome of the people of God,or the ordinances of the elders,are to be holden for a lawe. And as the breakers of the lawe of God: fo the contemners of the ecclefia-fticall ordinaunces,or cuftomes of the Churche,are to be punifhed . But yf anie man feem to be contencioufe, we haue no foche cuftome, nor yet the Churche of God.

Ad Cafu-lanum Epift.86. Oordinaun ces of the elders to be holden for lawes,wher fcripture prefcribeth not.

Thus ye fee,what be fainte Auguftines rules in foche matters , as be not expreffedlie determined by the fcriptures. Ye heare howe the decrees,com-

C　maundementes , and the cuftomes of the people of God(howe foeuer yt liketh this newe reformer to mocke and skorn them)by the minde of fainte Auguftine , are to be holden for hawes,and the contemners of them are to be punifhed.

Thefe matters with me feeme to haue weight, but with foche as can fwallowe a Camell, and choke with a gnatte, perchaunce they feem light enough. But yet howe a priuate perfon maie breake a common ordre, vni-uerfalie receaued,whiche is not againft the fcriptures,I knowe not . But of this matter for aunfwer to this Proclamer, I truft ther ys fufficientlie faied. Wherfore leauing yt , I will proceade further in the order of my matter cheifly pourpofed and intended.

THE EIGHT AND TWENTETH CHAP. BEGINNETH
to fpeake of the prophecies, and firft of the prophecie of the preifthead of Chryft after the ordre of Melehifedech.

D　Owe after the figures , whiche in a darke maner did as yt were painte the myfteries of Chryfte being applied to the fame , by ordre folowe the prophecies , whiche alfo fpake before of the fame myfteries. Among the whiche that Prophecie fhall be firft fpoken of, that aunfwereth the firft figure. Whiche figure was

E

of *Melchiſedech*,anſwerablie to whiche the Prophet Dauid prophecied thus:
*Iurauit Dominus,& non pœnitebit eum, tu es ſacerdos in æternum ſecundùm ordinem Melchiſedech.*Owre lorde hath ſworn,and yt ſhall not forthinke him. Thowe arte a preiſt for euer after the ordre of *Melchiſedech.*

*Pſal.*109.

That this prophecie ys ſpoken of Chryſte, he himſelf proueth in the Goſpell,wher we read that the Phariſeis being gathered to gether,Chryſt asketh them a quieſtion,ſaing : *Quid vobis videtur de Chriſto? Cuius filius eſt? Dicunt ei Dauid.Quomodò ergo Dauid in ſpiritu vocat eum Dominum, dicens: Dixit Dominus Domino meo, ſede à dextris meis, &c. Si ergo Dauid in ſpiritu vocat eum Dominum, quomodo filius eius eſt?* What thinke ye of Chryſt? Whoſe Sonne ys he? They ſaied vnto him : The Sonne of Dauid. Howe then dothe Dauid in ſpirit call him Lorde,ſainge:The Lord ſaied vnto my Lorde, ſitte thowe on my right hand,&c. Yf then Dauid in ſpirit call him Lorde howe ys he then his Sonne?

*Mat.*22.

By which allegacion of our ſauiour Chryſte yt ys manifeſt,that this pſalme ys to be vnderſtanded of him, whiche alſo hath ſome proofe of the Phariſeis ſo to be. For when they heard Chryſt alleadge this pſalme, and being learned in the lawe knewe that yt was prophecied of Meſſias, though they were ſo confounded, that they coulde not anſwer a woorde: yet they ſaied not that this pſalme ys not vnderſtand of Chryſt, whiche they wolde not haue ſpared to doo, yf in the common opinion of learned men yt had ben ſo vnderſtanded, raither then they wolde haue ſuſteined ſoche confuſion as to be put to ſilence. Wherfor by this yt maie appeare that the common opinion of the Iewes was alſo, that this pſalme was a prophecie of Chryſte. Amonge the whiche Iewes one *Rabbi Ionathas* a man of great authoritie among them, an *Rabbi Barachias* being writers bothe do expownd this Pſalme of Chriſte.

F

But what neadeth me ſeke for proof ſo farre of,ſeing that ſainɟe Peter in the Aɟes,and ſainɟe Paule in his firſt epiſtle to the Corinthians,and to the Hebrues maie ſuffice to proue this matter.

Sainɟe Peter in the Aɟes doth alleage the ſame pſalme vnderſtanding yt of Chryſt. Sainɟ Paule to the Corinthians applieth the ſame pſalme to Chryſte ſaing. *Oportet illum regnare, donec ponat omnes inimicos ſub pedibus eius.* He muſt reign,till he hath putte all his enemies vnder his feete.

G

*Aɟ.*2.

1.*Cor.*15.

But to the Hebrues he moſt fullie and plainlie teacheth the ſame,prouing firſt therby the excellency of Chryſt aboue the Angells, and ſaieth: *Ad quem autem Angelorum dixit aliquando : Sede à dextris meis, donec ponam inimicos tuos ſcabellum pedum tuorum?* Vnto whiche of the Angels hath he ſaied at anie time,Sitt thowe on my right hand, till I make thy enemies thy footeſtoole? All theſe alleadged do well proue this pſalme to be a prophecie of Chryſte.

*Hebr.*1.

But yet ſainɟ Paule proceading, commeth ſomwhat nearer to the pourpoſe, and applieth the verſe of this pſalme firſt aboue alleaged, vnto Chryſte in mo places then one, prouing therby the ceaſſing of the legall preiſthead,for that Chryſt was nowe commed the preiſte after the order of *Mechiſedech.*And firſt declaring that Chryſt did not vſurpe his preiſtheade, but that he was appointed to yt by God, he ſaied : *Sic & Chriſtus non ſemetipſum glorificauit vt Pontifex fieret, ſed qui locutus eſt ad eum,&c. Tu es ſacerdos in æternum ſecundùm ordinem Melchiſedech.* Euen ſo Chryſte alſo glorified not him ſelf to be made the high preiſt, but he that ſaid vnto him, &c. Thowe arte a preiſt for euer after the order of Melchiſedech.

H

*Hebr.*5.

And

A　And declaring the great benefitte,that came by him being the high preift to all beleuers,he faieth again: *Et confummatus factus eft omnibus obtemperantibus fibi caufa falutis æternæ, appellatus à Deo Pontifex iuxta ordinem Melchifedech.* And he being perfight , was the caufe of eternall faluacion vnto all them that obeied him, and ys called of God an high preift after the ordre of Melchifedech. `Ibid.`

Likewife he calleth him in the VI. chapiter. And the wholl VII. chap. he occupieth in applieng *Melchifedech* to Chryft, prouing by this prophecie, the abrogacion of the preifthead of the lawe,and fo confequentlie of the lawe yt felf. Wherfore he faied. *Yf nowe therfore perfection came by the preiftheade* `Hebr.7.` *of the Leuites (for vnder that preifthead the people receaued the lawe) what neadeth further, that an other preift shoulde rife to be called after the ordre of Melchifedech, and not after the order of Aaron? For yf the preifthead be tranflated, then of neceßitie muft the lawe be tranflated alfo, &c. For after this maner dothe he teftifie, Thowe arte a preift for euer after the order of Melchifedech. Then the commaundement that went before ys difanulled , bycaufe of weakeneffe and vnpro-* **B** *fitableneffe.*

And further declaring the excellencie of Chryftes preifthead aboue the preifthead of Aaron, he faieth: *For thefe preiftes were made withoute an othe , but this preift with an othe, by him that faied to him : The Lorde fware and will not repent him. Thowe art a preift for euer,after the order of Melchifedech.*

Thus as the lawe of nature hath in Melchifedech figured Chryfte, And the lawe of Moyfes by prophecie forefpoken yt: So hath the lawe of the Gofpell (as ye haue nowe learned by fainct Paule)fullfilled the fame, and moft plainlie and euidentlie proued yt fo to be.

Yf then Chryfte be a preift after the order of Melchifedech, we muft feke what the order of the preiftheade of Melchifedech ys, and wherin yt confifteth, And therbie fhall we knowe the preiftheade of Chryfte, & wherin yt confifteth.

Sainct Paule generallie declareth the order of a preift when he faieth: **C** *Omnis namque Pontifex ex hominibus affumptus , pro hominibus conftituitur in ijs,* `Hebr.5.` *quæ funt ad Deum , vt offerat dona & facrificia pro peccatis.* Euery high preift, that ys taken from amonge men, ys ordeined for men in thinges perteining to God,to offer giftes and Sacrifices for finne.

By whiche defcription of fainct Paule yt dothe appeare, that the order of preifthead ftandeth in two partes : The firft he teacheth when he faieth: *Pro hominibus conftituitur in ijs, quæ funt ad Deum.* He ys ordeined for men in thinges perteining to God . Wherby ys ment, the preaching to the people,and teaching them the lawes of God, and miniftring the Sacramentes to them, as yt was faied vnto Moyfes: *Efto tu populo in ijs quæ ad* `Exod.18.` *Deum pertinent , vt referas quæ dicuntur ad eum , oftendasque populo ceremonias & ritum colendi , viam per quam ingredi debeant , & opus facere.* Be thowe vnto the people to Godward, that thowe maift bringe the caufes vnto God. And thowe fhalt teache them ordinaunces and lawes, and fhewe them the waie,wherin they muft walke and the worke that they,muft doo.

`Ordre of preifthead ftandeth in two partes.`

D　The feconde parte of the order of preiftheade ftandeth in offring giftes, and facrifices for the finnes of the people.

Then they that be called of God , as was Aaron, and doo preach and teache one faith of God vnto the people, and offer vnto God one maner of facrifice,they be of one order of preiftheade. So that:thefe two muft concurre,or ells yt ys not a perfight order.For Elias the prophet of God,and the `3.Reg.18.`

preiftes

preiftes of Baall did offer one maner of thinge in facrifice (for they both of- **E**
fred oxen)yet they differed in preifthead. For Helias was the preift of God,
the other the preiftes of Baall. And why was this diffcrence? bycaufe they
taught not one faithe in one God,

Gen.14.
Leuit.8.
Heb,5.

Melchifedech and Aaron taught one God, and were bothe preiftes of
God. For Melchifedech was the preift of the moft high God, as the booke
of Genefis wittneffeth, and Aaron was called of God, as the booke of
Leuiticus, and fainéte Paule to the Hebrues teftifie. And yet they were
not of one order of preifthead, bycaufe their facrifices were not of one
maner.

By this then yt maie be taken for a trueth, that Chryft, not being a preift
after the order of Aaron, but after the order of Melchidech (whiche two
orders differed not in faith, but in maner of facrifice) ys fo called a preift
after the order of Melchifedech for the maner of the facrifice. For he muft
agree with Melchifedech in that thing, that maketh the difference betwixt
the order of Aaron, and the order of Melchifedech, and that was and **F**
ys in the maner of facrifice. For Aaron offred in blood, the other in bread
and wine.

Obiection.

But here the Aduerfarie will faie, that Chryft ys not likened to Melchifedech for anie facrifice by all the proceffe of fainéte Paule. But for
that Melchifedech was *Rex Salem*, kinge of Salem, and withall the preift of
God, and for that he was withoute Father, withoute Mother, hauing
neither beginning of daies nor ending, in thefe pointes he ys the figure
of Chryfte, who ys both king and preift, hauing no Father in earth, nor
mother in heauen, neither as concerning his Godhead anie beginning,
and as touching his Godhead and Manhead no endinge. And fo ys he a
preift for euer.

Principall
entent of
S.Paule in
his epift. to
the He-
brues.

To this I faie, that the thing that fainéte Paule principallie intended, ys
to be confidered. And then yt fhall eafilie be perceaued, why he did not
make reherfall of the maner of the facrifice of Melchifedech, nor mencion
of the doing of the fame in Chryfte. **G**

The principall entent of fainéte Paule in this place was to proue and
make manifeft the excellencie of Chryft and his preifthead, aboue Aaron
and his preifthead. Whiche excellencie in nothing more appeared then
in that, that Chryft was an euerlafting preift, and his preifthead euerlafting,
and not in the maner of facrifice. For yf he had alleaged that Melchifedech
did facrifice in bread and wine, The Hebrues wolde quickly haue faied,
that their facrifices in that refpeéte moche excelled, and had a moche more
glorioufe fhewe and cowntenance, then the facrifice of Melchifedech, being

VVhie S.
Paule fpa-
ke nothing
of she facri
fice of Mel
chifedech
in his epift.
to the Heb.

but bread and wine. And therfor fainéte Paule omitted to make mencion
of the facrifice, and choofe to fpeake of that, that mooft manifeftlie, and
alfo inuinciblie proued the excellencie of Chryft and his preiftheade aboue
the preift and preifthead of the lawe. And therfor emong other pointes.
declaring the excellencie of Chryft, as that he was made a preift with an
othe, other withoute an othe, laft as the cheifeft he reherfeth his eternitie
faing: *Among them (meening the preiftes of Aaron) manie were made preiftes by-* **H**
caufe they were not fuffred to endure by reafon of deathe: But this man bycaufe
he endureth euer, he hath an euerlafting preiftheade. Wherfore he ys able alfo euer
to faue them to the vttermoft, that come vnto God by him. Seing he euer liueth to
make interceffion for vs.

Heb.7.

Thus

A　Thus nowe ye maie perceaue that the obiection of the Aduerfarie ys aunfwered,when faincte Paules principall entente ys once knowen.

Yf by the facrifice of Melchifedech, the excellencie of Chryft might as
well haue appeared to the Hebrues (who as yet were foche, as *Quibus lacte
opus erat non folido cibo*, whiche had neade of milke, not ftrong meate, and
coulde not beare the myfteries of our faith) as by his eternitie, be you well
affured, Saincte Paule wolde not haue omitted yt. But bycaufe in the conceit of the Hebrues,their facrifices appeared to them more glorioufe, and
more excellent then the facrifice of Melchifedech: therfore faincte Paule
did not fpeake of yt.

But yet the Aduerfarie,who can not ceaffe to impugne the trueth, when
he feeth that he can not preuaill with his firft obiection, he hathe inuented
an other whiche ys foche one as men ouercommed with furie and malice
do make.Whofe reafon and knowledge being obfcured do fpeake they can
not tell what,and in that rage vtter as foen a falfehood as a trueth,and hauing
no fownde Iudgemet,faie good ys euell,and euell ys good,darkeneffe light,
B　and light darkeneffe.Their obiection ys this.

Melchifedech (faie they) did not offer bread and wine in facrifice, but he 　*Obiection*
mett with Abrahã retourning from the flaugter of the Kinges,and brought 　*of the Ad-*
furth bread and wine, as yt were to welcome Abraham homewarde from 　*uerfaries.*
the battaill.For the fcripture(faie they) hath not in that place of Genefis the
woorde *offerre*, to offer but *proferre*, to bring furth. For the text ys: *At verò
Melchifedech Rex Salem proferens panem & vinum*. And Melchifedech king of
Salem brought furth bread and wine,and bleffed him.

This obiection ys fo vain that yt ys raither woorthy to be exploded, then 　*Thanfwere*
with penne to be remembred, raither to be laught and hiffed at, of the
children in the fchooles,then to be anfwered and folued. Notwithftanding
that the vanitie of the fame maie the better appeare to the reader, and that
he alfo maie be fatisfied, yt fhall be anfwered both by Scriptures, and alfo
by the eldeft and nobleft learned men of Chryftes Parliament houfe.

C　Yt ys manifeft by that, that ys aboue faied, that one of the partes of the
function of a preift ys to offer facrifice. Nowe for afmoche as the Scripture,
when yt faied that Melchifedech brought furth bread and wine, and immediatelie added: *For he was the preift of the moft high God*, what dependance ys ther of this one parte of this fcripture to the other, or why fhoulde this
that he was the preift of the moft high God be added, as the caufe why he
brought furth bread and wine, but that he as the preift of God, had
facrificed that, that he brought furth? What direct caufe ys yt, that Melchifedech,bycaufe he was the preift of the moft high God, fhoulde bring
furth bread and wine? Yt ys nothing perteigning to the preiftheade to 　*Yt pertei-*
bring furth bread and wine, in the abfolute or bare refpecte of bread 　*ned not to*
and wine, but in the refpecte that bread and wine were the thinges, 　*Melchife-*
that he did vfe in facrifice, whiche he had at that time offred to God 　*dech his*
for a thankes geuing for the victorie of Abraham, fo yt apperteineth to 　*preifthead*
the preifthead. And this parte of the text (*for he was the preift of the moft* 　*to bring-*
D　*hig God*) maie very well be added as the caufe, as in verie dede 　*furth: but*
yt ys. Otherwife the bringing furth of bread and wine ys not apper- 　*to offre*
teining to the Preifthead, neither to be the preift of the moft high God 　*bread and*
ys or can be the directe and propre caufe of the bringing furth of bread 　*Eine.*
and wine.

　　　　　　　　Thys

This vnderftanding the verie connexion ofthe fcripture and dependéce of the fame, enforceth vs to take, and none other can be admitted. And thus the fcripture taken in his owne natiue fenfe, and then to faie, he brought furth bread and wine, doth nothing improue the facrificing of Melchifedech in bread and wine, as more at large yt fhall appeare to yowe, when we come to heare the Fathers.

Nowe for fomoche as Melchifedech did facrifice in bread and wine, and to facrifice ys one of the effentiall and neceffarie partes of preifthead, and Chryft ys a preift after the order of Melchifedech, of neceffitie he muft then doo facrifice withe bread and wine. This neceffitie fainct Paule affirmeth to the Hebrues. *Omnis namque Pontifex ad offerenda munera & hoftias conftituitur, vnde neceffe eft & hunc habere, quod offerat.* Euery high preift (faieth he) ys ordei-ned to offer giftes and facrifices, wherfor yt ys of neceffitie, that this man alfo haue fomwhat to offer.

Chryft exe-cuted his preifthead after the or-dre of Aa-ron vpon the Croffe, but after the ordre of Melchife-dech in his laft fupper.

Chryfte then beinge a preift after the ordre of Melchifedech, muft nedes haue fomwhat to offer after the maner of that order. But we neuer redde that he made anie mo oblacions then two. The one was vpon the croffe, when he offred his owne bodie to be flain, and that oblation was after the maner of Aaron. The other in his laft fupper, wher we muft nedes confeffe (except we will faie, that Chryft altogether neclected the preifthead ap-pointed him of God, whiche ys not to be faied) that he did execute the offi-ce of his preifthead after the order of Melchifedech, when taking bread and wine, he faid to his Apoftles: *Take eate, this ys my bodie: Take and drinke this ys my bloode.* Yf not then: let the Aduerfarie fhewe, when and wher Chryft did facrifice after the ordre of Melchifedech. Yf he did neuer facrifice after that ordre, then ys yt not true that he was a preift after that order, for fomoche as one cheif parte and office of preifthead ftandith in facrificing. But vn-doubtedlie he a was preift after that order, and in his laft fupper he fhewed him felf fo to be. When vnder the formes of bread and wine he offred his owne bodie and blood, an vnbloodie facrifice after the order of Melchife-dech. And thus moche for the proof of this matter by the Scripture.   G

THE NINE AND THIRTITH CHAP. PROCEA-
deth to proue the fame by fainct Ciprian and Ifychius.

Hat Chryfte did Sacrifice at his laft fupper after the order of Mel-chifedech: and therby was as well likened to Melchifedech, as by the eternitie of his preifthead: and that Melchifedech him felf offred bread and wine in facrifice (whiche three thinges the Aduerfaries denie) yt fhall be, by the great famoufe elders, that were nere to Chryfte, and whiche liued in the time, that the Churche hadde moft perfight knowledge of gods treuth, and therfore knewe the enacted and recea-ued treuth in the Parliament houfe of Chryfte, made fo plain and cui-dent, that the enemies fhall be confounded, and the Reader, yf he will fee,   H fhall perceaue that the Aduerfaries haue fpoken againft a moft manifeft treuth.

And firft we will heare the teftimonie of the holie Martyr Sainct Cy-prian. Who faieth thus: *Significata olim à tempore Melchifedech prodeunt Sacramenta, & filijs Abrahæ facientibus opera eius, fummus facerdos panem profert &*   *vinum*

Serm. de Cæna Do-mini.

A *vinum, Hoc eſt, inquit, corpus meum. Manducauerant, & biberant de eodem pane ſecun-*
dùm formam viſibilem, ſed ante verba illa cibus ille communis tantùm nutriendo corpori
commodus erat. Sed ex quo à Domino dictum eſt; Hoc facite in meam commemoratione,
Hæc eſt caro, & hic eſt ſanguis meus. Quotiescunque his verbis, & hac ſide actum eſt,
panis ille ſubſtantialis, & calix benedictione ſolemni conſecratus, ad totius hominis vi-
tam ſalutemque proſicit, ſimul medicamentum & holocauſtum ad ſanandas infirmitates
& purgandas iniquitates exiſtens. Manifeſtata eſt etiam ſpiritualis, et corporalis cibi diſtã-
tia: Aliud ſuiſſe quod prius eſt appoſitum, aliud quod à magiſtro datum eſt, et diſtributum.
The Sacramentes ſignified long agon from the time of Melchiſedech nowe
doo come abroad. And the high preiſt to the children of Abraham doinghis
woorkes, dothe bring furth bread and wine: This (ſaieth he) ys my bodie.
They had eaten and dronken of the ſame breade after the viſible forme. But
before thoſe woordes, that comõ meate was onelie meate profitable to nouriſh the bodie, but after the time that yt was ſaied of owre lord: *Thys do ye in*
the remẽbrance of me, This ys my fleſh, this ys my bloode. As often as yt ys doen withe

B theſe woordes, and this faith, *that ſubſtanciall bread and cuppe conſecrated by the*
Solemne benediction dothe proſitt and auaill to the health and life of the wholl man, being
bothe a medicen and Sacrifice, to heale infirmities and to pourge iniquities. Ther ys alſo
declared, the difference of the ſpirituall, and corporall meate. Yt was one
thinge that firſt was ſett before them and cõſumed, and an other thing that
was geuen of our Maſter and diſtributed. Thus farre S. Cyprian.

　　Ye ſee here a clere teſtimonie, bothe of the thing that ys in this place ſpeciallie inquired, that ys, of the applicacion of the bread and wine, whiche
Melchiſedech offred in figure, to the bread and wine whiche Chryſt
offred in veritie: and alſo of the thing that generallie ys inquired through
oute the wholl booke, whiche ys of the reall preſence of Chryſtes bodie in
the Sacrament.

　　Of the firſt ther neadeth no note to be made, for he ſaieth manifeſtlie,
that the Sacramentes ſignified from the time of Melchiſedech in the laſt
Supper of Chryſt came abroad. What they were he openeth ſaing: *And the*
high preiſt (meening Chriſt) bringing furth bread and wine, etc. Wherby yt muſt neades

C folowe, that the bread and wine whiche Melchiſedech vſed, was the figure
of the bread and wine with Chryſte occupied. And thus wher the Aduerſaries ſaie that Chryſt ys likened to Melchiſech for hys eternitie, and not
for his ſacrifice of bread and wine, howe moche therin they ſpeake againſt
the auncient faith of the Churche, thys holie Martir declareth, whiche thing
alſo, not onelie by this Authour but by other herafter ſhall be moſt euidentlie proued.

　　Nowe of the Reall preſence alſo, ſaincte Cyprian ſpeaketh verie plainlie.
As touching the whiche although ther might be taken here diuerſe notes:
yet I will at this preſent take but two. The one ys that he ſaieth, that before thoſe woordes (meening the woordes of Chryſt *This his my bodie,* whiche
be a litle before ſpokẽ) that bread was onelie meat to nouriſh the bodie. But
after yt was ſaied of Chryſte. *This do ye in remembrane of me: and, This ys my fleſh,*
And this ys my bloode: that ſubſtanciall bread cõſecrated by the Solẽne benediction, ys pro-
fitable to the health ãd life of the wholl mã, that ys, both of bodie, ãd of ſoule wheih

D both together make an wholl man. And howe yt doth proſite he declareth.
Yt ys (ſaieth he) both a medicẽ and a ſacrifice, to heale infirmities and to pourge iniquities.
　　Note well that he dothe not here in this place ſaie, that the faith one-
ly to beleue that Chryſt hath ſuffred for vs, or the benefittes and
merittes of Chryſtes paſsion, and death, whiche ys ſpirituall receauing,

O　　　　　　　　　　ys

Marginal notes:
Cõſecraciõ and ſacrifice plainlie auouched by S. Cyp.

Bread and wine offe-red by Melchiſe-dech were figures of that, whiche Chryſt offred in his laſt ſupper.

Two notes oute of S. Cipriã for the preſẽce of Chryſts bodie in the Sacra-ment.

ys both a medicin to heale infirmities, and a facrifice to pourge iniqui- E
ties (although neither he, ner we be ignorant of the vertue power, and effica
cie of thē) But he here faieth that the fubftanciall bread being cōfecrated, ys
the medicin and the facrifice. Wherby what ells dothe he meen, or cā meen,
but that that bread ys confecrated into his bodie, who ys our high Sacrifice, whiche hath pourged vs from our iniquities? *Lauit nos à peccatis noſtris*

Apocal. 1.
in fanguine fuo. He hath wafhed vs from our finnes in hys bloode . For nei-

The thing
that the
bread ys cō
fecrated in-
to, ys the fa
crifice that
pourgeth
oure iniqui
ties.
ther our faith in Chryft crucified, neither the merite of hys pafsion ys that
facrifice, for the one ys the mean to atteign to be partaker of that facrifice,
the other the effeċt of the fame facrifice, So that neither of them ys the facrifice yt felf: But the thinge that the fubftanciall bread ys confecrate into,
ys the facrifice that pourgeth iniquities. Ther ys nothing that ys or can be
that facrifice, but the bodie of Chryft. Wherfor the thing into the which the
bread ys confecrated ys the bodie of Chryft.

*Aliud in
the neutre
gendre fig-
nifieth a
reall diffe-
rence in
thinges .*
And for the confirmacion of this, take alfo the feconde note whiche ys
wher he faieth: *Aliud eft, quòd prius eft appofitum et confumptum: Aliud quod à magi-* F
ſtro datum,& diſtributum. Yt ys one thing that was firſt fett before them and
confumed: And an other thing that was geuē of our Mafter and diftributed.

Yt ys well knowen to learned men, that this woorde (*aliud*) in the neutre
gendre importeth a difference fubftanciall, from the thing that yt ys compared to, and fo the two thinges that be compared together, be of two different fubftances. And therfore for fomoche as the Father, the Sonne, and
the holie Gofte be three diftinċted perfons, the catholique faithe teacheth
vs to faie: *Alius eft Pater, alius Filius, alius Spiritus fanċtus.* The Father ys one, the
Sonne ys an other, and the holie Gofte ys an other. But formoche as they be
not diftinċted in fubftāce we maie not faie: *Aliud eſt Pater, aliud Filius, aliud Spi-*
ritus fanċtus. The Father ys one thing, the Sonne an other thing and the holie Goft an other thinge. But cōtrarie wife bicaufe thefe three be one in fub-

Ioan. 5.
*Vnum in
the neutre
gēdre figni-
fieth vnitie
of fubſtāce.*
Ioan. 10.
ftance, the Scripture teacheth vs thus: *Tres ſunt qui teſtimonium dant in cœlo , Pa-*
ter, Verbum,& Spiritus fanċtus,& hi tres vnum funt. Ther be three that beare witt
neffe in heauen, the Father, the Sonne and the holie Goft, and thefe three be
(*Vnum*) that ys one thing or fubftance not (*Vnus*) one perfon. So we reade in
the Gofpell: *Ego & Pater vnum fumus.* I and the Father be one, that ys in fub- G
ftance. So here where fainċt Cyprian faieth : *Aliud eſt quod appofitum , &c.*
Yt ys one thinge that was fett before them and cōfumed, and an other thing
that the mafter did geue and diftribute: he fheweth that thefe two thinges
were thinges fubftanciallie diſtinċted. For before yt was the fubftance of
bread, of the whiche he fpake in the beginning of the fentence whē he faied:
Manducauerāt de eodem pane fecundùm formam viſibilem. They had eaten of the
fame bread after a vifible forme.

But nowe after the folemne benediċtion yt ys an other fubftance, that
ys, the fubftance of Chryfte, whiche (as before ys faied) ys the medicin to
heale our infirmities, and the facrifice to pourge our iniquities. Yf ther were
the fame fubftance of bread ftill remaining after the confecracion by the folemne blefsinge , as was before, fo as ther were none other chaunge
but an accidentall chaunge , that ys (as the Aduerfaries faie) that
the bread before the woordes of Chryft fpoken ouer yt (For they abhorre to vfe the woorde, *confecracion*, as fainċte Cyprian dothe , and other H
holie Fathers) ys but comon bread, but after the woordes be fpoken yt ys
a facramentall bread, then this Authour wolde not faie: *Aliud eſt, yt ys an other*
thing. Whiche latin woord (*Aliud*) refpeċteth the difference of the fubftance

(as

A (as ys before faied) and ys as moch to faie , as an other thing in fubftance, or an other fubftance.

Wherfore to conclude, this holie Martir of Chryfte teacheth vs here, that the bread confecrated by the Solemne benediction, wher before yt was bread onelie to nourifh the bodie , yt ys nowe after the confecracion a thing profitable for the healthe and life of the wholl man, that ys, both of the bodie and of the foule, *being a medicin to heale infirmities , and a facrifice to pourge iniquities* . Which thing ys an other thing from the thing that yt was before, differing from that in fubftance. We muft nedes therfore affirme and profeffe that yt ys the verie bodie of Chryft fubftanciall and Reall.

Thebread, that before confecraciō ferueth to nourish the bodie one-lie, after cō fecraciō ys an other thing, whiche noxri-sheth the foule.

But that this maie appeare vnto yow to be the verie minde of fainte Cyprian , and not a fenfe of mine owne wrefting, as the Aduerfaries for the more parte will faie, when ells they coulde faie nothing, being put to fcilēce by force of the trueth, ye fhall heare an other place of the fame Authour.

B *At Melchifedech Rex Salem protulit panem & vinum (fuit enim facerdos Dei fummi) & benedixit Abraham . Quòd autem Melchifedech typum Chrifti portaret, declarat Spiritus fanctus in pfalmis ex perfona Patris ad Filium , dicens: Ante luciferum genui te. Iurauit Dominus , & non pœnitebit eum , tu es facerdos in æternum fecundùm ordinem Melchifedech . Qui ordo vtique hic eft de facrificio illo veniens , & inde defcendens , quòd Melchifedech facerdos Dei fummi fuit , quòd panem & vinum obtulit , quòd Abraham benedixit. Nam qui magis facerdos Dei fummi quàm Chriftus Iefus Dominus nofter , qui facrificium Deo Patri obtulit , & obtulit hoc idem , quod Melchifedech obtulerat, id eft , panem & vinum, fuum fcilicet corpus & fanguinem.* And a litle after yt foloweth: *Vt ergo in Genefi per Melchifedech Sacerdotem benedictio circa Abraham pofsit ritè celebrari , præcedit antè imago facrificij in pane & vino fcilicet conftituta. Quam rem perficiens , & adimplens Dominus , panem & calicem mixtum vino obtulit , & qui eft plenitudo veritatem præfiguratæ imaginis adimpleuit.*

Li. 2. Epi. 3. ad Cecil.

And Melchifedech King of Salem (faieth holie Cyprian) brought furthe bread and wine (For he was the preift of the moft high God) and he blef-
C fed Abraham. And that Melchifedech did beare the figure of Chryfte, the holie Goft in the perfon of the Father to the Sonne , dothe declare in the pfalmes faing : *Before the daie ftarre haue I begotten thee , Owre Lorde hath fworn , and yt shall not repent him , Thowe arte a preift for euer after the ordre of Melchifedech .* Whiche ordre alfo ys this cominge from that Sacrifice, and from thence defcendinge , that Melchifedech was the preift of the moft high God, that he offred bread and wine , that he Bleffed Abraham. For who ys more the preift of the moft high God , then our Lorde Iefus Chryfte , who did offer facrifice to God the Father. *And offred the verie fame that Melchifedech had offred,* that ys to faie , bread and wine , euen hys bodie and bloode . And after a fewe woordes , he proceadeth thus: That therfore the bleffinge aboute Abraham might laufullie be celebrated by Melchifedech the preift in Genefis, the ymage of the facrifice goeth before, appointed in bread and wine . Whiche thing owre Lorde perfecting and fullfillinge, hath offred the bread and the cuppe mixed with wine . And he that ys the fullneffe , hath fulfilled the
D trueth of the prefigurated ymage. Thus farre fainte Cyprian.

The ordre of Melchifedech came to Chrift, not onelie in that he was the highpreift, but in that he offred bread and wine the like facrifice.

What neadeth me here to faie any thing wher euery parte of the fentence ys fo plain, that yt clerelie and plainlie openeth yt felf? As touching the fpeciall matter of thys place, do ye not fee , that he faieth , Melchi-

O ii   fedech

Melchifedech was the figure of Chryft? Do ye not perceaue that he alfo **E**
faieth, that the holie Goft declareth the fame in the pfalme? Do ye not alfo
fee that Melchifedech was the figure of Chryft in three poinƈts, that ys, in
that he was the preift of the moft high God, in that he offred bread and wine,
and in that he bleffed Abrahā? Do ye not alfo fee, that this Authour applieth
thefe to Chryft, in that there was none more the high preift of God then
our Lorde Iefus Chryft, who offred facrifice vnto God the Father? And perceaue ye not that Chryft offred the verie fame, that Melchifedech, whiche
was bread and wine.

Wher (gentle reader) let me note by the waie for the fatisfieng
of my promeffe, that wher the obieƈtion of the Aduerfarie ys, that
Melchifedech did not offer in facrifice bread and wine, and for his
proof he faied that the text in *Genefis*, had not *obtulit, he offred*, but *Pro-*
tulit, he brought furth : Nowe note yf this Father vfeth not this woorde,
obtulit, he offred, faing that Chryft offred the very fame that Melchifedech did offer. And what he did offer, he alfo declareth faing: that yt was **F**
bread and wine.

S. Ciprian
by expreffe
woordes
faith Mel-
chifedech
offred.

What impudencie then ys ther in the Aduerfaries to improue that, that
fo auncient and fo famoufe a learned holie Martir fo plainlie teacheth, and
not he alone, but all the holie companie of the writers, of the which the tefti
monie of fome mo fhall be heard herafter.

As yow fee that Melchifedech did offer bread and wine, whiche was the
figure: So did our Sauiour Chryft(faieth Cyprian)*offer bread and wine in veritie*,
that ys, *hys bodie and bloode.*

Chrift of-
fred bread
and wine,
in veritie,
that ys, his
bodie and
bloode.

And that the Aduerfaries fhall not cauille, and faie: Wher Cyprian faieth,
Chryft offred his bodie and blood, yt ys not to be vnderftanded of any facrifice offred in the laft Supper, but of the facrifice of his bodie and bloode offred vpon the croffe: The fame fainƈt Cyprian ftoppeth the mouth of the
wicked in the other fentence before alleaged wher he faieth: The ymage of
the Sacrifice went before appointed in bread and wine, whiche thinges our
Lorde perfecting and fulfilling *offred bread and the cuppe mixed with wine*. And **G**
that we fhoulde not take occafion to ftomble with the Aduerfaries, taking
yt but for bread and wine, he addeth: *And he that ys the fulneffe hath fulfilled the*
veritie of the prefigurated image.

Do ye not heare that Chryft offred the facrifice in his laft fupper, of
the whiche the ymage went before in bread and wine? And doo
ye not heare that he offring bread and wine, did offer in that forte,
that he fulfilled the veritie of the prefigurated ymage? Whiche veritie
was(as fainƈt Cyprian faied be fore)that *he offred bread and wine, that ys, hys bo-*
die and bloode:

Learn then(thow Reader) of this fubftanciall piller, the fubftāciall faith
of Chryfts catholique Churche. And fuffer not thy felf to be caried awaie
with the Aduerfaries painted reafons, and glofes, hauinge a fhewe of trueth,
and godlineffe aboue, but vnder ther lurketh falfhead and Hypocrifie. But
abhorre them as fainƈte Paule dothe aduertife. For as the fifhe ys deceaued
by the faire bait, whiche outwardlie fheweth to be a thing of commoditie,
but inwardlie ys deftruƈtion and death, when fhe taketh yt: Euen fo the rea- **H**
fons of the Pfeudochriftians maie appeare to thee moft godlie and true, and
to haue the commoditie of eternall life, But inwardlie they contein deftruƈtion and death of the fowle, to the whiche they will drawe thee, except
thowe

A thowe shifte thy self of from that bait,whileſt thowe arte yet in the wauing water of this worlde.Therfore be warned and while thowe haueſt time loo ke to thy ſelf.

Nowe that we haue heard this noble learned Father of the one ſide of Chryſtes Parliament houſe,we will heare an other of the other ſide,whiche ſhall be Iſychius,who vpon Leuiticus toucheth this matter and ſaieth: *Et quod hoc eſt ſacrificium? Duæ decimæ ſimilæ conſperſæ oleo.Oportet enim ſcire perfeĉtam huma-* *In Leuitie.* *nitatem,& perfeĉtam diuinitatem contemperare,id eſt,in vnum conuenire in oleo , id eſt,* *li.6.ca.23.* *per eam,quam circa nos habet,compaſsionem.Sic enim ſacrificium odor ſuauitatis Domino inuenitur,ſapientibus nobis de eo , quæ digna ſunt. In quibus autem ſacrificium , & per quos agitur,quomodò celebratur intelligiblis agni oblatio , quod ſequitur oſtendit. Neque enim in ſanguine, neque per irrationabilia animalia ſacrificium à nobis Deus ſuſcipit , ſe-cundùm quod ſequentia demonſtrant.Ait enim :Liba quoque vini quarta pars hyn ,panem & polentam. Quia dubium futurum erat forſan, à quibus myſterium ſacrificij, quod per Chriſtum eſt, quod ſuperius diximus , celebratur : habes ecce intelligibilis Melchiſedech* B *oblationem,quæ in pane & vino perficitur,in qua quarta pars hyn in libis vini offertur ,vt per quartam Euangelij traditionem,quæ in libris quatuor eſt , per libationem verò Domi-nicum ſermonem ſignificaret,quum ait:Hic eſt meus ſanguis, qui pro vobis fundetur : ſine imminutione enim ſignificare legiſlatori viſum eſt Chriſti myſterium.* And what ys this ſacrifice?Two tenth deales of fine flower ſprinkled with oile . For we muſt knowe to contemper the perfeĉt manhead, and perfeĉt godhead , that ys to come together into one in oile,that ys , by that compaſsion ,whiche he hath toward vs.For ſo the ſacrifice ys fownde a ſwete ſauoure to our Lorde, when we vnderſtand of him thinges that be woorthie.In what thinges thys ſacrifice,whiche ys the oblacion of the intelligible lambe,ys,and by whome yt ys doen,howe yt ys celebrated,that that foloweth, declareth. For nei-ther by vnreaſonable beaſtes doth God receaue ſacrifice of vs , acording as the woordes that folowe de plainlie ſhewe.For he ſaieth:And the drinke of-fringe therof ſhal be of wine euen the fourte parte of an hyn,bread,and per ched corne.Bicauſe perchaunce yt might haue comed in doubte hereafter *Chriſt ſa-* of whome the myſterie of the ſacrifice whiche ys by Chryſte, which we ha- *crificing in* C ue ſpoken of aboue, ys celebrated , beholde thowe haueſt the ſacrifice of *bread and* the intelligible Melchiſedech,whiche ys full doen in bread and wine, in *wine was* whiche ſacrifice ys offred the fourth deale of the drinke offring of wine, *the intelli-* that by the fourth deale the tradicion of the Goſpell, whiche ys in foure *gible ſacri-* bookes,and by the drinke offring he wolde ſignifie the woorde of our Lord *fice.* when he ſaieth : *This ys my bloode , whiche ſhall be ſhedde yowe for.* And ſo yt pleaſed the Lawe geuer that yt ſhoulde fully ſignifie the myſterie of Chryſt Thus farre *Iſychius.*

In the whiche ſainge ye haue the wholl matter teſtified that we ſeke for. For wher in *Leuiticus* God commaunded an he lambe to be offred , and that the meat offring therof ſhoulde be two tenth deales of fine flower mengled with oyle to make bread , and the drinke offring ſhoulde be the fourth deale of an hyn of wyne whiche thing thys Authour *Melchiſe-* ſeking to Applie to the newe Teſtament , *Thowe haueſt* (ſaieth he)*the* *dech ſacri-* *oblacion or ſacrifice of Chriſt in the intelligle Melchiſedech aunſwering thys,whiche* *ficing in* D *ſacrifice was fullie and perfeĉtlie doen in bread and wine* Wherby he dothe not *bread and* onely teache vs , that Melchiſedech was a figure of Chryſte abſolutelie : *wine was* but that in ſacrificing bread and wine he was alſo the figure , and *the figure* Chryſt ſacrificing in the like thinges was the intelligle Melchiſe- *of Chriſt.*
O iii dech,

dech,that ys to faie,he whome Melchifedech fo doing did prefigurate.

In thefe fewe woordes then we maie firft learn thefe two thinges,which the Aduerfaries do denie,that ys, that Melchifedech did not onelie bring furth,but did alfo offer bread and wine in facrifice. And that Chryft the intelligible Melchifedech did alfo facrifice in bread and wine.

Ifychius ac knowled geth the prefence of Chryftes bodie and bloode in the Sacra.

But that none occafion fhoulde be geuen, either to the Aduerfaries to faie that Chryft gaue but bare bread and wine, or to the Reader to take fcruple bicaufe he faieth,that Chryft did facrifice in bread and wine, he ope-neth immediatelie what bread and wine yt was , faing : *by the drinke offring whiche was in wine,he wolde fignifie that of whiche Chryft faied:This ys my bloode , whiche fhall be fhedde for yow* .Wherby he deliuereth vs from that doubte , and tea-cheth plainlie the prefence of Chryftes blood in the Sacrament . Wher yf we acknowledge that,and that this Authour fo meneth that foche prefence ys ther,we maie alfo confeffe the prefence of his bodie in the other kinde, for fo the Authour alfo entendeth , as not onely in that , that ys aboue faied yt dothe appeare, but in that alfo, that foloweth yt ys manifeft and euident.

F

For thus he faieth:*Oblatio enim prafentium donorum,quam effe myfterium Vnige-niti oftendimus,reconciliauit nos Deo,& cibum nobis noua polenta praftitit.* The obla-cion of thefe prefent giftes,whiche oblacion we haue declared to be the my fterie of the onelie begotten fonne of God,hath reconciled vs to God , and hath geuen vs meate,of newe dried corne.

This oblacion that Ifychius fpeaketh of here,ys yt(as he faieth)*which re-conciled vs to God*,whiche oblacion ys not an other from that he fpake of be-fore,but yt ys the fame.The oblacion that he fpake of before was the obla-cion after the ordre of Melchifedech.Wherfore in the oblacion after the or dre of Melchifedech,was Chryft offred , who by his death reconciled vs to God.

Chryft then being facrificed,and therfore prefent,ys now alfo facrificed, and therfor prefent.For the table of Chryft that now ys(as Chryfoftome fai eth)being in no poincte inferiour to that,but being all one , As Chryft was ther in his facrifice verilie prefent:So ys he here verilie prefent.

G

Thus Although Melchifedech (as the Aduerfaries affirme)was a figure of Chryft in the eternitie of his preifthead:yet was he alfo(as by thefe Fathers before alleaged ys taught) the figure of him in the verie office of the preift-head in offring bread and wine:Melchifedech in his maner,in earthly bread and wine:Chryfte in his maner in heauenlie bread and wine , which ys hys verie flefh and bloode the bread and wine of euerlafting life.

THE THIRTITH CHAP. TREATETH OF THE
fame matter by fainct Hierom and Theodorete.

Ainct Hierō handeling the prophecie of Dauid fpeaking of the pre-ifthead of Chryft after the ordre of Melchifedech , geueth vs a no-table and moft clear teftimonie in this matter and faieth : *Superfluū eft nos de ifto verficulo velle interpretari,cùm fanctus Apoftolus ad Hebr.eos ple nifsimè difputauit.Ipfe enim ait:Ifte eft Melchifedech,fine patre,fine matre, fine genera-tione . Et ab omnibus ecclefiafticis dictum eft , quoniam fine patre dicitur fecundùm*

Hieron.in Pfal.110.

carnem ,fine matre dicitur fecundùm Deum . Hoc folùm ergo interpretemur : Tu es facerdos in aternum fecundùm ordinem Melchifedech . Hoc folùm dicamus, quare dixerit , Secundùm ordinem . Secundùm ordinem : Nequaque facerdos

H

eris

A *eris secundùm victimas Iudaicas, sed eris sacerdos secundùm ordinem Melchisedech. Quo-*
modò enim Melchisedech Rex Salem obtulit panem & vinum : sic & tu offeres corpus
tuum , & sanguinem, verùm panem, & verum vinum. Iste Melchisedech ista mysteria,
quæ habemus, dedit nobis. Ipse est, qui dixit : Qui manducauerit carnem, & biberit san-
guinem meum &c. Secundùm ordinem Melchisedech, tradidit nobis sacramentum suum.
Yt ys superfluouse for vs to go aboute to expownde this verse, seing the holie Apostle, hath fullie vnto the Hebrues treacted of the same. For he saieth:
This ys *Melchisedech* withoute father, withoute mother, withoute generaciõ.
And of all men of the churche yt ys saied, that he ys withoute father as concerning the fleshe: and withoute mother as concerninge his godhead. This
onelie therfore let vs interprete : *Thowe art a preist for euer after the ordre of Mel-*
chisedech. Let vs onelie saie, wherfore he saieth: after the ordre, After the ordre. that ys: *Thowe shalt not be a preist according to the sacrifices of the Iewes: but thowe*
shalt be a preist after the ordre of Melchisedech, For as *Melchisedech* king of Salem
did offre bread and wine : *So thowe also shalt offre thy bodie and bloode, the true*

B *breade and true wine .* This *Melchisedech* gaue vs these mysteries, whiche we haue . Yt ys he that hath saied: He that shall eate my flesh, and drinke my bloode &c. He after the ordre of *Meichisedech* hath deliuered vnto vs his Sacramẽ-
te . Thus farre sainćte Hierom.

    Nowe wher the Aduersaries being sore pinched with this figure of *Mel-*
chisedech laboure with might and main to cast mistes before the eies of mẽ,
to make thẽ beleue that they see in *Melchisedech* but onelie the figure of the
eternitie of Chryst, and not the figure of his preisthood and sacrifice, and
for that pourpose alleage sainćte Paule, treacting of the same to the Hebrues, and saie, that he doth ther onelie so applie it : I wishe yowe wolde well
note sainćte Hierom, howe as concerning the matter of the eternitie of
Chryst he saieth, that yt ys supperfluouse to speake of yt, bicause sainćte
Paule euen to the full hath clerly opened that matter to be Hebrues.

    But what then? Doth sainćt Hierom saie nothing to the explicacion and
applicacion of this figure? Yes, notwithstanding that full, and plain explicacion of sainćt Paule, he addeth also an expositiõ, not of that sainćte Paule

C had expownded, but of that, that sainćte Paule had left vnexpownded. And
therfor he saeth : *Hoc solùm interpretemur. Tu es sacerdos &c.* Let vs onelie expowde this : Thowe arte a preist for euer after the ordre of Melchisedech.
Why? ys this the text that ys fully handeled of sainćte Paule, and so clerlie
expownded to the Hebrues? Yt ys the same.

    Wherfore note that yn this litle werse, twoo thinges being conteined:
the one that Chryst ys a preist for euer, the other that he ys of the ordre of
Melchisedech: The first ys at large expownded by sainćte Paule: but the
other, that ys, the order of Melchisedech ys not expownded by sainćte Paule. Wherfor sainćte Hierom saieth immediately: *Hoc solùm dicamus, quare dix-*
erit secundùm ordinem. Let vs onelie declare this : Why he saieth after the ordre.
As who might saie, Sainćt Paule hath plentifullie saied of the eternitie of the
priestgood of Chryste. Wherfore yt were vain for me to speake of that :But
I will onelie speake of the order of the preisthood of Chryst. for that hath
not sainćt Paule spoken of.

D   And entring to shewe of what ordre of presthoode Chryst ys, he speaketh
in the persõ of God the Father and saieth: *Thowe shalt not be a preist after the or-*
dre of offrings of the Iewes sacrifices, but thowe shalt be a preist after the ordre of Melchise-
dech And howe he shoulde doo sacrifice after that ordre, he furtwith declareth. For as *Melchisedech* (saieth he) *king of Salem did offer bread and wine : So shalt*

S. Paule
tre acteth
fullie of the
eternitie of
Chrysts
preisthead
but not of
the ordre
after Mel-
chisedech.

O iiij   thowe

thowe alſo offer thy bodie and bloode, the true bread and true wine. A breif expoſition,   E
but as plain, as yt ys breif.

Nowe as ſainĉte Paule to the hebrues hath oponed the firſt parte for the
eternitie of the preſtheade of Chryſte: So here ſainĉte Hierom hath as touching this order, and ſacrifice opened the ſecond parte. wherin reader, firſt
note, that wher the Aduerſaries (as ys before ſaid in the laſt chapter) to denie the ſacrifice of Chryſt after the ordre of Melchiſedech, doo firſt denie
that Melchiſedech him ſelf did offer breade and wine, ſaing, that in Geneſis yt ys not readd of Melchiſedech: *Obtulit panem & vinum: he offred bread*

*Melchiſe-
dech offred
bread and
wine after
S. Hierom.*

and wine, but *protulit panem, & vinum* he brought furth bread and wine: Yet
ſainĉt Hierom knowinge the olde Teſtament, and well vnderſtanding the
hebrue toung ſaieth that Melchiſedech did offer bread and wine, and vſith
the latin woorde, *obtulit,* he offred, and not, *protulit,* he brought furth.
wherby we are taught that this ys the true mening, and vnderſtanding of
the place.

Further alſo, as we are taught that Melchiſedech did offer bread and wine:
So alſo are we taught (whiche ys in the ſecŏd parte to be noted) bothe that   F
Chryſt did offer, and what he did offer, he did offer after the ordre of Melchiſedech bread and wine, not bare bread and bare wine, as Melchiſedech
did in the figure, but his verie bodie and blood, the true bread and true
wine, as ſainĉte Hierom expreſſeth, wherbie we are taught not onelie the
verie preſence of Chryſtes bodie and blood in the ſacrament: But alſo that
he in his laſt Supper did offer the ſame bodie after the ordre of Melchiſedech.

Whiche for ſomoche as yt ys ſo plainlie ſpoken, I ſhall not neade either
to bring in anie other ſaing of the ſame ſainĉte Hierom to declare his minde more plainlie in this: or I my ſelf to tarie anie longer in opening of this
his ſainge, being all readie ſo plain, that yt can be made or ſpoken no plainer.

Onely this I ſhall deſire thee (gentle Reader) to call to thy memorie the
ende of the ſaing of ſainĉte Ciprian laſt alleadged in the chapiter before, and
compare yt to the ende of this ſaing, and I thinke verilie, yt will wonderfullie delight thee, to ſee the trueth not onely ſo painlie, but alſo with ſo
goodlie conſonannt agreement vttered and ſpoken. Sainĉt Ciprian ſaied: G
who ys more proprelie the preiſt of the moſt highe God, thā our Lorde Ieſus Chriſte, Who

*A plain
place for
maſter
Iuell.*

*offred a ſacrifice to God the Father, and offred the ſame that Melchiſedech offred, that ys,
bread and wine, euen his bodie, and bloode?* Sainĉte Hierom ſaieth: *As Melchiſedech
offred bread and wine: So ſhalt thowe offer thy bodie and blood, the true bread, and true
wine.* what goodlie conſent ys this? what plain maner of ſpeache ys this?
what more neadeth to be ſaied in this matter? Ys yt not cōſeſſed that Chryſt
offred in his laſt Supper his bodie, and bloode? I truſt the proclamer him
ſelf will graunt yt, and ſaie yt ys moſt plain. ffor who can doubt that theſe
woordes be ſpoken of the ſacrifice in the Supper, ſainĉt Hierom ſaing,
that this Melchiſedech (meening Chryſt) deliuered vs theſe miſteries &c.

Wherfor leauing further explicacion of this Authour we will heare
Theodorete, one of the other ſide of Chryſtes parlament houſe, who as
breiſlie as plainlie openeth the trueth of the matter whiche we ſeke, as yt
ſhall appeare in this his ſainge: *Antiquam genealogiam conſcribens diuinus Moyſes,
docuit nos, quòd Adam, cùm tot annos natus eſſet, genuit Seth. Ei cùm tot annis vixiſſet,*   H

*Theodore-
tus Dial 2.*

*finem vitæ accepit. Ita etiam dixit de Seth & Enos, & alijs. Melchiſedech et gene-
rationis initium, et vitæ finem ſilentio præterijt: Ergo ſi hiſtoria ſpectetur, nec initium
dierum, nec vitæ finem habet. Reuerà autem Dei filius nec eſſe cœpit, nec finem accipiet.*

                                           In

A *In ijs ergo maximis, et verè diuinis fuit Melchisedech figura Christi Domini. In sacerdotio autem, quod hominibus magis quàm Deo conuenit, Dominus Christus Pontifex fuit secundũ ordinem Melchisedech. Melchisedech enim fuit gentium Pontifex. Et Dominus Christus pro omnibus hominibus sanctum et salutiferum sacrificium obtulit ,* The godlie Moyses writing the olde genealogie, hath taught vs, that Adam when he was thus manie years olde, he begatte Seth, And when he had liued so manie yeares he made an ende of his life. Enen so also he saieth of Seth, and Enos, with other. As for the beginning of the generacion of Melchisedech, and the ende of his life he ouerpasseth yt with scilence. Wherfor if the historie be looked on, he hathe neither beginning of daies, nor the ende of life. So in verie dede the Sonne of God neither hathe beginning of his being, neither shall haue ending. In these great thinges then verie diuine, was Melchisedech a figure of our Lorde Chryst. In the preisthead also, whiche ys more mete or agreable for men then for God, our *lorde Chryst was an high preist after the ordre of Melchisedech.* For Melchisedech was the high preist of the gentiles. And **B** our lorde Chryst offred for all men an holie and holsom sacrifice. Thus moche Theodorete.

Whom ye do perceaue to testifie not onelie that Melchisedech was a figure of Chryste as concerninge his eternitie, but also as concerning his preisthead, and Sacrifice, which did appertein to him as man. By whiche Applicacion he conuinceth the *Eutichians,* who forsaking the catholique faith, whiche teacheth that in Chryst be two natures, that ys to saie, the perfecte nature of God, and the perfecte nature of man, and so confesseth Chryst to be verie God, and verie Man, folowed their master *Eutiches,* and taught (as in the Chalcedon Councell yt ys testified) that Chryste before the adunacion, was of two natures, but after the adunacion he was but of one nature, whiche was God, and therfore denieng Chryste to be man, confessed him onelie to be God. Wherfor folowing *Appollinaris, Valentinus,* and *Macedonius,* they wolde not receaue this common article of our faith : *Whiche was conceaued by the holie Goste , born of the virgen Mary.*

Chrystes offring of sacrifice after the ordre of Melchisedech ouerthroweth the heresie of Eutiches.

Nowe as these confessed Chryst to be God : So this Theodorete labou-**C** ring to proue him also to be man, bringeth in this figure of Melchisedech, whiche as by eternitie yt proueth him to be God , For eternitie, that ys, to haue no beginning, nor ending, farre surmounteth the created nature of man, and apperteineth to the increated nature of God : So by the preisthead of Melchisedech whiche was in Chryst (whiche being to base an office for God, doth proprelie appertein to man) he proueth Chryst to be a very Man.

Yf then the Aduersaries shall denie Melchisedech to be a figure of Chryst, as touching his preisthead and sacrifice, they shall take awaie the argument of this learned man, and helping the parte of the heretikes, shall weaken the parte of the catholiques. And so where by the full and true applicacion of the figure, Chryste ys proued to be both God and mã, by the onelie applicacion of the eternitie (whiche the Aduersaries wolde haue) he shall be proued onelie God.

Aduersaries exposicions maintein the heresie of Eutiches.

Nowe not onelie the argument of the matter proueth that this Authour brought in this figure cheifly to proue the manhead of Chryste, whiche **D** was the thing to be proued against *Eutiches,* and that by the preisthead of Melchisedech : But also his very plain woordes do proue the same. For whẽ he saieth : *In sacerdotio, quod hominibus magis quàm Deo conuenit, Dominus Christus secundùm ordinem Melchisedech Pontifex fuit .* In the preisthead whiche more

agreeth

agreeth to mē, thē to God our Lorde, Chryſte was an gigh preiſt after the or E dre of Melchiſedech. Leauing the eternitie of the Godhead of Chryſte, whe rof Melchiſedech was a figure in that he ys ouerpaſſed in the hiſtorie with oute mencion made either of his beginning or ending: He commeth to that parte, that proueth him a man, whiche was to be a preiſt after the ordre of Melchiſedech.

Office of a preiſt. What ys yt to be apreiſt, but to do the office of a preiſt? What ys the office of a preiſt? the office of a preiſt ys to offer Sacrifice to God for ſinnes (as ſaincte Paule wittneſſeth, whiche alſo this authour alleaging for his pourpoſe bringeth in thus: *Si eſt ergo ſacerdotum proprium offerre munera, Chriſtus autem, quod ad humanitatem attinet, ſacerdos appellatus eſt, non aliam hoſtiā, quàm ſuum corpus obtulit.* Yf then yt be ſolie apperteining to preiſtes to offer ſacrifice, and Chryſte as cōcerninge his humanitie, was called a preiſt, he offred no other ſacrifice but his own bodie.

Dial. 1.

Then maie we alſo conclude, that Chryſt being a preiſt after the ordre of Melchiſedech, and the office of a preiſt after the ordre of Melchiſedech ys F to offer ſoche ſacrifice as to that ordre apperteineth, therfor Chryſt offred ſoche ſacrifie as to that ordre apperteineth. Yt apperteineth to that ordre to offer bread and wine. Wherfore Chryſt ſacrificed in bread and wine. In bread and wine I ſaie, a kinde of foode of more excellencie, then the bread and wine whiche did figure yt, I meen with Theodoret, and ſainct Hierom, the bodie and blood of Chryſt, the true bread, and true wine, whiche feadeth vs to liue the true life. the life, that endureth and faileth not: *Qui manducat hunc panem viuet in æternum.* He that eateth this bread, ſhall liue foreuer.

Ioan. 6.

What neadeth me anie more to ſaie here, ſeing that bothe ſainct Hierom, and Theodorete do thus plainly and agreablie (as ye haue heard) declare, that Melchiſehech was a figure, as well of the preiſthead and ſacrifice of Chryſt, in that he offred ſacrifice to God in bread and wine: as of his eternitie, for he ys accompted withoute ffather, without mother, without beginning, or ending. G

But Reader, when thowe ſeeſt them ſo manifeſtlie, erre, and ſo maliciouſlie impugne that, whiche the holie Fathers doo teache, by ſo plain ſentence and expreſſe woordes as can not but be ſeen and perceaued, except wher malice blindeth, thinke with thy ſelf, that iuſt cauſe ys miniſtred vnto thee, to feare them and their ſainges in other matters. Thus much for thy aduertiſement by the waie, being ſaied, gentle Reader, I will for thy further inſtruction, and confirmacion of the matter bring yet mo wittneſſes of the trueth herof.

THE ONE AND THIRTITH CHAPITER CON-
cludeth this matter of Melchiſedech by ſaincte Auguſtin and Damaſcen.

A S ye haue allredie heard ſome auncient men of Chryſtes Parliament howſe agreablie teſtifieng the trueth of the figure of Melchiſedech, euen as yt hath ben enacted, and receaued from the beginninge of the ſame howſe: So ſhall ye heare one coople more of them doing the like, and ſo ſhall we ende the explica H cion of this prophecie of the pſalmiſt as touching the preiſthead of Chryſte after the ordre of Melchiſedech. Sainct Auguſtin writteh of the matter thus:

In Pſa. 33. *Erant ſacrificia antea Iudæorum ſecundum ordinem Aaron in victimis pecorum, & hoc in myſterio*

A   *myſterio. Nondum erat ſacrificium corporis & ſanguinis Domini, quod fideles norunt, &*
qui Euangelium legerunt, quod ſacrificiũ nunc diffuſum eſt toto orbe. Proponite ergo vobis
ante oculos duo ſacrificia : & illud ſecundùm ordinem Aaron, et hoc ſecundùm ordinem
Melchiſedech. Scriptum eſt enim, Iurauit Dominus, et non pœnitebit eum, Tu es ſacerdos
in æternum ſecundùm ordinem Melchiſedech. De quo dicitur, Tu es ſacerdos in æternum ſe-
cundùm ordinem Melchiſedech? De Domino noſtro Ieſu Chriſto. Quis enim erat Melchiſe-
dech? Rex Salem. Salem autem fuit Ciuitas illa, quæ poſtea (ſicut docti prodiderunt) Hie-
ruſalem dicta eſt. Ergo antequam ibi regnarent Iudæi, ibi erat ille ſacerdos Melchiſedech,
qui ſcribitur in Geneſi, ſacerdos Dei excelſi. Ipſe occurrit Abrahæ, quando liberauit Loth
de manu perſequentium, et proſtrauit illos, à quibus tenebatur, et liberauit fratrem. Et poſt
liberationem fratris occurrit ei Melchiſedech, (Tantus erat Melchiſedech à quo benedicere-
tur Abraham) protulit panẽ et vinum, et benedixit Abraham, et dedit ei decimas Abra-
ham. Videte quid protulit, et quem benedixit, et dictum eſt poſtea : Tu es ſacerdos in æter-
num ſecundùm ordinem Melchiſedech. Dauid hoc in ſpiritu dixit, longè poſt Abra-
ham. Temporibus autem Abrahæ fuit Melchiſedech. De quo alio loco dicit : Tu es
B   *ſacerdos in æternum ſecundùm ordinem Melchiſedech, niſi de illo cuius noſtis ſacrificium?*

    Ther were before, the ſacrifices of the Iewes after the ordre of Aaron in
the offringe of beaſtes, and that in myſterie. *The Sacrifice of the body and blood*   Sacrifice af
of our Lorde, the whiche the faithfull, and they that haue red the goſpell knowe,   ter the or-
was not yet. Whiche Sacrifice ys nowe diffuſed throughoute all the woorlde. Sette be-   dre of Mel
fore your eyes therfor the twoo ſacrifices, both that after the order of Aarõ,   chiſedech
and this after the ordre of Melchiſedech. For yt ys written : *The Lord hathe*   ys nowe
ſworne, and yt ſhall not repent him. Thowe arte a preiſt for euer after the ordre of Melchi-   diffuſed
ſedech. Of whom ys yt ſaied: *Thowe arte a preiſt after the ordre of Melchiſedech?* Of   troughout
our Lorde Ieſus Chryſte. who was this Melchiſedech? King of Salem. Salem   the worlde.
was before time, that ſame Cittie, which as the learned haue declared, was
afterwarde called Hieruſalem. Therfor before the Iewes reigned ther, the
preiſt Melchiſedech, who ys written in Geneſis the preiſt of the high God,
was ther. He mett with Abraham when he had deliuered Loth from the
hand of them, that did perſecute him, and he ouerthrewe them, of whom
he was holden, and deliuered his brother. And after the deliuerance of his
C   brother, Melchiſedech mette him (So great a man was Melchiſedech of whõ
Abrahã was bleſſed) he brought furth bread and wine, and bleſſed Abrahã,
and Abraham gaue him tithes. Beholde what he brought, and whom he bleſſed. And yt ys ſaied afterwarde, *Thowe arte a preiſt for euer after* the ordre of
Melchiſedech. Dauid ſpake this in ſpirit long after Abraham. Melchiſedech
was in the time of Abraham. *Of whom in an other place ſaieth he, Thowe arte a preiſt*
For euer after the ordre of Melchiſedech, But of him whoſe ſacrifice ye knowe? Thus farre
ſaincte Auguſtine.

    Ye haue here heard the diſtinction of the two orders of preiſthead, of
Aaron, and of Melchiſedech. Ye haue heard alſo the diſtinction of the two
ſacrifices. the one according to the order of Aaron, the other after the order
of Melchiſedech. What this ſacrifice after the ordre of Melchiſedech ys,
ſainct Auguſtin hathe declared wher he ſaied : *The ſacrifice of the bodie and*   Sacrifice
blood of our Lorde was not yet, whiche ſacrifice ys nowe diffuſed throughoute all   avouched.
the worlde.
D   What he meeneth when he ſaieth : *as yet the ſacrifice of the bodie and bloode of*
our Lord was not, and alſo whether this ſacrifice be after the ordre of Melchiſedech, in a breif ſentence of fewe woordes, he doth verie plainlie in an other
place open and declare. *Sublatum eſt ſacrificium Aaron, & cæpit eſſe ſacrificium, ſe-*
cundùm ordinem Melchiſedech *The ſacrifice of Aaron was taken awaie. And the ſacri-*
fice

fice after the ordre of Melchifedech beganne. By the which fentence yt ys manifeft, **E** that while the facrifice of Aarõ endured, this facrifice was not vfed. But whẽ, that was taken awaie, this facrifice began.

Likewife he hath taught alfo that the facrifice of the bodie and blood of Chryfte ys the facrifice after the ordre of Melchifedech. For wher before he faied *that the bodie and blood of our Lord was not yet*, And nowe he faieth, *that the facrifice of Melchifedech began, when Aarons facrifice was taken awaie*: What doth he ells fignifie, but that they be all one thing? that ys, that the bodie and blood of Chryfte be the facrifice after the ordre of Melchifedech. And fo conuertiblie that the facrifice after the ordre of Melchifedech, ys the bodie and blood of Chryfte. Which bodie and bloode be no wher ells offred in facrifice after the ordre of Melchifedech, but in the facrifice of the Altar, wher bread and wine be turned into the fame bodie and bloode. For the bodie of Chryfte vpon the croffe was a bloodie facrifice, perfected with bloodfhedding after the maner of Aarõ. Therfore the holie facrifice of the Altar, which (as fainct Auften faieth) ys nowe diffufed and fpredde through all the world **F** ys the verie bodie and blood of Chryfte.

Although this, that ys alleaged oute of fainct Auguftin, ys fo plain, that the Aduerfaries can not but fee the trueth, and fo ftrong, that they can not againft faie yt: Yet that they maie fee all this that ys fpoken confirmed, and made more plain, and that fo being confownded by the euident trueth, they maie geue ouer their erroure, and yelde vnto trueth, we will heare the fentence of the fame faincte Auguftine, treating of this fame matter in an other place. Thus yt ys. *Coram regno patris fui mutauit vultum fuum, & dimifit eum, et abijt, quia erat ibi facrificium fecundùm ordinem Aaron, et poftea ipfe corpore et fanguine fuo inftituit facrificium fecundùm ordinem Melchifedech. Mutauit ergo vultum fuum in facerdotio, et dimifit gentem Iudæorum, et venit ad gentes.* Before the kingdom of his Father he hath chaunged his cowntennce, and lefte him and went awaie. bicaufe ther was ther the facrifice after the ordre of Aaron. *And afterward of his bodie and blood he inftituted the facrifice after the ordre of Melchifedech.* He chaũged therfor his contenaunce in preifthead, and left the people of the Iewes, and came to the Gentiles. Thus fainct Auguftin.

Dooye marke what ys here faied? Yf ye doo, ye muft nedes vnderftand **G** yt, yt ys fo plain. For what can be more breiflie, and more plainlie faied, then *that Chryfte did inftitute a facrifice of his bodie and blood after the ordre of Melchifedech?* By this breif fentence manie thinges be aunfwered: Firft, where the Aduerfaries moft flaunderouflie haue faied, to bring the thing in hatred emongethe people, that the Pope made the holie Sacrament a facrifice to obfcure the glorie of Chryfte, and to diminifh the woorthineffe and merit of Chryftes facrifices vpon the croffe, and therwithall to bring the people into beleiff, that the Sacrifice of Chryfte vpon the croffe was not fufficient withoute this: And that without authoritie (*as this Proclamer faieth*) we offer vppe Chryft vnto his Father: And thus with a nombre of like lies, The Pope and the Papiftes were made Authours and founders of this facrifice. But baffhe and be afhamed thowe flaunderoufe mã, thowe Enemie of the trueth, and open thine eies to fee, and thine eares to heare what faincte Auguftine that holie Father, and learned doctour here teacheth, that ys, *that Chryfte did of his owne bodie and blood inftitute a facrifice after the ordre of Melchifedech,* **H** So that Chryft, euen by this bolie Fathers teftimonie, ys the inftitutour and founder of this bleffed Sacrifice, and not the Pope, neither the papiftes as thowe termeft them. But they be the humble receauers of this fame inftitucion of Chryft.　　Secon-

Sacrifice of the bodie and blood of Chryft in the Sacr. ys after the order of Melchifedech.

In Pfalm. 33. Cõcion. 3.

Not the Pope nor the Papiftes made the facrament a facrifice but Chryft him felf after S. Auguftin.

A　　Secondarelie, wher the Aduersaries haue saied that Chryste did not offer his bodie in sacrifice in his laſt Supper, this sentence alſo confuteth them. For ſaincte Auguſtine ſaithe here, that Chryſt did inſtitute a ſacrifice after the order of Melchiſedech . Nowe wher read we that Chryſte did ſacrifice after the ordre of Melchiſedech , but onelie in his laſt Supper ? Wherfore ſeing Chryſt did inſtitute a ſacrifice after that ordre , and did neuer execute the office of a preiſt of that ordre in viſible forme and maner (For other wiſe he dothe dailie) but in the laſt Supper : Then of neceſſitie yt muſt be , that in the laſt Supper he did ſacrifice.

Yt muſt of neceſſitie be graunted that Chryſt did ſacriſice in his laſt ſupper.

Thirdlie, for ſo moch as Chryſt did inſtitute this ſacrifice in his bodie and blood, yt muſt neceſſarilie folowe that Chryſtes bodie and blood be preſent in the Sacramēt. And as Chryſte did verilie make his bodie and bloode preſent in that ſacrifice in his laſt Supper inſtituted and offred : So dothe he verilie make his bodie and blood preſēt in the ſacrifice of the Altar, and that

B　　as often as the ſame ys duelie excuted and doen . For as he did in that Supper : So dothe he in euery miniſtracion of the bleſſed Sacrament duely miniſtred . For the Sacrament ys of no leſſe force, poour, wourthineſſe and dignitie nowe in the Altar, that yt was in the table, wher Chryſt himſelf viſiblie preſent did ſanctifie yt , as Chryſoſtome dothe teſtifie.

Non ſunt hæc humanæ virtutis opera , quæ tunc in illa cœna confecit ipſe quoque nunc operatur , ipſe perficit . Miniſtrorum nos ordinem tenemus , qui verò hæc ſanctificat & tranſmutat,ipſe eſt . Cum Diſcipulis (inquit) meis , facio Paſcha . Hæc enim illa non alia menſa eſt : hæc nulla re minor , quàm illa eſt .Non enim illam Chriſtus, hanc homo quiſpiam facit, ſed vtramque ipſe . Theſe woorkes be not of mans power, whiche he then did in that Supper,he doth nowe alſo woorke, he doth perfecte yt. we hold the ordre of miniſtres , but yt ys he, *that doth ſanctifie, trāſmute or chaūge theſe* things .With my diſciples (ſaieth he) do I kepe the Paſſouer.*This ys euen the ſame,not an other table.*This ys in nothing leſſer thē that . For Chryſt maketh not that table, and ſome other man this, but Chryſte bothe. Thus Chriſoſtom.

Chryſ.in 26 Matth.

Chryſt and not man doth conſecrate.

C　　Wherby we are taught , that as moche as was doen by Chryſt in his laſt Supper, ſo moche ys doen nowe . So moche as the Apoſtles receaued, ſo moche receaue we nowe . The reaſon ys(as Chryſoſtome ſaieth) that Chryſte, who did ſanctifie that table, doth alſo ſanctifie this our table , and this table ys in nothing leſſe, then that table was . In that table (as ſaincte Auguſtine in his laſt ſentence did teache) Chryſtes bodie was by himſelf ſacrificed , and ſo verilie preſent in that ſacrifice . Wherfor in this table likewiſe Chryſtes bodie ys verilie ſacrificed , and ſo verilie and realie preſent.

Sacrifice auouched.

But ſomwhat to ſaie of that, that maie be gathered of this ſaing of Chryſoſtom : Yf nothing were geuen to the Apoſtles (as the Aduerſaries teache) but a peice of Sacramentall bread, a figure of Chryſtes bodie : what nead all theſe compariſons betwixt table, and table . For yf the doctrine of the aduerſaries be true, we can haue no leſſe, except we ſhoulde eate courſe bread, wheras the Apoſtles eate fine bread. we can haue noleſſe I ſaie, then they had. A peice of bread eche of thē had:a peice of bread eche of

D　　vs hathe. Yf that bread were a figure , this bread ys a figure . What thing nowe then moued Chryſoſtom to trauaill ſo moche to ſett furth the equalitie of theſe two tables(ſo I terme thē for diſtinctiō of knowledge) ſeing ther cā be no inequalitie betwē them, eche of them hauing a peice of bread,and

P　　a cuppe

a cuppe of wine ? Be yowe well affured , Chryfoftom fawe moche caufe in the imperfection and weakneffe of the faith of men, whiche might thinke, that forfomoche as Chryft was then in vifible maner prefent at the Supper, and fo the Sacrament being of him felf confecrated and diftributed, that yt might be and was hys verie bodie: But nowe that he was afcended, and not in vifible maner prefent, with hys owne mouthe fpeaking, and with hys owne hand deliuering, they might thinke that ther was no foche wonderfull worke wrought, he being nowe from vifible feight abfent , as then when he was in vifible feight prefent.

And in dede foch an herefie did the Petrobrufians , and the Henricians holde (as *Petrus Cluniacenfis* teftifieth , who in the beginning of his booke written againft them, reherfeth the fainges of thofe heretikes in this wife: *Nolite, o populi, Epifcopis & presbyteris ceu Clero vos feducenti credere , qui ficut in multis, fic in altaris facrificio vos decipiunt, vbi corpus Chrifti fe conficere , & vobis ad veftrarum animarum falutem fe tradere mentiuntur: Mentiuntur plane. Corpus Chrifti femel tantùm ab ipfo Chrifto in cœna ante pafsionem factum eft, & femel, hoc eft , tunc tantùm Difcipulis datum eft. Exinde neque confectum ab aliquo, neque alicui datum eft.* Beleue not (o people) faied thofe heretikes, the Byfhoppes and preiftes or the cleargie begilinge yow. Which as in manie thinges: fo alfo they deceiue you in the office of the Altar, wher they lie vnto you , that they do confecrate the bodie of Chryft, and deliuer yt to you for your foules health. They lie plain lie. The bodie of Chrifte was once onelie made of Chryfte in hys laft Supper before hys pafsion, and once, that ys, then onelie was yt geuen to the Difciples. Since that time, was yt neither geué to anie, neither made of anie. Thus they.

Petrobru-
fians and
Henriciãs
their here-
fies.
Petr. Clu-
niacen.

Nowe ye maie fee, that the holie Goft did not without caufe moue hys holie organs to fpeake foche thinges before hand, as wherby the Succefsion of the catholique Churche , fhoulde finde the herefie aunfwered , before the faied herefie were fett furth abroad (The holie Gofte well knowing that foche euell wedes fhoulde fpring in the vineyarde of Chryfte) And yet this maie ye marke that herefie the further yt goeth , yt ys allwaie the woorfe as fainte Paule comparing yt to a Canker dothe verie well expreffe the condicion of yt, and by plain woordes fheweth the progreffe of yt thus: *Prophana autem & vaniloquia deuita . Multum enim proficient ad impietatem , & fermo eorum vt cancer ferpit.* As for vngodlie and vain talkes, auoide them . For they will encreafe to further vngodlineffe. And their wordes fhal crepe euen as dothe the difeafe of a Canker.

Herefie fur
der yt goeth
the woorfe
yt ys.
2. Tim. 2.

For the Petrobrufians being badde enough, yet they vpon the confideracion of Chryftes prefence in the laft Supper , graunted that he then made hys bodie, and that the Apoftles receaued his bodie. But neuer after was yt geuen to anie.

This was a verie euell cankre , but yt hath encreafed fince to fo moche vngodlineffe, and hath Cankrelike fretted fo fore , that nowe in our time men haue denied the bodie of Chryft to be confecrated and geuen , either by the preiftes or miniftres of the churche, or yet by Chryft him felf in the laft Supper. For he gaue (faie they) but the figure of hys bodie to hys Apoftles, as the miniftres doo nowe to the people.

But as Chryfoftome in hys fentence hath aunfwered the *Petrobrufians*: So hath he alfo aunfwered the *Oecolampadians, Caluiniftes* , and the reft of the vypers that brake oute of Luthers beallie (of the which *generacion this chalenger*

A　ys one)who like vipers in dede,whiche gnawe and frette their dames beallie to come from her,euen fo thefe impugning the doctrine of therFather,haue endeuoured , to deftroye bothe him and his doctrin to be ridde therof. *Qui verò hæc fanctificat & tranfmutat ipfe eft.Yt ys euen he(faieth Chryfoftom mee ning Chryft)that dothe fanctifie and tranfmute thefe thinges?*

chryft doth fanctifie ãd tranfmute the bread and wine.

Owre herefiarke of Englande,Cranmer faieth in his booke,that the creatures of bread and wine can not be fanctified.But by Chryfoftomes fentence they be fanctified in to fome other thing.Which ys fo in dede , and therfore he addeth,*& tranfmutat,and dothe tranfmute or chaunge them.* For Chryfte fanctifieng dothe chaunge the fubftance of the creatures of bread and wyne, into the fubftance of his bodie and blóode.

Tranfub-ftanciaciõ auouched.

For (as Origen faieth) the bread ys made in to an holier bodie . *Nos conditori rerum morem gerentes,pro eius in nos collatis beneficijs vbi & gratias diximus oblatis panibus vefcimur,qui vtique ex oratione & precibus in fanctius quoddam corpus conflantur, quod fanè fanctiores hos reddit , qui mente integriore hoc ipfo vtuntur .* We
B obeing (faieth Origen) the creatour of thinges, when we for the benefittes whiche he hath geuen vs,haue geuen him thankes,we eate the breades that be offred,whiche *by oracion and praiers,are made into a certain holier bodie,which maketh them holier,which with an wholl minde doo vfe the fame.*Thus Origen.

Orig.cont. Celf.li. 8. The bread ys turned into an holier bodie.

Do ye not heare that the breades that be offred be made into a certain holier bodie?And what a bodie ys yt?Soche a bodie as maketh thofe holier, whiche receaue yt withe a pure and godlie minde . What bodie ys yt , that we receaue hauing power to make vs holier,but the holie bodie of him,who ys owre fanctificacion,iuftificacion,and redemption?

Nowe here ys no place for the Aduerfaries comon glofe, to faie, that we receaue the bodie of Chryft fpiritually,whiche maketh vs holier that receaue yt,and therby to feclude the receauing of Chryftes bodie reallie .For he faieth that the breades,whiche be offred,be made into an holier bodie.And that bodie that ys made of the bread(I vfe fainte Ambrofe hys phrafe, *De pane fit corpus Chrifti*)maketh them holier,whiche receaue yt with a good and godly minde . Whiche bodie being foche that the bread ys turned
C or made into yt , muft nedes be the reall and fubftanciall bodie of Chryft.

Li.4 .de Sacramentis.

Vnderftande me not here , that I reiecte the fpirituall receauing of Chryft in the Sacrament . But I wifhe bothe the receauinges to go together . For as the receauing of Chryft reallie profiteth not withoute the receauing of him fpirituallie : So he can not receaue him fpirituallie, that beleueth not him to be receaued reallie . And therfor when oportunitie ferueth,as I wifhe bothe the receauinges to go together , fo muft they in dede go together, yfthe receauer will take and haue anie profitte therbie.

He can not receaue Chryft fpirituallie, whiche beleueth not that he receaueth him reallie

Albeit thefe might fuffice,that be hertofore alleaged to teftifie vnto vs, what ys the enacted and receaued trueth of Chryftes Parliament houfe as concerning the preifthead and facrifice of Chryft after the ordre of Melchifedech:yet that S.Auguftine maie haue one of the other fide of the houfe, that ys of the greke churche,ioined with him,I will bring yowe Damafcen,
D who in fewe woordes faieth thus:*Pane & vino fufcepit Melchifedech Abrahã ex cæde alienigenarum reuertentẽ,qui erat facerdos Dei altifsimi . Illa menfa hanc myfticam præfigurabat menfam,veluti & facerdos ille Chrifti veri facerdotis figurã præferebat,& imaginẽ.Tu es(inquit)facerdos in æternũ fecundùm ordinẽ Melchifedech.*With bread and wine did Melchifedech receaue Abraham returning from the flaughter of

Li.4.de de thod.fide. Melchifedech ãd his facrifice a figure of Chryft ãd his facrifice

the ſtraungers. That table did preſigurate this myſticall table, as alſo that E
preiſt did bear the figure and image of Chryſt the verie preiſt. Thowe arte
(ſaieth he) a preiſt for euer after the order of Melchiſedech. Thus Damaſcen.

*Table ſigni-
fieth ſacriſi-
ce as in S.
Paule.
1.Cor. 10.*
In whiche ſentence ye ſee the compariſon & applicacion of table to table,
of preiſt to preiſt, Damaſcen teaching the one to be figure of the other.
Wher I wolde that the Aduerſarie did note that the table of Melchiſedech, whiche all men of learning doo knowe, ys taken for the ſacrifice,
as in ſainct Paule, *ye can not be partakers of the table of God, and the table of Deuells alſo.* In whiche ſaing what ells ment ſainct Paule, but that the Corinthians coulde not be partakers of that, that was offred to God in ſacrifice,
and of that, that was offred in ſacrifice to Deuells alſo? The table of Melchiſedech (I ſaie) whiche ys the ſacrifice of Melchiſedech, did preſigurate the
table, that ys, the ſacrifice of Chryſte. *The ſacrifice (I ſaie) which he offred after the
ordre of Melchiſedech.*

Nowe ſee (o thowe Aduerſarie) the concorde and plain teſtimonie of the- F
ſe right auncient elders, and famouſe learned Fathers of Chryſtes Parliament houſe, howe all they, with one mouth as yt were, haue reported, what
was the receaued trueth in the houſe of Chryſt in their tymes, which tymes
were the times of pure and ſincere knowledge in this matter, a time whē ther
was no hereſie nor controuerſie to moue thē to writte of yt, but quietly and
godlie for the inſtruction of Gods people in the trueth of his faithe, and to
leaue certain both monumentes and munimentes of the ſame to the poſteritie, they haue expreſſed their faithe in this and other diuerſe matters. And
not onelie their priuate faith, but the vniuerſall faith of Chryſtes catholique
Churche. And left the ſame in writing for the ſtaie and confirmacion of
them that remain in the faithe and for the calling home again of them that
haue erred.

Therfore wher thowe erring from the true faith, haueſt taught that Melchiſedech did not offer bread and wine in ſacrifice, beholde that theſe Fathers by expreſſe woordes auouche the contrarie. Wher thowe haueſt alſo
defended, that Melchiſedech was not a figure of Chryſte as concerning hys
ſacrifice, ſee howe conſtantlie and vniformlie thowe arte impugned, all theſe G
teaching, that the ſacrifice of Melchiſedech, was a figure of Chryſtes ſacrifice, offred and doen by Chryſte after the ſame ordre. And what that ſacrifice
ys, they haue not left vndeclared, but by plain woordes they haue taught
that yt ys the bodie and blood of Chryſte, whiche bodie and blood of
Chryſte being offred in ſacrifice after the ordre of Melchiſedech (as by them
alſo yt ys affirmed) doth inuinciblie proue the verie reall preſence of Chry-
*Aug. cōt.
Iudæos.
The preiſt
head of
Chryſt ſhal
not be chaū-
ged.*
ſtes bleſſed bodie in the Sacrament, whiche dailie ys offred after the ordre
of Melchiſedech, and ſhall be to the woorldes ende. *Iurauit Dominus, & non pœ
nitebit eum.* Oure Lord hath ſworn, and yt ſhall not repent him. *Quid eſt* (inquit
*Auguſtinus) iurauit Dominus, niſi inconcuſſa veritate firmauit? Et quid eſt non pœnite-
bit eum, niſi hoc ſacerdotium nulla ratione mutabitur?* What ys yt (ſaieth ſainct Auguſtin) that our Lorde hath Sworne, but that with a moſt certen
trueth he hath made yt ſure? And what ys that: *Yt ſhall not repent him, but
that this Preiſthead by no meanes ſhall be chaunged?* Yf then (as ſainct Auguſtin ſaieth) this preiſthead ſhall not be chaunged, howe ſhall yt be H
continued?

Theophilacte one as yt were of the other ſide of Chryſtes parliament
houſe

A   houſe,being one of the greke Churche,ioineth with ſaincte Auguſtine and teacheth howe, expownding to the Hebrues theſe woordes: Thow arte a preiſt for euer, &c. *In æternum dicit, quia quotidiè offertur, vel in perpetuum offertur per Dei miniſtros oblatio, Chriſtum Dominum & Pontificem habens & ſa-crificium, qui ſeipſum noſtri ob gratiam ſanctificat, frangit, & tribuit*. He ſaieth for euer : *bycauſe he ys dailie offred*, or bycauſe by the miniſtres of God, ys for euer or continuallie offred the oblation *hauing Chryſt our lorde, being bothe the high preiſt, and the ſacrifice*, who doth for our ſake continuallie ſanctifie, breake,and geue him ſelf.

Theophila. in Epiſtola ad Hebr. Chryſt ys dailie offe- red by his miniſters and ſhall be ſo conti- nued for euer.

    Ceaſſe therfor to reuile and blaſpheme this bleſſed myſterie.For heauen and earth ſhall paſſe awaie, but the woorde of God abydeth for euer. Whi-che woorde of God ſaieth that this preiſthead and ſacrifice ſhall continue for euer. And therfore though yowe barke againſt yt, as do the dogges againſt the moone:Yet as the moone notwithſtanding abideth in her heaue, and goeth her courſe, and ſhall continewe : So ſhall this bleſſed myſterie

B   abide in his ſtate,and ſhall go forwarde and cōtinewe vntil the worlde ende, what ſo euer ye ſaie or doo,yt ſhall not be impared . But ye ſhall for your abominable doing,be not a litle decaied and afflicted.

    I wolde bring certain of the lower houſe (I meen of them that were after ſixe hondreth yeares after Chryſte) to geue their teſtimonie in this matter, but that yt wolde make this rude worke growe to a greatter volume, then I wolde wiſhe. Therfor for this place I will omitte them, and ende this matter of the prophecie of Chryſtes preiſtheade after the ordre of Mel-chiſedech, whiche hathe aunſwered the figure that did preſigurate the ſame . And proccade to ſpeake of the prophecie that aunſwereth the next figure.

THE TWO AND THIRTITH CHAPITER TO

proue the ſacrifice of our Shewe bread to be a continuall ſacrifice,as the olde shewe bread was,alleageth the prophecie of Daniel and reiecteth the falſe expoſitions of the Aduerſaries.

C

He figure that folowed next after the figure of Melchiſedech, was the figure of the Paſchall lambe, the accompliſſing of the whiche was doen(as yt was declared) in the laſt Supper, the which laſt Supper being doen after the ordre of Melchiſedech, the prophecie, that aunſwered the figure therto apperteining, aunſwereth alſo the figure of the Paſchall Lambe, forſomoche as the bodie of Chryſte ſacrificed after the ordre of Melchiſedech,and eaten in that Sup per,aunſwereth alſo the eating of the Paſchall Lambe in the olde teſtament, and ys our verie Paſchall Lambe in the newe Teſtament.

    And therfore being lothe to trooble the Reader,with the reading of that, of the which moche ys allreadie ſpoken, and (as I truſt) ſufficiently bothe in the handling of the figure of the Paſchall Lambe, and alſo of the ſacri-fice of Chryſt after the ordre of Melchiſedech : Therfor I ſhall go to the next figure,which ys the Shewe bread, and therunto applie ſoche prophe-

D   cies,as ſeme to aunſwere the ſame,ād maie wel be ioined to yt,as I haue doē in the ſetting furth of the preiſthead of Chryſte,after the ordre of Melchiſe-dech,with the prophecies therto apperteining.

    The Shew bread(if ye remembre what ys before ſaied) was a bread, that was both offred in facrifice, and eaten, but fo that none might eate of yt, but the preiftes, and foche as were clean, as by the ftorie of Dauid and Abime-lech yt did appeare. Whiche bread was not feldom offred, but as fooen as the olde was taken awaie, newe were offred, and putte in their place, fo that the table might not be withoute fhew bread : but yt was allwaies referued, and their remained. Nowe as the referuacion of that bread, was a figure of the referuacion of our bleffed bread (as ther yt was declared) So that bread being offred in facrifice, was a figure of our bread offred in facrifice. And as that bread was appointed to be a perpetuall facrifice, allwaies to continewe : So this facrifice ys appointed to be perpetuall, and to côtinewe vntill Chryftes côminge. Of the whiche Sacrifice, and of the continuance of yt, not onelie the Prophet Daniell, but alfo the Prophet Malachie hath prophecied.

Daniell (as the holie Fathers do expownde) fpeaking of the wickedneffe of the time of Antichrifte, amonge other euells that then fhall be wrought, he faied that the dailie facrifice fhall be taken awaie. At whiche time what dailie facrifice fhall ther be to be taken awai. but the facrifice of the chryftians?

For (as Petrus *Cluniacenfis* faieth) ther be in the worlde foure principall feétes: that ys, of the Iewes, the Sarazens, the paganes, and the Chryftians. The Iewes perfeuering in the carnall obferuacion of their carnall lawe, for fomoch as yt ys emong them receaued that onely in Hierufalem they muft honour God, do facrifice ther, and no wher ells. And nowe for fomoche as they are difperfed among nacions, and had no temple this fiften hondreth years, and for that God hathe not, fence the deuaftacion and fubuerfion of Hierufalem, fuffred them yett ther to dwell, therfor they vfe no facrifice. wherin alfo ys fullfilled the prophecie of Daniel, whiche faieth, that after a certain time after Chryfté ys flain, facrifice and meate offring fhall ceaffe amonge the Iewes. And what foeuer was after doen in the temple (as fainét Hierom faieth) *Non fuit facrificium Dei, fed cultus Diaboli.* yt was not the facrifice of God, but the woourfhipping of the Deuell. And this defolacion (faieth Daniell) fhall continewe to the ende. Wherby ys ment, that the abolifhing of the facrifice of the Iewes, ys perpetuall and for euer.

The *Sarazens* being deluded by the fhamefull impofture and deceipt of Mahomete, haue a certain mingled religion, vfing circumcifion, and certain lotions of the Iewes. And fo vfe a parte of Moifes lawe. They alfo confeffe that Chryft was born of a virgen, and that he liued holilie, and preached truely, and wrought manie miracles : But externall and fpeciall facrifice, wherbie their religion fhoulde be difcerned from other, they vfe none, but that certain howres on the night, and certain howres on the daie, they geue them felues to praier, and fpeciallie after meate.

The Pagans being a rude, groffe, and barbaroufe people, almoft vnkno-wen to the worlde, and neither knowing God, neither almoft theim felfes, dwelling farre of in the furtheft parte of the northe, and not knowing the names of the Idolls of other Idolaters, nor religion, what thing fo euer they firft mete in the morning, be yt horfe, hogge, Cowe, or calf, that fame for that daie doo they take, and honour for their God. So that they haue not *Deos perpetuos,* but *Deos Diarios vel horarios.* Gods for euer continuall, but daie Gods, and howre Gods, vnto whom yet they do no facrifice, but according to their ignoraunt educacion they liue withoute the knowledg of doing facrifice.

The

1 Reg. 21.
Shewe bread conti nuallie vpô the table of the Ta-bernacle applied to the Sacra-ment.

Petrus Cluniacen. côtra Pe-trobr.
Foure prin cipall feétes of religion in the worlde.

Daniel. 9.

Hieron in Daniel. cap. 9.

Pagans haue daie Gods, and howre Gods, and no certen God.

A　　The chriftians being called to the knowledg of the true liuing God, and of his fonne Iefus Chryfte, inftructed in his lawes, and taught the true maner of honouring and feruing him:knowe that all that haue ferued God frō the beginnig, haue not onelie ferued him with the facrifices of lawdes, praifes, praiers and obedience, whiche be thinges comon: but haue vfed alfo this fpeciall fign of feruice, as to offer fome extern facrifice to teftifie their duetie and right propre feruice to God. Whiche maner of feruice I call propre, for that yt can be don to none, but to God, or to fome thing taken for god.

Call to minde all the Fathers in the beginning, the Patriarkes, the Prophetes, and all other holie men knowing God, and ye fhall perceaue that all they befides lawdes, praifes praiers and other, did alfo teftifie their feruice to God, by their externall facrificing of fome of the fruictes of the earth. So did Abel,fo did Noe, fo did Iob, Abrahā, Ifaac,and Iacob, and manie other, as the bookes of the olde Teftament do teftifie.

B　　And Chryft him felf did not onelie offer his bleffed bodie a bloodie Sacrifice vpon the Croffe to God his Father,which all that do but taft the name of the religion of Chryft doo confeffe : But he alfo as the authour of the newe Teftament did firft offer to God his hodie and blood an vnbloodie facrifice in his laft fupper after the ordre of Melchifedech, ther and then inftituting the fame facrifice, and commaunding yt to be doen and continued in his Church,as yt ys allreadie proued.And fo(as *Irenæus* faieth)he taught the newe oblacion of the newe Teftament..
Chryft offred facrifice in his fupper,and comaūded yt to be cōtinued.

Nowe then feing that no fect in the worlde vfeth anie dailie facrifice, but we Chryftians: Yf we alfo had no dailie facrifice (as the enemies of Cod haue traueiled to compaffe) howe then fhoulde the prophecie of Daniel be fullfilled, that the dailie facrifice fhall be taken awaie ? yf ther be none, none can be takē awaie. But the Prophet faieth,that one fhall be takē awaie. wherfor ther muft nedes be a dailie facrifice,whiche for the fullfilling of the prophecie, muft be taken awaie.

Of this prophecie ys fainct Hierom an expowivder, who being more bu-
C　fied to refell the wicked expofitions of *Prophyrius*, and breiflie to open the true vnderftanding of the Prophete, then at large to fett furthe owre mifteries in plain woordes, faieth yet that, that ys fufficient to fatiffie anie man that ys not contencioufe, that this prophecie ys to be vnderftanded of the dailie facrifice of the chriftians, although not in fo expreffe woordes, as this time of controuerfie in this matter wolde require. Thus ys the text of the Prophecie · *Et à tempore quo ablatum fuerit iuge facrificium, & pofita fuerit abominatio in defolationem, dies mille ducenti nonaginta.* And from the time that the dailie or continuall Sacrifice fhall be taken awaie or put down, and the abominable defolacion fett vppe, ther fhall be a thoufande daies two hundreth and nintie.
Daniel 12.

Vpon this texte Hierom faieth thus: *Hos mille ducentos nonaginta dies Prophyrius in tempore Antiochi & in defolatione templi, dicit completos, quam & Iofephus,& Machabæorum (vt diximus) liber tribus tantùm annis fuiffe commemorant. Ex quo perfpicuum eft tres iftos & femis annos de Antichrifti dici temporibus, qui tribus & femis annis, hoc eft mille ducentis nonaginta diebus fanctos perfecuturus eft, et poftea corruiturus*
D　*in monte inclyto et fanclo.A tempore igitur quod nos interpretati fumus iuge Sacrificium, quando Antichriftus orbem obtinens, Dei cultum interdixerit, vfque ad internitionem eius tres et femis anni, id eft, mille ducenti nonaginta dies complebuntur.* Thefe thoufande two hundreth and ninetie daies, *Porphyrius* faieth, they were fullfilled in the
Hieron in Danielem.

time of *Antiochus*, and in the defolation of the temple, whiche bothe *Iofephus*, **E**
and the booke of the Machabees (as we haue faid) doo teftifie to be don in
three years onelie, Wherbie yt ys plain, thefe three yeares and a half to be
fpoken of the times of Antichryfte, who by the fpace of three years and a
half, that ys, a thoufande two hundreth and ninetie daies, fhall perfecute the
holie and faithfull chryftians, and after fhall fall downe in the famoufe and
holie hill. From the time therfore that we haue interpreted the dailie facrifice, when Antichryfte fhall for bidde the feruice of God, vnto his deftructiõ
ther fhall be fullfilled three years and a half, that ys to faie, a thoufand two
hundreth and ninetie daies. Thus moche S. Hierom.

Antichryft shall caufe the dailie facrifice to ceaffe.

Who yf we marke, interpreteth the greke woorde, and calleth yt *the dailie
facrifice*, and therwith remember that (as before by him ys faied in the expofition of the prophecie of the preifthead of Chryft after the ordre of Melchifedech) Chryft our Melchifedech offred his bodie and bloode, the verie
true bread, and true wine, and deliuered vnto vs thefe mifteries that we haue to vfe in the remembrance of him vntill he come to iudgement. Wherto **F**
yf we adde the expofition of this prophecie of *Daniel* that in the time of Antichrift the feruice of God fhall be byhim forbodden, what fhall we ells vnderftand by the dailie facrifice, but the facrifice of our Melchifedech, left with
vs to be vfed as our moft high feruice to God.

The dailie facrifice ys the facrifice of the bodie and blood of Chryft.

Which thing *Lyra* by verie plain woordes dothe declare expownding this
text of Daniell thus : *Hic Angelus inftruit Danielem de termino à quo incipiendi funt
prædicti tres anni cum dimidio, dicens : A tempore cùm ablatum fuerit iuge facrificium, id
eft, à tempore quo facrificium altaris ceffabit celebrari folemniter.* Here the Angell
teacheth Daniell the tyme from the whiche the three years and a half fhall
beginne, faing: from the time when the dailie Sacrifice fhall be taken awaie,
that ys, from the time in the whiche the facrifice of the Altar fhall ceaffe fo-
lemnelie to be celebrated, Thus *Lyra*.

As by the expofition of thefe Fathers yt doth appeare that the dailie Sacrifice ys the facrifice of the Altar, the Sacrifice of Chryftes bodie and
bloode, So herunto reafon alfo agreeth, and by yt we are alfo forced thus **G**
to vnderftand the prophete. For he can not be vnderftanded of the facrifice
of lawde, and praife, of the which S. Paule fpeaketh, *Per ipfum offeramus hoftiã
laudis femper Deo, id eft, fructum labiorum confitentium nomini eius.* By him (mening
Chryft) let vs offer facrifice of lawde allwais to God, that ys to faie, the
fruicte of our lippes confeffing his name. Of the whiche facrifice the prophet Dauid fpeaketh, faing · *Immola Deo facrificium laudis.* Ofer vppe vnto **God**
the facrifice of lawde.

Hebr. 13.

Pfal. 49.

Neither can yt be vnderftande of the facrifice of the mortificacion or affliction of our bodies, to the whiche S. Paule exhorteth vs, faing: *Obfecro
vos per mifericordiam Dei, vt exhibeatis corpora veftra hoftiam viuentem, fanctam, Deo
placentem.* I befech yowe by the mercie of God, that ye geue vppe your bodies as a liuelie and holie facrifice vnto God, and pleafing to him,

Neither can yt be vnderftanded of the facrifice of a contrite hearte, of the
whiche Dauid fpeaketh : *Sacrificium Deo fpiritus contribulatus*, A troobled fpirit
ys a facrifice vnto God. For all theife facrifices fhall be in vfe in the time of
Antichrift euen in the heat of his perfecution. For the Angell faied : *Eli-
gentur, & dealbabuntur, & quafi ignis probabuntur multi*. Many fhall be chofen, **H**
and purified, and fhall be tried as yt were fire. In foche men ther ys no
doubte but they will continuallie withe their humble praiers praife God,
and confeffing his faith, magnifie his holie name, and fo offer vnto God
the

Pfal. 50.

Daniel. 12

A the facrifice of lawde and praife as the fruictes of their lippes. They will alfo not onely mortifie and crucifie their bodies with all the luftes and concupifcence : but they will alfo at that time geue vppe their bodies to fuffer tormentes, yea and very deathe for the name of Chryft, and fo offer them as pleafaunt facrifices vnto God. Other fome ther fhall be, whiche feing the heauie, great, and violent perfecucion that fhall be vfed by Antichryft, and his miniftres will with Daniell confeffe their finnes, and the finnes of the people, and humbly with Dauid faie : *Peccauimus cum patribus noſtris, iniuſtè egimus, iniquitatem fecimus.* We haue finned with our Fathers, we haue don vniuftlie, we haue committed iniquitie.

Pfal. 105.

Seing then that Antichrift neither fhall nor can put downe or take awaie thefe facrifices, but that they fhall be vfed vnder his fwoorde, and in the middeft of his flammes and other tormentes : yt ys moft euident, that none of thefe be that dailie facrifice, that fhall be put downe. For thefe facrifices fhall be openly offred, and that dailie.

B Yt remaineth then that of neceffitie this prophecie muft be vnderftande of the dailie facrifice of the bodie and blood of Chryfte, whiche although fome godlie difpofed people maie percafe fecretlie vfe (as *Lyra* faieth) vt fhal for three years and a half ceaffe openly and folemnely to be celebrated.

Antichriſt
shall put
down the
daily ſacri-
fice of the
Altar.

And further of congruence yt maie be reafoned, yf the Fathers that haue ben in all ages before Chryfte, did knowe that yt was a thing acceptable and pleafing to God to offer extern facrifice to him : fhoulde not the Chryftiã know more, who liueth in the clear light, wher they liued in the fhaddowe? Yf thofe facrifices were a fwete fauour to God (as no doubte but they were fo for his fake whom they figured) howe moche fweter then ys our facrifice vnto him, offringe (as we do) Chryft him felf in facrifice ? Yf they gaue to God not onely the facrifices of lawdes and thankes, but alfo an extern facrifice of thankes, as yt were of an higher thanke for foche befittes as they receaued : fhall not the chryftian, who hathe receaued greater benefittes, incomparablie paffing thers, geue at the leeft as great thankes as they? Yf we fhall offre no other facrifice, then the facrifice of praife and thankes

C geuing and fochelike, the fathers did fo as well as we, and ouer and befides that they offred an extern facrifice of thãkes : What ingratitude maie yt well be thought then, that we receauing manie mo benefittes then they, fhoulde geue fewer thankes then they? Yt ys an euell proporcion, the mo and greater benefittes, the fewer and leffe thankes : the fewer and fmaller benefittes, the mo and greater thankes.

O lorde what obcecate, and blinde enemies of God were thefe, that coulde not fee thefe thinges, but wolde that we Chryftians hauing clerer knowledge then other, fhoulde leffe do their duetie then other, and receauing mo benefittes, fhoulde be leffe thankfull? And thus God fhoulde be robbed of his honoure, and the Chryftians withdrawed from doing of ther dueferuices. And then wolde yt fhortly come to vs, as yt came to them, who knowing God, haue not glorified him as God, neither were thankfull, but waxed full of vanities in their ymaginacions, and their foolifh hearte was blinded, when they cownted them felues wife, they became fooles.

Chryſtians
uſing no ex
ternal ſacri
fice are leſ-
ſe thãkfull
then the Fa
thers of the
lawe.

D

THE

THE THREE AND THIRTITH CHAP. OPENETH E
the prophecie of Malachie.

Ot onely the Prophete Daniel (as before ys faied) doth prophecie that ther fhall be a facrifice : but alfo Malachie, who plainlie declareth the reiecting of the facrifice of the Iewes, and the placing of a common vfed facrifice : *Non eft mihi voluntas in vobis, dicit Dominus exercituum, & munus non fufcipiam de manu veftra. Ab ortu enim folis vfque ad occafum magnum eft nomen meum in gentibus, & in omni loco facrificatur, & offertur nomini meo oblatio munda, quia magnum eft nomen meum in gentibus, dicit Dominus exercituum.* I haue no pleafure in yowe, faieth the Lorde of hoftes, And as for meat offring, I will not accept yt as your handes. For from the rifing vppe of the funne vnto the going downe of the fame, my name ys great emong the gentiles. yea in euery place fhall ther be facrifice doen, and a clean meat offring offred vppe vnto my name. For my name ys great among the Gentiles, faeth the Lorde of hoftes.

Malac.1

This prophecie hath moche tormented the Aduerfaries, and therfore all F their ingines, hookes, and all their fetches haue be fett vpon this place to drawe yt to their fenfe and pourpofe, but yt will not be, all will not ferue that they can doo. for trueth will fhewe yt felf, and preuaill. This prophecie in dede inuinciblie proueth the Sacrifice of Chryftes Churche, as hereafter fhall be fhewed. But firft let vs fee, howe the Aduerfaries wolde wreft this place, and let vs make yt plain to the reader, that the fence whiche they wolde haue the fcripture vnderftanded in, ys not the right and full fence, but a diftorted fence, a wrong fenfe, and foche a fenfe, as the place can not beare, a fenfe difagreing from the expofitions of all the holie Fathers bothe of the latin churche, and of the greke churche.

Proteftantes tormented with the prophecie of Malac. howe they wreft yt.

Oecolampadius in a booke that he did write of the Maffe vnto the Senate of Bafille, faieth that by this prophecie of the Prophet Malachie, was Prophecied, that the miniftres of the newe teftament fhoulde make a faithfull people oute of all nacions, as a pure and an holie oblacion and facrifice to God. And this (faieth he) ys the minde of the Prophet.

Oecolamp.

Martin Bucer not moche differing from him, in his aunfwer that he made G to *Latomus*, faieth that hy this Prophecie ys cheiflie promifed the preaching of the Gofpell, by the whiche God fhall be euery whear acknowleged, and the fruicte alfo of the fame preaching, that ys faithe, and the confeffing of the fame faithe. And he faieth alfo that by the incenfe and oblacion are to be vnderftanded the facrifices of chryften men, whiche be (faieth he) the praifing and calling on the name of God, wherunto ys allwaies annexed the geuing vppe of our felues to the will of God, and the declaracion of our thakefull minde towardes God, by the doing, and fhewing of loue and mercie to the poore. And thus dothe he expownde the Prophete.

Bucer.

Bullinger an other of the fame fecte aud forte, faieth that the lawde and prayfe of God his name ys the pure facrifice that the Prophete fpeaketh of.

Bullinger.
Urbanus Rhegius.

But *Vrbanus Rhegius* writing againft *Eckius* his mafter in his firftbooke faieth thus: The facrifice that Malachias prophecied of, ys the mortificacion of the flefh, and the calling on the name of God, with godlie prayer. And this was his phantafie, whiche fo I terme as I might the reft, for that eche of thē H hath vnderftanded the prophecie as him lifteth, and not as the full mening of the fame hathe required. And although other haue vttered their conceptes and coniecturs vpon this prophecie : Yet thefe being the ftandarde

bearers

A bearers of that wicked armie, that hath so malicioußie fowght againft Gods truthe,maie fuffice to be reherfed for this time, prefuppofing that the reft do folowe their ftanderd bearers.

But let vs nowe examin, and weigh their expofitions. Yf ye marke they do all agree in this, that this prophecie ys to be vnderftanded of the facrifice of praife and thanks geuing, which thei call the pure facrifice. Yt ys to be confidered here that Allmightie God by his Prophet declaring, that the facrifice of the Iewes, which was onelie doen in Hierufalem fhoulde be reiected, abolifhed,and lefte, fignified alfo, that an other facrifice fhoulde be fubftituted in the place of the fame, whiche fhoulde be a pure and clean facrifice, whiche fhoulde not be doen onlie in Hierufalem, as the other was, But in euery place.

Nowe as for the facrifice of a contrite heart, of lawde, praife, and thankes geuing, who doubteh but that they were vfed and offred of diuerfe holie *Pfal.50.* and vertuoufe men in the olde lawe, and well accepted? whiche thing Da-

B uid was not ignorant of, when he faied : *Sacrificium Deo fpiritus contribulatus,* *Pfalm.49.* *cor contritum & humiliatum, Deus,non defpicies.* A troobled fpirit ys a facrifice to God, a contrite and humble heart(o God) fhalt thowe not defpice. Of the facrifice of lawde Dauid alfo fpeaketh *Immola Deo facrificium laudis.* Offer to God the facrifie of lawde &c. praife . And in the fame Pfalm : *Sacrificium laudis honorificabit me.* Who fo offreth me thankes and praife,he honoureth me. *The hereticall expofitions of the prophecie of Malachie can not ftand.*

Therfore wher the Aduerfarie wolde,that thefe kinde of Sacrifices fhoulde be they,of the whiche the prophet Malachie fpake, that fhoulde come into the place of the facrifice of the Iewes, whiche God wolde abolifhe, their expofition can not ftande. For thefe can not nowe be placed as newe facrifices, whiche were placed and vfed from the beginning of the firft good man, that offred facrifice to God, Abel, who withe the facrifice of the fruictes of the earth,whiche he offred, offred alfo praife and thankes geuing to God, Thefe facrifices then be not newe placed,but being of olde time vfed, God wolde haue them fo continued.

Neither doo I meen that thefe be feparated from that facrifice, that God
C wolde place in ftead of the facrifice of the Iewes . For their ys no extern facrifice but yf yt be rightlie, and duely offred, yt bringeth with yt the facrifice of lawde and praife, and of other alfo. But that the Prophet dothe meen of thefe onelie, and not raither of fome extern facrifice to be vfed, offred, and frequented among the Chryftians : and that he ment not cheiflie and principallie of an extern facrifice , to be placed in the place of the Iewes extern facrifices, that ys moft vntrue . And that maie be perceaued by the difference of the newe facrifice from the olde. What ys that ? That yt fhall be a pure facrifice. *Sacrifice of laude feparated from the extern facrifice.*

Why, were not theirs pure facrifices before in the olde lawe ? Was ther not a facrifice of expiacion, and a daie of expiacion affigned , in the whiche the clenfing facrifice fhoulde be offred? Read the xvi chapter of *Leuiticus,*and *Leuit.16.* ther fhall ye finde that Allmightie God faeth thus : *In hac die expiatio veftri erit atque mundatio. ab omnibus peccatis veftris coram Domino mundabimini.* In this daie fhall be your expiacion and cléfing, and ye fhall be made clean from all your finnes before the Lorde.

D Was not this then a pure facrifice, that purified, and clenfed the people from all their finnes before God? Ys yt not a pure facrifice that ys a fwete fauoure to God? were not the facrifices of the olde lawe foche ? Doth not Moifes from Gods mouth fo terme them ? Yt can not be denied but the

scripture

scripture doth so call them. But as Chryste saieth, *Nemo bonus, nisi solus Deus.* **E**
Ther ys no man good but God alone. And yet again he saieth : *Bonus homo*

Luc. 18.
Matth. 12
God good
by nature
man by par
ticipacion.

de bono thesauro profert bona . The good Man oute of good treasure brin
geth furth good thinges : So though God alone of him self, and of his
diuine nature be onlie good : yet men be good also, not of them selues, nor
of their owne natures, but by participacion of the goonesse of God. So ther
ys one sacrifice whiche onely ys pure, for that yt ys pure of yt self, whiche
sacrifice ys the bodie and bloode of our Sauiour Iesus Chryst. Other sacrifices that be called pure and clensing sacrifices, they be so called by participacion, that they doo please God, and purifie men by the vertue and merite,
of that pure Sacrifice Iesus Chryst, who ys the lambe, that was slain from the

Apoc 13.

beginning of the worlde, geuing vertue to all sacrifices that were yet offred
from the beginninge of the worlde. And therfore when the Prophett putteth this difference to this sacrifice, that shall succead the sacrifices of the Iewes, that yt shall be a pure sacrifice : Yf yt were pure but by vertue of other,
as the sacrifices of the Iewes were, then were this woorde, pure, no woorde **F**
of difference, but raither a superfluouse woorde making no distinction betwen the two sortes of sacrifices. But for so moche as the Prophet hath put
yt as a difference, seing the other were pure by vertue of other, this must nedes be the sacrifice, that ys pure of yt self, whiche (as ys before said) ys the
bodie and bloode of Chryst.

Neither maie this nowe be drawen to that most blessed Sacrifice of the
bodie and blood of Chryst vpon the Crosse. For that Sacrifice in that maner
was offred in one place onelie, that was, vpon the mounte Caluarie : But this
Sacrifice (saieth God by the Prophet) ys offred in euery place. Wherfore of

Sacrifice of
the crosse
and of the
altar, al one
in substäce,
but diuerse
in maner.

necessitie this must be vnderstanded of the pure Sacrifice of Chrystes bodie
and blood offred on the Altar, which ys offred, not in Hierusalem, not on
Caluery, but in euery place, where Chryst ys knowë and receaued. Whiche
sacrifice although in maner of offring, yt differeth from that offred vpon the
Crosse : yet in substance yt ys all one.

Nowe ye maie perceaue, that the expositions of the städerd bearers of the **G**
wicked armie of the enemies of gods trueth, ys but a violët or a wrested exposition, and will not be born of the text.

THE FOVRE AND THIRTITH CHAP. EXPO-
wndeth the Prophecie of Malachie by Martialis, and Irenæus.

Hat the Aduersaries shall not saie that I am iudge in mine
owne cause, although I am certen that I builde vpon the rocke:
Yet to the better contentacion of the Reader, and more manifest confutacion of these Aduersaries, I will reporte the Iugement of the right auncient Elders of Chrystes Parliamët house,
as touching the enacted trueth of this matter by their owne woordes.

Sanctus Martialis a great auncient in Chrystes house as being one of Chry
stes disciples, and after the death of his and our master almost continuallie in
the Companie of the Apostle Peter, ys a notable wittnesse of this trueth,
and wourthie to be credited. This holie man maketh mencio of this prophe-

S. Martia-
lis Martyr
epist. ad
Burdegalë.
cap. 3.

cie of Malachie after this maner. **H**

Sacrificium Deo creatori offertur in ara, non homini, neque Angelo . Nec solùm in ara
sanctificata, sed vbique offertur Deo oblatio munda, sicut testatus est, cuius corpus &
sanguinem in vitam æternam offerimus, dicentes: Spiritus est Deus, & eos qui adorant eü,

in

A   *in ſpiritu & veritate oportet adorare.Ipſe enim corpus habens immaculatum,& ſine pec cato (quia conceptus eſt de Spiritu ſanĉto,natus ex Maria virgine)ipſum in ara crucis per miſit immolari. Quod autem Iudæi per inuidiam immolauerunt, putantes ſe nomen eius à terra abolere, nos cauſa ſalutis noſtræ in ara ſanĉtificata proponimus,ſcientes hoc ſolo remedio nobis vitam præſtandam, & mortem effugandam.* The ſacrifice ys offred vnto God our creatour on the altar , not vnto men , nor vnto Angell,nor onelie on halowed altar , *but euery wher yſ offred to God a pure ob lacion* , as he hath wittneſſed , *whoſe bodie and blood we offer to euerlaſting life,* ſainge:God ys a ſpirit, and they that adore him ,muſt adore him in ſpiritte and trueth.For he hauing an immaculate bodie,and withoute Sinne(for he was conceaued by the holie Goſt, born of the virgen Mary) he ſuffred that ſame bodie to be ſacrificed on the altar of the Croſſe. And that, that the Iewes did ſacrifice by enuie, thinking to abolifhe hys name from the earthe,we for cauſe of our health doo ſett furth in the ſanĉtified altar, know ing that *by this onelie remedie life ys to be geuen , and death to be driuen awaie.* Thus

Chryſtes bodie and blood ys of fred euerie wher,a pu re oblacion to euerla ſting life.

B   moche this holie Martyr Martialis.

     What a notable ſentence ys this?Do ye not ſee that he maketh mencion of the ſaing of the Prophet Malachie ſaing: *Euery wher ys offred the pure oblacion or ſacrifice?*And perceaue ye not that immediately he ſaieth , that *we offer the bodie and blood of Chryſt vnto euerlaſting life?*And that this his mening ſhould not be wreſted , nor myſtaken,he declareth what bodie of Chryſt we offer, and wher. The bodie of Chryſte whiche we doo offer , ys that bodie , that the Iewes offred by enuie : The place that we offer yt on, ys the ha lowed altar. The effeĉte that the Iewes ſought by the offring of Chry ſtes bodie,was to take life from him, and therby to abolifh his name from the earth:The effeĉt that we chryſtians ſeke by the ſacrificing of his bodie on the altar ys to magnifie hys name,and by that ſacrifice,as by the only re medye,to gett vs life,and to driue awaie death.

what bodie we offre, in what place and to what effeĉt

     Note well that this holie Martyr and auncient Father teacheth that pure doĉtrine,that the primitiue church of the Apoſtles did profeſſe, and teache. And iudge yf the church that nowe ys,which the Aduerſaries haue ſo vilely

C   reuiled,and ſo maliciouſly railed on,hath taught anie other doĉtrine , then this holie diſciple of Chryſte hath taught. The Churche hath taught, and doth nowe teache,that the bodie of Chryſt ys in the Sacrament of the altar reallie:This holie man teacheth that the ſame *whiche the Iewes crucified , we ſett furth vpon the holowed altar* . The Iewes crucified the reall bodie of Chryſte, Wherfore we ſett furth or ſacrifice Chryſtes reall bodie. The churche nowe teacheth that we offer the reall bodie of Chryſt on the altar : This holy man teacheth,that we offre the bodie and blood of Chryſt vnto euerlaſting life. And that we ſhoulde knowe that this ys a ſure doĉtrine grownded vpon a ſure fundacion he endeth hys ſentence thus : *Hoc enim ipſe Dominus Ieſus iuſſit nos agere in ſui commemorationem.* Thys (ſaieth he) hath our Lorde Ieſus commaunded vs to doo in the commemoracion or remem brance of him.

Chryſt cō maunded his bodie and blood to be offred

D   Weigh this ſaing with me,I beſech thee,gentle Reader.Manie of the wic ked teachers haue wounderfullie deceaued the ſimple people with this ſen tence of Chryſte,which this Father here alleageth,ſaing that Chryſt inſtitu ted this Sacrament for a memoriall or a remembrance of him. But a memoriall (ſaie they)ys of a thing that ys abſent ,and not of a thing, that ys preſent , wherfore Chryſte ys not preſent in the Sacrament. Yf he were , what neadeth anie other memoriall , but hys preſence?

A fond ob ieĉtion of the Aduer ſaries ,anſ wered by the holie Martyr Martialis.

     Q   A more

A more full aunfwer fhall be made to this, by the helpe of Gods grace, in the E
thirde booke, wher this matter fhall be treacted of more at large. But at
this prefent, this holy man onely fhall aunfwer. Whofe aunfwer, his grauitie,
holineffe, and auncientie ys foche, that they that flee not from gods grace,
to their owne fingular affeċtion, and opinion, fhall perceaue that in
yt ys foche pith and fubftance, that they maie well ftaie them felues vpon
the fame. For when the holie Father had declared the reall prefence
of Chryfte in the Sacrament, and that he ys offred in facrifice, then he added, that our Lorde Iefus commaunded vs fo to doo. Wherby what ells dothe he meen, but that as our Lord Iefus did confecrate, and facrifice his own
bodie, and gaue the fame alfo to hys Apoftles to eate in his laft Supper, as ys
allreadie declared: So doo we nowe confecrate and offre the fame bodie, and
receaue yt according to his commaundement and that in the remembrance
ce of his death?

Cap. 41.

Let mafter Iuell con-ferre this with hys priuate glo-fe vpon the fame text inhis fermõ fol. 34.

This I faie maie ferue and fuffice for an aunfwer to a man that ys not contencioufe, nor lifteth to make euery parte of his faith a doubte, and call yt F
into queftion. Thys man I faie, his auncientie in the Parliament houfe of
Chryft confidered, ys of authoritie more fufficient, and better to be beleued, then *Lutherus, Oecolampadius, Zuinglius, Caluinus* or our owne contrie men
Cranmer, Ridley, Latimer, or ther complices dead or liuing, whofe faings hauing
no grownde of auncient trueth, and fo of congruence none authoritie, yet
haue they ben (the more ys the pitie) to rafhlie beleued, to the cafting awaie
of manie a foule, and to thencreafe of the damnacion of the fpeakers.

But further to proceade to learn the enaċted trueth of this matter, I meen
the true vnderftanding of the Prophet Malachie: we haue an other auncient
elder of the fame houfe, *Irenæus* the difciple of *Polycarpus*, whiche *Polycarpus*
was difciple of S. Iohn the Euangelift, as *Eufebius* wittneffeth in the ecclefiafti
call hiftorie. And therfore ys this auncient Father not to be fufpeċted of hys
trueth, nor diftredited. Thus he writeth: *Sed et fuis Difcipulis dans confilium primi-*

Li. 5. ca. 5. Irenæus. Li 4. c. 32.

tias Deo offerre ex fuis creaturis, non quafi indigenti, fed vt ipfi nec infruċtuofi, nec ingrati
fint: eum, qui ex creatura panis eft, accepit, & gratias egit, dicens, Hoc eft corpus meum. Et G
calicem fimiliter, qui eft ex ea creatura, quæ eft fecundùm nos. fuum fanguinem confeffus eft,
& noui teftamenti, nouam docuit oblationem, quam Ecclefia ab Apoftolis accipiens in vni-
uerfo mundo offert Deo, ei, qui alimenta nobis præftat, primitias fuorum munerum in nouo
teftamento, de quo in duodecim Prophetis Malachias fic præfignauit: Non eft mihi volun-
tas in vobis dicit Dominus omnipotens, & facrificium non accipiam de manibus veftris,
&c. But alfo geuing inftruċtion to hys difciples, to offre the firft fruites of
the creatures to God, not as to one hauing nede, but that they fhoulde neither be vnfruiċtfull, nor vnthankfull, he tooke that bread whiche ys a creature, and gaue thankes, faing. *Thys ys my bodie:* And the cuppe likewife whiche

Chryft taught the newe facri-fice of the neweTefta-ment, the Church re-ceaued yt of the Apo-ftles.

ys a creature as we, *he confeffed to be hys bloode.* And of the newe teftament he
taught the newe oblacion, the whiche the churche receauing of the Apoftles, offreth to God in all the woorlde, euen vnto him, who geueth vs foode,
being the firft fruiċtes of his facrifices in the newe teftament. Of the whiche
emong the twelue Prophetes Malachie did this fpeake before hand: I haue
no pleafure in yowe, faieth the Lorde omnipotent, and I will take no facrifice of your handes. And fo furth he reherfeth the wholl fentence of
the Prophet. H

In the faing of this holie Elder of Chryftes houfe, yefe a goodlie agreement, with the other Elder before recited. For thys Elder teacheth that
Chryft of the creatures of bread and wine made hys bodie and bloode, and therwith

all

A *all inſtituted and taught the newe ſacrifice of the newe teſtament,* the whiche ſacrifice the Churche receauing of the Apoſtles , doth offre throughoute all the worlde , of the whiche the Prophet Malachie (ſaieth he)ſpake before.

Make nowe then compariſon betwen *Martialis* and *Irenæus* . *Martialis* teacheth the preſence of Chryſtes bodie in the Sacrament:*Irenæus* teacheth the ſame,ſaing that Chryſt confeſſed the bread and cuppe to be hys bodie and bloode.The other ſaied that the bodie and bloode of Chryſt were offred in ſacrifice:Thys man ſaieth that Chryſt confeſſing his bodie and blood to be preſent,taught a newe oblacion of the newe teſtament.The other ſaied that Chryſt commaunded vs ſo to doo:This man ſaieth that Chryſt taught the newe ſacrifice of the newe teſtament to the Apoſtles and that the Church receauing the ſame of the Apoſtes dothe offre yt to God troughoute all the worlde.The other alleaging Malachie,treateth of the ſacrifice of Chryſtes bodie and bloode:This man treating of the bodie and blood of Chriſt, the newe ſacrifice of the newe teſtament offred of the Churche throughout

B all the worlde,alleageth Malachie,ſaing,that he ſpake of the ſame.

S. Martia lis and Irenæus copa red toge ther in the ir doctrine of the Sa crament.

Aboue theſe goodlie notes of agreement betwē theſe two great anciēt Fathers,this ys in *Irenæus* ſpeciallie to be obſerued,that in ſaing that Chryſt taught the newe oblacion of the newe Teſtament,he geueth vs two goodly documentes for the mainteinaunce of the treuth of the catholique faithe, and the represſion of the falſe errours of the Aduerſaries,and maliciouſe reproches.

Two nota ble docu mentes out of Iren. wherby the gloſes of the Aduerſari es are re proued ād ouerthro wen.

And firſt,wher he ſaieth,that Chryſt taught a newe oblacion,yt confown deth all the expoſitions of the Aduerſaries ſo plainlie , that anie childe maie ſee that they are confownded.For wher they ſaie that by the pure ſacrifice that Malachie ſpeaketh of,ys vnderſtanded the ſacrifice of praiſe and thankes geuing,mercy to the poor,obedience to gods will ãd ſoche other, this Authour ſainge,that Chryſt taught a newe oblacion, of the whiche Malachie did ſpeake,doth clean ouerthrowe them.For theſe ſacrifices of the whiche the Aduerſaries make mencion,be not newe,but ſoche as haue ben vſed of godlie men from the beginning,as ys before touched.But Chryſte taught a

C newe oblacion that was aunſwerable to the newe teſtament , of the whiche yt was by Chryſt ordeined and appointed to be the oblacion . Nowe the newe Teſtament was ſo newe, that yt was neuer before in manifeſt form or maner.Wherfore the newe oblacion or ſacrifice was ſo like wiſe , and in like ſorte newe,that yt was newer before in verie dede,but in figure, as manie other thinges were.

The ſeconde document ys,wher he ſaieth that Chryſt taught a newe oblacion of the newe teſtament.Wherin he dothe deliuer vs frō the maliouſe ſlaunders of the Aduerſaries,whiche ſaie that yt ys an Idoll, a mere inuencion of the papiſtes,to make merchandies to emptie poour mens purſeis, and ſoche like railing ſlaunders.But nowe,reader, iudge thowe whether yt be ſo or no.nowe that thow haueſt heard the ſainges of theſe auncient holy Fathers,who ſaie that this newe ſacrifice of the newe teſtament was of the doctrine of Chryſte,was commaunded by him to be don , was receaued by the Church at the handes of the Apoſtles , and by and in the ſame Church ys offred throughout the wholl worlde.

D   Q ii   THE

THE FIVE AND THIRTITH CHAP. PRO-
ceadeth in the expofition of the fame Prophet by fainct Auguftin
and Eufebius.

VE haue hearde one cople of the auncient Fathers of Chryftes Parliament houfe, reporting what the true vnderftanding of the Prophecie of Malachie ys: Yt fhall not be, I truft, withoute profett to
heare the reporte of an other coople, to the entente the reader
maie fee fome plentie of good matter to be fatiffied withall, forfomoche as
the Aduerfaries haue powred oute aboute this prophecie, fo moche falfe and
naughtie matter to deceaue him withall.

And therfore me will procead to fett oute the trueth, and heare fainct
Auguftine what he faieth therin. *Dominus omnipotens dicit: Non eft mihi vo-*
Auguftin li. aduerfus Indæos. *luntas in vobis, & facrificium non fufcipiam de manibus veftris. Certè hoc negare non*
poteftis, o Iudæi, non folùm non facrificium non accipere de manibus veftris, locus enim
vnus eft loco Domini conftitutus, vbi manibus veftris facrificia iufsit offerri, præter quem
locum omnino prohibuit. Hunc ergo locum quoniam pro meritis veftris amififtis, etiam
facrificium, quod ibi tantùm licebat offerri, in locis offerre alijs non audetis. Et imple-
tum eft omnino, quod ait Propheta: Et facrificium non accipiam de manibus veftris. Nam
fi in terrena Hierufalem maneret vobis templum & altare, poffetis dicere in eis hoc effe
completum, quorum iniquorum inter vos conftitutorum facrificia Dominus non acceptat.
Aliorum verò ex vobis, atque in vobis acceptare facrificia, qui Dei præcepta cuftodiunt,
hoc non eft cur pofsit dici, vbi nullus omnino veftrum eft, qui fecundùm legem, quæ
de monte Synai procefsit, manibus fuis facrificium poffet offerre. Neque hoc ita
prædictum, & impletum eft, vt vos prophetica fententia refpondere permittat,
quia manibus non offerimus carnem, corde & ore offerimus laudem, fecundùm
illud in pfalmo: Immola Deo facrificium laudis, etiam hinc contradicit vobis, qui
dicit: Non eft mihi voluntas in vobis, &c. Deinde ne exiftimetis, non offerentibus vo-
bis, nec illo accipiente de manibus veftris, Deo facrificium non offerri, quo quidem ille
non eget, qui bonorum noftrorum nullius indiget, tamen quia fine facrificio non eft, quod
non illi fed nobis vtile eft, adiungit, & dicit: Quia ab oriente fole vfque in occiden-
tem nomen meum clarum factum eft in omnibus gentibus, & in omni loco facrificium
offertur nomini meo, facrificium mundum, quoniam magnum nomen meum in
gentibus, dicit Dominus omnipotens. Quid ad hæc refpondetis? Aperite oculos
tandem aliquando, & videte ab oriente fole, vfque in occidentem non in vno, fi-
cut in vobis erat conftitutum, fed in omni loco offerri facrificium Chriftianorum, non
cuilibet Deo, fed ei, qui ifta prædixit, Deo Ifraël. Vnde & alibi dicit Ec-
clefiæ fuæ: Et qui eruit te, ipfe Deus Ifraël vniuerfæ terræ vocabitur. Scrutami-
ni fcripturas in quibus putatis vos vitam habere æternam, & profectò haberetis, fi
Chriftum in eis intelligeretis & teneretis. Sed perfcrutamini eas, & ipfæ tefti-
monium perhibent de hoc facrificio mundo, quod offertur Deo Ifraël: non ab vna
gente veftra, de cuius manibus non fe fufcepturum prædixit, fed ab omnibus gentibus,
quæ dicunt: Venite, afcendamus in montem Domini, nec in vno loco, ficut præceptum
erat in terrena Hierufalem, fed in omni loco vfque in ipfam Hierufalem, nec fe-
cundùm ordinem Aaron, fed fecundùm ordinem Melchifedech. I haue no pleafure
in yowe faieth the Almightie Lorde, And facrifice I will none accepte
at yow handes, Certenly this ye can not denie, o yowe Iewes, that not
onely he doth not take facrifice of your handes (for therys one place, in
the place of God appointed, wher he hath comaunded facrifice to be offred with your handes, befide the which, he hath forbodden euery place.
Thys

A This place therfor for fomoche as for your defertes ye haue loft, that which was iaufull ther onely to be offred, in other places ye dare not offre. Beholde yt ys fulfilled that the Prophet faied: And facrifice I will not accept at your handes. Yf in the earthlie Hierufalem, ther were remaining a temple and an Altar for yow, ye might faie yt were fulfilled in wicked men. of the whiche wicked men being among yow God dothe not accept facrifice. But of other whiche be of yow, and among yowe, whiche kepe the commaundementes of God, he accepteth the facrifice. But this can not be faied, forafmoche as ther ys not one of yowe all whiche according to the lawe, that proceaded from mounte Synai, maye offre facrifice with hys handes. Neither ys this fo forefpoken and fullfilled that the fentence of the Prophet will fuffer yow to aunfwer, that though with our handes we offre not flefhe, yet with our heart and mouthe we offer lawde and prayfe, according to that in the pfalme. Offre vnto God the facrifice of lawde, From this place alfo he fpeaketh againft

B yow, who faieth: I haue no pleafure in yowe. Yet further, that ye fhoulde not thinke, that forfomoche as ye offre not, nor that he taketh no facrifice at your handes, that ther ys no facrifice offred to God the which in dede he nedeth not, who nedeth not the goodes of anie of vs, yet *bycaufe he ys not withoute facrifice*, the whiche ys profitable to vs, and not to him, he addeth and faieth: from the rifing of the funne to the going downe of the fame my name ys made honourable among the gentiles. And in euery place ys offred facrifice vnto my name, whiche ys a pure or clean facrifice. For my name ys great amonge the gentiles faieth the lorde Allmightie. What do ye awnfwer to thefe? Open yowr eyes once at the laft, and fee from the rifing of the Sunne to the going down of the fame, not in one place, as to yow yt was appointed, but *in euery place the facrifice of the Chryfhans ys offred*, not to euery God, but to him that fpake thefe thinges before hande, euen the God of Ifraell? Wherfore in an other place he faieth to hys Church: And he that hath deliuered thee, that fame God of Ifraell fhall be called the God of the whol earth. Search ye the fcriptures,

C for in them ye thinke ye haue eternall life. And truly ye fhoulde haue yt, yf in them ye wolde vnderftand Chryfte, and holde him. But fearche them through, and *they doo beare wittneffe of this pure Sacrifice, whiche ys offred to the God of Ifraell*, not of your owne nacion, of whofe handes he hath faied before that he will take no facrifice, but of all nacions whiche do faie: Come and let vs go vppe to the hill of our Lord neither in one place, as yt was commaunded in the earthlie Hierufalem: But in euery place, euen in Hierufalem yt felf. Neither after the ordre of Aaron, but after the ordre of Melchifedech, Thus moche S. Auguftine.

Whofe fainge although yt be long: yet I thought yt good whollie to afcribe yt, both bicaufe yt ys a goodly, liuely, and pleafaunt expofition of the place of the Prophet Malachie, and alfo that the dependence of the fentence might be feen, wherby great light ys geuen to the vnderftanding of the matter that yt ys alleaged for.

Of the whiche long expofition to make a breif collection of thinges ap-

D perteining to the declaracion of the matter whiche we haue in hande, thys ys to be obferued, that faincte Auguftine verie ftronglie, and pithilie prouing the reiection of the facrifices of the Iewes, faieth yet that ther muft be a facrifice to be offred to God not for hys neceffitie, who nedeth not our goodes:but for our owne vtilitie and profitte.And pro E uing yt by the Prophet Malachie that in euery place, ther fhall be facrifice offred to the name of God,he faieth, that that Sacrifice ys the Sacrifice of the Chryftians,which Sacrifice of the Chryftians he willeth the Iewes to o- pen their eies,and fee yt doen, from the rifing of the Sunne to the going down of the fame.Whiche maner of facrifice when he calleth yt the facrifi- ce of the Chryftians,he doth plainly fhewe that he meneth a fpeciall ma- ner of facrifice,peculiar and propre to the Chryftians,wher withe the Iewes be not acquainted.

*The facri-
fice of the
chryftians
ys a pecu-
liar and
fpeciall Sa-
crifice.*

For yf he had here ment the facrifice of lawde and thankes geuing, or foche like,the Iewes might haue faied that thofe be their facrifices, but whē he faied the facrifice of the Chryftians,he ment vndoubtedly their peculiar facrifice,as when yt ys faied : the Sacrifice of the Iewes did ceaffe at the coming of Chryfte, what ells ys ment but thefe facrifices,which were peculiar to the Iewes,then ceaffed.But as for the fpirituall facrifices, as the facrifice of a contrite heart,of a beleuing hearte ceaffeth not. But as they F were vfed of the faithfull Iewes beleuing Mefsias to come, fo maie they be vfed of the faithfull Iewes beleuing that he ys comed, wher as the other maie not,whiche be proprelie called the facrifices of the Iewes.

But this fcruple fainéte Auguftine dothe yet more plainlie diffolue , and fo plainlie that the Aduerfaries can not faie againft yt, neither the true ca- tholique,anye further doubte in yt.For S. Auguftine faieth to the Iewe. Searche the fcriptures through, whiche do beare wittneffe of this pure fa- crifice , whiche (faieth he)ys offred not in one place of Hierufalem , but in euery place not of one nacion of the Iewes,but of all nacions . And at laft touchinge the verye pithe: not(faieth he)after the ordre of Aarō,but after the ordre of Melchifedech. Note then the facrifice whiche he firft called the facrifice of the Chryftians,and after the pure facrifice, nowe he calleth yt the facrifice after the ordre of Melchifedech.

Nowe then,Reader,thowe maift perceaue what facrifice yt ys,that God fpake of by hys Prophete Malachie, that fhoulde be the pure facrifice, whiche fhoulde fuccead the facrifice of the Iewes, and be the facrifice of the Chryftians.Yt ys (faieth S.Auguftin) the *Sacrifice after the ordre of Melchi-* G *fedech.* What the facrifice after the ordre of Melchifedech ys , that our high preift after the ordre of Melchifedech did inftitute, yt ys before in the pro- phecie of Chryftes preifthead declared and teftified by graue and weightie authoritie,that yt ys the facrifice of Chryftes verie bodie and blood, the ve- rie true heauenly bread and wine.

Howe then ftandeth the expofitions of the Aduerfaries?Howe moche dothe their malicioufe falfhead appeare , who by their voluntary glofes laboured to take awaie from the minde of the Prophet,that, that was prin- cipallie by him entended and fpoken of , and onelie to place that was prefuppofed , and as yt were annexed . For thofe fpirituall facrifices before touched, with other like be prefuppofed as neceffarilie requi- red to concurre with extern facrifice , yf yt be duely and acceptablie offred.

*Li.1.cont.
Aduerfari
um leg. &
Proph.*

As notable a fainge as this hath fainéte Auguften in an other place alfo. Who fo lifteth to reade, fhall ther finde that , that fhall not repent him of H the reading.

Nowe muft we haue an other wittneffe of the other fide of the Parlament houfe agreable to fainét Auguftine . This fhall be *Eufebius* a
　　　　　　　　　　　　　　　　　　　　　　　　　　　　　　　great

A great learned man, and an awncient of the houfe of God, who faieth thus: *Mofaicis reiectis facrificijs, quod futurum erat, noftrum ipforum inftitutum diuinitus nunciat dicens: Quoniam ab ortu folis vfque ad occafum, nomen meum glorificatu eft in gentibus, & in omni loco incenfum offertur nomini meo, & hoftia munda. Sacrificamus igitur Deo altiffimo facrificium laudis. Sacrificamus Deo plenum, & horrorem adferens, & facrofanctum facrificium. Sacrificamus nouo modo, fecundum nouum teftamentum hoftiam mundam &c.* The Mofaicall facrifices being reiected, he doth by the reuelació of God fhewe our ordeinaunce that was to come, faing: From the rifing of the Sunne, to the going downe of the fame, my name ys glorified among the gentiles, and in euery place incenfe ys offred vnto my name, and a pure facrifice. *We doo facrifice therfore vnto the high God, the facrifice of lawde. We do facrifice to God a full and moft holie facrifice bringing horroure. We doo facrifice a pure facrifice in a newe maner, after the newe teftament.* Thus *Eufebius.*

Li. 1. Euãgel Demoft. ca 10.

Sacrifice of the Chriftians a full Sacrifice. and moft holy.

Do ye not fee this ancient Father howe he expowndeth the Prophet, and
B declareth that *we facrifice to God a pure facrifice in a newe maner after the newe teftament?* And declaring what facrifice yt ys, he faieth, *yt ys a full and moft holie facrifice bringing horroure.* What facrifice ys that, that ys a full facrifice, but the facrifice of Chryftes bodie? that ys a full facrifice in yt felf. All other facrifices, that euer were or fhall be, are not full, but all they muft take their fulneffe of this. And what facrifice ys moft holy but this, which maketh all other holie? In fo moche as holie Dionyfe the difciple of S. Paule, who was a man full of the fpirit of God faeth · *Neque enim ferme fas eft facerdotalis muneris myfteriu aliquod peragi, nifi diuinum iftud Euchariftiæ auguftifimumque facramentum compleat.* Neither ys yt almoft lawfull for anie mifterie of the preiftlie office to be doen, except this diuine and moft noble Sacrament of Chryfte do fullfill or ende yt.

Dionyf. Ec clefias. Hierar parte. 1 ca. 3.

And what facrifice ys yt that bringeth horroure with yt, but the Sacrifice that conteineth the high Maieftie of Chryft, whiche ys to be feared of all men? of the whiche fpeaketh Chrifoftome, faing: *Quando autem ille & Spiritu fanctum inuocauerit, facrificiumque illud horrore, & reuerentia pleniffimum perfecerit, communi omnium Domino affidue manibus pertractato, Quæro ex te, quorum illum in or-*
C *dine collocabimus?* When he hath called vpon the holie Goft (*faieth Chrifoftom, fpeaking of the preift that confecrateth*) and hath perfected that Sacrifice *moft full of horroure and reuerence, the commune or vniuerfall Lorde of all thinges being felt with handes*: I afke of thee, in the order of whome fhall we place him? Thus Chryfoftom.

Li. 6. de Sacerdocio.

Sacrifice full of horroure bicaufe the Lord of all ys ther handled.

Ye fee here that he calleth the facrifice of the Altar, *the facrifice moft full of horroure and. Reuerence*, and whie he dothe fo, he geueth caufe, for *that the vniuerfall Lorde being in the Sacrifice, ys fo prefent, that he ys handeled with handes.*

Who ys this Lorde in this facrifice, in an other place he dothe expreffedlie declare: *Ad fanctum & terribile facrificium properas, erubefce oblationis arcana. occifus propofitus Chriftus eft.* Thowe comeft (faieth Chrifoftom) vnto an holie and terrible facrifice: Baffhe at the fecrete thing of the oblació. Chryft that was flain ys fet furth.

De prodition. Iude. homil. 30.

Marke (reader) that in both fainges he calleth yt a facrifice: but in the
D firft fainge, a facrifice full of horrour and reuerence, in the fecond, an holie and a terrible facrifice. The caufe why yt ys full of horrour and reuerence ys by caufe the vniuerfall Lord of all ys ther in handling: Who ys this Lorde in the fecond fentence he openeth, faing: Chryft that was flain ys fett furth in facrifice. And therfor no meruaill though *Eufebius* did call yt a facri-

fice

fice bringing horroure, wher the maieftie of Chryfte ys (as Chrifoftom E hath wittneffed)

In that he faied, we facrifice, after the newe maner of the newe Teftamét what dothe he faie, but as *Irenæus* faied : *that Chryſt taught yt, that we doo facrifice, to be the newe facrifice of the newe Teſtament*. And the facrifice of the newe teftament ys, that the high preiſt of the newe teftament, being a preiſt after the ordre of Melchifedech doth fett furth, after that fame ordre. Whiche *facrifice* ys (as S. Hierom faieth) *his bodie and blood, the verie true bread, and true wine*.

Thus haue ye heard the wittneffe of S. Auguftine and *Eufebius* côfonnät and agreeing both the one to the other, and alfo to thofe that were before them alleadged and brought for the declaraciô of the true meening of the prophecie of Malachie.

THE SIXT AND THIRTITH CHAP. ENDETH
the expofition of Malachie by fainⷱe Hierom and Damafcen.

F

TO ende this proceffe in the expofition of the prophecie of Ma- lachie nowe in hande, leeſt I might be tediouſe to the Reader, I will onelie adde the teſtimonie of S. Hierom and Damafcen and of no mo at this prefent, trufting that thefe with thother before alleaged ſhall fatiffie thee, gentle Reader, and fullie in-

Hieron. in Malach.

ftruⷱe thee in the trueth of this matter.

S. Hierom vpon the Prophet Malachie faieth thus: *Propriè nunc ad facerdo- tes Iudæorum fermo fit Domini, qui offerunt cæcum & claudum, & languidum ad immo- landum, vt fciant carnalibus victimis fpirituales victimas fucceffuras: Et nequaquam tau- rorum hircorumque fanguinem thymiama, hoc eſt, fanctorum orationes Domino offerendas, & non in vna orbis Prouincia Iudæa, nec in vna Iudæa vrbe Hierufalem, fed in omni loco offerri oblationem nequaqnam immundam, vt à populo Ifraël, fed mundam vt in ceremo- niis Chriſtianorum.* Nowe the woorde of our Lorde ys proprely fpoken to the preiſtes of the Iewes, whiche bringe the blinde, the lame, and the ficke to be offred in facrifice, that they ſhoulde knowe that fpirituall facrifices ſhall folo- we their carnall facrifices, and that not the blood of bulls and of goattes, but G infence or fwete perfume, that ys, the praiers of the holie men ſhall be offred, and that not in Iewrie being one Prouince of the woorlde, neither in Hierufalem alone, the Cittie of Iewrie, *but in euery place ſhal be offred, not an vnclean facrifice*, as of the people of Ifraell, *but a clean oblacion as in the Ceremonies of the Chryſtians*. Thus moche of fainⷱe Hierom in the expofition of the Pro- phecie of Malachie nowe in hand. In the whiche prophecie ye maie percea- ue two thinges that ſhall be offred vnto God in euery place, that ys incenfe, and the meate offring.

Incenfe (faieth S. Hierom) ys the praiers of the holie, whiche ſhall not be offred to God in Hierufalem alone, but in euery place ſhall the faithfull offre that facrifice as the facrifice of thankes, lawdes, and prai- fe. So that kinde of facrifice by S. Hierom ys conteined vnder this woor- do incenfe.

Sacrifice of the chriſti ans Chry- ſtes bodie and blood.

The other that ys meat offring, *whiche ys the pure and clean facrifice, ſhall be dô* (as S. Hierom faieth) *in the Ceremonies of the Chryſtians*. Whiche Ceremonies contain the rites and facrifices of the Chryſtians. Among theife Ceremo- nies what ys ther that can be proprely called the pure or clean facrifice, but the pure facrifice of Chryſtes bodie and blood, whiche (as befor ys

H

faied

A faied)ys a pure facrifice in yt felf, ād of yt felf, and ys able to purifie all other.

That the bodie and blood of Chryfte be a facrifice among the chryftians, S. Hierom in this fame chapiter declareth. who fpeaking to Biffhopps, Preiftes, and Deacons, and other that necligentlie come to the Altar of God, faieth: *Offertis (inquit) fuper altare meum panem pollutum. Polluimus panem, id eft, corpus Chrifti, quando indigni accedimus ad altare, & fordidi mundum fanguinem bibimus.* Ye offer (faieth Allmightie God) defiled bread vpon mine Altar. We defile the bread, that ys, *the bodie of Chryfte* (faieth S. Hierom) when we being vnwourthie come to the Altar, and being filthie drinke the clean blood of Chryft. In this expofition of S. Hierom ys geuen vs to vnderftand not onelie that the bodie and blood of Chryft be the facrifice of vs that be chryftians, whiche we offer vpon the Altar: but alfo we are taught an other maner of expofition then the Aduerfaries teache: yea euen a clean contrarie. For they, where in the fcriptures or doctours they reade thefe woordes, the bodie of Chryft, they expownde yt to be bread a figure of the bodie of **B** Chryfte: contrarie S. Hierom declaring howe we offre defiled bread, and howe we defile yt, expowndeth the bread to be the bodie of Chryfte.

S. Hierom expowndeth the fcriptures contrarie to the Sacrvmētriet.

Neither can the Aduerfarie fhifte him felf from this faing of S. Hierom, with the inuented glofe of his owne head, that we defile and doo iniurie to the bodie of Chryfte, when we take the Sacramēt of his bodie vnworthilie. For he doth not onelie faie that by the bread ys vnderftanded the bodie of Chryft: but he alfo by moft plain woordes faieth, that we drinke his blood. He doth not faie that we defile the bloode of Chryfte, when we drinke the Sacramentall wine: but he faieth we defile the bloode of Chryft, when we being defiled doo drinke the fame. So that by fainct Hierō, we doo not take one thing, ād doo iniurie to an other, but receauing a pure thing whē we be defiled, we doo iniurie to the fame. Wherfore receauing the bread that ys the bodie of Chryft, we doo iniurie to the fame, receauing yt vnwourthilie, and drinking the pure blood of Chryft, we doo iniurie to the fame, yf we receaue yt, being vnpure our vnclean our felues,

Yf ther were not the bodie and bloode of Chryfte in the Sacramēt, wolde **C** S. Hierom, who in this place taketh vpon him to be an expofitour, which ys to make thinges clear and plain, that be darke and lie hidden, wolde he (tro we ye) fo handle the matter, that the thinges he fpeaketh of fhoulde implie more difficultie, more darkneffe, and harder maner of vnderftanding, then they had before? Yf ther were not the prefence of Chryft in the Sacrament S. Hierom wolde haue faied, we defile the bread, when we take that bread whiche ys the Sacrament of Chryftes bodie vnwourthilie: And we defile his blood when we take the Sacrament of yt vnpurely. And this were the plain maner of an expofitour to fpeake liuely, and plainlie to vtter the matter, with oute anie tropes or figures: but faing (as before ys faied) and fpeaking yt as an expofitour, we muft vnderftande, that he teacheth that the bread on the Altar ys the bodie of Chryfte, and that ther ys alfo his very bloode, whiche two be the facrifice of the Chryftians alfo after the minde of S. Hierom.

Damafcen alfo breiflie commeth to the point, and affirmeth all that ys faied by S. Hierom. For he fpeaking of the verie reall prefence of Chryftes **D** bodie in the Sacrament, and teaching that yt ys the facrifice that Malachie fpake of, faieth thus: *Hæc eft pura illa hoftia, & ir cruenta, quam ab ortu folis vfque ad occafum ipfi offerri per prophetā Dominus loquitur, corpus videlicet & fanguis Chrifti, in ftabilimentum animæ noftræ & corporis, inconfumptū, & incorruptum, non in feceffum abiens*

Damafc. li.4. ca.14.

abiens (abfit enim huiufmodi imaginatio) fed in noftram fuftentationem & conferuationē E
omnimodo nocumenti reparatio, fordis omnis purgatio. This ys that pure facrifice
and vnbloodie, that our Lorde fpeaketh by the Prophet, to be offred to
him from the rifing of the funne, to the going downe of the fame, that ys to
faie, *the bodie and bloode of Chryfte, vnto the inconfumed, and incorrupted ftablifhment
of our bodie and Sowle,* not going into feceffe (God forbidde that any foche
imaginacion fhoulde be) but yt ys a purgacion of all maner of filth, and a
reparation of all maner of hurte, vnto our fuftentacion and conferuacion.
Thus Damafcen this faing nede no expofition yt ys fo plain that euery childe maie perceaue, that the pure facrifice, that the Prophet fpeaketh of, *ys the
bodie and blood of Chryft,* which maie not be wrefted to be faied, that the facramentall bread (as the Aduerfaries terme yt) ys figuratiuely the bodie of
Chryfte. For this Authour excludeth all foche interpretacions, when he
faieth, *that the bodie and bloode, he fpeaketh of, goeth not vnto feceffe,* which can not
be verified of their bread, whiche they faie and confeffe that yt goeth into
feceffe. Wherbie ye maie perceiue that this Authoure, who ys an auncient F
of Chryftes Parliament houfe not to be contemned, reported to vs that
enacted trueth *that Chryftes bodie and bloode be reallie in the Sacrament,* and that
that bodie and blood ys alfo the facrifice, that was prpheciced of the Prophet
Malachie, to be the Sacrifice that fhould fucceade the facrifice of the Iewes,
and to be offred vnto the God of the Chryftians, wherby his bleffed name
fhoulde be glorified among them.

And thus this Authour agreing which the reft alleadged for the declaracion of this matter, whiche other be of the moft auncient and famoufe men
of Chryftes Churche, men of holy life, of great learning, and withoute cor
ruption of iudgement: methinke men fhoulde raither appoint them felues to folowe their iudgements, then the light and rafhe fainges of foche, as
neither integritie of life, neither incorruption of iudgement, nor auncientie of time doth commende: but raither the contraries of thefe do them
difcommend.

Nowe as ye haue hearde this prophecie: So haue ye heard other Prophe G
cies and figures, that did prophecie and figurate this bleffed Sacrament of
Chryftes bodie and bloode, duely, iuftlie, and truelie applied to the thing.
In the doing wherof I claime not creditte to be geuen to me, as to my felf,
for fo moche as Iam in the wicked time, in the time of corruption, in the
time of Controuerfie: But I claim creditte to be geuen to me for the trueths
fake whiche I folowe. Whiche trueth hath ben in auncient time, before this
time of corruption and controuerfie taught, beleued, and folowed. I claime
alfo creditte to be geuen to the holie aunciét Fathers, whom I haue alleaged,
who being in that pure time, when faith was purely taught, do cōmunicate
to vs foche doctrine as the Churche of God then had, whofe doctrine howe
moche yt ys different from the doctrine of this wicked teacher, that hathe
thus exclamed, and howe repugnāte his doctrine ys to the teaching of thefe
Fathers, yt ys as eafie to difcerne as darkneffe frō light, or white frō blacke.

Wherfore, gentle Reader, nowe being by me aduertifed after foche forte
as yt hath pleafed my lorde God to imparte his grace vnto me, yf thowe haueft not erred reioice in God, and be confirmed: Yf thowe haueft erred repent before God, and be reduced. And thus moche of the fcriptures of the H
olde Teftament.

THE

A   THE SEVEN AND THIRTITH CHAP. MAKETH
*a breif Recapitulacion of thinges before written, with thapplicacion
of them to the Proclamacion of the aduersarie, and
so concludeth this first booke.*

Lthough I am not ignorante (gentle Reader) that in the Psalmes
be diuerse other prophecies, whiche according to the minde of
saincte Hierom do speake of this blessed Sacrament and sacrifice of
Chrystes bodie and bloode, that shoulde be offred in the Churche
of Chryst, and of the whiche the poour in spiritte shoulde eate and be satisfied, as in the xxi. xxij. lxxj. cx. psalmes : Yet for that the figures of this Sacrament be allreadie aunswered by prophecies to them aunswerable : And
these that be lefte maie by iust occasion be spoken of hereafter, I shall for
the Readers ease, disauauntage my self of the allegacion of them to the setting furth of the matter here taken in hand by me to be defended, and so cō-
B clude this booke with a breif recapitulacion of some thinghes bfore saied to
the entent they maie be applied to aunswere some one or mo mēbres of the
Aduersaries proclamacion not yet spoken of.

I did of pourpose omitte to applie that ys saied, as aunswer to that parte
of his wicked proclamacion whiche yt doth fullie confute, by cause I wolde
not to moche trouble my processe, but thought yt best to reserue yt to this
place, as in other matters I haue also doen the like in this booke.

Wherfor that yt maie well be perceaued, that this that ys saied doth clean
ouerthrowe this mans doctrine, vnderstand first what ys his doctrine, Thus
in his proclamacion he crieth.

*Yf any one of all our Aduersaries be able plainlie and clerely to proue by soch authoritie of
the scriptures, the old Doctours, and Councells (as ys before saied) that the preist had then
authoruie to offre vpp Chryst vnto his Father, &c.* In which his proclamaciō he denieth the Sacrifice of the Churhe, which *ys the bodie and blood of our sauiour
Chryst* which (he saieth) the Churche hath none authoritie to offre to God
in sacrifice.

C   Against this his false doctrine, call to minde what ys in this booke saied *The deuell*
speciallie in the setting furthe of the prophecies of the preisthood of Chryst *hath bewit*
after the ordre of Melchisedech : of the prophecies of Daniel, and Malachie, *ched the*
wher (but that the deuell hath bewitched this man, and to his perdition hath *Proclamer.*
cast a mist before his eies, that he shoulde not see the trueth) he coulde not
ells but see, that the bodie and blood of Chryste were of him self offred
in his last supper, and ther and then instituted and ordeined to be offred and
continued in his Church as the memoriall of his passion and death. *Cyprian.*

S. Ciprian (as yt ys alleaged) saieth, that our Lorde Iesus offred the same
that *Melchisedech* offred, that ys bread and wine, *that ys to saie* (saieth he) *his
bodie and blood.*

Isychius saieth, that we haue the sacrifice of Chryst the intelligible *Melchise* *Isychius*
dech, whiche sacrifice was perfectlie doen in bread and wine, when Chryste
saied : *This ys my bloode, that shalbe shedd for yowe.*

S. *Hierom* saieth, that as *Melchisedech* offred bread and wine : so shall Chryste *Hieron.*
offred *his bodie and blood the true bread, and true wine.*

D   S. *Augustin* saieth, Chryst did institute the sacrifice of his bodie and *Augustin.*
blood according to the ordre of *Melchisedech* to succeade the sacrifice after
the ordre of *Aaron.*

Wher note that he saieth, Chryst did institute the sacrifice of his bodie
and

and bloode after the ordre of *Melchisedech* Yf he did institute the sacrifice, **E**
then ys ther authoritie by the same institution geuen to the Church to offre
the same . Whiche well appeareth by the saing of *Origen* whiche foloweth in
this processe.

Origen.   We (saith *Origen*) being obedient to the Creatour of thinges, when we
haue geuen thankes, we receaue the breades that were offred. *whiche be tur-*
ned into a certain holier bodie, whiche bodie trulie maketh them holier, that with a sownde
and pure minde vse yt.

The church   Note then that our obedience standeth not onely to eate the bread, but
must both   to eate the bread that ys offred, and therforre we must both offre and eate,
offre and   yf we will be obedient. Yf yt be our obedience to offer, then ther ys
eate.   commaundement geuen to offre . *Yf commaundement be geuen , then Au-*
thoritie also.

Theophila.   *Theophilact* saieth, that *the oblacion conteining Chryste our Lorde, Bishoppe, and Sa-*
crifice, ys continuallie offred by the ministres of God. Seing that Chryste ys offred
(as Theophilact saieth) by the ministres of God , yt ys euident that
yt ys doen with authoritie . For withoute authoritie can none offre him. **F**

S. Martia.   *Martialis* one of the disciples of Chryste, saieth, that *we for our health offre*
We offre on   *that vpon the holie Altar , that the Iewes did offre vpon the Crosse for enuie.* And yf ye
the altar,   require by what authoritie we do it, he saieth that our Lord cõmaunded vs
that the   so to doo, in the remembrance of him.
Iewes of-
fred on the   And yf ye will vnderstande howe the authoritie cometh ordrely to vs,
crosse.   to offre the bodie of Chryste to God the Father. *Irenæus* will teache you. For
Irenæus.   he saieth, that Chryste geuing instructions to his Apostles to offre sacrifice
to God, tooke the creature of bread and gaue thankes, and saied: *this ys my*
body. And the cuppe also he tooke, and confessed yt to be his bloode, *and so*
of the newe Testament taught the newe oblacion, whiche the Churche taking of the Apost-
les , offreth yt yn all the worlde to God according to the prophecie of Malachie.

     Can not nowe this Proclamer , or raither Blasphemer, see or perceaue
what authoritie the preist hath to offre Chryst to God the Father? Yt ys
deriued from Chryst to the Apostles, from the Apostles to the Church, and
so vsed through out all the worlde . S. Augustine saieth, *that the pure and clean*
Augustin   *sacrifice that Malachie speaketh of, that shall be offred in euery place, ys the sacrifice after* **G**
the ordre of Melchisedech . What the sacrifice after the ordre of Melchisedech
ys, by the minde of S. Augustin yt ys aboue declared, wher he saieth that
Chryst did institute the sacrifice of his bodie and blood after the ordre of
Eusebius   Melchisedech . *Eusebius* saieth, that the Mosaicall sacrifices being reiected,
Cæsarien.   the Prophet Malachie by the reuelacion of God , sheweth what ys our
ordeinaunce that was to come . *And therfore we sacrifice nowe to the most high*
God the sacrifice of lawde, We sacrifice to God a full and a most holie sacrifice bringing
horrour. We sacrifice a pure sacrifice, in a newe maner after the newe Testament.

     What this most holie sacrifice ys bringing horrour with yt, yt ys declred
Chrysost.   by Chrysostom saing : *Thowe commest to the holy and terrible sacrifice, Bashe at the*
secret thinge of the sacrifice, For Chryst that was slain ys ther setfurthe.

     The cause then why this sacrifice ys called the most holie sacrifice, Why
yt ys called terrible, Why yt ys saied to be full of horrour, ys, bicause Chryst
that was slain, ys in the sacrifice sett furth before vs . Chryst then being settfurth in our sacrifice. Yt ys to be saied after the minde of these holie Fathers, **H**
that Chryst ys offred in our Sacrifice.

Damascẽ.   Last of all to make the conclusion, Damascen saieth *that the bodie and blood*
of Chryst ys that pure and vnbloodie sacrifice that our Lord speaketh of by the Prophet
to be

A *to be offred from the east to the west.* Yf our Lorde spake yt, mete yt ys that yt be doen. And the doers haue good authoritie to do yt, seinge their Lorde hath so ordeined and commaunded.

Now Reader doest thow not see the great bragge of this yonge Goliath o-uerthrowen, See yow not plain scriptures, and doctours, and those the gra-uest and eldest, withe their plain and weightie sentences presse and crushe this hys puffed bladder, and thrust oute in hys seight the vanitie therin con-teined? Perceaue yow not by these holy Fathers that the preist hathe autho-ritie to offre vppe the bodie of Chryst to God the Father? whiche thing thys Proclamer in his stowt maner flattering him self, semed percase to ma-nie of his auditorie by his Proclamacion to haue ouerthrowen : But what so euer he or anie other withe him phantasied, both he and they maie per-ceaue that this blast was not against a reed wauing and bowing with the winde: but yt was against the sure and substancial piller, and grownded faith of Chrystes Churche, and against that sure builded house the catholique

B Churche builded vpon the Rocke, and therfore shaketh yt not, neither with the waues of the trooblesome sea : nor yet with soche blastes as this man bloweth.

Thus ye perceaue, here ys good matter shewed for that, that the catholi-que Churche teacheth: What bringeth he for that whiche he so stowtlie blowstereth? Yt ys with good authoritie nowe proued, that Chryst ys of-fred in the holie sacrifice: What proofe hath he that Chryst ys not so offred now but hys bare Proclamaciō? A meruailouse matter. He requireth scriptu-res, Doctours, and Councells, for that, that the catholique Church teacheth, and for that he teacheth and wolde haue receaued, he bringeth not one title And therin he doth but as he maie doo. For certé I am that he cã bring none

And here wiil I again ioin with him, that yf he can bring anie one suf-ficient authoritie, that shall directlie saie that the Churche maie not offer the bodie of Chryst in soche sorte as yt doth, I will geue hym the victorie. He requireth plain proof that the preist offreth Chryst: his requeft ys satified: the plain proof by expresse woordes ys made: Let him

C doo the like for hys doctrin yf he can.

But let him not trust to proue yt by the wresting of sainct Paule to the Hebrues, folowing Caluine, and other of his Fathers : For that will not serue hys turne.

As for Doctours, ther ys not one that will fauour hym and hys doctrine in thys poinct. For yf ther had bén anye, hys predeces-sour Cranmer, or he that was the authour of that booke, wolde in the fifte booke, wher he treacteth of the sacrifice, haue alleaged some one. But I saie, he had not one Doctour or Father, nor Councell by whom he impugneth the doctrine of the catholique Churche that Chryst ys offred in hys Churche. He wolde fayn Father hys do-ctrine vpon sainct Paules epistle to the Hebrues, but that scripture accepteth yt not as a laufull childe, but as a Bastarde begotten by some wicked parentes, and therfore refuseth yt. He ys moche en-combred laboring to deliuer himself from Chrysostome and other, but all in vain.

D Wherfore as this man, who sparing not stirreth ãd moueth (as the prouer-be saieth) euery stone to gett some helpe or finde some shifte for the maintei-naũce of his doctrine, could not gette one whollie to go with him, although he semeth to alowe *Lōbardus*, ãd *Nycen Coũcell:* yet he durst not so alleage thẽ as

R   that

that he wolde ſtand throughlie with them : So I beleue verilie , that this **E**
Proclamer can no more doo but (leuing the holy Fathers) ſing a litle
voluntarie falſe deskant vpon a ſcripture or two, as Cranmer did.

By this then thus moch maie be ſaied , that to ſaie that Chryſt ys not
offred in and of the Church,and the miniſtres therof, ys no catholique
doctrine , for that yt ys not taught of anie catholique Father . But
that the contrary ys a catholique doctrine,yt doth well appeare by a
nombre of catholique Fathers before alleadged,and ſhall more appeare to
yow by thoſe that ſhall be yet alleaged. For God be praiſed this trueth ys
not ſo ſlender that yt lacketh good wittneſſes , nor yet ſo barren that nothing can be ſaid of yt,but what I can inuent.But yt ys ſo full that to ſaie all
yt wolde fill an wholl volume . Wherfor in this place I ſhall of manie
produce but foure or fiue to be added in this recapitulacion, and ſo end this

booke. *Iuſtinus Martyr* of the Sacrifice of the Chryſtians ſaieth thus.*Deus ipſe*
ait: In omni loco in gentibus hoſtias acceptas grataſque immolari.Neque verò à quoquā ho-
ſtias Deus accipit,niſi à ſuis ſacerdotibus.Itaq; omnia ſacrificia,quæ ſuo nomine faciēda Ieſus
Chriſtus tradidit, id eſt,in Euchariſtia panis & poculi, quæ in omni loco à Chriſtianis fiunt,
præoccupatione vſus Deus ſibi grata eſſe teſtatur. God him ſelf ſaieth ,that of the

gentills acceptable and pleaſaunt Sacrifices in euery place ſhall be offred.
Neither trulie doth God accept Sacrifices,but of hys owne preiſtes. Wherfor all the ſacrifices whiche Ieſus Chryſt hath deliuered to be doen in hys na
me,that ys to ſaie,in the Sacrament of breade and the cuppe , *whiche ſacrifices*
*are doen of the Chriſtians in euery place,*God vſing preoccupacion wittneſſeth thē
to be acceptable vnto him.Thus Iuſtinus,of whom we maie learn, that the
Sacrifices of the Sacramēt are deliuered to vs by Ieſus Chryſt.So that the au
thoritie of this maner of ſacrificing cometh frō him,ād ys not of our ſelues

S.Hierom ouer and aboue that,that ys allreadie alleaged of him, ſaieth thus:
Quòd autem ait,Tu es ſacerdos in æternum ſecundùm ordinem Melchiſedech: myſterium in
verbo ordinis ſignificatur,nequaquam per Aaron irrationabilibus victimis immolandis,ſed
*oblato pane & vino,id eſt,corpore & ſanguine Domini Ieſu.*Wheras he ſaieth,Thow
arte a preiſt for euer after the ordre of Melchiſedech : our myſtery in the
woorde of order ys ſignified, not by Aaron in offring brutiſh ſacrifices : But
in offring bread and wine,that ys to ſaie, the bodie and bloode of our Lorde **G**
Ieſus. Thus ſainct Hierom.

Of Iuſtinus we learned,that the ſacrifices of the Chryſtians wer deliuered
vnto vs by Ieſus Chryſt.

Of S.Hierom we learn,that theſe ſacrifices be the bodie and blood of our
Lord Ieſus.So by theſe two,in moſt manifeſt ād plain woords we be taught,
that Ieſus Chryſt deliuered vnto vs the authoritie to offre in ſacrifice hys bo

die and bloode.

S.Ambroſe alſo teacheth vs the ſame leſſon ſaing thus: *Ego enim,Domine, me-*
mor venerandæ paſsionis tuæ accedo ad altare tuum,licet peccator,vt offerā tibi ſacrificium,
quod tu inſtituiſti,& offerri præcepiſti in commemorationē tui pro ſalute noſtra. For I , o

Lord,being mindefull of thy paſsion,come vnto thine Altar, although I be
a ſinner,*that I maie offre vnto thee,the ſacrifice that thowe dideſt inſtitute, and commaun*
de to be offred in the remembrance of thee for our health.

Thus holie Ambroſe,who maketh the matter oute of all cōtrouerſie, that
a preiſt hath authoritie to offre Chryſte in ſacrifice.And to declare what ſa- **H**
crifice , he ſaieth the ſame ſacrifice , that Chryſt did inſtitute . And
to lett yow vnderſtand by what authoritie he wolde offre yt, he ſaieth
by that, that Chryſt commaunded yt to be offred in the remembrance of
hym.

A　him. As this maie well inftructe the reader, what ys the plain and verie
trueth of this matter : So yt maie verie well compell the Proclamer,
to confeffe that this ys a plain fentence impugning his falfe doctrine, and
acknowleging other his ignorance or malice, fubmitte him felf to the trueth.

But yet let vs defcend a degree lower towardes our time, and fee what
was then taught. *Ifidorus*, who liued aboue nine hundreth years agon in
this matter geueth this teftimonie : *Sacrificium quod à Chriftianis offertur Deo
primum Chriftus Donunus nofter & magifter inftituit, quando commendauit Apoftolis corpus & fanguinem fuum priufquam traderetur, ficut legitur in Euangelio : Accepit
Iefus panem & calicem & benedicens dedit eis*. The facrifice that ys offred of the
Chryftians vnto God, firft our Lord and mafter Iefus Chryft did inftitute,
*When he gaue his bodie and blood to his Apoftles before he was betraied, as yt ys readde in
the Gofpell: Iefus tooke bread and the cuppe, and bleffing them gaue the fame vnto them*.

In thefe fewe woordes of this Authour we maie learn that Chryft did inftitute the facrifice of the chriftians. We maie learn that the thing that ys
B　offred in facrifice ys the bodie and bloode of Chryft. We maie learn to whô
yt ys offred, that ys vnto God. We maie alfo learn what time yt was inftituted: euen at that time, when Chryft tooke the bread and the cuppe, and
when he had bleffed them gaue them to his Apoftles. Whiche was in his laft
Supper. All thefe ioined to gether doo well beare the contrary propofition
to this mans proclamacion, that ys, that Chryft gaue authoritie to offre his
bodie and bloode vnto God.

A Confonante teftimonie haue we alfo of Haymo, who as he ys of good
auncientie: So ys he accompted a learned Authour. This man expownding
the epiftle of fainct Paule to the Hebrues, and declaring Chryft to be a preift
after the ordre of Melchifedech, faieth thus: *In cuius ordine facerdottj Chriftus factus eft facerdos, non temporalis, fed æternus, nec offerens victimas legales, fed inftar illius panem & vinum, carnem videlicet & fanguinem fuum, de quibus ipfe dixit: Caro mea verè
eft cibus, & fanguis meus verè eft potus. Ifta quoque duo munera, panem videlicet & vinum commifit Ecclefiæ fuæ in memoriam fui offerenda. Vnde patet facrificium pecudum,
perijffe quod fuit ordinis Aaron, & illud manere potius, quod fuit ordinis Melchifedech,
C　quia & Chriftus illud corroborauit, & Ecclefiæ fuæ tenendum reliquit*. In the ordre of
the preifthead of Melchifedech. Chryft being made not a temporall but an
euerlafting preift neither offring legall facrifices, but like vnto him (*meening
Melchifedech*) bread and wine, that ys to faie, his bodie and his bloode, of the
whiche he faieth: My flefh ys verilie meat, and my bloode ys verilie drinke.
*Thefe two giftes, that ys to faie, bread and wine he hath committed to this Churche to be
offred in the remembrance of him. Thus Haimo*.

Wherby yt yt manifeft that the Sacrifice of beaftes ys vanifhed awaie,
whiche was of the ordre of Aaron, and that that raither remaineth, which ys
of the ordre of Melchifedech, bycaufe Chryft alfo hath confirmed yt, and
left yt to his Churche to be kept and vfed. From whence the authoritie co-
met that the Church offreth the facrifice after the ordre of Melchifedech,
this Authour, like as the other before alleaged. hath declared that yt cômeth
from Chryfte. And opening what the Churche doth offer, he faieth that
Chryft did offre bread and wine, that ys (faieth he) his bodie and bloode, whi
che bread and wine he committetd to the Churche to be offred in the re-
D　menbrance of him.

Eycept that the calling of a man, a man: or an oxe, an oxe, be no
plain fpeaches, thefe fentences of thefe Authours in this matter, be plain
fpeaches, and plain fentéces. Yet to côclude this matter, we will heare a grecià

R　ij　　fpeaking

Ifydorus li.
1. de off. ca.
18.

Haymo in
5. ad Heb.

Plain fen-
tences for
mafter
Iwell.

E

speaking as plain as anye of these, whiche ys *Nicolaus Cabasila*, who although he be long: yet for hys plainesse he ys pleasaunt. And for that he ys a grecian we shall learn of him the faith that ys yet receaued in thatChurch, as before of long tyme yt hath ben. This authour shewing howe the blessed Sacrament ys consecrated, sacrificed, and ministred ther, saieth thus: *Cùm venerandam illam cœnam narrauit, & quomodò ante passionem ipsam dedit sanctis suis Discipulis, & quòd accepit calicem, & quòd accepit panem, & actis gratiis sanctificauit, & quòd dixit ea per quæ significauit mysterium, & cùm ea ipsa verba dixit, deinde procidit, & orat, & supplicat, diuinas illas voces ipsius vnigeniti seruatoris nostri etiam in donis propositis applicans, vt suscepto eius sanctissimo & omnipotente Spiritu conuertatur quidem panis in ipsum preciosum & sanctum eius corpus: vinum autem in ipsum immaculatum, & sanctum eius sanguinem. Hæc cùm orauit & dixit, vniuersum sacrificium peractum & perfectum est, & dona sunt sanctificata, & hostia integra & perfecta effecta est, & magna hostia & victima, quæ pro mundo mactata est, supra sacram mensam sita cernitur. Panis enim non amplius figura Dominici corporis, neque donum ferens imaginem veri doni, neque ferens aliquam descriptionem ipsius seruatoris passionum tanquàm in tabula: sed ipsum verum donum, ipsum sanctissimum corpus Domini, quod omnia illa verè suscepit probra, contumelias, vibices, quod crucifixum, quod interfectum, quod sub Pontio Pilato pulchrum testimonium confessum est, quod colaphis appetitum, quod contumelijs affectum, sputa passum est, & fel gustauit. Similiter & vinum ipse sanguis, qui exilijt occiso corpore, hoc corpus et sanguis qui ex Spititu sancto constitutus est, natus ex Maria virgine, qui sepultus est, qui resurrexit tertio die, qui ascendit in cœlos, & sedet ad dexterā Patris.*

F

When he hath declared that honourable Supper, and howe he gaue yt before hys passion to hys holie disciples, and that he tooke the bread, and tooke the cuppe, and geuing thankes sanctified them, and saied those woordes by the which he declared the mysterie. And when he hath spoken those woordes, then he falleth down and praieth, and maketh humble request, applieng those sainges of God the onely begotten Sonne our Sauiour, to the giftes sett furth, that hys Almightie and most holie Spirit being receaued, *the bread maie be turned into the self same precioufe and holie bodie of him, and the wine into the self same immaculate and holie bloode of him.* When he hath praied and saied these thinges, all the whol sacrifice ys throughlie doē and perfected, and the giftes are sanctified, and an wholl and perfecte host ys made. *And the great host and sacrifice whiche was slain for the worlde ys seen sett vpon the holie table.* For the bread ys no more a figure of our Lordes bodie, neither ys yt the gifte bearing the image of the true gifte, neither as in a table, but the very gifte yt self, the verie most holie bodie of our Lord, whiche verilie suffred reproches, contumelies, beatinges, which was slain, whiche confessed a goodlie testimonie vnder Ponce Pilate, which being buffited and with contumelies affected, suffred spitting and tasted gall. *Likewise the wine ys the self same blood that gusht oute of the slain bodie. This ys the bodie and bloode that was made by the holie Gost, borne of the virgen Marie,* which was buried, which rose again the thirde daie, whiche ascended into heauen, and sitteth at the right hand of God the Father. Thus moch this Authour, who as he hath verie plainly and fullie testified the sacrificing of Chrystes bodie in the holie table, So doth he immediately in the next chapter declare the commaundement of Chryst vnto the Apostles and the Church to doo the same, ād saieth thus: *Ipse dixit, Hoc est corpus meum, hic est sanguis meus. Ipse etiam iussit Apostolis, & per Apostolos vniuersæ Ecclesiæ hoc facere. Hoc enim (inquit) facite in meam recordationem. Non iusisset autem facere, nisi esset potestatem daturus vt possent hoc facere.* He saied, this ys my bodie, this ys my blood. *He also commaunded his Apostles, and by hys Apostles the vniuersall Churche*

G

H

this

Nich. Cabasila c. 27

The bread of the Sacrament ys turned into the verie bodie of Chryst, ād wine into his blood, and ys no figure of them.

Idē ca. 28.

A *this to doe. For do ye this* (faieth he) *in my remembrance.* But he had not commaunded them to doo yt, except he wolde geue thē power that they might doo yt. And in the end of this chapiter he faieth thus: *Dominus autem videtur, & contrectatur per veneranda, & facra myſteria, vt qui naturam noſtram & fuſceperit, & ferat in æternum. Hæc eſt facerdotij poteſtas: hic eſt facerdos. Etenim qui feipfum femel obtulit, & facrificauit, à facerdotio non ceſſauit, fed perpetuum hoc facrificij munus nobis obit: per quod etiam eſt aduocatus pro nobis ad Deum in æternum .* Owre Lorde ys feen and felt by the honourable and holie myſteries, as he who hathe bothe taken our Nature vpon him, and will beare yt for euer. Thys ys the power of the preiſthead: This ys the preiſt. *For he that hath once offred and facrificed him felf ceafeth not from hys preiſthead, but he dothe execute the perpetuall office of facrifice in vs, by the which alfo he ys Aduocate for vs to God for euer.*

Nowe this Authour (as other before haue don) hath taught vs both that Chryſtes bodie ys facrificed, and alfo that he hath commaunded hys Apoſtles, and by the Apoſtles all the Churche, to doo euen the fame. And therto he hath alfo geuen power to hys Church to offre Chryſt. For (as this Au-

B thour faieth) *except he had geuen powre to doe yt, he wolde neuer haue commaunded yt to be doen.* And that the verie bodie and blood be facrificed, and not onelie a peice of bread eaten in the remembrance of Chryſt, this Authour fo plainlie teacheth that this Proclamer can not auoid him : but as hys Father *Luther* did aunſwer faincte Iames epiſtle in the matter of iuſtificacion reiecting the fame epiſtle.

For firſt, to auoid the figures, tropes, and fignes , whiche the Aduerſaries comonlie caſt vpon this matter, this Authour faieth, *that by the Almightie powre of the Spirit of God, the bread ys turned into the very bodie of Chryſt,* and not into an image of Chryſt: *And the wine into hys immaculate bloode.*

Secondarely, to auoyd their figures, by expreſſe woordes he faieth : *that after the confecracion the bread ys no more a figure of our Lordes bodie,* neither ys yt an image of the verie thing: neither an onely defcription of Chryſt as a thing might be defcribed in a table: but yt ys the thing yt felf, euen the verie fame bodie that was crucified, and the felf fame bloode that yſhued out the fame

C crucified bodie. What can we haue more? What more plaineffe can be defiered? Ye fee that the bodie of Chryſt ys offred in facrifice: ye fee that powr, authoritie and commaundement ys geuen to the Church fo to do.

And nowe I doubte not, but the reader feeth good , plain, and fufficient matter to approue the doing of the holie catholique Churche , in this matter. And will , I truſt , iudge this Proclamer fufficientlie aunſwered by the beſt learned Fathers, as well of the greke church , as of the latin , and will therfore thinke yt right , that wher this Proclamer required but one plain fentence, hauing nowe a nombre, that he doo perfourme hys promeffe , and fubmitte him felf to the trueth , and fubſcribe to the catholique Churche, and become her childe again , whiche God of hys mercie bring to paffe in him.

For trulie the giftes that God hath placed in him confidered , I can not but loue him, and prayfe God in him, and wiſh that I might ioin with him: But whē I remember hys great fall into this wickedneffe, I pietie him,

D and vtterly deuide my felf from him , as my bownden duetie before God ys.

In this booke then as occafion hath ferued. I haue aunſwered foure peices or membres of hys proclamacion : The firſt , for the hauing of the fcriptures in the vulgar toung : The fecond , for Referuacion of the

Sacrament: The thirde, for the authoritie of the offring of Chryſt to hys Father. The fourth, for the preſence of Chryſtes bodie and blood in the bleſſed Sacrament.

    In the other bookes, by the helpe of God, ſhall be likewiſe aun-
ſwered ſome other partes of the ſame proclamacion as like
occaſion ſhall be miniſtred, whiche God graunt
maye be to hys euerlaſting prayſe and honour. Amen.

THE FIRST CHAPITER DECLARETH THE OFFI-

CES OF THE OLDE LAVVE, AND THE BENEFITTES OF

the newe Lawe, with an exhortation to fubmitte our vnderftanding to the knowledge of faithe, and therwith to
the beleif of the Sacrament.

EX per Moyfen data eft, gratia & veritas per Iefum Chriftum facta eft.
The Lawe (faieth faincte Iohn) was geuen by Moifes but grace
and trueth came by Iefus Chryft.

The Lawe (as faincte Paule declareth)had two offices, for the
which yt was geuen of God, by Moifes to the people. The one
B was to geue them knowledge of finne, and to reftreign them from yt.

Ioan. 1.
The lawe hath two offices.

The firft parte of this office S. Paule fpeaketh of to the Romans, faieng:
Per legem cognitio peccati. By the lawe cometh the knowledge of finne. For
(faieth he in an other place) *Peccatum non cognoui nifi per legem . Nam
concupifcentiam nefciebã, nifi lex diceret : Non concupifces.* I knewe not finne but by
the lawe. For I had not knowen what luft had ment, except the lawe had
faied : Thowe fhalt not luft.

Rom. 3.
Ibid. 7.

The feconde parte he fpeaketh of to the Galathians, wher, when he had
proued that the promiffe of the bleffing came not by the lawe, but by faith,
as being made foure hundreth and thirtie years before the lawe was geuen,
he moueth this queftion : *Quid igitur lex? wherfor then ferueth the Lawe?* As who
fhoulde faie, yf the lawe were not geuen, that by yt men fhoulde atteign to
iuftification, wherto then ferueth yt? what then ys the office of yt? He anfwereth : *Propter trangreffionem pofita eft .* yt was added for tranfgreffion, that
tranfgreffours takinge with the lawe the fpirit of feruitude in feare, might be
C witholden from the trangreffion of the fame Lawe, although the outwarde
obferuacion of yt, conferred not that iuftificaciõ to the obferuers therof, that
auaileth before God.

Galat. 3.

The other office of the Lawe was by liniamentes of figures and fhaddowes to leade the people to Chryft, as S. Paul faieth: *Lex pædagogus fuit in Chrifto.*
The Lawe was oure fchoolemafter to Chryfte . Wherfore our Sauioure
Chryfte willed the Iewes, who were not willinge to receaue him as the Meffias, being yet by the Lawe taught to knowe him, that they fhoulde repair to
the fcriptures of the Lawe, as to their fchoolmafter faieng : *Scrutamini fcripturas, in quibus putatis vos vitam habere æternam, & illæ funt, quæ teftimonium perhibent
de me .* Searche the fcriptures , in the whiche ye thinke to haue eternall life,
and they are they, whiche teftifie of me. Whiche Lawe vndoubtedlie did
fo teache them Chrifte by promiffes, figures, and prophecies, that they
coulde not pretende ignorance, but they muft nedes be fownde offendours
of malice, wherof the cheif ruler of the fchoole Moyfes wolde accufe them,
as Chryfte faieth to them: *Nolite putare quòd ego accufaturus fum vos apud patrem
D meum, eft qui accufat vos Moyfes, in quo fperatis, Si enim crederetis Moyfi, crederetis forfitan & mihi. De me etenim ille fcripfit.* Do not thinke that I will accufe yowe to
my Father, ther ys one that accufeth yowe, euen Moifes in whom ye truft.
For had ye beleued Moifes, ye wolde peraduenture haue beleued me, for he
wrote of me.

Ibid.

Ioan. 5.

Ibid. 5.

Of this office of the Lawe, that ys of the fchoole mafterfhippe of yt, Ho- **E**
we yt promifed Chryfte : Howe yt painted, and defchribed him by figures
and fhaddowes · Howe yt fpake of him by prophecies in the old teftament:
yt ys (as to the pourpofe of the matter, whiche ys nowe in hand, apperteineth) treacted of in the firft booke.

Nowe mindinge to feke the trueth of the fame matter in the newe Teftament, I am moche comforted and delighted, trufting with moche more facilitie and eafe to atteign the fame. And yet as not withoute pleafure mixed
with trauaill, I haue doen the like in the firfte booke, paffinge through the
thikkes (*as yt were*) and obfcure places of the Law, not all vnlike vnto an Hū-
ter, who painfullie beating the buffhes, and traueling through the Thickes,
yet not withoute pleafure feking his game, and comming to the goodlie
faire Lawnde, femeth to be moche eafed, and as yt were, releiued of a great
greif, and then with more delight and pleafure foloweth the fame. Euē fo nowe that I am comed to the beautifull Lawnd of the newe Teftament, wher,
for the fharpe priking busfhes of the feuitute and bondage of finne vnder **F**
the Lawe, and for the obfcure and darke thickes of figures, and fhadowes of
the fame, finding the goodlie pleafaunt Lawnde of grace and veritie by
Iefus Chryfte, I forgett my former trauaills, and with frefhe delight folowe
on my gamme.

The Gospel
hath two
commodi-
ties.

The Lawe had two offices not voide of incōmodities : The Gofpell hath
two benefittes, enriched with great cōmodities. The Lawe gaue knowledge
of finne : The Gófpell geueth grace for remiffion of finnes. the Lawe had
figures : the Gofpell hathe the veritie.

Ioan. 1.

He then by whome came this grace and veritie, *Iefus Chriſte*, who ys the
light of the worlde and lightneth euery man, that cometh into the fame,
geue the bright and clere beames of his knowledge vnto vs, both the writer,
and the reader, that beinge led by his grace, we maie come perfightlie to
his trueth and veritie, and cominge to the fame, we maie with all humilitie
and mekeneffe fubdue our vnderftanding to the feruice of faith. And fo learninge not to be wife in oure owne conceiptes, we maie embrace the trueth
of yt, earneftlie and vnfeignedlie beleuinge the fame trueth, and by beleuing alfo vnderftand yt. for *Nifi credideritis non intelligetis*, faieth the Prophete, **G**

Efay.7.

Except ye beleue, ye fhall not vnderftande. And therfor let vs all call to the
Authour of grace, and geuer of faithe with the Apoftles and faie: *Domine ad-*

Luc. 17.

auge nobis fidem. Lord encreafe our faithe, and I doubte not, but yf he fee that
we come to him, he will haue compaffion vpō vs, and renne and mete with

Luc. 15.

vs, and fall one oure neckes, and kiffe vs, and fo receauinge vs with moche
ioie and gladneffe, walke with vs on the waie, and interprete the Scriptures

Ibid.24.

vnto vs, and fo open oure eyes whiche were holden before, that we fhall
knowe him in breaking of the bread.

And here be aduertifed (Reader) that yf thowe be not with Chryfte in
the breaking of bread thy eies fhall neuer be opened to knowe Chryfte. For
faincte Auguftine fhewing that the eies of the two difciples that went in
Emaus were holden from the knowledge of Chryft, vntill the breaking of
bread faieth *Non enim incōgruenter accipimus hoc impedimentū in oculis corū à Satana*

Aguſt. de.
confenſu
Euāgeliſt.

fuiſſe, ne agnofceretur Iefus, fed tantùm à Chriſto, propter eorum fidem ambiguam facta
eſt permiſſio vſque ad facramentum panis, vt vnitate corporis eius participata, remoueri **H**
intelligatur impedimentum inimici, vt Chriſtus poſſet agnofci. We do not take yt incongruentlie, that this impediment in their eies (*mening the two diſciples that*

Luc.24.

went to Emaus) was of Satan, that Iefus fhoulde not be knowen. But onelie yt
was

A was permitted of Chryſte for their doubtfull faith ſake, vntill they came to the ſacramēt of breade, *that the vnitie of Chryſtes dodie beinge participated,* yt might be perceaued, that the impediment of the Enemie was remoued, that Chryſte might be knowen.

Agreablie to this alſo ſaieth *Theophilact vpon Luk. Inſinuatur & aliud quiddam, nempe quod oculi eorum, qui benedictum panē aſſumunt, aperiuntur, vt agnoſcant illum. Magnam enim & indicibilem vim habet C A R O D O M I N I.* An other thinge alſo ys here inſinuated, that ys, that the eies of them which do take the bleſſed breade, are opened that they maie knowe him (mening *Chriſte*) *For the flesh of oure Lorde hathe a great and vnſpeakable powre or ſtrenght.* Thus moche *Theophilacte.*

Thus although the two diſciples were in the companie of Chryſte, and hearde him interprete the ſcriptures vnto them : yet he was a ſtraunger vnto them, for they knewe him not. And verie well. For as they for lake of perfecte and full faith in him, were ſtraungers to him: So he agreablie as a ſtra-

B unger appeared vnto them. And euen ſo though manie haue hearde the interpretacion of ſcriptures, yea and can them ſelues interprete and vnderſtande manie of them, and can ſpeake and talke of Chryſte, as theſe diſciples did: yet be they ſtraungers to Chryſte, they knowe not Chryſte, for that they haue not a ſownde faith in the veritie of the Sacrament, and ſo in diuerſe other poinctes and matters of faithe. Whiche happeneth to all ſohe as will not be with Chryſte in the breaking of the breade.

For note well this (Reader) that whoſoeuer he be, that erreth in the matter of the Sacrament, he erreth in manie mo. So did *Luther* the Raiſer, and ſtirrer vppe of hereſies in oure time. So did *Oecolampadius, Zwinglius, Bullingerus, Bucerus,* and *Petrus Martir.* So did our contrie men , *Cranmer, Ridley, Latimer,* and *Taler.* So dothe this Chalenger, as his owne confeſſion in his ſermō well prouethe . So do ſoche as yet liue conuertlie, cloaking, and diſſemblinge their hereſies. So that though ſome other hereſie maie be alone in a mā: yet be well aſſured, the hereſie againſt the bleſſed Sacrament ys neuer alone in anie man, but accompanied with ſo manie other hereſies, as he that hath

C them becometh a ſtraunger to Chryſte, and for lacke of a ſownde faithe knoweth not Chryſte.

Come therfore, and ioin with Chryſte in the breaking of the breade, be partaker of the vnitie of Chryſtes bodie, that (as ſaincte Auguſtine ſaieth) the impediment of the Enemie, whiche letteth thee to knowe Chryſte, maie be remoued, and taken awaie. For *the flesh of Chryſte (as Theophilacte* ſaiethe)*hath an vnſpeakeable powre or ſtrenght,* ſoche power or ſtrenght that after the receipt of yt in due maner of faithe, and ſincere deuocion , yt will open thine eies, that thowe ſhalt knowe him trulie, whiche nowe, phantaſieng that thowe doeſt knowe him, knoweſt him but phantaſticall . Seing then this bleſſed Sacrament ys of ſoche great, and vnſpeakable vertue and geueth ſo great a benefitt , let vs heare the Authour of veritie, and of the Sacrament alſo, commending to vs the veritie of the ſame.

Theop . in Luc.ca.24

Soche as haue not a ſownd faith in the veritie of the Sacrament are ſtraungers to Chryſt.

Whoerreth in the Sacrament, erreth in many other matters of faithe.

Theffeſhof Chryſt in the Sacrament hath an vnſpeakable powr

THE

THE SECONDE CHAPITER EXPOVNDETH THE
fixt of fainĉte Iohn according to the letter.

Two nota-ble mencios made by Chryſt of the Sacra-ment.

THe holie gofpell teacheth vs, that the Authour of this bleſſed Sacramét made two notable mencions therof at two ſondrie times. The one was the promiſſe of the inſtitution of yt, with a declaracion of the befitte, that ſhoulde enſewe to men ther-bie, whiche ys ſett furth and declared in the ſixt chapiter of ſainĉte Iohn. The other was the plain and certen inſtitutio of yt in the laſt ſupper, accompliſhing the promiſſe before made. Of theſe two by the helpe of the Authour of them, with thaſſiſtance, and direĉtion of that his Spirit of trueth, whiche he hathe promiſed ſhoulde lead vs into all trueth, this boo ke ſhall tell the verie trueth.

And foraſmoch as by ordre the promiſſe goeth before the accompliſh-ment of the promiſſe, although ſainĉte Iohn, who ys the writer of yt, did write yt manie years after the other Euágeliſtes had written the laſt ſupper, yet will I, as yt was ſpoken of Chryſt firſt, before the other was doen, ſo firſt treaĉte of the ſame.

Oure Sauiour Chryſt being God and man, and knowinge (for that not-hing was hidden to him) all thinges, as well the preſent ſecrete thinges and thoughtes of man, as alſo the ordre and ſucceſſion of thinges to come, fore-ſeeing that the people wolde reſorte vnto him, and that mete occaſio ſhoul-de be geuen, and that the time wolde verie well ſerue for the preparinge of the mindes of ſoche as wolde beleue in him, to ſpeake of the high miſterie of the receauing of his bodie and bloode : he began with the great miracle of the multiplieng of fiue barlie loaues and two fiſhes. By the whiche miracle they being moued to conſider his great power, might the more eaſilie be in-duced to the beleif of the greate miracle of the geuing of his bleſſed bodie and blood in the Sacrament, as Chryſoſtome ſaieth : *Propterea id prius fecit mi-*

Chryſoſt. hom.45 in Ioan.

raculum, vt per illud non eſſent ampliùs increduli his, quæ poſtmodum diceret, Therfore (ſaieth Chryſoſtom) did he woorke this miracle firſt, that by yt they ſhoulde be no more vnbeleuing in thoſe thinges, whiche he wolde afterwarde tell them. For as the ſame Chryſoſtom ſaieth, *Ex eo, & hæc credere oportuit ei facilia faĉtu eſſe.* By that miracle yt behoued them to beleue, that theſe thin ges alſo were eaſie for him to do.

Ibidem.

This miracle then beinge doen as a preparatiue or induĉtion to the beleif of that great miracle, that afterward he wolde tell them that he wolde do : manie people did folowe him, though drawen by diuerſe Spirittes : Some by the heauenlie Spiritte mouinge the minde : Some by the fleſhlie Spiritte, moued of the bellie. whiche our Sauiour Chryſte did note when he ſaied :

Ioan. 6.

Sequimini me, non quia vidiſtis ſigna, ſed quia manducaſtis ex panibus, & ſaturati eſtis. Ye folowe me not bicauſe ye haue ſeen the miracles, but bicauſe ye haue eaten of the loaues, and were filled. And ſo proceding nearer to entre into the matter, whiche he cheiflie entended, ſaied vnto them : *Operamini non cibũ qui perit, ſed qui permanet in vitam æternam, quem filius hominis daturus eſt vobis.* Labour not for the meat whiche periſheth, but for that whiche endureth into euerlaſting life, whiche meate the Sonne of man ſhall geue vnto yowe.

The Iewes nowe by this aduertiſed, perceaued that they were moued to woorke for the heauenlie life, and therfore aſking howe they ſhoulde woor-ke the worke of God, receaued aunſwer, that yt was to beleue in him whŏ god had ſent. Yet nowe forgetting the miracle ſo lately doen in feading ſo
great

A great a multitude with ſo fewe loaues, for the whiche then they coulde ſaie: This ys the verie Prophete, whiche ſhoulde come into the worlde, and wolde haue taken him and made him king: they ſaied nowe vnto him: *Quod ergo facis ſignum, vt videamus, & credamus tibi &c.* What ſign ſhewest thowe nowe, that we maie ſee and beleue thee? What doeſt thowe woorke? Oure fathers did eate Manna in the deſert (as yt ys written) he gaue them bread from heauen to eate: Here our Sauiour Chryſte hauing iuſt occaſion, entreth into a large diſputation with thē whiche continueth to the chapiters end. In the whiche he maketh mencion of three ſundrie breades: that ys, of the bread *Manna*, of the bread the Sōne of God, and of the breade the fleſh of Chryſte. Whiche three breades, as they be diſtincted in nature: So dothe the Euangeliſt, diſtincte them, by the diſtinction of their times in the whiche they were geuen.

Three ſundrie breades mencioned by Chryſt. Joan.6.

And therfore ſpeaking of *Manna*, whiche was geuen long before, he dothe diſtincte yt by the time that ys paſt, ſaieng: *Patres veſtri manducauerunt Manna in deſerto.* yowre fathers haue eaten *Manna* in the wilderneſſe. By whiche ſaing ys declared not onelie a diſtinction and difference of the thing yt

1.
Ibid.6.

B ſelf, being *Manna*, but alſo of the time and place that yt was eaten of their fathers.

The ſeconde bread ys the Godhead of Chryſt, whiche as yt ys diſtincted from the firſt bread in ſubſtance: So ys yt diſtincted by the difference of the geuing of yt. And therfore our Sauiour Chryſte vttereth yt in the preſent tence, as then preſentlie geuen, ſaing: *Non Moyſes dedit vobis panem de cælo, ſed Pater meus dat vobis panem de celo verum.* Moyſes gaue you not that bread from heauen: but my Father geueth yowe the true bread from heauen,

2.

Where note that Chryſt ſaieth: *that his Father geueth the true bread.* He did not ſaie, *that he did geue, or will geue:* but preſentlie, *geueth.* And who ys this bread he declareth, ſaieng: *Ego ſum panis vitæ.* I am the bread of life. And whether this be ſpoken of his manhead, or of his godhead, he immediatelie openeth: *Qui venit ad me non eſuriet, & qui credit in me, non ſitiet in æternum.* He that cometh to me ſhall not hunger, and he that beleueth in me ſhall neuer thirſt. Beleif ys directed to none, as to beleue in them, but to God alone.

Beleif ys directed to God alone.

C We beleue in Ieſus Chryſt God and man, not by the conſideracion of his manheade alone do we beleue in him, but in that his Godhead and his māhead be ioined in vnitie of perſon, ſo as God and man ys one Chryſt. Wherfore in this place he muſt be vnderſtanded of neceſſitie to ſpeake of his Godhead.

The thirde bread he beginnith to ſpeake of when he ſaied: *Et panis quem ego dabo, caro mea eſt, quam dabo pro mundi vita.* And the bread whiche, I will geue ys my fleſh. whiche I will geue for the life of the worlde. In the whiche woordes he teacheth a manifeſt diuerſitie of this bread here ſpoken of, from the other ſpoken of before. For here by expreſſe woordes he nameth the bread his fleſh. whiche yet more plainlie he teacheth to be his verie reall and ſubſtanciall fleſh, when he ſaieth: *that he will geue them that ſame fleſh, whiche he will geue for the life of the worlde.* He gaue not his fleſh ſpirituallie to ſuffer death for the life of the worlde, But the verie reall fleſh of his verie bodie.

3.

Wher nowe note, that wher I ſaied before, that in this chapiter (beſides

D the bread whiche our ſauiour Chryſt fedde the people then with, miraculouſlie) ther were three breades ſpokē of by Chryſt: Theſe three breades be diſtincted not onelie with difference of time, as ys before declared, but alſo with the differēce of ſubſtāce, as being three ſeuerall and diuerſe ſubſtances, as in this ſequele it ſhall appeare.

As for *Manna*, that yt was a diuerſe ſubſtance from either of the other E
two, ye will eaſilie graunt me. That theſe other two be different in ſubſtance alſo, yt ys partlie proued allreadie, for that the one of the ſame ys the
God head of Chryſt, the proof wherof ys, that he moued the Iewes to beleue in yt. The other ys his fleſh. whiche he gaue for the worlde.

And here note that ſpeaking of the bread of his Godhead he moueth the
Iewes more then once to beleue in him. But ſpeaking of this other bread
he neuer moued the Iewes to beleue in yt, but allwais to eate yt. Ther he
ſaied: *Ego ſum panis vitæ.* I am the bread of life. Here (as yt were diſſeueringe
his fleſh, as being one of the ſubſtáciall partes of his perſon, from the wholl)
he ſaieth, *Panis &c. The bread whiche I will geue ys my fleſh,* whiche ys a different
Subſtance from the ſubſtance of the Godhead of Chryſt although bothe
theiſe Subſtances in Chryſt, be but one perſon.

As touching the difference of time in the geuing of theſe two breades:
The firſt ys geuen preſentlie, and therfore Chryſt ſaied: *Panis enim Dei eſt, qui
de cœlo deſcendit, & dat vitam mundo.* For the breade of God ys he, which com F
meth down from heauen, and geueth life vnto the worlde. Wher he allwais
ſpeaketh of the preſent time, ſaing: that he cometh and geueth life to
the worlde.

Nowe ſpeaking of the thirde breade, he ſpaketh of the time not preſent,
but of the time to come, ſaing: *The bread which I will geue.* So that as ther ys
two plain differéces of time, that ys the time preſent, and the time to come:
So be the two breades, two different Subſtances, the one being expreſſed as
the cheifer parte to be beleued on, the other as the inferiour parte, by the
name of fleſh to be eaten on.

This I dare auouche to be the verie natiue ſenſe, and the true vnderſtanding of this ſcripture, as ye maie perceaue the verie ſcripture yt ſelf enforceth vs to take this ſenſe, accordinge to the letter.

Neuer the leſſe that ye maie perceaue, that I will not arrogate to my ſelf
ſoche authoritie to expownde this ſcripture, as the Aduerſaries haue doen,
who haue ſo impudentlie vpon their owne head and authoritie taught, that G
Chryſt here ſpake no one woorde of his bodie and bloode in the Sacramét,
but onelie of his woorde and our beleif in the ſame: for the confirmacion
of that, which yt hath pleaſed god to be vttered by me, and the confutaciō
of that, that Satan hath moued the Aduerſaries to ſaie againſt the trueth, I
wil as hertofore ys doen, conſulte with certain of the elders of Chryſtes Par
liament houſe, and learn of them yf in that ſame houſe, ther ys acknowledged, and receaued any ſoche differences of breades in the ſixte chapiter of
ſaincte Iohn, as I haue declared or no. whiche differences when they ſhall
be by them auouched, I will vſe their teſtimonie and authoritie to expownde the reſt of the chapiter, that toucheth my matter cheiflie intended, and
not mine owne. Whoſe authoritie (Reader) yf thowe wilt not by thy affection ſo farre abaſe, that thowe wilte counteruaill the ſame with a bare ſaing
of a light Newling, and preferre him before ſo manie graue Auncientes, I
doubte not but thowe ſhalt ſe matter enough, to drawe thee to the auncié t,
and verie trueth, profeſſed and receaued manie hundreth years in the Churche of Chryſte.

H

THE

A THE THIRDE CHAPITER PROVETH BY THE
*doctours that the sixte of sainct Iohn speaketh as wel of the bread Chryftes flesh in
the Sacrament, as of the bread his Godhead.*

 Nd firft let vs fee the diftinction of breades. As for the breade whiche oure Sauiour Chryft multiplied and the breade *Manna*, which be manifeftlie diftincted in all mens knowledges, and of the whiche ther ys no Controuerfie, I fhall not nede to fpeake any more.

Of the other two breades, wher oure Sauiour Chryft began to enter difputacion of them, and in the beginning of the fame faied: *Ego fum panis vitæ.* Ther Chryfoftom in expownding the fame text, faieth: *Iam in myfteriorum traditionem deuéturus eft, et primùm de diuinitate fua fic difputat: Ego fum panis vitæ. Neque enim de corpore, hoc dictum eft, de quo circa finem inquit, Panis quem ego dabo, caro mea eft: Sed adhucde diuinitate. Etenim ille propter Deum Verbũ panis eft, quemadmodum hic panis, propter aduenientem ei Spiritũ, panis cæleftis efficitur.* Nowe will he (meening **B** Chryfte) come to the fetting furth of the myfteries, and firft of his Godhead, he faieth thus: *I am the bread of life.* For this was not fpoken of hys bodie of the which aboute the end he faieth: *The bread which I will geue, ys my flesh:* But as yet of his Godhead. For as that ys bread for God the Sonne: So ys thie breade made heauenlie bread, for the Spirit coming to yt. Thus moche Chryfoftom Ys not this a cler teftimonie? Do ye not fee here, a plain diftinctiõ of breads? This (faieth he) *I am the bread of life,* ys fpoken of the Godhead, and cõtinueth difputacion of yt, till he come to this text: *The bread that I wil geue ys my flesh.* And this (faieth he) ys fpoken of his bodie. And dothe not nowe the fixt of S. Iohn fpeake of the bodie of Chryfte in the Sacrament?

Note further that he faieth, as the Godhead ys bread for God the Sonne (*meening that the Godhead in Chryft ys God the Sõne*) So (*faieth he*) this bread (*meening the flesh of Chryft*) ys made the heauenlie breade for the fpirit coming to yt.

But I will not trooble thee (Reader) with manie woords in fo plain a mat ter. I will raither produce fome other one of the other fide of Chryftes Parliament houfe, to fee yf their teftimonie be agreable, and whether they be **C** taught of one Spirit, one true expofition of Chryftes Gofpell.

S. Auguften expownding the fame text (that Chryfoftõ faieth Chryft fpake of his bodie) writeth thus: *Determinat confequenter Dominus quomodò fe panẽ dicat, non tantùm fecundùm diuinitatẽ, quæ pafcit omnia, fed etiã fecũdùm humanã naturã, quæ eft affumpta à Verbo Dei, cum fubdit: Et panis quẽ ego dabo caro mea eft.* Owr Lord (faieth S. Auguftine) determineth confequentlie how he calleth him felf bread, not onelie after his Godhead, whiche fedeth all thinges, but alfo after his humane nature, which ys affumpted of the Sonne of God, whẽ he faied afterward: *And the breade whiche I will geue ys my flesh, &c.* Doth not here S. Auguftin agrea blie with Chryfoftome, teach a plain difference of the bread of the Godhead of Chryft, and the bread of his Mãhead? doth not he faie that Chryft in this text. *The bread which I will geue, ys my flesh,* dothe fpeake of his humane nature? Confider then (Reader) the authoritie and auncientie of thefe two great and famoufe Fathers of Chryftes Churche, and accept their iudgementes before thefe newfangled Inuentours, in the expofition of the fcriptures.

And now that ye haue heard thefe two of the higher houfe agreablie re **D** porting how the Church in their times vnderftood the fixt chap. of S. Ihon of the Sacramẽt: We will alfo heare fome of the lower houfe, ãd fome of thẽ not of the later daies, but of the aunciéts of that forte being well toward a thoufand years agone. Of the whiche we wil firft heare *Theophilacte* the folower,

(margin notes:)
Ioan. 6.
Chryfoft. homil. 44. in Ioan.

Chryftes Godhead and manhead diftincted as two breades.

lower of *Chryfoſtome* in manie thinges,whether he folowe him in this alſo or no.Thus he writeth vpon the ſame téxt.

Theophi-lact.in 6. Ioan.

*Manifeſtè autem nobis hoc loco,de communione corporis dicit. Nam panis (inquit) quem ego dabo,caro mea eſt,quam ego dabo pro mundi vita. Porro poteſtatem ſuam indicans, quòd non vt ſeruus,& minor patre crucifigendus,ſed voluntariè,inquit, Ego dabo carnem meam pro mundi vita.*Manifeſtlie doth Chryſt ſpeake vnto vs of the myſticall communion of hys bodie.*For the bread(ſaieth he)whiche I will geue yowe, ys my fleſh,which I will geue for the life of the worlde.* And ſhewing his power, that he ſhould be crucified not as a ſeruaunt,and leſſe then the Father,but willinglie he ſaieth:*I will geue my fleſh for the life of the worlde.*

Note here that *Theophilacte* doth not onelie folowe,and agree with Chry ſoſtome:but alſo he ſemeth to ſignifie,that yt was a clere matter,a plain matter,a matter receaued of all men of Chryſtes Churche in his time withoute controuerſie,when he ſaeth, that Chryſt in that text ſpake manifeſtly of the communion of his bodie.

A meruciloufe matter,that,that Chryſt did ſpeake ſo manifeſtlie, and of theſe Fathers was cõceaued ſo clerly:ſhoulde nowe a daies be taken of theſe peruerters of Gods ſcripturs ſo obſcurelie By this ye maie ſee that in the cler light they are blinde,and can not ſee. For blinde malicioufe ignorance hath vtterlie blinded them.Therfore an other daie,except in time they repente, they ſhall ſaie,and lamentablie confeſſe,as in the booke of wiſdom ys ſaied in the perſons of ſoch:*Errauimus à via veritatis,et iuſtitiæ lumẽ nõ illuxit nobis, &c. We haue erred from the waie of trueth,and the light of righteouſnes hath not ſhined to vs, and the Sunne of vnderſtanding roſe not vppe vpon vs.We haue wearied our ſelues in the waie of wickedneſſe,and deſtruction.Tedioufe waies haue we goen, but as for the waie of the Lorde we haue not knowen.*Whiche maner of lamentacion God auerte from them,and geue them grace in time to repent, that the Sunne of vnderſtanding maie riſe vpon theme.

To procead,and therby to trie whether ſoch as haue writen of late years, I mene, whiche were within theſe three hundreth years or ther aboute (whiche haue ben ſo vilie eſtemed of theſe ſingular phantaſied men of our time)did diſſent from theſe elders in the expoſition of this ſcripture : And whether the Church theſe two or three hundreth years laſt paſt, did otherwiſe vnderſtand the ſcriptures then the fathers did, by the hearing of ſome one we ſhall perceaue.

And to ſpeake here what I thinke,verilie I thinke the ſubtle and craftie conueighance of the Aduerſaries,and this Proclamer alſo,was and ys to contemne and deſpiſe theſe late authours, firſt, bicaufe they wer(as they ſaie) not eloquent, and therfore *Eraſmus* moche inueigheth againſt Lyra . Then theſe are not auncient,and therfor not to be alleaged.Laſt they open théſelues a litle more,and ſaie theſe authours are not,to be alleaged, but reiected bicauſe their doctrine ys not ſownd,but corrupted. And they haue corrupted(ſaie they)and peruerted,and deſtroied Gods woord with the inuentiõs of mẽ.And by this were al the learned writers,which were within theſe ſixe or ſeuen hũdreth years defaced and reiected as .*S.Tho.Aquinas, S. Bonauentura,Petrus Lombardus,Dionyſius Carthuſianus,Hugo Cardinalis,*Holcot, and N.Lyra, with a great nõbre mo of that age,which are not eſteemed, nor accepted as of authoritie,nor none that haue writen within the compaſſe of theſe thouſand years can be allowed by ſome of the Aduerſaries. And why was this? Bicauſe they wrote ſo plainlie, that they coulde not be wreſted.

As for other Fathers, that were before a thouſand years, though manye

Sap.5.

Fathers in olde time ſpake of the myſteries ſouertlie.

of

A of them did writte verie plain,as occasion did serue , when they did write
to christen men.Yet oftentimes when they did preache to the people , or
write to soche as were weake in faith , as in those daies the Churche was
mingled with those that had not receaued the faithe,then bicause *Perfectorũ
est solidus cibus*,strong meat ys for them that be perfecte,and *Paruulis in Christo
lac dandum*. To ionglinges in Chriſte milke ys to be geuen: therfor they of-
tentimes(as yt was neceſſarie,that the myſteries of our faithe , ſhoulde not
be vttered to them that coulde not beare them) did ſpeake of the ſame couertlie and cloſelie,and therfore they were fain oftentimes to knitte vppe
ther talke of the Sacrament, with this or like ſaieng: *Norunt fideles*,the faithful
do knowe.And by like occaſion did in manie places write obſcurelie in this
matter,and did not ſo manifeſtlie and plainly vtter yt, bicauſe ther was no
occaſion geuen them by hereſie in that matter,but all were of one minde in
yt,hauing moſt godlie peace and quietnes in the ſame.

B And therfore the Aduerſarie more delighted with obſcure places,which
he thinketh better to drawe to his ſence,then the plain places , whiche will
not ſuffer them ſelues to be drawen , hath laboured to reiecte ſoche as did
write , ſince the Churche was well ſettled and ſtaied, and might therfore
write plainly,what their faith taught them in this myſterie. But cheiſlie all
them that did write ſince the time of *Berengarius* , whiche vpon occaſion of
hereſie were enforced to write plainly in this matter. But God be prayſed
the eldeſt and auncienteſt Fathers , haue yet in diuerſe places written
ſo moche in plain maner , that yt ys able to conuince and ouerthrowe
the hereſies of the Aduerſaries , as partelie ye haue heard allreadie.

And yet for all the pretenſed auncientie they ſought,refuſing theſe learned men , that were within a thouſand years,yet one of them wolde alleage
an other,as *Bullinger* alleaged *Zuinglius* in his expoſition vpon ſainct Paules
epiſtles,whiche,*Zuinglius* was ſo holie and ſo auncient a father , that he was
ſlain in a ſedicion raiſed by him and his diſciples, againſt the magiſtrates of
hys contrie . And this ys as good a chaung,as the heretiks made in the begin
C ning of this wicked time of hereſie, when they putte the holy ſaincte and
Martyr *Policarpus*,that was ſaincte Iohn the Euangeliſtes diſciple,oute of the
kalender , and putt in the heretike Thomas Hutten , that was bournt
for hereſie.

Nowe notwithſtanding their craftie iniquitie in reiecting theſe good
catholique authours,I will vſe plain ſimplicitie in the accepting of them,that
the trueth which they profeſſe being auncient though the authours be of
late daies,and the conſonancie of theſe with the moſt auncient authours in
teaching and vttering the ſame trueth , maie be perceaued.
For yf theſe of late yeares agree with them of the olde time in the trueth,
and teache the ſame trueth that thother do,what ſhoulde lette vs to heare
them,and accepte them?Yf none ſhoulde be receaued but ſoche as were a
thouſand years ſince,and ſoche alſo as be of this our time,ſhal be refuſed,thē
preachers muſt ceaſſe.For of what more authoritie or credite ys he of, that
teacheth in the pulpet by ſpeaking, then he that teacheth by open writing?
Yf ye will not beleue me writing, ye will not beleue me preaching.Yf ye wil
beleue me preaching,for that I ſpeake the trueth by the ſcriptures, and aun-
D cient fathers:Beleue me alſo writing the trueth by the ſcriptures ād aunciēt
fathers.And yf theſe alowed writers of theſe later daies teach the trueth
by the ſcripturs,ād aunciēt fathers,thē muſt they neds be receaued.And ther
for trulie yt ys neceſſarie that they be alleaged , to thētent the trueth maie

*Heretikes,
how they
alleage the
fathers.*

*Like to like,
Zuinglius
ſlain in a re
bellion begõ
by himſelf.*

*Polycarp.
put out of
the Kalēder*

*Th'authori-
tie of late
writers ap
proued by
good rea-
ſons.*

be perceaued to be one throughout all, and that they being ioined with the **E**
aunciétes, yt maie be feé that the same trueth is taught now, that was taught
a thousand yeares agó before? And therfor haue I determined not to geue
place to this refusall of Heretiques, but to alleage the Authours of these later
yeares, that the cósonancie and vnitie of the trueth maie be perceaued in all
ages, and that ther ys no other trueth taught now, thé was taught in thePri
mitiue Church, and the time of the Apostles, yea, no other trueth, then was
taught by oure Sauiour Chryst himself, and by his holie Spirit, the Authour
of all trueth. Wherby the foule railinges, and slaunders, which bemost comó
lie in the mouthes of the enemies maie be taken awaie, and they of their vntrueth and malice woorthilie confownded. Thus moche I thought good to
saie, for that in this book I minde to vse the testimonies of these late writers
for thentent aboue specified.

And nowe therfore to *Theophilaéle* the Grecian, I shall ioin the learned do
étour *Nicolaus de Lyra* a latin Authour who writing vpon the sixt of S. Iohn
cometh to this text: *Et panis, quem ego dabo, caro mea est.* And the bread, whiche **F**
I will geue ys my flesh: and expowndeth yt thus: *Postquam egit de pane spiritua-*
Nico.Lira *li, qui est Verbum, hic consequenter agit de pane spirituali, qui est Sacramentum.* After he
in.6.Ioan. hath don (saieth this Authour, of Chryst) with the spirituall bread, which ys
the woorde: here consequentlie he treaéted of the spirituall breade, whiche
ys the Sacrament. What dothe this authour dissent from the Fathers? dothe
he not signifie that Chryste before the sentence so often alleaged, did speake
of the spirituall bread hys Godhead, which he calleth the woord? And doth
he not now saie, that in yt that foloweth Chryst speaketh of the Sacrament?

These be sufficient to declare the true vnderstáding of our Sauiour Chry
stes processe, and ordre in the sixte of S. Iohn. And for that ye perceaue the
same, aswell after the minde of Chryste, the verie texte so leading vs to vnderstand yt, as also after the minde of diuerse learned authours, I will nowe
procead to see the vnderstáding of diuerse textes of the rest of this chapiter,
that treaéte of the blessed Sacrament.

G

THE FOVRTH CHAPITER BEGINNETH A
further proof of the former matter by S.Cyprian and Euthymius.

His distinéction of these two breades last before mencioned perceaued, and being withall remébred, that at this text (*The bread,*
which I shall geue, ys my flesh, whiche I will gene for the life of the world)
Chryst began to speake of the Sacrament, and continueth the di
sputation therof to the ende of the chapiter: to proue the same
more manifestlie to the Reader, and withall to make yt clere, that that processe ys not of a figuratiue flesh, but of Chrystes verie propre flesh and bodie
I will beginne at the same text, and so descending to the last by a nombre of
the most auncient Fathers of Chrystes Parliament house, open both the one
and the other, I trust, to the full contentacion of the godlie Reader.

The firste that shall shewe hys minde of this matter shall be the holie Mar
tyr Cyprian, who saieth thus: *Panis vitæ Christus est, & panis hic omnium non est,*
sed noster est. Et quomodò dicimus, Pater noster, quia intelligentium, & credentium pater
est: sic & pané nostrú vocamus, quia Christus noster, qui eius corpus cótingimus, panis est. **H**
Hunc autem pané dari nobis quotidiè postulamus, ne qui in Christo sumus, & Eucharistiam
quotidie ad cibú salutis accipimus, intercedente grauiore aliquo delicto, dum abstenti, & nó
cómunicantes, à cælesti pane prohibemur, à Christi corpore separemur, ipso prædicante, &
mon ente:

A *monente: Ego sum panis vitæ,qui de cælo descendi.Si quis ederit de hoc pane viuet in æternum.Panis autè quem ego dedero,caro mea est, pro seculi vita.* The bread of life ys Chryst,and this breade ys not the breade of all men,but yt ys ours. And as we do saie,*Oure Father*,becaufe he ys the father of all that do beleue and vnderstande: Euen so also , *oure bread,call we,whiche touche his bodie* , bicaufe owre Chryste ys bread.This breade we dailie defire to be geuen vs,least we,which be in Chryst,and take the Sacrament dailie to oure meate of health , fome greuoufe offence coming betwene,while we being excomunicated, and not receauing be forbidden from the heauenlie bread, maie be feparated from the bodie of Chryfte,he himfelf openly faing and teaching : *I am the bread of life,whiche defcended from heauen.Whofoeuer shal eate of this bread shall liue for euer. The bread,which I will geue,ys my flesh for the life of the worlde.*Thus moch S.Cypriã

In this fentence,I doubte not but ye perceaue , that this holy Martyr applieth the fentences of the fixt of S.Iohn to the Sacramēt of Chryftes bodie and blood.According to whiche vnderstanding he calleth Chryst *our bread*, whom he fo calleth ,not onelie bicaufe of his Godhead, but alfo bicaufe he

S. Cyprian applieth the fixt of .S. Iohn to the Sacrament

B feadeth vs in the Sacrament with his bodie.For(faieth he) we *being in Chryfte, do receaue the Sacrament dailie to the meate of health.*But yf by finne we forbeare to receaue the heauenlie bread,we be feparated from the bodie of Chryfte. Wherby we maie perceaue that not onelie the fixt of S.Iohn ys to be vnderstanded of the Sacrament,But alfo when S. Cyprian calleth the Sacrament *the meat of health,the heauenly bread,and the bodie*: we are taught that in the Sacramēt ys the veric prefence of that bodie,to the which proprelie thefe goodlie titles maie be wourthilie applied.Whiche bodie can be none other but the bodie of Chryft God an man.

But forafmoch as the faith of this famoufe Father and holie Martyr Cyprian in this point hath ben notablie and manifeftlie declared in fentences before alleaged in the firft booke , and more herafter fhall be fpoken,I will not nowe trooble the reader,with any longer declaracion of the fame , but will ioin with *Cyprian* one of the other fide of Chryftes Parliament houfe, euen *Euthymius* a grecian,whofe fentence,Reader yt fhall not repent thee to

C hear,yf thowe defire to knowe the trueth. Vpon the text of S . Iohn before treacted of he maketh this expofition.

Euthymius in 6 .Ioan.

Duobus modis dicitur Chriftus effe panis,fecundùm diuinitatem fcilicet, & humanitatem.Poftquam ergo docuit de modo qui fecundùm diuinitatem eft , nunc etiam docet de modo,qui eft fecundùm humanitatem.Non autem dixit,quem do,fed quem dabo . Daturus namque erat in vltima cœna,quando fumptum panem,actis gratijs fregit , deditque Difcipulis,& ait, Accipite, & comedite: Hoc eft corpus meum. Chryfte ys faied to be bread two waies:that ys,after his Godhead,and after his manhead. Therfore when he had taught the maner whiche ys after his Godhead : Nowe dothe he alfo teache the maner whiche ys after hys manhead . For he did not faie,*which I do geue*,but *which I will geue.* For he wolde geue yt in the laft Supper,when thankes being geuen,he brake the bread which he had taken, and gaue yt to the difciples and faied:Take,eate, this ys my bodie.

What can the Aduerfaries faie againft fo manifeft , and fo plain a fentence?Do not their chekes waxe red for fhame?Ys not blind ignorance,or deue-

D lifh malice to be laied vnto thefe men, that either do not know the learning of fo manie great clerkes,or ells,yf they knowe , do fo maliciouflie, fo deuelifhlie preferre their owne arrogant phantafies and opinons, and prefume to faie the contrarie to that,fo manie,in foch fundrie ages,declaring alfo therby the whol cõfet of the church through al ages in the fame do affirme ãd teach?

whiche ys,that Chryſt did treact of,and promiſſe in ſixt of Iohn, the Sacra- **E**
ment of his bodie and bloode.

Now(gentle Reader) wilt thow beleue them in their matters,when they
be deprehended in ſoche notable falſhead,as all the Church doth reprehende them for.And yet their falſhead ſhall more appeare by other mo heraf-
ter.Wherby yt ſhall moſt clerely be perceaued,that they haue attempted a-
gainſt all trueth,to wreſt the ſixt chapiter of ſaincte Iohn , from the Sacrament. And ſo ſhalt thowe ſe howe farre they haue ſwarued,and doo ſwarue
from the treuth.

THE FIFTH CHAPITER PROCEADETH VPON
the ſame text,by ſaincte Auguſtin and Chryſoſtome.

Hat ye maie ſee more of the vnderſtāding of this text, an other
coople ſhall be produced to ſhewe yow howe this place of Ihō
ys vnderſtanded.The firſt of them ſhall be famouſe Auguſtine, **F**
who ſaieth thus:*Menſa ſponſi tui panem habet integrum, & poculum
ſanctū,quem panē,et ſi fractū,comminutumque vidimus,integrè tamen cum
ipſo ſuo Patre manet in cælis.De quo pane dicit:Panis quem ego daho,caro mea eſt pro mun
di vita.*The table of thy ſpouſe hath perfect or pure bread,and an holie cup-
pe.Whiche bread although we haue ſeen broken,and bruyſed on the croſſe:
yet yt abydeth with that his Father wholl in heauen. Of the whiche bread
he ſaieth : *The bread that I will geue ys my fleſh , whiche I will geue for the life of
the worlde.*

Auguſt.de cultura a- gri Domi- nici.

S.Auguſtine ſpeaking here to the ſpouſe of Chryſte,ſaieth,that the table
of her Spouſe or huſbande hath a perfect bread , The bread on the table of
Chryſte,what ys yt but the Sacrament?Of this bread whiche ys the Sacrament in the table of Chryſte,the ſame Chryſte(ſaieth S. Auguſtine) ſaieth:
*The bread whiche I will geue ys my fleſh.*By which woordes yt ys ineuitablie mani
feſt that that ſentence of S.Iohn ys ſpoken of the Sacrament.

But nowe whether yt be ſpoken of the Sacramēt,as of a bare ſigne,which
ſigne(as the Aduerſaries alleage)as other ſignes likewiſe,dothe but take the
name of the thing,that yt ys the ſigne of, or no,let vs ſearche by ſainct Augu **G**
ſtine here.Yt ys euident that ſaincte Auguſtine here teacheth,that yt ys ſpoken of the verie thing whiche ys ſignified, and not of the bare ſigne. For S.

All one bodie that was broken on the Croſ ſe, ys with the Father in heauen, and on the altar.

Auguſtine ſpeaking of the bread,and that of one bread,dothe declare yt to
be,and to haue ben in three ſundrie places,that ys,on the table,on the croſſe,and in heauen with his Father.The Sacrament,that ys, the externe ſigne,
was neither on the croſſe,neither ys in heauen.Wherfore yt ys the verie bodie of Chryſte which was vpon the croſſe, and ys with the Father in heauen,
that ys nowe on the table of Chryſte. For note the ſaing well,and ye ſhall
finde,that he ſpeaketh but of one bread.For when he had ſpoken of yt, as
being on the table,he ſpeaketh again of the ſame by the relatiue,ſaing:which
bread although we haue ſeen broken on the croſſe.

A relatiue(as the grammarian knoweth)maketh reherſall of a thing ſpokē
of before.Then when he ſaied ,*whiche*,he ſpeaketh of the bread on the table.
So that by S.Auguſtine,*that ſame bread,that ys on the table,ys yt whiche was broken
on the croſſe.And that that was broken on the croſſe,ys yt,that ys wholle ſitting in heauen* **H**
*with the Father.*Wherbie yt ys conſequent,that yt ys the ſame , and verie bodie of Chryſte that ys on the table,that was vpon the croſſe , and ys at the
right hande of God the Father . As ſaincte Auguſtine in fewe woordes
hath

A　hath pithilie touched that, that we here feke, namelie that this place of the fixt chapiter of fainҫte Iohn fpeaketh of the Sacrament, and yet not of the Sacrament as of a bare figne, but of the verie bodie of Chryfte, and of the fame dodie by the name of bread fpake the fentence, *The Bread whiche I will geue, ys my flesh*: So I breiflie haue touched and noted the fame to yowe, hafting to heare the fainges, and expofitions of Chryfoftome vpon the fame text.

　　Chryfoftome, after he had in his learned maner declared in his 44 home lie, that Chryfte fpake this texte of S.Iohn, which we treaҫt of nowe, of his bodie, when he cometh to the fame in his owne place, after he had reprehéded the Iewes for their incredulitie, and flacknes in the beleif of Chryftes woordes, faieth that they therfore tooke no profitte of them. *Illi tunc tempo-* *ris nihil ex ijs diҫtis, nos illius beneficij vtilitatem cepimus. Quare neceffariò dicendum quàm admiranda mifteria, & cur data fint, & quæ eorum vtilitas*. They at that time tooke nothing by thofe woordes, we haue taken the profitt of the benefitte, wherfore neceffarilie yt ys to be faied, howe wonderfull the mifteries be,

Chryfoft. hom.45. in Ioan.

B　and wherfore they be geuen, and what ys the profitt of them. Thefe woordes Chryfoftome fpeaketh vpon the woordes of Chryfte, *The bread which I will geue, ys my flesh*. In the whiche woordes forfomuche as Chryfte faied he wolde geue his flefh, Chryfoftom faieth, they be wonderfull myfteries, And therfore he wolde fearche the caufe why he gaue them, and what profitt co meth to vs by them.

　　And immediatelie as a caufe whie Chryfte gaue vnto vs this mifterie, the bread whiche ys his flefh: the faid Chryfoftom adioineth this fentence of fainҫte Paule: *Vnum corpus fumus & membra ex carne & offibus eius*. We are one bodie and membres of his flefh and of his bones. And that he wolde not be miftaken, but that thefe woordes be fpoken of the receipt of that breade that Chryfte gaue, whiche ys his flefh, he more plainlie vttereth his mening, expownding the former woordes thus: *Vt autẽ non folùm per dileҫtionẽ, fed reipfa in illam carnem conuertamur, per cibum id efficitur, quem nobis largitus eft.* That we fhoulde not onelie by loue, but in verie dede be turned into that

C　flefh, that ys brought to paffe by the meate whiche he hath graunted vs. Thus Chryfoftome.

　　And what meate did he graunte vs? euen that, that he frelie promifed to geue vs, a bread whiche ys his flefh. whiche flefh being oure heauenly and fpirituall meat contrary to the ordre of carnall foode, whiche receaued ys turned into vs, and not we into yt, turneth vs into the flefh of Chryfte, as yt was faied to fainҫte Auguftine: *Nec tu me mutabis in te, ficut cibum carnis tuæ, fed tu mutaberis in me*. Neither fhalt thowe chaunge me into thee as the meate of thy flefh: but thowe fhalt be chaunged into me. And this ys one caufe why Chryfte gaue vs this wonderfull mifterie as Chryfoftome right godlie termeth yt.

Chryftes flefh turneth vs into yt.

　　He addeth alfo an other caufe of the geuing of this great miftery vnto vs, whiche ys this: *Cùm enim fuum in nos amorem indicare vellet, per corpus fuum fe nobis commifcuit, & in vnum nobifcum redegit, vt corpus cum capite vniretur.* When he wolde fhewe furth his loue towardes vs, *by his bodie he mingled him felf with*

D　*vs*, and brought him felf into one with vs, that the bodie might be vnited with the head. Thus muche Chryfoft. Marke his woordes, that *Chryfte By his bodie hath* mingled himfelf with vs. whiche bodie ys not a phantafticall bodie, but his verie reall bodie, as the fame Chryfoftome after goodlie examples godlie fetting furth the matter, fpeaketh in the perfon of Chryfte.

The fame flesh and blood that Chryft tooke of ourna ture, he geueth vs againe.

Vester ego frater esse volui, & communicaui carnem propter vos & sanguinem, & per E
quæ vobis coiunctus sum, ea rursus vobis exhibui. I wolde be yowr brother, and for
yowr sakes I tooke flesh and bloode with yowe, and *by what thinges I was con-*
ioined to yowe, those thinges again I haue geuen vnto yowe.

Weigh this golden sentence with me (gentle Reader) I beseche thee,
weigh yt well, and see whether we receaue but a peice of bread in the holie
Sacrament or not. Yt ys most certen, that Chryste tooke not a phantasticall
bodie. as the *Maniches* here tofore saied, but a verie true bodie, of verie flesh
and verie bloode, and was in all thinges fownde a verie mã, saue onelie that
he lacked sinne, and hauinge soche flesh, and soche bloode, he must nedes
be ioined to vs as one of our nature and kinde, a verie man as we be. Yf thē
he gaue vnto vs those thinges, by the whiche he was conioined to vs, he was
conioined to vs by verie substanciall fleshe and bloode, wherfore he gaue
vnto vs his verie substanciall flesh and bloode. Yf he gaue (as the aduersarie
saieth) vnto vs his flesh but onelie in a sign, then he gaue not his verie flesh
in dede: But he was not conioined to vs by flesh and bloode in a signe onelie. Wherfore he giueth vs not his flesh and bloode in a sign onelie.

And again (as some other do saie) he geueth vs his flesh and bloode, that
ys the benefitte, the merite and grace of his flesh and bloode, and not his
verie reall flesh and bloode. I denie not but he geueth vs the merite of his
passion, suffred in his flesh, and shedinge of his most precioufe bloode, but
that ys not imparted and geuē to vs onelie in the Sacrament of his blessed
bodie and bloode: but also in other sacramentes. As in Baptisme we haue
remissiõ of sinnes, both originall and actuall, from the whiche we be washed
in his bloode: *Lauit nos à peccatis nostris in sanguine suo.* He hath washed vs from
oure sinnes in his blood: So haue we also in the sacramēt of penaunce, wher
also we haue remission of sinnes by the merite of Chrystes passion, And breif
lie all the sacramentes haue their efficacie, power and strenght of the merites
of Chrystes passion. So that to haue the meritie of Chrystes passion ys not
the propre benefitt that cometh to vs by the receipt of this Sacrament of
the bodie and bloode of Chryste, but ys a benefitt geuen to vs in the ministracion and due receauing of all other sacramentes. But the propre benefit
of this sacrament, ys to receaue the verie bodie of Chryste, as a singular G
pledge and token of his loue, who voucheth saif for the vnmeasurable loue
that he beareth to vs, not onelie to be with vs by his sign or token: but (as
vehement and perpetuall loue requireth) to be with vs by his verie presence,
and that we receauing him shoulde be turned into his fleshe wherby (as S.
Hilarie saieth) we are naturallie in him, as he ys naturallie in vs, being mēbres of his bodie, of his flesh and of his bones, yea ãd into that flesh, whiche
(as *Cyrill* saieth) ys *viuifica,* that ys, geuing life or making to liue euerlastinglie,
according to his owne promisse: *Qui manducat me, viuet propter me,* he that
eateth me shall liue by means of me.

These be the benefittes propre vnto this Sacrament (as Chrysostome
hath reherfed) who also procaading declareth the great and wonderfull excellencie of this Sacrament, and a nombre of other benefittes ensewing to
vs by the receipt of the same. Whose procesfe although yt be somwhat long:
yet for that yt declareth moste manifestlie the trueth of Chrystes presence in
the Sacrament, and most godlie commending the same, teacheth vs not H
onelie to reuerence yt in our heartes, and also by mouthe reuerentlie to
speake of yt (whiche bothe two haue moche decaied in thefe daies) but alfo moueth spirituall delectacion in the heart of the true chrystian, I trust yt
　　　　　　　　　　　　　　　　　　　　　　　　　　　　shall

A plain pla
ce of Chry-
sost. for the
Proclamer

Apocal. 1
Receipt of
Chrystes
merites not
propre to
one but cõ-
mon to all
sacramētes

E

F

G

H

A ſhall not be tedious to the Reader in readinge, And therfore ſhall I more gladlie take paines in the writing.

When Chryſoſtom had ſpoken moche of the fleſh of Chryſte, of whiche ſome parte ye haue nowe hearde, He cometh to ſpeake of his bloode, of the which ye ſhall nowe heare. Thus he writeth : *Hic ſanguis ſacit, vt imago in* *Chriſoſt:*
nobis regia floreat. Hic ſanguis pulchritudinem, atque nobilitatem animæ, quam ſemper ir- *ibid.*
rigat & nutrit, langueſcere non ſinit. Sanguis enim à cibo non fit repentè, ſed prius aliud
quiddam. Hic quàm primùm irrigat animam;eamque vi quadam magna imbuit. Hic myſti
cus ſanguis Dæmones procul pellit, Angelos & Angelorum Dominum ad nos allicit. Dæ-
mones enim cùm Dominicum ſanguinem in nobis vident , in fugam vertuntur, Angeli autē
procurrunt. Hic ſanguis effuſus vniuerſum abluit orbem terrarum, de quo multa Paulus
ad Hebræos proſecutus eſt. Hic ſanguis abdita , & ſancta ſanctorum purgabat. Quòd ſi
eius figura tantam habuit vim in templo Hebræorum, in medio Aegypto liminibus aſper-
ſus, longè magis veritas. Hic ſanguis aureum altare ſignificauit. Sine hoc Princeps ſacer-
dotum in penetralia ingredi non audebat. Hic ſanguis ſacerdotes faciebat. Hic ſanguis in

B *figura peccata purgabat, in qua ſi tantam habuit vim, ſi vmbram ita mors horruit, quan-*
topere quæſo, ipſam formidabit veritatem? Hic animarum noſtrarum ſalus eſt, hoc laua-
tur, hoc ornatur, hoc incenditur . Hic igne clariorem noſtram mentem reddit, & auro ſplē-
didiorem. Huius ſanguinis effuſio cœlum peruium fecit. Admiranda ſanè Eccleſiæ myſteria,
admirabile ſacrarium. Ex Paradiſo fons ſcaturiit, à quo ſenſibiles fluuij emanarent. A mēſa *The great*
hac prodiit, fons , qui fluxios ſpirituales diffundit. This blood maketh that the kinges *excellencie*
image dothe floriſh in vs. This bloode dothe neuer ſuffer the beautie and *of the blood*
nobilitie of the ſoule, whiche it dothe allwais water, and nouriſhe, to fade *of Chryſt*
or waxe fainte. Bloode ys not made of meate furth with, but firſt yt ys ſome *in the Sa-*
other thing . This bloode at the firſt dothe water the ſoule, and indewe yt *crament.*
with a certain great ſtrenght. This bloode driueth Deuells a farre of, and allureth vnto vs Angells, and the Lorde of Angells. When the Deuells ſee the
blood of our Lorde in vs , they are turned to fleight, but the Angells runne
furth to vs . This bloode bing ſhedde, did waſhe all the wholl worlde, of
the whiche Paule hath made a great proceſſe to the Hebrues. This bloode
did pourge the ſecrete places, and the moſt holie place of all. Yf then the fi-

C gure of yt had ſo great power in the temple of the Hebrues, and in Aegipte,
being ſprinkeled vppon the vpper poſtes of the dores, moche more the veritie. This bloode did ſignifie the golden Altar. Withoute this bloode the
cheif preiſt durſt not go into the inwarde ſecrete places. This bloode made
the preiſtes. This bloode in the figure pourged ſinnes, in the whiche if yt
had ſo great might and power, yf deathe ſo feared the ſhadow, how moche,
I praie thee, wil yt feare the veritie it ſelf. This blood ys the health of our
ſoules With this bloode our ſoule ys waſſhed, with yt ſhe ys decked, with
yt ſhe ys kindled. This bloode maketh our minde clerer then the fire, more
ſhining then golde . The effuſion of this bloode made heauen open. *Trulie* *The miſte-*
the miſteries of the Churche are wonderfull, the holie treaſour houſe ys wonderfull. From *ries of the*
Paradiſe a ſpring did runne , from thence ſenſible waters did flowe : from *Churche be*
this table commeth oute a ſpring whiche diffundeth and powreth oute ſpi- *wonder-*
rituall floudes . Hether to Chryſoſtom. *full.*

In the whiche proceſſe ye maie perceaue how moche this holie man eſtemed the bleſſed Sacrament. Euen ſo moche did he eſteeme yt, ſo moche
D did he regard yt, ſo moche he reuerenced it, that after ſo moche praiſe and
magnifieng of it, as a man beholding the vnſpeakable highneſſe of it, he
brake oute and ſaied. *Admiranda Eccleſiæ myſteria.* wonderfull be the miſteries
of the Churche.

Bud

E

Obiection

But perchaunce the aduerfarie will gladlie here fekea ftarting hole , as commonlie he dothe, when he is charged with the ineuitable trueth , and will faie that all thefe great praifes be not of the blood of Chryfte, whiche we faie ys in the Sacrament : but of the blood of Chryfte that was fhed vpõ the croffe.

Anfwere.
Bloode of
Chryft on
the croffe
and in the
Sacrament
all one.

To the whiche I aunfwer, that trueth yt ys, that all this praife ys of the blood of Chryft whiche was fhed vpon the Croffe. For I vnderftand the blood of Chryfte in the Sacrament, to be the fame, and none other, that did flowe oute of Chryftes fide vpon the Croffe. For as in the Sacrament ys the veraie fame bodie in fubftance, that was crucified vpon the Croffe: So ys ther the felf fame blood in fubftance that was fhed vppon the Croffe. But in maner diuerfe. Ther the bodie and blood of a man mortall: Here of Chryft immortall. Ther paffible : here impaffible : Ther vifible : here inuifible Ther fenfiblie perceaued : Here faithfullie beleued. Neuertheleffe I faie that Chryfoftom fpake all thefe praifes of the blood of Chryfte in the Sacrament, the praife of which ys the praife of the other, for that they be all one.

F

To proue
that he fpa
ke of the Sa
crament

But that my bare faing fhall not be fufficient authoritie to anfwere the vntreu faing of the Aduerfarie, and that I feke raither to fatiffie then to contende: Chryfoftom him felf fhal fufficiently aunfwer this, by his authoritie. And that both by that, that ys alleaged of him allreadie, and alfo by that, that foloweth the fame. Call therfore to remembrance the fentence of Chryfoftõ immediately preceading this long faing nowe laft alleaged, and let them be ioined together, and then by the dependance of the one to the other, ye fhall perceaue whether all this praife was directed. The fentence going before was this : *I wolde be yowre brother, and for yowr fakes I tooke flesh and bloode with yowe. And by what thinges I was conioined to yowe, thofe fame again haue I exhibited,* And thẽ entreth into this long praife, wherby when he fpeaking of the geuing to vs of his flefh and blood (of the whiche alfo he made a long difputacion before, and of the whiche the wholl homelie treacted) ioined this faing to it: wherof fhoulde he fpeake, but of that blood in this fentence, that he fpake of before in the other , and in the wholl homelie?

G

And alfo when he had fo greatlie and highly magnified the bloode of Chryft : Yet he declareth wherto he looked when he exclamed and faied: *Admiranda Ecclefiæ myfteria.* The mifteries of the Church are wonderfull. and then proceading declareth him felf manifeftlie to fpeake of the Sacrament, by a fimilitude faing : *From Paridife runneth a fpring, from the which floweth fenfible riuers : from this table goeth oute a wellfpring, whiche diffundeth fpirituall riuers.* all whiche woordes do clerely fhowe, that all this his proceffe, tendeth to the blood of Chryfte, as being in the Sacrament.

Partakers
of the blood
of Chryft
dwell with
Angells,

And although this aboue faied dothe fufficientlie proue this to be fpoken of the Sacrament : yet this that foloweth doth more proue yt, and maketh it fo clere, that yt can not be gainft faid. *Vt enim homo feruos fuos emit, & ornat: ita nos fanguine fuo Chriftus. Qui huius fanguinis funt participes, cum Angelis, & Archãgelis, & fupernis virtutibus commorantur, ipfam regiam ftolam Chrifti induti, fpiritualibus armis muniti. Sed nihil dixi, ipfum induti funt regem. Sed ficut purum eft, & admirabile, ita fi purè accefferis, ad falutem acceßifti, fiue praua confcientia , ad pœnam & fupplicium. Qui enim manducat, & bibit indignè SANGVINEM Domini, iudicium fibi manducat & bibit.* As a man (faieth Chryfoftom) dothe both buie his feruauntes, and deck them : euen fo dothe Chryft vs with his bloode . They that be partakers of this bloode, they dwell with Angells and Archaungells, and

H

with

A with the powers aboue, being cloathed with the kinglie garment of Chryſte, are defended with ſpirituall armour. But I haue ſaied nothing. They haue putte on the King himſelf. But as yt ys a great thing, and a wonderfull: euē
ſo if thowe come to it purelie, thowe haueſt comed to health or ſaluacion:
But if with an euell conſcience, thowe haueſt commed to pain and puniſhment. *For he that eateth, and drinked the blood of our Lorde vnwourthelie, eateth and
drinketh his owne damnation.* Thus Chryſoſtom.

*Note here,
thathe ſpea-
keth of the
Sacrament*

　　What can the enemie nowe ſaie? hath not nowe Chryſoſtome opened
him ſelf? and fullie, and plainly certified vs, that all this his communicacion
was of the bleſſed Sacrament? Dothe not his allegacion of ſainɛte Paule invinciblie proue yt? yf ſainɛt Paule in the place alleaged ſpake of the Sacrament, then Chryſoſtom that alleaged him ſpake of the Sacrament. and vndoubtedlie he did ſo.

　　Wherfore (chryſtian Reader) obſerve here and note that Chryſoſtom
dothe not onely vnderſtand the text of ſainɛte Iohn of the Sacrament: But
alſo that therwith, both by plain opening of the woordes of S. Paule by
B moſte goodlie and high praiſe, he teacheth vs that in the ſame Sacrament ys
the verie preſence of *Chryſtes bodie and bloode.* And in his ſo doinge teacheth
alſo all good chryſtian men highlie to eſteme, and greatlie to reuerence and
magnifie this wonderfull miſterie of Chryſtes bleſſed bodie and bloode, cō-
ſidering, and by faithe perceauing verie Chryſte God and man ther to be
preſent. And not ſo lightlie, ſo irreuerentlie, ſo vndeuoutlie to vſe it, as heretofore, euen before the time of hereſie, yt was vſed or raither abuſed. For
the whiche abuſe, I aſſure yowe, I earneſtlie beleue, that as in yt we did ſore
offende: So by it God hath ſore plagued vs. Let vs therfor be admoniſhed,
and learn to amend our ſelues.

*God plagu-
eth vs for
abuſe of the
Sacrament*

　　And the like I wolde wiſh the Aduerſarie to do, that wher he in this wicked time hath forſaken his faith, and with defiled mouthe hath railed in blaſ-
pheming this moſt holie Sacrament, and hath called the faitfull Chryſtians,
Idolaters, and robbers of God, robbing him of his honour, and geuing yt
to a peice of bread, he wolde nowe learn that he hath gon aſtraie. and that
C not the Catholique Chryſtians, but he and ſoche like haue ben Idolaters, and robbers of God his honour, not honouring him wher he was preſent, but with all vile means diſhonouring him, whiche he and they
maie repent.

*Honoura-
ble titles,
and great
effeɛtes of
the Sacra-
ment proue
the preſence
of Chryſt
therin.*

　　Wolde this famouſe and noble clerke holie Chryſoſtom haue ſo extolled
and magnified this Sacrament, ſo oftentimes calling it *blood,* and atributing
to yt goddes power *in fearing and driuing awaie of Deuells, in waſhing our ſowles, in
geuing remiſſion of ſinnes, in putting death to flight, in being our health,* and ſaluacion,
with a nombre of ſoche effeɛtes, as ye haue heard, yf it were but wine? Can
a cuppe of wine woorke ſoche wonderfull workes and effeɛtes? ys yt of ſoch
force and ſtrenght? if yt ſo be, the chamberlain of king *Darius* that tooke
vpon him to proue, that *forte eſt vinum,* wine ys ſtrong, wold not haue omitted ſo great praiſes of yt in his oracion, for it wolde haue made moche for
his pourpoſe. But ſurelie this ys ſpoken by Chryſoſtome of the verie blood
of Chryſte, whiche in dede hath this great might and power, or ells this
D great Father wold neuer ſo haue magnified yt,

　　And nowe thow that waſt once in Chryſtes faith, and haueſt runne aſtra
ie, return again, and magnifie this diuine Sacrament with Chryſoſtom,
and all other faithfull in Chryſte. Return, I ſaie, while the time ſerueth thee,
and while yt ys daie, for *Venit nox, quando nemo poteſt operari.* The night will
　　　　　　　　　　　　　　　　　　　　　　　　　　　　　come,

come, when no man can woorke. Therfore I do aduertife thee with fainct Paule, *Cum metu et tremore falutē tuam operare*, with feare and trembling woork thy faluacion. Return, and faie with the Prophet *Dauid* : *Errauifcut ouis quæ periit,quære feruum tuum Domine.* I haue erred like the fhepe that hath perifhed: feke thy feruannt o Lorde.

Philip . 2.
Pfal. 118.

And nowe although I haue a litle digreffed frō the right line of the proofe of the fixt chapiter of faincte Iohn, to be vnderftanded of the Sacrament: Yet I haue not digreffed from charitie, nether from the principall pourpofe of this booke, whiche ys to laboure to reduce them, that haue erred, to the trueth, and to confirme and comforth them that be in yt.

THE SIXT CHAPITER PROCEADETH IN THE
opening of the vnderftāding of the fame texte of faincte Iohn by Beda and Cyrillus,

Beda in 6.
Ioan.

He trueth of this matter ys foch,that ytys teftifiedād auouched by manie mo fathers,of the which we will heare firft *Beda* , and *Cirille*. *Beda* expowndeth the forfaid text of S.Iohn thus.*Hunc pa nē Dominus dedit,quādo myfteriū corporis et fāguinis fuis Difcipulis tradidit et quādo femetipfum Deo patriobtulit in ara crucis.Quòd verò dicit, pro mū di vita,nō debemus intelligere pro elemētis,fed pro hominibus qui mūdi nomine defignātur.* This bread (faieth *Beda*)our lord gaue,when he deliuered the mifterie of his bodie and blood to his difciples , and when he offered him felf on the Altar of the Croffe to God the Father . And wher he faieth: *for the life of the worlde,*we maie not vnderftād it for the Elemētes,but for mē, whiche by the name of the worlde are fignified. Thus haue ye Bedes expofitiō, whiche al thoug yt be breif and fhorte yet it ys plain and clere. As he text faeth that Chryft wolde geue twice a bread that fhoulde be his flefh : So Bede decla-reth two fundrie maners, and times for the geuing of the fame . Firft, wher Chryfte faied,*the bread which I fhall geue,*that(*faied Bede*)our Lorde gaue, whē he deliuered vnto his Difciples the mifterie of his bodie ād blood. The fecōd,wher Chryft faied,*which I fhall geue for the life of the world,*that bread (*fa-ieth Bede*)did our Lord geue whē he offred himfelf to God the Father on the altar of the Croffe.

Chryftes
bodie vpon
the croffe cal
led bread.

I nede not here to note that Bede expowndeth this text of the Sacramēt, wher the woordes are fo plain. But this I note that he calleth the flefh of Chryfte offred vppon the Croffe, bread, as well as the fame flefh deliuered to the difciples in the laft fupper. Wherby it appeareth,that wher the Aduer farie, when he findeth the Sacrament called bread, dothe take occafion to maintein his errour , and faie that it ys but bread,yt ys no good argument. Neither doth it any more conclude, that the Sacrament ys but breade, by-caufe it ys called bread, then that Chryftes bodie on the croffe ys but bread bicaufe it ys called bread. Chryfte calleth himfelf being whollie God and man (as Cirill faieth) bread. And therfor bothe the godhead and the man-head of Chryfte maie be called bread, and be of Chryfte him felf in the fixt of S. Iohn fo called. But yet therfore yt ys no good confequent that the bo-die of Chryfte fhoulde be but materiall breade . So likewife ys yt no good confequent, that the manhead of Chryfte fhoulde be but materiall bread. Yf then thefe two in the perfon of Chryfte be called breade, and yet be not materiall breade , why fhoulde not they being in the Sacrament be called bread , and yet be no materiall breade? But raither this ys to be faied, accor ding to the fainge of Chryfte in this place of S. Iohn, and alfo Bede expoun-

ding

A ding the fame,that as the flesh of Chryste vpon the crosse ys called bread,ād yet ys verie flesh:So ys the blessed flesh of Chryst in the Sacrament called bread,and yet ys yt verie flesh,Chryste so saing, that the breade whiche he wolde geue was his flesh.Thys his geuing,as ye haue heard Bede expownd, was vnto his disciples,vnto whom he gaue his flesh called breade.

As ye haue hitherto heard diuerse,whiche be of good authoritie, ād high eftimacion in Chryftes Church, which all haue expownded this text of S. Iohn,to be spoken of Chryftes bodie in the Sacrament, not as in figne , but by reall prefence:So God ayding,ye shall heare some other liuely and agrea- blie expownding the fame,Therfor now shal Cyrill also,a Father of the Gre ke Churche,geue his teftimonie.This man like himself,learnedly and godly expownding the fixt chapiter of S.Iohn faieth thus: *Antiquus ille panis figura,* *imago,vmbraque folummodò fuit nec quicquam præter quàm quòd corruptibile nutrimen-* *tum,ad modicum tempus exibebat.Ego verò fum ille panis viuus,ac viuificans in æternum.* *Et panis quem ego dabo,caro mea eft,quam ego dabo pro mundi vita. Vides vt paulatim*

B *magis magisque fe aperiat,& explicet mirificum hoc myfterium.Dixit fe panem viuum,et* *viuificantem,qui fe manducantes faceret corruptionis expertes,& donaret immortalitate.* *Nunc dicit panem illum carnē fuam effe,quam daturus erat pro mundi vita , & per quam* *nos illam participantes viuificaturus.Siquidem verbi viuificans natura illi ineffabili illo vnio* *nis modo coniunéla,viuificantem eandem effecit , & propterea participantes viuificat ifta* *caro,eijcit ab eis mortem,& interitum penitus expellit.* That olde bread was onelie a figure,an image,a shadowe,neither did yt geue vnto the corruptible bodie any thinge els,but a corruptible nutrimēte for a litle time.But I *(faieth Chrift)* am that liuing and quickning bread for euer.And the bread that I will geue ys my flesh,which I wil geue for the life of the worlde.Thow seieft,how by litle ād litle,he more ād more openeth himself,ād doth declare this wōderful myfterie . He hath faied that he ys the liuing,and quickning bread,whiche shoulde make the partakers of yt withoute corruption,and geue thē immor- talitie. Now he faieth *his flesh ys that bread, which he wolde geue for the life of the* *woorld.And by the which he wolde geue life to vs that do receaue the fame .* For truly that quickning nature of the Sonne of God conioined to that flesh , by

C that vnspeakable maner of vnion,hath made that flesh quickning,*and therfore* *doth this flesh quicken the partakers of yt.*For yt doth caft oute death from them, and vtterly expelleth deftruction.

I thinke yt not obfcure to yow to perceaue that Cyrill in this faing dothe both expownde this fentence of Chryst fo often allready fpoken of, of the flesh of Chryste in the Sacrament:And.alfo that he doth here, as he doth all moft euery wher in this chapiter,teache the verie prefence of Chryst in the fame.For after he had alleaged the faieng of Chryste , note that he doth ad- uertife vs,how Chryste doth open him felf,*and dothe plainlie fet furth this wonder* *full myfterie.*For wher before he faied that he himself was the bread, Now he doth more open himself,and faie *that hys flesh ys breade.* And that he fpeaketh of the flesh of Chryste in the Sacrament he declareth by that,that he faieth, that yt geueth life to them that be partakers of yt.For the propre partakinge of Chryftes flesh ys in the receauing of this holie Sacrament.

This being plainlie declared by Cyril who draweth by the line of cōcord with the reft of the ancièt fathers,as ye do perceaue,yt maie be knowē that

D on both fides of the Parliament houfe,God hath euer remained with one re ceaued truthe of this Sacrament.

(marginal notes:)
Cyrill.in 6. Ioan.

Chryftes flesh in the Sacrament geueth life to the recea uers.

THE SEVENTH CHAPITER ENDETH THE
expofition of this text by Theophilacte, and Lyra.

Orafmoche as ther remaineth more matter to profequute in the expounding of the reft of this fixt chapiter of fainéte Iohn , for the proof of the veritie of Chryftes reall prefence in the bleffed Sacrament: I fhall adde onelie two mo wittneffes to geue ther teftimonie of this text nowe in hande, and fo ending the expofition therof, proceade in my matter and pourpofe entended by like expofition of other mo textes in the fame chapiter.

Theophi-
laét.in fex-
tum Ioan.

The firft of thefe fhal be *Theophilaétus,* who expownding this texte geueth a plain teftimonie of the trueth. *Attende* (faieth he) *quòd panis,qui à nobis in myfte rijs manducatur,non eft tantùm figuratio quædam corporis Domini,fed ipfa caro Domini. Non enim dixit:Panis quem ego dabo,figura eft carnis meæ,fed caro mea eft. Transforma- tur enim arcanis verbis panis ille per myfticam benedictionem, & accefsionem fanéti Spi- ritus in carnem Domini.Et ne quem conturbet,quòd credendus fit panis caro , etenim in car- ne ambulante Domino,& ex pane alimoniã admittente,panis ille qui mãducabatur in cor- pus eius mutabatur,& fimilis fiebat fanétæ eius carni,& in augmentum & fuftentationem conferebat,iuxta humanum morem.Igitur & nunc panis in carnẽ Domini mutatur.Et quo- modò (inquit)non apparet nobis caro,fed panis?Vt non abhorreamus ab eius efu.Nam fi qui dem caro apparuiffet,infuauiter affecti fuiffemus erga communionem. Nunc autem conde-*

Chryftes ve
rie ffefh in
the Sacra-
ment,not
thefigure.

fcẽdẽte domino noftræ infirmitati,talis apparet nobis myfticus cibus,qualibus aliquando afue ti fumus. Take hede,that the bread whiche ys eaten of vs in the myfteries,ys not onelie a certain figuring of the bodie of our Lord , but the verie flefh of our Lord.For he did not faie:The bread which I wil geue,ys a figure of my flesh but,yt ys my flesh. For the bread ys *tranfourmed,*by the fecret woords of the my fticall benediétiõ,and coming of the holie Gofte,*into the flesh of our Lord.* And let yt not trooble any mã that the bread ys to be beleued flefh.For our Lord walking in the flefh,ãd receauing foode of bread,that bread which was eatẽ, was chaunged into his bodie,ãd was made like to his holie flefh and yt went to the augmentaciõ,and fuftẽtaciõ of him according to the maner of man.

How the
bread ys
turnedinto
ffesh, and
why flesh
ys not feen
in the Sa-
crament.

Therfore alfo now the bread ys chãuged into the flesh of our Lord. And how(faieth he) doth yt not appeare flefh,but bread? that we fhould not abhorre frõ eating of yt.For yf yt had appeared flefh we fhould not haue ben well affeéted to- wards the Cõmunion. But now our Lorde condefcending to our infirmitie the myfticall meat appeareth foche to vs,as we haue ben otherwife accufto- med vnto.Thus *Theophilaéte.*

By whom yt ys mofte manifeft,that this texte of S.Iohn yet in hand ys vnderftanded of the bleffed Sacrament. And further he moft plainly auou- cheth the reall prefence of Chryftes bodie in theSacrament,when he faieth, that the bread by the work of the holy gofte *ys transfourmed into the flesh of Chry fte,*wherby ye are not onelie taught withoute all obfcuritie and darkneffe of

Tranfub-
ftanciaciõ
auouched.

fpeache that the verie flefh of Chryfte,ys verilie and reallie prefent in the Sa cramẽt:But ye are alfo taught the maner how the flefh ys made prefent that ys by tranfubftanciation.which although he vtter by an other woorde , yet in effeéte yt ys all one.For wher as he faieth yt ys transformed , and euery creature hath two formes,an outward forme,and an inwarde , and he affir-

Forme na-
ture, effẽce
fubftance
all one.

meth , and declareth that the outward forme remaineth, when he faieth: yt appeareth bread,whiche alfo our fenfes iudge and perceaue,then yt muft nedes be,that this transformacion muft be of the inwarde forme . whiche inuarde forme(as learned men do knowe) for fomoch as *forma , natura,effen- tia ,* and *fubftantia* be all one , ys the nature and fubftance of the thing:

which

A whiche forme, nature, or substance being chaunged, that chaunge maie aswell be called transubstanciacion for the chaunge of substance, as transformacion for the chaunge of forme, forme and substance being all one verie thing.

And that he ment of the chaunge of the verie substance of the bread into the flesh of Chryst, he declareth by that he saieth: that as when our Sauiour walked here vpon the earth, and being a naturall man, did for his natural sustentacion eate bread, which bread was chaunged into the substance of hys flesh, and was so chaunged that yt was made like to his holie flesh, as *Theophila-ctes* woordes be: *Euē so now (saieth he) the bread ys chaunged into his flesh.* By which similitude he most plainlie teacheth, that as the substance of the bread which Chryste did eate, by natural dispositiō was substãciallie chaūged, into the substance of Chrystes flesh: So ys now the substance of bread by the operaciõ of the holie Gost chaunged into the substãce of Chrystes flesh . And to proue this he vseth the woordes of scripture noting to vs that Chryst did not saie: B *The bread which I will geue ys a figure of my flesh: but my flesh.* Yf then yt be not the figure of Chrystes flesh, and yet ys flesh, yt must nedes be hys verie naturall and substanciall flesh.

Neither ys this to be ouerpassed, and left vnnoted to the reader, that thys authour by a plain negatiue, denieth the false affirmatiue of the Aduersarie. For wher the Aduersarie saieth yt ys but a figure, This authour saieth, yt ys not onely a figure: And yet this woorde (*onely*) did *Oecolãpadius* put to of hys owne, in the trãslating. For the greke hath not that woorde, as the learned in that tounge haue noted. And wher the Aduersarie saieth by the negatiue, yt ys not flesh: This authour boldlie vsing the woorde and trueth of his master Chryst saieth the affirmatiue, that yt ys flesh. And thus (reader) thowe maist perceaue the great impudencie and shamelessnes of these Professours of heresie, that what the holie writers, and auncient authours do expressedlie affirme, that do they denie, and that, that the auncient Fathers doo manifestlie denie, that doo they affirme, what now ys to be iudged of these I leaue to thee Reader.

C The other whose testimonie shall finish the expositiõ of this text, shall be *Lyra*, one of the other side of Chrysts Parliamēt house, who albeit in time he be not aunciēt, yet in treuth he ys auncient, in the which he cõcordeth and agreeth euen with the most aunciēt, as yt shal appeare. Vpon this same text of S. Iohn so often repeated, without all maner of high speache, he writeth thus plainlie: *Sciendum quòd in sacramento Eucharistiæ continetur ipsum Verbum incarnatum. Et ideo ostendens qualitatē huius sacramenti, quatuor tangit: Primum est illud, quod est ibi sacramentū tantùm, scilicet species panis, cùm dicit: Et panis, &c. Secundum est, author huius sacramenti, qui est ipse Christus summus sacerdos. Sacerdos autē, qui est minister huius sacramenti tantùmodo profert verba, non in propria persona, sed in persona Christi. In aliis autem sacramentis vtitur minister verbis suis, vel verbis Ecclesie, quibus exprimitur actus quem facit, vt in Baptismo, cum dicitur: Ego baptiso te, &c. Sed in Sacramento refert solùm verba Christi, cùm dicit: Qui pridie quàm pateretur &c. et sequūtur postea verba Christi cõsecratiõe efficientia, & hoc notatur cùm dicitur: Ego dabo, &c. Tertium est, res significata, & cõtenta, scilicet verum Christi corpus, cùm dicitur: Caro mea est. Quartū est, res significata, sed non contenta, scilicet corpus Christi mysticum, quod coniungitur capiti per charitatem . Hoc autem sacramentum dicitur sacramentum amoris.* Thus moche *Lyra*. who D although he speaketh plainlie (as ys saied) yet fullie and trulie, so fullie and trulie, that he hath whollie set furth that faith that the whol Churche dothe professe, ãd so plainlie as here ys no obscure maner of speach for the Aduersa

rie to

Marginal notes:

Bread in the Sacra. chaunged into flesh, a plain saig for the Pro clamer.

Oecolam-padius falsifieth Theophilacte.

Nico. Lyra in 6. Ioã

to lurke vnder, and by a wicked glose to drawe to his sense and pourpose. **E**

Yt ys to be knowen (saieth *Lyra*(that in the Sacrament of thankes geuing, ys cōteined the verie Sōne of God incarnate. And therfor shewing the qua litie of the Sacrament, he toucheth foure thinges: The first, that ther ys one thing, whiche ys a Sacrament onelie, and that ys the forme of bread, whē he saieth: *And the bread, &c.* The seconde ys the Authour of this Sacrament, which ys Chryste himself the high preist. The preist whiche ys the mynistre of this Sacrament, doth onelie speake the woordes, not in his owne person, but in the person of Chryste. In other sacramentes the mynistre doth vse his owne woordes, or the woordes of the Churche, by the which the acte that he dothe ys expressed, as yt doth appeare in Baptisme, wher yt ys saied: I Bap tise thee. But in the Sacrament he doth onelie reherse the wordes of Chry ste, when he saieth. Who before the daie he suffred, &c. And after folowe the woordes of Chryste working the consecracion. And this ys noted when yt ys saied: *whiche I shall geue to yowe.* The thirde ys the thing signified, and contei ned, that ys the verie bodie of Chryst, noted when yt ys saied: *yt ys my flesh.* **F** The fourth ys the thing signified, ād not cōteined, ād that ys the mystical bo die of Chryste, the which ys conioined to the head by charitie. For this Sa crament ys called the Sacrament of loue.

This ys the exposition of Lyra . In the whiche that he doth vnderstand this text of the Sacramēt yt ys more manifest then I nede to note yt to yow, That he also in the same Sacrament teacheth to be the verie reall presence of Chrystes bodie. For in the first entrie he affirmeth *that the verie Sonne of God in* *Verie Sōne* *carnate ys in the Sacrament.* Whiche in the thirde note he groundeth vpon this *of God in-* woord of Chryste(*yt ys my flesh*)whiche flesh of Chryste)*saieth he*)ys the thing *carnate in* signified, and conteined. Yt ys signified by the Sacrament, that ys, a signe of *the Sacra.* an holy thing, whiche ys the formes of bread, and wine, And ys conteined being reallie present, as the verie substance vnder the same formes. In these two partes this Authour dissenteth not from other, that haue ben hitherto alleaged. For they all teach one doctrin. One thing in dede he teacheth here whiche the other alleaged for the exposition of this texte haue not taught, **G** which ys that he noteth in this texte, that Chryste dothe accompte himself the Authour and geuer of this Sacrament. Which in my iudgement he doth verie well take of these woordes of Chryste, *which I will geue &c.* By whiche woordes Chryste signifieth vnto vs, that he himself ys the doer, the woorker, and the geuer of this Sacrament which thing this authour more at large ope ning saieth: *Chryste ys the authour of this Sacrament, For he ys the heigh preist* . The preist that ys the minister doth but onely speake the woordes, and vse hys ministerie.

By the which woordes the vain saing of vain mē, which do deceaue the sim ple, and haue not passed to Blaspheme this holie mysterie, and shamefullie to slaunder the Church of Chryste, are made openlie to be knowen in their owne sorte as they be. For wher to drawe the simple from Chrystes holie sa *Preists ma* crament, and bringe the same most excellent mysterie in contempte to be de *ke God, Ca* rided of boies and Girlles, they wolde saie: doest thow beleue that God ys in *uill of the* the Sacrament? why? then the preist doth make him. And beleuest thow that *Aduersa-* the preist can make God? What? God made all the worlde, and he ys made **H** *ries opened* of none. With these and soche like the simple astoined and not seing what to aunswer, ys led awaie as the oxe to the slaughter.

THE

THE EIGHT CHAPITER DECLARETH BY
whose authoritie and power the Sacrament ys consecrate and Chrystes
bodie made present.

BVt that ye maie perceaue, that to saie the preist maketh God, ys the doctrine of the Deuel and hys disciples, who haue inuented soche lies, and slaunders to dishonour God, and his holy Sacrament, and to snare and entrappe the simple in heresie, and so finallie to cast thē headlong into perpetuall dānacion: I shall open, and declare vnto yow, what ys the verie true doctrine of Chrysts Churche in this matter.

margin: Preist maketh God, the doctrine of the Deuell.

The doctrine of Chrystes Church was declared vnto vs by the authour last alleaged in the chapiter before. Who saieth that Chryst ys the high preist and that he ys the authour and woorker of this Sacrament. This was the doctrine taught nowe in the latter daies, whiche vndoubtedlie was also taught in the auncient Churche, as yt shall appeare to yowe by the Fathers whiche shall be alleaged, which liued in diuerse ages.

B   Damascen an holie father and of good antiquitie, as touching this matter saieth thus: *Quemadmodum omnia quæ fecit Deus, Spiritu sancto cooperante fecit: sic & nunc Spiritus sancti operatione hæc supra naturam operatur, quæ non potest cognoscere, nisi sola fides. Quomodò fiet istud, dixit sancta virgo, quoniam virum non cognosco? Respondit Gabriel Archangelus: Spiritus sanctus superueniet in te, & virtus Altissimi obumbrabit tibi. Itaque si & nunc interrogas: Quomodò panis fit corpus Christi, vinum & aqua sanguis Christi: Respondeo & ego tibi, Spiritus sanctus obumbrat, & hæc supra sermonem & intelligentiam operatur. Panis autem & vinum Transsumuntur.* As all thinges that God hath made, he hath made them by the holie Gost woorking with him: Euen so nowe he woorketh these thinges aboue nature, by the operacion of the holy Goste. Whiche thinges no man can knowe but onely faith. Howe shall this thing be doen (*saieth the holy virgen*) seing I knowe not a man? The Archangell Gabriell aunswered: The holie Goste shall come vpon thee, and the power of the moste higheſt shall ouershadow thee. Therfore yf thowe al so aske nowe, *howe the bread ys made the bodie of Chryste, and the wine and water hys bloode,* I also aunswer thee. *The holie Gost ouershadoweth, and woorketh these thinges aboue speache and vnderstanding. The breade and the wine be transsumed.* Thus moche Damascen, who did write a booke of the faithe of the Church, in the which writing this saieng, that yowe haue now heard, he dothe sufficientlie geue yow knowledge what was taught to the faithfull people of hys time.

margin: Damasce. de orth. fid. lib. 4 ca. 14

margin: Howe the bread ys made the bodie of Chryſt.

In the whiche saieng also ye perceaue how reuerentlie he frameth himself toward the worke of God in this blessed and wonderful mysterie. And cer tifieth vs, that yf ye aske him howe the bread and wine, be made the bodie and blood of Chryste: he will aunswer *that the holie Goste aboue speache and vnderstanding woorketh these thinges.* In the whiche woordes we are not onelie admonished by his example to speake reuerentlie of the mysteries of Chrystes Church, but we are also taught that yt ys not man, that woorketh this wonderfull worke, or to vse the maner of speache that the Deuell teacheth his disciples, yt ys not the preist that maketh God, but yt ys the holie Goste, who aboue that, that man can speake or conceaue woorketh this wonderfull worke.

margin: A plain place for the presence and trā substanciation.

And though this be the principall thing, that in this authour ys at thys present to be sought: yet note also by the waie for the presence of Chryste in the Sacrament, that he bothe teacheth that the bread and wine be made the bodie and blood of Chryste, and also the mean howe that by the worke

of the holy Goſt ys brought to paſſe. *For the bread and wine be tranſſumed(ſaieth* E
he)that ys, turned, tranſmuted, chaunged, tranſelementated (as the fathers
ſaie) and as the Church nowe ſaieth, tranſubſtanciated, which ys as moche
to ſaie, as the ſubſtance of bread and wine, ys turned into the ſubſtance of the
bodie and blood of Chryſte.

Chryſoſt.
homil. 2. in
2. Tim.

Chryſoſtom(who liued long before Damaſcen, writeth alſo of this matter
thus: *Volo quiddam adijcere planè mirabile, & nolite mirari, neque turbemini. Quid verò*
eſt iſtud? Sacra ipſa oblatio, ſiue illam Petrus, ſiue illam Paulus, ſiue cuiuſuis meriti ſacer-
dos offerat, eadem eſt, quam dedit Chriſtus ipſe Diſcipulis, quamque ſacerdotes modò confi-
ciunt. Nihil habet iſta, quàm illa minus. Cur id? quia non hanc ſanctificant homines, ſed Chri
ſtus, qui antè illam ſacrauerat. Quemadmodum enim verba , quæ locutus eſt Chriſtus,
eadem ſunt, quæ ſacerdotes nunc quoque pronunciant : ita & oblatio. I will adde herevnto a certain thing plainlie wonderful, and meruail ye not, neither be trou-

Sacrifice of
the Maſſe
what preiſt
ſoeuer offre
yt, ys alone
with that,
whiche
Chriſt did

bled. And what ys that? *The holie oblacion, whether Peter, or Paule, or a preiſt of anie*
maner of life doo offer yt, yt ys euen the ſame that Chryſte gaue vnto hys diſciples, and that
the preiſtes doo nowe conſecrate: This hath nothing leſſe then that, why ſo? Bicau- F
ſe men doo not ſanctifie thys, but Chryſte , who did conſecrate that other
before. *Euen as the woordes that Chryſte ſpake, are the ſame whiche the preiſtes doo*
nowe pronounce: So alſo ys the oblacion. Thus moche Chryſoſtom. Whom ye haue
heard not onelie teaching that Chryſt dothe ſanctifie the table nowe , who
did hallowe the table in the laſt Super: but alſo with a plain negatiue denieng that men doo ſanctifie yt.

Whiche Chryſoſtom alſo in an other place ſpeaketh more plainly to
thys matter. The woordes ther maie be an expoſition of theſe woords
here, and be after the phraſe of ſpeache that ys vſed nowe a daies. And therfore I thinke yt expedient , to aſcribe them. *Nunc ille præſtò eſt Chriſtus,*
qui illam ornauit menſam , ipſe iſtam quoque conſecrat: Non enim homo eſt , qui pro-

Chryſoſt .
homil . 30 .
de produ.

poſita de conſecratione menſæ Domini corpus facit & ſanguinem , ſed ille qui pro
nobis crucifixus eſt Chriſtus. Sacerdotis ore verba proferuntur, ſed Dei virtute con-
ſecrantur & gratia. Hoc eſt, ait, corpus meum , hoc verbo propoſita conſecrantur.

Not man
but Chryſt
hiſelf doth
conſecrate.

The ſame Chryſte ys nowe preſent, whiche did beautifie that table , he
alſo dothe *conſecrate this* . For yt ys not man which with the conſecracion
maketh the thinges of the table, that be ſett furth, the *bodie and blood of our* G
Lorde, but he that was crucified for vs, euen Chryſte. The woordes are ſpoken by the mouthe of the preiſt, but they be conſecrated by the power of
God and grace. *This ys* (ſaieth he) *my bodie , with this woorde the thinges ſett furth*
are conſecrated. Thus Chryſoſtome.

Do ye not ſee the doctrine of the Church yet euery wher like? Do ye not
heare Chryſoſtō by directe woordes, aunſwer theſe ſlaunderouſe heretikes,
ſaing that yt ys not man that doth make the bodie of our Lord, and blood,
but he that was crucified for vs, euen Chryſte. Of whoſe woordes alſo, as be-

A plain
place for
the Procl.

fore of Damaſcē, learn not onelie who doth conſecrate, but alſo what ys doē
and conſecrated. Thys ys doen (ſaieth Chryſoſtome) that *Chryſte maketh the*
bread and wine, which be the thinges ſett furth, to be his bodie and blood. Here ys no mē-
cion of any figure or ſigne, but plain ſpeache they be made hys bodie and
blood, which thing all catholike fathers doo teache.

And that as well of the Latin Church, as of the Greke Church, we maie ſee
the trueth with full conſent and agreement teſtified, S. Ambroſe ſhall alſo H
be brought furth as a wittneſſe in thys matter. Who treacting of the bleſ-
ſinges of the Patriarkes, and among them of the bleſſing of Aſer and of the
myſterie of the ſame, for Aſer by interpretacion ys riches , ſaieth thus:

Qnis

A *Quis igitur diues, nisi vbi altitudo diuitiarum est sapientiæ & scientiæ? Hic ergo diues est, thesaurus huius pinguis panis, quem qui manducauerit, esurire non poterit. Hunc panem dedit Apostolis vt diuiderent populo credentium . Hodieque dat nobis eum, quem ipse quotidie sacerdos consecrat suis verbis . Hic ergo panis factus est esca sanctorum .* Who ys then riche , but he in whom ys the great deapth of of wisdom and knowledge? This riche man then ys the treasure of this fatte bread, which who shall eate , he can not hungar . This bread he gaue to his Apostles , that they shoulde diuide yt to the beleuing people . And nowe he geueth the same to vs , whiche he being the preist , dothe dailie with his owne woordes consecrate . This bread then ys made the meat of the holie . In these woordes sainðe Ambrose saieth that the preist doth consecrate, but what preist ys yt? the preist in whome ys the deapt of the riches of wisdom , and knowledge, of whom sainðe Paule speaketh to the *Collossians* , whiche ys Chryste . For ther ys none that can consecrate, with his owne woordes but Chryste . And with his woordes the consecracion ys doen, as sainðe Ambrose saieth in an other place: *Hoc igitur*

Amb . de Bened. Patriarch. c. 9

Christ doth dailie consecrat with his owne woordes.

B *astruamus, quomodò potest, qui panis est, corpus esse Christi ? Consecratione . Consecratio igitur quibus verbis est, et cuius sermonibus? Domini Iesu. Nam reliqua omnia, quæ dicütur, laus Deo defertur, oratione petitur pro populo, pro regibus, pro cæteris. Vbi venitur vt cõficiatur venerabile Sacramētü, iã non suis sermonibus vtitur sacerdos, sed vtitur sermonibus Christi. Ergo sermo Christi hoc conficit Sacramentum .* Let vs then teache this. How cã that, that ys bread be the bodie of Chryste? *By consecraciõ* By what, ãd whose woordes ys the consecracion? Of our Lord Iesus. For all the other things that be saied laude ys geuê to God, peticiõ ys made in praier for the people, for kinges and other. Whê the time ys comed that the honorable Sacrament shall be made, then the preist vseth not his owne woordes, but the woordes of Chryste. *Therfor Yt ys the woorde of Christe that maketh this Sacrament.*

Li. 4. de Sacra. cap. 4.

Cõsecraciõ how yt ys doen.

Thus moche S. Ambrose whose woords are so plain that I nede not by no tes vnto yow declare the same, ãd his testimonie so cõsonaunt and agreable with the Fathers before alleaged for this matter her hãdled, that ye maie eui dëtlie perceaue howe one trueth and the self same doctrine, hath bê cõstant

C ly taught in the diuerse ages in the whiche these Fathers liued.

A plain place of S . Amb. for master Iuell .

And to ascend a litle higher and nearer to the Apostles time, we will, for the full declaraciõ of this treuth and doctrine allready auouched, heare the testimonie of *Eusebius Emissenus* an auncient Father in Chrystes church, who saieth thus : *Inuisibilis sacerdos visibiles creaturas, in substantiam corporis & sanguinis, verbo suo, secreta potestate conuertit .* The inuisible preist , with his woord, by a secret power, turneth the visible creatures into the substance of his bodie and bloode. Thus *Eusebius* . Whome heare yowe here tomake the bodie of Chryste ? dothe not the inuisible preist, which ys onr Sauiour Iesus Chryste, and not the preist, who ys but the ministre? as the Auersaries maliciouslie blaspheme.

Eusebius Emis. in homil. pasch. Christ doth consecrate his own bodie by turning the substance of bread &c.

But leauing to thee (gentle reader) to weigh and consider, what maner of people they are, that haue feigned soche abhominable vntrueths, as to saie to deceaue with all, that the preist made God, and to iudge what credite aught to be geuen to soche, as with lies, slaunders, and blasphemies go aboute

D to maintein their detestable heresies, I will ioin one more of like auncientie to this *Eusebius* , and then, I trust, this maie satisfie thee in this matter. And this shall be *Cyprian* that holie martir , who speaking of euell receauers , saieth thus : *Melius erat illis mola asinaria collo alligata mergi in pelagus , quàm illota conscientia de manu Domini accipere , qui vsque hodie hoc*

Cypr. de cœna Dom.

T iiij   vera-

veracißimũ & ſanctißimũ corpus ſuũ creat,& ſanctificat,et benedicit, & piè ſumentibus E

Chriſt doth create,ſanc-tifie , and bleſſe his own bodie a plain ſaig of S.Cyp.
*diuidit.*Yt were better for thẽ, a milſtone tied to their neckes to be drowned in the ſea,then with an vnwaſſhed conſciẽce to take the morſell at the hãde of our Lorde, who vntill this daie, *doth create, and ſanctifie, aud bleſſe, and to the godlie receauers diuide, this his moſt true and moſt holie bodie.* Thus Cipr.

Do ye not ſee, and learn by this holy martir,who doth make the bodie of Chryſt in the Sacrament? *Oure Lord*(ſaieth he) *dothe enen till this time create, ſanctifie, and bleſſe this his moſt holie bodie .*

Note alſo againſt theſe ſigne makers, and figure feigners, that he ſaieth not,he createth a bodie: But his bodie,*Corpus ſuum.* and not an imaginatiue bodie: but *veraciſimũ,& ſanctiſimũ corpus ſuũ,*his moſt true,ãd moſt holie bo-die.And he did not onelie ſo do in his laſt ſupper(as the Petrobruſiãs ſaied) *ſed vſq; hodie creat.*vntill this daie he dothe create, ſanctifie and bleſſe this his moſt true and moſt holie bodie. Wherbie ys taught that Chryſte and none other dothe cõtinuallie create in that holie miniſtraciõ, ãd make his bodie.

Nowe ye haue heard, frõ the latter daies vntill the time of this holie mar F tir Cipriã and *Euſebius* before alleaged, who were nere to the primitiue chur

Supra.li.1. cap.31.
che,what hath bẽ taught as cõcerning this matter, in diuerſe ages, and that aſwell in the Greke Church, as in the Latin Churche. whiche ys, that Chryſte himſelf doth woorke this wonderfull worke of conſecracion, to make preſent in this bleſſed ſacrament his verie bodie and bloode, and not the preiſt, who (as Chryſoſtom hath taught) ſpeaketh the woordes, *but the power and grace of God dothe conſecrate the thinges.*

Wherfore (Reader) take hede of this wicked ſorte of people, who (as ye maie perceaue)haue not onelie,for the ſetting furthe of their wicked hereſies wickedlie ſlaundered the wholle Churche, and the holie miniſterie of the ſame. But alſo moſt impudẽtlie haue ſpoken the contrarie of that,that the fa mouſe learned holie Fathers haue taught . What trueth maie be thought to be in thẽ in other matters, by this ye maie coniecture.But nowe leauing this matter as ſufficientlie declared and proued againſt them : I will reſume my entended pourpoſe to expownde the ſixt of ſaincte Iohn, wherof ye ha-ue heard one texte, and the teſtimonie of diuerſe Fathers auouching the ſame to be vnderſtanded of the bleſſed Sacrament , and of the reall G preſence of Chryſtes bodie in the ſame . Nowe will I proceade to other textes in the ſame chapiter touching this matter.

THE NINTH CHAPITER EXPOVNDETH THE
next text that foloweth in ſainct Iohn.

Ioan.6.
He next text folowing in the ſixt chapiter of ſaincte Iohn ys this : *Litigabant ergo Iudæi adinuicem dicentes : Quomodò poteſt hic nobis car-nem ſuam dare ad manducandum ?* The Iewes ſtroue among them ſelues, ſainge : How can this felowe geue vs his fleſh to eate ? The Iewes vnto whom (as ſaincte Paule ſaieth) *vſque in hodiernum diem , cùm legitur*

2.Cor.3.
Moyſes , velamen poſitum eſt ſuper cor eorum . Vntill this daie , when Moyſes ys red , the veill ys putt vpon their heartes , their vnderſtan-dinges being carnall , and couered with ſo groſſe a veill , that they coulde not perceaue the ſpirituall talke of Chryſte , they ſtroue togeth- H er,and aſked howe he coulde geue them his fleſh to eate . They lac-

Eſay 7.
ked the right principle of the vnderſtanding of his matter,whiche ys faith: For *Niſi credideritis , non intelligetis .* Vnleſſe ye beleue,ye ſhall not vnderſtand

A They did not vnderſtand yt, bicauſe they did not beleue yt. No more ſhall they vnderſtande, vntill they turne vnto God by true beleif, as ſainŝe Paule ſaieth *Cùm autem conuerſi fuerint ad Dominum, auferetnr velamē de corde eorū*. Neuer theleſſe when they turne to our Lord, the veile ſhall be taken awaie frō their hearte. And then ſhall they not vſe this woordeof incredulitie, and doubtfullneſſe, whiche neuer paſſith from man, but in the wante of faithe, as ſaieth Chryſoſtom vpon this texte: *Quando ſubit quæſtio, quomodò aliquid fiat, ſimul ſubit & incredulitas. Itaque & Nicodemus perturbatus eſt inquiens, Quomodò poteſt homo in vētrē matris ſuæ iteratò introire et renaſci? Itidē & hi nunc: Quomodò poteſt hic nobis dare carnē ſuā ad manducandū? Nam ſi hic inquiris, cur non idem in quinque panum miraculo dixiſti, quomodò eos in tantum auxit? Quia tunc tantùm ſaturari curabant, inquies, non conſiderare miraculum. Sed res ipſa tunc docuit. Ergo ex eo & hæc credere oportuit ei facilia faŝu eſſe.* When the queſtion, *how*, cometh, ther cometh alſo incredulitie. Euē ſo Nichodemus was troubled ſaing: How can a man enter into his mothers wombe again, Euen ſo theſe nowe, how

B can this man geue vs his fleſh to eate, For yf thowe enquireſt this, why doeſt thowe not ſaie the like in the miracle of the fiue loaues, howe he encreaſed thē to ſo great a quantitie? Bycauſe then (*ye will ſaie*) they did onelie care to be filled with meat, not to conſider the miracle, but then the thing yt ſelf taught them, that the bread was multiplied. Therfore by that then yt behoued to haue beleued theſe thinges to haue ben eaſie to him to doo. Thus moche Chryſoſtom.

In dede (as this authour ſaieth) the Iewes hauing experiēce of Chryſtes power by that miracle wrought in bread for their bodilie ſuſtenaūce, might verie well haue beleued, that by the like power he might woorke this miracle alſo in bread, to turne the ſubſtāce therof into the ſubſtāce of his bodie, in a maner cōueniēt to be receaued for their ſpirituall ſuſtenaūce. but *Animalis homo nō percipit ea quæ ſunt Dei.* The naturall or carnall man dothe not perceaue the thinges of God. No more do our Pſeudochryſtians, who be woorſe thē the Iewes, for that they once beleued, and yet nowe be led awaie by diuerſe and ſtraūge doŝtrines, the cōtrarie wherof ſainŝt Paule coūſeileth thē in his

C epiſtle to the Hebrues. And for that they wolde not remain and continue in that faith, wherunto God had once called them, he ſuffreth them to be as groſſe and carnall in vnderſtanding, as the Iewes; and to vſe the like queſtion that the Iewes did, and ſaie, *Howe can the bodie of Chryſte be in the Sacrament, vnder ſo litle a peice of bread? And howe can we receaue the bodie of Chryſte in at our mouthes? And howe can Chryſte be in the Sacrament, that ys at the right hande of the Father? And howe can the bodie of Chryſte, being but one, be at once in ſo manie Altars?* All whiche queſtions do plainlie declare a lacke offaith to and of Gods workes and power, that he ys able to do and doth theſe thinges. For vnto all theſe queſtiōs the aunſwer ys: that they be doē by the power, and miraculouſe worke of God. Yf ye do proceade to aſke, wher finde yowe that God did ſaie, that he wolde woorke ſoche a miraculouſe worke by his diuine power? Ye heard yt euen nowe, that Chryſte ſaied: *The bread whiche I will geue ys my fleſh,* not a phantaſticall fleſh, not a Mathematicall, or a figuratiue fleſh (as Theophilaŝe expowndeth that texte) but that ſame fleſh, that I will (ſaieth Chryſt) *geue for the life of the worlde*, I will

D geue yowe that ſame fleſh to eate, that I will geue to be crucified vpon the croſſe, for the redemption of the worlde, and none other but euen the verie ſame.

Soche as beleued God, emonge the children of Iſrael, that they ſhoulde

posſe

Chryſ. homil.45.in Ioan.

1.Cor. 2. Falſe Chryſtias worſe then Iewes with their queſtioning howe.

The miraculouſe worke of the Sacrament promiſſed by Chryſt.

poſſeſſe the land of Canaan, when God had, ſaied they ſhoude ſo do, and not **E**
withſtãding the mightineſſe of the people that did inhabit that land, whiche
by the iudgemẽt of mẽ were ſo mightie, that it was vnpoſſible for the childrẽ
of Iſrael to vanquisſh them, as by their owne arme, yet did not miſtruſt,
but that God, that had ſaied yt, was able and wolde perfourme yt, theſe I
ſaie, enioied that land according to their beleif, and their faith was not fruſtrated of her expectacion. But ſoche as had heard the ſaing of God, and
conſidered how great a matter yt was, and howe farre exceading the power
of the Iſraelites to compaſſe, and vpon this conſideracion meaſured the
power of God, according to the meaſure of man, and ſo hauing a litle
faith, and moche doubte, began to queſtion: howe can we debel this people
ſo great, mightie, and ſtrong? and wolde not by an aſſured faithe leaue the
maner of the doinge and compaſing of yt to God, aſſuredlie beleuing that
no woorde of his ſhall fall to the grownde vnfulfilled, ſoche I ſaie, neuer came to vanquiſh the people, but vaniſhed awaie in their vnbeleif, and procu-
red Gods diſpleaſure vpon them, and died in the wildierneſſe.   **F**

Gods power   Wherfore ſeinge Chryſt hath ſaied, that he wolde geue vs that ſame fleſh,
ys not to be whiche he wolde gue for the life of the worlde, let vs not meaſure his power
meaſured by ours, to thinke that bicauſe we can not do yt, nor comprehende yt, or
by mans bicauſe yt miſliketh our naturall reaſon, therfor he can not do yt. But hũblie
reaſon. let vs vnderſtãd yt by faith, and not aske howe cã he geue vs his fleſh to eate?
but by faith cõfeſſe yt: *Quia omnia poſſibilia ſunt credẽti, & quæ ſunt impoſſibilia apud*
Marc. 9. *homines, poſſibilia ſunt apud Deũ. Quia nõ eſt impoſſibile apud Deũ omne verbũ.* All thin
Luc. 18. ges are poſſible to the beleuer. And ſoche thinges as are vnpoſſible with mẽ,
Jbid.1. are poſſible with God. For with God nothing ys vnpoſſible. And ſo leauing
to be a curiouſe ſearchers of gods wõderfull works, praiſe God ãd ſaie: *Tu es*
Deus, qui facis mirabilia. Thowe art God that woourkeſt meruailouſe thinges.
But for ſo moche as this texte declareth the incredulitie of the Iewes onelie
in this miſterie, and teacheth not the faith of a chryſten man neceſſarilie
to be had aboute the ſame, Therfore I haue decreed breiflie to ouerpaſſe yt, and by occaſion theroffom what to ſaie to the Aduerſaries.   **G**

THE TENTH CHAPITER PROVING AGAINST
the Aduerſaries, that the bodie of Chryſte maie be and ys in mo
places then one at once.

Ccaſion being here geuen by the doubtfull *how* of the Iewes
aſking, *Howe can this man geue vs this fleſh to eate?* to make mencion
alſo of the doubtfull *howe* of faitheleſſe Chryſtians, asking, *howe*
Chryſt, who ys at the right hand of the Father, can be in the Sacrament: And
howe the bodie of Chryſt being one, can be at one time on manie Altars: I
haue thought good here a litle to ſtaie, by faith theologicall to anſwere, not
the faith, but the doctrine Philoſophicall, both of the Proclamer, and alſo
of his Complices. For this ys a membre of his proclamacion: *whether the*
bodie of Chryſt ys, or maie be in a thouſand places or mo at one time. Whiche albeit in
ſenſe yt be coincident to thẽ other before mencioned: yet in vtterance yt **H**
ſheweth a more doubtfull countenance. For asking *whether Chryſtes bodie can*
be in a thouſand places at once, he doth both by the woorde, *thouſand,* moche declare his incredulitie to the miſteries of God, and by the ſame perſuadeth to
his hearers an impoſſibilitie,

And

A And for that this maner of queſtioninge ys a queſtiō on incredulitie, as the Iewes was, and ſpring bothe oute of vnbeleif, I haue thought good to ioin them to gether, and after the handling of the one, to handle the other.

And to them bothe to ſaie: As the Iewe remaining with in the cōpaſſe of his carnall vnderſtāding, coulde not atteign to the vnderſtāding of this matter, which was by faith, and yet poſſible, So theſe mē meaſuring Chryſte and his power by naturall knowledge, whiche ys but groſſe dregges and ſuddes, to the pure knowledge of faithe, they come in doubte, and aske a queſtiō as of a thinge vnpoſſible, when yet yt ys very poſſible.

But perchaunce ye will ſaie to me, yf it be a thinge ſo verie poſſible, howe dothe yt appeare to this mā and his likes vnposſible? I anſwere that yt appea reth to them vnposſible, bicauſe they leauing the knowledge of faith, are re-turned to the onelie knowledge naturall, and therby will they meaſure Chryſtes doinges in this matter. And for ſo moche as this appeareth vn-posſible to that knowledge, therfor they alſo ſaie that yt ys vnposſible. For allrhough, bycauſe they wolde ſeme to builde vpon faith, they do

Obiection with an-ſwer.
Faith iud-geth yt poſ-ſible, that reaſon iud-geth impoſ-ſible.

B ſometime alleage the article of our faith, that Chryſt aſcended into heauen an ſitteth at the right hand of God to Father, yet the grounde of their diſputacion, the force of their praclamacion, yea the ſhottanker of their re-fuge in this matter ys naturall reaſon, euen plain naturall philoſophie. That thowe maiſt ſee this (gentle Reader) I will for examp'e make one of their ar-guments, *that Chryſtes bodie can not be in the Sacrament.* Thus they reaſon.

He aſcended into heauē, and ſitteth at the right hand of God the Father. Ergo he ys not in the Sacrament.

Yf the true chryſtian ſaie, yt ys no good conſequence. For though yt be true that Chryſt beat the right hād of the Father. yet yt improueth not the preſence of Chryſt in the Sacramēt. For the catholique faith cōfeſſeth both that Chryſt ys preſēt with his Father in heauē, according to the article of the faithe, and alſo preſēt in the Sacramēt according to his worde, whē he ſaied: *This ys my bodie. This ys my bloode This do ye in remēbrance of me.* So that his preſen-ce in heauen, denieth not his preſence in the Sacrament, but he ys preſent in

C bothe, in maner conuenient to bothe.

Againſt this they replie and ſaie: Euery naturall bodie can be but in one place: Chryſt hath a naturall bodie: Ergo yt can be but in one place. But yt ys in heauē as in a place. Ergo yt ys ther and in no other place, Marke ye no-we, howe they flie to naturall phiſolophie as to their great ſtrenght, to main-tein their faithe? ys yt not a ſure peice of faith that ys builded vpon naturall philoſophie, and naturall reaſon, and not vpon the ſcriptures, the auncient fathers, or the vniuerſall receaued faith?

Sacramen-taries cheif growndes be naturall reaſous.

Perchāuce yt maie be ſaied, that I reaſon thus of my ſelf to deface the vali ditie of their matter: Well, to auoide this ymaginaciō, I will bring in the ve-rie argument of *Oecolampadius* , the great fownder, and prince of this ſchoole in our time, and the maſter of this Proclamer in this matter. Thus he reaſo-neth: *Si dicas, panis continet corpus, vide quid ſequitur. ergo panis locus erit, & vnum corpus erit in multis locis, & multa corpora in vno loco, & corpus in corpore etc.* Yf thow ſaieſt, the bread cōteineth the bodie, looke what foloweth, thē the bread ſhall

Oecolamp. De verbis coenæ Domi ni.

D be a place, ād one bodie ſhall be in many places, ād manie bodies in one pla-ce, and one bodie in an other. Thus *Oecolampadius.* Doo I nowe feign this ma-ner of reaſoning? Dothe not *Oecolampadius* reſorte to naturall phiſolophie, to prooue his hereſie, and impugne the faith catholique? Although in dede the argumēt proceadeth directlie againſt *Luther*, who taught the bread in the Sa-

crament

crament to remain with the bodie of Chryste(foche ys the agrement of the E
Father,ād the Sōne,of the master ād the fcholer,of *Luther*,ād *Oecolāpadius*,ād fo
of one of thē with an other)yet yt ys alfo againft the catholique faith , for yt
impugneth the prefēce of Chryfte in the Sacramēt. But howeʔas ys faied,by
naturall reafon. And fhall I faie why they prouē this their doctrin by natural
reafon ? In dede bicaufe yt ys fo farre vnknowen to the fcriptures that I
dare faie, they newer were, nor fhall be able to bring fruthe anie one fcripture to proue yt,and fo moche to diminifh the omnipotencie or allmightie
power of God.

De initiād			But to aunfwere *Oecōlampadius* for his naturall reafon, I thinke the faing of
myft.cap.9		fainfte Ambrofe to be a good anfwere.*Quid hic quæris naturæ ordinē in Chrifti cor-*
pore, cum præter naturam fit ipfe Dominus Iefus partus ex virgine? What fekeft thowe
(faieth fainfte Ambrofe) the ordre of nature in Chryftes bodie here,feing
the felf fame our Lord Iefus befides nature was born of a virgen. And to adde to fainfte Ambrofe faiēg,not onelie his birthe was befides nature,but ma
Naturall		nie other his actes:as his great learning ād wifdome declared in his difputa- F
order had		ciō with the doctours in the tēple,whē he was but twelue yeares of age, his
no place in	walking vpon the fea,his volūtarie death in geuing vppe his bleffed fowle at
many of		his owne pleafure , withoute force or violēce, as yt were, to thruft yt oute
Chryftes		and to caufe yt to departe . His refurrection and his afcenfion withall be as
doinges,		moche againft the ordre of nature , as his bleffed bodie to be in diuerfe
places,and as good argumentes maie the Aduerfarie finde in natural philofophie againft them as againft this . Whiche if he do or maie doo , fhall
Mahomets	we therfore denie Chryftes walking on the fea, his death, his refurrection,
patched re	and his afcenfion as theie do his prefence in the Sacrament. Then fhall we
ligion and	make a mingled faith, as the Turkes do.For as they kepe parte of Moyfes la-
the Sacra-	we, parte of Mohometes inuention : So we muft haue a faith partelie gro-
mentaries	wnded vpon the fcriptures, partelie on naturall reafon.But fo, that whē we
moch like.	will fcripture fhall rule naturall reafon, and when we lift naturall reafon
fhall commaunde and withftand both faith and fcripture . This ys a mad-
fetled faith.Wherfore thus moche to conclude with fainfte Ambrofe , *let vs* G
not feke the ordre of nature in Chryftesbodie, but let vs feke the ordre of faithe, and
cleaue to that.

But this proclamer wolde haue fome one fcripture doctour, or Councell,
that fhoulde declare that *Chryftstes bodie ys or maie be in a thoufand places or mo*
at one time.

In dede to aūfwer trulie,Imuft cōfeffe I finde neither fcripture,nor doctour
nor Councell teaching this matter in foche maner . For ther ys not one of
thefe that fpeaketh fo fondlie,ād fo vnreuerentlie,to prefcribe the omnipotencie of God a certen limitacion,and a ftinted nōbre ād that with foch a dif
fidencie vttered, as this Proclamer faieth,*in a thoufand places or mo* : fignifieng
therby an impoffibilitie,that yt ys vnpoffible forChryfte *to be in a thoufand pla*
ces at one time,fo in dede I finde not. But I finde thē with reuerence and faith,
withoute prefcription of nombre of places (for that they leaue to Gods wil)
faieng and teaching,that the bodie of Chryfte ys in diuerfe, or in manie places. And this (gentle reader)for thy fatisfaction fhall I, by the teftimonie of
diuerfe and manie of the moft auncient Fathers, laie before thee.

And here I confeffe , that this matter, by learned Fathers hath ben fo H
well laboured , that I can not bring in moche more, then they haue before
me gathered togecher . but that their confeffion of this treuth , and
their faith therin maie not be vnknowen to thee , I will not fticke hither

to

A to afcribe,that I find collected in other, raither then thowe fhouldeft be defrauded of fo moche good knowledge, and this fonde membre of this Proclamers proclamacion not fullie aunfwered.

And firft, to declare and proue this matter by the fcripture, I faie that our fauiour Chryfte taking the bread, and bleffing yt, made yt his bodie fainge: *Hoc eft corpus meum*, This ys my bodie. Whiche being doen, his bodie was at that time prefent in diuerfe places, as in his owne handes, in the handes alfo of euery of his Apoftles.

Mat.26.
Marc.14.
Luc.22.

That at that time he did beare or holde him felf in his owne handes, fainĉte Auguftin ys a notable wittneffe, fpeaking of king Dauid and applieng yt to Chryfte, faing: *Et ferebatur manibus fuis.Hoc verò fratres, quomodò poffit fieri in homine quis intelligat? Quis enim portari in manibus fuis? Manibus aliorum poteft portari homo, manibus fuis nemo portatur. Quomodò intelligatur in ipfo Dauid fecundùm literam non inuenimus,In Chrifto autem inuenimus. Ferebatur enim Chriftus in manibus fuis,quando commendans ipfum corpus,ait: Hoc eft corpus meum.* And he was borne in his owne handes. But bretheren howe this maie be doen

B in man,who can vnderftand? Who ys borne or caried in his owne handes? A man maie be caried in the handes of other men, in his owne handes no man ys borne.Howe yt maie be vnderftanded in Dauid himfelf accordinge to the letter,we finde not:But that yt maie be vnderftanded in Chryfte we finde. *For Chryft was borne in his owne handes when he,geuing furth the felffame bodie, faied:This ys my bodie.*

Auguft. in
Pfalm. 33.

Chryft in
his fupper
bare him-
felf in his
own handes

Ye haue here heard fainĉt Auguftin affirming that Chryfte caried him felf in his owne handes. Then this muft nedes folowe, that the felf fame bodie that did bear or carie, and the felf fame bodie that was born or caried,being but the verie one bodie of Chryfte, was then at one time in diuerfe places.And the fame one bodie of Chryfte being geuen furth to eche of his Apoftles,and they fitting in diuerfe places, argueth that the fame one bodie of Chryfte,was at one time in twelue fundrie places at the leaft. And as yt was then in fo manie: So maie yt be nowe in fewer or mo, according

C to the omnipotét pleafure of him that ys Lorde of nature,and naturall ordre and ys fubieĉte to neither of them,but ruleth and altereth them as to his wifdome femeth conuenient for the fetting furth of his honour,and glorie.

This was fo well knowen, and fo firmelie beleued of Sainĉte Bafill that holie Father,that hereunto agreablie he praieth in his Maffe thus:*Refpice Domine Iefu Chrifte,Deus nofter,de fanĉto habitaculo tuo,& veni ad fanĉtificandum nos,qui furfum Patri confides,& hic nobifcum inuifibiliter coes.Dignare manu tua forti dare nobis fanĉtum,& intaminatum corpus tuum, & preciofum fanguinem, & per nos peccatores populo tuo.* Looke o Lorde Iefu Chryft our God, from thy holie tabernacle, and come to fanĉtifie vs. Which fitteft aboue with thie Father,and arte with vs here inuifiblie, *vouchefafe with thie mightie hand to geue vnto vs thy holie and vndefiled bodie,and precioufe bloode,and by vs finners to thy people.*

Bafil.in fua
Liturgia.
Plain pla-
ces for the
Proclamer.

Chryfoftome in his maffe hath almoft the fame woordes,that he praieth *Refpice Domine Iefu Chrifte Deus nofter de fanĉto habitaculo tuo,& de fede gloriæ regni tui,& veni ad fanĉtificandum nos qui furfum cum Patre fedes, & deorfum nobis inuifibi-*

D *liter affiftis,Dignare tua potenti manu tribuere nobis immaculatum corpus tuum, & preciofum fanguinem, & per nos omni populo.* O Lord Iefu Chryfte our God, looke from thy holie tabernacle, and from the feat of the glorie of thy kingdom, and come to fanĉtifie vs,whiche fitteft aboue with theFather,and ftandeft by vs beneath inuifiblie, *vouchfaif with thy mightie hande to geue vnto vs thy vndefiled bodie,and precioufe bloode and by vs to all thy people.*

Chryf.in
fua Liturg.

　　　　　　　Y　　Thefe

Thése two holie Fathers, what foeuer naturall reafon or ordre wolde, not　E
withftanding they praied according to the ordre of faithe, and therunto according they confeffed, and acknowledged Chryfte both to be aboue with
the Father, and alfo prefent with vs in the Sacrament.

Although Chryfoftom dothe fo plainlie with Bafill teftifie the prefence
of Chryfte both with the Father in heauen, and with vs here in earth: yet more plainlie he dothe wittneffe the fame in an other place, fpeaking of the fa-

Chryfoft in crifice of Chryftes bodie offred in the Churche, and faieth: *Hoc autem facrifi-*
10. ad He. *cium exemplar eft illius. Idipfum femper offerimus, nec nunc quidem alium agnum, craftina*
hom.17. *alium, fed femper eundem ipfum. Proinde vnum eft hoc facrificium hac ratione. Alioquin*
quoniam in multis locis offertur, multi Chrifti funt. Nequaquam: Sed vnus vbique eft Chri-
ftus, & hic plenus exiftens, & illic plenus, vnum corpus. Sicut enim qui vbique offertur
vnum corpus eft, & non multa corpora: ita etiam & vnum facrificium. This facrifice
ys an exemplar of that, that Chryfte offred: *Euen the felf fame do we allwaies offer.*

The facrifi- Neither do we nowe offer one lambe, and to morowe an other, but allwais
ce offred in euen the felf fame. *Therfore ys this one facrifice, by this reafon.* Otherwife for that　F
manie pla- yt ys offred in manie places, ther be manie Chryftes. Not fo. But ther ys one
ces ys but Chryfte euery wher, bothe here being full and ther full, euen one bodie.
one Chryft. *And as he, that ys euery wher offred, ys one bodie, and not manie bodies: Euen fo alfo*
ys the facrifice one.

Weigh well this teftimonie of Chryfoftom, gentle Reader, and firft this
that he faieth: *That the facrifice of Chryftes bodie ys but one. For otherwife bycaufe yt ys*
offred in manie places, ther shoulde be manie Chriftes. In whiche woordes howe
plainlie dothe he faie that Chryfte ys offered in manie places? and yet not
manie Chryftes, but one Chryfte. This Father teacheth not like a naturall
Philofopher, but like a diuine Philofopher, a louer of the wifdom of Chryftes faith, according to the whiche, and contrarie to Philofophie, he confeffeth Chryftes bodie to be in manie places at once, and that with reuerence, and not with doubtfull admiracion, and exclamacion (*as this Proclamer*
doth) *to be in a thoufand places at once.* Althouh in his reuerent woordes ther ys
as moche implied, as the woordes folowing do well declare. Whiche alfo　G
good reader note. For he faieth: *vbique offertur, he ys euery wher offred*, and that
ys more then in a thoufand places. And although this mans herefie hath
fretted, and eaten in manie places, moche like a deadlie cankre: yet I beleue
Chryfte ys not fo forfaken, but he ys yet offred in mo then a thoufand places,
and fhall be, except our finnes fhall deferue that he be taken awaie from vs.
As for that that he faieth, that Chryfte ys our facrifice, and therfore prefent,
I will leaue yt withoute note, to be confidered in a place more conuenient.

As before ye haue heard S. Bafill and Chryfoftom vttering almoft all
one and the fame woordes of this matter: So fhall ye heare Saincte Ambrofe fpeaking almoft the fame woordes that Chryfoftome did. So be thefe
good Fathers linked together in one trueth, that they oftentimes fpeake all
one, and the fame woordes in one and the fame matter. Thus writeth
Ambr. in fainate Ambrofe : *Proinde vnum eft hoc facrificiuue. Alioquin hac ratione, quoniam*
10. Heb. *multis in locis offertur, multi Chrifti funt. Nequaquam : Sed vnus vbique eft Chriftus, &*
hic plenus exiftens, & illic plenus, vnum corpus. Sicut enim qui vbique offertur, vnum　H
Chryft of- *corpus eft, & non multa corpora: ita etiam & vnum facrificium.* Therfore this fa-
fred euerie crifice ys one. or ells by this reafon, for that yt ys offred in manie places,
wher ys but ther be manie Chryftes. Not fo but euerie wher one Chryft, both here being
one bodie, full and ther full, euen one bodie. *For euen as he that ys offred euerie wher ys one bo-*
and one fa- *die, and not manie bodies: Euen fo alfo ys the facrifice one.*
crifice.

I will

A I will not trouble yow with noting sainct Ambrose woordes, but what ys geuen yow to note vpon Chrysostom, note the same euen here likewise, and I will hast me to heare an other place of S. Ambrose wher he saieth thus: *Vidimus Principem sacerdotum ad nos venientem . Vidimus & audiuimus offerentem pro nobis sanguinem suum. Sequamur vt possumus sacerdotes, vt offeramus pro populo sacrificium, etsi infirmi merito, honorabiles tamen sacrificio, quia etsi nunc Christus non videtur offerre, tamen ipse offertur in terris, quãdo Christi corpus offertur.* We haue seen the high preist coming to vs . We haue seen and heard him offring for vs his bloode. Let vs priestes, as we maie, folowe, that we maie offre sacrifice for the people, although by merite we are weake: yet are we by the sacrifice honorable. For although Chryste ys not nowe seen to offer : *Yet ys he offred in earth, when the bodie of Chryste ys offred.*

Amb . in Psalm. 38.

Leuing all other thinges that maie be here noted, this ys not to be ouerpassed, that saincte Ambrose saieth, *that Christe ys offred in earthe.* But when ys he offred? When his bodie ys offred. Wherbie yt ys manifest, that as we maie confesse Chryste verilie to be in glorie : So maie we also confesse that

B he ys verilie in earth, for somoche as he ys ther offred in sacrifice . And so being verilie both in heauen and earth, that ys true, that we trauaill here to proue.

Chryst ys offred in earth, whẽ his bodie ys offred.

But that, that ys yet remaining to be saied in this matter, will not suffer me to tarie to note, and saie, what might be noted and saied here : For besides other thinges we haue yet to heare the goodly testimonie of S. Bernarde, who so plainlie teacheth this matter, and so godly, that yt were pitie the reader shoulde be defrauded of the reading of so notable a sentence.

Thus he writeth: *Sed vnde hoc nobis pijßime Domine , vt nos vermiculi reptantes super faciem terræ, nos inquam, qui puluis & cinis sumus te præsentem habere mereamur præ manibus, præ oculis, qui totus & integer sedes ad dextram Patris, qui etiam vnius horæ momento, ab ortu solis vsque ad occasum, ab Aquilone vsque ad Austrum præstò es omnibus, vnus in multis, idem in diuersis locis, vnde hoc, inquam? Certè non ex debito , neque ex merito nostro: sed ex voluntate tua, & dulcedinis tuæ beneplacito.* But howe happe-

C neth this vnto vs , O most mercifull Lorde : that we litle woormes creping vpon the face of the earthe, *maie haue thee present, before our handes, before our eyes, whiche all and wholle sittest at the right hand of the Father.* Which also in the minute of an howre, from the East to the West, from the North to the South arte present to all. *Thowe being one, arte in manie, and being the selffame arte in diuerse places,* from whence cometh this I saie? Trulie not of anie duetie, neither of our desert, but of thy will, and the pleasure of thy gentlenesse . Thus saincte Bernard.

Bernard. sermone de cœna Dom.

Chryst being one ys at one time in manie placæ.

See ye not howe this holie Bernard notwith woordes of skoffes and doubtfullnesse, but with godlie simplicitie, and reuerence confessing the veritie of Christes presence, both at the right hand of God the Father, and also in the Sacrament before our handes, before our eyes, and therof nothing doubting, woundereth at the great goodnesse and mercie of our Sauiour Chryste, howe he doth vouchsaif so moche to do for vs poour litle woormes creping vpon the earth. Suche was the simplicitie of faith, the humblenesse

D of minde in good Fathers, that beleuing the thing, they did agnise the great benefitt of God, wher this Proclamer puffed vppe with pride, reiecteth the simplicitie of faith, and contemneth the benefitt of God.

But contemning him that contempneth God, let vs heare more of this good Father, that honoured our Lord God. In the same sermon he hath also this saieng, speakinge to the Churche, whiche ys the Spouse of Chryst to stire

V ij her also

her alſo to agniſe this great benefitte of God , ſaing thus: *Gratulare ſponſa,gau-*
de incomparabiliter . Præſidentem habes,& rectorem ſponſum in præſentis exilij militia.
Pignus habes,arrham tenes, quibus fœliciter vniaris ſponſo in patria, glorioſa & amabilis
ſponſa. In terra ſponſum habes in ſacramento: in cœlis habitura es ſine velamento, &
hic & ibi veritas: ſed hic palliata , ibi manifeſtata. Gene thankes, O ſpouſe,reioice
incomparablie. In the warrefare of this preſent banniſhment,thowe haueſt

thy husband preſident, and ruler,thowe haueſt the pledge , thowe haueſt
thy earneſt money, by the whiche thowe maiſt as a gloriouſe and beloued
Spouſe be vnited and ioined to thy Spouſe in heauen with felicitie. In
earth thowe haueſt thy Spouſe in the Sacrament : In heauen thowe ſhalt
haue him withoute anie couert. *Bothe here,and ther ys the veritie.* But here couered,ther openly ſhewed.

    This ys a goodlie ſentence, and woorthie well to be noted , but this for
our pourpoſe ſpecialle , that the Churche hath her Spouſe Chryſt in earth
in the Sacrament,whiche in heauen ſhe ſhall haue in open viſion.Here verilie Chryſt,and ther verilie Chryſt,all the difference ys,that here he ys vnder F
couerture,ther manifeſtlie ſeen.

    To conclude, that the aduerſarie ſhall not reiecte ſainct Bernard for his
plain ſainge:yt ſhall be confirmed by the like ſaing of Chryſtom, who ſaieth

thus: *O miraculum,O Dei benignitatem , qui cum Patre ſurſum ſedet,in illo ipſo temporis*
articulo omnium manibus pertractatur, ac ſe ipſe tradit volentibus ipſum accipere ac com-
plecti. O miracle, O the gentle godneſſe of God,*he that ſitteth aboue with God*
the Father,euen in that ſame poincte of time ys handeled with the handes of all, and he
deliuereth him ſelf to them that will receaue him, and embrace him. Thus
moche Chryſoſtome.

    Beholde nowe(good reader)howe Chryſoſtom agreablie to the ſpeache
of ſainct Bernard, acknowlegeth the great goodneſſe of God , that Chryſt
whiche ſitteth at the right hand of the Father ys in that time, *meening the*
*time of miniſtracion,*in the handes of men. In that he ſaieth,he ys in the handes
of men,yt argueth a reall preſence, for the ſpirituall preſence can not be in
handes,but in heart.   G

Chryſtes
being in the
Sacr.ys mi-
raculouſe
contrarie
to the rules
of philoſo-
phie.

    To the proofe of this alſo yt maketh inuinciblie,that Chryſoſtome excla-
meth with reuerent wonder ſaing: *O miracle.*In this that he acknowlegeth yt
a miracle,he dothe acknowlege more then the bread to be a figure of Chryſtes bodie.For that ys no miracle to be wondered at. But he doth acknowledge the miracle to be , that Chryſte that ſitteth aboue with the Father,
ſhoulde alſo be in the Sacrament in the handes of men. This ys the miracle.
For this ys both aboue nature, and againſt nature, and doen by the onelie
power of God,and therfore ys a miracle.

    Thus then yt ys manifeſt by the humble lowlie , and faithfull confeſsion
of the faith of theſe holy fathers, that Chryſtes bodie miraculouſlie ys both
in heauen,and in earth in the Sacrament,and ſo in manie places at one time
notwithſtandinge the contemptuouſe exclamacion of this Proclamer, limi-
ting the power of God by an impoſsiblitie,as yt appeareth to his vnbeleuing
vnderſtanding,that the bodie of Chryſt ſhoulde be in a *thouſand places.*Which
his exclamacion was his beſt argument to bring the people from their fathe. H
Bnt yf he will acknowledge the miracle with Chryſoſtom, he ſhall perceaue
howe fooliſh his argument ys.

A **THE ELEVENTH CHAPITER PROVETH THAT**
*as two bodies maie be in one place: so the bodie of Chryst being one
maie be in diuerse places.*

S the Aduersaries to ouerthrow the worke of faith haue vsed
naturall philosophie: So to maintein their naturall philosophie,
they haue vtterlie denied the verie Gospell, the grownd of faithe. For wher the good catholique learned men of charitable
pitie laboured to bring them, from this their wicked errour, persuading the
not to cleaue to naturall reason, as therwith to measure, and streicten that,
which ys the bodie of the Sonne of God, exalted to be in vnitie of person
with the Godhead, as they wolde doo our bodies which be but naturall,
and earthlie bodies onelie, infinite degrees vnder the condicion of that
blessed bodie of Chryste: but to consider, that as the bodie of Chryst, though
yt be a naturall bodie, might be with an other bodie in one place at one
B time, whiche ys against naturall Philosophie and reason: So the same being
but one bodie, might be in diuerse places at one time, notwithstanding natu
rall reason and Philosophie.

To proue two bodies to be in one place at one time, the Gospell of saincte *Ioan.20.*
Iohn was alleged, wher we read: *Venit Iesus ianuis clausis, & stetit in medio eorum
& dixit: Pax vobis.* Iesus came the doors being shett, and stood in the middest
of them and saied: *Peace be with yowe.* This beinge testified of saincte Iohn, for
the miraculouse coming in of Chryste to his Apostles, proueth that he so
coming in, passed through doore or wall as his pleasure was to do, and so
doinge, ther was, contrarie to *Oecolampadius* saing, *Corpus in corpore, & duo cor-* *Cranmer*
pora simul. One bodie in an other, and two bodies together one place. *in his aunswer agaist
winch.*

I remembre, that this scripture was obiected by master Smith against
Cranmer: and for aunswere therunto thus saith Cranmer: *But peraduenture
Master Smith will aske me this question: Howe coulde Chryste come into the house, the*
C *doore beinge shett, except he came through the doore? To your wise question, master Smith,
I will aunswer by an other question. Coulde not Chryste come aswell into the house, when the*
doore was shette, as the Apostles coulde go oute of prison, the doore being shett? Coulde not *Act.5.*
*God wourke this thing except the Apostles must go through the doore, and occupie the
same place that the doore did?* In this aunswere by Cranmer made by questions,
as ther be two questions, so ther be two partes. But by the aunswering of the
first, the aunswering to the second shall be the easier.

The first questiō asketh: yf Chryst coulde not come as well into the house
the doores being shett, as the Apostles coulde go oute of prison the doore
being shett: whiche question I praie thee, Reader, well to weigh. Which yf
thow doo thowe shalt perceaue that to auoid this argument, and to deceaue *Cranmer*
the reader, he here vttereth a manifest and shamefull vntruthe, and abu- *falsifieth*
seth the Scripture for the maintenaunce of his heresie to wickedlie. For *the scriptu-*
he, to make the readers beleue that the coming in of Chryste into the house, *re to main-*
and the goinge of the Apostles out of prison, was of one maner, saieth that *tien his he-*
D the goinge oute of the Apostles, and the coming in of Chryste were bothe *resie.*
the doores being shett. Which ys verie false, and directlie against the truth of
the scripture. For as concerning the going oute of the Apostles out of prison,
Looke the actes of the Apostles, and ye shall finde, that they went not oute
the doors being shett, as this man vntrulie reporteth, but the doores
beinge open. Whiche thing the holie Goste lefte not vndeclared. For

V iij　　thus

thus shall ye reade ther : *The cheif preist rose vppe,and all they that were with him,* E
which ys the secte of the Saduces,and were full of indignacion,and laied handes on the
Apostles , and putt them in the common prison. But the Angell of our Lord by night
opened the prison doors and brought them furth, and saied. Go and stande , and speake
in the temple to the people all the woordes of life, When they heard that, they entred
earlie in the morning and taught. But the cheif preist came , and they that were with
him,and called a councell together,and all the elders of the children of Israell,and sent men
to the prison to fetch them , when the ministers came , and fownde them not in prison they
returned,and tolde,saing:The prison trulie we founde shette, with all diligence,and the ke-
pers standing withoute,before the doores,but when we had opened,we fownd no man within.

In this scripture first note,that when the Apostles were committed to prison,the Angell of God came by night and opened the doores of the prison
and not onelie opened the doores,but also brought the Apostles oute.Then
ys yt false that this man saieth,that the Apostles went oute of the prison the
doores being shett. Trueth yt ys that the doores were made fast again after
their departure.For the messengers, that came in the morning to fetche the F
Apostles reported that they fownd the doores shet with all diligence , and
the kepers standing before the doore.And herin wolde the holie Goste the
miracle to be noted, that the Angell opened the prison doores , and shett
them again,and brought furth the Apostles , and the kepers standing at the
doore perceaued not. But yet he wolde not this miracle of their going oute to be like the miracle of Chrystes Cominge in.For as touching the Apostles, the holie Goste plainly reporteth howe they went oute by the helpe
of the Angell opening the doores: But in Chrystes coming in ther ys no
Chryst en- meanes declared howe he came in , but yt ys absolutely spoken, *Venit Iesus*
tred into *ianuis clausis,*Iesus came,the doores being shette , signifieng that he came in
his Apost. more miraculouslie by the power of his Godhead, not requiring the aide of
the doores the opening of any dore.
being shett. But that ye maie perceaue that I do expownd and vnderstand this facte
and miracle of Chryste as the holie fathers doo, and that ye maie the better
credite the matter, ye shall heare howe they vnderstand this place of sain_te G
Iohan.

Chrysost. Chrysostom to proue the Mother of Chryste a virgen both before and
homil.de after his birth,alleageth this place,and saieth thus:*Sancta Maria,beata Maria,ma*
Ioan.Bapt. *ter et virgo.Virgo fuit ante partum,virgo post partum.Ego hoc miror, quomodò de virgine*
virgo natus sit, & post nationem virginis mater virgo sit.Vultis scire quomodò de virgine
natus sit, & post natiuitatem mater ipsa sit virgo? Clausa erant ostia, & ingressus est
Iesus.Nulli dubiũ quin clausa sint ostia:qui intrauit per ostia clausa,non erat phantasma,non
erat spiritus,verè corpus erat.Quid enim dicit?Respicite & videte,quia spiritus carnem,&
ossa non habet,sicut me videtis habere.Habebat carnes,habebat ossa,& clausa erant ostia.
Quomodò clausis ostijs intrauerunt ossa,& caro? Clausa sunt ostia,& intrat,quem intran-
tem non vidimus.Vnde intrauit? omnia clausa sunt,locus non est per quem intret,& tamen
intus est qui intrauit. Nescis quomodò factum sit, & das omnipotentiæ Dei: Da potentiæ
Dei,quia de virgine natus sit. The holie Marie,the blessed Marie , mother and
virgen, she was a virgen before birth,a virgen after birth.I merueil at this,
howe of a virgen , a virgen shoulde be born , and after the birth of a virgen, H
the mother shoulde be a virgen. Will ye knowe how he was born of a virgen,and after the birth,howe she was both mother and virgen?*The doores were*
shett and Iesus entred in . No man doubteth but that the doores were shette, He that
entred by the shett doors was no phantasie,he was no spirit, he was verilie a
bodie.For what saied he?Looke and see that a spirit hath no flesh and bones,
as ye

A as ye fee me haue. *He had flesh, he had bones, and the doores were shette, Howe did flesh and bones enter the doore being shette? The doores be shette,and he goeth in,whome we fawe not going in.How did he go in?all thinges are cloſſe,ther ys no place,by the which he might go in,and yet he ys within, that went in, and yt doth not appeare howe he went in.* Thowe knoweſt not,and doeſt referre yt to the omnipotencie of God.Geue this alſo to the omnipotencie of God,that he was born of a virgen.

Sainɕe Hierom vſeth the ſame argumēt,to the ſame pourpoſe and ſaieth: *Reſpondeant mihi,quomodò Ieſus ingreſſus eſt clauſis oſtijs,cùm palpandas manus,ⱪ latus conſiderandum,ⱪ oſſ a carneméque monſtrauerit, ne veritas corporis phantaſma putaretur: Et ego reſpondebo quomodò ſanɕa Maria ſit mater ⱪ virgo, virgo poſt partum, mater antequàm nupta.* Let them aunſwer me (ſaith ſainɕe Hierom) howe Ieſus entred in the doores being ſhette,when,leſte his bodie ſhoulde be thought a phantaſie,he ſhewed both fleſh and bones,and his handes to be felt,and his ſide to be conſidered:And I will aunſwer them,howe the holie Marie, maie be bothe a mother,and a virgen. A virgen before birth,a mother before ſhe was knowen of man.

Hieron. in Apologia, cont.Iouin.

B In bothe theſe Autours, we maie perceaue not onelie by their woordes, but alſo by the argument whiche they make,that the doores remained ſtill ſhette, both at the entring in of Chryſte in to the houſe, and after that he was entred in, wherbie they proue that the clauſures of the virginitie in the virgen Marie,remained cloſſe, both before the birth in the birth, and after the birth of Chryſte.Nowe yf the doores did open at the going in of Chryſte to his Apoſtles(*as ſome haue wickedlie taugt raither ſeking to ſhadow the miraculouſe worke of Chryſte,and to falſifie the ſcriptures,then they wolde forſake their erroure , or haue yt conuinced*)then coulde yt not proue that the clauſures of the virginitie of the mother of Chryſte,notwithſtanding his birth, remained allwais cloſed whiche (as ye maie perceaue)they intended to proue.

Yt maie be that the Aduerſarie being preſſed with the authoritie 'of theſe graue and learned fathers , will graunt that Chryſte went in to this Apoſtles the doores being ſhett,But yet he went not(*he will ſaie*)through the C doore,nor no other body,ſo as there ſhoulde be two bodies in one place at one time.That he went in the doores being ſhett he will graunte:But howe he went in,he can not tell.

To make this matter plain to the Aduerſarie and thee, Reader, we will heare Chryſoſtom in an other place,geuing ſome cauſe, how he might ſo go in.*Dignū autem dubitatione eſt,quomodò corpus incorruptibile formam clauorum acceperit, ⱪ mortali manu tangi potuerit.Sed hoc te non perturbet,hoc enim permiſſionis fuit.Corpus enim tam tenue ⱪ leue vt clauſis ianuis ingrederetur, omni craſſitudine carebat, ſed vt reſurreɕio crederetur,talem ſe exhibuit.Et vt ipſum crucifixum fuiſſe , ⱪ neminem alium pro eo reſurrexiſſe intelligas,proptereà cum ſignis crucis reſurrexit.* Yt yt woorthie of doubte,howe the incorruptible bodie did take the forme of the nailes, and coulde be touched with mortall hand.But let not this trooble thee, For this was doen of permiſſion.*For that bodie , being ſo ſubtile and light,that yt might entre in,the doores being ſhett,was void of all groſſneſſe.*But that the reſurreɕiō might be D leleued,he ſhewed him ſelf ſoche a one,and that thowe mighteſt vnderſtād, that yt waſeuē he that was crucified,and no mā ells did riſe for him,therfore he roſe with the figures and tokens of the croſſe.Thus moche Chryſoſtome.

Chryſoſt. homil. 86. in Ioan.

Chryſtes bodie was ſo void of groſſneſſe that yt might enter the doorea being ſhett

The cauſe whiche ys geuen here to helpe vppe the weakneſſe of oure faith the ſooner to beleue that Chryſte paſſed through the doore, ys, that he had after his reſurreɕion,a pure,clear,and ſubtile bodie, void of all corruption, and groſſneſſe,euen a ſpirituall bodie , that might to oure own iudgement

and reafon the eafelier fo do:and yet was yt a perfecte bodie of a man in fub-　**E**
ftance,and lineamentes.

But that he came in to his Apoftles through the doore,and howe, and by
what means he fo did,Chryfoftom by expreffe woordes in an other place
declareth,fpeaking in the perfon of Chryfte after this maner.　*Non eft meum*

Chryf.de
refurrect.
fermon.9.

meos ludificare phantafmate,vanam imaginem vifus fi timet, veritatem corporis manus
& digitus exploret.Poteft fortaßis aliqua oculos caligo decipere,palpatio corporalis verum
corpus agnofcat. Spiritus (inquit)carnem,& offa non habet,ficut me videtis habere.Quòd
*oftia claufa penetraui, fola eft virtus diuini Spiritus,non fola carnis fubftantia.*Yt ys not

Chryft en-
tred trough
the doores
that were
shett.

my propertie,myne to delude with a phantafie.Yf the feight feare a vain ima
ge,let the hand and fingar trie oute the veritie of the bodie. Perchaunce fome mift maie deceaue the eyes,let the corporall feeling acknowledge a true
bodie.A fpirit(faied he)hath not flefh and bones, as ye fee me to haue . *That I*
entred through the doores, that were shett , yt ys onelie the powre of the diuine fpirit not
*the onelie fubftance of the flesh.*Thus Chryfoftom.

As this place geueth goodlie inftruction to the reader : fo doth yt fullie,　**F**
and mighteilie ftoppe the mouthes of thē that fpeake wicked thinges againft
God,in denienge the miraculoufe workes of our Sauiour and mafter Chry-
fte.That Chryft with his perfecte bodie entred in to his Apoftles , Chryfoftom proueth by Chryftes owen faieng being in the middeft of them,when

Howe Chri
ftes bodie,
entred
through
the doores
shett.
Amb.in
Luc.li.10.
cap.14.

he faied:A fpirit hath not flefh and bones,as ye fee me haue.Howe this bodie, being a perfecte bodie of a man entred,he declareth when he faieth in
the perfon of Chryfte,that yt entred through the doores.Yf ye will learn by
what mean,he faieth , *yt was not by the fubftance of the flesh , but by the vertue or*
power of the Godhead,

Of this matter alfo fainct Ambrofe ys a goodlie wittneffe,who vpon the
Gofpell of fainct Luke faieth thus:*Habuit admirandi caufam Thomas, cum videret,*
claufis omnibus per inuia fepta corporibus inoffenfa compage Chrifti corpus infertum, &
ideo mirum quomodò fe natura corporea per impenetrabile corpus infuderit, inuifibili aditu,
vifibili confpectu, tangi facilis, difficilis æftimari. Thomas had a caufe to merueill
when he fawe(all thinges being fhet vppe and clofed) the bodie of Chryfte　**G**
by claufures,without all waies for bodie to entre,the walls being vnbroken,
to be entred in emong them.And therfore yt was wonder,howe the corporall nature paffed through the impenetrable bodie,with an inuifible coming,
but with uifible beholding,eafie to be touched , hard to be iudged. Thus
fainct Ambrofe.

Yf ye note this teftimonie, yt varieth not from Chryfoftom: For yt 'teftifieth that oure Sauiour Chryfte came in to his Apoftles , the doores being
fhett And that notwithftanding he went through the claufures of the
houfe,they not being broken. And herevpon,faieth fainctε Ambrofe ys the
great wonder, how his naturall bodie coulde entre through an impenetrable bodie.Wherby bothe thefe Fathers declare the trueth of the doctrine of
the Churche,that Chryfte thus entring,ther were two bodies in one place.

There be manie that beare verie plain teftimonie in this matter . But we
will heare but two mo onely- Whiche, *I fuppofe,*with thefe before alleaged,
being all men of foche grauitie,holineffe,authoritie,and learning, maie fuf-　**H**
fice,not onelie to counteruaill thefe fond bablers,void of like grauitie, holineffe or learning:but alfo with them,that haue any fparke of grace and wifdom, take foch effecte,as to caufe them flee thefe leude teachers , and to
hiffe them oute of all chryftian companie , forafmoch as they teache foche
learninge, as none of the holy Fathers doo teache, but foch raither as ys
contrarie

A   contrarie to them.   But let vs heare faincte Auguftine in this matter, thus
he faieth: *Nec eos audiamus,qui negant tale corpus Domini refurrexiffe , quale pofitum*   Auguſt. de
eſt in monumēto.Nec nos moueat,quòd clauſis oſtijs fubitò eum apparuiffe Difcipulis fcriptū   agone Chri
eſt,vt propterea negemus illud fuiffe corpus humanum, quia contra naturam huius corporis   ſti.cap.24.
videmus illud per clauſa oſtia intrare,omnia enim poſsibilia funt Deo . Si enim potuit ante
paſsionem clarificare illud ſicut ſplendorem Solis,quare non potuit & poſt paſsionem , ad
quantam vellet fubtilitatem in temporis momēto redigere,vt per clauſa oſtia poſſet intrare?   Chriſtes bo
Neither let vs geue eare to them, that denie the fame bodie to haue rifen,   die againſt
that was putte in the graue.Neither let yt moue vs, that yt ys written , that   the nature
fodenlie he appeared to his difciples, the doores being ſhett , that therfore we fhoulde   of a bo-
denie yt to be a mans bodie,bycaufe we fee yt againſt the nature of this bo-   die entred
die to *entre in through the ſhette doores.*For all thinges are poſsible to God. For   through the
yf he coulde before his paſsion make yt as clear as the brightneffe of the   ſhett doores
Sunne,why might he not after his paſsion alfo in a moment of time,bring yt
to afmoche a fubtilitie as he wolde, that he might entre in through the ſhett
doores?

B   Note here in faincte Auguftine,that where the Aduerfarie wolde not that
the bodie of Chryfte fhoulde be in diuerfe places for offending the lawe of
naturall ordre , he faieth , that Chryft againſt the nature of this bodie,
entred in through the ſhett doores,fo that the bodie of Chryfte maie not
be bownde to the lawe or ordre of nature, for that he ys the lord of nature,
not an onelie man,but a perfon that ys God and man,as Cirill faieth: *Clauſis*   Cyrill.in
foribus repentè Dominus omnipotentia fua,natura rerum fuperata, ingreſſus ad Difcipulos   Ʒoan.li.12.
eſt. Nullus igitur querat,quomodò corpus Domini ianuis clauſis penetrauit , cùm intelligat   cap. 53.
non de homine nudo, vt modò nos fumus , fed de omnipotente filio Dei,hæc ab Euangeliſta
defcribi. Nam cùm Deus verus ſit,rerum naturæ non fubiacet,quod in cæteris quoque mira-
culis patuit.   The gates being ſhett our lorde through his omnipotencie, the
nature of thinges beinge ouercomed,fodenly went in to his difciples. *Let no*   Chryſt ys
man therfore aske howe the bodie of our Lorde went through the gates beinge ſhett, foraf-   not fubieƈt
moche as he maie vnderſtand,thefe thinges to be defcribed of the Euange-   to lawe of
C   lift,not of a bare man, as we be nowe,but of the Allmightie Sonne of God.   nature.
Who forafmoche as he ys verie God, ys not fubieƈte to the lawe of nature.
Whiche thing did appeare in other his miracles alfo. Thus Cyrill.

        Nowe ye haue heard a fufficient nombre of holy learned Fathers, auou-
ching this great miracle of Chryfte,not as fome of the Aduerfaries faie, that
he came into his difciples after the doores were ſhett , after the maner of
other men:neither as fome other of them do faie, that he caufed the doores
or walls to open,and fo came in:neither that an Angell did open the doores
to him,as to the Apoſtles, that were in prifon:but that he being verie God,
gaue vnto that his manhead that fingular fubtilitie aboue all other , that yt
was not fubieƈt to nature(as Cirill faieth) but aboue nature,fo farre , and in
foche excellent degree,that yt might paffe through thofe doores,the doores
not broken (as faincte Ambrofe faied.

        In this matter, thus moch haue I laboured, both that the miraculoufe
worke of Chryft might not be obfcured, nor fhadowed by the malignitie of
D   men, and alfo that yt might be perceaued ; that in the workes of Chryfte
we maie not fo looke to the ordre of nature,to naturall reafon, or naturall
philofophie,that for the mainteinaunce therof, we fhall denie the worke of
Chryfte.Naturall philofophie,hath manie propofitions, that will not ſtande
with oure faith.For naturall philofophie teacheth that *mundus eſt perpetuus,*the   Gen.1.
worlde ys perpetuall or ouerlaſting: Faith teacheth, that: *In principio creauit*
                                                                Deus

*Deus cœlum & terram.*In the beginninge God created heauen and earth,and **E**
that therfore the worlde had a beginninge. And yt teacheth, alſo that yt
ſhall haue an ende. For *cœlum & terra tranſibunt,* heauen and earth ſhall paſſe
awaie.Of the whiche both, the Prophete ſaieth: *In principio Domine terram*
*creaſti, et opera manuum tuarum ſunt cœli:ipſi peribunt,tu autem permanes,&c.*Thowe
in the beginning(*O Lorde*)dideſt laie the fundacion of the earthe,and the hea
uens are the workes of thy hand.They ſhall periſh , but thowe doeſt abide.
Of the whiche matter alſo ſaincte Peter maketh plain declaracion. Likewiſe
naturall philoſophie teacheth, *quod vnum corpus non poteſt eſſe ſimul & ſemel in*
*diuerſis locis:*that one bodie can not be at one time in diuerſe places.But faith
teacheth vs(as yt ys declared in the laſt chapiter)that Chryſtes bodie ys and
maie be in diuerſe places.Naturall philoſophie teacheth , that *duo corpora non*
poſſunt ſimul eſſe in vno & eodem loco . Two bodies can not be together in one
place:Yet the Scripture teacheth(as ye haue heard the holie learned Fathers
vnderſtand them)that Chryſtes bodie entred in through the doore, and ſo
ther were two bodies at one time in one place.   **F**

Nowe therfore foraſmoch as theſe two,that ys,that the bodie of Chryſte
ys in diuerſe places,and that the bodie of Chryſte and the doore that he entred through were in one place , be the workes of God, let vs in the conſideracion of them, forgett naturall philoſophie,and remembre faith . That
theſe appertein to faith yt ys proued by a nombre of the holie Fathers, and
both theſe be acknowledged of them to be miraculouſe workes of Chryſte
aboue nature.And as theſe workes were verilie doen by Chryſte: So ys the
other mencioned in the chapiter before doen by Chryſte.

Wherfore (chryſtian reader) weigh well what in theſe two chapiters ys
ſaied,howe many holie and learned Fathers be alleaged,howe plainlie they
teſtifie the matter,and haue regarde to them,ſtaie thy ſelf by them , and be
not caried awaie with them that haue nothing to confirme their doctrine
but naturall philoſophie. For as touching the matter ſpoken of in this chapiter let the Aduerſarie bring anie one ſufficient Authour , that ſhall by expreſſe woordes teache the contrarie,and I will ioin with him.   **G**

THE TWELVETH CHAPITER AVNSWERETH
certain obiections that ſeme to impugne the catholique doctrine
of this matter.

Nothing ſo
true but he
reſie maie
impugne yt
Deut.6.
Hereſies a-
gainſt God,
and euerie
perſon in
the trinitie

Here ys nothing ſo true in all our holie faith,but ſome hereſie
maie be fownde to againſt ſaie yt,and argumétes deuiſed to im
pugne yt. Yt ys a moſt a certen trueth,that ther ys but one God
the ſcripture ſaieng:*Deus noſter Deus vnus eſt.* Owre God ys one
God. Yet ther were that taught that ther were two Gods, as *Apelles ,* and
*Manichæus.*Who taught that ther was a good God,and an euell. And for the
mainteinaunce of this their hereſie,had their argumétes whiche apparantlie
confirmed their ſainges.

Yt ys a verie treuth that Chryſt ys both God and man, and yet ther were **H**
that ſaied he was not God,as *Ebion* and *Cerynthus,* and ther were that ſaied he
was no man,as *Eutyches,*and *Dioſcorus .* Yt ys a certen trueth,that God the
Sonne ys God coequall , and conſubſtanciall to the Father , yet *Arius* ſaied
that he was a creature not equall to the Father in deitie, power or maieſtie.
Yt ys an infallible trueth that the holie Goſte ys God,yet *Macedonius* taught
that he

A that he was a creature. Yt ys a certen trueth that Chryste fuffred death for vs: yet ther were that faied that yt was Symon *Cyrinenfis*, of whome ther ys mencion made in the Gofpell, that he bare Chryftes croffe.

Thefe and an innumerable forte mo haue all apparant argumentes, to make a cowntenance, that their doctrines be true, and do intermingle in dede fome trueth with their falfhead as fainct Auguftine faieth : *Nulla porrò doctrina falfa,quæ non aliqua vera intermifceat*. Ther ys no falfe doctrine, that dothe not intermingle fome treuth, therbie the better to vtter their herefie.

Auguft ho. All falfe doctrine hath fome treuth admixed.

So of this matter of the prefence of Chryfte in heauen and in the Sacrament, apparant argumentes be made by other Aduerfaries to deceaue the people, which well weighed and examined, haue no force nor weight, to proue that they intended.

As for this Aduerfarie the Proclamer (as yt ys faied) made no argumente in his matter, for that he wolde haue the people receaue but his onelie bare proclamacion, wherfore to him the aunfwere ys foen made.

B But his great mafter *Oecolampadius*, heapeth vppe in dede a great nombre of Scriptures by quotacion onely, which (he faieth) he fhall not nede to alleage at large bycaufe yt ys an article of our faithe, that Chryfte fitteth at the right hande of the Father. Of the which fcriptures I will alleadge fome, that the reader maie both knowe them, and alfo perceaue that they be not againft the doctrine of Chryftes Churche as touching the reall prefence of Chryftes bodie and blood in the bleffed Sacrament.

Scriptures alleaged againft the prefence by Oecolamp.

In fainite Iohn his gofpell we finde written thus : *Iefus knowinge that this howre was comed, that he shoulde go oute of this worlde to the Father &c* . And in an other place thus: *A litle while (faieth Chryfte) and ye shall not fee me, and a litle while and ye shall fee me. For I go to the Father.* And in the fame place : *I went furth from the Father, and came into the worlde, again I leaue the worlde, and go to the Father.* Again in an other place: *And nowe I am not in the worlde, and thefe be in the worlde and I come to thee.* And in the Actes of the Apoftles: *This Iefus that ys taken from yow into heauen shall fo come as ye haue feen him going into heauen.*

Joan.13.

Ibid.16.

Jbid.

Act.1.

C Thefe and all other like fcriptures that teache vs of Chryftes going to his Father, of his exaltacion aboue all poures, and foche other, we reuerence the we accept them, we beleue them, we embrace them. For they teache vs that, which we doo confeffe, that Chryfte ys God, that he ys afcended, that he ys in glorie, But when we confeffe this, and beleue this, doth this take awaie this treuth, that Chryfte ys verilie prefent in the Sacrament? No in deed. For that ftandeth ftill as an vntouched truthe, neither impugning the other, neither impugned of the other. And therfore we confeffe both to be true. For he that faied : *Vado ad Patrem, I go to the Father:* faied alfo. *Hoc eft corpus meum. Hoc facite. This ys my bodie . Thus do ye.* Wherbie he bothe confecrated his bodie (for as Chryfoftome faieth, *Qui enim dixit Hoc eft corpus meum, & rem fimul cum verbo confecit.* He that faied, *This ys my bodie*, made the thing together with the woord) and alfo gaue authoritie to his preiftes to do the like. Whiche thing *Luther* denieth not.

Phil.2.

Arsicle of the Afcenfion impugneth not Chryftes prefence in the Sacr.

Chryfome. 51.in Mat.

D Then forafmoche as Chryfte willed that this myfterie fhall be continued, frequented, and vfed vntill his comminge, in the whiche myfterie by his power, ys his bodie, we maie not thinke anie contrarietie or repugnaunce in his woordes, but beleue that as he ys the verie truthe: So ys yt all treu that he hath fpoken. And as he ys allmightie: So ys he able to performe, and make good that he hath faied. And therfore aught

we to

we to beleue both that he ys in heaué, and also in the Sacrament, forafmoch **E**
as by his woorde, we learn his prefence in bothe.

Exãples of manie thin ges doen by our Sauiour Chryft abo ue and cou trarie to na ture.

Yf this our Sauiour Chryfte, wher naturall knowledge faieth, *Omne graue appetit deorfum*, euerie heauie thinge ys inclined downeward, coulde yet by his power make the earthlie bodie of Peter, whiche was a mere naturall bo-die, and therfore heauie, contrarie to his nature to walke vpon the fea, and when yt pleafed him to leaue him to his nature to fuffer him to finke, and beginne to drowne: can not he at his owne pleafure make that bleffed bodie of his, which ys fo excellentlie conceaued and born, and therwith vnited to the Godhead in vnitie of perfon, that although yt be a natu-rall bodie, yet yt doth furmounte, and ys aboue all nature, and naturall bodies: can not he, I faie, at his pleafure demife, lett downe, or abafe that his bodie to the ftate and condicion of a verie naturall bodie? and a-gain at his pleafure exalte and magnifie the fame aboue the ftate of a naturall bodie?

Matt. 4.

He did faft fortie daies and fortie nightes and eate no meat, whiche **F**
was aboue naturall ordre: In the ende of that faft he was hungrie, and therin he fubiected him felf to naturall ordre.

Ibid. 17.

He was transfigured in the Mounte where, as yt pleafed him, he fhewed his power, and made his face to fhine as bright as the Sunne, and his gar-mentes white as fnowe, whiche was aboue the ftate of a bare naturall man.

Ioan. 4.

An other time he was wearie of his iourneie, whiche was agreable to the nature of man.

Ibid. 18.
Ibid. 19.
Mat. 27.

The Iewes came to apprehend him, and with the voice of his mouthe he threw them all to the grownde: Again he abafed him felf, and fuffied him felf not onelie to be taken of them, whom he had fo eafilie ouer throwé, but alfo to be buffited, and to be fcourged, and finallie to be crucified. What fhall I ftand in the reherfall of thefe thinges, whiche be fo plentifull in the Gofpell? Therfore to conclude I will faie with Cyrille, we maie not thinke of the bodie of Chryfte, as of the bodie of a bare naturall man: but we muft thinke of that bodie, as of the bodie of the Sonne of God. **G**
Whiche for that yt ys fo, yt paffeth by infinitie degrees the ftate and condi-cion of one of our bodies.

Wherfore methinke the Aduerfaries be to ftreict, yea and cruell to the bodie of Chryfte, that wher, for caufes aboue faied, yt ys fo excellent a bodie, and yet for our fakes he made himfelf obedient to death euen to the death of the croffe, they will for all this excellencie, geue vnto yt no more prerogatiue, nor preuilege, then they will do to an other bodie, whiche ys an iniurie to that bleffed bodie. I wifh that the Aduerfaries fhould not onelie after the counfell of Cyrille thinke that yt ys the bodie of the Sonne of God, and leaue yt as a naturall bodie ioined to the Godhead: but alfo confider the fingular prerogatiues that yt hathe by the fame coniunction to the Godhead. And then fhall they fee howe that bodie maie, aboue the comon condicion of other bodies, through the power of the Godhead, be in fundrie places.

Cyrill. in 6.
Ioã ca. 14.

Although yt be not apperteining to the bodie of a man to geue life: yet **H**
Cyrill faieth that the bodie of Chryfte, for that yt ys ioined to that whiche ys life, yt geueth life. Thus he fpeaketh yt: *Quoniã Saluatoris caro Verbo Dei, quod naturaliter vitã est, coniũcta, viuifica effecta eft, quãdo eã comedimus tuuc vitã habemus in nobis, illi coniũcti, quæ vita effecta eft.* Bicaufe the flefh of our fauiour ioined to the
                                                                    Sonne

A Sonne of God,whiche ys naturallie life,ys made able to geue life: when we eate that fleſh,then haue we life in vs, being ioined to that fleſh , whiche ys made life.

See this great prerogatiue that Cyrill geueth to the fleſhe of Chryſte, for that yt ys ioined to the Godhead. Yf yt haue prerogatiue to geue life to them that receaue yt: can not God geue a leſſe prerogatiue to yt to be in diuerſe places?

Obiection.

Perchaunce yt maie be ſaied to me , that God can thus do: but we finde not that he doth yt.

To the former parte of this obiection I ſaie, that yf the Aduerſaries *Anſwer.* thought that God coulde do yt,then the Proclamer was to blame, to ſpeake of Chryſtes being in a thouſand places or mo,as therbie to ſignifie an impoſſibilitie. Again *Oecolampadius* wolde not laboure to bringe in ſo manie inconueniences vpon yt,yf yt appeared poſſible to him.

B To the ſecond parte I ſaie, that yt ys ſufficientlie ſhewed allreadie, that Chryſt cauſed his bodie to be in diuerſe places at one time, and that the holie Fathers of Chryſtes Churche,yea and that a good nombre teach, ſome of them that he ys both in heauen with his Father , and alſo in earth in the Sacrament:ſome that he ys in manie places , as yt ys declared in the tenth chapiter.

And thus although the ſcriptures alleaged by *Oecolampadius* ſeem , yf a man will onelie lean to naturall philoſophie , to be againſt the faith , that the catholique Churche teacheth:yet when thoſe ſcriptures be compared to other ſcriptures, and the Fathers well weighed and vnderſtanded : and the omnipotencie of God conſidered, and the excellencie of the bodie of Chryſte remembred,yt ſhall be perceaued that the Scriptures be not againſt vs,neither we againſt them. For they ſaie that Chryſte ys in heauen and ſo ſaie we : and yet neuerthèleſſe we ſaie that he ys in the Sacrament, and ſo ſaie they. Yf the Scriptures,that be alleaged , had ſaied that Chryſt ys in heauen onelie, and can be in no other place, then the Aduerſarie might haue triumphed. But ſaing that he ys in heauen , withoute anie excluſiues

C or exceptiues, ther ys no deniall implied in that his being,to a chryſtian man , but that he maie be beleued, to be alſo in the Sacrament. And this, I truſt,maie ſuffice to aunſwer all the Scriptures that be,or can be produced of the being of Chryſte in heauen , as therby to exclude and denie his preſence in the Sacrament.

Ther ys made an other obiection oute of ſaincte Auguſtine, who writeth thus: *Cauendum eſt,ne ita Diuinitatem aſtruamus hominis, vt veritatem auferamus corporis. Non eſt autem conſequens, vt quod in Deo eſt,ita ſit vbiqne vt Deus.* *Auguſt. ad Dardanum.* We muſt beware that we do not ſo affirme the deitie of man , that we take awaie the veritie of the bodie. For yt ys no conſequent, that that which ys in God,ſhoulde ſo be euery wher as God ys.Again in the ſame place. *Ieſus vbique per id quod Deus eſt : in cœlo autem per id quod homo.* Ieſus by that that he ys God , ys euery where:by that that he ys man,he ys in heauen.

For aunſwere to theſe places of Sainct Auguſtin firſt vnderſtand that one *Dardanus* wrote to Sainct Auguſtine to diſſolue this queſtion : whether Chryſtes manhead,for that yt was vnited to the Godheade in vnitie of per-

D ſon,was euerie whear as his Godhead ys.For aunſwere to whiche queſtion, emong other thinges S.Auguſtin wrote the propoſitions, which *Oecolampadius* alleageth againſt Chryſtes being in the Sacrament, and in heauen , for that by his iudgement, his bodie can not be in two places at one time.

S.Auguſtin bis placete to Dardan. declared.

　　　　　　　　　　　X　　　Wherfo-

Wherfore firste I wiſh yow to note,that S.Auguſtin in that epiſtle not ſpea- **E**
king of the Sacrament, the ſentences alleaged make not againſt the matter.

And although thys might ſuffice : yet for the better vnderſtanding of the matter , more ſhall be ſaied . Wherfore that a thing maie
be at one time in manie places, vnderſtand that yt maie be twoo waies.
The one ys by nature,the other by gifte.By nature to be in manie or all places at one time,yt apperteineth onelie to God, who by hys immenſitie ys
euery where,ſo that ther ys no place in heauen,in hel, in earth,or in the waters,in the which God ys not.And therfore he ſaieth.*Ego cœlum & terram im-*
*pleo.*I fill bothe heauen and earth.And again: *Cœlum mihi ſedes eſt , terra autem*
*ſcabellum pedum meorum.*Heauen ys my ſeat,and the earth ys my foote ſtoole.
After this ſorte,that ys,by nature,no creature can be in all places,but onelie
God.Wherfore *Didymus* by this did well make his argument to proue the ho
lie Goſte to be God,bicauſe of hys owne nature he ys euery wher,and ſo
can no creature be.

One thing
in manie
places at
one time
two waies.
Hiere. 23.
Eſai. 66.

Didym. de
Spiritu S.

The other waie that a thing maie be in manie places, not by nature , but **F**
by the gifte of God maie be in man.For nothing being vnpoſsible to God,
yt ys then poſsible to him,to geue hys gifte to hys creature, that yt maie be
in manie and diuerſe places at once,which maner of being ys in the Manhead of Chryſt,which manhead hath yt not of the own nature to be in manie places at one time, but by the gifte of the Godhead. And therfore the
argument of *Oecolampadius* ys nothing woorth.And yt ſemeth to me he did
not vnderſtand this difference of being in manie places at once,when he ar-
gued,that yf Chryſte coulde be in manie places at one time , by the like he
might be in al places,ãd ſo ſhould a creature become God , whiche ſomtime was no God, whiche ys a great abſurditie.

By this argumente yf yt were good, yt mighte be proued that Chryſtes
fleſh ys not quickning or geuing life,bicauſe yt apperteineth to God alone
to geue life.And ſo ſhoulde Chryſtes ſaieng be vntrue wher he ſaieth : *Qui*
*manducat meam carnem & bibit meum ſanguinem , habet vitam æternam.*He that
eateth my fleſh, and drinketh my bloode hath euerlaſting life. And Cyrille ſaieth,as ye haue heard,that the fleſh of Chryſte being made the fleſh
of the Godhead,whiche ys life,ys made alſo able to geue life. **G**

Ioan. 6.
Cyril. in 6.
Ioan. ca.14

But this ys verie true that the fleſh of Chryſte ys able to geue life.
Whiche thing ys aſwell onely perteining to God to do yt by nature, and
of himſelf,as yt ys to be in manie or all places . And yet Chryſtes fleſh hauing this powre to geue life ys not for all that , when yt ys conſidered in yt
ſelf,thought that yt ys God,for yt hath yt not of yt ſelf , but by the power
of the Godhead , wherunto yt ys ioined in vnitie of Perſon . No more ys
the bodie of Chryſte thought to be a God, bicauſe yt maie be in manie places at one time,bicauſe yt ys not ſo of the owne nature, but by the power
of the Godhead.

And this difference yt to be obſerued in all thinges that be geuen of God
to creatures,wherfore when Chryſt ſaied: *Nemo bonus,niſi vnus,Deus.* No man
ys good but God alone.Yt ys not therfore to be thought that euerie creature that ys good,ys furth with alſo God,for then all the creatures of God
be Gods, for they be all good,as the Scripture ſaeth : *Vidit Deus cuncta,*
quæ fecerat , & erant valdè bona. God ſawe all thinges that he had made, **H**
and they were verie good:but yt ys to be conſidered that that, that ys good
of yt ſelf ys God,and ſo ther ys none good but God alone . All creatures are
good by participacion of the goodneſſe of God,and therfor though they be
good:

God alone
good by na
ture,creatu
res by parti
cipacion.
Gen. 1.

A good: yet be they no Gods. And by this ye maie perceaue that the Church dothe according to the aduertifement of fainɗe Auguſtine. For yt dothé not fo deifie the manhead of Chryſte, that yt thinketh yt of the owne nature able to be in manie places, for then fhoulde yt take awaie the veritie of the fleſh or bodie of Chryſte. But as touching that nature in yt felf yt ys acknowledged to be in one place in heauen, but as touching the power of the godhead wherunto yt ys annexed, with the confideracion of the ordinaunce of the Sacrament, in the whiche ys appointed alfo the prefence of the fame bodie: yt ys beleued, that the fame one bodie ys in diuerfe and manie places at one time.

Vnto all this for the perceauing of a more difference betwene the nature of the Godhead, and the nature of the manhead in Chryſte, Note that the nature of the Godhead of yt felf ys fo in euery place, that yt hath not poffibilitie to be oute of anie place. The nature of the manhead of Chryſte though by the power of the Godhead yt ys and B maie be in diuerfe places at one time : yet yt hath allwaies a poffibilitie to be but in one place alone, and maie fo be and ys . By this alfo we maie fee that ther ys moche difference betwene the Godhead, and manhead, wherby we maie eafely, and clearlie perceaue, that though Chryſtes bodie be in manie places, yet we côfeſſe yt not to be the Godheade, but acknowledge yt to be the fleſh of the Sonne of God, and one of the natures of the perfon of Chryſte, and therfor an excellent bodie, and woorthie moche honour and eſtimacion. And thus moche for aunſwer and vnderſtanding of fainɗe Auſten in that epiſtle to *Dardanus*.

Godheade of Chryſt hath not poſſibilitie but to be euerie wher, his Manhead hath poſſibilitie to be fom wher.

And other obieɗion ther ys made oute of the fame epiſtle, whiche doth raither declare the malicioufe ignorance of the Aduerfarie, then make any thing againſt this trueth here defended. And if we fhall here write yt, euê as *Oecolâpadius* did, then fhall we alfo fee his fubtiltie and crafte. Thus yt ys to be fownde in his booke: *Spacia locorũ tolle corporibus, & nuſquã erũt: & quia nuſquam erũt, nec erũt. Tolle ipſa corpora qualitatibus corporũ, non erit vbi ſint, & ideò non alibi quã in cœlo corpore fatemur Chriſtũ.* Take the fpaces of places from bodies, and they C fhall no wheare be. And bicaufe they fhall no whear be, they fhall not be. Take thofe bodies from the qualities of bodies, ther fhall no place be fownde wher they maie be. and therfore we côfeſſe Chryſte in bodie to be no whear ells but in heauê. thus *Oecolâpadius.* Ye heare all this alleaged, as the wholl wer of S. Auguſtine, but yt ys not . For *Oecolâpadius* hath wickedlie patched on a côcluſiõ, as though it were fainɗe Auguſtines owne woordes, but yt ys not. He hath craftilie peiced yt, to deceaue the fimple. For thefe woordes(*And ther for we confeſſe Chryſte in bodie to be no whear but in heauen*) be the woordes of *Oecolampadius* and not of Sainɗ Auguſtin, Soche ys the fincereritie of thefe men, that they can not maintein ther euell and falfe matters, but with crafte and fubtletie.

Auguſtin. ad Dardã.

Oecolamp. falſifieth S. Auguſt. by a fubtile adicion.

Nowe to aunſwer fainɗe Auguſtines owne woordes, they be not ſpokế of the bodie of Chryſte, but they be ſpokế of naturall bodies vpon the earth, whiche be fubieɗ to earthlie qualities. Glorified bodies foch as Chryſtes bodie ys, are deliuered from earthlie qualities. For they are neither hote, nor colde, weet nor drie, wherfore yt maketh nothing for the Aduerfaries pourpofe D to alleadge fainɗe Auguſtine in this place, more then to declare, that blinde malice wolde be faing fomwhat, againſt the trueth, yt careth not what.

An other place ys produced onte of fainɗe Auguſtine and yt ys this: *Surſũ eſt Dominus, ſed etiã hic eſt veritas Domini. Corpus enim Domini in quo reſurrexit in*

Auguſtin. 30.Traɗ. in Ioan.

vno loco esse potest, veritas eius vbique diffusa est. Owre Lorde ys aboue, but hys **E**
veritie ys also here. The bodie of Chryste wherin he did rise maie be in one
place, but his veritie ys diffused euerie wher. Thus farre sainct Augustine.
That, that ys before saied doth fullie aunswere this. For we beleue that owre
Lorde ys aboue with the Father, and withall we beleue that his Godhead
ys euery wher. Yt ys not denied, but declared aboue also, that the bodie of
Chryst in whiche he did rise, maie be in one place. So that we dissent not
one title from sainct Augustin. *For though the bodie of Christe maie be in one place: yet yt ys not enforced that yt must of necessitie be in one place.* Nowe (gent
le Reader) thowe haueft seen the trueth of this matter testified by wittnes-
fes sufficient, thow haueft seen the obiections of the Aduersaries fullie dif-
solued. I wish thee nowe soche faith as Abraham had, wherbie he was iustified. Who hearing the promisse of God that his seed shoulde be as the

Gen. 13.
& 15.
Rom.4.

starres of heauen, and Sandes of the Sea, *fainted not in faith nor yet considered
hys owne bodie, whiche was nowe dead, euen when he was almost, an hondreth yeares
olde, neither yet that Sara was past childe bearing, he staggered not at that promisse of* **F**
*God through vnbelief, but became strong in faith, and gaue God the praise, being full cer-
tified, that he whiche had promised was also able to make yt good*: that thow likewise
knowing by faith whiche thowe haueft learned of the Fathers, as they haue
learned the same of the verie woorde of God, that Chryftes blessed bodie
ys in the Sacrament, and also in heauen, consider not nowe the naturall
ordre of thinges, as Abraham did not, neither of hys owne bodie neither
of hys wieues, but become strong in faith, and faint not, neither stagger at
the promisse of God through vnbelief, But consider and be fullie certified

Naturall
ordre had
no place in
manie of
Chryftes
doinges.

that Chryste, who hath spoken and saied: *This ys my bodie*, ys able to make yt
good. And he that againft the ordre of nature began ths life of man, for that
he was born of a virgen, and againft the same ordre withoute enforcement
gaue vppe his owne soule, and died at his owne pleasure, and that crieng
with a great voice, and likewise contrarie to the same nature rose from
death the third daie, passing through the ftone, for that hys monument was
fast closed: ãd the eight daie after (as yt ys teftified) passed through the doo-　**G**
res into his disciples, and finallie ending hys a boade vpon earth besides na-
turē ascended into heauen, that he appointing hys bodie to be here in the
Sacrament, and in heauen also, ys so to be beleued, though naturall ordre re-
peine. For seing he hath so appointed, yt ys so in verie dede.

THE THIRTENHT CHAPITER BEGINNETH THE

expofition of an other text in the fixt of S. Iohn.

I Will nowe leaue this matter of Chryftes being in manie places as sufficientlie treacted of and proued, and return to the
fixt chapiter of S. Iohn, and entre the expofition of the text ther
enfewing, whiche ys this. *Dixit ergo eis Iefus, Amen Amen dico vobis,
nifi manducaueritis carnem filij hominis, & biberitis eius fanguinem, non

Ioan.6.

habebitis vitam in vobis.* Iefus therfor saied vnto them: Verilie, Verilie I saie vn
to yowe, except ye eate the flesh of the Sonne of man, and drinke hys blood　**H**
ye shall haue no life in yowe.
Wheras the Iews through vnbelief, thought yt an vnpoffible thing for Chrift
to geue his flesh to be eaten, Chryft here aunfwering thē, declareth yt to be
poffible

A possible,and neceſſarie to be doen,yea and ſo neceſſarie,that except we eate his fleſh and drinke his bloode,we ſhal not haue life.For as man concerning his naturall life muſt haue two thinges neceſſarie to life;that ys, birth to beginne and entre life,and then foode to nouriſh and maintein the ſame,without the whiche yt can not be continued : So as concerning the ſpirituall life man muſt haue accordinglie his birth and foode: birth to be born and entre into that life , whiche birth ys baptiſme , whiche ys of ſuche neceſſitie,that as he ſpeaketh heare of the neceſſitie of the foode, ſo ſpeaketh he of the neceſſitie of this birthe ſaing to *Nicodemus* : *Amen,Amen dico tibi,niſi* *Ioan. 3.*
quis renatus fuerit ex aqua et Spiritu ſancto non poteſt introire in regnū Dei. Verilie,verilie,I ſaie vnto thee:Except a man be born again of water,and the holie Goſt he can not entre into the kingdom of God.Nowe when man by Baptiſme ys born in to the ſpirituall life,and hath begon yt,he muſt nedes haue foode to ſuſtein the ſame , or ells he ſhall not continewe life , whiche foode ys the bodie,and blood of Chryſte, a foode by Chryſte himſelf appointed, whiche yf we take not,we can not liue.And therfore he ſaieth : Except ye
B eate the fleſh of the Sonne of man,and drinke hys bloode,ye ſhall not haue life in yowe.

Hitherto the Aduerſarie will agree with me,expownding all that ys ſaied in his ſenſe of ſpirituall eating,and drinking of the fleſh and blood of Chry- *Corporall* ſte,with whō I will thus farre agree alſo, that ſoche as be of mature age,and *eating with* haue atteigned to the yeares of diſcrecion , except they eate the fleſh of *out the ſpi-* Chryſt,and drinke hys bloode ſpirituallie they ſhall not liue. For the corpo- *rituall ea-* rall eating withoute the ſpirituall eating ,ys not auailable.   But both theſe *ting auai-* together nouriſhe life in man , and make him luſtie and ſtronge in God. *leth not.* But that this texte extendeth not the neceſſitie therin mencioned, to the corporall eating and drinking of Chryſtes fleſh and blood alſo,which thys Aduerſarie affirmeth , that ys vntrue. He wolde haue no other receauing of Chryſte , but the ſpirituall receauing : bicauſe he wolde haue no other preſence but the ſpirituall preſence , but that this texte ſpeaketh alſo of the corporall eating and receauing of the reall and ſubſtanciall bodie of Chryſte in the Sacrament,the connexion and dependence of the Scriptu-
C res do proue.

For the firſt ſainge of Chryſte , whiche we haue allready expownded, (*that the bread whiche he wolde geue , ys hys fleſh, &c.* ſpeaketh of Chryſtes naturall fleſh to be geuen in the Sacrament , as ys allready declared, and ſufficientlie proued.   And this texte ſpeaketh of the ſame fleſh , as the connexion well proueth. Wherfore Chryſte here ſpeaketh alſo of the corporall eatinge of hys fleſh in the Sacrament.The neceſſitie of whiche eating ys ſoche,that yf we contemne that eating of yt,being(as ys ſaied)of mature age,and diſcrecion,we ſhall not haue life.

But that yt maie appeare,that the Church through oute all ages,hath euē thus vnderſtanded this texte, as I do, I will conuerte me to the ordre that I haue preſcribed to my ſelf, to heare the great auncient men , and learned Fathers of both ſides of Chryſtes Parliament houſe , both of the greke
D and of the latin Churche.   And although yt might ſuffice , for the vnderſtanding of all that ys here ſpoken of the Sacrament , for thatthey vnderſtoode the firſt text of the ſame , to proue that therfore the reſt whiche apperteineth to the ſame matter,muſt be euen ſo vnderſtanded: Yet for the full ſatiſſieng of the humble ſpirited reader , and the like confutacion of the arrogaunt,I will not refuſe the paines to aſcribe their
X iij   iudge-

iudgementes, both of this text, and of the reſt that folowe.

The firſt of this companie that ſhall be brought furth to wittneſſe, ys ſainct Cyprian, who alleaging this ſame text doth declare howe he vnderſtandeth yt, ſaing thus: *Quando ergo dicit in æternum viuere, ſi quis ederit de eius pane: vt manifeſtum eſt, eos viuere, qui corpus eius attingunt, & Euchariſtiam iure communicationis accipiunt: ita contrà timendum eſt, & orandum ne dum quis abſtentus ſeparatur à corpore Chriſti, procul remaneat à ſalute, comminante illo & dicente: Niſi ederitis carnem filij hominis, & biberitis ſanguinem eius, non habebitis vitam in vobis. Et ideò panem noſtrum, id eſt, Chriſtum dari nobis quotidie petimus, vt qui in Chriſto manemus, & viuimus, à ſanctificatione, & corpore eius non recedamus.* Therfore when he ſaieth *him to liue for euer, whoſoeuer ſhall eate of his breade:* As yt ys manifeſt that they do liue, whiche do touche this bodie and according to the right of partaking do receaue the Sacrament: Euen ſo contrarie wiſe yt ys to be feared and praied for, leſt while any man being accurſed, ys ſeparated frō the bodie of Chryſt, he maie abide and remain farre from health, he threatninge, and ſainge: *Except ye eate the fleſh of the Sonne of man, and drinke his bloode, ye ſhall haue no life in yowe.* And therfore we dailie deſire our bread, *that ys to ſaie, Chryſte,* to be geuen to vs, that we whiche do abide and liue in Chryſte, maie not departe from his ſanctification and bodie. Thus moche S. Cyprian.

In which ſainge firſt he manifeſtlie ſheweth that this text ys to be vnderſtanded of the Sacrament. For by expreſſe woordes he ſaieth, that they haue life, whiche by right of partaking do receaue the Euchariſt, or Sacrament (as I terme yt) for that the engliſh toung hath none apter terme for yt. And all men vſe the woord (*Sacrament*) to that ſignification in comon ſpeache. And as we do oftentimes by this tearm (*the Sacrament*) vnderſtand both the Sacrament, and the thing ſignified by the Sacrament : So dothe ſaincte Cyprian likewiſe in this place vnderſtand and meen both. For as when he had ſaied, that we ſhall haue life by partaking of the Sacrament. Euen ſo ſaieth he, yt ys to be feared, that when we be ſeparated from the bodie of Chryſte, that then we ſhall be farre frō health. Wherby yt ys plain that he ſpeaketh not onelie of the Sacrament, as of the ſacramentall ſignes : but he ſpeaketh raither of the Sacrament, as of the thinge ſignified and conteined in and vnder the ſacramentall ſignes, whiche by expreſſe woordes he calleth *the bodie of Chryſte.*

But that ye maie the better creditte the matter, not for my ſaing, but for his, ye ſhall heare him expownde him ſelf, that by this woorde, *Euchariſtia,* he meneth the bodie of Chryſte, *Illi contra euangelij legē, veſtrā quoq; honorificā petitionem, ante actam pœnitentiam, ante exomologeſin grauiſsimi atque extremi delicti factam, ante manum ab Epiſcopo & Clero in pœnitentiam impoſitam, offerre pro illis, & Euchariſtiam dare, id eſt, ſanctum Domini corpus prophanare audent.* They againſt the lawe of the goſpell, and alſo your honorable peticiō, before the penaunce was doē, before the cōfeſsiō of the moſt greuouſe, and extreme fawte made, before the hand was put on by the Biſhoppe, and the cleargie vnto penannce, dare offer for them and geue the Sacrament, that ys, *to prophane the holie bodie of our Lorde.* Thus Ciprian. In theſe woordes he plainly interpreteth him ſelf, and ſheweth that he taketh this woorde. *Euchariſtia,* for the bodie of Chryſte, and therwithall teacheth the reall preſence of Chryſtes bodie to be in the Sacrament. for yf yt be not in the Sacrament, yt can not by receauinge of the Sacrament be prophaned.

This then being preceaued, that ſaincte Ciprian vnderſtandeth this texte of the Sacrament, I will alſo call one of the greke churche, to geue vs knowledge

A ledge howe he expowndeth the fame, who fhalbe Theophilacte, thus he writeth : *Iudæi cùm audiuiſsent de eſu carnis illius diſcredunt. Ideò & verbum incredulitatis dicunt, quomodò. Nam quando cogitationes incredulitatis ingrediuntur animam, ingreditur ſimul quomodò. Propterea ipſe volens oſtendere quòd non ſit impoſsibile, ſed etiam valde neceſſarium, & non poteſt haberi vita niſi eius carnem comedamus &c. Oportet igitur nos cùm audiuerimus : Niſi comederitis carnem filij hominis, non habebitis vitam: in ſumptionibus diuinorum myſteriorum indubitatam retinere fidem, & non quærere, quo pacto?* The Iewes, when they had hearde of the eatinge of Chryftes flefh, they do not beleue. And therfor they faie the woorde of vnbeleif *Howe.* For when the thoughtes of incredulitie do entre the foule, ther entreth withall *Howe.* Therfore he willing to fhewe that yt was not impofsible, but euen very neceffarie, and that other wife life can not be had, except we eate his flefh &c. Therfore we muft when we heare: *Except ye eate the flesh of the Sonne of man ye shall haue no life* : in the receauinge the *Diuine* mifteries retein an vndoubted faith and not aske, *Howe or bywhat mean.* Thus moche Theophilacte.

Theophilact. in. 6. Joan.

Howe, the woorde of incredulitie.

Marke that he wolde, when we heare this texte: *Except ye eate the flesh &c.*
B we fhoulde haue an vndoubted faith. what vndoubted faith he meneth, he opened in his faing alleaged for the text before declared; wher he faied that the bread whiche Chryft wolde geue, ys not a figure of his flefh, but his verie flefh. For *the bread* (faieth he) *yt transformed into the flesh of oure Lorde.* This ys that vndoubted faithe, whiche Theophilacte wolde that we fhoulde haue, when we heare thefe woordes, *Except ye eate the flefh &c.* to beleue that in the Sacrament, we muft eate the flefh of Chryfte, or ells we fhall not haue life Neuerthelefe this necefsitie ys not foche, that all that doo not receaue the holie Sacrament actuallie, fhall not haue life : but all that do not in acte or pourpofe beinge of age agreable, or doo contemne the receipte of yt actuallie, they fhall not haue life. But foche as be of mature age, and doe of good deuocion pourpofe to receaue it, though they do not receaue yt actuallie, yet hauing a godlie faith, and not contemning the thing, they fhall by Gods mercie haue life. As Baptifme ys a facrament of great necefsitie, yet al that haue obteined life (*I meen life euerlafting*) were not baptifed in water according to Chryftes lawe, but fome in bloode, and all in pourpofe, none
C of them at the leaft contemning the Sacramēt, and therfore being fo newe born again they haue entred into the kingdom of God. But he that ys not born a newe, neither actuallie, nor in pourpofe, he fhall not entre into the kingdom of God.

Capite 7.

Moche goodlie matter offreth yt felf here, and diuerfe other authours ther be of the auncient time, whofe expofitions be right plain in this matter. Wherby the diligent Reader maie perceaue that the Aduerfaries haue not dealt fincerelie, whiche wolde go aboute to putte furth foche a falfe doctrine, and therwith fo feircelie reproue other men for wrefting of the fcriptures, when they them felues moft fhamefullie wreft them, plaiing the parte of an euell man, who will allwaies be accufing other men, and charging them with fautes, bicaufe he will feeme to be in no faute, but incupable, when he ys moft vicioufe, and moft woorthie reprehenfion.

THE FOVRTENTH CHAPITER EXPOVNDETH

the same texte by saincte Augustine, and Cyrill.

F eche side of Chryftes Parliament howfe, ye haue heard teftimonie, howe yt was ther determined and enacted, that this text fhoulde be vnderftanded of Chryftes verie bodie and bloode. We will yet proceade to heare fome mo of the fame houfe, of the which fainéte Auguftine fhall be firft. Who vpon the fame texte faieth thus, fpeaking to the Iewes: *Quomodò quidem detur, & quisnam modus fit manducandi iftum panem ignoratis. Veruntamen nifi manducaueritis carnem filij hominis, et biber.tis eius fanguinem, non habebitis vitam in vobis. Hæc non cadaueribus, fed viuentibus loquebatur.* Howe yt ys geuen, and what ys the maner of the eating of this breade ye do not knowe. Neuerthelefle except ye eate the flefh of the Sonne of man, and drinke his bloode ye fhall haue no life in yowe. This did he fpeake not to dead Carkafies, but to liuing men. Thus fainéte Auguftine.

Auguſt. tract. 26. in Ioan.

That the Iewes did not knowe the maner of the eating of Chryftes flefh in the Sacrament, fainéte Auguftine more plainlie, hadling this texte declareth. *Nifi quis manducauerit carnem meam, non habebit vitam æternam. Acceperunt illud ftultè, carnaliter cogitauerunt, et cogitauerunt quòd præcifurus effet Dominus particulas quafdam de corpore fuo, et daturus illis.* Except a man eate my flefh, he fhall haue no life. They tooke it, faieth fainéte Auguftine, foolifhlie, carnallie they thought yt, and they thought that our lorde wolde cutte certen peices from his bodie and geue them. This he.

Auguſtin. in Pfal. 98

Nowe the Iewes thus groffelie vnderftanding Chryfte had no pleafure in Chryftes doctrine: But yf they had vnderftanded that he by his diuine and allmightie powre might and wolde geue his flefh to be eaten verilie in the Sacrament, after an other maner, and not groffelie, as in that forte or maner as he walked and liued vpon the earthe, then the woordes of Chryfte wolde haue ben to them liuelie and pleafaunte, but they tooke them foolifhlie (faieth fainéte Auguftine) and carnallie. So that he vnderftandeth this faing of Chryfte, of the eating of the flefh of Chryft in the Sacrament, whiche ys one of the thinges, that we feke to proue, forafmoche as yt hath ben contrarilie taught of the Aduerfaries.

Auguſt. de Doct. Chriſt. li. 3 cap. 16.

But they perchaunce will faie, that though fainéte Auguftine do vnderftad this text of the Sacrament, yet he doth not therby teache the reall prefence of Chryftes bodie in the Sacrament · but raither the contrarie. For alleaging this text in a certain place he faieth that yt ys a figuratiue fpeache. *Si autem flagitium, aut facinus iubere, aut vtilitatem & beneficentiam videtur vetare, figurata locutio eft. Nifi manducaueritis carnem filij hominis, & biberitis eius fanguinem, non habebitis vitam in vobis, facinus, vel flagitium videtur iubere: figura ergo eft, præcipiens paßioni Domini effe communicandum, & fuauiter, atque vtiliter in memoria recondendû, quòd pro nobis caro eius crucifixa & vulnerata fit.* Yf the fcripture feme to commaû de anie euell dede or great offence, or to forbidde any profitte or well doing, yt ys a figuratiue fpeache. *Except ye eate the flesh of the Sonne of man, and drinke his bloode, ye shall not haue life in yowe,* Yt femeth to commaunde an euell dede or offence, wherfore yt ys a figure, commaunding to communicate the paffion of Chryfte, and fwetelie, and profitablie to kepe in memorie, that Chryftes flesfhe was crucified and wounded for vs.

This ys fainéte Auguftines faing, who (*as the Aduerfaries faie*) plainlie affirmeth that this faing of Chryft: *Except ye eate the flesh &c.* ys a figuratiue fpeache, whiche fo being, then the flefh of Chryft (*faie they*) ys but figuratiuelie eaten in the Sacrament   Tis

A   This argument haue the heretikes of our time borowed of *Berengarius* and his difciples, as alfo they did therefie yt felf, which of a good time laie all ruftie and vnknowen, vntill the Deuell raifed vppe thefe his furbyfhers, who haue newlie fkoured this herefie, and the argumentes therto apperteininge, and haue fett them furth to deceaue the people withall.

But as the argumęt was inuęted and made by the heretikes of that time, fo was yt aunfwered and folued by the good catholike Fahers at that fame time. Whofe aunfwers, and folucions be foche as they wipe awaie all the ftrenght that was thought to be in that argument. Among the whiche we will onclie for this prefent bring furthe the aunfwer, whiche was made by *Guitmundus*. who liued in the yeare of our Lorde 1060. and folued this argumente thus : *Ait beatus Auguftinus quòd Dominus videtur facinus, vel flagitium iubere, non quia facinus aut flagitium inberet, iubendo manducari carnem fuam. Sed videtur (inquit) iubere: illis videlicet, qui putauerunt quòd hoc iubendo, neceffariò etiam fe iuberet occidi, & membratim confcindi, atque ita demũ carnẽ eius crudã, vel coctã mãducari.*

B   *Proinde ergo figura eft (inquit) in hac locutione. Hic iã adgaudet fortaßis vmbraticus, hic iam obftrepit. Noli præpofterè vmbratice, noli præcipitãter gloriari. Cuius rei figura dicatur hic effe patiéter & diligéter aduerte. Figura ergo eft (ait Auguft.) præcipiens. Quid præcipiens? quid figurans? hoc enim figurat quod præcipit. Paßioni Domini (inquit) comunicandũ, et fuauiter atq; vtiliter in memoria recõdendũ, quòd pro nobis caro eius crucifixa, & vulnerata fit. Deo gratias. Quicquid igitur illud eft, quod Auguftinus hic figurã appellat, (Nam quid figuram dicat, in his eius verbis agnofci non difficilè poteft) non vtique corporis Domini, fed crucifixionis eius, & vulnerationis, hoc eft occifionis, noftræque communicationis cum ea, id eft vt imitemur Chriftum, & communicemus paßioni eius compatiendo, manifeftißimè figuram effe demonftrat : Paulo quoque Apoftolo concordante, qui ait, Quotiefcunque panem hunc manducabitis, & calicem Domini bibetis, mortem Domini annunciabitis donec veniat.* Sainéte Auguftine faieth, that owre Lorde feemeth to bidde an euel dede, or a great offence, not that he bidding his flefh to be eaten, did bidde anie euell dede to be doen or great offence, but that he femed to bidde, that ys to faie, to them whiche thought that he bidding this, did neceffarelie bidde his flefh to be flain, and to be cutte one membre from an other, and fo at

C   the laft his flefh either rawe or fodden to be eaten. Therfore (faieth he) ther ys a figure in this faing . Here nowe peraduenture the fhadowe man (*meening the heretike*) doth reioice, here nowe he maketh his noife. Reioice thow not, fhadow teacher, oute of ordre, reioice not to haftilie . Of what thing yt ys faied to be a figure patientlie and diligentlie take hede . Yt ys a figure (faieth fainéte Auguftine) commaundinge, what commaunding? or what figuring? (For yt doth figure that, that yt doth commaund) that we, faieth he, fhoulde partake the pafsion of oure Lorde, and fwetelie and profitablie kepe in memorie, that his flefh was crucified and wounded for vs. God bethanked. What foeuer yt be then that fainéte Auguftine here calleth the figure (for what he doth call the figure in thefe his woordes yt ys not fo harde to be knowen) *yt ys not the figure of the bodie of our Lorde, but of his crucifieng and wounding,* that ys, *of his death, and of owre communicating with the fame,* that ys to faie, *that we fhoulde folowe Chryft, and communicate his* pafsion, fuffring withe him, that doth he moft manifeftlie fhewe to be a figure, Paule alfo the Apoftle agreinge with him, who faieth, As often as ye fhall eate this breade, and drinke ths cuppe, ye fhall fhewe furthe the death of our Lorde vntil he come.

D   Thus farre Guitmundus.

In this aunfwer (which although yt be long, yet I thought yt neceffarie to bring yt not truncatelie, but whollie to fatisfie the Reader) ye maie perceane

that

that this Authour manifeftlie proueth that fainôte Auguftine faieth not that　E
the flefh and blood of Chryfte be figuratiuely in the Sacrament (whiche
the Aduerfarie cheiflie pretendeth and feketh) But fainôt Auguftine faieth,
that this fainge of Ghryfte (*Except ye eate the flesh of the fonne of man &c.*) ys a
figuratiue fpeache(For the eating and drinking of Chryftes flefh and blood
in the Sacrament ys a figure of Chryftes paffion and blood fheding for vs)
and a figne for the continuance of the thinge in our memorie, and alfo for
the mouing of vs to take our croffes, and to fuffer with Chryfte.

　Whiche thinge yet this Authour both more plainlie,and breiflie dothe
fett furth in that that foloweth, fainge: *Quòd fi quæramus, quid hic figuram Au-*

guftinus dixerit, nihil hic vtique tam congruè videtur occurrere, quàm id quod paulò fupe-
rius Doctor idem iam dixerat, id eſt celebratio corporis, & fanguinis Domini. Quas ob
res ſtultè, & infipientiſſimè Berengariani librum de Doctrina Chriſtiana nobis objiciũt,cùm
cibus altaris Domini, nufquam ibi figura, nufquam ibi fignum dicatur. Et quicquid illud ſit,
quod & fignum ibi vel figura dicitur, non vtique figura corporis & fanguinis Domini,
fed paſſionis Domini, & noſtræ communicationis cum ea, certiſſimè demonſtratur. Yf we*   F

aske what fainôte Auguftine here calleth the figure, ther ys nothinge here
that ys perceaued fo agreable to occurre, as that whiche a litle before the
fame doôtour had nowe faied, *that ys,* the celebracion of the bodie and bloode of our Lorde. For which caufe the Berengarians fooliflie, and moft vn-
wifelie do obieôte the booke of the chryftian doôtrine to vs, feing that the
meate of the Altar of our Lorde in no place ther ys called a figure, in no
place ther ys called a figne.And what foeuer ther ys called a figure or a figne
yt ys moft certenlie fhewed,not to be a figure of the bodie and blood of our
Lorde, but of the paffion of our Lorde, and of our communicating with the
fame. Thus moche Guitmundus.

　I nede not to note here to yowe anie thinge, wher euerie thinge ys fo
plain, neither after my rude maner to trauaill to faie any more for aunfwering this argument, where the aunfwere of this learned man ys fo full, that
yt hath fullie and perfeôtelie aunfwered the Aduerfaries, aud that by the fame fainôte Auguftine whom they obieôted, and oute of the fame booke,　G
oute of the whiche the obieôtion was taken. Yet raither to confirme the fainge of this learned man, then to open and declare that the hath faied, and
that the Aduerfarie maie perceaue, that yt was not the minde of fainôte
Auguftine, to make the Sacrament a bare figure voide of the reall prefence of Chryftes bodie and bloode, I will afcribe a fainge of the fame fainôte Auguftine, whiche femeth to allude to this his fainge here.
This yt ys.

Quamuis horribilius videatur humanam carnem manducare, quàm perimere, & huma
num fanguinem potare, quàm fundere : nos tamen mediatorem Dei & hominũ hominem
Iefum Chriſtum carnem fuam nobis manducandam, bibendumque fanguinem dantem, fide-
li corde, & ore fufcipimus. Although yt maie feeme to be more horrible to eate

the flefh of man, then to kill a man, and to drinke the bloode of man, then
to fhedde yt : yet we for all that do receaue the mediator of God and men
Iefus Chryfte, *geuing vs his flesh to be eaten with a faithfull heart and mouth, and his*
bloode to be dronken. Thus fainôte Auguftine.

　Remembre nowe (gentle Reader) the rule of fainôte Auguftine before　H
geuen for the vnderftanding of the fcriptures, and conferre this his fainge,
with that other, and ye fhall perceaue, that the figuratiue fpeache, that he
fpeaketh of ther, ys not foche as fhoulde take awaie the prefence of Chryftes
bodie and bloode in the Sacrament, and leaue but a bare figure, a figne, or
a token

Guitmũd .
Ibidem.

Berenga-
riãs foolish
lie obiected
S.Aug.So
do the Sa-
cramenta-
ries now.

Aug. cont.
aduerf. le-
gis &
Prop.ca.9

A a token of that bodie and blood, as the Aduerſarie wolde haue yt. For wher he ſaieth ther, that Chryſt, *willing vs to eate his fleſh, and drinke his bloode,* ſemeth to commaunde an euell dede to be doen, and therfore to be a figuratiue ſpe ache : here he ſaieth, that though yt ſeme to be an horrible facte, to eate the fleſh of man and drinke his bloode : yet do we with faithfull heart, and mouth eate the fleſh and drinke the bloode of the mediatour of God and man, whiche ys the man Ieſus Chryſte.

Ye ſee that though yt ſeme to be an horrible facte ſo to do : yet ſaincte Auguſtine here maketh not the figuratiue ſpeache ſoche, as to take awaie ihe reall preſence of the bodie and bloode of Chryſte from the Sacrament : but that we ſhoulde receaue the bodie and blood of Chryſt, and that not one-lie with a faithfull heart, whiche ſerueth for the ſpirituall receipt of Chryſtes bodie and blood, but alſo with a faithfull mouthe, whiche argueth a corpo-rall receipt of the bodie of Chryſt, as the Proclamer knoweth right well. And therfor I dare ſaie, this ſaing of ſaincte Auguſtine pincheth him euen by the conſcience. I ſaie then with *Guitmundus,* let not the Aduerſarie trium-
B phe to moche vpon his figuratiue ſpeache, as once I heard maſter Horn do in a ſermon by him made in the Vniuerſitie of Cambridge, wher after the maner of ſoche his likes, he abuſed the figuratiue ſpeache, and placed yt ther wher yt ſhoulde not be placed. For ſaincte Auguſtine did not ſo place this figuratiue ſpeache, as therby to diſplace the bodie and blood of Chryſte frō the Sacramente, whiche we muſt receaue with a faithfull hearte and mou-the · but he placed his figuratiue ſpeache, as *Guitmundus* noted to yow, that ys, in the ſwete and dououte remembrance of Chryſtes death and paſ-ſion, and in the crucifieng, and mortifieng of our fleſh with all his luſt and concupiſcence. Yf then the Aduerſarie be deſierouſe to haue figures in the Sacrament, let him not diuiſe ſoche a figure as neither Chryſte nor his ho-lie membres did acknowlege : but let him take ſoche and in ſoche place as by them be appointed, whiche bicauſe the Aduerſarie ſhall not lacke, let him vnderſtand that ther be manie.

This holie Sacrament ys (as ys ſaied) a figure of Chryſtes death and paſ-
C ſion : yt ys a figure teaching vs, that as Chryſte was crucified for our ſinnes, ſo ſhoulde we crucifie ſinne in our owne bodies. Yt ys a figure of rhe miſti-call bodie of Chryſt, the Churche. The formes of bread and wine, be figu-res of Chryſtes bodie and blood verilie being vnder the ſame formes. Fi-nallie bicauſe the woordes of Chryſte (*Except ye eate my fleſh, and drinke my bloo de*) in groſſe vnderſtanding after the ſownde of the letter, as the Iewes did rake yt, do importe that we ſhoulde (*as S. Auguſtine ſaieth*) eate his fleſh rawe, ſodden, or roſted by lumpes and peices, as we do fleſh from the ſhambles, after whiche maner we do not, nor maie not eate yt, therfore yt ys a figu-ratiue ſpeache, that we muſt eate yt, euen the ſame fleſh, and the ſame bloo de in ſubſtance, after a ſpirituall maner, that ys vnder the formes of the Sa-crament inuiſiblie, and thus yt ys a figure alſo. And bicauſe one thing ys re-ceaued not in his owne forme in ſenſible maner, but in the forme of an ot-
D ther thing, in this reſpecte yt ys figuratiuelie eaten.

Thus ye perceaue howe the ſainge of Chryſte ys a figuratiue ſpeache, and that by conference with S. Auguſtines own ſainge. Ye ſee alſo that the Sa-crament ys a figure of manie thinges, and yet ſo as the reall preſence of Chry ſtes bodie ys not taken awaie from the ſame, But ys ſo ther that we muſt (*as S. Auguſtine ſaieth*) receaue yt with owre mouth, whiche can not be but ve-rilie, and reallie.

Chryſtes bo diễd blood in the Sacr. to be recea-ued both with heart and mouth

Maſter Horns figu raciou.

The Sacra ment ys a figure in di uerſe reſpec tes, but not onelie a fi gure.

　　　　　　　　　　　　　　　　　　　　　　　　　And

And nowe I leaue this obiection as fullie aunſwered, and turne me to   **E**
the proceſſe of the matter, noting this to yowe for the ſame, that where yt
ys declared, that S. Auguſtine ſaieth that the ſainge of Chryſte ys a figuratiue
ſpeache, he vnderſtandeth this alleaged texte of the Sacrament, and of
the verie reall preſence of the ſame fleſh and bloode, as the woordes of
Chryſte do pourporte, ſpirituallie (as ys before ſaied) vnderſtanded.

Yt were not a litle to be meruailed, that ſo famouſe a man, ſo highlie learned, ſo conſtante in faithe, who, as ye haue alreadie hearde, and more ſhall,
hath ſo plainlie, ſo manifeſtlie, withoute all obſcuritie, taught the verie reall
preſence of Chryſtes bleſſed bodie and blood in the Sacrament, ſhoulde in
this place forgette his faithe, forgette his learninge, leaue his conſtancie, and
teache a contrarie doctrine, that Chryſte ſhould be there but as in a figu-
gure or ſigne. No, God be praiſed, as he ys a ſtrong piller of Chryſtes Chur
che: So he will ſtand conſtantlie and ſtronglie in the ſame, and will not be
drawen into the companie of the malignaunte Churche, whiche God hateth: but remain in the catholique Churche, whiche God loueth.   **F**

S. Auguſtine thus being declared, for the better vnderſtanding of this
ſcripture, I will heare one other, who ſhall open vnto vs howe he alſo vnderſtandeth the ſame. This ſhall be Cyrille, whoſe ſainge ys this: *Non poterat*

Cyrill in.
15. Joan.

enim aliter corruptiblis hæc natura corporis ad incorruptibilitatem & vitam traduci, niſi
naturalis vitæ corpus ei coniungeretur. Non credis mihi hæc dicenti? Chriſto te obſecro fidé
præbe dicenti: Amen amen (inquit) dico vobis, niſi manducaueritis carnem filij hominis, &
biberitis ſanguinem eius, non habebitis vitam in vobis. Audis apertè clamantem non habi-
turos nos vitam niſi ſanguinem eius biberimus, & carnem manducauerimus. In vobis ipſis
dicit, id eſt, in corpore veſtro. vita autem iure ipſa vitæ caro intelligi poteſt. The corrup-

The rece-
ipt of Chry
ſtes bodie
maketh
oure bodies
immortall.

tible nature of this bodie, can not otherwiſe be brought to incorruptibilitie
and life, excepte the bodie of naturall life ſhould be conioined to yt. Doeſt
thowe not beleue me ſaing theſe thinges? I beſeche thee beleue Chryſt ſainge. *Verilie verilie I ſaie vnto yowe, excepte ye eate the fleſh of the Sonne of man, and*
drinke his bloode, ye ſhall haue no life in yowe. Thowe heareſt him plainlie ſainge,
that we ſhall not haue life except we drinke his bloode, and eate his fleſh,   **G**
He ſaieth in your ſelues, that ys, in your bodie. That ſame fleſh of life by
right maie be vnderſtanded life.

In this ſaieng Cyrill nedeth no expoſitour, who ſo plainlie teacheth, that
this corruptible bodie coulde not atteign to incorruptibilitie and life, except
the bodie of naturall life ſhoulde be conioined to yt. what ys the bodie of

Chryſts
fleſh called
life, as be-
ing the
fleſh of
God, who
ys life.

naturall life he teacheth afterwarde, when he ſaied: *the fleſh of Chryſte maie*
of right be called life, bicauſe yt ys the fleſh of life, that ys, *of God,* who ys the verie
life of his own nature, by whom all other thinges, in the which he hath
putte a liuing ſoule, do liue. But he naturally liueth, that ys, of his owne
nature, not by life powred into him, as by him yt ys powred into vs,
but of him ſelf. Therfore Cyrill calleth the bodie of Chryſt, the bodie
of naturall life, bicauſe yt ys the bodie of God, who ys naturall life. Nowe note that he ſaieth, that this bodie of naturall lif, whiche ys the bo-

Chryſtes
bodie is ioi
ned to vs
by corpo-
rall receipt
not by ſpiri
tuall.

die of Chryſte, muſt be ioined to our corruptible nature, whiche ioining
ys not but by the corporall receipt of that bodie, and not by the ſpirituall
receipt, whiche ioineth not the bodie of Chryſt to our corruptible nature.
Therfore Cyrill proueth by this texte, that of very neceſſitie we muſt re-   **H**
ceaue the verie fleſh and bloode of Chryſte verilie, and reallie, as that yt
maie be ioined to this our corruptible bodie, that yt by the other maie haue
life and incorruptibilitie. Wherfor they that take awaie the one and leaue
vs but the other, do vs wronge.   Heare

Heare therfor what the fame Cyrill faieth in this fame chapiter : *Non ne-*
A *gamus nos recta fide charitateque fyncera Chryfto fpiritualiter coniungi, fed nullam no-*
bis coniunctionis rationem fecundùm carnem cum illo effe, id profectò pernegamus, idque
à diuinis fcripturis, omnino alienum dicimus . Quis enim dubitauit etiam fic Chri-
stum vitem effe, nos verò palmites, qui vitam inde nobis acquirimus ? Audi Paulum di-
centem, quia omnes vnum corpus fumus in Chrifto, quia etfi multi fumus, vnum tamen
fumus in eo, omnes enim de vno pane participamus . An fortaffis putat ignotam nobis
myfticæ benedictionis virtutem, quæ cum in nobis fiat, nonne corporaliter quoque facit,
communicatione carnis Chrifti, Chriftum in nobis habitare ? Cur enim membra fidelium
membra funt Chrifti? Nefcitis (inquit) quia mēbra fidelium, membra funt Chrifti ? Mem-
bra igitur Chrifti,meretricis faciam membra? Abfit. We do not denie(faieth Cyrill)
that we, by right faithe, and fincere charitie, fpirituallie be conioined to
Chryft, but that we haue no maner of coniunction withe him after the
flefh, that truly we vtterly denie, and faie that that ys altogether contrarie
to the fcriptures of God. For who hathe doubted Chryfte euen fo to be
B the vine, and vs to be the braunches, whiche from thence gett life . Heare
Paule faing that we be all one bodie in Chryft. For although we be manie,
yet we be one in him. For all we do partake of one breade. Or peraduentu-
ture doth he thinke that the power of the myfticall benediction ys vnkno-
to vs? the whiche when yt ys doen in vs, dothe yt not make, by the partaking
of Chryftes flefh, Chryfte corporallie to dwell in vs? Wherfore be the membres of the faithfull, the membres of Chryft? *knowe ye not* (faieth he) *that yowr*
membres be the membres of Chryft? shall I then make the membres of Chryst the membres
of an Harlotte? God forbidde. Thus moche Cyrill.

In the which faing, ye perceaue, he teacheth that we be ioined to Chryft
bothe fpirituallie and corporallie: Spirituallie, by faithe, and charitie: Corpo
rallie by the partakinge of Chryftes flefh in the Sacrament, *by the whiche* (as
Cyrill faieth) *Chryfte abideth in vs corporallie,* by the which faing, the doctrine of
the Aduerfarie ys quite ouerthrowen, who wolde haue no other receipte of
Chryftes bodie, but a fpirituall receipt, and detefteth the corporall receipt.
But ye haue heard S. Cyrill earneftlie denieng yt and conftantlie affirminge
C yt to be againft the fcriptures, that Chryft fhould not be ioined to vs corporallie, which corporall coniunction ys by the partaking of Chryftes flefh,
not in the myfterie of hys incarnacion (as fome haue feigned) for thē Chryft
tooke our flefh, but in the myfterie of the Sacramēt, which Cyrill calleth the
myftical benediction, wher we take Chryftes flefh.

In the incarnaciō Chryft tooke our flefh, ād by yt was ioined to vs: in the Sa
crament we take Chryftes flefh, and be ioined to him. In the incarnaciō he
tooke our flefh, and the miferies of the fame, finne onelie excepted, in the Sa
crament we take hys flefh, and the merites of the fame, hys fingular exaltaciō
excepted. In the incarnacion he did take: in the Sacrament he doth geue.
Which both, that ys, the taking of our flefh to him, ād the geuing of his flefh
to vs, Chryfoftome fpeaking in the perfon of Chryfte verie well and breiflie
declareth, faing: *Vefter ego frater effe volui,et cōmunicaui carnē propter vos,& fangui-*
nē. Et per quæ vobis coniunctus fum,ea rurfus vobis exhibui. I wolde be yow brother,
and for yowe I tooke flefh and bloode, and by what thinges I was cōioined
to yow, thofe haue I again geuen to yow. Thus Chryfoftom . And thus
D ye maie perceaue the falfe doctrine of thefe naughtie men, and ther
withe their bolde fhameleffnes, that wher the faings of the learned fathers
fo clerelie denie their onely fpirituall maner of the conioining of Chryfte to
vs, and auouche the corporall ioining by the fcriptures, and faie that thefe

mens

In 15. Joan
A plain
place of S.
Cyrill for
the procla-
mer.

We are ioi-
ned to
Chryft two
waies cor-
porallie ād
fpirituallie.

S. Cyrill dē
nieth that
we receaue
Chryfts bo
die onelie
fpirituallie.

Chryst by
his incarn.
ioined to vs
We by the
Sacra. ioi-
ned to him

Hom l.45.
in 6. Ioan.

mens ſainges be againſt the ſcriptures: yet they will peruerſedlie and arro-　E
gantlie proceade to maintein their hereſie,and geue no place eitherto the fa
thers,or to the ſcriptures.

I can not ceaſſe to merueill that they will perſiſt ſo obſtinatelie againſt ſo
plain a matter,ſo plainly vttered and taught by this holie and learned Father S.Cyrill.Wherfore,reader,weigh,and conſider well this that ys here
ſpoken,and yf thow haueſt ſtand in faith perſeuer, and geue thankes : yf
thow haueſt erred,return,and ſeke mercie.Chryſte caſteth none awaie that
come to hym.

THE FIFTENTH CHAPITER CONTINVETH
the expoſition of the ſame texte by Leo and Euthymius.

That right holie man Leo,the Pope,who was elected vnto that office,in the yeare of our Lord 443. ſo that he was aboue a thouſand
yeares agone,whoſe vertue and holineſſe was ſoche,that not onely
of the Synode of Chalcedon,wher were gathered 630. Byſhoppes,　F
he was highlie commended:but alſo of *Platina*, who wolde ſpeake no more
to the comendacion of popes,then trueth wolde beare him. This holie Father ſaieth thus: *Hanc confeſſionem,Dileĉtiſſimi,toto corde promentes, impia hæretico-*
rum commenta reſpuite,vt ieiunia veſtra,& eleemoſinæ nullius erroris contagio polluan-
tur.Tunc enim & ſacrificij munda eſt oblatio,& miſericordiæ ſanĉta largitio , quando hi
qui iſta dependunt,quid operentur,intelligunt.Nam dicente Domino . Niſi manducaueritis
carnem filij hominis,& biberitis eius ſanguinem,non habebitis vitam in vobis . Sic ſanĉta
menſæ communicare debetis,vt nihil prorſus de veritate corporis Chriſti, & ſanguinis am-
bigatis.Hoc enim ore ſumitur,quod fide creditur , & fruſtra ab illis Amen reſpondetur,à
quibus contra id,quod accipitur,diſputatur. Thys confeſſion , moſt well beloued,
vttering furth with all yowr heart,forſake the wicked cōmentes of heretikes,
that yowr faſtinges and allmeſſes be not defiled with the contagion of er-
roure.For then ys bothe the oblacion of the ſacrifice clean, and the geuing
of almeſſe holie,when they that doo theſe thinges , vnderſtand what they
doe.For when our Lord ſaieth.Except ye eate the fleſh of the ſonne of man,
and drink hys bloode,ye ſhall haue no lyfe in yowe.Ye ſhoulde ſo communi-　G
cate of the holie table,*that ye ſhoulde nothing at all doubte of the veritie of the bodie*
and bloode of Chryſt.For that ys taken and receaued by mouthe,which ys beleued in faithe.
And in vain ys *Amen* aunſwered of them,of whom,againſt that,that ys receaued,argument ys made.Thus moch Leo.

Who (as ye maie perceaue) ſo certenlie tooke this texte to be vnderſtanded of the Sacrament,and of the verie preſence of Chryſtes bodie in the ſame,that he vſeth yt for an authoritie to prooue the ſame,and ſaieth, that for
aſmoche as our Lord did ſaie yt,we ſhoulde nothing at all doubte of the veritie of Chryſtes bodie and bloode.

Wherby this alſo maie be gathered,that he vſing this as an authoritie againſt
heretiques,did vſe yt as a ſcripture receaued, and ſo vnderſtāded throughout
all the catholique,Church,which I ſaie,he vſed againſt heretikes,not againſt
them in the matter of the Sacrament(for ther were no ſoche in thoſe times,
but againſt *Eutyches* and hys diſciples,whiche moſt peſtilētlie taught,that the
nature of man,which the Sonne of.God did take of the virgen, was turned
into that nature of God.And ſo deſtroyed the cōiunĉtiō of the two natures　H
in that one perſō of Chryſt.Againſt the which hereſie this holie mā brought
this ſentence of ſcripture,as a ſentence receaued of all men for the veritie of
Chryſtes fleſh in the Sacrament,therwith to prooue,that foraſmoche as the
verie

Leo ſer. 6.
de ieiu.ſept
menſis.

A plain pla
ce of Leo for
M.Iuell.

The mou-
the recea-
ueth , that
faith bele-
ueth.

Eutiches
his hereſie.

verie flesh of the manhead of Chryste was in the Sacrament, Chryste had
A still the verie nature of man in him.

Thus ye maie perceaue, that the truthe of this matter of the Sacrament
that ys to saie, that Chrystes verie bodie and blood be reallie in the Sacrament, was in those daies so clear withoute doubte and controuersie, so substanciallie beleued, that yt was reputed esteemed, and accompted an authoritie sufficient to confute the heresie of *Eutyches,* and to defende and maintein the true catholique faithe, that in Chryste was both the natures of God
and man. Now yf the verie flesh and blood of Chryst were not trulie, verilie,
and reallie in the Sacrament, the matter of the Sacrament, coulde proue nothing against this heresie, but raither make with yt. But forsomoche as ther
ys the verie flesh of Chryste, yt proueth very well, that the verie nature of
man ys in Chryst, directlie against the heresie of *Eutyches.*

This alone, in my opinion, might suffice to reduce men from erroure, con
sidering that thys was a trueth thus receaued a thousand yeares agon, in
B the whiche time we be well assured that the Church was withoute errour
in this matter, and men so zelouse in the trueth of the catholike faith,
that an heresie did not so soone appeare and shewe yt self, but yt was furthwith impugned, as to the learned yt ys well knowen. But this matter of
the Sacrament was neuer yet impugned, of anie catholique writer, that hath
liued since Chryst (as the learned also do knowe) wherfore yt ought to be ta
ken as an vndoubted trueth.

But omitting to make any further prooff herof by thys authour, I will,
according to my ordre prescribed, ioin vnto him *Euthymius* a greke authour,
who in hys exposition of this texte geueth vs thus to vnderstand yt : saing:
Nisi comederetis carnem filii hominis , & biberitis eius sanguinem , non habebi-
tis vitam in vobis . Illi quidem hoc impossibile iudicabant , ipse verò omnino pos-
sibile ostendit , neque id tantùm , sed necessarium , quod etiam fecit ad Nicodemum.
Addit autem & de sanguine , significans de pane ac poculo , quæ , vt dictum est,
daturus erat Discipulis in vltima cœna. Except ye eate the flesh of the Sonne of
man and drinke hys blood, ye shall not haue life in yowe. They (*meening the*
C *Iewes*) thought this vnpossible: but he (*meening Chryste*) declared yt alltogether
to be possible, and not that onelie, but also necessarie. Whiche thing he also
did to Nicodemus. He speaketh also of hys blood, signifieng that he speaketh
of the bread and the cuppe, whiche he wolde geue (*as yt ys saied*) to his Disciples in his last supper. Thus *Euthymius.*

I haue thought good in this exposition first to note to yow, that thys authour (notwithstanding the wicked wresting of the Aduersarie) vnderstandeth thys scripture with the other holie Fathers, of the Sacrament. For
by plain woordes he saieth, that our Sauiour speaketh here of the bread and
cuppe, that he wolde geue in the last supper. And signifieng that he forgatt
not what he had saied in the same matter before, referreth himself to that,
that he had before saied, saing · *Sicut dictum est,* as yt ys allreadie saied.

For before he saied that Chryst ys called bread two waies, that ys, after
hys deitie, and after hys humanitie. Therfore after he had spoken of the
bread whiche ys hys deitie , nowe in thys place he speaketh of the bread
whiche ys hys humanitie, of the whiche bread he saied not : *whiche I do geue*
D *yowe, but I will geue yowe*: for he wolde geue yt in his last supper, but when?
when he tooke the bread, and after thankes geuen, brake yt , and gaue yt to
his Disciples, saing. *Take, eat, This ys my bodie .* And therfor yt ys withoute
al scruple or doubte, that seing Chryst speaketh here of the bread and

　　　　　　　　　　　Y ii　　　　　　cuppe

Reall pre-
sence so cer
tenlie bele-
ued that an
ciēt fathers
vsed yt for
authoritie
in cōfuting
of heresies.

Euth.in 6.
Joan.

Chryst cal
led bread
two waies.

cuppe,that he wolde geue in his laſt Supper,therfore theſe woordes be ſpo- **E**
ken of the Sacrament.

Neither maie the Aduerſarie here cauille vpon theſe woordes, bread and
wine,that this authour doth meen that in the Sacrament ys nothing but
bread and wine,as figurs of the bodie and blood of Chryſt. For ſo farre wide
was this from his meening,that he plainlie denieth the ſubſtance of the Sacrament to be a figure,ſigne or token of the bodie and blood of Chryſt , but
the verie bodie and blood of Chryſt,as ſhall better and more at large appea
re by this ſame authours expoſition vpon the xxvi.of Matthew , in the lviii.
chap.of this booke.

Euthimius
denieth
that, which
the Sacra-
ment aries
affirme, ä l
affirmeth,
that they de
nie.

So then thys ys firſt certen,that this ſixt chapter of S.Iohn ys by this authour vnderſtanded of the Sacrament,which ys one thing that ys denied by
the Aduerſaries. So likewiſe this authour denieng the ſubſtance of the Sacra
ment to be a figure or ſigne of the bodie and blood of Chryſt,but the verie
reall and ſubſtanciall bodie and bloode of Chryſt(for yf the ſigne or figure
be taken awaie,the verie ſubſtance muſt nedes be in place) the other parte **F**
that the Aduerſaries denie,ys by this authour affirmed , and what by the
Aduerſaries ys affirmed,by this Authour yt ys denied.

Thus(gentle Reader)thow maiſt perceaue the doctrine of the Aduerſaries to be directly contrarie to the doctrine of the holie Fathers . Whiche
thing when I conſider in the Proclamer, me ſemeth to ſee before me
hym , vpon whom this curſe of God ys fallen : *Wo be vnto them , that*
call euell good , and good euell , which make darkneſſe light , and light darkeneſſe,

Eſay. 5.

which make ſowre ſweet,and ſweet ſowre.Wo be vnto them,that are wiſe in their own ſeight,
*and thinke them ſelues to haue vnderſtanding.*For the Proclamer and hys complices,teaching obedience to the catholique Church to be euell , and diſobe-
dience to the ſame to be good, trueth to be darkneſſe , and falſhead to be
light:penitent life to be ſowre,and ſenſuall life to be ſwete,are they not vnder this curſe?Dothe not the Proclamer take the ſeconde curſe vpon hym
alſo,thinking himſelf wiſe in hys owne conceat ? Dothe not he thinke him- **G**
ſelf wiſe and to haue vnderſtanding, that contemneth all the learned men
that haue ben this thouſand year ? Standeth not he in hys owne conceat,
that ſtoutely derideth,ſkoffeth mocketh,and wickedlie abuſeth the learning
not of one or two,but of manie,not of ſoche as be obſcure , but of ſoche as
be famouſe,and haue ben of the Chryſtian church reputed and eſteemed as
learned?And finallie ys not he accurſed that ſaieth hereſie ys trueth , and
trueth hereſie?that trueth ys darkneſſe,and hereſie light?hys owne phantaſies truethes,and the truthes of the Fathers phantaſies?that ſaieth yea,when
they ſaie naie,and naie,when they ſaie yea But whether go I. Though grief
wolde yet again carie me awaie,I will ſtaie here,and return to my matter.

THE SIXTENTH CHAPITER ENDETH THE EX-
poſition of this text in hand by the Epheſine Councell.

Auing ſufficientlie proued by the ſentences and iudgementes
of diuerſe learned and holie Fathers,that the ſaing of our Sauiour Chryſt in the ſixt chapter of S. Iohn : *Niſi manducauer. &c.*
*Except ye eate the fleſh,&c.*ys to be vnderſtanded of the Sacramēt: **H**
nowe to knitte vppe and end my proceſſe of the ſame texte,
I thought good to alleage the epiſtle of the Epheſine Councel ſent to *Neſto-*
*rius,*in the which this text being alleaged,yt maie be perceaued by the iudge
ment

A ment of cc.Byſhoppes,both grekes and latines,how the ſaied text ys to be vnderſtanded.Which as Leo did alleage againſt *Eutiches*,So do theſe Fathers expownd the ſame againſt *Neſtorius*.As *Eutyches* denied the nature of man to remain in Chryſt: So did *Neſtorius* denie the nature of God to be incarnate. *Eutyches* ſaied that he was but one perſon,for that he was onelie God, and not man:*Neſtorius* ſaied that both the natures of God and man remained diſtinctlie,as to ſeuerall perſons,the Godhead not incarnated , the Manhead not deitated,as *Gregorie Nazianzen* termeth yt,and ſo implied he that Chryſt born of the virgen,was onelie man and not God.

Neſtorius and Eutiches, their hereſies.

Againſt the whiche blaſphemouſe hereſie,the Councell ſent him the epiſtle before ſaied,and in the ſame they write thus:*Neceſſariò & hoc adijcimus,annunciantes enim ſicut ſecundùm carnem,mortem vnigeniti filij Dei, id eſt, Ieſu Chriſti, & reſurrectionem eius, & in cœlis aſcenſionem pariter confitentes, incruentam pariter celebramus in eccleſijs ſacrificij ſeruitutem:ſic & ad myſticas benedictiones accedimus, & ſanctificamur,participes ſancti corporis, & precioſi ſanguinis Chriſti,omnium noſtrûm Redemptoris effecti:non vt communem carnem percipientes(quod abſit) nec vt viri ſanctificati , &*

B *verbo coniuncti ſecundùm dignitatis vnitatem,aut ſicut diuinam poſsidentis habitationem, ſed verè viuificatrice, & ipſius verbi propriam factam.Vita enim naturaliter exiſtens vt Deus,quia propriæ carni vnitus eſt,viuificatrice eam profeſſus eſt. Et ideò quamuis dicat ad nos,Niſi manducaueritis carnē filij hominis, & biberitis eius ſanguinē,non habebitis vitã in vobis:non tamē eam vt hominis vnius ex nobis exiſtimare debemus . Quomodò enim ſecundùm naturã ſuã,viuificatrix eſſe caro hominis poterit? Sed vt verè propriã eius factã, qui propter nos et.filius hominis factus eſt, & vocatus.* Neceſſarelie therfor this alſo we putte to,ſhewing furth the death after the fleſh of the onelie begottē Sō ne of God,that ys of Ieſus Chryſt,and confeſſing alſo the reſurrection and aſcenſion of him into the heauens,we do celebrate in the churches an vnbloodie ſeruice of Sacrifice.So alſo do we come vnto the myſticall benedictions,and be ſanctified,being made partakers of the holie bodie and precious ſe blood of Chryſte theRedemer of vs all not taking yt as comō fleſh(which God forbidde)neither as of a ſanctified mā,and ioined to the Sōne of God, after the vnitie of dignitie,or as poſſeſſing the diuine habitacion, but truly

C quickning or geuing life,and made the propre fleſh of the Sōne of God.For being naturallie life as God,bicauſe he ys vnited to hys owne propre fleſh,he hath profeſſed yt to be geuing life.And therfor although he ſaieth to vs:*Verilie verilie I ſaie to yow,except ye eate the fleſh of the Sōne of mã,ãd drinke hys blood ye ſhall haue no life in yow.* Yet we ſhould not eſteem yt as of a mā that ys one of vs, for how can the fleſh of man after hys owne nature be a quickning fleſh,or geuing life,but as made hys own propre fleſh,who for vs was made theSonne of man,and ſo called.Thus the Councell.

Epheſine Councellvn derſtandeth this text : Except ye eate &c. of the Sacrament and ſo did Neſtorius alſo.

Do ye not here ſee,howe that this holie Coūcel,which ys one of the four famouſe generall Coūcells,wold that we ſhould not take this text of S.Iohn, as *Neſtorius* did,to be ſpokē of the fleſh of Chryſt,as of the fleſh of a pure mā, but of the fleſh of Chryſte,as the verie owne propre fleſh of God , and that yt ſo taken and eaten doth geue life,being able ſo to doe, not for that yt ys of the nature of man,but bicauſe yt ys the fleſh of God.

Nowe maie yt not be ſaied that this ys to be vnderſtanded ſpūallie.For *Neſtorius* that ſaied that Chryſt was but a verie man,and grownded hymſelf

D moch vpon this text:*Except ye eate the fleſh of the ſonne of man.*and cōcluded therfore that he was but the Sonne of man,did not take the matter ſo fineliethat the fleſh of Chryſt was in the Sacramēt but merelie ſpirituallie,who had cōceaued ſo groſſe an opinion of Chryſt, that he was but a bare man naturallie.

Y iij   And

And therfor the Councell,who tooke the fame fcriptures to improue that, **E**
that *Neftorius* femed,to himfelf to haue proued,muft nedes vfe the fame fenfe
of the fcripture,as touching the fubftance of the thing that ys in difputacion
or ells they fhoulde nothing proue againft him.For yf *Neftorius* fpake of the
verie flefh of Chryft,and the Councell of the fpiritnall flefh of Chryft,what
coulde they conclude againft him,not fpeaking of the fame thing that the
other fpake of.And therfore vndoubtedlie they fpake of the verie reall flefh
of Chryft,which ys the own propre flefh of God. Whiche thing alfo the
woordes of the Councell do proue wher yt ys faied : *We come to the myfticall
benedictions,being made partakers of the holie bodie and precioufe blood of Chryft the Redemer of vs all , receauing yt not as common flesh,but as the flesh truly geuing life.*

Reall pre-
fence auou-
ched by the
Ephefine
Councell.

A plain
faing of a
Councell
for M.Iuel

Yt maketh alfo for this vnderftanding not a litle that Cyrill being prefident of the Councell,who(as before ye heard)doth plainlie affirme, that we
do not onelie by faith and charitie,fpirituallie receaue the flefh of Chryfte,
but alfo verilie and reallie,wolde not nowe,nor did not fpeake of the fpirituall receauing onelie,which onelie receauing of Chryft fpirituallie and not
otherwife in the Sacramet he did earneftlie denie, and ftronglie improue by **F.**
the fcriptures.And therfor yt ys moft euident that this texte nowe in hand
was vnderftanded by that Councell of the Sacrament, as being the very
reall bodie and blood of Chryft , whiche yf we receaue not , we
haue no life.

To this holie Councell I thinke yt vnfemlie to ioin anie one particular
man.Wherfore to ende here the expofition of this faid texte, I will onelie
adde to yt being an holie multitude,the practife of an other holie multitude
euen the auncient Church,who fo ftreictlie,and yet directilie for the fubftan
ce of the thing,did take this text to be vnderftanded of the verie reall and
fubftanciall flefh and blood of Chryft in the Sacrament,that they thought
yt a matter of neceffitie to miniftre the fame to infantes,as withoute receipt
wherof they thought they coulde not be faued.   The practife wherof we
finde to haue endured in the Affrican Church from the time of S. Cyprian
vntill the tyme of S. Auguftine at the leaft . By whiche yt ys manifeft that the Churche then vnderftood thys fcripture of the Sacrament,
and yet not of the bare Sacrament onelie , but of the verie flefh and **G**
bloode of Chryft ther reallie to be receaued , and not of yt fpirituall-
lie to be receaued , for that they well knewe , that ther lacked in thofe
infantes that knowledg, whiche neceffarilie ys required to the fpirituall
receauinge of Chryftes bodie , and therfor they did not receaue yt fpirituallie,but facramentallie.

The church
of Affrica
vnderftan
dingthe vi.
of S.Iohn of
the Sacr.
miniftred
yt to infan-
tes.

And though this practife of the communicating of infantes grounded
vpon this vnderftanding of this fcripture,was ceaffed, yet that the Churche
did ftill retein that vnderftanding, this well proueth, that *Petrus Drefenfis*
perfwading *Iacobellus de Praga* to minifter the Sacrament vnder bothe kindes,vfed this texte here expownded, as being vnderftanded of the Sacrament,by the comon confent of the Churche, for hys argument , which text
when *Iacobellus* had weighed, and confidered howe yt hadde ben alwaies
vnderftanded in the Churche,he began to perfwade the people, that they
aught of neceffitie,yf they wolde haue euerlafting life, to receaue the Sacrament vnder both kindes,as vnder whiche they fhoulde both eate hys flefh **H**
and drinke hys blood:of whiche matter more large difputacion fhall be made in the ende of this booke.wherfor I think yt not mete here to trouble the
reader with all, but to refer him thither, thinking yt fufficient for this place
to ad-

A　to aduertife him, that all the authours hertofore alleaged vpon this text, and all thefe holie fathers in the Ephefine Councell reprefenting the Churche, and the Chuch in the time of S. Cyprian, and fo to S. Auguftine, and from him to the time of *Petrus Drefenfis* and *Iacobellus*, and after ther time, in the time of foche as haue written vpon the gofpells, vntill the time of *Luther* did vnderftand this text, of the flefh and bloode of Chryft in the Sacrament, as their workes do well teftifie.

But thus moche maie I here well faie, that yt pitieth me to fee howe the people fuffer them felues to be deluded of thefe newe inuentours of difordres, and by them both to be drawen from true faith, and alfo to breake the vfuall ordre of the Churche, that wher our Sauiour Chryft faied by plain woordes : *Except ye eate the flesh of the fonne of man, and drinke his bloode, ye shall not haue life in yowe.* Whiche text (*as ye haue heard*) ys fullie proued to be ment of Chryftes veric bodie and bloode in the Sacrament, yet being inueigled by thaduerfaries doctrine hardlie beleue this mening of the Catholique Fathers to be true, and therfor wher the Aduerfaries maliciouflie perfwade thē,

B　that the miniftres of the Churche deceaued them, in geuing them the Sacrament but vnder one kinde, they are contented to encline and yelde vnto them. And fo wher before they did vnder one kinde, receaue the verie flefh and bloode of Chryfte, they are nowe contented vnder two kindes to receaue neither flefh nor bloode.

Both flesh and blood was before vnder one kind, now neither of both vnder two kindes.

THE SEVENTENTH CHAPITER EXPOVNDETH THE
next text folowing in the fixte of S. Iohn by fainƈte Augufine and Cyrill.

C　Owe will I proceade to the text folowing in S. Iohn, whiche, for afmoche as yt ys not moche difcrepant from that before, but as yt were an affirmatiue fequele of the fame, I will not troble the reader with long treaƈting vpon yt, but breiflie fhewe the meninge therof, and hafte me to other that contein more matter, not fo plainlie fpoken of before, as this hath ben. The text ys: *Qui manducat meam carnem, & bibit meum fanguinem, habet vitam æternam.* He that eateth my flefh and drinketh my blood, hath eternall life.

As the abfteining from the eating of the flefh and blood of Chryfte, caufeth lacke of life: So ys yt confequent that the feading on the flesfh and blood of Chryft caufeth the hauing of life. As the meat ys, foche ys the effecte and operacion of yt. Yf a man eate corruptible meate, yt will for a while maintein, but yt will not preferue from corruption. Yf a man feade on mortall thinges, yt can not preferue from mortalitie, but fuffer him to be mortall: So if a man feed on fpirituall thinges, and digeft them well, yt will make a man fpirituall. Yf a man feed of immortall thinges, yt will bring the like effeƈt, aud make a man immortall. For euery foode leaueth his effeƈt or operacion of nature in the thing that feadeth. Yf then we feede on Chryft, who ys life, he will leaue his effeƈt in vs, which ys life. And for fo moch as he ys the eternall and immortall life, he wil woork in vs according to his nature, that we fhall haue eternall and immortall life. And therfor he faieth:

Foode of Chryftes flesh caufe of immortalitie.

D　*Qui manducat meam carnem & bibit meum fanguinem habet vitam æternam.* He that eateth my flefh and drinketh my blood hath eternall life, he faieth not life onely, but eternall life. And (as Chryfoftome faieth) *Cùm dixiffet fi quis manducauerit*

Hom.46. in Ioan.

Y　iiii　*cauerit*

cauerit ex hoc pane non morietur inæternum , & credibile effet eos dicturos, quemadmo- **E**
dum fuperius, Abraham mortuus est, & Prophetæ mortui funt, & quomodò tu dicis, non
guStabit mortem inæternum? Refurrectionem ponit, per quam foluit quæStionem, quòd non
morietur in fine. When he had faied : whofoeuer fhall eate of this bread he
fhall not die for euer: and yt was credible that they wolde haue faied, as
they did before, Abraham ys dead and the Prophetes be dead, and howe
doeſt thowe faie he fhall not taſt deathe ? He putteth the refurrection by
the whiche he folueth the queſtion that he fhall not die in the ende . And
therfore he faieth : *Et ego refufcitabo eum in nouiſsimo die.* And I will raife him
vppe in the laſt daie.

But I will leaue my expofition to fee the mindes of the doctours vpon
Tract 26.
in Ioan. this fcripture. S. Auguſtine writeth thus : *Hanc non habet, qui istum panem non*
manducat, nec istum fanguinem bibit. Nam temporalem vitam fiue illo habere homines
poſſunt, æternam verò non poſſunt. Qui ergo non manducat eius carnem, nec bibit eius fan-
guinem non habet in fe vitam,& qui manducat eius carnem,&bibit eius fanguinem,habet
vitam æternam. Ad vtrunque autem refpondit, quòd dixit vitam æternam. Non ita est in **F**
hac efca, quam fustentadæ huius corporis vitæ caufa fumimus.Nam qui eam non fumpferit,
non viuet.Nec tamen qui eam fumpferit, viuet. Fieri enim potest, vt fenio vel morbo,vel ali
quo cafu, plurimi qui eam fumpferint moriantur:in hoc verò cibo & potu,id est,corpore &
fanguine Domini non ita est. Nam & qui eum non fumit, non habet vitam: & qui eum fu
mit habet vitam, & hanc vtique æternam. He hath not this life, that eateth not
this bread, nor drinketh this bloode, For withoute that meat, men maie haue the temporall life, but the eternall life they can not haue . He therfor
that dothe not eate his flefh, nor drinke his bloode, hath no life in him. And
he that doth eate his flefhe and drinke his bloode, hath life euerlaſting. He
hath aunfwered to both in that he hath faied(euerlaſting) Yt ys not fo in this
meate, whiche we do take to fuſtein the life of this bodie . For he that doth
not take yt fhall not liue, neither for all that fhall he liue that hath taken yt.
For yt maie be that manie with age, difeafe or fome other chaunce euen of
them that haue taken yt maie die. In this meat and drinke, that ys to faie, *in*
the bodie and blood of our Lorde, yt ys not fo. For bothe he that doth not take yt,
hath not life, and he that doth take yt hath life, yea and that eternall. This
Ibidem. ys faint Auguſtines minde vpon this text. Whiche although yt doth fpeake **G**
of the Sacrament, yet fome perchaunce will obiecte and faie, that S. Auguſtine immediately expowndeth him felf to fpeake of the miſticall bodie of
Chryſte, whiche ys his Churche,and not of the bodie of Chryſt in the Sacrament. For thus he faieth : *Hunc itaque cibum & potum focietatem vult intelligi*
corporis & membrorum fuorum, quod est Ecclefia in prædeStinatis, & vocatis, & iustifi-
catis, & glorificatis, fanctis & fidelibus eius . Quorum primum iam factum est : fecundu
& tertium, & factum est, & fit,id est,vocatio & iustificatio : quartum verò nunc in fpe
est, in re autem futurum est,id est, glorificatio. This meate and drinke therfor he
will to be vnderſtanded the focietie or felowfhippe of the bodie and his me-
bres, whiche ys the holie Churhe in the predeſtinated, and called, and iuſtified, and glorified fainctes, and his faithfull. Of the whiche the firſt vs nowe
doen, that ys to faie: predeſtinacion. The fecod and the thirde, ys both doe,
and ys in doing,and fhall be doen, that ys vocacion, and iuſtificacion : The
fourth ys nowe in hope, but in deed to come, that ys glorificacion. This ys
the fentence of S. Auguſtine, which in deed doth make plain mencion of **H**
the bodie miſticall of Chryſte , and expowndeth the meat that ys fpoken of to be the folowfhippe of the bodie and the membres , whiche ys
his Churche.

But

But what though S. Auguſtin in this place dothe expownde yt of the mi-
A ſticall bodie of Chryſte, ys that a good argument that yt ys not to be expownded of the holie Sacrament? and of the verie fleſh ther in conteined? S.
Paule ſaieth that Abraham had two Sonnes the one by a bond maiden, the
other by a free woman. whiche thinges (ſaieth he) are ſpoken by an allego-
rie. For theſe are two teſtamentes. Nowe ys yt for me to ſaie that they were
not two children in deed, but two Teſtamentes, or bycauſe S. Paule ſaieth
they are ſpoken allegorycallie, therfor they are not ſpoken hiſtoricallie, or
litterallie? Do ye not knowe that ſainᶜte Auguſtine him ſelf ſaieth, that
the ſcripture ys fertile and full of goodlie ſenſeis? Therfore though S. Auguſtine here expowndeth yt thus: Yet in other places he expowndeth diuerſe ſentences of this ſame chapiter of the verie bodie, and reall fleſh of Chryſt
in the Sacrament.

Wherfore this ys to be conſidered that S. Auguſtine in his treaᶜtiſes vpon
the ſixte of S. Iohn, knowing the people to whom he ſpake, then to be ſo-
B wnd in the faith of the Sacrament, and that ther was no controuerſie in all
the Churche of that matter, by the whiche he was occaſioned to ſpeake di-
reᶜtlie, diſinitiuelie, and more plainly of the ſame: he framed him ſelf to
ſpeake of that, that neaded, as of the maners, conuerſacion, and liuing of
the people, and not of that, that neaded not, as to inſtruᶜte them of the due
faithe to be had aboute this miſterie. For they knewe right well what yt
was. And therfore he did not go aboute to inſtruᶜte them *quid ſumerent, ſed
quàm bene ſumerent,* what they did receaue, but howe well they ſhoulde recea
ue yt. And therfor the moſt parte of his doing was here to moue them
that as they did according to ther faith receaue the bodie of Chryſte ſacramentallie: So alſo according to their duetie with godlie deuocion, holie conuerſation, and ſpirituall meditaciõ they might receaue him ſpirituallie
withoute the whiche maner of receipt, the other was nothing profitable,
but raither hurtfull and damnable.

And therfore in the end of the ſixt of S. Iohn ſhewing his pourpoſe to be
(as I haue ſaied) and that the people ſhoulde perceaue, that as he knewe,
C that they did beleue well: ſo alſo they might receaue well, he concludeth
the wholl matter thus: *Hoc ergo totum ad hoc nobis valeat, dileᶜtiſſimi, vt carnem
Chriſti & ſanguinem Chriſti non edamus tantùm in ſacramento (quod & multi mali)
ſed vſque ad ſpiritus participationem manducemus, & bibamus, vt in Domini corpore
tanquam membra maneamus, vt eius ſpiritu vegetemur, & non ſcandalizemur, etiamſi
multi modò nobiſcum manducant & bibunt temporaliter ſacramenta, qui habebunt in fine æterna tormenta.* All this therfor (*moſt wellbeloued*) let yt auaill to this ende,
that we eate not the fleſſh and bloode of Chryſt onelie in the Sacrament
(*whiche alſo manie euell men do*) but let vs eate and drinke to the participacion
or partaking of the ſpirit, that we maie abide in the bodie of our Lord as
membres, that we maie be made luſtie and ſtrong by his ſpirite, and not
be ſlaundered, though manie do eate and drinke with vs temporallie the
Sacramentes, whiche in the ende ſhall haue eternall tormentes. Thus
S. Auguſtin.

Here maie ye clerely perceaue the ſcope of S. Auguſtines treatiſes vpon
S. Iohn, that he wolde the people ſhoulde not onelie receaue the fleſh and
D blood of Chryſte in the Sacrament, ſacramentallie: but alſo by the partaking of the ſpirit, ſpirituallie. In which his concluſion, as ye maie perceaue,
that he teacheth two maner of receauinges: ſo wolde he both to be vnderſtanded in Chryſtes woords, and neither of them to be baniſhed as a thing

not

S. Auguſti
nes cheif en
tent in hys
treaᶜtiſes v
pon the ſixt
of S. Iohn.

The fleſh
of Chryſt
eaten in the
Sacr. of e-
uel men.

S. Auguſt.
doth ac-
knowledge
both ſpiri-
tual and
corporalre
ceauing.

not intended or ment by Chryſte. Wherbye ye maie perceaue the great　E
folie of the Aduerſaries, that bicauſe ſaint Auguſtine dothe exhorte vs to
the ſpirituall receauing of Chryſtes bodie and blood, therfore we muſt con
tempne the ſacramentall receauing therof : And yet ſaincte Auguſtin
wolde we ſhoulde do bothe, and teacheth aſwell the one as the other.

But ther doing herin ys moche like to their doing in the matter of iuſti-
ficatiō, that bicauſe ſainct Paule did ſo moche extolle faithe to the Romans,
therfore they contemned the woorkes of charitie ſett furth to the Corinthians. The effecte wherof hath well appeared in their practiſe : For not one-
Luther cō-
demned S.
James epiſt
ly *Luther* did cōdemne ſaincte Iames epiſtle for the ſettiug furth of workes:
but alſo he and his ſequaces haue maliciouſlie ſeparated, cutt of, and diuided them ſelues from the vnitie of Chryſtes Churche, and felowſhippe
with yt. And then being ſo ſeparated, haue withoute all meaſure and
ende, blaſphemed, railed at, and reuiled the ſame, and odiblie and cruellie
perſecuted yt, which was towardes them frendlie and blameleſſe. But God
kendle in them that be liuing the fire of his lowe, that by yt they maie re-　F
turne to vnitie, whiche by malice haue made lamētable diuiſion, not onelie
among the people, but betwen God and manie a ſoule.

And, Reader, beholde thow the trueth nowe laied before thy face, and
ſee that nowe taught of S. Auguſtin, that before thowe haueſt ſeen taught
by Chryſoſtom, and Cyryll. Chryſoſtome ſaied: *Vt autem non ſolùn per dilectio*
nem, ſed reipſa in ipſam carnem conuertamur, per cibum id efficitur, quem nobis largitus eſt.
That we ſhould not onelie by loue, but in verie deed be turned in to that
fleſh that ys brought to paſſe by the meate, whiche he hathe grauntedvs,
Wher note bothe our turning into Chryſt by loue, whiche ys the ſpirituall receauing, and our turning into his fleſh in verie deed, whiche ys by the
corporall receauing.

In.15.Ioā.
Corporal re
ceauing a-
uouched aſ
wel as ſpiri
tuall.
Cyrill ſaieth : *Non negamus nos recta fide charitatéque ſincera Chriſto ſpiritualiter*
coniungi: Sed nullam nobis coniūctionis rationem ſecūndū carnem cum illo eſſe, id profectò
pernegamus We do not denie, that we be conioined to Chryſte ſpirituallie
by right faith and ſincere charitie: But that we hawe no maner of coniuncti-　G
on with him after the fleſh, that we earneſtly denie . Note here a ſpirituall ioininge of vs to Chryſte , whiche ys by ſpirituall receauing,
and a carnall ioininge of vs to his fleſh, which ys by corporall receauing.

Nowe compare S. Auguſtine here to theſe, who ſaieth that we maie not
onely eate the fleſh, and drinke the blood of Chryſt in the Sacramēt (whiche
ys the corporall receauing) but we muſt eate yt euen vnto the participacion
of the ſpirit, which ys the ſpirituall receauing, And thus thow ſeeſt an vniforme doctrine, that we muſt bothe receaue Chryſt in the Sacrament reallie,
and alſo by faithe ſpirituallie. And therfor, *thowe Chryſtian,* ſuffer not thy ſelf
to be robbed of the one, ſeing that the exceading loue of Chryſte, as a pled
ge of the ſame, hath to thy endleſſe comforte lefte thee bothe.

And nowe what S. Cyrill ſaieth agreablie to S. Auguſtin vpon this text
Jn.15.Ioan
let vs heare : *Manet enim immaculata vtraque natura , & vnus ex vtriſque Chriſtus*
eſt, ſed ineſabiliter, & vltrà quàm poſsit mens humana intelligere . Verbum humanitati
coniunctum, totam in ſeipſum ita reduxit, vt indigentia vitæ poſsit viuificare, Sic interitum
à natura expulit, & mortem, quæ peccato plurimum poterat, deſtruxit. Quare qui carnem
Chriſti manducat , vitam habet æternam . Habet enim hæc caro Dei Verbum, quod natu-　H
raliter vita eſt. Propterea dicit, & ego reſuſcitabo eum in nouiſsimo die. Ego enim dixit, id
eſt, corpus meum quod comedetur , reſuſcitabo eum . Non enim alius ipſe quàm caroſua. Nō
id dico, quia natura non ſit alius, ſed quia poſt incarnationem in duos ſe diuidi filios minimè
patitur.

A *patitur. Ego igitur (inquit) qui homo factus sum per meam carnem in nouißimo die comedentes resuscitabo.* Bothe the natures (saieth he) abide inuiolated, and of them both ther ys one Chryst, but vnspeakeablie, and beionde, that mans minde can vnderstande. The Sonne of God conioined to the manheade hath so reduced yt whollie into him self, that yt ys able to geue life to thinges lacking life. So hath yt expelled destructiō from the nature of man, and death, whiche by sinne was very strong, yt hath destroied. Wherfore he that eateth the flesh of Chryste hath euerlasting life. For this flesh hath the Sonne of God, whiche ys naturallie life: Therfore he saiethe: *and I will raise him vppe in the last daie.* He saied I: that ys to saie, *my bodie that shall be eaten will raise him vppe.* He ys none other then his flesh. I do not saie that he ys none other in nature, but bycause after the incarnacion he suffreth not him self to be diuided into two sonnes. Therfor he saieth: I, whiche am made man by my flesh will raise them vppe in the last daie, whiche do eate me. Thus farre S. Cyrill.

Chrystes bodie receaued in the Sacr. shall raise our bodies to immortall life.

B　Although yt be moche wourthie to be noted, howe he declareth the flesh of Chryste to be able to geue life, Yet bicause I wolde not digresse so moche, to the greif of the reader, from the matter in hande, This onelie I note, that he maketh all this processe to proue that Chrystes flesh that was ioined to the Sonne of God in vnitie of person had power and did geue life (*as in the fourtenth chapiter more at large appeareth*) to the entent, that he wolde therby open the trueth of this saing of Chryste: *He that eateth my flesh and drinketh my blood shall haue eternall life.* Whiche saing of Chryst must be vnderstanded of the same flesh, whiche he hath proued to geue life, whiche ys the verie flesh of the Sonne of God, or ells all his processe were vain. For if the probacion be of the very naturall flesh of Chryst, and the scritpture be vnder standed of the spirituall flesh, what serueth the probacion, and all the processe of the naturall flesh? but that the scripture ys to be vnderstanded of the verie flesh of Chryst. he declareth in the next saing *And I will raise him in the last daie, I,* saieth he, that ys to saie, *my bodie that shall be eaten will raise him vppe.* Nowe the verie reall bodie of Chryste shall raise vppe the faithfull at the

C　last daie, wherfore that same bodie ys eaten. For yt ys all one bodie that ys eaten of the faithfull, and that shall raise vppe the faithful.

　Why the bodie of Chryst shall raise vppe our bodies, he geueth a reason in the fourtenth chapiter vpon the sixt of S. Iohn. *Oportuit enim certè, vt non solùm anima per spiritum sanctum, in beatam vitam ascenderet : verùm etiam vt rude hoc & terrestre corpus, cognato sibi gustu, tactu, & cibo, ad immortalitatem reduceretur.* Trulie yt must so haue ben, that not onelie the soule, by the holie Gost shoulde ascend into the blessed life, but also that this rude and earthlie bodie by a like natured tast, touching, and meat, shoulde be reduced to immortalitie. Wher note that as our spirit ys brought to the blessed life by the Spirit of God: so ys our dodie reduced to immortallitie by his bodie. Note further howe yt ys doen (*cognato cibo*) with a like natured meate, and soche ther ys none, that ys of like nature to vs, that can reduce vs to immortallitie, but the verie bodie of Chryst Therfore yt ys the verie bodie of Chryste that ys this our meat, whiche meat who so doeth eate, as yt becometh him to eate, shall haue eternall life.

Cirill. in. 6. Ioan ca. 14 Cause and maner of oure raising to immortalitie declared.

D

THE

THE EIGHTENTH CHAPITER BEGINNETH
the expofition of the next text in the fixt chap . of S. Iohn by
Origen and S. Ambrofe.

E

Ow foloweth in S. Iohn the fecond determinatiue fentence of the fubftance of this matter of the Sacrament. *Caro mea verè eft cibus, & fanguis meus verè eft potus.* My flefh ys verilie meat, and my blood ys verily drinke.

Joan.6.

Owre Sauiour Chryft fpeaking moche of the bread whiche his father gaue, as that: *Non Moyfes dedit vobis panem, fed Pater meus dat vobis panem de cælo verum* Not Moyfes gaue yowe bread from heauenbut my father geueth yowe from heauen the true bread. and that : *Panis Dei eft, qui de cælo defcendit & dat vitam mundo.* Yt ys the bread of God that cometh from heauen, and geueth life to the worlde : yet had he not determined, who was this bread, but at the laft he determined faing : *Ego fum panis viuus, qui de cælo defcendi.* I am the liuing bread, whiche defcended from heauen. So that F as here in thefe fainges he determined,fpeaking of the bread of his Godhaed that he was that bread whiche he hetherto fpake of , whiche bread was allreadie prefentlie geuen : So fpeaking of a bread that he wolde geue in the Sacrament,determined what yt was faing, that yt was his flefh , whiche flefh although he faied he wolde geue, and had fpoken moche of the eating of yt : yet he determined not what that flefh was vntill nowe. But nowe he faieth *yt ys verilie meate.*

Thaduerbe verè what force yt hathe and whie Chryft chofe to fpeake by yt.

Wher note that our Sauiour determining this thing, hath chofen raither to faie. *Caro mea vère eft cibus.* My flefh ys verilie meat, by the Aduerbe, then to faie, *Caro mea verus eft cibus* My flefh ys the verie meat : by the adiectiue, For the aduerbe hath a more force,and more fullie expreffeth the thing that yt fignifieth, than dothe the Adiectiue . As if I fhoulde faie : *Pium hoc opus operatus eft.* He hath wrought this godly worke. Yt hath not fo full and perfecte fenfe, as yf I faie : *Hoc opus piè operatus eft.* He hath wrought this worke godlic. For in the former fentence fpoken by the Adiectiue, ther ys but one G thing determined, that ys, that the worke was good , but not the doinge. but in the other bothe the worke and the doing ys determined to be good. For if the worke be godlie doen,both the worke, and the doing of the worke ys godlie. But if I faie: he hath doen a godlie worke: though the worke be fignified to be godlie : yet the doing maic be vngodlie. As, the Pharafeis did geue almeffe, whiche was a godlie worke, but bicaufe yt was doen to oftentacion, the doing of yt was not godlie.

Ouer and aboue this, an Aduerbe put to a verbe doth fullfill the fignificacion of the verbe. Wherfore put to a verbe fubftātiue yt doth fullfil the fignificaciō of the fame and more fullie doth fignifie the fubftance of the thing that ys ruled by the verbe, as, *Hic eft verus homo,* This ys a true man, doth not fignifie fo moche the fubftance, as to faie : *Hic eft verè homo*. This ys trulie or verilie a man . This doth fully expreffe the nature or fubftance of a man.

So likewife the Aduerbe here put to the verbe fubftantiue, dothe more fullie declare the Subftance of the thing. As tho he might faie : My flefh ys meat not by a metaphor,fimilitude,or figure: but yt ys verylie meat,that ys, H fubftanciallie meat, whiche fo fedeth vs, that *(as Chryfoftom faieth)reipfa conuertimur in carnem Chrifti.* in verie dede we are turned into the flefh of Chryft.

But we will heare the auncientes of Chryftes houfe vpon this text alfo, whether yt be thus to be vnderftanded or no, And firft *Origen,* who faieth
thus:

thus: *Lex Dei iam non in figuris,& in imaginibus,sicut prius:sed in ipsa specie veritatis*

A *agnoscitur.Et quæ prius in ænigmate designabantur,nunc in specie & veritate complentur.* ┃ *In Numer.*
The Lawe of God ys not nowe knowen in figures, and ymages (as before, *homel.7.*
but in plain trueth.And soche thinges as before were described or shewed
in a dark maner,nowe are they fullfilled in plain maner and trueth.

And what the thinges be,he after rehearseth of the which some be these:
*Antea in ænigmate fuit Baptismus iu nube,& in mari: nunc autem in specie regeneratio
est in aqua & Spiritu sancto.Tunc in ænigmate erat Manna cibus:nunc autem in specie ca-
ro Verbi Dei est verus cibus, sicut ipse dicit: Caro mea verè est cibus, & sanguis
meus verè est potus.* Before baptisme was in a darke maner,in the cloud, and
in the sea : Nowe regeneracion ys in plain maner, in the water and the ┃ *The flesh
of Chryst
meat in
plain ma-
ner.*
holie Gost. Then Manna was meat in a darke maner,but nowe the flesh
of the Sonne of God ys verie meat in a plain maner , As he him
self saieth : *My flesh ys meat in dede , and my blood ys drinke in dede .* Thus
Origen.

B　Nowe weigh with me (gentle Reader) that *Origen* saieth that the Gospell
hath not thinges in ymageis ād figures,ād shadowes,as the Lawe before had ┃ *The Gos-
pell hath
not the figu
res but the
verie thin-
ges.*
but soch thinges as were ther described by figures,in the time of the Gospell
are knowen in plain trueth,So that the Gospell walketh not in figures, but
in the trueth of thinges figured. Wherby *Origen* concludeth, that the flesh
of Chryst figured by Manna,that was meat to the Iewes, ys nowe not figu-
ratiuelie , but verilie the true meate of the Chrystians. And for his autho-
ritie vseth owre text nowe in handling, saing thus : As he saieth (mening
Chryste) My flesh ys meat &c . By which maner of his declaracion ys
yt not most plain that this ys no figuratiue speache. But that he vnderstan-
deth Chrystes saing as a plain assertion of a trueth, withoute any figure,and
that they be, the very thinges in dede, as the woordes do plainlie signifie?
yt ys most certen.

Perchaunce the Aduersaries will saie *we take the flesh of Chryst, as Chryst spea-
keth here to be verilie meat, spirituallie to be receaued in spirit , but not reallie to be recea-
ceaued of the bodie .* This aunswere conteineth two partes . one, that we do

C　receaue Chryst but spiritually : the other,that we do not receaue him re-
allie, and therfor we must receaue him in a figure.Whiche bothe be direct-
lie againft *Origen.*

For the first, *Origen* saieth,that the Iewes had baptisme spiritually,they also ┃ *The Sacra
mentaries.
onelie spiri-
tuull recea-
uing impug
ned by
Origen.*
did feed on Chryst spirituallie, and dranke his blood spirituallie, if we
fede of Chryst none other wise, wherin then doth the newe lawe excell
the olde? What hath the Sacramentes of the Chrystians, more then the fi-
gurs of the Iewes ? But of this more at large in the thirde booke For
the seconde, if we do not receaue Chryst reallie, then (as yt ys saied) we
must nedes receaue him vnder a figure . But *Origen* saieth that the lawe of
the Gospell ys not knowen nowe by figurs and ymages, but by the verie
trueth. In the lawe of Moyses Chryste was eaten in the figure Manna,
Nowe (saieth he) *the flesh of the sonne of God ys eaten in very plain maner .* What
ys that, but that yt ys eaten, reallie, verilie, trulie , and not in figure?
Yf the flesh of the Sonne of God , be eaten with vs in a figure, why doth
he saie,yt ys eatē in plain and opē trueth,and make soche difference betwixt

D　the Lawes?Why did he not raither saie, that yt ys in both lawes eaten in fi-
gure? But if ye marke him well, he appointeth figures to the olde lawe, and
denieth figurs in the newe lawe , and so teacheth that the flesh of Chryst
ys verilie eaten in the Sacrament . Wherby ys reiected the wicked

faing of this Aduerfarie proclamer, that we receaue Chryft none other wife in the Sacrament then the Iewes did in Manna, fauing that they receaued Manna as the figure of Chryft to come, and we our bread as the figure of Chryft that ys comed. For *Origen* faieth that we do not receaue Chryft in a figure. for the lame of God ys not nowe in figurs and images, but in veritie. And thus be the figures of the Auerfaries denied.

Further if we haue not, and eate not Chryft reallie, but in a figure of bread: then was the Lawe of Moyfes moche more excellent, then the newe in that refpecte. For Manna whiche came from heauen fo miraculouflie, and had fo many woonders aboute yt, as the fcripture doth declare, was by all means, and without all comparifon more excellent figure then a poour litle morcell of artificiall bread. Whiche hath no excellencie by mira cle or wonder, but ys a plain comon vfuall thing. All whiche vain confideracions are nothing but vntreuths, wherby the lawe of the Gofpell fhoulde raither be abafed, then duely magnified. Wherfor the fingular inuencions of priuate men lefte, I will creditte the woorde of Chryfte, and his holie infpired men declaring the fame, that the flefh of Chryft ys very meat in dede, feding our foules fpiritullie. wherby we are not inferiour to the Iewes. And ys receaued alfo corporallie for our incorporacion to Chryft, wherby we excell the Iewes.

S. Ambro
fe comēded

And nowe that we haue heard this great auncient thus vnderftanding this text of the very flefh of Chryft, not figuratiuely but verilie and truly, we will nowe heare alfo holy S. *Ambrofe* Bifhoppe of Millan, the mafter of S. Auguftin in Chryftes faith, whofe fame, learning, and holineffe ys knowen to all chryftendom, whofe auncientie ys great, for he liued aboute the year of our lorde 3 8 o. and therfor aboue eleuen hondreth years agon. Whom I thus now commend to thee, Reader, partlie for that he ys not in this ordre as yet alleaged, partelie that his fentēce maie the raither moue thee to creditte the trueth Thus he faieth: *Sicut verus eft Dei filius Dominus nofter Iefus Chriftus,*

li. 9. de Sacra ca. 1. A
plain place
of S. Amb.
for the Pro
clamer.

non quemadmodum homines per gratiam, fed quafi filius ex fubftantia Patris : Ita vera caro (ficut ipfe dixit) quam accipimus, & verus eft potus. As our Lorde Iefus Chryft ys the verie Sonne of God, not as men by grace but as a Sonne of the fubftance of the Father : Euen fo yt ys verie flefh (*as he him felf faieth*) which we do receaue, and very drinke . Thus he . Marke well this faing, and then fhall ye well perceaue the vnderftanding and mening of this fcripture, that yt neither fuffreth yt felf to be vnderftanded of the figure of the flefh of Chryft, neither of the fpirituall flefh of Chryft onely. But of the verie fubftanciall flefh of Chryft . For he maketh yt by fimilitude plain, that as Chryft ys the very Sonne of God, euen of the fubftance of the Father, Euen fo ys yt verie flefh that we receaue. whiche ys thus moche to faie : *As Chryft ys the very Sonne, of God : So ys this verilie flefh that we do receaue.* And as he ys the Sonne of the fubftance of the Father: So ys this flefh whiche we receaue of the fubftance of Chryftes flefhe.

As Chryft
ys the verie
Sōne of the
Father, fo
ys his verie
in flesh
the Sacr.

By whiche woordes of fainct Ambrofe the fonde phanfies of thefe phantaʃticall men be taken awaie. For here ys not alowed the figure of Chryftes flefh, but the thing in dede. not a fpirituall receauing of Chryft onely, but a reall and fpirituall receauing of the fubftanciall flefh of Chryfte. And thus ye maie fee the trueth of the faith to be had in this matter, vttered plainlie withoute any darke maner of fpeache, and fo ftronglie fet furth that yt can not be drawē to any other vnderftanding. And therfor I maie boldely

chalenge

A chalenge this fcripture from the heretikes,which fo euidentlie refufeth the figure,and fo plainly teacheth the reall and fubftanciall prefence of Chryft in the Sacrament.

THE NINETENTH CHAPITER PROCEA-
deth vpon the fame text by Eufebius Emif. and S.Auguftine.

Owe that ye haue heard two auncientes vnderftanding thys text nowe in haude,we will heare one other coople,of eche fide of Chryftes Parliamét houfe one,as the other were,ãd thefe agreyng in one minde,as the other did, which fhall be *Eufebius Emifenus,*and fainct Auguftin. Of the which *Eufebius* being the el der fhall fhewe hys minde,who in hys time was a great learned man, *as fainct Hierõ witneffeth,* and wrote many workes,as againft the Iewes, ãd alfo againft the gentiles,and vpon the Gofpells,and the epiftles of S. Paul alfo. Thys mã being fo profowndly learned,fo auncient in time (*as liuing aboute the yeare of our*

B *Lord.344.*fo famoufe in conftancie of faith,and holy in liuing,ys woorthie of credit. In a certain homelie alleaging this text he fheweth the fame to be vn derftanded thus: *Quia corpus affumptum ablaturus erat ab oculis,& illaturus fideribus, neceffarium erat,vt in die cœnæ facramentum nobis corporis & fanguinis confecraret, vt co leretur iugiter per myfterium,quod femel offerebatur in precium,vt quia quotidiana & in- defeffa currebat pro omnium falute redemptio,perpetua effet redemptionis oblatio, & per- ennis victima illa viueret in memoria,& femper præfens effet in gratia, vera, vnica, & perfecta hoftia,fide æftimanda,non fpecie,neque exteriori cenfenda vifu fed interiori affectu. Vnde cœleftis confirmat authoritas,quia caro mea verè eft cibus, & fanguis meus verè eft potus.* Bicaufe he wolde take awaie hys affumpted bodie from our eyes, and bring yt vppe into the heauens,yt was neceffarie,that in the daie of hys Sup per he fhould confecrate vnto vs the Sacrament of hys bodie and of hys blood,that yt might continuallie be woorfhiped in myfterie, that once for vs was offred in price,that bicaufe the dailie and inceffaunt redemption did renne for the health of all men,the oblacion of the fame redemption fhould be perpetuall,and that perpetual facrifice fhould liue in memorie,and alway

C be prefent in grace . *A true, one onelye , and perfect facrifice,* to be eftemed by faith,and not by outwarde forme,nor to be iudged by the outwarde feight, but by the inwarde affecte . Wherfor the heauenly authoritie confirmeth faing:that my flefh ys verilie meat , and my blood ys verilie drinke . Thus Eufebius.

In this fentence yt ys firft to be confidered, that this authour , declaring the caufe of the inftituciõ of the Sacrament,and of the continuãce of the fa me:and alfo inftructing vs how we fhoulde efteme yt,beleuing ther to be añ other maner of thing,then ther doth appear in outward feight, teacheth vs by the allegaciõ of this fcripture,that yt ys the verie flefh ãd blood of Chrift which we muft efteme by faith,and iudge by our inward affect. And therfor he faieth not,that Chryft doth faie,but that the authoritie of Chryft confir- meth yt fo to be,wherfor thys ys without all controuerfie,that this fcripture now in hand ys by this authour vnderftanded of the Sacrament.

D But here the Aduerfaries do triumphe,as allwais they doo when any au- thour fpeaketh anie woord,that maie by any wrefting be drawen to their vn derftanding,though in verie dede he ment nothing leffe. Firft, *they faie ,* that this authour doth not affirme that Chryft did confecrate hys bo- die and blood,but did confecrate the Sacrament of his bodie and blood. And after faieth again , fpeaking of the facrifice of Chryftes bodie

Eufeb. Emifen. homil.5 pafch.

Obiection of the Sa- cramenta- ries oute of Eufebius.

vpon

vpon the Croffe, that the euerlasting facrifice shoulde liue in memorie, and **E**
allwaies be prefent in grace. But note(*faie they*) that he doth not faie that
that he ys prefent in bodie, but in grace.

Annswer.

But ftaie a while (Reader) and be not troobled with thefe their notes. For
ye shall fee immediatelie that thefe notes shall be the notes of their côfufiô,
ād declaraciô of their falfe doctrin. For God be praifed, though this authour
ment, yea and did fetfurth the true faith of Chryft by this that ys allreadie
alleadged, whiche yet might be peruerted by myfvnderftanding of the malicioufe, who haue peruerted euen the very plain woordes of Chryft: Yet adioining immediatelie to this fentence more of this matter, he addeth woordes fo plain, that they will neither fuffer thêfelues, neither the woords which
the Aduerfaries haue gone aboute to wreft, to be fo vnderftanded as the Aduerfaries wolde haue them. His woordes immediatelie adioined to the fentence of Chryft by him alleaged, be thefe. *Recedat ergo omne infidelitatis ambiguū,*

Eufebius ibid.

*quandoquidem, qui autor eft muneris, ipfe eft teftis veritatis. Nam inuifibilis facerdos vifi-
biles creaturas in fubftantiā corporis & fanguinis fui verbo fuo, fecreta poteftate conuertit.* **F**
Let therfor al doubt of infidelitie go awaie, for truly he that ys the authour
of the gifte: he alfo ys the wittneffe of the trueth. *For the inuifible preift by a fecret
power, with hys woorde doth conuert or turne the vifible creaturs into the fubftance of hys
bodie and blood:* Thus he.

*The prefen
ce plainlie
auouched
by Eufeb.
againft
M. Iuell.*

What can the Aduerfaries now faie? Do ye not heare what this authour
ment by the fainges, whiche the Aduerfaries wolde wreft and peruert to
their wicked vnderftanding? Did not he as well ther as here (though not
with fo plain woordes) teache the treuth of this matter, that Chryftes bodie and blood ys in the Sacrament? Do ye not nowe perceaue that he allead
ged the text of S. Iohn, to declare that the flefh of Chryft was to be eftemed
by faith.

But I wolde the Aduerfaries, and all that be doubtful of the prefence of
Chryftes bleffed bodie and blood in the Sacrament, wolde regarde and
folowe the counfell of this auncient father, *to let all doubte of infidelitie departe
from them.* Which counfeill yf they wel weigh, was geuen for the beleue of **G**
a weightier and greater matter of faith, then to beleue that the bread maye
be or ys the figure of Chryftes bodie. A chryftian man shall do no great mat
ter to beleue foch a thing, which shall be no higher aboue reafon nor no mo
re repugnaunt therto then that ys. But the authour fpeaking thefe woordes
vpon the faing of Chryft, which ys our text now in hand, ment a greater mat
ter to be beleued, whiche reafon can not atteign to, whiche ys, that the flefh
and blood of Chryfte in the Sacrament(which thinges are eftemed by faith
ther to be, though not fo to be iudged by the outward feight) are verily
meat and drinke.

And to shewe vs by whome this great matter ys wrought he addeth: *Qui
authour eft muneris, ipfe eft teftis veritatis.* He that ys authour of the gift, he ys the

*Bread and
wine tur-
ned not in-
to Sacra-
mentall
bread and
wine but in
to the bodie
and bloode
of Chryft.*

wittneffe of the trueth. Chryft ys the wittneffe of the trueth, wherfore he ys
the authour of the gift, that ys of the Sacrament. And yet that he wolde certifie the weake beleuer, he teacheth by what meās the authour doth woork
this miraculoufe gifte and worke, faing: *Inuifibilis facerdos, &c. The inuifible preift
doth turne, the vifible creaturs* (of bread and wine) *into the fubftance of hys bodie and* **H**
bloode. Note that the bread and wine be turned, not to be a facramentall
bread, as the Aduerfaries wolde glofe yt, but into the fubftance of the bodie
and blood of Chryft.

O meruciloufe God what be they that will fticke ftill in the filthie mire
of de-

A of deteſtable hereſie,when they heare the trueth ſo plainly,ſo ſimplie,ſo ex-
preſly ſpoken and vttered,as they be not able to againſt ſaie yt, and that not
of one of this time , neither of the time ſince the hereſie againſt thys Sacrament beganne,but of one being aboue a thouſande years agon , when the
Church was in moſt godly and quiet peace in thys matter. Open yowr eyes
and ſee and beholde yowr filthineſſe,and in time ſeke to gett oute of yt.

Now that this authour being on the one ſide of Chryſtes Parliament hou
ſe,hath ſo manifeſtly declared this our text to be vnderſtanded of the very re
all and ſubſtanciall fleſh of our Saüiour Chryſt in the Sacrament , to be our
verie meat:we will heare the other,which ys S.Auguſtine, who vpon the ſame text ſaieth thus:*Cùm enim cibo & potu id appetant homines, vt non eſuriant,neque
ſitiant,hoc veraciter non præſtat niſi iſte cibus & potus,qui eos à quibus ſumitur immortales & incorruptibiles facit,id eſt,ſocietas ipſa ſanctorum,vbi pax erit,& vnitas plena atque perfecta.Propterea quippe ſicut etiam ante nos intellexerunt homines Dei , Dominus
Ieſus Chriſtus corpus & ſanguinem ſuum in eis rebus commendauit,quæ ad vnum aliquid
rediguntur ex multis . Namque aliud in vnum ex multis granis conficitur & conſtat:*

Tractatu
26. in Ioā.

B *Aliud in vnum ex multis acinis confluit.*Foraſmoche as by meat and drinke men
do this deſire,that they ſhoulde neither hunger,neither thirſt : this doth no
thing truly geue,but that meat and drinke, which maketh them of whom
yt ys receaued immortall and incorruptible,that ys,the feloſhippe of ſaincts,
wher ſhall be peace and vnitie full and perfight.Therfore truly (as alſo before vs the men of God haue vnderſtanded this) *our Lorde Ieſus Chryſt hathe
commended hys bodie and blood in thoſe thinges, which to one certen thing be brought of
manie.*For the one ys made into one of manie graines,and ſo conſiſteth : the
other cometh into one of manie grapes.Thus he.

Three thin
ges in the
Sacrament
to be conſi-
dered.

Yf ye call to remembrance what was ſaied of a certain authour vpon this
text:*The bread whiche I will geue,&c.* Yt will helpe yow well to vnderſtand S.
Auguſtin here.Yt was ſaied ther that in the Sacrament be three things: The
firſt ys the ſacrament onelie,which doth ſignifie or ys the ſign of an holie
thing,and that ys the forme of bread.The ſecond ys that that ys ſignified ād
coteined,which ys the verie bodie of Chryſt.The thirde ys ſignified but not

C coteined,which ys the myſticall bodie of Chryſt,that ys, the copanie of all
hys electe ioined to Chryſt the head by faith ād charitie,for the which thing
this ſacramēt ys called the ſacramēt of vnitie,bicauſe manie be made one,ād
ioined in vnitie:So yt ys called the ſacramēt of loue,bicauſe yt ſignieth that
by loue this vnitie ſhould be brought to paſſe.

Now forſomoch as theſe three thinges be in the Sacramēt,a mā maie ſpeak
of eche of thē ſeuerallie,and yet whē he ſpeaketh but of one,he denieth not
the other.So S.Auguſtin here ſpeaking of the ſocietie of Sainctes , ſpeaketh
of the thirde thing of the Sacramēt,but denieth not the other.   For by the
learning of the Aduerſaries:the Sacramēt ys as wel a ſacrament of Chryſtes
bodie brokē vpō the Croſſe , as yt ys of the vnitie of Chryſtes bodie myſti-
call.And that ye maie perceaue that S.Auguſtin excludeth not the bodie ād
blood of Chryſt frō the Sacrament but raither includeth yt , note , he ſaied
that *our Lord Ieſus Chryſt commended his bodie and blood in theſe thinges,which be made
one of manie,*that by the bread made of manie graines,nowe turned into one
bodie of Chryſt,and by the wine made of manie grapes, nowe turned into

D the bloode of Chryſt,all we(as S.Paule ſaieth)eating of this one bread, and
drinking of this one cuppe,might be one bodie in Chryſte, and eche of vs
one an others membres.

That S.Auguſtin denieth not the very preſence of Chryſt in the Sacramēt

(though here vpon S. Iohn he fpeaketh moch of the effect of the fame, the E confideracion wherof we haue declared in the expofition of the laft text before this) yt doth appear in a great nombre of places, of the whiche ma-nie haue ben allready alleaged, and mo by Gods helpe fhall be. As this:

Auguft. li.   *Hoc eft quod dicimus, quod modis omnibus approbare contendimus , facrificium Eccle-*
fente. Prof.   *fia duobus modis confici, duobus conftare: vifibili elementorum fpecie, & inuifibili Domini noftri Iefu Chrifti carne & fanguine, & facramento, & re facramenti, id eft, corpore Chrifti. Sicut Chrifti perfona conftat ex Deo & homine, cum ipfe Chriftus verus fit Deus, & verus fit homo. quia omnis res illarum rerum naturam & veritatem in fe con-tinet ex quibus conficitur : Conficitur autem facrificium Ecclefia duobus , facramento, & re facramenti : id eft, corpore Chrifti . Eft ergo facramentum , & res facra-*

Sacrifice of   *menti.* This ys yt, whiche we faie , whiche by all means we labour to
the Church   approue, that the Sacrifice of the Churche ys made by two means, and
confifteth   confiftes of two thinges , *of the vifible forme of the Elementes, and the inui-*
of the vifi-   *fible flesh and bloode of our Lorde Iefus Chryft,* the Sacrament, and the thing
ble formes   of the Sacrament, that ys to faie , *the bodie of Chryfte .* As the perfon of
of bread ād   Chryft ys of God and man, for as moche as he ys very God and very man F
wine and   For euery thing doth contein in yt the nature and trueth of thofe, thinges, of
the inuifi-   the whiche yt ys made. The Sacrifice of the Chruche ys made of two thin-
ble flesh ād   ges: of the Sacramēt and the thing of the Sacrament, that ys, the bodie of
blood of   Chryft. Thus farre S. Auguftin.
Chryft.

S. Auguft.   Doth he not here in this fentence teache the prefence of Chryftes bodie in
teacheth   the Sacramēt, yes, yf ye note wcl, he teacheth three thinges by expreffe wor-
three thiu-   des , whiche the Aduerfaries deinie, that ys, that the Churche hath a Sacri-
ges in one   fice, that therin ys a facrament, whiche he expowndeth to be the formes of
fentence   the Elementes, that ys, of bread and vine, that ther ys alfo prefent the ve-
againft the   rie bodie and blood of Chryft, which he calleth the thing of the Sacrament
Sacramen-   bicaufe yt ys the thing that the Sacrament doth fignifie . And bycaufe
taries.   men fhoulde not cauille faing that the bodie and bloode of Chryft be not
verilie prefent, but fignified : He declareth by the fimilitude of Chryfts perfon, that as verilie as Chryft being God and man hath both the nature of God and the nature of mam : So verilie hath the facrifice of the Sacra-ment, that ys, *the outwarde formes of bread and wine, and the bodie and blood of Chryft.* G

     Nowe if the Aduerfaries will faie, that in the Sacrifice of the Churche, ther ys not really either the formes of bread and wine or the verie bodie and blood of Chryft : then muft they likewife faie that in the perfon of Chryft, ther ys not reallie, either the nature of man or the nature of God, whiche both are to deteftable to be fpokē of the mouthe of a Chryften man. And fo trulie ys the other alfo. And yet not cōtented with this fimilitude, which ys abundantlie fufficient, he proceedeth to proue the fame by this faing *Euery thing* (faieth he) *conteineth in yt the nature and trueth of the thinges that yt ys made of.* The Sacrifice of the Churche ys made of the Sacrament and the bodie and blood of Chryft. Wherfore S. Auguftine thus concludeth vpon this reafon: *Eft igitur facramentū, & res facramenti corpus Chrifti .* Ther ys therfor the Sacra-ment, and the thing of the Sacrament, the bodie of Chryfte.

     In thefe wordes I fuppofe S . Auguftin hath fo plainly expreffed and declared his faith in this matter, that yt can not fuffer any other opinion iuftlie to be conceaued of him. For yf we that haue liued, and liue in this H time of peftilent herefie , wolde againft this herefie of the Sacrament, ftudie to deuife, to fpeake or write the plaineft woordes that might impugne this herefie, and declare fullie our faith, we can no more faie

                                                                  nor

A nor by better and plainer woordes do the fame, then fainéte Auguſtin hath here doen. Wherfore what fo euer he did ſpeake or write to any partie or parties according to the diſpoſition, and condicion of them, ſomtime ſpeaking of the miſticall bodie of Chryſt ſignified by this ſacrament, ſomtime onely of the ſpirituall receauing of Chryſt, ſomtime darkely for the maner of the audience: yet be well aſſured his faith can not be otherwiſe for the preſence then here ys declared, for ſomoch as theſe woordes can bear no other ſenſe nor mening then they in the outwarde face do ſhowe.

Therfore, *Reader*, be not caried awaie by the falſe cōmentes that naughtie men make of S. Auguſtins woordes. For though he ſpeake ſomtime obſcurelie, as yt maie appeare to haue a doubtfull vnderſtanding, as before we ende this chapiter of S. Iohn thowe ſhalt heare: yet for ſomoche as fainéte Auguſtin had but one faithe, whiche ys ſo plainly here profeſſed and ſett furth, be well aſſured that he neuer varieth or goeth from and againſt this. But I tarie to long vpon this, ſeing ther be diuerſe cooples mo to be hearde

B vpon this text.

THE TWENTETH CHAP. PROCEADETH
vpon the ſame text by fainét Hilarie and Euthymius.

S. Hilarye cōmended.

Ainéte Hilarie ys a great auncient of Chryſtes houſe liuinge aboute the 360 yeare after Chryſte, and not onelie auncient, but alſo right excellent in learning, and famouſlie conſtant in faithe. His ex cellencie in learning ys not onely teſtified by fainéte Hierom, who faieth he wrote manie learned woorkes, but alſo by *Rufinus*, who faieth he was accompted the great light in his time to all Fraunce, and Italie. His conſtancie in faith ys well declared, that notwithſtanding the Emperours and Princes, ād manie Biſhopps were the fauourers of the hereſie of the Arians: yet he neither moued with the fauour of mightie and great men, neither feared with their puniſhment, or baniſhment, did conſtantlie reſiſt the faied hereſie, and alſo wrote learned bookes againſt yt. This authour writteh thus:

Li. 8. de Trinitate.

C *Quæ ſcripta ſunt legamus, & quæ legerimus intelligamus, & tunc perfectæ fidei fungemur officio. De naturali in nobis Chriſti veritate quæ diſcimus, niſi ab eo diſcimus, ſtulte atque impiè diſcimus. ipſe enim ait: Caro mea verè eſt eſca, & ſanguis meus verè eſt potus. Qui edit carnem meam, & bibit ſanguinem meum, in me manet, & ego in eo. De veritate carnis, & ſanguinis non eſt relictus ambigendi locus. Nunc enim & ipſius Domini profeſſione, & fide noſtra verè caro eſt, et verè ſanguis eſt. Et hæc accepta atque hauſta id efficiunt, vt et nos in Chriſto, et Chriſtus in nobis ſit.* Let vs read thoſe thinges that be written, and ſoche thinges as we read let vs vnderſtand. and then ſhall we perfeételie do the office of our faith. Soche thinges as we learn of the natu-*Of the ve-* rall veritie of Chryſt in vs, except we learn of him, we learn fooliſhlie and *ritie of* vngodlie. For he doth faie: *My fleſh ys verilie meat, and my blood ys verilie drinke Chryſtes He that eateth my fleſh, and drinketh my blood dwelleth in me, and I in him.* Of the ve-*fleſh and* ritie of the fleſh and bood ther ys no place left to doubte. For nowe both by *Sacr. ther* the plain ſpeaking of our Lorde him ſelf: and by our faith yt ys verilie fleſh, *ys no doubt* and verilie bloode. And theſe taken and dronken do bring it to paſſe, that both we be in Chryſt, and Chryſt in vs. Thus he.

D Among many goodlie notes tobe gathered in this faing, three thinges will I breifly note. The firſt ys, that this our text ys vnderſtanded of the Sacrament, but not of the Sacrament as of a bare figure, but as conteining the thi g that yt dothe ſignifie, whiche thing ys the bodie and bloode of Chryſt

Z iiij   And

And this matter appeareth so plain, so euident and so certen to this great
learned and holy man, that by the instruction that faithe gaue him to vnderstande this scripture, he saied that *of the veritie of Chrystis flesh and bloode ther*
ys no place to doubte. And why was ther no place left to doubt? He sheweth
the cause: *For nowe* (saieth he) *by the saing of oure Lorde, and our faith, it ys verilie*
flesh and verilie bloode.

A plain sa-
ing for M.
Iuell.

O this was a blessed simplicitie, a godlie obedience, that curiously wolde
not aske with the Iewes, *howe yt should be flesh and bloode, and howe his flesh and*
bloode shoulde be meate, but reuerently captiuating his vnderstanding to the
obsequie of Chryst saieth : by cause Chryst did saie, *that his flesh was verilie*
*meate,*ther ys no place of doubte lefte, but that yt ys flesh in dede, and bloode in dede.

And in this saing yt ys not to be ouer slipped, that he saith: *that by the saing*
of our Lorde and our faith : So that he putteth our faith to the saing of Chryst,
not that our faith ys a woorker with the saing of Chryst to woorke the substance of the thing : but that as by the saing of Chryst, the thing in yt self
ys most certenly true : so by faith beleuing and accepting yt, yt ys certen
also to vs. For as Chryste hath died for the sinnes of the wholl worlde,
whiche in yt self ys most certen: So yet to all yt ys not so certen, but to soche
as by faith beleue and accepte yt. And so yt ys also certen to vs . Wherfor
though to S. Hilary by the faith that he gaue to Chrystes woorde yt was
very flesh and very blood: yet to heretikes that haue not soche faith as Hilary had, yt ys not the flesh and bloode of Chryst, not that yt ys not so
in dede, but vnto them yt ys as though yt wer not so. How moch then maie
they be abasshed at this saing of S. Hilary, who declareth that by his faith
he beleued yt to be the very flesh and blood of Chryst, and they like shamelesse obstinate men leauing the faith that S. Hilary had, and cleauing to their
owne inuented imaginacions and naturall reason, saie they can not beleue
yt. But God geue them a better minde.

Faith how
yt ys requi-
site in the
Sacrament

The second note ys, *that this verie flesh and verie bloode ys taken of vs, and droke*
*of vs,*whiche dothe teache vs the corporall receauing of Chryst in the Sacrament, corporall I saie in two respectes, that bothe we receaue his very reall
and substacial dodie, and that we with our bodie and into our bodie receaue that same self blessed bodie. So yt ys a corporall receipt in respecte of the
thing receaued, and of the receauer also,

Flesh and
blood of
Chryst ve-
rilie eaten
and dronke
in the Sacr.

This thing the same S. Hilarie in the same booke dothe open more at large, when he saieth : *Si enim verè verbum caro factum est, & nos verè verbum carnē*
cibo Dominico sumimus, quomodò non naturaliter in nobis manere existimandus est, qui &
naturam carnis nostræ iam inseparabilem sibi natus assumpsit, & naturam carnis suæ, ad
naturam æternitatis sub sacramento nobis communicandæ carnis admiscuit, Yf the worde
were verilie made flesh, and we receaue the woorde made very flesh in our
Lordes meat, howe ys yt to be thought that he doth not naturallie abide in
vs, who being born man hathe bothe taken the nature of our flesh vpon him
nowe inseparablie, and also vnder the Sacrament of his flesh to be comuni-
cated vnto vs, hath admixed the nature of his flesh to the nature of the eternitie? Thus he.

Hilar ibid.

Chryst na-
turallie in
vs by re-
ceipt of the
Sacra.

In the whiche saing what wolde we wishe to be more plainly spoken, thā
that the Sonne of God was made flesh, and that same Sonne of God
being made flesh, we receaue in the Lordes meate? Neither maie that glose
here be hearde that we receaue him verilie in the Sacrament but spiritually,
For that whiche foloweth in the text will not beare that glose. Whiche ys
　　　　　　　　　　　　　　　　　　　　　　　　　　　　　　　when

A plain
place of S.
Hilar. for
the Procla
mer.

he faieth : *Howe ys he to be thought not naturallie to abide in vs?* Marke well thefe

A woordes howe can Chryfte naturallie abide in vs, but by the receipt of his naturall flefh and bodie? The fpirituall receauing woorketh not a naturall abiding, but eche of them agreablie, the fpirituall receauing maketh a fpirituall abiding, and the corporall receauing of his naturall bodie maketh a naturall abiding of Chryft in vs. Wherfor if he be naturally abiding in vs by the receipt of his flefh in the Sacrament, that receipt ys agreablie of his very naturall and reall flefh into our naturall bodies, and then yt muft nedes be that we receaue Chryftes bodie really in the Sacrament.

The thirde note ys, that Chryfte thus receaued woorketh in vs this effect, that we therby be in Chryfte, and Chryft in vs, of the whiche maner of being, the text whiche foloweth in fainte Iohn, will geue vs occafiõ to fpeake more. Wherfor we will diffre yt till we come thither.

And now wil we come to *Euthymius* who in fewe woordes faith thus: *Caro*

In.6.Ioan.

mea verè eſt cibus. verus eſt cibus ſiue aptiſſimus, vtpote animã, quæ propriiſſima hominis

My fleſhys

B *pars eſt, nutriẽs. Et ſimiliter de ſanguine. Aut hoc dixit confirmans, quod nõ enigmaticè neq;*

verilie

parabolicè loqueretur. My flefh ys meat in dede. Yt ys the verie or moft apteft

meat:ys no

meate, as whiche nourifheth the foule, whiche ys the moft proprieft or

parabolical

wourthieft parte of a man. And likewife of the blood, Orells he faied thus

or figurati-

confirming that he did fpeake neither obfcurelie, nor parabolicallie. Thus

ue ſpeache.

Euthymius. Doeft thowe not perceaue (reader) that one fpirit was in the mouthe of all thefe holie and auncient Fathers? do they not agree in fenten ce? Marke well howe this Auncient Father expowndeth this text, remouing and denieng the figure, wherby he declareth him felf to vnderftand this text of the very reall flefh of Chryft, as Hilarie doth. *yt ys* (faieth he) *no parabolicall ſpeache : yt ys no figuratiue ſpeache*, but yt ys a plain fpeache fignifieng no other waies then the woordes fownde, that ys the very flefh and the very bloode, not the figure of them. Whiche maner of expofition thowe fhallt fee (Reader) in other that do folowe, efpeciallie in Chryfoftome and Theophilact. Wherfor comminge to them remembre this, and conferr thẽ to gether, and thowe fhalt finde good matter, and agreable to the trueth of

C this affercion.

THE ONE AND TVENTETH CHAPITER CONTI-
nueth the ſame expoſition by Chryſoſtome and Lira.

Heras ye haue hitherto hearde the fentẽces of the Fathers and auncientes of the higher houfe vpon this text nowe in hande : Herafter for the better declaracion of the confonãt doctrine of this trueth in all times, and for the more confufion of the Aduerfaries who fo malicioufly haue depraued the writers of the later time : I will as before ys promifed ioin to fome of the elder fort, fome of the yõger.

Of the whiche the firft coople fhall be Chryfoftome and Lira, the one a gre-

Homil.46.

cian and of the higher houfe, the other a latin and of the lower howfe (as

in Ioan.

ye haue heard) Chryfoftome vpon this text faieth thus: *Quid autem ſignat: Caro*

Chryſt in

mea verè eſt cibus, & ſanguis meus verè eſt potus? Aut quòd is eſt verus cibus, qui ſaluat

the ſixt of

D *animam : aut vt eos in prædictis confirmet, ne obſcurè locutum in parabolis arbitrarentur.*

S.Iohn ſpa-

What meneth this fainge: *My fleſh ys verilie meat, and my bloode ys verilie drinke*

ke not para

Either that this ys the true meat that faueth the foule, or ells that he might

bolicallie

confirme them leaft they fhoulde thinke that he had fpoken obfcurelie in

or obſcure-

parables

lie.

                 Wher

Wher note that Chrysostome saieth, that Chryst did speake these woor- **E**
des in plain speache, and not darkelie in paraboles. Whiche saing wonder-
fully confuteth the Aduersaries. For yf Chryst did not speake parabolicallie,
then he ment that the woordes shoulde signifie no other thing then in their
propre significacion they do signifie, and then must yt nedes be that Chryst
spake here of his very flesh and of his very blood with oute all obscuritie or
darke maner of speache by figures, tropes, similitudes or paraboles, whiche
the Aduersaries wolde here ensparse. *My flesh is meate in dede, and my blood is
drinke in dede,* ys no obscure speache, nor no figuratiue speache *(saieth Chrisostome)* let the Aduersaries then wrest and wring, and peruert the scriptures as
they list, I will creditt holy Chrysostom and the churche that he liued in
before anie of the Aduersaries, and their malignant church, whiche they liue
in. Yf the Proclamer will not saie that this ys a plain saing when ther ys no
parbole in yt: I knowe not what he will saie ys plain, these woordes being of
them selues so plain.

Nowe whether the exposition of *Lira,* who was of the latin Churche, and **F**
of the later daies, be consonant and agreable to Chrysostome or not let vs
heare. vpon the same text he saieth: *Hic ostenditur huius Sacramenti veritas. Christus
enim frequenter parabolicè Discipulis loquebatur. Et ideo, ne crederent quòd caro eius continere-
tur in hoc sacramento Eucharistiæ tantummodò sicut in signo, ideo hoc remouet dicens: Caro
mea verè est cibus, quia hic sumitur realiter, & non figuratiuè. Et eodem modo est de sanguine sub specie vini, & ideo subdit: Et sanguis meus verè est potus. Dicitur etiam caro
Christi verè cibus, & sanguis eius verè potus, quia reficiunt animam, quæ est immortalis.
Cibus autem corporalis tantùm reficit corpus quod est corruptibile.* Here ys shewed
(saieth Lira) the veritie of this Sacrament. For Chryst oftentimes did speake
to his disciples parabolicallie. And therfor leest they shoulde beleue, that
this flesh were conteined in this Sacrament onely as in a figure: he remoueth that, saing: *my flesh ys verily meat.* For yt ys here receaued really, and not
figuratiuely. And after the same maner ys yt of the bloode, vnder the forme
of wine. The flesh of Chryst ys also called meat in dede and his bloode drink
in dede, bicause they refresh the soule, whiche ys immortall. But corporall **G**
meat refresheth onelie the bodie, whiche ys corruptible. Thus he.

Remembre. Reader, the exposition of Chrysostome, wherin he saied two
thinges: The one that Chryst saieth, *that his flesh ys verily meat,* bicause yt saueth the soule: The other that Chryste so saied, *bicause he wolde confirme them
in the forsaied thinges that he did not speake in paraboles.* And nowe conferr this
authour to him, and see yf he speake anie other thing, but euen the same two
thinges that Chrysostom did. For wher Chrysostome saieth, *that yt ys the true
meat that saueth the soule:* This authour saieth, *that the bodie of Chryst ys called verily meate, and his bloode verily drink, bicause they refresh the soule, whiche ys immortall.*
Chrysostome saieth, that Chryst wolde shewe him self not to speake nowe
in paraboles: This authour more at large saieth, that bicause Chryst did ofte
speake parabolicallie, leaste they shoulde thinke or beleue, that his flesh were
conteined in the Sacrament, as in a signe onlie, therfor he remoueth that,
saing, that this flesh ys verily meat, bicause yt ys receaued really, and
not figuratiuely.

Thus ye see agreement betwen these authours, and one trueth spoken **H**
here amost by one maner of woordes of him that did write aboue a thousande yeares agone, and of him that did write not fullie three hundreth years
agon. Wherby ye maie perceaue that the same doctrine hathe ben continued and taught in these latter years by writers of late time. whiche was
                                                            receaued

*A a plain
saing of
Chrysost.
for M. Iuel.*

*Lira in 6.
Ioann.*

*The flesh
of Chryst
in the Sa.
eaten real-
lie, not fi-
gurat.*

A receaued and taught in the churche in auncient time, as touching thexposition of this scripture we haue in hande.

THE TVO AND TVENTETH CHAP. CONTInueth yet thexposition of the same text by S. Cyrill, and Dionise

AS in the chapter last before ye hearde one coople farre distant in time of ther lifes, but consonant in sownde of their faithe: So shall ye in this chapter heare an other coople, the one very auncient, the other of later time, likewise agreablie declaring their faith and opening the right sense of our text nowe yet in hande. This coople shall be *Cyrill* and *Dionise* the *Carthusian*. the one of the greke churche, the other of the latin churche, as they before alleadged were. S. Cyrill saieth thus : *Vmbram & figuram nosti? Disce ipsam rei veritatem. Caro enim mea (inquit) verè est cibus, & sanguis meus verè est potus. Rursus distinguit inter mysticam benedictionem, & Manna, aquarum fluenta ex lapide, & calicis sancti communicationem, ne magis Manna miraculũ admirentur, sed ipsum potius suscipiant, qui cælestis panis est, & æternæ vitæ largitor. Mannæ namque alimentum non æternam vitam, sed breue famis remedium attulit. Non erat ergo ille verus cibus. Sanctũ verò Christi corpus ad immortalitatem, & vitam æternam nutriens cibus est. Aqua etiam illa è petra ad momentum sitim corporalem leuabat, nec quicquam adferebat præterea. Non erat ergo potus ille verus, sed verus potus est sanguis Christi quo radicitus mors euertitur, & destruitur. Non enim hominis simpliciter sanguis est, sed eius, qui naturali vitæ coniunctus, vita effectus est.* Hauest thowe knowen the shadowe and the figure? Learn the verie trueth of the thing *My flesh*)saieth he) *ys meat in dede, and my bloode ys drinke in dede.* He doth again make a distinction betwixt the misticall benediction, and Manna : the streames of waters oute of the rocke, and the partaking of the holy cuppe : leaste they shoulde more esteem the miracle of Manna, but raither shoulde receaue him, the whiche ys the heauenly bread and the geuer of eternall life. For the foode Manna did not bringe eternall life : but a short remedie of hungar. *but the holie boodie of Chryste ys a meat nourishinge to immortalitie and eternall life.* That water also oute of the stone, did for a litle while ease the bodilie thrist : *but the true drinke ys the bloode of Iesus Chryst,* by the whiche death ys turned vppe by the rootes and destroied. *Yt ys not the blood of a bare man, but of him, who beinge conioined to the naturall life ys made life.* Thus farre sainct Cyrill.

Do ye not perceaue in these woordes that he speaketh as moch and the very same in sense, though not in woordes that Chrysostom did? He had treacted before of the paschall lambe, and therby moued the Iewes, to consider the Shadowes of Moyses lawe, wherby being instructed, they shoulde be the readier to vnderstande, these misteries of the newe testament, and therfor saieth : *Hauest thowe knowen the figure, learn also the very trueth of the thing.* what ys that? *My flesh ys meat in, dede and my bloode ys drinke in dede.*

Marke then (*Reader*) the figures were the Paschall lambe, Manna, and the water flowing oute of the stone : The veritie (saieth he) that these figures did prefigurate, ys that trueth that Chryst vttered, saing : *My flesh ys meat in dede.* Yf this be the veritie, then yt ys not a figure : yf yt be no figure, then Chryst speaking yt, spake neither parabole, nor figure, as the last coople hath also taught. And in this ye perceaue again the confutacion of the Aduersaries, that this ys spoke of Chrystes very flesh in the Sacramet, and that

ys

Li.4.ca. 16. in Ioã.

Figures of the olde Lawe, and veritie of the newe, be as the shadow ãd the thing shadowed.

yt ys no figuratiue fpeache as they wolde feign yt to be: but a fpeache teac-　**E**
hing the thinge to be reallie and verilie prefent,

But that I be not to tedioufe in tarieng to long vpõ euery authour, I will
faie no more of this mans teftimonie at this prefent, both for the caufe alleged, and alfo that through all the fixt chapiter of faincte Iohn, and allmoft
through all the gofpell of faincte Iohn, he ys not onely plentifull inma-
king mencion of this matter, but alfo as plain as he ys plentifull. And that
knowe the aduerfaries right well. Therfor we will heare what Dionife
Dionyf. Carthus in Ioan. 6.
who ys ioined to him doth faie: Thus I teade ther: *Caro mea verè eſt ci-*
bus, & ſanguis meus verè eſt potus. Hoc ait Saluator, ne putaretur parabolicè lo-
qui ſolito more, ita quòd carnem ſuam diceret panem, quia ſignificaretur per pa-
nem, & eſſet ſub forma panis ſolùm ſicut in ſigno: vel propter aliquam proprie-
tatem cum pane cibus diceretur, quomodò dicit Apoſtolus: Petra erat Chriſtus, que-
niam figurauit Chriſtum. Et Eſaias: Verè fœnum eſt populus, propter conuenien-
tiam quandam. Et infrà ait de ſeipſo Saluator: Ego ſum vitis vera. Ad inſinuan-　**F**
dum ergo quòd caro ſua ſit verè & ſubſtantialiter ſub ſpecie panis, veraciterque ſu-
matur à communicante: Sanguis quoque ipſius verè ſub ſpecie vini contineatur, &
recipiatur, adiecit: Caro mea, id eſt, corpus (ſumitur enim nunc caro, non prout
oſſa excludit, pro toto corpore, neruos, venas, & oſſa habente) verè eſt cibus,
animæ non corporis, quia non viſibiliter, nec corporaliter ſumitur, quamuis rerum
corpus ſumatur. My flefh ys verily meat, and my blood ys verilie diin-
ke. Thus faied our Sauiour leeft he fhoulde be thought after his cufto-
mable maner to fpeake parabolicallie, fo that he fhoulde call his flefh
bread, bicaufe yt fhoulde be fignified by the bread, and fhoulde be
vnder the forme of bread onelie as in a figne. Or that yt fhoulde be called
meat, for fome propretie that yt hath with bread. Euen as the Apoftle doth
The verie flesh of Chryſt vn- der the for- me of bre- ad, and his verie blood vnder the forme of vine.
faie: *The ſtone was Chryſt,* bicaufe yt figured Chryft. And Efaie: *Truly the people*
ys graſſe, for a certain agrement to the fame. And in the gofpell our Sauiour
faieth of him felf: *I am the true vine.* To infinuate therfor vnto vs, that his
flefh ys verilie and fubftãciallie vnder the forme of bread, and that yt ys truly
receaued of the cõmunicant, and his bloode alfo ys conteined in dede vn-　**G**
der the forme of wine, and ys receaued, he added: *My flesh:* that ys to faie, *my*
bodie (For flefh ys nowe here taken, not as yt doth exclude the bones, but
for the wholl dodie, hauing, finewes, vaines and bones) *ys verilie meat,* of the
foule, not of the bodie. For yt ys not taken or receaued vifible, nor corporallie, although the verie bodie be receiued. Thus moche Dionife.

Although I nede not here to note anie thing, wher euery fentéce, and peice
of the fame ys fo plainly laied furth to our vnderftanding: yet I haue thought
yt good not to ouerpaffe to aduertife thee (reader) that this authour, though
he fpeake thus plain: yet he diffenteth not frõ the auncíetes before alleaged,
namelie Chryfoftom and Cyrill. For as they faied that this faing of Chryft
ys no parable, nor figure nor darke fpeache: but conteining the veritie, and
the very thing in deed, that by figurs was perfigurated: So this authour drawing by the fame line faieth, that wher Chryft was accuftomed to fpeake
parabolicallie: yet to geue vs to vnderftand that yt was neither figure nor
parabole that he fpake of here, but that yt was his flefh verilie and fubftanciallie, that ys vnder the forme of bread and his bloode in verie dede,　**H**
that ys vnder the forme of wine. He faied, my flefh (whiche ys here taken
for the wholl bodie) this wholl bodie ys verilie meate.

Secondarely, where fome of them faied, yt was verie meat bicaufe yt faued
the foule: Some other faied yt was the meat of the foule, bicaufe yt brought

A to the foule immortalitie, and euerlasting life: so this Authour also saieth, that yt ys the meate of the foule, not of the bodie. Thus in these pointes ye see no dissencion betwixt the Authours of auncient time, and the Authours of the later time.

Yf ye obiecte that Chrysostome did vse no soche woordes as this Authour dothe. For Chrysostome, though he saied that yt was the very meat that saued the foule: yet he did not saie that this very meat was vnder the formes of bread and wine, as this man doeth.

Ys this, trowe yow, abhorring from the sainges of the auncient Fathers, though Chrysostom dothe not here speake yt by expresse woordes as this Authour doth? Dothe not Chrysostome saie that this ys no parabolicall speache? wherby what dothe he ells insinuate, but that ther ys the thing euen as yt ys spoken of Chryst: whiche ys the verie flesh the very meat of the faithfull? Yf this flesh be verilie ther, as most certenly yt ys, and we do see but the forme of bread, then yt ys ther vnder the forme of bread.

B But to declare vnto yow that this maner of speache and wordes ys not of late vsage, or of late or newe inuencion, harke what sainct Augustin saieth. *Caro eius est, quam forma panis opertam in Sacramento accipimus: & sanguis eius est, quem sub vini specie & sapore potamus.* Yt ys the flesh of him, whiche we receaue, couered in the Sacrament vnder forme of bread. And yt ys the blood of him, whiche we drinke vnder the forme and taste of wine.

Lib. sente. Prosp. A plain place for M. Iuell.

Do ye not heare in these woordes of Saint Augustine, the same forme of woordes, vsed by Dionise? Do ye not heare the forme of bread and wine? Do ye not heare that Chrystes flesh ys vnder the one, and his bloode vnder the other? Why then do ye sticke still in the mire? Why do ye not frame your selues to be obedient to the faith of Crystes Churche? Or do ye thinke that ye alone haue the true faithe, whiche the Churche had not in the time of sainct Augustine? Why do ye perseuere, deceauing the C simple, and vnlearned, feading them with lies in stead of trueth, with heresie in stead of faith, and with Scisme in stead of vnitie of Gods religion. Saie not nowe(*as yt hath ben your common slaunder*) that these late writers were full of corrupte doctrine. For ye see yet that they teache no other doctrine in this matter then the auncient Fathers did.

Formes of bread and wine a speache knowen to S. Augu.

And yet in this saing of sainct Augustine, ther ys one thing wourthie of note, that wher the Aduersaries trauailed to impugne this doctrine of Chrystes being in the Sacrament vnder the formes of bread and wine, by the alteracion or chaunge of the significacion of this woorde, *species*, saing that the woorde doth signifie the nature or kinde of a thinge, and not the outwaade forme: Let them here weigh well and consider saincte Augustines maner of speache, who taketh here this woorde, *species*, applied to the wine, in the same significacion that he taketh, *forma*, applied to the bread. But this woorde, *forma*, ys taken for the outwarde forme, wherfor this woorde, *species*, must nedes be so likewise.

Species and forma vsed both in one significaciō.

D And here also I wolde wish the vnlearned that haue erred in this matter that they wolde be aduertised by this good Father and learned man Dionise, that they will not abuse these sentences of the scripture: *Petra erat Christus.&, verè fœnum est populus:* The stone was Chryste. and, Truly the people ys grasse: to the maintenaunce of their errour, that bycause these be spoken figuratiuelie, therfor this also: *Caro verè est cibus:* My flesh ys *meate in verie dede.* Ys fpoken figuratiuelie. For yf ye will fo, then might ye **E** make thefe fentences : *Tu es Chriſtus filius Dei viui.* Thowe arte Chryſt the Sonne of the liuing God: *Et verè filius Dei erat iſte,* And *trulie this man was the Sonne of God:* ye might, I faie, make thefe fentences, figuratiue fpeaches, and fo confequentlie fubuert the fenfe of holie fcripture and all our faith.

Therfor vnderſtand by this Authour, that they be figuratiue fpeaches , or fpeaches fo vfed for fome agreableneffe of the thinges compared together, and do not ouertwartly turn that to impugne the trueth, that ys brought in example for the declaracion of the trueth , as I hearde a Reader do in Cambridge, who being willing to pleafe the worlde he liued in, be-

Schoole argumentes made for the opening of trueth, produced of a Proteſtant to cōfirme a falfe doctrine.

gan to impugne the prefence of Chryſt in the Sacrament, and the Maffe. And to make his matter good in apparaunce, he induced manie argumentes and delighted him felf very moche in them, as by whiche his matter was moche confirmed and ſtrengthed, as he thought. In the hearing of the argumentes, methought they were foche as I had readde, wherfor the lecture being ended, I repared to my ſtudie, and fuppofing I had readde thē in Dun- **F** ce, I tooke him in hande, and turned, and fownde them. Whiche as Dunce had moued againſt the truthe , to be folued for the better declaracion and opening of the trueth: So did this man bring them in againſt the truth , to confirme his falfe doctrine. So that foche argument as Dunce framed for an argument of impugnacion: this reader vfed yt as an argument of confirmacion. And fo I feare verilie, that manie feke good Authours , and what they finde in them to impugn falfheade , with that do they defende and fortifie the fame. Wherfor, reader , do not the like here, that what this Authour bringeth in for a better and further declaracion of the trueth, thowe take yt to impugne the trueth.

I thought yt good alfo not to omitte that this Authour faieth that we *receaue in the Sacrament the very reall, and wholl bodie of Chryſt, with veines , ſunnewes, and bones,* for that I haue hearde fome of the Iewifh Capharnaites aske, what *do we receaue Chryſtes bodie bones and all? Howe can yt come wholl in to my mouthe?* Ah thow man of litle faith, why doeſt thowe doubte, bicaufe thowe imagi- **G**

The prefence of Chriſtes bodie in the Sac. no more impoſſible thē many other his workes, which feme as impoſſible to naturall knowledge.

neſt with the Capharnaites no other prefence, but after the groffe corporall maner? But thowe erreſt fowllie. He ys ther fpirituallie, and yet verilie , and really, and no more to be thought impoffiblie to thee , than that that bodie was born of a virgen : then that yt walked vpon the fea : then that yt was transfigurated on the mount: then that yt rofe from death life: then that yt paffed oute of the graue the monument being ſtill faſt fhett and clofe : then that yt entred into the Apoſtles the doores being fhett: then that yt afcended into heauen: all whiche factes yf thowe meafure by naturall knowledge, they will feme as vnpoffible as the other. For naturall knowledge wondereth and faieth: howe coulde the bodie of Chryſt being a perfect bodie. Hauing fleſh and bones paffe oute of the fepulchre, the fepulchre not being opened but ſtill clofed and fhett? howe coulde that bodie hauing (as ys faied) fleſh and bones, enter into the difciples the doores ſtill being fhett? So doth yt alfo faie : Howe can a man receaue the wholl bodie of Chryſt with his mouth? But as thefe two former thinges be made poffible to thee by faith, **H** let this third fo be alfo . For yf thowe beleue them bicaufe the fcripture teacheth thee : beleue the fcripture and the holie Fathers alfo which teache thee, that this bodie of Chryſt ys fo prefent , and fo receaued . And yf yt be prefent, yt muſt nedes be that fame bodie that was born , that was crucified . But not as yt was born and crucified.

That

A That fame bodie in fubftance, not the fame in qualitie and condicion. But yet the verie fame wholl bodie. So did Chryftome teache that we fhoulde take yt faing thus: *Et quando id propofitum videris, dic tecum, propter hoc corpus non amplius terra & cinis ego fum, hoc corpus crucifixum, verberatum, morte victum non eft. Hoc idem corpus cruentatum, lancea vulneratum, fontes fanguinis & aquæ, vniuerfo orbi falutares fcaturiuit.* When thowe (faieth Chryfoftom fpeaking of the Sacrament) feift that thing fett furth, faie with thy felf, for this bodie I am no more earth and afhes. This bodie crucified and beaten, was not ouercomed with death. This fame verie bodie bloodied and wounded with a fpeare, hath lett runne oute fountains of water and bloode holfome to all the worlde. Thus he.

> *In 10.1Co. Hom.24.*

Note, Reader, that Chryfoftom willeth yowe, when ye fee the Sacrament fett furth, to faie with your felf. *This bodie being crucified, was not ouercomed with death. This fame verie bodie wounded with a fpeare, fent holfom ftreanies of water aud bloode to the worlde.* Wherby ye are taught, that the fame bodie ys in the Sacrament, that was crucified. And therfor are ye not willed to faie at the

> *The fame bodie ys in the Sacr. that was crucified.*

B feight of the Sacrament: This ys a figne, figure or token of the bodie, that was crucified: but this ys the felf fame bodie, and none other. For Chryfte hath but one bodie, and that fame one bodie ys in the Sacrament fubftanciallie, whollie and perfectlie.

And therfor as that Chryfte was incarnate we knowe, and by whofe worke yt was doen we knowe, but the maner howe that flefh was wrought we knowe not: That Chryft did rife from deathe, and that his foule was in Hell we knowe, but howe yt came to his bodie again we knowe not, yet by whom yt was doen we knowe: So, that Chryftes bodie ys in the Sacrament we knowe, and by whom yt ys wrought that yt ys ther we knowe, but howe yt ys ther, more then ys faied, we knowe not. Nowe yf ye will not beleue his bodie to be in the Sacrament, bicaufe ye knowe not howe yt ys ther, howe will ye beleue that Chryftes foule returned to his bodie, feing ye knowe not howe, yt came ther.

C Chryft made the water wine in *Cana Galilæa*, Bnt howe we knowe not. For he fpake no extern woord, neither did anie extern facte toward the turning of yt appeare more the that he did bid the minifters to drawe, and geue the ftewarde. The fiue loanes, and two fifhes the feuen loaues and the fewe fifhes we knowe to be multiplied, and by whom, but howe, whether by putting to of an other fubftance, or they the felues were encreafed, or otherwife, we knowe not. That *Lazarus* was dead, and fo certelie, that he being foure daies in the graue did ftinke, we knowe: but howe the foule came to that putrifieng bodie, and from whence, and howe that ftinkinge bodie was made hole and fwete, we knowe not, but by whome yt was doen we knowe.

> *Joan. 2.*
>
> *Ibid.6. Matt. 15.*
>
> *Joan.11.*

Therfor the maner of thefe and manie mo being wrought by the diuine power, for fomoche as the fcripture faieth that they were doen (though the maner of the doinge be vnknowen) we beleue them: So forafmoche as the fcripture faieth that the flefh of Chryft ys meate in deed and that we muft eate yt, yf we will haue life: Let vs beleue yt, though we knowe not howe yt

D ys fo made, nor can comprehende howe foche a bodie fhoulde entre into a mans mouth. Let vs not be curioufe in fearching the wonderfull workes of God. Yf he did faie yt, yt ys knowledge enough for a Chryftian man to beleue that yt ys fo. I tarie to long here, but the chryftian charitie I beare to them that haue erred, that they maie be reduced, and ftaied, hath thus caried me.

> *VVe maie not be curioufe in the workes of God.*

THE THREE AND TWENTETH CHAPITER

endeth the expofition of this text by Theophilact.
and Beda.

He laft coople, whiche fhall be brought furth for the expownding and vnderftanding of this text of S.Iohn, fhall be *Theophilact*. and *Beda*. Whome I will breiflie, alleage bicaufe I wolde be gone from this to other in fame chapiter. Theophilacte faieth thus: *Non enim nudi hominis caro est qua manducatur, fed Dei , & qua deificare valet, vtpote contemperata Deitati . Ista etia verè est cibus,eò quòd non ad paruum tēpus duret,neque corrumpatur ficut corruptibilis cibus:fed aterna vita fit fubfidium. Similiter et potus fanguinis Domini verè est potus quia non ad tempus fufficit fiti,fed femper abfque fiti conferuat,nec indigere permittit bibentem ficut et ad Samaritanam dicebat: Qui bibit ex aqua,quam ego dabo,non fitiet.Nam quifquis gratiam fancti Spiritus per fumptionem diuinorum mysteriorum fufceperit , neque famem fpiritualem, neque fitim patietur qualem incredulị .* Yt ys not the flefh of a bare man, whiche ys eaten, but of God, and whiche ys able to make vs as yt were F Goddes, as contemperated to the Godhead. This flefh alfo ys meat in very dede, bicaufe yt endureth not for a litle while, neither ys yt corrupted as the corruptible meat, but yt ys the helpe of eternall life , likwife alfo the drinke of the bloode of our Lorde ys drinke in dede, bicaufe yt fufficeth the thirft not for a time, but allwaies yt conferueth from thrift , and fuffreth not the drinker to lacke , as he faied to the Samaritane : He that drinketh of the water whiche I fhall geue him, he fhall not thirft, fo as do the vnbeleuers. Thus moche Theophilacte.

In 6. Joan.

I fhall not nede to trauaill here to fhewe that he vnderftandeth this text of the Sacrament. For that ys all readie made fo manifeft , that yt can not be denied. And for the prefence I will not trouble the reader to make any farther proofe or declaracion here, feing yt maie be well perceaued , by that that ys allreadie faied, what this Authours meening ys in this matter . I will therfor paffe him thus ouer, and come to Beda , who breiflie writeth thus: *Dixerat fuperiùs, Qui manducat meam carnem , & bibit meum fanguinem habet vitam* G *aternam . Et vt ostenderet quanta diftantia fit inter corporalem cibum , & fpirituale mysterinm corporis & fanguinis fui,adiecit: Caro mea verè est cibus , & fanguis meus verè est potus.* He had faied before he that eateth my flefh, and drinketh my bloode, hath euerlafting life. And to the intent he might fhewe howe great difference ys betwen the corporall meat , and the fpirituall myftery of his bodie and bloode, he added: *My flesh ys meate in dede.and my blood ys drinke in dede.* Thus Beda.

In Joan.

That this Authour vnderftandeth this text of the Sacrament, yt can not be obfcure to anie man, feing that he fo plainlie faieth, that Chryft to fhewe the differēce of corporall meat, and fpirituall myfterie of his bodie and blood added this faing: *My flesh ys meat etc.*

Howe the Sacr.ys a myfterie, and what a myfterie ys

And let no man take occafion to maintein his erroure againft the prefence of Chryfte in the Sacrament, bicaufe he calleth yt the myftery of Chryftes bodie and bloode. For a myfterie ys that couertlie conteineth a thing not by fenfeis or comon knowledge to be perceaued . So this my- H ftery conteineth the very bodie of Chryft as a thing fecretly hidden from the fenfeis, as Eufebius faieth: *Non exteriori cenfenda vifu,fed interiori affectu.* Not to be iudged by outwarde feight , but by inwarde affecte, that ys by faithe. Wherfor yt ys very well called a mifterie, for that yt conteineth the very bodie and Chryfte, whiche the fenfeis can not perceaue.

Hom.5. Pafch.

I might

A   I might, but for diffidence of the Aduerſaries, haue onelie named theſe Authours to be of one minde, whiche I haue hetherto brought in, for the ex poſition of this text. For they ioin ſo nere, that the allegacion of one ys but the reherſall of an other: But I content my ſelf with my pains, that the Aduerſaries maie ſee that we be on his trueths ſide: *Qui facit vnanimes habitare in domo:* Who maketh me of one minde to dwell in the houſe. For here among theſe (as ye haue hearde) ys ſoche agreement concorde, and conſent, ſo iuſtlie and ſo neerlie, that a man maie ſkant diſcerne the ſentence of one from an other, eſpecially by diſcrecion of matter.

Pſal.67.

And to conclude and knitt vppe this knotte, ye haue heard them all conſent in this, that this text of S. Iohn ys vnderſtanded of the bleſſed Sacramēt, whiche ys one cheif poincte we laboure to proue. And moſt of them teſtifie that Chryſte did not ſpeake yt figuratiuely or parabolycallie, but euen plain lie and withoute trope. So that ther being no figure, we maie ſaie that Chryſt ſpeakinge of his fleſh to be receaued in the Sacrament ſpeaketh of no figuratiue fleſh, but of his very fleſh in dede, whiche as yt ys ther reaallie, So ys

B   yt withoute all figure meat verilie and in dede.

THE FOVRE AND TWENTETH CHAP. BEGIN-

neth the expoſition of the next text in the ſixt of S. Iohn by ſainct Hilary and ſainCte Auguſtine.

He text that foloweth in the ſixte of ſainct Iohn ys: *Qui manducat meam carnem , & bibit meum ſanguinem in me manet & ego in eo.* He that eateth my fleſh and drinketh my bloode, dwelleth in me, and I in him. Foraſmoche as our Sauiour Chryſt had ſaied, that he that eateth his fleſh ſhoulde haue life eternall: and towarde the proof of that had ſaied that his fleſh was verie meate, not nouriſhing to the perpetuitie of the tēporall life, but nouriſhing to eternall life, wherof he had

C   ſpoken before. Nowe he proueth that, and declareth howe yt ys doen, ſaing: *He that eateth my fleſh, and drinketh my bloode, dwelleth in me and I in him.* As yt might be thus ſaied: He that eateth my fleſh, and *drinketh* my bloode, ys ioined to me, and dwelleth in me, being made one with me . But he that ys made one with me, for ſo moche as I am the very life, he alſo muſt haue life, and therfor he that eateth my fleſh &c. hath eternal life. For as the bodie of euery liuing creature, vntill the Soule be ioined to yt, hath no life, but being ioined to the Soule, whiche ys the beginning of life in naturall thinges, yt immediatelie liueth. So we hauing not that eternall life of our ſelues, but in the reſpect, being like the bodie without the Soule, yf we be ioined to the Authour of life, we ſhall liue by him, being made liuing by him, who ys life himſelf. Therfor being ioined and abiding in Chryſt, though we had not life, yet as the ſoule quickneth and geueth life to the bodie, being ioined to yt and abiding in yt, though before yt had none: So Chryſt quickeneth vs, and geueth life euerlaſting to vs, though we had no ſoche life before.

D   But for ſomoche as we ſpeake of our abiding in Chryſt, yt ys to be obſerued, that we abide in Chryſt two maner of waies, that ys, ſpirituallie, and naturallie, ſpirituallie by right faith, and ſincere charitie, as S. Cyrill doth tearme yt, and naturallie by the receauing of Chryſtes naturall fleſh, as S. Hilarie teacheth.

We abide in Chryſt two maner of waies.

Of theſe two maners of abiding in Chryſt the holy writers ſonderlie and

seueriallie doe write. Wherfor that ye maie perceaue this text to be vnder-
ſtad of both maners of a bidding of Chryſt in vs. I ſhall ioin two of the Latin
Churche, bycauſe they ſhew the differece moſt plainly, the one expownding
this text of our naturall abiding in Chryſt, whiche ys S. Hilarie : the other
of our ſpirituall abiding in Chryſt which ys S. Auguſtin. This will I do to
the etent that the errour of the Aduerſarie maie be ſeen, Who bycauſe ſainct
Auguſtin in ſome places doth expownde this ſcripture of the ſpirituall abiding of Chryſt in vs, or of vs in him, he furthwith not conſidering other places of other Fathers or of S. Auguſtine him ſelf, maketh a doctrine of the
one, and reiecteth the other: affirming the ſpirituall abiding of Chryſt in vs,
and denieng the naturall abiding, whiche ys wickedly doen, for ſomoche as
the catholike faith taught by the holie Fathers, yea and by S. Auguſtine him
ſelf, teacheth vs both to be doen by the receipt of the bleſſed Sacrament, yf
yt be woorthilie receaued.

Lib.8. de Trinit.　S. Hilarie ſaieth thus: *Quòd autem in eo per Sacramentum communicatæ carnis
& ſanguinis ſumus, ipſe teſtatur, dicens : Et hic mundus iam me non videt, vos autem me
videbitis, quoniam ego viuo & vos viuetis, quoniam ego in Patre meo, & vos in me, &
ego in vobis &c. Quòd autem naturalis in nobis hæc vnitas ſit, ipſe ita teſtatus eſt : Qui
edit meam carnem, & bibit meum ſanguinem in me manet, & ego in eo. Non enim quis
in eo erit, niſi in quo ipſe fuerit, eius tantùm in ſe habens aſſumptam carnè, qui ſuam ſumpſe-
rit.* That we be in him by the Sacrament of his fleſh, and blood being communicated, he himſelf withneſſeth ſaing: And this worlde doth not ſee me,
but ye ſhall ſee me, for I liue, and ye ſhall liue. For I am in my Father, and
yowe in me, and I in yowe. But that this vnitie ys naturall in vs, he hath wittneſſed ſaing: *He that eateth my fleſh and drinketh my bloode abideth in me and I in him.*
Ther ſhall no man be in him, but in whome he ſhall be, hauing onelie his aſ-
ſumpted fleſh in him, who hath taken his. Thus S. Hilarie.

Hereſie of the Arriãs.　Yt ys to be vnderſtanded that this holie man being baniſhed by *Conſtãcius
the Emperour,* who fauoured the hereſie of the Arrians, being nowe in exile,
wrote againſt the ſame hereſie. And foraſmoche as the Arrians denied God
the Sonne to be of the ſame ſubſtãce with God the Father and for that pour
poſe peruerted the ſcriptures that ſpake of the vnitie of God the Sonne in
ſubſtance with God the Father: as this: *Ego & Pater vnum ſumus: I and the Father
be one,* and ſoche other, ſainge : that they were not vnderſtanded of the vnitie
of God the Father, and God the Sonne in ſubſtance, that they being two
diſtincte perſons ſhoulde be one in ſubſtance: but of the vnitie of will, that
they two haue but one will: ſo that allwaies, what the Father willeth, that wil-

Naturall vnitie of Chryſt to vs by our re ceipt of his naturall fleſh.　leth the Sonne.

　Nowe to proue that they be one not onely in will but alſo in ſubſtance
this Authour vſeth the argument of the Sacrament, that foraſmoche as we
receauing the fleſh of Chryſte in the Sacrament, Chryſt therby ys in vs naturally: So foraſmoche as Chryſt ſaieth *I am in the Father, and yowe in me, and I
in yowe,* as Chryſte by taking of his fleſh ys naturallie in vs: So ys he naturallie in his Father. Nowe yf Chryſt be not naturallie in vs by the receauing of
the Sacrament (I meen of his fleſh in the Sacrament) then the argument of
S. Hilarie ys of no force or ſtrenght againſt the Arrians.

Lib.8. de Trinit.　That S. Hilarie vſeth the Sacrament for an argument in this matter,
ye ſhall perceiue by his owne woordes, whiche be theſe. *Si enim verè
Verbum caro factum eſt, & nos verè Verbum carnem cibo Dominico ſumimus:
quomodò non naturaliter in nobis manere exiſtimandus eſt? &c. Ita enim omnes vnum
ſumus quia & in Chriſto Pater eſt, & Chriſtus in nobis eſt. Quiſquis ergo naturaliter Patrem*

A *trem in Chriſto negabit,neget prius naturaliter vel ſe in Chriſto, vel Chriſtum ſibi ineſſe, quia in Chriſto Pater, & Chriſtus in nobis, vnum in ijs eſſe nos faciunt. Si verè igitur carnem corporis noſtri Chriſtus aſſumpſit,& verè homo ille, qui ex Maria natus fuit Chri-ſtus eſt,noſque vere ſub myſterio carnem corporis ſui ſumimus, & per hoc vnum erimus, quia Pater in eo eſt,& ille in nobis, quomodò voluntatis vnitas aſſeritur, cùm naturalis per ſacramentū proprietas perfectæ ſacramētum ſit vnitatis.*Yſ the Sonne of God in verie dede be made fleſh, and we in verie dede do receaue the Sonne of God being made fleſh in the Sacrament,howe ys he thought not naturally to abide in vs?&c. Euen ſo all we are one.For bothe the Father ys in Chryſte, and Chryſt in vs. Whoſoeuer therfore will denie the Father to be in Chryſt, let him firſt denie, that either Chryſt ys naturally in him, or he in Chryſt. For the Father being in Chryſt, and Chryſt in vs, do make vs one in theſe. Yf therfor Chryſt did take in verie dede the fleſh of our bodie, and that man, that was born of Marie be Chryſt in dede, *And we vnder the myſterie do take in very dede the fleſh of his bodie, and by this we ſhall be one* (For the Father ys in him and he in vs)howe ys the vnitie of will affirmed, ſeing the

B naturall proprietie by the Sacrament ys the Sacramēt of perfect vnitie.Thus farre ſainct Hilarie.

The Sonne of God ma-de fleſh ys receaued in the Sacra.

Do ye not ſee here howe he diduceth his argument from the receipt of the fleſh of Chryſt in the Sacrament, and that more then once ? Yf Chryſt in verie dede did take the fleſh of our bodie, and that man in very dede, that was born of Marie was Chryſt, and yf we in verie dede do receaue in the myſtery,the fleſh of his bodie,by this we ſhall be one,for the Father ys in him,and he in vs.

In whiche proceſſe this ye maie perceaue him to auouche,that as Chryſt being the Sonne of God ys naturallie in the Father:So ys Chryſt, by the receipt of his verie fleſh by vs,naturallie in vs. Whiche maner of naturall being in vs he proueth by this our text, that we haue nowe in hand, and ſaieth:that Chryſt by this text,doth witneſſe that he ys naturally in vs. And that this vnitie ys naturalll in vs, he himſelf (ſaith Hilarie) haith witneſſed

C ſaing: He that eateth my fleſh,and drinketh my blood, abideth in me, and I in him. So that ye maie perceaue that this text ys not onely vnderſtanded of the Sacrament,but by yt alſo ys taught, that Chryſt ys verilie,reallie, and in veri dede preſent in the Sacramēt.Who being ſo receaued of vs,ys(as this Author tearmeth yt)naturallie in vs.Who yet denieth not but that alſo we receaue Chryſt ſpirituallie,and he abideth in vs ſpirituallie.

Note here howe S.Hi larie vnder ſtood the 6. of S. John, and ſo iud-ge of the reſt of the Fathers.

Wher alſo note howe this aduerbe verily ys as well added to the preſen-ce of Chryſt in the Sacrament,as yt ys to the myſtery of his incarnacion, and to yt, that he was verily Chryſt. Wherby we are taught, thas as verilie as Chryſt was incarnated, and as verilie as he incarnated was Chryſt : So ve-rilie ys he preſent in the Sacrament,and ſo verilie do we therin receaue him.

As verilie as Chryſt was incor-nated: ſo verilie ys he in the Sacr.

But as we haue hearde this man teaching that Chryſt naturallie abideth in vs:So we will nowe heare Saincte. Anguſtine ſpeaking of the ſpirituall receauing,and ſpirituall adiding of Chryſt in vs: Thus he writeth : *Denique*

D *iam exponit quomodò id fiat,quod loquitur,& quid ſit manducare corpus eius, & ſangui-nem bibere. Qui manducat carnem meam, & bibit ſanguinem meum, in me manet, & ego in illo. Hoc eſt ergo illam manducare eſcam,& illum bibere potum in Chriſto ma-nere,& illum manentem ia ſe habere. Ac per hoc, qui non manet in Chriſto, & in quo non manet Chriſtus, procul dubio nec manducat ſpiritualiter eius carnem, nec bibit eius ſanguinem, licet carnaliter & viſibiliter premat dentibus ſacramentum corporis & ſan-guinis Chriſti. Sed magis tantæ rei ſacramentum ad iudicium ſibi manducat & bibit,*

Aug. tra. 26. in John

quia immundus præsumpsit ad Christi accedere Sacramenta, quæ aliquis non dignè sumit, *nisi qui mundus est. De quibus dicitur : Beati mundo corde quoniam ipsi Deum videbunt.* Nowe at the laft he expowndeth (faieth S. Auguftine) howe that maie be doen, that he fpeaketh , and what yt ys to eate his flefh, and drinke his blood *He that eateth my flesh, and drinketh my bloode,* abideth in me, and I in him. This therfore ys to eate his flefh, and to drinke his blood, to dwell in Chryft, and to haue him dwelling in him. And by this he that dwelleth not in Chryft, and in whome Chryft dwelleth not, without doubte he doth neither eate his flefh, nor drinke his blood fpirituallie , although carnallie, and vifiblie he preffe with his teeth the Sacrament of the bodie and bloode of Chryft. But raither to his damnacion, he eateth and drinketh the Sacrament of fo great a thing, bicaufe he being vnclean hath prefumed to come to the Sacramentes of Chryft, whiche anie man doth not receaue woorthilie, but he that ys clean of the whiche, yt ys faied: *Bleſſed be the clean in heart, for they shall see God.* Thus farre Sainct Auguftine.

S. Aug. pro duced of the Sacra. mentaries in a wrong fenfe.

This place and expofition of S . Auguftine hath ben brought furth by the Aduerfaries , as wherby they wolde improue the receipt of Chryftes very reall bodie in the Sacrament. But they are wide from the trueth. For S. Auguftine here determineth what maner of receauing he fpeaketh of, and faieth: *He that doth not dwell in Chryst , and in whom Chryst doth not dwell, withoute doubte he doth not receaue Chryste spirituallie.* So that he fpeaketh of the fpirituall receipt, whiche no good chriftian man denieth, but yt ys counted of all good men fo neceffarie, that without this, the reall receipt ys not profitable, but raither to the contrarie right hurtfull, yea verie damnable. Therfor wher Sainct Auguftin in the beginning of this his faing, faieth that *to dwell in Chryst, and to haue Chryst dwelling in vs, ys to eate his flesh, and to drinke his bloode :* He determineth that that ys to eat his flefh an to drinke his blood fpirituallie. And that we graunte. But that ther ys no other maner to eat his flefh and to drinke his blood then this fpirituall maner, that fainct Auguftine fpeaketh of here, that ys moft falfe.

Serm. 11. de Verbis Dom.

For the fame S. Auguftin expownding the fame text in an other place, declareth both this maner and the other alfo, faing: *Illud etiam quod ait: Qui manducat carnem meam, & bibit fanguinem meum, in me manet, & ego in illo, quomodo intellecturi fumus? Nunquid etiam illos hic poterimus accipere, de quibus dicit Apostolus, quòd iudicium fibi manducent & bibant, cùm ipfam carnem manducent, & ipfum fanguinem bibant? Nunquid & Iudas magistri venditor & traditor impius , quamuis primum ipfum manibus eius confectum Sacramentum carnis & fanguinis eius cum cæteris Difcipulis, ficut apertius Lucas Euangelista declarat , manducaret & biberet , manſit in Christo, aut Christus in eo? Multi denique qui vel corde ficto carnem illam manducat, & fanguinem bibunt, vel cùm manducauerint & biberint, Apostatæ fiunt, nunquid manent in Christo. vel Christus in eis? Sed est profectò quidam certus modus manducandi illam carnem, & bibendi illum fanguinem, quo modo qui manducauerit & biberit in Christo manet, & Christus in eo.* That alfo that he faieth, *He that eateth my flesh, and drinketh my blood, dwelleth in me and I in him.* Howe fhall we vnderftande yt?

Euell men do eate the flesh and drinke the blood of Chryst.

Maie we vnderftand them here of whom the Apoftle faieth: *that they eate and drinke to their damnacion, when they eate that flesh, and drinke that bloode?* And did Iudas alfo, that feller , and wicked betraier of his mafter, although he did (as Luke the Euangelift plainlie declareth) firft eate and drinke with the other difciples, the Sacrament of his flefh and blood, made with his owne handes, dwell in Chryft, and Chryft in him? To be brief, manie whiche either with feigned heart, do eate that flefh and drinke that bloode: or when they haue

eaten,

A eaten,and dronke,they becom Apoftaties,and forfakers of Chryftes religion do they abide in Chryft, or Chryft in them? But ther ys in dede a certain maner of eating that flefh, and of drinking that bloode, after the whiche maner he that eateth,and drinketh, dwelleth in Chryft,and Chryft in him. Thus farre S.Auguftin.

Do ye not here fee two maners of eatinge of the flefh of Chryft, and drinking of his bloode, the one to eate and drinke them verilie, which yf yt be doen with a feigned heart, or when they haue fo doen, they forfake Chryftes faith (as manie of late yeares haue doen and do in this matter of the Sacrament) they, though they haue receaued Chryftes very flefh and blood in the Sacrament: yet Chryft dothe not dwell in them. Then ther ys an other maner of eating Chryftes bodie(faieth S.Auguftin) which ys a fpirituall maner of receauing by true and right faith, and feruent charitie. And he that eateth Chryftes flefh after this maner,he hath Chryft dwelling in him, But (as yt ys before faid) he that eateth Chryftes flefh fpirituallie, hath Chryft dwelling in him fpiritually: But he that eateth Chryftes very flefh in the Sacrament with perfect faith,and godly charitie, he hath Chryft dwelling in him bothe naturallie(as S. Hilary faieth) and alfo fpirituallie (as S. Auguftin faieth) So that the one of thefe denieth not the other, neither ys anie of them by any catholique writers denied,but they be both raither wifhed,yea required,and commaunded. And bothe thefe maners of receauing iointlie vfed of the faitfull chriftian do augment the benefitt very moche.

> *Two maners of eating the flesh of Chryst.*

And here I wifh the Reader,diligently to note that S.Auguftin faieth that euell men do eate the flefh of Chryft, whiche inuincible proueth the reall and fubftanciall flefh of Chryft in the Sacrament. For otherwife the euell man can not eate the flefh of Chryft.

C Thus ye fee to what pourpofe I haue ioined thefe two holie learned Fathers together though they be both of the latin Churche, that ye maie perceaue the abiding and dwelling of Chryft in vs to be not onelie fpirituall by faith and charitie,but alfo natural by the receauing of Chryftes very flefh in the Sacrament. And that thone of thefe maners ys not to be onlie affirmed as a treuth,and thother denied as an erroure,but bothe to be receaued and beleued as a treu catholike doctrine auouched and taught by holie Fathers, whiche expownde this text of fainct Iohn nowe in hande bothe to meen te naturall abiding of Chryft in vs,as fainct Hilary hath here doen,and alfo the fpirituall abiding, as fainct Auguftin expownded yt.

> *Two waies of dwelling in Chryst, that ys spirituallie and naturallie.*

THE FIVE AND TWENTETH CHAPITER
proceadeth in the expofition of the fame by Chryfoftom and fainct Gregorie.

D Hrifoftome very breiflie expowndeth this text on this wife. *Qui manducat meam carnem,& bibit meum fanguinem, in me manet, & ego in eo.Quod dicit, vt cum ipfo fe admifceri oftendat.* He that eateth my flefh,and drinketh my blood, dwelleth in me and I in him. Whiche he faieth,that he might fhewe himfelf to be mingled with him.

> *Hom.45. in Joan.*

What he meeneth by this(*mingled*) yf ye remember what ys alleadged of him before,that fhall ye foon perceaue,and vnderftande therwith that Chrifoftom according to our two maners of receauing, maketh mencion of two

maners

Ibid.

maners of being in Chryſt, ſaing thus: *Vt autem non ſolùm per dilectionem , ſed* **E**
reipſa in illam carnem conuertamur,per cibum id efficitur, quem nobis largitus eſt. That
we ſhoulde(ſaieth Chryſoſtom) not onelie by loue,but in very dede be turned into his fleſh,that ys doen by the meat whiche he hath graunted vs.

Two ma-
ners of
being or
dwelling in
Chryſt.

Wher note that he teacheth, that we be turned into Chryſte two maner
of waies:by loue,whiche ys the ſpirituall maner, by the whiche we be ſpiritually in Chryſt,euen dwelling in him(as ſaincte Iohn ſaieth) *Deus charitas eſt*
& qui manet in charitate in Deo manet,& Deus in eo. God ys charitie,and he that
dwelleth in charitie ,dwelleth in God,and God in him:And alſo in verie dede, when we woorthilie eate his fleſh,whiche ys our hauenly meate,by whiche meate(ſaieth Chryſoſtom) yt ys brought to effect , and that not by an
imaginacion,but in very dede.

Thus ye perceaue that theſe be two ſondrie effectes, to dwell in Chryſt
ſpirituallie, and to dwell in him in very dede(as Chryſoſtom ſaieth)or natu-
rallie(as S.Hilary ſaieth)whiche two ſondrie effectes, haue two ſondrie cau-
ſes:whiche be to eate Chryſtes fleſh ſpirituallie,and to eate id reallie , or in **F**
verie dede. So that ye maie perceaue,that this ys not an horrible matter , as
the Proclamer with blaſphemouſe exclamacion pretendeth yt to be, when
ſo manie auncient Fathers ſo plainly ſpeake of yt.

Greg.in
Iob cap. 6.

But nowe come we to S. Gregorie ioined with Chryſoſtom who vpon
Iob ſaieth thus: *Natus Dominus in præſepi ponitur, vt ſignificaretur , quòd ſancta ani-*
malia,quæ ieiuna diu apud legem inuenta ſunt,incarnationis eius fœno ſatiarentur. Præſepe
natus impleuit,qui cibum ſemetipſum mortalium mentibus præbuit , dicens : Qui comedit
carnem,& bibit ſanguinem meum, in me manet , & ego in eo. Owre Lorde being
born ys laied in the maunger that yt ſhoulde be ſignified,that the holie beaſtes,whiche long vnder the lawe were fownde faſting,ſhoulde be filled withe
the heie of his incarnacion. Being borne he filled the maunger , who gaue
him ſelf meat to the mindes of the mortall , ſainge : He that eateth my fleſh
and drinketh my bloode,dwelleth in me,and I in him.Thus S. Gregorie.

In this ſentence ye heare that Chryſt gaue himſelf meat to mortall men,
and that according to our text:he that eateth my fleſh,and drinketh my bloo **G**
de &c. Whiche text as ye haue hearde of other fathers before alleaged , ys
to be vnderſtanded of the eating of Chryſtes fleſh in the Sacrament.

Obiection
oute of S.
Gregorie
aunſwered.

But yf the Aduerſarie reclame and ſaie, that S.Gregory ſaieth Chryſt gaue himſelf meat to the mindes of the faitfull,and that therfor he meneth not
of anie corporall receipt for the minde taketh none ſoche. Therto I ſaie that
trueth yt ys,that ſainct Gregorie ſaieth that Chryſt geueth himſelf meate,to
the mindes of the mortall: but I praie you, howe take ye the minde here?
do ye not take yt for the ſoule? and do not all the holie writers ſaie, that the
fleſh of Chryſt in the Sacraemt ys the meate of the ſoule?dothe not Chryſoſtom ſaie,that yt ys *verus cibus qui ſaluat animam.* Yt ys the very meat in dede
that ſaueth the ſoule?Why then,what do ye winne by this that ye ſaie, yt ys
the meat of the ſoule , ſeing that the holie Fathers haue ſo plainly teſtified,
that the very ſubſtanciall bodie of Chryſt being in very dede receaued in
the bleſſed Sacrament ys the meat of the ſoule?What then doth S. Gregorie
helpe your cauſe, ſeing he ſaieth none otherwiſe then they which haue **H**
ouerthrowen your cauſe?

And that yow ſhall perceaue,that he agreeth with the reſt acknowledging
two maner of receiptes of Chryſtes bodie and blood as they doo, ye ſhall

Greg.inHo
mil.Paſch.

heare him open himſelf. *Quid namque ſit ſanguis agni,non iam audiendo,ſed bibendo*
didiciſtis,qui ſuper vtrumque poſtem ponitur, quando non ſolùm ore corporis,ſed etiam ore
cordis

A　*cordis hauritur.*For what the bloode of the lambe ys,ye haue not onely learned by hearing,but alſo in drinking.Which blood ys putt on bothe the poſtes when yt ys not onely dronken with the mouth of the bodie, but alſo with the mouth of the heart.

Se ye not here S. Gregorie when he ſaieth,the bloode of the lambe ys dronke both with the mouth of the bodie and with the mouth of the heart? Doth he not plainlie diſtinᶜte and diſſeuer, theſe two receiptes , as the receipt of the bloode of the lambe with the mouth of the bodie to be the corparall receipt, and with the mouthe of the heart to be the ſpirituall receipt,which although they be diſtinᶜted receiptes: yet he wiſhed them in this homelie to be ioined together, for then we ſhall be ſure to haue the blood vpon both our poſtes to our more ſauegarde againſt the deſtroier. Yt maie be but vpon one poſte for as he ſaieth not moche after : *Qui ſic Redemptoris ſui ſanguinem ſumit vt imitari paſsionem eius necdum velit,in vno poſte ſanguinem poſuit.* He that doth ſo receaue the blood of his Redemer,that as yet, he will not folowe his paſsion,he hath put the blood vpon one poſte.

Chryſtes blood drok with mouth of bodie and mouth of heart.

B　Thus we vnderſtande by S. Gregorie not onely two maner of receiptes of Chryſtes fleſh and bloode, but alſo we be taught by him that they maie concurre,and be both doen at once.And alſo that the corporall receipt maie be withoute the ſpirituall,as alſo the ſpiritual maie be without the corporal.

THE SIX AND TWENTETH CHAPITER CONTI-
nueth this expoſiton by S. Cyrill and Lyra.

O adde yet mo wittneſſes howe this text ys to be taken, S. Cyrill expowndeth yt in this wiſe:*Qui manducat meam carnem , & bibit meum ſanguinem, in me manet & ego in eo.Vnde conſiderandum eſt,quòd non habitudine ſolùm qu.e per charitatem intelligitur, Chriſtum nobis ineſſe, verùm etiam participatione naturali.Nam quemadmodum ſi quis igne liquefaᶜtam ceram,alij cer.e ſimiliter liquefaᶜt.e ita miſcuerit,vt vnum quid ex vtriſque faᶜtum videatur:Sic communicatione corporis & ſanguinis Chriſti,ipſe in nobis eſt,& nos in ipſo.Non poterat enim aliter corruptibilis h.ec natura corporis,ad incorruptibilitatem , & vitam traduci,niſi naturalis vit.e corpus ei coniungeretur.*Owre Sauiour Chryſt ſaieth.He that eateth my fleſh,and drinketh my bloode,dwelleth in me,and I in him . Wherupon (ſaieth Cyrill) yt ys to be conſidered,*that not onelie by inwarde diſpoſition, whiche ys vnderſtanded by charitie,Chryſt to be in vs:but alſo by naturall participation.*For as yf anie man wolde men.le waxe that ys melted by the fire , with other waxe that ys likewiſe melted,ſo that of both ther maie be perceaued to be made one:*So by the parta king of the bodie and bloode of Chryſt,he ys in vs,and we in him.*For this corruptible nature of the bodie,coulde not otherwiſe be brought to incorruptiblitie and li fe,except the bodie of natural life ſhoulde be conioined to yt. Thus Cyrill.

Jn Ioan. cap.15.

Two waies of Chryſtes being in vs: that ys ſpirituallie, and naturallie.

What can the Aduerſaries ſaie to this Authour?ys ther no other receipt of Chryſts bodie,but a ſpirituall receipt?yes, this auncient father, as the other auncient fathers haue doen before,ſaieth,that *Chryſt ys not in vs onely by charitie,* wherbie he vnderſtandeth the ſpirituall maner, *but alſo by naturall participacion,* that ys ,by the eating and drinking of naturall fleſh and bloode.And that this ſhoulde not be taken for a phantaſie he ſaieth that Chryſtes fleſh ys ſo in vs,

D　and we in him,as two waxes melted and put together be made one. So alſo (*as S.Hilarie ſaieth before*)as God the Sone,and God the Father be one in ſubſtance · So we by this receipt of Chryſt be one with him, and by him alſo ioined to the godheade. I nede not to note then to yow that Cyrill vnderſtandeth this text of the bleſſed Sacramēt,wher the woordes wholie fownde to that pourpoſe.The reall preſence alſo ys ſufficiétly taught,when he ſaieth that

A plain place of S. Cyrill for the proof.

that we do partake the naturall flesh and bloode of Chryst, whose naturall　E
flesh ys not nor can be receaued, but wher yt ys reallie present. The effect of
of this also proueth the receipt, bicause we be not onely in minde affection,
and soule ioined to Chryst: but also by our natural flesh, receauing his natural flesh.　This sentence alone trulie, yf a man hath not solde himself ouer to
he Deuell, to be blinded, ys sufficiēt to moue and stirre anie heart to accept
the the true catholike faith. But yf men wil not see what shal we saie? who ys
blinder thē he that will not see? God yet illumine their heartes, that they cal
not darknesse light, and light darknesse.　To proceade in our matter, to this
anciēt Father of the higher house shal be ioined Lira ne of the lower house
to shewe his vnderstāding of this text. Thus he saieth writing vpon yt: *Hic pro*
bat quoddā suppositū. Dixerat enim, quòd māducatio dat vitā. Istud probat hic, quia illud, per

Lyra in 6.
Ioan.

qnod aliquis vnitur principio viuificatiuo, illud dat vitā. Hoc patet in vita corporali etc. He
re he proueth a thing supposed. For he had saied, that the eating of this flesh
geueth life. This he pueth here. For that by the whiche a mā ys vnited to the
principle that maketh thinges to liue, geueth life.　This appeareth in the cor-　F
porall life. By this Sacramēt, a mā ys vnited to Chryst, who ys the beginning
of the spūall life. And this ys yt that ys saied: *He that eateth my flesh and drinketh*
my bloode, dwelleth in me and I in him. that ys to saie, he ys vnited to me.　This Au
thour pceadeth as yow haue hearde him beginne, wher he taught that Chry
stes flesh was so verilie meat, that yt was in the Sacramēt not as in a sign, but
reallie and in very dede. To the whiche flesh of Chryst (saieth he) we be vnited
by the Sacramēt, that ys by the receauing of the Sacramēt, wherin being real
lie Chrystes verie flesh we be vnited to the same. For yf yt be not ther, we can
not be vnited to yt by the Sacramēt. For an vniō ys the making of two things
or mo, one, whiche thinges must be present so to be vnited.　Wherfor the
bodie of Chryst ys reallie in the Sacramēt or ells ther can be no vniō. What
maner of vnion ys wrought by the Sacramēt S. Hilary hath taught vs, that yt
ys a natural vniō, that ys, an vniō of Chrystes natural flesh and substāce, and of
our natural flesh and substāce, whiche both by this Sacrrmēt be made one, so
that Chryst dwelleth in vs, and we in him. Yf anie of the Aduersaries wolde　G
take occasiō to obiect (*as they wil doo as wel vpō a woorde, as a whol sentēce*) that this
Authour saieth, that Chryste ys the beginning of the spūal life, wherfor we
be ioined to him spirituallie, for the hauing of that spūal life, and not corporal
life: it ys very manifest, I saie, that we liue not corporally by the Sacramēt but
this corporall life ys mainteined by other foode. But the life that we haue by
the receipt of Chryst in the Sacramēt ys the eternal life, whiche ys called the
spūal life, as distincted frō the corporal and temporal life. *Temporalē vitā sine illo*
habere homines possūt, æternā verò omnino nō possūt. Men maie haue (saieth S. Augu.)
the tēporal life withoute the Sacramēt but the eternall life by no means can
they haue. For this meat suffreth the tēporal death to come to vs, but (*as Chry-*
sostom saieth) yt expelleth death, meening the eternall death. Of the whiche S.
August. saieth. *Quantū pertinet ad mortem istā visibilē et corporalē, nunquid nos nō mori-*

Aug. tract.
n Ioan. 26.

mur, qui māducamus panē de cælo descendentē? Sic sunt mortui et illi, quemadmodū et nos su
mus morituri. Quantū attinet, vt dixi, ad mortē huius corporis visibilē atq; carnalē. Quantū
attinet ad mortē illā de qua terret Dñs quia mortui sunt patres istorum. Manducauit Manna　H
et Moyses, manducauit Manna et Aaron, māducauit Manna et Phinees, manducauerant ibi
multi, qui Dño placuerunt et mortui non sunt. For somoche as doth pertein to this vi
sible and corporal death do not we die, which do eate the bread descending
from heauen? So also be they dead, euen as we also shall die. for somoche as perteineth to the visible and corporall death of this bodie, as
I haue saied, for somoche as perteineth to that death from the whiche our
Lor-

A Lorde doth feare vs,that the fathers of thefe be dead, Moyfes alfo did eate Manna,and Aaron did eate Manna, and Phynees did eate Manna , manie did eate ther whiche haue pleafed God and be not dead , Thus moche S.Auguftine.

In all whiche fainges ye perceaue that by the receipt of Chryft in the Sacrament,we haue life, not corporall and temporall , but eternall . Neither by yt do we efchape temporall and corporall death but eternall death, So that yowe fe the eternall life,fet againft vifible, corporall , and temporall life,as a fpirituall life,whiche fpirituall and eternall life ys by faith and holy conuerfacion anfwerablie begonne in this life,in owre inwarde man, and in our bodies by the receipt of Chryftes liuing flefh *(as he himfelf faieth) Ego refufcitabo eum in nouifsimo die.*I will raife him in the laft daie. *Ego*(faieth Cyrill) *id eft corpus meum quod comedetur, refufcitabo eum.* I, that ys , my bodie, whiche fhall be eaten,fhall rayfe him vppe in the laft daie. And again he faieth : *Ego ergo, qui homo faƈtus fum,per meam carnem in nouifsimo die comedentes refufcitabo,* I therfor

B (faieth S.Cyrill in the perfon of Chryft)who am made man,by my flefh will raife the eaters of the fame in the laft daie.So that Chryft ys he by whome, being vnited vnto him we fhall haue that eternall and fpirituall life,that kno weth neither corruption nor ende.

Chryftes bodie, fnall raife our bodies;

THE SEVEN AND TWENTETH CHAP. ABIdeth in the fame expofition by Theophilaƈt , and Rupertus Tuicien.

Heophilaƈte vpon the text nowe in hande faieth thus : *Hoc loco difcimus Sacramentum Communionis.Nam qui edit,& bibit carnem & fanguinem Domini,in ipfo manet Domino,& Dominus in ipfo. Contemperatio enim fit noua,& fuper rationem, ita vt fit Deus in nobis , & nos in Deo. Non audis terribilem auditum?Non Deum nudum manducamus,tangi enim nequit,& incorporeus eft,& neque occulis,neque manibus apprehendi poteft . Iterum nudi hominis caro nihil prodeffe poteft.Sed quia Deus vniuit fibi carnem fecundùm ineffa*-

C *bilem contemperationem,viuifica eft & caro, non quòd in Dei naturam tranfierit (abfit) fed ad fimilitudinem candentis ferri,quod & ferrum manet,& ignis oftendit operationem: fic ergo & Domini caro manens,caro viuifica eft,ficut Dei caro.*In this place we learn the Sacrament of Cõmunion.*For he that eateth and drinketh the flesh and blood of our Lorde,dwelleth in the fame our Lord,and our Lord in him.*For ther ys a newe con temparacion made,and that aboue reafon,fo that God fhoulde be in vs, and we in him.Doeft thowe not heare a terrible hearing?We do not eate bare God,for he can not be touched , and ys withoute bodie, and can neither with eyes,nor with handes be apprehended. Again the flefh of a bare man nothing profiteth, but God hath vnited to himfelf this flefh after an vnfpeakable contemperacion,yt ys flefh caufing life , as the flefh of God , not that yt ys gone into the nature of God *(God forbidde)*but to the likeneffe of fierie Iron,whiche ftill remaineth Iron,and fheweth the operacion of fier: So therfor the flefh of our Lorde alfo,remaining ftill flefh , ys quickning or caufing to liue,as the flefh of God. Thus moche Theophil.

Not God alone , fpiri tuallie but the flesh of Chrift verilie and alfo corporallie recea ued in the Sacr.

Who in the firft front of his fentence teftifieth by expreffe woordes , that

D this text ys to be vnderftanded of the Sacrament.For he faieth:*that in this place we learn the Sacrament of Cõmunion.*In the reft he trauaileth to fett furth the excellencie of Chryftes flefh, prouing that yt ys able to giue life, for that yt being vnfpeakeably cõtemperated with the Godhead,as Iron ys with fier

The flesh of Chryft geueth life and yet re- maineth ftill natu- rall flesh.

whiche

which hath the operacion of fire, and yet ys still very naturall Iron : So the **E**
flesh of Chryst hath the power to giue life as the flesh of God: and yet yt remaineth still very naturall flesh.

All which processe why hath he made, but to declare to vs, that the flesh
of Chryst being receaued of vs (*for that therbie Chryst dwelleth in vs, and we in him*)
we haue that in vs, whiche ys able to giue vs life, bicause (*being the flesh of God*)
yt hath soch powre. And so he doth not onely testifie, this scripture to speak
of the Sacrament, but also he testifieth the very flesh of Chryst, that ys ioined to the Godhead, to be ther present, and so receaued and eaten to giue
life. Of the which matter he hath so manifestly allreadie vpon the scriptures
before alleaged spoken his faith that yt can not here be called in question
whether yt be so vnderstanded of him in this place or no. Wherfor I leaue
this authour as one most plainly shewing himself, and for the further exposition of the text I will heare the testimonie of *Rupertus* who making a conference betwixt the godlie assured and certen promesse of Chryst, and the
wicked and false promesse of the serpent to our Mother Eue, saieth thus:

Rupertus   Quáto enim suauior est hæc vox (Qui mandacat meam carnem, & bibit meum sanguinem, **F**
Tuicien.   in me manet & ego in illo) illectione illa, qua Serpens susurrauit: Comedite, & eritis sicut
dij? qui vtique de suo non dabat, sed rapinam facere suadebat. Hic autem non qualecunque
suum, sed suam carnem, & suum sanguinem dat. In illis qui non credunt, & non credentes,
ore tamen, Sacramentum percipiunt, cibus & potus iste operatur iudicium. Howe moch
more pleasaunt ys this voice (*He that eateth my flesh and drinketh my blood, dwelleth*
in me and I in him) then that enticement, whiche the serpent whispered. Eate
and ye shall be as Goddes? Who yet gaue nothing of his owne, but moued them to do robberie. But this (*mening Chryst*) geueth not euery maner
thing of his, but euen his flesh and his blood. In them that beleue not, and
yet not beleuing, with their mouth receaue the Sacrament, this meat and
drinke vnto them woorketh iudgement. Thus *Rupertus.*

As in other, so in this authour ye maie perceaue, that he vnderstandeth
this scripture (*as the rest do*) of the Sacrament. For he saieth that *they whiche*
withoute faith receaue the Sacrament, receaue yt to iudgement. Whiche saing as yt delighteth me, and reioiceth me, for that I see soche concorde, consent, and
agreement among the Fathers, and Chrystes Parliament house, all affir- **G**
ming and teaching, against the false perswasion of the Aduersarie, that this
sixt chapter of S. Iohn ys vnderstanded of the blessed Sacrament: So yt greueth me to see the whyspering of the serpent so farre to haue preuailed v-
pon the Sonnes of Adam, that they crediting him in his ministers, and without due faith receauing the Sacrament, receaue their iudgement to condem
nacion, as this authour also saieth.

Rupertus   As for the presence of Chryst in the Sacrament, ther ys none that ys
most plain   familiarely acquainted with this authour, but knoweth that the confesseth
lie auou-   and auoucheth the verie reall presence of Chryst in the Sacrament
cheth the   not onelie in this place, when he saieth, that Chryst geueth vs no small thing
presence.   of his, but he geueth vs hys flesh and his blood : But also vpon this chapter in manie places. Of the whiche for the better creditt to be geuen
by the reader, I will here bring in one, and hereafter diuerse other shall
Li.6.co-   be brought furth. Thus he saieth : *Proinde cunctis figurarum vel similitudi-*
ment.in E-   num nebulis amotis, non corpus quodlibet, non corpus Christi quod est Ecclesia, sed illud cor- **H**
uang.Ioan.   pus Domini, quod pro nobis traditum est, nos manducare, & illum sanguinem, qui pro
nobis fusus est in remissionem peccatorum, nos bibere, indubitanter credimus. Et quod fecit
ipse, hoc idem in comemorationem ipsius scimus, et benè scimus nos facere, id est, carnê ipsius
manda-

A _manducare,& sanguinem bibere._ Therfor all clowdes of figures and similitudes remoued,we vndoubtedlie beleue that we receaue,not euerie bodie,not the bodie of Chryst (whiche ys the Churche) _but the same bodie of our Lorde that was betraied for vs,and that same bloode that was shed for vs in the remission of Sinnes ._ And we knowe,and knowe well,that we do euen the same verie thing in the remembrance of him,that he himself did,that ys,that we do eate hys flesh,and drink hys bloode.Thus he.

Hath not this Authour taught the presence of Chryst in the Sacrament plainlie enough?I Suppose he hath spoken so plain that he shall be shent for his laboure,and gett litle good will of the Proclamer,but hatred (_For veritas odium parit,_ trueth causeth hatred)and so shall be cast oute as a man not woorthy to be heard,and yet a man aswell learned,and aswell estemed,as the Proclamer,ād not yesterdaie born,but one that liued almost fiue hūdreth years agone.Well in this hys plain maner of writing,ād testifieng of the faith that was in the Church in those daies let vs examin him, what he doth saie , that

B other Fathers haue not saied before.First he saith that we must remoue , all clowdes of figures and similitudes,as touching the substance of the Sacrament.So that the substance of the Sacrament ys not a figure or a similitude of the bodie of Chryst,but the verie bodie of Chryst yt self. Hath not Origen and Chrysostome saied as moche before,and diuerse other ? And when thys Authour remoueth figures from the Sacrament,doth not he thē both impugn the clowdie doctrine,and the obscure shadowes of the Aduersaries figures,signes,and tokens,and teacheth that the verie substance of Chrystes bodie and blood ys present in the Sacrament?He saieth that we receaue no other bodie in the Sacrament,but that bodie of Chryst , that was betraied for vs,and that same blood that was shedd for vs:The like woordes speaketh Chrysostome,as before ys alleaged more then once or twice , and herafter more shall be.Thus then we maie conclude that this Authour both vnderstandeth the sixt of sainct Iohn of the Sacrament,and that also in yt he confesseth withoute figure the very bodie of Chryst.

C

THE EIGHT AND TVENTETH CHAP. EN-

deth the exposition of this text by Haymo,and Euthymius.

Vfficient testimonie being produced for the right and ttue vnderstanding of this text, I haue determined nowe to ende the same with this one onely coople mo,whom I will breiflie alleadg and ouerpasse.The first of these shall be Haymo,who alleaging this scripture declareth well howe yt ys to be vnderstanded. For speaking of the flesh and bodie of Chryst,he saieth thus:_Sicut illa caro corpus Christi est,ita iste panis transit in corpus Christi.Nec sunt duo corpora,sed vnum corpus. Diuinitatis enim plenitudo,quæ fuit in illo replet & istū panē,& ipsa diuinitas Verbi quæ implet cœlū et terram, & omnia quæ in eis sunt,ipsa replet corpus Christi,quod à multis sacerdotibus per vniuersū orbē sanctificatur.Et facit vnū Christi corpus esse.Et sicut ille panis & sanguis in corpus Christi trāseunt :ita omnes qui in Ecclesia dignè comedūt illud,vnū corpus Christi sunt, sicut & ipse dicit:Qui māducat carnē meam,& bibit sanguinē meū,in me manet,& ego in eo._

D As that flesh ys the bodie of Chryst: euen so this bread passeth in to the bodie of Chryst.Neither be they two bodies,but one bodie.For the plenitude or fulnesse of the Godhead that was in him,doth also fil thisbread,ād the sāe Godhead of the Sōne of God,which doth fil heauē ād earth ād al things that

Bb ii   be in

Rupertus his saing conferred with other more aūcient fathers

Haim . in. 10.1.Cor.

The God head of the Sonne filleth the bodie of Chryst sanctified by the preistes

be in them,the fame doth fill the bodie of Chryft,which ys fanctified of ma- **E**
nie preiftes through all the worlde,and maketh yt to be one bodie of Chrift.
And as that bread and blood do paffe into the bodie of Chryft : Euen fo all
that do woorthilie in the Church eate yt,they are one bodie of Chryft, as
he himfelf faieth:He that eateth my flefh,and drinketh my bloode dwelleth
in me,and I in him,Thus farre Haymo. I do merueill howe the Aduerfarie
could haue the face to denie this , the fixt of S. Iohn to be vnderftanded of
the Sacrament,feing that foch a nombre with fo great confent do not onely
in generall woordes faie that yt ys vnderftanded of the Sacrament , but do
alfo expownde euery fentence particularly,as hytherto(gétle Reader)thowe
maift perceaue euen to this authour . Who when he had declared the
wholl matter of the Sacrament,as firft howe the bodie of Chryft fhoulde
be in the Sacrament, which,he faieth,ys by that that the bread paffeth into
the bodie of Chryft,which ys doen by the turning of the fubftance of the
bread into the fubftance of the bodie of Chryft:vnto thys he addeth and
teacheth by whom thys merueiloufe worke ys wrought and doen , faing: **F**
that yt ys doen by the power of the Godhead,euen the fame that was fullie
in Chryft : euen the fame that filleth both heauen and earth , that fame
ys fullie , faieth he , in the bodie of Chryft, whiche ys fanctified of manie preiftes.

The bodie   And here note,Reader,againft the carnall difputers that allthough he faie,
of Chryft   that the bodie of Chryft be confecrated of manie preiftes through the whol
confecrated   worlde:yet he faieth not that they be manie bodies of Chryft, but onely
of manie   one bodie.And fheweth alfo howe that ys brought to paffe , and who ys
preiftes ys   the woorker of yt. *The Godhead* (faieth he) *that ys fullie in Chryft , maketh thys to*
but one bo-   *be one bodie.* Thus when he had fhewed howe great a thing the Sacrament
die.   ys in yt felf,then he beginneth to fhew what yt ys towarde vs , and what yt
woorketh in vs yf we receaue yt woorthilie. *As the bread (faieth he) ys become*
the bodie of Chryft: So all they that woorthilie eate the fame are the bodie of Chryft.
And to proue this, he alleageth the faing of Chryft, whiche we haue in
hande : *He that eateth my flesh , and drinketh my blood , dwelleth in me,*   **G**
and I in hym.

So then in this difcourfe yt ys eafilie perceaued , that he teacheth the
bread to be turned into the bodie of Chryft, that the bodie of Chryft ys in
the Sacrament,and not alone,but with the Godhead in yt , and fo perfect
God and man:that though the bodie of Chryft be côfecrated of manie prei-
ftes:yet by the powre of the Godhead yt ys wrought, to whom nothing ys
vnpofsible. Finallie that we receauing this bodie of Chryft in the Sacrament, according to Chryftes faing, we maie dwell in Chryft, and he
in vs. And thus yt ys manifeft that thys Authour vnderftandeth thys
text of the Sacrament.

In Matth.   Now this being plain , we will breiflie heare hys yocke felówe, whom
26.   for thys time we make *Euthymius.* Thus writeth he.*Si(inquit)de vno corpore , &*
fanguine omnes fideles participamus,omnes vnum fumus per ipfam horum myfteriorum
participationem,& in Chrifto omnes,& Chriftus in omnibus.Qui edit(inquit) meam car-
The flesh   *nem,& bibit meum fanguinem,in me manet,& ego in eo.Verbum fiquidem per affum-*
that the Sô   *ptionem carni vuitum eft,hæc rurfus caro vnitur nobis per participationem.* Yf all we(fai-
ne of God   eth *Euthymius*)do partake of one bodie,and one blood,all we are one by parti **H**
tooke by in   cipacion of thefe myfteries and we be all in Chryft,and Chryft in vs all . *He*
carn.ys vni   (faieth Chryft) *that eateth my bodie,and drinketh,*my blood, dwelleth in me and
fed to vs by   I in him.For trulie the Sonne of God by taking of flefh vpon him, ys vnited
the Sacra.   to the

A to the flesh:*Again this flesh ys vnited to vs by participacion.*Thus Euthym.

This sentence ys but short, but yt ys effectuouse. But hasting to ende the exposition of this text, I will note here but one thing, leauing the rest to the diligent reader to consider. The thing that I note, ys that this Authour saieth that the flesh, whiche the Sonne of God by assumption did vnite to him, *that flesh again ys vnited to vs by participacion.* Wherin I note that the same flesh that was vnited to the Sonne of God , the very same and none other ys vnited to vs. The verie naturall flesh was vnited to the Godhead. Wherfor the verie naturall flesh of Chryst ys vnited to vs by participacion. That yt ys the same flesh, this Authour well sheweth when he speaking of the flesh vnited to the Godhead saieth: *Hæc rursus caro :* This flesh again : not this flesh spirituallie, but this flesh that was vnited to the Godhead , which was naturall flesh. The mean how this flesh ys vnited to vs he saieth ys by participacion. Wher do we participate yt? in the Sacrament. Then this flesh ys in the Sacrament.

A plain proof of the presence against the proclamer:

B **THE NINE AND TWENTETH CHAP. EX**

powndeth the next text that foloweth in the sixt of S. Iohn, by sainct Augustin and sainct Cyirill.

He text that foloweth in the sixt of S. Iohn ys this: *Sicut misit me viuens Pater, & ego viuo propter Patrē. Et qui māducat me, & ipse viuet propter me.* As the luing Father sent me, and I liue for the Father: Euē so he that eateth me shall liue by the means of me. Not mindinge to tarie vpon this, as to declare how we eating Chryst do liue by him, for that this ys (I trust) sufficientlie declared allready, I will no more nowe trauaill but to shewe that , that yet was not declared , namelie howe Chryst liueth by the Father, Whiche matter S. Augustine dothe so well open that yt satisfieth me: and so, I trust, yt will do the Reader.

Ioan. 6.

Thus he saieth vpon the same text: *In qua sententia, si recte accipiuntur hæc verba, ita dixit: Sicut me misit viuens Pater, & ego viuo propter Patrem: & qui manducat me,*

C *& ipse viuet propter me. Ac si diceret vt ego viuam propter Patrem, id est, ad illum tanquam ad maiorem vitam meam referam, exinanitio meā fecit, in qua me misit : vt autem quisquam viuat propter me, participatio facit, qua manducat me. Ego itaque humiliatus viuo propter Patrem: ille erectus viuit propter me. Si autem ita dictum est, Viuo propter Patrem, quia ipse de illo, non ille de ipso est, sine detrimento æqualitatis dictum est: Nec tamen dicendo, Et qui manducat me, ipse viuet propter me, eandem suam, & nostram æqualitatem significauit, sed gratiam Mediatoris ostendit.* In whiche sentence, if these woordes be rightlie taken, thus he saied: *As the liuing Father sent me, and I liue for the Father: Euen so he that eateth me, liueth by the means of me.* As though he should saie, that I liue for the Father, that ys, that I referre my life to him as to a greater, the abasing or demission of my self made yt, in the whiche he sent me . But that anie man liueth by me, the participacion maketh yt, in the which he eateth me. I therfore humbled do liue for the Father: and he exalted liueth by the means of me. Yf yt be so saied, I liue for the Father, bicause the Sonne ys of the Father, and not the Father of the Sonne: yt ys saied withoute detriment of the equalitie. Neither yet saing : and he that eateth me , liueth by the means of me , hath he signified hys equalitie and owrs to be all one,

Aug. trāc. 26 in Ioan.

D but he hath shewed the grace of the Mediatour. Thus farre S. Augustin.

In whose sentence ye see howe the saing of Chryst maie be vprightlie vnderstanded, either of his Godhead, or of his manhead . Of hys Godhead yt

maie be faied,*I liue for the Father*,not that the Sonne,who ys born equal to the　E
Father,and ys from euer with the Father, being one in nature and fubftance
with the Father, ys made better then he was by the Father,but he liueth for
the Father, as being of the Father, born of the Father, and yet not after the
Father in time, neither leffe or inferiour to the Father in deitie, who ys
equall God with God the Father, born from euer before all times. Of his
Manhead yt ys alfo vnderftanded, who being a creature, was inferiour to
the Father, and therfor in that refpect faied: *Pater maior me eft*, The Father ys
greater then I. who being fo was bettered by the Father,and liued by the
Father the fountain of all life in all liuing creatures.

　　And that I breake not the ordre that I haue hitherto obferued, I will ioin
to faincte Auguftine being of the one fide of Chryftes Parliament houfe,
faincte Cyrill an auncient of the other fide of the houfe, who faieth thus:
Sicut mifit me Pater , & ego viuo propter Patrem , & qui manducat me , vi-
uet propter me . Cùm miffum fe dicit Filius , nihil aliud quàm incarnatum fe, vult
fignificare . Confueuit autem Chriftus quæ vim excedunt humanam , ea Patri tribue
re . Humiliauit enim feipfum factus homo , & ideo conuenientem homini menfuram
non recufat . Pater (inquit) qui manet in me ipfe facit opera . Patri ergo etiam
incarnationis operationem , quæ vim excedit humanam , vt folet , accommodat. Hoc
ergo eft quod dicit : Quemadmodum ego factus fum homo voluntate Patris,& viuo prop
ter Patrem . quia fcilicet è vita , quæ fecundùm effentiam eft , naturaliter , emanaui,
& genitoris naturam ad vnguem conferuo , vt & ego naturaliter vita fim: ita qui
manducat meam carnem ipfe viuet propter me, totus ad me reformatus, qui vita fum, &
viuificare poffum . Se verò manducari dicit , cùm fua caro manducatur , quia Verbum
caro factum eft, non naturarum confufione , fed ineffabili illo vnionis modo . As the
liuing Father hath fent me , and I liue for the Father : Euen fo he that
eateth me,fhall liue by the means of me . When the Sonne faieth that
he ys fent , he will nothing ells fignifie , but himfelf to be incarnated
For Chryft hath vfed to attribute foche thinges as exceade the power
of man , to the Father . He hath humbled him felf being made man,
and therfor he doth not refufe the meafure conuenient to man . Therfor the worke of the incarnacion,which paffeth the powre of man , he doth
(as he was woute) applie yt to the Father.This ys yt therfor that he faieth　G
Euen as I am made man by the will of the Father,and do liue for the Father, bicaufe I haue
flowed oute naturally of that life,which ys of very nature,and I do conferue the nature of my
Father in euery poincte,fo that I am alfo naturallie life: Euen fo he that eateth my flesh ,he
*fhall liue by me alltogether reformed vnto me who am life,and am able to make to liue.*He
faieth himfelf to be eaten , when his flefh ys eaten.For the woorde ys
made flefh not by confufion of natures , but by an vnfpeakeable maner of
vnion.Thus farre S. Cyrill.

　　As the text doth fpeake of two maner of liues,that ys of the life of
Chryft by the Father , and of the life of vs by Chryft: So doth this authour declare, both that Chryft flowing from the nature of the Father,
who ys life him felf , and hauing and being the fame very nature : ys
life him felf, and liueth by the Father , and alfo that we eating him,
for fomoche as he ys the very life, fhall liue by him.Wher note that Cyrill
faieth that Chryft faieth him felf to be eaten , when his flefh ys eaten . wherby he fignifieth to vs that the flefh of Chryft ys verilie eaten.　H
For yf yt were fpoken of the fpirituall eating of beleife,he wolde not tranf-
ferre yt from the Godhead , to the whiche moft proprely yt doth appertein , that we fhoulde beleue in yt , and referre yt to the flefh of
Chryfte

In 6. Joan.
cap. 18.

Chryft
vfeth to at-
tribute to
the Father
foche thin-
ges as ex-
cead mans
power.

Chryft ys
eaten when
his flesh ys
eaten.

A Chryfte onelie, or fo applie yt to yt, as by yt to come to whole Chrifte.
As a man maie faie, I am whole when either hand, or head or fome membre,
or parte of the bodie ys made whole, whiche ys proprely made whole in
dede, or as a man maie faie, I do fee, I do heare, when proprelie the eie
doth fee, and the eare dothe heare, or the foule raither doth fee and heare
by the eie and eare : So Chryft (*as Cyrill faieth*) doth faie him felf to be eaten, when his flefh ys eaten, to whom yt apperteineth proprely to be eaten,
and not to the God head.

For (as *Theophilacte* faieth) *Deum nudum non manducamus, tangi enim nequit, &* *In.6.Joan,*
incorporeus eft, & neque oculis neque manibus apprehendi poteft. We do not eate
bare God, for he can not be touched, and he hath no bodie, neither can he
be apprehended with eies nor handes, So then as the fpiritull eating of *As to the*
Chryft by beleife moft proprely doth appertein to the Godhead, and by *Godheadto*
yt ys applied to the wholl perfon of Chryft : So to the flefh of Chryft yt *be beleued:*
apperteineth moft proprely to be verily and really eaten, and by yt (*for fo* *So to the*
moche as the Godhead ys infeparablie annexed to yt, (as Cyrill faieth(*non enim abeft* *flefh yt pro*
B *Vnigenitus, the onely begotten fonne of God ys not abfent frō yt*) we do faie that wholl *prelie ap-*
Chryft ys eaten, euen as of Chryft we do learn, who (as Cyrill hath noted) *to be eaten.*
doth faie: *Qui manducat me,* he that doth eate me, not diuiding the Godhead
from the manheade, but me, that ys wholl Chryft.

Being thus then, made manifeft, that by this text alfo Chryft taught vs
the eating of his verie flefh, whiche can not otherwife be then in the Sacrament, wherbie yt ys confequent that this text ys to be vnderftanded
of the Sacrament: I will procead to feke the vnderftanding of other textes folowing.

THE THIRTETH CHAP. BEGINNETH EXPOSITION
of the next text by fainct Ambrofe and Chryfoftom.

T foloweth in the fixte chapiter of fainct Iohn : *Hic eft panis*
qui de cælo defcendit, non ficut manducauerunt patres veftri Manna in
deferto , & mortui funt. Qui manducat hunc panē viuet in æternū. This
ys the bread that camme down from heauen , not as yower
Fathers did eate Manna and are dead. He that eateth of this *Ioan.6.*
bread, fhall liue euer. Owre fauiour Chryft, who began to declare this great miftery to the Iewes , and notwithftāding their murmuring,
did open to them not onely, that yt was poffible, that his flefh fhoulde be
eaten, but alfo neceffarie, and nowe in the laft fentence as in other before he
had made mencion of the fame, and had declared the benefit , and great
commoditie that fhoulde enfewe to them that wolde eate his flefh, namely
that they fhoulde haue life euerlafting: Nowe as yt were after a difputacion
he maketh a conclufion or determinaciō of the matter, faing: *This ys the bread*
that came from heauen.

The Iewes (*as in the beginning of this fixt chapiter, yt doth appeare*) although
they had feen the great miracle of our Sauiour Chryft wrought in the multiplieng of the bread, and in feading fo great a multitude whith fo fewe loaues, that then they could faie, this ys the very Prophet, whiche fhould come
D into the worlde, wherby they ment *Meffias,* and therfor wolde then haue
made him a king : yet fhortly after like an vnthankfull and vnmindefull peo
ple of that notable fact doen in the prefence of fo manie, woorthy truly neuer to haue ben forgotten, forgetting this great woonder, required to fee

E

some notable sign at Chryftes hand, as though they had neuer feen anie, and therfor faied: *Quod tu facis fignum, vt videamus & credamus?* What sign sheweft thowe, that we maie fee and beleue? And then to make their bragge they faied: *Patres noftri manducanerunt Manna in deferto, ficut fcriptu eft: Panem de cælo dedit eis.* Owre fathers haue eaten Manna in the wildernefse, as yt ys written he gaue them bread from heauen to eate.

To determine directly againft them, and that they fhoulde perceaue, that Manna was but a figure of this very bread, that camefrom heauen (For Manna gaue not life to the eaters of yt, but this bread doth) therfor he faied Not as yower fathers did eateManna and be dead, but he that eateth of this bread fhal liue for euer.He wel declareth what death their fathers died, who did eat Manna, that ys the euerlafting death, not all that did eate Manna died that death but their fathers in vnbelief. And as they through vnbeleif died an euerlafting death : fo they that fhall eate this bread with true beleif fhall liue an euerlafting life. But yt fhall be to the pourpofe to heare the holy Fathers how they vnderftad this text.of the which the firft coople fhall be fainct *Ambrofe* and *Chryfoftom.*Sainct *Ambrofe* faieth thus : *Reuera mirabile*

F

eft quòd Manna Deus plueret patribus, & quotidiano cœli pafcebantur alimento. Vnde dictum eft : Panem Angelorum manducauit homo. Sed tamen illum panem qui manducauerunt in deferto mortui funt. Ifta autem efca, quam accipis, ifte panis viuus, qui de cælo defcendit vitæ æternæ fubftantiam adminiftrat. Et quicunque panem hunc manducauerit, non morietur in æternum. & corpus Chrifti eft. Truly yt ys merueiloufe that God did rain Manna to the fathers, and that they were fedde withe the dailie foode from heauen. Wherfor yt ys faied: Man hath eaten the bread of Angells. but for all that they that haue eaten that bread in defert, are dead. This meat that thowe takeft, this bread of life, that came downe from heauen, doth miniftre the fubftance of euerlafting life, and who fo euer fhall eate this bread, he fhall not die for euer, andyt ys he bodie of Chryft. Thus farre he.

What this bread ys that defcended from heauen, and what the profit and benefitt of yt ys, fainct Ambrofe hath in this his faing declared, the bread ys the bodie of Chryft (faieth he) whiche bodie ys the meat that the faithfull doth take, and the benefite of this fo taken ys euerlafting life.

G

Wherfor fainct Ambrofe being fo plain, I will bring in his yocke folowe Chryfoftome, who hath *(according to the counfell of fainct Paule)* not caried the yocke with the vnfaithfull, but with the faithfull, whiche ys the yocke of Chryft, whiche, as he himfelf faieth, ys fweet. Thus he faieth : *Dicit*

ergo : Qui manducat carnem meam in morte non peribit, neque damnabitur. Sed non de communi dicit refurrectione (fiquidem omnes refurgent) fed de clara illa & gloriofa quæ præmium meretur. Patres veftri manducauerunt Manna in deferto, & mortui funt. Qui manducat hunc panem, viuet in æternum. Frequenter idem repetit, vt auditorum animis imprimatur. Vltima enim hæc erat doctrina, vt refurrectionis, & vitæ æternæ fidem confirmaret. Quocirca poft vitæ æternæ promifsionem refurrectionem proponit, poftquam illa futuram oftendit, & hoc vnde conftat? à fcripturis, ad quas eos femper relegat, vt inde erudiantur. Cùm autem dare vitam mundo dicit, in æmulationem eos adducit, vtfi aliorum bono mouentur, nolint ipfi excludi. Frequenter autem Mannæ meminit, & differentiam conferendo ad fidem allicit. Nam fi pofsibile fuit vt quadraginta annos fine mefsibus & frumento, & aliis ad victum neceffarijs viuerent, longè magis nunc cùm ad maiora venerint. Nam fi in illis figuris fine labore expofitum colligebant : nunc profectò magis, vbi nulla mors, & veræ vitæ fruitio. Vitæ autem vbique meminit. Nam eius trahimur cupiditate, & nihil fuauius quàm non mori.Etenim in veteri Teftamento longa vita, & multi

E

dies

dies promittebantur : Nunc verò non simpliciter vitæ longitudo, sed vita sine fine promit-

A *titur* He saieth therfor, he that eateth my flesh, shall not perish in death, neither shal be damned. But he doth not speake of the common resurrection (for all shall rise) but of that clere, and glorioufe, whiche deserueth rewarde. Yower fathers haue eaten Manna in the wildernesse, and be dead. He that eateth this bread shall liue for euer. he doth often repete the same, that yt might be ymprinted in the mindes of thearers. This was the last doctrine, that he might confirme the faith of the resurrection, and euerlasting life: wherfor after the promisse of eternall life, he proueth the resurrection, after he had shewed that yt was to come. And from whence doth his appeare? by the scriptures, vnto the whiche he doth allwaies send them, that from thece they might be taught. When he saieth yt to geue life to the woorlde, he bringeth them to folow, that if they be moued with the profit or commoditie of other, they wolde not be excluded. Often he maketh mencion of Manna, and conferiring the difference, allureth them to faith. For if yt were

B possible that they shoulde liue fortie years withoute haruestes, and other necessares to their liuing: *moch more nowe when they are comed to greater things.* For if in these figures they did gather withoute labour the thing sett furth, or made ready to their handes, nowe truly moche more, wher ys no death, and the fruicion of true life. Of life he maketh mencion euery where. For we be drawen with defire therof, and nothing ys more pleasaunt, then not to die. For in the olde Testament long life, and manie daies were promised: Nowe not simplic lenght of life, but life withoute ende ys promised: Thus he.

We cometo greater thi ges in the Sacr. then the Iewes did in Mã na.

Albeit Chrysostom in this sentence maketh no great mencion of the Sacrament in open and expresse woordes: yet folowing the sense in the beginning of this part of this chapter, whiche by his iudgement ys of the Sacrament, if yt be well considered he saieth sufficiently: as also wher he saieth that yf yt were possible for the Iewes to liue fortie yeare without harueft or corne *moche more nowe when we be commed to greater thinges.* Manna was a great miracle as sainct Ambrose saieth, and if they did well receaue yt, they did

C receaue spirituallie Chryst. Then if our Sacramet be (*as the Sacramentaries saie*) a peice of bread, whiche ys no like thing to Manna, the one being from heauen by miracle, the other by common courfe from the hand of the artificer withoute any miracle or wonder, and in the receipt of yt Chryst spiritually receaued, as in the receipt of Manna, howe then be we comed to greater thinges then the figure of Manna was, seing that in both Chryst ys receaued but spirituallie. And Manna ys from heauen by God, the bread from the earth by the baker.

Mãna and the Sacrament com pared.

Wherfor by these woordes of Chrysoftome that we be comed to greater thinges, ys signified to vs that the Sacramet coteineth a woorthier thing, and a thing of greater miracle, then Manna was, whiche also was a miraculoufe thing, which thing conteined in the Sacrament ys the very bodie of Chryst, of the whiche Manna was the figure, of the whiche more shall be saied in the thirde booke. But here to be short if the reall presence of Chryftes bodie be not in the Sacrament, then ys Manna a woorthier and greater thing then yt by al meanes, as by that, that ys allready saied yt maie appeare.

D And so shall Chrysoftome be reproued of an vntrueth for that we are not comed to greater thinges, But I shall sooner refuse the sainges of these aduersaries, then I will the sainges of Chrysoftome, and so I trust, will the wife reader.

THE

THE ONE AND THIRTITH CHAP. PROCEA

deth in the the expofition of the fame text by S. Hierom
and S. Cyrill.

Hieron. ad
Hedibiq.2

Et vs heare the teſtimonie of an other coople for the vnderſtanding of this text. S. Hierom ſaith : *Si ergo panis, qui de cœlo deſcendit , corpus eſt Domini, & vinum quòd Diſcipulis dedit ſanguis illius eſt noui Teſtamenti, qui pro multis effuſus eſt, in remiſſionem peccatorum, iudaicas fabulas repellamus, & aſcendamus cum Domino cœnaculum magnum ſtratum, atque mundatum, & accipiamus ab eo ſurſum calicem noui Teſtamenti , ibíque cum eo Paſcha celebrantes, inebriemur ab eo, vino ſobrietatis. Non enim eſt regnum Dei eſca, & potus, ſed iuſticia & gaudium, & pax in Spiritu ſanctò . Nec Moyſes dedit nobis panem verum , ſed Dominus Ieſus, ipſe conuiua , & conuiuium, ipſe comedens, & qui comeditur .* Yf therfor the bread that deſcended from heauen, *be the bodie of our Lorde,* and the wine that

The bread
that deſcen
ded from
heauen ys
the bodie
of our Lor-
de.

he gaue to his Diſciples *be his blood of the newe Teſtament,* whiche was ſhed for manie in remiſſion of ſinnes, let vs repell and caſt from vs Iudaicall fables, and let vs aſcende with our Lorde in to the great parlour paued and made clean, and let vs from aboue take of him, the cuppe of the newe Teſtament, and ther celebrating with him the Paſſeouer, let vs be ſatisfied of him, with the wine of ſobrietie. For the kingdom of God ys not meat, and drinke, but righteouſneſſe, and peace, and ioie in the holy Goſt. Neither did Moyſes geue vs the true bread, *but our Lorde Ieſus , he ys the feaſter, and he ys the feaſt, he ys he that eateth , and ys eaten .* Thus farre S. Hierom.

Chryſt ys
the feaſt
and the
feeſter.

By theſe woordes we are after the vnderſtandinge of S . Hierom , fullie enſtructed what the bread ys, that our Sauiour Chryſt ſpeaketh of when he ſaied: *This ys the bread that deſcended from heaue.* Yt ys (ſaieth S. *Hierom*) the bodie of our Lorde, and the wine ys the bloode that was ſhed for manie in the remiſſion of ſinnes. By the which woordes he doth not onelie teache vs , that this ſcripture ys to be vunderſtanded of the Sacrament, but by the ſame alſo he hath teſtified with other holie Fathers the preſence of Chryſtes bodie in the Sacrament. For in the beginning he ſaied, *that the bread that deſcended from heauen ys the bodie of our Lorde,* and to ſhewe vs wher he ment yt to be, in the ende he ſaieth, *that not Moyſes did geue the true bread, but our Lorde Ieſus, he ys the feaſter and the feaſt, he ys he that doth eat, and ys eaten .* Wherby he well ſheweth that that bread ys the bodie of our Lorde, which ys in that holie feaſt, wher our ſauiour Chryſt ys the feaſter, and he him ſelf alſo ys the meat and drinke of the feaſt, and ſo the wholl feaſt. In the whiche as he doth in his membres, being the head of them, eate the bleſſed meat of that holie feaſt: So yt ys euen he, euen his very dodie, and bloode that ys ther eaten and dronken. Wherfor ſoch a noble feaſter being preſent, and ſo holie meat being ther eaten, the Church right well with goodlie concorde, and conſent ſingeth : *O ſacrum conuiuium , in quo Chriſtus ſumitur.* O holie feaſt in the which Chryſt ys receaued.

But the prolixitie of this matter, if yt ſhoulde be woorthilie folowed, calleth me backe, and moueth to ſtaie and heare the other that ys ioined to ſainctie Hierom, whiche ys S. Cyrill, who ſaieth thus : *Non enim prudenter, quæ ad breue tempus ſufficiunt, hoc nomine appellabuntur, nec panis erat ex Deo, quem maiores Iudæorum comederunt, & mortui ſunt. Nam ſi de cœlo & ex Deo fuiſſet, liberaſſet à morte participantes . Contrà verò corpus Chriſti , panis de cœlo eſt, quia æternam comedentibus vitam largitur* Thoſe thinges which for a ſhort time ſuffice ſhall not wiſely be called by this name. Neither that bread, which the elders of the Ie-

wes

A wes did eate, and be dead, was of God. For if yt had ben from heauen and of God, yt had deliuered the partakers of yt from death. Contrary wife the bodie of Chryſt ys the bread from heauen, For yt graunteth the eaters eter nall life. As S. Hierom ſaied that the bodie of Chryſtes ys the bread that deſcended from heauen : So by like woordes ſaieth S. Cyrill here And that we ſhoulde knowe what he meneth, he applieth the figure of yt eaten by the elders of the Iewes, whiche did not giue life, whiche was Manna, vnto the bodie of Chryſt, whiche being eaten doth giue life eternall. Wherfor Manna being a figure of Chryſtes bodie eaten in the Sacramēt, yt muſt ne- des folowe that he vnderſtandeth this ſcripture of Chryſtes bodie in the Sa- crament, of the whiche no man that hath redde Cyrill can doubte, whoſe wholl proceſſe ys ſo plain in the matter.

THE TWO AND THIRTETH CHAP. ENDETH THE
expoſition of this text by ſainƈe Auguſtin and Theoph.

B Owe let vs heare as breifly one coople mo and then we ſhall leaue this text. S. Auguſtin ſaieth thus : *Hic eſt panis, qui de cœlo deſcendit, vt illum manducando viuamus, quia æternam vitam ex nobis habere non poſſumus. Non ſicut (inquit) manducauerunt patres veſtri Manna & mortui ſunt. Qui manducat hunc panem viuet in æternum.* *Quòd ergo illi mortui ſunt, ita vult intelligi, vt non viuant in æternum. Nan temporaliter profeƈò, & hi moriuntur, qui Chriſtum manducant, ſed viuunt in æternum, quia Chriſtus eſt vita æterna.* This ys the bread that deſcended from heauen, that we eating him maie liue. For we can not of our ſelues haue eternall life. Not (ſaieth he) as yower Fathers haue eaten Manna, and are dead, he that eateth this bread, ſhall liue for euer. That they then be dead, thus he wolde yt ſhoulde be vnderſtanded, that they liue not for euer. For tēporallie the ſe truly ſhall alſo die, which do eate Chryſt, but they liue for euer. For Chryſt ys eternall life. Thus farre he.

Traƈ. 26. in Ioan.

What gloſes the Aduerſaries do here vpon S. Auguſtins ſaing inuent, I C leaue them to their the ſame inuencion. But for ſomoche as Chryſte him ſelf and S. Auguſtin expownding Chryſtes ſaing, doth applie the figure of Man- na and the eating of yt to this bread that came from heauen, and Manna by all the Fathers iudgementes ys the figure of the holie Sacrament, yt ys manifeſt that therfor this ſcripture ys to be vnderſtanded of the Sacrament.

Whiche *Theophilaƈ,* who at this preſent ys ioined with S. Auguſtin, will by expreſſe woordes declare. *Patres veſtri comederunt Manna in ſolitudine. Hoc ſæpe & multum verſat in ore, vt perſuadeat hominibus. Nan ſi poſſibile fuit quadraginta annis ſine meſſe, & ſemente paſci homines, & conſeruari illorum vitam, multò magis nunc conſeruabit naturam ſpiritualem meliori pane Dominus, carne ſua, quæ abſque ſemine viri ex virgine conſtituta eſt.* Yower fathers haue eaten Manna in the wilderneſſe. Thys (ſaieth *Theophilaƈ*) oftē and moche he ſpeaketh, that he might perſwade men. For yf yt were poſſible men to be fedde, and their liues to be conſerued fortie yeares, withoute ſowing or harueſt, moche more nowe ſhall our lorde with a better bread, that ys, his fleſh, which without the ſeed of man ys ma- D de of a virgen conſerue our ſpirituall life. Thus he.

In 6. Ioan.

Obſerue, as ys before noted, that the applicacion of the figure argueth the thing figured here to be ſpoken of, which thing ys the Sacrament. And for the veritie of the ſame, yf this authour had nothing ſpoken here expreſ-
ſelie:

felie : yet that whiche he hath hitherto vpon this part of the fixt of S. Iohn E
allreadie declared,wolde and maie fufficiently fhewe his minde vpon this.

Oure lord But, God be praifed, he doth verie plainlie here alfo open the matter . For
feadeth vs when he had faied that our Lorde wolde feed vs with a better bread, expo-
with a bre- wnding yt , that ys (faieth he) his flefh . And that he wolde not make yt an
ad which imaginarie flefh, he faieth *that he feedeth vs with the fame flesh , whiche withoute the*
ys his flesh. *feed of man was born of the Virgen,* Whiche maner of fpeache ys fo plain that I cã
A plain fa- not but merueill that men will fuffer them felues to be feduced, and led
ing for the awaie by vain men, when foche auncient Fathers do teache them in foche
Procla. forte, that they haue nothing to kepe them felues from the trueth, but felf
will,and malice.

THE THREE AND THIRTETH CHAP. PROCEADETH
to the next text in the fixt of Jainſle Iohn.

Itherto our Sauiour Chryſt fpeaking of this great miftery of the F
eatinge and drinking of his flefh and bloode, doth here nowe
make an ende of the fame. And therfor, faieth the Euangelift to
declare the fame : *Hec dixit in Sinagoga docens in Cpharnaum.* Thefe
Joan.6. thinges faied he in the Sinagog as he taught in Capharnaum.
But for afmoche as manie hearning this doctrine of Chryft were not edi-
fied, but offended therwith, as manie of our faint Chryftians are, whofe
Sacramēta maner of incredulitie, and hardneffe of beleif, with Chryftes proceeding to
ries of oure reforme the fame , as the Euangelift fetteth yt furth, our Capharnaites,
time are through vnbeleif of that that Chryft fpake to the better declaracion of his
Capharnai- doctrine, haue taken to the more occafion of their doubte , eroure , and
tes. ruine , feing that they wolde fo take his woordes to turne them againft him
felf, and with them to impugne that trueth that he hath taught, and left
in his Church to remain and continue vntill he come: we fhall by his grace
take thefe fcriptures from them , and by like proceffe, as hertofore ys vfed
fhewe the true vnderftanding of them, that all men maie perceaue that thefe G
Heretikes Aduerfaries haue raither fought occafion to be raither enemies of Gods
call their. trueth then fauourers of the fame. whiche name they moche vfurpe, cloa
phantafies thing them felues with fhepes cloathinge, but inwardlie they are very wol-
gods woord ues. outwardlie they euer crie Gods woorde , when in dede they vtter
and their their inuencions grownded vpon affection , raither to pleafe the peoples
lies,trueth. phantafies , then fullfill Gods pleafure . So they crie the trueth, the trueth,
when they in very dede fet furth lies , and herefie to impugn and deftroie
the trueth.

And as they that mifliked the doctrine of Chryft were of his Difciples:So
thefe nowe that miflike the fame doctrine were of his Difciples, but nowe
abierunt retro poſt Satanam, they are gone back after Satan. And as the difciples faied when they heard this doctrine : *Durus eſt hic fermo,quis poteſt eum*
audire ? This ys an hard faing , who can abide the hearing of yt : So
thefe men faie that yt ys an hard faing, and they can not abide the hearing of yt.

But as fainct Auguftin faied by the Difciples, which firft fpake thefe woor H
Ang in des : So maie yt be faied by their difciples,who in thefe daies do folowe thẽ:
Pfal.98. *Ipfi erant duri non fermo.* They were hard, and not the woorde . But as he faieth
in an other place : *Si Difcipuli durum habuerunt iftum fermonem,quid inimici ?* Yf the
Difciples counted this woorde harde, what do the enemies ? Yf thofe that
did

A did knowe and folow Chryſt of late daies do accõpte yt an hard ſaing , that we ſaie according to Chryſtes doctrin, that we do eate his very fleſh in the Sacrament,what maie the Iewes,and Infideles do? But yf Chryſt did labour to abduce the Iewes from the figures and ſhaddowes,and adduce them to the very thing and trueth:moche more they that haue profeſſed Chryſt, ſhould be brought from figures, and learn to knowe the trueth of figures, which ys nowe in the newe teſtament. Which was Chryſtes pourpoſe , though they lept backe,as *Theophilact* ſaieth ſpeaking of the proceſſe of Chryſtes doctrine as concerning this myſterie.*Quod lucrum ex his verbis?imò plurimum, & maximũ. Nam quoniam memores erant ſubinde cibi corporalis,oſtendens eis quia omnia illa figura erant,& vmbra:Quæ autem ab ipſo nunc introducuntur, veritas ſunt. eius gratia hæc dicit, & ſpiritualis cibi recordatur, vt faciat eos à ſenſibilibus aliquantum remergere, cõtemnereque figuras & vmbras,& accurrere ad veritatem. Sed illi cùm nihil poſſent intelligere, quod ſupra ſenſum eſt,meliores non fiunt,ſed magis reſiliunt,& dicunt:Durus eſt hic ſermo, hoc eſt aſper,& qui ſuſcipi nequeat. Quis enim cùm carnalis ſit,poſſet ſuſcipere ſpiritualem*

Theophi-
lact in 6.
Ioan.

B *cibum,& panem qui de cœlo deſcendit,& carnem,quæ comeditur, &c. Nam quia carnem audierant,putabant quòd eos cogeret carnis & ſanguinis fieri deuoratores : quia autem nós ſpiritualiter intelligimus,neque carnium voratores ſumus, imò ſanctificamur per talem cibum.* What aduantage or gain of theſe woordes? very moche and great . For for that they were often mindefull of bodilie meat,Chryſt ſhewing that all thoſe thinges were but a figure,and a ſhaddowe:but ſoche things as by him were brought in were the trueth,for this cauſe he ſaied theſe thinges,and remembreth the ſpirituall meate,that he might make them ſomwhat return from ſenſible thinges,and to contemne figures , and ſhaddowes . But they when they can vnderſtand nothing that ys aboue the ſenſe is they are made neuer the better,but they leape ãd ſaie:*This ſaing ys harde,* that ys,vnpleaſaunt to ſenſuall knowledge,and which can not be receaued. For what ys he who when he ys carnall,can receaue ſpirituall meat and the bread, that deſcẽded frõ heauen,and the fleſh which ys eatẽ?for bicauſe they had heard him ſaie (*fleſh*)they thought that he wolde compell them to be deuourers of fleſh ãd blood.But bicauſe we vnderſtand the ſpirituall meat,we are not the deuourers of fleſh,but raither we are ſanctified by ſoch meat.Thus moch Theoph.

Carnall mẽ
vnderſtan-
ding no
thing aboue
ther ſenſies
leape backe
from the
vnderſtan-
ding of the
Sacr.

C Who geuing a cauſe why this doctrine of Chryſt ſemed hard to them ſaieth,yt was bicauſe they coulde not vnderſtand anie thing , that was aboue the knowledge of the ſenſeis:Euen ſo our ſenſuall and carnall men vnderſtanding not howe Chryſtes verie bodie ſhould be in the Sacrament , vnleſſe yt ſhoulde occupie the place of a bodie,neither be eaten vnleſſe yt ſhoulde be felt with our teeth,as other fleſh,and ſoch like after the groſſe knowledg of the ſenſeis,they leape backe and ſaie:yt can not be doen, yt ys a thing vnpoſſible,and who can abide to heare yt? But yf they wolde(*as Theophilact ſaieth*)vnderſtand aboue the ſenſes that ther ys the very reall body of Chryſt, which ys yet a ſpirituall meat,and not take yt ſo groſſlie and carnallie , but yet verilie and ſpiritually,they ſhould not be groſſe deuourers of fleſh , but yet eate the verie fleſh of Chryſt, not with teeth percing and hurting that, which ys liuing impaſsiblie , and yet with the mouth receauing that fleſh faithfullie.

Carnall vn
derſtãding

THE FOVR AND THIRTETH CHAP. BEGIN-
*neth the expofition of this text: Si ergo videritis, &c. by fainct Augu-
ften and fainct Cyrill.*

Wre Sauiour perceauing fome of hys owne Difciples , and other
who heard him fo plainlie fpeaking of the eating and drinking of
his flefh and bloode, to be offended, bicaufe thei phanfied that he
wolde haue them groflie to deuoure his flefh, ãd drinke his blood,
to lead and bring them from this ther groffe vnderftanding he faied : doth
this offended yowe. *Si ergo videritis filium hominis afcendentẽ vbi erat prius?* What
and if ye fhall fee the Sõne of man afcẽde vppe thither wher he was before?

Or we entre to fhewe the expofition of this text, as to know to what pour
pofe, or wherfore Chryft fpake thefe woords to the Iewes, and how he doth
aunfwer their incredulitie to his woordes, or diffolue their errour: this ys to
be examined, how Chryft doth faie that *the Sonne of man fhall afcend wher he was
before.* Yt ys knowen to all that profeffe Chryft, being of difcrecion , that
Chryft as man was born of the Virgen in earth, and was neuer in heauen before he fpake thefe woordes. *Howe then doth he faie, that the Sonne of man fhall afcende wher he was before?*

As I haue learned of S.Auguftine howe to diffolue this doubte : So do I
thinke yt mete that ye do, for that his authoritie ys great , and his faings be
weightie, In this matter thus he reafoneth. *Illud non negligenter prætereundum eft,
quod ait: Si ergo videritis filium hominis afcendentem vbi erat prius? filius hominis Chriftus
ex virgine Maria. Ergo filius hominis hic cœpit effe in terra, vbi carnem affumpfit ex terra. vnde propheticè dictum erat: Veritas de terra orta eft. Quid ergo fibi vult quod ait: Cùm
videritis filium hominis afcendentem vbi erat prius? Nulla eft quæftio fi ita dixiffet: Si videritis filium Dei afcendentem vbi erat prius: Cum verò, filium hominis, dixit, afcendentem
vbi erat prius, nunquid filius hominis in cœlo erat, priufquàm in terra effe cœpit? Hic quidem dixit vbi erat prius, quafi tũc non ibi effet quando hæc loquebatur. Alio autem loco ait:
Nemo afcendit in cœlum, nifi qui defcendit de cœlo, filius hominis, qui eft in cœlo. Non dixit
(erat) fed filius (inquit) hominis, qui eft in cœlo. In terra loquebatur, & in cœlo fe effe dicebat. Quò pertinet nifi vt intelligamus, quod etiã priftino fermone commendaui charitati ve
ftræ, vnam perfonã effe Chriftũ, Deum & hominẽ, non duas, ne fides noftra non fit Trinitas
fed Quaternitas. Chriftus ergo vnus eft. Verbum, anima & caro, vnus Chriftus, filius Dei,
& filius hominis vnus Chriftus. filius Dei femper: filius hominis ex tempore. tamen vnus
Chriftus fecundùm vnitatem perfonæ in cœlo erat, quando in terra loquebatur. Sic erat filius
hominis in cœlo, quemadmodum filius Dei erat in terra, filius Dei in terra in fufcepta carne:
filius hominis in cœlo in vnitate perfonæ.* That ys not necligently to be ouerpaffed
that he faieth: *What and yf ye fee the Sonne of man afcending wher he was before?* The
Sonne of man, Chryft of the Virgen Marie. Therfore the Sonne of man began here in earth, wher he tooke flefh of the earth. Wherfor yt was fpoken
by the Prophet: *Trueth fhall fpring oute of the earth.* What meneth then that he
faieth, *when yow fhal fee the Sonne of man afcende wher he was before ?* Ther were no
queftion yf he had faied: What yf yow fhal fee the Sõne of God afcẽd vppe
wher he was before? but when he faied the Sonne of man to afcende wher he
was before, was the Sonne of man in heauen, before he begã to be in earth?
Here he faied, where he was before , as though he were not then ther, when
he fpake thefe woordes. In an other place he faieth. No man afcendeth vppe to heauen, but he that came down from heauen, euen the Sonne of man
which ys in heauen He did not faie (*which was*) but the Sonne (faieth he) of
man which ys in heauen. He fpake in the earth, and he faied he was in heauen

Ioan.6.

Aug. tract
27. in Ioan

*Howe chrift
the Sõne of
man was in
heauẽ whẽ
he fpake in
earth.*

A uen.To what powrpofe yt ys,but that we maie vnderſtand, which I haue alreadie declared to yowr charitie,that Chryſt God and man ys one perſon,
not two,leaſt our faith be not a trinitie,but a quaternitie? Chryſt therfor ys
one.The Sonne of God,the ſoule,and the fleſh one Chryſt. The Sonne of
God,and the Sonne of man one Chryſt.Chryſt the Sône of God euer: the
Sône of mã in time:Yet for al that one Chryſt after the vnitie of perſõ was
in heauen,when he ſpake in earth.The Sonne of man was ſo in heauē,as the
Sonne of God was in earth.TheSonne of God was in the earth in the recea
ued fleſh:the Sonne of man was in heauen in the vnitie of perſon.Thus farre
ſainct Auguſtine.

Although this ſentéce be ſomwhat lõg:yet if ye weigh yt wel, yt ſhall not
repétyow of the reading of yt.For in yt ye maie ſee the doubt fullie diſſolued
for the being of Chryſt the Sône of mã in heauē,who thē preſentlie ſpake in
earth:and howe he was before in heauē,who was born in time in the earth.

Nowe this doubt being diſſolued,let vs ſeke the vnderſtanding of the ſcri-
B pture we haue to expownde,which in a great parte we ſhall do,yf we knowe
wherfor Chryſt here made mencion of his aſcenſion into heauen , ſeing he
was now in ſetting furth howe his bodie ſhould be eaten in earth.The cauſe
why he maketh here mencion of hys aſcenſion ys declared by the ſame S.
Auguſtine,who vpon this text ſaieth thus:*Quid eſt hoc?Hinc ſoluit illos , quos noue
rat.Hinc aperuit vnde fuerant ſcandalizati; hinc planè ſi intelligerent. Illi enim putabant
eum erogaturum corpus ſuum:Ille autem dixit aſcenſurum ſe in cœlum vtique integrũ.Cùm
videritis filiũ hominis aſcendentẽ vbi erat prius,certè vel tũc videbitis,quia nõ eo modo quò
putatis,erogat corpus ſuũ.Certè vel tunc intelligetis,quia gratia eius non conſumitur morſi-
bus.*What if yow ſee the Sône of man aſcend vppe wher he was before?what
ys this (ſaieth S.Auguſtine)By this he ſolued them,whom he had knowen. By
this he hath opened wherby they were offended,by this plainly if theywold
vnderſtand.For they thought that he wolde deale furth hys bodie,but he ſai
eth that he wolde aſcende into heauen,and that wholl.*When ye ſhall ſee the Sô
ne of man aſcende vppe wher he was before,*certenlie euen thẽ ſhall ye ſee,that not
after that maner that ye thinke,he geueth oute his bodie,certenlie euen thẽ
C ſhall ye vnderſtande,that his grace ys not conſumed by morſels.

Do ye not here ſee the cauſe,why Chryſt ſpake of his aſcenſion ? S.Auguſtin
hath opened yt vnto yow. They thought that Chryſt wolde haue geuen his
bodie in lumpes or peices among them. Therfor to plucke thẽ frõ that groſſe and carnal vnderſtanding,he telleth them before that he wil leaue no part
nor peice of his bodie behinde , but he will whollie aſcende into heauen
with an wholl bodie.

But let not now the Aduerſarie,neither the weake man take anie occaſiõ
of errour,wher none ys iuſtly geuen,that bicauſe S.Auguſtin ſaieth that the
Diſciples thought that he wolde geue his bodie emõg thẽ,and Chryſt ſaied,
he wolde aſcend vppe wholl,that therfor by no means Chryſt geueth hys
bodie vnto vs in the Sacramẽt.For if by no means,then he geueth yt not ſpi
rituallie neither,and ſo were the doctrine of the Aduerſaries ouerthrowen.
But that he geueth not his verie real bodie in the Sacramẽt,although the Ad
uerſaries wolde haue yt ſo onely to be vnderſtanded:yet yt doth not ſo meẽ
but,as S.Auguſtin ſaieth,*non eo modo,quo putatis,erogat corpus ſuum,*not after ſoch
D maner as yowe thinke he geueth oute his bodie.So that he denieth not the
geuing oute of Chryſtes bodie,but the maner of the geuing oute of hys bo-
die.And what maner doth he denie ? that maner that the groſſe Diſciples
thought,which maner S.Auguſtin more plainly declareth in an other place

*why Chriſt made men-
cion of hys aſcenſion in
the vi. of S.?ohn.*

*Tract. 27.
in Ioan.*

In Psalm.
98.

saing:*Tunc autem, quando Dominus hoc commendans, de carne sua locutus erat , & dixe-* E
rat : Nisi quis manducauerit carnem meam non habebit in se vitam æternam , scan-
dalizati sunt quidam ex septuaginta, & dixerunt: Durus est hic sermo. Quis potest eum
intelligere? & recesserunt ab eo, & amplius cum eo non ambulauerunt . Durum illis vi-
sum est quod ait : Nisi quis manducauerit carnem meam , non habebit vitam æternam.
Acceperunt illud stultè , carnaliter illud cogitauerunt , & putauerunt , quia præ-
cisurus esset Dominus particulas quasdam de corpore suo, & daturus illis , & dixerunt:
Durus est hic sermo. Then, saieth S. Augustin, when our Lord setting furth thys

Capharnai
tes how thei
vnderstood
Chryst car
nallie.

had spoken of his flesh, and had saied: *Except a man eate my flesh, he shall not haue*
in himself life euerlasting. Certain of the seuentie Disciples were offended and
saied: *This ys an hard saing. Who can vnderstand yt?* And they went from him,
and walked no more with him. Yt semed harde to them, that he saied : *Except*
a man eate my flesh, he shall not haue in himself life euerlasting. They tooke yt foolish-
lie, carnallie they thought yt. And they thought that our Lord wolde cut
certain peices from hys bodie and geue to them, and they saied: *This an harde*
saing. Thus S. Augustin. F

Here ye perceaue after what maner the Disciples thought that Chryst
wolde geue them his bodie to eate, and this maner doth sainct Augustin
denie, not the maner that the Chrystian faith teacheth but onely that ma-

S. Aug. de
nieth not
the geuing
furth of
Chrystes bo
die reallie,
but the gros
se maner
conceaued
of the Dis-
ciples.
Obiection
out of S.
Aug. aun
swered.

ner, that the grosse Disciples thought, and therfor S. Augustin saith : *Non*
eo modo quo putatis, not after that maner, that yowe thinke , so that S. Augustine in this place dothe neither denie the geuing oute of Chrystes bodie
verilie, ãd reallie, to be receaued: nor yet the maner côuenient to the geuing
oute of the same, which now the catholique Church throughout the world
vseth: Wherfor let neither the weake man wauer for thys, neither the Aduersarie triumphe thinking his heresie to be confirmed, and himself to haue
gotten the victorie. *Ne ante victoriam canat triumphum,* Leaft he make a triumphe before the victorie.

But yet the Aduersaries will saie that S. Augustin doth not teache
here the presence of Chrystes bodie reallie, but spiritually, that ys by grace,
for he saieth plainlie that then when the Sonne of man ys ascended vppe G
wher he was before , we shall perceaue that his grace ys not consumed
with morsells. Wher he teacheth the presence of Chryst by grace, not by
reall presence.

This reason or argument ys as good here as yt ys in some other places of
S. Augustins workes, wher bicause he speaketh of the spirituall receauing of
Chryst, therfore ye will clean expell the reall receauing of hys bodie . And
thus might some other Heretique contrarie, take some other place of
S. Augustin, where he speaketh of the reall presence, and therby contend
against yow that ther ys no spirituall presence. But an vpright reader
shall, as ys before saied, finde in S. Augusten both maners of the presence
of Chryst in the Sacrament, that ys a reall presence, and a spirituall presence , and agreablie therunto , a reall receauing of the same bodie,
and a spirituall.

But that the reader maie perceaue that this ys true that I haue saied,
that S. Augustin teacheth the reall presence of Chrystes bodie in the

Aug. serm.
ad Neoph.
A plain pla
ce of. S.
Aug for
M. Iuel.

Sacrament, harken howe sainct Augustin taught as yt were the yonge
scholers in the faith of Chryst in this matter . Thus he taught them: H
Hoc accipite in pane quod pependit in cruce . Hoc accipite in calice , quod effu-
sum est de latere Christi. Erit enim illi mors, non vita, qui mendacem putauerit Chri-
stum. Take ye this in the bread, that did hang on the crosse. Take this in
the

A the chalice, that was fhedde oute of the fide of Chryft. He fhall haue death not life that thinketh Chryft a Lyar.

What ys ther to be thought here but that S. Auguftine teaching yonge fcholers wolde fpeake in plain woordes, and plain fentence, that the yong learners might perceaue the thing to be as yt ys fpoken, and not vfe to them obfcure figures, and tropes? For in thefe do not they vnder-ftand what ys to be beleued. Yf therfor Chryft were in the Sacrament but as in a figure, then wolde fainct Auguftin haue taught thefe yong ones thus : Take ye, this bread, as a fign, token or figure of Chryftes bodie, and when ye fee yt broken, remembre that Chryftes bodie was broken vpon the Croffe for yowe. And likewife, take thys wine as a fign, or token of Chryftes bloode fhedde for yowe vpon the Croffe. But vnderftande that yt ys not in verie dede the bodie and blood of Chryft, but fignes and to-kens of them. Thys were a maner of fpeache mete to teache yong ones, yf the trueth of the thing were agreable, but bicaufe the trueth ys not fo, therfore S. Auguftin taught them by foche plain fpeache, as the truth wolde

B beare, that ys, that they wolde take in the Sacrament that bodie that hanged vpon the Croffe, and in the cuppe that blood that was fhedde oute of Chryftes fide.

Chryft yt made a liar when his woord ys not beleued

Yea and that they fhoulde fo take he addeth a cominaciõ that they fhould take death and not life, which think Chryft a lyar. Why? What faied Chryft? *Take eate, thys ys my bodie.* He then that dothe not beleue Chryft herin, but fai-eth yt ys not his bodie, but a figure of hys bodie : he ys the Aduerfarie of Chryft, the reprouer of Chryft. And he maketh Chryft a lyar, as S. Auguftin faieth and therfor fhall haue death and not life.

In time therfor take hede yf thow beeft in errour, thow canneft not make Chryft a lyar, but thow thy felf fhalt be fownde a lyar. And therfore thowe fhalt not be admitted to the bleffed companie of the mafter of the trueth: but to the curfed and damnable companie of the Father of lyes. Repēt thee therfore of thine herefie, and embrace the trueth, that by yt thowe maift atteign to the true life.

C Nowe to this learned Father fhall be ioined S. Cyrill, who faieth thus: *Ex imperitia multi qui Chriftum fequebantur, verba ipfius non capientes, perturbaban-tur. Nam cùm audiffent: Amen, amen dico vobis, Nifi comederitis carnem filij hominis, & biberitis eius fanguinem, non habebitis vitam in vobis: Ad immanes ferarum mores vocari fe à Chrifto arbitrabantur, incitariſque vt vellent crudas hominis carnes manducare, & fanguinem bibere, quæ vel auditu horribilia funt, nondum enim myfterij huius formam & difpenfationem pulcherrimam cognouerant. Illud etiam adhoc cogitabant : Quomo-dò caro huius hominis, æternã nobis vitam largietur? aut quomodò ad immortalitatē addu-cere poterit ? Quæ cùm intelligeret is, cuius oculis omnia nuda funt, atque aperta, alia eos re mirabili ad fidem impellit. Fruftra (inquit) o vos, propter verba mea conturbamini. Quòd fi credere non vultis vitam vobis à meo corpore dari, quid fa-cietis, quando in cœlum me volare confpicietis ? Non enim afcenfurum me folum-modò profiteor, ne rurfus quomodò id fieri poffit quæratis, fed oculis etiam ita fieri veftris cernetis. Quid ergo hoc videntes, dicetis : Annon erit hoc magnum veftræ dementiæ argumentum ? Si enim putatis carnem meam vitam vobis affer-re non poffe, quomodò tanquam volucris in cœlum afcendet ? quomodò per aëra volabit : hoc enim fimiliter generi humano impofsibile eft. Quod fi præter na-*

D *turam caro mea in cœlum confcendet, quid prohibet ne fimiliter præter natu-ram viuificet ?* For lacke of knowledg manie that did folowe Chryft not vnderftanding his woordes were troobled. For whē they heard: *verily verelye*

Ca. 22. fup. 6. Ioann.

Capharnai tes howe thei vnder ftood Chryft. Ioan. 6.

Except ye eate the flesh of the Sonne of man, and drinke hys blood , ye shall not haue life in E
yowe. They thought themselues to be called of Chryst to the cruell maners
of wilde beastes, and to be moued that they shoulde eate the rawe flesh of a
man, and drinke hys bloode, whiche thinges are horrible euen to heare.
They had not yet knowen the goodly forme and dispensacion of this
mystery. Moreouer also they thought: Howe should the flesh of this man
graunt vs eternall life? or howe can yt bring vs to immortalitie ? Whiche
thinges when he did vnderstand, vnto whose eyes all thinges are naked and
Chrystes   open, with an other merueilouse thing he driueth them to the faith. O
flesh besi-   yowe *(saieth he)* vainlie are ye troobled for my woordes . For yf ye will
de nature   not beleue life to be geuen yow of my bodie, what will ye do when ye shall
ascendedin   see me flie vppe into heauen? I do not saie that I will onely ascende into hea
to heauen: uen, least yow aske again howe that maie be doen: but ye shall euen so see
beside natu   yt with yowr eyes. What therfore wil ye saie seing this? shal yt not be a great
re yt geueth   argument of yowr madnesse? Yf ye thinke that my flesh can not bring life
life in the   vnto yow, how shall yt as a flieng thing ascende into heauen ? howe shall yt
Sacra.   flie by the ayer, for this likewise ys vnpossible to mankinde? Then yf my flesh F
shall go vppe into heauen beside nature, what dothe let that yt likewise beside nature maie not geue life. Thus moche S. Cyrill.

     Yow maie in this goodlie and liuely expositiō perceaue two vain though
tes, that the grosse Disciples had, one that they shoulde after the cruel maner
Two vain   of wildes beastes, eate the rawe flesh of Chryst, as yt were tearing yt, or cut-
thoughtes   ting yt oute by peices, and so Chrystes blessed flesh , as other thinges that
of the Ca-   be eaten, to be consumed. The other vain thought was how that flesh, which
pharn.   they accompted but as the flesh of a naturall man onely, and not as the flesh
of God ioined to the Godhead in vnitie of person, and therfor supposed yt
to be a mortall, and a corruptible flesh, howe *(I saie)* that mortal and corruptible flesh coulde geue vnto them immortalitie, and incorruption.

     Nowe to answer bothe these vain thoughtes, and to reforme thē, Chryst
saied: *what yf ye see the Sonne of man ascende vppe wher he was before?* By which one
saing he answereth bothe their thoughtes, and teacheth as concerning the
first, that wher they thought, that his bodie shoulde be cutte or torne in peices, that they had an euell vnderstanding. For yt shoulde ascende vppe into G
heauen, and that wholl, *as S. Augustine saied.* And that they might the better
beleue yt, they shoulde see yt, as S. Cyrill here saieth. The other vain thought
ys also answered in that he saieth his bodie shall ascend vppe to heauen,
which ascension ys aboue the order of nature. Therby instructing them,
that as his bodie aboue the course of nature shoulde ascende : So yt aboue
the course of nature shoulde geue life. How the flesh of Chryst shoulde geue life S. Cyrill heretofore hathe declared vpon the sainges of Chryst , that
yt ys by the eating of Chrystes flesh. And therfor he saied of the power of
Chrystes flesh: *Non verbo solùm verumetiam tactu mortuos excitabat, vt ostenderet*
In 6. Joan   *corpus quoque suum viuificare posse. Quodsi solo tactu suo corrupta redintegrantur: quomo-*
cap. 14.   *dò non viuemus, qui carnem illam & gustamus & manducamus? Reformabit enim omni-*
no ad immortalitatem suam participes sui. Ne velis iudaicè quomodò quærere, sed recor-
dare quamuis aqua naturaliter frigidior sit: aduentu tamen ignis frigiditatis suæ oblita,
æstuat. Chryst did not with his woorde onelie, but also with hys touching he
did rase dead men, that he might shewe, that his bodie also coulde geue life. H
Yf then with his onely touching corrupted things are made sownde again,
how shall not we liue, which taste and eate that flesh ? He will withoute all
doubte reforme the partakers of him to this immortalitie . Neither do tho-
                                                         we

A we after the Iewes maner aſke, *howe* : but remembre that though the water naturallie be colde : yet by the coming of the fire to yt, hauing forgotten her coldneſſe, waxeth hote. So that by S. Cyrill here yowe maie perceaue that the fleſh of Chryſt, which the vnbeleuing Diſciples did thinke coulde not geue life, doth geue life to them, that receaue and eate yt.

Let not the Aduerſaries nowe caſt in ther comon gloſe, that Cyrill ſpeaketh of the ſpirituall receauing and eating of Chryſtes fleſh For he teacheth more then in one place, that we are ioined to Chryſt not onely ſpirituallie, but alſo after the fleſh, by the eating of the ſame verie fleſh. And to this pourpoſe alſo tendeth this his diſputacion in this ſentence laſt alleadged, that he wolde proue the fleſh of Chryſt to geue life by the corporall touching of yt, and therfor yt geueth life to vs that corporallie do taſt and eate the ſame. And therfor let not the Sacramentarie aſke, *howe*, For as Chryſt aſcended aboue the courſe of nature of man : So he geueth him ſelf in the Sacrament to be eaten aboue the order and courſe of the nature B of man.

And nowe ye maie perceaue, wher the Aduerſaries haue abvſed this ſcripture to proue that ther ys no reall preſence of Chryſt in the Sacrament, by cauſe they ſaie that Chryſt by this text minded onelie to pluck the Diſciples from their groſſe thought of the carnall eating of him, to a ſpirituall maner of eating, and therfor here ys no reall fleſh to be eaten. Wherupon they charge vs, not onely with the name, but alſo with the groſſe erroure of the Cpharanaites, that we (like as they did) do go farre wide from the true mening of the ſcripture. But they are ſo buſie in charging vs with the groſſe carnalitie of the Capharnaites, and ſo curiouſe in ſifting of their ſpiritualytie, which they ſifte ſo long and ſo finely, that they let all the fine flower of Chryſtes heauenlie bread fall from them, and kepe nothing but the bare branne of the ſignifieng ſign in their owne hande, which in dede ys the groſſe bread they feed on.

The Sacramentaries ſifte the Sacra. ſo fine that they leaue nothing but the brã for themſelues.

For, as ye haue heard, neither S. Auguſtin, nor S. Cyrill do ſo expownC de yt that ther ys no reall preſence of Chryſt in the Sacrament, but that Chryſtes minde was onely to remoue the carnall and groſſe maner of eating whiche the Capharnaites had conceaued, of the whiche maner bothe theſe fathers haue made mencion. But as for the maner of our eating, ys no ſoche groſſe and beaſtlie maner, as Chryſt wolde remoue from the Capharnaites, but yt ys ſoche a maner as ys bothe reall, and yet ſpirituall, taught vnto vs by our Sauiour Chryſt himiſelf, and teſtified by his holie Churche and ſet furth by the holie Fathers of the ſame, as yowe maie perceaue by S. Auſten and S. Cyrill, who although they reproue the maner of the Capharnaites: yet they commende to vs the maner vſed and receaued in the Churche.

Cc iiij　THE

THE FIVE AND THIRTETH CHAP. PROCEADETH E
in the expofition of the fame text, and endeth yt by
Euth. and Petrus Cliniacen.

In 6. Ioan.

Owe hauing heard one coople of the elder houfe expownding this text: we will heare one coople mo onely, expownde the fame, and fo ende yt, and paffe to the next. *Euthymius* expownding this fcriptu te writeth thus: *Si ergo videritis filium hominis afcendentem vbi erat prius, quid dicetis? Loquitur de futura fui in cœlum affumptione. Afcendentem, quoad humanitatem: vbi prius erat, quoad diuinitatem. Qui enim poteft hanc carnem reddere cœleftem,*

As eafie for Chryft to make his flesh meat in the Sa. as to make it to afcēd.

poteft vtique ipfam cibum hominum efficere . What yf ye fee the Sonne of man afcende vppe wher he was before, what will ye faie? faieth *Enthymius* He fpeaketh of the affumption of him felf in to heauen, to come. what if ye fee him afcending? *Afcending vppe,* as touching his humanitie, *where he was before,* as touching his deitie. *For he that can make his flesh heauenly, can alfo make the fame meate of men.* Note I praie yowe, that this authour by the poffibilitie of F the worke of Chryft to make his flesh heauenly concludeth the poffibilitie to make the fame the meat of men, not groffie after the rude phantafie of the Capharnaites, but verilie and reallie after the pleafure of Chryft.

Argument of the afcēfion vfed by Chryft Io.vi ys vain to proue the Spirituall eating, but good to proue the reall eating of his flesh.

And that this authour meneth of the reall flesh of Chryft to be the meat of men, yt dothe moft euidenlie appeare by his argument deduced wpon the poffibilitie of Chryft in making his flesh heauenlie. For yf he had fpoken of Chryftes flesh to be eaten fpirituallie, ther neded no foche argument vpō poffibilitie to be made vpon his veric reall flesh. For the flesh of Chryft was fpirituallie the meate of the holie fathers in the olde lawe. Wherfor that neded not to be proued poffible, which fo manie yeares had ben in vfe: but that was nedefull to be proued to be poffible, which before was not in vfe, whiche was that the verie flesh of Chryft shoulde be eaten of men reallie.

Yf the faing and mening of Chryft had ben, that the Iewes shoulde haue eaten his flesh fpiritually onelie, as the Aduerfaries wolde haue yt, this argu ment of his afcenfion shoulde not haue neaded, but he might haue faied to them: As I gaue yower fathers Manna from heauen, that they eating yt shoulde alfo fpiritually eate me in a figure that I was then to come: So nowe ye shall eate a peice of bread, and drinke a cuppe of wine, in a figure, and for the remembrance of me, that I am comed, and haue fuffred for yowe. This maner of eating of Chryftes flesh as yt was vfed of the good and beleuing Iewes, and well knowen to them both in Manna, and in the Pafchall lambe: So if Chryftes mening had bē to no further matter of eating his flesh but in foche fort, they wolde neuer haue ftaied, and fticked fo moche at yt. But he ment the receipt of his flesh in dede. And therfor he verie well bringheth the poffibilitie of two workes vpon one thing, namely that yt ys as poffible for Chryft to make his flesh the meate of men, as yt was to make the flesh whiche was earthlie nowe to be hauenly, And fo this Authour concludeth that the flesh of Chryft ys as reallie eaten of men, as yt ys made heauenlie of Chryft: But Chryft hath made yt heauenly . wherfore he maketh yt to be eaten reallie.

G

H

Petrus Cluniacen.

Of this fcripture *Petrus Cluniacenfis* maketh a verie goodlie expofition paraphrafticallie: *Si videritis filium hominis afcendentem vbi erat prius. Spiritus eft qui viuificat, caro non prodeft quicquam, hoc eft, quia me hominem, inter homines videtis,*
nihil

A *nihil de me adhuc, quod ad hoc Sacramentum spectat, plusquam de alio homine sentire potestis. Et ideo carnaliter sapientes velut per frusta concisam carnem meam me vobis velle dare creditis. Sed postquam in cœlum ascendero, postquam hanc carnem, de qua agitur, adhuc mortalem, in Deum glorificauero, tunc intelligetis, quia Spiritus est qui viuificat, hoc est spiritualliter intellecta, accepta viuificant. Caro autem non prodest quicquam, quia carnaliter intellecta mortificant. Dabo enim carnem meam hominibus, non more cadauerum detruncandam, minuendam, consumendam, quia sic accepta caro mea non prodesset quicquã, sed dabo eam absque dolore diuidendam, absque imminutione partiendam, absque consumptione comedendam, quia Spiritus est qui viuificat, & quia sic accepta, & intellecta caro mea vitam non mortalem, sed æternam percipientibus donat.* What if ye see the Sonne of man afcende vppe where he was before? Yt ys the Spirit that quickneth, the flefh profiteth nothing, that ys, bicaufe ye fee me a man among men, ye can nothing more vnderftand of me (*for fomoche as apperteineth to the Sacrament*) then ye can of an other man. And therfore vnderftanding carnally, ye beleue that I will geue my flefh to yowe, as cutt in lumpes

This ysthe maner of our Sacramentaries.

B or peices, but after that I afcende into heauen, after that I fhall glorifie this flefh, of the whiche we nowe fpeake, being yet mortall, into God: then ye fhall vnderftand, that yt ys the Siprit that quickneth, that ys, that thefe my woordes fpiritually taken do quicken, but the flefh profitteh nothing. For carnally vnderftanded they kill. I will geue my flefh vnto men, not after the maner of dead karkafes to be cutt in peices one from an other, to be diminifhed, to be confumed, For my flefh fo taken fhould not profitt anie thing, But I will geue yt withoute greif to be diuided, without diminucion to be parted, withoute confumption to be eaten. For yt ys the Spirit that quickneth. And my flefh fo taken and vnderftanded, yt geueth to the receauers, not mortall life, but eternall. Thus farre *Petrus Cluniacen.*

This ys the faith of all catholikes

In this Authour as in the other before, ye fee that expowndeh he not this faing of Chryft of his afcenfion into heauen, that the reall prefence of his bodie fhoulde not be in the Sacrament: but onely Chryft made mencion of his afcenfion to pull them from that groffe maner of eating of his flefh, that they thought he wolde geue them lumpes or peices of that his vifible flefh

why Chriƒt made mencion of hys aƒcenƒion John.vi.

C in carnall and groffe maner, as a man wolde geue a peice of beof or mutton to one to eate. And that his bodie fo eaten fhoulde be dead, and fo finally confumed, and therfor, yt felf as they thought being mortall, they merueiled howe yt fhoulde make the eaters of yt ymmortall, and howe yt being eaten and fo confumed, and ended fhoulde make the eaters of yt continue for euer and to haue none ende. To reforme this their vain and groffe ymagination, he tolde them of his afcenfion. But for his prefence in the Sacrauient, as the holie Churche beleueth and teacheth, his verie bodie in vifible forme ys afcended, and yet the fame verie bodie in fubftance ys prefent inuifiblie in the Sacrament, and ys wholly receaued of euery receauer. Whiche maner this authour dothe very well feetfurth when he faied in the perfon of Chryfte: *I will geue my flesh to men not after the maner of dead karkafes to be cutt in peices, to be diminished, to be confumed* (for my flefh fo taken fhoulde nothing profitt) *but I will geue my flesh withoute greif to be diuided, withoute diminucion to be parte, dwith oute confumption to be eaten.* Thus ye maie perceaue that though the groffe maner of the vnbeleuing difciples be reprehended: yet the faithfull

D maner of the beleuing Chryftians ys approued, and therby alfo as the wrefting of this fcripture ys efpied: So ys their herefie by the fame (truly nowe declared and expownded) reiected and refufed. Wherfore I will nowe leaue this fcripture and go to the next.

THE

THE SIX AND THIRTTETH CHAP. TREACTETH E
of the next text by S. Austen and Chrysostom.

Poan.6.

Piritus est qui viuificat, caro non prodest quicquā.yt ys the spirit that quickneth, the flesh profitteth nothing . This text the Aduersaries haue not a litle triumphed on, and haue made yt so familiar, that boies and girles, coulde blatter this against Chrystes presence in the Sacrament. *The flesh profiteth nothing .* My saing therfor left aparte, I will laie the sainges and expositions of the Fathers before the reader, and then shall ye see whether these wicked schoolemasters haue not well taught their wicked scholers, and yonge ympes, to blaspheme Chrystes blessed flesh, saing that yt profiteth nothing, and also howe well they wrest the scripture, and violentlie plucke yt and teare yt, as yt were, from the natiue sense. The first coople to shewe vs the exposition of this text, shall be S. Augustine and Chrysostom.

Tract.27. in Ioan.

S. Augustine saieth thus : *Quid est quod adiungit: Spiritus est qui viuificat , caro* F *non prodest quicquam? Dicamus ei (patitur enim nos non contradicentes, sed nosce cupientes) O Domine magister bone, quomodò caro non prodest quicquam, cùm tu dixeris, Nisi quis manducauerit carnem meam, & biberit sanguinem meum, non habebit in se vitam? An vita non prodest quicquam? & propter quid sumus, quod sumus, nisi vt habeamus vitam æternam, quam tua carne promittis? Quid est ergo, Non prodest quicquam ? Caro non prodest quicquam, sed quomodò illi intellexerunt. Carnem quippe sic intellexerunt, quomodò in cadauere dilaniatur, aut in macello venditur, non quomodò spiritu vegetatur. Proptè sic dictum est: Caro non prodest quicquam, quomodò dictum est : Scientia inflat. Iam ergo debemus odisse scientiam? Absit. Et quid est, Scientia inflat? sola sine charitate. Ideo adiunxit : Charitas verò ædificat. Adde ergo scientiæ charitatem, & vtilis erit scientia, non per se, sed per charitatem. Sic & nunc ,Caro non prodest quicquam, sed sola caro. Accedat Spiritus ad carnem quomodò accedit charitas ad scientiam, & prodest plurimùm . Nam si caro nihil prodesset, Verbum caro non fieret, vt habitaret in nobis. Si per carnem multu nobis profuit Christus, quomodò caro nihil prodet? Sed per carnem spiritus aliquid pro salute nostra egit. Caro vas fuit, quod habebat attende, non quod erat. Apostoli missi sunt, nunquid caro* G *ipsorum nihil nobis profuit? Si caro Apostoloru nobis profuit, caro Domini nihil potuit prodesse ? Vnde enim ad nos sonus verbi, nisi per vocem carnis ? Vnde filius ? Vnde conscriptio? Ista omnia opera carnis sunt, sed agitante Spiritu tanquam organum suum . Spiritus ergo est qui viuificat. Caro non prodest quicquā. Sicut illi intellexerunt carnem : non sic ego do ad manducandum carnem meam.*

A long sentence of S. Augustine, but as profittable and pleasaunt, as yt ys long, whiche I bring whollie that the reader shoulde not be defrauded of the right meninge of S. Augustine vpon this scripture, and that the Aduersaries shoulde not haue occasion to reprehende that in vs, that so often they haue offended in, namelie to bring in a sentence of an Authour truncately so moch as apparantly wolde serue for their poupose, but not so moche as wolde trulie open the right mening of the Authour in that matter. In this sentence thus alleaged ye shall perceaue the full minde of S. Augustin, for so moche as he thought necessarie to be saied for the explication of Chrystes minde in this scripture. Thus maie S. Augustines woordes be englished:

Spirit how yt quickneth, and flesh howe yt profiteth nothing.

What ys yt then that he adioineth: *Yt ys the Spirit that quickneth, the flesh pro-* H *fiteth nothing?* Let vs saie vnto him, he suffreth vs, not against saing, but desiring to knowe: O Lorde, good master , howe doth the flesh profitt nothing, seing thowe hauest saied : *Except a man eate my flesh, and drinke my bloode, he shall haue*

A haue no life in him? Doth not life profitte anie thing? And for what be we, that we be, but that we maie haue eternall life, which thowe promiseſt by thy fleſh? What ys yt then that the fleſh profiteth nothing? The fleſh profitteth nothing, but as they vnderſtoode yt. They did ſo vnderſtande the fleſh, as yt ys torne in the dead karkas, or as yt ys ſolde in the ſhambles, not as yt ys quickned withe the ſpiritt. Therfore yt ys ſo ſaied: *the fleſh profitteth nothing*, as yt ys ſaied: *that ſcience doth puff vppe or make prowde*. Shall we nowe therfore hate ſcience? God forbidde. And what ys yt: Science doth puff vppe? Alo ne withoute charitie. Therfore he adioined: *Charitie edifieth*. Adde therfore to ſcience charitie, and ſcience ſhall be profitable, not by yt ſelf, but by charitie. So alſo nowe the fleſh profitteth nothing, but the fleſh alone, let the ſpirit come to the fleſh, as charitie cometh to ſcience, and yt profiteth very moche. For if the fleſh ſhould profitt nothing, the *woorde* ſhoulde not haue ben made fleſh, that he might dwell among vs. Yf Chryſt by the flesſh hath profitted vs moche, howe doth the fleſh profitt nothing? But the ſpirit by the fleſh hath doen ſomwhat for our healthe. The fleſh was the veſſell, what

B yt had attend, not what yt was: The Apoſtles were ſent, did not their fleſh profitt? yf the fleſh of the Apoſtles did profitt vs, coulde the fleſh of our Lord nothing profitt? Frō whence came the ſownde of the worde to vs, but by the voice of the fleſh: from whence the ſtile? from whence the writing? All theſe workes be of the fleſh, but the Spirit mouing yt as his organ. Ther fore *yt ys the Spirit that doth quickeneth, the flesh profiteth nothing*. As they do vnderſtande the fleſh: So do not I geue my fleſh to be eaten. Thus farre S. Auguſtine.

The preſen ceof Chriſts fleſh in the Sacr. after the catholi que faith.

Nowe weigh, gentle Reader. whether the fleſh of Chryſt doth profitte anie thing or no. Nowe weigh alſo whether this ſcripture doth any one iotte ſpeake or make againſt Chryſtes bleſſed fleſh in the Sacrament. The catholique faith teacheth not that the fleſh of Chryſt ys geuen in the Sacramēt as peices or lumpes of fleſh betorn oute of a dead karkas, neither that the fleſh of Chryſt ys there as yt ys in the ſhambles, nor that yt ys a pure naturall fleſh without the ſpiritte, not the fleſh of a perſon that ys onelie man, for

C ſo vnderſtanded as they did vnderſtand yt, ſaith S. Auguſtine, yt profiteth nothing. But the fleſh of Chryſt of the good catholiques ys beleued to be in the Sacrament, not as the fleſh of a pure man, but as the fleſh of God: not diuided from the Godhead, but inſeparablie euermore conioined tò the ſame, not groſſly as in the ſhambles but ſpirituallie, and yet verilie and reallie, as a diuine fleſh in miſterie, not torn as oute of a dead karkas by peices to be geuē abroade to the people, but (*as Petrus Cluniacenſis ſaieth*) yt ys parted, euery mā without diminuciō euerie one receauing whol Chryſt. Neither yt ys eatē, that therby yt ys cōſumed, but yt ys eatē and yet euer remaineth (*as the Church ſaieth*) *Nec ſumptus, abſumitur*. neither being receaued yt ys cōſumed.

The flesh of Chryſt receaued as the flesh of God profiteth moch.

This ys the catholique faith againſt the whiche this ſcripture doth nothing ſpeake, but raither with yt, For as S. Auguſtine ſaieth: The fleſh of Chryſte taken as yt ys quickned with the Spirit, that ys, with the Godhead, and as the fleſh of God, yt profiteth moche, which fleſh ys ſo taken of the faithfull. And therfor the Sacramentaries maie be aſhamed and moche repent of ther wicked blaſphemie, wherwith they haue blaſphemed the true catholique faith of Chryſte, calling yt the groſſe and vain imaginacions of

D the Capharnaites, with ſoche like impieties: ſeing that the faith ys pure, perfeċt and agreable to godds woorde, and nothinge agreeing with the vanities of theſe groſſe men. After whoſe groſſe maner as the fleſh profiteth nothing:

Chryſt ge-
ueth his
fleſh in ſub-
ſtance veri-
lie, but not
in rude ma-
ner groſſe-
lie.

nothing : So after that maner Chryſt doth not geue his fleſh, as S. Auguſti- **E**
ne in the perſon of Chryſt concludeth his expoſition, ſainge : *Sicut illi intelle-*
xerunt carnem, non ſic ego do ad manducandum carnem meam. As they did vnderſtande the fleſh, ſo do not I geue my fleſh to be eaten. In the whiche wordes
ſainct Auguſtin dothe inſinuate to vs that Chryſt dothe geue vs the ſame
his fleſh to eate, but not after that maner For the ſubſtance ys not here de
nied of the thing that ys geuen, but the maner, whiche he ſignifieth plain
lie when ſaieth : *As they did vnderſtande fleſh : ſo do I not geue my fleſh.* of
the whiche this foloweth well : I do geue my fleſh, but not as they
vnderſtande yt.

The like we yſe in common ſpeache, as whē we ſaie : we be no ſoch men as
yowe take vs to be : we graunt the ſubſtance of the thing, that we be men :
but ſaing (*no ſoche men*) we denie but the condiciō or maner of the thing, and
not the thing yt ſelf. So he ſaing : I do not geue my fleſh as they did vnderſtand, the maner onely ys denied, but the thing ys raither admitted, and
affirmed.
                                                             F

I am compelled to leaue S. Auguſtine, leaſt I ſhoulde be to tediouſe to

Chryſoſt.
hom.46. in
Ioannem.

the reader and turne, me to his yockfelowe in this place, Chryſoſtom,
who handling this ſcripture ſaieth thus : *Quid igitur caro non prodeſt quicquam?*
Non de ipſa carne dicit, abſit, ſed de his qui carnaliter accipiunt, quæ dicuntur. Quid autē
eſt carnaliter intelligere? ſimpliciter vt res dicuntur, neque aliud quippiam excogitare.
Non enim ita iudicanda ſunt quæ videntur, ſed myſteria omnia interioribus oculis conſide-
randa, hoc eſt, ſpiritualiter. Qui non manducat meam carnem, & bibit meum ſanguinem,
non habet vitam in ſemetiſpo. Quomodò nihil prodeſt caro, ſine qua nemo poteſt viuere?
Vide quòd ea particula, Caro non prodeſt quicquam, non de ipſa carne, ſed de carnali audi-

Caro non
prod. ys
not ſpoken
of the fleſh
of Chryſt,
as being
the fleſh of
God.

tione dictum eſt. What then? Doth the fleſh profitt nothing? He ſpeaketh yt
not of that fleſh (God forbidde) but of theſe that carnally take theſe thinges, that be ſpoken. But what ys yt to vnderſtande carnallie? Plainlie as the
thinges be ſpoken, neither to thinke anie other thing. Not ſo are thinges
that be ſeen to be iudged : But all miſteries are to be conſidered with the inwarde eies. that ys ſpirituallie He that doth not eate my fleſh, and drinke **G**
my bloode, hath no life in him ſelf. Howe dothe the fleſh profitte nothing
withoute the whiche no man can liue? See, that that particle (*the fleſh pro-*
fiteth nothing) ys not ſpoken of that fleſh, but of the carnall hearinge. Thus
Chryſoſtom,

He needeth no expoſitour to open and expownd his expoſition. For at
the firſt ſeight he maketh yt manifeſt, that this ſaing of Chryſt : *The fleſh pro-*
fiteth nothing, ys not to be vnderſtanded of the fleſh of Chryſt. *Non de ipſa car-*
ne dictum eſt yt ys not ſpoken of that fleſh of Chryſt, *ſaieh he*. And in the ende
of his ſaing again he ſaieth : *Vide quòd ipſa particula, Caro non prodeſt quicquam, non*
de ipſa carne dictum eſt. See that, that particle (*the fleſh profiteth nothing*) ys not
ſpoken of that fleſh, mening the fleſh of Chryſt. What vngodly ſchoolemaſ
ters and impudent be theſe that teache their vngodly diſciples ſo to vnderſtand this ſcripture, as two of the moſt famouſe Fathers of Chryſtes Church
vnderſtand yt (*as ye heare*) to the plain contrarie. Thei ſaie the fleſh of
Chryſt ys not in the Sacrament, for the fleſh profiteth nothing : But that
the fleſh of Chryſt ys in the Sacrament, and ſo being receaued doth profitte
bothe theſe Fathers and other alſo, haue, and ſhall hereafter teſtifie againſt **H**
them. Therfor I will not trooble thee, Reader, with anie longer inueighing
againſt them, more then ordinarie proceſſe by me intended ſhall inueigh.
Whiche I truſt ſhall be ſoche, that euery authour that ſhall be brought, ſhall
                                                     impugn

A impugn their wicked doctrine, and maintein the true faith of Chrysts catho
lique Churche, I will therfore proceade to induce mo wittnesses.

THE SEVEN AND THIRTETH CHAP. PRO-
ceadeth vpon the same text by Theophilact and S. Bernard.

Heophilact geueth a breif testimonie of hys vnderstanding of
this text, writing thus: *Spiritus est qui viuificat: Caro non prodest
quicquam. Quoniam (vt sæpe diximus) carnaliter exponentes ea quæ dicebantur à Christo, offendebátur, dicit quia spiritualiter intelligenda sunt, quæ
dicútur à me, hoc est prodesse. Caro autē, hoc est, carnaliter illa exponere, nihil
prodest. Sed offendiculi occasio fit. Sic ergo illi qui carnaliter audiebāt, quæ à Christo dicebā
tur, offendebantur.* Yt ys the Spirit that quickneth, the flesh profiteth nothing.
For that (as we haue ofté saied) that they expownding those things carnallie
B which were saied of Chryst, were offended, he saied that they are spiritually
to be vnderstanded, that be saied of me, that ys to profitte. But the
flesh, that ys carnallie to expownde, doth nothing profitte, but ys
made occasion of offence or flaunder. So they that carnallie did
heare those thinges, whiche were spoken of Chryst were offended.
Thus *Theophilact.*

In whiche woordes ye se nothing spoken against the flesh of Chryst in
the Sacrament. He bendeth not himself to expownde this scripture against
yt, as Chrystes enemies haue doen: but he bendeth himself to expownde yt
So as Chrystes very minde maie be opened vnto vs. Which was to teache
the Capharnaites spirituallie to vnderstande Chrystes woordes, which he spa
ke of the eating and drinking of hys flesh and bloode. Whiche woordes yf
they were vnderstanded spirituallie they did profit. Yf they were vnderstanded carnallie, they did not profitte. But he doth not saie that Chrystes *Obiectiõ of*
flesh in the Sacrament profiteth nothing. But here will the Sacramenta- *the Sacra-*
ries obiect and saie, this ys the thing that we wolde, that Chrystes woordes *mentaries*
                                                  for the spi-
C shoulde be taken spirituallie, that the eating whiche Chryst speaketh of, *rituall ea-*
shoulde be taken not for a corporall ot carnall eating, but for a spirituall *ting.*
eating, which ys (beleuing) ād his flesh not for that carnall flesh of hys naturall bodie, but for hys spirituall flesh, that ys for the meritte, benefitt, vertue
or grace that cometh to vs by hys naturall flesh. And therfor the papistes
(as they terme them) vnderstanding these woordes of Chryst carnally, as to
saie, that they do eate Chrystes very flesh really in the Sacrament, are verie
Capharnaites, and the flesh profiteth them nothing.

Ye saie very well, and ye seem in yowr owne conceit to haue made a strõg *Thãswer to*
argument. But weigh well the authour that ye haue grownded yowr *the former*
argument vpon. Yt ys *Theophilact*, who saieth that Chrystes woordes *obiect.*
must be vnderstanded spiritually. And euen so saie all the Catholiques,
whom yt liketh yow to call Papistes and Capharnaites. And what ys the
spirituall vnderstanding of Chrystes woordes by *Theophilact?* that we should
onely beleue Chryst to haue died, and shedde hys bloode for vs? and that
we be partakers of the meritte of the same? Call to minde howe he
D expownded these woordes of Chryst: *Panis quem ego dabo caró mea est.*
The bread that I will geue ys my flesh: and ther shall ye perceaue the vnderstanding of Chrystes woordes, that he meneth of. He saieth ther these woordes. *Take heed that the bread whiche ys eaten of vs in the mysteries ys not onely a*

figure of our *Lordes* bodie , but the *very flesh of our Lorde* . For he did not *faie,The* **E**
bread that I will geue ys a figure of my flesh, but yt ys my flesh . And howe yt cometh to paffe that this bread fhoulde be the very flefh of Chryft , and

Spirituall vnderſtanding what yt ys.
by whom yt ys fo compafed and wrought , the fame *Theophilact* furthwith
declareth.*That bread(faieth he)ys transformed with the fecrett woordes by the myſti*
call benediction, and the coming of the holy Goſt,into the flesh of our Lorde. Thys ys
the fpirituall vnderftanding of *Theophilact,* which ys in dede a fpirituall vnderftanding. For yf that be fpirituall that ys wrought hy the worke of
the Spiritt of God , and that ys aboue the reafon of man , and ys not
with in the compaffe of fenfuall knowledge , but ys apprehended and
knowen onely by faith,then ys this a fpirituall vnderftanding. That yt ys
wrought by the Spiritt of God, this Authour doth teftifie, that yt ys abo
ue naturall reafon,yt ys manifeft. For ther ys no naturall mean vfed in the
doing of yt . That yt ys not within the compaffe and the knowledge
of the fenfeis, this Authour alfo doth ther fhewe . *And howe* (faieth
he) *ys yt,that yt doth not appeare flesh to vs , but bread ? That we shoulde not* **F**
(faieth he)abhorre from the eating of yt . For yf yt shoulde haue appeared flesh , we
shoulde haue had no pleafure to the Communion . But nowe our Lorde condefcending to
our infirmitie , the myſticall meat appeareth foche , as we haue ben otherwife accuſton
med withall.

   This flefh then of Chryft ys not feen of vs.And fo trulie ys yt not perceaued of anie fenfe.And therfor for fomoch as yt ys perceaued by no ſeſe, but

Serm.ad in fances.
that faith ys of hearing,in that refpect yt maie alfo be called fpirituall.What
ys knowen in the Sacrament by fenfes and what aught to be knowen by
faith S.Auguftin alfo teacheth faing:*Quod videtis in altari panis & calix eſt, quod*
etiam oculi veſtri renuntiant.Quod autem fides poſtulat inſtruenda,panis eſt corpus, calix
eſt fanguis.Poteſt animo cuiufpiam cogitatio talis fuboriri.Dominus Iefus Chriſtus nouimus
vnde carnem acceperit,de Virgine Maria fcilicet, nutritus eſt, creuit,fepultus eſt , refurre
xit,coelum afcendit,illuc leuauit corpus fuum, vnde venturus eſt iudicare viuos & mor
tuos.Ibi eſt modò fedens ad dextram Patris,quomodò ergo panis corpus eius? vel quod ha
bet calix,quomodò eſt fanguis eius? Iſta ideo,fratres, dicuntur facramenta , quia in eis aliud
videtur,aliud intelligitur. Quod videtur fpeciem habet corporalem, quod intelligitur fru
*ctum habet fpiritualem.*That ye do fee in the aultar, yt ys bread and the cuppe, **G**
which alfo yowr eyes do fhewe yowe,but that faith requireth to be inftru

A plain faing of S. Auguſt.for the Procla mer.
cted , the bread ys the bodie , and the cuppe ys the bloode.But in the minde of fom
bodie foch a thought maie ryfe.We knowe from whence our Lorde Iefus
Chryfte hath taken flefh,that ys,of the virgen Marie, he was nourifhed, he
did growe , he was buried , he did rife , he hath afcended into heauen , thither he hath lifted vppe hys bodie from whence yt fhall cóme to iudge the quicke and the dead . Ther ys he howe fitting at the
right hande of the Father. Howe then ys the bread hys bodie ? or that
the chalice hath , howe ys yt hys bloode ? Bretheren , therfore thefe
thinges be called Sacramentes , bicaufe ther ys one thing feen in them,
and an other vnderftanded. That whiche ys feen hath a corporall forme
that which ys vnderftanded hath a fpirituall fruit or profyt. Thus farre
faint Auguftine.

   In the whiche woordes S. Auguftin doth plainly open what ys iud

Senfes and faith iudge diuerfelie.
ged to be in the Sacrament by the iudgement of the fenfeis , and what by **H**
the iudgement of faith. The eyes iudge yt bread, and a cuppe of wine ,but
faith iudgeth that,that the eyes haue iudged bread,to be the hodie of Chrift
and that , that by the fenfeis ys iudged wine , to be the blood of Chryft.
                                                                        Then

A Then yf the bodie of Chryſt be not knowen in the Sacrament by anye o-
ther knowledge,then by the knowledg of the faith , then yt ys no carnall
knowledge,but a ſpirituall knowledg: yſſo,then we vnderſtande Chryſtes
woordes ſpiritually and not as the Capharnaites carnallie(*as the Sacramētaries
do ſlanderously charge vs*) but like lowlie ſubiectes vnto our maſter Chryſt,
ſtriuing againſt our naturall knowledge,and though euen by faith we can
not comprehende the wholl myſterie:yet for that he hath ſaied yt we beleue yt ſo to be,as *Algerus* werie well to this pourpoſe ſaieth.

Dum in myſterio , quod non eſt apparet , quod eſt occultatur , fidei lucta propo-
nitur , vt meritum augeatur . Dum contra hoc quod videtur , credens quod non vide-
tur , de credita intus veritate , de ſuprata exterius falſitate , duplicem aſſequitur gra-
tiam . Cætera enim Chriſti miracula , cùm ſint inſidelibus in ſignum vt cōuer-
tantur , hoc ſolùm fidelibus datur ad meritum , vt illo erudiantur , In illis enim
quæ Deus in extrinſeca materia fecit , roboratur fides . In hoc autem ſolo quod ex
ſeipſo facit,fides exercitatur , vt victa,et inuicta facilius coronetur.Victa , inquam,ne
B *comprehendat , ſed inuicta , ne diffidat , dum exteriores quidem ſenſus obiecta panis,*
& vini ſpeciem , colore , odore , & ſapore , ipſum quod fuerat mentiendo , panem
& vinum quod non eſt nituntur inſtruere. Interior autem intellectus ipſum quod eſt,
corpus ſcilicet Chriſti conterаplans nec comprehendere ſufficiens,non tamen deſiſtit credere.

Algerus li.
2 ca.3.

While in the myſterie that that ys not appeareth,that that ys,ys hidden,bat-
taill vnto faith ys propownded,that meritte maie be encreaſed , while that
againſt yt that ys ſeen,beleuing yt that ys not ſeen of the beleued inwardly
veritie,of the ouercomed outward falſitie,ſhe getteth duble grace.For other
miracles of Chryſt,wher they be to the vnfaithfull for a ſign, that they maie
conuerte,this alone ys geuen to the faithfull to merite, that by yt thei maie
be taught.In thoſe miracles , that God did make in an owtwarde matter,
faith ys ſtrenghtned.In this alone that he maketh of himſelf, faith ys exerciſed,that being ouercomed , and vnouercomed, ſhe maie be more eaſilie
crowned.I ſaie ouercomed that ſhe can not comprehende , vnouercomed,
that ſhe diſtruſt not , while the outward ſenſeis by the formes of bread and
wine obiected,the coloure,the ſauour and the taſte,falſly ſaing to be yt that
C yt was, doo laboure to affirme yt bread and wine,which yt ys not. But the
inwarde vnderſtanding,beholding yt,that yt ys,that ys to ſaie, the bodie of
Chryſte,neither being able to comprehende yt , ceaſſeth not yet to beleue.
Thus farre *Algerus.*

Faith ouer
cōmed and
not ouerco-
med in the
miſterie of
the Sacr.

Thus farre be we from the Capharnaites that wher they reſtedwithin the
cōpaſſe of carnall knowledg ād vnderſtanding,we flie to the height of faiths
erudicion,and ſo leauing carnall knowledge,mete for the ſenſeis,we accept,
and cleaue to that ys ſpirituall,according to the inſtruction of faith.Therfore
ſeing that nothing ys taught of the catholique Church,or beleued,as cōcer-
ningChryſts very bodie in the Sacrament,that cometh vnder natural know
lege,either of reaſon,or of the ſenſeis:what blinde malice ys ther in the Aduerſaries to call vs carnall Capharnaites, who iudged of Chryſt no otherwiſe then by naturall reaſon and ſenſeis? Yf they will ſaie , that we be carnall , bicauſe we beleue Chryſtes diuine fleſh miraculouſlie by the diuine power to be in the Sacrament,and verilie to be receaued of the faith-
full:then maie they call vs carnall bicauſe we beleue the ſame fleſh to be
D vnited to the Godhead in vnitie of perſon, and nowe to be exalted aboue
all creatures,and to be at the right hande of God the Father. For what more carnalitie ys yt to beleue the bodie of Chryſt to the in the Sacrament,
then to beleue the ſame bodie,to be at the right hand of God the Father?

Cpharnai-
tes iudged
only by rea
ſon and ſen
ſes.

For as the power of God woorketh the one:So yt woorketh the other.And E
as by the fcriptures we be certified of the one:So be we therby alfo certified
of the other.And therfor as all faith concerning Chryftes bodie,as hys incar
nacion,paffion, refurrection, and afcenfion, ys fpirituall and not carnall,
though yt be aboute Chryftes.flefh:So ys the faith beleuing the fame flefh
to be in the Sacrament,a fpirituall faith.And the beleuers in that refpect, be
likewife fpirituall,and not carnall.

To beleue Chryftes flefh to be in the Sacr. ys a fpiritu all faith.

And Albeit yt were neceffarie of this to haue faied more,for that the Aduerfaries haue moch delighted themfelues with their fpiritualitie, and haue
moche flattered themfelues to be by this their herefie right fpirituall, when
in dede they,be therby verie carnall(*herefie being a worke of the flesh*) and haue
thought themfelues with this alone clean to abolifh the name of the catholique Church,and the memorie of the fame from the earth,the contrary effect wherof they haue feen:yet for that I fee the matter fo to fall oute that
this rude booke will excead the quantitie and proporcion by me intended
to the more trooble of the reader,and for that I haue ben longer vpon*Theo-* F
philact then I minded:I will breiflie touche his yockefelowe S. *Bernarde* and
fo ende this chapter.

Thus writeth S.*Bernarde.Quis non illic vehementer cupiat pafci,& propter pacem,*
& propter adipem , & propter fatietatem?Nihil ibi formidatur,nihil faftiditur, nihil de-
ficit.Tuta habitatio Paradifus:dulce pabulum,verbum:opulentia multa, nimis æternitas.Ha
beo & ego verbum,fed in carne:& mihi apponitur veritas,fed in Sacramento . Angelus
ex adipe frumenti faginatur,& nudo faturatur grano:me oportet interim quodam facra-
menti cortice effe contentum,carnis furfure,literæ palea,velamine fidei. Et hæc talia funt,
quæ guftata adferunt mortem,fi non primitijs Spiritus quantulumcunque accipiant condi-
mentum.Prorfus mors mihi in olla,nifi ex prophetæ farinula dulcoretur. Denique abfque
Spiritu,& Sacramentum ad iudicium fumitur,& caro non prodeft quicquam,& litera oc
cidit,& fides mortua eft:fed Spiritus eft qui viuificat,vt viuam in eis. Who defiereth
not earneftlie ther to be fedde,both for peace,and for the fatte, and for fatie
tie?Ther ys nothing feared,nothing loathed,nothing lacking. Ther ys Paradife a faif habitacion:the woorde,a fwete foode:eternitie,great abundance. G
I alfo haue the woorde,but in the flefh:and the veritie ys fett before me,but
in the Sacrament.The Angell ys fedde of the fatte of the qwheat,and ys filled or fatisfied with the open corne in feight. In the mean while I muft be
contented with a certain barke of the Sacrament, with the branne of the
flefh,with the chaffe of the letter,with the veil or couering of faith, and thefe thinges be foche that being tafted they bring death, yf of the firft fruites
of the Spiritte thei take not fome maner of feafoning,my death ys furely in
the potte except yt be made fweete with the Prophetes meall . Laftly
withoute the Spirit the Sacrament alfo ys taken to condemnacion : and
the flefh profiteth nothing at all:and the letter killeth : and faith ys dead:
but yt ys the Spiritte, that geueth life , that I maie liue in them . Thus
moche S.Bernarde.

Bernard. ferm.33.in Cant.

The veri- tie ofChri- ftes flefh ys fetfurth be fore vs in the Sacr.

Who in this chapiter,fhewing the great difference betwixt this prefent
life and the bleffed life to come, openeth the commodities of the one , and
the incommodities of the other:the perfection of the one,and the imperfection of the other, among which to our pourpofe he faieth: *that Paradife ys* H
a faif habitacion , Ther the Sonne of God ys the fweete foode . Wherunto comparing the ftate of this life , he faieth : *I alfo haue the woorde the Sonne*
of God , but in the flesh : the veritie ys fettfurth before me , but in the Sa-
crament.

A　Here firſt note that the veritie ys ſettfurth in the Sacrament, and not a bare figure : and yet this Sacrament, though yt hath the veritie yet yf yt be receaued withoute the Spirit, yt ys (ſaieth ſ.inct Bernard) receaued to con- demnacion. For the fleſh profiteth nothing . But yt ys the Spiritt that ge- ueth life. The ſpirit, as before ye haue ben taught of Chryſoſtom and Cy- rill, ys taken two maner of waies: either for a ſpirituall vnderſtanding in be- leuing, and therbie vnderſtanding the verie fleſh of Chryſt to be verilie in the Sacrament, not after a groſſe maner to be cutte oute to vs in Lumpes (*as the Capharnaites vnderſtood yt*) but ſpirituallie, and yet verilie, vn- ſpeakeablie, and yet crediblie by the worke of Gods powre euen verie wholl Chryſt: orells for the fleſh of Chryſt as a diuine or godlie fleſh vni- ted to the ſpirit, whiche ys the Godhead, and ſo becomed nowe ſpirituall, and quickning, able to geue life, for that yt ys the fleſh not of a ſole man, but the fleſh of God.

Spirit take two maner of waies.

Nowe, ſaieth S. Bernard, the veritie ys in the Sacrament, the verie fleſh of Chryſt ys ther receaued, but yf yt be receaued withoute the ſpirit (*as ys decla-*
B　*red*) the fleſh alone profiteth nothing, yf ye ioin the ſpirit to the fleſh (*as ſainct Auguſtin willeth yow*) the fleſh profiteth moche . For to take the fleſh alone, and ſo to vnderſtand carnallie, the fleſh profiteth nothing. Thus maie ye perceaue howe holie Bernarde with the reſt agreeth, that he placeth not ſo the ſpiritte, that he expelleth the fleſh of Chryſt from the Sacrament, as the Aduerſarie doth, but he ioineth the veritie of the fleſh and the ſpirit toge- ther , and ſo ſtand they in moche amitie, and do greatly profit the beleuers.

THE EIGHT AND THIRTETH CAAP. EN-

deth the expoſition of this text by Euthymius and Lyra.

C　Owe fearing with prolixitie to be tediouſe, I will breiflie heare the teſtimonie of one coople mo expownding this text nowe in hand, and ſo end the ſame. *Euthymius* writeth thus: *Spiritus eſt qui viuificat. Spi- ritum nunc vocat intellectum ſpiritualèm eorum quæ dicta ſunt. Similiter & car- nem intelligere ea carnaliter. Non enim de carne ipſius quæ viuificat, nunc ſermo eſt. Ait ergo: Hæc ſpiritualiter intelligere vitam præbet, quam ſuprà dixi: carnaliter verò intellige- re non prodeſt quicquam .* Yt ys the Spiritte that quickneth . He calleth the Spirit nowe the ſpirituall vnderſtanding of thoſe thinges that be ſpoken. Li- kewiſe the fleſh carnallie to vnderſtande. For nowe he ſpeaketh not of hys fleſh that quickneth. He ſaieth therfore to vnderſtand theſe thinges ſpiri- tuallie, yt geueth life, whiche I ſpoke of before. But carnallie to vnderſtand them yt profiteth nothing.

Euthy. in 6 Ioan.

I ſhall not nede to note the woordes of this Authour, for all the authours yet alleadged drawe ſo iuſtly by one line, that allmoſt they ſpeake all one maner of woordes, euen from the firſt to the laſt, aſwell the later writers, as the moſt auncient . For this man with Chryſoſtom and Auguſtine ſai- eth : that this ſcripture : *the fleſh profiteth nothing* : ys not ſpoken of the fleſh of Chryſt, which doth quicken : but of carnall vnderſtanding, of
D　the whiche ye haue not a fewe times hearde. He ſaieth alſo that theſe woor- des, *the Spiritt dothe quicken*: are to be vnderſtanded of ſpirituall vnderſtanding of the woordes of Chryſte ſpoken of this myſterie, what the ſpirituall vn- derſtanding of Chryſtes woordes be, this authour hath ſhewed throuhoute

this proceſſe.But breiflie vpon theſe woordes of Chryſte : *My fleſh ys meat in* E
*dede:*This(ſaieth he)Chryſt ſaied,confirming that he neither ſpake in darke
maner of ſpeache, neither in parables.Then(as ther was delared, aſwel vpon
Chryſt as alſo vpon this Authour)yf ther be no darke maner of ſpeache nor
parable in thoſe woordes of Chryſt:then we eate Chryſtes very fleſh reallie,
and not in a figure,which yet ſo taken and vnderſtanded , ys ſpirituallie taken and vnderſtanded after this Authour,and other,which likewiſe haue vnderſtanded yt,as before appeareth.And the like ſhall yow perceaue in the
Authour that foloweth,who ys Lyra,who for an expoſition of this ſcripture
writeth thus:

*Lyra in 6.
Ioan.*

Spiritus eſt qui viuificat.Quia dixerat carnem ſuam eſſe cibum neceſſarium ad ſalutem,
& ipſi intelligebant hoc,acſi daretur in propria ſpecie,ſicut laniatur,vel veditur in macello,
quod eſt horribile,ideo tollit hunc intellectu,dicens: Spiritus eſt qui viuificat , quaſi dicat:
Verba quæ dixi ſpirituale habent ſenſum,& ſic viuificant.Caro aute non prodeſt quicquam,
quia caro Chriſti manducata eo modo quo intelligebant,non eſſet vtilis,ſed magis horribilis.
Yt ys the ſpiritte that quickneth,the fleſh profiteth, nothing. For bicauſe he
had ſaied,that hys fleſh ys a neceſſarie meat to ſaluacion,and they did vnder- F
ſtande yt,as though yt ſhoulde be geuen in his owne forme, as yt ys cut and
ſolde in the Shambles,which ys horrible,therfor he taketh awaie that vnderſtanding,ſaing:Yt ys the ſpiritte that quickneth,as who ſhoulde ſaie.The
woordes that I haue ſpoken haue a ſpirituall ſenſe,and ſo they quicken , but
fleſh profiteth nothing,for the fleſh of Chryſt eate after that maner,that they
did vnderſtand,ſhould not be profitable,but raither horrible. Thus *Lyra.*

In this expoſition ye doe alſo ſee the groſſe maner of the Capharnaites,
who(*as ye haue hearde*)thought the fleſh of Chryſt ſhould be geuen vnto the,
as ytys cutt or ſolde, in the ſhambles,in his own propre forme and maner,
that ys as verie peices of fleſh both in ſeight and ſubſtance,to be refuſed. For
this maner of vnderſtanding ys groſſe and carnal,and therfore theſe woords
muſt haue ſaieth this Authour a ſpiritual ſenſe.What ſpiritual ſence alſo this
Authour vnderſtandeth of Chryſtes woordes,yt appeareth well in the expo
ſition of theſe woordes of Chryſt: *My fleſh ys meat in dede,&c.*Wher this Authour ſaieth,as before ys alleadged that by this text wasſhewed the veritie of
the Sacrament.For Chryſt did often ſpeake to hys Diſciples in Parables, ad G
therfor leaſt yt ſhould be beleued that hys fleſh ſhoulde be conteined in the
Sacrament onely as in a ſigne,therfore to remoue this,he ſaieth : *My fleſh ys*
*meat in dede,*for here yt ys taken reallie,and not figuratiuelye . Marke that he
ſaieth reallie,and yet he accompteth this a ſpirituall vndetſtanding , as yt ys
in dede,as before ys declared,though the Aduerſaries ſifting yt ſo finely vntill they make yt nothing,ſaie that we be carnall,carnallie vnderſtanding the
woordes of Chryſt.But God bring them from ther carnall hereſie.

THE NINE AND THIRTETH CHAP. BE-

ginneth the expoſition of the next text by ſainct Augu-
ſtin,and Cyrill.

Owe we come to the laſt ſcripture that treacteth of this matter in
the ſixt of ſainct Iohn,which being appendent , hath almoſt the ſame vnderſtanding that the laſt ſcripture before hath. *Verba quæ ego lo-* H
*cutus ſum vobis,ſpiritus & vita ſunt.*The woordes that I haue ſpoken to
yow are ſpirit and life.I will not detein the reader,but euen furthwith heare
the Fathers expownd this ſcripture.

And

A And firſt S. Auguſtin, who writeth thus : *Quid eſt ſpiritus & vita ſunt? Spi-*
ritualliter intelligenda ſunt. Intellexiſti ſpiritualliter ? Spiritus & vita ſunt. Intellexiſti
carnaliter? etiam ſic illa ſpiritus & vita ſunt, ſed tibi non ſunt. What ys yt: *The woor-*
des that I haue ſpoken to yowe, are ſpirit and life ? They are ſpiritually to be vnderſtanded. Haueſt thowe vnderſtanded them ſpirituallie? They are ſpiritt
and life. Haueſt thowe vnderſtanded them carnally? Euen ſo alſo are they
ſpiritt and life, but to thee they be not. Thus he.

What S. Auguſtine meneth by carnall vnderſtanding ye haue hearde
more then once by his owne woordes alleaged. that ys, to vnderſtand that
we ſhoulde eate the fleſh of Chryſt in the verie forme and maner of
fleſh cutt oute to vs in morſelles or peices, as fleſh ys cutte oute and
ſolde in the ſhambles. And not onely ſo, but to take yt as the fleſh of an
onely naturall man and not as the fleſh of the Sonne of God, and to be of
that weake and baſe degree, that yt ſhoulde be mortall, and conſumptible,
not able to geue life euerlaſting to them that ſhoulde woorthilie eate yt, neit
her for euer to endure, and continue and neuer to haue ende. This (if yowe
B haue marked the ſainges of S. Auguſtine, Chryſoſtom, and Cyrill) ys to
vnderſtand Chryſt carnallie Which maner of vnderſtáding ther ys no good
chryſtian hath. But theſe woordes of them are vnderſtanded ſpirituallie.

And what ys the ſpirituall vnderſtanding of this proceſſe of Chryſt, for
the eating of his fleſh, yt hath ben by manie places of S. Auguſtin alled-
ged, declared. But at this preſent to be ſhort, theſe his woordes maie
declare. *Caro eius eſt &c.* Yt ys his fleſh, whiche we take couered vnder
the forme of bread, and his bloode, whiche we do drinke vnder the
forme, and taſte of wine. This ys the ſpirituall vnderſtanding of S. Auguſtin, as concerning the ſubſtance of the Sacrament, although ther
be an other maner of ſpirituall vnderſtanding, whiche both he and all
the holie Fathers, and all good catholique men doo beleue, receaue, and
approue, and do not denie this ſpirituall maner, but both muſt be ioined,
and concurre in euery good chryſtian man, yf time and condicion will ſerue,
as before ys ſaied.

Sup.ca. 22

Spirituall
vnderſtan-
ding of the
Sacrament

C Nowe what S. Cyrill ſaieth, whom here we place with S. Auguſtine, Let vs heare: *Verba quæ ego locutus ſum vobis, ſpiritus & vita ſunt.*
Totum corpus ſuum viuifica ſpiritus virtute plenum eſſe oſtendit. Spiritum enim
hic ipſam carnem ſuam nuncupauit, non quia carnis naturam amiſerit, & in ſpi-
ritum mutata ſit. ſed quia ſummè cum eo coniuncta, totam viuificandi vim hauſit.
Nec indecenter hoc dictum quiſquam exiſtimet. Nam qui Domino conglutinatur,
vnus cum eo ſpiritus eſt. Quomodò igitur caro ſua vna cum eo non appllabitur? Hu-
iuſmodi ergo eſt, quod dicitur : Putatis me dixiſſe viuificum natura ſui eſſe terre-
ſtre, & mortale hoc corpus, ego verò de ſpiritu & vita locutus ſum. Non enim natura car-
nis ſecundùm ſe viuificare poteſt, ſed virtus ipſius ſpiritus, viuificantem carnem reddidit.
Verba ergo quæ locutus ſum, id eſt, ea quæ locutus ſum vobis, ſunt ſpiritus & vita, qua ipſa
etiam caro mea viuit, & viuifica eſt. The woordes, which I haue ſpoké vnto yowe
are ſpiritt and life. He ſheweth all his whol bodie to be full of the quickning
power of the ſpiritte. For he calleth here the ſpiritte his verie fleſh, not that
yt hath leſt of the nature of fleſh, and ys chaunged into a ſpirit : but bicauſe
being excellently conioined with him, yt hath taken the wholl power to
D quické. Neither let anie man thinke this, to be ſpoké vndecétlie. For he that
ys ſurely ioined to our Lorde, ys one ſpirit with him, howe then ſhall not his
fleſh be called one with our Lord? Yt ys therfor after this faſhió that ys ſaied:
ye thinke me to haue ſaied, this mortall and earthlie bodie of the owne na-

Ca. 24. in
6. Joan.

The verie
fleſh of
Chryſt cal-
led ſpirit.

ture to be quicking or geuing life. but I haue ſpoken of ſpiritt and life . For **E**
the nature of the fleſh yt ſelf cã not geue life. But the power of the Spiritt,
hath made the fleſh geuing life. The woordes therfor that I haue ſpoké,that
ys, the thinges that I haue ſpoké vnto yowe,are ſpiritt and life, by the which
the ſame my fleſh alſo doth liue , and ys quickning. Thus farre S. Cyrill.

    In whiche woordes, yt ys eaſie to be perceaued that wher S . Auguſtine
before expownding theſe woords of Chryſt,ſaied,that they are to be vnderſtanded ſpirituallie,this authour, as yt were expownding him and the woordes of Chryſt,ſaieth,that ſo they are to be expownded ſpirituallie,not by an
expoſitiõ of a ſingular imagined ſpirituall maner of vnderſtanding,that ſhall
be ſo ſpirituall that yt ſhall vtterly denie Chryſtes fleſh , but the verie reall
and naturall fleſh of Chryſt , for that yt ys ſo inteirlie ioined to the God
head, which Cyrill here calleth the Spirit, yt ys ſoche a ſpirituall fleſh that
yt maie be called alſo the Spirit , as S. Hierom alſo for like conſideracion,
and for that yt ys ſo exalted, calleth yt the diuine fleſh So that S. Cyrill vnderſtãdeth Chryſt, that wher he ſaied, *the woordes that I haue ſpoken to yowe are* **F**
ſpirit and life: yt ys thus to be vnderſtãded,that the fleſh of Chryſt ys ſpirit and

Sacramen-
taries are
Capharnai
tes.
life. And therfor the Aduerſaies ſeme to be carnall and groſſe,that wher the
ſe holie Fathers vnderſtãde the verie fleſh of Chryſt to be a ſpirituall fleſh for
cõſideracions aboue ſpecified,they maliciouſlie and deſpitefullie to the great
derogacion of ſo high a miſterie, call vs Capharnaites,as though we ſhoulde
receaue nothing but carnall fleſh , the fleſh of an onelie bare naturall man,
and not the fleſh of Chryſt, whiche being inſeparablie ioined to the God
head, and therfore the very fleſh of God,endewed with the power of the ſa

The fleſh
of Chryſtys
both natu-
rall and ſpi
rituall.
me Godhead to geue life , ys called both Spirit ãd life,and ſo ys bothe very
naturall,and yet ſpirituall fleſh. And therfor the catholique people receaue
Chryſtes verie reall fleſh ſpirituallie,bicauſe yt ys a ſpirituall fleſh,and alſo by
cauſe yt ys knowen with a ſpirituall knowledg, not with the knowledg of naturall reaſon,nor with the knowledge of carnall ſenſeis,but with the ſpiritual
knowledge of faith, which beleueth that in the Sacrament, that reaſon can
not comprehende, nor the ſenſes perceaue.

    And ſo as,*Algerus* ſaieth . *Etſi ſciri non poteſt : credi poteſt, quia quod vide-*
Alger li.2.
cap.3.
tur non materiale corpus panis eſt , ſed ſpecies corporalis . Quod autem intelligitur **G**
Chriſtus eſt , qui omnia quæcunque vult in cœlo & in terra poteſt. Sicque dum exteriorum
ſenſuum teſtimonio non acquieſcit , nec interiori inquiſitione comprehendens , de veritate
tamen non titubat , ſit per Dei gratiam vt in tali ſuo agone fides noſtra exerceatur,
exercendo augeatur , augendo perficiatur, perfecta coronetur . Although yt can not
be knowen: yet yt maie be beleued, for that that ys ſeen ys not the materiall bodie of bread, but the forme of bread, but that that ys vnderſtanded ys
Conflict of
faith with
reaſon and
ſenſes.
Chryſt, who can doe all thinges that he will in heauen and in earth, and ſo
while man doth not agree to the wittneſſe of the outwarde ſenſes , neither
by the inwarde inquiſition cõprehending,doth not yet doubte of the trueth
yt ys doen by the grace of God that faith in ſoche her conflicte ys exerciſed, in exerciſing ys encreaſed, in encreaſing ys perfected, and being perfect ys crowned. Thus *Algerus·*

    So farre wide then ys the catholique faithe from carnalitie in beleuing
and recauing Chryſtes very bodie in the Sacramét vnder the forme of brea-
de(*as this authour ſaieth*) that our faith hath a great battaill and conflicte with **H**
reaſon and the knowledg of ſenſeis, whiche conflicte if we proceade to continue,our faith by ſoche exerciſe ſhall be perfected,and in the ende by Gods
mercie for this trauaill crowned. Therfor that this crown maie be obteined
God

A grauntall catholique people ftronglie to côtinue the fight of this battaill, ãd all Sacramétaries to leaue their carnall herefies, and to come to this fpiritual faith and battaill therof, that they alfo with vs maie be crowned.

THE FOVRTETH CHAP. ENDETH THE EXPO
fition of this text and fo of the proceffe of the fixt of S. Iohn by Euthymius and Lira.

Owe one coople mo and then we end this fcripture, and this proceffe of the fixt of fainct Iohn. The coople fhall be *Euthymius,* and *Lyra. Euthymius* faieth thus: *Verba quæ ego loquor vobis fpiritus & vita funt, Spiritualia & viuifica funt. Oportet namque non fimpliciter ea intueri, id eft carnaliter intelligere, fed aliud quippiã imaginari, & interrioribus oculis ea afpicere tanqã mifteria. Nã hoc eft fpiritualiter intelligere.* The woordes that I haue fpokè to yowe, are fpirit and life, that ys, they are

B fpirituall and quickning.For we mnft not fimplie beholde thé,that ys,carnal lie to vnderftande,but ymagen fome other thinge,and with the inwarde eies beholde thefe thinges as mifteries. For this ys fpirituallie to vnderftand. Thus he.

Ye maie perceaue thys author ftill to proceade and continue in one maner of vnderftanding and allwaies declaring one fpirituall maner of Chry ftes flefh in mifterie, wher thinges maie not be taken, as they appeare fimplie, but confidering that they be mifteries, ther muft be confidered fome other thing ther to be préfent, which ys to be beholden not with the outwarde eye, but with the inwarde eie, whiche thing ys the verie bodie of our Sauiour Iefus Chryft by faith ther in verie dede, as verilie to be beleued, as the outwarde forme be by the fenfeis verilie to be feen.

All violent mocions (faieth he Philofopher) be flacke or flowe in the beginning, and quicke in the ending, fo man violétly moued to vertuoufe and godlie,dedes goeth flacklie and flowlie in the beginning,but whé he approcheth to the end,he maketh moche fpede to come to yt And euè fo I mifelf

C drawing to the ende of the expofition of the matter of the Sacramét by the fixt chapter of S.Iohn,make haft to the ende,as though bothe I in the writing ãd the reader in the reading were violély caried in this verteuoufe worke ãd bufineffe,ãd nowe as yt were with a natural defire runne haftilie to the ende.

Wherfor as I haue breiflie ouerpaffed this laft authour,fo will I his yockelowe,which in this place ys *Lira,* who faieth thus: *Verba quæ ego locutus fum vobis,de carne mea mãducãda,fpiritus & vita funt. quia fpiritualé habét intellectũ.nec mirũ, quia funt à Spiritu fancto.Ifta tamé fpiritualitas non eft fic uccipiéda, quia caro Chrifti fit in facraméto Euchariftiæ tantũ modò ficut in figno, vt dixerũt aliqui hæretici, quia eft ibi realiter, vt dictũ eft, fed quia mãduetur caro Chrifti in hoc Sacraméto quodã fpiritualli modo, in quantũ fpecies vifibiles atterũtur, & comeduntur, & fpiritus ex virtute Dei carni vnita reficitur.* The woordes whiche I haue fpokè vnto yow,of my flefh to be eaten, they are fpirit and life, for they haue a fpirituall vnderftanding.And no merueill. For, they be of the holie Goft. This fpiritualitie for all that, ys not fo to be taken that the flefh of Chryft ys onely in the Sacrament as in a figne, as certain heretiques did faie, for yt ys ther reallie,as yt ys faied, but bycaufe

D the flefh of Chryft ys eaten after a certain fpirituall maner, forfomoche as the vifible formes are bruifed and eaten, and the fpirit by the power of God vnited to the flefh ys refrefhed.

In this fentence of this authour ye fee the fpiritual maner of the flefh of

Chryft

Chryst in the Sacrament whiche the Sacramentaries had diuised, plainlie re- **E**
iected, as hereticall, and the right spirituall maner taught, which ys, that the
flesh of Chryst ys reallie vnder the formes of bread and wine, ãd so receaued.
Whiche maner of presence, and receipt ys called spirituall for diuerse causes,
of the whiche this authour reciteth diuerse. One ys, that this presence of

.1.　　Chryst ys wrought by the holy Spirit of God. And therfore as workes doen

.2.　　by Gods Spiritt are called spirituall of the woorker: so ys this being wrought
by the holie Spirit, called spirituall. An other cause ys, that the bodie of
Chryst, although yt be verilie present, yet yt ys not perceaued by anie corpo
rall knowelege, but onelie by the spirituall knowledg of faith. Wherfore as
all thinges not atteigned vnto by corporall knowledge but by spirituall, are

.3.　　spirituall: So ys this whiche (as before ys saied) ys by faith beleued, but not
of naturall knowledge comprehended, An other cause this authour rehearseth. Whiche ys, that our spirit by the vertue and power of God, vnited to
the flesh ys refreshed. As the refection wher with the bodie ys refreshed ys
a corporall refection: so the refection of the spirit ys a spirituall refectiõ. For- **F**
asmoche then as our spirit ys by this meat refreshed, yt ys a spirituall refecti
on. And in his last cause this authour toucheth an other cause whie yt ys spiritual, though he do not so expresse yt. And that ys, by cause the powre and
spirit of God, (whiche ys the Godhead) ys vnited to this flesh, which diuine
Spirit so being vnited, and made one with the flesh in the vnitie of person,
not in the vnitie of nature, maketh this flesh a spirituall flesh, though neuer
the lesse yt be also the verie naturall flesh of man.

Nowe, gentle Reader, wher the Aduersaries wolde haue wrested, and per-

Heretiques
malicïouse,
arrogant
and impu-
dent.

uerted this chapter of S. Iohn, to haue not ben vnderstãded of the Sacramēt
whether they were obcecated, and blinded through malice, nowe iudge-
Whether also they were not arrogant, whiche contemning the authoritie of
so manie noble famouse, and auncient Fathers, as ye haue hearde nowe faith
fullie alleaged, wolde seke and procead most arrogantly to preferre their
owne vain and false Commentes and gloses, before the others expositions.
Whether also they were not impudent, shamelesse, yea and clean past shame
that so boldie wolde commēd their lies to the people, not onelie, by their **G**
sermons, but also to their continuall shame with their pennes in their
bookes, as a most substanciall and godlie trueth, when so manie godlie
and auncient wittnesses reclamed by their testimonies, and conuinced them
to be lies.

Doctrine
flïeng the
comon re-
ceaued vn-
derstãding
of the
script. ys to
be suspectd.

Wherfor nowe, Reader, being aduertised beware of them, and learn, as ye
haue iust cause, to mistrust them, and flie from them. And cleaue to that cõ-
panie wher ye see the auncient trueth taught by auncient fathers as here ye
haue doen, And not by prowde arrogant will, as the other haue doen, flie
from the trueth. Their doctrine ys to be suspected that flie from the common vnderstanding of the scripture receaued in the Churche, as yt ys nowe
to be perceaued that these singular men haue doen by their single sigularitie.
As our Sauiour Chryst saied to the Iewes: *Si non venissẽ, & locutus eis non fuissẽ,*

Ioan.cap 5.　*peccatũ non haberent. Nunc autem excusatiõcm non habent de peccato suo.* Yf I had not
comed and not spoken vnto them, they shoulde haue had no sinne but nowe
they haue no excuse of their sinne. Yf then soche as haue heard the woorde
of Chryste teaching thē his promesse of the geuing furth of his verie bodie **H**
and bloode, and do not beleue yt, haue no excuse to saue them frõ eternall
dãnacion : moche more when they haue the same woorde expownded and
declared by the holie Churche, of the whiche the holie Gost ys the master,

the

A the guide,and leader in to all trueth, and yet wil perſiſt in peruerting the ſcriptures,and through arrogancie will credit none but them ſelues,they be not onely voide of all excuſe, but their damnacion ys greatlie encreaſed.

Wherfore ye that haue erred, ſtaie, and looke vppe in time, beholde all the chryſtiã worlde profeſſing Gods true faith and religiõ, and come to the ſame.Lurke not in the corners of darkeneſſe, whiche will bring yowe to extreã darkneſſe,but com to the light,which Chryſt hath lefte in his Churche, which ſhall lighten yowe the waie to that light, that euer hath ſhewed and ſhined,and neuer was darkned nor ſhadowed.

THE ONE AND FOVRTETH CHAP. BEGIN-
neth the expoſition of theſe woordes of Chryſt: This ys my bodie,
after the minde of the Aduerſaries.

Reate and manifolde are the maliciouſe inuencions and deuiſeis of the graund enemie of mankind againſt the ſame. Whiche enemie perceauing man to be in that ſtate to come and enioie the glory and felicitie that he was fallé frõ,enuied him,and ſubtellie

B vnder the conntenáce or pretéte of a cõmodtie,brought him to a moſt miſerable incõmoditie:vnder the colour of their aduaũcemét,dignitie,and great exaltaciõ, he wrought vnto thẽ their deieẽtiõ,ouerthrowe, and dãnacion.*Ye shall not die*(ſaieth the enemie to the womã)*but God doth knowe,that the ſame daie that ye eate therof yower eies shall be opened,and ye shal be as Gods knowing good and euel.* **Gen.3.**
To whiche his perſwaſiõ and falſe aſſertiõ the womã geuing place by to light creditte, ſeing alſo the fruit of the tree to be deleẽtable and pleaſaunt to the eies, not regarding the certé and moſt true woorde of her Lorde God, who before had ſaied,*that in what daie they did eate of the tree of the knowledge of good and euell,that they shoulde die the death,* ſhe tooke of the forbidden fruit,and did eate therof, and gaue to her huſbande, who did eate of yt alſo, and ſo not beleuing the woorde of their Lorde God, but tranſgreſſing his commaundemét they were not onely expelled oute of that pleaſaunt garden of Paradiſe,but alſo being fallen vnder the heauie burden of gods wrathe and iuſtice, were nowe baniſhed from the eternall felicitie, and glorie of heauen, and made

C bonde to hell and euerlaſting damnacion. **Ibid. 2.**

Euen ſo the ſame enemie ſeing the chryſtiã people redemed with Chryſtes moſt precheuſe bloode and reſtored to that felicitie and ioie, whiche by his meãs he had once cauſed thẽ to loſe, ãd that they were nowe quiet,ãd in godlie order in the eartlie Paradiſe of Chryſts Church,he not bearing their happineſſe in the vnitie of faith and godlie cõuerſaciõ,hath vſed his like ſubtletie and craft to make vs trãſgreſſe the cõmaundemét of our lorde God,as he did our firſt Parétes,to the entét he wolde cauſe vs to be baniſhed frõ the inheritãce of the glorie of God, wherunto by Chryſtes bloode we are made free. And will ye ſee howe like his ſubtilties be: Owre firſt Parentes had an order appointed to thẽ what meat they ſhoolde eate in the Paradiſe wher they liued:The builder of our Paradiſe hath appoinẽted vs what the meat ſhall be that we ſhall eate, ſaing :*Take, eate, this ys my bodie*. The enemie tempted them to breake their order about their meat and foode: he tempteth vs to breake our order about our meat and foode.Their meat was the fruit of eueric tree in Paradiſe,ſauing the tree of knowledge of good and **Gen.2.**

D euell, God ſaing:*Of euerie tree that ys in the gardé thowe ſhalt eate,but as touching the tree of knowledg of good and euell thowe ſhalt not eate of yt*:Owre meat in the Paradiſe of Chryſtes Churche,ys his verie bodie and bloode he him ſelf ſaing:*Take eate,this ys my bodie. Take,drinke, this my blood.*The enemie not withſtãding gods owne

Temptaciõ of our firſt parentes, and of Chriſtians in theſe daies compared.

owne faing to our Parétes: *In what daie foeuer ye eate of that tree, ye shall die the death,* E
he directlie côtrary faied: *Ye shall not die.* The fame enemie notwithftãding
Chryftes owne faing: *This ys my bodie This ys my blode:* directlie côtrarie faieth: *yt
ys not his bodie, yt ys not his bloode: yt ys but a peice of bread, but a cuppe of wine, figures, fignes, or tokés of his bodie, and his bloode,* and to côpaffe that this his perfwafion and
affertiõ maie be receaued, as to our firft parétes he faied: *that yf theie did eate of
that fruict they shoulde be as Gods knowing both good and euell, preteding a great cõmodi-
tie:* fo nowe he faied: *Efteem this no better thẽ a peice of bread, ãd a cuppe of wine, and
not as the bodie and bloode, of Chryft.* For fo (foramoch as Chryftes bodie ys in heauen and
therfor can not be here) ye shall not cõmitte idolatrie whych ys yower great commoditie.

And as to the furtherance of the temtacion of owre Parétes the pleafing
of their fenfeis in feing the fruict fair and pleafaunt , and not regarding the
woorde of their Lorde God, did moche prouoke thẽ: fo in this our tẽptaciõ
he willeth vs, not regarding the woorde of Chryft our Lorde God, to folowe the pleafant iudgemẽt of our fenfies. And for fomoche as we fee nothing
but bread and wine, we taft nothing but bread and wine, we feell nothing F
but bread and wine: Therfore we muft beleue nothing to be ther but bread
and wine. By whiche maner of iudgement, we are moche prouoked the foo
ner to affent to his temptacion.

Nowe if we fo affent, and eate of the meate, which the enemie perfwadeth
vs to eate of, and not of the meat whiche our Lorde and God hath appoincted, we fhall not onely be expelled oute of this Paradife, of Chryftes Church
by the Angell of God: but alfo being difherited frõ the inheritãce of heauẽ,
which Chryft our Sauiour by his blod hath bought vs to, we fhall be cõdẽp-
ned to that pain that we were once redemed frõ, ãd fo eternallie become mi
ferable with him, vnto whofe wordes we wolde geue credditte before the
woordes of our Lorde God. As nowe ye perceaue howe like the tẽptacions
be: fo maie ye perceaue howe like the rewarde of the affẽting or agreing to
the tẽptaciõ of the enemie ys. Yf therfor ye will auoide the rewarde, which
ys pain eternal, withftãd the temptacion, whiche beginneth the thrall.

*Two thin-
ges which
aught to
moue vs to
refift the
temptatiõs
of the Sa-
cramenta-
ries.* A mong manie other, two thinges (methinketh) fhoulde with the affiftẽce of G
gods grace, moche moue yowe to withftãd his wicked tẽptacions in this be
half: the one ys, that as in the firft tẽptaciõ to our firft parentes he fpake the
plain côtrarie of that God had fpoke: fo in this his tẽptacõ he fpeaketh the
verie contrarie to that that Chryft our Lorde God hath fpoken. For Chryft
faied: *This ys my bodie:* But Sathã faieth: *yt ys not his bodie.* Now whẽ anie thing
ys taught, that ys manifeftlie repugnant to the woorde of our Lorde God
(who cã fpeak nothing but trueth) except we be woorfe bewitched then the
Galathians were, we muft nedes deme and iudge that doctrine to be falfe coming from Sathan the father of lies, vutrueth and falfhod. And being falfe,
what ells ys to be doen but to withftande and reiecte yt?

*Sectes of
Sacramen-
taries.
Bereng.
Wicleff
Io. Hus.* The other thing that aught to moue vs to withftãd this tẽptaciõ, ys, that
the woordes of his doctrine be not confonant nor agreable . For befides his
diuerfe and côtrarie fpirit, which he breathed into *Berengarius,* the firft publique and open impugner of this bleffed mifterie (as yt ys faied in the prcface
of this book) into *Wiceff,* and *Hus:* he hath in this our time poured oute manie contrarie fpitites, and meruelouflie fhewed himfelf the authour of diffẽ-
tion, and repugnant doctrine in the fame mifterie . But for that I might be H
iudged partiall in the report of this diuerfe doctrine, I will not vfe mie owne
woordes but the woordes of Luther, Satans cheif and firft Commiffionar in
this maner of proceading, and of Melancthon his right ofspring, and defen-
dour of his doctrine.   Luther

A　Luther in his breif confession, noting the diuerse, and repugnant spirittes, that reigned amongest the Sacramentaries, saieth in this maner : *At the first these men were well warned of the holie Gost , when that vpon that one text they diuided them selues into seuen spirits, eche one differing allwaies from the other.* First *Carolstadius* wold haue the text so, that *this ys my bodie,* should signifie : *here sitteth my bodie.* Then *Zwinglius* saieth, that that coulde not be well saied , no, though the Father of heauen had reueiled yt. Therfor being moued with an other holie spirit of his own thus he turned the text : *Take, eate, this signifieth my bodie.* The thirde, *Oecolampadius,* brought furth his third holie spirit, which turned that text into an other hew, as thus : *Take, eate, this ys the token of my bodie .* The fourth, *Swenckfeldius,* thinking to make his stench to smell as muske brought vs furth of his holie spirit this rule : These woordes, *this ys my bodie , must be remoued from oure seight .* For they do let vs of the spirituall vnderstanding . The fifth holie spirit, being but excrementes of that other, doth thus read that text. *Take and eate, that which ys deliuered for yowe in this my bodie.* The sixt holie spirit saieth, *Take and eate , this ys my bodie in remembrance ,* as

B　though Chryst had saied; *Take and eate, this ys the monument of my bodie.* The seuenth holie spirit, *Ioannes Campanus,* bringeth this exposition : *Take and eate this ys my breadie bodie, or bodie of bread.* Beside all these , an other spirit flieth aboute (For the Deuell ys an holie , and great spirit) whiche persuadeth men that herein ys no article of oure faith , and therfor we aught not to contend of this matter , but leaue yt free to euery man to beleue herein what he list. Thus farre Luther.

See ye not by Luthers one woordes seuen, and in thend of his collection one mo to make eight dissonant, and disagreable doctrines vpon these woordes of Ghryst : *This ys my bodie ?* See ye not Sathan diuided against Sathan? See ye not his ministres plaing at crosse wasters for the victorie? Be persuaded then, that wher soche contencion, soche strife, soche Battaill ys amongest men, springing all oute of one Gospell, that in that Gospell ys no treuth. But we haue not yet seen the ende.

C　Melanchton the right ofspring, and heire of the Lutheran doctrine, was not onelie intoxicated with a diuerse spirit from his Father , and master Martin Luther, in the ende of his life, but also reporteth that among the Lutherans them selues , ther were fiue Sacramentaries sectes, or heresies. For some (saieth he) be of *Helhusius* minde: some of *Sarcerius* minde: some other folowe the ministers of Breme: and some *Ioachimus Morlinus:* other also he alleageth , whose opinion ys , that Chrystes bodie maie be in euery place. Whiche sectes being fiue in nombre, yf ye put them to the eight enombred by Luther, they make thirtene.

Thus by their own report yt ys to be perceaued that the woordes of Sathans doctrine be not of one sownde, of one agreement, but his spirit hath breathed into his disciples vpon these fewe woordes of Chryst di: uerse and and plain repugnant expositions and doctrines.

To these thirtene diuerse doctrines, yf we adde and putto the expositions of Luther himself, Melanchton and Caluine, whiche esteemed

D　them selues as the lightes of the worlde , we shall make vppe sixtene diuerse expositions , and doctrines of this matter settfurth by Sathans disciples.

As for Luther, yt ys euindent that he expounded Chrystes woordes farre vnlike to *Zuinglius, Oecolapadius,* or anie of that line, yea vnto *Berengarius* himself

Eight disagreing spirittes amõg the Sacramentaries nombred by Luther.
Carolstad.
Zwinglius.
Oecolamp.
Swenckfel.

Ioan. Cam

Fiue sectes of Sacramẽ taries amõg the Lutherans nombred by Melanct.

Chrystes woordes wrested to sixtene diuerse senses by the Protestants,

For he faieth they muſt be thus vnderſtãded:*This ys my bodie*,that ys, *this bread ys my bodie.*　E

*Melanĉth.
His muta-
bilitie.* Melanchton in his later daies(as yt ys common to heretiques to growe worſe and worſe) forſooke Luthers ſpirit, and taſted of *Zwinglius* ſpirit, but ſo as he wolde in ſoch wiſe correct him,that he wolde make him a newe ſpirit.And therfor he wolde haue this ſenſe vpon Chryſtes woordes, *This ys my bodie,that ys,This ys a participacion of my bodie*, whiche newe interpretacion (ſaieth Staphilus)ys plainlie a newe Sacramentaries hereſie.

Io. Caluine Laſt of all the doctrine of Caluine ſwarueth from all theſe, teaching that Chryſt ys geuen to vs reallie,but not corporallie , as though the ſenſe of Chryſtes woordes might be:*This ys my bodie*,that ys,*This ys the verie ſubſtance of my bodie,but it ys not my bodilie ſubſtance.*

Thus aboute the ſenſe of Chryſtes woordes ye haue among theſe Egyptians ſeen a merueillouſe varietie,who creping and groping in their palpable darkneſſe tooke that for trueth,that Sathan ſuffred to come firſt to their hand,by which mean euerie one of them vttered that for trueth, that in his F darkneſſe he had lighted on.But among all note howe by *Swenckfeldius*,Sathã wolde haue berieued yowe not onelie of this Sacrament, but of all other, and not onelie of them,but of the ſcriptures alſo. This ys a miſerable progreſſe,this ys the right building of Babell,wher the tounges of men be confownded,that a mãn can not vnderſtand his neighbour, neither can the catholike vnderſtand the proteſtant,nor the proteſtant,the proteſtant.

But nowe returning to my pourpoſe again,I wiſh that to be perceaued in this proceſſe whiche before I ſpake of to be noted, the better to withſtand Sathan in his temptacions againſt the true doctrine and faith, namelie that his doctrine ys not conſonant,nor agreable in yt ſelf, but diſſonant and repugnant,ſome of his diſciples teaching that the bodie of Chryſt ys in the Sament with the bread,ſome that the bodie of Chryſt ys in the Sacrament in and vnder the bread:other ſome that the bread ys the bodie of Chryſt:other of the contrarie maner denieng the preſence of Chryſt in the Sacrament, but yet diuerſlie,ſome of them teaching that the Sacrament ys but a ſigne G of the bodie of Chryſt:other ſome that the bread ys a figure of the bodie of Chryſt:other that it ys the powre vertue,or efficacie of the bodie of Chryſt: other that Chryſt ys reallie exhibited vnto vs,but not bounde nor excloſed in the bread:other(whiche be the worſte ſort) teaching that ther ys neither bodie nor Sacrament.

In which diuerſitie,and contrarietie of doctrines,yt ys eaſelie to be perceaued not onely how moche diſſonant they are frõ the doctrine and woordes of Chryſt: but alſo howe farre diſagreing they are among them ſelues. Whiche faut perceaued,I thinke him more then bewitched that will geue credittre to anie of them,forſomoche as ther ys no man but knoweth that in the doctrine of God ys concordé agreement. And forſomoch as in theſe other doctrins ther ys none agreement,but repugnance and contrarities, yt ys certen that they be not of God.
Beſides this what proof haue anie of all theſe either in the ſcriptures or holie Fathers,that this ſaing of Chryſt:*This ys my bodie*,ſhoulde be vnderſtãnded H as eche of them ſtowtly ſeeme to auouche,and that after their ſondrie maners?They be contrarie one to an other , yet eche of them perſwade their diſciples that they teache the true woorde of God.And yet the ſcriptures of God beare no ſoche contrarie ſenſeis.
Nowe therfor,Reader,ſtaie thie ſelf,and chooſe raither to beleue Chryſt, then Sa-

A Sathan who goeth aboute to deceaue thee, as he did thie firſt parentes, who through light creditte neclecting what God had ſaied, and beleuing what the ſerpent ſaied, fell into preuaricacion and were condemned. Thus moche then being ſaied of Sathans maner of temtacion to abduce and lead awaie men from the faith of Chryſt, and of his ſondrie and manie inuented falſe expoſitions diſagreeng and clean repugnant euen amongeſt them ſelues, of theſe woordes of Chryſt, *This ys my bodie:* I ſhall nowe addreſſe my ſelf, firſt ſomewhat to ſaie of thinges apperteining to the true vnderſtanding of thoſe woordes, and afterwarde open to youe he right vnderſtanding of the ſame woordes by the moſt auncient and holie Fathers of Chryſtes Church, wher ye ſhall perceaue not a repugnance, as in Sathans ſchoole, but concorde and agrement meit for Chryſtes ſchoole.

THE TWO AND FOVRTETH CHAP. BEGINNETH
the expoſition of the woordes of Chryſt after the catholike
maner with certain proofes of the ſame.

B   AS ye haue hearde Sathā teaching his ſcholers with moche contrarietie, ſtrife, and repugnance, to expownd or raither to expunɡ cte the woordes of Chryſt and to pertiert them, as yt hath pleaſed the ſame ther maſter to moue them, ſome one waie, ſome an other, but neuer one of them the right waie: ſo ſhall ye nowe heare the diſciples and ſcolers of Chryſt, and of his holie ſpirit, with all agremē t, concor- and peace expownde yowe the ſame woordes of Chryſt, after the learniug of their maſter, not ſome one waie, and ſome an other waie: but all one waie, as yt were with one mouthe ſpoken. Yt ſhall moche cōmende this goodlie amitie and concorde of this ſchoole, yf we firſt in the entrie of this declaracion ſhall heare howe the cheif, and higheſt ſcholers of this ſchoole do agree in the reporte of theſe woordes of Chryſt whoſe expoſition we ſeke.

The cheifeſt ſcholers reporters of theſe woordes be the three Euangeli-
C ſtes, Matthew, Marke and Luke, and the Apoſtle Paule. S. Matthew reporteth   *Mat. 26.*
yt thus: *Ieſus tooke bread and when he had bleſſed it, he breake it, and gaue it to the diſciples, and ſaied: Take, eate, this ys my bodie. And he tooke the cuppe, and thanked, and gaue it them, ſaing: Drinke ye all of this. This ys my bloode whiche ys of the newe teſtament, whiche ys ſhedde for manie for the remiſſion of ſinnes.*

S. Marke agreablie teſtifieth the ſame thus: *Ieſus tooke breade, and bleſſing*   *Mar. 14.*
he brake it, and gaue to them and ſaied. Take, eate, this ys my bodie, and he tooke the cuppe, and when he had geuen thankes, he tooke it to them. And they all dranke of it, and he ſaied to them: This ys my bloode of the newe teſtament, whiche ys ſhedde for manie.

S. Luke reporteth yt after this maner. *And whē he had takē bread he gaue thākes*   *Luc. 22.*
and brake it, and gaue it vnto them ſaing: This ys my bodie, whiche ys geuen for yow. Likewiſe alſo when he had ſupped he tooke the cuppe ſaing. This cuppe ys the newe Teſtament in my bloode, whiche ys ſhedde for yowe.

With this teſtimouie of S Luke agreeth S. Paule thus: *Owre Lorde Ieſus,*   *1. Cor. 11.*
the ſame night that he was betraied toke bread, and when he had geuen thankes he brake
D *it and ſaied: Take ye and eate, this ys my bodie, whiche ys broken for yow. This do in remembrance of me. After the ſame maner alſo he tooke the cuppe when ſupper was doen ſaing: This cuppe ys the newe teſtament in my bloode. This do as often as ye drinke yt in the remembraunce of me.*

Thus ye ſee firſt theſe foure highe ſcholers of Chryſtes ſchoole conſonātlie and agreablie reporting the doctrine of their maſter namelie that *he tooke*

Tropes and figures patched to Chrystes woordes excluded.

bread and after he had geuē thankes or blessed yt gaue yt to them, saing: take, eate, this ys my bodie. Of the whiche ye see not one making anie one title or mencion of tropes figures, or significacions, whiche the Aduersarie wolde patche vnto this text to cōfownde the saing, and mening of Chryste, and to shadowe his great mercie and loue toward vs, in leauing vnto vs so high a mysterie, as a pledge of his great loue to owre endlesse consolacion and comforte. Wher thē haue they these their tropes, what grounde haue they for them? In dede they haue none. But nowe to cōfirme this doctrine of these scholers of Chryste, S. Iohn a great scholer of the same schoole dothe make an inuincible proofe. For he reporting the promisse of Chryste, that he wolde geue vnto his Aposties a bread that shoulde be his flesh, euē the same flesh that he wolde geue for the life of the worlde, vttereth the same simplie and plainlie. Whiche promisse was fullfilled no ells wher, but in the last supper whē he saied. *Take, eate, this ys my bodie,* wherfore these woordes, *this ys my bodie,* are simplie ād plainlie whith oute tropes and figure so to be vnderstāded, as they maie answer the promesse.

The sixte of S. Iohn being vnderstanded of the bodie and blood of Chryst, the woordes of the supper must of necessitie be so likewise.

F

As for the vnderstanding of these woordes of the promisse and the rest adioined to the same in the sixt of S. Iohn, yt ys allready made euident, that theye are to be vnderstanded of Chrystes verie bodie and bloode. And for that, that processe must and ys necessarilie so vnderstanded, of like necessitie must these woordes of Chryst be so vnderstanded. For S. Augustine, Chrysostome and diuerse other testifie one thing to be spoken of in the sixte of S. Iohn, and in the last supper. Wherfore as the sixt of S. Iohn speaketh without tropes and signes, of the verie bodie and bloode of Chryst: So also do these woordes of the supper of Chryst.

Yt maketh also an euident proofe for this pourpose that S. Paule, who taught the Corinthians the vse of the supper of our Lorde, did neuer teache them that yt was but a figure of the bodie of our Lorde, but simplie that yt was the bodie of our Lorde. The proof of this ys easie, for he taught thē none otherwise thē he wrote to thē. He wrote none other meeninge or vnderstanding of the woordes of Chryste, but euen as they were of Chryst spokē, whiche was withoute trope or figure, wherfor S. Paule taught them without

G

trope or figure. Yt ys not like that so woorthie an Apostle and teacher wolde in so perilouse a matter (wher on the one side, yf Chrystes presence be not there, Idolatrie might by occasion of the woordes sownding as they do, sooē be cōmitted, and on ther side, yf the presence of Chrystes bodie as the woordes do sownde, be verilie ther, necligence in omittinge of duetie might be admitted, yt ys not like (I saie) that he wolde leaue a matter of weight and perill vndeclared and not opened. Wherfore sithen he so taught and wrote the woordes of Chryste in no other sense then they were of Chryst spoken, yt dothe well folowe that they must be so vnderstanded. Theie were spoken of Chryst whithoute any trope or figure, wherfore yt appeareth that of S. Paule they were vnderstand whithoute trope or figure.

The same among infidells of the christiā religiō in the primitiue Church, proueth the presence.

That the woordes of Chryst are to be vnderstanded withoute trope or figure not onelie the faith of Chrystes Churche, whiche shall be hereafter declared, but also the same grounded vpon the same faith spred thoroughout among the infidells and heathen in the primitiue Churche dothe well

H

proone yt. Yt ys not vnknowen to soche as haue trauailed in the histories that the Chrystians were moche hated and abhorred, for that they were famouslie reported to eate the flesh of men, and of children. And being so reputed, were with more cruelltie sought, and drawen to tormentes, and Martyrdome. Among the whiche the holie

woman

A woman and conſtant Martyr *Blandina*, ſaied to them that were aboute her: *Multũ erratis,o viri,quòd putatis infantum vſceribus veſci eos, qui ne brutorum quidẽ animaliũ carnibus vtuntur*. Ye are deceiued,o ye mẽ,that ye thinke thẽ to eate the bowells of children,which vſe not to eate the fleſh of brute beaſtes. Attalus alſo being ſore tormented,when he ſawe the people delighted with the ſmel of his fleſh being roſted,ſaied vnto them.*Ecce,hoc eſt hominis comedere, quod vos facitis,quod à nobis velut occultũ inqniritis facinus,quod vos aperta luce committitis*. This Lo that you do,ys to eate men, whiche as a ſecret wickedneſſe ye enquiere amonge vs,whiche ye committe in the open light.

The heathen,as yt ys ſuppoſed, knowing the chryſtians to aſſemble , and hearing that in thoſe aſſembles they did eate the fleſh of a man,and not knowing the myſterie,ſuſpected that they killed either men or children for that pourpoſe,when in dede they eate the fleſh of Chryſt.Who(as ſainct Androwe ſaied) when his veryfleſh ys eaten of the people , and his blood dronke: yet doth he ſtill remain wholl and ſownde vndefiled,and aliue.

Yt prooneth well alſo this ſame, that Auerrois the Philoſopher ſaieth of
B the Chryſtians:*Mundum peragraui,varias ſectas inueni,& nunquam tam ſatuam repperi ſectam,ſicut eſt ſecta Chriſtianorũ.Quoniam Deum ſuum,quem colunt, deuorant dentibus*. I haue walked ouer the worlde,I haue ſownde diuerſe ſectes, and yet did I neuer finde ſo fooliſh a ſecte as the ſect of the Chryſtians.For they deuoure with their teeth,whom they honoure as God.Yt was knowen to all the worlde,that the Chryſtias honoured Chryſt as theirGod.Wherfor yt ys caſie to perceaue , that the ſame was that they receaued and eate Chryſt. And foraſmoche as the heathen reputed Chryſt but as a verie man,and were ignoraunt of that great myſterie of the coniunction of the Godhead and manhead in vnitie of perſon in Chryſt,they ſaied that the Chryſtians did eate the fleſh of man.By whiche voice other ſome, as in a multude yt often happeneth, myſvnderſtanding yt,and taking yt abſolutelie,reported the Chryſtians as before ys ſaied, that they did eat ſecretlie the fleſh of men and children.

C   With this ſuſpicion yt ys not vnlike that the Iewe was ledde of whom S. Amphilochius maketh mencion:who being deſierouſe to ſearche and knowe the ſecrett myſteries of the chryſtians,at the time that S. Baſille ſhoulde go to the holie miniſtracion,feigning himſelf a chryſtian, entred among the Chryſtians, and when the Sacrament was broken by the handes of S.Baſill, he ſawe thẽ a childe diuided,and whẽ with other he came to the cõmunion, the Sacrament deliuered vnto him was made fleſh,and the cuppe was full of bloode,of whiche bothe reſeruing ſome token, he went home and ſhewed yt to his wief,and for declaracion tolde her what he had ſeen with his eyes. Whervpon beleuing the myſteries of the Chryſtians to be merueilouſe and wonderfull, the next daie he came to S.Baſill,and deſired to be baptiſed,and made a chryſtian.

Thus we maie perceaue,that the workes of God be great and merueillouſe,who vnto this Iewe but ſuſpecting the chryſtians to eate fleſh and drinke bloode in their myſteries made yt ſoch to him as he ſuſpected yt to be and
D to appeare ſoche to his ſeight as yt was couertlie to other in verie dede. But he ſawe yt with his bodilie eye for his inſtruction,that the true Chryſtian ſeeth with his faithfull eye to his ſaluacion.

But to return to our firſt matter,ſo great was the fame that the Chryſtians did eate mãnes fleſh in their myſteries , that to deliuer thẽ frõ the enuie that was cõceaued,againſt thẽ for the ſame *Iuſtinus* the holie martyr was enforced

Ee iij   in his

Euſeb.li.ς.
cap.2.
Blandina.

Ibid.cap.3.
Attalus.

Lib. de paſſione eius quem ſcripſerunt presbyteri & Diacones Achaia.

S.Amphil.
in vita Baſilij.
A iewe induced to be a Chryſtiã by a miracle of the Sacramẽt.

in his Apollogie made vnto *Antonius Pius* to reueil and declare vnto him all　E
the wholl order of the mysteries of the chryftians, and what was their faith
therin, whiche thing was not vfed in thofe daies to be declared to anie prophane man and infidel, but allwaies kept fecrette, fo moche as yt might be.
And yet vpon this enforcemét this *Iuſtinus* declared the matter fo plainlie, as
no man of his auncientie to foche men more plainlie, as fhortlie here after
ye fhall perceaue.

　As thefe thinges then hitherto faied do proue by the fame that Chryſt ys
prefent in the Sacrament, and fo confequentlie that the woordes of Chryſt,
haue ben and fo ought to be vnderſtanded in their propre fenfe withoute
trope or figure: So wolde I wifh them of all chryftians in thefe daies to be receaued. And as by thefe thinges we maie be moued. So by other reafons we
maie from the contrarie vnderſtanding be diffwaded. Among manie of whiche I wil bring but one or two, that *Rupertus* doth make and the firſt ys this.

*Rupert. li.
.6. in ʒoan.
Apoca.22.*

*Nonne Ioannes Euangeliſta dicit in Apocalipſi: Si quis appofuerit ad hæc, apponet fuper illũ
Deus plagas fcriptas in libro iſto. Et fi quis diminuerit de verbis prophetiæ libri huius, au-　F
feret Deus partem eius de ligno vitæ, & de ciuitate fanĉta, & de ijs quæ fcripta funt in libro
iſto? Nunquid minùs timenda eſt hic illa maledĉio, vt non detrahamus, vel apponamus
quidquam verbis dicentis, Hoc eſt corpus meum, quod pro vobis tradetur: Hic eſt fanguis
meus noui teſtamenti, qui pro multis effundetur, in remiſsionem peccatorum? Cùm enim illo
dicente: Hoc eſt corpus meum, nos fubauditionem appofuerimus dicentes, figuratiuum, vel
per fimilitudinem diĉtum: Cùm inquam illo dicente: Hoc eſt corpus meum, nos dixerimus,
hoc fignificat corpus meum, nonne multum eſt quod apponimus, vel praua demutatione de-
trahimus, & fenfum generamus, quem tantus Author Deus & homo nufquã eſt locutus,
nec afcendit vnquam in cor eius?* Dothe not the Euangeliſt Iohn faie in the Apo-
calipfe: *Yf anie man fhall adde vnto thefe thinges, God fhal adde vnto him the plagues,
that are written in this booke. And yf anie man fhall minifhe of the woordes of the booke of*

*To the
woordes of
God maie
nothing be
added nor
diminished*

*this prophecie, God fhall take awaie his parte oute of the booke of life and oute of the holie
citte, and the thinges whiche are written in this booke?* Ys this maledĉió or curfe leffe
to be feared here, that we diminifh not or putte any thing to the woordes
of him that faied: *This ys my bodie, whiche fhall be deliuered for yow. This ys my bloode*　G
of the newe teſtament, whiche fhall be fhedde for manie in the remiſsió of finnes? For when
he faieth: *This ys my bodie:* we fhall putto an vnderſtanding, faing a figuratiue
bodie, or that yt ys fpoken by a fimilitude, when I faie, he faieth. *This ys my bodie:* we fhall faie this fignifieth my bodie, ys yt not moche that we putto his
woordes, or by an euell chaunge take from them, ahd make a fenfe, whiche
fo great an Authour God and man, in no place hath fpoken, neither at anie
time did yt afcende in to his heart? Thus *Rupertus.*

　This ys the firſt reafon of this Authour, whiche yf yt be well weighed, and
the thing well confidered, howe moche we by figures, tropes, and fignificacions, do alter and chaunge, howe moche we putto in woordes and diminifh
in fubſtance, howe the expofition denieth, that the text affirmeth : we haue
good caufe to feare the malediĉtion of God fpoken by S. Iohn, who beareth
not foche expofitions denieng what he hath faied, nor foche glofes confown
ding his text. Wherfore we maie well be diffuaded from foche expofitions,
or rather deprauacions, and the rather that their ys no warrant to beare vs　H
fo to expownde thefe woordes of Chryſt, as of the circumſtance of the place maie be perceaued, whiche this Authour vfeth as an other reafon to moue
vs not fo to vnderſtande Chryſtes woordes of his fupper as the Aduerfarie
dothe expownde them. And thus he faieth.

　Cùm obijcit quis fuisque fcriptitat in fedulis, quod itidem dixerit eadem veritas. Ego fum
vitis

A *vitis,tam audacter,quã imperitè in argumentum mendosum illud attrahit,cum statim sub-*
sequentia verba dicentis: Sicut palmes non potest ferre fructum à semetipso nisi manserit in
vite:sic nec vos nisi in me manseritis,manifestè per similitudinem compellant intelligi, præ-
sertim cùm non signanter dixerit:Ego sum hæc vitis:sicut signanter dixit , Hoc est corpus
meum,hic est sanguis meus,apposita protinus descriptione veræ proprietatis, de corpore in-
quiens,quod pro vobis tradetur,de sanguine autem,qui pro multis effundetur. Igitur ne ve-
niant super nos plagæ nouißimæ,neque apponimus,neque diminuimus quicquam diuinæ de-
finitioni,vel descriptioni,quam incarnatum Verbum ore proprio deprompsit. Imo quia per-
fecta charitas foras mittit timorem,non tam plagarum timore,qunm veritatis amore, confi-
temur,quia panis iste corporeus,postquam signauerit eum Pater, & vinum hoc expressum
acinis præsentibus mox vt eodem signo signatum est per manus ecclesiæ dicentis: vt nobis
corpus & sanguis fiat dilectißimi filij tui,Domini nostri Iesu Christi,etc. vsque in memoriã
mei facietis: corpus & sanguis eius qui huius traditionis author est,& hoc sacrificium ipse
*Christus est,cuius paßione vt sacrificium fieret à Deo Patre in veritate signatum est.*Whē
one obiecteth,and writeth yt also in his bookes euen as boldlie as vnlearned
lie that the same trueth(mening Chryst)saieth also,*I am a vine*:he draweth yt

B into a false argument,seing that the woordes immediately folowing of him
saing thus:*As the braunche can beare no fruit of him self,except he abide in the vine: So
neither can yowe except ye abide in me:*Do manifestlie enforce that saing to be vnde by a similitude,speciallie for that he did not with a singular demonstraciõ
saie:*I am this vine:*as with a singular demonstracion he saied:*This ys my bodie,this
ys my bloode:*Wherunto furthwith he put the description of the true propertie
of eche of them,of the bodie saing:*whiche shall be deliuered for yowe*,of the blood
also , *whiche shall be shedde for manie.* Therfor that these later plagues come
not vpon vs, we neither diminish,nor put to any thing to the diuine definition or discription,whiche the Sonne of God incarnate hath spoken or vttered with his owne mouthe.But raither, bycause perfecte charitie casteth oute feare,not so moche for the feare,as for loue of trueth we do confesse, that
this bodil.e breade,after the Father hath blessed it,and this wine pressed oute of these present grapes, as sooen as yt ys blessed by the handes of the

C churche saing:that yt maie be made to vs the bodie and bloode of thy most
beloued some Iesus Chryst,and so furth vntill ye come to these woordes, *ye
shall do yt in the remembrance of me*,that yt ys the bodie and bloode of him,who
ys the Authour of this tradicion,and that this sacrifice ys Chryst him self,by
whose paßion yt was blessed of God the Father in verie dede, that yt might
be made a sacrifice.Thus farre he.

   Two thinges I thinke,good gētle Reader,in this reason of this Authour to
note to thee : The one ys that where the Aduersarie bringeth furth certain
places of the scripture, whiche be vnderstand by tropes:as wher Chryste
saieth:*I am a vine,I am the dore*,and soche like,therby to prooue that these woor
des of Chryst.*This ys my bodie*:shoulde so be vnderstande also(whiche in dede
proueth nothing)this Authour declareth that the circumstance of these places,doth compell vs so to vnderstand them,as in the opening of this text:*I am
a vine*,he hath declared. So this scripture also:*I am the doore*, the woordes of
Chryste immediately folowing teache vs that they are to be vnderstande by

D a similitude,for streight waie he saieth: *By me who soeuer entreth he shall be saued,
and shall go in,and go oute, and finde foode.*So that we haue Chrystes owne warrant so to vnderstand them.But to vnderstande the woordes of Chrystes sup
per in like maner, vieue the place,ye shall finde no title in the texte, to cause
yt to beare the Aduersaries sense.So that they haue no other warrãt but wil-
full and naturall reason,whiche warrant ys not allwaies sufficient and alowe

                         Ee iiij   able

*These woor-
des ʃ am a
vine. Ioan.
15. are pro
ued by the
circuʃtance
to be a simi
litude.*

Ioan.10.

*Willfull or
naturall
reaʃon ys no
ʃufficient
warrant
allwaies in
the court of
faith,*

able in the courte of faith.Wherfore as thefe fcriptures be to be vnderftan- **E**
ded by a trope, bicaufe the circumftance ther fo teacheth: So are the other
woordes in their propre fenfe to be vnderftanded, bicaufe the circumftance
fo teacheth.

For declaracion of whiche matter, I maie deuide the feconde note into
two partes. The one ys, to note the enunciacion of bothe fcriptures. For
though Chryft faied, *I am a vine*:yet he did not particularly take a braunche
of a vine,and faie, *I am this vine,or this vine ys my bodie*: but vfed the generall
woorde,and faied *I am a vine*.But fpeaking of the myfterie of his bodie,he did
not vfe that maner of fpeache ,faing,*I am bread*,whiche maner of phrafe maie
feeme well to beare a trope,yf anie circumftâce had ben adioined to declare
and open the fame:But leauing the generall woorde of bread , and particularlie taking a peice of bread in his handes,and blefsing,and geuing thankes,
faied with a particular and fpeciall demonftracion:*This ys my bodie*. As thefe

two propofitions fpoken of an olde man.*I am a childe*,and by fpeciall demon-
I am a vi-
ne:and this
ys my bodie
be no like
fpeaches.
ftracion to this childe faing:*This ys my childe*:haue a great difference. The firft **F**
being fpoken by a fimilitude, for that reafon witte vnderftanding and fenfeis being decaied in him,he maie faie.I am a childe,that ys,*like a childe*, The o-
ther being fpoken of his owne childe,and importing not a fimilitude , but a
naturall fubftance of him in the childe:So thefe propofitions:I am a vine,and
this ys my bodie:haue great difference : The one being fpoken by a fimilitude
bicaufe Chryft ys like a vine:The other by certen demonftracion of fubftance,for that that Chryft made demonftracion vnto was his verie fubftance

The fecond parte of the note ys that the circumftance of the fcripture reiecting figures,and tropes dothe mightilie prooue the fenfe of that place to
be propre,and not figuratiue or tropicall.For the propretie (faieth he)apper
teining to the bodie (*whiche can not be applied to the figure*)ys furthwith added,
whiche ys that the thing ys there,whiche fhall be deliuered for manie. And
that ys in the cuppe,whiche fhall fhed in the remifsion of finnes,whiche can
be nothing ells, but the bodie and bloode of Chryfte.Who onelie gaue his
bodie to be crucified,and his bloode to be fhed for owre redemption. **G**

This ys my
bodie. no fi-
guratiue
fpeache.
Thus then ye perceaue that thefe woordes of Chryft:*This ys my bodie*:we-
re fpoken of him withoute the putting to of anie trope,figure or figne. They
are left to vs written by the three holie Euangeliftes,whithoute any mêciô
of trope or figure. They were fo taught by S.Paule to the Corinthians,and
afterwarde fo writtê.The promiffe of Chryft,wherin he faied:*The bread, which*
I will geue ys my flesh,which I will geue for the life of the worlde,was plainlie whithoute any trope fpoken. Yt ys fo reported of the Euangelift S. Iohn. Yt ys fo expownded of all the auncient doctours,and fo fhewed what the woordes be,
teaching the perfourmance of that promiffe.

Ye perceaue alfo the fame of the communion of the Chryftians emong
the infidels to be not by a figure of flefh,but by verie flefh in dede.Ye percea
ue emong Chryftians the beleif of the Sacrament,to be the flefh of Chryft,
to be fo commonlie receaued and beleued,that younge babes in thofe daies
coulde fpeake yt. Ye perceaue that yt ys not laufull for vs to putte to , or
to take awaie from the woorde of Chryft. For yf we do, we fall into the **H**
daunger of Gods malediction,and other plagues. All thefe confideracions,
and manie mo fhewe vnto vs that we fhoulde take the woordes of Chryfte,
as they be of him fpoken:yf ye put to anie of thefe woordes,*fignum* or *figura*,
Token or figure,ys not that put to that Chryft fpake not? and do ye not fo
fall into the daunger of Gods plagues ? Ouer and befides this ye perceaue
that

A that the circumftance of the fcripture refufeth tropes and figures and enforceth to accept the propre fenfe onelie.

Wherfore chryftian Reader, beware of that flattering contenaunce and deceiptfull lieng of the olde ferpent Sathan: flie the hiffing of the vipers: be not caried awaie with light creditte, as our firft parentes were therby to creditte the deuel, and difcreditte God. But knowe the one to be thie enemie, and feare him: knowe the other to be thy Lorde God, thy Sauiour and Redemer, and embrace him,

Of the which matter harke farder to the godlie faing of *Rupertus : Accipe, inquit, & comedite, Hoc eft corpus meum. Et alibi: Qui manducat carnem meam, & bibit fanguinem meum, in me manet & ego in eo . Cùm hæc dicit agnus Dei, oportunè nobis ad memoriam recurrit illud: quod dixit ferpens, imo per ferpentem Diabolus, hoftis humani generis. Accipite & comedite, & eritis ficut dij. Optimæ, & fpectabiles valdè propofitiones. Ille ferpens erat: ifte agnus eft. Ille vetus peccator, ifte antiquus creator. Ille fpiritu Diaboli falfum fibilans: ifte fpiritu Dei verum euangeliȝans. Ille de ligno non fuo raptor optulit: Ifte de corpore & fanguine fuo largitor dedit. Ille quod non habebat mendaciter promifit, eritis*

B *(inquiens) ficut dij: Ifte quod habebat, quod femper naturaliter habet , fideliter dedit vt fimus dij, dum manet ipfe in nobis: Illi tandem nephandifsimè creditum eft plufquam Deo: Creditur è contrario huic Deo, fi non plus, at faltem quantum creditum eft illi Diabolo. Creditum eft enim, quod illi pomo ineffet, quod non videbatur, fcilicet vis deos efficiendi: Credatur huic Sacramento ineffe quod non videtur, videlicet, veritas carnis & fanguinis , valens efficere nos corporales Vnigenito filio Dei. Hoc enim ratio vel ordo, iuftitiæ expofcit . Accipite ergo (inquit) & comedite. Accipere eft fideliter credere, cum gratiarum actione diligere, compatienti affectu corporis huius traditionem, & fanguinis huius effufionem refpicere . Hoc fieri non poteft, nifi priùs reijciatur id, quod ab illo malè acceptum eft. Illud igitur mendacium execrantes, hanc veritatem accipite, approbate, amplectimini, & contra cibum mortis, panê comedite vitæ eternæ & calicem bibite falutis perpetuæ.* He faieth (mening Chryft) take and eate, this ys my bodie, and in an other place: He *that eateth my flesh and drinketh my bloode, dwelleth in me and I in him.* When the lambe of God faieth thefe thinges yt cometh in due time to our memorie, that the ferpent faied , or

C raither by the ferpent, the Deuell, the enemie of man kinde: *Take and eate, and ye shall be as Gods.* Goodlie and verie notable propofitions. He was a ferpent: this ys a lambe. He an olde offender: this an auncient creatour. He by the fpirit of the Deuel hiffing oute an vntrueth: this by the fpirit of God preaching a trueth. He a theecf gaue of the fruit that was not his: This a right geuer, gaue of his owne bodie and bloode. He falfely promifed that that he had not, ye fhall (faieth he) be as Gods: This trulie gaue that he had, whiche allwaies naturallie he hathe, that ys, that we maie be Gods, forfomoche as he dwelleth in vs. Vnto him neuer the leffe moft wickedly was geuen more credit then to God: Vnto this côtrarie wife let credit be geuen being God, yf not more, yet at the leaft as moche creditte as was geuê to the Deuell. For yt was beleued, that to be in that apple whiche was not fein, that ys to faie, power to make Gods: Let yt be beleued to be in the Sacrament , that ys not feen, that ys to faie, *the veritie of the flesh and bloode of Chryft, able to incorporate vs to the onely begottê Sonne of God.* Thus moche reafon, or ordre of iuftice dothe require. Take ther-

D fore, faieth he, and eate. To take ys faithfully to beleue, with thankes geuing to loue, with a compatient affection to beholde the deliuerance of this bloode. This cã not be doen, except that be reiected, that of the enemie was euel receaued. Detefting therfor that lie, receaue, approue, and ébrace this trueth, and againft the meat of death, eate ye the bread of euerlafting life, and drinke the cuppe of euerlafting faluacion

Thus

Conference of Chryftes woordes and the ferpents.

To take Chryftes bodie, what yt ys.

Thus being by this good Father admonifhed of the true vnderftanding   **E**
of Chryftes woordes, I will nowe make the fame plain before thine eyes by
the teftimonie of a nombre of holie Fathers, to the whiche, good Reader, I
praie thee geue good heede.

THE THREE AND FOVRTETH CHAP. BEGINNETH
to proue the vnderftanding of Chryftes forfaied woordes not to be figuratiue by the
authoritie of the Fathers. And first by Alexander and Iuftinus.

Orfomoche as the mifunderftanding of the woordes of the fupper
of Chryft hath and doth maintein great and lamētable contencion
among foche as profeffe Chryftes name, and the right vnderftādïng
of the fame ought to be the occafion of the reftitucion of peace, and concorde: Let yt not greiue thee (gentle Reader) though I tarie fomwhat long vpon
this text, in producing manie holie Fathers of Chryfts fchoole. who fhal teache vs howe thefe woordes, *This ys my bodie*, were ther taught to be vnderftan-   **F**
ded, and therby fhall do vs to witte, what ys the enacted trueth of Chryftes
Parliament houfe, as touching this matter nowe among chryftian men in
controuerfie. For the plain declaracion wherof I fhall produce manie of the
eldeft Fathers, and fewe I truft, that do treact of thefe woordes, being of any
fame or authoritie fhall be omitted. And for a fpeciall note to difcerne the
trueth from falfheade, the fcholers of Chryft from the fcholers of Sathan, and
the graue and conftant ftaied Senatours of Chryftes Parliament houfe, from
the light, and vauering whifperers of the Conciliables of Sathan: Marke and
note well that as in the one and fourteth chap. ye haue pceaued, the fectes of
Sathan are merueillouflie diffected, and by great and fowle contencion amōg
them felues diuided: So fhall ye perceaue that Chryftes difciples are vnited
all of one minde all of one vnderftanding, all fpeaking one thing in full peace and perfect concorde: Remembre that the high fcholers and cheif noble
men of Chryftes Parliament honfe (I meen the foure Euāgeliftes and S. Pau
le) fo agree that among them there ys no one title fpoken of the Aduerfaries   **G**
tropes and figures: but euery one of them teftifie the matrer plainlie, leauing
the woordes in their propre fenfe. So fhall ye fee all this noble companie of
Fathers doo. Let vs then in Chryftes name heare them vtter, what ys the ena
cted trueth of the vnderftanding of Chryftes woordes.

Although ther are right auncient Fathers, that doo verie notablie declare,
and teftifie the prefence of Chryftes bodie and bloode in the Sacrament, as
Martialis the difciple of Chryft: *Ignatius* the difciple of S. Iohn the euangelift,
Dionyfius Arcopagita, the difciple of S. Paule, with diuerfe other: yet the eldeft
that I finde after the Euangeliftes and S. Panle, treacting of the woordes of
Chryft are *Alexander and Iuftinus*, of the whiche although *Alexander* be the elder: yet for that by him occafion ys geuen to fpeake of fome matter more at
large, I fhall firft produce *Iuftinus.*

This holie martyr, for anfwer and defence of the Chryftians, who were
flaundered, that they fhoulde eate mans flefh, wrote to the Emperour *Anto-*
nius Pius, and among other thinges declareth what ys the religion of the chri   **H**
ftians aboute the Sacrament, and what faith they were taught to haue of yt

Iuftin.
Apolog. 2.

and faieth thus: *Cùm autem is qui preeft gratias egerit, & totus populus approbauerit*
hi qui vocantur apud nos Diaconi diftribuunt vnicuique præfentium, vt participent de pane
in quo gratiæ actæ funt, & de vino & aqua, & ijs qui non funt prefentes deferunt. Atque
hoc alimentum apud nos vocatur Euchariftia. De quo nulli alij participare licitum eft, nifi qui
cr. dit

A　*credit vera esse,quæ docentur à nobis,et qui lauacro in remissionem peccatorū & in regene*
rationem lotus est.& sic viuit , sicut Christus tradidit.Neque vt commune panem &com-
mune poculū hæc suscipimus:sed quemadmodum per verbum Dei incarnatus Iesus Christus,
seruator noster,& carnem & sanguinem habuit:Sic & verbi sui oratione , consecratum
gratiarum actione alimentum,ex quo caro nostra,& sanguis per transmutationem aluntur,
ipsius incarnati Iesu Christi & carnem,& sanguinem esse edocti sumus. Apostoli enim in
commentarijs suis,quæ Euangelia vocantur,sic ipsis præcipisse tradiderunt . Cùm accepisset
panem,gratijs actis,dixisse:Hoc facite in mei commemorationem,Hoc est corpus meum. Et
poculum similiter cum accepisset,& gratias egisset,dixisse:Hic est sanguis meus , & solis
ipsis impartisse. When the preist hath ended his thankes geuing, and all the
people haue saied *Amen*, they whom we call Deacons distribute to euery
one then present to be partakers of the bread,wine, and water consecrated,
and carie part to them that be absent.And this ys the foode whiche among
vs ys called *Eucharistia*.Wherof yt ys laufull for no man to be partaker,except
he beleue those thinges to be true,that be taught vs:And be baptised in the
water of regeneracion in remission of sinnes,and so liueth as Chryst hath

Bread, wi-
ne and wa-
ter consecra
ted in the
primitiue
churche

B　taught.For we do not take these as common bread and wine:but like as Iesus Chryst our Sauiour incarnated by the woorde of God had flesh and
blood for our saluacion, *Euen so we be taught that the foode,* (wherwith our flesh
and bloode be nourished by alteracion)*when yt ys consecrated by the praier of his*
*woorde to be the flesh and bloode of the same Iesus incarnated.*For the Apostles in those their bookes,whiche be called Gospells,teache that Iesus did so commaun
de them,when he had take bread,and geuen thankes saied,*Do this in my remē-*
*brance,This ys my bodie,*And likewise taking the cuppe when he had geuen than
kes,saied:*This ys my bloode,*and gaue them to his Apostles onelie.Thus moche
holy Iustine.

Bread and
wine after
consecracio̅
be the bodie
and blood
of Chryst.

In this Authour be many thinges woorthie note. But omitting them all
I shall onely note that, that he ys at this time alleaged for, namely for the
right vnderstanding of Chrystes woordes in their propre sense, withoute figure or trope.For the which,note well that he saieth,that we be taught that

C　the foode (*mening the bread, wine and water*) after the consecracion ys the flesh
and bloode of Iesus incarnate.He saieth not that they were taught,that they
were signes,tokens or figures of the flesh of Iesus,neither that they be onely
called the flesh of Iesus.Ye maie then perceaue what the teaching and doctri
ne of the primitiue church was:ye maie well see,that they were plainly taught
that the bread wine and water,be the flesh and bloode of our Sauiour Iesus.

And herwith all note howe certen this doctrine was.Yt was as certen,and
sure,as the mysterie of the incarnacion of Chryst. For (saieth this Authour)
Like as Iesus Chryst our Sauiour incarnated by the woorde of God,had flesh
and bloode for our saluacion: Euen so we be taught,the breade wine and
water,after the consecracion,to be the flesh and bloode of the same Iesus.

Doctrine
of the reall
presence as
certen as
the incar-
nacion to
the primiti-
ue church.

Weigh this(gentle Reader) and marke these woordes well that euen as
we be taught as a principle of our faith,to beleue that Iesus Chryst in his incarnacion had flesh and bloode:euen so we be taught the foode of the holie
Sacrament to be the flesh and bloode of the same Iesus.But howe doth this

D　Authour proue that this doctrine was so taught?By this proof For the Apo-
stles(saieth he)in their workes,whiche they call Gospells do teache, that our
Lorde Iesus so commaunded them,saing(*when he had taken breade and geuen than-*
kes)doe this in the remembrance of me. This ys my bodie. And likewise taking the cuppe,
when he had geuen thankes saied:This ys my bloode.

In this proof of this Authour ther be two thinges to be noted. The one
againſt

against the blasphemouse reproche of the Aduersaries and this Proclamer,　**E**
whiche saie that yt ys an inuencion of the papistes to teache Chrystes flesh
and bloode to be in the Sacramēt. But this Authour saieth, that the Apostles
taught that our Sauiour Iesus did commaunde them so to doe. So thar yt ys
his commaundement and tradicion, an not the papistes inuencion, but yf
they will accompt Iesus Chryst for this his so doing to be a papist, Then in
dede they maie saie, yt ys the inuencion of a papist.

　　The other note ys for the applicacion of the woordes of Chryst to the
Sacramēt. Ye haue perceaued that we be taught, that the foode of the Sacrament ys the flesh of Iesus Chryst. Ye perceaue also that the same Iesus Chryst
so cōmāded, as the Apostles haue taught in their Gospells. But wher ys that
cōmaundement in the Gospells? This ys the commaundement. *Doe this in the
remembrance of me. This ys my bodie, this my bloode.* By these woordes we are commaunded to doe the thing. By these woordes we are taught what the thing
ys. The thing (as this authour saieth) ys the flesh and bloode of Iesus Chryst
incarnated. And this thing also he saieth, we are taught by these woordes.　**F**
Wherfore these woordes are to be vnderstanded of the flesh and bloode of
Iesus Chryst.

*Doctrine of
the primiti
ue churche,
and the
churche
since and
nowe com-
pared.*　　Nowe looke well vpon the doctrine of Chryst and his primitiue Church:
compare them to the doctrines of the catholike Church that nowe ys, and
see yf they be not agreable: Trie yf they be not all one. Chryst saieth, after
he had blessed the bread and the wine: *This ys my bodie, This ys my bloode.* This
Authour saieth, that they were taught in the primitiue Churche, that the
bread and wine with water, after cōsecraciō be the flesh and bloode of Iesus
incarnated. The catholike Churche, that hath ben, and nowe ys, teacheth
that the bread and wine on the Altar after the consecracion be the bodie
and bloode of Chryst. Wolde ye desire anie more agreement? wolde ye desire anie better concorde?

*A plain pla
ce for M.
Iuell.*　　And wher the Proclamer requireth anie one auncient Authour that teacheth plainlie Chrystes verie reall presence, wolde he haue anie plainer speache, then that whiche he impugneth in vs? This Authour saieth that, that we　**G**
saie, and speaketh as plainlie as we speake, as by the conference of both a
childe maie perceaue. Let the Proclaimer then be ashamed of his rash proclamacion, and with mature and sobre beliberacion and iudgement let him
agnise the doctrine of the primitiue Churche, and so shall he confesse with
vs the reall presence of Chrystes bodie in the Sacrament, whiche nowe wickedlie he hathe impugned.

　　But here ys not be ouerpassed the exceading crafte and vntrueth of Cranmer, one of the Fathers of this Proclamer in the corrupting, falsieng., and
abusing of this Authour *Iustinus.* And that yt shall not be laied to my charge
that I misreporte him. I will faithfullie ascribe his, woordes as they be written in his booke. Thus he writeth. *Iustinus a great learned man, and an holie Martyr
the eldest Authour that this daie ys knowen to write anie treactice vpon the Sacramentes,
and wrote not moche after one hundreth yeares after Chrystes ascension. He writeth in his
seconde Apologie, that the bread, water and wine in this Sacrament are not to be taken as
other common meates and drinkes be, but they be meates ordeined pourposely to geue than-　**H**
kes to God, and therfore be called Eucharistia, and be called also the bodie and bloode of
Chryst, and that yt ys laufull for none to eate or drinke of them, but that professe Chryste,
and liue according to the same, And yet the same meate and drinke (saieth he) ys chaunged
into our flesh and bloode and nourisheth our bodies.*

　　These be his verie woordes, and in this maner dothe he report *Iustinus.*
　　　　　　　　　　　　　　　　　　　　　　　　　　　　　Whiche

A Whiche reporte howe yt agreeth with *Iustinus* owne woordes, the reader by conference shall easilie perceaue. And therfor omitting manie falsheades and other fawtes by him here admitted, I wil nowe touche but two, whiche be intollerable, and doen with to moche impudencie. The one ys that he reporteth this Authour as though he shoulde saie, that the Sacrament ys but called the bodie of Chryst, wher this Authour saieth no soche woordes But saieth plainly, that the bread and wine after the consecracion be the flesh and blood of Iesus incarnate, and that the people were in his daies so taught. The other ys, the misplacing of the sentences of the authour, to make them serue his pourpose. For wher Iustine saieth that the foode of bread, wine and water, werwith our bodies be nourished, when they be consecrated by the praier of his woorde be the flesh and bloode of Iesus. And so before the consecracion of them, he teacheth, that they be creatures meet to nourish our bodies. and to that vnderstanding doth so place them. Cranmer, or the Authour of that booke pleaceth them as creatures meet to nourish vs after the consecracion, therby signifieng, that they be but creatures

B of bread, wine and water after the consecracion as they were before. But howe falsely that ys doen, not onely this translacion, but also the translaciõ of *Petrus Nannius* declareth, whiche for the better opening of the trueth I will here also ascribe: Thus he translateth that parte of *Iustinus.Non enim vt quemuis panem, neque vt quemuis potum, ista omnia accipimus, sed quemadmodum per verbum Dei incarnatus est Iesus Christus saluator noster, & carnem & sanguinem pro nostra salute assumpsit: ita quoque per preces verbi illius, cibũ ex quo caro nostra et sanguis per immutationē aluntur cũ bedictus fuerit, Iesu ipsius incarnati, carnē et sanguinē dicimus esse.*

Neither do we take all these thinges, as euery other bread, neither as euery other drinke. But euẽ as IesusChryst our sauiour by the woorde of God was incarnated, ãd for our health tooke flesh and bloode: euẽ so haue we learned that foode of the whiche our flesh and bloode by immutaciõ are nourished, whẽ yt ys blessed by the praiers of his woordes, *to be fleshe and bloodo Iesus incarnate.* In whiche translacion, as in the other ye see, that the nourishmẽt of the foode, of breade, wine and water, ys put before the consecracion, which Cranmer vntrulie wolde place after the consecracion, for the pourpose befo

C re saied and therby also to denie transubstanciacion. But Iustine to declare the great worke of God, wrought in and by the consecracion, saieth, that yt ys soche foode before the consecracion as we be nourished with, but when yt ys consecrated, *yt ys the flesh of Iesus incarnated.*

The like maner of speache vseth both S. Ambrose and S. Augustine, saing: *Antequam consecretur panis est, vbi autem verba Christi accesserint, corpus est Christi.* Before yt be consecrated yt ys bread, but when the woordes of Chryst haue comed to yt, yt ys the bodie of Chryst. S. Augustine thus: *Ante verba Christi quod offertur panis dicitur: vbi Christi verba deprompta fuerint, iam non panis dicitur, sed corpus appellatur.* Before the woordes of Chryst, that whiche ys offred ys called bread: but when the woordes of Chryst are spoken, yt ys not nowe called bread, but yt ys called the bodie.

Thus Reader, thowe maist see, the sleight of Cranmer and his falsifieng of the holie doctours, by him. The like in diuerse places of this booke shalt thowe finde prooued in *Oecolampadius*, whom Cranmer folowed, and also in this

D Proclamer who foloweth Cranmer. Soche and soo good ys the quarrell that they maintein, that withoute falsifieng, wresting, or truncating of the holie Fathers their doctrine can haue no good shewe, Wherof thowe nowe being aduertised, and in them the matter being well prooued, trusting

Ff that

Two false sleights of Cranmer noted in thallegacion of Iustin.

Petrus Nannius

Amb. li.4. de Sac.ca.5 Plain sainges for M. Iuell. Augu. de verbis Do. serm.8.

that yt will geue thee occasion to looke er thowe leape: I will leaue Iuftine, and call in *Aleander* an holy martyr, who liued not long after Chryft euen in the time of *Ignatius* and *Polycarpus*.

Thus writeth *Alexander*. *In facramentorum oblationibus, quæ inter miſſarum ſolemnia Domino offeruntur, paſsio Domini miſcenda eſt, vt eius, cuius corpus & ſanguis conficitur, paſsio celebretur, ita vt repulſis opinionibus ſuperſtitionum, panis tantùm & vinum aqua permixtum in ſacrificio offerantur. Non debet enim vt à patribus accepimus & ipſa ratio docet, in calice Domini aut vinum ſolum, aut aqua ſola offerri, Sed vtrumque permixtum, quia vtrumque ex latere eius in paſsione ſua profluxiſſe legitur. Ipſa verò veritas nos inſtruit, calicem & panem in ſacramento offerre, quando ait: Accepit Ieſus panem, & benedixit, deditque Diſcipulis ſuis, dicens (Accipite & manducate: Hoc eſt enim corpus meum, quod pro vobis tradetur. Similiter poſtquam cœnauit accepit calicem, deditque Diſcipulis ſuis, dicens: Accipite & bibite ex eo omnes. Hic eſt calix ſanguinis mei. qui pro vobis effundetur in remiſsionem peccatorum. Crimina atque peccata, oblatis ijs Domino ſacrificijs delentur. Idcirco & paſsio eius in iis commemoranda eſt, qua redempti ſumus, & ſæpius recitanda, & hæc Domino offerenda. Talibus hoſtijs delectabitur, & placabitur Dominus, & peccata dimittet ingentia. Nihil enim in ſacrificijs maius eſſe poteſt quàm corpus & ſanguis Domini. Nec vlla oblatio hac potior eſt, ſed hæc omnes præcellit Quæ pura conſcientia Domino offerenda eſt, & pura mente ſumenda, atque ab omnibus veneranda. Et ſicut potior eſt cæteris, ita potiùs excoli & venerari debet.*

In the oblacions of the Sacramentes, whiche in the ſolemne doinges of the Maſſes be offred, the paſsion of our Lorde ys to be intermedled, that the paſsion of him, *whoſe bodie and bloode ys conſecrated*, maie be celebrated, ſo that, the ſuperſticions of opinions repelled, onely bread and wine mixed with water maie be offred. For ther aught not (as we haue receaued of our Fathers, and alſo reaſon yt ſelf dothe teache) either wine alone, or water alone to be offred in the cuppe of our Lorde: but bothe mixed together, bycauſe yt ys redde that both in the time of his paſsion did flowe oute of his ſide. The verie trueth yt ſelf doth teache vs to offer bread and wine in the Sacrament, when he taking the bread, and bleſsing yt ſaied: *Take ye and eat, This ys my bodie, whiche ſhall be deliuered for you. Likewiſe when he had ſupped, he tooke the cuppe, and gaue yt to his diſciples, ſaing: Take ye, and drinke ye all of this: For this ys the cuppe of my bloode, whiche ſhall be ſhedde for yow in remiſsion of ſinnes.* Theſe ſacrifices being offred to our Lorde, crimes and offences are wiped awaie. Therfor his paſsion alſo by the whiche we are redemed, ys in theſe to be remembred, and often to be recited, and yt alſo ys to be offred to our Lorde. For with ſoche ſacrifices our Lorde will be delighted, and appeaced, and will forgeue great ſinnes. Among all ſacrifices nothing can be of more eſtimacion then the bodie and bloode of Chryſt. Neither ys ther any oblacion moreoworthie. But this doth precell all. Whiche ys to be offred to our Lorde with a pure conſciéce, and with a pure minde to be receaued of al, and woourſhipped. And as yt ys more woorthie then other: Euen ſo yt aught more woorthilie to be honoured and woourſhipped. Thus farre Alexander.

Who alleaging the woordes of Chryſt: *This ys my body.* And *this ys my bloode*, doth by other his woordes therwith declare that they are not to be vnderſtanded by figure or trope: but in their propre ſenſe. And among manie notes, that maie here be made, I will take, but three to prooue the ſame.

The firſt ys that he confeſſeth the preſence of Chryſtes bodie, and bloode in the Sacrament, for that he agreablie to holié Iuftine, who ſaied

that

Margin notes

Alexand. 1 epiſt. 1.

Maſſe.

Neither wine alone nor water alone aught to be offred in the ſacrifice

Among all ſacrifices none of more eſtimacion then the bodie and bloode of our Lorde.

Three notes plainlie impugning three articles of the Proclamer.

A *that the bread and wine after the confecracion be the bodie and bloode of Iefus incar-* **Reall pre-**
nated : He, I faie , agreablie faieth , that *the bodie and bloode of him ys* **fence auou-**
in the Maffe confecrated. Whofe pafsion ys ther celebrated. The pafsion of Chryft **ched.**
ys in the Maffe celebrated · wherfore his bodie and bloode be ther confe-
crated:Who foeuer confeffeth Chryftes bodie to be confecrated on the aul
tar,confeffeth that confecracion to be doen by thefe woordes of Chryft:
This ys my bodie , &c. Wherfore who foeuer confeffeth foch confecracion,
confeffeth the woordes to be vnderdanded withoute figure and trope. This
Authour confeffeth foche confecracion . Wherfor he confeffeth foche
vnderftanding.

And here by the waie note, that this aunciant olde Authour hath that
maner of phrafe and fpeache that the catholike Churche at this daie vfeth,
namelie when he faieth: that the bodie and bloode of Crhyft be confecrated in the Maffe,and not the maner of fpeache of the Aduerfarie , faing that
yt ys made a facramentall bread, a figure,figne, or token of Chryftes bodie.
He hath no foche woorde,no more hath anie one of all thefe fathers,and ho-
B ly doctours,that fhall be alleaged in that fenfe and vnderftanding, that the
Aduerfarie moft vntruly bluftereth abroade. And yet euery learned catholike man confeffeth the Sacramét to be a figure but foche a figure as denieth
not the reall prefence of Chryft.

The fecond note to prooue the woordes of Chryfte to be vnderftad with **Sacrifice**
oute figure,ys that alleaging thefe wooordes, *This ys my bodie,This ys my bloode:* **propiciato-**
immediatelie he faieth: By thefe facrifices offred offences and finnes be wi- **rie auou-**
ped awaie,by whiche woordes calling thofe thinges,whiche Chryfte before **ched.**
fpake ofin the woordes of the Supper, facrifices, and that foche facrifices,as
put awaie finnes,and we haue no facrifice to put awaie finnes,but the Sacrifice of Chryftes bodie and bloode. Yt ys more then manifeft,that the vnderftandeth the woordes of Chryft in theirpropre fenfe ofthe bodie and blood
ofChryfte,and not of the figure of his bodie, for that ys no facrifice to putte
awaie finnes.

That he calleth the bodie and bloode of Chryfte in the Sacrament of the
aultar,facrifices , the woordes folowing in the fame proceffe do well prooue
C and declare,when he faieth: *Nihil in facrificijs maius effe poteft , quàm corpus &*
*fanguis Domini.*Among the facrifices ther ys nothing greater, then the bodie
and bloode of our Lorde, And that he fpeaketh this of the facrifice and oblacion of Chryftes bodie and bloode in the Sacrament of the aultar, yt ys
made certen by the woordes that do folowe, whiche be thefe: *Nulla oblatio* **Sacrament**
potior eft,fed hæc omnes præcellit , quæ pura Domino confcientia offerenda eft, & pura **of the aul-**
*mente fumenda.*There ys no oblacion woorthier then this , but this excelleth **tar ys a fa-**
all other, whiche ys to be offred to our Lorde with a pure confcience , and **crifice.**
to be receaued with a pure minde . Among the Chryftians ther ys no facrifice to be offred,and with pure minde to be receaued,but the facrifice offred
on the aultar.And thus of necefsitie yt foloweth , that this Authour graunteth the prefence of Chryftes bodie in the Sacrament, and that yt ys a facrifice, and that the woordes of Chryftes fupper are to be vnderftanded without figure.

The thirde note ys,that when he had taught that the facrifice muft be of **Adoracion**
D fred with a pure cófcience,and receaued with a pure minde, he teacheth alfo **of the Sa-**
that yt muft be woourfhipped and honoured,and that with no lowe degree **crament**
of woorfhippe and honour,but as this facrifice(*faieth he*)doth precel al:fo it ys **auouched.**
aboue all to be honoured . By whiche doctrine yt maie appeare,that yf the

thinge of the facrifice dothe excell all other, and ys aboue all other to be ho- E
noured, and the onely facrifice of Chryftes bodie and blood excelleth all
other ys to be honoured: that then that bleffed bodie and blode are there
prefent to be honoured, wher they be offred. They be offred wher they be
receaued, they be receaued in the Sacrament, wherfore they are to be honoured in the Sacrament.

Now when all this difputacion of this holie Father ys graunted vpõ thefe
woordes of Chryft: *This ys my bodie, this ys my bloode*: yt can not be but that
thefe woordes of Chryft, muft be vnderftanded fimplie and plainly in their
propre fenfe withoute figure or trope. And thus to conclude for thefe two
great Seniours of Chryftes fchoole and Parliament houfe: ye perceaue that
they vfe Chryftes woordes in ther propre fenfe. And alfo thervpon teftifie
to vs the enacted trueth of Chryftes very prefence in the holy Sacrament,
whiche ys the cheifeft matter here fought.

THE FOVRE AND FOVRTETH CHAP. BY
occafion of the woordes of Alexander treacketh of the adoracion F
and honouring of Chryftes bodie in the Sacrament.

BVt occafion being geuen by this holie Father *Alexander* to fpeake
of the adoracion of Chryftes bodie in the Sacrament: I can not
ouerpaffe fomewhat more to faie of yt, to the confutacion of the
moft impudent and blafphemoufe vntrueth fpoken and vttered by this

Proclamers
woordes a-
gainft ado-
racion reci-
ted and cõ-
futed.

Proclamer, for thus he faieth: *Chryft that beft knewe, what aught to be doen herein,*
when he ordeined, and deliuered the Sacrament of his bodie and bloode, gaue no com-
maundement, that anie man should fall dowen to it, or woourshippe it. S. Paule that tooke
the Sacrament at Chryftes hande, and as he had taken it, deliuered it to the Corynthians,
neuer willed adoracion or godlie honour to be geuen vnto it. The olde doctours and holie
Fathers of the Churche S. Cyprian, S. Chryfoftom, S. Ambrofe, S. Hierom, S. Auguftine,
and others that receaued the Sacrament at the Apoftles hands, and as it maie be thought,
continued the fame in fothe forte, as they receaued it, neuer make mencion, in any of all their
bookes of adoring or woourshipping of the Sacrament. Yt ys a verie newe deuife, and as it ys
well knowen, came but lately into the Churche, oboute three hundreth yeares paft, Honorius G
then being Bishoppe of Rome, commaunded the Sacrament to be lifted vppe, and the peo-
ple reuerentlie ta bowe dowen vnto yt. After him Vrbanus the fourth appoincted an holie
feaft of Corpus Chrifti. And graunted oute large pardons to the kepers of it, that the people
shoulde with the better will reforte to the Churche and kepe it holie. This ys the greateft
antiquitie of the wholl matter, aboute three hundreth yeares ago it was firft fownde oute,
and putte in practife. But Chryft and his Apoftles the holie Fathers in the primitiue Chur-
che, the Doctours that folowed them, and other godly and learned men what foeuer for the
fpace of a thoufand and two hundreth yeares after Chryftes afcenfion into heauen, this
woourshipping of the Sacrament, was neuer knowen nor practifed in any place within
the wholl catholike Churche throughout the wholl worlde. Thus moche the Proclamer.

Whẽ I readde thefe his woordes, I ftaied as one aftoined, confidering that
they coulde not proceade from anie man, but either by ignorance, or ells by
peruerfe malice, that wittinglie wolde, al fhame fet apparte, vtter foche an vn
trueth as the meã learned, I fuppofe, of all the catholike Churche knoweth it
foto be. And the more did I merueill that it was fo impudẽtly fetfurth with a
repeticiõ, as therbie with moch boldneffe to auouche the matter. Nowe for H
that the Authour of the woordes ys not vnlearned, I coulde not affcribe thẽ
to ignorance. And confidering his callinge ther fhoulde be in him no foche
peruer-

A peruerſe malice.But remembring howe Macedonius,Neſtorius, and diuerſe ſoche other leauing the doctrine of the catholike Church and the mocion of the ſpirit of God in the ſame, and folowing the doctrine of priuate men, according to the mocion of the ſpirit of Sathan did forget their calling, and peruerſedlie vſed them ſelues:So likwiſe I perceaue this man doth, the more ys the pittie.

But that we maie perceaue howe farre wide he ys from the trueth, we will examen his woordes.His firſt argument ys.*that Chryſt neuer gaue commaundement to woourſhippe the Sacrament.Ergo:yt ys not to be doen.* To this,firſt I ſaie to him,as to one exerciſed in ſchooles that an argument of negatiues concludeth nothing. But for more large declaracion, to the vnderſtanding of the Reader:yt ys not redde in the Goſpell,that Chryſt commaunded anie bodie to adore him while he here liued in the earth : yt ys therfore a good argument that he was not to be adored? The three wiſe men of the eaſt came with their giftes,and offringe them,adored the babe Chryſt. They had no commaundement of Chryſt ſo to do,ſhoulde they not therfore haue doen yt?

B or did they offende in ſo doing? Diuerſe that were cured of Chryſt came and adored him,but not commaunded of Chryſt ſo to do.Yt ys not redde in the Goſpells that the Apoſtles during their familiare conuerſacion withe Chryſte before his paſsion, that they fell down and adored him. Shall we therfore frame an argument that Chryſt in his mortall ſtate was not to be adored,bycauſe the Apoſtles be not readde to haue adored him ? And that Mary Magdalen,the woman of Canaan,and the Leeper that did adore him, did offende? Yt ys a faint kinde of argumentacion. I will in like maner reaſon with this diſputer in his owne kinde of diſputacion:Chryſt gaue the Sacrament of his bodie to his Apoſtles onelie,and gaue no commaundement that all people indifferentlie ſhoulde receaue the ſame,as nowe they doe, Wherfor yt aught not to be doen.

Yf this argument be good,then ys his good.But the trueth ys, this argument ys naught,and ſo ys his,but this diſputer knewe well what ſchoole he

C was in, he was certen that ther was no reſpondent, that preſentlie wolde return his argument into his lappe.I beleue, he wolde not for ſhame haue made ſoche argument in a ſchoole,except yt had ben to haue occupied the time,while he might haue ſtudied a better, or ells for lacke of other kinde of argumentes,in the matter that he impugneth,as I dare ſaie he dothe here,as yt well appeareth in the proceſſe of his diſputacion. For the next argument ys of like force,but of more vntrueth,this yt ys: *S. Paule that tooke the Sacrament at Chryſts hand,an as he had taken yt deliuered yt to the Corynthians neuer willed adoracion or godly honour to be geuen to yt.*

Leauing this argument,as a thinge of no force to conclude that the Authour therof intendeth,let vs examen the trueth of yt. This Proclamer firſt alleaging Chryſtes inſtitucion,wherin he ſaieth, Chryſt made no mencion of adoracion,ioineth S,Paule to yt,as one receauing of Chryſt no other order then in the miniſtracion of Chryſt was vſed, and deliuered alſo to the Corynthians no other,nor no more then Chryſt did, whiche thing howe

D falſe and vntrue yt ys S. Paule him ſelf ſhall declare. S.Paule deliuered to the Corynthians,that the vnwoorthie receauer ſhall be giltie of the bodie and bloode of our Lorde: Chryſt who to vſe the woordes of this Proclamer, knewe beſt what aught to be doen when he inſtituted this Sacrament,gaue no ſoche lawe. Sainct Paule geueth a rule or commaundement that, a man muſt examine him ſelf, and ſo eate of that bread : Chryſt in the

The negatiue argumēt of the Proclamer concludeth nothing.

The proclamers argumēt oute of S.Paule faileth for wāt of trueth.

inftitucion gaue no foche commaundement, but raither admitting Iudas to E
the receipt of the holie myfteries whofe wicked intentes and pourpofes were not vnknowen(neither was he ignorant,that he nothing examined himfelf) femed to practife the contrarie of that S.Paule fetteth furthe to be ob-
ferued.Wherfor this difputer referring the maner and all other circumftances of the deliuerie of the Sacrament by Sainct Paule to the Corinthians,to
the maner and circumftances of the deliuery of the Sacrament by Chryft
in his fupper,ys foulie deceaued in his argument:taking therin, as yt dothe
appeare,an vntrueth for a trueth, and fo deceauing his Auditorie, geueth
them chaffe for good corne.

　　Thus ye maie perceaue that S. Paule deliuered diuerfe doctrines to the
Corynthians concerning the receipt of the holy Sacrament, which Chryft
ys not fownde by the teftimonie of anie of the Euangeliftes to haue deliuered to his Apoftles,and yet who being a chryftian doubteth that yt ys the

S.Paule
willed ado-
racion to be
geñe to the
Sacramẽt.

doctrine of God,and of our Sauiour Chryft? In this argument this difputer
alfo faieth,that S. Paule neuer willed adoracion,or godlie honour to be ge- F
uen to the Sacrament,yf he fpeake of the woorde adoracion, I confent vnto
him,for trueth yt ys that S.Paule hathe not thefe woordes : *Adore the Sacrament*.But yf he fpeake of the thing? I diffent from him.For that I iudge to be
vntrue. Manie thinges are fpoken of in verie dede,when the propre vocable
appropriated to the fame thing to fignifie yt to a mans vnderftanding ys not
fpoken or vttered.As yf I faie:*Plato was a reafonable liuing creature*.Though I applie not the propre vocable of a man to Plato : yet to the vnderftandinge I
fignifie as moche in deed,as yf I had called him a man : So though S. Paule
fpeake not in the deliuerie of the Sacrament to the Corynthians , of thefe
woordes,*adoration or honour*: yet he fpeaketh of the thing in deed. For when

Yt ys great
honour to
the Sacra-
mẽt to exa-
men our fel
ues er we
prefume to
receaue yt.

he geueth this rule: *Probet feipfum homo.Let a man examen him felf, and fo let him
eate of that bread,and drinke of that cuppe* : Dothe he not will vs to geue mofte
fingular honour to the Sacrament? What more honour can be doen,then to
fee that our faith towarde the Sacrament,be firme and ftable, voide of all fi-
niftre opinions,thinking nothing of fo great a myfterie, but that,that ys fe- G
melie? Howe great an honour do we to the Sacrament alfo , that to receaue
yt,we examen and fearch our confciences, and what we finde filthie, and
fowle we purifie,clenfe and make clean by earneft contricion, by pure confefsion and humble penaunce.

Ad Ian.
Epift. 118.

　　S.Auguftine faieth:*Placuit enim Spiritui fancto, vt in honorem tanti Sacramenti in
os Chriftiani prius Dominicum corpus intraret,quam exteri cibi*.Yt hath pleafed the ho
lie Goft, that in the honour of fo great a Sacrament the bodie of our Lorde

Yf corporal
abftinence
be to Gods
honour,
moch more
fpirituall
abftinence.

fhoulde entre the mouth of a chryftian before worldlie meates.Yf the holie
Goft doeth efteme yt as doen to the honour of the Sacrament, to receaue yt
fafting before al meats:how moch more ys it to the honour of the Sacramẽt,
that we fafting from all vices,from all horrible finnes and crimes come with
pure confcience hongring and thirfting righteoufneffe,to receaue in the Sacrament the Lorde and geuer of righteoufneffe?Yf any honour be doen to
God by corporall abftinence or fafting,howe moche more ys doen , by fpirituall abftinence from finne?　　　　　　　　　　　　　　　　　　　　H

　　But the Aduerfarie will faie , that this honour ys not doen to the Sacra-
ment,but to God,and to his grace receaued in the receipt of the Sacrament.
Wherunto I faie, that the verie woordes of S. Paule ouerthroweth this
faing: For S. Paule by expreffe woordes fpeaketh of the Sacrament faing:
Let a man examen himfelf, and fo let him eate of that bread,and drinke of that cuppe.
　　　　　　　　　　　　　　　　　　　　　　　　　　　　　　　　　　He

A He saieth not: *Let him examen himself, and so he shall receaue the grace of God, and the vertue of the meritte of Chryftes pasion and deathe.*whiche ys a matter moche and almoft generallie taught thorowoute all the Gofpell. For what ys more taught then remifsion of sinnes to true penitentes by the vertue of Chryftes pafsion?But here S. Paule fpeaketh of the Sacrament by a fpeciall maner, and therfor faieth: *And so let him eat of that bread, and drinke of that cuppe.*

For more manifeft proof of this, note, that S. Paule referreth the honour or difhonour, that ys doen by woorthie or vnwoorthie receauing, not immediately to the grace of God, or meritte of Chryftes pafsion: But to the Sacrament, and therfor faieth. *Itaque quicunque manducauerit panem & biberit calicem Domini indignè, reus erit corporis & fanguinis Domini.* Who foeuer therfore fhall eate the bread, and drinke the cuppe of our Lorde vnwoorthilie, he fhall be giltie of the bodie and bloode of our Lorde, fo that the vnwoorthie receauing ys referred to the bread and the cuppe of our Lorde. Wherfore yt ysmanifeft, that as the woorthie or vnwoorthie receauing ys referred to

B the Sacrament : fo ys the honour or difhonour doen by the fame referred alfo to the Sacrament. Wherfor then S. Paule teaching the chryftian people to examen them felues, and to prepare them felues that they maie be woorthie receauers of fo woorthie a Sacrament, taught them in that to honoure the Sacrament.

Vnto all this, this maie be added, that forafmoch as S. Paule, taught the Corynthians and by them all Chryftian people, the prefence of Chryft in the Sacrament, that he might well teache them to honour him in the Sacrament. For wher Chryft ys verilie prefent, ther ys no daunger but the chryftian maie their honoure him. That S. Paule teacheth the prefence yt fhall be made manifeft to yow in the thirde booke, wher the fcriptures of S. Paule fhall be more at large handled. Wherfor to auoide prolixitie I leaue to fpeake anie more of them here. But this maie be faied here, that forafmoche as the woordes of Chryfte, whiche we haue nowe in hande do teache vs the

C prefence of Chryft in the Sacrament, that we maie alfo honour Chryft in the Sacrament. And to conclude againft this Proclamer, ye maie perceaue by that, that ys faied, that S. Paule taught vs to honoure the Sacrament.

1. Cor.11. Honour or dishonour doen by the receauer ys referred to the Sacrament by expreffe woordes of S. Paule.

THE FIVE AND FOVRTETH CHAP. PROVETH BY
the same doctours that the Proclamer nameth, that the Sacrament ys to be honoured.

Fter this man had abufed the fcriptures to make fome fhewe of his wicked pourpofe, he vfed his like fynceritie in naming certain doctours, whiche doctours (as he faieth) neuer make mencion in anie of their bookes of adoring or woourfhipping of the Sacrament.

To declare the trueth of this man, we will firft produce them, whome he
D hath named as making for him, and afterwarde fome other. Among thofe whome he nameth Chryfoftom ys one. A merueiloufe thing to fee the impudencie or ignorance of this man. He nameth Chryfoftome as one who in his bookes maketh no mencion of the honouring of Chryft in the Sacrament, and yet among all the learned Fathers that writte, ther ys none that maketh more often and more plain mencion of that matter then he doth

To bring manie of his testimonies the condicion of this rude booke will
not suffer, for yt wolde therby growe to great. Wherfore one or two places
shal be brought, whiche shal so clerelie ope this matter that I beleue, Reader,
thowe wilt meruecill, that this Proclamer durst for shame name Chrysostome as one that maketh no mencion of the honouring of Chryst in the Sacrament. In one place thus he saieth. *Cùm autem ille & Spiritum sanctum inuo-*

Chrys.de sa cerd.li.6.

cauerit, sacrificiumque illud horrore ac reuerentia plenisimum perfecerit, communi omnium
Domino manibus assiduè pertractato: quæro ex te, quorum illum in ordine collocabimus?
Quantam verò ab eo integritatem exigemus? quantam religionem? Considera enim quales
manus illas administrantes esse oporteat, qualem linguam, quæ verba illa effundat. Deni-
que qua anima, non puriorem, sanctioremue conueniat esse animam, quæ tantum illum, tam-
que dignum spiritum receperit. Per id tempus, & Angeli sacerdoti assident, & cælestium
potestatum vniuersus ordo clamores excitat, & locus Altari vicinus in illius honorem
qui immolatur, Angelorum choris plenus est. Id quod credere abundè licet, vel ex tanto illo
sacrificio, quod tum peragitur. Ego verò & commemorantem olim quendam audiui, qui
diceret senem quendam virum admirabilem, ac cui reuelationum mysteria multa diuinitus
fuissent detecta, sibi narrasse, se tali olim visione dignum a Deo habitum esse, ac per illud
quidem tempus derepentè Angelorum multitudinem conspexisse, quatenus aspectus hu-
manus ferre poterat, fulgentibus vestibus indutorum Altare ipsum circundantium. Deni-
que sic capite inclinatorum, vt si quis milites, præsente Rege stantes videat, id quod mihi ipse
facilè persuadeo. When he (*mening the preist*) hath called vpon the holie Gost,
and hath perfected that sacrifice, most full of horrour and reuerece, when
the vniuersall Lorde of all thinges ys in his handes handeled, I aske of thee,
in what order of men shall we place him? howe great integritie shall we require of him? howe great religion or godlinesse? Consider also what hands
those aught to be, that doe ministre: What maner of tounge, that speaketh

*Angells at-
tende vpon
the preist
in the time
of oblacion,
and a visiō
therof she-
wed to an
olde man.*

those woordes (*mening the woordes of consecraciō*) last of al that it ys meet that that
soule be purer and holier then anie other soule, that receaueth him so great,
and so woorthie a spirit. At that time the Angells also geue attendance
to the preist, and all the wholl order of the heauenlie powers sing praises, and
the place nighe to the Aultar, in the honour of him, that ys then offred in
sacrifice ys full of Angells, which thing a man maie fullie beleue, for that
great sacrifice that then ys doen. Trulie I also did once heare a certain man
reporting that an olde woorshippefull man, vnto whome manie secre-
tes were by Gods pleasure reuciled, declared vnto him, that God did
vouchesaif to shewe him soche a vision, and that, at that time, as farre as the
sieght of man might beare yt, he sawe sodenlie a multitude of Angells cloathed in bright garmentes compassing the Aultar aboute, and afterwarde
so bowing downe their heads, as yf a man shoulde see soldiours stand when
the king ys present. Whiche thing I easely beleue. Thus Chrysostome.

In this saing easie yt ys to perceaue, howe honorably he thinketh of the
Sacrament, and what honoure he thinketh yt of. For that the Sacrament,
ys so honourable, he knoweth not wher to place the preist that dothe conse-

*The vniuer-
sall Lorde
of all hand-
led by the
preist.*

crate yt. He questioned, what hands they aught to be, that handle the vniuersall Lorde of all thinges: What toung that aught to be, that speaketh the
mightie woordes of consecracion: howe pure that soule aught to be, that
receaueth so woorthie a thing, yea he acknowlegeth the Sacrament to be so
honourable, that he saieth that the Angells in the time of the ministracion

*Angells ho-
noure the
Sacram.*

of yt, doe assist the preist, and attend, and for confirmacion of this, he bringeth in a vision of an holie man, who sawe Angells in bright garmentes
stand aboute the Aultar, and bowing downe their heades to honour the Sa-
cra-

A crament. Whiche thing Chryſoſtom ſaieth, he did beleue. Yf man for the miniſtracion of the Sacrament be ſo honourable, yf yt be ſoche as Angells do honour yt, howe moche aught man to honoure yt?

That man aught to honour yt, the ſame Chryſoſtome in the ordre of the Maſſe by him ſethfurth, by his owne practiſe declareth, wher we finde his praier, and after his praier, his rule for the honouring of this Sacrament. Thus we read ther: *Qui ſupra vnà cum Patre ſedes, & hic vnà nobiſcum inuiſibili-* Chryſ.in *ter verſaris: Dignare potenti manu tua nobis impartiri impolutum corpus tuum & pre-* Liturg. *cioſum ſanguinem tuum, & per nos toti populo. Deinde ſacerdos adorat, & Diaconus in eo, in quo eſt loco, ter ſecretò dicentes: Deus propitius eſto mihi peccatori. Et populus ſimiliter. Omnes cum pietate & reuerentia adorant.* Thowe that ſitteſt aboue with the Father, and alſo arte with vs here inuiſiblie, voucheſaif with thy Preiſt dea mightie hand to geue vnto vs thy vndefiled bodie, and thy precioſe con and all blood, and by vs to all the people. This ys his praier. After this praier he ge- the people ueth this rule: Then the preiſt adoreth, and the Deacon alſo in the place, adored the that he ys in thrice, ſaing: *God be mercifull vnto me ſinner:* And all the people Sacr. in
B likewiſe with godlineſſe and reuerence doo adore. Chryſ.time

Perceaue ye not in this ſaing, Chryſt both to be aboue with his Father, and alſo here with vs? See ye not the rule of Chryſoſtome, that the preiſt, the Deacon, and all the people did adore before they receaued the Sacrament? Theſe places might ſuffice to anie man, that ys not contencioufe. But that the Reader maie ſee plentie of matter, to ſtaie him, and to confounde the Proclaimer, that ſo vntreuly reporteth of the holie Fathers we will heare one place more of Chryſoſtom whiche ys this: *Chriſtus ſuam carnem dedit* Homil.24 *nobis, vt ea ſaturemur, quo nos in ſui amorem plurimum allexit. Ad eum igitur cum feruore* 10.1.Cor. *accedamus, & dilectione quàm vehementiſsima ne grauius ſubeamus ſupplicium. Quanto enim maius beneficiū accipimus, tanto magis puniemur, quàdo eo indigni apparebimus. Hoc corpus in præſepi reueriti ſunt Magi, & viri impij, & barbari, longo itenere confecto, cum timore et tremore plurimo adorauerunt. Imitemur igitur barbaros, nos qui cæloru ciues ſumus. Illi enim, cùm id præſepe, & tugurium tantùm, neque eorum quidquam, quæ tu nunc intue-ris, viderent, ſumma acceſſerunt reuerentia & horrore. Tu verò non in præſepi id, ſed in Altari, non mulierem, quæ in vlnis teneat, ſed ſacerdotem præſentem, & Spiritum per*
C *abundè ſuper propoſito diffuſum ſacrificio vides. Nec ſimplex, vt illi, corpus vides, ſed et eius potentiam & omnem agnoſcis adminiſtrationem, & nihil eorum quæ per ipſum facta ſunt ignoras, & diligenter initiatus es in omnibus. Excitemur, horreſcamſque, & maiorem quam barbari illi præ nobis feramus pietatem.* Chryſt gaue vnto vs his fleſh, that with yt we might be fedde, wherby he moche alleured vs into his loue. Let vs therfor with feruencie, and moſt vehement loue, come vnto him, leeſt Chryſt we ſuffre a more greuoufe condemnacion. The greater benefit we take, the hath geuen more ſhall we be puniſhed yf we be fownde vnwoorthie of yt. This bodie vs his fleſh did the wiſe men, and men without God, and barbarouſe, reuerence, and to feede vpō woourſhippe. And after they had ended a long iourneie with moche feare and tremblinge, did adore yt. Let vs therfor at the leeſt folowe the example of theſe barbarouſe, we that be the cittizens of the heauens, for they when they ſawe that maunger and cottage onelie, and did not ſee anie of theſe thinges whiche thowe doeſt nowe beholde, they came with great reue-rence and horrour. *But thowe ſeeſt not that bodie in the maunger, but in the aultar,* That ſame
D *thowe ſeeſt not a woman that holdeth yt in her armes, but thowe ſeeſt the preiſt preſent* body on the *and the Spirit plentifullie powred vpon the propoſed ſacrifice.* Neither doeſt thowe aultar that ſee a bare bodie, as they did, but thowe knoweſt all his power and rule, was in the and thowe art ignoraunt of nothing that ys doen by him. But thowe art maunger.

dili-

diligently inſtructed in all poinctes. Let vs be ſtirred vppe and feare, and　E
let vs declare a more godlineſſe then thoſe barbarouſe men. Thus moche
Chryſoſtom.

Nowe haue we hearde three teſtimonies of Chryſoſtom. In the firſt, we
were taught his faith as touching the honouring of the Sacrament, whiche
he ſaieth to be ſo honourable, that not onely men, But alſo Angells doo honoure yt. In the ſecond, he declared the practiſe or execution of the honouring of the Sacrament, by him ſelf, his miniſters, and his people before the receipt of the ſame Sacrament. In the thirde he geueth generall
exhortacion to all men to do the ſame. And therunto prouoketh by the
example of the three wiſe men that came to honour Chryſt at his birth, teaching vs that we honour the ſame bodie in the aultar, that they did in the
maunger. Theſe places being plain enough let vs leaue them and heare
Sainct Ambroſe who ſaieth thus, evpownding a verſe of the Prophet Dauid.

Amb. de
Spiritu S.
li. 3. ca. 12.
We adore
the fleſh of
Chryſt in
the myſte-
ries.

Per ſcabellum terra intelligitur, per terram autem caro Chriſti, quam hodie quoque in
myſterijs adoramus, quàm Apoſtoli in Domino Ieſu, vt ſuprà diximus, adorarunt: Neque
enim diuiſus eſt Chriſtus, ſed vnus. By the footeſtoole ys vnderſtanded the　F
earth: by the earth ys vnderſtanded the fleſh of Chryſt, whiche nowe alſo
we adore in the myſteries, whiche the Apoſtles (as before we haue ſaied)
did adore in our Lorde Ieſus: Neither ys Chryſt diuided, but one.

what thinke you (gentle Reader) doth not Sainct Ambroſe plainlie enough
teſtifie, and teache the adoracion of Chryſt? who, that ye ſhall not be caried
awaie with the wicked gloſes of heretiques, which to robbe Chryſte of his
honoure in the moſt holie and bleſſed Sacrament, ſaie that thowe muſt
adore Chryſt in heauen, teacheth you by expreſſe woordes that the fleſh
of Chryſt ys to be adored and honoured in the Sacrament, whiche he
calleth the myſteries, wher he affirmeth the ſame fleſh to be, that the Apoſtles
did adore in our Lorde Ieſus.

Nowe after S. Ambroſe, we will heare S. Auguſtine, who in diuerſe places teacheth vs to adore Chryſt in the Sacrament. But yt ſhall be beſt firſt
to laie before you that place of Sainct Auguſtine at the lenght whollie
and plainly, whiche this Proclamer with ſleight doth truncately, and
by peice meale touche, that yt might appeare to his readers, and heares　G
that that place of Sainct Auguſtine nothing impugned his doctrine, whiche in deed doth plainlie ouerthrowe yt. This ys the wholl place of Sainct
Auguſtine. *Adorate ſcabellum pedum eius, quoniam ſanctum eſt. Sed videte fra-*

Aug. in
pſal. 98.

tres, quid nos iubeat adorare. Alio loco ſcriptura dicit: Cœlum mihi ſedes eſt, terra
autem ſcabellum pedum meorum. Ergo terram iubet nos adorare, quia dixit alio loco
quod ſit ſcabellum Dei. Et quomodò adorabimus terram, cùm dicat apertè ſcriptura:
Dominum Deum tuum adorabis. Et hic dicit: Adorate ſcabellum pedum eius? Expo-
nens autem mihi, quid ſit ſcabellum pedum eius, dicit: Terra autem ſcabellum pedum
meorum. Anceps factus ſum, timeo adorare terram, ne damnet me qui fecit cœlum
& terram. Rurſum timeo non adorare ſcabellum pedum Domini mei, quia Pſalmus
mihi dicit: Adorate ſcabellum pedum eius. Quæro quid ſit ſcabellum pedum eius, &
dicit mihi ſcriptura: Terra ſcabellum pedum meorum. Fluctuans conuerto me ad
Chriſtum, quia ipſum quæro hic, & inuenio, quomodò ſine impietate adoretur terra,
ſine impietate adoretur ſcabellum pedum eius. Suſcepit enim de terra terram, quia
caro de terra eſt, & de carne Mariæ carnem aſſumpſit. Et quia in ipſa carne hic
ambulauit, & ipſam carnem nobis manducandam ad ſalutem dedit. Nemo autem carnem　H
illam manducat, niſi priùs adorauerit, inuentum eſt, quemadmodum adoretur tale ſcabellum
pedum Domini & non ſolùm non peccemus adorando, ſed peccemus non adorando.

Adore

A Adore ye the footestoole of his feete, for yt ys holie. But marke ye bretheren what he commaundeth vs to adore? In an other place the scripture saieth: *Heauen ys my seat, and the earth ys my footestoole.* Then he commaundeth vs to adore the earth. For he hath saied in an other place, that yt ys the footestoole of God. And howe shall we adore the earth, seing the scripture open-lie saieth: *Thowe shalt adore thy Lorde God.* And here saieth: *Adore his footestoole?* And expowdding to me what ys his footestoole, he saieth : *The earth ys my footestoole.* I am doubtfull, I feare to adore the earth leest he damne me that made heauen and earthe. Again I feare not to adore the footstoole of my Lorde, bycause the Psalme saieth to me: *Adore his footestoole.* Thus wauing vppe and downe, I turne me vnto Chryst (*for I seke him here*) and I finde howe withoute impietie the earth maie be adored: howe withoute impietie his footestoole maie be adored. For he tooke earth of earth, for flesh ys of the earth, and he tooke flesh of the flesh of Marie. And bicause he liued here in the same flesh, and the same flesh he gaue vs to eate to our saluacion, and no man eateth that flesh, eycept he first adore yt, yt ys

B perceaued howe soche a footestoole of our Lorde maie be adored. And we shall not onely not sinne in adoring yt, but we shall offende in not ado-ring yt. Thus haue ye hearde S. Augustine at lenght.

The flesh born of the Virgen ys geuen vs to eate, whi-che we must also adore or ells we do offende.

Yf ye haue marked, ye maie perceiue a goodlie and pleasaunt discurse, howe he trieth oute the footestoole of God, and howe yt maie be ado-red. The footestoole of God at the last he findeth to be the flesh of Chryst the same flesh that he here liued in, the same flesh also that he geueth vs to eate: This flesh then ys the footestoole of God. This footestoole ys to be adored (saieth Sainct Augusten) that in heauen yt aught to be adored at all times no man doubteth. But forasmoche as the same footstoole, the same flesh of Chryst ys geuen vs to be eaten, we must also remembre our duetie before we receaue yt, that we adore yt, and honoure yt. For yf we do not honour yt, omitting then our duetie we offende saieth Sainct Augu-stine. This flesh we receaue in the Sacrament, wherfore we must honour yt

C in the Sacrament.

Yf Sainct Augustin ment not this adoracion to be doen to the Sacra-ment, he wolde neuer haue spoken of this flesh of Chryst as eaten in the Sacrament, but as exalted in glorie, and sitting at the right hande of the Father. Yt ys an easier waie to induce vs to honour a thing for that yt ys in heauen glorified, then for that yt ys here in earth receaued. But bicause this adoracion of the Sacrament, was in vse among chrystians, and gaue him light to vnderstande the Prophet Dauid, Therfor he spake of yt. That the adoracion was in vse, yt appeareth in sondrie places of the whiche I shall bring furth one or two.

Sainct Augustine declaring the godlinesse of his mother, lieng in her death bedde, saieth thus of her. *Illa imminente die resolutionis suæ non cogi-tauit corpus suum sumptuosè contegi, aut condiri aromatibus, aut monumentum ele-ctum concupiuit aut curauit sepulchrum paternum · Non ista mandauit nobis, sed tantummodò memoriam sui ad altare tuum fieri desiderauit, cui nullius diei præter*

Li.9.confe. cap.13.

D *missione seruierat, vnde sciret dispensari victimam sanctam, qua deletum est Chi-rographum, quod erat contrarium nobis, qua triumphatus est hostis.* She when she perceaued the daie of her departinge to be at hand, she had no care to haue her bodie sumptuouslie buried, or to be spiced with swete spi-ces, neither did she couet a speciall monument, or cared to be buried in

her owne

her owne contrie. She did not charge vs with thofe thinges, but fhe desiered, that her memorie might be made at thie aultar, which fhe withoute anie daies missing had serued, from whence fhe knewe that holie sacrifice to be difpensed, by the which the obligacion that was againft vs was cancelled, wherbye the enemie also was ouercomed. Thus he.

The mother of S. Augu. serued the aultar dai-lie.

In this that Sainct Auguftine to the comendacion of his mother before God and the woorlde, saieth, that fhe dailie did serue the aultar, I wolde learn of the Proclamer, what seruice yt was that fhe did, was yt not the seruice of Chryft her Lorde God, and redemer that fhe did: yea trulie: And why did fhe yt at the aultar, and not in heauen, as the Proclamer wolde that we fhoulde onely dooe? Bicaufe fhe knewe (as Sainct Auguftine witnesseth) that Chryft owre sacrifice was from thence difpensed and miniftred: So wher this Proclamer denieth the presence of Chryft in the Sacrament, Sainct Auguftine confesseth that same Chryfte to be there that cancelled the writing that was againft vs, and so made vs free. And wher the Proclamer difcommendeth them and crieth oute againft them that honour Chryft in the Sacrament, Sainct Auguftine writeth yt to the perpetuall commendacion and praife of his Godlie mother. The Proclamer wolde yt fhoulde neuer be vfed: Sainct Auguftin declareth that his mother dailie did vfe yt. And as fhe, so likewife her doinge argueth the vfe of the like honowringe and seruing of Chryft amonge and chryftian people.

Aultar.

S. Auguft. plain a-gainft the Proclamer.

Befides this the opnion that manie had of the chryftian people, who, not knowing the hidden myfterie of Chryftes presence in the Sacrament, saied that they did honour Ceres and Bacchus, Gods, among the gentiles, dothe prooue the vfe of the honouring of Chryft in the Sacrament. For yf the chryftians had doen no more but eate their bread and drinke their wine, foche reporte had not rifen of them. But bicaufe they were perceaued to honoure the Sacrament therfore they were so reported.

The fame that the Chryftias did honour Ceres and Bacchus, proueth their ado-racio of the Sacr. in the primitiue Church. Cont. Fau. li.2.cap.13

Of this fame opinion, fame and reporte, speaketh Sainct Auguftin, writing againft *Fauftus*, sainge: *Quomodò ergo comparas panem, & calicem noftrum & parem Religionem dicis errorem longè à veritate difcretum: peius defipiens quàm nonnulli, qui nos propter panem & calicem, Cererem & Liberum colere exiftimant?* Howe doeft thowe compare our bread and wine, and saeft errour farre diuided from the trueth to be like religion, plaing the foole woorfe then manie, whiche for the bread, and the cuppe thinke vs to honour *Ceres* and *Bacchus*.

And again in the fame place he saieth: *Sicut a Cerere & Libero Paganorum Dijs longè abfumus, quamuis panis & calicis Sacramentum, quod ita laudaftis, vt in eo pares nobis effe volueritis, noftro ritu amplectamur: ita patres noftri longè fuerunt à Saturniacis catenis, &c.* As we are farre from *Ceres* and *Bacchus*, the Gods of the Pagans, although after the maner of our religion we honoure the Sacrament of bread and wine, whiche ye haue so praifed, as in yt, ye wolde be equall to vs: Euen so our Fathers were farre from the bondes of Saturn, although for the time of the Prophecie, they haue obferued the vacacion of the Sabboth. Thus the vfe of the honouring of the Sacrament in and before the time of Sainct Auguftine being perceaued, we will heare one place more of him, and so for this matter ende him.

After the maner of oure religio we honoure the Sacr. saieth S. Auguft.

Thus

A　Thus he writeth: *Edent pauperes, & faturabuntur. Quid edunt? Quod fciunt fideles. Quomodò faturabuntur? Imitando pafsiones Domini fui, & non fine caufa accipiendo precium fuum, &c. Diuites quid? Etiam ipfi edunt, fed quomodò edunt? Manducauerunt, & adorauerunt omnes diuites terræ. Non dixit manducauerunt, & faturati funt: fed manducauerunt, & adorauerunt. Adorant quidem Deum, fed humanitatem nolunt exhibere fraternam. Manducant illi, & adorant: Manducant ifti et faturantur, tamen omnes manducant.* The poour fhall eate and be fatisfied. What eate they? That the faithfull do knowe. Howe fhall they be fatisfied? In folowing the pafsions of their Lorde, and taking their price not in vain. What do the riche? They alfo eate, but howe do they eate? *All the riche of the earth haue eaten, and haue adored.* He faied not, they haue eaten, and be fatisfied. But they haue eaten and haue adored. They doe in deed adore God, but they will not fhewe furth brotherlie humanitie. They doo eate, and adore, thefe doe eate and be fatisfied: yet all doo eate, hitherto he.

In pfal. 41.

B　As the fcripture ioineth eating and adoring together, faing: *They haue eaten, and adored:* So Sainct Auguftine, expownding the fcripture, and declaring that the thing that ys eaten, ys our price, a thing knowen to the faithfull (*which our price, and thing knowen to the faithfull ys the bodie of Chryft*) he ioineth alfo adoracion to the fame. And fo bothe by the Scripture, and by Sainct Auguftine, eating and adoring be referred to the Sacrament.

Eating and adoring both referred to the Sacrament

Whiche thing although he dothe plainlie enough here fetfurth: yet handling the fame fcripture in an other place, he doth more plainly open the matter, faing: *Neque enim fruftra ita diftincti funt, vt de pauperibus fuprà diceretur: Edent pauperes, et faturabuntur. Hic verò: Manducauerunt, et adorauerunt omnes diuites terræ. Et ipfi quippe adducti funt ad menfam Chrifti, et accipiunt de corpore et fanguine eius: fed adorant tantùm, non etiam faturantur, quoniam non imitantur. Manducantes enim pauperem, dedignantur effe pauperes, quia Chriftus pro nobis paffus eft, relinquens nobis exemplum, vt fequamur veftigia eius.* Neither are they

Ad Honoratū Epi. 129.

C　withoute pourpofe fo diftincted, that before of the poour yt fhoulde be faied: The poore fhall eate, and fhall be fatisfied. And here: *All the riche of the earth haue eaten, and haue adored.* For they alfo are brought to the table of Chryft, and they receaue of his bodie, and his bloode. But they doe adore onelie, they are not alfo fatisfied for that they folowe not. For they eating the poour man (*meaning Chryft*) they difdein to be poour. For Chryft fuffred for vs leauing vs an example, that we fhoulde folowe his fteppes.

The poore eat and are fatisfied the riche eat and adore onlie.

Among Chryftian people Sainct Auguftin findeth two fortes: Some that be riche, that ys, not leauing worldely affections, but riche in heart, not humble in fpirit, not fubmitting them felues to the fweet yocke of Chryft, and yet beleuinge, and therfor when they eat poour Chryfte, when they receaue of his bodie and blood they knowe by faithe what they receaue, and they adore and honoure Chryfte, whom they receaue. But they are not fatisfied. An other forte ther be, whiche be called poour and they contemning, at the leeft labouriug to fuppreffe wordly affections

Two fortes of chryftiā people.

D　not being riche in defire of heart, but poour and humble in fpiritte, taking their croffe and fo folowing Chryft, do walke vnder his holie yocke. Thefe receauing poour Chryft, eating of his bodie and drinking of his bloode, they doe not onelie adore, but alfo they be fatisfied, they are filled. For they folowe Chryfte, and their conuerfacion declareth that the iuice of this foode, the grace and vertue of that bleffed meate appeareth in their

Gg　　actes

actes,in their deedes, in their liuinges, that they haue well fedde and be E
satisfied. In which twoo fortes of men,who feith not howe Sainct Auguftine teacheth both the prefence of Chryft in the Sacrament,and the adoracion of the fame when the chryftian people receaue him.

The au-
thours na-
med by the
Proclamer
make a-
gainft him.

Thus nowe ye maie perceaue,that euen of thofe Authours , whiche the
Proclamer did name,as making no mencion of adoracion or woourfhipping
of the Sacrament in their bookes, ye maie perceaue, I faie, that they make
foche plain mencion of yt, as yt not onely ouerthroweth his peftilent doctrine, but alfo geueth him iuft occafion to rubbe his forehead for verie fhame that he fhoulde fo vntruely bothe fpeake and write.

THE SIXT AND FOVRTETH CHAPITER,
prooueth by other Doctours, that the Sacrament
ys to be adored.

Haue firft in his matter of adoracion produced fome of thefe
Authours,whiche the Proclamer named. Nowe for fomoche as F
after the naming of them, by a generall terme,he fpake the like
of other doctours,I fhall alfo alleadge fome of thefe other, that
by them yt maie appeare,that he fpake as vntrulie of thefe comprifed vnder
his generall tearme,as he did of them,whom he reherfed by fpeciall names.
And yet merueill yt ys that almoft anie one of them fhoulde fpeake of the
adoracion of Chryft in the Sacrament,forafmoche as all they vniuerfallie
and conftantlie beleuing Chryft verily and reallie to be in the Sacrament,
did prefuppofe,that he fhoulde ther be adored,they well vnderftanding the

Deut.6.

fcripture geuinge this commaundement. *Dominum Deum tuum adorabis.* Thy
Lorde God fhalt thowe adore . By the whiche as we be commaunded to
honour him for that he ys God:So haue we commaundement in the pfalme

Pfal.96.
Heb.1.
Mat.2.
Ioan.9.
Mat.15.
Luc.24.

10 adore his wholl perfon God and man, as Sainct Paule to the Hebrues
teacheth vs to vnderftand yt.*Adorate eũ omnes Angeli eius.*Adore him al ye his
Angells.Thus they being taught,and by the doctrine of the Gofpell perceauing the fame by the three wife mẽ of the eaft,that came from farre contries,
to Bethleem, by diuerfe alfo that were cured of Chryft, more ouer alfo by G
the Apoftles them felues being with Chryft in Galilee,to be practifed, and
put in vfe,they coulde not otherwife take yt,But wher foeuer by faith they
were taught Chryft to be,their to adore him. For Chryft ys Chryft wher-
foeuer, or after what maner fo euer he be in heauen,or in earthe,vifible or
inuifible . Wherfor all the chryftian worlde certenly beleuing Chryft to
be verilie in the Sacrament,did withoute all fcruple adore and honoure him
in the Sacrament.

That the Chryftian orbe did fo beleue,yt fhall appeare to yow by the teftimonie of diuerfe in diuerfe ages . To beginne at our age and fo to afcend
we will firft heare *Erafmus* a man of moft fame in this age. Who faicth thus.

Erafmus
ad Cõradũ
Pellicanũ,

Hactenus cum om ibus Chriftianis adoraui Chriftum pro me paffum,in Euchriftia. Nec
adhuc video quicquam cur debeam ab hac opinione recedere. Nullis humanis rationibus
abduci potero, à concordi fententia Chriftiani orbis. Plus enim apud me valent illa
quinque verba : In principio creauit Deus cœlum, & terram: quàm omnia Ariftotelis,
cæterorumque Philofophoʒum argumenta, quibus docent mundum carere initio . Quid
autem adferunt ifti, cur tan impiam támque feditiofam fententiam profitear? Rationes
ftupeʒ funt : Semel fuftulit carnem ne effet offendiculo. Non admirati funt, non ado-
rauerunt Apoftoli : Iubemur effe fpirituales, quafi caro fic exhibita officiat fpiritui.
H

Caro

A *Caro est sed nullis obnoxia sensibus, & tamen hoc ipsum pignus est diuinæ erga nos charitatis, solatium est expectationis.* Hitherto with all chryften men I haue in the Sacrament adored Chryft that fuffred for me. Neither do I yet fee anie thing, why I fhoulde go from this opinion. With no humane reasons can I be fedde awaie from the full agreement of the chryftian orbe. For thofe fiue woordes: *In the beginning God created heauen and earth:* are of more weight with me, then all Ariftotles and other Philofophers argumentes, with whiche they teache the worlde to haue no beginning. What doe thefe men bring, why I fhoulde profeffe fo wicked and fo fedicioufe a doctrine? Their reafons are friuoloufe. *He tooke awaie his flesh that yt shoulde not be an hinderance to vs: The Apostles did not woonder at yt, they did not adore yt: we are commaunded to be spirituall,* as though the flefh fo geuen to vs, as yt ys, fhoulde hinder vs to be fpirituall. *Yt ys flesh in deed, but not subiecte to the senseis.* And yet the fame verie thing ys the pledge of the loue of God towardes vs, and the comforte of oure expectacion. Thus *Erafmus.*

Erafmus Rot. his fentence of adoracion.

Ye fee nowe this mans profefsion, he adored Chryft in the Sacrament.
B Ye heare him faie that all chryften people did the like. Ye fee that yt was not a priuate opinion of fome one contrie. But yt was the faith and religion of the wholl Chryften worlde, whiche can not be deceaued in fo weightie a matter. Ye fee in this Authour a conftancie (which I wish to be, and wolde God yt were in all chryften men) that he wolde not by mens reafons be led awaie from that, that was fullie agreed vpon thoroughout all and fo receaued. Note with all on the other fide what iudgment he hath of the contrarie doctrine, whiche this Proclamer fetteth furthe in this behalf. Firft he faieth that he feieth nothing, why he fhoulde go from the faith of the catholique Churche, as not to adore Chryft in the Sacrament. Secondlie he accompteth the doctrine of the Aduerfarie, contrarie to this, to be wicked and fedicioufe. The reafons alfo (faieth he) whiche they make to maintein their doctrine are but vain and friuoloufe: So that as ye fee the doctrine of the Aduerfarie wicked and fedicioufe, not pithie, and weightie, neuer of all
C chryftian people agreed vpon, and receaued: So maie ye fee the catholique doctrine godlie and of one fort, fo fubftanciall, and well grownded that all the chryftian orbe hath refted vpon yt, and at all times, vntill the time of *Luther* and *Oecolampadius,* hath in all places with great confent and concorde accepted yt, and approoued yt,

Eraf. Rot. his iudgment of the Sacramentarie doctrine against adoracion.

A good nombre of yeares, more then foure hondreth before *Erafmus,* was *Algerus,* who alfo teftifieth that the prefence of Chryftes bodie in the Sacrament, was receaued of all the catholique Churche, and fo beleued. Thus writeth he: *Idem quod Christus de veritate corporis sui testatur, & Petrus & (quia pro aliis loquebatur) cum eo & alij Apostoli. Quid ergo de veritate corporis & sanguinis Christi in Sacramento dici potest certius, nisi forte eam ipsam oculis videre velimus? In quo tamen nec ipse Dominus nobis deesse voluit, sed modicæ fidei nostræ per omnia consuluit. Quamuis enim ipsius Christi & tot sanctorum testimonijs & vniuersalis etiam Ecclesiæ catholica fide, quæ ab initio conuersionis suæ ita credidit,*
D *& ita saluata est, sufficienter astructum sit, quòd vera Christi caro verusque sanguis in mensa Dominica immmoletur, ne quis tamen peruersor aliter intelligeret, aut exponeret, facta sunt à Deo congrua huic nostræ fidei miracula quando, vel vbi, vel quibus reuelare dignatus est, huius mysterij secreta. Quæ nimirum facta esse non ignorabit, quifquis studiosius sanctorum patrum gesta legerit, quæ testantur sacramentum corporis & sanguinis Domini, oblata panis & vini specie, carnem & sanguinem naturali sua specie, sicut esse solet, exhibuisse. Cùm ergo præteriti &*

Algerus.

G ij   *præsentes*

præsentes fideles vbique terrarum hoc credant, & astruant, si hæc vniuersalis Ecclesiæ   **E**
fides vera ad salutem non extitit: aut nunquam catholica fuit, aut perijt. Sed aut non
fuisse, aut perijsse Ecclesiam, nemo catholicus consenserit. Nam cùm Ecclesia, & Pro-
phetia, & Euangelijs instituta sit, vbi est quod Abrahæ veritas promisit: In semi-
ne tuo benedicentur omnes gentes? Itémque vbi est, quòd eadem veritas Apostolis
ait: Docete omnes gentes, qui crediderit, saluus erit? Cùm enim omnes gentes ita
se credere glorientur, si salutis benedictione carent, vtrobique veritas Dei, & in pro-
phetia, & in Euangelio periclitatur. Euen the same that Chryst did testifie of
the veritie of his bodie, did Peter testifie also, and hicause he spake for
the other Apostles, the other Apostles testifie with him. What then can
more assuredlie be saied of the veritie of the bodie and bloode of Chryst
in the Sacrament, except we wolde see the verie same flesh with our eies?
In whiche thing yet our Lorde hath not left vs, but hath in all poinctes
holpen our litle faith. For although by the testimonies of Chryst him
self, and so manie holie men, and also by the catholique faith of the vni-
nersall Churche, which from the beginning of her conuersion hath so

The vniuer beleued and ys so saued, yt be sufficiently taught or auouched that the ve-
sal Church rie flesh of Chryst, and his verie bloode be sacrificed in our Lordes table:
from the leest yet anie ouerwhart man shoulde otherwise vnderstande or expownde
beginning yt, ther haue ben doen of God certain miracles agreable to this our faith
of her con- when, or wher, or to whom he hath vouchesaif to reuele the mysterie.
uersion ha- Which truly to be doen no man shall be ignorant, that shall read the wor-
the euer be- kes of the holie Fathers, whiche do testifie, that the Sacrament of the bodie
leued the and bloode of Chryst *(the formes of bread and wine taken awaie)* to haue shewed
presence yt self flesh and blood in his naturall forme, as yt ys wont to be. Seing
and sacri- then the faithfull that be past and goen, and they also that be nowe liuing
fice. in euery place of the worlde do this beleue, and this teache: Yf this faith
of the vniuersall Churche be not a true faithe to saluacion, then either the
The church Church was neuer catholique, or ells yt hath or ys perished. But that the
neuer yet Church hath not ben, or that yt hath decaied or perished, no man that ys
perished. catholique will consent. For, forsomoche as the Churche was sette vppe
bothe with Prophecies and Gospells, wher ys that that the trueth promised
to Abraham: *In thy seed shall all nacions be blessed?* Likewise also wher ys that   **G**
that the same trueth saieth to the Apostles: *Teach all nacions, he that shall be-*
leue shall be saued? Forasmoch then as all nacions glorie, that they so beleue, yf they atteign not the blessing of saluacion, the trueth of God in
both partes, both in prophecie, and in the Gospell ys in daunger. Thus
farre *Algerus.*

By whose testimonie ye see that the vniuersall Church professed this
faithe of the presence of Chrystes bodie and bloode in the Sacrament,
which faith was good to saluacion, or ells we must saie that ther was neuer
anie catholique Church, or ells yf ther were anie, that yt ys decaied, perished
and goen. Which maie not be saied. For Chrystes Churche abideth
for euer. And as all the Churche beleued Chryst in the Sacrament to
be present: so no doubte they adored him ther, whom they knewe ther
to be present.

Before this Authour was *Paschasius* more then twoo hundreth yeares.
Who reporteth the same faith vniuersallie to be professed in the Chur-   **H**
che of Chryst vntill his time of all that trulie beleued in Chryst. Thus
he writeth. *Discant diuinis verbis in omnibus acquiescere, & in nullo de ijs dubitare,*
quia vsque in præsens, nemo in ijs errasse legitur, nisi qui de Christo errauerit.
Qui

A *Quin potiùs admiremur profundißimum Dei confilium, quòd magni confilij Angelus inftituit, qui vult omnes faluos fieri homines. Admiremur, & laudemus atque intelligamus in his, quòd beatus Hilarius intellexit, quo artificio (vt ita loquar) nos Chriftus in fe collegit, vel quo myfterio vnum in fe nos effe naturaliter voluit, non per concordiam folummodò voluntatis, fed & per naturam carnis fuæ, & fanguinis. Ideo verum eft, quod Ambrofius ait fanctißimus: Quia ipfa eademque caro eft, & fanguis quam accipimus & communicamus, quæ nata eft de Maria,& quæ pro nobis pependit in cruce. Vnde fi quis negat hoc ita effe, quia Sacramentum vocatur, erit ei, ficut fanctus Auguftinus teftatur,mors non vita, qui mendacem putauerit vitam. Et quia Chriftus fuum dicit effe corpus, fuumque fanguinem, non oportet,etfi carneis non videmus oculis, quod credimus mente dubitare in aliquo. Audiuimus quid fanctus Cyrillus cum vniuerfis coepifcopis in Ephefo congregatis fentiat, Quid Græcia cum ijfdem, quid Ægyptus, & fanctus Hieronymus presbiter. Et ideo quamuis ex hoc quidam ex ignorantia errent: nemo tamen adhuc eft in aperto, qui hoc ita effe contradicat, quòd totus orbis credit & confitetur. Quapropter charißime, nihil in hoc dubites myfterio quod veritas Chriftus de fe largitus eft nobis, quia etfi fedet in dextra Patris in cælis, non dedignatur fuo fa-*

B *cramento, quotidiè per manus facerdotis, vt vera hoftia non infidèliter fed fidèliter immolari.*

Let them learne to agree to the woorde of God in all thinges,and in no one poinct to doubte. For vnto this prefent, no man ys redde to haue erred,but he that hath erred aboute the perfon of Chryfte. But raither let vs reuerence the depe fecrettes of God, whiche the Angell of great fecret hath inftituted,who will all men to be faued. Let vs honoure, and praife, and alfo vnderftand in thefe thinges, that Sainct Hilarie hath vnderftanded,by what workmanfhippe or cunning (yf I maie fo fpcake) Chryft hath gathered vs into him,or by whatmyfterie he wolde vs naturally to be one in him,not onely by concorde of will: but alfo by the nature of his flefh and bloode. *Therfor yt ys true that the moft holie Ambrofe faied, that yt ys the fame verie flefh and bloode,whiche we receaue and communicate,whiche was born of Marie, and which hanged for vs vpon the Croffe.* Wherfore who foeuer denieth this fo to be

Notable proues of the reall prefence.

C bicaufe yt ys called a Sacrament,yt fhall be to him, as Sainct Auguftine dothe teftifie,death and not life,that will thinke life to be a liar. And bicaufe Chryft doth faie yt to be his bodie and bloode, although we doe not fee yt with our flefhlie eies,that we beleue with owre minde , we maie not doubte of yt in anie point. We haue hearde what S. Cyrill with all his felowbifhoppes gathered together in *Ephefus,* dothe beleue : what Grece doth with them:What Aegipt,and alfo Sainct Hierom the preift.And therfore although fome maie erre of ignorance : ther ys no man yet hitherto that openlie againft faieth this fo to be, whiche the worlde dothe beleue and confeffe. Wherfore,derely beloued, doubte nothing in this myftery, which Chryft the trueth hath of him felf graunted vnto vs. *For although he fitteth at the right hande of his Father in heauen, he difdeineth not dailie by the handes of the preift in the Sacrament, as a true facrifice, not vntrulie to be facrificed.* Thus farre *Pafchafius.*

Chryft fitteth in heaué, and yet ys dailie facrificed by the preift.

See ye not the faith of the prefence of Chryftes bodie and bloode in

D the Sacrament ftande vntouched, and not fhaken with anie herefie againft faing yt openlie vntill the time of this writer? Perceaue ye not Sainct Hilarie, Sainct Ambrofe, Sainct Auguftine, Sainct Cyrill, with all the Bifhopps in the Councell at *Ephefus,* whiche were foure hundreth and eightene, Sainct Hierom alfo, all Grece and Aegipt, and finallie that the wholl worlde in this writers time did fo beleue, and fo confeffe? The

　　　　　　　　　　G iij　　　　　caufe

The Procla
mer impu-
gneth ado-
racio of the
Sacr. bicau
se he bele-
ueth not
reall pre-
sence.

caufe why the Proclamer denieth the Sacrament to be adored, ys that he denieth alfo Chryftes bodie and bloode to be ther. But yf that blindeneffe of herefie taken from his heart, he coulde by pure and clere faith fee that bleffed bodie ther, ther ys no doubte but he wolde adore yt, Euen fo for-afmoche as all the worlde with godlie confefsion acknowleged Chryftes prefence in the Sacrament, euen the fame that was born of Marie, as Sainct Ambrofe faieth, whiche Chryft ys of all Chryftians humblie to be adored, and honoured, who can doubte but that they, wher they beleued him to be, ther they honoured him?

Before this Authour was Leo, more then foure hundreth yeares. For he liued aboute the yeare of owre Lorde 452. and fo more then eleuen hun-dreth yeares agone: in whofe time what the faith of Chryftes Churche was in the matter of the bleffed Sacrament, ye fhall heare him reporte. *Separen-*

Leo Epi. 22
ad Coſtant.

tur huiufmodi a fanctis membris corporis Chrifti, neque fibi catholica libertas infidelium iugum patiatur imponi. Extra enim domum diuinæ gratiæ, & extra Sacramentum ha-bendi funt falutis humanæ, qui negantes naturam noftræ carnis in Chrifto, & Euangelio contradicunt & Symbolo reluctantur. Nec fentiunt fe in hoc præruptum fua obcæca-tione deduci, vt nec in pafsionis Dominicæ nec in refurrectionis veritate confiftant, quia vtrumque in faluatore vacuatur, fi in eo noftri generis caro non creditur? In quibus isti ignorantiæ tenebris, in quo hactenus defidiæ torpore iacuere, vt nec auditu difcerent, nec lectione agnofcerent, quod in Ecclefia Dei in omnium ore tam confonum eft? vt nec ab infantium linguis veritas corporis & fanguinis Chrifti, inter communis Sacramenta fidei taceatur? quia in illa myftica diftributione fpiritualis alimoniæ hoc impertitur, hoc fumitur, vt accipientes virtutem cæleftis cibi, in carnem ipfius, qui caro no-ftra factus eft, tranfeamus.

Eutyches
and Diofc.
their heref.

Let foche maner of men be diuided from the holie membres of Chryftes bodie, neither let the catholique libertie fuffre the yocke of infidelitie to be putte vpon yt. Theie are to be accompted oute of the houfe of Gods gra-ce, and oute of the Sacrament of mans health, whiche denieng the nature of our flefh in Chryft, do bothe fpeake againft the Gofpell, and ftriue againft the Symboll. Neither do they perceaue them felues through their blinde-neffe to be brought into foche daunger, that they can not abide in the ve-ritie, neither of our Lordes pafsion, neither of his refurrection. For both thefe be voide in our Sauiour, yf the flefh of our kinde be not beleued in him. In what darkeneffe of ignorance, in what fluggifhnes of flothe hath thefe men hitherto lien in, that neither by hearing they coulde learn, nei-ther by reading they coulde knowe, that in the Churche of God, in the mouthe of all men ys fo agreablie fpoken, that not afmoche as of the toun-ges of infantes, the veritie of the bodie and bloode of Chryft, among the Sacramentes of the common faithe, ys vnfpoken of? For in that myfticall diftribution of the fpirituall foode, this bodie ys geuen furth, this bodie ys receaued, that receauing the vertue of that heauenly meate, we maie be ma-de his flefh, who was made our flefh, Thus Leo.

Veritie of
the bodie
and bloode
of Chryft
fpoken of
by the toun
ges of babes

Of this Authour alfo being both auncient and holy ye perceaue yt tefti-fied that the veritie of the bodie and bloode of Chryft in the Sacrament was fo certenly beleued, and fo commonlie receaued, that yt was not onelie confeffed by the mouthes of all men, but alfo yt was fpoken by the mouthes of babes. And here with all note that this Authour doth merueill at *Eutyches* and *Diofcorus* and their adherentes, howe they coulde denie Chryft to be a verie man, feing that all Chryftian people confeffed
the

A the naturall bodie of Chryft God and man to be in the Sacrament. For confefsing the veritie of his bodie and bloode, which thinges be not of the nature of the godhead, yt muft nedes folowe that they confeffe the nature and bodie of his manheade, and fo Chryft to be very man.

Thus ye maie perceaue that the prefence of Chryftes verie bodie and bloode in thofe daies was reputed, efteemed, and beleued, fo certen, fo fure, and fo vndoubted a matter of faith, that learned men did vfe yt as a ftronge argument to confute and conuince diuerfe herefies. For as this Authour did vfe yt againft the heretikes of his time: So did *Irenæus* and *Hylarius* (whiche were long before him) againft the heretiqu⸱s of their times. Whiche they wolde neuer haue doen, yf in their times alfo the prefence of Chryft in the Sacrament had not ben a clere matter oute of all controuerfie, and receaued of all, afwell heretiques, as catholiques as a fubftanciall poinct of their faithe, whervpon an argument might be well grownded.

The reall prefence fo certenlie be leued that auncient Fathers ma de argumēt therof to cō fute here- fies.

Nowe ye haue hearde the prefence of Chryftes bodie teftified to haue
B ben receaued of all the chryftian Churche, from this our time to the time of Leo and before his time (as by Pafchafius yt ys aboue reported) to the time of Sainct Hilary. And fo to the time of *Irenæus*, who was the difciple of Polycarpus (as Sainct Hierom witneffeth) which *Polycarpus* was difciple of Sainct Iohn the Euangelift, fo neare was this man to the Apoftles time.

In catolog. fcript.

This difcourfe haue I made afcending from our time to the primitiue Churche, to prooue by confent of the wholl Churche the prefence of Chryftes verie bodie and bloode in the Sacrament. Whiche proof being made, yt ys eafie to prooue the adoracion of Chryft in the Sacrament. For Chryft being verilie ther, adoracion muft nedes folowe.

Reall pre- fence pro- ued, adora- cion muft nedes folo- we.

Nowe let this Proclamer who fo blafphemouflie hath denieth Chryft to be adored in the Sacrament (which his deniall ys for that he alfo de-
C nieth Chryft to be in the Sacrament) Let him, I faie, bring foche a difcourfe, to prooue by foche plain teftimony that Chryft ys not in the Sacrament, and I will not onelie denie to adore the Sacrament, but I will fubfcribe to him, to denie alfo the prefence, which I knowe for all his bragges he can neuer doe. Wherfore he vfeth in that kinde of wifdome himfelf wifhelie. For what he lifteth to denie, he doth denie, and prouing nothing of that he fhoulde affirme, he driueth the catholique Churche to prooue that that fhe affirmeth. A fleight he vfeth fome time (as partely ys declared and more hereafter fhalle) to touche a woorde or twoo of an Authour wreftinge them to his pourpofe, but plain proof, as this ys, he maketh none, neither dothe he to my remembrance, bringe furth three authorities of the doctours in all his fermon wholl and full, but mutilated and truncated.

G iiij　　T H E

D

THE SEVEN AND FOVRTETH CHAPITER
proceadeth in the proofe of the adoracion of the Sacrament by doctours.

AS in the laſt chapiter I haue prooued the preſence of Chryſt in the Sacrament, therby to inferre the adoracion of the ſame: So will I here prooue adoracion, therby to inferre the preſence. For as the preſence prooued, yt ys but foolerie to denie adoracion: So adoracion prooued, yt ys but vain to denie the preſence. Ye haue hearde yt ſufficientlie prooued by ſoche as the Proclamer named not to haue ſpoken of yt: nowe we ſhall bring other, of the whiche Sainct Dionyſe the diſciple of Sainct Paule, as of manie learned men he ys thought, whome alſo this Proclamer alleageth, ſhall be firſt. Who declaring the order of the miniſtracion of the holie Sacrament, maketh this praier to the

Dion. Are. Ecclefiaft. Hiera 3. parte. ca. 3. S. Dionyſe adored the Sacram.

ſame. *O diuinum penitus, ſanctumque myſterium, obducta tibi ſignificantium operimenta ſignorum dignanter aperiens, nobis palàm atque apertè luceſce, noſtroſque ſpirituales oculos ſingulari & aperto tuæ lucis fulgore imple.* O verie godly and holie myſterie, opening fauourablie the coueringes of ſignifieng figures, wherwith thowe arte couered, ſhewe thy ſelf to vs openlie and apertlie, and fill our ſpirituall eies, with the ſingular, and clere brightneſſe of thy light.

The peticions that be here made well weighed and conſidered, as to deſire our ſpirituall eies, owre vnderſtanding, our minde to be illumined, well clerely and perfectlie to ſee, to beleue and vnderſtand, the wholl ſecret myſterie of the Sacrament: what ys yt but an adoracion, and acknowleging of that thing to be God of whome we deſire ſoche thinges (for ſoche thinges can no creature geue nor graunt) and a plain ſubmiſſion of our ſelfs as to God to obtein that we deſire, as onely of him, whiche ys one of the cheifeſt partes of adoracion? Theſe kinde of peticions made this holie Dionyſe vnto the Sacrament. For vnto yt he directed his woordes, ſainge: *O verie godlie and holie myſterie.* Yt doth verie well appeare then that he adored the holie Sacrament not as a bare ſigne figure or token, but as conteininge very Chryſt God and man vnder thoſe ſignes and tokens: Neither can the Proclamer drawe this praier to Chryſt in heauen. For he ys not ther in a myſterie, but in clere and open viſion. But this ys directed to Chryſte very preſent in myſterie, whiche maner ys not ells where but in the Sacrament. Wherfore this praier and honour was made and doen to the Sacrament.

As in Dionyſe we finde adoracion of the Sacrament practiſed and lefte to vs as an example to folowe: So a moche like thing finde we reported of Gregorie Nazianzen. And this yt ys: *Quid igitur magna, & maximis digna*

Greg. Naz in epitaph. Gorgoniæ ſororis: Gorgonia proſtrate before the aultar calleth on him whom ſhe woourſhipped on the aultar

faciebat anima, & quodnam aduerſus infirmitatem remedium habebat? Iam enim occultum proditur, quum iam de omnibus alijs deſperaſſet, ad omnium confugit medicum, noctiſque captata ſolitudine, quum illi morbus paruas conceſſit inducias, ante altare cum fide procubuit, ac illum quem ſuper altare venerabatur, magna voce, ac omni inuocauit conanime, eique miracula cuncta, quæ olim fecerat in memoriam reduxit. What then did the ſoule, both great and woorthie of great thinges: what remedie had ſhe againſt the ſickneſſe? Nowe the ſecrete thinge ys opened. When ſhe had diſpared of all other, ſhe flieth to him that ys the phyſition of all men, and hauinge the ſolitarineſſe of the night, when the diſeaſe had geuen her a litle reſpitte, ſhe proſtrated her ſelf with faith before the

aultar

A aultar , and with a great voice and all her might fhe called vpon him whome fhe woourfhipped vpon the aultar , and vnto him fhe reherfed all the miracles,that of olde time he had doen. Thus Nazianzen,

In whome befide other thinges,this maie ye note, that this holie woman laie proftrated before the aultar,and called vpon him,whom fhe woourfhipped vpon the aultar . This maketh mightilie againft the Aduerfarie , who denieth Chryft anie other wher, or in anie other place to be honoured but in heauen.For his woman did honour him vpon the aultar, wher fhe laie proftrated as before, Chryft her Lorde God ther prefent.

This alfo ys not to be ouerpaffed, that this holie and auncient Authour reporteth this facte of this holie womã to her perpetuall praife,as did S.Ambrofe the facte of his brother Satyrus for the hanging of the Sacrament at his necke, in the whiche he repofed his hope of his faiftie, whiche according to his truft was not fruftrated,but had good effecte.

By the reporte of Nazianzen we maie perceaue two thinges: The one that he being a great learned man, an auncient and catholique Father B wolde praife nothing that was againft the true honour of God, and the vprightneffe of the catholique faithe . Wherfor we maie be affured that to lie proftrate before the aultar , and ther to call and praie vnto him that ys woourfhipped vpon the aultar , ys no idolatrie, nor againft the true honour of God(as this Proclamer,moche to Gods difhonour teacheth) but ys right good and acceptable honour.

The other ys that we compare the doctrine and doing of this holy man and of the Proclamer together: Sainct Gregorie teacheth Chryft to be honoured vpon the aultar : This Proclamer no wher but in heauen.Sainct Gregorie with grauitie praifed his fifter for fo honouring of Chryft: This Proclamer with mocking and taunting derideth and difpraifeth them that do fo honoure Chryft. Sainct Gregorie by all mens iudgementes as he was auncient:fo ys he iudged to be catholique and to fauoure Chryfte, and the catholique Churche: This Proclamer as he ys of thefe daies,and but younge of age, fo diffentinge from this holie Father maie well be iudgd the enemie of Chryft, and his catholique Churche. And as we haue C faied of Sainct Gregorie : So maie we faie of Sainct Ambrofe, who commendeth in his brother the great faith, affiance, and truft that he had in the holie Sacrament. For what more honour, what higher honour, can we do to God,then to fetle our faith, our hope and our truft in God,acknowledging him one not onely able and of power to helpe vs,to deliuer and faue vs from all perills and daungers, that maie happen to vs,but alfo affuredly truft that he will fo doe? Thus Sainct Ambrofe to the praife of his brother reporteth that he did to the Sacrament , as before ys at large declared. Seinge then this Proclamer difpraifeth that that holy Ambrofe did praife ,yt ys eafie to perceaue, what ys to be thought of him,and which of their doctrins ys to be embraced,and whiche of them ys to be folowed euerie good chryftian will foen determine.

Gre.Nazi. and the Proclamer cõpared in their doctrines.

In this matter alfo ys *Eufebius Emifenus* a goodlie witneffe writing thus. *Quia corpus affumptum ablaturus erat ab oculis noftris , & fideribus illaturus neceffarium erat , vt nobis in hoc die Sacramentum corporis , & fanguinis confecraret, vt coleretur iugiter per myfterium, quod femel offerebatur in precium .* For that D he wolde take awaie his affumpted bodie from our eyes and carie yt into the heauens , yt was neceffarie that in this daie he fhoulde confecrate the Sacrament of his bodie and bloode , that yt might continuallie

Euf. Emif. Hom.paf.

be

be honoured by myfterie, that once was offred for our price. Thus he.

Eufeb. Em.
directlie a-
gainst the
Proclamer.

Nowe wher the Proclamer faieth, that Chryft did inftitute the Sacrament onely that yt fhoulde be receaued in the remembrance of his death: This Authour faieth that bicaufe the vifible prefence of his bodie fhoulde be taken from vs, he did inftitute the Sacrament that the fame his bodie might continuallie be honoured by myfterie. And forfomoch as yt ys fo, he exhorteth vs fo to doe; fainge: *Cum reuerendo altari cæleftibus cibis fatiandus atcedis, facrum Dei tui corpus & fanguinem fide refpice, honora, mirare, mente continge, cordis manu fufcipe, & maximè hauftu interiori affume.* When thowe comeft to the reuerend aultar to be fatisfied with heauenly meates, looke with faith vpon the bodie and bloode of thy God: Honoure yt, woonder at yt, touche yt with thy minde, receaue yt with the hand of thy heart, and cheiflie receaue yt with the inwarde draught. This Authour in this his exhortacion, firft teacheth vs what we fhall beholde by faithe, when we come to the reuerende aultar, the bodie (faieth he) of our God. Wherby he teacheth the prefence of our Lordes bodie in the Sacrament, whiche in dede by faith onely ys ther to be feen, and not by fenfeis, except yt pleafe God by miracle to fome fo to reuele yt, as we reade that fundrie times he hath fo doen.

Eufeb. ibi.

Eufeb. bid-
deth vs ho-
nour the Sa
crament.

F

But let not the Proclamer walkinge in his darke miftes of his figures, faie that Chryft ys in the Sacrament, as in a figure, bicaufe this Authour faieth, that we by faith muft beholde him, and thervpon triumphe that this Authour ys on his fide. For this cauille ys auoided by the woordes that fhortlie after folowe, whiche be thefe: *Sicut autem quicunque ad fidem Chrifti veniens ante verba Baptifmi, adhuc eft in vinculo veteris debiti, ijs verò memoratis mox exuitur omni fece peccati: ita quando benedicendæ verbis cæleftibus creaturæ facris altaribus imponuntur, antequam inuocatione fummi nominis confecrentur, fubftantia eft illic panis & vini, poft verba autem Chrifti, corpus & fanguis Chrifti.* As anie man cominge to the faith of Chryft before the wooordes of Baptifme, ys yet in the bands of the olde debte, but when the woordes be fpoken ys furthwith deliuered from all the dregges of finne: Euen fo when the creatures that are to be bleffed with the heauenly woordes are putte vpon the holie aultars, before they be confecrated by the inuocacion of the moft high name, ther ys the fubftance of bread and wine: but after the woordes of Chryft, the bodie and bloode of Chryfte. Thus *Eufebius.* This his fainge clean diffolueth the cauill of the Aduerfarie. For though before the woordes of Chryfte yt be bread and wine: yet after the woordes yt ys the bodie and bloode of Chryfte.

A plain
place for
M. Juell.

G

Thus the minde of Eufebius being declared that Chryftes bodie and bloode be in the Sacrament after the confecracion, yt foloweth in his exhortacion (as meit ys we fhoulde doe) *Honora,* honoure yt. When by foche an auncient holie Father we be moued and aduertifed to honour the bodie of our God, and that not onelie in heauen, but when we come to the reuerende aultar, wher after the woords of Chryfte ys the bodie and bloode of Chryft, ys yt meit (fuppofe ye) to leaue fo auncient doctrine, and to cleaue to the newfangled inuencion of this Proclamer? After this he faieth: *mirare,* that ys merueill or woonder. As who might faie, that the bodie of thy Lorde God ys in the Sacrament, the fenfeis of man can not perceaue yt, his imaginacion can not compaffe yt, his might and power can not woorke yt: his reafon can not comprehende yt, therfore with reuerence and honour merueill and wonder at yt. Remembre that to God nothing ys

Reall pre-
fence and
adoracion
plainlie a-
uouched by
Euf. Emif.

H

vnpof-

A　vnpofsiblie. Remember the workes of God be merueillouſe: And therfor reuerentlie woonder and faie:*Tu es Deus qui facis mirabilia.*Thowe arte the God whiche doeſt merueillouſe thinges.

Nowe yf ther were but a figure,but bread and wine, ſignes and tokens of the bodie of Chryſt,what neaded this Authour to aduertiſe euery chryſtian man,and faie: *Mirare*,merueill . Ther was neuer man that bidde the Iewes merueill at the Paſchall lambe,bycauſe yt was a figure of Chryſte , ther was neuer man bidde wonder at Iſaac,at Ioſeph, at Ionas, at the braſen ſerpent, and ſoche other bicauſe they were figures of Chryſte: but the merueill ys here at the ineffable and vnſpeakeable worke of God, who aboue all mans deuiſe maketh preſent by his allmightie power the bodie and bloode of his Sonne our Sauiour Chryſt.

Figures of thinges be not merueil louſe but the bleſſed Sacram. ys merueilouſe

This therfore toucheth the wicked faing of *Oecolampadius*, who thinking verie baſely of this Sacrament`, denieth anie ;miracle to be wrought in yt. whoſe faing howe falſe yt ys, this Authour who willeth vs to merueill at yt doth declare, for no wiſe man willeth men to merueill wher no thinge ys B　to merueilled at. Wherfore in this Sacramēt ſomething ys wrought wher at we maie iuſtlie merueill,whiche ys in dede the merueillouſe worke of God to make preſent the bodie of Chryſte our Sauiour.

But I ſee,I ſtande to long in the alleadging of the Fathers,wherfor leauing theiſe auncientes,whiche haue taught vs the practiſe of the primitiue Churche in the adoracion of the holie Sacrament, we will among manie of the later time, heare but holie Bernarde,to ſee the agreement of the two times. *Chriſtus enim pridie quàm pateretur, Diſcipulis ſuis huius ſacramenti formam praſcripſit, efficaciam exhibuit. Cùm adhuc cænaretur ſurrexit à cæna: Diſcipulorum pedes Dominus vniuerſorum lauit : Dehinc ad menſam regreſſus ordinat ſacrificium corporis & ſanguinis ſui. Chriſtus in cæna illa munerans & munus , cibans & cibus, conuiua & conuiuium, offerens & oblatio. Obſtupeſcentes admiramini , nulli Angelorum, nullis ſpiritibus ſupernis,ſed hominibus , nec tamen omnibus : ſed ordini veſtro tantùm mandatam eſſe tanti ſacramenti celebrationem in altari , quod Chriſtus fecit manibus ſuis in cæna Paſchali. Quid facis indigne ? quid facis homo ingrate? Adora deuotiùs,& recole frequentiùs in Sacramento altaris ſalutem mundi pro te paſſam.* Chryſte the C　daie before that he wolde ſuffer preſcribed to his diſciples the forme of this Sacrament : he declared the efficacie of yt . When they were yet at ſupper,he roſe from the ſame and being the Lorde of all waſhed the feete of his diſciples. After that being returned to the table he ordeined the ſacrifice of his bodie and bloode. In that ſupper Chryſt was the geuer and the gifte:the feeder and the foode:the feaſter and the feaſt, the offerer and the offeringe. Wonder ye therfor and merueill, for to none of the Angells,to none of the heauenly ſpirittes:but to men , neither yet to all men, but onely to your order was appoincted the celebracion of ſo great a Sacrament in the aultar, which Sacrament Chryſt made with his handes in the Paſchall ſupper, what doeſt thowe,thowe vnwoorthie man ? What doeſt thowe,thowe vnthankfull man? In the Sacrament of the aultar, adore deuoutely , remember often the health of the worlde , that ſuffred for thee.

Bernar. de dign.ſacer.

Chryſt in his ſupper, the geuer and the gifte,the feeder and the foode , the feaſter and the feaſt, the offerer and the offering.

Of this Sainct Bernarde we maie firſt learn (as he did of the Euangeliſt D　Sainct Iohn)Chryſtes order both in the preparacion of his Apoſtles towarde the inſtitucion of the holie Sacrament,and alſo what he himſelf did in the ſame inſtitucion· He prepared his Apoſtles towarde the inſtitucion not onely ſignifieng to them by the waſhing of their feet , that they and
　　　　　　　　　　　　　　　　　　　　　　　　　　all

Waſhing of the Apoſtles feet what yt ſignifieth.

all chryſtians, that will come to this holie myſterie, muſt be pure and clean from all wordlie, vnclenlie, and eartlie affections: and alſo humble meke and lowly, not onely to God with all ſubmiſsion, being readie to obey his holie commaundements, but alſo by penance for the tranſgreſsion of anie of them, and therwith meke and lowly one to an other. Yf I (ſaieth he) haue waſhed your feete being your Lorde and maſter, yowe alſo aught to waſh one an others feet. For I haue geuen yowe an example, that as I haue doen, ye ſhoulde ſo doe.

Joan.13

Thus moch doen for the preparacion of his Apoſtles and all Chryſtians: he returneth to the inſtitucion of the Sacrament. In the which what he did S. Bernarde alſo declareth. He did (ſaieth he) ther inſtitute the ſacrifice of his bodie and bloode, and of his bodie and bloode ther ys no other ſacrifice, but the ſame his bodie and bloode. And that he ſo did S. Bernarde teacheth by the woordes immediatelie folowing. For he ſaieth, that in that ſupper. Chryſt was the geuer and the gifte: The feeder and the foode: The feaſter and the feaſt: The offerer, and the offering.

F

Marke well, gentle Reader, theſe propre ſpeaches. For as they contein a notable declaracion of the trueth : So alſo be they not ſpoken withoute imitacion of holie auncient doctours. For the firſt, yf Chryſt him ſelf were in his ſupper, the geuer, the feader, the feaſter, and the offerer (as moſt certenlie he was) then was he alſo the thing that was geuen, he was the foode or meat that was eaten, he was the wholl feaſt, he was the oblacion. What ys Chryſt him ſelf but God and man ? Then was Chryſt God and man ſo geuen of him ſelf in the laſt ſupper. Theſe maner of ſpeaches be vſed of S. Hierom, S. Ambroſe, and S. Auguſtine.

Hieron. ad Hedib. q. 2 Amb. orat. præpar. ad miſſam. Augu. in pſal. 33. conc. 1.

S. Hierom ſaieth thus : Dominus Ieſus ipſe conuiua & conuiuium, ipſe comedens, & qui comeditur. Owre Lorde Ieſus he ys bothe the feaſter, and the feaſt, he ys the eater, and that which ys eaten. Sainct Ambroſe praing to Chryſt ſaieth: Tu es ſacerdos & ſacrificium, mirabiliter & ineffabiliter conſtitutus. Thowe arte the preiſt and the ſacrifice, wonderfullie and vnſpeakeablie appoincted. Sainct Auguſtin ſpeaking of Chryſt, ſaieth. Ferebatur manibus ſuis. He was born in his owne handes. Then Chryſte bearing him ſelf in his owne handes, was bothe the bearer, and that was born.

G

Theſe I haue broughtin, that the Reader might perceaue that S Bernarde hath not framed ſoche maner of ſpeaches of his owne inuencion, but hath taken thē of the Farhers by imitacion, Whiche maner of ſpeaches I haue the more willingly ſetfurth at large, bicauſe they doe verie well, and godly declare the true catholique faithe, they mightilie ouerthrowe the hereſie of the Aduerſarie they alſo confirme and comfort the true chryſtian, notablie prouinge vnto vs the preſence of Chryſt in the Sacrament.

Chryſt in the Sac. de-uoutlie to be adored.

This preſence of Chryſt by S. Bernarde ſo ſetfurth, then he putteth vs in minde of our duetie ſainge: Adore in the Sacrament, the health of the worlde that ſuffred for thee. Obſerue diligently that he willeth thee to adore Chryſt in the Sacrament, whiche woordes be directlie againſt the woordes of the Proclamer, who willeth thee not to adore Chryſt in the Sacrament, but onely in heauen.

H

Nowe Reader, wher the Proclamer ſaied, that Sainct Ambroſe, Sainct Auguſtine, Sainct Chryſoſtome made no mencion of the adoracion of Chryſt in the Sacrament, thowe haueſt hearde them plentifullie teſtifieng the contrarie. Wher alſo he ſaied that no other doctours made mencion of yt, thowe haueſt hearde diuerſe declaring the contrarie. And not

onely

A onelie thefe doctours: but alfo thowe haueft heard S. Paule theaching vs to honoure Chryft in the Sacrament. Thus thowe feeft a nombre of wittneffes produced for the declaracion of the catholique faith: for the wicked doctrine of the Proclamer thowe feeft not one. As I haue redde this Proclamer in this matter: fo haue I redde *Oecolampadius* the great fownder of this doctrine in this our time, and I affure yow that neither in the one or the other of the did I finde anie authoritie of fcripture or doctour fullie and trulie alleaged for the maintenaunce of their doctrine. Trifling argumentes of negatiues and vntrueths they haue a fewe : other haue they none.

And here in this matter to conclude I will ioin this yffue withe the Proclamer : let him bringe but one auncient catholique doctour that by expreffe woordes, fhall faie as he faieth, that Chryft ys not to be adored in the Sacrament, and I will fubfcribe to him. But I am verie fure that he can bring not one. Yf he can bring none what madneffe ys ther in him that fo Goliath like reuileth the holie catholique Churche, and willeth her childeren to B forfake her, not to creditte her, not withftanding that fhe hath moche and good authoritie that fhe buildeth vpon, but to cleaue to him, to folowe his phantafies, to creditte his bare fainges without al authoritie. But how moch more madde fhall theie be, that neclecting the godly order of the Churche, contemning the religion therin by long times and manie hondreth yeares continued: not weghing the graue ad weightie autoritie of fo manie holie learned Fathers, fhall rafhlie committe their faithe to foche one, as bringeth nothing to grownde a faith vpon, but as ys faied, negatiues, and vntrueths. For this ys the fleight of this man he crieth oute vpon the Churche for the proofe of her doctrine, and in the mean while he bloweth oute his doctrine withoute all authoritie.

God ope the eies of all chryftia me well to fee yt, and fo to confider yt, that they maie efchewe yt. Great occafion ys geue the fo to doe when they feing him auochinge foche an vntrueth as this ys, that none of the doctours make mencion of the honouring of Chryfte in the Sacrament, fhall fee fo manie as nowe be alleaged, make plain mencion of yt befide manie other not here C alleaged. Yf ther were no mo vntreuthes in him but this (*as ther be to manie*) yt were enough to aduertife one that had regarde to God, and to the health of his foule, to looke twice er he leape once. Thus moch being faied for the admonicio of the reader, I wil addreffe me to examine the reft of his woords.

Iffue ioined with the Proclamer vpon adoracion.

THE EIGHT AND FOVRTETH CHAP. CON-
*futeth the reft of the Proclamers woordes before reherfed
againft the honouring of Chryft in the
Sacrament.*

S the twoo wicked iudges when they had once by their carnall luftes corrpted their iudgement, did not fpare to teftifie a wicked vntrueth againft the innocent and godlie *Suzanna*, and that before all the people, and being fo entred into fhamelefneffe proceaded to auouche the fame before the holie prophet Daniell: So this Proclamer, whe he had corrupted his iudgement in the matters D of faithe, and vttered an vntrueth againft the innocent and godlie *Suzanna* the Churche the fpoufe of Chryft, and that before a famoufe people, he fo entered into fhamelefneffe, that he proceaded to auouche the fame before God bi writing to his more codemnacion. And nowe being malicioulie fett

Hh　paffeth

paſſeth from vntrueth to vntrueth euen by yonde meaſure. For to theſe vntreuthes allreadie confuted thus he addeth ſpeaking ſtill againſt the adoracion of Chryſt in the Sacrament. *Yt ys (ſaieth he) a verie newe deuiſe, and as yt ys well knowen , came but late into the Church. Aboute three hundreth yeares paſt, Honorius then being Bishoppe of Rome, commaunded the Sacrament to be lifted vppe, and the people reuerently to bowe downe to yt.*

M. Iuell.

Yt ys (ſaieth he) a verie new deuiſe. Yf he had ſpoken of the doctrine, whiche he himſelf teacheth, that we ſhould not adore Chryſt in the Sacrament, he had ſpoken a trueth: For among all that confeſſed Chryſt to be God ād mā, and Chryſtes bodie to be preſent in the Sacrament, Luther was the firſt that fondlie erred in that poinct. And among them that denied Chryſt to be verilie and really in the Sacrament, *Oecolampadius* ys the firſt, that *(by the reporte of the learned)* hath in writing ſetfurth, with trifling perſwaſions, and vain argumentes of negatiues, the impugnacion of the adoracion of Chryſt in the Sacrament. Wherfore this hys vntrue ſaing againſt Chryſtes honoure, and the doctrine and doing of the catholique Church, maie trulie be turned into hys owne lappe againſt him and ſoch like blaſpemers and deprauers, that this his and their doctrine, that Chryſt ſhoulde not be woorſhipped in the Sacrament, ys a verie newe deuiſe, and ys *(as yt ys well knowen)* but lately comed in. For in dede yt came in by *Luther* and *Oecolampadius* , who were both late enough and ſooen enough, yea to ſoone, but that they were the inſtrumentes of Sathan, ſoche as God permitted for the puniſhmet of the ſinnes of the people.

Luther ād Oecolamp. Firſt deniers of adoracion of the Sacr.

But to our pourpoſe, that hys ſaing againſt the adoracion of Chryſt in the Sacrament ys vntrue, not onely the Fathers of the primitiue Church before alleaged doe prooue: but alſo the practiſe and doing of the thinge : As Chryſoſtome in his Maſſe, *Gregory Nazianzen* of his ſiſter, S. Ambroſe of hys brother, S. Auguſtine of his mother do declare. All which are before alleaged, and were aboue a thouſand years agone, ſo true ys this mans ſaing that yt ys but a new deuiſe. Wherunto yf ye adde the commaundement of God, to adore Chryſt: and the rule of S. Paule for our examinacion before we receaue, ye ſhal perceaue howe farre wide this man ys from all trueth in thys matter, and how auncient the adoracion of the Sacrament ys, and how new the denial of the ſame ys. Yt ys ſo newe I ſaie, that before *Luther* and *Oecolampadius* ther ys none fownde to haue written yt: although ſome infected with the hereſie of *Berengarius* and *Wicleff* maie be thought in corners to haue whiſpered yt, as by *Ioannes Rokizana* yt maie be gathered, who writeth thus: *Sacerdotes debent verbo & exemplo docere populū vt contremiſcant, adorando & colendo, & ſummum ac viuacem reſpectum habendo circa hæc diuiniſſima, & ineffabilia myſteria. Ex quo patet error dicentium quod corpus Chriſti, vel Sacramentum, ſolùm ſit nobis datum ad manducandum, & ſanguis in calice ſolùm ad bibendum , & non ad colendum ſiue adorandum. Sed patet quod inaniſ & fatua ſit irriſio eorùm, qui luminum accenſionem corā Dominico corpore in ſacramento derident, dicentes: quia Deus eſt lux, & non egens lumine. Nam in veteri lege etiam Domini mandato lucernæ ſiue luminaria in candelabro diſpoſita coram panibus propoſitionis, qui fuerunt figura tantùm corporis in Sacramento, exardebant, multo magis decens eſt vt hoc in præſentia tanti ſacramenti fiat. Si nempe decens eſt & honeſtum (teſte Hieronimo ad Riparium) vt lumina ardeant coram corporibus & oſsibus ſanctorum: Etſi decens fuit temporibus primorum ſanctorum, vt lampades mortuis chriſtianis fidelibus accendantur, vt hæc deſcribit Chryſoſtomus ſermone quarto ſuper epiſtolam ad Hebræos: multo magis decens honeſtū, & ſanctū eſt, vt lumina corā tā deiſico, et diuino corpore Chriſti accēdātur:* The preiſtes aught to teach the people both with exāple and

Ioan. Rokizana tract. de 7 . Sacr. cap. 12.

A and woorde, that they in adoring and woorſhipping and hauing an high ād, liuelie reſpe&t aboute theſe moſt godlie and vnſpeakable myſteries, doe feare and tremble. Wherby ys manifeſt the errour of thē that wickedlie ſaie, that the bodie of Chryſt or the Sacrament was onelie geuen to be eaten, and the blood in the cuppe onelie to be drunkē, and not to be woorſhipped or ado red . But yt ys manifeſt that their ſkorning ys vain and fooliſh, which doe mock the lighting of lightes before the bodie of our Lord in the Sacramēt ſaing: that God ys light himſelf, and neadeth no other light . For in the olde lawe euen by the cōmaundement of our Lord lightes that were ſett in the cādleſticke did burn before the ſhew breades, which were onelie a figure of our Lordes bodie in the Sacramēt: moch more ys yt comely that this be doē in the preſence of ſo great a Sacrament. For trulie if yt be comelie ād honeſt (*S. Hierom being wittneſſe vnto Riparius*) that lightes doe burn before the bodies or bones of ſain&ts: And if yt were comely in the time of the cheif holie mē, that lampes ſhould burn before the faithful Chryſtians that were dead, as

B Chryſoſtō deſcribeth theſe thinges in his fourth ſermon vpon the epiſtle to the Hebrues, moch more ys yt comely, honeſt, ād holie that lights ſhouldbe lighted before ſo diuine ād godly bodie of Chriſt. Thus moch this Authour.

Who although he were otherwaies naught himſelf, yet vnderſtanding ſo me ſoch ſecrett talke againſt the honouring of the bleſſed Sacrament he hath earneſtly laboured and learnedly, to extin&t the ſame. So (*as before ys ſai-ed*) though ſome haue in their corners murmured againſt the honouring of the Sacrament: yet ſure I am that none beleuing Chryſt, God and man, did openly write that Chryſt was not to be adored in the Sacrament, vntill the times of *Luther* and *Oecolampadius*, none neither catholique nor heretique. And therfor I ſhall returne the woordes of this Proclamer trulie to him, whiche he vntrulie hath publiſhed to the worlde, that this ys the greateſt antiquitie of the wholl matter: About fortie yeares agon yt was firſt fownd oute, and putt in pra&tiſe by *Luther*, and *Oecolampadius*, that the Sacrament might not be honoured. But Chryſt and his Apoſtles, the holy Fathers in

C in the primitiue Church, the do&tours that folowed them, and other lear-ned and godly men, whatſoeuer for the ſpace of xv. hondreth years and and odde after Chryſtes aſcenſion into heauen, neuer taught this do&trine, that the holie and bleſſed bodie of Chryſt in the Sacrament ſhoulde not be honoured, neither was yt pra&tiſed within anie place within the catholique Church of Chryſt throughoute the wholl worlde. And thus nowe be theſe woordes true, whiche before vttered by the Proclamer, were yerie falſe.

Greateſt antiquitie of denial of adoraciō of the Sacr. ys but fourtie years.

And nowe wher he ſaieth that *Honorius* was the firſt that commaunded the Sacrament to be honoured, in caſe yt were true, as yt ys allready proued to be falſe: yet ys the do&trine of the honouring of the Sacrament moche more auncient then this his do&trine, that wickedly denieth yt. For that by hys owne confeſsion was begon by *Honorius* three hondreth years agon: This do&trine but aboute fortie years agon. *Honorius* was neuer diffamed of hereſie: *Luther* and *Oecolampadius*, diffamed and condemned for hereti-ques. The honouring of the Sacrament was receaued, of the wholl Churche, and quietly continued thoſe three hondreth years at the leaſt

Honouring of the Sacr. vniuerſaly receaued but neuer yet vniuer-ſallie deni-ed in the Church.

D euen by this mans owne rekning : The contrarie do&trine was neuer yet receaued of the wholl Churche, and therfore neuer one howre quietlie continued. Thus moch aduantage haue we vpon the woordes of his owne confeſſion.

But he saieth that *Honorius* commaunded the adoracion of the Sacramēt, **E**
I graunt he did: But what of that? Will he therbie inferre, that bicaufe he
commaunded yt, that yt was neuer in vfe before? A verie fond kinde of argument, And yet, as fonde as yt ys, moch vfed in the Schoole of the doctrine
of thys Proclamer, from whence no doubte he hath learned fo to difpute.
For euen in like maner the flefhlie forte of them difpute to maintein their
fhamefull aboade with their women. Yt ys (faie they as this Proclamer faieth) a new deuife, yt ys as new fownd holie daie, that preiftes fhoulde not
marrie. For yt was but of late daies inuented by *Vrban and Gregorie.*

Nowe trueth yt ys, that thefe Popes made decrees that preiftes fhoulde
not marrie, but doth this proue that yt was neuer forbidden before? No tru
lie. For Siluefter long before them made a decree that yf a preift did marrie af
ter he had receaued holy orders he fhould be depriued of his office ten years,
but yf he difobediently kept his woman, and wolde not fubmitte himfelf to
the lawe, he fhould be condempned for euer : fhall we yet nowe here reft,
and faie that *Siluefter* was firft fownder of this matter, bicaufe yt ys fownd **F**
that he made foche a decree? Naie. *Calixtus* was before him, who made a like

decree. *Prefbyteris, Diaconis, Subdiaconis, & Monachis concubinas habere, feu matrimo-
nium contrahere pœnitus interdicimus. Contracta quoque matrimonia ab huiufmodi perfo-
nis difiungi, & perfonas ipfas ad pœnitentiam debere redigi, iuxta facrorum Canonum de-
finitionem iudicamus.* We vtterly forbidde : preiftes, Deacons, Subdeacons
and monkes to haue concubines, or to marrie. We iudge alfo the matrimo-
nies contracted of foch perfons to be diffolued or vndoen, and the perfons
themfelues to be fett to penaunce, according to the definition of the
holy Canons.

For this decree fome haue ben angrie with *Calixtus*, and haue fathered
the prohibition of preiftes mariages vpon him, but yet they haue erred.
For they might haue perceaued that he in this his decree referreth the
penaunce of the married preiftes, Deacons and other, to the holy Canons.

So that ther was an other decree for that pourpofe before *Calixtus*, and that
was the decree of the Canon of the Apoftles. For foche a Canon haue they **G**
made, which ys thus: *Ex his qui cœlibes in clerum peruenerunt, iubemus, vt lectores
tantùm, & cantores, fi velint, nuptias contrahant.* Of them that becomed fingle into the cleargie, we commaunde that readers onely, and
the finging men, yf they will, doe marrie. And an other like, which ys

this. *Qui duxit viduam, aut diuortio feparatam à viro, aut meretricem, aut an-
cillam, aut aliquam quæ publicis fit mancipata fpectaculis, Epifcopus, presbyter
aut Diaconus, aut denique ex confortio facerdotali effe non poteft.* He that hath
married a widowe, or a woman diuorced from her husbande, or an harlott,
or a bond maiden, or a anie that ys accuftomed to plaie in enterludes, can
neitherbe Bifhoppe, preift, nor Deacō, nor be of the cōpanie of the preiftes.

By this breif difcourfe ye maie perceaue the Fathers of the later
times made decrees of that was in vfe in the Apoftles time, wher vnto they
were enforced, by the wickedneffe, and licencioufe life of men in their times, not to make newe deuifes, but to caufe the olde auncient lawes to be
obferued and kept.

Ther be decrees made in thefe later daies for the fafting of Lent, bothe
by Councells and Popes. As for example to produce one. In the eight **H**
Councell of Tolett, thus we finde declared : *Illis qui aufu temerario quadrage-*

*fimæ dies contemnunt, nec voracitatis ingluuiem frenant, & (quod peius eft) Pafchalia fe-
fta, illicitorum efuum perceptione profanant, ex hoc adeò acerrimè interdicitur, vt*
quifquis

A　*quiſquis ſine ineuitabili neceſſitate atque fragilitate, & euidenter languore, ſeu etiam im-poſsibilitate ætatis diebus quadrageſimæ eſum carnium præſumpſerit attentare. non ſolùm reus erit reſurrectionis Dominicæ, verumetiam alienus ab eiuſdem diei ſancta commu-nione. Et hoc illi cumuletur ad pœnam, vt ipſius anni tempore ab omni eſu carnium abſti-neat, quia ſacris diebus abſtinentiæ oblitus eſt diſciplinam.*　　Vnto them that pre-ſumptuouſlie contemne the daies of Lent, neither do refrein the exceſſe of their greadineſſe, and that which ys wooeſt of all, do prophane the Ea-ſter ſolemnities, with the eating of vnlaufull meates : from hencefurth we ſtraightlie commaunde , that whoſoeuer withoute ineuitable neceſſitie and weakneſſe , and euident ſickneſſe , great weakenſſe of age , ſhall preſume in the daies of Lent to eate fleſh , he ſhall not onely be gil-tie of the reſurrection of our Lorde , but ſhall be alſo excommunica-ted from the holie Communion of that ſame daie . And thys ſhal be ad-ded to his farther pain, that that yeare he ſhall abſtain from all eating of fleſh , bicauſe in the holy time of Lent, he forgotte the diſcipline of abſtinen-ce. Thus the Councell.

B　In the which Councell the faſt of Lent ys commaunded, as ye per-ceaue , but this proueth not that yt was but then begonne , and that yt ys a newe deuiſe. For S. Hierom, who liued moch aboue twoo hüdreth years before that Councell ſaieth thus: *Nos quadrageſimam ſecundùm traditionē Apoſto-lorum ieiunamus.* We faſt the Lent according to the tradition of the Apoſtles.

Hieron. ad uerſus Mõ tan.

But this faſt of Lent (not withſtanding that yt ys the tradicion of the Apo ſtles) hath ben in diuerſe Councels ſince the Apoſtles, and long after their time commaunded, bicauſe in proceſſe of time the deuociõ of the people de caied, as yt doth to moch in theſe our daies, Wherbie the decrees of the Apo ſtles being contēned *(as nowe alſo they be)* yt was neceſſarie by a newe cõmaun dement to reuiue and confirme the ſame, and ſo cauſe them to be continued which ells had ben omitted. Euen ſo *Honorius* perceauing the deuociõ of the people to be decaied, and their regard of the bleſſed Sacrament, through the wicked doctrine of *Berengarius(which yet, as yt maie be thought, laie ſmoldering in pu-trified and rotten* poſtes and ſtickes) to be moche abated , to reuiue that that

The queen that nowe ys commaũ ded Lent tobe faſted and yet yt was in vſe before.

C　ſo long had continued, he gaue commaundement to honoure the Sacramēt as the like maie be doē, whē the catholique faith ſhal be reſumed in Englõd. Thus ye maie perceaue both how fõd and weake the argument of the Pro-clamer ys, and therwith howe falſe and vntrue.

After this yt liketh him to dallie and ſolace himſelf in alleadging certain ſcholaſtical doctours, as S. *Thomas. Dunce, Durande, Holkot* and other , not in re-prouing their learning by learning *(which he can not doe)* but reprouing yt with mocking and ſkorning *(which ys in deed eaſie to doe)* The Summe of all that long diſputacion ys onely to make the matter appeare to the worlde, that yt ys a daungerouſe thinge to honour the Sacrament, for that the people can not diſcerne the accidentes or the outwarde formes of the Sacrament, from the bodie of Chryſte, and therfore maie ſoen committe idolatrie in honouring the outward formes in the ſtead of Chryſtes bodie.

Mocking and skor-ning eaſie kindes of confutaci-on.

Yt ys a woorld to ſee thys man, that when he hath no ſubſtácial argument to make againſt the matter derectlie, he ſeketh oute daũgers to bring himſelf ãd the people into more daũger. For wher yt ys our duetie to honour our ſa

D　uiour Chryſt, wherſoeuer we know him by faith to be. to auoide his inuēted daunger, he wold haue vs, by omiſsiõ of owr duetie, to rūne into a certē daũ-ger, ãd to auoide ſoch abuſe as he imagineth, to take away the thing yt ſelf, as *Licurgus* did, who ſeing wine to be abuſed, for that mē took exceſſiuelie of yt,

Hh iii　　cauſed

caufed all the vines in the contrie to be cutte dowen , that ther fhoulde be **E**
no wine. So this man for an abufe that he phantafieth , he wolde take a-
waie the thing.

Like Phan tafie ioined with aua- rice pulled down all Abbeis in England.
By like phantafie he might alfo moue vs not to honoure Chryft in hea-
uen.But moche more yt might feem to haue moued the Apoftles and other
that were conuerfaunt with Chryft in the flefh,and beleuing in him honoured him.What daunger were they in that feing the humane bodie of Chrift,
and percafe not fufficientlie difcerning the humanitie from the deitie , nor
fully perceauing the vnition of thefe two natures in the vnitie of perfon,nei
ther yet well vnderftanding how the bodie of Chryft ys to be adored , and
howe yt ys not,howe the deitie was in that perfon of Chryft , and howe to
be confidered,and yet did adore him?Al thefe poinctes, as yt maie be gathe
red by the peticion of Philippe,were not well vnderftanded of the Apoftles
themfelues.For when he faied:*Domine,oftende nobis Patrem,et fufficit nobis*, Lord
fhewe vs the Father, and yt ys enough for vs:yt femeth that he had not that
confideracion of the Deitie,that faith required.

And further by the aunfwer of Chryfte, yt femeth that the Apoftles did **F**
not yet knowe Chryft.For he faied:*Tanto tempore vobifcum fum , & non cogno-
uiftis me?*Haue I ben fo long time with yowe, and haue ye not knowen me?
Yf they that had ben fo long conuerfaunt withe Chryft,and fo long traded in
the fchoole of Chryfte did not know Chryft, how did the three wife men of
the eaft,the woman of Chananie,the man born blind reftored to his feight,
with other which did adore Chryft without reproche? Did they (trowe ye)
know Chryft,feing the Apoftles did not know him?Did they(*trowe ye*) vnder
ftand this quidditie of faith,how the flefh and bodie of Chryft was to be ado
red,and howe yt was not to be adored?And yet were not they in the fimpli
citie of their faith well accepted?

And to come nearer to anfwer this man,do all Chryftian people, which at
this prefent daie adore Chryft in heauen,vnderftand this quidditie,how the
flefh of Chryft being a creature,maie be adored with Godlie honoure ? To
adore the Godhead of Chryft with godlie honour,yt ys a plain matter , but
to adore the manhead, to adore the naturall flefh of a natural man, to adore
a verie man with God,I thinke the Difciples of this Proclamer, who not vn- **G**
derftanding howe the accidentes be fownded in the Sacrament,nor how to
difcern them frõ the bodie of Chryft,that ys couered with thefe accidentes,
therfor flie from the honouring of Chryft in the Sacrament,for feare of cõ-
mitting Idolatrie,were neuer fo well taught by ther mafter , well to vnderftand thefe quiddities aboue mencioned.Will he alfo therfore,that they not
vnderftanding thefe thinges,fhould alfo flie the honour of Chryft in heauẽ?
I thinke verilie yt will therto growe at the laft as yt doth allreadie break out
among the Caluiniftes. For doth not *Richerus* forbidde to praye to Chryft,
Richerus a Caluinift forbiddeth to praie to Chryft.
leaft we fhoulde honour hys humanitie with godly honoure ? Hath he
not faied that he ys to be accompted an heretique that faieth that Chryft
muft neceffarely be praied vnto?See yowe not howe Satthan goeth aboute
by prettie means to take awaie Chryft from yowe? Among the Caluiniftes,
as nowe among yowe,he began to take awaie the adoracion of Chryft in the
Sacrament,but nowe he taketh awaie the adoracion of Chryft in heauen.
Take heed therfor Sathan ys fubtle. **H**

He faieth that the fchoolemen make a doubte of the adoracion of the Sa-
Damafcen li 4.ra. 3.
crament,bicaufe the vnlearned maie cõmitte Idolatrie , yf they happen to
woorfhippe the outward formes or fhewes of bread,ãd geue honour to that
in ftead

A in stead of Chrystes bodie. Damasen saieth, that the flesh of Chryst, the humanitie of Chryst ys not in some consideracion to be adored, and if they
so adore and honore yt they committe Idolatrie. shall all the vnlearned
christians therfore, bicause they maie committe Idolatrie in adoring Chrystes flesh and bodie, geue ouer their dueties, and ceasse to honour Chrystes
bodie in heauen? Yf daungers maie withdrawe vs from the matters of our
faith, and the doing of our duetie in the same, forsomoche as in manie mat
ters of faithe, manie daungers maie happen, manie matters of our faith must
be omitted and forsaking.

*Phanticall
daungers
maie not
drawe vs
from oure
faith and
duetie do-
ing.*

Among the daungers that maie happen in matters of faith, this man to
disswade his hearers and readers from the faith, bringeth in one other, abou
te the consecracion of the holy Sacrament. *what (saieth he) if yt happned the
preist not to consecrate? what if he leaue oute the woordes of consecracion and neuer speake
them? or what if the preist haue no minde or intencion to consecrate?*

As this man goeth aboute to shake the fundacion and building of this Sa
crament, which ys (as S. Dionise saieth) the perfection all other Sacramen-
B tes: So his bothers and likes haue goen aboute to shake the fundacion of
the sacrament of Baptisme. For *Brentius* saieth that baptisme ys good and
maie be ministred withoute the forme of the woordes of Baptisme. But yt
shall be best, that I ascribe his owne woords, that I be not thought to misreport him. Thus he writeth: *Christus non collocauit fundamentum Baptismi super
certis literis, sillabis, aut dictionibus, nec alligauit nos ad certa verba (non enim instituit
magiam, quæ ad certam verborum formam, aut ritus alligata est) sed instituit cœlestia sacramenta, quæ constant sua ipsius sententia & voluntate, his vel illis verbis significata.
Itaque si quis post recitationem Symboli Apostolici in Baptismo diceret ad baptisandū hæc
verba: Audiui iam ex te confessionem fidei tuæ, quòd credas in Deum Patrem omnipoten-
tem creatorem cœli & terræ, Et in Vnigenitum Filium eius Dominum nostrum Iesum Chri
stum, & in Spiritum sanctum. In hanc igitur confessionem, & fidem, intingo te in aquam
seu perfundo te aqua, vt hoc signaculo certus fias, te insertum esse in Iesum Christum,
& communionem omnium bonorum. Vade ergo in pace: Hic certè Baptismus verè
esset Baptismus.*

*Brentius
in explica-
tione Bap-
tismi.*

C Chryste hathe not settled the fundacion of Baptisme vpon certen letters
sillables, or woordes. For he hath not instituted magike, that ys to saie, incan
tacion, sorcerie or witchcrafte, which ys bownden to certen form of woordes or ceremonies: but he hath instituted heauenly sacramentes, whiche
are established by his owne will and sentence, signified by these or these
woordes. Therfor if anie man after the rehersall of the *Symbole* or *Creed* of the
Apostles in Baptisme shoulde saie these woordes to him that ys to be baptized: *I haue now heard of thee, the confession of thy faith, that thowe beleuest in God the Fa
ther allmightie maker of heauen and earth: And in his onely begotten Sonne our Lord Iesus
Chryst: And in the holie Gost. Vpon this confession therfor and faith, I dippe thee in the
water, or I washe thee with water, that by this signe thowe maist be made certen, that
thowe arte inserted or engraffed into Iesus Chryst and into the cōmunion of all good thinges &c. Therfor go thie waie in peace. Certenly this Baptisme shoulde be verilie Baptisme.*

*Berentius
impugneth
the forme
of Baptis-
me.*

Ye see here howe this man reiected the woordes of Baptisme, and ac-
counted yt sorcerie and supersticion to be bownde to a certen forme
of woordes in the ministracion not onely of this but of other sacramentes.
D Yt ys lamentable to see the wickednesse of these men, howe they labour to
weaken all the fundacion of our faithe, and wolde make vs viode of all
certentie in the ministracion of Chrystes Sacramentes.

But to returne to our Proclamer and to aunſwer him with his owne learning (for *Brentius* and he be of one religion and doctrine, or ells Sathan ys
diuided in him ſelf)ſeinge that to vſe a preſcript forme of woordes in the Sa
crament ys ſuperſticion, and Magicke, what nedeth he to make any doubte
whether thoſe formes (*whiche the holy auncient Fathers call the woordes of conſecracion*) be vſed or no? as though ther were daunger if they were omitted, where by the learning of his ſchoolefelowe *Brentius*, to omitte them ys raither
religion, then daunger. For if the woordes of the forme of Baptiſme maie
withoute daunger be omitted, why maie not the woordes of conſecracion
withoute daunger be omitted?

Thus hitherto I haue aunſwered this Proclamer with the doctrine of his
owne ſchoole, that yt maie appeare to the reader, howe wicked and deteſtable the doctrine ys, and howe yt confowndeth all order, and all certentie of
the miniſtracion of ſacramentes in Chryſtes Church, leauing a man ſo recea
uing theſe Sacramentes vncerten and doudtfull, whether he hath receaued
either the one Sacrament or the other.

Proteſtan-
tes admitt
ſome two
Sacramen-
tes, ſome
three ſome
foure ſome
neuer one.

I wolde here reherſe mo daungers that might likewiſe happen in the miniſtracion of the other ſacramentes if I knewe of what religion this man
were. For ſome of them admitte but two Sacramãtes, ſome three, ſome foure
ſome neuer one, ſo diuerſe be they in their opinions, ſo vnſtable ys the profeſsion of their religion. But contenting my ſelf with theſe that be reherſed,
fearing that he will admitte no mo, though the catholike church admitte ſeuen : I will nowe open the doctrine of the catholique Church in theſe two,
for aſmoch as ys here to be ſaide.

And firſt for the Sacrament of Baptiſme, thus teacheth the holy catholique churche, that the inuocacion of the holie Trinitie, maie not be omitted,
as wittneſſeth S. Baſill: *Neminem impellat ad errorem, illud Apoſtoli, quòd nomen
Patris, ac ſancti Spiritus in baptiſmatis mentione ſæpe omittit. Neque ob id putet nominum
nomenclaturam non neceſſe eſſe obſeruari. Quicunque (inquit) in Chriſtum baptiſati eſtis,
Chriſtum induiſtis.* That the Apoſtle in the mencion of baptime doth often
omitte the name of the Father, and the holy Goſt, let yt driue no man to er
roure. Neither for that let him thinke, that yt ys not neceſſarie the naming
of their names to be obſerued.

Baſill. de
ſpiritu ſact
ca. 12. For
me of Bap-
tiſme neceſ-
ſarilie re-
quired in
that Sacra.

And again he ſaieth : *Oportet immortalem manere traditionem in viuifica gratia da
tum. Qui enim liberauit vitam noſtram ex corruptione, poteſtatem renouationis nobis dedit.
Quæ poteſtas inexplicabilem cauſam habet, & in myſterio abſtruſam, verùm magnam
animis ſalutem adferentem. Quare addere quid, aut detrahere, palàm eſt elapſus à vita
æterna. Si igitur ſeparatio Spiritus in Baptiſmate à Patre & Filio, periculoſa eſt baptizan-
ti, & inutilis Baptiſmum ſuſcipienti, quomodò nobis tutum eſt à Patre & Filio diuellere
Spiritum ſanctum? Fides & Baptiſma duo ſalutis modi ſunt inter ſe cohærentes, & inſepa-
rabiles. Fides enim perficitur per baptiſmum: baptiſmus verò fundatur per fidem & per
eadem nomina vtraque res impletur. Sicut enim credimus in patrem, & Filium, & Spiritum ſanctum: ſic etiam baptizamur in nomine Patris, & Filij & Spiritus ſancti.*

¶ibidem.

Faith and
baptiſme
two inſepa-
rable me-
anes of ſal-
uacion.

The tradition geuen in the quickning gracemuſt abide vnmoued. He that
deliuered our life from corruption, gaue vs the power of renouacion, which
power hathe an inexplicable cauſe, and hidden in miſterie but, yet bringing
great health to our ſoules. Wherfore to putt to, anie thing, or to pluck awa
ie anie thing, yt ys an open fall from euerlaſting life. Yf therfor the ſepara-
cion of the holie Goſte in Baptiſme from the Father and the Sonne, ys peri-
Louſe to the baptizer, and vnprofitable to him that receaueth baptiſme,
howe can we ſafelie from the Father and the Sonne diuide the holy Goſt?

Faith

A Faith and Baptiſme be twoo meanes of healthe conioined together, and in ſeparable. For faith ys perfected by Baptiſme, and Baptiſme ys founded by faith and by the ſame names bothe theſe thinges be fullfilled . As we beleue in the Father, and the Sonne, and the holy Goſt : ſo are we baptiſed in the name of the Father , and the Sonne, and the holie Goſt Thus farre S. Baſill.

Damaſcē.
li.4 ca. 10.

Damnaſcen alſo ſaieth : *Quemadmodum ſemel completa eſt Domini mors :* ſic ſemel oportet Baptizari iuxta Domini verbum : In nomine Patris , & Filij , & Spiritus ſancti, inſtructos confeſsionem, Patris, & Filij, & Spiritus ſancti. As the deathe of our Lorde was once doen: So muſt they, that be taught the confeſsion of the Father, the Sonne, and the holie Goſte, be once baptiſed according to the woorde of our Lorde : In the name of the Father , the Sonne, and the holie Gſte. Thus Damaſcen.

Manie other Fathers maie be brought, but theiſe two maie at this time ſuffice , which both do declare that not onely the confeſsion of the Father,

B and the Sōne, and the holy Goſt muſt be had in Baptiſme: but alſo ouer and beſide the partie to be baptized muſt be baptized in the name of the Father, and the Sonne, and the holy Goſte, as by the well weighing of their ſainges yt ſhall be eaſie to perceaue.

But nowe by cauſe *Brentius* teacheth that the woordes of the forme of Baptiſme be not neceſſarie, and yt maie be that this Proclamer thinketh euē the ſame , and herein ſome light heades leauinge the doctrine of the auncient church will folowe *Brentius* his doctrine , and will not baptiſe in the name of the Father, and of the Sonne, and of the holie Goſte, which (as S. Baſill ſaieth) ys periloufe to the baptizer, and vnprofitable to the baptiſed, ſhall we therfore reiect and caſt awaie the Sacrament of Baptiſme, bicauſe ſoch perills and daungers maie happen in the miniſtracion of yt, as this man wolde that we ſhoulde Chryſtes bodie and bloode in the bleſſed Sacramēt bicauſe daungers maie happen in the honouring of the ſame? As for the conſecracion of the Sacrament , yt ys taught vs alſo hy the catholique Church, that yt ys doen by the power of God woorkinge at the due pronunciacion

C of the woordes of Chryſt, as wittneſſe *Euſebius Emiſenus , Chryſoſtome,* and *Ambroſe* with a nombre of other,

This perill I fear falleth vpon manye in Englond in theſe daies.

But this Proclamer ſaieth, that yt ys knowen that ſome preiſtes haue manie yeares lefte oute the woordes of conſecracion. Yt ys plain then (ſaie I) that the bodie of Chryſt ys not preſēt in the Sacramēt, bicauſe the inſtituciō ys not obſerued. Then yt foloweth (*as the proclamer ſaieth*) that ther ys daunger. Ther ys daunger in dede to the wicked preiſt, who pretending in outwarde face to do that, that Chryſt hath appointed, and dothe yt not in deed. But to the people ſimplie beleuing the miniſtre to doe that, that to his miniſterie apperteineth, and perceauing nothinge to the contrarie, ther ys no daunger to them in doing their duetie, though the naughtie man the preiſt doe not his duetie. And wher the Proclamer ſaieth that yt ys knowen that preiſtes haue ſo doen : I thinke if yt be ſo, yt ys knowen to him of him ſelf and of his likes, who of peruerſe mindes being corrupted in their faith haue committed ſoche impietie in dede to their greater and more greuouſe damnacion, but not to the hurte of the people if they knewe yt not . And

What daū-ger to the preiſt, and what to the people if the woodes of Conſecracion be left vnſaied.

D here alſo to ſaie, I beleue that if any catholique preiſt had ben knowen to this man, ſo to haue doen (as he ſaieth) he wolde without all dowbte to the helpe of his cauſe (wher vnto he hath none) haue named him . But foras moche as he ſpeaketh yt of him ſelf, and his conſpired complices, which ſecretly

E

cretly *Conuenerunt in vnum adnersus Dominum, & aduersus Christum eius,* haue conspired againſt our Lorde, and againſt his annoincted, when they durſt not vtter, what they had wickedly conceaued : he ys aſhamed to name him ſelf to haue committed ſo heinouſe a facte. Yf yt be not ſo, yt ys like to be a feigned matter to ſupplie, when certen and true matter lacketh.

Bnt to returne to the matter, and to moue the ſame ſcruple to him, that he moueth againſt the catholique Churche : What if ſome that miniſtre the communion after the ſorte that ys nowe receaued, do neither ſpeake the woordes of Chryſt vpon the bread (For *Richerus* a Caluiniſt reiecteth the woordes of conſecracion, as not nedefull to be ſpoken, or munbled, as his terme ys, vpon inſenſible creatures) neither entende to make anie ſacramentall bread : what then do your people receaue? Yf they receaue no ſacramēt (as yt ys none, if bothe woordes and intencion be lacking) then they receaue no promiſſe, they receaue no remiſſion of ſinnes, nor ſoch other benefittes (for the promiſſes be annexed to the ſacramentes) howe are they then deceaued? Howe then ys the Sacrament of Chryſtes bodie and bloode in

F

due forme miniſtred? Howe ys the death of Chryſt ſhewed furthe according to Chryſtes mindē, whiche muſt be ſhewed furth, when we eate that bread and drinke that cuppe, as S. Paule teacheth vs: *As often as ye ſhall eate of this breade, and drinke of the cuppe:* he ſaieth not bread generallie, but this breade, mening the bread of the Sacrament? Thus if men ſhall improue the great matters of religion, withe *why, what,* and *howe,* and inuented daungers and abuſes, your owne religion, whiche yowe magnifie as moſt ſure and good, maie be proued vnſure and weake. To be ſhort, all his argumentes grownded vpon (*if* and *and*) are to no pourpoſe . For if maketh no certen argument. Wherfore leauing them as ſufficiently touched, I ſhall reuert to matter of more ſubſtance, and proceade in the allegacion of the fathers for the expoſition of Chryſtes woordes nowe in hande.

THE NINE AND FOVRTETH CHAP. PROCEA-
deth in the vnderſtanding of Chryſtes woordes by Irenæus, and Tertullian.

G

Llthough betwen *Iuſtine* and *Irenæus,* ther were ſome holy Fathers, that haue left behinde them goodly teſtimonies, for the proofe of Chryſtes very preſence in the Sacrament: Yet I finde none that doe alleage Chryſtes woordes, and therby geue vs light to vnderſtand them, vntill welcome to *Ireneus,* who writeth thus : *Sed & Diſcipulis ſuis dans conſilium primitias Deo offerre ex ſuis creaturis, non quaſi indigenti, ſed vt nec ipſi infructuoſi, nec ingrati ſint, eum qui ex creatura panis eſt accepit, & gratias egit dicens: Hoc eſt corpus meum. Et calicem ſimiliter, qui eſt ex ea creatura quæ eſt ſecundum nos, ſuum ſanguinem confeſſus eſt, & noui teſtamenti nouam docuit oblationem, quam Eccleſia ab Apoſtolis accipiens in vniuerſo mundo offert Deo.* Geuing alſo inſtruction to his diſciples (the authour ſpeakethe of Chryſte) to offre to God the firſt fruictes of his creatures, not as to one hauing nede, but that they ſhoulde be neither vnfruictfull , neither vnthankfull , he tooke that breade , whiche ys a creature, and gaue thankes ſaing : *This ys my bodie.* And the cuppe likewiſe , whiche ys a creature as we be , he confeſſed to be his bloode, and of the newe Teſtament, taught a newe oblacion, whiche the Churche receauing of the Apoſtles offreth to God in all the worlde. Thus *Irenæus.*

H

who when he had declared howe allmightie God inſtituted and appointed

Irenæus li. 4. cap. 32. cont. hereſ.

Sacrifice of the newe Teſtament inſtituted ād taught by Chryſt in conſecracio of his bodie and blood.

A &ted facrifices and oblacions in the olde teftament, as thinges to be geuen to him not as to one that neaded foche thinges or giftes, but for the exerci-fing of their obedience and faithe, in the whiche God ys delighted, not yet that God had anie profitt, or aduantage therbie, but that they doing thefe thinges, profitt and aduantaie might enfewe to them from, God, for whofe commodities fake God did inftitute them. So he declareth that in the newe Teftament alfo, the people of the fame might exercife their faith and obe-dience, and therbie pourchafe gain and profitte , and for benefittes recea-ued be fownde thankfull, Chryft alfo taught his Apoftles to offre facrifice. And what the facrifice ys he teacheth faing that yt ys his bodie made of the creature of bread, and his bloode, made of the creature of wine. Howe this thinge ys brought to paffe he fheweth when he faieth : that *Chryft tooke the bread, whiche ys a creature and gaue thankes faing : This ys my bodie : And likewife the cuppe, which alfo ys a creature, and confeffed yt to be his bloode.* In whiche woordes, wher he hath expreffedly faied, that Chryft confeffed yt to be his bloode, and the like ys ment of the bread tobe his bodie: what more plain fpeache

New facri-fice of the newe Tefta-ment, what yt ys.

B wolde we defire of anie authoure? Yf Chryft confeffed yt to be his bodie, and his confeffion ys allwaies true, howe then ftandeth the fainge of the Aduerfarie that yt ys not his bodie? Shall we doubte of the trueth of Chry-fte? as S. Ambrofe faieth : *Ipfe Dominus Iefus teftificatur nobis, quod corpus fuum ac-cipiamus & fanguinem : Nunquid debemus de eius fide,& teftificatione dubitare?* Owre Lorde Iefus teftifieth vnto vs, that we receaue his bodie and bloode: ought we to doubte of his truth and teftimonie?

Li.4.de Sa-cramēt c.6

　　Seing then this authour faieth, that Chryft confeffed his bodie and bloo de to be prefent and that by thefe woordes : *This ys my bodie. This ys my bloode:* yt ys plain that he vnderftandeth them in their propre fenfe, withoute figu-re or trope, and fo acknowledgeth the very reall prefence of Chryftes bodie ād blood in the Sacramēt. For farder proof wherof, the woordes that imme-diately in the fame authour doe folowe do make very moch, wher he faieth, *Et noui Teftamenti, nouam docuit oblacionem* : And of the newe Teftament he taught a newe oblacion. This newe oblacion of the newe Teftament, ys

Ireneus auoucheth both reall prefence ād facrifice.

C the bodie and bloode of Chryfte, as before in the firft booke ys declared and prooued. And here to the pourpofe farder to faie, yf the facrifice that Chryft inftituted to be the newe oblacion of the newe teftament, were but a peice of Sacramentall breade, yt were no newe oblacion. For then yt we-re the fame that Melchifedech offred, who offred bread and wine in facrifi-ce as a figure. Wherfore if this facrifice be but bread and wine, a bare figure, then yt ys no newe oblacion.

　　In the leuiticall lawe alfo we finde bread and wine offred in the facrifice. The fhewe bread alfo was offred in facrifice. Wherfor of neceffitie yt muft be vnderftand of an oblacion and facrifice not hertofore accuftomed to be offred, whiche by that reafon maie be called a newe oblacion, which ys none other but the verie bodie and bloode our Sauiour Chryfte . Which al-though yt were figuratiuelie offred before of Melchifedech in materiall breade and wine: yet nowe in the newe teftament, yt ys offred as neuer be-fore, not in figure but in verie dede, the verie bodie and blood of Chryft him felf, the heauenly breade, and heauenlie wine anfwering the bread and

D wine of Melchifedech, as the thing the figure. And fo yt ys a newe oblaciō inftituted to be offred in the newe Teftamēt. Wherfor alfo Chryft to fhewe the adaptaciō of the figure to the thing, and the figure therin to be fullfilled, tooke bread and wine, and confecrating them into his bodie and bloode,
　　　　　　　　　　　　　　　　　　　　　　　　confeffed

confeſſed them (*as this authour ſaieth*) to be his bodie and bloode, that the **E**
figure might be manifeſtlie ſhewed ther to be termined in that heauenly
bread and wine, the verie thing figurated by that figure.

Yf the malice of the aduerſarie will go aboute to peruerte this plain ſainge and teſtimonie of his authour : ſainge : that allthough Chryſt did confeſſe the bread and wine to be his bodie and bloode, yet yt foloweth not
that they were ſo in dede. This were a merueilouſe ſaing, that Chryſt ſhoulde confeſſe a thing to be in plain maner of ſpeache withoute anie circunſtance, leading vs to an other ſenſe: and yet in deed not to be ſo. But that
he ſhall not ſo wickedly auoide the trueth vttered here by this authour, he
ſhal heare an other teſtimonie of the ſame, in the whiche, as befote he ſaied
that Chryſt confeſſed the bread and wine to be his body and bloode : ſo
here the authour affirmeth them to be the bodie and blode : Thus he ſaieth

Quomodò conſtabit eum panem in quo gratiæ aƈæ ſunt, corpus eſſe Domini ſui, & calicē
ſanguinis eius, ſi non ipſum fabricatoris mundi filium dicant? &c. Quomodò autem rurſum
dicunt carnem in corruptionem deuenire, & non percipere vitam, quæ à corpore Domini
& ſanguine alitur? Howe ſhall yt be manifeſt, that bread in the whiche than
kes be geuen, to be the bodie of their Lorde, and the cuppe of his bloode, yf
they ſaie that he ys not the ſonne of the maker of the worlde? &c. And a-
gain, howe ſaie they the fleſh to come into corruption, and not to receaue
life, whiche ys nouriſhed of the bodie and bloode of our Lorde?

Ther be here in this teſtimonie twoo notes, wherby as the aduerſarie ys aunſwered and conuinced : ſo ys the trueth notablie ſettfurth
and confirmed.

The firſt ys, that he ſaieth that the bread, in the whiche thankes are geuen, ys the bodie of our Lorde, and the cuppe ys the cuppe of his bloode.
The bread in the which Chryſt gaue thinkes, was the bread which the
Euangeliſtes ſaie that Chryſt tooke in his handes, and gaue thankes ſaing:
This ys my bodie. Chryſt then might verie well confeſſe yt to be his bodie,
ſeing (*as Irenæus ſaieth*) yt ys his bodie . So that of this authour we
learn yt not onely to be called and confeſſed the bodie of Chryſt, **G**
bnt alſo to be, and that not in obſcure woordes, but in plain and euident ſentence.

The other note ys, that our fleſh ys nouriſhed of the bodie and bloode of
our Lorde . Wherby the erroure of the Aduerſarie teaching that Chryſt ys
onely ſpiritually and not reallie receaued in the Sacramēt ys ouerthrowen
and fownde falſe. For by that ſpirituall maner our fleſh ys not nouriſhed,
wherfor of neceſsitie the other maner, that ys , Chryſtes verie reall bodie
muſt be in the Sacrament receaued. Yt ſhal helpe yowe the better to percea
ue the minde of this authour as concerning the reall preſence of Chryſt
in the Sacrament, if ye doe vnderſtande wherfore he wrote this, that ys
here alleaged.

Vnderſtand therfore that by this place laſt alleaged he impugneth **two**
hereſies : the one was that Chryſt was not the Sonne of God that made the
worlde, but that he was a man liuing in Iewrie, who did not onelie diſſolue
the lawe and the Prophetes , but alſo all the workes of that God, that made
the worlde. The other taught that the ſoule onely ſhall be ſaued, and liue
euerlaſtinglie, and not the bodie, for that yt being a groſſe thing, made of **H**
the earth, yt ys not poſsible, that yt ſhoulde atteing to euerlaſting life. **To**
confute theſe two hereſies *Irenæus* growndeth him ſelf vpon the Sacrament,
as a matter certen, euident, plain, and knowen aſwell of the heretiques,

againſt

*Irenæus li.
5.cont. He
reſie.*

*A plain
ſaing of Ire
næus for the
Proclamer*

*Oure fleſh
ys nouriſ-
hed of the
bodie and
blood of our
Lord.*

*Two here-
ſies cōfuted
by one ar-
gument
grownded
vpon the
Sacr.*

A against whom he disputed, as of the true catholique Chrystians.

Nowe against the first heresie, he proueth Chryst to be the Sonne of God by that that they confessed the bodie of their Lorde, to be in the Sacrament. For yf he whose bodie ys in the Sacrament were not the Sonne of him that made the worlde, but a bare naturall man, howe coulde a man of hys owne powre compasse that his bodie should so be? and howe coulde yt be the bodie of their Lorde, yf he were not the Sonne of God? So all the weight of this argument standeth and resteth vpon the presence of Chrystes bodie in the Sacrament. Nowe denie the presence with thys Proclamer, and then the argument maketh nothing against the heresie, and so the argument which this holie Father thought to be stronge shall be but weake. But who can doubte of the true knowledge of this auncient Father? When he grownded hys argument vpon the presence of Chryst in the Sacrament, he was sure that hys grownde was fast and good. Yf the Sacrament were nothing but a figure, what more proofe coulde be grownded vpon yt then

B vpon anie other figure of the olde lawe?

The second heresie he also impugneth by the receipt of the bodie and bloode of Chryst in the Sacrament.   For wher that heresie denied the bodie of man to be able or like to atteign to life euerlasting, this holie man proueth that yt shall. For howe can yt (saieth he) but receaue life, seing yt ys nourished by the bodie and bloode of Chryst? as though he might haue saied, as sainct Cyrill saieth : *Quoniam Saluatoris caro Verbo Dei, quod naturaliter vita est, coniuncta, viuifica effecta est. quando eam comedimus tunc vitam habemus in nobis illi coniuncti, quæ viuifica effecta est.* Bycause the flesh of our Sauiour ioined to the Sonne of God, whiche ys naturally life ys made quickning or geuing life, when we eate that flesh, then haue we life in vs. For (as he saieth in an other place : *Non poterat aliter corruptibilis hæc natura corporis ad incorruptibilitatem & vitam traduci, nisi naturalis vitæ corpus ei coniungeretur.* This corruptible nature of our bodie coulde not otherwise be brought to incorruptibilitie and life, except the bodie of naturall life should be ioined to yt.

C. So then ye maie nowe likewise perceaue the force of this argumente of *Irenæus* to consist vpon the corporall receipt of the bodye of Chryst in the Sacrament, whiche (as *Cyrill* saieth) being the flesh of life, and incorruption when yt ys ioined to our corruptible and mortall flesh (*whiche maner of coniunction ys by none other mean doen, but by the Sacrament*) yt maketh this naturall bodie of our to be apte to incorruption and life. Yf in the Sacrament we doe not receaue the verie reall bodie of Chryste, but a figure of the bodie, whiche geueth not life to our bodies, howe standeth the argument of *Irenæus* ? what trueth ys ther in the saing of *Cyrillus* ? howe shall these our mortall and coruptible bodies be made immortall and incorruptible, yf the flesh of life, the flesh of our Lorde Chryst be not ioined to our flesh?

And here note, Reader, that these maner of speaches of these two authours improue the phantasie and erroure of the Sacramentaries, and inuinciblie proue the true catholique doctrine of the Churche. As touching the false doctrine of the Sacramentaries, wher yt teacheth that we o-

D nely receaue Chrystes bodie spirituallie, that ys, the meritte and vertue of Chrystes passiõ ãd death, this receipt toucheth not our bodies, this spirituall Chryst ys not ioined to our flesh, but this receipt toucheth our soules, thys

Ii   spirituall

Cyrill in 6. Ioan. ca 14

In 15. Ioan Our corruptible bodie can not atteign to incorrup. and life, except the bodie of Chryst be ioined to yt

The nourishing of our flesh to incorruptibilitie by the flesh of Chryst proueth inuinciblie the reall presence.

spirituall Chryst ys ioined to spirittes. But these authours saie that the flesh and bodie of Chryst ys receaued and so ioined to our flesh and bodies. Which receipt and coniunction proueth inuinciblie that for as moch, as the spirituall receipt ys ioined onely to the foule that ther must nedes be an other receipt of the reall and substanciall flesh and bodie of Chryste, whiche maie be ioined to our substanciall flesh and bodies. And so shall the argument of *Irenæus* be of great force and strenght, against the heretiques, against whome he disputed: So ys the testimonie of Cyrill true: So ys the doctrine of the catholique Church fownd auncient substanciall and well grownded: So ys the doctrin of the Sacramentaries improued and fownd false as yt ys in dede.

Plain pla-ces and ar-gumentes against M. Iuell. And wher the Proclamer required but one plain place of anie one auncient doctour, he hath nowe one, not onely plain, but also strong and mightie, so ouerthrowing the green wrought walls of hys late inuented heresie, that well he maie hang vppe some painted cloathes, paincted like strong walls, whiche maie deceaue simple eies, and weake seightes, but they shall be in dede but painted cloutes. This *Irenæus* ys not onely taken of the catholiques to be (as I haue saied) plain and strong, but also of heretiques. For *Melancthon* against *Oecolampadius* this proclamers late fownder alleageth the same *Irenæus* as one most plain and auncient, and ther for not to be against saied.

Thus hauing brought furth an auncient scholer of Chrystes schoole, and a graue counseilour in Chrystes Parliament house, who hath declared vnto vs the true doctrine of Chrystes schoole, and the enacted and receaued trueth of his Parliament house, that the woordes of Chryst teache vs the presence of his verie bodie in the Sacrament, and that they are to be vnderstanded in their propre sense: Now foloweth Tertullian a man verie nere the time of *Irenæus*, whome the Aduersaries seme to make the patrone of their figuratiue doctrine, but yt shall be well perceaued, that *Tertullian li.4.cont. Marc.* he ys against them and fauoreth them not. Thus he writeth. *Professus itaque se concupiscentia concupiscere edere Pascha, vt suum (indignum quippe vt quid alienum concupisceret Deus) acceptum panem, & distributum Discipulis, corpus suum illum fecit, dicens : Hoc est corpus meum id est, figura corporis mei. Figura autem non fuisset, nisi veritatis esset corpus .* When Chryst therfore had saied, that *Chryst made the bread his bodie, saieth Tertull.* with desire he desired to eat the Passouer, as his owen (for yt was vnsemelye that God should desire anie straunge thing) the bread that was taken and distributed to hys disciples, he made yt his bodie, sainge : *This ys my bodie*, that ys to saie, a figure of my bodie. But yt had not ben a figure, except yt were a bodie of trueth.

August. li. Aduers. Heres.c.28 Heresie of Marcion As *Irenæus* against *Valentinus*: So *Tertullian* against *Marcion* vsed hys argument taken of the Sacrament. Marcion the disciple of *Cerdon (whose heresies S. Augustine reherseth)* wickedlie taught as hys master did, that Chryst had no very true bodie, when he was here conuersant vpon the earth, but a phantasticall bodie. Nowe *Tertullian* to proue that he had a verie true bodie, bringeth in the institucion of the Sacrament, sainge, that Chryst made the breade that he tooke and distributed to hys disciples, hys bodie, saing : *This ys my bodie* . Wherbie as he stronglie proueth by Chrystes owne facte, who made the breade hys bodie, and by his owne woorde (who saied of the same that he had so made : *This ys my bodie*) that Chryst had a verie bodie, Whiche coulde not well haue proued the pourpose of *Tertullian*, yf that, that he made hys bodie, and said

and said

E

F

G

H

A and faied to be hys bodie, had not ben a verie bodie . Euen fo faing that Chryft made the bread hys bodie , when he faied : *Thys ys my bodie* , prooueth againft the Sacramentaries bothe the prefence of Chryftes verie bodie in the Sacrament, and alfo that the woordes of Chryft are to be taken in their propre fenfe.

But here reclaimeth the Aduerfarie, and faieth that not withftanding this that ys faied, *Tertullian* addeth and faieth that yt ys a figure of hys bodie . I wifhe that the Aduerfarie wolde here ioin with me, as I will with him , that both of vs accept the wholle faing of *Tertullian*, as yt ys here alleaged , and that he whofe doctrine repugneth againft anie parte of yt , to confeffe that hys doctrine ys not good, and he that confeffeth the whol, that hys doctrine be accepted as fownde and good. Let vs then open the partes of *Tertullian* his faing.

Ther be in yt twoo partes: The one ys that he faieth , that Chryft made the bread that he tooke in hys handes hys bodie: The other that he faieth:
B *This ys my bodie*, that yt ys to faie, *a figure of mi bodie*. I nowe require of the Aduerfarie , whether he will receaue the firft parte of *Tertulians* faing, that Chryft made the breade his bodie? Certen I am that neither he, nor anie other Sacramentarie doth graunt that. For if Chryft made the breade hys bodie *(as by the teftimonie of this authour yt ys moft certen that he did)* then ys hys very bodie certenlie and verilie in the Sacrament. Which they all denie, as by declaracion of the fainges of fome of their capitans yt fhall appeare.
Zuinglius writeth thus : *Cùm panis & vinum illius amititiæ fymbolum fint , qua Deus humano generi per filium fuum reconciliatus eft, illa non æftimamus pro materiæ præcio, fed iuxta fignificate rei magnitudinem, vt iam non fit vulgaris panis, fed facer, nec panis tantùm nomen habeat, fed corporis Chrifti quoque , imo fit corpus Chrifti fed appellatione , & fignificatione , quod recentiores vocant facramentaliter .* Forafmoche as bread and wine be the token of the frendfhippe, by the which God by hys Sonne was reconciled to mankinde, we weigh not thefe thinges for the woorthineffe of their matter, but according to the greatneffe of the thing fignified : that nowe yt be not cōmon bread, but holie, neither that yt haue
C onelie the name of bread, but alfo of the bodie of Chryft: yea that yt be the bodie of Chryft, but by name onely, and fignificacion, whiche the younger men call facramentallie. Thus he.

Ye fee that this Sacramentarie, wolde not haue the Sacrament to be eftemed for the fubftance of yt, wherbie he denieth the prefence of the fubftance of Chryftes bodie. In the ende he alfo faieth that yt ys the bodie of Chrift but he correcteth or raither corrupteth himfelf faing : that yt ys fo by name and fignificacion onelie, and not by trueth, and fubftance.
Oecolápadius alfo faieth thus · *Barbaries plus quàm Scythica, vel Diomedea eft, in panis in volucroceu in ænigmate ipfam hofpitis carnē quærere. Rufticitas eft non obferuare nec cogno fcere in quo hofpes beneuolentiā fuam doceat, & pro fpirituali carnalem requirere cœnam.* Yt ys more then fcythicall or diomedicall Barbaroufneffe , in the couering of breade to feke the flefh of Chryfte, yt ys groffe inciuilitie not to regarde and knowe wherin Chryft teacheth hys beneuolence, and for a fpirituall to require a carnall fupper. And here *Oecolampadius* alfo denieth that *Tertullan* affirmeth. For he faieth yt ys a barbaroufneffe or rudeneffe to feke the flefh
D of Chryft in the Sacrament : but *Tertullian* (whom I often repete) faing that Chryft made the bread hys bodie geueth vs not a rude, but a godlie doctrine to feke the flefh of Chryft in the Sacrament,

(margin notes)
Tertullian opened and deliuered from the Sacramentaries.

Zuinglius ad illutrif. Germ. prin cipes.

Jn expofit. verborū cœ na. Dom.

Bullinger also faieth thus:*Commemoratio ac symbolum est corporis veri, non ipsum* **E**
Bullingerus in 2.Act. *corpus.* Yt ys a remembrance and a token of the verie bodie, not the verie bo
die yt felf. What nede I trouble the reader with the fainges of anie moe of
them, feing yt ys certen, that the wholl rable of them, and this Proclamer alfo denieth that, that Tertullian faieth, and abhorreth to faie as he faieth, that
*Chryst na-
med not o-
nelie, but
made the
bread hys
bodie.* the breade ys made the bodie of Chryft. And note well that Tertullian faieth not, that yt ys named or called the bodie of Chryft, but in plain expreffe
woordes faieth, that yt ys made the bodie of Chryfte. And nowe yt ys plain
that the aduerfarie receaueth not this parte of *Tertullian* hys faing: but al the
catholique church euer hath and doeth receaue yt, confeffing yt with thys
man and S. Cyprian, who folowed him, and highlie embraced him, and S.
Ambrofe, which both vfe the like woordes, that the breade ys made the bodie of Chryfte. Cyprian in this maner: *Panis quem Dominus Difcipulis edendum*
*Cypriā. de
cœnaDom.* *porrigebat non effigie, fed natura mutatus omnipotentia verbi factus est Caro.* The bread
that our Lord gaue vnto hys difciples, chaunged not in outwarde forme, but
in nature, by the omnipotencie of the woorde ys made flefh. S. Ambrofe in **F**
*Amb.li.4.
de Sacr.c.4
Bread ys
made the
flesh of
Chryst.* this forte: *Panis iste, panis est ante verba facramentorum, vbi accefferit confecratio de pane fit caro Chrifti.* This bread ys breade before the woordes of the Sacramen-
tes: but when the confecracion ys comed to yt, of the bread ys made the
flefh of Chryfte. In all thefe ye fee this maner offpeache, that bread ys made
the flefh or bodie of Chryft. Which maner fullie excludeth the onelie figure
and includeth the verie fubftanciall prefence of Chryftes bodie.

   Thus moch being faied of the firft parte of *Tertullians* faing: Let vs alfo haue a fewe woordes aboute the feconde parte. The fecond parte (*yf yowe remember*)ys that calleth yt a figure of Chryftes bodie. This parte the Aduer-
farie(*ther ys no doubte*)receaueth though he receaue yt not well, according to
the minde of the authour. The catholique alfo receaueth yt, and receaueth
yt well. For he receaueth yt according to the minde of the authour. Howe
fhall the reader perceaue that? Thus fhall he perceaue yt.

*The right
waie to vn-
derstand a
catholique
authour.*   He that fo vnderftandeth a catholique authour, that he make him not repu
gnant to himfelf, nor to other his likes, he vnderftandeth the authour well, **G**
and receaueth him well. But he that fo vnderftandeth an authour that he ma
keth him contrarie, and repugnant to himfelf, and other learned authours
which be his likes, he vnderftandeth the authour euell, and receaueth him
euell. The catholique receaueth this parte of *Tertullian*, wher he faieth yt ys a
figure of Chryftes bodie, and graunteth yt, and alfo folowing *Tertullian*, teacheth that yt ys a figure, but fo that the prefence of Chryftes bodie be not
denied, which the firft parte (as aboue ys faied)teacheth. And therfor though
*The Sacr.
a figure but
not onlie a
figure.* yt be a figure: yet not onely a figure, but alfo the bodie with yt. The Aduerfarie receaueth this parte of the authour vnderftanding yt as *Oecolampadius*
dothe. *quod panis affumitur in fignum tantùm*, that the bread ys taken for a figne
onlie, denieng therbie the prefence of the bodie. And fo maketh the authour not onelie repugnante to himfelf, but alfo to other holie writers. To
himfelf thus: For wher he faied, that Chryft made the bread his bodie, nowe
*Oecol. de
verbis cœn.* vnderftanding by the figure, the Sacrament to be onely a figure or figne of
Chryftes bodie and not the bodie yt felf, the bread ys not made hys bodie.
And fo fhall the authour denie in the fecond parte of his faing, that he
thaught in the firft, which maie not be allowed, and therfor he receaueth **H**
and vnderftandeth the authour euell. And fo to other whiche be auncient as he ys, that authour fhoulde be repugnant, as to S. Ambrofe. S. Cyprian,
to *Irenæus, Iuftinus*, and *Alexander* which all teache(as before ys declared) that
                                                                              the

A the Sacrament of Chryftes bodie and blood conteineth the very bodie of Chryft,and ys not a bare figure or figne onely.

For the better vnderftāding of this matter,I wifh thee,reader,to perceaue that for fomoch as to our pourpofe apperteineth,a figure maie be taken two maner of waies.One waie as yt ys a figne or token of a thing abfent in dede, but prefent in figure or fign. As a ring geuen of a man to his louing fpoufe, ys a figne or token of remembrance of him being abfent. An other waie a figure maie be taken as of a thing abfent in maner and condicion foche as fomtime yt hath ben in,but prefent in verie deed and fubftance.As the fpoufe beholding her verie husbande,and feing the skars and tokens of wounds that he fuffred for her defence and fauegarde,and of his children an hers: ys brought in remembrance of his louing kindneffe,and of the daungers fufteined for hir fake. In which cafe although the fubftāce of the man be prefent: yet to his wife he ys a figure and token of remembrance of himfelf abfent in condicion of a man nowe in fight,and daungered with fore and depe woondes.For nowe he ys no foch mā, but whol ād fownd,and a perfect mā.

eA figure maie be taken two waies.

eA figure maie be of a thing prefent in fubftance.

B Nowe wher *Tertullian* faieth that the Sacrament ys a figure of Chryftes bodie,yt ys true after the fecond maner of acception of a figure. For Chryftes bodie nowe prefent in the Sacrament,and ther by faith certenlie and af furedlye feen and beholden,ys a figure and a token of remembrance to hys fpoufe the Church of his afflictions,paffions,and woundes fuffred vpon the Croffe for her fauegarde and deliuerie,which bodie although yt be fubftanciallie prefent:yet in that maner of a pafsible, and fuffring bodie yt ys not nowe prefent.*Caro carnis, & fanguis facramentum eft fanguiuis. vtroque inuifibiliter fpirituali & intelligibili fignatur Domini Iefu Chrifti corpus vifibile & palpabile,plenum gratia omnium virtutum,& diuina maieftate.* The flefh,faieth S.Auguftin,ys a Sacrament of the flefh,and the blood ys a facrament of the bloode. By both which being inuifiblie fpirituall and intelligle ys fignified the vifible and pal pable bodie of our Lord Iefus Chryft,full of grace and all vertues,and diuine maieftie.Thus moche he.Here do we learn of S. Auguftine that the bodie of Chryfte and blood in the Sacrament being vnder the formes of bread C and wine inuifible,fpirituall,and intelligible,be figures of the fame bodie vifible and palpable.

The Sacr. ys a figure of a thing prefent.

Auguft.li. fentē.Prof.

The inuifible bodie of Chryft in the Sacr. a figure of the fame vifible, &c.

Let not this then feme incredible to thee(gentle Reader) feing **S**.Auguftinē teftifieth yt by fo plain woordes,and the fcriptures alfo teftifie vnto vs that Chryft was made in the likeneffe of men:and yet was he neuertheleffe a very naturall and fubftancial man,and that he ys the very image of the Father,and yet he ys of the fubftāce of the Father alfo.So that as we are taught, that Chryft ys made to the likeneffe of men, and ys alfo a verie man , and ys the image of the fubftance of the Father,and yet of the verie fubftance of the Father alfo:So we be taught that the Sacrament ys a figure and the thing yt felf alfo.For we faie the bodie of Chryft vnder the forme of breade, and his bloode vnder the forme of wine,to be a figure of that bodie that fuf fred vpon the Croffe,and of the blood ther yffuing oute of the fame bodie, and diuided from yt.And yet neuer the leffe to be the fame very bodie in fubftance that hanged vpon the Croffe,and the fame blood in fubftance that ranne oute of that bleffed bodie. And therfor *Tertullian* might verie well call yt a figure as before he called yt the bodie of Chryft , for yt D ys both.

Philip. 2.

This fhall farder appeare by two places of S.Auguftin,in the which fpeaking of one thing , he calleth the Sacrament in one the figure of

the

the bodie of Chryste : in the other he calleth yt or price or Redemption, **E**
which ys as moche to saie as the bodie of Chryst. Thus he saieth speaking
of *Iudas* the traditour.*Cùm Christus eius cogitationes non ignoraret, eum tamen adhi-*
buit and conuiuium , in quo sui corporis & sanguinis figuram Discipulis commendauit.
When Chryst was not ignorant of the thoughtes of Iudas : yet he had him
present at the feast,in the which he commended to hys Disciples the figure
of hys bodie and blood. Here ye perceaue that sainct Augustine calleth the
Sacrament the figure of Chrystes bodie and bloode . In an other place he

Aug.in
Psalm.3.

saieth thus:*Tollerat ipse Dominus Iudam,Diabolum,furem,& venditorem suum . Sinit*
accipere inter innocentes Discipulos,quod norunt fideles,precium nostrum . Owre Lorde
himself doth suffre *Iudas*,a deuell, a theef,and his seller, he suffreth him to
take among the innocent Disciples , that the faithfull knowe, our price or
redemption.

Epist.162.
Iudas recea
ued the bo-
die of christ
which ys
our price.

　Nowe marke that what in the other sentence he called the figure of Chry
stes bodie,here he calleth yt our price or redemption,which ys Chryst him
self as sainct Paule testifieth:*Qui factus est nobis sapientia,& iustitia,& sanctificatio*
*& redemptio.*Who ys made to vs wisdom,and righteousnesse,and sanctificacion,and redemption.Yf the Sacrament be but a bare figure : yf yt be but **F**
bread and wine,yt ys not then our price,yt ys not then our redempcion as
S.Augustine saieth yt ys. By this then yt ys manifest that the bodie and
blood of Chryst in the Sacrament being our price and redempcion, be the
figures of the same bodie and blood of Chryst crucified for our redemptiō.
And therfor yt maie rightly be called both the bodie of Chryst, and the figure of the bodie of Chryste.

　Wherunto agreably saieth *Theophilact*:*Attende quòd panis qui à nobis in myste-*
rijs manducatur,non est tantùm figuratio quædam carnis Domini ,sed ipsa caro Domini.
Note or take head that the bread, whiche ys eaten of vs in the mysteries,
ys not onely a certain figure of the flesh of our Lorde,but the flesh yt self of
our Lorde.　Thus by this declaracion of sainct *Augustine* and *Theophilact*
ye maie clerely see and perceaue , the right and true vnderstanding of
Tertullian,who according to the Chrystian and catholique faith taught that
Chryste made the bread hys bodie,wherby he conuinceth hys Aduersarie
Marcion.And after to his farder confutacion(*for that a figure, must nedes be a fi-*
gure of a bodie) he saieth also that yt ys the figure of Chrystes bodie, **G**
and so confesseth bothe the verie bodie,and the figure of the bodie.

In 6.Ioan.
Bread of
the Sacra.
verie flesh
A plain
saing for
M. Iuell.

　This vnderstanding of *Tertullian* must nedes be good and vpright. For
after this maner he agreeth with himself both in this place and other , as
wher he saieth:*Caro corpore & sanguine Christi vescitur , vt anima de Deo saginetur.*
The flesh eateth the bodie and bloode of Chryst, that the soule maie be
made fatte with God.Wher in plain woordes he saieth that man,not by spiritte,but by his flesh eateth,not a peice of bread a signe or figure onely of
Chrystes bodie,but yt eateth Chrystes verie bodie and bloode yt self. After this vnderstanding also he agreeth with sainct *Augustine* , and *Theophilact*,
and other holy Fathers, as partely ye haue before hearde , and shall herafter
plentifullie heare.And thus vnderstanded he agreeth to be shorte with the
wholl catholique Churche,which alwaies hath and doth teache the bodie
of Chryst both to be a figure,and the thing yt self in veritie. Wherfore neither *Tertullian*,neither sainct Augustine in these places alleaged neither a-
gainst *Amantus*, be either refused or denied but accepted and embraced. **H**
For the Churche doth acknoledge as moche as they saie, and they with the
Churche doe acknowledge the Sacrament to be bothe.

Li . de re-
sur.carnis.
A plain sa-
ing for the
Proclamer

　　　　　　　　　　　　　　　　　　　　　　　　　　　　　　But

A　But let the Aduersarie bringe but one auncient authour that saieth as he doeth, that yt ys *figura tantùm*. onely a figure, and therwith saieth as he dothe that the reall and veric bodie of Chryst ys not in the Sacrament, and then I will saie he hath doen somwhat. Hetherto all they haue doen nothing to effecte to prooue their matter, but onely made some cowntenance and ap-parance in woordes to deceaue the people, and to plucke them from the catholique faith. For wher their doctrine ys that the Sacrament ys a figure onelie, when they reade this woorde (*figura*) in *Tertullian*, S. *Augustine*, or anie other authour they runne awaie with yt, and violentlie wrest yt ma-king their auditorie beleue, that the authour saie as they saie. And that ys false. For the authours saie no not one of them that yt ys onely a figure, which ys the thing that the Aduersarie must prooue, and that shal he neuer doe.

No catholi-ke authour saieth that the Sacr. ys onelie a fi-gure.

　Wherfor Reader, looke to thy self, and be not deceaued, marke well whiche parte saieth as *Tertullian* saieth, and folowe that parte. *Tertullian* sa-ieth, that the breade ys made the bodie of Chryst, so saieth the catholique, B　so saieth the holie Churche, but that denieth the Aduersarie. *Tertullian* saieth that yt ys a figure of the bodie of Chryst, so saieth the catholique, so saieth the holie Churche, so after a maner saieth the Aduersarie, but the maner ys soche, that though in the woorde (*Figure*) yt seemeth so to saie, and to haue agreemēt with *Tertullian*: yet in sense yt denieth the wholl. For neither dothe the Aduersarie agree vpon the thing that ys the figure, neither dothe he saie as *Tertullian* dothe saie, that yt ys a figure, but with an exclusuie, that yt ys a figure onely, which as yt ys more then *Tertullian* saieth : so yt ys more then ys true. and thus trusting ye clerely, and fullie perceaue, who agreeth and who dissenteth from this auncient Father of the primitiue Church, I en-de with him, and proceade to heare other,

THE FIFTETH CHAP. ABIDETH IN THE EX-
position of the same woordes by S. Cyprian, and Athanasius.

C　Ot long after *Tertullian* was S. Cyprian, who being a senior in Chrystes schoole, and an auncient in his Parliament house, will shewe vs the faith taught and continued in that schoole, and the trueth enacted and receaued in that Parliament house: Thus he writeth : *Significata olim à tempore Melchisedech prodeunt sa-cramenta, & filiis Abrahæ, facientibus opera eius, summus sacerdos panē profert & vinū Hoc est* (inquit) *corpus meum &c.* The sacramentes signified long agon frō the time of Melchisedech come nowe abroade, and the high preist to the childe-ren of Abraham doinge his workes, bringeth furth bread and wine. *This* (*saieth he*) *ys my bodie*. They had eaten of the same bread after the visible for-me, but before those woordes, that cōmon meate was onely meate to nou-rishe the bodie, and ministred the helpe of the corporall life. But after that our Lorde had saied : *Doe this in my remembrance, This ys my flesh, and this ys my bloode* : As often as yt ys doen with these woordes, and this faith, that sub-stanciall bread and cuppe consecrated by the solemne benediction doth pro-fitte to the health and life of the wholl man, being both a medicen and a sa-crifice, to heall infirmities, and to pourge iniquities. Thus he.

Cypry. de cæna Dom, vide sup. li. 1.cap. 29.

D　What sense the woordes of Chrystes supper haue, this holy Ciprian dothe manifestlie declare, who rehersing them saieth : *but after that our Lorde had saied : This doe in the remembrance of me : This ys my flesh, and this ys my bloode, that substanciall bread and cuppe consecrated doth profitte the wholl man , that ys , both the bodie and soule of man, for so moche as yt ys a medicen to heale the infirmities of them,* and a sacrifice to pourge their iniquities. In the Sacrament after the woordes of Chryst spoken what can be saied to be , that profiteth both bodie and soule, and ys a medicen and also a sacrifice, what I saie, can ther ells be that shoulde be these great workes but the bodie and blode of Chryste? Yt ys that bodie that ys our medicen: yt ys that bodie that ys our sacrifice. Wherfore S. Cyprian mening that after the woordes of our Lorde, that bodie and blode ys in the Sacramēt, inuinciblie proueth againſt the proclamer the presence of Chryſtes bodie and that the woordes of our Lorde be not to be vnderſtand figuratiuely, but proprely in their owne sense.

S. Cyprian saing that the bread and cuppe after the cōsecraciō, ys a medicine to heal infir. and a sacrifice to pourge iniquit. proueth inuincible the reall presence of Chryſts bodie.

And this ys not to be ouerpaſſed, what differēce this authour maketh be twixt the cōdicion of the bread before the words of Chryſt spokē, ād after the woords. *Before the woordes* (saieth he) *yt ys cōmon meate meet onelie to nourish the bodie, but after the woordes yt ys, as ye haue hearde, profitable both for bodie and soule:*

Benefites at tributed to the Sacra.

This alſo ys to be noted that this authour speaking of theſe great benefittes doth not attribute thē to faithe, nor to the vertue of the paſſiō of Chryſte, nor to the ſpirituall bodie of Chryſt, or receipt of that (although all theſe be neceſſarie for that withoute thē the befittes before mēcioned cā not be obteined) but dothe attribute thē to the ſame meat nowe in the Sacrament after conſecraciō, which before the conſecracion was corporal meate. Owre faith, the vertue, grace, or meritte of Chryſtes paſſiō were neuer corporall meate, wherfore this authour speaketh not of thē . And therfore we maie conclude, that yt ys the bodie of Chryſt into whoſe ſubſtance, the ſubſtāce of breade that before Chriſtes woordes was able onelie to ſuſtein the bodie nowe after the wordes ys turned into the ſubſtāce of Chryſt, whiche ys able to comforte both bodie and soule, and ys become the ſubſtanciall breade, geuing and mainteining our ſubſtāciall life, whiche ys the euerlaſting life.

In the firſt booke c.29.

Of this place of S. Ciprian, foraſmoche as I haue more at large ſpoken in the opening of the figure of Melchiſedech, I ſhall deſire the reader, if he wol de ſee what maie be more ſaied vpon yt, to reſort thither , wher, I truſt, he ſhall finde matter to the better opening of this place.

But yet that yt maie be fullie perceaued that S. Cyprian in this place meneth as ys ſaied, that the verie bodie of Chryſt ys in the Sacrament, and that ſoche was his faith, and that Chryſt ſo taught, and his ſchoole ſo learned: we will heare an other teſtimonie of the ſame S . Cyprian in the ſame treactice, that this ſentēce before alleaged ys in , which ys this. *Noua eſt huius Sacramēti doctrina, & ſcholæ euangelicæ hoc primū magiſteriū portulerunt, & doctore Chriſto primū hæc mūdo innotuit diſciplina, vt biberēt ſanguinē chriſtiani, cuius eſum legis antiquæ authoritas diſtrictiſßimè interdicit. Lex quippe eſu ſanguinis prohibet: Euangeliū præcipit vt bibatur. In quibus mādatis hoc maximè diſcernere debet chriſtiana Religio, quòd ſanguis animaliū, à ſanguine Chricti per omnia differens, tēporalis tantū habet viuificationis effectū, & vita eorum finem habet ſine reuocacione conſtitutū.* The doctrine of this Sacrament ys newe, and the euangelicall ſchooles firſt brought furth this maner of teaching, and Chryſt being the teacher this learning firſt was knowen to the worlde, that chryſtian men ſhoulde drinke bloode, the eating wherof the authoritie of the olde lawe did moſt ſtrictlie forbidde . The Lawe for biddeth the eating of bloode : The Goſpell commaundeth that yt be dronke. In whiche commaundementes this moſt cheiſtie aught the chryſtian religion to diſcerne that the bloode of beaſtes by all means differinge from the blode of Chryſt hath onely the effect of temporall releif, and

Cypr. de cæna. Dom. A plain place for M. Iuell.

The lawe dyd forbidde the eating of blood, the Goſpell cōmaundeth yt.

the

E

F

G

H

A the life of them hath an ende appoincted withoute reuocacion . Thus he.

I wishe the (*gentle reader*) againft the blafphemies of the Aduerfaries, to weigh well euery parte of this faing of S. Cyprian. The Aduerfarie faieth that the doctrine of the Sacrament, ys the Papiftes diuife, and their inuencion : But S. Cyprian teacheth vs firft that yt ys a newe doctrine, he teacheth vs in what fchoole yt was firft, taught. *In the fchoole* (faieth he) *of the Gofpell*, he teacheth vs who was the fchoole mafter, who was the firft teacher of yt, *Chryft* (faieth he) *was the firft teacher of yt, he firft did notifie yt to the worlde.* But if ye afke what ys this newe doctrine: He faieth that yt ys a newe doctrine of the Sacrament that chryftian men fhoulde drinke bloode. Yf ye proceade and afke whether they muft drinke verie blood: He faieth verie blood. For yt ys foche bloode as the lawe did forbidde to be eaten. And that affuredlie was verie bloode. Wherfore this ys verie bloode. Yf ye queftion farder, if the chryftians muft drinke verie bloode, whofe bloode muft they drinke? He anfwereth, Chryftes bloode, as in the comparifon of the com-

Doctrine of the real prefence howe yt ys called newe.

B maundementes of the two lawes (the olde lawe forbidding bloode, the newe lawe commaunding bloode) yt ys euident, to be feen, that he faieth newe lawe commaundeth the bloode of Chryft to be dronke.

In this then ye maie perceaue that the doctrine of the prefence of Chryftes bodie and blood in the Sacrament ād the real receipt of the fame ys not the inuencion or deuife of the Papiftes, but yt ys as this holie Father and martir of Chryfte, and therfore a good fcholer of Chryft, faieth, who knewe the learning of his mafter wel, yt ys faieth he, the doctrine of Chryfte, yt ys his ordeinance, yt ys his inuencion, diuife, and inftitucion. Wherfore they maie bafhe, and be a fhamed, yea they maie tremble for feare to fee them felues fallen into that impietie, that the Iewes were, who feinge Chryfte cafting oute the dumbe fpiritte oute of a man, malicioufelie and wickedlie afcribed the miraculoufe worke to *Belzebub*, whiche was doen by the power of God in Chryft: So they wickedly afcribe this inftitucion of the Sacramét this doctrine of the prefence of Chryftes bodie and bloode in the fame (whiche ys the miraculoufe worke of God) to the Papiftes, at yt pleafeth

Doctrin of the real prefence ys no new inuention of the Papiftes.

Luc. 11.

C them to terme them. But here maie ye learn that Chryft ys the firft teacher of this doctrine. And this fhall we make more euidentlie to appeare to yowe by the woordes of this authour.

And firft where he faieth, that the doctrine of the Sacrament ys newe This doth plainly and ftronglie reiecte the figure and Tropes of the Aduerfaties from the Sacrament. For if the Sacrament be but the figure and not the thing : howe ys yt, or howe can yt be a newe doctrine? To offre bread and wine as figures of Chryfte, we finde Melchifedech in the lawe of nature to haue fo doen. That the people of the Iewes did eate Manna, and breade from heauen, and dranke the water of the rocke, as figures of Chryftes bodie and blood, yt ys more manifeft , then can be denied . The two tenth deales of fine flower made in cakes, and the wine alfo that was offred for a drinke offring, ftinted in Leuiticus by the meafure of a fourt deale of an hyn were offred as figures of Chryfts bodie and bloode, as *Ifichius* witneffeth, fo that to haue bread and wine, or to eate and drinke foche thinges as figures of Chryftes bodie and bloode, yt ys no newe doctrine. Yt was in the lawe

Gen. 14.
Exod. 16.
1. Cor. 10.

Li.6.ca.23

D of nature, yt was in the lawe of Moifes. Wherfore yt can not be a newe doctrine. The newe doctrine then ys to receaue the verie thing of thefe figures verilie, reallie, and prefentlie, whiche in dede ys a newe doctrine, neuer taught to be vfed and parctifed, before Chryft taught yt, yea and com-

maunded

maunded yt. When and wher did he teache yt? Before his pafsion at his **E**
laft fupper, and (*as Cyprian termeth yt*) in the fchoole of the Gofpell. Wher in
the Gofpell then finde we this new doctrine or commaundement? The
doctrine we finde (as before ys declared) in the fixt of S.Iohn. *Panis quem ego*
dabo, caro mea eft, quam dabo pro mundi vita. The breade, that I will geue yowe,
ys my flefh, whiche I will geue for the life of the worlde. And that which fo
loweth in the fame chapter concerning the Sacrament.

　　The commaundement we finde in the three other Euangeliftes and in S.
Paule. *Accipite, & comedite, hoc eft corpus meum. Bibite ex hoc omnes. Hic eft calix*
Matth.26 *fanguinis mei.* Take and eate. This ys my bodie, drinke ye all of this, This ys the
Mar. 14. cuppe of my bloode. Cyprian faieth that Chryft firft taught that men fhoul
Luc.22. de drinke bloode, and that the fchoole of the Gofpell did firft fett yt furth,
1.Cor. 11. and alfo the Gofpell did commaunde yt. But in all the Gofpell we finde no
foche commaundement, but this that ys nowe faied. Wherfor thefe woordes
doe commaunde vs to drinke the verie bloode of Chryft, and not the onely
figure of yt. Whiche being fo yt prooueth the verie reall prefence of Chry- **F**
ftes bodie and bloode in the Sacrament, and thefe commaundements in
the woordes of Chryftes fupper, to be literall and not tropicall.

　　Nowe foloweth *Athanafius*, whome for that he was not long after Cyprian, I haue coopled with the fame, as a famoufe auncient father of the greke
Athanafi- churche, with an holie famoufe martir of the Latin church. Thus writeth
us li. de fide *Athanafius. Corpus eft ergo cui dicit: Sede à dextris meis. Cuius etiam fuit inimicus Dia-*
vt citatur *bolus, cum malis poteftatibus, & Iudæi, & Greci, per quod corpus Pontifex & Apofto-*
à Theodo- *lus fuit & dictus eft, per id quod tradidit nobis myfterium dicens: Hoc eft corpus meum,*
ret.Dialo- *quod pro Vobis frangitur. Et fanguis noui teftamenti non veteris, qui pro vobis effunditur*
go 2.Incon- *&c.* Yt ys therfore a bodie to the which he faied: *Sitte on my right hande,* whofe
fufns. enemie was the Deuell, with the euell powers and the Iewes, and the grekes. By whiche bodie he both was in dede, and was called an high preift,
and an Apoftle, by that mifterie that he deliuered vs faing: *This ys my bodie,*
which ys broken for yowe, and the bloode of the newe Teftament, not of
the olde, whiche ys fhed for yowe. The Godheade hath neither bodie nor **G**
bloode, but man, which he did take of the virgen Mary.

　　Theodorete, who in his fecond dialoge laboureth to prooue two diftincted natures without confufion, that ys, the nature of God and the nature of
man, eche of them full and perfight ioined, but not commixed in vnitie of
perfon in Chryft owre fauiour, alleageth this faing of *Athanafius*, wher in
Athanafius touching both natures, doth moft abide to prooue the nature of
man to remain in Chryft. And to prooue that, he proueth that Chryft had
a verie mans bodie, and that by two argumentes: The firft ys that where
Dauid in the pfalme prophecied that Chryft fhoulde be exalted to fitte on
the right hand of God the Father, and therfor faied: *The Lorde faied to my Lor-*
de, fitte thowe on my right hand. This coulde not be faied but to a bodie. But
Chryft as God, had neither bodie nor bloode. Wherfore yt ys fpoken to
Chryft as man. The other argument ys after this forte Chryft by that that
he deliuered vnto vs the mifterie of his bodie and bloode, was in dede, and
fo alfo was called an high preift. But in the deliuering of this mifterie he faied
This ys my bodie, This ys my bloode. And the Godhead of Chryft hath neither **H**
bodie nor bloode: Wherfor he fpake hy his verie mãheade which had both
bodie and bloode) *This ys my bodie: This ys my bloode.*

　　In both thefe argumentes, this ys principallie entended, to prooue
Chryft a verie man by that that he had a verie bodie. Nowe to our pourpofe

A　in the feconde argument to proue that he had a bodie, by that that Chryſt faied: *This ys my bodie*: doth yt not proue that this authour vnderſtãdeth Chryſte to haue ſpoken this by his very bodie? yf the ſhoulde not ſo doe, what ſhoulde yt helpe his matter that he entendeth to prooue, to bring in this ſaing of Chryſt : *This ys my bodie*, yf yt be not ſpoken of his bodie?

To prooue that this auhour, dothe ſo vnderſtande this place of Chryſt, as ſpoken of his verie bodie this maketh yt moſt certen, and yt maie not be againſt ſaied. S. Auguſtine faieth, and yt ys a rule among all the learned diuines , that in the diſputacion of matters of faithe all ſcriptures muſt be alleaged in their literall ſenſe. Foraſmoche then as this ſcripture ys alleaged in the diſputacion of an highe matter of faithe (as ye haue hearde) yt muſt be taken ãd vnderſtãded in the literal ſenſe. The woords are takē to prooue that Chryſt had a verie bodie . Wherfore in the literall ſenſe they are ſpoken, and vnderſtand of his verie bodie. Thus ye maie perceaue that figures ſignes, tokens, and tropes, are not admitted by this authour to geue vs the true ſenſe and mening of theſe woordes.

Scriptures muſt be alleaged in their literal ſenſe in matters of faith

B　And thus moche maie we here note (as I haue before touched) that the beleif of the preſence of Chryſtes verie bodie in the Sacrament was in the auncient churche of Chryſte ſo faithfullie receaued, ſo generallie accepted, ſo highlie eſteemed, that the learned Fathers grownded their argumetes againſt heretikes vpon the matter of the Sacrament, as vpon a principle of faith. This haue yowe ſeen in *Irenæus* : This haue yowe ſeen in *Tertullian*: This ſame ye ſee in *Athanaſius* . Whiche as yt aught to be an occaſion of an aſſured ſtaie, and confirmacion of our faithe in the ſame matter in the Sacrament : ſo wiſhe I that yt maie be a reuocacion of the Proclamer, and all other walking in erroure with him to the verie faith of the Sacrament, that Chryſt maie by the mouthe of all that profeſſe his name, be in his Sacramentes praiſed and magnified , euen according to his holie will and pleaſure.

THE ONE AND FITITETH CHAP. SHEWETH
C
the minde of Iuuencus, and Euſeb. Emiſen vpon the woordes of Chryſt.

Monge the Latines that doe open vnto vs the vnderſtanding of the woordes of Chryſtes ſupper, the next that I finde to S. Ciprian ys *Iuuencus* the preiſt, a chryſtian Poete in Spain , who in Verſe geueth a notable and a plain vnderſtandinge of Chryſtes woordes . He ys verie auncient ; he did write a good nombre of yeares aboue xii hundreth yeares agone. Thus faieth he.

Iuuencus lib.4. Euangelice hiſtor.

> *Hæc vbi dicta dedit, palmis ſibi frangere panem,*
> *Diuiſumque dehinc tradit ſanctumque precatus,*
> *Diſcipulos docuit proprium ſe tradere corpus.*
> *Hinc calicem ſumit Dominus, vinoque repletum*
> *Gratis ſanctificat verbis, potumque miniſtrat.*
> *Edocuitque ſuum ſe diuiſiſſe cruorem.*
> *Atque ait, hic ſanguis populi delicta remittet.*
> *Hunc potate meum &c.*

D　Of theſe verſeis, this maie be the ſenſe in engliſh . When Chryſte had thus ſaied, he tooke bread in his handes, and when he had geuen thankes, he diuided yt to his Diſciples, and taught them, that he deliuered vnto thē

Chryſt deliuered to his Apoſtles his own bodie.

　　　　　　　　　　　　　　　　　his

his owne bodie. And after that our Lorde tooke the cuppe filled with wine **E**
he fanctifieth yt with thankes geuing, and geueth yt to them to drinke, and
teacheth them that he hath geuen them his blood, and faieth: *This bloode shall
remitte the Sinnes of the people. Drinke ye this my bloode &c.*

This Authour fetting furth the hiftorie of the Gofpell in verfe, and therwith oftentimes geuing vs with the hiftorie the fenfe and vnderftanding of
yt, dothe euen fo here . For he dothe not onely faie that Chryft faied,
Thys ys my bodie , but geueth the vnderftanding of yt, faing, *that Chryft taught
his Apoftles that he deliuered vnto them his owne bodie*. In whiche maner of fpeache
note this alfo, that he faieth not onelie, that Chryft deliuered them his
bodie : But addeth this woorde (*owne*) and faieth that he taught them, that
he deliuered to them his owne bodie. Whiche maner of fpeach hath foche
force and ftrenght with yt, that as yt declareth the catholique faith and geueth great teftimonie of the fame : fo yt beateth and driueth awaie the wicked glofe of onely figures and fignes, inuented by the Aduerfaries to peruert the trueth. For what more plain teftimonie wolde we defire for the vn- **F**

A plain fa-
ing for the
Procla.

derftanding of Chryftes woordes, then to faie, that when Chryft faieth: *Take
eate, this ys my bodie, that he taught his Apoftles, that he gaue them his owne* bodie?
Thus maie yow fee that for the catholique faith yow haue plain teftimonie,
for the herefie of the Aduerfarie, yow haue not one woorde . For I affure
yowe of this, as partlie before ys faied, ther ys not one catholique writer,
neither olde nor yong, from Chryft to *Berengarius* that euer taught or wrote
that the Sacrament ys onely a figure or figne of the bodie of Chryft. And
therfor (*Reader*) looke to thie felf, be not caried awaie from Chryftes faith
with onely bragges and glofing woordes voide of all good proofe. But raither fettle thy felf wher thowe findeft the trueth fett furth to thee with fimplicitie and plainneffe commended with moche proofe and authoritie.

But hauing yet manie mo wittneffes let me haft me to bring him, that ys
appoincted to be this authours yockfelowe, to declare the continuance of
the vnderftanding of Chryftes woordes in the greke churche, as the other
hath doen in the latin churche. This ys *Eufebius Emifenus*, who by the fuppta- **G**
cion of learned men, liued in the fame time that *Iuuencus* did . He writeth
thus : *Recedat omne infidelitatis ambiguum, quoniam quidem qui author eft muneris, ipfe
eft etiam teftis veritatis. Nam inuifibilis facerdos vifibiles creaturas in fubftantiam corporis & fanguinis fui verbo fuo, fecreta poteftate conuertit, ita dicens : Hoc eft corpus meū.*

Eufeb.
Emif. Ho-
mil. 5 . Pa.
Vifible bre
ad and wi-
ne turned
into the fub
ftance of
the bodie
and blood
of Chryft

Et fanctificatione repetita, Accipite, & bibite, ait, Hic eft fangnis meus. Let all doubte of infidelitie or vnbeleif departe. For truly he that ys the authour of the
gifte, he alfo ys the wittneffe of the trueth. For the inuifible preift by his fecret power, dothe with his woorde conuert or *turne the vifible creatures into the
fubftance of his bodie and bloode*, faing thus: *Take and eate, This ys my bodie.* and the
fanctificacion repeted : *Take and drinke* (faieth he) *this ys my bloode,*

In this faing of *Eufebius* ther ys no foche darke maner of fpeache that the
reader nede to doubte of the true prefence of Chryfte in the Sacrament, or
howe to vnderftand the woordes of Chryftes fupper, feing that he fo plainlie faieth, that Chryfte (whom he calleth the inuinfible preift) with his po-

Reall pre-
fence and
tranfubftā-
tiaciō, plain
lie auouc-
hed by En
feb. Emis.

wer and woorde, faing *This ys my bodie, This ys my bloode,* turneth the vifible
creatures of bread and wine into the fubftance of his bodie and bloode. Yf **H**
they be turned into the fubftance of his bodie and bloode, as by the teftimonie of this authour they trulie be, then thefe woordes *Corpus, & fanguis,*
bodie and blode, in the fainges of Chryft doe not fignifie the figures of the
bodie and bloode of Chryft, but the fubftance of the bodie and bloode of
　　　　　　　　　　　　　　　　　　　　　　　　　　　　　Chryfte

A Chryſte,into which ſubſtance to make the bodie and blood verilie preſent, the creatures of bread and wine be turned,and ſo Chryſt ſaing,*This ys my bo-die,this ys my blood*:yt ys aſmoch as he had ſaied,This ys the ſubſtāce of my bo die,this ys the ſubſtance of my blood. This doctrine ys ſo certen,ſo ſure,and ſo true,that this authour gaue exhortaciō and admoniciō in the beginning of his ſaing,that in this matter ther ſhould be no doubte,all vnbeleiſe ſhould departe,and ſo faithfullie to beleue Chryſtes woordes,that foraſmoch as he ys the authour of all trueth,and ſaieth:*This ys my bodie,This ys my blood*,vndoub tedly ſo to take yt.

Beſide this doctrine of faith of the preſence of Chryſtes verie ſubſtanciall bodie and blood in the Sacrament,this authour alſo teacheth the meā how God woorketh yt,and ſaieth,that yt ys doen *by turning the creatures of bread and wine into the ſubſtance of the bodie and blood of Chryſt*,which turning or chaunging of one ſubſtance into an other,as the holy Fathers do diuerſly terme, ſo-me of thē calling yt a conuerſion or turning,ſome of thē mutaciō or chāu-

B ging,ſome communicacion or tranſlacion,ſome tranſelementaciō:ſome trāſ mutacion:ſo the Church fullie and liuelie to expreſſe the thing that ys doen, and therby the better to repell the hereſies that haue riſen and encōbred the Church ſince the time of *Berengarius*,hath tearmed yt *Tranſubſtanciatōn*,which terme importeth no more in this matter,then tranſmutacion,or tranſelemen tacion,but yt ſowndeth and openeth the thing that yt ſignifieth more liue-lie, and ſuffreth notthe heretiques to wreſt yt as they doe the other. Which ys the cauſe that manie be ſo greuouſlie offēded with the terme.But bicauſe theProclamer doth lightlie ouerpaſſe yt I will not tarie lōg vpō yt.But in the allegaciō of theFathers,as thei ſhal make mēciō of it,ſo ſhal I breleiſlie not it.

And yet that the reader ſhall not thinke that that matter ys ſo barren,that nothing can be ſaied of yt,or being deſielrouſe to learn ſhould be fruſtrate of his deſire,ād expectaciō.I ſhall ſomewhat here ſaie of yt,deſiering withal that as they do read the doctours that ſhall be hereafter alleaged , they will note in them what they ſhall finde, as therunto I ſhall geue thē occaſion in euerie one that doth ſpeake of this matter.And for that we haue taken occa-

C ſiō of this authours woordes to ſpeake of yt,we wil firſt heare what he ſaieth farder of yt,that yt maie fullie appeare to the reader, that yt ys not reputed of him as a doubtful matter,but as a certen and ſubſtācial ſure matter.Wher fore let him vnderſtand that to the more full declaracion of this that ys be-fore ſaied, the authour immediatelie addeth this that foloweth : *Ergo vt ad nutū Domini præcipientis,repentè ex nihilo ſubſtiterint alta cœlorum,profunda flucluū,va ſta terrarum:ita pari potentia in ſpiritualibus Sacramentis,verbo præbetur virtus & rei ſeruit effectus.Quanta itaque,& quàm celebranda vis diuinæ benedictionis operetur , & quomodò tibi nouū & impoſsibile videri non debeat, quòd in Chriſti ſubſtantiam terrena & mortalia cōmutantur,teipſum,qui iam in Chriſto es regeneratus,interroga.*Therfor as at the will of our Lord cōmaunding,ſodenlie of nothing, the heightes of the heauens,the deapths of the waters,the greatneſſe of the earth were in ſubſtā ciall being:Euen ſo in the ſpirituall Sacramentes vnto the woorde ys geuen vertue or power, and the effect ys brought to paſſe.Therfore how great and notable things,the power of the diuine benediction maie woork,and howe yt ſhould not ſeme to thee as newe or impoſſible that earthlie and mortall

D things are cōmuted or chāuged into the ſubſtāce of Chryſt,aske of thy ſelf, who art now regenerate inChryſt.Thus *Euſebius*.Who,to proue that,which he had before ſaied,that the viſible creaturs of bread ād wine are turned into the ſubſtāce of the bodie ād blood ofChryſt,bringeth this argumēt:that as at

Tranſub-ſtanciaciōn treactedof.

Euſeb. E-miſſ. ibid.

How the bread and wine betur ned into the bodie ād blood, &c.

as the cōmaundement of God hys onelie woord, soden̄lie the heaues, the wa- E
ters, and the wholl worlde was made of nothing: So by like power he woorketh in the Sacrament, to make the substance of his bodie and blood of the
substance of the bread and wine.

An other argument he bringeth by the chaunge that God maketh of a
man in Baptisme, that he that was a straunger and a banished mā from God,
yea and dead before God, sodenly ys reuiued, and of a banished man ys
made a frende, and of a straunger ys made an adoptiue Sonne of God. Wher
by he wolde not haue yt thought impossible, but that earthlie and mortal
thinges, as the bread and wine in the Sacrament, maie be and are chaunged
into the substance of Chryst.

Euseb. ibid

In the same homelie to this pourpose also he maketh this perswasion: *Nec*
dubitet quispiam primarias creaturas nutu diuinæ potētiæ, præsentia summæ maiestatis in do
minici corporis posse transire naturā, cùm ipsum hominem videat artificio cœlestis misericor-
diæ Chrysti corpus effectum. Neither let anie man doubte that by the commaun-

Chaunge of
the bread
and wine
into the bo-
die &c. ys
not to be
doubted of

dement of the diuine power by the presence of his high maiestie, the former
creatures (*mening bread and wine*) can passe or be chaunged into the nature of
the bodie of our Lordes bodie, seing that he maie see man himself by the F
workmanshippe of the heauenlie mercie, made the bodie of Chryst.

Eused ibid.

And ther again yt foloweth immediatelie: *Sicut autē quicunque ad fidē Chri-*
sti veniens ante verba Baptismi adhuc in vinculo est veteris debiti, ijs verò memoratis, mox
exuitur omni fece peccati: ita quādo benedicendæ verbis cœlestibus creaturæ sacris altaribus
imponuntur, antequàm inuocacione summi nominis consecrentur, substantia est illic panis &
vini, post verba autē Chrysti, corpus & sanguis Chrysti. Quid autē mirū est, si ea quæ po-
tuit verbo creare, verbo possit creata conuertere? As anie mā coming to the faith of

Before the
woordes of
Chryst ther
ys the sub-
stance of
bread, af-
ter, the bo-
die of
Chryst, a
plain saing
for M. Iuel

Chryst, before the woords of Baptisme ys yet in the bād of the old debt, but
as soen as they be spoke furthwith he ys deliuered frō al filth of sinne: Euen
so when the creatures are sett vpō the holie altars to be blessed with the hea
uely woords, before they be cōsecrated with the inuocaciō of the most high
name, ther ys the substāce of bread ād wine: but after the woords of Chryst,
the bodie ād blood of Chryst. What woōder ys yt, if he that could create
these things with his woord, cā now being created turn thē with his woord.

And he addeth: *Imo iā videtur minoris esse miraculi, si id quod ex nihilo agnoscitur cō*
didisse, iam conditū in melius valeat cōmutare. Yea raither yt semeth to be a lesse mi- G
racle, if that, that he ys knowen to haue made of nothing, he can now when
yt ys made chaunge yt into a better thing. Thus moch Eusebius. Whome ye
see by diuerse goodly examples, and meās teaching the presence of Chrysts
bodie in the Sacrament, by the turning or chaunging of the bread and wine
into the substance and nature of the bodie and blood of Chryst.

But yt shall doo well to heare some other besides him, what testimonie they
geue in this matter, that therbie the reader maie haue more full instruction,

Greg. Nis-
se. sermone
cathechit.
de diuinis
sacramen,

Among these we wil first heare Gregory Nissen the brother of Basil, who sai
eth thus: *Sicut autē qui panē videt, quodāmodò corpus videt humanū, quoniā panis in cor-*
pore existens corpus euadit: ita diuinū illud corpus, panis nutrimentū accipiēs, idē quodāmmo-
dò erat cum illo cibo (vt diximus) in eius naturā immutato. Quod enim cuiusque carnis pro-
prium est, id etiam illi conuenisse confitemur.　Nam & corpus illud pane sustentabatur,
corpus autem, propterea quod Deus Verbum in illo habitauit, diuinam obtinuit dignitatem.
Quamobrē rectè nunc etiam Dei verbo sanctificatum panē, in Dei Verbi corpus, credimus im H
mutari. As he that seeth bread, in a maner seeth the bodie of a mā, for bread be
ing in the bodie becometh a bodie: Euen so that bodie of God taking the
nutriment of bread, was in a maner all one with the same meat that was (as

wc

A we haue faied)chaunged into the nature of his bodie.For that that yspropre
to euery man,that fame do we confeffe to haue apperteined to him. For
that bodie alfo was fufteined with bread,but that bodie , for that God the
Sonne did abide in him,yt obteined the dignitie of God,wherfore nowe alfo doo we very well beleue the bread fanctified by the woord of God,to be
chaunged into the bodie of the Sonne of God.Thus he.

Let not this efcape thee,reader,without diligent note,that this authour
doth not onelie faie that the factifiedbread ys chaûged into the bodie,of the
Sône of God,but he faieth alfo(as yt were in the perfô of the wholChurch)
that we beleue yt fo to be. Wherbie we be aduertifed that,ytys a matter of faith,and not a matter of opiniô.Yt ys not lauful for euery mã to think
what he lift in yt,but yf he will be amôg the faithfull he muft without difcep
tacion humblie accept and embrace what faith commaûdeth to be beleued.
But let vs alfo heare S.Ambrofe,who writeth thus.*Fortè dicas:Aliud video,quo*
modò tu mihi afferis,quòd Chrifti corpus accipiam?& hoc fupereft, vt probemus. Quantis
B *igitur vtimur exemplis,vt probemus hoc non effe quod natura formauit fed quod benedictio*
confecrauit,maioremque vim effe benedictionis,quàm naturæ,quia benedictione natura ipfa
mutatur?Virgam tenebat Moyfes,proiecit eam,& facta eft ferpens.Rurfus apprehendit cau
dam ferpentis,& in virgæ naturã reuertitur.Vides igitur prophetica gratia bis mutatã effe
*naturam ferpentis,& virgæ.*Peraduenture thow maift faie:*I fee an other thing,how*
doeft thow affure me that I take the bodie of Chrift? And this remaineth for vs to
prooue.How manie examples therfore doe we vfe,that we maie prooue that
this ys not yt that nature hath formed,but that the benediction hath confecrated,and that greater ys the power of benediction then of nature. For by
benediction nature yt felf ys chaunged.Moyfes did hold a Rodde, he caft yt
down,ãd it was mad a ferpét.Again he taketh the tail of the ferpét ãd yt retur
neth into the nature of the rod.Thow feeft thê by the grace of the prophet
the nature of the Serpét ãd the rod twice to be chaûged.Hetherto S. Ambr.

After which woordes and diuerfe other examples brought in to prooue
nature in the Sacrament by the benediction to be clean chaunged , he maketh this argument.*Quodfi tantum valuit humana benedictio vt naturam conuerteret,*
C *quid dicimus de ipfa confecratione diuina,vbi verba ipfa Domini faluatoris operantur?Nam*
*facramentû iftud quod accipis Chrifti fermone conficitur.*Yf then the benedictiô of mã
was of fo great power,that yt chaunged nature,what faie we of the verie con
fecracion of God,wher the verie woordes of owre Lord and Sauiour doe
woorke?For this Sacrament which thow receaueft,ys confecrated by the
woorde of Chryft.

Yt were to long to reherfe all the exãples and argumêtes that S. Ambro
fe maketh to prooue this mutacion or chaunge that we fpeak of. Wherfore
but one more of him,and then we will heare fome other one. Thus he maketh an other argument.*De totius mundi operibus legifti , Quia ipfe dixit & facta*
funt,ipfe mandauit & creata funt.Sermo ergo Chrifti qui potuit ex nihilo facere,quod non
erat,non poteft ea quæ funt in id mutare,quod non erant ? Thow haueft readde of he
workes of all the world:that he faied,and they were made,he comaûded ãd
they were created.The woorde of Chryft then that could of nothing make
that that was not,can yt not chaunge thefe things that be into that,that they
were not ? *Non enim minus eft nouas rebus dare, quàm mutare naturas* . Yt ys no
D leffe thing to geue newe natures to thinges , then to chaunge natures.
Thus farre S. AmbrofeWhome for that yt ys manifeft to what pourpofe he
tendeth,namelie to proue the nature of bread and wine after the confecracion to be chaûged into the nature of the bodie and bloode of Chryft,

Kk ii   I will

Tranfubft.
beleued of
the aunciêt
fathers.

Ambr.de
his qui ini-
tian .ca.9.

Benedictiô
what powr
yt hath.

Amb.ibid.

Amb.ibi.

I will not trauaill to open him, but leaue him to the confideracion of the rea　E
der, and heare fome other.

Chryfoftome faieth thus: *Non funt humanæ virtutis hæc opera. Qui tunc ifta in illa*
Homil. 83.
in Matth. *cæna conferit, ipfe nunc quoque operatur, ipfe perficit. Miniftrorum nos ordinem tenemus
Qui verò hæc fanctificat, & tranfmutat ipfe eft .* Thefe workes be not the workes
of mans power. He that then in that fupper made or confecrated thefe thinges, he now alfo woorketh, he perfecteth yt, we are in the place of mynifters,
but yt ys he that doth fanctifie and tranfmute thefe thinges. Thus of Chryfo
ftom we learn alfo that in the Supper of Chryft the bread and wine are fanctified and tranfmuted, and that by the power of Chryft, who fanctified and
tranfmuted them in that fupper, which he did celebrate and kepe for the inftitucion of this, forfomoch as he ys the dooer of this, as he was of that, he ys
the woorker of both.

After Chryfoftome foloweth Cyril, and teacheth vs the fame leffon, faing
Cyrill. ad
Calofirium thus: *Viuificatiuum Dei Verbum vniens feipfum propriæ carni, fecit eam viuificatiuâ. Nunquid igitur, & cùm in nobis vita Dei eft, Dei Verbo in nobis exiftente, viuificatiuum erit no*　F
*ftrum corpus? Sed aliud eft fecundùm participationis habitudinem nos habere in nobis Dei
filium: aliud ipfum fuiffe factum carnem, id eft, corpus fumptum ex alma Virgine proprium
corpus effeciffe. Decebat ergo eum noftris quodammodò vniri corporibus, per facram eius
carnem, & preciofum fanguinem, quæ accipimus in benedictione viuificatiua in pane, & vino. Ne enim horreremus carnem & fanguinem appofita facris altaribus, condefcendens
Deus noftris fragilitatibus, influit oblatis vim vitæ, connertens ea in veritatem propriæ carnis, vt corpus vitæ quafi quoddam femen viuificatiuum inueniatur in nobis .* The liuing
Sonne of God vniting himfelf to his owne flefh, made yt alfo liuing. Nowe
then forafmoche as the life of God ys in vs (the Sonne of God being in vs)
fhall our bodie alfo be able to geue life? But yt ys an other thing for vs to haue the Sonne of God in vs, according to the ordre of participacion : And an
other thing the fame Sonne of God to haue ben made flefh, that ys to faie, to
haue made the bodie taken of the pure Virgen, his own bodie. Yt was nede
full that he fhould be vnited to our bodies by his holie flefh, and precioufe
blood, whiche we take in the liuely benediction in bread ad wine. For lefte　G
we fhould abhorre flefh and blood put vpon the holy altars, God condefcen
ding to our fragilities, he putteth into the thinges offred the power or ftrêgt
of life, turning them into hys very flefh, that the bodie of life maie be fownd
in vs as a quickning feed, able to make vs to liue . Thus moche S. Cyrill.

As of other we haue learned that God by his power doth chaunge the
fubftance of the bread and wine into the fubftance of hys bodie and blood:
fo do we learn of this holie father the caufe whie yt pleafeth God fo to dooe.
*Yt ys (faieth he) that God condefcending to our weakneffe, forafmoche as we abhorre to
eate flefh and drinke blood, yet that he wolde be vnited vnto vs by hys flefh, and therbie
imparte life to vs in maner conuenient for vs, as yt hath by that yt ys vnited to the Sonne
of God, he by hys power woorketh in the bread and wine fo, that he turneth them into hys ve
ry flefh and bloude, that in that maner takinge hys verie flefh and blood, we might haue
them as the feedes of life, and fo growe to life.* Thus breiflie vnderftanding the minde
Euthym. in
26. Matth of Cyril, we go on to *Euthymius,* who faieth in this matter thus: *Quemadmodum
fuper naturaliter affumptam carnem deificauit (fi ita loqui liceat) ita & hæc ineffabiliter
tranfmutat in ipfum viuificum corpus fuum, & in ipfum preciofum fanguinem fuum, & in
gratiam ipforum.* As he fupernaturallie did deifie (yf yt be leefull fo to fpeak)　H
hys affumpted flefh: Euen fo vnfpeakablie doeth he tranfmute or chaunge
thofe things (mening the bread and wine) into hys very liuing bodie, and into hys
verie precioufe blood, and into the grace of them. Thus ye here alfo in this
authour

A   authour yē ſee a tranſmutacion of the bread ād wine into the verie bodie ād verie blood of Chryſt, and that as adſuredlie as he deified the fleſh that he tooke of the Virgen.

A moch like teſtimonie geueth *Remigius* ſaing: *Caro quam Verbum Dei Patris aſſumpſit in ʋtero virginali in ʋnitate ſuæ perſonæ, & panis, qui conſecratur in Eccleſia, ʋnū corpus Chriſti ſunt. Sicut enim illa caro corpus Chriſti eſt: ita iſte panis tranſit in corpus Chriſti, nec ſunt duo corpora, ſed ʋnū corpus.* The fleſh which the Sōne of God the Father tooke in the virgens wombe in the vnitie of hys perſon, and the bread which ys cōſecrated in the Church are one bodie of Chryſt. For as that fleſh ys the bodie of Chryſte: ſo this bread paſſeth or ys chaunged into the bodie of Chryſt, and yet they are not two bodies, but one bodie. Ye ſee yt alſo in this authour teſtified, that the bread conſecrated in the church ys the bodie of Chryſte, ye ſee alſo how yt ys doen. For (ſaieth *Remigius*) the bread goeth, paſſeth or ys chaunged into the bodie of Chryſte, and that as adſuredlie as the fleſh which he tooke of the virgen was hys verie bodie: ſo ys this bread made hys verie bodie. Yf men wolde haue plain ſpeach and plain aſſeuera

B   cion of matters of faith, I iudge this to be ſo plainly ſpokē, that they will not leaue anie man in doubte, but him that will not be reſolued.

The like plaineſſe ſhall ye find in Damaſcen, who ſaieth thus: *Corpus ſecundùm veritatē coniunctū eſt diuinitati, quod ex ſancta virgine corpus eſt, non quòd ipſum corpus aſſumptū ex cœlo deſcenderit, ſed quòd ipſe panis & vinū tranſmutantur in corpus & ſanguinē Dei. Si autē modū requiris, quo pacto id fiat, ſat ſit tibi audire, quoniā per Spiritū ſanctū, quemadmodū ex ſancta Deipara, ſeipſo, & in ſeipſo Dominus carnē ſuſtentauit, & nihil amplius cognoſcimus, quàm quod verbū Dei verū eſt, & efficax & omnipotens, modus autē inſcrutabilis.* That bodie that ys a bodie born of the holie virgē, ys in verie dede ioined to the Godhead, not that that aſſūpted bodie cometh down frō heauē, but that that *bread and wine be tranſmuted into the bodie and blood of God.* Yf thow require the maner how yt ys doen, let yt ſuffice thee to heare that by the holie Goſte, euen as of the holie mother of God our Lorde by himſelf, and in himſelf did make vppe a fleſh, and we know no more then that the woorde of God ys trewe, and effectuouſe, and the maner ys inſcrutable.

C   Thus moch Damaſcen.

This authour doth not onelie teſtifie to vs that the verie bodie ād blood of Chryſt be in the Sacramēt, but alſo opening the maner how yt ys doen, declareth that yt ſhould be ſufficient for vs to vnderſtand that the bread and wine be *tranſmuted* into the bodie and blood of Chryſt by the operacion of the holie Goſte, and that as adſuredly as the ſame bodie was by him framed in the virgens wōbe. And with this (ſaieth he) ſhould we be contented, knowing that the woorde of God ys true, and omnipotent, ād therfor effectuou ſe, adſuredly woorking that that yt ſaieth, though the maner of the doing of yt be inſcrutable.

A teſtimonie not moch vnlike to this geueth alſo *Theophilact*, ſaing in this ma ner. *Non enim dixit Dominus: Panis quē ego dabo figura eſt carnis meæ, ſed caro mea eſt. Transformatur enim arcanis verbis panis ille per myſticā benedictionē, & acceſsionē ſancti Spiritus in carnē Domini. Etne quē conturbet, quòd credendus ſit panis caro. Etenim & in carne ambŭlante Domino, & ex pane alimoniā admittente, panis ille qui manducabatnr, in corpus eius mutabatur, & ſimilis fiebat ſancta eius carni, & in augmentū & ſuſtentationē cōferebat iuxta humanū morē. Igitur & nunc panis in carnē Domini mutatur.* Owr Lord

D   did not ſaie, the bread that I will geue ys a figure of my fleſh, but yt ys my fleſh. For yt ys transformed with the ſecret woords by the myſtical benedic tiō, ād thecoming to of the holie Goſt into the fleſh of our lord, ād let yt not

          Kk   iii   trooble

[margin notes:]

Remig. in 1. Cor. cap. 10.

fleſh of the Sonne of God and the cōſecrated bread one bodie.

Plain ſainges for M. Iuell.

Damaſc. li. 4. ca. 14.

Bread and wine tranſmuted into the bodie and bloode ſo God.

Thinges ſpokē of God muſt be beleued though the maner of doing be vnknowen.

Theoph. in 6. Ioan.

Bread, which Chryſt gaue no figure but fleſh.

trooble anie man that the bread ys to be beleued flefh. For when owre Lord **E**
A plain fa- walked in the flefh, and tooke fuftenaunce of bread, that bread that he too-
ing for M. ke was chaunged into hys bodie, and was made like to his holie flefh, and
Juell. yt gaue encreafe and fuftentacion according to the maner of mans nature.
Therfor now alfo ys the bread chaunged into the flesh of our Lord.

　　Agreablie writeth *Pafchafius*, with whome we will ende, being certen by
the fupputacion of learned men, that he was an hondreth yeares before
Pafchafius *Berengarius*, and therfore before anie publique controuerfie in this matter of
li. de corp. the Sacrament, thus he writeth: *Spiritus fanctus , qui hominem Chriftum in vtero*
& fang. *virginis fine femine creauit, etiam ipfe panis ac vini fubftantiam carnem Chrifti & fangui-*
Dom. *nem inuifibili potentia per facramenti fui fanctificationem operatur, quamuis nec vifu exte-*
riùs , nec guftu faporis comprehendatur. Sed quia fpiritualia funt, fide & intellectu pro cer-
to, ficut veritas prædixit, pleniffimè fumuntur . Quòd in veritate corpus & fanguis fiat
No man *confecratione myfterij, nemo qui verbis diuinis credit, dubitat.*　　The holie Goft who
that bele- withoute feed created the man Chryft in the wombe of the Virgen , he alfo
neth the with his inuifible powre by the fanctificacion of his Sacrament, woorketh
woordes of the Subftance of bread and wine into the flefh and bloode of Chryfte, al-
God doub- though neither by the feight outwardlie, neither by the taft of the fauoure **F**
ieth of the they can be comprehended, but bicaufe they be fpirituall thinges, they are
bodie of by faith and vnderftanding moft fullie of afuertie receaued, as the trueth
Chryft in did before faie yt. *That in verie dede the bodie and blood ys made by confecracion of*
the Sacr. *the myfterie, non man that beleueth the woordes of God doubteth.*

　　Hauing now alleaged a good nõbre to teftifie that the fubftãce of bread ãd
wine be chaũged or turned into the fubftãce of the bodie ãd blood of Chrift
Tranfub- (whiche turning of fubftance into fubftance the Church calleth *Tranfubftanciacõ*) foraf
ftantiaciõ moche as they are plain and euident teftimonies, not encombred with dark
what yt ys. fpeaches, as I content my felf to produce no mo: fo, I truft, thefe maie fuffice
anie man, confidering howe auncient they be, to caufe him to fetle and fixe
How the Fa- his faith in the matter of the Sacrament, and not to wauer or doubte.
thers pro- 　　In thefe doctours and authours this ys to be confidered, that *Eufebius, S.*
ue Tranfub *Gregorie* , and *fainct Ambrofe*, whiche be the firft, doe proue this turning of
ftantiacion fubftances by the great workes of Gods might and power . As *Eufebius* by
to be a mi- the creacion of the high heauens, the huge and depe waters or floudes, the **G**
raculoufe great and vaft earth, and by the great worke of God in chaunging a man
work of God that was deteftable and filthie in finne, that was bonde to the wofull and
Eufe. Emif. miferable bond of damnacion, that was a ftraunger to God, and an enemie,
that God maketh him pure and clean from all that filthineffe , and fetteth
him in the ftate of innocencie, deliuereth him from the bond , and maketh
him free to the kingdom of heauen, and of a ftraunger and an enemie maketh him a domeftical, and a fonne adoptiue.
S. Gregorie 　　S. Gregorie by that worke of God that he caufed bread and other naturall foode to be chaunged into that merueiloufe bodie conceaued by the
holie Goft, and ioined to the Godhead in vnitie of perfon, whiche was not
a common bodie, but the bodie of God. And for that yt hath God abiding
in yt, yt ys exalted to the dignitie of God, which in dede well weighed ys a
merueiloufe worke of God.
S. Ambrofe S. Ambrofe by the chaunging of the nature of a rodde into a Serpẽt, and of
the nature of the ferpent into the rodde again, ãd by a great nõbre of other
works of God. which their maner of teaching geueth vs to vnderftãd, that this **H**
turning or chaũging wrought by God in the Sacr. ys no fmall work, but foch
a worke, as ys and maie be accompted amonge the great workes of God,
　　　　　　　　　　　　　　　　　　　　　　　　　　　　　　among

A among thofe workes that be myraculoufe, that be wonderfull, foche as mans witte and vnderftanding can not atteign vnto but by faith, And ther fore in the Sacrament ys an other maner of worke wrought by God, then to make the bread and wine to be fignes and tokens of remembrance that Chryft hath fuffred an died for vs, for that ys not among the miraculoufe and wonderfull workes of God.

    S. Cyrill in fitting furth this matter findeth, (as yt were) a neceffitie, that this chaunge a fore faied fhoulde be bicaufe the flefh of Chryft, whiche ys hable to geue life to our naturall flefh, might by the receipt of the fame in the Sacrament, make owre mortall bodies to liue, being once raifed vppe to liue euerlaftinglie.   *S.Cyrill.*

    Remigius ioineth the worke of the incarnacion with the worke of God in tranfubftanciacōn. *Damafcen* doth the like, and with all teacheth that as the holie Goft wrought in the wombe of the virgen the incar- nacion of Chryft, by turning her fubftance into the fubftance of Chryft: fo in the Sacrament he woorketh the tranfubftanciacion by turning the   *S. Remig. Damafcen.*

B fubftance of the bread and wine into the fubftance of Chryftes bodie and bloode. *Theophilact* and *Pafchafius* do the like, with other good and ne- ceffarie inftructions.   *Theophil. Pafchaf.*

    Thus ye maie fee that as they teache the thing certenlie to be doen: fo doe they afcribe yt to the power of God, to the woorke of the ho- lie Goft, they fo efteem yt, fo magnifie yt, that they accompt yt and enombre yt among the great and miraculoufe workes of God. As meruei- loufe and miraculoufe yt ys in dede, that the fubftances of bread and wine fhoulde be turned into the fubftance of the bodie and bloode of the Sonne of God.

    But to appoint a thing to be a figure, to be a fign or token of remembrāce ther neadeth not foch fpeciall power of God, nor foch fpecial worke of the holie Goft. For manie thinges haue ben appoincted to be fignes and tokens of remembrance of Gods benefittes, whiche the writers and learned men did neuer accōpte among the miraculoufe and wonderfull workes of God.   *Appoin- ting of figu res ys no fpe ciall mira- culoufe wor ke of God.*

C As the twelue ftones whiche God commaunded *Iofue* that people fhoul- de laie in an heape in remembrance that the twelue Tribes paffed vnder *Iofue* through Iordane with drie foote to go to *Hiericho.* Though this were a tokē of the remembrence of a miraculoufe and a wonderfull worke and benefitt of God doē to the people of Ifraell: yet the laing together of the xii ftones was neuer accompted as a miraculoufe worke of God.   *Iofue.4.*

    To come to thinges that were figures of Chryfte, as to the Brafen Serpēt, whiche Chryft applieth to him felf, as a figure of him felf to be crucified, though yt were both a token of the great benefitt of God to the people of Ifraell in releiuing them of the plague that he had fent amonge them, and alfo a figure of Chrift to be crucified, wherbie the faithfull fhoulde be relea- fed of the plague of euerlafting damnacion: yet this ferpent was not of lear- ned men in Chryftes Churche magnified and exalted among the great mi- raculoufe workes of God.   *Num.21. Ioan.3.*

    The Pafchall Lambe that was both a token of remembrance to the Iewes of the benefittes that they receaued in their paffage oute of Aegipt, and alfo a figure of Chryft, and that a notable liuelie figure: yet ys ther no chriftian   *Exod.12.*

D writer that accompteth the killing or eating of that lambe as a miraculoufe worke of God in yt felf.

    To come nearer to the maner, the *Catechumeni* that ys, the newlie in-
Kk iiii   ftructed

structed in chriftes faithe, but not baptifed, of the whiche ther were a great **E**
nombre in the primitiue Church, they receaued a bread whiche S. Augufti
ne calleth a Sacrament, and accompteth yt an holie meate, yea holier then
other meates, although yt be not (*faieth he*) the bodie of Chryft. And yet
this bread accompteth he not (though yt be a Sacrament to them and an
holie figne) amonge the miraculoufe workes of God. no more then the
Church did the holie bread, whiche the people receaued on certain daies.
Wherfor if the Sacrament were but a fign or token onelie (as *Oecolampadius*
faieth yt ys) then yt fhould be but as the bread of the Catechumeni the newe conuerted to Chryft, and as the holie bread of Chriftian people, whiche
S. Auguftine accompteth but as an holie thing, and yet referred yt not into
the nombre of the miraculoufe workes of God. No more wolde thefe holie
and auncient Fathers, which I haue alleaged, fo haue efteemed the Sacrament and fet yt furth by the great workes of God as a miraculoufe worke
requiring faith, to be beleued to contein more than reafon can conceaue or
fenfeis iudge. And therfor the holie fathers haue traueiled to ftaie and confirme the faith of the Chryftians by examples of workes doen miraculouflie
by Gods power, accompting this as one of the fame kinde or forte. **F**

This being well weighed and confidered by the Fathers in the Lateran
Councell, wher were affembled no fmall nombre of learned men as well
of the greke church, as of the latin, as the Patriarkes of Hierufalem and Con
ftantynople, Archebifhoppes 70. Bifhoppes 400. of other Fathers 92. with
the Ambaffadours of the Grecian and Romain Empire, and the Oratours of
Hierufalem, Fraunce, Spain, Englonde, and Cypres, for the declaracion and
confirmacion of the faith in this matteir accordinge to the doctrine of the
holie Fathers, and to the confutacion of the wicked doctrine of *Berengarius*
at that time yet lurking in corners, this Canon was ther agreed vpon and fet
furth. *Verum Chrifti corpus & fanguis in facramento Altaris fub fpeciebus panis & vini
veraciter continentur, tranfubftantiatis pane in corpus, & vino in fanguinem poteftate
diuina*. The verie bodie and blood of Chryfte are verilie and truliei conteined vnder the formes of bread and wine in the Sacrament of the aultar, the
bread and wine being tranfubftanciated into the bodie and bloode by the
power of God, Thus the Councell, whiche was celebrated aboue thre hon- **G**
dreth yeares agone.

Nowe Reader thowe feeft the learning and faith of Chryftes Church in
this matter of tranfubftantiacion. not onelie nowe in thefe daies profeffed,
taught and beleued through oute all Chryftendome, but alfo aboue three
hondreth yeares agon in the great and generall Councell Lateran. and fo
by Fathers teftified before and vppewarde vntill ye come to the primitiue
church. Wherfor minding here after to touche yt more as occafion fhall be
miniftred, I think this for this time fufficient to moue anie man to haue a regarde to his faith, that hath not folde him felf ouer to liue vnder herefie difobedience and finne. Nowe therfor I returne to my pourpofe.

*August.
de peccator
merit. & re
miff. holie
bread vfed
in the pri-
mitiue
Churche.*

*Figures cõ-
tein what,
reafon can
conceaue,
the Sacr.
what faith
muft bele
ue.*

*Concil. La-
teran. cap.
1. de fide
cathol.*

THE

A   THE TWO AND FIFTETH CHAP. OPENETH
the mindes of Sainct Basill and Sainct Ambrose vpon the
woordes of Chryst

Hinke not (*gentle reader*) but that ther be manie lefte not here alleaged, as *Optatus, Dionisius Alexandrius, Hilarius, Origen*, and other, which geue goodlie teftimonie for the veritie of Chryftes bodie in the Sacrament. But here we alleadge none but foche as treacting of thefe woordes of Chryft, *This ys my bodie, This ys my bloode*, doe geue vs their doctrine, for the true vnderftanding of them. wherfor the other omitted, this ordre hath brought vs to S. Bafill in the greke churche, and to S. Ambrofe in the latin church.

S. Bafill, to whom this queftion was moued: with what feare, what maner of faith or affured certentie, and with what affection the bodie and blod of Chryft fhoulde be receaued, made this aunfwer: *Timorem docet nos Apofto-* B *lus dicens: Qui edit & bibit indigné iudicium fibiipfi edit ac bibit. At verò certitudinis perfectioné inducit fides verborū Domini, qui dixit : Hoc eft corpus meum, quod pro vobis datur: Hoc facite in meam cōmemorationé.* The Apoftle teachethvs the feare, faing: He tht eateth and drinketh vnwoorthilie, he eateth ād drinckethvnto himfelf iudgement. But the perfection of certitude induceth the faith of the woords of our Lorde, who faied: *This ys my bodie, whiche ys geuen for yowe. Doe this in the re membrance of me.* Thus moch S. Bafill for aunfwer to the queftion.

For the better vnderftanding of which aunfwer, confider that this queftion ys propownded as of them that were vnlearned, and wolde be fimplie inftructed in the faithe of Chryft, to the inftruction of whiche kinde of people S. Bafill appointed him felf in the folucion of this queftion, and other. Wherfor yt ys to be thought that in this folucion he taught the fimple and plain trueth. Nowe then teaching them that thefe woordes : *This ys my bodie*, doe inftruct them what faith they fhoulde haue in the receipt of the Sacrament, what dothe he but teach that thefe woordes muft be taken as they fownde, and fo by them to haue this faith, that Chryftes verie bodie ys in C the Sacrament, according as the woordes doe fownde? For confider, wolde this holie man, trowe ye, teache the people to grownde their faith vpō thefe woordes, if their faith fhoulde not be grownded ypon them as they lie, but vpon this fenfe : this ys a figure of my bodie? Yf the faith of the people of the Sacrament aught to be none other, but that yt ys but a figure of the bodie, and not the bodie yt felf, wolde he haue moued them to beleue the woordes as they be fpoken, and not haue taught the true fenfe, that they aught to grownde their faith vpon in dede? No chryftian will fo thinke of fo woorthie a man, as this was. And therfor ye maie perceaue that this holie man vnderftoode Chryftes woordes fimplie in propre fenfe, and taught therbie the very prefence of Chryftes bleffed bodie and bloode in the Sacrament, as before ys faied, and fhall be plentifullie declared in the thirde booke.

Nowe foloweth S. Ambrofe, in whome I finde foche copie, and foche plentie of plain and euident places to open and declare the right and true, vnderftanding of this fcripture. *This ys my bodie*: that as a man comming into D a goodlie garden garnifhed, adorned, and pleafantlie furnifhed with all delectable and fwete flowres, can not tell which flower to take firft : Euen fo I beholding S. Ambrofe and the plentie of goodlie liuely places in him, I knowe not whiche to take firft But bicaufe he ys fo plain in gods treuth,
and

Bafil.quaft compend. explic. qu. 172.

S. Bafill how he taught the fimple to beleue of the Sacrament

Ca.25.37. 44.

S. Ambr. booke of Sacr. reiected of Occo lāp. as S. Ia mes epiftle by Luther, for their plaintrueth and *Veritas odium parit*, trueth cauſeth hatred : he gotte himſelf ſo moche **E** hatred for this his plain treuth, that had not the catholique Churche ſtande his good Mother, he had ben caſt oute of the doores by *Oecolampadius*, as S.*Iames*, epiſtle had ben by *Luther*, for his plain ſpeaking for god workes. But God be praiſed, as by her bothe theſe were approued : ſo (*God aiding*) by her they are conſerued.

A mong ſoche plentie therfor as I haue ſaied, and as yt ys well knowen to them that be learned we will gather a flower or twoo, for the mainteinã-ce of the côfortable ſinell of the trueth, of the which this ſhall be the firſt: *Antequam conſecretur panis eſt, vbi autem verba Chriſti acceſſerint, corpus eſt Chriſti. Denique audi dicentem: Accipite, & edite ex eo omnes, Hoc eſt corpus meum. Et ante verba Chriſti calix eſt vini & aquæ plenus, vbi verba Chriſti operata fuerint, ibi ſanguis efficitur, qui plebem redemit.* Before yt ys conſecrate yt ys bread, but when the woordes of Chryſte haue comed to yt, *yt ys the bodie of Chryſt*, Heare him ſainge : *Take and eate, this ys my bodie.* And before the woordes of Chryſt, yt ys a cuppe full of wine and water, but when the woordes of Chryſte haue **F** wrought, *ther ys made the bloode that redemed the people.*

What can the Aduerſaries ſaie to this place of S. Ambroſe? What can the Proclamer ſaie, yf he folowe not his Father *Oecolampadius* and reieɛt S. Ambroſe? Can they for ſhame ſaie that the woordes of Chryſt are ſpoken by a figure, wher they be ſo plainlie expownded by this notable Father of the verie thing? Doe ye not heare that after the woordes of Chryſte be ſpoken vpon the bread, yt ys the bodie of Chryſt, and again that after the woorking of the woordes of Chryſte, ther ys made in the cuppe the bloode that redemed the people? Here ys no figure ſpoken of. He ſaieth not, that yt ys a figure of the bodie, and a figure of the bloode, but he ſaied, they be the bodie and the bloode, yea and that ſo verilie, that he ſaieth, *yt ys the bloode that redemed the people.*

As yt ys woonderfull, ſo ys yt pittifull, that men will ſtill remain in blinde hereſie, when the trueth ys ſo ſimplie and plainlie vttered, and that of ſo excellent a Father, that they can not denie yt, but malciouſlie to contein **G** them ſelues in that miſerable ſtate, will refuſe the worke, and ſaie yt ys not S. Ambroſe worke, and yet they knowe that S. Auguſtin himſelf wittneſſeth that S. Ambroſe wrote ſoche bookes of the Sacramentes, and ther be none but theſe. But yt ys but a bare ſhifte when they be ouercomed of the trueth to denie the authour, and be not hable to prooue that they doe.

But lett vs returne to S. Ambroſe, and gather an other of his flowers. Thus he ſaieth in an other place : *Tu fortè dicis, meus panis eſt viſitatus. Sed panis iſte, panis eſt ante verba ſacramentorum, vbi acceſſerit conſecratio, de pane fit caro Chriſti.* Thowe peraduenture ſaieſt, my bread ys vſuall or common bread. But this bread before the woordes of conſecracion ys bread, but when the conſecracion hath comed vnto yt, of the bread ys made the fleſh of Chryſt. And again he ſaieth in the ſame chapiter. *Sed audi dicentem: Ipſe dixit, & faɛta ſunt, ipſe mandauit & creata ſunt. Ergo tibi vt reſpondeam, Non erat corpus Chriſti ante conſecrationem. Sed poſt conſecrationem, dico tibi, quòd iam eſt corpus Chriſti. Ipſe dixit & faɛtum eſt, ipſe mandauit, & creatum eſt.* But heare one ſaing: He hath ſaied and they were made, he hath cômaunded and they were created. Therfor that **H** I maie aunſwer thee. *Yt was not the bodie of Chryſt before the conſecracion, but after the conſecracion* (I ſaie vnto thee) *that nowe yt ys the bodie of Chryſt.* He hath ſaied, and yt ys made, he hath commaunded and yt ys created.

I nede not explane S. Ambroſe in this place neither. For as the parentes

Ambr.li.4 de Sacr. cap.5.

Plain ſaïgs of S.Amb. for the Procla.

Ambroſ. ibid. li. 4. cap.4.

Amb. ibid

What plainer woords câ the Proclamer require.

of

A of the blinde born fonne faied of him : *Aetatem habet, ipfe pro fe loquatur*. He hath age, let him fpeake for himfelf, fo S. Ambrofe hath foche grace, foche learning, and withall foche plain fpeache, that he fpeaketh fufficently for him felf, and for Gods caufe, whiche he openeth, and that ther ys nothing here to be defired but an humble reader. And if ye will not beleue him, yet beleue him, to whom he referreth yowe, that ys Chryft. For he faieth : *Ipfe Dominus Iefus teftificatur nobis, quòd corpus fuum accipiamus & fanguinem. Nunquid debemus de eius fide & teftificatione dubitare?* Owre Lorde Iefus him felf teftifieth vnto vs, that we receaue his bodie and bloode, fhall we doubt of his trueth and teftificacion?

Ambr. ibid. ca.5.

Nowe let vs compare the doctrine of S. Ambrofe, with the doctrine of the Aduerfaries. S. Ambrofe faieth that Chryft himfelf doeth teftifie that we receaue his bodie and bloode: The Aduerfaries faieth that we doe not receaue the bodie and bloode of Chryft, But breade and wine the figures of the bodie and blood of Chryft. whom fhall we here beleue? Chryft and S. Ambrofe, or the Aduerfaries? The choife aught foen to be made. And therfor

S. Ambr. doctrine and the Sa cramenta- ries copa- red togct her.

B yt ys lamentable to fee howe Sathan hath preuailed, and caufed the Aduer faries to call that in queftion and doubt, which Chryft himfelf teftifieth to be the verie trueth. Yf yt were not the trueth, S. Ambrofe, be ye well affu- red, wolde not fo haue reported yt. But yf Chryft had teftified to vs, that we in the Sacrament receaue but a figure, S. Ambrofe wolde not haue repor- ted that we receaue Chryftes bodie. For as ther ys great difference betwen thefe two thinges : fo be the doctrines greatlie different. And S. Ambrofe who in thefe his bookes laboured to teache the thrueth, and to deliuer men from doubte, was not of foche groffe iudgement nor fo rude in vtterance, but he coulde well iudge betwene the thing and the figure, andfo vtter his iudgement, that his fpeache fhoulde not fownde one thing, and his mening fhoulde be an other. for that were not the waie to deliuer from doubte but raither to bring into doubte, not a waie of inftruction, but raither a waie of deftruction.

But here to conclude this parte, for as moch as S. Ambrofe faieth, that

Figure of the Sacrme taries ex- cluded fro Chryftes woordes.

C Chryft hath teftified by thefe woordes, *This ys my bodie*, that we in the Sacra- mèt after the woords fpokè receaue his verie bodie, thei are not to be vnder ftaded withe anie figure or trope, but fimplie, ad plainlie in that fenfe that theic are fpoken. Wherfore yt maie be by this perceaued that the Aduerfa- ries figuratiue fpeache hath no place, as they vnderftande yt, in this faing of Chryfte. But this ys raither to be faied that his interprife in fo wrefting and abufing of Chryftes woordes ys wicked and deteftabele. For yf that fenfe might haue ben here vpon thefe woordes placed, who can doubte that S. Ambrofe fo often reherfing them, wolde not in one place or other, haue re ported the true fenfe, and faied yt had ben but a figne. But forafmoche as in no place he fo doeth, but continuallie and conftantlie faieth, yt ys the bodie of Chryft, let no man doubte of the trueth of that that he tea cheth, but embracing that let him flie the feigned figures.

Confecra- cion the ter me of the Papiftes vfed of S. Ambr. feri oufite.

In thefe fainges alfo of S. Ambrofe, this ys breiflie to be touched with a note, that wher the Aduerfarie in fkorne, when he happeneth to fpeake of this woorde (*confecracion*) for the moft parte addeth (*as the Papiftes teare yt*)

D yet ye perceaue that yt ys vfed of S. Ambrofe, and not fknorned. And howe fo euer yt liketh him to dallie and trifle withe that woorde, yet S. Ambrofe in fo weightie a matter dothe vfe the woorde feriouflie. And if for that he vfeth this woorde, the Aduerfarie will alfo accompte him for a papift, I had

leuer

leuer be a Papiſt wiht the one, then an heretique with the other. But yt ys **E**
time to call in an other coople.

THE THREE AND FIFTETH CHAP. CONTINV-
eth in the expoſition of Chryſtes woordes by Gregorie Niſſen.
and S. Hierom.

S a man permitted to come into a councell chambre, and admitted, through ſpeciall fauoure, to talke withe eche of the counſelours, and haue their ſenerall aduertiſementes howe he ſhall
ſafelie beare him ſelf in the ſtate that he ys called vnto : or as a
man deſierouſe to be reſolued in a matter of learning, entreth
an aſſembley of learned men, and gentlie receaued heareth their ſeuerall
iudgementes vttered with great and full agreement, to his full reſolucion,
and contentacion, can not be but therwith moche delighted : ſo I truſt, the
reader being as yt were in Godes counſell chambre, or in Gods Schoole, **F**
and hearing the aduertiſementes and iudgementes of Gods counſelours
and learned men ſo ſeuerallie, and yet ſo agreablie vttered to his full and
perfect reſolucion, I truſt, I ſaie, he ys delighted, and the more for that all
theſe with whiche he hath conference (and yet for a good nombre ſhall haue) be all verie auncient, and with in the compaſſe of ſixe hondreth yeares after Chryſt. Wherfor let vs in Gods name proceade with delight and
pleaſure to heare the other that remain to be conferred with all for they be
(as ys ſaied) a good nombre of the bothe auncient, and learned, and though
all be not auncient, yet all learned and approued.

Of theſe auncientes that remain the firſt ys Gregorie Niſſen. the brother
of S. Baſill and therfor in the greke church meet next to folowe him. This
ys his iudgement in this matter. Thus he writeth. *Qua ex cauſe panis in eo corpo*
Greg. Niſ- *re mutatus in diuinam virtutem tranſiit, eadem de cauſa idem nunc fit. Vt enim illic verbi*
ſen.inſerm. *Dei gratia ſanctum efficit illud corpus, cuius firmamentum ex pane conſtabat, & ipſum*
catathetico *etiam quodammodò panis erat : ſic panis, vt ait Apoſtolus, per verbum Dei, & oratio-* **G**
de diuinis *nem ſanctificatur, non quia comeditur, eo progrediens, vt Verbi corpus euadat, ſed ſtatim*
ſacram. *per verbum in corpus mutatur, vt dictum eſt à Verbo. Hoc eſt corpus meum.* By what
cauſe bread in that bodie chaunged paſſed into the diuine vertue, by the ſame cauſe that ſame thinge ys nowe doen. For as ther the grace of the Sonne
of God made that bodie, whoſe ſubſtanciall nutriment was of bread, and
yt alſo in a maner was bread, ſo alſo this bread (*as the Apoſtle ſaieth*) ys ſanctified by the woorde of God and praier, not tending to this point that bicau
ſe yt ys eaten yt ys the bodie of the Sonne of God, but that furthwith by
the woorde yt ys chaunged into the bodie, as yt was ſaied of the Sonne, *This*
ys my bodie

By this authour, who vndoubtedlie geueth a notable teſtimonie for the
Three here- veritie of the Sacrament, be ouerthrowen three hereſies in the ſame matter.
ſies ouer- Of the whiche, *Luther* or at the leaſt the *Lutherans* did ſettfurth one, which
throwen by was that the Sacrament was the bodie of Chryſt if yt were receaued, and to
one ſaing of him that receaued yt, yt was the bodie of Chryſt, otherwiſe yt was not. An
Gregor. other ys ſett furth bothe by *Luther,* and all the *Lutherans,* and by *Oecolampadius*
Niſſen. and all the *Oecolampadians,* and by this Proclamer, whiche ys that the bread **H**
and wine be not chaunged into the ſubſtance of the bodie and bloode of
Chryſt, of the whiche we haue ſomwhat at large ſpoken before. The thirde
ys ſettfurth by *Carolſtadius, Oecolampadius* and their diſciples, and alſo by this
Proclamer,

A Proclamer , whiche ys that Chryftes fubftanciall bodie ys not verilie prefent in the Sacrament . Againft thefe three , this authour teacheth vs very good documentes according to that, that the catholique Churche now teacheth.

And nowe for the firft that the *Lutherans* doo teache, wher they faie that in the Sacrament ys the bodie of Chryft to him that receaueth the Sacrament, otherwife yt ys not the bodie of Chryft , this authour hath direct woordes to the contrarie, wher he faieth . *Hic panis fanctificatur per verbum Dei,& orationem, non quia comeditur eo progrediens vt verbi corpus euadat.* This bread ys fanctified by the woorde of God and praier , not tending to this poinct that bicaufe yt ys eaten, therfore yt ys the bodie of the Sonne of God. So that yt ys not receauing , or not receauing, eating or not eating that caufeth the prefence of Chryftes bodie in the Sacrament, but the power of God with the woorde of Chryft , as before ys faied . The caufe of fo great a worke as to make prefent the bodie of Chryft , dependeth not of fo fimple and weake caufe as the will of man,

B whiche yt fhould dooe if yt fhould depende vpon the receipte. For yf the man wolde receaue yt, then were yt the bodie of Chryfte: yf he wolde not receaue, yt were not the bodie of Chryft, fo willing and not willing fhoulde make bodie or no bodie after that fonde opinion.

But to adde fomwhat befide the authoritie of this auncient Father, which ys more then fufficient to conuince fo vain and foolifh an herefie, what apparance haue they of anie fcripture or holie writer (*For fubftanciall grownde in anie of them both they haue none*) to make fome fhewe or counteinance , for the maintenance of their herefie? yt ys certen that they haue none. Nowe then fhall we not condemne them by their owne iudgement, wherwith they haue trauailed in manie thinges to condemne the catholique Church ? What ys defined , decreed or determined by the Churche, if ther be not manifeft fcripture for the fame, yt ys condemned of them, as a tradicion of man, and a doctrine of Sathan. But this their

C doctrine hath no manifeft fcriptures. Wherfore yt ys a tradicion of man, and a doctrine of Sathan. Thus as *Aman* was hanged vpon the fame Galowes that he had made for innocent *Mardochæus*: So ys their wicked doctrine ouerthrowen with their owne iudgement , and vanquiffed with their owne fwoorde.

But what fhall I occupie the time, and trooble the reader in refelling this fonde herefie, feing(as a litle before ys declared by *Eufebius*) that the inuifible preift , Chryft , by his power with his woerde doeth turne the vifible creatures into the fubftance of his bodie and bloode. Chryfoftome alfo faieth , that the preiftes be in the place of the mynifters of God , but yt ys Chryft that doeth fanctifie, and chaunge the fubftances of bread and wine . And breiflie to faie, fainct Ambrofe in the laft chapiter , *Euthymius* , *Damafcen* , and *Theophilact* in the chapter before, doe teftifie that the worke of confecracion ys doen by the power of God , by the acceffion of the holie Goft, and by the woorde of Chryft fpoken by

D the preift in the perfon of Chryfte. As yt ys alfo teftified in the Florentine Councell wher yt ys thus declared : *Forma huius facramenti funt verba Saluatoris , quibus hoc conficit Sacramentum . Sacerdos enim in perfona Chrifti loquens hoc conficit Sacramentum . Nam ipforum verborum virtute fubftantia panis in corpus Chrifti,& fubftantia vini in fanguinem conuertuntur.* The forme of this Sacrament be the woordes of our Sauiour by the whiche he

---

Side notes:

What warrant haue the Lutheras for this

Receauing or not receauing caufeth nor prefence , nor abfence of Chryftes bodie in the Sacr.

Lutherans doctrine hauing no apparat fcripture ys ouerthrowen by ther owne argument.

Concilium. Florent.

Trāsubstā | confecrateth this Sacrament. For the preist speaking in the person of Chryst E
tiacion. | doeth confecrate this Sacrament. *For by the vertue of those woordes, the sub-*
stance of bread , ys turned into the bodie of Christ , and the substance of wine
into hys bloode. Thus the Councell . By whiche woordes, as by the woordes of them also before alleaged, yt ys manifestly declared that the power
of the confecracion of the bodie of Chryst, ys not depending of the will of
the receauer, but of the power of God, of the worke of the holie Gost, and
of the vertue of the woordes of Chryst, spoken by the preist in the person
of Chryste.

And as this fonde heresie semeth to be mother of that heresie that impugneth reseruacion: so that, that ys before saied for the defence of reseruacion,
will also impugne this heresie here nowe spoken of. Wherfore I referre the
reader to that place, wher he findinge plentie of proofe that the Sacrament
maie be reserued, and being reserued , that yt still remaineth the bodie of
Chryst, this wicked doctrine that teacheth, that yt ys but the bodie of Chryst
when yt ys in vse, shalbe ouerthrowen, and prooued (*as it is*) a false and a de- F
uellish doctrine.

The other heresie which ys settfurth both by the *Lutherans* and the *Oeco-*
lampadians, ys that the substance of bread and wine be still remaining in the
Sacrament, and not chaunged into the bodie and bloode of Chryst.

Diuision | And, yet here by the waie vnderstand this, that though they agree in this
among the | poinct, yet here Sathan ys deuided againft Sathan , and his kingdom also,
Proteftan- | as kingdom against kingdom. For Luther graunteth the prefence of Chry-
tes. | stes bodie: *Oecolampadius* denieth the prefence of Chryftes bodie, and in this
they are more then enemies. But in the other (as ys faied) they doe agree.
And as in this they agree amonge themselues: So in the fame they difagree, from the true faith, from the catholike Church , and from Gregorie
Niffen, whom we haue nowe in hand. For by expreffe woordes he affirmeth
that the fubftance of the bread ys chaunged into the bodie of Chryst. The-
Greg. Niff. | fe be his woordes fpeaking of the bread before the confecracion . *Hic panis*
in vita | *ftatim per verbum in corpus mutatur.* This bread ys by the woorde furthwith G
Moifeos. | chaūged into the bodie. Who fo lifteth maie read the like faing of the fame
authour in his booke of the life of Moyfes.

Neither doeth he here meen of foche a chaunge as the Aduerfarie dreameth of, that yt ys chaunged to be called the bodie of Chryfte , whiche
proprely ys no chaunge, but raither an addicion. But this authour meeneth
of a fubftanciall chaunge as hys woords doe moft plainlie declare, which he
vfeth to proue this chaunge. For thus he faieth: *Qua ex caufa panis in eo corpore*
mutatus in diuinam virtutem tranfiit, eadem de caufa idem nunc fit . By what caufe
bread in that bodie chaunged, paffed into the diuine vertue: euen fo by the
fame caufe the verie fame thing ys now doen.

For the better weighing of this faing of the authour, confider firft , that
Chryfte was and ys bothe God and man , confider that the bodie of man
was fo ioined to the Godhead in vnitie of perfon, that Chryft God and man
was one perfon, one Chryfte. Confider then that this bodie by this merueiloufe coniunction ys the bodie of God. Nowe this bodie liuing here vpon H
the earth, although as yt liued fortie daies and fortie nightes wihout foode:
fo yt might haue liued fortie wekes, and fortie moneths, yet as yt was a naturall bodie: So yt liued in natural order, and did eate foode. This foode which
by a generall terme ys called bread, allthough yt were but comon meate,
euen foche as the Apoftles, and other did eate, yet this comon bread eaté of
Chryfte

A Chryst,was chaunged in the bodie of Chryst into the substance of the bodie
of Chryst,and became now the substance of his bodie, and being so yt came
to be the substance of the bodie of God.

Nowe saieth Gregorie Nissen by what cause the bread was chaunged into the bodie of Chryste , and became the substance of the bodie of God,
which(*as I take yt*)he meneth by these woordes (*diuine vertue*) euen by the same cause,the same thing ys nowe doen. Yf the same thing be doen nowe
then the bread ys chaunged into the substance of the bodie of God,for that
ys the thing that was doen then.Wherfor good reader,note this wel,that he
saieth,*the same thing ys doen nowe*,wherbie the dreame of the Aduersarie ys dissolued,that the bread ys chaunged but in name. For that was but a cauill,
and in dede but a bare shifte to auoide the force of the trueth.And what the
thing ys that nowe ys doen , thys authour tolde when he saied : *Panis*
mutatur in corpus per verbum . The bread by the worde ys chaunged into the bodie.

As bread
while
Chryst li-
ued was
turned into
his diuine
flesh : so no
we in the
Sacr.

B   Seing then this auncient Father teacheth vs, that in Chrystes bodie the
substance of bread was chaunged into the substance of that diuine bodie,
and by example of that,teacheth the like to be nowe doen in the Sacrament
that as in the one ther was a chaunge of one substance into an other: so in
this ther ys a chaunge of one substance into an other,that ys, once again to
saie,of the substance of bread and wine,into the substance of Chrystes bodie and blood:why maie not this turning,chaunging or transmuting of substances into substances be called transubstantiacon , seinge yt ys so in dede?
Whie,I saie,maie not the same terme by the Church be vsed liuelie to expresse a treuth , and to auoide an heresie, as in the time of the Arrians,
the Church for the confutacion of that heresie , was enforced to vse this
terme(*consubstantialitie*)therby to declare that God the Sonne was and ys of
one substance with God the Father? A newe mischeif must haue a newe remedie and for a newe sore,a newe salue must be fownde. So as for the Arrians,whiche was then a newe mischeif and a newe sore in the Churche,
these tearmes (*consubstanciall and consubstancialitie*)were by the holie Gost de-

C uised in the same:So when *Berengarius* began this newe mischeif and sore a-
gainst the Sacrament,teaching that ther was no chaunge of the substance of
bread into the substance of the bodie of Chryste , which sore the Church
had not felt before,the same Churche perceauing that all the termes that
the holie Fathers had vsed to expresse this chaunge (as *turning , chaunging,*
mutacion,transmutacion,transumption,transelementacion)did not suffice,but the Deuell wolde by his ministers dallie with them to deceaue Chrystian soules,
and impugne the holie Chrystian faith:the Church I saie,by the holie Gost
deuised to vse this tearme (*transubstanciacion*)to declare fullie the thing that
ys doen,whiche ys the chaunge of one substance into an other, and so to o-
pen the true faith,by the same to defende the faith,and to sett yt for a salue
and a remedie against that sore, and mischeif,that the Deuell had newely
caused to springe.

As the
woord Con
stātialitie
in the time
of Arius :so
Trāsubstā
tiacion in
the time of
Berēg. was
taught by
the holie
Goste

And as in the time of the Arrians , ther was no newe thinge deuised in
faith , though a newe tearme was settfurth : so nowe no thing ys newlie deuised but onelie the tearme,fullie to declare,and make vs vnderstand

D that thing that was before .   Wherfore the newnesse of the tearme
shoulde not offende,speciallie being setfurth by no particular man , but by
a generall consent, so that yt be not a prophane noueltie, prophanelie,

abducinge men from an auncient trueth to a newe inuented falſheade and **E**
ſo by a newe terme, newely commended to vs, to ſupplant vs. But a ne
we tearme to expreſſe an olde trueth hath ben in the beginning of
the Churche, and maie alſo nowe be well vſed, as S. Auguſtine ſa-

A newe tearm to expreſſe an old treuth vſed in the primi tiue church and maie ſo be nowe.

ieth: *Audite Apoſtolum ſalubriter admonentem. Prophanas, inquit, verbo-rum nouitates deuita, Multum enim proficiunt ad impietatem, & ſermo eorum, vt cancer ſerpit. Et non ait ſolùm verborum nouitates, ſed addit, Prophanas. Sunt enim & doctrinæ religionis congruentes verborum nouitates. Sicut ipſum no-men Chriſtianorum, quando dici cæperat, ſicut ſcriptum eſt (In Antiochia enim primum poſt aſcenſionem Domini ſic appellati ſunt Diſcipuli, Sicut legitur in Actibus Apoſtolorum) Et Xenodochia, & Monaſteria, poſtea appellata ſunt nouis nominibus, res tamen ipſæ & ante nomina ſua erant, & religionis verita-te firmantur quæ etiam contra improbos defenduntur. Aduerſus quoque impietatem*

Aug.tract. 96.in Ioan.

Arrianorum hæreticorum nouum nomen patres (Homouſion) condiderunt, ſed non rem nouam tali nomine ſignauerunt, Hoc enim vocatur Homouſion, quod eſt ego **F**
& Pater vnum ſumus, vnius videlicet eiuſdemque ſubſtantiæ. Nam ſi omnis nouitas pro-phana eſſet, nec à Domino diceretur: mandatum nouum do vobis, nec teſtamentum appella-ret nouum, nec cantaret vniuerſa terra canticum nouum. Heare the Apoſtle holſom-

Some newe woordes be agreable to good religiō

lie admoniſhing: *Prophane nouelties of woordes* (ſaieth he) auoide. They doe moche aduaunce impietie, and their woorde fretteth like a kanker. And he doeth not ſaie onely nouelties of woordes : but he addeth : *Prophane.* For ther be nouelties of woordes alſo agreable to the doctrine of religion as the na me of Chryſtians, when yt firſt began to be ſpoken of, as yt ys writ-ten (For ſo firſt in Antioche after the aſcenſion of our Lorde were the Diſciples called, at yt ys redd in the Actes of the Apoſtles) And Hoſpitals and Monaſteries afterward were called with newe names, the thinges them ſelues for all that were before theſe their names, and are eſtabliſhed with the veritie of religion, and are alſo defended againſt wicked men, Againſt the impietie or wickedneſſe alſo of the Heretiques the Arrians, the

Homouſion what yt ſig niſieth.

Fathers made the newe tearme (*Homouſion*) but by that name they did not ſignifie a newe thing. For *Homouſion* ys called the ſame that this ys : *I* **G**
and my Father be one : that ys to ſaie, of one and the very ſame ſubſtance. For if euery noueltie were euell yt ſhoulde not be ſaied of our Lorde : I geue yow a newe commaundement, neither ſhoulde his teſtament be called ne-we, neither ſhoulde the wholl earth ſing a newe ſong. Thus moch S. Augu ſtin. Wherfor this tearm of tranſubſtanciation, which the Aduerſarie calleth newe, although yt hath bē in vſe more then three hondreth years, by the minde of S. Auguſtine ys not to be reiected. But for ſomoche as the thing whiche yt ſignifieth ys auncient, as *Homouſion* againſt the Arrians : ſo this a-gainſt the Sacramentaries ys of all faithfull people to be accepted. But what doe I tarie ſo long vpon this matter ſeing moche ys ſaied of yt allreadie, and more ſhall by waie of note as occaſion ſhall be geuen.

The thirde hereſie ys alſo by this authour refelled, in that he teaching the bread to be chaunged by theſe woordes of Chryſt : *This ys my bodie.* teacheth both the reall preſence, and alſo the woordes to be vnderſtand withoute fi-gure or trope, as the Aduerſaries wolde haue them vnderſtanded. That he ſo doeth yt ys eaſie to be perceaued by his owne woordes, whiche he vttereth in this maner. *Panis ſtatim mutatur in corpus, vt dictum eſt à Verbo : hoc eſt corpus me-* **H**
um. The bread ys furthwith chaunged by the woorde into the bodie, as yt ys ſaied of the Sonne of God. *This ys my bodie.*

But what neadeth to tarie anie lōger to ſaie more for the opening of this au
thours

A thour, where euerie parte of yt ys fo opē of yt felf,that a childe maie fee yt? I will therfor leaue him,and heare the minde of his yocke felowe,whom we haue in this place appointed to be.S.Hierō,who writeth thus:*Nos autem audia mus panē,quem Dominus fregit,dedítque Difcipulis fuis effe corpus Domini faluatoris, ipfo dicente ad eos:Accipite,& comedite,Hoc eſt corpus meū:& calicē illū effe,de quo iterum locutus eſt.Bibite ex hoc omnes:Hic eſt fanguis meus noui teſtamenti,qui pro multis effun-detur.Iſte eſt calix,de quo in Propheta legimus:Calicē falutaris accipia· & alibi:Calix tuus inebrians quàm præclarus eſt.Si ergo panis qui de cœlo defcendit,corpus eſt Domini,& vi num quod Difcipulis dedit fanguis illius eſt noui teſtamēti,iudaicas fabulas repellamus,&c.* But let vs heare that bread which our Lord brake and gaue to hys Difciples to be the bodie of our Lord our Sauiour,forafmoch as he faied vnto thē·*Take and eate,This ys my bodie.*And the cuppe to be that of the which again he faied: *Drinke ye all of this.This ys my blood of the newe Teſtament,which shall be shedd for manie* This ys the cuppe of the which we read in the Prophete:*I wil receaue the cuppe of faluacion.*And in an other place.*Thy cuppe inebriating ys verie noble.*Yf therfore the bread that defcended frō heauen ys the bodie of our Lord,and the wine

B which he gaue to his Difciples ys his blood of the newe Teſtament, let vs repell the Iewifh fables.Thus moch S.Hierom.

   For the better vnderſtanding of this faing, yt ys to be confidered that a certain vertuoufe woman named *Hedibia* fent to fainct Hierom to be refol-ued in certain queſtions. Among the which fhe defiered to be inſtructed how the faing of Chryſt in S. Matthew; was to be vnderſtanded, wher he faied:*I will not from hencefurth drinke of this generacion of the vine , vntill that daie in whiche I shall drinke yt newe with yow in the kingdome of my Father.* To the anfweringe wherof he declareth vnto her, firſt, the fond opinion of fome that vpon that place inuented a fable, that Chryſt fhoulde reign a thou-fand yeares corporally in which time of his reign, he fhoulde drinke wine and fo fhoulde be fullfilled hys faing,that he wolde drinke no more wine vntill he dranke yt in the kingdom of his Father, in the whiche he fhoulde then reign. But fainct Hierom well vnderſtanding howe great and howe weightie a matter was fpoken of in the place,wher from thefe woordes were

C taken,namely of the bodie and blood of Chryſt, and being greued that yt being fo great a worke of God,fo great a benefitt to man , fhoulde be inter-mengled and obfcured,with foche vain inuentions of foche fables, he ope-neth the true fenfe of the place and moueth the good woman *Hedibia* that all foche phantafies reiected and forfaken,fhe fhoulde regarde the woordes of Chryſt and credit them and that the bread and wine that Chryſt fpake of in that place were no foch thinges as vpon which foch vain fables fhould be grownded , but they were the bodie and bloode of Chryſt, forafmoch as he that can fpeake but trueth faied:*Thys ys my bodie .Thys ys my bloode.*

   Now cōfider with me yf Chryſt had geuē to hys Apoſtles but Bread ād wi ne,as figures of hys bodie and blood,wolde S.Hierō being required to geue the true vnderſtāding of the fcriprure,ād he taking vpō him fo to doe, wold he(trowe ye)haue faied,Let vs vnderſtād that the bread which our Lord gaue to his Difciples washis bodie,ād that the wine which he gaue was hys blood exceptwe fhould beleue ād vnderſtād thē,fo to be in dede?Were this an ope ning of the true vnderſtanding of the fcriptures? Were yt not raither an hi-

D ding or a darkning of the fcriptures,to bid vs to beleue one thing,ād the fcri pture biddeth an other?He biddeth vs beleue that yt ys the bodie ād blood of Chryſt,that Chryſt gaue to his Apoſtles,ād the fcriptur(as the Aduerf.fai eth)biddeth vs beleue that they be but figurs.Wold S.Hierō,being alwaies

Marginal notes:

Hieron.ad Hedid q.2

The bread which our Lord gaue was his bo-die, ād the cuppe hys blood.

Herefie of the Mille-naries.

S. Hierom his woordes weighed ād conferred with the do ctrine of the Proteſtātes

an enemie to herefie, teache foche an herefie ? Wolde not he raither (if E
the trueth had ben fo) haue taught this vertuoufe woman the trueth of the
matter that fhe fought at his hand, and faied vnto her : This vnderftand, that
the bread and wine, which Chryft gaue to his Apoftles, were but figurs of
the bodie and bloode of Chryft, and not the thinges themfelues? And alleaging Chryftes woordes : *This ys my bodie, This ys my bloode*, wolde he not (if
they had ben fo to be vnderftanded) haue faied; thefe woordes are fpoken
by a figure, they be figuratiue fpeaches, and are thus to be vnderftanded: this
ys a figure of my bodie, this ys a figure of my bloode? To inftructe thé that
wolde learn the true vnderftáding of this fcripture (if yt were fo to be vnder
ftanded) this were the right waie of teaching. But here ys no foche woorde:
here ys no foche maner of teaching. And yt ys to be thought, that S. Hieró
was not ignorant howe to teache, neither was he ignorát of the trueth, that
in this place fhoulde be taught. Wherfor feing he knewe the trueth, and kne
we howe to teache yt, and nowe he was in place to teache and had good oc
cafion, being (as ys faied) therunto required, forfomoche as he willeth vs to
vnderftande that the bread and wine, whiche Chryft gaue to this Apoftles,
were his bodie and bloode, and the caufe why we fhoulde fo vnderftáde thé F
ys the woorde of Chryft, faing: *This ys my bodie, This ys my bloode* : Let vs thinke
and beleue that the trueth of this matter ys, that his bodie and bloode be pre
fent verilie in the Sacramét, and that the woordes of Chryfte are to be vnderftanded withouté figure fimplie and plainlie as they lie.

And that yt ys the bodie of Chryft, the woordes which S. Hierom vfeth
as the conclufió of the matter, dothe alfo prooue. For thus he concludeth:
*Si ergo panis, qui de cælo defcendit &c. Yf then the bread that defcended from heauen be
the bodie of our Lorde, and the wine that he gaue to his Difciples be his bloode of the newe
teftamét, let vs caft awaie Iewish fables*, As who might faie, forafmoche as thefe
woordes of Chryft fpeake of no cheering nor banquetting, that the Iewes
doe dreame fhall be in Chryftes worldlie kingdom, but they fpeake of the
bread which Chryft gaue to his Apoftles, which they faie to be his bodie,
and of the wine, which they faie to be his bloode, therfor let vs caft awaie
foche vain fables, and cleaue to the true vnderftanding of Chryftes woordes, and beleue that the bread and wine be Chryftes bodie and bloode. G
And therfor looking for no foche worldlie kingdom, nor kinglie palace of
Chryft here vpon the earth : *Afcendamus cum Domino cænaculum magnum ftra-
ftum, atque mundatum, & accipiamus ab eo furfum calicem noui teftamenti, ibíque cum
eo Pafcha celebrantes, inebriemur ab eo vino fobrietatis* : Let vs (faieth S. Hierom)
go vppe with our Lorde into the great dining chambre allreadie prepared
and made clean, and ther let vs receaue of him aboue, the cuppe of the newe teftament, and ther with him celebrating the Paffouer, let vs be fatisfied
with the wine of fobrietie.

I can not here withoute forowe and greif paffe thefe laft woordes of S.
Hierom, but note to thee (gentle reader) the malicioufe doing of the
Proclamer, who impugning the prefence of Chryftes bodie and bloode in the Sacrament, trauaileth to prooue that his wicked doctrine by
fome of the holie fathers, whome he wolde wreft to make them faie, that
Chryft ys onelie to be adored and honoured in heauen, as wherbie
yt might appeare, that his prefence were onelie ther. Among the whiche, H
full euell fauoredlie he bringeth in thefe laft woordes of S. Hierom, cut-
tinge them of from the middeft of the fentence, and leauing oute that
that goeth before, whiche (as ye haue heard) maketh alltogether againft him,
and

*Nomenciõ
of figurati-
ue fpeache
in S. Hierõs
woordes.*

*The Pro-
clamer cut-
teth of the
woordes of
Sain. Hie-
rom, to de-
ceaue his
auditorie.*

A　and alfo that that foloweth, whiche (as ye fhall heare) doeth make againſt him likewife . And ſnatcheth truncatelie theſe fewe woordes, and maketh a falſe fhew with them as well as he can to deceaue his Auditorie. Thus yt foloweth in S. Hierom ymmediately woorde for woorde, *Non enim eſt regnū Dei, cibus & potus, ſed iuſticia, & gaudium, & pax in Spiritu ſanĉto. Nec Moyſes dedit nobis panē verū, ſed Dominus Ieſus, ipſe conuiua & conuiuium. ipſe comedens & qui comeditur. Illius bibimus ſanguinem, & ſine ipſo potare non poſſumus. & quotidie in ſacrificiis eius de genimine vitis veræ, & viueæ Sorec, quæ interpretatur electa, rubentia muſta calcamus, & nouum ex iis vinum bibimus de regno Patris, nequaquam in vetuſtate literæ, ſed in nouitate ſpiritus cantantes canticum nouum, quod nemo poteſt cantare niſi in regno Eccleſiæ, quod regnum Patris eſt.* For the kingdom of God ys not meat and drinke, but righteouſneſſe ād ioie, and peace in the holie Goſt. Neither did Moyſes geue vs the true bread, but our lorde Ieſus, for he ys both the feaſter, and the feaſt, he ys he that eateth and ys eaten. His bloode drinke we, and withoute him we can not drinke, and dailie in his ſacrifices of the generacion of the true Vine, and of the wine of *Sorec,* whiche by interpretacion ys

Hierō ibid

Chryſt ys the feaſter ād the feaſt whoſe blood we drinke in his ſacrifices.

B　called choſen, doe we preſſe ruddie newe wines, and oute of theſe we drinke the newe wine of the kingdom of the Father, not in the oldeneſſe of the letter, but in the neweneſſe of the ſpiritte ſinging a newe ſong, which no mā can ſinge, but in the kingdom of the church, which ys the kingdom of the Father. Thus moche S. Hierom.

Who in refelling of the Iewiſh fables declareth that in the kingdom of Chryſt fhall be no matter of wordlie cheering. For (faieth he) *the kingdom of God ys not meate and drinke.* And returning to the right cheer of Chryſtes king dom, he compareth yt with the cheer of Moyſes, and faieth that Moyſes gaue vs not the true bread, but our Lorde Ieſus. Whie did not Moyſes geue the true bread, ſeing that the bread that he gaue was a miraculouſe bread, a bread that came from heauen, and the bread that Chryſt gaue was no miraculouſe bread, but yt was common vſuall bread, made here by the hand of man vpon earth? Yf ye ſaie that the bread of Chryſt was a figure of Chryſt: ſo was the other alſo, and more liuely thē this for manie cauſes, whiche in the

C　thirde booke fhall be declared.

But if ye will learn the true cauſe, why our Lorde Chryſt gaue the true breade, and Moyſes did not, learn of S. Hierom, who teacheth vs that yt ys bicauſe Chryſt geueth vnto vs not an onelie figure of him ſelf, but bothe the figure and him ſelf alſo. For in the feaſt that Chryſt maketh, he ys he, that both maketh the feaſt (as S. Hierom faieth) and alſo the meat of the feaſt. So thē he geueth him ſelf who in dede ys the verie bread of life, he geueth vs the true bread that Moyſes coulde not geue. For Moyſes gaue the figure of yt, but he gaue not the thing, And therfore he gaue not the true bread.

Cap. 12.

Note then that Chryſte ys the feaſter, for he biddeth vs to the feaſt, and faieth: *Take and eate.* He ys the meate alſo of the feaſt, for appoincting the meat he faieth, *This ys my bodie.* And thus ye maie perceaue that S. Hierom ioineth with the woords of Chryſt: And farder he faieth by expreſſe woordes, comminge to the poinĉt of the drinking of Chryſtes wine in the king dome of his Father: *Illius bibimus ſanguinem:* We drinke his bloode. But where drinke we yt? *In ſacrificiis eius:* In his ſacrifices. Howe come we by this wine

A ſaing of S. Hierom, opened.

Ioan. 15.

D　of his, whiche ys his bloode? *In ſacrificiis eius de geminine vitis veræ rubentia muſta calcamus,* In his ſacrifices we preſſe oute of the true vine the ruddie newwine. Who ys the true vine? Chryſt, who ſaied : *Ego ſum vitis vera.* I am the true wine. Howe preſſe we oute this newe ruddie wine oute of the generacion

of this true wine? By speaking the woordes of Chryst, as he hath comaun- E
ded, by which (as S. Ambrose saieth) *that, that ys in the cuppe, ys made the bloode*
that redemed the people. But in what place muste we drinke this newe wine?
Nouum bibimus vinum in regno Patris : We drinke this newe wine in the
kingdom of the Father. For soche as be in this kingdom maie be partakers
of Chrystes wine dronken in his sacrifices. Other maie not. *Habemus al-*
tare ,de quo edere non habent potestatem , qui tabernaculo deseruiunt. We haue an aultar of whiche they maie not eate that serue the tabernacle. For they singe
not a newe song, but remain in the olde letter. None can sing this newe song
but they that be in the kingdom of the Churche, whiche ys the kingdom of
the Father, saieth S. Hierom.

By this then ye maie perceaue not onelie the answer of S. Hierom to
the questio of *Hedibia*: but also his assertion for the presece of Chryst in the
Sacrament. For he saieth not in all this discourse that Chryst geueth vs a figure of the true bread, but the true bread yt self. We haue not a figure of
the meat of Chryst, but the meat yt self: we drinke not a figure of Chrystes
bloode, but we drinke his blood, saieth S. Hierom. And therfore this Pro-   E
clamer did seke to doe to moche violence to S. Hierom to cutt of a peice of
him, and shewing yt to his audience, to make them beleue, that S. Hierom
was on his side, as he saied, when al that ys before saied, and all that cometh
after in S. Hierom reclameth, yea and fighteth against him. Thus ye
haue hearde twoo great clerkes of Chrystes schoole, and the same also
two great Seniours of Chrystes Parliament house testifieng the enacted
trueth of the presence of Chryst in the Sacrament, and the vnderstanding of the woordes of his supper. Weigh them well, and consider them
throughlie.

THE FOVR AND FIFTETH CHAP. TESTIFIETH
the vnderstanding of the same woordes by Isichius and
S. Augustin.

Lthough *Isichius* be in the phrase of woordes somwhat darke : yet I wolde not omitte him, both for that he ys gra-   G
ue, auncient and learned, and his testimonie also verie effectuouse and good. Vpon *Leuiticus* writing on this text: *Qui*
comederit de sanctificatis per ignorantiam, addet quintam partem cum
eo, quod comedit, & dabit sacerdoti in sanctuarium. He that eateth of the holie thinges vnwittinglie, he shall put the fifte parte therunto, and geue vnto the preist, the halowed thing, thus he saieth : *Sancta sanctorum sunt pro-*
priè Christi mysteria , quia ipsius est corpus de quo Gabriel ad virginem dicebat:
Spiritus sanctus superueniet in te, & virtus Altissimi obumbrabit tibi, ideo quod na-
scetur ex te sanctum, vocabitur filius Dei. Sed & Esaias, sanctus Dominus, &
in altis habitat, in sinu videlicet Patris. Ab hoc enim non solùm alienigenas , &
inquilinos ,& mercenarios , sacrificio prohibuit, sed nec per ignorantiam percipere prace-
pit. Per ignorantiam autem percipit, qui virtutem eius, & dignitatem ignorat, qui
nescit quia corpus hoc, & sanguis est secundùm veritatem , sed mysteria quidem perci-
pit,nescit autem mysteriorum virtutem. Ad quem Salamon dicit, vel magis Spiritus,qui in
eo est: Quando sederis vt comedas cum principe, diligenter attende qua posita sunt ante te.
Apertè & ipse côpellens,& cogens eum,qui ignorat addere quintá parté. Hac enim quinta   H
addita, intelligere nos intelligibiliter diuina mysteria facit. Quid sit autem quinta pars, ipse
te verba legis latoris docere possunt , ait enim : Addet quintam partem cum eo, quod
comedit

Amb.li.4
de Sa.ca.5

Hcb.13.

Leuit. 22.

Isych. in
Leuit.li.6.
ca.22.

A comedit. *Et quomodò eius quod iam comedit, & côsumpsit addere quis quintã potest? Neq; enim aliud, aut aliunde, sed de ipso, & cum eo, vel sicut lxx, super ipsum iubet addi quintam. Ergo quinta eius super ipsum, sermo est, qui prolatus est ab ipso Christo super Dominicum mysterium. Ipse enim liberat nos ab ignorantia, remouetque nos additus, carnale quippiam & terrenum de sanctis arbitrari : sed diuinè ea & spiritualiter accipi sancit, quod quinta propriè nominatur, quia qui in nobis est diuinus spiritus, & sermo quem tradidit, qui in vobis sunt componit sensus, & non solùm nostrum gustum producit ad mysterium, sed & auditum, & visum, & tactum, & odoratum, ita vt nil in eis minori rationi, & infirmæ menti proximum, de ijs videlicet, quæ valdè superna sunt, suspicemur.* The most

Receauing of the Sacr. by ignoráce what yt ys.

holie things proprelie are the mysteries of Chryste. For yt ys his bodie, of the whiche Gabriel saied to the Virgen : The holie Gost shall come vpon thee, and the power of the highest shall ouershadowe thee. Therfore that holie thinge, that shall be born of thee shall be called the Sonne of God. And Esaias also : the Lorde ys holie and dwelleth on the heightes, that ys to saie, in the bosome of the Father. From this Sacrifice he doeth not

B onely forbidde straungers, and hired seruantes but he commaunded also that yt be not receaued by ignorance. *He receaueth yt by ignorance, that knoweth not the power and dignitie of yt, that knoweth not that yt ys the bodie and bloode in verie dede, but receaueth the misteries, and knoweth not the power of the misteries.* Vnto whõ Salomon saieth or raither the holie Goste that ys in him : *When thowe sittest to eate with a Prince, diligentlie attende what thinges are sett before thee :* He also compelling and constreigning him that ys ignorant to putto the fifte parte. This fifte part putto maketh vs easilie to vnderstand, the diuine and mystical thinges. What that fifte parte ys, the woordes of the Lawgeuer can teache thee for he saieth : he shall putto a fifte part with that that he hath eaten. Howe can a man putto a fifte parte that that he hath eaten and consumed? Neither maie he putto anie other thing, or had from anie other wher, but he commaundeth a fifte parte to be putto, of that, and with yt, or (as the seuentie interpretours saie) vpon yt. Then the fifte part of him vpon him, ys the woorde whiche was spoken of Chryst him self vpon our Lords mysterie.

C That woorde deliuereth vs from ignorance, and being putto, causeth vs to thinke no earthlie or carnall thing of the holie thinges, but maketh them to be taken diuinely and spirituallie. Whiche thinge proprelie ys called the fift part, bicause the spirit of God that ys in vs, and the woorde whiche he deliuered, settleth the wittes that be in vs, and bringeth furth to the mysterie not onelie our taste, but also our hearing and seeing and feeling and smelling, so that of these thinges whiche be verie high, we can not surmise anie base or grosse matter. Hitherto *Isichius.*

In whome I finde manie thinges woorthie to be noted, of the whiche some I shal breiflie touche, leauing other to be weighed of the reader. First yt ys certen, that he speaketh here of the bodie of Chryste in the Sacrament, whiche he calleth *the most holie thing,* and also a *sacrifice.* As of the holie thinges sacrificed in the Leuicall lawe, straungers and hirelinges might not receaue : no more maie they that be straungers to Chryste receaue of this holie thing. Besides this, no man might eate of that sacrifice vnwittinglie or ignorantlie : no more aught anie to eate of this owre sacrifice ignorántlie. Who doeth eate of this holie thing ignorátlie? *He* (saieth *Isichius*) *that knoweth not the*

The Sacramēt a most holie thing and a sacri fice.

D *power and dignitie of that, that he receaueth, who knoweth not yt to be a verie bodie, and blood in verie deede.*

Note well then these woordes, that the misteries of Chryst the Sacramēt of Chryst, ys his verie bodie and blood in dede. Yf yt be the bodie and blood

in

of Chryst in dede, wher ys nowe the bread and wine that the Aduersarie so E moche talketh of? wher be the onely figures and signes? As signes oftentimes be tokens of thinges that be not in dede: so these sainges of the Aduersaries be signes of a thing that they wold haue brought to passe, and yet yt ys not in dede, For all their talke in this sorte of this matter, ys but vain, fond, and withoute grownde. Here ye see in this auncient authour that we haue good grownd. For he saieth yt ys the bodie ād blood in verie deed. Let the Proclamer bring one of like aunciētie saing that yt ys not the bodie and bloode in dede, and as before I haue ioined with him, so will I nowe again that I will subscribe, Yf he can not, let him performe his promesse and subscribe to the catholique Churche. For here ys one that by expresse woordes saieth that the Sacrament ys the bodie and blloode in verie deed. wherbie the onelie figure of the Aduersaries ys excluded.

A plainpla ce for the Proclamer and issue ioi ned with him ther- vpon.

And here maie the Proclamer and all that ioine with him in this matter see their state, whiche ys the state of ignorance. For he (saieth this authour) *that receaueth thys Sacrament, and knoweth not the power and dignitie of yt, and that yt ys* F *the dodie and bloode in deed* (as the Proclamer and his complices doe) *he receaueth yt in ignorance.* I wish yt maie please our mercifull Lorde God to haue mercie vpon them, and to open their eies that they maie see their owne ignorance, and with humilitie mollifie their stonie hartes, that vain singularitie and pride forsaken, they maie humblie receaue the commaundement of God figuratiuelie spoken, and plainlie expownded by this authour, that their ignorance maie be remoued from them. What ys the commaundement of God that they shoulde doe? They must (*saieth allmightie God*) putto a fifte parte vpon the holie thing, and that will make them clerelie to vnderstand Gods misteries. This fifte part (*saieth Isichius*) ys the woorde that was spoken of Chryst himself vpon the mysterie of God. What woorde that was, yt ys doubted of neither partie, neither of the catholiques, neither of the aduersaries to be this: *This ys my bodie: This ys my blood. Ipse liberat nos ab ignoratia:* That woorde (*saieth Isichius*) deliuereth vs from ignorance.

Protestan- tes not ta- king the Sacr. to be the bodie and blood of Chryst in verie de de, receaue yt by igno- rance.

Nowe remembre that the ignorance ys, that a man receaueth the Sacra- G ment, and knoweth not the power and dignitie of yt, whiche power and dignitie ys, that in yt ys the bodie and bloode of Chryst in verie dede. This ignorance ys remoued by this woorde: *This ys my bodie This ys my bloode.* bicau se this woorde simplie without any trope or figure, teacheth that in the Sacrament ys the bodie and blood. Ioin then the woordes of this authour to gether. He saied before that the bodie and bloode be in the Sacrament in verie deed, and he saieth that these woordes of Chryst doe make vs cle rely to vnderstand yt, wherfor these woordes are to be vnderstanded as spoken of the bodie and blood of Chryst in deed, and not of the figu- re of them.

Ignorance of the Sa- crament what yt ys, and howe yt ys remo- ued.

Yf ye will yet heare more, and be more fullie certified of the trueth of this matter, this authour, as other did that be allreadie alleaged teacheth who ys the woorker of yt, and by what mean yt ys brought to passe. For proceading in the exposition of the text, he saieth thus: *Quicunque ergo san-ctificata per ignorantiam comederit, ignorans eorum virtutem (sicut diximus) addet quin-tam eius super eo, & dabit sacerdoti in sanctuarium. Sanctificationem enim mystici sacri-ficij, & à sensibilibus ad intelligibilia, translationem siue commutationem, ei, qui verus* H *est sacerdos, videlicet Christo oportet dari, id est, ipsi de eis miraculum cedere, & imputa-re. quia per eius virtutem, & prolatum ab eo verbum, quæ videntur, tam sanctificata sunt, quàm cunctum carnis excedunt sensum.* Whosoeuer therfor shall eate the holie

A lie thinges by ignorance, not knowing their power (*as we haue faied*) he fhall putto a fifte parte of yt vppon yt, and fhall geue yt vnto the preift into the fanctuarie. For the fanctificacion of the mifticall facrifice, and the tranflaciõ or commutacion from fenfible to intelligible thinges, muft be geuen to him that ys the true preift, that ys to faie, to Chryfte, that ys to geue and impute the miracle wrought in thefe thinges to him, bicaufe by his power, and the woorde fpokẽ of him the things that are feen, are fo fanctified as they paffe al the witte of man. Thus he.

Chaunge of fefible thinges to intelligible in the Sacr. muft be geuẽ to Chrift

See ye not here who ys the dooer of this matter? perceaue ye not who woorketh this miracle? The dooing of all this(*faieth Ifichius*) muft be referred, and imputed to Chryfte. For he by his power, and the woorde fpoken of him, fanctifieth the vifible bread and wine as yt paffeth mans witte to knowe. Let vs here then firft vnderftand, that if the bread and wine were but made figures of Chryftes bodie and bloode, fignifienge to vs that as thefe feed the bodie: fo Chryft feedeth the foule, yt were not a matter paffing mans witte. But mans witte maie well atteign to perceaue that in foch forte,

Bread and wine fo fanctified in the bleffed Sacr. as yt paffeth mãs witte.

B they maie be figures. Wherfor ther ys a greater matter wrought in the bread and wine then that, whiche we maie perceaue by that he faieth, that they be fainctified. By which woorde ys not onelie refelled the wicked faing of Cramner, that bread and wine can not be fanctified, but alfo ther ys geuen a farder matter to confider in the worke of Chryfte. Wherfor vnderftand again that this fanctificacion declareth the mean howe this worke ys brought to paffe that ys wrought. For by this fanctificacion ther ys wrought (as the termes of this authour be) a tranflacion or a commutacion from fenfible thinges to intelligible, that ys ftom breade, which ys perceaued by fenfeis, to the bodie of Chryft, which ys in this maner not perceaued by fenfeis. Which tearmes importe that, that the Churche calleth *Tranfubftantiacion* For when ther ys a tranflacion commutacion or chaunging of thinges fenfible to thinges not fenfible (which ys a chaunge of one thing of one nature or fubftance, into an other thing of an other nature or fubftance) what

Tranfubftantiacion proued by Ifych.

C fhoulde let that yt maie not be called *Tranfubftantiacion?*

But what doe I tarrie in thefe thinges fullie and effectuouflie teftified by this authour. For he hath thaught vs that Chryftes bodie and bloode be in the Sacrament in verie deed: he hath taught vs that to be wrought by the tráflacion or commutacion of the bread and wine into the fame bodie and blood of Chryfte, he hathe taught vs that Chryft ys the woorker of yt by his power, and by the woorde fpoken of him. Finallie he teacheth that by the woordes of Chryft we are clearlie taught the prefence of his bodie in the Sacrament, and fo by confequent we are taught, that they be no figuratiue fpeaches.

Thus moche being faied of *Ifichius*, and teftified by him: let vs alfo heare S. Auguftine, who at this time ys ioined with him. Thus writeth he in this matter vpon the 33 pfalme, treacting a ftorie of king Dauid, and applieng yt to Chryft. *Et ferebatur in manibus fuis. Hoc verò, fratres, quomodò poffet fieri in homine, quis intelligat? quis enim portatur manibus fuis? manibus aliorum poteft portari*

Auguft. in Pfal. 33 concion.

D *homo, manibus fuis nemo portatur. Quomodò intelligatur in ipfo Dauid, fecundum literam non inuenimus: In Chrifto autem inuenimus, ferebatur Chriftus in manibus fuis, quando commendans ipfum corpus fuum ait: Hoc eft corpus meum, ferebat enim illud corpus in manibus fuis.* And he was caried in his owne handes. Bretheren howe this can be doen in a man, who can vnderftande? Who ys born is his owne handes In the handes of an other, a man maie be born: in his owne handes no man

Chryft bare his bodie in his owne hãdes, whẽ he faied: This ys my bodie.

ys

ys born. howe yt maie be vnderſtand in Dauid himſelf according to the　E
letter we finde not : but in Chryſt we finde yt. He was born in his owne
handes, when geuing furth the ſame his bodie, he ſaied : *This ys my bodie.* For
he did beare that bodie in his handes, Thus farre he,

For aſmoch as S. Auguſtiye by diſcuſſion did finde that the woordes,
whiche he treacted of coulde not be vnderſtanded literallie in Dauid, euen
ſo as yt coulde not be perfourmed in him, that he being but a man ſhoulde
beare his own bodie in his owne handes, no more coulde yt, or can yt be per
fourmed in anie other pure naturall man. Therfor enforced to make a far
der ſearche he had recourſe to Chryſt, who was more then a naturall man,
and in him at no other time dothe he finde yt perfourmed and fullfilled ac
cording to the letter, but when he gaue furth his bodie to his Diſciples,
ſaing : *This ys my bodie.* Yf then yt was at that time fulfilled in him according
to the letter, when he ſaied: *This ys my bodie,* and if then he caried his owne
bodie in his handes, then this ſcripture alſo muſt ſo be vnderſtanded, or ells
what ſhoulde yt make to the pourpoſe? For Chryſt did not carie his bodie　F
in his owne hands, yf he caried but the figure of his bodie-

Wherfor the wreſting that *Oecolampadius* maketh vpon theſe woordes of
S. Auguſtine : *Ipſe ſe portabat quodã modo cùm diceret : Hoc eſt corpus meũ.* He did
beare him ſelf after a certain maner, when he ſaied : *This ys my bodie :* will not
ſerue to prooue that he did beare him ſelf onely in a figure. For if S. Augu
ſtine had vnderſtand the woordes of bearing of a mans bodie in his owne
handes, to be to bear the figure of his bodie, he wolde not haue ſaied that
he coulde not finde yt in Dauid. For who doubteth but that Dauid might
haue born a figure of himſelf in his owne hand, and ſo maie anie other natu
rall man. And Chryſt bare his owne figure in his hand when he had the Pa
ſchall lãbe in his hand. And therfor in that maner of vnderſtanding, yt might
be fownde to be doẽ in Dauid, and in other mẽ . But this maner of bearing
was ſoche as coulde not be doen in Dauid, or anie other being onely a natu
rall man, but onely in Chryſt God and man. Who aboue the power of man
by his great diuine power coulde cõpaſſe that, that man by no meanes can　G

reach vnto. Wherfor hauing the bread in his handes, and by his allmightie
power, and woorde ſaing: *This ys my bodie:* he turned that bread into his bo
die, and ſo in that certein maner after S. Auguſtines woords and mening, he
did beare his owne bodie in his owne handes. And ſo was this fullfilled in
Chryſt according to the letter. And therfor as to the verifieng of the letter,
yt muſt nedes be that Chryſt caried verilie him ſelf in his owne handes : ſo
to the verifieng of that acte yt muſt nedes be, that theſe woords: *This ys my bo
die:* muſt be vnderſtanded in their propre and literall ſenſe.

Thus then yt ys euident, that forſomoche as Chryſt bare him ſelf in his
owne handes in geuing furth the Sacrament to his Apoſtles, that this verie
bodie ys born alſo of his miniſtres nowe in the Sacrament geuẽ furth to his
faithfull beleuers. For (as Chryſoſtome ſaieth) this table of Chryſt nowe vſed

according to his inſtituciõ, ys nothing inferiour to the table that Chryſt him
ſelf ſatte perſonallie at. For as Chriſt did ſanctifie that table: ſo doeth he this.
And therfor we muſt otherwiſe thinke of this Sacramẽt, thẽ we doe of other　H
thinges, whiche doe ſhew furth Chryſt to vs, to the which the aduerſarie of
tẽtimes doth compare this Sacrament, to abaſe and diminiſh the dignitie of
the ſame.

For although the Apoſtles by their woorde and epiſtles did ſhewe furth
Chryſt: yet neither the one nor the, other ys called the bodie of Chryſt but
　　　　　　　　　　　　　　　　　　　　　　　　　　　　onely

A onelie that that ys confecrated by the woordes of Chryſt in the aultar as S.Auguſtine ſaieth.*Potuit Paulus ſignificando prædicare Dominum Ieſum Chriſtum,ali ter per linguam ſuam,aliter per epiſtolam, aliter per ſacramentum corporis & ſanguinis eius.Nec linguam quippe eius,nec membranas,nec atramentum,nec ſignificantes ſonos lingua editos,nec ſigna literarum conſcripta pelliculis, corpus Chriſti & ſanguinem dicimus, ſed illud tantùm,quod ex fructibus terræ acceptum,& prece myſtica conſecratum, ritè ſumimus ad ſalutem ſpiritualem in memoriam pro nobis Dominicæ paſsionis , quod cùm per manus hominum ad illam viſibilem ſpeciem,producitur, non ſanctificatur vt ſit tam magnum ſacramentum,niſi operante inuiſibiliter Spiritu Dei.*Paule might by ſignifieng preache our Lorde Ieſus Chryſt,or ells by his tonge,or ells by epiſtle, or ells by the Sacrament of his bodie and blood,yet doe we call neither his toung, nor his parchement,nor inke, nor the ſignifieng ſowndes ſettfurth by the tounge,nor the markes of the letters written together in skinnes , the bodie and bloode of Chryſt,but onely that,whiche being taken of the fruictes of the earth,and by the myſticall praier conſecrated,we receaue to our ſpiritual healthe in the remembrance of our Lordes paſsion ſuffred for vs.   Whiche

B thing when yt ys brought by the handes of men to that viſible forme , yt ys not ſanctified that yt maie be ſo great a Sacrament , but by the Spirite of God woorking inuiſiblie.Hitherto ſainct Auguſtin.

Auguſt. de Trin.li. 3.cap.4.

Bread and wine are not ſanctified to be ſo great a Sacrament but by the inui ſible worke of God.

Of whome ye ſee that we are taught, that thoug Chryſt be by diuerſe meanes ſettfurth and preached,as by ſcriptures,preachinges,and by the Sacrament:yet theſe thinges be not all of like degree.For ther ys none of theſe called the bodie of Chryſt,but onelie the bread that ys conſecrated by the myſticall praier,that ys,by the woordes of Chryſt:*Thys ys my bodie*:that onelie ys called the bodie of Chryſte.

Nowe Oecolampadius wolde, that bicauſe ſainct Auguſtin ſaieth , that Chryſt ys preached by ſcripture, woorde,and Sacrament , that theſe three be of one ſorte, no more being in the Sacrament, then in the other two. But note I praie thee (*gentle reader*) howe he abuſeth ſainct Auguſtin to proue that hys wicked ſainge . Of this place of ſainct Auguſtin

C nowe alleadged he taketh onely thus moche : *Paule might by ſignifieng preache our Lorde Ieſus Chryſt , otherwiſe by hys toung , otherwiſe by epiſtle , otherwiſe by the Sacrament of his bodie and blood .* And vpon thys he growndeth hys argument , and wolde be ſeen well to haue confirmed hys doctrine . But all the reſt of ſainct Auguſtines woordes whiche folowe , whiche ouerthrowe all his building he craftelie lefte oute . For yt foloweth : *Yet doe we call neither his toung , neither his epiſtle , nor his writinges the bodie of Chryſte : but onely we call that the bodie of Chryſte , that ys taken of the fruictes of the earth , and ys by the myſticall prayer conſecrated , that doe we call the bodie of Chryſt .* All thys doth he leaue oute.Soche was the ſynceritie of the man in alleaging the holie Fathers. So good ys the cauſe that he defended,that the doctours muſte be mutilated and brought oute in peice meall,or ells yt coulde not ſtand.

Oecolamp. craftilie abuſeth S. Auguſtin.

Not toung nor writing nor ſoche other ſhewing furth Chryſt be called his bodie but bread and wine conſetrated.

Ys yt not merueilouſe,that he coulde bring this place of ſainct Auguſtin, whiche although the firſt peice taken alone ſeemeth ſomwhat to ſownde to his pourpoſe: yet the wholl taken together ys alltogether againſt him? Alas that euer anie man wolde ſo deceaue the people of God , and by

D ſoche frawde and abuſe of the holie writers make them to embrace erroure in ſtead of trueth,weigh the place throughlie,and yowe ſhall perceaue howe yt mainteineth the catholique trueth of the preſence of Chryſtes boin the Sacrament verie moch . Ye haue nowe heard,that neither the worde

written,nor the woorde ſpoken,though Chryſt be preached by them, be **E**
called the bodie of Chryſt,but onely the Sacrament ys called the bodie of
Chryſt.And why yt ys called the bodie of Chryſte,he declareth:Not bicau
ſe (ſaieth he)by the handes of man yt ys brought to be a viſible forme,but bicauſe yt ys ſanctified and made ſo great a Sacrament by the inuiſible woorking of the holie Goſte.

Note theſe two poinctes,that S.Auguſtine ſaieth *that the bread ys ſanctified,*
*and made ſo great a Sacrament.*And again that he ſaieth *yt ys ſo ſanctified and made*
by the,inuiſible worke of the holie Goſte. Ther ys great difference betwixt the ſancti
ficacion of the Sacrament yt ſelf,and the ſoule of man, that receaueth the
Sacrament.

Oecolamp.
and Cran-
mer their
hereſies.

Now *Oecolampadius* and Cranmer ſaie that the Sacramentes being dumbe
creatures receaue no ſanctificacion,but onely the ſowles of men. They ſaie
alſo that the holie Goſt woorketh not in the thinges that be the Sacramentes,but in the men that receaue the Sacrametes.Thys they ſaie bicauſe they
wolde auoid the preſence of Chryſte in the Sacrament,which ys made ther **F**
preſent by ſanctificacion of the bread.But againſt theſe their ſaings S. Augu
ſtin ſaieth:that the ſame bread that ys made by the handes of men ys ſanctified,and receauing ſanctitie,ys made ſo great a Sacrament.Againſt them alſo

S. Augu-
ſtin plain
againſt Oe
colamp. ād
Cranmer.

he ſaieth,that the holie Goſte woorketh inuiſiblie in the bread.I wolde now
learn of the Aduerſaries,what S.Auguſtine meneth by calling the Sacramet
ſo great a Sacrament,and what worke yt ys that the holie Goſte woorketh
inuiſiblie in the bread?The woorkes of the holy Goſt be no trifles . Yt ys
great and miraculouſe that he woorketh.And what he woorketh S.Iames in
his Maſſe, S. Baſill alſo and Chryſoſtom in their Maſſes, by their humble
praiers doe declare.

Diuus Iac.
in Miſſa.

S.Iames thus:*Spiritum tuum ſanctiſsimum demitte nunc Domine in nos,& in hæc ſan-*
cta dona propoſita,vt ſuperueniens ſancta,& bona, & glorioſa ſua præſentia ſanctificet,
& efficiat hunc panem corpus ſanctum Chriſti tui,& calicem hunc precioſum ſanguinem
*Chriſti tui.*Sende downe now(o Lord)thy moſt holie Spirit vpon vs, and vpon
theſe holie giftes ſettfurth, that he coming ouer them , maie with his holy
good,and gloriouſe preſence,ſanctifie,and make this bread the holie bodie of
thy Chryſt,ād this cuppe the preciouſe blood of thy Chryſt.Thus S.Iames. **G**
S.Baſili and Chryſoſtome haue the like woordes.

See ye not nowe then howe the bread ys ſanctified ? See ye not what ys

Bread ſan-
ctified con-
trarie to
Cranmers
aſſertion ād
Oecolamp.

the worke of the holie Goſte ? Perceaue ye not howe that S.Auguſtine vpō
good cauſe called the Sacrament,ſo great a Sacrament?ys yt not a great Sacrament in whieh by worke of the holie Goſt ys made preſent the bodie of
Chryſt?To haue hidden this trueth Oecolampadius by peice meall brought
in S.Auguſtine.But now ye haue ſeen the catholique faith well teſtified,the
falſhead of the Aduerſaries detected,and(to return to oure matter, and to
conclude)ye perceaue this Sacrament by myſtical praier,which ys by Chryſtes woordes,to be conſecrated,the effecte of which conſecracion being the
bodie of Chryſte(as ys ſaied)the woordes muſt nedes be taken without figuratiue ſenſe.

Thus,if my iudgement faill me not,ye haue hearde two other noble men
of Chryſtes ſchoole,and Parliament houſe,very plainlie teſtifieng the enacted trueth of the vnderſtanding of Chryſtes wordes,yea ſo plainly that yt cā **H**
not but moch confirme the good Chryſtian,and confute the Pheudochri-
ſtian.But to go forwarde,I will ende with theſe two, and call other two.

THE

THE FIVE AND FIFTETH CHAPITER
tarieth in the expofition of the fame woordes by Chry-
foſtom and Sedulius.

Ow among the learned Fathers of the greke church,we are deſ
cended to Chryſoſtome,of whome I maie ſaie, as before ys ſaied of S.Ambroſe,that he ys ſo full of godlie teſtimonies, teſtifieng to vs the true vnderſtanding of Chryſtes woordes, that as
I knowe not whiche of them firſt to take:ſo doe I merueill that
they being ſo manie,the Proclamer coulde for ſhame ſaie, that ther ys not
one auncient doctour that maketh for the catholique faith of the Sacra-
ment.Thus Chryſoſtō expownding theſe woordes of owre Sauiour Chryſt
in the xxvi of Matthew,ſaieth.*Credamus vbique Deo,nec repugnemus ei, etiamſi ſen-*
ſui,& cogitationi noſtræ abſurdum eſſe videatur , quod dicitur,ſuperet & ſenſum,& ra- | Chryſ.in.
tionem noſtram ſermo,quæſo,ipſius,quod in omnibus, & præcipuè in myſteriis faciamus, | 26 Math.
B *non illa quæ ante nos iacent ſolummodò aſpicientes,ſed verba quoque eius tenentes. Nam* | hom.83.
verbis eius defraudari non poſſumus,ſenſus verò noſter deceptu facillimus eſt.Illa falſa eſ
ſe non poſſunt,hic ſæpius ac ſæpius fallitur.Quoniam ergo ille dixit.Hoc eſt corpus meum:
nulla teneamur ambiguitate,ſed credamus,& oculis intellectus id perſpiciamus. Let vs in | Gods word
euerie place beleue God,and let vs not ſtriue againſt him,although that that | euen cōtra
he ſaieth,ſeem to our ſenſe and thought vnlikely.Let hys woorde (I beſeche | rie to ſen-
yowe)ouercome bothe our wittes and reaſon,which thing let vs doe in all | ſes muſt be
thinges,but cheiflie in the myſteries,not onely loking on thoſe things, whi- | beleued.
che lie before vs,but alſo regarding hys woords.For by hys woords we can
not be deceaued our ſenſe ys eaſie to be deceaued:they can not be falſe:this
our ſenſe ys often and often deceaued.Foraſmoche them as he hath ſaied:
*This ys my bodie:*Let vs be holden with no ambiguitie or doubte,but let vs beleue,and with the eies of our vnderſtanding,let vs verilie ſee yt . Thus farre
Chryſoſtom.

In this ſaing yt ys to be perceaued howe he laboureth,that in this matter
of the Sacramēt we ſhould diſcredit our ſenſeis,ād creditte Chryſts woords.
C And foraſmoche as he ſaied.*This ys my bodie:*thouh yt paſſe our reaſon to com
prehend the worke of God in making preſent the bodie of Chryſt, and our
ſenſeis can not of themſelues atteign to perceaue the ſame bodie:for neither | But yt paſ-
our eies doe ſee yt,neither our taſt diſcern yt, neither our féeling or other | ſeth not rea
ſenſes perceaue yt:yet (ſaieth'Chryſoſtome)we maie not doubte of yt,but bele- | ſon to make
ue yt to be the bodie of Chryſt,bicauſe he ſaied yt was ſo. | preſent a ſi
| gure of his
Nowe conſider with me,if the woordes of Chryſt had an other ſenſe,thē | bodie.
they doe outwardlie purporte,as that they ſhoulde teache vs,that yt ys but
a figure of Chryſtes bodie, and not the bodie yt ſelf, wolde Chryſoſtom
(trow ye)in this his open ſermon wil the people to beleue,and not to doubt
of the trueth of the woords,as they be ſpokē,and wold not raither firſt vtter
the true ſenſe and vnderſtanding of them yf anie other were, and then perſwade the people of that ſenſe not to doubt?Yt ys an euel maner of teaching
to will the people to beleue the woordes of ſcripture as they lie, and are not | Chryſo. wil
ſo to be vnderſtanded,but in a ſenſe moche different from that.Yt ys not the | leth Chry-
maner of Chryſoſtom ſo to teache, wherfore for ſo moche as he willeth | ſtes woor-
D them not to doubte,but to beleue the woordes as they be ſpoken (whiche he | des to bevn
dothe in that, that he teacheth no other ſenſe) yt ys manifeſt that theſe woordes | derſtāded
are to be vnderſtanded in their propre ſenſe withoute the Aduerſaries | as they be
figure. | ſpoken.

Reall pre-
sence auou-
ched by
Chryso.

Jn 14.
Marc. hõ.
51.

Chryst sa-
ing.This ys
my bodie.
with the
woorde
made the
thing.

And that Chrysostome himself did so vnderstand them, thys proueth that he in sondrie and manie places of his workes, treating of these woords of Chryst: *Thys ys my bodie*: he neuer addeth this sense: *Thys ys a figure of my bodie*: But euer leaueth them in the sense that they be spoken, and in some place by expresse woordes, in some place by plain circumstance, he declareth the verie presence of Chrystes bodie in the Sacrament. By expresse woordes, as wher he saieth: *Qui dixit: Hoc est corpus meum, & rem simul cum verbo confecit.* He that saied : *Thys ys my bodie :* He with hys woorde made the the thing also.

I wishe these fewe woordes of Chrysostom to be well marked, that they neuer fall from memorie, but maie allwaies be reteined as a rule to vnderstand him in all places wher he speaketh of the Sacrament of Chrystes bodie and blood. For yf Chryst with hys woorde made the thing also that he spake of, and the thing that he spake of was hys bodie, then with the speaking of hys woorde he made hys bodie. This then being trueth (as Chryso stome here teacheth) yt can not be denied, but that by expresse woordes he teacheth the presence of Chrystes verie bodie in the Sacrament.

Figure of
the Sacra-
mentaries
wiped awa
ie by Chry
sost .

And thus by Chrysostome ys clerely wiped awaie the hereticall figuratiue vnderstanding of these woordes of Chryst: *Thys ys my bodie.* For the Aduersaries wolde haue yt so a figure as of a thing absent. *But Chryst* (as Chrysostome saieth) *made the thing together with the woorde.* Wherfore as the woorde was present: so was the thing present. Yf the thing be present, then the figure of the Aduersaries can not here be admitted.

Plain pla-
ces of Chry
sost for the
Pooclamer
Chrys. ibi .

Vpon the certentie of which presence, the same Chrysostome in the same homelie thus taught hys people. *Quando igitur sacerdotem corpus tibi prebere videris, noli sacerdotis, sed Christi manum ad te porrigi arbitrari.* Therfore when thow seest the preist geue thee the bodie, thinke not the hand of the preist, but the hand of Chryst to be put furth to thee . And that the people shoulde geue full creditte to this trueth, he vseth this perswasion in the same homelie: *Qui enim maius, id est, animam suam pro te posuit, quare dedignabitur suum tibi tradere corpus? Audiamus igitur tam sacerdotes quàm alij, quàm magna, quàm admirabilis res nobis concessa est. Audiamus, oro, & perhorrescamus, carnes suas nobis tradidit, seipsum immolatum nobis proposuit. Quam igitur satisfactionem offeremus, cum tali pabulo nutriti peccemus? cum Agnum comedentes in lupos conuertamur? cum ouinis carnibus refecti, vt leones rapiamus ?* He that hath geuen a greater thing for thee, that ys to saie, his life, why will he disdein to deliuer hys bodie to thee ? Let vs therfore heare, bothe preistes and other, howe great and wonderfull a thing ys graunted vnto vs. Let vs heare (I praye yowe) and let vs feare . *He hath deliuered vnto vs hys flesh : himself offred hath he putte before vs.* What satisfaction then shall we offre, that being nourished with soch foode, doe sinne? When eating the lambe, we are turned into wolues? when satisfied with shepes flesh, we rauine as lions? Thus farre Chrysostom.

Note well this perswasion of his. *Yf Chryst hath vouched saif to geue his life for thee, will he not vouchesafe to geue his bodie? he hath geuen his life for thee, whiche ys a great matter, will he not geue thee his bodie, whiche ys not so great a matter?* After that we haue considered this perswasion, let vs somwhat more depelie weigh this place of Chrysostom, and we shall finde yt so euident in declaring the presence of Chrystes bodie in the Sacrament, that Sathan himself can not well open hys mouthe against yt, moche lesse hys mynisters. For if they will glose this place of Chrysostom, they must bestowe a great nombre of figures vpon yt. For here be manie plain woordes and tearmes

Tearmes
to plain for
figuratiue
speaches.

A mes , *as his bodie* , *his flesh a great and a woonderfull thinge* , *himself offred*
settfurth before ꝟs : *soche foode* , *the lambe*, *the flesh of the shepe* , whiche doe
declare vnto vs the presence of Chrystes bodie . And therfore as ys
saied , they must be darkened with manie figures and mystie gloses, yf
they shall be peruerted to the Aduersaries corruption of the trueth.
And trulie yt were wonderfull that Chrysostom preaching to the people wolde vse so manie plain tearmes, and leaue them as sownding in their
owne significacion,when in verie dede (as the Aduersaries saie , and wolde
bear vs in hand) they doe all signifie figuratiuelie.

　　But let vs yet a litle deapelier consider the wholl place , and tearmes of the same . And first as touching the perswasion , let vs weigh
the comparison that ys made in the same by this authour to declare the
great loue , and mercie of Chryst towardes vs,wherin he compareth the
life of Chryste,whiche he gaue for vs, to his bodie which he geueth to vs.
Nowe if the Aduersarie by the bodie,will vnderstand a figure of the bodie,
howe vnmeet a comparison will he cause Chrysostom to make , as to com-

B pare a bare figure to the life of Chryst?Or who will thinke that Chrysosto-　*Figures be*
me wolde vse soche a great matter as the life of Chryst geuen for vs, to per-　*no wonder-*
swade vs to beleue so small a matter , as that Chryst geueth vs a peice of　*full things.*
bread a figure of his bodie after the sense of the Sacramentarie ?
But that yt can not beare that sense,the woordes that folowe doe well proo
ue.For he saieth,that the thing that ys geuen vnto vs,ys *a great and a wonder-*
full thing. Yf yt be but a figure yt ys no great thing.For figures haue ben sin
ce the beginning,and for the most parte not esteemed as great things in the
respect that they were figures.

　　Yf the Aduersarie will saie that Chrysostom speaketh of the bodie of
Chryst spirituallie receaued,whiche ys a great thing : Yet yt will not helpe　*wonderfull*
him to wrest Chrysostom to him.For albeit the bodie of Chryst spirituallie　*what ys pro*
receaued be a great thing·yet yt ys not proprelie woonderfull . For that ys　*prelie.*
proprely woonderfull that ys not in vse , but rare , seldom , and almost not
seen(as saieth) sainct Augustine. Nowe to receaue the bodie of Chryst

C spirituallie ys no rare matter , for yt hath ben in vse from the be-　*Spůall re-*
ginning of the worlde, yt was comon to the holie Fathers and Patriar-　*ceipt onelie*
ches in the lawe of nature.Yt was in vse among the faithfull Iewes , and so　*of Chryst*
among the faithfull Chrystians (though not among the false Chrystians)　*ys not won-*
yt ys no straunge matter, and therfore not a woonderfull thing , though　*derfull.*
a greate thing. But to receaue Chrystes bodie bothe spirituallie and reallie , that ys both a great thing and a woonderfull thing , woonderfull I
saie,for that yt was neuer in vse the bodie of Chryst reallie to be receaued
before Chryst saied:*Take,eate,this ys my bodie*, at whiche time he did institute
and ordein yt so to be receaued. Before Chryst did so by his woorde insti-
te,the worlde neuer knewe this maner of receipt,yt was neuer in vse, neuer
in practise.And therfore yt ys a wonderfull thing,not onelie for that yt exceadeth the compasse of reason,and passeth the reache of the senseis that a
naturall bodie shoulde in soche maner be receaued,but also for that before
Chrystes institucion yt was neuer in vse.

　　But what needeth me to trauaill so moche in declaring this , when the　*Spůall and*
　　　　　　　　　　　　　　　　　　　　　　　　　　　　　　　　　　real receipt
D authour himself openeth what the great and wonderfull thing ys that he　*together of*
speaketh of heare , saing in the same place : *Audiamus oro & perhor-*　*Chrystes bo*
*rescamus , carnes suas nobis tradidit,seipsum immolatum nobis proposuit.*Let vs heare,I　*die ys won-*
beseche yow , and let vs feare , *He hath deliuered to vs his flesh, himself offred*　*derfull.*
　　　　　　　　　　　　　　　　Mm iii　　　　　　　　　　　hath

hath he sett before vs. Thys ys the great thing that he spake of, this ys the woon **E** derfull thing that ys geuen to vs, which he meneth of, the flesh of Chryste, Chryst himself sett before vs. Which thing that we shoulde well geue heed vnto, and perceaue the greatnesse and wonderfullnesse of yt, he preuenteth vs with hys aduertisement saing: *Let vs heare and feare,* whiche kinde of aduertisement neaded not, if yt were but a peice of breade.

And note here that Chrysostome to the entent the thing might fullie be perceaued according to the trueth, and his mening in the same, he did not content himself onelie to saie that *Chryst hath deliuered vnto vs his flesh* : but he addeth, that *Chryst sett himself offred before vs,* wherbie are remoued all the figures and tropes, whiche the Aduersaries to the corruption of the trueth, wolde here haue putto. For yf Chrysostome had saied no more , But that Chryst hath geuen to vs his flesh, then wolde Sathan by his ministers hanged on one of his comon seales, as this woorde, *figuratiuelie,* or *spirituallie,* and so made yt to haue appeared, that yt ys his euidence . But the holie Gost, being a good schoolemaster, hath taught hys scholer Chrysostom so to frame his woordes, that if the enemie wolde go aboute to falsifie them by putting to, one of his comon seales, yet his falhead shoulde needes appeare. **F** For when Chrysostome had saied, that Chryst had deliuered vnto vs hys flesh, he immediately added, as an exposition of those woordes , *himself hath he setfurth before vs.* By whiche woordes the matter ys made plain for yf Chryst himself be sett before vs, then ys the bare figure taken awaie and denied . Yf he be sett before vs, then ys he not onely spiritually receaued. For spirituall receipt ys in vs, and not before vs. Chryst by the doctrine of the Aduersarie ys within vs, and not in the Sacrament before vs: but Chrysostom saieth that he ys before vs, and speaketh of the being of Chryst in the Sacrament. Wherfore he himself ys in the Sacrament before vs, and so ys excluded the onely spirituall maner, whiche ys the other seale of the Aduersarie, and the reall presence ys proued whiche ys the doctrine catholique.

The farder certentie also of this matter ys added when he saieth , *that we eate the lambe,* wherby he meneth the Lambe, that taketh awaie the sinnes of the worlde, Iesus Chryst, that innocent Lambe figured by the olde Paschall **G** lambe. Likewise saing, that *we eat the flesh of the shepe* , he meneth the flesh of Chryst, who ys he, *Qui tanquam ouis ad occisionem ducebatur, & tanquam agnus coram se tondente obmutescebat, & non aperiebat os suum,* who as a shepe was ledde to be slain, and as a lambe before the sherer did holde his peace, and did not open his mouthe.

Finallie that in all this discourse he speaketh of the verie reall presence of Chrystes bodie in the Sacrament, and that we verilie and substanciallie receaue yt, and be nourished with yt, his last woordes doe inuinciblie prooue. In whiche mouing a question vpon the woordes before saied, he saieth: *Quam satisfact. &c.* what maner of amendes, or satisfaction shall we make to him , that being in sinne, doe receaue soche foode ? that being wolues doe eate the lambe? that being lions , doe rauine the flesh of the shepe ? Nowe certen yt ys both by the doctrine of the Catholique , and the Protestant , that the sinner eateth not the bodie of Chryst spirituallie , wherfore yt must needes be, that soche as being wolues and lions in wickednesse of life , and doe yet **H** by the doctrine of Chrysostom eate the flesh of the lambe, and deuoure the flesh of the shepe, forasmoch (as ys saied) that they doe not eate the flesh of Chryst spirituallie , that they eate yt in the Sacrament reallie and substanciallie

Sathäs seales can not be hanged to Chrysostomes woordes.

Esay.53.

Sinners receaue the bodie of Chryst in the Sacr. not spiritu allie, but yet reallie.

A ſtanciallie, For this ys well knowen to the Aduerſatie that the euell man can not receaue Chryſtes bodie but in the Sacrament. But Chryſoſtom ſaieth that the euell man receaueth the bodie of Chryſt, Wherfor in the Sacrament.

Thus, if my iudgement fail me not, Chryſoſtom hath by expreſſe woordes taught vs the reall preſence of Chryſt in the Sacrament, Nowe we ſhall heare him teach the ſame by circunſtance, but ſo plainlie and euidently that yt can not be againſt ſaied. The circunſtance conſiſteth in the compariſon of the Paſchall Lambe, and in the woordes of Chryſte in the ſixt of S. Iohn by whiche both he prooueth theſe woordes of Chryſt: *This ys my bodie* : to be ſpoken in their propre ſenſe, and to teach vs the reall preſence of Chryſt in the Sacrament. The woordes be theſe: *Præcipuam eorum ſolemnitatem diſſoluit, & ad aliam menſam horroris plenam eos conuocat, dicens : Accipite , & comedite, Hoc eſt corpus meum. Quomodò igitur turbati non ſunt hoc audientes? quia multa & magna de hoc antea audierant.* He diſſolueth their cheif Solemnitie, and to an other table full of terriblenesse he calleth them, ſaing: *This ys my bodie.* Howe then

B were they not troobled hearing this? bicauſe he had ſpoken manie and great thinges of this before. Thus he.

Reall preſence auouched of Chryſoſt, bi circunſtãce

Chryſ. homil.83. in 16. Math.

In this ſaing two thinges breiflie noted, I paſſe to the next place. The firſt ys, that the other table wherunto Chryſt did call his Apoſtles was full of terriblenesse or trembling, whiche ſheweth that ther was in that table, aboue the table of the Paſchall lambe, from the whiche they were called, ſome thing that was of ſoche maieſtie, that yt was to be feared, whiche thing was not in the other table. In the other table was the Paſchall lambe a liuelie figure of Chryſt our Paſchall lambe, and in yt Chryſt was figuratiuely eaten. And although yt were their cheifeſt ſolemnitie : yet Chryſoſtom doth not call yt a fearfull table. Yf then in that ſolemne table ther was the figure of Chryſt, and Chryſt was ther figuratiuely eaten, and yet that table was not terrible or ful of horroure: then in the table of Chryſt ys not onelie a figure of Chryſt, and Chryſt figuratiuelie eaten, but ther ys a great matter ther that maketh this table to be fearfull. What ys that ? *Hoc eſt corpus meum. This ys my*

C *bodie.* For Chryſoſtom ſaieth, that when Chryſt called them to this table he ſaied : *This ys my bodie.* Yf theſe woordes *This ys my bodie,* did no more but cauſe the figure of Chryſtes bodie to be in the table of Chryſt, and ſo Chryſte to be eaten in a figure as he was in the table of the Paſchall Lambe, thẽ this table had ben no more full of horroure then the other. But for ſo moche as by that ſainge of Chryſt, the table was full of horroure, yt argueth(as before yt ys alleaged oute of Chryſoſtome) that he ſo ſaing *with the woorde made alſo the thing.* ſo that as he ſpake the woorde preſentlie, ſo the thing, that ys, his bodie was ther preſentlie. For the ſaing of the woorde, and the making of the thing went iointlie togeather. Wherby then as yt doth plainly appeare that the bodie of Chryſt was preſent in that table : ſo alſo dothe yt appeare that the bodie being made preſent at the ſaing of theſe woordes: *This ys my bodie* : that theſe woordes are to be taken and vnderſtanded in their propoſe ſenſe.

Table of the old Paſchal lambe not terrible as onelie bnt a figure the table of Chryſt ys terrible ãd therfor more then a figure.

The ſecond note ys, that wher Chryſoſtome moueth a queſtion, ſaing: *how were not the Apoſtles troobled when they heard Chryſt ſaie, Take, eate, This ys my*

D *bodie?* He aunſwereth that they were not troobled bycauſe they had heard him ſpeake manie and great thinges of this thing before. Wher this ys to be noted that Chryſt did not ſpeake moche of this matter but onely in the ſixt of ſainct Iohns Goſpell. Nowe yt ys allready prooued that ther Chryſt ſpake of

ke of his flesh and his bloode. Then if he speaketh here of that, that he spake E
of ther, then he saing : *This ys my bodie, this ys my bloode,* speaketh here of his
verie flesh and verie bloode. And so these woordes must be vnderstanded in
their propre sense.

Crāmers argument against the Sacrament

And here ys to be remēbred that the authour of Cranmers booke growndeth an argument (as he supposeth, vpon a good grownde, but in verie dede
yt ys vpō the sande) againſt the Sacrament, saing: that if Chryſt had made his
bodie in the Sacrament yt being so great a woorke, so great a misterie,
yt ſhoulde haue ben declared either by Chryſt himſelf ſhewing the verie thing so to be, or by the Euangelistes in proceſſe of the ſtorie, or

Sacramentaries denie the vi.ofS. Iohn to speake of the Sacr.that yt shouldap-peare amatter of no weight.

of the cirumſtance: But for somoche as the Goſpell ſaieth no more but
breiflie without all preuiall diſpoſition to the doing of the thinge, and
without all circumſtance, that *he tooke bread and gaue thankes and brake yt,
and gaue yt to his Diſciples, ſaing : Take, eate, This ys my bodie &c .* Therfor
(ſaieth he) ther ys no ſoche thing of beleife ther . for aboute other
thinges to be beleued, either Chryſt him ſelf, or the Euangelistes doe
ſtand in the declaracion, as in the matter of the incarnacion and birth of
Chryſte, of his baptiſme, of his paſſion and death, of his reſurrection of F
his aſcenſion and ſoche other. Wherfor (ſaieth he) their ys no ſoche great
worke of faith wrought in the Sacrament.

Cranmers spirit and Chryſoſtomes compared.

But ſee howe the ſpirit of erroure blinded this man, and whether he
led him . Yf he had ben led by the ſame ſpirit that Chryſoſtom was
led by, he ſhoulde haue ſeen that, that Chryſoſtom did ſee . Chryſo-
me (as ye haue hearde) ſaied , that Chryſt had ſpoken manie and great
thinges of this Sacrament before to the Apoſtles , and therfor nowe
when Chryſt went to the perfourmance of his promiſſe made before,
and in fewe woordes ſaied : *Take , eate , This ys my bodie :* Theie were
mindefull of his promiſſe made before, and of his great inſtruction geuen vnto them for their beleif in that behalf . ſo that being ſufficientlie inſtructed, and therfor redilie prepared, when Chryſt ſpake the
woorde , and commaunded them to eate his bodie, they were not
troubled, for their faith was ſtaied . So that Chryſoſtom coulde ſee manie
and great thinges that Chryſt had ſpoken of this matter: But this other man G
blinded with the great miſt of hereſie, coulde ſe nothing, wher Chryſoſtom
ſawe manie thinges, and great thinges.

Therfor yowe that be yet , or haue ben ſeduced , here by this great piller of that ſect be aduertiſed, that if he being a learned man, and
yet the wicked ſpirit ſo blinded him that wher Chryſoſtome ſaied, that
Chryſt did ſpeake manie and great thinges of this Sacrament, whiche
yet this learned man coulde not ſee one of them , yowe that be learned ſee one of yowr beſt learned mē blinded, and beware in time. But yowe
that be vnlearned, of this moche more doe yowe beware. For yf the learned
be deceaued by the Deuell and blinded, and led oute of the waie of trueth,
moche more the vnlearned maie be deceaued and blinded, as was yowr
firſt fownder in this our time, *Luther* by name, who ſaied that the ſixt chapiter of S. Iohn, was whollie to be ſet a part, as in whiche ther was no
ſillable that ſpake of the Sacrament . Yet Chryſoſt. ſaieth Chryſt ſpake
manie and great thinges of the Sacramēt. And in all the Goſpell ther ys no-
place that ſpeaketh of yt before the ſupper, but the ſixt chapter of S. Iohn. H
Wherfor Luther gropeth alſo in the darke and can not ſee one ſillable of S.
Iohns ſixt chapter ſpeaking of the Sacrament, which ſpeaketh moche of yt.

Whiche

A   whiche thing alſo ys by expreſſe woordes teſtified of S. Auguſtine, who ſaieth thus ſpeaking of the ſupper of Chryſt . *Ioannes de corpore & ſanguine Domini hoc loco nihil dixit, ſed planè alibi multo vberiùs de iis Dominum locutum eſſe teſtatur.* Iohn ſpake nothing in this place of the bodie and bloode of our Lorde, But in an other place he plainly teſtifieth that our lorde verie plentifullie ſpake of theſe thinges . Wher note breiflie by the waie that S. auguſtine ſaieth not, that S. Iohn ſpake of the Sacrament of Chryſtes bodie and bloode, but of the bodie and bloode of our Lorde by expreſſe and plain woordes, and therwith ſignifieth the ſame bodie and blood to be ſpoken of both in the ſixt of S. Iohn , and in the other Euangeliſtes, wher they treacte of the laſt ſupper of Chryſt . And thus ye haue perceaued the authour of that booke not onely blinded, but alſo directlie ſaing contrarie to Chryſoſtome in theſe two places iointly alleaged , and alſo to S. Auguſtine, And therfor once again I wiſh yow to be warned, that ſeing the ſainges of your cheif maſters be clean contrarie to the ſainges of the cheif maſters of Chry-

B   ſtes Church, beware of them, ſuſpect them, flie farre from them. Ye haue good cauſe ſo to doe yf yowe conſider the matter well.

And now to yowr farder inſtruction in this poinct, and to the more confutacion of the aduerſaie and declaracion of the trueth , I will craue yowr pacience to heare one other place of the ſame Chryſoſtom, wherin ye ſhall both more plainly perceaue both that the vi of Iohn, and alſo the woordes of the ſupper doe manifeſtlie ſpeake of the bodie and bloode of Chryſt in the Sacrament. Thus he writeth : *Hac de cauſa deſiderio deſideraui hoc Paſcha vobiſcum comedere, qno vos ſpirituales faciam . Ipſe quoque bibit ex eo, ne auditis ;verbis illis dicerent : Quid igitur ſanguinem bibimus, & carnem comedimus? ac ideo perturbarentur. Nam & quando prius de iis verba fecit multi ſolummodò propter verba ſcandalum paſſi ſunt. Ne igitur tunc quoque id accideret, primus ipſe hoc fecit, vt tranquillo animo ad com municationem myſteriorum induceret.*For this cauſe with deſire haue I deſiered to eate this paſſeouer with yowe, by the whiche I maie make yowe ſpiritual. He alſo dranke of yt , leſt when they had heard theſe woordes they ſhoulde ſaie, what therfor doe we drinke bloode, and eate fleſh? And ther for they

C   ſhoulde be troobled. for when he did firſt ſpeake of theſe thinges alſo, manie alonlie for his woordes were offended . Leſt therfor that alſo ſhoulde then happen, he himſelf firſt did this thing, that with quiett minde he might iuduce them to the partaking or communicacion of the myſteries . Thus moche Chryſoſtome.

In whiche ſaing I will firſt note to yowe for the ſixt of S. Iohn, that after I maie the more at large open his minde to yowe for the preſence : That Chryſt ſpake of his bodie and bloode in the ſixt of S. Iohn, theſe woordes of this authour doe teach vs wher he ſaieth: *Quando de iis prius verba fecit, multi ſolummodò propter verba ſcandalum paſſi ſunt.* When he firſt ſpake of theſe thinges manie euen alonely for the woordes were offended . Wherby yowe maie perceaue that Chryſoſtome ſheweth here that Chryſt ſpake before of this myſterie of his bodie and bloode in that place, wher manie onelie were offended for the woordes. Wher that was yt ys clere to all men that can read the Goſpell, that yt was ther, wher they ſaied, *Durus eſt eſt hic ſermo, quis poteſt eum audire?* This ys an harde ſaing, who can abide yt? wher yt ys manifeſt

D   that they were (according to Chryſoſtoms ſaing) offended onely for the woordes of Chryſt, whiche made them to ſaie that yt was an hard ſaing. So that wher Chryſoſtom in the other ſentence ſaied that Chryſt had ſpoken great thinges of this myſterie, but opened not in what place , here by cir-
                                                                    cumſtan

Aug.li.3° de Conſeuſe Euang.

Chryſt ſpake of his bodie and blood plentifullie in the ſixt of S. Iohn.

Chriſ. homil.83. in. 26.Math.

Chryſt ſpake of his bodie and blood in the Sacramēt Ioā.6.

Ioan.6.

cumſtance he ſheweth the certen place.

This I thought good firſt to note, that being ioinctlie ſpoken of after the other, the firſt might be corfirmed by this, in that that this openeth the place of the ſpeaking of yt. And this by that manie ſomwhat be explained in that yt declareth, that Chryſt ſpake ther manie and great thinges which in this place be not ſo farre reported.

Ther ſeemeth betwixpt theſe two places of Chryſoſtom to be a contradiction, the diſſolucion of whiche ſhall bringfurth ſome good matter meit for this place. The contradiction ys this: in the firſt ſentence ſaing : *Quomodò igitur turbati non ſunt diſcipuli hoc audientes?* howe were the diſciples not troobled hearing this? he geueth vs to vnderſtand, that the Apoſtles were ſo ſtaied and confirmed, that when Chryſt ſpake to them comaunding them to eate his bodie, they wete not, neither coulde be troobled . In this ſentence he ſaieth thatChryſt did firſt drinke of his bloode leſt they ſhoulde ſaie: *wherfor then doe we drinke blood and eate fleſh? and therfor ſhoulde be troobled* . Wherby contrariwiſe he ſemeth to inſinuate that they were not perfect, but wolde haue ben troobled.

But theſe two ſainges well weighed, ther ſhall be fownde no contradiction, but raither ſtrong euident matter for the opening of the trueth nowe declared. Wherfor this ys to be noted, that in the firſt ſentence Chryſoſtom ſpake of the faith of the Apoſtles as concerning this miſterie. And as touching their faith they were not troobled at the ſtraunge ſownde ofChryſtes woordes, who bid them take and eate his bodie and drinke his blode, who otherwiſe if they had not ben ſtaied in faith, being fullie inſtructed, and fullie perſwaded, they wolde haue ben troobled at the hearing of ſoche woordes, but they were reſolued, and therfor wolde not depart and go backe from Chryſte, as other diſciples did, but when Chryſt aſked them : *will yowe alſo go awaie?* They anſwered: *Domine ad quem ibimus? verba vitæ æternæ habes.* Lorde to whom ſhall we go? Thowe haueſt the woordes of euerlaſting life. They had taken a good taſt in the woordes of Chryſt, though they were repugnaunt to their naturall knowledge. Wherfor they ſubdewed their naturall knowledge to the heauenly and ſpirituall knowledge, and ſo perceaued euerlaſting life in his woordes. Therfore hearing this newe and ſtraunge voice, *Take, eate, This ys my bodie. Drinke, this ys my blood,* that yt was ſo in dede, as Chryſt ſpake they beleued moſt certenlie. And therfor in faith they were not troobled. For if they had, they wolde haue vttered their doubte with a (*Quomodò*) howe, as they did that were troobled and ſaied : *Quomodò poteſt hic nobis dare carnem ſuam ad manducandum?* Howe can this felowe geue vs his fleſh to eate? And as our men in theſe daies trobled likewiſe in faith doe ſhewe their doubte with a (*Quomodò*) with an howe, asking howe can Chryſt be in the Sacrament? with manie ſoche like queſtions. But theApoſtles were deliuered from this trooble. and therfor (ſaieth Chryſoſtom) they were not trobled, that ys, they were not troobled in faith. That he meneth they were not troobled in faith, his woordes doe declare, when he asketh, *howe were not the Apoſtles troobled hearing theſe woordes?* So that their troble ſhoulde be vpon the hearing of Chryſtes woordes. But foraſmoche as faith ys of hearing, and by hearing Chryſt before they had conceaued faith, therfor faith by the hearing of theſe woordes, which before by hearing were beleued, was not nowe troobled. Whiche alſo this Chryſoſtome ſaieth in his anſwer geuing a cauſe why they were not trobled. *Quia multa & magna de hoc antè diſſeruerat.* Bicauſe he had ſpoken manie and great thinges of this before . ſo

that

A that by the hearing of thefe manie and great thinges they were nowe quieted in faith.

In the feconde fentence wher he fheweth a thing to be doen by Chryft
left they fhoulde be troobled, he doth not fpeake of their trooble in faith,
but of their trooble that mighthaue happened in the execuciõ of their faith,
that ys, in the receauing of that bodie and bloode whiche they beleued ther
to be reallie prefent, and as verie flefh and verie bloode to be receaued. *The Apoft-*
Wherfor yt ys to be noted that the Apoftles beleued in the Sacrament to *les beleued*
be not a bare figure, as of thing abfent, but they beleued the verie bodie *the real pre-*
and bloode of Chryft really prefent. The proofe of this by Chryfoftom ys *fence of*
this: Yf they had beleued yt to be but a figure, and in very dede bread and *Chryftes*
wine, then in the receipt of yt they wolde not haue ben troobled. For vnto *bodie and*
bread and wine they were accuftomed as their vfuall foode. But forafmoch *blood in the*
as they beleued yt to be the verie flefh and verie blood of Chryft, the re- *Sacr.*
ceipt wher of being both ftraunge, and to oure nature lothfome, and
fpeciallie the flefh and blood of a man (*as Theophilact faieth*) therfor as they *Chryft to*
B were not troobled in the beleuing : fo that they fhoulde not be trobled in *induce his*
the receauing of yt, Chryft, to induce them by his example, and to remoue *Apoft.*
the lothfomneffe of nature abhorring to eate the flefh of man, and to drinke *without*
his bloode, did drinke firft, *vt tranquillo animo* (faieth Chryfoftom) *ad commu-* *lothfomnef-*
nicationem myfteriorũ induceret. That he might induce them with a quiet minde *fe to eat his*
to receaue the mifteries. Cõfider with yowr felf, if they had beleued yt to be *flefh, and*
but bread, whie fhould thei not receaue yt with quiet mind? yf yt were wine *drinke his*
why fhoulde they not drinke yt quietlie. And if they were foche thin- *blood, did*
ges, what needed Chryft to drinke before them, to induce them, and *firft eat ãd*
to quiet them? Did they neuer eate bread before? Did they neuer drinke *drinke thẽ*
wine before? *himfelf.*

Perchaunce the Aduerfaries will faie that they neuer eate bread, and drã-
ke wine in that fort before. For nowe they did eate bread, and drinke wine
as the figures of Chryftes bodie and bloode. Ys this a fufficient caufe to troo
ble them? Had they neuer before eaten any thing as the figure of Chryft?
C Had they not euen a litle before eaten the Pafchall lambe, a verie liuely figu
re of Chryft? Had they not hearde, that Melchifedech did eate and drinke
bread and wine in the figure of Chryfte? Had they not heard that Manna
was eaten, and the water of the rocke dronken in the figure of Chryft? Was
this matter fo ftraunge to them, that they fhoulde be trobled? No, yt was
not this. but yt was for the eating of the flefh, and drinking of the blood of
Chryft, whiche for that that yt was neuer in vfe before yt was very ftraunge
to them, and for that yt was againft nature yt was lothfome, and therfor
they might verie well haue ben troobled. That this ys the caufe Chryfoftome by plain woordes declareth faing: *Chryft did drinke firft of yt left, when*
they had heard the woordes of Chryfte, which were thefe: Eate, This ys my bodie. Drinke,
This ys my bloode: they fhoulde faie, what doe we eate flefh and drinke bloode? and therfor
they fhoulde be troobled.

Note that he faieth, that the Apoftles wolde haue faied, *whi doe we eat flefh* *Trooble of*
and drinke bloode? In the whiche woordes he doth plainlie expreffe their faith *the Apoft.*
that they beleued yt to be flefh and bloode. And bicaufe they did certenlie *fhoulde ha-*
D beleue yt to be flefh and bloode, and that they fhoulde fo haue receaued yt, *ue ben bi-*
yt might haue ben a caufe to trooble them. Therfor Chryfoftom addeth: *Ac* *caufe they*
ideo perturbarentur. And therfor they fhoulde be troobled. Therfor, that *knewe they*
ys, bicaufe they fhoulde eate the flefh, and drinke the blood of a man. *fhould eate*
　　　　　　　　　　　　　　　　　　　　　　　　　　　　　　　　For *verie flefh.*

Fot that ys the caufe that Chryfoftom doeth affign, of their trooble.

That whiche foloweth alfo moche helpeth the declaracion of this matter, that when Chryft (*faieth Chyfoftom*) did fpeake of thefe thinges before manie for the woordes alonelie were offéded. In that he faieth that they we re offéded for the wordes alone, he geueth vs to vnderftád, that the Apoftles fhoulde not nowe haue bé offended fo, but for the doing, that where Chryft before did fpeake of the geuing of his flefh, nowe he did both fpeake of yt, and geue yt in dede. And fo in the receipt of yt in dede, they fhoulde haue ben offended. But (faieth Chryfoftom) *that that might not happen, he dranke firft,* that they animated, and comforted by his example, might with a quiett minde, neither thinking yt ftraunge neither lothfome, receaue the mifteries, in the whiche (as a miftery requireth) was hidden a thinge not open to fenfeis, whiche was the bodie of Iefus Chryfte. Nowe ye haue heard the minde of Chryfoftom vpon the woordes of Chryft, and howe he vnderftandeth them yowe maie perceaue, and by the fame alfo yowe maie knowe both howe he did beleue, and howe alfo the Apoftles, who firft tooke this mifterie at Chryftes hand, did beleue.

And nowe forafmoche as I haue taried long vpon Chryfoftom (but not without profitt to the reader, as I truft) I will with the more expedition breiflie, ouerpaffe the breif faing of *Sedulius,* who at this time ys ioined to Chryfoftom, as his yockefelowe, to teftifie the true vnderftáding of Chryftes wordes in the latin churche, as Chryfoftome hath doen in the greke churche. Thus he faieth· *Accipite, hoc eft corpus meũ. quafi dixiffet Paulus: Cauete ne illnd corpus indignè comedatis, dũ corpus Chifti eft.* Take, this ys my bodie, as though Paule had faied, *Beware that ye eate not that bodie vnworthilie, forafmohe as yt ys the bodie of Chryfte.* Thus moche he.

Who expownding the woordes of Chryft vttered by S. Paule to the Corinthians dothe by expreffe woordes geue vs to vnderftande thé in their pro pre fenfe, as fpeaking of the verie bodie, and of no figure or trope. For if they were fo to be vnderftáded, this learned man taking vpon him the office of an expofitoure, and fo to expownde the woordes of Chryft, and the mening of S. Paule, in the alleaging of them, wolde haue taught nowe that theie are to be vnderftáded by a figure, as an expofitour aught to doe. But forasmohe as he teacheth that they are vndeftanded of Chryftes bodie, as in opening S. Paules minde yt doeth wel appeare, yt can not otherwife be but the woordes of Chryfte are to be taken fimplie, as teaching vs that Cryfte and S. Paule fpake of the very bodie and not of the bare figure of yt. This mã was both learned and auncient, not moche aboue foure hondreth years after Chryfte who as by learning he was not voide of good knowledg: fo by auncientie he was not voide of true faith. Wherfot we muft nedes confeffe, that this doctrine ys according to the true faith, and fo confequentlie acknowledge that yt ys the true faith to beleue Chryftes verie bodie in the Sacrament.

Thus, Reader, thowe haueft heard thefe twoo noble men of Chryftes Parliament howfe openinge to vs the enacted trueth of the vnderftanding of Chryftes woordes, bothe of them teftifieng the prefence of Chryftes bodie by the fame woordes, and no one title of the Aduerfaries figures and fignes, and that fo plainlie and euidentlie, that methinke the Proclamer fhall doe me wronge if he fubfcribe not to this trueth, for fomoche as he hath promifed fo to doe vpon the feight of anie one plain place in fcripture, Councell or doctoure. Chryfoftom, I am fure, ys fo plain and with all fo euident, and ftrong againft the wicked affertion of the Proclamer, that he fhall neuer be able

Margin notes:

Sedul. in 11 prim. Cor.

A plain place for M. Iuell.

Sedulius cõmended.

The Proclaër muft fubfcribe to the catholique doctrin of the Church if he will kepe promeffe.

A able with all his engins,and falſe ſhiftes that he had to withſtand his force.
But yf hys mouthe will not for pride confeſſe the trueth, his conſcience , I
doubte not,accuſeth him as confownded.

THE SIX AND FIFTETH CHAP. ABIDETH
in the expoſition of the ſame woordes by Theophilus and Leo.

Ow(gentle Reader) coming towardes the ende of theſe famou
ſe and noble men of Chryſtes higher houſe , of Parliament , I
meen of ſoche as were within ſixe hondreth years after Chryſt,
I truſt thowe wilt not fainte to proceade and ſee the ende. And
to thy more eaſe,I alſo, as a man trauailing in iourneie and coming towarde the ende,being deſicrouſe of the ſame taketh courage to him,
and maketh the more haſt to atteign his deſire:Euen ſo I nowe drawing to
the ende,will be ſhorter then I haue ben,and ſo make haſt that I maie obtein
B that,that I deſire.

And nowe of thoſe fathers that remain *Theophilus* Archibiſhoppe of *Ale-*
xandria,ſhall be the firſt that in our matter ſhall geue his teſtimonie.   This
man writing againſt *Origen*,for that he ſaied that the deuells ſhall be ſaued at
the laſt,ſaieth thus.   *Conſequens eſt,vt qui priora ſuſceperit,ſuſcipiat & quæ ſequun-*
tur.   Et qui pro Dæmonibus Chriſtum dixerit crucifigi,ad ipſos quoque dicendum ſuſci-
piat , Hoc eſt corpus meum,& accipie,Hic eſt ſanguis meus.Si enim pro Dæmonibus cru-
cifigitur(vt nouorum dogmatum aſſertor affirmat) quod erit priuilegium , aut quæ ratio,
vt ſoli homines corpori eius ſanguiníque communicent , & non Dæmones quoque pro-
*quibus in paſſione ſanguinem ſuderit.*Yt ys conſequent,that he that receaueth the
firſt thinges,ſhoulde alſo receaue thoſe thinges that folowe.   And he that
doeth ſaie Chryſt to be crucified for Deuels, alow alſo to be ſaied vnto thē:
This ys my bodie,and *Take,this ys my bloode.*For yf Chryſt ſhall be crucified alſo
for Deuells,as the auoucher of newe doctrines doeth affirme, what ſhall be
the priuilege, or what reaſon that onely men ſhoulde communicate
the bodie and bloode of him, and not Deuells alſo for the whiche in his paſ
C ſion he did ſhedde his bloode?hitherto *Theoph.*

Who improuing the opinion of *Origen* before mencioned, ſaieth that if the
bodie of Chryſt ſhoulde ſuffre for Deuells, and his blood ſhoulde be ſhedde
for thē,then vnto thē he ſhoulde haue ſaied, as he hath to his Apoſtles, and
all faithfull men : *Take, eate, This ys my bodie, Take and drinke, This ys my blood.*
Whiche argumēt, as yt doth confute the errour of *Origen*, for that yt ys meit
that all they that be partakers of the redemption purchaced by the bodie
and blood of Chryſt, ſhould alſo be ſoche, as to whō in time conuenient, yt
might be ſaied : *Take eat, This ys my bodie.Take drinke, This ys my blood .* Whiche
thing to Deuells ys not ſaied: ſo alſo yt doeth impugn the errour of our Ad
uerſarie in that that no mencion being made of figures and tropes, the wor
des of Chryſt be left in their owne propre ſenſe, teaching vs that we muſt ta
ke and eate, his verie bodie, and drinke his verie bloode.

And that they doe ſo teache vs by the minde of this authour , the woordes
that folowe in his ſecond argumēt doo well prooue. For the better percea-
ving wherof,vnderſtād firſt (as the trueth of the catholique faith ys)that De
D uells be not redemed by the paſſion of Chryſt, neither be they,nor can be
partakers of the vertue and benefitt of the ſame. Nowe to receaue Chryſt
ſpirituallie , ys to receaue the grace and fruict of this paſſion . When
then in his ſecond argument this authour ſaieth that the Deuells be not

N n   par-

Origen his
hereſie.

Theop. A
lexand . li.
2.paſch.

Deuells be
not rede-
med by
Chryſtes
paſſion,but
if they
might rece
aue him
ſpirituallie
they ſhoul-
de be parta
kers of his
merittes.

partakers of Chryftes bodie and bloode, as men be, he doeth not fpeake of E
the fpirituall receipt, for then he fhoulde make his argument of that thing,
whiche he hath to impugne, whiche ys againft all kinde of difputacion.
Wherfore the receipt of Chryftes bodie being but in two maner of fortes,
that ys either fpirituall, or corporall: feing he doeth not meen of the fpiritual
maner, yt muft nedes be vnderftanded of the corporall maner.

Deuells cā
not be par-
takers of
Chriſtes bo
die reallie.

For the better vnderftanding of this, I will frame hys argument to yowr
vnderftanding in this forre, Soche as maie be partakers ef Chryftes verie
reall bodie, maie be partakers of Chryftes fpirituall bodie : But onely men
and not Deuells be partakers of Chryftes reall bodie (for vnto them and not
to thefe yt ys faied: *Take eat, this ys my bodie, &c*) Wherfore men onely and not
Deuells be partakers of Chryftes fpirituall bodie, yf Deuels can not be parta
takers of Chryftes bodie fpirituallie, then can they not be faued. Thus then
ye maie perceaue that this authour vnderftandeth both thefe places of fainct
Matthew, and fainct Paule, of the verie bodie of Chryfte in the Sacrament,
and not of the figure of yt.
F

Errour of
Origen.
Theoph.li.
1.Paſch.

And that he did certenly fo without all doubte, an other place of his in
the firft booke will make yt manifeft, wher refuting one other erroure in
Origen, faing that the holie Goft woorketh not in dumbe thinges : he faieth
thus. *Dicit Spiritum ſanctum non operari in ea, quæ inanima ſunt, nec ad irrationabilia peruenire. Quod aſſerens non recogitat aquas in baptiſmate myſticas, aduentu Spiritus ſancti con-
ſecrari, panemque Dominicum, quo ſaluatoris corpus oſtenditur, & quem frangimus in ſan-*

The bread
of the Sacr.
ys conſecra-
ted by the
coming of
the holie
Goſt.

*ctificationem noſtri, & ſacrum calicem, quæ in menſa collocantur, & vtique inanima ſunt,
per inuocationem & aduentum Spiritus ſancti ſanctificari .* He faieth that the holie
Goft neither cometh to vnreafonable thinges, nor woorketh in thofe thinges whiche be without life. Which when he faieth he remembreth not the
myfticall waters in baptifme by the coming of the holie Gofte to be confecrated, and the bread of our Lord, in the whiche the bodie of our Sauiour ys
fhewed, and whiche we breake to the fanctificacion of our felues : And the
holie cuppe, whiche be fett vpon the table, and be withoute life, to be fanctified by inuocacion, and the coming to of the holie Gofte. Thus moche *Theo*
phil. Doe ye not fee that the bread and wine be fanctified by the coming of
the holie Goft, in the whiche by his worke ys fhewed, when yt ys fanctified, the bodie of our Sauiour? Doe ye not fee alfo that this ys doen by inuo-

Homil.30.
de prod.ʒn
dæ.Homil.
5.paſch.
Theop. in
6.Ioan.

cation ?　And what ys this inuocacion but the woordes of confecracion
fpoken vpon the bread and wine, by the which, as Chryfoftom, *Euſebius Emiſ.*
Theophilact, and other doe faie, the bread and wine be confecrated, they be
turned into the fubftance of the bodie and bloode of Chryft, fo adfu-
redlie, that although yt femeth bread, yet in verie deed yt ys the flefh
of Chryft.

Iren.li. 4.
cont. here-
ſies.Baſill.
de ſpiritu
ſancto cap.
27. Cyrill.
in 15.Ioan.

The woordes of confecracion be of the Fathers diuerfly named . *Irenæus*
calleth them *vocationem Dei* , the calling of God . S. Bafill and *Theophilus*
call them: *inuocationis verba:* the woordes of inuocacion or calling vpon. S. Cyrill calleth them and the Sacrament alfo, *Myſticam benedictionem,* the myfticall
benediction, and fo furth. Which all teache vs that by thofe woordes, and by
the worke of the holie Goft , of the bread and wine be made the bodie and
bloode of Chryft. *Vbi acceſſerint Chriſti verba* (faieth S. Ambrofe) *de pane fit corpus*
Chriſti. When the woordes of Chryft haue comed to the bread, ofthe bread
ys made the bodie of Chryft. Euen fo this holie father *Theophilus,* no doubte,
H

Li.4.de
fac.ca.4

but as he vfed the fame woordes aboute the matter of the Sacrament , as
other holie fathers did : fo did he profeffe and teache the fame faith
that

A that they did,whiche being oute of doubte,we maie affirme that this authour by the woordes of Chryſte teacheth the preſence of Chryſtes bodie, and ſo vnderſtandeth them in their propre ſenſe, withoute the Aduerſaries figure.

This then being plain,let vs alſo heare the holie Father *Leo* Byſhoppe of Rome, of whoſe holineſſe, and woorthineſſe, the generall Councell of Chalcedon,geueth notable teſtimonie.This holie man allthough he doth not make expreſſe mencion of the verie woordes of Chryſte:yet he maketh relacion to them,and ſheweth vs the mening of them.Thus he ſaieth: *Ieſus conſilij ſui certus,& in opere paternæ diſpoſitionis intrepidus,vetus teſtamentum conſummabat,& nouum Paſcha condebat.Diſcumbentibus enim ſecum Diſcipulis ad edendam myſticam cœnam,cùm in Caiphæ atrio tractaretur,quomodò Chriſtus poſſet occidi; ille corporis & ſanguinis ſui ordinans ſacramentum,docebat,qualis Deo hoſtia debet offerri, nec ab hoc quidem myſterio traditore ſubmoto.*Ieſus being at a poinct with himſelf and readie to doe the worke of his Fathers diſpoſition,he finiſhed the olde Teſtament,and made a newe paſſouer.For he ſitting downe with his Diſciples

B to eate the myſticall ſupper,when they in the houſe of Caiphas were treating howe Chryſt might be ſlain,he ordeineing the Sacrament of his bodie and bloode,taught what ſacrifice ſhoulde be offred to God, *Iudas* the traditour not being remoued from this myſterie.Thus farre *Leo.*

In this ſentence, where this authour ſaieth that Chryſt did ordein the Sacrament of his bodie and bloode, and taught what ſacrifice ſhoulde be offred to God,he doeth vnderſtand theſe woordes of Chryſt (*Thys ys my bodie,which ſhall be geuen for yowe.* And *This ys my blood,which ſhall be ſhed for the ſinnes of manie*)literally,by whiche woordes he did both ordein the Sacrament of his bodie and blood,and declared alſo that the ſame hys bodie and blood ſhould be offred for the ſinnes of the woorlde.But here the Aduerſarie will ſaie,that this authour ſaieth not that Chryſt by thoſe woordes of his ſupper did make really preſent his bodie and blood,but did ordein a Sacrament of his bodie and bloode,whiche maner of ſpeache maketh for him verie moch. Let the Aduerſarie ſtaie a litle,and he ſhall perceaue that this authour ma

C keth nothing for him.And firſt lett him conſider that the learned of the catholique Church,and other alſo whiche be vnlearned,who doe profeſſe acknowledge and beleue the verie reall and ſubſtanciall preſence of Chryſtes bodie and blood in the Sacrament,doe cōmonlie call the ſame, ſomtime the Sacrament of Chryſtes bodie and blood:ſomtime the Sacrament of the aul tar,whiche their maner of tearning or calling doth not empayr their faith, neither proue that they take yt for a Sacrament onelie. Euen ſo although this authour call yt the Sacrament of Chryſtes bodie and blood,yt proueth not that he meneth yt to be a ſacrament onelie,as the Aduerſarie doeth teache,but bothe a ſacrament,and the thing yt ſelf alſo, as yt ys in *Tertullian* before declared.

And that this authour ment not of the ordeinaunce of a bare Sacramen. , but of the thing yt ſelf alſo , hys ſaing in the ſame ſermon written a litle before this laſt alleadged place , doeth fullie teſtifie. Thus he writeth : *Vt vmbræ cederent corpori , & ceſſarent imagines ſub præſentia veritatis , antiqua obſeruantia nouo tollitur ſacramento , hoſtia in ho

D ſtiam tranſit , ſanguinem ſanguis excludit , & legalis feſtiuitas , dum mutatur , impletur.* That the ſhadowes ſhoulde geue place to the bodie, and the images ſhould ceaſſe in the preſence of the trueth,the olde obſeruance ys taken awaie with a newe ſacrament , one ſacrifice paſſeth into an other,

Nn ii   one

Leo prim. Serm.7.de paſſio.Do.

Chryſte in his ſupper taught what ſacrifice ſhoulde be offred to God.

Obiectiō of this woord. Sacrament of Chryſtes bodie and blood.

Aunſwer

Leo.ibid.

InChryſtes ſupper ſacrifice foloweth ſacrifice, and blood excludeth blood.

one bloode excludeth an other, and the legall solemnitie, when yt ys chaun E
ged, ys fulfilled. Thus Leo.

For the better vnderstanding of this saing of the authour, yt ys to be obserued that he doth compare the solemnitie of the olde iudaicall Passouer to
the newe Passouer solemnely begonne by Chryst in his last supper. Whiche
thing maie well be perceaued by the last woordes of the authour, wher he
saieth as the conclusion of all that he had before spoken : *& legalis festiuitas,
dum mutatur, impletur*: And the legall solemnitie, when yt ys chaunged, ys fulfilled. The legall solemnitie, was the feast of the Paschall lambe. This feast
was chaunged and then fullfilled, when Chryst in stead of that lambe being
the figure, made his solemne feast, and gaue his owne bodie and bloode,
the bodie and blood of the right, and verie true lambe of God, that taketh
awaie the sinnes of the worlde, of which matter more ys saied in the first
booke. In the whiche feast (saieth the authour) *that the shadowes shoulde geue
place to the bodie, and the images shoulde ceasse in the presence of the trueth, the olde
obseruance ys taken awaie with a newe sacrament.* Marke then, in the legall solemnitie was the shadowe: in Chrystes supper the bodie, in the legall solemnitie
were the Images: in Chrystes feast was the presence of the trueth, that ys,
the verie thing signified by the image, which ys the bodie and bloode of
Chryst, not nowe in figure, but in verie deed.

See ye not nowe then what ys in Chrystes supper ? Ys ther not
the bodie of the shadowe, and not the onelie shadowe ? Ys ther not
the verie thing and not the image ? Ys not the bodie of the shadowe
and the verie thing of the image the bodie and blooode of Chryst?
Then the verie bodie and bloode of Chryst be in hys supper. Thus
maie ye perceaue what he ment, when he saied that Chryst did ordein the Sacrament of hys bodie and bloode, not a Sacrament voy-
de of hys bodie and bloode, but a Sacrament conteining hys bodie
and bloode.

Will ye see this again plainlie taught ? This authour saieth, *that
the olde obseruance ys taken awaie with a newe Sacrament. But* what ys thys
Sacrament ? Yt ys a sacrament, that ys a sacrifice remouing and ending the sacrifice of the Paschall lambe, and others of that nature. G
Yt ys a Sacrament wherin ys bloode excluding the bloode of legall sacrifices. *Hostia in hostiam transit, sanguis sanguinem excludit,* one sacrifice passeth
into an other sacrifice : one bloode excludeth an other bloode. The
sacrifice of the olde lawe passeth into the sacrifice of Chrystes bodie
and ther endeth, and the bloode of Chryst excludeth and putteth
awaie the bloode of the sacrifice of the olde lawe, and so ys the sacrifice of
that bloode ended.

Thus maie yowe perceaue, that when this authour saied, that Chryst ordeined the Sacrament of hys bodie and bloode, that he ment not onely
the institucion of a bare Sacrament, but also the consecracion of the bodie
and bloode of Chryst lieng hidden vnder the formes of bread and wine
in the same Sacrament. Whiche ordeinance and consecracion was doen
by the woordes of Chryst, when he saied· *Take, eate, This ys my bodie.* And
Take, drinke, this ys my bloode. And so the woordes teache the verie presence of
Chrystes bodie and blood in the Sacrament, and not a naked figure.

Yf thus moch satisfie not the reader forsomoch as ys here saied of and vpo H
this authour, as I trust yt maie anie that ys not contenciouse, yf he desire to
see more of this authour, let him reparie to the sixt of sainct Iohn, and
to the

*In Chrystes
supper ys
the verie
bodie and
not the sha
dow.*

*Chryste in
his supper
did not in-
stitute a
bare Sacra
ment onelie*

A   to the beginning of this proceſſe vpon the woordes of the Supper, and he ſhall ſee more, wherfore remitting the reader to thoſe places, I ſtaie to ſaie anie more vpon this coople, but haſt me, according to my promeſſe to heare an other coople.

THE SEVEN AND FIFTETH CHAP. PRO-
ceadeth in the expoſition of the ſame woordes by ſainct Cyrill and ſainct Gregorie.

Hough yt be moche that ys allready ſaied vpon theſe fewe woordes of Chryſt, and maie well ſuffice to teache the trueth of this matter: yet that the arrogancie of the Proclamer maie be beaten down, and his vntrueth againſt gods trueth well perceaued, we ſhall yet bring in one or twoo cooples mo of the higher houſe of Chryſtes Parliament, and then deſcend to other of the lower B   houſe.

Of the higher houſe ther yet remaineth holy Cyrill, whoſe faith in the Sacrament, although yt maie well be knowen to vs by hys manie and ſondrie ſentences both in the firſt booke, and in this vpō the vi. of S. Iohn alleadged: yet that the faith of the catholique Church maie be diſcerned from errour and hereſie, with which titles ſome heretiques wold defame the ſame, we wil heare him teache vs the faith that ought to be had and geuen to the woordes of Chryſt, and howe we ſhall vnderſtand them, euen as he taught *Caloſyrius*, to whom he wrote vpon the woords of Chryſt in this maner: *Non dubi*   Cirill ad *tes, an hoc verum ſit, eo manifeſtè dicente. Hoc eſt corpus meum: ſed potius ſuſcipe verbum*   *Caloſyriū.* *ſaluatoris in fide. Cùm enim ſit veritas, non mentitur.* Doubt not whether this be true   *Chryſtes* or no, ſeing that he manifeſtlie ſaieth: *This ys my bodie*: But raither receaue the   *woordes* woord of our Sauiour in faith. For he foraſmoch as he ys tureth, he lieth not.   *manifeſt*   *and with-*

Weigh theſe fewe woordes of S. Cyrill well (gentle Reader) and firſt that   *out doubt.* he willeth *Caloſirius* not to doubte whether this that Chriſt manifeſtlie ſaied: *This ys my bodie*: be true or no. For in that he willed him and by him all chry- C   ſtians not to doubte, what ells willeth he but that al errour, hereſie, opinion, wandering, wauering and colde faith ſhoulde be remoued, and firme, ſure,   S. Cyrill and faſt faith ſhould be geuen to the woordes of Chryſt : *This ys my bodie,*   *ſheweth* whiche woordes he ſaieth be manifeſt. Yf they be manifeſt, then they haue   *the Pro-* no obſcure ſenſe: then they muſt be taken in the ſenſe that manifeſtlie lieth   *clamer* open before vs. That ſenſe ys the grāmaticall ſenſe. Then the figuratiue ſenſe   *plain woor* ys taken awaie. For that ſenſe, as the woordes be nowe ſpoken, ys not mani-   *des.* feſt, but obſcure. Then alſo muſt the Proclamer ſubſcribe. For by the iudge- mente of S. Cyrill the woordes of Chryſt be manifeſt. Yf they be manifeſt, as vndoubtedlie they be, then ther ys one ſcripture that manifeſtly teacheth the preſence of Chryſtes bodie.

Again ſainct Cyrill ſaieth, that foraſmoche as Chryſt ys the trueth, he lieth not : but he taking the bread and wine, ſaied : *This ys my bo- die.* Therfore he being the trueth and lieng not, the thinges were as he ſaied, then were they his bodie and bloode. For ſo ſaied he that they were. Yf the bread and wine, he ſaing, *Thys ys my bodie. This ys my bloode* : were not D   made by his allmightie power and woorde the bodie and blood of Chryſt (theſe woords being ſpoken by demōſtraciō of certain ſingular things in nature without anie circūſtance to declare anie other ſenſe vpō theſe woordes, then in the firſt hearing they ſownde to haue) Yf, I ſaie, theſe creatures

Nn iii   remain

remain ftill in their nature and fubftances, and be but figures of Chryftes E
bodie and blood , then I faie, that Chryftes woordes were not true.
For he faied that they were his bodie and bloode . And by the opinion
of the Aduerfarie,they be not fo, but bread and wine figures of Chryftes
bodie and blood.

Forafmoche as my cheef pourpofe ys to helpe and ftaie them in their
faith that be vnlearned,to whome quiddities in learning be raither trooblefom then pleafaunt or profitable,I haue determined not to difpute with the

The Pro-
clamer to
difgrace
our faith
plaieth
with indiui-
dũ vagum.

Proclamer in anie quidditie, or ells I wolde fomwhat haue faied to him , for
that yt liketh him to dallie,and to aske where we finde that this woord (*hoc*)
in englifh(*this*)poincteth not the bread,but *indiuiduum vagum*. For if yt fhall
be his phantafie to difgrace the trueth before the comon people by plaing
with fome quidditie,that they can not vnderftand, he maie fo foen difgrace
our faith in the holie and bleffed Trinitie.For if he lyft fo to plaie,he might
moue matter of the diftinction and relacion of the perfons, and by foche
toieng bring the people to ftagger in their faith in the bleffed Trinitie,as by F
this mockerie of the demonftracion, he wolde make them fall from their
faith of the bleffedSacrament. Yt were conuenient that as the people fhould
be taught fimplie,to beleue in God the Father , God the Sonne, and God
the holie Goft,and not to be troobled with the learned quiddities of the
generacion of the Sonne, of the fpiracion as touching the holie Gofte , of
the procefsion of the fame from the Father and the Sonne, and with the
diftinction and relacion of the perfons:fo fhoulde they be taught fimplie to
beleue as the fcripturs doe teache,and the holie fathers doe declare and ex-

People are
fimplie to
be taught
not with
Quidditi-
es.

pownde the fame,that the bodie and bloode of our Sauiour Chryft, euen
full Chryft,God and man,after the confecracion,which (as before ys declared)ys doen by the fecrett power of God,by the worke of the holy Gofte
at the pronunciacion of Chryftes woordes by his fufficient mynifter, ys verilie,reallie,fubftanciallie,and naturally prefent in the Sacrament, and not
to be troobled with demonftracions with accidentes,with fubftances, with
placing of that bodie circumfcriptiuelie,definitiuelie, by the maner of fub- G
ftance,or by the maner of quantitie.For thefe matters are for learned men to
difpute, not for good Chryftian vnlearned people to call in queftion of be-
leue.In the fchooles yt had ben a meit matter to difpute: in the pulpitie yt
was no matter to teache to edifie.But yt liked him to talke of foche quiddities,bicaufe by their obfcuritie and darkeneffe,they being vnpleafaunt vnto
the people fhoulde the more myflike them ,and by that means haue the
redier waie to deface the catholique faith,and to fett vppe his herefie.But I
minding for that litle that in me ys,to maintein that holie faith ofChryft my
Sauiour that ys taught in his catholique Churche,I will leaue thefe quiddities,and fimplie treact of the thing,that we haue in hande. And therfore
nowe returning to Cyrill,from whom I haue a litle digreffed , I faie with

Cyrillus
i bidem.

him,that Chryft being trueth,and faing:*This ys my bodie*, yt muft nedes be as
he faied,and fo fimplie we muft beleue the bodie and blood ofChryft,accor
ding to his woorde to be prefent in the Sacrament.

Chryft tur-
neth the
bread into
his owne
verie flesh.

Whiche thing,as he faied here that Chryft manifeftlie faied *Thys ys my*
bodie:So he manifeftlie in the fame epiftle after a fewe lines , doth open and
declare to be true,wher he thus writeth:*Ne horreremus carnẽ et fanguinẽ appofita* H
facris altaribus, cõdefcendẽs Deus noſtris fragilitatibus,influit oblatis vim vitæ,cõuertẽs ea
in veritatẽ propriæ carnis, vt corpus vitæ quafi quoddã femẽ viuificatiuũ inueniatur in nobis
That we fhoulde not loath flefh and bloode fett vpon the holie aultars,God
con-

A condefcending to our fragilities hath powred into the thinges offred the power of life *conuerting or turning them into his verie owne flesh,* that the bodie of life maie be fownde in vs, as a certain quickning feede.

For that I haue vpon this place of Cyrill faied fomthing allreadie, I will nowe no more but note vnto yowe, howe manifeftlie, howe apertlie, and howe plainlie he teacheth vs not onely that the bodie of Chryft ys in the Sacrament : but alfo the meanes howe yt ys ther, which ys that *God turneth the bread fett vpon the holie aulanrs into his verie flesh.* After this he rendreth to vs two caufes of the goodneffe of God towarde vs, and fhewed in this Sacrament. the one ys , that though yt be flefh in dede: yet (as *Euthymius,* and *Theophilact* alfo doe faie) God confidering or condefcending to our infirmities, maketh yt not to appeare vnto vs that that yt ys in dede, but yt appeareth ftill to vs as yt was before, as bread and wine. The other caufe whie we receaue the verie flefh of Chryft (though not in the forme of flefh) ys, faieth Cyrill, that the bodie of Chryft, whiche in an other place he calleth the bodie of life, **B** might be in our bodies, as the feede of life, to communicate life vnto vs, and fo make vs by vertue therof, to liue euerlaftinglie.

Two caufes whie the fubftã-ce in the Sacr. being flesh appeareth not.

Nowe if the Sacrament were but a figure, and not the bodie of Chryft, as the Aduerfarie faieth, howe coulde Cyrills faing be true, that God turneth the offred thinges into his flefh? Again if in the Sacrament we receaue not the bodie of Chrufte, howe then ftandeth Cyrills fainge, that the bodie of Chryft, to the intent yt maie be the feed of life ys fownde in vs ? Yt maie then well be perceaued, that the doctrine of the Aduerfarie teaching that Chryftes bodie and bloode be not in the Sacrament, ys peftilent, perniciou- fe and vntrue, not onely in that yt ys repugnant to the doctrine of this holie Father, and others before alleadged, but alfo to the verie woorde of Chryft, who plainlie faieth: *This ys my bodie,* and the Aduerfarie faieth, *yt ys not his bodie But a figure of his bodie.*

The flesh of Chryst receaued in the Sacr. ys the feed of euerla-sting life.

But yt ys time that we heare S. Grogorie whom we haue appoincted to ioin with S. Cyrill, to declare what was the faith of the latin church in his **C** daies. Thus he writeth: *Debemus itaque præfens feculum, vel quia iam confpicimus de fluxiffe, tota mente contemnere, quotidiana Deo lachrimarum facrificia, quotidianas carnis & fanguinis eius hoftias immolare. Hæc namque fingulariter victima ab æterno interitu animam faluat, quæ illam nobis mortem Vnigeniti per myfterium reparat. Qui licet refurgẽs ex mortuis iam non moritur , & mors ei vltrà non dominabitur : tamen in feipfo immorta-liter, atque incorruptibiliter viuens, pro nobis iterum in hoc myfterio facræ oblationis immo-latur, Eius quippe ibi corpus fumitur, eius caro in populi falutem partitur , eius fanguis non iam in manus infidelium, fed in ora fidelium funditur. Hinc ergo penfemus, quale fit pro no-bis hoc facrificium, quod pro abfolutionè noftra paffionem Vnigeniti filii fui imitatur . Quis enim fidelium haberè dubium poffit in ipfa immolationis hora ad facerdotis vocem cælos ape riri? in illo Iefu Chrifti myfterio Angelorum Choros adeffe? fummis ima fociari: terrena cæle ftibus iungi? vnum quoque ex vifibilibus, & inuifibilibus fieri?* We aught therfor, forafmoche as we fee this prefent worlde to haue comed to nothing , with all owre minde to contemne yt , and to offre vnto God the dailie facri- fies of teares , the dailie facrifices of his flefh , and bloode . This fin- gular facrifice faueth the foule from euerlafting deftruction , whiche reneweth vnto vs by mifterie the death of the onelie begotten Sonne.

Grog. li. 4 dialog. ca. 58.

Dailie facri-fice of Chry-ftes bodie and blode ys to be of-red,

D Who allthough rifing from death, dieth no more , and death fhall neuer more haue lord fhippe ouer him : yet in himfelf liuing immortallie , and in corruptiblie, he ys offred again in this mifterie of the holie oblacion for vs. *Ther trulie his bodie ys receaued , his flesh to the health of the people ys geuen abroede: his*

bloode ys nowe shedde, not into the handes of the *vnfaithfull: but into the mouthes of the* **E**
*faithfull.*By this thē let vs weigh what maner of sacrifice this ys for vs, whiche
for our deliuerance dothe allwais folowe the passion of the onely begotten
Sonne. What faith full man can doubte in the time of that sacrificing,
at the woorde of the preift, the heauens to be opened, in that misterie
of Iesus Chryfte? companies of Angells to be present? vnto high thinges
lowe thinges to be coopled? to heauenlie thinges earthlie thinges to be
ioined? one thing also of inuisible and visible thinges to be made? Thus
moche S. Gregorie.

Yt maie perchaunce be faied, that though this place of S. Gregorie doeth
moche prooue the verie presence of Chryftes bodie in the Sacrament, yet
yt teacheth not the vnderftanding of Chryftes woordes: *This ys my body:*
whiche ys the matter that I nowe take in hande to declare, Trueth yt ys,
that the woordes of Chryft be not here recited by expreffe woordes, but
they are heare vnderftanded and the true vnderftanding of them ys also he- **F**
re settfurth. for the vnderftanding wherof I firft note vnto yowe this fenten
ce of Gregories authoritie: *What faith full man* (faieth he) *can doubte in that time
of immolacion at the voice of the preift the heauens to be opened &c.* what voice of the
preift yt ys at whiche the heauens be opened, the companies of angells be
present: high thinges are coopled to lowe thinges: but that voice of the

The heauē woordes of Chryft fpoken by the preift, in the perfon of Chryft: *This ys my*
lie bodie of *bodie, This ys my blood?* For vnto that time (*faieth S. Ambrofe*) the preift vfeth
Chrift ys his owne woordes, but then he vfeth not his owne woordes but the woor-
ioined to des of Chryft. at the whiche voice all thefe wonderfull thinges are doen.S.
the earthlie Gregorie then by this voice of the preift vnderftandeth thefe woordes of
formes of Chryft vttered by the preift. The true vnderftanding of whiche woordes he
bread and teacheth when he faieth: that at the fpeaking and pronunciacion of them,
wine at the *vnto high thinges, lowe thinges are coopled: vnto heauenly thinges, earthlie thinges are*
pronouin- *ioined* What be thefe high thinges and heauenly thinges coopled and ioined
cing of the to lowe thinges and eartlie thinges, but the heauenly and glorioufe hodie
woordes of and bloode of our Sauiour Chryft? whiche by his diuine power turning the **G**
Chryft subftances of bread and wine into the fubftance of the fame his bodie and
bloode and being in the Sacrament vnder the earthlie formes of bread and

Irenæus li. wine, he being high and heauenly ys ioined and coopled to lowe and earth
4 .ca.34. lie thinges.

After this maner the holie martir *Irenæus* did settfurth the holie Sacramēt
for he faieth : *Qui eſt à terra panis precipiens vocationem Dei iam non communis panis*
eſt, fed Euchariftia, ex duabus conſtans rebus, terrena, & cœlefti. The bread, whiche

Amb.ora. ys of the earth, receauing the vocacion of God (*that ys the woordes of confecraci-*
prepar. ad *on*) ys nowe not common bread, but (*Euchariftia*) a good grace of God being
Miſſam. compact of two thinges, earthlie and heauenlie. S. Ambrofe alfo hath euen
the fame woordes, that S. Ghregorie hath, faing: *vbi fumma imis iungutur.* Wher
Heauenlie high thinges be ioined to lowe thinges.
and earth-
lie thinges Yt fhall moche helpe the fetting furth of the trueth, if we maie, confer-
of the Sacr. ring with the doctrine of the aduerfaries, difcuffe what ys this heauenlie or
difcuffed high thinge that ys ioined in the Sacrament, with the eartly thinge, And he
what they re we muft according to the doctrine of *Irenæus,* firft confeffe and agree, that
be, by confe thefe twoo thinges, of the whiche the Sacrament ys made, are twoo perma **H**
rēce of th'ad nent thinges, twoo thinges ftanding and abiding.
uerfar.
doctrine, Nowe the aduerfaries doctrine feking by all means to difplace and remoue Chryft from the Sacrament feigneth manie thinges to be the heauenlie
parte

A parte of the Sacrament, which in dede will not ftand with the doctrine of *Irenæus*. In fome place yt faieth that the grace of God which cometh to the receauers of the Sacrament, ys the heauenly parte of the Sacrament. This can not ftand as part, for grace ys the effect of the Sacrament, and not the parte. And grace therfor muft be and ys in the receauer and not in the Sacrament, as a part therof. For if grace were in the Sacrament as a part of the Sacrament, then either vnwoorthie men receauing the Sacramet, receaue grace alfo, (which ys not to be faied) or ells yt muft be faied, that forafmoche as they receaue not grace, they receaue no Sacrament: for a thing ys receaued when yt ys whollie receaued. And thus fhall they be vncerten when the Sacrament ys miniftred.

Grace ys not one of the partes of the Sacr. but the effecte.

Of fome yt maie be faied that bicaufe the Sacrament ys called the bread of thankes geuing, that thankes to God ys the heauenly parte of the Sacrament. This alfo can not be. For this ys well knowen to all men that haue but reafon, that thankes geuing ys either in him that geueth them, or in him that receaueth them, and not in the bread, for yt neither geueth nor recea-

B ueth thankes.

Thankes geuing ys not thone parte of the Sacr.

Yf they faie, bicaufe, S. Auguft. faieth, *Accedit verbū ad elementū, et fit Sacramentū,* that ys, the woorde cometh to the element, and yt ys made a Sacrament: that therfor the woorde ys the heauenly part of the Sacrament. That alfo can not be faied of the Sacrament allreadie confecrated. for the woorde ys raither the caufe of the Sacrament, then the part, bicaufe the woorde ys not a permanent thing. but thefe partes of the Sacrament muft be twoo permanent or conftant thinges as *Irenæus* faieth,

The woorde ys not that one part of the Sacrament.

Yf they will flee to this fhifte and faie, that though the woorde be not a permanent thing: yet the fanctrificacion that ys doen in the bread by the woorde remaineth, and that ys the heauenly part of the Sacrament. This alfo euen by their owne learning can not ftande. For *Oecolampadius* and *Cranmer*, and all the rable of that Sect teache conftantlie that dumbe thinges be not partakers of fanctificacion.

Sanctificacion of the creaturs cā not be the heauenlie part of the Sacram. by the doctrine of the aduer.

Nowe what ells they can feign to maintein their euell matter I can not

C deuife. but of thefe no one will ferue. Wherfor leauing them, we will hearewhat the catholique faith teacheth to be the heauenly part of the Sacramet whiche thing we maie eafilie doe, trauailing no farder then to S. Gregorie whom we haue nowe in hande. For we haue heard him faie that *Iefus Chryft liuing in himfelf immortallie, and incorruptiblie, ys offred for vs in the holie myfterie, wher his bodie ys receaued, wher his flesh ys geuen abroade to the people, wher the bloode ys not shedde vpon the hādes of the vnfaithfull, but into the mouthes of the faithfull.* Here maie yowe fee the heauenly parte of the Sacrament what yt ys. Yt ys verie bodie and bloode of Chryft that ys geuen in the holie mifterie to the people yt ys the high thing coopled to lowe thinges: yt ys the heauenlie thing ioined to earthlie thinges: yt ys that one inuifible thing that ys made one with vifible thinges.

The heauēlie part of the bleffed Sacrament what yt ys

And here note that this place of S. Gregorie can not be wrefted to the onely fpirituall receauing of Chryftes bodie, but yt muft be vnderftande of the corporall receipt. For he faieth, that the blood of Chryft in the Sacramen ys powred into the mouthes of the faitfull, whiche maner of receipt ys

D corporall, euen the receipt of Chryftes verie reall and fubftanciall bloode. The other receipt ys onely in the foule, and can not be receaued of the bodie. Wherfor we maie conclude that he fpeaketh here of the corporal receipt of Chryftes bloode, whiche thing alfo ys confirmed by that he accompteth

Corporall receauing of the bodie and blood of Chryfte auouched by S.Greg.

compteth all one bloode that was shed vpon the handes of the vnfaith F full, and into the mouthes of the faithfull. That, that was shed vpon the handes of the vnfaithfull Iewes in the pasfion of Chryst, was Chrystes verie reall and fubstanciall bloode, wherfor that, that ys receaued by the mouthes of the faithfull, ys Chrystes verie fubstanciall bloode. Thus by S. Gregorie we are taught that Chrystes verie bodie and bloode, be verilie in the Sacrament, whiche fo being the catholique doctrine ys, that Chrystes bodie and bloode be the heauenly parte of the Sacrament.

But of both partes diftinctlie fainct Bernarde, whom onely at this time I will produce, dothe verie learnedly fpeake, treacting of the Sacrament in this maner *Quemadmodum species ibi videntur, quorum res, vel subftantiæ ibi esse non creduntur: fic res veraciter, & subftantialiter creditur, cuius fpecies non cernitur. videntur enim fpecies panis & vini, & subftantia panis & vini non creditur. Creditur autem fubftantia corporis, & fanguinis Chrifti, & tamen fpecies non cernitur.* As the formes be

ther feen whofe thinges or fubftances be not beleued, ther to be: fo a thing ys verilie and fubftanciallie beleued, whofe forme ys not feen. For the forme of bread and wine ys feen, and the fubftance of bread and wine ys not beleued: the fubftance of the bodie and bloode of Chryft ys beleued, and yet F the forme ys not feen. Again in the fame fermon he writeth thus: *Quod autē videmus fpecies eft panis & vini, quod autem fub fpecie illa credimus, verum corpus eft, & verus Chrifti fanguis. quod pependit in cruce, & qui fluxit de latere.* That that we fee ys the forme of bread and wine: but that we beleue vnder the forme ys the verie bodie and verie bloode of Chryft, that did hang vpon the crofse and that flowed oute of his fide. Thus he,

Nowe ye haue feen the twoo partes of the Sacrament fo plainly expresfed, as nothing can be defired more plain. In the Sacrament (faieth S. Bernarde) be the formes of bread and wine, and the fubftance of the bodie and bloode. Thefe twoo thinges be the twoo partes of the Sacrament. The bodie and blode of Chryft be the heauenly parte: the formes of bread and wine be the earthlie part. The bodie and bloode of Chryft be the high thinges the formes of bread and wine be the lowe thinges. Thefe heauenlie and high thinges of Chryftes bodie and bloode, and the lowe and earthlie thinges of the formes of bread and wine ioined together make the Sacrament G according to the fainges of the holie martir *Irenæus*, of S. Ambrofe, and S. Gregorie.

And nowe fuppofing that the mindes of thefe two noble men of Chryftes Parliament houfe, I meen S. Cyrill and S. Gregorie, be fullie opened, and declared as touching the vnderftanding of the woordes of Chryftes fupper, whiche in all poinctes agreeth with the reft, I will leaue them, and call in the laft coople of this companie of the higher houfe.

THE EIGHT AND FIFTETH CHAP. ENDETH
*the expofition among the eldeft Fathers by Euthymius,
and Ifidorus.*

Hough yt hath ben a painfull worke for me to gather fo manie authours of the eldeft Fathers of Chryftes Churche, vpon this one text of Chryft: yet yt comforteth me and releiueth H me of my paines to fee and beholde the mercie and goodnesfe of God towardes his Churche, who by his foreknoweledge forefeing that the childeren of *Ifmael* wolde perfecute, and vexe the childeren

A ren of *Sara* and *Ifaac*, did in time of peace prouide weapons, and in time of plentie laied vppe ſtore, that the children of *Sara* the children of the Church might haue plentie of weapons, and prouiſion to withſtande the aduerſaries and defende their mother.

In the time of peace as concerning the matter of the holy Sacrament, when no cōtrouerſie was moued vppō yt, his holie Spiritt directed the pennes of a nombre of holie men then to write that, that nowe (as ye haue perceaued and yet more ſhall) defendeth the holie faith of Chryſt and his ſpouſe the Church. of the which ther yet remaineth one named *Euthimius*, a famouſe man in the Greke Churche, who as he ys auncient, learned and holie: ſo ys his weapon verie ſharpe againſt the Aduerſarie, yt will in dede perce the falſe patched coate of Chryſtes enemie in this matter of the Sacrament Thus he writteh : *Sicut vetus teſtamentum hoſtias & ſanguinem habebat : ita*

Euthym. in 26. Math.

B *ſanè & nouum, corpus videlicet et ſanguinē Domini. Non dixit autem: Hæc ſunt ſigna corporis mei, & ſanguinis mei: ſed, Hæc ſunt corpus meum, & ſanguis meus. Oportet ergo non ad naturam eorum quæ proponuntur reſpicere, ſed ad virtutem eorum. Quemadmodũ enim ſupernaturaliter aſſumptam carnem deificauit(ſi ita loqui liceat)ita & hæc ineffabiliter tranſmutat in ipſum vinificum corpus ſuum, & in gratiam ipſorum. Habent autem ſimilitudinem quandam, panis ad corpus, & vinum ad ſanguinem. Nam & panis & corpus terrea ſunt : vinum autem & ſanguis aerea ſunt & calida. Et quemadmodum panis conſortat : ita & Chriſti corpus hoc facit, ac magis etiam, corpus & animam ſanctificat. Et ſicut vinum Lætificat : ita & ſanguis Chriſti hoc facit, & inſuper præſidium efficitur.* As the olde teſtament had ſacrifices and blood: ſo trulie hath the newe teſtament alſo, that ys, *the bodie and bloode of our Lorde*. He did not ſaie: *Theſe be ſignes of my bodie and bloode, but theſe thinges be my bodie and bloode*. We muſt therfor not looke to the nature of thoſe thinges that be ſettfurth but to the vertue of them. For as he did ſupernaturallie deifie *(if a man maie ſo ſpeake)* the fleſh that he tooke vpon him : Euen ſo doeth he vnſpeakeablie tranſmute theſe thinges into the ſame his quickning bodie, and into his owne preciouſe bloode, and into the grace of them. The bread hath a certain ſimilitude to the bodie, and the wine to the bloode. For bothe the bread and the bo-

Plain ſainges for the Proclamer

C die be of the earth. But the wine and bloode be of the aier and hotte. And as bread doeth comfort: ſo doeth the bodie of Chryſt alſo, and moreouer alſo yt doeth ſanctifie both bodie and ſoule. And as wine doeth make glad de : ſo doeth the blood of Chryſt alſo, and aboue that yt ys made a defence. Thus farre *Euthym*.

I will not nowe trooble yowe with manie notes here, the authour ys ſo plain of himſelf that he neadeth not to be noted. And yet euery ſentence ys woorthie to be noted. But for that that ys to the pourpoſe of our proceſſe here, namelie for the hauing of the true vnderſtanding of Chryſtes woordes I can not paſſe, but wiſh thee (good reader) if thowe haueſt noted yt, yet to turne backe and note yt again, that the wicked expoſition of the Aduerſarie ys by expreſſe and direct woordes denied and reiected. So ſownd and good ys that doctrine that an holie father writing aboue a thouſande yeares paſt by the computacion of ſome doeth flatlie denie yt. The Aduerſarie confoundeth the text of Chryſte, and ſaieth *this ys a figure of my bodie* : This learned Father expowndeth the woordes of Chyſt, and ſaieth : *Chryſt ſaieth not theſe be*

Figuratiue gloſe of the Sacramentaries flatlie denied.

D *ſignes of my bodie and bloode, but theſe be my bodie and blode.* And to remoue all cauills he doeth immediatelie ſhewe howe theſe thinges become his bodie ād blood. As Chryſte *(ſaieth this authour)* did ſupernaturally deifie the fleſh that he tooke vpon him : euen ſo vnſpeakeablie doeth he tranſmute theſe thin-

ges

ges into his owne verie bodie, and into his owne verie preciouse boode.

O mercifull God what ys the malicioufe blindneffe of thefe men, that fee their doctrin confuted a thoufand years agon, and yet arrogantlie perfift in yt, and to the encreafe of their damnacion, laboure to drawe manie foules with them to withftande fo manifeft a trueth. Yf the Proclamer will not *Euthymius with a plain nega tiue deni eth the proclamers affirmati- ue.* faie that this ys a plain fentence, whiche by a plain negatiue denieth his affirmatiue, and teacheth that the facrament ys not a figne or a figure of Chry ftes bodie, but the bodie yt felf, wher the Aduerfarie faieth yt ys a figure and not the bodie: I can not but faie that his feight faileth him, being corrupted with a verie euell humoure, fo that he can not iudge betwixt rough and plain, crooked and ftreight.

And here again confider that this holy father *Euthymius* writeth thefe wor des vpon the woordes of Chyrft, expownding them to geue vs the true mening, fenfe and vnderftanding of them. Wherfor we maie verie well conclude, that the woordes of Chryft are to be vnderftanded withoute figure or trope, accordinglie as this learned auncient hath taught. 　F

Perchaunche the Proclamer will faie that although this authour denieth a figure in Chryftes woordes: yet he doeth not as by him ys requefted in his proclamacion, faie plainlie by expreffe woordes that Chryftes naturall bodie ys in the Sacrament. To fee the vanitie of this fhift, let vs fearche howe manie thinges be called Chryftes bodie, and by applicacion we fhall perceaue, that yt can not otherwife be but that this authour fpeaketh of the naturall bodie of Chryft.

Foure thin ges called the bodie of Chryft. Ther be foure thinges that be called the bodie of Chryfte: The figure, the Churche, the meritt, fruit, or vertue of his paffion, and his bodie naturall. The figure ys called the bodie of Chryft. For S. Auguftine faith: that figures oftentimes haue the names of the thinges of the whiche they are figures, This maner of bodie ys not here to be vnderftanded, for yt ys by expreffe woordes denied, of this authour. Yt ys not the Churche, which S. Paule calleth the bodie of Chryft. For to all men yt ys euident, that the Sacrament ys not the Churche, other wife then bicaufe the Sacrament ys a 　G figure of the Churche. Yt ys not the fpirituall bodie of Chryft, I meen the meritte, vertue, and grace of Chryftes paffion. For the bread and wine can not be tranfmuted into yt, as the Aduerfarie him felf doth graunt. Yt remaineth then that yt muft nedes be fpoken of the naturall bodie of Chryft. And wher of neceffitie one thing muft be vnderftanded, and none other can ther be vnderftanded, that place muft nedes be called plain.

Plain tear mes for proof of re- all prefece. To be fhort, wher a thing ys fpoken of and if yt can not be applied to the figure of the thing, yt muft nedes be applied to the thing yt felf, fpeciallie when the circumftance fhall alfo fully prooue the fame, as here yt doeth. For the tranfmutacion of the bread and wine into the thing, and thefe terms: *his owne verie bodie, and his own verie bloode,* with the comparifons of the propreties of the breade and wine to the propreties of the bodie and bloode of Chryft, maketh the matter fo plain, that yt can not be but confeffed fo to be but as a man in a bringht Sunne fhining daie will maliciouflie faie that the Sunne fhineth nott.

But what doe I ftande fo long vpon fo clere a place? Yt ys time that the other that fhall declare the faith of the latin Churche be produced, who fhall 　H *Ifidorus cō mended.* be *Ifidore.* This *Ifidore,* although he be not with in fix hondreth yeares of Chryft: yet he ys verie neare, For he liued the yeare of our Lorde 626, I haue yet produced him to make vppe the coople with *Euthymius,* both that he

ys

A ys the eldeſt of the latin Church of them that remain, and treat of the woordes of Chryſt, and alſo that he ys one that liued before anie controuerſie was riſen in the matter of the holie Sacrament. Wherfore I might produce him as a ſufficient and a meet wittneſſe in this matter. this ys his teſtimonie . *Sacrificium quod à Chriſtianis Deo offertur primum Chriſtus Deus noſter & magiſter inſtituit, quando commendauit Apoſtolis corpus & ſanguinem ſuum priuſquam traderetur ſicut legitur in Euangelio : Accepit Ieſus panem & calicem, & benedicens dedit eis.* The ſacrifice that ys offred of the chryſtians vnto God, Chryſt our Lorde and Maſter did firſt inſtitute, when he gaue to his Apoſtles *his bodie and bloode,* before he ſhoulde be betraied , as yt ys redd in the goſpell : *Ieſus tooke the bread and the cuppe , and bleſſing them gaue them vnto them.* Thus Iſidor.

In this breif ſaing of this authour ye learn not that Chryſt gaue vnto his Apoſtles a figure of his bodie and bloode, but that he gaue them his bodie and bloode. We be here alſo aduertiſed of the time, that yt was before he ſhoulde be betraied (as yt ys readde in the Goſpell) whiche was in his laſt ſupper, at which time (as this authour maketh mencion) he tooke the

B bread and the cuppe, and bleſſing them, gaue them to this Diſciples. Great ys the prowe of the bleſſing of Chryſt. And as the power ys great, ſo ys the effect anſwerablie great .He bleſſed the fiue loaues, ad two fiſhes and by that bleſſing they ſo multiplied as they fedde fiue thouſande people. And when they were ſatisfied ther were gathered vppe twelue baskettes full of the frag metes that they had lefte. He bleſſed vii loaues and a fewe fiſhes, and by the power of his bleſſing they were ſufficient not onely to feede and ſatisfie foure thouſande people, but alſo to fill ſeuen baskettes after they had doen. Great therfor, I ſaie, ys the power of Chryſtes bleſſing. Wherfor taking in his laſt ſupper the breade and the cuppe and bleſſing them, he wrought therby ſoche and ſo great an effect, that he ſaied: *This ys my bodie : This ys my bloode.* This great effect ys aunſwerable to ſo great a power. Yf by this bleſſing he had made the bread and wine onelie figures of his bodie and blode, and not his verie bodie and bloode, the effecte in reſpect had ben very ſmall. For manie thinges were figures without the expreſſe bleſſing of God : The lambes

C the calues, the oxen that were ſlain in the lawe of Moyſes. The braſen Serpent, as Chryſt him ſelf teſtifieth, was a figure of himſelf exalted vpon the Croſſe . And yet we read not that yt was bleſſed to be made a figure, yt ys therfor but a vain dreame of the aduerſarie and an abaſing of Goddes power, and a derogacion to his honour, to ſaie that Chryſt bleſſing the breade and wine did no more but make the figures of his bodie and bloode. Therfor acknowleadging the great power of Chryſtes bleſſing with this holie *Biſhopp Iſidore,* let vs ſaie as he ſaieth, that Chryſt gaue to his Apoſtles after he had bleſſed the bread and wine, not nowe bread and wine in ſubſtance, but the bodie and bloode of himſelf, according to the trueth of his owne ſaing : *This ys my bloode.* As who might ſaie, before I bleſſed yt, yt was bread and wine : but nowe that I haue bleſſed yt, and by my bleſſing chaunged yt, nowe I ſaie to yowe : *Take and eate : This ys my bodie : Take and drinke this ys my bloode.*

This like maner of vnderſtanding (as ys before declared) hath both S. Ambroſe, and S. Auguſtin , when they ſaied : *Non erat corpus Chriſti ante conſe-*

D *crationem , ſed poſt conſecrationem dico tibi, quòd iam corpus eſt Chriſti.* Yt was not the bodie of Chryſt before the coſecracion: but after the conſecracion, I ſai to thee, that nowe yt ys the bodie of Chryſt.

Thus nowe ye ſee the conſonant teſtimonie of this Father of the latin
                                        Oo   Churche,

Iſydor . de offic. eccle. cap.18.

Chryſt inſtituedthe ſacrifice of fred of the Chryſtiās.

The bleſſing of Chryſt of great force and power.

Matth. 14
Ioan.6.
Matth. 15

Effect of Chryſtes bleſſing of the breade

Ioan. 3.
To ſaie Chryſt made but a figure of hys bodie by bleſſing the bread ys a derogacion of his powr and honour

Amb. li.4. de Sac. c.4
Aug.de verbis Do. ſerm. 28.
Conſent of doctrine among the holie and auncient faþers.

Church,with *Euthymius* of the greke Church,and of thefe twoo with all the F
reft,and of all among them felues,which all as yt were with one mouth, as
yt becometh foche auncient fathers,and noble men of Chryftes high Parliament houfe,and right fcholers alfo of his bleffed fchoole , though they
were in diuerfe places, half of the greke Churche , and half of the latine Churche , and diuerfe times , fome in the verie beginning of the
Churche , fome two hundreth , fome three hundreth , fome foure' hundreth years after other,and yet in faith and in agreement in the fame,in the
vnderftanding alfo of the woordes of Chryftes fupper,they fpeake as they
were but one mouthe,and in one time and place, all confeffing vpon thefe
woordes of Chryft the verie prefence of his reall bodie,and not one confeffing yt to be a figure,*Tertullian* onely excepted, who yet fo doeth not after
the maner of the Aduerfaries doctrine,but after the maner of the catholique
doctrine,which (as ther at large ys declared)teacheth that the Sacrament ys
bothe the figure and the thing yt felf.

Nowe therfore(Reader)feing thowe feeft fo great confent and agreement of fo manie auncient learned Fathers,euen of the eldeft of the Church F
of the whiche diuerfe haue teftified their faith by their bloodes, and be holie Martirs of Chryft,diuerfe holie confeffours and fainctes in heauen , and
all vertuoufe and good, vpon whofe authoritie, next vnto the fcriptures, the
Canons of the holie Apoftles,and the holie generall Councells,the Church
doeth fownde and buill their faith and religion in all poinctes of the fame,
honouring and reuerencing them,and fubmitting themfelues to them and
their iudgementes as children to fathers and fcholers to mafters : fubmitte
alfo thy felf to them,confent to them,agree with them,and beleue with the,

Let all the Proteftātes bring furth if they can, when anie contrie did whollie opē lie and qui etlie profef fe foche reli gon as they nowe preac he.

that thowe maift be faued with them.   Remembre whether thowe be Englifh man,or Frenche man,Germain,Flemming or Saxon . that when thie
contrie firft receaued Chryft,yt receaued this faith,in this yt hath continued,in this thy fathers were baptifed,in this they liued,in this the moft parte
of them died , and in this , hope ys , that they be faued .   Bringe furth yf thow can , yf euer (till nowe of late daies) thy contrie
profeffed foche faith (yf yt maie be called faith) yf euer yt vfed foche maner of religion , yf euer they did fo often chaunge their pro-
feffion . Yf no foche prefident can be fhewed , yf this waie be a waie G
that thowe neuer faweft before, why wilt thowe vpon the phantafie of nouelties be caried awaie?Call to thy minde the good aduertifement of fainct
Paule,who faieth : *Be not caried awaie with diuerfe and ftraunge doctrines.*   Forgett
not that when *Luther* firft began hys peftilent herefie , he acknowleged

Heb.13 Diuerfities of religiō in thefe daies howe they began.

the prefence of Chryftes bodie in the Sacrament , fo did his difciples
alfo , till within fewe daies hys Difciples *Carolftadius*,*Zuinglius* , and *Oecolampadius* , fell from him , and began a newe waie , and taught that
Chryftes bodie was not in the Sacrament . Befides thefe , oute of Luther came the *Anabaptiftes*,and a nombre moo of other fectes fo that in diuerfe contries,fo manie free cities:fo manie Dukedomes,fo manie lordfhips,
almoft fo manie faithes , or raither opinions , and fo manie diuerfe coun-
tenances of religions.   In Englonde in the time of King Henrie the eight,

Mutacions of religion in Englōd.

ther began a newe countenance of religion:In the firft yeare of the reign of
his Sonne King Edwarde, an other countenance: within twoo yeares after euen in the time of the fame king hys reign, an other countenaun- H
ce.And that ys nowe in thys fame Realme varieth from them all.

Perceaue then that the doctrines that be nowe fettfurth by the Proclamer

A mer,as they be ftraung,fo be they diuerfe,fo be they variable,fo be they chaungeable.The doctrine,that was before this kinde of people troubled theChurch,was not diuerfebut one,not ftraunge,but of auncient continuan ce, not caufing warre,debate,tumultes,and infurrections in Realmes: diui- fions,diffentions and contencions betwixt neighbours:But as touching re- ligion great quietneffe,ioifull peace, and amiable concorde,not onely in Citties and townes:but alfo in all free cities, Lordfhipps, Dukedomes and realmes of *Europe*.Remembre again that (as S.Paule faieth) *God ys not the God*   1.*Cor*. 14. *of diffention but of peace*. Wher then thow feift peace,thither diuerte,ther fetle thy felf:ther abyde:among thefe holie Fathers thow feift peace in this mat- ter of the Sacrament:among the other,ther ys difcord as thow haueft percea ued in the xli. chapter of this booke , leaue the one and cleaue to the other, and the God of peace be withe thee.

B ## THE NINE AND FIFTETH CHAPITER

beginneth the expofition of the fame text by the fathers of the later

daies,and firft by Damafcen,andHaymo.

Haue hitherto vfed the teftimonies of the auncientes and Fa- thers of Chryftes Churche,naming them noble men of the hi- gher houfe of Chryftes Parliament,for that they be all within or verie neare fixt hundreth years of Chryft,whiche the Procla- mer,can not refufe,except he will faie,as the great herefiark *Lu-*   *Luthers* *ther* faied.*Non curo mille Cyprianos,nec mille Auguftinos*:I care not for a thoufand   *prowde con* Cyprians,nor a thoufand Auguftines.By the teftimonie of all whiche the   *liefathers.* woordes of Chryft are deliuered from the myftie and clowdie figures of the aduerfaries,and are placed and adourned with the auouching of the bright and clere prefence ofChryftes bleffed bodie and blood.And fo ysthe Proclamer plentifullie confuted by foche holie fathers as he himfelf can not refufe.And the faith of the catholique Church by the fame ys as fullie main- C teined and declared.

And although the Proclamer by Luciferane pride, femeth (as yt ys in the englifh prouerbe) to correct *magnificat*,I meen,to correct theChurch,and the faith of the fame,and to be a iudge vpon all the learned men, that haue ben thefe nine hundreth years,and by his iudgement withoute anie fufficient Commiffion to condemne them,to deface them, and not to efteem their fainges,learning or authoritie,wherin he foloweth the *Manichees* and other, which for the mainteinaunce of their herefieswolde accept foche fcriptures as they liked,and foche as they liked not they wolde refufe:Yet forafmoche as the Church hath allowed them,and their doctrine ys agreable to the el- der Fathers:I will call a companie of them,both that their doctrine maie be conferred with the elders before alleadged,and fo to be approued: and alfo that by them we maie know the enacted trueth of the true vnderftanding of   *TheProcla* Chryftes woordes,in the lower houfe of Chryftes Parliament, wherby the   *mer moc -* Aduerfaries herefie maie be more manifeftlie confuted,and the faith of the   *keth holie* good Chryftian more confirmed and ftaied.And although yt liked the Pro-   *åd learned* D clamer in his high pride to folace himfelf with the mocking of the learning   *fathers.* of *Siluefter*,*Ifidore*,*Innocentius* the thirde,*Gerfon*,*Durand*, *Holkot*,*S.Thomas*, *Dunce*, *Fisher* , and other , and made their argumentes as foolifhlie as he lifted , therbie to commende himfelf and his doctrine to foche as were

Oo ii   light

light,whiche yet was and ys difcommendable to them that be graue, fobre, and wife,yet in the ende ye fhall fee that thefe men fhall confute him, and ouerthrowe him in the iudgement of them whome gods grace hath not forfaken. For who ys he that ys wife,and, as the wifeman faieth,hath his eies in his heade,that feith not to moche arrogancie in that man, that taketh vpon him in open audience to deride mocke and skorne holie auncient learned men? of which fome of them be Sainctes in heauen,fome of them liued with great fame of learning aboue a thoufand yeares agon , fome eight or nine hundreth years agon,fome three hundreth years agon or ther aboute. All which are but babes and punies in his feight.

A lamentable time to fee preachers in pulpittes mocke Sainctes in heauen.

But I will not intermedle this worke of the heigh and great matter of the Sacrament,with foche vain toies of mockeries,but they fhall be referued to fome other more meit place,as either to a Chriftenmaffe skaffold, and fo a plaier by a plaier,or ells to the *Paruife* in Oxforde,a paruife toie, by a paruife boie to be aunfwered. Wherfore conuerting my felf to the matter,I wil produce Damafcen,as the firft and eldeft of this companie of the lower houfe, whiche I haue felected and chofen among all other to expownde vnto vs Chryftes woordes. This Damafcen although he be placed in the lower houfe,as in confideracion that the aduerfarie doeth not accept or regarde hys authoritie:yet he liued more then eight hundreth yeares agon,and therfore ys woorthie to be hearde. Thus he writeth vpon the woordes of Chryft: *Propofitionis panis,vinum & aqua per inuocationem,& aduentum fancti Spiritus,fupernaturaliter tranfmutantur in corpus & fanguinem Chrifti , & non funt duo , fed vnum , & idem .* The fhewe bread , the wine and the water by the inuocacion and the coming of the holie Goft are fupernaturallie tranfmuted into the bodie and bloode of Chryft,and they be not twoo,but one and the verie fame.

F

Damafcen li.4 ca.14.

And after a fewe woordes of exhortacion in the fame matter , he faieth thus of the fame breade and wine . *Non eft figura panis & vinum corporis & fanguinis Chrifti (abfit enim hoc credere)fed ipfum corpus Domini deificatum, ipfo dicente,Hoc eft meum (non mei corporis figura)fed corpus, non figura fanguinis,fed fanguis. Et ante hoc,ipfis Iudæis:Quoniam nifi manducaueritis carnem filij hominis, & biberitis eius fanguinem,non habebitis vitam in vobis. Caro mea verè eft cibus, & fanguis meus verè eft potus . Proinde omni cum timore & confcientia pura, & indubitabili fide accedamus.* The bread and wine ys not a figure of the bodie and blood of Chryft(*God forbidde we fhoulde beleue that*)but yt ys the verie bodie of our Lorde deified,himfelf faing:*This ys,not a figure of my bodie, but my bodie, not a figure of my bloode,but my bloode.* And before this he faied to the Iewes,that *except ye eate the flefh of the Sonne of man,and drinke his bloode , ye fhall haue no life in yowe.My flefh ys verilie meat, and my bloode ys verilie drinke .* Therfore with all feare and pure confcience , and vndoubted faith let vs come vnto yt.

G

Bread and wine not a figure of the bodie and blood of Chryfte

In thefe fewe woordes of Damafcen ye fee foure thinges taught : The tranfubftanciacion: The prefence of Chryftes verie bodie and bloode, with a plain deniall of the aduerfaries figure : The applicacion of the fixt chap. of fainct Iohn to thefe woordes of Chryft : And finallie an exhortacion for owre due coming to the receipt of the fame bodie and blode. Of tranfubftanciacon we haue allreadie fpoken , and that by the autho ritie alfo of this man amonge other Fathers . wherfore I will not tarie vpon yt , onely I wolde that the reader fhoulde be aduertifed, that though the Aduerfarie doe fo moche exclame againft the thing:

H

yet

A yet the learned Fathers according to the catholique faith of Chryftes Church, doe plainlie and agreablie teache the fame, and therfore, I wolde wifh that by repeticion of the fame, yt maie remain in memorie, wherbie, as meit yt ys, their authouritie declaring the trueth with great agreement and confent, maie be regarded and efteemed, and the arrogant falfheade of the Aduerfarie teaching vntruethes and herefie, maie be vtterlie condemned and forfaken, and thus ouerpaffing this matter as not principallie here fought, I will come to that, that ys here cheiflie intended.

For the whiche I wifh yt to be well noted, that this Authour expownding the woordes of Chryft: *This ys my bodie* (the feking of the expofition of whiche woordes ys our trauaill) doeth plainlie by expreffe woordes denie, refufe and reiect, the fonde expofition of the Aduerfarie, and teacheth that thefe woordes are to be vnderftanded in their propre fenfe. And therfore faieth, *that yt ys not a figure*, mening that yt ys not a bare figure of a thing abfent in fubftance, and onelie prefent in figure, but yt ys (faieth he) the

B verie bodie.   And this ys not to be ouerpaffed, that to this expofition he addeth thefe woordes: *God forbidde that anie man fhoulde fo beleue*, whiche maner of woordes we vfe in matters that be periloufe, daungeroufe, and horrible, and matters to godwarde, wher the thing ys moche offending God, and prouoking his heauie difpleafure, yre and indignacio. Wherbie maie be perceaued the great daunger that ys enfewing to them that fo beleue, and the great neceffitie of the right beleif, that ys, to beleue that the Sacrament ys not a bare figure, but the verie bodie of Chryft.

Thus once again to aduertife yowe, ye fee that wher the Aduerfarie faieth, *This ys my bodie*, that ys (faieth he) a figure of my bodie : This learned authour faieth, God forbidde yowe fhould fo beleue. *Yt ys not* (faieth he) *a figure of the bodie of Chryft, but his bodie, not a figure of the blood of Chryft but his blood in deed*. This expofition as yt ys diffonaunte and repugnaunte to the expofition of the Aduerfaries: fo ys yt confonaunte and agreable to the doctrine and expofition of the elders.

C In the next chapter before this, yowe fawe the expofition of *Euthymius* vpo thefe woordes of Chryft, not vnlike vnto this, but altogether like bothe in woordes and fentence, yt ys not (faieth he) a figure of Chryftes bodie, but his bodie, not a figure of hys bloode, but his bloode. Wherfore Reader, when thowe feeift the authours agree, and agreyng faie the contrarie of that, that the Aduerfarie teacheth, thowe maift be well adfured, that the doctrine of the Aduerfarie ys falfe. Wherfore feing yt plain before thine eyes, flee the falhead, and cleaue to the trueth.

The third note alfo maketh for the declaracion of this matter that he alleaging the fixt of fainct Iohn, referrethyt to the Sacrament in the fame fenfe that he vnderftoode Chryftes other woordes, which ys, as *Theophilact* alfo vpon the fame fixt of fainct Iohn faieth, *Non figura carnis, fed caro mea eft*. Not a figure of my flefh but yt ys my flefh. So that by thefe authours the fixt of S. Iohn perteineth to the Sacrament, notwithftanding the contrarie faing of *Luther* and *Oecolampadius*, and other of that rable. In which chapter ys promi-

D fed the geuing not of a figure of his flefh, but his verie flefh, And as yt was ther promifed verilie to be geuen: fo was the fame to the accomplifhment of the fame promeffe in verie dede deliuered and receaued, euen the verie flefh and verie blood of Iefus Chryft, and not the onelie figure of them.

Oo iii   The

Figuratiue expofitions of the Sacr. flatlie denied.

Euth. in 26. Matt. Doctrine of the Sacramentarie contrarie to the fathers.

The fourte note alſo, whiche ys for the due receauing of the Sacra- **E**
ment, geueth alſo light to the vnderſtanding of the preſence of Chryſtes
verie bodie in the Sacrament. But for that the conuenient place to ſpeake
of this matter ys in the thirde booke, we ſhall not here trooble the reader
with all.

We haue nowe ſeen a goodlie, and an euident teſtimonie teſtifieng howe
Chryſtes woordes were vnderſtanded in the greke Church: we will likewiſe
heare one that ſhall declare the vnderſtanding of them in the latin Church.
Who ſhall be Haymo, who vpon theſe woordes of Chryſt writeth thus:

Haymo in *Expletis ſolemnijs veteris Paſchæ, tranſit Dominus ad ſacramenta noui Paſchæ demonſtran-*
26. Matth *da, Poſtquam cœnauit dedit eis panem, & vinum in myſterio videlicet corporis, & ſan-*
guinis ſui: Quia enim panis cor hominis confirmat, & vinum anget ſanguinem in homine,
meritò idem panis in carnem Domini mutatur, & idem vinum in ſanguinem Domini tranſ-
fertur, non per figuram, neque per vmbram, ſed per veritatem. Credimus enim quia in ve-
ritate caro eſt Chriſti, ſimiliter & ſanguis. The Solemnities of the olde paſſeo-
Breadchau- uer being fullfilled, our Lord goeth to ſhewe the ſacramentes of the newt
ged into the Paſſouer. After he had ſupped he gaue them breade and wine in myſte-
bodie, and rie, that ys of his bodie and bloode. Bicauſe bread doeth make ſtrong the **F**
wine into heart of man, and wine encreaſeth blood in man, therfor the ſame bread ys
the blood of verie well chaunged into the fleſh of Chryſt, and the ſame wine ys transfer-
Chryſt not red into the blood of our Lorde, not by figure, nor by ſhadowe, but by tru-
in figur but eth. *For we beleue that in verie dede yt ys the fleſh of Chriſte, and likewiſe that yt ys hys*
in trueth. *bloode.* Thus moch *Haymo.*

Yowe ſee nowe here in the latin Church, alſo a goodlie teſtimonie, and a
clere expoſition of Chryſtes woordes, ſo clere and plain, that I ſhall not
nede to trauaill to open the ſame, but onely I haue thought good to note
to thee, Reader, the goodlie order that this authour obſerueth in his expoſition. Firſt he ioneth our newe Paſſouer to the olde, as the verie trueth
to the figure, whiche being in place the figure vaniſheth awaie. Wherbie yt
ys conſequent, that yf the Paſſouer whiche Chryſt did inſtitute were the
trueth, whiche the olde paſſouer did preſigurate, that the newe Paſſeouer
was a true thing in dede, and not a bare figure. For otherwiſe ſhoulde the
figure be the figure of a figure, and not of a trueth, which ys againſt the na- **G**
ture of a figure.

And when he had thus ioined the trueth to the figure, he declareth whē
yt was doen, ſaing that after he had ſupped he gaue them bread and wine in
the myſterie of his bodie and bloode. Then proceading he geueth a cauſe
whie Chryſt vſed bread and wine in this myſterie of his bodie and blood bicauſe (ſaieth he) the materiall bread comforteth the heart, and the materiall
A chaun- wine encreaſeth the blood, therfor to ſignifie that as theſe twoo things doe
ge in the woorke ther effectes in our material bodies: ſo thy being tranſmuted and
Sacr. in tru chaunged into heauenlie bread and wine of Chryſtes bodie and blood the
eth not in bread of the life, they woorke the like effect ſpirituallie in our ſoules. And
figure. foraſmoche as he had ſaied that the bread and wine be turned and chaunged into the bodie and bloode of Chryſt, he immediatelie teacheth howe
yt ys chaunged. *They are chaunged (ſaieth he) not by figure, nor by ſhadowe, ſed per*
veritatem, but in verie dede, whiche ys aſmoche to ſaie, as yt ys chaunged
or turned into the verie fleſh and blood of Chryſt in verie dede, and **H**
not into a bare Sacramentall bread as the Aduerſarie tearmeth ys.

Now as I haue doen with Damaſcē, ſo will I with this authour firſt cōferr
this dictrine with the doctrine of the elders to ſee howe they agree, and
after

A after, the doctrine of the aduersarie, both that yt maie appeare which of the best agree with the auncient Churhe, and whether ther be anie iust cause why the Aduersarie shoulde reiect this authour or his likes . This authour saieth that the bread ys chaunged into the bodie of our Lorde, and the wine into his bloode, doeth not among the elders, the great elder *Gregorie Nissen* vse the like woordes? *Quamobrem* (saieth he) *rectè nunc etiam Dei verbo sanctifica-tum panem, in Dei Verbi corpus credimus immutari.* Wherfor we doe nowe also verie well beleue the bread that ys sanctified by the woorde of God, to be chaunged into the bodie of the sonne of God.

Greg. Nis-sen. serm. cathec . de diuinis Sa-cramen.

See ye not then that the doctrine which *Haymo* here teacheth of the trans mutacion, chaunging, or turning of the bread into the bodie of Chryst which nowe the Church tearmeth, *Transubstantiacion*, ys an auncient doctrine and if yowe will conferre them diligentlie, ye shall haue occasion to thinke that this authour *Haymo* did in this matter folowe *Gregorie Nissen*, their sainges be so like. For as Gregorie maketh this matter of the chaunging of the bread into the bodie of Chryst no matter of doubte, or an opinion, but a

Transubsta ciacon, that ys, chaunge of bread ād wine into the bodie and bloode of Chryst, a matter of faith.

B sure and certen matter of faith and beleif. for he saieth, *Credimus immutari,* we beleue yt to be chaunged into the bodie of our lorde : so *Haymo,* when he had saied that the bread ys chaunged into the flesh of Chryst, and the wine into his bloode, saieth, *Credimus quia in veritate caro est Christi, similiter & sanguis,* we beleue that in verie dede yt ys the flesh of Chryst, and likewise his blode. So that ye maie perceaue not onely a concorde and consent of doctrine bet wixt them, but also an imitacion.

And here I wish these wooordes well to be noted, that the vnstablenesse of men in their faith might be také awaie. For the more ys the pitie, so moch hath the Deuell gotten by the worke of his ministres, that diuerse men in these daies be not ashamed to saie , we can not tell what to beleue. Other some will saie, I will beleue none of them all , vntill they agree better. as though yt were sufficient for them to liue withoute faith, and that they might be saued, without the profession of their faith, forgetting the saing

Faith howe yt ys deca-ied in these daies.

C of S. Paule: *Sine fide imposibile est placere Deo.* withoute faith yt ys not possible to please God. And again: *Corde creditur ad iusticiam , ore autem confessio fit ad sa-lutem .* The hearte beleueth vnto righteousnes, but the confession of faith by mouthe ys doen to saluacion. Let them vnderstande that this time ys a time of probacion, a time of triall, who will abide by their faith and who will be caried awaie from yt. But although yowr teachers in this time saie : *Non cre-dimus immutari,* we beleue not the bread and wine by the woorde of God to be chaunged into the bodie and bloode of Chryste, yet turne yowr eies to the olde auncient churche, haue yowe recourse thither, and see *Gregorie Nis fen* and after him *Haymo* saing: *Credimus immutari*, We beleue that the bread and wine be chaunged into the bodie and bloode of Chryst, and they be nowe in verie dede the flesh of Chryst, and likewise his bloode . and so a-bide in the faith of the auncient churche, what soeuer ys nowe taught yowe to the contrarie.

Hebr . 11. Rom . 10.

This time a time of probacion.

By this conference ye maie perceaue, that *Haymo* agreeth with the aun-cient elders, as concerning the chaunging of the bread and wine into the bodie and bloode of Chryst. Yf ye will conferre him in that he saieth, that **D** this chaunge ys not doen by figure, or shaddow , but in verie dede: yowe haue *Euthymius* and Damascen at hand, which both denie the Sacrament to be onely a figure. Yf ye will conferre the doctrine of the Aduersarie to the do-doctrine of these Fathers ye shall perceaue that what the Fathers affirme,

Sacramen-taries denie that the fa-thers affir-me and af-firme that they denie.

the Aduerſarie denieth, and what the Fathers denie, the Aduerſarie affir- E
meth. The holie Fathers affirme that the bread and wine be chaunged : the
Aduerſarie denieth yt. The holie Fathers denie that the Sacrament ys onlie
a figure, the Aduerſarie ſaieth that yt ys a figure onely. See yowe not then
that the Aduerſarie ys directlie contrarie to the holie Fathers? What hope
of true learning then ys ther to be had, wher and of whome the fathers of
trueth are denied, contraried and againſt ſaied.

But to conclude for the matter that ys here ſought, this authour ſpeaking
theſe woordes as an expoſition vpon the woordes of Chryſt and teaching
vs, that the bread and wine be chaunged into the bodie and bloode of Cryſte, and that by no figure, nor ſhadowe, but in verie dede, yt ys manifeſt that
theſe woordes of Chryſte, be to be vnderſtanded withoute figure, and that
they teache vs that in the Sacramēt ys the verie bodie, and the verie bloode
of Chryſte in verie dede. Wherfor leauing this as a moſt plain matter, we
will call an other coople.

THE SIXTETH CHAP. PROCEADETP IN
the expoſition of the ſame text by Theophilact,
and Paſchaſius.

F
F this coople that ſhall nowe geue ther teſtimonie for the true vnderſtanding of Chryſtes woords, Theophilact, as he ys the ſeniour ſo
ſhall he be the firſt that geueth teſtimonie. Expownding the woor
des of Chryſt, thus he writeth vpõ the ſame woords: Dicens: Hoc eſt
corpus meum, oſtendit quod ipſum corpus Domini eſt panis, qui ſanctificatur in altari &
non reſpondens figura. Non enim dixit. Hoc eſt figura, ſed hoc eſt corpus meum. Ineffabili
enim operatione transformatur, etiãſi nobis videatur panis. Quoniã infirmi, ſumus & abhor-
emus crudas carnes comedere, maximè hominis carnem, ideo panis quidem apparet, ſed caro eſt. Saing : This ys my bodie, he doeth declare that the bread which ys ſancti
fied in the aultar ys the verie boodie of our Lorde, and not a figure anſwering to yt. For he did not ſaie, This ys a figure of my bodie : but this ys my bodie,
For yt ys transformed by an vnſpeakeable operacion, although yt appeare
bread. For aſmoche as we be weake, and doe abhorre to eate rawe fleſh
ſpeciallie the fleſh of a man, therfor yt appeareth bread, but yt ys fleſh.
Thus Theophilct.

As they that be obſtinate in this hereſie againſt the bleſſed Sacrament
when they reade this expoſition, their conſciences be, I dare ſaie, touched
and preſſed with the ſame to their great greif : euen ſo doe I merueill that
they be ſo ſolde ouer to voluntarie and malicioſe blindeneſſe in hereſie,
that ſeing not onelie the true faith and expoſition taught ſo clerelie and euidentlie, that they be not able with any good apparant anſwere to auoide,
will yet ſtubburnlie to their greuouſe damnacion, perſiſt and abide ſtill in
their hereſie. But let vs veiue the ſaing of Theophilact. In him we finde theſe
foure thinges taught : Firſt the preſence of Chryſtes verie bodie in the Sacra
ment. For he ſaieth that the bread that ys ſanctified in the aultar, ys the very bodie of our Lorde.

The ſecond ys a flatt and a plain deniall of the figuratiue ſpeache, that
the Aduerſarie wolde haue in the woordes of Chryſte. For this authour ſaieth that Chryſt did not ſaie : This ys a figure of my bodie : but my bodie . and ſo
the figure ys denied, that ſo ſtoutlie and with violence ſhoulde be here
thruſt in.

Thirde

*Theoph. in
26. Math.*

*The bread
ſanctified
on the aul-
tar ys the
verie bodie
of Chryſt ãd
not onelie a
figure.*

*Foure thin
ges plainlie
auouched
by Theoph.
againſt the
Sacram.*

*1.
Reall pre-
ſence affir-
med.*

*2.
Figure de-
nied.*

A   Thirdelie here ys taught howe the fanctified breade ys made the body
of Chryft: yt ys transformed (faieth he) by an ineffable operacion,although
yt appeare bread vnto vs. In thefe fewe woordes he teacheth vs three thinges : firft that the bread ys trasformed, whiche ys all one as if he had faied
tranfubftanciated. for in the bread ther be two formes, the inwarde forme,
and the outwarde forme. Nowe this authour faieth that the outwarde forme
of bread remaineth ftill . For he faieth that yt appeareth vnto vs as
bread . Yt ys confequent then that feing here ys a transformacion,
which ys a chaunge of a forme , that the inwarde forme of breade
ys chaunged. The inward forme of the bread ys the fubftance of yt (*Subftantia* and *forma* being all one) wherfor he faing that yt ys transformed, faieth
that the Church faieth, that yt ys tranfubftanciated· The fecod that he teacheth ys that transformacion or tranfubftanciacion ys doen,*ineffabili operatione*
with an vnfpeakable maner of woorking,by which he doeth both teach that
this chaunge of the bread into the bodie of Chryft ys againft *Oecolampadius,*

B a woonderfull and a miraculoufe worke, fo miraculoufe that though we beleue yt to be doen, yet not being able to comprehende yt, how yt ys doen,
we are not able to faie how yt ys doen , ad therfor vnfpeakable. For nothing
can well be fpoken that ys not knowen: and alfo that this chaunge againft
the Aduerfarie ys not a facramentall chaunge, for that trasformacio or chau
ge ys not vnfpeakable . For we both comprehende the doing of yt,and we
are alfo able to fpeake yt, and therfor not vnfpeakeable. And if then this traf
formacion be vnfpeakeable, yt ys a moche greater and higher chaunge,then
to chaunge the vfe of a peice of common breade, to the vfe of Sacramentall bread.

   The fourth that ys here taught, ys why the bread being transformed, yt
doeth yet ftill appeare breade, as though yt were ftill bread in fubftance . yt
ys (faieth the authour)bicaufe we are weake, and doe abhorre to eate rawe
flefh,cheiflie of a man,therfor yt appeareth bread. So that by this we are war
ned of the great goodneffe of God and mercie towardes vs, in that he fo
mercifullie confidereth our weake ftate and condefcendeth to oure infir-

C mitie , and yet as touching the Sacrament , though for gods mercifull
confideracions yt appeareth breade,yet in verie dede(as this authour faieth)
yt ys flefh.

   Nowe to kepe our order, for that *Theophilact* ys of the lower houfe, and
with in the compaffe of the time, that the Aduerfarie prefcribeth againft,
Let vs alfo conferre his doctrine with the doctrine of the Fathers, whiche
be of the higher houfe to make proof howe they agree. Wher he faieth that
the bread which ys fanctified in the aultar ys not a figure,but the verie bodie
of Chryft, although the Aduerfarie him felf maie confeffe that *Chryfoftom,*by
that that ys alleaged oute of him in this booke and in manie other places,
doeth likewife plainlie and fullie confeffe the fame prefence of Chryfte in
the Sacrament : yet that I maie be fhort and with one authour fhewe yowe all that *Theophilact* faieth,I wil conferre him with S.Cyrill. whom ye hear
de but late alleaged, who vfeth almoft the fame woords that S. Cyrill did, fo
near that in this place I maie raither call him the imitatour of Cyrill, then
of Chryfoftom. Thus ye haue him ther alleaged : *Ne horreremus carnem & fan*

D *guinem appofita facris altaribus, codefcendens Deus noftris fragilitatibus,influit oblatis vim
vitæ , conuertens ea in veritatem propriæ carnis.*That we fhoulde not abhorre flefh
fett vpon the holie aultars, God codefcending to our fragilities powreth into the thinges offred the powre of life, turning the into his verie owne flefh.
Thus Cyrill.   Nowe

[margin notes:]
Tr afubfta
tiacion a-
uouched.

The work
of theSacr.
ys miracu-
loufe·

Forme of
bread why
yt remai-
neth.

ca. 55.

ca. 57.

Cyrill.ad
Calofir.

Theophi-
laƐt,and S.
Cyrill,com
pared in
their do-
Ɛtrine of
the Sacr.

Nowe if yowe wil conferre them, wher *TheophilaƐt* faieth that the bodie
of Chryſt ys in the altar, *Cyrill* faieth that fleſh and bloode ys on the holie
altars.wher*TheophilaƐt* faieth that the bread ys transformed by the vnſpeakea
ble worke of God:*Cyrill* faieth that God turneth yt into his verie owne fleſh.
TheophilaƐt faieth that bicauſe we are weake, God conſidering our weakneſſe
ſuffreth the outwarde formes of breade to remain : *Cyrill* faieth that leeſt we
ſhoulde abhorre fleſh and blod vpon the holie aultars, he put into the bread
and wine which be the thinges offred. the power of life, whiche ys the fleſh
of Chryſte,whiche he calleth the fleſh that hath power to geue life. Thus ye
fee a goodlie agrement,be twixt *TheophilaƐt* and *Cyrill*. Soche was the conſtãt
faith of this learned authour that not onelie vpon the ſixt of S. Iohn, and
the x x v i of S. Matthewe, as ye haue nowe hearde, he doeth teache the pre
ſence, and denie the Sacrament to be a figure, and côfeſſeth the transforma
cion of the bread into the fleſh of Chryſt, but alſo he doeth the like vpon S.
Marke, Whoſe ſaing I will aſcribe, not onelie for that yt maketh for the
matter of the Sacrament as the other doe : but alſo that ſoche cauill as the   F
Aduerſarie wolde make ther vpon maie be remoued. Thus he writeth ther.

Theophil.
in 14.
Matth.

*Quum benedixiſſet, hoc eſt gracias egiſſet, fregit panem, id quod etiam nos facimus preces
adiungendo, Hoc eſt corpus meum, hoc (inquam) quod ſumitis.Non enim figura tantùm &
exemplar Dominici corporis panis eſt, ſed in ipſum côuertitur corpus Chriſti,Dominus enim
dicit : Panis, quem ego dabo, caro mea eſt, non dixit figura carnis meæ eſt , ſed caro mea
eſt. Et iterum : Niſi ederitis carnem filii hominis. Et quomodò (inquis) caro non videtur?
O homo, propter noſtram infirmitatem iſtud fit, quia enim panis & vinum ex iis ſunt quibus aſſueuimus, ea non abhorremus . Idcirco miſericors Deus noſtræ infirmitati condeſcendens ſpeciem quidem panis & vini ſeruat, in virtutem autem carnis & ſanguinis tranſelementat.* When he had bleſſed, that ys, when he had geuen thankes, he brake

Figure of
of the Sacr.
flatlie de-
nied.

the breade, whiche thing alſo we doe, adioining praiers: This ys my bodie, this I ſaie,that yowe receaue. For the breade ys not onelie a figure and
an exemplar of owre Lordes bodie, but yt ys turned into the verie bodie of
Chryſte. For our Lode ſaied : *The bread that I will geue yowe ys my fleſh.* He did
not ſaie, yt ys a figure of my fleſh, but yt ys my fleſh. And again except ye   G
eate the fleſh of the Sonne of man &c. But thowe ſaieſt, howe ys not the
fleſh ſeen? O man, this ys doen for our weakneſſe· For bicauſe bread and wine be of theſe thinges whiche we be accuſtomed vnto, we doe not abhorre
them, therfor oure mercifull God condeſcending to our weakneſſe,*he kepeth
the forme of bread and wine, but he doeth tranſelementate them into the vertue of his fleſh
and bloode.* Thus *Theoph.*

Yt were ſuperfluouſe, to make anie notes vpon this place, ſith euerie par
te ys ſo plain, and therwith ſo like the other before alleaged, that what ys

Cauille of
the Sacra-
mentaries
vpon the
woord (ver
tue)

ſaied ther,maie be applied to this, and ſoche notes as be ther maie be referred alſo to this. Onelie I ſhall remoue the cauill of the Aduerſarie, whiche
he wolde grownde vpon theſe woordes of *TheophilaƐt,* wher he ſaieth, that
God trãſelementated the bread ãd wine into the vertue of his fleſh ãd bloode. By this ſentence , and ſpeciallie by this woorde (*vertue*) wolde the Ad
uerſarie wreſt all the ſainges of this Authour, that wher he ſaieth, that God
tranſmuteth, transformeth,turneth or chaungeth the bread and wine into
his fleſh and bloode, they are (*ſaieth the Aduerſarie*) to be vnderſtanded of the
vertue of his fleſh and bloode, and not of the fleſh and bloode them ſelues.   H

Oecol. de
verb. cœnæ
Dom.

For this ys his ſaing : *Panem & vinum conuertuntur dignè comedentibus non in corporalem præſentiam,ſed in virtutem carnis & ſanguinis Chriſti.* The bread and wine are
turned, to them that woorthilie eate, not into the corporall preſence, but
into

A into the vertue of the flesh and bloode of Chryste.

Let vs nowe weigh this their violent expofition. They faie that the bread *Sacramēta* and wine be turned into the vertue of the flesh and bloode of Chryste. yt *ries teache* ys a pretenfed rule among them, that nothing maie be taught withoute *cōtrarie to* fcriptures. What fcripture haue they to proue this their faing? Wher finde *their owne* they in all the fcripture that the bread ys turned into the vertue of Chryftes *rules.* flesh? Certen I am, they haue no one title. and yet they teache nothing, they faie, but the fincere woorde of God. but vnder foche coolour of finceritie they vtter manie vntrueths, as we fhall prooue this to be one. Firft their owne doctrine ys (as before ys faied) that thefe dumbe and infenfate creatures are not partakers of fanctificacion or holineffe. But the vertue of Chryftesflefh ys not onelie an holie thing, but alfo the caufe of fanctificacion and holineffe. wherfor bread and wine being infenfate creatures, are not par takers of yt muche leffe can they be turned into yt.

To prooue this we will open fomeparte of the vertue of Chryftes flefh. *Vertue of* for yt ys great and large, and hath manie partes, But the bread and wine cā *Chryfts* B be turned into none of them. The vertue of Chryftes flefh ys to vnite vs to *flesh* the fame his flefh, as S. Hilarie faieth. The vertue of the fame flefh ys to make Chryft naturallie to abide in vs, as he alfo faieth. The vertue of the fame flefh *Hilar.li.8,* maketh vs membres of Chryftes bodie, as faieth *Irenæus.* The vertue of the *de Irini.* fame flefh, which ys quickning and making to liue, or geuing power of life, maketh our flefh after the refurrectiō to liue euerlaftinglie, as faieth S.Cyrill. *Iren. li. 5.* Chryfoftom reherfing the vertues of Chryftes bloode, amonge a great nom- *aduerf he-* bre, which were to long to reherfe, faieth thus: *Hic fanguis facit vt imago in no-* *ref.* *bis regia floreat : hic animarum noftrarum falus : hoc lauatur, hoc ornatnr, hoc incenditur,* *hic igne clariorem mentem noftram reddit, & auro fplendidiorem.* This bloode caufeth *Cyrill in* the Kinges ymage to florifh in vs : this bloode ys the faluacion of our foules, *15.Ioan.* with this fhe ys wasfhed, with this fhe ys beautified: with this fhe ys enkind- *Chrifo.hŏ.* led : this bloode maketh our minde more clear, and more gliftering then *45 in Ioan.* golde. To be fhorte the vertue of the flefh and bloode of Chryfte ys our re- demption, iuftificacion, and faluacion. Be the bread and wine turned into C thefe vertues, or into anie one of thē? yf the breade and wine can receaue no holineffe, can they receaue thefe vertues?

As by this ye maie perceaue that their doctrine ys neither confonant and agreeable within yt felf, nor yet fownde and good: fo fhall yt be made plain *Sacramen-* to yowe that yt will not agree with *Theophilact.* whom they labour to wreft. *taries do-* They faie that the bread and wine be turned into the vertue of Chryftes *ctrine con-* flefh and blood, and not into the flefh and blood yt felf: yf the bread be tur *ferred with* ned into the vertue, and not into the flefh, then ftandeth this propoficion *Theophi-* of theirs, that the bread and wine be ftill but figures. But howe ftandeth that *lact.* their faing with the fainge of *Theophilact,* who by expreffe woordes faieth: *Non eft figura. Yt ys not a figure?* Again, faing that the bread ys not turned into the flefh : howe agree they with *Theophilacte,* who faieth alfo by expreffe woordes: *Panis conuertitur in ipfum corpus Chrifti.* The bread ys turned into the verie bodie of Chryfte. or into the bodie of Chryft yt felf? Whiche woor- des haue great force, and limite this turning of the breade folie and onelie into the flefh of Chryfte. I meen wholl Chryfte him felf, and no other thing D for him. Again, yf the breade be not turned into the flefh of Chryft, howe agreeth yt, with that *Theophilacte* faieth, that although yt appeare bread: yet yt ys flefh?

Tus then ys maie perceaue that this Authour by expreffe woordes denied
the

the breade to be a figure,and also affirmed the same bread to be turned into
the bodie of Chryst yt self,and that the Sacrament ys flesh,though yt appea
re breade. What impudencie than, What shamelesnes ys ther in these men,
that after so plain and manifest asseueracion of the turning of the bread, and
wine into the bodie and bloode of Chryst, made by this authour not in one
place as a thing vnaduisedly spoken, or sodenlie fallen from him, but with
good deliberacion both vpon S. Matthew, and vpon the sixt chap. of S.
Iohn, and ther also more then once, and here likewise vpon S. Marke, denieth the figure, and affirmeth the turning of the bread to be into the verie
bodie of Chryst. yet nowe they wolde vpon one woorde drawe him violentlie to theeir wicked pourpose,and make him(as yt werewith one breath)
to saie yea and naie to one thing, and in one sentence to denie and again to
affirme the same.

But that we maie once ende this matter, and let yowe perceaue the true
vnderstanding of this woorde of *Theophilact*. which the Aduersarie abuseth:
ye shall vnderstand that the woorde (*Vertue*) in that place ys taken for the
flesh of Chryst, and not for the vertue as diuided from the flesh of Chryst.
Which thing first the processe of *Theophilact* doeth well prooue, and among
other this that he saieth , that although yt appeare bread : yet yt ys flesh.
which maner of speach prooueth inuinciblie the presence of Chrystes flesh.
which presence ys no otherwise there but by turning of the substance of
bread into yt.

*Vertue and
power take
for the flesh
of Chryste
Tractatu
26.in Ioan.*
Besides this the holie doctours vse this woorde (*Virtus*, vertue) and this
woorde (*Vis power*)for the flesh of Chryst in the Sacrament. As for the first
yt appeareth in S.Augustin,and the other in Cyrill. S.Augustyn saieth thus:
*Aliud est sacramentum, aliud virtus sacramenti, quam multi de altari accipiunt, & mo-
riuntur, & accipiendo moriuntur.* The Sacrament ys one thing : the vertue of the
Sacrament ys an other.which vertue manie doe receaue from the aultar and
doe die, and in receauing doe die. By the death that S. Augustine here speaketh of he meneth dánacion euerlasting. For immediatelie he saieth: *vnde di
cit Apostolus: Iudicium sibi manducat & bibit.* Wherfore the Apostle saieth: he
eateth and drinketh his owne damnacion.

In which his woordes this partickle (*the Vertue of the Sacrament*)ys not taken
for the vertue of Chrystes flesh as distincted and diuided from the flesh of
Chryst, but yt ys taken for the verie flesh of Chryst yt self, which we knowe
and beleue allwaies to be full of vertue whersoeuer yt be. Yf the Aduersarie
will take here the woorde (*Vertue*) in S. Augustine, as not signifieng the flesh
of Chryst, but onelie the merittes and benefittes of Chrystes flesh, which
be grace, remission of sinnes, iustificacion and saluacion, then yt shall folowe
that a man maie at one time receaue grace and displeasure, iustificacion and
condemnacion. saluacion and damnacion. For S. Augustine saieth : *that manie in receauing the vertue of the Sacrament doe die.* that ys be damned. Nowe if in
receauing the vertue of Chrystes flesh, which ys saluacion they also receaue
death which ys damnacion, then they receaue at one time both saluacion
and damnacion, which ys vnpossible. Wherfor (*Vertue*)in this place neither
ys nor can be taken as the aduersarie wolde haue yt , but for the flesh of
Chryst, whiche being vnwoorthilie taken and receaued causeth in dede
damnacion, as the text of S. Paule by S. Augustin alleaged doth teache.
of the which we shall treact more at large in his owne place in the thirde booke.

The other also vsed by S. Cyrill signifieth not the power of life, as separated

A rated from the flesh of Chryst, whiche ys(as S. Cyril faieth)*Caro vitæ*, the flesh of life: and *Corpus vitæ*, the bodie of life: but yt signifieth that liuelie flesh yt self. For when fainct Cyrill(as a litle before ye haue heard) had faied that God powreth into the offred thinges(mening the bread and wine) the power of life, howe that ys doen, or what he meneth by that, he immediatelie declareth faing: *turning thofe thinges into his owne verie flesh and bloode:* As who might haue faied: He powreth into the offred thinges the power of life, whé he turneth them into his owne flesh and bloode.

Thus trusting that *Theophilact* ys fullie deliuered from the wresting of the the Aduersarie, and that the falfhead of the fame Aduersarie, ys here detected and the catholique trueth opened and defended: I will ende with him, and call in *Paschafius*, who ys of the other fide of Chrystes Parliament house, who will verie aptelie come in this place to aunfwer the Aduersarie, who wolde in-fteade of Chryftes bodie place the vertue of his bodie. For he vpon Chry ftes woordes faieth thus: *Cœnantibus autem illis, accepit Iefus panem, benedixit ac fre-*

Plain pla-ces of Paf-chafius a-gainft the Sacramen-taries.

B *git, deditque Difcipulis fuis & ait: Accipite & comedite, Hoc eft corpus meum. Audiant qui volunt extenuare hoc verbum (corpus)quòd non fit vera caro Chrifti, quæ nunc in fa-cramento celebratur in Ecclefia Chrifti, neque verus eius fanguis.* When they were at fupper Iefus tooke bread, he bleffed yt and brake yt, and gaue yt to his Dif-ciples and faied: *Take and eate, this ys my bodie.* Let them heare that will extenua-te or abafe this worde(*bodie*) that yt ys not the verie flesh of Chryft, that ys nowe celebrated in the Sacrament in the Church of Chryft, neither that yt ys verie bloode,

Pafchafius li. de corp. et fang. Dom.

And a litle before he faieth vpon the fame text: *Nec ita dixit, cùm fregit & de dit eis panem: Hæc eft, vel in hoc myfterio eft quædam virtus, vel figura corporis mei, fed ait non fictè: Hoc eft corpus meum . Et ideo hoc eft, quod dixit, & non quod quifque fingit.* Neither did he faie, when he brake the bread, and gaue yt them: This ys, or in this myfterie ys a certain vertue or figure of my bodie: but he faieth plainlie, *This ys my bodie. And therfore yt ys yt, that he faied, and not that that euery man feigneth.*

C And yet again after a fewe lines he faieth: *Vnde miror quid velint nunc quidam dicere non in re effe veritatem carnis Chrifti & fanguinis, fed in facramen to, virtutem quandam carnis, & non carnem: virtutem fanguinis, & non fan-guinem: figuram, & non veritatem : vmbram, & non corpus.* Wherfore I woonder what fome men doe meen to faie that ther ys not in dede the ve-ritie of the flesh and bloode of Chryfte·but in the Sacrament, to be a cer-tain vertue of the flesh and not the flesh, the vertue of the bloode and not the bloode, a figure and not the veritie, a fhadowe and not the bodie.

What fhall I trooble the reader with doing of that, that ys allreadie doen? As *Euthymius, Damafcen, Haymo,* and *Theophilact,* doe auouche the prefence of Chryftes bodie in the Sacrament, and as yowe haue hearde them denie the Sacrament to be onelie a figure: fo doth this authour agree with them, and denieng with them the Sacrament to be a figure, fhadowe or vertue or Chryftes bodie, teacheth as they doe, the verie prefence of Chryftes bodie in the Sacrament, and that by vertue of Chryftes woordes, who faied (*This ys my bodie*) Wherupon again he faieth: *Hoc eft corpus meum,*

Pafchaf. ibid.

D *& non aliud quàm quod pro vobis tradetur. Et cùm calicem porrigeret : Hic eft (inquit) calix noui Teftamenti, qui pro vobis effundetur in remifsionem peccatorum . Nec dum itaque erat fufus, & tamen ipfe porrigitur in calice fanguis, qui fundendus erat. Erat quidem iam in calice, qui adhuc tamen fundendus erat in precium.*

*Et ideo ipfe idemque fanguis iam erat in calice,qui & in corpore,ficut & caro, vel corpus in pane.T his ys my bodie,*and none other but euen the fame that fhall be deliue-red for yowe. And when he gaue them the cuppe,he faied: *This ys the cuppe of the newe Teftament,whiche shall be shed for yowe in the remifsion of finnes.* Yt was not

The fame blood in the cuppe, that was to be shedd.

yet fhed,and yet the fame bloode was geuen in the cuppe , that was to be fhed.*Yt was trulie nowe in the cuppe,that was to be shed in redemption.* And therfore euen the verie fame blood was nowe in the cuppe, that was in the bodie, euen as yt was the fame flefh or bodie that was vnder the bread.   Thus far re Pafchafius.

As this authour agreeth with other aboue named,for that he ther faied: fo for this that he here faieth he agreeth with fainct Auguftine. For as this man faieth that the bodie and blood, which was geuen to the Apoftles,was euen the fame that was to be deliuered to death,and to be fhed for the re-miffion of finne,and fo all one with his owne bodie fitting among them in vifible forme:fo(as ye haue heard)fainct Auguftine faied,that Chryft caried

F

Aug in Pfal.33. conc.1.

himfelf in his owne handes,when he gaue furth his bodie to his difciples, and faied,*Take eate,this ys my bodie.* And fo the bodie that did carie , and the bodie that was caried,was all one bodie of Chryfte.So nowe to conclude, yt ys manifeft,that as faint Auguftine in that place taught the verie prefen-ce of Chryftes bodie in the Sacrament,and the woordes of Chryfte to be vnderftanded withoute figure in their propre fenfe:fo doth this authour al-fo.Wherfor this being plain I ende,and go to an other coople.

THE ONE AND SIXTETH CHAP. CONTI-

nueth the expofition of the fame woordes by Oecumenius,
and Anfelmus.

Owe of the lower houfe we haue hearde two cooples , whiche al-though they be fo placed, yet are they both of good antiquitie(the yongeft of them,which ys *Pafchafius,* being almoft feuen hundreth

G

yeares agon)and alfo foche as aught to be receaued for that they were a good time before *Berengarius* began the controuerfie of the bleffed Sa crament.Thefe that folowe be foche as were after the controuerfie was mo ued by *Berengarius:*yet foche as haue ben in eftimacion, price and reuerence both in the greke Church and in the latin Churche,and foche, whofe doc-trine the Churche hath approued , and receaued. Wherfore reafon and good order wold (notwithftanding the arrogancie of the Aduerfaries, who haue appointed them felues iudges vpon the Churche,to which they aught to be fubiectes, and fo refufe foche as they lift) that they that loue the Church of Chryft,and wifh to be,or be membres of the fame , fhoulde ac-cept,whome the Church accepteth,and approue, whom the Churche ap-prooueth,The teftimonie then of thefe we will heare, that to the confuta-ciö of the enemie,yt maie appeare that they are vniuftlie reiected of thē,whē they teache as the fathers doe. And therwithall we fhall fee the trueth of the Sacrament fetfurth and commended vnto vs,to the great comfort (*I truft*)of foche as loue the catholique faith, and the honoure of that bleffed

H

Oecum in 11.Prim. Corr.

Sacrament.

Among thefe therfore that yet remain,*Oecumenius,*one of the greke church, who ys accompted to haue liued aboute foure hondreth and feuentie years agon, writeth thus vpon Chryftes woordes:*Erant quoque in veteri teftamento po cula*

A *cula in quibus libabant vbi etiam, poſtquàm victimas immolaſſent, ſanguinem irrationabilium excipientes poculis libabant. Pro ſanguine igitur irrationàbilium, Dominus proprium
ſanguinem dat, & bene in poculo, vt oſtendat vetus Teſtamentum anteà hoc delineaſſe.*
Ther were alſo in the olde Teſtament cuppes in the whiche they did ſacrifice, wherin alſo after they had offred their ſacrifices, receauing the bloode
of vnreaſonable beaſtes, they did ſacrifice yt in cuppes. Therfore for the
bloode of vnreaſonable beaſtes, our Lord geueth his owne blood. And well
in a cuppe, that he might ſhewe the olde Teſtament to haue delined this be
fore. Thus *Oecumen.*

Our Lorde
geueth his
owne blood
in a cuppe.

Beſides the aptacion and applieng of the thing figurated to the figure, in
the whiche this authour meneth, that as verilie as the bloode of vnreaſonable beaſtes was receaued in cuppes, ſo verilie alſo haue we the bloode of
Chryſt in cuppes, beſides this I ſaie, his ſpeache and maner of woordes are
to be weighed. The figure of Chryſtes bloode ys not his owne bloode.
Wherfore ſainge that Chryſt geueth vs his owne bloode, he remoueth the
aduerſaries figure. For the one importeth proprely the thing yt ſelf: the other
B a figure or token of the ſame.

And yet farder to conſider the verie woordes of this authour, wher geueth Chryſt his owne bloode vnto vs? He ſaieth: *In poculo.* In the cuppe. Yf
then yt be geuen vs in the cuppe, yt ys not the bloode of Chryſt ſpirituallie,
for that ys not receaued in cuppes, but in the ſoule of man. Being than Chryſtes own bloode, and receaued in a cuppe, yt muſt nedes be the bloode of
Chryſt reallie, to the which yt well apperteineth, for ſomoche as Chryſt
hath ſo appointed yt, to be receaued in a reall cuppe, for that yt ſelf ys a
reall thing. Beſides this, the authour ſaieth that yt aunſwereth the figure verie well, that the bloode of Chryſt ys in a cuppe, bicauſe the figure had ſo, as
yt were foreſaied that yt ſhoulde ſo be, in that that the bloode of beaſtes was
offred in cuppes. Then Chryſt geuing his own bloode in the cuppe to hys
Diſciples, and ſaing: *Drinke ye all of this. This ys my blood:* did ſpeake theſe woordes in their propre ſenſe. And as he did them, ſo did he vndoubtedlie theſe,
This ys my bodie. And thus by this authour we haue like teſtimonie, as by other
C before alleaged.

Chryſtes
blood ys not
conteined.
in cuppes
ſpirituallie

We ſhall nowe likewiſe ſee what agreable teſtimonie *Anſelmus* will geue,
who ys appointed to geue the ſame for the latin Church, as *Oecumenius* hath
doen for the greke church. Thus he writeth: *Sic enim habemus in euangelijs: Accepit Ieſus panem, benedixit, fregit, deditque Diſcipulis ſuis dicens: Accipite, & manducate
ex hoc omnes. Hoc eſt enim corpus meum, quod pro vobis tradetur. Quando in manus accepit panis erat, ſic enim dixit: Accepit panem, & per illam benedictionem panis factus eſt
corpus Chriſti, non tantùm ſignificatiuè, ſed etiam ſubſtantiuè. Neque enim ab hoc ſacramento figuram omnino excludimus, neque figuram ſolam admittimus. Veritas eſt, quia
corpus Chriſti eſt: figura eſt, quia immolatur, quod incorruptibile habetur. Conſideremus verba Domini. Manducate (inquit) ex hoc omnes. Hoc enim, quod vobis trado ad manducandum eſt corpus meum. Et vt certi eſſent, quod reuera eſſet corpus Chriſti, ſigna expreſſit,
quibus hoc dignoſcerent. Hoc eſt, inquit, corpus meum, quod pro vobis tradetur. Si hoc corpus, corpus Chriſti non ſubſtantiuè, ſed ſignificatiuè tantùm fieret, hoc figura corporis Chriſti tantùm exiſteret. Nihil ad figuram, quod ſequitur: Quod pro vobis tradetur. Nec panem
nominauit poſtquam panem benedixit, ſed corpus: nec vinum nominauit poſtquam vinum
benedixit, ſed ſanguinem. Igitur, ſicut fides catholica credit, panis qui offertur ſacerdoti ad
D ad conſecrandum, per ſacerdotalem conſecrationem fit corpus Chriſti non ſignificatiuè tantùm
ſed ſubſtantiuè.*

Anſel. li.
de offic.
dini.

Thus haue we in the Goſpells: Ieſus tooke bread, he bleſſed yt, he brak yt,

and gaue yt to his Diſciples,ſainge:Take and eate of this all. For this ys my
bodie,which ſhall be deliuered for yowe.When he tooke yt into his handes yt was bread.For ſo the Euāgeliſt ſaieth·he tooke bread,and bythat bleſ
ſing the bread ys made the bodie of Chryſt,not onelie ſignificatiuelie , but
alſo ſubſtantiuelie.Neither doe we from the Sacrament alltogether exclude
the figure,neither doe we admitte the ſole figure.Yt ys the veritie, bicauſe
yt ys the bodie of Chryſte:Yt ys a figure bicauſe yt ys offred in ſacrifice,that
ys incorruptible.Let vs conſider the woordes of our Lorde:He ſaieth : *Eate
ye all of this.For this,whiche I deliuer yowe to eate,ys my bodie.*And that they ſhoulde
be certen,that in verie dede yt was the bodie of Chryſt,he declared certen
tokens , by which they ſhoulde perceaue yt. *This ys my bodie (ſaieth he)that
shall be deliuered for yowe.*Yf this bodie ſhoulde be made the bodie of Chryſt figuratiuelie and not ſubſtanciallie,yt ſhoulde be onelie a figure of the bodie
of Chryſt,that that foloweth,perteineth nothing to a figure, which ys this,
that ſhall be deliuered for yowe.Neither did he name yt bread, after that he
had bleſſed the bread,but his bodie:neither did he after he had bleſſed the
wine,name yt wine,but his bloode.Therfor, as the catholique faith doeth
beleue,the bread that ys offred to the preiſt to be conſecrated by the preiſtlie conſecracion ys made the bodie of Chryſt,not ſignificatiuelie,but ſubſtā-
tiuelie.Thus moch *Anſelmus.*

    Whome ye ſee to drawe by the ſame line,that all the reſt of the fathers
haue doen.Ye ſee in this expoſition,as yt ſhoulde be among ſoche as be of
the houſe of God,an vniformitie,a conſent,and a goodlie agreement in the
vtterance of this one trueth,being a weightie matter of our faith. Ye ſee not
here as among them that haue ſeparated them ſelues frō the houſe of God,
as the *Lutherans,*the *Zuinglians* or *Oecolampadians* and *Caluiniſtes,*who ſo contend
ſtriue and diſſent among them ſelues,that that the one ſide affirmeth the o-
ther ſide denieth.So amonge theſe ther ys yea and naie, yt ys,and yt ys not.
But among all them that be produced oute of Gods Parliament houſe ,a-
mong theſe that learned their leſſons in Chryſtes ſchoole, ther ys no ſoche
diſſention.What one affirmeth,the other denieth not. And what one denieth,the other afirmeth not.For wher other before haue taught,that inthe
Sacrament after conſecracion, ther ys the bodie and blood of Chryſt, as
ſainct Ambroſe,and ſainct Auguſtine·ſo doeth this authour ſaie, that by the
conſecracion ys made the bodie and bloode of Chryſt. And wher by a
nombre yt was before taught,as by *Euthymius, Damaſcen, Haymo , Theophilact,*
and *Paſchaſius,*that the Sacrament ys not a figure onely. This authour teacheth vs euen ſo,and withall geueth vs the plain catholique vnderſtanding
of theſe fathers(whiche thing ys alſo declared vpon the place of *Tertullian*)
that the Sacrament conteineth both the bodie of Chryſt verilie, reallie, and
ſubſtanciallie·and alſo the figure of the ſame bodie.

    Wherunto to adde alſo ſomthing at this preſent, ſainct Auguſtine ge-
ueth a goodlie, and a moſt plain teſtimonie therof,ſaing: *Corpus Chriſti & veritas & figura eſt : Veritas dum corpus Chriſti & ſanguis in virtute Spiritus
ſancti ex panis & vini ſubſtantia efficitur : figura verò eſt, quod exteriùs ſentitur.*
The bodie of Chryſt ys bothe the veritie and the figure. Yt ys the veritie for that the bodie and bloode of Chryſt,by the power of the holie Goſte,ys made of the ſubſtance of bread and wine:butthat ys the figure, that
ys outwardlie perceaued.

    Agreablie to this ſaieth Hilarius, Biſhoppe of Rome next vnto Leo the
firſt.*Corpus Chriſti quod ſumitur de altare figura eſt,dum panis & vinum videntur extrà,*
veritas

*Bread how
yt ys made
the bodie of
Chryſt.*

*Circumſtā
ces in Chri
ſtes woords
declaring
the Bleſ.
Sacr.to be
his Verie bo
die.*

*Sacramen-
taries diſ-
ſent among
them ſelues
tholie fa-
thers agree
in one doc
trine.*

*De conſec.
diſt.2.ca.
vtrum*

*Both figure
and veritie
in the Sacr.*

A *veritas autem,dum corpus & sanguis Christi interius creditur.* The bodie of Chryst that ys receaued of the aultar ys a figure, for that the bread and wine be seen outwardlie:But yt ys the trueth,for that the bodie and bloode of Chryst be beleued inwardlie.

Wher then these fathers saie that the Sacrament ys not a figure of the bo die of Chryst but the bodie yt self: they vnderstand that yt ys not onelie a figure.   A figure yt ys,but yt ys the bodie also, whiche thing this authour *Anselm*, dothe verie well in fewe woordes vtter when he saieth : *Neque ab hoc sacramento figuram omnino excludimus,neque figuram solam admittimus.* We doe not from this Sacrament exclude alltogether a figure:neither doe we admit te onelie a figure. This then ys the catholique faith, that the holieSacramēt ys both a figure, and also the verie bodie of Chryst.

By this authour also, who doeth expownde Chrystes woordes ys the tri fling sophisticall argument solued, whiche an Aduersarie made against Chry stes presence in the Sacrament, vpon these woordes of Chryst.   The argu-

B ment was this:Chryst tooke bread, he blessed bread, he brake bread. Wher- fore he gaue to his Disciples bread.Yf he gaue them bread , then he gaue them not his bodie.

In this argument the Aduersarie vseth the woordes,as though by the ac- tes, whiche the verbes expresse, nothing had ben doen. *He saieth Chryst did ta- ke bread,and blessed bread.* By that that Chryst did take bread, ys declared one acte, and when he did blesse the bread, he did an other acte, whiche the Ad- uersarie passeth ouer, as though Chryst in blessing had done nothing . By whiche Sophisme he maie aswell prooue Chryst to haue deliuered no sacra- ment, as no bodie. For(as they saie) he deliuered that, whiche he took : but he tooke bread no sacrament: therfor he deliuered bread no sacrament. But what did Chryst when he blessed the bread? Though the Aduersarie wolde so ouerpasse yt:yet this authour telleth vs what he did. For he saieth: *Accepit panem,& per illam benedictionem panis,fit corpus Christi.* He tooke bread, and by that benediction the bread ys made the bodie of Chryst.Nowe then wher the Aduersarie reasoneth and saieth:Chryst tooke bread , and blessed

C bread,and brake bread,and therfore gaue bread,he hideth what acte Chryst did when he blessed the bread.For by that blessing the bread was made the bodie of Chryst.So that he might and did truely saie, take and eate, This ys my bodie.Therfor the argument ys nothing but a false Sophisme . For in dede he tooke bread into his handes but after he had once blessed yt ,and saied , this ys my bodie , he deliuered no breade, but his bodie, according to the trueth of his woorde.   Other thinges woorthie of note ther be in this authour, but hauing declared that, that sufficeth to the pourpose for the expownding of Chrystes woordes, I leaue the rest to be considered by the reader, and will hast me to bring in an other coople.

M.Pilkin- tons sophi- sticall ar- gument in thopen dis- putaciō hol den inCam bridgie a- gainst the blessedSac.

Effect of Chrystes blessing of the bread.

THE TVO AND SIXTETH CHAP. ABIDETH

in the expofition of the fame woordes by Rupertus, and Nico-
laus Methonen.

Ishing that the reader fhould fullie perceaue the defcent of
the faith of the Sacrament, howe yt ys deduced frō Chryſt
to the Fathers, and fo from age to age, and from time to ti
me, euen vnto this our time, and therwith howe the woordes of Chryſt are to be vnderftanded, euen from Chryſtes
time of the fpeaking of thē vntill this our time: forſomoch
as I haue paſſed fo neare to our time, I will with thy pacien
ce(gentle reader)go on, vntil I bring the within a verie litle of this our time.
In Gods name then let vs proceade and go to the time of *Rupertus*, who ys
thought to haue liued the year of our Lord MCCXXIIII. ād fo about CCCCXXXVIII.
agon, of whome we fhall learn what faith was in the latin Churche in his time as concerning the bleſſed Sacrament, and howe the woordes of Chryſt
were vnderftanded. Thus he writeth: *Cœnantibus, id eſt, ſedentibus adhuc in cœna*
qua manducauerant carnes agni, carnes Paſchæ veteris, accepit panem, & benedixit. Panem
communem accepit, ſed benedicendo longè in aliud quàm fuerat tranſmutauit, vt veraciter
diceret ſic: Hoc eſt corpus meum, quod pro vobis tradetur. Item vini ſubſtantiam accepit,
ſed itidem gratias agendo, vel benedicendo ſic in aliud vertit, vt diceret veritas, quæ non
mentitur: Hic eſt ſanguis meus noui Teſtamenti, qui pro multis effundetur. Sed non vide-
tur oculis carnis, non ſentitur guſtu oris, quòd panis ille caro factus ſit: quòd vinum illud in
ſanguinem verſum ſit. Nimirum ſi videretur color, aut ſentiretur ſapor carnis, & ſan-
guinis humani, homini non plus ſalutis, ſed plurimum adferret horroris. Being at fupper,
that ys, fitting yet at fupper in the whiche they had eaten the flefh of the
lambe, the flefh of the olde Paſſouer, he tooke bread and bleſſed yt,
he tooke comon bread, but bleſſing yt, he did tranfmute yt into a
farre other thing, than yt was, that he might trulie faie : *This ys my bo-*
die, which shall be deliuered for yowe . He did alſo take the ſubſtance of wine,
but likewiſe geuing thankes or bleſſing, he did ſo turne yt into an other
thinge, that the trueth which lieth not, might faie: *This ys my bloode of the newe*
Teſtament, whiche shall be shedde for manie . But yt ys not feen with the eies of
the bodie : yt ys not perceaued by the taſte of the mouthe, that, that bread
ys made the flefh of Chryſt, that that wine ys turned into bloode. For
trulie yf the cooloure of the flefh and bloode of man fhould be feen, or the
taſte fhoulde be perceaued, yt fhoulde bring no more health to a man, but
yt fhoulde bring moch loathfomneſſe. Thus moche *Rupertus*.

In this authour as in *Anſelmus*, who went laſt before him in the laſt chapter, ys declared the vertue and power of the benediction of Chryſt when he
bleſſed the bread and wine in his holie fupper. For as *Anſelmus* ſaied, that by
the bleſſing of the bread and wine, they were made the bodie and bloode of
Chryſt: So this authour faieth, that Chryſt bleſſing the bread, did tranfmute
or chaunge yt into a farre better thing, Whiche thing was ſoche that Chryſt
might trulie ſaie by yt: *This ys my bodie, whiche ys geuen for yowe*. Neither let this
feem ſtraunge to the Aduerſarie, that theſe two authours faie, that by the
bleſſing of Chryſt the bread and wine be chaunged or turned into the
bodie and blood of Chryſt. For yt ys not a ſainge yeſterdaie inuented, but yt ys a ſainge, of the great Fathers, the auncientes and
pillers of the Church. Howe moche doeth ſainct Ambroſe ſpeake of this
thing

Rup de ope
rib. lib.3.

Yf Chryſt
bleſſing the
bread tranſ
mutedyt in
to a better
thing, M.
Pilkintons
argument
bealeth.

Effect of
Chryſtes
bleſſing of
the bread.

A thing? how large a difcourfe doeth he make of yt? treacting of the bleffed
Sacrament, and prouing by examples of the fcripture, howe the grace and
blefsing of God doeth chaunge the nature of one thing into an other thing.
He faieth thus. *Quantis igitur vtimur exemplis, vt probemus non hoc effe, quod natura
formauit, fed quod benedictio confecrauit, maioremq́ue vim effe benedictionis, quam naturæ,
quia benedictione etiam natura ipfa mutatur?* Howe manie examples haue we to
proove, that this ys not yt that nature formed, but yt that the blefsing hath
confecrated, and that the power of the blefsing ys greater then the power
of nature. Bicaufe that by the blefsing nature yt felf ys chaunged. And after
manie examples ther produced to that pourpofe, he maketh this conclufion
*Quodfi tátum valuit humana benedictio, vt naturá cónerteret, quid dicimus de ipfa cófecratio
ne diuina, vbi verba ipfa Domini faluatoris operátur?* Yf thē the blefsing of mā were
of fo great force that yt might turn or chaunge nature : what faie we of the
diuine confecracion, wher the verie woordes of owre fauiour doe woorke
them felues? Thus S. Amb.

*Amb.li.de
imit.myft.
cap.9.*

*Power of
blefsing grè
ater thē po-
wer of natu
re.*

B   And thus maie we perceaue the great power of Chryftes blefsing to be
foche, that not onelie yt maie, but yt doeth alfo chaunge the nature of one
thing into an other, as the nature of bread and wine in the Sacrament, into
the verie nature of the bodie and bloode of Chryft, verilie and fubftanciallie. And therfor this chaunge wrought and doen by the blefsing of Chryft
for fomoche as yt ys a turning or chaunging of one nature or fubftance
into an other nature or fubftance, yt maie verie well beare the name of
Tranfubftanciacion . For that name doeth liuelie declare the acte that ther
ys doen.

*Tranfub-
ftanciacion
auouched.*

Holie Cyrill alfo confidering that the great worke of God, whiche maketh
prefent in the Sacrament the bodie and bloode of Chryft, ys doen by the
denediction of God, doeth commonlie in his workes call the bleffed Sacrament the mifticall benedictiō. As then this authour hath taught no other
wife then he heard his Fathers fpeake before him, of the power of Chryftes
blefsing: no more doeth he in teaching the prefence of Chryftes bodie and
bloode, although our fenfeis can not perceaue the fame prefence. For (faieth
C he) though the bread be made the flefh of Chryft, and the wine be turned
into his bloode: yet neither doe we fee yt, neither taft yt fo to be. By whiche
his teaching he doeth well aduertife vs of the office of faith that aught to
be in vs, which grownded vpon the woorde of God, beleueth what yt teacheth, though no one of our fenfes geue vs anie aide ther vnto. And here ys
rebuked the groffe maner of *Cranmer* , who faieth that faith teacheth nothing againft the fenfeis. and therfor for fomoche as we fee no flefh nor bloo
de, nor taft none in the Sacrament, ther ys none in the Sacrament. But I
will not nowe tarie to refell that groffe and fenfuall erroure of the fenfeis,
forafmoche as I doe more at large fpeake of yt in an other place . Therfor I
will no more doe here, but by conferring of the doctrine of this authour,
with the doctrine of the Fathers, fo by that waie improoue the doctrine
of *Cranmer*. Yt ys not faieth this authour, feé with our eies, nor tafted by our
mouthes, that the bread ys made flefh, nor that the wine ys turned into
bloode, for yf yt fhoulde fo be, yt fhoulde nothing encreace our faluacion,
but yt fhoulde bring moch loathfomneffe. And therfor yt ys fo the flefh
D and blood of Chryft. as yt maie be meit for our vfe, and fufficient alfo for
our faluacion. Agreablie to this ye haue heard declared oute of S. Cyrill. Le
eft we fhould loath flefh and blood fett vpon the holie altars, God condefcending vnto our weakneffe, powred into the offred thinges the power of

*Cranmers
groffe fen-
fuall here-
fie impro-
ued.*

*Cyrill. ad
Calofyr.
Chryftes
owne verie
flefh in the
Sacrament*

Pp iiii   life,

life, turning the fame into *the treuth of his owne flesh.* Here ye fee Chryftes ow- **E**
ne flesh taught to be in the facrament, but fo as no fenfe perceaue the fame,
leaft we fhoulde loath yt, if fhe fhoulde fee yt or taft ys as verie flesh . Damaf
cen alfo hath the like fainge, and *Theophilact* in diuerfe places. but one of the
fhall fuffice for all.Bycaufe we are weake and loath to eate rawe flesh, fpecial

Theophil. lie the flesh of man, therfor *yt appeareth bread, but yt ys flesh* Note this laft part
of *Theophilactes faing,yt appeareth bread but yt ys flesh.* Are we not taught by this

Faith tea-
cheth one
thing 'and
fenfes an o-
ther. that faith teacheth vs one thing,and the fenfeis teache vs an other thing? Yt
appeareth bread : What ys that? Owre feight iudgeth yt to be breade, owre
taft iudgeth yt to be breade, owre taft iudgeth yt to be breade and fo furth
of other fenfeis, But yt ys flesh. For owre faith grownded vpon the certen
and infallible truthe of Chryftes woorde, beleueth and knoweth yt (bicaufe
he faieth : *This ys my bodie*) to be his flesh . Nowe our fenfeis teache yt to be
that, that yt ys not. For they teach that yt ys bread, wher faith teacheth that
yt ys flesh in dede.Vain therfor ys *Cranmers* fainge, vain alfo be they that faie
bicaufe they fee not,nor taft no flesh nor bloode, they will beleue none to **F**
be ther. As they be fenfuall men: fo they frame to themfelues a fenfuall
faith. But God make them once rightlie fpirituall.

And nowe to our pourpofe yowe haue feen a conference and a plain agree
ment, betwixt this authour and other in thefe two poinctes. Finallie he expowndeth the woordes of Chryft of the verie prefence. for (faieth he) *the*
bread ys chaunged into that thing,that Chryft maie trulie faie:This ys my bodie. And fo the
wine ys turned into that thing,that he maie trulie faie by yt : This ys my bloode. Thefe woordes with that that ys aboue faied, prooue moft fufficientlie that
the woordes of Chryft are to be vnderftanded withoute figure metaphor, or trope.

This being thus plain we will fee what his felowe will doe. who ys *Nico-*

Nicolaus
Methan. *laus Methanenfis.* Thus he writeth : *Quis ille qui conculcat filium Dei ? Nonne qui fan-*
guinem eius ingratus abrogat, nec admittit? & veracis ab omnique mendacio alieni oris
trrditionem & mandatum nihili facit, Hoc eft corpus meum dicentis, & hic eft fanguis
meus, &, nifi manducetis carnem filii hominis, & bibatis eius fanguinem, non habetis vi- **G**
tam in vobis? Quid hæfitas? Quid omnipotenti impotentiam attribuis? Nonne ipfe eft, qui
ex nihilo omnia vt effent fecit?Vnus trium perfonarum diuinitatis, qui poftremis incarnatus
eft, & panem in fuum corpus tranfmutari iufsit. Quid requiris caufam & ordinem natu-
ræ panis tranfmutationis in Chrifti corpus,& aquæ vinique in fanguinem cùm fupra naturã,
rationem mentem & cogitationem ex virgine fit natus? Non credes itaque nec mortuorum

he treadeth
vnder foot
the Sonne
of God,that
b.leueth
not his bo-
die and
blood to be
in theSacr. *refurrectionem, nec in cælos eius affumptionem, & alia Chrifti miracula fupra naturam mé-*
tem,& cogitationem eminentia. Who ys he that treadeth vnder foote the Sonne
of God? ys yt not he that as an ingrate and vnkinde man, dothe abrogate
his bloode and will not alowe yt? and fetteth nothing by the commaundement and tradicion of that true mouthe, which ys all wide from all vntrueth, faing: *This ys my bodie*: And, *this ys my bloode,* And *except ye eate the flesh of*
the Sonne of man, and drinke his bloode, ye haue no life in yowe ? What doeft thowe
doubte?What doeft thowe attribute impotencie to the omnipotent ? Ys yt
not he that made all thinges of nothing? one of the three perfons in god
head, who in thefe laft times was incarnated, and commaunded the bread
to be tranfmuted into his bodie. What doeft thow require the caufe ãd order of the tranfmutacion of the natuae of bread into Chryftes bodie, and of **H**
the water and the wine into the bloode , fithen that he aboue nature, reafõ,
vnderftanding and thought was born of a virgen? Thowe wilt not then beleue neither the refurrection of the dead, nor the affumption of him into
heauen,

A heauen, nor other miracles of Chryſt being aboue the reach of nature, vnderſtanding and thought . Thus farre he.

Ye haue nowe hearde an other wittneſſe, but not telling yowe an other tale diuerſe from him that he ys coopled with, or frō anie here before alleaged. In the maner of the vtterance of his teſtimonie he doeth ſomwhat, like vnto *Chriſoſtome*, ſpeake with wonder and admiraciō that men ſhoulde doub te of the preſence of Chryſtes bodie in the Sacrament, ſeing that Chryſtes owne mouth hath ſpoken yt. Wherin he wel declareth that this faith in this matter was ſo firme, ſo ſure, and ſo ſtable, that yt was a matter of wonder to him, that anie man coulde not beleue yt, that had ben brought vppe in Chryſt, in ſomoche that he reputeth the misbeleuers of this Sacrament, of the nombre of thoſe that treade Chryſt vnder foote, vpon whome, as S. Paule ſaieth, ſhal come heauie and greuouſe puniſhmentes-

He teacheth vs, as *Gregorie Niſſen*, Chryſoſtom and manie mo haue taught that the bread ys tranſmuted or chaunged into the bodie of Chryſt. In the ſetting furth wherof he vſeth almoſt S. Ambroſe ſentence and woordes. S.

Ambr .li. de myſt.c. 9.

B Ambroſe ſaieth: *Quid hic queris naturæ ordinem in Chriſti corpore, cùm preter naturam ſit ipſe Dominus Ieſus partus & virgine?* What doeſt thowe here ſeke the order of nature in the bodie of Chryſt, ſith the ſame Lorde Ieſus Chryſte was beſide nature conceauued of a virgen ? This authour ſaieth, what doeſt thowe ſeke the cauſe or ordre of the tranſmutacion of the nature of breade, into the bodie of Chryſt, and of the wine and water into his bloode, ſith he aboue nature, and reaſon was born of a virgen? So farre wide was yt from the mening of this authour to varie from the mindes of the auncient fathers, that he vſeth their woordes. To end, yt ys eaſie to perceaue that this man teaching tranſmutacion, or tranſubſtancion, and ſoche creditte to be geuen to the plain woorde of Chryſt for the verie preſence of his bodie in the Sacrament, vnderſtandeth Chryſtes woordes withoute figure, as alſo *Rupertus* did?

THE THREE AND SIXTITH CHAP. TARIETH IN
C *the expoſition of the ſame wordes by Innocentius, and Germanus.*

IN this proceaſſe we are deſcended to *Innocētius* the thirde, who liued the yeare of our Lorde. 1300. and therfor about 362 years agon. In this matter he writeth thus : *Agnus Paſchalis ſiue dubio fi gurabat Dominicum corpus : ſed panis azimus ſincerum opus. Sicut autem Ioannes Baptiſta qui dixerat : Eccè agnus Dei, per adiunctum determinauit: Ecce qui tollit peccata mundi: Sic & Chriſtus qui dixerat , Hoc eſt corpus meum, per adiunctum determinauit : quod pro vobis tradetur. Sicut ergo corpus Chriſti veraciter tradebatur : ſic verè demonſtrabatur, non in figura, quæ iam ceſſauerat, ſed in veritate quæ iam aduenerat.* The paſchall lambe without doubte, was a figure of our Lordes bo die, but the vnleauened breade ſignified a ſincere worke As Iohn the Baptiſt who ſaied: *Behold the lambe of God,* by a clauſe adioined did determine yt ſaing: *Behold him that taketh awaie the ſines of the worlde :* So Chryſte, who had ſaied, *This ys my bodie :* by a clauſe adioned determined the ſame, ſaing : *which ſhall be deliuered for yowe.* Therfor as the bodie of Chryſt was verilie deliue red : ſo was yt verilie demonſtrated, not in a figure, whiche nowe had ceaſſed, but in trueth which nowe was comed.

Innocen.de offic. Miſſ.

The bodie of Chryſt both deliue red and de monſtrated not in figur but in trueth.

D This authour minding to expownde Chryſtes woodes, doeth firſt declare, that

re that the Paschall lambe, wherof we haue at large spoaken in the first boo- **E**
ke, was vndoubtedlie a figure of Chrystes bodie wherbie the geueth vs to
vnderstand, that nowe the figure being taken awaie (which can not other
wise be ceassed but by the cominge of the veritie) that nowe the bodie
of Chryst ys not onelie as in a figure, as yt was in the paschall lambe,
but yt ys nowe in veritie. He prooueth yt by Chrystes owne woorde, who saied and spake nothing but trueth : *This ys my bodie* . That he
spake yt by his owne naturall and substanciall bodie , he prooueth by
the determinacion that he put to yt, which was this : *Which shall be deliuered*
for yowe. This particle added determineth his sainge to be of his naturall bo-
die.For he deliuered not his figuratiue bodie,neither his spirituall bodie,nor
his misticall bodie. Wherfor yt was spoaken of that bodie, whiche might be
deliuered for the sinnes of the worlde, whiche was onelie his owne naturall bodie.

Then he concludeth vpon these two partes, that as Chrystes bodie was verilie deliuered to deathe : so was yt verilie spokē of Chryst in the supper not
in a figure, which ys nowe past and hoen, but in veritie, which ys comed.

Figure of
the Sacra-
mentaries
flatlie de-
nied.

To be shorte, as he breiflie concludeth the true th: so with asmoche breui- **F**
tie he excludeth the vntrueth. He sendeth the emptie figure, to the olde
Lawe : he appointeth the fullnesse of the veritie in the newe Lawe . Thus
the Aduersaries figure being also denied by this authour, as yt hath ben by
manie other, the conclusion maie be made, that Chrystes woordes are
to be vnderstanded not figuratiuely, but in their propre sense simplie and
literallie.

Germanus
episc. Con-
stantin.

Nowe on the other side shall geue testimonie the holie man *Germanus,*
Bishoppe of Constantinople,who did write an exposition vpon theMasse of
the greke church, wher in he writeth thus: *Ipse dixit: Hoc est corpus meum : hic*
est sanguis meus. Ipse & Apostolis iussit, & illos vniuersæ Ecclesiæ, hoc facere. Hoc enim
ait, facite in meam commemorationem. Non sanè id facere iussisset, nisi vim inditurus fuis
set, vt id facere liceret. He saieth, *This ys my bodie:this ys my blood*: He also commaunded the Apostles, and by them rhe wholl Church, this to doe. For saieth
he, *This doe ye in the remembrance of me.* Trulie he wolde not haue commaunded them so to doe,except he had geuen them powr that thei might doe yt. **G**

What ys their power afterwarde he declareth saing : *Spiritus sanctus, qui se-*
mel egressus est, & in posterum non dereliquit nos, sed est nobiscum & erit in perpetuum
æuum, hæc per manum sacerdotum & linguam mysteria conficit.Ac non sanctum Spiritum
dumtaxat misit Dominus noster vt maneat nobiscum, sed & ipse policitus est se mansurum
nobiscum vsque ad consummationem seculi. At Paracletus inconspicuus adest , quia ipse
The holie
Gost confe-
crateth the
Sacr.bythe
hand and
toungof the
preistes. *corpus non gestauit: Dominus verò, & conspicitur, & tangi se patitur per tremenda &*
sacra mysteria, vt qui nostrā naturā acceperit, eamque gestet in secula. The holie Gost,
who once came furth to vs,and neuer hereafter doeth forsake vs,but shal be
with vs for euer to the worldes ende, dothe consecrate these misteries by
the hand and tounge of the preistes. And our Lorde hath not sent his holie
Spiritte, that he onelie shoulde abide with vs: But he himself also hath promised to dwell with vs, vnto the ende of the worlde . The holie Gost ys
with vs, but not seen, bicause he had no bodie. But our Lord ys both seen,
and suffreth himself by the fearfull and holie misteries to be touched, as one
that hath taken our nature vpon him, and will beare yt for euer.

The power thē of the ministres of Chryst ys that they be the instrumētes of **H**
holie Goft,by whose hād ād toung these mysteries be cōsecrated. In that he
saieth the holie Goft doeth woork this great work by the toūg of the preist,
he meneth

A he meneth at the pronunciacion of Chryftes woordes by the' mouthe of
the preiftes, at the whiche the holie God inuifiblie woorketh the prefence of Chryftes bodie and bloode agreablie to the woordes of Chryft　*Li.4.de*
fpoken by the preift in the perfon of Chryft, faing : *Thıs ys my bodie.* For　*Sacr.,*
vntill that time (faieth S . Ambrofe) the preift vfeth his owne woordes, but nowe (faieth he) he vfeth not his owne woordes, but the woordes of Chryft,

That the holie Gofte woorketh this confecracion of the bodie and bloode of Chryft yt ys not a fewe times teftified before. But Damafcen by moft
plain woordes declareth the matter, faing: *Quemadmodum quæcunque fecit Deus,*
Spiritu fanƈto cooperante fecit: fic & nunc spiritus fanƈti operatione , hæc fuper naturam
operatur, quæ non poteſt capere nifi fola fides. Quomodò fiet mihi iſtud, dicit fanƈta virgo,
quoniam virnm non cognofco? Refpondit Gabriel Archangelus · Spiritus fanƈtus fuperue-
met in te , & virtus Altıſsimi obumbrabit tibi. Et nunc interrogas, quomodò panis fit cor-
pus Chriſti, & vinum & aqua fanguis Chriſti. Refpondeo tibi & ego : Spiritus fanƈtus
B *obumbrat, & hæc operatur fuper fermonem & intelligentiam.* As all that god hath
made, he hath made them the holie goft woorking with him : euen fo now　*The woork*
by the worke of the holie Gofte he woorketh thefe thinges (mening the có　*of the holie*
fecracion of the bodie and blood of Chryft) aboue nature, which thinges　*Goſt in the*
nothing can perceaue but onelie faith. Howe fhall this be doen to me (fa-　*Sacr.ys a-*
ieth the holy Virgen) for I knowe not a man ? The Archangell Gabriell　*boue natu-*
anfwereth : The holy Goft fhall come vpon thee, and the power of the hie-　*re,and vn-*
gheft fhall ouerfhadowe thee. And nowe thowe afkeft howe the bread ys　*derſtãding*
made the bodie of Chryft, and the wine and water the bloode of Chryft.
And I alfo aunfwer vnto thee, The holie Goft ouerfhaddoeth and woorketh
thefe thinges aboue that can be fpoken, and aboue all vnderftanding.

Agreablie to this S. Auguftine alfo fpeaking of the Sacrament, and of the
worke of the holie Goft therin faieth : *Quod cùm per manus hominnm ad illam vi-*　*Auguſt.li.*
bilem fpeciem perducitur, non fanƈtificatur vt fit tam magnum facramẽtum, nifi operante　*3.de Trin.*
inuifibiliter Spiritu Dei. Whiche thing (mening bread) when by the handes of　*cap.4.*
men yt ys brought to that vifible forme , yt ys not yet fanƈtified that yt
C maie be fo great a Sacrament but by the inuifible worke of the Spiritte
of God?

In this then that this authour faieth that thefe mifteries of the bodie and
bloode of Chryft be wrought by the holie Goft, ye perceaue that he teacheth none otherwife then the other holie Fathers of the Church . And by
this alfo by the waie maie we learn reuerentlie to fpeake of this bleffed Sacrament, for fomoche as yt ys no trifeling toie of mans inuenciòn, but yt ys
the worke of the holie Gofte, who woorketh no trifles but matters of weight agreable to his maieftie. Whiche thing this authour alfo after the ma-　*The Sacra*
ner of Chryfoftome doeth verie well teache in the later parte of his faing,　*mentes of*
when he calleth the Sacramentes of Chryftes bodie and blood, *Tremenda &*　*Chryſtes bo*
facra myſteria. fearfull and holie mifteries. They are not fearfull and holie, ex-　*die ãd blod*
cept fomthing be in them that ys of yt felf fearfull and holie . Bread and wi-　*be holie ãd*
ne being figures of Chryftes bodie and bloode, be no more fearfull, then　*fearfull my*
the bread and wine of Melchifedech, or the fhewe bread in the temple,　*ſteries.*
whiche was eaten of Dauid and his men without anie feare . Ther ys therfor
D in this holie mifterie more then a figure, whiche ells can be nothing but the
verie thing that ys figured , which ys Chryft our Lorde and God, who ys
to be feared of all fainƈtes, the pfalme fainge : *Timete Dominum omnes fanƈti eius.*
Feare yowr Lorde all ye Sainƈtes.

In

In the ende this authour declaringe the difference of the being and abidinge of Chryst and the holie Goste withe vs maketh this difference. The holie Gost (saieth he) for that he had no bodie, for he was not incarnated, ther for though he be with vs, yet he ys not seen: Chryst for that by his incarnacion he tooke a bodie vpon him, he ys bothe seen, and also suffreth himself to be touched, but howe? By the holie and fearfull misteries. Then by the holie and fearfull misteries Chryste ys bothe seen and touched. Yt ys so, For so saieth Chrysostome: *Ipsum vides, Ipsum tangis, Ipsum comedis.* Thowe seist him, thowe touchest him: thowe eatest him, thowe desierest to see his garmetes, but he deliuereth himself to thee, not that thowe shouldest onelie see him: but also that thowe maist touche him and also haue him with thee.

A Cauill of the Sacramentaries.

But here laboureth the Aduersarie to laie a snare to entrappe the reader, and to make him mistake Chrysostome. For (saieth the *Aduersarie*) we touche and eate Chryst in the Sacrament as we see him. But wet see him onelie by faith, wherfor we touche and eate him but by faithe. And so ys the presence of Chryst merelie spirituall and not corporall.

An answer

Yf this argument were good, he might proue by the same that there were no creature. And thus he might, frame his argument. Euerie creature as concerning his beinge ys as yt ys seen. But no creature ys seen to haue corporall Substance, wherfor no creature hath corporall Substance. Or thus, to come nearer to him in his owne termes: We touche and eate our meat at the table as we see yt: But we see no substance of meate. Wherfor we eate no substance of meat. Thus one fond argument maie be perceaued by an other. And so perceaued to be fond, to let yt so go as sufficientlie aunswered.

A thing ys saied to be seen, whe the outuard formes are onelie seen, bicause the substace ys inuisible

But for the contentacion of the reader this shall be saied: As naturall knowledge teacheth that euerie creature hath a substance: so yt teacheth that that substance ys inuisible. Therfor though we see no substauce, but the outwarde formes of creatures: yet being assured by this knowledge, that ther ys vnder those formes a substance, we saie that we did see or touche this or that creature, and the saing ys true: Euen so when spirituall knowledge, which ys faithe, teacheth vs that the holie Sacrament hath a substance, and that substance ys inuisible. And therfor though we see but outwarde formes of bread and wine. yet being assured by this spirituall knowledge that ther ys vnder those formes the substance of the bodie and bloode of Chryst, we saie verie well, that we see Chrystes bodie, and touche his bodie, and eate his bodie, when we see, touch, and eate these formes in due maner after that the consecracion ys doen, faith geuing vs certen and assured knowledge of the being of Chrystes substance vnder those formes as naturall knowledge doeth for the substances of naturall creatures vnder their formes. And therfor nowe wher the Aduersarie saieth, that we eate Chryst as we see him, though in naturall things yt be not proprely true, for their we eate both the substace and the outward formes, yet see but the outwarde formes, in maner aboue saied: yet for that the substance ys certenly vnder those formes, by a mean yt ys truly saied, that we see and eate soche a thing: so in this heauenlie matter of the Sacrament, we both eat and see presentlie the verie presence of Chrystes bodie in substance, our senseis subiecting them selues as well to the knowledge of faith, as they doe to the knowledge of nature, and truely saie that we see and eate the substance of the body of Chryst. And by this was the comon sainge of the faithfull people vsed generallie in the church, when they had seen the Sacrament: I haue seen my Sauiour, I haue seen my redeemer, and soche like, as in naturall things we

Spirituall knowledge teacheth the substance of Christs bodie and blood to be vnder ther formes of bread and wine as wel as naturall knowledge the substances of natu rall thinges vnder their formes.

saie:

F
G
H

A faie·we haue feen a man,a woman,a beaft,a tree,an herbe , when we haue
neither feen the fubftance of man,woman,beaft,tree,nor herbe , but onelie
the outwarde formes of them.

But to protracte this difputacion no lóger,I wil ende yt with the argument
of this authour , which maie be vttered in this maner . Chryft ys continuallie with vs , and fo ys the holie Goft,but they be after diuerfe maners,the one to be feen,the other not to be feen, wherfore the one corporallie,the other fpiritually.The proofe maie be this: Yf Chryft be with vs
but fpirituallie in the Sacrament,then ys he with vs no otherwife., than the
holie Goft ys. But Chryft ys with vs in an other diuerfe maner then the
holie Goft ys , in foche a maner as he maie by his fearfull and holie myfteries be feen, whiche diuerfe maner to fpirituall maner muft be the corporall maner .   Wherfore he ys with vs corporallie.   And this moft vndoubtedlie was the mening of this authour. For ther ys no doubte of the
fpirituall prefence of the holie Goft in the myniftracion of the Sacra-
B mentes neither yet of Chryft .   But ther muft be an other maner of
Chryftes being with vs befides that maner , or ells the being of the holie
Goft and Chryft muft be all one , and not different.   The contrarie wherof this authour teacheth.Wherby alfo,as by that , that ys before faied , yt
maie be perceaued,that the woordes of Chryft be of him vnderftanded in
their propre fenfe.

Difference
of the being
of Chryft
with vs,ãd
of the holie
Gofte.

THE FOVR AND SIXTETH CHAPITER

Sheweth the expofition of Petrus Cluniacen.and Beffa-
rion vpon the fame.

C Owe that our proceffe ys comed fo near to our time we will
ende with this coople,that fhall be produced of the whiche
the firft ys the good and vertuoufe learned man *Petrus Cluniacen-*
*fis,*of whofe vertue and learning not onelie his writing ys a
good wittneffe,but alfo holie fainct Bernarde in fondrie epiftles written doeth verie well teftifie the fame. This man thus expowndeth
the woordes of Chryft: *Dic Domme teftator noui & æterni Teftamenti, vtrum Te-*
ftamentum hoc vnius diei(ficut ifti dicunt)effe volueris, an potius æternum effe decreueris.
Audiant ifti,non me,fed te,vt conuertantur non ad me,fed ad te.Quid ergo ? In cœna vl-
tima,quam cum Difcipulis tuis vetus Pafcha nouo commutans celebrafti, accepifti panem,
gratias egifti,fregifti,dedifti Difcipulis tuis. Sed quid dixifti ? Accipite , hoc eft corpus
meum , quod pro vobis tradetur.   Et quid addidifti? Hoc facite in meam comme-
morationem .   Similiter & calicem poftquam cœnafti: Hic eft fanguis meus noui Te-
ftamenti, qui pro vobis & pro multis effundetur in remifsionem peccatorum. Audiftis?
Nolite fieri fimulachra quæ oculos habent & non vident,aures habent, & non audiunt.
Audiftis hoc non à quolibet doctore ,fed ab illo,de quo Pater clamans præcipit : Ipfum
audite . Audiftis eum dantem corpus , fed quod corpus ? Sunt enim corpora cœ-
leftia , & terreftria.   Et quicquid vifui , auditui , olfactui,guftui, hic fubiacet ,cor-
pus eft.   Vnde ne putaret quis animalis cuiuslibet hoc effe corpus , aut hominis cu-
iuslibet , ad excludendum omne aliud fenfibile vel infenfibile corpus , poftquam dixit:
D *Accipite, hoc eft corpus,adiunxit,meum.   Suum ergo non alterius corpus Difcipulis de-*
dit . Rurfus ne alicui cogitatio occulta fubreperet , potuiffe creare in manibus
fuis , corpus , quod fuum quidem effet ,fed tamen, quod ipfe erat, non effet , addidit.
Quod pro vobis tradetur.Ac fi diceret,nolite dubitare , nolite hoc vel illud vobis fingere,

Petr. Clu-
niacen.con
tra. Petro-
brufianos.

                                                Q q   nolite

nolite , nolite aliud & aliud cogitare, quia hoc eſt corpus, non alterum , aut alterius ſed E
meum,non permutatum vel nouiter creatum,ſed quod pro vobis tradetur , pro vobis cru-
cifigetur , pro vobis morietur . Sic & de calice : Hic eſt ait ſanguis , non bo-
uis , aut arietis , non agni aut cuiuſlibet hominis , ſed meus,non alius, aut noua crea-
tione productus,ſed qui pro vobis fundetur,flagellis prouocatus,clauis extortus , lancea ex-
cuſſus. Saie therfore , o Lorde,the teſtatour of the newe and euerlaſting teſtament,whether this teſtament be of one daie,as theſe men ſaie,thowe wol
deſt yt to be,or whether thowe haueſt decreed yt to be an euerlaſting Teſta
ment.Let theſe men heare,not me,but thee,that they maie be turned not to
me,but to thee,what then was doen?In the laſt ſupper whiche thowe dideſt

Chryſtega
ue to hys
Apoſt .not
the bodie of
an other,or
his bodie
newlie crea
ted but that
ſame bodie
that should
be deliue-
red.

celebrate,with the Diſciples,chaunging the old paſſouer for the new,thow
thookeſt bread , thowe gaueſt thankes,thowe brakeſt yt,and gaue yt to the
diſciples. But what ſaideſt thowe ? *Take this ys my bodie , which shall be deliuered*
for yowe . And what dideſt thowe adde vnto yt? *This doe ye in my remem-*
brance. Likewiſe the cuppe alſo after thowe haddeſt ſupped,ſaing : *This ys*
my bloode of the newe Teſtament which shall be shedde for yowe, and for manie in the re-
miſsion of ſinnes. Haue yowe hearde?Be not made dead images, which ha- F
ue eies and ſee not,eares and heare not.Ye haue heard this not of euery tea
cher,but of him,of whome the Father ſainge commaunded : Heare him.
Ye haue heard him geuinge a bodie, but what bodie ? Ther be heauenlie bodies,and earthlie bodies,and what ſoeuer ys here ſubiect to the ſeight,
hearing , ſmelling , taſting or touching , ys a bodie . Wherfore leaſt anie
man ſhoulde thinke this to be a bodie of anie comon man , or anie other
naturall creature,to exclude all other bodies ſenſible or inſenſible , after he
had ſaied : *Take this ys a bodie ,* he adioined this worde (*mine*) he gaue
then his owne bodie to his Diſciples , and not the bodie of anie o-
ther . Again leaſt anie priuie thought ſhoulde come to anie man , that
he might haue created in his handes a bodie that ſhoulde be his in deed,
but not that ſhoulde be yt that he was himſelf : he added : *Whiche shall*
be deliuered for yowe . As who ſhoulde ſaie?: doubte yowe not , feign yowe
not this or that to yowr ſelf,thinke not an other thing,and an other thinge.
For thisys the bodie,not an other,or of an other,but mine,not permuted,or
newlie created,but that which ſhall be deliuered for yowe,ſhall be crucified G
for yowe:ſhall die for yowe.So likewiſe alſo of the cuppe:*This ys ,* ſaieth he,
bloode,not of an oxe,nor of a Ramme,nor of a lambe, or of anie man , but
mine,not an other,or produced by a newe creation , *but which shall be shedde*
for yowe , prouoked by skoorges , extorted with nailes , thruſt oute with a
ſpeer.Thus moch this authour.

To this expoſition to adde anie thing as therbie to make yt plain to the rea
der,I thinke yt ſuperfluouſe.Yt ys allreadie ſo plain as no man in my iudgement,can make a more plain expoſition.Onelie I will open the cauſe , why
he wrote this.Ther was a ſect of heretiques begonne by one *Peter de Bruys,*ād
one *Hericus,*whoſe diſciples were called *Petrobruſians* and *Hericians.*Theſe had

Phanſies of
Heretiques
called the
woorde of
the Lorde.

inuented a newe phantaſticall hereſie,as yt ys propre to all ſoche men,to ma
ke their phantaſies matters of faith,and euerie of their phantaſies ys the pure,and ſincere woorde of the lord.Theſe had (I ſaie) inuented this phantaſie
that Chriſt alone at his laſt ſupper did cōſecrate his bodie and blood,ād gaue
yt to ys diſciples,ād they al receaued his bodie ād blood.But ſince that time
was yt neuer,nor yet ys receaued of anie man.Againſt theſe men did thys H
holie father write,againſt whome taking the ſword of the Spiritte, which ys
the woorde of God,he fought with them with yt,and ouerthrew rhē by the
                                                                            the

A the woorde of Chryst that saied:that the blood which he gaue in the cuppe
to his disciples, was the bloode of the euerlasting Testament , wherupon
taking an argument, he saieth in the beginninge: Saie, o Lord, the testatour
of the newe testamenr,whether this testament be of one daie, as these men
saie thow woldest yt to be, or whether thow haueft decreed yt,to be an euer
lasting testament.

An other argument he maketh also of the commaundement of Chryste,
who saied:*This doe ye in the remembrance of me.* Wherby Chryst geuing them
commaundement to doe that that he had doen,and he by their owne confes-
fession consecrated his bodie(wherin theye are more gentle to Chryste,thē
the Aduersaries and the Proclamer) The argument ys good that soche, to
whom the authoritie ys deriued doe that that Chryst did, that ys,doo confecrate his blessed bodie and bloode.I write thus moche,that ye maie percea
ue into what varietie and diuersitie of phantasies men doe fall in,that beginne to withstande Gods holie faith,of which varietie I haue allreadie spoken

B in the xli.chapter of this booke,wherunto yf ye add this phantasie,then shal
yowe perceaue howe manie contrarie phantasies Sathan can deuise vpon
thesefoure woordes of Chryst:*This ys my bodie*.And can, as ys saied,vtter thē
all to the people for the pure woorde of God.

But to return to this authour,as by these argumentes he hath ouerthrowen the heresie of the *Petrobrusians*: so with these and the plain exposition of
Chrystes woordes,he conuinceth all the other wicked phantasies , and leaueth Chrystes woordes in their propre and natiue sense,figures and tropes
not remembred.I shall not nede to conferre him,with the auncient and elder Fathers,the conference of other saing as he doeth, maketh good that he
hath saied,as yt did theirs which were cōferred with him. Wherfor omitting
that cōference with his seniours, I shall bring in his iuniour to be cōferred
with him,who ys *Bessarion* Patriarch of Constantinople and Cardinall,who
liued the yeare of our Lorde.1471.Wherfore not fullie one hondreth yeares
agon.And yer(as his disputacion in the Florentine Councell against the gre
kes,and his booke against *Marcus Ephesinus* doe proue) he was an excellent

C learned man,in this matter thus he writeth:*Nemo est quem lateat, quemadmodum*   *Bessarion*
panis & vini in corpus & sanguinem Christi in instanti facta transubstantialitas, huma-   *li.de Sacr.*
nam omnem excedit facultatem,ingensque opus est & certè diuinum:ita etiam huius Sacra   *Euchar.*
menti efficientia verba instar ipsius Sacramenti , eximiæ cuiusdam virtutis esse debe-
re. Christi verò diuinis verbis nihil esse potentius, nihil efficacius esse posse manifestum
est . Quamobrem fateri necesse est,Dominicis illis verbis, & nullis alijs diuinum hoc
facramentum confici posse. Nec enim diuinissima per diuinam potentiam confici ne-
gauerit quispiam , nec verbis Christi nihil efficacius esse ,cùm non modò homo ,ve-
rumetiam Deus sit,creatorque omnium,qui solo nutu cuncta produxit , qui verbo ægros
curauit,mortuos suscitauit,cæteraque miracula fecit,quæ in Euangelio recitantur. Ther ys
no man but knoweth how that the trāsubstanciacion of the bread and wine,
doen in an instant into the bodie and bloode of Chryst, doeth exce-   *The Sacra*
de all power of man , and ys a great and verie worke of God : Euen   *ment maie*
so also the efficient woordes of this Sacrament shoulde be of some great   *be consecra*
power , like as the Sacrament ys. Nowe yt ys manifest that nothinge   *ted by noo-*
can be more mightie,more effectuouse then the diuine woordes of Chryst.   *ther woords*

D Wherfor we must nedes cōfesse,that this diuine Sacram,maie with no other   *then with*
woords be cōfecrated,thē with those woords of our Lord,Neither will anie   *these : Hoc*
man denie these most holie thinges to be cōfecrated by the diuine power,   *est cor.etc.*

neither that anie thing ys more mightie in woorke then the woordes of E Chryſte, ſithen he ys not onely man, but alſo God the creatour of al things, who at his onelie pleaſure produced all thinges of nothing, who with his woorde healed the ſicke, raiſed the dead, and did other miracles, whiche be written in the Goſpell.

Not the merites of man, but the power of God con ſecrateth the Sacr.

And within a fewe woordes he ſaieth thus: *Panis & vini in corpus & ſangui nem tranſmutatio non petentium meritis, ſed eius potentia, qui ex nihilo cuncta produxit, per ſacerdotem tanquam per inſtrumentum quoddam efficitur.* The tranſmutacion of the bread and wine into the bodie and bloode ys doen not through the me rittes of the peticioners, but by the preiſt as by a certain inſtrument, through the power of him that brought oute all of nothing.

Of this authour, as of all the reſt, we learn the power and mightie worke of Chryſtes woordes, God and man, by which the bread and wine be tranſ muted and chaunged into the bodie and blood of the ſame owre maſter ãd Sauiour Ieſus Chryſt. And wher tranſmutacion and tranſubſtanciacion ys F confeſſed and taught(as this author confeſſeth bothe)ther ys the Aduerſa ries figure denied, and the propre ſenſe of Chryſtes woordes, and not the fi guratiue ſenſe admitted and alowed.

But we ſhall heare him with his owne woordes declare himſelf. Thus he ſaieth: *Corpus eſt duplex: Verum alterum, alterum myſticum. Et verum quidem eſt, quod in hoc diuino Euchariſtiæ ſacramento conſecratur, atque conficitur, ſub viſibili ſpecie panis ac vini. Hoc idem eſt cum eo corpore, quod fuit ex beata Virgine Spiritus ſancti obum bratione conceptum. De quo ipſe Dominus in exhibitione ſacramenti, cum nobis ſenſibilē pa nem vinumq́; oſtendiſſet, ait, Hoc eſt corpus meũ: & hic eſt ſanguis meus. Deinde addidit: Quod pro vobis traditur, & qui pro vobis effunditur in remiſſionē peccatorũ. Myſticũ autē eius corpus eſt Eccleſia, & congregatio fideliũ.* Chryſt hath two bodies: A true bo die, and a myſticall bodie. The true bodie ys yt, that ys cõſecrated and made in this diuine Sacrament, vnder the viſible forme of bread and wine. This ys all one with that bodie, that was by the ouerſhadowing of the holie Goſte, conceaued of the bleſſed virgen. Of which bodie our Lorde himſelf in the geuing furth of the Sacrament, when he had ſhewed to G vs ſenſible bread and wine, ſaied. *This ys my bodie, and this ys my blood.* Then he added: which ys deliuered for yowe, and whiche ys ſhed for yowe in the remiſſion of ſinnes. But his myſticall bodie ys the Church, and the congre gacion of the faithfull.

The true bodie of Chryſte vn der the for me of bre ad.

And afterward by expreſſe woordes denieng the Aduerſaries figure, ſaieth thus: *Cauendum autem, ne quis propterea quòd Euchariſtiæ myſterium figura eſſe dicitur, dicere aut omnino ſuſpicari audeat, non eſſe verum Domini corpus. Abſit tanta blaſ phemia à fidelium mentibus.* Yt ys diligentlie to be taken heed vnto, that no man, bicauſe the Sacrament ys called a figure, be ſo bolde to ſaie, or by anie meanes to thinke that yt ys not the verie bodie of our Lorde. God forbidde ſo great a blaſphemie, from the mindes of the faithfull. Thus farre he. In whiche ſaing(as before diuerſe times ys ſaied)the authour according to the catholique faith, teacheth that the Sacrament ys both a figure, and the bo die of Chryſt. But bicauſe yt ys a figure therfore (*as the Aduerſarie ſaieth*) yt ys not the bodie of Chryſte? *That blaſphemie* (ſaieth this good man) *God kepe from the mindes of the faithfull.* Beholde Chryſtian reader) that to ſaie, that the Sacrament ys a figure, and not the verie bodie of Chryſt, H yt ys a blaſphemie. O mercifull Lord, howe moche blaſphemie then ys ther nowe committed? God of his mercie preſerue ſoche as yet haue not, that they neuer ſpeake blaſphemie againſt ther Lorde God in this

A great blaſphemie to ſaie or thinke the Sacr. ys not the bo die of our Lord.

matter,

A matter,and call again foche as haue, that his heauie indignacion fall not vpon vs.

I fee I haue taried long vpon thefe fewe woordes of Chryft. And therfore although I might haue brought furth manie moo of the lower houfe (as the learned knowe ther be manie) yet I haue of them také but fixe cooples, remembring that I had a good nombre of the higher howfe, and they my-niftred moche occafion of matter,vpon which I had better will to tarie , bi-caufe the Proclamer aloweth their authoritie.Who in dede, if he will looke well vpon himfelf,and will thinke no more of himfelf then ys meet, nor take more vpon him then becometh him,fhoulde not with fkorn and contume-lie reiect anie of thefe of the lower houfe,nor difalowe foch learned men,as he doeth,and foche a nombre and of fo long time, and fo manie yeares , ex-cept he doeth yt vpon like policie,as fome men doe, who myftrufting their caufe, refufe manie to go vpon their queftes, bicaufe they fhall be fownde giltie. I haue, I faie, taried long vpon this fhort text, and fewe woordes of Chryft, bicaufe the mifunderftanding of them (whiche ys the mainteinance

B of their herefie, and the mother and damme of all the wicked opinions in this matter) maie be taken awaie and the true vnderftanding, whiche ys the grownde of true faithe, and the verie fowntain and liuelie well fpring of whollfom doctrine , maie be ftaied, fettled, and with like mindes of men to be receaned . For he that hath the true vnderftanding of the woor-des of Chryft can not lightlie erre in the matters of the Sacrament. And he that mifunderftandeth them,for the moft parte erreth in all matters,that be moued by euell men againft the bleffed Sacrament.

Mifunder ſtāding of Chryſtes woordes mother of all the here ſies of the Sacramen-taries.

Nowe ye haue heard, firft the three holie Euangeliftes and S . Pau-le reporting in one maner thofe woordes of Chryft : ye haue heard ele-uen cooples of Chryftes higher howfe of parliament of eche fide, that ys , both of the greke Churche , and latine Church , men not ob fcure , but moft famoufe among all writers that haue written vpon thefe woordes of Chryft, not onelie in learning , but in auncien-tie , in holineffe , and in grauitie : ye haue heard fixe cooples of

C Chryftes lower howfe of Parliament , chofen alfo of both fides of the howfe , men alfo in their times famoufe both in learning , in holineffe of life , and in my iudgement moft woorthie men . I faie a-monge thofe that I coulde finde that did treact of the woordes of Chryft , by waie of expofition . In the proceffe alfo ye haue hearde the propofitions or faynges of the catholiques and of the aduerfarye as touching the vnderftanding of thefe woordes of Chryft, wherin ftandeth the controuerfie . The catholiques haue twoo faynges : The one that the woordes of Chryft are to be vnderftanded withoute figure : The other whiche foloweth vpon that , that Chryft fpake of his verie bodie. The Ad-uerfaries contrarie wife haue two fainges : the one that Chryftes woor-des are to be vnderftanded with a figure : The other that Chryft did not fpeake thefe woordes of his verie bodie.The catholique, vpõ his fainges gro wndeth this trueth,that Chryftes verie bodie,and verie bloode after the cõ-fecracion, be reallie and fubftanciallie in the Sacrament, and fo geuen to the receauers.The aduerfarie vpon his fainges growndeth his erroure,that Chry

Catholi-ques howe they vnder ſtand Chry ſtes woor-des

Sacramen-taries howe they vnder ſtād them.

D ftes verie bodie and blood be not reallie and fubftanciallie in the Sacramét, but in the Sacramét ys onelie a figure of the bodie,and ys geué to the recea-uers as a figne or toké of Chryft.As cõcerning which cõtrouerfie yt ys nowe

　eafie

easie to be saied:first for the first parte of yt that neither the holie Euangeli- **E**
stes,neither sainct Paule,nor anie of all the holie Fathers of the higher house,hathe taught or saied as the Aduersarie dothe teache and saie, that Chrystes woordes are to be vnderstanded figuratiuelie,I meen,that the Sacramēt
ys onelie a figure,I saie not one. But contrarie wise a nombre of them by
expresse woordes denie that Chrystes woordes are so to be vnderstanded,
and that the Sacrament ys a figure onelie.And for the better memorie to be
had of them,I shall make a breif epiloge of their sainges:*Chrysostom* vpon the
the sixt of sainct Iohn saieth that Chryst did not speake these woordes : *My*
flesh ys verilie meat:obscurelie or in parables.Yf not so:thē plainlie and withoute figure.*Euthymius* vpon Chrystes woordes saied:*He did not saie, these be si-*
gnes of my bodie and bloode,but these thinges be my bodie and bloode. *Damascen* saied:
The bread and wine ys not a figure of the bodie and blood of Chryst. God
forbidde that anie man shoulde so beleue.*Haymo* saied: That same bread ys
chaunged into the flesh of our Lorde,and the wine ys transferred into the
bloode of our Lorde,not by a figure,nor by a shadowe,but by trueth or in
verie dede.*Theophilact* saied,that the bread that ys sanctified on the aultar ys   **F**
the verie bodie of our Lord,and not an aunswering figure. For Chryst did
not saie,this ys a figure,but thys ys my bodie. The like saiethhe vpon sainct
Iohn,that yt ys not a figure but the bodie.*Paschasius* saied, that he merueiled
what they ment that saied,that in the Sacrament was not in verie dede the
flesh of Chryst and his blood,but the vertue,the figure and not the veritie,
the shadowe,and not the bodie.*Anselmus* saied,Chryst tooke bread , and by
his blessing of yt,the bread was made the bodie of Chryst,not onelie signifi
catiuelie,or by significacion,but substantiuelie or in substance. Neither doe
we(*saieth he*)from this Sacrament,alltogether exclude the figure, neither doe
we admitte the onelie figure.*Innocentius* saied:As the bodie of Chryst was verilie deliuered:so was yt verilie demonstrated,not in a figure , whiche nowe
had ceassed: but in trueth which was nowe comed . *Bessarion* saied:that we
be not so bolde,that bicause the Sacrament ys called a figure,that we either
saie or thinke that yt ys not the verie bodie of Chryst.God kepe(*saieth he*) so
great a blasphemie from the mindes of men,by which woordes he denieth
the onelie figure to be in the Sacrament without the presence.All these stād   **G**
directlie against the Aduersarie.For wher he saieth,that the Sacrament ys a
figure onely,they saie yt ys not onely a figure by plain woordes. And forasmoche as S.Augustin and Hillarie doe teach that the Sacrament ys both the
figure,and the veritie,maie they not be adnombred to this companie, as denienge the onelie figure,forasmoch as with the other they affirme as well
the presence as the figure.   And in that they doe so, they denie the onely figure.

   Thus ye see the first proposition of the Aduersarie by so manie wittnesses
denied,and the proposition of the catholique Church affirmed.Yf the Aduersarie for all these can bring anie one catholique writer that ys auncient,
and approued,that doeth saie,as he saieth,that the Sacrament ys onely a figure,I for my part shall confesse the trueth to be on hys side. Yf he can not
bring one,as I am sure he can not, and the catholique Church for the trueth
that she teacheth bringeth so manie,what madnesse ys ther in him that will
still persist in his phantasie , for the maintenance wherof he hath no   **H**
authoritie.
   But let vs gather as breif an epiloge for the proposition of the catholiques
which ys,that Chryst in these woords:*This ys my bodie*:spake of his verie bodie.
                                                     Although

An Epilo-
ge of aut-
hours deni-
eng the Sa-
cramenta-
ries figure.

Chrysost.in
6. Ioan.

Euthy.in
26. Math.

Damascen
li.4.cap.14

Haim. in
26.Math.

Theophi-
lact in 26·
Math.

Paschasius
lib.de corp
& sang.
Domini.

Ansel.li.de
offic. diui.

Innocēt. 3.
li de offi.
Miss.

Bessariō. li
de sacra.
Eucha.

Augusf.
Hilar.

An Epiloge
of authours
affirming
the reall
presence.

A Although yt be allreadie fufficientlie prooued and declared by that yt ys not a figure onelie, and fo importeth that Chryft fpake of his bodie: yet that the matter maie be plentifullie plain before yowr face, I fhall take the like pain in this, as I haue doen in the other. *Iuftinus*, who ys the firft, faied : that as Iefus Chryft our Sauiour had flefh and bloode for our faluacion : euen fo we are taught, the foode,wher with our flefh and blood be nourifhed by alteracion, when yt ys confecrated by the praier of his woode, to be the flefh and blood of the fame Iefus incarnated. *Irenæus* faied, that Chryft tooke bread,whiche ys a creature,and gaue thankes fainge: This ys my bodie. and the cuppe likewife,whiche ys a creature as we be, he confeffed to be his bloode, and of the newe Teftament taught a newe oblacion.*Tertullian* faied,that the bread which Chryft did take and geue to his difciples,he made yt his bodie. Cyprian faied : after our Lorde had faied, *This doe in the remembrance of me. This ys my flesh and this ys my bloode*, that fubftanciall bread and cuppe, as often as yt ys doë with thefe woords,and this faith,that fubftancial bread and cuppe confecrated by the folemne benediction doth profitt to the health and life

B of the wholl man,being alfo a medicin and a facrifice to heale infirmities and to pourge iniquities.*Iuuencus* faied, when Chryft tooke bread in his handes and had geuen thankes,he diuided yt to his Difciples,and taught them,that he deliueredvnto them his owne bodie. And that he tooke the cuppe and fanctified yt, and gaue yt to them to drinke, and taught them, that he gaue them his bloode, and faieth drinke this bloode. *Eufebius Emifenus* faied, The inuifible preift turneth the vifible creatures into the fubftance of his bodie and blood, by his fecret power with his woorde,faing : *This ys my bodie.* And the fanctificacion repeted, take and drinke (faieth he) *This ys my bloode.* Again he faieth : when the creatures are fett vpon the holie aultars to be bleffed with the heauenlie woordes,before they be confecrated with the inuocaciõ of the moft high name ther ys the fubftance of bread and wine,but after the woordes of Chryft the bodie and bloode of Chryfte. S. Ambrofe faied, be-

C fore yt ys confecrated yt ys bread, but when the woordes of Chryft haue cõ med to yt, yt ys the bodie of Chryft. And before the woordes of Chryft yt ys a cuppe full of water and wine, but when the woordes of Chryft haue wrought,ther ys made the bloode that redemed the people. Gregorie niffen faied: the bread by the woorde ys chaunged into the bodie, as yt was faied of the woorde (*mening Chryst*) This ys my bodie. And again he faieth: we doe beleue that the bread fanctified by the woorde of God, ys chaunged into the bodie of the Sonne of God. S. Hierom faied: Let vs vnderftand that the bread which our Lorde gaue vnto his Difciples, ys the bodie of our Lorde and Sauionre,forafmoch as he faied: *This ys my bodie.*ãd that the cuppe ys that, of the whiche again he faied : *Drinke ye all of this, This ys my blood of the newe Tefta ment.* Ifichius faied: he receaueth the facrifice by ignorance,that knoweth not the power and dignitie of yt, that knoweth not that yt ys his bodie and bloode in verie dede, but receaueth the mifteries, and knoweth not the power of thẽ.S. Auguftine faied: that Chryft was born in his owne handes, when geuing furth that fame his bodie he faied: *This ys my bodie.* For he did beare that bodie in his handes . *Chryfoftome* faied : Forafmoche as he hath faied : this ys my bodie, let vs be holden with no doubte, but let vs beleue, and with the eies of our vderftanding let vs verilie fee yt. Again he faied:He

D that faied : *This ys my bodie*, alltogether with his woorde,he made the thing alfo. *S. Cyrill* faied : Doubte not whether this be true or no, fith he manifeftlie faieth : this ys my bodie, but raither receaue the woorde of our Saiouur

Q q iiii   in

Iuſt.apo log 2.

Iren. cõtra hæreſ. li. 4. ca. 32.

Tertulli.4 cont. Mar cion. Cypr.de cæ na Dom.

Iuuenc.li.4 hiſto,euãg.

Eufebius Emiſ.hom. 5.Paſch.

Amb li.4 de facr.cas

Greg.Niſſ. ſer.cathec. Hier.ad Hed. qn.2 Iſich.in Le uit li.6. ca. 22. Ang. in Pſalm.33. con.1. Chryſoſt hom.83.in 26 Math. hom. 51.in 14 Marc Cyril. ad Caloſyriũ.

in faith. For he forafmoche as he ys the trueth, he lieth not. S. *Gregorie* faied: E

Grego.li.4.
Dial.ca 58

Chryft ys offred for vs in this mifterie of the holie facrifice. Ther trulie his bodie ys receaued, his flefh to the health of the people ys geuen abroade, his blood ys nowe fhedde, not vpon the handes of the vnfaithfull, but into the mouthes of the faithfull. And again: whiche of the faithfull can doubte in that time of the facrifice, at the woorde of the preift the heauens to be ope-ned in that mifterie of IefuChryft côpanies ofAngells to be prefét, vnto high thinges lowe thinges to be coopled, vnto heauenly thinges earthlie thin-ges to be ioined, one thing alfo of inuifible and vifible thinges to be made. *Ifidor* faied: The facrifice that ys offred of the Chryftians vnto God, Chryft

Ifidorus de effi.eccl.ca 18.

our Lorde and mafter did firft inftitute, when he gaue to his Apoftles his bo die and bloode before he wolde be betraied, as yt ys redde in the Gofpell: Iefus tooke bread and the cuppe, and bleffing them gaue, them to them.

Thus haue I breiflie tocuhed fo moche as maie ferue to prooue the fe-cond propofition of the catholiques: Yf anie defire to fee anie more of thefe authours, let him repair to their chapters and ther fhall he fee them at large. And nowe ye fee that as by manie wittneffes the figure in the firft propofi-tion was denied: fo by all thefe, that Chryft in his woordes fpake of his ve- F rie bodie, yt ys here affirmed. And yet all thefe notwithftanding, yf the Ad uerfarie can bringe furth but one auncient Father that by expreffe woordes faieth, as he faieth that Chryft in his fupper did not fpeake of his bodie or that his bodie after côfecraciô duelie doê, ys not in theSacrament, I will ioi ne with him. The Proclaimer more arrogantlie thê trulie, faieth of the catho

The brag-ge of the proclamer.

lique Churche, and that with repeticiô, faing: *once againI faie* (as therby with boldecountenance to beare oute his fal fhood and vntrueth) *that of all the woor des of the holie fcriptures: of all the examples of the primitiue Churche: of all the olde fat-hers, of all the anncient doctours in thefe caufes, they haue not one,*

Nowe iudge whether he be true or no, and what credditte ys to be geué vnto him in other matters, that fo fhameleflie fpeaketh in this. To the far-der proofe of the trueth of Chryftes fubftanciall prefence in the Sacrament alfo, befide that that ys faied of manie of the authours feuerallie, I haue tre-acted of tanfubftancion, wherfor I remitte the reader thither, and nowe ha-ning but one fcripture in the Euangeliftes to fpeake of, I will breiflie touche G yt, and fo finifh this fecond booke.

THE FIVE AND SIXTETH CHAP. TREACTETH
of the bread bleffed and geuen by Chryft to the two difciples in Emaus, and prooueth by Theophilact and Bede that yt was the Sacrament.

Luc.24.

IN the gofpell after fainct Luke we read that Chryft ioining him felf to two of his Difciples goinge to *Emaus*, whê he cam thither he fatte downe with them, *And tooke bread and bleffed, and brake yt, and gaue yt to them, and their eies were opened and they knewe him.* And

The bread geuen to the Difci-ples in E-maus was Chryftes bleffed bo-die.

thefe Difciples returned with ioie to Hierufalem, and tolde the Apoftles, what was doen in the waie, and howe they knewe him in the brea king of bread. This bread that was here bleffed, and broke, and geuen to the Difciples, the holie learned men do teftifie not to be common bread, but to be by the bleffing of Chryft made the bread of life, euen his owne bodie. H Wherfor feinge yt ys fo vnderftâded, I thought yt apperteining to that pour pofe that I haue taken in hande, to fee the mindes of the holie fathers in yt.

And

A And at this time to afcende, I will beginne with *Theophilact*, who writeth thus vpon the fame fcripture : *Infinuatur autem & aliud quiddam, nempe quod oculi* | *Theophil.* *eorum, qui benedictum panem affumunt, aperiuntur, vt agnofcant illum. Magnam enim* | *in 24.Luc.* *& indicibilem vim habet caro Domini.* An other thing alfo ys geuen vs to vnder-ftande, that ys, that the eies of thē,which doe take the bleſſed bread, are ope ned, that they maie knowe him *(mening Chryſt)* For the fleſh of Chryſt hath a great and *vnſpeable power.* Thus he.

By this authour yt doeth not onely appeare that Chryſt gaue vnto the two difciples his bodie, but yt ys alfo euident. For when he had firſt faied that their eies were opened that receaued the bleſſed bread,fo well that they might knowe Iefus, immediatelie opening what this bleſſed bread was, he faieth : For the fleſh of Chryſt hath an *vnſpeakeable power.* The bleſſed bread then bleſſed of Chryſte to be geuen to the Difciples was fo of him bleſſed by the teſtimonie of *Theophilact* that yt was made the fleſh of Chryſt. Whiche he prooueth by the effecte. For although Chryſt had walked with them fo
B moche waie, and had conferred with them,and had rebuked their flackneſſe of faith, and finallie had interpreted the fcriptures vnto them, beginning at Moiſes, and fo paſſing through all the Prophetes, that had written of him: | *The Difci* yet all this bleſſed and holie taulke, his liuely interpretacion of the fcripturs, | *ples in E-* his bleſſed and mightie voice, whiche fownding in the eares of the Iewes, | *maus kue-* that came with *Iudas* to apprehende him,did throwe them downe to the gro | *we not* wnde, did not make theſe Difciples to knowe him as Chryſt,vntill they had | *Chryſt vn-* eaten of the bleſſed bread, whiche he bleſſed for them and gaue to thē, and | *till they* their eies were opened, and they knewe him .By this great effect then yt ys | *had eatē of* manifeſt,that yt was a greate thinge,that was geuen them,a thing of moche | *the bleſſed* power and vertue, euen that fame fleſh in fubſtance, that anoincted the eies | *bread.* of him that was born blinde, and gaue him his feight. That fame fleſh nowe opened their eies,that nowe they might knowe him,whom before by other diuerfe meanes (as ys faied) they did knowe.

To this grecian we fhall ioin *Bede*, one of the latin Churche, who vpon | *Beda in 24* the fame place faieth thus :*Certi myſterij cauſa factum eſt,vt eis in illo alia oſtendere-* | *Luc.*
C *tur effigies, & fic eum non niſi in fractione panis agnoſcerent, ne quiſquam ſe Chriſtum ag* *nouiſſe arbitretur,ſi eius corporis particeps non eſt, id eſt, Eccleſiæ, cuius vnitatem in ſacra-* | *No mã kno* *mento panis commendat Apoſtolus, dicens: Vnus panis, vnum corpus multi ſumus,vt cùm* | *weth Chry* *eis benedictum panem porrigeret, aperirentur oculi eorum, vt agnoſcerent eum.* Bicauſe | *ſte except* of a certain miſterie yt was doen that an other likeneſſe or forme fhoulde be | *he be a mē-* fhewed to them in him and fo they fhoulde not knowe him but in the brea- | *bre of his* king of breade, leeſt anie man might thinke him felf to haue knowen Chryſt | *bodie,that* yf he be not partaker of his bodie,that ys,of his Churche. The vnitie wherof | *ys,of his* the Apoſtle fetteth furth in the Sacrament of bread, faing : *All we being manie* | *Churche.* *are one bread, and one bodie:* that when he gaue to them the bleſſed bread,their eies fhoulde be open, that they might knowe him . Thusfarre *Bede.*

Of whome we learn that yt was not doen as a matter to no pourpofe,that Chryſt fhewed him felf vnto them in a ſtraunge likeneſſe, but to open a mi-fterie, which ys,that no man can knowe Chryſt, except he be a membre of his Churche, and be in the vnitie therof. And that they might be in that vni tie, he gaue them the bleſſed bread, whiche ys the Sacrament of vnitie , and
D then were their eies opened,and they knewe him. Thus as *Theophilact* faied by expreſſe woordes, that Chryſt gaue them his fleſh wherbie to open their eies,fo *Bede* faieth, that he gaue them the bleſſed bread, whiche ys the Sa-crament of vnitie,mening that bleſſed bread that *Theophilact* calleth the fleſh
of

of Chryſt, whiche (ſaieth he) he gaue them and then their eies were opened. **E**
Of bothe theſe then we are taught, that Chryſt gaue vnto the two Diſciples
in *Emaus* not comon and bare bread, but the Sacrament.

THE SIX AND SIXTITH CHAP. PROOVETH
the ſame by ſainct Auguſtine and Chryſoſt.

S *Theophilact* ys the folower of *Chryſoſtome* ſo ys *Bede* of *S. Auguſtine*. Wherfor as we haue heard the mindes of theſe two as diſciples : ſo will we heare the mindes of the other as maſters. S. Au
guſtine writing of the conſent and agremēt of the Euangeliſtes
ſaieth thus of this matter : *Non enim incongruenter accipimus hoc im-*

Auguſt. de
conſens.
Euang. li. 3
cap. 25.

*pedimentum in oculis eorum à Sathana fuiſſe ne agnoſceretur Ieſus, ſed tantùm à Chriſto
propter eorum fidem ambiguam facta permiſſio vſque ad ſacramentum panis, vt vnitate
corporis eius participata, remoueri intelligatur impedimentum inimici vt Chriſtus poſſet ag-
noſci* .

The bread
that Chriſt
bleſſed and
deliuered to
the diſciples
in Emaus
was the B.
Sacram.

We doe not incongruentlie take this impediment in their eies to ha **F**
ue ben doen by Sathan, that Ieſus ſhoulde not be knowen. But of Chryſt yt
was onelie permitted for their doubtfull faith vntill they came to the Sacrament of bread, that *the vnitie of his bodie being participated*, yt might be perceaued that the impediment of the enemie was remoued, that Chryſt might
be knowen. Thus moch S. Aug.

Of whome this ys without difficultie to be learned that the bread that
Chryſt bleſſed, and gaue to the Diſciples was the Sacrament. For ſo by that
name doeth he call yt. Wherunto when he addeth the effect, that after the
receipt of that Sacrament, the impediment of Sathan was remoued, their
ſight was illumined, and Chryſt before vnknowen, was then well knowen:
he doeth ſignifie vnto vs that they ther receaued him that ys the true light,
that lighneth euery man that cometh into the worlde. Whiche thing more plainlie Chriſoſtom doeth opē, vpon Mathew thus ſaing: *Quia de ſanctis cœ-*

Chryſoſt.
hom. 17. in
Matth.

*pimus dicere, non eſt tacendum, quin aliud eſt ſanctificatio, aliud ſanctificatum. Sanctifica- **G**
tio enim eſt quod alterum ſanctificat. Sanctificatum autem alterum ſanctificare non poteſt,
quāuis ipſum ſit ſanctificatum. vt puta ſignas panem tuum quem manducas, ſicut ait Paulus, Sanctificatur enim per verbum Dei & orationem. Sanctificaſti eum, non feciſti ſancti-
ficacionem. Quòd autem ſacerdos de manu ſua dat, non ſolùm ſanctificatum eſt, ſed etiam
ſanctificatio eſt, quoniam hoc ſolùm non datur quod videtur, ſed etiam illud quod intelligitur. De ſanctificato ergo pane licet animalibus iactare, & infidelibus dare, quia non ſancti
ficat accipientem. Si autem tale eſſet, quod de manu ſacerdotis accipitur, quale eſt quod de
menſa manducatur, omnes de menſa manducarent, & nemo de manu ſacerdotis acciperet.
Vnde Dominus non ſolùm in via benedixit panem, ſed de manu ſua dedit Cleophæ & ſocio
eius. Et paulus nauigans non ſolùm benedixit panem, ſed de manu ſua porrexit Lucæ &*

Sanctifica-
ciö and the
thing ſancti
fied be di-
uerſe.

cæteris Diſcipulis ſuis. Bicauſe we haue begon to ſpeak of holie thinges, yt ys not
to be left vnſpoken, but that ſanctificacion ys one thinge, and the thing ſanctified ys an other. Sanctificacion ys that ſanctifieth an other thing, but the
thing ſanctified can not ſanctifie an other thing, allthough yt be ſanctified,
as for example, thowe makeſt a croſſe vpon thy bread, whiche thowe eateſt,

The bleſſed
Sacr. a ſanc
tified thing
and ſancti-
ficaciö alſo.

as S. Paule ſaieth, *Yt ys ſanctified by the woorde of God and praier* : Towe haueſt
ſanctified yt, but thow haueſt not made ſanctificaciö . But that *the preiſt geueth
frō his hāde, yt ys not onely a ſanctified thing, but alſo yt ys ſanctificacion.* For not onelie **H**
that ys geuē that ys ſeen, but alſo that that ys vnderſtanded. Then yt ys lau-
full to caſt of the ſanctified bread to beaſtes, and to geue of yt to infidels,
bicauſe yt doth not ſanctifie the receauer. But if that which ys taken of the
hand

A hand of the preist were soche a thing as that, that ys eaten of the boorde, all wolde eate of the boorde, and no man wolde receaue of the preistes hand. Wherfor our Lorde also, did not onelie blesse the breade in the waie but gaue with his owne hand to *Cleophas* and his felowe. And Paule sailing did not onelie blesse the bread, but also with his hand gaue to Luke and his other Disciples. Thus farre he.

In this place of Chrysostome three thinges are, as concerning the matter of the Sacrament to be noted. The first ys, that he saieth, that yt that the preist geueth with his hand *ys not onelie a sanctified thing, but also sanctificacion yt self,* that ys, both a thing made holie, and also the thing yt self that doeth make holie. In that he saieth that the thing that the preist geueth with his hand, ys yt that sanctifieth other thinges, or maketh other thinges holie, what ells can be vnderstanded but Chrystes blessed bodie, who ys our sanctificacion, iustificacion and redemption, as saieth S. Paule, who being ther, sanctifieth the woorthie receruers? Forasmoche nowe as Chrysostome saieth that this sanctificacion, this thing, that maketh other thinges holie ys geuen by the

B preistes handes and yt can not be vnderstanded of Chryst spirituallie receaued, for that ys not geuen by the preistes hand, I wolde the Aduersarie wolde answere directlie, wher this sanctificacion resteth? wher yt ys, whether yt be in the bread or in the preist. For sith he saieth that yt ys geuen by the hand of the preist, yt must be either in the preist, that geueth yt, or in the thing that ys geuen. No man will saie that that great power to sanctifie other ys in the preist. for yt ys the propre acte of God, as he himself withnesseth, saing: *Ego Dominus qui sanctifico vos.* Yt ys I, yower Lord, whiche doe sanctifie yowe. So that the preist doeth not the acte, he sanctifieth not, but he deliuereth the sanctificacion . Yf in the Sacrament were nothing but bread (as the aduersarie teacheth) this sanctificacion coulde not by his owne doctrine be in yt . For the bread beinge a dumbe creature ys not apte to receaue sanctificacion, as he saieth. Then yt remaineth that the Aduersarie must of force confesse, that sith ther ys a thing geuen by the hand of the preist, in whiche resteth this sanctificacion, and yt ys prooued that yt neither can be the preiste, nor the bread, yt can be none other but the bodie of

C Chryst in the Sacrament, whiche neuer being separated from the God head ys euen he, that sanctifieth vs.

And this ys not to be ouerpassed that Chrisostom saieth that that, whiche the preist geueth ys both a sanctified thing, and the sanctificacion also, wherby he doth fullie open both partes of the Sacrament , namely what yt was as bread and wine, whiche nowe being sanctified, are therby turned into sanctificacion yt self, that ys, into the bodie and blood of Chryste, Of the whiche thing in effect S. Augustine saieth : *Qui cùm per manus hominum ad illam visibilem speciem perducitur, non sanctificatur vt fiat tam magnum sacramentum , nisi in visibiliter operante Spiritu Dei.* Whé the bread by the handes of men ys brought to that visibile forme , yt ys not sanctified, that yt maie be made so great a Sacrament, but by the inuisible worke of the holie Gost.

In that he saieth yt ys sanctified, he openeth the first woorde of Chrysostom, who calleth yt *sanctificatum,* a thinge made holie. In that he saieth that yt ys made so great a Sacrament by the inuisible worke of the holie Gost: he openeth the other woorde of Chrysostome calling yt sanctificacion. For

D by the worke of the holie Gost yt ys sanctified to be the bodie of Chryste, who (as ys saied) ys our sanctificacion , that ys, he that sanctifieth vs . And for affirmacion of the geuing of this sanctifieng thing by the hand of
　　　　　　　　　　　　　　　　　　　　　　　　　　　　the

A plin place for reall presence against M. Iuell.

Exod. 31.

Bothe partes of the Sacr. opened.

*Not onelie
that which
ys seen, but
also that
which ys
vnderstan-
ded ys geuē
in the Sacr.*

Esay.7.

the preist, Chryfoftom addeth thefe woordes: *Quoniam hoc folùm non datur,* E
quod videtur, fed etiam illud quod intelligitur. For not onelie that, that ys feen,
ys geuen, but that alfo that ys vnderftanded: vnderftanded I faie by faith,
and not by reafon. For that vnderftanding muft in this matter of the Sacrament be placed, of the which yt ys faied: *Nifi credideritis, non intelligetis.* Except
ye beleue, ye fhall not vnderftand.

The fecōd note of Chryfoftome ys, to the matter here fought, that Chryft
bleffed the bread in the waie, he meeneth at *Emaus*, and gaue yt with his
hand to *Cleophas* and his felowe. By whiche geuing with the hand, he meeneth the Sacrament, as before by the geuing of the preiftes hand, as he by
expreffe woordes doeth declare immediatelie, after this aboue alleaged,
wher he thus faieth, declaring what ys ment by that that ys geuen by
the hand: *Quod autem de manu porrigitur, nec animalibus dandum, nec infide-*
libus porrigendum, quia non folùm fanctificatum, fed etiam fanctificatio eſt, &
fanctificat accipientem. As for that, that ys geuen by hand, ys neither to
be geuen to beaftes, nor deliuered to infidels. for yt ys not onelie a F
*The bread
bleſſed in
Emaus,
both a fanc
tified thing
and fancti-
cacion.*
fanctified thing, but alfo yt ys fanctificacion, and doeth fanctifie the receauer.
In this then that he faieth that that, which ys geuen by the hand ys both a
fanctified thing, and alfo fanctificacion, he declareth that the bread which
Chryft bleffed, and brake, and gaue with his hand to the two difciples in
Emaus, was a fanctified thing, and the fanctificacion yt felf alfo, whiche
(as before ys faied) ys the bleffed Sacrament conteining Chryftes bodie
owre fanctificacion.

The third ys, that Chryfoftom faieth the like of the breaking of the
the bread by S. Paule, when he was in the fhippe failing towardes
Act.27.
Rome, wherof mencion ys made in the actes of the Apoftles, whiche
blesfing and geuing of bread he faieth to be foche as was that, that
Chryft gaue in *Emaus.* yf yt fo were, then ther was geuen alfo the
Sacrament.

There be that fo vnderftand that other place of the Actes of the a-
poftles, of the facrament alfo, wher yt ys faied: *Et erant perſeuerantes in* G
Act.2.
doctrina Apoſtolorum, & communicatione fractionis panis, & orationibus. They
were continuing in the doctrine of the Apoftles, and communicacion of
breaking of bread, and in praiers. Wher forfomoche as the breaking of
*Certain pla
ces of the
actes of the
Apoſtles
vnderſtan
ded of the
Sacr.*
bread ys ioined with doctrine and praier, whiche be the workes of Chryftians in their affemblies, in the feruice of God, yt ys moft like that yt ys
fpoken of the miniftracion of the Sacrament, as one of the cheif thinges
meit to be doen in foche affembles. As for that place of S. Luke ye fee
teftified to be vnderftanded of the Sacrament. The firft place alfo of the
Actes here alleaged ys by Chryfoftom fo vnderftanded alfo. So ys the other
place by men of right gooh fame in learning, whiche I omitte to auoide
prolixitie.

THE

A THE SEVEN AND SIXTETH CHAP. PROOVETH
*by the scriptures and practises in the last chappiter handeled that
the communion vnder one kinde ys laufull
and good.*

T ys a membre of the Proclamacion made by this Proclamer, that yf anie man can shewe by the scriptures, by the example of the Primitiue Churche, or by anie olde catholique doctour, that the Sacrament was ministred vnder one kinde during the time of sixe hundreth yeares next after Chryst, that he wolde geue ouer and subscribe. Nowe forasmoche as I trust euen by the iudgement of other, I haue in other matters conteined in his Proclamacion doen as moche as in the same he hath required: I will also doe the like in this matter of the ministracion of the Sacrament vnder one kinde, that he also maie doe as moche as he hath promised, wherunto iust and good occasion ys ministred vnto me by these scriptures, whiche in these two last chapiters be treacted of. Wher first ye hearde *The Sacr. deliuered by our Saui our Chryst vnder one kinde.*

B the breaking of bread mencioned in Sainct Luke, to be a deliuerie of the Sacrament, and not left barelie so, but also to be a deliuerie of the bodie of Chryst. And this deliuerie ye redd and perceaued to be doen but in one kinde, that ys, of bread. And this deliuerie was not doen by anie priuate man but euen by Chryst himself, euen vpon the daie of his resurrection.

Yf the Proclamer will saie, as *Melancthon* saieth, that yt ys spoken by *Senecdochen*, by the parte for the wholl, he hath saied yt, but he hath not prooued yt. Yt ys no scripture yf he so saie, yt ys but an inuencion of his owne head to auoide a scripture. But that that we saie ys the scripture, and we saie neither more nor lesse, then the scripture, as we also doe vpon these woordes of Chryst: *This ys my bodie.* Yf then we speake the scripture, and for the better vnderstanding of the scripture, we bring furth the auncient learned men both of the greke and latin Churche to expownde the scripture, and they teache vs but of the ministracion of the Sacrament vnder one kinde

C also: What remaineth for vs to doe, but so to accept and vnderstand the scriptures as we read them, and finde them expownded vnto vs?

Nowe then wher the Proclamer saieth, that the institucion of Chryst and *The Proclamers obiection of Chrystes institucion for receauing vnder bothe kindes aunswered. Marc. 16. Mat. 28. Chrystes ministracio͂ of the Sacr. first vnder bothe kindes after vnder thone proueth either of bothe to be laufull.* the woordes of S. Paule maie seme sufficient to a Chrystian man, to receaue the Sacrament no otherwise then vnder bothe kindes, bicause Chryst did so institute yt, and S. Paule to the Corynthiansso reporteth yt. Yt maie in dede seem sufficient for that time, and for the condicion of soche persons as then receaued. As this ordeinaunce of Chryst forbidding his Apostles to go amo͂ge the gentiles, when they were sent furth to preach, was a good ordeinaunce, and shoulde haue bownde vs to the obseruacion of yt, yf afterwarde he had not saied: *Ite, prædicate euangelium omni creaturæ,* And: *Euntes docete omnes gentes.* Go ye and preach the gospell to euerie creature. And again: Go and teache all people: Euen so yf Chryst had not ministred the Sacrament in one kinde after his institucion, whiche was in both kindes, the saing of the Proclamer might haue seemed to haue had some force. But nowe seing the sa-

D me Chryst that first ministred the holie Sacrament vnder both kindes, hath nowe ministred the same vnder one kinde, yt ys a moche beter argument to prooue that both maners maie be vsed, then that onelie the first maner shoulde be vsed, vnlesse the Proclamer will condemne the second ministracion of Chryst, bycause yt differeth from the first,

　　　　　　　　　　　　　　R r　　　　But

But yf yt be laufull for vs to folowe euerie acte of Chryst doen for our example and inftruction, then we maie receaue vnder both kindes, and we maie laufullie receaue vnder one kinde, but diuerfely. For as Chryft when he did inftitute yt, did yt as a folemne action of or for the memoriall of his pafsion and death, whiche by his minifters fhoulde be frequented in his Church, vntill he came again, and therfor though the nombre that beleued both men and women was great, yet he called none to this maner of miniftracion but the. XII. Apoftles who were preiftes, fignifieng therby that all preiftes, that fhoulde in his Church doe this folemne action before his people for the memoriall of his pafsion and death, fhoulde doe yt vnder both kindes, as therby to fignifie vnto the faithfull, that in the pafsion of Chryft, the blood of that bleffed bodie was feparated and diuided from that bodie, and ran oute plentifull to wafh awaie our filthie finnes: Euen fo they that be preiftes, and accordinge to the office of preiftes, doe this publike minifterie in the fetting furth of this memoriall of Chryftes death, muft according to Chryftes inftitucion haue and receaue the bleffed Sacramentes vnder both kindes. Whiche thing the catholique Churche neuer hath nor doeth pretermitte, but inuiolablie obferueth, hauing ther in, as yt ys meit a fpeciall regarde to Chryftes inftitucion.

Preiftes doing the folemne action of the memoriall of Chryftes pafsion in their maffes aught to receaue vnder both kindes.

In the other time of Chryftes miniftracion of the Sacrament of his bodie to the twoo difciples, as the Gofpell maketh no mencion that yt was doen as a folemne action of or for the remembrance of Chryftes pafsion or death, but raither as a mean to woorke them a benefit, to remoue the impediment of Sathan, whiche letteth them to knowe Chryft, and fo to open their eies that they might knowe him, and therfor receaued the Sacrament but vnder one kinde: Euen fo priuate perfons that for their fpirituall côforte in Chryft, for the enkendling of the fire of Gods loue in them, for the godlie exercife of their faith, for their incorporacion into Chryft, for their ftrenght and defence againft the affaultes and temptacions of the enemie, or in extreames for their voiage meate the better to walke ther iourneie, doe receaue the bleffed Sacrament, maie verie well, according to Chryftes example receaue yt vnder one kinde, as thofe difciples did. Wherfor all Bifhoppes, all preiftes, and all other of the cleargie, whenfoeuer they receaue as priuate perfons, that ys, when they doe not that publique miniftracion and folemne action of Chryftes memoriall for and before the Churche, then doe they, as all other doe, receaue vnder one kinde, contenting them felues in their fo doinge by the example of Chryfte as ys afore faied.

Priuate perfons for their fpirituall côfort maie laufullie receaue vnder one kinde as the difciples did in Emaus. Bifhoppes preiftes and all of the clergie not doing the publique action, receaue vnder one kinde.

As Chryft by his doinges hath left vs an example what we maie laufullie doe as concerninge the receipt of the bleffed Sacrament, by whiche the Proclamer ys anfwered, for that part of his obiection, that obiecteth Chryftes inftitucion: So fhall we nowe anfwere for that he obiected of Sainct Paule, *He faieth that the woordes of Sainct Paule are fufficient alfo to prooue that the Sacrament aught to be receaued of all men vnder both kindes.* Yt ys a plain matter that Sainct Paule maketh no fpeciall inftitucion of the Sacrament, but onely maketh a reherfall of Chryftes inftitucion, then this parte of his obiection maie be aunfwered with that that ys faied to his obiection of Chryftes inftitucion, forfomoche as this ys but a reherfall of that. But yet fhal we to the furtherance of the trueth make a farder aunfwere.

Proclamers obiection of S. Paule for receauing vnder both kindes aunfwered.

Wherfor vnderftand that although S. Paule did deliuer to the Corynthians the inftitucion of Chryft as then deliuered vnder both kindes: yet
S. Paule

A S. Paule teacheth not, that of necefsitie yt muft allwaies be vfed in both kindes and no other. For yf he had taught yt with an exclufiue excluding all other maner but this, yt had fome force. But fo he doeth not. The fcope of S. Paules doctrine refteth in thefe two poinctes: that the Sacrament be re ceaued in the remembrance of Chryftes death: And that yt be receaued woorthilie. Wherfor I faie, that fo farre wide yt was from the minde of S. Paule, by his doctrine there taught to forbidde the receipt of the Sacrament vnder one kinde, that as Chryft did to his two difciples in Emaus, fo did S. Paule to Luke and his felowes in the fhippe (as Chryfoftome witneffeth) geue the Sacrament vnder the one kinde of bread. Although thefe actes of Chryft, and Sainct Paule are fufficient to prooue that the receipt of the Sa crament vnder one kinde ys laufull and good, in maner aboue faied: yet the fame maie alfo appeare by the other place of the actes alleaged in the laft chapiter. Wher alfo mencion ys made that the Sacrament was miniftred vn der one kinde, namely of bread, no title of mencion made of the other kinde. And befide the good catholique men that doe vnderftand this place of the

B Sacrament, the *Waldenfes* alfo did fo vnderftand yt.

The fcope of S. Paule touching the Sacra. 1.Cor. 11.

Then fith the multitude of the faithfull euen immediatelie after the co ming of the holie Goft, did receaue the Sacrament vnder one kinde, yt ys manifeft that yt maie without offence be doen and vfed nowe in Chryftes Churche, and maie not be reputed, as yt ys of the Proclamer, for an vn laufull facte. For he that impugneth the Churche for doing of that, that the fcripture fheweth the example, and faieth that the acte of the Churche ys vnlaufull, impugneth the fcriptures, and importeth that they be vnlaufull.

Acto.2.

Thefe actes of Chryft and Sainct Paule', and the doinge of the multitude in the feconde of the actes, doe not abbridge the firft inftitucion of Chryft, or take yt awaie, as his feconde ordeinance in fending his Apoftles to prea che taketh awaie the firft: but they doe raither teache, that oute of the folem ne action of Chryftes memoriall, whiche muft be doen vnder both kindes of him that doeth that action, other maie verie well receaue the Sacrament

C vnder one kinde. And as yt maie be doen bycaufe the fcriptures faie, yt hath ben doen: fo fhall yt appeare to euerie faithfull man that yt ys well doen, yf he trulie conceaue and vnderftand what ys doen.

Acto.2.

In the catholique faith yt ys taught, that after the confecracion, as by ma nie yt ys allreadie teftified, in the Sacrament vnder the forme of bread ys the verie bodie of Chryft, and vnder the forme of wine the verie bloode of Chryft, not in this, bloode withoute a bodie: nor in that, a bodie withoute bloode. For Chryft, as Sainct Paule faieth, rifing from the dead, nowe dieth not, death fhall no more haue lordfhippe ouer him. Nowe yf the bodie were withoute bloode, yt coulde not be liuinge and fo fhoulde death be in the bodie of Chryft again, wherfor yt ys a bodie with bloode, and fo a liuing and a perfight bodie, as the holie Martyr Cyprian teftifieth yt to be, fainge: *Panis ifte communis in carnem & fanguinem Domini mutatus procurat vitam* This comon bread chaunged into the flefh and blood of our Lorde procureth life. The bread then chaunged into the flefh and blood of Chryft, teacheth

D vs that yt ys not flefh alone, but yt ys both flefh and bloode: So likewife vnder the forme of wine ys not the bloode of Chryft onelie but the bodie alfo. Wherof we haue the teftimonie of the auncient Martyr *Irenæus*, who faieth thus: *Calicem qui eft creatura, fuum corpus confirmauit.* He affirmed the cuppe, whiche ys a creature to be his bodie. So that vnder eche of the kin des yfverilie and fubftanciallie the bodieand bloode of Chryfte: For where a

Cypr. de cænaDom, Vnder for meof bread both flefhe and bloode of Chryft. Iren lib.5. Vnder for me of wine the bodie of Chryfte.

R r ij   liuelie

liuelie bodie ys, ther muſt be bloode alſo: And where bloode ys, ther muſt **E**
be fleſh and veines alſo, as *Irenæus* ſaieth: *Sanguis non eſt niſi a venis, & carnibus,*
& à reliqua, quæ eſt ſecundum hominem, ſubſtantia. Bloode ys not but of the veines and fleſh, and the other ſubſtance, whiche ys as man. Wherfor I ſaie that
vnder eche of theſe kindes ys the bodie of Chryſt.

Iren. ibid.

Whiche thing alſo S. Bernarde teacheth by expreſſe woordes in his ſermon of the ſupper of our Lorde, ſainge: *Idipſum, ô Chriſtiane, de vino ſentias, id*
honores in vino, quod ſcilicet de panis ſpecie ſenſiſti, & in ea honoraſti. Vnderſtande
euen the ſame (o chryſtian) of the wine honour that in the wine, that thowe
dideſt vnderſtand of the forme of bread, and dideſt honoure in yt.

Bern. ſerm.
de cœn.

And wher Melancton ſaieth, that this neceſsitie that where the bodie ys,
there muſt be bloode, and where the blood ys, ther of neceſsitie muſt be the
bodie: ys but mens inuencions and tradicions hauing a contenance of
trueth, but not the thing: Thowe ſeeſt (Reader) that we ſtand not vpon phantaſies, but we ſtande and ſtaie vpon the authoritie of the great auncient Fathers, and holie Martyrs. Sainct *Irenæus*, S. Cyprian, and S. Bernarde, who **F**
teache what in this poinct ys to be ſaied. And therfor Melancton, and his
likes ſainge that the one kinde ys but half the Sacrament, and diuiding
Chryſte confeſſe him not to be whollie vnder eche kinde cleaueth to his
phantaſies, and ſingular deuiſes, and foloweth not the doctrine of the
Fathers.

But we ſainge *Vale* to Melancton and his inuencion we cleaue to the ſubſtanciall, and auncient doctrine of the Fathers, and by that we conclude,
that the bodie and bloode of Chryſt ys neceſſarelie vnder eche kinde, as
whollie and perfectlie vnder the one as vnder the other. And foraſmoche as
the godhead ioined to Chryſt in vnitie of perſon ys inſeparable from the
manhead, therfor yt foloweth of neceſsitie alſo that the bodie being vnder
eche kinde the godhead that hath taken to yt ſelf the ſame bodie, ys with
the ſame bodie vnder eche kinde, and ſo vnder eche kinde ys wholl Chryſt
God and man. And being ſo, he ys there with all his giftes, graces, merittes,
and vertues. Wherfor he that receaueth the Sacrament vnder one kinde, re- **G**
ceaueth woll Chryſt, God and man. And yf he receaue yt woorthilie, receaueth him with his giftes and graces, according to the meaſure of the gift
of Chryſt.

Wholl Chri-
ſte being
vnder eche
kinde, the
people be
not defrau-
ded recea-
uing but o-
ne kinde.

Nowe then perceauing what ys doen in the receipt of the Sacrament,
vnder one kinde, namelie that ther ys receaued wholl Chryſt God and man
with all his giftes and graces as fullie and perfectlie, as yf both kindes were
receaued, ſo that the receauer ys nothing defrauded of the effect of the Sacrament: yt maie be perceaued that ſo to receaue ys well doen and lauſullie
doen. Yf yt be then asked, whic Chryſt did inſtitute the Sacrament vnder
both kindes, yf yt be ſufficient to receaue the one: the aunſwer ys made
before, that he did inſtitute the Sacrament vnder bothe kindes to be frequented as the ſolemne memoriall of his paſsion, and death, in the preſence
of his Churche. yet he himſelf miniſtred vnder one kinde to declare that to
priuate men he leaueth yt indifferent to receaue vnder one or bothe. Thus **H**
moche ys ſaied vpon the ſcripture for the receauing of the bleſſed Sacrament
vnder one kinde.

Whie Chriſt
inſtituted
the Sacr.
vnder bo-
the kindes

THE

A

THE EIGHT AND SIXTETH CHAPITER,

prooueth the same receipt vnder one kinde to be laufull
by the auncient practise of the
Churche.

S the enemies of Chryſtes Churche in the ſubuerſion
of *Boemia*, reioiced that they had ſownde oute (as they
thought) ſome notable errour in the Churche, whiche
ys(as they wolde haue yt vnderſtanded) directlie againſt
the ſcriptures, namelie the receauing of the Sacrament
vnder one kinde, againſt this ſainge of Chryſt in Sainct
Iohn. *Except ye eate the fleſh of the Sonne of man, and drink his blood, ye ſhall not
haue life in yowe.* So the Aduerſaries of Chryſtes Church in theſe our daies
likewiſe reioice, and in their owne conceipt triumphe againſt the ſame,
ſaing that yt erreth, and doeth directly both againſt the plain inſtitucion
of Chryſt, who did inſtitute the ſame Sacrament vnder two kindes, and ſo

B gaue yt furth to be receaued: and alſo againſt the vſe and example of the
primitiue Churche, which did miniſter the ſame manie hundreth yeares
after Chryſt vnder both kindes.

Among theſe the Proclamer ſingeth a part, and ſaieth, *that the Communion vnder both kindes was vſed throughoute the wholl Churche ſixe hundreth yeares
after Chryſtes aſcenſion without exceeption.* But for the proofe of this his ſainge
he bringeth in but a litle fragment of *Gelaſius* an olde Father of the Churche, and a Biſhoppe of Rome, whiche ys this: *Diuiſio vnius eiuſdemque myſterij ſine grandi ſacrilegio non poteſt peruenire.* The diuiſion of one verie myſterie, can not be doen withoute great ſacriledge.

*Proclamers
obiection of
the practiſe
of the primi-
tiue chur-
che.*

But as the one parte of their wicked ſlaunder ys allreadie declared to be
vntrue, for that to receaue the Sacrament vnder one kinde, as ys ſaied, ys
not againſt the ſcriptures: So ſhall yt be made as plain that the other ys
as vntrue, forthat ye ſhall euidentlie ſee the practiſe and examples of the

C primitiue Churche in diuerſe ages to haue vſed the Sacrament vnder one
kinde.

But firſt we ſhall aunſwere the obiection, that the Proclamer maketh
by *Gelaſius.* For the whiche yt ys to be vnderſtanded, that the hereſie of the *Manicheis*, whiche began in the time of *Felix* the fiue and twenteth Biſhop of Rome after Sainct Peter, in the yeare of our Lorde two hundreth, ſeuenteth and two: continued to the time of *Gelaſius*, who ruled the
Church of Rome, the yeare of our Lorde four hundreth, neinteth and foure
whiche hereſie, as Sainct Auguſtine did with great labour, and like learning
impugne: ſo did diuerſe holie Fathers, and rulers of Chryſtes Church trauail, for yt did moche vexe the Church, to repreſſe and vtterlie to extinguiſh yt.

*Gelaſius his
meening
opened.*

Nowe in the time of *Gelaſius*, ther were manie of them in Rome, who
vſinge diſſimulacion to cloake their hereſie, came among the Chryſtian
people to the receipt of the Sacrament. But for that they beleued that

D Chryſt had no verie naturall bodie of man born of the Virgen Marie, but
a phantaſticall bodie, therfor they contented them ſelues to receaue the
Sacrament vnder the forme of bread, they wickedlie phantaſieng yt, as a
memoriall of the phantaſticall bodie of Chryſt. But when they ſhoulde
come to receaue the Sacrament vnder the forme of wine, they conueighed

*Manicheis
howe they
diſſimuled
in receauig
the Sacr.*

　　them

Eutychians their herefi

them felues awaie, bicaufe, they beleued that the bodie of Chryft, which as ys faied, they did take to be phantafticall, had no bloode. And therfor they wolde receaue no Sacrament of his blood. The Eutychians alfo denieng the humane nature to abide in Chryfte, and therfor to haue anie perfect naturall bodie in the Sacrament, ioined at that time with the Manicheis, and with like difsimulacion contenting them felues to receaue the Sacrament vnder the forme of bread, as the Sacrament of a certain diuine, and heauenlie bodie, they, as the other did, fledd from the receipt of the other kinde, phantafieng no blood to be in foche a bodie.

Of whiche their wicked doinges, *Gelafius* hauing intelligence to the intent they might be difcerned and well knowen from the true Chryftians, and fo to be deprehended, he made a like decree, as before him, for the fame pourpofe, and againft the fame men, did the holie Father Leo the firft, Bifhopp of Rome not manie yeares before *Gelafius*. The verie woordes of which Leo to the better vnderftanding of the matter, I thinke verie

Leo fer. 4. de quadr.

neceffarie to afcribe, and they be thefe: *Abducant fe Sacramento falutis humanæ & Chriftum Dominum noftrum, ficut in veritate carnis noftræ denegant natum, ita mortuum verè, & refurrexiffe non credunt, & ob hoc diem falutis noftræ, & lætitiæ noftræ fui ieiunij mœrore condemnant. Cumq́ue ad tegendum infidelitatem fuam noftris audeant intereffe mysterijs, ita in Sacramentorum communione fe temperant, vt interdum tutius lateant. Ore indigno Chriſti corpus accipiunt fanguinem autem redemptionis noftræ haurire omnino declinant. Quod ideo veftram volumus fcire fanctitatem, vt vobis huiufmodi homines & ijs manifeſtentur indicijs, & quorum depræhenfa fuerit facrilega fimulatio, notati & prodita, à fanctorum focietate, facerdotali authoritate pellantur.* They with drawe them felues from the Sacrament of the health of man. And as they denie Chryft our Lorde to be borne in the veritie of our nature: So dóe they not beleue him to haue ben verilie dead, and rifen again. And therfor doe they condemne

Manichies fafted on the fundaie

the daie of our health and gladneffe, with the fadneffe of their fafting. And when to couer their infidelitie, they are fo bolde to be at the miniftracion of our mysteries, to the entent they maie be the longer vnknowen, they tempre themfelues fo in the communion of the Sacramen-

A plain pla ce for reall prefence a gainſt the Proclamer

tes, *That with vnwoorthie mouthe they receaue the bôdie of Chryſt, but to drinke the bloode of our redemption they vtterlie refufe.* Whiche thing we will your holineffe to vnderftande, that thefe maner of men by thefe tokens maie be knowen, and whofe facrilegall difsimulacion ys perceaued being difclofed, and noted they maie be by the preiftlie authoritie banifhed from the focietie or felowfhippe of true Chryftian people.

In thefe woordes ye maie learn the herefies of the Manicheis, ye maie perceaue their wicked difsimulacion, ye maie vnderftand the verie caufe whie they wolde not receaue the Sacrament vnder the forme of wine, finallie ye maie perceaue to what pourpofe bothe kindes were commaunded to be receaued, namely that foche cloaked heretiques might by foche means be difclofed and knowen.

Gelafius.

Nowe *Gelafius* fucceading this man, and finding this offpringe of vipers not yet deftroied, he folowed him in pronowncing againft them, as he did folowe him in time and gouernement, and faied thus: *Comperimus autem, quòd quidam fumptâ tantùm facri corporis portione, à calice facrati cruoris abſtineant, qui procul dubiò (quoniam nefcio qua fuperſtitione docentur aſtringi) aut integra Sacramenta percipiant, aut ab integris arceantur, quia diuifio*

vnius

A *vnius eiufdemque myfterij fine grandi facrilegio non potest peruenire*. We certenlie finde, that certain men, when they haue receaued the porcion of the
holie bodie, they doe abftein from the cuppe of the holie bloode, who
forafmoche as I knowe not by what fuperfticion they are taught fo to be
witholden, let them without all doubte either receaue the wholl Sacramentes, or ells let them be forbidden from the wholl. For the diuifion
of one verie myfterie can not be doen withoute great facriledge. Thus he,

Porcion of the holie bo die and cup pe of the ho lie blood.

Nowe yf ye will referre this fentence of *Gelafius* to the fentence of Leo,
ye fhall perceaue that *Gelafius* writeth not againft the doing of the catholique Churche receauing the Sacrament vnder one kinde. But againft
the Manychies, who by their herefie diuided the bleffed myfterie of
Chryft, and teaching that he had but a phantafticall bodie, denied anie
verie blood to be in yt, And therfor in their diffembling maner receauing one kinde as a Sacrament offoche phantafticall bodie, as they phantafied him to haue, they refufed the other kinde as a Sacrament of his bloode, and fo in their conceat they diuided the bloode from the bodie, and fo

B diuided the myfterie, whiche (as Gelafius faieth) can not be doen withoute great facrilege, which thing euery good catholique affirmeth and
embraceth.

For yf ye will call to remembrance, yt ys declared in the laft chapiter
that the catholique Churche teacheth that the verie bodie and bloode of
Chryft, euen wholl Chryft, God and man ys vnder eche kinde, fo that we
make no diuifion of the bodie from the bloode, or of the bloode from the
bodie: or of the godhead from the manheade, or of the manhead from the
godhead, but we teache the wholl verie bodie, and the wholl verie bloode,
whol God, and wholl man iointelie to be in thefe Sacramentes of Chryftes bodie and bloode, albeit the one ys more principallie the Sacrament
of his bodie, and the other more principallie the Sacrament of his bloode.

Doctrine of the catholi ke churche touching eche kinde of the Sacr.

Weigh then therfor that thefe fainges were not fpoken againft Catholiques, but againft heretiques, that by their wicked herefie diuided the
C bloode of Chryft from his bodie, phantafieng him a bodie withoute bloode, whiche in dede ys a great facriledge: Seing then yt ys fpoken againft
foche maner of heretiques, whie doeth this Proclamer fo wreft and wring
this Authour to make him appeare to the vnlearned that he fpake againft
the catholique vfe of one kinde in the Churche, when the Authour hath
not one title againft yt? Bothe kindes were commaunded to be vfed. But
whie? Not that one kinde were not fufficient, but that thofe heretiques
(as Leo faieth) might therby be knowen, and therfor was yt expedient at
that time to be commaunded to the confutacion of that herefie, as in the
Councells of conftance, and Bafill yt was expedient to be doen vnder one
kinde for the confutacion of foche herefies, as Wycleff, and Huffe, had
raifed.　And as thefe thinges haue ben altered as yt hath ben thought
good to the Churche for the wealth of Gods people, and the confutacion
of his enemies: So ys this commaunded but for a time, and maie be
altered as occafion fhall ferue, but not by euerie priuate man, but by the
D Church onelie.

But will ye befides all this wrefting of this Authour fee alfo the
fynceritie or raither the falfe fleight of this Proclamer, who to deceaue his audience, wolde not faithfullie bring in the whol faing of the Authour, as I haue nowe doen. But brought in half a skore of the laft

woordes, and left oute (I thinke I maie faie) of verie pourpofe an wholl skore that go before, bycaufe they made fo moche againft him, that he durft not for fhame bring them whollie in.

For in the former woordes be two thinges verie plainlie taught againft him.   The firft ys the verie reall prefence of Chryftes bodie and bloode, in that he fo reuerentlie calleth the Sacrament vnder one kinde *the por-cion of the holie bodie, and the other he calleth, the cuppe of the holie bloode*. As this ys fpoken reuerentlie: So ys yt fpoken plainlie.   For when he faieth that they abftein from the cuppe of the holie bloode, he plainlie teacheth that the content of the cuppe ys holie bloode, which holie blood ys not mere fpirituall. For that, as yt ys diuerfe times faied, ys not conteined in extern or outwarde materiall veffells, but in the inwarde fpirituall veffells.

And although this one parte of the Authours fainge, whiche the Pro-clamer left oute, doeth prooue the reall prefence : Yet marke an other as affectuall as this, whiche ys, that he faieth, that thefe wicked men, thefe Manychies, againft whome he pronownced this fentence, did receaue the holie bodie.   Of the whiche men alfo *Leo* faied: *Ore indigno Chrifti corpus accipiunt*. They with vnwooorthie mouthe, receaue the bodie of Chryft. Yf they receaued the holie bodie, forfomoche as they did not, being euell men, receaue the holie bodie fpirituallie, yt argueth inuinci-blie that they receaued the holie bodie corporallie.

The feconde thing, that he teacheth ys, the he calleth not thefe two kindes, *Sacramentum*, a Sacrament : But *Sacramenta*, Sacramentes, in the plurall nombre : Signifieng therbie that eche of them ys an wholle Sa-crament.   And by this be aunfwered the fonde fainges of the Aduerfarie, whiche he vfeth againft the catholique Church fainge, that her preiftes geue vnto the people but half a Sacrament, or a peice of a Sacrament, a truncate Sacrament, and foche like. Wher by this Proclamers Authour, at the leaft by him produced, yt ys manifeft that the people receauing one kinde receaue an wholl Sacrament, and not a peice: They receaue wholl Chryft and not half, or a peice of Chryft.

By this then yt maie be perceaued that the Authour whiche the Pro-clamer hath truncatelie alleaged againft the catholique Churche, beinge whollie produced and trulie vnderftanded maketh all together againft him. Soche ys the fynceretie of the man in the handling of the doctours, that bringing in ten woordes that femed, but in dede made nothing for him, he left oute thirtie that directlie made fo moche, and fo plainlie againft him, that I dare faie, he was afhamed, and his confcience moche rebuked to bring them in. But why fhoulde not he vfe his falfe fheift in them nowe as well as Melanchton did his falfe corrupcion before?

He than being thus fullie aunfwered: we will nowe fee the practife of the Churche for the receauing vnder one kinde, that his trueth maie as

well be perceiued in this, as his falfheade ys in the other. For introdu-ction wher vnto yt ys to be vnderftanded, that in the primitiue Chur-che were manie, and great perfecucions moued againft the Chryftians, by reafon of whiche they coulde not but feldome come together to com-mon praier, and miniftracion of the Sacramentes, wherfor the preift at foche time as they might meet deliuered them of the Sacrament wrapped in fair limen cloathes to carie home with them, that where they coulde not when they wolde receaue the Sacrament at the hand of the preift in

their

A their common affemblies, yet they might fecretlie at home receaue yt by their owne handes. And this coulde be none other, but the Sacrament vnder the forme of breade.

The plain practife wherof we finde declared by Tertullian, who writing to his wief, and diffwading her from the marriage of anie infidell after his deceaffe, vfeth her priuate receipt of the Sacrament, as a thing to diffwade her bie, faing: *Non fciet maritus, quid fecretò ante omnem cibum guſtes? & fi fciuerit, panem, non illum credit effe qui dicitur.* Shall not thy husbande, knowe what thowe doeſt eate fecretlie before all meat? and yf he doe knowe yt, he will not beleue yt to be that bread, that yt ys faied to be. As who might faie-wher ye vfe in the morninges fecretie, and faſting to receaue the Sacrament, whiche I being a chryſtian man, and your husband ye maie verie well doe, but yf I die either by naturall death or by perfecucion for my faith, which in this time ys like, yf after my deceaffe, ye marrie with an infidell, will not he (thinke yow) perceaue what yow doe fecretlie receaue when ye be fa-ſting, and fo perchaunce forbidde ye fo to doe, or yf he fuffre yow : yet

B this incommoditie and greif ye fhall haue, that where ye take yt, and be-leue yt (as yt ys in dede) a great myſterie, he wil not regarde yt, neither will he beleue yt to be anie other thing then breade. By this then yt ys manifeſt, that this was a practife of the primitiue Churche to recea-ue the Sacrament vnder one kinde, that was vnder the forme of breade, whiche might beſt be referued, and that they did yt fecretlie alone withoute anie nombre of Communicantes, as hereafter alfo more at large fhall be fhewed.

For this priuate maner of the receipt of the Sacrament Sainct Bafill ge-ueth a notable teſtimonie. Who writing to a godlie woman, that for the reuerence that fhe bare to the bleffed Sacrament feared to receaue the fa-me into her handes, as then the vfe was, and to carie yt home (as yt ys faied) in a fair linnen cloathe, and to referue yt to receaue when deuocion fhould moue her, withoute the miniſtracion of the preiſt, faieth thus. *Illud autem*

C *in perfecutionis temporibus neceſsitate cogi quempiam, non præfente facerdote, aut miniſtro Communionem propria manu fumere, nequaquam effe graue fuperuacaneum eſt demonſtrare. Proptereà quòd longa confuetudine hoc ipfo rerum vfu confirmatum eſt. Omnes enim in eremis folitariam vitam agentes, vbi non eſt facerdos, Commu-nionem domi feruantes, à feipfis communicant. In Alexandria verò & in Aegypto vnufquifque eorum, qui funt de populo, plurimùm habet Communionem in domo fua. Semel enim facerdote facrificium confecrante, & diſtribuente, meritò participare, & fufcipere, credere oportet. Etenim & in Ecclefia facerdos dat partem, & accipit eam is, qui fufcipit cum omni libertate, & ipfam admouet ori propria manu. Idem igitur eſt virtute fiue vnam partem quis accipiet à facerdote, fiue plures partes fimul.* As for that not to be a greuoufe thing in the times of perfecucion, anie man to be enforced, with his owne hande to receaue the Communion, the preiſt or Deacon not being prefent, yt ys more then neadeth to prooue, for bicaufe the fame thing ys by a long cuſtome, and by the verie vfe of thinges eſtablifhed and confirmed. For all they that in

D the wildernefle Lead a folitarie life, referuing the Communion in their houfes, wher ther ys no preiſt, they communicate them felues. In Alexandria and in Egypt euerie one of the people for the moſt parte haue the Sacra-ment in their houfes. When the preiſt hath once confecrated the fa-crifice, and diſtributed yt, we muſt beleue that we doe receaue, and
partici-

Li. 2. ad vxorem.|
Practifes of the pri-mitiue churche prouing af-well reall prefence, as referuacion and priua-te or fole re-ceipt of the bleffed Sac.

Baf. Epiſt. ad Caf. pat.

In Alexan-dria and Egypt peo-ple had the Sac. in their priuate hou-fes referued

participate the fame. For in the Churche alfo the preift geueth parte, and he that receaueth yt, taketh yt with all libertie, and with his owne hand putting yt to his mouthe. Yt ys therfor all one thing in vertue of power, whether a man take one parte of the preifte or manie partes together. Thus moche he.

Omitting to note vnto yow here in Sainct Bafill. howe the Sacrament was referued in the houfes of the Chryftian people to receaue as their deuocion moued them, which inuinciblie and moft plainlie affirmeth and prooueth that the Aduerfarie denieth, namelie that the Sacrament ought to be referued: I wifh yow to note for that that ys before faied, that Sainct Bafill faieth, that in the times of perfecucion the people receaued the Sacrament at home by them felues, when they had once receaued yt at the preiftes handes. And this Sainct Bafill wifheth to be taken as no ftraunge thing, for that they in Alexandria and Egypt, yea and all foche as liued folitarelie in wilderneffe had the Sacrament at home with them, and did communicate them felues. Which thing was not latelie practifed, but yt ys a thing eftablifhed and confirmed by auncient vfe and cuftome long before the time of Sainct Bafill. And being long before Sainct Bafill I truft the Aduerfarie will graunt that yt was an accuftomed practife of the primitine Churche to referue the Sacrament, and to receaue yt vnder one kinde, for that in thofe whotte contries foche fmall porcions of wine will not be kept conuenientlie in their owne kinde foch long time, as they were forced to referue the Sacrament in the wilderneffe and ells wher.

Yf yow defire a more plain teftimonie for this receipt vnder one kinde

Cypr fer.5. de lapfis.

harken to Sainct Cyprian, who writeth thus: *Præfente ac tefte meipfo, accipite quid euenerit. Parentes fortè fugientes, dum trepidi minus confulant fub nutricis alimento paruulam filiam reliquerunt. Relictam nutrix detulit ad magiftratus. Illi ei apud idolum quò populus confluebat, quòd carnem necdum poffet edere per ætatem, panem mero mixtum (quod tamen & ipfam de immolatione pereuntium fuperat) tradiderunt. Recepit filiam poftmodum mater. Sed facinus puella commiffum tam loqui & indicare non potuit, quam nec intelligere prius potuit, nec arcere. Ignoratione igitur obreptum eft, vt facrificantibus nobis, eam fecum mater inferret. Sed enim puella mixta cum fanctis, precis noftræ & orationis impatiens, nunc ploratu concuti, nunc mentis eftu fluctuabunda iactari, velut tortore cogente, quibus poterat indicijs confcientiam facti in fimplicibus adhuc annis, rudis anima fatebatur. Vbi verò folemnibus adimpletis calicem Diaconus offerre præfentibus cœpit, & accipientibus cæteris, locus eius aduenit, faciem fuam paruula inftinctu maieftatis diuinæ auertertere, os labijs obturantibus premere, calicem recufare. Perftitit tamen Diaconus, & reluctanti licet, de Sacramento calicis infudit. Tunc fequitur fingultus, in corpore atque ore violato Euchariftia permanere non potuit. Sanctificatus in Domini fanguine potus de pollutis vifceribus erupit.*

Of a child that receaued of the wine offred to idolls, ãd afterward the B. Sac.

Heare what happened my felf being prefent and witneffe. The parentes of a childe flienge by chaunce, while in their feare they tooke not good adwifemeut, lefte their litle daughter at nourcing. The nource brought the litle one fo left vnto the officers. They before an idolle, wher the people were gathered, did deliuer vnto the fame litle one, bicaufe yt coulde not as yet for lacke of age eate flefhe, a foppe dipped in the wine, whiche remaineth of the immolacion or facrifice of the idolaters. Afterward the mother receaued her daughter. But the girle coulde not fpeake, and declare the offence comitted. euen as before fhe coulde not vnderftand yt, nor withftand and let yt, yt fell oute therfor by ignorance, that while we were doing facrifice, the

mother

A mother brought her in with her. But trulie the girle being among holie
people,and not able to abide our supplicacions and praiers, sometime was
constreigned to crie oute, somtime with vehement greifes of minde tossed
here and there,and euen as the tortoure had forced her, the ignorant soule
by soche tokens as she coulde,did knowleg or confesse the conscience of the
facte in these her tender yeares.And when the solemne seruice was fullfilled
the deacon began to offre the cuppe to them that were present, and other
receauing yt,her place came to receaue . The litle one euen by the mocion *The Sacr.*
of the diuine maiestie , turned awaie her face,stopped her mouthe with hol- *was mini-*
ding her lippes together,and refused the cuppe. The deacon notwithstan- *stred to this*
ding persisted, and euen against her wil powred in to her of the Sacramēt of *childe vn-*
the cuppe.Then ensewed boakinge and vomit. The Sacrament coulde not *der one kin-*
abide in that defiled bodie and mouth, The sanctified drinke in the bloode *de.*
of our Lorde,brust oute of the polluted bowells.Thus farre he.

　　For the better vnderstāding of S.Cyprian obserue that in his time, and so
to the time of S.Augustt.yt was in vse to ministre the Sacramēt vnto infantes
B being chrystened, as to other of persight ageʔAnd yet yt was to this childe
ministred not vnder both kindes,but vnder the forme of wine onelie. For yf
yt had ben ministred before vnder the forme of bread,the like effect shoulde
haue folowed in the childe that folowed vpon that other kinde,bothe kindes
being of one vertue might and power. Wherfor yt was ministred vnder one
kinde,that was vnder the forme of wine,

　　Of this maner of ministraciō vnder one kinde we finde a goodlie testimonie also of the practise of the Churche in the time of Chrysostome,reported
in the historie of *Sozomenus* in this maner. *Ioanne Constantinopolitanam Ecclesiam* *Eccl. hist.*
optimè gubernante, vir quidam è Macedoniana hæresi, vxorem eiusdem opinionis habebat. *li.8.cap. 5.*
Hic,cùm Ioannem quomodò de Deo sentiendum esset, docentem audisset,dogma illius lau-
dabat,& vxorem quoque vt secum sentiret hortabatur. Cùm verò illa magis nobilium
mulierum sermonibus,quam illius consuetudini obtemperaret, & post frequentes admoni-
tiones vir illius nihil effecisset: Nisi(inquit) in diuinis consors fueris,neque in vitæ communio-
C *ne posthac eris.Mulier hoc audito,& consensum simulatè policita,rem eam famulæ cuidam*
communicat,quam fidam sibi esse iudicabat, illiusque opera ad fallendum virum vtitur.
Circa tempus autem mysteriorum (sciunt initiati quid sit quod dico) illa quod accepit con-
tinens,quasi oratura procumbit.Famula astans clanculum illi dat,quod secum in manu attu-
lerat . Hoc cùm dentibus admoueretur in lapidem congelascit . Mulier perterrefacta,
metuens ne quid sibi mali propter eam rem,quæ diuinitus acciderat, contingeret , ad Episco-
pum cursu contendit,ac seipsam prodens lapidem ostendit , adhuc morsi vestigia habentem
& materiam incognitam , coloremque admirabilem ostendentem, simulque veniam cum
lachrimis petens,viro suo consensuram se policetur. Quodsi hoc cuipiam incredibile videtur
lapis iste testis est, qui etiamnum inter clinodia Ecclesiæ Constantinopolitanæ asseruatur.

　　In the time of the good gouernement of the church of Constantinople by *The histo-*
Iohn Chrysostome, a certain man of the heresie of the Macedonians had a *rie of a wo-*
wief of the same opinion. This man when he had hearde Iohn Chrysosto- *man that*
m teaching what was to be thought of God,he commended his doctrine, *receaued a*
and exhorted his wief, that she also shoulde be of his minde.But when she *stone.*
D did more regarde the woordes of noble women , then his conuersacion or
maner in faithe , and after manie admonicions her husbande had doen no
good in her,he saied vnto her: *Except in the matters of God thowe be a companion*
withe me , thowe shalt not hereafter be a partaker of liuing with me. The woman
when she had heard this , and had dissimulatelie promised to consent vnto
　　　　　　　　　　　　　　　　　　　　　　　　　　　　　　　　　him,she

E

him she tolde the matter to a certain woman seruant whom she iudged to be trustie vnto her, whose helpe she vsed to begile her husbande. Aboute the time of the mysteries (they that be taught the faith, knowe what I saie) she keping still that she had taken, falleth downe, as though she wolde praie. Her woman seruant standing by her geueth vnto her priueily, that she had brought in her hande: which thing when she had putte to her teeth yt congealed into a stone. The woman being astoined, fearing least some euell shoulde happen her for that thing, which by Gods power had chaunced, she goeth with spede to the Bishoppe, and accusing her self, she sheweth the stone, hauinge yet the markes or printes of her bitinge, and shewing an vnknowen matter and a merueillouse coloure, and withall desiering with teares forgeuenesse she promiseth to agree to her husbande. Yf this thing seeme to anie man incredible, this stone ys witnesse of the matter, whiche vntill this daie ys kept in the Churche of Constantinople.

This woma̅ recaaued vnder one kinde onelie

As this historie ys notable: so for the pourpose yt ys euident that the Sacrament was ministred vnder one kinde, that was vnder the forme of breade. For the woman takinge that in her hand, and not minding to receaue yt kept that still and tooke some other thing of her seruant to eate, and so thought to haue begiled her husbande, so their was but one kinde receaued.

F

To be short, as of the learned yt ys testifieth, the maner of receauing vnder one kinde, whiche ys vsed in all the latin Churche vpon good fridaie, on whiche daie the preist receaueth the host consecrated vpon Mawndie Thursdaie, hath ben so vsed from the primitiue Churche. Wherbie as by that that ys before saied also, yt doeth well appeare, that the receauing vnder one kinde, hath ben practised in the primitiue Churche, notwithstanding the false reporte of the Proclamer. Wherfore, Reader, be not deceaued with soche bragges of vntrueth. For though he hath saied yt, he neither doeth nor can prooue yt, but stand thowe to the doctrine of the catholique Churche, who what she teacheth, she prooued to be true, as by this matter thowe doest perceaue.

The maner of receau̅ig vnder one kinde vpon good fridaie vsed in the primitiue Churche.

G

Thus hauing nowe ended the scriptures of the Gospell, with thankes to God, we ende this seconde booke, praing that yt maie be to his honour, and to the profitte of the Readers.
Amen.

A

THE THIRDE BOOK.

THE FIRST CHAPITER ENTRETH BY PRE
*face into the firſt text of ſainᵉte Paule that toucheth the Sacra-
ment and expѡndeth yt according to
the letter.*

Idymus, of whome, for that he was a famouſe learned man, ſainᵉt Hierom deſiered to be taught and inſtruᵉted, in his firſte booke of the holie Goſt (whiche worke ys tranſlated by ſainᵉt Hierom) conſidering howe great a matter yt was to treaᵉte of diuine thinges, and that therfor they aught with reuerence to be vſed, he ſaieth thus: *Omnibus quidem, quæ diuina ſunt, cum reuerentia, & vehe-*

B *menti cura oportet intendere.* We muſt with reuerence and great care, diligent-lie looke vnto all thinges that be diuine. Wherfore mindinge by Gods ay-de, to proceade in treaᵉting of the bleſſed Sacrament of the bodie and bloode of Chryſt, and of the preſence of the ſame our Sauiour IeſusChryſt, werie God and verie man in that Sacrament, with other matters therunto apperteining, whiche be in deed diuine matters, I wiſh not onelie vnto my ſelf in the writing, but alſo to the reader in the reading, that reuerence, that to eche of vs apperteineth.

And for my parte conſidering what I haue allreadie writen as con-cerning the holie ſcriptures, that they be harde and darke, ſo that (as ſainᵉt Hierom ſaieth) *Sine præuio & monſtrante ſemitam ingredi non poſſumus,* withoute a fore guyde and a ſhewer, we can not entre the right path of them. And for ſomoche alſo as ther ys (*the more pitie*) ſo great controuerſie of the matter to be treaᵉted of: I will not be ſo raſhe and irreuerent to the ſcriptu-res, to handle them, wreſt them, and abuſe them after mine owne phanta-

C ſie, but I will (as *Irenæus* aduertiſeth) haue recouerſe to the eldeſt churches, and learn of them the truth, and true mening of ſoche ſcriptures, as be cal-led in queſtion aboute the matter of the ſaid Sacrament, of the whiche I ſhall nowe treaᵉte. *Quid enim? & ſi quando de aliqua quæſtione modica deceptatio eſſet, nonne in antiquiſſimas oportet recurrere eccleſias, in quibus Apoſtoli conuerſati ſunt, & ab eis de præſenti quæſtione ſumere, quod certum, & rei liquidum eſt.* What? yf at anie time ther be a deceptacion of a litle matter, muſt we not runne or haue recourſe to the eldeſt churches in the whiche the Apoſtles were conuerſant, and of them to take that that ys certen and plain? Thys holie Father geueth ſo moche vnto the auncient Fathers, that yf ther were no ſcriptures he ſaieth, we ſhoulde folowe the ordre of tradicion, whiche the Apoſtles haue deliuered vnto them. *Quid autem ſi neque Apo-ſtoli quidem ſcripturas reliquiſſent nobis, nonne oportebat ordinem ſequi traditionis, quem tradiderunt his quibus committebant eccleſias?* What (ſaith *Irenæus*) yf neither the Apoſtles had lefte vs ſcriptures, did yt not behoue vs to folowe the order of tradition, whiche they deliuered vnto thoſe, to whome they committed the churches? Thus *Irenæus.*

D In whiche ſentence of this holie Martyr we are not onelie taught, that we aught to repare to the Fathers to haue our doubtes diſ-ſolued, and ſo to learn of them howe the Scriptures are to be vn-derſtanded but alſo for tradicions that be not written in the ſcriptures,

S ſ   for

li.1. de Spi ritu ſanᵉto.

Diuine thinges are with reue-rence anᵈ diligence to be hãdled.

Before in the begin-ning of the firſt booke.

ſrẽ.li.3. ca 4.

Doubtes in controuerſi es wher to be diſſol ued.

Ibidem.

Tradicion yt to be folo wed.

for the reporte of whiche, as wel as for foche as be in the fcriptures, we muft **E**
credit the Fathers. So that yt ys of this holie martyr to be learned, howe
moche the elders are to be efteemed, howe moche to be credited, and howe
for certen knowledge of thinges that be in doubte and controuerfie they
muft be confulted with, which were in the auncient church before the controuerfie was euer moued. Of the whiche matter we reade a like counfell in
the tripartite hiftorie . Therfore as heretofore I haue not vfed mine
owne iudgement or phantafie in the expofition of foche fcriptures as
do fpeake of this myfterie by me treacted of : No more will I hereafter in foche as fhall be brought oute of S. Paule for the proof and confirmacion of the trueth of the matter of the bleffed Sacrament and the
myniftracion therof.

And firft, to take the places and fentences here to be handled, in order as
they are written by fainct Paule, we will beginne with this : *Nolo enim vos*
ignorare fratres, quoniam patres noftri omnes fub nube fuerunt, & omnes mare tranfierüt,
& omnes in Moyfe baptizati funt in nube & in mari, & omnes eandem efcam fpiritua-
lem manducauerunt, & omnes eundem potum fpiritualem biberunt, bibebant autem de
fpirituali confequente eos petra, Petra autem erat Chriftus. Brethren I wolde not
that ye fhoulde be ignorant how that our fathers were all vnder the clowde,
and all paffed through the Sea, and were all baptifed vnder Moyfes in the
clowde and in the fea, and did all eate of one fpirituall meate, and did all
drinke of one fpirituall drinke, and they dranke of that fpirituall rocke that
folowed them, whiche rocke was Chryft.

Yt fhall not be without profit, for the better vnderftanding of this fcripture, yf we do fearch the caufe why fainct Paule maketh rcherfall of foche
benefittes, as the Iewes receaued at the hand of God, at their departure
oute of Egypte, and in the defert. The caufe ys bothe breiflie and clerelie
declared by Chryfoftom, who asketh the queftion, and foluethyt thus:
Quare, & vnde incidit in hanc hiftoriam ? Increpabat eos qui temerè, & non
requifiti ad Idola ingrediuntur, pollutam comedentes menfam, & tangentes Idolo-
thyta . Et cùm oftendiffet, quòd duplex damnum illi inde fuftinerent, nam & **G**
infirmiores offendebant, & ipfi Dæmoniorum participes erant, & cùm per prædicta
fatis fpiritus eorum humilaffet, & docuiffet: oftendit fidelem fpectare, non folùm quæ
fua funt, debre, fed & quæ multorum. Volens eis incutere timorem, veterem hiftoriam
eis recenfet. Siquidem & illi magna de fe fentiebant, quafi fideles, & ab errore libera-
ti, & fcientiam affecuti, ineffabilium facramentorum participes effecti, necnon
& ad regnum cœlorum vocati. Volens ergo declarare quòd illorum nulla fit vtili-
tas, nifi adfit vita tantæ gratiæ refpondens, ex veteri hiftoria ipfos erudit. Wherfore, and from whence fell he into this ftorie? He did rebuke them whiche
rafhlie, and not being required, did enter in to the Idolls, eatinge the defiled table, and touchinge thinges offred to Idolls: And when he had fhewed
that they by yt did fuffer double harme. For they bothe offended the weak,
and thy themfelues wer partakers of Deuells. And when by the forfaied
thinges he had fufficientlie humbled their fpirittes, and had taught them.
He declareth that the faithfull aught not onely to looke to thofe thinges that appertein to himfelf: but alfo to thinges that appertain to o-
ther manie . Nowe willing to ftrike feare into them, he rcherfeth
the olde hiftorie vnto them. For they alfo did thinke moche of themfel- **H**
ues, as that they were become faithful and deliuered from errour, ad had ob
teined the knowledge of the vnfpeakeable facramentes, and made partakers of the fame, and alfo that they were called to the kingdom of heauen.

Which fa-
thers are to
be cofulted
within con
trouerfies.

Li.9.ca.19

1.Cor. 10.

Homel .in
dictü A-
poftli Nolo
vos ignor.

Why S.
Paule re-
herfeth the
benefittes
that the Ie
wes recea-
ued,
1.Cor. 10.

good religiö
without
good life
not auaia-
ble.

A uen. Willing therfore to declare, that of thefe thinges ther ys no profitte except ther be a life aunfwering to fo great grace: he doth teache them oute of the olde hiftorie. Thus moch Chryfoftom.

In whiche fentence ye perceaue the caufe of the reherfall of the benefittes geuen to the Iewes, and fo in that place recited by fainct Paule to be to put the Corinthians in feare, and to difwarde them from euell by the example of the Iewes, who notwithftanding the receipt of fo manie benefittes, for that they were ingrate and difobedient, not feking by an aunfwerable life to pleafe their Lord God, as he by foche benefites did pleafure them, God in them had no pleafure, but plagued them, and ouerthrewe them in the defert. Euen fo the Corinthians, who had receaued the verie thinges and true benefittes, as the Sacrament of Baptifme, the holie Goft, and had eaten the bodie of Chryft, and dronken hys bloode. Whiche benefittes wcre figured by the benefittes geuen to the Iewes, that yf they wolde be prowde, vnthankfull, and difobedient, and wolde not lead a life wourthie their vocacion, that God wolde after the gift of fo manie benefittes and

Benefites of the Iewesas they were fi gures of our benefites, fo their pla- gues of our plagues.

B fo great, as their demerittes required, haue no pleafure in them, but plague them and ouerthrowe them, as he did the Iewes. For as their benefitteswcre figures of our benefittes: So their plagues and punifhmentes, we figures of our plagues and punifhmentes, as Chryfoftom faieth: *Quemadmodnm enim dona figuræ funt, ita & fupplicia.* Wherfore fainct Paule faieth: *Hæc autèm in figura facta funt noftri, vt non fimus concupifcentes malorum ficut & illi concupierunt.* Thefe are figurs or examples vnto vs, that we fhoulde not luft after euell thinges as they lufted.

In 10. 1.Cor.hom 23.

Here by the waie to note, by thefe fcriptures ys ouerthrowen the wicked herefie of them whiche haue taught, that yf a man beleue in Chryft, and haue receaued hys facramentes, howe wicked fo euer hys life be, he fhall be faued. For here ye perceaue that though the Corinthians had receaued the faith and the facrament annexed to the fame: yet yf ther life and con uerfacion were not agreable and aunfwerable, that they fhoulde fall into Gods difpleafure, and neither faith, neither facramentes fhoulde auaill them

Faith with out woorks fufficet hnot in perfons of difcretiõ

C as Chryfoftome doth expownde.

The caufe thus knowen why fainct Paule recited thefe thinges, yt were not amiffe to knowe what thinges they were, and what commoditie or benefitt happened vnto the Iewes by thefe. Thefe thinges in nombre be foure: *The clowde*, the Sea, Manna, and the water that flowed oute of the rocke. Of thefe foure *Efdras*, reciting vnto God hys benefittes fhewed and doen, faieth thus: *And the readde Sea dideft thowe diuide before them in fundre, fo that they went through the middeft of the Sea drie shooed, and their per- fecutours threweft thowe in to the depth as a ftone in mightie waters, and leddeft them on the daie time in a clowdie piller, and on the night feafon in a piller of fire, to shewe them light in the waie that they went. Thowe gaueft them bread from heauen when they were hongrie, and broughteft furth water for them oute of the rocke, when they were thrftie.*

Foure bene fites of the Iewes nom bred.

2.Efd.9.

The diuifion of the read fea, wherof *Efdras* firft maketh mencion, fhall be perceaued to be a great wonderfull worke of God, and a great benefitt to the Ifraelites, yf the hiftorie of the fame be confidered.

The read Sea.

D In the booke of *Exodus* we read, that when Pharao king of Egypt, had, according to gods commaundement fent vnto him by Moyfes, permitted the children of Ifraell to departe oute of Egypte: he being a man of wicked heart, when they were goen, with might and force

Exod-14.

prepared to folowe them, and to perfecute them. Whofe mighttie armie, **E**
and great nombre of horfes and chariettes, when the Ifraelites fawe pour-
fewing them : and with all confidering the great ftrait that they were in,
hauing *Pharao* and his hofte behind them at their backe , and the readd
fea before them : So that ther appeared vnto them nothing but wofull diftreffe , and ineuitable perill of death, they were fore afraied and
caried oute to God. *And Moyfes ftretched oute his hand ouer the read Sea, and*
God caried awaie the Sea, by a verie ftrong eaft winde all that night , and made the Sea
drie land , fo that the children of Ifraell went through the middeft of the Sea
with drie feet , hauing the waters as a wall vnto them , bothe on the right hand,
and on the lefte . And the Egyptians folowed after them into the middeft of the
Sea , and God caufed the waters to return vpon them , and drowned them with
their horfes , and chariettes . For whiche great wonder Moyfes fange in

Exod. 15.

prayfe to God: *Flauit fpiritus tuus , & operuit eos mare , fubmerfi funt quafi*
plumbum in aquis vehementibus. The winde blewe, and the Sea couered them,
they fanke like lead in the mightie waters. *Filij autem Ifraell ambulauerunt*
per ficcum in medio ieius . But the children of Ifraell went on drie land in
the myddeft therof. **F**

The clow-
de.

As ye maie perceaue by this, what a great worke of God, and howe great
a benefitt to the Iewes yt was that fainct Paule in thefe fewe woordes fpake (that all paffed through the redde Sea)So was yt likewife that he faied,
that all the Fathers were vnder the cloude. Of the beginning of this clowd

Exod. 13.
& 14.

we read alfo in *Exodus* that when the children of Ifraell departed oute of
Egypt, that theyr iourney fhould not be vncerten, and they wander without
ordre, the Lord went before them by daie in a piller of a clowde to lead
them the waie, and by night in a piller of the fire to geue them light , that
they might go both by daie and by night. The piller of the clowde depar-

Benefites
of the Clow
de.

ted not by daie, nor the piller of fire by night oute of the fight of the people. This clowdie piller was not onelie a guide and a leader vnto the people: but yt was alfo a bullwarke of defence. For when *Pharao* with hys armie
did perfecute the children of Ifraell, the aungell of God, whiche went before the hofte of Ifraell, remoued and began to go behinde them. And the
clowdie piller, that was before the face of them began to ftand behind thē, **G**
and came betwen the hoft of the Egyptians, and the hofte of Ifraell. Yt was

Num.9.

alfo a darke clowde, and gaue light by night, and all night long the one came not at the other. Thys clowde did not onely nowe ferue for the commo
ditie of the Ifraelites: but further on their iourney in the wilderneffe, yt
was a great benefitt vnto them, as we read in the booke of *Nombres*, wher we
learn that yt *couered the Tabernacle allwaie by daie, and the fimilitude of fire by night.*
And yt happened that when the clowde abode vpon the tabernacle from euen vnto
the morning , and was taken vppe in that morning then they iourneied . Or yf the
clowde taried two daies, or a moneth, or a long feafon vpon the tabernacle, and remained theron , the children of Ifraell aboad ftill and iourneied not . And as fooen as the clowde was taken vppe they iourneied . Of thys clowde alfo fpeaketh the Prophet Dauid in the pfalme, reck
ninge yt amonge other as a great benefitte of God geuen to the Ifrae-

Manna.

lites, *Expandit nubem in protectionem eorum , & ignem vt luceret eis per noctem.*

Exd. 16.

He fpred oute a clowde to be a couering, and fire to geue them light in **H**
the night feafon.

Thus this goodlie benefitt fomwhat opened and declared, we fhal do the
like aboute the next, which ys Manna. Of the whiche we read , that the
xv. daie

A xv. daie of the feconde moneth, after the departing of the children of Ifraell oute of the lande of Egypte , the wholl multitude of the children of Ifraell murmured againft Moyfes and Aaron in the wildernefle, and the children of Ifraell faied vnto them: *wolde to God we had died by the hande of the Lorde in the lande of Egypte, when we fett by the flesh pottes, and when we did eate bread our bellies full. For ye haue brought vs out into this wildernesse to kill this wholl multitude with honger . Then faied the Lorde vnto Moyfes: Be holde , I will rain breade from heauen to yowe, and the people shall go oute and gather daie by daie.*

And in the fame chapiter yt foloweth: *And in the morning the dewe laie rownde aboute the host, And when the dewe was fallen, beholde yt laie vpon the grownde in the wildernesse fmall and rownde, and when the children of Ifraell fawe yt, they faied euery one to his neighbour: yt ys Manna. For they wist not what yt was. And Moyfes faied vnto them this ys the bread, which the Lord hath geuen yowe to eate.*

Thus God fedde the children of Ifraell in the wildernefle, wher they did neither fowe ne reape with this bread from heauen, of the whiche they
B had no lacke. This ys the meate that fainct Paule fpeaketh of that all the fathers did eate of . This ys yt that ys fpoken of in the Pfalme . *Et pluit illis Manna ad manducandum, & panem cæli dedit eis.* He rained downe Manna alfo vpon them for to eate , and gaue them foode from heauen . Of the wounders of this bread more fhall be faied in the next chapiter.   *Pfalm. 77.*

The laft benefitt recited of fainct Paule in this place ys, that they all dranke of one drinke that came oute of the rocke. Of this miraculoufe drinke we read, that when the children of Ifraell were in *Raphadim* wher was no water, the people thirfted, and therupon murmured againft Moyfes and faied: *Why haueft thowe brought vs oute of Egypt , to kill vs , and our children, and our cattell with thyrst ? And Moyfes and Aaron at the commaundement of God gathering the people together, Moyfes tooke the rodde wher with he fmote the riuer in Egypt and the redd Sea, and fmott the rocke twice, and the water came oute of the rocke abundantly, and the multitude dranke, and their beastes alfo .* And this was a miraculoufe worke of God, and a great benefitt to the Iewes. Dauid the Pro-
C phet enombreth yt fo among other the benefittes of God, doen for hys people faing: *Interrupit petram in eremo, & adaquauit eos velut in abyffo multa. Et eduxit aquam de petra , & eduxit tanquam flumina aquas.* He claue the harde rocke in the wildernes , and gaue them drinke therof as yt had ben oute of the great deapth, he brought waters oute of the ftonie rocke, fo that yt gufhed oute like the riuers . Nowe thefe foure thinges conteined in fainct Paules fentence being opened and knowen what they be , and howe they were miraculoufly wrought for the commoditie and benefitt of the children of Ifraell, and wherfor fainct Paule did enombre them : the letter of the faied fentence maye be perceaued.   *Pfalm. 77.*

Mater of the Rocke.

Exod. 17 Num. 20.

Sf iii   THE

THF SECONDE CHAPITER SHEWETH

*what thefe foure thinges doen in the olde lawe did figure in
the newe lawe.*

S thefe foure thinges before reherfed, were verilie doen in the olde lawe: So are they figurs of thinges verily doe in the newe lawe. The figure muft be like the thing figured in fome poincts, but not in all. Neither muft yt be in all poinctes vnlike, For then yt can not be a figure, as Chryfoftom faieth: *Neque omnino alienum oportet effe typum à veritate. Alioqui non effet typus: Neque omnino adæquari veritati, quia alioqui & ipfa veritas foret, fed oportet manere in fuo modo, & neque comprehende-re omnem veritatem: neque omni veritate deftitui. Nam fi totum contingat, iterum ipfa eft veritas: Si autem à toto deftituatur, & nulla fit fimilitudo confequenter non poteft effe figu-ra.* Neither muft the figure altogeter be vnlike or not agreable to the trueth, or ells yt fhould not be a figure. Neither maie yt altogether be like vnto the trueth, for then yt fhoulde be the trueth yt felf. But yt muft abide in his own maner, and neither in all thinges aunfwer the trueth, neither in all things be vnlike the trueth. For yf it aunfwer al, yt ys again, the trueth yt felf: but yf yt be deftitute of al, ad ther be no fimilitude of cofequece yt ca not be a figure.

Homilia in dictu Apoft Nolo vos ignor.

A figure what a thig yt muft be.

In feking therfore of what thinges in the newe Teftament, thefe thinges be the figures: yt fhall be neceffary to obferue, with what thinges they will moft aptlie agree in fimilitude, and yet not in all partes. This fhall be the better doen, if we firft laie before vs foche thinges as be in the figure. And for fo moche as fainct Paule in the reherfall of thefe figures, maketh firft mencion of the clowde faing that all our Fathers were vnder the clowde, we alfo fhall firft fpeake of that.

Commodi-ties of the Clowde.

As touching the whiche, I wifh that yowe call to yowr remembrace that that was fpoken in the laft chapter, yt was ther declared, that the clowd was a leader of the people in their iourney, fo that they wandred not in vncerte waies, but folowing the clowde they walked the right waie, euen both in their flight oute of Egypt, and alfo in the wilderneffe. Yt alfo defended them from the tyrannie of *Pharaò*, and his hoft, ftanding betwixt them and their enemies, fo that their enemies might not come to them to hurte them. A clowde alfo defendeth from the violent heat of the funne, and mitigateth the rage of the fame, moch alfo refrefheth the laboring man with the fhadow of yt. A clowde alfo geueth dewes ad rain to moyft the earth, wherby the good lie and pleafant fruites of the earth are brought furth. Thefe being the pro-perties, let vs fearche to what thing they maie be moft aptlie applied vnto in the newe Teftament.

Among all to no one thing maie they better agree, than to the holie Goft, as a learned writer faieth, expownding this place of fainct Paule: *Quod enim il-lis nubes protegens, conducens, ac refrigerans: id nobis Spiritus fanctus, actionum noftrarum Dux, & protector, libidinumque moderator, & extinctor.* That that the clowde de-fending, conducting, and refrefhing was vnto them, that vnto vs ys the holie Goft, the guide and protectour of our doinges and the temperer and extin-guifher of our vnlaufull luftes.

The clowd applied to tho holie Goft, as the figure to the thing figured.

By the clowde the children of Ifraell were ledde in their waie oute of Egypt through the wildernes to the land of promiffe : By the holie Goft we are guided oute of the feruitude of the Deuell, and finne, through the defert of this worlde and life, to the land of euerlafting blef-fe. By the clowde they were defended from the Egyptians : By the holie

A holie goſt we are preſerued and defended, from the armie of ſinnes and wic kedneſſe. Vnder the clowde they reſted refreſhed, and comforted them ſel ues after their labours and trauaills in ther iourney, and otherwiſe in battaill: vnder the holie Goſt, after we haue ſomwhat trauailed in the iourney of this life, and after conflictes and battaills had againſt the aſſaultes of the great Pharao the Deuell, the tentacions of ſinnes, we reſt and be refreſſhed and comforted by his grace, and made ſtrong by his bleſſed helpe to trauaill again and fight a newe fight. Oute of the clowde cometh ſwete and pleaſant dewes, and goodlie ſhoures of rain, wherby the earht ys moiſted, and ma de luſtie to bring furth good fruicts: From the holie Goſt, cometh the ſwete and pleaſaunt dewes of grace, and goodly ſhoures of godlie inſpiracion, wherby man ys made luſtie to bring furth good and godlie workes, and vertueouſe exerciſes to the glorie of God, and good example of his neigh bour. The clowd defendeth frō the heat of the Sūne ād mitigateth the raige of the ſame : The holie Goſt defendeth from the heat of filthie concupiſcen ce and luſt, and mitigateth the raig of them. In this cōpariſon then yt maie

B be perceaued, howe aptlie the one anſwereth the other : ſo that we maie very well call the cloude the figure of the holie Goſt, of the whiche yet more ſhall be ſaied, wherbie the matter ſhall more clerely appeare to the reader, hereafter.

The ſeconde benefitt that S. Paule reherſeth ys that the fathers, did paſſe *Tract. 45.* through the redde ſea. The redde Sea (as S. Auguſtine declareth) ſignifieth *in Joan.* Baptiſme: *Mare rubrum ſignficat baptiſmum. Moyſes ductor per mare rubrum, ſignificat Chriſtū. Populus tranſiens, ſignificat fideles. Mors Aegyptiorum ſignificat abolitionem pec-* *The reade torum.* The redde ſea ſignifieth Baptiſme. Moyſes the leader through the red *Sea a figure* de ſea ſignifieth Chryſt. The people paſſing through yt ſignifieth the *of Baptiſm.* faithfull. The death of the Egiptians ſignifieth the aboliſhing of ſinnes. Thus he.

In whiche ſaing of S. Auguſtin, we perceauing the thinges doen in the olde Teſtament to ſignifie thinges doen in the newe Teſtament, maie alſo by applicacion of the one to the other, perceaue howe anſwerable the one

C ys to the other, Whiche yet in ſome parte S. Auguſtine more clerely ope neth in an other place : *Rubet mare rubrum : Baptiſmus vtique Chriſti ſanguine con-* *ſecratus. Hoſtes ſequentes à tergo moriuntur : peccata præterita. Ducitur populus per deſer-* *Cōt. Fauſt.* *tum : baptiſati omnes nondum perfruentes promiſſa patria, ſed quod non vident, ſperando* *& per patientiā expectando tanquam, in deſerto ſunt.* The redde Sea ys redd, likewi ſe Baptiſme conſecrated with the bloode of Chryſt. The enemies folowing die be hinde their backe : the ſinnes paſt are deſtroied. The people ys ledde through the deſert : all the baptiſed not yet enioieng the promiſſed contrie, but hopping, and through pacience looking for that they ſee not, they are as in the deſert. Thus moche S. Auguſtin.

Chryſoſtome alſo moſt manifeſtly ſetteth furth this figure, applieng yt to baptiſme, as to the thinge by yt figured. And firſt he diligentlie noteth howe S. Paule to euery of theſe figurs, whiche the fathers receaued addeth this woorde (*all*) ſaing: all our fathers were vnder the cloude, and all did paſ ſe the Sea, and all were baptiſed vnder Moyſes, and all did eat of one ſpiri tual meate, and all did drink of one ſpiritual drink: In the which he noteth a *In dictum* great ſimilitude ād anſwearableneſſe of the things figured to the figures, and *Apoſt.*

D after applieng yt to the pourpoſe ſaieth: *Volens enim declarare, quod ſicut in Eccleſia* *Nolo vos* *nō eſt diſcrimē ſerui & liberi, neque ciuis & aduenæ, neque ſenis & adoleſcentis, neque in-* *ignor.* *ſipientis & ſapientis, neque priuati & principis, neque mulieris & viri, ſed omnis ætas*

S ſ iiii   omnis

omnis dignitas, & vnaquæque natura in Baptismum descendit, etiam Rex & pauper ea-   **E**
dem purificatione vtuntur. id quod maximum nostræ præsertim nobilitatis est argumentum.
Nam similiter & mendicus, & purpuram gestans ad mysteria admittuntur. neque in sacra
mentis maior istius quam illius est respectus : sic & in veteri conuenienter, omnes posuit.
Neque enim dicere potes quòd Moyses per aridã, Iudæi per mare transierunt, neque quòd
abundantes per vnam, & indigi per aliam viam, neque mulieres sub sereno, viri sub nube
fuerunt, sed & sub mari omnes, & sub nube omnes, & in Moysen omnes,. Nam transitus
ille futuri Baptismi tipus erat. Oportebat igitur primum figuram illam benè omnia figura-
re, quòd omnes ipsam tenerent, sicut & hic omnes ex æquo participes sunt. He willing to
declare, that as in the Churche ther ys no difference of bond man and free
man, neither of contrie man and straunger neither of olde man, and young
man, neither of vnwise man, and wise man, neither of priuate man and prince, neither of woman and man: but euery age, euerie dignitie, and euery nature equallie descendeth into the font: both king also and poour mã vse one
purificacion, The whiche thing ys a great argument cheiflie of our nobilitie.   **F**
For bothe the begger and he that weareth purple be in like sorte admitted
to the misteries, neither in the sacramentes ys ther any more respecte of this,
then of the other. So in the olde he hath conuenientlie vsed the woord (al)
for neither canst thowe saie that Moyses did passe by the drie land, and the
Iewes by the sea, nether that they which were riche passed by one waie and
the neady by an other, neither the wemen vnder the clere, and the men
vnder the clowde: but that they were all vnder the sea, and all vnder the
clowde, and all vnder Moises, for that passage was a figure of Baptisme to
come . Yt behoued therfor that the figure shoulde figurate all thinges
well, that all shoulde be vnder the lawe, euẽ as here all be equallie partakers.
Hetherto Chrysostom.

  Whom as ye perceaue to affirme that the passage through the red Sea
was a figure of baptisme : so haue ye also perceaued the one very liuely applied to the other, for that parte, and for so moche as they were compared
together . For whiche afterward coming to the very poincte of the thing,
he directly applieth the figurs to the things figured in theselfs. *Et poterimus te*   **G**
docere quomodò vetus ad nouum Testamentum habeat cognationem, & ille transitus ad
nostrum baptisma. Nam ibi aqua: & hic aqua . Lauachrum hic: & ibi pelagus. Omnes
hic in aquam ingrediuntur, & ibi omnes, Iuxta hoc similitudo est. Postea vis cognoscere
colorum veritatem? ibi quidem liberati sunt ex ÆEgipto per mare: hic autem ab Idolola-
tria, & ibi quidem Pharao submersus est: hic autem Diabolus. Ibi ÆEgyptii submersi:
hic autem vetus homo peccatis defoditur. And we can teache thee *(saieth Chrysostom)*
howe the olde Testament agreeth to the newe, and that passage with our
baptisme. For ther was water and here ys water. Here a wishing place, and
ther the Sea : All here entre into the water, and all ther . According to this
here ys similitude. Wilt thowe afterwarde knowe the trueth of the colours?
Ther they were deliuered oute of Egipt by the Sea, here frõ Idolatrie. Ther
Pharao was drowned, here the Deuell. Their Egiptians were drowned, here
the olde man with his sinnes ys buried.

  In this although Chrysostom hath sufficientlie shewed the agreement
and similitude of the figure of Baptisme with Baptisme yt self: Yet he staieth
not, but proceadeth by like applicacion to shewe the excellencie of the effecte or operacion of the one aboue the other, sainge thus : *Vide cognationem*   **H**
figuræ ad veritatem, & veritatis excellentiam. Vbi igitur est affinitas figuræ ad veritatem?
Omnes ibi, hic omnes. Per aquam sunt ibi, & hic per aquam. A seruitute liberati sunt illi,
& nos à seruitute liberati sumus, sed non ab eadem omnes. Nam illi quidem à seruitute
ÆEgytio

A *Aegytiorum, nos vero à seruitnte Dæmonum. Illi quidem à seruitute Barbarorum, nos ve-*
rò à seruitute peccati. ad libertatem venerunt illi, & nos, sed non ad eandem. Nam nos ad *The good*
multo clariorem. Beholde (saieth he) the likelihood of the figure to the trueth *lie effectes*
and the excellencie of the trueth. Wher then ys the affinitie of the figure to *of Baptis-*
the trueth? All ther, and all here. By water ther, by water here. They are de- *me.*
liuered from seruitude, and we are deliuered from seruitude, but not all frõ
one or the same seruitude. For they were deliuered from the seruitude of
the Egiptians : but we from the seruitude of Deuells. They from the seruitude of barbarouse people, but we from the seruitude of sinnes. They came to
libertie, and we also, but not to all one . For we came to a moche more honourable libertie. Thus farre Chrysostom.

    Nowe that ye haue hearde him speaking so moche and so plainly
declaring this figure of Baptisme, I thinke yt for me vain and superfluouse to adde anie thinge to his sainges as to make the matter more clere
and plain, wher all ys allready so manifest, except I wolde attempt to
putte some more light to the bright sunnie beames , whiche were me-

B re folie.

    Wherfor leauing this figure sufficientlie opened and declared we shall do
our endeuour to make that plain that foloweth in S. Paule, wher he saieth: *Doubtes*
Et omnes in Moyse baptisati sunt in nube, & in mari. And all were baptised vnder *that maie*
Moyses in the clowde and in the Sea. These woordes be somwhat obscure *rise of S.*
and dobtfull. For yf the clowde (as before ys saied) were a figure of the holy *Paules wor*
Gost, and the redde Sea of Baptisme, and Moyses of Chryst : Howe then be *des.*
they baptised in all these three? Again, seing that the redde Sea onely in this
scripture ys appointed as the figure of Baptisme, why nowe dothe he seem
to ioin all three as the figure of baptisme? Moreouer if this be but a figure of
Baptisme, why dothe he teache, that the childeren of Israell were baptised,
as though yt were very baptisme in dede, and not the figure? Yt semeth also
to haue some scruple that he saieth they were baptised in Moyses, as though
that Moyses were the institutour of Baptisme.

    These doubtes will be solued , if yt be remembred that to baptisme, besi- *The same*
C des the partie to be baptised and the vertues in him requisite, ther be three *doubtes sol*
principall thinges necessarilie to be had : that ys, Chryst the institutour and *ued.*
authour of the sacrament, or his ministre for him, or other depute in time of *Three thin*
necessitie to pronounce the prescribed forme of woordes of baptisme : The *ges necessa*
holie Gost, the woorker of grace in the ministracion of the sacrament : And *relie to be*
the water for the matter of the sacrament. That Chryst ys the institutour yt *had in Bap*
ys manifest, for he was first baptised him self in the floode of Iordan of Iohn *tisme.*
the Baptiste. Yf anie obiecte that not Chryste but Iohn did institute baptisme. for he did baptise in the wildernesse before Chryste was baptised or she *Math . 3.*
wed him self openly to the worlde. For yt ys written : *Exibat ad eum Hierosoli-*
ma, & omnis Iudæa, & omnis regio circa Iordanem, & baptisabantur ab eo in Iordane.
Hierusalem and all Iewrie and all the contrie aboute Iordane, went oute to
him, and were baptised of him in Iordan. Yt ys true that Iohn did baptise before Chryste, but he baptised not then with the baptisme of Chryste of the
whiche Chryst was the institutour: but he baptised with the baptisme which *Act. 19.*
was called the baptisme of Iohn, as yt ys in the Actes of the Apostles. So that
there were two Baptismes: the Baptisme of Iohn, and the Baptisme of Chryst
D The distinction of the whiche the saied Iohn maketh sainge : *Venit fortior me* *Mar. 1.*
post me, cuius non sum dignus procumbens soluere corrigiam calceamentorum eius. Ego
baptiso vos aqua, ille baptisabit vos Spiritu sancto . There commeth one stronger
                then

then I am after me, whose shooe latchett I am not woourthie to stoupe dow
ne and vnloose. I haue baptised yowe with water, but he shall baptise yowe
with the holie Gost.

Act.19.
The baptis
me of Chrisł
and of Iohn
distincted.

This distinction appeareth also in the Actes of the Apostles : wher we
reade that Paule came to *Ephesus*, and fownde certain disciples and saied vnto them : *Haue ye receaued the holie Gost, since ye beleued? And they saied vnto him,*
we haue not heard of the holie Gost, whether their be anie or not . Wherwith then were ye
baptised? And they saied, with Iohns Baptisme. Then saide Paule, Iohn verilie baptised
with the baptisme of penaunce, saing vnto the people that they shoulde beleue on him,
whiche shoulde come after him, that ys on Chryste Iesus , when they heard this they were
baptised in the name of our Lorde Iesus,

Thus then yt doth manifestlie appeare that the Baptisme of Iohn was not
the verie Baptisme, but raither a figure or a preparacion to the verie baptisme

Homil.12.
in Matth.

whiche ys the Baptisme of Chryst (as Chrysostome saieth) *Vide igitur quàm di-*
ligenter hæc expresserit. Cùm enim dixisset, quia venerit prædicare Baptisma pœnitentiæ,
intulit : in remißionem peccatorum, quasi diceret : Ego illis confiteri peccata sua, & pœni-
tentiam agere persuasi, non vt castigarentur omnino, sed vt dignius postea remißionis dona
susciperent. Nisi enim se ipsos ante damnassent, neque sanè gratiã requisissent. Non quæren-
tes verò gratiam, neque remißionẽ profectò assecuti fuissent . Ita istud Baptisma alterius, id
est, Christi Baptismatis præparatio est, & idcirco dicebat vt crederent in aduenïetem post

The Baptis
me of Iohn
preachedre
mißion of
sinnes, and
prepared
men to the
baptisme of
Chryst.

eum. See therfor howe diligentlie he hathe expressed these thinges , When
he had saied, that he came to preache the Baptisme of penance, he inferred:
in remission of sinnes. As who shoulde saie : I haue perswaded them to confesse their sinnes, and to do penance, not that they shoulde be all together
amended but that they might more wourthilie afterwarde receaue the giftes of remission. For except they had before condemned them selues they
had neuer sought for grace, and not seking for grace, truly they had neuer
obteined remission. so this Baptisme was the preparacion of an other Baptis
me, that ys of the Baptisme of Chryst. And therfor he saied that they shoulde beleue in him, that was coming after him. Thus he.

In this saing of Chrysostome two thinges are to be obserued : first that he
saith that the Baptisme of Iohn was a preparaciõ to the Baptisme of Chryste.
The seconde (whiche ys a proofe that yt was not very Baptisme, but a figure

G

or a preparacion) that yt did not remitt sinnes, Whiche thing although
Chrysostome doth here saie, yet more expressedlie he saith yt in the same
homelie : *Qua verò de causa ad baptisandi est missus officium? Et hoc nobis idem Bapti-*
sta declarat, dicens : quoniam venerit in regione Iordanis prædicans Baptisma pœnitentiæ in
remißionem peccatorum. Et certè remißionem peccatorum non habebat. Hoc enim munus il
lius baptismatis erat, quod postea Christus instituit. in hoc enim vetus noster homo cruci-
fixus est, ac sepultus. & ante crucem nunquam prorsus extitit remißio peccatorum. siqui-

The baptis
me of Chrisł
gaue remis
sio of sinnes
the baptis-
me of Iohn
not so,
whiche ouer
throweth
the doctrin
of Caluine.

dem vbique ipsius hoc sanguini deputatur. Idem enim istud Paulus affirmat : Sed munda-
ti estis, inquit, sed sanctificati estis, non per Baptisma Ioannis sed in nomine Domini
nostri Iesu Christi, & spiritu Dei nostri . Et alibi ipse dicit : Ioannes quidem præ-
dicauit baptismum pœnitentiæ , & non ait remißionis, sed vt crederent in aduenï-
entem post eum . For what cause was Iohn sent to the office of baptising? Thus
also the same Baptist declareth, saing : *that he came in the region of Iordane pre-*
aching the Baptisme of penaunce in remißion of sinnes . And truly this Baptisme
had not remission . For this gifte apperteineth to the baptisme, whiche
Chryst afterward did institute · In this baptisme our olde man was cruci-

H

fied and buried. and before the crosse, ther was vtterly no remissiõ. For trulie
this euery wher ys deputed to his bloode . For euen the same dothe Paule
affirme

A affirme : *But ye are clenfed : but ye are fanctified, not by the baptifme of Iohn, But in the name of our Lorde Iefus Chrift, and by the Spirit of our God.* And in an other place he faieth : *Iohn did preache the baptifme of penaunce , and he doth not faie of remiſsion : but that they shoulde beleue in him , that was comming after him .* Thus farre Chryfoftom.

By all this that ys faied of Chryfoftome yt ys eafie to be perceaued that Chryftys the inftitutour of Baptifme, that ys auailable before God for the remiſsion of finnes. And that Iohn Baptifed to penaunce, therby to prepare men, that they baptifed with the Baptifme of Chryfte, might receaue remiſsion of their finnes, for fomoche as they were penitent. Of thefe woourdes maie be gathered thefe differences of thefe two baptifmes . The baptifme of Iohn was a figure and preparacion of and to the very effectuall Baptifme of Chryft : The baptifme of Chryft the thing prepared for, and the true thing by figure fignified. The Baptifme of Iohn was in water : The Baptifme of Chryft in water and the holie Gofte. The Baptifme of Iohn was in water to

B penaunce: The baptifme of Chryfte in water and the holie Goft to the remiſsion of finnes. The Baptifme of Iohn was included in the Baptifme of Chryft, as the leſſer thing in the greater: The Baptifme of Chryft conteined the Baptifme of Iohn, as the woorthier thing maie conteine the vn woorthier, and can neithier be included nor conteined of yt.

Differéces of the Baptifme of Iohn, ãd of Chryfte.

Chryfte then the inftitutour of this Sacrament who leadeth vs from the Tirannie of the Satanicall Pharao, and the feruitude of finfull Egipte, and bringeth vs through the miraculoufe fowntain, to walke through the defert of this worlde to the heauenly lande of promiſſe ys as neceſſarilie required as Moyfes was to lead the people oute of Egipt through the fea into the deferte, to iourney to the earthlie land of promeſſe, who was the figure of Chryfte, as S. Auften hath teftified . Wherfor the thing figured muft nedes aunfwer the figure.

As Chryft the inftitutour ys neceſſarilie required: fo alfo ys the holy Goft,
C and the water, Chryft him felf teftifieng: *Nifi quis renatus fuerit ex aqua & Spiritu fanĉto, non poteft introire in regnum Dei.* Except a man be born a newe of the water and the holy Goft, he can not entre into the kingdom of God. Nowe then thefe three, that ys Chryft the holy Goft, and the water, being neceſſarilie required to the effectuall Baptifme , whiche ys the thing figured : The other three alfo , as Moyfes , the clowde , and the fea, muft nedes concurre in the figure, fullie to fignifie , that ys here fullie required .

Ioan 3.

The Iewes vnder Moyfes were baptifed in the clowde and the fea in the darke maner of a figure : The Chryftians in the holie Goft and the water in the clere maner of the trueth, as *Origen* faieth. *Antea in enigmate fuit Baptifmus in nube, & in Mari: Nunc autem in fpecie regeneratio eft in aqua & Spiritu fanĉto.* Before Baptifme was in a darke maner, in the clowde and in the Sea: But nowe in clere maner regeneracion ys in the water and in the holie Goft. This thē that ys faied wel weeghed and confidered the doubtes before moued are clerely folued, and the text thus farre expounded.

Homil. 7. in Numer.

THE

THE THIRD CHAPITER EXPOWNDETH

the refidue of the text : Et omnes eandem efcam
fpiritual &c.

IT ys to be reteined in memorie, that (as in the firft chapter ys faied) S. Paule in this fentence did reherfe certain benefittes of God beftowed vpon the Iewes, as figures of greater benefittes, that God hath and dothe beftowe vpon the chryftians. What the clowde and the fea did to the commoditie of the Iewes, yt ys ther declared: Likewife what Manna, and the water flowing oute of the rocke.

The feconde chapiter began to declare what thefe great workes and won ders of God in the olde lawe, did figure in the newe lawe, and finifhed three of them, that ys, what Mofes, and what the clowde, and what the read fea did fignifie. Nowe ther remaineth to be declared what Manna and the wa- ter of the rocke did fignifie, and of what thinges in the newe Teftament they be figurs.   F

In this declaracion yt apperteineth to me to mēbre, that in the firft booke in the 22 chapter, wher by ordre thefe two fhoulde haue ben declared, vpon confideracion that S. Paule did make mencion of them, and that I wolde not be greuoufe to the reader with the reading of one matter twice: I diffe- red yt, and referued yt to this place. Wherfor I muft, I faie, remēbre in the declaraciō of thefe two, to kepe foche ordre, as I wolde haue doen ther, and as I did with the reft of the figures ther declared. The ordre was by fcriptu- res of the newe Teftament and doctours to declare what thinges the figu- res did prefigurate. That doen, to declare what prophecies were of the fa- me, and them according to the minde of the holie Fathers to applie to the thing prophecied.

Omnes (faieth S. Paule) *eandem efcam fpiritualem manducauerunt*. All did eat of one fpirituall meat. What this one meate was, of the whiche they did all eate, yt ys before declared, that yt was Manna. Whiche thing alfo Chryfo- G ftome doeth teftifie: *Quia dixit de mari, et de nube, & de Moife: Adiecit preterea: Et omnes eundem fpiritualem cibum comederunt. Sicut tu (inquit) à lauachro aquarum af- cendens, ad menfam curris : fic & illi à mari afcendentes, ad menfam venere nouam, & admirabilem. De Manna loquor*. By caufe he had fpoken of the clowde, and of Moyfes: He alfo added: And they haue all eaten of one fpirituall meate. As thowe (faieth he) cominge vppe frō the wafhing place of the waters, doeft haft the to the table: fo they alfo cominge vppe from the fea, came to a newe and a woonderfull table, I fpeake of Manna.

In thefe woordes ye perceaue Chryfoftome to expownde this fame one meate, whiche all the Fathers did eate of after they had paffed through the red Sea, to be Manna. Agreablie wherunto S. Auguftin alfo fpeaking of this text of S. Paule, whiche we haue nowe in hande faieth thus: *Quando autē man-* dncauit Manna populus Ifraël? Cùm tranfiffet mare rubrum. When did the people of Ifraell eate Manna? When they had paffed through the red fea. And a litle af ter he faieth : *Si ergo figura maris tantum valuit, fpecies Baptifmi quantum valebit? Si quod geftum eft in figura, traiectum populum ad Manna perduxit, quid exhibebit Chriftus in veritate Baptifmi fui traiecto per eum populo fuo?* Yf then the figure of the H Sea was of fo great force : of what force fhall the veritie of the Baptifme be? Yf that was doen in figure did bring the people that was ledde ouer vnto Manna: what will Chryft in the veritie of his baptifme geue vnto his people led

Tract. 11. in Ioan.

A led and cõducted by him? Manna then, as by the holy Fathers we are taught was the meate that all the Fathers did eate of.

But yt ys to be conſidered whie ſainct Paule did call yt ſpirituall meat, ſeing yt was ſenſible and corporall, and did corporallie feade: He dothe ſo call yt, bicauſe yt was miraculouſlie geuen vnto them, as ſainct *Thomas* in the expoſition of this ſame text ſaieth: *Vocat eam ſpiritualem, cùm eſſet corporalis, & miraculosè fuit data.* He calleth that meat ſpirituall, when yet yt was corporall, bicauſe yt was miraculouſlie geuen. The like cauſe why yt was called ſpirituall, doth Chryſoſtome alſo aſſign: *Quamuis quæ dabantur in ſenſu perciperentur, ſpiritualiter tamen dabantur, non ſecundùm naturam conſequentium, ſed ſecundùm muneris gratiam.* Although thoſe thinges whiche were geuen were perceaued in ſenſe or ſenſiblie: yet they were geuen ſpirituallie, not according to the courſe of nature, but after the gifte of grace: For although Manna were a corporall thinge: yet yt was made by God in the cloudes by his eſpeciall worke cauſing yt to fall, as yt were dewe vpon the earth, whiche thing we ſee not

B to be doen by common courſe of nature, for that the like ys not nowe done. So that yt maie well be called a ſpirituall, meat bicauſe yt had no naturall cauſe.

As their meat whiche God ſent them in the deſert was ſpirituall: ſo was alſo ther drinke in the deſert ſpirituall. Wherfore ſainct Paule ſaieth: *Et omnes eundem potum ſpiritualem biberunt.* And all drank of one ſpirituall drinke. Thys drinke ys called ſpirituall, bicauſe yt was miraculouſlie geuen them oute of the rocke, by the powre and worke of the ſpirituall rocke which was Chryſt, as S. Paule immediatelie declareth: *Bibebant de ſpirituali conſequente eos petra: Petra autem erat Chriſtus.* They dranke of that ſpirituall Rocke that folowed them. The Rocke was Chryſte. Yt ys moch againſt nature that an harde and a drie ſtone ſhoulde bring furth ſtreames of water, that ys both ſofte and moiſt. So ys yt againſt nature, that the great rocke, whiche once gaue them water ſhoulde folowe them, through the deſert, and geue them drinke ſufficient for ſo great a multitude of people, at all times and places. But as the ſpi-

C rituall Rocke Chryſte by his great powre and work gaue them guſſhing ſtreames of water in great plentie to ſerue their neceſsitie in that place oute of a materiall ſtóne or rocke: So did that ſpirituall rocke alſo, and not that materiall rocke, folowe them in their iourncie through the deſert, and gaue them drinke ſufficient to ſatiſfie their neceſsitie. Whiche thing ſainct Paule very plainly by expreſſe woordes ſaieth: *Bibebant de ſpirituali conſequente eos petra.* They dranke of the ſpirituall rocke that folowed them, *Petra autem erat Chriſtus,* but that Rocke was Chryſt. Note that ſainct Paule ſaieth not, they dranke of that materiall rocke: but they dranke of a ſpirituall rocke, whiche folowed them, which ſpirituall Rocke was Chryſt.

I wiſhe this to be well noted here bicauſe Oecolampadius the Archenemie of the Sacrament of the bodie and blood of Chryſt, affirmeth this text of ſainct Paule (*the rocke was Chryſt*) to be a figuratiue ſpeache. And vſeth yt for his probaciõ to proue the ſaing of Chryſt (*This ys my bodie*) to be alſo a figuratiue ſpeache. Nowe forſomoche as this text ys here to be expownded being nowe in handling, yt ys meet that yt be not onelie expownded in the natiue ſenſe, but alſo deliuered from all adulterine and violent expoſitions

D whiche the ſaied Oecolãpadius wolde wreſt yt vnto, for a further miſcheif. Let vs therfor heare his woordes, and examin his expoſitiõ and ſee yf the text of the ſcripture will beare yt. His woordes be theſe: *Tẽpus eſt vt probemus verba cœne Dominicæ eodẽ tropo dicta, quo illa quæ Apoſtolus dixit: Petra autẽ erat Chriſtus, hoc eſt*

Tt   *Petra*

Tho. Aqui ʃn. 10. Cor.

ʃn. 10. 1. Cor.

Manna why it was called a ſpirituall meat.

Water of the rock. why yt was called ſpirituall drinke.

Oecolãp. abuſeth S. Paules wordes: Thē rock was Chryſte

Oecolãp. in Expſitiõ Hoc eſt. Corpus.

*petra ſignificabatChriſtum,vel erat figura Chriſti.*Yt ys time(*ſaieth he*)that we proue **E**
the woordes of the Lordes ſupper,to be ſpoken by the ſame figure, by the
whiche the woordes which the Apoſtle ſaied are ſpoken:*The rocke was Chryſte,*
that ys to ſaie,the rock ſignified Chryſte:or the rocke was a figure of Chriſt.
Thus he.

Theſe wor
des:The
rocke was
Chryſte cã
not be expo
wnded by
a Trope.
　　Yf *Oecolampadius* will haue the woords of Chryſt,*This ys my bodie,* vnderſtan
ded with the ſame ſenſe that theſe woordes of S.Paule,*The rocke was Chryſt,*are
to be vnderſtanded,I ſhall ioin with him.For the woordes of S. Paule are to
be vnderſtanded withoute trope.And by that parte of his argument , ſo are
the woordes of the Lordes ſupper (as he termeth them) wherin I ſaie, I ſhall
ioin with him.That the woordes of S.Paule are to be vnderſtanded without
trope,yt ysmanifeſt,for he calleth not Chryſte the materiall rock,but theſpi
rituall rock,ſaing,that they dranke all of the ſpirituall rocke,which ysChryſt.
So that this ſentence: Chryſt ys the ſpirituall rocke, of the whiche the Iewes did drinke neadeth no tropicall or figuratiue ſenſe to be expownded **F**
by.Neither in this place and maner as S.Paule ſpeaketh yt,can yt beare a figuratiue ſenſe, as *Oecolampadius* wolde patche and peice one to yt,but the
plain literall ſenſe.

Chryſo.in
10.1.Cor.
　　To this vnderſtanding of this text, as the ſcripture yt ſelf enforceth vs ,ſo
ys alſo Chryſoſtome a wittneſſe,writing vpon this text thus : *Cùm dixiſſet
quòd potum ſpiritualem bibebant,addidit:Bibebant enim de ſpirituali conſequente eos petra,& adiunxit:Petra autem erat Chriſtus.Non enim ipſius petrae natura aqua* (inquit)
*ſcaturiebat.Siquidem ante etiam ſcaturiiſſet,ſed alia quaedam ſpiritalis petra, omnia opera-
ta eſt,hoc eſt Chriſtus,qui praſens vbique omnia fecit miracula. Ideo dixit , conſequente.*
When he had ſaied that they dranke ſpirituall drinke,he added:*They dranke
of the ſpirituall rocke, that folowed them ,*and ioined to yt : *That rocke was Chryſte.*

Chryſte
was theſpi
rituall not
the materi-
allroſk,ãd
therfor no
figure ys in
S.Paules
ſaing.
For not the nature of that ſtone (*ſaieth he*) flowed oute water , for then yt
wolde haue flowed oute before that time, but an other certain ſpirituall
ſtone wrought all theſe thinges, that ys, Chryſt being preſent euery wher
did all the miracles,and therfor he ſaied,*that folowed.*Hitherto Chryſoſtome **G**
Whoſe woordes geue plain teſtimonie to the woordes of ſainct Paule:
Chryſt was the roke , not the materiall rocke,for than *Oecolampadius* trope muſt
nedes haue taken place.But he ſaieth that Chryſte was that ſpirituall rocke
of the whiche they dranke, and therfore no trope can be admitted here.
And to proue that ſainct Paule ment that Chryſt was that ſpirituall rocke,
Chryſoſtome noteth ſainge·*Ideo dixit,Conſequente:*Therfor ſaied Paule,*whiche
folowed::*as who might ſaie,for ſo moche as ſainct Paule ſaieth that the Iewes
dranke of a ſpirituall rocke,whiche ſpirituall rocke was ſoche one as did folowe them.But no other rocke did folowe them ſaue Chryſt:wherfore Chry
ſte was the ſpirituall rocke, ſo that we maie conclude that this propoſition
ys to be vnderſtanded grammaticallie or literallie,and not tropicallie or figu
ratiuelie.Yf then *Oecolampadius* laie his fundacion of his building to proue

Scriptures
alleaged by
Oecolãp.to
proue hisfi
guratiue
ſpeache.
the woordes of the Lordes ſupper to be figuratiue vpon a wrong vnderſtanding of the ſcriptures:will he not(*trowe ye*)make his building of the ſame nature,that ys,that theſe woordes of Chryſt ſhal be wrong vnderſtanded alſo?
Which thing(I doubte not)but ye will credite,when ye ſhall perceaue how
wel he frameth other ſcriptures to his building.

　　Proceading in his profe he ſaieth:that yt ys comõ in the ſcripturesthat the **H**
figures of thinges ſhall be named with the names of the thinges of whiche
they be figures.To proue this he bringeth in the fierie tounges,which appea
red vpon the Diſciples : The doue whiche appeared vpon Chryſt at hys
　　　　　　　　　　　　　　　　　　　　　　　　　　　　　　　Baptiſm

A Baptifm.The breathing of Chryſt vpon his Apoſtles:and the ſaing of Chryſt
that Iohn was Helias,al whiche he ſaieth,be figures,as the fierie tounges,the
doue,and the breathing of Chryſt were tokens or figurs of the holy Goſt:
and Iohn a figure of Helyas.

Oecolamp.
his abuſing
of the ſcrip
tures ope-
ned.

Wher firſt note howe he abuſeth the ſcripturs, and laboureth to blinde
and deceaue the reader.   For wher he, pretending to proue this ſaing of
Chryſte (*This ys my bodie*)to be figuratiuely ſpoken,bringeth in theſe reherſed
places:ther ys not one of them that hath the like enunciacion or maner of
ſpeache,as the ſaing of Chryſt hath.Neither ys the fiery tounges, the doue,
or the breathing of Chryſt named in the ſcriptures to be the holie Goſt, as
the other thing ys named to be the bodie of Chryſt.And that this maie manifeſtlie appeare,I will ſimplie bring in euery of the ſcriptures of theſe places

Act.2.

The firſt ys in the Actes of the Apoſtles where we reade thus:*Factus eſt re-*
pentè de cœlo ſonus tanquam aduenientis ſpiritus vehementis, & repleuit totam domum
vbi erant ſedentes,& apparuerunt illis diſpartitæ linguæ,tanquam ignis,ſeditque ſuper ſin-
*gulos eorum.*And ſodenly ther came a ſownde from heauen,as yt had ben the

B comminge of a mightie winde,and yt filled all the houſe wher they ſatte.And
ther appeared vnto them cloauē tounges,like as they had ben of fire, and yt
ſatte vpon eche of them.*This ys the text.*Note nowe what Chryſoſtome ſhall

In.2. Act.

ſaie vpon this this text *Viſæ ſunt(inquit)illis diſpartitæ linguæ, velut igneæ. Rectè vbi-*
que additum eſt,velut,ne quid ſenſibile de Spiritu ſuſpicareris,velut igneæ(inquit) & ve-
lut flatus.Nec enim ventus erat ſimpliciter per aerem diffuſus.Ac tamen cum Ioanni de-
beret innoteſcere Spiritus velut columbæ ſpecie in caput Chriſti venit. Nunc verò cum tota

Fierie toun
ges are not
ſaied to be
the holie
Goſt.

*multitudo conuertenda eſſet ad fidem,venit in ſpecie ignis.*And ther were ſecn (ſaieth
he)to them cloauē tounges as fiery.Yt ys in euery place added(*as*) that thow
ſhouldeſt ſuſpecte nothing ſenſible of the ſpirit. As fiery (ſaieth he) and as a
winde.Neither was yt the winde ſimplie diffuſed by the aier.And alſo when
the holy Goſt wolde be knowen to Iohn,he came in the forme of a doue
vpon the headde of Chryſte,but nowe when all the multitude was to be
conuerted to the faith,he cam in the ſhape or forme of fire. Thus Chryſoſt.

C Now albeit he hath in the ende of his ſentence reſolued vs for the maner
of the cominge down of the holie Goſte in the likeneſſe of a doue : yet will
we heare the ſcripture,that the agrement of the doctour and the ſcripture

Luc.3.

manie appeare together.S.Luke ſaieth *Ieſu baptiſato,& orante apertum eſt cœlum,*
& deſcendit Spiritus ſanctus corporali ſpecie ſicut columba in ipſum. When Ieſus was
baptiſed,and did praie,the heauē was opened,ād the holie Goſt came down
in a bodilie ſhape like a doue vpon him.In this text,as ye perceaue that the

The doueys
not ſaied to
be the holie
Goſt.

holie Goſt came downe like a doue,but neither that the doue was the holie
Goſt,neither the holie Goſt the doue:ſo ye perceaue that Chryſoſtome a-
greeth,ād ſaieth nothing cōtrarie to the ſcripture.But as the ſcripture ſaieth
that the holie Goſt came down like a doue:ād that the ſownd was, as yt had
bē the cominge of a mightie winde,ād the cloauē toūges as thei had bē of fire:
So Chryſoſtom noteth in euery place to be this woord(*as*)wherbi eys taught
raither the likelihead of the thinges ther to be,then the very things thēſelus.

The thirde thing that *Oecolampadius* reherſeth ys the breathing of Chryſt:

Ioan.23.

vpon his Apoſtles:In the Goſpel of S.Iohn we read that Chryſt thus ſaied to
his Apoſtles.*As my Father ſent me,euen ſo I ſende yowe alſo.And when he had ſaied*
thoſe woordes, he breathed on them, and ſaied vnto them : Receaue ye the holie Goſte.

D In whiche facte of Chryſt,although the holie Goſt to the fullneſſe of his gif-

Ibid. 16.

tes were not geuen , for that Chryſt ſaied ; *Niſi abiero Paracletus non*
veniet ad vos , ſi autem abiero mittam eum ad vos . Except I go the

Tt ii   comforter

comforter ſhall not come to yowe: but yf I go awaie I will ſende him to **E**
yowe. At the whiche coming he promiſed them ſaing: *Accipietis virtutem ſu-*
peruenientis Spiritus ſancti in vos. Ye ſhall receaue powre after the holie Goſte
ys comed vpon yowe: yet nowe they receaued certain giftes of the holie
Goſte as Chryſoſtom wittneſſeth: *Non erraret quiſpiam ſi tunc eos poteſtatem quan*
dam & gratiam ſpiritualem accipiſſe diceret, non tamen vt mortuos ſuſcitarent, & vir-
tutes oſtenderent, ſed vt peccata dimitterent. Differentes enim ſunt gratiæ Spiritus. Quare
addidit : Quorum remiſeratis peccata remiſſa ſunt, oſtendens quod virtutis genus largiatur.
A man ſhoulde not erre yf he ſaied, that they did receaue a certain power
and ſpirituall grace, not yet that they ſhoulde rayſe the dead, and ſhewe
wonders, but that they ſhoulde forgeue ſinnes . The graces of the Spirit
are different wherfore he added : *Whoſe ſinnes ye remitte , they are remit-*
ted, declaring that he graunted a kinde of power.　Thus Chryſoſtome.
By this then yt ys manifeſt that at that breathing Chryſt gaue vnto his Apo
ſtles the holy goſt.

Let vs nowe examin the fourth ſcripture , which *Oecolampadius* alleageth
to proue a trope in Chryſtes woordes, whiche ys that Chryſt ſaied of Iohn **F**
the Baptiſt, that he was Helias. The woordes be theſe: *Omnes Prophetæ ac ipſa*
lex vſque ad Ioannem prophetauerunt, & ſi vultis recipere, ipſe eſt Helias, qui venturus
erat. All the Prophetes and the lawe yt ſelf hath prophecied vnto Iohn. And
yf ye will receaue yt: This ys Helias whiche was for to come: For the better
vnderſtanding of this text yt ys to be noted that the Iewes vpon the prophe
cie of Malachie, which prophecieth that Helias ſhal come before the Iudgement of Chryſt, miſtaking and myſunderſtanding the ſame, that he ſhoulde
come before his coming into fleſh, were in doubte whether Iohn the Baptiſt
were Helias, and therfore ſent Meſſengers vnto him asking, whether that he
was Helias or no. Wher in dede the prophecie ſpeaketh of the coming of He
lias before the ſeconde coming of Chryſte, whiche ſhall be to iudgement, as
the woordes do declare. *Beholde* (ſaieth allmightie God by the Prophet) *I will*
ſende yowe Helias the prophet before the coming of the great and fearful daie of the Lorde.
He ſhall turne the heartes of the fathers to their children, and of the children to ther fathers
that I come not and ſmite the earth with curſing.

Two things in this prophecie ther be, which do teache vs, that Helias ſhal **G**
be the percurſour of the iudgement of Chryſte, and not of his natiuitie. The
one ys that he ſhall come before the daie of the great and fearfull Lorde.
Chryſte at his natiuitie came, as *Rex pacificus*, a king a peacemaker: he came as
Rex manſuetus, as a lowlie kinge, as Zacharie prophecied that he ſhoulde do:
Reioice (ſaieth he) *greatlie, thowe daughter of Syon, be glad o daughter Hieruſalem . For*
lo, thy king cometh vnto thee, euen the righteouſe and ſauiour, lowlie and ſimple ys he, he ri-
deth vpon an aſſe, and vpon the fole of an aſſe. This to be fulfilled in Chryſte the ho
lie Euangeliſts do wittneſſe. At his birth alſo, as the prophet willeth Syon, ād
Hieruſalē to reioice: ſo the Angell appearing to the ſheperds, ſaied . *Beholde I*
bring yow tidinges of great ioie, that ſhall come to all people. And ſtreit waie ther was with
the Angel a multitude of heauenlie ſoldiers praiſing God and ſaing. Glorie to God on hight
and peace on the earth, and vnto men a good will. By this yt doth well appeare that
the firſt coming of Chryſt ys not fearful but peaceable, lowlie, and Ioyfull.

The ſeconde thing be noted ys that the Prophet, *ſhall come to turn the*
heartes of the fathers to the Sonnes , &c. Leſt when that Lorde cometh **H**
he ſmite the earthe with curſing. Chryſt at hys firſt coming , came
not to ſmite puniſh and curſe , as he himſelf not a fewe times doth
teſtifie : *Non veni vt iudicem mundum , ſed vt ſaluificem mundum .* I came
　　　　　　　　　　　　　　　　　　　　　　　　　　　　　　　　　　not

Act o .1.

In .20. Ioā.

The holie
Goſt was
geuen by
Chryſtes
breathing.

Math 11

Opinion of
the Iewes
of the co
ming of He
lias.

Mala. 4.

Zacha . 9.

Math. 21.
Mar. 11:
Luc. 19.
Ibid. 2.

The firſt co
ming of
Chryſte
was ioifull.
the ſecond
ſhall be ter
rible.

A   not to iudge the worlde, but to faue, the world. Again: *Venit filius hominis quære re, et faluum facere, quod perierat* . The Sonne of man came to feke and faue *Luc.19.* that that had perifhed. In fo moch that when his Difciples moued him, that fire might defcende from heauen to confume the Samaritanes , that wolde not receaue him, he faied: *The Sonne of man came not to deſtroye, but to faue mens li- fes.* All whiche places declare, that Chryft at hys firft coming , came not to *Luc.9.* iudge, nor to punifh, but to feke, and faue.

But hys feconde coming in dede fhall be fearfull and terrible. For then he fhall come to iudgement, at which time yf the heartes of the people be not turned, he fhall then be a feuere iudge, and fhall greuouflie fmite the wicked neffe of men, and fhall pronunce the fentence of curfing vpon earthlie men *Matth.25* faing: *Go ye curfed into the euerlaſting fire, whiche ys prepared for the Deuell and hys Angells.* Of thys iudgement ye maie read in fainct Matthew more at large. Forfomoche then as Chryft at that his feconde coming fhall be a fearfull Lorde, and fhall fmite the earth with curfing: yt muft nedes be that Helias B   muft be a precurfour of that coming and not of the firft. Nowe for that the Iewes where in that errour that they loked that Healias fhoulde come befo- re that Meffias fhoulde come in to the worlde, Chryft faied vnto them : *Si vultis recipere ipfe eſt Helyas, qui venturus erat.* Yf ye will receaue yt , this ys Helias which was for to come. Whiche woordes. Euthymius expowndeth thus : *Si vultis recipere, quod futurum effe dictum eſt, de hoc tempore, ipfe eſt He-* *In 1.Math lias, qui venturus erat, vtpote ipfum illius miniſterium perficiens* . Yf ye will receaue that that ys fpoken to be doen hereafter, to be of this time prefent: *He ys He- lyas whiche was for to come,* as one perfourming euen his very mynifterie and office.   As who might faie, Wher as ye thinke that Helyas (who fhall be the percurfour of my feconde cominge to prepare the heartes of the peo- ple, that they maie efchape my terrible iudgement) ys the precurfour of this my firft cominge , to prepare the heartes of the people to receaue me and my faith , as touchinge that office , yf ye will fo take yt, Iohn ys Helias. For to that office ys he by the prophetes appointed, as Helyas C   ys to the other.

So that in this maner of fpeache Chryft did but anfwer the opinion of the Iewes, and therfor did not affertiuelie faie , that Iohn was Helias, but *Chryſt did* with a circumftance: yf ye will receaue yt . whiche thing alfo ys noted of *not afferti-* Chryfoftome : *Significauit autem Ioannem Heliam effe , et Heliam Ioannem.* *uelie faie Vtrique enim vnam adminiſtrationem fufceperunt , et præcurfores ambo conſtituti* *that Iohn funt . Quare non dixit : hic eſt profecto Helias : fed fi vultis fufcipere , hic eſt.* *was Helias* He fignified Iohn to be Helias, and Helias Iohn. For bothe they haue taken one adminiftracion, and both be made percurfours. Wherfor he did not faie this ys verilie Helias. But yf ye will fo take yt, this ys he. Thus Chryfoft.

Neither ys yt the propre fenfe or vnderftanding of this propofition, that Iohn ys a figure of Helias, or Iohn ys a figne or token of Helias: as by this he wolde proue the other faing of Chryft : *This ys my bodie* to be vnderftan- ded, for that this ys fpoken with a circumftance, and as yt were with a condi- cion, and not fimplie as Chryft faied: *This ys my bodie.*

Now to applie all thefe other fcriptures, which *Oecolampadius* hath brought in : Marke diligetlie, I befeche thee, good Reader, yf anie of them all be of like D   fpeach as thefe woordes: *This ys my bodie.* The fcripture faieth not : *The doue ys the holie Goſte:* neither dothe yt faie that either the breathing into the Apoft- les, or the fierie tounges be the holie Goft, But farre otherwife , as ys allrea- die faied , and farre vnlike to this maner of fpeache : *Thys ys my bodie:*

For the one ys fpoken by a liklihead, and therfore vfed with this terme, as, **E**
the other by the very fubftance, and therfore expreffed with this woorde, *ys*.
And yet withall note howe yt pleafeth God, that as he made *Balaams* Affe
to fpeake to the reproche of her mafter: fo yt pleafeth him to woorke in this
man, who, through malice made dumbe to fpeake the trueth, willinglie, but
yet vnwittinglie hath broughtin thefe fcriptures, whiche being confidered and weighed make nothing againft the trueth, but moche for the
trueth.

Oecolãp. likned to balaams affe.

And firft wher he began his building with our text. *Petra erat Chriftus.*
The rocke was Chryft : whiche he faied was a figuratiue fpeache : yt ys
proued that ther ys none but a plain fpeache, for the fpirituall rocke was
Chryfte. Therfore yt ftandeth well to be applied to the catholique trueth,
that as the rocke was not figuratiuelie, but verilie Chryft : fo the fubftance of the Sacrament of the aultar ys not figuratiuely, but verilie
the bodie of Chryft. And as the holie Goft was verilie vnder a corporall forme like a doue, and verilie prefent with the fierie tounges : and alfo
verilie geuen to the Apoftles with the breathing of Chryfte : fo ys the bo- **F**
die of Chryft verilie, and trulie vnder the corporall formes of bread and wine, as the holie Gofte vnder the forme of a doue : and verily alfo geuen to
the faithfull, as the holie Gofte to the multitude. And vnder that corporall
forme as trulie receaued of the Chryftians, as the holy Goft was by the
breathing of Chryft, receaued of the Apoftles. So that ther ys a conformitie and great likelihead betwixt thefe fcriptures, and moueth the Chryftian
very ftronglie to beleue the prefence of Chryftes bodie in the Sacrament.
For as we are taught to beleue that the holie Gofte was vnder a corporall forme, bicaufe the fcripture faieth, that the holy Goft defcended in a corporall forme : fo are we taught to beleue, that Chryftes bodie ys vnder the forme of bread, bicaufe the fcripture faieth, that
Chryft bleffing the bread faied : *Thys ys my bodie*, and fo of the reft.
And as the fcripture faieth not that the doue, or the tounges were the holie
Gofte : No more dothe yt faie that the forme of bread ys the bodie of
Chryft. But as the fcripture teacheth that with thefe formes the verie thinges be geuen, and not the bare fignes onelie : fo are we taught that with the **G**
the forme of bread ys geuen the very thinge fanctified whiche ys the
verie bodie of Chryft himfelf fainge: *Take, eate, This ys my bodie.*

Prefence of the holie Goft vnder the forme vf the doue with the fierie tounges and breath of Chryft, conferred with the prefece of Chryft in the Sacr.

Thus maie ye perceaue, howe goodlie God hath fett furth hys myfteries, that one maie aptlie be conferred with an other, as that therby the
faith of the weake maie be moche holpen, and the faith of the ftrong
moche comforted and delighted, and the more when they maie fee howe
God turneth the weapons of the enemies vpon them felues, and fo withe
their weapons defendeth vs.

　　　　　　　　　　　　　　　　　　　　　　THE

A   THE FOVRTH CHAP. BEGINNETH TO DE
clare by the holie fathers of what thinges
Manna and the water be
figures.

Owe this text of S. Paule being truly expownded, according to the mindes of the holie catholique fathers, and deliuered from the violent wresting of the Aduersarie : yt ys time and place conuenient, that we seke of what things these two yet not applied that ys Manna, and the water, be figures of . That they be figures yt ys most certen: but of what thinges yt ys in controuersie. The Aduersarie affirmeth Manna to be onely of the woorde of God a figure, as wherby the soule of man ys fedde, as the Iewes were in desert: But the good catholique teacheth that yt ys not onely a figure of the woorde of God, but also of the bodie of Chryste in the Sacrament, wherwith man ys fedde to euerlasting life, and made strong to walke through the desert of

B this worlde, to the heauenlie lande of promisse . And for further openinge of this matter, vnderstand that one *Irenæus* wrote an epistle to S. Ambrose as king whie God did not rain Manna from heauen as he did to the Iewes. S. Ambrose answering him, treacteth not onelie of Mana yt self, but also of that whiche was figured by yt. And so in that processe, declareth, that not one- *Ad Irenæ um epla 62* lie the worde of God ys a spiritual Mana, but also the bodie of Chryst in the Sament ys Manna . Thus writeth S. Ambrose : *Quæris à me cur Dominus Deus Mannapluerit populo patrum & nunc non pluat. Si cognoscis, pluit. & quotidiè pluit de cœlo Manna seruientibus sibi. Et corporeum quidem illud Manna hodie plerisque in locis iuuenitur.   Sed nunc non est res tanti miraculi quia venit quod perfectum est. Perfectum autem panis de cœlo, corpus ex virgine, de quo satis Euangelium te docet. Quanto præstâ- tiora sunt hæc superioribus: Illud enim Manna, hoc est, panem illum, qui manducauerunt, mortui sunt. Hunc autem panem qui manducauerit, viuet in æternum . sed est spirituale Manna, hoc est plumia spiritualis sapientiæ, quæ ingeniosis & quærentibus de cœlo infundi- tur, & irrorat mentes piorum, & obdulcat fauces eorum.* Thowe askest me, why the

Quãto præ stantiora sunt hæc su perioribus.

C Lord God did rain Manna to the people of the Fathers, and nowe he doth not rain. Yf thow knowest, he raineth now, and dailie he raineth Manna frõ heauen vnto them that serue him. And in diuerse places the same corporall Manna ys nowe fownde, but yt ys not nowe a thing of so great miracle. for that ys comed that ys perfecte . But that perfecte ys the bread from heauē, *Howe moo he more ex cellent are these then the other aboue re- herfed?* whiche ys the bodie born of the virgen, of the whiche the gospell sufficient lie teacheth. Howe moche more excellent are these, then the other aboue reherfed ? Who soeuer did eate that Manna, that ys, that bread, they are dead. But this bread whosoeuer eateth, shal liue for euer. But this ys a spiritual Manna, that ys the spirituall rain of wisdom, whiche ys powred into them from heauen that be wittie, and do seke yt, and yt dothe dewe the mindes of the Godlie , and maketh swete their Iawes . hitherto S. Ambrose.

Of whom we maie learn as ys before saied, that not onelie the woord and *Oecolap. his shaful abusing of the aunciet Fathers, namelie of S. Ambr.* wisdom of God ys called Manna, but also the bodie of Chryste whiche was born of the virgen, whiche he calleth perfecte Manna. And here yt ys not to be ouerpassed that *Oecolampadius* the enemie of this Sacrament, who of indu-

D rate malice, wrote a booke against the same, in the whiche to the entent he might more easilie deccaue the vnlearned and simple, as to make them bele- ue that the holie fathers were of his side, he vseth to alleage diuerse of thē,

T t iiii   but

but fo that fomtime he doth wreft them fhamefullie, fome time he falfifieth them, fomtime he corrupteth them: fomtime he truncateth them : fomtime alleaging them and taking vpon him trulie to reporte them, he doth muty late them in the middeft of their fainge, as impudenilie and wickedlie he doth vfe S. Ambrofe here in this place laft alleaged, of the whiche, for that he perceaued yt made againft him, he left oute a fentence, whiche I haue noted in the margen both the latin and the englifh, to the entent ye fhoulde perceaue the fentence alone, and with all fee howe that wicked man ioined the reft of the fentence to gether, mutilating and cutting this awaie. This ys the finceritie of heretikes in handling of matters of faith and religion . And thus maie ye fee what credite they be wourthie of. By this ye maie perceaue alfo whether they offende of ignorance, of fimplicitie, or ells of deuelifh ma lice. Ys not this deuelifh malice, that feing a fentence in the middeft, that impugneth his herefie, he cutteth yt of, and peiceth yt together again, as though ther were nothing lacking? Did not his confcience (*trowe ye*) repre hend him whe he did yt? Ys not he the childe of his father Sathan, that feeth and perceiueth that this waie ys naught and wicked , and yet by gile and crafte will trauaill to induce men into yt, and bringing manie to damnaciõ, aggrauate his owne, euen as his father doth.

I haue thought good (*reader*) here to aduertife thee of their impoftures, that though they fett oute their doctrine with neuer fo good a countenance of holineffe, learning, and confent, or teftimonie of holie Fathers: yet be well affured that vnder the faire countenaunce of the enemie of mankinde tempting our mother Eue ther was a mortiferoufe ferpent, vnder his fwete woordes, which to well liked the hearer, was moft bitter falfhood and vn trueth. In that goodlie pleafaunt and delctable aple was cruell and horrible death and damnacion: fo in their faire countennance ye fhall finde ferpenti ne infection, in their woordes falfhead, errour, and herefie, and in the ta king of their doctrine or confenting to yt plain damnacion. But nowe that ye maie perceaue howe moche this fentence whiche denelifhlie he cutt of, dothe impugne his doctrine, and make for the trueth, I will fomwhat open the fame, and fo fhall ye perceaue that of fett pourpofe, and of very ma lice he left yt oute.

Vnder the fweet woor des of Here tiques lieth bitter poifõ of falfhead

S. Ambrofe anfwering *Irenæus*, faieth, that Manna nowe a daies, though yt be fownde in many places, at this prefent time yt ys not a thing of fo gre at miracle. He addeth the caufe: bicaufe (*faieth be*) that ys nowe comed that ys perfect. as who might faie: The figures of the lawe, though manie of thé, when they were in vfe, were great thinges, and femed to be merueiloufe: yet when the thinges came, of the whiche they were figures, they were not fo merueiloufe: like as the light of a torche in the night time , femeth to be a great light a very perfect light: yet in the daie the brigth beames of the Sunne fhining, and gliftering, yt ys but an vnperfecte and almoft no light: fo the figures of the olde lawe compared to the thinges figured in the newe lawe. Wherfor Manna being but a figure of that perfect thing the bodie of Chryft: when that once came in place Manna appeared to be but an vnper fect thinge.

When S. Ambrofe had made this comparifon of the figure to the thing figured, and fawe the perfectiõ of the one, and the impefection of the other the excellencie of the one, and the weakneffe or bafeneffe of the other, he brought in this fentéce which, *Oecolãpadius* left oute: *Quanto funt præftãtiora hæc fuperioribus* : Howe moche more excellent are thefe then the other aboue re herfed?

A herſed? howe moche more excellent ys the bodie born of the virgen, our ve
rie true Manna, and the right bread of heauen, whiche we feade vpon in the
Sacrament , then Manna whiche the Iewes did eate? And here note
again (*gentle reader*) that this wicked man, and other his complices, who
denie (*as ye perceaue*) the preſence of Chryſt in the bleſſed Sacrament do alſo
as wickedly teache, that the Sacramentes of the newe lawe geue no grace.
And to maintain theſe two euell and wicked opinions, they take the third
againſt the trueth, that all Chryſtes Churche receaued, whiche ys that the
Sacramentes of the newe lawe are of no more excellencie, then the Sacramentes of the olde lawe· For yf they ſhoulde graunt that they were more
excellent, then muſt they nedes alſo admitte the Sacrament of Chryſtes bodie and bloode to be more thē a bare ſign, figure or token of his bodie. And
ſo muſt be enforced to graunt the preſence. Nowe bycauſe *Oecolampadius* im
pugneth that preſence, and fowde in S. Ambroſe, that he taught, that the
thinges of the newe teſtament, are more excellent, then thinges of the olde,
and ſawe that he was preſſed with the weight of S . Ambroſe his argu-
B ment, he had no better ſolucion then clean to leaue yt oute, and ſo to ſhippe yt ouer.

Sacramēta ries to ma- in tein their hereſie de- nie the ex- cellencie of the Sacra- mentes of the newe la we.

Oecolamp. his beſt ſolu cion to S. Amb. argu met.

I truſt ye perceaue, that this litle ſentence of S. Ambroſe, left oute by *Oecolampadius*, dothe not a litle impugn his peſtilent doctrine, whiche he mainteined againſt the preſence of Chryſtes bodie in the bleſſed Sacrament, and
alſo ouerthroweth by plain woordes his hereſie againſt the excellencie of
the Sacramentes of Chryſtes Churche, wherbie I think yt maie wel appeare
of what wicked pourpoſe he left yt oute. And as in this he ys deprehended
to be a falſarie: ſo I doubte not but he ſhall be fownde the like herafter in
the ſentences, and ſainges of other holie fathers.

Nowe to proceade with S. Ambroſe, yt ys euident, that he calling the bo
die of Chryſte born of a virgen the perfect thing in compariſon of Manna,
whiche he meneth to be the vnperfect thing, (*as euery figure ys, in reſpecte of the
thinge figured*) that he doth vnderſtande Manna, to be the figure of our true
Manna, the bodie of Chryſt, our heauenly foode, and verie bread geuē frō
C heauen : whiche ys not ment of the bodie of Chryſte abſolutely, as the bodie onelie born of the virgen, but of the bodie born of the virgen, and geuē
vs in ſacrament to fede on, to our ſpirituall comfort . which thing S. Ambroſe ſignifieth in that ſame epiſtle, wherwith alſo *Oecolampadius* wolde not
medle, but coulde ouerpaſſe yt as yt were a thing in a miſt which he coulde
not ſee. *Oriente autem iuſticiæ ſole, & ſplendidioribus Chriſti corporis & ſanguinis ſacra-
mentis reſulgentibus ceſſarent inferiora, & perfecta illa ſumenda populo forent.* The Sun
ne of rightwiſneſſe appearing, and the bright Sacramentes of Chryſtes bodie and bloode ſhininge , the inferiour thinges ſhoulde ceaſſe, and thoſe
perfect thinges ſhoulde be taken of the people . Thus S. Ambroſe.

Manna, a figure of the bodie of Chryſt.

By whiche he dothe not onelie teache vs, that the ſacramentes of Cry-
ſtes bodie and blood are the perfect things, and the figures therof inferiour
thinges : but alſo that the bodie and blood of Chryſt, as in Sacramentes
(*whiche Sacramentes for the preſence of that bodie and bloode are bright and ſhining Sacramentes*) ys the clere light, of the whiche Manna, was the figure and the
ſhadowe. In whiche maner of ſpeache yt ys notable howe S. Ambroſe doth
magnifie this moſt wrouthie and excellent Sacrament, I wiſh yt of the Rea-
D der to be cōſidered. Yf that bleſſed Sacrament were but a bare ſign or figure
(*as they terme yt*) why ſhoulde yt be called of S. Ambroſe the bright and ſhining Sacrament aboue Manna? wher as yf yt were not for the preſence of

S. Ambro. his magni- ſieng of the bleſſed Sa. argueth it to be more thē a figure

him

E

him that ys the light of the worlde Manna in and hundreth partes were more wonderfull more excellent and farre ſurmounting the figure or ſigne of Chryſtes bodie, as here after ſhall moſt clerelie appeare vnto yowe. Wher fore we are not onely taught by S. Ambroſe that Manna was the figure of the bodie of Chryſt: but alſo that the ſame bodie ys preſent in the Sacramẽt of his bodie and bloode wherby yt ys made a wonderfull an excellent, and a bringt ſhining Sacrament.

Neuer the leſſe the ſame S. Ambroſe teacheth vs that the woorde of God, whiche he calleth the rain of ſpirituall wiſdom, ys alſo a ſpirituall Manna, whiche vndoubtedlie well and dewlie taken feadeth the ſoule. *Non in ſolo pane viuit homo, ſed in omni verbo, quod procedit de ore Dei.* Man liueth not by bread

Deut.8.
Math.4.
Thre kindes of Manna.

onely, but by euery woorde whiche proceadeth from the mouth of God. So that of S. Ambroſe yt maie be learned, that ther be three kindes of Mãna. Manna whiche God rained frõ heauen to the people in the deſerte, whiche ys the figure: Manna the bodie of Chryſt in the Sacrament, which duely taken feadeth both bodie and ſoule to euerlaſting life. And Manna the worde of God. whiche illumineth, nouriſheth and feadeth the ſoule, and moyſteth yt with the dewe of gods wiſdom, and maketh man wiſe in God. This

F

doctrine ys not diſſonant from the Goſpell for in the ſixte of S. Iohn, we are taught that Manna the figure was geuẽ to the Iewes, and that yt figured not onelie the woord, and the Godhead of Chryſt, but alſo his manheade whiche both are called the breades of life, as in the ſeconde booke ys declared. The declaracion of the figure, and applicacion of yt to the thinge figu-

Ioan.6.

red ys plainlie ſettfurth by Chryſte when the Iewes ſaied vnto him: *Patres noſtri manducauerunt Manna in deſerto.* Owre Fathers haue eaten Manna in the deſert. To whom Chryſte, minding to bring them frõ the bread Manna whiche did but nouriſh the bodie to the mainteinance of the corporall life, whiche bread and life in reſpect of the heauenly bread and euerlaſtinge life, be no true bread and true life, to him ſelf the true bread, and geuer of true life, ſaied: *Non Moiſes dedit vobis panem de cœlo, ſed Pater meus dat vobis panem de cœlo verũ.* Moyſes did not geue yowe breade from heauen: but my father geueth yowe the true bread from heauen. This text *Euthymius* verie liuely and plainlie expowdeth: *Quia putabant Manna eſſe panem ab eo, quod cœlum propriè appellatur, eò*

G

quòd ſcriptum eſſet, Panem de cœlo dedit eis, corrigit erroneam eorum opinionem. Nam ibi

In.6.Ioan.

ſcriptura impropriè aerem vocauit cœlum. Quemadmodum etiam dicuntur, volucres cœli Et rurſum: Intonuit de cœlo Dominus. Ait ergo: Non Moyſes dedit tunc nationi veſtræ panem, qui de cœlo propriè ſit: ſed Pater meus nunc dat vobis panem ab eo quod propriè cœlum appellatur. Nam ſicut Pater propriè dicitur cœleſtis: ita & filius cœleſtis, & pro-

Heauen ta-
ken for the
aier.

priè panis, vtpote cor hominis confirmans. Bicauſe they thought Manna to be bread from that that ys proprelie called heauẽ, bicauſe yt ys written: *He hath geuen them bread from heauen:* He doth correcte ther erroniouſe opinion. For the ſcripture ther called the aier vnproprelie heauen. as alſo the birdes be called the birdes of heauen. And again: *The Lorde thondered oute of heauen.* He ſaieth therfore, Moyſes did not geue then vnto yower nacion bread whiche ys from that whiche ys proprelie called heauen: but my Father geueth yowe nowe bread from that ys proprely called heauen. Eor as the Father ys called heauẽly: euẽ ſo the Sonne ys heauẽly, and called breade as cõfirming the heart of Man. Thus *Euthymius.* In whiche expoſitiõ this ys firſt taugh, that wher the ſcripture ſaieth, that God gaue the Iewes bread frõ heauẽ yt ys not

H

ment that he gaue thẽ that breade or foorde of Manna frõ heauẽ in dede, but frõ the aire, whiche in diuerſe places of the ſcriptures ys called heauen, as in

exam-

A the exãples yt ys ſhewed, ãd diuerſe other places maie likewiſe be prodnced.
A gain, vpon this ys taught the excellencie of Chryſt the thing figured aboue the figure. For wher the bread of the Iewes was but frõ the aier, our bread
Chriſte ys from heauen in dede, and not from heauen as a comon heauenlie thing, but from heauen as a thing heauenlie, as the Father ys heauenly
and withall not as a cõmon bread, but as a bread that ys proprelie called,
and ys heauenlie bread in verie dede, bicauſe yt confirmeth and maketh
ſtrong the heart of man. And yet immediatelie by expreſſe woordes this authour declareth as a cauſe why that Mãna was not the trewe bread, and ſpea
keth yt in the perſon of Chryſt: *Siquidem panis ille figurątiuus erat, me (inquit) præ*
figurans, qui ſum ipſa veritas. For that bread was a figuratiue bread, preſigura-
ting me (ſaieth *Chryſt*) whiche am the treuth yt ſelf. Here vnto agreablie
alſo ſaieth Chryſoſtome: *Panem autem ſimpliciter, & non verum illum appellat, non*
quòd falſus eſſet in Manna miraculum, ſed quòd figura eſſet, non veritas. He calleth yt
onelie bread and not the true bread, not that in Manna was a falſe miracle,
B but bicauſe yt was a figure and not the veritie. Nowe then as in the woordes of Chryſt comparing and alſo preferring him ſelf before and aboue the
bread that the Iewes had vnder Moiſes in the deſert, he declareth him ſelf
to be the thing figured by that breade, and that bread to be the figure: ſo
haue ye hearde theſe learned men expownding this ſcripture to teache the
like or raither the verie ſame.

Yf nowe the aduerſarie will obiecte and ſaie, that Manna was a figure of
the Godhead, but not of his Manhead, and ſo conſequentlie not of his bodie, for that theſe textes and ſcriptures ſpeake of the deitie or God head of
Chryſt, and not yet of his humanitie, as *Euthimius*, whom we haue alleaged,
doeth alſo teſtifie, expownding this ſaing of Chryſt: *Ego ſum panis vitæ.* I am
the bread of life. *Panis viuificans, & qui, vt dictũ eſt, dat vitã æternã. Nã ea proprie di*
citur vita quæ æterna eſt. Quæ enim ad tẽpus durat, nõ vita eſt, ſed vitæ imago. Panem autẽ
vitæ ſuã vocat diuinitatẽ. Siquidẽ ipſa panis eſt, quæ de cælo deſcendit. I am the bread of
life, the bread that maketh to liue, ãd which (as yt ys ſaied) geueth eternal lif.
C For that proprelie ys called life, which ys euerlaſting. That that endureth but
for a time yt ys not life but an image of life. The bread of life he calleth his
Godhead. For yt ys the bread that deſcended from heauen. Thus *Euthim.*

Yt ys true that all that Chryſte hath ſpoken of him ſelf hitherto, ſithen
he began to ſpeake of Manna, ys ſpoken of his Godhead. For ſo dothe Chry
ſoſtome alſo wittneſſe. And therfor we accept that that *Euthimius* ſaieth, and
graunt the ſame. But then I wold ye wẽt to the next line of *Euthymius*, ãd read
what he addeth to this ſentence, that ys nowe oute of him alleaged. Yt foloweth ther immediatelie: *Tandem verò etiam corpus panem vocat.* Afterwarde alſo
he calleth his dodie bread. Whiche he doth when he ſaieth: *And the bread*
whiche I will geue ys my fleſh, whiche I will geue for the life of the worlde. vpõ the which
text he ſaieth: *Duobus modis Chriſtus dicitur eſſe panis, ſecundùm diuinitatem ſcilicet*
& humanitatem. Poſtquam ergo docuit de modo, qui ſecundùm Diuinitatem eſt, nunc etiã
docet de modo, qui eſt ſecuudùm humanitatẽ. Two maner of waies Chryſte ys ſaied
to be bread, that ys to ſaie, after his Godhead and after his Manheade. Ther
fore after he hath taught of the maner whiche ys after his Godhead, nowe
alſo he teacheth of that maner whiche ys after his Manhead.
D Thus then yt ys manifeſt, Chryſte him ſelf teaching, and *Euthimius*, Chryſoſtom, with diuerſe other ſo declaring as ye maie ſee in the ſecond booke,
wher the ſixt chapter of S. Iohn ys by a nombre of learned Fathers expown
ded, that Chryſtes bodie ys called bread, and yerie well, both for that by
that

Manna was frõ the aier Chriſte our bread ys from hea uen.

Manna a figure of Chryſte oure bread. In 6. Ioan. hom. 44.

Iohn. 6. Euthim. ibi dem.

Euthim.

Chryſte cal led bread two waies.

Ioa:1.6.

that name yt aunſwereth the figure : And alſo as Manna ſedde the Iewes E
ſo in a more excellent maner the bodie of Chryſte ſeadeth the Chryſtians
he him ſelf witneſſing and ſpeaking of his owne bodie thus : *Qui manducat*
hunc panen, viuet in æternum . He that eathe this bread ſhall liue for euer.

Ibid.6

And here I can but merueill at the maliciouſe blindneſſe of *Oecolampadius*,
who trauaileth by all means to proue that the bodie of Chryſt ſeadeth not
the ſoule, and ſo wolde make Chryſt contrarie to him ſelf bothe in this ſentence laſt alleaged, and alſo in this ſentence wher he ſaieth : *Caro mea verè eſt*
cibus, & ſanguis meus ve rè eſt potus. My fleſh ys meat in dede, and my bloode
ys drinke in dede. But *Oecolam*. wolde haue that the ſoule ys ſedde onely
whith the worde of God, and faith and therfor ſpeaking of the fleſh of
Chryſte, he ſaith : *Neque opus eſt carnem in ipſam ingredi animam* . *Quod ne imagina-*
remur ſatis cauerat Dominus , *dicens: Caro non prodeſt quicquam*. Neither yt ys nedefull that the fleſh entre into the ſoule. whiche thing that we ſhoulde not ima
gen the lord did diligently prouide ſainge : *The fleſh profiteth nothinge·* And yet
Chryſte ſaieth: *Except ye eate the fleſh of the Sonne of man, and drinke his blood, ye haue* F
no life in yowe.

In the
xxxvi.
chap. &c.

I am loath (as in the prouerbe yt ys ſaied) *Actum agere.* to doo that thing
that ys doen all readie , and ſo with prolixitie and tediouſnes to greue the
readie. Wherfor all theſe ſcriptures of the ſixt chap. of S. Iohn being ſufficiently declared in the ſecond booke, and among other, this text whiche
Oecolampadius bringeth, in whiche ys (*The fleſh profiteth nothing*) ther truly by
S. Auguſtine. Chryſoſtom Theophilact and other expownded and declared
to be of an other maner of ſenſe, then he deuiliſhlie wolde wreſt yt to : and
ther alſo being ſhewed howe the fleſh of Chryſt ſeadeth and profiteth the
ſoule very moche : I ſhall referr the reader thither, wher he ſhall finde *Oeco-*
lampadius fullie aunſwered, and matter ſufficient, *I truſt*, wherwith he him ſelf
ſhall be ſatiſſied . Wherfor nowe I will but touche a woorde of *Oecolampa-*
dius wher he ſaieth : that the inwarde man ys ſedde by faithe. Yt ys a maner
of ſeede that I haue not redd in anie autentike authour. But this maie be,

Inward mā
ys fedde by
faith the
gloſe of Oe
colāp. tou-
ched.

and ys red that Chryſt and his woorde receaued by faith, doth feed the ſou G
le, but not faithe yt ſelf. Neither haue I red anie catholique authour that
teacheth that the fleſh of Chryſt entreth in to the ſoule, as yt liketh *Oecolam-*
padius whith his feigned ſpeache to dallie, or raither as a man in darkneſſe
goeth he can not tell whether: ſo he in this darkneſſe of hereſie ſpeaketh he
can not tel what, and wandereth he can not tell whether.

Ioan.6.

But to conclude this parte that the ſixt chapter of S. Iohn, or raither
Chryſte in that chapter teacheth, that Manna ys a figure of his bodie in the
Sacramēt, as before yt ys taught to be a figure of his God head, Marke what
Chryſt ſaieth in that parte, wher (*Chryſoſtom ſaieth*) he ſpeaketh of his bodie:
He that eateth me, ſhall liue by the means of me, This ys that bread, which came down frō
heauen. Not as yowr fathers did eate Manna and are dead. He that eateth this bread ſhall
liue euer. In whiche woordes of Chryſte ys made a iuſt compariſon of him
ſelf the thing figured to Manna the figure. of the whiche (as Chryſoſtom

Homil.46.
in Ioan.

ſaieth) he often maketh mencion, as yt were by yt to allure them to the faith.
This ys his ſentence : *Frequenter autem Mannæ meminit , & differentiam conferendo*
ad fidem allicit. Nam ſi poſſibile fuit, vt quadraginta annos, ſine meſſibus , & frumento,
& aliis ad victum neceſſarius viuerent. longè magis nunc cùm ad maiora venerint. Nam H
ſi in illis figuris ſine labore expoſitum colligebant, nunc profectò magis , vbi nulla mors, ſed
veræ vitæ fruitio. Often he maketh mencion of Manna and conferring the dif
ference, allureth them to faith. For yf yt were poſſible that they ſhoulde liue
fourtie

A fourtie years , without harueft, and corne and other neceffaries to their liuing: moche more nowe when they are come to greater thinges. For yf in
thofe figures they did gather withoute labour the thing made readie to ther
handes: nowe truly moch more, wher ys no death, but the fruycion of the
true life. Thus moche Chryfoftome.

*Why Chry-
fte made fo
often men-
cion of Mã-
na 90.6.*

In whofe faing as yt firft offreth yt felf: fo yt ys firft to be noted, that Chrift
often maketh mencion of Manna, but to what pourpofe? that by conferring
of himfelf and Manna, as the thing, and the figure, he might allure thẽ to the
faith of him, vnto whom the lawe, and all the figurs of yt did lead them . An
other that Chryfoftome by expreffe woordes calleth yt a figure. For(*faieth
he*) yf in thofe figurs they withoute laboure did gather that, that was readie
laied before them: moch more now, &c. By which he meneth Manna, which
God raining from heauen, and fo being prepared withoute their laboure,
they did but gather yt, and had fufficiẽt to ferue their neceffitie. Thus, *I truft*,
yt ys manifeft that Manna ys a figure of the bodie of Chryft, bothe by the
B woordes of Chryft himfelf in the fixt of S. Iohn, and alfo by holie learned
men in the expofition of the fame chapiter fo teaching vs , wherfore nowe
leauing yt we will repair to our text of S. Paule, and feke howe yt ys taken
their of the auncient Fathers. Likewife what the water that flowed oute of
the ftone, whiche for the moft parte are ioined together, did fignifie.

THE FIFTE CHAP. TEACHING THAT MAN-
*na and the water of the ftone were figures of the bodie and blood of Chryft by
Origen, and S. Ambrofe.*

C S our Sauiour Chryft hath taught, that Manna was a figure of
his bodie: And as he laboured with the Iewes by yt to make thẽ
to vnderftande him, and from yt the fign and figure of him , to
lead and bring thẽ to him the thing fignified and figured : fo S.
Paule trauaileth with his Corinthians by figures to vnderftand
the verities, as well of verie benefites by figurs of benefites , as of verie plagues by the figurs of plagues, that they fhould not be puffed vppe with pride, neither led with a negligẽce of holie life, now that they be vnder Chryft,
and haue receaued the great gift of the newe byrthe by baptifme, and haue
ben fedde with the bodie and blood of Chryft. For yf they did, thefe great
giftes notwithftanding, God wolde haue no pleafure in them, no more then
he had in manie of the Iewes, whiche were vnder Moyfes, and were baptifed
in the clowde and in the fea, and did eate of one fpirituall meat, and drink of
one fpirituall drinke, whiche were figures of thefe benefittes , but he wolde
caft them of as he did the Iewes. For they were ouerthrowen in the wilderneffe, of the which more at large was fpoken in the firft chapter. Wherfore I
will not now detein the reader but entre to the pourpofe, and heare the mindes of the fathers what they thinke of thefe figures, and whether they be figurs of figures, and fignes of fignes, or ells figures of verie things , and fignes
of thinges now prefent, and not abfent.

In this proceffe *Origen* for that he ys right auncient fhall firft be heard: *Mo-*
D *do enim cum Moyfes venit ad nos & coniunctus eft noftra Aethyopiffæ , lex Dei iam
non in figuris, & in imaginibus ficut priùs, fed in ipfa fpecie veritatis agnofcitur. Et quæ
priùs in ænigmate defignabantur, nunc in fpecie & veritate complentur. Et ideo ille qui fpecies figurarum, & ænigmatum differebat, dicit: Scimus quoniã patres noftri omnes
fub nube erant, & omnes mare tranfierunt, & omnes in Moyfe baptifati funt, in Nube, &*

*Origen. ho-
mil 7s in
Num.*

in mari, & *omnes eandem escam spiritualem manducauerunt,* & *omnes eundem potum spiritualem biberunt, biberunt autem de spirituali consequente eos petra, Petra autem erat Christus. Vides quomodo ænigmata legis absoluit Paulus,* & *species ænigmatum docet.* Nowe

Yf Chryst be nowe receaued in figure, he ys receaued as in Moyses lawe in darke maner.

when Moyses came vnto vs, and was ioined to this owre Ethyopisse, the law of God ys not nowe knowen in figurs and images as before yt was, but in the plain forme of trueth. And soche things as before were appoincted in a dark maner, now they are fulfilled in plain formād trueth. And therfor he, who declared the plain formes of darke thinges, saieth: *We knowe that all our Fathers were vnder the clowde, and all passed through the Sea, and all were baptised vnder Moyses in the clowde and in the Sea, and all haue eaten one spirituall meat, and all haue dronke one spirituall drinke. They dranke of that spirituall rocke that folowed them. The rocke was Chryst.* Thowe seest howe Paule openeth the darke thinges of the lawe, and teacheth the plain formes of the darke thinges. And after he had shewed of the rocke, the clowde and the sea, he cometh to Manna and saieth. *Tunc in Aenigmate erat Manna cibus: nunc autem in specie caro Verbi Dei est verus cibus, sicut ipse dicit: Caro mea verè est cibus,* & *sanguis meus verè est potus.* Then in a darke maner Manna was meat: but nowe in plain and open maner, the flesh of the Sonne of God ys the true meat, as he himself saieth: My flesh ys meat in dede, and my bloode ys drinke in dede. Thus farre *Origen.*

In the whiche saing of *Origen* ther ys nothing (*as me thinketh*) to be desiered, either for the expresse maner of affirming Manna to be a figure of the bodie of Chryst, or ells for the presence of Chrystes bodie in the Sacrament. For yf the Iewes in eating Manna did figuratiuelie receaue Chryste, that ys, did eate Manna as a figure of Chryst, whiche *Origen* calleth the darke maner, then yt must nedes be that the Chrystians, who receaue Chryst in plain maner (*as*

Chryste ys not nowe receaued of the chrystians as he was of the Iewes: for then in figure nowe in veritie.

Origen termeth yt) must receaue Chryst verilie, that ys, not figuratiuelie onelie, which ys the dark maner, but verilie, that ys, substanciallie, and reallie, which ys the true and very maner, or ells yt were all one to *Origen,* and ther were no difference betwixt a clere maner and a darke maner, which were to moche absurditie to affirme. Yt can not therfor by the minde of *Origen* be saied that the Chrystians in receauing the Sacrament receaue but a sign or a figure of Chryst. For they shoulde them receaue him in a darke maner onely, and so shoulde Chryst be all one waie, meat to the Iewes, and to vs. Whiche ys not true, for he was meate vnto them figuratiuely, but to vs verilie, according to his owne sainge, which *Origen* alleageth: *My flesh ys meat in dede, and my bloode ys drinke in dede.* And so ys yt true that the very flesh and blood of Chryste ys reallie and verilie receaued in the Sacrament.

To *Origen* shall be ioined that the holie reuerend Father sainct Ambrose, who declaring howe the Chrystian people reioice and glorie in the excellency and honour of the table of Chryste, geueth to this matter a goodlie

Ambro. in psal.110.

testimonie. *Ille ergo antè despectus, iam præferor, iam anteponor electis. Ille ego antè despectus populus peccatorum, iam habeo cœlestium sacramentorum veneranda consortia, iam mensæ cœlestis honore suscipior. Epulis meis non pluuia vndatur, non terræ partus laborat, non arborum fructus. Potui meo non flumina quærenda, non fontes. Christus mihi cibus est: Christus mihi potus. Caro Dei cibus mihi,* & *Dei sanguis est potus. Non iam ad satietatem mei annuos expecto prouentus: Christus mihi quotidie ministratur. Non verebor ne qua mihi cœli intemperies, aut sterilitas ruris immineat, si pij cultus diligentia perseuerat. Non iam coturnicum pluuias mihi opto descendere, quas antè mirabar. Non Manna, quod antè cibis omnibus præferebant, quia qui Manna manducauerunt patres, esurierūt. Meus cibus est, quem qui manducauerit, non esuriet. Meus cibus est, qui non corpus impinguat, sed confirmat cor hominis, fuerat mihi antè mirandus*

panis

A *panis de cœlo.Scriptum est enim:Panem de cœlo dedit eis manducare,sed non erat verus ille panis,sed futuri vmbra.Panem de cœlo illum verum, mihi seruauit pater .* Euen I (saieth S.Ambrose in the person of the newe become faithfull Chrystians)before despised now I am preferred,nowe I am sett before the chosen. Euen I before a despised people of sinners,now I haue the woorshippefull companies of the heauenlie sacramentes.Now I am aduaunced to the honour of the heauenlie table. The raign ys not powred downe for my meat, the spring of the earth laboureth not,neither the fruicts of the trees.To my drinke neither riuers are to be sought,nor wells.*Chryst ys my meat, Chryst ys my drinke. The flesh of God ys my meate,the bloode of God ys my drinke.*Now for my satietie,I looke not for yearlie profittes.*Chryst ys euerie daie myniftred vnto me.*I will not feare leeft anie waie the vntemperatnesse of the heaue,or the barennesse of the earth come vpō me, yf the diligence of Godlie tillage do continue. I desire not now the raynes of quaills to descende vnto me,the whiche before I wondred at:NotManna, which before they preferred before all other meates.For the fathers whiche haue eaten Manna,haue hungred. My meate ys which fatteth not the bo-

Plain sain-
ges of S.
Ambrose
for the Pro
clamer.

B die,but yt maketh stronge the heart of man. Before the bread from heauen was merueiloufe to me,for yt ys written:he hath geuen them bread frō heauen to eate,but the bread which was not the true bread,but the shadowe of the bread to come.The Father hath kept for me that true bread from heaue. Hitherto S.Ambrose.

Of whome first,that ys here to our pourpofe we maie learn,that Māna was a figure of Chrystes bodie in the Sacramēt,for he saieth,that ytwas a shadow of the true bread,which true bread the Father of heauen hath kept for him. What this true bread ys he also sheweth,saing:Chryst ys my meate, Chryst ys my drink.And that these hys woords should notbe misvnderstāded bythe simple,or wrested by the wicked,he addeth as yt were an expositiō what he meneth by Chrystе,and saieth:*The flesh of God ys my meat, the blood of God ys my drinke.*And yet for that yt was forseen by the holie Goft, that the Aduersarie wold wreft these woordes, though they were thus plainly spoken,to eschew

Mana was
a figure of
Chryftes
bodie in the
B.Sacram.

yt he addeth where the flesh of the Sonne of God , and the bloode of the C Sonne of God,be hys meat and drinke,saing: *Iam habeo cœlestium sacramentorum veneranda consortia.Iam mensæ cœlestis honore suscipior.*Nowe (saieth he) haue I the worshippefull companies of the heauenly Sacramentes. Nowe am I aduanced to the honoure of the heauenlie table. In the heauenly table then , wher he hath the woorshippefull companies of the heauenly Sacramentes,ther receaueth he the true bread,that the father hath kept for him: ther receaueth he his meat,which ys the flesh of God, ther receaueth he his drinke,which ys the bloode of God. Which woordes do moft euidentlie proue vnto vs,that in the heauenly Sacramentes of Chryftes bodie and bloode myniftred in that heauenly table ,ys this wourthie and excellent meat Chryft,euen hys verie flesh,and hys verie bloode.

The flesh of
God oure
meat,the
blood of
God oure
drink , and
that on the
table.

In this breif opening of S.Ambrose woords (*which maie as well be perceaued of the vnlearned Chryftiā,as of the learned*)I haue not,Iam sure,diffentet frō the minde of S.Ambrose,no more haue I gone frō his woords,that the trueth might as yt ys appeare.*Oecolāpadius,*Whofe cōscience was cawtherifed hauing a prе- tēce of sinceritie in handling,of the scripturs,ād theFathers,but not in dede, as ye perceaued before:so shal ye nowe again, perceaue how wickedlie he D hath abufed S.Ambrose in wrefting him to his wicked pourpofe.

Oecol. hys
wrefting of
S.Ambro-
fe opened.

In this same fermon wher thefe woordes be written,which as ye perceaue be very plain, and of that force, that they coulde not well be wrefted by

V ii   the

the craftie engines of *Oecolampadius,*imme diatelie after folowe otherwoords, **E**
whiche he perceauing that he might wre st,left oute all this that ys before al
leadged,and tooke onely this thatfolowe th,whiche when yt ys applied to
this that ys before reherfed,then iudge(*R eader*)whether yt be not violentlie
wrefted from the true mening of faint A mbrofe or no.Thus he alleadgeth:

Ambr. ibid.

Mihi ille panis Dei defcendat de cœlo,qui dat vita m huic mundo.Non Iudæis, non Synago-
gæ defcendit, fed Ecclefiæ defcendit, fed populo minori . Nam quomodò Iudæis defcen-
dit panis, cùm omnes qui illum manducarunt, hoc eft, quem Iudæi putarunt Ma-
nna , in deferto mortui funt ? Quomodò Synagogæ defcendit , cùm omnis Synagoga
interierit , & æterno ieiunio fidei defecerit ? Denique fi accipiffent panem verum,
non dixiffent : Domine , femper da nobis panem hunc. Quid petis Iudæe vt tribuat
tibi ? Panem , quem dat quotidie , dat femper , in teipfo eft vt accipias hunc pa-
nem . Accede hunc panem , & accipies eum. De hoc pane dictum eft : Omnes qui
fe elongant à te peribunt . Si elongaris ab eo peribis . Si appropinquaris viues . Hic
eft panis vitæ . Qui vitam manducat , mori non poteft. Quomodò enim moritur, cui
vita cibus eft? Quomodò deficiet,qui habet vitalem fubftantiam? Accedite ad eum , &
fatiemini , quia panis eft. Accedite ad eum & potate, quia fons eft. Accedite ad eum
& illuminemini, quia Lux eft . Accedite ad eum & liberemini , quia vbi Spiritus
Domini , ibi libertas . Accedite ad eum & abfoluimini, quia eft remiffio peccatorum.
Qui fit ifte quæritis? Audite ipfum dicentem : Ego fum panis vitæ,qui venit ad me non
efuriet , & qui credit in me non fitiet vnquam. Audiftis eum,& vidiftis eum , &
*non credidiftis ei,ideo mortui eftis.*That bread of God defcend vnto me from heauen whiche geueth life to the worlde.He hath not defcended to the Iewes,
not to the Synagoge:but he hath defcended to the Church:he hath defcen
ded to the inferiour people. For howe hath that bread defcended to the
Iewes,feing that all that haue eaten yt,that ys,whome the Iewes thought to
be Manna in the wildernefle,are dead?Howe hath he defcended to the Synagog,feing that all the Synagog hath perifhed,and with the hungar or faft
of faith hath failed or decaied?Yf they had receaued the trewe bread , they
had not faied:*Lorde geue vs allwaie this bread.*What doeft thowe aske , O Iewe,
that he fhoulde geue vnto thee?The bread whiche he geueth to all, whiche
he geueth dailie, whiche,he geueth alwaies,yt ys in thy felf,that thow maift
take that bread Come vnto this bread,and thowe fhall receaue yt . Of this **G**
bread yt ys faied:*All that make themfelues farre from thee,fhal perifh.*Yf thow make
thy felf farre from him,thow fhalt perifh:yf thow drawe neer to him, thowe
fhalt liue. This bread ys the the bread of life.He that eateth life, can not die
Howe can he die vnto whome life ys meate?Howe fhall he faill that hath
that liuelie fubftáce?Come vnto him ád be filled,for he ys the foode.Come
vnto him and drinke,for he ys the well.Come vnto him and be lightned,for
he ys the light.Come vnto him and be made free.*For wher the Spirit of God ys,*
*ther ys fredome.*Come vnto him and be abfolued,for he ys the remiffion of fin
nes.Who thys ys do ye aske?Heare him faing:*I am the bread of life , he that co-*
*meth to me fhall not hungar,and he that beleueth in me fhall not thirft at anie time.*Ye ha
ue heard him,ye haue feé him,ád haue not beleued him.Therfor ye are dead

Thus moche of S.Ambrofe ys alleaged of *Oecolampadius,* whiche for that
yt hath none of thofe expreffe woordes,which be in the reft of S. Ambrofe,
which I haue before alleadged.Therfor he tooke this part of S. Ambrofe,
that he might the better wreft yt,and left that whiche I haue alleaged , bi- **H**
caufe he could not fo well blind the eie of his reader with the wrefting of yt.

Nowe what wolde ye thinke of a man that fo vfeth anie holie authour,as
to bring him againft a matter , or raither as feming to fpeake againft a
matter

A matter, who in dede ſpeaketh nothing againſt yt, but in the next line ſpeaketh ſo manifeſtlie, and ſo plainlie with yt, that the wreſter, ys aſhamed, and dare not bring him furth, and reporte that, that there he ſaieth, but knowing that he ys for the trueth, will bring him furth as though he were againſt the trueth? There ys no other thing but that he ys an Angell of Sathan tranſforming himſelf into the Angell of light, and by ſwete woordes enttappeth the heartes of the ſimple, and of ſoche as be not ware and circumſpecte. And therfore yowe muſt thinke that yt ys neceſſarie to be vigilant, and by earneſt prayer to deſire the Lord of all Spirittes to geue yowe grace to diſcern betwixt ſpirittes, I meen, betwixt the ſpirit of trueth, and the ſpirit of errour, and ſo to flie the euell and cleaue to the good. And when ye ſee ſoche wicked wreſters ſo to abuſe the authours, thinke as ye haue iuſt cauſe, that their matter ys naught, who ſeke by ſoche naughtie meanes to maintein yt.

B Nowe I wiſh that yf the reader be learned he wolde read theſe two allegacions in ſainct Ambroſe: yf he be not learned reade them as they be here alleaged. For ſo moche as *Oecolampadius* alleadgeth foloweth in ſainct Ambroſe immediately after that, that I alleadged, euen as yt doth here. Nowe ioin them together as one (as they be in dede) and then iudge yf they teach not the preſence of Chryſt in the Sacrament, and Manna to be a figure of the ſame, howe ſoeuer *Oecolampadius* wolde wreſt yt to the contrarie.

This alſo by the waie ys to be noted, that where this and the reſt of the Aduerſaries of Gods trueth, teache that ther ys no difference betwxit the Sacramentes of the olde lawe and the newe, as touching anie more excellencie or woorthineſſe in the one then in the other, but that the one ſignified Chryſt to come, the other as comed: that ſainct Ambroſe here noteth a more difference, ſaing that Manna was not the true bread, but our bread ys the true bread, that was a ſhadowe, our the very thing: that gaue not life, our geueth life. Be not theſe differences ſhewing the one more excellent then the other? Did not *Origen* alſo in his ſaing ſignifie moche difference whe he ſaied C that Manna was meate in darke maner, and nowe the fleſh of the Sonne of God ys true meat in a plain maner? Yf the balance be in a true mans hand, the one will weigh moch more then the other, euen as moche as the bodie more then the ſhadowe.

Difference betwene Manna ãd the bleſſed Sacrament

Thus ye haue heard the minde of *Origen* and S. Ambroſe in theſe three pointes, that ys, that Manna ys a figure of the bodie of Chryſte: that the bodie of Chryſte ys preſent in the Sacrament: and that the thinges of the new Teſtament are of more excellencie, then the thinges of the olde Teſtament. In particular, I meen of that thing that they haue ſpoken of. A place ſhall be had that they ſhall be ſpoken of vniuerſallie. In the mean while as I do paſſe through the Authours, as they do touche yt, ſo yt ſhall be noted, and ſo likewiſe of the other two.

THE SIXTH CHAPITER DECLARETH THAT E
Manna was a figure by the testimonie of saincte Cyprian,
and Chrysostom.

He holy Martyr S. Cyprian, whose faithe ys well to be perceaued in the matter of the Sacrament by hys plain and manifold godlie sainges in the first and second booke alleaged, wil also be a notable wittnesse for the same here. In the first booke he hath moft clerely declared vnto vs, the figures that were there fpokē of, as of *Melchisedech* and the Paschal lābe: fo here also as plainly as breiflie he toucheth this figure faing: *Huius panis figura fuit Manna, quod in deserto pluit. Sic vbi ad verum panem in terra promissionis ventum est, cibus ille defecit.* Of this bread, Māna was a figure, which rained in the desert. So when we came to the true bread in the land of promesse, that meat ceassed. That the bread which he fpeaketh of here, of the which he faieth that Manna was the figure, ys the holie bread of the blessed Sacrament, yt ys more manifest, than that yt can be denied. For this his Sermon, wherin these woordes be written, being of the supper of our Lorde, he onely treacteth of yt.

This will also be proued not onely by the sentence on the whiche this de F pendeth and hangeth: but also very manifestlie, where he openeth himfelf in the ende of the sermon by expresse woordes, faing: *Sed & nos ipsi corpus effecti, Sacramento & re Sacramenti capiti nostro connectimur, & vnimur. Singuli alter alterius membra ministerium dilectionis proinuicē exhibentes, communicamus charitate, participamur solicitudine, eundem cibum manducantes, & eundem potum bibentes, qui de spiritali profluit petra, & emanauit. Qui cibus & potus est Dominus noster Iesus Christus.* But we our felues alfo (faieth Cyprian) being made his bodie by the Sacrament and the thing of the Sacrament, we are connected and vnited to our head, euery one being membres one of an other, we communicate in charitie, we are par takers of one care, eating of one meate, and drinking of one drinke, whiche did flowe oute of the fpirituall ftone. *Which meat and drinke ys ower Lord Iesus Chryst.* Thus moche S. Cyprian. In this faing yt ys manifeft that he alludeth to the fame text of S. Paul, that we haue in hand, for he vfeth the very woordes of S. Paule faing: that we eate all of one meat, and drinke all of one drink, whiche drinke did flowe oute of the fpirituall ftone. I nede not to conferre G the one to the other, for he that knoweth the one dothe well perceaue the other. But what this one meat ys that we all eate of, and what this drinke ys that flowed oute of the fpirituall ftone, of the whiche we all drinke, he furth with expowndeth and faieth: *Which meat, and drinke ys our Lord Iesus Chryst.* A more plain fpeache can not be defired.

As the Iewes did eate of one Manna, and dranke of one water flowing out of the ftone: fo all we Chryftians eate one meate, and drinke one drinke the bodie and blood of Chryft. The bodie of Chryft being the one meat figurated by the one meat of the Iewes, whiche was Manna. The blood of Chryft being the one drinke of the Chryftians, figurated by the one drinke of the Iewes, whiche did flowe oute of the ftone, as the bloode flowed oute of the fpirituall ftone, *the bodie of our Lord and Sauiour Chryst Iesus.* For as the Euangelift faieth, *vnus militum lancea latus eius aperuit, & continuò exiuit sanguis & aqua.* One of the foldiers with a fpere thruft him into the fide and furthwith there came oute blood and water.

This clere teftimonie of S. Cyprian can not be darkned with the comon H obfcure glofe of the Aduerfaries, as to faie that our Lorde Iefus Chryft ys our meat fpirituallie . We confeffe (as before) that Chryft ys our fpirituall
meat

A meat, and that we fede vpon him fpirituallie, and we wifh and praie that all chryftians will fo frame their liues, and conuerfacions, that they maie dailie fede on him fpirituallie. But with all we confefle and beleue, that we recea him reallie, and fubftanciallie in the Sacrament, as S. Cyrill faieth, whofe phrafe ys not vnlike this that we haue nowe faied. Thus he writeth: *Non nega-* *mus nos recta fide, charitateque fincera Chrifto fpiritualiter coniungi : fed nullam nobis* *coniunctionis rationem fecumdùm carnem cum illo efle, id profecto pernegamus, idque à di-* *uinis fcripturis omnino alienum dicimus.* We denie not but that we are ioined to Chryft fpirituallie by right faith, and fincere charitie: But that we haue no maner of coniunction with him after the flefhe, that in verie dede we vtter-lie denie, and faie yt to be farre wide from the fcriptures. And a litle after: *An fortaßis putat ignotam nobis mifticæ benedictionis virtutem efle? quæ cùm in nobis fiat* *nonne corporalliter quoque facit comunicatione carnis Chrifti, Chriftum in nobis habitare?* Dothe he thinke peraduenture that the vertue of the mifticall benediction ys vnknowen to vs? whiche when yt ys doen in vs, dothe yt not make alfo by the comunicacion or receauing of Chryftes flefh, Chryft corporallie

B to dwell in vs?

Cyrill. in 15 Joan.
Chryftes bodie ys re ceaued bothfpiritu allie and reallie.

Nowe therfor with S. Cyrill confesfing both maners of receauing and fea-ding of Chryft, we do not with the Aduerfaries fo confefle the one, that we denie the other. wherfor not denieng, but affirming with the holy martir Ciprian, we faie that we receaue Chryft verilie, and that our lorde Iefus Chryft, as Cyprian fpeaketh yt, ys our meate, and his bloode our drinke real-lie, and fubftanciallie.

And that S. Cyprian fo meneth yt will withoute all fcruple appeare mani-feftlie to the reader, yf he will confider, and vnderftande, where he fpeaketh thefe woordes. They are fpoken in a fermon that he made of the fupper of our lorde, whiche fermon being made to fetfurth that thing that yt was made for, muft, and doth feth yt furthe as yt ys. And fo by the figure of the Pafchall lambe, and by the figure of Melchifedech he declareth the veritie of Chryft in the Sacrament, of the whiche moche ys faied before, both in the firft booke, and in the feconde, where inuinciblie by S. Cyprian ys pro-ued the prefence of Chryfte in the Sacrament. In the whiche matter S. Cy-

C prian ys fo plain in this fermon that the Aduerfarie hath no better euafion then of his owne authoritie to faie that yt ys not S. Cyprians fermon, as he doth for the like caufe make a like folucion to the bookes of S. Ambrofe of the facramentes, faing they be none of his. And therfor weigh well the reft of the fermon, and what ys faied of him in the other bookes here before and ye fhall fee what faith he profefleth as concerning the Sacrament, and howe he wolde be vnderftanded here.

A fhort folucion of the Sacra-mentaries.

But that the vnlearned reader maie not be referred to a place vnknowen to him, or enforced to fufpend his iudgement in this matter, yt fhall vpon this prefent fentence of S. Cyprian be manifefted and declared vnto him. This ys in this faing of S. Cyprian to be confidered, that he teacheth the ef-fecte and comoditie of the Sacrament, and by what mean we atteing to yt. The effecte ys that we be made the bodie mifticall of Chryfte, we be knitte and vnited to him, as to our head, we be made membres one of an other in this mifticall bodie. Thefe effectes whiche happen vnto vs by the re-ceipt of the Sacrament, yf they be well confidered and weighed, they

D be verie excellent and great. The mean to atteign to them S. Cyprian alfo here declareth when he faieth: by the Sacrament, and the thing of the Sacrament, what the Sacrament ys, and what the thing of the

Effectes of the blefled Sacr. and the means to atteing them.

Vv iiii   Sacra-

Sacrament ys, and what ys the difference betwixt them both, S. Auguſtin **E**
Li.ſenten. teacheth vs ſaing: *Hoc eſt quod dicimus, quod modis omnibus approbare contendimus,*
Proſper. *ſacrificium Eccleſiæ duobus modis confici, duobus conſtare, viſibili elementorum ſpecie, &*
vide ſup. *inuiſibili Domini noſtri Ieſu Chriſti carne, & ſanguine, & ſacramēto, & re ſacramēti, id*
cap.19. *eſt, corpore Chriſti &c.* This ys yt (ſaieth S. Auguſtine) that we ſaie, that by all
means we labour to proue, the ſacrifice of the Churche to be made two wa-
ies, to be of two thinges : of the viſible forme of the elementes, and the in-
Aplain pla uiſible fleſh and blood of our Lorde Ieſu Chryſt : both the Sacrament, and
ce for the the thing of the Sacrament, that ys to ſaie, the bodie of Chryſte. Euen as the
Proclamer perſon of Chryſt ys of God and man, for as moch as he ys very God, ād verie
man. For euery thing conteineth the nature and veritie of thoſe thinges, of
whiche yt ys made. The ſacrifice of the Churche ys made of two thinges, of
the Sacrament and the thing of the Sacrament, that ys to ſaie, of the bodie
of Chryſt. Yt ys therfor the Sacrament and the thing of the Sacrament, the
bodie of Chryſt. Thus moche S. Auguſtin.

Of whome ye haue heard (except my iudgement faill me) a verie plain **F**
declaracion of the ſacrifice of the Churche, and of the Sacrament and of the
Sacrifice of thinge of the Sacrament. But leauing here to ſpeake of the Sacrifice, and re-
the Church ſeruing yt to ſome other more mete place, we will onelie ſpeake of that that
auouched. this place requireth, that ys, for ſo muche as S. Cyprian ſaieth, that we be
connected, knitt, and vnited to Chryſte our head by the Sacrament, and the
thing of the Sacrament, to marke and learn by S. Auguſtin, what ys ment
therby. The ſentence of S. Auguſtin ys plain therin, that the Sacrament ys
the viſible forme of the elementes. As for example: Euen as the viſible for-
Sacrament me of the element of water, when the woorde cometh to yt, ys the ſacra-
and thing ment of Baptiſme: So be the viſible formes of bread and wine, when the wor
of the Sacr. de ys comed to them, the Sacramentes of the bodie and blood of Chryſte.
what they Beſide this there ys alſo the thing of the Sacrament. Whiche S. Auguſti-
be. ne ſaieth, ys the bodie and blood of Chryſte. Nowe when S. Cyprian ſaieth
that we be knitte and vnited to Chryſt our head by the Sacrament, and the
thing of the Sacramēt: What ys yt ells, but we are vnited (as S. Cyrill ſaieth) **G**
by the Sacrament and the bodie and bloode of Chryſte, and that (as ye
heard S. Cyrill ſaie before) not onelie ſpirituallie, but alſo corporallie, receauing his very fleſh?

Yf of S. Cyprian we aſke howe we are knitte to Chryſt our head by his
bodie and bloode, whiche ys the thing of the Sacrament: He alſo aunſwereth like vnto S. Cyrill, ſainge : *Edentes, & bibentes, eundem cibum & potum , qni*
cibus & potus eſt Dominus noſter Ieſus Chriſtus. Eating, and drinking the ſame
meat, and drinke, whiche meat and drinke ys our lorde Ieſus Cryſte. Nowe
then ye perceaue that S. Cyprian taketh the meat and drinke, that S. Paule
ſpeaketh of, not for the figures of the bodie and blood of Chryſt, of the
whiche we haue the very preſence in the Sacrament. whiche as yt ys declared by him very plainly : So I doubt not but Chryſoſtom will as plainlie de
clare yt, ſo that there ſhall be no place for the enemie to lurke in. Chryſoſtom
Homil .in making a ſpeciall homelie vpon the woordes of S. Paule , whiche be nowe
dictum. A- in hande, declareth both the figures and the thinges figured by expreſſe
poſt. Nolo woordes, ſaing thus : *Dixi enim quod oportet veritatem habere excellentiam quandā* **H**
vos ignor. *ſupra figuram. Vidiſti de baptiſmate quæ figura, & quæ veritas . Age, oſtendam tibi &*
menſas, & ſacramentorum communionem ibi delineari, ſi non iterum petis à me totum, ſed
ſic requiris, quæ facta ſunt, ſicut par eſt in adumbratione & figuris videre. Igitur quia dixit
de mari, & de nube, & de Moyſe, adiecit preterea : Et omnes eundum ſpiritualem cibum
come-

A *comederunt. Sicut tu (inquit) à lauachro aquarum afcendens ad menſam curris : ſic & illi à mari aſcendentes ad menſam venere nouam, & admirabilem, de Manna loquor. Et iterum ſicut tu admirabilem habes potum ſalutarem ſanguinem : ſic & illi admirabilem habuerunt poculi naturam.* I haue ſaied (ſaieth Chriſoſtom) that the trueth muſt haue a certain excellencie aboue the figure. Thowe haueſt ſee of Baptiſme, whiche ys the figure and whiche ys the veritie. Go on I ſhall ſhewe thee the tables and the cõmunion of the ſacramentes there to be in a darke maner ſet furth, yf thowe do not again aske all of me, but ſo requireſt thoſe thinges that be doen, as yt ys mete in the ſhadowing and figures to ſee. Therfor bicauſe he had ſaied of the Sea, and of the clowde and of moyſes, he added fardermore: *And all haue eaten one ſpirituall meate.* as thowe (ſaieth he) aſcending from the bathe or waſhing of waters doeſt runne to the table. So they alſo going vppe from the ſea, came to a newe, and a merueiloufe table, I ſpeake of Mãna, and again as thow haueſt a wonderfull drinke, *the wholſome bloode:* ſo they alſo had a wonderfull nature of drinke. Hitherto Chryſoſtome. Who hath declared euery part of theſe matters, that here are to be ſett furth.

The trueth muſt haue an excellencie aboue the figure.

B   In the beginning of his ſaing he confowndeth the Aduerſarie in that he ſo plainlie ſaieth, that *the veritie muſt haue a certain excellencie aboue the figure.* Thẽ foraſmoche as Baptiſme ys the veritie, and the ſea the figure, Baptiſme ys more excellent then the ſea: Likewiſe Manna and the water being the figure of the Sacrament of the bodie of Chryſt, and of his bloode. then the Sacrament of the bodie and blood of Chryſte ys more excellent then Manna, for the veritie ys more excellent then the figure. That Manna and the water be figures of the Sacrament, he dothe moſt manifeſtlie declare when he ſaieth : *I will ſhewe thee the tables, and the cõmunion of the Sacramentes ther to be in figurs ſett furth.* And proceeding to ſhewe whatSacramentes be ſettfurth there, he dothe applie the one to the other ſaing : *As thowe coming vppe (ſaieth he) from the ſoute of baptiſme, runneſt to the table. So they from the ſea to Manna . As thowe haueſt a wonderfull drinke, whiche ys the wholſom bloode of Chryſt : ſo they the water of the ſtone.*

Oure drinke the whol ſome blood of Chryſte.

   In this ys plainly taught, whiche be the figures, whiche be the verities. **C** The Sea, Manna, and the waters be the figures: Baptiſme, Chryſtes bodie and Chryſtes bloode be the verities. For although Chryſoſtom in the applicacion of Manna doth but put the table as the veritie. what he ment by the table he well declareth in the applicacion of the water to the veritie where he ſaieth : *As thowe drinkeſt wonderfull drinke the wholſome bloode, So they the water.* Wherby as in this by expreſſe woordes he declareth the bloode to be the veritie of the water being the figure : ſo by the table wherin that holie Sacrament ys miniſtred, he ment the bodie of Chryſt, whiche after a fewe lines he opẽly ſpeaketh ſaing : *Sicut autem dixit, quòd omnes per mare tranſierunt : Sic nobilitatem Eccleſiæ præfigurauit cùm dixit : Eundem cibum ſpiritualem comederunt . Hoc idem rurſus inſinuauit : Sic enim in Eccleſia, nou aliud corpus diues, aliud verò pauper, neq; alium quidem ſanguinem ille, alium autem iſte. Sic & ttunc non aliud quidem accipiebat diues Manna, alium verò pauper, neque alterius ſontis iſte particeps erat, alterius verò in digentioris ille.* As he hath ſaied that all haue goen through the ſea : ſo he hath perfigurated the nobilitie of the churche when he ſaied : *They haue eaten all one ſpirituall meat.* he hath inſinuated the ſame again, for ſo yt ys in the Church

Riche and poore eate all one bodie, and drinke all one blood.

D For the riche man receaueth not one bodie, and the, poore man an other, neither he one maner of blood and this an other. So alſo then the riche mã did not take of one Manna, and the poore man of an other, neither was this man partaker of one fountain, and he of a woorſe.

                               In

In this faing Chryfoftome making an other comparifon betwixt the figu-re and the veritie, he fheweth what he ment by the table in the place firft al-leaged. For here he calleth yt the bodie, faing, that the riche man doth not receaue one bodie, and the poore man an other : no more then the riche man did receaue one Manna, and the poore man an other : but as all eate one Manna in the figure : So all indifferentlie eate one bodie in veritie. For the poore lazar receaueth that fame bodie of Chryft that the kinge dothe. Whiche by the waie to note, I wifh all men of power and honour to remé-bre and confider that God contemneth not the miferable and wretched, but receaueth all, and difpifeth none but the wicked. And as he ys no acceptour of perfons in the receipt of his Sacramentes, no more ys he in the receauing to his glorie. For poour *Lazarus* was in the bofom of Abraham when the great riche man was in tormentes. **E**

But to return to our matter . Chryfoftome yet in the fame home-lie declaring why S. Paule maketh mencion of thefe thinges . faieth: *Sed cuius gratia horum memoriam adfert beatus Paulus ? Ob caufam quam princi-pio vobis dixi , vt difcas , quòd neque Baptifma , neque peccatorum remifsio, neque fcientia , neque facramentorum Communio , neque facra menfa , neque frui-tio corporis , neque participatio fanguinis , neque aliud horum prodeffe nobis pote-rit , nifi vitam rectam , & admirabilem , & omni peccato liberam habeamus.* But wherfor doeth S. Paule make mencion of thefe thinges ? for the caufe whiche I tolde yowe in the beginninge, that thowe fhouldeft learn , that neither Baptifme , neither remiffion of finnes, neither know ledge , neither the cómunion of the facramentes , neither the holie ta-ble , neither the fruicion of the bodie, neither the partaking of the blood, neither anie thing of thefe can auaill vs, except we haue a life right and comé dable, and free from all finne. Thns Chryfoftom. **F**

Chry. Jbid.

Neither the fruitiõ of Chryftes bodie nor the parta-king of hys blood auai-leth with-out good lif

In whiche his faing ye perceaue how plainlie he teacheth the receipt of the bodie and bloode of Chryft in the Sacrament reallie and in very dede and not figuratiuelie or fpirituallie. And this ys the proofe of yt. *For he faieth that the receipt of the bodie and blood of Chryft profiteth nothing, ex-cept we haue a godlie life withal .* Nowe the fpirituall receauing of Chryft includeth a godlie life with all . For to receaue Chryft fpirituallie ys hauing the remembrance of Chryftes pafsion and death to receaue him by faith and charitie, whiche can not be withoute a godlie life . For whe re perfect faith , and perfecte charitie ys , ther ys a man of perfecte and holie life , and he that ys of that forte receaueth Chryft fpirituallie. But here Chryfoftom fpeaketh of the receipt of the bodie of Chryft with-oute holie life . whiche muft nedes be fpoken and ment of the bodie of Chryft in the Sacrament . Whiche as yt was receaued by *Iudas*, he being then a wicked man : fo maie yt be receaued of other that be wicked , and not of holie life , but then (as Chryfoftome faieth) yt profiteth nothing, but yt raither hurteth moche , as here after fhall be faied. **G**

Chryftes bo die maie be receaue re-allie, and yet not fpi-rituall.

All though ye haue had here clere teftimonie of Chryfoftome in this matter : yet he ys more plain in an other place, expownding the fame fcripture and applieng yt to the veritie ,thus :*Quæ autem fequntur fa-cram menfam fignificant . Nam quemadmodum tu corpus Dominicum manducas: ita & illi Manna manducauerunt . Et ficut tu fanguinem bibis : ita illi aquam de petra biberunt.* Thefe things that do folowe do fignifie the holie table. For as thowe doeft eate the bodie of our Lorde: fo they alfo haue eaten Manna and **H**

Jn 10.1. Cor . hom. 23. Chryftians eate the bo die of Chrift as the le-wes did Manna.

and

A   and as thowe drinkeſt bloode: ſo they haue dronke the water of the ſtone. And again in the ſame homelie, ſpeaking of the benefittes, whiche God gaue to the Iewes, as Manna, and the water in figures of the benefittes of his bodie and bloode, whiche he geueth vnto vs, and ſhewing him to be the geuer of them bothe, ſaieth in the perſon of S. Paule. *Qui enim illa illis prebuit (inquit) hic & hanc præparauit menſam. Et ipſe idem, & illos per mare, & te per baptiſma adduxit. Et illis Manna, & aquam: & tibi corpus & ſanguinem dedit.* He that prepared (ſaieth he) thoſe thinges to thē, to theſe hath he alſo prepared this table. And euen the very ſame hath brought them through the Sea: and the through Baptiſme. And vnto them he gaue Manna and the water : *and vnto thee, the bodie and bloode.*

What can the Aduerſarie once ſaie againſt theſe ſo clere and manifeſt teſtimonies for the trueth? What blinde gloſe or maliciouſe interpretacion can he bring to make theſe ſainges anie thing looke towarde him? Yf the Iewes receaued the figure, and we the veritie : what baſer or lower thing ys yt thē

B   the bodie of Chryſt? Yf the Aduerſarie ſaie, that we receaue Chryſt ſpirituallie, ſo did they in the receipt of Manna alſo : I meen all they that receaued well. What then receaue we more nowe in, or with the veritie vnder Chryſt in the Goſpell, then they did with their figures vnder Moyſes in the lawe? Yf they proceade and ſaie that we receaue the Sacramentall bread as a figure of Chryſt : ſo receaued the Iewes Manna as a figure of Chryſt. Yf in euery place the figure, wher ys the veritie? Yf ther a figure and here a figure, yf ther Chryſt ſpiritually, and here ſpirituallie, and no more in the one, then in the other, what then ſignifieth the veritie? and wher ys the veritie?

   Farder (as ye hearde Chryſoſtome before ſaie) the veritie muſt haue excellencie aboue the figure, yf then we haue the veritie (as Chryſoſtom alſo ſaieth) then of neceſſitie yt muſt folowe, that yf the Iewes had the figure of Chryſt in Manna, and yf the goode receauers with the figure Manna, receaued alſo Chryſt ſpirituallie, that we muſt haue a certen excellencie with

C   our veritie, whiche be none other, but the preſence of him that ys the veritie in dede, whiche ys Chryſt. For we haue a figure with the Iewes, and a ſpirituall receauing, with the Iewes, and in theſe we be equall, and on our parte ther ys no excellencie. This therfore ys the excellencie, that where they had the figure : we haue both figure and the thing figurated, whiche ys the bodie and bloode of Chryſte.

   Of theſe two authours then, as of the other, ye perceaue theſe three thinges auouched, whiche were before mencioned, that ys Manna, and the water, to befigures of Chryſtes bodie and blood, and that ſame bodie and bloode be in the Sacrament, and that ther ys an excellencie in the thinges prefigured aboue the figures, as to the veritie yt apperteineth aboue the figure.

THE

Yf the chriſtiā receaue Chryſte but in figure ſpirituallie, as the Iewe did wher ys thē the veritie,

THE SEVENTH CHAP. PROCEADETH TO DE-
clareth the fame by faincte Hierom and fainct Cyrill.

E

Hen I confider with my felf, howe long the veritie of the prefence of Chryftes bodie in the Sacrament hath ben receaued and beleued : howe not in one corner of the chryftian orbe (as nowe the Aduerfaries of this trueth do occupie) but throughoute in all places, where Chryfte was profeffed, as well in the eaft Chruch, as the weft churche, in the greke churche, as in the latin Churche, this trueth was embraced, the Sacrament moch reuerenced, Chryft God and man there truly and highlie honoured : the fame alfo by the greateft, graueft, and holieft learned men taught and preached, and in their bookes by the teftimonie of their handes teftified, and to all the worlde comended : I can not ceaffe to merueill howe men of this our time be bewitched and infatuated to leaue so fure an anker, while they be in the trooblefom fea of this worlde, and take holde of a feather, in the whiche there ys no fuertie nor ftaie, but raither great occafion of prefent perill and deftruction. They be not alltogether vn-

Proteftan-tes compared to the dogge in the fable.

like the dogge in the fable, who fwimming through the water, and hauing a good bone in his mouthe fawe the fhadowe of the fame in the water, and foddenlie withoute confideracion leauing his good bone, fnatched at the fhadowe to haue caught yt, and fo loft for the fhadowe, the fubftancial thing: So thefe men fwimming through the trooblefome water of his worlde, and hauing in their mouthes the fubftanciall woorde of trueth that was able to feed them, feing the fhadowe of this vain doctrine, whiche like a fhadowe appeareth to be fomwhat, but ys nothing in dede, they let the catholique and fubftanciall doctrine fall from their mouthes and catche the fhadowe. But as long as they haue but the fhadowe their feeding will be fo bare, or raither nothing, that their foules which fhoulde be fedde withe the true woorde of God, fhall perifh with famine, yt encreafeth my merueilling and woondering, that they feing thefe graue fathers, and learned writers fo manifeftlie teaching the trueth, yet as men addicted to fwear to the woordes of their wicked mafters, they moue not from their phantafies. What then? Shall we ceaffe to call vpon them? Naie, God forbidde. S. Paule although he well fawe the ftif neckes of the Iewes, that they wolde not bowe to the faith , yet he faied : *Quamdiu fum gentium Apoftolus, minifterium meum*

F

G

Rom. 11.

honorificabo, fi quomodo ad æmulandum prouocem carnem meam, & faluos faciam aliquos ex illis. As long as I am the Apoftle of the gentiles I will magnifie mine office yf by anie mean I maie prouoke them whiche are my flefh, and might faue fome of them. God graunte the charitie of S. Paule to all, whom God hath called to the offiice of teachers, that they maie magnifie their office, and call vpon the people continuallie, that fome maie be faued, though damnacion to them that be called, and will not heare be the more greuoufe. Wherfor although thefe two coople in the chapiters before alleaged, might fuffice to certifie vs of the true vnderftanding of this fcripture of S. Paule, and of the matters depending vpon the fame : yet to the entent I maie by a nombre of woorthie wittneffes, all with one confent, and as yt were with one mowthe teftifieng the auncient receaued treuthe, prouoke fome to folowe: I will by gods helpe produce three or foure cooples mo that fhall teache al one trueth though they were not all in one time, but fome fiue hundreth yeares after the other, and fome more and fome leffe.

H

The

A   The firſt coople of theſe ſhall be S. Hierom and S. Cyrill, whoſe fame and auncientie, I nede not nowe to ſett furth. For I haue of yt allready ſaied and they are alſo well knowen. But for that Sainct Hierom ys the elder, his ſentence ſhall be firſt hearde. Expownding this ſcripture he ſaieth thus: *Et omnes eandem ſpiritualem eſcam manducauerunt &c. Manna figura corporis Chriſti fuit.* And all did eate of one ſpirituall meate. Manna was a figure of the bodie of Chryſte. Although theſe woordes be full enough and teache that that ys here ſought, for ſaing that Manna was a figure of the bodie of Chryſt they teache, that as the Iewes did eate Manna as the figure: So nowe the figure being gon we eate the bodie of Chryſt as the veritie of that figure, yet more at large he openeth the wholl matter ſomwhat after ſaing: *Omnia enim quæ in populo Iſraël illo tempore facta ſunt in figura, nunc in nobis in veritate celebrantur. Sicut enim illi per Moyſen ex Ægipto liberati ſunt: Sic nos per quemlibet ſacerdotem vel doctorem de ſeculo liberamur. Deinde chriſtiani facti, ducimur per deſerta, vt per exercitium contemptus mundi & abſtinentiæ in obliuionem nobis eant Ægypti voluptates, ita vt neſciamus ad ſeculum repedare. Cùm verò Baptiſmi mare tranſimus, tunc*

B   *nobis Diabolus cum ſuo exercitu tanquam Pharao demergitur. Deinde Manna cibamur,& potum accipimus de Chriſti latere emanantem. Claritas quoque ſcientiæ tanquam columna ignis in nocte ſeculi demonſtratur, & in tribulationis æſtu, diuinæ conſolationis nube protegimur.* All thinges (ſaieth S. Hierom) whiche in that time were doen in the people of Iſraell in figure, nowe they are celebrated in vs in veritie. As they by Moyſes were deliuered oute of Egypte: So we by euery preiſt and doctour are deliuered from the worlde. Then being made Chryſtians we are ledde through the deſertes, that by the exerciſe of the contempt of the worlde, and of abſtenence, the fleſhlie pleaſures of Egypt maie be of vs forgotten ſo that we ſhall not knowe to go backe again into the worlde. When we paſſe through the ſea of Baptiſme then the Deuell with all his armie, euen like as Pharao was, ys drowned. Thē we are fedde with Manna, *and take drinke flowing oute of the ſide of Chryſte.* The brightneſſe alſo of knowledge ys ſhewed in the night of the worlde, as the piller of fire, and in the heat of tribulaciõ, we

C   are defended with the clowde of diuine conſolaciõ, Thus moche S. Hierom.
    In whom we ſee the wholl applicacion of the figurs mencioned in Sainct Paule to the thinges figured, whiche thinges as by other before, ſo by him they are cailed, *veritates,* the verities. And therfore he ſaieth in the beginning of his ſentence thal all thinges doen in the Iewes in figures, are fulfilled in vs in veritie. So that ſoche thinges as we haue, whiche were prefigured in the Iewes, they be not with vs bare ſignes or figures as they were with them. But although they be figures in ſome reſpecte: yet they are alſo verities, and the very thinges in dede. Wherfor as Moyſes was a figure of Chryſt, and nowe again we haue not a figure of Chryſt, but Chryſt himſelf as the veritie, or verie thing of the figure: and as the ſea was the figure of Baptiſme, and nowe we haue not an other figure of Baptiſme, but Baptiſme yt ſelf in very dede: And as the clowde was a figure of the holie Goſt, and nowe we haue not an other figure of the holie Goſt, but the holie Goſt in very dede: ſo *Mãna,* as S. Hierõ ſaieth here, being the figure of the bodie of Chryſt, of like conſequēce

D   yt muſt folowe, that nowe we hauing the veritie of the figure, haue not an other figure of the bodie of Chryſte, but the very bodie of Chryſte in dede, that as the Iewes did verilie eate *Mãna,* and drinke verilie the water as the figures of the bodie and bloode of Chryſt. *So as Chryſoſt. ſaied in the laſt chap. thowe doeſt verilie eate his bodie and drinke his bloode.* Wherfore alſo S. Hierom, in this applicacion of the figures to the verities, coming to Manna, ſaieth: *Cibamur Manna, et potum accipimus de latere Chriſti emanantem.*   Xx   We

Hieron. in 10.1.Cor.

We drinke drinke flowing oute of the ſide of Chryſt.

As we haue not nowe Moyſesbut Chryſte in dede, not a figure of Baptiſme, but Baptiſme in dede, not the holie Goſte in figure but in dede. So not the figure of Chryſtes bodie, but his bodie in dede. Hierõ. ibi.

We are fedde(faieth he) with Manna, but that ye fhoulde vnderftand him of E
the true Manna the bodie of Chryfte, he addeth : *And we take drinke flowing*
oute of the fide of Chryst.

What drinke flowed oute of that bleffed fide? yt ys well knowen to be
the precioufe bloode of our Sauiour Chryft. So that ye fee that Sainct Hierom, as he dothe yt godlie, and learnedlie: So alfo fimplie and plainlie, and
faithfullie confeffeth and teacheth, that as the Iewes did eate Manna, and
dranke the water of the ftone: So we eate the veritie of that figure, and drinke the veritie of that figuratiue water, whiche be the verie bodie and bloode
of the fpirituall ftone Iefus Chryft.   And note that the mafters of figures
can not place their figure in Sainct Hieroms woordes. For he contented
not himfelf to faie onelie the bloode, but to declare the realitie and fubftance in dede, he faied: the bloode that flowed oute of Chryftes fide, not a figure, but that bloode in dede.

But peraduenture the Aduerfarie will reiecte this authoritie, bicaufe yt
ys doubted of fome, whether yt be Sainct Hieroms worke or no, that this F
authoritie ys taken oute of.   Whether yt be or no, two thinges moue me
to regarde and efteem the authoritie.   The firft and the cheifeft, bicaufe yt
ys a catholique faing, not difagreing from the like fainges of the good catholique and auncient Fathers.   The fecond, bicaufe yt ys no newe worke,
but of foche auncientie, that yt might, as yt appeareth, be afcribed to Sainct
Hierom, yf yt be not his in dede.

But that the Aduerfarie fhall not cauill that we alleadge Sainct Hierom,
where in dede yt ys not Sainct Hierom: we will alleadge SainctHierom, that
he fhall not refufe to be Sainct Hierom.   And this ys his faing: *Si panis,*

Hieron. ad
Hedibiam.
queft. 2.

qui de cælo defcendit, corpus eſt Domini, & vinum, quod Difcipulis dedit, fanguis illius
eſt noui Teſtamenti, qui pro multis effufus eſt in remiſsionem peccatorum, Iudaicas
fabulas repellamus. Yf the bread that defcended from heauen be the bodie of
our Lorde, and the wine, that he gaue to his difciples, be his bloode of the
newe Teftament, whiche was fhedde for manie in remifsion of finnes : let
vs caft awaie Iewifhe fables. And again a litle after: *Nec Moyfes dedit nobis* G
panem verum, fed Dominus Iefus, ipfe conuiua, & conuiuium, ipfe comedens & , qui
comeditur. Illius bibimus fanguinem, & fine ipfo potare non poſſumus. Neither hath
Moyfes geuen vs the treu bread, but our Lorde Iefus. He ys bothe the feafter
and the feaft : He ys bothe the eater, and he that ys eaten. We drinke his
bloode, and withoute him we can not drinke. Thus S. Hierome.

For that both thefe places do applie the figure to the thing figured, that
ys, Manna to the bodie of Chryft the true bread, whiche Manna in the fixth
of Sainct Iohn ys called the bread from heauen, and likewife in diuerfe places, therfor I thought them meet for this place. In the firft vnder a condicionall tearme, he teacheth a plain affercion, that the bread that defcended
from heauen ys the bodie of our Lorde, and the wine that he gaue to his
Difciples ys his bloode, whiche ys a plain maner of fpeache affirming
the prefence of Chryft, and not a figuratiue fpeache fignifieng his abfence.
In that he faieth that our Lorde Iefus bodie ys the bread that defcended H
from heauen, he declareth the veritie of Manna the figure to be the bodie
of Chryft. For when the Iewes had faied to Chryft: Owre Fathers did
eate Manna in the defert, in whiche woordes they fpake of the figure:

Ioan. 6.

Chryft anfwering, ioined them both together and faied : *Non Moyfes dedit*
vobis panem de cælo, fed pater meus dat vobis panem de cælo verũ. Moyfes hath not ge
uẽ you bread frõ heauẽ. But my Father geueth you the true bread frõ heauẽ.
                                                                         And

A And after fpeaking of the bread whiche ys his bodie, and applieng yt to the figure he faieth: *Hic eft panis qui de cœlo defcendit. Non ficut manducauerunt patres veftri Manna, & mortui funt. Qui manducat hunc panem viuet in æternum.* This ys the bread that defcended from heauen, Not as your Fathers haue eaten Manna in the defert and be dead. He that eateth this bread fhall liue for euer.

Nowe then Sainct Hierom faing that the bread that defcended from heauen, ys the bodie of owre Lorde Iefus: He teacheth againft the Aduerfarie, that the fixt of Sainct Iohn fpeaketh of the Sacrament, and alfo auoucheth that the veritie of the figure Manna, ys the bodie of Chryft.

The like alfo he doth in the next fentence, faing, *That not Moyfes, but our Lorde Iefus gaue vs the true bread.* And that by this true bread, whiche Chryft gaue vs, he meneth his bodie in the bleffed Sacrament, yt ys inuinciblie proued by that that he adioined: He ys the feafter and the feaft, yt ys he that eateth and ys eaten. As Chryft in his laft fupper was bothe he that prepared the feaft (as Cyprian faied) *Et confumpto agno quem antiqua traditio proponebat, in-* De cœna Domini.

B *confumptibilem cibum magifter apponit Difcipulis.* And when the lambe was confumed whiche the olde tradicion did fet furth, the mafter fet before his difciples inconfumptible meate: and one that did partake of the feaft, as among diuerfe other Chryfoftome faieth fpeaking of the cuppe of his bloode, *Ipfe* In 26. Ma. Hom. 83. *quoque bibit ex eo, ne auditis verbis illis, dicerent: Quid igitur fanguinem bibimus, & carnem comedimus? ac ideo perturbarentur.* He alfo dranke of yt himfelf, lefte when they had heard thofe woordes, they fhoulde faie: What then do we drinke bloode and eate flefh? and therfor fhoulde be troubled. So was he the feaft himfelf, I meen the meat of the feaft, whiche as he then gaue yt fitting at his laft fupper with his Apoftles: So geueth he yt nowe. For, as Chryftome Hom. 30. faieth, he ys nowe prefent, and fanctifieth. So that this table that ys dailie de prodit. miniftred ys in nothing inferiour to that table of his laft fupper: *Hæc enim* Hom. 83 in *illa, non alia menfa eft: hæc nulla re minor quam illa eft.* This ys euen the fame ta- Matty. ble and not an other: this ys in nothing leffe then that.

C And as Sainct Auguftin faieth, that he ys the preift that doth offre, and De ciu. Dei the offring, or oblacion that ys offred: So ys he, he that eateth, as Sainct li 10. ca. 20 Hierom faieth, and he that ys eaten.

Thus Reader, thowe doeft not onelie perceaue the euident and ftrong teftimonie of Sainct Hierom againft the Aduerfarie. But alfo thowe perceaueft the goodlie concorde and agreement of the Fathers together, fo mightilie knit together in the plain confefsion of Gods trueth, that yf a legion of enemies were confpired together they coulde not by all their pulling and wrefting drawe them into their parte.

And yet to fortifie this trueth, not for yt felf, but for the Reader, we will Cyr. ca, 19, nowe heare Sainct Cyrill, whome we promiffed to ioin with S. Hierom. in 6. Joan, Thus he faieth: *Non enim prudenter quæ ad breue tempus fufficiunt hoc nomine appellabuntur, nec panis erat ex Deo, quem maiores Iudæorum comederunt, & mortui funt. Nam fi de cœlo, & ex Deo fuiffet, liberaffet à morte participantes. Contrà verò corpus Chrifti panis de cœlo eft, quia æternam comedentibus vitam*

D *largitur.* Thofe thinges whiche fuffice but for a fhort time, fhall not well be called by this name. Neither was yt bread from God, whiche the elders of the Iewes haue eaten and be dead. For yf yt had ben from heauen and of God, yt had deliuered the partakers of yt from deathe. *But contrary wife the bodie of Chryfte ys the bread from heauen, for yt graunteth euerlafting life to the eaters.* Thus he.

Thisys a breif and a plain testimonie, in the whiche mencion ys made of **E** the figure, that ys, of the bread whiche the elders of the Iewes did eate, whiche bread was Manna: and of the thing figured, whiche ys the veritie, whiche by expresse woordes he calleth the bodie of Chryst. So that agreablie to all that before hath bē spokē, he teacheth, that the thing figured by Māna was not a figure or a signe of the bodie of Chryste, but the verie bodie of Chryst in dede. For as in diuerse places before alleadged oute of the same Cyrill, yt dothe well appeare that he ys no figurer, but a plain a auoucher of the presence of Chrystes bodie in the blessed Sacrament, and that we receaue the same bodie reallie and substanciallie, as amonge a great nombre

Cyr.ca. 14 in 6. Ioan. When we eate the flesh of Chryste we haue life in vs.

this maie be one: *Quoniam saluatoris caro Verbo Dei, quod naturaliier vita est coniuncta, viuifica effecta est, quando eam comedimus, tunc vitam habemus in nobis, illi coniuncti, quæ vita effecta est.* Forasmoche as the flesh of our Sauiour being ioined to the Sonne of God, who naturally ys life, ys made hable to geue life. *When we eate the same flesh,* then we haue life in vs being ioined to yt that ys made able to geue life. Thus S. Cyrill.

Ioan. 14.

F

In this saing ye perceaue that the flesh of Chryst ys hable to geue life, bycause yt ys ioined to the Sonne of God in vnitie of person, whiche ys naturally of yt self very life, he him self testifieng: *Ego sum via, veritas, & vita.* I am the waie, the trueth and the life. Therfor we eating the same flesh that hath life, we also haue life.

In this here ys no voide woorde of figure, he saieth not that we shall haue life, yf we eate the figure of his flesh, for the figure hath no life in yt, *but yf we eate the flesh.* And yf ye will weigh yt, ye shall perceaue no consecucion nor dependence to be in the saing of S. Cyrill, yf prouing the flesh of Chryst to geue life, he shoulde will vs to eate the figure of his flesh, and so by yt to haue life, for that ys not proued. For what consequence ys this, the flesh of Chryst geueth life, ergo we eating the figure of yt haue life? Naie, the consequence of Cyrill, as he speaketh and meneth yt, hath a good consecucion

The flesh not the figure geueth life, wherfor we eate the verie flesh to haue life

after this forte. The flesh of Chryste ys quickninge, or making to liue, therfore he that eateth yt shall be made to liue: So that yt can not be denied, **G** but he speaketh of the verie reall flesh of Chryst to be eaten, and not of the figure of yt. And thus Cyrill speaking of the bread whiche was the figure addeth therunto the veritie of the figure, whiche ys the verie bodie of Chryste, and not an onely figure of the bodie. And nowe this coople thus being hearde to agree with the rest before them, we shall make like triall of an other coople.

THE EIGTH CHAP. PROCEADETH IN DECLA-
racion of the same by Saincte Augustin & Oecumenius.

Aincte Augustin whom all good chryftians haue in great reuerence for his fingular gifte of knowledge, whiche God by his holie spiritte had exceadinglie powred into him, as by the same gifte of **H** knowledge he ys in all matters of the chryftian faith copiouse and plentiful: so ys he in this matter, nowe in hand. But of manie places to bring some let vs first see howe he speaking of the younglinges or nouices in the faith, doth compare Manna the figure to the bodie of Chryste the thing figured. Thus he saieth. *Cathecumeni iam credunt in nomine Christi, sed Iesus non se credit eis, id est, non eis impertit corpus & sanguinem suum*

A *suum. Erubescant ergo quia nesciunt. Transeant per mare rubrum. Manducent Manna vt quomodò crediderunt in nomine Iesu, sic se ipsis credat Iesus.* The learners of Chryftes faith nowe beleue in the name of Chryfte, but Iefus committeth not himfelf to them, *he doth not impart or geue to them his bodie and blood.* Let them be afhamed therfor bicaufe they knowe not. Let them go through the read fea. Let them eate Manna, that as they haue beleued in the name of Iefus, fo Iefus maie committe him felf to them. Thus moche Sainct Auguftine.

For the better vnderftanding of whofe faing, yt ys to be knowen, that in the primitiue Churche, foche, whofe heartes god had touched to receaue the holie faith of Chryft, were for a time vnder the handes of teachers to be inftructed in the principles of faith. During whiche time, as they were not baptifed vntill they had fufficient knowlege of faith, and beleued according to their knowledge: no more did they receaue the bleffed bodie and blood of Chryfte. Nowe (as yt maie appeare) fome of thefe learners, that beleued in Chryfte, did not encreace and profitte fo well in faith that they might be B admitted to be baptifed, and to receaue the bodie of Chryfte. Of the which S, Auguftin therfor to quicken them, faied that they beleued in Iefus Chryfte, but Iefus did not yet committe him felf to them. What he ment by that he faied, *that Iefus did not committe him felf to them*, he immediatelie openeth when he faieth: *That ys* (faieth he) *he geueth not them his bodie and bloode.* Wherfor rebuking them he faieth: Let them be afhamed that as yet they be no better learned in Chryfte. Let them fo beleue that they maie paffe through the read fea, and maie eate Manna.

Nowe to applie this faing directlie to our pourpofe, this ys without al doubt that S, Auguftine in the ende willing the Cathecumeni to paffe through the read fea, and to eate Manna, moued them to be baptifed, and to receaue the holie Sacrament. Wherbie yt ys euident that he by Manna vnderftanding the bleffed Sacrament accompteth Manna the figure of yt. For yt ys common by the name of the figure to vnderftand the thing figured. As C Chryfte ys called the lambe that ys flain from the beginning of the worlde and fo yt ys in other figures. But yf yowe will knowe what oure Manna ys in verie dede, S, Auguftine opened yt in expreffe woordes, when he faied, that Iefus gaue them not his bodie and blood. See then the comparaifon of the figure to the thing figured, fee the thing figured to be the bodie of Chryfte. But of this place of S. Paule S. Auguftine more at large treacteth in another place.

When he had fhewed howe Sainct Paule, expownded the ftone to be Chryft, he proceadeth to enquire what the other thinges did fignifie. *Iam* *Auguft. de vtilit. pæn.* *ergo lumine illato, quæramus quid cœtera fignificent. Quid fibi voluit mare, nubes Manna, hæc enim non expofuit. Sed Petra quid oftendit. Per mare tranfitus, Baptifmus eft. Sed quia Baptifmus, id eft falutis aqua, non eft falutis, nifi Chrifti nomine confecrata, qui pro nobis fanguinem fudit, cruce ipfius aqua fignatur, & vt hoc fignificaret, ille Baptifmus mare rubrum fuit. Manna de cœlo apertè ab ipfo Domino exponitur. Patres veftri (inquit) manducauerunt Manna in Eremo, & mortui funt. Quando enim viuerent? Figura enim pronuntiare vitam* D *poffet, vita effe non poffet. Manducauerunt (inquit) Manna & mortui funt, id eft, Manna, quod manducauerunt, non illos potuit de morte liberare, non quia Manna mors eis fuit, fed quia à morte non liberauit. Ille enim à morte liberaturus erat, qui per Manna figurabatur, de cœlo certè Manna veniebat. Attende quem figurabat. Ego fum (inquit) panis viuus qui de cælo defcêdi.* Nowe, faieth S. Auguft. the light being brought in, let vs feke what the other thinges do fignifie. What the clowde the fea, and *Manna* do meen.

For thefe thinges he hath not expownded. But what the ftone was he hath **E** fhewed. The pafsing through the fea ys Baptifme. But bicaufe Baptifme, that ys to faie, the water of health ys not of healthe excepte yt be confecrated in Chryftes name, who fhed his blood for vs, the water ys bleffed with his croffe, and that *Manna* from heauen ys plainlie expownded of our Lorde himfelf: *Your Fathers* (faieth he) *haue eaten Manna in the Wilderneffe* , and they be dead. When fhoulde they liue? A figure maie prenunciate life, but yt can not be life. *They haue eaten* (faieth he) *Manna and be dead*, that ys to faie, *Manna*, that they did eate, coulde not deliuer them from death, not that *Manna* was death vnto them, but bicaufe yt deliuered not from death. He fhoulde deliuer from death, who was figurated by *Manna*. The *Manna* trulie came from heauen. Marke whom yt figured: *I am* (faieth he) *the liuing bread whiche came downe from heauen*. Thus farre S. Auguftine:

A figure geueth not life, but the bleffed Sac. geueth life. ergo, yt ys more then a figure.

In whofe woordes ye fee a goodlie applicacion of the figures to the thinges figured. Howe well and aptelie the redde fea figured Baptifme, whiche ys made redde in vertue by the bloode of Chryft, Sainct Auguftine moft **F** godlie hathe declared. And he hath doen no leffe in the applicacion of *Manna* to Chryfte in the Sacrament. Marke (faieth he) whom *Manna* did figure. Yt figured him, who faied: *I am the bread of life, whiche came downe from heauen*.

That Chryft fpake thefe woordes ther ys no doubte. But whether he fpake them of his bodie in the Sacrament the Sacramentarie will make a doubte. But that S. Auguftine meent that the bodie of Chryft in the Sacrament ys the thing figured by *Manna*, he himfelf doth fo plainlie open in an other place, that we are deliuered from doubte therof. Thus he faieth.

Lib. queft. No. et vet. teft. queft. 65.

Manna typus eft efcæ fpiritualis, quæ refurrectione Domini veritas facta eft in Euchariftiæ myfterio. *Manna* ys a figure of that fpirituall meat, whiche in the refurrection of our Lorde, was made the veritie in the Sacrament. In whiche woordes ye fee the iuft applicacion of the figure to the thinge figured. *Manna* ys the figure: the bodie of Chryft in the Sacrament ys the thing figured and the veritie.

Manna howe yt was called a fpirituall meat and the water of the rock a fpiritual drinke

Let yt not trooble the Reader, that he calleth yt the fpirituall meat, as **G** though therby were not affirmed the verie reall prefence. But remembre that S. Paule calleth *Manna* a fpirituall meat, although yt were corporall, and the water alfo he calleth fpirituall, althoug yt were likewife corporall, not that he wolde fo teache them to be fpirituall, that they were not in very dede corporall, but bicaufe they were miraculouflie and wonderfullie, not by the ordinarie power and worke of God, whiche he dailie worketh in the producing and conferuing of his creatures, but by a fpeciall, and vnwonted maner, geuen to the people of Ifraell. Wherfore yt liked S. Auguftin, as he might very well, to call yt, beinge the veritie, a fpirituall meate, as Manna the figure was called fpirituall meat. Wherby the one better anfwereth the other. And in dede as Manna was fent to the Iewes befide the courfe of nature: So was Chryft fent to vs befide the courfe of nature. And as yt was made meat to them merueillouflie: So ys the bodie of Chryft in the Sacra- **H** ment made meat for vs merueiloufly. And thus both thefe be fpirituall meates, although the bodie of Chryft more fpirituall, both for that after his refurrection his bodie was glorified and indewed with the giftes of immortalitie, agilitie, impafsibilitie, fubtilitie, and claritie: and alfo for that in the Sacrament yt ys beholden by faith, and not by fenfes whiche ys a fpirituall maner. Thus then yt appeareth very manifeftly, that the bodie of Chryft ys and maie be called for diuerfe confideracions a fpi-

The bodie of Chryft in the Sacr. howe yt ys called a fpirituall meat.

rituall

A rituall meat, and yet be neuer the leſſe a corporall ſubſtance.

That thus in this place, yt ys to be vnderſtanded to be a ſpirituall meate and not after the maner that the Aduerſarie wolde haue yt wreſted, the very woordes of Sainct Auguſtin enforce: For he ſaied that this ſpirituall meat ys in the myſtery or Sacrament. The ſpirituall maner that the Aduerſarie wolde here violentlie intrude and thruſt in, ys not, nor can not be in the Sacrament, but in the receauer, who by faithe and charitie receaueth after that ſpirituall maner, whiche faith and charitie be not in the Sacramentall bread (as they tearme yt) but in the man the receauer of yt. Of the whiche ſpirituall meat the bread ys a ſigne or a figure as they teache, ſaing, that as they receaue that bread to nouriſh the bodie: So they ſpiritually receaue Chryſt to nouriſh the ſoule: So that that ſpirituall meat of the whiche they ſpeake, ys not in the Sacrament. Therfor yt ys to be concluded, that he ſpeaketh of the naturall meat of Chryſtes bodie, whiche ys, according to the minde of this holy Father, and the doctrine of the catholique Churche verilie, really, ſubſtanciallie in the Sacrament and yet neuer
B the leſſe ſpirituallie, in maner aboue declared.

In this matter diuerſe other places might be brought in, but for that I wolde not wearie the Reader, but raither delight him with the hearing of ſome other, and that conuenient place might be had for Oecumnnius, we ſhall ceaſſe with thus moche of Sainct Auguſtine, and heare the ſaid Oecumenius vpon the ſame text of Sainct Paule. Thus he writeth. *Comederunt nempe Manna, ſicut nos corpus Chriſti. Potum ſpiritualem, hoc eſt, aquam è rupe ſiue petra ſcaturientem biberunt, quemadmodum nos ſanguinem Chriſti.* They haue (ſaieth Oecumenius) eaten Manna, as we the bodie of Chryſt: They heaue dronke a ſpirituall drinke, that ys, water running oute of a rocke or a ſtone, as we the bloode of Chryſte. Thus he.

Oecumen.
1.Cor.10.

A plain ſaing for the Procla.

This ys but a breif expoſition, but yet wonderfull weightie, and mightie to ouerthrowe the enemie. Methinke I ſhoulde nothing ſaie here to ope the matter, wher all ys ſo plain, but to declare that I wonder that men will or can
C be ſo deluded in a matter ſo clerely taught, as yt ys here. I merueill alſo howe malice can preuaill, or howe yt can ſhewe yt ſelf againſt ſo manie feſt a trueth by ſoche expreſſe woords vttered, that no miſtes or clowdes of wicked gloſe can wreſt, but in ſoche wiſe as yt maie very well be perceaued.

But to come to the pourpoſe, this ys firſt to be noted in this Authour, that he applieth the figure to the veritie in both partes, that ys Manna to the bodie of Chryſt, and the water to the bloode of Chryſt. In the whiche ye maie perceaue howe well he agreeth with Sainct Auguſtin, with whom he ys here ioined, and howe both they agree with them, that be before alleadged, whiche all haue taught that Manna and the water be figures of the bodie and bloode of Chryſte, and that not of the bodie and bloode of Chryſt abſolutelie withoute reſpecte, but of the bodie and bloode of Chryſte as eaten and dronken, whiche ys onely in the Sacrament, as touching the corporall eating of his bodie. Obſerue alſo for the preſence of Chryſtes bodie in the Sacrament, howe this Authour ſpeaketh withoute
D tropes, withoute figures, or anie ſoche like ſpeach, and in moſt plain maner ſaieth. *That they did eate Manna, as we the bodie of Chryſte: they dranke of the water of the rocke, as we the bloode of Chryſt.*

Reall preſence and corporall receipt of Chryſtes bodie auouched.

In the whiche comparaiſon I wolde learn of the Aduerſarie howe this aduerbe of ſimilitude ſhoulde agree with his ſpirituall maner, as concerning the eatinge of yt, as this Authour ſpeaketh yt, taking as they be in dede

Xx iiij　　Manna

Manna for the figure, and the bodie of Chryſt for the veritie. Yf the bodie　E
of Chryſte the veritie be eaten but ſpiritually, then Manna was not eaten
corporallie but ſpirituallie, whiche ys to wide from the trueth. For they did
eate Manna, as we the bodie of Chryſt, then yt foloweth that we eate the
bodie of Chryſt corporallie. For they did eate Manna corporallie. What
folie wolde theſe maſters of moſt folie, laie in theſe holie Fathers, that wher
(yf the hereticall aſſertion be true) we receaue not Chryſtes very bodie,
but the figure of yt or ſigne, they as Chryſoſtom, Sainct Hierom, and this
Authour expownding, and by their expoſitions taking vpon them to ſett
furth to vs the true mening, and right vnderſtanding of this ſcripture of
Sainct Paule geue vs no light of vnderſtanding, but raither darkeneſſe, no
true mening but a wrong mening, no right vnderſtandinge, but a miſvn-
derſtanding, and that ſo periloufe, as therbie they bring vs into the daunger
of Idolatrie? For they ſhoulde teache vs (as the heretikes wolde haue yt)
and ſaie, that as the children of Iſraell did eate Manna a figure of Chryſt:
So we eate the Sacramentall bread as a figure of Chryſt. As they the good　F
Iewes receauing the figure, receaued Chryſt by faith ſpiritually: So we receauing the Sacramentall bread as a figure, receaue likewiſe by faith Chryſt
ſpirituallie. As they receaued Manna corporally, but not Chryſt corporallie, but onely ſpirituallie: So we receaue the bread corporallie, but Chryſt
not corporallie, but onely ſpirituallie,

Noᵘ catholi-
que doctour
teacheth
the Sacr. to
be onelie a
figure.
　　This ys the hereticall pure, and ſyncere doctrine, and yet this maner and
forme of doctrine, yf yt be fownde in anie one of all the holie Fathers,
that haue taught ſynce Chryſt in anie time or age, I will leſe my credite
and geue the victorie. So pure ys ther doctrine and ſpirituall that yt cometh not vnder our ſenſeis, either to be ſeen, or hearde, as the doctrine of the
Fathers. But the Fathers teache that we receaue the very bodie of Chryſt,
and they putte no trope nor figure to yt, Wherfore they expownding the
Scriptures are to be vnderſtanded as they ſpeake.

　　When Chryſoſtome expowndeth this text of Sainct Paule, he vſeth
no other maner or phraſe of woordes in his expoſition, but this: *Ille illis*　G
Manna & aquam, & tibi corpus & ſanguinem dedit. He (mening God) gaue vnto
them Manna and water, and vnto thee his bodie and bloode.

　　Yf God geueth not vnto vs the bodie and bloode of Chryſt verilie, as
the woordes in their true ſignificacion do purporte, why dothe he not by
plain woordes ſo ſaie vnto vs, in an expoſition, whiche ſhoulde be all cleare and plain?

Note well
theſe plain
ſentẽces, rea-
der for thy
ſtaie.
　　Sainct Hierom alſo ſaied not, we are fedde with the figure of Chryſtes
bloode, whiche yf yt had ben none other, ther ys no doubte but in his
expoſition of the ſcripture he wolde ſo haue ſpoken yt. But he ſaied: *Et po-*
tum accipimus de latere Chriſti manantem. And we receaue drinke flowing oute
of the ſide of Chryſt. Wherby what ells can be ment, but that we receaue
the very bloode of Chryſt that flowed oute of his ſide, and not the bare
figure? Whiche might moche better haue ben expreſſed by other woordes, then by ſo plain liuelie woordes as theſe be, whiche vttereth the very　H
thing mightilie, and not the figure.

　　So alſo this Authour expownding the ſcripture therby to geue vs the
true vnderſtanding, doth not teache that we take but a figure. Whiche he
ſhoulde haue doen yf the trueth were ſo. But by plain woordes ſignifieng
the verie thing he ſaieth, that *the Iewes did eate Mãna, as we the bodie of Chryſt. And*
they dranke water of the ſtone as we the bloode of Chryſt. What ſhall we nowe
then

A then doubte of the matter? Coulde not thefe holie men and learned Fathers as well knowe to fpeake as *Oecolampadius, Zwinglius, Bullinger, Bucer, Peter Martyr, Cranmer or Iuell?* Were yt not to ftraunge that yf yt were but a figure, that none emong fo manie fhoulde fo expownde yt, and declare yt? Yf ther were no more but this yt might fufficientlie ftaie anie man not deftitute of grace to beleue that the Sacrament ys not onely a figure, but yt conteineth alfo the very bodie and bloode of Chryft, as the woordes of thefe Authours be, whiche bodie and bloode be the verities of ther figures Manna, and the water of the rocke.

THE NINTH CHAP. PROCEADETH IN
the declaracion of the fame by *Haimo*, and
Theophilact.

B Itherto we haue ben bufied in the teftimonies of foche as be of the moft auncient. Nowe we will defcend to fome of later time: and yet not yefter daie born, but foche as were well towarde a thoufand yeares agon, and therfor before *Berengarius* time, before the time of controuerfie in the Sacrament. Whom as their time doth nothing difcommend: So their learning ioined with holie life hath gotten them moche eftimacion. The coople we meen here to produce, be *Haimo*, and *Theophilact*. whiche both haue trauailed to expownde the epiftles of Sainct Paule. Wherfore we can not miftruft, but that they will geue vs that expofition, and vnderftanding of them, that the holie Churche had in their times, as the other auncient Fathers before alleadged haue doen. For howe foeuer yt be in this our time, yt was reputed and accompted with the holie men, a great and an horrible offence to diffent or depart from anie thing, that the Churche had receaued, accepted, approued or allowed. And therfor they wolde not by anie meanes, admitte that, wher-

C by they fhoulde be fownde to varie from the faithe of the Churche.

Nowe then being fure that they report to vs the faith of the Churche, as yt was receaued then, and comparing it to the auncient Church, the faith of whiche we haue hearde by foche as hetherto haue ben alleaged, ye fhall be fure that ye fhall not be deceaued of the very true auncient faith. Nowe therfore let vs heare thefe two, and firft Haimo.

He expowndeth the text of Sainct Paule nowe in hande, on this wife: *Et omnes eandem fpiritualem efcam manducauerunt. Et omne eundem potum &c. Manna, quod de cælo, id eft, de ifto aere eis datum eft: Et aquam, quæ de Petra fluxit, dicit fpiritualia effe, vel quia fpiritualiter intelligenda funt, fignificabant enim corpus & fanguinem Domini, quod modò confecratur, & percipitur in Ecclefia, vel quia non mundana lege, & confuetudine parata funt.* Manna whiche was geuen them from heauen, that ys from this aier, and the water whiche flowed from the ftone he faieth to be fpirituall, either bicaufe they are fpirituallie to be vnderftanded. *For they fignifie the bodie and blood of our Lorde, whiche ys nowe confe-*

D *crated, and receaued in the Churche:* Or ells bicaufe they were prepared not after the lawe and cuftome of worldlie thinges. Hitherto Haimo.

In whofe expofition ye haue to perceaue two caufes whiche he affigneth wherfor the Apoftles called Manna and the water fpirituall meat, and fpirituall drinke. The one was, that they be fpiritually to be vnderftanded. What the fpirituall vnderftanding of them ys he declareth. They did fignifie

Haimo
1.Cor.10.

The bodie and bloode of our Lorde are cõfecrated in the church gnifie(faieth he)the bodie and blood of Chryſt. In the whiche he agreeth **E** with the reſt before alleaged, that Manna and the water were figures of the bodie and blooode of Chryſt.

But nowe to come to the poinct of the controuerſie, of what bodie of Chryſt were they figures, of his bodie corporall, or ſpirituall? Attend, and marke well what he faieth. *They ſignified* (laieth he) *the bodie and bloode of our Lorde, whiche ys nowe conſecrated, and receaued in the churche.* In this ſaing the doubte ys diſſolued, and the matter ys opened. For yt ys the very bodie of of Chryſt reallie and ſubſtanciallie in the Sacrament, that was figured by Manna. And this ys proued by the woorde *Conſecrated*, whiche he vſeth ſaing the bodie and blood of Chryſte, be conſecrated in the bleſſed Sacrament.

Conſecracio̅ what yt ys.

Although this woorde (*Conſecracion*) be a woorde that the Aduerſaries can not abide: yet yt ys more manifeſt then that they can denie, that yt ys a woorde from whoſe vſe the graue and auncient Authours did not alhorre, but did vſe yt, as yt ys beforeſaied, and declared oute of Chryſoſtome, Sainct Ambroſe and other, wher alſo yt ys taught **F** by Chryſoſtome, what conſecracion ys, whiche (*to vſe his tearmes*) ys to make the bodie and blood of Chryſt of the thinges ſett furth vpon the table. Wherby he meneth the bread and wine, where alſo he declareth, who doth conſecrate, and by what woordes the conſecracion ys doen.

De pro. Iu. Hom. 30.

As touching him that doth conſecrate, he ſaieth yt ys not man, but Chryſte himſelf, who was crucified for vs. By what woordes conſecracion ys doen he ſheweth thus. *Hoc eſt, ait, corpus meum. Hoc verbo propoſita conſecrantur.* This ys(ſaieth he, mening Chryſt) my bodie. With this woorde (ſaieth Chryſoſtom) the thinges ſettfurth, that ys the bread and wine are conſecrated. But where vnto are they conſecrated? into the bodie and bloode of Chryſt, as Chryſoſtom hath ſaied.

Lib. 4. de Sac. cap. 4.

And herevnto alſo Sainct Ambroſe ys a witneſſe who ſaieth. *Non erat corpus Chriſti ante conſecrationem, ſed poſt conſecrationem, dico tibi, quod iam corpus eſt Chriſti. Ipſe dixit, & factum eſt, ipſe mandauit & creatum eſt* Yt was not the **G** bodie of Chryſt before the conſecracion. But after the conſecracion, I ſaie to thee, that nowe yt ys the bodie of Chryſte: He hath ſaied, and yt was made, he hath commaunded and yt was created.

The cauill of ſacrame̅tall bread impugned.

And leeſt the Aduerſarie ſhoulde cauille, and ſaie, that the bread after the woordes come to yt, ys Sacramentall bread, and therfore yt maie take vpon yt the name of the thing, of whiche yt ys a Sacrament, and ſo meneth Sainct Ambroſe. To this maie be ſaied, that that gloſe ys to violent for ſo plain woordes. For yt ys to be thought that Sainct Ambroſe wolde not haue ſaied with ſoche a vehement maner of ſpeache, that yt ys the bodie, yf yt ſhoulde be but called the hodie, and not be the bodie in dede. For this maner of ſpeache(I ſaie vnto thee, that nowe yt ys the bodie of Chryſt) importeth an other maner of force of the thing that ys ſpoken of to be ſo in dede, then to be ſo called.

Amb. ibid.

And that he ment no leſſe then he ſaied, his owne woordes in the ſame **H** chapiter proue, where obiecting againſt him ſelf in the perſon of a weake man, at the ſeight of the Sacrament he ſaieth thus. *Tu fortè dicis, meus panis eſt vſitatus: Sed panis iſte, panis eſt ante verba Sacramentorum, vbi acceſſerit con- ſecratio, de pane fit caro Chriſti.* Thowe perchaunce ſaieſt: Yt ys my vſuall bread, But this bread before the woordes of the Sacramentes ys bread, but when the conſecracion cometh to yt, of the breade ys made the fleſh of Chryſt.

In theſe

A In thefe woordes of Sainct Ambrofe, yt maie well be perceaued, that he meneth that the bodie of Chryft ys in the Sacrament fubftanciallie, and not that the Sacramentall bread (as they tearme yt) ys onely fo called. For the flefh of Chryft ys made of the bread, the fubftance of the bread being turned into the fubftance of the flefh of Chryft by the Almightie power of God thorough the worke of the holie Goft, as Sainct Cyprian teftifieth. *Panis quem Dominus Difcipulis edendum porrigebat, non effigie fed natura mutatus, omnipotentia Verbi factus eft caro.* The bread whiche our Lorde gaue to his difciples to eate being chaunged not in outwarde forme, but in nature, by almightineffe of the woorde ys made flefh. Sainct Ambrofe faieth the flefh of Chryfte ys made of the bread: Sainct Cyprian faieth, that the bread by the allmightineffe of the woorde ys made flefh.

De cœna Domini.
The bread chaunged in nature ys made flesh.

And that this fhoulde not feme vnpofsible, though yt be wonderfull. Theophilacte maketh a very apte fimilitude: fainge: *Et ne quem conturbet quod credendus fit panis caro. Etenim & in carne ambulante Domino, & ex pane alimoniam admittente, panis ille qui manducabatur, in corpus eius mutabatur, &c.*

B And let yt not troble anie man, that the bread ys to be beleued flefh. For when our Lorde walked in the flefh, and receaued the foode of bread, the fame bread whiche was eaten, was chaunged into his bodie, and was made like vnto his holie flefh, and yt auailed to his augmentacion, and fuftentacion, after the maner of man. Therfor nowe alfo the bread ys chaunged into the flefh of our Lorde. And howe, faieth he, dothe yt not appeare flefh, but bread? That we fhoulde not abhorre from the eating of yt.

Whie'ther appeareth not flesh in the Sacr.

What can be faied againft thefe fo manifeft and fo plain teftimonies? Maie we not, or raither aught we not to faie as thefe holie famoufe, and learned men do, raither then to faie as a fewe phantafticall heretiques, and Apoftaties do? Let vs beleue thefe pillers of Chryftes Churche, and beleuing them, feke to be faued as they be.

Thus haue ye hearde enough, I fuppofe, to declare vnto yowe, that by confecracion, whiche Haimo fpake of, the bodie of Chryft ys in the Sacra-

C ment. And therfor Manna, as he faied, fignifieng the bodie of Chryft confecrated, fignifieth the very reall and fubftanciall bodie of Chryft. And thus hauing opened the minde of this authour, who as he ys agreable to the holie auncient Fathers before alleadged: So ys he plain and pithie to the readers and ftrong, and mightie to debell the Aduerfaries, I will come to heare Theophilacte expownde the fame place of Sainct Paule. Thus he writeth, *Vt enim nos aqua Baptifmi perfufi corpus dominicum manducamus: Sic & Manna illi mari traiecto, in efum funt vfi: Et quemadmodum ipfi Domini fanguinem bibimus; Sic illi erumpentem e percuffo lapide aquam biberunt.* As we wafhed with the water of Baptifme, do eate our Lordes bodie: So they hauing paffed through the fea, vfed Manna for their foode. And as we drinke the bloode of our Lorde: So they dranke the water that gufhed out of the fmitten Rocke. Thus Theophilacte.

A plain faing for M. Iuell.

Thefe two teftimonies be fo like in fenfe and phrafe, that they might raither be iudged to come oute of one minde, and oute of one mouthe

D them from two men, different in time, diftant in place, and contrie. But God, who ys not, as Sainct Paule faieth: *Diffentionis Deus, fed pacis, & vnitatis.* The God of diffention: but of peace and vnitie: who by his holie fpirit wrought that *Multitudinis credentium erat cor vnum, & anima vna.* The multitude that beleued were of one heart, and of one foule, made them being of one faith to fpeake one thing, as he did his foure holy Euangeliftes

1. Cor. 14. The spirit of vnitie among catholiques.

who

Who although they did write in diuerſe times and places:yet they agreed **E** in vnitie of one trueth.

　　But they that can not content them ſelues with that ordre and condicion that God hath placed them in, but being puffed vppe with the ſpirit of pride, go aboute to buyll the tower of Babell to get them a name, God by his ſpirit of humilitie and vnitie not working withe them, their tounges are diuided, and diſſention ys among them,they agree not, they ſpeake not of one thing:as yt ys eaſie to ſee in the ſchoole of confuſion, euen an other Babell the Tower of the wicked name of Luther. Among whoſe diſciples was nor ys the ſpirit of vnitie,neither were nor be yet that multitude of one heart,nor of one ſoule,but of diuerſe. Luther he ſpake with one toung, and ſaied, the verie bodie of Chryſt was in the Sacrament reallie and ſubſtanciallie: *Oecolampadius* he ſpake in an other toung contrarie to his Maſter, and ſaied that Chryſtes bodie was not ther, but as in a ſign. Some other of Luthers diſciples ſaied that Magiſtrates and rulers muſt be obeied : Some of them had other tounges and ſaied that we are **F** called to libertie, and therfor we be all equall, and owe no obedience to Man. Some tounges ſaied that children muſt be chryſtned again. Some other tounges ſaied naie. Some tounges ſaied that ther were but two Sacramentes : Some ſaied their were three: Some otherwiſe with a nombre of diuiſions not onely among the multitude : but among them ſelues. I meen that one of them in all places, and at all times did not agree with him ſelf,but here ſaied this,in an other place clean contrarie, as hereafter by the helpe of Gods grace,more at large ſhall be ſhewed.

Pſal.67.　　But God (*qui facit habitare vnius moris in domo.* Who maketh men to be of one minde in the houſe) maketh men that dwell in his houſe of his holie Churche to be of one toung, of one minde, to beleue one thing,and to ſaie one thing. Therfor let theſe men of Babell go, theſe men of confuſed tounges,and let vs heare the people of agreement.

　　Ye ſee I ſaie,howe Theophilacte agreeth with Haimo, and yf ye aſcende to Oecumenius, to Chryſoſtome and other, ye ſhall ſee ſoche agrement **G** in ſenſe, ſoche likneſſe in woordes that a man might ſaie, that they were all ſpoken, not of diuerſe men,but of one man.Conferre them together,Reader and trie my ttueth:

The Iewes eate Māna we our Lordes bodie. They dranke water: we the bloo de of Chriſt　　I ſhall not nede to trooble thee with many woordes to open the ſaing of Theophilacte, for yt ys ſo euident and plain that yt nede no expoſitour. Onelie I wiſh,that for the pourpoſe that he ys alleadged,that ye note firſt,that he compareth Manna, and the water to the bodie and bloode of Chryſt as the figures to the verities, in that he ſaieth: *As we eate our Lordes bodie.So they Manna. As we drinke the biood of our Lorde. So they drinke the water of the Rocke.*

　　That by the bodie and blood of Chryſt,he meneth the bodie and bloode in the Sacrament, whiche he moſt manifeſtlie affirmeth, and by expreſſe *Cap.lx.* woordes denieth the onelie figure of the Aduerſarie ſo wickedlie auouched, yt appeareth in his expoſition of this ſaing of Chryſt, *This ys my* **H** *bodie*, in the ſix and twenteth of Sainct Matthew, and in the fourtenth of Sainct Marke, whiche bothe be alleageth in the ſeconde booke in the expoſition of the ſame ſaing of Chryſt.

Theoph. in 6.Ioan.　　Likewiſe alſo dothe he vpon the vj. of Sainct Iohn wher he ſaieth thus. Marke that the bread , which ys eaten of vs in the myſteries ys not onelie a figure of the bodie of our Lorde but the fleſh yt ſelf of our Lorde.For he

did

A did not faie the bread, whiche I will geue, ys a figure of my flesh. But yt ys my flesh.

In this sentence yt perceaue Theophilacte not onelie auouching the verie substanciall presence of Chrystes flesh in the Sacrament, whiche ys the catholique doctrine: but also denieng the figure whiche ys the hereticall doctrine. What wicked obstinacie ys this, that wher this Authour denieth yt to be a figure, they affirme the contrarie: and wher he affirmeth the substanciall presence of Chrystes flesh, they denie yt? Yf the Aduersaries had but one soche place to denie the presence (as certen I am they haue none) they wolde triumphe moche against the trueth. But hauing none to denie that, that they denie, but manie to denie that they do affime, yt ys most deuellish arrogancie to stand in yt. *Reall presence auouched, and the hereticall figure denied.*

But let vs heare Theophilact in an other place, treacting of Manna, and the Sacrament. *Patres vestri comederunt Manna in solitudine. Hoc sæpe & multùm versat in ore, vt persuadeat hominibus. Nam si possibile fuit quadraginta annis sine messe & semente pasci homines, & conseruari illorum vitam, multo magis nunc* B *nostram spiritualem meliori pane Dominus carne sua, quæ absque semine viri, ex virgine constituta est.* Your Fathers haue eaten Manna in the Wildernesse. This (saieth Theophilact speaking of Chryst) he hath moche and often in his mouthe, that he might persuade men. For yf yt were possible men to be fedde fortie yeares without harnest and sowing, and their life to be conserued, moche more nowe he shall conserue our spirituall life with that better bread his flesh, which withoute seed of man was born of the virgen. *In 6. Joan.*

In this ye perceaue the comparaison of the figure to the thing figured, which thing figured ys not a peice of bread, of no better sorte, condicion or dignitie then Manna. But yt ys a better bread saieth Theophilacte, that ys the thing figured, which ys not an onelie figure of the flesh, as the Aduersary wolde glose yt, but yt ys the flesh of Chryst in very dede. For yt ys the same flesh that was born of the virgen withoute seed of man. Albeit more might be saied oute of Theophilacte, who ys both plain and plentifull in C in this matter: yet trusting that this maie suffice a Chrysten reader, I will ceasse, and come to the last coople vpon this texte.

THE TENTH CHAP. PROCEADETH
vpon the same text by Rupertus, and Rich. Holkot,
and endeth with Gagneius.

Erceauing that in these former allegacions, I haue ben somwhat long, being desierouse that the Reader shoulde well perceaue the faith of these auncientes, and learn the trueth of them to the condemnacion and vanquishing of the falshead of heresie, in the opening of these three, for that they be not of great auncientie, but yet of most substan-
D ciall trueth, I shall to ende this text make with them a short conclusion.

Rupertus, who ys a learned writer, and so reputed and accepted of learned men, writing vpon Exodus, and treacting of Manna saieth thus vpon this text. *Nec qui plus collegerat habuit amplius, nec qui minus parauerat reperit minus. Hoc pro virtute cibi & spiritualis potus, id est, corporis & sanguinis Christi sciendum & firmiter tenendum est, quia non pro quantitate portionis, quam ore percipit* *Rupert. in Exod.*

Yy   secundum

secundùm visibilem speciem panis & vini, alius plus, alius minus consequitur de gra- E
tia spiritus viuificantis: sed singuli iuxta id quod possunt edere congregant, id est,
quod possunt credere, remissionem peccatorum percipiunt, & vitam æternam. Si-
cut enim pater qui primus peccauit, cuius nos iniquitatem portauimus, non pro quantita-
te morsus sui, siue pomi quod momordit, sententiam, vel damnationem iustam accepit,
tantúmque illi valuit pomum vnum momordisse, quantum quicquid pomorum in ar-
bore illa fuit deuorasse, ad condemnationem infidelitatis, & inobedientiæ: Sic è con-
trario quisque nostrum, non pro quantitate portiunculæ viuifici panis quæ frangitur illi,
quam ore sumit, aut dentibus terit, gratiam vel vitam accipit, sed tantùm illi valet ad
consequutionem Iustitiæ exiguum quid percipisse, quàm valeret, si totum quod obla-
tum est, proprio solus ore perciperet. Rectè ergo sancta Christi Ecclesia panes non valdè
grandes, sed exiguas ad conficiendum corpus Christi componit similas & valdè tenues.
Neque vini multum sed exiguum quid infundit, quia sicut iam dictum est, nec qui
plus collegit habuit amplius, nec qui minus parauerat repperit minus. Vnto him that
had gathered moche ther remained nothing ouer: and to him that had
gathered litle, ther was no lacke. This ys to be knowen and firmely to be F
holden for the vertue of the spirituall meate, and drinke, that ys to saie,
of the bodie and bloode of Chryst, that not for the quantitie of the porcion
which anie man taketh with his mouthe according to the visible forme
of bread and wine one getteth more, an other lesse of the grace of the
quickning spirit: but euery one acording to that, that they can eate, do
gather, that ys, according as they can beleue, they receaue remission of
their sinnes, and life euerlasting. As our Father which first offended,
whose iniquitie we haue borne, not for the quantitie of his bitte or mor-
sell, or eils of the apple whiche he bitte, hathe he receaued sentence, or
iust damnacion. For yt had ben as moche for him to haue bitten one
apple to the condemnacion of his infidelitie and disobedience, as to haue
deuoured all the apples on that tree: So contrary wise euerie one of vs
receaueth grace or life, not for the quantitie of the litle porcion of the
quickninge bread whiche ys broken vnto him whiche he receaueth with his
mouthe, or bruseth with his teeth. But asmoche yt shall auaill him to G
the obteining of righteousnes to haue receaued a litle porcion, as yt shoulde auaill him yf he alone shoulde receaue with his owne mouthe, all that
ys offred. Therfore the holie Churche of Chryst doth well, whiche maketh not great loaues to consecrate the bodie of Chrysti, But small cakes,
and thinne. Neither dothe she occupie moche wine but a litle. For as yt
ys saied, vnto him that had gathered moche, remained nothing ouer,
and to him that had gathered litle, ther was no lacke. Thus farre
Rupertus.

Who expownding the sixtenth Chapiter of Exodus, in the whiche ys
declared the feding of the children of Israell with Manna, expowndeth
in the same the miraculouse worke of God, which Moyses declareth to be
doen in the gathering of the same Manna, whiche was that where they
were commaunded, that they shoulde euery Man gather a certain measure called a Gomer, whiche shoulde suffice a man, yf anie gathered for H
gredinesse or otherwise, anie more then his measure, whiche God ap-
appoincted him, yet he had no more, yf he gathered lesse then the measure
yet he had ynough.

This Authour applieng this worke and miracle of God in Manna to the
Sacrament, as to the thing figured, he declareth howe answerablie, God
woorketh nowe in the thing figured, to the figure, teaching as great a mi-
racile in

A　racle in the one, as in the other in that refpect of hauing more or leffe. Allthough as touching the fubftance of them, the one fo farre exceadeth the
other, that ther ys no comparaifon. By whiche yt ys moft manifeft, that he
taketh Manna to be a figure of Chryft in the Sacrament.

That he beleued Chryft to be in the Sacrament he doth well open in
this his applicacion where he faieth, that the receipt of the vertue of the
fpirituall meat, and drinke, whiche ys the bodie and bloode of Chryft,
ys not to be proporcioned, according to the quantitie of the vifible formes of bread and wine. In the whiche woordes, he plainlie declareth, that
the meate of the Sacrament figured by Manna, ys the bodie and bloode
of Chryft.

But here the Aduerfaries will faie that this Authour ys on ther parte. *Obiection of fpirituall meat and drinke an- fwered.*
For he calleth yt fpirituall meate and drinke, wherby he meeneth the fpi-
rituall receipt of Chryftes bodie fpirituallie, and not corporallie. Call to
remembrance, what ys faied of this in the eighte chapter of this booke
wher ther be caufes affigned vpon the faing of S. Auguftin, why the bo-
B　die of Chryfte ys called fpirituall meat, and yt fhall anfwer the Aduerfarie fullie.

And yet I fhall adde the faing of Sainct Ambrofe to the vtter difcom-
fiting of the Aduerfarie, whiche teacheth the bodie of Chryft to be in the
Sacrament. For he declaring Manna to be the figure of yt, proueth by
that, and by an other excellent reafon, that the bodie of Chryft in the Sa-
crament ys a fpirituall bodie: *In Sacramento Chriftus eft, quia corpus eft Chrifti:* *Aubr. de myft. ca.9.*
*Non ergo corporalis efca, fed fpiritualis eft. Vnde Apoftolus de typo eius ait: quia patres
noftri efcam fpiritualem manducauerunt, & potum fpiritualem biberunt. Corpus
enim Dei, corpus eft fpirituale. Corpus Chrifti, corpus eft diuini fpiritus.* In the Sacrament ys Chryft, for yt ys the bodie of Chryft, yt ys not therfor corporall meat. Wherfor the Apoftle alfo faieth of the figure of yt, that our Fathers haue eaten fpirituall meat, and dronken fpirituall drinke? The bodie
of God ys a fpirituall bodie. The bodie of Chryfte, ys the bodie of the diui-
C　ne fpirit. Thus moche Sainct Ambrofe.

Firft teaching the prefence of Chryft in the Sacrament, he contenteth
not himfelf fo to faie, but to preuent the obiection of the Aduerfarie, who *Chryfte ys the fubftan ce of the bleffed Sac.*
will elude this, and faie that Chryft ys in the Sacrament as in a fign, he faieth
not onely that Chryft ys in the Sacrament, but he faieth alfo that the bodie
of Chryft ys the Sacrament, the fubftance of bread and wine being chaunged into the fubftance of the bodie and bloode of Chryfte, the onely formes of bread and wine remaining. And after he hath thus taught, he inferreth, that therfor yt ys no corporall meat, but fpirituall meate. And to
proue this, he maketh as yt were two argumentes: The firft ys that forafmoche as the figures of yt were by Sainct Paule called fpirituall meate,
and fpirituall drinke, moche more maie yt be called fpirituall meat, and
fpirituall drinke. The feconde argument ys that the bodie of God ys
fpirituall, and the bodie of Chryft ys the bodie of God, wherfor the bodie of Chryft ys fpirituall.

D　Thus ye fee that as Sainct Auguftin (as yt ys before in the eight Chapiter alleadged) calleth the very reall and fubftanciall bodie of Chryft in
the Sacrament fpirituall. So alfo doth Sainct Ambrofe, not that yt ys
not a very bodie, but bicaufe in diuerfe refpectes yt ys fpirituall, as Sainct
Cyrill alfo faieth: *Totum corpus viuifica fpiritus virtute, plenum effe oftendit.* *In 6. Joan.*
Spiritum enim ipfam carnem nuncupauit, non quia naturam carnis amiferit, & in fpi-

ritum mutata fit : fed quia fummè cum eo coniuncta, totam viuificandi vim haufit. E
Nec turbari propter hoc decet. Nam qui Domino conglutinatur, vnus cum eo fpi-
ritus eft, quomodò igitur caro fua vna cum eo non appellabitur? He fheweth that

The flesh of Chryfte called a fpi rit, and fo a fpirituall flesh.

all his bodie ys full of the quickning power. For he calleth his flefh the
fpirit, not that yt had loft the nature of flefh, and ys chaunged into the fpirit,
but bicaufe yt ys fo nerelie ioined with him, yt hath taken into yt all power
to make to liue. Neither ys yt decent any man to be troubled for this. For
he that ys faft ioined with God, ys one fpirit whithe him. Howe then fhall
not his flefh be called one with him? Thus moche Sainct Cyrill.

Of whome we maie learn that Chryft him felf called his flefh a fpirit, and
therfore yt maic well be called fpirituall, and yet faieth Sainct Cyrill, though
yt be fo called, yt hath not loft the nature of flefh, but ys both flefh and fpirit. And therfor well called of thefe Authours a fpirituall flefh, a fpirituall
bodie, a fpirituall meate, and yet allwaies being a very fubftanciall bodie,
and a naturall flefh.

By thefe Authours yt ys made manifeft to you, that when they or other F
do call the bodie of Chryft in the Sacrament, a fpirituall bodie, or a fpirituall flefh, or as *Rupertus* doth, a fpiritual meate: yt ys not furthwith after
the Aduerfaries minde, to be made fo fpirituall, that ther fhall remain neither bodie, nor meat, but that by a fpirituall vnderftanding by faith we
muft vnderftand yt a verie bodie, verie flefh, and yet fpirituall for manie
caufes here and before declared. And that this Authour ment euen fo
yt appeareth well. For when he had called yt fpirituall meat, he furthwith
expownded yt and faied, *that ys to faie, the bodie and bloode of Chryft.* whiche
bodie and bloode he wolde fo to be fpirituall, not that yt fhoulde be abfent
from the Sacrament, but raither to be the fubftance of the Sacrament,
whiche he doth well infinuate, when he faieth, that we receaue not the fpirituall meat of the bodie and bloode of Chryft according to the quantitie
of the vifible forme of bread and wine. He faieth not according to the quantitie of bread and wine, whiche woordes might include their fubftances, but
faieth after the maner of the fpeache of the catholique faith, according to G
the quantitie of the vifible formes of bread and wine fignifieng the fubftaces
of thē to be abfent bicaufe they be chaunged and maketh mencion onely of
the formes. And that this was his faith, he by moft plain woordes declareth,

Rupert. in Exo. ca. 10

in his expofition vpon the fame booke of Exodus, faing thus: *Quomodò verbum*
à fummo demiffum caro factum eft, non mutatum in carnem, fed affumendo carnem. Sic
panis & vinum, vtrumque ab imo fubleuatum fit conpus Chrifti & fanguis non mu-
tatum in carnis faporem, fed affumendo inuifibiliter vtriusque diuinæ fcilicet & hu-
manæ, quæ in Chrifto eft immortalis fubftantiæ, veritatem. Proinde ficut hominem qui
de virgine famptus in cruce pependit, rectè & catholicè Deum confitemur: Sic vera-
citer hoc quod fumimus de fancto altari Chriftum dicimus, agnum Dei prædicamus. As

As rightlie as we côfef- fe Chryfte to haue ben crucified, fo rightlie we côfeffe him to be in the Sacr.

the Sonne of God coming down from the high was made flefh, not
being chaunged into flefh, but by taking flefh vpon him, So bread and
wine both lifte vppe from the loweft ys made the bodie and bloode of
Chryfte not chaunged into the tafte of flefh, or into the horriblenefse of H
bloode, but inuifiblie taking the veritie of bothe the immortall fubftances, whiche be in Chryft, that ys to faie both of God and man. Therfor
as we rightly and catholikely confeffe the man whiche being born of the
Virgen hanged on the croffe to be God: So this that we receaue at the
holie aultar, we trulie faie to be Chryft, we openly confeffe yt to be the lambe of God. Thus Rupertus.

　　　　　　　　　　　　　　　　　　　　　　　　　This

A   This faing nedeth no commentarie. Wherfor breifly note, gentle Reader, that he faieth, that the bread and wine be made the bodie and bloode of Chryft.   Note that the bread and wine haue the veritie of the fubftances of both natures of Chryft.   Note that as catholikely as we confeffe Chryft, to be God : So catholikely do we confeffe yt that we receaue at the holy aultar to be Chryft, and the lambe of God.   Alfo yf the aultars be holie, as this Authour faieth they be.   Yt can be no holie dede to pull them down with defpite as Germanie and Englond haue doen.

Aultars ho lie.

      This I truft, fufficeth to open this Authours faith as concerning the prefence of Chryft in the holie Sacrament. Wherfor nowe leauing him, his folowe fhall be hearde, who ys Holkot an englifh man, who writing vpon the booke of wifdom faieth thus.   *Per Manna in facra fcriptura figuratur fignanter Euchariftiæ Sacramentum. Sicut enim filij Ifraël tranfeuntes per defertum verfus terram à Domino promiffam cibi refocillabantur alimento, ita nos per mundum ad cœlum pergentes corporis & fanguinis Chrifti quotidiano viatico recreamur.* By Manna in the holie fcripture, the Sacrament ys notablie figured. For as the

Holkot in li fap.cap.16

Manna a notable figure of the Sacrament

B children of Ifraell going through the defert towarde the land promifed vnto them of God they were recreated with the foode of that meat : Euen fo we going through the worlde to heauen, are recreated with the dailie iourneing meat of the bodie and bloode of Chryft.

      Of this Authour though he be of the later daies, we learn no other thing in this matter, but euen the verie fame that the great auncientes haue before taught and auouched. So that I can not perceaue why the mafters of wickednefle, fhoulde reiect him and foche other, but onely of malice for there plain teftimonie. As all that before be alleaged haue taught Manna to be a figure of the Sacrament: So doth this Authour likewife. As they haue auouched the prefence of Chryftes bodie in the Sacrament. So doth this Authour alfo. For he faieth that we are fedde in this worlde in our iourneie to heauen warde with *the bodie and bloode of Chryst.*

      Nowe ye haue hadde thefe matters reported and teftified to yowe by
C twelue witneffes, whiche be fufficient by the lawes yf yt were in matter of life and death, as in dede this ys, for they that beleue this, as they haue teftified, maie haue life: but they whiche do not fhall die the death.   They haue teftified that Manna ys a figure of the Sacrament, they haue teftified that in the fame Sacrament ys Chryft verilie, and therwithall fome of them by expreffe woordes haue teftified the excellencie of this Sacrament, aboue the Sacramentes of the olde lawe, and in effecte fo haue they euery one. For fainge that we haue the veritie, wher they hadde but the figure, yt declareth as moch excellencie in owres aboue theirs, as ys of the bodie aboue the fhadowe.   Thefe be not twelue bare witneffes, but they are fubftanciall witneffes, all being of Chryftes Parliament houfe, and moft of them of the higher houfe, I meen of them that were aboue nine hundreth yeares agon, who teftifie vnto vs no other, but that trueth and faithe, whiche then was receaued as an enacted trueth.   Wherfor Reader, contemne not their teftimonie, contemne not their aunciencie, and with all neclect
D not thy faluacion, but yf thowe will yt obtein, heare thefe witneffes reuerently, beleue them faithfullie, abide in that beleif conftantly, and yf all other poinctes of life and faith be in thee agreablie, thowe fhalt, no doubte, liue perpetually.

      Nowe finallie to conclude and fhet vppe the expofition of this text: I haue thought good to adde the thirtenth witneffe, who fhall be *Gagneius*

                                          Yy iij   a man

a mān of the later daies, but not to be contemned but woorthilie for his **E**
learning to be receaued. Whom for that he breiflie expowndeth the wholl
text of Sainct Paule here treacted of, I haue placed him in the laft place, for
the Readers better remembrance. Thus hewriteth. *Admonet hoc capite Paulus*

Gagneius
in Paulum
1.Cor.`10.

Corinthios, ne de donis à Deo perceptis efferantur. Futurum enim vt per elationem
hanc atque alia peccata, ijs donis excidant, & à Chriſto eijciantur idque exemplo Iu-
dæorum docet. Quos, licet in figura, similibus tamen donis ab eo affectos probat, ſed
hinc tamen ob ſua delicta excidiſſe. Sicut enim Corinthij in ſpiritu ſancto & aqua bap-
tiſati, veri Pharaonis ſeruitutem excuſſerunt, Chriſti carne paſti, & eius ſanguine potati
ſunt : Ita patres Iudæi excuſſa Pharaonis ſeruitute, & tranſgreſſo marı rubro, quodam
modo in mari & nube baptiſati ſunt, ſimilitudinarie ſcilicet : Quod enim illis nubes pro-
tegens, conducens, ac refrigerans, id nobis ſpiritus ſanctus actionum noſtrarum dux &
ptotector, libidınumque moderator & extinctor. Quod illis mare, hoc Corinthijs aqua
Baptiſmatis. Corinthij Chriſti carnem manducabant: illi figuram eius Manna, quam ſpi-
ritualem vocat eſcam, quod miraculosè cœlitus deſcenderit. Corinthij Chriſti ſanguinem
bibebant. Iudæi ſpiritualem potum, quem miraculosè petra ſudit, biberunt, neque tamen **F**
tot affecti beneficijs præter duos tantùm, in terram promiſſionis peruenerunt, ſed in de-
ſerto proſtrati ſunt ac mortui. Qua in re figura noſtri fuere, vt ſcilicet à vitijs illorum
abſtıneamus, alioquin in deſerto perpetuæ vaſtıtudinis perituri, neque veram promiſ-
ſionis terram ingreſſuri.   Paule doth admoniſh the Corynthians in this cha-

A notable
conference,
of the figu-
res and the
thinges figu-
red, and of
the benefi-
tes of bothe

piter that they be not prowde of the giftes whiche they haue receaued of
God. For yt maie come, that by this pride and other ſinnes, they maie fall
from theſe giftes, and be caſt oute from Chryſt. And that he teacheth by the
example of the Iewes, whom he proueth to haue had the like benefittes although in figure: and yet by their ſinnes to haue fallen from them. For as the
Corynthians baptiſed in the holie Goſt and water brake of the ſeruitude of
the verie Pharao after they were fedde with the fleſh of Chryſt, and had
dronken this bloode: Euen ſo the Fathers the Iewes, hauing broken the ſeruitude of Pharao, and paſſed through the read ſea, after a certain maner
they were baptiſed in the ſea and the cloud, that ys to ſaie, ſimilitudina-
relie. For what the clowde was vnto them, defending, conducting, and **G**
refreſhing them : that vnto vs ys the holy Coſt, the guide of our doinges
and protectour, and of our euell luſtes the moderatour and deſtroyer.
What the ſea was vnto them : that vnto the Corynthians was the water
of Baptiſme. The Corynthians did eate the fleſh of Chryſte: they did
eate Manna the figure of yt which he calleth ſpirituall meat, bicauſe yt mira-
culouſly deſcended from heauen. The Corynthians dranke the bloode of
Chryſt: the Iewes dranke the ſpirituall drinke, whiche the Rocke miraculouſlie powred owte. And yet for all that being indued with ſo manie benefittes, they came not into the lande of promeſſe, two onely excepted, but
they were ouerthrowen in the deſert, and dead. In the whiche they were a
figure of vs that we ſhoulde abſtein from their vices, or ells we ſhall periſh in
the Wilderneſſe of euerlaſting vaſtitie, and not entre the true land of promiſ
ſe. Thus moche Gagneius.

Whom ye ſee not onely applieng Manna and the water of the Rocke as fi- **H**
gures of Chryſtes bodie and bloode, and affirming the verie preſence of thē
bothe, but alſo fullie and throughly expownding the text to the perfect vnderſtanding of S. Paule, and in nothing diſſenting, but conſenting to the ena
cted trueth of Chryſtes Parliament houſe, with the other before alleaged.
And nowe thus moche of the figure Manna, and of the expoſition of the
text of S. Paule conteining the ſame.

THE

A

THE ELEVENTH CHAPITER, DECLA-
*reth the prophecies of the Sacrament vnder the names of Manna
and the water of the Rocke.*

Lthough of this bleſſed Sacrament ther be manie prophecies, as in the firſt booke yt ys declared yet of yt, as
aunſwerable vnto this figure there be not manie. The prophet Dauid in the pſalme maketh mencion of yt ſaing: *Pſalm. 77.*
*Et mandauit nubibus deſuper, & ianuas cæli aperuit. Et pluit illis
Manna ad manducandum, & panem cæli dedit eis. Panem Angelorum manducauit homo.* He commaunded the clowdes aboue, and opened the
doores of heauen. He rained down Manna alſo vpon them for to eate, and
gaue them foode from heauen. So man did eate Angels foode. Of this alſo he
ſpeaketh again: *Et pane celi ſaturauit eos. Dirupit petram,et fluxerunt aquæ,abierunt in
ſicco flumina.* And he filled thē with the bread of heauen. He opened the Rocke of ſtone, and the waters flowed oute, ſo that riuers ran oute of drie pla-   *Applicaciō*
B ces. Theſe wonderfull factes doen by the hand of God for his people the   *of Manna*
children of Iſraell, the Prophet Dauid reherſeth not as an hiſtoriographer   *and the wa-*
vpon onely reſpect that they were doen, as they be reported, but that they   *ter to the*
ſhall be doen ſpirituallie vpon his people the faithfull Chryſtians, whiche be   *bleſſed Sac.*
his verie children of Iſraell, as Sainct Paule ſaieth to the Romains. And for
this cauſe ys he called a prophet, For he wrote all his Pſalmes and Prophecies of Chryſt, and his Churche, as Sainct Auguſtin ſaieth, So that by this
he prophecieth, that as the children of Iſraell were fedde in the deſert with
Manna a foode from heauen: So the children of Iſraell the Chriſtians ſhall   *Rom. 4.*
be fedde with the verie Manna from heauen, euen the bodie of Chryſt.
And as vnto them water flowed oute of the Rocke : So vnto the Chryſtians
oute of that ſtone, vpon whome the Churche ys buylded, whiche ſtone
God did ſtrike for our ſinnes, as Sainct Paule ſaieth, flowed water and bloode, of the whicch ther ys ſoche plentie, that yt ſufficeth for all the worlde to
C drinke of yt, yf they will.

Vpon this text S. Hierom ſaieth: *Sed & fontem Baptiſmi, atque martyrij eadem*   *In pſai. 77.*
*petra oſtendit. De latere enim eius cùm percuſſus eſt, ſanguis & aqua proceſsit. Quod
Baptiſmum & martyrium, figurauit,* But the ſame ſtone alſo ſheweth oute the
fountain of Baptiſme, and of martyrdome. For oute of his ſide, when he was
ſtriken, came furth bloode and water, whiche did figure Baptiſme and martyrdome. And vpon the other text of Dauid, applieng that as a prophecie,   *Pſal. 77.*
he ſaieth *Panem cæli dedit eis, panem Angelorum manducauit homo. Ipſe homini*   *Hier. ibid.*
*cibum præbuit, qui dixit : Ego ſum panis vitæ, qui de cælo deſcendi, qui manduca-
uerit ex hoc viuet in æternum.* He gaue them foode from heauen, ſo hath man
eaten the foode of Angells. He himſelf hath geuen meat to man who
ſaied: *I am the bread of life, whiche came down from heauen. He that ſhall eate of that
breade ſhall liue for euer.*

In the whiche woordes S. Hierō expownding the Prophet declareth to what
ende the woordes of the Prophet did tende, namely that ther ſhoulde be
D an heauenly Manna geuen to the ſpirituall children of Iſraell, whiche Manna was Chryſt the bread of life, whiche thing S. Hierom vpon the Prophet
in an other place, more plainlie doth opē. The Prophet ſaieth: *Pane cæli ſatura-*   *Pſal. 104.*
uit eos. With the bread of heauē he filled thē: And S. Hierom ſaieth. *Sicut enim
illi de cœlis fluēte Māna refecti ſunt: Ita nos hodie in eccleſia corpore agni accepto reficimur.
Diſrupit Petrám & fluxerunt aquæ, etc. Percuſſus eſt enim lapis ille pretioſus angu-*

laris, & immensos nobis protulit fontes , qui nostros errores abluunt , & ariditates **E**

We be fed with the bo die of the lambe. *irrigant,* As they were fedde with Manna flowing from heauen : So we nowe in the Churche, are fedde with the bodie of the lambe being receaued. He brake the stone , and the waters flowed oute. For that precioufe corner stone was smitten, and he brought furth to vs vnmeafurable fowntaines, which wash awaie our errours, and water our drinesse.

August. in psal.77. Sainct Augustin alfo vpon the fame psalme geueth a moch like expoficion . *Qui enim mandauit nubibus desuper , & ianuas cœli aperuit , & pluit illis Manna ad manducandum , & panem cœli dedit eis , vt panem Angelorum manducaret homo . Qui cibaria misit eis in abundantia , vt satiaret incredulos , non est inefficax dare credentibus verum ipsum de cœlo panem , quem Manna significabat , qui verè cibus est Angelorum , quod Dei Verbum corruptibiles , incorruptibiliter pascit , quòd vt manducaret homo , caro factum est , & habitauit iu nobis.* He that commaunded the clowdes aboue and opened the doores of heauen , and rained down Manna to them to eate and gaue them bread from heauen, that man might eate the bread of Angells, who fent to them meat in abundance , to fill the vnbeleuers, he ys not vnable to geue vnto the beleuers the true bread from heauen, whiche Manna did fignifie, which ys the meat of Angells in dede, whiche Sonne of God feedeth the corruptible incorruptiblie, who, that man might eate, was made flesh, and dwelled amongvs. **F**

As Sainct Hierom and Sainct Augustin be well agreing in the expofition of the fainges of the Prophet Dauid: So alfo Caffiodorus, a man well towarde their time, in nothing diffenteth from them, expownding the fame pfalme of Dauid. Cafsiod. in Pfal.77. *Et pluit illis Manna ad manducandum. Pluit dixit , vt ostenderet escæ nimiam largitatem , quæ tanquam pluuia de cœlo descendit. Et ne dubitares, quæ fuerit illa pluuia , sequitur. Manna manducare . Manna interpretatur, quid est hoc? quod sanctæ communioni decenter aptamus quia dum admirando cibus iste perquiritur , corporis dominici munera declarantur . Addidit : Panem cœli dedit eis. Quis est alter panis cœli, nisi Christus Dominus , vnde cœlestia spiritualem escam capiunt , & delectatione inestimabili perfruuntur ? Denique sic sequitur : Panem Angelorum manducauit homo . Panis ergo Angelorum bene dicitur Christus , quia æterna ipsius laude pascuntur . Neque enim corporalem panem Angeli manducare credendi sunt , Sed illa contemplatione Domini , quia sublimis creatura reficitur , verùm hic panis in cœlo replet Angelos , nos pascit in terris.* **G** And he rained down Manna vnto them to eate. He faied (rained) that he might shewe the great plentie of the meat which like vnto rain came down from heauen. And that thowe shouldest not doubte, what that rain was , yt foloweth. To eate Manna. Manna ys interpreted, what ys this? Whiche we verie well Manna what yt ys by interpretacion. applie to the holie communion . For while this meat ys gotten with woondering, the giftes of our Lordes bodie be declared. He added: *He gaue them bread from heauen.* Who ys the other bread from heauen , but Chryst our Lorde, of whome heauenly thinges do receaue spirituall meat, and ioifullie vfe inestimable delectacion. Then yt foloweth thus : *Man hath eaten the bread of Angells:* Chryst than ys well called the bread of Angells, bycaufe they are fedde with his euerlasting lawde and praife. Neither are Angells to be thought to eate corporall meat, but with that contemplacion of our Lorde, with the whiche the high creature ys fedde they are fedde. *But* **H** *this bread filleth Angells in heauen, yt feedeth vs in the earth.* Thus farre Caffiod.

The testimonies of thefe Authours, whiche here be produced vpon the Prophet Dauid, are fo confonant and agreable that I differe to make anie note of them vntill we heare one mo , who fhall be Titelman, a writer vpon
the

A the Pfalmes not to be contemned,though he be of the later daies. Whom I ioin with the better will to thefe auncientes, that yt maie well appeare to the Reader, that thefe later writers, being agreable and nothing diffenting from them, the falfe flaunders of the Aduerfaries be but vain, and without caufe moued.　This Authour in his annotacions for the Hebrue and Caldeie toung faieth that the bread, whiche in our conimunion text ys called *Panis Angelorum*, the bread of Angells, in the Hebrue, as Sainct Hierom, and other do tranflate yt, ys called *Panis fortium & robuftorum.* the bread of ftrong and mightie men.　And giuing two caufes why yt ys fo called, he putteth this for one: *Aut forte propter fignificationem panis viui illius tempore gratiæ mundo defcenfuri defuper, cuius non dubium eft, Manna corporeum fuiffe figuram, panis fortium aut robuftorum dictus intelligatur, quia is, cuius typum gerebat, panis viuus de cœlo mittendus, confortaturus erat corda fumentium in vitam æternam, iuxta quod apud Ioannem Saluator teftatur, dicens: Qui manducat hunc panem viuet in æternum, & qui manducat me, & ipfe viuet propter me.* Or ells this bread maie be vnderftanded to be called the bread of the

B ftrong and mightie, for the fignificacion of that liuely bread that fhoulde defcend from aboue to the worlde, of the whiche bread without doubte that corporall Manna was a figure, for that liuing bread to be fent from heauen, of the whiche the other was the figure, fhoulde make ftrong the heartes of the receauers to euerlafting life, according to that our Sauiour teftifieth in Sainct Iohn, faing: *He that eateth this bread shall liue for euer. And he that eateth me, shall liue through me.* Thus moche this Authour.

Nowe ye haue hearde thefe Authours with great concorde expownding the Prophet Dauid. And forfomoche as their fainges, here, be euen like to them that before are faied vpon Sainct Auguftine, to auoide prolixitie, I fhall raither geue a breif note vpon their fainges then long to ftand vpon them This ys to be obferued in them all, that they applie this Prophecie to Chryft, as the foode of heauen, the very liuing bread, that geueth foche ftrengh to them, that duely eate therof, that they liue for euer, which

C foode ys receaued in the Sacrament of his bodie and bloode.　For Sainct Hierom applieng yt to Chryft, as the foode of mans foule, alleageth the fixt Chapiter of Sainct Iohn, which Chapiter, as yt ys inuinciblie proued in the fecond booke, treacteth of the Sacrament. Wherof alfo Sainct Hierom ys ther a witneffe, as a great nombre mo be.　And for the more plain proofe of this in the expofition of the hundreth and fourth Pfalme he faieth by expreffe woordes, that we be fedd with the bodie of the lambe, as they were with Manna, whiche plain maner of fpeache leaueth vs in no doubte what faith Sainct Hierom was of, and howe he vnderftandeth the Prophet Dauid.

And thus confidering howe long, I haue ben vpon this one text of Sainct Paule, and remembring howe manie mo ther remain likwife to be expownded, I fhall leaue the reft of the Authours here alleaged, to be weighed by the Reader and in the next chapiter make an ende of that that vpon this fcripture ys to be faied.

D

THE

Titell.in annot fuper Pfal.77.

THE TWELTH CHAPITER, PROVETH BY

occasion of that that ys saied, with farder Authoritie that the Sa-
cramentes of the newe lawe are more excellent, then the
Sacraments of the olde lawe.

FOrasmoche as all the Anthours alleaged for the exposition of the text of Sainct Paule nowe laſt handled and treacted of, doo all together conſpire and agree in this trueth, that Manna was the figure, and the bodie of Chryſt, whiche we receaue in the Sacramēt, the veritie: and the veritie allwais ys more excellent in good thinges then ys the figure, euē as moche more excellent, as the bodie of a man ys aboue the ſhadowe: Yt muſt nedes then of neceſsitie folowe, that the Sacraments of the newe lawe, whiche be the thinges figured by the figures of the olde lawe, muſt as farre exċel them, as the veritie doth the figure, and as the bodie doth the ſhadowe. For further proof of this conſider, as yt ys declared at large in the firſt booke and yt ys S. Auguſtins rule alſo, that all euell thinges figured by figures of the olde lawe, are moche woorſe, then the figures by the whiche they are figured, Soo all good thinges figured, are moche better, and more excellent then the figures. Yf then the Sacramentes and ſacrifices of the olde lawe be figures of the Sacramentes and ſacrifices of the newe, as in dede they be, then muſt the Sacramentes, and ſacrifices of the newe lawe be moch better then the Sacramentes or ſacrifices of the olde lawe. Yf moche better, then more excellent. And nowe note that yf yt were ſo (as the Aduerſaries falſlie doe teache) that the bodie of Chryſt were not preſent verilie in the Sacramēt and that the other Sacramentes of Chryſtes Churche (as the conſtant and true doctrine of the ſame Churche ys to the contrary) did not geue grace, then were the Sacramentes of the olde lawe not onely as excellent as the Sacramentes of the newe lawe, but by all means paſsing and excelling them.

Good thin-
ges figured
better then
the figures.

And bicauſe this ſhall not be declared, and proued by examples, that be ſtraunge to our matter, we will bring furth an example with in the limites of our matter, euen of Manna yt ſelf, the figure of our Sacrament. What great miracles and wonders were in that Māna, the booke of Exodus doth declare, whiche for the better vnderſtāding of thē, that are not exerciſed in the ſcriptures, are collected and ſetfurth by Roffenſis, and they be in nombre twelue.

Twelue wō-
ders in Mā-
na declared
Roff. lib. 1.
cap. 12.

1. The firſt ys, that howe moche ſoeuer anie hadde gathered, yet he had no whit more then the meaſure, that God had appoincted them to gather.

2. The ſecōd, that he that gathered leſſe thē the meaſure appoincted, he had aſmoche when he caried yt home, as he that had gathered the iuſt meaſure.

3. The thirde, yf they had kept any porcion vntill the next daie, yf yt were not the Sabboth daie, yt wolde haue putrified.

4. The fourth, although yt might ſo quickly and ſhortly putrifie: yet yt was kept in the Arcke a great nombre of yeares, and putrified not.

5. The fift, yf yt were laied in the Sunne, yt wolde melt, yf before the fire, yt wolde be very harde.

6. The ſixte, although yt did euerie other daie orderly fall from heauen, yet vpon the Sabboth daie ther fell none.

7. The ſeuenth, although other daies in the weke, whether they gathered more or leſſe, yet they had but one meaſurefull called Gomer: vpon the daie next before the Sabboth to ſerue them two daies, bicauſe they were forbidden to gather vpon the Sabboth daie, they had home with them two meaſures full.

The

A   The eight, he that that daie gathered more or leſſe, had no more nor 8.
leſſe then his two meaſures, when he came home.

The ninthe, although in ſo great a multitude, ther were of diuerſe ſto- 9.
mackes, diuerſe appetites, ſome eating more, ſome leſſe: yet that meaſure ſuf-
ficed the ſtrong ſtomaked, and was not to moche for the weake ſtomacke.

The tenth, vnto them that were good yt taſted to euery one according 10.
to his deſire.

The eleuenth, although to the godly yt was a moſt pleaſaunt taſte: yet 11.
to the vngodly yt was lothſom.

The twelth, the children of Iſraell were fedde fourtie yeares with this 12.
Manna in the Wilderneſſe.

As theſe miracles be conteined in the ſcriptures, as in *Exodus, Numeri,*   *Exod.16.*
and in the booke of wiſdom : So they are alſo ſetfurth by holy writers, to   *Num.11.*
the ſettingfurth of Gods glorie in his wonderfull workes. Of diuerſe of   *Sap.16.*
theſe Chryſoſtome maketh mencion ſaing : *Et hoc vtique mirabile: Tentauerunt*   *Chryſoſt.in*
tunc aliqui per tempus illud, plus quàm opus fuerat, colligere, & nullum auaritiæ   *dictum A-*
B *ſuæ fructum accipiebant. Et quamdiu æqualitatem colebant manſit Manna, quod Man-*   *poſt. Nolo*
na erat. Poſtquam autem auari plus habere deſiderauerunt, auaritia mutauit Manna   *vos ignor.*
in vermem. Quamuis hoc non cum detrimento aliorum faciebant. Non enim rapiebant
ex alimento proximi, cùm plus colligerent, attamen cùm plus deſiderarent condemnati
ſunt . Nam tametſi neminem alium iniuria affecerunt, tamen ſibi ipſis maximè no-
cuerunt, hoc colligendi modo auaritiæ ſtudentes, atque ſic ſimul erat cibus, & diuinæ
agnitionis inſtructio, ſimul & paſcebat corpora & erudiebat animam. Neque paſce-
bat ſolùm, ſed à laboribus liberabat, non enim opus erat iungere boues, neque trahere
aratrum, neque ſulcos ſecare, neque ad annum expectare : ſed menſam habebant
ſubitò appoſitam, ſemper recentem, & quotidie nouam, rebusque ipſis diſcebant Euange-
licum illud præceptum, non debere ſolicitum eſſe in craſtinum. Nulla enim vtilitas ipſis ab
hac ſolicitudine proueniebat . Nam qui plus colligerat corrumpebatur & peribat, &
auaritiæ argumentum ſolùm dabat. Inſuper ne putarent illum imbrem iuxta naturæ
conſuetudinem eſſe, nihil talium in die Sabbati fiebat, Deo duo illa ipſos docente, quòd
C *prioribus diebus ipſe mirabilem, & priorem pluuiam operabatur, & per diem illum*
abſtinebat, vt inuiti etiam diſcerent illo die feriari. And this alſo was merueiloſe.
Some proued in that time to gather more then was nede, and of their couetouſneſſe they tooke no profit. And as long as they tooke their equall
proporcion, that that was Manna did abide Manna. But after the couc-
touſe deſiered to haue more, auarice turned Manna into a woorme, although they did this withoute hurte of other, when they wolde gather more
they did not violentlie take awaie any parte of their neighbours foode, and
yet for all that whē they deſiered more they were condemned, For although
they did not wrong an other man : yet after this maner of gathering geuing their mindes to auarice, they did moche hurte them ſelues. And
ſo yt was both meat, and alſo an inſtruction of the knowlege of God. Yt did
bothe feed the, bodie and teache the ſoule. Neither did yt onely feede,
but yt alſo deliuered them from labours. For they had no nede to yocke
their oxen, to drawe their plough, nor to cutte oute furrowes, neither
D to tarie a yeare, for the croppe, But they had a table quicklie ſett furth
and made readie, freſh and dailie newe. And by the ſame thinges
they did learn the Euangelicall commaundement, that they ſhoulde
not be carefull for to morowe. For of this carefullneſſe ther came
no profet to them. For he that gathered more, yt was corrupted, and periſhed, and gaue onely a rebuke of their greadineſſe or couetouſneſſe. Moreouer

ouer, that they shoulde not thinke that shower or rain to be according to   **E**
the custome of nature, vpon the Sabboth daie ther was none soche. God
teaching them these two thinges, who was the worker of that merueilouse
rain in the other daies, and that he vpon that daie absteined, that they
shoulde learn whether they wolde or no to kepe holy daie. Thus farre
Chrysostome.

    In this he hath declared that Manna was no naturall effect of naturall
custome and ordre, but by the speciall worke of God, who caused yt, as yt
pleased him to rain down from the clowdes to them. He saieth also that vpō
the Sabboth daie, God rained not Manna to the people, signifieng that euery other daie he did. For the maner of the gathering of yt he teacheth that
they that gathered more then was nede, they had no profitte af their couetousnesse, whiche ys, as the text of Exodus saieth, that he that gathered moch
to him their remained nothing, howe moche so euer through gredie desire

Mānakept
vpon the
Sabboth
daie remai-
ned good,
vpon other
daies not.

he gathered, he had no more but his measure. As touching the ordre of the
keping of yt, yf they kept yt as yt shoulde be kept, as vpon the Sabboth daie   **F**
they might kepe yt, then as Chrysostome saieth, Manna did abide Manna.
But yf anie other daie of couetousnesse they wolde kepe of yt vntill the next
daie, then Manna wolde not abide Manna, but Manna was turned into
woormes,

    S. Augustin also, to omitte the rest, speaketh in one place, of one miracle

of yt mencioned aboue, that ys, that yt tasted to them according to their
desire: *In primo populo vnicuique Manna secundùm propriam voluntatem in ore sapiebat.*
In the first people Manna tasted in euery mans mouth according to his
owne will.

    By this ye perceiue howe manie miracles God wrought in Manna, so that
yt might verie well be called a merueilouse thing. And truly for the great
workes that God wrought in yt, and for the nombre, whiche also ys great,
as being doen in one thing, yt maie well be reputed and esteemed an excellent thing.

Manna
farre excel-
leth the Sa-
cramenta-
ries sacra-
mētal bread

    Cōpare nowe our Sacrament with this figure, as the Aduersarie doth cal   **G**
yt a Sacrament, whiche then ys but bread taken to signifie or to be a token
or figure of Chrystes bodie, and thē what ys yt? ys yt anie more then a plain
peice of artificall bread made by mans hande? ys yt in any respecte wonderfull? ys ther anie one miraculouse worke of God in yt like as in Māna? ys not
Manna by all means more excellent, and farre exceadinge this Sacrament?
Certenly yt farre excelleth, and exceadeth yt, wher the catholique faith teacheth that the lawe had but shadowes, and the Gospell the verie thinges. Yf
the highest, the cheifest, the excellentest Sacrament that ys in the Gospell
whiche as Sainct Dionyse Areopagita saith, ys the Sacrament of the bodie
and bloode of Chryst, be so base and bare. and maie no better compare
with his figure, than that yt ys a signe or token of Chrystes bodie : then
must Sainct Paule his doctrine to the Hebrues, and the doctrine of the catholique Churche be turned into the contrarie saing, that ys, that the Gospell hath the shadowes, and the lawe the very thinges. For as our Sacramēt ys   **H**
a figure of Chrystes bodie, so was Māna. As we receauing that peice of bread
maie receaue Chryst spirituallie: So did the Iewes receauing Manna, receaue
Chryst also spirituallie. And aboue this, Manna hath a nōbre of excellences,
and our bread hath none. So that yf we receaue this doctrine of the Aduersarie that our Sacramētes be of no more excellēcie thā the Sacramētes of the
olde lawe: we also admitte this that the Sacramēts and figures of the olde lawe farre

A　farre excell owers.For the excellencie of a sacrament or a figure ſtādeth ſpeciallie in three poinctes, in the excellencie of the thing that yt ſignifieth or figureth:In the fulneſſe and liuelineſſe of the ſignificacion: And in the work of God aboute the ſame figure.

As touching the firſt,yt ys very plain that king Pharao was a figure of the Deuel:theEgyptians his people were figures of ſinnes:the ſeruitude that the children of Iſraell were in vnder this king and his people,was a figure of the ſeruitude of man vnder the Deuell and ſinne.Theſe three,although they be figures,and iuſtlie do figure the thinges by them figured:yet they be not accompted excellent figures,bicauſe the thinges by them figured be not excel lent.Contrariwiſe *Melchiſedech* for that he ys a figure of Chryſt, as S . Paule declareth to the Hebrues,ys accompted and reputed an excellent figure,bycauſe the thing figured ys excellent.A figure ys as the image of a thing . An image(as comon experience teacheth)ys regarded and eſtemed according as the thing ys,whoſe image yt ys. As the image of a king, of the ſubiectes

B　of the ſame King ys moche regarded, for that yt ys the image of their King. And as they honour and loue their Kinge:So will they vſe his image.So like wiſe *Melchiſedech* being the figure and image of Chryſt,ys an excellent,figure bicauſe Chryſt ys excellent.

The ſecond poinct moche commendeth the excellencie of the figure alſo. For although *Iſaac* were a goodlie figure of the paſſion of Chryſt : yet the Paſchall lambe ys reputed the more excellent figure,for that yt more liuelie dothe declare the thing therbie ſignified , then thother did. For altho *Iſaac* was the onely Sonne of his Father,as Chryſt of his Father,and bare the wodde to the place of ſacrifice , as Chryſt his croſſe to the place of hys death:yet the lambe bicauſe yt was ſlain in dede, and the bloode of yt caſt vpon the poſtes of the doores defended the inhabitantes from the hand of the Angell that ſtrooke the Egyptians,and for that , vpon the death of the lambe the people departed oute of Egypte,and were deliuered from the ſer uitude of King Pharao,and his people,which figured the death of Chryſt in

C　dede,and the effectes of the ſame . For as the innocent lambe died and ſhedde his blood without gilt or offence:ſo the innocent lambe Chryſt died and ſhedde his bloode without gilt or offence.As the blood defended the Iſraelites from the ſtriker:ſo the blood of Chryſt being caſt vpon vs , defendeth vs from the wrathe of God,vnder the whiche we were born ,ād apeaceth the ſame,that yt ſtriketh vs not to death,as the Egyptians were of the Angell.As the Iſraelites vpon the death of the lambe were deliuered from the ſeruitude of Pharao,and his Egyptians:ſo we Chryſtians vpon the death of our lambe Chtyſt were furthwith deliuered from the ſeruitude of the De uell and ſinne.Therfore, I ſaie , the lambe ſo liuely and ſo fullie ſignifieng Chryſt,who ſuffred for vs and pourchaſed owre redemption,ys more excellent figure than *Iſaac.*

The thirde poinct alſo muſt of neceſsitie be admitted. For where the workes of God be and ſpecially miraculouſe workes, the mo they be, and the more miraculouſe,the more excellent the thing ys about the which ſoche workes be doen . Yt was a miraculouſe worke that *Eliſabeth* being an olde woman , and paſt childe birth , in her age ſhoulde

D　conceaue and bring furth Iohn the *Baptiſt* : but yt was more miraculouſe , that a maide withoute man ſhoulde conceaue and bring furth a childe.And therfore this conception ys more excellent than the other,but thys increaſeth theexcellēcie,that here be mo miracles thā in the other.For inthis cōceptiō was cōceaued God ād mā:in the other mā onelie.But that this excellécie maie appeare betwixt two figures,I shall bring exāple of two figures of the Sacramēt.As yt ys sufficiētly proued in the first book,the Shew bread was a figure of the Sacramēt.And as yt ys here proued,Manna ys a figure of the same.The Shew bread was but plain artificiall bread, about the whiche was no speciall work of God,but soch as ys aboute all other thinges,formed and made to the conseruacion of man:Aboute Manna ther was no artificiall worke,but a speciall worke of God,and that beside the naturall custome and ordre.Wherfore Manna ys the more excellent figure in that respect.For the one was made by man,the other was wrought by God.Aboute the one also was no miracle,aboute the other were manie miracles,and therfor in that respect yet more excellent.

Cōparison of the B. Sacr.to the figure Manna.

In these three poinctes yf cōparison be made betwixt our Sacramēt and Māna,yf our Sacramēt haue not the presence of Chrystes bodie,then Manna farre excelleth.For first our Sacrament being a figure of Chryst,and not conteining Chryst,as the Aduersarie saieth,nothing exceadeth Manna:For Manna was a figure of Chryst also.So that as touching the thing figured ther ys no excellencie.For they be figures of one thing.

In the second poinct,which ys the liuely significacion and ful figuracion of the thing signified,and figured,Manna moche excelleth the Sacrament. For as Chryst was a bread frō heauen:so was Manna a bread from heauen . As Chryst descended frō heauen that his people might feed vpon him to euerlasting life:so Manna descended frō heauen,that the people might feed vpon yt,to the mainteinance of their life.As Chryst ys aboue naturall ordre sent vnto vs by God the Father:so was Manna aboue naturall ordre sent to the Israelites from God,as by Chrysostome yt ys before testified.

Now yf cōparison be made betwixt the Sacrament and Chryst,the Sacrament ys nothing so liuely a figure so fullie figuring Chryst , as Manna hath doen.For Chryst ys a bread frō heauen:the Sacrament a bread frō the earth as Irenæus saieth,and as oure cōmon knowledge testifieth.Chryst ys our food to euerlasting life:the Sacrament(in respect that yt ys a Sacrament)feedeth vs not to the sufficiēt mainteinaunce of this life, as Manna did the Israelites. Chryst was sent to vs aboue naturall ordre,as also Manna was:the Sacramēt by natural and artificiall ordre.Who then seith not that Māna in all respects more liuely and more fullie signifieth and figureth Chryst, then our Sacrament doth.Wherfor yt maie then well be saied,that Manna ys the more excellent figure.

As touching the third poinct,ther can be no controuersie,but that Māna was alltogether miraculouse our Sacrament in no poincte miraculouse, yf yt contein not the presence of Chrystes bodie and blood. About Manna were manie miraculous woorkes of God,aboute our Sacrament not one. Manna was frō heauen:our Sacramēt frō the earth.Manna wrought by the especial worke of God:our Sacrament by the cōmon work of man.Manna besides naturall order:our Sacrament,by naturall and artificiall ordre.Manna tasted in euery mans mouth as he listed: our Sacrament but as bread and wine.Māna although yt putrified being kept more then one daie in the weke daies: yet yt remained vnputrified vpō the Sabboth daie.And although being reserued after the Sabboth daie yt wolde putrifie:yet of the same reserued in the goldē pott in the Arke,ther remained manie years vnputrified , swete ād good. Owre bread and wine neither putrifieth sooner,neither remaineth lōger thē other bread,and wine after the comon ordre doth.

A Yt ys then a moſt plain matter, that yf our Sacramēt be robbed of the real preſence of Chryſtes bodie and blood that yt ys in nothing more excellent thē the figure of yt. But contrariwiſe the figure in all reſpects ys moch more excellent then yt, as by that that ys ſaied, yt doth manifeſtly appeare. Wherfore the Aduerſarie muſt of neceſsitie graunt one of theſe two: that either in the Sacrament ys the preſence of Chryſtes bodie, and ſo ys yt more excellēt then the figure Manna: or ells denieng the preſence, graunt that our Sacrament ys not equall but a baſer and inferiour Sacrament, to Manna . But to graunt that a Sacrament of the newe lawe ys inferiour or baſer, then a Sacrament of the olde lawe, ys a plain abſurditie: wherfore ſo ys that likewiſe, that yt floweth oute of: that ys, that ther ys no preſence of Chryſt in the Sacrament. Yt muſt then of very neceſsitie be concluded, that Chryſtes bodie ys verilie in the Sacrament.

Yf our Sa꞉ haue not the reall preſence of Chryſtes bodie and blood, yt ys moche ba꞉ ſer figure then Mãna

THE THIRTENTH CHAP. PROVETH THE
the ſame by ſcriptures and doctours.

B Oche hath ben the malice of Sathan againſt God and hys Chryſt, and againſt his beloued church, that to hinder the honoure of God, to ſhadowe or abaſe the woorthineſſe of the mediacion of Chryſt, and to drawe men from ſaluacion he ceaſſeth not hys laboure and induſtrie, he ſleapeth not frō his inuencions and deuiſes, he ſpareth not hys engines and waies: but buſsier ys he to impair and deſtroie, then we be to repair and ſaue. Wherfore as before the coming of Chryſt, he drewe mē from the true honour of God to Idolatrie, and therin deceaued the very Iewes, whiche were ſpeciallie called to the true knowledge of God. So to abaſe the woorthineſſe of his annointed after his coming, he ſtirred vppe diuerſe wicked membres, as *Cerinthus, Ebion, Sabellius, Paulus Samoſatenus, Marcion, Arrius, Neſtorius, Eutiches,* and a great nombre mo of like rable. By ſome of the which he impugned his Godhead, and by other ſome he impugned his manhead, and withall miſerablie tormented and diuided hys church, to the loſſe of many a ſoule: So nowe in theſe daies he hath inuented ſome other engins : as wher

Luther allowed two ſacramētes Melācthō three The Saxons four re. Poſtellus ſix Suenckfeldius neuer one.

C Chryſt had inſtituted ſacramentes by the which as by certain inſtrumētes or conductes the merit of his paſsion in ſondrie ſortes ſhoulde come and be applied vnto his people, and by the whiche the people ſhould haue moch comforte: he hath to ſett furth his engins ſtirred vppe other diſciples and wicked mēbres, as *Luther, Oecolampadius, Caluine. Zuinglius, Bucer, Brentius Cranmer, Radley, Iuel,* and a filthy nōbre of ſoch like, by the which he hath not onelie by ſome of thē laboured to take awaie three of thē, by other ſome foure of them , by other ſome fiue of thē, by other ſome all of thē: but alſo ſoch ſinall nombre as ſome of thē do ſuffer to remain, they be by thē ſo robbed, and ſo ſpoiled, that neither are they greatlie to the honour of God and Chryſt , neither to the profect or comfort of his people. For when generallie they teach that the ſacramentes geue no grace to the receauers of thē, litle ys God honoured in his ſacramentes, litle ys his people holpen by receapt of thē. As when ſpeciallie they ſaie, Baptiſme waſſheth not or taketh not awaie originall ſinne , and that the Sacrament conteineth not the verie ſubſtanciall bodie of Chryſt, but onely a bare ſign or token of yt, what commoditie , or aduantage can

D come to vs oute of ſoch ſpoiled ſacramentes left ſo bare and ſo poore that they can geue a man nothing. But yet though theſe ſacramentes be ſo ſpoiled, they are not in very dede ſpoiled to the faithfull catholique, but vnto him they are riche, and plentifull geuing that meaſure of grace, that God

Luther꞉ in aſſert.꞉art. 2.

Zz ii   through

through the merite of Chryſtes death,hath appointed to be geuen to them **E**
that faithfullie,and woorthilie receaue them.For as Manna taſted in euery
mans mouth according to his deſire:ſo the Sacramēt ſauoureth to life accor
ding to the faith of the receauer.But vnto theſe wicked ;robbers and ſpoilers
of ſacramentes, which through vnbelief eſteme them no better then S.Paul
did the ſacramentes and Ceremonies of the olde lawe,which he called:weak
and vnprofitable ordinaunces,to them they are as though they were poore,
for that they lacking faith robbe and ſpoile théſelues of ſoch benefit ād grace
as might come vnto them by the ſacramentes,which now through their vnbeleif ys not geuen vnto them.

Of the high and moſt noble Sacrament of Chryſtes bodie and bloode, I
merueill that the Aduerſaries feared not ſo blaſphemouſly to abaſe yt, as to
ſaie that ytys a Sacrament no more excellent thé, theSacramentes of the old
lawe.In ſo ſaing note with me I praie thee, gātle reader,what opiniō or eſtimaciō he hath ofChryſtiā religion.As before ys ſaied, S.Paule calleth the ce
remonies of the olde lawe,weake ād vnprofitable ordinaũces.Yf then the or
dinātes of the Chryſtian religiō be of no more excellencie, then the ordinances of the Moſaycall religion,then wher no difference of excellencie ys, **F**
the things maie equallie be eſtemed.And ſo by this eſtimaciō and iudgemēt
all the ſacramētes and ordeinances of the new lawe,for that they are no bet
ter,then the ordeinances of the olde lawe, are weake,ād vnprofitable ordei-
nances.For wher equalitie of condicion and ſtate ys,ther maie well be equalitie in denominacion.What then ys our Chryſtian religion,yf yt be no better adorned and magnified,then with weak and vnprofitable ordeinances?

Yf they will ſaie that as long as the thinges were not cōmed which they
figured,ſo lōg they were not vnprofitable: but whē Chryſt was once cōmed
and they ceaſſed any longer to figure or ſignifie, thē their office being doen
and expired,they were vain and vnprofitable,and ſo S. Paule ment of them:
But as for our ſacramentes they do their office ſtill,for they figure and ſignifie thinges doen by Chryſt that ys comed, as the other did of Chryſt to co-
me.And therfore they be not vnprofitable ordeinances.

Although this ſolucion hath ſome coloure,yet yf the Aduerſarie will look
in S.Paule to the Hebrues he ſhall finde him calling the lawe,and the ordei- **G**
nances of the ſame weake and vnprofitable euen when they did their office,
ād figured Chryſt to come,bicauſe they brought not the obſeruers of the ſame to perfection.The commaundement that went before (ſaieth S.Paule)
ys diſalowed,bicauſe of weakneſſe,ād vnprofitableneſſe,for the law brought
nothing to perfectiō.To the which pourpoſe he ſaieth again. The lawe hauing the ſhadowe of good thinges to come,and not the very facion of the
thinges théſelues,can neuer with theſe ſacrifices which they offre, make the
cōmers therunto perfect.So then the cauſe why S.Paule calleth the ordeinances of the lawe weak and vnprofitable was bicauſe they brought not the
obſeruers of thé to perfectiō and not bicauſe they ceaſſed to ſignifie and to
figure.And what difference betwixt weake and vnprofitable,as here S.Paule
calleth thé:and weake and beggarly as he termeth thé to the *Galathians?*Thé
yf theſe ordeinances in the time of their vſe, before the coming of Chryſt
were weake and vnprofitable,or weake and beggarlie, and our ſacramentes
be no better then they,then our ſacramentes be as they be weake and vnpro **H**
fitable or weake and beggarly.

That our Sacrament of Chryſtes bodie and blood ys no better then the
Paſchall lābe *Oecolamp.*by expreſſe woords doth cōfeſſe,ſaing:*Panis autē noſter*
agno

A　*illorum ſpiritualium eſt præcioſior. Propterea non magis prædicandus.* Owre bread ys not more precioule then the lambe of thoſe ſpirituall, therfor no more to be prai-　*Oecolamp.*
ſed. This then being the wicked doctrine of the Aduerſarie, this wicked con-　*in Expoſi*
cluſion ys deduced out of the ſame that our Sacramentes of the new lawe,　*verbor. Cæ*
be but weake and vnprofitable, as the Sacramentes and ordeinances of the　*na Dom.*
olde lawe were. O wicked blaſphemie, o deteſtable ſaing, geuing occaſion of
contempt of the wholl religion of Chryſt. A ſaing more like to ouerthrowe
the honour of God, the deuocio of mã, the coforte and hope of all Chryſtiãs
and ſo conſequently all the whol religion, then to edifie anie one of theſe.

　Yf the Aduerſaries had not minded the plain ſubuerſion and deſtruction
of the Chryſtian religion, though they had robbed the holie ſacramentes of
their efficacie, ãd made thẽ (as they do) as bare as the ordinances of the lawe:
yet they might haue comended thẽ iuſtly and truly aboue the other, bicauſe
theſe did ſignifie Chryſt preſent, and were inſtituted by Chryſt himſelf.

　Eſaie was an holie Prophet, and an holie martyr, who ſo liuely, ſo plainlie
B　and clerely preacheth of Chryſtes natiuitie, and paſſion that of ſome he ys
thought more mete to be called an Euangeliſt, then a prophet. Hierimie alſo
was an holie prophet, ſo holy that he was ſanctified in his mothers wombe,
who alſo excellently prophicied of Chryſt. Daniel ys knowen of all men to
be an notable holy prophet, who as certenly appointed the time of Chryſt
as a man wold haue appoincted to a thing with his ſingar: And yet Iohn the
Baptiſed ys called of Chryſt not onelie a Prophet, but more then a Prophet,
and why? bicauſe the other did prophecie certenly of Chryſt, but this man
did pointe to him with his ſingar ſaing: *Ecce agnus Dei, ecce qui tollit, &c.* Behold　*Ioan. 1.*
the lambe of God, behold him, which taketh awaie the ſinnes of the world.

　Chryſoſtome alſo aſſigneth an other cauſe, why Chryſt called S. Iohn mo-
re then a Prophet: *Quum dixiſſet Prophetis illum eſſe maiorem, quare maior ſit oſtẽdit.*　*In Matth.*
Cur igitur maior Prophetis Ioannes? quoniam propinquior erat Chriſto venturo. Mittã enim　*homil. 38.*
(inquit) Angelũ meũ ante faciẽ tuã. Qui autem ante faciem eſt, is proximus eſt. Nam quem-
admodum maiori dignitate hi ſunt, qui proximè Regibus deambulantibus ordinantur: ſic &
Ioãnes in ipſo aduentu conſtitutus, maiore gratia fulſit. When he had ſaied that he was
C　more then a Prophet, he ſheweth why he ys more. Therfor then ys Iohn more then a prophet? Bicauſe he was nearer to Chryſt to come. *For I ſhall ſend (ſai-*
eth he) *my Angell before thy face.* He that ys before the face, ys neareſt. For as
theſe are in greater dignitie, which are neareſt placed to kinges when they
walke: ſo alſo Iohn appoincted in the coming of Chryſt, ys more honorable.

　Oecumenius treating the ſame text ſaieth moch like, adding alſo an other cauſe: *Sed quid exiſtis videre? Prophetam? vtique dico vobis, & excellentiorem propheta ex-*
cellentiorem, hoc eſt, maiorem. Deinde dicit in quo maiorem, videlicet in eo quòd venerit cir-
ca Chriſti aduentum. Nam maiores aliis inter præcones ſunt hi, qui prope Regem præcedunt.
Poteſt etiam dici excellentior propheta, quia eum quem vidit prophetabat, quod nulli con-
tigit prophetarum. Nec vidit tantùm verùm etiam baptiſabat. But what went ye furth
to ſee? a Prophet? yea I ſaie vnto yowe, and one more excellẽt thẽ a Prophet,
more excellẽt, that ys greater. Then he ſaieth in what he ys greater, that ys, in
that, that he came aboute the coming of Chryſt. For among the foregoers
theſe be the greater, which go next before the King. He maie alſo be called
the more excellent Prophet, bicauſe he prophecied him, whome he ſawe.
D　Whiche happened to none other of the Prophetes. Neither did he
onely ſee him, but he alſo baptiſed him. Thus he. So the Sacramentes and
figures of the lawe, for that they figured Chryſt to come, they are woorthie
of the name of figures of Chryſt, but the Sacramentes of the newe

　　　　　　　　Zz iij　　　　lawe

lawe, forſomoche as ſome of them, were figures of Chryſt preſent, and other E
of them figures of his benefites wrought by his paſſion and blood ſhedding
nowe allreadie purchaſed and doen, and were alſo all by him inſtituted and
ordeined, as the Councell of Trydent, and other haue before that defined,
they muſt nedes for theſe reſpectes, and conſideracions be more excellent
then the Sacramentes of the olde lawe. The Sacrament of Chryſtes bodie
and blood, as no Chryſtiã dowbteth but that yt was immediately inſtituted
of Chryſt himſelf: and figured and ſignified him in ſubſtance their preſent,
though yt had a farder reſpect, and ſignificacion to the maner, as to be a figure of Chryſt crucified: ſo yt can not be denied but yt muſt be more excellent
Sacrament then the Paſchall lambe, wherunto *Oecolampadius* compareth yt,
and ſaieth that yt ys no more precioufe, neither more to be praiſed then yt,
whiche figure was immediately inſtituted by *Moyſes*, allthough mediately
by God, and figured Chryſt to come, wheras this Sacrament figured Chryſt
preſent, and was immediately of him inſtituted.

Nowe yf Iohn the Baptiſt was counted more then a prophet, bicauſe (*as
Chryſoſtome ſaieth*) he was nearer to Chryſt then other prophetes, then by that
reſpect, this Sacrament muſt be more excellent then the Sacramentes of the F
olde lawe, bicauſe yt ys nearer to Chryſt, then other of the olde lawe. And if
Iohn were the more excellent prophet (*as Oecumenius* ſaieth) bicauſe he ſawe
Chryſt preſent whom he prophecied. then likewiſe this Sacrament muſt be a
more excellent ſacrament, bicauſe he was preſent whom yt figured.

Chryſt ſaieth to the Iewes: Abraham *pater veſter exultauit vt videret diem me-*
Ioan.8. *um, vidit, & gauiſus eſt.* Abrahã yowr father reioiced that he might ſee my daie
In Joan ca. he ſawe yt and was gladde. *Exultauit (ſaieth Oecumenius)ſine concupiuit,* he reioiced
8. or deſiered to ſee the daie of Chryſt. The daie of Chryſt that Abraham deſie
red to ſee, was the daie of his paſſion (as Chryſoſtome ſaieth) in the which he
reioiced to ſee the redemption of mankind. He ſawe yt in the oblacion of
the ramme that ſupplied the place of his onelie Sonne Iſaac, and he
Inloã ca 8. was gladde. For (as *Oecumenius* ſaieth) *Didicit quod ſicut ipſe non peper-*
cit filio ſuo dilecto propter Deum : ita neque Deus parciturus eſſet filio ſuo dilecto pro-
pter hominem. Et quemadmodum ille portauit ligna holocauſti ſui:ita & ipſe portaturus
eſſet lignum mortis ſuæ. Veruntamen ſicut illo non paſſo ſuppoſitus eſt aries:ita & hoc ma G
nente impaſſibili, humanitas eius occiſa eſt. He learned, that as he did not ſpare his
beloued Sõne for god ſake: euë ſo neither wolde God ſpare his ſonne for mãs
ſake. And as he bare the woodde of his ſacrifice: ſo alſo he ſhoulde beare the
woodde of his paſſion. But as he not ſuffring a ramme was put in his ſtead:
Math .13. ſo this (*mening his Godhead*) abiding impaſſible his manhead was ſlain.

As *Abraham* did ſee Chryſt: ſo no doubte manie other holy fathers and
prophetes did ſee him, and yet thinking themſelues more happie and bleſſed
yf they might haue ſeen Chryſt in the fleſh, did earneſtly deſire the ſame, as
Chryſt ſaieth: *Multi prophetæ & iuſti cupierunt videre, quæ videtis, & non viderunt,*
& audire quæ auditis, & non audierunt. Manie prophetes and righteouſe men ha
ue deſiered to ſee thoſe thinges which ye ſee, and haue not ſeen them, and to
heare thoſe thinges which ye heare, and haue not hearde them. But aboue
them all. *Veſtri beati oculi, quia vident, & aures veſtri, quia audiunt.* Bleſſed are yowr
eies, for they ſee, and yowr eares, for they heare.

In 13. In theſe woordes Chryſt declareth the beleuers in him, and the ſeers of
Math.ho- him, to be more happie, then they that onely beleued, and ſawe him not, H
mil.46. with the bodilie eie, as Chryſoſtome ſaieth, expownding theſe woordes of
Chryſt. *Multi prophetæ & iuſti cup. &c. Aduentũ ſcilicet meũ, præſentiã, miracula, vocẽ.*

Hic

A *Hic enim non solùm perditis illis eos antéponit, verùm etiam prophetis ac iustis præstantiores eos asserit, atque beatiores. Quare ita? Quoniam non solùm ista aspiciunt, quæ illi non viderunt, verùm etiam quæ illi videre cupierunt isti oculis cernunt. Nam fide illi etiam intuiti hæc fuerunt, sed isti multo clarius omnia perspexerunt.* Manie prophetes and righteousse men haue desiered to see those thinges whiche ye see, and haue not seen them, and to heare those thinges whiche ye heare, and haue not hearde them, that ys to saie *(saieth he in the person of Chryst)* my coming, my presence, my miracles, my preaching Here he doth not onely preferre them before those lost or damned men, but also he affirmeth them to be more excellent and blessed then the prophetes, and the righteousse men. And why so? for that they do not onely see those thinges whiche thother sawe not, but also those thinges which they desiered to see, these men sawe with their eies. For they also by faith did beholde these thinges, but these moche more clerely did see all thinges. Thus Chrysost.

Yf then they that sawe Chryst in the flesh, were moch more blessed, and excellent, then the prophetes which sawe him onely by faith: howe then **B** shoulde not the Sacramentes instituted by Chryst in the flesh, and vsed of him in the flesh, and signifieng him, and his merites being preset in the flesh, be more excellent then the sacramentes of the olde lawe, which in a darke maner and a farre of signified him onely to come. And again, if they that sawe Chryst in the flesh were more blessed by the sentence of Chryst, then the prophetes, and righteousse men, whiche desiering to see him, did not see him: howe than standeth the saing of *Oecalampadius,* who wickedly trauailed almost in all pointes to make the olde lawe and the Sacramentes therof, nothing inferiour to the newe lawe, and the sacramentes therof, saing: *Absit vt spirituales, qui sub lege erāt Messiámque expectabant, fide pauperiores nobis fuerint, quibus manifestatus est.* God for bidde, that they which were spirituall vnder the lawe, and did looke for Messias in faith, shoulde be poorer then we, vnto whom he ys manifested? And howe again standeth this saieng of *Oecolampadius,* whiche within a fewe lines foloweth, with the saing of Chryst before mencioned? *Neque Patriarchis fideles nostri beatiores sunt, quos æquauit fides, non reddunt inferiores sacramenta.* Neither be our faithfull more blessed then **C** the Patriarches, for those whom faith maketh equall, sacramentes can not make inferiour.

In expas. verborum Cænæ.

Chryste saieth they are more blessed: *Oecolampadius* by expresse contrarie woordes saieth naie. What heticall impudencie ys this, to denie that that Chryst affirmeth? That the holie Patriarches were excellent in faith, and as constantly beleued that Messias shoulde come, as they that sawe him in the flesh beleued that he was comed, no man of sownd minde will denie And yet although in that part they might be equall: yet yt ys no good argument, that in other thinges and respectes the faithfull Chrystian shoulde not excell. For as Chryst hath taught, that they that beleued in him, and bodilie sawe him, were more blessed, then they that onely beleued him to come: so they that receaue the sacramētes in faith presentlie, which Chryst hath instituted, are in that respect more blessed then they, which in faith onelie beleued that soche shoulde be instituted and neuer sawe them, nor receaued.

Oecolāp. denieth that Chryst affirmeth.

But see howe this matter carieth me awaie? by this yet yt maie be perceaued, that though the sacramentes of the newe lawe did not conferre grace **D** (as the Aduersaries wolde haue yt) but were bare signes, and that the fathers of the olde lawe were equall in faith with the Chrystians in the newe lawe: yet if Sathan the master of vntrueth and heresie had not with malice

Zz iiii   blinded

blinded the fight of this his fcholer, and other his likes, he and they might   **E**
well haue feen, that both the facramentes of the newe lawe excell the facramentes of the olde lawe : and that the faithfull of the newe lawe excell the
faithfull of the olde lawe, though not in all, yet in diuerfe refpectes, as yt
ys faied.

THE FOVRTENTH CHAP. PROCEADETH IN
the proof of the fame by the fcriptures and doctours.

Nd nowe that the facramentes of the newe lawe do excell the
facramentes of the olde lawe, yt fhall by moft manifeft teftimonie be proued. And firft for that our fpeciall difputacion ys of
the bleffed facrament of Chryftes bodie and bloode we fhall
firft deliuer that from the malicioufe blafphemie of the Aduerfaries, and proue the excellencie of yt aboue other of the olde lawe. And fo
generalie proue the excellencie of all our facramentes. For the fundacion of   **F**
the proof of the excellencie of the facrament of Chriftes bodie and blood,
I will take the woord of him, who ys the fundació of all Chryftians, vpó whó
they muft all builde, which ys Chryft. who moft plainly declareth the excel
lencie of this Sacrament in the fixt of S. Iohn. And to the fortifieng of this
matter, for that the Aduerfarie moft arrogantly faieth (*but he proueth yt not*)
that the fixt chap. of S. Iohn ys not to be vnderftanded of the Sacrament,
before I produce the authoritie of Chryft in that place, vnderftand (gentle
Reader) that I do not onely faie yt, but in the feconde booke, yt ys auouched, and inuinciblie proued by the teftimonie of a nombre, namely by *Ori-*
gen, Cyprian. Eufebius Emiß. Hierom, Chryfoftom, Hilarie, Ambrofe , Damafcen, Au-
guftin, Cyrille, Euthimius, Gregory, Theophilact, Petrus Cluniacen. Guitmundus, Dioni-
fius Carthufian. Lira, and in fewe woordes to comprehende a greater nombre
then all thefe, by the *Ephefine Councell,* in the whiche were two hondreth
learned Fathers . By the teftimonie of thefe yt ys ther proued that in
the fixt of S. Iohn Chryft fpeaketh of the Sacrament of his bodie and   **G**
bloode.

    To this alfo maie be added the cómon and vniforme confent of the chry-
ftian Church, before this fciffure was made in the time of *Luther,* and Oecolampadius, and the other like Angells of Sathan, whiche with one mouthe
as yt were, taught that chapter to be vnderftanded of the Sacrament. This
alfo maketh good proof of the fame, that when the herefie of the Comunion vnder both kindes was firft raifed in *Bohemia,* they grownded the neceffitie of that matter vpon this text of that chapiter : *Except ye eate the flesh of the*
fonne of man, and drinke his bloode, ye shall haue no life in yowe . For the repreffion of
whiche herefie , as the heritiques vnderftoode that chap . of the Sacrament : fo did no Catholique impugn the fame , but graunted and accepted yt as a true vnderftanding . Whiche then they wolde not haue doen if
yt had ben otherwife to be taken : yf yt had, as that herefie was condemp
ned by a generall Councell : fo fhoulde that vnderftanding haue ben condemned likewife.

    To ende this proof, that the reader maie fee fome authoritie, in this place   **H**
prefentlie, and not to feke farre for yt, we fhall heare S. Auguftin, who fpeaking of the maundie of Chryft, faieth : *Ioannes de corpore & fanguine Domini hoc*
loco nihil dixit. Sed planè alibi multo vberius de iis Dominũ locutum fuiffe teftatur . Iohn
faied nothing in this place of the bodie and blood of our lorde . But plainly

                                                                 iij

Marginal notes:

Joan.6.

De confen
fu Eunnge-
lift.li.3.c.1
The vi.of
S.Iohn fpea-
keth of the
bodie and
blood of
Chryfte.

A in an other place, he teſtifieth that our lorde hath ſpoken of yt very plentifullie. Ye heare S. Auguſtin plainlie ſaing, that though S. Iohn ſpeaketh nothing in that place of the Sacrament, yet in an other place (ſaieth he) he ſpeaketh plentifullie of yt, We read in no place of S. Iohns Goſpell that he ſpeaketh plentifullie of Chryſtes bodie and blood in the Sacrament but in the ſixt chapiter, Wherfor S. Auguſtine vnderſtandeth the ſixt chapter of S. Iohn to ſpeake of the bodie and bloode of Chryſt.

In theſe woordes alſo of S. Auguſtin yt ys not to be ouerpaſſed, but by the waie to be noted, that he ſaieth not that S. Iohn ſpeaketh of the Sacrament, figure or ſign of the bodie of Chryſt, but plainlie he calleth yt the bodie and bloode of Chryſt, and ſaieth that S. Iohn ſpeaketh of them in the ſixt chap. This then being certen, and euident, that the woordes of Chryſt in the ſixt of S. Iohn, as by Chryſoſtom and *Euthymius*, by S. Auguſtin and *Teophilact* they are diſtincted, be ſpoken, and vnderſtanded of his bodie and blood, according to the diſtinction: we ſhall bring in the woordes of Chryſt, for the proof of this that ys here to be prooued.

B Thus Chryſt ſaieth : *Non ſicut manducauerunt patres veſtri Manna, & mortui ſunt. Qui manducat hunc panem, viuet in æternum.* Not as yowr Fathers did eat Manna, and be dead, he that eateth this bread ſhall liue for euer. In the whiche ſaing of Chryſt we are taught two thinges. The firſt that Manna ys a figure of our heauenly Manna (I meen of Chryſt in the Sacrament our moſt pleaſant foode) as the compariſon of the one to the other made by Chryſt him ſelf doth well proue, and as at large yt ys teſtified by the teſtimonie of manie Fathers in the. 4. 5. 6. 7. 8. 9. and tenth chapiters of this booke. The ſecond thing ys the excellencie of our Manna the bodie of Chryſt in the Sacrament, the thing figured by the other Manna. Whiche excellencie Chryſt very manifeſtlie declareth when he ſaieth that the eaters of Manna are dead: but the eaters of this Manna in the Sacrament, ſhall not onely liue, but they ſhall liue for euer. *Ioan. 6.*

Thexcellécie of the B Sacr. aboue Manna.

As life in naturall thinges ys moch more excellent then death: ſo that which geueth naturall life ys moche more excellent, then that whiche geueth yt not life. As betwixt life and death ther ys no iuſt cõpariſon, both for **C** that *inter ens, & non ens nulla eſt comparatio,* betwixt ſome thing and nothing ys no compariſon, and alſo for that no compariſon can be grownded wher ys no poſitiue: ſo betwixt temporall life and eternall life ys no compariſion, for that, as S. Gregory ſaieth, *Temporalis vita æternæ vitæ comparata mors eſt po tius dicenda, quàm vita.* The temporall life compared to the eternall life ys raither to be called death them life. Then the eternall life ſo farre paſsing the temporal life, as life doth death : how moch then ſurmounteth the Manna of the chryſtians the Manna of the Iewes, wher as this geueth but temporall life, the other eternall, as ſaieth S. Auguſtin: *Manna de cælo aperiè ab ipſo Domino exponitur. Patres veſtri (inquit) manducauerunt Manna in deſerto & mortui ſunt. Quã do enim viuerent? Figura vitam prænunciare poſſet, vita eſſe non poſſet. Manducauerunt (inquit) Manna & mortui ſunt, id eſt, Manna quod manducauerunt, non illos potuit de morte liberare, non quia ipſum Manna mors eis fuit, ſed quia à morte non liberauit. Ille enim liberaturus erat à morte, qui per Manna figurabatur. De cælo certè Manna veniebat. Attende quem figurabat : Ego ſum (inquit) panis vinus, qui de cælo deſcendi.* Manna from heauen ys plainly expownded of our lorde himſelf. Yowr fathers (ſaieh he) **D** haue eaten Manna in the wilderneſſe and are dead. for when ſhoulde they liue? A figure maie foreſhewe life: but yt can not be life. *They haue (ſaieth he) eaten Manna and are dead,* that ys to ſaie, Manna which they haue eaten could

Gregorius.

Mãna the figure gaue but téporal life: Mãna the thing eternall life

A figure maie fore ſhewe life but yt can not be liſe.

not

E

not deliuer them from death not that, that Manna was death vnto them, but bycaufe yt deliuered them not from death. He fhoulde deliuer them from death, who was figured by Manna. Certenlie that Manna came frō heauen: Take hede whom yt did figure. *I am* (faiethe he) *the liuing bread, whiche defcen-ded from heauen,* Thus farre S. Auguftin.

Seing then that Manna the figure, whiche rained to the Iewes coulde not deliuer from death, as here yowe haue heard S. Auguftin teftifie: and Manna the bodie of Chryft, the thing figured, and conteined in our Sacramēt doth deliuer from death, and therfor of confequent geueth eternall life, as Chryft him felf alfo auoucheth in the text alleaged : yt can not otherwife be con-cluded, but that our Sacrament of Chryftes bodie and bloode ys incompa-rablie excelling Manna and anie other facrament that in the olde lawe did figure Chryft. As here by the comparifon which Chryft hath made betwixt Manna and his bodie, the excellencie of the one aboue the other ys eafie to be difcerned : fo nowe fhall we fee the like handling of the figure, and the ve ritie by the holy fathers.

(margin: Our Sacr. geuing life farre excel leth Mānа that gaue not life.)

F

Holy Cyprian fheweing the meting and applicacion of the olde Pafchall lābe. which was a figure of our new Pafchall lābe declareth moft plainlie the excellencie of the one aboue the other. *Cæna difpofita inter facramentales epulas obuiarunt fibi inftituta noua, & antiqua. Et confumpto agno, quem antiqua traditio pro-ponebat, inconfumptibilem cibum magifter apponit Difcipulis . Nec iam ad elaborata im-penfis & arte conuiuia populi inuitantur, fed immortalitatis alimonia datur, à comunibus cibis differens , corporalis fubftantiæ retinens fpeciem, fed virtutis diuinæ inuifibili efficiē tia probans adeffe præfentiam.* The fupper being ordined, emong the Sacramen-tall meates, ther mett together the newe and the olde ordinances, and the lambe which the olde tradiciō did fett furth being confumed, the mafter fett before his difciples inconfumptible meate . Neither are the people bidden to feaftes prepared with charges and conning : *but the foode of imortali-tie ys geuen , differing from comon meates , reteining the forme of corporall fub-ftance but prouing by inuifible woorking , the prefence of the diuine power to be prefent.* Thus S. Cyprian.

(margin: Cyprian de cœna Do.)

(margin: The incon-fumptible meat geuē to the Apo ftles both conteined the prefēce of diuine power, and alfo retei-ned the for me of corpo rall fubftan ce.)

G

As in this fentēce ye fee the applicaciō of the ordināuces of the old law to the newe: fo maie ye eafilie perceaue that the one farre excelleth the other. The meat whiche was geuen according to the olde ordeinaunce was confu-med: but the meat whiche was geuen according to the new ordeinance, was inconfumptible. That, that ys of a limited power, and finite, yt maie haue a certain degree of excellencie, cōpared to thinges of like condiciō but whē yt ys cōpared to a thing that ys infinite, yt maie not ftād in comparifon, for *Finiti ad infinitum nulla eft comparatio,* of a thing finite to a thing infini-te ther ys no comparifon . Wherfore the inconfumptible meat of ōur lambe in our Sacrament fo farre excelleth (being infinite) that the con-fumptible meat of the olde lawe (being finite) maie not ftande with yt in comparifon.

H

Again S. Cyprian calleth our Sacramēt the foode of immortalitie, the Pafchall lambe of the Iewes was none foche. Wherfore our Sacrament by all meanes excelleth that facramēt of the Iewes. S. Cyprian alfo applieng our Sacrament to the figure of the fame vfed by Melchifedech, doth moft plain lie declare the excellencie of yt : *Significata olim à tempore Melchifedec prodeunt facramenta, & filiis Abrahæ facientibus opera eius fummus facerdos panē profert, & vi-num : Hoc eft (inquit) corpus meum. Manducauerant , & biberant de eodem pane fecun dùm formam vifibilem. &c.* The facramentes fignified in the olde time , from

(margin: Cyprian ibidē vide fup.l.1. cap. 39.)

the

A　the time of Melchifedech come nowe furth, and the high preift to the children of Abraham doing his woorkes, bringeth furth breade and wine. *This ys* (faieth he) *my bodie.* They had eaten, and dronken after the vifible forme of the fame bread. But before thofe woordes that common meat was profitable onely to nourifh the bodie, and did miniftre helpe to the corporall life. But after yt was faied of our lorde. *This do ye in the in the remembrance of me, This ys my flesh, and this ys my bloode,* as often as yt ys don with thefe woordes, and this faith, this fubftanciall bread and cuppe confecrated with the folemne benediction, yt doth auail to the health and life of the wholl man, *and ys both a medicin and facrifice, to heale infirmities and to pourge iniquities.* Thus moche S. Cyprian.

Sacrifice propitiatorie.

But forafmoch as thefe two fainges are handled in the firft booke, wher the figure and the thing figured be at large opened: I thinke yt not meete anie more of them here to faie, then toucheth this prefent matter, whiche they do wonderfullie fet furth. Yt ys more then manifeft that the facrifices

B　of the olde lawe were not of that force, power, and vertue to pourge or take awaie finnes, S. Paule faing: *Impoßibile eft fanguine taurorum, aut hircorum auferri peccata.* Yt ys vnpoßible finnes to be taken awaie with the bloode of bulls and goates. But this owre facrifice of the newe lawe, whiche ys the flefh and blood of Chryfte, ys auailable to the wholl mā, that ys to the health both of the bodie and foule of man. *For yt ys a medicin to heale infirmities and a facrifice to pourge iniquities.* Yf this then be not a notable excellencie, whiche the holie martir Cyprian geueth vnto this glorioufe and blefled Sacrament aboue the excellencie of thefe figures, I knowe not what excellencie ys. But the matter requireth to haue other holy Fathers to fpeake what they thinke in this matter.

Hebr.10. The blood of bulls and goates in the olde lawe did not take awaie finnes: but the facrifice of the newe lawe pourgeth iniquities.

S Ambrofe, for that he fpeaking of this matter, affirmeth the like operacion and effect of this Sacrament, as S. Cyprian did, he fhall be ioined vnto him Thus he faieth: *Ipfe Dominus Iefus teftificatur nobis, quod corpus fuum accipiamus & fanguinem. Nunquid debemus de eius fide & teftificatione dubitare? Iam redi me*

C　*cum ad propofitionem meam. Magnum quidem & venerabile quod Manna Iudæis pluit è cœlo. Sed intellige quid eft amplius, Manna de cœlo, an corpus, Chrifti? Corpus Chrifti vtique, qui author eft cœli. Deinde Manna qui manducauerit, mortuus eft, qui manducauerit hoc corpus fiet ei remißio peccatorum, & non morietur in æternum.* The Lorde Iefus him felf (faieth S. Ambrofe) teftifieth vnto vs that we receaue his bodie and bloode, awght we of his teftificacion and trueth to doubte? Nowe come again with me to my propofition. Yt ys a great thing trulie, and venerable that he rained Manna to the Iewes from heauen. But vnderftand, whiche ys the greater, Manna from heauen, or the bodie of Chryft. The bodie of Chryft trulie, who ys the authour of heaue. Farder he that hath eatē Manna hath died: he that eateth this bodie, he fhall haue remiflion of finnes, and fhall not die for euer. Thus farre S. Ambrofe.

Li.4. de facrams cap.5

Manna a creature frō heauen moche inferiour to Chrifte the authour of heauen.

Doeft thowe not, Reader, in this goodly faing fee the great excellencie of the Sacrament aboue Manna, as thow dideft in S. Cyprian aboue the Pafchall lambe, and the facrifice of Melchifedec? Doeft thowe not alfo note the goodly argrement, of thefe two, in commending vnto vs the great and woorthie effectes of this Sacrament? by the whiche yt doth withoute all contro-

D　nerfie, woonderfully excell all the facramātes and facrifices of the olde lawe. As S. Cyprian applieng the bodie of Chryft to the Pafchall lambe, called yt the inconfumptible meat, wherby yt excelleth the figure whiche was confumed: So S. Ambrofe, applieng the bodie of Chryft to Manna as to his figure,

Effectes of the S. Sacr. prouing the excellencie of yt.

gure, faieth, that though Manna came from heauen, Yet Chryſt who ys the **E**
authour of heauen ys more excellent. As S. Cyprian called the bodie the
foode of imortalitie : So S. Ambroſe faieth that he that eateth this bodie, he
ſhall newer die As S. Cyprian faieth that yt ys a ſacrifice to pourge iniquites :
So S. Ambroſe faieth, that he that eateth this bodie, his ſinnes ſhall be remitted. Theſe goodly effectes were not in the ſacramentes and ſacrifices
of the olde lawe. Wherfore they being in this Sacrament, yt excelleth
them all.

Yf thowe aske why, or howe theſe effectes be in this Sacrament : I anſwe
Colloſſ.2. re, bicauſe he ys ther verily ſubſtancially, and reallie *in quo inhabitat omnis pleni-*
tudo diuinitatis corporaliter, in whom dwelleth all the fullneſſe of the deitie cor
Joan.3. porally : and vnto whom *Non ad menſuram dat Deus Spiritum*. God geueth not
his Spirit by meaſure : *Et cui data eſt omnis poteſtas in cœlo, & in terra.* And to whō
Math. 28. ys geuen all power in heauen, and in earth, whoſe fleſh *comuncta ei, quæ natura-*
liter vita eſt, viuifica effecta eſt, being ioined vnto that, whiche naturally ys life, **F**
Cyrillus. ys made alſo able to giue life, as S. Cyrill faieth.

Of this his preſence in the Sacrament, for that that Chryſt him ſelf faieth,
and teſtifieth vnto vs that we do receaue his bodie, we ſholde not, neither
we aught (as S. Ambroſe faieth) to doubt of his wittneſſe and trueth. Of the
whiche, as alſo of farder teſtimonie to the proof of the excellencie of the Sacrament, he faieth in an other place : *Conſidera nunc, vtrum preſtantior ſit panis An*
Ambro
ſius De ini-
tiand myſt
ca.9. *gelorum, an caro Chriſti, quæ vtique eſt corpus vitæ. Manna illud è cœlo : hoc ſupra cœ-*
lum. Illud cœli : hoc Domini cœlorum. Illud corruptioni obnoxium, ſi in diem alterum ſerua-
retur : hoc alienum ab omni corruptione, Quod quicunque religioſe guſtauerit, corruptionem
ſentire non poterit. Illos ad horam ſatiauit aqua : te ſanguis diluit in æternum. Iudæus bibit,
& ſitit : tu cùm biberis, ſitire non poteris. Et illud in vmbra : hoc in veritate. Et poſt
pauca, Cognouiſti præſtātiora : potior enim lux, quàm vmbra, veritas, quàm figura, corpus
authoris, quàm Manna de cœlo. Conſider nowe whether the bread of Angells
ys more excellent or the fleſh of Chryſt, whiche ys alſo the bodie of life. That
Manna was from heauen : this aboue heauen. That of heauen : this of the
lorde of heauens. That ſubiect to corruptiō, yf yt were kept till the next daie : **G**
Manna
proued
moche infe
riour to the
B. Sacr. by
S. Amb. his
cōpariſon. this free from all corruption, whiche whoſoeuer ſhall taſt deuoutely ſhall
not be able to feele corruption. Vnto them water did flowe oute of the rock
vnto thee bloode oute of Chryſt. Them did water ſatisfie for a litle time : thee doth
blood waſh for euer. The Iewe dranke, and thirſteth : thowe, when thowe
haueſt dronke, canſt not thirſt. And that was in ſhadowe : this in treuth. And
after a fewe wordes he faieth : Haueſt thowe knowen the more excellent?
The light ys more excellent thē the ſhadow. The veritie, then the figure. The
bodie of the authour, then Manna from heauen. Thus S. Ambroſe. Nede
we anie plainer teſtimonie, for the proof of this our matter in hande? I thin
ke the holy Goſt directed the penne of S. Ambroſe, to anſwere and confute
the wicked aſſertion of Oecolampadius. for this ſo ouerthroweth his hereſie,
as though yt had ben nowe written in theſe daies to confute him.

But perchaunce the Aduerſarie will ſaie, that this maketh nothing againſt
him, for here S. Ambroſe ſpeaketh not of the Sacrament, but of the bodie of
Chryſt, as ſuffring for vs, to woorke our redemption. To this ther maie be
manifolde anſwers made. Firſt that Manna ys not proprely a figure of Chryſt **H**
Obiection. as ſuffring, but of Chryſt as feeding vs. For Manna deſcended from heauen
to feed the Iſraelites, and not to ſuffer for them. ſo Manna being the foode
Thanſwer from heauen of the people of God, ys a figure of owre heauenly foode
Chryſt in the Sacrament. Farder alſo yt ys well knowen that S. Ambroſe in
                                                                              that

A   that booke treacteth of myfteries and facramentes, wherfore in this place yt ys moft like, that he treacteth of the Sacrament. Finallie the plain woordes of S. Ambrofe inuincible proue the fame. For immediatelie, and iointlie to this fentence laft alleadged he obiecteth to himfelf as nowe the Aduerfarie doth in thefe daies vnto vs, and faieth, *Forte dicasialiud video, quomodò tu mihi affe ris, quòd Chrifti corpus accipiam? Et hoc nobis fupereft adhuc vt probemus, quantis igitur vtimur exemplis, &c.* Perchaunce thowe maift faie: I fee an other thing, howe doeft thowe faie vnto me, that I receaue the bodie of Chryft? And this remaineth yet vnto vs to proue. Howe manie examples maie we therfore vfe? Let vs prooue this not to be that thing, whiche nature hath formed: but that the blefsing hath confecrated, and the power of the blefsing, to be greater then of nature. For by the blefsing nature yt felf ys chaunged. Moyfes did holde a rodde, he caft yt down, and yt was made a ferpent. Again, he tooke the taill of the ferpent, and yt returned into the nature of the rodde. Thowe feeft therfore euen by the propheticall gra-

B   ce, nature to be twice chaunged, both of the ferpent, and of the rodde. The riuers of Egypt did runne with a pure courfe, and fodenly oute of the veines of the fountaines ther began blood to breake oute, fo that ther was no drinke in the riuers. Again, at the praiers of the Prophet the bloode of the floodes ceaffed, and the nature of the water returned. The people of Ifraell were compafed aboute on euerie fide, on this fide with the Egyptians, on the other fide with the fea. Moyfes lift vppe the rodde, the water deuided yt felf, and congealed in maner of walls, and fo betwen the waters ther appeared a foote path Iordan turned backward againft hys nature, he returned into his well fpring. Ys yt not clere then that the nature either of the waueis of the fea, or of the courfe of the riuer hath, ben chaunged? The people of the fathers did thirft. Moyfes touched the ftone, and water flowed oute of yt. Did not grace woorke befides nature, that a ftone fhoulde powre oute water, whiche nature had not? and after other mo. examples he concludeth thus: we perceaue therfore grace to be of greater

C   power then nature. And yf mans blefsing was of foche force that yt might turne nature, what fhall we faie of the diuine confecracion, wher the verie woordes of our Lord and fauiour do woorke? For this Sacrament whiche thowe receaueft ys made by the woorde of Chryft. Yf then the woorde of Helias was of fo great power, that yt might putt down fire from heauen: fhall not the woorde of Chryft be able to chaunge the natures of the ele- mentes? Thowe haueft readde of the workes of all the worlde, that he hath faied, and they were made: he hath commaunded, and they were created. The woorde of Chryft then, which coulde of nothing make that that was not, can yt not chaunge thofe thinges that be into that they were not? Yt ys nolefle matter to geue vnto thinges newe natures, then to chaunge natures. Thus moch S. Ambrofe.

    In this anfwer as pithie and plain, as yt ys long, the Aduerfary ys not one ly fullie aunfwered, but we are alfo inftructed in three thinges: The firft that concerneth this matter ys, that in the applicacion of the veritie to the figure, he vnderftandeth the veritie of the figure Manna to be the bodie of Chryft in the Sacrament, by the which he taketh the Sacrament to

D   be moche more excellent then the figure, which although in euery parte of his fentece he toucheth, yet in this he moft plainly declareth yt, whe he faith *The light ys more excellent then the fhadowe: the veritie, then the figure.* And expown-

Ambr. ibid. vide fup. li. 2. ca 51.

The B. Sa. ys not that, that nature hath for- med, but that the blefsing hath confe- crated.

Confecra cion of the B. Sacr. of what force yt ys.

Three no- tes out of S. Ambr.

ding which ys the light and veritie, which ys the shadowe and figure, he addeth: *The bodie of the authour, than Manna from heauen.*

    The seconde thing that he teacheth, ys howe, and bywhat meanes the bo
die of Chryst ys in the Sacrament, which he declareth to be in two poinctes:
The one ys that yt ys doen by consecracion, which ys doen by the woord of
Chryst. Wherfor he saieth: *We perceaue grace to be of greater power then nature.* For
yf the benediction of a man was of so great power, that yt might turne nature: what shall we saie of the diuine consecracion yt self, wher the verie woor
des of our Lord and Sauiour do woorke? As who might saie. Yf Moyses did
cast downe the rodde, and yt was turned into a serpent, and tooke yt vppe a-
gain and yt was turned into a rodde: and soch like. Yf *Helyseus* did make the
axe against his nature to swimme aboue the water: Yf *Helyas* by his woorde
caused fire to descend from heauen. Yf the woorde of these men but seruantes did woork soch wonders: how moch more maie the woorde of the Lord
and master of these men woorke? The second poinct ys, that he sheweth by
what means the woord of Chryst woorketh the presence of his bodie in the
Sacrament, that ys (*saieth he*) by the chaunging of the natures of the creatures, into the nature of his bodie ād blood, which he signifieth when he saieth
Yf the woorde of *Helyas* was of soch power, that yt might bring down fire frō
heauen, shall not the woorde of Chryst be of soch power, that yt maie chaun
ge the natures of the elementes? And again: the woorde of Chryst that
coulde of nothing make that that was not: can yt not chaunge those thinges
that be, in to that thing that they were not? The meā then by the which the
woorde of Chryst maketh the bodie of Chryst present in the Sacrament ys
by chaunging the natures of bread and wine into the nature of his bodie ād
blood, which bicause the chaunging of natures, ys the chaunge of substances, therfor the Church doth call yt *Transubstanciacion*, forsomoch as the nature or substance of one thing ys chaunged by Gods power into the nature or
substance of an other thing.

    The thirde thing that we are taught of S. Ambrose (which also ys didu-
ced of these two) ys the verie presence of Chryst in the Sacrament. Which
so being (as most certenly yt ys) we maie conclude, that this ys incomparablie
a more excellent Sacrament, then either Manna or the Paschall lambe, notwithstanding the saing of the Aduersarie.

    And although S. Augustin saieth, that *Sacramenta in signis diuersa, in re tamen
quæ significatur paria sunt.* Sacramentes in signes being diuerse: in the thing yet
that ys signified they are like: Yet that taketh not awaie the excellencie of
this Sacrament. For although Manna and the Paschall lambe did signifie the
same Chryst that our Sacrament doth, and so in that respect of significacion
be like: yet for that the other sacramentes did but signifie, and this Sacramēt
doth both contein and geue that yt doth signifie, therfor yt doth farre excell them.

    To this that ys saied, although yt be sufficient to proue that, that ys here
entended: yet yf the reader will adde the saing of S. Ambrose in the eight
chapter of the booke last alleaged (whiche to auoide tediousnesse I ouerpasse) and wil remembre what the saied S. Ambrose saieth in the fourth chap
ter of this booke, and Chrysostom in the sixth chapter, and *Theophilact* and
Haymo in the ninth chap. and other treacting of *Manna* and the bodie of
Chryst, of which he shall find diuerse from the fourth chapter to the eleuēth
chapiter of this booke, I doubte not but he shall see so moche, that he will
merueill that euer anie heretike could so shamelesly teach soch wicked doctrine

*In the con-
secracion of
the B. Sac.
the woordes
of our Saui
our do woor
ke.*

*Transub-
stanciation
what yt ys.*

*Difference
betwē Mā
na and the
blessed Sac.*

A trine, fo repugnant to the catholique faith, and fo direct contrarie to the fain ges of fo manie holy Fathers being wittneffes of this trueth, but aboue all that they fhoulde fo blafphemoufly difhonour the facramentes of God, and his Chryft. Who for the fetting furth of his honour, and for owre helpe and comfort in the perigrinacion of this life, that we maie haue ftrenght againft owre enemies, whiche cruelly lie in wait for vs, and our affured hope of the mercie of God in the ende of our iourney, hath inftituted thefe facramé tes and by them woorthilie vfed and receaued hath geuen vs manie benefit-tes, of all which, as alfo of Gods honour, they wolde robbe both him and vs. But, Reader, beware of them, and be not led awaie with foch doctrines, as were born but yefterdaie. But cleaue to that ys tried, receaued, approued, and teftified manie hondreth years, of the whiche thowe fhalt learn that the Sacramentes of Chryft and of the newe lawe are moch more excellent, then the facramentes of the olde lawe.

B   ## THE FYFTENTH CHAPITER PROVING

all our Sacramentes generallie to be more excellent then
the facramentes of Moyfes.

S ye haue heard by fufficient teftimonie, that the bleffed Sa crament of Chryftes bodie and bloode ys more excellent, then Manna and the Pafchall lambe, the figures of the fame, of the which I haue fpeciallie treacted, bicaufe this wholl rude woork ys cheifly fettfurth for the commendacion of the trueth of the fame Sacrament: Nowe that the other facramentes be not left in the handes of the enemies, and by them fpoiled ad ouer moche wronged, fomwhat alfo fhall be breiflie faied, wherby they maie be knowen as they be, and be deli-uered from the handes of their enemies, who falfelie report of them, and de-uelliflie trauaill to difhonour them.

C   Among all the facramentes next vnto this bleffed and moft honorable Sa crament of Chryftes bodie and blood, yt ys to be merueiled that they could fo vnreuerentlie fpeake of the facrament of Baptifme, which was fo inftitu-ted and commended to the Chryftian worlde, as no facrament more folem-nelie. At the fetting furth of this Sacrament Chryft himfelf being prefent, and baptifed, the voice of the Father was heard faing: *This ys my wel beloued Son ne, in whom I am well pleafed:* heauen was opened, and the holy Goft was feen in the forme of a doue defcending from heauen and abyding vpon Chryft. So that in the miniftracion of this facrament was prefent the Father, the Sonne and the holie Goft. Which noble prefence femeth to bring with yt fome mo re noble gift than a bare fign, or token, as the wicked faie that yt ys. But what fhall I nede to ftand to declare the woorthineffe of this facrament a-gainft thefe enemies of God, feing that heauen and the wholl Trinitie, tefti-fieth againft them.

Baptifme inftituted by Chryfte and comme ded by the wholl Tri-nitie.

   Wherfore leauing to fpeake any more of this facrament fpeciallie, or of the other particularlie for feare of prolixitie, and for that yt ys fpoken D   of here but by occafion, we fhall heare faint Auguftin fpeaking of them generallie: *Prima facramenta quæ obferuabantur, & celebrabantur ex lege, prænunciatiua erant Chrifti venturi, quæ cùm fuo aduentu Chriftus impleuiffet, abla-ta funt, & ideo ablata funt, quia impleta. Non enim venit legem foluere, fed adimplere.*

Aug. cò̄t. Fauft ü li. 19 cap. 13.

Et alia sunt instituta, virtute maiora, vtilitate meliora, actu faciliora, numero pauciora. **E**
The first sacramentes, which were obserued and celebrated of the olde lawe

were forefhewers of Chryft to come, the whiche when in his coming he
had fulfilled, they were taken awaie, and therfor taken awaie bicaufe they
were fullfilled. For he came not to breake the lawe, but to fullfill yt. And o-
ther were inftituted greater in power, better in profitt, eafier to be done, and
fewer in nombre. Thus S. Auguftin.

Obferue gentle reader, thefe woordes. *He faieth that after the facramentes of*
the olde lawe were taken awaie, ther were other inftituted, which were greater in power, and
better in profitte. Wher in be they greater in power, but in this that the facramentes of the olde lawe had no power but to fignifie onely: our facramentes haue power not onely to fignifie, but alfo to geue that that they fignifie? As the Sacrament of Chryftes bodie fignifieth the fame bodie, and yt
geueth alfo to the receauer the fame bodie that yt fignifieth. And as Baptifme fignifieth by the wafhing of the bodie, the clenfing of the foule: fo yt geueth remifsion of finnes both originall, and actuall, by taking awaie of
of which, the foule ys pourged, clenfed, and wafhed from all her filthineffe. **F**
And fo in other Sacramentes, what they fignifie, that they geue, yf ther be
no ftoppe nor let in the receauer. And therfor as they in geuing that they
do fignifie, be in power greater then the Sacramentes of the olde lawe, for
they coulde but fignifie, but to geue that that they fignified they had no power: So to vs warde in that they geue vs foche benefittes as they fignifie
they are more profitable. The Aduerfarie maketh no more difference betwixt the Sacramentes of the olde lawe and newe, but that they fignified
Chryft to come, and owers Chryft that ys comed, in the whiche ther appeareth to me no difference either in power or in profit. But S. Auguftine maketh a great difference. For he faieth that our Sacramentes are greater in
power, and better in profit. Howe fo euer the Aduerfarie will vnderftande
S. Auguftin, yf he will anie other waie make our Sacramentes better and
profitablier then the Sacrametes of the olde lawe, he muft nedes alfo graunt
that they be more excellent then thofe. Nowe therfor he muft either denie
S. Auguftin, or ells graunt that he hath before denied, and faie that our Sacramentes be more excellent.

G

To the confirmacion alfo of this matter maketh moche the common con
fent of learned men vpon the difinition of a Sacrament. Thus do they defi-

ne yt: *Sacramentum eft facræ rei fignum, ita vt imaginem gerat, & caufa exiftat.* **A**
Sacrament ys a figne of an holy thing in foche maner that yt maie beare the
image, and be the caufe. In the which definition are put the two offices of a
Sacrament of the newe lawe. The one office ys to be a figne, but not onelie

a figne, but an euident, or a liuely fign, hauing fome properties or condicions
like to the thing that yt fignifieth, fo that yt maie fignifie yt euidentlie as the
image of a man fignifieth a man. The other office ys that yt be the caufe
of the thing that yt fignifieth not a caufe of the being of yt, but a caufe of the
effectuall woorking of yt, in him that receaueth the Sacrament. As for exam
ple. Baptifme ys an euident fign of the wafhing of the foule, and beinge miniftred ys a caufe that the wafhing of the foule ys effectuallie wrought, and
doen. For yf Baptifme be not either in facte, or in vowe, howe moche foeuer
otherwife the partie beleueth, the foule ys not clenfed from finne. Wherby
yt ys euident that Baptifme ys a caufe effectuall.

H

But here ys to be noted, ther be (as to the pourpofe fufficeth) two caufes effectuall, one principall, the other inftrumentall. As for example.

The

A The foule ys the principall caufe efficient of the feight of man: The eye ys the organ or inftrumentall caufe efficient of the feight. So bothe be caufes, but the foule the principall, the eye the inftrumétall, fo called, bicaufe yt ys the orgá or inftrumét, by which the foule doth fee. So in the geuing of grace which cometh to man by the facramentes. God ys the principall caufe efficient of that benefitt or gift or grace, for he ys the geuer, he ys the doer: the facrament ys his inftrument or organ, by the whiche yt hath pleafed him to take ordre to woorke his gracioufe pleafure and to giue his gift of grace to men. So that as the foule (yf the eie be not altered from his due ordre that nature hath appointed) infalliblie, and moft affuredlie dothe fee by the eie: fo God yf the facramentes be miniftred in that ordre that he hath appointed them, infalliblie, and moft certenly he woorketh and geueth his grace to the receauers by them yf the receauers put no ftoppe nor lette to the entrie of the grace of God into them.

Two effec-tuall caufes one princi-pal, the o-ther inftru-mentall.

B Nowe wher the Aduerfaries make exclamacion for that we faie, that the facramentes of Chryft geue grace, and faie that we robbe Chryft of hys honour, and committe Idolatrie in geuing the fame to dumbe creatures, as to bread and wine, water, oyle, and foch other, ye maie perceaue howe litle they fee or vnderftand, or ells blinded by malice, will not fee or vnderftand. For although yt be fo faied and trulie faied, what catholike learned man yet faieth not with all, that God geueth grace by hys facramentes? And who ys ignoraunt of this faing, that the facramentes are effectual by the merit of Chryftes pafsió, ád blood fheding? And who being learned and catholike faith not that Baptifme of yt felf hath no foch power to geue grace, but the power of Chryft which afsifteth his facramentes geueth yt according to his paét or promeffe made in the inftitucion of the facramentes. So that when foeuer the facramentes be duely myniftred to woorthie receauers, vndoubtedlie the grace, which they fignifie ys alfo geuen. In the whiche they geue the principalitie to God Chryft our Sauiour, to whom they geue their due honour, and yet withall confefsing and acknowleging Gods ordeinance, that he by his facramentes hath taken order to geue his grace, faie, that the facramentes as gods organs, do geue grace.

Sacramen-tes of the newe law how they geue grace.

C And this maner of fpeach ys common, to afcribe the effeéte of the caufe principall, to the caufe inftrumentall. For Chryft himfelf abhorreth not from yt, but vfeth yt. As when he faieth: *Veftri beati oculi, quia vident, & aures, quia audiunt*. But bleffed be yowr eyes, for they fee, and your eares for they heare. Chryft was not ignorant, that their foules did fee and heare, as the caufe principall, and yet he afcribeth the effeét to the eye and to the eare, by the which as by her organs, fhe doth fee and heare.

The fcripture alfo vfeth both thefe maner of fpeaches. Sainét Paule faieth: *Secundùm fuam mifericordiam faluos nos fecit per lauacrum regenerationis & renouationis fpiritus fanéti*. According to his mercie he hath faued vs by the fowntain of regeneracion, and the renouacion of the holie Goft. In the whiche maner of fainge, fainét Paule declareth that our faluacion commeth from God, as from the caufe principall, and by Baptifme, as the caufe inftrumentall. Sainét Peter fpeaking of the Arke of

Tit.3.

D Noe, in the whiche Noe and his children were faued, as the figure of Baptifme by the which we are faued faieth: *Nunc fimilis formæ faluos vos facit Baptifma*. Nowe in like maner baptifme faueth yowe. In which maner of fpeach doth not fainét Peter afcribe faluacion to Baptifme? Yet was not he ignorant

1.Pet.3.

Aaa iii   who

who was,the principall cauſe of our ſaluacion.Nowe what ys yt to ſaie that baptiſme ſaueth vs,but that baptiſme geueth vs grace of remiſſion of our ſinnes?what then do we offende to ſpeake as the ſcripture doth, and to ſaie that the ſacramentes geue grace?Doth S.Peter robbe God and Chryſt of his honour,bicauſe he doth aſcribe ſaluacion to baptiſme?No:no more do the the Churche in ſaing that ſacramentes geue grace.Both be vprightlie ſpo ken,and Gods honour vprightlie ſaued.

Yf then (as S.Paule ſaieth) we be ſaued by Baptiſme, and (as S. Peter ſai eth)Baptiſme ſaueth vs:and by the ſacramentes of the old lawe no man was ſaued,neither did they ſaue anie man (*Nam neminem ad perfectum adduxit Lex*, for the lawe brought no man to perfection) then yt maie be conclu ded, that our ſacramentes are more excellent,then the ſacramentes of the olde lawe.

Neither can *Oecolampadius* hys wicked gloſe ſtand to peruert the true de finicion of a ſacrament.*Cauſa non ad efficientiam,ſed ad ſignificantiæ euidentiam refer ri debet.*Cauſe (ſaieth he)ought to be referred not to the efficiencie,or woor king of the effect,but to the euidence of ſignificacion.For as Roffenſis both well and learnedlie ſaith againſt him.This woorde cauſe ys not referred to the euidence of ſignificacion,but to the efficacie, or ells (ſaieth he) this parti cle of the definicion(*& cauſa exiſtit,and ys the cauſe*)were ſuperfluouſe. For by that particle that the definicion hath (*vt imaginem gerat,that yt beare the image*) the euidence of ſignificacion ys ſufficientlie expreſſed.To haue anie thing ſu perfluouſe in a definicion ys a great inconuenience among learned men. Wherfore nothing in this definicion being ſuperfluouſe,yt muſt nedeſſtand that the ſacramentes be cauſes effectuall,and being ſo they excell the ſacra mentes of the olde lawe.For wher they were but onelie ſignifieng, owre are (as the definicion teacheth)both ſignifieng and effectuall. *Nam efficiunt quòd ſignificant*,For they bring that to effecte which they ſignifie.

But let vs heare ſainct Auguſtine teaching the difference of theſe ſacramen tes,for he nothing diſſenteth from this that ys ſaied, but moche confirmeth yt.Thus he ſaieth *Oportunè non ex noſtra,ſed Dei diſpenſatione factū eſt,vt modò au diremus ex euangelio,quia lex per Moyſen data eſt,gratia & veritas per Ieſum Chriſtum facta eſt.Si enim diſcernimus duo Teſtamenta,nec eadem promiſſa , eadem tamen plera que præcepta. Nam non occides . Non mœchaberis . Non furaberis . Honora patrem & matrem· Non falſum teſtimonium dixeris.Non concupiſces res proximi tui,& non con cupiſces vxorem proximi tui,& nobis præceptum eſt, et quiſquis ea non obſeruauerit, de uiat, nec omnino dignus eſt qui accipere mereatur montem ſanctum Dei , de quo dictum eſt: Quis habitabit in tabernaculo tuo , aut quis requieſcet in monte ſancto tuo? Innocens manibus & mundo corde.Hæc dicimus,fratres chariſſimi,vt omnes de nouo teſta mento diſcatis,non inhærere terrenis, ſed cœleſtia adipiſci.Diſcuſſa ergo præcepta, aut om nia eadem inueniuntur,aut vix aliqua in euangelio quæ non dicta ſunt à prophetis.Præcepta eadem , Sacramenta non eadem , promiſſa non eadem . Videamus quare præcepta eadem : quia ſecundùm hæc Deo ſeruire debemus. Sacramenta non eadem, quia alia ſunt ſacramen ta dantia ſalutem , alia promittentia ſaluatorem . ſacramenta noui Teſtamenti dant ſalu tem : ſacramenta veteris teſtamenti promiſerunt ſaluatorem . Quando ergo iam teneas promiſſa , quid quæris promittentia ſaluatorem iam habens ? Hæc dico teneas promiſſa, non quòd iam accepimus vitam æternam , ſed quia iam venit Chriſtus, qui per Prophetas præ nunciabatur . Mutata ſunt ſacramenta,facta ſunt faciliora,pauciora, ſalubriora.*In good ſeaſon yt ys doen,not of owre,but of the diſpenſacion of God,that nowe we ſhoulde heare oute of the Goſpell that the lawe was geuen by Moyſes , but grace and veritie was doen by Ieſus Chryſte . Yf we diſcern the two

teſtameu

Oecolāp. his wicked gloſe of the woord cau ſe cōfuted.

Roffen.li.2 aduerſus Oecolāp. cap.29.

Aug.inpro log.pſal.73

Cōpariſon of the lawe and the goſ pell and of their ſacra mentes.

A testamentes, ther be not the same promisses, but there be manie of the same cōmaundementes. For thowe shalt not kill. Thowe shall not cōmitte adulte rie. Thowe shalt not steale. Honour thy father and thy mother. Thowe shal not speake false wittnesse. Thow shalt not desire thy neighbours goods. And thowe shalt not desire the wief of thy neighbour: yt ys to vs also cōma unded. And whosoeuer shall not obserue them, he goeth oute of the waie, neither by anie meanes ys he woorthie to take the holie hill of God, of the which yt ys saied: *who shall dwell in thie tabernacle, or who shall rest in thy holie hill?* *He that ys* innocent of his handes, and of a clean heart. These thinges we saie (derely beloued brethered) that all yowe that be of the newe testament maie learn not to cleaue to earthly thinges: but to geit heauenly thinges. The cōmaundentes therfor discussed, either they are all fownde to be the same or ells scarce anie in the Gospell, whiche were not spoken of the Prophetes. The cōmaundementes be all one: The sacramentes be not all one. The promesses be not all one. Let vs see why the cōmaundementes be all one. bicause according to these we aught to serue God. The sacramentes be

B not all one. For they be other sacramentes geuing saluacion, and other promising a Sauiour. The sacramentes of the newe Testament geue saluacion: The sacramentes of the olde testament haue promised a Sauiour. Forasmoch then as thowe nowe holdest the promisses, what sekest thowe nowe, hauing the Sauiour, the thinges that do promesse? I saie (*holdest the promesses*) not bicause we haue nowe receaued eternall life : but that nowe Chryst ys comed, whiche was spoken of before by the Prophetes, the sacramentes are chaunged, they are made easier, fewer, holsomer, and better. Hither to S. Augustin.

Sacramentes of the newe lawe geue saluacion.

Ys yt not woonderfull that euer men can be so impudent, so shamelesse to speake the contrarie of so manifest a matter, so clerely, and so plainly vtte red and spoken by soche an notable father, as S. Augustin ys? He hath vsed no circumlocution, no figures, no darke maner of speache, but as yt ys learnedly, so ys yt truly and plainlie cōmended vnto vs. Let me, I beseche thee gentle reader, with thy patience, (although yt be as I saied, so plainly spoke

C of S. Augustin, that except a man will be a trunke, he can not but perceaue yt) a litle more to the confusion of the Aduersarie, weigh the partes of this saing, that touch our matter. wher as S. Augustin saieth that the sacramentes be not all one of the newe and olde testament: the Aduersaries will agree with him and vs. But they saie that although they be diuerse in their matters of the sacramentes : yet in this they be like. for they do all but signifie, the one sorte Chryst to come, the other Chryst allreadie comed, so that ther ys no difference betwixt them, neither ys the one sorte better then the other, more then ys spoken. This ys the assertion of the Aduersarie. Let ys nowe heare the assertion of S. Augustine, he saieth that the sacramentes be diuerse. Ther be some geuing saluacion : othersome but promising the Sauiour, and opening eche sort, he saieth : *The sacramentes of the newe Testament geue saluacion: The sacramentes of the olde Testament haue promised the Sauiour.*

Assertion of the Aduersarie touching the Sacramētes cōferred with S. Aug. his indgement of them.

D O mercifull God ys ther no difference betwixt these sacramentes, more then the Aduersarie hath saied? Ys the one sorte no better then the other? Among scholers, a pettite, yf he be asked, will answer that ther ys great difference. Yt ys a great difference betwixt geuing and not geuing, And that that geueth saluacion ys in manie degrees better then yt that doth but figure or signifie yt to come. S. Augustine saieth that our sacramentes geue saluacion, wheras the other of the olde Testament by figures did but promisse.

Wherfore our facramentes be better. Yf better, then more excellent. That **E**
they be better S. Auguſtin by expreſſe woordes affirmeth afterwarde ſaing:
The facramentes are chaunged , they are made eaſier, fewer, holſomer,and better.

What nowe can the Aduerſarie ſaie? Ys ther no difference, wher the ſacramentes of the newe lawe are holſomer, and better then the other ſacramentes? Ys ther, I ſaie, no difference betwixt theſe facramentes but Oecolampadius difference? Yes, they are better and holeſomer then the other,
and therfor more excellent, yea ſo moche our facramentes excell the other,
that S. Auguſtin in that ſame prologe, comparing the facramentes together,

Aug. ibid   calleth the facramentes of the olde lawe childrens plaies or games in reſpect
of our facramentes. For this ys his ſaing : *Numquid quoniam puero dantur quædā*
puerilia ludicra, quibus puerilis animus auocetur, propterea grandeſcenti non excutiuntur è
manibus, vt aliquid iam vtilius tractet quod grandem decet? Non ergo quia illa quaſi ludi-

Sacramen-   *cra puerorum Deus per nouum teſtamentum excuſſit de manibus filiorum vt aliquid vtilius*
tes of the   *daret grandeſcentibus, propterea priora illa non ipſe dediſſe putandus eſt .* For ſo moch **F**
olde lawe   as vnto a childe ther be geuen certain childeſh plaies or trifles, by the which
compared   the childiſh minde maie be called awaie, are they not therfor taken oute of
to childrens   his handes when he waxeth bigger, that he maie handle ſome other thing
trifles: Sa-   more profitable , as yt becometh a bigger : No more therfor God by-
cramentes   cauſe he hath taken the thinges as childrens plaies oute of the handes
of the newe   of his ſonnes by the newe teſtament, that he might geue the ſomthing more
lawe to   profitable nowe being waxen greater, ys he to be thought not to hauegeuen
things of   thoſe former thinges.
profit.

In this ſaing S. Auguſtin likeneth the facramentes of the olde lawe in reſpect of the facramentes of the newe lawe vnto childrens games, and our facramentes he likeneth to the thinges of more profett, which are to be
geuen to the ſonnes of God, when they waxe of more age, knowledge, and ripeneſſe . And ys not this a great difference? Are not then the
facramentes of Chryſt moch better and more excellent, then the facramen
tes of Moyſes?

Nowe being teſtified that they be better, yt ys to be inquired in what **G**
thing, howe, or by what mean they be better: as before yt ys ſaied, they are
the better for that they geue that, that they ſignifie, As the Sacrament of
Chryſtes bodie and blood ſignifieth the bodie and blood, and conteining
the ſame geueth yt alſo, For in this that yt conteineth the very preſence of
the bodie of Chryſt ſtandeth the excellencie of the Sacrament. for ells howe
can a bare, peice of bread, hauing no other office but that yt ys a ſign of Chry
ſtes bodie, be better or excell ether the paſchall lambe, or Manna, the one
being ſo liuely a figure, the other ſo beautified with many miracles? Wherfor we muſt nedes graunt the preſence of Chryſtes bodie to be in the Sacra
ment, wherby the Sacrament excelleth thoſe other two of the olde lawe be
they neuer ſo gloriouſe, or alſo ſo miraculouſe. For the glorie of this bleſſed
bodie paſſeth the glorie of the other, and the miracles of this preſence, paſſeth all the miracles of Manna. And ſo the reſt, for that they geue that they
ſignifie, and the olde facramētes did but ſignifie and not geue, therfore they
be better and profitabler, and more excellent.

I will nowe oute of this that ys ſaied , gather the condicion of bothe **H**
theſe kindes of facramentes, and laie them before thy face (*Reader*) and ſo
end this matter, leauing the iudgement of yt to thee . The facramētes of the
olde lawe did but ſignifie : the facramentes of the newe lawe, do both ſignifie and alſo geue that, that they ſignifie. The olde facramentes did promeſſe

ſalua

A saluacion : the newe sacramentes do geue saluacion. The olde sacramentes were but childrens plaies, thinges vnprofitable, but for children to dallie withall : The newe sacramentes be profitable thinges not meet to be in the handling of children, but of soche as be well waxen and of knowledge and discrecion. Finally if ther were anie health, vertue or goodnesse in the olde sacramentes: yet the sacramentes of the newe lawe are (to vse the woordes of S. Augustine) *virtute maiora, vtilitate meliora, salubriora, feliciora.* greater in power, better in profett, holsomer, and better. And nowe as of a matter treacted of beside my pourspose this maie suffice.

THE SIXTENTH CHAP PROCEADETH TO
the next text of sainct Paule whiche ys . Calix
cui Bened.

B Hauinge intended to sett furth in this booke the exposition of soche scriptures as be in the epistles of S. Paule, which speake of the Sacrament of Chrystes bodie and bloode, to searche oute the vnderstanding of the fathers, whether they speake of yt as taking yt for a bare signe, or figure of the bodie and bloode of Chryst : orells as a Sacrament conteining the thing that yt signifieth : I haue thought good, if anie scriptures do come betwixte soche, not to trooble the Reader with the exposition of them, for that they be impertinent to owre matter, but ouerpassing them to go to the next text to our matter apperteining. Wherfor hauing now doen the scriptures in the beginning of the tenth chapiter, I passe ouer to this text : *Calix benedictionis, cui benedicimus, nonne communicatio sanguinis Christi est? Et panis, quem frangimus, nonne participatio corporis Domini est?* ys not the cuppe of blessing which we blesse partaking of the bloode of Chryst? ys not the breade whiche we breake partaking of the bodie of Chryst.

C For the better vnderstãding of this text yt ys to be obserued, that S. Paule trauailing to abduce the Corinthians from certain vices and euells, whiche he hath remébred vnto them, to haue ben in the Iewes, and for the whiche they were punished of God, enombring thé particularly, and among other, noting Idolatrie, dehorteth them from yt sainge : *Fugite ab Idolorum cultura.* Flie frõ the honouring of Idolls: And for that the Corinthians were moche defiled, and moche offended other by their resorting to the banquettes of Idolls, and partaking of the *Idolathites*, they thinking that for asmoche as they had learned that vnto the chrystian all meates are clean, that they might do so, S. Paule doth not onely dehorte them from yt, but also by argument taken of the sacrifices of the Iewes, and of the partaking of the same, whiche might not stand with the partaking of *Idolathites*, proueth that they maie not be partakers of the sacrifice of the chrystians, and of the sacrifice of Idolaters.

Sacrifice of the church proued by S. Paule.

And here entring to speake of an high misterie of the chrystian religion, whiche ys not to be spoken to the weake and the carnall, but to the wise and spirituall, as in this epistle he testifieth saing : *Animalis homo non percipit ea quæ sunt Spiritus Dei.* The naturall man perceaueth not the thinges that belong to the spiritt of God. Wher of the one he saieth thus : *Et ego fratres, non potui loqui vobis, quasi spiritualibus, sed quasi carnalibus, tanquam paruulis in Christo, lac vobis potum dedi, non escam. Nondum enim poteratis.* And I coulde not speake vnto D yowe, bretheren, as vnto spirituall, but as vnto carnall. Euen as vnto babes in Chryst, I gaue yowe milke to drinke, and not meat for ye were not thé strõg

1. Cor. 2.

Ibibid. 3.

And

And of the other he speakith thus : *sapientiam loquimur inter perfectos.* We speake wisdome among them that are perfect. Euen so nowe entending to speake of an high wisdome he warneth them with this saing : *vt prudentibus loquor. vos ipsi iudicate quod dico.* I speake vnto them that are wise, or haue discrecion. Iudge ye yowr selues what I saie. *Ys not the cuppe of blessing, whiche we blesse, she partaking of the bloode of Chryst? Ys not the breade, whiche we breake partaking of the bodie of our Lorde.* As who might saie : For as moch as ye are called to the chrystian religion, and be made partakers of the misteries of the same, and are nowe becomed wise in Chryst Iudge ye as wise men, what I saie: do not ye, drinking of our Lordes cuppe in our sacrifices, partake of the blood of our Lorde Chryste, and eating of that bread of the chrystian sacrifice do ye not partake of the bodie of our Lorde ? yt must nedes so be. For all that be partakers of sacrifices, are partakers of yt, to whom the sacrifice ys offred.

This I proue vnto yowe: Consider and remembre the sacrifice of the carnall Israelites : Aare not they whiche eate of the sacrifices, whiche were offred emong them partakers of the aultars? euen so yowe partaking of the sacrifices of Idolls, which sacrifices are offred to deuells. But I wolde not that ye shoulde be ioined in felowshippe with Deuells. for if ye so be, ye sustein great dammage and losse, and what ys that ? Ye can not be partakers of Chryst. For ye can not drinke of the cuppe of oure Lorde, and of the cuppe of Deuells. Ye can not be partakers of the table of the sacrifice of our Lorde, and of the sacrifice of Deuells. Wherfore if ye desire to be partakers of our Lordes bodie and bloode, in eating of his bread, and drinking his cuppe in his sacrifice, leaue to be partakers of the sacrifices offred to Idolls, Wherby ye are made partakers, and be ioined to Deuells. For as ther ys no companie betwixt light and darknesse : so ys ther no agreement betwixt our Lorde God, and the Deuell neither maie God and *Beliall* dwell together. And as he that beleueth hath no part with the infidel, neither rightcousnes felowshippe with vnrighteousnesse, no more dothe the temple of God agree with Idolls,

As in this maner of periphrasis the wholl minde of S. Paule in this place ys settfurth and made clere and plain, howe and by what perswasiõ he laboured to diswade the Corinthians from *Idolothites*: So also yt ys manifest that in his sentences in the processe of this chapiter, whiche he vseth as argumentes grownded vpon the Sacrament, that he vnderstandeth no trope or figure of the bodie and blood of Chryst, but the very thinges thē selues in very dede. And as he by that the carnall Israelites eating of their sacrifices were partakers of the same, proueth that eaters either at our lordes table, or at the table of Deuells be partakers of the same: So doth he as well accompt that, that ys vpon the table of our Lorde to be a sacrifice, as either the sacrifice of the Israelites offred to God: or of the gentiles offred to Deuells.

Yf yt be not so, what awaileth, or of what force ys the argument, diduced from the sacrifices of the Iewes? For if the eating of the sacrifice of the Iewes maketh them partakers of the aultar, what proueth that that either *Idolothites* of the table of Idolls, or the cuppe and bread of our Lorde his table doth make either the receauers of the one, or of the other partakers of the if that bothe the one, and the other be not sacrifices, as that ys, frõ the whiche the argument ys diduced, and vpon the whiche yt ys grownded ? yt ys an euell maner of disputacion to go aboute to proue like effectes of vnlike causes: but of like causes to proue like effectes yt ys a good maner of disputacion, if due ordre and circumstance be obserued.　　　　To

A To make the matter plain, what ys the caufe that the Ifraelites were made partakers of the aultar? the anfwer ys bicaufe they did eate of the facrifice. Again, to applie to the other : what ys the caufe that the chriftians be partakers of the bodie and bloode of Chryft? fhall the anfwer be bicaufe they eate a peice of bread? and drinke a cuppe of wine? no: the caufes be not like, and that caufe can not make vs partakers of the bodie and bloode of our Lorde. What ys the caufe then? That, that ys like the other whiche ys this: Bicaufe the chryftians do eate of the facrifice, therfor they be partakers of the facrifice, whiche ys the verie bodie and bloode of Chryft. For fo fainge, ther ys a good argument to be made from the liklihood of the caufes in eche of thê to the like effectes of eche of them. As thus to faie : The Ifraelites, bicaufe they did eate of the facrifice, they were partakers of the Aultar: So the Corinthians bicaufe they did eate of *Idolathites* whiche were facrifices of Idolls, they were partakers of Idolls. Of like maner the chriftians bicaufe they eat of the facrifice of Chryft, they be partakers of the bodie and blood of Chryft.

As the Ifraelites and infidels had their facrifices, fo the chryftians haue their facrifice euê the bread and cuppe of bleffing.

B And thus the difputacion of S. Paule ys of force, and prouerh well his entêt. And that S. Paule did afwell take the bread of our Lorde, and his cuppe to be a facrifice of the chryftians, as the, *Idolathites*, of the Corinthians to be the facrifice of the Infidells, euen this doth ftrongly proue yt, that he fetteth the table and the cuppe of our Lorde, againft the table and cuppe of deuells. Ye *can not (faieth he) drinke of the cuppe of our Lorde, and the cuppe of Deuells. Ye can not be partakers of the table of our Lorde, and of the table of Deuells.* In the whiche maner of fpeache as by the cuppe, and table of Deuells he vnderftandeth the facrifice doen to Deuells : fo muft yt nedes be, that by the table and cuppe of our Lorde, he vnderftandeth the facrifice doen to our lorde. As yt might in plain maner thus haue ben faied : Ye can not eate and drinke of the facrifice that ys offred vnto God, and of the facrifice that ys offred to Deuells. For except they were both facrifices, the fetting of the one againft the other were of no great force.

C And again , yf S . Paule did not afwell take the cuppe and table of our Lorde to be a facrifice, as the cuppe and table of Deuells to be a facrifice, he wolde not haue vfed like termes to them bothe, but as he had vnderftâded a difference or diuerfitie in the thinges: fo wolde he haue vfed a diuerfitie in woordes and tearmes, to expreffe and declare the fame. But for fomoche as he vnderftanding therby the facrifice of deuells called the fame the cuppe and table of Deuells, yt ys manifeft that he calling the meat of our Lorde by the like terms vnderftood the thing alfo to be like, that ys to bê a facrifice.

The cuppe and table of oure Lorde takê for the facrifice of oure Lorde

In this opening of the text (gentle Reader) thowe perceaueft two thinges to be here learned of S. Paule. The one ys the prefence of Chryftes bodie and bloode in the Sacrament : the other ys that the fame bodie and blood be a facrifice.

Reall prefence and facrifice proued by S. Paule.

But that yt maie appeare to yowe that this ys not my owne, dreame, or phantafie in thus vnderftanding S. Paule, but the comõ fentence of the Fathers of Chryftes Parliament houfe, we fhall for triall therof, and for better fetting furth of Gods trueth and the faith catholique heare the fainges of a good nombre of them, And firft of the auncient Father Chryfoftom. who

In, 10. 1. Cor.

D expownding this text faieth thus: *Maximè his fibi verbis, & fidem facit, & horrorem. Eorum autem huiufmodi eft fententia. Quod eft in calice, id eft, quod à latere fluxit, & illius fumus participes. Calicem autem benedictionis appellauit, quoniam cùm præ manibus eum habemus, cum admiratione, & horrore quodam inenarrabilis doni, laudamus*

bene-

benedicentes, quia sanguinem effudit, ne in errore permaneremus. Neque tantùm effudit, **E**
sed nos omnes eius participes effecit. Itaque si sanguinem cupis (inquit) noli Idolorum aram
brutorum animalium cœde, sed meum altare, meo sanguine aspergere. Quid hoc admirabi-
lius? Dic quæso, quid amabilius? Hoc & amantes faciunt, cum amatos intuentur, alienorū
cupiditate allectos propriis elargitis suadent vt ab illis abstineant. Sed amantes quidem in
pecuniis, vestibus, possessionibus hanc ostendunt cupiditatem: in proprio sanguine nemo vn-
quam. Christus autem & in hoc curam & vehementem in nos dilectionem ostendit. With
these woordes he doth gette greatly vnto him self both creditte and feare.
Of those woordes this ys the mening: *That, that ys in the chalice ys yt, that flowed*
from the side, and we are partakers of yt. But he hath called yt the cuppe of blef-

A plain
saing of
Chrysostō
for the Pro
clamer.

sing. For when we haue yt before our handes, with admiracion, and certein horrour of the vnspeakeable gift, we laude blessing, that he hath shedde
his bloode, that we shoulde not abide in errour. Neither hath he onely shed
de yt, but he hath made vs all partakers of yt. Therfore if (saieth he) thowe **F**
doest desire blood, do not sprenkle the aultar of Idolls with the slaughter of
brute beastes, but sprenkle mine aultar with my bloode. Saie I praie thee:
What ys more merueilouse then this? What ys more louing? This do louers
also, whē they see these whom they loue allured with desire of straunge thin
ges, when they haue geuen frely to them of ther owne, they moue thē that
they abstein from the other. But louers shewe this desire in money, in appa-
rell, in possessions, but in his owne blood no man at anie time hath doen yt.
But Chryst in this also hath shewed his care, and vehement loue towardes
vs. Thus moche Chrysostom.

Note here
that this ys
the mea-
ning of St
Paules
woordes,
that that
ys in the
chalice,
which flow
ed out of
Chryctes
side.

God for euer and allwaies be praised, who, although yt be his pleasure,
that his church shall be vexed and tried with the fire of tribulacion (as at this
present yt ys miserablie afflicted, shaken, and torne) yet he leaueth yt not
destitute of sufficient staie and comforte of trueth, wherby yt maie bothe de
fende yt self, and impugne the enemie, as in this authour expownding this
scripture we maie well perceaue. Doste thowe, reader, marke the expositiō
of the text? S. Paule saieth: *Ys not the cuppe of blessing, whiche we blesse, a partaking*
of the bloode of Chryst? Chrysostome saieth: of these woordes this ys the mea- **G**
ning: *That, that ys in the cuppe ys yt that flowed oute of the side, and of yt we are parta-*
kers. Yf this be the meaning of S. Paule, why then walke we in errour in this
matter? Why wander we in the mistes, and darke clowdes of tropes, and figures and significacions? wher Chrysostom expownding the scripture and
minding to shewe vs the verie vnderstanding and plain mening of yt, teacheth, that not a trope, figure, or sign of the bloud of Chryst ys in the cuppe,
but the bloode of Chryste that flowed oute of his side.

In the whiche exposition we maie in clere maner see and beholde the verie, trueth euen the right catholique faith so sett furth, that ther ys no helpe
for the aduersarie to cloke his heresie withall. The proclamer requireth one
plain sentence, to proue the reall presence of Chryste in the Sacrament:
what more plain speache wolde anie man desire to be spoken in this matter,
as wherbie to geue him perfect instruction in the same, than to saie: *that, that*
did flowe onte of the side of Chryst, ys in the chalice.

Yf the aduersarie with forced violence wolde thrust into Chrysostō woor
des his comon glose, that the figure of yt, that did flowe oute of Chrystes
side ys in the cuppe, then shoulde he make Chrysostome an vntrewe man. **H**
For Chrysostome saieth, that that, which he saied vpon that scripture, was
the mening of the woordes of S. Paule. Now if the Aduersarie will expownd Chrysostom with an other mening, then either Chrysostome did not

geue

A geue vs the true meaning of S. Paule, which ys not to be thought, or ells the Aduersarie reporteth vntrulie of him, whiche ys his common practise. For so farre wide ys yt that these two meninges should be one that the one saieth yea, the other saieth no, thone saieth yt ys, thother saieth yt ys not, the one ys an heresie and thother a truthe. So fare I saie be these from being one that for these two sentences, this lamentable diuision, and greuouse contencion in the Churche ys raised by heretiques.

What ys a mening, but a simple and plain opening and declaracion of a woorde or sentence of a mans conceipt, or speache doubtfullie or darkly conceaued or spoken before? Wherfor Chrysostom saing that this was the mening of S. Paules woordes, did by plain woordes simplie declare the same

This then being the true mening of S. Paules woordes, what trueth was ther in the saing of Cranmer or the Authour of that booke, who alleaging this text abused yt to a cleane contrarie vnderstanding? Thus he saieth: *Neither that wine made of grapes ys his verie bloode, or that his bloode ys wine made of grapes, but signifie vnto vs, as S. Paule saieth, that the cuppe ys a communion of Chrystes*

S.Paules woordes a-bused by Cranmer.

B *bloode.* Howe wickedlie and vntrulie this ys spoken, and howe this scripture ys drawen to a false vnderstanding, this exposition of Chrysostom dothe wel proue, as other also hereafter shall do.

That he wolde haue no soche mening vpon these his woordes, as the Ad-uersarie wolde yll fauouredlie peice and patche vpon them, his like maner of speache in an other place declareth, where he saieth: *Reputate salutarem san-guinem quasi è diuino, & impolluto latere effluere, & ita approximantes labijs puris accipite.* Regarde or esteme the holsome bloode, as to flowe oute of the di-uine, and vndefiled side, and so coming to yt, receaue yt with pure lippes Whiche woordes forsomoch as he spake them in a sermon to the common people, he spake them in plain maner, in that sense, as they sownded to the hearing of the people, which was that they shoulde accompte the cuppe of our Lord to be his blood. And therfore they shoulde come and drinke yt euen as oute of his side, as who should saie, yt ys all one. In this also that he willeth them to take yt with pure lippes, he teacheth the reall presence. For

Chrysost. ser. de Euch in Enceniis The bloode of Chryst in the Sacr. how yt ys to be estemed.

C the spirituall maner of Chrystes blood ys not to be receaued with lippes, but with heart and soule. Wherby yt ys plain, that Chrysostom wolde his woords no otherwise to be vnderstanded, then they were spoken. Wherfore not to tarie long vpon this saing of Chrysostom, whiche ys so plain that eue-ry childe maie vnderstande yt, I wish yt onely to be imprinted in the memo-rie of the reader, that ys of him saied, which ys (again to repeat yt) that yt that ys in the cuppe, ys yt that flowed oute of the side, and of yt we are partakers.

As by this we are taught the trueth of the presence of Chryst in the Sa-crament: So in the rest of his sainges vpon the same text, he teacheth vs, that yt ys a sacrifice. Thus he saieth: *In veteri testamento cùm imperfectiores essent quem idolis offerebant sanguinem, eum ipse accipere voluit, vt ab idolis eos auerteret. Quod etiam inenarrabilis amoris signum erat. Hic autem multo admirabilius, & magnificentius sacrifi-cium præparauit, & cùm sacrificium ipsum commutaret & pro brutorum cæde seipsum of-ferendum præciperet.* In the olde Testament, when they were more vnperfecte, to the entent he wolde turne them from Idolls, that blood, which they of-

Chrysost. in 10. i . Cor.

Chryste commaunded himself to be offred,

D fred vnto Idolls he himself, wold accept, which also was a token of an inenar rable loue. *But here he hath prepared a moch more woonderfull, and magnificall sacrifi-ce, both when he did chaunge the saied sacrifice, and for the slaughter of brute beastes com-maunded himself to be offred.*

Bbb   In this

In this faing of Chryfoftom, ther be two notable notes to be obferued, which as they do moche declare and confirme the catholique doctrine: So do they as plainly, and as mightilie ouerthrowe the wicked herefie of the Aduerfarie. The firft ys, that declaring the great loue of God towarde the vperfect people of the olde lawe, that to turn them from Idolatrie he was contented to accept to be offred to him in facrifice foche bloode of brute beaftes, as they offred to their Idolls, when he cometh to the facrifice of the newe lawe, he faieth that here he hath prepared a moche more woon-derfull, and magnificall facrifice. What I praie thee, Reader, coulde be fpo-ken more plainlie againft the wicked affertion of the Aduerfarie, teaching that the facrifices of the newe lawe are nothing more excellent, then the facrifices of the olde lawe, then to faie *that Chryft here in the newe lawe hath pre-pared a moche more woonderfull and magnificall facrifice?* Which woordes Chry-foftom fpeaketh fetting the facrifices of both lawes together, and therfore they were fpoken, in comparifon of the facrifices, of the ol-de lawe.

> *God prepa red a moch more won-derfull and magnificall facrifice for the newe Tefta ment then was in the olde.*

And to the intent that the Aduerfarie being here fore preffed with the woordes of Chryfoftom fhall not with his common glofe cloake him felf, and gette a fubterfuge, faing that Chryfoftom fpake of the facrifice of Chryft vpon the croffe, which he graunteth to be moche more excellent then the facrifices of the olde lawe, the feconde note of the faied Chryfoftome fhall clerely wipe awaie his glofe, and difapoint him of his cloake. Wherfor obfer-ue that when he faied that Chryft prepared this woonderfull facrifice, he opened the time alfo when he did prepare yt. *He did* (faieth he) *prepare this woonderfull facrifice, when he did chaunge the facrifice of the olde lawe and when he com-maunded himfelf to be offred.* When did he thefe two thinges? Reader yf thowe marke, here be two thinges: the one ys that Chryft chaunged the facrifice: the other that he commaunded himfelf to be offred. When did he thefe two thinges? In his laft fupper when (as fainct Cyprian faieth) *obuiarunt fibi inftituta noua & antiqua, & confumpto agno, quem antiqua traditio proponebat, inconfumptibi-lem cibum magifter apponit Difcipulis.* The newe and the olde ordeinaunces mett together and the lambe, which the olde tradicion did fettfurth being confumed, the mafter did fett to his difciples inconfumptible meate.

> *•A plain faing for M. Iuell.*

> *Cyp. de Cæ.*

> *De prodi-tion Iudæ.*

So that for this lambe of the olde tradicion he gaue nowe inconfump tible meate to his Difciples, whiche was his bodie and bloode, whiche was the veritie of that fhadowe as Chryfoftom faieth : *Ille agnus futuri agni typus fuit , & ille fanguis, Dominici fanguinis monftrabat aduentum, & ouis illa fpiritalis ouis fuit exemplum. Ille agnus vmbra fuit : hic veritas. Sed poftquam fol iufticiæ radiauit, vmbra foluitur luce, & ideo in ipfa menfa, vtrumque Pafcha, & ty-pi, & veritatis celebratum eft.* That lambe was the figure of the lambe to come. And that bloode fhewed the coming of the bloode of our Lord, and that fhepe was an example of the fpirituall fhepe, that lambe was the fhadowe: this the veritie. But after the Sunne of righteoufneffe did fhyne with beames, the fhadowe was taken awaie with the light. And therfore in that table bothe the paffeouer of the figure, and of the trueth was celebra-ted. Thus he.

> *Bloodof the Paf-chall lābe figure of the bloodof Chryfte in the Sacr.*

In which faing ys declared, that the olde lambe was a figure of our lambe Chryft, whiche were together in the table, as two paffeouers, the olde and the newe. But when the newe paffeouer, whiche was the bodie of Chryft ther confecrated, was fettfurth ther as a newe paffouer, whiche he calleth the fonne of righteoufneffe, then the olde Paffeouer was taken

awaie

A awaie, and this placed in the stead. Then was the olde sacrifice chaunged, and a newe sacrifice appointed. So that ys true that S. Augustin saieth: *Aliud est Pascha, quod Iudæi celebrant de oue, aliud autem quod nos in corpore & sanguine Domini celebramus.* Yt ys an other Passouer that the Iewes do celebrate with a shepe: and an other, whiche we celebrate in the bodie and bloode of Chryst.

Cont. lite-ras Petilia

Yt cã not be saied that Chryst did chaung the sacrifice of the olde lawvpõ the crosse, for that sacrifice was after the maner of the sacrifices of the ordre of Aaron, a bloodie sacrifice, as they were. But this chaunge of sacrifice must nedes then be, when the shewing of the chaunge of preisthead was. For (as S. Paule saieth) *Necessarium fuit secundùm ordinem Melchisedec alium surgere sacerdotem, & non secundùm ordinem Aaron dici.* Yt was necessarie, that an other preist, shoulde rise to be called after the order of Melchisedech and not after the order of Aaron. Chryst neuer shewed himself a preist after the order of Melchisedec but in the last supper, in the which he sacrificed after that order.

Heb. 7.

B Wherfore then was the olde sacrifice chaunged, when this newe preist after the ordre of Melchisedec did shewe himself in sacrificing. The trueth of this ys well proued by the seconde note in the saing of Chrysostome, whiche ys that he commaunded himself to be offred. Let al the volume of the Gospell be turned and searched, and in no place shall ye finde that Chryst commauñded himself to be offred, but in the last supper, when he had instituted this holie sacrifice of his and bodie and blood. Then he saied. *Hoc facite:* This do ye. By which woordes he gaue cõmaundement to all, to whõ cõmission of this holie ministraciõ should be geué, that they should doe that that he had doẽ.

In that high and woonderfull institucion he did three thinges, that ys, he consecrated his blessed bodie and blood, he offred yt in sacrifice after the ordre of Melchisedech, and receaued yt with his Apostles. Wherfore saing and commaunding that his preistes shoulde that do that he then did, forsõmoch as among other his doinges he did then offre sacrifice. Therfore he cõmaunded that he himself should be offred. And thus yt maie be perceaued that C Chrysostom looked to this place when he saied that Chryst commaunded himself to be offred.

Three nota-ble thinges doen by Chryst in the institu-cion of the B.Sacr.

Li.4.ca.32

Of this same sentence and minde be a nombre of the holie Fathers. *Irenæus* saieth: *Eum qui ex creatura panis est, accepit, & gratias egit, dicens: Hoc est corpus meũ: Et calicem similiter, qui est ex ea creatura, quæ est secundùm nos, suum sanguinem confessus est. Et noui Testamenti nouam docuit, oblatione, &c.* He took the bread (saieth *Irenæus* speaking of Chryst) which ys a creature, and gaue thankes saing: *This ys my bo-die.* And the cuppe likewise, which ys a creature as we, he confessed to be his blood. And of the newe Testament, he taught a newe oblacion, &c.

In primæo-ration. præ-par.

S. Ambrose also in his praier saieth: *Ego enim Domine memor venerandæ passio-nis tuæ, accedo ad altare tuum licet peccator, vt offeram tibi sacrificium, quod tu instituisti, & offerri præcepisti in commemorationem tui pro salute nostra.* I Lorde mindefull of thy woorshippefull passion, come vnto thy aultar, although a sinner, to offer vnto thee, the sacrifice, which thow hauest instituted and commaunded tõbe offred in the remembrance of thee for our health.

The Pro-clamer ma-ie her learn that Chryst cõmanded his bodie to be offred in sacrifice.

Ye see these two graue and auncient wittnesses testifieng with Chrysostõ that Chryst commaunded this sacrifice which he instituted to be offred. D What the thing ys that we offre Chrysostome by moste plain woordes declareth, when he saieth that Chryst commaunded himself to be offred: So that Chryst himself ys our oblacion, and sacrifice, which we offre not vpon our owne inuencion, but vpon his holie, and most louing commaundement.

By this latter part then of Chryſoſtome his ſaing,the two other partes before noted be well proued.For by that,that Chryſt hath commaunded vs to
offre him in our ſacrifice,yt ys moſt clere,that our ſacrifice ys more excellent
then the ſacrifice of the olde Teſtament:yt ys manifeſt alſo ,that he ſpake yt
not of his ſacrifice made vpon the croſſe,but of the ſacrifice inſtituted in his
laſt ſupper,wher and when the olde ſacrifices were taken awaie,and this one
placed for them all,which Chryſoſtom well taught,when he ſaied : *for the
ſlaughter of beaſtes,he commaunded himſelf to be offred.* So that he commaunded
himſelf to be offred,when the ſacrifices were chaunged . But the ſacrifices
were chaunged in the laſt ſupper,wherfore in the laſt ſupper he commaunded himſelf to be offred.

THE SEVENTENTH CHAPITER PROCEA-
deth vpon the ſame text by the expoſition of Chryſoſtom
and ſainct Hierom.

Lbeit this text ys verie plainlie expownded by Chryſoſtom,and
that,that by me was affirmed by the ſame his expoſition fullie　F.
confirmed,namely that S.Paule here ſpeaketh of the preſence of
Chryſt in the Sacrament,and therwith alſo teacheth that yt ys
the ſacrifice of the Chryſtians:yet that the trueth maie be the
better eſteemed,as yt ys plentifull in yt ſelfe,ſo ſhall yt be ſetfurth by plentie
of wittneſſes.And wher Chryſoſtom expownding the firſt parte of the text,
hath confeſſed the catholique faith of the preſence of the blood of Chryſt in
the cuppe with theſe plain woordes,that yt ys that which flowed oute of the
ſide,which ys ſo ſpoken,as the Aduerſarie can not once open his mouth to
ſpeake againſt yt:And in confeſsing the bloode,ther ys no doubte but he al
ſo dothe like of the bodie.Yet foraſmoch as he proceadeth and expowndeth
the other parte of the text,which ſpeaketh of the partaking of the bodie : I
ſhall not for the commoditie of the reader,and the ſetting furth of Godes
trueth ſpare my laboure to ſhewe furth the ſame.

1 Corin.10　　The reſt of the text ys: *Et panis quem frangimus nonne communicatio corporis Chri-*
ſti eſt? And the breade whiche we breake,ys yt not a communicacion of the　G
of the bodie of Chryſt?Although the vulgar engliſh bibles doth otherwiſe
ingliſh this text:ſaing that the breade that ys broken ys a partaking of the
bodie:Yet I being aduertiſed by Chryſoſtom that communicacion includeth more than participacion:I engliſh yt as I maie with this woorde (com-
Chryſoſt.in　municacion) according to his inſtructiō,which ye ſhal perceaue in his ſaing.
10. 1. Cor.　Thus he ſaieth.*Quare non dixit participatio?quia amplius quiddam ſignificare voluit,*
& multam inter hæc conuenientiam oſtendere . Non enim participatione tantum &
Comunica-　*acceptione,ſed vnitate communicamus. Quemadmodum enim corpus illud vnitum eſt*
cion ys a　*Chriſto : ita & nos per hunc panem vnione coniungimur. Sed quare addit,quem fran-*
nearer con　*gimus ? Hoc in Euchariſtia videre licet : in cruce autem minimè , ſed omnino*
iuction the　*contrà . Os enim eius (inquit) non conteretur . Sed quod in cruce paſſus non eſt , id*
participa-　*in oblatione patitur , & propter te frangi permittit.* Ys not the bread whiche we
cion , ther-　breake ; a communicacion of the bodie of Chryſt ? Why did he not ſaie a
for the tran　particpacion or partaking ? Bicauſe he wolde ſignifie ſome more thing,and
ſlacion of　ſhewe a great agreement betwixt theſe thinges. We doe not communicate
the engliſh　by partaking and receauing onelie,but alſo by vnitie . For as that bodie　H
bible ys to　was vnited to Chryſt : Euen ſo we by this breade are ioined together
be miſliked　in an vnion. But wherfore dothe he adde:*which we breake ?* This maie yowe
　　　　　ſee

A ſee in the Sacrament:in the croſſe not ſo,but alltogether contrarie . For (ſaieth he)his bone ſhall not be broken.But that he ſuffred not in the croſſe, that he ſuffreth in the ſacrifice , and permitteth for thee to be broken. Thus he.

In this liuely expoſition of Chryſoſtom,whiche ſo I call bicauſe he leaueth no woorde vnquickned and made as yt were aliue to mans vnderſtanding,he geueth vs three worthie inſtructiõs.And firſt,he geueth a cauſe why *Three nota* S.Paule calleth this a communicacion raither then a participacion , bicauſe *ble inſtruc-* (ſaieth he)by the receipt of this myſterie we are ioined together in one *tions out of* with Chryſt,as his bodie was ioined vnto him.Whiche vnion neither parti *Chryſoſt.* cipacion nor receauing do expreſſe or ſignifie.For we maie partake or receaue a thing,and yet not be made one with yt . But duely communicating the bodie of Chryſt,we are made one with yt.   For communication ys ei- *Communi-* ther a making of one thing common to manie,or to make manie to be one *caciõ what* thing,and all one with yt,and yt one with them. Of this more in the expoſi- *yt ys.*

B tion of the next ſcripture.

The ſeconde note ys that where he ſaieth,that as that bodie was vnitedto Chryſt:So by this bread we are ioined together in an vnion. Where he inſtructeth vs again of the preſence of Chryſt in the Sacramẽt,before by his blood,here by his bodie,and yet in eche parte full Chryſt.That this maie ap peare plain vnto the reader,as yt ys true in yt ſelf,vnderſtande this, that the bodie ofChryſt ys vnited to him reallie,verilie,and ſubſtanciallie,and not ſpi tuallie.Yf then ther be an vnion of Chryſt and vs,as of him and his bodie, then yt muſt be an vnion reall,but this maner ofvnion can not be but by a reall communicacion,wherfore we do reallie communicate with the bodie of Chryſt.This ys confirmed to vs by the ſaing of Chryſoſtõ,when he ſaieth, *that we be ioined together in vnion by this bread.* A bare peice of bread can no more make vs one ſubſtanciallie with Chryſt,than a peice of beof, or anie other victuall . Wherfore this bread that he ſpeaketh of ys the bread , and the foode ofhis verie bodie which duely receaued , maketh vs to be in Chryſt,and Chryſt,as S.Hylary ſaieth,naturallie,and as S.Cyrill ſaieth, ſub-

C ſtanciallie in vs.

The thirde note alſo both confirmeth this that here ys ſaied of the pre- *Realpreſen* ſence , and alſo that ys before ſaied of the ſacrifice. For here by expreſſe *ce and ſacri-* woordes he dothe ſo tearme yt. For he ſaieth thus:that,that he ſuffred not *fice both a-* in the croſſe,that he ſuffreth in the ſacrifice,and permitteth to be broken for *nouched.* thee.In the which woordes he declareth two diſtinct beinges ofChryſt:one vpon the croſſe:the other in ſacrifice.For he maketh no difference either of Chryſt,or of his ſubſtance,or of his being.But euen the ſame that ſuffred not to be broken vpon the croſſe,euen the ſame ſuffreth in the ſacrifice,and permitteth to be broken for thee.Yf the verie ſame be in this ſacrifice, that was vpon the croſſe,then we muſt nedes confeſſe him to be as verilie preſent, in the ſacrament,as vpon the croſſe.And the ſame ſo preſent,for that he ys our onely and euerlaſting ſacrifice,to be our ſacrifice.Yf we aske where he ys a ſacrifice,Chryſoſtome anſwereth,ther to be a ſacrifice,where he permitteth to be broken.He ys broken in the Maſſe vpõ the aultar,wherfore he ys their in ſacrifice.

D   But here vnderſtande that although Chryſoſtom ſaieth that Chryſt ſuffreth , and that the Sacrament ys broken: yet he meneth not that anie violence ys doen to that bleſſed bodie, or that yt ys affected with greif, pain,or paſsion (for yt being paſſed all theſe miſeries , yt ys nowe an impafsible bodie,and what violence foeuer anie cruell heart wolde inferre to yt:yet yt being impafsible no pain can be inflicted to yt. Neither think this to be a ftraunge fpeache feing that Chryft himfelf,when he was in hys pafsible bodie,and gaue his pafsible bodie to his Apoftles impafsiblie,faied: *Take,eate,This ys my bodie,whiche ys broken for yowe.*For although he fo faied : yet in geuing oute of his bodie,he fuffred no violence nor pain.And as that brea king wrought no greif to his bleffed bodie then : no more doth yt nowe. For the fame woundes that he bare in his pafsible bodie pafsiblie,he beareth the fame after his refurrection and now ftill impafsiblie.

And nowe that ye haue hearde. Chryfoftome declaring vnto yowe the vnderftanding of this fcripture in the whiche he hath in no darke fpeache, but in plain maner with expreffe woordes taught the prefence of Chryftes bodie and blood in the Sacrament, and yt alfo to be a facrifice , and that by this fcripture:we fhall nowe leaue him for this place,and heare S. Hierom.

Hieron. in deci.1 Cor.

Who for this time fhall be ioined with Chryfoftome,that one veritie maie be teftified on both fides of Chryftes Parliament houfe S. Hierom ys but fhoit,and this ys his expofition.*Calix benedictionis, ideo primum calicem nominauit, vt pofsit de pane latius difputare,nonne communicatio fanguinis Chrifti eft? ficut ipfe faluator dicit.Qui manducat carnem meam,& bibit fanguinem meum,in me manet , & ego in eo.*The cuppe of blefsing which we bleffe:therfore hath he firft named the cuppe,that he maie more at large difpute of the bread:ys yt not a communi cacion of the bloode of Chryft?As our Sauiour himfelf faieth: *He that eateth my flesh,and drinketh my bloode,dwelleth in me and I in him.Thus S.Hierom.*

This ys his breif expofition vpon this firft parte of S.Paules text , whiche ys not fo bare and hungrie,but that yt bringeth good foode with yt, to nouriſh and comfoite the faith of a Chryftian man in this matter of the Sacrament.For when he cometh to the pith of the fentence whiche ys this:ys yt not a communicacion of the blood of Chryft:he addeth this for an expofition to yt:as our Sauiour himfelf faieth:*He that eateth my flesh and drinketh my blood dwelleth in me and I in him:*as who might faie: yt ys foche a communicacion of the blood of Chryft, that who fo doth communicate of yt fhall haue that benefitt,that Chryft himfelf fpake of faing:*He that eateth my flesh,and drinketh my bloode,dwelleth in me, and I in him .* That he alleaging this fcripture of Chryft to expownde the faing of S.Paule doth fignifie vnto vs, that S.Paule ys to be vnderftanded,to haue fpoken of the verie bloode of Chryft in the Sacrament,he that hath redde fainct Hierom , howe he vnderftandeth the fixth chapter of fainct Iohn,whofe authoritie hath ben vfed in the feconde booke for the fame pourpofe,fhall not nede to doubte. But that the reader fhall not be driuen to feke farre for the triall herof, fainct Hierom fhall be produced,alleaging this fame verie faing of Chrift in the fixth of faint Iohn,

In pfalm. 109.

Wherin he fhall clerely fee and perceaue the true vnderftanding of yt, after the minde of faint Hierom.Thus he faieth vpon the pfalme . *Quomodò enim Melchifedech Rex Salem, obtulit panem & vinum:fic & tu offeres corpus tuum,& fanguinem tuum,verum panem,& verum vinum . Ifte Melchifedec ifta myfteria quæ*

Sacrifice of Chryfte in his fupper and Melchifedec's compared.

habemus dedit nobis . Ipfe eft qui dixit: Qui manducauerit carnem meam , & biberit fanguinem meum: fecundùm ordinem Melchifedec tradidit nobis facramentum fuum. For as *Melchifedec* King of Salem hath offred bread and wine : fo fhalt thowe offre thy bodie and bloode , the true bread , and true wine.This *Melchifedec* hath geuen vs thefe myfteries which we haue.Yt ys he that hath faid:*He that shall eate my flesh, and drinke my bloode : according to the ordre of Melchifedech he hath deliuered vnto vs his facrament.* Hitherto S. Hierom.

Do   H

A   Do ye not fee that ourMelchifedech dothe offre the true breade and true wine his bodie and bloode, not after the ordre of Aron vpon the croffe, but after the ordre of Melchifedec? And hath not he geuen vs thefe mifteries? And doth not he of thefe mifteries after the minde of S. Hierom, faie : *he that eateth my flesh, and drinketh my bloode dwelleth in me, and I in him?* By this then yt ys euident that the faing of S. Paule referred and expownded by this, ys vnderftanded, of the true wine, the bloode of Chryft, as this ys.

The other text alfo ys but breiflie touched and folowed thus : *Et Panis quē frangimus nonne cōmunicatio corporis Domini eſt? Itaꝗ panis Idololatriæ, Dœmonum participacio eſſe monſtratur.* And ys not the bread which we breake a communicaciō of the bodie of our lorde? Euen fo alfo the bread of Idolotrie ys a partaking of Deuells. Albeit this expofitiō in the firſt feight and face femeth not moche to faie to the maintenaunce of the catholique faith, as touching the matter of the Sacramēt: yet if yt be well weighed, yt fhall be fownde to make moch. And for the better weighing of yt, yt fhall be neceffarie, that yt be called to memorie, that before ys faied in the laſt chapiter, that the caufe why mē be

B   made partakers of Deuells, ys that they do eate of foche meates as be offred in facrifice to Deuells. for ther ys no meat accompted to make men in that felowfhippe, what meat foeuer yt be (in that onely refpect that yt ys eaten) but onely that that ys offred to Deuells.

Nowe then, when in the expofition the probacion ys that as the eating of the breade, which ys broken ys a communicacion of the bodie of Chryft: So the bread of Idolatrie ys a participacion of Deuells: muft not both thefe be vnderftanded of the thinges offred in facrifice? yf not, what auaileth the applicacion of the one to the other? Howe can S. Paule proue the Corinthians to be partakers of Idolls, but by the partaking of *Idolathites?* Wherfor this expofitour folowing S. Paule bringeth his argument from the facrifice of Chryfte as a thing cleare and manifeft to the Corinthians. As who might faie : As the partaking of the bread of Chryft in facrifice maketh vs partakers of the bodie of our Lorde: So the partaking of meates offred in facrifice to Deuells, maketh vs partakers of Deuells. And thus ther muft be a facrifice vnderftanded in both fides, afwell in the one, as in the other. Which being

C   fo, yt muft nedes be confeffed, that the bread which S. Paule fpeaketh of here by the whiche we are made partakers of the bodie of Chryft, ys a facrifice, and in that yt ys a facrifice, yt neceffarily foloweth, that yt ys the very bodie of Chryft, whiche ys owre onely facrifice. And thus yt maie be perceaued that this fhort expofition well weighed, had good matter in yt to cōmende and fettfurth the catholique faithe, and to teache the prefence of Chryft in the Sacrament, and yt alfo to be the facrifice of chryftians. And nowe that yow haue hearde the expofitions of thefe two, we will proceade to heare other two vpon the fame fcripture.

Hierom.
Ibid.

An argumēt growñ ded vpon the facrifice by S. Hierom.

Bbb iiii   THE

THE FICHTTENTH CHAP. PROCEADETH IN

*the expofition of the fame text by fainct Augufin and
Damafcen.*

E

*Aug. côt-
inimic. le-
gis & Pro-
phet.*

Ainete Auguftine openeth the minde of S. Paule thus : *Nolo vos focios Dæmoniorum fieri: eos quippe ab Idololatria prohibebat. Propter quod eis ofté
dere volebat, ita illos fieri focios Dæmoniorum, fi Idolothita facrificij manducauerint,quomodò Ifraël carnalis focius erat altaris in templo, qui de facrificiis man
ducabat. Hinc enim cæpit, vt boc diceret: Propter quod, dilectiffimi mihi, fugite ab idolo
rum cultura. Deinde fecutus oftendit ad quod facrificium debeant iam pertenere, dicens:
Quafi prudentibus dico, iudicate vos quod dico. Calix benedictionis quem benedicimus non
ne communicatio eft fanguinis Chrifti? Et panis quem frangimus, nonne communicatio eft
corporis Domini? &c.* I will not that ye be made felowes of Deuells . He did
truly forbidde them from Idolatrie. For the which thing he wolde declare
vnto them, that they fhoulde euen fo be made felowes of Deuells if they
did eate Idolathites of the facrifice, as the carnall Ifraell, whiche did eat of
the facrifices in the temple, was felowe of the Aultar. By occafion of that he
began, that he wolde faie this: wherfor my moft beloued, flee from the honouring of Idolls. Afterwarde folowing, he fheweth to what facrifice they
aught now to pertein faing: I fpeake as vnto wife men, iudge what I faie: *ys
not the cuppe of blesfing whiche we bleffe a cômunicacion of the bloode of Chryft? And
ys not the bread which we breake a comunicacion of the bodie of our Lorde?* Thus farre
S. Auften.

F

*S. Aug.
calleth the
bread and
cuppe of the
B.Sacr.a
facrifice.*

This expofitiô yf yt be well marked,âd côpared to the expofitiô of this text
of S.Paul which ys in the xvi chap. of this book,yt fhall be perceaued,that yt
doth iuftly agree with the fame, âd moch alfo côfirme yt. But leauing all o-
ther things therin côteined,âd onely to touch that,that to this matter apper
teineth this ys here to be noted in S.Auguft.that he faieth this to be the min
de of S.Paule,that he labouring to bring the Corinthians from *Idolothites*,by
the whiche they were made felows of deuells, he willed them to flee from
them, as (nowe being of the calling they be of) hauing nothing to do with
them. And therfore leauing the facrifices of Idolls (*faieth S. Auguftin*) he
fheweth them to what facrifice they fhoulde nowe pertein . And what facrifice ys that? euen the cuppe of bleffing, whiche we bleffe, and the
bread which we breake, by the which we are made partakers of the bodie
and blood of Chryft.

G

*Sacrifice a-
uouched by
S.Paule af-
ter the vn-
ftanding of
S. Auguft.*

By the which woords who feith not that the minde of S.Paul ys afterthe
mening of S.Auguftin,that the Sacramét of Chryftes bodie âd blode ys a fa
crifice,vnto the which,as he wolde thé theCorinthiãs:So aught al Chryftiãs
to pertein?For S. Auguftin faing,that S.Paul by thefe woords: *ys not the cuppe
of blesfing, which we bleffe a partaking of the blood of Chryft &c.* did fhew thé the facri
fice vnto the whiche they did nowe pertein, what can be faied but that he
ment yt to be a facrifice? That S. Auguftine taketh yt to be a facrifice, as yt
ys moft plainlie fhewed in the firft booke,So in this alfo hereafter yt fhall be
made fo euident, that yt fhall not be denied.

Damafcen, whom here we will ioin with S. Auften, although he doth
not by waie of expofition folowe the letter of S. Paule : yet treacting of the
Sacrament, he expowndeth the tearmes,namelie participacion and cômunicacion, whiche here S. Paule vfeth and applieth to the Sacrament,of Chryftes bodie and bloode. And forfomoche as the expofition of thefe termes
geueth a great light to the clere vnderftanding of the minde of S. Paule,

H

as

A as whether he ment that the Sacrament were a bare figne of the bodie and blood of Chryft, or ells verilie conteining the fame: I thought to bring in that his faing.

And wher as this holie Sacrament, for that yt ys of infinite vertue can not fufficientlie be expreffed: deuoute and godlie men, minding, as the meafure of our weakneffe in the capacitie of fo great mifteries wolde permitte and fuffer to fignifie fome parte of yt, haue called yt by fondrie and diuerfe names. of the whiche Damafcen remembring fome doth thus faie of them.

Damafcen li.4. ca.14

Et fi quidam exemplaria corporis, & fanguinis Domini panem & vinum vocauerunt vt deifer vocauit Bafilius: non tamen poft fanctificationem dixit, fed priufquam fanctificaretur ipfa oblatio, ita vocabant. Participatio etiam dicitur. Nam per ipfam Iefu diuinitatem participamus. Dicitur & comunio, & eft reuera, quia comunicamus per ipfam Chrifto, & participamus eius carne & Diuinitate, & quia comunicamus, & vnimur inuicé per illã.

Although fome haue called the bread and wine exemplaries of the bodie and bloode of our Lorde, as the godly man Bafill hath called yt: yet they did not fo after the fanctificacion, but before the oblacion was fanctified

B they did fo call yt. Yt ys alfo called a partaking. For by yt we partake the God head of Iefus. Yt ys alfo called a Comunion, and yt ys in verie dede, for by yt we comunicate with Chryft, both that we partake his flefh and God head, and alfo that by yt we be vnited one with an other. I nede not to tarie, to open this faing of Damafcen, whiche lieth fo open and plain that the fimpleft maie fee the true vnderftanding of yt. And wher S. Paule here fpeaketh of the partaking and of the comunicacion of the bodie and bloode of Chryft, which as before ys noted, fome wolde wickedly corrupte faing that the breade and the cuppe are fignes that we partake, and communicate the bodie and bloode of Chryft : *This man faieth that we partake both the flefh, and Godhead of Chryft.*

Bread and wine called exeplaries of the bodie and blood of Chryfte before fanc tificacion, but not after.

And that we fhoulde not thinke him to fauoure the hereticall expofition of the Aduerfarie, he declareth the catholique faith, and alfo reiecteth the contrarie opinion in that he diffolueth that, that of the Aduerfarie might be taken for an argument againft the trueth. For although (faieth he) fome haue

C called yt the exemplaries of the bodie and bloode of Chryft, that ys (faieth he) before the confecracion or fanctificacion, not after the fanctificacion: fignifieng to vs that after the cofecracion they be the verie thinges themfelues, that ys the verie bodie and blood of Chryft, and not the exemplaries fignes, or figures of them. This authour ys to plain and to ftrong to be wrefted or by violence to be drawen to make any countenannce towarde the fignes and figures of the Aduerfaries. For in the fame very chap. expownding the woordes of Chryftes : *This ys my bodie*, he faieth thus : *Hoc eft meum, non figura corporis, fed corpus. & non figura fanguinis, fed fanguis.* This ys not the figure of my bodie, but my bodie and not the figure of my bloode, but my bloode, wherby he plainlie denieth the Deuells expofition fettfurth by the Aduerfarie. And yet in the ende of the fame chapter he calleth the Sacrament exemplaries, but in foche forte and maner, as he affirmeth withall the verie prefence. For this ys his faing : *Exemplaria autem futurorum dicuntur, non vt non exiftentia verè corpus & fanguis Chrifti, fed quoniam nunc quidem per ipfa participamus Chrifti Diuinitatem : tunc autem intellectualiter per folam vifionem.* They are called

An argument of the Sacramentaries foluted by Damafcen.

Damafc. ibid.

Damafcen ibidem.

D the exeplaries of thinges to come, not as not being the bodie and bloode of Chryft verilie : but that we nowe therby partake the God head of Chryft: but then intellectuallie by onely vifion.

By whiche fainges, as the reader dothe clerelie fee, that damafcen fo
conftant

conftantlie doth teache and affirme the prefence of Chryft in the Sacramēt, that he vtterly reiecteth the figures of the Aduerfarie: So maie he well vnder ftande, that the faied Damafcen fpeaking of the participacion of the flefh of Chryft, and his Godhead, of the whiche participacion S. Paule maketh mencion, fpeaketh of the verie participacion of wholl Chryft, God and man verilie, and not figuratiuely. And forafmoche as this ys fo plainly taught byDamafcen that the Aduerfarie can by no meās coulour yt, nor by anie fhift or fleight of falfhoode auoide yt, I wolde to God that he wolde fee his erroure, and calling to God to geue him the fpirit of humilitie, he wolde fo humble him felf, that he wolde confeffe his faied errour, knowing this that yt ys bothe more eafie, and more profitable to be a litle confownded here, then to be fo greatlie confounded before the iudgement feat of Chryft, in the feight of his Angells and Sainctes, and all the woorlde, at the daie of his fearfull and terrible generall iudgement.

THE NINETENTH CHAP. CONTINVETH
the expofition of the fame text by Ifidore and
Oecumenius.

Einge that of necefsitie I muft be fhorter, for that moche ys yet to be faied, as the one of the wittneffes in the laft chapiter hath direct lie affirmed the prefence the other the facrifice: So will we heare two breiflie auouching the like. The firft fhall be *Ifidorus* who fpeaking of this text nowe in hande geueth a brief and clere expofition of the fame in this wife: *Panis quem frangimus corpusChrifti eſt, qui dicit: Ego fum panis viuus, qui de cœlo defcendi, vinum autem fanguis eius eft. Et hoc eft, quod fcriptum eft: Ego fum vitis vera.* The breade that we breake ys the bodie of Chryft, who faieth:I am the bread of life, whiche came down frō heauē. But the wine ys his blood, and this ys yt, that ys written. *I am the true vine.*

In thys expofition that the text might be plain to the reader, wher S. Paule faied : *The bread which we breake ys a communicacion of the bodie of Chryft:* This authour geuing the vnderftanding of yt faieth,*that the bread which we breake ys the bodie of Chryfte.* And that he wolde haue yt taken for the verie bodie: he faieth, that yt ys the bodie of Chryft, who faied: *I am the bread of life.* And who he was, the fixt chap. of S. Iohn declareth that yt was verie Chryfte. no figuratiue Chryfte. And what the cuppe of blefsing dothe contein he fullie declareth when he faieth : *The wine ys his bloode.* whiche maner of fpeache ys fo plain, and ftandeth fo directlie againft the faing of the Aduerfarie, that as for the plaineffe of'yt I neither can nor nede to faie anie thing to make yt more plain: fo can I but woonder, that men can erre that either knowe or haue readde thefe holie fathers except they be puf fed vppe with foche pride, and be brought to foche fingularitie in ther owne conceat, that they contempn all mens iudgementes,fainges,and learning befides their owne of what faith,trueth,aunciétie,holineffe or learning fo euer they be, as this Ifidore, who liued well near a thoufande yeares agō, and was famoufe in all the chryftiā orbe, and as a ftrong piller ftoode againft the Arrians whiche then were mightie in Spain, and hath left learned wor kes as teftimonies of his learning and godly zeale,ys not to be difdained,but to be reuerenced.

And although for his learning and aunciétie he ys to be credited: yet he ys
the

margin notes:
Ifidor. li.of fic.ca.18.
The bread that we breakysthe bodie of Chryft etc.

A the more fo to be for that to eche part of his faing he alleageth the fcripture. For as to the firft part he alleageth the fixt of S. Iohn : fo to the other parte he alleageth the fainge of Chryft in the xv. of S. Iohn, wher he faieth: *I am the true vine.* For in dede as he ys the true vine : fo cometh oute of him the true wine. The earthlie wine helpeth to maintein the earthlie life, whiche as S. Gregorie faieth, compared to the eternall life, ys raither to be called death then life. But the heauenly wine that cometh out of the true vine nou rifheth to euerlafting life, whiche ys the true life. And bicaufe we be by faith inferted, and griffed into Chryft, this bleffed wine, whiche ys the Iuice of that true vine, ys of vs, as of braunches of the fame vine, receaued, and fo maketh vs his liuely braunches, not onely fpirituallie by faith : but alfo by nature, whiche thing holie Cirill doth very liuely open and declare . *Annon conuenienter dici poteft, vitem humanitatem eius, & nos palmites, propter identitatem naturæ. Eiufdem enim naturæ vitis & palmites funt. Ita & fpiritualiter, & corporaliter nos palmites, & Chriftus vitis eft.* Maie not the manheade of Chryft be very wel

B called the vine? and we the braunches, for that we be all of one nature? for the vine and the braunches be of one nature · So both fpirituallie and corporallie , Chryft ys the vine, and we be the braunches . Thus Cyrill.

Wherfore *Ifidore* to proue that, that ys in the cuppe, to be the bloode of Chryfte, as the wine or iuice whiche fhoulde be receaued of vs the naturall braunches of Chryft the true vine, did very well alleadge the fainge of Chryft : *I am the true vine.* And by this alfo yowe maie perceaue the minde of S. Cyrill, that we be not onely of one Spirit with Chryft by faith, but we be alfo of one nature with him. not onely that he hath taken our nature vpon him, wherby he ys one with vs, but that we receaue his naturall flefh and bloode, wherby we are of one nature with him. This his natural flefh and bloode we receaue not but in the Sacrament . Wherfor the Sacrament con teineth the naturall flefh and bloode of Chryfte.

C And nowe that we haue hearde *Ifidore,* who was of the latin churche, fo breifly and plainly expownde this text : we will alfo heare *Oecumenius,* who was of the greke churche, howe he breifly expowndeth the fame He faieth: *Poculum vocat benedictionis, poculum fanguinis Chrifti, quod benedicimus, quod præ ma nibus habentes benedicimus eum, qui gratiosè fanguinem fuum nobis largitus eft .* He cal leth the cuppe of the bloode of Chryft the cuppe of bleffing whiche we bleffe , whiche hauing before vs we bleffe him , who hath grauntcd vs his bloode,

Is not this as plain an expofition, as yt ys breif? ys yt not wonderfull that anie man wolde open his mouth againft a trueth fo plainlie vttered as this ys? Here maie ye fee what maner of cuppe yt ys that S. Paule calleth the cuppe of bleffing. Yt ys (faieth this authour) *the cuppe of the bloode of Chryfte.* And when he hath expownded to yowe what yt ys, than he geueth yowe a caufe why yt ys called of S. Paule the cuppe of bleffinge, being in dede the cuppe of Chryftes bloode. Yt ys fo called (faieth he) becaufe hauing yt before vs, we bleffe and geue thankes to him that hath graunted vs his bloode. and woorthily we bleffe him, both for that he hath commaunded vs that as oftē as we eate of that breade and drinke of that cuppe, we fhoulde fhewe furth

D his death vntill he come : and alfo for that befides an infinite nombre of benefittes, whiche he hath pourchafed vnto vs by his paffion and bloode fhedding, ther ys graunted vnto vs, as a pledge of his vnfpeakable loue towar des vs (as this authour faieth) his bloode. For afmoche then as the cuppe of

bloode

bloode conteineth his bloode, who hath wrought vs fo great mercie, and

The cuppe of the blood why yt ys called the cuppe of blefsing. quickneth in vs the liuelie remembrance of the fame, we are prouoked to lawde, praife, and bleffe him, by whom thefe mercies were wrought, and therfor yt ys very well called the cuppe of blesfing, that ys to faie, the cuppe that moueth ftirreth, and prouoketh to bleffe Chryft our Sauiour, whofe bloode yt ys.

And here, Reader, to commend this trueth better to thee, I meen, that the cuppe which S. Paule calleth the cuppe of blesfing, that yt ys (as this authour faieth) the cuppe of Chryftes bloode, call to thy remembrance the faing of Chryfoftome what he faied expownding this text: dothe not he faie this ys the meening of S. Paule, *that, that ys in the cuppe, ys yt that flowed oute of the fide?* Nowe this ys a cõmon maner of fpeache, that the veffell ys named by the thing that yt conteineth, as a cuppe conteining wine, ys called a cuppe of wine a cuppe conteining water ys called a cuppe of water. Nowe whẽ Chryfoftom faieth, that the bloode that flowed oute of the fide of Chryft, ys in the cuppe: and *Oecumenius* faieth, that yt ys the cuppe of bloode, what difference ys ther in the thinge, that they fpeake of? ys yt not all one? Ther for thowe maift fee that thefe authours agree and haue confent bitwixt thẽ. For this authour though he differ in maner of fpeach from Chryfoftom: yet in the thing that they fpeake he faieth euen the fame that he dothe. And nowe as for thefe two wittneffes *Ifidorus* and *Oecumenius* let not the Aduerfarie attempt to corrupt them with his wicked glofe, for they be allreadie alleadged, and again fhall be withe foch euident and ftrong fentence declaring their faith, that they can not be altered.

THE TVENTETH CHAP. PROCEADETH
vpon the fame text by Haymo, and Theo-
philaéte.

His being true that our Sauiour Chryft faieth, *In the month of two or three wittneffes ftandeth all trueth:* thefe that be alleaged might fuffice to teftifie this trueth that I haue taken in hand to fett furthe, Neuertheleffe for that yt hath pleafed him who ys the verie trueth him felf, who neded no teftimonie, to call twelue, and when one of them the childe of perdicion perifhed, to haue an oiher chofen that the nombre of twelue. might be continued, yt fhall like me to-folowe his example, and as I haue doen in the expofition of the firft text of S. Paule, wher I haue produced twelue wittneffes, to do the like here in the expofition of this text. And allthough the trueth of this matter ys foche that being fpoken of him that ys the trueth him felf, as ys faied, yt nedeth no other commendacion : yet to the confufion of the enemie, and the comforte of the fauourer and louer of gods catholique faithe, twelue be and fhall be cauled, that yt maie be feen howe largely this trueth hath ben fpred and receaued and in what diuerfitie of times yt hath ben euer cõtinued, as I do not hing doubte, but yt fhall be continued to the worldes ende.

But to go a boute that, that here ys entended, that the reft of this nombre which remain maie geue alfo their teftimonie, and fhewe their mindes *Theoph. in 10. prioris ad Corin.* in the vnderftanding of S Paule, we fhall firft heare *Theophilaéte*, whofe expo fition of this text ys this : *Calix benediélionis, hoc eft, gratiarum aélionis. In manibus namque habentes, gratias ei haud dubiè agimus, qui noftri gratia fanguinem fum effuderit, dignatufque nos fit, bonis ineffabilibus . Non enim participatio dixit, fed vt plus ali-*
quid

A *aliquid exprimat, summam scilicet coniunctionem. Quod autem dixit, tale est. Sanguis enim iste, qui calice continetur, ille est, qui Christi è latere profluit. Hunc ipsi cùm sumimus participamus, hoc est, Christo coniungimur.* The cuppe of blessing, that ys, of thankesgeuing. For hauing him in handes, we geue vndoubtedlie thankes vnto him, who for owre sake hath shed oute his bloode, and hath esteemed vs woorthie of vnspeakeable giftes. He did not saie *participacion* but *communicacion*, that he might expresse somwhat more, that ys to saie, a most near coniunction. But that that he hath saied ys after this maner. *This bloode whiche ys conteined in the cuppe, ys the same that flowed oute of the side of Chryste.* This when we take we participate, that ys to saie, we are conioined to Chryst . Thus *Theophilact.*

Cōmunica-tion vsed of S. Paule to expresse a nearer coniūction betwen Chryste and vs then participacion cā signifie.

Yf thow, reader, desierest to be instructed howe this text ys to be vnderstanded, and what ys the verie minde of sainct Paule, yf euer man did clerely expownd yt, no man more plainlier then this, although Chrysostom and Oecumenius, as plainly and almost by the same woordes. Consider therfore this exposition well and credit yt, and thowe shalt atteign to the true sense

Theophi-lact cōmen ded.

B and mening of sainct Paule . Ther ys nothing to be desiered in this man, that ys necessarilie required to one to whome creditte shoulde be geuen. He ys so auncient that he was before anie controuersie as touching the presence of Chryst in the Sacrament, for he was before *Berengarius*. And after the councell of *Sisimius* in the tripartite historie they are to be called to the decision or dissolucion of a controuersie, whiche wrote before that controuersie was risen, and forsomoche as this authour did so, therfore he maie well be called to this matter. That he ys vncorrupted, I suppose, the Aduersarie will depose . For yt ys knowen to all men learned that *Oecolampadius* did translate him owte of greke into latin, whose sinceritie and dexteritie in the doing of anie soch matter, they that be of that side, can not asmoche as once suspect. And although he hath in other places offended, and vitiated him: yet here he hath not . Learning ther lacketh none in this authour for that he doth ys by imitacion of Chrysostom, whose sentences and matters being setfurth at lenght, this man doth collect, and in a breif maner

C settfurth. By which fact as we be sure that that ys setfurth ys learned matter: So be we sure that the setterfurth ys without all doubte learned, for soch a worke can not be doen of an vnlearned man. And besides that the voice of all learned men doth with moch estimacion, and praise so commende him. And therfore he ys so reputed, esteemed, and taken. Breiflie ther was neuer yet authour that euer yt happened me to read, that did either for learning, trueth, or anie other soche like matter, make as moch as a note of anie reprehension, or declared anie thinge, that was to be desiered in *Theophilact*. Therfore seing all thinges be in him, that are required to be in an authour, he ys withoute all exception woorthie of creditte, and in this matter as a wittnesse maie iustlie be produced.

The same blood that flowed oute of the side of Chryste, ys in the cuppe, euen by the min de of S. Paule.

In this exposition then wher no tropes, no signes, no figures of the blood of Chryst be admitted, but the presence of the verie bloode taught to be in the cuppe, yea and the verie same that flowed oute of the side of Christ what can we or maie we ells do but so take yt, that ys, that sainct Paule, when he saied: *The cuppe of blessing, which we blesse ys a partaking of the bloode of Christ,*

D spake of no figure, nor by no figure: But of the substanciall bloode of Chryst to be verilie in the cuppe of blessing, whiche we also take and receaue, and so be verilie partakers of the bloode of Chryste, and partaking yt be conioined to Chryst, as this authour saieth.

And here ys to be noted that *Theophilact*, doth not here fpeake as fhewing his owne minde but opening vnto vs the minde and meaning of fainctPaul, and therfore faieth: *Quod autem dixit tale eſt.* That he faied ys this, or after thys maner, as who fhould faie, this ys yt that he faied. So that this expofition ys to be taken as the woordes of S. Paule, for that yt dothe declare the minde and meaning of S. Paule.

PeterMartir.his wreſting of Theophil. vpon the woorde. (vertue)

Neither ys *Peter Martyr* to be hearde, who wolde peruert all the negatiues of *Theophilact*, wherbie he denieth in fondrie and diuerfe places, that the Sacrament ys onely a figure of Chryſtes bodie, as in the xxvi of S. Matthew, in the xiiii. of fainct Marke, in the vi. of fainct Iohn, and ther auoucheth the verie reall prefence by expreffe woordes: The faied Peter Martyr wolde I faie, taking a fmall occafion of a woord vpon the xiiii. of S. Marke by violent

Vide ca. 60.li.2.

preffing, euen turne the face of theophilact backwarde, and make him looke an other waie, and to fpeake a directe contrarie fentence to that, that he fpake within ten lines before.

In the xiiii. of S. Marke to proue the woordes of Chyſt: *This ys my body*, to be no figuratiue fpeach he bringeth in the faing of Chryſt in the vi. of S.

Theoph. in 14.Marci.

Iohn, and faieth thus: *Dominus enim dicit. Panis quem ego dabo, caro mea eſt, non dixit figura eſt carnis meæ, ſed caro mea eſt. Et iterum: Niſi ederitis carnem filii hominis, & quomodò, inquis, caro videtur? O homo propter noſtram infirmitatem iſtud fit. Quia enim panis & vinum ex his ſunt, quibus aſſueuimus, ea non abhorremus. Idcirco miſericors Deus noſtræ infirmitati condeſcendens ſpeciem quidem panis & vini ſeruat in virtutem autem carnis & ſanguinis tranſelementat.* Owre Lord faieth: *The bread that I wil geue*

The flesh of Chryſte in the B.Sacrament appeareth not for oure in firmities ſake.

ys my flesh He faied not yt ys a figure of my flefh, but yt ys my flefh. And again: *Except ye eate the flesh of the Sonne of man.* And howe(*ſaieſt thow*) ys not the flefh feen? O man this ys doen for our infirmitie. For bicaufe bread and wine be of thefe thinges, vnto the which we haue ben accuftomed we doe not abhorre them. *Therfor our mercifull God condeſcending to our infirmitie, dothe kepe the outwardes formes of bread and wine, but he turneth the ſubſtance into the vertue of fleſh and bloode.*

Here wolde Peter Martyr (as ys faied) wreſt *Theophilact* that he wolde haue no reall prefence, and therfore that we receaue not the verie flefh and blood of Chryſt in the Sacrament, but the vertue of them. But, Reader, I ha ue afcribed the full fentence of *Theophilact*, to the entent that thow maiſt fee, that if anie foch fenfe fhould be gathered of him, yt maie well appeare to thee, that yt ys violentlie wreſted, and not truly according to the minde of the authour alleadged, nor expownded.

And for proof of this, firſt obferue and note, that *Theophilact* bringeth in, the faing of Chryſt to proue that ther ys no figuratiue fpeach, and therfore he faieth, that Chryſt did not faie, that the bread which he wolde geue was a figure of his flefh, but his flefh. Yf *Theophilact* will not haue yt the figure of Chryſtes flefh, but his flefh in dede, how ſtandeth Peters expofition, who wolde no flefh, but the vertue of the flefh, ãd fo denieng the verie flefh, wold

Trãſelemẽ tacion vſed of Theophi lact.more fullie to ex preſſe the chaunge in the Sacrament:

haue yt a bare figûre, which *Theophilact* hath fo oftẽ denied? And think yowe that foch an authour wolde in fo fewe lines denie a figure and graunt a figure? Secondly note that *Theophilact* faieth that for our infirmitie our mercifull God *doth tranſelementate into the vertue of the fleſb and bloode,* wher I wolde learn of this man what ys the propre fignificacion of this verbe (*tranſelementare*) ãd yf yt be to chaunge, then what ys chaunged? As I can perceaue, this verbe cometh of this woorde (*Elementũ*) which fignifieth an Element, and fo yt fhould fignifie to chaunge Elementes. As the philofophers do teache, the

natural

A naturall conſtitucion of naturall thinges that be compownded ys of the fower Elementes as of foure principles, yet not as primere, of the whiche the
thing hath his beinge, but as concurring to the due order and diſpoſition of
the thing, without the which the naturall thing can not abide in his being.
As fleſh and bone be of the earth, ſwet and moyſtnes of the water, breathing
of the aier, and the naturall heate of the fire. Euen ſo the principles of other
thinges, whether they be in learning, or religion be called *elementa* Elementes. As in learning the letters of the Alphabete be called Elementes. Likewiſe in religion as ſainct Paule ſaieth to the hebrues. *Etenim cùm deberetis magi-*   *Hebr.5.*
ſtri eſſe propter tempus, rurſum indigetis vt vos doceamiui quæ ſunt elementa exordij ſer-
monum Dei, & facti eſtis quibus lacte opus ſit non ſolido cibo. For when as concerning
the time ye ought to be teachers, yet haue ye nede again that we teach yow
the firſt Elementes or principles of the woorde of God, and are become ſoch
as haue nede of milke, and not of ſtronge meate. In which ſentence wher he
ſaieth that they had need to be taught the elementes of the woorde of God
B he meneth the principles of religion. And thus the beginninges of all ſoche
thinges maie be called elementes.

Nowe to applie this to our pourpoſe, what be the principles of bread
and wine? be they not their ſubſtances? Then, when *Theophilact* ſaith that he
doth tranſelementate, ys yt not to be ſaied that he doth chaunge their principles, or elementes? But their principles be their ſubſtáces, wherfor he doth
chaunge their ſubſtances.

Although (yf I be not deceaued) this ys ſpoken according to the rule of   *An earth-*
learning: yet if this ſhould miſlike the Aduerſarie: yet he muſt nedes graunt   *lie creature*
that ſome thing ther muſt be, that muſt be chaunged. And then I wolde learn   *can not be*
of him what this ys that ys chaunged into the vertue or grace of the fleſh of   *tranſelemē-*
Chryſt as the Aduerſarie here taketh this woorde (virtus) to be vnderſtáded?   *ted into ſpi-*
Yt was neuer readde that euer anie thing earthlie coulde be primarelie chaũ   *rituall ver-*
ged into the vertue or grace a qualitie ſpiritual. Wherfor no ſoch chaunge cã   *tue.*
here be made as the Aduerſarie wold feign to be. But that an earthly ſubſtáce
maie be turned into the ſubſtáce of Chryſt not onelie we are taught yt by
C that that he tooke fleſh of the virgé Mary: but alſo as our *Theophilact*, to proue
this that here ys to be proued, ſaieth: the foode which our Sauiour Chryſt
tooke vpõ the earth was chaunged into his bodie ãd was made like to his ho   *Of this mat-*
lie fleſh. Wherfore wher *Theophilact* ſaieth here that this tranſelementacion   *ter ſee mo-*
ys into the vertue of the fleſh and blood of Chryſt, he meeneth into the ve   *re in the ſe-*
rie fleſh, as though yt had ben ſaied: *In veritatem carnis & ſanguinis Chriſti*, into   *cond booke*
the veritie or trueth of the fleſh and blood of Chryſt.   *cap.lx.*

And that this was his mening this proueth: firſt that in the ſame ſentence
he ſaieth, *that God condeſcending to our infirmitie, kepeth the outwarde formes of bread*
and wine, ſignifieng that the formes remaining the ſubſtance ys chaunged . For
yf the outward formes remain, and the ſubſtance (as they ſaie) be not
chaunged, what then ys tranſelemented, or chaunged ? The ſeconde
proofe ys, that *Theophilact*, ſpeaking of the verie ſame matter vpon the ſixt of
S. Iohn, doth by open and plain woordes proue this that I haue ſaied, for
better declaraciõ wherof I will bring in his wholl ſentence. *Non enim dixit*
panis quem ego dabo figura eſt carnis, ſed caro mea eſt. Transformatur enim arcanis ver-
D *bis panis ille per myſticã benedictionē & acceſsionem ſancti ſpiritus in carnē Domini. Et ne*   *Theoph. in*
quē cõturbet quod credēdus ſit panis caro. Etenim in carne ambuláte Domino, et ex pane ali-   *6. Ioannis.*
moniã admittēte, panis ille qui mãducabatur, in corpus eius mutabatur, et ſimilis fiebat sãctæ
eius carni et in augmētũ, et ſuſtentationē cõferebat iuxta humanum more. Igitur et nũc panis

*in carnem domini mutatur.*For he hath not faied,the bread which I will geue, ys **E** a figure of my flefh,but yt ys my flefh.For that bread by the myfticall blef- fing and coming to of the holie Gofte, with the fecret woordes ys tranffor- med into the flefh of owre Lorde.And leeft yt fhoulde troble anie man, that the bread ys to be beleued flefh:when owre Lorde walked in the flefh , and tooke foode of bread, that bread that was eaten was chaunged into his bo- die,and was made like vnto his holie flefh and yt went vnto the encreafing and fuftentacion after the condicion of the nature of man.Therfore now al- fo the bread ys chaunged into the flefh of our Lorde.Thus *Theophil.*

In this faing,ye fee not the figure only of Chryftes flefh denied in the Sa- crament, but withal the very flefh affirmed , and the wholl matter howe yt cometh to paffe declared.In the fetting furth wherof, wher as vpon S.Marke he faied,that the bread was chaunged into the vertue of the flefh of Chryft, he expownding the fame faieth,yt ys transformed into the flefh of Chryft. And that yt might appeare to yowe,that this chaunge was a chaunge of the fubftance of bread into the fubftance of the flefh of Chryft,he bringeth in a fimilitude of the food which Chryft did take being conuerfant here vpon the earth after the maner of men,which foode was fubftanciallie chaunged **F** in to the fubftance of the bodie of Chryft,and therupon concludeth , that therfore nowe alfo the bread ys chaunged into the flefh of Chryft. Whiche conclufion muft contein as moch as the premiffes of the argument, that as the foode which Chryft receaued was fubftancially chaunged into the fub- ftance of the bodie of Chryfte,fo now the bread by the myfticall benedic- tion, and coming of the holie Goft,with the fecrett woordes ys fubftancial lie chaunged into the fubftance of the flefh of Chryft.

In this proceffe of the declaracion of the minde of *TheophilaƐt,*ys not one ly ouerthrowen the wicked wrefting of Peter Martyr,but alfo the veritie of the Sacrament fo fenfiblie as yt were opened,that,as I fuppofe,ther ys no pla ce of doubte left to make a Chryftian to doubte in. For yf ye will conferre the expofition of S.Paule nowe here brought in, with the other fainges , yt alone will fufficiently teache a man the perfeƐt catholique faith aboute the Sacrament of Chryftes bodie and bloode.

Wherfore fo moch being fpoken of the minde of *Theophilaƈt,*in the which **G** I haue taried longer then I entended,I will nowe haft me to inferre. *Haymo,* who ys placed here with this grecian,*Theophilaƈt,*to declare the faith of the la tin Church in his time.This haymo thus expowndeth this text of fainƈtPaul: *Et panis quem frangimus in altari,nonne participatio corporis domini est? vtique, primùm confecratur,& benedicitur à facerdotibus & fpiritu fanƈto,& deinde frangitur:cum iam, licet panis videatur,in veritate corpus Christi est.Ex quo pane quicunque communicant,cor pus Christi edunt* And the bread which we do breake in the aultar, ys yt not a partaking of the bodie of our Lord?Yt ys fo.Firft yt ys confecrated, and blef fed of the preiftes and the holie Goft,and afterwatd ytys broken . And al- though nowe yt feemeth bread,in verie deed yt ys the bodie of Chryft, of the which bread whofoeuer do communicate , they do eate the bodie of Chryft.Thus *Haymo.*

Here ye fee an other expofition of S. Paule his text, whiche although yt differ from the other in woordes:in the thing that they fpeake of,they fullie agree.*TheophilaƐt* faied that the blood that ys in the cuppe ys the fame that **H** flowed oute of the fide of Chryft,fo that he teaching the prefence of the ve- rie blood of Chryft in the Sacrament,teacheth by the fame the verie pre- fence of the bodie of Chryft . So this man teaching the very prefence of the

A　of the bodie of Chryſt by the ſame,teacheth alſo the preſence of the verie bloode of Chryſt.The ord er alſo howe the bread ys turned into the bodie of Chryſt ys here teſtified.as yt was of *Theophilact*.For he ſaied that the bread ys trãsformed by the myſticall benedictiõ,and the acceſſe of the holie Gõſt: This man ſaieth,that yt ys conſecrated and bleſſed of the preiſtes and the ho lie Goſt.*Theophilact* ſaieth, that God chaungeth the bread into the fleſh of Chryſt,the outward formes remaining ſtill:This man ſaieth, that allthough yt ſeeme bread,in verie deed yt ys the bodie of Chryſt.Wherby we maie ſee the goodlie conſent,and agrement,that the God of vnitie and peace woorketh in them that do loue and embrace his trueth.*Theophilact*,alſo ſaieth that the bloode of Chryſt ys in the cuppe: This man ſaieth, that the bodie of Chryſt ys in the aultar.Whiche bothe maner of ſpeaches proue a reall preſence.For the ſpirituall preſence ys neither in the aultar,neither in the chali ce,but in the ſoule of man.

B　Hitherto by all theſe auncientes,we can learn none other but that ſainct Paule in this ſcripture ſpake of the verie reall and ſubſtanciall preſence of Chryſtes bodie and blood in the bleſſed Sacrament.And therfor receauing this ſaied bleſſed Sacrament we are partakers of the ſame bodie and bloode of Chryſte.

THE ONE TWENTETH CHAPITER PRO
ceadeth yet vpon the ſame text by Anſelmus,and Bruno.

Owe that we haue heard S.Paule expownded by the auncient elders,and learned writers,that be of all ſtudentes of the Chry ſtian faith,to be reuerenced and ſo receaued:to bring the matter euen home to our time,for that the later writers be ſo contemned and without iuſt cauſe of the aduerſarie reiected ,ſome of them ſhall be produced,that triall maie yet be made,whether they agree with theſe elders,or diſſent from them. And firſt Anſelmus his expoſition

C　ſhall be hearde,thus he writeth:*Panis quem frangimus eſt participatio corporis Domini,quia ipſe panis quem multis diuidimus,eſt verum corpus Domini.Et qui de illo accipiũt de corpore Domini accipiunt,atque fiunt etiam ipſi,quod accipiunt.* The bread that we breake ys partaking of the bodie of our Lorde,for that bread,which we diuide to manie ys the very bodie of our Lorde.And they that do take of yt *they receaue the bodie of our Lorde*,and they alſo be made that , that they receaue. Thus Anſelmus.

Anſel mus in De ci.1.Cor.

The bread diuided to many ys the bodie of our Lord.

This expoſition diſſenteth not from the expoſitions of the elders, but as they taught that S.Paule ſpeaketh here of the very bodie of Chryſt, ſo doth this man alſo.For ſaieth he,the bread which we diuide to manie ys the very bodie of our Lord,wherfor they that receaue yt, receaue the bodie of our Lord.And with S.Auguſtine expownding yt that S.Paule ſaieth, that yt ys a communicacion of the bodie of our Lorde,he ſaieth that they that receaue the bodie of Chryſt,are made that,they receaue.For they , that receaue yt duely,are made membres of the myſticall bodie of Chryſt.

D　But in this expoſition the reader ys to be aduertiſed that this authour,ſaing that the bread which we geue to manie ys the bodie of Chryſt,meneth, not as *Luther* doth,that the materiall bread in the Sacrament,ys the very bo die of Chryſt. For after the conſecracion whẽ we diſtribute the holie Sacramẽt their ys no materiall bread,but he that ys the heauẽli bread,who ſaiẽth. *Ego ſum panis vitæ.Et panis quem ego dabo,caro mea eſt,quam dabo pro mundi vita.*

Ioan.6.

　　　　　　　　　　Ccc iii　　I am

I am the bread of life,and the bread which I ſhall geue ys my fleſh , which I
will geue for the life of the worlde.So that we diſtribute in the Sacrament
no other bread but that bread . Wherfore he ſaied very well , that that
bread ys the very bodie of Chryſte.

Not minding to trooble the reader,with long declaracion where the authours for their plaines in ſentences nede none ſoch,I ſhall leaue Anſelmus,
and call the good holy man *Bruno*,who was more then foure hundreth years
agon.who vpon this texte maketh this expoſition:*Calix benedictionis,id eſt,quem*
ipſe Deus benedicit,& conſecrat,& cui nos benedicimus per officium noſtrum . Deus enim
hoc efficit per ſacerdotem miniſtrum.Hic itaque calix, nonne eſt communicatio ſanguinis
Chriſti?id eſt,nonne per ſanguinem aſſumptum vnimur Chriſto,ipſíque conformamur? Et pa
nis,id eſt, verum corpus Chriſti,qui ſub ſpecie ſola panis accipitur,panis dico,quem nos in al-
tari frangimus, vt quod vnum eſt in veritate,licet ita videatur,ſcindi tamen non poteſt,hic,
inquam,panis quem frangimus,nonne eſt participatio corporis Domini?id eſt,nonne per hoc
corpus,Deum in nobis capimus?eumque nobis incorporamus? Ideo in duabus ſubſtantiis,cor-
poris ſcilicet & ſanguinis,ſacrificium Deus hoc inſtituit, vt per carnem in altari traditam
oſtenderet ſe redimere carnem noſtram per hæc ſacramenta in incorruptionem quandoque
transferendā:& per ſanguinē,quē tradit,inſinuaret ſe ſimiliter redimiſſe animā noſtrā.Ad
quod de anima inſinuandū,quia re incorporali vti non potuit,dignè per ſanguinem,qui ſedes
animæ dicitur,animā figurauit.Hæc in duas partes diſtribuit, vt diuerſas partes eius.Qui enim
vel ſanguinem tantùm,vel corpus ſolùm, totū accipit.Qui vtrumque accipit, nō magis per
vtrūq;quā per alterā accipit. Quod corpus ſicut vera caro Chriſti eſt ſub ſpecie panis,ita per
ſolā ſpeciem atteritur, diminuitur,in partes diuiditur,cùm in veritate incorruptibile,indiui-
ſibile,impotens diminui permaneat. The cuppe,of bleſſing, that ys to ſaie , whiche
God himſelf doth bleſſe,and which we by our office do bleſſe (*for God doth*
this by his myniſter the preiſt)therfor this cuppe,ys yt not a communicacion of
the blood of Chryſt?that ys,are we not,by the bloode receaued vnited to
Chryſt,and conformed to him?And the bread,that ys to ſaie , the bodie of
Chryſt , which ys taken vnder the forme of bread alone,the bread I ſaie,
which we breake in the aultar,as which ys one in verie dede,although yt ſemeth ſo to be,yet yt can not be diuided, this bread I ſaie,which we breake,
ys yt not partaking of the bodie of our Lorde?that ys to ſaie , do we not by
this bodie receaue God into vs?and incorporate him vnto vs? Therfor God
hath inſtituted this ſacrifice in two ſubſtances, that ys, of his bodie and his
bloode,that by the fleſh diliuered in the aultar he wolde ſhew himſelf to haue redemed our fleſh by theſe ſacramentes ſomtime to be trāſferred into in-
corruption.And by the blood whiche he deliuereth he wolde inſinuate him
ſelf to haue redemed our ſoule. Vnto the which thing of the ſoule to be inſinuated,forſomoche as he could vſe no corporall thing,woorthilie by blood
(*which ys called the ſeat of the ſoule*)he hath figured the ſoule. Theſe thinges he
hath diſtributed into two ſubſtances,that he ſhoulde vnderſtand his diuerſe
partes.For he that receaueth the blood onely,or the bodie,he taketh all.He
that receaueth bothe receaueth no more by bothe then by one. Which bodie as the very fleſh of Chryſt ys vnder the forme of bread:ſo by the onely
outewarde forme ys yt bruiſed,diminiſhed,and diuided into partes,when in
very deed yt doth abide incorruptible,indiuiſible,and not able to be dimi-
niſhed.Thus farre Bruno.

In this expoſition both catholique and learned are manie thinges, woorthie of note,whiche yf I ſhoulde all touch,I feare I ſhoulde tarie the reader
to long.Wherfore leauing them to his diſcuſſion I will onely breiſly touche
them,that appertein to our principall pourpoſe to be learned of S. Paule,
of the

Bruno in
dec.1 Cor.

By the bo-
die of Chriſt
receaued in
the B. Sac.
we be incor
porated to
him:and by
his blood we
are vnited
to him .

He that re
ceaueth one
lie vnder o-
ne kinde,re
ceaueth as
moch as he,
that recea-
ueth both,
Chryſt be-
ing perfect
lie in both.

A of the whiche firſt to ſpeake of the bread, whiche S. Paule ſaieth, that we breake, whether yt be vnderſtãded to be materiall bread, or bread the bodie of Chryſt, this authour expownding S. Paule, and opening his minde to vs ſaieth. *that yt ys the bodie of Chryſt, taken vnder the forme bread.* And of the cuppe of bleſſing, he ſaieth : *that we receaue the bloode by the whiche we are vnited to Chryſt* In that he teacheth, S. Paule by the bread and the cuppe to ſignifie the bodie and blood of Chryſt, as he agreeth with the olde fathers before alleaged, as by conference ye ſhall eaſilie perceaue: So in that he teacheth that we receaue the ſame bodie and bloode vnder the formes of bread and wine, though not in their ſentences, here vpon this text alleaged, yet in other places, they are in this matter verie plain. S. Ciprian ſaieth: *The bread whiche our Lorde gaue vnto his Diſciples, chaunged, not in outwarde ſhape, but in nature, by the allmightineſſe of the woorde ys made fleſh.* Yf the nature of the bread be chaunged, and by the all mightineſſe of the woorde of God made fleſh: the outwarde formes remaining ſtill, what ys yt, but that ther ys the fleſh of Chryſt vnder the outwarde forme of bread, that remaineth vnchaunged.

Doctours teaching the bodie ãd blood of Chryſt to be vnder the formes of bread and wine.

B   S. Auguſtine alſo ſaieth *vnder the formes of bread and wine, whiche we ſee, we honour thinges inuiſible,* that ys to ſaie, *the fleſh and bloode of Chryſt.* Again he ſaieth: *Yt ys his fleſh whiche we receaue, couered vnder the forme of bread. And yt ys his bloode, which we vnder the forme and taſt of wine do drinke.* And *Theophilact* ſaieth: *Yt dothe appeare or ſeem bread, but yt ys fleſh.* All whiche what do they ells but plainly teache that the bodie and bloode of Chryſt be in the Sacrament vnder the formes of bread and wine, So that in this poinct this authour teacheth nothing diuerſe or different from the auncient Fathers.

Li. Senten. Proſperi. Ibidem. In 26. Matth.

    Again wher he ſaieth that God hath inſtituted this ſacrifice in two ſubſtances, that ys of the bodie and bloode of Chryſte, as diuerſe other haue before doen, teaching that S. Paule in this proceſſe, doth take the bodie and bloode of Chryſt in the Sacrament, as a ſacrifice: ſo dothe this authour alſo. Wherfor ſeing in theſe poinctes he ſwarueth nothing from the doctrine of the Fathers, I ſee not why anie man, vpon willfull arrogancie ſhoulde reiecte him, but receaue him as a wittneſſe of the catholique faith declaring vntô vs the faith of the Churhe in his time, whiche ys none other but ſoche as was in the time of the Fathers, as the compariſon or conference of this authours and their teachinges doth very well proue.

C

    Nowe wher the Proclamer by an article of his proclamacion importeth, that we can not ſhewe one doctour, that ſaieth that the outwarde ſhewes or formes of bread and wine remain withoute their ſubſtances: Although yt hath ben ſufficiently proued in that place, wher we haue treaicted of tranſubſtancion: yet here by occaſion of theſe authours alleadged we maie note the ſame again. For when S. Cyprian ſaieth, that the bread ys chaunged in nature, but not in outwarde ſhewe, what doth he ſaie, but that the outwarde ſhewe remaineth, ãd that the ſubſtance of bread ys chaunged. And when S. Auſten ſaieth of the Sacrament that yt ys the fleſh and blood of Chryſt that we receaue vnder the formes of bread and wine, dothe he not ſaie the ſame that S. Cyprian ſaied? except the Proclamer will ſaie, that vnder the formes of bread and wine, ther be bothe the ſubſtances of the bodie and blood of Chryſte, and alſo the ſubſtances of the bread wine withall, whiche ys to great an abſurditie. And to be ſhorte, when *Theophilact* ſaieth that yt doth appeare bread, but yt ys fleſh: And *Haymo* ſaieth, that yt ſemeth bread, but in verie dede yt ys the bodie of Chryſte: And this authour ſaieth, that yt ys the fleſh of Chryſt vnder the forme of bread: All which what do they

Here maie he ſee moo then one or two, yf he liſt to ſee aſfirming the bodie of Chryſt to be vnder formes of bread and wine.

D

ells teache but that ther be in the Sacrament the outwarde ſhewes of bread and wine, and the ſubſtance of Chryſts bodie and bloode, and not the ſubſtance of bread and wine.

See the ma
lice of the
Prorcl. ſee
in what de
peſſeape of
hereſie he
lieth, that
can not, or
will not ſee
all theſe
doctours.
See ye not thē, howe great a ſmooke the Proclamer wolde make withou te anie fire? See ye not howe greate reproache he wolde laie to the Church withoute iuſt cauſe? See yowe not howe greatt bragges he maketh withoute anie grownde to buill then vpon? Or raither ſee ye not howe he hath prouoked matter to be ſhewed to his ſhame? So that euery man that readeth this maie well ſaie yt ys a ſhame for him to ſaie that the catholikes haue nothing to ſhewe for that they teache: when ther ys ſoche plentie produced to proue and confirme that they ſaie. But as for him ſelf he hath nothing that ys of any ſubſtanciall authoritie, to maintein his ſainges, but reſteth onely vpon his bare bragges, and his owne priuate authoritie. Neither do I doubte, but the Proclamer him ſelf knoweth yt. Manie mo maie in this matter be produced. Feare not then, Reader, neither be thowe caſt in doubte, to continewe the olde auncient ſaing of the church, that thowe haueſt ſeen in the Sacrament Chryſt vnder the formes of bread and wine, for ſomoche as tho we ſeiſt S. Cyprian S. Auguſtin, whiche were aboue a thouſand years agon and other, whiche were eight hondreth, ſeauen hondreth. and foure hondreth yeares agon, ſaie that yt ys ſo. Wherby we maie conclude againſt this article of this Aduerſaries proclamacion, that in the Sacrament, after the conſecracion remain the outwarde ſhewes of bread and wine, withoute their ſubſtances, but not withoute the ſubſtances, of the bodie and bloode of Chryſt.

THE TWO AND TWENTETH CHAP. ENDETH
*the expoſition of this text by Dioniſe, and
Gagneius.*

Dioniſius
Eartha. in
10.1. Cor.
Y T ſhall auaill to declare the continuance of conſent of doctrine in all ages, if we alſo heare the expoſition of Dioniſe the Carthuſian, who was ſomwhat nearer to onr time then the other were. Thus he expowndeth S. Paule his ſaing: *Calix benedictionis. id eſt, contentum in calice, vt pote ſanguis Chriſti, per quem ſanguinem benedicimur, id eſt, dona gratiarum conſequimur, cui calici ſeu ſanguini benedicimus, id eſt, quem conſecramus, cùm per prolationem ſacrorum verborum, à nobis conuertitur vinum in ſanguinem Chriſti. nonne communicatio ſanguinis Chriſti eſt? id eſt, nonne veraciter eſt ſanguis Chriſti, nobis comunicatus ſeu datus, facienſque nos comunicationem habere cum Chriſto, incorporando nos ei, & faciendo nos participes meriti ſuæ ef fuſionis. Et panis quem frangimus, id eſt, corpus Chriſti conſecratum ex pane, quem panem conſecratum cuius dimenſiones ſeu ſpecies frangimus porrigendo eum fidelibus : nonne participatio corporis Chriſti eſt ? id eſt, nonne vtique eſt corpus Chriſti verè acceptum à nobis, faciens nos vnum cum Chriſto, qui ait : Qui manducat meam carnem, & bibit meum ſanguinem, in me manet, & ego in eo?* The cuppe of bleſſing, that ys, the thing

Comunica-
cion of the
blood, ys
when the
blood of
Chryſt ys
verilie ge-
uen to vs.
conteined in the cuppe that ys to witte the bloode of Chryſt by the which blood we are bleſſed, that ys, we obtein giftes of graces, whiche cuppe or bloode we bleſſe, that ys, we conſecrate, wher by the prolacion of the holy woordes, the wine ys turned into the bloode of Chryſt, ys it not a Commu nicacion of the bloode of Chryſt? that ys, ys not the bloode of Chryſt verilie communicated or geuen, to vs, and making vs to haue a communiō with Chryſt, incorporating vs to him, and making vs partakers of the meritte of

his

Participa-
cion of the
bodie ys li-
kewise as of
the bloode
ys saied.

A his effusion ? And the bread whiche we breake, that ys, the bodie of Chryst consecrated of bread, which bread consecrated, whose dimensions and formes we breake, geuing yt to the faithfull : ys yt not a partaking of the bodie of Chryst? that ys, ys yt not also the bodie of Chryst verilie taken of vs, making vs one with Chryst, who saieth: he that eateth my flesh and drinketh my bloode abideth in me, and I in him? Thus mouch Dionise.

In this as in the other expositions, as ye see moche plainnesse : so ye se no parte of S. Paule his sentence left vnexpownded. But yet as truly: as simplie and plainlie. That in the cuppe S. Paule meent to be the very bloode of Chryst, yt ys so plainlie here spoken, as yt nedeth no addicion, for better declaracion. In the whiche his exposition, that he agreeth with all that hitherto haue ben induced, the matter being so clere, I trust, ye will be easilie perswaded, for anie futher proof to be made by me for the same. And therfor leauing this authour to the discrecion of the reader farder to be considered, we will descende a litle lower to one of this our time, and ther ende the exposition of this text of S. Paule .

Ioann. Gagneius in de-
cim.1.Cor.

B This shall be *Ioannes Gagneius*, who treating of this text, dothe thus open the same. *Calix benedictionis. cui benedicimus. id est, quem cum gratiarum actione sumimus, nonne communicatio sanguinis Christi est? id est, nonne calicem Christi sumentes, ac sanguinem illius bibentes , cum illo communicamus , & cum illo commercium nobis esse declaramus ? Et panis quem frangimus, id est, corpus Christi quod sub speciebus panis sumimus , nonne participatio corporis Domini est , id est, nonne declarat nos partem habere cùm corpore Domini, & in illud consentire?* The cuppe of blessing which we blesse, that ys, whiche we receaue with thankes geuing, ys yt not a Commucacion of the blood of Chryst? that ys, do not we taking the cuppe of Chryst and drinking his bloode communicate with him? and declare vs to haue an entredoing with him ? And the bread whiche we break, that ys, the bodie of Chryst, which we vnder the formes of bread do receaue , yt ys not a participacion of the bodie of our Lorde : that ys, dothe yt not declare vs to haue part with the bodie of our Lorde, and into yt to consent? Hitherto *Gagneius* Who although he wrote but last daie : yet he agreeth in the expownding of S. Paule with them that wrote aboue thousand yeares agon. And teacheth **C** (as they did) that S. Paule in this place spake of the very reall presence of the bodie and bloode of Chryst in the Sacrament, which we receaue, and by the which we are made partakers of the same bodie and bloode . For wher S. Paule saieth: The bread whiche we breake, that ys to saie (saieth this authour) the bodie of Chryst which we receaue vnder the forme of bread, maketh vs to haue part with the bodie of our Lorde,

Communi-
cacion and
participati
on of Chry
stes bodie
and blood
what they
be,

Nowe, *reader*, if thowe wilt gather together the expositions of all these famouse Fathers and learned men, which to shewe thee , the vnderstanding of S. Paule vpon this text, I haue here alleaged, and laie, them in a breif before thy face, thowe shalt, I suppose, see soche a plain declaracio of the trueth so euident, so manifest, so clere, so consonant, so agreing, and so consenting one with an other, although spoken in diuerse ages, in sondrie churches, and in moche difference of times, that I thinke, thowe wilt wonder with me that euer men coulde be so stubbornlie blind that they will not see an opé treuth whiche can not be so couered, and hidden, with their deuelish glooses, but **D** yt will allwaie lie aboue of all men readie to be seen.

A breif re-
hersall of
the docto-
urs allea-
ged for
this text.

Chrysostt.

Chrysostome saieth that this ys the meening of S. Paule, *that that which ys in the cuppe, ys yt that flowed oute of the side.* S. Hierom saieth, *that we partake of the bloode of Chryst, as he him self saieth: He that eateth my flesh and drinketh my bloode &c.*

Hieron

which

Whiche faing of Chryſt (as ther ys declared) ys ſpoken of the eating of the **E**
verie bodie of Chryſt and drinking of his verie blood. wherfor S. Hierom ſo
vnderſtãdeth S. Paule: *Damaſcen*, who can not abide theſe woordes of Chryſt

Damaſcen.

(*This ys my bodie*) to haue a figuratiue ſenſe, ſaieth, that in the participacion,
and the communion of the bread *we partake the fleſh of Chryſt and his Godhead
alſo.* S. Auguſtin ſaieth that S. Paule ſpeaking this text did ſhewe them to

Auguſt.

what ſacrifice they ſhoulde pertein, which was to the ſacrifice wherby they
ſhoulde be partakers of the bodie and bloode of Chryſt. Oecumenius ſaieth

Oecomen.

that *S. Paule calleth the cuppe of the bloode of Chryſt, the cuppe of bleſſing.* So that he
taketh yt for a cuppe of Chryſtes bloode. *Iſidore* ſaieth that the bread whiche

Iſidorus.
Theophil.

we breake, ys the bodie of Chryſt. He ſaieth not yt ys called, but yt ys the
bodie. *Theophilact* ſaieth *that the blood whiche ys cõteined in the cuppe, ys the ſame that
flowed oute of the ſide of Chryſt.* Haymo ſaieth, that the bread whiche we breake
in the aultar, although yt ſeem bread in very dede, *yet yt ys the bodie of Chryſt?*

Haymo.
Anſelm.
Bruno.

Anſelmus ſaieth, that the bread whiche we brake, and diuide to manie *ys the **F**
verie bodie of our Lorde, Bruno* ſaieth, *are we not by the bloode receaued, vnited to Chryſt*
and ys not the bread, that ys, the very bodie of Chryſt, *whiche ſemeth to be bro
ken, and ys not in deed, do not we by this bodie receaue God into vs?* and incorporate

Dionyſ.

him to vs? *Dionyſe* ſaieth, *that, that ys conteined in the cuppe ys the bloode of Chryſt.* by
the which bloode we are bleſſed, So that yt ys verilie the bloode of Chryſt
geuen vnto vs, makingvs to haue communion with Chryſt, and tobe partakers of the merittes of the effuſion of the ſame his bloodd. And laſt *Gagneius*

Gagneius.

ſaieth: that the bread whiche we breake that ys to ſaie, the bodie of Chryſt
whiche we receaue vnder the forme of bread, doth yt not declare vs to haue
parte with the bodie of our lorde?

Doth anie of theſe twelue finde anie trope or figures in the ſaing of S.
Paule? No, they do all teach yt to be a plain ſpeache, and a plain aſſercion of
the verie bodie of Chryſt, and not a bare ſign of yt. And here to conclude
this matter, and to make an ende of this expoſitiõ of this text, I haue thought
good to heare the minde of the right godlie, and learned Father *Roffenſis*,

*Roffen. in
proem. li. 5*

who, as all thinges that he did, ſo doth he handle this text learnedly and pi- **G**
thilie. Thus he ſaieth: *Poculum benedictionis cui benedicimus, nonne communicatio ſanguinis Chriſti eſt? Panis quem frangimus, nonne communicatio corporis Chriſti eſt? Quid hic
audimus? figuras ne corporis, & ſanguinis Chriſti? Nequaquam. ſed veritatem corporis
& ſanguinis, quibus nos verè communicare Paulus aſſerit. Profectò ſi figuram ſolam hic in-
dicaſſet Paulus, non adeo frequenter hæc (nulla vſpiam figurarum habita mentione) vo-
caſſet corpus, & ſanguinem Domini. Sed nec arbitratur Oecolampadius, nos per panem et
vinum ſuum. communicare corpori & ſanguini Chriſti, ſed fidem ſolam huius communicationis cauſam eſſe contendit. Et certè qui fieri poteſt vt merus panis, aut vinum eam effica-
tiam habeat, vt nos veri corporis & ſanguinis Chriſti reddat participes? Quare conſentane-
um eſt vt quum huius panis eſu, & liquoris eius, qui in poculo eſt potatione, verè corpori,
& ſanguini Chriſti communicamus, eiuſdem corporis, & ſanguinis veritatem hic adeſſe,
ceu compertiſſimum habeamus.* The cuppe of bleſſing, whiche we bleſſe, yt ys not

*S. Paule in
all his pro-
ceſſe of the
Sacra.
maketh not
one title of
mencion of
anie figure.*

a communicacion of the bloode of Chryſt? the bread whiche we breake, ys
yt not a communicacion of the bloode of Chryſte? What heare we here? Figures of the bodie and bloode of Chryſt? Not ſo, but the veritie of the bodie
and bloode of Chryſt, which Paule affirmeth vs verily to cõmunicate. Truly
yf Paule had iudged here to be an onely figure he wolde not ſo often haue **H**
called theſe thinges the bodie and bloode of Chryſte, no mention in anie
place beinge made of figures. But neither *Oecolampadius* doth thinke, that we
by his bread and wine do cõmunicate with the bodie and bloode of Chryſte, but

A   ste, but he doeth earneſtlie affirme that faith alone ys the cauſe of this cõmu
nicacion. And ſuerely howe can yt be doen, that the very bread and wine
maie haue that efficacie, that yt maie make vs partakers of the bodie and bloo
de of Chryſte? Wherfore yt foloweth agreablie, that ſeinge by the eating of
this bread, and drinking of that liquor whiche ys in the cupp we doe verilie
comunicate the bodie and bloode of Chryſt, that we haue yt for moſt aſſured knowledge, that here ys preſent the veritie of the ſame bodie and blood.
Thus farre Roffenſis.

    I praie thee, *reader*, weigh well the ſaing of this reuerend Father, and tho-
we ſhalt perceaue that here ys made an argument ſo pithie and ſo ſtrong
that all the Aduerſaries power can not ſtande againſt yt. For ſeing the Aduerſarie him ſellf affirmeth that by the receipt of his Sacramentall bread, we
be not partakers of the bodie and blood of Chryſt, which ys true, and S.
Paule ſaieth, that by this bread and this drink, we be made partakers of the,
yt muſt nedes be that this bread, and drinke, whiche the Apoſtle ſpeaketh of,
ys the verie bodie and bloode, whiche duely receaued make vs verilie parta-
B   kers of Chryſt: Yf the Apoſtle had not ment this bread and this drinke to
be the verie bodie, and verie bloode of Chryſt, he wolde not ſo plainlie
haue tearmed them, but in ſome place he wolde haue called them figures.
But ſo he calleth them not in anie place, but allwaies by the propre names of bodie and bloode. Wherfor to ende and conclude with all theſe
Fathers thus expownding S. Paule, ther ys (as he ment) the verie bodie
and bloode.

THE THREE AND TWENTETH CHAP. BEGIN-
nith the expoſition of this text: Quoniam vnus
panis &c:

In the text of S. Paule yt foloweth : *Quoniam vnus panis & vnum*
corpus multi ſumus, omnes, qui ex eodem pane, et eodē calice participamus.
By cauſe that though we be manie : yet we are one bread and
C   and one bodie, in aſmoche as we all are partakers of one bread
and of one cuppe. Foraſmoche as this text dependeth vpon the
other nowe laſt expownded, and ys inferred as a expoſition of that, that the
Apoſtle ſpake of ther, namely of owre participacion and communion with
Chryſt, and with our ſelues, and ſpeaketh of the ſame bread and the ſame
cuppe, that ys ſpoken of ther: Therfor yt ys manifeſt that yt muſt haue the
ſame vnderſtanding, as yt had, I meen, that the bread and the cuppe be not
taken for bare figures of the bodie and bloode of Chryſt, but for the things
them ſelues, the very bodie and bloode. And wher the Apoſtle ſpeaketh of
our communion with Chryſt, yt ys to be noted that we haue a double com
munion with him. One ys ſpirituall, whiche we come vnto in baptiſme
through the worke of the holie Goſt. of the whiche S. Paule ſpeaketh to
the Corinthians, ſaing: *In vno ſpiritu omnes nos in vnum corpus baptizati ſumus, ſiue*
Iudæi, ſiue gentiles, ſiue ſerui, ſiue liberi. By one ſpiritt are we baptiſed to make one
bodie, whether we be Iewes, or gentiles, whether we be bonde or free. And
again to the Romans : *Multi vnum corpus ſumus in Chriſto. ſinguli autem alter alterius*
D   *membra,* We being manie, are one bodie in Chryſt, and euery man emonge
vs, one and others membres.

    And other corporall: whiche we come vnto by the receipt of his bodie
and bloode in the Sacrament, of whiche S. Paule ſpeaketh here. By the firſt

we

An argu-
mēt grown
ded on S.
Paule to
auouche
the reall
preſence:

1. Cor. 16.

Communiõ
with Chriſt
ys t wo wa-
ies.

1. Cor. 12.

Rom. 12.

we are admitted, and as yt were gaffed into the misticall bodie of Chryst, to **E**
be membres of the same: by the other we are nourished as with an necessarie foode to growe and to waxe strong and to be made lustie membres of the same bodie, which thing cometh better to passe, for that by this receipt we are incorporated to Chrystes bodie, and receaue with all manie goodlie benefittes of spirituall nutriment, and spirituall health. For as manie meates are both nutritiue, and also holsome, according to the naturall qualities of the same, yf the partie that receaueth them be well disposed in bodie, and not troubled with deseases, by reason of yll humours: So the foode of Chrystes bodie and bloode, ys bothe nutritiue and holsome, according to the good qualities of mercie, grace, and goodnesse, yf the receauour be not euell disposed by the reason of viciouse humours, But in this these two foodes do differ. For the earthlie foode being receaued ys incorporated to the receauer, and made one with him. But this heauenly foode being duely receaued doth incorporate vs to yt: *Nec tu me mutabis in te sicut cibum carnis tuæ: sed tu mutaberis in me.* Neither shalt thow chaunge me into thee, as a me at of thy bodie: but thowe shalt be chaunged into me.

As ther ys then a spirituall communion, wher by we are ioined to Christ, **F**
and spiritually made one with him: so ys ther a corporall communion, by the whiche we are ioined to Chryst, and corporallie made one with him. Yf yt were not so, why then hath the Apostle taught vs the communion that we haue with Chryst by the holie gost, and Baptisme, and nowe teacheth vs of an other communion whiche we haue with Chryst, by the receipt of his bodie and bloode? Yf they will saie that yt ys no other neither of anie other effect, then the other by Baptisme and the holy goste: then we maie saie to them, that then yt ys vainly instituted, for thar yt ys superfluouse, seing that this communion ys doen before and ys sufficient for the wholl life of man. But that maie not be saied. for God woorketh nothing in vain. Wherfor seing that S. Paule doth saie that all we, that do eate of that one bread, and drinke of that one cuppe be made one bread and one bodie, ther ys an other vnion in the whiche we are ioined all together, than yt, that we were ioined in be fore by faith, and Baptisme.

We haue a spirituall communion with Chryste by baptisme and a corporall by the Sacr. of his bodie and blood.

For yt ys to be thought that none cometh to receaue this Sacrament, but **G**
soche as be perfect in faith ad be baptised. Wherfore in the primitiue church, and so to the time of S. Augusting, the *Cathecumeni*, that ys, the younge scholers or learners of faith, were not suffred to receaue this Sacrament, but in stead therof they receaued other bread blessed, as our people now doe, whe they doe not communicate, they receaue holie bread. And the being baptised, and hauing faith, the Aduersarie will not denie, but that they be membres of Chrystes misticall bodie, and haue that spirituall communion that ys doen by faith. Wherfor (as before ys saied) either by the receipt of the bodie and blood of Chryst, they come into an other communio: or ells they receaue that that they had before. But here the Reader ys to be aduertised, that as they that receaue the spirituall vnion by Baptisme, receaue yt not but with codicion: So none can receaue this corporall vnio to Chryste, but with codicion. The Sacramentes be receaued of manie, but not profitablie, as touching the finall effect to all that receaue, but to some.

Holie bread receaued instead of the B. Sacrament.

Chryst hath died not onely for our sinnes, but for the sinnes of all the **H**
worlde, yet all atteign not remission of sinnes, whiche ys the effecte of the same death: And as God geuing vs Chryst, gaue vs all thinges with him: yet all receaue not all thinges: Euen so though by the receipt of Chrystes bodie

in

A in the Sacrament,we be as yt ys faied vnited and incorporated toChryft,yet not all:for the benefittes which God geueth vnto vs,manie of them haue cõ dicions annexed,as the benefittes before recited haue . For as touching re- miſsion of finnes all they ſhall haue yt,that will obſerue the condicion decla red by S.Iohn:*Si ambulauerimus in luce,ſicut & ipſe eſt in luce,ſocietatem habemus ad-* *inuicem,& ſanguis Ieſu Chriſti filii eius emundat nos ab omni peccato.* Yf we ſhall walke in light,as he alſo ys in light,we haue felowſhippe together,and the bloode of Ieſus Chryft the Sonne of him clenſeth vs from all finne . Eternall life ys geuen to vs by Chryft,but ther ys a condicion annexed.*Si vis ad vitam ingre-* *di ſerua mandata.*Yf thowe wilt entre into life kepe the commaundementes. Vnitie with Chryft,as that Chryft ſhall dwell in them,and they in him, that do eate the fleſh of Chryft,and drinke his bloode,ys promiſed to them that ſo doe,but not without a condicion,that ys,that they doe eate yt woorthi- lie.Iudas eate the fleſh of Chryft,and dranke his bloode,as hereafter ſhall be ſhewed.But yet he obteined not the promiſſe,he enioied not the effecte,for not Chryft,but Sathan abidde in him as the Goſpell teſtifieth. Wherfore S.

1.Ioan.1.

B Paule faied not,that yowe all be one bread,and one bodie,but manie.For in dede as manie as ſhall woorthilie receaue that one bread,and drinke of that one cuppe,all they ſhall be one bread,and one bodie,both with Chryft,and within themſelues.But the euell receauers not ſo.

    This alſo ys not to be ouerpaſſed,that ſainct Paule faieth, that we all eate of one bread,and drinke of one cuppe. Which in my iudgement proueth very moche,that he tooke not this bread for bare materiall bread(as the Ad uerſarie doth)for then yt were not true. For all do not eate of one bread. For the grekes eate leauened bread, and the latines fine and vnleauened bread. In the catholique Church ys geuen to euerie communicant a ſon- drie bread. In the ſciſmaticall church they haue not throughout all one bread,but in euery conuenticle a ſondrie bread , and ſomtime in the ſame conuenticle diuerſe breades . For yt were a meruailouſe bread that ſhoulde ſuffice them all in all their wicked congregacions. And as before ys noted,their bread hath no ſoche vertue,as ſainct Paule dothe attribute vnto this bread,and this cuppe,which ys to make vs one bodie with Chriſt.

C Wherfore yt can haue no other vnderſtanding but that the bread which S. Paule ſpeaketh of ys no materiall bread , but yt ys the heauenly bread of Chryſtes bodie,which being but one ys eaten of euery faithfull , and ſuffi- ceth for all.For he ys not ſo receaued in one aultar,that he ys not , nor can not be in an other.But(as ſainct Bernarde faieth ſpeaking to Chryft in the Sacrament)*vnius horæ momento,ab ortu ſolis,vſque ad occaſum,ab aquilone vſque ad* *auſtrum,præſto es omnibus,vnus in multis, idem in diuerſis locis.* In the moment of one howre from the riſing of the Sunne to the going downe of the ſame, from the North to the Sowthe thowe art at hande,which arte one in manie places,and the very ſame in diuerſe places.

In ſermone *De cana.*

    For (as Chryſoſtome faieth) *Quoniam in multis locis offertur , multi ſunt Chriſti?* *Nequaquam.Sed vnus vbique eſt Chriſtus,& hic plenus exiſtens,& illic plenus, vnũ cor-* *pus.*For that Chryft ys offered in many places,be ther many Chryſtes ? not ſo,but euery wher one Chryft,being full here,and full ther , all one bodie. So that wher S.Paule faieth,that they are one bodie , and one bread , that

In deci . 1. *Corn.hom.* *17.*

D doth partake of that ſame one bread,and that ſame one cuppe,yt ys not very fied,nor can be verified of anie other,but of Chryft the true bread , whiche (as ys ſaied)being one bodie , one Chryft , ys euerie where full Chryſte,

here full,and ther full,of the whiche one all doo partake,and so by that one   **E**
they all are made one,I meen as manie as do duelie receaue yt,as ys before
saied.For by the receipt of that one bodie,they growe to be onebodie,both
with the bodie,that ys receaued,and also among themselues.

THE FOVR AND TVENTETH CHAP. PRO-

ceadeth vpon the same text by Chrysostom,and
S.Augustine.

AS among philosophers yt ys vnseemlie to auouche anie thing
withoute reason:so among diuines speciallie in matters of controuersie,yt ys vnsemelie to auouche anie thing withoute autho
ritie,wherfor to doo that,that to a diuine ys seemlie,and withal
to geue aduertisement to the Proclamer, who in his sermon
powreth oute manie of his hereticall deuises in matter of controuersie with
oute authoritie,although,I haue not hitherto without authoritie , but with   **F**
authoritie expownded this text of S.Paule yet returning to my former order heretofore in other scripturs vsed,I will proue the same exposition to be
good,by farder authoritie of the fathers,coopled together oute of the latine
and greke church.In which processe I will beginne with Chrysostome,who
thus expowndeth the same text of S.Paule:*Quoniam vnus panis,& vnum cor-*
pus multi sumus.Quid enim appello,inquit, communicationem? Idem ipsum corpus sumus.
Quid nam est panis?Corpus Christi. Quid autem fiunt,qui accipiunt? Corpus Christi , non
multa,sed vnum corpus.Nam quemadmodum panis ex multis grauis vnitur,vt minime gra
na appareant,sed tamen grana sunt,verùm incerta discretione coniuncta:sic & inuicem &
Christo coniungimur.Non enim ex altero corpore tu, ex altero ille educatur, sed ex eodem
omnes.Ideo subdit:omnes qui de vno pane participamus . For being manie we are
one bread and one bodie.What do I(saieth he) call comunicacion?We are
the very same bodie. What ys the bread?The bodie of Chryst.what be they
made that receaue yt? the body of Chryst, not manie but one bodie. For
as bread ys made one of manie cornes, though they do not appeare cornes,
but yet they be cornes,yet without certen difference ioined together : So   **G**
we both within our selues,and with Chryst are ioined together . For thowe
art not fedde or nourished of one bodie,and he of an other , but all of one
and the selffame.Therfore he addeth : all whiche do partake of one bread.
Thus moch Chrysostome.

    In these woordes ye see the minde of Chrysostome vpon sainct Paule,
and therwith ye maie see the minde of S.Paule himself. For in the first entrie of the exposition Chrysostom moueth not the question in hys owne
Three thin
ges learned
oute of S.
Paule. person,but in the person of sainct Paule. For after this maner he moueth
yt:*What doe I call*(saieth he)*communicacion?*mening sainct Paule, so that , that
ys here spoken , ys after the minde of sainct Paule.
Therfore of sainct Paule we maie here learn three things,as he ys opened of
Chrysostome.The first ys, what ys communicacion . What yt ys we are
taught , for yt ys to be all one bodie.For when S.Paule had saied,ys not the
bread which we break a communicacion of the bodie of our Lorde?And
shewing that yt ys a communicacion,and withall what a communicacion yt   **H**
ys,added:For we being manie eating of one breade , and drinking of one
cuppe,are one bodie and one bread . As though he had saied : we eating
one bodie,are made the same bodie . And thus yt cometh to passe that
                                          Chryso-

A Chryfoftome faieth,that cōmunicacion,ys,we be all one bodie.

The fecond thing,what that ys,by the eating wherof we are made one bodie. Chryfoftom expownding S. Paule asketh this queftion : *What ys the bread that S. Paule here fpeaketh of.*He aunfwereth that yt ys the bodie of Chryft Note then,Chryftian Reader,that by Chryfoftom yt ys euident that S. Paul here by the bread ment not materiall bread, but the true bread , the verie bodie of Chryfte,which ys euen that one bread,of the whiche though we be manie,we maie all receaue,and by yt being one,we all maie be made one both with yt,and within owre felues,whiche can not be doen by materiall bread.

And here this ys not to be ouerpaffed,that fome one either of malice , or ignorance hath corrupted and falfefied Chryfoftome in this place,that wher in the greke Chryfoftom asketh:*what ys the bread* he altered yt in tranflation faing:*what dothe the bread fignifie?*For the triall of this I haue not onelie feen diuerfe bookes in the which this queftion ys thus corrupted,but other alfo

B in whiche yt ys corrected,and befides I haue conferred with diuerfe well learned in the greke toung,whofe greke bookes being feen yt was in them all fownde thus:*what ys the bread?*and not *what fignifieth the bread?*Soche ys the falfhead of Sathan and his Angells to corrupt the doctours to maintein their herefie.And yet yf yt might fo haue ben iuggled in,the deuell had ben begiled.For yt coulde not beare the fenfe that S. Paule fhoulde aske what materiall bread did fignifie,but what the woord bread did in that place fig-nifie.Wherunto when S. Paules aunfwer had ben added that that woorde bread did fignifie the bodie of Chryfte had yt not made againft Sathan ftil? But nowe that the trueth of the queftion ys:what ys the bread?and the aun fwer ys,that yt ys the bodie of Chryfte,ys not Sathan nowe laied flatt vpon his backe , and Chryftes prefence in the holie Sacrament moft plainlie taught,fo plainlie,that the Proclamer,if he will open his eies,maie here fee a plain place to induce him into the plain trueth,whiche trueth Chryfoftom in that,that foloweth in this expofition dothe verie clerelie commende and

C fetfurth?

Thus yt foloweth there *Non enim fimpliciter corpus fuum tradidit fed cùm prior carnis natura,à terra formata,à peccato mortalis facta,à vita deferta effet,aliam(vt ita di-cam)maßam,& fermentum induxit hoc eft carnem fuam,natura quidem eandem, verùm à peccato liberam,& vitæ plenam,quam omnibus tribuit,vt participes fierent , vt ea nu-triti,& priore abiecta,quæ mortua erat,per hanc menfam viuentem , & immortalem, comifceremur.*He hath not fimplie deliuered his bodie,but wher the firft natu-re of the flefh,being formed of the earth,was by finne made mortall, and of life forfaken,he brought in (as I might faie) an other lumpe and leauen, that ys,his flefh,in nature the fame,but free from finne,and full of life,which he hath geuen to all,that they maie be made partakers , that being nourif-hed with yt,and the firft,whiche was dead caft awaie, by this liuinge and immortall table,we fhoulde be mixed together.Thus Chryfoftom.

Doeft thowe not fee here Reader what bread yt ys that we be partakers of,by the which we be mixed together,to be this one bodie ? Chryfoftome hath plainly taught that yt ys the flefh of Chryft in nature all one with our flefh,but that yt ys free from finne,ād full of life,which Chryft hath brought

D in an geueth to vs to the intent we fhoulde be partakers of yt.And that ther fhould remaln in this matter nothing doubtfull,but all fcruple taken awaie, as that this flefh fpoken of here fhoulde not be drawen to the flefh v-pon the croffe,or to the fpirituall flefh , or figuratiue flefh , or anie foche

Ddd ii　　　　　other

Chryfoftō corrupted by the trāf latour.

Chryftes flesh of one nature with our,but free frō finne but ful of life ys ming led with vs to deliuer vs frō finne ād to make vs immor-tall. The immor tall table ys the immor-tal foode of the table, that ys Chri ctes flesh wher with we are nou rished to immortali-tie.

other:he doth by expreſſe woordes declare,that he ſpeaketh of the fleſh of **E**
Chryſt on the table.For(ſaieth he)he hath geuen vs thys fleſh,that webeing
nouriſhed with yt,by this liuing and immortall table we ſhoulde be mixed
together.Ther ys none(I thinke)ſo infenſate,or withoute vnderſtanding
but he knoweth what Chryſoſtom meneth by the table. He meeneth the
meat of the table.Nowe this meat of the table,ys not(as the Aduerſarie dreameth)a peice of dead bread,but yt ys a liuing,and an immortall meat (*as*
Chryſoſtome termeth yt)whiche ys the fleſh of Chryſt, of whiche he ſpake before,ſaing,that yt was free from ſinne, and full of life.   Calling yt then
before full of life,and here liuing and immortall , there ſaing, that of yt
we are made partakers,and here by yt,we are mixed together : ther that by
yt we are nouriſhed, and here calling yt the meat of the table,argueth beſides the continuance of the ſentence (which proueth the ſame)that he ſpake
of one thing,whiche ys the fleſh of Chryſt,which ys on the table,by the nutriment of which we are partakers of that one bread,and ſo be made one bo
die and one bread.And nowe reader,that thowe haueſt hearde Chryſoſtome ſo plainlie expownding ſainct Paule,we will leaue him and heare ſainct **F**
Auguſtine,for he alſo geueth an vnderſtanding of this text on this wiſe:
Quia Chriſtus paſſus eſt pro nobis,cōmendauit nobis in iſto ſacramento corpus & ſan-
guinem ſuum. Quod etiam fecit & nos ipſos. Nam & nos ipſius corpus facti ſumus,
& per miſericordiam ipſius quod accipimus nos ſumus . Bicauſe Chryſt hath ſuffred
for vs he commended vnto vs in this Sacrament his bodie and bloode,

Auguſt.
feria.2.
Paſch
Chryſt
hath cōm̄-
ded to vs
his bodie
and blood
in the Sacr.

whiche alſo he hath made our ſelues. For we alſo are made his bodie , and
by his mercie thatwe receaue we be.In thisſhort ſaing he hathdeclared both
the mean by the which we are made the bodie of Chryſt,and that we be the
bodie of Chryſt.Firſt he openeth the mean ſaing,that bicauſe Chryſt hath
ſuffred for vs,he hath commended vnto vs in this Sacrament his bodie and
bloode. Note the ſpeache of ſainct Auguſtin,he ſaieth not that Chryſt hath
commended vnto vs,bicauſe he hath ſuffred for vs, a figure for a memoriall
of that his paſſion:but he ſaieth by plain woqrdes,*that Chryſt commended to vs*
his bodie and bloode.And applieng the cauſe to the effecte afterwarde he ſaieth:
By his mercie we be that we receaue. Which in plain ſpeache ys, that bicauſe we
receaue the bodie of Chryſte, therfore by his mercie we be the bodie of **G**
Chryſt.   And to moue vs to abide in this bodie of Chryſt,he proceadeth:
Dic mihi,quid eſt,ex quo viuis? Spiritus tuus viuit de corpore tuo,an corpus ex ſpiritu tuo?
Reſpondet omnis qui viuit:Ex ſpiritu viuo. Qui autem hoc non poteſt reſpondere , neſcio
an viuat. Quid reſpondet omnis qui viuit:Corpus vtique meum viuit de ſpiritu meo.
Vis ergo viuere et de ſpiritu Chriſti ? In corpore eſto Chriſti. Nunquid enim corpus
meum viuit de ſpiritu tuo?Meum viuit de ſpiritu meo,et tuum de ſpiritu tuo. Non po-
teſt viuere corpus Chriſti niſi de ſpiritu Chriſti: Inde eſt quod exponens Apoſtolus Paulus
hunc panem,vnus panis(inquit)vnum corpus ſumus. Tell me , what ys that of the
which thow liueſt? dothe thie ſpiritt liue by thie bodie, or thie bodie by the
ſpiritt?Euerie one that liueth anſwereth:I liue by my ſpiritte. He that can
not this anſwere,I can not tell whether he liueth.what doth euerie one anſwere that liueth?My bodie liueth by my ſpirit.Wilt thow alſo liue by the
Spiritt of Chryſt?Be in the bodie of Chryſt.For doth my bodie liue by thie
ſpiritte? My bodie liueth of my ſpiritt,ād thy bodie of thie ſpiritt.The bodie
of Chryſt can not liue but by the Spiritte of Chryſt . Therfore yt ys
that the Apoſtle Paule expownding vnto vs this bread , ſaieth : we   **H**
being manie are one bread,and one bodie.Thus ſainct Auguſtine.In whom
as we haue goodlie inſtruction for our faith : ſo we haue the like for our
                                                                conuer-

A conuerſacion. But not to be tedioufe to the reader, S. Auguſtin ſhall be left withoute note here vnto him to his farder cōſideracion of this his ſaing, for that by yt that ys ſaied, yt ys eaſie to perceaue the wholl minde of him in this matter.

THE FIVE AND TWENTETH CHAPITER

proceadeth vpon the ſame text by Damaſcen and Haymo.

S the Aduerſarie vſeth all the craft ſubtletie and falſhead that he can, to deceaue the ſimple, and to abduce him, to lead him awaie and to carie him a farre from the flocke and folde of Chry ſte to the entent he ſhall not deſire to come home again, and yf he do: yet for the diſtance, he ſhall not finde the waie to come, as a ſhepe, if he be caried but a litle waie from the flocke, that he went in, he

B will make great ſhift to return to yt again: if he be caried farre of, he neither deſiereth neither for his ſimplicitie can find the waie to return, therfore the Aduerſarie (Iſaie) cōtenteth not himſelf to bring the ſimple a litle oute of the waie from the faith into one onelie erroure or hereſie: but he will carie and lead him a great waie out of the right waie, by manie ſteppes, and manie paſſes, that ys into manie errours and hereſies. For ſeldome hath yt ben ſeen, that the Deuell bringeth a man into one onelie hereſie, but into Diuerſe, wherwith that common enemie oftentimes will ſo delight him, that he ſhall haue no deſire to retnrn home again, or ells through plain ſimplicitie, not perceauing the falſhead of hereſie, or by malice blinded, he ſhall be as yt were plainlie ignorant, not able to finde the waie to return: but ſo ſhall remain in a ſtraung place, and then (which ys the woorſt of all) he ſhall thinke himſelf at home, when he ys fardeſt of. Therfore, I ſaie, ſeing the Aduerſarie hath ſo moch falſhead to bring men to ſoch great blindneſſe, in to ſo great calamitie and miſerie of their ſoules, yt ys our parte to ſeke all the helpe of trueth to reduce them that be ſtraied, and to ſtaie them that be at home, that

C they periſh not in that lamentable daunger, neither ſuffre them to come to yt. Wherfore although this trueth of our naturall, and corporall commu- nion with Chryſt be allreadie ſufficiently proued, and teſtified: yet that the reader ſhall perceaue that yt ys not a doubtfull matter, and teſtified of a few, but a certen matter of aſſured trueth, and generallie receaued, and teſtified of manie: we ſhal go forwarde in producing of mo, and of theſe Damaſcen ſhall be the firſt, who ſaieth thus.

Quia ex vno pane participamus omnes, vnum corpus Chriſti, & vnus ſanguis, & inui- cem membra efficimur, concorporati Chriſto exiſtentes. Omni igitur virtute obſeruemus, ne participemus participatione hæreticorum, neque tribuamus. Nolite enim ſancta dare canibus, inquit Dominus noſter, neque ſeminare margaritas veſtras ante porcos, vt non participes er- roris, & malæ fidei eorum efficiamur, atque condemnationis. Si enim omnino vnio eſt ad Chriſtum, & ad inuicem: omnino & omnibus comparticipantibus nobis ſecundùm electio- nem vnimur. Nam ex electione vnio ipſa fit, non ſine noſtra ſententia, ac deliberatione. Om- nes enim vnum corpus ſumus, quoniam ex vno pane participamus, &c. Bcauſe we do all partake of one bread, we are made one bodie of Chryſt, and one blood,

D and membres one of an other, being cōcorporated vnto Chryſt. Let vs ther- fore obſerue with all our powre, that we partake not with the partaking of heretikes, neither that we geue vnto thē. For our Lord ſaieth *Geue not the holie thinges to dogges, neither ſowe precioufe ſtones before hogges,* that we be not partakers

The Ad- uerſarie lea deth the ſimple into manie er- rours that holden by them he ſhall not find the wa ie home again.

Damaſcē. li.4.ca.14.

Ddd iii their

their errour,and euell faith and condemnacion.For if the vnion be whollie E
to Chryſt,and whollie one to an other,we be alſo vnited to al that after our
election be comparteners with vs.For that vnion ys doen by election, not
without oure ſentence and deliberacion. For we all are one bodie,bi-
cauſe we partake of one bread,as the Apoſtle of God ſaieth : Thus farre
Damaſcen.

 Although occaſion be here geuen to note manie thinges : yet for that I
will not trooble the reader with mo notes then be neceſſarilie appertinent:
I will here make but onely two notes.The firſt ys that this authour, according to the text of ſainct Paules epiſtle,ſaieth:that bicauſe we partake of one
bread,we are one bodie of Chryſt.Wherin the Aduerſarie ſtill ys impugned.
For although this authour with all good catholique men confeſſeth,that we
be vnited to Chryſt by faith:yet with them alſo he affirmeth that we be neuertheleſſe vnited to Chryſt by a corporall vnion,for that we do partake his
very bodie and blood.Whiche he noteth when he ſaieth that we be concor
porated vnto Chryſt.Which concorporacion he doth not attribute to faith, F
but to the partaking of that one bread,although by faith we are ſpirituallie

Damaſcē.
li.4.ca.13.

vnited to Chryſt.

 Of which cōcorporacions,this authour maketh a plain diſtinction in an
other place ſaing:Noṅ ſimpliciter,& fortuito ad orientem adoramus,ſed quia ex viſibili,& inuiſibili,id eſt,intellectuali & ſenſibili conflati ſumus natura,duplicem adoratiōe
conditōri noſtro offerimus,vt & mente pſallimus,& corporalibus labiis:& baptiẓamur

We are vni
ted to our
Lord two
waies.

aquā & ſpiritu:& dupliciter Domino vnimur,myſteriis participantes,& gratia ſpiritus.
Not ſimplie,and by chaunce we do adore vnto the eaſt:But bicauſe we are
made of a viſible and inuiſible,that ys to ſaie,of an intellectuall and ſenſible
nature,we offre vnto our maker a dooble adoracion, as we do both with
minde and corporall lippes ſing:and are baptiſed both with water and ſpi-
rit:and to maner of waies we are vnited vnto our Lorde, partaking of the
myſteries,and by the grace of the ſpiritt.Thus Damaſcen.

 Do ye not ſee that we are two waies vnited to our Lorde ? Are we not
vnited to him by the participacion of the myſteries(which myſteries be the
Sacramentes of Chryſtes bodie and Chryſtes bloode)and by the grace of G
the ſpritte?This doth this authour plainlie teache. Wherfore conſider hys
grownde,that we be made of a viſible and inuiſible nature and ſhould therfore by bothe theſe partes honour God.And ſo by means conuenient both
theſe partes ſhoulde be vnited to God,the inuiſible parte by grace of the ho
lie Goſt,as by faith and charitie:the viſible parte by that that ys of like natu-

In.6. Ioan.
ca.14.

re,that ys by the bodie and blood of Chryſt.

 For as S.Cyrill ſaieth:Oportuit enim certè,vt non ſolùm anima per ſpiritum ſanctum in beatam vitam aſcenderet,verumetiam vt rude,atque terreſtre hoc corpus cognato,
ſibi guſtu,tactu,& cibo ad immortalitatem reduceretur.Truelie yt behoued,that not
onelie the ſoule by the holie Goſt ſhould aſcende into the bleſſed life : But
that alſo this rude and earthlie bodie with a taſte,touching,and meat of hys

Both bodie
and ſoule of
man relei-
ued by Chri
ſte,and ho-
we yt ys
doen.

nature,ſhould be reduced to immortalitie.Thus S.Cyrill.

 As both the viſible,and inuiſible, the mortall and immortall partes of
man had need of releif, and bothe theſe moſt conuenientlie might be releiued by his like in nature,therfore Chryſte,hauing the likes of theſe two
in his perſon,that ys to ſaie,the immortall nature of the Godhead and the H
mortall nature of man(which mortall nature being ſtill the ſame nature,
was chaunged in his condicion,and by the immortall Godhead was made
alſo immortall)was by theſe two his partes able to amende the

imper-

A imperfection of our two partes. For wher the foule had infirmitie by finne, he was able as God to faie : *Remittuntur tibi peccata tua*. Thy finnes be forgeuen thee.

By this parte wher the foule was fpoiled of fpirituall giftes, and impouerifhed for lacke of the fame, he was able to enriche her, and adorne her, with the firft and cheifeft giftes, as with faith, hope, and charitie.

As touching our other parte, yt receaued great and fingular benefittes by the like parte of Chryft, I mean by his bodie. For by his bodie be cured manie difeafes, he raifed the dead, and wrought great wooders, by his bodie *Jn 6. Joon ca.14.* now immortall he maketh our mortall bodies duely receauing the fame, to come, at the time by him affigned, to immortalitie, as S. Cyrill faieth : *Non verbo folùm, fed & tactu mortuos excitabat, vt oftenderet corpus quoque fuum viuifica re poffe. Quod fi folo tactu fuo corrupta redintegrantur, quomodò non viuemus, qui carnem illam & guftamus, & manducamus? Reformabit enim omnino ad immortalitatem fuam,*

B *participes fui. Ne velis iudaicé (quomodò) quærere, fed recordare quamuis aqua naturaliter frigidor fit: aduentu tamen ignis frigiditatis fuæ oblita æftuat.* He did not by his woorde onelie allwaies raife the dead: but alfo with his touching, that he might declare that his bodie alfo was able to quicken or geue life Yf then by his onely touching the corrupted thinges are reftored: howe fhall not we liue whiche do tafte and eate that flefh? He fhall whollie reforme to his immortalitie, foche as be partakers of him. Neither afke thowe Iuefhlie (*howe*) but remébre that although the water be naturallie colde, yet by the coming to of fire, forgetting her coldneffe yt waxeth hote. Thus S. Cyrill. So then according as *Damafen* faied, as to our duetie yt apperteineth to honour God with the two partes of our compownded bodie, both fpirituallie, and corporallie: So God of his mercie helpeth bothe thefe partes, geuinge to eche of them giftes vniting vs fpirituallie to him by faith and charitie, and corporallie by his bodie and bloode receaued in the Sacrament, By the which (as S. Cyrill hath faied) he will reforme this mortall bodie of oure to his immortalitie.

C Therfore, Reader, looke to thie felf, and be not feduced withe the herefie of the Aduerfarie. Weigh well the fainges of the holie and auncient Fathers, and for lacke of faith leefe not thefe goodly giftes of excellencie, Yt ys an excellent thing to be ioned to God and Chryfte, and to be as one with him. Which thowe fhalt be if thowe haueft a perfight faith, and fo receaue that bleffed bodie of Chryft.

But yt ys time that I fhewe the feconde note in the faing of *Damafcen*. The feconde note ys his admonition that we beware with all diligence that we do not communicate with heretiques. neither miniftre the Sacrament vnto them, For if we do we partake of their euell faith and condemnacion. This admonicion, as yt ys good: fo ys yt neceffarie to be kept. For yt ys agreable to the fcriptures. For as this place of S. Paule to the Corinthians, doth forbidde them, that they fhoulde not be partakers with Idolaters in their *Idolathites*, for then they fhoulde entre into felowfhippe with Deuells: fo doth yt forbidd vs to be partakers with heretiques. For if we do we entre into felowfhippe with them, we feem to confent to their wicked herefie, and fo to be *2 Ioan.* partakers of the fame, wherfor S. Iohn gaue ftreict charge, faing: *Si quis venit ad*

D *vos, & hanc doctrinam non adfert, nolite eum recipere in domum, nec aue ei dixeritis:* Yf any man come vnto yowe, and bring not this learning, receaue him not to houfe, neither bidde him God fpede.

So farre wide was yt frõ the minde of the Apoftle that we fhoulde entre
　　　　　　　　　Ddd iiii　　　　　　　into

Communiõ aught not to be had with hereti ques.

into the houſe of God with heretiqnes, and their to ioin with them in the   E
partaking of ſacramentes, that he wolde that we ſhoulde not receaue them
into our houſe, neither as moche as to bidde them God ſpede. And ſhewing
the cauſe of this his commaundement ſaieth: *For he that biddeth him God ſpede*
ys partaker of his euell dede: And to the entent this his admonicion ſhoulde be
the better regarded, and the daunger of the breach therof well knowen to
them, and feared, he concludeth thus: *Beholde I haue tolde yowe before, that ye*
ſhoulde not be aſhamed in the daie of our Lorde., In this ſaing of S. Iohn yt ys eaſie
to perceaue that yt ys daungerouſe to ioin with heretiques, and ſpeciallie in
the communion of ſacracmentes. For if we do, we ſhall be confownded in
the daie of our Lorde.

2 Teſſalo 3.

Yf S. Paule did earneſtly require the *Theſſalonians* and that in the name of
our Lorde Ieſus Chryſte, they ſhoulde with drawe them ſelues from euery
brother that did walke inordinatelie, and not after the tradicion whiche
they had receaued, ſhoulde we not withdrawe our ſelues frō them, which
do not onelie walke inordinately but do with all that in them lieth laboure   F
to ſubuert the wholl order of Chryſtes Churche, and with all violence and
blaſphemie impugn not onelie the tradicions which they haue receaued,
but the Sacramentes and miſteries of the true religion, and the wholl faith
of Chryſt?

1 Cor. 5.

S. Paule willeth that with fornicators, adulterers, dronkers, and idolaters we ſhoulde not aſmoch as eate meate. Therfor with the other yt ys withoute doubte, that we ſhoulde haue no felowſhippe, nor medle with them,
and ſpeciallie in the communion of ſacramentes. And as yt ys not lauſull for
the true chryſtian to communicate with them in the ſacramentes of the catholique Churche: no more ys yt lauſull for him to communitate with anie
in the newe forged ſacramentes of the congregacion of heretiques, for like
perill enſeweth vpon bothe.

Heretiques
how, they
muſt be
auoided.

But let not the reader take me that I meen that they, which ignorantlie
not knowing them to be ſoche, incurre anie ſoche daunger, if they communicate with them: But I meen of them who knowing ſoch to be heretiques,
will yet communicate with them. They vndoubtedlie incurre the daunger.   G
For when they be knowen to be ſoche and will not be reformed, S. Paule
willeth them to be auoided. *Hæreticum hominem poſt vnam & alteram admonitio*
nem deuita, ſciens quia ſubuerſus eſt, qui eiuſmodi eſt, & delinquit, cùm ſit proprio iudicio

Tit. 3.

condemnatus. A man that ys an Heretique after the firſt and ſecond admo
nicion auoid, knowing that he who ys ſoch ys peruerted, and ſinneth euē dā
ned by his own iudgement.

Eccl. hiſt.
tripar. li. 4.
ca. 39. & li.
5. ca. 30

According to this rule the people knowing *Macedonius* to be a notable
heretique did both men and women ſo auoid him, that they wolde
not, although enforced with great and cruell tormentes, once communicate with him, as in the Tripartite hiſtorie yt ys more at large
declared.

Can. 45.

In the primitiue Churche this matter was ſo ſtraightlie obſerued, that by
the Canons of the Apoſtles ys was ordeined, that Byſhoppe, preiſt or Deacon, which did but onely praie with heretiques, ſhoulde be putte from the
comunion. if they ſuffred them to do anie thing as clerkes, they ſhoulde for
their ſoche permiſſion be depriued from their office. Although ther be ma-   H
nie hiſtories declaring this auoiding of the communion of heretiques to haue ben moche practiſed: yet I omitte them, for that this maie ſuffice to be
ſpoken as but by occaſion of the note of the woordes of *Damaſcen*, whiche

although

A although breiflie, yet with dumbe scilence I coulde not ouerpasse yt, perceauing the note to be verie necessarie for this time.

In. 10. 1. Cor.

And nowe here shall be place for *Haymo*, whom I haue thought good to ioing with *Damascen* bicause his sentence ys but short, and yet doth plainlie expresse the minde of S. Paule. Thus he saieth, *Diuinitas Verbi, quæ implet cœlum & terram, & omnia quæ in eis sunt, ipsa replet corpus Christi, quod à multis sacerdotibus per vniuersum orbē sanctificatur, & facit vnū corpus Christi esse. Et sicut ille panis et sanguis in corpus Christi transeunt : ita omnes, qui in Ecclesia dignè comedunt illum, vnum corpus Christi sunt, sicut & ipse dicit : Qui manducat carnem meam, & bibit sanguinem meum, in me manet, & ego in eo .* The Godhead of the Sonne which filleth heauen and earth and all that in them ys, that same filleth the bodie of Chryst, the whiche ys sanctified of manie preistes, throughoute all the worlde, and maketh one bodie of Chryst to be. And as that bread and bloode do passe into the bodie of Chryst : euen so all that in the Church do woorthilie eate yt, they are one bodie, as he himself saieth : *He that eateth my flesh, and drinketh my blood, dwelleth in me and I in him'.* Thus moche *Haymo.*

The God head filleth the bodie of Chryste, which ys sanctified of the preist.

B Do ye not in these fewe lines see these two thinges, that ys, that in the Sacrament ys the verie bodie of Chryst and his verie blood: and also that all they which do woorthilie receaue the same, that they are one bodie of Chryst? As concerning the first, yt ys woorthie of note to see howe he doth settfurth the excellencie of the Sacrament, whiche I wish the reader more diligentlie to obserue, that the wickednesse of the Angells of Sathan maie be the better perceaued. Beholde howe litle so euer they esteem yt, or howe barelie so euer they terme yt : yet this authour saieth, that the Godhead of the Sonne of God doth fill the bodie of Chryst that ys sanctified of the preistes through oute all the worlde. So that he doth not take yt for a bare peice of breade, neither for the bodie of Chryst in consideracion of his humanitie onely, but as the bodie of Chryst vnited to the Godhead in vnitie of person, ād so of Chryst perfectly God and mā. And this ys the excellencie of the Sacrament in dede, howe barelie soeuer they sett yt furth.

The excellēcie of the blessed Sacrament.

And if they will reiect this authour so sainge, by cause he was (as some ac compt) within the compasse of these thousand yeares : In dede if he were not a full thousand years agone, he ys verie neer . But who geueth this wicked generacion authoritie to reiecte him nowe at their pleasure, whom the churche hath so long approued and receaued ? And what saieth he that the holie elders before a thousande years saie not ? As touching that he saieth, that God ys in the Sacrament what ys he of the elders that treacteth of this misterie and saieth yt not?

C

Haymo his doctrine cōferred with the elder fathers.

Among other Chrysostome most plainly doth saie yt euen vpon this chapiter, in this maner : *Absterge ab omni sorde animam tuam . Præpara mentem tuam ad horum mysteriorum perceptionem, Etenim si puer regius purpura & diademate ornatus tibi ferendus traderetur, nonne omnibus humi abiectis eum susciperes? Verùm nunc cùm non hominis regium puerum, sed vnigenitum Dei filium accipias , Dic queso, no horrescis? & omnium secularium rerum amorem abiicis ?* Make clean thy soule from all filthinesse, prepare thy minde to the receipt of these misteries. For if the kinges childe decked with purple and diademe were deliuered to thee to be born, woldest not thowe, all other thinges cast down on the grownde, receaue him? But nowe when thowe takest not the childe of a king a man, but the onelie begotten Sonne of God, tell me, I praie thee, arte thowe not afearde? and castes awaie the loue of all worldlie thinges?

In deci. 1. Cor. homil. 24.

The onelie begotten Sonne of God ys receaued in the B. Sacr.

D

In this sentence Chrisostome being in exhortacion that men shoulde prepare

pare

pare them felues woorthilie to receaue the bleffed Sacrament, doth he not **E**
by plain woordes tell them, that they receaue the onelie begotten Sonne of
God? S. Cyrill alfo faieth : *Qui Chrifti carnem manducat, vitam habet æternam. Ha-*
cap. 15. in   *bet enim hæc caro Dei Verbum quod naturaliter vita eft.* He that eateth the flefh of
6.Ioan.   Chryft, hath euerlafting life. For this flefh hath the Sonne of God, whiche
The flesh of   ys life naturallie. As the fentences of thefe two Fathers be, that the Sacra-
Chryft in   ment conteineth and hath the bodie of Chryft, and the Godhead alfo, and
the Sacr.   fo verie Chryft God and man : fo ys the concorde fentence of all the reft of
hath the Sô   the holie auncient fathers. But to fhewe that *Haymo* ys agreable to the catho
ne of God   lique and auncient faith, thefe two maie fuffice.
ioined to yt

    Nowe yt were a meruailoufe kinde or maner of teaching, if thefe fathers
ment, that in the Sacrament were no prefence, but that yt ys a bare fign or fi
gure, that they wolde teache that yt ys the verie onelie begotten Sonne of
God, as Chryfoftom doeth. And that yt ys the flefh of God, that hath the
Godhead ioined to yt (as S. Cyrill faieh) and neuer as moche as once to te
ache that yt ys not Chryft in dede, or onely a figure of him. Can anie man **F**
whofe head and iudgement the madde fpiritt hath not infected and corrupted, thinke, that thefe being reputed holie, vertueoufe, and larned men
wolde allwaies by thefe tearmes fo haue taught, and the trueth to be clear,
the côtrary by the negatiue? wolde they allwaies haue faied: yt ys the bodie
of God, yt ys the bodie of Chryft, yt ys his flefh, yt ys his bloode : if the
trueth were by the negatiue, as the Aduerfarie faieth, that yt ys not fo? Wol
de they haue faied yt ys fo, if the trueth were to faie, yt ys not fo? Yt ys not
to be thought in them. For all their trauaill was to plant Gods trueth in the
heartes of people, and to roote oute errour ãd herefie.wherfore (as ys faied)
obferue howe this authour fetteth furth the excellencie of the Sacrament,
which ys doen agreablie to the fentence of the Fathers, and therfore repute
thowe yt foche a thing, as of foche men yt ys commended vnto thee, and
not as by thefe inuentours of mifcheif yt ys difcommended to thee. This
thing being thus manifefted to thee (Reader) the other note (whiche ys,
that all that do woourthily receaue the Sacrament be one bodie of Chryft) **G.**
can not be obfcure.For as Chryft taking vpon him our flefh and our bloode,
ys one with vs: fo we again receauing his flefh and his blood woorthily, are
one with him. And nowe of the expofitions of thefe two vpon this text, this
maie fuffice.

THE SIX AND TWENTETH CHAP. PROCEA-
deth vpon the fame text by S. Cyrill, and
S .Thomas.

Hough the plentie of teftimonies maie, and (as I am fure) doth
offende the Aduerfarie, (for the more teftimonie againft him,
the more confufion) yett I doubt yt not, but on the other fide
yt dothe afwell delight and alfo comforth the catholique chryftian. Therfor we fhall not refufe to heare S. Cyrill,howe he vn
derftandeth S. Paule in this text. In diuerfe places he maketh mencion of
this text, very plainly declaring howe he vnderftandeth yt, but moft plainly
vpon the xvii. chapter of S. Iohn wher he faieth thus : *Cùm trinitas vnum na-* **H**
Cyril. in 17   *tura fit, confideremus quomodò etiam nos ipfi inter nos corporaliter, & cum Deo fpiritua-*
Ioan.   *liter vnum fumus. Ex Dei patris fubftantia, vnigenitus prodiens, & totum in fua natura*
genitorem poffidens, caro factus fecundùm fcripturam eft, feque ipfum naturæ noftræ, inef-
                                   fabiliter

A *fabiliter coniunxit atque vniuit. Qui enim natura Deus est, verè homo factus est: non Theo-*
phorus, id est, Deum in se per gratiam habens, vt mysterii vim ignorantes contendunt, sed
verus deus simul & homo est. Sic quæ inter se plurimum distant secundùm naturam in vnp
seipso coniunxit, & naturæ diuinæ nos participes effecit. Communicatio enim Spiritus &
(vt ita dicam) mansio, primum in Christo fuit , & ab eo in nos penetrauit, cùm homo fa-
ctus, ipse templum suum proprio spiritu perunxit, atque sanctificauit. Origo ergo & via
qua Spiritu sancto participamus, & Deo vniti sumus, Christi misterium est. Omnes enim
in illo sanctificamur. Vt igitur inter nos & Deum, singulos vniret, quamuis corpore simul
& anima distemus, modum tamen adinuenit consilio Patris, & sapientiæ suæ congruen-
tem. Suo enim corpore credentes per Communionem mysticam benedicens, & secum, & in-
ter nos, vnum corpus effecit. Quis eos qui vnius sancti corporis vnionem in vno Christo vni-
ti sunt, ab hac naturali vnione alienos putabit? Nam si omnes vnum panem manducamus,
vnum omnes corpus efficimur: Diuidi enim , atque seiungi Christus non patitur. idcirco etiā
Ecclesia corpus Christi facta est, & nos singuli membra Christi, secundùm Paulū, vni enim
Christo per corpus suum coniuncti, quoniam in nobis illum, qui est indiuisibilis, accepimus,
ipsi potius, quam nobis membra nostra accommodantur.

B   Forasmoche as the Trinitie in nature ys one, let vs confider howe we our
felues among our felues corporallie, and with God fpirituallie are one. The
onelie begotten coming oute of the fubftance of God the Father, and pof-
feffing in his nature, the wholl Father according to the fcripturs , was made
flefh, and vnfpeakeablie conioined and vnited himfelf to our nature. He that
in nature ys God, ys verilie made man, not hauing God in him by grace (as
they that knowe not the power or vertue of the mifterie do contende) but
he ys very God, and alfo very man. So he hath conioined things to gether
in him felf being one, which in nature betwixt them felues, are very moche
different, and hath made vs partakers of the diuine nature. The communicacion, and (as I might faie) the dwelling of the fpirit was firft in Chryft, and
from him hath comed into vs , when he being made man, throwly anoin- By the B.
ted and fanctified his temple, with his owne fpiritt. The originall therfore, Sacrament
and the waie by the whiche we participate the holie Goft, and be vnited to Chryfte
God ys the mifterie of Chryft· For in him we are all fanctified. Therfor that maketh vs
he might vnite euery one betwixt our felfes and God, (all though both in one bodie
C bodie and foule we differ moch) yet he fownd awaie agreing to the counfell in his bodie
of the Father and his wifdom, for bleffing the beleuers by the mifticall com- and among
munion, he hath made vs in his bodie, one bodie both with him felfe , and our felues
alfo emong our felues. For who fhall thinke them ftraunge from this natu-
turall vniō, whiche by the vnion of one holie bodie are vnited in one Chryft.
For if we do all eate one bread we are all made one bodie. For Chryft fuffreth vs, not to be difioined, and diuided. Therfore the churche of ys made
the bodie of Chryft , and euery one of vs the membres of Chryfte, after S.
Paule, being conioined to one Chryft by his bodie, for that we haue receaued him in vs, who ys indiuifible, our membres be raither appropriated to
him then to vs. Thus farre S. Cyrill.

Ye haue hearde the long faing of this woorthie Father, and yet in my iudgement, as pleafant and profitable, as yt ys long. For he hath made a full
difcourfe of the vnion of vs to God. For plain declaraciō wherof, this if yowe
haue marked maie be perceaued, that firft he hath taught the vnitie of God
the Sonne in nature with God the Father. Secondarelie, the vnion of the
D nature of God, and the nature of man, in the perfon of Chryft , whiche although they were fo different and diftant : yet he ioined them together in
him felf in vnitie of perfon, when he became man . Thirdlie , the vnion of
                                                                                    men

men ſenerall and diſtincte in perſons, which although they be diſtante and **E**
different both in bodie and ſoule : yet he fownde awaie agreing bothe to
the counſell of the Father, and his owne wiſdome alſo, to vnite them by the
vnion of his holie bodie in a naturall vnion, and ſo they become one bodie.
And to proue this he taketh this text of S. Paule, which ys now in had, ſaing.
Nam ſi omnes vnū pane manducamus, vnū omnes corpus efficimur. For yf we all eate of
one breade, we are all made one. So that as he gaue the cauſe of the vnitie
of the Father and the Sonne in Godhead, which was for that they be one in
nature. And as he ſhewed the mea of the vniō of the naturs of God and ma,
whiche was brought to paſſe by the miſterie of the incarnaciō: So he taught
the communion of vs among our ſelues, and with Chryſt to be by that, that
we all receaue that his one bodie. And that ther ſhoulde be no inuention ad
ded to peruert the trueth of his intent and pourpoſe, he ſaieth : that we are
all with his bodie by the miſticall communion made one bodie . By which
his ſaing yt ys moſt euidentlie to be perceiued that he teacheth not onelie **a**
communion by a bare ſacrament, but a communion by the verie bodie of
Chryſt in the ſacrament. Which cōmunion alſo ys not a ſpiritull cōmunion **F**
onelie, but a naturall communion by the receipt of the naturall bodie of
Chryſt, whiche he ſignifieth by plain woordes, when he ſaieth : *Quis enim
eos, qui vnius ſancti corporis vnione, in vno Chriſto vniti ſunt, ab hac naturali vnione alienos putabit?* Who ſhall thinke them ſtraunge from this naturall communi-
on , which by the vnion of one holie bodie are vnited in one Chryſt?

I truſt, I ſhall not nede any more to note vpon this allegacion, but that
by this yt maie well be perceaued howe he vnderſtandeth the text of S. Pau
le to be ſpoken of communion of Chryſtes bodie and bloode, by the
which, beſides the communion ſpirituall, whiche ys by faith and charitie, we
communicate naturallie with Chryſt, by the receipt of his naturall bodie in
the Sacrament.

And that S. Paule ment that we do ſo communicate yt appeareth moſt
euidentlie by this holie father, who reaſoning againſt one that ſaied the con
trarie whoſe hereſie the wittneſſes of iniquitie, the newe maſters of our time, haue neuely ſkoured, and ſett abroade as ſale ware to the worlde , as **G**
they haue a nombre mo, did thus write : *Verùm quoniam nnlla nos ratione, humanitati Chriſti poſſe tribuere iſta, arbitratur, quoniā fide ac dilectione non carne, illi coniungimur: Age pauca de hoc dicamus, ac peruerſe ab eo ſacrarum litterarum ſenſum exponi
oſtendamus . Non tamen negamus nos recta fide , charitateque ſincera Chriſto ſpiritualiter coniungi : ſed nullam nobis coniunctionis rationem ſecundùm carnem cum illo eſſe , id
profectò pernegamus, idque à diuinis ſcripturis omnino alienum eſſe dicimus. Quis enim dubitauit Chriſtum etiam ſic vitem eſſe, nos verò palmites, qui vitam inde nobis acquirimus?
Audi Paulum dicentem, quia omnes vnum corpus ſumus in Chriſto: Quia & ſi multi ſumus, vnum tamen ſumus in eo . Omnes enim vno pane participamus ,* But
foraſmoche as he ſuppoſeth that we by no means can applie this to the
humanitie of Chryſt, for that we are conioined to him by faith and charitie,
and not by fleſh. Go to, let vs ſaie a fewe woordes of this matter , and lett
vs ſhewe the ſenſe of the holie ſcripturs peruerſly to be expownded of him.
Yet for all that we denie not that we be ioined ſpirituallie to Chryſt by
right faith and ſincere charitie, but that we haue no maner of coniunction
with him after the fleſh, that truly, we vtterlie denie, and we ſaie that to be **H**
alltogether contrarie to the diuine ſcriptures . For who hathe doubted
Chryſt alſo ſo to be the vine, and we the braunches, whiche from thence
gett life vnto vs ? Heare Paule ſaing, that we all are one bodie in Chryſt,
　　　　　　　　　　　　　　　　　　　　　　　　　　　　　for

*By receipt of the bo-
die of Chry-
ſte all woor
thie recea-
uers are
made one.*

*Coīmuniō
and vnion
both ſpiri-
tuall and
naturall by
the B. Sa.*

*Cyrill. in 15
Ioan. ca. 6.*

*Coīunction
of vs to
Chryſte by
faith and
charitie ſpi
rituallie,
by his fleſh
naturallie
both auou-
ſhed.*

A for alltho we be manie: yet we are one in him. For we do all partake of one bread.

Do ye not here fee that S. Cyrill bringeth in this text of S. Paule, to proue that we haue not onely a commvnion fpirituall with Chryfte, but alfo a communion after the flefh? What plainer expofition can be defired for the vnderftandinge of the fcripture, then that fenfe in the whiche yt ys alleadged in argument to conuince an herefie ? And if fainct Cyrill did iudge him peruerflie to expownde the fcriptures that faied, that we had no corporall communion with Chryft, but onelie fpirituall, what fhall we faie of the fautours of the like vntrueth? Shall we not faie, that they alfo peruerflie, expownde the fcriptures? And fhall we not woorthilie repute them as corrupters of Godes trueth, and deceauers of his people, whiche fettfurth that to them for a trueth whiche was fo manie hondreth yeares agon reproued as a falfheade, and fo of all catholiques, and good Chryftians holden and eftemed ? no doubte but God will fo declare yt, when

The Procla mer and his felowes fetfurth that for a trueth now, which S.Cyrill re puted an he refie.

B yt fhall pleafe him to take his time to ouerthrowe their building. Endure yt can not. For they haue builded vpon the fandes, and not vpon the rocke. In the mean time let them blufter oute their ftinking doctrine, as yt fhall pleafe God to fuffer them, for the punifhment of our finnes, for the triall of the conftancie of hys faithfull, and for the excercife of their pacience, to the honour and glorie of God. But *veritas vincet.* The trueth fhall ouercome, and *veritas Domini manet in æternum.* The trueth of our Lord abideth for euer. Yt maie be impugned, but ouerthrowen yt can not be. What the trueth ys in this matter, I truft yt maie eafilie be perceaued, and yet ther lacke no wittneffes for the better declaracion of the fame.

S. Thomas a man approued as learned and holie of all the church, hath trauailed in the expofition of the fcriptures, and that not withoute his immortall laude and praife. He ys a woorthie wittneffe in this matter. And for the fuller vnderftanding of him, we will heare his expofition on bothe the textes iointlie as they lie one depending of the other. Thus he

C faieth: *Et panis quem frangimus, id eft, fumptio panis fracti in altari noune participatio corporis Domini eft? faciens nos vnum cum Chrifto? quia fub fpecie panis, fumitur corpus Chrifti. Deinde cum dicit: Quoniam vnus panis, &c. oftendit quod omnes fumus vnum in corpore eius myftico, & tangit duplicem vnitatem : primam incorporationis, qua in Chriftum transformamur, aliam vitæ & fenfus, quam à Chrifto capite accipimus, quafi diceret: Per hoc patet quod vnum fumus cum Chrifto, quoniam vnus panis vnione fidei, fpei, & charitatis, & vnum corpus multi fumus, per fubminiftrationem operum charitatis: Corpus fcilicet illius capitis, qui eft Chriftus. Multi dico: fcilicet omnes qui de vno pane, id eft, corpore Chrifti, & vno calice, id eft, fanguine participamus, digna participatione. fci licet fpirituali, non tantùm facramentali.*

S.Thomas Aqui. in dect.1.cor.

And the bread which we breake, that ys to faie, the receauing of the bread broken on the aultar, ys yt not a partaking of the bodie of our Lorde making vs one with Chryft? For vnder the forme of bread ys receaued the bodie of Chryft. Thé whé he faieth: *For we are one bread, &c.* he fheweth that we are all one in his myfticall bodie, ād he toucheth a double vnitie: The firft ys the vnitie of incorporacion, by the whiche we are transformed into Chryft.

Vnder the forme of bread ys receaued the bodie of our Lorde.

D The other ys of life, ād feeling, which we take of Chryft our head. As who might faie, by this yt ys manifeft that we are one with Chryft. For we being manie are one bread, bi the vnió of faith hope, ād charitie: And one bodie bi

the

the fubminiftracion of the workes of charitie, that ys to faie : the bodie of **E**
that head, which ys Chryft. I faie, manie, that ys to faie, all we that do partake
of one bread, that ys to faie, of the bodie of Chryft, and one cuppe, that ys to
faie of the bloode of Chryft, with a woorthie participacion, not onely facramentall, but alfo fpirituall. Thus moch S. Thomas.

In whofe expofition we finde nothing diffonant from the elders, but in all
consonāt. The elders before alleadged haue expownded the bread and the
cuppe whiche we partake of, to be the bodie and blood of Chryft : fo doth
this S. Thomas. They haue taught that S. Paules minde ys, that by that participacion we are made one bodie with Chryft : and the like teacheth he alfo.
Thus as God ys the God of peace and concorde: fo in his houfe ys agrement
and confent, in the fubftanciall poinctes of our faith and religion : And this
ys a trueth hetherto conftantlie, as yt were, with one mouthe taught that
the bread broken in the aultar or table of Chryft, ys his bodie, and all we
woorthilie receauing yt, are by the fame incorporated to Chryft and made
one bodie with him.   Wherfore, we fhall nowe leaue thefe, and heare **F**
other.

S. Thomas
his doctri-
ne confonāt
to the el-
ders.

THE SEVEN AND TVENTETH CHAPITER
proceadeth vpon the fame text by Euthym. and Hugo.

S God hath builded his church vpon a Mounte to be feen of all
men: fo hath he caufed his trueth to be profeffed of manie, that
yt might be knowen to all men. He fent his Apoftles into all
the woorlde to preach the Gofpell to euery creature. He hath
appointed learned men in euery parte of the worlde to geue
the true vnderftanding of the fame to euery creature. Praifed therfore be his
holie name, that wher now Sathan hath fent his wicked myniftres to corrupt
the trueth of the Gofpell, and to lead vs from the true vnderftanding of the
fame, our mercifull Lorde God hath prouidentlie before prouided foche teachers, by whom we maie not onelie fee the falfhead of the wicked : but alfo **G**
haue fufficient knowledge and teftimonie to rebuke, detect, and conuince
their vntrueth, and their deuelifh fetting furth of the fame, and to kepe vs in
in the right waie that we erre not with them, if we will geue eare to good ād
holfome doctrine. And therfore feing God hath fent foche plentie of good
authours yt were pitie, but that they fhoulde be brought furth, wherby God
in his trueth maie glorified, and his people in the fame edefied.

Euth. in 26
Matth.

Of all thefe that remain firft cometh to hande the learned grecian *Euthy-*
mius, who withoute all darke maner of fpeache openeth to vs the true vnderftanding of S. Paules faing. Thus he writeth: *Quemadmodum panis confortat:*
ita & Chriſti corpus hoc facit, ac magis etiam, corpus & animam fanctificat. Et ſicut vi-
num lætificat: ita & ſanguis Chriſti hoc facit, & inſuper præſidium efficitur. Quodſi de
vno corpore & ſanguine omnes fideles participamus, omnes vnum ſumus per ipſam horum
myſteriorum participationem & in Chriſto omnes, & Chriſtus in omnibus. Qui edit
(inquit) meam carnem, & bibit meum ſanguinem, in me manet, & ego in eo. Verbum ſi-
quidem per aſſumptionem carni vnitum eſt, hæc rurſus caro vnitur nobis per participatio-
nem. As bread doth comforte, fo doeth the bodie of Chryft alfo this, and
more, yt fanctifieth both bodie and foule. And as wine dothe make gladde: **H**
Euen fo the blood of Chryft doth this alfo, and moreouer yt ys made a defence. And if all the faithfull do partake of one bodie and bloode, we are all
one by the fame participacion of the myfteries . For all be in Chryft,

Flesh vni-
ted to the
Sonne of
God by af-
fumption,
the fame v-
nited to vs
by partici-
pacion.

                                                                    and

A and Chryſt in all,*he that eateth* (ſaieth he) *my fleſh, and drinketh my bloode, dwelleth in me and I in him* . For truely the Sonne of God ys vnited to the fleſh by aſſumption. Thys fleſh again ys vnited to vs by participacion . Thus Euthym.

I nede not (as to me yt ſemeth) to ſaie anie thing to the opening of this authours minde. For he ys both plain in himſelf, and alſo plainlie dothe open the minde of ſainct Paule vnto vs. Whoſe ſentence he ſetteth furth in the plain tearmes, and leaueth the tropes. For wher ſainct Paule ſaieth, *that we that eate of one bread, and drinke of one cuppe are one bodie . He ſaieth that we that partake of one bodie and bloode are made one.* So that wher the text calleth yt bread: the expoſitour calleth yt the bodie, and what the text calleth the cuppe, that this authour calleth the bloode . Wherfore the true mening muſt be taken, as the expoſitour doth expownde yt. For ſomoche then as the expoſitour doth expownd the bread and the cuppe, calling them the bodie and the blood: yt can not be auoided but that yt ys ſo, except the Ad-uerſarie will ſaie that the text expowndeth the expoſition. For vnto that ſen

B ſe that he wolde wreſt all the authours vnto , the text ys more nearer then the expoſition. The aduerſarie wolde haue yt bread , and the text calleth yt bread. The Aduerſarie wolde not haue yt the bodie of Chryſt: but this au-thour ſaieth yt ys the bodie of Chryſt.   Wherfore to the ſenſe of the Ad-uerſarie the text ys more clere then the expoſition. And ſo yt cometh to paſ ſe (as before ys ſaied) that the text expowndeth the expoſition, whiche ys af-ter the maner of other of their doinges. For they turn the catte in the pan-ne, and make light darkneſſe, and darkneſſe light.

But thowe, *Reader,* be thowe ſure that Chryſt who hath promiſed his ho-lie ſpiritte to his Church, *which ys the pillour of the trueth,* hath not left yt contra tie to his promiſſe deſtitute of this guide of trueth theſe thouſand yeares, but yt was that Spiritt, that did leade the minde and the penne of theſe holy Fathers to vnderſtand and perceaue the true ſenſe of the ſcriptures, and ſo to write yt to vs.

C God hath left vnto vs bread, euen the holie ſcripture to feede vs with-all : but as he bidde his Apoſtles to breake the breade , that he had bleſſed for the fiue thouſand people : ſo by his myniſtres in the church he hath commaunded the bread of the ſcripture to be broken to the people , and what ys yt to breake yt but to expownd yt . And why ſhoulde they expownd yt , yf their were not places to be opened, and cleared by expoſition? And therfore I ſaie theſe holie fathers, being appoin-ted to breake this bread of the woorde of God vnto vs, ther ys no doubte but as they had learned of the maſter of trueth, ſo they brake yt truly vnto vs, and haue geuen vs the true vnderſtanding of yt. And therfore the bread, and the cuppe expownded by ſo manie to be the bodie and bloode of Chryſt, yt muſt nedes be true that by ſo manie; and ſo manie yeares hath with concorde and conſent, withoute contradiction, ben preached , taught, and written.

D This alſo ys not to be ouerpaſſed, that thys Authour leaueth yt not vntaught howe we are made all one in Chryſt , bicauſe (ſaieth he) we do all partake of one bodie and bloode , we are all made one by the participacion of the myſteries . So that although he well knewe that we are all made one in Chryſt by faith and charitie : yet he alſo ſaieth , that we are made one by the participacion of the myſteries . And that yt ſhoulde moſte manifeſtlie , well be

Ecc ii   be

Bread and cuppe in S. Paule meē thebodie ãd blood, &c.

Ioan. 6. Bread of the woord of God how yt ys broke.

be perceaued what maner of vnion this ys , of the whiche he speaketh **E**
here,when he had alleaged the saing of Chryst: *He that eateth my flesh,and drin-*
keth my blood,dwelleth in me,and I him:mening therby to proue this vnion,he by
most plain woordes openeth the same,saing.*The Sonne of God ys vnited to the*
flesh by assumption:this flesh again ys vnited to vs by participacion , wherby yt ys very
manifest that we are vnited to Chryst by the vnion of his flesh.For that flesh

Chryst was vnto the whiche the Sonne of God was vnited,that same ys vnited to vs.
vnited to So that,as Chryst was vnited to vs by taking of our flesh in his incarna-
vs by his in cion,and so was made one with vs:In like maner,we are vnited to him by
carnacion, the taking of his flesh in the Sacrament , and are therby made one with
we be vni- him.   Wherfore note that he saieth not,that we are in the receipt of the
ted to him Sacrament vnited to Chryst by faith , but by participacion of his flesh.
by partici- And yet this authour was not ignorant,that we are also vnited to Chryst by
pacion &c. faith.But minding to open the peculiar commoditie of this mysterie he teacheth that by flesh we are vnited to Chryst.

Consider therfore,*Reader*,that wher the Aduersarie trauaileth to obscure
and hide the benefittes of God whiche he geueth to the woorthie receauers **F**
of his blessed and honourable Sacrament: we on the other side labour to
open and declare them vnto thee,that thowe maist according to thy duetie
more reuerentlie prepare thee to the recept of them, and also more thankfullie accept them. For we teache thee by the authoritie of these scriptures
and holie fathers alleaged , that thowe woorthilie receauing the Sacrament doest not onely enioie the vnion vnto Chryst by faith (*whiche onely*
vnion the Aduersarie teacheth)but also the vnion by the flesh of Chryst , by the
which thow arte verilie vnited to him,being nowe of his flesh,as he by his in
carnacion ys of thy flesh,as this authour hath saied.

The natu- These two poinctes then,I trust,be made clere,that in the Sacrament ys
ral flesh of the very substanciall and naturall bodie of Chryst, and that the woorthie
Chryst in receauers of yt are vnited and incorporated to Chryst, spirituallie by faith:
the B.Sac. and also naturallie by the flesh of Chryst . Whiche coniunction ys
couseth na- taught of sainct Cyrill to be so necessarie,that he thinketh that our mortall
tural vni- bodie coulde not atteign to immortalitie yf yt shoulde not be so ioined
tie of vs to to this liuing and immortall flesh of Chryst . *Non poterat aliter corruptibilis* **G**
Chryste. *hæc natura corporis ad incorruptibilitatem & vitam traduci , nisi naturalis vitæ corpus*
ei coniungeretur . This corruptible nature,of the bodie (saieth he) coulde not
Cyrill. 15. otherwise be brought to incorruptibilitie and life , except the bodie of na-
cao.in 6. turall life shoulde be ioined to yt.   And (*saieth he*)if thowe beleuest not me
Ioac. saing these thinges , I beseche thee beleue Chryst,saing : *verilie I saie*
vnto yowe,Except ye eate the flesh of the Sonne of man,and drinke his bloode,ye shall haue
no life in yowe.

Whether that sainct Cyrill here speaketh of this naturall coniunction of
the naturall bodie of Chryst, to our naturall and corruptible bodie yt
ys more manifest then yt nedeth either probacion or declaracion.
As for *Euthymius* yf the Aduersarie wolde wrest him , and corrupt him , yt
can not be suffred. For wher he speaketh these woordes here alleadged,
within a verie fewe lines before he speaketh of the transmutacion of the
bread and wine into the bodie and bloode of Chryst, and therwith expownding the woordes of Chryst:*This ys my body*:denieth by expresse woordes , anie figure to be in these woordes of Chryst. Wherfore as he ys a **H**
stowte auoucher of the trueth of the catholique Churche , and a mightie
vanquisher of the Aduersarie,so can not he by anie engine be drawen from
                                                                    after-

A his affertion.But the Aduerfarie maie waxe red for fhame,when he fhall fee
fo manifeft teftimonie againft him,that he can not once open his mouth to
auoide yt.

And nowe that this grecian hath fo notablie teftified the trueth,and opened the verie true faith of Chryftes Parlament houfe,what yt was in his time,and before:Beholde here cometh one of the latine church, being of
thefe later daies, which,to trie concorde and confent in faith to be in both
their fides,and in both their times and ages, fheweth what was profeffed
throughoute the latin church in his time,who in the expofition of this text
of S.Paule faieth thus:*Dico quod vnum fumus cum Chrifto, per fumptionem facramenti Euchariftiæ,Quoniam omnes quidem participamus,id eft.participes efficimur , vel quoad
fpeciem,vel quoad effectus cómunionem. vnde benè dicit participamus,propter diuifionem,
quæ fit aliquando in fpecie panis, vel propter effectus diuerfos, quos habent ipfi fumentes.
Aliam enim gratiam recipit ille,aliam ille fumendo dignè Sacramentum illud.Qui de vno
pane,id eft,de corpore Chrifti· & de vno calice,id eft,de fanguine Chrifti, licet multi fumus*

B *participamus. Non dicit omnes,quia non omnes , qui fumunt hoc facramentum effectum*   HugoCard
illius recipiunt,& ideo non funt vnus panis,quo reficiatur Dominus,nec vnum corpus cum   in Dec.1.
Chrifto.Licet (inquam)multi,tamen fumus vnus panis per vnionem fidei, fpei, & charita-   Cor.
*tis . Quæ vnio initiatur in fide,& confummatur in charitate. Et vnum illius capitis,
quod eft Chriftus.*   I faie that we are one with Chryft by the receipt of the
Sacrament of the aultar . For we do all partake ,that ys to faie , we are
made partakers,either as touching the forme or ells as touching the effect
of the communion. Wherfore he faieth well,that we partake, for the diui-   All we par
fion whiche ys doen fomtime in the forme of bread , or ells for diuerfe ef-   take of one
fectes whiche the receauers haue. For he receaueth one grace , and he an   bread.that
other,receauing the Sacrament woorthilie,which although we be manie,   ys thebodie
do partake of one bread,that ys to faie, of the bodie of Chryft, and of one   of Chryfte
cuppe,that ys,of the blood of Chryft. He doth not faie, all,for all that do   and of one
receaue this Sacrament do not receaue the effect of yt . And therfore   cuppe that
they be not one bread, with the whiche our Lorde maie be fedde, nei-   ys theblood
ther one bodie with Chryft. Although(I faie)we be manie : yet we are   of Chryft.

C one bread by the the vnion of faith,hope and charitie,which vnion ys begó
ne by faith,and ys confummated by charitie,and we are one bodie of that
head which ys Chryft.

In this authour as in the reft before alleadged owre two cheif poinctes,
whiche are here fought,are plainly taught. For he dothe bothe teache the
prefence of Chryftes bodie in the Sacrament:and alfo that by the receipt of
that bodie,we are made one with Chryft.As touching the firft,as the other
authour laft before alleadged,expownded thefe woordes(*The bread , and the
cuppe*)to be the bodie and bloode of Chryft:fo this authour likewifeexpown
deth the bread and the cuppe to be the bodie and Bloode of Chryft:Wher
fore betwixt them ys goodlie confent,foche as although they were fo farre
diftant in time and place:yet in this they be not a finger breadeth a fondre,
but euen iointlie together.I nede therfore no more to trauaill in this , the
matter ys clere in yt felf.

The other poinct ys likewife as plainlie fettfurth to vs.For in the firft entrie
he faieth,that by the receipt of the Sacramét,we are made one with Chrift,
D yf by the Sacrament,then not by faith onely:yf by the Sacrament, not by
bare bread. For onelie bread can not make all Chryftians, wher-
foeuer they be abiding, to be one with Chryft, and among them felues.
And the Aduerfarie himfelf faieth that bread hath no foche powre.

And all Chryſtians can not be made one, but by that that ys one thing to vs all, of the which all we be partakers. And in the Sacramēt can nothing be imagined to be one to all the Chryſtiā church, of the which all they cā be par kers, but the bodie of Chryſt. Wherfore in the Sacrament ys the bodie of Chryſt of the which all Chryſtians receauing woorthilie be(as this authour ſaieth) made one in Chryſt.   **E**

In this vnion we are not onelie one bread: but alſo, by S. Paule, one bodie. Which diſtinction of vnion, this authour ſemeth to refer or applie to the ſeuerall vnions before treacted of: as to the vnion ſpirituall by faith , and to the vnion naturall of vs to the naturall bodie of Chryſt . As touching the firſt, he ſaieth, that although we be manie: yet we are all one bread, by the v- nion of faith, hope and charitie. As for the ſeconde, he ſaieth that we are one bodie of that head, which ys Chryſt. The fitſt ys mere ſpirituall, and ys and maie be doen withoute the Sacrament , although not ſo certenly, nor ſo perfectlie.

For *Dionyſius Areopagita* ſaieth: this Sacrament ys *omnium ſacramentorum con-*   **F**
ſummatiſſimum, of all Sacramentes yt ys moſt conſummate, both for that yt ys ſo perfect in yt ſelf, and alſo for that yt perfecteth all other Sacramentes , as the ſame Dyoniſe alſo more at large ſaieth: *Dicimus ergo cætera ſacrarum rerum ſi gna, quorum nobis ſocietas indulgetur, huius diuinis profectò , conſummantibuſque muneri- bus perfici. Neque enim fermè fas eſt ſacerdotalis muneris myſterium aliquod peragi niſi diuinum iſtud Euchariſtiæ auguſtiſſimumque ſacramentum compleat.* We ſaie therfore, that the other ſignes of holie thinges, the ſocietie of the whiche ys geuen to vs, to be perfected by theſe diuine and conſummating giftes. Neither ys yt laufull allmoſt anie myſterie of the preiſtlie office to be full doen, except this diuine Sacrament and moſt full of maieſtie do finiſh or per- forme yt.

Wherfore as by Chryſoſtom and other yt maie be perceaued, in the pri- mitiue church they that were baptiſed, were brought frō baptiſme to the re- ceipt of the bleſſed Sacrament of Chryſtes bodie as therbie to be perfected in Chryſt, and certenly to be vnited to him bothe by faith , and alſo by hys bleſſed bodie. Although then by faith we be ſpirituallie vnited to Chryſte   **G**
without the Sacrament: yet(as yt ys ſaied) we be not ſo certenly vnited, as when this noble Sacrament, which perfecteth other Sacramentes cometh al ſo, but ſpirituallie vnited we be.

Nowe as touching the ſeconde vnion, whiche this authour ſpeaketh of, yt ys not likewiſe mere corporall as the other ys mere ſpirituall, but yt ys ſo corporall, as yt ys neuertheleſſe ſpirituall. According as the bodie of Chryſt ys, which we receaue, which although yt be a verie true and perfect bodie, yet yt ys ſpirituall, as S. Ambroſe ſaieth: *Corpus enim Dei corpus eſt ſpiritale. Corpus Chriſti corpus eſt diuini ſpiritus.* The bodie of God, ys a ſpirituall bodie. The bo- die of Chryſt ys the bodie of the diuine ſpiritte. Yt ys alſo ſpiritually recea- ued for that yt ys doen onely by the knowledge of faith, and not of anie ſen- ſe. Although the office of ſenſeis, and alſo of the bodie be required to the re ceipt therof.

So then as the bodie of Chryſt ys ſo corporall, as yt ys alſo ſpirituall, and the receipt of the ſame bodie ſo corporall, as yt ys neuertheleſſe ſpirituall!: ſo alſo the vnion brought to effect by the ſame receipt, yt ys verilie corpo-   **H**
ral, altho withall yt ys ſpiritual. This vniō he ſignifieth vnto vs, whē he ſaieth that we be the bodie of that head which ys Chryſt. For as cōcerning the ſpi ritual vniō, he ſaied before, that we are al one bread, ād therfor for the corpo ral vnion

A vnion he faieth that we be one bodie. For proof wherof that he fo plainly ment, the allegacion of S. Paule to the *Ephefians* declareth which he bringeth to open the true fenfe and mening of S. Paule here. For (faieth he) we are membres of his bodie, of his flefh and of his bones. whiche woordes that they be vnderftanded of our corporall vnion with Chryft, yt ys more manifeftlie declared by *Iræneus*, then by the Aduerfarie yt can be denied. *Li. 5. ad-uerf. heref.*

Thus hetherto of fo manie auncient and learned authours, ye haue heard no diffonante, but a confonante voice, all fownding one thing, that by the receipt of the bleffed bodie of Chryft in the Sacrament we be vnited to Chryft, and made one with him.

THE EIGHT AND TWENTETH CHAP. PROceadeth vpon the fame text by *Oecumenius*, and *Anfelmus*.

B

Reade in the fourth booke of the Kinges, that the King of *Syria*, who was in warre againft the King of Ifraell, for fomoche as he vnderftoode that *Elifeus* the Prophet difclofed to the kinge of Ifraell the fecrett counfells, intentes, and pourpofes of the faied King of *Syria*, that he fent an armie of men to the cittie wher the Prophet laie to take him. And when the feruante of the Prophet went furth in the morning and fawe fo great a multitud with horfes and chariottes com paffing the cittie rownde aboue, he cried, and faied, *Alas mafter, what shall we dooe?* The Pprophete faied vnto him: *Feare not, here be mo with vs them with them*. And when the Prophete had praied, the eies of his feruaint were ope ned, and he fawe the mowntain full of horfes, and chariottes of fire rownde about the Prophete. *4. Reg. 6.*

As the Prophete was thus ftrenghtned with fo great a multitude, that his enemies were not able to preuaill againft him, though his feruante knewe yt not, and therfor feared and cried: Euen fo the verie prophet of God in the
C Churche of Chryfte, who hath geuen him felf ouer to the feruice of God, that he ys fullie become the man of God, therfore ys lightned and illumi- ned with the wholfome knowledge of the catholique faith, wherby he feeth God and his holie will and pleafure, he doth well fee that though the Kinge of *Syria* hath now moued warre againft the King of Ifraell: that ys, Sathan againft Chryft the Kinge of verie Ifraell, and his catholique kingdom his Churche: and hath for the better expedicion of his pourpofe fent an armie to kake awaie the prophete and godlie learned man, that he fhoulde not warne the people of Ifraell of the affaute of Sathan, whiche he entendeth to moue by herefie, fchifme, diuifion, and fubuerfion of all good ordre in the Churche of Chryfte: He doth, I faie, well fee, that the prowde and cruell kinge ys not able to carie him awaie oute of the kingdom of Chryft, into his kingdome. For he ys compafed abowte with a moft mightie armie of the no ble foldiers of God, all the holie catholique fathers, godly writers, and no- ble Martirs, whiche ftand by him mightilie in the confeffion of Chryftes ho lie faith, whiche nombre being infinite, he maie (as euery learned catholi-
D que alfo maie) vnto the vnlearned faithfull man, the feruante of God, faie, *Feare not, ther be mo with vs, then with thefe enemies of Ifraell, with thefe Aduerfaries of* Chryftes Churhe. And for that thefe Aduerfaries when they knewe the tru eth, wolde not abide in the trueth: *and when they knewe God, wolde not glorifie*

Rom. 1.

him as God, but they haue vanished awaie in their owne thoughtes , and saing them selues E
to be wise, they are become verie fooles. So that as their likes the people of the hoft
of *Syria*, were ftriken with blindneffe:fo , *obscuratum est insipiens cor eorum.* their
foolifh heart ys blinded. So that nowe blinder then Molls, they faie, light
ys darkneffe, and darkneffe light. And thus being blinde are contented to
be caried in to the handes of their enemies, as the *Syrians* were.

But God of his mercie woorke mercifullie with them, that they perifh
not in the handes of their enemies in the end, but that yt maie pleafe him,
that they maie be deliuered by the charitable mean of the Prophet of God,
by the minifterie of the catholique preacher, and that for his perfecucõ they
maie fuftein no other affliction, but that they maie eate in the middeft of
the cittie, the bread of the Ifraelites , the bread of the true chryftians the
bodie of Chryfte in the holie Sacrament, and fo ceaffe anie more to perfequute Ifraell , but to become one with thê, in that forte, that *Multitudinis cre-*

Acts 4.

dentium fiat cor vnum, & anima vna in Domino. Of the multude of them that beleue, ther be but one heart, and one foule. An ende they fhall haue, for to F
continue God will not fuffre them, and if their demerites fo require (as nowe ours do to be afflicted with them) God will withholde that mercie
from them, that they maie not come to that ende, which before I haue defiered for them: Oh Lorde, howe miferable then fhall be the ende?

Wherfore, Chryften reader, be of good cheer, and feare not. For though
they haue worldlie might and power on their fide: yet they can not preuaill
againft vs. *For ther be mo on our fide, then on theirs.* All the holie writers be with
us, of which thowe haueft hearde a good nombre, and yet thowe fhalt heare
moo, which fhall not fpeake in darke maner, fo as thowe maift be doubtfull
what they meen, or howe they be to be taken and vnderftanded , thowe
fhalt heare them in fo clere maner teftifie the trueth , that yt fhall be eafie to faie : this ys their meening, and thus they are to be vnderftanded.

And for triall herof, here ys firft the teftimonie of *Oecomenius* to be hearde.
Which ys this vpon the text of S. Paule nowe treacted of. *Vnus panis, & vnũ*

Oecum. in
deci. 1 Cor.

corpus fumus. Nam ex vno pane omnes participamus . Rationem addit , quomodò corpus
Chrifti efficiamur. Quid enim (inquit) eft panis? corpus nempe Chrifti. Quid autem effici- G
ciuntur hi, qui participant ? Corpus fanè Chrifti. Nam participantes corpus Chrifti nos quo-
que illud efficimur. Quoniam vnus panis eft Chriftus. Ex multis namque grauis (vt exem-
pli gratia loquamur) vnus panis factus eft, & nos multi, ex ipfo vno participantes, efficimur
vnum corpus Chrifti: Quoniam enim vetus noftra caro corrupta eft fub peccato, opus nobis
fuit noua carne We are one bread, and one bodie, for we do all partake of

Note howe
Oecum. fo-
loweth the
woordes of
Chryfoftom
before allea
ged, faing
what ys the
bread, and
anfwereth,
the bodie
of Chryfte.

one bread. He addeth a reafon (faieth *Oecumenius*) howe we are made the
bodie of Chryft. What (faieth he) *ys the bread? Verilie the bodie of Chryft.* And
what are they made that do partake? truelie the bodie of Chryft. For we par
taking the bodie of Chryft, are alfo made the fame. For Chryft ys one bread.
for of manie granes (As for example we maie fpeake) one bread ys made. and
we being manie partaking of that one, are made one bodie of Chryfte, forafmoche as our olde flefh was corrupted vnder finne, we had nede of a newe
flefh. Thus he.

In my iudgement I nede not anie thinge vpon this expofition to faie, as
wherby to make yt clere or plain, for that yt ys fo plain of yt felf: but yet in
confideracion that I write not to the learned , but to helpe the vnlearned, H
to whom nothing can be to plain, I will fomwhat faie, therbie at the leeft
to miniftre occafion to the reader, the better to note what this authour doth
faie. S. Paule immediatelie before this text, had faied: that the bread whiche

we

A we breake ys a communicacion of the bodie of our lorde. by the whiche woordes (as alſo Chryſoſt. did note) S. Paule wolde teach, that neer coniunction and vnion of vs, to and with Chryſt, whiche ys no leſſe then that we be made the bodie of Chryſt. Then S. Paule proceading to this text which we haue nowe in hande, this authour ſaieth that wher before he had ſaied, that we be made the bodie of Chriſt, *Here he geueth a reaſon howe we are made the bodie of Chryſt.*

Among philoſophers yt ys accompted vnſemelie to affirme anie thing without a reaſon. the ſcripture alſo willeth vs to be readie to geue an anſwere to euerie one that asketh vs a reaſon of that hope that ys in vs. So when S. Paule (as this authour implieth) had taught, that we be made the bodie of Chryſt, here he geueth a reaſon, howe we be made the bodie of Chryſt. And that this reaſon of S. Paule maie the better appeare vnto vs: the authour firſt openeth the partes of yt to vs. For wher S. Paule in his reaſon ſaieth: that we do all eate of one breade: to open what that bread ys, he asketh a queſtion, ſaing: what ys the breade? he ſolueth the queſtion furthwith and

B ſaieth: verilie yt ys the bodie of Chryſt.

1.Pet.

Note this then, Reader, that the bread whiche S. Paule ſpeaketh of here, ys the bodie of Chryſte. And note farder that he ſaieth not yt ys a figuratiue bodie, but he ſaieth yt ys the bodie of Chryſt verilie. Wherbie the Aduerſaries ſignes and figures are cutte of, and in this ſentence of S. Paule ther ys no place for them. For yf yt be verilie the bodie of Chryſt, yt ys not figuratiuelie his bodie.

Yf the Aduerſarie wolde ſeke ſome ſhifte to helpe to hide and couer his falſhoode and wickedneſſe, and ſaie that the bread, whiche this authour asketh this queſtion of, and ſolueth yt to be the bodie of Chryſt: ys the congregacion of the faithfull, whiche he will graunt to be the very bodie of Chryſt miſticall. This gloſſe will not ſerue him, but raither declare him to be a violent wreſter of this authour, as he ys of manie other mo. For this authour ſpeaketh of the bread that ys partaké and receaued, and not of vs which do partake and receaue yt. For when he had declared the bread to be the

C bodie of Chryſt, then immediatelie he asketh: what be they made that do partake yt? So that yt ys moſt manifeſt that he ſpeaketh diſtinctlie bothe of the bread that ys partaken, Whiche bread ys the bodie of Chryſt, and that verilie, and alſo of the partakers, who be made his miſticall bodie therby. See then, Reader, what a plain document this ys, howe mightilie yt confirmeth the catholique trueth, and confuteth the Aduerſeries hereſie. Weighe yt well, and thowe ſhalt perceaue good grownde to ſtaie thie ſelf vpon. Conſider that the authour ys an auncient writer of the Greke churche, and for that which he hath written, he was neuer by anie godlie writer impugned. No man hath inueighed againſt him, for his aſſercion of Chryſtes preſence in the Sacrament. *Oecolampadius, Zwynglius, Carolſtadius,* and that rable, they haue not onelie ben impugned, but alſo their wicked hereſies in this poinct, haue ben in manie and ſondrie Councells condemned er they tooke vpõ them by the mocion of Sathan, to pull them oute of that filthie and ſtinking pitte, wher they and manie other hereſies laie buried. And nowe yet again they and their hereſies againſt the bleſſed Sacrament, haue ben newlie by a generall Councell condemned. This authour ſtandeth vpright, clean vntou

D ched and vndefiled.

The reall bodie of Chryſte partaken: the miſticall bodie the partakers.

Catholique fathers agree all in one.

Conſider that he expownding the text of S.Paule laſt before this treacted of, that ther he called the cuppe of bleſſing, the cuppe of the bloode of Chryſt.

Chryſt. So that as ther he taught the preſence of Chryſtes very bloode. ſo **E**
here he agreablie teacheth the preſence of his bodie. Ther ys not in his mou
the, neither in the mouthe of anie of the other catholique fathers, whoſe
doctrine we folowe, bothe yea and naie, but onelie yea.

In the mouthe of *Luther,Oecolapadius*, and other, ther ys both yea, and naie,
yt ys ſo, and yt ys not. For *Luther* hath not onelie preached and taught the
preſece ofChryſtes bodie in the Sacrament, as the catholique Churche doth
but hath alſo writte yt euen ſo: Again he hath preached, taught, and written
moche againſt that that the catholique Church dothe teach. In this he agre
eth with the catholique churche, that he teacheth the veric reall preſence of
Chryſtes bodie in the Sacrament : But in this he varieth, that he ſaieth, the
bread ys the bodie of Chryſt, and the wine ys his bloode.

Heretiques   And here note that heretiques falling fro the catholique church, as they
diſſent fro diſſent and varie from yt: ſo do theye amonge them ſelues. For hereſie ys
the church election ſo they though they take occaſion by ſome one or other to folowe
and among ſome deueliſh doctrine: yet they will haue in diuerſe thinges a ſpeciall choi-
them ſelues ce, neither agreable with the catholique Churche, neither with theſe hereſi-
arkes who they folowe. As *Luther,* who ys a great folower of *Wicleff.* hath not **F**
choſen to folowe him in his aſſertion of the Sacrament as he left yt, but hath
Luther.   a peice of his propre phanſie, as he thought yt good. For wicleff affirming
the preſence of Chryſt in the Sacrament, but denieng tranſubſtanciacion,
taught, that the bread remained with the bodie of Chryſt, ſo that ther was
both the ſubſtance of bread, and the ſubſtance of the bodie of Chryſt in the
Sacrament. But *Luther* varieth from this, and chooſing to folowe his owne
inuencion, ſo affirmeth the preſence of Chryſt, that he wolde auouche the
Oecolapad bread to be the bodie of Chryſt.

Nowe *Oecolampadius* the diſciple ſometime of Luther hath in this mouth
both yea and naie. For he ſomtime both taught and preached, yea alſo did
write, that Chryſtes bodie was reallie preſent in the Sacrament, euen as the
catholique Churche doth teache. Afterwarde being by his owne election
the diſciple of *Luther* he beganne to haue a peice of a naie in his mouthe to
that, to the whiche before he had ſaied yea. And finallie, as his maſter *Luther*
chooſe to varie from his Maſter *Wicleff,* and to folowe his owne phantaſie: **G**
ſo this *Oecolampadius* choſe to varie from his Maſter *Luther,* and to folowe his
phantaſie. For he neither with his maſter, neither his graunt M. *Wicleff* wolde phantaſie as they did, but all together the contrarie, teaching that ther
was no preſence ofChryſt in the Sacrament, but as in a ſigne or figure. In the
whiche he was ſo vehemet, that he wrote againſt his maſter *Luther,* and that
veric earneſtlie. So that in theſe mens mouthes ye maie perceaue ther hath
ben yea and naie : Their mouthes were ſoche ofthe which S. Iames ſpeaketh that oute of them cometh bothe bleſſing and curſing. They are ſoche
ſpringes as oute of the whiche come waters both ſalte and freſh : bitter and
ſwete: So that as ther ys no ſtaie in them ſelues: ſo can no man be ſtaied by
them, in any good certentie.

The maſters whom God hath appointed in his catholique Churche, they
be not inconſtant, they be not double tunged, with yea and naie in one mat
ter, they ſaie not nowe this, and then that. The maſter ſaieth not one thing,
and the ſcholer an other. The peſtilence and deſtruction of comon wealths
whiche be diſcorde, contencion, and diuiſion, ys not among them, But **H**
Malach.2. as allmightie God ſaied by his Prophet Malachie of *Leui* . *Lex veritatis*
fuit in ore eius . & iniquitas non eſt inuenta in labiis eius : In pace & æquitate
ambu-

A *ambulauit mecum.* The lawe of trueth was in his mouthe, and ther was no wickednesse fownde in his lippes, he walked with me in peace and equitie, and did turne manie one awaie from their sinnes. This (as S. Hierom saieth) being the description of the office of a perfight preist, agreeth very well to these holie preistes of the stocke of spirituall *Leui,* our auntient Fathers and writers, in whose mouthes was the lawe of trueth and they walked with God in peace and equitie, and turned manie from their sinnes.

The office of a perfight preist. in three poinctes.

This being the office of a perfight preist, and *Luther,* and his complices taking vpon them to reforme the state of the wholl Church, as though they were the masters of perfection : let vs make a proof how yt will agree with them. The first point of this office ys that the lawe of trueth shoulde be in their mouthes. But this poincte ys not in them. For besides that the catholique Church argueth and reproueth them of most detestable falshead and heresie, they among them selues do reproue one an other of fasheade and vntreuth. *Oecolampadius* writing against Luther, and so his wholl sect of Sa-
B cramentaries against the sect of the Lutherans, wherin the one conuincing the other of vntrueth, they make this true, that the lawe of trueth ys not in their mouthes.

1.

2.

An touching the secõd which ys, that a preist should walke with God in peace and equitie, in this also they are to farre wide : For ther yt not onely a great lacke of peace betwixt God and their conscience : But also they be fixed in deadlie warre against his holy spouse, the church. Whiche they haue most cruellie diuided, cutt and mangled. They haue throwen dowen her houses, destroied her aultars, spoiled her treasures, prophaned her ornamentes, contemned and cast oute her sacramentes, violated and broken her lawes, infringed her liberties, derided her ceremonies, and with one woorde to ende, euerted all her orders. What peace ys in them that woorke these horrible troubles, and destructions? of all warres this ys the most cruell, this passeth fire and swoorde.

Hauocke made in the churchs by heretiques.

In the thirde poincte, whiche ys that a preist shoulde turne manie from iniquitie, they are clean contrarie. For they turn manie, not from but to iniquitie. For preistes (which as S. Hierom saieth) shoulde be so pure in preist
C lie chastitie, that they shoulde abstein from all vnclean worke both in their bodies and their mindes spirituallie, for that they are ministres to consecrate the bodie of Chryst they should be free from all errour of filthie thought are nowe by these masters of wickednesse turned to all carnalitie and corrup tion of licenciouse life. And that they shoulde haue no conscience of their wicked doinges, they cloake whoordom with matrimonie. After this sorte religiouse men are poluted, virgens consecrate to God are defiled and so all virginall chaistitie almost vtterlie (wher they reign) abandoned. Praier ys shortened, fasting ys not regarded, obediéce to auncient order ys extingnished. What shall I stand in rehersall of the wickednesse wherunto men be nowe induced? As the time will not suffice, no more will my heart abide for wo to rehearse the heapes of euells that be nowe laied open for men frelie to runne to. These be to manie which be allreadie rehearsed to proue that these masters of wickednesse do so litle stoppe men from iniquitie, that they open wide gates for them to passe frely to yt. And yet I wolde to God
D ther were no mo but these. Thus by these three poinctes of the descriptiõ of the office of a preist described by God him self, for somoche as they be not fownde in these aboue mencioned men, yt maie well appeare that they be not of the nombre of gods preistes, as the other holie fathers be vnto whom

3.

these

thefe three poinctes be well applied, as in whome they were fownde. E

But I fee howe I am digreffed, I will recall my felf backe, and go forwarde in my matter in farder opening of the notes of the expofitiō of this authour, and committe the redreffe of thefe euells vnto God, whom I befeche not to deale with vs accordinge to owre finnes, nor to our iniquites, but that his mercieis maie fooen come vpon vs. For we are become in life and religion verie miferable.

Ye haue heard the authour before alleaged clerelie teftifieng the prefence of Chryftes bodie, which he fo opened bicaufe the reafon of S. Paule might the better appeare vnto vs howe we be made the bodie of Chryft. And ther fore that doen, he entreth to the opening of S. Paules reafon with this que ftion faing: *What be they made that do partake?* He aunfwereth: *Truelie the bodie of Chryft.* And geuing the reafon whie they be fo made, he faieth: *For we par-taking the bodie of Chryfte, are alfo made the fame.*

Note then what ye do partake, and what by the fame partaking ye are ma de. Ye partake the bodie of Chryft, not a peice of materiall bread, and by F the partaking of that bodie of Chryft, ye are made the bodie of Chryfte. In this faing yt ys geuen vs to confider (as by other yt ys allreadie faied) that not onely by faieth, but alfo by the receipt of the bleffed Sacrament, we are

Owre natu rall flesh corrupted by finne ys repaired bi the ioinnig of Chryftes naturall flesh ther vnto.

ioined and vnited to Chryft, whiche vnion, for that yt ys doen by the verie bodie of Chryfte, yt ys corporall a vniō. Whiche corporall vniō this authour dothe manifeftlie declare and prooue to vs by his laft fentence, when he faieth: *For fomoche as our olde flesh was corrupted vnder finne we had nede of a newe flesh.* Wher withoute all controuerfie he fpeaketh of our naturall flefh that was corrupted. Wherfore then to repaire this naturall flefh corrupted, yt was neceffarie to haue a naturall flefh vncorrupted and foche ther ys none in that refpecte but the flefh of Chryft. Wherfore yt ys that flefh that muft be ioined to owre flefh, to releiue the nede of yt, and fo vniting vs to yt redu-ce vs (as S. Cyrill faieth) to incorruption and immortalitie, whiche fhall come to our flefh by that vncorrupted and immortall flefh.

But of this authour vpon this fcripture here ys enough, yt ys time nowe breiflie to heare his yockfelowe of the latin church, which fhall be *Anfelmus* G

Anfelm. in deci. 1 Cor.

who expowndinge this text faieth thus: *Dominus corpus & fanguinem fuum in eis rebus commendauit, quæ ad vnum aliquid rediguntur ex multis. quoniam aliud in vnum ex multis granis conficitur: aliud in vnum ex multis acinis confluit. & ob hoc communica-tio corporis & fanguinis Chrifti focietatem fanctorum defignat, & facit, vbi pax erit, & vnitas plena, atque perfecta. Propter quæ omnia recte dicimur omnes vnus panis, & vnū corpus, quia & omnes de vno pane corporis Chrifti participamus. Quod enim quifque fuã partem ex hoc pane percipit, fignificat quia vnusquifque iuxta menfuram fuam, particeps fit huius gratiæ. Sicut autem vnus panis Dominici facramenti, vnum corpus Chrifti efficit in ecclefia: fic panis Idolatriæ Dæmonum participatio eft. Et ficut omnes, qui de vno pane, ac de vno calice Domini fumimus, vnum corpus efficimur: ita fi cum idolatris de facrificio eorum fumimus, vnum corpus efficimur. Qui comedit idolothitum vnum cum Dæmone fit, ficut qui comedit corpus Chrifti, fit vnum cum Chrifto.* Owre Lorde hath geuē furth his bodie and blood in thofe thinges, whiche of manie thinges are brought into one certen thinge. For the one ys made of manie granes into one thing and the other oute of manie grapes into one thing, And therfore the cōmu-nicacion of the bodie and bloode of Chryfte, doth fignifie and make alfo H the focietie of fainctes, where fhall be peace and alfo full and perfect vnitie. For all whiche thinges we are all well called one bread, and one bodie bicau fe we all do partake of the one bread, and of the bodie of Chryft. That eue-

rie

A euerie one dothe take his parte of this bread, yt fignifieth that euerie one
accordinge to his meafure ys partaker of this grace. For as that one breade
of our Lordes Sacrament, maketh one bodie in the Churche : So the
bread of Idolatrie ys the partaking of Deuells. And as all we whiche receaue of one bread, and one cuppe, are made one bodie : Euen fo yf with
Idolaters we receaue of their facrifice, we are made one bodie. For he
that eateth of that that ys offred to Idolls, ys made one with the Deuell:
as he that eateth the bodie of Chryft, ys made one with Chryft. Thus
moche *Anfelmus.*

In whome maie be perceaued, a moft godly concorde, and agreement,
with his yockfelowe *Oecumenius*. For as he taught that we partaking the
bodie of Chryft, are made one bodie in Chryft : So dothe this Authour
teache alfo. For declaracion wherof as alfo for a note for the better vn-
derftandinding of Sainct Paule, obferue that where Sainct Paule faieth.
All we are one bread, and one bodie, which do partake of that one bread. This Authour expownding what that one bread ys, doth not faie that yt ys materiall

*The one
bread that
manie be
made one
by ys the
bodie of
Chryfte.*

B or Sacramentall breade, but with expreffe woordes he faieth that yt ys the
bread of the bodie of Chryft.

And let not the Aduerfarie thinke that he maie wreft this faing to the
fpirituall bodie of Chryft, after his wicked maner and cuftome. For neither
the euident and plain fentences of this Authour whiche are before alleaged, in the whiche ys declared the very reall prefence of Chryft in the Sacrament, neither this expofition will fuffre yt. For where he expowndeth,
The one bread, in Sainct Paules faing to be the bodie of Chryft : afterwarde
he calleth the fame the bread of our Lordes Sacrament. So that the bread
of the bodie of Chryfte being the breade of our Lordes Sacrament, we are
plainlie taught that he fpeaketh of the bodie of Chryft in the Sacramēt. For
the fpirituall maner whiche the Aduerfariē fpeaketh of, neither ys, neither cā
be in the Sacrament but in the receauer, Wherfor the other before fpoken
of muft nedes be true.

C And for our vniō to Chryft agreablie as before ys taught, he teacheth here.
For in the ende he faieth: He that eateth Idolathites ys made one with the
Deuel, as he that eateth the bodie of Chryft ys made one with Chryft. Wher
by yt ys plain that this Authour teacheth that vniō to be made by the recea
uing of the bodie of Chryft in the Sacrament, for of yt he fpeaketh, as before
ys proued. We are vnited to Chryft, not onely after the maner wherwith we
are by faith and charitie vnited, but by that fpecial maner, that before ys declared oute of S. Cyril, and other, whiche ys a natural and fubftancial vnion,
Whiche vnion cometh to vs by the nature and fubftance of the flefh of
Chryfte receaued in the Sacrament, as Chryft ys one with vs by the taking.
vpon him our flefh in his incarnacion.

THE NINE AND TWENTETH CHAPITER,
*treacteth of the fame text by Theophilact and Dionyfe, and
endeth with Remigius.*

D Owe to finifh the expofition of this text in hande cometh the laft
coople to make vppe the nombre of twelue, whiche nombre as yt
ys taken, and reputed as fufficient by the lawes to determine
matters of great controuerfie, and weight, yea euen for the life, and
death of man: So yt maie fuffice to anie reafonable man to determine this

Fff　　matter

matter nowe called in controuerfie by euell men, whiche of yt felf ys a moft **E**
plain matter, and fo hath ben accepted thefe fiftene hundreth yeares, al-
thought a fewe light fculkers haue fomwhat murmured, and whifpered
againft yt in corners: yet yt hath allwaies preuailed, and fhall vndoubtedlie
nowe alfo, albeit that Sathan fo mightilie impugneth yt, and that with fo
great an Armie, as the like to this time was neuer feen.

But to fpeake in the boldeneffe of faith with S. Paule. *Deus pacis conteret*
Rom.16.   *Satanam fub pedibus veftris velociter.* The God of peace fhall treade Sathan vnder your feete fhortlie.

And therfor Reader, be ftrong in faithe, and feare not though the Aduer-
Pfal.36.   fary glorie a litle while, thowe fhalt fee yt come to paffe, that thowe maift
faie with the Prophet Dauid . *Vidi impium fuperexaltatum, & eleuatum ficut*
Cedrus Libani, & tranfiui, & ecce non erat. Quæfiui eum, & non eft inuentus locus eius.
I myfelf haue feen the vngodlie in great power, and flowrifhing like a green
baie tree, and I went by and lo, he was gon, I fought him but his place coulde not be fownde.

Indich.13.   *Holofernes* was mightie ouer the people of God in *Bethulia*. He gloried **F**
moche, and fpake great woordes, but howe foddein and fhort was his de-
1. Reg. 17.   ftruction? *Goliath* defied the hoft of the liuing God, he reuiled and railed
vpon Ifraell, and God fuffred him a certain time : but yet was he by litle
Dauid, whom he contemned foen ouerthrowen, and Ifraell that daie had
great and ioifull victorie vpon *Goliath* and all the Philiftines. Therfore let
neither their glorie difmaie thee, or put thee in doubte, neither feare put
thee from this faith, but remembre the faing of S. Paule, *Oportet hærefes effe*
1. Cor. 11.   *vt qui probati funt, manifefti fiant in vobis.* Ther muft be herfeis or fectes among
yowe, that they, which are perfecte among yowe, maie be knowen. Not (as
Sedulius in   *Sedulius* faieth) *quod hærefes Deo placeant, fed quòd per eas fideles exerceantur, vt qui*
Dec.1.Co.   *Deo noti funt, hominibus manifeftentur.* Not that herefeis pleafe God, but that the
faithfull maie be exercifed, and that they whiche be knowen to God maie
alfo be knowen to men. Stand therfore ftronglie in the battaill of thie Lord
God, abide pacientlie his pleafure, abide thie triall in this exercife, and God
will turne yt to thie glorie. And for thie better ftaie, and conforth read the **G**
holie writers in whiche thowe fhalt finde that, that fhall moche ftrengthen
thie faith.

Let vs nowe therfore proceed, and heare howe Theophilact vnderftan-
In Dec.   deth Sainct Paule. Thus he faieth vpon this text . *Cùm itaque vnum fumus,*
1.Cor.   *quopacto inter nos charitate feruata, non in vnum inuicem cohæremus, præfertim cùm*
Paulus dicat, eò nobis Dominus proprium corpus impertitur, vt fibi nos copulet, &
nexu quodam mutuo, nos reddat propinquiores ? At vbi prior illa carnis natura prauis eft
facinoribus corrupta, & vitæ cæleftis eft effecta expers, fuam nobis Deus contulit, no-
ftræ afsimilem, quæ & peccato careret, & vitam largiretur, vt eius effecti participes,
& fibi admifceremur, & vitam duceremus innoxiam, vtpote qui vnum effemus cum
S.Paule   *Chrifto corpus adepti.* Forafmoche therfore as we be one, why by keping of
faieth that   charitie among vs, do we not cleaue together in one ? fpeciallie feing that
our Lorde   Paule faieth, that our Lorde therfor imparteth to vs his owne bodie that he
imparteth   might coople vs vnto him, and make vs nearer together by a bande or knot- **H**
to vs his   te among our felues. And wher that firft nature of our flefh was corrupted,
owne bodie   and was made voide of the heauenly life, he gaue vs his, being like vnto our
the whiche fhoulde both lacke finne, and fhoulde geue life, that we being ma
de partakers of yt, we fhoulde bothe be mixed with him, and alfo leade an
harmeleffe life, as whiche haue gotten one bodie with Chryft. Thus he.

Among

A　　Among other thinges woorthie of note in Theophilact, to trooble the Reader with no mo then appertein to the declaracion of the matters, whiche be here to be decided, two onely fhall be noted. As for the prefence of Chryfte in the Sacrament, as he doth euerie wher: So dothe he here moft plainlie teache the fame. Owre incorporacion alfo to Chryft by the receipt of the fame bodie with other Fathers before alleaged he doth profeffe and acknowledge.

As for the firft, this Authour perfwading vs to the vnitie of loue and charitie, induceth for his cheif and great argument for that pourpofe that we fhoulde fo be, bicaufe our Lorde hath imparted his owne bodie to vs, to the entent we fhoulde be one. And yf the Aduerfarie wolde blinde the fimple reader, that this Authour meneth, that he gaue vs his owne bodie vpon the croffe for our redemption, yt ys true in dede that our Sauiour Chryfte gaue his bodie for vs to the death of the croffe. But that this Authour ment here of that his geuing of his bodie, that ys moft falfe. For he fpeaketh of that maner of the geuing of the bodie of Chryft, that S. Paule fpeaketh of in

B this fcripture, which he expowndeth. And here Sainct Paule fpeaketh of the geuing of Chryft, as he ys geuen in the Sacrament, as the wholl proceffe of Sainct Paule doth well proue. So that this Authour expownding Sainct Paule, fpeaketh as Sainct Paule doth of the Sacrament. Then fpeaking of the Sacrament this Authour faieth, that Chryft geueth vs his owne bodie therin.

And here by the waie note, that he faieth not this as of him felf, but faieth that Sainct Paule faieth fo. Wherhie he fignifieth that this text of Sainct Paule fpeaketh not of materiall bread fignifieng or figuring the bodie of Chryft, but of the verie reall bodie of Chryft, and therfore faieth, that he *Argument* imparteth to vs his owne bodie. He geueth vs not his owne bodie yf we *vpon the* haue but a peice of bread. For the bread ys but a fign or figure of the bo- *woorde* die of Chryft, not prefent to be geuen, but abfent. So that wher the Aduer- *(bread) in* farie buyldeth (as he thinketh) his ftrong towers and bullwarkes againft the *S. Paule re-*

C veritie of this bleffed Sacrament vpon this and other places of Sainct Paule, *felled.* of the whiche fome be allreadie treacted of, and the reft by the helpe of Gods grace hereafter fhall be: faing that yt ys but bread bicaufe Sainct Paule calleth yt bread, ye maie well perceaue what a falfe grownde he taketh, and howe vnfure his buylding ys. For this Authour faieth, that Sainct Paule in this place faieth, that Chryft geueth vs his owne bodie, wherby yt ys euident, that though Sainct Paule calleth the Sacrament bread, yet he meneth not nor vnderftandeth therbie materiall breade, as the Adueafarie dreameth, but meneth that yt ys that breade which ys Chryft, in that fenfe that Chryft calleth himfelf, when he faied. *Panis quem* *ego dabo, caro mea eft, quam dabo pro mundi vita.* The bread whiche I will geue *Ioan. 6.* ys my flefh, whiche I will geue for the life of the worlde. This fentence, as Chryfoftome, Theophilact, and manie mo (as yt ys declared in the feconde booke) do teftifie, ys fpoken of the Sacrament, and then wolde I afke the Aduerfarie, whether Chryft calleth him felf materiall bread here

D or no. Yf he fhoulde aunfwer that he did fo, then the faing of Chryft muft nedes haue this fenfe: that materiall bread, which I will geue ys my flefh. And fo fhall he bothe graunt a prefence of Chryftes flefh in the Sacrament, and alfo condefcend to Luthers herefie, who faieth that this ys a good and true propofition: This bread ys my bodie, and this wine ys my bloode.

Yf he faie, yt that ys not taken there for materiall bread, but in the gene- **E**
rall fignificacion for foode, as the fcripture calleth Manna: as when yt faieth:

Pfal. 77. *Panem cæli dedit eis, panem Angelorum manducauit homo..* He gaue them bread
of heauen, Man hath eaten the bread of Angells. Of the which in the
Ioan. 6. fame fignificacion Chryft faieth: *Non Moyfes dedit vobis panem de cœlo*. Moyfes
S. Paule cal- did not geue yow bread from heauen. Whie then maie not Sainct Paule
leth the bo- fpeaking of the Sacrament, vfe the fame terme in the fignificacion, that
die of Chry- his mafter Chryft did, when he fpake of the fame Sacrament, and yet
ſte bread, the fame not to be taken for material bread, but for foode, as yt was in
as Chryſte the fenfe of his mafter? Sainct Paule was no foche difciple to varie
called him- and chaunge the fignificacion of a woorde, wherby he fhoulde varie from
felf in the 6 his mafter in fenfe. For he well knewe the minde of his mafter; as he
of S. Iohn. faied. *Nos fenfum Chrifti habemus*. We vnderftand the minde of Chryft.
1. Cor. 2. Yf then Chryft vfed this woorde *Panis*, not for materiall bread, but for
foode, when he fpake of the Sacrament, that he wolde geue furth, and
leaue to vs: will not (trowe ye) his chofen veffell, who vnderftandeth the **F**
minde of his mafter, when he fpeaketh of the fame thing that his mafter
fpake of, and vfeth the fame woorde that his mafter did, will not he vfe the
woorde in the fame fignificacion that his mafter did, to kepe the minde of
his mafter, and not to varie from yt? He fhoulde haue varied from the
minde of his mafter all the heauen wide (as they faie) yf he fhoulde take
this woorde, *panis*, for materiall bread. For then this great myfterie of
our incorporacion to Chryft, and this great benefit of the incorruptibilitie
and immortalitie of our flefh and bodie, which cometh to vs by the partaking of Chryftes flefh, fhoulde be attributed to a peice of materiall bread.
Which thing what ys yt but plain idolatrie, geuing the diuine honours of
Chryft to a creature, a dumbe peice of bread? Wherfor to ioin with this
learned Authour we muft faie (for that otherwife we can not trulie faie)
that Sainct Paule faieth here that Chryft imparteth to vs his owne bodie,
And fo Sainct Paule fpeaketh here of no materiall bread, but of that high
and godlie foode, the bodie of our Lorde and Sauiour Iefus Chryft. **G**

The argu- Wher then nowe ys the force of the herculeoufe argument of the Ad-
ment of the uerfarie, who by this proceffe of Sainct Paule wolde proue that the Sa-
Sacramēta- crament ys but bread. bycaufe Sainct Paule calleth yt bread after the confe-
rie ouerthro- cracion. For he fpeaketh (faieth he) of the bread broken to the vfe of the
wen, for S. communion, whiche ys after confecracion. Wherfor feing Sainct Paule
Paule fpea- calleth yt bread after the confecracion, yt ys after the confecracion
keth not of but bread.
materiall
bread. Yf this woorde bread were not vfed in the fcripture in an other fignificacion then for materiall bread, and were not alfo of our Sauiour Chryft
him felf fpeaking of this Sacrament otherwife vfed, as yt ys declared, the argument might feem to haue force but nowe yt ys to vain: yt ys as good
an argument as the heritique might make that denied the Sonne of God
to be incarnate, bycaufe the fcripture faieth directlie againft him. *Verbum*
caro factum eſt, The woorde was made flefh: that bycaufe, *Verbum*, fignifieth **H**
a materiall woorde, therfor he fhall argue that yt doth none otherwife fignifie ther, and fo as he thinketh ouerthrowe the faith of the incarnacion of
the Sonne of God, and maintein his herefie, as this Aduerfarie wolde ouerthrowe the faith of the prefence of Chryft in the Sacrament, and by this
woorde, bread, maintein his herefie. But as the one hath fmall force or
ftrenght, fo hath the other.

Wherfor

A   Wherfor nowe leauing this note in this Authour as which mightilie de-
stroieth one of the fundacions of the Aduersarie, and confirmeth the catholique faith, I will in fewe woordes touche the other note, whiche ys for our
incorporacion to Chryste, by partaking of his bodie in the Sacrament, whiche incorporacion he so plainly setteth furthe, that yf his saing be considered, verie fewe woordes shall nede to explain yt.

Note therfor that thus he saieth: *And where that first nature of our flesh was*
corrupted, and was made voide of that heauenlie life, he gaue vs his nature of flesh, being
like vnto owers, the whiche did both lack sinne, and shoulde geue life, that we being made
partakers of yt, we shoulde be mixed with him.

Doest thowe not Reader, see here that he saieth, that Chryst hath geuen
vs the nature of his flesh, not the figure of his flesh, but the nature of yt, the
substance of yt, but to what pourpose hath he geuen vs his naturall flesh? he
declareth, to this pourpose that we shoulde be partakers of yt. Yf we pro-   *What pro-*
cead and aske, what commoditie or profitte haue we by the partaking of his   *fitte we ha-*
flesh? He aunswereth by the partaking of his flesh we are mixed with him in   *ue by parta*
B soche sorte that we receauing his bodie, and nowe being ioined to the same   *king Chry-*
the great vertue and poower of that bodie turneth our bodies into his bo-   *stes flesh.*
die, So that nowe we are be come one bodie of Chryst.

Neither let the grosse Capharnait saie, that yf all faithfulll and woorthie
partakers of the Sacrament be one bodie of Chryst, that then Chryst hath
an huge great bodie: but let him remembre that the naturall man hauing
twentie children, euery one of them ys his flesh and bloode, and yet the
Father ys neuer the greater: So, manie of the faith becoming the flesh of
Chryst by partaking of the Sacrament, yet the flesh of Chryst ys nothinge
bigger of the person of Chryst. And howe soeuer this Aduersarie listeth
grosselie to dallie in soche diuine mysteries: yet this ys the trueth, as by this
Authour ye haue perceaued yt clerelie to be testified, and the like shall you
see in him that foloweth: who ys Sainct Dionise, who expowndeth this text
of Sainct Paule, almost woorde by woorde in this maner. *Quoniam vnus*   *Dionysius*
C *panis per proprietatem, & vnum corpus mysticum vnitate fidei, spei & charitatis,*   *Carthus.*
cuius corporis caput est Christus, multi sumus, videlicet, omnes qui de vno pane, & de
vno calice participamus: id est, de singulari & vero corpore, & sanguine reficimur, &
Sacramentum tantum dignè recipimus. For we are one bread by propertie and
one bodie mysticall by the vnitie of faith hope and charitie of the which
bodie Chryst ys the head, we being manie, that ys to saie, all we whiche do
partake of one bread and one cuppe, that ys, all we whiche be refreshed of
the singular, and verie bodie and blooode of Chryst, and worthilie receaue
so great a Sacrament. Thus Dionyse.

In this exposition let this be diligentlie noted against the Aduersarie,
that the bread which all we receaue, and by the whiche we are made
all one bread and one bodie: yt ys not materiall bread, but the singular, and verie bodie and bloode of our Sauiour Chryst, and so did
Sainct Paule meen yt, as this Authour agreablie with all other before
alleaged, dothe testifie, expownding and declaring the minde of Sainct
D Paule.

Wher then ys the great argument that the Sacrament shoulde be no-   *Argument*
thing but bare bread, Bycause Sainct Paule calleth yt breade? What   *of the woor*
bread yt ys, and what the cuppe conteineth not onely this Authour, but   *de (bread)*
also one, many hondreth yeares elder then he doth declare. Whiche   *ouerthrowē*
auncient Authour shall ende the exposition of bothe these last textes,
                              F ff iij   and

and ioin them together. Thus he faieth: *Calix benedictionis cui benedicimus,* E
nonne communicatio sanguinis Christi est? Idcirco primùm calicem nominauit, quia de pa-
ne postea plus erat disputaturus.Calix autem benedictionis dicitur, qui benedicitur à sacer-
dotibus in altari . Appellatur & ipse calix communicatio, quasi participatio , quia omnes
communicant ex illo partémque sumunt ex sanguine Domini,quem continet in se. Et panis
quem frangimus in altari, nonne participatio corporis Domini est? vtique, primùm conse-
cratur , & benedicitur, à sacerdotibus & spiritu sancto, & deinde frangitur , cùm iam
licet panis videatur in veritate corpus Christi est. Ex quo pane quicunque communicant,
corpus Christi edunt.Quoniam vnus panis,subaudis Christi,& vnum corpus, Christi, multi
*sumus qui comedimus illum panem.*The cuppe of blesing whiche we blesse, ys yt

not a communicacion of the bloode of Chryst?Therfor did he first speake of
the chalice,bicause he wolde afterwarde more at large treacte of the bread.
Yt ys called the cuppe of blesing bicause yt ys blessed of the preistes on the
aultar.The same cuppe also ys called the cōmunicacion, for that yt ys a participacion, bicause all do communicate of yt, and do partake of the bloode
of our Lorde whiche the cuppe conteineth in yt self.And the bread,whiche F
we breake in the aultar ys yt not a partaking of the bodie of our Lorde?Yt ys
so,for first yt ys consecrated of the holie Gost , and of the preistes and afterwarde yt ys broken,when nowe although yt seem to be breade,yet in verie
dede yt ys the bodie of Chryst , of the whiche breade as manie as do cōmunicate,do eat the bodie of Chryst,yt ys one bread of Chryst, and one bodie
of Chryst,and we being manie do eate the same bread.Thus moche *Remigius*
Who being aboute the yeare of our Lorde 511. liued before this our time
aboute 1050.Whose confession yet of the veritie of the presence of Chrystes
bodie in the Sacrament, ys as plain as yf yt had ben made in this our time.
What can be more plainlie spoken then to saie that the cuppe conteineth
the bloode of Chryste?Who can better opē the trueth then to saie,although
yt seem breade:yet in verie deed yt ys the bodie of Chryst?and so moche he
saieth therbie not onely declaring his owne faithe,but also the faith of the
Church he liued in.　Nowe reader when thowe seest so auncient and with
all so euident testimonie of and for the trueth, laie hande to yt and be not G
caried, awaie with the vain woordes of this Proclamer. And thus ending
this text we will go to an other.

THE THIRTETH CHAPITER BEGINNETH THE

exposition of this text . Ye can not drinke of the cuppe of oure Lorde,and
of the cuppe of Deuells,By S.Cyprian and Chrysost.

Orasmoche as in the sixtenth chapiter of this booke . Wher I began the exposition of this disputacion of Sainct Paule with the Corynthians , the dependence of these scriptures,the one of the other
and also the minde of Sainct Paule ys opened , what he here intendeth: I
will not trooble the Reader with that argument again in this place, but remitte him thither.Onelie this I wish him to obserue that Sainct Paule di-
swading the Corynthians from Idolathites vseth three means to doe the H
same.

S.Paule v-
seth three
meanes to
diswade the
Corynthiās
frō Idola-
thites.

One ys the declaracion of the greuouse punishment of the Iewes whiche they susteined for Idolatrie . Whiche being laied before their faces, they might be moued to flye the like offence, for feare of like
pain .

The seconde ys vpon the communion of the bodie and bloode of Chryst
that

A　that wher by the communion of that, that they did communicate they were
vnited to yt, which they did communicate. And vnited they coulde not be
bothe to Chryst, and to deuells. Therfor forsomoche as by the communion
of Chrystes bodie and bloode, they were vnited to him, they must forbeare
the communion with deuells by Idolathites, by which they shoulde be separated, and diuided from Chryst again.

　　The thirde ys (as Sainct Thoms saieth) by the similitude of the legall sacri
fice, whiche Sainct Paule bringeth in as an argument of like, to prooue this
communion or participacion, when he saieth: *Nonne qui edunt hostias, partici-*
pes sunt altaris? Are not they whiche eate of the sacrifice partakers of the
aultar?

　　To ioin the partes of the similitude together, and to make yt fullie to
appeare, thus Sainct Thomas doth sett yt furth: *Are not they whiche eate of*　*Thomas*
the sacrifices, partakers of the aultar, as they whiche eate of the flesh of Chryst are par-　*Aqui. in*
takes of the bodie of Chryst? Forasmoche as eche of these be so, and Chryst and Baall can not　*dec. prima*
dwell together, neither can we serue two masters. Therfor as a perfect conclusion he　*Cor.*
B　inferreth and saieth. *Non potestis calicem Domini bibere, & calicem dæmoniorum.* Ye
can not drinke of the cuppe of our Lorde, and of the cuppe of Deuells.
Where note this conclusion depending vpon the premisses, must include
in yt tearmes of the same significacion that were in the premisses. Forasmoche then as the premisses spake of the partaking of sacrifices: yt must nedes
be that Sainct Paule speaking here of the partaking of the table of our
Lordre, and of the table of deuells, speaketh of the sacrifice of our Lorde,
and the the sacrifice of deuells.

　　That he teacheth the bread and wine to be a sacrifice, yt shall be opened　*Sacrifice*
to yow, after the exposition of the doctours, although this ys sufficietlie testi-　*auouched*
fied before from the sixtenth chapiter vnto this place : yet that yt maie well　*by S. Paule*
be perceaued of the Reader, that my saingys agreable to the holie Fathers
and that this text was spoken of Sainct Paule, as of the sacrifice of the bodie
and bloode of our Lordre on the aultar, the holie Fathers shall be brought
C　furth as before they haue ben vpon the other scriptures, by whose testimonie this matter shall be made clere.

　　And for that Sainct Cyprian rebuketh the same offence, that Sainct Paule
doth, and vseth the same woordes that Sainct Paule doth, wherby the
true mening and vnderstanding maie the better be perceaued, we shall first　*Cyp. ser. 5.*
let his saing be hearde. This yt ys. *Contra euangelij vigorem, contra Domini, ac*　*de lapsis.*
Dei legem, temeritate laxatur incautis communicatio, irrita & falsa pax, periculosa
dantibus & nihil accipientibus profutura, Non quærunt sanitatis pænitentiam, nec veram
de satisfactione medicinam. Pænitentia de peccatoribus exclusa est. Grauissimi, extremíque
delicti memoria sublata est. Operiuntur morientium vulnera & plaga lætalis altis & pro-
fundis visceribus infixa dissimulato dolore contegitur. A diaboli aris reuertentes ad san-
ctum Domini, sordidis & infectis nidore manibus accedunt. Mortiferos idolorum cibos
adhuc penè ructantes, exhalantibus nunc etiam scelus suum faucibus, & contagia funesta
redolentibus Domini corpus inuadunt, cùm occurat scriptura diuina, & clamet & dicat.　*Leuit. 7.*
Omnis mundus manducabit carnem, & anima quæcunque manducauerit ex carne salutaris
D　*sacrificij, quod est Domini, & immundicia eius super ipsum & peribit anima illa de*　*1. Cor. 10.*
populo. Apostolus item testetur, & dicat: Non potestis calicem Domini bibere, &
calicem dæmoniorum. Non potestis mensa Domini communicare, & mensa dæmoriũ.
Against the force of the Gospell, against the lawe of our Lorde and God,
through the rashnesse of some, communicacion ys frelie geuen to the necligent, being a false peace and of no force, yet perilouse to the geuer, and

which shall nothing profitte the receauer. They seke not the penance of **E** healthe,neither the true medicen of satisfaction,penance ys excluded from sinners,the memorie of the extreame and most greuouse offence ys taken awaie. The woundes of them that be dieng be couered, and the deadlie plague stricken into the depe bowells ys with a dissimuled sorowe hidden. Returning from the aultars of the Deuell with filthie and infected handes with the sauoure they come to the holie thing of our Lorde, *Theie yet almost breathing owte the deadlie meates of idolls their chekes puffing oute euen yet their mischeuouse dede, and smelling of the deadlie infection, they violently come vpon the bodie of our Lorde,* When yet the scripture of God cometh against them,and crieth and saieth *Euery clean person shall eate the flesh.* But *yf anie eate of the flesh of the holsome sacrifice, which belongeth to our Lorde hauing his vncleannesse vpon him, the same soule shall perish from among his people.* The Apostle also witnesseth and saieth. *Ye can not drinke the cuppe of our Lorde, and the cuppe of Deuells: Ye can not communicate of the table of our Lorde,and of the table of Deuells:* Thus moche Sainct Cyprian. **F**

Who being moche offended with the necligence of soche preistes,as did admitte them to the receipt of the holie Sacrament,which had defiled them selfes with Idolathites,before they had sufficientlie doen penance,and made amendes for the same,rebuketh them both,the preistes for that they suffred yt,and the receauers,for that they presumed to receaue yt. Whose rebuke, yf you marke,ys verie sore,sharpe,and terrible, whiche of so graue,and god-lie holie martyr shoulde not haue ben doen,yf the thing that they receaued had ben but a peice of breade. For soche graue men as holie Cyprian was did with moche grauitie and godlie wisdome rebuke offences with iust mea-sure, a small faulte gentlie and easilie,a great faulte seuerely and sharpelie. Wherfor this rebuke of S. Cyprian being sharpe and sore,yt argueth that their offence was great, and so in dede yt was.For they being so filthilie de-filed,presumed to come to receaue the blessed bodie of Chryst. *For they yet smelling of the deadlie infection* (saieth S.Cyprian of the eating of the Idolatites) *came violently vpon the bodie of our Lorde, to receaue yt.* By whiche his woordes as **G** ye maie perceaue, ther was a great offence committed, iustly deseruing so great a rebuke: So maie ye perceaue, that by the table of our Lorde spoken of by S.Paule,he vnderstandeth the bodie of our Lorde. So that when S. Paule saieth:*Ye can not be partakers of the table of our Lorde,* yt ys asmoche to saie: as ye can not be partakers of the bodie of our Lorde. In this then the one parte heretofore in the former processe taught, ys confirmed namely that S. Paule rightly vnderstanded, taught the presence of Chrystes bodie in the Sacrament.

I shall not nede to make farder proof of this,seeing that yt ys manifest, that S.Cyprian correcting them that being defiled with Idolathites did pre-sume to receaue our Lordes bodie, dothe touche them with the saing of S. Paule:*Ye can not be partakers of the table of our Lorde.* Whiche texte in dede shoul de nothing touche them,yf the thing that S. Cyprian spake of,were not the same that S.Paule spake of.And so contrarie wise yt ys manifest then that S. **H** Cyprian speaking of the euell receauing of the bodie of Chryst,that S.Paule also spake of the bodie of Chryste,and so both of them of the very presence of Chrystes bodie in the Sacrament.

The other parte also,namely that he speaketh of the bodie of Chryst, as of a sacrifice,ys also easie in him to be pceaued.For to what pourpose ells shoul de Sainct Cyprian alleadge that place of Leuiticus forbidding the vnclean perso

Leuit.7.

1.Cor, 10.

A perſon to receaue anie parte of the ſacrifice of our Lorde, but that that prohibition being ſpoken of the ſacrifice that was the figure, ſhoulde directlie be applied to the ſacrifice which ys the thing, which ys the bodie of Chryſt our ſacrifice, and ſo teache vs that euery vnclean perſon ys forbidden to eate of this holie ſacrifice? For to that pourpoſe did S. Cyprian alleadge that text, as a ſcripture by the which we are forbidden to be partakers of our Lordes ſacrifice, yf we be ioined in anie folowſhippe with Sathan. I minde not to ſtande long vpon this matter, for that I haue ſaied moche of yt allreadie, both in the firſt booke, and alſo in this booke. Wherfore thus leauing Cyprian, I will call in Chryſoſtom, as one of the other ſide of Chryſtes parliament houſe, of whoſe iudgement in the matter of the Sacrament, ſoche a nombre of his ſainges being produced, I truſt the Reader ys not ignorãt, of the whiche alſo diuerſe produced vpon this Epiſtle of Sainct Paule, whiche we nowe treat of, be ſo plain and clere, that none can be deſiered more clere.

But for that vpon this text I finde him not by expreſſe woordes ſpeaking ſo plainlie as the matter maie fullie appeare to the Reader, for the opening
B of the matter that ys here to be ſpoken of, I will produce him where he ſpeaketh of the ſame ſenſe, that S. Paule doth, and withall openeth our matter very plainly. Thus he writeth : *Quomodò ſacrum videbimus Paſcha? quomodò* *Chry.hom.* *ſanctum ſuſcipiemus ſacrificium? quomodò mirabilibus communicabimus myſterijs, lingua* *11. ad pop.* *illa, qua Dei legem conculcauerimus? lingua illa, qua animam contaminauerimus? Si nemo* *Antioch.* *namque purpuram regalem manibus accipere inquinatis auderet : quomodò Dominicum* *corpus lingua polluta ſuſcipiemus? Iuramentum enim maligni : Sacrificium verò Domini:* *Quæ igitur communicatio luci ad tenebras, vel quæ conuenientia Chriſto ad Belial?* Howe *Sacrifice* ſhall we ſee the holie Eaſter? howe ſhall we receaue the holie ſacrifice? howe *plainly a-* ſhall we communicate the wonderfull myſteries with that tounge, whiche *uouched* we haue contemned the lawe of God withall? with that toung wherwith *with reall* we haue defiled our ſoules? For yf no man wolde be ſo bolde, with defiled *preſence.* handes to take the kinges robe: howe ſhall we with a defiled toung receaue the bodie of our Lorde? Swearing ys of the wicked. The ſacrifice ys of our
C Lorde. What folowſhippe then ys ther betwixt light and darknes? or what agreement betwixt Chryſt and Beliall? Thus Chryſoſtom·

Who diſwading the people from vain and ſuperfluouſe ſwearing (*Wher-* *Swearing* *vnto wicked cuſtom, hath at theſe daies alſo to moche brought our people*) ſaieth in *to moche* effect, that they can not receaue, and become partakers of the bodie of our *vſed.* Lorde, with the ſame toung, with whiche they blaſpheme Gods holy name, and contemne his holy lawe. Whiche ys euen the ſame that S. Paule ſaieth here: ye can not be partakers of the table of our Lorde, and of the table of Deuells.

And here note that as S. Paule by the table of our Lorde vnderſtandeth the ſacrifice of our Lorde, of the whiche the wicked can not be partakers: So here Chryſoſtome by expreſſe woordes ſaieth, that the wicked blaſphemour can not be partaker of the ſacrifice of our Lorde: By the whiche ſacrifice he vnderſtandeth the bodie of Chryſte.

For the better perceauing wherof, note that he tearmeth the holie Sacra- *Excellent*
D ment with theſe tearmes. He calleth yt, *the holy ſacrifice.* He calleth yt, *the won-* *titles of the* *derfull myſteries.* He calleth yt, *the bodie of our Lorde:* He calleth yt, *light:* Yea he *bleſſed Sac.* calleth yt *Chryſt himſelf.* By whiche tearmes he declareth vnto vs the excellencie of the Sacrament, as in which ys the very preſence of Chryſtes bodie, verilie and ſubſtancially, whiche ys alſo our ſacrifice. Theſe two partes we ſhall breiflie open in this Authour.

The

Reall pre-
fence proued
by Chryſo.

The verie reall preſence he teacheth when he ſaieth : *Howe ſhall we with* E
a defiled toung receaue the bodie of our Lorde ? Yt ys manifeſt that with our
mouth and toung we can receaue nothing,but that that ys ſubſtancial,and
corporal,but with theſe(*ſaieth Chryſoſt*,)we receaue the bodie of Chryſt.Wher
for we receaue the ſubſtācial and corporal bodie of Chryſt.And therfor this
being well knowen to the Aduerſarie , he with might and main , denieth
that we receaue the bodie of Chryſt with hande or mouth , but onely
with heart . But howe ſhamefullie he doth yt thowe maiſt perceaue , both
by this famouſe and notable Authour , and alſo by Sainct Cyprian , by
Sainct Ambroſe, Sainct Auguſtin , and a nombre mo . Which do plainly
by expreſſe woordes ſaie , that the bodie of Chryſt ys receaued both with
hand and mouthe.But nowe to ſtaie vpon our Authour this one maie ſuffice
againſt the Aduerſarie that he by expreſſe woordes ſaieth , that we receaue
the bodie of our Lorde with our mouth and tounge.

Sacrifice
proued by
Chryſoſt.

For the other parte alſo he teacheth that the ſame bodie of Chryſt ys
a ſacrifice : For he asketh : *Quomodò ſanctum ſuſcipiemus ſacrificium ?* Howe F
ſhall we receaue the holie ſacrifice ? Nowe yf ye compare theſe two ſainges of Chryſoſtome together, namely that we receaue the bodie of our
Lorde with our mouthe , and that euen ſo alſo we receaue the woonderfull ſacrifice : yt ſhall be withoute all doubte eaſie to peaceaue, that
this woonderfull ſacrifice ys the bodie of owre Lorde , and that theſe two
ſainges be ſpoken of one thing . And thus theſe two partes ſtande clere
being here auouched by Chryſoſtom , that both ther ys the very corporall
preſence of Chryſt in the Sacrament , and that the ſame bodie ſo being in
the Sacrament, ys our ſacrifice.

Cranmers ge-
nerall rule
refuted.

By this ſaing of Chryſoſtome ſhall ye perceaue howe vain the generall
rule of Cranmer (*Or of him that ſettſurth that booke in his name*) ys, who
in his fifte booke treating of the ſacrifice ſaieth, that the ſacrifice of the
preiſtes, and the people , ys onely a ſacrifice gratulatorie, that ys of thankes geuing, and a ſacrifice commemoratiue remembring the bodie of
Chryſt,that ſuffred,but not hauing Chryſt reallie,and ſubſtanciallie preſent. G
And this ys his aunſwer to the Nycen Councell , and to *Petrus Lombardus*
and ſo generallie to all.

Sacrifice
gratulato-
rie,or of
thankes ge-
uing.

But nowe conſider what ys the nature of a ſacrifice of thankes geuing, or
as he calleth yt gratulatorie. A ſacrifice gratulatorie ys not receaued of
vs,but offred and geuen of vs and from vs . For we geuing thankes to God
our hauenly Father, that he ſo loued vs, that he ſpared not his owne Sonne
but for our ſakes deliuered him to ſuffer moſt cruell death for vs . And to
that his Sonne alſo we gauing thankes, that he hath vouchedſafe to waſh
awaie our ſinne with his bloode , and to cancell the obligacion that was a-
gainſt vs,wherby he hath made vs free from ſinne, hell, and death , and hath
made vs heires to the kingdom of his Father,and coheirs with him of the ſame kingdom?we offer a ſacrifice of thankes geuing.But this maner of ſacrifice aught to be geuen frō our heartes to our Lorde God,and to our Sauiour
Ieſus Chryſt:And ys ſo,yf yt be reuerently and deuoutlie doen of vs . H

Sacrifice of
the aultar.

This ſacrifice of the aultar ys ſoche a ſacrifice,that yt ys receaued, of vs,
ſaieth Chryſoſtom. Nowe ther ys a great difference betwixt theſe two thinges, of the whiche the one we maie in diuerſe reſpectes both offre , and alſo
receaue: The other we can onely but offre . An other difference ther ys
alſo.The ſacrifice of thankeſgeuing, ys no wonderfull ſacrifice . For yt ys
no wonder,but a duetie to geue God thankes , for his manifold benefittes.

But

A But the ſacrifice of the aultar(as Chryſoſtō ſaieth)ys a woonderfull ſacrifice.

In an other place he calleth yt alſo an holie,and a terrrible ſacrifice: This *Homil.30.* ſacrifice of thankes geuing ys holy but yt ys not terrible. Many ſoche other *De prodſt.* tearmes he geueth to the ſacrifice,whiche will not be applied to the ſacrifi- *Iudæ.* ce of thankes geuing . But to be ſhort,by theſe fewe differences yt ys eaſie to perceaue,that the generall rule of Crāmer,that he wolde al the doctours, wher they call the Sacrament , a ſacrifice , ſhoulde be vnderſtanded to haue ſpoken onelie ofthe ſacrifice gratulatorie, will not ſtand. For the ſainges of the holie doctours, can not beare that rule, as hereafter ſhall appeare more clear to yowe.

Wherunto euen in this place alſo, the concluſion of Chryſoſtoms ſainge geueth good light,and plain vnderſtanding . For after he had declared that the blaſphemouſe mouthe can not receaue the ſacrifice of our Lorde : he ſetteth theſe two together , and ſaieth : *An othe ys of an euell,* The *ſacrifice ys of our Lorde*. What folowſhippe betwixt light and darkneſſe , and what agree- ment betwixt Chryſte and Beliall? In whiche maner of ſpeache yf yow

B note, as blaſphemie,darkneſſe, and Beliall be of one ſide, and ſignifie one thing:So ys the ſacrifice of our Lorde,light, and Chryſt ſett on the other ſide, and ſignifie one thing. So that our ſacrifice ys here alſo called light, and Chryſt himſelf. Whiche names can not be attributed to Cranmer his ſacrifice of thankes geuing, but to the ſacrifice of Chryſtes bodie. Whiche ys in verie dede that thing, that both ys and maie be called the ſacrifice of our Lorde,light and Chryſt. Of the whiche I nede to make no proofe to a true Chryſtian.

This then being prooued,that Chryſoſtom teacheth here the preſence of Chryſtes bodie in the Sacrament,and that the verie ſame ys the ſacrifice of our Lorde:Let ys return to our text, and ſomewhat more open yt, for the better vnderſtanding of yt in all the proceſſe that foloweth , and of the doctours alſo that ſhall be produced for the expoſition of the ſame.

Wher Sainct Paule ſaieth here: *Ye can not drinke of the cuppe of Owre Lorde,* *S.Paules*

C *and of the cuppe of Deuells :* Ye *can not be partakers of the table of our Lorde , and of* *woordes he* *the table of Deuells.* He dothe not ſpeake theſe as abſolute negatiues , but as *re are to be* condicionall. For he meneth not that they coulde not do ſo in verie dede, *vnderſtan-* but that they coulde not ſo do,yf they wolde do well . For he welll knewe *ded, with a* that the Corynthians went both to the table of Chryſt, and alſo to the ta- *condicional* ble of Idolls. And to diſwade them from the table of Idolls, he ſaieth that *negatiue,* they can not without the offence of God partake of bothe tables . Ther ys *not with an* a ſaing: *Hoc poſſumus,quod de iure poſſumus.* That maie we doe, whiche we maie *abſolute.* do by the lawe.Euen ſo maie yt be ſaied on the other ſide. *Hoc non poſſumus,* *quia de iure non poſſumus.* This we can not doe , bicauſe we can not doe yt by the lawe . Whiche maner of ſainge implieth not an abſolute negatiue, vtterlie denieng the facte to be doen:but(as ys ſaied) a condicionall negati- ue,that yt can not be doen by the lawe.

For S. Cyprian,who rebuketh them that impenitently came defiled with eating of Idolls meat, to eate of the meat of our Lordes table , and ſaieth

D alſo to them with Sainct Paules ſentence . Ye *can not be partakers of the table of* *our Lorde, and of the table of Deuells:* Yet he accuſeth them, that they ſo were, aud in facte they did ſo:but to Gods pleaſure, and the wealth of their ſoules, they coulde not do ſo. For yt ys proprely ſaied, that we maie doe that,that we maie doe well.And that we can not doe, whiche we can not doe well. To this ſenſe alſo Chryſoſtome by his interrogatiue including ſoch a negati- ue,ſaied:

ue faied: *The blafphemers of Gods name coulde not with the fame mouth and toung that they blafphemed with, receaue the bodie of our Lorde, receaue the facrifice of our Lorde.* Whiche his fainge yet rebuketh them bicaufe they did fo. Wherfore yt ys not a negatiue abfolute.

Origenes.

A like fainge ys ther afcribed to Origen, for yt ys vncerten whether yt be his worke or no, oute of the which yt ys taken, and yt ys this. *Multa porrò & de ipfo Verbo dici poffunt, quod factum eft caro cibusque verus, quem qui comederit, viuet in æternum, quem nullus malus poteft comedere.* Manie thinges alfo maie be faied of the Sonne of God himfelf, that yt was made flefh, and verie meat, whiche whofoeuer fhall eate, fhall liue foreuer, whiche no euell man can eate. Thus moche Origen.

A place of Origen ope ned.

As S. Paule and S. Cypriane faied, that they that were parteners of Idola-thites coulde not be partakers of our Lordes table: And as Chryfoftom faied, that vain fwearers by Gods holie name, coulde not with the fame mouthe, and tounge receaue the holy facrifice, whiche ys the bodie of our Lorde, whiche ys the table that S. Paule and S. Cyprian fpake of in whiche their fainges they haue made mencion but of two vices, that fhoulde let them from the partaking of the holie and bleffed meate of our Lordes table: So Origen declareth that all vices that be mortall, and whiche make a man an euell man, do diuide him from the fame table. And faieth that foche a man can not eate of the meat of our Lorde, not that foche a one doth not eate yt, but that foche a one dothe not eate yt to his profitte, but raither to his condemnacion, bycaufe with the offence of God he doth abufe the bo-die of Chryft, with moche irreuerence, ioining yt, as yt were in the houfe of his bodie with Sathan: betwixt whom and Chryft, as betwixt God and Be-liall, ys none agreement.

1. Reg. 5.

A liuely argument wherof ys declared in the firft booke of kinges, where we read that the Azotyans hauing the Arke of God, put yt into the temple of Dagon. And forafmoche as they accompted yt as the Arke of the God of Ifraell, of whofe great might and power they had heard moche, they fet yt by their Idoll Dagon. But in the morning when the Azotians came into the temple, they fownde Dagod lieng grooueling vpon the grownde. They fet him vppe again, and the next daie coming into the temple, they fownde him lieng before the Arke of God like a trunke, caft downe to the grownde, his head and palmes of his handes cutte of. By this ys fignified vnto vs, that although yt pleafed God through his great fufferance fo to be abufed, as to be ioincd with Sathan, Beliall, or Dagon: yet to declare that he ys offended withall he throweth down Dagon, and caufeth him to be fownde lieng like a ftocke, or trunke, and with all ftriketh the people with a great glague. By this then (as by that that ys before faied) yt maie be perceaued; howe this fcripture of S. Paules epiftle ys to be vnderftanded, and the doctours alfo, whiche haue ben hetherto alleaged for the expofition of the fame, or fhall hereafter be alleaged.

THE ONE AND THIRTETH CHAP. ENDETH
the expofition of this text by Theophilact and Anfelmus.

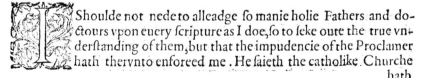

Shoulde not nede to alleadge fo manie holie Fathers and do-ctours vpon euery fcripture as I doe, fo to feke oute the true vn-derftanding of them, but that the impudencie of the Proclaimer hath thervnto enforeed me. He faieth the catholike Churche

hath

A hath not one scripture nor doctour for them, but yt ys and shall be made manifest, that yt hath not one in dede alone, but yt hath all the scriptures, and holie doctours, that treacte of the blessed Sacrament. But bicause vpon this tenth chapiter of Sainct Paule a long exposition by diuerse, and manie doctours ys allreadie made, by whom being made plain howe these scripturs going before are to be vnderstanded, yt ys the easier to perceaue the vnderstanding of this nowe in hande, depending of them, therfor I will cutt of some parte of my pourpose, and nowe vpon this text bring in but one coople more, of the which Theophilact shall be the first, Who for that that S. Paule willed the Corinthians to consider the Iewes, who vsed to offre sacrifices and be partakers of the aultar to the entent that they being chrystians might perceaue that of soche sacrifice as they offred, they were partakers by expresse woordes openeth and declareth what S. Paule ment that the Corinthians were partakers of. Thus he saieth: *De Iudæis namque nil intu-* *Theoph. in Dec.1.Cor.*
lit, quod de eo participarent, sed Altaris sunt participes dixit, in quo, quod immolandum
fuisset, impositum igni consumebatur. De Christi autem corpore haud quaquam res ita se
B *habet, sed Christi corporis fuit participatio. Non enim altaris sumus, sed Dominici corpo-*
ris ipsi participes. Of the Iewes he saied nothing, that they shoulde partake of   *We are par-*
yt (meninge the sacrifice) but he saied that they are partakers of the aultar.   *takers euen*
vpon the which aultar that, that was to be offred in sacrifice, when yt was   *of the bodie*
put vpon yt, yt was consumed with fire, But of the bodie of Chryst the mat-   *of our Lord*
ter ys not so: but ther was a participacion of the bodie of Chryst. For we are   *offred on*
not partakers of the aultar. But we are partakers euen of the bodie of our   *the aultar.*
Lorde. Thus moche Theophilact.

In whome this cometh woorthilie to be noted that S. Paule speaking of   *VVhie S.*
the sacrifices of the Iewes, doth not name anie thing by speciall name wher-   *Paule saied*
of they shoulde be partakers, but onely vseth the generall tearme of the   *not, that the*
aultar, saing that they be partakers of the aultar. And whie? bicause in some   *Iewes were*
of these Sacrifices yt was ordeined that they shoulde be burnt, and consu-   *partakers of*
med. And therfor he saied not that they shoulde be partakers of the thing   *their sacrifi-*
C offred but of the aultar. But when he spake of the bodie of Chryst (saieth   *ces as the*
Theophilact) he did not handle the matter so, but by expresse and speciall   *chrystians*
woordes saied allwais that ther was a partaking of the bodie of Chryste. No-   *of theirs.*
we yf the bodie of Chryst by his ascension were absumed frō vs, as the sacrifice of the Iewes was consumed from them by fire, so that we did no more
by no nearer partaking by presence receaue Chryst, then they did their sacrifices: by the mening of Theophilact yt shoulde seme, that S. Paule
wolde haue saied of the chrystians that they are partakers of the aultar, as
the Iewes, and not by speciall woorde haue saied, they are partakers of the
bodie of Chryst.

Nowe in the disputacion of S. Paule yt ys plain to see that speaking of the
sacrifice of the Chrystians, he nameth, wherof they are partakers. As when   *1.Cor. 10.*
he saieth: *The cuppe of blessing, which we blesse, ys yt not a partaking of the blood*
of Chryst? And the bread whiche me breake, ys yt not a partaking of the bodie of Chryst.
Wher by speciall woordes he nameth the thinges their receaued and par-
D taken. But speaking of the sacrifices of the Iewes throughoute all the disputacion he nameth no speciall thinge, but vseth (as I saied) the generall terme
of the aultar. Wherby we maie conclude with Theophilactes woordes.
Non enim altaris sumus sed Domini corporis ipsi participes. We are not partakers of
the aultar, but we are partakers of the bodie of Chryste. Yf the bodie of
Chryste were absent from the sacrifice, we shoulde be by Theophilactes

iudgement partakers of the aultar: but bicauſe the bodie of Chryſt ys preſent E in the ſacrifice, and ys the ſacrifice yt ſelf, that ys offred, therfore are we partakers of the bodie of Chryſt. By which proceſſe of Theophilact yt ys plain to be perceaued that he vnderſtandeth Sainct Paule here to haue ſpoken of the verie bodie and bloode of Chryſt, of the whiche we are verie partakers. Of this who can doubte, that remembreth his expoſition of the firſt text of this diſputacion of Sainct Paule wher he ſaieth, ſpeaking of him. *That, that he ſaied, ys after this maner: This bloode that ys conteined in the cuppe, ys euen the ſame that flowed oute of Chryſtes ſide. This bloode when we receaue, we do partake, that ys, we are ioined to Chryſt.*

The bloode of Chryſte ys not onely in heauen, but alſo in in the chalice.

Who can doubte of the faith of this man, and howe he vnderſtandeth Sainct Paule, that ſo plainlie expowndeth him? He ſaieth that we receaue, not a figure onely, but the bloode of Chryſte. And this blood ys not onely in heauen, whether onely, the Aduerſarie ſaieth, we muſt by faith lift vppe our eyes and heart, but yt ys conteined (ſaieth Theophilact) in the cuppe, wher alſo by faithe we muſt beholde yt. And this ys not onely a Sacrament of Chryſtes bloode, ſo called bicauſe Sacramentes haue the names F of thinges wherof they are Sacramentes, but yt ys (ſaieth Theophilacte) euen the ſame bloode that flowed oute of Chryſtes ſide, and not a thing bearing the name of the bloode of Chryſt

Nowe Chryſtian Reader, iudge yf the Aduerſarie haue not plain authoritie againſt him, that wher he wolde that yt ſhoulde be prooued, that Chryſtes naturall and ſubſtanciall bodie ys in the Sacrament. Yf that bodie vpon the crooſſe, oute of the whiche for mannes redemption did plentifullie flowe oute bloode, were naturall, foraſmoche as this bloode in the holie Sacrament ys euen the ſame bloode, yt muſt nedes folowe, that the naturall bodie, and naturall blood of Chryſt, ys in the Sactament.

Why ſtand I ſo long vpon ſo clere a matter, ſeing that *Anſelmus* who ys ioined with him to ſhewe the faith of the latin churche, as Theophilact hath doen of the greeke churche, ys euen as plain as he? Thus expowndeth he

Anſel. in 10. 1. Cor.

Sainct Paule. *Non poteſtis calicem Domini, in quo ſanguis eſt eius, bibere, & calicem G Dæmoniorum, in quo vinum eſt ſacrilegæ ſuperſtitionis. Nec poteſtis menſæ, id eſt, altaris Domini, in quo corpus eius eſt, participes eſſe, & menſæ, id eſt, altaris Dæmoniorum.* Ye can not drinke the cuppe of our Lorde, in the whiche ys his bloode, and the cuppe of Deuells, in whiche ys the wine of ſacrilegall ſuperſticion. Neither can yow be partakers of the table, that ys of the aultar of our Lorde, in the whiche ys his bodie, and of the table, that ys, of the aultar of Deuels. Thus he.

In this Authour, who liued within xvi. yeares of fiue hundreth yeares agon, ye ſee a very plain expoſition, fullie agreing, yea allmoſt vſing the ſame woordes that Theophilact did. Who was liuing almoſt three hundreth yeares before him. Which Theophilact vſeth the woordes of Chryſoſtome, who liued more then foure hundreth yeares before Theophilact. Whoſe ſaing ye ſhall finde in the xvi. chapiter of this booke. I ſaie in this Authour here alleadhed, ye haue a plain expoſition of Sainct Paules woordes. For firſt, he expowndeth what S. Paule meneth by the cuppe of our Lorde, and H ſaieth that yt ys the cuppe of our Lorde, bicauſe the blood of our Lorde ys in yt. Then teaching what he meneth by the table of our Lorde he ſaieth, he meneth the aultar of our Lorde. Whiche ys ſo called bicauſe the bodie of our Lorde ys vpon yt. So that as the cuppe ys called the cuppe of our Lorde, bicauſe his bloode ys in yt: So ys the table called the aultar of our Lorde,

bicauſe

A bicause the bodie of our Lorde ys vpon yt. I thinke these woordes be plain enough, wher by expresse woordes ys taught the presence of the very bodie and bloode of Chryst in the Sacrament, and that in no other sorte of woordes, then Theophilact before him, and Chrysostome before him, as ye haue hearde did teache.

Peraduenture ye will saie he expowndeth the table to be an aultar, which cometh in but of late daies, and ys a terme not vsed amonge the auncient doctours. That bothe the woorde and the thinge, was in vse in the time of the auncient doctours, yt shall be made manifest to thee, gentle Reader, and that euen from the Apostles.

A proof of the vse of aultars euē frō the Apostles time.
Dion. Are. eccles. Hie. par 3. ca. 3

Sainct Dionyse the disciple of S. Paule declaring the order of Chrystes Churche in his time, among other declaracions of the blessed Sacrament, maketh mencion of the same sett vpon the aultar, saing thus: *Sed & illud sacratius intuere, quod impositis altari venerabilibus signis, per quæ Christus signatur & sumitur, adest protinus sanctorum descriptio.* But reuerentlie beholde that, that when the honorable signes be put vpon the holy aultar, by the whiche

B Chryst ys both signified and receaued, furthwith their ys a description of sainctes. In these woordes ye perceaue bothe the name of the aultar, and the vse of yt. For the vse of yt was to put vpon yt the holie Sacrament, for the whiche vse sake, this auncient holie Father called yt the holie aultar. Whiche wolde be noted of thē, who in these our daies, geue the aultar moche baser tearmes, yf I shall saie no woorse of them. And herwithall note that this Authour doth not onely call this Sacrament honourable, but also furthwith addeth the cause, for bicause (saieth he) Chryst ys bothe signified, and receaued. So that by the outwarde formes he ys not onely signified, but also verilie vnder them receaued. Of the which two partes of the Sacrament we haue more at large spoken before.

Of the aultar and the vse of the same also Sainct Ambrose maketh mencion saing: *Ego Domine memor venerandæ passionis tuæ accedo ad altare tuum licet peccator vt offeram tibi sacrificium quod tu instituisti, & offerri præcepisti in commemo-*

Amb. orat. præpar.
Aultar and sacrifice both mēcionedby S. Amb. and vsed.

C *ratione tui pro salute nostra.* I (o Lorde) being mindefull of thy honourable passiō come vnto thine aultar allthough a sinner, to offre vnto thee the sacrifice that thowe didest institute and commaunde to be offred in the remembrance of thee, for our health. Here maie ye perceaue that S. Ambrose came to the aultar, of whom also ye maie learn the vse of the aultar, for he came to offre sacrifice vpon yt, so that the vse of the aultar was to haue sacrifice offred vpon yt, which thing S. Ambrose his facte dothe well declare. For so holie a man as he was wolde not abuse the aultar. Wherfore yt dothe well appeare that yt ys the right vse of the aultar.

The name and the vse of the aultar ys likewise declared vnto vs by his disciple S. Augustine, who shewing the godlie zeale of his Mother lieng on her death bedd, and what she desiered to be doen for her, saieth. *Illa imminente die resolutionis suæ, non cogitauit corpus suum sumptuosè contegi, aut condiri aromatibus, aut monumentum electum concupiuit, aut curauit sepulchrum patrium. Non ista mandauit nobis, sed tantummodò memoriam sui ad altare tuum fieri desiderauit, cui nullius diei*

Aug. lib. 9. cōfes. ca. 13

D *prætermissione seruierat, vnde sciret dispensari victimam sanctam, qua deletum est chyrographum quod erat contrarium nobis.* She, the daie of her death being at hand, was not mindefull to haue her bodie sumptuously buried, or to be spiced with spices, nor coueted to haue a solemne monument, neither desiered to be buried in her owne contrie. These thinges did she not commaunde vs, but onely desiered she to be remembred at thine aultar, which she withoute

Aultar serued wher sacrifice was done.

Ggg ij　　　anie

anie daies omifsion had ferued, from whence fhe knewe that facrifice to be　**E**
defpenfed, by the whiche the hand writing was put oute that was againft vs.

Thus of Sainct Auguftine alfo ye heare the name of the aultar and the
vfe. The vfe ys like as ye haue hearde in S. Ambrofe, that ys, to offre facrifice
vpon. For S. Auguftins mother knewe that that facrifice was defpenfed or
geuen from the aultar whiche redemed vs and wafhed vs from our finnes
in his bloode, whiche euery true Chryftian will confeffe to be the bodie of
our Lorde Iefus Chryft.

The fame S. Auguftine alfo ys a plentifull withneffe of this matter of the

The Procla-
mers falfe
fleight in
his allega-
cion of S.
Auguft.

aultar, ad *Cafulanum*. And in his fermon to the infantes, of whiche place alfo
the Proclamer in his fermon maketh mencion : but with foche fleight, and
craftie falfheade, as I can not ouerpaffe yt, but note yt to the Reader. For
firft, wher S. Auguftine vfeth the plain terme or name of the aultar, this
man not liking that name corrupted S. Auguftine and putteth in to the
place of yt the name of table. Secondly wher S. Auguften plainly teacheth
the prefence of Chryftes bodie and bloode. He to deceaue his audience
bringeth three or foure woordes of the place to make them beleue that S.　**F**
Auguften reputed the Sacrament but as a peice of breade, and leaueth oute
all the reft. But I fhall firft alleadge S. Auguftine as his owne woordes be.

Aug. ferm.
ad infant.

Thus he writeth : *Hoc quod videtis in altari Dei, etiam transacta nocte vidistis.*
Sed quid effet, quid fibi velit, quam magnæ rei Sacramentum contineret, nondum au-
diftis. Quod ergo vidiftis panis est, & calix, quod vobis etiam oculi veftri renunciant.
Quod autem fides veftra poftulat inftruenda, panis est corpus Chrifti, calix fanguis. Domi-
nus nofter Iefus Chriftus nouimus vnde acceperit carnem, de virgine Maria, infans
lactatus eft, nutritus eft, creuit, ad iuuenilem ætatem peruenit, à Iudæis perfecutionem
paffus eft, in ligno fufpenfus eft, in ligno interfectus eft, fepultus eft, tertia die refurrexit,
quo die voluit in cœlum afcendere, illuc leuauit corpus fuum, vnde est venturus vt iudicet
viuos & mortuos, Ibi est modò fedens ad dextram Patris : Quomodò est panis corpus
eius? & calix, vel quod habet calix, quomodò est fanguis eius? Ista fratres ideò dicuntur
Sacramenta, quia in eis aliud videtur, aliud intelligitur. Quod videtur fpeciem habet
corporalem, quod intelligitur, fructum habet fpiritualem. This that ye fee in the

Wher S.
Aug. here
nameth the
aultar, the
Proclamer
a fhamed
of fo honou-
rable a na-
me calleth
yt a table.

aultar of God, ye did alfo fee yt the laft night. But what yt was, what yt　**G**
ment, of howe great a thing yt conteineh a Sacramet yet haue not yet hearde. That then that ye haue feen ys bread and a cuppe, whiche thing alfo
your eyes doe tell yow: but that your faith requireth to be inftructed, the
bread ys the bodie of Chryft, and the cuppe his bloode. Owre Lorde Iefus
Chryft, we knowe from whence he tooke flefh, euen of the virgen Marie,
being an infant he fucked: he was nourced, he grewe, he came to the age of
a young man, he fuffred perfecucion of the Iewes, he was hanged vpon the
croffe, vpon the croffe he died, he was buried, the thirde daie he rofe, what
daie he wolde he afcended into heauē: Thither did he cacrie vppe his bodie
from whence he will come to iudge the quicke and the dead : Ther ys he
nowe fitting at the right hand of God the Father. Howe ys the bread his
bodie? and the cuppe, or that ys in the cuppe, howe ys yt his bloode? Thefe
thinges bretheren are therfore called Sacramentes, bicaufe in them one
thing ys feen, an other thing ys vnderftanded. That that ys feen hath a　**H**
corporall forme, that ys vnderftanded, hath a fpirituall profitte. This
ys the wholl faing of Sainct Auguftine. The Proclamer alleadgeth
him thus : *Quod videtis in menfa, panis est.* That ye fee in the table, ys
bread.

In whi-

A　In whiche his allegacion firſt ye maie perceaue, that wher Sainɛt Auguſtine putte and vſed this woorde, aultar. This man to make him appeare to haue ſaied to his pourpoſe, was contented to corrupt him, and falſifie him, in ſtead therof to put his woorde, table. In dede yt coulde not but haue ſownded to his ſhame in ſoche a wiſe and learned audience yf he ſhoulde haue alleaged Sainɛt Auguſtine making mencion of the aultar, and not onely calling yt the aultar, but alſo the aultar of God, the whiche aultar with the mencion and wholl remembrance of yt, he hath laboured to deface, and vtterlie to wipe awaie. What ye maie thinke and iudge of the doɛtrine of this man, that to maintein yt dothe ſo manifeſtlie falſifie the doɛtours, and dare not alleadge them as they be written, but as he liſteth him ſelf, I leaue to be conſidered. What ſynceritie alſo he vſeth ſo truncatelie alleadging Sainɛt Auguſtine, that wher he taught the twoo partes of the Sacrament, namely the outwarde corporall forme, and the inwarde ſubſtance of Chryſtes bodie and bloode: the one knowen by the eye of the bodie, the other by the vnderſtanding of faith, this man ſnat-
B　cheth the firſt parte, and renneth awaie with yt, leauing the other parte behinde him, and ſo truncating Sainɛt Auguſtin deceaueth the people, and abuſeth the holie doɛtour. I ſhall not nede to geue farder aduertiſement here. Sainɛt Auguſtine as he did write, and as this man alleageth him lieth before yow, ye maie compare them, and trie the trueth. Wherfore I will leaue to ſpeake of them anie more and proceade in my matter.

　　As of theſe Fathers before alleaged we haue learned that in the primitiue Churche the aultars were in vſe: So nowe learn withall what in thoſe daies was thought of them that did abuſe aultars. To geue vs vnderſtanding in this matter, we will heare. *Optatus*, the holie auncient Biſhoppe, who liued before Sainɛt Auguſtine, Sainɛt Hierom, or Sainɛt Ambroſe, and was almoſt xij. hondreth yeares agon. This learned Father and Biſhoppe writing againſt the Donatiſtes who threwe downe the aultars, and ſpoiled the Churches, ſaieth thus: *Quid eſt tam ſacrilegum quam altaria Dei, in*
C　*quibus & vos aliquando obtuliſtis, frangere, radere, & remouere, in quibus vita populi, & membra Chriſti portata ſunt, quo Deus omnipotens inuocatus ſit, quo poſtulatus deſcendit Spiritus ſanɛtus, vnde à multis pignus ſalutis æternæ, & tutela fidei, & ſpes reſurreɛtionis accepta eſt? Altaria, inquam, in quibus fraternitatis munera non iuſſit ſaluator poni, niſi quæ eſſent de pace condita. Depone, inquit, munus tuum ante altare, & redi, priùs concorda cum fratre tuo, vt pro te poſſit ſacerdos offerre. Quid eſt enim altare, niſi ſedes corporis & ſanguinis Chriſti? Hæc omnia furor veſter, aut raſit, aut fregit, aut remouit. Quid vobis fecit Deus, qui illic inuocari conſueuerat? Quid vos offenderat Chriſtus, cuius illic per certa momenta, corpus & ſanguis habitat? Quid vos offenditis etiam vos ipſi, vt altaria frangatis, in quibus ante nos per longa temporum ſpatia, ſanɛtè (vt arbitramini) obtuliſtis? Hoc modo Iudæos eſtis imitati. Illi iniecerunt manus Chriſto in cruce: à vobis percuſſus eſt in altari, De quibus apud Dominum Helias Propheta quærelam deponit, ijs enim locutus verbis, quibus & vos inter alios ab ipſo accuſari meruiſtis, Domine, inquit, altaria tua confregerunt. Dum dicit tua, indicat quia res eſt Dei, vbi Deo aliquid à quocumque oblatum eſt.* What ys ſo great ſacrilege, as to breade
D　raſe, and remoue the Aultars of God, in the whiche yowr ſelues ſomtyme haue offred: in whiche the praiers of the people and membres of Chriſt were born: wher allmightie God ys called on: wher the holy Spirit deſired deſcendeth. from whence of manie the pledge of euerlaſting health: and the ſauegarde of faith: and the hope of reſurreɛtion ys taken? the Aultars Iſaie, on

　　the

Aultar of God.

S. Auguſt. truncatlie alleaged by the Proclamer to deceaue the people and to robbe the B. Sacr. of the preſence of Chriſte.

Optatus li. con. Donatiſt.

3. Reg. 19.

See here the vſe, the regard, the eſtimation and reuerẽce of aultars in the auncient churche.

the which our fauyour commaunded the offrings of the bretheren not to be **E**
put, except foche as were feafoned with peace . *Laie downe*, (faith he) *thy of-*
fring before the Aultar.and go firft and agree with thy brother , that the preft maie offer
for thee. What ys the Aultar but the feat of the bodie and bloode of Chryfte? But all theife hath yowr furie either raced, broken, or remoued and taken

Aultar
what yt ys,
ãd the fpoil
of aultars.

awaie . what had God doen to yowe, who was wount ther to be called on?
What had Chryft offended yowe, whofe bodie and bloode fomtime dwelleth ther ? what doe yowe yowr felues offende yowr felues, to breake thofe
aultars in the whiche a long time before vs ye haue offred, as ye thinke,
godlie . By this ye haue folowed the iewes . They fmitte Chryft vpon the
croffe : of yowe he ys fmitten on the aultar, of whome the Prophet *Helias*
maketh cõplaint to our lordre. For he fpeaketh foche woordes, wher with
yowe alfo are woorthie to be blamed . Lorde (faieth he) they haue broken
downe thine aultars. When he faieth(,*Thine*) he declareth that that thing
ys gods or belongeth to God, wher anie thing of ani man ys offred to God,
thus moch *Optatus* . Who was not born yefterdaie to tell vs the fafhion of
religion in the latter daies . But he telleth vs the religion of the auncient **F**
Churche , whiche was almoft twelue hondreth yeares agone at which

Let the Pro
clamer and
his felowes
fee and faie
howe they
agree in
their doings
with the the
auncient
church
wherof in
woordes
they bragg
fomocke .

time he liued and in that tyme yt was thought that ther coulde be no
greater facriledge then to breake and pull downe the aultars.

In thofe daies (as by this authour yt maie be perceaued) yt was religion
to faie that the aultar ys the feat of the bodie and bloode of Chryft. Wherby as the prefence of the verie bodie and blood in the Sacrament maie euidently be perceaued to haue ben faithfullie beleued and taught : So maie
yt that the aultars , for that they were accompted the feat of the bodie and
bloode of Chryft, were reuerently vfed . Yt ys eafie alfo to perceaue howe
that in thofe daies the vfe of the aultar was to offer vpon, as ye maie perceaue by hys allegacion of Chryfts fainge. Yf then to pull downe and deftroie aultars be fo heynoufe and great an offence , that ther ys no facrilege greater than yt , and thys was fo thought aboue eleuen hondreth years
agon , I wifh them that finde them felues giltie of foche facts to haue confideracion of their dooings , yf they haue anie regarde to the iudgments **G**
and aduertifements of the anncient Fathers . Yf they will not creditte
their iudgements let them creditte the iudgements of God. who in times
paffed hathe euedently declared the fame . Wherfore as ye haue hearde
the vfe of the aultars teftified by diuerfe Fathers , and the abufe of them alfo
reputed as an heinoufe crime and offence , yea more heinoufe then facrilege: So fhal ye nowe perceaue the contemptuoufe abufe of them to haue ben
fore and greuouflie punifhed of God, therby well appearinge foche abufe

Lib·6.cap.
23.
The impu-
dens fact of
Iulianus in
piffing a-
gainft the
holie aul-
tar.

moche to offend him.

In the tripartite hiftorie we reade that in the tlme of *Iulianus Apoftata*, one
called *Iulianus* beinge the ruler of the eaft parts vnder the fame wicked
Iulian then Emperour, entred in to a church, and piffed againft the aultar.
The woordes of *Theodorete* be thefe : *Iulianus præfectus impudenter contra facrum*
altare minxit, quem cùm Euzoius prohibere tentaret, eum ille percuſsit in capite . Iulian
the prefident impudently piffed againft the holie aultar, whom when *Euzoius* **H**
wolde haue forbidden, he ftrooke him vpon the heade. Here by the reporte
of this authour, ye fee the impudente facte of this wiked *Iulianus*, wher by the
waie note that the authour calleth yt an impudent facte, and alfo calleth the
aultar an holie aultar.

And

And nowe heare the punifhint of this facte. The authour reporting the wiked doinges of the faied *Iulianus*, and of one *Felix* together, fhewinge both their punifhiments faieth thus: *Sed pro ijs impietatibus vefanifque præfump-tionibus non poft multum pænas exacti funt. Nam repente Iulianus fæuo morbo correptus viferibus putrefactis interijt. & excrementa non per meatus egeftinos emittebat, fed fce-leftum os, quod blafphemijs miniftrauerat, organum huius excretionis eft factum.* But for all thefe wickedneffes, and furiofe prefumptions, they within a litle whi-le after, fuffred paines. For *Iulianus* being fodenly taken with a fore difeafe his bowells being putrifieddied, and he did not voide the excrements by the lower parts of his bodie. But the wiked mouthe, that had ben an inftru-ment to blafphemies, was nowe made an organ of excretion. Thus moche the ecclefiefticall hiftorie.

In whiche, as before we fawe the offence of the man: So nowe perceaue we the punifhmēt. *Arrius* was a blafphemoufe heretique whofe heinoufe of-fence, was (by his death inflicted of God) declared to all the worlde, to be to God very greuoufe, and difpleafaunt, and yet yt was not more greuoufly

B punifhed then this. For.that man though he in eafing of nature, by gods plague powred oute with thexcrements the bowells of his bodie, and fo died a fylthie deathe: Yet this man, whofe bowells, by the like plague of God were putrified, and rotten in his bodie, and therby God fo difpofing, the filthie and ftinking excrements, that fhoulde haue ben voided by the lo-wer parts of his bodie wer voided and powred oute at his mouth, and fo dieng, died yet a filthier deathe, then thother. Yf then the contemptuou-fe abufe of aultars were fo greuoufly punifhed of God, and the reuerent vfe of aultars was neuer reproued, eafie yt ys to iudge that the well vfers of aultars, are of God praifed, and the abufers of them, of God difpraifed. the vfe of aultars of God and auncient Fathers well liked the abufe of thē moch mifliked.

But once, to finifh this matter, and to returne to our text, and to *Anfelmus* whofe expofition we alleaged: ye maie by this that ys faied well peceiue
C that both the name of the aultar, and alfo the vfe of yt, ys comed to vs from the primitiue churche. So that this authour *Anfelmus* ys not the firft authour of yt. But he fpeaketh of yt as he hath learned of the Fathers. And therfo-re dothe verie well expownde the table of our lorde in S.Paule, calling yt the aultar. For the aultar in deed ys the table of our lorde, wherin ys the meat of the bodie of Chryft whiche ys the facrifice of our lorde. of the which the faithfull people be partakers, and wher vpon we feede, to repayre this corruptible flefh that yt maie once come to incorruption, ad from mortalitie to immortalitie.

Neither onelie are we moued by the expofition of this authour to vn-derftande S. Paule to fpeake of the aultars: but alfo to vnderftand him to haue fpoken of the facrifice of the fame aultar of Chryft. for that therin he implieth the facrifice of Chryfts bodie and blood, by caufe an aultar generaly ferueth to beare a facrifice: wherfor particularlie the aultar of Chryft ferueth to beare the facrifice of Chryft. To this vnderftanding
D of S. Paule the verie letter leadeth: S. Paules own argument made to the Corinthians enforeth. For when he faieth vnto them: *Ye can not drinke the cuppe of our lorde, and the cuppe of deuells: ye can not be partakers of the table of our lorde, and of the table deuells.* In bothe parts he calleth yt indifferentlie
Ggg iiij   the

the cuppe. So that to the veſſell of our Lordes table he geueth no other ter- E
me then he doth to the veſſell of the table of Deuells. Yf then yt be the
cuppe of the Deuells bicauſe yt was offred to Deuells, in ſacrifice : then ys
the other the cuppe of our Lorde, bicauſe yt ys offred to him in ſacrifice.
Likwiſe for the ſecond ſentence: Yf the table of Deuells, be ſo called bicauſe yt ſerueth to the ſacrifice of Deuells : Euen ſo muſt the table of our Lorde be ſo called, bicauſe yt ſerueth to the ſacrifice of our Lord.

Thus then ye ſee that of the verie letter, and of Sainct Paules argument, yf yt ſhall haue anie force by the compariſon, whiche he here
maketh, that as he ſpake of the ſacrifice of Deuells on the one ſide : ſo he
ſpake of the ſacrifice of our Lorde on the other ſide. For as Hilarie ſaieth.

Hilar de
Trinit li. 8 *Omnis compariatio ad intelligentiæ formam præſumitur, vt id, de quo agitur, ſecundùm
exemplum propoſitum aſſequamur.* Euery compariſon ys taken to the forme
of vnderſtanding, that we maie atteign yt that ys ſpoken of according to
the example that ys propoſed.

Nowe yf Sainct Paule making his compariſon ſhoulde in one parte
ſpeake of one thing, and in the other parte of an other thing, howe ſhoul- F
de the compariſon healpe our vnderſtandinge ? Wherfore according
to Sainct Paules example we vnderſtand him ſpeaking of the cuppe of our
Lorde, to haue ſpoken of yt, as of the bloode of Chryſt offred in ſacrifice (of the whiche, as before ys ſaied we be partakers) as in the ſame example ſpeaking of the cuppe of Deuells, he ſpeaketh of yt as of a ſacrifice
offred to Deuells, of the whiche Idolaters are partakers. Otherwiſe what
ſhoulde the cōpariſon auaill, when betwixt a thing offred in ſacrifice and
a thing not offred in ſacrifice ther ys no proporciō. Wherfor as the exāple
ys vnderſtāded of a thing ſacrificed: So muſt the thing compared to the exāple be vnderſtanded of a thing ſacrificed, that ther maie be proporcion and
ſimilitude betwixt the thinges ioined in cōpariſon. Then muſt yt be concluded that as Sainct Paule ſpake of ſacrifice in the example : So ſpake he
of ſacrifice in the thing compared to the example. And ſo yt ys euident
that the bodie and bloode of Chryſt in the Sacrament, of which we are
partakers, after the minde of Sainct Paule, ys a ſacrifice.   G

To this yf ye adde the ſainges of Sainct Cyprian and Chryſoſtome in
the laſt chapiter, and the expoſitions of all the doctours vpon theſe textes
of Sainct Paule: *The cuppe of bleſſinge, &c.* and, *The bread which we break, &c.*
Which ye ſhall finde before alleaged in this booke, whiche all ſo ſhewe
the minde of Sainct Paule, as that he ſpake not onely in theſe places of
the bodie and bloode of Chryſt in the Sacrament, as ther verilie preſent:
But alſo as yt ys a ſacrifice, ye ſhall yf ye will, eaſilie perceaue and vnderſtand the trueth of the matter, that Sainct Paule in this diſputacion withe
the Corynthians, treacted of the bodie and bloode of Chryſt in the Sacrament as of a ſacrifice. To the vnderſtanding of whiche trueth moche
light ys added by that ys declared, that the auncient Fathers of the primitiue Churche accepted both the name and the vſe of an aultar, whiche

Aultar and
Sacrifice be
correlati-
ues. argueth a ſacrifice. For a ſacrifice, and an aultar be (as yt were) Correlatiues : So that whether yt be extern or interne ſacrifice, yt hath an- H
ſwetablie an aultar, ſo that we maie ſaie: Yf here be an aultar yt preſuppoſeth to doe ſacrifice on. Yf we ſaie, here ys a ſacrifice, yt preſuppoſeth to be doen on an aultar. This the Aduerſarie knewe right
well. Wherfore to compaſſe his pourpoſe to take awaie the ſacrifice he
remo-

A remoued and tooke awaie aultars. But what foeuer the Aduerfarie hath doen,yt ys plainly prooued,that the primitiue Churche vfed bothe,and had both in honoure and reuerence.

THE TWO AND THIRTETH CHAP. VPON OCCA-
fion that yt ys prooued, that the primitiue Church vfed the aultar, and reputed the bodie and bloode of Chryft to be a Sacrifice, begin-neth to treact of the fame facrifice, whiche we commonlie call the Maffe.

S the Sacrament of Chryftes bodie and bloode ys(as *Dio-nyfius Areopagita* faieth) of all Sacramentes moft excellent, and moft honorable, perfecting and confummating al other Sacramentes: Euen fo ys ther none that Sathan more cruellie perfecuteth by his minyfters in thefe our daies than this. For of all the partes or membres of this B he leaueth none vntouched and not impugned:The prefence he vtterly de-nieth: tranfubftanciacion he derideth: Adoracion as Idolatrie he detefteth referuacion he contemneth:Communion either priuate (as he tearmeth yt) or vnder one kinde, he flieth and defpiceth:The facrifice as a peftilence he abhorreth and hateth:the hatred,wherof he hath fo fixed, and fiered in the heartes of his difciples, that not onely the thing, as the facrifice yt felf, and the Ceremonies thervnto apparteining: but the very name ys vnto them fo odioufe,as nothing can be more odioufe. This facrifice and the wholl mini-ftracion of the fame ys called the Maffe, whiche howe yt hath ben mocked and skorned, what raiginges and railinges haue ben vfed againft yt, yt ys raither to be Iamented,then reherfed.After the whiche forte this Proclamer bendeth himfelf cheiflie to inueigh againft the Maffe.

But forafmoche as S.Paule hath taught vs that the bodie and bloode of Chryft be our facrifice, and the Fathers of the primitiue Churche did fo re-C ceaue yt and beleue yt : by breaking and drinking of which in the aultar of our Lorde, they trufted faftlie and infeparablie to be vnited to Chryft:I will fomwhat more fpeciallie (being thus as ys faied occafioned) fpeake of the fa-me facrifice and the miniftracion of yt. And firft of the name. Secondly of the wholl miniftracion.Thirdly of certain partes of the Canon, whiche the Proclamer impugneth. Forthlie of the valeu of yt to the quicke and dead.

Maffe the woord how yt cometh.

As for the name,I can but meruell what they meen that fo furioufle rage againft yt, confidering that yt was not yefterdaie begon or inuented : but vfed in the primitiue Churche, and from the primitiue Churche in the fame fignificacion as yt ys at this prefent daie. For this woorde, Maffe, whiche ys vfed in the englifh tounge : And *Miffa*, whiche to fignifie the fame ys vfed in the latin tounge, be (as the learned in the tounges faie) Hebrue woordes. In the whiche toung of this woorde (Mas) cometh Miffa, whiche in fignificacion ys all one with the greeke woorde (Liturgia) infomoche that yf a man wolde tranflate or interprete this woorde (Miffa) D into greke, he can haue no meeter woorde, then this woorde (Liturgia) liuely, and fully to aunfwer, and expreffe his fignificacion . Likewife yf a man will interprete or tranflate this woorde (Liturgia) into the He-brue toung he can haue no apter terme then this woorde, Miffah . And yf yowe will tranflate both thefe into the latin tounge,yt fhallbe rightlie

and

and iustly doen by the woorde (*officium*) as yt signifieth our duetie in doing **E**
Missa.   sacrifice and diuine seruice to God.

Liturgia.
Officium.

And although these woordes, *Missa, Liturgia*, and *officium*, be of more large significacion : yet haue they ben by great auncient Fathers of Chrystes Churche restreigned, and limited to signifie onelie our sacrifice, and seruice to God. Wherfore in the greke Churche the Masse of Sainct Basill war called *Liturgia*, the Masse of Sainct Chrysostom was called *Liturgia*. So ys this woorde, *officium*, vsed in Sainct Lukes Gospell wher he speaketh of *Zacharias* the preist and father of Sainct Iohn Baptist : *Et factum est, vt impleti*

Luc.1.   *sunt dies officij eius, abijt in domum suam.* And when the time of his seruice was expired, he went home. In whiche sainge this woorde, seruice, ys taken for the sacrifice and diuine seruice doen in the time of his course in the temple. And that this woorde *Missa*, whiche the latines haue borowed of the Hebrues, hath ben vsed of the Fathers of the latine Churche, for the sacrifice and seruice of God, whiche we cal Masse, fewe that haue vsed to readd those Fathers be ignoraunt.

And here to beginne with that holie Leo the first, who was, as ye haue **F**
before hearde, more then a thousand yeares agon, he willing two Masses to be had in one daie for the commoditie of the people, saieth thus : *Necesse*

Leo epi. 79   *est vt quædam pars populi sua deuotione priuetur si vnius tantùm Missæ more seruato sacrificium offerre non possunt, nisi qui prima diei parte conuenerint.* Yt must nedes be that some parte of the people shall be hindred of their deuocion, yf the maner of one Masse onely being kept, none can offre sacrifice, but they that come together in the first parte of the daie. By this saing of Leo, we are taught, two thinges : The one ys, that Masse here ys taken for the common sacrifice and seruice of the people to God. Which ys easie to be perceaued by that he saieth that a great part of the people shoulde be hindred of their deuocion, and shoulde not offre sacrifice, yf ther should be but one Masse. For the Masse being a common seruice and sacrifice to God, ys or ought by ioinct affection and deuocion of the people to the preist (who ys the common ministre of the Churche, and offreth for them all) to be offred of them all. And therfore the preist saieth plurallie, *offerimus*, we offre. And when he **G** hath doen he likewise saieth plurallie, *obtulimus*, we haue offred. And this common offring or sacrifice ys commonly called Masse.

The other ys that ther maie be mo Masses then one in a Church on one
Ther maie daie. Whiche nombre of Masses in one church, the Proclamer impugneth
be mo mas- by a membre of his proclamacion, and chargeth the catholique Church
ses then one with an abuse in that ther haue ben in one Churche mo Masses than one
in one chur in one daie. Yf he saie that yt was doen that the people might communica-
che and one te : I content me, let yt be so (though the trueth ys, ys was doen that all the
daie. people might sacrifice) Then for communion ther maie be no Masses then one in one daie. Then yf ther be fiue ten, or twentie communions in one daie ther maie be fiue, ten, or twentie Masses in one Church in one daie. For why not aswell twentie as two, and those aswell for thoffring of sacrifice, as for communion? what scripture hath the Proclamer to the contrarie? But thus moche oute of the principall matter by occasion, as the like shall **H** happen again when we shall alleadge *Telesphorus*.

But nowe as touching the name of Masse, we finde yt also vsed of
Ambrosius Sainct Ambrose. For he saieth of him self : *Ego mansi in munere, missam*
epist.33. *facere cepi, orare in oblatione Deum, vt subueniret.* I did abide in my office:

I began

A I began to faie Maffe : to praie God in the facrifice, that he wolde helpe. In which faing Sainct Ambrofe vfeth the name of Maffe to expreffe to vs the facrifice of God, that he began to doe. Whiche by plain woordes he openeth when he faied, he began Maffe to praie God in the facrifice to helpe. So that to faie Maffe, was to offre facrifice, and the oblacion of yt to make praier to God.

So familiare was the name of the Maffe, that as yt ys thought, Sainct Ambrofe making two godly praiers to be faied before Maffe, he entitled them : the praiers preparatiue before Maffe. Yt ys not vnlike that the name of Maffe was familiar in Sainct Ambrofe daies, feing yt was in vfe in the time of *Telefphorus*. Who being the feuenth Byfhoppe of Rome after Sainct Peter, was wellnigh three hundreth yeares before Sainct Ambrofe. This man made a ftatute that in the feaft of the natiuitie of our Lorde there fhoulde three Maffes be fonge. The firft, at midnight, when Chryft was born in Bethleem : The feconde, in the morning, when he was feen of the fhepards. The thirde, aboute the howre, that Chryft fuffred

B his paffion. And ye maie perceaue that yt was the Maffe nowe in vfe for a great parte of yt, calling the Maffe the wholl Ceremonie, that was by this man appoincted. For by him, was *Gloria in excelfis*, commaunded to be fonge before the facrifice fhoulde be offred. From this mans time who liued more the fourten hundreth yeares agon, not onely the name of Maffe hath ben in the Churche : But alfo on the daie of the Natiuitie of our Lorde, three Maffes haue ben vfed in the Church. For fome proofe wherof we haue Sainct Gregorie, who vpon the Gofpell of Sainct Luke readde that daie in the Churche, making an homelie or fermon to the people faieth thus. *Quia miffarum folemnia ter hodie celebraturi fumus, diu de Euangelica lectione loqui non poffumus.* Bicaufe this daie we muft fing three folemne Maffes, we can not long fpeake of the Euangelicall leffon. That this hath ben alfo obferued in thefe later daies, ther ys no doubte. Then feing yt hath ben folemnely obferued fo long time, to fing three fo-

C lemne Maffes vpon the daie of Chryftes birth, who can be fo blinde not to fee the name to haue ben from the primitiue church vfed?

Nowe here by the waie note howe true the article of the Proclamer ys, wher in he auoucheth that yt can not be fhewed, that mo Maffes then one were faied in one daie. Yt ys I fuppofe, laufull to haue mo then one on a daie, when firft we finde yt by fo auncient, and fo holie a Martyr commaunded, and that fo nere to the beginning of the Churche. Secondarely, for that Leo gaue ordre that in one daie, and in one Church mo Maffes fhould be celebrated then one. Thirdlie, we maie iudge yt laufull, forafmoche as we finde yt fo obferued to Sainct Gregories time. In all which time, who can doubte the Churche to haue ben in good perfection. And yf the Churche did repute yt well doen that time: Yf fo manie learned men, as were in that flowrifhing time, whiche was for the fpace of foure hundreth yeares, in the which time liued: Tertullian, Cyprian, Hylary, Hierom, Ambrofe, Auguften, and a nombre of men

D both famoufe in holineffe of life, and excellencie of learning did practife the fame, did obferue, and folowe the fame : What maie we, or can we faie, but yt ys laufull to haue mo Maffes faied then one in one daie, and in one Churche? For yf three be commaunded, to be faied : Why maie not fiue be faied ? Why not ten ? Why not

fiften

Telefphor.
Three maffes commaunded to be doen on Chryftmaf fe daie. 140 yeares agő.

Greg.hom.

not fiftene, and so furth, wher the nombre of preistes and denocion of the **E** people suffice and require.

Thus ye maie see howe the Proclamer bragging of the primitiue Churche, ys confownded by the primitiue Churche. He wolde with woordes of the primitiue Churche, bleer the eyes of men, when the doinges of the same Church shall cause them to see him ouerthrowen. And thus by shamefull speakinge against the trueth he geueth occasion to his owne shame, to haue the trueth shewed, And here also yt ys to be obserued, that this impugnacion of the nnmbre of Masses can not procead oute of anie godly or vertuouse principle. For yf yt be godly, and to our ductie apparteining highlie to esteeme Chrystes passion and death for oure redemption therin wrought, to rendre to God and our Sauiour Chryst, most humble heartie and often thankes, and often also to doe that solemne memoriall that Chryst himself hath appoincted to be doen, all whiche be doen in the *Masse*, what shoulde let, or what likelie or apparaunt dissuasion can this Proclamer make that the Masse shoulde be seldomer, and not raither oftener doen? Soche **F** doctrine as moueth to vertue, to the setting furth of Gods honoure, ys to be embraced. Soche as dissuadeth from vertue, and causeth a decaie of deuocion, and slacknes of our ductie in remembring of Chrystes passion, and death and thankes geuing for the same, ys not onely to be suspected, but to be iudged euell deuelish and abhominable. And truelie in this ys a farder

matter entended by Sathan and his mynisters, then ys yet opened. But this maie be coniectured, that where they beginne to diminish the memorie of Chryst they will afterwarde clean extinguish yt. And so at the last alltogether wipe Chryst from all memorie.

But to returne to our cheif pourpose: Although this sufficeth to prooue the name of Masse, the vse of Masse, and the vse of moo Masses then one in one daie and one place, to be right auncient, yet we shall ascende somwhat higher, and come nearer to the Apostles time. Before *Telesphorus*, was *Sixtus*, who commaunded that when the preist began the solemne action of the Masse (wherby ys ment the praiers going before the consecracion) the peo-**G** ple shoulde singe *Sanctus, Sanctus &c*. Whiche we see to this daie obserued

in the Masse, where yt ys vsed. Before *Sixtus* was Alexander the Martyr, a Roman borne, and aboute the yeare of our Lorde cxix. Byshoppe of Rome. Who made soche a decree, as I finde yt in the summe of decrees. *In sacrificio missarum, panis tantùm & vinum aqua mixtum offeratur*. In the sacrifice of Masses, let onely bread and wine mixed with water be offied.

This man being a Roman borne, an auncient of the Churche, and an holie Martyr withe his plain speach of Masse presseth the Aduersarie so sore that he ys fain to flie to his common solucion. Whiche ys to denie the Authour. In whiche his doing he doth not degenerate from his sore graunde Fathers. Marcion for the maintenance of his heresie reiected the olde Testament and the Prophetes, all the Euangelistes sauing Sainct Luke. The Manicheis also reiected the olde Testament. Martin Luther reiected the Epistle of Sainct Iames. The Sacramentaries reiecte Sainct Ambrose bookes of the Sacramentes. And why haue all these denied **H** these bookes? Bycause they be directlie against their heresies and do confute them. So, I saie, the Aduersary denied Alexander, bicause he maketh so expresse, and plain mencion of Masse, whiche he wolde ouerthrowe.

But

A But let vs fee what proofe he hath to prooue that *Alexander* did not make this aboue mencioned conftitucio, *Bicaufe* (faieth he) *The churche in the time of Alexander, did not knowe this woorde Maffe. And therfore yt ys like not to be his fainge.*

This faing fhall be diuided in to two partes, and to aunfwer the firft parte of yt, I faie, yt ys a merueiloufe thing, that he will faie of him felf withoute all authoritie, yea euē againft plain authoritie, that the Church did not knowe this woorde Maffe, when by authoritie the contrarie ys prooued. Yf he will refufe yt, let him counteruaill yt withe like authoritie, and then we fhall geue him place. But naked woordes without proofe in matters of controuerfie are not of weight able to prooue any thinge. For the fecond parte, wher he faieth : yt ys therfore like not to be his fainge: I muft faie that oute of a fainct antecedent, commeth but a weake confequent. Euerie likelihoode hath not the verie veritie, no more hath his. And therfore in cafe yt were like (as he faieth) yet yt proueth not.

Alexan.his authortie approued and deliuered frō the cauile of the Aduerf.

But to prooue that this ys the faing of *Alexander*, we will vfe neither bare woordes, neither fainct likelihoods. But authoritie, and probable matter. For authoritie we haue a councell holdē more then fex hōderth yearesagon, whiche teftifieth this to be the faing of *Alexander*. and neuer yet againft faied by anie councell that fince hath ben celebrated, or by anie famoufe learned catholique man. Probable matter we haue, that for afmoche as the name of Maffe was in vfe in the time of S. Gregorie, as ys allreadie teftified. In the time alfo of *Felix* the fourth who was before S. Gregorie, in whofe time the vfe of the thing yt felf with the name was fo moch in vfe, that he made a decree that no preift withoute a great neceffitie fhoulde faie maffe but in places halowed and dedicated to God, wher by yt ys clere that yt was vfed alfo before his time. Nowe yf the name of Maffe or the thing were fo ftraung in that time, as the Aduerfarie wolde beare vs in hande, ther fhoulde no foch commaundement haue ben made to will the preiftes to celebrate onely in churches, For by this reftraint yt maie be coniectured,

Conc. Conftantino. 6.

Felix quartus epiftola. ad Epifc.

C that yt was commonlie vfed in prophane places, I meen in their houfes, no neceffitie enforcing them therto, but their owne priuate deuocion.

Nowe yf I were in the Aduerfaries cafe and fhoulde perceaue the vfe and continuaunce of the Maffe, and the name of yt to haue continued but for fo long time as from *Felix* hitherto, which ys almoft a thoufand yeare. I fhoulde be afhamed to take vpon me, to reprehende the doing of the wholl chriftian worlde fo long vfed, and the iudgement of fo manie holie and learned men, as in fo moche time haue liued: And contemning all them to fetfurthe mine owne phantafie. But pitie yt ys to beholde, he doth not onely fo, but (arcogancie fo leading him) he reproueth the wholl chriftian worlde and all the Church and learned men that haue ben thefe eleuen hondreth, and three fkore years and more. For euen by his owne confeffion yt ys euident that the name of Maffe hath ben in vfe fince foure hondreth years after Chrift. For thefe be his woordes towardes the ende of his fermon : *I affure yowe Bretheren, in the time of Peter and Iames, neither was ther*

The Proclamer him felf graunteth the name of Maffe to haue ben vfed from four hundreth years after Chrifte.

D *anie man that euer heard the name of Maffe. For Miſſa was neuer named vntill foure hundreth yeares after Chrift. And yet then was yt no Priuate Maffe neither.* By whiche woords yt ys euident that he acknowlegeth the name of Maffe to haue ben vfed, from foure hundreth years after Chrift, and yf yt hath continued but fo long, what arrogancie maie be thought in him? Not onelie arrogancie, but manifeft vntrueth maie be perceaued in him. For yt ys all-

Hhh   ready

vſe within one hundreth 'and a fewe yeares after Chryſt . For better declaracion wherof, we haue ſhewed the vſe of yt in the time of S. Gregorie and *Felix* . But yet here ys not the beginning of the matter . For as ye haue hearde *Leo*, who was before this *Eelix*.and *S . Ambroſe, who was before, do make expreſſe* mencion of yt . *Theleſporus* alſo 'and *Sixtus* that were verie nere the time of *Alexander* (as yt ys before ſhewed) made decrees for the Maſſe.

Seing then yt ys prooued that the name of Maſſe was in vſe from owre time to *Sixtus*, who was next Biſhoppe of Rome to *Alexander* : ys ¦yt not a probable matter , or raither dothe yt not prooue in dede, that yt was in vſe in the time of the ſame *Alexander* . For when *Sixtus* made the addicion of *Sauctus* to the Maſſe, yt preſuppoſeth that the Maſſe was before his time. Yf before his time then neades in the time of *Alexander*,who went next before him.

Nowe Reader thowe ſeiſt ſubſtanciall proofe againſt the Aduerſarie wherby ys prooued this to be the ſaing of *Alexander?* as ſome accompt the fifte Biſhoppe of Rome after Sainct Peter, whom the Aduerſarie wolde reiect by cauſe he ſo planlie impugneth his hereſie . But this being thus prooued, the trueth appeareth that the name of Miſſe hath bē in the Churche aſſuredlie withoute all double more then fourtene hondreth years. And yf vaingloriouſe pride did not to moche preuaill in the Aduerſarie, ſoche reuerence ſhoulde be geuen to antiquitie , and ſpeciallie to ſo holy a Martir as he was, that that ys ſaied of him with the approbacion of the wholl Churche ſhoulde be embraced and humblie receaued, and not arrogantlie and contemptuoſlie reiected and deſpiſed . And yet this ys to be thought of ſo holy and auncient a Martir, that he himſelf wolde not inuent a noueltie of himſelf but raither that he tooke yt of his Fathers as the maner of his writing doth in good parte prooue.

And nowe that we haue driuen the matter thus farre, let vs here reſt with S. Auguſtins rule and counſell, whiche ys this : *Illa quæ per orbem vniuerſa obſeruat Eccleſia , datur intelligi vel ab ipſis Apoſtolis , vel à plenarijs Concilijs , quorum eſt in Eccleſia ſaluberima authoritas , ſtatuta retineri .* Soche thinges as the wholl Churche through the worlde dothe obſerue, we maie vnderſtand that they are retined as ordeined either of the Apoſtles them ſelues : or ells of generall councells , whoſe authoritie ys in the Churche moſt holſome or profitable . Then foraſmoche as the name of Maſſe ys reteined through all the Churche, For that which the Grekes call *Liturgia*, the Latines call Miſſa , and in the engliſh tounge both be called Maſſe , and that name was not appointed by anie generall councell, but was in vſe before the firſt generall councell that was holden , we maie ſaie by S. Auguſtines rule , that yt cometh from the Apoſtles.

And nowe wher ys the great aſſurance that this Proclamer made vnto yowe , wen he ſaied . *I aſſure yowe Bretheren , that the name of Maſſe was neuer named vntill foure hondreth years after Chryſte?* And among vs engliſh men I wolde ſee what other name either the Proclamer, or anie other learned or vnlearned man , can ſhewe to haue ben in this realme generallie vſed ſince yt receaued the faithe , but onelie this name . Yf thei haue none other name but this : and this name they receaued when they firſt receaued the faithe as ingliſh men, and haue from that time till within theſe fewe late yeares continued the ſame : What nowe moueth the engliſh man to reiecte that name that he receaued withe his faithe ? With the greif of

my

Ad Ianua.
epus.118.

This his
falſe aſſu-
rance de-
clareth
both vn-
treuth, and
arrogancie.
vntreuth
for yt was
in vſe be-
fore foure
hondreth
yeare:arro-
gancie that
confeſſing
the vſe for
Mc.years,
he dothe
nowe reiect
yt.

A my heart I tell the caufe : The caufe ys that he reiecteth the faithe that was
firft receaued . And therfor I feare that the englifh man reiecting the faith,
wherby he was firft made a chriftian man , and the names of thinges to that
faithe apperteyning, he will alfo reiect Chryft, and the name alfo of a chriftian man . But God of his mercie turne his face from our finnes, and turne vs home again to him, that we perifh not in our vnfaithfullneffe : but by
his grace acknowledging our offence, we maie euerie one of vs determe
with the prodigall Sonne and faie: *Surgam & ibo ad patrem meum , & dicam ei:*　Luc. 15.
Pater peccaui in cœlum & coram te iam non fum dignus vocari filius tuus &c. I will
arife and go to my Father, and I will faie to him: Father I haue finned againft
heauen, and before thee: I am not woorthye to be called thy Sonne. Whiche determinacion God graunt fhortely to come to paffe.

THE THREE AND THIRTETH CHA-
piter treacteth of the Maſſe
B
yt felf.

Orafmoche as Maffe hath a larger and ftraiter acception or figni-　*Maſſe
ficacion : meet yt ys that both be declared, that yt maie be difcer-　hath two
ned whiche of them yt ys that proprely ys called Maffe . Of Maf-　ſignifica-
fe in his large fignification the Proclamer, though more like a Si-　tions.*
cophant, then a man of true and fincere reporte, faieth, that yt confifteth
in foure partes . Yf he had added the fifte, or if in the holie confecracion,
he alfo vnderftandeth holy oblacion he hath declared what Maffe ys in
the large fignification . For the holie praiers that go before confecracion,
oblacion, and receauing. and that folowe them : holie doctrine alfo as the
epiftle, the Gofpell and other fcriptures ther placed and readde, with all
the Ceremonies therunto apperteining added and putto of diuerfe holy
C Fathers, to encreafe, nourifh, and conferue the deuocion of the people,
for the more reuerend vfe of the Sacrement to the honour and glorie of
God (whofe honour ys moche mainteined by the reuerend handling of his
mifteries) are not proprelie called Maffe, but largelie forafmoch as they be
annexed and ioined to that that proprely ys called Maffe, and be not the
Maffe yt felf . For the Maffe yt felf ys the holie confecration of the bodie　*Maſſe
and bloode of Chryft, the holie oblacion and offringe of the fame, in the　prophelie
memoriall and remembrance of his paffion and death with humble and　what yt ys.*
lowlie thankes, lawdes, and praifes for the fame, and holie receauing, of
that bodie and bloode fo confecrated . This ys yt that proprely ys called
the Maffe, bicaufe thus moche ys inftituted of Chryft him felf . For he in
his laft Supper when he had confecrated and offred his bleffed bodie and
bloode, he faied. *Accipite, comedite . Hoc in mei memoriam facite* . Take and
eate, do this in remembrance of me . So that confecracion oblacion with
thankfull remembrance of Chryftes deathe, and holie receauing, of his　*Ambr.de
D bleffed bodie be the thinges that proprely be called the Maffe . Nam per　Sar. lib. 4.
reliqua omnia quæ dicuntur, Laus Deo defertur, oratione petitur pro populo, pro Regi-　cap.4.*
bus, pro cæteris . Vbi venitur vt conficiatur venerabile Sacramentum, iam non ſuis ſermonibus ſacerdos, ſed vtitur ſermonibus Chriſti. For by all the other thinges that be
faied (faieth Sainct Ambrofe) lawde and praife ys geuen to God, praier
Hhh ij　　ys ma.

ys made for the people, for kinges, and for other, but when the honorable **E** Sacrament shall be consecrated, then the preist vseth not his owne woordes, but the woordes of Chrift. So moche then as ys of Chryftes inftitucion, ys properly called the Maffe, by the propre fignification. And the reft that of godlie men ys added for confideracions before mencioned, ys generaly called the Maffe by a general fignificacion.

Baptifme vfed in two fignificacions.   As baptifme proprely ys no more, nor proprelie extendeth yt felfe anie farder then to the wafhing of the bodie in the name of the Father, and of the Sonne, and of the holie Goft. and to the wafhing of the Soule from finne by grace geuen in the miniftracion of the fame Sacrament : yet the wholl miniftracion and praiers afwell before batifme as after vfed in the fame, by a generall fignificacion ys called Baptifme . So ys the confecracion and oblacion of the bodie of Chryft with all praiers and Ceremonies either going before or folowing the fame, by generall fignificacion called Maffe.

This breif defcription of the Maffe being made, let vs examin the partes of yt, whiche of them or howe manie of the be againft the woorde of God, **F** and the example or practife of the primatiue Church (as yt ys pretended) that yt maie be perceaued what iuft caufe the Proclamer hath fo moche to exclame againft the Maffe.

Parts of the Maffe.   The firft parte ys confecracion. This parte for that by yt ys taught the prefence of Chryftes bodie and bloode, whiche the Proclamer can not abide, ys one caufe why he reiecteth the Maffe, But howe iuftly he doth it yt maie be perceaued through oute all this booke, in which ys prooued the prefence, whiche the catholique Church teacheth, and the figure ys improued, whiche the Aduerfary mainteineth.

An other parte ys oblacion or facrifice, wherin the Churche offreth Chryft to God the Father according to the commaundement of the fame owre maifter Chryft in the memoriall of his paffion and deathe . That this parte ys not againft the fcriptures, and the holy Fathers yt ys allready proued in the declaracion of the prophecies of *Melchifedech*, *Daniel*, and *Malachie* in the firft booke, wherunto ys made an addicion, whiche thowe fhalt **G** finde in the xxxvij.chapiter of that fame booke, fufficient I truft to aunfwere and fatisfie anie reafonable man.

An other parte ys receauing of the Sacrament. In the whiche twoo thinges do offend the Proclamer : The one ys that the people do receaue vnder one kinde : The other that the preift receaueth alone . Whether the receauing vnder one kinde be againft the Scriptures, or the practife of the Primitiue Churche, yt ys difputed, and the trueth declared in the feconde booke from the lxiiij chap. to the end of lxvijchap. As for the receauing whiche the Proclamer termeth priuate, yt fhall be hereafter treacted of.

In doctrine, which ys an other parte, I knowe not what fault he can finde. In praier the firft and laft parte of the Maffe he findeth two faultes. The one that praier ys made to fainctes : The other that praier ys made for the dead, for thefe two we fhal haue recourfe to the primitiue Churche, and the- **H** re make triall whether the Church doth well in fo doing : or the Aduerfarie euell in denieng the fame to be laufull and good.

Nowe for the firft parte of the Maffe whiche ys confecracion, I will not moche otherwife here treact of yt, but onelie laing furth the practife of
the

A   the Apoſtolique and primitiue Churche therin, compare the doinges of the catholique Churche nowe therwith, that yt maie be perceaued howe iuſtlie yt foloweth the example therof . As for the effect of conſecracion, whiche ys the preſence of Chryſtes bodie, ther neadeth here no ſpeciall treactice, for that the woll booke treateth therof ſo fullie, that yf the Proclamer will finde fault in the Maſſe forthat the preſence ys taught ther to be, he maie in other places of this worke finde ſufficiét matter for the proofe of the preſence whiche yf yt will not ſatiſfie him, neither maie a fewe woordes here ſpoken moche helpe him.

As for the ſeconde parte, whiche ys the oblacion or ſacrifice of Chryſtes bodie, as before yt ys declared, that yt ys offred according to the will and commaundement of Chryſt himſelf, and that by the teſtimonie of the Scripturs, as they be vnderſtáded of a nombre of the moſt auncient Fathers, and by diuerſe other graue authorities: So ſhall yt be nowe ſet furth and cómended to yowe by the practiſe of the Primitiue Churche . Whiche we haue differred to this place.

B   And foraſmoche as the Proclamer to extenuate and abaſe the honorable eſtimacion of the Maſſe, whiche yt ought to haue in the heartes of the people, doth for ſhame, and with ſhame conceale the names of ſoche auncient Authours as do teſtifie that both Sainct Peter and Sainct Iames ſaied Maſſe, the one at Rome the other at Hieruſalem, and doth alſo to bring the matter in contempt aſke by waie of ſkorn, *whie raither we ſaie not* *that Chryſte him ſelf ſaied Maſſe, for that were the neerer waie to bring the Maſſe in* *creditte:*I ſhall by good and ſufficient authoritie ſhewe that not onelie Sainct Peter and Sainct Iames, but alſo Chryſte him ſelf did ſaie Maſſe. And ſo beginning at Chryſt deſcende to three or foure hundreth yeares after Chryſt, and ſhewe the practiſe of the Churche . And for this time I will ouerpaſſe the farder mocke and ſkorn that he maketh againſt the bleſſed Maſſe, aſking *whie we doe not raither ſaie that Aaron and his chapleins ſaied Maſſe,* *For in dede* (ſaieth he) *as yt hath ben vſed,the Churche hath had moch more of the*

Whē truth and learning ſerueth not, mocking and ſkorning be their beſt argumētes.

C   *Robes of the Ceremonies , and of the ſacrifices of Aaron, then of the inſtitucion or or-* *deinance of Chryſte .* For yf I ſhoulde touche him for that, I ſhoulde cauſe him to be perceaued to impugne and in that behalf to ſkorne the miniſtracion of the Communion . For that ys miniſtred in coapes and other ſoche garmentes as before were vſed in the Churche, and he himſelf refuſeth not to weare Aarons garment for a Biſhoppericke. So well agreeth his doing and his preaching together . And thus ſcoffing at the garmentes that be nowe yet vſed, he ſeemeth to me not to like this order of Religion that he liueth in, but raither to reprooue this as he doth the other: For in this poinct by his iudgement they holde both of Aaron.

Arons garment worne for a Biſhopperke, and the Comunion miniſtred in a cope.

But letting this paſſe I will returne to my matter, and wiſh the Reader to remembre, what this woorde Maſſe doth ſignifie, as yt ys declared in the laſt chapiter and therwith to haue in minde, as yt ys ſaied in this chapiter, that Maſſe ys the action of the conſecracion, oblacion and receauing of the bodie and bloode of Chryſt, and ſo vnderſtanding Maſſe, I

Chryſte ſaied Maſſe.

D   ſaie that Chryſt did ſaie Maſſe .For he in his laſt Supper did inſtitute Maſſe, and did ther conſecrate his bodie and bloode, and offred them in ſacrifice, and gaue them to his Apoſtes to be receaued, and commaunded that ſo yt ſhoulde be doen in the remembrance of his paſſion and death. In this matter who liſteth to be ſatisfied (forſomoche as one auncient Au-

Epiſt. li. 2.
Epiſt. 3.
thour maie ſatisfie a man) let him reade the Epiſtle of *Sainct Ciprian* to *Ceci-* E
lius, and he ſhall ther finde euery parte of the Maſſe here reckned, to be doen
by Chryſt.

Firſt for the conſecracion he ſaieth thus : *Vt in Geneſi per Melchiſedech Sa-*
cerdotem benedictio circa Abraham poſſit ritè celebrari, præcedit antè imago ſacrificij
in pane & vino ſcilicet conſtituta. Quam rem perficiens & adimplens Dominus panem
& calicem vino mixtum obtulit, & qui eſt plenitudo veritatem præfiguratæ imaginis
adimpleuit . That the benediction in Geneſis by *Melchiſedech* the preiſt might
be celebrated accordinglie aboute Abraham, the image of the Sacrifice appoincted in bread and wine goeth before . Which thing our lotde perfecting and fullfilling offred bread and the cuppe mixed with wine, and
he that ys the fullneſſe , hath fullfilled the veritie of the preſigurated
image.

Holy Ciprian teacheth here that the bread and wine offred by *Melſchi-*
ſedechi, were the preſigurated ymage of the veritie fullfilled by Chryſt.
What the veritie ys he doth in the ſame epiſtle declare when he ſaieth:
Obtulit hoc idem quod Melchiſedec obtulerat, id eſt panem & vinum, ſuum ſcilicet F
corpus & ſanguinem . He did offre euen the ſame that *Melchiſedech offred,*
that ys to ſaie, bread and wine, that ys to witte, his owne bodie and blode.
Chriſt then fullfilling the veritie of *Melchiſedechs* bread and wine , made
bread and wine his bodie and bloode , which fullfilling of the veritie,
and making the bread and wine his bodie and bloode, what ys yt ells,
but that we call conſecracion ? This bodie ſo conſectated, ys offred of vs
in ſacrifice, as the ſame Sainct Ciprian diſputing againſt them that vſed
onelie water in the Sacrifice, teſtifieth and ſaieth : *Quærendum eſt enim ipſi*
quem ſint ſecuti . Nam ſi in ſacrificio quod Chriſtus eſt, non niſi Chriſtus ſequendus
The Sacri-
fice in the
Maſte
ys Chryſte
himſelf.
eſt : vtique id nos obaudire , & facere oportet, quod Chriſtus fecit, & quod facien-
dum eſſe mandauit . Yt muſt be aſked, whome they haue folowed .
For yf in the Sacrifice whiche ys Chryſt, none ys to be folowed but
Chryſt, we muſt then obey and doe that that Chryſt did, and that he commaunded to be doen.

Marke well theſe woordes : that in the Sacrifice whiche ys Chry- G
ſte, none ys to be folowed But Chryſte . The ſacrifice then that the
chriſtian Churche in the time of holie Ciprian did offre was the bodie of Chryſt , yt was Chryſt him ſelf . *In the Sacrifice* (ſaieth he) *whiche ys*
Chryſt.

That the Churche ys commaunded by Chryſt to offre this ſacrifice, in
the remembrance of him, the ſame Sainct Ciprian by moſt expreſſe and
plain woordes doth teache, ſaing : *Quodſi nec minima de mandatis Dominicis*
licet ſoluere : quanto magis tam magna r tam grandia, tam ad ipſum Dominicæ paſſio-
nis & noſtræ redemptionis Sacramentum pertinentiâ, fas non eſt infringere, aut in aliud
quàm quod Diuinitus inſtitutum eſt, humana traditione mutare ? Nam ſi Ieſus Chri-
ſtus Dominus & Deus noſter, ipſe eſt ſummus ſacerdos Dei Patris, & ſacrificium
ipſe primus obtulit, & hoc fieri in ſui commemorationem præcepit, vtique ille Sacerdos
vice Chriſti verè fungitur, qui id quod Chriſtus fecit, imitatur . Et ſacrificium verum
& plenum tunc offert in Eccleſia Deo Patri, ſi ſic incipiat offerre, ſecundum quod ipſam H
Chriſtum viderit obtuliſſe . Yf then yt be not laufull to breake the leaſt of
the commaundementes of our Lorde, howe moche more yt ys not laufull to infringe or breake thinges ſo great, ſo weightie, ſo apperteining to the
verie Sacrament of the paſſion of our Lorde, and of our Redemption, or
ells

A　ells by mans tradicion to chaunge yt into anie other thing, then that that by God was inftituted. For yf Iefus Chryft our Lord and God yf he be the high preift of God the Father, and he firft did offre this facrifice, and commaunded this to be doen in the remembrance of him: that preft doth the office of Chryft trulie, that doth folowe that, that Chryft hath doen. And then dothe he offre in the Churche vnto God the Father a true, and a full facrifice, yf he fo beginne to offre, as he hath feen Chryft him felf to haue offred. Thus moch S, Ciprian.

The fame facrifice that Chrifte did ys commaunded to be offred in his church.

　　Manie thinges are in this faing of Ciprian to be noted whiche I fhall breiflie touche and paffouer, Firft, yt ys to be obferued, that to alter the inftitucion of Chryft ys a great and a weightie matter, whiche he accompteth to be altered, when either water alone or wine alone ys yfed in the mini ftracion, and not both together mixed. Wherin I wifh the Aduerfarie to weigh whether he offende not in a weightie and a great matter, when he breaketh and altereth the inftitution of Chryft, as Sainct Ciprian faieth, in that he vfeth but wine alone in the miniftracion. And farder obferue

B　that yf to take awaie wine or water from the miniftracion be a great and a weightie matter, howe moche greater and more heinoufe matter ys yt to take awaie the bleffed boodie of Chryfte from the Sacrament? Which Sainct Ciprian teacheth not onely in this place but in diuerfe other, as before maie be feen, that Chryft afwell inftituted his bodie and bloode ther to be prefent, as he did the matters of bread wine and water ther to be vfed. And yet in thefe two poinctes to alter the inftitucion of Chryft the Proclamer thinketh yt no great matter.

The Communions in Englond teftifie the breach of thefe ordonances and mo to.

　　And here by the waie to note, yt ys merueiloufe to beholde howe the Deuell bewitcheth this man. For he findeth great fault with the Church, and wolde make thofe which he reputeth faultes to be as Mowntaines in the feight of the people, as the vfing and wearing of ornamentes in the miniftracion, the fpeaking of the woordes of confecracion high or lowe, and foch other: And yet the deniall of the prefence of Chryftes

C　bodie and bloode to be in the Sacrament, he accompteth yt but a fmall matter.

　　In the Apologie of the Churche of Englonde, which femeth an arrowe that came oute of the fame quoiuer that this Sermon did, and to be both feathered whith the feathers of one Goofe, of like maner, and coolor, I meen, of phrafe and matter, fo near and fo like are they or raither the fame, that a man maie well thinke, they be one mans boltes. In that Apologie, I faie, the Authour being fo defiroufe to hide and cloake the famoufe and notable diffention in weighty matters of Faith betwixt *Luther*, and *Zwinglius*, faieth that they were both good and excellent men, and they did not (faieth he) varie in great matters of faith, as of iuftificacion, and foche like, but they varied in a litle matter, a matter of no great weight. And yet that litle matter was the matter of the Sacrament. For *Luther* taught the prefence of Chryftes bodie in the Sacrament. But *Zuinglius* denieth yt, as this proclamer dothe. And fo that, which Sainct Cy-

The Appologie and the Proclamacio both like bolts.

D　prian accompteth a great and a weightie matter: this man being blinde on the one fide can perceaue yt but a fmall matter, but opeining his eies to the other fide he feeth yt to be a great and horrible faulte. For the miniftres of Chryftes catholique churche teaching according to Chryftes inftitucio and woorde, faing this ys my Bodie, that his bodie ys in the Sacramet, are

by

by this man not a litle exclamed at . For here are we Papiſtes : here are **E**
we Capharnates : Here are we Idolaters , and the Authours of deſtable Idolatrie : here are we makers of Gods : here are we blaſphemers : here are we
the Robbers of Gods honour, and what are we not that euell ys, ſo great
and wicked ys our offence teaching Chryſtes bodie in the Sacrament , and
yet the ſame in Luther was but a ſmall matter . Soche ys the parciall Iudgement of this man.

But howe ſoeuer he iudgeth , holie Ciprian iudgeth him and all ſoche
as he ys greuouſe offenders and brakers of the inſtitucion of Chryſt , that
doe ſo alter Chriſtes inſtitucion, that wher yt pleaſed him of the abun-
dant and vnſpeakeable loue that he beareth to vs , to ordein his owne blef-
ſed bodie to be miniſtred vnto vs in the holie Sacrament, as a pledg of
that ſame his loue to our great conſolacion and comforte , and to our
great benefitt both in bodie and ſoule : they will miniſtre and geue vnto vs not his bodie, but a peice of bread and a cuppe of wine . But that
Chryſt did geue furth his owne bodie and bloode, and not bread and wine ye haue before heard yt declaretd . For Chryſte fulfilled that in veritie **F**
(ſaieth Sainct Ciprian) that *Melchiſedeth* did in figure . *Melchiſedech* offred
bread and wine : Chryſt perfecting that figure offred bread and wine , that
ys (ſaieth holy Ciprian) *his bodie and bloode* . Note then that Sainct Ciprian expownding the fullfilling of the figure of bread and wine offred
by *Melchiſedech* ſaieth not that Chryſt offred bare bread and wine , but
bread and wine, that was his bodie and bloode . wiche bleſſed bread and
wine of his bodie and bloode being made preſent by his allmightie power , by the turninge of materiall bread and wine into his bodie and
blood ys the right fullfilling of the figuratiue breade and wine offred by

Tertull.cō.
Martionē.
Conſecra-
cion the
woorde
vſed by
Terrul.

Melchiſedech . *Ita nunc ſanguinem ſuum in vino conſecrauit , qui tunc vinum in ſangui-*
ne figurauit . So nowe (ſaieth *Tertulian*) he hath conſecrated his blood in wine , who then figured wine in his blood . Thus then ye perceaue that
Chryſt did conſecrate his bodie and bloode , whiche woorde of conſecracion ye ſee that Tertulian abhoreth not, although yt miſlike manie in theſe
daies , but vſeth yt as the Church nowe vſeth yt, and ſaieth that Chryſt did **G**
conſecrate his bloode in wine.

An other note we haue whiche ys this, that Ieſus Chryſt our lorde and
God the high preiſt of God the Father did firſt offre this ſacrifice . In
whiche woordes we are taught not onelie that he did in his laſt Supper
offre a Sacrifice, but that he did then offre a Sacrifice, that was neuer offred before . Let vs therfor difcuſſe and ſearche what ſacrifice that was.
Yt was not a ſacrificie of figuratiue bread and wine, For that alſo was offred by *Aarons* preiſtes : yt was not a ſacrifice of thankes geuing onelie,
For that was both in the lawe of nature , and by the lawe of Moiſes , and
alſo by Chryſt diuerſe times doen . What ſacrifice was yt then ? was yt
a ſacrifice after the ordre of *Melchiſedech* ? Yt was a ſacrifice after the
ordre of *Melchiſedech* . But yt maie be ſaied that that ſacrifice was of-
red by *Melchiſedech* thouſand of years before Chryſt , ſo that Chryſt was
not the firſt that did offre after that maner, wherfor yt ſhoulde appea- **H**
re , that yt was not that maner of ſacrifice . True yt ys, that *Melchiſedech*
offred ſacrifice in bread and wine, as yt ys proued in the firſt booke.
But *Melchiſedech* offred bread and wine in figure , Chryſt offred after
the ſame ordre , bread and wine in veritie . What did he offre in veritie?

A ritie ? That that the bread and wine of *Melchifedech* did figure , what did yt figure ? Yf figured the verie bread and wine of Chryftes bodie and bloode . Then Chryft offred in facrifice his bodie and blood . True yt ys. And this facrifice was neuer offred before Chryft himfelf did offre yt. For neuer man did offre yt before in veritie , though *Melchifedech* and other did offre yt in figure. For as Sainct Ambrofe faieth : *Chriftus formam Sacrificij peren-nis inftituens, hoftiam fe primus obtulit , & primus docuit offerri*, Chryfte inftitu-ting the forme of the euerlafting facrifice , he firft offred him felf a facrifice, and firft taught yt to offred.

Chryfte in his laft Sup-per offred his bodie and blood in facrifice.

Ambro. in præfattion Miffe in cana Dom.

And that Chryft did offre his owne bleffed bodie in facrifice Sainct Ci-prian hath taught vs . For firft he faied that Chryft offred bread and wine, that ys (faieth he) his bodie and bloode , and nowe teaching howe yt ys of-fred , he faieth that yt ys offred in facrifice . Thus, yf I be not deceaued, the matter ys plain that Chryft did offre hys bodie in his laft Supper in facrifice. And yf the Aduerfarie can fhewe what facrifice yt was ells that Chryft did firft offre, yt maie fomwhat make for him . yf he can not (as I am fure he can

B not) let him geue place to the trueth taught by the holie Fathers in the aun-cient Curche.

Thus moche then for this note being faied, let vs farder confider what ys faied of this holie Father . He faieth not onely that Chryft did firft offre this facrifice , but he faieth alfo: *Et hoc fieri in fui commemorationem præcepit*. And he commaunded this to be doen in the remembrance of him . Here I wolde learn of the Aduerfarie which fhall be the fubftantiue to the Pronowne *This* , yt ys manifieft to him and to all that haue but their grammer rules, that this woorde, *Sacrificium*, ys the Subftantiue . Then muft yt of neceffitie folowe that our lorde and God Iefus Chryft hath commaunded vs to offre this facrifice in remêbrance of him , that he offred in his laft Supper, whiche facrifice ys his bleffed bodie and blood . Wherfore I wifhe this to be well noted , that howfoeuer the enemies of Chryft doo raile at the catholi-que Churche , and at the miniftres of the fame, for that they doo tea-

We are cô-maunded by Chryfte to offre the fame facri-fice that he offred.

C che that in the Maffe they offre facrifice to God : yet we are fo com-maunded to doo by the authoritie of Chryfte , as here by holie Ciprian ye fee yt teftified.

Neither ys this to be ouerpaffed , but diligentlie to be noted , that wher the fame enemies of Chryft in their fondrie workes doo triumphe againft certain learned catholique men , for that they faie that power ys geuen to Chryftes Churche to offre facrifice by thefe woordes of Chryfte , *This doe ye in the remembrance of me* : for afmoche as holie Ciprian faieth , that Chryft hath commaunded vs to offre his bodie in facrifice , and before him fo faied *Irenæus* , and after him fo faied Sainct Ambrofe , and diuerfe other holie lear-ned Fathers, I wolde learn of them , what place ells in the fcripture ther ys wherupon thefe auncient Fathers , dooe grownde thefe their fainges. But let them mocke and skorn at Chryftes trueth as the Pharifeis and Scribes did at him felf, yet as Chryft remained, and remaineth, and fhall for euer remain, and fhall condemne the wiked generacion : So dothe and fhall this trueth

D remain to their condemnacion.

And howefouer they will laboure to obfcure yt : yet the holie do-ctours , who verie well knewe by the doctrine of the primitiue Chur-che , howe the fcripture ys to be vnderftanded , fhall allwaies open the fame, and make yt clere . As nowe Sainct Cyprian in declaring

the

the commaundement of Chryſt , doth almoſt ſpeake the verie woor- E
des of the commaundement. Chryſte ſaied : *Hoc facite in meam commemo-*
rationem . This doe ye in the remembrance of me . Ciprian ſaieth :
he commaunded this ſacrifice to be doen in the remembrance of him .
Sainct Ambroſe likewiſe growndeth himſelf vpon theſe ſaine woordes of
Chryſt, when he ſaied : *I lorde being mindfull of thy honorable paſſion , come vnto*
thine aultar, although vnwoorthie and a ſinner, that I maie offre vnto thee the ſacrifice, that
Ambr.ora-
tione prae-
par.ad
Miſſam.] *thowe dideſt inſtitute , and commaundeſt to be offred in the remembrance of thee* . The
ſame alluſion haue other Fathers alſo'. So that yt ys as clear as the daie light
amonge the auncient doctours, that Chryſt by theſe woordes commaunded
his Churche to offre his bodie and bloode in ſacrifice.

Nowe once to ende the notes that maie be made vpon Sainct Ciprian,
and to ſtoppe the mouthes of them that ſpeake wicked thinges , as ſaieth
the ſpalmiſt : Note well the laſt parte of Sainct Ciprians ſainges, and ye ſhall
ſee , that both Chryſt did offre ſacrifice in his laſt Supper and that we alſo
do offre ſacrifice , yf we doe obſerue, and kepe the inſtitucion of Chriſt . For
Sainct Ciprian ſaieth : *Sacerdos vice Chriſti verè fungitur , ſi id quod Chriſtus fecerit* F
imitatur . & ſacrificium verum & plenum tunc offert in Eccleſia Deo Patri, ſi ſic incipiat
offerre ſecundùm quod ipſum Chriſtum viderit obtuliſſe . The preiſt doeth truelie
exerciſe the miniſtracion of Chryſte , yf he folowe that that Chryſt hath
doen , and then doeth he offre in the Churche vnto God the Father a true
and full ſacrifice , yf he ſo beginne to offre , as he hath ſeen Chryſt to haue
offred . In which ſentence this maie be noted , firſt that Chryſt did offre ſacrifice in the laſt Supper', which the Aduerſarie denieth . Secondarely , that
the Church folowing the inſtitucion of Chryſte , offreth to God , a full and
a true ſacrifice, whiche alſo the Aduerſarie denieth . By this then ye perceau-
ue theſe two partes of the Maſſe , that ys, holie conſecracion, and oblacion,
to be doen by Chryſt in his holie miniſtracion.

As for the thirde , whiche ys holy receauing, ther ys no controuerſie betwixt vs and the Aduerſarie . Yt ys more then neadeth to be ſpoken of, that
both Chryſt him ſelf, and all the Apoſtles preſent at the borde of Chryſt,
did eat of that holie oblacion or ſacrifice . Theſe three being the ſubſtanciall G
partes of the Maſſe , and the verie true Maſſe in dede , and being by Chriſt
inſtituted, ordeined, and appoincted, as yowe haue perceaued, what can we
ells ſaie, but that Chryſte ys the Authour of the Maſſe, that he inſtituted the
Maſſe , and that he ſaied Maſſe ? Yf anie deſire to be better ſatisfied in theſe
two partes namely conſecracion and oblacion, for the firſt let him repaire to
the ſecond booke , and ther from the xli chapiter to the ende of the booke
he ſhall finde enoughe to ſatisfie him . For the other in the firſt booke from
the xxxiij chapiter to the ende of that booke he ſhall likewiſe finde that maie
content him.

THE

H

A   THE FOVR AND THIRTETH CHA.

piter sheweth, the vse of the Masse vsed and practised
by the Apostles.

He Masse (as ys saied, and proued) being instituted by Chryste, and by him also cōmaunded to be practised and vsed of his Church: yt shall be expedient and necessarie that we see how and in what maner that his commaundement was executed, and his institucio̅ practised, first, by the Apostles, and after by the holie Fathers of the primitiue and auncient Churche. For they well knowing Chrystes verie minde, their doinges are to vs a perfect expositio̅ and declaracio̅ of the same. Wherfore minding to see them, they shall yet so be seen, as both the practise of the Masse of the catholique Church nowe in vse, and the practise also of the Schismaticall Churche maie be plainlie laied furth and compared to the former practises, that therbie triall maie be made, whether of these two agree or

B   disagree with the Apostolique and primitiue Churche. Yf we of the catholique Churche dissent either from Chrystes institution, or from the Apostles and Fathers as touching the substanciall parts of the Masse or anie other weightie matter of the faith, let vs suffre the reproche? Yf the Proclamer and and his complices haue swerued from them, let them repent and seke gods mercie. This I promisse before God, that I will laie furth the matter as simplie for the declararatio̅ of the trueth, as I can deuise, that the fault maie be fownd wher yt ys.

And before I enter to declare this practise. I wish the reader to be aduertised, and to haue this for a generall rule, that wher in this Processe we shall treact of the Masse and call yt the Masse of S. Peter, of S. Andrewe, of S. Iames, of S. Clement. or S. Dionise Masse, S. Basills Masse, Chrisostomes Masse, S. Ambrose Masse, and soche other, that we doe not neither ys yt so to be taken, that these distinctions be vpon the propre significacio̅ of the Masse that

C   ys, that these Masses be distincted in the substanciall parts of Masse : as that the Masse of S. Peter shoulde be substanciallie distincted from the Masse of S. Iames, and the Masse, of S. Iames substanciallie different from the Masse of S. Basill, and so furth. But the difference ys taken of the generall acception or significacio̅ of Masse, that ys, that they be different in extern thinges, as in some ceremonies, in praiers, and in other gestures or maners, but not in intern or inwarde substanciall thinges. For in them all ye shall finde one thing onely consecrated, one thing onelie offred in sacrifice, one thing onelie receaued. And therfore in Consecracion, oblacion, and receauing they being not different, But all one, are not called S. Peters Masse, nor S. Iames Masse and so furth: But Chrystes Masse. For these thinges be of his institucion, and not of theirs. The diuersitie of Ceremonies, praiers, and other maners, ys of the̅ by the magisterie of the holie Gost instituted, and not of Chryste. In this processe then be diligent to see the agreement in the substanciall matters of ministracion, be yt either Masse or Communion, and yf anie be

D   fownde to varie in the substanciall partes from the doctrine of the Apostolique and primitiue Churche, discredit them, and reiect them : and soche as shall be fownd to retein like doctrine in inthose parts to the primitiue Churche receaue them, and embrace them. So vpright and indifferent will I be, that other thing then trueth will, I will not require.

And that the matter, as yt ys confessed on either part, maie clerlie appear,

Masse of the Apostles and Fathers, and that ys vsed nowe in the Church, all one in substance.

pear, and as yt were lie flat before yowe, vnderſtand, that the catholique, **E**
Churche reteining the name of Maſſe, confeſſeth yt, as ys ſaied, to be a conſecracion and oblacion of the bodie and blood of Chriſte in the memoriall
of his paſſion and dath, to the releef and comforte both of the liuing, and
of the dead, and the holie receauing of the ſame bleſſed bodie and blood.
And although the Proclamer and his complices moche raill againſt the
name of Maſſe: yet the thing that they ſhoote at and wherwith they are moſt
greiued ys the preſence of Chriſtes bodie and blood, and the ſacrifice of
the ſame, Take awaie theſe two, and they will not force what name ys put to
yt. But fraſmoche as the catholique Churche teacheth theſe things, and theſe be they that the Aduerſarie impugneth, yf we can ſhewe theſe two things
to haue ben vſed of the Apoſtles, and their diſciples, and the Fathers of the
primitiue church we ſhall caſelie prooue them to haue vſed Maſſe, whiche
thing by Gods helpe I doubte not to doe. And doing this, I muſt to eche
of theſe adde one other thing, as it were an handmaidden to wait vpon
them. For to conſecracion, muſt be added intencion: and to ſacrifice, praier
for acceptacion. Fo ſo ſhall we ſee a great part of the order of the Apoſto- **F**
lique and primitiue Churche in this holie miniſtracion: vnderſtand therfor
that of theſe four, that ys, of the two principals, and their hãdmaides, we wil
ſeuerallie treact after this order. Firſt, of conſecration: then of the intencion of the conſecratours: after that of oblacion, laſt of praier for acceptacion of the ſame. In treating of euerie of whiche I will laie to the practiſe
of the Apoſtolique and primitiue Churche the doinges of the catholique
Church in theſe daies, and of the ſchiſmaticall Churche, that iuſt triall maie
be made whiche agreeth withe the Apoſtles and Fathers, which diſſenteth from them.

    To enter into this matter, let vs firſt ſee the maners of the miniſtration
of the Apoſtles. And foraſmoche os the Proclamer with a certain skof or
ſkorn of (ſome ſaie) beginneth with the cheif Apoſtle S. Peter, ſaing that
ſome ſaie, he ſaied Maſſe at Rome: I will alſo firſt beginne with him. And
albeit, as ys ſaied, yt ys ſpoken with ſkorn that he ſaied Maſſe: yet yf yt be
well weighed, the ſkorn turneth to the Proclamers owne head. For yf ſo- **G**
me ſaie that he ſaied Maſſe, and none ſaie the contrarie, I meen among the
catholique writers, then that S. Peter ſaied Maſſe, bicauſe yt ys of ſome affirmed, yt ys a trueth: And that he ſaied no Maſſe whiche this Proclamer
ſaeth, bicauſe yt ys of no catholique writer affirmed, ys an vntreuthe. And
thus (though in skorn) he hath confeſſed more for the trueth, then he ys hable
to bring to maintein his vntrueth. For yf we haue ſome to ſaie for vs, and
he none to ſaie for him, whoſe cauſe ys beſt, yt ys caſie to iudge.

    That S. Peter ſaied Maſſe at Rome I can not doubt, for that he and S.
Paule being the ſownders of the Churche ther, as *Irenæus* witneſſeth and
Peter being ther Biſhoppe reſident xxv years, as bothe *Euſebius*, and S. Hie-

*Irenæus li.3
cap.3. Eu-
ſeb. eccl.
hiſt. lib. 3.
cap.2. Hie-
ron. li. eccl.
ſcriptorū.
Hugo de S.
Vict. lib.2.
de Sac.
part. 8.
cap. 14.*

rom do teſtifie, yt maie not be thought of ſoche an Apoſtle, ſo feruentlie
profeſſing, and folowing Chriſte, for ſo long time to haue neclected that
part of his duetie. And that he ther ſaied Maſſe yt proueth well, that before
being reſident at Antioche he ys of diuerſe teſtified ſo to haue doen. Wher- **H**
for yt well foloweth that he ſaing Maſſe at Antioche, wher he was firſt reſident, did the like at Rome, wher (as *Irenæus* ſaieth) he ſownded the churche,
and was all the reſt of his life reſident.

    That he ſaied Maſſe at Antioche *Hugo de S. Victorys* a plain wittneſſe, who
ſaieth thus. *Celebᵞatio Miſſæ in cõmemoratione paſſionis Chriſti agitur, ſicut ipſe præcepit
Apoſtolis,*

A *Apoſtolis,tradens eis corpus & ſanguinem ſuum dicens,Hoc facite in meam commemora-*
*tionem.*Hanc *Miſſam beatus Petrus Apoſtolus primus omnium Antiochiæ dicitur celebraſ-*
*ſe,in qua tres tantùm orationes in initio fidei dicebantur.*The celebracion of the Maſſe
ys doen in the commemoracion of the paſſion of Chryſte,as he commaun-
ded the Apoſtoles,deliuering vnto them his bodie and blood,ſaing:*This doye*
*in remēbrāce of me.*This Maſſe S.Peter the Apoſtle ys ſaied firſt of all to haue ſai
ed at*Antioche,*in the which in the beginnig of the faith ther were oneli three
praiers ſaied.Thus moche he.In whom beſides his teſtimonie that S. Peter
ſaied Maſſe at *Antioche,*yt ys alſo teſtified and taught,that Chryſte did inſtitute the Maſſe,in the which he deliuered his bodie and blood. And that yt
ſhoulde not be left in doubt what Maſſe S. Peter ſaied , this authour ſaieth
that he ſaied this Maſſe wherin ys deliuered the bodie and blood of Chryſt,
whiche ys the Maſſe of the catholique Church.

*S Peter ſai
ed Maſſe at
Antioche.*

    A moch like teſtimonie geueth *Remigius.*But yt ſhal ſuffice to heare the te
ſtimonie of *Iſidorus,*who ys the eldeſt of theſe three,for he liued more then
B   nine hundreth years agon,who ſaieth thus:*Ordo Miſſæ vel orationum,quibus ob-*
*lata Deo ſacrificia conſecrantur,primùm eſt à ſanćto Perro inſtitutus.*The ordre of the
Maſſe or of the praiers,with the which the ſacrifices offred to God are conſe
crated,was firſt inſtituted of S.Peter.Thus *Iſidorus.* In whiche his ſaing yt ys
to be noted,that he maketh not S.Peter the inſtitutour or authour of the
Maſſe.For(as yt ys ſhewed in the firſt booke) he doth attribute that to
Chryſte,but he maketh him the authour of a certain ordre of the Maſſe, and
of praiers to be ſaied at the conſecracion,oblacion, and myniſtracion doen
in the Maſſe , but not of the Maſſe yt ſelf.Thus moch being ſaied to aunſwer
the Proclamer for S.Peters Maſſe,let vs nowe procead.

*Iſid.li.1.de
off.ecl.cap.
15.*

Cap.vltim.

    Yt maie perchaunce ſeem ſtraunge to the Proclamer,to ſaie that S. Paule
ſaied Maſſe:but that he did ſo, to the faithfull Chryſtian conſidering the
weight of that,that ſhall be ſaied,yt ſhall be made manifeſt.Yt ys therfore to
be remembred that Maſſe,as yt ys taken in the propre ſignificacion ys no
more , but the conſecracion oblacion , and receauing of Chryſtes bleſ-
C   ſed bodie and bloode. Maſſe largelie taken ys both the conſecracion,
oblacion,receauing,and alſo a certain ordre of rites,ceremonies,praiers, and
reading of ſcripturs added therunto.Nowe that S.Paule did conſecrate the
bodie of Chryſt and ſacrificed the ſame his doćtrin in the x.and xi.of his epiſtle to the Corinth.hath and ſhal ſo declare the ſame,that the Proclamer by
no honeſt mean ſhall denie yt,this being preſuppoſed that he did as moche
as he taught.But he taught the bodie and blood of Chryſt to be conſecrated
and ſacrificed.Wherfor he did the ſame,yf he did that,then ſaied he Maſſe as
of Chryſt yt was inſtituted.But to this inſtitucion S.Paule alſo (as S . Peter)
added a certain maner and ordre of praiers and ceremonies,and therfore yt
maie be ſaied,that he ſaied Maſſe in the large maner of the acceptiō of Maſſe
That he made a certain ordre,his own woordes will proue yt. For when he
had trauailed to reduce the Corinthiãs to the right inſtituciō of Chryſt,that
ys,to the honourable maner of the myniſtracion of his bodie and blood,
which ys the conſecraciō,oblaciō,and godlie receauing of the ſame , in the
ende of all he ſaieth:*Cetera cùm venero diſponā.*Other things I ſhal ſett in ordre
when I come,As who might ſaie:I haue now geuē inſtrućtiōs as touching
D   the ſubſtancial parts of the Maſſe aboute the well doing of the whiche lieth
the great weight:I haue put yow in mind of the verie inſtituciō of Chryſt: I
haue taught yow how ye aught to examin yower ſelues, before ye come to
receaue that bleſſed bread the bodie of Chryſte.I haue let yowe vnderſtand
what horrible daunger abideth thē,that vnwoorthilie receaue that bodie ād

*S.Paule
ſaid Maſſe*

1.Cor . 11.

Iii   drink

drinke that blood: and that ye might perceaue fome forefhewe and feel (as **E** yt were) a foretafte of the wrath and difpleafure of God vpon them, that vn-woorthilie receaue the bodie and blood of Chryfte, I haue certified yowe, that forfoche vnwoorthie receauing God hath plagued manie with diuerfe difeafes, and ficknefles, yea and manie with death. Thus haue I inftructed yowe in the weightie pointes of this honorable mynistracion. As for the extern maner of ceremonies and praiers to be vfed therat after the maner of fome other Churches, to bring yowe to one forme, when I come, I fhall ma-ke that ordre for yowe.

That thus S. Paule did meen, the expofitours of the fcriptures beare wit-neffe. Hugo Cardinalis faieth thus: *Cætera neceffaria ad fumptionem Euchariftiæ, et* *ad ordinationem ecclefiafticam, cùm venero difponam.* Other thinges neceffarie for the receipt of the Sacrament, and the ordeinance of the Church, I fhall dif-pofe and fet in ordre when I come. But though this expofition maie like the quiett man: Yet yt ys like not to pleafe the contentioufe Sacramentarie. Wherfore we will heare S. Hierom who breiflie faieth thus : *Cætera de ipfius* *myfterii facramento, cùm venero difponam.* Other thinges as concerning the facra-ment of that myfterie when I come. I fhall take ordre for them. Thus **F** S. Hierom.

The neceffarie, fubftanciall, and weightie parts of the Sacrament being fpoken of in the, x. and xi. chapters, yt ys eafie to gather and perceaue, that here he fpeaketh of the ordeinance of the rites ceremonies, and praiers tobe doen aboute the mynistracion. But that all cauille of the Aduerfarie maie vt terlie be remoued, the plain expofition, and fentence of S. Auguftine fhall be heard vpon this place, who faieth thus. *Vnde datur intelligi, quia multum erat vt in* *epiftola totum agendi ordinem infinuaret, quem vniuerfa per orbem obferuat Ecclefia , ab* *ipfo ordinatum effe quòd nulla morum diuerfitate variatur.* Wherbie yt ys geuen tobe vnderftanded, that yt was to moche that in an epiftle he fhoulde declare all that ordre of mynistracion, which the vniuerfall Churche throughout the worlde taketh to be ordeined of him, forafmoch as yt ys not by anie diuerfi-tie of maners varied, or altered.

Yf then S. Paule deliuered to the Corinthians both the fubftanciall parts of the Maffe, as ys faied, and alfo by this teftimonie of S. Auguftine deliuered **G** vnto them the ceremonial part, that ys, the ordre and maner of celebracion, and mynistracion, what can we ells faie, but that he deliuered and taught the the ordre of Maffe? And that he did fo, S. Auguftines wordes prooue inuinci blie. For he faieth, that he fpeaketh of that ordre which the vniuerfal Church obferueth. But the vniuerfall Church obferueth the ordre of Maffe. Wherfor yt ys the ordre of Maffe that S. Paule fpeaketh of. And what fhould we think but that thefe two cheif Apoftles ãd the other alfo fhould fetfurth the ordre of the mynistracion of the Sacrament, the ordre of the Maffe, fith that Chrift inftituting the thing, left the ordre and maner of the mynistracion to them, as S. Auguftine ys a ftrong and a plain wittneffe faing: *Non præcepit quo deinceps* *ordine fumeretur, vt Apoftolis, per quos ecclefias erat difpofiturus, feruaret hunc locum.* Chryfte gaue no commaundement after what ordre yt fhoulde afterwarde be receaued, bicaufe he wolde leaue that place to his Apoftles, by whom he wolde fett his Church in ordre.

In this faing of S. Auguftin note that Chryft inftituting the holie mynistra **H** cion, did, as ys faied, onelie inftitute the fubftanciall parts of the Maffe the thing yt felf, and not the ordre and maner how yt fhould be doen. Wherbie maie be perceaued the vanitie of the railing of the Aduerfarie againft Chryft

catholi-

A catholique Churche for the rites and ceremonies vfed in the Maffe . For (faieth he)Chryfte commaunded no crouching no kneelinge , nor no foche dumbe ceremonies as the,Papiftes doo vfe.Yt ys true he commaūded none foche,but he left the ordre of them to his Apoftles,that they in thofe matters fhould take ordre.Wherfor the Aduerfarie maie not drawe the Church to do nothing more in the holie myniftracion,then Chryfte did.Fot fo,asby S.Auguftine yt maie be perceaued,Chryfte himfelf wolde not,but he wolde haue an ordre and maner therin,whiche he wolde fhoulde be made by hys Apoftles,and Churche,wherfore let not the Aduerfarie vfe anie more his vain argumēt:Chryft did not this,or,Chryft did not that,therfor we fhould not doo yt.For foch doings he lefte to the ordre of his Church. And forafmoch as he fo did we muft with reuerent obedience accept and regard, that by her ys ordeined.

　　And now feing that Chryfte hath lefte foch ordre by other then by himfelf to be made,what fhould yt offend theProclamer to hear that S.Peter,ād
B S.Paule did make a certain ordre,and certain praiers to be vfed in the Maffe, and fo likewife S.Andrew,S.Iames,S.Dionyfe,S.Bafil,and S.Chryfoftō,and other,by reafon of whiche ordeinaunces and praiers by them feuerallie made they fhould be called S.Peters Maffe.S.Andrews Maffe,S. Iames Maffe, and fo furth.

As S.Peter and S.Paule are teftified to haue faied Maffe,So ys S.Andrew the　*S. Andre*
brother of S.Peter,who after he had with moch trauaill and manie miracles　*as Apoft.*
preachedChryftes faith in *Scythia* in Europe,which contrie happened to him　*ad Aegeā.*
when the Apoftles diuided thēfelues to preach throughout the woorld. He came to *Patras* in Grece,wher being refifted by Aegeas the Proconfull , and
by him apprehēded,in geuing an accōpt of his doinges,faied thus to the fa-　*S. Andrew*
me Aegeas: *Omnipotenti Deo,qui vnus & verus eft Deus,ego omni die facrifico , non*　*offred facri*
thuris fumū,nec taururū mugientiū carnes,nec hircorū fanguinē fed immaculatū agnū qnoti-　*fice dailie.*
die in altari crucis facrifico,cuius carnes poftqaam omnis populus credentiū manducauerit,
& eius fanguinē biberit,agnus qui facrificatus eft,integer perfeuerat & viuus.Et cùm ve-
rè facrificatus fuerit & verè carnes eius manducatæ fint à populo,& verè fanguis eius fit
C *bibitus:tamen(vt dixi)integer permanet.& viuus.*Vnto the AllmightieGod,which ys one and the verie God,euery daie do I facrifice,not the fmook of franken cenfe,neither the flefh of roaring bulls, nor the blood of kiddes , but an vn defiled lābe do I dailie offre in facrifice in the aultar of the croffe.whofe flefh after that all the beleuing people haue eaten, and haue dronken his bloode, the lābe that ys facrificed doth remain wholl, and aliue.And when he ys ve rilie facrificed,and his flefh verilie eaten of the people,and his blood verilie drōnken,yet for all(as I haue faied)he doth remain wholl,and vndefiled and aliue.Thus he.

Although in this faing of S.Andrew here ys no menciō made of the woord　*Maffe*
Maffe:yet he hath reported himfelf to haue doē that thing that he fhould ha　*what yt ys.*
ue doē,yf he had faied that he faied Maffe.For call to remēbrance what we haue faied Maffe to be:yt ys to confecrate the bodie and blood of Chryfte, to offre the fame in facrifice,and to receaue yt. Thefe three S. Andrewe re porteth himfelf dailie to haue doen.For he faieth that in the aultar he facri ficed the immaculate lambe,&c. Wherbie declaring the bleffed and innocēt
D lambe Chryfte to be on the aultar,he declareth the confecracion: and faing that he did on the aultar facrifice yt,he doth open the facrifice , and expref fedlie alfo confefsing the receipt,the wholl three parts of theMaffe be confef fed to haue ben by him doen.

Nowe let not the Aduersarie reiect the saing of S. Andrew as of none E authoritie, for yt hath ben in the Churche receaued manie hundreth years, and written in an epistle by the preistes and deacons of *Achaia*, of the passió of S. Andrewe, and to this daie of no catholique to my knowlege reproued. To these three Apostles, we shall adde one other Apostle S. Iames by name, whom with the skoff of somsaie this Proclamer wolde haue made his audience beleue that he had neuer saied Masse at Hierusalem, as he wolde haue persuaded that S. Peter neuer did at *Antioche*, or at Rome. But afterward correcting himself, as a man waking oute of a sheape or dreame, and better aduised, perchaunce not knowing when he preached his sermon that the Masse of S. Iames was a broad in print, but before he penned yt coming to knowledge, he corrected his Some saie spoken in his dreame and vnaduisedlie, ád being now waking and better aduised chaungeth his phrase, and saieth that yt ys constantlie affirmed that S. Iames saied Masse at Hierusalem. And finallie he himself confessing the same and magnifieng and highlie extolling yt by soche comparison as yt liketh him to make, he abaseth, depresseth, and F dispraiseth the Masse of the catholique Church that ys nowe vsed, but howe, well he handleth the matter thowe shalt hereafter vnderstand.

S. Iames Masse allo wed and praised by the Procla mer.

Let vs nowe examen the Masse of S. Iames, and see whether his maner of consecracion agreeth with ours. *Dominus Iesus ea r..te qua tradebatur, vel potius seipsum tradebat pro vita & salute mundi, accipiens panem in sanctas, immaculatas, inculpabiles & immortales manus suas, in cœlum suspiciens, ac tibi Deo & Patri ostendens, gratias agens, sanctificans, frangens dedit nobis Discipulis suis dicens: Accipite, comedite, Hoc est corpus meum, quod pro vobis frangitur, & datur in remissionem peccatorum.* Oure Lord Iesus the same night that he was betraied, or raither in the which he deliuered himself for the life and saluacion of the worlde, taking bread into his holie, vndefiled, innocent, and immortall handes, looking vppe into heauen, and shewing yt vnto thee God and Father geuing thankes, sanctifieng, and breaking, gaue yt vnto vs his Disciples saing: Take, eate, this ys my bodie which ys broken for yowe, and geuen in the remission of sinnes. Then he tooke the cuppe and saied: *Similiter postquàm cœnauit accipiens calicem, & permiscens ex vino & aqua, & aspiciens in cœlum, ac ostendens tibi Deo & Patri gratias agens, sanctificans, benedicens, implens Spiritu sancto, dedit nobis Discipulis suis, dicens: Bibite ex hoc omnes. Hic est sanguis meus noui Testamenti, qui pro vobis, & multis effunditur & datur in remissionem peccatorum.* Likewise he after he had supped taking the cuppe and mingling yt with wine and water, and looking vppe into heauen, and shewing yt to thee God and Father, geuing thankes, sanctifieng, blessing, filling yt with the holie Gost, he gaue yt vnto vs his Disciples, saing: Drinke ye all of this. This ys my bloode of the newe Testament, which for yowe, and for manie ys shed and geuen in the remission of sinnes.

S. Iames di rected his speache in the cósecra cion to God the Father

Chryst mix ed his cuppe with wy ne ád water

This was his maner of consecracion. And forasmoche as all the holie Apostles preached one Chryste, one faith one religion, and did all see Chryste setting furth this one institucion, yt ys to be thought in so weightie a matter, that they all vsed one forme, which maie well be proued to be this, for that S. Iames being an Apostle wolde not in this high ministracion varie or dissent from other Apostles, but vse the same ordre and maner that they did. Nowe then let the Masse of the catholiques, and the Communion (as yt H ys tearmed) of the Schismatiques, be compared to his maner of consecració that triall maie be made, which of the two ioineth neareft vnto yt, and best agreeth with yt. S. Iames approching to the holie consecracion abideth in

Chryst befo re the conse cracion of his bodie lifted vppe his eies, and gaue tháks to his Fa ther.

deuoute

A deuout praier,and proceeding in his pourpofe directeth his wholl talke to God the Father,as Chryfte in his propre perfon before the fame confecracion did,both lifting vppe his eies,and geuing thãks to the fame his Father. The catholique Church euen fo approching to the holie confecracion abideth and continueth in deuoute praier,and proceeding in the fame pourpofe directeth all her woordes to God the Father after the example of the Apoftles Maffe,thus faing:Who the daie before he fuffred,tooke bread into his holie ãd honorable hãdes,and lifting vppe his eies vnto thee,God his father allmightie,ãd alfo geuing thankes he bleffed yt,&c.In the which woords by the waie note,that as in the Maffe of the Apoftles thefe woordes were vfed as directed to God the Father:*He lifted vppe his eies,and gaue thanks to the God ãd Father:* So in the Maffe of the catholique Church yt ys faied to the Father: *He lifted vppe his eies into heauen vnto thee God his Father allmightie,*and to thee geuing thankes bleffed yt,&c.Wherin ys made direction of woordes to God the Father,as was in the Apoftles Maffe.And here alfo this maie be noted that the rule of the Apoftles Maffe was,that when the preift came to the con

The maner of the Apoftles and catholique preifts incõ fecracion.

B fecracion,folowing the example of Chryft,who tooke the bread into his holie handes,he tooke alfo the bread into his handes:So the preift of the catholique Church coming to the confecracion,taketh the bread into his handes, and foloweth both the example of Chryfte,and of his Apoftles.
Now the mynifter of the Schifmaticall Cõmuniõ approching to,I cã not tel what(for that church not bearing the name of cõfecracion,I know not how to terme their doings)hyftorically reherfeth the woordes ofChryfts fupper, not as Chryft himfelf and his Apoftles did directing his cõmunicaciõ toGod the father,but paffeth furth as one that wolde tell a tale,faing thus:*Who inthe fame night that he was betraied,tooke bread and when he had geuen thankes,he brake yt,ãd gaue yt,to his Difciples,faing:Take,eate,this ys my bodie,which ys geuen for yowe , doe this in the remembrance of me.*In thefe woordes ye fee nofoch direction of fpeach to God the father,as Chryfte and his Apoftles made , and as the catholique Church vfeth folowing thẽ.The mynifter faieth,not to the Father thefe wordes:he looked vppe into heauen to thee,God and father, and geuing thee thanks,but onelie maketh a bare reherfall of the hyftorie.Yt ys euident then

The maner of new my-nifters in their Com-munion.

Woordes of the Cõmu-nion.

C that in this part,the fchifmaticall church foloweth not the maner of the A-poftolique Church,but the catholique Churche doeth.
The rule of the Apoftolique Churche was to take the bread that fhoulde be confecrated into their handes:The breach of rule in the Schifmaticall Church that they take not the bread into handes,but let yt lie on the table, as though they had nothing to do withall.In this alfo they fall not onelie from the order receaued of the Apoftles,but alfo from the doing of Chryft, who (as in S.Iames Maffe yt ys faied)tooke bread into his holie immaculate handes,&c.before he did confecrate yt.And allthough the woordes of the Euangeliftes be nõt fo full as to faie that he tooke bread into his handes:yet in that they,and S.Paule alfo faie that he tooke bread,yt importeth as moch as S.Iames faieth,that he tooke yt into his handes.

Conference of the A-poftles and new myni-ftres in con fecracionof the bread.

The conference thus farre being made aboute the bread and confecra-cion of the bodie of Chryfte:let vs procead to make conference alfo aboute the wine,and the bloode.Firft,as touching the wine,yt ys manifeft that the Apoftles vfed to mixte yt with water . For yt ys in the Maffe of

D fainct Iames faied , that Chryfte tooke the cuppe and mixed wine with water,&c.The catholique Church both Latines,and Grekes in all ages preparing the cuppe of our Lorde forthe holie myniftracion mixeth,

Conference of the fame in the con-fecraciõ of the wine.

water

water with wine in the same cuppe. The Schifmaticall Communion (if yt maie be so well termed, as to call yt a Communion, when in dede yt ys raither a disunion) dissenteth here from the doing of Chryste, of the Apostles, and of the primitiue Churche, for in yt ys not vsed to mixe water with wine.

　　The Euangelistes saie, that Chryste likewise tooke the cuppe, that ys, as he tooke the bread into his holie handes: so tooke he the cuppe into his holie handes. The preist in the catholique Church folowing Chrystes example, and the Apostles, and Fathers of the primitiue Church taketh the cuppe into his handes before he confecrateth yt. The mynister of the Shifmaticall Church herein also foloweth not the doing of Chryste, nor of the Apostles and primitiue Churche, but letteth the cuppe stand as a straunger to him, not taken into the handes. Chryste entring towarde the consecracion of his blood continueth his communicacion to his Father with thankes geuing. The Apostles beginning the same direct their woordes to God the father, as yt ys seen in the Masse of sainct Iames, wher they speake to him saing. Geuing thankes to the God and Father. The primitiue Churche did

Woordes of the Masse. the like. The catholique Church folowing Chryste, the Apostles, and primitiue Churche entreth the consecracion of the blood with these woordes: *In like maner after he had supped taking this cuppe into his holie and honourable handes, geuing thee also thankes, he blessed yt, and gaue yt to his Disciples, &c.*

　　In whiche woordes yt ys easie to perceaue that the catholique Churche continueth her praies to God the Father, and directeth her speach to him, as Chryste the Apostles, and the primitiue Churche did. The late fownde Churche, as aboute their sacramentall bread: so aboute their sacramentall wine leauing the maner vsed of Chryste, the Apostles, and the primitiue *Woordes of the Commu nion.* Churche, proceadeth onelie historicallie reherfing the woordes of Chryste thus: *Likewise after supper he tooke the cuppe, and when he had geuen thankes he* [1] *gaue yt to them, saing: Dirnke ye all of this , &c.* In whiche maner howe moche soeuer the Proclamer braggeth for himself and his Churche, that they folowe Chryste, and the primitiue Churche, yt maie be perceaued that these are but woordes, For their doinges doo almost in nothing agree. But let vs see more of the consecration of the cuppe of our Lord.

　　The Apostles did not onelie saie that Chryste gaue thankes to his Father, but also that he did sanctifie and blesse yt. The catholique Churche folowing them saieth likewise that he gaue not onelie thankes, but also that he blessed yt, The Proclamers Church saieth no more but that he gaue thanks, and liketh not to saie that Chryst blessed yt, or sanctified yt. And wote yow whie? Bicause they feared that the trueth might be sooner perceaued, that by the blessing and sanctificacion of Chryste, his verie bodie and blood were confecrated (as they were in dede) which by all shiftes and meanes they labour, to hide. But I wishe the wholl woordes of S. Iames Masse not onely to be well noted, but also continuallie to be remembred, that he saieth that *Chryste gaue thankes, he sanctified, he blessed, and fylled the cuppe with the holie Gost.* *Woordes of S. James. Masse.* For these woordes not onelie impugne the wicked assertion of the Sacramentarie, but also commende to vs the excellencie of the B. Sacrament, and proue the presence of that blessed bloode whiche the catholique Churche teacheth there to be present. For who can saie that after these great doings of Chryste, of sanctificng, blesing and filling with the holie Gost, that ther ys nothing ells made but a bare hungrie figure?

This godlie acte of Chryste the Apostles and Fathers foloweing, as S. Iames

A in his Maſſe, S. Baſill, and Chryſoſtom in their Maſes, did not onelie make mencion of his bleſſiing and ſanctifieng, but did them ſelues ſign and bleſſe the Sacrament, as in their Maſſes yt ys plain to ſee. Which acte of Chryſt, of the Apoſtles ād fathers, the catholike church embrancing ſigneth with the ſign of the croſſe, and bleſſeth the Sacrament, ſignifieng the ſanctificacion their doen to be doen by the power of him that by his croſſe ſanctified all the faithfull. But theſe wicked bretheren of the late fownd Church geue as fewe termes of excellencie to yt and vſe as fewe geſtures and actes ſignifieng bleſſing and ſanctificacion, as they maie, that the eſtimacion of that gloriouſe Sacrament maie be impaired.

Conference of the catholeque authoritie of preiſts withe the lacke of authoritie of newe miniſters.

Thus nowe ye haue ſeē the conference made, ye ſee the catholique Churche in euerie poinct agreing with Chryſte, withe Apoſtles, and with the priſtiue Churche. Contrarie wiſe ye ſee the newe fownd Churche allmoſt in all pointes diſagreing. Finallie I thinke yt expedient that as I haue here ſpoken of conſecracion, and conferred the doing of the catholique Churche, and of the newe Churche, with the Apoſtolique and primitiue Churche:

B So to ſaie a fewe woordes of the preiſt of the one, and of the miniſter of the other. And here not moche to tarie the reader, yt ys to be remēbred that Chryſte, when he had inſtituted this diuine and noble Sacrament, willing yt to be continued gaue his Apoſtles, and in them to all their ſucceſſours power, authoritie, and commaundement to doo that, that he had doen. By which commaundement euery catholique preiſt duelie executing this miniſtracion, doth conſecrate the verie bodie and blood of Chryſte, by vertue of Chryſtes ordeinance, and woordes duelie pronouced.

Newe miniſtres haue no autho ritie to conſecrate.

The miniſtres of the newe churche not being of the catholique ſucceſſion, as they haue no ſoche power, authoritie or cōmaundement from Chryſte to conſecrate his bodie and blood, and as their monſtrouſe heades neither can geue them ſoche, neither mindeth that they ſhoulde doe anie ſoche thing, but raither as they finde yt bread and wine ſo to let yt remain, and ſo to receaue yt: they do not ſo reherſing Chryſtes woordes, conſecrate his

C bleſſed bodie, no more then they doo that read thoſe woordes vpō the booke in their cōmon ſtudies. For if the hiſtorie of Chryſtes ſupper reherſed of a miniſter not endewed with laufull authoritie, deſcending to him by catholique ordre, did conſecrate then ſhoulde conſecracion haue ben doen in manie a querulouſe and contenciouſe dinner, and ſupper, aſwell in Tauerns as ells wher, wher the like woords haue ben ſpokē and reherſed of men of as good authoritie for that pourpoſe, as the miniſtre. Be not deceaued therfor (gentle readers) to thinke that of ſoche mens hands yowe receaue the bodie of Chryſte. Yt ys to moche that yowe receaue ther ſchiſinaticall bread: yt were lamentable therwith alſo to committe Idolatrie.

Addias hiſt. Apoſt. li.7.

S. Matthew ſaied Maſſe.

And now although this might ſuffice to prooue the Maſſe to haue ben vſed of the Apoſtles, yet for thy better cōnfirmaciō (gentle reader) I ſhall ad de the teſtimonie of *Abdias* Biſhoppe of *Babilon*, and a Diſciple of the Apoſtles who writeth thus of the Maſſe and death of S. Matthewe. *Cumque reſpondiſſent amen, & miſteria Domini celebrata & Miſſā ſuſcepiſſet omnis Eccleſia, retinuit ſe vt iuxta altare, vbi corpus ab eo fuerat Chriſti confectum, illic martyriū Apoſtolicū exulta ret.* And when all had ſaied Amen, and all the Churche had receaued the Maſſe, and the miniſteries that were celebrated, he ſtaied him ſem ſelf, that

D by the aultar, wher the bodie of Chryſte was by him cōſecrated, ther ſhould his martidom be ſolemniſed, Thus ther. In this place ye heare plain menciō made of the Maſſe doen and celebrated by S. Mathewe, whiche if the Aduer farie wil feke to auoid, as put in by the tranflatour: yet he can not denie thefe E two thinges, whiche be in effect equiualent, that ys, the aultar, and the confecracion of the bodie of Chryfte. Nowe if he did clerebrate at the aultar, and on the aultar did confecrate the bodie of Chryfte, yt foloweth that he did celebrate the Maffe.

And here I wifh thefe two thinges to be well noted, forfomoch as they were written of one that was difciple to the Apoftles, and did write diuerfe bookes of their liues. The one ys, that S. Matthew did celebrate at the aultar: the other that he did confecrate the bodie of Chryfte. Yf thefe two were to be writté as in vfe thé, yt maie eafelie be iudged who doth offéd: he that doth vfe both in thefe daies, or he that refufeth both. And wher the Proclamer as ys of late faied prouoketh fo moche to the primitiue Churche, iudge nowe again, Reader, how well yt liketh him to folowe the order of the primitiue Churche, whé he abādoneth and flieth frō thefe two thinges, as frō a ferpét, and yet both vfed, as ye perceaue, of the Apoftles and the PrimitiueChurch.

Hauing nowe faied fufficiétlie for the vfe of theMaffe in the Apoftles time, to cōclude this chapter, this maie be faied, that as yt pleafed our SauiourChri F fte to cōmend to the worlde the trueth of his holie Gofpell principallie by foure Euāgeliftes, and S. Paule his chofé veffell: So yt hath pleafed him to cō méd the trueth of the holie miniftracion of his bodie and blood called the Maffe, by foure Apoftles, namelie S. Peter, S. Andew, S. Iames, and S.Matt hew and alfo by S.Paule. He of his mercie graūt that as by the Euangeliftes his Gofpell was receaued and beleued: fo by the teftimonie and doinges of thefe Apoftles the trueth of the bleffed miniftracion maie be embraced.

THE FIVE AND THIRTETH CHAPTER SHE-
weth the maner of confecracion vfed and practifed by the
Difciples of the Apoftles and the Fathers of the
primitiue and auncient Church.

Auing nowe faied of the confecracion vfed in the Apoftles time, and to yt cōferred the maner of confecracion of the cathollque Church that now ys, ād the difordred maner of the fchifmatical G chuȓch: yt fhall geue good light to the atteigning of the trueth yf we fee allfo the order of the fame confecracion vfed of the eldeft fathers of the priuitiue Churȼh. Amōg the whiche, as among the Apoft les we began with S. Peter, and S. Paule fo fhall we here beginne with their difciples S. Clement, and S. Dionife. That S. Clement faied Maffe, and con fecrated the bodie and blood ofChryfte in the fame maner that S.Peter, and the reft of the Apoftles did, not onelie his Maffe, which ys extant, and the woordes of confecracion ther in conteined, but alfo *Nicolaus Methonen*: by expreffe woordes doth teftifie yt. Whofe woordes for the clere declaraci- on of the matter I fhall at large alleage. Thus he faieth: *Offerimus pané perfectú viuum, fiue corpus Chrifti quod perfectum etiam poft paßionem permanfit & integrum. Neque enim os eius contritum eft, & à diuina vita infeparabile, planè quale ipfe primus no- fter ac magnus Pontifex & facrificus victimáque fuis ipfius Difcipulis tradidit, iíque denuo, qui ab initio fuis ipfis oculis verbum intuiti funt, eíque miniftrarunt, catholicæ Ecclefiæ ab extremis ad extremos vfque orbis terrarum limites tradiderunt: Omnes quidem, Hierofoli- mitanæ, vbi & D.Iacobus primi magníquePontificis frater ac fucceßor myfticá incruentáq; liturgiam expofuit. Petrus autem et Paulus Antiochenfi. Paulus verò peculiariter orbi vni- uerfo. Marcus Alexandriæ. Ioannes & Andreas Afiæ & Europæ. Omnesque vniuerfæ* H Eccle

A *Ecclesiæ vbicunque sit per eam, quā S. Clemens conscripsit liturgiam, tradiderunt, in qua hæc ita ad verbum habentur : Memores igitur eorum quæ propter nos passus est, gratias agimus tibi omnipotens Deus, non quantum debemus, sed quantum possumus, vt eius statutū adimpleamus. In qua enim nocte tradebatur, accipiens panem in sanctas & immaculatas suas manus & eleuatis oculis ad te Deum & Patrem suum fregit, deditque nobis dicens : Accipite ex eo, comedite, hoc est corpus meum, quod pro multis comminuitur in remißionem peccatorum. Similiter & calicem ex vino & aqua temperatum sanctificauit deditque nobis dicens : Bibite ex eo omnes. Hic est sanguis meus, qui pro multis effunditur in remißionem peccatorum. Hoc facite in meam commemorationem,*

We offre a perfect liuelie bread, that ys, the bodie of Chryste, whiche *The bodie* remained alſo perfect and wholl after his paſſion, for ther was no bone of *of Chryste* his brokē, and plainlie ſoche bodie as oure high and great Biſhoppe, who ys *offred in* both preiſt and ſacrifice, deliuered to his owne Diſciples, was from the diui *the Maſſe.* ne life inſeparable, and they again, whiche from the beginning did withe their eies ſee the Sonne of God, and did wait vpon him, deliuered the ſame

B to the catholique Churche, euen from one ende of the worlde to an other: euen all of them at Hieruſalem, wher alſo S. Iames the brother and ſucceſſour of that cheif and great Biſhoppe ſettfurth the miſticall and vnbloodie *The Maſſe* ſacrifice, or Maſſe. Peter and Paule at Antioche, but Paule peculiarly to the *of S. Cle-* wholl worlde. Mark at Alexandria. Iohn and Andrew in Aſia and Europe. *mēt the ſa-* And all of them deliuered yt to the vniuerſall Churche, wher ſoeuer yt be, *me that all* by that ſame Maſſe, whiche S. Clement ſetfurth, in the which theſe woor- *the Apoſt* des be had woord for woorde Being mindefull of thoſe thinges, whiche he *les vſed.* ſuffred for vs, we geue thee thankes, Allmightie God, not aſmoche as we aught, but aſmoche as we can, and we fullfill his ordinance, In the night that he was betraied taking bread into his holie and vndefiled hands, and lifting vppe his eies vnto thee God and his father, he brake yt, and gaue yt vnto vs, ſaing : Take of yt, eate, This ys my bodie whiche ys broken for ma nie in the remiſſion of ſinnes. Likewiſe alſo the cuppe mixed with wine and water, he ſanctified and gaue yt to vs ſaing drinke ye all of this. This ys my blood, which ys ſhed for manie in the remiſſiō of ſinnes. This doe ye in the

C remembrance of me. Thus moche this authour.

I haue produced this part of the Maſſe ſetfurth by S. Clement vnder the authoritie and teſtimouie of this man, both for that he being of the greke churche ys not to be ſuſpected of Papiſtrie by the euell bretheren, and alſo liuing ſome hundreth years agon ys to be thought the freer from corruption. And albeit I iudge this that he ſaieth that Peter, Paule Iames and all the Apoſtles ſaied the ſame Maſſe that S. Clement afterward vſed and commen ded alſo to the churches, to be a verie notable ſaing, euen ſo notable that both catholique and proteſtant maie well note yt, the catholique for ioie ſeing the catholique religion well teſtified: the proteſtant for furie and greif ſeing his vntrueth impugned, and his falſhed detected: yet I ſhall in conſideracion that of this matter moche ys ſaied in the laſt chapter, ouerpaſſe yt, and applie my ſelf to that, that ys in this chapter to be ſpoken of. This then in this place ys to be noted that the Maſſe that S. Clement vſed ys euen the ſame that Peter, Paule and all the Apoſtles did vſe. Thi s Maſſe vſeth not an hiſtoricall narracion in the reherſall of the woordes of Chryste at the conſe-

D cracion, but entring into yt by praier made to the heauenlie father, abideth and continueth in the ſame, vſing the like directiō of woordes, as were vſed in the Maſſe of S. Iames, as by conferēce yt ſhall be eaſilie perceaued. This alſo here, as in S. Iames Maſſe, yt to be noted, that the cuppe of Chryste

was

was not a cuppe of wine onelie, but yt was a cuppe of wine mixed with **E**
water.

S. Proclus
tractatu
de tradi. di-
uina litur-
giæ.

But perchaunce the Aduersarie will demaunde howe we prooue that yt
ys S. Clements Masse. God be praised we lacke no proues. for besides this
Grecian, whom we haue allreadie produced, we haue an other Grecian
Proclus Bishoppe of Constantinople who liued aboute 1100 years agon testifieng that manie did setfurth the Masse in writing emong whiche he nõb-
reth sainct Clement. his woordes be these. *Multi quidem & alii diuini pastores,*
qui Apostolis successerunt, ac Ecclesiæ doctores sacrorum illius diuinæ liturgiæ mysteriorum
rationem explicantes, scriptis mandatam Ecclesiæ tradiderunt. In quibus primi & clarissi-
mi sunt beatus Clemens, summi illius Apostolorum Discipulus, ac successor, qui sacrosancta
illa mysteria à sanctis Apostolis sibi reuelata in lucem edidit, & D. Iacobus, qui in sortem
Ecclesiæ Hierosolimitanæ administrandæ vocatus fuit, quique huius primus Episcopus à
primo illo & summo Pontifice Christo Deo nostro constitutus est. Manie other godly
pastours also, whiche succeded the Apostles and doctonrs of the church, set
ting furth the order or maner of the Godlie Masse of the diuine misteries **F**
left yt vnto the Churche in writing. Amõg the whiche the cheifest and most
famouse be S. Clement the Disciple of him that was cheifest of the Apostles,
and successour, who did setfurth these holie misteries, as they were deliuered or taught vnto him of the Apostles: And S. Iames who was called to ru
le the churche of Hierusalem, who also was ordeined the first Bishoppe of
that cheif and high Bishoppe Chryste our God. Thus he. In this testimonie
ye heare that not onelie S. Clement did setfurth the ordre of Masse, but
other doctours, and pastours of the church also, and that not by their owne
authoritie, but as they had learned of the Apostles, And note here also an
euident testimonie for the Masse of S. Iames, wherof we haue spoken in the
last chapter.

Nowe to proceade, to heare more of the maner of consecracion in the
primitiue Church. S. *Dionisius Areopagita* Disciple to S. Paule, as S. Clemẽt
was to Peter, that he saied Masse yt ys more euident, then nede to be declared. His booke of the *ecclesiasticall hierarchie* ys extant, wherin the wholl order **G**
of Masse ys at lenght setfurth and declared. But forsomoche as that booke to
the learned ys well knowen, and to the vnlearned although he were alleaged, yet for his obscuritie he wold be still vnknowen, I haue thought good
here to ouerpasse him as a witnesse famouslie knowen, ãd bring in other mo
re plain, and yet right famouslie knowen. Among the whiche holie Basill
shall be first, who in his Masse vsed this forme of consecracion, entring into

Bassil.in
Miss.

yt by praier made to the heauenlie father, in the whiche he thus spake
of Chryste.

Chryst too-
ke the bre-
ad and cup-
pe mixed
withe wine
and water
in to his
hands and
blessed and
sanctified
them.

Debens enim exire in voluntariam & beatiss. & viuificam, suam mortem in nocte
qua tradebat seipsum pro mundi vita, accipiens panem in sanctis suis & immaculatis mani-
bus, & ostendens tibi Deo & Patri gratias agens, benedicens, sanctificans, frangens, dedit
sanctis suis Discipulis & Apostolis, dicens: Accipite & manducate, hoc est corpus meũ,
quod pro vobis frangitur in remißionem peccatorum. Similiter & calicem de genimine vi-
tis accipiens, miscens, gratias agens, benedicens, sanctificans, dedit sanctis suis Discipulis &
Apostolis dicens: Bibite ex hoc omnes. Hic est sanguis meus noui Testamenti, qui pro vobis
& pro multis effundetur in remißisnem peccatorum. Hoc facite in meam commemoratio-
nem. Willing to go furth to his voluntarie and blessed death geuing life, in **H**
the night in the whiche he deliuered himself for the life of the world, taking
bread in his holie and vndefiled hands, and shewing yt to thee God and
Father, geuing thankes, and blessing sanctifieng breaking, he gaue yt to his
holie

A holie Difciples and Apoftles, faing. Take and eate, this ys my bodie, whiche ys broken for yowe in the remifsion of finnes. Likewife alfo taking the cuppe of the iuice of the wine, mixing, geuing thankes, blefsing, fanctifieng he gaue yt to his holie Difciples, and Apoftles faing drinke ye all of this. This ys my blood of the newe Teftament whiche fhall be fhedd for yowe and for manie in the remifsion of finnes. This do ye in the remembrance of me. Thus moche in the Mafse of S. Bafill.

Whiche if ye conferre and compare to the confecracion vfed by S. Iames *Chryfoft in* and S. Clement, fo moche fhall yt fee them agree that ye fhal iuftilie faie that *Miff-* they be all one. Therfor leauing him to be confidered with the notes made vpon S. Iames and S. Clement, we fhall procead to fee what maner of confecracion was vfed in S. Chryfoftoms Mafse. Chryfoftom (as the reft before mencioned) entreth into yt with praier made to the Father, and coming to fpeake of our Lorde and Sauiour Iefus Chryfte inftituting this moft holie and noble facrament, faieth : *Qui veniens, completo pro nobis omni myfterio, nocte qua tradebatur, magis autem tradebat feipfum pro mundi vita, panem accipiens cum fan-*

B *ctis fuis & immaculatis & impolutis manibus, cùm gratias egiffet, benedixit, fanctificauit, & frangens fanctis fuis Difcipulis & Apoftolis tribuit dicens : Accipite, & comedite, hoc eft corpus meum, quod pro vobis tradetur in remifsionem peccatorum . Similiter autem & calicem poftquam cænauit dicens: Bibite ex hoc omnes . Hic eft enim fanguis meus noui teftamenti, qui pro vobis & pluribus effundetur in remifsionem peccatorum .* Who coming, when all the mifterie for vs was fullfilled, in the night in the whiche he was be traied. or raither in the whiche he deliuered him felf for the life of the worlde, taking bread with his holie, vndefiled and impoluted hands, when he had heuen thankes, he blefsed yt, fanctifieng yt, and breaking yt, gaue yt to his holie Difciples, and Apoftles, faing : Take, and eate, this ys my bodie, whiche fhall be deliuered for yowe in the remifsion of finnes . Likewife alfo the cuppe after he had fupped faing : Drinke ye all of this. This ys my blood of the newe teftament. whiche fhall be fhedd for yowe and for manie in the remifsion of finnes. Thus moche in Chryfoftomes Mafse for the confecracion, whiche that yt agreeth with all before alleaged, yt ys eafie to perceaue.

C But that the Proclamer feem not with his fkoff of fomfaie to weaken or *S. Bafill ad* call into doubt the authoritie of the Mafse of S. Bafill, and S. Chryfoftom, *Chryfofto* as I haue by authoritie proued the Mafses of S. Peter S. Iames and other *not the* Apoftles, and alfo of S. Clement, by good and fufficient authoritie : fo alfo *firft fown-* fhall I doo thefe two of S. Bafill, and S. Chrfyoftom. And here I wifh the rea *ders of* der firft to be aduertifed that S. Bafill and S. Chryfoftom did not make the *Mafse but* ordenaunce of the Mafse as the firft fownders of the ordeinance, for that, as *fetters* ye haue heard, was doen by the Apoftles, and vfed by S. Clement, and fo by *furth of* liueall tradicion brought to the time of thefe two fathers. But the Mafse of *foche order* the Apoftles being verie long as the holie Father *Proclus* witneffeth, and the *ther in as* deuocion of the people waxing fhort, and colde, thefe holie Bifhoppes Ba- *ceaued by* fill and Chryfoftom were compelled to bring yt into a fhorter forme of pra- *tradicion.* iers and ceremonies (the fubftance allwaies ftanding and abiding) which fo being fetfurth were called the Mafses of Bafill and Chryfoftome, fo that not *Proclus* the lack of an ordeinance of Mafse, as though ther were none before, moued *vbi fupra.* them to make this ordre, but the lacke of deuocion in the people, as yowe

D fhall perceaue by the teftimonie of the auncient Father Proclus thus reporting. *Pofteri, abiecta fidei firmitate & feruore, negotiis huiufce feculi & curis mundi mancipati & immerfi, Miffæ longitudinem (vt dixi) pertæfi, vix conueniebat ad audien-*
                                                                              dæ

da Domini verba. Quare D. Basilius medica quadam ratione vsus, breuiorem eam & concisiorem reddidit. Haud multò post Pater noster Ioannes, cui aurea lingua cognomen dedit curam ouium, vt pastorem decet magna alacritate animi suscipiens, ac hominum naturæ socordiam, atque ignauiam prospiciens, fibras omnes & radices huius prætextus sathanici prorsus auellere voluit. Quare multa præcidit, & vt breuior esset constituit, ne sensim homines libertatem & ocium maximè amplectentes fallacibus, & furiosis Aduersarii sermonibus decepti ab hac Apostolica & diuina traditione deficerent, quod multis sæpe accidisse variis in locis ad hunc vsque diem deprehendimus. Men of later daies leauing the feruencie and fowndnesse of faith being feruilelie geuen, and drowned in the businesse and cares of this world, as I haue saied being wearie of the lenght of the Masse, they skantlie assembled or came to heare the woord of our Lorde. Wherfor S. Basill vsing the waie of a good phisition, made yt breifer and shorter. Not long after, our Father Iohn, whose golden toung hath geuen him a Surname, taking vpon him the charge of the shepe as yt becometh a good sheperd, beholding the slacknesse and sluggishnesse of the nature of men, he wolde vtterlie remoue or pluck awaie all the rootes and small stringes of this intencion of Sathan. Wherfor he cutt of manie thinges, and ordeined that yt shoulde be shorter, leste by litle and litle men embracing libertie and idlenesse, and by the deceiptfull and furiouse woordes of the Aduersarie deceaued, shoulde fall from this diuine and Apostolique tradiciõ, which thing euen vnto this time we haue perceaued to happen to manie. Thus moche he, in whom yowe perceaue plain testimonie to be made both of the Masse of S. Basill, and of S. Chrysostom. And not that onelie, but also (as I haue noted) yowe maie perceaue the cause whie these two holie men made these ordeinances of Masse.

Last of all yt ys to be noted, as well woorthie yt ys so to be, that the Masses of these two holie Fathers, be not newe Masses, but they be both euen that same Masse, that by the diuine and Apostolique tradicion, was first setfurth and commended to the catholique Churche to be practised, but that by these men, the small deuocion of the people ther vnto enforcing them, they be drawen shorter. Wherbie we maie learn howe the auncient Churche did retein, and abide in the tradicions of the Apostolique and primitiue Churche, and did for no other pourpose make the order of the Masse receaued from the Apostles shorter, but to kepe the people, that they shoulde not for lack of faith and deuocion by the temptacion of Sathan fall from the diuine and holie tradicion of the Masse, as nowe by the like means Englond hath doen.

Of these Masses as also of the Masse of S. Iames, we haue yet not one or two, or twentie witnesses onelie, but we haue a nombre euen the wholl, vi Councell of Constantinople, wher the Fathers making a canon against the *Armenians* and *Hydroparastæ,* whiche semed to misunderstand Chrysostome, for the true vnperstanding of the matter saic thus of Chrysostom : *Non docet sanctus Pater per solum vinum oblationem fieri, quandoquidem & suæ Ecclesiæ, vbi est illi pastoralis administratio tradita, aquam vino miscendam tradidit, quando incruentum peragi sacrificium oportet, & precioso & honorando nostri redemptoris sanguine & aqua contemperationem attendens, quæ in totius mundi viuificationem effusa est, & peccatorum redemptionem. Et in omni Ecclesia vbi spiritalia luminaria refulserunt, hic ordo diuinitus traditus seruatur.* The holie Father teacheth not that the sacrifice shoulde be doen with wine alone, forasmoche as he gaue order to the Churche wher he was Bishoppe that water shoulde be mingled with wine, when the vnbloodie sacrifice ys to be doen considering the cõtemperacion of the perciouse and hono-

Note the decaie of deuocion the cause of the shortning of the Masse by S. Basill ad Chrysost.

Tradiciõ of the order of Masse obserued frõ the time of the Apostles.

Cõcil. Cʃtã tin.sext. cã 32.

Wine and water why they were mixed in our Lordes cuppe.

A honorable blood and water which was shedde for the life of the worlde,and the remission of sinnes.And in euerie Church wher spirituall lights did shine,this order setfurth by diuine tradicion ys kept.

In that the Councell saieth that Chrysostom gaue order to the Churche wher he was Bishoppe,to mengle water with wine:they vnderstand his Masse,wherin soch order was vsed.And let the Proclamer and all his complices note this saing well,that this order setfurth by diuine tradicion was kept in euery Church wher spirituall lights did shine:wherby maie be gathered that in Englond wher this order ys contemptuouslie banished,ther be no spiri-tuall lightes,but carnall and earthlie smoking Turffes.Of S.Iames and S. Basill thus yt foloweth in the same Councell:*Nam et Iacobus Domini nostri Iesu Chri sti secundùm carnem frater,et BasiliusCæsariensis Archiepiscopus,cuius gloria omnem terra rum orbem peruasit,mystico nobis in scripto tradito sacrificio,ita peragendum in sacro myste rio ex aqua et vino sacrum poculum ædiderunt,et qui Cartagine conuenerunt ita apertè tra diderunt* . Iames the brother of our Lorde Iesus Chryste after the flesh , and

B Basill the Archbyshoppe of *Cesaria*,whose prayse ys gon throughout all the worlde,in the mysticall sacrifice deliuered vnto vs in writing,did setfurth the holie cuppe so to be vsed with water and wine.And the holie Fathers which were together at the Councell of Cartage did euen so apertlie and openlie setfurth. Thus the Councell.

Here now in the whol, ye see that not onelie S.Iames,and S.Basil,and also Chrysostõ did setfurth the holie mynistraciõ in writing,but also taught that the cuppe in the same mynistracion should be mixed with water and wine as a diuine tradicion coming from the Apostles,which tradiciõalthogh vsed of the Apostles,and receaued of the auncient Fathers, this Proclamer and his felowes doe reiect.And yet to bleer the eies of mē he ys euer prouo king to the Apostles and the Primitiue Church,when yet he himself will not come near yt.And here,reader,consider,that if this Proclamer intended the restitucion of religiõ to the maner of the Apostles ãd the primitiue Church, whie doeth he not obserue this,which he can not denie ther to haue ben ob serued,and by the Councels of Cartage,and Constantinople decreed accor

C dinglie to be receaued?But yt ys not the primitiue Church that he trauai-leth for to be regarded,but yt ys his phantasie and will that he seeketh to be receaued.God geue him a better minde.

This also ys not to be ouerpassed that the Councel of Constantinople testi-fieng that S.Iames did setfurth in writing the holie mynistracion, doth call yt by the name of Sacrifice,saing that he did setfurth the mysticall sacrifice, which name the Proclamer abhorreth.But what do I tarie so long aboute the settingfurth of these wittnesses,seing ther be diuerse other that testifie the same?As *Nicolaus Methonen.S.Bernard.Algerus,Bessarion*, and other whom for breuitie sake,I thinke yt sufficient to haue named.

Nowe,Reader,wher the Proclamer in the second place that he speaketh of S.Iames,saieth that we constantlie affirme that S.Iames saied Masse,I pra-ie thee,maie we not so doo,and doo truelie?And yf he and his complices saie the contrarie,shall they not saie falselie?we haue wittnesse and good au-thoritie to maintein that we saie:He deskanteth voluntarilie with manie dis cordes all oute of tune.For he singeth without his rule,hauing nothing well

D alleaged to maintein what he saieth.Thie parte therfore shall be, Reader,to lean and cleaue to that side that growndeth yt self vpon substanciall authori tie, and not vpon phantasie and willfull affection.

Mixing of water with wine in the holie myni-stracion ys a diuine tra dicion.

Masse cal-led a sacrifi ce by the Counc.of Constatin.

But yt ys time that we also see the maner of confecracion vfed in the lati- **E**
me Church in time of the auncient Fathers of the fame, of the whiche one
maie nowe fuffice for all, whiche one fhall be S. Ambrofe, who thus reporteth yt: *Vis scire quia verbis cœlestibus consecratur? Accipe quæ sunt verba . Dicit sacer-*

*dos: Fac nobis (inquit) hanc oblationem ascriptam, rationabilem & acceptabilem , quod est
figura corporis & sanguinis Domini nostri Iesu Christi. Qui pridie quàm pateretur, in sanctis
manibus suis accepit panem, respexit ad cœlum ad te sancte Pater omnipotens æterne Deus,
gratias agens benedixit, fregit, fractumque Apostolis suis & Discipulis tradidit , dicens:
Accipite, & edite ex hoc omnes. Hoc est enim corpus meū, quod pro multis confringetur. Si
militer etiam calicem postquàm cœnatum est pridie quàm pateretur accepit, respexit ad cœ
lum ad te sancte Pater omnipotens æterne Deus, gratias agens benedixit, Apostolis et Discipulis suis tradidit, dicens: Accipite, et bibite ex eo omnes: Hic est enim sanguis meus.* Wilt
thow know that the Sacrament ys confecrated with heauenlie woordes?

Marke what be the woordes. The preift faieth: Make this oblacion (faieth he)
alowed, reafonable and acceptable, which ys a figure of the bodie and blood
of our Lord Iefus Chryfte. Who the daie before he wolde fuffer, tookebread **F**
in his holie handes, and looked vnto heauen to thee holie Father allmightie
euerlafting God, geuing thankes, he bleffed yt, he brake yt, and brokē he de
liuered yt to his Apoftles and Difciples faing. Take ye, and eate ye of this all.
For this ys my bodie, which fhall be broken for manie. Likewife alfo the daie
before he wolde fuffre, he tooke the cuppe after they had fupped, he looked
to heauen vnto thee Father, allmightie euerlafting God , geuing thankes he
bleffed yt, and gaue yt to his Apoftles and Difciples faing: Take and drinke
ye all of this. For this ys my blood.

Hitherto S. Ambrofe hath opened the praier vfed in the Church immediatelie before the confecracion, and the confecracion alfo. Which doen he
maketh a certain expofition of yt, and faieth thus: *Vide, omnia illa verba Euange
listæ sunt, ad Accipite siue corpus, siue sanguinem, inde verba sunt Christi. Vide singula: Qui
pridie (inquit) quàm pateretur, in sanctis manibus suis accepit panem. Antequàm consecretur panis est, vbi autem verba Christi accesserint corpus est. Christi : Denique audi dicentem: Accipite, & edite ex eo omnes, hoc est corpus meum. Et ante verba Christi calix est vi
ni & aquæ plenus, vbi verba Christi operata fuerint, ibi sanguis efficitur, qui plebem rede-* **G**
mit. Marke, all thofe woordes be the woordes of the Euangelift vnto thefe
woordes: Take either bodie or blood, frō hencefurth they be the woords of
Chryfte. Note enerie thing: Who (*faieth he*) the daie before he wolde fuffer
tooke bread in his holie handes. Before yt ys confecrated yt ys bread: when
the woordes of Chryfte haue comed to yt, yt ys the bodie of Chryfte. For
hear him faing: Take and eate ye all of this, This ys my bodie . And before
the woordes of Chryft yt ys a cuppe full of wine ãd water, whē the woords
of Chryft haue wrought, ther ys made the blood that redemed the people.

Now of S. Ambrofe ye haue heard the praier preparatiue to the cõfecracion: Ye haue heard the cõfecracion yt felf, which be the woords of Chryft:
Ye haue heard the effect of confecracion, as yt was beleued of the holie catholique Church before ãd in the time of S. Ambrofe, ãd of S. Ambrofe him
felf, as his owne woordes not onelie here, but in diuerfe ãd fondrie other
places do declare. Who among other expownding the *Pater nofter*, faieth thus

*Memini sermonis mei cùm de sacramētis tractarē, dixi vobis, quòd ante verba Christi quod
offertur, panis dicitur, vbi Christi verba deprōpta fuerint, iam non panis dicitur, sed corpus ap* **H**
pellatur. I remēbre my faing, whē I treacted of the Sacr. I faied vnto yow that
before the woords of Chryft, the thing that ys offred, ys called bread: when
the woords of Chrift be vttered, now yt ys not called bread, but ys called the
bodie of Chryft. The like woordes hath S. Auguftine.   Nowe

A Now what the maner of confecracion hath ben among the Fathers of the primitiue and auncient Church,as we haue learned yt in the laſt chapter by foure Apoſtles,and S.Paule:ſo in this we haue learned yt by foure Fathers, and S.Dionyſe the Diſciple of S.Paule,all which doe well agree,that yt maie well be perceaued that *Proclus* ſaied:that yt ys all one confecraciō of one Maſſe varied in ſhortneſſe or lenght in ſome praiers or extern ceremonies or geſturs onelie,for the variacion of the maners of the people, but not in the ſubſtanciall parts.For proof wherof,note (gentle reader,as before ys ſaied) that as S.Iames,and S.Clement directe their communicacion in praier to God the Father:ſo doth S.Baſill,Chryſoſtom,and S.Ambroſe,ſo alſo doth the catholique Church:The ſchiſmaticall Church of the Proclamer and his felowes doth not ſo,but reherſeth hiſtoricallie the woordes of the ſcripture.

Yf yt ſhould be asked whie the Proclamer and his likes refuſe to folowe herin the auncient maner of the primitiue Church,the imitaciō , of whiche they ſo moch pretend,and ſo often haue yt in their mouth:yt ys eaſie to aunſwer that they ſo doo,bicauſe innouaciō (which delighteth ytſelf with thown inuencions and deſiereth nouelties,and liketh allmoſt nothing that before

B was fownded ād ſetled by the Fathers,which alſo pleaſeth the people thurſting chaunges of thinges)occupieth their heades. Other cauſe whie they ſhoulde not kepe the ſame forme maner and order of confecracion , as the Apoſtles,their Diſciples,and the Fathers did:whie they ſhould not cōtinew their peticion and praier in the time of conſecraciō,to god the father,as they did:whie theie vſe not ſoch phraſe and maner of woordes as all, or moſt , or ſome of thē did:whie they put not water to the wine,as all they did,I cā none aſſign.But to conclud,hitherto yt maie be perceaued that the catholique Church in nothing varieth from the Apoſtolique primitiue and auncient Church,and that the hereticall Church in nothing,as touching confecraciō agreeth.

THE SIXE AND THIRTETH CHAP. DEclareth what was the intencion of the *Apoſtles* and Fathers in and aboute the confecracion in the Maſſe.

C He order by me appointed now requireth,that we ſearch what was the faith ād intenciō of the Apoſtles and Fathers of the primitiue Church aſwell Grekes as Latines in and about the cōſecracion.Yt ys a world to ſee how the Proclamer like a commō ieſter trifleth with ſoch a weightie matter . Ah mercifull God, that wiſe men can not ſee the deueliſh wicked intēts of this heretical brood. *Brentius* and *Caluine* contemne the woordes of the formes of Sacraments:The Proclamer mocketh and skorneth the intencion of ſoch as myniſtre the ſacraments.Yet when theſe two be taken awaie,what ſacrament haue yowe? But that I tread not oute of my path,leauing to entre the diſputacion of intencion and faith generallie in all ſacraments,I will onelie here declare the intencion of the confecracion of the B.Sacrament by the practiſe of the Apoſtles and fathers.And without all circumſtances breiflie to entre into the matter,we will firſt ſee the intent,and faith of S.Iames,what he thouht to be wrought in the confecracion of the Sacrament.Which his goodlie praier wil fullie declare wherin he praieth thus: *Miſerere noſtri Deus omnipotens,miſerere no-*

D *ſtri Deus ſeruator noſter,miſere noſtri Deus ſecundùm magnam miſericordiam tuam,⁊ de mitte ſuper nos,et ſuper hæc dona propoſita,Spiritum tuum ſanctiſsimum,Dominum viuificum,vnà tecum Deo Patre,et vnigenito Filio tuo,aſsidentem,ſimul regnantem,conſubſtantialem,ac cœternū,qui locutus eſt in lege et Prophetis,et in nouo tuo teſtamento,qui deſcen-*

dit in specie columbæ super D.n. Iesum Christum in Iordanis fluuio , & mansit super eum,
qui descendit super Apostolos tuos in specie ignearum linguarum in cœnaculo sanctæ & glo-
riosæ Syon in die Pentecostes: Ipsum spiritum tuum sanctiss. demitte nunc quoque Domine
in nos,& in hæc dona sancta proposita, vt superueniens sancta, et bona, et gloriosa sua præsen-
tia sanctificet, et efficiat hunc panem corpus sanctum Christi tui, et calicem hunc preciosum
sanguinem Christi tui, vt sit omnibus ex iis sumentibus in remissionem peccatorum, et in vitã
æternam. Haue mercie vpon vs, o God allmightie, haue mercie vpon vs, o God
our Sauiour, haue mercie vpon vs, o God according to thie great mercie, and
send downe vpon vs, and vpon these proposed giftes thy most holie Spiritt

S. Iames be-
leued by
the worke
of the holie
Gost, the
bread and
wine to be
consecrated
into the bo-
die ãd blod
of Chryste.

our liuing Lorde sitting, and reigning , and euerlasting together with thee
God the Father, and thy onelie begotten Sonne, who hath spoké in the law,
and in the Prophets, ãd in thie new testament, which came down in the shape of a doue vpon our Lord Iesus Chryst in the floud of Iordane, ãd abidde
vpon him, who came downe vpon thy Apostles in the shape of fierie toungs
in the parlour of the holie and gloriouse Syon in the daie of pentecost: The
same thy most holie Spiritt o Lorde sende down also vpon vs and these holie
proposed gifts, that he coming vpon them maie with his holie good and gloriouse presence sanctifie and make this bread the bodie of thy Chryst, ãd this
cuppe the preciouse blood of thie Chryst, that yt maie be to all that receaue
of yt, remission of sinnes, and life euerlasting, &c.

Allthough in this praier of S. Iames manie things might be fownd woor-
thic of note: yet yt shall suffice for this present that we obserue that he vpon
the consecracion had the same maner of intent and faith that the catholique
Church now hath, that ys, that the bread and wine set vpon the aultar, by the
miraculouse woork of the holie Gost be made the bodie ãd blood of Chryst.
Which thing ys so liuelie and fullie spoken and vttered , that yt nedeth no
farder declaraciõ. This onelie maie be added that yf ther were no more doé
by the consecracion, but that the bread and wine be made a sacramentall
bread and wine, that ys, onelie figurs and tokens of the bodie and blood of
Chryst, S. Iames wold neuer haue so earnestlie praied for the coming down
of the holie Gost to sanctifie that bread and wine, he knowing that the bread
and wine might without the speciall sanctificacion of the holie Gost verie
well be figurs of Chrystes bodie and blood, as manie other things were in
the olde lawe. Neither wolde he haue praied that the holie Gost by his holie
presence should make the bread and wine the bodie and blood of Chryste,
yf he had entended or beleued Chrysts institucion to haue but figures . Yt were in my iudgement a mockrie of God to desire , that the bodie and bloode of Chryste might be ther, and wolde not haue yt in dede,
but onelie the figurs of yt. But whie do I saie so moch in so plain and clere a
mater.

As ye nowe perceaue by S. Iames his praier that his entent and faith was
that Chrystes verie bodie and verie blood were consecrated on the aultar:
so shall ye see that S. Clement came to the aultar with, the same faith, and entent, wherupon he praied thus: *Rogamus vt mittere digneris sanctum tuum Spiri-*
tum super hoc sacrificium , testem passionum Dom . Iesu , vt efficiat panem hunc
corpus Christi tui , & calicem hunc sanguinem Christi tui . We praie thee
that thowe wilt vouchsafe to send thie holie Spirit vpon this sacrifice,
a wittnesse of the passions of our Lorde Iesus , that he maie make
this bread the bodie of thie Chryste , and this cuppe the blood of thie
Chryste. Thus moche S. Clement. Yf in anie place the faith and intent of
holie

A holie men maie appear, that fhoulde yt moft cheiflie doo in their holie praiers deuoutlie andfimplie powred oute in the feight of God. S. Clement then making his deuoute praier in the holie diuine myniftracion of this bleffed and glorioufe Sacrament, and deficring God that the holie Goft might be fent to make by his diuine power the bread and the wine vpon the aultar the bodie and blood of Chryft, his intent and faith was that yt fhould fo be. No man will faie that he praied againft or contrarie to that, that he beleued, and intended. His faith therfore and intent was, that by confecracion ther was made prefent the bodie and blood of Chryfte. As in the laft chapiter I referred the reader to S. Dionyfe to fee his myniftracion in his booke: fo doe I here alfo. And therfore the practife of the Apoftles perceaued by S. Iames, and of their Difciples by S. Clement, thinking that yt will do well to vnderftand the like in the Fathers, that by the receauing and continuall practife of the fame one thing in diuerfe times, in diuerfe churches, and of diuerfe Fathers, the more adfured and perfect knowledge maie be had, and fo occafion

S. Clement beleued the bread and wine to be made the bodie and blood of Chryfte by the work of the holie Gofte.

B maie be taken for the reader to ftaie, and confirme himfelf in the veritie of Chryftes Sacrament: we fhall defcend to the Fathers that were more then two hundreth years after them, to make trial whether they kept like order as the Apoftles and their Difciples did, or varied from them.

And in this proceffe we will firft fee what S. Bafill intended, and what he beleued to be wrought in the Sacrament, what he intended and beleued his owne praier will liuelie and fullie declare. Thus in his Maffe, he praieth : *Te poftulamus, & te obfecramus fanĉte fanĉtorum beneplacita tua benignitate venire Spiritum fanĉtum fuper nos, & fuper propofita munera ea, & benedicere ifta, & fanĉtificare, & oftendere panem quidem iftum, ipfum honorificum corpus Dom. Dei, et faluatoris noftri Iefu Chrifti: quod autem eft in calice ifto ipfum fanguinē Dom. Dei & faluatoris noftri Iefu Chrifti, qui effufus eft pro mundi vita.* We befech and defire thee, o moft holie of al holie that by thie wellpleafing goodneffe thie holie Spirit maie come vpon vs, and vpon thefe propofed giftes, and to bleffe and fanĉtifie them, and to fhewe this bread to be the verie honorable bodie of our Lord God and Sa-

S. Bafill by the fanĉtifi cacio of the holie Goft beleued the bread and wine to be made

C uiour Iefus Chryfte. And that ys in this cuppe the verie blood of our Lord God and Sauiour Iefus Chryfte, which was fhedde for the life of the world. Thus moch S. Bafill.

Chryfts bodie and blood.

Yf ye call to remembrance the maner of S. Iames his praier in his Maffe, and compare yt to this, fo litle difference ys ther betwen them, that they might be thought all one, fo well doo they agree in woordes, fo well in faith that as thei fpeake all one thing: fo they beleued all one thing, namelie the confecracion of Chryftes bodie and blood to be wrought in the holie myniftracion by the worke of the holie Goft. And yet thus moche hath S. Bafill more then S. Iames, that he doth not onelie defire that the bread and wine maie be made the bodie and blood of Chryfte, but that the holie Goft will make thē *ipfum corpus, et ipfum fanguinē Domini,* the verie felf fame bodie ād blood of our Lord. So that ther ys no doubt, but that in the Maffe, he beleued by the cōfecracion, the bodie and blood of Chryft to be made verilie prefent. That the reader be not lōg deteined frō the pleafure ād godliedelight that he maie cōceaue ād haue by the heauenlie harmonie of the iuft cōfent ād agreemēt of the holie fathers breiflie laied together: we will alfo heareChryfoftō,

D ād by his own woords learn of him, what intēciō and faith he had about the myniftraciō of the bleffed Sacr. Thus he like vnto other praied : *Precamur et fupplicamus, vt mittas Spiritum fanĉtum tuum fuper nos, et fuper hæc appofita munera, et fac panem iftum quidem preciofum corpus Chrifti tui, et quod in calice, eft*

Chryfoft. in Miffa.

preciofum fanguinem Chrifti tui,permutans ea fanƈto Spiritu tuo. We praie and befe- **E**
che thee,that thowe wilt fende thy holie Spirit vpon vs, and vpon thefe
gifts fetfurth,and make this bread the precioufe bodie of thy Chryfte , and
that ys in this cuppe the precioufe blood of thy Chryfte,permuiting or chaũ
ging them by thine holie Spirit. Thus farre Chryfoft.

Yt ys not hard to perceaue either his agreement will other before alleaged , or his like intencion and faith when he vfeth the fame maner of woordes that they did,and the like requeft or praier? fauing that wher they defiered the bread and wine to be made the bodie and blood of Chryfte by the
high and great woorke of the holie Goft,he declareth alfo by what meã the
holieGoft doeth yt,faing: *Permutans ea fpiritu tuo fanƈto,*chaunging them by thy
holie Spirit,mening that yt ys doen by the holie Goft chaunging the bread
and wine into the bodie and blood of Chryfte.

To procede by as manie in this matter as we did in the other treaƈted of
in the laft chapiter,we muft than alfo heare S. Ambrofe , who declareth the
faith and intent of the Latine Church aboute the confecracion faing thus:
Vis fcire quia verbis cœleftibus confecratur? Accipe,quæ funt verba.Dicit facerdos, Fac no- **F**
bis(inquit)hanc oblationem afcriptam,rationabilem,& acceptabilem,quod eſt figura cor-
*poris & fanguinis Do.n.Iefu Chrifti.*Wilt thow knowe that the Sacrament ys con
fecrated with heauenlie woordes? Marke what be the woordes. The preift
faieth . Make this oblacion (faieth he) allowed, reafonable and acceptable
which ys a figure of the bodie and blood of oure Lord Iefus Chryfte.

As S. Ambrofe willeth yowe to marke the woordes of the praier of the
preift,wherby ye maie perceaue,what intent and faith was in S. Ambrofe and
in the holie Fathers, that myniftred and confecrated the holie Sacrament in
thofe daies: So wifh I yowe to marke them that ye maie conferre them,with
the praier of the catholique Church that now ys, declaring the intent and
faith of the fame.The praier of the Church ys thus: *Facere digneris hanc oblatio-*
nem,tu Deus omnipotens,in omnibus quefumus,benediƈlam,afcriptam,ratam rationabilem,
*acceptabilemque,vt nobis corpus & fanguis fiat filii tui Do.n.Iefu Chriſti.*Vouchfafe,we
befeche thee,o God Almightie,to make this oblacion bleffed,allowed , approoued,reafonable and acceptable,that yt maie be made vnto vs the bodie
and blood of thy beloued Sonne oure Lord Iefus Chryfte. **G**

Yf ye note the firft part of this praier yt agreeth almoft woord for woord
with the praier of S. Ambrofe,yf ye note the fecond part, wher yt faieth and
defiereth that yt maie be made the bodie and blood of our Lord IefusChrift
yt agreeth with S.Iames S.Clement.S.Bafill and Chryfoftom,all whiche de
fiered the like.So that the praier of the catholique Church declaring the intent and faith of the fame agreeth fullie with the Apoftolique,primitiue,and
auncient Church,euerie one of them defiering that the bread and the wine
maie be made the bodie and blood of oure Lord I efus Chryfte.But the intencion withoute faith of the newe feigned Church ys fooen perceaued to
diffent and difagree from all thefe princes,pillers,and Fathers of the Church
for foch a countenaunce of praier they make.*Heare vs,o mercifull Father, we be-*
feche thee,and graunt that we receauing thefe creatures of bread and wine according to thie
Sonne our Sauiour Iefus Chriſts infticucion in remembrance of his death and paßion , maie
*be partakers of his moſt bleffed bodie and blood.*Thus they. Here firft let vs , before
we haue of other,make conference of this praier with the praiers of the Apo
ftles,and primitiue Church,and then after we fhall examen the treuth of yt, **H**
and of their intent.

Remembre, gentle reader, obferue and note, that S. Iames, S. Clement.
S.Ba-

Chryfoftõ
beleued the
bread and
wine by fan
ƈtificaciõto
be the bo-
die ãd blod
of Chryfte.
Li.4.de Sa
cram. ca.5

The praier
in the Maſ
fe now vfed
agreethj
with the
Apoftoli-
que ãd pri-
mitiue
church.

woordes of
theCommu
nion.

A in remembrance of his death. Yf anie place be, yt muſt be the place of the
S. Baſill. S. Chryſoſtom. S. Ambroſe and ſo of all the Churche which they
liued in both greks and latines for the ſpace of foure hundreth years immediatlie after Chryſte, praied not that they might receaue the creatures of
bread and wine, but that the creaturs of bread and wine might be made the
bodie and blood of Ieſus Chryſte. Wherfor the newe Church making to
them ſelues a newe fownd praier, ſo farre diſſenteth here from the Apoſtolique and primitiue Churche, that I can not proprelie make a conference bet
wene them, but raither ſhewe the great difference of them . The Apoſtoli-
qne and primitiue Churche deſire the bread and wine maie be made the
bodie and bloode of Chryſte: The newe Churche, that the bread and wine
maie remain to be receaued, and ſo of conſequent contrarie to the other
church, deſiereth that they maie not be made the bodie and blood of Chry
ſte. See ye not then howe farre theſe two praiers are different? They are ſo
farre different as two contraries, euen as yea and naie, I will, and I will not:
ſo neerlie and iuſtlie doth this newe fownde Church folowe the primitiue
B Church, of the which this Proclamer ſo moche braggeth. The Apoſtolique
and primitiue Churche deſiereth not to receaue the creatures of bread and
wine in the B. Sacrament, but the verie bodie and blood of Chryſte, as their
plain woordes do plainlie teſtifie : This erring Churche deſiereth not by ex
peſſe woordes to receaue the verie bodie and blood of Chryſte in the Sacrament, but the creaturs of bread and wine, and then to be made partakers of
the bodie and blood of Chryſte, but howe, or whiche waie, wher or by what
means, what maner of bodie, ſpirituall or corporall, reall or phantaſticall,
they ourpaſſe with ſilence. Thus ſtill ye ſee, that they in all theſe weightie
matters alltogether diſſent frō the Apoſtolique and primitiue Churche, and
do no leſſe varie from yt then they do from the catholique Churche nowe
being, whiche they ſo feercelie perſecute.

    And that they ſo doo, this ſhall well prooue yt, that neuer yet did anie
catholique Father or authour, greke or latin, young or olde vſe this phraſe
of woordes of theirs, either in praier, ſermon or writing . Whiche if yt had
C ben agreable, yt muſt nedes haue ben fownde in ſome of them, and learned
of ſome of them. But this newe praier of this newe churche ys ſo newe, that
the like of yt could neuer vntill this newe degeneraciō be ſeen heard or kno
wen. Yf yt were let the Proclamer, and all his complices learned and vnlearned bring furth ſome preſident. Yf they can, I will ioin this iſſue with
them, that I will praie and receaue with them . Yf they can not, as I am ſure
they can not, let them praie and receaue with vs. We haue brought furth pre
ſidents for oure praiers : let them bring furth preſidents for theirs, I prouoke them to yt.

    Thus moche being ſaied of the difference of the praier of the newe Chur
che from the praier of the Apoſtolique Churche : let vs nowe examen the
trueth of the ſame praier. Their praier hath theſe woordes : *that we receauing
theſe they creaturs of bread and wine, according to thy ſonne our Lord Ieſus Chryſts inſtitucion in remembrance of his deathe &c.* I wolde learn of the maſters of this Churche, wher that inſtitucion of Chryſte ys, that we ſhoulde eate the creatures
of bread and wine in remembrance of his death . The proclamer requireth
D ſome plain and expreſſe ſentence of the Catholiques to proue what they affirme againſt his articles : I require of him and his companie ſome plain ſentence in the ſcriptures to prooue that, that he and his companie affirme, that
Chryſte by expreſſe woordes cōmaunded vs to eate bread and drinke wine

The praier of the newe Church va rieth from all the praiers of the Apoſtoliq̃ ād primitiue Churche

The praier of the newe Cōmunion neuer vſed nor heard of before

What au toritie hath the Procla me or all the Prote-ſtants to ſhewe, that the eating and drin-king of bre-ad and wi-ne ys of Chryſts in-ſtitution

in remembrance of his death. Yf anie place be, yt muſt be the place of the   E
inſtitucion of the Sacrament, in whiche place although yt be teſtified that
he tooke bread in his holie hands : yet yt teſtifieth withall that he ſanctified
and bleſſed the ſame bread, and when he had ſo doen, yt was ſo farre chaunged from the nature of bread, that Chryſt who ys the trueth, and in whoſe
mouth was no guile might and did boldlie ſaie, *Take and eate*, not a peice of
bread, but *my bodie, euen the ſame that ſhal be deliuered for yowe.* And likewiſe of the
cuppe he ſaid: *Take ād drinke ye, this ys,* not a cuppe of wine, but euē *my blood that
ſhall be ſhedd for yowr ſinnes and the ſinnes of manie* . This eate ye, and this drinke
in the remembrance of me. What ſhould they eate? That that he tooke vnto
them. what did he take vnto them? The Euangeliſts do teſtifie : *Take eate,
this my bodie.* They ſhoulde drinke in the remēbrance of him . What ſhoulde
they drinke- That alſo that he did take them . What did he take them ? The
Euangeliſts likewiſe declare . *Drinke ye all of this,* ſaieth Chryſte , *for this ys my
blood of the newe teſtament &c.* Here be the woordes of the inſtitucion . Here

*By Chryſts
inſtitucion
we ſhoulde
receaue his
bodie and
bloode in
remēb &c.*

ys inſtituted that the bodie and bloode of Chryſte ſhould be receaued in   F
the remembrance of his paſſion and death, that bread and wine ſhoulde be
ſo receaued, here ys not one title. Chryſte ſaied not, eate this bread, and
drinke this wine in my remembrance . Wher then be we commaunded to
receaue the creaturs of bread and wine according to the inſtitucion of Chry
ſte, yf yt be not commaunded here? As touching the inſtitucion of Chryſte,
yt ys at the full treacted of in the ſecond booke, wher be produced xii cooples of the higher houſe of Chryſtes Parliament, and vi cooples of the lower

*The newe
church
chargeth
Chryſt
with an
vntrueth.*

houſe, of the which a great nombre declare the verie ſubſtance of Chryſtes
bodie and blood to be verilie diſpenſed and geuen in the Bleſſed Sacrament
and a good nombre of them denie the ſame Sacrament to be a figure onelie. Yf yt be not a figure, then ys yt not bread and wine : Yf yt be not then
we eate not bread and wine, as they ſaie, according to Chryſts inſtitucion.
Beholde thē the impudencie of theſe mē ſee their notable vntrueth, that fear
not before mē onelie (which in ſo weightie a matter were to moche) but alſo
as yt were) euen to the face of God to make a ſtoute lie againſt his onelie   G
begotten ſonne charging him with that, that they be not hable to prooue.
But that this their vntrueth wher with they charge our Sauiour Chryſt maie
more fullie appeare, and the trueth of the catholique Churche clerelie be
ſeen, ye ſhall not onelie when ye come to the next chapter, note what ys
doen according to Chryſts inſtitucion, but alſo here the practiſe of the Apo
ſtolique and primitiue Churche ſhall teache yowe, what Chryſte inſtituted
to be receaued for the remembrance of his death. S. Iames praied thus in
his Maſſe : *Miſericors Deus dignum me fac gratia tua vt citra condemnationem particeps
fiam ſancti corporis, & precioſi ſanguinis in remiſsionem peccatorum &c.* O mercifull
God make me by thie grace wourthie that withoute my condemnacion, I
maie be made partaker of thie holie bodie, and precioſe blood, to the remiſſion of ſinnes. S. Baſill thus : *Nullum noſtrum ad iudicium aut condemnationem
facias accipere ſanctum corpus & ſanguinem Chriſti tui.* Make none of vs to iudgement or condemnacion to receaue the holie bodie and bloode of thie
Chryſte. S. Chryſoſtom praied thus : *dignare potenti manu tua tribuere nobis imma
culatum corpus tuum & precioſum ſanguinem, & per nos omni populo.* Vouchſafe with   H
thy mightie hand to giue vnto vs thie vndifiled bodie and thie precioſe
blood, and by vs to all the people. Thus they,

   Yt ys not to be doubted, but that all theſe, and the Churche that they liued in receaued the ſacrament according to Chryſtes inſtitucion . But theſe
creaturs

creaturs of bread and wine omitted, they shewe thē selues by expresse woordes, to receaue the bodie and bloode of Chryste. Wherfor Chrysts institucion ys to receaue his bodie and blood, and not the creaturs of bread and wine. And that they speake not of the spirituall bodie onelie, but of the reall bodie in the blessed Sacramēt, two thinges in these fathers prooue yt inuinciblie. The one ys in S. Iames and S. Basill. They both desire that they not to cōdēnaciō maie receaue the holie bodie ād precioufe blood of Chryst. That bodie thē ys here receaued, that maie be receaued both to saluaciō and damnacion. The spirituall bodie can be receaued but to saluacion, the reall bodie both to saluacion and damnacion, wherfor they receaue the reall bodie of Chryste, that maie be receaued to condemnacion. The other ys in Chrysostom, who desiereth Chryste that he wold vouchsafe both to imparte vnto him his bodie and blood, and also by him and the preists to the people. Wher vpon we maie thus reason: That bodie was receaued of Chrysostom and the preistes, which by them also might be deliuered to the people, But the reall bodie of Chryste, and not the spirituall might by them be deliuered to **B** the people. Wherfore Chrysostom and the preists receaued the reall bodie of Chryste. That the spirituall bodie of Chryste, or Chryste spirituallie cā not by the preists be deliuered to the people, yt ys so manifest that yt nedeth no probacion, yt standeth thē certē and sure that Chrysostome receaued the verie reall bodie of Chryste.

To conclude then this disputacion vpon the principall part of that, that here ys intended: S. Iames, S. Basill. S. Chrysostom receaued that, that was according to Chrysts institucion to be receaued in the remembrance of his death: But they receaued not the creaturs of bread and wine, but the verie reall bodie of Chryste: Wherfor they receaued according to Chrysts institucion his verie reall bodie in the remembrance of his passion and death. Yt ys euident then that yt ys not Chrysts institucion to receaue the creaturs of bread and wine in the remembrance of his death, wherfor we maie conclude that the pretensed praier of the late erected Churche hath a foule and a wicked vntrueth in yt, and for the maintenance of an abhominable heresie, doth vntruely report and saie of our Sauiour Chryste, and that not one- **C** lie to the world, but euen, as yt were to the face of God.

Of intēciō of the newe ministres.

Nowe remaineth the last thing appointed here in this chapter to be spoken of, which ys the intencion and faith of the ministers of this newe Churche, in the whiche a fewe woordes, maie and shall suffice. The intencion and faith of this Church ys not onelie perceaued by their cōmon professiō: but also by this their praier. Their common professiō denieth the presence of Chrysts bodie in the Sacrament, their praier confirmeth the same. For desiering to receaue the creaturs of bread and wine, they exclude the bodie and blood of Chryste into whose substance (as Euseb. Emis. saieth) the inuisible creaturs are turned. Vnderstand that in this newe fownded Church be two sorts of ministres that doo minister this Communion. One sorte ys of preists, whiche laufullie consecrated in the catholique Churche, haue fallen to heresie, who although they haue authoritie by their holie orders to consecrate the bodie and bloode of Chryste: yet nowe hauing neither right intencion nor faith of the catholique Churche, they consecrate not. The other sort ys of **D** ministres made after the schismaticall maner. These men though they wolde vnwiselie haue intencion to consecrate: yet laking the laufull authoritie they neither do nor can consecrate, but (as yt maie be iustlie though)

Two sortes of ministres of the Communion.

thought) hauing neither autoritie, nor due faith and intencion they neither   E
receaue nor diftribute to the people anie other thing then bread and wine.
Whiche their doing and intencion compared to the Apoftolique and primi
tiue Churche fooen fheweth yt felf to be nothing like yt, to haue nothing to
do with yt, nor nothing to folowe yt.

The condicion of this matter being foche, what cafe be thofe preifts in,
whiche hauing catholique authoritie and catholique faith, and thinke but
well of the catholique mifteries and religion, for feare, or for liuing fake, leaue that they knowe to be good, and doo that they knowe to be euell? What
trembling hearts fhall they haue before the terrible iudgement feat of God,
when their owne confciences fhal accufe them, faing: we were called to ferue the aultar, we had authoritie geuen vs to confecrate Chryfts bodie and
blood according to his holie inftitucion, we might haue offred the fame in
facrifice to the memoriall of Chryfts death, to the côfort of our owne foules,
and releiff of manie. We might haue receaued that bleffed food to the nutriment of our foules to euerlafting life. Thus might we haue fpent our time
in the feruice of God, thus might we haue liued in our calling, wher omit-   F
ting all thefe, we haue ioined with fchifmatiques and heretiques, and ben
as yt were in armes againft Chryftes ordeinance, againft his catholique
Church and the holie religion of the fame, wo be to vs, wo be to vs, what
fhall we doo? This or foche like or moche more bitter and greuoufe accufa-
tion will yowr confciences make againft yowe. Awake therfor and looke a
bout yowe in time. Yt ys yet the time of mercie, the time of iuftice will come in whiche repentance fhall come to late.

Thus hauing here to fpeake of intencion and faith, for that I fee yowe in
countenance to decline form the excucion of that intencion and faith that
fhoulde be feen in yowe, and profeffed of yowe, I haue a litle digreffed from
my principall intencion to ad monifh yowe to return to yowr deutifull intencion. And here to conclude with yowe as I do with fchifmatiques and
heretiques, whiche ys a greif to my heart that I maie fo doo, I faie that hauing intent to receaue the creatures of bread and wine in the Sacrament, ye
fullfill not Chryfts inftitucion, neither do ye folowe the intencion and
faith of the Apoftolique Churche, neither of the primitiue and auncient   G
Church.

The mife-
rable ftate
of catholi-
que preifts
folowing
the fchifme

THE SEVEN AMD THIRTETH CHAPITER
*treacteth of the oblacion and facrifice of the Maffe as
yt was vfed of the Apoftles and
Fathers.*

O moche being all readie fpoken of the oblacion and facrifice of
the Maffe, I fhould not nede, but that the fpeciall order here taken fo requireth, to fpeake anie more of the fame. I minde therfor
no otherwife here to treact of yt, but onely as I haue doen in the
matters of confecracion and intenciõ to fhewe furth the practife of the Apoft
les and fathers vfed in their Maffes. And here firft for the practife vfed a-
mong the Apoftles, we will fee what was doen by S. Iames being well affured that he did in this weightie matter of faith no otherwife then all the reft
of the Apoftles did. For what he did, all they did: and what they did he did   H
foche was their confpiracion, common confent, vnitie and agreement.
In his Maffe immediately after confecracion, thus he proceded: *Memores igi
tur &*

Iacob.in
Miff.

A *tur & nos peccatores paßionum eius viuificarum, crucis salutaris ac mortis, sepulchri & resurrectionis à mortuis tercio die, ascensionis in cælos, & asseßionis eius ad dextram tuam Dei Patris, & secundi, gloriosi, & tremendi eius aduentus, cùm veniet cum gloria ad indicandum viuos & mortuos, cùm reddet vnicuique secundùm opera eius, offerimus tibi, Domine, hoc sacrificium verendum & incruentum, orantes ne secundùm peccata nostra nobiscum agas.* We sinners also therfor mindefull of his liuelie passions, of his holsom crosse and death, buriall and resurrection from the dead the third daie, of his ascension into the heauens and of his sitting at the right hand of God the Father, and of his second, gloriouse and fearfull coming, when he shall with glorie come to iudge the quicke and the dead, when he shall geue to euery one according to his workes: We offre vnto thee, o Lord, this dreadfull and vnbloodie sacrifice, praing that thowe do not with vs according to our sinnes.

　　In this part of S. Iames Masse we maie perceaue three thinges. The first that Chrysts bodie ys offred in sacrifice: The second, that yt ys offred in re-
B membrance of his passion and death, resurrection, ascension &c. The third, that yt ys doen for the remission of sinnes.　For the first, yt ys to be noted that immediatelie after consecracion, by the which ys wrought the presence of Chrysts bodie (*as ys saied*) hauing yt present he furthwith saieth: *We offre vnto thee, o lord, this dreadfull and vnbloodie sacrifice*. This saied S. Iames immediatelie vpon the consecracion, when nothing ells was before him to offre but the bodie of Chryste. Wherfor he then offred the bodie of Chryste.

　　To this vnderstanding manie things do enforce vs in the woords of S. Iames. first, that he vseth the demonstratiue (*thus*) saing this sacrifice, whiche spoken at the aultar vpon the consecracion of Chrystes bodie, whiche ys the verie true sacrifice, signifieth vnto vs, that he offreth yt. Farder, that he calleth the sacrifice whiche he offreth a *dreadfull sacrifice*. What sacrifice, that by man can be offred to God, ys dreadfull, but onelie the bodie of Chryste, the bodie of God and man? whiche for the maiestie of Godhead, wherunto this bodie ys ioined in vnitie of person ys dreadfull, other sacrifices what soeuer, be not of themselus. Wherfor the dreadfull sacrifice that he offred was the
C bodie of Chryste. Lastlie, he calleth yt an vnblooddie sacrifice. Whiche verie well agreeth with the sacrifice of Chrysts bodie offred on the aultar. For that bodie being nowe glorified ys impassible, and immortall, and neuer shall shedd blood to be sacrificed by death again, but ys nowe offred to the Father with remembrance of that passion and death, and blood shedding, whiche he once suffred, and shall neuer suffre again, and ys so set before the face of his Father to procure vs mercie of the remission of oure sinnes, and to obteign for vs the grace of God, and the giftes of his holie Spirit.

　　Nowe the oblacion perceaued in this holie Apostle, and by him in all the Apostles: let vs descend to the Disciple of the cheif Apostle, to see in him whether he and other Disciples did in the Masse make oblacion and offre sacrifice as the Apostles did. This man (S. Clement I meen) euen as S. Iames did, immediatelie after the holie consecracion praied thus: *Memores igitur paßionis eius, mortis, resurrectionis, reditus in cœlos, & futuri eius secundi aduentus, in quo veniet iudicaturus viuos & mortuos, redditurusque cuique secundùm opera sua, offeri-*
D *mus ibi Regi & Deo secundùm eius institutionem panem hunc, & hunc calicem, gratias tibi per eum agentes, quod nos dignatus fueris astare, coram te, & tibi sacrificare.* Being therfor mindefull of his passion, death, resurrection, ascension into heauen, and of his second coming, in the whiche he will iudge both quicke and dead

and

and will geue to euerie one according to his workes : We offre vnto the **E**
King and God according to his inftitucion this bread and this cuppe, geuing thee thanks by him, that thow haueft vouchfafe vs to ftand before thee,
and to offre facrifice to thee. Thus S. Clement.

S. Clement offred Chryfts bodie and blood in facrifice.

Let not the good Chryftian be difmaied, nor the Sacramentarie triumphe that he faieth we offre this bread, but let them both vnderftand, that as
our Sauiour Chryfte in the vi of S. Iohn, and S. Paule in the x of the firft to
the Corinth. whiche ys allreadie declared, and in the xi of the fame, whiche
here fhall be declared, doo call the bodie of Chryfte bread: So doth S. Clement here. For proofe wherof haue recourfe to the praier of S. Clement in
the laft chapter before and fee his faith what he beleued to be in the Sacrament, wher ye fhall finde him defiering that the holie Goft maie be fent, who
maie make the bread the bodie of Chryfte and the wine the blood of Chryfte. Yf then the bread by the worke of the holie Goft be made the bodie of
Chryft, then ther ys no other bread there after confecracion to be offred in
facrifice but the bread of the bodie of Chryft and the cuppe of his blood. **F**
Neither can the Sacramentarie with all his wrefting malice vnderftand this
of materiall bread. For this that ys here offred, ys offred according to the in
ftitucion of Chryfte: but as the Sacramentarie can not but confeffe, Chryfte
neuer inftituted materiall bread to be offred in facrifice . Wherfor yt can
not be vnderftanded of materiall bread . Yt ys euident then that S. Clement offred Chryfts bodie , and blood the verie true bread, and true wine
in facrifice.

S. Bafill offred the like facrifice to S. Ja. ãd S. Clem.

This being made plain, we fhall defcende to S. Bafill and fee what he did,
whether he offred in his Maffe or no. He as S. Clement, immediately after
the confecracion continued his holie taulke to God, faing on this wife : *Memores ergo, Domine , & nos falutarium eius paßionum , viuificæ crucis, triduanæ fepul-
turæ, ex mortuis refurrectionis, in cælum afcenfionis, in dextra tua Dei Patris feßionis, &
gloriofæ ac terribilis fecundæ eius præfentiæ, tua ex tuis tibi offerimus.* We alfo therfor,
o Lorde, being mindfull of his holfom paffions, liuelie croffe, three daies
buriall, his refurrection from the dead, his afcenfion into hauen, his fitting
at thie right hand, God and Father, and of his glorioufe and terrible fecond **G**
prefence : we offre thine to thee oute of thine. Thus he.

See ye not here, as in S. Iames and S. Clement an oblacion of the bodie
and bloode of Chryfte, whiche be thinges of God, confecrated of his creaturs bread and wine, and fo offred vnto God? Hitherto then ye fee the holie
Fathers, to haue offred Chryftes bodie and blood, and therfor in their woor
des and writings not to haue abhorred the tearmes of offring, or making ob
lacion and facrifice, as the newe brothers do.

Chryfofto-me offred facrifice in Maffe.

But for farder proofe of the practife of the Sacrifice we will procede and
fee what Chryfoftom did in his Maffe. For he keping the order before mencioned immediatelie vpon the confecracion addeth this praier : *Memores igitur falutaris huius mandati & omnium eorum, quæ pro nobis facta funt, crucis, fepulchri,
refurrectionis, ad cælos afcenfionis, feßionis ad dextram, fecundi & gloriofi rurfus aduentus, tua ex tuis tibi offerimus .* Remembring therfor this holie commaundement
and all thofe thinges that haue ben doen for vs as the croffe buriall, refurrection, afcenfion into heauen fitting at the right hand, the feconde and glo
rioufe coming again : we offre thine vnto thee of thine owne. Thus ther. **H**

Yt can not be that they that fo iuftlie agree in woordes and fentéce fhoulde varie and dyfagree in fence and vnderftanding. Wherfor Chryfoftom, as
the other did, did in his Maffe offre facrifice. I labour not here to feke the

deapth

A deapt of this matter, for that I haue done allreadie in diuerse places of this worke, but I cheiflie seke by the woordes of these Fathers to declare that all they did offre sacrifice. What they offred, and to what effect, yt ys and shalbe declared, and, as yt maie for this place suffice, by S. Ambrose yt shall be made euident, what he and the auncient Church in his time did offre. Wherby also we shall be assured what the former Fathers did offre, this being certen that holie Ambrose did nothing contrarie to the holie faith of the primitiue Church. Thus he reporteth, of the practise of the auncient Church of his time and before: *Sacerdos dicit: Ergo memores gloriosissimæ eius passionis, & ab inferis resurrectionis, & in cœlum ascensionis, offerimus tibi hanc immaculatam hostiam rationabilem hostiam, incruentam hostiam, hunc panem sanctum, & calicem vitæ æternæ*. Being therfor mindful of thie most glorioufe passion, and resurrection from death, ad ascension into heauen, we offre vnto thee this vndefiled sacrifice, reasonable sacrifice, vnbloodie sacrifice, this holie bread and cuppe of life euerlasting.

S. Ambro-se and the church that he liued in of-fred sacrifi-ce in the Masse.

B 　　Doo ye not here see by the testimonie of S. Ambrose that the preist did offre sacrifice in the remembrance of Chrysts passion, resurrection and ascension? But note and marke well what maner, of sacrifice: An immaculate or vndefiled sacrifice, a pure sacrifice. What sacrifice ys yt that man can offre to God, that he maie boldlie so tearm and call? No pure man dare so farre presume of his owne doings of offrings to God. This pure and vndefiled sacrifice then can be none other, but that pure and innocent lambe of God, that purifieth and clenseth vs by taking awaie the sinnes of the worlde, euen Iesus Chryste his verie bodie and blood. Which maner of vnderstanding the later woordes of this offring sentence doeth also enforce vs to take, determining this pure and vndefiled sacrifice to be the holie bread on the aultar lieg before the preist, in that he saieth: *hunc panem sanctum*, this holie bread, and that he tearmeth the cuppe to be the cupp of euerlasting health. For as the bread ys holie, and the fountain of holinesse, from whence to vs floweth all holinesse: so ys the cuppe the cuppe of euerlasting health. For *sanguis Iesu Christi emundat nos ab omni delicto.* The blood of Iesus Chryst doth clense vs from all sinne, and so pourging the grosse and filthie humoures of sinne, which make the

Note here what maner of sacri-fice was of-fred in the Masse.

1. Ioan.1. Ibid.6.

C soule sicke geueth vs euerlasting health, and wher euerlasting health ys, ther ys euerlasting life. And so cometh to passe that Chryst saieth : *Qui manducat meam carnem, et bibit meum sanguinem, habet vitam æternã.* He that eateth my flesh and drinketh my blood hath euerlasting life.

　　Thus then maie yt be perceaued, that this holie bread and cuppe of life euerlasting, ys the holie vndefiled and vnbloodie sacrifice, which S. Ambrose testifieth to be offred in the Church, which (*as ys saied*) well considered and weighed, and these tearms: the vndefiled and vnbloodie sacrifice, and the holie bread and cuppe of life euerlasting, compared and ioined together as meening one thing (as they doo in dede) cã signifie no other thing to vs but the verie bodie and blood of oure Lord and Sauiour Iesus Chryst, offred as the vndefiled and vnbloodie sacrifice of his Church.

Chrysts bo-die in the Sacr. ys the vnbloodie sacrifice of the Church

　　And Reader in case the Aduersarie wold bleer thine eie, expownding thys woord of S. Ambrose Masse, *panem sanctum*, holie bread, to be the sacramétall bread, and the bread of their holie cõmunion, so to delude thee, and to elude the argument, and to auoide the presence of Chrysts blessed bodie in the Sacra-

D ment· yet the woords adioined, which be, that the cuppe ys called the cuppe of euerlasting life, do ãd shal so streict him, that he cã not but vnderstand thé of the bodie ãd blood of Chryst, ãd not his sacramétal bread, and cuppe. For the one bi the cõfession of *Oecolãp.* ãd *Crãmer* cã receaue no holines being a

LII　　　　　dumbe

dumbe creature, and the other wil be confessed of all men, yf yt be but a cup   **E**
pe of wine, that yt ys not the cuppe of euerlasting life. Yt remaineth then
that they are vnderstanded of the bodie and blood of Chryst, which be the
holie bread, and cuppe of euerlasting life, and the vndefiled and vnbloodie sa
crifice of the Church. Hitherto ye haue perceaued that S. Ambrose agreeth
with S. Iames, S Clement, S. Basill, and S. Chrysostome in this poinct, namelie in the oblacion of sacrifice.

And now that by S. Ambrose yt ys perceaued that he and the Church that
he liued in did offre sacrifice, and that that sacrifice was the bodie and blood
of Chryst, ther remaineth now that we conferre with him and the rest, the
doing of the catholique Church now in their Masse, and of the hereticall
congregacion in the Comunion, as they vntruelie tearm yt. The catholique
Churche as in the practise of all the Fathers yt was vsed, immediatelie after
the consecracion ys doen proceadeth thus saing: *Vnde & memores nos Domine,*
serui tui, sed & plebs tua sancta eiusdem Christi Filii tui tam beate passionis, necnon & ab
inferis resurrectionis, sed & in cælos gloriosæ ascensionis, offerimus præclaræ maiestati tuæ
de tuis donis ac datis, hostiam puram, hostiam sanctam, hostiam immaculatam, panem san-
ctum vitæ æternæ, & calicem salutis perpetuæ. Wherfore, o Lord, we thie seruantes,   **F**
and the holie people also being mindeful of the blessed passion of the same
Chryste thie Sonne, and of his resurrection, and also of his gloriouse ascensio
into heaue, we offre to thie excellet maiestie of thie gifts, and graunts a pure
sacrifice, and holie sacrifice, an vndefiled sacrifice, the holie bread of euerlasting life, and the cuppe of euerlasting saluacion. Thus the Church.

Wher ye perceaue that as S. Iames. S. Clement S. Basill, and other did offre sacrifice and that in the remembrance of Chrysts passion, resurrection,
&c. So dothe the catholique Church now likewise offre in this praier, which
forasmoch as yt dependeth of somthing going before, vnderstand, that as in
the Masse of S. Iames and the other, so in this Masse rehersal ys made of this
comaundement of Chryst: *Do ye this in remembrance of me.* Wherupo this praier,
wherin in euerie of these Masses oblacio ys made of the sacrifice of Chrystes
bodie and blood, ys furthwith added as the fulfilling of that comaundemet,
and therfore saieth: *Wherfor we mindeful, o Lord, of the blessed passion, &c.* Whiche
ys asmoch to saie, forasmoch as thie Sonne our Lord and Sauiour hath com   **G**
maunded vs to offre in sacrifice his blessed bodie and blood in the remebra-
ce of that death, which he did once suffre in that bodie, ad of other his great
and woderfull actes that he did in the same, as his resurrectio, ascension, &c.
Therfor, o Lord, according to this thy Sonne his comaundemet, being mind
full of those great ad wonderful actes, we offre vnto thee this holy sacrifice.

And here by the waie let the Proclamer note, that wher he wold be certi
fied, wher we be commaunded to offre Chryst in sacrifice, he maie by all
these Masses be taught that we are so comaunded by Chrysts owne woord,
wherupo, if he wil see, he maie perceaue that oblacio ys made of the bodie ad
blood of Chryst in eche of the, euen by his comaudemet as ys allreadie saied

That the bodie and blood of Chryst ys the sacrifice that ys here offred yt
maie suffice to repete a fewe words of S. Sames our first witnesse, ad of S. Am
brose our last witnesse for the profe of the same, this being oute of all doubte
that the Fathers betwe the dissented not fro the. S. Iames saied: *Offerimus tibi,*
Domine, sacrificiu verendu, et incruentu. We offre vnto thee, o Lord, this dreadful ad   **H**
vnbloodie sacrifice. This sacrifice being dreadfull and vnbloodie ca be none
other, as ther yt ys proued but the bodie of Christ. And in that he calleth yt
an vnbloodie sacrifice, he beateth downe the grosse hereticall obiection
                                               of the

Woords of
the Canon
in the Mas
se.

we be com-
maunded
to offre
Chryst in
sacrifice.

Sacrifice of
fred by S.
Iames.

A of the enemies of Chrysts euerlasting sacrifice, saing: that if he be offred in sa
crifice, he must be slain again, and his blood as often shedd, as he ys offred,
wher the faith of all holie Fathers acknowlegeth, yt to be an vnbloodie sacri
fice, for that no violence ys now wrought to the shedding of Chrysts blood.
S. Ambrose saieth: *Offerimus tibi hanc immaculatā, rationabilē, incruentā, hostiā.* We of
fre vnto thee this pure reasonable and vnbloodie sacrifice. And determining
what this sacrifice ys he addeth: *Hunc panē sanctum, & calicē vitæ æterna.* This holie blood, and cuppe of euerlasting life. In that he calleth yt a pure sacrifice, he allu
deth to the Prophet *Malachie* calling yt an vnbloodie sacrifice, he foloweth S.
Iames: in that he calleth yt the holie bread, and the cuppe of the euerlasting
life he perfectlie determineth yt to be the blessed bread of Chrystes bodie,
ād the cuppe of his blood geuing euerlasting life. Now the catholike Church
embracing the faith of the Apostles and Fathers, saieth as they saied, and
doeth that they did. For as S. Ambrose saied we offre this pure sacrifice, so sai
eth the catholique Church now, we offre this pure sacrifice. As S. Ambrose
B saied, we offre this holie bread and cuppe of life euerlasting. So saieth the Church, we of
fre the bread of euerlasting life and the cuppe of euerlasting saluacion. Thus ye see howe
iustlie he catholike Church in this our time foloweth in this point the faith
and doing of the anciēt Church. But now the degenerating church maketh
no one title mencion of offring Chryst in sacrifice, neither wold that her my
nisters should haue soch intent, therfore can therbe no comparison here ma
de of her faith and doing. For comparison must be made betwen two thinges
or mo that be or haue a being. For *Inter ens & non ens nulla est comparatio.* Betwen a thing that ys, and that that ys not ther ys no comparison. Thus thenwe
maie ende this part that the new Church not offring sacrifice neither kepeth
Chrystes institucion, neither foloweth the practise of the Apostolique primi
tiue, and auncient Church, but omitteth the commaundement of Chryst in
his institucion, and dothe clean contrarie to the examples of the Apostles,
and holie Fathers.

Sacrifice was offred in Masse by S. Ambr.

The catholike church now offring sacrifice in Masse folweth Chryst his holie Apostles, ād the primitiue Church the newe Church offring none do cōtrarie to them all.

C ## THE EIGHT AND THIRTETH CHAPTER TREA-
teth of the praier for acceptacion of the oblacion or sacrifice made in the
Masse, and vsed aswell by the Apostles as the Fathers.

Owe remaineth to shewe what maner of praier was vsed of the
Apostles and of their Disciples, and of the primitiue Church after the offring of sacrifice in Masse, for the acceptacion therof.
The holie Apostles and Fathers thought yt not enough onelie
in bare maner to offre the sacrifice to God: but also their condi
cion considered thought yt apperteining to their duetie most humblie by
denoute praier to craue and desire at Gods hād that their seruice in so doing
might be mercifullie accepted. And her to obserue the ordre before vsed we
shall first see how the Apostle S. Iames made his praier to God for the acce
ptacion of his seruice in offring of the sacrifice. Thus he praied: *Pro oblatis &
sanctificatis, preciosis, supercœlestibus, ineffabilius, immāculatis, gloriosis, tremendis, horren-
dis, diuinis donis Dom. Deo nostro oremus, vt Dom. Deus n. acceptis iis in sanctum & super
cœleste, mentale, & spiritale altare suum, in odorem spiritalis fragrantiæ, rependat ac mittat*
D *nobis diuinā gratiā et donū sanctiss. Spiritus: Oremus.* Let vs praie to our Lord God for
these offred ād sāctified, preciouse heauēlie, vnspeakable, immaculate, gloriou
se, fearfull, horrible, diuine gifts: Let vs praie that our Lord God accepting
these into his holie ād heauēlie, mētall ād spirituall aultar to the sauour of spi

Jacob. in Missa.

tuall fragrance or fweetneffe, maie geue again and fend to vs the diuine gra-   E
ce, and the gift of the moft holie Spirit. Thus he ther.

S. Clement after he had offred facrifice praied thus. *Rogamus vt propicio ac fe*
reno vultu refpicias fupra hæc propofita dona coram te, tu qui nullius indiges Deus, & tibi
complacitum fit in eis ad honorem Chrifti tui, &c. O God, which neadeft no other
mans goods we befeche thee, that with a merciful and pleafant countenance thow wilt looke vpon thefe prefent gifts fet before thee, and that thowe
maift be well pleafed with them to the honour of thy Chryfte.

In Miſſa
Apoſt.

S. Bafill praied thus: *Dominum poftulemus pro oblatis & fanctificatis, honorificentif*
fimis muneribus Domini Dei noftri & commoditate bonorum noftrarum animarum, vt cle
mentiſſ. Deus, qui accepit ea in fancto & fuper cælefti, intelligibili altari in odorem fuauita-
tis emittat nobis gratiam et communionem fancti fui Spiritus. Let vs defire our Lorde
for the offred and fanctified moft honourable gifts of our Lord and God, ãd
the commoditie of the goodneffe of our foules, that our moft mercifull God
who hath receaued them in his holie and heauenlie and intelligible aultar
in the fauour of fweetneffe, maie fend vnto vs the grace and communion of   F
his holie Spirit. Thus he.

Baſil. in
Miſſa.

S. Chryfoftom foloweth S. Bafill, and after the oblacion of facrifice praieth
thus: *Pro ablatis et fanctificatis preciofis donis Dominum deprecemur, vt clemens Deus, qui*
ea fufcepit in fancto cœlefti intelligibili altari fuo mittat nobis propterea gratiam, et donum
fancti fpiritus. For the offred ãd facctified precioufe gifts, let vs praie to ourLord
that our merciful God, who hath receaued thé in his holie ãd heauélie intelligle aultar, maie féd vs therfore grace, ãd the gifte of the holieGoft. Thus he.

Chryſoſt.
in Miſſa.

I wifh that all thefe alleaged Fathers praing to God for the acceptacion of
their feruice in the offring of facrifice, might be fo diligétlie noted, that their
phrafe maie hereafter be remébred. For yf they be well noted, they feme in
maner of fpeach to praie for their facrifice, which maner of fpeach S. Ambro
fe alfo vfeth, and after him the catholique Church S. Ambrofe in this maner.
Petimus et precamur vt hanc oblationem fnfcipias, in fublimi altari tuo per manus Angelo-
rum tuorũ, ficut fufcipere dignatus es munera pueri tui iufti Abel, et facrificiũ Patriarchæ
noftri Abrahæ, et quod tibi obtulit fummus facerdos tuus Melchifedec. We defire and
praie thee that thow wilt receaue this oblaciõ bi the hãds of the Angels into
thy high aultar, as thow haueft vouchefafe to receaue the gifts of thie childe
Abell, and the facrifice of our Patriarch *Abraham,* and that, which thie preift
Melchifedech did offre vnto thee. The catholique Church maketh the like
requeft in this maner: *Supra quæ propitio ac fereno vultu refpicere digneris, et accepta*
habere, ficuti accepta habere dignatus es munera pueri iufti tui Abel, et facrificium Patriar
chæ noftri Abrahæ, et quod tibi obtulit fummus facerdos tuus Melchifedec, fanctum facrifi-
cium, immaculatam hoftiam. Vpon which things, vouchefafe to looke with a mer
cifull and pleafaunt countenance, and to accept them, as thow dideft vouche
fafe to accept the gifts of thie child Abel the iuft, and the facrifice of our Patriarch Abraham, and that which thie high preift Melchifedec did offre vnto
thee, an holie facrifice, ãd an vndefiled hofte. And immediatelie yt foloweth
thus: *Supplices te rogamus, omnipotens Deus, iube hæc perferri per manus fancti Angeli*
tui in fublime altare tuum, in confpectu diuinæ mãieftatis tuæ, vt quotquot ex hac altaris par-
ticipatione, facrofanctum Filij tui corpus et fanguinem fumpferimus omni benedictione cœle
fti repleamur et gratia, per eundem Chriftum Dominũ noftrũ. We mekelie befech thee
(o allmightie God) cõmaunde thefe to be caried by the hands of thie holie   H
Angells vnto thie high aultar in the feight of thy diuine maieftie, that as manie of vs as do by this participacion of the aultar, receaue the moft holie bodie and blood of thy Sonne, maie be fulfilled with all heauenly blefsing
and

Ambr. li. 4
ca. 6. de
facr.

Woordes in
the Maſſe
nowe vſed.

G

A　and grace by the fame our Lord Iefus Chryft.

Thefe be the praiers that the Proclamer in his fermon derideth, mocking withall the godlie doings of the catholique Church. Here he triumpheth, here he fheweth his trifling toies and merie côceates to delight himfelf, âd foch as were of light heads and gracelefle heartes in his audience, Here his diffembled grauitie failing, he fhewed himfelf in his owne colours, euen like a man of his profefsion, that ys to mifconftrue, to mifunderftand, to wreft, to diftort to adulterate foch things as they read, and yet fhameleflie with bolde countenaunce to vtter yt, to compafle therbie a mifcheif. But that he be no otherwife charged then his own woordes will require we fhall reporte them as they be. Thus he faieth as touching thefe praiers.

Moreouer the preift defiereth God fo to accept the bodie of his Sonne Iefus Chrift as he once accepteth the facrifice of Abell, or the oblaciô of Melchifedec. Yt ys knowê that Abell offred vppe of his fruict of his flocke a lâbe or a fhepe, and that Melchifedec offred vnto Abrahâ and his côpanie returning frô the battaill bread and wine. And think we that Chrift the Sonne of God ftandeth fo farre in his Fathers difpleafure that he nedeth a mortal and B *miferable man to be his fpokefmâ to procure him fauour? or think we that God receaueth the bodie of his onelie begotten fonne none otherwife, then he once receaued a fhepe or a lâbe, at the hands of Abel? or then Abrahâ receaued bread and wine of Melchifedec? Yf no: why doth the preift then make this praier in the Canon immediatelie after confecraciô? Supraquæ propitio ac fereno vultu refpicere, digneris, & accepta habere, ficuti accepta habere dignatus es munera pueri tui iufti Abel, & facrificiû Patriarchæ noftri Abrahæ, & quod tibi obtulit fummus facerdos tuus Melchifedec,* that ys to faie: Looke down with mercifull contenâce vpô thefe facrifices (that ys, the bodie of Chryft thy Sône, and the cuppe of his blood) and vouchefafe to receaue thê, as thow fomtime vouchfafeft to receaue the oblaciôs of the child *Abel* the iuft, and the facrifice of our Patriarch Abrahâ, and that thing that was offred to thee by thy high preift *Melchifedec.* Befides this he defiereth that an *Angell* maie come, and carie Chryfts bodie awaie into heauen. This ys the praier that he maketh: *Iube hæc perferri per manus fancti Angeli tui in fublime altare tuum.* What a fable ys this that Chryft should be born vpon an Angel, and fo caried vppe awaie into heauen? Thus moch the Proclamer.

How faie yow? Haue not feen him plaie his part? Haue ye not feen a mer-
C　ueloufe mockrie of Gods holie myfteries? Haue ye not heard the phrafe of the praiers of the holie Apoftles, âd of their Difciples, of the âunciêt Fathers of the primitiue Church âd of all the catholike Church derided âd fkorned? For thus fkorning âd abufing the praiers of the canô of the Maffe vfed now in the catholique Church, he fkorneth and abufeth the praiers of all thê a forefaied. For the praiers of the Canon contein their woordes, âd are côpiled of thê. The beginning of thefe woordes produced by the Proclamer, that ys, *Supra quæ propitio ac feren, &c.* ys taken oute of S. Clement, who praied thus: *Rogamus vt propitio ferenoq; vultu refpicias fuper hæc doua.* The Church faieth: vpô which vouchefafe, with a mercifull and pleafed countenâce to looke vpô, &c. S. Clement faied: *We befeche thee that with a merciful and pleafed countenaunce thow wilt look vpon thefe gifts or facrifices,* that that foloweth in the praier of the Canon yt ys whollie in S. Ambrofe, fauing that yt ys ther diuided as yt were into two praiers, that S. Ambr. côprehêdeth in one. For wher in the praier of the Churche yt foloweth thus: *& accepta habere ficuti accepta, &c.* And vouchefafe to receaue thefe, as thow vouchfafeft to receaue the gifts of Abel the iuft, and the
D　facrifice of our Patriarch Abraham, &c. yt ys in S. Ambrofe woorde for woorde in effect. For thus he praied. *Petimus & precamur vt hanc oblat, &c. fupra.* We defire âd praie thee that thow wilt receaue this oblaciô by the

　hands

The woordes of the Proclamer
See what blind iudgment blind malice pronounceth of all the chryftian world

The praiers of the Canô of the Maffe be the praiers of Fathers of the primitiue Church.

handes of the Angels into thie high aultar as thowe vouchsafest to receaue **E**
the gifts of thy childe *Abel* the iust, and the sacrifice of oure Patriarch Abraham, and that, that thie high preist *Melchisedec* offred vnto thee.   See ye not nowe that the catholique Church vseth the verie same woordes that S.Ambrose and the auncient Church in his time did vse? well let vs procede to see and compare the rest.

The Church goeth further in the Canon and praieth thus: *Suplices te roga-mus omnipotens Deus iube hæc perferri, &c.* We humblie beseche thee, o Allmightie God, that thowe wilt commaunde these sacrifices to be caried by the hands of thy holie Angell into thie high aultar in the seight of thine diuine Maiestie S.Ambrose praieth, thus: *Petimus et precamur, vt supra.* We desire and praie, that thow wilt receaue this sacrifice by the hands of the holie Angells into thie high aultar.

Nowe ye see the praier of the Canon of the Masse vsed in the catholique **F**
Churche, with which the Proclamer hath fownd soche fault, ye see also the praiers of S.Clement and S.Ambrose, and by conference ye perceaue them so to agree, that the woordes of the praier of the Church nowe be none other then the woordes of S.Clement and S.Ambrose. Maie yt not then be truelie saied, that the Proclamer deriding and skorning the praier of the

Church nowe vsed, dothe deride and skorn S. Clement and S . Ambrose and the church that they liued in? But let vs consider the great enormities and abuses that the Proclamer pretendeth to be in these praiers of the Canõ in the Masse. Ther be in all three principall and horrible blasphemies, as he feigneth ãd setteth thē furth, cõmitted in these praiers: The first is, that Christ should so stand in the displeasure of his heauenlie Father that he nedeth a mortall and miserable man to be his spokesman. The second, that the bodie of the onelie begotten Sonne of God should in no better wise be receaued of the father then a lambe at the hands of *Abel.* The third, that desire ys made that an Angell maie come and carie awaie Chrysts bodie into heauen.

As touching the first, hath the Proclamer no more learning and knowledge in the phrasis of the scripturs and doctours , then here   his railing blas-

phemie declareth? Or wher the Fathers in the scriptures vpon the oblacion of their sacrifices were yt oxe, calf, kidde, or lambe made their praiers for ac-**G**
ceptacion, will he also mock them and saie that they vnsemelie praied to God to receaue an oxe, calf, kidde or lãbe at their hãds, or that they praied for soch brute beasts as they offred to be receaued into his fauour? But to discusse this point within the list and compasse of oure owne matter: When S. Iames in his Masse praied as ys before alleaged, saing: *For these offred, and sanctified, preciou se, heauenlie, vnspeakeable, immaculate, gloriouse, dreadfull, horrible, diuine gifts, let vs praie that oure Lord accepting these into his holie heauenlie mentall and spirituall aultar, vnto the sauour of spiritnall fragrance:* And when S.Basill saied: *For the offred and sanctified moste honorable gifts of oure Lorde and God, let vs praie:* And when Chrysostom likewise saied: *Let vs praie to oure Lorde for the offred and sanctified preciouse gifts:* wher vndoubtedly by these sanctified, preciouse, dreadfull offred gifts , they vnderstood and ment the bodie and blood of Chryst, ther on the aultar offred in sacrifice: Wil the Proclamer, I saie, mock all these and other holie Apo stles ãd Fathers, and skorning their phraseis saie that they praie to God the Father for the bodie of his Sonne Iesus Chryst to be accepted?   Ys this the learning and grauitie wherwith a matter of so great importance of so great, **H**
weight, of so long continaunce, of so great estimacion, reuerence and honou re, shal be ouerthrowē? Maie so great a mysterie of christiã religiõ be without

scriptu

A scripture againſt ſaied, without autoritie cõuelled withoute graue reaſõ impugned, without ſtrõg argumẽt cõuinced,ãd without formall proceſſe clean defaced.Truſt me,gẽtle reader,inal his vehemẽt inuectiue againſt this part of the Canon of the Maſſe, he hath impugned yt with no other good learning or authoritie,no other graue reaſon or argument, then onelie gibing mockes. This ys one that ys woorthie to occupie the place of a Biſhoppe, this ys one that ys reputed a famouſe preacher : this ys a Iuell to helpe to plucke down the Churche of Chryſte and to ſett vppe the Sinagog of Sathan, that can with a falſe feigned skoff ſeeme to ſticke down all that ſtand in his waie doctours, Fathers, Biſhopps, Diſciples,Apoſtles, and all. Can anie chryſtian heart thinke that S. Iames S. Clement S. Baſill S. Chryſoſtom,S. Ambroſe, and all other holy fathers vſing theſe alleaged praiers, did thinke thẽ ſelues ſpokeſmen to intreate the Father for Chryſte? Yſyt can not be thought of them, howe can yt be thought of the catholique Churche vſing the ſame praiers.

Mockes ãd skoffes the onely argumentes of the Procla mer in this matter.

B To conclude therfor this firſt part againſt the maliciouſe mocke of the Proclamer,I ſaie, that yſ the Apoſtles and Fathers vſing this maner of phraſe in their praiers were ſpokeſmen to the Father for Chryſt his Sonne, then ys the Church ſo nowe likewiſe: yſ they were not, no more ys the Churche. The Apoſtles and fathers, and the Church did allwaies and doth well know Chryſte, as he ys the onelie begotten, ſo ys he the welbeloued Sonne of the Father. They beleue, they teache and preache that yt ys he, in whõ the Father ys wel pleaſed: yea they beleue that in him the Father ys ſo wel pleaſed, that whatſoeuer thei aske of theFather in his name,he wil geue yt thẽ.Wher vpon the churche in this praier making humble inteceſſion (as the Apoſtles and fathers before haue doen) not for Chryſt,but by Chryſte,not to procure fauour for him, but to procure mercie to them ſelues from God the Father, cocludeth their peticions and requeſts in theſe ſame praiers, whiche the Proclamer skoffinglie abuſeth, with theſe woordes, *Per Chriſtum Dominum noſtrum.*By Chryſte oure Lorde,which ys as moche to ſaie: All this we deſire for Chryſte our Lorde his ſake. In this firſt part then behold the ſlaunderou ſe vanitie, and ſo let vs examine the next pretended fault.

The mening of the Curche in the firſt po incte.

C In the ſeconde he accuſeth the Churche that yt wolde Chrſtes bodie no better to be accepted of the Father, then the ſacrifice of *Abel,* of *Abraham,* of *Melchiſedec.* Abel, Abraham, and *Melchiſedec* were men acceptable to God, whoſe ſacrifices were alſo acceptable, not for the thinges them ſelues that were offred by them, as a ſhepe a ramme, bread, wine , for of theſe thinges as God hath no nede being the Lorde of the wholl earth and all that ys therin: ſo of them, as of them ſelues he hath no pleaſure. In theſe ſacrifices then not the things but the ſeruice of them which offred thoſe thinges, was acceptable and pleaſaunt vnto God.Abel offred ſacrifice to God, ſo alſo did Cain. But *reſpexit Dominus ad Abel, & ad munera eius . ad Cain autem & ad munera. eius non reſpexit.* God did looke vnto *Abel* and to this gifts, but vnto *Cain* and to his gifts he did not looke. He looked firſt to *Abel* him ſelf,then to his gifts He behelde his hartie deuocion and for that looked to his ſeruice in his due tifull ſacrifice:he ſawe in *Cain* a ſlackneſſe or coldeneſſe of deuocion,wherfor he neither looked fauorablie to him nor to his ſeruiſe in offring ſacrifice.

2. Anſwer io te the ſecõd fault.

God looked not on the thing offred in the old e ſaciſices,but on the deuoclõ of the offerers.

D *Noẽ* offred ſacrifice and God ſmelled a ſwete ſauoure, ſaith the ſcripture, not that God was delighted with the kitchẽ ſauour of burnt meate as here the Proclamer might in his licenciouſe maner skoff at the phraſe of the ſcripture as he doth at the phraſe of the catholique Churche, but God ſmelled

the fwete fauour of his deuoute and duetifull feruice. As God then was not **E**
defiered by *Abel* to receaue his fhepe in to heauen, nor by *Melchifedec* to take
vppe thither bread and wine, nor by *Abraham* to take the ramme that he of
fred, but that their humble feruice and obedience therby fhewed and decla
red might [be accepted : So the Churche defiereth not that her facrifice
whiche ys Chryfte might be accepted (being moft acceptable in yt felf, and
all other made acceptable by yt) but that her deuocion, humble feruice and
obedience in doing that facrifice maie be foche, that yt maie be accepted as
was the feruice of *Abel*, of *Melchifedec*, and of *Abraham* in the offring of their.

Jacob.in
Miff.

In this fame fenfe praied the Apoftolique and primitiue Churche. S. Ia
mes in this maner: *Refpice in nos, o Deus, & ad noftrum hoc rationabile obfequium in*
tuere, idque accipe vt Abel dona accepifti, Noë facrificia, Moyfis & Aaronis facerdocia
Samuelis pacifica, Dauidis pænitëtiã, Zachariæ incenfum. Looke vpõ vs, o Lord, and be
hold this our refonable feruice, ãd receaue the fame as thowe dideft receaue
the gifts of *Abel*, the facrifices of *Noe*, the preiftlie oblaciõs of *Moyfes* ãd *Aarõ*,
the peace offrings of *Samuel*, the penance of *Dauid*, the inceufe of *Zacharie*.

S. Bafill in his Maffe praied almoft with fame woordes : *Refpice in nos, Deus*
F
Bafil.in
Miff.
& vide fuper feruitutem noftram hanc, & fufcipe eam ficut fufepifti Abel munera, Noe,
facrificium, Abrahæ horocauftum, Moyfes & Aronis facrationes, Samuelis hoftias pacifi-
cus, ficut fufepifti de fanctis tuis Apoftolis verum iftud myfterium, fic & ex manibus no-
ftris peccatorum fufcipe munera ifta in benignitate tua Domine. &c. Looke vpon vs, o
God, and looke vpon this our feruice, and receaue yt, as thow dideft receaue the prefentes of *Abel*, the facrifice of *Noé* the burnt offring of Abraham,
the oblaciõs of *Moyfes* and Aaron, the peace offrings of *Samuel*, euen as
thowe haueft receaued this true mifterie of thie holie Apoftles, fo, o Lord,
receaue thefe facrifices of oure hands being finners, in thy benignitie.

S. Ambrofe and the auncient latin Churche that he liued in, as ye haue
heard yt allreadie teftified, vfed a moche like phrafe. *We befeche thee, o Lorde,*
faieth he, *vouchfafe to receaue this facrifice as thowe haueft vouchedfafe to receaue the*
gifts of thy childe Abel the iuft, the facrifice of our Patriarche Abraham, and that whiche
thy high preift Melchifedec did offre vnto thee.

The feruj-
ce in doing
of facrifice
ys defierd
to be accep
ted, not the
facrifice yt
felf.
Thus haue ye nowe feen the praiers for acceptacion of facrifice, that were
praied by the Apoftles, vfed of the greke Church, receaued of the auncient
latin Churche, and cõtinued by the catholiq; Churche euë to this our time.
G
Nowe did S.Iames ãd the Apoftles praie for the acceptaciõ of Chryfte their
facrifice? Did S.Bafill and the greeke Churche defire that the bodie of Chry
fte might no otherwife be accepted thë the facrifices of *Abel, Noë, Abrahã,* &c.
Did S. Ambrofe ãd the fathers of the latin Church for thefe xiihũdreth years
fo bafely think of the woorthineffe of Chryfts bodie and facrifice, that they
thought a fhepe, an oxe or bread ãd wine as acceptable as the bodie of Chrift?
No, they thought nothing fo, but thei defiered (as ys faied) that their feruice
in offring this facrifice might be accõpted as the feruice of thofe other was
accepted. This acceptiõ thë hath refpect to the offrers, ãd not the facrifice off.

And that the Proclamer fhall not faie, that this expofition ys feigned by
me, let him vnderftãd that this fame expofitiõ hath ben made by diuerfe lear
ned fathers fome hundreth years agon, of the whiche for profe I will alleage
the faing of one whiche fhall be Hugo de S. victore, who expownding the ca
Lib. 2.de.
eccl.off.ca.
33.
non of the Maffe, vpõ, this praier which the Proclamer by his mooking fo blaf
H
phemouflie abufeth and derided faieth thus: *Quafi per gradus fcalæ afcëdens cõme*
morat munus Abel pueri, facrificiũ Abrahæ Patriarchæ, oblationë Melchifedec facerdotis, qui
in pane & vino fpeciæ veri facrificii elegãter expreffit, ficut Abrahã veritatë in filio, et Abel
innocentiæ munus in agno. Quod dicit: Sicuti accepta habere dignatus es munera, &c. non

A *optat similiter acceptari oblationes (hæc enim multo est acceptabilitor) sed offerentes.* As one going vppe by the steppes of a ladder he maketh mencion of the gifte of *Abel* his childe, of the sacrifice of *Abraham* the Patriarch, and of the oblacion of *Melchisedec* the preist, who in bread and wine did well setfurth the figure of the true sacrifice, as *Abraham* the veritie in his Sonne, and *Abel* the gift of innocentie in a lambe. That he saieth : As thowe haueft vouched safe to accept the gifts of thy childe *Abel* &c. he desireth not the oblacions or sacrifices to be in like accepted (for this sacrifice ys moche more acceptable) but the offerers. Yf of this vnderstanding the Proclamer wolde see more he maie read Gabriell and other whiche treacte of the Canon of the Masse, and he shal see so moch that he maie haue iust cause to be ashamed of his vain ãd wicked saings and false imaginacions againft the godlie doings of Chrysts catholique Churche. To conclude then this seconde parte also yt ys euidēt that the Churche desiereth not the sacrifice of Chryfte to be equallie taken with the sacrifices of *Abel, Abraham. Melchisedec,* but raither the offerers of

The mening of the Churche in the secõ de poinct.

B thefe sacrifices, that ys, that the preist and people offring this sacrifice maie so do yt, as bothe they and their feruice in so doing maie please God and be accepted as were *Abel, Abraham, Melchisedec,* and their feruice in offring their sacrifices to God.

                                                  £.

The third faulte that the Proclamer falselie (I wil not saie folishlie) pretēdeth to be in the Canon, ys, that (as he fableth) desire ys madē that an Angel maie come and carie Chryftes bodie awaie into heauen. Ys not this a fonde deuised toie of a man pretending grauitie? Did euer man as moche as dreame anie soche phantafie that had his witts not intoxicated with the poison of herefie, and his heart not fiered with the furiouse flames of malice? Ah good Lord, who wolde haue thought that euer soche time wolde haue comed, that a Chryftian man shoulde be so depelie drowned in herefie, that by force of malice therof he shoulde blowe oute soch blafts of contempt of honorable antiquities, and soche horrible blafphemie againft Gods bleffed facrrfi ce, and minifterie and that in so honorable audience, and not so to ceaffe, but afterward in printe to publish the fame to the notice of the worlde? or that

Anfwere to the thirde fault.

C chryftian people coulde euer haue patientlie heard foche vain inuēted toies so farre vide from all good reafon and learning, foche wicked vntruethsfo farre abhorring from all godlie pitie and religion? or that euer they shoulde like to read them? So farre hath this Proclamer presumed, so clean hath he caft awaie all reuerence and femelie iudgement of all holie forefathers and their doinges, folowing therin *Melhoferus, Zuinglius* and foche like, that he iudgeth them infenfate men and verie fooles, and thinkes him felf onelie wife.

    But that thowe (gentle reader) maie, not by my woordes onelie, but by good fubftanciall matter iudge thefe malicioufe false imaginacions to be his inuēted toies void of all learning and rrueth, and afwell impugning and skor ning the phrafe of holie fcripture and auncient fathers, as of the catholique Church in thefe daies, vnderftand that the fcriptures haue this maner of fpeache that an Angell doth carie oure praiers into the feight of God. For the Angell *Raphaël* faied vnto the holie father *Tobias, Quandò orabas cum lachrimis, & fepiliebas mortuos &c. ego obtuli orationem tuam Domino.* when thowe

D dideft praie with tears and dideft burie the dead &c. I did offre or prefent thy praier to God.

    Nowe will the Proclamer here skoff at the faing of the Angell *Raphaël* and aske in his hiftrionicall maner whether he caried *Tobies* praiers in a cart or a

Tob. 12.

wheleba

whelebarow, or will he aske him whether God could not knowe the praiers **E**
of *Tobie* except he had brought them vppe into his feight? Soche fond friu‑
loufe queftions might he afwell here moue againft the faing of the Angel
in the holie fcripture, as he doth againft the fame maner of fpeache in the
Canon of the Maffe.

*S. Ambro-
fe praied in
this poinct
as the Chur
che doth no
we.*

S. Ambrofe, as before ys feen, declareth that he and the Churche wher
in he liued, vfed the like maner of fpeache in their praier within the Canon
of the Maffe, faing thus: *We defire and praie thee, that thow wilt receaue this facrifice into thie high aultar, by the hands of thie holie Angells.* Nowe did S. Ambrofe
and the Churche that he liued in defire by this maner of praier as the fkof-
fing Proclamer fableth, that their facrifice (whiche was he bodie of Chryfte)
might be caried à waie into heauen by Angells? Was S. Ambrofe of fo fmall
learning and knowledge, or of fo litle witte and vnderftanding as to iudge
or think that? Naie, the lacke of learning knowledg witte and grace alfo ys rai
ther in the Proclamer, who of fo learned and holie a man, and of the wholl **F**
Churche withall, fo rafhlie and wickedlie iudgeth. S. Ambrofe fo praieng
foloweth the maner of fpeache vfed in the fcriptures, and the Churche nowe
vfing the fame phrafe foloweth both the fcripturs and S. Amhrofe, and
the auncient Churche, wherfor in the vfing of foche phrafe ther ys no
foche fable entended, as the Proclamer maliciouflie pretendeth and
feigneth.

*Of the mi-
nisterie of
Angells.*

But that the right fenfe of this phrafe maie be here more fullie declared:
vnderftãd, that, as S. Paule faieth, the Angells of God are all miniftring fpirit
tes fent to helpe thẽ, that fhal atteing the inheritance of faluacion. In the old
law they did to *Abraham*, to *Ifaac*, to *Iacob*, to the parents of Sampfon, and to

*Gen.22.
ibid.28.
Iudic.13
Tob.3.4.5

Ibid.10.11
12.*

diuerfe other innumerable minifteries. To holie *Tobie* the Angel *Raphael* was
the minifter to conduct his fonne to *Raguel* in *Rages.* and ther to him he was
the counfailour, not onelie to take *Sara* to wieff, but alfo by chaiftvfage of
her, and by other means to reftreign and debarre the wicked affaulting and
molefting fpirit, that infefted that houfe. To the fame father *Tobie* the Angell fo miniftred that his feight was reftored. His praiers alfo and other good **G**
dedes he did prefent in the feight of God.

*Luc. 1.
ibid Ma.2.
Act. 5 8.*

In the newe teftament the Angell *Gabriell* was the meffenger of the ioifull
conception of the Sauiour of the world. An Angell was the Meffenger to
Zacharias to tell him before of the birth of his fonne Iohn the Baptift. An
Angell was meffenger to the poore fheperds to geue them to vnderftand
that they had a Sauiour born. An Angell attended vpon Peter and opened

*Euerie mã
hath a pro
pre Angell*

*Pfal.90
Math.18,*

*Bern.fer.7
in Cant.*

the doores of the prifon, guided him oute and dimiffed him in fafetie. What
fhall I ftand to enombre the nõbre of the places of fcripture to this matter
apperteining, whiche be allmoft immunerable? This ys certen, that both
men and children haue their Angells to kepe them, helpe them, and to offre
vppe their praiers to God for them. *Angelis fuis mandauit de te &c*. He hath
commaunded his Angells (faieth the Pfalmift) to attende thee, that they ma
ie kepe thee in all thie waies, they fhall carie thee in their hands, that thowe
hurt not thy foote with a ftone. And for children Chryfte gaue monicion
faing: *Nolite fcandalizare vnum ex his pufillis.* Do not offend one of thefe litle

*Angells of-
fre vppe
our praiers
to God.*

ones. I faie vnto yowe that their Angells do allwaies fee the face of my Fa- **H**
ther which ys in heauen.

Diuerfe of thefe fcripturs are treacted of by S. Bernard and expownded
to the fame fenfe that I haue alleaged them for. Of the place of *Tobie* thus he
faieth: *Credimus Angelos fanctos aftare orantibus, offerre Deo preces & vota hominum*
vbi

A *vbi tamen ſine ira & diſceptatione leuari puras manus perſpexerint . Probat hoc angelus ita loquens ad Tobiam: Quando orabas cum lachrimis &c.* We beleue that the holie Angells be preſent with them that do praie to offre to God the praiers and deſires of men, wher they ſee clean hands to be lifted vppe withoute wrath and diſceptaciõ. This doth the Angell prooue thus ſpeaking to Tobie: when thowe dideſt praie with tears and dideſt burie the dead &c. I did offre thie praier beforeGod. And vpõ the ſaing of thePſalmiſt he ſaieth thus: *Quantã tibi debet hoc verbum inferre reuerentiam, adferre deuotionem, conferre fiduciam? Reuerentiã pro præſentia, deuotionem pro beneuolentia, fiduciam pro cuſtodia. Cautè ambula, vt videlicet cui adſunt Angeli &c.* Howe moche reuerence, howe moche deuocion, howe moche truſt aught this woorde to bring to vs? Reuerence for the preſence, deuocion for beneuolence, truſt for their cuſtodie, walke wiſelie foraſ moche as Angells be preſent. *Adſunt, & adſunt tibi, non modò tecum, ſed etiam pro te. Adſunt vt protegãt, adſunt vt proſint.* They are preſent, and vnto thee they are preſent, not onelie with thee but alſo for thee. They are preſent to de-

B fend, they are preſent to profitt thee, and to doo thee good. That the ſaing of Chryſte teacheth that Angells attend young children, S. Bernad doth alſo wittneſſe thus: *Parum eſt, quod facis Angelos tuos ſpiritus, facis & Angelos paruulorum. Denique, Angeli eorum ſemper vident faciem Patris .* Yt ys but a ſmall matter to thee, o God, that thowe makeſt thie Angells ſpirits, thowe makeſt thẽ alſo the Angells of litle children.

To conclude with S. Bernarde ſpeaking of the miniſterie of Angells aboute vs in the ſeruice of God, thus he ſaieth: *Attendite principes veſtros cùm ſtatis ad orandum, vel pſallendum, & ſtate cum reuerentia, & diſciplina, & gloriamini quia Angeli veſtri quotidie vident faciem Patris , nimirum miſsi in miniſterium propter nos, qui hæreditatem capimus ſalutis, deuotionem noſtram in ſuperna ferunt, referunt gratiã.* When ye ſtand to praie or to ſiñg praiſes to God, remembre your rulers (*mening Angells*) and ſtand with reuerence and good ordre, or ſemelie maner, and reioice that your Angells do dailie ſee the face of the Father . For they being ſent in miniſterie for vs, which receaue the inheritance of ſaluacion, do carie vppe our deuoute ſeruice into heauen, and bring vs again grace.

C That Angells then be preſent with vs, that they kepe vs, that they helpe vs , that they carie vppe oure praiers and deuoute ſeruices and offre them to God, notwithſtanding the Proclamers apiſh mockrie, yt ys euident both by ſcripturs and Fathers.

But that the reader maie vnderſtãd howe they offre our praiers, and what ys therby ment, and to the intent alſo that both he maie be deliuered from all ſcruple of that matter, and the Proclamers vntrue feigning vpon this place of the Canon, perceaued to be all together againſt the minde of the Chur che, as a thing neuer by anie of them ther thought or ſpoken, I ſhall for this time produce one of the ſame Churche, expownding the ſame praier of the Canõ whiche the proclamer ſo ſhamefullie abuſeth and wickedlie wreſteth to a deueliſh ſenſe. This ſhall be the reuerend Father *Hugo de S. Victore*, who expowndeth yt thus: *Sacrificium per manus Angeli perferri nihil aliud intelligimus, quàm ipſum cooperari noſtræ deuotioni. Cooperatur autem nobiſcum pro nobis orando, modóque inenarrabili et inuiſibili bona mentibus noſtris ſuggerendo.* The ſacrifice to be cã ried by the hands of the Angells, we vnderſtand to be no other thing , but

D the Angell to woorke with our deuocion . He woorketh with vs both praieng for vs, and alſo by a merueiloufe and inuiſible maner putting good things into our mindes.

The Angell then, after the minde of the Churche, to carie oure ſacrifice,

ys

Idem ſer 11 in pſal. 90.

ibidem

Idem ſer 7. in Cant.

Angells what miniſteries they do for vs.

li. 2. ca. 34. de offic. eccl

ys to helpe vs by godlie fuggeftion to doo our feruice therin humblie and E
deuoutlie, and by faith and charitie effectuallie, and therin to praie with vs
and for vs, that our doing maie be acceptable and pleafant in the feight of
God. This ys and euer hath ben the minde of the Churche in this praier of
the Canon. And here will I ioin iffue with the Proclamer, that yf he bring
furth anie one catholique writer, be he neuer fo flender, neuer fo vnlearned,
neuer fo auncient, or neuer fo young, that faieth that the praier of the Canō
ys to be vnderftanded as he hath moft vainlie and falfelie (after his hereticall maner folowing *Melhoferus*) feigned and diuifed, I will yelde to him and
faie, that the wholl Church hath offended: yf he can bring no one (as certen
I am he can not) and I dare faie he himfelf knoweth that he can not, let him
blufh and be afhamed of this his wicked toieng: and let the reader fee his vanitie, and beware of his falfe hereticall fubtiltie, knowing that this ys but a
vain imagined, and malicioufe diuifed vnderftanding of heretiques, neuer af
moche as once dreamed of any good catholique.

 And here I faie farder to the Proclamer, that yt can not be but that he F
hath vttered this feigned vnderftanding either of ignorance or of malice. Yf
of ignorance, yt ys to moche fhame for him occupieng the place of a Bifhoppe fo fierelie and in foche audience to impugn that he ys ignorant of: Yf of
malice (whiche ys more like) then muft yt nedes be of the Deuell, who fo
leadeth men, that although they knowe the trueth, he maketh them maliciouflie to impugn and depraue yt, they knowe to be the trueth, and fo to
fpeake directlie againft their knowledge, and their confciences. By whiche
of thefe the Proclamer hath thus depraued the godlie praiers of the Churche, I will not here certenly pronownce, but leaue yt to his confcience,
whiche I dare faie, doth greuouflie accufe him. Thus thefe praiers being deliuered frō wicked vnderftanding, and opened according to the true mening:
and fo finallie confecracion, intencion, oblacion, and acceptacion by full
declaracion from the Apoftles and Primitiue Churche, proued, I fhall here ceaffe of them any farder to treact, and go to other Matters of the
Maffe.

 G

THE NINE AND THIRTETH CHAPT. TRE-
acteth of the value of the Maffe to the quicke and
the dead

Ow foloweth the fourth thing I pourpofed to fpeake of, namelie of the value of the facrifice for the quicke and the dead. For
the whiche alfo I will haue recourfe to the time of the Apoftles
and the Fathers of the primitiue Churche, as here tofore I haue
doen in the proof of matters reproued by the Aduerfaries, and
the proclamer. Yf yt fhall be made euident that S. Iames in his Maffe, S. Ba
fill in his Maffe S. Chryfoftom in his Maffe, and other auncient Fathers in
their writings doo faie that the facrifice of the Maffe auaileth all that be faith
full both the quicke and the dead, and not one can be brought that denieth
yt, reafon wolde that oure caufe fhoulde be approued and alowed, and the
caufe of the Aduerfaries difprooued and difalowed. And for that the Aduer
faries will fooner graunt yt to be profitable to the quicke then to the dead, H
and the proof of the value of yt to the dead, proueth well the value to the
quicke, I fhall ftand the more vpon yt, and fo by proof of the one, make
good the other.

 And

A   And firſt to ſee what was doen of and among the Apoſtles, we will ſee
what was doen in S.Iames Maſſe,thus praied he:*Recipe munera hæc propoſita per
tuam benignitatem,& fac vt oblatio noſtra grata et acceptabilis ſit,per Spiritum ſanctum
ſanctificata,in propitiatione peccatorum noſtrorum,& eorum,quæ populus per ignorantiã
admiſit,& in requiem animarum eorum,qui ante nos dormiunt,vt & nos abiecti,& peccatores,& indigni ſerui tui,digni habiti,qui ſine dolo miniſtremus ſancto altari tuo,merce-
dem,accipiamus fidelium & prudentium diſpenſatorum,gratiamque inueniamus et miſericordiam in die illa tremenda retributionis tuæ iuſtæ et bonæ.*Receaue through thy mer

S.James
praieth
both for the
quick and
the dead

cifulneſſe theſe giftes of our handes which be ſinners, ãd graunt that our ob
lacion maie be pleaſing and acceptable,ſanctified by the holie Goſt,vnto the
forgeueneſſe of our ſinnes,and of thoſe which thy people hath cõmitted by
ignorance,and vnto the reſt of the ſoules of them,which ſleape before vs, ãd
that we alſo abiectes and ſinners,and thy vnwoorthie ſeruantes, maie be accõpted woorthie,which maie without gile myniſter at thie holie aultar, and
that we maie receaue the rewarde of the faithfull and wiſe ſtewardes,ãd that
B we maie finde grace and mercie in that fearfull daie of the iuſt and good re-
warde.Thus moch S.Iames Maſſe.

. Not minding to tarie vpon the beginniug of the praier,wher ye maie per
ceaue that like maner of praier ys vſed,as in the laſt chapter ys ſpokẽ of,name
lie that this ſacrifice maie be receaued gratefullie acceptably, &c. Whiche I
doe but touche, wiſhing yt to be noted the better to perceaue the malice
of the Proclamer,who (as ye haue heard)reproueth and skorneth that in the
Church,that was vſed of the Apoſtles.I minde not,I ſaie,to tarie, but to haſt
me to note theſe thinges,that now we haue to ſpeake of,namely that the ſacrifice of the Maſſe ys auailable both to the quicke ãd the dead,which both
be here teſtified,whẽ the Apoſtle praieth that this ſacrifice maie be pleaſing
and acceptable vnto the remiſſiõ of ſinnes,ãd to the reſt of the ſoules of thẽ
that ſleape before vs.Doe not theſe woordes teach vs,that S.Iames took this
for a ſacrifice propiciatorie,whẽ he deſiereth that the ſacrifice maie be accep
ted to the propiciaciõ of our ſinnes?And did he not thinke yt auailable to
the dead,whẽ he praieth that yt maie be to the reſt of the ſowles of thẽ that
C be dead? The woordes be ſo plain,that yt can not be deuied.

And as Caiphas,though he were an euel Biſhoppe ſpake one trueth of the
death of Chryſt:ſo the Proclamer though he be an euell mã ſpake one trueth of S.Iames Maſſe.For he ſaieth that S.Iames Maſſe ys full of knowledge.
Yf yt be full of knowledge by the teſtimonie of the Aduerſ.thẽ feare thowe
not,whether thow be catholike or other,to ſaie that this ys good knowledg,
that the ſacrifice of the Maſſe ys aualeable to the quick ãd the dead.For ſoch
ys the knowledge in S.Iames his Maſſe.And that thow maiſt be farder aſſured that the Apoſtles taught praier and the Maſſe to be profitable to the
dead,harken firſt what *Dionyſe* the Diſciple to ſainct Paule,ſaieth for the one,
and what Chryſoſtome teſtifieth for both. S. *Dionyſe* deſcribing the maner
of the buriall and exequies vſed in his time and before his time in the
churche,for parte of yt ſaieth thus:*Accedens venerandus Antiſtes , precem ſacram
ſuper mortuum peragit,precaturque diuinam clementiam vt cuncta dimittat,per infirmitatem humanam admiſſa , peccata defuncto , eumque in luce ſtatuat , in ſinibus Abrahæ , Iſaac , et Iacob , in loco vbi aufugit dolor et triſticia , et gemitus.*
D The reuerẽde Biſhoppe coming,maketh holie praier vpon the dead,and prai
eth the goodneſſe of God,that he wold forgiue the dead perſon al hys ſinnes
which he hath through infirmitie committed,and that he will place him in
the place of light in the Boſomes of Abraham , Iſaac,and Iacob , in the

S.James
Maſſe ys
full of know
lege euẽ by
the iudge-
ment of the
Proclamer

Dionyſ ec-
cleſ.Hier.
cap 7.par-
te prim.

Praier for
the dead v-
ſed in S.
Dioxyſe
time.

Mm m   place

place frō whēce flieth forowe, heauineſſe ād morning. Thus moch S. Dyniſe.

See yowe not praiers here made for the Sinnes of the dead? See yowe not peticion made for him that he maie come to the place of light, to the place wher he maie feell neither forowe nor heauineſſe? Yf this maner of praier was vſed in the time of the Apoſtles, in whoſe time this Dionyſe liued, what ſhall we thinke, but that S. Iames being one of them, praied for the dead as the other Apoſtles did.

Obiection.

Perchaunce yt maie be ſaied that yf the Apoſtles had thought yt neceſſarie to praie for the dead they wolde haue left yt writtē in ſome of their epiſtles. To this I ſaie, that yt neaded not. For firſt amōg the Iewes yt was before the coming of Chryſt in vſe, to praie and offre ſacrifice for the dead, as the ſecōd booke of the *Machabies* doeth teſtifie. Which booke although the Aduerſarie

August. de cura pro mortu. Lib. vni-uerſ.fid. Iu dæorum.

doeth reiect: yet S. Auguſtin ſaieth yt ys in the Canon of chriſtē men. And *Antonius Margarita* one conuerted frō a Iewe to a Chryſtian man, in a booke that he made of the faith of the Iewes, declareth the praier that they made for the dead which ys not moch vnlike to this praier of S. Dionyſe. And ouer he ſaieth that they haue a booke wherin be writtē the names of them that be dead, which thrice in a yeare be redde and ſo praied for. Which order ys yet amongeſt them. ſo that then neaded not.

Clemens epiſt. i. Hom. 3. Philip.pri.

As for the Gētiles although they vſed funerall obſequies: yet for that they were vngodlie after the heathē maner, the Apoſtles gaue thē commaunde-ment by tradicion to burie their dead, and to praie for thē after the chryſtiā maner. Of the which cōmaundement S. Clement maketh mēciō, how yt was geuē by S. Peter. And ſo doth Chryſoſtome that yt was doē by the Apoſtles. For he ſaieth thus: *Non fruſtra ab Apoſtolis ſancitū eſt, vt in celebratione venerandorū myſteriorū memoria fiat eorū qui hinc deceſſerunt. Nouerunt illis multū hinc emolumenti fie ri, multū vtilitatis. Stante ſiquidē vniuerſo populo manus in cœlos extendente, cœtu itē ſacer dotali verendoque poſito ſacrificio quomodò Deū non placaremus pro iſtis orantes?* Y twas

The Apoſt les decreed that the dead ſhould be praied for in the Maſſe.

not but to good pourpoſe decreed of the Apoſtles that in the celebracion of the honourable myſteries (wherby he meneth the Maſſe) a memorie or re-mēbrance ſhould be made of thē that haue departed hence. They knew that moch commoditie ſhoulde come from thence to thē, and moch profit. For all the people ſtanding, and holding vppe their hāds into heauē, the cōpanie alſo of preiſtes, and the fearfull ſacrifice being ſettfurth, how ſhall we not ap-peaſe God praing for theſe? Thus Chryſoſtome.

As before ye haue ſeen the praier of the Apoſtle S. Iames praing for the dead: ſo now ye ſee yt teſtified by Chryſoſtome that the Apoſtles cōmaūded the dead to be praied for in the celebraciō of the holie myſteries, whiche ys the Maſſe, wher the holie and bleſſed bodie and blood of Sauiour Chryſt ys ſetfurth in the ſeight of the Father: wherby his paſſiō ād death being liuelie remēbred, ād hūble peticiō in the preſence therof, and for the meritte therof by the preiſtes ād people being made, yt cā not be (ſaieth Chryſoſt.) but that God will be appeaſed ād merciefor the ſoules obteined. For (as S. Cypriā ſai eth) *In huius præſentia nō ſuperuacuè mēdicāt lacrimæ veniā, nec vnquā patitur cōtriti cordis holocauſtū repulſam.* In the preſence of this (vnderſtād ſacrifice) teares doe adſu rediebegge pardō, neither doeth the ſacrifice of a cōtrite heart at anie times ſuf

Cypr.ſerm. de cœna.

fre repulſe. Therfor in this ſentēce Chryſoſtome doeth not onelie teſtifie the dead to be praied for by the decree of the Apoſtles, but alſo that they are to be praied for in the celebracion of the honourable myſteries. Which myſte-ries after, when he ſpeaketh of the praiers of the preiſtes, ād the people, he cal leth the fearfull ſacrifice, wherbie ys fullie taught that this holie celebracion

A lebracio̅ ys a sacrifice.Finallie howesoeuer the Deuel hath bewitched some, that they in their death beddes make speciall request not to be praied for when they be dead, and at the buriall of the dead praier ys abandoned : yet of S.Chrysostom we maie learn,that yt ys highlie beneficiall to the dead, that the preistes and the people shoulde in the presence of the blessed sacrifice,which ys Chrystes bodie and bloode,praie for the dead.But let vs go to S.Basills Masse,and see whether he did therin praie for the dead.In his Masse *Basil.in* I finde, this praier:*Nos aute̅ oēs de vno pane & de vno calice participantes,coadunari* *Missa.* *Spiritus sancti co̅munione,& nullu̅ nostru̅ ad iudiciu̅ aut condemnatione̅ facias accipere sanctu̅ corpus,& sanguine̅ Christi tui:Sed vt inueniamus misericordiā & gratiā in cœtu omniu̅ sanctoru̅, qui à seculo tibi placuerunt, Auoru̅,Patru̅,Patriarcharu̅,Prophetaru̅,Apostoloru̅ Euangelistaru̅,Martyrum,Confessorum,Doctoru̅,& omnis spiritus iustorum fine̅ in fide ha bentium.Præcipuè sanctæ & intemeratæ,benedictæ dominatricis nostræ, Dei genitricis , & semper virginis Mariæ,sancti Ioannis præcursoris & Baptistæ,Sancti illius , cuius memoriam facimus,& omnium sanctorum tuorum, quorum postulationibus visita nos Deus.*

B *Et memento omnium dormientium in spe resurrectionis vitæ æternæ,& refrigera eos vbi* *S.Basil pra* *visitat lux vultus tui.*Make all vs partaking of one bread and cuppe to be made *ied in his* one together in the Communion of the holie Goste,and make none of vs *Masse* to receaue the holie bodie and blood of thy Chryst, to iudgement and *the dead,* condemnacion,but that we maie finde mercie and grace in the companie of *and made* all sainctes which haue pleased euen from the time of owre Graunfathers, *intercessio̅* Fathers,Patriarches,Prophetes,Apostles , Euangelistes , Martyrs , Confes- *to Sainctes* sours,doctours,and of the spirittes of all righteouse men hauing their ende in faith,speciallie of the holie and vndefiled our blessed Ladie,the Mother of God,and euer virgen Marie,of sainct Iohn the forerunner,and Baptist , and of that Sainct whose memorie we make this daie,and of all thie sainctes , by whose praiers visite vs (o God)And remembre all them that sleape in the ho pe of resurrection of euerlasting life,and refresh them,wher the light of thy countenaunce comforteth.Thus fare S.Basill.

 , In this praier yt not onely request made for them that be deade,whiche *Iacob in* ys one thing among other for the whiche the Aduersarie raileth at the *Missa.* C Masse:But ther ys also intercession made to sainctes,which ys an other mat- *S.James* ter that misliketh him therin,which intercession also ys in the Masse of sainct *made inter* Iames.For thus shall yowe finde ther:*Commemorationem agamus sanctissimæ, im-* *cession to* *maculatæ,gloriosissimæ,benedictæ Dominæ nostræ Matris Dei,& semper virginis Mariæ,* *Sainctes* *ac omnium sanctorum,& iustorum,vt precibus atque intercessionibus eorum, omnes misericordiam consequamur.* Let vs make a commemoracion of the most holie, vndefiled,most gloriouse,our blessed ladie the Mother of God,and perpetuall virgen Marie, and all holie and iust men,that by their praiers and intercessions,we maie all obtein mercie.

 See ye not peticion here made that by the intercessions and praiers of all sainctes and iust men mercie maie be obteined.Nowe yf the knowledge of S.Iames Masse teacheth vs the consecracion of the bodie and bloode of Chryst,yf yt teach vs the same bodie and bloode ther to be offred in sacrifice:yf yt teach vs yt to be auaiable to the quicke and the dead: yf yt teache vs the intercession of Sainctes : and yf the same thinges be in the Masse nowe vsed in the Churche , howe happened yt that the Procla-D mer coulde make that to be ignorance in our Masse , that ys know - ledge in sainct Iames Masse, sithen ther ys one knowledge in them bothe? Yf yowe will knowe how yt happened,I shall shewe yowe.Yt happened by the same mean that he in an other comparison saieth, that sainct *Iames in hys*   Mmm ii   *Masse*

Maſſe preached and ſetfurth the death of Chryſt:but they in their Maſſe(ſpeaking of the **E**
catholique Church) *haue onelie a nombre of dumbe geſtures , and Ceremonies , which
they themſelf vnderſtande not,and make no maner mencion of Chryſtes death.* The mean

that he ſpake this by was the ſpiritt,but wilt thow aske me what ſpirit? For
ther be two ſpirittes: *Spiritus veritatis,qui docet omnem veritatem:* The Spiritte of
trueth that teacheth all trueth:And *Spiritus mendax in ore propheta,* the lieg ſpiritt in the mouth of the Prophet.To the queſtion then I ſaie, that yt can not
be the ſpiritt of the trueth,that teacheth all trueth.For that ſpirit can teach
and vtter nothing but trueth,ād with vntrueth he medleth not.But yt ys the
lieng ſpiritte,who although ſomtime he vtter a trueth:yet ytys to maintein
an vntrueth,and to ſett a countenance of a trueth vpon an vntrueth , and ſo
by that countenance of trueth,to make ſale of his bragge and vntrueth.

For in the compariſon vnder this trueth that S. Iames in his Maſſe prea-

ched,and ſetfurth the death ofChryſt,he vttereth three vntrueths againſt the
catholique Church.Firſt,he ſaieth that they in their Maſſe haue onely a nō- **F**
bre of dūbe geſtures and ceremonies . How farre wide this ys from the trueth yt ys eaſie to perceaue by his one teſtimonie. For he ſaieth that in the
Maſſe ys holie praier holic doctrine of the woorde of God, holie conſecracion,and holie receauing.But contemning his teſtimonie ther ys(*as in S . Iames Maſſe*)the ſacrifice of lawd es,and thankeſgeuing:ther ys thc holie ſacrifice of Chryſtes bodie,with praiers for all ſtates and ſoch other:ther ys a re-

membrance of Chryſtes frendes,the holie Apoſtles and Martyres,and Saine
tes, to the ſettingfurth of Gods honour in them , who ſo mercifullie hath
wrought in them,that in their weake bodies,he wolde woorke the ſtronge
confeſsion of his holy name,euen to the ſheding of their bloodes for the ſame,ther ys charitable praier for the ſoules departed,according to the tradicion of the Apoſtles:all which be more thē onelie dūbe geſture s,ād ceremo
nies,wherfor by this he ys conuinced to haue ſpokē and writtē an vntrueth.

The ſeconde vntruethys that he ſaieth that we oure ſelues vnderſtāde not
theſe dūbe geſtures and ceremonies.This ys not onely an vntrueth. For he
knoweth that ther be learned Fathers,that haue written bookes of the ceremonies of the Maſſe,and farder haue declared what euerie p cercell or peice **G**
of the garmētes that the preiſt doeth weare in myniſtracion doe ſignifie and
haue fullie ād plainlie expounded euerie part of the Maſſe and the canon of
the ſame,as *Iſidorus,Rabanus,Hugo de Sancto Victore,*Gabriel, Hoiffmiſter ād Ga
retius with other. But yt ys alſo arrogantlie ſlanderouſe,For he generallieac
cuſeth the wholl Church of ignorāce,therbie ſeking to winne to himſelf the
praiſe of ſingular knowledge,and to blott all other before him with the groſ
neſſe of ignorance,to make himſelf to be ſeen wiſe,and all other to be reputed as fooles but *dicentes ſe eſſe ſapientes ſtulti facti ſunt.*

The thirde,which ys ſo manifeſt an vntrueth,that euen a plain mā wolde
by plain woorde call yt a lie,as he maie doe the reſt before mencioned , ys
that the Maſſe maketh no maner of mencion of Chryſtes death.Who wolde

hauing knowledge ſo ſaie except he were ſo farre paſt ſhame , that he regarded not what he ſaied?Who wolde ſo ſaie that were not forced by Deuelliſh
malice,that wittinglie he wolde impugne the trueth and ſaie that not to be
that ys,and that to be that ys not?What ys he that knoweth not, that the
Maſſe ys the memoriall of Chryſtes paſsion and death?Why ys the conſecra **H**
cion,and oblacion of the bodie of Chryſt doē,but to the remēbrance of his
paſsiō ād death?Farder whē the preiſt ſaieth,*that the daie before our Lord Ieſus
ſuffred,he tooke bread into bis holie hādes,and gaue thankes and ſaied,take, eate, this ys my
bodie*

A bodie which shall be geuen for yowe: maketh he no mencion of Chrystes death? When he saieth also, *This ys my bloode of the new testament which shall be shedde for yowe and for manie*: ys ther no mencion made of Chrystes passion and deth? what hath the newe Communion to settfurth the death of Chryst more thē this? but in the Masse besides this, when the bodie and blood of Chryst be lifted vppe, as once that same his bodie was vpon the crosse: ys ther not a liuelie mencion made of his exaltacion vpon the crosse, and of his death? whē the preist in doing of this speaketh the woords of Chryst, *As often as ye doe this ye shall doe yt in the remembrance of me*: ys ther not good occasiō geuē to remembre Chrystes passiō, and death by the rehersall of his owne cōmaundemēt?

After all this the preist immediatelie praieth and saieth: *Wherfore we Lorde being mindefull of the passion, resurrectiou, and ascension of oure Lorde, offre vnto thie ro-ble maiestie this pure sacrifice*: and be these woordes spoken without anie menciō of Chrystes death, wher his passion, resurrection and ascencion be called to minde, and spokē by expresse woordes? Ys not the prophecie of S. Peter fulfilled in this man and his likes when he saieth: *Erunt in vobis magistri mendaces, qui*

2. Peter. 2.

B *introducent sectas perditionis, &c.* Ther shall be among yowe lieg masters which shall bring in sectes of perdiciō, denieng the God, that bought thē, bringing vpon thē selues hastie perdiciō? But leauing his vntrueths ād slaūders to him self, and wishing this onelie here to be noted that soch vntrueths come not frō a good spirit, I will returne to holie Basill, of whose spirit ther ys no doubte, and remember that he in his Masse doeth both make intercession to Sainctes, and doeth also praie for the soules of them that be departed.

Chrysostome also in his Masse praieth likewise in this maner. *Offerimus tibi rationabile hoc obsequiū pro fideliter dormientibus, pro patribus & pro auis nostris, interuenientibus Patriarchis Prophetis, Apostolis, Martyribus, confessoribus, et omnibus sanctis.* We offre vnto the this reasonable seruice for thē that sleape in faith, for our Fathers and great graundfathers, the holie Patriarches, Prophetes, Apostles, Martyrs, and confessors, ād all sainctes praing for vs. And shortlie, after he praieth thus again: *Sancti Ioannis Baptistæ prophetæ & præcursoris, sanctorū & nominatissimorū Apostolorū, et sancti huius cuius memoriā agimus, et omniū sanctorū supplicationibus*

Missa Chrisost.

Chrysostō desierethintercessiō of Sainctes ād praieth for the dead.

C *visita nos Deus, et memor esto omniū in Domino dormientiū, in spe resurrectionis vitæ æternæ ac requiem præsta eis, vbi lumen vultus tui superintendit.* By the supplicaciō or praiers of S. Iohn the Baptiste the prophet and forerunner, ād of the holie ād mostfamouse Apostles, ād of this Sainct whose memorie we make, o God viset vs, ād be mindfull of all that sleape in our Lord, in hope of the resurrectiō of euerlasting life, ād geue thē rest wher the light of thy coūtenance ouerlooketh all. As in the other, so in Chrysostōs Masse yowe see oblaciō made for the dead, yowe see praier made for thē to obtein thē rest, ād that also by the intercessiō of Sainctes. By this then ye maie perceaue the maliciouse and slaunderouse railing of the Aduers. againft the Church, who saieth that the Papistes haue made the Masse a sacrifice for the quicke ād the dead, to the entēt they might make their merchandise therwith, and so robbing the people fill their purseis, with soule pence. But ye see yt not inuēted of the Papistes as the Ad-uersarie termeth the catholike Chrystiās, but ye see yt vsed ād practised of the Apostles and the holie Fathers in their Masses, and so deliuered to vs.

Aug. li. de heres. Aerius accōpted an heretike denieng the sacrifice of the Masse to auail the dead.

D Now as we haue seen the practise of the aunciēt Church, for the doing ād affirming the thing: so let vs see the practise of the same for deniēg ād refusing the thing. S. Augustine, and before him *Ephiphanius*, declare that ther was one called, *Aerius*, who as our newe masters doe nowe a daies, denied the sacrifice of the Masse to be profitable to the dead, for the whiche and

certain other doctrines,he was of the holie learned Fathers nombred amõg **E**
heretiques,and of the Church so esteemed and reputed. The practise of the
Church then vpon them that denied the sacrifice of the Masse to be auailable to the dead,was to esteem them, and repute them as heretiques, and
Concil.Car　this estimacion and reputacion was before the time of *Epyphanius,*ãd S.Aug.
tha.4.

Let vs now proceade and see yet a litle farder. In the fourth Councell of
Cartage,in the which S.Augustine was one,soch a decree was made:*Qui oblationes defunctorum,aut negant ecclesiis,aut cum difficultate reddunt, tanquam egentium
necatores,excommunicĕtur,*they which denie vnto the church the oblacions of
the dead,or ells doe slacklie paie thẽ,let them as the slears of the neadie be
excommunicated.

What shal I stand longer in so plain a matter,sithen the practise declared
vnto vs by holie Cyprian,doth both teach vs that sacrificewas offred for the
dead as to ther releif, ãd that to some yt was denied,as a pain inflicted?Thus
in a certain epistle we finde this practise to be reported,*Episcopi antecessores nostri religiosè cõsiderantes,&salubriter prouidẽtes censuerũt ne quis frater excedẽs,ad tutelã
Gip. li.*　*vel curam clericũ nominaret.Ac si quis hoc fecisset,non offerretur pro eo,nec sacrificium pro* **F**
epist.9.　*dormitione eius celebraretur.Neque enim ad altare Dei meretur nominari in sacerdotum
prece,qui ab altari sacerdotes,& ministros suos leuitas auocare voluit.Et ideo Victor,cùm
contra formam nuperin concilio à sacerdotibus datã, Geminiũ Faustinum ausus sit actorem
constituere,non est quo pro dormitione eius apud vos fiat oblatio,aut deprecatio aliqua
nomine eius in ecclesia frequentetur, vt sacerdotũ decretum religiosè, & necessariè factum,
seruetur à nobis.*The Bishoppes our predecessours,godlie considering and hol-
If yt be the　somlie prouiding,made a decre,that no brother departing this life should ap-
anltar of　poincte anie one of the cleargie to be his Gardiã.And if anie did so,neither
God what　shoulde oblacion be made for him,nor sacrifice celebrated for his death.Nei-
a wicked de　ther doth he deserue to be named in the praier of the preistes at the *Aultar,
de ys yt to*　*of God,*that wold call awaie the mynisters,the preistes and Deacons from the
throwthem　aultar.And therfor sithen *Victor*contrarie to the order of late geuen oute by
downe?　the preistes in the counsell,hath ben so bolde to cõstitute *Geminius Faustinus,*
the preist his Gardian,their ought not among yowe,anie oblacion to be made for his death,or that anie praier should be vsed in the Church in his name
that the decree of the preistes godlie and necessarely made maie be kept of **G**
vs.Thus moch S.Cyprian.

The denial　Of whom as we maie learn the decree and practise of the Church before
of praier for　his time,that soch as made preistes their Gardians, for the punishment of
the dead of　their so doing,ther should neither sacrifice nor praier be doen or made for
fending　them in the Church after their death:so maie we verie well perceaue, that
proueth the　for them that died in the obedience of the Church ther was both sacrifice
vse therof　and praier offred and made for them at their burialls, and so after their
to be good.　deaths were remembred in the praiers of the preistes. Bi the same also are we
instructed that as the deniall of oblacion,sacrifice and praier was to the pain
of them that were dead:so was the doing of the same to the emolument releif and profitte of them that were dead.

What shall I nede after so manie practises of the holie Apostles, of the pri-
Amb. ad　mitiue Church,and of the Church in the time of the auncient Fathers to set
Faustin.　furth the practise of the Church in the time of S.Ambrose, who writing an
epistle of cõforth to*Faustinus,*for the death of his sister saieth,that he thinketh
Li.9.Cõfes　her not so moch to be lamented,as with praiers to be releiued : not moche **H**
ca.13.　to be made sad with tears, but raither with oblacions to be commended
to God?Or of S.Augustine,whose mother(as before ys saied)desiered in her
　　　　　　　　　　　　　　　　　　　　　　　　　　　　　death

A death bedde tobe remembred at the Aultar, which ys, ther to be praied for? whiche her doing being recited of S. Auguſtine to her immortall laude, and praiſe, well proueth the thing to be according to the order of the church that then was, and alſo that to deſire to be praied for after death ys well doē and woorhie of praiſe. And if they be woorthie of praiſe that ſo deſire, what be they that deſire not to be praied for, or they that deride the pra ier for the dead, or take awaie the order of praing for them? yt ys eaſie to iudge.

The practiſe of the churche in this matter being ſo farre brought furth as to the time of S. Auguſtine, I ſhall therin nowe no farder encombre the rea der, but ſtaing vpon a place or two of the ſame S. Auguſtin, end this chapter In one place thus he ſaieth: *Orationibus verò ſanctæ Eccleſiæ, & ſacrificio ſalutari, & eleemoſinis quæ pro eorum ſpiritibus erogantur, non eſt dubitandum mortuos aduuari, vt cum eis miſericordius agatur, quam eorum peccata meruerunt. Hoc enim à patribus tra ditum vniuerſa obſeruat Eccleſia, vt pro eis qui in communione corporis & ſan guinis Chriſti defuncti ſunt, cùm ad ipſum ſacrificium loco ſuo commemorantur, oretur, ac* **B** *pro illis quoque id offerri commemoretur.* Yt ys not to be doubted, that the deade by the praiers of the holie Church, and the holſom ſacrifice, and the almoſes whiche are geuen furth for their ſoules, be holpen, that they maie be more mercifullie dealt withall then their ſinnes haue deſerued. For this as deliue red of the Fathers the vniuerſall Chuhch doeth obſerue, that for thē which are dead in the communion of the bodie and bloode of Chryſt, praiers ſhoulde be made, when at that ſacrifice they are remembred in their place, and that remembrance be made, that that ſacrrfice alſo ys offred for them. Thus he.

In this ſaing of S. Auguſtine firſt note the maner of his ſpeache. that yt ys not to be doubted but the dead are holpen with the praiers of the holie Churche, with the holſom ſacrifice, and with almoſe. Yf by the iudgement of S. Auguſtin yt ys not to be doubted, mercifull God, whie ys yt called in queſtion at the bare ſaing of a railing heretique, and not onelie called in queſtiō, but vtterlie denied, and almoſt with ſkorne hiſſed oute of the Chur che of Inglonde?

C Secondlie, note that in the time of S. Auguſtine, the vniuerſall Church did receaue this order of praing for the dead. For aſmoche as the vniuerſall churche did accept yt in S. Auguſtines time, and before *(for they receaued yt of the Fathers)* and then was the flowriſhing Church both in holineſſe of life, and excellencie of learning howe dothe nowe a peice of the church that ys in holineſſe farre vnlike, in learning moche inferioure, reiect and contemne that, that (as ys ſaied) the wholl church hath in the auncient time reuerent lie receaued?

Thirdlie, marke what was receaued, namely that bothe praier ſhoulde be made for them that died in the Communion of Chryſtes bodie and bloode, and alſo that ſacrifice ſhoulde be offred for them. This doctrine S. Auguſti ne ſaith, ſhoulde not be doubted of: yea yt ys ſo certen a doctrine that in an other place he ſaieth yt can not be denied. Thus he writeth: *Neque negandū eſt defunctorum animas pietate ſuorum viuentium releuari, cum pro eis ſacrificium media toris offertur, vel eleemoſinæ in eccleſia fiunt.* Neither ys yt to be denied, but that the ſoules of the dead are releiued by the godlineſſe of their frendes liuing, **D** when the ſacrifice of the mediatour ys offred for them, or ells almoſe dedes be doen in the Churche. Yf by the iudgement of S. Auguſtine yt be not to be denied, then yt ys a doctrine to be receaued and holden of a good chry-

Mmm iiii   ſtian.

Auguſt. de Verbis Ap. ſerm. 32.

Praier, ſa crifice, and almoſe pro fitable to the dead, deceſſing in the Coion of the bo die ād blod of Chryſte.

Praier for the dead baniſhed out of Eu glond.

The vni uerſal Chur che in and before the time of S. Auguſt. praied for the dead.

Auguſt. in Enchi. ca. 110.

Sith yt can not be deni ed but that praier for the dead ys good yt can not againbe denied. but they be nau ght that ſa ie yt ys euel

ſtian. And wicked maie he be iudged that reiecteth yt, contemneth yt, and **E**
derideth yt. The time ſhall come that ſoche ſhall deſire to be refreſhed as
did the riche glotten, but they ſhall not be heard.

But that I maie once make an ende of this matter of the value of the Maſſe to the dead, though a iuſt volnme might be made of that that therin maie
be ſaied: yet this maie ſuffice to him that will be ſatisfied. For firſt ys ſhewed
that the praier and ſacrifice for the dead, was vſed of the Apoſtles . For
proof wherof ys produced the praier of S. Iames Maſſe, and to confirme
that, ther ys added both the teſtimonie of Chryſoſtom, and alſo the maner
of praing for the dead deſcribed by S. Dioniſe S. Paules Diſciple. Afterwarde for the farder declaracion of the practiſe of the Churche the authorities
of the Maſſes , aſwell of S. Baſill as of Chryſoſtom be alleaged. And that
the continuance and generall receipt of this practiſe maie be perceaued to
be good, and the refuſall of yt to be euell, aſwell in the greke Church as in
the latin, *Epiphanius* and S. Auguſtine be brought furth as wittneſſes teſtifien
ge that *Aerius* mainteining the cōtrarie doctrine, was reputed eſteemed and
nombred among heretiques. Againſt ſoche like perſons did the Councell of **F**
Carthage publiſh a decree. And that this practiſe might moſt clerelie be per
ceaued to be frequented in the churche, the decree reported by S. Cyprian,
and the practiſe of the ſame decree by S. Cyprian vpon *Geminius Fauſtinus and*
Victor ys added, which inuinciblie prooueth praier and ſacrifice to be vſed
for the dead in the holie auncient churche.

Finallie for the proofe of the countinuāce of this ſacrifice from the Apoſt
les time to the time of S. Ambroſe and S. Auguſtine not onely mencion ys
made what S. Ambroſe wolde haue doē towarde and for *Fauſtinus* ſiſter, and
what was doen of S. Auguſtines Mother, but alſo two places be alleaged, in
the which the certentie of this matter ys ſo taught, that yt ys neither to be
denied nor doubted . And good cauſe whie we ſhoulde neither denie yt,
nor doubte of yt. For yt was receaued ād obſerued of the vniuerſal Churche.

Nowe, reader, when thowe ſeiſt this matter ſo plainlie and ſo euidentlie
teſtified to thee, that thus yt hath ben taught, thus yt hath be doen : thus yt
hath ben vſed : and yet all this not withſtanding , that the Aduerſarie rai-
geth and raileth againſt yt, and that, that by theſe Fathers was taught to be **G**
hereſie of him to be taught to be averitie : that the Apoſtles and Fathers
commaunded to be vſed, that he commaundeth to be refuſed : that the holie Fathers had in reuerence, that he hath in contempt, I ſuppoſe, thowe
neadeſt no farder aduertiſement, but when thowe ſeiſt him ſo ſtowtlie, ſo ar
rogantlie, and therfor hereticallie impugn this being ſo certen a trueth, thowe maiſt iuſtlie thinke, that he ys not ledde of the ſpiritt of trueth, who med
leth not (as ys ſaied) with falſheade, but he ys ledde with the lieng ſpiritt.
And therfor iuſt cauſe haueſt thowe to ſuſpect all that he ſaieth, and to no
parte of yt to geue creditte as ſpoken of him, but as ſpoken of other whoſe
doctrine agreeth with the doctrine of the Spiritt of trueth, taught in his
ſchoole the holie Churche.

Yſſueioined
with the
proclamer
for praier
for the de-
ad.

And nowe to ende, I will ioin this yſſue: yf either the proclamer, or anie
other of his adherentes can bring anie one catholique and auncient Father,
that ſaieth that ſoche as departe in the faith of Chryſt, are not to be praied
for, or that ſacrifice ys not to be offred for them, or that charitable almoſſe
doeth not profitt thē: Let them I ſaie bring one aunciēt and catholiq; Father **H**
ſo writing, and I dare and will not onely for my ſelf, but for aſmanie as be ca
tholique and learned, promiſſe that we will ſubſcribe.

Again

A   Again, reader I beseche thee, if thowe be learned marke : if thow be vn-learned enquire if euer anie Aduersarie in anie booke made anie argument of authoritie againſt this matter, other then mocking, lieng, denieng, and reprooving by voluntarie reaſon, and will warrant : if thowe wilt weigh and marke, thowe ſhalt finde none. Yf then in that ſide ys nothing but willfullnes: and on this ſide thowe ſeiſt graue auncient and weghtie authoritie: call vnto God for his grace, and ſtaie wher authoritie ys, and flee from thence wher noiſom wilfullnes reigneth.

THE FOVRTETH CHAP. TREACTETH OF
priuate Maſſes(as the Proclamer tearmeth them)and ſolueth his argumentes.

B   Auing nowe ſomwhat ſaied of two principall partes of the Maſ-ſe, namelie conſecracion and oblacion: ther remaineth the thirde principall parte to be ſpoaken of, whiche ys receauing. As touching that the Sacrament ſhoulde be receaued ther ys no controuerſie, betwixt vs and the Aduerſarie. For on both ſides yt ys affirmed that yt ſhoulde be receaued. But the controuerſie ys aboute the maner of receauing. Which ſtandeth in two poinctes: The one whether of neceſſitie yt muſt be receaued vnder both kindes: The other whether of neceſſitie yt muſt be receaued of mo then one at once. Of the firſt we haue ſpoken at large in the ſecond booke. Of the other ſhall be teacted here.

  In this matter, for that the catholique Church permiteth preiſtes in their common miniſtracion to receaue the bleſſed Sacrament alone, and ſeke men for their neceſſitie to doe the like, yt liketh the Proclamer (as yt hath doen other his likes)with might and main to accuſe the Church of tranſgreſ-ſion and breach of Chryſtes ordinance. And here we be all that euell ys, for our ſo doinge. Here the Proclamer triumpheth vpō vs in his own conceipt, preſſing and cruſhinge vs, as he ſuppſeth, euen to the grownde, ſo lowe,

C that he thinketh we ſhall neuer be able to ſtand on foote again againſt him, and hath (as to him appeareth) ſo ſtopped our mouthes with ſcriptures and the practiſe of the primitiue Churche, and the authorities of auncient Fathers, that we ſhall likewiſe neuer be able to open our mouthes againſt him. But as Horace ſaieth : *Parturiunt montes, naſcetur ridiculus mus* : ſo here be great bragges, but we ſhall haue but colde roſte : here ys a great cowntenance, but ſmall ys the force.

  Chryſte (ſaieth he) miniſtred not to one alone, but to all the twelue Apoſtles. Paule commaunded that one ſhoulde tarie and wait for an other, *Inuicem expectate.* S. Clement willed that ſo manie hoſtes ſhoulde be offred vpon the Aultar, as might be ſufficient for the people, S. Dioniſe ſaieth that the preiſt when he had receaued himſelf and deliuered the holie communion to all the people, geueth God thankes and maketh an ende of the miſteries. *Iuſtinus* the holie Martir ſaieth that in his time the Deacon exhorted the people that they will be partakers of thoſe thinges that be laied furth before the S. Ambroſe rebuketh his people that were then growen necligent in receauing the lordes ſupper, and vſed to excuſe the matter for that they thought

D them ſelues not woorthie, ſaing to them : *Yf thowe be not woorthie euery daie, thē art thowe not woorthie once in a yeare.* And again S. Ambroſe expownding theſe woordes of S. Paule: *Alius alium expectate,* writeth thus : He commaunded them to tarie one for an other, that the oblacion of manie maie be celebra-ted

The Prtclamer his arguments againſt ſole receauing.

E

ted together, and so be ministred vnto them all. S. Hierom, S. Augustine, and the ecclesiasticall historie, wittnesse, that vntill that time comonlie euery where, but speciallie in Rome, the people vsed to comunicate euery daie. *Leo* wrote to *Dioscorus* Bishoppe of *Alexandria*, and willed him, that wher the churche was not able to receaue all the people to comunicate together, that the preist shoulde ministre two or three communions on one daie, that as the people came in, and had once filled the Churche: so they shoulde recea ue the communion, and afterwarde geue place to other. S. Hierom writing vpon the elementh chapter of S. Paules first epistle to the Corinthians saieth that the supper of the Lorde muste be common to all the people. For Chryste gaue his Sacramentes to all his Disciples that were present. These be the Proclamers scriptures, these be his Doctours, these be his authorities.

And nowe, gentle Reader, weigh with one, what force these authorities haue, to proue that he intendeth. His intent ys to prooue that of necessitie ther must be mo communicantes then one at euery place and time, wher and when yt happeneth Masse to be saied. Nowe these places prooue no soche necessitie, onelie they prooue that the Sacrament in the beginning was ministred to the people, that were disposed to receaue, and therby he maie prooue that manie maie receaue, and that the Sacrament ought to be comon to all that will orderlie desire to receaue. And that yt can not be denied to soche as so require yt, bicause Chryste hath instituted yt be a comon Sacrament of all his faithfull, that be meet and able to receaue yt, to be receaued, as he hath also instituted Baptisme. For these sacramentes were not instituted for Kinges, Princes, Bishopps and the mightie of the earth onlie, but answearablie to their figures, for all people. For as all the Iewes, as well high as lowe, riche and poore did all (as S. Paule saieth) passe through

F

the Read Sea, and all did eate of one meat and all drinke of one drinke: so (as Chrysostom saieth) yt ys in the churche. *Non aliud quidem corpus diues, aliud vero pauper, neque alium quidem sanguinem ille, alium autem iste. Sic & tunc, non aliud accipiebat quidem diues Manna, aliud vero pauper, neque alterius fontis iste participes erat, alterius vero indigentoris illle.* For so yt ys nowe in the Churche. For he riche man receaueth not one bodie, a poore man an other, neither he one maner of bloode, and this man an other. So also then the riche man did not eate of one Manna and the poore man of an other, neither of one fowntain was this man partaker, and of a woorse the other man. So these two sacramentes, I saie, are common to all, bothe Baptisme, and the Sacrament of Chry stes bodie and bloode·

G

And to this pourpose saied S. Hierom, wher the Proclamer allcageth him, that the supper of our lorde must be common to all people. For Chryst ga ue his sacramentes equallie to all his Disciples, that were present, and not to the pourpose that the Proclamer alleageth yt, whiche ye maie perceaue by this woorde (*equallie*) wherby ys signified that Chryst gaue his bodie and bloode as well to the inferiour Apostles, as to the higher, and so equallie to all.

And here note that the proclamer in his translacion left oute this woorde equallie, and saied thus: that Chryst gaue his sacramentes to all his disci ples that were present, minding by that phrase of woordes to make yt appea re that all that be present must communicate, whiche was not saincte Hie roms minde, but raither after the minde of S. Paule to shewe that both the supper of the riche, and the Sacrament of Chryste shoulde be common to all that were present equallie, as Chryst made his supper of the paschall lambe

H

and

A and the supper of his bodie blood common to all his Disciples, equallie geuing yt as well to the lower, as to the higher. But soche ys the sleight of this man.

But to returne: Baptisme ys a common sacrament for all, Nowe shall we saie that we maie not ministre yt to one alone, but to manie at once? Naie: the communitie of yt standeth well if all receaue yt, though but one at once receaue yt. But yowe vrge and saie, that he bringeth the practise of the primitiue and auncient Churche, that yt was receaued of manie. To this first I saie that he maie doe the like for the ministracion of the sacrament of Baptisme. Yt ys knowen to all that be learned, that ther were in the primitiue Churche two speciall assigned times for Baptisme: Easter and whitsontide, at which times not one alone, but manie were baptised, and commonlie in that time Baptisme was ministred to manie, and not to one alone. But yet no good argument can of that be deduced that Baptisme ys not to be ministred, but to manie together, and not to one alone. So though he bring manie practises of the Church, that manie did receaue the sacrament together,

B yet yt prooueth not that yt can not be receaued of one alone at one time. For though the Sacrament be common, yt nothing hindereth the communitie of yt (when all maie and doe receaue yt) though but one at one time doe recaue yt. And so receaued yt maie verie well be called, and ys in dede a communion, forasmoche as one thing ys made common to all, and one thing ys receaued of all, and in that one thing all the receauers being manie be made one. And therfor dothe the Proclamer against all trewth call the Masse, wher one alone doeth receaue, a priuate Masse. For the thing ther receaued ys yt, by which all we be made one.

Again I saie, these allegacions prooue well the deuocion and godlie zeale of the people in the primitiue churche, whiche I wish were like nowe in our people, but they prooue no lawe. For if yt had ben a lawe that the people as often as Masse was saied, shoulde communicate, Fabianus the nineteth Bishoppe of Rome and holie Martir, who liued aboute the yeare of our Lorde two hundreth fourtie and two, and therfor in the pure time, wolde not haue made a lawe, that the people shoulde receaue the Sacrament at the

C leest thrice in a yeare, that was, at Easter, Whitsontide and Chrystenmasse. And yet after this the deuocion of people decaing, and waxing colder and colder, that lawe was remitted, and a newe decree made, that the people shoulde once in the year, at Easter, receaue the Sacrament, whiche ys yet obserued.

Nowe I wolde aske of the Proclaimer whether holie Fabian when he ordeined that the people shoulde communicate thrice in the yeare, ment that the preist also shoulde saie Masse but thrice in the yeare. And whē the other decree was made, that they shoulde receaue once in the yeare, whether yt was ment that the preist shoulde also saie Masse but once in the yeare: yf he saie yt was so ment, the practise of the churche prooueth the contrarie. For Chrysostom saieth: *Nonne per singulos dies offerimus? offerimus quidem, sed ad recordationem facientes mortis eius.* Doe we not euerie daie (saieth he) make oblacion? we make oblacion in dede, but doing yt to the remembrance of his death. And who doubteth but the holie fathers of the latin Churche did the like?

D yf he saie that he ment not but that the preist might oftener saie Masse, then yt ys manifest that he ment that the preist might saie Masse without communicantes. For none by lawe, but preistes, were bownde oftener to receaue then thrice in the yeare, and afterwards once in the yeare. Thus maie ye

percea-

perceaue, that all thefe alleadged authorities prooue not that the preift maie not, if he be difpofed, receaue alone, when none of the people will but they fhewe vs the godlie deuocion of the people in thofe daies (as ys faied) and the diligence of holie Bifhoppes and preiftes in rebuking the flackeneffe of the people in receauing, wherunto ferueth the place of S. Ambrofe alleaged by the Proclamer, and not to that he maketh the cowntenance of.

Likewife he alleageth againft the order of the Churche the decree of that holie man and auncient Father *Leo* Bifhoppe of Rome, But howe fincerelie and truelie I fhall caufe thee to vnderftande, when I haue produced the verie woordes of the fame *Leo* and the woordes of the Proclamer, and conferred them together. Thefe be the woordes of the Proclamer: *Leo writing vn to Diofcorus the Bifhoppe of Alexandria, gaue him this aduife, that when the church was fo litle, that yt was not able to receaue all the wholl people to communicate together, then the preift fhoulde miniftre two or three communions in one daie, that as the people came in and had once filled the churche fo they fhoulde receaue the communion, and after geue place to other.* Thus the Proclamer.

In reporting of this authour firft note this in the Proclamer, that alleadging S. *Clement*, *Dionife.* *Iuftine*, *Ambrofe* and *Hierom* in this matter, he alleadgeth them in the latin tonge as being bolde by fleight to make them appeare to his hearer or reader, that they made fomwhat for his caufe and pourpofe. And being defieroufe to haue a nombre of authours for the better commendacion of his matter, he wolde alfo alleage *Leo*. But here he folowed his auncient Father Cranmer, who alleaging certain Authours, alleadged foche as he might with fome cowntenance wreft, in the latin tonge: other, whiche he coulde not well wreft he wolde reporte as yt pleafed him in the inglifh toung, but fo as apparantlie they fhoulde feme to be of his fide, when in dede they were alltogether againft him Euen fo this man, not daring for verie fhame, to alleage *Leo*, with his owne woordes, reporteth him as he wolde haue had him to faie, and not as he faied in dede. The verie woordes of leo be thefe: *Vt autem in omnibus obferuantia noftra concordet, illud quoque volumus cuftodiri, vt quum folemnior feftiuitas conuentum populi numerofioris indixerit, & ad eam tanta multitudo conuenerit quam recipere bafilica fimul vna non poßit, facrificii oblatio indubitanter iteretur, ne his tantùm admißis ad hanc deuotionem, qui primi aduenerint, videantur hi, qui poftmodum confluxerint non recepti, cùm plenum pietatis atque rationis fit, vt quoties bafilicam, in qua agitur, præfentia nonæ plebis impleuerit, toties facrificium fubfequens offeratur. Neceffe eft autem vt quædam pars populi fua deuotione priuetur, fi vnius tatùm Miffæ ordine feruato, facrificium offerre non poßint, nifi qui prima diei parte conuenerint. Studiofè ergo dilectionem tuã & familiariter admonemus, vt quod noftræ confuetudini, ex forma paternæ traditionis infedit, tua quoque cura non necligat, vt per omnia nobis & fide, & actibus congruamus.* That our religion maie in all thinges agree we will that this be kept, that when a folemne feaft fhall caufe a great nombre of people to come together, and to that folemne feaft fo great a multitude fhall come, as one Church can not receaue at once, that the oblation of the facrifice be without all feare doen again, leeft thefe whiche came firft being admitted to this feruice, they that came afterwarde maie feme not to be receaued, fithe yt ys right godlie and reafonable, that as often as the churche wher the feruice ys doen ys replenifhed with a newe people, fo often the facrifice folowing be celebrated. Yt muft nedes be that fome parte of the people fhall be hindered of their deuocion, if the order of faing of one Maffe being kept, none can offre facrifice, but they whiche come together in the firft

Note this falfe tranf-lacion of M. Iuell.

A common fleight of heretiques to alleage the fathers wher they maie wreft them or els to falfifie them.

Leo epla 79. ad Diof coru.

In ftead of oblacion of facrifice at Maffe the proclamer hath comu nicate and Communio and for fo often he hath twice or thrice.

A firſt parte of the daie. Diligentlie therfor and familiarlie we aduertiſe yowr louing gentleneſſe, that the thing which hath remained in our cuſtome, by forme of tradicion of our Fathers, thy care wolde not neclect, that in all thinges, bothe in faith and doinges we maie among our ſelues conſent and agree.

Theſe be the verie woordes of _Leo._ Thys ys the place which the Proclamer taketh in hande to reporte. Iudge now I ſaie, gentle Reader, whether he hath truelie reported him or no. And firſt wher he alleadged _Leo_, to prooue his communion, vieue well, I praie thee, the authour and obſerue diligentlie yf ther be in him anie one woorde of communion or communicantes, and thowe ſhalt perceaue that ther ys no mencion made therof. What trueth then ys to be thought either in the man, or in the cauſe that he defendeth, when to maintein yt, he ys fain to falſifie the authours that he alleageth? Ys yt not lamentable to ſee his ſhameleſſe boldeneſſe that he wolde wittinglie vtter in an honorable audiéce, and alſo publiſh the ſame in printe to an wholl realme that he knewe to be falſe and clean otherwiſe, then was the in-

B tent or minde of the authour which he alleaged? That yt was not the minde of the authour thowe ſhalt eaſilie perceaue: For firſt, wher the Proclamer vſeth theſe woordes communicate and communion, The authour hath theſe woordes, _the oblacion of the ſacrifice, and the ſacrifice._ Nowe bicauſe the Proclamer hateth this woorde ſacrifice as a ſcorpion, as being applied to the holie Sacramét of Chryſtes bodie and blood, therfor to eaſe his maliciouſe affection, and to delude his hearers and readers, yt liked his Chryſtian ſinceritie, properlie tearmed hereticall malignitie, to corrupt and falſifie the authour, and reporte ſoche matter to be in him, as ther ys in dede no woorde toward yt in him, I mene to that ſenſe and vnderſtanding.

Again thowe ſeiſt that in all that ſermon (yf yt be woorthie of that name) his cheifeſt pourpoſe ys to inueigh againſt that holie myniſtracion, whiche ys called the Maſſe in ſo moch that he ſaieth that this name, _Maſſe_, was not in vſe manie years after Chryſt, which ys before improoued, yet in this authour _Leo_ euen in this place: whiche he alleaged, ther ys expreſſe and liuelie mencion made of the Maſſe, and he calleth yt Maſſe, that thys

C man calleth Communion. And theſe twoo woordes, _ſacrifice_ and _Maſſe_, vſed of this authour, cauſed (as I haue ſaied) thys man to falſifie the authour, ſo that he durſt not alleadge him as he wrote, but as yt might ſerue to helpe hys wicked cauſe. To ende this note of the falſifieng of this authour by this Proclamer, this alſo ys to be obſerued and marked, howe God ſuffreth Sathan and his Diſciples to be blinded, that they ſhall bring furth and alleadge places, whiche being well weighed, and taken as they lie according to the minde of the authour, ſhall not onely ouerthrowe their matter (as this authour in teſtifieng both ſacrifice and Maſſe) but ſhall alſo geue and myniſtre occaſion, that theyr falſhead, their corruption of authours, their blinding of the people, ſhall be perceaued, as nowe allreadie yt hath ben perceaued in ſainct Hierom, and this authour, and ſhall more hereafter in thys matter.

But the Proclamer proceadeth and prooueth by the Maſſe booke, that ther ſhoulde be a Communion, bicauſe the preiſt ſaieth, _oremus_,

D _Let vs praie._ I ſee this man wolde plaie ſmal game raither then he will ſet out, he wolde content himſelf with ſome ſlender ſhewe or countenaunce

Marginal notes:

See here the impudencie of the Proclamer.

See here his falſe ſleight.

Sacrifice and Maſſe cauſe the Proclamer to falſifie Leo.

of proofe,raither then mainteining an euell matter to feem to be deftitute E
of all proofe.I praier thee(good reader)weigh with me what proof ys yt of
the communion of the Sacrament that the preift faieth (*oremus*) *Let vs praie*?
what dependance ys ther of that woorde to proue the communion of the

Sacrament?Yf he can by that woorde prooue the communion of the Sacra-
ment:he maie doe the like in the Sacrament of Baptifme,and in other facra
mentes alfo,for ther the preift faieth (*Oremus*)*Let vs praie*.Yf by yt he had trauailed to proue a communion in praier, he had doen right, but to abufe yt
to prooue the necefsitie of the Communion of the Sacrament in foch forte
as he meneth,yt ys raither a declaracion of his malice againft the churche,
then anie proofe of his pourpofe.

That ther ys a Communion in praier,the other woordes of the preift,
whiche he alfo alleageth for hys pourpofe , doe manifeftlie declare.

The preift (faieth he) *faieth : The Lorde be with yowe , and the people aun-*
fwer : And with thie fpirit . Doe ye not fee here howe the preift and
the people ioin themfelues together , one praing for the other ? Whiche
maner of Communion ys alfo liuelie fettfurth by that that he after- F
warde produceth oute of the order of the Maffe . *The preift* (faieth
he)*turneth him to the people and faieth : Orate pro me fratres , & forores.*
Praie for me brothers and fifters. Here(as before ye haue perceaued and fhall
hereafter perceaue)he vfeth a fleight,he durft not for fhame tell yowe , why
the preift defiereth the people to praie for him, but as traitours clippe the
kinges coin,and deceaue the people , fo he clippeth manie of the places

whiche he alleageth to deceaue gods people . But that his falfhead
maie be perceaued,and the caufe knowen why the preift defiereth the people to praie for him,I fhall laie before yowr eies the wholl praier . Thus he
praieth . *Orate fratres & forores pro me , vt meum pariter & veftrum acceptum fit*
omnipotenti Deo facrificium: Whiche ys thus moche to faic in englifh : Praie
for me brothers and fifters,that my facrifice and yowr maie be accepted of

our Lord God.
Se ye now his fleight?Ys here anie praier for the communion whiche he
intendeth?Doe thefe woordes proue that the preift can not receaue alone?
Ys ther anie mencion made here of that his communion ? Doe ye not per- G
ceaue that with two or three woordes he wolde blere yowe eyes, and (as
the inglifh prouerbe ys)make yowe beleue that the Moone ys made of a
green cheefe ? The defire of the preift ys not,that all they that be prefent
wolde receaue the Communion:but that they wil praie that their common
facrifice maie be acceptable to God. This with the bringing in of two or
three woordes,wolde this man craftelie haue concealed,and fuppreffed, being (as I fuppofe)afhamed,and grudged in confcience to letyowe know the
verie thing required to be praied for,which ys the acceptacion of the facrifice,which facrifice he and his complices doe wickedlie denie.

Thus ye fee that he wolde claime helpe of the Maffe booke,which in dede
doeth him no other helpe but open his fhame.Yt doeth vs thus moch helpe,
that hereby we learn two *Communions*:The firft ys of praier:the fecond of fa-
crifice.For in thefe two all that be faithfullie and deuoutlie prefent, lifting
vppe their heartes to God,and ioining with the preift in godlie affection, be
communicantes:And fo yt commeth to paffe,that both the praier and the
facrifice made and offred by the preift, as by the common mynifter of the H
Church,ys common to all the people of gods church.

I will not ftand vppon this being fo plain, but leaue yt to the farder
confide-

A consideracon of the Reader, and come to his conclusion of the Masse booke wher he saieth shus: *And to conclude the preist, by his owne Masse booke ys bidden to saie these woordes immediatelie after the Agnus Dei.* Hæc sacrosancta commixtio & con- *The Procl.* secratio corporis & sanguinis Domini nostri Iesu Christi fiat mihi & omnibus sumentibus salus mentis & corporis. That ys to saie: This commixtion and consecracion of the bodie and blood of our Lorde Iesus Chryst be vnto me and to all that receaue yt, health of bodie and soule.

I perceaue this man repeth his profession. For yt ys apperteining to meof his calling either to diminish and take awaie, or to adde and put to somwhat *The An-* from or to most of the sentences that they alleage. For where before he cutt *swer.* of from the places which he alleaged here he putteth to For wher the Masse booke hath but these woordes. Hæc sacrosancta commixtio corporis & sanguinis, &c. He putteth in this woorde (*consecratio*) which the booke hath not. But o-uerpassing yt, let vs see the force of the argument that he maketh oute of our owne Masse booke (as he tearmeth yt) and verie well. For in dede yt ys our

B booke, that abide and remain in the catholique Church, not his, that hath cutte himself of, from yt, and ys become a cast awaie. But our Lord chaunge his minde, that the lost shepe maie be fownde and brought home to the fol-de again.

The praier ys that the comixtion of the bodie and blood of Chryst maie be to the preist, and to all that receaue, health of bodie and soule. Vnderstad that the preist ys the common mynister of the Church, wherfor doing the co- *The comon* mon mynistracion he comonlie praieth for all that doe receaue generally, he *praier of* stricteth not his praier for a fewe, neither doeth he limitte yt, or bownde yt *the Church* withtime and place, but he leaueth yt comon, and vttereth yt with an vniuer *ys not for* sall. He praieth not that the bodie and bloode of Chryst maie be health of *one angle,* soule and bodie to the onely that receaue with him at that time and in that *but for the* place (which ys the thing the Proclamer laboureth to proue (but in vain) *wholl vni-* but he praieth for all that receaue indifferenlie either in that place and time, *uersall* or anie other. Whether yt be now or at anie other time, in that place, or in a- *Church* nie other place in Fraunce, or in Italie, in Spain or in Germauie in Englodor

C in Hierusalem, whersoeuer the catholique Church ys, and the Sacrament ca tholiquelie receaued.

But be yt that the preist had praied with limitacio of time ad place, ad de-siered that yt might be halth of soule and bodie to all that receaue with him in that place and time, what offence should the preist comitte, yf when none wolde receaue with him, he receaued alone? or howe can the Proclamer pro ue a necessitie by yt, that neades ther must be mo then the preist? or that at that time and place the preist can not receaue alone? Yf the Church charita-blie wishing that some people shoulde receaue the holie Sacrament withthe preist, had made soch a praier, coulde the Proclamer turne this charitie to a necessitie? Will he turne the charitie of the Church wishing vertue, godlines se, and deuocion in the people to a necessitie, that bicause the people wil not vse this of necessitie the preist shall not? Ys this good learning? Ys this hys good doctrine ys this his holie religion? Yt ys as moch to saiethat yf the peo ple waxe colde in deuocio, so shall the preist to: Yf the people slacke their de uocion, so shall the preist to: yf the people neclect the seruice of God, so shall

D the preist to. Yf the people omitte to rendre most humble thankes to God and our Sauiour Iesus Chryst for our redemption, so shall the preist to. Finallie if the people will but twice or thrice in the yeare celebrate that sole ne memorie of Chrysts passio and death as (the more pitie yt ys) the most of

them doe yt not fo often,no more fhal the preift alfo.Thus fhall yt come to   **E**
paffe that the deuociō ād duetie of the preift,fhall hang vpon the will of the
people.Thus the preiftes that fhould be the falte of the earth,the light ofthe
woorlde,whofe light fhould fo fhine before men,that they feing their good
workes,might glorifie their Father which ys in heauen,fhall neither be falt,

Math. 5.
light,nor geuers of good exāple to prouoke them to doe the memoriall of
Chryftes death,but when the people will.Yt ys a ftraunge doctrine, that yf
the people will not ferue God,the preift fhall not.But who ys he that wife ys
that feeth not the vanitie of yt,and whether yt tendeth?Hitherto, I truft ye

*As odioufe
as Popes be
to Proteſtā
ts they can
alleage
theirdecres
wher they
thinke
good.*
perceaue that how great fo euer the countenaunce was made by thefe allegacions before alleadged,that yet the force ys verie fmall.

But nowe come the great argumentes, nowe come they, which can not
be auoided(*as the Proclamer fuppofeth*)fo great ys the force of them.Where to
his places before alleadged I faied and doe faie,they are raither examples of
vertue for the people,and not lawes of necefsitie for the preift,nowe he produceth lawes,as the Canons of the Apoftles,and the decrees of Bifhoppes **F**
of Rome,which how odible foeuer they be,and haue ben to this Proclamer
and his complices:yet nowe in this matter,they are fain to praie aide of thē.
Firft he alleageth a Canon of the Apoftles in this forte.*Fideles qui ecclefiam in-*

Canon. 19.
See this Ca
nō cut of in
the mid
deſt.
*grediuntur,& fcripturas audiunt,& Communionem fanctam non recipiunt, tanquàm ec-
clefiaſticæ pacis perturbatores à Communione arceantur.*Soch Chryftian men as come
to the church and heare the fcriptures, ād doe not receaue the holie commu
nion,let them be excommunicated,as men that difquiet the Church.

In the alleaging of this Canon he kepeth his profefsion as he did in other
by him before alleaged,that ys to cutte them of,and to mangle foch places
as he alleageth,and not to bring thē wholl as they lie,wherof,reader, I make
thee iudge.This ys the Canon.*Omnes fideles,qui conueniunt in folemnibus facris ad
ecclefiam,fcripturas Apoſtolorum,& Euangelium audiant.Qui autem non perfeuerarint
in oratione vfque miſſa peragitur,nec fanctam Communionem percipiunt,velut inquietudi-
nes ecclefiæ mouentes,conuenit communione priuari.*All the Chryftian men that in the
folemne feruice come together to the Church let them heare the fcriptures
of the Apoftles and the Gofpell.And foche as continue not in praier vntill **G**
Maffe be all doen,nor doe receaue the holie Communion , yt ys meet that
they be excommunicated , as foch as moue difquietneffe to the Church.

*The Pro-
clamer al-
leaging
this Canō
cheiflie
againſt the
Maſſe lea-
ueth oute
the woorde
Maſſe in
the fame.*
Now conferre this with that he hath alleaged,and ye fhall perceaue that
he hath varied in diuerfe poinctes.But of thofe I will touch but one. In this
fermon he cheiflie bendeth himfelf to impugn the Maffe,wherin(malice blin
ding his heart) he findeth by his iudgement manie horrible faultes , of the
which he fpeciallie chofeth fower,againft the which with might and main,
that ys to faic,with as moch falfhead as he can,he doeth inueigh.And amōg
thefe foure,as ye perceaue,he trauaileth very fore againft that,that the preift
fhoulde receaue alone.And to improue that receipt he pretendeth that thys
Canon did mightilie make for him.But when he redde yt and fawe in the fa
me Canon mencion made of the Maffe,which he impugneth,that the people fhould continue in praier vntill yt were all doen , for hindering of hys
caufe,though his cōfcience were touched,he vfed his cōmon fleight,and for
fhame durft not fpeake the Canō as yt laie,ād fo with more fhame wrote yt,
ād caufed yt to be printed,that all mē might fee ād perceaue his finceritie,ād **H**
true dealing in alleaging the Fathers and writers , which ys (as ye perceaue)
to corrupt them,to falfifie thē,and to leaue oute,ād cutte of what liketh him.

But to aunfwer that part of the Canon,that he alleageth , as fo ftronglie
ma-

A making for him: I saie firſt that he doeth myſtake yt and miſunderſtand yt. For the Canon ys not made for the good catholique people that doe communicate with ail good Chryſtians in praier, and when deuocion ſerueth them in the receipt of the holy Sacramēt, but yt ys made againſt licenciouſe and yet diſſembling heretiques and ſchiſmatiques, who then (as manie haue of late doen) came to the Church among good Chryſtiãs, ãd yet being there wolde neither cōmunicate with them in praier, neither in the receipt of the holie Sacrament. Againſt ſoch (I ſaie) as wolde neither in praier, nor in Sacrament communicate with the good Chryſtians, that theie ſhould be excommunicated, was the Canon made.

The true mening of the Apoſtles Canon miſunderſtanded by the Proclamer.

And, Reader, I doe not feign this vnderſtanding of my own head, I haue authoritie right good for me, that ys right auncient, which ys the Councell of Antioche, which Councell hauing the ſame Canon allmoſt woord for woord expowndeth yt to the ſame vnderſtanding that I haue. Theſe be the woords of the Councell. *Omnes qui ingrediuutur ecclēſiā Dei, & ſcripturas ſacras audiunt, nec*

Concil. Antioch.

B *communicant in oratione cùm populo, ſed pro quadā intēperantia ſe à perceptione ſanctæ cōmunionis auertunt, ij de eccleſia remoueantur, donec per confeſſionē pœnitentiæ fructus oſtendant, & precibus indulgentiā conſequantur, Cum excōmunicatis autē non licet communicare, nec cum ijs, qui per domos conueniunt deuitantes orationes eccleſiæ, ſimul orandū eſt.* Al that come to the Church of God, and heare the holie ſcriptures, and doe not cōmunicate with the people in praier, but for a certain wantonneſſe doe auerte thē ſelues frō the receipt of the holie communion, let theſe men be remoued frō the church, vntill by confeſſiō they ſhewe the fruictes of penaunce, and through praiers doe obtein pardon. With excōmunicate perſons yt ys not lawfull to communicate, neither maie we praie with ſoch as go from houſe to houſe ſhunning the praiers of the Church.

The canon was made againſt wãton heretikes ãd Schiſmatiques, whocoming to the churche wolde not for a ſingularitie cōmunicatei ther in praier or in ſacrament with the faithfull.

This ys the Canon of the Councell of Antioche, which ye ſee to be the verie ſame, and all one with the Canon of the Apoſtles, or raither the expoſitiō of yt. In the whiche yt ys plain to perceaue that yt was ſpoken againſt ſoche as were ſingular and wanton in their own conceiptes, diſdeining to cōmunicate with the people of God, either in praier, or in the receipt of the Sacram. but onelie they wolde come to the church to heare the ſcriptures redde. To C meet with ſoch as will not praie with the Church, the Canō forbiddeth the catholique perſon to praie with thē. By this then ye maie perceaue that the Canō ys to be vnderſtãded of thē that both refuſed to cōmunicate with the faithfull people in praier and ſacrament, vpon wantō ſingularitie as contemning the receaued ordre of the Church, and as Sciſmatiques and heretiques gadded from houſe to houſe, and fled the Church: and not of good Chryſtiã people that abſtein not for anie ſoch pourpoſe.

Secōdarelie to ſaie, yf the Proclamer wil not admitte or alow this true vnderſtãding, grownded (as yowe perceaue) vpō authoritie, but cleaue to hys falſe vnderſtãding of the Canō, grownded vpō his onelie phantaſie, what maketh the Canō ſo vnderſtãded, either againſt the Maſſe, or againſt the Churche, or againſt the preiſt? What one woord findeth he in this Canō that proueth the Maſſe to be naught, if the people doe not cōmunicate? By what parte of the Canō cã he reprehēd the Church, if the whol cōgregaciō receaue not? which peice of the Canō doeth prohibitt the preiſt to receaue alone yf none other deſire to receaue with him? Weigh wel the Canō ãd ye ſhall perceaue euen D after his own vnderſtãding, that ther ys a lawe of correctiō for the people, if they wil not receaue with the preiſt: but ther ys no woord againſt the preiſt, if he receaue without the people. The law ys againſt the ſlackneſſe of the peo

The Canon of the Apoſtles forbideth notthe preiſt to receaue alone

and not againſt the godlie deuocion of the preiſt. Thus his greateſt argument being ſo eaſilie ſolued, and his crafte in the alleaging of the ſame detected, as with more eaſie we maie ſolue the other: ſo ſhall we therin perceaue his more falſheade.

Calixtus (ſaieth he) *Biſhoppe of Rome not long after the Apoſtles time geueth oute the like commaundement, in the ſame behalf. His woordes be theſe: Peracta conſecratione omnes communicent, qui noluerint eccleſiaſticis carere liminibus. Sic enim Apoſtoli ſtatuerunt, & ſancta Romana tenet eccleſia. That ys (ſaieth he) when the conſecracion ys doen, let euerie man receaue the Communion, vnleſſe he will be put of from the entrie of the Church. For this thing haue the Apoſtles ordeined, and the holie church of Rome continueth the ſame.*

The decree of Anacletus abuſed. by the Proclamer.

In this alleaged place be mo vntrueths then one vſed by the Proclamer. Firſt he doeth father yt vpon *Calixtus*, wher in dede yt ys the decree of *Anacletus*. But this ys not ſo great a matter. I wolde eaſelie pardon that fault, yf ther were no woorſe in him. But he committeth two great faultes here beſides that. For he doeth both diſtort abuſe and wreſt the place, and alſo (as he hath doen diuerſe other) he doeth mutilate yt, and cutte yt of by the knees (aswe ſaie) and bringeth yt not whollie as yt lieth. I will therfor bring the whol place, that yowe maie both perceaue, how moch he hath of a deueliſh pourpoſe left oute, and alſo plainlie ſee howe vntruelie he wreſteth yt to a falſe ſenſe. This ys the place as yt ys alleaged oute of *Anacletus* by Bartholemew Caraza in the ſumme of the Coūcels: *Sacerdotes quando Domino ſacrificant non ſoli hoc agere debent, ſed teſtes ſecum adhibeant, vt Domino in ſacratis Deo locis perfecte ſacrificare probentur, iuxta illud Deuteron.12. Vide ne offeras holocauſta in omni loco, quem videris, ſed in loco quem elegit Dominus Dens tuus. Epiſcopus Deo ſacrificans teſtes ſecum habeat, et plures quàm alius ſacerdos, cum quo peracta conſecratione, omnes miniſtri communicent, qui noluerint eccleſiaſticis carere liminibus. Sic Apoſtoli ſtatuerunt, et ſancta Romana tenet eccleſia.* The preiſtes when they doe offre ſacrifice vnto our Lord, they ſhall not doe yt alone, but they ſhall haue wittneſſes with thē, that they maie be proued to doe ſacrifice to our Lorde perfectlie in places dedicated vnto God, according to the ſaing of Deuteron. the xii. chapter: *Take heed thowe offre not ſacrifice in euery place that thow ſeeſt, but in the place that thy LordGod hath chooſe.* A Biſhoppe doing ſacrifice to God let him haue mo witteneſſes with him then an other preiſt, with whome, when the cōſecracion ys doen, let all the myniſters communicate, they that will not, ſhall be forbidden to entre into the church.

This ſame place of *Anacletus* ys alſo alleadged in the ſecond diſtinction hauing the ſame ſenſe, in lenght, that this hath in Summe or in breif. Nowe firſt iudge of the ſinceritie of the Proclamer in alleaging the Fathers, whether he doeth as yt becometh one that taketh vpon him to correct all the worlde, and to preache the trueth, which in his iudgement, was before lacking. Ys this ſinceritie to bring three or foure woordes of the ende of a ſaing, which maie be wreſted to his pourpoſe, and to leaue oute all that goeth before? Secondlie, for the vnderſtanding of the place, he hath voonderfully abuſed his audience before whom he preached yt, and all ſoche alſo as haue or ſhall happen to read the ſame ſermon nowe imprinted and diuulged. For in the epiſtle of *Anacletus* yt ys decreed thus: *Epiſcopus Deo ſacrificans teſtes ſecum habeat, in ſolemnioribus diebus aut ſeptē, aut quinque, aut tres Diaconos, qui eius oculi dicūtur, & ſubdiaconos, atq; reliquos miniſtros ſecū habeat.* The Biſhoppe doing ſacrifice vnto God, let him in the ſolemne daies haue either ſeuen or ſiue, or three deaeons whiche be called his eies, and ſubdeacons and other myniſtres. And then yt foloweth that the Proclamer alleageth: *Peracta conſecratioue omnes communicent*, when the conſecracion ys doen let all communicate. So that thys decree can

Anacletus epla.1.

E

F

G

H

A can not be vnderſtāded of all the people,but onelie of all thoſeDeacons,and Subdeacons,and miniſtres which ſhoulde attende vpon the Biſhoppe in the time that he offreth ſacrifice to God, which ys as moche to ſaie, as when he ſaied Maſſe. The decree ſaieth not: when the conſecracion ys doen let all the people communicate : but let all, that ys, all they aſſiſtent to the Biſhoppe in the miniſtracion, the Deacons the Subdeacons, and the miniſtres let them communicate and if they will not, let them be prohibited to entre the churche.

That this ſhoulde be vnderſtanded as ys ſaied yt doeth well appeare by the relacion of this decree to the doctrine of the Apoſtles. So (ſaieth the decree) haue the Apoſtles taught. In dede in their canons they haue ſo taught. For this ys one of their Canons. *Si quis Epiſcopus, aut Presbiter, aut Diaconus, vel quilibet ex ſacerdotali catalogo, facta oblatione, non communicauerit, aut cauſam dicat, vt ſi rationabilis fuerit, veniam conſequatur, aut ſi non dixerit, communione priuetur.* Yf anie Biſhoppe or preiſt, or deacon, or anie other of the clergie, when the conſecracion ys doen doe not communicate, either let him ſhewe a cauſe, that if yt be reaſonable he maie be pardoned, or if he ſhewe none, let him be excōmunicated. Thus the ApoſtlesCanon.

Canon. 9. Apoſtol.

B

The cauſe why this Canon was ſo made, was not for the neceſſitie of the thing, that the ſacrifice were not perfect, or the Maſſe not good in yt ſelf, if the cleargie aſſiſtent did not communicate, but that they abſteining might be occaſion of offence to the people of ſuſpicion againſt him that did offre the ſacrifice, that he had not wel doe yt, as the words immediatelie ſolowing in the ſame Canon doe plainlie declare. *Si non dixerit:cōmunione priuetur, tanquā qui populo cauſa læſionis extiterit, dans ſuſpicionem de eo qui ſacrificauit,quod recte non obtulerit.* Yf he ſhewe no reaſonable cauſe why he abſteineth let him be excom municated, as one that ys cauſe of offence to the people, geuing ſuſpicion of him that did ſacrifice, that he had not well offred yt.

Thus nowe ye ſee howe this man hath abuſed this decree of *Anacletus*, vn derſtanding yt of all that be preſent, where yt ys to be vnderſtanded onelie of them that attend vpon the Biſhoppe in the time of the holie miniſtracion, and that alſo on ſolemne daies. In this poinct onelie he hath not

C abuſed this decree, but in this alſo, that by yt he intended to prooue the Maſſe an euell thing, ād to be naught if ther were no communicates beſides the preiſt, and that maſſe ought not to be ſaied withoute communicantes, and finallie that the Church ys wicked ſo abuſing yt, where in dede ther ys no one ſillabe, in that decree to prooue theſe or anie one of them, or anie parte of one of them. For as in the anſwer to the tenth Canon of the Apoſtles by them alleaged, yt was ſaied: ſo yt maie be ſaied here, that be yt yt were vnderſtanded that all the people ſhoude communicate, as he wolde ha ue yt (but vntruelie) yet in this decree he findeth no prohibition that the preiſt ſhall not offre ſacrifice, nor receaue him ſelf, if the people will not, he findeth not either here or ells wher, that the maſſe ys naught, if ther be no mo communicantes in that place but the preiſt. Wherfor we maie conclude that all that he hath in this poincte alleaged hath but a ſhewe of woordes and no proofe in dede of that that he alleadged yt for.

As for the ninthe Canon of the Apoſtles yt alſo after the right vnderſtan ding proceadeth not of neceſſitie, but of condicion. For if they or anie of

D them, that attend vpon the Biſhoppe in the time of miniſtracion, haue reaſo nable cauſe to ſaie whie they abſtein, they maie abſtein. And poſſible yt might be that when the Biſhoppe had but three attendante vpon him or

foche like fmall nōbre, they might all haue caufe to abftein. And fo yt ys plain ⟨E⟩
that this Canon geueth vs to vnderftand that wher a nombre ys affembled
at the miniftracion, if all the nombre haue iuft caufe to aftein from the recea
ving of the Sacrament, that the Bifhoppe or preift fhall neuer the leffe proceade to receaue alone. For the facrifice muft be receaued. And fo by this
Canon the preift alone maie receaue, though in that place ther be none to
communicate with him. But whether all or no, certen yt ys that fome of the
attendantes might abftein, and fo yt foloweth ineuitablie, that fome might
be prefent, and not receaue.

*Priuate
Maffe
vfed in the
time of
Chryfoft.*

And thus ye maie perceaue that wher the Proclamer faieth that he wolde
make yt plain to yowe by the moft auncient writers, that were in and after
the Apoftles time, and by the order of the firft and primitiue church, that
then ther coulde be no priuate Maffe, yt was a faing more full of oftentacion
and bragge, then of trueth. For though he hath heaped a forte of places: yet
ther ys no one fentence in anie of them, that prooueth that ther coulde be
no priuate Maffe And fo farre from trueth ys this his faing (that in the auncient Churche was no priuate Maffe, I mene a Maffe with fole receauing)
that in the Maffe of Chryfoftom ys a plain rule geuen, what was to be doen ⟨F⟩
whē the preift receaued alone, and what whē the people receaued with the
preift. But yt ys like, the Proclamer had not learned fo farre as to knowe this.

*Iffue ioined
with the
Proclamer
for priuate
Maffe.*

And here to knitte vppe all that he hath faied, or can faie in this matter,
whiche he tearmeth priuate Maffes : This I faie, that if he can bring furthe
anie one fcripture, auncient councell, or catholique doctour that faieth, that
that Maffe, that ys faied withoute a nombre of Communicantes in the fame
place, ys naught, or that yt ought not to be faied, except ther be mo then
the preift to receaue, or that ther ys prohibition for the preift to receaue alo
ne: or anie penaltie in anie catholiq; lawe affigned for the preift that doeth
receaue alone : or anie like decree forbidding a ficke man to receaue the
Sacrament, except fome receaue with him : Let him (I faie) prooue thefe,
or fome one of them by expreffe woordes in maner aboue faied, and I will
not onelie fubfcribe, but I will agnife my felf his fcholer during our two naturall liues.

TAE ONE AND FOVRTETHT CHAP. PROO-

*ueth that the Maffe maie be faied and the Sacrament receaued
withoute a nombre of communicantes at one time
in one place.*

Pfal. 33.

S yt ys not fufficient for a man to decline from euell : but alfo to
doe good, the fcripture fo ioining them together, and faing : *De
clina à malo, & fac bonum.* decline from euell and doe good. So
yt ys not fufficient for a man onelie to flie herefie, but he muft
alfo profeffe the trueth. Wher then I haue in this laft chapiter
opened the craftie falfhed of the Proclamer and folued his argumētes which
in dede be not woorthie to be called argumētes for that they haue no force

*Rom. 10.
Soche ther
be maie no
we in Eng-
lond.*

to impugn that that they are forged for, and therby geuen occafion, as I my
felf doe flie that wicked doctrine, that other men maie doe the like : fo will
I nowe profeffe the tueth of that matter that other men maie doe the fame.
Manie in this time of temptacion embrace parte of the faing of S. Paule : ⟨H⟩
Corde creditur ad iufticiam, but the greater nōbre (the more ys the pitie) ftādeth
not to the other part: *Ore confeßio fit ad falutem.* Thei beleue well in heart : but
they

A they feare with mouth to confesse the fame to faluacion. They turne the admonicion of Chryst vppe fide downe. Chryst faieth: *Nolite timere eos qui oc-* *Math. 10.* *cidunt corpus, animam autem non possunt occidere, fed illum potius timete, qui potest & animam & corpus mittere in gehennam.* Feare not them that fleie the bodie, but can not fleie the foule: But raither feare him who can caft both bodie and foule into hell fire. But they faie in their dedes, feare him that killeth the bodie, and regarde not him that hath power to kill both bodie and foule. For lamentable yt ys to faie, foche ys the loue of manie to the life of the bodie, and to worldlie honour and wourfhippe, and to the tranfitorie baggage of this worlde, that for the conferuacion of thefe, man ys feared, and God the lorde of all power and maieftie neclected. God graunt vs to heare the voice of the caller, that calleth and faieth: *Venite filii audite me, timorem Domini doce-* *Pfal.33.* *bo vos*. Come ye children and heare me. I will teach yowe the feare of our Lorde. Yf we feare him and loue him as to our duetie apperteineth, we fhall neither feare nor be afhamed to confefle him and his holie faith be-

B fore men.

S. Paule thought all thinges in the worlde, as filth or dunge, fo that he *Worldlie* might winne Chryst, but we are contented to lefe Chryst, fo that we maie *cares kepe* wine the worldlie mucke, and filth, for fauegarde of the which, wher Chryst *men from* in his laft fupper, inftituting the facrifice of his bodie and bloode to be of- *God.* fred and frequented of his faithfull in the remembrance, and for the high and folempn memoriall of his pasfion and death, and we haue heretofore fo receaued yt, and in heart ftill receaue yt: yet nowe we ioin with them, that hate yt, we go with them that raill at yt, and abandoning yt with them we doe as they doe. But mans folie fhall come to an ende, and the trueth of our Lorde abideth for euer.

To take awaie this trueth of Chryftes facrifice Sathan hath taught his Difciples that the Sacrament was inftituted to none other ende and pourpofe but onelie to be receaued, and not to be offred. And to make that apparante all their and his endeuoure ys to prooue that yt muft be receaued of manie. And that that receipt maie be compaffed, and the facrifice defaced, they

C exclame againft the Maffe. But when they haue all faied and doen, the Maffe fhall be holie and good. and this fhall be a trueth, that a preift faing Maffe, or anie other Man godlie difpofed ficke or holle, maie receaue the holie Sacrament alone.

For proofe of this, firft, I vfe this reafon. All thinges forbidden vs to doe *Reafons for* (as the Aduerfarie faieth) be conteined in the fcripture: But in the fcripture *fole recea-* yt ys not conteined that anie man ys forbidden to receaue the Sacrament *uing grown-* alone. Wherfor by the woorde of God man ys not forbidde to receaue the *ded vpon* Sacrament alone. Then maie we alfo reafon thus: What foeuer ys not for- *the Peotes-* bidde by Gods woorde as touching matters of faith the Aduerfarie faieth *tants do-* we maie lawfullie doe yt: To receaue the Sacrament alone ys not forbidden *ctrine.* by Gods woorde, Wherfor we maie laufullie doe yt. But leauing reafons, al though they be of foche force that the Proclamer can not with ftand them, and doe alfo ouerthrowe his falfe doctrine: I fhall vpon and after the reherfall of his owne woordes, prooue by authoritie, that the Sacrament maie be receaued of one perfon alone, which ys the contrarie of that that he wold

D maintein and defende, but all in vain.

He vfeth a certain preoccupacion and faieth thus: *Perhappes their maie be* *fome that will faie. We graunt thefe thinges be fpoken of the commuuiõ in the olde doctours:* *but ther be as manie thinges or moo fpoken by them, of the priuate Maffe, and all that yowe* *diffemble*

diſſemble and paſſe by. I knowe ſoch replies haue ben made by diuerſe . Thus moche **E**
the Proclamer.

Theſe woordes haue two principall partes: Firſt ys, that the catholiques
do graunt, that theſe thinges which the Proclamer hath alleaged, be ſpoaken
of a communion. The ſeconde, that ther be as manie thinges or mo ſpoken
of the priuate Maſſe by the holie doctours, which he diſſembleth or paſſeth
by. In dede the catholiques graunt both theſe partes, and ſaie that they be
both true . As for the firſt, we ſaie, wher manie of the people in the primitiue Churche, and for the ſpace of foure or fiue hundreth yeares after, were
well diſpoſed, deuoute and well and godlie affected to the often receipt of
the holie Sacrament . For the continuance wher of, the holie Fathers the
Biſhopps and the preiſtes did trauaill with lawes and decrees, with exhortacions, yea and ſomtime as occaſion was geuen by exprobacions to trade the
people in the ſame (which thing wolde to God the people wolde again
bring in vſe, and frequent in theſe daies) to the great honour of God, and **F**
ſingular comforte of their owne ſoules health: yet we ſaie that all this prooueth not, that ther ys anie lawe, decree, commaundement or ordinance,
that the preiſt in time of miniſtracion, or anie other faithfull at time conuenient, maie not receaue alone. And as we ſaie that this prooueth not, ſo we
ſaie that yt neuer can nor ſhall be prooued by the Proclamer, and all his
adherentes , but that the bleſſed Sacrament maie verie well be receaued
of one alone.

Marke he
re a ſleight
of the Pro-
clamer.

For the ſeconde part of his ſaing, wher he ſaieth that we ſaie, that ther be
as manie thinges ſpoken by the holie doctours of priuate Maſſe whiche he
diſſembleth and paſſeth by : yt ys alſo true, that ther be ſo. And therfor the
more ſhame for him, that, he diſſembleth them. And here marke his ſleight:
He ſaieth that ther be places in the olde doctours for the matter that he calleth priuate Maſſe, but which of theſe did he alleadge and anſwere. He crafti
lie conueigheth him ſelf awaie from them ſaing: I knowe ſoche replies haue
ben made by diuerſe. And by theſe woordes he bleereth the eies of his ſimple Readers, and filleth the eares of his audience, as though he had made
ſufficient aunſwer to them all, wher in dede he toucheth no one ſillable **G**
of them.

The catho
lique doctri
ne and pra
ctiſe ys that
the Sacra-
ment hath
ãd maie be
receaued of
or of one ma
nie at once·

But Reader, thowe ſhalt perceaue that we will vſe no ſoche diſſimulacion
nor ſleight with thee , but as we haue ſolued his argumentes without anie
great laboure, for in dede ther was no weight in them : So ſhall we nowe
open the trueth vnto thee ſimplie without all coolour of ſleight or crafte,
and that by good and ſufficiēt authoritie, as thowe ſhalt well perceaue. Firſt
to certifie thee of the trueth : The trueth ys that the people did often and
moche communicate togeather in the primitiue and auncient church. And
yet neuertheleſſe , trueth yt ys, that bothe the preiſt and other alſo vpon oc
caſion did often and moche receaue alone. Of the which two practiſes this
trueth maie be gathered, that the bleſſed Sacrament maie laufullie be receaued of manie together, and maie alſo laufullie be receaued of one alone, the
firſt ys prooued by that, that the Proclamer hath alleaged: The ſeconde ſhall
be prooued by that that I will alleadge.

And firſt I will vſe the teſtimonie of *Iuſtinus* whome both Cranmer and
this Proclamer doe pitifullie abuſe, and truncatelie alleadge . But alleaging **H**
no more then this mã alleageth euen in this matter, ye ſhall perceaue howe
he goeth aboute to deceaue them, that ther did heare him preache, or ſhall
happen to reade his ſermon. Thus he alleageth *Iuſtinus* in his ſaied ſermon.

Diaconi

A *Diaconi distribuunt ad participandũ vnicuique præsentiũ ex consecrato pane, vino & aqua. Illis verò, qui non adsunt deferunt domum.* The Deacons deliuer of the consecrated bread and wine and water, to euerie one that ys present. And if ther be anie awaie, they carie yt home to them. Vpon this peice of this authour thus alleaged, the Proclamer bringeth in these his woordes : *Here also we finde a Communion, but no priuate Masse.* Note well (good Reader) what this man findeth in this authour, and then shalt thowe perceaue whether he be clere or corrupted in seight, or not raither alltogether blinded.

In these woordes that Iustine saieth, *that the Deacon deliuereth to euerie one that ys present of the consecrated bread wine and water,* I graunt that he findeth a Communion : But in the other parte, when the same authour saieth : *And if anie be awaie, they carie yt home to them :* What findeth he ther? Ys he so blinde that he can not see the Sacrament caried home to them that be absent? Can he not see that to euerie one of these that were absent, and had the Sacrament brought home to them, that yt was brought that they shoulde receaue yt? And when euerie of these to whome the Sacrament was brought, did

B seuerallie receaue yt in their houses, what was yt then? howe will he terme yt, was yt priuate, or a common receipt? What findeth he here? What seeth he here? Can he not finde that the people that were at home did seuerallie receaue it in their houses, as the people assembled did receaue yt at the time of the ministracion ? Yt ys most like that this man looked onely vpon this matter with his left eie, as manie a fletcher doeth vpon a crooked bolt, and not with his right eie. And so likewise when he did write yt, he forgatt the counsell of Chryste, and by like made his left hand of coũsell what the right hand did. But whoso will with the right eie looke vpon this place of this holie Martir *Iustine,* shall finde that trueth that before I testified, that in the primitiue and auncient churche the people did receaue both in nombre and alone.

Perhapps the Proclamer being by this place of *Iustine* driuen to his shiftes, will saie that yt was (notwithstanding that some of the people did receaue at home) a right communion, for that both they and the people being at the ministracion, did all receaue of one consecrate bread. Will yowe see what a

C bare shift this ys? And to ioin with him in his owne termes, I will aske him, whether by this one consecrate bread he mean one loaf of bread, or one Sacramentall breade. He can not speake of one loaf of bread. For in the primitiue Church when the nombre of people did receaue, one loaf coulde not suffice. Yf he speake of one sacramentall bread, or one consecrated bread, *as Iustine doth tearin yt,* ys not the bread consecrated to daie, and the bread consecrated to morowe all one consecrated bread? all one sacramentall breade, ys yt not allwais one Sacrament? Ys not the sacrament of Baptisme ministred to daie, and ministred to morowe all one Baptisme? forasmoch as S. Paule saieth : *Vnus Dominus, vna fides, vnum Baptisma.* Ther ys one lorde, one faith, and one Baptisme. Likewise ys not the bread consecrate in the morning, and at noone all one consecrate bread? And to saie more at large, ys not the bread consecrated in the Supper of Chryst by Chryst him self, and the bread consecrated nowe by his minister, and that shall be consecrated in the last daie of the worlde all one bread? yf yt be not so, why saieth S. Paule, that we are all partakers of one breade? The reason why yt ys one breade, Chry-

D sostome sheweth, speaking of the table of Chryst consecrated by the minister, saing : *Hæc enim illa non alia mensa est. Hæc nulla re minor quàm illa est. Non enim illam Christus, hanc homo quispiam facit, sed vtramque ipse.* This ys euen the same,

not

The Sacrament was seuerallie and solie receaued of thẽ to whom yt was caried home, and therfore priuatelie, as the proclamer vseth the tearmi.

Homi 83 in 26. Math.

E

not an other table: This in no poinct ys leffer then that. For Chryft did not fanctifie that, and this an other man, but Chryft did fanctifie both: So that the reafon whie yt ys one bread, ys by Chryfoftom, bicaufe yt ys fanctified and confecrated by one Chryft . Yf then yt be a communion bicaufe they receaue all of one confecrated bread, and S. Paule faieth *that we all doe eate of one bread* , in fomoch that by yt we are made one bread and one bodie : ys yt not one Communion that the Apoftles , and the faithfull that nowe be, and fhall be in the laft daie of the worlde , haue, made , doe and fhall make? Yf yt be fo, then among true Chryftians receauing as becometh them the holie Sacrament , ther ys no priuate communion. Priuate communion ys among priuate men, foche as cutte them felues of frome the vniuerfall churche, and eate of one peice of bread to daie, and of and other to morowe, as heretiques doe, and doe not all eate of one breade, as the faithfull doe.

Priuate Cõ munion ho we and wher yt ys.

This Proclamer alleageth *Leo* Bifhoppe of Rome , that vpon confideracion that the churche being litle, and not able to receaue the people , ther might be three communions in one daie, in one churche. I wolde nowe knowe whether they that receaued at the firft, Second , and thirde communion, whether they did all communicate together or no. Yf they did not, then were they not all of one communiõ, whiche ys not to be faied: Yf they did, and did not receaue of one cõfecrated bread, nor at one time, yt fhoulde folowe, that cõmunion dependeth vpon fome other thing, then one bread, time, or miniftracion. And in dede fo yt doeth: For yt depédeth of one thing made common to vs all, and which all we being faithfull doe receaue, in the whiche we are made one, and knitte together as membres of one bodie, which thing ys the bodie and blood of Chryft, which ys that one bread, that S. Paule fpeaketh of and faieth that all we partake of, whiche ys in dede the bread of life nowrifhing vs to euerlafting life.

F

I haue taried to long vpon this place, in opening the vanitie of this mans doctrine, and the longer, that yt might be perceaued, that he alleaging this holie man was fo blinded, that he wolde not afwell fee the one trueth as the other, but brought yt as an argumét to reproue the church, wher yt reproueth him felf, and to confute the trueth wher yt confuteth his herefie. But let vs heare other teftimonies, and firft of *Tertullian*, who liued in the time of *Seuerus* the Emperour, in whofe time the chryftian religion not yet being receaued of the Princes of the worlde, the chryftians liued vnder great and fearfull prefecucion , by reafon wherof, though the people were right godlie affected , and well difpofed to the feruice of God , and the receipt of the blefled Sacrament : yet they coulde not freely make their affemblies when they wolde . Wherfor at foch time as they came together the Bifhopps and paftours wold to foch as were right godlie and holie chyftians deliuer the blefled Sacrament to carie home with them , to receaue yt at home, at foche time as they might, bicaufe they coulde not otherwife when they wolde.

G

For the which pourpofe, as by S. Cyprian , S. Bafill, and S. Hierom yt maie be gathered, the godlie brought with them , either a faire cleã linnen cloath, or a prettie boxe to carie yt home in. The like yt appeareth that *Tertullians* wief did. For he difwading her from the Marriage of anie gentile or heathen man after his decefle, and knowing that fhe did fecretlie receaue the Sacramét at home, ãd wolde alfo doe the like though fhe maried an infidel vfed this for one part of his difwafion . *Non fciet maritus , quid fecretò*

H

ante

A *ante omnem cibum guſtes?etſi ſciuerit,panem non illum credet eſſe qui dicitur.* Shall not thy husbande knowe,what thowe doeſt ſecretlie eate before all meat ? And if he knowe yt he will not beleue yt to be that bread, that yt ys called. As who might ſaie:As I being yowr housband doe know that yowe doe receaue the Sacrament ſecretlie:So yt can not be but an heathē man being yowr husband ſhall perceaue alſo that yowe doe receaue yt ſecretlie. Wherby yt ſhall come to paſſe that either he will reſtreign yowe from that libertie, that nowe ye vſe in yowr ſecretē receipt,or ells taking,and beleuing yt not to be that bread that yt ys,he will with irreuerencie abuſe yt.In this ſaing of *Tertullian* yt ys eaſie to be perceaued,that his wief did ſecretlie receaue the Sacrament at home,yf ſecretlie then with no nombre,So theſe woordes of *Tertullian* ſauer of the receipt of the Sacrament by one alone.

Tertulliãs wief receaued the B. Sacr. alone or ſolie,or priuatelie

S Baſill alſo,as before ys mencioned,geueth a notable teſtimonie in this, matter,who writing to a notable godlie matrone,who for the great reueren ce ſhe bare to the bleſſed Sacrament,feared and thought yt vnſemelie to re-

B ceaue yt at her owne hand in her owne houſe,withoute the deliuerie of the ſame by the preiſt or the Deacon,ſaieth thus:*Communicare per ſingulos dies, & participare de ſacro corpore & ſanguine Chriſti pulchrum & valdè vtile eſt,ipſo manifeſtè dicente:Qui manducat meam carnem,& bibit meum ſanguinem habet vitam æternam. Quis enim ambigit,quin frequens vitæ participatio nihil aliud ſit quàm pluribus modis viuere?Nos idcirco quater in ſingulis hebdomadis communicamus:in die Dominico,in quarto die hebdomadæ:in Paraſceue,& in Sabbato,ac in aliis diebus,ſi qua memoria fuerit ſancti alicuius.Illud autem in perſecutionis temporibus neceſſitate cogi quempiam non præſente ſacerdote,aut miniſtro,communionem propria manu ſumere nequaquam eſſe graue,ſuperuacaneũ eſt demonſtrare,propterea quòd longa conſuetudine hoc ipſo rerũ vſu confirmatum eſt. Omnes enim in eremis ſolitariam vitam agentes,vbi non eſt ſacerdos, Communionem domi ſeruantes,à ſeipſis communicant. In Alexandria verò & in Aegypto, vnuſquiſque eorum qui ſunt de populo,plurimùm habet communionem in domo ſua. Semel enim ſacrificium ſacerdote conſecrante,& diſtribuente,meritò participare & ſuſcipere credere oportet. Etenim & in eccleſia ſacerdos dat partem,& accipit eam is qui ſuſcipit cum omni liberta te, & ipſam admouet ori propria manu.Idem igitur eſt virtute, ſiue vnam partem acci-*

Baſil epiſt. ad Cæſariã patrici.

C *piat quiſquam à ſacerdote,ſiue plures partes ſimul.*To communicate euerie daie,and to be partaker of the ſacred bodie and bloode of Chryſte , yt ys a goodlie thing and verie profitable. For he himſelf manifeſtlie ſaieth : He that eateth my fleſh, and drinketh my blood hath euerlaſting life. For who doubteth but that the often receipt of life ys nothing ells but manie waies to liue? We therfore doe communicate foure times in the weke : on the Sondaie, the Vedniſdaie,the Fridaie,and the Satterdaie, and on other daies yf ther be the memorie of anie Saincte.That yt ys no greuouſe thing anie man in the time of perſecucion to be enforced when ther ys no preiſt nor Deacon preſent,to take the communion with hys owne hande,yt ys more then neadeth me to declare,foraſmoche as yt, by the verie practiſe of the thing yt ſelf , ys eſtabliſhed and confirmed by a long cuſtome . For all they that liue ſolitarie liues in the wilderneſſe , wher ther ys no preiſt , hauing the Sacrament at home, they communicate by themſelues . In Alexandria , and in Egypte euery one of the people for the moſt part hath the Sacrament in his owne houſe . We muſt beleue that after the

Ermets ãd holie men liuing in wilderneſſe receaued the Sacr. by themſelues.

D the preiſt hath once conſecrated and diſtributed the ſacrifice, we maie well be partakers of yt , and take yt. For in the Church alſo the preiſt geueth part, and he that doeth receaue yt, doeth freelie and boldlie take yt,

Ooo   and

and putt yt to his owne mouth, with his owne hand. Yt ys all one in vertue **E**
or power, whether anie man take one part of the preiſt, or manie partes together.

Thus moch at lenght haue I written oute of ſainct Baſill, that manie thinges maie be perceiued in one ſaing. In this yowe maie perceaue his faith as
touching the preſence of Chryſtes bodie and blood in the Sacrament, which
ys ſo farre wide that he beleueth yt to be a onelie figure that he called yt the
ſacred bodie and blood of Chryſte. In this ye maie alſo perceaue that he vnderſtandeth the ſixt of S. Iohn of the bleſſed Sacrament. In this ye maie perceaue that he beleued not the Sacrament to be a dead peice of bread, foraſmoch as he tearmeth and calleth the ſame life. In this ye maie perceaue the
godly diſpoſition and deuocion of the people, that did cōmunicate foure times euerie weke, and oftener if anie feaſt of anie Martyr happened. In thys
alſo ye maie euidentlie perceaue, that in the time of perſecucion (as before
ys ſaied vpon *Tertullian*)yt was of long cuſtome vſed, euerie man in his owne
houſe to receaue the Sacrament. For farder proof of this ye perceaue here al **F**
ſo, that they which liued ſolitarie liues in the wilderneſſe, though they had
no preiſt nor Deacon with them, did communicate by themſelues.

Now to lead a ſolitarie life, What ys yt ells but to liue ſole, to liue in a caue
or denne, as *Paule* and *Antonie* did, alone, and ſo whollie geuing themſelues to
praier and godlie contemplacion, for their exerciſe therin did often receaue
the Sacrament, which they had readie by them. In this alſo ye maie perceaue
howe vntruelie the Proclamer hath heretofore ſetfurth his matter, when he
ſaieth, that all the catholique Church of Chryſt vſed the communion as he
vnderſtandeth yt, that ys, that none receaued yt alone. And to amplifie hys
matter he ſaieth *the Indians the Arabians, the Armenians, the Grecians, and as manie as
bare the name of Chryſt, haue kept and continued the ſame amongeſt themſelues, from the
firſt time they receaued the Goſpell, vnto this daie, ād neuer receaued, nor vſed priuate Maſ
ſe.* For yowe here ſee yt teſtified by S. Baſill, whoſe creditte farre ſurmoūteth
the creditte of the Proclamer, that in *Alexandria* and *Egypt*, euerie one of the
people had the Sacramēt in his houſe. And whie had they ſo, but that euery **G**
one by himſelf might ād did receaue yt in his own houſe? Thus ye maie perceaue that ratling oute his amplificacion he ratled beiond the trueth, and en
ded his matter with an vntrueth, and ther he reſteth. But the trueth ys, as S.
Baſill doeth teſtifie, that the people in the primitiue Church did often recea
ue the B. Sacrament alone. But to ende with ſainct Baſill, wher the Aduerſarie ſaieth, that the Sacrament was onelie inſtituted to be receaued, and not
to be offred, and therfor doth allwaies call yt the Sacrament or Communion, or the Lordes ſupper, but neuer ſacrifice, for that name he abhorreth as
the name of *Beelzebub*, in S. Baſill yt maie be perceaued, that yt ys called a ſacrifice. And here I wiſh that, as ſainct Baſill doth call yt both Sacrament, and
ſacrifice, ſo the Aduerſarie wolde alſo, and as he teſtifieth yt to be receaued
both of manie together, and of ſome alone: ſo he wolde alſo beleue bothe
and knowe as well the one to be true as the other, and not maliciouſlie to
diſſemble the one, and confeſſe the other.

Yt ys not vnlike to this that ſainct Hierom teſtifieth to haue ben vſed in
Rome in his time, in the time of perſecucion. Thus he ſaieth : *Scio Romæ hanc*
eſſe conſuetudinem, vt fideles ſemper Chriſti corpus accipiant, quod nec reprehendo, nec pro- **H**
bo. Vnuſquiſque enim in ſuo ſenſu abundat. Sed ipſorum conſcientiam conuenio, qui eodem
die poſt coitum communicant, & iuxta Perſium, noctem flumine purgant. Quare ad Marty
res ire non audent? Quare non ingrediuntur eccleſias? An alius in publico, alius in domo
Chriſtus

Hieroc.
Apola.
ad uerſus
Iuni.

A *Chriſtus eſt?quod in eccleſia non licet,nec domi licet. Nihil Deo clauſum eſt , & tenebræ*
*quoque lucent apud Deum.Probet ſe vnuſquiſque & ſic ad corpus Chriſti accedat.*I know
at Rome this to be the cuſtome,that the faithfull doe alwaies receaue the bo
die of Chryſte,which thing I neither reprehended nor alowe . Euerie man
doeth abunde in his owne ſenſe. But I call their conſcience to iudgement
which after the duetie of matrimonie doe euen the ſame daie communicate,
and according to the ſainge of *Perſius*,they clenſe the night with the floode,
Why dare they not go to the Martyrs? Why doe thei not entre the churchs?
Ys ther one Chryſt in the open place,and an other Chryſte at home? That,
that ys not laufull in the Churche, ys neither laufull at home . Ther ys
nothing ſhett from God, yea the verie darkeneſſe ys bright before him. *Let*
euerie man examin himſelf,and ſo let him come to the bodie of Chryſt . Hitherto Sainct
Hierom.

As S.Baſill reproued the Proclamer of vntrueth,ſo doeth S.Hierõ of craft.
The Proclamer ſaied that S.Hierom wittneſſeth that vntill that time , commonlie euerie where but ſpeciallie at Rome, the people vſed,to communica

B te euerie daie:but craftelie he ſuppreſſeth the maner howe and where, wher
vpon reſteth all the cõtrouerſie. The people of Rome in dede did alwaies cõ
municate,but howe?in the Church allwaies? Naie, but often in their houſes,
and S.Hierome ſaieth that ſome of them,when they had doen the office of
matrimonie,and durſt not go to the Church to the commune receipt of
the Sacrament,nor to the memorialls of Martyrs,they wolde yet receaue at
home in their owne houſes,wher they had allwais the Sacrament readie,for
their which doing S.Hierom rebuketh them,asking whether ther be one
Chryſt in the Church and an other at home.

In this ſaing then of S.Hierome we maie perceaue that the Chryſtiã peo
ple of Rome did both receaue the Sacrament,ſomtime priuatelie at home,
and ſomtime alſo openlie in the Church,wherbie the aſſertion of the Proclamer ys reprooued.In this ſaing alſo are we taught, what ys in the Sacrament,not bread,but Chryſt.For ſaieth S.Hierom,ther ys not one Chryſt re
ceaued at home, and an other in the Churche , but euery where one
Chryſt.

C And here I wiſh the Sacramentaries to diſpute with S.Hierom howe the
bodie of Chryſt maie be in diuerſe places.For here yt ys euident by S. Hieroms owne woordes,that yt ys one Chryſt that ys receaued in the Churche
and at home. And if he maie be in two places,he maie be in two thouſand,
and ſo furthe.In this ſaing alſo we maie learn to vnderſtande ſainct Paule cal
ling the Sacrament (in the eleuenth chap. of the firſt epiſtle to the Corinthians)bread,as wher he ſaieth: *Let a man examine himſelf , and ſo lett him eate of*
that bread,and drinke of that cuppe, that by that bread he meneth the bodie of
Chryſt.For S.Hierom vſing the ſame text,and vttering the right vnderſtanding of the ſame,ſpeaketh yt thus: *Let euery man examine himſelf,and ſo let him co*
*me to the bodie of Chryſt.*So that ſainct Paule by bread ment not material bread,
as the Sacramétaries wolde haue yt,but the verie bodie of Chryſt,the bread
of euerlaſting life.

In this ſaing alſo ys geuen an admonicion to maried perſons,that although
matrimonie be honorable,and the office of the ſame duelie doennot diſplea

D ſant to God:yet as S.Paule willeth a man to abſtein frõyt,when he will geue
himſelf to praier.And as Dauid ãd his men might not eate of the ſhew bread
except they had a certain time before abſteined from ther wieues Euen ſo

The Pro
clamers
ſleight in al
leaging S.
Hierom.

The act of
matrimo
nie for prai
er and re
ceipt of the
B.Sacram.
to be for
born.

sainct Hierom rebuketh them that after soch acte with their wi=ues,did presume to receaue the holie and blessed Sacrament.Yf theywhich did vse their owne laufull wieues,were fownde woorthie of reprehension , bicause they did not dispose themselues to abstein when they entended to receaue:howe great rebuke ys to be laied on our preistes,who by their office being appoincted allwaies to mynistre or receaue,when they be called on, doe come frō their filthie doinges not with their laufull wieues,but with their cloaked euell wemen,to mynister or receaue? What,trowe ye,wolde S. Hierom haue saied of them?Let the pretensed maried preistes well warke sainct Hierom his saing vpon the epistle of sainct Paule to *Titus*. And thus leauing vnto them the matter farder to be considered , I will in my pourpose proceade, and after sainct Hierom who hath testified the maner, howe the people of Rome did communicate by themselues in their houses,we will heare howe the preistes in Grece did the like in their churches.

Chrys.in
cap. 1 ad
Eph.ho. 3.
The people
did not dai
lie receaue
though
Chrysost.
did dailie
saie Mas
se, Wherfo
re in that
respect he
saied hedid
in vain of-
fre sacrifice
at the aul-
tar.

Chrysostome for that he perceaued the godlie deuocion of the people,as touching the receipt of the Sacrament,to waxe colde,he earnestlie rebuked his people,as I wish that our Bishopps,and Pastours shoulde doe theirs, and to their reproache saied thus:*Frustra habetur quotidiana oblatio, frustra stamus ad altare.Nemo est qui simul participet.*The dailie oblacion or sacrifice ys doen in vain,we stand at the aultar in vain.Ther ys no man that will partake with vs. In this saing of Chrysostome these two thinges maie be perceaued that by Chrysostom and his preistes the dailie sacrifice was offred in the Church of Constantinople,that ys,that Masse,was dailie saied ther.For he saieth.*Quoti diana habetur oblatio.*The dailie sacrifice ys doen,which ys to saie , that euerie daie the sacrifice ys offred.The other that although Masse were dailie saied, yet manie times none did communicate with him that did offre the sacrifice And therfor he saied:*Nemo est qui simul participet.*Ther ys none that will take parte of the sacrifice.Wherbie yt ys euident that in the greke Church Masse was saied though ther were no communicantes with the preist.

Obiection,
with answ.
The bodie
and bloode
of Chryste
consecrated
to two ends

Neither let the Aduersarie grownde his sandie argument vpon this woorde (*Frustra*)for nothing ys absolutelie doen in vain that atteigneth anie end that yt was ordeined for.Nowe wher the holie consecracion of Chrystes bodie and blood ys cheiflie and principallie doen for two endes:The one that yt should by an vnblooddie maner in the name of the wholl Church be offred vnto God our heauenly Father in sacrifice representatiue,ād cōmemora tiue of that his blody sacrifice offred vpō the crosse,The other thatyt should be receaued when yt ys offred.Yf yt haue these two endes,as alwaies yt hath for after yt ys cōsecrated,yt ys allwaies receaued,Thē hauing the endes that yt was ordeined for,yt can not be saied absolutelie to be doen in vain.In some respect yet yt maie be saied to be doen in vain:as in the godlie entent of Chrysostom,who of godlie zeale to prouoke his people,to receaue the blessed Sacrament,did by himself and his preistes,dailie offre the solemne sacrifice,which forasmoch as he did yt to the pourpose that they should cōmunica te,and yet did not,he might verie well saie that his pourpose was frustrated, and that,sithen they came not,hys doing in that respect was vain. And that this was hys mening his woordes doe well declare. For when he had saied that the dailie sacrifice was doen in vain, and that he stoode at the aultar in vain:he addeth the cause:For(saieth he)ther ys none that will partake with vs.As who might saie:In this respect that we looke that the people shoulde communicate and yet none will come,we stand in vain at the aultar.

That he ment not that the holie oblacion was absolutelie vain yf
the

A the people did not communicate, yt ys more plain then that yt neadeth anie probacion. For firſt yf yt were ſo, wolde ſo great a learned man, ſo holie a mã, either haue offred the ſacrifice himſelf, or cauſe yt to be offred dailie, whẽ he knewe yt to be doen in vain? Secondlie, howe can he ſaie that holie myniſtracion to be doen in vain, wher himſelf confeſſeth in the conſecracion ſo great a miracle to be doen? ſo great beneuolence of God to be ſhewed to mankinde, that in the ſame time of conſecracion Chryſt that ſitteth aboue with the Father, ys nowe in the handes of men? Again, doeth he mean yt to be doen in vain, that ſaieth that the myniſtracion ys ſo high, ſo excellent, and ſo honourable, that Angels in that time doe accompanie the preiſt, and that the heauenlie powers be aſſembled together in the honoure of him that ys ther offred? *li.3. de ſacerd.* *Ibid.li.7.*

Farder, doeth he thinke this ſacrifice to be doen in vain, that ſaieth we offre the ſame ſacrifice that Chryſt offred? Moreouer, ys yt like that he taketh yt to be doen in vain wher praier ys made for princes, for rulers, and for all **B** that doe acknowledge Chriſt? wher alſo praier ys made for peace, for health, for wealth, for proſperitie, and for the helpe and releif of all that be ſicke, in pain in captiuitie, and in pryſon? wher all the heauenly powers doe praie for vs with the preiſt? *Hom.17. ad Hebr.* *Idem.in Liturgia.* *Sermon in Enceniis Serm.3.ad Philip.*

Finallie, yt can not be ſaied that he thinketh yt to be in vain, that ſaieth that the Apoſtles did know that moche releif and moche profitte cometh to the ſoules departed by the oblacion of this holie ſacrifice. Wherfor I conclude that he ſpake yt to be vain, not abſolutelie but in reſpect of his pourpoſe and deſire, which was fruſtrated bicauſe the people did not communicate.

That the Sacrament maie be receaued alone without a nõbre of communicantes, the hiſtorie eccleſiaſticall alſo proueth inuinciblie. For ther we read that one Serapion being ſicke, ſent his ſeruant to the preiſt, deſiering that he wolde myniſtre the Sacrament to him, that he might depart. The preiſt being ſicke and not able to go himſelf, and yet loath but that the man ſhoulde receaue the Sacrament or that he died, in this neceſſitie ſent of the Sacrament by the meſſenger, which when yt was brought, the ſicke man recea **C** ued yt withoute anie to communicate with him, which maie well be ſaied, both for that the hiſtorie maketh no mencion of anie communicantes, and alſo that, as the hiſtorie teſtifieth, the quantitie of the Sacramẽt that was ſent was verie litle not able to ſuffice anie nombre. By this then yt maie be perceaued, that in the auncient Church yt was not reputed or taken as an heynouſe crime to receaue the Sacrament alone, as now the Proclamer wold make yt, but yt was thought good and commendable when occaſion ſerued. *Euſeb.li.6. ca.34.* *Serapion being ſick receaued the Sacramẽt alone.*

A moch like teſtimonie for this matter haue we of S. Auguſtine, wherof mencion ys made before, which ys, that a certein man hauing hys houſe infeſted with euell ſpirittes, came to ſainct Auguſtin houſe S. Auguſtin being abſent, and deſiered of hys preiſtes that they wolde eaſe him of that moleſtacion. One of them went, and ſaied Maſſe ther, and praied earneſtlie and the euell ſpirittes ceaſſed anie more to trooble the houſe. Here we perceaue the Sacrifice to be offred, Maſſe to be ſaied, but we heare no woorde of a communiõ. As by this that ys hitherto ſaied yt maie be perceaued, that the preiſt **D** myniſtring, or anie other perſon maie receaue the bleſſed Sacrament, withoute anie other communicantes, according to the practiſe of the primitiue and auncient Church: ſo ſhall yt now be declared by auncient lawes and decrees that the people were by lawe, bownd but to heare Maſſe, and not allwaies to receaue.

Soter that was the eleuenth Bifhoppe of Rome after S.Peter,and liued a- **E**
boute the yeare of our Lorde lxiii.made this decree. *Nullus presbyterorum Miſ*
ſarum ſolemnia celebrare præſumat,niſi duobus præſentibus,ſibique reſpondentibus,& ipſe
tertius habeatur,quia cùm pluraliter ab eo dicitur,Dominus vobiſcum,& illud in ſecretis:
Orate pro me:apertiſsimè conuenit,vt ipſius reſpondeatur ſalutationi. Let none of the
preiſtes preſume to celebrate the ſolemne office of the Maſſe, except ther be
two preſent and anſwering him,ſo that he maie be the thirde,for when yt ys
plurallie ſaied of him:Owre Lorde be with yowe, and in the ſecretes : Praie
for me,yt ys moſt manifeſtlie conuenient, that his ſalutacion be anſwered.
Here ye ſee yt commaunded that ſome be preſent at the Maſſe, but not alwaies to communicate,but anſwere the ſalutacion of the preiſt.

In a Councell alſo thus we finde yt decreed:*Miſſas die Dominico ſecularibus*
totas audire,ſpeciali ordine præcipimus,ita vt ante benedictionem ſacerdotis,egredi populus
non præſumat,quodſi fecerint ab Epiſcopo publicè confundantur. We commaunde the
ſecular people by ſpeciall order,vpon the ſondaie to heare the wholl Maſſe.
So that the people preſume not to go furth before the benediction of the **F**
preiſt.And if they doe,let them be openlie rebuked of the Biſhoppe.Here
we finde ſoch order commaunded as the catholique church,for all the weſt
part of yt,obſerued,namelie that the people ſhoulde heare Maſſe euerie ſon
daie,but of communion here ys no title,A like decree we finde in an other
councell in theſe woordes.*Cùm ad celebrandas miſſas in Dei nomine conuenitur,popu*
lus non ante diſcedat,quàm Miſſæ ſolemnitas copleatur,& vbi Epiſcopus non fuerit, bene-
*dictionem à ſacerdote percipiat.*When they be come together in the name of God
to celebrate Maſſe,the people maie not departe before the ſolemnitie of the
Maſſe be fulfilled.And wher ther ys no Biſhoppe preſent let them receaue
the benediction of the preiſt.This decree commaundeth no more but that
the people ſhall not departe vntill Maſſe be doen,of the communion therys
no woorde.

S.Auguſtin alſo made this ordeinaunce,as yt ys to be ſeen in the firſt diſtinction of conſecracion in theſe woordes.*Et hoc attendendum, vt miſſæ peculia-*
res,quæ per dies ſolemnes à ſacerdotibus fiunt,non ita in publico fiant,vt propter eas populus
à publicis miſſarum ſolemnibus,quæ hora tercia canonicè fiunt , abſtrahatur , ſed ſacerdotes **G**
qui in circuitu vrbis , aut in eadem vrbe ſunt,& populus in vnum ad miſſarum publicam
celebrationem conueniant . And this ys to be obſerued,that the peculiar Maſſes
that be ſaied of the preiſtes vpon the ſolempn daies be not ſo openly doen,
that for them the people be not drawen awaie from the publique ſolemnitie
of Maſſes, whiche be canonicallie doen the thirde howre . But the preiſtes that dwell aboute the cytie,or within the ſame citie,and the people alſo
ſhall come together to the publique celebracion of Maſſes.Thus he.

In this ordeinance ye firſt perceaue that peculias Maſſes were ſaied in one
citie,beſide the high or common Maſſe,to the which the people might ſo reſorte,as that they might not be letted or withdrawen fro the high Maſſe.Ye
ſee again,that both the preiſtes that had ſaied Maſſe,and the people that had
heard the,were appoincted neuer the leſſe to come to the high Maſſe.Now
if none maie be preſent(as the Aduerſarie teacheth)but ſoch as will commu
nicate,and theſe preiſtes hauing ſaied their peculiar Maſſes,and ther commu
nicated muſt yet be preſent at the high Maſſe by S. Auguſtines ordeinance,
yt foloweth that the doctrine of the Aduerſarie ys contrarie to the ordei- **H**
naunce of S.Auguſtin.And although the name of Maſſe be ſo odiouſe to
the Proclamer : yet ye maie perceaue yt was not ſo to ſainct Auguſtine,
bus he aloweth both peculiar Maſſes and high or publique Maſſes, at bothe
the

Soter vnde
cimus Ro.
Epiſ.Epiſt.
ſecund. ad
Epiſcop.Ita
lia.

Concil.A.
gathen. &
habetur de
conſecr.
Diſt.1.

Concil. Au
relian.

Aug.de
conſe.Diſt.
1.cap.Et
hoc.

A the whiche although the people might and aught to be : yet ther ys no com maundement for them al to communicate as in his ordeinaunce yt ys to be perceaued.

What fhall I nede anie more to faie in this matter, fith yt ys manifeft by manie practifes of the primitiue and auncient churche, that both priftes at the miniftracion and other perfons as well wholl as ficke did and therfor maie nowe receaue the blefled Sacrament alone, withoute a nombre of cõmunicantes? And therfor to returne part of the Proclamers woordes home to him and his complices, again I faie, O mercifull God, who wolde thinke ther coulde be fo moche wilfullineffe in the heart of man, fo maliciouflie, fo flaunderouflie to caluminate the Churche , for that fhe like a good mother doeth fuffer her children to take their blefled and holie foode of Chryftes bodie and blood either by nombre or by one alone , as deuocion and occafion fhall ferue, fith that both maners haue ben allwaies practifed as before ys prooued?

B Wherfor we maie trulie faie: *O Iuftine, o Tertullian, o Bafill. o Hierom, o Chryfoftom. o Auften, o Leo, o auncient councells, if we be deceaued, ye are they that haue deceaued vs.* But fure we are, that we are not deceaued, but we reft in the trueth that ye haue taught vs. But alas whofe heart wolde yt not greiue to fee the blafphemie of the Proclamer againft Chryft and S. Paule, and his deteftable flaunder of the holie doctours, whom he chargeth to haue taught him his Scifmes, diuifions, and herefies? Ys Chryft who ys the trueth, the miniftre of herefie? Ys Paule the doctour and Apoftle of the gentiles, the teacher of Scifmes? Be the holie doctours and Fathers of Chryftes Church, who haue ben paftours and feaders of Chryftes flocke, and kepers of the fame with in his folde, in vnitie and peace, the authours of diuifions, and difperfions of the fhepe of Chryft? Naie, yt ys Sathan the firft lie maker, the father of lies and vntrueth , the authour of diuifion betwixt God and man, that hath taught him herefie, Scifme and diuifion, whofe wicked infpiracion (the more ys the pitie) he foloweth. For neither Chryft, nor Paule, not *Iuftine* nor *Bafill*

C &c. hath taught that the celebracion or miniftracion of Chryftes Sacrament ys not godlie or good, if ther be not manie communicantes at yt, But they haue taught, that manie maie receaue yt, and that manie did receaue yt, and that one alone maie receaue yt, and that diuerfe alone did receaue yt , and both to be true.

And nowe to ende this matter, as the Proclamer hath doen all that he can, and yet, by no autoritie (as ys faied) hath prooued that a preift or anie other maie not receaue alone: fo I faie, that neither he, nor all his complices, though they be ioined all together, fhall euer bring furth anie expreffe place of fcripture, Councells, or doctours, that doeth by commaundement forbidde a well difpofed chryftian to receaue the Sacrament alone . And thus the three principall partes of the Maffe being auouched by fcriptures Councells, and doctours: I fhall confirme the fame by miracle, wrought by God, in the blefled Sacrament in the Maffe time.

THE TWO AND FOVRTETH CHAP. PROO-
neth the trueth of thefe matters of the Sacrament by that
yt hath pleafed God to confirme the fame
with miracles.

Llthough the cominge of Chryft into the flefh was moft certenly taught by promiffes, figures, and prophecies (as before in
the firft booke ys faied) yet the fame his coming his conception, his birth and abode with vs, was commended vnto vs, by
manie portentes, miracles, and woonders, which the Gofpell
doeth declare : Euen fo yt hath pleafed the goodneffe of God well knowing
owre infirmitie and weakneffe, to deale with vs in the matter of the Sacrament of the bodie and bloode of the fame his Sonne Iefus Chryft. The certen trueth wherof although by figures, prophecies, and by the liuelie woor
de of Chryft himfelf yt be certenlie commended vnto vs: yet to the confir- F
macion of the fame trueth to vs warde, which otherwife in yt felf ys moft
certen, yt hath, I faie, pleafed him to confirme the fame trueth to vs by diuer
fe miracles, that we maie be affured, though reafon, though fenfes, though
hell gates wolde arife againft yt, this ys and fhall be a trueth, and euer endure a trueth.

3 Reg. 18.

In the time of *Elias* the Prophett when God and his holie faith and religion (as nowe yt ys with vs) was fo farre forfaken that none were fownde, that
openlie for the feare of the king and wicked *Iefabell* wolde profeffe the fame,
although fome laie in caues and dennes, as nowe I truft ther doe fome, faith
fullie feruing God, *Elias* moued by the fpiritt of God to haue the religiõ and
faith of God difcerned frõ the religion of *Baall* wolde the triall of the fame
fhoulde be made by fomme miracle from heauen. Wher vnto the Kinge and
the people agreed, that if anie miracle were doen on *Baalls* fide he fhoulde
be taken for God, and his religion receaued : yf on *Elyas* fide : his God and
his religion fhoulde be embraced. The preiftes of Baall laied on their facrifice, they called on their God in their maner, no fire came from heauen, no
miracle was doen. After that they had doen, *Elyas* prepaired the facrifice, he G
called on his God, fire came from heauen, and burnt the facrifice. Wherupõ
the people feing the miracle, cried : *Dominus ipfe eft Deus, Dominus ipfe eft Deus*.
Owre Lorde ys God, owre Lorde ys God. Euen fo nowe the minifters of
Baall haue peruerted Chryftes faith and religion. The people in outwarde
countenance for feare of lawes haue forfaken the fame : They are nowe
taught that Chryft ys not reallie in the Sacrament duelie miniftred : They
are taught that his bodie ther ys not to be honoured, They are taught, that
the bleffed Sacrifice of Chryftes bodie and bloode ys nothing auailable either to the quicke or to the deade, with foche other.

Chryft ys
not in the
facramen-
tall bread
of the newe
miniſters,
but he ys in
the B. Sacr.
duelie mini
ſtred by a
preiſt.

Nowe let them fearch all hiftories of antiquitie, and fhewe anie one miracle that God hath wrought either in the time of Berengarius : of *Wicleff*, and
Huffe, of *Zwinglius Oecolampadius*, or of this Proclamer for the confirmacion
and declaraciõ of that their faith, and if they doe, we fhall faie that their faith
ys good : Yf theie doe not, and we doe : let them yelde and faie that owre
waie ys good. For like yt ys the trueth ther to be, wher yt pleafeth God to
confirme the fame by miracle : And like yt ys no trueth to be on the contra- H
rie fide wher God doth not vouchfaffe at anie time to commende yt by fome miracle?

Nowe the catholique Church teacheth the prefence of Chryftes bodie
in

A in the Sacrament : The Aduersarie teacheth no bodie, but the figure of the bodie. The catholique Church teacheth Chryftes bodie in the Sacrament to be honoured : Luther and the Sacramentaries teache that yt ys not to be honoured. The catholique Church teacheth that Maffe ys to be vfed : Luther and the Sacramentaries teache that yt ys to be abhorred. Nowe as *Elyas* willed the preiftes of *Baall* , firft to confirme their waie with miracles : So lett the Lutherans and the Sacramentaries , bring furth firft fome Miracle.

As for miracles for the confirmacion of their doctrine as touching this matter of the Sacrament, I neuer did nor coulde heare or reade of anie , but onelie of one, which ys a miracle meet for the doctrine. Of whiche miracle Luther himfelf ys the reporter, *Ionas* his difciple being interpretour in his *Luther.* booke of priuate Maffe, wher he faieth thus: *Ego coram vobis reuerendis patribus & fanctis, confeßionem faciam, date mihi abfolutionem bonam, quæ vobis (opto) quamminimum noceat. Contigit me femel fub mediam noctem fubito expergefieri. Ibi Sathan mecũ cæpit eiufmodi difputationem. Audi (inquit) Luthere, doctor perdocte . Nofti te quinde-*

B *cim annis celebraffe Miffas priuatas penè quotidiè. Quid fi tales Miffæ horrenda effent Idololatria? Quid fi ibi non adfuiffet corpus & fanguis Chrifti, Sed tantùm panem & vinum adoraffes, & aliis adorandum propofuiffes?* I will before yowe reuerend and holie Fathers. make a confeffion, geue me a good abfolucion, which I wifh maie nothing hurte yowe. Yt happened me once at midnight fodenlie to be wa- *Sathan ap-* kened. Ther Sathan beganne this maner of difputacion with me . Hearken *peared to* (faieth he) thowe well learned doctour Luther. Thowe knoweft that by the *difputed* fpace of thefe fiftene years, thowe haueft faied priuate Maffe all moft euerie *with him* daie. What if foche priuate Maffes were abhominable Idolatrie? What if *of priuate* ther hath not ben prefent the bodie and blood of Chryft, but that thowe *Maffe.* haddeft honoured onely bread and wine and haddeft fett yt furth to other to be honoured? Thus moch Sathan to Luther.

In which talke Sathan goeth aboute to confirme three pointes of their doctrine, that ys, that Chryftes bodie and bloode be not in the Sacrament, but onelie bread and wine : That Chryft in the Sacrament ys not to be adored: And that priuate Maffes are not to be vfed. See ye not nowe what a miracle

C here ys, that Sathan wolde vouchefaf to fpeake with Lurher at middenight? ys not this doctrine moche confirmed nowe, that Sathan hath perfwaded yt ? who knoweth not that Sathan perfwadeth to herefie, not to the right faith? to euell, not to good? to falfhoode, not to trueth ? Wherfor chryftian reader, if thowe wife be, flee that he perfwadeth thee vnto , and embrace that he difwadeth thee from.

And thus to a good chryftian this doing of Sathan maie be occafion of confirmacion in faith. For wher Sathan difwadeth Luther from the Maffe, *Ioan.8.* from the beleif of the prefence of Chryft in the Sacrament, from the honou ring of Chryft ther, we maie be certen and fure that the Maffe ys good, that the prefence of Chryfte in the Sacrament, and the honouring of him ther be holfom and good doctrines . For he being (as Chryft faieth) a liar , and *1.Pe.5.* a manifleer from the beginning : feketh not to teache vs the trueth, nor to helpe to faue ys, but raither (as S. Paule faieth) he being our aduerfarie goeth aboute like a roaring lion feking whome he maie deuoure, whom God graũt vs ftronglie to withftande in faith. Thus I faie, occafion ys geuen vs to be cõ

D firmed in that faith from the whiche Sathan wolde difwade vs.

But as touching the matters which Sathan wolde perfwade by his deuelifh apparition to Luther, if ther were no more faied, a wife reader wolde

by

by thefe fewe woordes eafelie perceaue, howe good and true the doctrine
of the Proclamer ys, which ys foche as Sathan perfwaded, and euen the verie fame. This being all the miracles that I can finde of the confirmacion of
the Proclamers doctrine, I maie thus conclude, that forafmoch as this doctrine ys fetfurth by the apparition and perfwafion of Sathan, and not by
God, that yt ys Sathans doctrine and not gods.

　　Nowe for the catholique doctrine let vs fee if God hath befides his figures, prophecies, plain fpeaches of his onelie begotten Sonne Iefus Chryft,
and the great nombre of affertions, declaracions, and expofitions of moft
holie famoufe, auncient and learned Fathers, fhewed anie miracles for the
confirmacion of the trueth of the bleffed Sacrament. And Firft let vs fee for
the prefence of Chryft in the Sacramēt. Sathan perfwaded Luther that ther
ys not prefent the bodie and bloode of Chryft, but bread and wine let vs
trie the trueth therof by Gods worke.

In vita Ba.
The bleffed
Sacr. deliue
red to a Ie-
we was ve-
rie flesh ād
verie·blood
in feight
　　Amphilochius an holie Bifhoppe, who liued within the compaffe of foure
hondreth yeares after Chryft and therfor a good nombre of yeares, more
then eleuen hondred agone, writing the life of S. Bafill, teftifieth that a cer
tain Iewe defieroufe to fee the mifteries of the chryftians, came among an
infinite multitude to the churche wher S. Bafill faied Maffe. And feigning
himfelf to be a Chryftian, and being among them at S. Bafills Maffe, fawe in
the handes of S. Bafill a childe diuided. Neuer the leffe when the time of the
communion came, he ftoode among other to doe as they did and when the
Sacrament was deliuered vnto him, yt was yerie flefh: And when the cuppe
was brought to him, yt was verie bloode : of whiche both as he might keping fome parte, when he came home he fhewed them to his weif, and tolde
her what he had feen with his eies. Whervpon beleuing that the mifteries of
the chriftians were woonderfull, the next daie he went to S. Bafill, and tolde
him all the wholl matter, and defiered him that he might withoute delaie be
chriftened and fo he was, and all his houfholde.

　　Yt ys redd alfo in the liues of the Fathers, that ther was a certain olde mā,
who although he were a great man : yet he was fimple and did erre in the
matter of the Sacrament, and faied that the confecrated bread which we doe
receaue ys not the naturall bodie of Chryft, but a figure of yt . This his errour when two auncient men did vnderftand and knowe that his life and cō
uerfacion other wife was good, they thought that he did yt innocētlie, and
fimplie. And therfor they went to him and reherfed his errour to him . He
graunted that he did fo faie. They perfwaded him that he fhould not fo bele
ue, but as the catholike Church doeth . We *(faie they)* beleue that that bread
The bleffed
Sacr. deli-
uered to a
doubting
chryftian
appeared
flesh.
ys the bodie of Chryft, and that cuppe his bloode in verie dede, and not in
figure. But as in the beginning God taking a litle earth, made man to his
owne image, and no man can faie but that man, although he be made of the
earth he ys the image of God : Euen fo the bread, by caufe he faied: *This ys*
my bodie: we beleue that yt ys verilie his bodie. The olde man faied : except
I maie know yt fo to be in verie dede, yowr reafons can not fatisfie me:Then
they faied : Let vs geue our felues to praier this weke, that God maie vouchfaffe to reueill this myfterie vnto vs. After their praier they three came
to the church. And when the time came that they fhoulde receaue, the one
lie porcion of the Sacrament deliuered to that olde man, was verie bloodie
flefh, whiche when he fawe he was afearde and cried, faing: I beleue that
the bread that ys on the aultar ys thie bodie, and the cuppe ys thy bloode.
And furthwith the flefh in his hand was made breade, and fo he receaued
yt, and gaue thankes to God.　　　　　　　　　　　　　　　　　Let

A Let not the Aduersarie by skorning trauaill to reiecte this miracle or auoi
de the force of yt by slaunder, saing that some papist hath inuented yt. For
as yt ys testified, this was doen, as the last rehersed miracle was, with in the
compasse of foure hundreth yeares after Chryst, at whiche time yt were to
moch wickednesse for the Aduersarie to think anie vain inuencions to haue
ben deuised for the maintenance of the treuth of the Sacramet.

I omitte to alleadge here soche miracles, as S. Cyprian and S. Ambrose
reporte aboute the blessed Sacrament, for that I haue made some mencion
of them allreadie, and again by occasion shall. Manie goodlie miracles also
be reported by S. Gregorie, and manie were doen in his time, aboute this
blessed Sacrament, whiche were to long to reherse. These two therfor shall
suffice to helpe vs to perceaue and vnderstand Gods pleasure and his
holie trueth as concerning the presence of Chrystes bodie in the blessed
Sacrament.

B Sathan perswaded Luther not to honoure the bodie of Chryst in the Sacrament, but what the Churche hath doen frõ the Apostles time, and what
the holie Martirs and learned Fathers teach in this matter yt ys declared in
the secõd booke: Besides whiche knowledge so left vnto vs of God, we shall   *Optatus li.*
perceaue gods pleasure by miracle, that the blessed Sacrament shoulde be ho   *2.cont Do-*
noured. In the which matter yt ys verie notable that *Optatus* reporteth of the   *natist.*
Donatistes, who being cruell heretiques, so farre missliked what was doen
by the catholiques, that violentlie inuading their Churches, they commaun
ded the Sacrament to be geuen to the dogges. But the iudgement of God   *Dogges af-*
not suffring so heinouse an offence to be vnpunished, so great contumelie to   *ter their*
the dishonour of the blessed Sacrament, to be vnreuenged : The dogges   *eating of*
vnto their owne masters whom before they loued and defended, nowe be-   *the Sacra-*
ing enemies, fell on them as on straungers or theues, and with all violence   *ment woro*
as though they had neuer knowen them, waxed feirce on them and woro-   *wed their*
wed them, God herby (as I take yt) signifieng vnto vs that as rabbish men   *Masters*
forgatte their duetie and honoure to their Lorde God: so the vnreasonable   *that cast*
creatures forgatt their loue to their masters.   *yt vnto*
   them.

C Whether they haue offended and displeased God, that in this our time
haue as wickedlie abused the Sacrament, as did these Donatistes, they maie
by this miracle easilie perceaue. And this maie we perceaue also, that as the
dishonouring of the Sacrament offendeth and displeaseth God, and therfor
he punissheth yt, So in the honouring of the Sacrament, neuer anie Idolatrie was committed, for we neuer readd yt punished. Let anie of the Aduersaries, if they can bring furth anie one sufficient example, that euer anie one
was punished of God, for honouring Chryst in the Sacrament, and then
they haue doen somwhat, but they neuer coulde yet, nor neuer shall, so
weake ys their cause.

Against the Masse also Sathan perswaded Luther, and good cause whie.   *Sathan his*
For by the Masse his power as well in extern or worldly thinges as in intern   *power aba-*
or spirituall thinges, ys ouerthrowen. For worldlie thinges we haue the te   *ted by the*
stimonie of S. Augustine, who as before ys mencioned, testifieth that by the   *vertue of*
offring of the sacrifice of the bodie and blood of Chryste (whiche ys the   *the Masse.*
Masse) the wicked power of the Deuell molesting the house of a certain mã,
D and moche disquieting his familie and seruants, was clean driuen awaie,   *Aug li.22.*
and the house after wel quieted.   *De ciuit.*
   Dei.ca.8
Howe moche then so euer they crie oute against Masse, howe great ab ho
minacion soeuer they make yt to saie that the sacrifice of Chrystes bodie ys
offred

offred by the preiſt : howe moche foeuer Sathan and his diſciples wolde extenuate the vertue and power of yt : yet in ſpite of their teeth they muſt heare S. Auſten ſaie, that the preiſt offred the ſacrifice of Chryſtes bodie. And what ys yt to offre the ſacrifice of Chryſtes bodie, but to ſaie Maſſe? And to ſaie Maſſe ys to offre this ſacrifice. And wher Sathans Angells troobled the houſe of this man to the great hurt bothe of his ſeruantes and of his cattaill, when Maſſe was ſaied in the houſe, the power of Sathan was put to fleight. Yowe maie perceaue then, that yt ys not without cauſe, that Sathã ſtirred vppe his miniſtres ſo cruellie and fiercely to crie oute, to raill, and to rage againſt the bleſſed and holie Maſſe. For being deuoutlie and godlie doen, yt weakeneth his power, yt withſtandeth his malice, yt abateth his tirannie, and diminiſheth his kingdom . And by this ye maie conſider howe acceptable a thing the Maſſe ys that at once ſaing the Deuel and his Angells were driuē awaie. Yf the Maſſe were ſo deteſtable before God as they wolde make yt, God wolde at the doing of yt haue cauſed mo Deuells to come to the houſe, raither than by the doing of yt to putte them to fleight. Thus maie yowe perceaue that God commendeth to vs the goodneſſe of the Maſſe by miracle.

Sermon. de Baptiſ. In ſpirituall thinges yt alſo abateth the power of the Deyell, for yt diminiſheth the force of temptacion (as ſaieth S. Bernard) *Duo enim illud ſacramentũ operatur in nobis, vt videlicet & ſenſum minuat in minimis, & in grauioribus peccatis tollat omnino conſenſum. Si quis veſtrum non tam ſepè modò, non tam acerbos ſentit iracundiæ motus, luxuriæ, aut cæterorũ huiuſmodi gratias agat corpori, & ſanguini Domini quoniã virtus ſacramenti operatur in eo .* Two thinges that Sacrament woorketh in vs, that in leſſer ſinnes yt diminiſheth the feeling, and in greater ſinnes yt taketh awaie conſent. Yf anie of yowe doe not ſo often nowe feele ſo bitter mocions of wrathe, of enuie, of lecherie, or ſoche other, let him geue thankes to the bodie and bloode of ower lorde. For the vertue of the Sacrament woorketh in him. Thus the bodie and blood of Chryſt in the Sacramēt with ſtandeth the furie of Sathan and his Angells both in outewarde thinges and inwarde thinges.

Three thinges to be attended in the bleſſ. Sacr. Nowe let not the Aduerſarie cauill that bicauſe S. Bernarde ſaieth here that the vertue of the Sacramēt woorketh, that he vnderſtandeth not Chryſt him ſelf to be geuen in the Sacrament, but the vertue. For S. Bernarde with all catholiques acknowlegeth three thinges in the Sacrament, the outwarde formes, the bodie and bloode of Chryſt, and the ſpirituall grace which three he profeſſeth in a ſermon ſaing . *Tria in ſacramento Altaris attendere debes , ſpeciem panis, veritatem carnis, virtutem gratiæ ſpiritualis. vſque ad ſpeciem panis ſenſus pertingit exterior: ad veritatem carnis fides interior : ad virtutem gratiæ ſpirituallis charitas* Bernardus ſermon. de Cana Dom *ſuperior.* Three thinges thowe oughteſt to attende in the Sacrament of the aultar: The outwarde forme of bread : The veritie of the fleſh : the vertue of ſpirituall grace. Vnto the outwarde forme of breade reacheth the outwarde ſenſe: Vnto the veritie of the fleſh the inwarde faith: Vnto the vertue of the ſpirituall grace, perfeſt charitie . So that in the Sacrament ys both the bodie of Chryſt, vnto whome we muſt geue thankes and the vertue of the ſpirituall grace therin receaued, for the whiche we aught to geue thankes.

The pleaſure of God being by his miraculouſe workes ſhewed to be other wiſe, yea euen contrarie to that that yt pleaſed Sathan to perſwade Luther as touching the preſence of Chryſt in the holie Sacrament, and the hououringe of him in the ſame, with or ſeruice and duetie in the holie ſacrifice of

the

A the Maſſe: we will ceaſe to ſaie any more vpon the woordes of S. Bernard.

But if yowe deſire to be aduertiſed of ſome notable practiſe, call to remē- *Paul Dia-* brance the hiſtorie of the noble matrone of Rome, who by Sathans tentaciō *con.* encōbred and in (faith as manie be now a daies) blinded that could not bele- ue the verie bodie ād blood of Chryſte to be in the bleſſed Sacramēt, but co- ming to the Maſſe ād ioining in cōpanie with other to receaue, whē in the de- liuery of the Sacrament to her, ſhe heard theſe woordes: The bodie of our Lorde Ieſus Chryſte, awail thee to the remiſion of ſinnes, ſhe ſimiled, which when S. Gregorie perceaued and by examinaciō vnderſtoode her vnbeleue, he and the people praied and after praier going again to the aultar, and ta- king the Bleſſed Sacramēt in his hand, to the helpe of the faith of that womā and the confirmacion of the faith of the people, yt was of the one and of the other ſeen as a verie bloodie fleſhly litle fingar. Wherupon S. Gregorie wil- led her to remember the ſaing of Chryſt: *The bread which I will geue yowe, ys my flesh.* Which ſo being ſeen, and praier made by S. Greg. and the people, that

B yt might be reduced to the forme that yt might be receaued, yt came furth- with ſo to paſſe, and ſhe thus of an vnfaithfull made a faithfull receaued the bleſſed Sacrament, as other faithfull had doen. Thus ſhe holden captiue in lacke of faith in the forts of Sathan, was by the holie myniſtracion of Chryſt at the Maſſe deliuered from the ſame.

And now that we haue made reporte of one miracle, doen in the time of S. Gregorie, we will touche one or two mo reported by hym and ſo ende this matter of proof. Thus writeth S. Gregorie: *Non longè à noſtris fertur tempori-* *Greg. hom.* *bus factū, quòd quidā ab hoſtibus captus, longè tranſductus eſt. Cumque diu teneretur in vin-* *37.* *culis, eum vxor ſua, cùm ex eadem captiuitate non reciperet, extinctum putauit. Pro quo iam* *velut mortuo, hoſtias hebdomadibus ſingulis curabat offerri. Idem ergo vir longo pòſt tem-* *pore reuerſus, admirans valdè, ſuæ indicauit vxori, quod diebus certis, hebdomadibus ſingu-* *Apriſoners* *lis, eius vincula ſoluebantur. Quos videlicet dies eius vxor, atque horas diſcutiens, tunc eum* *cheines loo-* *recognouit abſolutū, cùm pro eo ſacrificiū meminerat oblatū.* Y t ys ſaied to be doen not *ſed by ver-* long before our time, that a certain man take of his enemies was caried into *tue of the* a farre contrie, and whē he was lōg kept in priſon, ſo that he could not come *Maſſe.*

C home to his wief, ſhe thought that he had bē dead. For whō as for one being dead, ſhe cauſed wekelie ſacrifice to be offred. The ſame mā after a lōg while returning home, greatlie wondring declared vnto his wief that certain daies euerie weke his bandes were looſed: Which daies and howres, whē his wief had well remembred, ſhe perceaued him then to be looſed from his bandes when ſhe cauſed ſacrifice to be offred for him. Thus he.

In this miracle reported by S. Gregorie, this maie we firſt perceaue, that *Maſſe for* the order of the vniuerſall Church was to praie for the dead, and to offre ſa- *the dead* crifice for them, which thing moued this woman ſuppoſing her husband in *before S.* captiuitie to haue bē dead, to cauſe the ſacrifice of Maſſe to be celebrated for *Gregories* him certain daies euery weke. Again this ys to be obſerued, that Chryſts ſa- *time.* crifice being offred for that man as for one that was dead, was not ouerpaſ- ſed or let fall from the mercifull ſeight and hearing of God, as a thing doē in vain, but miraculouſlie, wher yt was offred to looſe the bandes if a dead mā *Gregorius* (he being a liue) yt looſed the bādes of a liuing man. Which thing S. Grego- *ibidem.* rie verie godlie alſo doeth note vpō the ſame miracle, by theſe woords: *Hinc*

D *ergo, fratres chariſſimi, hinc certa conſideratione colligite, oblata à nobis hoſtia ſacra, quantā* *Vertue of* *in nobis ſoluere valeat ligaturā cordis. ſi oblata ab altero, potuit in altero ſoluere vincula cor-* *the Maſſe.* *poris.* Of this thē deareli beloued, of this doe yowe certēlie gather, how moch the holie ſacrifice offred of vs, maie looſe the bāde of cōſciēce, if being offred of one, yt might in an other loſe the bādes of the bodie.   Ppp   The

The fame S.Gregorie alfo reporteth an other miracle doen by one Aga E
petus,a verie holie and averteoufe man by the report of diuerfe writers,and

A miracle doen in the Maſſe vpon a dumbe and lame man.

Bifhoppe of Rome before the faied Gregorie.Yt happened the faied Agapetus go to Conftantinople to the Emperour Inftinian. Vnto whome, as he trauaiLed in the waie,was brought one being both lame and dumbe to be cured,who was fo fore taken,that he coulde neither fpeake anie woorde,nor was able to rife from the grownde. When the holy man vnderftoode, that they that brought him had faith in God,that God by him wolde cure the defeafed man,he prepared himfelf to Maſſe,and doing the folemne feruice of the fame,he offred vppe the facrifice in the feight of allmightie God, whiche being doen,he went from the aultar,and tooke the lame man by the hand,and in the feight of all the people,he lifted him vppe,and fette him on his feete.And when he had putte the bodie of oure Lorde in the mouthe of the dumbe man,that tounge that long before had ben bownde,and could not be framed to fpeake a woorde nowe ys loofed,and the man can fpeake, and with all his frendes reioice and praife God.

F

In this miracle I will not encombre the reader with manie notes,but this onelie I wifh to be marked,that the Maſſe ys holie and the power of the ble fed Sacrament ys great,for when after the Maſſe yt touched the dumbe tong yt made yt furthwith to fpeake.Now reader of manie,I haue produced a few miracles to the entent thow maift perceaue,and be aſſured,that if the doctri ne of the prefence of Chryfte in the Sacrament were wicked capharnaites doctrine(as the Aduerfarie tearmeth yt)or the facrifice of Chryft on the aul tar were the robberie of Gods honour,or the wholl myniftracion of the holie and bleſſed Maſſe were filthie ftinking abhominacion , as gods enemies abhominablie tearmeth yt,God wolde neuer commende yt to vs with fo manie miracles.And hereunto if thow adde the lowlie and reuerent feruice doen of the holie Angels vnto the bleſſed Sacrament,in the time of the Maſ fe,as yt ys teftified of Chryfoftome,S.Ambrofe,and S.Gregorie,thowe fhalt not nede(I fuppofe)to feare to folowe the faithe of the holie Church in beleuing,neither to doe the duetie,and fhewe thine obedience with them in honouring,nor to leaue thie charitie at the Maſſe time , but for the quicke G
and the dead allwaies to be praing. For why fhall man feare to confeſſe Chryftes prefence,wher the Angells doe acknowledge yt? Why fhall man ftaie to doe moft humble honoure,wher Angels vfe moft lowlie obeyfaunce? Why fhall man forfake and flee from that as from a ferpent,wher Angels are defieroufe to be prefent?

Looke therfore to thy felf(o Chryftian man)and ioin with Angell pro-
Iſſue ioined with all Sacramenries that the Maſſe was neuer by anie catholique called ?Idolatrie.
uoking thee to thy duetie,and confent not to Sathan though he call the Maſ fe,Idolatrie.For this I will aſſure thee,that the Maſſe was neuer fo termed but by Sathan.And here I will make this iſſue with Sathan and the Proclamer, and all the reft of Sathans difciples,that although the Maſſe hath ben in vfe by the Proclamers owne confefsion,more then eleuen hundreth yeares a-gone.For he faieth,although falfelie,that the name of Maſſe began but foure hundreth years after Chryfte,yet they neuer haue nor neuer fhall finde anie one approued catholique authour either within the compaſſe of thofe foure hundreth years or fince that faieth as they doe,that the Maſſe ys Idolatrie. Yf none faie yt the he and his coplices fpeake yt of them felues,*& qui ex propriis loquitur,mendaciu loquitur.*Finallie to conclude for our faith,that yt ys to H
gods pleafure,we haue befides the fcriptures and Fathers, the teftimonie of miracles.Let nowe the Proclamer,if he can,bring furth one miracle for the
confir

A   confirmaciō of his religion.Yf he can not,let him learn to know himſelf, and hys companie, to be the preiſtes of Baall vnder *Iezabel*. And let him confeſſe the catholikes the preiſtes of God with Elyas the Prophett.

Neither, reader, be thowe diſſuaded or oute of countenance , if thow ſee anie of Sathans ſcholers mocking or skorning at theſe miracles , whiche ys their maner of folowing of argumentes, when other wiſe they can not auoi de that ys ſaied. For vnderſtand and marke well, that none of theſe by me al-leaged, were yeſterdaie doen, but they were all doen before and in time of S. Gregorie. And therfore vpon the poinct of a thouſand yeares and vppe-warde, and are reported and teſtified by right graue and holie men. I knowe that theſe miracles will and haue ſpited the rebellioufe enemies of God, and his Chryſt. For the Phariſeis coulde not abide the miracles, that Chryſt him-ſelf did, but wickedlie ſaied: that in *Beelzebub* prince of Deuells he caſteth oute Deuells.   The *Arrians* not bearing miracles confirming the faith of Chryſt, which they impugned, either derided them, or ſaied they were feig-ned miracles, or flatlie , though the matter were neuer ſo euident denied

B   them, as in S. Ambroſe yt maie be at large ſownde teſtified.So for that theſe miracles commende and côfirme the catholique faith, which our heretiques nowe impugn, they will with the Phariſies, with the *Arrians* and with *Melanc thon*, and *Vadian* for ſpite mocke, and skorn at them, call them feigned miracles or denie flatlie anie ſoch to haue ben doen. But conſider thowe the repor-ters: Theie be ſainct *Amphiloch*, S. *Optatus*, S. Ambroſe, S. Chryſoſtom, S. Au-guſtine, and S. Gregorie, whiche all be in time auncient, in life famouſely ho lie, in learninge with moche commendacion excellent, of the Church euer receaued, and therfore of a vain man not to be reiected. Great ys the diffe-rence betwixt the creditte of a nombre exalted to glory, and of ſome yet liuing in ſinfull miſerie.Ther ys great oddes betwixt them , whoſe doctrine hath allwaies ben approued, and thoſe whoſe doctrine ys allwais reproued. To be ſhort, yt ys more wiſdom to beleue an holie ſainct reporting , then a wicked heretique denieng. For that then theſe miracles be reported of ſoche as be reputed holie ſainctes, yt ys verie meet, and moſt ſaiftie for vs to bele-

C   ue them.

Sermen. 9 1 de inuent. corp. Ger-uaſ. & Pro tha.

THE THREE AND FOVRTETH CHAPT. MA-

keth recapitulaciō of the conferences of the Maſſes of the Apoſtles and Fathers of the primitiue Church, and of the catholique Church that nowe ys, with a breif confutacion of the conference made by the Proclamer betwen , the Maſſe of S. Iames and that ys now vſed.

D   Oraſmoch as a matter difcourſed at large, being drawen into a compendiouſe and breif forme ys ſooner atteigned, and better kept in memorie: therfore, and for that alſo I wold take iuſt occa-ſion to open and ſhewe the folies vanities , and ſhamfull vn-trueths of the conference that the Proclamer hath made betwē the Maſſe of S. Iames, and the Maſſe nowe vſed of the catholique Church: I will, as yt were into a breif Summe collect that ys ſaied, and make a ſhorte recapitulacion of that, which of neceſsitie both for the opening of the mat-ter, and for anſwering of the Proclamer, I was compelled more at lenght to

setfurth. The Proclamer diuided the Masse into foure parts: into holie doc- **H**
trine, holie praier, holie consecracion, and holie Communion. Of the first,
which ys holie doctrine, I mene the Epistle and Gospell, but that they shoul
de be red and vsed in the Masse ther ys no controuersie, therfore haue I entred no disputacion therof. In the other three ther be by the Proclamer and
his likes, controuersies moued, which ye haue heard by sufficient good au-

A breif col thorities discussed and dissolued.
lection of   And here breiflie to repete the parts as we haue treated of them, we ha-
the conferē ue first to speake of Consecracion. Consecracion, as yt ys vsed nowe in the
ces of the catholique Churche, hath ben by me conferred to the consecracion
Masse now vsed by the Apostles and Fathers, and ys fownd in all substanciall parts to
vsed and of agree. The schismaticall mynistracion in most of them disagreeth. The
the new cō- intencion of the Apostles and Fathers in and vpon consecracion ys shewed,
muniō with wherin they are perceaued to haue beleued, that by their due consecracion,
the Masse the verie bodie and blood of Chryste by the almightie power of God and
of the A- vertue of his woord were made present in that blessed Sacrament. Wherun
postles and to the faith and intencion of the catholique Church being conferred, yt ys
Fathers. fownd fullie to agree. The schismaticall Church alltogether dissenteth and **F**
disagreed.

Sacrificev-   Vpon their consecracion the Apostles and Fathers made in the remembrā
sed of the ce of Chrysts passion, death, resurrection, ahd ascension, an oblacion or sacri
Apostles. fice of the same bodie to God the Father according to the institucion and or
abhorred of deinance of Chryst. The doing of the catholique Church in this poinct ys
the Sacra- conferred and fownd agreable. The schismaticall church ys so farre wide frō
mentaries. folowing the Apostles and Fathers, that yt can not abide to hearc soch sacrifice asmoch as once named or spoken of.

     The catholique Church in the Masse maketh humble supplicacion and
peticion for the mercifull acceptacion of their sacrifice, which maner of sup-
plicacion the Proclamer most fondlie ād vndiscretlie derideth and skorneth.
But by conference yt ys fownde that the catholike Church foloweth therin
the phrase of scriptures, Apostles and Fathers, and dothe altogether as ys
fownd to haue ben doen by them, so neerlie that yt praieth with the same
woordes that the Fathers did. The Schismaticall congregacion as yt folow- **G**
eth not the Apostles and Fathers in making this oblacion or sacrifice so con
temneth yt their praier for acceptacion.

     Thus moch being saied of Consecracion, intencion, oblacion, and accepta-
Praier for cion, we descended to the praiers in the Masse, wherin be two things which
the dead v- the Schismaticall church impugneth that ys, praier for the dead, and inuoca
sed of the cion of Sainctes. As for that the catholique Church praieth for the dead, the
Aposts ād doing therof ys conferred to the doings of the Apostles and Fathers, and yt
the cathols ys fownd that they praied for the dead in their Masses, and that they gaue
que Church ordre to frequent and vse praier for the dead, wherfore yt ys euidēt that the
despised of catholique Church in so doing foloweth thē, and obserueth their ordre ap-
the Schism. poincted. The Schismaticall Church cā not wel be cōferred herin, for yt vtter
lie abandoneth all praier for the dead so that yt hath not one title for that
pourpose, and wher nothing ys, no comparison can be made.

     Inuocacion of Sainctes vsed in the Masse, ys also conferred with the doings
Inuocacion of the Apostles and Fathers, ād fownd to haue ben doen by thē in their Mas
of Sainctes ses. The Schismaticall Church as in this yt flieth the doing of the catholique **H**
likewise. Church: so doth yt flie the doing of the Apostolique and primitiue Church
whose doctrine and example the catholique Church holdeth and foloweth.

Finallie

A   Finallie we come to holie Communion, wher the catholique Churche
ys accufed and charged in two poinctes heinouflie to offende. The one that
the preift tarieth not allwais for fome nombre of communicants: The other,
that to foche as do communicate at times, but one kinde ys myniftred. For
thefe two poincts, as for the other before, the auncient prefidents of the primitiue and auncient church are fought, and laied furth, and no commaunde
ment fownde forbidding the preift in his Maffe, or anie other man ficke or
wholl to receaue alone. And the practife alfo of the fame Church fheweth
that oftentimes one kinde onelie was receaued, and none offence therin iud
ged. Whervnto the vfe of the catholike Church being cõferred, yt ys fownd
to be agreable and to do that that in the primitiue Churche was practifed.
The Schifmaticall Church vnder pretence of fingular obedience , commit-
ting great difobedience, and vnder the countenance of fincere imitacion v-
fing a wicked innouacion, neither communicateth vnder one kinde, nor alone, thinking that of necefsitie yt muft fo be, and cõtemneth the auncient pra
B   ctife of the primitiue Church and moft fiercelie accufeth the wholl Churche
for thefe thoufand years of the tranfgrefsion of Chryftes inftitucion and
commaundement.

*Sole Com-
munion ãd
vnder one
kinde vfed
in theprimi
tiue church*

   Thus ye maie fee that the Maffe of the catholique Church for the fubftan
ciall parts, and poinctes of yt being conferred to the Maffe of the Apoftles
and Fathers of the primitiue and auncient Church, ys fownd to be fullie a-
greable, and the Communion of the Schifmaticall Church in all poincts di-
fagreable. Yf the Maffe had difagreed or diffented in anie fubftanciall poinct
thow maift be well affured(gentle Reader) that the Proclamer wolde not
by fo flender, fo impertinent yea and fo vntrue conferences , haue gone a-
boute to improue and difgrace yt, as he doeth. He conferred yt with the Maf
fe of S. Iames but in foch forte, that yf he had neuer made pithier oracion in
the difputacion at the *Paruis* in Oxforde, I ween he fhoulde neuer haue ben
alowed for a generall Sophifter . But God be praifed that his catholique
Churche ys fo appoincted , that the enemies can not finde anie
weightie matter iuftlie to repugn or reproue yt . But let vs fee his con-
C   ferences.

   S. Iames(faeth he)*faied Maffe in the common toung, as the people might vnderftand   1
him: They faie their Maffe in a ftraunge toung, that the people fhould not knowe what they
mene.* This ys the firft peice of his conference. The man lackt good ftuff to
beginne his worke, when he ys fain in the firft fhewe of all to place foch pelf.
Confider, I praie thee, gentle reader, that yf yt fhoulde be in queftion whether *Plato* were a man, and his enemie fhoulde come in and faie , he was no
man bicaufe he fpake latin, yt were but a fond argument and all together impertinent. For the matter to be tried ys aboute the fubftance of *Plato* , and
not aboute anie accident, and the enemie growndeth vpon the accident
and leaueth the fubftance : So the queftion here ys whether the Maffe be
good or no, which ys about the fubftance of the thing , and he cometh in
with an argument of an accident , that yt ys faied in latin , and therfore
yt ys not good, what ys this to the pourpofe? Manie a thing ys good in yt
felf, though yt be not of all vnderftanded. The feuen liberal Sciéces be good
though they be not vnderftanded of all men. The holie fcriptures be good in
D   themfelues though all men vnderftãd them not. Yea, euen nowe when they
be in the vulgar toung they will not fpeake fo familiarlie no not to the
mynifters, that euerie mynifter maie vnderftand them : and yet they be
                                             Ppp   iii   good.

good.So ys the Maſſe likewiſe good though all the people vnderſtand yt E
not. This argument therfore proueth nothing againſt the Maſſe.　Yt he
wolde rightlie haue proceaded he ſhoulde haue proued no Maſſe to be or
that that ys called Maſſe to be in ſubſtance not good,before he ſhoulde improue yt,for being ſaied in an vnknowen toung (as he tearmeth yt)for yt ys
meet yt be diſputed whether the thing be,before yt be diſputed whether yt
be of this maner or that.Againſt his firſt compariſon therfore we maie conclude,that as S.Iames Maſſe ſaied in the hebrue toung,was in yt ſelf godlie
and good,though the greke or latin being at the ſame vnderſtand not what
was ſaied:ſo the Maſſe nowe ſaied in the catholique Churche in the latin
toung though the engliſh or frenche man vnderſtand yt not,yet yt ys godlie
and good in yt ſelf.

2　　　His ſecond compariſon ys:*S.Iames ſpake oute the woordes of conſecracion : They
in their Maſſe ſuppreſſe the ſame woordes,and kepe them cloſe*. Hetherto the Proclamer plaieth ſmall game.　He had leuer in a weightie matter ſpeake ſome
trifling woord,then ſaie nothing.　Malice will caſt duſt or what ſoeuer cometh to hand at his enemie in want of better weapon.Here ſemeth a bare F
Armarie wher ſo weake a weapon ys bent againſt that,whiche with all force
he wolde ouerthrowe.He hath ſmall fauts to obiect againſt the bleſſed Maſſe,when lowd ſpeaking or ſofte ſpeaking ys made a faute.As before　ys ſaied,

The primi-
tiue church
praied ma-
nie praiers
of the Maſ-
ſe ſecretlie.
what ys this to the ſubſtance of the Maſſe?As the Maſſe ſaied , ys as good as
the Maſſe ſonge,ſo ys the Maſſe ſoftelie ſpoké in ſubſtáce as good as the Maſ
ſe lowdlie ſpoken.Ys not yowr owne Communion as good ſaied as ſonge,
yf ther were anie goodneſſe in yt?or ys yt not as good ſaied in a great congregacion wher ſome ſtand ſo farre of as they can not heare the woordes
of conſecracion whiche in that caſe are ſpoken as in ſofte ſilence to them,
as yt ys being ſong in a ſmall congregacion where all the people maie heare?
Were all the Maſſes in the auncient Church throughlie oute ſpoké alowde?
Let the Proclamer looke the bookes,and he ſhall finde yt otherwiſe. Did S.
Baſill in his Maſſe pronounce the wholl action of côſecracion with a lowde
voice?No,when he began the Canon to entre toward conſecracion he
praied ſecretlie,and the rule ys prefixed at the beginning of the praier:*Ponti-*
*fex ſecretè.*The Biſhoppe praieth this ſecretlie.By imitacion wherof I thinke G
yt receaued throughout the catholique Churche to praie the praiers of the
Canon ſecretlie.And when S.Baſill came to the conſecracion , did he ſpeake
the wholl proceſſe with a lowde voice?No,part he ſpake with a lowde voice,
part with a ſecret or ſoft voice,but this moch the Proclamer did not knowe
percaſe whé he obiected this ſecrette ſpeaking for a fault:Yf he did,he obiec
ted yt more of malice then of trueth or wiſdom.　Howe ſhender then thys
compariſon ys , and of what weake force yt ys ,yt maie eaſilie be perceaued.

3　　　The thirde compariſon ys this *S.Iames in his Maſſe myniſtred the Communion to*
the people:They in their Maſſe,receaue themſelues alone. This compariſon in ſome
vnderſtanding ys true,in ſome yt ſmelleth of vntrueth. Yf yt be vnderſtanded particularlie and not generally that ys,that S.Iames ſomtimes when he
ſaied Maſſe myniſtred the Communion to the people, yt ys true . And ſo yt
ys true that the catholique Church ſomtime myniſtreth the Sacrament to
to the people when Maſſe ys ſaied.　Yf yt be vnderſtanded generallie, H
that ſainct Iames at all times when he ſaied Maſſe myniſtred the Communion to the people, yt ſmelleth,I ſaie,of an vntrueth , and ſo ſhall ſtand and
be reputed , vntill the Proclamer proue yt.For I ſee ſo litle trueth , in
　　　　　　　　　　　　　　　　　　　　　　　　　　　　　　　　　　him

A in him, that withoute some better authoritie then his owne bare woorde, I can not beleue him in this matter. And that I thus doo, I haue euen in this matter good cause. For as I finde that in the Churche of Constantinople Masse was dailie saied, when the people did not communicate: so doe I finde a rule made in the auncient Churche, what the preist shoulde doo, when ther were no communicantes. Wherbie being euident that Masse was saied without communicantes, yt smelleth, as I saied, of an vntrueth, that S. Iames ministred the communion to the people allwaies, when he saied Masse. And for somoche as yt so doeth, yt raither declareth the malice of him that wolde somwhat saie against the holie Masse, thē that of certen knowlege he can auouche anie thing against yt.

Masse saied withoute communicants

In Missa Chrysost.

Nowe cometh the fourth comparison, whiche ys of asmoch force as this last was, and yet yf anie force be in all his heape of comparisons, yt ys in the se two. This ys the comparison : *S. Iames in his Masse ministred the communion to the people vnder both kindes: They in their Masse minister the Sacrament vnto the people in one kinde onelie.* A proposition framed in an argument, and not conteining
B the wholl trueth of the matter disputed, maie well be reiected wherfor in consideracion that the Proclamer trauaileth to improue euerie Masse in the whiche the Sacrament ys not ministred vnder both kindes, allegeth S. Iames Masse, as in which S. Iames did allwaies geue the Sacrament to the people vnder both kindes, this allegacion ys to be reiected as insufficient for yt ys onelie saied but not proued, and so he maketh his conclusion vpon his premisses, before the parts of his argument be graunted. Naie Sir, tarie a while and proue that S. Iames allwaies when he saied Masse ministred the Sacrament to the people vnder both kindes. And if yowe proue yt not, as I knowe yowe can not, yt shall be cast into the bagge of your vntrueths, among your other store. That S. Iames did not allwaies minister the Sacrament vnder both kindes I haue not onelie a vehement presumption, but the practise of the primitiue and auncient churche whiche wolde infringe and breake no necessarie order fullie perswadeth me so to beleue, forasmoche as in the tyme of *Tertullian*, who was near to the Apostles in the time of S. Cyprian, who was not long after him, in the time of S. Basill and other, the Sacramēt
C was diuerse times ministred vnder one kinde.

Yt ys euidēt by diuerse histories that the blessf. Sacr. hath ben ministred vnder one kinde in the primitiue Churche

But let vs see an other of his comparisons the fifte comparison ys this. *S. Iames in his Masse preached and setfurth the death of Chryste : They in their Masse haue onelie a nombre of dumbe gestures and ceremones whiche they themselues vnderstand not, and make no maner of mencion of Chrysts death.* Hitherto he hath made conferences impertinent and slender: nowe for lacke of soche pelting store, he ys fain to bodge vppe a fewe moo euen with flatt lies. I tolde yowe before his store of stuff was not great, and that his armarie was not well furnished with weapons and nowe yt doth appeare. Ye haue seen the best stuf and sharpest weapons, nowe ys he driuen to this shifte to sett vppe Skarecrowes in stead of men, I meen vntrueths in stead of trueths to skare awaie simple men frō the blessed Masse as the Skarecrowes do the simple fowls and birdes from the corne, eche of thē making the poore creatures to thinke them to be that in dede they be not. That S. Iames setfurth the death of Chryste I well allowe, and willinglie confesse but that the Masse of the catholique Churche
D ys none other then he reporteth, yt ys to manifest an vntrueth. And that my saing maie be iustified in the seight of all men, yt shall be made euident that ther be here in this one place three vntrueths packt together. Firste he saieth that the Masse of the catholique Churche hath onelie a nombre of dumbe

4.

5.

Amalicion sesslaunder.

Three vntrueths in one copari-son of the Proclamers.

Ppp iiii　　gestures

gestures and ceremonies. Secondlie, that we our selues vnderstand them **E** not. Thirdlie, that the Masse maketh no mencion of Chrysts death.

1   As for the first, what face had he so to saie, sith ther be diuerse Fathers some of two or three, some of foure or fiue, some of seuen and eight hundreth yeares agon, whiche haue written in this matter, and haue geuen a reason of euery ceremonie in the Masse, and declared what euery of them do signifie, of whiche I haue named some alreadie, so that they be not dumbe ceremonies, but liuelie signifieng vnto vs godlie things, which here to reherse ys nowe no place. But as to his shame ther hath ben mencion made allreadie of some Fathers writing of these things : so shall ther hereafter, yf I be prouoked, to his more shame and confusion, a greater nombre be produced and the ceremonies also opened and declared. In the mean while this maie be to his shame, and the confusion of his vntrueth that notwithstanding so manie authours haue written and declared these things, that he either ignorantlie or malicioullie saieth nowe that they be dumbe ceremonies. And yet to adde to these, this maie I saie, first, that in case we coulde not geue **a** **F** reason of euery ceremonie, might not the Proclamer, if he were godlie disposed, as well beare yt, as the Fathers of the Primitiue Churche who saied that of the gesturs and ceremonies then vsed, fewe coulde geue a reason or vnderstanding. Secondlie, that the gesturs and ceremonies of the Masse, are an hundreth folde more liuelie then the gesturs of their barren cōmunion.

2.   His second vntrueth being more arrogant, then reprochefull ys in this first vntrueth answered. For wher he arrogantlie condemneth the wholl Church for this thousand year, that yt did not vnderstand the ceremonies of the Masse, besides that his saing ys verie false, for that diuerse fathers haue (as I saied) written therof, he wolde be demaunded what proof he hath to maintein this his maliciouse arrogant saing. Howe proueth he that all the Church did not vnderstand the ceremonies of the Masse? Had he commission from God to examine al the Churche that hath ben since the Masse was receaued? Hath he examined all the holie Martirs, all the holie Confessours the Bishopps, Doctours, Fathers, and all other holie learned men, that haue **G** ben in all this time? Yf he hath not, howe dare he thus arrogantlie to pronounce and condemne them of ignorance. O vane arrogant man. But let vs examine his third vntrueth.

    In the third vntrueth he ys as impudent and shamelesse as he ys in the second arrogant. He saieth that the Masse maketh no maner of mencion of Chrysts death, wher yt doth not onelie contein the memoriall of Chrysts death by the consecracion, oblacion, and receauing of his blessed bodie and blood according to his institucion in his last supper, but also by outward ornamentes and gesturs expesseth all or most of the circumstances of his passion, as the albe with whiche the preist ys cloathed, signifieth the white garment that Chryste was sent in from *Herode*: the vestment signifieth the garment that he was mockt in, in the howsse of *Pilate*: the crosse vpon the vestiment signifieth the crosse of Chryste which the preist beareth on his back going to the aultar, in significacion that Chryste bare his crosse vpon his backe to the place of execution. And as Chryste was there lifted vpon the crosse: so hys bodie and blood consecrated on the aultar are ther to the liuelie remembrance of the same his eleuacion, eleuated, speaking (as yt were) **H** to vs this : As ye see this bodie and blood here lifted vppe distinctlie and sunderlie apart, so was this bodie once lifted vppe for yowe vpon the crosse, wher the side of the same bodie being peirced the blood for your redempti

on

A on ran oute and was diuided apart from the bodie as here ye fee yt apart
For the like admonicion the preiſt eleuating the blood of Chryſte ſaieth : *As often as ye dooe this, ye shall doo yt in the remembrance of me*. That
the Proclamer then ſaieth , that the Maſſe maketh no maner of mencion of Chryſts death, ys ſoch and impudent vntrueth , that a plain
man will tearme yt a ſhamefull falſe lie . This place ſuffreth me not
to anſwere euerie of his compariſons full . Wherfor I ſtaie my ſelf here,
where moche more might be ſaied, and will breiſlie touche the reſt of his
compariſons.

His ſixt compariſon ys this . *S. Iames Maſſe was full of knowlege : Their Maſſe*   **6.**
ys full of ignorance. As vain gloriouſe men, hauing not plentie of victualls
in their larders , for their glories ſake will inuent ſome toie to ſupplie
a diſh and furniſh the ſeruice , ſo this man ys nowe fain to runne to
his Rethorike to make vppe a ſhewe of compariſons . But remembre,
gentle reader , that in the conferences , and compariſons whiche I
haue made at large , I haue declared the ſame knowlege that was in
B S, Iames Maſſe , to be in the Maſſe of the catholique Churche that
ys nowe , foraſmoche as in ſubſtance they be all one. S . Iames Maſſe
hath the knowlege of the conſecracion of the bodie and blood of Chryſte : ſo hath the Maſſe of the Churche nowe the conſecracion of the
bodie and blood of Chryſte . In S . Iames Maſſe , the oblacion of
them was made in the memoriall of Chryſts death: In the Maſſe nowe the oblacion of them ys made in the remembrance of his death.
In S . Iames Maſſe was knowlege to offre the bodie and blood of Chryſte and to make praier for the liuing and dead : in owre Maſſe ys the
like. In S . Iames Maſſe was the knowlege of the receipt of the ſame bodie
and blood : in our Maſſe ys the ſame bodie and bloode receaued. Howe then ſaieth this man that our Maſſe ys full of ignorance ? Let him
ſhewe, if he can what knowlege was in S . Iames Maſſe that ys not in the
Maſſe of the Churche . Be well aſſured , Reader, that he can not . For
as the Maſſes are in ſubſtance one and not diuerſe : ſo be they in knowlege
one and not diuerſe . But this diſhe he deuiſed for yowe oute of his Re-
C thorike, of the ſame confection ys the next , whiche ys his ſeuenth compariſon , and ſaieth thus:

S . Iames Maſſe was full of conſolacion : their Maſſe ys full of ſuperſtition.   **7.**
Here ye maie ſee his gifte of amplificacion . For he hath made a lar-
ge ſhewe in tearmes , and done nothing in dede. I praie yowe , what
conſolacion was ther in Sainct Iames Maſſe that ys not in the Maſſe
nowe ? and what ſuperſtition ys in this, that was not in that ? When
yowe haue declared theſe two , and proued that yowe haue declared,
then yowr amplificacion ſhall be ſomwhat in dede . In the mean while yt ſhall ſtand for a fume of vain woordes to helpe to fill vppe yowr
vain ſermon.

As for yowr eight compariſon doth yowe ſmall honeſtie, yt ſheweth   **8.**
yowe were nere driuen, when yowe bring that in, for a newe compariſon , that was brought in before. For what difference betwixt yowr third
compariſon, wher yowe ſaied that *S . Iames miniſtred the Communion in his Maſſe*
D *to the people* , and this , which with certein alteracion of woordes yowe
make to appeare an other compariſon, when yowe ſaie. *When S. Iames*
ſaied Maſſe the people reſorted to receaue the Communion , wher in effect
                                                                                              yt

E

yt ys all one. But particularlie to faie to this comparifon, what ys this againft the goodneffe of the Maffe, that the people reforte not to receaue? yowr comparifon ys altogether againft the people that come not to receaue, as they did in the time of S. Iames, and not againft the Maffe, although yowe wolde haue yt fownde againft the Maffe, fo furioufe ys the rage of yowre herefie to impugne the fame, that yt forceth yowe blindlie to hitte other, when yowe thinke to fticke at yt. Yf yowe had faied, that when S. Iames faied Maffe, the people reforted to receaue the bodie and blood of Chryfte, but now when the Communion ys faied they come to receaue a bare mor- fell of bread, and a fippe of wine, yowe had made a newe comparifon and a true.

4.

Finallie he concludeth his comparifons thus : *And to conclude S. Iames in his Maffe had Chryfts inftitucion: They in their Maffe haue wellneer nothing ells but mans in uencion.* This comparifon femeth couertly to denie the inftitucion of Chryfte to be in the Maffe, but plainlie yt doth yt not, fearing that then yt fhoulde be reiected as a plain lie. For yt ys allreadie proued that in the Maffe ys the inftitucion of Chryfte. Wher he faieth, that yt hath wellneer nothing but mans inuencion : yf he tearme all things that the holie Goft hath appointed to be fett furth by men, the inuencions of men, I can not fkill of his inuen-

F

The order of the Maffe was left to be difpofed by the Apoftles

cions. For certen I am that of the Maffe, as yt hath ben receaued, no more but confecracion, oblacion, and communion ys of the inftitucion of Chry- fte, the reft by the inftitucion of the holie Goft, was added by the Apoftles and holie men. For, as S. Auguftine faieth, Chryfte did not inftitute or ap- poinct after what maner his fupper fhoulde be celebrated, but he left that to his Apoftles by whom he wold fet his Churche in order. Wherfor the maner of the Maffe being ordeined and appoincted at the inftruction and mocion of the holie Goft, and the appoinctment of Chryfte. yt becometh not the Proclamer fo to abufe yt, and difcredit yt with foche tearmes, cal- ling the contents therof the inuencions of men. A man in whom were regar de of God, and his holie Church, wolde not fo irreuerentlie, and fo contemp tuouflie fpeake of thinges, that yf they had not ben ordeind by the Apoftles and men Apoftolique, but had ben onelie made by godlie and vertueoufe Bifhoppes, and had continued in eftimacion and reuerence more then a thoufand years, might yt not haue be comed the proclamer reuerentlie alfo to haue receaued them, and fo haue tearmed them accordinglie? Yf his Cō munion had but one hundreth years of reuerend eftimacion, he wolde not a litle triumphe of yt. But letting that paffe as yt ys, he endeth his compari- fons thus: *Soche differéce yowe maie fee betwen S. Iames Maffe and their Maffe.* Soche ys the differéce for anie thing that he in thefe comparifons hath faied, that as before he was borne they were in fubftance all one : fo be they ftill, and fo will remain when he fhall be rotten.

G

Subftácial differéces of the Maffe and the newe Cōmunio

But where I haue made comparifons betwen S. Iames Maffe, and the Communion of the Churche of this Proclamer and his complices, yowe maie fee manifeft and great differences, not by my woordes, not by toies of rethoricall inuencion, not by vntrueths, but in the things them felues, in their fubftanciall poincts, in matters of weight and trueth. For foche ys the difference betwen S. Iames Maffe (whiche ys the Maffe of all the holie Apo les and fathers, and of the catholique Churche that hath ben or nowe ys, for in fubftance all ys one) and the newe Cōmunion of the newe Churche, that firft wher the Maffe fetting furth the matter of the Sacrament doth vfe bread, wine and water, the newe Communion vfeth no water, wherin yt

H

doth

A doth neither folowe the Apoftles, nor fo well and liuelie fet furth the death of Chryfte, as the Maffe. For as oute of the fide of Chryfte yffued oute bothe blood and water, fo the Maffe in the latine Churche at the putting in of the water into the chalice, faith thus : *of him be this water bleffed, oute of whofe fideo ran oute both blood and water.* And the greke Church faieth, thefe woordes of the fcripture : *Et vnus militum lancea latus eius aperuit, & continuò exiuit fanguis & aqua.* And one of the Soldiers perced his fide with a fpeer, and furth with ther went oute blood and water: both well minding that bleffed welfpring of Chryfts fide, oute of the whiche ran that clenfing water and blood that wafhed awaie the filth of our finnes. Here yowe fee one difference in fubftance.

The Maffe of the Apoftles, Fathers, and catholique Churche (as ys faied) had intencion, and beleued that they folowing Chryfts inftitucion fhoulde confecrate the bodie and blood of Chryfte : The newe Communion of the newe Churche hath no foche intencion nor beleueth, no nor mindeth B nor pourpofeth to confecrate the bodie and blood of Chryfte according to his inftitucion. The Maffe, as before ys faied, foloweth the inftitucion and cōmaundement of Chryfte, who commaunded faing: *This do ye in the remem.* and confecrateth as he did, his verie bodie and blood: The newe Communion, neither confecrateth the bodie and blood of Chryfte, neither abideth the name of confecracion, fo farre ys yt from that Church either to obeie Chryfte, or to folowe the church of his Apoftles and Fathers. The Maffe according to Chryfts inftitucion and commaundement, as ys proued, offreth his bodie and blood in facrifice to the Father, in the remembrance of his paffion and death. The newe Communion not onelie abhorreth this to do, but alfo detefteth both the name of facrifice, and the name of him that hath authoritie to do yt, that ys, A preift. The Maffe afwell of the Apoftles as other offreth the fame facrifice, as yt ys alfo proued, for the liuing and the dead. The newe Communion of the newe Churche, deriding both, offreth neither for the one nor for the other. The Maffe of the catholique Churche defiereth the aide and intercefsion of bleffed Sainɛts to commen-C de their feruice and praiers to God: The newe Churche fkorneth yt, and vfeth yt not in their Gommunion. The Apoftles and fathers with great reuerence and lowlie humbleneffe came to an aultar femelie, as meit yt was, adorned to do this bleffed oblacion and memoriall of Chryfts death. The minifter of the newe Communion commeth Tapfter like to a pelting table onelie to eate and drinke and to deliuer to a fewe mo a bare peice of bread and a cuppe of wine : fo that the Apoftles, and catholique Churche in their Maffe fedde them felues and the people with the bleffed bodie and blood of Chryfte the fatt and the fine flower of the heauenlie wheat, and thefe feed them felues and the people with chaf and bran in refpeɛt, euen a bare peice of bread, and a cuppe of wine. Soche differéce ys ther, and foche maie yowe fee betwixt the Apoftles Maffe, and the newe communion. And thefe defferences be in weightie matters and fubftanciall poinɛts, foche as the doing or refufing of them, bringeth life or death, heauen or hel, faluacion or damnacion.

Wherfor, Reader, looke well to thie doings, ther ys no dallieng in Gods, D matters. For the Maffe ther haue ben brought furth without all haulting or colouring, withoute all diffembling and lieng the auncient prefidents of the Apoftles, of their Difciples and of the Fathers of the Apoftolique and primitiue Churche, as plainlie, as truelie, and as fimplie, as they be commended

to

E

to vs by the books of our elders. As for the comparifons of the Proclamer, befides, that they be but voluntarie deskant, they are toies, colours of Rethorik, cloaked vntrueths, fetfurth withoute all authoritie. Nowe therfor, which ys to be embraced, whether the Maffe commended to vs by fo good authoritie, great antiquitie, long and reuerend continuance: or the newe Communion fet furth without good authoritie and of no antiquitie, and neuer yet reuerentlie continued, yt ys of him that hath either grace or wifdom eafie to be perceaued. Wherefor trufting that I haue fufficientlie inftructed and warned the reader aboute the Maffe, I ende and go forwarde in my matter.

THE FOVRE AND FOVRTETH CHAPT. RETVR-
ning to the expofition of S. Paule, expowndeth this text. As
often as ye shall eate of this bread &c. by S Hye
rom and Theophilact.

F

Doo here omitte the inftitucion of the Sacrament declared by S. Paule to the Corinthians, as he had receaued the fame of our Lorde, for that in the feconde booke thofe woordes of Chryfte, and that his inftitucion ys largelie fpoken of and expo wnded by a great nombre of holie learned Fathers. Wherfor I thought yt wolde be to tedioufe to the reader, and fuperfluoufe for me to ex pownde the fame woordes here a gain.

I come therfor to the woordes immediatelie folowing in S. Paule. *As often as ye shall eate of this bread, and drinke of the cuppe, ye shall shewe furth the death, of oure Lorde vntill he come.* For that this text hath ben woonderfullie abufed and by foche abufe manie of the fimplie haue ben deceaued, and caufed otherwife to thinke and beleue of the bleffed Sacrament, than the trueh ys, I haue thought yt good to open the true vnderftanding of the fame fcripture to the reader, that he being inftructed maie withdrawe his foote from the fnares of Sathan, and well efpie his falfhoode, and fo efchewe foch erroure, as he wolde entrappe him into.

G

Two argu-
ments of
the Sacra-
mentaries
grownded
vpon S.
Paule.

Vpon this text the miniftres of Sathan haue grownded two argumentes againft Chryftes reall prefence in the bleffed Sacrament. The one ys (*as theie faie*) that by this fcripture yt ys manifeft, that the Sacrament ys inftituted for a memoryall of Chryft: A memoriall ys of a thing that ys abfent. Wherfor the Sacrament ys a memoriall of Chryft that ys abfent and not prefent. For (*faie they*) what neadeth a thinge prefent, anie memoriall? yt will caufe yt felf to be remembred. The Sacrament then being a memoriall of Chryft, argueth Chryft not to be prefent in the Sacrament, but to be abfent. The other argument ys, that S. Paule calleth the Sacrament not the bodie of Chryft but calleth yt bread. For he faieth that as often as ye fhall eate of this bread, and faieth not, as often as ye fhall eate the bodie of Chryft in the Sacrament wherfor (*faie they*) the Sacrament ys but breade and not the bodie of Chryft.

Solucions
of the fame
argn.

As touching the firft, yt ys not true that Chryft did inftitute this Sacrament as a memoriall of him felf or of his bodie, but of his paffion and death fuffred in his bodie. which thing S. Paule here by expreffe woordes doeth teache faing: *As often as ye shall eate this bread, and drinke this cuppe ye shall declare or fetfurth the death of our Lorde.* So that the eating and drinking of this Sacrament ys not for a remembrace or a memoriall of the bodie of Chryfte

H

in

A in yt felf, as the Aduerfarie falfelie pretendeth, but ys (as ys faied) a memorial of the paſſion and death ſuffred, as ys faied, in that bodie, which paſſion and death be once doen actuallie, ād neuer ſhall ſo be again in that gloriouſe bodie, but onely in myſterie. Wherfor the paſſion and death whoſe memoriall ys celebrated in that ſolemne inſtitucio̅ of Chryſtes Sacrament ys and euer ſhall be abſent, and neuer preſent. And ſo ys the Sacrament the memoriall of a thing abſent and not preſent, which thing ys the paſſion and death of Chryſte.

Receipt of the B.Sac. ys not a memoriall of Chryſts bodie but of his paſsion and death.

As touching their ſecond argument, true yt ys that S. Paule calleth the Sacrament bread, but will the Aduerſarie therupon induce that S. Paule meneth materiall bread? euen bakers bread? Though he wolde ſo induce: yet he neither doth nor can ſo prooue yt, nor neuer ſhall. Bread he calleth yt, but what bread? euen ſoch as Chryſt the inſtitutour of the Sacrament called yt whe̅ he ſaied: *Panis que̅ ego dabo, caro mea eſt, quam dabo pro mundi vita.* The bread

B that I will geue, ys my fleſh, which I will geue for the life of the world. Wherfor S. Paule did not barelie call yt bread, but with an article, ſaing: *This bread.* As who might ſaie: As often as ye ſhall eate of this bread, which ys no common bread, but the bread of the fleſh of Chryſt, which as he gaue yt for the life of the worlde: So he did according to his promiſſe, geue yt vs to eate in the Sacrament, that we ſhoulde alwaies haue that his paſſion and death in minde. Therfore ſo often as ye eate of this bread, be ye mindefull of Chryſtes paſſion, and remembre his death ſuffred for yowr redemption. Wherfor the wholl Chryſtian church aſwell the greke church as the latin immediatelie after the conſecracion (as before ys declared) doe ſaie this in effect. *Were therfor(o Lorde)being mindefull of the paſsion of thy ſonne our Lord Ieſus Chryſt doe offre vnto thee, &c.* The wholl catholique Church by open profeſſion of their ductie in the holie myniſtracion declareth their obedience, and the fulfilling of Chryſtes commaundement, in that they offring and receauing the bleſſed ſacrifice of Chryſtes bodie and bloode, be mindefull of the paſ-

C ſion and death ſuffred in that ſame bodie, at the effuſion of that precioufe blood. Thus ye ſee howe they abuſe this ſcripture. For both S. Paules owne woordes, and alſo the practiſe of the wholl Church, doth declare that the holie Sacrament was inſtituted as a memoriall of Chryſtes death, and that yt ys not co̅mon bread, by S. Paules owne woords, but yt ys (as ys faied) a ſpeciall and ſingular bread noted with an article.

Ioan 6. S. Paule calleth the Bl. Sacr. bread but he addeth withal the article this, to ſignifie a ſpeciall bread.

Woords of the Cano̅ in the Maſſe.

But that this trueth maie be proued, and therby their falſhead the more confuted, I will alſo as I haue vpon other textes produce the expoſitions, ād vnderſtanding of holie Fathers and doctours, that yt maie be fullie perceaued how this ſcripture ys to be vnderſtanded, not by phantaſie, but by their fownde doctrines. And firſt we will heare faint Hierom vpon the ſame text, who ſaieth thus: *Ideo hoc ſaluator tradididit Sacramentum, vt per hoc ſemper commemoremus quia pro nobis eſt mortuus. Nam & ideo cu̅m accipimus à ſacerdotibus com monemur, quia corpus & ſanguis eſt Chriſti, vt beneficiis eius non exiſtimemur ingrati.* Therfor our ſauiour deliuered this Sacrament, that by this we ſhoulde allwaies remembre that he died for vs. For therfore alſo when we receaue yt, we are warned of the preiſtes, that yt ys the bodie and blood of Chryſt, that we be not thought to be vnthankfull for his benefittes.

Hieron.in. 11.1. Cor.

What S. Paule calleth bread, S.Hieron calleth yt the bodie of Chryſte.

D If this ſaing of S. Hierom be well noted, thoſe two thinges, which I before taught, ſhall be fownde to be taught of him alſo. I taught, according to faint Paule, that the Sacrament was inſtituted for the memoriall of Chryſtes paſſion and death, ſaint Hierom ſaieth that Chryſt therfore gaue furth

the Sacrament,that we ſhould allwaies remembre that he died for vs,ſo that **E**
yt ys the death of Chryſt that ys to be remembred.I ſaied that though ſainct
Paule in this text vſeth this woord bread:yet he meneth not materiall bread
but the heauenly bread the bodie of Chryſt:ſo ys he vnderſtanded of ſainct
Hierom.For he ſaieth,that when we receaue the Sacrament, we are admoniſhed that yt ys the bodie and blood of Chryſt.So what ſainct Paule in the
text calleth bread,that S. Hierom in the expoſition calleth the bodie and
bloode of Chryſte.Nowe who doubteth but the expoſitions of holie doctours be to explain that that ſemeth in the text not to be plain,and ſo plainlie and clerely to open the trueth and the true meaning of the text. Forſomoch then as ſainct Hierom doeth ſo here:we muſt nedes ſaie that by this
woorde(bread)in this text of S.Paule , ys vnderſtand the bleſſed bread of
Chryſtes bodie.

Theoph.in
11.1.Cor. To S,Hierom,we ſhall ioin *Theophilact*,to declare howe this ſcripture was
vnderſtanded in the greke Church.Thus he writeth:*Hoc facite, quoties biberi-*
tis,in meam commemorationem.Per poculum iſthuc(inquit)memoriam facis Dominicæ paſ- **F**
ſionis.Quid tu igitur ſolus bibis & inebriaris,tremendo iſto calice omnibus ex æquo tradito?
This doe as often as ye ſhall drinke in the remembrance of me.By this cup-
pe(ſaieth he)thowe makeſt a memoriall of our Lordes death, why thē doeſt
thow alone drinke,ād arte dronkē ſeeing that this fearfull cuppe ys equallie
deliuered to all.Thus *Theophilact*.

Cuppe of
our Lorde
a fearfull
cuppe. Se ye nōt that the cuppe of our Lordes table ys receaued in the remembrance of his death?But yt ſhall not be without profit to learn of him whie
he calleth our Lordes cuppe,a fearfull cuppe.Yf yt be but a cuppe of wine(as
the Aduerſarie ſaieth)yt ys not fearfull but pleaſaunt. Why yt ys a fearfull
cuppe yt ys declared of the ſame *Theophilact* expownding the text immediatelie going before,which ys this:*Likewiſe when he had ſupped he tooke the cuppe,ſa-*
ing:This cuppe ys the newe teſtament in my bloode,vpon this text he ſaieth thus: *Fue-*
runt & in veteri Teſtamento calices ſiue pocula,quibus ſanguinem brutorum poſt victi-
mam oblatam libarent.Pro ſanguine itaque brutorum,qui vetus Teſtamentum veluti ſigil-
lo conſignabat,meum ego nunc ſanguinem pono,nouum Teſtamentum eo ſeu ſigillo muniens.
Ne turberis igitur ſanguinem audiens.Nam ſi irrationabilium ſanguinem pecorum accepiſti
*in veteri Teſtamento:quanto potius nunc diuinum?*Ther were in the olde Teſtament **G**
alſo cuppes or pottes in the which after the ſacrifice they ſhould offre the
bloode of brute beaſtes.Therfor for the blood of brute beaſtes, whiche did
ſigne the olde Teſtament as with a ſeale, I nowe ſetfurth before yowe my
bloode , ſigning therwith the newe teſtament as with a ſeale. For yf thowe
haueſt receaued the blood of vnreaſonable beaſtes in the olde Teſtament,
howe moch raither maiſt thowe now receaue the blood of God?

In this expoſition I wiſh yt to be noted,howe the authour in the perſon
of Chryſt ſpeaketh,ſaing:For the bloode of brute beaſtes I put before thee
A plain
place for
the Procla
mer. my bloode.Seiſt thowe then whie he calleth the cuppe of our Lorde a fearfull cuppe?Yt ys bicauſe owre Lorde in that cuppe putteth before thee hys
owne bloode.And what blood ys yt?Ys yt the blood of a pure or onelie
man? Naie ſaieth *Theophilact*,yt ys the bloode of God. *For*(ſaieth he) *yf in the*
olde teſtament the blood of vnreaſonable beaſtes was receaued, moch more nowe receaue
*thowe the blood of God.*Perceaue thē that yt ys the blood of God that ys in the
cuppe of our Lord.Wilt thowe fullie perceaue whie yt ys fearful?Cōſider ād **H**
vnderſtād that ſoch is the coniunctiō of the Godhead with the manhead in
Chryſt,that wher the māhead ys or any part of yt(if now yt maie be parted)
there

A ther ys alſo the Godhead. In the death of Chryſt, the ſoule was parted from
the bodie: the ſoule deſcended into hell, the bodie laie in the graue: the
Godhead was whollie with the Soule deſcended into hell, yt was alſo whollie with the bodie lieng in the graue: Euen ſo wher the blood of Chryſt ys,
forſomoch as Chryſt ys both God ād mā, that blood ys the blood of God al
ſo ād ſo ther ys the blood of God ād mā, which now being inſeparable both
from the manhead and the Godhead of Chryſt, wher the blood of God ys,
ther ys alſo God himſelf.　Nowe then foraſmoch as in the cuppe of our
Loord ther ys the blood of God (as *Theophilaƈ* ſaieth) and where the bloode
of God ys, ther of conſequence ys alſo God: doth not *Theophilaƈ* well in calling yt a fearfull cuppe? who maie not well feare to approche ſo near vnto
hys Lorde God, and the more that he knoweth his owne filthineſſe, and ther
by his vnwoorthineſſe? As nowe yowe knowe whie the cuppe of oure Lorde
ys fearfull: ſo, what ſo euer the Aduerſarie bableth to the contrarie, ye haue
learned that in owre Lordes cuppe ys not bare wine but the bleſſed
blood of God.

B 　What ſhall I neede to alleadge anie mo of the ſainges of *Theophilaƈ*, ſeing
he hath allreadie opened the trueth that we ſeke for namelie that the Sacrament ys a memoriall of Chryſtes paſsion and death, and ys alſo the ſame bo　*Theoph.*
die and blood of Chryſt that ſuffred. Yf any man will deſyre anie other place　*Ibid.*
let the ſame vnderſtande that *Theophilaƈ* expownding this place, *as often as ye*
ſhall eate this bread, and drinke of this cuppe, ye ſhall ſhewe furth the death of our Lorde　*What we*
vntill he come, ſaieth thus: *Eo affeƈtu debetis eſſe imbuti, perinde quaſi in illa ipſa eſſe*　*aught to*
tis Chriſti cæna, & ab ipſo Chriſto acciperetis ſacrum iſtuc. Illa enim ipſa cæna eſt, & illam　*thinke in re*
ipſam mortem annunciamus. Ye ſhould be of the ſame minde, or ſo be haue yowr　*ceauing the*
ſelues, as though ye were in the ſelf ſame ſupper of Chryſt, and ſhoulde take　*Bl. Sacr.*
of Chryſt himſelf this holie thing. Yt ys euen the ſame verie ſupper, and we
ſhewe furth the verie ſame death. Yf ye will learn of *Theophilaƈ* what Chryſt　*What*
gaue in his laſt ſupper, expownding Chryſtes woordes reherſed by S. Paule,　*Chryſt de-*
he ſaieth thus: *Ille verò in cōmune, & generatim omnibus dixit: Accipite, edite, idque*　*liuered in*
corpus ſuum, quod pro omnibus ex equo fregit, in mortem tradens. But he in cōmon and　*his laſt ſup*
generallie ſaied to all: *Take, and eate, yea and that his bodie,* which he brake equal-　*per.*
C lie for all deliuering yt to ſuffer death. Thus *Theophilaƈ*.

　Here ye perceaue by him, that Chryſt gaue his bodie in his laſt ſupper.
And if this doe not ſatisfie yowe, know that this *Theophilaƈ*, as before ys ſhewed in the ſecond booke, and ells wher, wher he expowńdeth S. Matthewe,
Marke, Luke, and Iohn, ſaieth that Chryſt gaue in his laſt ſupper, his verie bo
die, ād not an onely a figure of his bodie. By all this then yt ys euident, that
Theophilaƈ vnderſtandeth by the woorde bread in S. Paule, the bodie of
Chryſt, and not materiall bread, and that that bread and cuppe are to be eaten and dronken of, not in the remembrance of that bodie in yt ſelf,
but in the remembrance of the paſsion and death ſuffred in the ſame bodie.

THE FIVE AND FOVRTETH CHAP. ABIDETH E

in the expofition of the fame text by fainct Bafill and Rupert.

Wolde haue ftaied my felf, ãd ceaffed to haue produced aniemo authours for the expofition of this text:but well knowinge that manie(as is faied)haue abufed it and deceaued manie,I thought yt expedient,and neceffarie for the helpe of the vnlearned,fomwhat more to faie vpon yt,by the expofitions of S. Bafill and *Rupertus.* And whether we take a peice of bread in the remembrance of Chrift, or whether we receaue the bodie and blood of Chryft in the remembrance that he fuffred for vs in that bodie,and fhedde that precioufe blood,we will firft heare S.Bafill,who writeth thus:*Oportet accedentem ad corpus & fanguinem Domini,ad rememorationem eius,qui pro nobis eft mortuus, ac refurrexit,non folùm purum effe ab omni inquinamento carnis ac fpiritus,ne ad iudicium edat,ac bibat, fed & euidenter oftendere & exprimere memoriam eius qui pro nobis mortuus eft,ac refurrexit.* Yt behoueth him that cometh to the bodie and blood of our Lorde to the remẽbrance of him that hath died for vs,and rifen again,not onely to be pure from all vnclenneffe of bodie,and foule,leaft he eate and drinke to his owne condemnacion,but he muft alfo euidentlie fhewe and declare the memorie of him that hath died for vs and rifen again.Thus moch S.Bafil.

Nowe wher S.Paule faieth,that as often as we eate of that bread,anddrinke of that cuppe we muft declare the death of Chryft:S.Bafill faieth that he that commeth to the bodie and blood of Chryft muft remembre him that died for vs.So that what S.Paule in termes called,this bread and this cuppe, S.Bafill geuing vs to vnderftand what S.Paule meneth by thefe termes fpeaketh by plain woordes,calling thofe thinges as they be in dede, the bodie and blood of our Lord. Likewife yt maie be perceaued that S. Bafill folowing S.Paule teacheth that the Sacrament ys a memoriall of Chryft as fuffring for vs,ãd not of Chryft in himfelf or abfolutelie without refpect of paffion and death fuffred for vs,which ys afmoch to faie as a memoriall doen in the remembrance of Chryftes pafsion and death agreablie to the fainges of other before alleadged.

Rupert alfo,whom we ioin at this prefent with S.Bafill,doeth euen likewife vnderftand S.Paule.Thus he writeth:*Sacramentum hoc,quo mors eius annunciatur(quemadmodum Apoftolus dicit:quotiefcunque manducabitis panem hunc, & calicem bibetis,mortem Domini annunciabitis donec veniat)quando debuerat condi & dari,nifi fub ipfius articulo pafsionis.* This Sacrament by the which the death of our Lord ys declared(as the Apoftle faieth:*As often as ye fhall eate this bread, and drinke of thys cuppe ye fhall fhewe furth the death of our Lorde vntill he come)* when fhould yt be made,and geuen furth,but euen at the verie poinct of the fame pafsiõ ? In thys faing of *Rupert,* the one parte of our faing,namely that theSacrament ys a memorial ofChryftes death ys clerely by expreffed woords teftified. The other part,that in the Sacrament the verie bodie and blood ys eaten and dronken to and for the memoriall of the fame death ys not here manifeftlie fpoken? Wherfor we fhall heare him in an other place vttering his knowledg in thys matter.Thus he faieth:*Quod fecit ipfe,hoc idem in commemorationem ipfius fcimus , et bene fcimus,nos facere,id eft carnem ipfius manducare,& fanguinẽ bibere.* That which Chryft himfelf did,we know and we wel know that we doe euen the verie fame thing in the remembrance of him that he did,that ys to eate his flefh and drinke his bloode.

Marke now the learning of Chryftes catholique Church,note nowe well what we eate and drinke in the remembrance of Chryftes pafsion and

Bafilius de Baptifmo.

A plain place for the Proclamer

What S. Paule calleth bread, and cuppe S.Bafil calleth the bodie ãd blod of our lord.

Rupert . in cap. 26. Matth,

Rupert . in 6.Joon. we eate the flefh and drinke the blood of Chryft in the remembrance of his death.

A and death.Iudge nowe whether S.Paule ment materiall bread as the Sacra
mentaries wolde haue yt to be vnderftanded,and not raither the heauenlie
bread of Chryftes bodie to be eaté in the remébrance of his paffió ád death.

I haue now produced but fower,two of the greke Church and two of the
latin Church,to geue vs vnderftanding what we ought to remébre in the re
ceipt of the Sacrament,and what in that Sacrament we doe receaue,wheru-
pon they all conclude that we receaue the bodie and blood of Chryft in the
remembrance of his death,and fo S.Paule ys to be vnderftáded in this place.
Now let all the whol rable of theAduerfaries fide bring furth but two,wher
as we might(as the Aduerfarie himfelf knoweth) haue brought manie mo,
which for the auoiding of more prolixitie, wherin we haue allreadie offended we doe ouerpaffe and omitte, that fhal by expreffe woordes expownde
S.Paule in this place;that he ment not the bodie of Chryft,but plain materiall bread:Let them,I faie,bring but two catholique,approued authours,ád
they fhall haue the victorie.So weake ys their caufe befides their owne affe-

*All the ra-
ble of the
Sacramen-
taries can
not bring
one coople
of catholike
authours
that faie S.
Paule fpa-
ke here of
materiall
bread.*

B ueracion,that yt ys verie certen they can not bringe one.

Although then this ys a trueth receaued of all the holie Fathers of Chryftes Church,and ys the doctrine of S. Paule , that the bodie and blood of
Chryft be receaued according to commaundement in the remembrance of
his paffion and death,and fo yt alfo cometh to paffe,that the bodie ofChrift
euen the felf fame bodie in fubftance vnder the formes of bread andwine,ys
a figure of the felf fame bodie hanging vpon the croffe,and fuffring paffió ád
death:yet *Oecolampadius* after his Sicophants maner,he himfelf either of mali
ce not willing to knowe,or ells plainlie ignorant, doeth accufe the learned
men of Chryftes Church of ignorance,that they make the bodie of Chryft
both the exemplar and the thing exemplified,the figure,and the thing figura
ted,the fign and the thing fignified,for that (faieth he) relacion muft be betwixt two thinges diftincted,and not of one thing to ytfelf.For euery relati
ue muft haue a correlatiue.

*Inexpofitió
verborum
cænæ.
Obiectió of
Oecolamp.*

To anfwere him for that I write to the vnlearned to inftructe them in the
faith,I will not vfe the quiddities of fchooles,neither with fchoole tearmes
C fo darken the matter,that the reader fhall not vnderftand me, but I will vfe
plain examples.And firft,wher *Oecolampadius* faieth:that relacion muft be betwixt two thinges diftincted,did he not knowe that in the diuine perfons
were fundrie relacions grownded vpon the one nature of God.But to come
to examples in Chryft of whome we nowe difpute,was not Chryft tranffigu
red in the mount,and fhewing himfelf in a glorionfe maner, was he not an
exemplar or figure of himfelf now in glorie,and of his glorioufe cominge to
iudgement?*Theophilact* faieth that *Dignitas fecundi aduentus in fplendore faciei Chrifti ineffabili claruit* . The dignitie or excellencie of the fecond cominge of
Chryft did appeare in the vnfpeakable brightneffe of the face of Chryft . So
that Peter Iohn and Iames fawe now in his firft coming an image of the glo
rie of Chryft that he fhall come in his fecond coming.Then maie we fee that
the felf fame bodie in fubftance after one maner,maie be an exemplar or figure of the fame bodie after or in an other maner. Chryft fhewed his bodie
to *Thomas*,and other the Apoftles with the fignes and tokens of his woundes,was not that bodie now immortall and impaffible an exemplar of the
D fame both mortall and paffible?

*The nn-
fwer.*

Matth.17.

*Theoph. in
17.Math.
Chryft one
and the fa-
me in fub-
ftace hath
ben,ys and
fhalbe a fi-
gure of him
felf in diuer
fe maners.*

The fcripture faieth,that the wicked fhal in iudgement fee Chryft,whom
they pricked and perced.For(as Chryfoftom faieth)he fhall appeare with his
croffe and woundes in the face of the worlde.This ys his faing: *Sed cur cùm*

*Chryfoft.
hom.de cru
& latrone*

*cruce veniat videamus,scilicet vt hi,qui eum cruci fixerunt,suæ sentiant dementiæ cæcitatem & ideo dementiæ eorum signum portatur . Ideo Propheta ait . Tunc lamentabuntur tribus terræ,videntes accusatorem,& agnoscentes peccatum.Et quid mirum est, si crucem portans adueniet,quando & vulnera corporis ipse demonstrat.Tunc enim(inquit) videbunt quem compunxerunt.Et sicut post resurrectionem Thomæ voluit diffidentiam commutare, & illi clauorum loca monstrauit,& laterum vulnera declarauit,& dixit: Mitte manum tuam,& vide,quoniam spiritus carnem & ossa non habet:sic & tunc ostendet vulnera, crucemque demostrabit,vt istum ostendat illum esse qui fuerat crucifixus.*But whie he co
meth with a crosse, let vs see,forsooth that they that crucified him maie per

*Chryst shal
come to iud
gemēt with
the signe of
the crosse
ād the prin
tes of the
woondes he
suffred.*

ceaue the blindenesse of their madnesse. And therfor ys the signe of their
madnesse caried.Therfore the Prophet saieth:*Then shall all the tribes of the earth
mourne seing the accuser,and they acknowleging the sinne.*And what wonder ys yt yf
he come bringing a crosse,seing that he himself doeth shewe furth his woun
des.*For then (saieth he)shall they see whom they haue pricked.*And as after the resur
rection he wolde amende the lacke of beleif in *Thomas,*and did shew him the
places of the nailes,and opened the woundes of his sides,and saied:*Put furth
thy hande and see,that a spiritt hath not flesh and bones.*So then also shall he shewe
his woundes,and shall openlie setfurth his crosse in seight,that he maie shew
this man to be him that was crucified.Thus Chrysostome.

 Seing then Chryst shall côme to the generall iudgement withwoundes ād
crosse representing the state and condicion of himself somtime a passible ād
a mortall man,he yet now being impassible,and immortall,and being soche
an examplar of himself,as he shall cause the faithfull vpon the remembrance
of that seight to reioice that they embraced his faith and receaued the bene
fett of their redemption wrought and doen vpon the crosse, and by the suffring of the woundes nowe ther shewed:and the wicked contrariwise vpon
the same seight to waile and mourne that through their madnesse they contemned him,by whom they now perceaue they might haueben saued:Why
maie not the same bodie in the Sacrament cause the faithfull nowe to their
comforte as well to remembre the passion and death and their redemption
wrought by yt,and so to be a memoriall to them,as yt shall be both to the
faithfull and wicked at the daie of iudgement?At the daie of iudgemēt that
same bodie shall be a memoriall and an examplar of yt self,yt being the same
verie bodie in substance that yt was,but chaunged in maner,as ys saied?why
maie not the same bodie be now likewise to vs that be faithful,who by faith
see yt as certenlie though in a darke maner,as then we shall see yt with open
face?Of these kindes of examples ther be manie in the scriptures,but to him
that will be satisfied these be sufficient.For by these yt ys made euident,that
that Chryst in one maner of being,maie be a figure of himself in an other
maner of being.Wherfore Chryst in the Sacrament vnder the formes of
bread and wine, maie right well be and ys a figure of himself hanging vpon
the crosse,and suffring for our redemption.Thus ye see the true vnderstanding of this scripture laied before yowe,oute of the holie doctours, and the
cauills of the Aduersarie solued,which be against the same.Now to the next
scripture.

THE

A
THE SIX AND FOVRTETH CHAP. BEGINNETH
the expofition of this text : Who foeuer therfor shall eate
of this bread, and drinke of the
cuppe &c.

S ye haue feen the fcripture laſt handeled recouered from the wreſting and wicked abuſing of the Aduerſarie : ſo by Gods grace ſhall yowe ſee this that foloweth. Thus ymmediatelie ſaieth S. Paule. *Itaque quicunque manducauerit panem hunc & biberit calicem Domini indignè, reus erit corporis & fanguinis Domini.* Whofoeuer therfor ſhall eate this bread, and ſhall drink of the cuppe of our Lorde vnwoorthilie, ſhall be giltie of the bodie and bloode of our Lorde.

After the Apoſtle had declared the inſtitucion of the honorable Sacrament, and ther vnto had added the caufe of the fame, namelie that yt ſhoulde be doen in the remembrance of Chryſtes paſſion and death, that neither the Corinthians to whome he wrote, who abuſed the fame Sacrament, neither other chryſtians ſhoulde thinke them felues to haue doen to God, their high and due feruice if they onelie had receaued the fame Sacrament as the memoriall of Chryſtes paſſion and death, other circumſtances not regarded, he goeth aboute to open vnto them two maner of receiptes, and the rewardes apperteining vnto them : that ys to ſaie, an vnwoorthie receipt, and condempnacion for the rewarde of yt : and a woorthie receipt, and grace ād glorie for the reward of yt. Forafmoch thē as their ys foch diffe rence in receauing, meet yt ys that the difference be knowē, that we maie diſ cerne, who ys a woorthie receauer, and who ys an vnwoorthie receauer. As woorthineſſe and vnwoorthineſſe be contraries, and therfor the one ys kno wen by the other : So the woorthie receauer being knowen yt ſhall be eaſie to knowe the other.

B

C

TWoo thinges are required to a woorthie receauer, true faith and per-fight charitie. For as *Ignatius* ſaieth : *Fides eſt principium vitæ. Charitas eſt confummatio. Hæ duæ fimul iunctæ, & in vnitate factæ Hominem Dei perficiunt.* Faith ys the beginning of life. Charitie ys the confummacion. Theſe two ioined toge-ther and made in one, doe perfect a man of God. As the one of theſe with-oute the other doth not make a perfect mā in God : ſo the one without the other dothe not make a woorthie receauer. But if both be ioined together in the receipt of the Sacrament, then ys that man a woorthie receauer. Faith here ſpoken of ys not a peiced or patched faith, that beleueth one part of the catholique faith, and refuſeth and other, but yt ys a true and an wholl faith. Wherfor heretiques be no woorthie receauers. Charitie here, ys not taken for that loue that a man flattereth him felf to haue when he thinketh he lo-ueth his neighbour : but for that charitie that S. Paule ſpake of, when he ſa-ied : *Qui diligit, legem impleuit.* He that loueth hath fullfilled the Lawe. This loue cauſeth a man to ioin in vnitie with God and man. Yt cauſeth obedi-ence to an ordinarie power. Yt cauſeth a man alfo to flee all corrupt licencio-uſe, and voluptuouſe life. Wher this charitie ys not, be his faith neuer ſo ſownde he ys no woorthie receauer. Wherfor Scifmatiques and contem-ners of ordinarie power, and voluptuouſe or corrupt liuers be no woor-thie receauers.

D

Thus moche being ſaied of woorthie and vnwoorthie receauers, ther re-maineth two other thinges in S. Paules woordes to be ſpoken of the one ys

Ignatius epla ad E-pheſios.
Faith and charitie to gether ma-ke woorthie receauers of the bleſſ. Sacr.

Twothings to be confi-dered in S. Paules woordes

E what ys receaued, the other the peine inflicted for vnwoorthie receauing. The thing to be receaued ys signified when he saieth: *This bread, and the cuppe of our Lorde.* The peine , that he shall be giltie of the bodie and blood of our Lorde.

For the first, what the bread and the cuppe of our Lorde ys, yt was opened in the exposition of the last scripture, that S. Paule ment therby the bodie and bloode of our Lorde. Whiche exposition shall here again be verified and iustified by a nombre of holie Fathers to the entent the trueth receaued in Chrystes Parliament house maie be well knowen, and the vntrueth of the aduersarie as well perceaued and seen.

The second, whiche ys the pein inflicted to the vnwoorthie receauer forasmoche as yt shall be plainlie opened and declared by soche auncient writers, as I shall alleage, I will to auoide prolixitie omitte to speake of yt my self and referre the Reader , to the expositions of the Fathers, For the whic **F** he consideracion also forasmoche as S. Paule repeteth this text again, I haue thought good for the ease of the reader, to ioin them together in exposition onelie letting him vnderstand the difference betwixt them, that in this text, the pein (as ys saied) of the vnwoorthie receauer ys declared, in the other both the pein and the cause also ys opened. Of both whiche full declaracion shall be made by the Fathers.

The Sacra mentaries abuse S. Paules woordes in two poinctes. But before I entre into the exposition of these Fathers I wish the Reader to vnderstand that the Aduersarie hath also abused this scripture in two poinctes : The one that bycause S. Paule calleth the Sacrament bread . Therfor yt ys after yt ys consecrated materiall bread: the other, whiche ys more stowtelie then trulie mainteined , they saie that euell men doe not receaue the bodie of Chryst in the Sacrament . These their wicked assertions by Gods grace shall be plainlie ouerthrowen. For yt shall be ineuitablie proued, that by the bread and cuppe that S. Paule speaketh of ys vnderstanded and meat the bodie and bloode of Chryst, whiche being by S. Paule receaued of euell men, yt must necessarilie folowe that euell men receaue the bodie of Chryst in the Sacra. And here maie we see the miserable strictes, that men teaching an vntreuth be brought vnto, who for the maintenace of that vntrueth are **G** enforced to fall into manie moo. For the damnable heresie inuented against the presence of Chryst in the Sacrrment, they are compelled to denie the plain woordes of S. Paule, as ye shall in the processe perceaue. But let vs heare the holie Fathers agreeablie shewing their learninges and faith in vnder standing S. Paule, of the whiche the first coople shall be saincte Cyprian and Origen.

Cypr. li. 3. epist. 15. S. Cyprian writing to certain Martirs and confessours, and lamenting the rash admission of certain that had offended to the recipit of the holie Sacrament, writeth thus of them so had admitted the offendours. *Illi contra euangelii legem, vestram quoque honorificam peticionem, ante actam pænitentiam, ante exomologesin grauissimi atque extremi delicti factam ante manum ab Episcopo & clero in pænitentiam impositam, offerre pro illis, & Eucharistiam dare, id est, sanctum Domini corpus prophanare audent , cùm scriptum sit : Qui ederit panem , aut biberit calicem Domini indignè, reus erit corporis & sanguinis Domini.* They against the lawe of the Gospell, and yowr commendable peticion, before they had doen penannce , before they had made confession of their most greuouse and extreame offence, be **H** fore anie hand was putt vpon them , of the Bishoppe and the cleargie vnto penance, they were so bolde both to offre for them , and also to geue vnto them the Sacrament, which ys as moch , as to prophane the holie bodie of

our

A our Lorde. Forafmoch as yt ys written : *He that eateth the bread and drinketh the cuppe of our Lorde vnwoorthilie, shall be giltie of the bodie and blood of our Lorde.* Of this holie Father and martir, S. Cyprian, if yowe will learn what ys to minifter the Sacrament to anie vnwoorthie perfon, *ytys* (faieth he) *to prophane to holie bodie and blood of our Lorde.* That yt ys prophaned in fo doing he prooueth by this fcripture of S. Paule : *He that eateth and drinketh vnwoorthilie shall be giltie of the bodie and bloode of our Lorde.*

　A thing ys prophaned, when yt being holie ys occupied aboute vnholie or cōmon vfes. As a church dedicated to God to be made a ftable. The ornamentes of the fame to be applied to the vanitie of mans pride, as to make beddes hanginges or cooſhinges. The plate of yt, as king *Balthafar* did with the plate of the temple to make them veſſells for the bankettes of men . So the bodie of our Lorde, faieth S. Cyprian, ys prophaned forafmoch as yt being holie, ys caſt into an vnholie thing, whiche ys the vnwoorthie receauer. Now if by the bread fpokē of in S. Paules fentēce were not vnderftāded the bodie of our Lorde, to what pourpofe ſhould S. Cypriā alleadge that text,

B as therby to prooue the bodie of Chryſt prophaned. That thing ys prophaned that ys deliuered and fo abufed. Yf thē not the bodie of our Lorde be deliuered in the Sacramēt, but mere materiall bread, than ys the bread prophaned and not the bodie. But Cypriā faieth the bodie ys prophaned, wherfore the bodie ys deliuered·

　And here I wiſh the minifters of Chryſtes Chürche to take hede, and to be verie circūfpeꝗ, that they looke well to whō they miniſtre this holie Sacramēt, leeſt they be dot onelie giltie of the prophanaciō of the holie bodie of our Lorde: but alfo be in verie dede, not feeders, but deceauers, not deliuerers frō finnes, but heapers and increacers therof, as S. Cypriā faieth in the fame epiſtle. *Ea enim cōcedere quæ in pernitiē vertāt, decipere eſt. Nec erigitur ſic lapſus, ſed per Dei offenfam, magis impellitur ad ruinam.* To geue or graunt thofe thinges that turne to a mans deſtruꝗiō ys to deceaue. Neither ys the offēder fo fett in good ſtaie, but by the offēce of God, he ys more impelled to ruine. Which offēces,

C I meē as well of the miniſtre deliuering, as of the vnwoorthie receauer receauing, being well weighed of Chrifoſtome howe weightie, ād burdenoufe thei be, he faieth thus of the deliuerie of the Sacramēt. *Non permittā iſta fieri animam prius tradam meam quam Dominicū alicui corpus indignè. Sanguinemꝗ; meū effundi potius patiar, quamfacratiſsmum illum fanguinē præterqā digno cōcedā.* I will not fuffer thefe thinges to be doē, I will firſt deliuer vppe mi life, rhē I will deliuer the bodie of our Lorde to anie bodie vnworthilie: And I ſhall fuffer my bloode raither to be ſhedde , than I will geue that moſt holie bloode to anie other then to a worthie receauer.

　Howe moche maie the fentences of thefe two graue auncient Fathers moue foche as be in the place of miniſtracion. Let them take heed that miniſtre to heretiques. Let them take heed that miniſtre to fcifmatiques. Let thē take heed that miniſtre to foche as they knowe to be in finne or in the pourpofe of finnes: They were better with . Chryfoſtom to deliuer vppe their liues, and ſhed their bloode, then to foche to deliuer the bleſſed bodie and moſt holie bloode of our Lorde.

　Here with all, good Reader, note, that Chryfoſtome alludinge to this our text of S. Paule, and opening what S. Paule fpake of ther, and what he ment

D bi the bread and the cuppe, calleth yt neither bread nor figure nor figne, but by plain and expreſſe woordes calleth yt with tearmes of honoure, that ys, *owre Lordes bodie ād his moſt holie blood.* Again note if the bodie of our Lorde were
　　　　　　　　　　　　　　　　　　　　　　　　　　　　receaued

The praꝗiſeof prophanaciō ys lamentablie to be ſee in Englond.

li. 3. epla. 15.

Chryfoſt: hom 83. in. 26. Matth.

receaued onelie bi faith (as the Sacramétaries doe faie) fo that yt ftood vpõ E
the will of the receauer, according as he will meafure his faith, not vpon the
power of God, and his woorde vfed in the confecracion: then wolde not
Chryfoftom faie that he wolde not deliuer the bodie and blood of our Lorde, for yt fhoulde not lie in his power to deliuer yt, yf he haue yt not in the
Sacrament to deliuer. But let thefe Sacramentaries faie their phantafies and
let vs that loue Chryftes true faith folowe yt in the holie fathers, and let vs
with Chryfoftom beleue, that the minifters of Chryftes Church maie deliuer vnto vs the bodie and blood of Chryft. Whiche then muft nedes be in
the Sacrament.

Orig ho.6
in diuerf.

But yt ys time to heare *Origen* S.Cyprians yockfelowe in this place, what
light he geueth vs to vnderftand S. Paule. Thus he writeth: *Quando fanctum*
cibum, illudque incorruptum accipis epulum, quando vitæ panè & poculo fueris, manducas
& bibis corpus & fanguinem Domini, tunc Dominus fub tectum tuum ingreditur. Et tu er-
go humilians temetipfum, imitare hunc Centurionem & dicito: Domine non fum dignus vt
intres fub tectum meum Vbi enim indignè ingreditur, ibi ad iudicium ingreditur accipienti.
When thow takeft the holie meate, and that vncorrupte bankett whé thowe
receaueft the bread and cuppe of life, then our Lorde entereth vnder thie F
roofe, and thow humbling thie felf, folowe this *Centurio* ãd faie: Lord I am not
woorthie, that thow fhouldeft enter vnder my rofe wher he entreth vnwor
thilie, ther he entreth to the condemnacion of the receauer. Thus Origen.

Who willing the chryftian man to be a woorthie receauer of the holie
Sacrament, he doeth firft declare the greatneffe, the holineffe and excellencie of the Srcrament, and what he receaueth. Which doen as a meã to make
a man to humble him felf he moueth him, to the intent that he maie be a
woorthie receauer, to folowe the humbleneffe or humilitie of *Centurio* in
acknoweleaging, and confesfiinge his vnwoorthineffe, and the raither to cõpaffe this he feareth him from vnwoorthie receauing with the terrour of S.
Paules fainge, whiche nowe we haue in hand, faing: where he vnwoorthilie entreth he entreth to the condemnacion of the receauer. In the whiche
his godlie admonicion and exhortacion ye maie firft perceaue with what
woordes he doeth extoll the bleffed Sacrament, with foche woordes trulie
that if the bodie of Chryft were not ther, they coulde not fo be applied. G
But he was certen of that bleffed prefence, and therfor he faied: when thowe takeft this holie meate, when thowe receaueft this vncorrupt bankett,
when thowe enioieft this bread, and cuppe, thowe eateft and drinkeft the
bodie and bloode of our Lorde. Secondlie, ye maie perceaue that receauing
the facrament ye receaue not a bare peice of bread, but the bodie of Chryft.
For then (faieth *Origen*) owre lorde entreth in vnder thy roofe, mening that
he entreth the houfe of thie bodie. Thirdlie, ye maie perceaue that the fame
our Lorde as he maie entre into our houfe of our bodie woorthilie', as he
did into the houfe of *Centurio*: fo maie he (faieth *Origen*) entre into owre
houfe of our bodie vnwoorthilie· And if he fo dooe, yt ys to the damnacion of the receauer.

What S.
Paule cal-
leth the
bread Ori-
gen calleth
it the bodie
of our Lor-
de.

Nowe conferre S. Paules faing and *Origen* togeather. S. Paule faieth, he
that eateth this bread and drinketh this cuppe vnwoorthilie &c: *Origen* faieth
wher our Lorde entreth vnwoorthilie &c: So that, what S. Paule calleth
bread, and the cuppe of our Lorde, *Origen* openinge and declaring the minde of S. Paule, calleth yt as yt ys in dede, our Lorde. Thus for the vnderftã H
ding of this text of S. Paule whiche the Aduerfarie hath wickedlie abufed,
wrefted, and diftorted taking the Apoftle to haue fpoken of verie materiall
bread

A breade : ye fee thefe two pillers of the Church, and auncient Fathers of Chryftes Parliament houfe teach the true vnderftanding receaued in that houfe in their time, which was verie near the primatiue church, that S. Pau le did not ther fpeake of materiall bread, but of the bodie of owre Lorde, the heauenly bread.

Likwife the Aduerfarie hath taught, that euell men receaue not the bodie of Chryft, ye fee that thefe two Fathers do auouche that euell men doe receaue the bodie of our Lorde. For S. Cyprian faieth that to geue the Sacrament to an vnwoorthy man, ys to prophane, not the Sacramentall bread (as the Aduerfarie tearmeth yt) *but the holie bodie of our Lorde.* So that yt ys the bodie of our Lorde being a moft holie thing that ys prophaned , bicaufe yt ys geuen to an euell man, which ys an vnwoorthie thing. *Origen* faieth alfo by expreffe woordes, that wher our lorde entreth vnwoorthilie, he entereth to the condemnacion of the receauer teaching plainlie that our lorde entreth into the vnwoorthie man. Chryfoftome alfo, whome by occafion I

B haue in this chapter alleadged, faing that he will raither yelde his life , and fhed his bloode, than he will geue the bodie of our Lorde and his moft holie bloode to an vnwoorthie man: fignifieth that yt maie be geuen to an vnwoorthie man. Yf nothing were deliuered but bread and wine, what neded Chryfoft for fmall a matter raither to fpend his bodie and bloode the to deliuer yt? Perchaunce fome one maie obie& , that *Origen* ys otherwife to be vnderftanded in this place, then ys here declared, bicaufe he in an other place by expreffe woordes faieth , that an euell man can not eate the bodie of Chryft. To this obie&ion anfwere ys made in the xxx chap. of this booke, whether for the auoiding of prolixitie, I remitte the Reader, and procead to heare moo of the auncient Fathers of Chryftes Parliament houfe, to the en tent, that we maie perfe&lie learn the ena&ed trueth of the vnderftanding of S. Paule in this place.

S. Cyprian and Origē teache that euell mē receaue the bodie of Chryſt.

THE SEVEN AND FOVRTETH CHAPT. PROCEA-
deth in the vnderſtanding of the ſame by
ſainct Baſill and ſainct Hierom.

C

FOr fomoche as nothing doth more declare the trueth of anie matter called in controuerfie in matters of our faith, then doeth the confonant, and accorde teftimonie of maie holie learned Fathers, of fundrie times, places and ages, as well of the greke churche , as the latin churche : Therfor fhall I proceade to bring furth mo of the holie auncientes of Chryftes Parliament houfe, that their agreement and concorde maie be perceaued in the vnderftanding of S. Paule. In the whiche, gentle Reader, truft me, thowe fhalt finde fo great confent, and fo euident matter, that this alone fhall fuffice, to bring thee or ftaie thee in the matter of the bleffed Sacrament, to beleue Chryftes verie reall prefence ther, if Gods grace hath not forfaken thee, that thowe wilt willfullie or obftinatelie refufe to fee the clear beames of the Sunne.

Wherfor to go to our matter note well this fainge of S. Bafill who asketh this queftion, whether yt be withoute daunger, that anie man not beinge

D clean from all filthineffe of bodie and Soule, maie eate the bodie and drinke the bloode of our Lorde : wherunto he maketh this anfwere : *Quoniam Deus in legè ſupermam pænam conſtituerit contra eum , qui immundicia audet contingere ſanĉta, ſcriptum eſt enim, figuratè quidem illis, ad noſtram verò commonefaĉtionem. Et locutus*

Baſil.li. dē Baptiſ. 2. ques. 93.

eſt

eſt Dominus ad Moyſen, Dic Aarone & filiis eius, vt attendant à ſanctis filiorum Iſraël, &
non contaminabunt nomen meum, quicunque ipſi ſanctificant mihi, Ego Dominus. Dic ipſis
in familias ipſorum : Omnis homo, qui acceſſerit ab omni ſemine veſtro ad ſancta quæcun-
que ſanctificauerint filii Iraël Domino, & immundicia ipſius in ipſo: anima illa extermi-
nabitur à facie mea. Ego Dominus. Tales minæ propoſitiæ ſunt côtra eos qui ſimpliciter acce-
dunt ad ea quæ ab hominibus ſanctificata ſunt , Quid verò quis dixerit contra eum, qui in
tantum ac tale myſterium audèt? Quanto enim plus templo hic eſt, iuxta ipſam Domini vo
cem , tanto grauius & horribilius in inquinamento animæ audere contingere corpus Chri-
ſti, quàm attingere arietes aut tauros? Sic enim Apoſtolus dixit : Quare qui ederit panem,
& biberit poculum Domini indignè reus erit corporis & ſanguinis Domini. Vehementius
autem ſimulque horribilius proponit ac declarat condemnationem per repetitionem dum ait:
Probet autem vniusquiſque ſeipſum, & ſic ex pane hôc edat, & ex poculo bibat. Qui enim
edit & bibit indignè, iudicium ſibi ipſi edit ac bibit, non diiudicans corpus Douini. Si verò
qui in ſola immundicia eſt (immundiciæ autem proprietatem figuratè ex lege diſcimus) adeo
horrendum habet iudicium, quanto magis qui in peccato eſt, & contra corpus Chriſti audet,
horrendum attrahet iudicium? Foraſmoche as God in the lawe hath ordeined ſo

greate a pain againſt him, that in his vncleanneſſe ys ſo bolde to touche the
holie thinges. For yt yt written figuratiuelie to them, but for aduertiſement
to vs . *And our Lorde ſaied vnto Moyſes, Saie to Aaron and his ſonnes , that they take*

A plain pla-
ce for thr
proclamer
both for
the preſence
and the ex-
cellencie of
the bl. Sacr.
aboue the
Sacramēts
of the olde
lawe.

heed of the holie thinges of the children of Iſraël , and whatſoeuer they ſhall ſanctifie vnto
me, they ſhall not defile my holie name, I am the Lorde. Saie to them, and to their families:
Euerie man that ys of yowr ſeed , and cometh to the holie thinges, what ſoeuer they be that
the childeren of Iſraell ſhall ſanctifie to the Lorde, and his vneleneſſe be vpon him, that ſou
le ſhall be putte awaie from my face. I am the Lorde. Soche threatinges are ſettfurth
againſt them that onelie come to thoſe thinges that be ſanctified of mē. But
what will a man ſaie againſt him that ys ſo bolde to come with his vnclen-
neſſe to ſo greate a miſterie? Looke howe moche greater this *(mening Chryſt*)
ys then the temple, according to the verie ſaing of our Lorde : *So moche more*
greuouſe and horrible ys yt in the filthineſſe of his ſoule to be ſo bolde to touche the bodie of
Chryſt, as to touche râmes or bulls For ſo the Apoſtle hath ſaied: wherfor he
that eateth the bread âd drinketh the cuppe of our Lorde vnworthilie, ſhall

begiltie of the bodie and blood of owre Lorde. But more vehemēlie, âd alſo
more horriblie he doeth ſettfurth and declare the condemnacion by repeticion, when he ſaieth : *Let euery man examin himſelf and ſo let him eate of this bread,*
and drinke of this cuppe. For he that eateth and drinketh vnwoorthilie , he eateth and drin-
keth his condempnacion, making no difference of our Lordes bodie . Yf then he that ys
in vncleanneſſe onelie (the propertie of which figurated vncleānſſe, we haue
learned of the Lawe) hath ſo horrible iudgement, howe moche more he
that ys in ſinne, and dareth to preſume vpon the bodie of Chryſt, ſhall drawe vnto him ſelf horrible iudgement? Thus moche S. Baſill.

Whoſo doeth but ſuperficiallie note this ſaing of his maie eaſilie perceaue the difference betwixt the lawe and the Goſpell: Betwixt the vncleanneſſe ſo reputed in the lawe, and ſinne reputed for vncleanneſſe in the Goſpell, and figured by the vncleanneſſe in the lawe. But cheiſlie the difference betwixt the ſacrifice of the olde lawe, and the partaking of them , and the ſacrifice of the newe lawe , and the partaking of yt: the excellencie alſo of this aboue that, ând therunto agreablie, and to the ſolucion of his queſtion, the greatneſſe of iudgement and côdempnacion to the euell partaker of the

holie ſacrifice of the Goſpell aboue the pain of the euell partaker of the ſacrifice of the lawe.

But leauing the firſt twoo differences and to ſpeake of the other twoo, for
that

A　that they appertein directlie to the matter that we haue to speake of ye shall note that they be conteined breiflie, in this one sentéce wher he saieth: Howe moche greater Chryst ys then the temple, so moche more greuouse and horrible pain remaineth for them that being defiled in the soule, dare touche the bodie of Chryst, than doeth them that touche but Rammes, and bulls? In whiche woordes the sacrifices of both lawes are expressed. The sacrifice of the olde lawe were Rammes, and bulls: The sacrifice of the newe lawe ys the bodie of Chryst. The euell or vnworthie partakers of the sacrifices of the lawe were soche as were vnclean with vncleánesse described in the lawe: The vnwoorthie partakers of the Sacrifice of the Gospell are soche as with deadly Sinne or the pourpose of yt, being defiled in Soule, doe presume to receaue Chrystes bodie in the holie Sacrament. The pain of an vnwoorthie partaker of the Sacrifices of the lawe was death corporall: The pain of an vnwoorthie receauer of the sacrifice of the newe lawe (which ys the bodie of Chryst) ys death eternall. This he prooueth by the scriptures of S. Paule, whiche we nowe haue in hand. For (saieth he) S. Paule saieth, *Whosoeuer shall eate the bread and drinke the cuppe of our Lorde vnwoor-*

B　*thilie, shall be giltie of the bodie and bloode of our lorde.*

　　Nowe, gentle Reader, weigh with me I paraie thee, that wher S. Basil saied that so greuouse and horrible condemnacion shall fall vpon them, that with vncleannesse of soule presume to touche the bodie of Chryst, howe doth he prooue the same by this sainge of S. Paule, yf by the bread and cuppe therin spoken of, be not vnderstand the bodie and bloode of Chryst? Yt ys therfor most certé that holie Basil so aleading S. Paule, vnderstood him by the bread and cuppe to haue most assuredlie mét that blessed bread of Christes bodie, and the cuppe of his holie bloode in the Sacrament. Basill was not so base in learning, nor so simple in iudgement, that he speaking of the vnworthie receauers of Chrystes bodie, wolde for the confirmacion of his sainge alleadge a text that speaketh but of a peice of bread, and nothing to his pourpose. No, he was of an other maner of learning and grauitie of iudgement.

C　As this text by his iudgement, ys vnderstanded of the bodie and bloode of Christ: So ys the other also, which (saieth he) S. Paule speaketh by repetició. Vpon the which text he maketh like exposition, as he did of the other before, but in more compendiouse maner, saing thus: *Si verò qui in sola immundicia est, adeo horrendum habet iudicium, quanto magis qui in peccato est, & contra corpus Christi audet, horrendum attrahet indicium?* Yf he that ys in the vncleanesse of the lawe onelie hath so horible iudgement, howe moche more he that ys in sinne, and dare presume vpon the bodie of Chryst shall drawe vnto him horrible iudgement? In the wiche who seeth not that he, as one expownding and declaring S. Paules wordes, geueth vs to vnderstand that S. Paule by the bread meneth the bodie of Chryste? For wher S. Paule saieth, *He that eateth this bread vnwoorthilie eateth his owne damnacion*: S. Basill saieth: *He that presumeth vpon the bodie of Chryst shall haue horible Damnacion.*

　　A moche like questió the same S. Basil moueth in the same booke, which also openeth the trueth of our matter. This ys the questió. Whether yt be wi-

D　thoute daunger that he that ys not pure in heart from an euell conscience and vncleannesse of life maie doe the office of a preist. In the aunswere of which questió he saieth thus: *Dominus dicens: plus templo hic est, erudit nos quòd tanto magis impius est, qui audet tractare corpus Domini, qui dedit semetipsum pro nobis oblationem, & hostiam in odorem suauitatis, quantum corpus vnigeniti filij Dei excedit, arietes, & tauros, non in comparationis ratione, Incomparabilis est enim excellentia.*

Rrr　　Owre

Yf Chryste be receaued in the bl. Sace. but spirituallie, howe can the sinner presume vpon the bodie, which he nor will nor cã receaue?

S. Basill vnderstandeth Sainct Paule to speake of the bread of Chrysts bodie.

*Let fchif-
maticall ãd
irreuerent
preifts note
well this
faing of S.
Bafill.*

Owre lorde faing: This man ys greater then the temple (*mening him felf*) tea- E
cheth vs that he ys fo moche the more wicked that ys fo bolde to handle
the bodie of our Lorde, who gaue him felf an oblacion and facrifice of fwete Sauour, as moche as the bodie of the onelie begotten Sõne of God doeth
excead Rammes, and Bulls, not by the mean of comparifon. For the excellencie ys incomparable. Thus ther. Of Sainct Bafill in this place we learn,
that the office of preifts ys not (as the Aduerfarie faieth) to handle a peice
of Sacramentall bread : but to handle the bodie of our lorde. euen the fame
bodie that the fame lorde gaue an oblacion and facrifice to God the Father
in the Sauoure of fwetenesse. And as that bodie incomparablie exceadeth
Rammes and Bulls, whiche were figures of that bleffed bodie : So doeth
yt incõparablie excead a peice of bread, being alfo but a figure of that bodie.

And here Reader if thowe be defieroufe to knowe the trueth, note and
marke well, howe great condemnacion commeth to them, that vnwoortilie
handle the Sacrament, aboue them that vnwoorthilie handle the facrifices
of the olde lawe ãd Teftament: They are (*Saieth Sainct Bafill*) as moche more
wicked, as the bodie of the onelie begotten Sonne exceadeth Rammes and F
bulls. Yf the vnwoorthie receauer of the Sacrament be fo moche more
wicked aboue the vnwoorthie receauers of the Sacrifices of the olde lawe,
as the bodie of the onelie begotten Sonne of God exceadeth Rammes and
bulls : yt prooueth well that the receauer of the Sacrament, receaueth the
bodie of the onelie begotten Sonne of God, or elles why fhoulde he be fo
incomparablie wicked, yf he did not wickedlie receaue that bodie? Soche incomparable wickedneffe, fo greuoufe, and exceading condemnacion can not
be but vpõ the abufe of an incõparable thing, which ys the bodie of Chryft,
and not Sacramentall bread. The receipt of Sacramentall bread, ys but a receipt of a figure : The receipt of a figure, though yt be euell ys not incomparablie wicked. Wherfor the receipt of the Sacramentall bread though yt be
euell receaued ys not incomparablie wicked : but the receipt of the Sacrament, yf yt be euell, ys incomparablie wicked. Wherfore the receipt of the
Sacrament ys not the receipt of Sacramentall bread.

*Yf the
bleff. Sacr.
be but afi-
gure as the
Sacramẽts
of the old
lawe were,
whie do the
euell recea-
ners offend
fo incompa-
rablie?*

And here plainlie to faie yf the Sacrament were but a figure of the bodie G
of Chryft and did not contein the fame, whie fhoulde the receauer of yt be
more wicked, and fuffer more greuoufe and horrible damnacion, then they
that receaued the figures of Chryft in the olde lawe? And here Reader vnderftanded that by the doctrine of the Aduerfarie, the Sacramentes of the
newe lawe, are no better, then the Sacramentes of the olde lawe. Which yf
yt be true, wheer ther ys equalitie betwixt the thinges themfelues : ther ys
the abufe, I mean the vnwoorthie receauing equall alfo. But to an equall
abufe iuftice inflicteth an equall pain. Wherfor for the abufe of the Sacrmen-
tes of both lawes, ther fhoulde be equall pain. But the pain for the abufe of both Sacramentes are not equall. For the pain of the abufe of this
Sacrament exceadeth the other as farre, as the Sonne of God exceadeth Rã-
mes, and bulls. Wherfor the Sacramentes alfo are not equall. By that then
that the pain of the vnwoorthie receauinge of the bleffed Sacrament, fo farre exceadeth the pain of the abufe of the Sacramentes of the olde lawe : yt H
maie well be perceaued that this Sacrament incomparablie excelleth the
other. And for as moche as S. Bafill teacheth them to be as farre different,
and as farre to paffe the one the other, as the Sonne of God exceadeth Rammes, and bulls, yt ys euident that the thinges them felues be euen the fame
that he fpeaketh of, as abufed by euell receipt. Wherbie alfo yt muft nedes folowe,

A lowe, that the bodie of the Sonne of God ys receaued of euell men in the bleff.Sacrament.

　But that ye maie heare him by moft plain woordes teache as moche harken what he faieth in an other place : *Si verò is qui fratrem propter cibum offendit à charitate excidit, fine qua & magnorum donorum & iuftificationum operationes nihil profunt : Quidnam dixerit quis de eo, qui ociofe, & inutiliter edere audet corpus, & bibere fanguinem Domini noftri Iefu Chrifti ?* Yf he that for meate offendeth his brother falleth from charitie, whitoute the whiche both the woorkes of great giftes, and alfo of iuftificacions doe nothing auaill, what fhall a man faie of him that idely and vnprofitablie dareth to eate the bodie and drinke the bloode of our lorde Iefus Chryft ? What can the Aduerfarie faie to this? Be not thefe woordes plain? Saieth not Bafill that a man maie eate the bodie and drinke the blood of Chryft ydelie,and vnprofitablie? And who can eate the bodie of Chryft, and drinke his bloode vnprofitablie, but the euell and finfull man ? For of the good receauer Chryft faieth : *Qui manducat meam carnem, & bibit meum fanguinem, habet vitam æternam.* He that eateth mi flefh and
B drinketh my blood,hath euerlafting life.

Bafil. de Bapt. li. 1. cap. 3.

A plain place that euell men maie eate the bodie of Chryfte and drinke his blood.

But vnprofitablie.

Ioan.6.

　But I haue taried long vpon Sainct Bafill : I will therfor be fhort aboute Sainct Hierom, who ys placed with Sainct Bafill to fhewe the enacted trueth of the vnderftanding of Sainct Paule in the latin Church, as the other hath doen in the greke Churche. Thus writeth Sainct Hierom vpon this verfe of the pfalme : *Adhuc èfcæ eorum erant in ore ipforum, & ira Dei defcendit fuper eos.* While the meat was yet in their mouthes the wrathe of God fell vpon them. *Hæc de his qui Deum paft acceptnm Manna dereliquerunt. Nam nunc in Ecclefia fi quis carne & fanguine Chrifti reficitur, & declinat ad vitia, nouerit iudicium Dei fibi imminere, ficut Paulus Apoftolus ait : Qui acceperit corpus & fanguinem Domini indignè, reus erit corporis & fanguinis Domini.* Thefe woordes be fpoken of them, that did forfake God, after they had receaued Manna. For nowe in the Church yf anie man be fedde with the bodie and bloode of Chryfte and doeth decline to vices, let him knowe that the iudgement of God ys at
C hand, as the Apoftle Paule faieth : *He that taketh the bodie and bloode of our lorde vnwoorthilie,fhall be giltie of the bodie and bloode of our lorde.*

Hieron. in Pfal.77.

A plain expofition of S.Paules woordes for the Proclamer.

　Marke here the faing of Sainct Paule reported by Sainct Hierom, and fo fhalt thowe fee the verie minde and true vnderftanding of Sainct Paules fentence, whofe vnderftanding we nowe feke. S. Hierom faieth,that S.Paule faieth thus:*He that taketh the bodie and bloode of our Lorde vnworthilie,fhal be giltie of the bodie and bloode our lorde.* In dede, as yt ys allreadie often reherfed, the woordes of Sainct Paule be not foche : yet Sainct Hierom faieth he faieth fo, bicaufe in verie dede, the authour faieth that, that Sainct Paule doeth mcen. As when Chryft did faie : *Deftroie this Temple, and in three daies I will reedifie yt,* The Iewes according to the outward fownde of the woordes, faied:that he fpake that faing of their verie Temple. But the Euangelift well knowinge the minde of his mafter,faied : *Hoc autem dicebat de templo corporis fui.* This he faied, of the temple of his bodie Nowe yf a man fhoulde faie, that Chryft faied. Deftroie ie or kill this my bodie and in three daies I will raife
D yt vppe again,he fhall with the Euangelift faie the trueth of Chryftes faing, though Chryftes woordes were not the fame woordes : yet Chryft did fo faie bicaufe he did fo mcen : So likewife here doth Sainct Hierom. Sainct Paule fpeaketh of bread, as Chryft did of the Temple. The Iewes tooke him to haue fpoken of the verie materiall temple, as the Sacramentaries doe Sainct Paule of materiall breade But as the Euangelift teftifieth that

Ioan.2.

　　　　　　　　　　　　　　Rrr ij　　he

he saied yt of the temple of his bodie: so Sainct Hierom testifieth, that Sainct **E** Paule spake this of the bread, which ys Chrystes bodie. And so sure was S. Hierom by the instruction of the holie Gost, and by the doctrine of the holie catholique Churche, that this was the true meening of Sainct Paule, that he boldlie saied, and with all holie Fathers agreablie, that Sainct Paule saied: he that eateth and drinketh the bodie and blood of our Lorde vnwoorthilie, shall be giltie of the bodie and bloode of our Lorde. This then being the saing of Sainct Paule, the Sacramentarie saing that he doeth speake of materiall bread, and not of the bodie and bloode of our Lorde, they lie vpon S. Paule, misreport him, and slaunder him, to maintein therwith their blasphemouse and pestilent doctrine. These two Fathers thus being heard, we will procead to heare other vpon this scripture.

THE EIGHT AND FOVRTETH CHAP. ABIDETH
in the exposition of the same text by Chrysostom, and
saincte Augustine.

F

YT liked the holie Euangelist Luke to the great commendacion of the Apostolique Church to reporte of yt thus : *Multitudinis credentium, erat cor vnum, & anima vna*. Of the multitude that beleued ther was one heart, and one sowle. For in dede as God ys one. So hath he appointed one faith, one baptisme to ioin all his faithful together, in one, and so of manie membres to make one bodie. This one bodie he wolde to haue one minde For the whiche Chryste also before his departure did most earnestlie praie to his heauenlie Father sainge : *Pater sancte, serua eos in nomine tuo, quos dedisti mihi, vt sint vnum, sicut & nos*. Holie Father kepe them in thy name, whome thowe haueft geuen me, that they maie be one, as we be one. By this vnitie, soche as the Father hath geuen to Chryst are knowen. For they, as they haue one God, and one baptisme, so haue they one faith, one minde, and one religion. *Deus est, qui habitare facit vnanimes in domo*. Yt ys God **G** that maketh men of one minde to dwell in the house of his Churche. Contrariewise soche as be not of Chryst, soche as the Father hath not geuen vnto him, they haue forsaken the house of God, bicause they will not be of one minde with them that be of the house, neither yet within them selues. They haue not one faith, one minde, nor one Religion. Let vs therfor laboure and trauaill to staie and settle our selues, wher we finde vnitie. Hitherto seking the vnderstanding of Sainct Paule by Sainct Ciprian, *Origen*, Basill, and Sainct Hierom, we finde an vnitie in them, all sainge as yt were one thinge, we shall therfor make farder triall, and call in an other coople, whiche shall be Chrisostom, and S. Augustine.

Chrysost. hom.45.in Ioan.

Thus writeth Chrisostome : *Qui enim manducat & bidit indignè sanguinem Domini, iudicium sibi manducat & bibit. Nam si qui Regiam purpuram coinquinant, haud secus quàm qui scindunt puniantur: Quid mirum, si qui immunda conscientia Christi corpus accipiunt, idem supplicium subeant, quod qui clauis eum cruci affixerunt*. He **H** that eateth and drinketh the bloode of our Lorde vnwoorthilie, eateth and drinketh his owne condemnacion. For yf they whiche defile the kinges purple robe, are punished as they which cutte the same : what merueill yf they which an vnclean conscience receaue the bodie of Chryst, suffer the same punishement, that they did which crucified him vpon the crosse.

Chrysost. vttered the woordes of S. Paule as S. Hierom did.

In

A   In this fainge of Chrifoftome firft note that he alleaging Sainct Paule vfeth not the woordes of bread and cuppe, whiche be in Sainct Paules fentence, but vfeth the woordes ment by them, namelie the bloode of our Lorde, and vfing that, he vnderftandeth alfo the bodie. For the bloode ys not withoute the bodie. For wher Sainct Paule faieth : He that eateth and drinketh the bread and cuppe of our Lorde : Chrifoftome expownding what therby ys ment of Sainct Paule, faieth: he that eateth and drinketh the blood of our Lorde &c. So by bread and cuppe in Sainct Paule, ys vnderftanded the bodie and blood of Chryft by the expofition of Chrifoftome. Wherin he agreth with Sainct Hierom, and others before alleadged, whiche doe likewife fo expownde the fame.

Note again that Chrifoftome proceading by a fimilitude, to open and declare the faing of Sainct Paule, faieth: *What merueill then yf they which with an vnclean confcience doe receaue the bodie of Chryft be punifhed as they whiche crucified Chryft ?* Wherin be two good leffons geuen vs for the confirmacion of our faith, and the true expofition of Sainct Paule, The one ys, that the bodie of

B   Chryft ys receaued in the Sacrament. Whiche woordes of Chrifoftome being vttered, as an expofition of Sainct Paule, declare that Sainct Paule fpeaking of the bread of our Lorde, vnderftoode therby the bread of Chryftes bodie, the heauenlie bread, and not the Sacramentall bread, whiche ys earthlie breade. His woordes be not obfcure, but plainlie he tearmeth yt the bodie of Chryft. The feconde leffon ys, that the bodie of Chryft being reallie and fubftaciallie in the Sacramēt, ys receaued both of good and euell men. Of the good ther ys no doubte. Of the euell alfo that yt ys receaued, Chrifoftom here by the woordes of S. Paule, doeth expreffedlie teache. For faing: *What merueill yf they which with an vnclean confciēce doe receaue the bodie of Chryft:* he doeth bothe open what Sainct Paule meant by vnwoorthie receauing, whiche ys (faieth he) to receaue with an vnclean confcience : And what the thing ys, whiche ys vnwoorthielie receaued, that ys (faieth he) the bodie of Chryft. By this then yt ys made clere againft the Sacramentarie, that euell

C   men maie, and doe receaue the bodie of Chryft.

And that the clerenesse of this matter maie be perceaued to the full what Chrifoftom beleued in yt, we fhall bring furth a place our two of the fame Chrifoftome, wherin he doeth plainly affirme that *Iudas* the proditour receaued the bodie of Chryft with the other Apoftles in the laft Supper. Thus in one place writeth Chrifoftom : *Cùm manducarent & biberent, accepit panem & fregit, & dixit: Hoc eft corpus meum. Agnofcunt quid loquor, qui funt diuinis confecrati myfterijs. Et iterum, accepit calicem, & dixit: Hic eft fanguis meus, & præfens erat Iudas ifta Chrifto dicente: Ifte eft fanguis meus. Dic Iuda quem triginta denarijs vendidifti ? Ifte eft fanguis, dè quo ante cum Pharfæis paĉta fecifti? O Chrifti mifericordia, O Iudæ dementia Ille eum triginta denarijs pacifcebatur vt venderet:& Chriftus ei fanguinem quem vendidit, offerebat, vt haberet remifsionem peccatorum, fi tamen impius exiftere noluiffet. Nam affuit Iudas, & illus facrificij communicationem meruit.* When they did eate and drinke, he tooke bread and brake yt, and faied: *This ys my bodie.* They that be confecrated to the diuine mifteries,

D   knowe what I fpeake. And again he tooke the cuppe, and faied: *This ys my bloode.* And Iudas, was prefent when Chryft faied thefe woordes. Saie Iudas, ys this he, whom thowe foldeft for thirtie pence ? Ys this the bloode for the whiche thowe madeft a bargain before with the Pharifies ? O the mercie of Chryft. O the madneffe of Iudas. He bargained that he might fell him for thirtie pence : *And Chryft offred him the bloode which he had*

Rrr iij   folde,

Two notes oute of Chrifoft. againft the Sacramentaries.

Euell men receaue the bodie of Chryfte.

Chrifo. hom. 30. de prodit. Iudæ.

Chryfte gaue to Iudas the blood that he had folde.

folde, that he might, haue remiſſion of his ſinnes, yf he wolde not haue had　Ｅ
ben wicked. For *Iudas* was preſent, and was partaker of that ſacrifice. Thus
farre he.

　In theſe woordes that Chriſoſtō ſaieth that Chryſt offred *Iudas* the blood
that he ſolde, ys both taught vs the preſence of Chryſtes bodie and bloode
in the Sacrament, and alſo that euell perſons doe receaue the ſame. For as
Iudas : ſo all like vnto *Iudas*. And let theſe woordes (*gentle Reader*) be well
noted of thee, that Chriſoſtome ſaieth, that Chryſt gaue *Iudas* the
blood that he ſolde. Yf he gaue him that he ſolde, he gaue him his
verie blood, and not the figure of his bloode. For not the figure, but
he blood yt ſelf was ſolde. Wher alſo in the ende of this place nowe
alleaged, Chriſoſtom ſaieth, that *Iudas* was preſent at the laſt Supper,
and was partaker of the Sacrifice, theſe twoo pointes nowe here inquired, are reuiued, and the trueth of them to vs confirmed. For the ſacrifice offred in the laſt Supper by Chryſt, was the ſacrifice of his bodie,
as before in the firſt, and ſecond, and alſo in this thirde booke yt ys
euidentlie prooued, and here alſo by Chriſoſtom ſignified. Wherbie　Ｆ

we are taught that the bodie of Chryſt ys preſent in the Sacrament, and
ſo *Iudas* being a partaker of that ſacrifice, was (*though he were a traditour and
a wicked man*) a receauer of the bodie of Chryſt. Which being ſo, yt maie be
concluded that euell and wicked men maie receaue the bodie of Chryſt in
the Sacrament.

　Allthough this that ys produced oute of Chriſoſtom maie fullie ſatisfie anie man, for that yt ys euident and plain : yet that yt maie be perceaued by that he ſpeaketh the ſame in ſondrie places, that yt was a trueth
aſſured and commonlie receaued, I will touche a place or two moo of his.
Of the whiche this ys one. *Nullus igitur fictus accedat, nullus fucato animo tantis
audeat myſterijs proximare ne condemnetur, & ſententiam mereatur, & quod Iudas ſu-
ſtinuit patiatur. Nam in illum poſt communicationem'menſæ Diabolus intrauit, non quia*

*contempſit Dominicum corpus, ſed quia impudentia Iudæ & malignitas mentis, vt aduer-
ſarius in eo habitaret, effecit.* Let therfore no feigned man come, let none be
ſo bolde with a counterfeit minde to come neare ſo great miſteries, leſt he　Ｇ
be condemned, deſerue ſentence, and ſuffre that that *Iudas* ſuffred. For after
he had partaken of Chryſtes table, the Deuell entred into him, not that he
contemned the bodie of our Lorde, but bicauſe the impudencie of *Iudas*,
and the miſcheif of his minde had cauſed that the Deuell ſhoulde dwell
in him.

　Wher Chriſoſtome ſaieth that after *Iudas* had receaued, the Deuell not
contemning the bodie of Chryſt, entred into him : what ells therby doeth
he teach, but that *Iudas* receaued the bodie of our Lorde. For yf he did not
receaue yt, Chriſoſtom neded not to declare that the Deuell entred
not vpon contempt of the bodie of Chryſt, For what contempt ſhoulde he ſeme to make to the bodie of Chryſt, by entring into *Iudas* yf
the bodie of Chryſt entred not into that perſon before. Yf anie contempt
ſhoulde appeare to be in that entrie, yt ſhoulde be that that wicked Aduerſarie, and miſerable damned creature ſhoulde preſume to entre to　Ｈ
that place wher his Lorde and maſter had ſo latelie entred. But (ſaieth *Chriſoſtome*) he did not ſo entre, as contemning the bodie of our lorde, but raither to the puniſhement of his deteſtable treaſon, doen and committed
againſt his maſter. And for his preſumption then vſed, that he being deſi-
led

A led with soche trecherie, wolde with dissimuled holinesse and loue receaue into his filthie and sinfull bodie, that pure and innocent bodie. And so the Deuell entred as a subiect whom God suffred for the torment of *Iudas* his mischeif, and not as a Lorde by power to contemne the Lorde of all Lordes ther entred.

Chrif. hom. 83.in 26. Math.

Alike sentence hath he in an other place whiche ys this : *Cænantibus autem eis, accepit Iesus panem & benedixit, atque fregit, & dedit Discipulis suis. O cæcitatem proditoris, qui cùm ineffabilibus mysterijs communicasset, idem permansit, & diuina mensa susceptus in melius commutari noluit, quod Lucas significauit dicens: Quia post hoc introiuit in eum Satanas, non quia dominicum corpus despiceret, sed quia proditoris stoliditatem irridebat.* When they were at Supper Iesus tooke bread, and blessed yt, and brake yt, and gaue yt to his disciples. O the blindenesse of the traditour, who when he had taken of the vnspeakeble misteries, he remained the same man, and being allowed at Gods table, he wolde not be chaunged into better, whiche thing Luke signified sainge: that after that Sathan entred into him not bicause he despised the

B bodie of our Lorde, but bicause he skorned the leudnesse of the traditour.

Here again ye see, as before, that the Deuell despised not the bodie of our Lorde receaued of *Iudas*, though he entred into him after yt. That he had receaued yt, these woordes of Chrisostom goinge a litle before, doe well declare, when he saieth : *When Iudas had taken of the vnspeakeable misteries, he remained all one man.* Whiche be the vnspeakeable misteries? not a peice of bread, and a cuppe of wine, receaued as signes and tokens of the bodie and bloode, For so these Sacramentes be not vnspeakeable misteris, but the matter ys well able to be spoken of, as other figures of the olde lawe were, whiche by the doctrine of the Aduersarie be as good as this, and this no better then they. Yf then the figures of the olde lawe were not vnspeakeable misteries (*as in dede they were not*) then be these figures of bread and wine no vnspeakeable misteries. Yf bread and wine as

C onelie figures be no vnspeakeable misteries, and *Iudas* in Chrystes Supper receaued vnspeakeble misteries then he receaued not bare bread and wine. Yt remaneth then that he receaued the bodie and blood of Chryst vnder the formes of bread and wine, whiche in dede be vnspeakeable misteries. For neither can reason atteign the knowledge of the worke of the holie Gost herein, nor toung speake and expresse the same, but onelie faith, as *Damascen* saieth : *Deus spiritus sancti operatione hæc super naturam operatur, quæ non potest capere, nisi sola fides.* God by the operacion of the holie Gost woorketh these thinges aboue nature, wich thinges onely faith can vnderstand. Wherfor thus speaking of the holie misteries, we manie well call them vnspeakeable misteries, whiche vnspeakeable misteries, Chrisostom saieth that *Iudas* did receaue.

Sacramentall bread and wine be not vnspeakeable misteries.

Damasc. li.4.ca.14.

The like are we taught of Sainct Augustine, but we will first heare him geue vs his vnderstanding of the saing of Sainct Paule which he doeth without all circumstance euen by plain woordes, as other haue doen before him. Thus he writeth against the Donatists. *Quisquis autem in hac Ecclesia*

D *bene vixerit, nihil ei præiudicant aliena peccata, quia vnusquisque in ea proprium onus portabit, sicut Apostolus dicit. Et quicunque corpus Christi manducauerit in dignè, iudicium sibi manducat, & bibit. Nam & ipse Apostolus hoc scripsit.* Whosoeuer shal liue wel in this Churche, other mens sinnes shall nothing hinder him. For in her

August. epistola cont. Donatist. post collation. S. August reporteth the woordes of S. Paule as S. Hier. and Chryso. did before.

Rrr iiii euerie

euerie man ſhall beare his owne burden, as the Apoſtle ſaieth. *And in her who-* **E**
ſoeuer ſhall eate the bodie of Chryſt vnwoorthilie, eateth and drinketh his owne condēnacion.
For the Apoſtle himſelf hath written this.

Note in this ſainge howe Sainct Auguſtine vttereth the ſainge of Sainct
Paule, he ſaieth not whoſoeuer eateth the bread, but as an expoſitour, whoſe
office ys to geue light to the text, yf anie part of yt be darke, and to geue the
true ſenſe of woordes that maie be diuerſelie vnderſtanded he expowndeth
the text and openeth yt, and plainlie teacheth vs that by bread ys vnderſtanded the bodie of Chryſt　. Wherfore by plain wordes he ſpeaketh
Sainct Paules ſentence, ſainge : *Whoſoeuer ſhall eate the bodie of Chryſte vnwoor-*
hilie &c.

Thus maie ye ſee the true vnderſtandinge of this ſcripture and by yt maie
ye learn that Sainct Auguſtine vnderſtoode that in the Sacrament ys the
verie bodie of Chryſte, and that euell men though to their condemnation

Cont. dona-
tiſt. lib. 5
cap. 8.

receaue the ſame. of whiche bothe, Sainct Auguſtine ſaieth again . *Sicut enim*
Iudas cui buccellam tradidit Dominus, non malum accipiendo, locum in ſe Diabolo præbuit:
ſic indignè quiſque ſumens Dominicum Sacramentum, non efficit, vt quia ipſe malus eſt, **F**
malum ſit, aut quia non ad ſalutem accipit, nihil accipiat. Corpus enim Domini, &
ſanguis Domini nihilominus erat etiam illis, quibus dicebat Apoſtolus : Qui manducat
& bibit indignè iudicium ſibi manducat & bibit. As Iudas to whome our Iorde gaue
a morſell, not taking an euell thing, but euell takinge the thinge, gaue pla-

Hell gates
cā not pre-
uail againſt
theſe pla-
ces, let the
Proclamer
well conſi-
der them.

ce to the deuell in himſelf : So anie man receauinge vnwoorthiely our Lordes Sacrament, cauſeth not, bicauſe himſelf ys euell, that yt ſhoulde be euell:
or bicauſe he receaueth yt not to ſaluacion, that he receaueth nothinge.
For yt was neuertheleſſe the bodie of our Lorde, and the bloode of our Lorde alſo vnto
then to whom the Apoſtle ſaied : *he that eateth and drinketh vnwoorthily eateth and drin-*
keth his owne condemnation. Thus moche Sainct Auguſtine.

Yt ys nowe to be remembred that the Aduerſarie denieng the reall and
ſubſtanciall præſence of Chryſtes bodie in the Sacrament, ys compelled for
the mainteinaunce of that his wicked hereſie, to ſaie that Chryſtes bodie ys
receaued ſpirituallie, that ys, that the grace, the vertue, and the meritte of
Chryſtes paſſion ſuffred in the ſame his bodie, ys receaued. And for that the- **G**
ſe benefittes be not receaued of an euell man, as beinge an euell man, therfor
he mainteineth an other wicked hereſie againſt the ſcripture, and the holie
Doctours, that euell men receaue not the bodie of Chryſt. For the confutacion of whiche euell doctrine, as the liuelie and plain ſentences of holie Fathers haue ben produced: So nowe ſpeaketh S. Auguſtine as plainlie againſt

Ao vnto
Iudas yt
was the
verie bodie
and blood
of Chryſte
that he re-
ceaued So
yt ys to all
other yll re-
ceauers.
Augu. in
Ioan tract.
26.

yt. For he contented not himſelf onelie to ſaie that euell men receaue the Sacrament of our Lorde, *Whiche woordes the Aduerſarie wolde haue wreſted to his*
pourpoſe, but by expreſſe woordes he ſaieth that ys was the *bodie of our Lorde,*
and the bloode of our Lorde vnto them alſo, of whom the Apoſtle ſaied : he that eateth,
and drinketh vnwoorthilie &c. Nowe what they be that receaue vnwoorthilie,
yt neadeth no declaracion, being manifeſt that they be euell men. And thus
by S. Auguſtine yt ys taught, that the verie bodie of Chryſt beinge in the
Sacrament, ys receaued of euell men: And although this place of S. Auguſtine ys ſo euidentlie gainſt them: yet in an other place he preſſeth them ſo **H**
ſtrictlie, that they haue no refuge, and yt ys this. *Quantum autem pertinet ad illam*
mortem, de qua terret Dominus, quia mortui ſunt patres eorum. Manducauit Manna &
Moiſes, manducauit Manna & Aaron : manducauit Manna & Phinees, mandu-
cauerunt & multi, qui Domino placuerunt, & mortui non ſunt. Quare ? quia viſibi-
lem cibum ſpiritualiter intellexerunt, ſpiritualiter eſurierunt, ſpiritualiter guſtauerunt, vt
ſpiritualiter

A *Spiritualiter satiauenter. Nam & nos hodie accepimus visibilem cibum. Sed aliud est Sacramentum, aliud virtus Sacramenti, quam multi de altari accipiunt, & moriuntur, & accipiendo moriuntur. Vnde dicit Apostolus: Iudicium sibi manducat & bibit.* As touching that deathe, of the whiche our Lorde saieth: that their Fathers be dead: Moises also did eate *Manna*, and *Aaron* did eate *Manna*, and *Phinees* did eate *Manna*, and manie did eate, whiche pleased our Lorde, and they died not. Whie? Bicause they vnderstoode a visible meate spirituallie: They did spirituallie hungar yt, they did spirituallie eate yt, that they might be spirituallie satisfied. And we also this daie haue taken a visible meate. But the Sacrament ys one thinge, and the vertue of the Sacrament an other thing, whiche vertue manie doe receaue at the Aultar and doe die, and in receaueing yt doe die. Wherfor saieth the Apostle: *He eateth and drinketh his damnacion.* Thus farre he.

Note here the distinction that S. Augustine maketh betwixt the Sacrament, and the vertue of the Sacrament sainge, that the Sacrament ys one thinge, and the vertue of the Sacrament an other. Then of the vertue of the
B Sacrament he saieth, that manie receaue yt at the Aultar, and doe die. meaning according to the saing of the Apostle, that receauing yt vnwoorthilie they die in the Soule, eating and drinking their owne damnacion. Nowe wolde yt be learned of the Aduersarie, howe he will vnderstand S. Augustine in this woorde (*Vertue*.) First certen yt ys, that yt ys not taken for the Sacramentall bread. For that ys the other membre of the distinction. Then must yt either be taken for the vertue of the passion of Chryst, or for the bodie of Chryst yt self. For in the Sacrament be no more but these three to be receaued: The Sacrament, the bodie of Chryst, and the vertue of his passion. Yt can not be taken for the vertue of Chrystes passion, for that ys not nor can not be death and damnacion to the receauer in the receauing, but life and saluacion. This vertue that S. Agustine speaketh of ys soche, that manie doe die in the receauing of yt. Yt remaineth then that by this vertue of the Sacrament, ys vnderstanded the bodie of Chryst, whiche manie by vnwoor-
C thie receauing doe wickedlie abuse, and so receauing kill their soules, and die the deathe that *Iudas* did.

Vertue of the blessed Sacr. what yt ys, and that euell men receaue yt.

What shall I tarie in the rehersall of Sainct Augustines sainges that touche this matter? They were euough to make a iust volume. Wherfor omitting manie, I will ende with one, whiche also expowndeth this our text: Thus he saieth: *Recordamini vnde sit scriptum: Quicunque manducauerit panem, aut biberit calicem Domini indignè, reus erit corporis & sanguinis Domini. Et de ijs erat sermo, cùm Apostolus hoc dicerit, qui Domini corpus velut quemlibet alium cibum indiscretè, negligenterque sumebant'.* Remember from whence yt ys written: Whosoeuer shall eate the bread, and drinke the cuppe of our Lorde vnwoorthieli, shall be giltie of the bodie and bloode of our Lorde. For when the Apostle saied this, he spake yt of them, *Whiche receaued the bodie of our Lorde vndiscreetlie and negligentlie*, as they wolde doe anie other meat.

August. in Ioan. tra. 6

Marke this well that Sainct Augustine saieth plainlie that Sainct Paule spake this of them that negligentlie and vndiscreetlie receaued, not
D a peice of Sacramentall bread, but the bodie of our Lorde. Then yt ys manifest that the bodie of our Lorde ys receaued in the Sacrament, and that yt ys also receaued by the testimonie of Sainct Augustine of negligent and vndiscreet persons, whiche make no differéce of the bodie of our Lorde. To make no differéce, saieth S. Augustine., ys, *non discernere à ceteris cibis diuinũ corpus.* to make no differéce of the bodie of our Lorde from other meates, but euen
as we

as we wolde with polluted cōsciences eate prophane meates,ād with pourpo- **E** se of sinne,without repentāce or pourpose of amendmēt of life , receaue our bodilie foode,so receaue the bodie of our Lorde. In whiche fewe woordes again S. Augustine teacheth the bodie of Chryst to be receaued of euell persons.Thus ye haue the mindes of Chrysostome and Sainct Augustine in the vnderstāding of S.Paule, which bothe vnderstand him to haue spoken of the bodie of Chryste,as the catholique Churche teacheth, and not of Sacramētall bread,as the malignaunt Churche feigneth. Thus moche being doen we shall with like spede heare other that remain,that the trueth of Chrystes faith maie be seen to the confusion of the enemie.

THE NINE AND FOVRTETH CHAP. CON-
tinueth the same exposition by Isichius and.
Sedulius.

Ainct Augustine writing against the Manicheis (in whiche sect he was by the space of nine years pietifullie deteined, and deluded) **F** perceaued after his conuersion one great cause of the continuance of manie in that heresie, to be , that they wolde not heare the holie learned doctours and Fathers of the Churche . Wherfor to remoue them

Aug.de mo- from that euell minde , he thus wrote to them : *Audite doctos catholicæ Ecclesiæ*
rib.Eccl. *Viros tanta pace animi,& eo voto, quo ego vos audiui. Nihil opus erit nouem annis,quibus*
cap.25. *me ludificastis.Longè omnino,longè beuiore tempore , quid intersit inter veritatem vanita-* *temque,cernetis.* Heare ye the learned men of the catholique Churche, with so moche quiettnesse of minde, and with that desire, that I heard yowe . Ther shall not nede the nine yeares , in the whiche ye mocked me . In a shorter time , yea in a moche shorter time shall ye see,what difference ys betwixt veritie and vanitie. Euen thus doe I wish that they that haue ben deluded with vain perswasions,and haue ben therbie insnared and entrapped in the heresie of the Sacramentaries, wolde with as good will heare the learned Fathers of Chrystes Churche , as they haue hitherto hearde them, that haue deceaued them.And I nothing doubte but yf they will so doe , ād with deuoute praier **G** to God for grace assistent , and with humblenesse of minde , enkindled with feruent desire(all affection sett aparte) Learn and knowe the verie trueth,but that they shall sooen discerne betwixt veritie and vanitie.

The Pro- Sixe nowe haue ben alleadged of the auncient and right famouse Fa-
clamer re- thers, whiche all with great and goodlie consent , haue expownded the
quired one woordes of Sainct Paule, to be vnderstanded of the bodie of Chryst . Whi-
plain sentē- che expositions be not settfurth with obscurities in doubtfull maner , as they
ce,he hath maie seme to be vnderstanded diuerse waies (whiche maner of sentences the
had nowe Aduersarie doth produce to maintein his heresie) But they are clere plain,
these sixe and easie to be vnderstanded in their right sense, so , that they can not be
and manie drawen to anie other sense . And therfor let the Proclamer looke well vpon
mo before, these expositions of these sixe Fathers past, and he shall perceaue that they
ād herester by expresse woordes teache that the bodie of Chryst ys in the Sacrament,
yet mo and ther receaued both of good and euell men, whiche thinge he shall see **H**
shal haue. also taught of sixe other or mo . And therfor let him for shame recant, and call in again his arrogant sainge , that the catholique Churche hath not one scripture, nor one doctour . For I doubte not but by the iudgement of them that shall reade this worke , that his sainge shall be prooued to be as false as vain.

A　Of thefe that yet remain to be alleaged, the firft coople fhall be *Ifichius* and *Ifich. in*
Sedulius. Ifichius hath this fainge: *Propter quod fanctuarium eius paueamus, vt nec cor-* *Leuit ca.*
pus noftrum polluamus, nec ad corpus Chrifti, in quo eft omnis fanctificatio(in ipfo enim *26.*
omnis plenitudo inhabitat diuinitatis) fine fubtili dijudicatione noftri, temerè accedamus,
fed potius nofmetipfos probemus, reminifcentes eius qui dixit : Quicunque manducauerit pa- *Ifich. vn-*
nem aut biberit calicem Domini indignè, reus erit corporis & fanguinis Domini. Wher- *derftādeth*
for let vs feare his holie place, that we neither defile our owne bodie, nor ra- *S. Paule to*
fhlie come to the bodie of Chryft, in the whiche ys all fanctificacion (For in *haue fpoken*
him abideth the fullneffe of the Godhead) withoute diligent examinacion *of the bodie*
of our felues. But raither let vs trie our felues remembring him that faied: *Who* *of Chryfte,*
foeuer fhall eate the bread, ād drinke the cuppe of our Lorde vnwoorthielie, fhall be giltie of
the bodie and bloode of our Lorde.

Howe this Authour vnderftandeth S. Paule, yt ys withoute great ftudie
to be perceaued. For he exhorting vs to come with great examinacion of
our felues, with puritie and cleanneffe of bodie and foule to the receipt of
Chryftes bodie, vfeth for the place of his authoritie the fainge of S. Paule no-
B　we in hand : *Whofoeuer eateth the bread, and drinketh the cuppe of our Lorde vnwoor-*
thielie, fhall be giltie of the bodie, and bloode of our Lorde. Wher in (as the other Fathers haue doen before) what Sainct Paule calleth the bread of our Lorde,
that doeth he by explaining woordes, call the bodie of Chryfte. And that
we fhoulde not take yt for a figuratiue bodie, but for the verie true and felf
fame bodie of Chryft, and therwith to ftirre vs to haue the more regarde to
our duetie, as with all honour and reuerence to come to yt, he faieth that in
that bodie dwelleth the fullneffe of the Godhead, that ys, as *Theophilact* fa- *Theoph. in*
ieth, *Si quid eft Deus Verbum in ipfo inhabitat,* That that ys the Sonne of God *2.cap. ad*
dwelleth in him. And farder expowndinge the fame, faieth: *Ne autem cùm au-* *Coll. ff.*
dis, habitauit, exiftimes quòd ageretur, aut impelleretur ficut Prophetæ (commorabatur
enim & in illis Deus, iuxta illud, inhabitabo in ipfis, & inambulabo) adiecit: corporaliter,
hoc eft, non energia vel operatio quædam, verùm fubftantia, ac veluti corporatus, & vna
hypoftafis exiftens cum affumpto. Leaft thowe (when thowe heareft this woorde *Exod. 29.*
C　(dwelleth)fhouldeft thinke that he fhoulde be moued or led, as the Prophe- *2.Cor.6.*
tes were(for God dwelled in them alfo accordinge to that faing I will dwell
in them, and I will walke a mong them) he added, *Corporally,* that ys, not a
certain force or operacion, but a fubftance, and as corporated and being one
perfō with the nature affumpted. Cyrill alfo by the teftimonie of *Theophilact,*
expownding thefe woordes, geueth great light to the vnderftanding of them
by an example and faieth this : *Vel hunc ad modum intelligere iuxta Diui Cyrilli fen-* *Cyrill.*
tentiam poteris : Perinde ac ia corpore immoratur anima (immoratur autem ipfi corpori ef-
fentialiter, & indiuifibiliter, ac citra mixturam) cæterum ipfa quidem anima per mortem
à corpore feparatur, Deus autem Verbum, nunquam ab affumpta carne feparatus eft, ve-
rum etiam in fepulchro aderat, ipfam incorruptibilem feruans, animæque, apud inferos prædi-
cans fine donans captiuis remifsionem. Ye maie alfo according to the minde of S.
Cyrill thus vnderftand yt, that as in the bodie dwelleth the foule, (but yt
dwelleth in the bodie effentiallie, and indiuifiblie, and that withoute the
commixtion of the two natures.) But yet the foule yt felf ys feparated from
D　the bodie by death. But God the Sonne ys neuer feparated from the flefh
whiche he hath taken, but he was with yt bothe in the graue keping yt from
corruption, And with the Soule declaring or geuinge remifsiō of finnes vnto
them that were in captiuitie. Thus farre he.

By all this ys ment that the verie Godhead ys fubftanciallie in Chryft, as
the foule ys fubftāciallie in the bodie, fo that we come to that bodie of Chryft
in

in the whiche dwelleth fullie, that ys to faie , fubftanciallie, the Godhead, **E**
which Chryftys God and man . And for fomoche as we come to fo woorthie a perfon , meet yt ys that we compownde our felues accordinglie . In
this Father then this maie we learne as in the other allreadie alleadged , that
S. Paule fpeaketh of the bodie of Chryft, and ys fo to be vnderftanded . For
ells when he moueth vs to prepare our felues as to come to the bodie of
Chryft , what fhoulde yt appertein to the pourpofe to alleadge Sainct Paule
yf Sainct Paule did not, or doe not fpeake of the fame thinge that he ys alleadged for? What ys yt to the pourpofe to alleadge Sainct Paule fpeaking
of a peice of bread, to prooue that we muft examine or felues before we receaue Chryftes bodie? Betwixt the bodie of Chryft and a peice of bread ther
ys no comparifon Likewife are we taught here that euell men maie receaue

Euell men
receaue the
bodie of
Chryfte.

the bodie of Chryft . For if they coulde not , why fhoulde he dehort them
from foche receipt? Vain yt were to moue a man not to doe a thing, whiche
ys vnpoffible to be doen. Yt were ftraung to perfwade a man not to pull dowen heauen with his handes. He were to be fkorned that wolde moue men
to eate the ftarres. And whie? Bicaufe he fhoulde moue them to doe that, that **F**
ys vnpoffible to be doen. Euen fo yf euell men can not receaue the bodie of
Chryft (as the Aduerfarie teacheth) what vanitie ys yt for this holie Father
and other his likes, to make fo manie and earneft exhortacions, that men
fhoulde not receaue the bodie of Chrifte vnwoorthilie? Forfomoche then as
thefe graue wife , and learned Fathers gaue vs fo manie godlie exhortacions,
fo manie vertueoufe admonicions that we fhoulde not receaue the bodie
of Chryfte vnwoorthilie, yt ys moft certen, that we maie fo receaue yt . And
yf fo, then euell men maie receaue the bodie of Chryft.

To *Ifichius* ys ioined *Sedulius*, who in euery parte, affirmeth what the other
hath taught . For he faieth thus vpon thefe woordes of Chryft recited of S.
Paule: *Take ye, This ys my bodie. Qnafi dixiffet Paulus : Cauete ne illud corpus indignè co-*
medatis, dum Corpus Chrifti eft. Indignè hoc comedetis: fi pauperes confundatis, fique efcam
aliquam ante fpiritualem & Dominicam Cænam comedatis . As though the Apoftle **G**
had faied: Beware ye that ye eate not that bodie vnworrhilie, forfomoche as
yt ys the bodie of Chryft . Ye fhall eate this bodie vnwoorthilie yf ye con-
fownde the poour, yf alfo ye eate anie other meate before the fpiritual meat,
the Supper of Lorde. Thus *Sedulius* . Wher Sainct Paule faieth: he that eateth
this bread vnwoorthilie &c. This man faieth that Sainct Paule in that wholl

Sedulius
faieth that
S. Paule
fpake of the
bodie of
Chryft.

proceaffe fpake of the bodie of Chryft. And therfor (faieth he) when S. Paule
had recited the woordes of Chrift: *Take ye, and eate . This ys my bodie* : yt was as
moche, as though the Apoftle had faied: *Beware that ye eate not that bodie vnwoor-*
thilie. for fomoche as yt ys the bodie of Chryft. In fewe woordes then yt ys euidét and
plain that the Apoftle theer fpake of the bodie of Chryft , whiche thing that
yt fholude be perceaued to be voide of all doubte , this Authour not conté-
ted with once fpeaking of the bodie , faieth with an addicion : *For yt ys the bo-*
die of Chryft. Whiche maner of fpeache maketh an affurance vnto vs that yt ys
fo. This alfo ys to be obferued , that as he faieth that S. Paule teacheth vs the
prefence of Chryftes bodie, that he alfo geueth vs an admonicion that we be

The bodie
of Chryfte
maie be re-
ceaued of
vnwoorthie
perfons.

ware that we receaue not that bodie vnwoorthilie. Wherby (as before ys no- **H**
ted) what ells ys geuen vs to vnderftande but that that bodie maie be receaued of vnwoorthie receauers. Whiche ys as moche to faie, as euell men maie
receaue the bodie of Chryft.

Nowe let not the good Chriftian be brought in doubte with the vain argument of the Sacramentaries, who doe reafon thus: *The Spiritt of Chryft ys all-*
vaies

This argumens was made to me in the Bishop of Elies house by one yet liuing.

Ciprian, serm. de Cana.

Solucion of the argument by S. Ciprian.

God and his Spirit in his creatures two waies.

Luc. 2.

Aug. cont. Gesconiũ.

A waies with his bodie or ys not. We maie not, saie that yt ys not for that the spiritte of Chryst ys inseparable from him. Yf then yt be allwaies with him, then the euell man receauing Chrystes bodie, receaueth also his Spiritte. And so shall the Spiritte of God be in sinners, whiche ys not to be saied. This vain argument shall the substanciall and pithie sainge of the holie Martir Ciprian clean dissolue and wipe awaie, who saieth thus. *Sacramenta quidem quantum in se est, sine propria esse virtute non possunt. Nec vllo modo diuina se absentat maiestas mysterijs. Sed quamuis ab indignis se sumi, vel contingi Sacramenta permittunt, non possunt tamen Spiritus esse participes, quorum infidelitas vel indignitas tantæ sanctitati contradicit. Ideoque alijs sunt hæc munera odor vitæ in vitam, alijs odor mortis in mortem. quia omnino iustum est, vt tanto beneficio priuentur gratiæ contemptores, nec indignis tantæ gratiæ puritas sibi faciat mansionem.* The Sacramentes trulie formoche as in them ys, can not be withthoute their propre vertue. Neither doeth the diuine maiestie, by anie meanes absent yt self from the misteries. But although the Sacramentes suffre them selues to be touched or receaued of the vnwoorthie: they for all that, whose vnbeleif or vnwoorthinesse doeth withstand so great holinesse, can not be partakers

B of the Spiritt. And therfor are these Sacramentes vnto some the sauoure of life vnto life, and vnto other the sauour of death vnto death. For yt ys allwaies meet, that the contemners of grace shoulde be destituted of so great benefitte, and that so excellent grace shoulde not dwell in vnwoorthie persons, Thus S. Cipriam.

Of whome we learn that allthough the diuine maiestie absenteth not yt self from the Sacrament: yet the vnwoorthie receauers be not partakers of the grace of the Spiritte, bicause yt ys vnmeet that the cõtempners of grace, shoulde haue grace abiding in them. For the more full vnderstanding of this, note that God and his holie Spiritt be in creatures two sondrie waies: that ys, by presence, and by grace. By presence God ys in manie places and creatures, where he ys not by grace. God by presence ys in hell among the damned soules, but he ys not among them by grace. Chryst was in the house of *Zachæus* by grace: But he was in the house of *Caiphas* and

C *Pilate* by presence, and not by grace. Chryste was in the middest of the Iewes by presence, but he was in the middest of his Apostles also by grace. The Apostles receaued the presence of Chryst with his grace in his last supper: Iudas receaued the presence of Chryst withoute his grace in the same Supper. And so yt cometh to passe that the same Chryste, who was sett to be a fall, and an vprising of manie in Israell, ys by the receipt of his bodie in the Sacrament, as Sainct Ciprian saieth, to some a sauoure of life, to life: and to other some a sauoure of death to deathe. For the same flesh and blood, whiche ys to some receauers (as Chryst saieth) euerlasting life, ys to other some, (as Sainct Paule saieth), euerlasting deathe.

Of the whiche saieth Sainct Augustine: *Quid de ipso corpore, & sanguine Domini vnico sacrificio pro salute nostra? Quamuis ipse Dominus dicat: Nisi quis manducauerit carnem meam, & biberit sanguinem meum, non habebit in se vitam: Nonne idem Apostolus docet etiam hoc perniciosum malè vtentibus fieri? Ait enim: Quicumque manducauerit panem, vel biberit calicem domini indignè, reus erit corporis & sanguinis Domini.*

D What shall we saie of the verie bodie and bloode of our Lorde, the onely sacrifice for our Saluacion? of the whiche although our Lorde himself doeth Saie: *Except a man doe eate my flesh, and drinke my bloode he shall not haue life in himself*: Dothe not the Apostle teache that the same also ys hurtfull to them that doe vse yt euell? For he saieth: *Whosoeuer shall eat the bread, or drinke the cuppe of our Lorde vnwoorthilie shall be giltie of the bodie and blood of our Lorde,* By this then I

S ſſ　　trust

truſt yt be made manifeſt and plain, that Chryſt and his Spiritt maie of euell **E** receauers be receaued as touching his preſence, but of ſoche by grace he ys not receaued, bicauſe they be not meet veſſells for grace, forſomoche as they doe contemptuouſlie reiect yt, and by ſinfull life withſtande yt. But yet the ſame receaue the verie preſence of Chriſt. The good receaue Chryſt outwardlie in the Sacrament and inwardlie by grace, and ſo the fruict, which ys life: The euell receaue him outwardlie in the Sacrament, but not inwardlie by grace, and ſo forgoinge life, they, for their abuſe gett death, whiche ys euerlaſting damnacion.

THE FIFTETH CHAP. SHEVVETH THE
vnderſtanding of the ſame text by Effrem,
and Primaſius.

S the mercifull goodneſſe of God whiche by the teſtimonie of the Prophete Dauid, endureth for euer and euer vpon the that feare him, ys declared by innumerable his workes wrought in **F** the creacion, redemption, and conſeruacion of man: So the trueth of God, Whiche by the teſtimonie of the ſame Prophete, abideth for euer, and reſteth vpon ſoche as be humble ſearchers of the ſame, ys teſtified by nombers of wittneſſes. Wherfor the nombre of wittneſſes beinge manie, that maie be produced for the true vnderſtanding of Sainct Paule in this text, I coulde not contein, but oute of ſo manie, yet bring ſome moe. Of the whiche I minde here to bring *Effrem* and *Primaſius*, men of great antiquitie. And for that they were of Chryſtes Parliament houſe, and therfor well knowing the enacted trueth of the vnderſtanding of S. Paule in their times, they are the better to be beleued.

This holie Father *Effrem*, writing of the daie of iudgement, and ſpeakinge of the woorthie and vnwoorthie receauinge of the Sacrament, maketh relacion to Sainct Paule, ſainge: the vnpure receauer to receaue the ſame to his confuſion in the daie of iudgement, as the pure receauer to his com-

D. Effrem tract de die Judic.

fort and glorie. Thus he writeth: *Si procul eſt à nobis Siloë, quo miſſus eſt cæcus, ſed* **G** *precioſius calix ſanguinis tui plenus vita & lumine nobis in proximo eſt, tanto propinquior, quanto qui acceſſerit fuerit purior. Hoc igitur nobis reſtat, miſericors Chriſte, vt pleni gratia & illuminatione ſcientiæ tuæ, cum fide, & ſanctificatione accedamus ad calicem tuũ, vt proficiat nobis ad remiſſionem peccatorum, non ad confuſionem in die iudicij. Quia quicumque myſterijs tuis indignus acceſſerit, ſuã animam ipſe condemnat, non ſe caſtificans vt cæleſtem regem, atque immortalem Sponſum in ſui pectoris puriſſimum ſuſcipiat Thalamum. Nam anima noſtra ſponſa eſt, immortalis ſponſi. Copula, autem nuptiarum, cæleſtia Sacramenta ſunt, quia cùm manducamus corpus eius, & ſanguinem bibimus, & ipſe in nobis eſt, et nos in eo. Attende ergo tibimet ipſi frater, feſtina thalamũ cordis tui iugiter virtutibus exornare, vt manſionem cum benedicto Patre ſuo faciat apud te. Et tunc coram Angelis, & Archangelis erit tibi laus, & gloria, & gloriatio, et cum magna exultatione, & gaudio ingredieris in Paradiſum.* Yf Siloe whether the blinde man was ſent, be farre from vs: *Yet*

A. plain ſaing of holie Effrem for the Proclamer.

the precioſe cuppe of thie bloode being full of life and light, ys neare to vs, yea ſo moche the nearer, as he that cometh to yt ys the purer. This then, o mercifull Chriſt, **H** remaineth vnto vs, that we being full of grace, and the illuminacion of thie knowledge, come vnto thy cuppe with faith and holineſſe of life, that yt maie auaill vs to the remiſſiõ of ſimes, and not to our confuſion in the daie of iudgement. For whoſoeuer being vnwoorthie cometh to the miſteries, he condemneth his owne ſoule, not purifieng himſelf, that he might into the moſt

pure

A pure or clean chambre of his breaſt receaue the heuenlie kinge and immortall Spouſe. For our ſoule ys the Spouſe of the immortall huſbãd: The coopplinge of the Marriage be the heauenly Sacramentes. *For when we doe eate his bodie, and drinke his bloode, both he ys in vs, and we in him.* Take heede to thy ſelf therfor, Brother, haſt thee to adorne the bride chambre of thy heart continuallie with vertues, that with his bleſſed Father he maie make his manſion with thee. And then ther ſhall be to thee before Angells and Archangells praiſe and glorie, and with great ioie and gladneſſe ſhalt thowe entre into Paradiſe. Thus farre holie *Effrem*.

We eate the bodie and drinke the blood of Chryſte.

Ye haue hearde a long teſtimonie, but as godlie, as long: and as true, as godlie. Ye haue heard that the cuppe of the blood of Chryſt, ys neare at hand with vs. Yf yt were not in the Sacrament, (as the Sacramentarie ſaieth yt ys not) then were *Syloë* being vpon the earth nearer vnto vs, then the bloode of Chryſt, which by their ſaing ys neuer vpon the earth, but allwaies in heauen. This cuppe of bloode maie not be vnderſtanded by a figure, as to ſaie we haue at hand a cuppe of wine, whiche ys the figure of Chryſtes bloode. For

Cuppe of blood near to vs.

B the woordes of ſingular praiſe, whiche this Authour addeth vnto the cuppe of the bloode which he ſpeaketh of, can not be applied, nor verified in the figuratiue cuppe. The cuppe that this Authour ſpeaketh of ys, as he tearmeth yt, a precioul̃e cuppe: A cuppe of wine in this reſpect ys not precioul̃e. This cuppe ys full of life and light: the figuratiue cuppe, by the Aduerſaries owne ſaing, hauing no holineſſe, hath neither life nor light. This cuppe the Authour by plain tearmes, calleth the cuppe of Chryſtes bloode: The other ys not ſo, but a figure of Chryſtes bloode. By all theſe titles then of ſingular praiſe yt ys euident that this Authour iudged the precioul̃e cuppe of Chryſtes verie bloode to be neare at hand with vs, and ſo teacheth the verie preſence of Chryſt in the bleſſed Sacrament, who in dede ys full of life and light he trulie ſainge of him ſelf: *Iam the life. Iam the light of the worlde.*

This Authour alſo openeth the minde of S. Paule, ſaing: that whoſo commeth to the miſteries of Chryſt vnwoorthilie, doeth condempne his owne

Bread in S. Paule ys not materiall bread.

C ſoule. He geueth the cauſe why: For (*ſaieth the Authour*) he doeth not receaue that heauenly king and immortall bridegrome into the bride chambre of his heart being purified and clenſed, but fowlie araied & defiled. The thing then receaued in the miſteries of Chryſt, called of S. Paule the bread of our Lorde, ys not materiall bread, but yt ys Chryſt the heauenlie bread, the verie heauenlie kinge and immortall bridegroome of our ſoules, as this Authour declareth. For immediatelie declaring that Chryſt ys ioined to our Soules, as the bridegroome to the bride, he ſaieth that yt ys doen by the Sacramentes. For (ſaieth he) *when we eate his bodie, and drinke his bloode then he dwelleth in vs, and we in him.* In dede in the receipt of Chryſtes bodie in the Sacrament ys wrought the perfect coniunctiõ betwixt Chryſt and vs, yf he be therin receaued as he aught to be receaued. For then we are not onelie conioined to him ſpirituallie by faith and charitie, but alſo (as Chriſoſtom, and S Cyrill ſaie) naturallie. For both we be in him by that he tooke our nature into him in his incarnation, And he ys in vs by that we take his naturall bodie in

D the holie miniſtracion. Wherfor reaſon wolde, duetie wolde, and loue alſo wolde, that as he ioined our nature to that glorioul̃e perſonne the Sonne of God in deitie, that we alſo ſhoulde trauaill and labour to ioin again that his bleſſed bodie to our nature, adorned with vertue ãd lifes puritie. Of this coniunction moche ys ſaied in the beginning of this booke, and more ſhall be ſaied, God willing in the ende.

Primasius
n Apocal.

Wherfor nowe ouerpassing yt, I hast to heare what *Primasius* will saie, to helpe vs to vnderstand S. Paules sainge nowe in hande. Thus he writeth: *Qui edit meā carnem, & bibit meum sanguinem, in me manet, & ego in co. pro eo ac si diceret: qui sic edent, vt edenda est, & sic bibent, vt bibendus est sanguis meus. Multi enim cùm hoc videantur accipere, in Deo non manent, nec Deus in ipsis. quia sibi iudicium manducare perhibetur.* He that eateth my flesh, and drinketh my blood dwelleth in me, and I in him. As yf he shoul saie: they that so shall eate my flesh as yt ys to be eaté, and shall so drinke my bloode, as yt ys to be dronken. For manie wen they are seen to receaue this Sacrament neither dwell they in God, nor God in them bicause they are wittnessed to eat and drinke their owne damnation.

The vj. of
S. John ād
S. Paule
speak of one
thing.

Primasius in this place alleadged expowndeth two scriptures, the one oute of the vj. of S. Iohn: the other, whiche we nowe haue in hand oute of S. Paule. Oute of the vj. of S. Iohn, wher Chryste saieth. *He that eateth my flesh, and drinketh my bloode, dwelleth in me, and I in him*: Ys not so to be vnderstanded, that what soeuer he be, and in what state or condicion soeuer he be, in sinne or oute of sinne, delighting in sinne or detesting Sinne, penitent or impenitét viciouse, or vertuouse, yf he eate the flesh of Chryst, and drinke his blood that he dwelleth in Chryst and Chryste in him: But yt ys to be vnderstāded, that he that eateth the flesh of Chryst, and drinketh his blood, as yt ys to be eaten and dronken, that ys, with sownde faith, with perfect charitie, with puritie of minde and cleannesse of conscience, that then he dwelleth in Chryst, and Chryst in him. To prooue this he hath recourse to S. Paules sainge, that manie doe eate the flesh of Chryst, and drinke his bloode, that doe eate and drinke ther owne damnacion. by whiche his allegacion he also expowndeth howe that Scripture ys to be vnderstanded. Whiche of him that will well weigh the allegacion shall be easelie perceaued.

First, yt ys to be considered that the vj. S. of Iohn, oute of the whiche he alleageth this scripture (as yt ys allreadie invinciblie prooued) speaketh of the verie flesh and verie bloode of Chryste. Secondlie, yt ys to be noted that he expowndeth this text, and saieth that yt ys not to be vnderstanded indifferentlie of all men to dwell in Chryste, and Chryst in them, that do eate his flesh and drinke his bloode : but of them that eate and drinke them as they aught to be eaten and dronken, and alleadgeth for his proof our text of S. Paule. Whiche so being alleadged, prooueth that he vnderstandeth S. Paule ther to haue spoken of the same thing that the vi. of S. Iohn spake of. But the vj. of S. Iohn spake of the flesh and bloode of Chryst in the Sacrament. Wherfor by this Authour so doeth S. Paule here. And so yt foloweth by S. Paule and this Authour that euell men maie eate the fleshe of Chryst, and drinke his blood, in whome yet neither Chryst shall dwell, nor they in Chryste. But they for their presumption presuming with a filthie Soule to receaue so pure a bodie, shall suffre their iust condemnacion. Thus by these two Fathers, as by other before alleadged, yt ys testified that the very presence of Chrystes bodie ys in the Sacrament, and that the same ys receaued of euell men, though to their condempnacion.

THE ONE AND FIFTETH CHAP. ABIDETH IN H
the exposition of the same text by Cassiodorus, and Damascen.

IT Ys moche for the probacion and confirmacion of the trueth, to see the goodlie consent and agreement emong the holie Fathers of Chrystes parliament house. Wherfor perceauing *Cassiodorus* to ioin

the

A the vj. of S.Iohan whith S.Paule, as *Primasius* did, as hauing both one vnder-ftāding.I haue thought good,of this coople , that here fhall be brought furth, firft and next to *Primasius* to place *Cassiodorus* , that yt maie more liuely be per-ceaued,that of them ys by me reported.

This *Cassiodorus* in his commentaries vpon the pfalmes expowndinge this verfe fpoken as a prophecie of Chryft: *Thow arte a preist for euer, after the ordre of* *Melchisedech:*writeth thus:*Cui potest veraciter, et euidenter aptari nisi Domino & fal-uatori, qui corpus & sanguinem suum in panis ac vini erogatione salutariter consecrauit? Sicut ipse in Euangelio dicit:Nisi manducaueritis carnem filij hominis, & biberitis eius fan-guinem non habebitis vitam in vobis . Sed in ista carne & sanguine,nil cruentum, nihil cor-ruptibile mens humana concipiat (ne sicut dicit Apostolus: Qui enim corpus Domini indi-gnè manducat,iudicium sibi manducat)sed viuificatricem substanciam, atque salutarem,& ipsius verbi propriam factam,per quam peccatorum remissio,& æternæ vitæ dona præstan-tur* . Vnto whome maie this be trulie and euently applied,but vnto our Lor-de and Sauiour ? Who in the geuing furth of bread and wine to our health, confecrated his bodie and bloode,as he in the Gofpell faieth : *Except ye eate the flesh of*

B *the Sonne of man,and drinke his bloode, ye shall not haue euerlasting life.*But in this flefh and bloode let not the minde of man conceaue anie thinge groffe,anie thing corruptible , leaft, as the Apoftle doeth faie, he that eateth the bodie of our Lorde vnworthilie eateth his owne condempnacion:but let man conceaue yt to be a fubftance geuing life and faluaciō,and foche a fubftance as ys made the verie owne fubftance of the Sonne of God himfelf,by the whiche remif-fion of finnes and the giftes of euerlaftinge life be geuen.

Ye haue nowe heard the weightie and pithie fainge of the holie Senatour *Cassiodorus* . Who as for his wifdome was woorthilie called to be a Senatour to geue counfell in worldly affaires ⁖ So for his godlineffe and learninge he ys a Senatour of Chryftes houfe in heauenlie thinges.In thefe fewe woordes he hath vttered manie truethes and geuen vs manie inftructions.Firft,he vtte-reth this trueth, that Chryft in his laft Supper did confecrate his bodie and his bloode.Whiche his fainge, as yt declareth and fetteth furth the trueth of

C the catholique faith:So yt openeth and declareth , and therwith impugneth the vntrueth of the herefie of the Sacramentaries . Secondly, wher he faied that Chryft had to our health confecrated the fame his bodie and blood , he proueth yt by Chryftes faing in the vj.of S. Iohn,wher he faieth:*Except ye eate the flesh of the Sonne of man, and drinke his blood ye shall not haue life in yowe:* Wherby yt ys manifeft, that as by the forbearinge to eate the flefh of Chryft we leefe the benefett of euerlafting life : So by eatinge the fame, as yt ys to be eaten, we obtein life euerlafting. Whiche being fo,his fainge ys affirmed and proo-ned wher he faied, that Chryft to our health and faluation confecrated his bodie and blood in his laft Supper . For, hauinge euerlafting life by the ea-ting of that his bodie confecrated in his laft Supper, we maie iuftlie faie that yt was confecrated to our faluacion. Thirdlie by that , that the vj.of Iohn ys fo alleaged, yt prooueth well that the fame fpeaketh of the bodie and blood of Chryft , that fhoulde be confecrated by him in his laft Supper , to ower health and faluacion, as ys faied. Forthlie,we are inftructed and taught what

D we aught to conceaue and thinke of that bleffed bodie and flefh of Chryft fo confecrated.We maie not thinke yt a phantafticall bodie, as *Marcion* and *Mā-nicheus* did,or the bodie of a mere man,as did *Ebion* and *Cerynthus*, againft whi-che heretiques,as S. Hierom faieth, S. Iohn firft was moued to write his go-fpell , therby moued to open, declare and fettfurth the deitie or godhead of Chryft, whiche herefie afterward notwitftanding S. Iohns Gofpell, and Epi-

ftles

Marginal notes:

Cassiodor. in versu: Tues sacer-dos &c.

Chryste cō-secrated his bodie and blood.

What we shoulde thinke of the bodie of Chryste cō-secrated.

ſtles (as *Philaſter* wittneſſeth) was ſettfurth by *Theodotus*, who was condemned **E** by *Victor* then Biſhoppe of Rome, who was the thirtenth Biſhoppe ther after S. Peter, as the compuracion of ſome doeth teſtifie:

Two natu‐res in Chri‐ſte, but not two perſos.

Neither maie we thinke, that bicauſe ther be in Chryſt two natures, that ther be alſo in him two diſtincted perſons, as did *Neſtorius*, ſo that the nature of man in Chryſt ys ſo diſtincted and diuided frō the Godhead, that yt hath no ſoche coniunctiō with the Godhead, as that yt by the reaſon of the vnitie of perſon, ſhoulde either be called the Sonne of God, or the propre and ve‐rie fleſh of God, but rhe Sonne of man onelie. For all theſe thought yt a cor‐ruptible fleſh, the fleſh of a pure man, and not the fleſh of the Sonne of God, as yt ys in dede, but we muſt thinke yt, as this Authour teacheth, that yt ys a ſubſtance quickning vs to ſaluacion and euerlaſting life, foraſmoche as yt ys made the verie owne and propre fleſh of the Sonne of God, by the whiche we haue remiſſion of ſinne, and life euerlaſtinge.

And this alſo are we taught of holie Cyrill, who geueth alſo a reaſon, whie the fleſh of God ſhoulde geue life, ſainge thus: *Quoniam ſaluatoris caro, verbo Dei*

Cyrill. in 6. Joan. cap. 14.

quod naturaliter vita eſt, coniuncta, viuifica effecta eſt, quando eam comedimus, tunc vitam **F** *habemus in nobis illi coniuncti, quæ vita effecta eſt.* Foraſmoche as the fleſh of our Sauiour being ioined to the Sonne of God, who naturallie ys life, ys made geuing life, when we eate that fleſh, thē haue we life in our ſelues, for aſmo‐che as we ar ioined to yt, whiche ys made life.

Thus then maie we perceaue that not onelie corrupt maners, but alſo cor‐rupt faithe, otherwiſe conceauing or phantaſinge of Chryſtes bodie then the catholique Faithe teacheth, diuideth vs from Chryſt, and maketh vs vn‐woorthie receauers of that bleſſed bodie. Yf they be accompted amonge euell receauers, that otherwiſe thinke of the bodie of Chryſt, then ys to be thought of yt: What ys to be thought of them, that wher Chryſt promiſed, that the bread, which he wolde geue ſhoulde be his fleſhe, whiche he wolde geue for the life of the worlde, and by expreſſe woordes, for the perfourmāce of the ſame promeſſe, takinge bread, ſaied plainlie: *This ys my bodie:* And S, Pau‐le (as the wholl companie of the Fathers hitherto haue teſtified, and mo yet ſhall teſtifie) ſaieth that in the Sacrament ys the bodie of Chryſt, what, I ſaie, **G** ys to be thought of them, that will not thinke Chryſtes bodie to be his bo‐die, but withe the *Ebionites* and *Cerinthians* will make Chryſt no God, with the *Manicheis* will (make him but a phantaſticall figure, and with the *Neſtorians*, will, as they made a diſtinction betwixt the two naturs, leauing the nature of man deuided and diſtincted from the Godheade, ſo make the holie Sacra‐ment diſtincted from Chryſt? wher in verie dede, as God and man ys one Chryſt: So the bleſſed Sacrament as touchinge the Subſtance, and Chryſt ys all one. the Subſtance of the Sacrament being none other but the verie ſub‐ſtance of Chryſt. Theſe euell receauers, and abuſers of Chryſtes holie Sacra‐ment, as they abuſe the thinge yt ſelf: So by ſlanderouſe tearmes doe they abuſe them that well vſe the ſame. For the true Chriſtians that honour God, call they Idolaters : Soche as acknowledge Chryſtes verie bodie in the Sacrament, call they groſſe Capharnaites: And ſoche as beleue the ſub‐ſtance of bread by the omnipotencie of God to be chaunged, and made **H** the ſubſtance of Chryſte, they call Papiſtes . But God geue them a better minde, and the catholiques plentie of pacience, patiently to ſuffre their railinges, ſo long as God for our correction, will permitte the ſame to continue.

　　　　　　　　　　　　　　　　　　　And

A And nowe to return to our matter, this finallie ys to be noted in our Authour, that alleging our text of Sainct, Paule, he vseth not the woordes of Sainct Paule, but the meaning and vnderstandinge. Thus he alleageth Sainct Paule : *Qui enim corpus Domini indignè manducat, iudicium sibi manducat.* For he that eateth the bodie of our Lorde vnwoorthilie, eateth his owne iudgement. Note well that he saieth not, he that eateth the bread, but he that eateth the bodie of our Lorde, expownding what bread Sainct Paule spake of in that scripture, the bread, I saie, of Chrystes bodie, as oftentimes yt ys allreadie saied. What can be saied more plainer? wolde the Proclamer haue anie plainer speache then this? Let him note the woordes, and the circunstance also, and weigh yt well, and he shall finde yt so plain, that all his engines and wrestinges, and all his subtilties', with the aide of all his complices, shall not be able to withstand the plain trueth of yt.

Cassiod, howe he vttereth Sainct Paules woordes.

But Let vs heare *Damascen* speaking as plainlie, as he, and by like woordes openinge to vs the true mening of Sainct Paule. This *Damascen* setting

B furth the vertue, goodnesse, and power of the Sacrament, saieth thus: *Si aurum offendat adulteratum, per iudicialem correptoriamque ignitionem purgat, vt non in futuro cum mundo damnemur : Curat enim morbos, & omnimoda damna, quemadmodnm dicit Apostolus : Si nos vtique iudicaremus, non vtique iudicaremur. Cùm iudicamur autem à Deo, corripimur, vt non cum mundo condemnemur. Et hoc est quod dicit : Quare qui participat corpus & sanguinem Christi indignè, iudicium sibi ipsi manducat, & bibit. Per illud purgati vnimur corpori Domini, & spiritui eius & efficimur corpus Christi. Nam spiritus viuificans est caro Domini, quia ex viuificante spiritu concepta est. Quod enim natum est ex spiritu, spiritus est. Hoc autem dico non auferens corporis naturam, sed viuificationem, & diuinitatem eius ostendens.* Yf yt finde golde that ys corrupted, by iudiciall and correptorie fieringe yt pourgeth yt, that we be not in time to come condemned with the worlde. For yt cureth diseases, and all maner of hurtes, as the Apostle saieth. Yf we wolde iudge our selues, we shoulde not be iudged, but when we are

C iudged of God, we are chasticed, that we shoulde not be damned with the worlde. And this ys yt that the Apostle saieth : *Wherfor he that receaueth the bodie and blood of Chryste vnwoorthilie, he eateth & drinketh his owne damnacion.* We being purged by that, are vnited to the bodie of our Lorde, and to his Spiritt, and are made the bodie of Chryste. For the flesh of our Lorde ys a quickning Spiritt, bicause yt was conceaued by the quickninge Spirite. For that that ys borne of the Spiritte, ys a Spiritte. This doe I saie not taking awaie the nature of the bodie, but declaring his Godhead and power to geue life. Thus he.

Damascen. li.4.ca. 14.

Damascen. vttereth the woordes of S. Paule as other elders before.

Leauing diuerse good and godlie notes in this sainge of Damascen to be considered, by the Reader, I hast me to note those thinges that be to the pourpose of this present cause. Of the whiche the first and cheifest ys, that he alleaging the sainge of Sainct Paule, shewinge vs the exposition of the scripture, and geuing vs the vnderstanding of the same, and the right meninge of Sainct Paule, speaketh yt by these woor-

D des. He that receaueth the bodie and blood of Chryst vnwoorthilie, eateth and drinketh his owne damnacion. In whiche maner of speache, as an expositour aught to doe, by vnwrestable woordes he declareth what Sathan wolde wrest, and soo by plain woordes calleth that, that Sainct Paule calleth the bread, and cuppe of our Lorde,

the bodie and blood of Chryst, he right well knowing that they be fo in **E**
verie dede.

I truft the Proclamer will not here vpon this Authour caft the ftinking
mift of his figure, confidering that yt ys an expofition. And the nature of an
expofition ys to be plainer then the thing expownded. And although both
the text, and the expofition fpeake the trueth: yet he knoweth that what the
text oftentimes fpeaketh obfcurely or doubtfullie, that muft the expofition
fpeake plainlie, clerely, and manifeftlie. Whefor he muft nedes confeffe, that
this Authour fhewing the minde of S. Paule, and expownding the bread and
the cuppe to be the bodie and bloode of Chryft, that yt ys plainlie fo. And
wher diuerfe of the adherẽts of this Proclamer beare great Stomacke againft
this Authour for his plain trueth in manie matters, Lett both him and them
knowe, that as in all pointes of this matter the wholl catholique Churche
hath alowed him: So ys he agreable to all that hitherto haue ben alleaged in
the expofition of S. Paule, which all be right auncient, or hereafter fhall be alleaged, though they be not fo auncient.

A Breif note alfo can I not but make of Damafcen, wher he faieth, *that we* **F**
being pourged are by the receipt of the bodie of Chryfte vnited to the fame bodie and to his
Spiritt, and are alfo made his bodie. For as by thefe fewe wordes the trueth ys opened, and the great commodities that come to vs by the woorthie receipt of
the Sacrament declared : So ys the vain argument of the Aduerfarie before
moued, fullie folued and anfwered. The trueth ys, that both good and bad
receauing the Sacrament, doe receaue the bodie of Chryft. Commodities
ther come none, but to the woorthie receruer, whiche cõmodities be three.
The firft ys, that we be vnited to the bodie of Chryfte, of the whiche moche
ys faied in this booke vpon the tẽth to the Corinthians. The fecond benefitt
ys, that we be alfo vnited to his holie Spiritte. The thirde ys, that we be made
the mifticall bodie of Chryfte. Thefe three commodities and benefites doe
we enioie by the receipt of the Sacrament, faieth this authour. But when?
when (*faieth he*) we being pourged doe receaue yt. For otherwife we receaue
not foche commodities, but we receaue great and notable incommodities
For we receaue (*faieth S. Paule*) our owne damnation. Then wher the Aduer- **G**
farie boyleth vppe his violent argument, that wher Chryft ys, ther his Spirite
ys alfo, And fo yf euell men receaue in the Sacrament the bodie of Chryft,
they receaue his Spirite alfo : Yt ys true, that they receaue Chryft and his
Spirite as touching their prefence, but not as touching grace. For although
they receaue his prefence, yet forfomoch as they be not (*as this Authour faieth*)
pourged, they receaue him not to grace. For neither be they vnited to the
bodie of Chryft, neither to his holie Spirite, neither be they therby made
members of Chryftes miftical bodie. for (*as Primafius hath faied*) they eate not
that flefh as yt ys to be eaten, nor drinke that blood, as yt aught to be dronke.
For in dede yt ys not to be eatẽ and dronkẽ, but of foche as be clenfed and
pourged from finne by penaunce, and be clerelie voide of pourpofe to
finne again, And to foche yt bringeth thefe three commodities, and manie
moe, to the other nothing, but they them felues woorke their owne dam- **H**
nacion.

Thus gentle Reader, thowe maift perceaue, that yf with the
minde of the holie Fathers of Chryftes Parliament houfe, thowe wilt
reade the Scriptures, and by them learn to vnderftande the fame,
thowe fhallt not onelie not be deceaued, but alfo in all matters
of controuerfie be fettled and ftaied, and clerelie fee the toies and
phan-

*Woorthie
receauers
of the bleff.
Sacr. What
benefitts
they haue.*

*Vnwoor-
thie recea-
uers what
they rece-
ue.*

A phantafies of the Aduerfaries to be maliciouflie, and deuelliflie forged and inuented.

THE TVVO AND FIFTETH CHAP. ENDETH THE
expofition of this text by Theodoret, and Anfelmus.

Itherto none be produced to fhewe vs the minde of S. Paule, but foch as by the teftimonie of diuerfe writers, were a thoufãd years agon and more, faue this laft alleadged *Damafcen*, whome fome fo place, as he had not liued full nine hundreth yeares agon. But be yt that he were fo, yet he ys of foche antiquitie, as he maie verie well be called as wittnefse in this matter, for that he was before this controuerfie was raifed in the Churche, I meen, before the time of *Berengarius*, Before whofe time, I am fure the Aduerfaries can make no prefcription, nor yet fince, but by ftartes as Sathan might gett occafion and minifters nowe and then to difturbe gods Churche. Whiche, I take, ys fuffred of God bothe to correct our euell liues : and alfo to ftirre vs to feke the knowledge of gods

Whie God fuffreth Sathan nowe to wexe his Church with herefies.

B trueth. Whiche although we had, as yt were an vpper face of the knowledge of yt : yet through necligence we did not wade to the deapth of yt.

But be yt, that *Damafcen* were not nine hundreth years agon : yet the promifse of Chryft being confidered that he wolde be with his, Churche to the ende of the the worlde, ãd that he wolde alfo fende his holie fpirite into the fame his Churche, that fhoule lead yt into all trueth : As yt ys to moche fhame for the Aduerfarie to faie that all this time fince *Damafcen* taught Chryftes promefse hathe failed : So yt ys as moche fhame to faie that all this time his owne doctrine hath ben fuppreffed.

In dede I wolde thinke that this Proclamer fhoulde doe that, that all his progenitours coulde neuer yet doe, yf he coulde fhewe that doctrine of the Sacrament that he profefseth to haue ben receaued vniuerfallie and quietly but one hũdreth yeares : yea one half hundreth years : yea one twentie years or yf he can not doe that, as I am fure he can not, Let him fhewe yt receaued

The Proclamers doctrine hath no prefidẽt, that yt hath ben quietly receaued.

C and cõtinued, as ys faïed, but one yeare. Yf he can make no foche prefcriptiõ of his doctrine, he ys to blame to reiect the catholique doctrine, which by manie of their confeffions hath ftand thefe thoufande yeares, and to obtrude, vnto vs his doctrine, that neuer was yet ftaied quietlie one yeare. Yf euer his droctrine was vniuerfallie receaued yt coulde neuer withoute great and notable trooble to the wholl Churche be taken awaie. Let him then fhewe, when, by whome, and by what meanes yt was taken awaie, by the authoritie of anie autentique hiftorie or catholique authour, and thẽ he fhall doe fomwhat, but that fomwhat will neuer be doen. Seing then the doctrine of the prefence of Chryft in the Sacrament hath vniuerfallie ben recaued fince the time of *Damafcen* vntill the time of this herefie : as we fhoulde be madde, men to receaue fochenoueltics of fo fmall ftaie or holde : So ys the Proclamer more madde fo to moue vs. *Damafcen* then teaching that, that all the Chriftian worlde receaued, and that alfo long before the controuerfie was moued, can not be iuftlie reiected, but ys to be regarded.

D These being twelue in nombre, are fufficient to be a queft and to geue their verdicte vpon this matter. Whiche all finde that S. Paule here fpake of rhe bodie and blood of Chryft in the Sacrament, no mencion being made of material bread. Whiche fo being, yt ys eafie by the fame verdicte to pronownce, that to faie that Chryftes bodie and bloode be not in the bleffed Sacrament, ys wicked herefie.

In

In this queftion I might alfo haue placed holy *Cyrill*, *Leo*, *Theodorete*, and
other, whiche to auoid prolixitie I haue yet omitted. But forfomoche as the
Sacramentaries haue fo fhamefullie abufed *Theodorete*, as though he fhoulde
fauour fome parte of their herefie, and wolde by his auncient authoritie deceaue the people, as *Cranmer* doeth in his booke, I haue thought good to recal
that I intended to haue omitted, and breiflie, as by a glawnce, to let yowe
vnderftande, what he thinketh of S. Paule in his eleuenth chap. to the Corinthians, and what S. Paule ther ment, and what *Theodorete* himfelf thought
of Chryftes prefence in the Sacrament, to the intent that fuche as reade, be
not deceaued withe gaie glofing wordes, finely vttered in the ftead of trueth.
Thus he writeth vpon our text of S. Paule : *Hic eos quidem pungit, qui laborabant*

*Theodo-
red in 11.
1.Corb.*

*ambitione.Pungit autem eum quoque,qui fuerat fornicatus, & cum eis illos,qui eorum,quæ
Idolis immolata erant,fuerant abfque vllo difcrimine participes.Præterea autē & nos,qui cũ
mala cõfcientia audemus diuina Sacramēta percipere.Illud autē:erit reus corporis et fangui-
nis:hoc fignificat, quod quēadmodum tradidit ipfum Iudas, ipfi autē infultarunt, &eũ pro-
bris ac contumelijs affecerunt Iudæi:ita cum ignominia & dedecore afficiunt,qui fanctiffimũ
eius corpus immundis manibus accipiunt , & in pollutum, et inceftum os immittunt.* Here
he toucheth them that were ambitioufe. He toucheth him alfo that had cõmitted fornicacion with his Fathers wief. And with them alfo he toucheth
them that without anie difference were partakers of thefe thinges that were
offred in facrifice to Idolls. Befides them alfo he toucheth vs, whiche with

*Theodore-
te vnder-
ftandeth
S. Paule to
fpeake of
the bodie of
Chryfte.*

an euell confciēce dare receaue the diuine Sacramētes. As for that he faieth:
that he fhall be giltie of the bodie and blood of our Lorde : fignificth this:
that as Iudas betraied him, and the Iewes mocked and reuiled him : Euenfo
doe they diflonour, and difwoorfhippe him that *with vnclean handes receaue his
moft holie bodie* and put yt into a filthie and defiled mouth.

Ye fee here this fcripture by *Theodorete* expownded : ye perceaue that the
vnwoorthie receauers of the Sacrament are giltie of the bodie and bloode of
Chryft, as Iudas that folde him, or the Iewes that mocked and fkorned him.
And whie? not that they eate a peice of bread, but bicaufe they receaue the
moft holie bodie of Chryfte with vnclean handes, and put yt into a defiled

*The bodie
of our lord
receaued
with hand
and mouth,
clean or vn-
clean.*

mouthe. Note then that *Theodorete* doeth not onelie faie that the moft holie
bodie of Chryfte ys receaued,but that yt ys receaued with handes and mou-
the.Which argueth inuinciblie the reall ãd fubftanciall prefence of Chryftes
bodie in the Sacrament. Farder yt ys to be noted, that he faieth not onelie
that the bodie of Chryft ys receaued with hands and mouthe,but alfo with
vnclean haudes, and defiled mouthe · Whiche vnclean and defiled handes
and mouthe are not taken for foche as be vnclean in feight before man, but
for foche as be by finne vnclean before God. Wherby ys plainlie taught that
finners and euell men receaue the bodie of Chryft.

Yf yt be not plainlie enough taught here,heare yt taught of the fame *Theodorete* expownding S. Paule a litle before.where fpeaking of Chryftes Supper

*Theod. fu-
per. Ego
enim ac-
cepi à
Dom.
A plain
fentence of
Theodorete
againft the
Proclamer.*

he faieth thus:*Sacram illam , & ex omni parte beatam noctem in memoriam reuocauit,
in qua & typico Pafchati finem impofuit,& verum tipi archetypum oftendit, & falutaris
Sacramenti portas aperuit.& non folum vndecim Apoftolis, fed etiam Iudæ proditori preciofum corpus & fanguinem impertit* . He calleth again to memorie that holie and
by all meanes bleffed night, in the whiche he did geue an ende to the figuratiue paffouer,And did fhewe furth the true patern of the figure, ãd alfo opened the gates of the holfome Sacrament, And gaue not onelie to the Eleuen
Apoftles,but alfo to *Iudas* the triditour,his precioufe bodie and bloode.

Note that Chryft gaue to Iudas not onelie his bodie, for then wolde the
Sacra-

A　Sacramentarie wreſt yt to the figure of his bodie : But he gaue him his precioufe bodie, whiche ys his owne verie reall and fubftáciall bodie. For other,
precioufe bodie for the vnaptneffe of Iudas he coulde not geue him.

Thefe places of *Theodorete*, I haue for that they were verie plain, a litle touched, that the Reader maie fee , that howfoeuer yt hath liked the Sacramentaries to abufe him: yet he fauoureth, not their herefie. For here being not in
the heate of difputació, but a fobre expofitour of S. Paule he teacheth not one
lie by plain woordes that Chryftes moſt holie bodie ys in the Sacramèt: but
to the confirmacion of the fame faieth , that he gaue the fame holie and precioufe bodie and bloode vnto *Iudas* . Which can not be yf the fame bodie be
not reallie, verilie, & fubftanciallie in the Sacrament . Let not them therfor
triumphe vpon him in places that be obfcure , which by fome meanes maie
be wreſted : but let them fee and beholde his faith and the trueth in places
that can not be wreſted.

But yt ys time that we heare his yockfelowe, whome at this time oute
of the latin Churche, we haue appoincted *Anfelmus*, who liuing near the time
B　of *Berengarius*, can well teſtifie, what the catholique Churche taught againſt
his peftiferoufe doctrine. This man expownding Sainct Paules epiſtle to the
Corinthians writeth thus vpon our text nowe in hand . *Quandoquidem autho-*
ritate Domini Iefu probauimus , panem illum effe corpus eius , & vinum fanguinem eius,
atque celebrandum vel accipiendum effe myſterium illud in commemorationem mortis
ipfius : itaque quicumque homo , fiue diues, fiue pauper , fiue clericus, fiue Laicus , mandu-
cauerit panem Domini hunc , & biberit calicem Domini indignè , reus erit corporis & fan-
guinis Domini . Indignè manducat & bibit , qui hoc myſterium aliter celebrat , vel accipit
quàm à Chriſto traditum eſt . Ideo fit reus corporis & fanguinis Domini , id eſt , dabit pæ-
nas mortis Domini . Indignè manducat & bibit , qui fine debita reuerentia facram Eucha-
riſtiam percipit . Indignè manducat , & bibit , qui non prius per pænitentiam purgatus ad
hoc Sacramentum accedit . Hoc eſt enim indignè accipere , fi eo tempore accipiat , quo de-
bet pænitentiam agere , fit igitur reus corporis & fanguinis , id eſt , non purgationem , fed
maculam culpæ pro qua pereat , trahit , ex eo quod malè accipit bonum Sacramentum cor-
C　*poris , & fanguinis Domini .* Forafmoche as we haue by the authoritie of our
Lorde Iefus Chryſt prooued that bread to be his bodie , and the wine his
bloode, and that that mifterie ys to be celebrated or receaued in the remembrance of his deathe : Therfor what man foeuer he be , whether he be
riche or poour , clerke or laie man , that fhall eate this bread of our Lorde,
and drinke the cuppe of our Lorde vnwoorthilie, fhall be giltie of the bodie
and bloode of our Lorde . He doeth vnwoorthilie eate and drinke, that
otherwife doeth celebrate or receaue this mifterie, then yt ys of Chryſt
deliuered . Therfor ys he made giltie of the bodie and blood of our Lorde,
that ys , he fhall be punifhed as giltie of the death of our Lorde . He eateth
and drinketh vnwoorthilie, that withoute due reuerence receaueth the holie
euchariſt . He eateth and drinketh vnwoorthilie, that cometh to this Sacrament before he be pourged by penaunce. For this ys to take yt vnwoorthily
yf anie man receaue yt at that time, in the whiche he ought to doe penáuce.
he ys made therfor giltie of the bodie and blood of Chriſt, that ys, he getteth
D　not purgacion of his offence, but blémifhe , for the whiche he maie be damned by that he doeth euell receaue the good Sacrament of the bodie and
blood of our Lorde.

Manie are the thinges that here maie be noted in this Authour,
But fearing the prolixitie of the worke , and tedioufneffe that maie
happen to the Reader being continuallie occupied in one kinde of
　　　　　　　　　　　　　　　　　　　　　　　　matter

Theophi-
lact. in 11.
1. Cor.

Anfelm. in.
11. 1. Cor.

Who be
vnwoorthy
receauers
of the Blef.
Sacram.

matter, and not delighted with some varietie whiche of manie ys desiered: **E**
I will but note our principall matters, that are of his text of Sainct Paule to
be learned, whiche (as before ys declared)are but two, and so ouerpaffe the
rest. The one that Sainct Paule here speaking of the Sacrament, and calling
yt *the bread of our Lorde*, and somtime with and article, *this bread* : mente not
common bread, but a speciall bread that ys, as often before ys saied, the heauenly bread of Chryftes bodie, whiche ys the bread of our Lorde in verie
dede. For in him onely confisteth the power to make this bread, and to geue
yt to the people. The other, that God suffreth this heauenlie bread of Chryftes bodie, to be receaued of sinners. As touching the Frst, the presuppo-
fall or caufe why a man shoulde be giltie of the bodie and bloode of Chryfte, when he doeth vnwoorthilie receaue the Sacrament ys, saieth *Anselmus,*
bicaufe by the *authoritie of our Lorde Iefus yt ys proued, that this bread that we fpeake*
of here, ys his bodie, and that the wine here alfo fpoken of in the vfe of the Sacrament ys
bis bloode.

Note I praie yowe, that this Authur saieth, that yt ys prooued of Sainct
Paule by the authoritie of our Lorde Iefus, that the bodie of the same our **F**
Lorde Iefus ys in the Sacrament, formoche as the bread and wine ther,
ys no other but the bodie and bloode of Chryft. And doe not onelie as
by tranfcourfe lightlie reade thefe woordes, but earneftlie note that he
saieth, yt ys proued by the authoritie of our Lorde Iefus. Yf yt be proued by
him, who can improoue yt? Yf he saie yt, who can denie yt? Yf he fo teache
y t, why shall we otherwife beleue yt?

Let the Proclamer nowe, let all the Sacramentaries, whiche be his com-
panions, bringfurth one Authour that faieth that yt ys proued by the woordes of our Lorde Iefus that the bread and wine of the bleff. Sacrament be
not the bodie and blood of our Lorde Iefus, but onelie figures of the fame
bodie and bloode, and not the thinges themfelues, and shewe the place as we
doe, and they shall haue the victorie. But let them painte their matters as well
as they can to bleer the eyes of the fimple, yet *Vincit Veritas,* the trueth ouer-
cometh. And fo shall yt in the ende faull oute, that they shall be perceaued
to be deftitute of trueth. For their vntrueth shall be confownded by the **G**
trueth. Though vntrueth for a time gett the vpperhand, and be mainteined
by the princes and mightie of the earthe, for that their fenfuall libertie ys not
by her reftreined, but by her in that refpect, they are moche pleafured : yet
as all vanitie faileth, vadith and vanifheth : So yt being of the fame kinde shall
fall awaie and confume as the fmooke, and the fauourers of the fame shall be
as the duft, which the winde bloweth awaie from the face of the erathe.

But lo, while I am a litle paffed the compaffe of the ringe, my fecond matter knocketh and calleth me again, wherin breiflie to touche moche matter:
this Authour maketh three fortes of euell and vnwoorthie receauers. The
firft ys of them that doe otherwife celebrate or receaue this holie mifterie,
then yt was deliuered of Chryft. In the whiche forte as he touched the *Be-*
rengarians, whiche were in his time: So doeth he the *Oecolampadians* and the *Ca-*
luinifts of this our time, whiche both otherwife celebrating, and otherwife
receauing this holie mifterie, then yt was of Chryft inftituted, they make the **H**
felues vnwoorthie receauers. Chryft inftituted his bodie to be diftributed ad
geuen in this holie refection: They geue and receaue a peice of bread, and a
cuppe of wine. Chryft inftituted a facrifice to be celebrated: They celebrate a
beare toke of remembrance. Wherfor by the iudgement of this Authour, they
altering Chryftes inftitucion, are accompted among the euell receauers.

An

What bread S. Paul fpake of.

The bleff. Sacra.ys proued by- our Lorde Iefus, to be his bodie.

Three for- tes of euell receauers.

A   An other forte ys of them that receaue the holie Sacrament without due reuerence: Of this forte be all the *Lutherans* who although they côfeſſe the verie preſence of Chryſtes bodie in the Sacramêt: yet they denie anie honour or woorſhippe to be doen vnto yt. Which fond and infatuate doctrine, I câ but woonder at, wel knowing that wherſoeuer Chryſt ys either in heauê or in earth, he ys (as Chryſoſtome ſaieth) woorthie of moſt high honoure, ãd if God hath ſo exalted him and geuen him a name, which ys aboue all names, that in the name of Ieſu euery knee ſhal bowe, both of thinges in heauê, and things in earth, and thinges vnder the earthe: by what authoritie câ or will man will or cômaunde no honour to be doen to him? but of this we haue allreadie ſpooken, wherfore ſtaing anie more to ſaie of yt here, I come to the third ſorte of receauers, which ys (ſaieth this authour) of them that preſume to come to the receipt of the bleſſed Sacrament before they haue pourged thê ſelues, and clenſed their conſciences by penance. Of this forte be all they who well beleuing, yet not well liuing, come with the filthineſſe of ſinne allreadie cômitted, yet remaing vpon them, or ells with pourpoſe of ſinne to be committed, by which both they make themſelues vnwoorthie receauers.

Philip. 2.

3

B   Here nowe ye ſee a varietie of euel receauers, and yet (ſaieth this authour) that they all receaue the Sacrament. And the Sacrament (ſaieth he) by the authoritie of our Lord Ieſus ys proued to be the bodie ãd the blood of Chryſt. Which thing this authour yet by more expreſſe woordes teacheth in the expoſition of the other text, wher S. Paule as by repeticion ſaieth: *He that eateth and drinketh vnwoorthilie, eateth and drinketh his owne damnacion:* ſaing thus: *Ideo prius ſe diſcutiat & purget. Quia qui manducat & bibit indignè, id eſt ſine ſui examinatione, iudicium ſibi manducat & bibit. Sicut enim Iudas cui buccellam tradidit Dominus non malum accipiendo, ſed malè accipiendo, locum in ſe Diabolo præbuit: ſic indignè quiſque ſumens Dominicum Sacramentum, vt quia ipſe malus eſt, malum ſit quod accepit, aut quia non ad ſalutem accipit, nihil acceperit, corpus enim Domini, & ſanguis Domini nihilominus eſt, ſed ille accipit hoc non ad vitam, ſed ad indicium, quia non diudicat corpus Domini, id eſt, non diſcernit quàm ſit dignius omnibus creaturis hoc corpus, quod videtur eſſe panis. Si enim cogitaret hoc corpus eſſe Verbo Dei perſonaliter vnitum, & vitam ac ſalutem eorum eſſe, qui hoc dignè accipiunt, non præſumeret indignus accipere, ſed dignum ſe præpararet.* Let him therfor firſt examine himſelf, and pourge himſelf. For he that eateth ãd drinketh vnwoorthilie, that ys without examinacion of himſelf, eateth aud drinketh his owne damnacion, making no difference of the bodie of our Lord. For as Iudas to whome our Lorde gaue a morſell, not taking an euell thinge, but taking'yt in euell maner, gaue to the Deuell a place in himſelf: ſo whoſoeuer receaueth the Sacrament of our Lorde vnwoorthilie, cauſeth not, bicauſe he ys an euell man, that thing which he hath receaued ys euell, or bicauſe he receaued yt not to ſaluacion, that he receaued nothing (For yt ys neuertheleſſe the bodie of our Lorde, and the blood of our Lord) but he taketh this not to life, but to condemnaciou, bicauſe he maketh no difference of the bodie of our Lord, that ys, he diſcerneth not howe moch more woorthie this bodie, which ſemeth to be bread, ys aboue all creatures. For if he had in minde that this bodie ys perſonallie vnited to the Sonne of God, and to be the life and ſaluacion of them that doe receaue yt woorthilie, the vnwoorthie wolde not preſume to receaue yt, but he wolde prepare himſelf to be woorthie.

Anſelm. ibid.

The bleſſ. Sacr. ys the bodie and blood of Chryſt though euell men receaue yt.

C

D   See ye not, that the bleſſed Sacr. ys neuertheleſſe the bodie and blood of our Lord vnto thê that take yt not to life but to condênacion? yt ys ſo plain that I nede to ſaie no more but to conclude with thys authour, and all the reſt hitherto alleaged, that ſainct Paule here ſpeaketh of the bodie

of Chryſt, and teacheth the ſame to be verilie receaued of euell and vnwoor
thie receauers. Yt ys not vnknowen to the Proclamer, but of the lower houſe of Chryſtes Parliament, I might haue brought manie moe both grecians
and Latines: as *Haymo, Bede, Photius, Oecumenius. Thomas de aquino, Lyra, Dionyſe, Hu
go,* and *Eraſmus,* and as manie as haue within the compaſſe of theſe nine hun
dreth yeares, either written vpon S. Paules Epiſtles, or alleaged him in the
matter of the Sacrament oute of the eleuenth of the firſt epiſtle to the Corin
thians. For they all vnderſtand S. Paule both to haue ſpoken of Chryſtes bo
die in the Sacrament, and that the ſame bodie ys oftentimes receaued of
euell men.

But amonge ſo manie, I can not ſtaie my ſelf, but I muſt heare one of them,
and the raither for that he ys a grecian, and ſo being no Papiſt, he maie be
heard with more indifferent eare. Yt ys *Oecumenius,* who vpon the woordes
of S. Paule ſaing, that the vnwoorthie receauer ſhall be giltie of the bodie

Oecum. in
11.1. Cor.

and bloode of our Lorde, ſaieth thus: *Quod ait, reus erit corporis & ſanguinis : hoc
indicat, quòd quemadmodum Iudas eum tradidit. Iudæi verò in ipſum, debacchati ſunt : Ita
ipſum ignominia afficiunt, qui ſanctiſsimum ipſius corpus manibus impuris ſuſcipiunt (veluti
Iudæi tunc eum tenuerunt) & execrando admouent ori. Per hoc quod frequêter ait, corporis
& ſanguinis Domini, manifeſtat, quod non ſit nudus homo, qui immolatur, ſed ipſe Dominus, & factor omnium, vt videlicet per hoc eos terreat.* That he ſaieth: he ſhall be gil-

*The bodie
of our Lord
maie be re-
ceauedwith
vn pure
hands and
execrable
mouth.*

tie of the bodie and blood of our Lorde: he ſheweth this, that, as *Iudas* betraied him, and the Iewes raiged againſt him, euen ſo doe they diſhonour
him, that with vnclean handes(as then the Iewes did holde him) doo receaue his moſt holie bodie, and put yt to their curſed or deteſtable mouthe. By
that, that he often ſaieth: the bodie and blood of our Lorde : he manifeſtlie
declareth, that yt ys not a pure or onelie man that ys offred, but euen our
Lorde himſelf, the maker of al things, that therby he might make thê afraied.

What ys in the Sacrament, which ys deliuered into the handes and mouthes of men, by this authour ye maie perceaue. For yt ys (ſaieth he) the moſt
holie bodie of our Lorde, which moſt holie bodie ys receaued both with vn
clean handes, for that the conſciences of ſoch receauers be vnclean, and with

*S. Paule
doth often
call the
bleſſ. Sacr.
the bodie
and blood
of our lord*

deteſtable mouthes, for that their mouthes ſpeaking wicked thinges, are dete
ſtable before God. Yf yowe will ſee more of the trueth of this matter : note
that he ſaieth, that S. Paule doeth often call the Sacrament, *the bodie and bloode
of our Lorde,* but will ye knowe why he doeth ſo? Not to make vs beleue that
yt ys not the bodie of Chryſt (as this Proclamer wolde beare vs in hande)
but that he wolde, as this authour teſtifieth, manifeſtlie teache vs, that yt ys
a verie bodie, and not the onelie figure of a bodie: a bodie, which ys not the
bodie onelie of a man, but the bodie of our Lord God, who ys the maker of
all thinges. Yf the Proclamer deſire to haue one that by expreſſe woordes,
doeth teach the verie preſence of Chryſtes bodie in the Sacrament. Let him
beholde a nombre now brought to expownde S. Paule, which al not onelie
of their own faith affirme ſoch preſence, but alſo teach that ſainct Paule affi-
med the ſame. And therfor if ther be anie treuth in the ſame Proclamer let
him nowe forſake his wicked hereſie, and according to his promeſſe, let him
ſubſcribe to the veritie. For that being nowe oftentimes doen, that he required but once to be doen, as iuſtlie I maie, ſo doe I clame the performance of
his promeſſe. Well reader whatſoeuer he, witholden either with ſhame or
with malice ſhall doe in this matter againſt the trueth, and moſt like alſo a-
gainſt his conſcience: yet thow hauing regarde to thie duetie before God,
and to the ſaluacion of thie ſoule, beholde thow with indifferent eies theſe

ſomanie

A fo manie plain manifeſt,and expreſſe places:tarie and abide·vpon them:vieue them and conſider them well,and yelding to trueth,thow ſhalt by gods gra ce,if thow humblie craue yt,come to yt,but yet thowe ſhalt ſee more of S. Paule.

THE THREE AND FIFTETH CHAP. BEGIN-

neth the expoſition of the next text of S.Paule,which ys,Let euery man examin himſelf,and ſo let him eate,&c.

I N S.Paule yt foloweth.*Probet ſeipſum homo,& ſic de pane illo edat, & de calice bibat.*Let therfore a man examine himſelf: And ſo let him eate of that bread,and drinke of that cuppe.The great peril and daunger that ſhall come to vnwoorthie receauers of that bleſſed bodie and blood being by S.Paule declared, he imedia telie ioineth therunto,as a falue to a deadlie ſore,a godlie admonicion, that to auoide foche daunger as maie enſewe,or to remedie the hurt, if yt be all-

B readie take euery mã that will receaue this bleſſed Sacramẽt,ſhoulde firſt cõ-ſider what yt ys, and vpõ conſideracion therof examine him ſelf,whether he be a woorthie perſon to receaue yt or no. But vnto this text we ſhall geue moche light , if we open what yt ys for man to examine himſelf, and when he hath ſo doen , howe he ſhall knowe when he ys woorthie or vnwoorthie. Firſt, yt ys expedient, that the ſtate of man ,wherin he aught to be before God , be knowen,for the ſtate knowen, yt ſhall be eaſier for man,to make examinacion of himſelf, wherher he be in the ſtate nere to yt,or farre from yt. The ſtate that man aught to be in before God in this fraill life cõſiſteth in two partes in vpprightneſſe of faithe and in puritie or cleneſſe of life. As touching faith the Apoſtle ſaieth : *Sine fide impoßibile eſt placere Deo* . withoute fatth yt ys vnpoſſible to pleaſe God . For (as he ſaieth again) *Accedentem ad Deum oportet credere.*He that will come to God muſt beleue. Wherfor Chryſt being as touching the birth of his manheade in his owne contrie did not ther manie miracles , for that the vnbeleif of the people, whiche ſhoulde

C haue comed to him by beleif, did let him, and ſtaie . For (ſaieth the Euangeliſt Mathew) *Nonfecit ibi virtutes multas , propter incredulitatem illorum* he did not manie miracles ther bicauſe of their vnbeleif. But wher faith was , ther Chryſt wroght his miracles bowntifullie. Wherfor when the *Centurio* came vnto Chryſt, as an humble and faithfull ſuiter for the he-alth of his ſeruant that laie ſicke of a palſie, and vpon the mercifull anſwere of Chryſt , who ſaied that he wolde come and cure him:The *Centurio* ſtrong in faith ſaied : *Lorde I am not woorthie than thowe ſhouldeſt entre vnder my roofe, but onelie ſaie the woorde , and my ſeruant ſhall be holle :*Chryſt was ſo delighted with his faith that he did not onely praiſe yt ſaing : *I fownde not ſo great faith in Iſrakell:*But alſo for the health of the ſicke man he ſaied to the *Centurio : Go thy wa-ies, as thowe haueſt beleued, ſo be yt vnto thee.* and his ſeruant was healed in the ſelf ſame howre.

The woman alſo that had the bloodie flixe , was ſo ſtrong in faith that ſhe ſaied with in her ſelf: yf I maie touche but the hemme of his veſture onelie I ſhall be wholl,whervpon immediatelie ſhe bothe receaued the benefett of health at Chryſtes hãde and alſo the praiſe of her faith,Chryſt ſaing to her

D be of good comforte daughter: thy faith hath made the ſafe.Chryſt alſo be-holdinge the faith of the womã of *Canaan,*did not onelie praiſe the ſame ſain-ge : *O woman great ys thie faithe .* But alſo for the health of her daughter ſaied

Ttt ii   vnto

Marginal notes:
To examin our ſelues what yt ys and howe yt maie be doen.
Hebr.11.
Ibidem.
Faith ho-we neceſſa-rie yt ys.
Math. 13.
Math.8.
Wher faith ys there God woor-keth.
Math.9.
Math.15.

Heb. 11.
The force of faith.

vnto her:*Be yt vnto thee as thowe hauest defiered*,and her daughter was healed, **E**
euen at the fame time. What fhall I ftand in this large campe of faith, and
in the woorthineffe therof,of the which the wholle bible from *Genefis*, to
the laft of the *Apocalips* doth continuallie make mencion?wherfor I wil with
S.Paule conclude in fewe woordes,faing with him:*The holie faithfull by faith
haue fubdewed kingdomes,wrought righteoufneffe, obteined the promiffes,ftopped the mou
thes of Lions,quenched the violence of fire,efchaped the edge of the fwoorde,oute of weaknef
fe were made ftronge,waxed valiaunt in fight,turned to fleight the armies of the alientes,
the wemen receaued their dead raifed to life again.*

    Thus maie we fee howe neceffarie faith ys,withoute the which man can
not come to God : Thus maie we fee howe bowntifullie God woorketh

Math. 17.

wher faith ys : Thus maie we finallie fee the great might, and power
of faithe, which ys foche , that yt maketh all thinges pofsible to the
beleuer.For to him that beleueth, nothing ys vnpofsible,faith Chryft.

Want of faith howe yt hinde- reth good effects.
Marc. 9.

    Nowe as faith woorketh thefe wonders: fo the lacke of faithe hyndereth
all thefe wonders. The Apoftles attempted to deliuer a man,that was poffef
fed of a Deuell,and coulde not,wherupon the Father of him , brought him
to Chryft faing:Mafter,I brought my Sonne to thie Difciples,and they coul **F**
de not caft the Deuell oute of him.When Chryfte had caft the Deuell oute,
the Difciples came fecretlie to him,faing:*Whie coulde not we caft him oute ? Iefus
faied vnto them,bicaufe of yowr vnbeleif.*Vnbeleif then was the hinderance of this
great worke that might haue ben doen by the Apoftles. Faith made Peter
walke vpon the fea:vnbeleif made him finke,wherupon he heard atChryftes
mouthe.*Modicæ fidei,quare dubitafti?*O thow of litle faith,wherfor dideft thow
doubte?Vnbeleif fo moche difpleafethChryfte that after the refurrection he
rebukedthe two Difciples that went from Hierufalem to *Emaus* , and with
fharpe woordes faied vnto them:O ye fooles,and flowe of heart to beleue al
that the prophetes haue fpoken.S.Marke alfo faieth that Chryft appearing

Matth. 14 & Mar.16.

to the eleuen as they fatte at meate,caft their vnbeleif in their teeth, and rebuked the hardneffe of their heart,bicaufe they beleued not them, whiche
had feen,that he was rifen from the dead.

    To thus moch,the *Arrian*,the *Nouatian*,the *Pelagian*,the *Berengarian*,the *Wy-
cleffeft*,the *Lutheran*,the *Oecolampadian*,the Caluinifte,and the *Anabaptift* , will **G**
agree,and euerie one of thefe will faie, that faithe muft be had , and eche of
them will faie,that he hath that faith that pleafeth God , and yet being all
voide of vpright faith,they varie in faithe,as did the *Pharifeies* , and *Sadduceis*,
that ys hauing fome peice, but miffing the wholl.

The catho- lique faith defcribed.

    This faith therfor wolde be knowen,as alfo of whome yt fhoulde be lear-
ned. Yf ye will knowe this faith,in fewe woordes yt ys the faith that we
call Apoftolique, and catholique, Apoftolique defcending by continuall
fuccefsion from the Apoftles,as yt were from to hand hand , euen vnto vs
that now liue.Catholique as vniuerfallie receiued,profeffed , and beleued
throughoute the chryftian orbe,not reigning in one corner,or in one realm,
by the priuate inuencion of one priuate brain,and mainteined by the priuate affection of one prince,but generallie and vniuerfallie of all Chryftian
princes, ofall Chryftian Realmes, ofall Chryftian men , and that not for
twentie or fortie years , as the new faith in Germanie,and in Englond but
in all times not nowe receaued , and now difproued , as the Lutherans **H**
doctrine, but euer without interruption continued . This faith maie not
be deuifed , newly inuented or vpon affection appoincted,but yt muft be
learned . *Fides ex auditu* , faith cometh by hearing faieth Paule, beinge
                                        called

A called to be the fingular vefell of God,was yet fent by Chryftes commaundement to *Ananias*,to learn of him what he fhoulde doe. *Hic dicet tibi , quid te* *Act.9.* *oporteat facere.*He fhall tell thee what thow muft doe. *Cornelius* a godlie man and fearing God,although he might haue ben taught of the Angell that appeared vnto him,yet he was not,but by the fame Angell was willed to fende to *Ioppe* for S.Peter to come to him.And he (*faieth the Angell*) fhall tell thee what thow oughteft to doe.Marke learned of S.Peter, Luke of S.Paule, of the which a longer difcourfe ys made in the firft book.So that this faith I faie *Cap.7.* muft by Gods ordeinaunce be learned of the elders,not deuifed by newe inuentours.

The faith, if yt maie be fo tearmed, which *Luther* taught,wher learned he *Wher lear-* yt?was there anie elder at that daie in all the worlde , that taught him that *ned Luther* phantafticall faith?did he not of his owne priuate head newlie skowre fome *and his ra-* of the herefies of *Wicliff* and *Huffe*,and fome deuifed neuer hearde of before? *ble their* Who in all the Chriftian orbe,when Luther had griffed(as he faied)a right, *faith.*
B a true and a perfect faith,taught *Carolftadius*,*Zuinglius*,and *Oecolampadius* a contrarie faith to *Luther*,as to teache that Chryftes bodie ys not in the Sacrament?Let *Carolftadius* bring furth one Chryftian realme that fo taught him: or one Church,or one allowed Father or elder then liuing, that fo taught. But forfomoch as he cã not,yt maie be cõcluded,that as well his faith, as the faith of *Luther* ys not learned of the Fathers by fuccefsion,but partelie boro wed of fome other heretique by priuate election,partlie deuifed by a newe inuention,and fo a faith not continued,but both inuented,and interrupted, and therfor neither Apoftolique,neither catholique.The ftate of man then in the vpprightneffe of faith,muft be in the faith Apoftolique,and catholike, and not in hereticall faith,which ys no more a faith in dede , then a painted man ys a man. A man ys vpright in faith whê he difcrediteth nothing that ys conteined in the holie faith Apoftolique and catholique.

The other parte of the ftate of mans life before God ys puritie and cleanneffe of life,which parte who fo can(*Faith,as ys faied prefuppofed*) atteign vnto, ys bleffed,Chryft faing:*Beati mundo corde,quoniam ipfi Deum videbunt.*Bleffed be
C the clean in hearte,for they fhall fee God.

This cleanneffe ftandeth in two poinctes:in the efchewing the filthinef- *Puritie of* fe of finne:and in adourning our felues with vertues,in declining from euel *life ftãdeth* and doing of good,as the pfalme faieth,*Declina à malo, & fac bonum.* Decline *in two pa-* or forfake euell,and doe good.For yt ys not fufficient to a good life to flie *inéts.* finne onelie,but alfo to doe good.And therfore the holie Gofte hath with *Pfalm.33.* a copulacion coopled and linked them together allwaies.

Nowe thus moch of the ftate of mans life knowen,yt ys the eafier to perceaue what S.Paule meeneth by the examinacion of themfelues.To examine our felues ys to trie and prooue,to fearch to call our felues to accompte, firft whether we ftand fownde in faith,according to the counfell of S.Paule in an other place,*Vos metipfos tentate fi eftis in fide,ipfi vos probate .* Prooue yowr felues whether ye be in faith or not examine yowr felues.This triall ys made, when we examining our felues,whether we difagree or diffent from anie one article of the catholique faith,finde our felues neither varieng from , nor doubting of anie of them.
D In the fecõd part,we muft thus examine our felues,firft whether anie finne be by vs allreadie committed, or anie pourpofe remaining in vs for anie to be committed.Yf anie be cõmitted,the fame muft by heartie cõtriciõ, hum- *2.Cop. 13.* ble and plain confefsion , true and faithfull penaunce be wiped awaie.

Yf anie pourpofe be in vs to finne, that muft be cutt of and detefted, and by **E** like means(as ys before faied)clean forfaken, knowing that euery finne to the which confent of wil ys geuen, though yt be not doen in facte, ys reputed before God, and ys in dede a full finne.

Thus moch not onely the catholique Church hath willed to be doen, as S.Cyprian and S.Auguftine are plentifull wittneffes. But alfo the *Lutherans* Conuenticles. For in their confefsion of the cheif articles of their faith, thus they faie: *Confefsio in ecclefiis apud nos, non eft abolita. Non enim folet porrigi corpus Domi*

ni nifi antea exploratis, & abfolutis. Confefsion ys not with vs in our churches abolifhed. For the bodie of oure Lorde ys not wount to be geuen, but to foche as before be diligently fearched and examined and abfolued.

When we be thus farre goen we muft examine our felues of our deuocion, regarde and reuerence to the thing that ys to be receaued. For ells we fhall receaue to our owne condemnacion, for that, as S.Paule faieth, we make no difference of the bodie of our Lord, from other common meates. Thus moch being faied for our examinacion and preparacion before we come to the receipt of this high myfterie, we haue therin neither varied from the doctrine of Chryft neither from the doctrine of S.Paule, nor of the holie **F** Fathers of the Church. The doctrine of Chryft fhall furth with be fhewed. The doctrine of S.Paule and the Fathers fhall be opened in all the proceffe folowinge,

Joan.6.
Chryfte in-
ftructed his
Apoftles
in the faith
of the bleff.
Sacrament
before he
inftituted it

Chryfte fetting furth this high myfterie of his bodie and blood, declared that yt was neceffarie to haue both faith and puritie of life. Firft, as touching faith, that his Apoftles fhoulde be therin prepared and made readie, he did not onelye inftructe them fullie long before he miniftred the thing to them that they fhoulde knowe what yt was that they fhould receaue, but alfo induced them to the fame faith by a miracle wrought alfo in bread, that as thei knewe by the power of his godhead the fiue loaues to be multiplied to the fatisfieng of fiue thoufand people, and to the leauing yet of twelue baskettes full of fragmentes of the fame loaues, fo they fhoulde(this being doe in their feight)with the more eafe be brought to beleue, that he by the fame power coulde make of bread his bodie. Wherupon though manie of the Difciples not beleuing Chryft did forfake him and came no more at him (as manie ha **G** ue doen in thefe daies)yet the Apoftles by the miracle being prepared, and by Chryftes owne doctrine inftructed in the faith of this myfterie, abode with him and faied-*Domine ad quem ibimus? Verba vitæ æternæ habes.* Lorde vnto whom fhall we go? Thowe haueft the woordes of euerlafting life.

Thus being by Chryftes inftruction made perfect in the faith of this myfterie, thei came(*as Chryfoftom faieth*) quietlie to the receipt of yt, being nothing troobled with the woordes of Chryft when he faied: *Take eate this ys my bodie. Take, and drinke this ys my blood*, for that(*faieth he*)they had before hearde manie and great thinges of this myfterie. By this then yt ys manifeft that to the receipt of this Sacrament, faithe ys neceffarelie required..

Chryfte ga-
ue inftructi-
on of the pu-
ritie of life
requiredin
the recea-
uers of the
bleff. Sacr.

Likewife are we by him admonifhed of the puritie of life. For when he wolde geue furth this bleffed Sacrament, he rofe from the fupper of the Pafchall lambe, and laied afide his vpper garmentes, and being girded with a towel wafhed his Difciples feete fignifieng therby, that all that come to receaue this Sacrament muft before be clenfed and purified from all finfull **H** affections.

And here to faie by the waie, yf this Sacrament contein no more, the did

A the Paſchall lambe, but that both this and that be onely figures of Chryſt: and ſo the Lambe as good a Sacrament as this : why did Chryſt leaue this ſolempn Ceremonie of wasſhinge his Diſciples feet vndoen before the eating of the Paſchall lambe, and differred yt vnto the receipt of this Sacrament? Yt hath alſo conſideracion why he wolde nowe waſhe his Diſciples feete, who before cōtrarie to the maner of the Iewes, not onelie ſuffred, but alſo defended his Apoſtles for the eatinge of their meate with vnwasſhed handes.

The other part of puritie of life, whiche conſiſteth in the adourning of our ſelues with vertuouſe and godlie actes, was not left vntaught of Chryſt, but when he ſaied : *This doe ye in the remembrance of me* : he bothe willed that godlie acte to be doen, and alſo that we ſhoulde be mindefull of his death and paſſion, and of his great loue towordes vs in ſuffring of the ſame, and therby to be moued, not onelie to render vnto him moſt humble and lowlie thankes, but for his ſake for the proporcion of owre posſibilitie, to practiſe the like charitie, and ſhewe the like loue to our bretheren. Nowe he that

B hath ſuche charitie what lacketh he to the ſufficient furniture of his ſoule with all godlie vertues neceſſarie?

But a merueilouſe matter, as godlie, a thing as yt ys, for a man to examine himſelf, as plain as yt ys, bothe by Chryſtes doinges, and S. Paules woordes, that yt ſhoulde ſo be : yet Sathan coulde gett a miniſter to teache that no other preparacion neadeth for the receipt of the Sacramēt, but one ly faith. Ys ther moche hope of trueth to be repoſed in him, that ſo teacheth? ys not the religion to be ſuſpected, or raither deteſted, that ys ſettfurth by ſoche a patrone? yet this ys the doctrine of *Luther*, who ys the fownder of this newe religion, the inuentour of this faith, the ſetter vppe of the woorde, the reſtorer, as they ſaie, of trueth, and the bringer of light. But Sathan and his miniſter alſo knewe well howe to winne the people. They knew that libertie was a goodly bait to catche them withall. Wherfor to deliuer the people from the trooble of contricion, and heauineſſe for ſinnes, to make them free from the heauie yocke (as yt ys taken) of confesſion, to eaſe them

C of the laboure of praier, to disburden them of the care of godlic life, Sathan by his miniſter Luther teacheth, that to the receipt of the Sacrament ther neadeth no other examinacion or preparacion, but onelie that they beleue that they ſhall receaue grace, and that ys ſufficient.

Libertie à baite of the Deuell, ſetfurth by his miniſters luther and his likes.

But that I maie not be thought to miſreport him, at my pleaſure, I will reherſe his owne woordes, whiche be theſe : *Magnus error eſt eorum, qui ad ſacramentum Euchariſtiæ accedunt, hinc innixi quod ſint confeſſi, quòd non ſint ſibi conſcii alicuius peccati mortalis, quòd præmiſerint orationes ſuas, & præparatoria: Omnes illi iudicium ſibi manducant, & bibunt. Sed ſi credant, & confidant ſe gratiam ibi conſecuturos, hæc ſola fides facit eos puros & dignos.* Great ys the erroure of them that come to the Sacrament truſting to this, that they be confeſſed, that they knowe not them ſelues giltie of anie mortall ſinne, that they haue ſaied their praiers before, that they haue prepared them ſelues : All they doe eate and drinke, their owne condemnacion. But if they beleue and truſt that they ſhal there obtein grace, this faith alone maketh them pure and woorthie receauers.

Luth. in Aſſert Acti. 15.

Haue ye not hearde the ſame ſerpent nowe ſpeaking to chryſtian people, that in paradſe ſpake to owre firſt parentes? Haue ye not heard him likewiſe

D encountteringe with his negatiue, the affirmatiue of Chryſt and S. Paule, as he did the affirmitiue of God, who ſaied : *In what day ye eate of this fruict, ye ſhall die :* : he contrariwiſe ſaing : *Ye ſhall not die?* Haue ye not heard that

Ttt iiii   Chryſt

Chryſt vſed that ſolemne preparacion of waſſhing the feet of his Diſciples, **E**
before he wolde miniſter vnto them the Sacrament of his bleſſed bodie and
blood? Saied not Chryſt after that waſſhing : *Iam vos mundi eſtis* : Nowe ye
are clean? Did he not alſo then prepare them to humilitie and lowlineſſe,
whiche ys moche required in all that receaue the Sacrament? *Yf I* (ſaith
Chryſte) *haue waſſhed yowr feete being Lorde and Maſter, then ought yowe alſo to waſſh
one an others feete, I haue geuen yowe an example, that as I haue doen, euen ſo that ye doe.*
Ys not lowlineſſe a neceſſarie vertue to a receauer of this Sacrament? yt ys
not meet that a man knowe his owne filthineſſe before he receaue and ther
fore go to Chryſte to be waſſhed with the water of his grace? Ys yt not cō-
mendable that we ſaie with the *Centurion: Lorde I am not woorthie that thowe entre
vnder my roofe?* Ar we not ſo moued to doe by the olde Father Origen? Ouer
and aboue all this alſo we are willed by. S. Paule to examine our ſelues, and
yf we doe not, we ſhall eate and drinke our owne condemnacion : And
yet this beaſt, this Serpent ſhameth not to ſaie clean cōtrarie, that yf ye con
feſſe yowr ſinnes, yf ye finde yowr ſelf clere from all mortall ſinne yf before **F**
ye receaue, ye geue yowr ſelf to praier, yf ye vſe ſoche prepatiues, then ye
eate and drinke yowr owne condempnacion, Who euer heard ſoche doctrine? What eares can abide yt? And yet this ys the doctrine of him that
lightned the worlde with the knowledge of the trueth, as blinde men
call yt.

Joan. 13.

Math. 8.

But perchaunce ſome Lutheran in defence of his Patriarche will ſaie that
S. Paule willing a man to examine himſelf ſpake onely as Luther doeth of
the examinacion of faithe. To trie this let vs haue recourſe to the letter of S.
Paules epiſtle and there ſee what moued him to write this . That moued
him to write this, that moued him to write the wholl proceſſe of the Sacramēt in the ſame eleuenth chapter. He wrote to the Corinthians in the matter of the Sacrament, for that they coming to the receipt therof admitted
diuerſe faultes and abuſes in maners, but not in faith. For firſt of all (ſaieth
S. Paule) *when ye come together into the congregacion , I heare that ther ys diſſention a-
mong yowe.* Ther ys alſo an other faulte that euerie man beginneth a fore to
eate his owne ſupper. And beſides this in the eating of yowr Supper , ther **G**
ys litle charitie. For one ys hungrie, and an other ys dronken, in the whiche
their doinge they ſemed to deſpiſe the congregacion of God and ſhame the
poor that of pouertie had nothing to eate . And for theſe cauſes when ye
come together, the ſupper of our Lorde can not be eaten (ſaieth S. Paule)
Of faithe here ys no one title. For S. Paule fownde no fault in the Corinthians as touching the matters of faith aboute the Sacrament, but aboute
their maners in receauing of yt. And therfor as touching maners he ſaied: *Let euery man examine him ſelf, and ſo let him eate of that bread and drinke of
that cuppe.*

What mo-
ued S. Pau
le to write
of the Sa-
crament to
the Corinth

Ye ſee then that S. Paule moued by the euell maners of the Corinthians,
and not by their euell faith was moued to entre the treactiſe of the Sacrament, wherfor therin he correcteth their maners, and not their faith. S. Pau
le then trauailing to remoue diſſenſion, and to plant concorde, to remoue
glottonie and to plant temperance : to remoue pride whiche the riche had
in the ſhewe of their great ſuppers, and to plant humilitie: to remoue lacke
of mercie whiche was in the riche , they being dronke , while their poor **H**
were right hongrie, and to plant pitie : to remoue diſdain and contempt,
and to plant ſeemly regarde, ſaing alſo that theſe vices being in place, the
ſupper of our Lorde coulde not well, and as yt ought , be eaten, did he not
pre-

S Paule cor
rected the
maners of
the Corinth
and not
their faith.

A prepare the Corinthians and in them all chryſtians to the woorthie receipt of the Sacrament, did he not herein folowe the example of his maſter Chryſte, goinge aboute to wasſh awaie the filthineſſe of their feet, that ys of their earthlie and carnall affections.

But what ſtand I ſo long in ſo open a matter? Finallie wher Luther ſaieth that if we haue faith, that we ſhall receaue grace ther, that grace alone maketh vs pure and woorthie receauers: Firſt, I maie aske him by what rule he ſpeaketh this? wher ys his ſcripture for yt? Might the *Corinthians* (trowe ye) being in the caſe that they were in, and hauing, as they had faith, might they I ſaie, receaue grace? Yf they might then, S. Paule was not true, that ſaied they ſhoulde receaue condemnacion.

But to looke ſomwhat nearer to this ſaing of Luther, yt wolde haue ben defined, and determined, ſeing ther be ſo manie faiths nowe a daies, by whiche faith a man ſhoulde receaue this grace. Yf he ſaie by the faith that he him ſelf hath framed, the *Carolſtadins, Zwinglians,* and *Oecolampadius* will denie that. Yf *Oecolāpadius* will ſaie, by his faith that he hath deuiſed: the *Swenck*-

B *feldians,* who denie all Sacramentes, denie that. Yf *Caluine* will chalenge yt to his faith that he hath inueuted, the Anabaptiſtes will not abide that. Thus leauing vs in vncertenties, as manie others of his likes doe in other matters, he concludeth nothing.

In the ende, foraſmoche as the Apoſtle ſpeaketh of the vnwoorthie receauer ſignifieng therby, that ther ys a woorthie receauer yt apperteineh to owre pourpoſe to diſcuſſe, yf anie man maie be a woorthie receauer yt ys plain that a ſinner ys no woorthie receauer. And S. Iohn ſaieth: *Yf we ſaie that we haue no ſinne we deceaue our ſelues, and ther ys no trueth in vs:* yea ſo manie be our ſinnes, that the Prophet Dauid ſaieth: *Yf thowe Lorde will be extreame to marke what ys doen a miſſe, oh Lorde who maie abide yt?* as who might ſaie, no man can abide yt. And therfor concluding all liuing men vnder ſinne, ſaieth: *In thie ſeight, o Lorde, ſhall no man liuinge be iuſtified.* Yf no man liuinge can be iuſtified, then no man lining vs woorthie to receaue this bleſſed miſterie. What nowe then ſhall we ſaie to S. Paule, that appointeth woorthie recea-

C uers? Yt ys the minde of S. Paule to pronownce who ys an vnwoorthie receauer: but he deſcribeth not the woorthie receauer. For in dede ſpeaking of woorthineſſe in the propre ſignificacion of yt, no man that liueth, be he neuer ſo iuſt, no though he were an Angell, yea, if he were an Archanngell, yf he were of the higheſt of the Angells as of *Cherubines* and *Seraphines* can be accompted woorthie in that maner, to receaue this high and heauenlie miſterie. For proprelie that man ys woorthie of an other thing, when he him ſelf or his deſertes be equiualent, and doe fullie aunſwere the goodneſſe of the thinge, wherto yt ys referred, as in our cōmō ſpeache we ſaie that foure pence be woorth a grote. And the woorkman ys woorthie his wages: in this kinde of woorthineſſe no man ys or can be woorthie.

An other kinde of woourthineſſe ys by reputacion, or acceptacion, when one ys accepted as woorthie, whē in very dede he ys not. As a queē to marie a lowe ſubiect. A noble womā to marrie her ſeruāt betwē whō, whē cōpariſon ys made, ther ys neither birth, nor honour, nor liuing, nor dominiō nor richeſſe in the mā that can cownteruaill the womā, yet for ſomoch as yt liketh her ſo to accept him, by her acceptaciō he ys made nowe woorthie of her, who of himſelf before was not. Euē ſo our mercifull Lorde God, in po-

D wer, wiſdome ād goodneſſe infinite, betwixt whō and vs ſinfull creaturs ther ys no cōpariſon, makinge through his great mercie of ſinners, iuſt mē, and of
vnwoor-

Woorthie or vnworthie receauers of the bleſſ. Sacr. who be.

1. Joan. 1.

Pſal. 130.

Woorthineſſe proprelie what yt ys.

vnwoorthie woorthie, when he feith vs in our weake maner endeuour our **E**
felues to accomplifh his holie will : when he beholdeth howe we prepare
and adonrne the tabernacle of owre hearte, being holden with moche defire ther in to receaue him, yt liketh him, though we maie ftill crie, Lorde I
am not woorthie that thowe fhouldeft come vnder my roofe : yet he accep
teth vs vpon foche preparacion as woorthie to his mercifull contentacion, and to our health and faluacion. Thus the text in part opened, and the
deteftable herefie of Luther fomwhat touched, I fhall for the farder expofition of the one , and the ftronger confutacion of the other after my
accuftomed maner repair to the holie Fathers , and vnderftand alfo therin
their mindes.

THE FOVRE AND FOVRTETH CHAP. BEGIN-
neth the expofition of the Fathers vpon the fame
text with fainct Hierom and
Chryfoftome.

IN the allegacion of the Fathers that nowe fhall be produced, **F**
to geue vs the vnderftanding of this text , bicaufe manie be alleaged vpon the laft fcripture , and this dependeth vpon that,
and fo the one fullie expownded, the other ys the eafier to be
perceaued, I fhall be the fhorter, both in the nombre and alfo
in the abiding vpon them . The firft coople that commeth to my hande ys
S. Hierom and Chryfoftom. S. Hierom expownding the epiftles of S. Pau-

Hieron.in. le, for the expofition of this text hath thus moche: *Si in lintheum vel vas fordi-*
ii. i. Cor. *dum non illud mitterè audet, quanto magis in corde polluto? quam immundiciam Deus fu-*
per omnia execratur, & quæ fola iniuria eft eius corpori. Nam & Iofeph ille iuftus prop-
terea findonè munda inuolutum in fepulchro nouo corpus Domini fepeliuit, præfigurans cor-
S.Hierõ ex *pus Domini accepturos tam mundam mentem habere, quàm nouam.* Yf a man dare not
powndeth putte that bodie into a filthie veffell or cloath, howe moche more in a defi-
S.Paule to led heart? which vncleanneffe God aboue all thinges detefteth, as which ys
fpeake of the onelie wronge that nowe can be doen vnto his bodie . For therfor did
the bodie of Iofph alfo the righteoufe, wrappe the bodie of our Lorde in a clean fheet, and **G**
our Lord. fo buried yt in a newe Tumbe, prefiguring that they that fhoulde receaue
the bodie of our Lorde, fhoulde haue bothe a newe and a clean minde. Thus
moch S. Hierom.

In whome firft we haue to obferue, that expowndinge S . Paule, who in
this place calleth the Sacrament breade, and not abfolutelie bread, but with
an article (*that bread*) expowndeth yt to be the bodie of our Lorde, whiche
alfo he doeth in an other place, by fo expreffe woordes that yt can not be
denied. In his apologie againft Iouinian he thus vttereth S. Paule faing:
Probet fe vnufquifque, & fic ad corpus Chrifti accedat. Let euerie man examine him
felf, and fo let him come to the bodie of Chryfte (faieth S.Hierom)yt were
not an expofition but a confufion of the trueth, yf he fhoulde call that the
Hieron. bodie of Chryft, that ys but breade . But yt ys more then euident in all
Apolo pr. that place of S, Hierom, as the circunftance alfo inuinciblie prooueth, that
lib. aduerf. he vnderftandeth S. Paule ther to haue fpoken of the bodie of Chryft, and
Iouinianũ. of no earthlie breade.

In the ende of this expofition, he doeth not onelie cõfirme this trueth of **H**
Chryftes verie prefence, but alfo he infirmeth and againft faieth the wicked
affertion of *Luther.* He faieth that Iofeph burieng the bodie Chryft in a clean
fheet

A sheet, and a newe Tumbe, prefigured that they that shoulde receaue the bodie of Chryst, shoulde haue both a clean and a newe minde. For the presence, marke that he saieth by plain woordes, that we receaue the bodie of Chryst. Against *Luther*, who wolde haue no other preparacion in vs in the receipt of the bodie of Chryst but onelie faithe, he saieth that they that will receaue the bodie of Chryst, must haue bothe a clean and a newe minde. wherbie what ells ys ment, but that we must clense owre consciences from dead workes, whiche putrifie and stinke in our sowles, and so leauinge the olde man, we must be renewed in spiritte of our minde, and be cloathed with the newe man, whiche after God ys shapen in righteousnesse and true holinesse.

Let the pro clamer see here howe plainlie S. Hierom vttereth S. Paules meninge.

But let S. Hierome open him self, who expownding this text of S. Paule *Whosoeuer eateth this bread, and drinketh the cuppe of oure lord vnwoorthilie, shall be giltie of the bodie and bloode of our lorde* : saieth thus : *Sicut scriptum est, Omnis mundus manducabit. Et iterum: Anima quæ manducauerit immunda, exterminabitur de populo suo*

B *Et ipse Dominus ait : Si ante altare recordatus fueris, quia habet frater tuus aliquid aduer sum te relinque munus tuum antè altare, & vade reconciliari fratri tuo. Prius ergo perscru tanda est conscientia, si in nullo nos reprehendit, & sic aut offerre, aut communicare debemus. Quidam sane dicunt, quia non indignum, sed indignè accipientem reuocet à sancto. Si ergo dignus indignè accedens retrahitur : Quanto magis indignus, qui non potest accipere dignè ? Vnde oportet ociosum cessare a vitiis vt sanctum Domini corpus, sanctè accipiat.* As yt ys written *Euery clean man shall eate, and again: That soule that shall eate being vnclean, shall be putt from amonge his people. And our Lorde him self saieth : Yf thowe remembre being before the aultar, that thie brother hath anie thing against thee, leaue thy gift before the aultar, and go to be reconciled to thy brother.* Therfore the conscience ys first to be searched, yf yt doe in nothing reprehende vs, and so we aught either to offre or communicate. Ther be some that saie, that he doeth not here forbidde the vnworthie man from the holie thinge, but him that receaueth vnwoorthilie. Yf the woorthie cominge vnwoorthilie be for bidden, howe moche more the vnwoorthilie that can not receaue woorthilie? Wher

Hier.in 11 1.Cor.

Howe men aught to prepare themselues to receaue the bless. Sacr.

C fore the euell doer must ceasse from vices, that he maie hololie receaue the holie bodie of our Lord. hitherto S. Hierom. Who in euery parte improoueth the pestilent doctrine of *Luther*, First, by the olde Testament, whose ex tern cleaenesse or vncleannesse being commaunded or forbidden in the eating of the holie thinges of the same lawe, be figures of spirituall cleannesse or vncleannsse of our consciences, required or prohibited in the receipt of the holie misteries in the newe lawe, So that, as ther was required an outwarde cleannesse in the bodie. So here ys required an inwarde clean nesse of conscience.

Besides this he beateth him downe with the plain and mightie authoritie of Chryst him self, who hathe geuen vs this order, that being at the aultar, and remembring that our brother hath anie matter against vs, we must first be reconciled to our brother, or that we can dooe anie thinge at the aultar, or offre sacrifice or receaue the holie Sacrament. Ys not this a notable preparacion commaunded by our M. Chryste? what can *Luther* and all his Disciples saie to this? Ys ther here nothinge required but faithe? ys not here full and perfect reconciliacion commaunded? Ys not here a discussion and

Men aught to prepare theselues be for the receipt of the bless. Sacr. euen by Chryst rule

D examinacion of our consciences in calling to minde and remembrance yf anie greif be betwixt vs and our brother? Yt ys so certenly. Wherfor S. Hierom concludeth sainge : *Therfor first ys the conscience to be searched, yf yt dooe not reprehende vs, then maie we either offre or receaue.* yf the conscience be to be searched

ched for foche matters of offence before we receaue, wher ys Luthers one- **E**
lie faith that will make vs woorthie receauers? Luther faieth we maie not fearche, whether we finde our felf giltie of anie offence or not : S. Hierom
not onely faieth that our confciences are to be fearched, but he alfo faieth
that the euell dooer muft ceaffe from vices that he maie receaue the holie
bodie of our Lorde holilie, in which woordes, note (geatle Reader) bothe
thy preparacion before thowe receaue, and alfo what thowe doeft receaue.
Thy preparacion ys to ceaffe from vices wherunto manie things appertein:
the thinge that thowe receaueft ys the holie bodie of our Lorde.

But S.Hierome hath faied fufficientlie both for the trueth of the prefence
and alfo againft *Luthers* licencioufe doctrine. Wherfore we will nowe heare
Chryfoftome dooe the like. He alfo expowndeth this text of S. Paule and
faieth thus : *Probet feipfum homo, quod & in fecunda inquit : Vofmet tentate fi eftis in*
fide : ipfi vos probatè non quemadmodum nunc facimus, temporis gratia accedentes, magis
Chryfoft in
11. 1. Cor. *quàm animi ftudio, neque vt præparati ad vitia noftra expurganda, compuctionis pleni acce*
dimus : fed vt in folemnitatibus fimus quando omnes adfunt, confideramus. Sed non ita **F**
Paulus præcipit. Sed vnum tempus nouit quo accideremus, communicationis & confcientiæ
puritatem. Let a man examin himfelf. Whiche thinge alfo he faieth in the feconde epiftle: *Proue yower felues yf ye be in faith.* doe ye yowr felues examine
yowr felues. Not as we dooe nowe, comminge raither for the times fake,
then for anie earneft affectiõ or defire of the minde. Neither doe we come
as full of compunction prepared to pourge oute our vices, but our confideracion ys, vpon that that all the people be affembled to gether, that we
alfo maie be in the folemnities. But Paule doeth not fo commaunde, but he
knewe one time in the whiche we fhoulde come, that ys, the puritie or cleanneffe of communicacion and confcience.

That we fhoulde not come to the receipt of the holie Sacrament, but
when we be prepared, and haue pourged oute oure vices by compunction
and repentaunce he declareth by an apt fimilitude, fainge : *Nam fi fenfibili*
nunquam communicamus menfa, fi febre laboramus, & malis humoribus abundamus, ne
perderemur : longè magis hanc tangere nephas eft, abfurdis cupiditatibus impediti, quæ fe-
bribus grauiores funt. Cùm autem abfurdas dico cupiditates, etiam corporum dico, & pecu **G**
niarum, & iræ, & fuccenfionis, & omnes fimpliciter abfurdas. Quæ omnia accedentem
exhaurire oportet, & ita purum illud attingere facrificium non pigrè difponi, & miferè
cogi propter folemnitatè acccedere, neque rurfum compunctum, & præparatum impediri,
eo quòd non fit folemnitas. Solemnitas enim operum eft demonftratio, animæ puritas, vitæ
certitudo, quæ fi habueris, femper celebrarè poteris folemnitatem, & femper accedere. Pro-
pterea (inquit) probet autem feipfum homo, & fic edat. For if we be ficke of a feuer,
This wholl
fentence im
pugneth lu
thers wic-
ked affertiõ and doe abunde with humours, we wolde neuer be partakers of the cõmon
diett left we fholde be caft awaie moche more yt ys wicked to touche, this
table, beinge entangled with odioufe luftes, whiche be forer then the feuers
When I fpeake of naughtie and odioufe luftes or defires, I fpeake alfo of the
luftes and defires of owre bodies, and of moneie, and of wraithe, and of
anger, and plainlie of all luftes that be naught. All whiche he that cometh
to receaue, muft ridde awaie, and fo receaue that pure facrifice not to be
flouthfullie difpofed, nor miferablie to be compelled to come for the folemnitie. Neither again beinge penitent and prepared, to be letted, bicaufe ther
ys no folemnitie. Solemnitie ys an enident declaracion of good woorkes, the **H**
puritie of foule, the affuredneffe of life. Whiche thinges if thowe haueft, tho
we maift allwaies celebrate a Solemnitie, and allwaies come to the recept of
the Sacrament, therfor he faieth, let a man examine himfelf and fo lett him
eate. Thus farre Chryfoftome.   In

A   In thefe woordes the faing of Luther ys alfo (as by S. Hierom) detected to be deuelifh and wicked. Luther will haue no preparacion of a man to come to receaue the Sacrament. But iudge thow, reader, whether we be not earneftlie admonifhed by Chryfoftome to be prepared: whether we be not wil led to caft awaie all the luftes of the bodie, of couetoufneffe, and foch other: whether we fhoulde not be penitent. For (faieth he) all that will receaue muft as a man labouring of a feuer, and full of humours not receaue, vntill he hath pourged himfelf. But when he hath pourged himfelf then he maie eate of the meat that before he might not. Manie goodlie occafions trulie be geuen for exhortacion to godlie receauing, farre otherwife then *Luther* hath geuen, which to auoide prolixitie, I leaue to the confideracion of the reader wifhing him yet to vnderftand, what yt ys that Chryfoftome moueth vs to receaue. Yt ys (faieth he) *purum illud facrificium*, that pure facrifice. What ys, or can be, that pure facrifice but the bodie of Chryfte? Wherfor by Chryfoftome yt ys the bodie of Chryft, that we receaue.

Chryf. Ho. oportet hæ-refies, &c.

B   But thow fhalt heare himfelf fpeake yt in plain woords, in an homely wher he faieth, thus moch of this matter. *Deinde vbi multum difputauit de his, qui indigné communicant myfteriis, eofque repræhendiffet grauiter & demonftraffet quòd idem fuppli cium paffuri effent, quod ij qui Chriftum occiderant, fi fanguiné eius & corpus abfque proba cione & temerè accipiant, rurfum ad propofitam materiâ fermoné conuertit.* Then when he hath difputed moch of thofe which vnwoorthilie receaue the myfteries and had greuouflie rebuked thé, and had declared that they fhould fuffre the fame punifhment, that they did, which had flain Chryft, if thei receaue the bo die and blood of Chryft rafhlie withoute anie examinaciõ, he turneth again his communicacion to the matter in hand.

Daunger of the vnwoor thie recea-uing of the bleff. Sacr.

Note this then well, that by expreffe and plain woordes, Chryfoftome faieth, that we fhall fuffre the fame pain, that they which crucified Chryft, if we rafhlie without examinacion of our felues receaue the bodie and blood of Chryft. Wherby he teacheth that we receaue the bodie of Chryft in the Sacramét, ãd that which ys more, ãd ys the great proof of the reall ãd fubftãcial

C   prefence of Chryftes bodie ãd blood in the bleffed Sacr. that euell men receaue yt, which argueth that prefence ther to be by the affured power of God, at the due pronunciaciõ of his woord, according to the catholike faith, grownded vpon Gods holie woorde. And not to depende vpon the vncerté vnadfured, and fleight faith of the receauer, according to the phantafticall do ctrine of the Sacramentaries, grownded and fownded vpon no one title of Gods woord, but onelie vpon their own pleafures and phanfies. Let this Pro clamer if he cã, if he cã not, let him praie aide of his likes, and bring furth one fcripture, that teacheth this doctrine that faith onelie maketh Chryft prefent vnto vs in the Sacr. and that he ys not verilie and reallie prefent in the Sacr. as ys faied, and he fhall haue the victorie. Yf he cã not let him for fhame, let him yelde, let the trueth haue the victorie. Better yt ys for him a litle here to be confownded, then to fuffre euerlafting confufion, in the worlde to come.

Sacramen-taries doc-trine ys without all grownd or authoritie of fcripturs

But to return to our matter, I wolde here ende, but that I thinke yt moche pitie to kepe from the knowledge of the godlie reader, fo godlie a leffon as Chryfoftome hath in this matter, conteining both faithfull inftruction, and godlie exhortacion. Thus he writeth: *Confidera nunc quanta illi veteris facrificii par-*

D   *ticipes vitæ frugalitate vtebantur. Quid enim ii non faciebant, omni tempore purificabantur. Et tu ad falutaré hanc hoftiam acceffurus, quam angeli ipfi cum tremore fufcipiut, vé tantam circúfcribis téporú ambitu? Qua fróte teipfum fiftes ad Chrifti tribunal præfenté, qui impuris manibus ac labiis, fic impudenter ipfius corpus aufus fis attingere. Regem vtique non eligas*

Hom. 3. in Epift. ad Eph.

Vvu   *exofcu-*

exofculari,fiquidem os tuum olet grauiter:& regem cœlorum impudens exofculari,anima E
tua tam vitiis olente?atrox sanè contumelia eſt res huiufmodi,dic tu mihi:Num eligas illo-
tis manibus ad tam venerabilem victimam accedere?Non puto,quin, vt coniicio, malis
prorfus tibi temperare ab aditu,quam fordidis accedere manibus·At interim in paruo tam
religiofus cum fis,animam autem habens cœno vitiorum fqualentem accedis,& audes im-
pudens contingere?Etiamfi ob manuum fordes ad tempus quis contineat,fed ad animam om-

Sacrifice of
*ni eluuie vitiorum repurgandam,totus interim redeat.*Confider nowe what great god
the aultar　lineſſe of life the receauers of the olde facrifice did vfe, what did they not?
honourable　They were alwaies purified,and doeſt thow coming to this healthfome fa-
to Angels.　crifice,which the angells thefelues doe with trembling honour,doeſt thowe
measure fo great a thing with the compaſſe of time?with what countenaûce
wilt thow ſtand before the iudgement feat of Chryſte , who haueſt ben fo
bolde,with impure and vnclean hands and lippes fo impudentlie to touche
his bodie?Thowe woldeſt not,if thowe haddeſt a ſtinking mouthe, take vpõ
thee to kiſſe the kinge:And doeſt thowe,thow impudent man, kiſſe the king
of heauens,thy foule fo fore ſtinking with vices and finnes ? This maner of F
thing ys a cruell reproache.Tel! me woldeſt thow take vpon thee to come
to this honorable facrifice with vnwafhed hands?I thinke not.But as a geſſe
thow haddeſt leuer altogether forbeare to go to yt,then to come to yt, with
filthie handes.And whileſt thowe arte fo religioufe in a fmall thing dareſt
thow(thowe impudent man)touche this,hauing a foule defiled with the filthineſſe of finnes?Although a man for the vncleanneſſe of his handes doe
witholde himfelf for a time,but yet to clenfe his foule frõ the peſtilent ſtinking finke of vices,let him whollie gêue himfelf.Thus he.

　　Thow haueſt heard,reader,a notable godlie faing ofChryfoſtome.Thow
1
Three po-　maiſt therin,as I haue faied,finde faithfull inſtruction,and godlie exhortaciõ.
inĉts of in-　As concerning inſtruction,thow art inſtructed here in three poinĉtes ? Firſt,
ſtruction in　that Chryſtes verie bodie ys in the Sacrament.Which thow art taught by
Chryfoſt.　expreſſe woordes,when he faieth to the finful man: dareſt thow with vncleã
woordes·　hands and lippes impudently touche his bodie?wherin he teacheth that the
bodie of Chryſt ys fo prefent in theSacrament,that yt ys touched both with
hands and lippes whẽ yt ys receaued,which maner of receauing argueth the
corporall fubſtance of Chryſt to be prefent,which maie be touched accor- G
ding to Chryſtes owne fainge:*Palpate,& videte quia fpiritus carnem & oſſa non*
*habet,ficut me videtis habere.*Feel and fee,that a Spirit hath not fleſh and bones
as yt fee mẽ to haue.Again wher he faieth to the like man : *Thowe woldeſt not*
take vpon thee,with a ſtinking mouthe to kiſſe the kinge. And dareſt thowe kiſſe the kinge
*of heauens,thy foule fo ſtinking with vices?*Marke yt well,So certenlie ys the bodie
of Chryſt prefentlie touched,that he calleth the fame the King of heauens.
What wife,godlie,or learned man making fermons to the people , wolde e-
uer call the Sacramen(if therin were nothing but a peice of bread)the bodie
of Chryſt,and the king of heauens,and fo leaue yt to them to beleue, if yt
2
were not as he calleth yt?Yt were not to teach but to deceaue:not to edifie,
The bodie　but to deſtroye.Wherfore vnderſtand that by the doctrine and inſtruction
of Chryſte　of Chryfoſtome,the verie bodie of Chryſt,the verie kinge of heauens , ys in
maie be tou　the Sacrament receaued into our handes and lippes.
ched and re
ceaued of　　　The feconde poinĉt of inſtruction confirmeth the firſt, whiche poinĉt ys
him that　that men defiled in foule maie yet receaue with their handes and mouthes H
hath a　the bodie of Chryſt,the king of heauens.Which poinĉt although he doeth
filthie foule.　open and declare throwoute the wholl proceſſe:yet fpeciallie when he faieth:*dareſt thowe not kiſſe the King if thow haueſt a ſtinking mouthe.And dareſt thowe kiſ*
fe

A *se the king of heauens thy soule stinking with filthie and stinking vices?* By which woordes he fullie teacheth that men defiled, and corrupted in soule, maie yet (though to their condemnacion) receaue the bodie and blood of Chryst. But vpon this bicause moch ys allreadie saied, and this ys so plainlie testified by Chrysostome, I will not tarie.

The thirde point of his instruction, that also confirmeth the presence ys: that he saieth that the Sacrament ys a sacrifice, which he doeth in the beginning of his saing, wher alluding to the preparacion of the receauers of the sacrifices of the olde lawe, he saieth, they clensed purified, and ordred theselus. *And wilt thow* (saieth he) *come to this holsome sacrifice, which Angels with trembling doe honoure,* by the measure of time? Meaning that the people should not come to receaue vpō this onelie pourpose, that yt ys a solemne feast, but vpō this that they be pure and clean in conscience, frō all filthinesf of sinne. Wher ye see that Chrysostome doeth not onelie call yt a sacrifice, but also saieth yt to be soch a sacrifice as Angels with trembling doe honoure, which Sacrifice ys not our sacrifice of thankesgeuing (as the Sacramentaries doe feign) for that **B** ys no soch thing, as wherunto the Angels should doe honoure, or in the presence ofwhich thei should treble: No, this sacrifice ys soch, as vnto the which being in yt self honourable: yet we maie come to yt with vnwashed hands, saieth Chrysostome, wherfor yt ys of an other sorte, which ys in dede the Sacrifice of Chrystes bodie and blood, which ys alwaies to the Angels honourable. He geueth also godlie exhortaciō, which whollie consisteth in the preparaciō of our selues, to pourge and clense our selues from all filthinesse of euell liuing, or viciouse affectiō. To this he persuadeth bi the exāple of them, that were partakers of the sacrifices of the olde lawe, which purified and clēsed themselues, and kept theselues clean in that time. By the exāple also of a man, that will not presume, for bicause he hath a stinking mouth, to kisse the King, that we moch more hauing stinking soules should not presume to receaue Chryst our King. And thirdly by example of extern reuerence doe to the Sacrament in the time of Chrysostome, at which time the people receauing the Sacramentes into their handes, vsed not so to receaue, but they had wa**C** shed their hāds before. By all which exāples he moueth the receauers of this blessed, holie, and diuine Sacrament, to pourge theselues, to clense their consciences, to purifie their soules frō the stinking sinke of vices, and so with all cleannesse of bodie and soule to come to the receipt of the mysteries. In all which proceasse, howe moch he varieth and dissenteth frō the wicked doctrine of Luther, yt ys more manifest then I nede to open yt. For Luther reiecteth all cōfession of sinnes which ys our clensing and pourging : regardeth not our examinaciō as touching life despiceth and cōtēnethour praiers ād preparacion, onelie a certain faith he wold haue which he saieth sufficeth.

But this holie Chrysostome, as a right Chrystiā mā ought to doe speakinge and writing to Chrystiā mē, presupposeth faith. Wherfor speaking no woord of yt, whollie laboureth to haue Chrystian receauers to be diligent in preparacion of themselues, to be chaste in bodie, pure in soule, clean in conscience vncorrupted in heart, in pourpose diuerted frō vice, whollie cōuerted to vertue. This is the doctrin of exhortaciō geuē bi holie fathers ofChrists church. Wherfor embrace yt, reader, for yt ys fowded vpō a sure stone. As for the doctrine of *Luther* a father ofSathās Synagog, yt ys a doctrin meit to be breathed **D** oute of Sathan. For wilt thow see the subtilitie of Sathan? Whē he had corrupted the faith of *Luther* in no small nombre of articles, by whiche corruption he was nowe before God, as hauing no faith, feeringe leest by the doinge

3 Sacrifice auouched.

Chrysost. exhorteth to preparacion contrarie to Luthers doctrine.

The subtle craft of the Deuell aboute Luther and so in other like.

of good woorkes,doen with godlie zeale and deuocion,God might be pro
cured to haue mercie vpon him,and reduce him from his heresie, as diuerse
haue ben,thought yt good,as he spoiled him of his faith:so to spoill him of
his good woorkes also,and to bringe that to passe, he breathed into him,
that onely faith sufficeth, wherby good woorkes neclected, and his painted
faith being nothing he and his Disciples shoulde be clean destituted and naked both from faith and workes,so that nothing should remain in them for
God to woorke vpon,but that Sathan shoulde be assured of them, and haue
the wholl possession of them.Wherfore,reader,flie the snares of the deuell,
and hauinge faith,studie to be fruictfull in good woorkes also,that thy master and Saviour maie vouchesafe to come with his Father and the holie Spiritt to dwell and abide in thee.

THE FIVE AND FIFTETH CHAP. PROCEA-
deth vpon the same text by Isichius and sainct Augustine.

Auing in consideracion the detestablenesse of *Luthers* sainge,ad
to what licenciousnes,yt maketh a redie open waie,how lightlie yt entrappeth the sensuall person,how directly also yt standeth against S.Paules owne woordes,that we haue now in hande,how yt swarueth from the doctrine of all holie Fathers, and
writers,I can not contein,but I must somwhat more saie in yt,that where yt
ys sufficientlie confuted by two noble Fathers of the Church yt maie be per
ceaued by a more nombre,more fullie doen.I haue therfor intended to produce an other coople of Chrystes house,which be *Isichius* and S. Augustin
by whose testimonie,I doubte yt not,the matter shall be made verie clere.

Isich in 26 Leuitic.
Isichius writeth thus:*Probet autem seipsum homo,& sic de pane illo edat, & de calice
bibat.Qualem probationem dicit?id est,vt in corde mundo atque conscientia, & pœnitentiam eorum,quæ deliquit intendenti,participetur sanctis ad ablutionem peccatorum suorum.*
Let a man examine himself,and so let him eate of that bread, and drinke of
that cuppe . What maner of examinacion doeth he speake of?yt ys this,
that in a clean heart and conscience,and to him that mindeth to doe penaun
ce for those sinnes,that he hath offended in,thee Sacrament shoulde be geuen to holie persons,to the washing awaie of their sinnes.

In this breif saing of *Isichius*,note I praie yowe,that asking vpon the woordes of S.Paule,what examinacion he wolde we shoulde make , He aunswereth that we shoulde be of clean heart,and conscience,and of minde to doe
penaunce for our sinnes,before we receaue,but of *Luthers* faith he speaketh
Penaunce, clean heart and conscië ce necessa- rie to the receauers of the blessf. Sacr.
no one woorde so that teaching soch examinacion to be made,he consown-
deth clean *Luthers* doctrine.*Luther* saieth we must make no preparaciõ by con
fession,which ys a parte of penaunce,this authour saieth that we must doe
penaunce for those offences that we haue committed.*Luther* saieth that we
maie not search whether we finde ourselues giltie or no:this authour saieth
that we must be clean in heart and conscience,which can not be knowe but
by soch search.What shall I saie more,but that *Luthers* wicked doctrine ys in
euery parte contrarie to the wholsome doctrine of the Fathers,euen as a mã
wolde of a sette pourpose take a vieue of their sainges, and maliciouslie saie
the contrarie of all that he findeth them to haue saied:Which thinge ye shal
more manifestlie perceaue,when ye shall heare the saing of S.Augustine also produced for the vnderstanding of S Paule.From whom bicause I wil not
long detein yowe,his saing shall be furthwith ascribed.

Thus

A Thus he writeth:*Ab iis,pietas Domini noſtri Ieſu Chriſti nos liberet, & ſeipſum edendum tribuat,qui dixit:Ego ſum panis viuus,qui de cœlo deſcendi.Qui manducat meam carnem,& bibit meum ſanguinem habet vitam æternam in ſeipſo.Sed vnuſquiſque antequam corpus & ſanguinem Domini noſtri Ieſu Chriſti accipiat,ſeipſum probet, & ſecundum Apoſtoli præceptum,ſic de pane illo edat,& de calice bibat.Quia,qui indignè mandu cat corpus & ſanguinem Domini,iudicium ſibi manducat,& bibit, non diiudicans corpus Domini.Quando enim accipere debemus,anteà ad confeſsionem, & pœnitentiam recurrere debemus,& omnes actus noſtros curioſius diſcutere,& peccata obnoxia ſi in nobis ſenſeri- ſerimus,cito feſtinemus per confeſsionem,& veram pœnitentiam abluere,ne cum Iuda proditore Diabolum intra nos celantes pereamus,protrahentes & celantes peccatum noſtrum de die in diem.Etſi quid mali aut nequam cogitauimus,de eo pœnitentiam agamus, & velo citer illud de corde noſtro eradere feſtinemus.*The greate mercie of our Lorde Ieſus Chryſt,deliuer vs from theſe things,and geue himſelf to be eaten,who ſaied: I am the bread of life,which came dowen from heauen.*He that eateth my flesh, and drinketh my blood,hath euerlaſting life in himſelf.*But let euery man before he re

Auguſt. ad Iulian. Epiſt.111.

B ceaue the bodie and blood of our Lord Ieſus Chryſt,examine himſelf,and ſo according to the commaundement of the *Apoſtle,let him eate of that bread, and drinke of that cuppe.For he that vnwoorthilie eateth the bodie and blood of our Lorde, eateth and drinketh his own condēnaciō making no differēce of the bodie of our lord.*Therfor when we ſhall receaue, we aught before to haue recourſe to confeſsion and penaunce,and moſt diligentlie ſearch all our actes and doings.And if we ſin de anie ſinnes in vs woorthie of puniſhment,let vs ſpedelie haſt by confeſſion and true penaunce to waſhe them awaie, leeſt we with Iudas hidinge the deuell within vs,doe periſh by that we doe protracte and hide our ſinne from daie to doe,ād if we haue thought anie euell or vnhappineſſe,let vs doe penance for yt,and make haſt quicklie to wipe yt clean from our heartes. Thus moch S.Auguſtine.

The receauer of the bleſſ. Sacr. muſt prepa re himſelf, by cōfeſſiō.

Ye haue now heard howe we ſhould examine our ſelues S.Hieron. Chry ſoſtome,and Iſichius,gaue vs like inſtruction in generall woordes,but S.Auguſtine hath touched the matter with ſpeciall woordes.For he expownding howe we ſhall examine or ſelues according to S.Paules precept,ſaieth:that if

C we minde to receaue the holie Sacrament we ought before to haue recourſe to confeſsion and penaunce,and ſo moſt diligentlie ſifte and ſearch al our doinges.The doctrine of S.Auguſtine and other fathers ys now heard as tou ching our examinaciō:the doctrine of Luther ys alſo knowen.Iudge nowe I beſeche thee(gētle reader)how he agreeth with thē. Ys he not in euery title plainlie repugnaunt to them?He wolde haue no preparacion before we,receaue.All they,as with one mouthe,exhorte vs to great and diligent prepara ciō.He wold haueno cōfeſsiō:S.Auguſtine by expreſſe woords requireth cō feſſion and penance.Luther ſaieth,yf we prepare our ſelues by confeſsion, penance,and other good workes,we receaue our condemnacion:S.Paule ād the holy fathers ſaie,if we doe not examine our ſelues and prepare our ſel ues we receaue or owne condemnacion.

Luther ys herein direc tliecōtrarie to the fathers to S. Paule and to Chryſte.

Haueſt thow not heard the ſerpēt againe or raither the deuel in the Serpēt contrarieng Gods owne woords,ād his holie ſaincts?Wherin they ſaie,yea, he therin ſaieth naie:and wherin they ſaie naie,therin he ſaieth yea. I wolde to God that all they that haue geuen their eares to the hiſſing of this Serpēt

D and haue ben therby allured to fall from the auncient faith and godlie reli gion of Chryſtes Church,wolde but weigh the doctrine of him in this par te(although he hath manie other poinctes as wicked,and as loathſome ād ab hominable as this)that thei might perceaue what ſtone their faith,ys builded

Vvu iii   on

on, what a fownder, ād patrone they haue of their new religiō. Yf ther were   **E**
no more but this, yt wold make me afraied to folowe soch a Schoolemaster.

As Luther ys here touched by S. Augustine, so ys the Proclamer also. For
as Luther will no confession to be made before receipt of the Sacrament,
no more will he and his complices, as the practise in the Church of Englōd
dothe well declare? wher, by their meanes confession of sinnes ys so abandoned, that allmost ther ys no woorde of yt. Not onelie in this ys the Procla
mer touched, but in one other poinct also wherin Luther ys not touched,
and that ys in the presence of Chryst in the blessed Sacrament, wherin the
Proclamer ys woorse then *Luther.* S. Augustin expownding S. Paules woords

*Note here
howe S. Au
gustine vt-
tereth S.
Paules
woordes*

speake the by clain woordes: *Let euerie man before he receaue the bodie and blood of
our Lorde Iesus Chryst, examine himself, according to the precept of S. Paule.* Perceaue
then that by S. Augustine yt ys the precept of S. Paule to examine our selues
before we receaue the bodie and blood of Chryst, and not before we recea
ue a peice of bread, and drinke a cuppe of wine. So that here again as in diuerse other before, we see that S. Angustine expownding S. Paule calleth yt
the bodie and blood of Chryst, that S. Paule calleth the bread and cuppe of   **F**
oure Lord, teaching that by that same bread and cuppe, S. Paule ment none
other thing, but our heauenlie bread and cuppe, the bodie and bloode of
ower Lord Iesus Chryst, I trust he can not saie, but S. Augustine hath here
spoken plain enough, yf he hath not, I wolde he had taught him to speake
plainer.

But to returne to our pourpose: yt ys well to be perceaued that S. Augustine teacheth here two thinges, which the Proclamer refuseth, that ys, the
presence, and confession, of which both robbinge the people, he hath with
all robbed them of godlie deuocion and feare, and opened the gate to them,

*Two great
euells com-
mitted by
putting a-
waie of cō-
fession.*

to let them runne headling to all licenciousnesse, and abhominable liuinge.
Among manie euells which they committe in putting awaie confession, two
in my iudgement be notable. The one ys that they wolde make the ordeinaunce of God voide, and his authoritie vain: The other that the simple passe and ende their liues withoute repentance.

As touching the first certen yt ys that God hath in his Church made thys
ordeinaunce, and therto hath geuen his power that sinnes shoulde be remitted. This ordeinaunce he did with a Solemnitie. For he first breathed vpon   **G**
his Apostles, and when he had so doen, he saied: *Accipite Spiritum sanctum, Quorum remiseritis peccata, remittūtur eis, & quorum retinueritis retēta sunt.* Receaue yowe

Joan.20.

the holie Gost, whose sinnes ye remitte, they are remitted, and whose sinnes
yowe retein, they are reteined. Beholde in the doing of this ordeinaunce
the holie Gost ys first geuen to the Apostles, and after the gift of the holie
Gost the authoritie to remitte sinne ys solemnelie geuen. Now if confession
be taken awaie, and sinnes by the mynisters be not forgeuen in the people,
then ys the ordeinaunce voide, then ys the authoritie vain. For wher, when,
or howe doe they exercise this powre of Chryste in the remission of sinnes,
yf they doe yt not vpon penitētes? how shal they know penitentes but by cō
fession? Confession then taken awaie, yt must nedes folow that the ordeinaū
ce of God ys voide, and that his authoritie ys vainlie geuen to his Churche.

S. Augustine saieth that for our fragilitie, God ordeined penaunce. These be

*August. ad
Julian.
comit epla.
111.*

his woordes: *Ordinauit nobis pœnitentiam propter fragilitatem nostram. Ideo debemus
nostras cōsessiones veraciter confiteri, et fructus dignos facere, id est, præterita ne iteremus, se
cundùm iussionem Denm timentis sacerdotis. Qui sacerdos vt sapiens, & medicus, primùm
sciat curare peccata sua, et postea aliena vulnera detergere, et sanare, & non publicare.*   **H**

Nos

A *Nos sequamur perquiramus, & cum talibus consilium salutis nostræ ineamus, vt non perdamus hæreditatem cœlestem, quam nobis Dominus ab initio mundi præparauit, si seruiamus ei in iusticia, & sanctitate, & puritate cordis, & charitate non ficta.* God in consideracion of our fragilitie hath ordeined for vs penaunce. Therfore we aught to confesse our confessions trulie and doe the worthie fruictes of penaunce, that ys, accordinge to the commaundement of the preist fearing God, that we committe not again our sinnes past. Whiche preist let him first knowe, as a wise man and good phisitian to cure his owne sinnes, and after to wipe clean, and to heale other mens woondes, and them not to publishe. Let vs folowe, let vs searche, and with soche let vs entre some holsome talke of our healthe, that we leese, not our heauenlie inheritance, whiche God hath prepared for vs from the beginninge of the worlde, yf we serue him in holinesse, and rightwisonesse, and puritie of heart and charitie not feigned, hitherto S. Augustine.

Confession aught to be made trulie

Se ye not that pennaunce ys gods ordeinaunce mercifullie appointed for our fragilitie? Se ye not what S. Augustine inferreth to be doen on our

B behalf vpon that ordeinaunce? Therfor (saieth he) must we trulie confesse our confessions. And that the hissing serpent shoulde not deceaue thee, sainge: that he speaketh of confession onelie to be doen to God, he by expresse woordes saieth yt must be doen to the preist, by whoise commaundement we must doe the woorthie fruicts of penaunce. Wher again note that he saieth that the preist hath or aught to haue these three poinctes: to make clean the woondes of our Sinnes (vnderstand by godlie counsell and whosome doctrine, and iniunction of penaunce) to heale them (vnderstand by the authoritie of absolucion) Thirdlie, not to publishe them, but to kepe most secrete all thinges in confession disclosed. I maie conclude then that to take awaie confession ys to make gods ordeinaunce voide, and his authoritie geuen for the remission of sinnes, to be geuen in vain.

Three things perteining to a gostlie father.

The other notable euell ys that the simple people passe their liues, yea, and manie ende the same withoute penance. Confession beside manie other commodities, had these two: Yt was occasion that fewer sinnes amonge younge people were committed: And yt was an occasion also to call the

C selues to an accompte for soche as they had comitted. And vpon the remembrance of them, and vpon farder and speciall exhortacion, admonicion and Counsell geuen vpon particular offences, and seuerallie applied in the same confessions, by the discreet hearers of the same, to make them to vnderstand the grauitie of their offences, and ther with and by, to make them earnestlie penitent, and so to cause them with sythes and humble prostracions, and other exercifes of penitent persons, to receaue the great mercie of God, whiche mercie so receaued vndoubtedlie they obteined.

Two great commodities of cofessio.

But nowe confession beinge abandoned, youthe withoute feare or shame fal to all kinde of vices, wherby vice nowe excesiuelie abundeth. Contrition for soche vices before God ther ys none. The gauitie of sinnes, otherwise then worldlie shame leadeth ys not discerned. The accopte that soche people call themselues to before God either yt ys merueilouse slender, or none at all. Penaunce ys not seen, Sackcloath and herecloath, be not in vse Fastinge ys derided and skorned. Praier ys shortned, and almost banished. Charitie ys all most dead for cold. The teares of Peter and Mary Magdalene

Penance banished oute England.

D are dried vppe, they washe not our faces. Alas what speake we of these bitter woorkes of penaunce, when we heare not in these daies from a penitent heart, as moche as this poour voice of the publicane. *O God be mercifull to me a*

ſinner? Or this one voice of Kinge Dauid, *Peccaui, I haue ſinned*. But the younge **E**
man and the maidé, the Mã ãd the wief, yea, the auncient father, ãd the matrone paſſe oute the moueth and the yeare, yea, and yeare, after yeares, the
firſt in wanton and licencioſe life, the next in ſtouteneſſe of Manhode, in qua
relinge, in fighting, in robbinge, in ſlainge, in deceauinge, and wrong
doinge: The thirde in auarice, and greadie gettinge and kepinge, wher
in euery ſtate pleaſinge them ſelues, they go furth, amendment of life
not nitended, neither mercie deſiered.

Luc.13. Nowe for ſomoche as Chryſt ſaieth: *Niſi pœnitentiam egeritis, omnes ſimiliter
peribitis.* Except ye doe penaunce, ye ſhall all periſhe: what maie we more
fear to enſewe vpon the greateſt nombre but perdicion, loſſe and damnacion ? But God who ys riche in mercie, and who (as S. Paule
Ehp.2. ſaieth) for his great loue, wherwith he loued vs, when we were
dead by ſinnes, quickned vs together in Chryſt, and raiſed vs vppe together
with him, and made vs to ſitte to gether with him among them in heauen,
in Chryſt Ieſu : he nowe quicken vs and raiſe vs vppe again from the deathe **F**
of hereticall and ſinfull life, and make vs by true faith, ãd true penaunce to
ſitte to getheher with him in the vnitie of his Churche amonge them that
be ſettled in faithe and charitie in his catholique Church, which ys (though
yt be yet vpon the earth) the kingdome of heauen, as Chryſt in the goſpell
Math.25. doeth teſtifie.

But that I ſeeme not (as yt ys in the proverbe) to daunce oute of the daunce, or forgetting my limittes to walke oute of my compaſſe, and ſo leauing my principall matter, to wander in digreſſions (although this matter
be apperteinent neceſſarelie, vnto the principall matter in dede) I ſhall ende
this matter of côfeſsion with theſe fewe woordes, truſtinge that God will
geue me grace and time to ſpeake more of yt in an other place. But yet reader forgett not thowe, that yt ys the mean of thy preparacion, as S. Auguſtine hath taught thee, yf thowe wilt come to receaue the bodie and bloode
of thy Lorde Ieſus Chryſt. Whiche bodie and bloode thowe haueſt alſo
hearde the ſame S. Auguſtine auouchinge to be receaued in the holie **G**
Sacrament.

THE SIXE AND FIFTETH CHAP. ENDETH
*the expoſition of this text, By Theodoret,
and Anſelm.*

Ell perceauing that manie, and thoſe of the cheifeſt and
moſt famouſe men of Chryſtes Parliament houſe, haue
ben nowe produced to teſtifie vnto vs the enacted trueth
of the right vnderſtandinge of S. Paule, I haue thought yt
good, not to troble the reader, with the allegacion of manie mo vpon this text but haue ſtaied my ſelf with one coo
ple onelie, although the Proclamer him ſelf knoweth that
mo might be produced. In the producinge of which, I can not cômitte but
one of them (as cômlie here to fore I haue doen) be of the later daies (whiche I tearme the lower houſe) that the doctrine of the later daies maie be
côferred with the doctrine of the auncient daies whiche being perceaued to
be all one the malice of the Proclamer and his likes maie be the more per- **H**
ceaued, and their confuſion more euidentlie daclared. This coople thê ſhall
be Theodorete and Anſelme.

Theodorete one of the higher houſe, whoſe teſtimonie ye haue hearde
vpon

A vpon the laſt text before this in the laſt chapter of the expoſitiõ of the ſame text, moſt manifeſtlie teſtiſienge the preſence of Chryſtes bodie in the Sacrament, ſo manifeſtlie that he ſaith, that yt ys receaued with handes and mouthes. Whiche inuinciblie argueth the verie reall and ſubſtanciall preſence of Chryſtes bodie. For their offices ſerue not to the receipt of the ſpirituall bodie . This Teodorete then knowinge what a great gift of God yt ys for a ſinfull mortall man to receaue the bodie of his Lord, vpon this text of S. Paules ſainge: *Let euery man examin himſelf, and ſo let him eat of that bread, and drinke of that cuppe* ſaieth thus: *Sic tui ipſius Iudex vitam tuam exactè iudica : conſcientiam ſcrutare, & examina & tunc dominum ſuſcipe.* So thowe beinge thine owne iudge, exactlie iudge thine owne life, ſearche and examine thine owne conſcience, and then receaue the gift. Thus Theodorete.

Theodoret in. 11. 1Cor

As who might ſaie, foraſmoche as euerie act of man, beinge Good or euell ſhall be iudged either by man himſelf, or ells by God, yf man preuent not the iudgement of God, and in God ther ys a mercifull bowntifullneſſe in geuinge, as in man ther aught to be a ſemelie duetie in receauinge , therfore
B ſeinge God geueth vs ſo great a gifte as the bodie of his owne dere Sonne, and our parte ys to be ſownde pure, clean, vndefiled, and withoute offence at the ſame receipt, let euerie one of vs before we receaue that gifte of God, preuent the iudgement of God, and enter into iugement with owre ſelues, and be our owne iudges . Let vs looke ſtrictlie vpon our life: let vs examine our conſciences, and ſee whether we be meete to receaue the gift or no. To be ſhorte our life and conuerſacion muſt be iudged our conſciences muſt be examined and ſearched, before we can receaue this bleſſed gift of God, the bodie of his Sonne Ieſus Chryſt. Yt maie verie well be called his gifte. For in dede yt ys a thinge that ys his, and not owres, but as geuen to vs yt cometh from him , and not from vs: yt ys inſtituted by him, and not by vs: the wholl title and intereſt, the full right and propretie ys in him, and not in vs. Seing then the gifte ys his, and the gifte ſo woorthie and ſo great, meete yt ys that we receaue yt ſeemelie.

But yt will be, that the aduerſarie will thinke, that I preſume to farre vpõ
C this authour, that wher he calleth the Sacrament but the gifte of God, I call yt the bodie of Chryſte. Let the aduerſarie vnderſtande that I neither ſwarue from the trueth nor from the minde of the authour. For beſides that he ſaieth here vpon S. Paule, he in an other place expowndeth him ſelf what he meneth by the gifte, and ſaieth thus talkinge in a dialoge, and asking a queſtion: *Quid appellas donum, quod offertur poſt ſanctificationem? Orth. corpus Chriſti, & ſanguinem Chriſti. Era . Et credis te fieri participem Chriſti corporis & ſanguinis? Orth. Ita credo.* What after ſanctificacion doeſt thowe call the gift that ys offred? The aunſwere: I call them the bodie of Chryſt and the bloode of Chryſte. The queſtion. And doeſt thowe beleue thy ſelf to be made partaker of the bodie and bloode of Chryſte? The aunſwere. So I beleue. Thus *Theodorete.* Ye maie perceaue then that I callinge the gift, the bodie of Chryſt, doe folowe the minde of the authour, who both did ſo call yt, and ſo beleue yt to be, as after in the ſame dialoge yt ys eaſie to ſee. In this authour then, as in other before alleadged we finde plain and ſufficient matter bothe againſt *Luther*, and againſt the Proclamer. Againſt *Luther.* For the authour ſaieth we muſt exactlie iudge our life and ſearche and examine our conſcience whiche
D (as ye haue hearde ofter then once) *Luther* ſaieth yt aught not to be doen, onelie faith ys to be had. Againſt the Proclamer he teacheth that the bodie and blood of Chryſt be in the Sacracrament, and more againſt him he ſaieth
that

Thedorit Dialog . 2.

A plain place for the proclamer both for real preſence, and ſacrifice.

that they so beleued, and adored as beinge those thinges that they beleued.   **E**

Thus hauinge but, as yt were glaūced by the notes of the sainges of this authour, and a litle touched the aduersarie by conference of the doctrine of eche side: I passe to Anselme, as to one of the lower house, of whome we shal learn what doctrine was professed in that house and whether yt was dissona unt to the doctrine of the fathers in the vnderstanding of S. Paule. Thus wri teth he vpon this text of S. Paule: *Nemo præsumat accedere indignus. Sed homo, id est rationabiliter agens, probet, id est, discutiat, & examinet prius seipsum, qui etiam ex eo quod homo est, sine peccato non est. Probet autem seipsum, id est, vitam suam inspiciat & cōsideret, an dignè possit accedere vel non. Rarò enim inueniri potest quisquā ita magnus & iustus, vt in eo per discussionem, non inueniatur aliquid quod debeat eum à corporè & san guine Domini tardare, nisi confessus fuerit illud & per pænitentiam deleuerit. Probet se, & sic, id est, postquam se probauerit, edat de pane illo, & bibat de calice, quia tunc ei prode- rit.* Let no man beinge vnwoorthie presume to come, but let the man, that ys to saie, the reasonable dooer, examine, that ys searche and trie first him self who also for that that he ys a man, he ys not withoute sinne. But let him examine himself, that ys, let him beholde his owne life, and considre yt, whe ther he maie come woorthilie or no. For seldon maie anie man be fownde   **F** so great and iust, that in him cā nothinge be fownde, that maie staie him frō the bodie and bloode of owre Lorde. Except he confesse yt and by penawn ce wipe yt awaie. Let him examine himself and so, that ys, after that he ha- the examined himself, let him eate of that bread and drinke of that cuppe. for then yt shall doe him good. Thus farre *Anselmus.*

This ys a plain exposition, but as godlie, and true, as ys ys plain. What can the Aduersarie reprehend in this expositiō? wherin dissenteth he from the auncient Fathers, in expownding S. Paule? They all saie that the exami- nacion of our selues that S. Paule speaketh of here, ys a triall or a searche, an entringe, into iudgement with owre owne liues and conuersations vpon the testimonie of our owne consciences, whether we be clean from sinne or no, and so saieth he. S. Augustine saieth that if anie thing be amisse in vs, we must by confession and penaunce put yt awaie, the like saieth this au thour. All the rest vnderstand S. Paule to haue spoken here of the bodie and bloode of Chryst: and so doeth he. Wherin then ys the quarrell of the Ad-   **G** uersarie? bicause he and his companie speake to plain. They can not be wre- sted. For to saie that they dissent in the doctrine of faithe from the auncient fathers, yt ys to impudent an vntrueth.

To conclude ye haue nowe hearde these three last cooples expownding S. Paule, and they all determe that ther must be an examinacion in life and maners and a semelie preparaciō of our selues before we receaue the blessed Sacrament. Wherin they ouerthrowe the Satanicall doctrine of Luther, who wolde haue no examinacion, no confession no preparaciō. Again they all vn derstand S. Paule to haue spoken of the bodie and bloode of Chryste in this processe. Wherfore the heresie of the Proclamer and of the rest of the Sacra mentaries, whiche they wolde fain grif here vpon S. Paules woordes, ys plu cked vppe by the rootes for soche wicked plantes maie not growe vpon soche godlie stockes.

And as touching this matter of the presence of Chrystes bodie, if ther were not so plain testimony for yt in S. Paule and the holie writers as ther ys: yet   **H** the holie and great preparacion, that they exhort vs to, and the heauie sen- tence of euerlastinge drmnacion thretened vnto vs for lacke of the same pre- paraciō, if we wolde not shutte vppe the eies of our vnderstandinge, wolde

cause

Anselm. in
11. 1 Cor.

The prepa-
racion that
we are com
maunded
to make for
the receipt
of the B.
Sacr. and
the daun
ger of vn-
worthie re
ceauing ar
gueth the
real presēce

A cause vs easelie to perceaue a moche greater matter to be in the Sacrmēt thē a poour peice of bread ād a poour bare cuppe of wine. Who euer hearde or redd soch spirituall and heauenlie preparaciō, for the recept of a simple earth lie, and as they themselues tearm yt, vnholie peice of bread? Whoeuer readd soche preparaciō commaunded for the eatinge of a bare sign or figure? Who euer readde damnacion appointed for lacke of preparacion to the receipt of anie figure? Let all the volumme of the olde testamēt, wher all thinges were doen in figures be searched, and ye shall neuer finde either soche preparacion, or soche pain inflicted for vnsemelie receauing of anie soche figure. Vieue the three principall figures, as *Manna*, the Paschall lambe, and the shewe bread, and see what preparacion ys ther commaunded, what pain to the euell receauers ys ther inflicted. As for *Manna* the seconde booke of Moyses declareth that although yt were so miraculouse a figure and that in manie respectes as before ys declared, yet ther was no other preparacion required of the people but onelie that they shoulde gett Baskettes, and gather

Exod. 16.

B yt. The pain also inflicted for the abuse of yt, as the thinge yt self was tempo rall, so was yt. They were commaunded that they shoulde not kepe yt vntill the next daie, except yt were the Sabboth daie, yet some of them kept yt, and therfore they were punished. For yt putrified, and waxed full of woormes. The Paschall lambe although yt were so liuelie a figure of Chryste, yt had no other preparacion But this. Of this maner saieth God shall ye eate yt with yowr loines girded, and yowr shooes on yowr feet, and yowr staues in yowr handes. And ye shall eate yt in haste. This preparacion was but ciuill and worldlie here ys no spirituall preparacion commaunded: here ys no clensinge of the conscience required. The Shewe bread also had none other preparacion, but that the preistes might when newe were putt vpon the aultar take the olde and eate them. Pain for the abuse of them we read none.

Exod. 12.

Perchaunce ye will saie, that in the offringes of sacrifices and in soche as did take parte of the Sacrifices, ther was required a preparacion. Trueth yt

C ys, what doeth that helpe the cause of the Sacramentaries, who denie the Sacrament to be a sacrifice? well yet for that the catholique faith teacheth yt to be the chrystian Sacrifice, we will accept the sacrifices of the olde lawe as beinge figures of the sacrifice of the newe lawe, and the preparacions ther as figures of preparacions in this lawe. In the olde lawe in dede we finde pre paracion commaunded both for the preistes that did offre soche sacrifice, and for them also whiche were partakers of those sacrifices. For the preistes we read this commaundement geuen to Moyses: *Facies labium æneum cum basi sua ad lauandum, ponesque illud inter Tabernaculum testimonii & altarè & missa aqua lauabunt in ea Aaron & filii eius manus suas, & pedes, quando ingressuri sunt tabernaculum testimonii, & quando accessuri sunt ad altare, vt offerant in eo thymiama, Domino, ne forte moriantur.* Thowe shalt make a lauer of brasse, and his foote also of brasse, to wash with all, and shalt putt yt betwen the tabernacle of wittnesse and the aultar, and putte water ther in. For Aaron and his sonnes shall washe their handes and ther feet ther in, euen when they go into the tabernacle of wittnesse, or when they go vnto the aultar to ministre, and to burne the Lordes offringe they shall washe them selues with water leest they die.

Exod. 30.

Leuit. 22.

D And again we finde thus ordeined of God, *Omnis homo qui accesserit de stirpe vestra ad ea, quæ consecrata sunt, & quæ obtulerunt filii Israël Domino, in quo est immun ditia, peribit coram Domino.* Whosouer he be of all yower seed that goeth to the holie thinges, whiche the children of Israell halowe vnto the Lorde hauin-

what

ge his vncleanneſſe vpon him, he ſhall periſh . Here we finde a preparacion   E
and a pain alſo inflicted to them that omitted ſo to prepare them ſelues. But
what were all theſe preparacions? They were (as S. Paule termeth) worldlie
holineſſe, wasſhinges and iuſtifienges of the fleſh whiche clenſed not the cõ-
ſcience. *In the time of the lawe* (ſaieth S. Paule) *were offred giftes and ſacrifices , that*
coulde not make the miniſtre perfect, as perteining to the conſcience, with onelie meates and
drinkes, and diuerſe waſhinges and iuſtifienges of the fleſh, whiche were ordeined vntill
the time of reformacion . For as ther ſacrifices that were then offred did not take awaie ſinnes and ſanctifie the conſcience, *For yt ys vupoſsible* (ſaieth S. Paule)
with the bloode of goates and calues ſinnes to be taken awaie, but onelie ſanctified men
and purified men, as touching the purifienge of the flesſh, as he again ſaieth,
no more did thoſe preparacions touche the conſcience, but onelie were doẽ
for an outwarde cleanneſſe . For reaſon will geue that that thing , that the
preparaciõ ys doen for, ſhould be of more force, value and vertue, then the
preparacion in yt ſelf yf then the ſacrifices them ſelues purified not the conſciences of men, moche leſſe the preparacion. The pain alſo that was infli-   F
cted to ſoche as omitted this preparacion, what was yt? yt was but deathe tẽ
porall, whiche hath no compariſon with death eternall.

    Nowe the preparacion required before the offring of the ſacrifice of our
Lorde, and before the partaking of the ſame in the newe Teſtament, ys an
exacte and a pure pourging and cleanſinge of our conſciences. And our pain
for our preſumption to receaue this ſacrifice without due preparacion, ys
not as yowe hearde, deathe temporall, but euen ſoche (as Chryſoſtome, and
Theodorete ſaie) as they ſuffre, whiche crucified Chryſte, whiche ys death
euerlaſtinge. Nowe as our preparacion, whiche conſiſteth in pourging and
clenſing of our conſciences, farre ſurmounteth the wasſhing of the fleſh:
And as our pain neclectinge this preparacion ys the loſſe of euerlaſting life,
whiche aboue all meaſure paſſeth the loſſe of this tanſitorie life : Euen ſo
muſt yt nedes be, that the thinge that we prepare for, muſt aboue all meaſure paſſe and exceade in woorthineſſe the figures and ſacrifices, that they in
the olde lawe made preparacion for.

Obiectiõ of
ſpirituall
preſence by
faith.

    But they will ſaie, that we by faithe make Chryſt, who ſubſtanciallie ſit-   G
teth at the right hand of his Father, as verilie preſent at the receipt of the Sacramentall breade and wine, and ſo we receaue Chryſtes bodie and blood
verilie, but yet ſpirituallie.

The an-
ſwer.

    In dede they ſaie yt, but they prooue yt not. But how ſoeuer they ſaie yt,
and howe ſoeuer they painct and coolour their euell ſainges, with goodlie
gloſinge woordes : certen yt ys that this they ſaie, that the fathers of the
olde Teſtament receaued Chryſte as well as we, and that there ys no more
in our Sacramentes, then was in theirs, but that their Sacramentes were figures of Chryſte to come, and owers be figures of Chryſte as nowe comed.
But to them I ſaie, yf we haue no more in our Sacramentes then they had,
why are we required to make anie other preparacion then they did ? Whie
preparare we ſo diligently our conſciences, wher they were required but to
purifie their fleſh? Again as touching the puniſhmẽt they make God vniuſt,
For if the thinge receaued of the fathers and vs hath no difference in value,
whie hathe yt a difference in pain? Yt ſtandeth not with the iuſtice of God,
the offence beinge all one to puniſhe to offenders, one with euerlaſting dea-   H
the : the other but with temporall death. And yet ſo muſt yt nedes be, yf the
ſaingcs of the Sacramentaries were true. But thowe maiſt ſee Reader, into
what inconueniences their dreames , and phantaſies bring them .   Wher
                                                         fore

A fore I fhall wifhe the reader, to confider that thys our preparacion being fo farre aboue the preparacion of the olde lawe, teacheth vs that we receaue a thing, farre aboue that, that they receaued in that lawe. And foralmoche as the punifhment of our prefumption ys euerlafting deathe, that yt argueth that we prefume to abufe the euerlafting Maieftie of our Lord God, and Sauiour Iefus Chryft, bicaufe (as fainct Paule faieth) we make no difference of our Lords bodie. In dede if we examine not our felues before we receaue, but go to yt with filthie côfciences, thê go we to yt as to other meates, and fo make we no difference betwixt our Lordes bodie and other meates. And for this our irreuerencie we woorthilie fuffre the pain teftified by fainct Paule, that ys, we eate and drinke our owne damnacion, yea fo great ys the offence of vnwoorthie receauing, that God doeth not onelie punifh yt eternallie, but alfo by diuerfe means temporallie, as thow fhalt fee yt plainly teftified in the text that foloweth.

B THE SEVEN AND FIFTETH CHAP. EXPOVNdeth this text: *For this caufe manie are weake and ficke, &c. By Origen and fainct Ambrofe.*

T foloweth in the text of S. Paule: *Ideo inter vos multi imbecilles, & infirmi, & dormiunt multi.* For this caufe manie are weak and fick among yowe, and manie do die. S. Paule rebuking the vn charitable, the vngodlie, and vndeuoute maner of the Corinthians in cominge to the receipt of the holie Sacrament, of the which fomwhat ys before faied, did plainlie teache them and affure them that foch vnwoorthie receauers fhould be eternallie côdem ned, as they that vilanouflie and cruellie putte Chryft to death. For as they did with all fpite fpitte vpô him, pietifullie araie him, mocke him, fkorn him, âd as they thought, with all fhame and reproache difwoorfhippe âd difhonour him, âd repute him but as a vile, abiect, and a caftawaie amôg the chil drê of mê: Euen fo they that come to receaue his bleffed bodie âd blood, as thei wold come to receaue a peice of the carkaffe of an oxe, lâbe, calf, orfhepe

C hauing no regarde to the cleanneffe and puritie of their côfciences, they doe as moch, and as wickedlie abufe, difwoorfhippe and difhonour that his bleffed bodie, as the Iewes of whome we fpake of before. For what more contumelie, what more inurie, can be doen to the bodie of Chryft, then to be caft into a finfull ftinking bodie more filthie or lothfome in his feight, then anie donghill or finke. The grauitie than of the offence, with the greuoufe painof condemnacion due to the fame declared, to make thê better creditt the fame, he induceth them by prefent examples of the punifhment of foche perfons in this prefent life, fainge: *For this caufe many amonge yowe are weake, and feke, and manie doe die.* As who might faie: think not that I dallie with yowe, behold and fee euen amonge yowr felues, howe God fheweth a preamble or image of his fearfull iudgement which I haue fpoken of. For euen for this vnwoorthie receauing of the bodie and biood of hys Sonne our Lorde Iefus Chryfte, he hath ftricken manie with weakneffe, manie with fekeneffe, and manie with death.

D The literall expofition being thus breiflie touched as wherby yt maie be perceaued, howe this text doeth depende of the other, âd ys ioined with the fame we wil (as heretofore ys doê) heare the Fathers of Chryftes Parliamêt houfe, therby alfo to trie, whether the catholike Church that now ys, côfent with thê, or diffent frô thê, or the Procla. âd his côpanie agree or difagree.

Xxx　　　　Of

Of thefe Fathers the firſt coople ſhall be *Origen* and ſainct Ambroſe . *Origen* **E**

Origen . in
Pſalm. 37.

ſaieth thus: *Iudicium Dei paruipendis? & commonentem te Eccleſiam deſpicis? Communi care non times corpus Chriſti, accedens ad Euchariſtiam quaſi mundus, & purus, quaſi in te nihil ſit indignum, & in iis omnibus putas quod effugies iudicium Dei. Non recordaris illud quod ſcriptum eſt, quòd propterea in vobis infirmi, & ægri, & dormiunt multi. Quare mul ti infirmi? Quoniam non ſeipſos diiudicant, neque ſeipſos examinant, neque intelligunt, quid communicare Eccleſiæ, vel quid eſt accedere ad tanta, & tam eximia Sacramenta. Patiun tur hoc quod febricitantes pati ſolent, quum ſanorum cibos præſumunt, ſibimetipſis inferentes exitium.* Setteſt thow litle by the iudgement of God? And deſpiceſt thow the

Origen in
plain words
calleth the
bleſſ. Sacr.
the bodie of
Chryſt.

Church admoniſhing thee? Thow arte not a feard to communicate the bo die of Chryſte, coming to the *Euchariſt*, as a clean and a pure man, as though ther were no vnwoorthie thing in thee: and in all theſe, thow thinkeſt that thow ſhalt eſchape the iudgement of God. Thowe doeſt not remembre, that which ys written: that for theſe thinges, ther be manie among yowe weake, and ſicke, and manie doe die. Whie be ther manie ſicke? Bicauſe they iudge not themſelues, neither examin themſelues, neither doe they vnderſtande **F** what yt ys to communicate with the Church, or what yt ys to come to ſo great, and ſo excellent myſteries. They ſuffre that that men whiche be ſick of agues, are wont to ſuffre, when they eate the meates of wholl men and ſo kill themſelues.

Origen rebuking here the euell doings of ſome men, Who not fearing the iudgement of God, nor the admonicion of the Church preſumed as though they had ben in clean ſtate of life to come to receaue the bodie of Chryſt: putteth them in feare with this ſaing of ſainct Paule that for this cauſe ther be amonge you manie weake , and ſick, and manie doe die. Wherin note that Origen ſaieth, that the cauſe of theſe plagues ys the vnwoorthie recea uinge of the bodie of Chryſt by expreſſe woordes. He neither calleth yt Sa cramentall bread, nor figure nor ſigne, but euē as yt ys, the bodie of Chryſt. And for that yt ys ther vnſpeakeablie, and yet moſt aſſuredlie, he afterwarde calleth yt, ſo great, and ſo excellent myſteries.

A myſterie
what yt ys,
and howe
the bleſſed
Sacr. ys a
myſterie.

A myſterie ys wher ſomthing lieth hidden, that ys not by open meanes, or common knowledge perceaued. Foraſmoch then as Chryſt verilie being **G** in the Sacrament ys not perceaued by the common knowledg of the ſenſeis, nor of naturall reaſon, but by the ſpeciall knowledge of faith yt ys verie well of *Origen* called myſteries. And foraſmoch as Chryſt therin being, ys ſo great and ſo excellent, therfor verie well doeth he call them myſteries great and excellent. And here this ys to be noted, that he calleth yt not a myſterie as being but one, but he calleth yt myſteries as being two . For although yt ys ſomtime called ſingularlie, a Sacrament or a myſterie as one thing, of the vnitie of the thing ſignified and conteined, which ys the bodie of Chriſt: yet as touching the thinges that doe ſignifie, and conteine, which be the formes of bread and wine , vnder which both, Chryſt ys verilie and whollie , they are right well called myſteries plurallie, bicauſe they be two kindes, and vn der eche kinde Chryſt fullie, and therfore eche of them well called a Sacra ment and a myſterie.

Euell mē re
ceaue the
bodie of
Chryſt in
the B. Sacr.

In all this ſainge, this alſo maie be noted , that euell men receaue the bodie of Chryſte, but ſpeciallie, when he ſaieth: that euell men doe as men ſicke of agues, who will preſume to eate holl mens meat , wherby he **H** plainlie teacheth , that euell men eate the ſame meate in the Sa crament, that good men doe, But good men receaue the bodie of Chryſt: wherfor

A wherfor so doe euell men also, but to contrarie effectes. For as the holl man eating his meate continueth his life, and the sicke man eating the same procureth or causeth his owne death: Euē so the worthie receauer receauinge the bodie of Chryst getteth life, wher the vnwoorthie receauing the same getteth him euerlasting death. Thus maie we of this auncient father of Chrystes Parliament house learn the trueth, that Chrystes bodie ys in the Sacrament. Thus maie we learn, that forbicause euell men do abuse yt vnreuerentlie receauing yt, that the plagues of God, as sicknesse, weaknesse, and deathe, come vpon them . Thys being true, God plant in the heart of euery man, that hath professed the name of Chryst, to professe also hys holie faith , and reuerentlie and thankfullie to accept this great and confortable benefitte of Chrystes presence with vs in the Sacrament, and yt honourablie to vse.

O Lorde, what mishappe haue we , that after so long continuance of the faith of Chryst we shoulde nowe in the later daies , fall from that reuerent and honourable vsage of this blessed Sacrament , that was v-sed in the primitiue Churche , when the faith was not so dilated , so

B spred, so establisshed , as nowe for the long continaunce of yt, yt aught to be : And yet then was yt had in great reuerence , and honourablie vsed.

But amonge manie testimonies that maie be produced, bicause we are nowe hearing the doctrine of *Origen*, we will also but heare hys testimonie in this matter. He exhorting the people, that hearinge the woorde of God they should vse great diligence, that, that they had once learned , shoulde not by necligence fall from their memorie: vseth the example of their re-garde of the holie Sacrament, and saieth: *Volo vos admonere religionis vestræ exemplis. Nostis, qui diuinis mysteriis interesse consuestis, quomodò cùm suscipitis corpus Domini cum omni cautela & veneratione seruatis, ne ex eo parum quid decidat, ne consecrati muneris aliquid dilabatur. Reos enim vos creditis, & rectè creditis, si quid inde per neccligentiam decidat. Quodsi circa corpus eius conseruandum, tanta vtimini cautela, & meritò vtimini, quomodò putatis minoris esse piaculi verbum Dei neclexisse , quàm corpus eius?* I will admonishe yowe withe the examples of your owne religion, ye , that haue ben wount to be at the mynistracion of the diuine mysteries , knowe,

C howe, *when ye receaue the bodie of our Lorde*, ye geue heed with all warenesse and honoure that no litle porcion of yt should fall down , that no parte of the consecrate thing should slippe awaie, ye beleue yowr selues to be giltie, and ye beleue well, yf anie of yt should fall from yow through neccligēce. Yf than ye vse so great warenesse and diligence aboute the conseruing of his bodie, and yowr vse therin ys good: howe thinke yowe yt a matter of lesse offence, to haue neglected the woorde of God , then his bodie? Thus moche *Origen*?

In this testimonie ys no mention made of the Aduersaries figure, sign or Sacramentall bread, but here ys plain declaracion of the catholique faithe, *Origen* saing and declaring to the Chrystian people of his time by expresse woordes that they receaued *the bodie of Chryst*. But note withal which ys most

E cheiflie to our pourpose here, that not onelie the people did vse the same bodie of Chryst reuerentlie and honorablie, but also *Origen* doeth both well alowe ther so doing, and commendeth and praiseth thē for the same also. And here note farder that the people had the blessed Sacr. in so great reuerēce, that they beleued thē selues to haue cōmitted a great offence (ād *Origē* saieth they beleued yt wel) yf by their necligēce anie part of the Sacr. had fal len from them to the grownde by which their reuerend vsage , as we maie

Orig. homil 13. in Exod

See what warenesse was vsed in the primitiue Chnrch in receauing the bodie of our Lorde.

A plain saing for the Procla.

E

clerelie perceaue and fee , that they beleued ther to be the verie bodie of
Chryſte,to the whiche they gaue this reuerence and honour:So by the ſame
ys the vnreuerend vſage of our Sacramentaries moch reprehended.Remem-
bre their doings,ãd conſider their vſages, and cõpare them with the doings
and vſageis of the auncient Chryſtian people,in the time of *Origen*.Owre Sacramentaries cauſed that the bread which was left at their comuniõ ſhould
not be honourablie but prophanelie vſed.For in ſome places the myniſter
had that that was left:in ſome places the pariſh clerke:in ſome places a peice
of yt was deliuered to him that ſhoulde the next ſondaie prouide the bread
for the communiõ.And euerie of theſe put this bread into his boſom ǫr pur
ſe,as beggers doe their lumpes and fragmentes into their bagges and wallet-
tes without all reuerence or regarde,and carieng yt home with like irreuerencie vſed yt in no otherwiſe then other common bread, geuing yt to their
wieues and children,the cruſtes to their dogges and cattes,the crommes ro
their pullen .   O Lord howe farre ys this vſage from the vſage of the primitiue Church?The good people that thẽ were(as thow haueſt heard)thought
yt a great offence,yf yt did but fall from them to the grownde.

F

And *Pius* the ninth Biſhoppe of Rome after S.Peter,and liued aboute the
yeare of our Lord cxlvii vpon conſideracion of the great excellencie of the
Sacrament as wherin ys verilie the bodie of our Sauiour Chryſte, and vpon
the regarde of ſoche due reuerence as apperteineth to vs to yeald to the ſame,appoincted ſondrie penaũces, ãd faſtings to ſoch as by whom anie parte
of the blood of Chryſt ſhould happen to diſtil or to be ſhedde:But theſe peo
ple of our daies neither regarde falling to the grownde nor ſhedding,no, as,
yt ys ſaied,they ſpare not to geue yt to their dogges.By which ſundrie maners yt ys eaſie to be perceaued that the faithes of theſe people be ſundrie.
The people of the primitiue church(as by their regard, reuerence, and honoure to the B.Sacrament,yt maie be perceaued) beleued the preſence of
Chryſtes bodie and blood to be ther, wher they beſtowed ſoche reuerence
and duetie:The companie of Sacramentaries,as their irrenerent vſage well
declareth,beleue no reall preſence of Chryſtes bodie in the Sacrament. For
to yt they denie all honoure and reuerence.Yf the primitiue Church had be
leued as theSacramentaries doe,whie gaue they that honour to yt,that theſe doe not?or raither whie doe not the Sacramentrries honour the Sacramẽt
as they of the primitiue Church did?Yf ye wil know the cauſe,yt ys(though
they bragge moch of the primitiue Church)bicauſe they varie and diſſent
from yt,bothe in faith and maners.Howe can they trulie ſaie,that they folowe the primitiue Church when yt ys here ſo manifeſt, as yt can not be a-
gainſt ſaied,that they not onelie diſſent from yt by their doctrine, but alſo
doe thinges euen clean contrarie to that , that was doen in the primitiue
Church?They with all irreuerencie contemning the leauings of the Sacrament wher the primitiue Church vſed honourablie to repoſe them and reſerue them in the holie placea(as S.Clement gaue cõmaundement)and alſo
had great regarde,and reuerence to yt,wher theſe men (as ye haue hearde)
fede their families with yt, as with prophane bread. Wherfore to conclude
this matter with ſainct Paule, I maie ſaie, that they be giltie of the bodie and bloode of owre Lorde , bicauſe they make no difference
betwixit yt and common or prophane meates , but indifferently eate
the one and the other.

G

H

But I tarie to long vpon *Origen*,yt ys time that S.Ambroſe alſo were heard
                                       Vpon

*See the vſe
of the Com-
munion
bread in
the newe
Church.*

*De conſec.
Diſt.2.*

*Difference
of the pri-
mitiue and
ſchiſmati-
cal church
in vſe of
the Sacr.ãd
in faith.*

*Clemens
Epiſt.2.*

*Ambr.in
11.1.Cor.*

A Vpon this text thus he faieth:*Vt verum probaret,quia examen futurum eft accipientium corpus Domini,iam hic imaginem iudicii oftendit,in eos qui inconfideratè corpus Domini acceperant,dum febribus,& infirmitatibus corripiebantur,& multi moriebantur , vt iis cæteri difcerent,& paucorum exemplo territi emendarentur non inultum fcientes corpus Domini negligenter accipere,& eum quem hic pœna diftulerit,grauius tractari, fore , quia contempfit exemplum.* To proue that ther ys a iudgemét to come of them, that receaue the bodie of our Lord,he doeth now fhewe a certain image of the fame iudgement vpon them,which without due confideraciõ had receaued the bodie of our Lord forafinoch as they were punifhed with feuers , and ficknefles,and manie died:that by thefe men other might learn,and they fea red with the example ofa few might be amended: knowing that to receaue the bodie of our Lorde necligentlie ys not left vnpunifhed, but yfhis punifh ment be differred that he fhal be more greuouflie handled hereafter,bicaufe he hath contemned the example.

S. Ambr. vnderftan deth S. Paule io fpeak of the bodie ofour Lord.

As *Origen* hath doen before:fo S. Ambrofe here agreablie declareth that
B feuers , ficknefles , and death alfo haue by gods punifhment fallen vpon them , that vnwoorthilie haue receaued the bodie of our Lorde. In which his declaracion of fainct Paules minde this ys alfo euident to be feen,that he bothe confeffeth the bodie of Chryft in the Sacrament: and alfo that the fame bodie of Chryft hath ben receaued of euell men. Nowe foche prefence as the Aduerfarie teacheth can be but of good men receaued,wherfor fainct Ambrofe here and *Origen*,and diuerfe other before allea ged for the expofition of fainct Paule, teaching vs that euell men receaue the bodie of Chryfte,yt muft nedes neceffarilie folowe that ther ys befides the fpirituall maner(which onelie the Aduerfarie teacheth) an other maner of reall and fubftanciall prefence,by which the euell man receaueth the verie fubftance of the bodie of Chryft verilie land in dede. Which being (*as yt ys in dede*) a moft certen trueth teftified by manie holie doctours , and graue Fathers,of the Church,the contrarie affertion of the Aduerfarie,muft neds be iudged an hereticall vntrueth.Wherfor Chryftian Reader,be not decea ued with vain glofes of light Sacramentaries,but ftaic thie felf vpon the fu
C re and agreable expofitiõs of the holie Fathers,ãd beleue no leffe but thow cominge wher the Sacrament ys duelie miniftred,according to Chryftes inftitucion,and receauing the fame,that thow receaueft the verie reall and fub ftanciall bodie of Chryft. But now yt ftandeth thee in hande , to fee howe thowe receaueft yt,with what faith,with that deuocion, and with what re uerence. For this holie father fainct Ambrofe(as other before) teacheth vs after the minde of fainct Paule,that we muft come to this moft holie Sacra ment with deuocion,feare and reuerence.For fhewing fainct Paules minde, who willeth vs to examin our felues , he faieth vpon the fame thus : *Deuoto animo,& cum timore accedendum ad communionem docet , vt fciat meus reuerentiam fe debere ei,ad cuius corpus fumendum accedit.*He teacheth vs to come to the com munion with a deuoute minde,and with feare,that the minde maie knowe yt felf to owe reuerence vnto him,whofe bodie yt cometh to receaue. Thus moche he.

Ambr. in 11. 1. Cor. Reuerence is due to him whofe bodie were ceaue.

What foeuer Luther hath faied againft our preparacion for our feemelie coming to the receipt of the bleff.Sacrament:what foeuer the Aduerfaries
D the Sacramentaries and the Proclamer faie againft the holie and bleffed bo die of Chryft in the Sacrament fekinge by termes,as by Sacramentall bread, by figure,by an holie figne,and foche like,to deface yt,and yet with foch ho lie tearmes to cloake their vnholie herefie,and loathing by expreffe words to

S. Ambr. andOrigen vfe plain tearmes for the Procla

call yt the bodie of Chryſt: yet this holie Father and Biſhoppe. S. Ambroſe E
in bothe theſe places alleadged, and *Origen* in his ſainges, in this chapter produced calleth ſhe Sacrament ſixe or ſeuen times by plain woords, *the bodie of
our Lorde*, the doubtful tearmes of the Aduerſarie left, as by which they could
not ſo liuelie expreſſe and ſhewe furth the trueth.

To ende with theſe two Fathers of Chryſtes Parliament houſe we maie
perfectlie by them vnderſtand, that God puniſheth vnwoorthie receauers
of the bodie of Chryſt, ſome temporallie, by feuers ſickneſſes, ād death: ſome
eternally by perpetuall damnacion. Wherbie as by the greuouſneſſe of the
puniſhmētes we maie learn the greuouſneſſe of the offence: So by the great
neſſe of the offence, we maie learn the greatneſſe, of the bleſſed Sacrament, in
the receipt of which no ſoch offence coulde be committed, if he were not
ther preſent, whoſe maieſtie being great, maketh the offence great.

THE EIGHT AND FIFTETH CHAP. ENDETH
the expoſition of the ſame text by Theophilact. F
and Anſelm.

Oraſmuche as the matter treacted of by S. Paule in this text ys apperteinent, and dependeth of the matter ſpoken of before, in the
which we haue proceaded at the lenght, therfor I haue determined
to content my ſelf with the two Fathers, in the laſt chapter produced, by whome we maie learn the enacted trueth of the vnderſtanding of
this text in the higher houſe, and with two other Fathers of the lower houſe
who ſhall open vnto vs alſo the vnderſtanding of the ſame in the lower houſe, which two ſhall be *Theophilact*, and Anſelme.

Theophilact writeth thus: *Accipite demonſtrationē ex iis, quæ apud vos contin-*
*gunt. Hinc enim ſunt immaturæ mortes, diuturnǽque ægritudines, & morbi, eò quòd multi in
dignè aſſumant. Quid igitur? Qui non ægrotant, & ad extremam vſque ſenectam ſeruan-
tur incolumes, nonne peccant? Peccant ſanè. Sed non huius temporis pænæ ſolæ indignè acce-
dentibus deſtinatæ ſunt, ſed in futuro quoque ſeculo.* Take ye a demonſtracion of thoſe
thinges which happen among yowe. For bicauſe manie do receaue vnwoor- G
thilie, therfor ther be haſtie deathes, and long diſſeaſes and ſickneſſes.
What then? They that are not ſick but to their extearm age are kept in health, doe they not ſinne? They ſinne trulie, but not the onelie paines of this
time are apointed to vnwoorthie receauers, but ther be alſo in the world to
cōme more harde, and more greuouſe puniſhmentes repoſed.

As the Iudgementes of God be merueilouſe, and incomprehenſible, ſo dee
pe alſo that no man can reache vnto the profunditie therof: ſo are they alſo
vpright, iuſt and full of equitie, geuing to euery man according to hys
workes. By whiche he puniſheth ſome in this life, but not eternallie, ſome
eternallie, but not in this life temporallie: ſome both temporallie, and eternallie. So likewiſe of them that by vnwoorthie receipt contemne and foulie
abuſe the bleſſed Sacrament ſome by ſickneſſes, and diſeaſes are puniſhed
who humblie receauing the ſame, and repenting their former doings, and
amending their liues, God temperinge hys iuſtice with mercie puniſheth them but in this life. Other ſome ther be that abuſing the holie Sacrament by vnwoorthie receipt, and continuing the ſame doe yet ſome H
good workes, though not in the right ordre of good workes, ſoche God of
hys mercie puniſheth not temporallie, but differring the puniſhment, puniſheth thē eternallie. Some being of moſt beaſtlie and deteſtable life,
and

A and continuinge in the fame without repentance as men euen folde ouer to finne, and touched with ficknefle will not hūblie receaue the fame as Gods mercifull punifhment to the amendmēt of life, but raither heapinge euells vpō euells doe murmure ād grudge, yea ād with all violēt impaciēcie blafphe me his holie name, ād reprooue his correctiō with manie vnfemelie woords, manie foche are punifhed both temporallie ād eternallie. Thus by *Theopilacte* then we maie learn, that to vnwoorthie receauers of the blefl. Sacrament foche punifhmentes haue ben inflicted of God, wherby (as ys faied) maie be perceaued, that as the offence ys great, fo yt ys doen againft him, who ys great, euen Chryft our Sauioure and redemer, whofe blefled bodie being prefent in the Sacrament ys by wicked receauers moche abufed. I ftand not to declare the faith of *Theophllact* as touchinge the prefence. For yt ys more then manifeft, that he that denieth the Aduerfaries figure in the Sacrument confefleth the prefence, whiche this authour doeth in diuerfe places expo-wndinge the fcripturs, as in this worke alfo yt maie be feen,

B   Wherfor leauinge him we will heare *Anfelmus*, who vpon this text folo-winge S. Ambrofe and vfinge his woordes, writeth thus, as fpeakinge to the Corinthians in the perfon of S. Paule : *Quia indignè manducatis hoc corpus, & fanguinem bibitis, ideo funt inter vos multi infirmi, qui graui morbo languent: & imbecilles qui diuturna inualitudine torpent & dormiunt etiam multi, id eft fomno mortis funt occupa ti, vt verum probaret, quia examen futurum eft accipientium corpus Domini. Iam hic imaginem iudicii oftendit in nonnullis qui corpus illud inconfiderate acceperant, dum ægrota tionibus, & longis inualitudinibus tenerentur, & multi morerentur, vt in eis cæteri difcerēt fe non impunè corpus Domini negligenter accipere, & paucorū exēplo cæteri territi emenda rentur, fcientes quia grauiores pœnas in futuro feculo propter hanc culpā ipfi forent paffuri, fi non corrigerentur.* Bicaufe ye doe eate ād drink his bodie and blood vnwoorthi lie, therfor ther be amōg yow manie fick of greuous ficknefle, ād weak which faint with lōg difeafe, ād manie alfo fleape, that ys, they are preuēted with death. To prooue that a iudgemēt or condēnaciō fhall come of thē that re-ceaue the bodie of ourLord, he doeth now fhew the ymage of the iudgemēt in manie, whiche had incōfideratelie reaeaued that bodie, forafmochas they

Anfelm. in. 11. 1. Cor.

C were holden with fickneffes, and long weaknefle and manie died, that by them other fhoulde learn, that they fhoulde not receaue the bodie of our Lorde negligentlie withoute punifhment, and other feared with the example of a fewe, fhoulde be amended, knowinge that theie fhall fuffre more gre-uoufe paines in the worlde to come for this offence, except they were amen ded. Thus he.

The Corin thians did eate and drinke the bodie and blood of ourLord vnworthi-lie.

    We learn here of *Anfelmus*, that the fickneffes, difeafes and deathes that happened amonge the Corinthians, were bicaufe thei receaued not onelie the Sacrament, or (*as the Sacramentaries tearme yt*) the Sacramentall bread vn-worthily, but bicaufe they did inconfideratelie receaue the bodie of our Lorde. In whiche maner of faithe, and fpeache this authour foloweth not his owne devife, but the graue doctrine and iudgement, of S. Ambrofe who fe fainge he doeth here alleage. And fo by them bothe yt ys manifeft that the bodie of Chryft ys receaued in the Sacrament, that euell men alfo recea ue yt ther, whiche prooueth the reall and fubftanciall prefence of Chryftes bodie, and that foche euell receauers for that they doe moche iniurie to that

D pure and vndefiled bodie ofChryft caftinge yt into their bodie defiled with moche filth of finne, doe oftētimes fuffre the pains in this life and alfo in the liue to come.

    Of the difpleafure of God againft euell receauers, as S. Paule maketh

proofe by demonſtracion, and experience of the ſame in his time: ſo doeth **E**
alſo S. Cyprian for the like in his time, who bringeth three or foure exáples
of Gods wrath againſt them that beinge defiled with ſinne did preſume to
approache to, or receaue the holie bodie of Chryſt. The firſt example is of a
childe, whiche beinge put to a Nource did taſt of a ſoppe of bread, whiche
was offred vnto Idolls. And when the mother hauinge this childe in her ar
mes came to the Churche amonge chriſtian people, and the Sacrament a-
monge other, was alſo offred to the childe, the child (who I ſaie, had taſted
of Idolls meat) turned awaie her face from the Sacrament, ſhe ſtopped her
mouthe and helde her lippes harde together, ſhe refuſed by anie mean to
touche the cuppe of the bloode of Chryſte. Yet though ſhe did thus ſtriue,
the deacon gaue her of the Sacrament. Whiche when ſhe had once receaued, furth with ſhe fell to boking and vomiting for (as Cyprian ſaieth) *in corpore, atque ore violato Euchariſtia permanere non potuit. Sáctificatus in Domini ſangui
ne potus, de pollutis viſceribus erupit. Tanta eſt poteſtas Domini, tanta maieſtas.* In a defiled mouthe and bodie the Sacrament coulde not abide. The ſanctified drin- **F**
ke in our Lordes bloode braſt oute of the defiled bowells. So great ys the
power of owre Lorde, ſo great ys his maieſtie.

By this example maie we learn, howe moche yt offendeth God, that the
bodie of Chryſt ſhould be receaued vnwoorthilie of one that hathe knowledge and reaſon. Immediatelie after this, S. Cyprian maketh reporte of a
woman that was of age, knowledge, and reaſon, ſainge that ſoche one when
he was offringe the ſacrifice priueilie ſtole in among other, and receauing
the Sacrament, not as meat to comforte her, for that ſhe was vnwoorthie,
but as a ſworde to deſtroie her, and takinge as yt were deadly poiſon in to
her mouthe and breaſt, ſhe begá to be merueilouſelie vexed, and diſquieted,
and ſo ſuffringe the heauie puniſhment of her offence, pantinge and tremblinge ſhe fell downe dead. So (ſaieth he) was not her euell offence left long
vnpuniſhed. But ſhe that thought by her cloaking and diſſemblinge of her
offence to haue deceaued man, felt God to whome all thinges be knowen,
the reuenger and puniſher of the ſame.

An other woman ther was alſo, who receauing the Sacrament into her **G**
handes kept the ſame, and carienge yt home, putte yt into her coaſer. But
to vſe the woordes of S. Cyprian, *Cum arcam ſuam in qua Domini ſanctum fuit
manibus indignis tentaſſet aperire, igne inde ſurgente deterrita eſt, ne auderet attingere.*
When ſhe wolde with vnwoorthie hands open the coaſer, wherin was *the
holie thinge of our Lorde,* ther ſprang oute a fire, wherby ſhe was caſt in ſoch feare that ſhe durſt not touche yt. Vpon this example this maie we note, that if
God wolde not ſuffre the woman, foraſmoche as ſhe was vnwoorthie, not
as moche as to open the coaſer, wher the holie thinge of our lorde was laied, howe moche leſſe will he beare yt that a licenciouſe filthie liuinge man ſhoulde touche the thing yt ſelf, eate yt, and caſt yt into his ſinfull bodie?

An other merueilouſe thinge doeth S. Cyprian report of the bleſſed Sacrament, Ther was (ſaieth he) a certain defiled or ſinfull man, who beinge
preſent when the Sacrament was celebrated by the preiſt (ſo doeth S. Cyprian
tearme the holie miniſtracion) he preſumed priuielie with other to receaue, but
he coulde not eate the holie thinge of God nor handle yt. For when he **H**
had opened his hande to ſee what he had receaued, he fownde nothinge
but aſhes. This in dede ys a meruertouſe thinge, wherby ys declared that
God ys not willing, that his holie Sacrament ſhoulde be receaued of a filthie

*Cyp.ſer. 5.
de. lapſis.*

*She might
haue recea
ued the ne-
we Commu
nion with
out anie ſo-
che troble.*

*A woman
receauing
the B. Sa.
vnvvorthi
lie ſtricken
vvith death*

*Amá vn-
vvoorthilie
receauing
the bleſſ. Sa
in his hand
vvhé he ope
ned his had
ther vvas
nothing
but aſſhes*

A   thie sinner,forasmoche as sodenlie yt pleaseth him to chaunge yt into asshes he him self departing from yt.

Serm.5 de lapsis.

But let vs heare what S.Cyprian him self noteth vpõ this miracle of God *Documento vnius ostensum est, Dominum recedere cum negatur, nec immerentibus prodesse ad salutem quod sumitur, cum gratia salutaris in cinerem sanctitate fugiente mutetur.* By the example of one yt ys declared, that our Lorde departeth when he ys denied,nether doeth yt , that ys receaued profitte the vnwoorthie to saluacion or healthe,when the holsome grace,holinesse departinge awaie, ys chaunged into asshes.

This note of S. Cyprian ys notable in dede, and for that yt ys so , I wishe yt so to be noted of the reader, that yt neuer fall from his memorie . First, let the euell man note that at the receipt of the Sacrament bicause in life and conuersation God ys denied that he departeth and goeth awaie. But let the faithfull herby learn , that owre Lorde ys present with his Sacramẽt, who as he departeth from the wicked so he abideth to be receaued of the vertuouse ãd godlie. This also ys not to be ouerpassed, that the holie Martir B   saieth, that yt,that ys receaued, profiteth not the vnwoorthie to saluacion. For by that he saieth, yt profiteth not the vnwoorthie, he argueth that yt profiteth the woorthie, or ells we must saie that the state bothe of the woorthie, and vnwoorthie ys equall, whiche if yt so were,S. Ciprian did but vainlie saie, that yt did not profitte the vnwoorthie,

Yf then one thinge be receaued in the Sacrament that profiteth the good and auaileth not the euel, we must first graunt, that the good and the euell receaue one thinge, profiting the one, and hurting the other . Nowe wolde yt be learned of the Sacramentarie,what one thing that ys in the Sacrament that ys receaued, that profiteth and hurteth . The Sacramentarie leaueth no more in the Sacrament by his doctrine, but Sacramentall bread, and Sacramentall wine, whiche both (saieth he) remain in their substance and nature,so that ther ys no other thinge (taking thing for substance) but the substance of bread and wine: Certen yt ys, that as God suffereth the Sunne to shine vpon good and euell, and raineth vpon the iust and vniust : So do C   the he suffre the substance of bread and wine to feede and nourish both good and euell,as well to profitte the wicked as the rightwise,no more (measure beinge obserued) to hurt the one then the other . Yf than the substance of bread be so indifferent,that yt profiteth as well the wicked as the good the substance of bread ys not the thinge , that holie Cyprian saith to be in the Sacrament, which onelie profiteth the good , and hurteth the euell, yf yt be receaued . Wherfor yt doeth necessarelie folowe,that ther ys an other thing in the Sacrament, than the substance of bread, whiche ys the bodie of Chryst, as the holie fathers before alleaged haue confessed , and the holie Churche catholique professeth and beleueth.

Nowe ye haue heard the presence of Chrystes bodie and bloode taught by S. Paule in the epistle to the Corinthians : ye haue heard yt testified, yea and auouched by a nombre of auncient holie Fathers: ye haue hearde yt E   prooued that by the testimonie as well of S. Paule,as the Fathers yt ys plain and euident, that the euell and vnwoorthie receaue the same bodie of Chryst in the bless. Sacrament that the good and woorthie doth : Ye haue heard paines both temporall and eternall appoincted to soche vnwoorthie receauers : Ye haue seen great difference of the pains of the vnclean receauers of the figures of the olde lawe, and of the vnwoorthie receauers of the Sacrament of the newe lawe, wherby also ys inuinciblie prooued a great

differen-

difference of thinges receaued in both lawes. For in the olde lawe Chryſt was receaued figuratiuely: In the newe lawe he ys receaued verilie. In the olde lawe onelie ſpirituallie: In the newe lawe of good people bothe ſpiritu allie and ſubſtanciallie. Thus moche beinge doen if grace be at hande with the reader ther ys enough doen to expell the Sacramentaries hereſie, and to moue to receaue the catholique veritie. Wherfore although ther be other ſcriptures in S. Paule, I will not ſtand and abide vpon them, as hitherto I haue doen vpon other, but I will touche them and ſo ende.

THE NINE AND FIFTETH CHAP. TREAC-
teth of theſe woordes of S. Paule. We are membres
of his bodie, of his fleſh, and of his
bones, by Irenæus and
Hylarius.

IN the epiſtle to the Epheſians, S. Paule exhorting men to loue　F their wieues, willeth them ſo to loue them, and nouriſh them, as Chryſt doeth his Churche. And for proof that they ſhoulde ſo doe, he ſaieth that no man at anie time hath hated his owne fleſh, but nouriſheth and cheriſeth yt as Chryſt doeth his Chur che. For we are ſaieth he mẽbres of his bodie, of his fleſh and of his bones. Whiche ſainge foraſmoche as the great auncient Father *Irenæus* doeth vn-derſtande of the fleſh, bodie and bloode of Chryſt in the Sacrament, I haue thought good to lett the reader perceaue the ſame.

Thus he writeth : *Quomodò carnem negant eſſe capacem donationis Dei, quæ eſt*

Iræn. li. 5. *vita æterna quæ ſanguine & corpore Chriſti nutritur, & membrum eius fit, quemadmo-dum & Apoſtolus ait, in ea, quæ eſt ad Epheſios epiſtola : Quoniam membra ſumus cor-poris eius, de carne eius, & de oſsibus eius, non de ſpirituali aliquo, & inuiſibili homine dicens hæc (ſpiritus enim neque oſſa, neque carnes habet) ſed de ea diſpoſitione, quæ eſt ſe-cundùm hominem, quæ ex carnibus & neruis & oſsibus conſiſtit, quæ de calice, qui eſt ſan guis eius nutritur, & de pane, qui eſt corpus eius augetur?* Howe denie they the fleſh to be hable to receaue the gift of God, whiche ys euerlaſting life, *whiche ys*

A plain ſa-ing of Iren. againſt the Proclamer *nouriſhed with the bodie and blood of Chryſte,* and ys made a membre of him, as the　G Apoſtle alſo ſaieth in the epiſtle to the Epheſians : *For we are membres of his bo-die, of his fleſh and of his bones :* not ſpeaking theſe woordes of any ſpirituall or inuiſible man, but of that diſpoſition, whiche ys after the nature of man whiche ys of fleſh, Sinnewes and bones, whiche ys nouriſhed of the cuppe, whiche ys his blood, and ys encreaſed by the bread whiche ys his bodie. hitherto Iren.

For the better vnderſtanding of this ſainge, the occaſion whie he wro-te this ys to be declared, although this Irenæus were ſo auncient and ſo neare to the time of the Apoſtles, that he was the diſciple of Policar-pus, whiche Policarpus was the diſciple of ſainct Iohn the Euangeliſt : yet

The fleſh of mã shall haue euer-laing life bi cauſe yt ys nouriſhed with the fleſh of Chryſt. before and in his time were riſen manie heretiques as *Symon Samarites*, who other wiſe ys called *Symon Magus:* Menander, Carporates, Baſilides, *Cerinthus Ebion*, and *Marcion* : whiche fowlie and diuerſlie erringe aboute the perſon of Chryſt, ſome of them alſo denienge the reſurrection, ſainge that owre earthlie and groſſe fleſh coulde not be partaker of ſaluacion. Aga inſt whiche hereſies Irenæus wrote fiue bookes, and in the fiſte booke　H amonge other thinges impugning that hereſie that ſaied that owre fleſh coulde not enioie euerlaſtinge life, prooueth that yt maie and ſhall

And

A by that yt ys nourished with the fleshe and bloode of Chryste. And therfora sketh a question sainge : howe denie they our flesh to be partaker of the gifte of God, whiche ys euerlastinge, whiche flesh ys nourished with the bodie and blood of Chryst, and ys made a membre of him ? That our flesh ys nourished by the bodie and blood of Chryst, and therby also made a membre of him : he prooueth yt by this Scripture of S. Paule, that we be membres of his bodie, of his flesh and of his bones.

And here note howe goodlie he confirmeth the catholique faith, and howe mightilie he ouerthrowe the heresie of the Sacramentarie. The Catholique saieth that the wholl man bothe bodie and sowle taketh benefitte, and ys nourished by the bodie and bloode of Chryste : The Sacramentarie saieth, that onelie the inwarde man, the spirituall man ys spirituallie nourished by faith. But this false glose ys here by expresse woordes reproued and conuinced. S. Paule (saieth *Irenæus*) speaketh not this of anie spirituall or inuisible man, but of the verie naturall man, which ys made of flesh sin-

B newes, and bones whiche naturall man ys nourished, and augmented by the cuppe, whiche ys the bloode of our Lorde, and the breade whiche ys the bodie of our Lorde. Yt ys manifest then against the Sacramentarie, yt ys manifest against the Proclamer, that the naturall man doeth eate and drinke the naturall bodie and bloode of Chryst wherby also yt ys manifest, that the naturall bodie and bloode of Chryste be in the Sacrament, For if they were not, howe coulde they so be receaued?

Again yt ys manifest, that not onelie the inwarde man, the inuinsible or spirituall man receaueth the bodie and bloode of Chryst, but also the outwarde, the visible and naturall man. And for the full and perfect vnderstanding of this, note well the cheife grownde of this auncient holie Father Irenæus. His pourpose ys to prooue, that our flesh although yt be a mortall thinge, shall receaue immortallitie : although yt be earthilie, yt shall receaue an heauenly and euerlastinge life: howe proueth he that? By that that our mortall flesh receaueth the immortall flesh and bloode of Chryst, and therby nourished shall in his time atteign to immortalitie ād life euerlastin-

C ge. Consider then that the argument of this holie father against this heresie, to prooue that our bodies shall rise, and that they at the same resurrection, shall atteign to immortallie, ys, that we receaue the bodie ād blood of Christ by the whiche (yt beinge immortall, and also able to geue immortalitie) we shall be made immortall, and receauers of euerlastinge life. The Sacramen tarie then denienge that we receaue the bodie of Chryst into our bodies, denieth the argument of this holie Father, and tectlie also denieth owre resurrection and immortalitie (which to manie of them haue allreadie apertlie doen) and robbeth vs of one great article of our faith, and of our cheif and high comforte, that we hope to haue in our resurrection. For (as S. Paule saieth) *Si in hac vita tātum, in Christo sperātes sumus omnibus hominibus, &c.* Yf in this life onelie, we beleue on Chryst, then are we of all men most miserablie. Yf then they will robbe vs of the mean to atteign to this resurrection and immortallitie, whiche mean ys the very receipt of the bodie and blood of Chryst, they shall also robbe vs of the effect. For the cause being taken awaie the effect also must be taken awaie : as the cause beinge admitted, the effect

D must necessarie folowe. For the cause of the immortalitie of our flesh ys the coniunction of the immortall flesh of Chryst with owre, whiche ys doen by the receipt of the same in the Sacrament.

Of these two Chryst ys a full wittnesse, for the first he saieth. *Nisi mandu-*
caueritis

Both bodie and soule haue benefite by the bodie of Christe.

The outward naturall man receaueth the bodie and blood of Chryste.

The Sacramentaries denieng the receipt of Chrysts naturall bodie into our, denie withall the argument of Iren. ād of consequent the immortallitie of our bodies after resurrect.

1. Cor. 15.

caueritis carnem filii hominis, & biberitis eius sanguinem non habebitis vitam in vobis
Except ye eate the flesh of the Sonne of man and drinke his blood, ye shall
haue no life in yowe, wherby ys testified that the receipt of the bodie and
blood taken awaie from vs, immortalitie and euerlastinge life ys also taken awaie.

ibid.

For the other, Chryst also testifieth: *Qui manducat meã carnem & bibit meum*
sanguinem, habet vitam æternam. He that eateth my flesh and drinketh my blood
hath euerlastinge life. Wherby ys taught that the receipt of the bodie and bloode of Chryst, ys the cause and mean of and to euerlasting life.

But that the Aduersarie shall not cauill and saie, that I speake moche in
this matter at mine owne libertie, and ther vnto expownde the scripturs by
mine owne authoritie: he shall heare the holie Father Cyrill affirme as mo-

Cirill in 15
ca. Joan.

che as I haue saied, and expownde the scripturs to the same sense. Thus he
writeth : *Non poterat aliter corruptibilis hæc natura ad incorruptibilitatem, & vitam*
traduci, nisi naturalis vitæ corpus ei coniungeretur. Non credis mihi hæc dicenti? Christo, te
obsecro, fidem præbe dicenti : Amen, amen (inquit) dico vobis : Nisi manducaueritis car
nem filii hominis, & biberitis eius sanguinem, non habebitis vitam in vobis. Qui manducat
meam carnem, & bibit meum sanguinem habet vitam æternam. Audis apertè clamãtem
non habituros nos vitam, nisi sanguinem eius biberimus, & carnem manducauerimus. In
vobis autem ipsis, dicit, id est, in corpore vestro. Vita autem, iure ipsa vitæ caro intelligi po-
test. Hæc enim nos in nouissimo die suscitat, & quomodò, dicere non grauabor. Caro vitæ
facta Vnigeniti caro, ad virtutem vitæ traducta est. Non potest igitur morte superari.
Propterea in nobis facta, interitum à nobis expellit. Non enim abest ab ea vnigenitus Dei
filius. Vnde quia vnus est cum carne sua, Ego (inquit) suscitabo eum. This corruptible

Oure, cor-
ruptible na-
ture could
not atteign
to incorrup-
tibilitie
but by the
receipt of
the incor-
ruptible
flesh of
Chryste.

nature of owre bodie could not other wise be brought to incorruptibilitie
and life, except the bodie of naturall life shoulde be ioined to yt. Beleuest
thowe not me sainge these woordes? I praie thee then beleue Chryst sainge
Verilie verilie (saieth he) *I saie vnto yowe, except ye eate the flesh of the Sonne of man,*
and drinke his bloode, ye shall haue no life in yowe. He that eateth my flesh, and drinketh
my bloode hath euerlastinge life. Thowe hearest him openlie saing that we shall
haue no life, except we drinke his bloode, and eate his flesh. He saieth : *in*
yower selues : that ys, in yower bodie. By life, maie of right be vnderstanded, that
flesh of life. For this flesh shall raise vs vppe in the last daie. And howe,
yt shall not greiue me to tell. The flesh of life being made the flesh of the
onelie begotten Sonne of God ys brought to haue the power of life. Yt
can not therfor be ouercomed of deathe. Wherfor that flesh beinge in vs,
expelleth deathe from vs. For the onelie begotten Sonne of God ys not
absent from that flesh. Wherfore bicause he ys one withe his flesh, he saied
I will rayse him vppe.

Se ye not here plainlie affirmed by sainct Cyrill, and that by those places of the vi. of sainct Iohn, that this corruptible nature of owre bodie, can not atteign to immortalitie and life, except the bodie of Chryst,

The flesh
can not be
subiect to
mortalitie
that duelie
receaueth
the flesh of
immortali-
tie.

whiche he calleth the bodie of life, be conioined to yt. To returne then, the argument of *Irenæus* ys of great force. For in dede, that
flesh can not be subiecte to mortalitie, that receaueth the flesh of Chryst,
whiche geueth immortalitie. But once to ende with *Irenæus*, I wishe the
Reader to be aduertised of two thinges : The one that wher *Irenæus* and S.
Cyrill saie, that by the receipt of the bodie of Chryst we receaue immortalitie, he maie not thinke them to speake against the scripture whiche saieth,
Quis est homo, qui viuit, & non videbit mortem? What man ys he, that liueth,
and

A and fhall not die?And again the penall fentence of God ys:*Puluis es, & in pul*
*uerem reuerteris.*Thowe arte duft,and into duft fhalt thowe returne. For they
fpeake not of this worldlie life, but of the heauenlie life,that fhall be geuen to man after the refurrection . At the whiche, forafmoche as man
fhall be raifed,this temporall deathe ys properlie in the fcriptures called
a fleape . Whiche immortalitie ys not promifed to all that receaue the
bodie of Chryft,no more then faluacion ys to all them ,that beleue and be
Baptifed, although Chryft faie: *Qui crediderit, & baptifatus fuerit faluus erit.*
Who that fhall beleue,and be baptifed,fhall be faued:But to foche as woorthilie receaue,and fo perfeuer to the ende.For *Qui perfeuerauerit in finem, hic fal-*
uus erit. He that perfeucreth to the ende this man fhall be faued.

Howe and
when this
immortali-
tie shall be
geuen.

   The other ys, that wher *Irenæus* faied, that owre flefh ys nourifhed by
the flefh of Chryft, yt ys not to be vnderftanded, that that bleffed flefh
ys turned or chaunged after the maner of other earthlie meates into the
fubftance of our flefh and bloode , but raither that yt turneth vs into
B yt, as yt was faied to Sainct Auguftine . *Nec tu me mutabis in te, ficut*
cibum carnis tuæ: fed tu mutaberis in me. Neither fhallt thowe chaunge or
turne me into thee , as the meate of thie flefh, but thowe fhallt be turned
or chaunged into me. Yt doeth alfo nourifh vs, in thar yt geueth vs
foche fuftentacion of life as yt hath .Earthlie meates whie are they receaued, but that they fhoulde geue fuftentacion of this earthlie life ?So this
hauenlie meate ys receaued to geue vs fuftentacion of the heauenlie
immortall life . As by the one then we are nourifhed to liue this
mortall life : So by the other are we nourifhed to liue the immortall life.

The flesh
of Chryste
ys not tur-
ned into our
fubftance,
but raither
turneth vs
into yt.

   Again by the receipt of this holie flefh are we made the membres of
Chryft incorporated to him , and made one with him,whiche thinge the
great and learned Father Hilarie teacheth . Wherby this text of fainct Paul
ys moche opened and declared.Which thing(although he doeth not fpeake
of the verie woordes of S.Paule)moued me to ioin him with *Irenæus* in this
C place,his woordes be thefe:*Eos,qui inter Patrem & Filium voluntatis ingerunt vni-*
tatem,interrogo vtrum ne per naturæ veritatem hodie Chriftus in nobis fit , an per con-
cordiam voluntatis? Si enim verè Verbum caro factum eft, & nos Verbum carnem
factum cibo dominico fumimus,quomodò non naturaliter manere in nobis exiftimandus eft,
qui et naturam carnis noftræ iam infeparabilem fibi homo natus affumpfit, et naturam car-
nis fuæ ad naturam æternitatis fub facramento nobis communicandæ carnis admifcuit? Ita
enim omnes vnum fumus,quia in Chrifto Pater eft,et Chriftus in nobis eft.Quifquis ergo na-
turaliter , Patrem in Chrifto negabit , neget prius non naturaliter , vel fe in Chrifto
vel fibi Chriftum ineffe , quia in Chrifto Pater , et Chriftus in nobis , vnum in iis
effe nos faciunt . Si verè igitur carnem corporis noftri Chriftus affumpfit , et verè
homo ille,qui ex Maria natus fuit,Chriftus eft, nofque verè fub myfterio carnem corporis
fumimus , et per hoc vnum erimus , quia Pater in eo eft , et ille in nobis.
I afke them ,that bringe in the vnitie of will betwixt the Father and the
Sonne,whether Chryft be in vs now by the agreement of will or by the veritie of nature. *For if the woorde was verilie made flesh,and we verilie receaue the*
woorde made flesh in our Lordes meat , howe ys he to be thought not to
abide in vs naturallie , who being born man , did both take our na-
D ture nowe infeparable vpon him , and alfo vnder the Sacrament of the communicating of hys flefh , vnto vs , hath admixed the
nature of his flefh to the nature of eternitie ? And fo we be all
one . For the Father ys in Chryfte , and Chryfte ys in vs.

We verilie
receaue the
woord ma-
de flesh in
our Lordes
meat.

Whofoeuer then fhall denie the Father to be naturallie in Chryfte let him
firft denie either himfelf to be naturallie in Chryft, or Chryft to be in him.
For the Father being in Chryfte, and Chryfte in vs maketh vs in thefe to be
one. Yf than Chryft hath verilie taken vpon him the flefh of our bodie : and
that man that was borne of Marie, be verilie Chryfte: *And we alfo in the Sacra-*
ment doe verilie receaue the flefh of his bodie, we fhall by this alfo be one. For the
Father ys in him, and he in vs. Thus moch S. Hilarie.

We verilie
receaue the
flesh of
Chryfte in
the Sacr.

For better vnderftandinge of whome, yt ys to be noted that he
wrote againft the peftiferoufe herefie of the Arrians, who taught that the
Sonne of God the fecond perfon in deitie was a creature, and was not
all one with the Father in nature, in deitie, eternitie and equalitie, but was
leffe then the Father, and onelie one with him in the vnitie of agreement or
confent of will. Againft this peftilent doctrine did faint Hilarie write,
prouing the Sonne of God to be naturallie in the Father, and the Father naturallie in the Sonne. And for that this wicked fect to prooue their wicked
doctrine made a falfe argument vpon our vnitie with God, fainge that
Chryft was one with God as we be, but our vnitie with him ys but by
fubmifsion ãd confent of will: therfor (faie) thei foch and none other ys this
alfo. To improoue and diffolue this falfe and lieng argument, he prooueth
that our vnitie with God ys not by confent of will onelie, but alfo by nature which vnitie ys made and wrought by the receipt of Chryftes naturall
flefh and blood in the Sacrament, Wherfore faint Hilarie thus reafoneth:
Si verè verbum, &c. Yf the woorde was verilie made flefh, and we verilie receaue the woorde made flefh in our Lordes meate, howe ys he not to be
thought naturallie to abide in vs, who hath bothe taken vpon him, beinge
made man, the nature of our flefh nowe infeparable, and alfo vnder the Sacrament of communicating his flefh vnto vs hath admixed the nature of
his flefh?

Arrius his
herefie

Chrifte too
ke oure
flesh in the
myfterie of
his incarna
cion, and ge
ueth vs the
fame in the
myfterie of
his Sa. and
fo ys natura
lie in vs, ãd
we in him.

By whiche argument he doeth not onelie go aboute to prooue that
the Father ys naturallie in Chryft, but moft plainlie teacheth alfo
that we receaue Chryftes verie naturall flefh in the Sacrament, and that,
by that receipt, Chryft ys naturallie in vs. By which two poinctes he
conuinceth directlie the wicked affertion of the Sacramentaries, who a-
gainft all trueth that maie be learned in fcriptures, and the moft auncient
Fathers, teache, that neither Chryftes verie naturall flefh ys receaued in
the Sacrament, neither that Chryft ys naturallie in vs, but onely fpirituallie. The contrarie wherof ys not onely by this Authour in plain
woordes taught, but alfo by Chryfoftome and faint Cyrill, as before ys
fhewed. That faint Hilarie intended by his difputacion to confute the
Arrians denieng Chryft to be naturallie in vs, and alfo the holie Goft (as yt
maie be thought) left the fame to confute the Sacramentaris, yt doeth verie
well appeare by a conclufion that he maketh vpon the fame difputacion thus fainge : *Hæc idcireo à nobis commemorata funt, quia volunta-*
tis tantùm inter Patrem & Filium, vnitatem hæretici mentientes, vnitatis noftræ
ad Deum vtebantur exemplo, tanquam nobis ad Filium, & per filium ad Pa-
trem obfequio tantùm ac voluntate religionis vnitis, nulla per Sacramentnm &
fanguinis naturalis communionis proprietas indulgeretur, cùm & per honorem no-
bis datum Dei filii, & per manentem in nobis carnaliter Dei filium, & in eo no-
bis corporaliter, & infeparabiliter vnitis, myfterium veræ ac naturalis vnitatis fit
prædicandum . Thefe thinges are for this caufe fpoken of vs, that
hereti-

G

H

A heretiques vntruely faing the vnitie betwixt the Father and the Sonne to be onelie the vnitie of will vfed the example of our vnitie with God, as though we being by obedience and will in religion onelie vnited to the Sonne, and by the Sonne to the Father, no proprietie of naturall communion fhoulde be geuen by the Sacrament of the flefh and bloode, fithen that both by the honour of the Sonne of God geuen to vs, and by the Sonne of God carnallie abidng in vs, and we being corporallie, and infeparablie vnited in him, the myfterie of the true and naturall vnitie ys to be declared. Thus moch he.

By thefe woordes as S. Hilarie improoueth the Arrians faing that Chryft ys not naturallie in vs, fo doeth he the Sacramentaries teaching the fame. And thus maie we fee the finceritie of them, who doe maintein the peftilent doctrine of the Arrians. And that that was confuted and reprooued as herefie twelue hondreth yeares agon, ys nowe with a litle falfe skouring and colouring, folde to the people for trueth. *The Sacramentaries ioin with the Arrians in deniengnatural vnion betwe Chryft and vs by the bleff.Sa*

B   The Proclamer hath promifed that he wolde fubfcribe yf we coulde bringe furth but one, that by plain woordes coulde teache the trueth of foche articles, as he Proclamed. Here nowe be two both right auncient and famoufe : The firft faieth, *that ower flesh ys nourished withe the cuppe*. He faieth not as the Sacramentarie doeth, *with the cuppe of the Lorde*, but he fpeaketh as the catholique Churche doeth, fainge: *With the cuppe, whiche ys the bloode of oure Lorde*. Neither vfeth he the hereticall phrafe, fainge that *our flesh ys nourished with the Sacramentall bread*, but the phrafe of Chryftes Churche, fainge that *our flesh ys nourished with the breade, whiche ys the bodie of our Lorde*, calling them by expreffe woordes, *the bodie, and bloode of Chryste*. Ys not this a plain fpeache ? The other faieth, that as trulie as the Father ys naturallie in the Sonne : So trulie ys Chryft naturallie in vs by the receipt of his naturall flefh in the Sacrament. Whiche fpeach ys alfo fo plain, that except men will not fee, or will not heare, or hearinge will not vnderftand, they can not choofe but fee, heare, and vnderftand a merueilloufe plain trueth. Whiche trueth was fo euident plain, famoufe and notorioufe in the time of thefe Fathers, that they might vpon the fame, grownde and frame ftrong argumentes againft great and famoufe herefies, as nowe ye perceaue thefe Fathers to haue doen. *A plain faing for the Procla.*

As God the Father ys naturallie in the Sōne fo ys the Sōne by his naturall flesh receaued in the bleff. Sacr.naturalie in vs.

C

To conclude then feinge the one of thefe Fathers, faieth that we be nourifhed with the flefh of Chryft, by the receipt of the fame in the bleffed Sacrament: And the other, that by the fame receipt Chryft ys naturallie in vs, and we naturallie one with him, we maie verie well faie with fainct Paule, that we are membres of his bodie, of his flefh and of his bones.

THE SIXTETH CHAP. TREACTETH VPON

this text of sainct Paule to Hebrues : He haue

an Aultar, &c.

IN the xiii.chapter of S.Paules epiftle to the Hebrues , we finde this fainge: *We haue an Aultar, of the which yt ys not laufull for them to eate that ferue in the tabernacle.* Whiche faing I finde fo expownded that by the Aultar ys vnderftanded the bodie of Chryft in the Sacrament. So that the fenfe of thofe woordes maie be thefe: We haue the bodie of Chryft in the Sacrament of the whiche yt ys not laufull for anie Iewe, refting and abidinge in the lawe of Moyfes to eate. That thus yt ys to be vnderftanded I haue wittneffes, but I will not trooble the reader with manie, but onelie produce a coople , which bothe be grecians. And they be *Ifichius*, and *Theophilact*, the one of the higher houfe and the other of the lower . *Ifichius* faieth thus expownding a text of Leuitic. *Omnem fanguinem reliquum Vituli, fundi circa bafim altaris holocaufti, quod eft in tabernaculo teftimonii, præcepit. Altare holocauftomatis rurfus Chrifti corpus intelligamus. Sicut enim ipfe Sacerdos, & facrificium eft, fic altare eft. Quia autem intelligibile altare corpus Domini, & beatus Paulus intelligit, ipfo dicente, cognofce. Ait enim: habemus Altare, de quo edere non habent poteftatem , qui tabernaculo deferuiunt : corpus videlicet Chrifti, dicens, De illo enim comedere Iudæis fas non eft.* He comaunded all the reft of the blood of the calfe to be powred oute aboute the foote of the Aultar of the burnt facrifice, which ys in the Tabernacle of wittneffe. Let vs again vnderftande the Aultar of the burnt Sacrifice to be the bodie of Chryfte. For as he ys the preift and the Sacrifice: fo ys he the Aultar alfo. That fainct Paule alfo doeth vnderftand the intelligle Aultar, the bodie of Chryft, know by his owne faing. For he faieth, *We haue an Aultar of the which yt ys not lauful for them to eate, that doe ferue in the Tabernacle*, that ys to faie , the bodie of Chryft, fainge that of yt, yt ys not laufull for the Iewes to eate. Thus moche *Ifichius.*

I nede not here moch to faie to open the place, for yt ys open enough of yt felf, and can not well be wrefted, but that in the literall fenfe yt muft be vnderftanded of the bodie of Chryft, in that maner that the Iewe obferuing yet the Lawe, maie not eate him. Whiche maner ys onelie by his reall prefence in the Sacrament, except we fhall euell fauourablie (as Hooper did) expownde *edere* for *credere*, to eate, that ys, to beleue. And then the fenfe muft be: that we haue an Aultar, which ys Chryftes bodie , on the whiche the Iewes that doe obferue the lawe of Moyfes maie not beleue. Whiche fenfe as yt ys verie falfe, fo yt ys verie cruell. God forbidde but that the Iewes fhoulde beleue on Chryft, as manie a thoufand of them haue doen , as the Actes of the Apoftles, and diuerfe other hyftories doe teftifie. The like fenfe fhall this fcripture haue, yf we vnderftand yt with the Sacramentarie of the fpirituall prefence of Chryft and the fpirituall eating of him. So that a diligent reader maie in this place perceaue into what ftrictes, and what inconueniences foche wreftinge expofitours doe bringe themfelues, who leauing the true, fownd, and perfect expofitions of the Fathers, cleaue to their owne inuencions, which be foche, as although they like well the inuentours : yet they neither like nor well agree, with the fcripturs, nor withe the true and ca

catho-

Ifich. in leuit. li. 1. c. 4

The aultar ofthewhich the Iewes maie not eate ys the bodie of Chryft.

Hoopers glofe edere. i. credere.

Theophil. in 13. ca. epift ad Hebrues.

F

G

H

A   tholique expofitours of the fame.But let vs heare *Theophilact* alfo vpon the fame text,Thus he faieth:*Quoniam dixerat non obferuandos effe cibos , ne videantur noftra defpicatui habenda,quod obferuatione careant,Nos (inquit) obferuationem , habemus , veram haud eam, quæ fit in huiufmodi cibis,fed fuper altare , fiue incruenta hoftia viuifici corporis,huius enim vt fint participes,ne pontificibus quidem legalibus permittitur,tantifper dum tabernaculo deferuiunt , hoc eft , legalibus vmbris , & figuris , quæ tranfeunt,ac diffoluuntur.*Forafmoche as he had faied , that regarde of meates fhould not be had,leaft our thinges might feeme to be defpiced , bicaufe they had no regarde or reuerence. We (*faieth he*) haue reuerend regarde, but not that that was vpon thefe maner of meates,but vpon the Aultar or the vnbloodie facrifice of the liuinge bodie. For of this Sacrifice to be partakers,yt ys not permitted,no not to high preiftes of the lawe as long as thei ferue in the tabernacle,that ys,as long as they ferue the fhadowes and figures of the lawe,which paffe awaie,and are diffolued.

Note well thefe tearms the aultar , the vnbloodie facrifice, the liuing bodie, &c.

Here again by *Theophilact* as before by *Ifichius*,ye fee this text vnderftanded of the bodie of Chryft in the Sacrament.He calleth yt the vnbloodie Sa

B   crifice as the holie Nicen Councell did.   And that thofe woordes alfo of the vnbloodie Sacrifice fhoulde not be drawen by the Sacramentaries , the enemies and diftroyers of this Sacrifice,to the facrifice of lawdes,and thankefgeuinge,as Cranmer doeth in his booke of Sacrifice,he addeth,and fullie calleth yt the vnblooddie facrifice of the liuing bodie,or more proprielie, of the bodie that geueth life,or maketh to liue,which ys not , nor can be anie other but the bodie of Chryft,which(as in the laft chapter ys faied) beinge ioined to the Godhead,and made the bodie of God(which ys life yt felf) ys able to geue life,and to make other to liue.And therfor ys here of *Theophilact* verie well called:*Viuificum corpus:*the bodie that ys able to make to liue. But note that we fpeake not here of this tranfitorie , and pafsing life , but of the permanent and euerlafting life.

In the woordes of S.Paule,this alfo ys to be noted,that allthough in hys time the faith was largelie fpred , as in Rome , in *Corinthus*,in *Galatia*,in *Ephefus*, in *Theffalonia*,in *Colloffis*,in *Laodicea* ,yea (as he himfelf to the Romans doeth teftifie)from Hierufalem rownde aboute all the coaftes vnto *Illiricum*,

C   he filled all the contries with the Gofpel: yet nowe writing to the Hebrues he faieth notplurallie we haue manie Aultars,but fingularlie we haue an Aultar.For the Church of Chryft hath but one Chryft,and one vnblooddie Sacrifice,as Chryfoftome faieth,*Vna eft hæc hoftia,& non multæ:* This facrifice ys one,and not manie.For we doe not offre one lambe to daie,and an other to morowe,but allwaies the fame one facrifice.*Proinde(faieth he)Vnum eft hoc facrificium,*Therfore this facrifice ys one,yt hath alfo but one Aultar, as S. Hierom doeth teftifie faing:*Vnum effe altare in ecclefia,& vnam fidem,& vnum baptifma Apoftolus docet.Quod hæretici deferentes,multa fibi altaria fabricati funt,non ad placandum Deum,fed in delictorum multitudinem,propterea leges Dei accipere non merentur, cùm eas quas acceperant,antè contempferint.Etfi quid dixerint de fcripturis, nequaquam diuinis verbis,fed Ethnicorum fenfibus comparandum eft. Ifti multas immolant hoftias, & comedunt carnes earum,vnam Chrifti hoftiam deferentes,nec comedentes eius carnem, cuius caro cibus credentium eft, quicquid fecerint , facrificiorum ordinem ritumque fimulantes , fiue dederint eleemofinam , fiue pudicitiã repromittant, fiue humilitatem fimulèt, fictifque blãditiis fimplices quofque decipiãt,nihil de huiufmodi facrificiis Dominus fufcipiet.*

D   The Apoftle teacheth,to be in the Church one Aultar,one faith and one baptifme,which the heretikes forfakinge,haue framed to thefelus manie Aultars

The facrifice of the Churche of fred in a thoufand places ys but one and the fame facrifice. Hier.lib.3. in Ofeam. cap.8.

not to appeafe God, but to the heaping vppe of multitude of finnes.
Wherfore they are not woorthie to receaue the lawes of God, forafmoch as
the lawes which they had receaued, they had before contemned. And yf
they faie any thinge of the fcriptures, yt ys not to be compared to the woordes of God, but raither to the fenfeis of Ethnickes. Thefe men offre manie facrifices, and doe eate the flefh of them, forfakinge the one facrifice of
Chryft, and doe not eate his flefh, whofe flefh ys the meat of the beleuers.
Whatfoeuer they doe diffemblinge the order and rite of facrifices, whether
they geue almofe, whether they vowe chaiftitie, whether they diffemble hu
militie, or whether with feined flatteries thei deceaue the fimple, God taketh
nothing of foch maner of facrifices. Hitherto S. Hierom.

Whom yf we marke well we maie learn that he by this woorde (*aultar*)
vnderftandeth Chryft, as fainct Paule doeth in this fcripture produced oute
of the epiftle to the Hebrues. For where fainct Paule to the Ephefians faieth
Vnus Dominus, vna fides, vnum baptifma, &c. One Lord, one faith, one Baptifme:
S. Hierom faieth, that S. Paule teacheth that we haue but one aultar, takinge
the one aultar for our one Lorde Chryft.

Heretiques of oure ti- me wel def- cribed by S. Hieron.

But note with all howe liuelie he defcribeth the heretiques of our time,
by the painting of the heretiques of and before his time. For heretiques in
all ages be heretiques, and heretiques be like heretiques. He faieth that the
heretiques did forfake the one aultar of the Church, and framed to themfelues manie aultars. So in this our time they haue forfaken the one aultar of
Chryftes Church, and framed to themfelues manie aultars. For firft *Luther*
forfaking the aultar of Chryftes Church, framed himfelf an other aultar.
But *Carolftadius, Zuinglius*, and *Oecolampadius*, not likinge either the aultar of the
Church or of Luther, framed to thefelues after their phatafie an other aultar.
The *Anabaptiftes* framed themfelues an other aultar after their deuife. The
Swenckfeldians mifliking all that was doen before them framed after their con
ceit a newe aultar altogether fpirituall. The *Caluiniftes* thinking to paffe them
all, haue inuented an other maner of aultar, euen altogether after the maner of the *Arrians* aultar, or not moch vnlike, as *Richerus* Caluines preacher
hath in Fraûce plainly declared. Al whiche aultars (as ours alfo in Englond
with like diuerfitie) haue not ben to appeafe God, but raither to heape vppe   G
the multitude of iniquities to the great prouocacion of hys yre, wrath,
and indignacion againft vs. Wherbie they being puffed vppe, with the vanitie of their mindes, and contemning the lawes of God, whiche before
they had receaued, are nowe reiected, and not thought woorthie of the
lawes of God, and therfor as men corrupted in iudgement, like mê in furioufe feuers, who miflike in tafte and appetite all thinges that be holfome, and
profitable and vehementlie defieroufe of thinges vnholfome, and noifome,
reiect all the holfome lawes, the holie religion, the catholique faith, the
orders, rites, and Ceremonies, vnder whiche they were born, in the
whiche thei were baptifed, in the which they liued, whiche they receaued, and profeffed, whiche with moche peace, moche concorde,
were manie nombres of years eftablifhed, holden, obeied, and reuerenced, and haue defire to haue no other faith, religion, con-
Soch be the phanfies of men of this time. ftitucions, ordeinannces or lawes, but foche as they can prefentlie
inuent and deuife. So great ys their defire, to alter, chaunge and
make newe thinges, that they wolde leaue nothinge that they fown-   H
de in vfe, But why God fuffreth them to doe this, fainct Hyerom
declareth, bicaufe he thinketh them vnwoorthie to receaue his lawes,
foraf-

A forafmoche as they haue contemned the lawes, whiche before they had receaued.

As touchinge their allegacions of the fcriptures, S. Hierom faieth, that their vnderftanding of them ys no better, than to be compared to the fainges of Ethnickes. For hauinge the letters or woordes of the fcriptures, and not the true fenfe, howe moche foeuer they bragge of the woorde, of the Lorde, they haue not the woorde of God, as yt doeth well appeare in their handlinge of the vi of S. Iohn, the xxvi of S. Mathew, the x and xi chapt. of the firft epiftle of S. Paule to the Corinthians, the fift to the Ephe, the thirtenth to the Hebrues and other, whiche in this booke we haue taken from their violent wreftinge, and tirannoufe captiuitie, and haue reftored them to the libertie of the concorde and true vnderftandinge of Chryftes Churche, as yt hath ben taught to vnderftande the fame by the magifterie of the holie Goft, the right and appoincted Schoolemafter of the fame Churche, by our Lorde and God Iefus Chryfte.

Force of the fcripturs falfelie alleaged by heretikes.

B To proceade in the fainge of S. Hierome, he faieth that they doe not eate the flefh of Chryft, whiche fainge howe true yt ys, with the greif of my heart I faie yt, yt ys to well knowen. For what thinge doe they more deteft and ab horre then to beleue and confeffe Chryftes bodie and verie naturall flefh to be in the Sacrament, and there to be receaued? And therfor to the intent, that they wolde not eate his flefh, they haue altered Chryftes inftitucion, they haue altered his faith, they haue abandoned his holie feaft of his bleffed bodie and bloode, and haue in place of yt inuented a poour bare receauing of a drie peice of bread, and a fippe of wine. And beinge as they be, yt ys well. For the flefh of Chryft ys not meate for them, but yt ys the meate (as S. Hierô faieth) of beleuers. Finallie what foeuer this kinde of people doeth whether they faft (as they doe not) for faftinge by them ys exiled, or praie, whiche by them ys almoft to nothing fhortened, or vowe chaftitie, whiche they runne fo faft vnto, that they hate all that doe not marrie, as the greater nombre of them ys married, and foche of them as doe not marrie, doe yt for the like holineffe that was in *Iouinian*, not for perfection of life, but for quiett neffe and eafe, and to auoide thencombrances that maie happê by a fhrewed

This yt a chaungefor the woufe.

Fafting for meritte ys punifhable by ftatute.

C weif. For thorowoute they condemne the vowe of chaftitie, though S. Hierom, S. Ambrofe, S. Auguftine, Chryfoftome, and all holie writers highlie efteem and commende the fame. But to ende, what good dedes foeuer they flatter them felues to doe, as by their diffembled humilitie to fhewe them felues lowlie, or by fweet and flatteringe woordes to deceaue the fimple, God (S. Hyerome faieth) receaueth no part of foche their facrifices.

Seinge then their doinges are accepted of God in no better part, I wifh all men to leaue their vanitie, and walke in the veritie, to leaue herefie, and to walke in faith : to leaue their inuented toies, and to walke in gods eftabli fhed, and long continued lawes : to leaue their manie aultars framed vpon diffent, and diuifion, and to cleaue to the one aultar of Chryftes catholique Churche, whiche ys our helpe and protectiô: to leaue their houngrie cheer

E of bare bread, and wine, and to enioie the roiall feaft of Chryftes bodie and bloode : to leaue their colde maner of faftinge, and praier, and to acquainte them felues with fharpe fafting and feruent deuocion : to leaue their pretenfed matrimonie, and to delight in pure chaiftitie, to leaue their licencioufe maner of life, and come to the trade of a penitent life. For in the ende *Veritas liberabit*, trueth will deliuer. And then, when confcience fhall be fett before the iudgement feat of God, in the daie, *when he fhall iudge the fecrettes of men, the*

                              Yyy iiii   *vnto*

vnto them that be rebells, and that doe not obeie the trueth but folowe vnrightwifnes, shall come indignacion and wrathe, tribulacion, and angnishe vpon the foule of euery man, that doeth euell (as faith S. Paule) and as he faieth to the Iewe firft, and alfo to the gentile: fo faie I, to the chryftian firft, and alfo to the infidell: *but to euery man that doeth good shall come praife, honour, and peace.* God therfore that hath once called vs to his holie faith, confirme and eftablifh foche as haue not yet fwarned from yt, and reduce, and bringe home again foche as haue wãd red like loft fheape, that we be maie all be of the nombre of them, that fhall receaue praife, honoure, and peace, whiche God of his mercie graunt Amen.

THE ONE AND SIXTETH CHAPITER
maketh a recapitulacion of that, that ys doen in this worke.

Owe gentle Reader, haue I goen thorowe all thofe fcriptures, that treact of the holie Sacrament, fpeciallie foche as be commonlie alleadged either by the catholiques to proue the fame, or by the Aduerfaries to improoue yt. In the hãdling of which fcriptures, fo litle haue I geuen to mine owne iudgement, that yt beinge fuppreffed, I haue (as meit yt ys and as I wolde wifh all that liue in this time of controuerfies to doe) geuẽ place to the iudgementes of the learned fathers of Chryftes Churche in all ages. In the fetting furth of which Fathers, I haue in fundrie places and matters cõferred the doctrine of the elder, and the younger together, that the concorde that ys betwixte thẽ might fullie be perceaued. This being trulie and faithfullie doen, the iudgement wher of I referre to the catholique Churche, and fubmitte both my felf, and this ys my worke to the correction of the fame, yt maie and doeth eafilie appeare and maie clerelie be feen, howe vain the bragge of the Proclamer ys, who wolde haue but one fcripture, one doctour, or one Councell produced for the teftimonie of the trueth of the catholique faith, And nowe ther be, fo manie fcriptures, doctours, and Councells brought furth that ther ys not one left to bolftar vppe his herefie The fcriptures which he and his complices pretend to haue in their ‡poffeffion are by the iudgement of the Fathers of Chryftes Parliament houfe prooued neuer to be theirs, but are and haue ben allwaies in the poffeffion of the catholique Churche.

Confidre, Reader, howe manie fathers of the greke churche be here produced, as *Dionife, Iuftyne, Irenæus, Origen, Gregorie Nazianzen, Bafill, Chrifoftom Cyrill*, with other of the elder fort, which although they were of one Churche: yet they were of diuerfe times, fome of them with in one hundreth yea re after Chryft, fome two hundreth, fome three, and yet all thefe agree in one trueth of the prefence of Chryftes bodie in the bleff. Sacrament,

In the latine Churche were *Alexander, Tertullian, Cyprian, Hilarie, Optatus, Hierom, Ambrofe Auguftine*, and other, whiche although they were farre diftaunte, manie hundreth of miles from the fathers of the greke Churche: yet in confent and agreement together in this matter they ioin and go together.

Of the greke churche again be produced other, that were manie yeares after the other Fathers before reherfed, as *Theodorete, Euthimius, Damafcen, Theophilact, Oecumenius*, and *Beffario* with other, whiche although they liued in gre at diuerfitie of ages, hauinge manie hundreth yeares pafsing betwixt them: yet they liued in the vnitie of faith and religion.

Again

A   Again alſo in the latine Churche anſwerablie to theſe were produced, *Gregorie, Beda, Haymo, Anſelme, Paſchaſius, Thomas de Aquino, Lyra,* and *Dioniſe,* with other, whiche alſo liuinge with moche difference of times, and diuerſitie of places, were yet with the eldeſt, and the midleſt, and with the lateſt all of one minde.

And here note that theſe authours, as they doe, according to the rule of *Vincentius Lirinen.* alltogether teache Chryſtes preſence in the Sacrament, ſo doe they yt manifeſtlie, commonlie, and continuallie For *Origen, Baſill. Chryſoſtome, Cyrill, Theodoret, Euthymius,* and *Theophilact,* whiche be the greater writers of the grecians, are not produced once onely, neither ſpeaking obſcurelie: but they are often and manie times, and that with ſpeache moſt plain and manifeſt, and that commonlie, in euerie weightie matter of the booke. Likwiſe be the Fathers of the latine churche, whiche in euery place beare agreable teſtimonie to the Fathers of the greke churche. And for aſmoche as theſe fathers haue expownded the ſcriptures to vs, that doe treact of the **B** Sacrament and doe therin agree, yt ys meete for vs to accept that ſenſe and vnderſtanding, that by the handes of ſo manie Fathers ys ſo conſonantlie deriued to vs. All they vnderſtande them of the preſence of Chryſt in the bleſſ. Sacrament: wherfor yt ys meete that we alſo vnderſtand them ſo, and not onelie yt ys meete but we aught and are bownde to doe ſo.

Nowe therfor let the Proclamer turne his Hiſtorie of *Mitridates* vnto his owne heade and his likes, who lainge wicked ſeige to the citie of Gods Church, wolde beare the citizens in hand, that the armie of the holie learned Fathers and doctours of Chryſtes Churche were on their ſide. But God be praiſed, the contrarie nowe appeareth. For this holie armie ys comed down, and haue ioined with Gods citizens, and haue vanquiſhed Mitridates, and his companie, and deliuered the citie from their cruel tirannie of hereſie, and haue declared themſelues to all the worlde, that they be frendes of Gods citie, and defenders of the ſame, and aduerſaries to *Mitrydates* the Proclamer and vanquiſhers of the ſame. For we haue not by bragge, onelie ſaied that the ſcriptures, doctours, and Councells be on our ſide (as this *Mitrydates,* this proclamer did) But we haue euidentlie, and inuinciblie prooued **C** yt in dede. *Giezi* the lieng and leprouſe ſeruante of *Heliſeus* coulde not, when his maſter was compaſed aboute with the theues of *Syria,* ſee anie that were on his maſters ſide, but againſt his Maſter he ſawe manie, yet in verie dede, there were mo on the Prophets ſide, then on the *Syrians* part. as after yt was well declared: So this *Giezi,* this Proclamer, the lieng leprouſe ſeruant ſeeth not what a noble companie ys on Chriſts ſide, but on the *Syrians* ſide the enemies of Chryſte he ſeeth multitudes.

For hitherto beinge blinded with ambition, and (as *Giezi* did) lieng for ſome gain, or promotion, he hath ſince fallen into the deapth of the ſpirituall leprey, which S. Auſten calleth hereſie. Leproſi (ſaieth he) *nou abſurdè intelliguntur, qui ſcientiã veræ fidei non habentes, varias doctrinas profitentur erroris. Nulla porro falſa doctrina eſt, quæ non aliqua vera intermiſeat. Vera ergo falſis inordinatè permixta in vna narratione, vel diſputatione hominis, tanquam in vnius corporis colore ſignificant lepram, tanquam veris falſiſque colorum fucis humana corpora variantem atque maculantem.* The lepres are verie well to be vnderſtanded thoſe, whiche not ha- **D** uinge the knowledge of the true faith, doe profeſſe diuerſe doctrines of errour. For their ys no falſe doctrine, whiche hathe not ſome true thinges medled with yt. True thinges therfore inordinatelie permixed with falſe thinges in one narracion or diſputacion of a man, as yt were appearing in

the

the coloure of one bodie, doeth fignifie the leprey altering and defiling **E**
the bodies of men as yt were with true and falfe fhewe of coloures.

By thefe means then this man was fo blinded that he could not fee one
fcripture, one doctour nor one Councell, on Chryftes fide, or on his trueths fide. But on the enemies fide, on herefies fide, he could fee an wholl
armie. But I compare this armie vnto the people that were with in the walls
of *Hierufalem*, at the time of the deftruction of the fame, whiche, as *Iofephus* de
clareth, were not onelie plagued by peftilence, and famine at the hande of
God, and with fwoorde and fire at the handes of their enemies without the
walls, but alfo they being with in the walls plagued them felues with great
debates, difcordes, infurrections, and mortall warres. So that the flaughter
was as great within, as yt was withoute. Euen fo this armie hath ben moche
plagued at Gods hande, yt hath raifed moche fedicion and tumulte bothe
in *Germanie, Frannce*, and Englonde, euen within their owne walls, yt hath bē
from time to time perfecuted with fwoorde and fire, and the heade capitai-
nes haue not agreed among thē felues, as in thefe our daies yt ys more then **F**
manifeft that they doe not.

This armie therfor, though yt be fuffred : yet as touching the caufe, they
are not to be feared, For we ftanding with our Prophete, our caufe can not
faill, and when yt fhall pleafe owre Prophete, the armie, that was with *Heli-
zeus*, fhall ioin with vs, and deliuer vs, whiche armie haue among them no
diuifion, no difcorde, ther be amongeft them no inwarde warres, no infurrections, no tumultes (as be amongeft the other) but of them all ther ys
one heart and one mouth. What one faieth all faie, what one denieth
all denie.

On the other fide, looke howe manie citties, howe manie contries, fo
manie doctrines, fo manie faiths, fo manie religions: yea almoft howe manie
heades, fo manie opinnions. Howe doeth Luther agree with *Oecolampadius*?
howe doeth *Melancthon with Bullinger*? yea howe doeth *Luther* agree with him
felf or *Melancthon* with himfelf? As for their difagreinge with the holie fathers, yt ys to manifeft. The holie fathers teache the prefence of Chryft in
the Sacrament, they denie yt. They teache that the facrifice of Chryftes **G**
bodie ys to be offred for the quicke and the dead : thefe denie yt. They teache almofe and praiers to be auailable to the dead : thefe denie yt. To this
yf yowe adde the gates, that they open to all licencioufe libertie, as the taking awaie of Confefsion, the contempt of penāce, the mocking of fafting,
the common maner of diuorcing and marieng again, the voluptuoufe taking
of women to preifts without all difcrecion, be fhe maide or widowe, yf no
worfe, the indempnitie of vfurie, yt were enough and to moche to offend
an honeft heart, but to heare foche things.

Yt were to long a repeticion to reherfe all the licencioufe doctrines, that
be fettfurth againft godlie and vertuoufe liuing. But yf ther were no more
but thefe two euells laft reherfed, in them, namelie their diffenting from
the fathers and their geuing of libertie to vicioufe liuing, yt wer enough to
geue anie man iuft occafion to fufpect, yea and vtterlie to forfake their
doctrine.

In the other fide, forafmoche as the Catholiques embrace the doctrine
of the Fathers, and teache vertueoufe liuing, as penaunce, contricion, con- **H**
fefsion, and fatisfactiō, charitable lending, chaift matrimonie in maried peo
ple, pure chaiftitie in preiftes and religioufe perfons, fafting and foche other
iuft occafion ys geuen to credite them, and to folowe them.

God

God nowe of his mercie open the eies of all his people, that hauing a
breif shewe of the teachers of trueth and vntrueth, of verteuouse liuinge,
and of licéciouse liuinge, maie by his grace take the one, and leaue
the other, folowe the good, and leaue the euell, and so framing
their lifes, to liue in the true faith, and good life, maie by
his mercie atteign to the euerlasting life with
him, to whome, be all honoure and
glorie worlde withoute
ende Amen.

*Volumen hoc ab eximio viro M. n. Thoma Heskins, De præsentia corporis
& sanguinis domini, Anglico idiomate conscriptum, perlectum est a viris illius idiomatis & sacræ Theologiæ peritissimis, quibus sicut ipsi authori meritò id
tribuendum esse iudico, vt ad vtilitatem gentis anglicæ euulgetur:*

*Ita testor et iudico Cunerus Petri de Brouwershauen Pastor sancti
Petri Louanij, 4. Iulij anno 1565.*

FINIS.

THE CHEIF AND MOSTE MAT-
ters conteined in this booke. wher nomber of
booke ys omitted, ye be referred to
the next before.

A.

Arons garment worn for a Bishoprick. lib.3.cap.33.
Abstinence from sinne honoureth God. lib.2.ca.44.
Adoracion of the B. Sacrament taught by S.Paule. lib.2.cap.44. by Alexander.cap.43.by S.Augustin.cap.45. by S.Dionyse.ca.47.by Eusebius Emiss.ib. by S.Bernarde. ibid.
Adoracion practised by Angells.lib.2.ca.45. by preist deacon, and people in the Greke Church: by S.Ambrose in the latin Churche: by S.Austens mother. ca. 45.by Erasmus, and al chrysten people.ca.46.by Gorgonia cap.27.
Adoracion impugned, and denied, by Iuther.lib.2.cap.48. by the Proclamer. cap. 46. by wicked doctrine. ibid.
Adoracion proued by the same doctours, that the Proclamer alleaged against yt. li. 2.cap.45.
Adoracion aught to be doen before we receaue. ibid.
Adoracion vsed in and before the time of S. Austen. ibid.
Adoracion in the primitiue Church infamed by infidells for idolatrie. ibid.
Adoracion ys to be alowed wher the presence ys admitted. li.2.cap.46.
Adoracion neuer by catholique writer denied. cap.47.
Adoracion first denied about xl. yeares past. cap.48.
Adoracion not to haue ben vsed before the time of Honorius ys vntrue. ibid.
Aerius denieng the sacrifice of the Masse to auaill the dead condemned for an heretique aboue a thousand years agon. lib.3. ca.39.
Ale geuen in stead of wine in a Communion lib.1.cap.26.
Alexanders authoritie approued. li.2.ca.32.
Alfonsus nombreth xiij. heresies against the B.Sacrament. in Prolog.
Algasia moued doubtes of scripture to S. Hierom. lib.1.cap.4.
Aliud in the neuter gendre signifieth difference insubstance. ca.29.

Almaricus a Sacramétarie condéned.in Pro.
S.Ambrose vnderstandeth S. Paule to speake of the verie bodie of Chryste.li.3.ca.57
Ambrose corrupted by Oecolapadius.ib.ca.5
Ambrose his doctrine compared with the Sacramentaries. lib.2.ca.52.
Ambrose commended the faith of his Brother Satyrus in the B.Sacramét. li.1.ca.24.
Ambr.geueth three instruct. li.3.ca.14.
Ambr. offred sacrifice in the Masse. cap. 37. he praied as the Church doth. ibid.
S.Andrewe offred the dailie sacrifice. ca.34.
Angells attend vpon the preist in the time of sacrifice. li.2.ca.45.
Angells appoincted to euerie man, and offre our praiers to God. li.3.ca.38.
Antichryste shall cause the dailie sacrifice to ceasse. lib.1.cap.32.
Appologie, and proclamació both like bolts. lib.3.cap.33.
Apostles vnderstood not Chrystes owne woordes. li.1.ca.1.
Apostles learned of Chryste. cap.7.
Apostles decreed that the dead should be praied for at Masse. lib.3.cap.39.
Argument of Chrysts ascension in the vi. of S.Iohn proueth the reall presence in the Sacrament. li.2.ca.35.
Argument of Theophil.to proue the bread made flesh. lib.3.cap.20.
Arrogancie mother of errour. lib.1.cap.4.
Ascension of Chryste improueth not the presence in the Sacrament. li.2.ca.12.
Asseurance of mercie promised to man before full sentence pronownced against him. li.1.cap.9.
Auncient and godlie customes are not to be left for the bare saing of a protestát.ca.25.
Aultars holie.li.3.cap.31. testified by Optatus, and S.Austen, and abuse of them punished. ibid.
Aultars in vse in time of S.Cyprian.ib.ca.39
Aultars from the Apostles time. cap.31.
Aultar wherfor yt serueth. ibid.
Aultar and sacrifice correlatiues ibid.
S.Austen to Dardan. opened li.2.cap.12.
Austens cheif intent vpon the vi.of S.Iohn. lib.2.cap.16.

(.:.)   Austen

Auften teacheth three things in one fenten-
ce againſt the Secramentaries.ca.19.
Auften anknowlegeth both ſpirituall and cor
porall receauing.   ca.16
Auften produced by the Sacramentaries in
wrong ſenſe.   ca.24.
Auften againſt Oecolamp. and Cranmer.
ca.54.
Auftens aſſertions conferred with the iudge
ment of the Aduerſa.   li.3.ca.15
Auften calleth the bread aud cuppe of our
Lorde a ſacrifice.   ca.18.
Auften trulie underſtanded·   li.2.ca.54
Auften vttereth S.Paules wootdes expreslie
of the bodie and blood of Chryſte. li.3
ca.55.
S.Auften corrupted by the Proclamer. li.3.
ca.31.
Authoririe of late writers proued good by
good reaſon.   li.2.ca.3.
Authoritie ys to be obied wher corruption
of life ys.   li.1.ca.6.

B

Baptiſme receaued of all indifferentlie. li.3.
cap.2.
Baptiſme and the read ſea compared.   ibid.
Baptiſme of chryſte and Iohn moch differēt.
ibid.
Baptiſme inſtituted by chryſte and commended by the wholl Trinitie   li.3.ca.14
Baſill and Greg.Nazian. how they atteigned
the knowlege of the ſcripturs . lib.1.
ca.7.
Baſill howe he taught the ſimple to beleue of
the Sacram·   li.2.ca.52
Baſill and Chryſoſtom not fownders of the
Maſſe, but ſetters furth of ſoche order as
they fownd recēaued by tradicion . lib.3.
cap.35.
Baſill beleued the bread and wine to be made the bodie and blood of Chryſte.
ca.36.
Baſill offred the bodie and blood of chryſte
in ſacrifice   ca.37.
Baſill in his Maſſe praied for the dead and to
ſainćts.   ca.39
Benediction, what power yt hath. li.2. ca. 51.
& ca.62.
Benefitts and plagues of the Iewes, figurs of
our benefitcs and plagues.   li.3.ca.1
Berengarius the firſt open impugner of the
B.Sacrament condemned in foure Coun-
cells.prolog.
Berengarius recanted and abiured ibid
Berengarius neither excellēt in learning nor

commendable in life.ibid.
Berengarius fooliſhlie obiected S. Auſten as
the Sacramentaries do nowe.li.2. cap.
14.
Bertramus wrote obſcurelie and ſuſpiciouſlie
of the Sacr. prolog.
Blaſphemie to ſaie the B.Sacr.to be onely a
figure.   li.2.ca.64
Bleſſing of Chryſte, what force yt hath
cap.58.
Bleſsing of more power then nature. cap.
62.
Blood of Chryſte on the croſſe and in the
Sacr.all one.   li.2. ca5.& li.3.ca.20.
Blood in the chalice the ſame that was ſhedd
on the croſſe.   li.2.cap.60
Blood of Chryſte in the Sacr.howe to be eſte
med.   li.3.ca.16
Blood of the Paſchall lambe a figure of chry-
ſtes blood in the B.Sacr.ibid.
Bodie of chryſte ioined to vs by corporall re
ceipt, not by ſpirituall onelie. li.2.cap.
14.
Bodie of chryſt conſecrated of manie preiſts,
all one bodie.   ca.28.
Bodie of chryſte inuiſible in the Sacrament,
a figure of the ſame bodie viſible. ca.49.
Bodie of chryſte demonſtrated ād deliuered
not in figure but in veritie.   ca.63.
Bodie of chryſt howe yt ys called a ſpirituall
meat.   li.3.ca.8
Bodie of the lambe chryſt fedeth vs.   ca.11
Bodie of chryſt vnder forme of bread.ca.26.
Bodie of chryſte conſecrated to two endes.
cap.41.
Bookes of ſcripture ſealed to manie. li.1.ca.5
Bread of the newe communion differeth not
from common bread.li.1.ca.17.howe the
ſame ys nowe vſed.   li.3.ca.47.
Bread broken in the Sacrament the medicin
of immortalitie.   ii.1.ca.17.
Bread by the omnipotencie of the woord ys
made fleſh ibid.& li.3.ca.9. 20
Bread and wine chaunged into the bodie
and blood of chryſte, not in figure but in
veritie.li1..ca.21.li.2. ca.59.60.51.
53.
Bread and wine offred by Melchiſedec
figurs of that which chryſt offre in his
ſupper.   li.1.ca.29
Bread turned into an holier thing .
cap.31.37.
Bread taken three waies in the vi. of Iohn.
li.2.ca.2.
Bread howe yt ys turned into fleſh , and why

fleſh ys not ſeen in the Bleſſ. Sacrament.
li. 2. cap . 7. 8. 19 . 57 & li . 3.
cap.20.

Bread that defcended from heauen ys the bodie of our Lord. li 2.ca.31

Bread whiche Chryfte deliuered no bare figure but flefh. ca 51.53

Bread and wine fo fanctified in confecracion, as yt paffeth mans witte. cap. 54.

Bread geuen to the two Difciples in Emaus was the bodie of Chryfte. cap. 65. 66.

Bread whiche we breake ys the bodie of Chryfte lib.3.ca.19.27.

Bread femeth to be in the Sacrament but yt ys flefh li.3,ca.20

Bread diuided to manie ys the bodie of our Lorde li.3.ca.21.

Bread, and cuppe in Sainct Paule the bodie, and bloode of Chryfte. lib.3.cap. 27.50.

Brentius impugneth the forme of Baptifme lib.2.cap.28.

C.

Canon of the Apoftles corrupted by the Proclamer, li.3.ca.40

Canon forbiddeth not the preift to receaue aloue ibi.

Capharnaites vnderftood Chryfte carnallie lib. 2. cap. 34. had twoo vain thoughts ibid.

Carnall vnderftanding ys by reafon and fenfes onelie cap.37

Carnall men vnderftanding nothing aboue their fenfes, leape backe from the vnderftanding of the myfterie of the Sacrament cap.33

Caffiodorus howe he vttereth Sainct Pauleswoordes li.3.ca.51

Catholique preifts folowing the Schifme be in miferable cafe. lib.3.cap.36.

Catholique faith defcribed cap.53.

Chaftitie required in preifts. lib. 1. cap. 22.

Chryfte turneth the malice of heretiques to the profitte of his Churche. prolog.

Chryfte dwelleth in vs corporallie not onelie fpirituallie in Prolog. item lib.1.cap. 14.lib.3.cap.23.& 26

Chryftes reall prefence in the Sacrament a receaued doctrine in all the chryftian Churche. prolog.

Chryftes Parliament houfe the catholique Church ibid.

Chryftes interpreting of the fcripture proueth the difficultie. li.1.cap.7.

Chryfte not Salomon the feed promifed to

Dauid cap.9

Chryfte and Sampfon compared ca.10

Chryftes paffion conferred to the prophecies therof. lib. 1. cap. 11. item his refurrection and afcenfion ca.12.

Chryftes bodie and bloode an euerlafting facrifice . cap.13.item 31. lib.3.cap. 36. a dailie facrifice. ibi.

Chryfte ys offered of his Church, and his Church of him. lib. 1. cap.18. item lib.3.cap.36

Chryfte and Melchifedech compared lib.1. cap.13.

Chtyfte offred bread, and wine that ys his bodie and blood. ca.29

Chryftes oblacion after the order of Melchifedech ouerthroweth the herefie of Eutyches cap.30

Chryfte offred facrifice in his fupper, and commaunded yt to be contiuued. li.1.ca. 32.34.item lib.3.cap.33

Chryfte commaunded him felf to be offred lib.3.cap.16

Chryfte offred euerie wher ys but one bodie and facrifice lib.2.cap.10

Chryfte gaue his owne bodie to his Apoftles . cap. 50. 64. he geueth himfelf to be eaten in the Sacrament, lib. 1. cap. 14.

Chryftes woordes : This ys my bodie, be not figuratiue. lib. 2. cap. 42. 43. 44. & fequent.

Chryfte verie bodie in the bleffed Sacrament not the figure onelie. lib. 1. cap. 21. item lib. 2. cap.7. item lib. 3. cap.7. & 59.

Chryfte geueth vs the fame flefh by whiche he was ioined to vs, or tooke of our nature.lib.1.cap.14.item lib.2.cap.5

Chryfte ys ioined to vs corporallie. lib. 1. cap.14.

Chryfte and the Pafchall lambe compared lib.1.cap.15.

Chryft in our paffouer verilie perfectlie.lib. 1.cap.16.19. in the Iewes paffouer vnperfectlie cap.17

Chryfte yf he be receaued but fpirituallie then ys our paffouer all one with the Iewes paffouer cap.19

Chryfte firft eate, and dranke his bodie,and blood,and then gaue to his Apoftles.and whie.lib.1.cap.16.item lib.2.cap.55.

Chryfte gaue inconfumptible meat, the Sacramentaries confumptible meat. li.1. cap.17.

Chryfte confecrated his owne bodie. lib.3. cap.51. and commaundeth the fame to be confecrated.li.1.ca.20.the preift confecrateth

(.:.) ij

consecrated Chrysts bodie.　　ibid.ca'.18

Chryste did three notable things in the institution of the blessed Sacrament. lib.3 cap.16.

Chryste commended to vs his bodie, and blood　　　　　　　　　24

Chryste in the lawe presented in figure represented in the Gospell in veritie. lib.1. cap.18

Chryste ys nowe receaued in veritie li.3.ca. 5.& 59.

Chrystes verie bodie set before vs in earth. lib,1.ca.18.

Chryste the onelie begotten Sonne of God receaued in the blessed Sacrament ibid.& lib.3.ca 25

Chryste verilie vpon the aultar lib.1. cap. 18.

Chryste geueth his owne blood in the cuppe lib.2.cap.61

Chryste turned the bread into his bodie and the wine into his blood lib.1. cap. 20. he made the bread his bodie. lib.2. cap.49.

Chryste saing, this ys my bodie, with the woorde made the thing　　　　cap.55

Chryste not man doth consecrate lib. cap. 20.31

Chrystes woordes (this do ye) be referred to the substance not to the maner. lib.1. cap.27

Chrystes maner in ministring hath no commaundement. ca.26. neuer synce vsed. ibid.

Chryste left the maner of ministracion to be ordered of his Apostles cap.26. & lib.3. cap.34.

Chryste in his supper bare himself in his hands　　　　　　lib.2.cap.10.54

Chryste geueth his flesh in substance verilie not in maner grosselie.　　　ca.36

Chryste in his supper the geuer and the gifte.　　　　　　　　ca.47.53

Chryste the meat that we all feed on. lib.3 cap.6.

Chryste ys the substance of the blessed Sacrament.　　　　　　cap.10

Chrystes bodie as verilie receaued in the Sacrament as yt ys beleued to haue hanged on the crosse.　　　　　　　ibid.

Chrystes blood in the Sacrament shed vpon the soldiours garments　　lib.1. cap. 24

Chrystes bodie receaued with mouth both of bodie and soule.li.1.cap.20.li.2.ca.14. 25.

Chrystes flesh ys not disgested as other mea-

tes.lib.1.cap.14. yt turneth vs into yt.li. 2.ca.5.lib.3.ca.59.

Chryst ys not there receaued spirituallie, where he ys not beleued that he maie be receaued reallie　　　li.1. cap.31.

Chryste doth sanctifie, and transmute the bread and wine.　　　ibid. See bread.

Chrystes bodie vpon the crosse called bread li.2.ca.6

Chryste doth blesse sanctifie, and diuide his holie bodie to the receauers. lib.2. cap 8.

Chrysts flesh in the Sacrament geueth life to the woorthie receauers li.2.cap.6. li.3.cap.7.

Chryste in all receauers naturallie : in good receauers both naturallie and spirituallie lib.2. cap.20.24.25. lib.3. cap.6.

Chryste as verilie in the blessed Sacrament as he was verilie incarnated lib.2.cap. 24.

Chryste by his incarnacion ioined to vs : we by the Sacrament ioined to him, lib.2. cap.14.28. item lib.3. cap.27. 59.

Chrystes bodie shall raise our bodies lib.2. cap.26.

Chryste feadeth vs with a bread, whiche ys his flesh.　　　　　　ca.32

Chryste moued the Iewes to beleue in his godhead, and to eate the flesh of his manhead.　　　　　li.2.ca.2

Chryste by the Sacrament maketh vs one with his bodie, and among our selues.li. 3.cap.26.

Chryste instructed his Apostles in the faith of the blessed Sacrament before he instituted yt　　　　　cap.56

Chryste spake plentifullie of his bodie and bloode in the sixt of Sainct Iohn. lib.2. cap.55.

Chrystes institucion ys to receaue his bodie and bloode in the remembrance of his death.　　　　　　li.3.cap.36.

Chrysts bodie ys not in the Sacramentall bread of the communion.　　cap.42

Chryste whie he instituted the Sacrament vnder two kindes　　　lib.2.ca.67

Chryste being whollie vnder eche kinde, the people be not defrauded receauing but thone　　　　　　ibid.

Chryste saied Masse.　　　li.3.cap.33

Chryste taught the newe sacrifice of the newe Testament lib.1. cap.34.37. item lib.2.ca.56.58.

Chryste and not the pope made the Sacrament

ment a facrifice   li 1.câ. 31

Chryfte muft of neceffitie be graunted to haue offred facrifice in his fupper.   ibid.

Chryfte ceaffeth not to excute his perpetuall preifthead and facrifice.   cap.37

Chryfte offred euery wher ys but one bodie, and one facrifice   li 2.cap.10

Chryfte both in heauen and earth in veritie ibid.

Chryftes being in the Sacrament ys miraculoufe contrarie to the rules of philofophie   ibid.

Chryfte bodie vpon the croffe, in heauen, and on the aultar all one. lib. 2. cap. 15. & 22.

Chryfte the Sonne of man, howe he was in heauen, when he fpake in earth. lib. 2. cap. 34.

Chryfts godhead and manhead diftinéted as two breades   ca. 3. & 15.

Chryft fitteth in heauen, and yet ys dailie facrificed by the preift   ca. 46

Chryftes bodie on the aultar that was in the maunger   ca. 45.

Chryfte why he made mencion of his afcenfion in the vi. of Sainét Iohn. cap. 34. 35.

Chryftes flefh befides nature afcended into heauen, and befides nature geueth life in the bleffed Sacrament.   ca. 34.

Chryftes woordes wrefted to xvi. diuerfe fenfes by proteftants.   ca. 41

Chryfte was the fpirituall rocke, not the materiall and therfor ys ther no figure in Sainét Paules fpeache.   lib. 3. cap. 3

Chryfte before the confecracion of his bodie, lift vppe his eies, and gaue thankes to his Father.   li. 3. ca. 34

Chryfte tooke the cuppe of wine mixed with water into his handes, and bleffed, and fanétified them.   cap. 35

Chryfts blood not onelie in heauen but alfo in the chalice   ca. 25

Chryfte entred in to his Apoftles the doores being fhett.   li. 2. ca. 11

Chryfte fhall come to iudgement with the fign of the croffe and prints of his woundes.   li. 3. ca 45.

Chryfte howe he ys, hath ben, and fhall be a figure of himfelf.   ibid.

Chryft what he deliuered in his fupper. ca. 44.

Chryftians eate the flefh of Chryfte, as the Iewes did Manna.   li. 3. ca, 6

Chryftians vfing, no external facrifice, are leffe thankfull then the Iewes.   lib. 1. ca. 32.

Chryftians receauing but a figure as the

lewes, wher ys then the veritie. lib. 3. cap. 6

Chryftians come to a greater thing in the Sacrament, then the Iewes did in Manna li 2. ca. 39

Chryfoftome calleth that blood, whiche Sainét Paule calleth the cuppe lib. 2. cap. 27. he beleued the bread and wine, by fanétificacion to be made the bodie and bloode of Chryfte.   lib. 3. ca. 36.

Chryfoftome offred facrifice in Maffe, cap. 37. defiered interceffion of Sainéts, and praied for the dead.   ca. 39

Chryfoftom impugneth Luther denieng preparacion to be nedefull before the receipt of the bleffed Sacrament. ca. 54

Chutche offring facrifice in the Maffe foloweth Chryfte his Apoftles and the primitiue Churche.   ca. 37

Church muft both offre and receaue. lib. 1. cap. 37

Churche vfeth miniftracion for referuacion, as Sainét Clement ordeined. cap. 24.

Church falfelie charged with erroure by M. Iuell   ibid.

Church referuing the bleffed Sacrament for the ficke offendeth not   cap. 27

Churches vniuerfall obferuacion to be obeied and be kept.   ibid.

Churche teaching the fcripturs to be fcripturs teacheth the vnderftanding of them alfo.   cap. 20

Churche of Afrik vnderftood the vi. of S. Iohn of the Sacrament.   lib. 2. cap. 15

Sainét Clements faing opened lib. 1. cap. 24.

Clement offred Chryfts bodie and bloode in facrifice. lib. 3. cap. 37. he beleued the bread and wine by the holie Goft to be made the bodie and bloode of Chryfte cap. 36

Cloude a figure of the holie Gofte   cap. 2

Communion with Chryfte two waies ca. 23 fee vnitie.

Communion fpirituall by Baptifme corporall by the Sacrament   cap. 23. 26

Communion vnder one kinde lib. 2. cap. 37.

Communion with heretikes maie not be. lib. 3. cap. 25

Communion in praier   ca. 40

Communion bread of the newe Church howe yt ys vfed. 47. the bodie of Chryfte ys not there   *2

Communicacion ys a nearer coniunétion them participacion.   cap. 17. 20.

Communicacion what yt ys ibid. item ca. 22

    Comon

Comon praier of the Churche ys for the wholl Church. ca.40.

Comfort fmall wher confciéce ys confownded. prol.

Conference of Chryftes woordes, and the ferpents. li.2.ca.42.

Confeffion hath three commodities. li.3.cap.55. yt ys to be made truly ibid.

Confecracion what yt ys lib.3. cap.9. how yt ys done. li.1. ca.20.31.li. 2. ca.8. what ys the force. li.3.ca.14.

Confecracion the woorde vfed by S. Ambrofe.lib.2.cap.52. by Tertullian. lib.3. cap.33.

Confecracion vfed by the Apoft.and that ys vfed nowe in the Church, all one.ca.34 35.

Confecracion and facrifice auouched by S. Cyprian. li.1.ca.29.

Confecracion and facrifice abolifhed in the Church that the minifters maie more frelie kepe wemen. ca.22.

Councells of more force then Parliaments cap.25.

Cranmers glofeth without warrant vpon Chryfoft. lib.1.ca.18.

Cranmers fenfuall fentence of faith. cap.16.

Cranmer glorioufe woordes to cloake euel mening. cap.21.

Cranmer falfifieth the fcripture. li.2.ca.11. he falfifieth Iuftine. ca.44.

Cranmer vfeth two falfe fleights in alleaging of Iuftine. ibid.

Cranmers herefie improued. li.2.ca.62.

Cranmers generall rule refuted. lib. 3. cap.30.

Creature earthlie can not be chaunged in to a fpirituall vertue. cap.20.

Cuppe of blefling what yt ys, ãd why yt ys called. ca.19.

Cyprian and Origen teache that euell men receaue the bodie of Chryfte. cap.46.

Cyril denieth that we receaue Chryfts bodie onelie fpiritually. lib.2.cap.16.26.

cap.54.

Death to him that will not heate the preift. lib.1.cap.6.

Decaie of deuociõ caufe of fhortning of the Mafle. li.3.cap.34

Dcrees made againft preifts Mariages. lib. 2.cap.28

Defire of the eating of the flefh of Iob applied to the eating of Chryfts flefh lib. 1. cap.14.

Difference betwen the bodie of Chryfte and fhewe bread. ca.22

Difference of being of the holie Goft with vs, and of Chryft. lib.2.ca.63.

Difference betwen the primitiue Church, and the catholique Church nowe in the vfe of the B. Sacrament. lib.3.cap.57.

Diuerfe hiftories of fcripture prouoke to finne being not godlie vnderftanded and vfed. li.1.ca.2.

Diuine things are wirh reuerence and diligence to be handled. li.3.ca.1.

Doctrine of the primitiue Churche conferred with the Churche nowe. lib. 2. cap.43.

Doctrine of the Sacramentaries conferred with the Fathers. lib.1. cap.21. contrarie to the Fathers. li.2. ca.59.

Doctrine of the reall prefence howe yt ys called newe. lib.2.cap.50. and that yt ys not inuencion of the papifts.

Doctrine flieng the common receaued vnderftanding of the fcripture ys to be fufpected. ca.40

Dogges cruellie vourowed their Mafters, that vnreuerentlie had caft the B. Sacrament vnto them. li.3.ca.43

Doubtes in the lawe of God, wher to be diffolued. lib.1.cap.6.item lib.3.cap.1.

Difciples in Emaus knewe not Chryft before the eating of the bread. lib. 2. cap.65.

Drinke whiche we drinke in the B. Sacrament flowed oute of the fyde of Chryfte. lib.3.cap.7.

D.

E.

Damafus pope difdenied not to learn of S. Hierom. li.1.ca.8.

Damafcen vnderftanded S. Paule to fpeake of the vtrie bodie of Chryft. Cor. 11. li.3.cap.51.

Dailie facrifice of Chryftes bodie and bloode to be offred. li.2.ca.57.

Dailie facrifice fhall ceafle by Antichryft. li.1. cap.32.

Daunger of vnwoorthie receauers. lib. 3.

Effecte of chryfts blefling of the bread, and of the woordes of confecracion. lib.1.cap.26.li.2.cap.61.& 62.

Effect of the B. Sacrament euerlaft. life.lib.2 cap.6.30.& lib.3.cap.7.

Effects of the bl. Sacrament prouing the excellencie therof, and meanes to atteing the fame. lib.3.cap.6.& 14.li.2.cap.5.

Effectual caufes two. cap.15

Epiftle to the Romaines full of obfcure places.

ces, li.1.ca.4

Ephesine Councell vnderstood the vi. of S. Iohn of the Sacrament. lib. 2.cap.15.

Erasmus calleth the errour of Berengarius impudent.prolog.errour of the Proclamer therfor arrogant. ibid.

Erasmus his iudgement of the blessed Sacrament. ibid.

Errour of Origen. li.2.ca.55

Errour in the Sacrament bringeth manie other errours. li.2.ca.1

Eucharist called the holie bodie of our Lorde by S. Cyprian. ca.13

Eutiches his heresie. ca.68.

Euthymius denieth that, which the Sacramentaries affirme ad affirmeth that they denie li.2.ca.15.

Euery chrystian maie not dispute of God.li. 1.cap.7.

Euell men eate and drinke the bodie and bloode of Chryste . li.2.cap.16.24. lib.3. cap.46.49.52.54.57.

Euell receauers three sorts. cap.52

Euells two committed by putting awaie of confess. cap.55.

Examinacion of our selues what yt ys, and howe to be doen. ca.53.

Excellencie of Sacramets standeth in three points cap.12

Excellencie of the blessed Sacrament aboue Manna. cap.14. item 25. excellent titles therof. cap.30

Exhortacion to preparacion by Chrysost. ca.54

F.

Fabianus made a lawe that the people should-de communicate thrice in the year lib. 3 cap.40.

Faith howe yt ys requisit to the receauing of the blessed Sacrament .lib.2.cap.20.lib.3 cap. 53

Faith that beleueth the flesh of Chryste to be in the blessed Sacrament a spirituall faith li.2.cap.37.

Faith aboue senses aud reason and teacheth manie things contrary to them.lib.1.cap. 16.& lib.2.cap.39.62.10.

Faith ouercomed , and not ouercomed in the mysterie of the Sacrament. lib.2.cap. 37.

Faith iudgeth possible that reason iudgeth impossible. cap.10.30

Faith and Baptisme inseparable means of saluacion . ca.48

Faith without woorks sufficieth not in persons of discrecion li.3.ca.1

Faith nourished by the bodie and bloode of

Chryste. lib.2.ca.49

Faith catholique described. li.3.ca.53

False Chrystians more woorthie reproche then Iewes. lib. 1. cap. 19. item lib. 2, cap.9.

False doctrine hath some trueth admixed. cap.12

Fame of the chrystian rites among infidells, proueth the presence. ca.42

Fasting for merit punishable by statute. lib. 3.ca.60

Fathers learned of their elders lib.1.cap.7

Fathers in the primitiue Churche spake of the mysteries often couertlie . lib. 2. cap.3

Figurs of Chrystes incarnacion. li.1.ca.10

Figurs be not in all points comparable ibi.

Figures of the blessed Sacrament foure cap. 15.

Figurs in good things not so good as the things figured:in euell things not so euell ibid.

Figuratiue passouer, and the true passouer both on one table ca.18

Figurs of the olde lawe, and veritie of the newe lawe , be as shadowes, and the thing shadowed li.2.ca.22

Figurs of things be not merueillouse but the Sacrament ys merueillouse ca. 47

Figure taken two waies cap.49.

Figurs contein what reason conceaue, the Sacrament , what faith beleueth . cap. 51.

Figure of the Sacramentaries excluded from Chrysts woordes lib. 2.cap. 51. 52. wiped awaie by Chrysost.cap.55.denied cap.58. 59.60.62.

Figure what yt must be li.3.ca.2

Figure geueth not life , but the blessed Sacrament geueth life, ergo &c. cap.8

Figurs and things figured compared. cap. 10.

Figure maie forshewe life, but yt can not be life. ca.14

Flesh of Chryste in the Sacrament hath an vnspeakeable power. lib.2.ca.1

Flesh of Chryste called life , as being the flesh of God , who ys life . ca.14

Flesh and blood of Chryste both vnder one kinde in the catholique maner of ministracion :neither of both vnder two kindes in the hereticall Communion . cap. 16.

Foode of Chrystes flesh cause of our immortalitie lib.2,cap.17 . 26. item lib.3 cap.24.58.59.

Flesh of Chryste meate in plain maner lib.2. cap.18.lib.3.cap.5

Flesh of Chryste geueth life and yet remaineth still naturall flesh. cap.27.

Flesh profiteth nothing Iohn vi. ys not spoken of the flesh of Chryste, for that profiteth moche. cap.36.

Flesh of Chryste both naturall and spirituall cap.36.lib.3.cap.10.

Flesh of the Sonne of God and the consecrated bread one bodie. cap.52.

Flesh of Chryste appeareth not in the B. Sacrament for our infirmities sake. lib.2.ca.7.8.19.57.lib.3.ca.20.

Flesh vnited to the Sonne of God by assumtion, the same vnited to vs by participacion. li.3.cap.27.

Flesh of Chryste called spirit. li.3.ca.10.

Flesh of Chryste receaued in the B.Sacramēt seed of euerlasting life. li.2.ca.57.

Forme, essence, nature, substance, all one. lib.2.cap.7.

Formes of breade and wine a speache knowē to S.August.ca. 22. and forme of bread remain. cap.60.

Foure thinges called the bodie of Chryste. ca.58.

Foure benefitts of the Iews nōbred.li.3.ca.1.

G.

Gelasius his meaning opened. li.2.ca.68.

Gelasius truncatelie alleaged by the Proclamer, auoncheth two thinges whiche he concealed. ibid.

Genesis not red of the Iewes before thirtie yeares of age. li.1.ca.2.

Germanes acknowlege the reall presence. prolog.

Good religion professed withoute good life not auailable. li.3.ca.1.

God appointed no vain figure. li.1.cap.24.

God and his spirit in his creaturs two waies. li.3.ca.49.

God good by nature, man by participacion. li.1.cap.33.li.2.cap.12.

God plagueth vs in these daies for the abuse of the bl. Sacrament. lib.2.ca.5.

God punisheth some tēporallie, some eternallie, some both waies. li.3.ca.58.

Gods woorde conttarie to senses must be beleued. li.2.ca.55.

Gods order in his Church for doctrine.lib.1.cap.6.

Gods order inuerted. ibid.

Godhead of Chryste hath not possibilitie but to be euery where: his manhead hath possibilitie to be somwhere. li.2.ca.12.

Godhead of the Sonne filleth his boddie sanctified by the preist. lib.2.cap. 28.lib.3. cap.25.

Gospell hath two commodities. li.2. cap.1.

Gospell hath not the figurs, but the verie things, ca.18.

Gospell commaunded the eating of blood: the lawe did forbidde yt. ca.50.

Gospell and lawe compared. li.3.cap.15.

Grekes affirme the real presence. prol.

H.

Heresie maketh man enemie to God. prol.

Heresie by arrogancie moche preuaileth.lib.1.cap.5.

Heresie the farder yt goeth the worse yt fretteth. cap.31.

Heretiques haue moued warre against the church.prolog.

Heretiques agree in conspiring against the Church. li.1.cap.8.

Heretiques why they are, not to be folowed. ibid.

Heretiques barke against the trueth, as dooges against the Moon. cap.16.

Heretiques build there faith vpon reason and senses. ibid.

Heretiques howe they alleage the fathers. lib.1.ca.21.li.2.ca.3.

Heretiques haue no faith but opinions.li.1. cap.21.

Heretiques refuges in reasoning of the Sacrament. ibid.

Hereticall Councells allwaies repressed. ca.25.

Hereticall expositions of the prophecie of Malch. cap.33.

Heretiques call their phansies Gods woorde li.2.ca.33.

Heretiques must be shunned. li.3. ca.25.

Heretikes of oure time wel described.ca.60.

Heretiques like men in feuers. ibid.

Heretiques saings cōpared to the saings of Ethnikes. ibid.

Hierom of praga condemned.prolog.

S. Hierom howe he learned the scripturs.li.1.ca.7.et.8. he expowndeth the scripturs contrarie to the Sacramentaries.ca.39.

S. Hieroms saing opened li.2.ca.57.he expowndeth S. Paule of the bodie of Chryste. li.3.ca. 44.

S.Hilarie vnderstandeth the vi.of S.Iohn of the Sacram .li. 2.ca.24.

Holie Gost consecrateth the B· Sacr. by the hande and tung of the preist li.2.ca.63.

Holie Gost woorketh the consecracion aboue our vnderstāding.li.1.ca.20. li.2 ca.63.

Holie bread vsed in the primitiue church.li.2.ca.51.li.3 .ca.23.

Honour due to God wherin yt consisteth.li.1.ca.18.

Honour or dishonour doen by the receauer ys referred to the Sacr.li.2.ca.44.

Hono-

Honorable titles,and great effects of the Sa. li.2.ca.5.

Hoopers glofe. li.3.ca.60.

Hornes figuracion .li. 2.ca.14.

How,the queftion of the faithleffe anfwered li.1.ca.20.li.2.ca.13.

I.

Iames and Iohns epiftles of few vnderdaded li.1.ca. 5.

S.Iames in his Maffe did three notable thinges.li.3.ca.37. he offred facrifice ibid. he praied for the quicke and dead. ca.39. he maketh intercefsion to Sainéts.ibid.

S. Iames in confecracion directed his fpeche to God the Father.ca.34.

S.Iames Maffe full of knowledge,as the pro clamer graunteth ca.39.

Ignorance as bold as blind.li.1.ca.5.

Ignorance of the B.Sa. what yt ys,and howe to be remoued li.2.ca.54.

Immortalitie when and howe yt fhal be geué li.3.ca. 59.

Intencion of the Apoftles and fathers in the miniftracion, of the catholiques now, and of the newe minifters.ca.36.

Iohn Wicleff, and Iohn Huffe condemned. prolog.

Iofeph and Chryfte compared.li.1. ca. 10

Ifaac a figure of Chryfte. ibid.

Ifichius acknowlegeth the prefence of Chriftes bodie and blood in the B. Sa.ca. 29.

Iewes did eate Manna : we oure lordes bodie. They dranke water of the rocke : we the blood of Chryfte.li.3.ca 9.

A Iewe by a miracle in the S. Sacrament indu ced to be a chriftian.   li. 2.ca. 42.

Iffue ioined with the Proclamer, for the prefence li.1.ca.21.li.2.ca.. 54. for referuacion.li. 1.ca.25..26.for facrifice.li.1. ca.37. for adoracion.li.2.ca 47.for priuateMaffe li.3.ca.40. for praier for the dead.ca.39.

Iudas receaued the bodie of Chryfte which ys oure price.   cap.49.

Iuell falfifieth.   li.3.ca.46.

L

Latine church hath , and doeth confeffe the reall prefence prolog.

Laie men for praier commaunded to abftein from their wieues.li.1.ca. 21.

Lawe of Moyfes had two offices.li.2. ca. 1.

Lent faft commaunded ca 48.

Libertie a bait of the deuell.li.3.ca.53.

Luther condemned . prolog.

Luther contrarie to him felf. li. 1. ca.7. his prowd bragges and lies. ibid.

Luther his ftraunge doctrin.ca. 8.and his pride.ibid.

Luthers fond opinion of the prefence. ca. 25.

Lnther condemned Sainét Iames epiftle.li. 2.ca. 16.

Lutherans doctrine hauing no apparance of fcripture ys ouerthrowe euen by their ow ne argument.ca.53.

Luthers prowde contempt of the holie learned fathers.ca.59.

Luther wher he learned his faith .li. 3. ca. 53.

Luther ys contrarie to S. Paule,to Chryfofto and the fathers.ca.54.

M

Mahomets patched religion and the Sacramentaries moche like.li.2. ca.10.

Manna why yt was called a fpirituall meat.li. 3.ca.3.8.

Manna a figure of Chryfte ca.4.5. applied to the Sacr.ca.11.12.

Manna three kindes, ca.4.

Manna had xii wonders.ca.12.

Manna what yt ys by interpretacion . ca. 11.

Manna and the Sacr. compared.li.2.ca.30.li 3.ca.10. 11.12.

Manna moche inferiour to the B.Sacr.ca.5. 14.but more excellent then the facramentall bread.ca.12.

Manna was from the aier,Chryfte from heauen ca.4.a creature : but Chryfte the creatour.ca.14.

Manna the figure gaue but temporall life: Manna the thing geueth eternall life. ibi.

Manna gathered more then was commaunded corrupted.   ca.12.

Man eatheth the bodie of Chryfte .li.1.ca.16

Marie Chryfts mother by nature,and aboue nature.   li.1.ca.13.

Maffe taken two waies li. 3.cap.33.and what yt ys proprelie.   ibid.& cap 34.

Maffes in the primitiue Church varied in maner from Chryfts doing.   cap.27.

Maffe of S.Iames alowed by the Proclam. cap.34.

Maffe of the Apoftles, fathers, and of the Churche nowe all one in fubftance. ibid.

Maffe called a facrifice in the Councell of Conftantinop.   ca.35.

Maffe fetteth furth the death of Chryfte more liuelie then the newe communion.cap. 39.

Maffe the woorde howe yt cometh. cap. 32. and in yfe within CCCC.hundreth years after Chryfte euen by the Proclamers confeffion.   ibid

Maffes mo then one maie be faied in one Church and one daie .ibid.three faied on

Chryft maffe daie fourtene hūdreth years agon.ibid.

Mafters and teachers of the fcripture muft be had and confulted li. 1.ca.7.

Matters of doubt are to be referred to the preifts.ca.6.

Matthew and Luke feme to varie in the genealogie of Chryfte.ca.3.

Meate of Chryftes fupper differeth from cōmon meates. ca. 17 .

Melanchthon his mutabilitie.li.2. ca.41.

Melchifedech and his facrifice treacted of and compared to Chryfte and his facrifice.li.1.ca.30. 31.

Membres onelie of Chryftes bodie knowe Chryfte.li.2. ca. 65.

Memories and monuméts of holie and worthie men defaced.li.1. ca.21.

Minifters of the newe church can not confecrate.li.3. ca.34.

Minifters of two fortes. ca.36.

Minifterie of Agells aboute men.ca.38.

Miracles wrought iu the bleffed Sa. li. 1.ca. 24.li.3.ca.42.

Mifunderftanding mother of herefie . li.1. ca.7.

Mifunderftanding of Chryftes woordes cau feth all the herefies of the Sacramentaries li.2.ca.64.

Mocks and skoffs the onelie arguments of the Proclamer againft the Maffe.li. 3. ca. 38.

Mother of Chryfte, and of Sampfon compared.li.1.ca. 10.

Mouth receaueth that faith beleueth. li. 2. ca.15.

Mifteries of religion not common to all mē. li.1.ca.7.

Myfteries of the church wonderfull . li. 2. ca. 5.

Myfterie what yt ys, and howe the B. Sacr.ys called a myfterie.li.3.ca.57.

My flesh ys verilie meate Iohn vi. no figuratiue fpeache li.2.ca.20.21.

N

Naturall order had no place in manie of Chryfts doings.li.2. ca.10. & 12.

Naturall vnitie of Chryfte to vs.li. 2.ca. 24. fee vnitie.

Naturs two in Chryfte, not two perfons.li.3 ca.51.

Nature corrupted could not be brought to incorruption but by the incorruptible bo die of Chryfte.li.3.ca.59.

Neftorius and Eutiches herefies.li.2.ca.15.

Newe lawe requireth a new prefthead.li.1.ca 13.

Newe mynifters maner in their comunion. li.3.ca.34.

Newe church chargeth Chryfte with an vntreuth.ca.39.

Nothing fo true but herefie maie impugn yt li. 2.ca.12.

O

Obedience to be fhewed euen wher corruption of lifeys   li.1.ca.6

Obedience of the newe church how yt ftandeth.   ca.25.

Obiection oute of Tertullian. li. 1. ca. 16. oute of S. Auften ca.19.item ca. 23.oute of S. Clement ca.24.oute of Chryfoftome li.1.ca.5.oute of S.Aug.ca.14 oute of Eufeb.Emif.ca.19 oute S.Gregorie.ca. 25 oute of S.Aug.ca.34 oute of.Tertull.ca. 29.oute of Leo.ca. 56.oute of Rupert.li.3 ca.10.

Obiction of the Aduerfarie folued . li. 1. ca. 18.

Obiection oute of S. Hierom folued. ca,22.

Obiection vpon Melchifedec anfwered. ca. 28

Obiection of Chryfts being in diuerffe places·li 2.ca.12.

Obiection of the fpirituall eating of Chryft. ca.37.

Obiections of the Proclamer againft adoracion.   cap.44.

Obiection vpon S. Bafill. folued by damafcen.   li.3.ca.18.

Obiection vpon the woord bread in S.Paul. cap.29.item other obiections oute of S. Paule.   ca.44.

Obiection of the Proclamer againft fole receauing.   ca.40

Obiection of Oecolamp.   ca.45.

Ocolampadius denieth that Chryfte affirmeth.li.3.ca.13.his wicked glofe cofuted ca.15.

Oecolamp.condemned.prolog.

Oecolamp.contradictions.   li·1.ca.23

Oecolamp.falfifieth Theophila.li. 2. ca. 12. and S.Aug.ibid.his wrefting and abufing of S.Auguft.   ca.54.

Oecolamp.abufeth S. Paules woords: The rock was Chryft.   li.3.ca.3

Oecolamp.wrefteth the fcripture ibid . he mutilateth S.Amb.   ca.4.

Office of preift to expownd the fcripture. li.1.   ca.6

Office of confecracion inftituted by Chryfte as Luther confeffeth.   ca.20.

Offring of bread ād wine, not bringing furth of yt perteineth to the preifthead of Melch. fedech.   cap.18

Olde lawe had but figurs, new lawe hath the verie things.   li.1.ca.15.21

Olde

Olde Paſchall lambe the ſhadowe , our Paſchall lambe the thing. ca.18

One thing in manie places two waies.lib. 2.
ca.12.

One aultar,one faith one bapt.in the church
li.3. ca.60

One bread that manie are made one by,ys
the bodie of Chryſt. li.3.ca. 28.

Opinion of the Iewes of the coming of Elias
lib.3. ca.3

Order of God inuerted. li.1.ca.6

Order of preiſthead in two poinⳓs. ca.28

Ordeinances of elders to be holden for lawes,wher ſcripture preſcribeth not.ca.27.

Origen opened. li.3.ca.30.

Origen in plain woordes calleth the Sacr.the
bodie of Chryſte. li.3.ca. 5.

P

Pagans haue daie Gods and howre Gods.
li.1.ca.32.

Partakers of Chryſtes blood dwell with Angels. li.2.ca.5.

Parts of the Sacr. ca.56.

Paſſion of Chryſt ſettfurth with the prophecies of yt. li.1.ca.11

Paſchal lambe had two notable things.ca.15

Paſſouer of the chryſtians more excellent thē
the Paſſouer of the Iewes ibid.

Paule by bread ad cuppe ment the bodie and
blood of Chryſte by the vnderſtanding of
Chryſoſt.li.1.ca.27.li.3.ca. 16. & 24.of S
Aug.ca.15. of Oecumenius and Iſidor. ca.
19.of Theophilaⳓt.ca.20.of Anſelme ca.21
of Euthymius.ca.37.of S. Hierō.ca.44.of
S.Baſil.ca.45.of Origen. ca.46.

S.Paule why he ſpake not of the ſacrifice of
Melchiſedec in the epiſt.to the Hebrues.
cap.18.

Paules woordes:the rocke was Chryſte, can
not be expownded by a trope. li.3.c.3

Paules woordes abuſed by Cranmer. ca.16

Paule in all his proceſſe of the Sacr. maketh
no litle mencion of anie figure. ca.22.

Paule ſaieth that our Lorde imparteth to vs
his owne bodie. ca.29

Paule ād the vi.of S.Iohn ſpeak of one thing.
ca.50.

Paule doth often call the Sacr. the bodie of
our Lord. ca.52

Penance aud clean conſcience neceſſarie for
the receauers of the Sacr. ca.55.

Peter ſaied Maſſe at Antioche. ca.36.

Peter de Bruis his hereſie. prolog.

Peter Martyr howe he wreſteth Theophilaⳓt.
and his gloſe ouerthrowen.li.3. ca.20.

Philippe ſent by the holie Goſte to expownd
the ſcripturs to the Eunuch,which argu-
gueth the difficultie therof. li.1.ca.1.

Plagues for breaking of Gods order in relig.
cap.6.

Polycarpus put oute of the caléder.li.2.ca.3

Praⳓtiſes of the primitiue church prouing a
ſwell reſeruacion,as ſole receauing.li.2.ca.
68.li.3.ca.40.

Praⳓtiſe of prophanacion lamentable to be
ſeen in Englonde.li.3.ca.49.

Praier neceſſarielie required to vnderſtand
the ſcripture.li.1.ca.7.

Praier of the canō in the Maſſe agreeth with
the fathers. The newe communion diſa-
greeth.li.3.ca.35.36.38,

Praier for the dead and almoſe profitable ād
vſed in the primitiue church, ca.39

Preiſts office none maie doo but he that ys
called li.1.ca.7

Preiſts ought to be reuerenced for their offi
ce. li.1.ca.18

Preiſts muſt conſecrate offre , and receaue.
ca.22.

Preiſt muſt allwaies haue thē B.Sacr. reſerued for the ſicke. ca.35.

Preiſthead of chryſte ſhall neuer be chaunged. cap.31

Preiſt maketh God,the cauil of the deuel.li.2
ca.8.

Preiſtes doing the ſolemne aⳓtion of the memoriall of chryſt in the Maſſe aught to receaue vnder both kinds:Preiſts not doing
the ſame and other receaue vnder one
kinde. ca.67

Preparacion for the worthie receipt of the
B.Sacr.commaunded:and the daunger of
vnworthie receipt declared , argueth the
reall preſence. li.3.ca.56

Preſence of chryſts bodie in the B. Sacr.li.1.
cap.17. 18.& paſſim per totos tres libros.

Preſence of chryſt in the Sacr. no more impoſſible then other of his workes and doings. li.2.ca.22.

Preſence of the holie Goſte vnder the forme
of the doue and chryſtes preſence in the
Sacr.compared. li.3.ca.3.

Preſuptuouſe teachers. li.1.ca.7.

Priuate perſons maie receaue vnder one kin
de. li.2.ca.67.

Priuate communion proprelie what and whe
re yt ys. li.3.ca.41.

Priuate Maſſe vſed in the time of chryſoſt.ib.

Proclamacion of a newe Goliath.prolog.

Proclamer to be pitied ibid . he denieth all,
and proueth nothing. li.1.ca.20

Proclamer impugneth reſeruacion withoute
reaſon or autoritie. li.1.ca.27.

Proclamer ſettfurth that nowe for trueth,
which S.Cyrill aboue a thouſand years a-
gon reputed an hereſie.li.3.ca.26.he truncateth

cateth S.Hierom.li.2.ca. 53. he falſifieth S.Auguſt.li.3.ca.37.he abuſeth Anacletus ca.4.

Proclamer ſkorneth the Maſſe. ca. 33. & ſequ. he findeth three faults in the Canon therof ca.38.

Proclamer braggeth of the primitiue Churche in woordes, but refuſith yt in dedes. ca.32.

Proclamer iudgeth maliciouſlie of all the chryſtian worlde.ca. 38.

Proclamers ſleight in alleaging S .Hierom. ca.41.

Profitts cōming to vs by receauing of Chryſts fleſh.ca. 39.

Prophanacion of holie things what yt ys.ca. 46.

Promeſſe of gladd tidings to Abraham. li. 1. ca.9.

Prophecie not geuen to all.ca.1.

Prophecie of the ſtocke of Chryſte and incarnation.ca.11

Proteſtants of euerie ſect chalenge to them the woord of God, and the name of the church. ca.25.

Proteſtants tormented with the prophecie of Malach.ca.33.

Proteſtants compared to the dogge in the fable.li.3.ca.7.

Puritie of life in two points.ca.53.

R

Raſh readers, and arroganr teachers.li. 1. ca.7.

Reall bodie partaken: myſticall bodie partakers.li.3. ca.28.

Reall preſence li.1.ca.14.16. 29. &c.li.2.ca 15.20.43.46.49.& ſequent. li.3. ca.5.8.& alijs.

Reall preſence and ſacrifice proued by S.Paule.li.3.ca 16.17.22.30. proued by Chryſoſt. ca.36.by Theodoret. ca.56.

Receipt of Chryſts bodie both ſpirituall and corporall.li.1.ca.14.li.3.ca.23.26.

Receipt of Chryſts merits not propre to one Sacrament, but cōmon to all li.2.ca.5

Receipt of Chriſts bodie maketh our bodies immortal.li. 2. ca. 14.ſee bodie and fleſh.

Receauing by ignorance what yt ys.ca. 54.

Receauers of the B.Sa. muſt prepare the ſelfes, and howe .li.3.ca.55. muſt abſtein frō the act of matrimo.ca.41.

Read Sea a figure of Bapt.ca.2.

Repreſent what yt ſignifieth li. 1. ca. 18.

Reſeruacion of the Sa. in the Apoſtles tyme li.1.ca.24 and after in the primitiue church ibid.&.ca.25 26.27.li.2.ca.68.

Reſeruacion not againſt the inſtitucion of Chryſt.li.1.ca.26.agniſed by the nicē Coū

cell.ca.25.deniers ther of accurſed ibid.

Reſeruacion in priuate houſes li. 1. ca. 24.in the ſhippe ibid.

Riche and poor eate all one bloode. li. 3. ca.6.

Richerus a Caluiniſt forbiddeth to praie to Chryſte.li.2.ca.48.

Right waie to vnderſtand a caholique authour.ca.49.

Roffenſis neuer yet anſwered prolog. his ſaings alleaged li.3.ca.12. & 32.

S

Sacrament hath honourable titles . li. 1. ca. 17. yt conteineth the thing woorthie of moſt honour.ca.18.

Sacrament reſerued. ca. 24. 25.&c.ſent to a ſicke man ibid.caried home to ſoche as we re abſent.ca.27.

Sacrament a figure not of the bodie of Chryſte, but of his death.li.2.ca.14.&. li.3.ca. 44.

Sacrament a figure in diuerſe reſpects, but not onelie a figure. li.2.ca.14.li.3.ca.8.

Sacrament conteineth three things li. 2. ca. 19.li.3.ca.42.

Sacrament a myſterie howe and what a miſterie ys.ca.23.

Sacrament hath two parts, and whiche thei be.ca.57.ahd two offices.ca.15.

Sacrament maie be conſecrated by no other woordes, then theſe Hoc eſt corp.ca.64.

Sacrament a ſanctified thing and ſanctificacion.ca. 66.

Sacrament deliuered by Chryſte in his ſupper vnder both kindes: in Emaus vnder one kinde proueth both to be laufull . ca. 67.

Sacrament myniſtred vnder one kinde by S. Cypr.ca.68.receaued ſo of a woman ibid. and vpon good fridaie. ibid.

Sacrament and the thing of the Sacrament. li.3.ca.8.

Sacrament if yt haue not the preſence of Chryſts bodie ys inferiour to Māna.ca.12

Sacraments diuerſlie nombred by the proteſtans.ca.13.

Sacrament geuing life farre excelleth Manna ca.14. yt ys inconſumptible meat.ibid.

Sacraments of the new law better, &c.ca.15 ſacrament defined.ibid.

Sacraments of the newe lawe geue grace.ib. and ſaluacion.ibid . compared to the olde lawe by S. Auguſt.ibid.

Sacram. proued by our lord to be his bodie. li.3.ca.53.

Sacrament caried home and receaued as deuocion ſerued, and lickwiſe reſerued of holie men in wilderneſſe ca.41.

Sacra-

Sacramét deliuered to a Iewe appeared flesh and likewise to an other.ca.42.

Sacramentaries condemned by eight Councells prolog. their glofe vpon S. Cyprian ouerthrowen li 1.ca.17.

Sacramentaries make two maner of prefence ca.21.they take awaie the fatte and fwete of the blefl. Sacr.ca.26.they ftomble at a ftrawe and leape ouer a blocke.ibid. their cheif grownds be naturall reafons. li.2. ca.19.

Sacramentaries denie that the fathers affirme, and affirme that they denie . ca. 59. they teache contrarie to their own rules. ca.60.they denie the excellencie of the Sacraments of Chryfte.li.3.ca.4.

Sacramentaries maintein the herefie of Eutyches li.1.ca.30.and of the Aarrians.li.3.ca 59.and denieng the receipt of Chryftes naturall flefh feme to denie the immortalitie of our flesh after refurrection. ibid.

Sacrifice after the order of Melchifedec nowe diffufed throughout the worlde . li.1. ca.31.

Sacrifice auouched.ibid.propiciatorie li.'ca. 43.li.3 ca.14.

Sacrifice of lawde or gratulatorie feparated from extern facrifice .li.1. ca. 33 .li.3. ca.30.

Sacrifice of the croffe , and of the aultar all one in fubftance,but diuerfe in maner.li.1 ca.33.

Sacrifice of the chryftians,a peculiar and fpeciall facrifice ca . 35. a full and moft holie facrifice. ibid. full of horrour honorable to Angells li.3.ca.54. immaculate. ca. 37. the bodie and blood of Chryfte. li. 1.ca. 36.inftituted by Chryfte.ca.31.32.& .li.2. ca.49.56.li.3.ca.33.& alibi.

Sacrifice of the Maffe of what preift foeuer offred, ys one with that Chryfte offred. li. 2.ca.8.offred in manie places ys all one facrifice.ca.10. item li.3.ca.33.& 60.

Sacrifice of the church confifteth of the vifible formes of bread and wine and of the inuifible flefh.&c.li2.ca.19.li.3.ca.6.

Sacrrifice of the church proued by S.Paule. li.3.16.after the vnderftanding of S.Aug. ca.18.29.

Sacrifice of Chryfte in his fupper and Melchifedec compared.li.1.ca.13.30.31.li.3. ca.17.

Sacrifice and Maffe caufed the Proclamer to falfifie Leo. ca.40.

Sampfons conception and Chryftes compared.li.1.ca. 10.

Sáctificacion,and a fanctified thing be diuerfe li.1.ca. 66.

Sathás finall marke he slooteth at.li.3.ca.31

Sathá appeared toLuther and difpured with him of the Maffe.ca.42.

Sathans power abated by vertue of the Maffe.ibid.

Satirus faued from drowning by power of the Sa.and his faith commended by S.Ambrofe therin li.1.ca. 24.

Sectes of religion principal in the world foure.li.1.ca.32.

Sects of Sacramentaries fixteen.li.2.ca.41.

Sedulius faieth that S. Paule fpake of the bodie of Chryfte.li.3.ca.49.

Serapion being being ficke called for the Sà. and receaued alone.li.3.ca.41.

Shewe bread a figure of the Sa .and applied to the Sa.li.1.ca.22.23.24. appointed for three things ibid . continuallie vpon the aultar.ca.23.

Schoole arguments made for the opening of the trueth produced by a Proteftant to confirme a falfhead li.2.ca.22

Scriptures to be hard proued by vii arguméts li.1.ca.1.

Scriptures muft be ftudied with moche labour.ca. 5.

Scripturs muft be learned of the fathers. ca. 7.they muft be full of doubtes,and maie be drawen to diuerfe fenfes.ca.6.& 7.8.

Scripture the ftorehoufe of God, and why God wolde the fame fhoulde be heard.ib.

Scripturs alleaged by Oecolamp.againft the prefence.li.2.ca.12.

Scripturs muft be alleaged in the literall fenfe ibid ca.50.

Sonne of God made flefh ys receaued in our lords meat li.3.ca.59.

Sonne of God troaden vnder foote whé his bodie and blood are not beleued to be in the Bl.Sa.li.2.ca.67.

Spirit howe yt quickneth, and flefh howe yt Profiteth or not. ca.36.

Spirit taken two maner of waies. ca.37.

Spirit of vnitie among catholiques: fpirit of diuifion among Proteft.li.3.ca. 9.

Spirituall receauing not figured by the Pafchall lambe.li.1.ca.19.

Spirituall vnderftanding what yt ys.li. 2.ca. 37.& 39.63.

Spirituall and reall receipt together wonderfull.ca.55.

Spirituall knowlege afwell teacheth the fubftance of Chryft bodie and blood to be vnder the formes of bread and wine,as naturall knowlege the fubftance of naturall things to be vnder their formes.ca.63.

Stercoranits of our time li.1.ca.14.

Storehoufe of God not commón to all.ca.7.
Stra

Straunge doctrines not to be folowed. li. 1.ca.8.

Subftance of Sacraments muft be obferued the maner maie be altered.ca. 26.

Subftance of a thing faied to be feen, when onelie the outwarde forme ys feen. li. 2. ca.63.

Synners receaue the bodie of Chryfte reallie but not fpirituallie.ca.55.

Sixtene fects of Sacramentaries and other like.ca. 41.

Swearing to moche vfed now a daies. li. 3. ca.30.

T

Table of Chryfte pourgeth li.1.ca.23.

Table fignifieth facrifice in S .Paule. ca. 31. item li.3.ca. 16.

Table of Chryfte terrible · of the olde Paffo uer not fo. li.2.ca. 55

Table of our lord, the bodie of our lorde.li. 3.ca.30.

Teachers meet or not meet to be folowed. li.1. ca.8.

Temtacions of oure firft Parents and men in thefe daies compared.li.2. ca.41.

Tertullian in one faing ouer throweth three affertions of the Sacramentaries li. 2. ca. 42.the fame opened and deliuered from their fleights.ca.49.

Tertullians wief receaued the Sa. fecretly, and alone.li.3.ca. 41.

Theophilact auoucheth three things againft the Sacramentaries.li.2.ca.60.

Three maner of doings touching fcripture. li.1.ca.26.

Tradicion to be folowed li.3.ca.1.

Tranfubftanciacion auouched li.1. ca. 31. li. 2.ca.7.51. beleued of the fathers . ibid. what it ys.ca.53.li.3.ca.14.proued bi Ifich li.2.ca. 54.& 57.item treacted of li. 2. ca. 59.60. 62.

Trueth muft haue an excellencie aboue the figure . li . 3 . ca.

W

Water of the Rocke whie yt was called fpi rituall. li.3.ca.3.

Waldo, and waldenfes. prolog.

Wanton lufts of Byfhops and preifts repro ued.li.1.ca.22.

Wafhing of the Apoftles feet what yt fignifi eth.li.2.ca.47.

Verè the Aduerbe, what force yt hath. li. 2. ca.18.

Verie flefh of Chryfte vnder forme of bread ca.22.the fame called fpirit ca. 39.

Veritie of Chryfts flefh fetfurth before vs in the Sa.ca.60.

Victor excõmunicated the Churches of Afia li.1.ca.24.

Willfull reafon no fufficient warrant allwa ies in the court of faith.li.2.ca. 42.

Wyne mixed with water in Chryfts cuppe.li 1.ca.20.26.li.2.43. li. 3.ca. 34. 35.yt ys a diuine tradicion fo to be vfed, and why yt ys. ibid.

Wyfe men , by hearing maie be wifer. li. 1. ca.8.

Woman ftricken to death for vnwoorthie re ceauing of the Bl.Sacr. li.3.ca.58.

Wonderfull what ys proprelie.li.2.ca.55.

Worke of the Sa. miraculoufe.ca.60.

Woorthie receauers and vnwoorthie what they receaue.li.3.ca.51.52.53.woorthinef fe proprelie what yt ys ibid.

Worldlie cares kepe men from God. li. 3. ca. 40.

Vntrueths vttered by the Procla · three in one place.ca. 39.

Vnbloodie facrifice, the liuelie bodie of chri fte, the aultar whiche the Iewes maie not eate.ca.60.

Vnitie with Chryfte two waies li.1.ca.14.li.2 ca.10.14.24.li.3.ca.23.

Faultes in printing.

In this long worke (gentle Reader) there can not a fewe faultes be committed in the or thographie , both bicaufe the printers were vnskilfull of oure language , and for that the ouerfeer coulde not be allwaies readie at the preffe to make corrections . In confideracion wherof, and that I haue not tyme my felf to gather all, I praie thee of gentleneffe to beare ther with , and for thy skill to correct after thefe fewe examples. God be euer withe thee.

In the prolog the firft line : read, haue moued: in the xv . lyne : for primatiue , primitiue and fo in other places.

In the booke firft amende the nombres of the leaues, as, for vii. viii .xi .xvi.lx.&c.ii.iii. iiii .viii .xl &c.then of the chapters,for thirtene,fourtene,&c.read thirtenth,fortenth &c. aud for nine and thirteth.read nine and twenteth.

And let the binder looke to the order of the Ternions , for the fignatorie letters be fome wanting: fome myfplaced.

Finis.